Contemporary Authors

Contemporary Authors

A BIO-BIBLIOGRAPHICAL GUIDE TO
CURRENT AUTHORS AND THEIR WORKS

CLARE D. KINSMAN

Editor

volumes 13-16

first revision

GALE RESEARCH COMPANY • THE BOOK TOWER • DETROIT, MICHIGAN 48226

CONTEMPORARY AUTHORS

Published by
Gale Research Company, Book Tower, Detroit, Michigan 48226
Each Year's Volumes Are Cumulated and Revised About Five Years Later

Frederick G. Ruffner, *Publisher*   James M. Ethridge, *Editorial Director*

Clare D. Kinsman, *Editor*
Cynthia R. Fadool and Alexander James Roman, *Associate Editors*
Jane Bowden, Robin Farbman, Christine Nasso,
Nancy M. Rusin, Adele C. Sarkissian, and
Frank Michael Soley, *Assistant Editors*
Laura Bryant, *Operations Supervisor*
Daphne Cox, *Production Manager*

EDITORIAL ASSISTANTS

Frances Carol Locher, Norma Sawaya, and Shirley Seip

PREFACE

VOLUME 13-16, FIRST REVISION

This volume represents a complete revision and a consolidation into one alphabet of biographical material which originally appeared in *Contemporary Authors*, volumes 13-14, published in 1965, and volumes 15-16, published in 1966. The revised material is up-to-date, in most cases, through early 1975.

In preparing the revision, the following are the major steps which have been taken:

1) Every sketch has been submitted to the author concerned, if he is still living, and all changes requested which were within the scope and purpose of *Contemporary Authors* have been made.

2) If an author has failed to submit changes or to approve his sketch as still correct, the editors have attempted to verify present address, present position, and the bibliography. A symbol (†) has been used to indicate those sketches appearing in this revision which have not been personally verified by their subjects.

3) Additional research has been done on the bibliographies of many authors, both to pick up publications which were not included in the previous versions of their sketches and to assure that all recent works have been included.

4) "Sidelights" have been added to many listings for prominent authors whose sketches did not include this material previously, and "Sidelights" for numerous other authors have been revised substantially.

As a result of these editorial procedures, the amount of new material in this volume is substantial, and, even after the deletions described below, the revised volume contains more pages of text than did the two original volumes.

Series of Permanent Volumes Established for Retired and Deceased Authors

A series of Permanent Volumes has been established as an adjunct to *Contemporary Authors*, in order to avoid reprinting in the future the sketches of authors which will normally not require further change.

Therefore, the editors are omitting from this revision and from future revisions two classes of authors—first, persons now deceased, and second, persons who are approaching or who have passed normal retirement age and who have not reported in revising their listings that they have published books recently or have work in progress.

Authors at retirement age and without recent works who nevertheless have books still in print would usually be retained in the revised regular volumes, in the expectation that they may produce additional work.

Cumulative Index Should Always be Consulted

As always, the cumulative index published in alternate volumes of *CA* will continue to be the user's guide to the location of an individual author's listing. Authors not included in this revision will be indicated in the cumulative index as having appeared in specific original volumes of *CA*, and as having their finally revised sketches listed in Permanent Volume 2.

The editors believe that this revision plan will prove to be not only convenient but economical, as well, since it removes from the revision cycle material which no longer needs periodic review and reprinting. As always, suggestions from users on revisions or any other aspect of *CA* will be welcomed.

CONTEMPORARY AUTHORS

† Indicates that author has not personally verified the entry in this edition

AARON, Daniel 1912-

PERSONAL: Born August 4, 1912, in Chicago, Ill.; son of H. J. and Rose (Weinstein) Aaron; married Janet Summers, August, 1937; children: Jonathan, James, Paul. *Education:* University of Michigan, A.B., 1933; Harvard University, Ph.D., 1943. *Home:* 85 Washington Ave., Northampton, Mass.

CAREER: Harvard University, Cambridge, Mass., instructor, 1936-39; Smith College, Northampton, Mass., 1939—, began as instructor, became professor of English. Visiting professor, Bennington College, 1950-51, University of Helsinki, 1951-52, University of Warsaw, 1962-63. Also taught at Amherst College, Yale University, Barnard College, University of Wyoming, and other institutions.

WRITINGS: Men of Good Hope: A Story of American Progressives, Oxford University Press, 1951; (editor) *America in Crisis: Fourteen Crucial Episodes in American History*, Knopf, 1952; (with Richard Hofstadter and others) *The United States: The History of the Republic*, Prentice-Hall, 1957, 3rd edition, 1972; (editor, with Alfred Kazin) *Emerson: A Modern Anthology*, Houghton, 1959; (with Hofstadter and others) *The American Republic*, two volumes, Prentice-Hall, 1959, 2nd edition, 1970; *Writers on the Left*, Harcourt, 1961; (editor) Robert Herrick (1868-1938), *The Memoirs of an American Citizen*, Harvard University Press, 1963, (editor) Paul Elmer More, *Shelburne Essays on American Literature*, Harcourt, 1963; (editor) Newton Arvin, *American Pantheon: Essays*, Delacorte, 1966; (editor with R. H. Bremner) *Essays on History and Literature*, Ohio State University Press, 1966; (compiler) *The Strenuous Decade: A Social and Intellectual Record of the 1930's*, Anchor Books, 1970; (with Richard Hofstadter) *The Structure of American History*, 2nd edition, Prentice-Hall, 1973; *The Unwritten War: American Writers and the Civil War*, Knopf, 1973. Contributor to *Partisan Review, Hudson Review, Kenyon Review, Reporter, New Republic, New York Times Book Review, New Leader, New England Quarterly, American Heritage*, and other publications.†

*   *   *

AARONOVITCH, Sam 1919-

PERSONAL: Born December 27, 1919, in London, England; married L. G. J. Walmsley; children: four. *Educa-*

tion: Oxford University, D.Phil. *Home:* 19 Bromwich Ave., London N.6, England.

CAREER: Writer.

WRITINGS: Crisis in Kenya, Lawrence & Wishart, 1947; *The American Threat to British Culture*, Arena Publications, 1953; *Monopoly*, Lawrence & Wishart, 1956; *The Ruling Class*, Lawrence & Wishart, 1961; *Economics for Trade Unionists*, Lawrence & Wishart, 1964; *Big Business: Concentration and Mergers in the United Kingdom*, Macmillan, in press.

WORK IN PROGRESS: A book, *Economics of Modern Capitalism*; studies in oligopoly pricing and financial characteristics of large mergers in the United Kingdom.

*   *   *

ABBE, Elfriede (Martha) 1919-

PERSONAL: Born February 6, 1919, in Washington, D.C.; daughter of Cleveland (a professor and editor) and Frieda (Dauer) Abbe. *Education:* The Art Institute of Chicago, student, 1937; Cornell University, 1947, University of Florence, 1960, and University of Padua, 1961. *Home:* 24 Woodcrest Ave., Ithaca, N.Y.

CAREER: Sculptor and graphic artist, with work in permanent collections of National Gallery of Art, Boston Museum of Fine Arts, Henry E. Huntington Library and Art Gallery, New York Public Library, and other libraries and universities of United States, Canada, and England. Exhibitor at seven one-man shows, 1960-65; represented in Middle East tour of the Kerlan Collection, sponsored by U.S. Department of State, 1952, London Chappel Exhibition in England, 1963, U.S. Intelligence Agency Printing Exhibition on five continents, 1964. Commissions include "Hunter" for New York World's Fair, 1939, "Explorer" (wood carving) for McGill University Library, other wood and marble sculptures for libraries and churches, and city seals. *Member:* National Sculpture Society, Allied Artists of America, Phi Kappa Phi. *Awards, honors:* Tiffany fellowship, 1948; Hunt Foundation grant, 1961; Gold Medal, Pen and Brush Club of New York, 1964.

WRITINGS: (Self-illustrated) *The Plants of Virgil's Georgics*, Cornell University Press, 1965; (editor) George Waldo Abbe, *Letters of George Waldo Abbe and Charlotte Colgate Abbe*, Arnold Print Co., 1968; *Shore Imprints,*

Abbe Press, 1970; *An Introduction to Hand-Made Paper*, Southern Vermont Art Center Press, 1972.

Illustrator: *Aesop's Fables*, privately printed by Elfriede Abbe, 1950; *Rip van Winkle*, privately printed by Elfriede Abbe, 1951; *Prometheus Bound*, privately printed by Elfriede Abbe, 1952; (also designer and printer) *The American Scholar* (limited edition), Cornell University Press, 1955; (also designer and printer) *Garden Spice and Wild Pot-herbs* (limited edition), Cornell University Press, 1955; (also designer and printer) *The Significance of the Frontier in American History* (limited edition), Cornell University Press, 1956; (also designer and printer) *Seven Irish Tales* (limited edition), Cornell University Press, 1957; *The Revelation of St. John the Divine*, privately printed by Elfriede Abbe, 1958; (and translator) Puplius Vergilius Maro, *The Georgics of Virgil*, [Ithaca], 1966.

BIOGRAPHICAL/CRITICAL SOURCES: American Artist, April, 1960.†

*   *   *

ABERLE, Kathleen Gough   1925-
(Kathleen Gough)

PERSONAL: Born August 16, 1925, in Yorkshire, England; came to United States in 1955; daughter of Albert (an agricultural engineer) and Eleanor (Umpleby) Gough; married David F. Aberle (an anthropologist); children: Stephen Daniel. *Education:* Girton College, Cambridge, B.A., 1946, M.A., 1949, Ph.D., 1950. *Politics:* Socialist. *Home:* 3325 Storey Blvd., Eugene, Ore.

CAREER: Lecturer in anthropology at University of Manchester. Manchester, England, 1954-55, Wayne State University, Detroit, Mich., 1959-60; Brandeis University, Waltham, Mass., assistant professor, 1961-62; University of Oregon, Eugene, research associate in anthropology, 1963—. Field work in villages of Kerala, India, 1947-49, 1964, in villages of Tanjore, India, 1951-53. *Member:* American Anthropological Association, British Association of Social Anthropologists, Royal Anthropological Institute of Great Britain and Northern Ireland.

WRITINGS: Under name Kathleen Gough: (Co-author with David M. Schneider) *Matrilineal Kinships*, University of California Press, Berkeley, 1961; (editor with Hari P. Sharma) *Imperialism and Revolution in South Asia*, Monthly Review Press, 1973. Articles in anthropological journals.†

*   *   *

ABERNATHY, M(abra) Glenn   1921-

PERSONAL: Born November 25, 1921, in Birmingham, Ala.; son of James Robert and Esther (Vines) Abernathy; married Nancy Katherine Perry, September 6, 1949; children: Mabra Glenn, Jr., Thomas Duncan, Richard Comer. *Education:* Birmingham-Southern College, B.S., 1942; University of Alabama, M.A., 1947; University of Wisconsin, Ph.D., 1953. *Religion:* Methodist. *Home:* 41 Dinwood Circle, Columbia, S.C. 29204. *Office:* Bureau of Governmental Research, University of South Carolina, Columbia, S.C. 29208.

CAREER: Assistant city manager in Mountain Brook, Ala., 1947-48; University of Alabama, University, instructor in political science, 1948-49; University of South Carolina, Columbia, assistant professor, 1951-60, associate professor, 1960-64, professor of political science, 1964—, director of Bureau of Governmental Research, 1972—. Vis-

iting associate professor, University of Wisconsin, 1959-60. *Military service:* U.S. Army Air Forces, meteorologist, 1942-46; became captain. *Member:* American Political Science Association, American Association of University Professors, Southern Political Science Association. *Awards, honors:* Russell Award for Creative Research, University of South Carolina, 1963, for *The Right of Assembly and Association*.

WRITINGS: The Right of Assembly and Association, University of South Carolina Press, 1961; *Civil Liberties Under the Constitution*, Dodd, 1968, 2nd edition, 1972. Contributor of articles to *Alabama Law Review*, *Cornell Law Quarterly*, and *South Carolina Law Quarterly*.

WORK IN PROGRESS: Research on administrative law and processes.

*   *   *

ABRAHAM, Willard   1916-

PERSONAL: Born May 18, 1916, in Chicago, Ill.; son of Edward (in retail sales) and Sadie (Weiss) Abraham; married Dale Wiener, June 13, 1948; children: Edward, Andrew, Amy Rebecca. *Education:* Illinois Institute of Technology, B.S., 1940; Chicago Teachers College, M.Ed., 1942; Northwestern University, Ph.D., 1950. *Office:* Department of Special Education, Arizona State University, Tempe, Ariz. 85251.

CAREER: High school teacher in Chicago, Ill., vocational guidance editor of *Chicago Times*, Chicago, Ill., and associate editor of *Vocational Trends* prior to 1942; Roosevelt University, Chicago, Ill., associate professor of education, 1946-53; Arizona State University, Tempe, professor of education and chairman of department of special education, 1953—. Delegate to White House Conference on Education, 1955; consultant to White House Conference on Children and Youth, 1960, 1970. Educational adviser for two series of reading films for *Encyclopaedia Britannica*, 1952-54; consultant for *Our Wonderful World* (children's encyclopedia), 1955-57; chairman, Special Education Advisory Committee, Arizona State Department of Public Instruction; educational director, Learning, Inc.; chairman, Steering Committee for the Gifted in Arizona. *Military service:* U.S. Army, 1942-46.

MEMBER: National Society for the Study of Education, Association for Supervision and Curriculum Development, American Psychological Association, National Education Association, American Personnel and Guidance Association (professional member), International Reading Association, National Society for Programmed Instruction, Council for Exceptional Children (member of executive committee; governor-at-large), American Association of University Professors, Arizona Education Association, Phi Delta Kappa. *Awards, honors:* Faculty Achievement Award, Arizona State University, 1965.

WRITINGS: Your Post-War Career (textbook), U.S. Army, 1945; *Get the Job!*, Science Research Associates, 1946; *A Guide for the Study of Exceptional Children*, Sargent, 1956; (contributor) John R. Green and Harry F. Steelman, editors, *Epileptic Seizures*, Williams & Wilkins, 1957; *A New Look at Reading*, Sargent, 1957; *Barbara: A Prologue*, Rinehart, 1958; *Common Sense about Gifted Children*, Harper, 1958; (contributor) Bruce Shertzer, editor, *Working with Superior Students*, Science Research Associates, 1960; (contributor) James F. Magary and John R. Eichorn, editors, *The Exceptional Child*, Dryden Press, 1960; *The Slow Learner*, Center for Applied Research in Education, 1964; *A Time for Teaching*, Harper, 1964.

Author of booklets and pamphlets. Contributor to *Encyclopedia of Vocational Guidance*, 1948, *Childcraft*, 1964, *World Book*, 1975, and of more than ninety articles to *This Week*, *Today's Health*, *Family Circle*, *Library Journal*, various educational and psychological journals. Syndicated newspaper columnist for Copley News Service; columnist for *Arizona Republic*.

*   *   *

ABRAHAM, William E. 1934-

PERSONAL: Born May 28, 1934, in Lagos, Nigeria; son of Samuel and Effie (Anaman) Abraham; married Adelaide M. Yorke, July 26, 1960; children: Henry Edisa, Kwesi Edisa, Kofi Edisa. *Education:* University College of Ghana (now University of Ghana), B.A., 1957; Oxford University, B.Phil., 1959, M.A., 1959. *Politics:* Humanist. *Religion:* Christian. *Office:* Department of Philosophy, University of California, Santa Cruz, Calif. 95060.

CAREER: University of Liverpool, Liverpool, England, lecturer in philosophy, 1959-60; All Souls College, Oxford University, Oxford, England, fellow, 1959-62; University of Ghana, Legon, associate professor, 1962-64, professor of philosophy, 1964-70, pro-vice-chancellor, 1965-66; Macalester College, St. Paul, Minn., professor of philosophy, 1969-73; University of California at Santa Cruz, professor of philosophy and board chairman, 1973—. Fellow and member of advisory council, Hansberry College of African Studies, Nigeria, 1959-63; governor of School of Oriental and African Studies, University of London, 1960-66; member of Committee to Review Pre-university Education in Ghana, 1964. Andrew Mellon lecturer, Indiana University, 1969; visiting professor, University of California at Berkeley and Stanford University, 1972. Member of board of directors, Ghana Publishing Corp., 1964-66. Chairman, Presidential Commission of Inquiry into Trade in Ghana, 1965; member of Presidential Commission, Ghana, 1965. *Member:* Ghana Academy of Sciences (vice-president, 1962-66).

WRITINGS: The Mind of Africa, University of Chicago Press, 1962; (contributor) Roger Bannister, editor, *Prospect: The Schweppes Book of the New Generation*, Hutchinson, 1962; (contributor) *The Works of Amo*, Halle University Press, 1964. Translator of several other works. Contributor to *Times Literary Supplement*, *New Society*, *Mind*, *Studia Leibnitiana*, *Nous*, *Phronesis*, and other journals.

WORK IN PROGRESS: Leibniz and His Critics; *The Theory of Necessary Truth*; *Ghana: The Nkrumah Years*; *The Pre-Socratics*.

*   *   *

ABRAMS, Richard M. 1932-

PERSONAL: Born July 12, 1932, in Brooklyn, N.Y.; son of Nathan (an insurance agent) and Ida (Levine) Abrams; married Marcia Lee Ash, August 14, 1960; children: Laura Susan, Robert Samuel, Jennifer Sharon. *Education:* Columbia University, A.B., 1953, A.M., 1955, Ph.D., 1962. *Home:* 422 Michigan Ave., Berkeley, Calif. 94707. *Office:* Department of History, University of California, Berkeley, Calif. 94720.

CAREER: Columbia University, New York, N.Y., instructor in history, 1957-60; University of California, Berkeley, assistant professor of history, 1962—. *Member:* American Historical Association, Economic History Asso-

ciation, Organization of American Historians, Newcomen Society in North America. *Awards, honors:* Newcomen Award in Business History for article, "Brandeis and the New Haven Merger Revisited," in *Business History Review*, 1962.

WRITINGS: The Issue of Federal Regulation in the Progressive Era, Rand McNally, 1963; *Conservatism in a Progressive Era: Massachusetts Politics, 1900-1912*, Harvard University Press, 1964; (editor with Lawrence W. Levine) *The Shaping of Twentieth-Century America: Interpretive Essays*, Little, Brown, 1965, 2nd edition, 1971; *Issues of the Populist and Progressive Eras, 1892-1912*, University of South Carolina Press, 1970; (editor) Louis D. Brandeis, *Other People's Money and How the Bankers Use It*, Peter Smith, 1971; (contributor) William E. Leuchtenburg, editor, *The Unfinished Century: America since 1900*, Little, Brown, 1973. Contributor to professional journals.

WORK IN PROGRESS: Research on government-business relations in the United States, and foreign policy.

*   *   *

ADAMCZEWSKI, Zygmunt 1921-

PERSONAL: Born May 27, 1921, in Bydgoszcz, Poland; came to United States in 1951, naturalized in 1957; son of Stanislaw (a jurist) and Izabella (Gouth) Adamczewski; married Melanie Hafele, March 15, 1951; children: Eva Danuta, Jan Zygmunt. *Education:* Attended University of Innsbruck, 1945-46; University of London, B.A. (honours), 1951; Columbia University, A.M., 1952; Harvard University, Ph.D., 1956. *Home:* 27 Royal York Rd., St. Catherines, Ontario, Canada. *Office:* Department of Philosophy, Brock University, St. Catherines, Ontario, Canada.

CAREER: Harvard University, Cambridge, Mass., teaching fellow, 1954; Long Island University, New York, N.Y., visiting instructor, 1955; Montana State University, Missoula, assistant professor of philosophy, 1956-62; University of Waterloo, Waterloo, Ontario, associate professor, 1962-67, professor of philosophy, 1967-69; Brock University, St. Catherines, Ontario, professor of philosophy and chairman of department, 1969—. *Military service:* Polish Army, 1938-39; became ensign. *Member:* American Philosophical Association, Canadian Philosophical Association.

WRITINGS: The Tragic Protest, Nijhoff, 1964; (contributor) James M. Edie, editor, *New Essays in Phenomenology*, Quadrangle, 1969; (contributor) John Sallis, editor, *Heidegger and the Path of Thinking*, Duquesne University Press, 1970. Contributor to *Diogenes*, *Journal of Philosophy*, *Journal of Existentialism*, *Chicago Review*, *Man and World*, *Philosophy East and West*.

WORK IN PROGRESS: The Question of Ethics in Our Time.

*   *   *

ADAMS, Clifton 1919-
(Jonathan Gant, Matt Kinkaid, Clay Randall)

PERSONAL: Born December 1, 1919, in Comanche, Okla.; son of Cleveland Alexander and Julia (Hendrix) Adams; married Gerry Griffeth, September 29, 1948. *Education:* Attended University of Oklahoma. *Politics:* Independent. *Home and office:* 1116 Marlboro Lane, Oklahoma City, Okla. 73116. *Agent:* Paul R. Reynolds & Son, 599 Fifth Ave., New York, N.Y. 10017.

CAREER: Former professional jazz drummer; free-lance

writer, 1948—. *Military service:* U.S. Army, 1942-45; became sergeant; received five battle stars. *Member:* Western Writers of America, Oklahoma Historical Society.

WRITINGS—All published by Gold Medal Books, unless otherwise indicated: *The Desperado*, 1950; *A Noose for the Desperado*, 1951; *The Colonel's Lady*, 1952; *Whom Gods Destroy*, 1953; *Two Gun Law*, 1954; *Death's Sweet Song*, 1955; *Gambing Man*, 1956; *Law of the Trigger*, 1956; *The Race of Giants*, Dell, 1956.

Killer in Town, Dell, 1960; *Stranger in Town*, Doubleday, 1960; *The Legend of Lonnie Hall*, Berkley, 1960; *Day of the Gun*, Ballantine, 1962; *Reckless Men*, Doubleday, 1962; *Hogan's Way*, Berkley, 1962; *The Moonlight War*, Gold Medal Books, 1963; *The Dangerous Days of Kiowa Jones*, Doubleday, 1964; *Doomsday Creek*, Doubleday, 1964; *The Hottest Fourth of July in the History of Hangtree County*, Doubleday, 1964; *The Grabhorn Bounty*, Doubleday, 1965; *Shorty*, Doubleday, 1966; *Concannon*, Doubleday, 1972; *Hard Times and Arnie Smith*, Doubleday, 1972; *The Badge of Harry Cole*, Ace Books, 1973; *Biscuit-Shooter*, Manor Books, 1973; *The Last Days of Wolf Garnett*, Ace Books, 1973; *Once an Outlaw*, Ace Books, 1973; *Tragg's Choice*, Ace Books, 1973; *The Hard Time Bunch*, Doubleday, 1973; *Hassle and the Medicine Man*, Doubleday, 1973.

Under pseudonym Jonathan Gant: *Never Say No to a Killer*, Ace Books, 1956; *The Long Vendetta*, Avalon, 1964.

Under pseudonym Matt Kinkaid: *Hardcase,* Avon, 1953.

Under pseudonym Clay Randall: *Six Gun Boss*, Random House, 1952; *When Oil Ran Red*, Random House, 1953; *Boomer*, Pocket Books, 1957; *The Oceola Kid*, Gold Medal Books, 1963; *Hardcase for Hire*, Gold Medal Books, 1963; *Amos Flagg—Lawman*, Gold Medal Books, 1964.

WORK IN PROGRESS: A bibliography of the Southwest, underway for five years and "no end in sight."

SIDELIGHTS: "At one time my output was divided almost equally between westerns and mystery fiction, but since 1960 I have settled definitely on the history of the Southwest as a backdrop for my novels, thanks largely to W. Foster-Harris, head of the professional writing section of the School of Journalism at the University of Oklahoma.

"Major passions: Sport cars, rare books (especially those relating to Southwest literature and history), and the classical guitar, the study of which consumes a great part of my time away from the typewriter."†

*   *   *

ADAMS, Robert P.   1910-

PERSONAL: Born April 21, 1910, in Detroit, Mich.; son of William Henry and Florence (Gossard) Adams; married Roberta England, October 8, 1932 (divorced, 1960); married Marjorie W. Ford, June 10, 1961; children: (first marriage) Robert William, Claire Wentworth. *Education:* Oberlin College, B.A., 1931, graduate student, 1931-32; University of Chicago, Ph.D., 1937. *Politics:* Independent. *Religion:* Unitarian Universalist. *Home:* 3180 Northeast 82nd St., Seattle, Wash. 98115. *Office:* Padelford Hall, GN-30, University of Washington, Seattle, Wash. 98195.

CAREER: Michigan State University, East Lansing, 1937-47, began as instructor, became associate professor of English; University of Washington, Seattle, associate profes-

sor, 1947-66, professor of Renaissance English literature, 1966—. *Member:* Modern Language Association of America, Renaissance Society of America, American Association of University Professors, American Civil Liberties Union, Caxton Club (Chicago), Queen City Yacht Club (Seattle). *Awards, honors:* Folger Shakespeare Library, fellow, 1956, senior fellow, 1971-72; Newberry Library, senior fellow, 1964-65.

WRITINGS: The Better Part of Valor: More, Erasmus, Colet, and Vives on Humanism, War, and Peace, 1496-1535, University of Washington Press, 1962; (contributor) U. M. Ellis-Fermor, editor, *Jacobean Drama*, Methuen, 5th edition, 1965; (contributor) *Pacific Coast Studies in Shakespeare*, University of Oregon Press, 1965.

Monographs—published by University of Washington Independent Studies: *Shakespeare*, 1967; *Shakespeare's Comedies and Histories*, 1967; *Shakespeare's Tragedies*, 1967; *Utopias and Social Ideals*, 1967; *Renaissance Drama Exclusive of Shakespeare*, 1969; *Shakespeare: An Introduction*, 1970; *Shakespeare to 1603*, 1970; *Shakespeare after 1603*, 1973.

Contributor to library and literature journals, 1941—.

WORK IN PROGRESS: Reason versus Passion in Jacobean and Twentieth Century English Tragedy; *Chapman's Original "Bussy D'Ambois": A Critical Study*; *The Abuse of Greatness: Shakespeare, Greville, Marston, Chapman, and Ben Jonson, ca. 1596-1603*; *The World's a Stage: An Approach to Renaissance English Drama Exclusive of Shakespeare*, the latter two for University of Washington Press.

AVOCATIONAL INTERESTS: Travel in northern Europe, photography, yachting (power and sail).

*   *   *

ADAMS, Thomas F.   1927-

PERSONAL: Born August 30, 1927, in Springfield, Mo.; son of Charles Henry (a mortician) and Marguerite (Kibbe) Adams; married Nora Ann Chambers, February 4, 1946; children: Thomas Jr., Norina, Brian. *Education:* Studied at San Francisco Conservatory of Music, 1947-48, Orange Coast College, 1955-56, California State College (now University), Long Beach, part time, 1956—. *Home:* 1333 South Arapahoe Dr., Santa Ana, Calif. 92704.

CAREER: Santa Ana Police Department, Santa Ana, Calif., 1954—, now lieutenant. Instructor in subjects related to police work at Santa Ana College, 1959-61, Orange Coast College, Costa Mesa, Calif., 1961—, and at California State Colleges (now Universities), Long Beach and Los Angeles. *Military service:* U.S. Navy, 1944-46. *Member:* International Association of Polygraph Examiners (treasurer, 1962-64), Orange County Peace Officers' Association.

WRITINGS: Training Officers' Handbook, Thomas, 1964; *Law Enforcement: An Introduction to the Police Role in the Community*, Prentice-Hall, 1968, 2nd edition, 1973; *Police Patrol: Tactics and Techniques*, Prentice-Hall, 1971; (compiler) *Criminal Justice: Readings*, Goodyear Publishing Co., 1972; (with others) *Criminal Justice: Organization and Management* (text edition), Goodyear Publishing Co., 1974. Contributor of about thirty-five articles to *Police* and *Arizona Sheriff*.

WORK IN PROGRESS: A series of articles on areas of police responsibility for *Arizona Sheriff*, for later publication in book form.†

ADAMSON, David Grant 1927-

PERSONAL: Born November 8, 1927, in Oxford, England; son of Pierre Duncan (a dentist) and Katharine (Tracy) Grant-Adamson; married Barbara Parrott, October 11, 1958; children: Alisoun (stepdaughter), Alexander, Oliver. *Education:* "Virtually nil—three years at a British public school." *Politics:* Liberal. *Home:* 186 Second St. Extension, Avondale, Salisbury, Rhodesia. *Office: Daily Telegraph,* Fleet St., London E.D. 4, England.

CAREER: Daily Telegraph Ltd., London, England, education reporter, *Daily Telegraph,* 1956-57, Paris correspondent, *Daily Telegraph,* 1958, deputy diplomatic and Commonwealth correspondent, *Sunday Telegraph,* 1960-63, central African correspondent for both daily and Sunday papers, 1964—. Broadcaster on Middle Eastern topics. *Military service:* Royal Marines, 1945-47; became lieutenant.

WRITINGS: The Kurdish War, Allen & Unwin, 1964, Praeger, 1965. Writer of television scripts.

WORK IN PROGRESS: A novel; research in African rebel or freedom movements and their histories.

SIDELIGHTS: Adamson was in Algeria during the revolt, in the Congo during the United Nations intervention, and has traveled in South America, Cuba, and the Middle East. He views journalism as a series of enterprises rather than a career in the accepted sense, and finds it "an excellent job for a slightly choleric egocentric."†

*   *   *

ADAMSON, Gareth 1925-

PERSONAL: Born May 10, 1925, in Liverpool, England; son of William John (a manufacturer) and Isobel (Hughes) Adamson; married Jean Elizabeth Bailey (a free-lance artist), October 5, 1957; children: Leo, Gabrielle, Kate. *Education:* Edinburgh College of Art and Architecture, student, 1944-46; Goldsmiths' College, University of London, National Diploma in Design (illustration), 1951. *Politics:* Liberal. *Religion:* Roman Catholic. *Home:* 1 Bailiffgate, Alnwick, Northumberland, England. *Agent:* London Authors, 8 Upper Brook St., London W. 1, England.

CAREER: Hunt Partners Ltd. (packaging), London, England, research designer, 1952-53; Cravens Advertising Ltd., Newcastle upon Tyne, England, creative chief, 1953-57; free-lance author and illustrator of children's books, 1957—. *Awards, honors:* First prize from British Broadcasting Corp, and North East Association for the Arts, for a television play, 1965.

WRITINGS—Illustrated by wife, Jean Adamson; all published by Blackie & Son except as indicated: *Topsy and Tim's Monday Book,* 1959; *Topsy and Tim's Tuesday Book,* 1959; *Topsy and Tim's Wednesday Book,* 1960; *Topsy and Tim's Thursday Book,* 1960; *Topsy and Tim's Friday Book,* 1961; *Topsy and Tim's Saturday Book,* 1961; *Topsy and Tim's Sunday Book,* 1962; *Topsy and Tim's Foggy Day,* 1962; *Neighbours in the Park,* Harrap, 1962; *Topsy and Tim at the Football Match,* 1963; *Topsy and Tim Go Fishing,* 1963; *Topsy and Tim's Bonfire Night,* 1964; *Topsy and Tim's Snowy Day,* 1964.

Author and illustrator: *Old Man up a Tree,* Abelard, 1963; *Mr. Budge Builds a House,* Brockhampton Press, 1963; *Three Discontented Clowns,* Abelard, 1966; *Mr. Budge Buys a Car,* Brockhampton Press, 1968; *Mr. Budge Builds a House,* Chilton Book Co., 1968; *Harold, the Happy Handyman,* Harvey House, 1968; (with wife, Jean Adamson) *Family Tree,* A. Whitman, 1968; *Machines at*

Home, Lutterworth, 1969; (with J. Adamson) *Hullo, Topsy and Tim,* Blackie & Son, 1971; (with J. Adamson) *Surprises for Topsy and Tim,* Blackie & Son, 1971; *People at Home,* Lutterworth Press, 1972; (with J. Adamson) *Topsy and Tim's Ups and Downs,* Blackie & Sons, 1973.

Illustrator: Charles Hatcher, *What Shape Is It?,* Brockhampton Press, 1963; Charles Hatcher, *What Size Is It?,* Brockhampton Press, 1964, Duell, Sloan & Pearce, 1965.

WORK IN PROGRESS: A history of domestic equipment from about 1800, for children, for Lutterworth Press.

SIDELIGHTS: Adamson's artistic interests include cartoon and animated puppet films (he and his wife have devised a method of puppet animation but haven't had time to develop it), and architecture. The Adamsons live in a house built in 1725 on the site of the old Baliff Gate, precisely ten paces from Alnwick Castle.†

*   *   *

ADDISON, William Wilkinson 1905-

PERSONAL: Born April 4, 1905, in Bashall Eaves, West Riding, Yorkshire, England; son of Joseph (a farmer) and Jane (Wilkinson) Addison; married Phoebe Dean, April 3, 1929. *Education:* Attended schools in Lancashire, England. *Home:* Ravensmere, Epping, Essex, England.

CAREER: Writer and bookseller. Justice of the peace, 1949; chairman of Epping bench, 1955; verderer of Epping Forest, Essex, England, 1957; Magistrates' Association of England and Wales, member of council, 1959—; deputy chairman, 1966-69; chairman, 1970—; former member of government committees dealing with the treatment of offenders. *Member:* Archaeological Society (council, 1949; president, 1964-67), Society of Antiquaries (fellow), Royal Historical Society (fellow).

WRITINGS: Epping Forest: Its Literary and Historical Associations, Dent, 1945; *The English Country Parson,* Dent, 1947; *Essex Heyday,* Dent, 1949; *Suffolk,* R. Hale, 1950; *English Spas,* Batsford, 1951; *Worthy Dr. Fuller,* Dent, 1951; *Audley End,* Dent, 1953; *English Fairs and Markets,* Batsford, 1953; *Thames Estuary,* R. Hale, 1954; *In the Steps of Charles Dickens,* Rich & Cowan, 1955; *Essex Worthies,* Phillimore, 1972; *Wanstead Park,* Corporation of London, 1972. Writer of journal articles on sociological subjects.

WORK IN PROGRESS: Research on church dedications and various aspects of Epping Forest and Essex history.

*   *   *

ADKINS, Dorothy C. 1912-
(Dorothy Adkins Wood)

PERSONAL: Born April 6, 1912, in Atlanta, Ohio; daughter of George Hoadley and Pearl (James) Adkins; married David L. Wood, 1959. *Education:* Ohio State University, B.Sc. in Education, 1931, Ph.D., 1937. *Home:* 122 West Second Ave., Plain City, Ohio 43064. *Office:* 2633 Neil Ave., Columbus, Ohio 43204.

CAREER: University of Chicago, Chicago, Ill., assistant examiner, Board of Examinations, 1936-38, research associate in psychology, 1938-40; U.S. Social Security Board, Washington, D.C., chief of research and test construction unit, 1940-44; U.S. Civil Service Commission, Washington, D.C., chief of social science testing, 1944-46, policy consultant to examination division, 1946-48, chief of test development section, 1948; University of North Carolina, Chapel

Hill, professor of psychology, 1948-66, chairman of department, 1950-59; University of Hawaii, Honolulu, professor of educational psychology and researcher, 1966-74; Consulting and Publishing, Inc., Columbus, Ohio, 1974—. Part-time supervisor, North Carolina Merit System Council, 1956-58; member of cooperative research advisory committee, U.S. Office of Education, periodically, 1958—.

MEMBER: American Psychological Association (fellow; recording secretary, 1949-52; member of board of directors, 1956-58), Psychometric Society (president, 1949-50), North Carolina Psychological Association (president, 1951-52), Southeastern Psychological Association (secretary-treasurer, 1964-67), Scholaris, Pi Mu Epsilon, Gamma Psi Kappa, Pi Lambda Theta, Sigma Xi.

WRITINGS: (With others) *Construction and Analysis of Achievement Tests*, U.S. Government Printing Office, 1948; (contributor) E. F. Lindquist, editor, *Educational Measurement*, American Council on Education, 1951; (with Samuel B. Lyerly) *Factor Analysis of Reasoning Tests*, University of North Carolina Press, 1952; (under name Dorothy Adkins Wood) *Test Construction*, C. E. Merrill, 1960; *Louis Leon Thurstone*, Educational Testing Services, 1962; (under name Dorothy Adkins Wood) *Statistics: An Introduction for Students in the Behavioral Sciences*, C. E. Merrill, 1964, 2nd edition, 1974. Contributor of articles and reviews to professional journals. Assistant managing editor, *Psychometrika*, 1937-50, managing editor, 1950-56, member of editorial board, 1956-72; associate editor, *Educational and Psychological Measurement*, 1940-52, member of board of cooperating editors, 1953—; editorial consultant, *Public Personnel Review*, 1955-58.

*   *   *

ADLER, Jacob H(enry) 1919-

PERSONAL: Born March 26, 1919, in Evansville, Ind.; son of Hiram J. and Jessica (Oberndorfer) Adler; married Emily Rowe, June 1, 1952; children: Jennifer, James. *Education:* University of Florida, B.A., 1939, M.A., 1947; Harvard University, A.M., 1948, Ph.D., 1951. *Religion:* Presbyterian. *Home:* 1523 Summit Dr., West Lafayette, Ind. 47906. *Office:* Department of English, Purdue University, Lafayette, Ind. 47907.

CAREER: University of Kentucky, Lexington, 1949-50, 1951-69, started as instructor, professor of English, 1965-69, chairman of department of English, speech, and dramatic arts, 1964-69; Purdue University, Lafayette, Ind., professor and head of English department, 1969—. Fulbright lecturer in India, 1960-61. *Military service:* U.S. Army, 1942-46; became technical sergeant; received Bronze Star. *Member:* Modern Language Association of America, National Council of Teachers of English, Midwest Modern Language Association, American Association of University Professors, American Society for Eighteenth Century Studies, Johnson Society of the Central Region.

WRITINGS: (Contributor) *South: Modern Southern Literature in Its Cultural Setting*, edited by Louis J. Rubin, Jr. and Robert D. Jacobs, Doubleday, 1961; (contributor) *Graham Greene: Some Critical Considerations*, edited by Robert O. Evans, University of Kentucky Press, 1963; *The Reach of Art: A Study in the Prosody of Pope*, University of Florida Press, 1964; *Lillian Hellman*, Steck-Vaughn, 1969. Contributor of articles on modern drama, eighteenth-century English literature, and literary criticism to scholarly journals.

WORK IN PROGRESS: Article on Samuel Johnson's

prosody to appear in *Studies in the Literary Imagination*; major current interest is influence of Ibsen on later dramatists.

*   *   *

AHERN, Margaret McCrohan 1921-
(Peg O'Connell)

PERSONAL: Born February 16, 1921, in New York, N.Y.; daughter of John and Margaret (O'Connell) McCrohan; married Edward Ahern (a postal superintendent), July 16, 1947; children: Michael, Maripat, James, Joanne, Edward, Jr. *Education:* Attended Harrison Art School, 1939-40, American Academy of Art, 1941-43, Chicago Academy of Fine Arts, 1943, and Chicago Art Institute. *Religion:* Catholic. *Home:* 1901 South 18th Ave., Maywood, Ill. 60153.

CAREER: New World, editorial cartoonist, 1943-45; freelance cartoonist and illustrator, 1950—; National Catholic Welfare Conference Features, cartoonist, 1958—. Cartoonist for television panel, "Cartuno," 1950-51, for monthly strips, "Beano" and "Angelo," for syndicated panel, "Speck the Altar Boy," 1954—, and for syndicated panel, "Our Parish," the last under pseudonym Peg O'Connell. *Member:* West Suburban Art Guild.

WRITINGS: Speck the Altar Boy, Doubleday, 1958; *Presenting Speck the Altar Boy*, Doubleday, 1960; *A Speck of Trouble*, Doubleday, 1964; (under pseudonym Peg O'Connell) *Our Parish* (cartoons), John Knox, 1968.

Illustrator: Velma Neiberding, *Sugar and Spice*, Catholic Home Journal Press, 1949; William Gillooly, *Mickey the Angel*, Newman, 1953; V. Neiberding, *Nice Guy*, Catholic Home Journal Press, 1954.†

*   *   *

AINSWORTH, Norma
(Norma Paul Ruedi)

PERSONAL: Born in Clinton, Mo.; daughter of Paul J. and Minnie Lee (Morris) Ruedi; married Freedom H. Ainsworth (president of Ainsworth Development, Inc.), July 31, 1954. *Education:* Lindenwood College, A.B.; Southern Methodist University, M.A.; postgraduate study at University of Missouri and New York University. *Religion:* Episcopalian. *Home:* 27 West Tenth St., New York, N.Y. 10011. *Office:* Scholastic Magazines, Inc., 50 West 44th St., New York, N.Y. 10036.

CAREER: Columnist and feature writer for newspapers in Missouri and Texas, 1932-35; teacher in high school and college, Bolivar, Mo., 1935-43; Colorado State University, Fort Collins, an assistant editor, 1943-44; U.S. Department of the Interior, radio assistant, later chief of editorial section, Bureau of Reclamation, 1944-49, director of publicity, Bureau of Land Management, 1949-54; publicity director for various civic groups, Salisbury, Md., 1954-58; Mac-Fadden Publications, New York, N.Y., managing editor of *True Experiences*, 1960-61; Scholastic Magazines, Inc., New York, N.Y., fiction editor of *Practical English* and *Co-ed*, 1961-62, fiction editor of books and magazines, secondary school level, 1962-67, editor of manuscript department, 1967—. *Member:* Authors Guild, American Association of University Women, Mystery Writers of America (chairman, juvenile awards, 1963-64, and 1973; member, board of directors, 1973; secretary, 1974); Alpha Sigma Tau.

WRITINGS: (Under name Norma Paul Ruedi) *If Dreams*

Came True and Other Poems, Avondale Press, 1927; (editor) *Hit Parade of Mystery Stories*, Scholastic Magazines, 1963; (editor) *14 Favorite Christmas Stories*, Scholastic Magazines, 1964; (editor) *The Last Bullet and Other Stories of the West*, Scholastic Magazines, 1965; (editor) *A Matter of Choice and Other Stories for Today*, Scholastic Magazines, 1965; *The Case of the Crying Child* (juvenile mystery), Action Books, in press. Contributor to *Writers' Yearbook*, 1964. Articles, short stories, and poetry have appeared in magazines and newspapers, including *Alaska Sportsman*, *Farm Journal*, *Saturday Review*, *Ozarkian*, *Popular Mechanics*, *Writer*.

* * *

AITKEN, A(dam) J(ack) 1921-

PERSONAL: Surname rhymes with *taken*; born June 19, 1921, in Edinburgh, Scotland; son of Adam (a coal miner) and Alexandrina (Sutherland) Aitken; married Norma Manson, June 19, 1952; children: Kenneth, Christine, Matthew, James. *Education:* University of Edinburgh, M.A. (first class honors), 1947. *Office: Dictionary of the Older Scottish Tongue*, 27 George Sq., Edinburgh, Scotland; and Department of English Language, University of Edinburgh, Edinburgh, Scotland.

CAREER: University of Edinburgh, Edinburgh, Scotland, assistant lecturer on the English language, 1947-48; research fellow at Universities of Glasgow, Aberdeen, and Edinburgh, Scotland, 1948-54, assisting Sir William Craigie on *A Dictionary of the Older Scottish Tongue*; lecturer at Universities of Glasgow and Edinburgh, 1954-65; University of Edinburgh, honorary senior lecturer, 1965-71, senior lecturer on the English language, 1971—. *Military service:* British Army, Royal Artillery, 1941-45; became sergeant. *Member:* Scottish Text Society (member of council, 1962—), Scottish National Dictionary Association (member of council, 1960—), Association for Scottish Literary Studies (chairman of language committee, 1971—).

WRITINGS: (editor with William Craigie) *Dictionary of the Older Scottish Tongue*, University of Chicago Press, Volume III, 1964, (editor) Volume IV, 1973; (editor with Angus McIntosh and Hermann Palsson, and contributor) *Edinburgh Studies in English and Scots*, Longman, 1971; (editor with R. W. Bailey and Neil Hamilton-Smith) *The Computer and Literary Studies*, Edinburgh University Press, 1973; (editor) *Lowland Scots*, Association for Scottish Literary Studies, 1973.

Contributor: Roy A. Wisbey, editor, *The Computer in Literary and Linguistic Research*, Cambridge University Press, 1971; H. Scholler and J. Reidy, editors, *Lexicography and Dialect Geography*, Franz Steiner Verlag (Wiesbaden, Germany), 1973; Raven J. McDavid, Jr., and Audrey R. Duckert, editors, *Lexicography in English*, New York Academy of Sciences, 1973; *Tavola Rotonda sui Grandi Lessici Storici*, Accademia della Cousca (Florence), 1973. Contributor of articles and reviews to *Scotsman*, *Scottish Genealogist*, *Scottish Historical Review*, *Scottish Literary News*, *Times Literary Supplement*, and other journals. Consultative member of the editorial committee of *Dictionary of Modern English Pronunciation*, 1972.

WORK IN PROGRESS: Volume V of *A Dictionary of the Older Scottish Tongue*; with Paul Bratley and Neil Hamilton-Smith, "The Older Scottish Textual Archive," a computer-readable archive of Older Scottish texts; contributions to *Collins English Dictionary*.

SIDELIGHTS: Aitken's chief modern languages are French and Icelandic.

* * *

AKERS, Charles W(esley) 1920-

PERSONAL: Born April 2, 1920, in Indianapolis, Ind.; son of Ira R. (a minister) and Mary B. (Lowe) Akers; married Eleanor Marie Emery (an elementary teacher), August 12, 1948; children: Marcie, Carolyn, Jeffrey. *Education:* Eastern Nazarene College, A.B., 1947; Boston University, A.M., 1948, Ph.D., 1952. *Religion:* Presbyterian. *Home:* 538 Clair Hill Dr., Rochester, Mich. 48063. *Office:* Department of History, Oakland University, Rochester, Mich.

CAREER: Eastern Nazarene College, Wollaston, Mass., 1948-59, became professor of history; Quincy Junior College, Quincy, Mass., director, 1959-60; Geneva College, Beaver Falls, Pa., professor of history, 1960-66; Oakland University, Rochester, Mich., professor of history, 1966—, chairman of department, 1968-71. *Military service:* U.S. Navy, 1942-46. *Member:* American Historical Association, Colonial Society of Massachusetts.

WRITINGS: Called Unto Liberty: A Life of Jonathan Mayhew, 1720-1766, Harvard University Press, 1964.

* * *

ALBRAND, Martha 1914-
(Other pseudonyms, Katrin Holland, Christine Lambert)

PERSONAL: Given name, Heidi Huberta; born September 8, 1914, in Rostock, Germany; came to United States, 1937; naturalized, 1947; daughter of Paul and Paula Freybe; married Joseph M. Loewengard, 1932; married second husband, Sydney J. Lamon. *Education:* Studied under private tutors and at schools in Italy, France, Switzerland, and England. *Religion:* Lutheran. *Agent:* Robert Lantz, 114 East 55th St., New York, N.Y. 10022. *Office:* 953 Fifth Ave., New York, N.Y. 10021.

CAREER: Began as journalist in Europe; had first book published at age of seventeen; used pseudonym Katrin Holland, 1930-40, and pseudonym Martha Albrand, 1940—. *Member:* P.E.N. *Awards, honors:* Le Grand Prix de Literature Policiers for *Desperate Moment*.

WRITINGS—Under pseudonym Martha Albrand: *No Surrender*, Little, Brown, 1942; *Without Orders*, Little, Brown, 1943; *Endure No Longer*, Little, Brown, 1944; *None Shall Know*, Little, Brown, 1945; *Remembered Anger*, Little, Brown, 1946; *Whispering Hill*, Random House, 1947; *After Midnight*, Random House, 1948; *Wait for the Dawn*, Random House, 1950; *Desperate Moment*, Random House, 1951; *Challenge*, Random House, 1951; *The Hunted Woman*, Random House, 1952; *Nightmare in Copenhagen*, Random House, 1954; *The Mask of Alexander*, Random House, 1955; *The Liden Affair*, Random House, 1956; *The Story That Could Not Be Told*, Hodder & Stoughton, 1956; *The Obsession of Emmet Booth*, Random House, 1957; *A Day in Monte Carlo*, Random House, 1959; *Meet Me Tonight*, Random House, 1960; *A Call from Austria*, Random House, 1963; *A Door Fell Shut*, New American Library, 1966; *Rhine Replica*, Random House, 1969; *Manhattan North*, Coward, 1971; *Zuerich/AZ 900*, Holt, 1974.

Under pseudonym Katrin Holland: *Man spricht uber Jacqueline*, Ullstein, 1930; *Wie macht Man das Nur!*, G. Stalling, 1930; *Unterwegs zu Alexander*, Ullstein, 1932; *Die silberne Wolke*, Ullstein, 1933 (translation by June Head published in England as *The Silver Cloud*, Nicholson & Watson, 1936); *Girl Tumbles Out of the Sky*, Nicholson & Watson, 1934; *Babbett auf Gottes Gnaden*, Ullstein, 1934; *Das Frauenhaus*, Orell Fussli, 1935; *Das Madchen, das niemand mochte*, Ullstein, 1935; *Youth Breaks in*, Nicholson & Watson, 1935; *Sandro irrt sich*, Orell Fussli, 1936; *Einsamer Himmel*, Orell Fussli, 1938; *Carlotta Torrensani*, Orell Fussli, 1938; *Vierzehn Tage mit Edith*, Orell Fussli, 1939; *Helene*, Orell, Fussli, 1940.

Under pseudonym Christine Lambert: *The Ball*, Atheneum, 1961; *A Sudden Woman*, Atheneum, 1964.

Contributor of short stories to *Ladies' Home Journal*, *Town and Country*, *Saturday Evening Post*, and other magazines.

SIDELIGHTS: Most of the Martha Albrand mystery stories ran as serials in the *Saturday Evening Post* before publication in book form. Many of them have been translated into German, Danish, Italian, French, Swedish, Arabic, and other languages. The film rights to both *The Sudden Woman* and *No Surrender* were sold. *Avocational interests:* Travel, dogs, gardening, fishing.

*   *   *

ALCORN, Marvin D.   1902-

PERSONAL: Born August 10, 1902, in Helena, Okla.; son of George W. (a farmer) and Pearl (Wheeler) Alcorn; married Ruby Miller, May 22, 1926; children: Richard. *Education:* Southwestern College, Winfield, Kan., A.B., 1925; Columbia University, M.A., 1931; University of Southern California, Ed.D., 1942. *Religion:* Protestant. *Home:* 4808 Atlanta Dr., San Diego, Calif. 92115. *Office:* San Diego State University, San Diego, Calif. 92115.

CAREER: High school teacher and principal, and superintendent of schools in Kansas, 1925-38; San Diego State University, San Diego, Calif., 1941-43, 1946—, now professor of education. Conductor of summer tours to Europe, 1960, 1963, and world tour, 1966. *Military service:* U.S. Naval Reserve, 1943-46; became lieutenant commander. *Member:* American Educational Research Association, National Education Association, Phi Delta Kappa.

WRITINGS: (With Richard Howseman and Jim Schunert) *Better Teaching in Secondary Schools*, Henry Holt, 1954, (with J. S. Kinder and J. R. Schunert) 3rd revised edition, Holt, 1970; *Issues in Curriculum Development*, World Book, 1959.

WORK IN PROGRESS: A series of paperbacks on such subjects as planning for instruction and discipline.†

*   *   *

ALDAN, Daisy   1923-

PERSONAL: Born September 16, 1923, in New York, N.Y.; daughter of Louis (a designer) and Esther (an actress; maiden name, Edelheit) Aldan; married Richard Miller (a publisher), marriage now annulled. *Education:* Hunter College (now of the City University of New York), B.A., 1943; Brooklyn College (now of the City University of New York), M.A., 1948; graduate study, New York University. *Home:* 325 East 57th St., New York, N.Y. 10022; and 15 Bannhollenweg, Dornach 4143, Switzerland.

CAREER: Actress on a regular dramatic program, Columbia Broadcasting System, 1930-57; also actress in stock theater, playing many classical roles; School of Art and Design, New York, N.Y., teacher of English, creative writing, literature, speech, and films, 1948-73; Ecole Libre des Hautes Etudes (French University of New York), member of Faculte des Lettres; publisher, small press, 1953—. Teacher of creative writing, Emerson College, Sussex, England, summer, 1971, Rudolf Steiner Institute, Spring Valley, N.Y., summer, 1973 and 1974, and Goetheanum, Switzerland, 1974. Member of board of directors, Folder Editions. *Member:* P.E.N., World Congress of Poets, Poetry Society of America (former member of executive board), Academy of American Poets, Poetry Forum, Film-Makers' Cooperative. *Awards, honors:* Herman Ritter award; Plymouth Drama Festival award; DeWitt American Lyric Poetry Award, 1967; National Foundation of the Arts poetry prize, 1968; first prize for poetry, Rochester Festival of the Arts, 1969; Poetry Forum award, 1970; Litt.D., University of Karachi, 1970.

WRITINGS—Poetry: *Poems, by Daisy Aldan* (pamphlet), Rumyon Press, 1946; *The Destruction of Cathedrals and Other Poems* (with a preface by Anais Nin), Two Cities Press, 1963; *The Masks Are Becoming Faces* (pamphlet), Goosetree Press, 1964; (with Stella Snead) *Seven: Seven* (poems and photographs), Folder Editions, 1965; *Or Learn to Walk on Water*, Folder Editions, 1970; *Journey*, Folder Editions, 1970; *+1=1: An ESP Poetry Experience with Elaine Mendlowitz*, Folder Editions, 1970; *Breakthrough: Poems in a New Idiom*, Folder Editions, 1971; *Love Poems of Daisy Aldan*, Barlenmir House, 1972; *Stones*, Folder Editions, 1973.

Translator: Stephane Mallarme, *A Throw of the Dice Never Will Abolish Chance*, Tiber Press, 1959; Albert Steffen, *Selected Poems*, Volume I, Folder Editions, 1968; *Some Poems of Albert Steffen*, Satyabrata Pal (Calcutta), 1969; (with Elly Simons) Steffen, *The Death Experience of Manes* (a play in verse), Folder, 1970; Rudolf Steiner, *The Soul Calendar*, Anthroposophic Press, 1974.

Editor: *A New Folder: Americans: Poems and Drawings* (with a foreword by Wallace Fowlie), Folder Editions, 1959; *Poems from India*, Crowell, 1969.

Poetry is represented in twelve major anthologies, including: *New Orlando Poetry Anthology*, edited by A. Vrbovska and others, New Orlando Publications, 1968; *Adam Among the Television Trees: An Anthology of Verse by Contemporary Christian Poets*, edited by Virginia R. Mollenkott, Word Books, 1971; *Fifty-Three American Poets of Today*, edited by Ruth W. Diamant, R. West, 1973; *Twentieth-Century American Women Poets*, edited by Laura Chester, Rising Tides, 1974.

Contributor of poems to *Botteghe Oscure*, *Trace*, *Epos*, *Literary Review*, *Poetry*, *New York Times*, *Locus Solus*, *Between Worlds*, *Massachusetts Review*, *Beat Coast East*, *Coastlines*, *Proteus Quarterly*, *Dimension*, *Imago*, *Poet and Critic*, *Two Cities*, and other periodicals. Contributor of translations to anthologies. Translator, into French, of the short stories of Anais Nin, published in Canada, Belgium, and France. Editor, *Folder Magazine of Literature and Art*, 1953-59; American editor, *Two Cities* (Paris-New York), 1961-62.

WORK IN PROGRESS: Translating from Swedish the work of Edith Sodergran; a novel.

SIDELIGHTS: Miss Aldan's major interests are contemporary international poetry, philosophy (particularly metaphysics), criticism, teaching, and travel. She has visited Africa, the Orient, and Central America. Having lived in Switzerland and France for three years, she now divides her time between New York and Dornach, Switzerland. She has studied painting and eurythmy. Many of her poems have been presented in programs with eurythmists in new experimental art forms. Her poems have appeared in major periodicals in Switzerland, England, France, Spain, Italy, and India.

Miss Aldan lectures extensively and has given poetry readings in the United States, France, Switzerland, and India. She may be heard on five recordings in the Library of Congress collection of American poets, as well as on three recordings of her own poems in the Lamont Poetry Collection of Harvard University. Her recordings include: (With Anais Nin) *Un Coup de des jamais n'abolira le hasard* (title means "A Throw of the Dice Never Will Abolish Chance"), her translation of *Selected Poems of Albert Steffen*, and works from *Folder* magazine.

Miss Aldan was chosen by Cornell University's literary magazine, *Epoch*, as one of the fifty best poets writing in America today. She was also included in the Doubleday ballot of the five hundred greatest living American writers.

She has directed, written, and photographed two original films, and has given an extensive course in films.

BIOGRAPHICAL/CRITICAL SOURCES: Mademoiselle, January, 1961; *New York Times Book Review*, March 8, 1964; *India News*, October 20, 1964; *India Morning Standard*, November 20, 1964; Valerie Harms, editor, *Celebration with Anais Nin*, Magic Circle Press, 1973.

* * *

ALEXANDER, Charles C(omer) 1935-

PERSONAL: Born October 24, 1935, in Cass County, Tex.; son of Charles Comer (an educator) and Pauline (Pynes) Alexander; married JoAnn Erwin, June 2, 1960; children: Rachel Camille. *Education:* Lamar State College of Technology (now Lamar University), B.A., 1958; University of Texas, M.A., 1959, Ph.D., 1962. *Politics:* Independent Liberal. *Home:* 8 Ann, Athens, Ohio 45701.

CAREER: University of Houston, Houston, Tex., instructor, 1962-64, assistant professor of history, 1964-66; University of Georgia, Athens, associate professor of history, 1966-70; Ohio University, Athens, professor of history, 1970—. Visiting associate professor, University of Texas, 1968-69. *Member:* Organization of American Historians, American Historical Association, Southern Historical Association, Phi Alpha Theta, Phi Kappa Phi, Pi Sigma Alpha. *Awards, honors:* L. R. Bryan, Jr. award of Texas Gulf Coast Historical Association, 1962, for *Crusade for Conformity: The Ku Klux Klan in Texas, 1920-30*.

WRITINGS: Crusade for Conformity: The Ku Klux Klan in Texas, 1920-30, Texas Gulf Coast Historical Association, 1962; *The Ku Klux Klan in the Southwest*, University of Kentucky Press, 1965; (with Loyd S. Swenson) *This New Ocean: A History of Project Mercury*, U.S. Government Printing Office, 1966; *Nationalism in American Thought, 1930-1945*, Rand McNally, 1969; *Holding the Line: The Eisenhower Era, 1952-1961*, Indiana University Press, in press. Contributor to *Phylon*, *Mid-America*, *Business History Review*, and *Arkansas Historical Quarterly*.

* * *

ALEXANDER, Colin James 1920-
(Simon Jay)

PERSONAL: Born April 10, 1920, in Lincolnshire, England; son of William Arthur (a doctor) and Linney (Thurlow) Alexander; married Bessie Susan Lee, March 24, 1948; children: Simon, Michael. *Education:* University of Otago, M.B. and Ch.B., 1944, M.D., 1964. *Home:* 49 Richard Farrell Ave., Remueva, Auckland, New Zealand. *Office:* 127 Grafton Rd., Auckland, New Zealand.

CAREER: Auckland Hospital, Auckland, New Zealand, radiologist, 1950-62; Mater Misericordiae Hospital, Auckland, New Zealand, radiologist, 1962—. *Military service:* New Zealand Army, 1945-47; served in Italy and Japan; became major. *Member:* British Medical Association, Royal Australasian College of Radiologists, Royal New Zealand Yacht Squadron, Pinnacle Ski Club. *Awards, honors:* Rouse traveling fellowship, Australasian College of Radiologists, 1964.

WRITINGS—Under pseudonym Simon Jay: *Death of a Skin Diver*, Doubleday, 1964; *Sleepers Can Kill*, Doubleday, 1968.

* * *

ALEXANDER, Edward 1936-

PERSONAL: Born December 28, 1936, in Brooklyn, N.Y.; son of Harry and Sarah (Levy) Alexander; married Leah McClement, July 3, 1958; children: Rebecca Frieda, David Morris. *Education:* Columbia University, B.A. (cum laude), 1957; University of Minnesota, M.A., 1959, Ph.D., 1963; University of London, postgraduate study, 1961-62. *Politics:* Liberal. *Religion:* Jewish. *Home:* 2117 Ravenna Blvd., Seattle, Wash. 98105.

CAREER: University of Washington, Seattle, instructor, 1960-64, assistant professor, 1964-67, associate professor, 1967-69, professor of English, 1969—. *Member:* Phi Beta Kappa. *Awards, honors:* Fulbright fellowship to University of London, 1961-62; American Council of Learned Societies fellowship, 1966-67; Guggenheim fellowship, 1974-75.

WRITINGS: Matthew Arnold and John Stuart Mill, Columbia University Press, 1965; (editor) *John Stuart Mill: Literary Essays*, Bobbs-Merrill, 1967; *John Morley*, Twayne, 1972; *Matthew Arnold, John Ruskin, and the Modern Temper*, Ohio State University Press, 1973.

WORK IN PROGRESS: A study of the literature of the Jewish holocaust of World War II; a study of Isaac Bashevis Singer.

SIDELIGHTS: Alexander has a reading knowledge of French, Spanish, Hebrew, and German.

* * *

ALEXANDER, Ian W(elsh) 1911-

PERSONAL: Born January 18, 1911, in Edinburgh, Scotland; son of George (a businessman) and Catherine Fleming (Welsh) Alexander; married Foscarina Pollitzer, December 23, 1935. *Education:* University of Edinburgh, M.A., 1932; University of Bordeaux and University of Paris, research, 1932-34, 1936-37. *Home:* Menai Dale, Siliwen Rd., Bangor, Caernarvonshire, Wales. *Office:* University College of North Wales, Bangor, Caernarvonshire, Wales.

CAREER: University of Edinburgh, Edinburgh, Scotland, lecturer in French, 1938-46; University College, University of St. Andrews, Dundee, Scotland, lecturer and head of department of French, 1946-51; University College of North Wales, Bangor, professor of French and Romance studies, 1951—, dean of Faculty of Arts, 1958-60. Former external examiner to Universities of Edinburgh, Leeds, and

Sheffield, and for higher degrees, Oxford, St. Andrews, Durham, Belfast, Sussex, and Melbourne. *Member:* Modern Humanities Research Association, Modern Language Association (president, North Wales branch, 1951—), Royal Institute of Philosophy, Association Internationale des Etudes Francaises, Societe Britannique de Philosophie de Langue Francaise, Society for French Studies, Association of University Teachers, Franco-Scottish Association (chairman, Dundee branch, 1946-51), British Society for Phenomenology (president, 1967-72; vice-president, 1972—). *Awards, honors:* Officier de l'Ordre des Palmes Academiques (France); Carnegie Research scholar, 1932-34; Carnegie Research Fellow, 1936-37; D.Litt., University of Edinburgh, 1949; G. T. Clapton Memorial Lecturer, University of Leeds, 1967.

WRITINGS: (Contributor) *Studies in Romance Philology and French Literature Presented to John Orr*, Manchester University Press, 1953; *Bergson, Philosopher of Reflection*, Bowes, 1957; (contributor) *Studies in Modern French Literature Presented to P. Mansell Jones*, Manchester University Press, 1961; (contributor) *Studi in Onore di Carlo Pellegrini*, Societa Editrice Internazionale (Turin), 1963; (contributor) T. V. Benn and others, editors, *Currents of Thought in French Literature*, Blackwell, 1965; (contributor) Anthony Thorlby, editor, *Penguin Companion to Literature, Vol. 2*, Penguin Books, 1969, 2nd edition, 1972; (contributor) *Linguistic Analysis and Phenomenology*, Macmillan, 1972; (contributor) *Mouvements Premiers: Etudes critiques offertes a Georges Poulet*, Corti, 1972; *Benjamin Constant: Adolphe*, Arnold, 1973. Also contributor to *Actes du Premier Colloque de la Societe Britannique de Philosophie de Langue Francaise*, 1962.

WORK IN PROGRESS: Research in the philosophy of Gabriel Marcel and in contemporary French philosophy, particularly phenomenology, existentialism, and structuralism.

SIDELIGHTS: Alexander is fluent in French and Italian; he has lived periodically in France and Italy.

* * *

ALFRED, William 1922-

PERSONAL: Born August 16, 1922, in New York, N.Y.; son of Thomas Richard (a bricklayer) and Mary (Bunyan) Allfrey. *Education:* Brooklyn College, B.A., 1948; Harvard University, M.A., 1949, Ph.D., 1954. *Politics:* Democrat. *Religion:* Roman Catholic. *Home:* 31 Athens St., Cambridge, Mass. 02138. *Agent:* Toby Cole, 234 West 44th St., New York, N.Y. 10036. *Office:* Kirkland House, H-14, Cambridge, Mass. 02138.

CAREER: Harvard University, Cambridge, Mass., instructor, 1954-57, assistant professor, 1957-59, associate professor, 1959-63, professor of English, 1963—. Judge, National Book Awards, 1969. *Military service:* U.S. Army, 1943-47. *Member:* Mediaeval Academy of America, Modern Language Association, Dramatists Guild. *Awards, honors:* Amy Lowell travelling poetry fellowship, 1956-57; Brandeis University Creative Arts Award, 1959; National Institute of Arts and Letters grant.

WRITINGS: (Co-editor) *Complete Prose Works of John Milton*, Yale University Press, Volume I, 1953; *Agamemnon* (a verse play in four acts; first produced in Princeton, N.J., at McCarter Theatre, October 27, 1972) Knopf, 1954; (contributor of translation) *Medieval Epics*, Modern Library, 1963; *Hogan's Goat* (play; produced on Broadway

at American Place Theatre, 1965; musical version with title "Cry for Us All," produced on Broadway at Broadhurst Theatre, April 8, 1970), Farrar, Straus, 1966; (editor with others) *The American Literary Anthology/1*, Farrar, Straus, 1968. Also author of television script, "Hogan's Goat" (based on his play), produced by Public Broadcasting Service, October 11, 1971. Assistant and associate editor, *American Poet*, 1942-44.

WORK IN PROGRESS: Translating Old English poetry, for Random House; a book of Middle English poetry and Anglo-Latin poetry, for Random House; two additional plays, "Hogan" and "The Curse of an Aching Heart."

SIDELIGHTS: Alfred told the *New York Times*: "I would like a theater that belongs to the whole people. And by that I mean a theater where you can have complicated things being talked about and yet not in complicated ways. One of the things that I find most distressing nowadays is that there is a division between the theater of entertainment and the theater of contemplation. And I wish the two could be forged together in some way.... It really is that I want the theater to have the force and attraction of television and yet include the kind of thing that [Harold] Pinter is doing."

Hogan's Goat, rewritten four times, took nine years to complete because teaching made great demands on his time.†

* * *

ALGREN, Nelson 1909-

PERSONAL: Born March 28, 1909, in Detroit, Mich.; married (divorced, 1939); currently married. *Education:* University of Illinois, B.A., 1931. *Home:* 1958 West Evergreen, Chicago, Ill.

CAREER: Salesman (sold coffee door to door for a time) and migratory worker in the South and Southwest during the Depression; worked at a gas station in Rio Hondo, Tex., 1933, which eventually led to the writing of his first published story; worked briefly for a W.P.A. writers' project; worked on venereal-disease control for the Chicago Board of Health; edited, with Jack Conroy, an experimental magazine called *The New Anvil. Military service:* U.S. Army, 1942-45; medical corpsman. *Awards, honors:* National Institute of Arts and Letters fellowship, 1947, and Newberry Library fellowship, both for the writing of *The Man With the Golden Arm*; National Book Award, 1950, for *The Man With the Golden Arm*.

WRITINGS: Somebody in Boots (novel), Vanguard, 1935, with new preface, Berkley Publication Corp., 1965; *Never Come Morning* (novel), Harper, 1942; *The Neon Wilderness* (stories), Doubleday, 1947; *The Man With the Golden Arm* (novel), Doubleday, 1949; *Chicago, City on the Make*, Doubleday, 1951, 3rd edition, Angel Island Publications, 1961; *A Walk on the Wild Side* (novel), Farrar, Straus, 1956; *The Chateau at Sunset, or, It's a Mad World, Master Copperfield*, 1959; *Who Lost an American?*, Macmillan, 1963; (editor) *Nelson Algren's Own Book of Lonesome Monsters*, Lancer Books, 1962, Bernard Geis, 1963; *Notes From a Sea Diary: Hemingway All the Way*, Putnam, 1965; *The Last Carousel* (a collection), Putnam, 1973. Contributor to *Story*, *Nation*, *Life*, *Saturday Evening Post*, *Atlantic*, and other publications.

SIDELIGHTS: Called the "poet of the Chicago slums" by Malcolm Cowley, Algren has been thus described by Chester E. Eisinger: "He is the poet of the jail and the whorehouse; he has made a close study of the cockroach, the drunkard, and the pimp, the garbage in the street and the spittle on the chin. He has a truly cloacal vision of the American experience.... The poetic quality of his writing comes in part from the impressionistic way in which he sees reality. He has an acutely developed feeling for mood, and he chooses his details in an artful, sometimes artificial, way to give us the atmosphere of halflight in which his characters live.''

He prefers to write about ''living'' situations instead of about the past, and he told his *Paris Review* interviewers that, unlike Saul Bellow, whom he admires, he tends to rely more on the stomach than on the intellect. ''I always think of writing as a *physical* thing,'' he says. Eisinger writes: ''The physical quality in his writing—it is significant that he works out in a gym preparatory to writing—emphasizes the belly-head distinction which he himself makes. His allegiance is to the feelings. He is indifferent to ideas, even uncomfortable with them.''

Algren has lived among and writes about the underdogs of American society. He writes, he says, out of ''a kind of *irritability* that these people on top should be contented, so absolutely unaware of these other people, and so sure that their values are the right ones. I mean, there's a certain satisfaction in recording the people underneath, whose values are as sound as theirs, and a lot funnier, and a lot truer in a way.''

Algren feels that American writers do not work out of a tradition. ''The thing is that here you get to be a writer differently,'' he once said. ''I mean, a writer like Sartre *decides*, like any professional man, when he's fifteen, sixteen years old, that instead of being a doctor he's going to be a writer. And he absorbs the French tradition and proceeds from there. Well, here you get to be a writer when there's absolutely nothing else you can do.''

Algren does not know many writers; he believes that ''a writer shouldn't be engaged with other writers, or with people who make books, or even with people who read them. I think the farther away you get from the literary traffic, the closer you are to sources. I mean, a writer doesn't really *live*, he observes.''

At one time Algren was ''engaged with'' another writer, becoming friend and traveling companion to Simone de Beauvoir (''I showed her the electric chair and everything.''). He appears in her roman a clef, *The Mandarins*, about which he has said: ''The first time I read it I didn't recognize who the man was.... I should have been flattered, but that's not the way it was.''

The writers he admires include Stephen Crane, Dostoevsky, Hemingway (Hemingway once said that, next to Faulkner, Algren was the best contemporary American writer), and Faulkner (''I can get lost in him awful easy. But he's powerful.''). With typical frankness he once called Washington Irving, Henry James, and Nathaniel Hawthorne ''the dullest writers that ever walked in shoe leather.'' He scoffs at the intrigues of critics, saying that they have not influenced his work because he doesn't read them, and adds: ''I doubt anyone does, except other critics.... I got a glimpse into the uses of a certain kind of criticism this past summer at a writers' conference—into how the avocation of assessing the failures of better men can be turned into a comfortable livelihood, providing you back it up with a Ph.D.... I know, of course, that there are true critics, one or two. For the rest all I can say is 'Deal around me.''

Algren most frequently does his writing at night, at a type-writer, working slowly (it took him three years to write *The Man With the Golden Arm*), rewriting after every five pages or so, writing in drafts that get increasingly longer.

His *Paris Review* interviewers noted that his ''good-humored nonchalance . . . is at once uniquely American and, in the latter-day sense, quite un-American: his tie, if he ever wore one, would very likely be as askew as his syntax often is. He is a man who betrays no inclination whatsoever towards politeness, but he has a natural generosity and compassion. To talk with Algren is to have a conversation brought very quickly to that rarefied level where values are actually declared.''

Ohio State University acquired Algren's personal papers in 1966.

The Man With the Golden Arm has been filmed, and also produced as an off-Broadway play; *Walk on the Wild Side* was made into a film in 1962.

BIOGRAPHICAL/CRITICAL SOURCES: Writers at Work, first series, edited by Malcolm Cowley, Viking, 1958; *Fiction of the Forties*, by Chester E. Eisinger, University of Chicago Press, 1963; *Atlantic*, October, 1964; *Conversations With Nelson Algren*, by H. E. F. Donohue, Hill & Wang, 1964; *Nelson Algren: A Checklist*, compiled by Kenneth G. McCollum, Gale, 1973; Carolyn Riley, editor, *Contemporary Literary Criticism*, Volume IV, Gale, 1975.†

* * *

ALISKY, Marvin (Howard) 1923-

PERSONAL: Surname is accented on first syllable; born March 12, 1923, in Kansas City, Mo.; son of Joseph A. and Bess June (Capp) Alisky; married Beverly Kay, June 10, 1955; children: Sander Michael, Joseph Martin. *Education:* University of Texas, B.A., 1946, M.J., 1947, Ph.D., 1953; Instituto Tecnologico de Monterrey, Monterrey, Mexico, certificate, 1951. *Office:* Department of Political Science, Arizona State University, Tempe, Ariz. 85281.

CAREER: National Broadcasting Co., southwest and midwest stations, newscaster, 1947-50; Indiana University, Bloomington, assistant professor of journalism and government, 1953-57; *Christian Science Monitor*, Boston, Mass., correspondent in Latin America, 1957-62; Arizona State University, Tempe, associate professor, 1957-60, professor of journalism and political science, 1960-72, professor of political science, 1972—, chairman of department of mass communications, 1957-66, director of Center for Latin American Studies, 1966-72. First Smith-Mundt visiting professor in Central America, 1960; visiting fellow in politics at Princeton University, 1963; visiting professor at University of California at Irvine, summers, 1971, and 1972. U.S. delegate to UNESCO Conference on Communications, Quito, Ecuador, 1960. Former judge of broadcasting scripts for Grand Prix of Radio-Televizione Italiana de Rome; currently member of committee for Maria Moors Cabot Inter-American Journalism Awards. *Military service:* U.S. Navy, 1944-45. *Member:* American Political Science Association, Inter-American Press Association, Hispanic Society of America, Western Political Science Association, Sigma Delta Chi (co-founder of Phoenix professional chapter and former president).

WRITINGS: Latin American Journalism Bibliography, Fondo de P.I., 1958; (with others) *Modern Journalism*, Pitman, 1962; (with John C. Merrill and Carter Bryan) *The Foreign Press*, Louisiana State University Press, 1964, 2nd edition, 1970; (contributor) B. G. Burnett and K. F. Johnson, editors, *Political Forces in Latin America: Dimensions of the Quest for Stability*, Wadsworth, 1968, revised edition, 1970; *Who's Who in Mexican Government*, Arizona State University, Center for Latin American Studies, 1969; *Uruguay: A Contemporary Survey*, Praeger, 1970; (contributor) M. C. Needler, editor, *Political Systems of Latin America*, Van Nostrand, 1970; *Guide to the Mexican State of Sonora*, Arizona State University, Center for Latin American Studies, 1971; *Government of the Mexican State of Nuevo Leon*, Arizona State University, Center for Latin American Studies, 1971; *Peruvian Political Perspective*, Arizona State University, Center for Latin American Studies, 1972. Writer of radio scripts for National Broadcasting Co. Contributor of some two hundred articles to *Reporter*, *New Mexico Historical Review*, *Arizona Highways*, and other journals. Editor of *Latin American Digest*, 1966-72; associate editor, *Intellect*, 1974——.

* * *

ALLEN, Dwight W(illiam) 1931-

PERSONAL: Born August 1, 1931, in Stockton, Calif.; son of John W. and Valera F. (Fisher) Allen; married Carole J. Swall, April 12, 1953; children: Douglas Bruce, Dwight Dennis, Dana Lee, Carla, Cheryl. *Education:* Stanford University, A.B., 1953, M.A., 1957, Ed.D., 1959. *Politics:* Non-partisan. *Religion:* Baha'i Faith. *Home:* Route 3, Amherst, Mass. 01002. *Office:* School of Education, University of Massachusetts, Amherst, Mass. 01002.

CAREER: Athens College, Athens, Greece, instructor, 1953-54; teacher in secondary school, 1957-58; Stanford University, School of Education, Stanford, Calif., research associate, 1959-62, assistant professor, 1962-65, associate professor of education, 1965-67; University of Massachusetts, Amherst, dean of School of Education, 1968——. Educational consultant to more than fifty school bodies in United States and abroad. Junior Statesman Foundation, trustee, 1960——, president, 1963-66; chairman of planning coordination committee and consultant, U.S. Office of Education, 1967. *Military service:* U.S. Army, 1954-56. *Member:* Association of Colleges and Schools of Education in State Universities and Land Grant Colleges, American Association for the Advancement of Science, American Educational Research Association, National Council for the Social Studies, National Education Association, National Society of College Teachers of Education, National Society for the Study of Education, American Teachers Association, California Teachers Association, Phi Delta Kappa.

WRITINGS: (With R. N. Bush) *A New Design for High School Education: Assuming a Flexible Schedule*, McGraw, 1964; (with Donald D. Bushnell) *The Computer in American Education*, Wiley, 1967; (with Kevin Ryan) *Microteaching*, Addison-Wesley, 1969; (with James Cooper and others) *Model Elementary Teacher Education Program: Final Report*, Bureau of Research, U.S. Department of Health, Education, and Welfare, 1969; (editor) *The Teacher's Handbook*, Scott, Foresman, 1971; (editor with Jeffrey Hecht) *Controversies in Education*, Sounders, 1974. Contributor to education journals.

WORK IN PROGRESS: Building a Performance Curriculum; research in high school organization, particularly flexible scheduling and other innovations such as team teaching, non-graded programs, and self-instruction; research in teacher education, particularly the development of micro-teaching.

SIDELIGHTS: Member of Baha'i pilgrimages to Israel, 1963, Japan, 1965; also traveled in southern Africa, 1963, and has made a number of trips in Canada and Mexico.†

* * *

ALLEN, Francis A(lfred) 1919-

PERSONAL: Born October 25, 1919, in Kansas City, Kan.; son of Oliver Boyd (a clergyman) and Justa L. (Wingo) Allen; married June F. Murphy, February 16, 1947; children: Neil W., Susan L. *Education:* Cornell College, Mount Vernon, Iowa, A.B., 1941; Northwestern University, LL.B. (magna cum laude), 1946. *Religion:* Protestant. *Home:* 414 Huntington Pl., Ann Arbor, Mich. 48104. *Office:* University of Michigan, Ann Arbor, Mich. 48104.

CAREER: Admitted to Illinois bar, 1950. Legal secretary to Chief Justice Fred M. Vinson, U.S. Supreme Court, 1946-48; Northwestern University, Evanston, Ill., assistant professor, 1948-50, associate professor of law, 1950-53; Harvard University, Cambridge, Mass., professor of law, 1953-56; University of Chicago, Chicago, Ill., professor of law, 1956-62; University of Michigan, Ann Arbor, professor of law, 1962-63; University of Chicago, professor of law, 1963-66; University of Michigan, Ann Arbor, dean of Law School, 1966-71, professor of law, 1971——. Salzburg Seminar in American Studies, member of faculty, 1963. Economic Stabilization Agency, special counsel, 1951; Attorney General's Committee on Poverty and the Administration of Federal Criminal Justice, chairman, 1961-63. Illinois Sex Offenders Commission, chairman of citizens advisory committee, 1952-53; Illinois Criminal Code of 1961, chairman of drafting committee; Family Court of Cook County, member of citizens advisory committee, 1962. Holmes Lecturer, Harvard University, 1973. *Military service:* U.S. Army Air Forces, 1942-45; became sergeant.

MEMBER: American Bar Association, American Law Institute (council member, 1969——), American Correctional Association, National Council on Crime and Delinquency, American Society for Legal and Political Philosophy, Illinois Academy of Criminology (president, 1961-62), Phi Beta Kappa. *Awards, honors:* Arthur von Briesen Medal of National Legal Aid and Defender Association for distinguished contribution to the cause of legal aid, 1953; honorary J.D., Cornell College, 1958; Guggenheim fellowship, 1971-72.

WRITINGS: (Contributor) Hermann Mannheim, editor, *Pioneers in Criminology*, Stevens, 1960; (contributor) C. R. Sowle, editor, *Police Power and Individual Freedom*, Aldine, 1962; (contributor) W. Petersen and D. Matza, editors, *Social Controversy*, Wadsworth, 1963; *The Borderland of Criminal Justice*, University of Chicago Press, 1964; (editor) Freund, *Standards of American Legislation*, new edition, University of Chicago Press, 1965; *Crimes of Politics: Political Dimensions of Criminal Justice*, Harvard University Press, 1974. Contributor to legal and criminological periodicals. Editor-in-chief, *Illinois Law Review*, 1942-43; associate editor, *Journal of Criminal Law, Criminology, and Police Science*, 1950——.

WORK IN PROGRESS: Research into nineteenth-century movements for reform of penal law in the United States, for forthcoming book.

SIDELIGHTS: Allen told *CA*: "I have been particularly concerned with the impact of what I call 'the new knowledge' on the values expressed in the legal order, especially the values of individual right and volition...." He has reading knowledge of French.†

ALLEN, Robert J. 1930-

PERSONAL: Born December 20, 1930, in New York, N.Y.; son of William J. and Margaret Allen; married June 2, 1962; children: Barrie Jean. *Education:* Villanova University, B.S., 1952; St. Paul's College, Washington, D.C., B.A., 1959; New York University, M.A., 1964, graduate study, 1964—. *Home:* 203 West 90th St., New York, N.Y. 10024. *Office;* National Council of Catholic Men, 405 Lexington Ave., New York, N.Y. 10017.

CAREER: Missionary Priests of Saint Paul the Apostle, seminarian, 1955-59; National Council of Catholic Men, New York, N.Y., television producer for network (Columbia Broadcasting System) religious series, "Lamp unto My Feet" and "Look Up and Live," 1960—. Actor in summer stock at Glen Cove, N.Y., 1952; producer, writer, and director of public service radio and television programs for Paulist Broadcasters, 1957-59. *Military service:* U.S. Navy, Special Services officer, 1952-55. *Awards, honors:* Catholic International Cooperation Program Award for television series on Latin America, "Not by Faith Alone," 1965; Catholic Broadcasters Gabriel Award for television film on Chile, 1965.

WRITINGS: (Editor) *Four Contemporary Religious Plays*, Paulist Press, 1964. Writer of three television documentaries for "Look Up and Live," Columbia Broadcasting System, 1963-64. Contributor of articles, including photo-essays and personality profiles, to magazines, 1958—.†

*   *   *

ALLEN, Thomas B(enton) 1929-
(Tom Allen)

PERSONAL: Born March 20, 1929, in Bridgeport, Conn.; son of Walter Leo (a salesman) and Catherine (Reilly) Allen; married Florence MacBride (a potter), June 5, 1950; children: Christopher, Constance, Roger. *Education:* Fairfield University, student, 1947-49; University of Bridgeport, B.A., 1955. *Politics:* Democrat. *Religion:* Unitarian Universalist. *Home:* 7820 Custer Rd., Bethesda, Md. 20014. *Agent:* Philip G. Spitzer, 111-25 76th Ave., Forest Hills, N.Y. 11375. *Office:* National Geographic Society, M. St. NW, Washington, D.C. 20036.

CAREER: Bridgeport Herald, Bridgeport, Conn., reporter, 1947-51, 1953-56; *New York Daily News*, New York, N.Y., feature writer, 1956-63; Chilton Co. (publishers), Philadelphia, Pa., managing editor for trade books, 1963-65; National Geographic Society, editor-writer, book service, 1965—. Instructor in freshman English, Montgomery College, 1969-70; lecturer in creative writing, U.S. Naval Academy, 1972, 1973. *Military service:* U.S. Navy, 1951-53.

WRITINGS: (Under name Tom Allen; with Harold W. McCormick and William Young) *Shadows in the Sea: The Sharks, Skates, and Rays*, Chilton, 1963; *The Quest: A Report on Extraterrestrial Life*, Chilton, 1965; (with Garbus) *Living in Washington: A Moving Experience*, Westover, 1972; (editor) *The Marvels of Animal Behavior*, National Geographic Society, 1972; *The Last Inmate* (novel), Charterhouse, 1973; *Vanishing Wildlife of North America*, National Geographic Society, 1974. Also author of numerous newspaper features, U.S. newspapers and overseas publications, Chicago Tribune-New York Daily News Syndicate, 1956-63.

Contributor; all published by National Geographic Society:

Greece and Rome: Builders of Our World, 1968; *The Age of Chivalry*, 1969; (and editor) *Vacationland U.S.A.*, 1970; *Wilderness U.S.A.*, 1972. Also contributor to Encyclopaedia Britannica's *Book of the Year*, 1968.

WORK IN PROGRESS: We Americans; Watching Jefferson, a novel.

*   *   *

ALLEN, William Sheridan 1932-

PERSONAL: Born October 5, 1932, in Evanston, Ill.; son of William Sheridan (a lawyer) and Rose (Brahm) Allen; married Luella Stinson, June 10, 1955; children: Caitilyn, Jefferson, Rebecca, Claire. *Education:* University of Michigan, A.B., 1955; Free University of Berlin, student, 1954; University of Connecticut, M.A., 1956; University of Goettingen, graduate study, 1957; University of Minnesota, Ph.D., 1962. *Politics:* Socialist Party. *Home:* 164 Woodward Ave., Buffalo, N.Y. 14214. *Office:* History Department, State University of New York, Buffalo, N.Y. 14214.

CAREER: Bay City Junior College, Bay City, Mich., instructor in history, 1958-59; Massachusetts Institute of Technology, Cambridge, instructor in humanities, 1960-61; University of Missouri, Columbia, assistant professor of history, 1961-67; Wayne State University, Detroit, Mich., associate professor of history, 1967-70; State University of New York, Buffalo, professor of history, 1970—. *Member:* American Historical Association, American Association of University Professors, American Civil Liberties Union, Congress on Racial Equality.

WRITINGS: The Nazi Seizure of Power: The Experience of a Single German Town, 1930-35, Quadrangle, 1965.

WORK IN PROGRESS: Editing and translating *The Memoirs of Albert Krebs, Gauleiter of Hamburg, 1926-28*; *The Socialist Underground in Nazi Germany, 1933-39*.

SIDELIGHTS: The *New York Times Book Review* called *The Nazi Seizure of Power* "a grass-roots history, all the more vivid because of this fact. As a pioneer work it may signalize a badly needed new departure in the study of recent history."

*   *   *

ALLENTUCH, Harriet Ray 1933-

PERSONAL: Born October 9, 1933, in Rochester, N.Y.; daughter of Philip and Lena (Kravetz) Ray; married Arnold Allentuch (an educator), June 10, 1956; children: two. *Education:* University of Rochester, B.A., 1955; Radcliffe College, M.A., 1956; Columbia University, Ph.D., 1962. *Home:* 49 Fairview St., Huntington, N.Y. 11743.

CAREER: Columbia University, New York, N.Y., lecturer in French, 1957-60; Queens College of the City University of New York, Flushing, N.Y., instructor in French, 1960-64; State University of New York at Stony Brook, assistant professor, 1964-70, associate professor of French, 1970—. *Member:* American Association of Teachers of French, Modern Language Association of America, Phi Beta Kappa.

WRITINGS: Madame de Sevigne: A Portrait in Letters, Johns Hopkins Press, 1963.

*   *   *

AMAMOO, Joseph Godson 1931-
(Joseph Kambu)

PERSONAL: Born August 29, 1931, in Swedru, Ghana;

son of Joseph Godson (a businessman) and Agnes (a businesswoman, maiden name Otoo) Amamoo; married Breid McArdle, May, 1963; children: Josephine, Samia. *Education:* Achimota College, student, 1945-50; University of Ghana, student, 1952-56. *Politics:* Moderate left. *Religion:* Methodist, "but rather catholic in outlook." *Home:* 11 Lexington Way, Barnet, Hertfordshire, England.

CAREER: Ghana Review (government weekly), Accra, Ghana, assistant editor, 1956-57; *Ghana Times* (daily), Accra, Ghana, correspondent in London, England, 1957-61; Ghana High Commission, London, England, public relations adviser, 1961; Ghana ambassador (first) to Hungary, 1962-63; currently attached to Office of the President, Accra, Ghana. Broadcaster on African affairs. *Member:* Institute of Journalists (United Kingdom), Royal Society of Arts (fellow), Royal African Society, Society of Authors, Hungarian Journalists' Association, P.E.N.

WRITINGS: The New Ghana, Pan Books, 1958; *Ghana Republic Souvenir*, Newman Neame, 1961; *Constitutional Proposals for Post-Coup Africa*, A. & C. Black, 1967. Contributor to *New Commonwealth*, *African Affairs*, *Ghana Daily Graphic*, *Ghana Evening News*, *African World*, *Tribune* (London).

WORK IN PROGRESS: Crusade in Africa.

AVOCATIONAL INTERESTS: Photography, reading, classical music, opera, country walking, watching boxing and wrestling.†

*   *   *

AMMERMAN, Robert R(ay)   1927-

PERSONAL: Born September 5, 1927, in Buffalo, N.Y.; son of John Raymond (an accountant) and Frances Mura (Pettit) Ammerman; divorced; children: Robert Thompson. *Education:* Swarthmore College, A.B. (highest honors), 1952; Princeton University, graduate study, 1952-53; Brown University, M.A., 1954, Ph.D., 1956. *Home:* 6308 Raymond Rd., Madison, Wis. 53711. *Office:* Department of Philosophy, University of Wisconsin, Madison, Wis. 53706.

CAREER: University of Wisconsin, Madison, instructor, 1956-57, assistant professor, 1957-61, associate professor, 1961-66, professor of philosophy, 1967—. *Military service:* U.S. Army, 1945-48. *Member:* American Philosophical Association, Phi Beta Kappa. *Awards, honors:* Honorary research fellow, Birkbeck College, University of London, 1965.

WRITINGS—Editor: (With M. G. Singer) *Introductory Readings in Philosophy*, Scribner, 1962; *Classics of Analytic Philosophy*, McGraw, 1965; (with Singer) *Belief, Knowledge, and Truth*, Scribner, 1970; (with Claudia Card) *Religious Commitment and Salvation*, C. E. Merrill, 1974. Contributor to journals.

WORK IN PROGRESS: Research on Ludwig Wittgenstein.

*   *   *

ANDERS, Leslie   1922-

PERSONAL: Born January 22, 1922, in Admire, Kan.; son of Ray L. and Bertie (Hasson) Anders; married Mardellya Soles, October 17, 1942; children: Geraldine, Charlotte. *Education:* College of Emporia, A.B. (summa cum laude), 1949; University of Missouri, A.M., 1950, Ph.D., 1954. *Politics:* Republican. *Religion:* Presbyterian. *Home:* 213

West South St., Warrensburg, Mo. 64093. *Office:* Central Missouri State University, Warrensburg, Mo.

CAREER: U.S. Army, Office of the Chief of Engineers, Baltimore, Md., military historian (civilian) in Historical Division, 1951-55; Central Missouri State University, Warrensburg, assistant professor, 1955-58, associate professor, 1958-63, professor of history, 1963—. *Military service:* U.S. Army, 1940-45; became technical sergeant. *Member:* American Military Institute, American Association for State and Local History, American Association for the United Nations, Missouri State Historical Society, Missouri Council for the Social Studies, Missouri State Teachers Association, Phi Kappa Phi, Scabbard and Blade.

WRITINGS: The Ledo Road, University of Oklahoma Press, 1965; *The Eighteenth Mission*, Bobbs-Merrill, 1968; *Education for Service: Centennial History of Central Missouri State College*, Intercollegiate Press, 1971. Contributor to military and historical journals.

WORK IN PROGRESS: A history of the Twenty-first Missouri Volunteer Infantry, 1861-65.

*   *   *

ANDERSON, David D(aniel)   1924-

PERSONAL: Born June 8, 1924, in Lorain, Ohio; son of David J. (an analyst) and Nora (Foster) Anderson; married Patricia Ann Rittenhour (a librarian), February 1, 1953. *Education:* Bowling Green State University, B.S., 1951, M.A., 1952; Michigan State University, Ph.D., 1960. *Home:* 1625 Cooper Ave., Lansing, Mich. 48910. *Office:* 240 Bessey Hall, Michigan State University, East Lansing, Mich. 48824.

CAREER: Michigan State University, East Lansing, 1956—, began as instructor, now professor of American Literature. University of Karachi, Fulbright lecturer, 1963-64. American delegate to International Congress of Orientalists and to International Federation for Modern Languages and Literatures. *Military service:* U.S. Navy, Amphibious Forces, 1942-45; served in European theater. U.S. Army, Artillery, 1952-53; became first lieutenant; received Purple Heart, Silver Star, five battle stars. *Member:* American Studies Association, Modern Language Association of America, Society for the Study of Midwestern Literature (founder). *Awards, honors:* Michigan State University book manuscript award, 1961, for "Sherwood Anderson and the Meaning of American Experience"; Michigan State University Distinguished Faculty Award, 1974.

WRITINGS: Louis Bromfield, Twayne, 1964; *Critical Studies in American Literature*, University of Karachi, 1964; (contributor) R. L. White, editor, *The Achievement of Sherwood Anderson*, University of North Carolina Press, 1966; *Sherwood Anderson*, Holt, 1967; *Brand Whitlock*, Twayne, 1968; *The Black Experience*, Michigan State University Press, 1969; *Abraham Lincoln*, Twayne, 1970; *The Literary Works of Abraham Lincoln*, C. E. Merrill, 1970; *The Dark and Tangled Path*, Houghton, 1971; *Sunshine and Smoke*, Lippincott, 1971; *Robert Ingersoll*, Twayne, 1972. Also author of serial published in *Vision*, May-September, 1964. Contributor to *Encyclopedia of World Literature of the Twentieth Century*, 1969, and 1971. Contributor to *Mark Twain Journal*, *Michigan History*, *Personalist*, *Artesian*, *Stylus*, *Yale Review*, *American Literature*, *Literature East and West*, and *Pakistan Review*. Editor, *University College Quarterly*, *Midamerica I*, 1974.

WORK IN PROGRESS: Woodrow Wilson for Twayne; *Ignatius Donnelly* for Twayne; *The Mind of the Midwest.*

SIDELIGHTS: Anderson has traveled and lectured throughout the Far East, Near East, and Europe, and is competent in German and French. Avocational interests: Lincoln and the Civil War; liberal politics; collecting art objects and coins.

* * *

ANDERSON, Einar 1909-

PERSONAL: Given name is pronounced A-nar, with long "a"; born August 21, 1909, in Winter Quarters, Utah; son of Einar and Nena (Bjarnson) Anderson; married Ann Etem, August 25, 1934; children: Joann (Mrs. Michael Van Buskirk). Education: Attended public schools in Spanish Fork, Utah. Politics: Republican. Religion: Protestant. Office: Voice of Calvary, 1101 South Main, Burbank, Calif. 91503.

CAREER: Standard Brands of California, San Francisco, salesman, 1936-41; Alice of California, San Francisco, salesman, 1941-56; Peterson Manufacturing Co., Glendale, Calif., West Coast sales manager, 1956-61; Voice of Calvary, Burbank, Calif., Bible teacher and evangelist, 1961—. Has lectured on the Bible in England, Scotland, Canada, and throughout the United States.

WRITINGS: Mormonism, Moody, 1956; I Was A Mormon, Zondervan, 1964; Inside Story of Mormonism, Kregel Publications, 1973. Contributor to evangelistic periodicals.

WORK IN PROGRESS: Paul's Revelation: The Answer to Mormonism.†

* * *

ANDERSON, George L(aVerne) 1905-

PERSONAL: Born February 27, 1905, in Blue Rapids, Kan.; son of Anders (a miller) and Mary (Pittman) Anderson; married Caroline Miek, June 8, 1928; children: Marianne (Mrs. John E. Wilkinson), James L. Education: University of Kansas, A.B., 1926, M.A., 1930; University of Illinois, Ph.D., 1933. Home: 1702 University Dr., Lawrence, Kan. Office: Department of History, University of Kansas, Lawrence, Kan.

CAREER: Colorado College, Colorado Springs, Colo., instructor, 1934-37, assistant professor, 1937-43, associate professor of history, 1943-45; University of Kansas, Lawrence, associate professor, 1945-49, professor of history and chairman of department, 1949—. Member of Board of Higher Education, United Lutheran Church in America (now Lutheran Church in America), 1946-62. Member: Agricultural History Society (president, 1958), Organization of American Historians, Kansas State Historical Society (president, 1961), Kiwanis Club (Lawrence; president, 1956).

WRITINGS: General William J. Palmer: A Decade of Colorado Railroad Building, 1870-1880, Colorado College Studies, 1936, 2nd edition, 1963; (editor) Issues and Conflicts: Studies in Twentieth Century American Diplomacy, University of Kansas Press, 1959; General William Jackson Palmer: Man of Vision (booklet), Colorado College, 1960; (editor) A Petition Regarding the Conditions in the C. S. M. Prison at Columbia, S.C., University of Kansas Library, 1962; Kansas West, Golden West, 1963; The Widening Stream: The Exchange National Bank of Atchison, 1858-1968, Lockwood Co. (Atchison, Kan.), 1968; Variations on a Theme: History as Knowledge of the Past, Coronado Press, 1970; Essays on Public Lands: Problems, Legislation, and Administration, Coronado

Press, 1971; (contributor) John G. Clark, editor, The Frontier Challenge: Responses to the Trans-Mississippi West, University Press of Kansas, 1971; Four Essays on Railroads in Kansas and Colorado, Coronado Press, c.1971. Member of board of editors, Mississippi Valley Historical Association (now Organization of American Historians), 1957-60.†

* * *

ANDERSON, Martin 1936-

PERSONAL: Born August 5, 1936, in Lowell, Mass.; son of Ralph and Evelyn Anderson; married Annelise Graebner, September 9, 1965. Education: Dartmouth College, A.B. (summa cum laude), 1957, M.S., 1958; Massachusetts Institute of Technology, Ph.D., 1962. Residence: New York, N.Y. Office: Hoover Institution on War, Revolution, and Peace, Stanford University, Stanford, Calif. 94305.

CAREER: Columbia University, Graduate School of Business Administration, New York, N.Y., assistant professor of finance, 1962-65, associate professor of business, 1965-68; special assistant to President Nixon, 1969-71; Stanford University, Hoover Institution on War, Revolution, and Peace, Stanford, Calif., senior fellow, 1971—. Director of research for Nixon presidential campaign, 1968. Military service: U.S. Army Security Agency; became second lieutenant. Member: American Finance Association, American Economic Association, Phi Beta Kappa.

WRITINGS: The Federal Bulldozer: A Critical Analysis of Urban Renewal, 1949-1962, M.I.T. Press, 1964.†

* * *

ANDERSON, Matthew Smith 1922-

PERSONAL: Born May 23, 1922, in Perth, Scotland; son of Matthew Smith (a shopkeeper) and Elizabeth (Redpath) Anderson; married Olive Ruth Gee (a university teacher), July 4, 1954; children: Rachel Elizabeth, Harriet Jane. Education: University of Edinburgh, M.A. (first class honors in history), 1947, Ph.D., 1952. Politics: "Unpolitical conservative." Religion: Presbyterian. Home: 45 Cholmeley Crescent, Highgate, London N6 5EX, England. Office: London School of Economics and Political Science, Houghton St., London WC2A 2AE, England.

CAREER: University of Edinburgh, Edinburgh, Scotland, assistant lecturer in history, 1947-49; London School of Economics and Political Science, University of London, London, England, assistant lecturer, 1949-53, lecturer, 1953-61, reader, 1961-72, professor of international history, 1972—. Historical adviser to Great Britain-USSR Historical Exhibition, London, 1967. Military service: Royal Air Force, 1942-45; became pilot-officer. Member: Royal Historical Society (fellow), Economic History Society, Society for Nautical Research, Society for Army Historical Research.

WRITINGS: Britain's Discovery of Russia, 1553-1815, St. Martin's, 1958; Europe in the Eighteenth Century, 1713-1783, Holt, 1961; The Eastern Question, St. Martin's, 1966; Eighteenth-Century Europe, Oxford University Press, 1966; The Great Powers and the Near East, 1774-1923, E. J. Arnold, 1970, St. Martin's, 1971; (contributor and editor with R. M. Hatton) Studies in Diplomatic History, Shoe String, 1970; The Ascendancy of Europe, 1815-1914, Rowman & Littlefield, 1972; British Parliamentary Papers Relating to Russia, 1800-1900: A Critical Commen-

tary, Irish University Press, 1973; *Peter the Great*, Thames & Hudson, in press. Contributor to *American Slavic and Eastern European Review*, *English Historical Review*, *Slavonic and Eastern European Review*, *Bulletin of the Institute of Historical Research*, and other journals.

WORK IN PROGRESS: The Historiography of Eighteenth-Century Europe for Harper.

SIDELIGHTS: Anderson speaks French and has reading knowledge of German, Spanish, Italian, and Russian.

*   *   *

ANDERSON, Roy 1936-

PERSONAL: Born June 11, 1936, in North Shields, Northumberland, England; married Elizabeth M. Duncan, September 17, 1960 (died, 1961); married Sylvia M. E. Sillett, August 31, 1963; children: Michael John, Neil Richard. *Religion:* United Reformed Church. *Office:* Evening Post, Mark Rd., Hemel Hempstead, Hertfordshire, England.

CAREER: Evening Chronicle, Newcastle upon Tyne, England, reporter, 1952-56, sub-editor, 1958-60; *Daily Nation*, Nairobi, Kenya, East Africa, sub-editor, 1960-61; *Evening Chronicle*, sub-editor, 1961-63; *Sunday Sun*, Newcastle upon Tyne, chief sub-editor, 1963-65; *Evening Post*, Reading, England, deputy chief sub-editor, 1965-66; *Sunday Sun*, assistant editor, 1966-69; *Evening Chronicle*, assistant editor, 1969-70; *Sunday Sun*, acting editor, 1970; *Evening Chronicle*, deputy editor, 1970-71; *Evening Post*, Luton, England, deputy editor, 1971—.

WRITINGS: White Star, Stephenson & Sons, 1964; *The Violent Kingdom*, Graham, 1971.

WORK IN PROGRESS: Great British Ships.

*   *   *

ANDERSON, Roy Allan 1895-

PERSONAL: Born March 15, 1895, in Melbourne, Australia; son of Albert William and Margaret (Linklater) Anderson); married Myra Elsa Wendt, 1920; children: Allan W., Tui Myra, Hilary. *Education:* Studied at Australasian Missionary College, Jones College (at that time affiliated with University of Melbourne), and University of Southern California. *Home:* 11600 Anderson St., Loma Linda, Calif. 92354. *Office:* Division of Religion, Loma Linda University, Loma Linda, Calif. 92354.

CAREER: Seventh-day Adventist Church, pastor and evangelist in South Australia Conference, 1918-20, North New Zealand Conference, 1920-26, Queensland Conference, 1926-30, South England Conference, 1930-36, and Southeast California Conference, 1936-38; La Sierra College, Riverside, Calif., teacher, 1938-41; General Conference of Seventh-day Adventists, Washington, D.C., editor of *Ministry*, 1941—; Andrews University, Berrien Springs, Mich., lecturer, 1958-66; Loma Linda University, Loma Linda, Calif., lecturer and instructor, 1967—. *Member:* Royal Geographical Society (fellow), Phi Chi Phi. *Awards, honors:* D.D. (honorary), University of Southern California, 1962.

WRITINGS: The Shepherd-Evangelist, Review and Herald, 1950; *Unfolding the Revelation*, Pacific Press Publishing Association, 1953, revised edition, 1974; *Preachers of Righteousness*, Southern Publishing, 1963; *Secrets of the Spirit World*, Pacific Press Publishing Association, 1966; *Faith That Conquers Fear*, Southern Publishing, 1967; *Love Finds a Way*, Southern Publishing, 1967; *A Better World*, Southern Publishing, 1968; *The God-Man: His Nature and Work*, Review and Herald, 1970. Contributor of articles to magazines and journals, including: *Review and Herald*, *Ministry*, *Signs of the Times*, *These Times*, *Australian Signs*, *Australasian Record*, *Scope*, and *Advent Survey*.

WORK IN PROGRESS: Three books, *All Eyes on Israel: Doomsday or God's Day?*, *The Coming Glorious Rapture*, and *Unfolding the Prophecies of Daniel: Making Worship Joyful*.

AVOCATIONAL INTERESTS: Music, photography, and writing.

*   *   *

ANGELL, Richard B(radshaw) 1918-

PERSONAL: Born October 14, 1918, in Scarsdale, N.Y.; son of Stephen LeRoy (a realtor) and Mary Alice Angell; married Imogene Lucille Baker, June 4, 1949; children: John Baker, Paul McLean, James Bigelow, David Bradshaw, Kathryn Elizabeth. *Education:* Swarthmore College, B.A., 1940; University of Pennsylvania, M.G.A., 1948; Harvard University, M.A., 1948, Ph.D., 1954. *Religion:* Society of Friends. *Home:* 1247 East Maple Rd., Birmingham, Mich. *Office:* Department of Philosophy, Wayne State University, Detroit, Mich. 48202.

CAREER: Florida State University, Tallahassee, acting assistant professor of philosophy, 1949-51; Wheaton College, Norton, Mass., visiting lecturer, 1952; Washington and Jefferson College, Washington, Pa., assistant professor of philosophy, 1953-54; Ohio Wesleyan University, Delaware, assistant professor, 1954-58, associate professor, 1958-63, professor of philosophy, 1963-68. Wayne State University, Detroit, Mich., professor of philosophy, 1968—, chairman of department, 1968-73. Visiting professor and acting head of department of philosophy, Wells College, 1962-64. *Military service:* U.S. Army, 1942-45; became captain; received Bronze Star and five campaign stars for service in Europe. *Member:* American Philosophical Association, Mind Association, Association for Symbolic Logic, American Association of University Professors. *Awards, honors:* National Science Foundation, research grants.

WRITINGS: Reasoning and Logic, Appleton, 1964. Contributor to *Journal of Philosophy*, *Mind*, *Journal of Symbolic Logic*, *Analysis et Logique* (Belgium), and *Nous*.

WORK IN PROGRESS: Research on the logic of subjunctive conditionals, and on the foundations of logic.

*   *   *

ANGRESS, Werner T(homas) 1920-

PERSONAL: Born June 27, 1920, in Berlin, Germany; son of Ernst Hermann (a banker) and Henny (Kiefer) Angress; married second wife, Mildred Rapp, June 14, 1964; children: (first marriage) Percy George, Dan Rainer; (second marriage) Miriam Lorraine, Nadine Marianne. *Education:* Wesleyan University, Middletown, Conn., B.A., 1949; University of California, Berkeley, M.A., 1950, Ph.D., 1953. *Home:* 117 Tuthill St., Port Jefferson, N.Y. 11777. *Office:* Department of History, State University of New York, Stony Brook, Long Island, N.Y. 11790.

CAREER: Wesleyan University, Middletown, Conn., instructor in history, 1954-55; University of California, Berkeley, instructor, then assistant professor of history, 1955-63; State University of New York at Stony Brook,

Long Island, associate professor of history, 1963-69, professor, 1969—. *Military service:* U.S. Army, 1941-45; became master sergeant; received Bronze Star, Purple Heart, Combat Infantry Badge, and Parachutist Wings. *Member:* American Historical Association, American Association of University Professors, Leo Baeck Institute (fellow). *Awards, honors:* Ford Foundation Fellow, 1954-55; State University of New York, University Faculty fellowship, 1969-70, for study abroad.

WRITINGS: Stillborn Revolution: The Communist Bid for Power in Germany, 1921-1923, Princeton University Press, 1963; (contributor) *Deutsches Judentum in Krieg und Revolution*, J. C. B. Mohr, 1971. Contributor of articles and reviews to scholarly journals in the United States, England, and West Germany.

WORK IN PROGRESS: Jews in German Politics, 1912-1922.

SIDELIGHTS: Angress is competent in German, French, and Dutch.

* * *

ANSTEY, Roger T(homas) 1927-

PERSONAL: Born February 1, 1927, in Maidenhead, England; son of John Frank (a railway official) and Ethel Mary (Thomas) Anstey; married Avril M. L. Gurney, August 11, 1954; children: Charles, Rosalind, Louise. *Education:* St. John's College, Cambridge, B.A. (honors in history), 1950, M.A., 1952; University of London, Ph.D., 1957. *Religion:* Methodist. *Home:* Hood's Place, Kingston, Canterbury, England.

CAREER: University College (now University of Ibadan), Ibadan, Nigeria, lecturer in modern history, 1952-57; University of Durham, Durham, England, lecturer, 1958-66, reader in modern history, 1966-68; University of Kent, Kent, England, professor of modern history, 1968—. Visiting professor, University of British Columbia, 1966-67; broadcaster of talks on African topics, British Broadcasting Corp. *Military service:* Royal Navy, 1945-48. *Member:* African Studies Association of the United Kingdom, Royal African Society.

WRITINGS: Britain and the Congo in the Nineteenth Century, Clarendon Press, 1962; *King Leopold's Legacy: The Congo Under Belgian Rule, 1908-60*, Oxford University Press for Institute of Race Relations, 1966; (contributor) L. H. Gann and P. Duignan, editors, *Colonialism in Africa*, Vol. 2, Cambridge University Press, 1970; *The Atlantic Slave Trade and British Abolition 1760-1810*, Macmillan, 1974; (contributor) R. W. Fogel and Stanley Engerman, editors, *Race and Slavery in the Western Hemisphere*, Princeton University Press, 1974. Contributor to *Encyclopaedia Britannica* (1974), *International Review of Missions, Economic History Review, English Historical Review, African Historical Review, Etudes d'Histoire Africane*, and *The Times.*

WORK IN PROGRESS: A book on the slave trade and suppression, and on the relationship of religion and reform in the nineteenth century.

SIDELIGHTS: Anstey has traveled widely in the Congo, and has lectured in a number of American and Canadian universities.

* * *

ANTHONY, Robert N(ewton) 1916-

PERSONAL: Born September 6, 1916, in Orange, Mass.; son of Charles H. and Grace (Newton) Anthony; married second wife Katherine Worley, August 4, 1973; children: (first marriage) Robert Newton, Victoria Stewart. *Education:* Colby College, A.B., 1938; Harvard University, M.B.A., 1940, D.C.S., 1952. *Residence:* Waterville Valley, N.H. 03223.

CAREER: Harvard University, Business School, Boston, Mass., 1940-42, 1946—, professor of business administration, 1956-63, Ross Graham Walker Professor of Management Control, 1963—, Leatherbee Lecturer, 1967; U.S. Department of Defense, assistant secretary, comptroller, 1965-68; U.S. Price Commission, special assistant and systems coordinator, 1971—. Consultant to comptroller, U.S. Air Force, Washington, D.C., 1951-52; president, Management Analysis Center, Inc., 1955-63; International Management Development Institute, member of original faculty, 1957-58, member of advisory board, 1961-65, 1968—; member, Stanford University Executive Development Program, 1962. Consulting editor, Richard D. Irwin, Inc., 1969—. Trustee of Lexington Savings Bank and of Colby College, 1959—; member of boards of directors of Technical Audit Associates (formerly Systems Audit Corp.), 1969-72, Carborundum Co., 1971—, and Warnaco, Inc., 1972—; member of nominations board, Ohio State University Accounting Hall of Fame, 1959-65. *Military service:* U.S. Navy, Supply Corps, 1941-46; became lieutenant commander; received CINCPAC Letter of Commendation with ribbon.

MEMBER: American Accounting Association (president, 1973-74), National Association of Accountants, Federal Government Accountants Association, American Institute of Certified Public Accountants, American Society for Public Administration, Academy of Management (fellow), Phi Beta Kappa, Pi Gamma Mu, Harvard Business School Club (member of board of directors, 1966—). *Awards, honors:* Baker scholar, 1940; M.A., 1959, and L.H.D., 1963, from Colby College; Distinguished Leadership award, Federal Government Accountants Association, 1967; Distinguished Public Service medal, Department of Defense, 1968; Colby Brick, 1972.

WRITINGS: (With Ross G. Walker) *Budgetary Control* (series of lectures), Harvard Business School, 1941; *Questions, Problems and Cases in Practical Controllership*, Irwin, 1949.

Management Controls in Industrial Research Organizations, Division of Research, Harvard Business School, 1951; (with DeWitt C. Dearborn and Rose W. Kneznek) *Spending for Industrial Research, 1951-52*, Division of Research, Harvard Business School, 1953; *Shoe Machinery: Buy or Lease?*, National Shoe Manufacturers Association, 1954, revised edition, 1955; (editor) *Proceedings, Automatic Data Processing Conference*, Division of Research, Harvard Business School, 1956; *Management Accounting: Text and Cases*, Irwin, 1956, 4th edition, 1970; (with Samuel Schwartz) *Office Equipment: Buy or Rent?*, Management Analysis Center (Boston), 1957; (editor) *Papers on Return on Investment*, Division of Case Reproduction and Distribution, Harvard Business School, 1959.

(With John Dearden) *Supplementary Cases and Problems of Management Accounting*, Irwin, 1960, 3rd edition (with J. Sinclair), published under title *Accounting Problems and Cases*, 1970; (with R. Masson and P. Hunt) *Cases in Financial Management*, Irwin, 1960; *Essentials of Accounting*, Addison-Wesley, 1964; *Management Accounting Principles*, Irwin, 1965, 2nd edition, 1970; *Planning and Control*

Systems: A Framework for Analysis, Division of Research, Harvard Business School, 1965; (with Dearden and Richard Vancil) *Management Control Systems*, Irwin, 1966, revised edition, 1972; (with James S. Hekimian) *Operations Cost Control*, Irwin, 1967; (with R. V. Matessich) *Harvard-Falle aus der Praxis des betrieblichen Rechnungswesens* (title means "Harvard Cases in the Practice of Management Accounting"), Bertelsman Universitatsverlag, 1969.

Plaid in Management Accounting, Irwin, 1970; (with Glenn A. Welsch) *Fundamentals of Financial Accounting*, Irwin, 1974; (with Welsch) *Fundamentals of Management Accounting*, Irwin, 1974.

Contributor: D. B. Hertz, editor, *Research Operations in Industry*, King's Crown Press, 1953; (author of introduction) Edward C. Bursk, editor, *The Management Team*, Harvard University Press, 1954; A. H. Rubinstein, editor, *Coordination, Control and Financing of Industrial Research*, King's Crown Press, 1955; Bursk, editor, *Planning the Future Strategy of Your Business*, McGraw, 1956.

Thomas J. Hailstones, editor, *Readings in Economics*, South-Western Publishing, 1962, 2nd edition, 1969; (with R. T. Sprouse) Harvard Business School Accounting Round Table, *The Measurement of Property, Plant, and Equipment in Financial Statements*, Harvard Business School, 1964; (author of introduction) James S. Hekimian, *Management Control in Life Insurance Branch Offices*, Division of Research, Harvard Business School, 1965; Lee Richardson and Harold A. Wolf, editors, *Readings in Finance*, Appleton, 1966; Maneck Wadia, *The Nature and Scope of Management*, Scott, Foresman, 1966; Robert K. Jaedicke and others, editors, *Research in Accounting Measurement*, American Accounting Association, 1966; William E. Thomas, editor, *Readings in Cost Accounting, Budgeting, and Control*, South-Western Publishing, 3rd edition, 1968, 4th edition, 1973.

K. Fred Skousen and Belverd Needles, editors, *Contemporary Thought in Accounting and Organizational Control*, Dickenson, 1970; Lawrence S. Rosen, editor, *Topics in Managerial Accounting*, McGraw, 1970; Alfred Rappaport,editor, *Information for Decision Making: Quantitative and Behavioral Dimensions*, Prentice-Hall, 1970; Eugene F. Breghan, editor, *Readings in Managerial Finance*, Holt, 1971; James D. Edwards and Bernhard C. Lemke, *Administrative Control and Executive Action*, C. E. Merrill, 2nd edition, 1972.

Contributor to management and accounting journals, including *Harvard Business Review*, *Accounting Review*, *Management Accounting*, *Public Administration Review*, and *Quarterly Journal of Economics*. Member of board, *Harvard Business Review*, 1947-60; member of editorial board, *Journal of Machine Accounting*, 1958-60, and *Management International*, 1961-68.

SIDELIGHTS: Some of Anthony's books have been translated into Italian, Spanish, Portuguese, Dutch, Afrikaan, Turkish, Japanese, and Chinese.

* * *

ANTONCICH, Betty (Kennedy) 1913-

PERSONAL: Born December 1, 1913, in Seattle, Wash.; daughter of Harry Phillip (a lumberman) and Francese (Nickels) Kennedy; married Michael A. Antoncich (a realtor), June 28, 1941; children: Michael A., Jr., Gay (Mrs. John Conroy), Franci (Mrs. Roger Fawley), Steven. *Education:* University of Washington, Seattle, B.A., 1936, Secondary Teaching Credential, 1937. *Politics:* Democrat. *Religion:* Roman Catholic. *Home:* 17 Upper Circle, Carmel Valley, Calif. 93924. *Agent:* McIntosh & Otis, Inc., 18 East 41st St., New York, N.Y. 10017.

CAREER: High school teacher of English in Eatonville, Wash., 1936-40, and in Monterey, Calif., 1947-51; Playtime Nursery School, Carmel Valley, Calif., owner and teacher, 1951—; junior high school teacher of speech and drama in Salinas, Calif., 1966-74. Member of board, Carmel Valley Community Center.

WRITINGS—Youth books: *Cliffhouse Mystery*, McKay, 1964; *Mystery of the Chinatown Pearls*, McKay, 1965.

WORK IN PROGRESS: A teenage mystery, *Secret of the Old Ghost Town*; two one-act plays, "Postmark Love," and "It Looks Like a Wonderful Summer."

* * *

ANTONY, Jonquil 1916-

PERSONAL: Born October 5, 1916, in London, England; daughter of Bertram (a medical doctor) and Frances (Ash) Soper; married John Wyse (an actor), 1941. *Education:* Attended high schools in South Africa and in Worthing, Sussex, England. *Politics:* Labour. *Religion:* Church of England. *Home and office:* 14 Rugby St., London W.C.1., England. *Agent:* Joyce Weiner, 127 Gyre Ct., London N.W. 1, England.

CAREER: Started writing scripts for British Broadcasting Corp., London, England, in 1937, doing serials, plays, and features, including (in more recent years) a daily radio serial, "The Dales," which she originated and wrote, 1948-63; now a free-lance writer. *Member:* Screenwriters and Television Guild, Society of Authors, Institut Napoleon.

WRITINGS: (With Lesley Wilson) *The Robinson Family*, Art and Education Publishers, 1948; *Sense and Sensibility* (three-act play adapted from Jane Austen's novel), Samuel French, 1949; *The Malindens*, Longmans, Green, 1951; *Mrs. Dale's Bedside Book*, Macdonald & Co., 1951; *Mrs. Dale At Home*, Macdonald & Co., 1952; *Paradise Square*, Macdonald & Co., 1952; *Mrs. Dale: Ten Years in the Life of a Doctor's Family*, British Book Service, 1958; (with Robert Turley) *The Dales of Parkwood Hill*, British Book Service, 1959; *Hark! Hark! the Ark!*, Constable, 1960; *Mrs. Dale's Friendship Book*, Constable, 1961; *Eaglemania*, Heinemann, 1965; *Dear Dr. Dale*, Dent, 1970; (compiler) *The Siege of Paris and Commune*, Grossman, 1970. Contributor to *Daily Telegraph* (London), *Housewife*, and other periodicals and newspapers.

WORK IN PROGRESS: A biography of Madame Fanny Bertrand, wife of Napleon's grand marshal.

AVOCATIONAL INTERESTS: Animals, country life, reading, theater, and France.†

* * *

APPEL, Benjamin 1907-

PERSONAL: Born September 13, 1907, in New York, N.Y.; son of Louis and Bessie (Mikofsky) Appel; married Sophie Marshak, October 31, 1936; children: Carla, Willa, Marianna Consideration. *Education:* Attended University of Pennsylvania, 1925-26, New York University, 1926-27; Lafayette College, B.S., 1929. *Politics:* "Utopian." *Home:* Roosevelt, N.J.

CAREER: Writer, 1929—, with some short stints during

depression years as bank clerk, farmer, lumberjack, tenement house inspector, and other positions. During World War II worked as aviation mechanic; served with various government agencies, including U.S. Office of Civilian Defense, and War Manpower Commission, 1943-45; special assistant to U.S. Commissioner for the Philippines, 1945-46, with simulated rank of colonel in Manila. Visiting author at University of Pennsylvania, spring, 1974. *Member:* Authors Guild, P.E.N.

WRITINGS: Mixed Vintage (poems), Richard G. Badger, 1929.

Brain Guy, Knopf, 1934; *Four Roads to Death*, Knopf, 1935; *Runaround*, Dutton, 1937; *The Power House*, Dutton, 1939.

The People Talk (nonfiction), Dutton, 1940; *The Dark Stain*, Dial, 1943; *But Not Yet Slain*, Wyn, 1947.

Fortress in Rice, Bobbs-Merrill, 1951; *Plunder*, Gold Medal, 1952; *Hell's Kitchen* (short stories), Lion Books, 1952; *Dock Walloper* (short stories), Lion Books, 1953; *Sweet Money Girl*, Fawcett, 1954; *Life and Death of a Tough Guy*, Avon, 1955; *We Were There in the Klondike Gold Rush* (juvenile), Grosset, 1956; *We Were There at the Battle for Bataan* (juvenile), Grosset, 1957; *The Raw Edge*, Random House, 1958; *We Were There with Cortes and Montezuma* (juvenile), Grosset, 1959; *The Funhouse*, Ballantine, 1959.

The Illustrated Book About South America, including Mexico and Central America (juvenile), Grosset, 1960; *A Big Man, A Fast Man*, Morrow, 1961; *Shepherd of the Sun*, Obolensky, 1961; *With Many Voices: Europe Talks About America*, Morrow, 1963; *A Time of Fortune*, Morrow, 1963; *Hitler, From Power to Ruin*, Grosset, 1964; *Ben-Gurion's Israel*, Grosset, 1965; *Man and Magic*, Pantheon, 1966; *Why the Russians Are the Way They Are* (juvenile), Little, Brown, 1966; *The Age of Dictators* (juvenile), Crown, 1968; *Why the Chinese Are the Way They Are* (juvenile), Little, Brown, 1968, revised edition, 1973; *The Fantastic Mirror: Science Fiction Across the Ages* (juvenile), Pantheon, 1969; *Why the Japanese Are the Way They Are* (juvenile), Little, Brown, 1973.

Short stories anthologized in *O. Henry Memorial Award Prize Stories* and O'Brien's *Best Short Stories*, 1934, 1935, and in *Best Short Stories 1915-39*. Contributor of essays on writers of the 1930's and short stories to magazines, such as *Carleton Miscellany, The Literary Review*, and *New Letters*.

SIDELIGHTS: Appel first wrote for the "little" literary magazines of the 1930's, reflected on the background of his youth (the "Hell's Kitchen" area of Manhattan) in his first novel, *Brain Guy*, and has since developed novels around politics, race relations, and the Philippines, and has written nonfiction on other contemporary subjects. *Avocational interests:* Fishing.

*   *   *

APPLEMAN, Philip (Dean) 1926-

PERSONAL: Born February 8, 1926, in Kendallville, Ind.; son of William Russell (a manufacturer) and Gertrude (Keller) Appleman; married Marjorie Haberkorn (a playwright), August 19, 1950. *Education:* Northwestern University, B.S., 1950, Ph.D., 1955; University of Michigan, A.M., 1951; University of Lyon, Fulbright scholar, 1951-52. *Home:* 123 South Jefferson St., Bloomington, Ind. *Office:* English Department, Indiana University, Bloomington, Ind. 47401.

CAREER: Indiana University, Bloomington, Ind., 1955—, began as instructor, became professor of English, 1967. International School of America, Columbus, Ohio, instructor in world literature and philosophy, 1960-61, instructor and field director, 1962-63, now member of academic advisory committee. Visiting professor, State University of New York College at Purchase, 1973, and Columbia University, 1974. *Military service:* U.S. Army Air Forces, 1944-45. U.S. Merchant Marine, 1946, 1948-49. *Member:* Modern Language Association of America (chairman of English Section II, 1966), National Council of Teachers of English, College English Association, American Association of University Professors (member of National Council, 1969-72), Poetry Society of America, Academy of American Poets, P.E.N., Phi Beta Kappa.

WRITINGS: (Editor with William A. Madden and Michael Wolff, and contributor) *1859: Entering an Age of Crisis*, Indiana University Press, 1959; *The Silent Explosion*, Beacon, 1965; *Kites on a Windy Day* (poems), Byron Press, 1967; *Summer Love and Surf* (poems), Vanderbilt University Press, 1968; *In the Twelfth Year of the War* (novel), Putnam, 1970; (editor) *Darwin* (critical anthology), Norton, 1970. Contributor of critical articles and reviews to scholarly periodicals; contributor of poems to *Harper's, Yale Review, Partisan Review, New Republic, Nation*, and other periodicals. Founding editor, *Victorian Studies*.

WORK IN PROGRESS: A new volume of poems and a novel.

SIDELIGHTS: Appleman has traveled in Europe and Africa, and twice around the world for International School of America. He is competent in French.

*   *   *

APPLEY, M(ortimer) H(erbert) 1921-
(M. H. Applezweig)

PERSONAL: Surname originally Applezweig, legally changed, 1961; born November 21, 1921, in New York, N.Y.; son of Benjamin and Minnie (Albert) Applezweig; married Dorothy Gordon, June 5, 1942 (divorced, 1969); married Mariann Berg Hundahl, January 10, 1971; children: Richard Gordon, John Benton; stepchildren: Scott Hundahl, Eric Hundahl, Heidi Hundahl. *Education:* City College (now City College of the City University of New York), B.S. in Social Science, 1942; University of Denver, M.A., 1946; University of Michigan, Ph.D., 1950. *Politics:* Democrat. *Religion:* Unitarian Universalist. *Home:* 80 William St., Worcester, Mass. 01609. *Office:* Clark University, Worcester, Mass. 01610.

CAREER: Instructor in psychology at University of Denver, Denver, Colo., 1945-47, University of Michigan, Ann Arbor, 1947-49; Wesleyan University, Middletown, Conn., assistant professor of psychology, 1949-52; Connecticut College, New London, professor of psychology and chairman of department, 1952-60; Southern Illinois University, Carbondale, professor of psychology and chairman of department, 1960-62; York University, Toronto, Ontario, professor of psychology and chairman of department, 1962-66, dean of faculty of graduate studies, 1965-67; University of Massachusetts, Amherst, professor of psychology and chairman of department, 1967-69, dean of graduate school and coordinator of research, 1969-74, associate provost, 1973-74; Clark University, Worcester, Mass., president, 1974—. Secretary, Connecticut Board of Examiners of Psychologists, 1959-60. Consultant to Electric Boat Division of General Dynamics, U.S. Naval Medical Research

Institute, other organizations. President, New London Child Guidance Clinic, 1956-58. *Military service:* U.S. Army Air Forces, 1942-45; became staff sergeant.

MEMBER: American Psychological Association (fellow), American Association for the Advancement of Science (fellow), Canadian Psychological Association (honorary fellow; member of board of directors, 1965-68), New England Psychological Association (president, 1973-74), Sigma Xi. *Awards, honors:* National Science Foundation faculty fellow, 1959-60; Fulbright fellowship in Germany, 1973.

WRITINGS: (Under name M. H. Applezweig) *Psychological Stress and Related Concepts: A Bibliography*, U.S. Office of Naval Research and Connecticut College Press, 1957; (contributor) B. E. Flaherty, editor, *Psychophysiological Aspects of Space Flight*, Columbia University Press, 1961; (with C. N. Cofer) *Motivation: Theory and Research*, Wiley, 1964; (editor with R. Trumbull) *Psychological Stress: Issues in Research*, Appleton, 1967; *Psychology in Canada*, Queen's Printer, 1967; (editor) *Adaptation Level Theory*, Academic Press, 1971. Contributor to *Annual Review of Psychology*, *Journal of Abnormal and Social Psychology*, *Journal of Experimental Psychology*, and other psychology journals.

*   *   *

ARAKI, James T(omomasa)   1925-

PERSONAL: Born June 18, 1925, in Salt Lake City, Utah; son of Hikotaro (a priest of Izumo sect of Shinto) and Kotomi (Tanaka) Araki; married Janet Yamada, August 18, 1957; children: Dale Makoto, Kenneth Toshio, Melinda Eiko, Melissa Yoko. *Education:* University of California, Los Angeles, B.A., 1954; University of California, Berkeley, M.A., 1958, Ph.D., 1961. *Office:* University of Hawaii, Honolulu, Hawaii 96822.

CAREER: University of California, Los Angeles, instructor in Japanese, 1961-62, assistant professor of Oriental languages, 1962-64; Fulbright research professor in Osaka, Japan, 1964-65; University of Hawaii, Honolulu, professor of Japanese literature, 1965—. *Military service:* U.S. Army, 1944-48, 1951-52; became first lieutenant. *Member:* American Oriental Society, Association for Asian Studies, Phi Beta Kappa.

WRITINGS: The Ballad-Drama of Medieval Japan, University of California Press, 1964; (translator with Delmer M. Brown) *Studies in Shinto Thought*, UNESCO, 1964; (translator and author of introduction) Yasushi Inoue, *The Tempyo Rooftile*, University of Tokyo Press, in press. Contributor to *Books Abroad* and *Monumenta Nipponica*.

WORK IN PROGRESS: Research in eighteenth- and nineteenth-century Japanese fiction for a book, *Edo Sketches in Japanese Fiction*.

*   *   *

ARBUCKLE, Dugald S(inclair)   1912-

PERSONAL: Born June 28, 1912, in Estevan, Saskatchewan, Canada; became U.S. citizen, 1952; son of John Finley and Margaret (Sinclair) Arbuckle; married Margaret May Redmond, October 10, 1942 (divorced, 1972); children: Donald Redmond, Margaret Ann, Mary Elizabeth, Jane Katherine, Judith Ellen. *Education:* University of Alberta, B.Sc., 1940, B.Ed., 1942; University of Chicago, Ph.D., 1947. *Home:* 101 Billings St., Sharon, Mass. 02067. *Office:* Boston University, Boston, Mass. 02215.

CAREER: Certified psychologist. Teacher in Alberta, 1931-43; International Harvester Co., Chicago, Ill., educational consultant, 1946-47; Boston University, Boston, Mass., started as assistant professor, 1947, professor of education and director of counselor education, 1953—. Harvard University, Cambridge, Mass., psychological associate, 1959-60; visiting professor at thirty other universities and colleges, 1951-65. Consultant to U.S. government agencies and to universities. *Military service:* Royal Canadian Air Force, 1943-45; educational officer.

MEMBER: American College Personnel Association, American Personnel and Guidance Association (past president), Student Personnel Association for Teacher Education (past president), American Social Hygiene Association, American Academy of Psychotherapists, National Vocational Guidance Association (professional member), American Psychological Association (fellow), Association for Counselor Education and Supervision (past chairman, North Atlantic region), National Education Association, American Educational Research Association, American Association of University Professors, New England College Personnel Seminar Group (past chairman), Massachusetts Council on Teacher Education (past president), Massachusetts Society for Social Hygiene (past president), Massachusetts Psychological Association, Phi Delta Kappa, Alpine Club of Canada.

WRITINGS: Industrial Counseling, Bellman, 1949; *Teacher Counseling*, Addison-Wesley, 1950; *Student Personnel Services in Higher Education*, McGraw, 1953; *Guidance and Counseling in the Classroom*, Allyn & Bacon, 1957; *Counseling: An Introduction*, Allyn & Bacon, 1961; *Pupil Personnel Services in the American School*, Allyn & Bacon, 1962, new enlarged edition published as *Pupil Personnel Services in the Modern School*, 1966; *Counseling: Philosophy, Theory, and Practice*, Allyn & Bacon, 1965, 2nd edition, 1970; (editor) *Counseling and Psychotherapy: An Overview*, McGraw, 1967. Contributor to professional journals.†

*   *   *

ARCHER, H(orace) Richard   1911-

PERSONAL: Born September 13, 1911, in Albuquerque, N.M.; son of Richard Reece and Martha Julia (Briglieb) Archer; married Margot Hanko, January 26, 1936. *Education:* University of California, Berkeley, B.A., 1940, Certificate of Librarianship, 1941, M.A., 1943; University of Chicago, Ph.D., 1954. *Home:* Sabin Dr., Williamstown, Mass. 01267. *Office:* Chapin Library, Williams College, Williamstown, Mass. 01267.

CAREER: Book shop assistant and manager in Los Angeles, Calif., and order librarian at University of California, Berkeley, while continuing education; University of California, Los Angeles, supervising bibliographer at W. A. Clark Memorial Library, 1944-52, curator of graphic arts, 1952-53; R. R. Donnelley & Sons Co., Chicago, Ill., librarian, 1954-57; Williams College, Chapin Library, Williamstown, Mass., librarian, 1957—, lecturer in graphic arts, 1965—. University of Southern California, visiting summer instructor, 1960; visiting lecturer at University of Oklahoma, summer, 1956, University of Michigan, summer, 1962, Simmons College, spring, 1965, University of Illinois, summer, 1969, State University of New York at Albany, 1968-73. Founder, owner, and operator of private press, Hippogryph Press, 1951—.

MEMBER: American Library Association (council, 1962-

65; chairman of rare books section, 1962-63), Bibliographical Society of America, American Association of University Professors, Society of Private Printers, Private Library Association, William Morris Society, Phi Beta Mu, Society for Italic Writing, Printing Historical Society, Society of Printers (Boston), Typophiles (New York), Library Company of Philadelphia, Faculty Club of Williams College (vice-president, 1962-63), Grolier Club, Zamorano Club, Rounce and Coffin Club. *Awards, honors:* Printing Award of Merit from Society of Typographic Arts, 1956.

WRITINGS: (Contributor) *William A. Clark Memorial Library: Report of the First Decade, 1934-1944*, University of California Press, 1946; (contributor) *Library Trends*, University of Illinois Library School, 1958; (editor) *Rare Book Collections: Some Theoretical and Practical Suggestions for Use by Librarians and Students*, American Library Association, 1965. Contributor to *Encyclopedia of Library and Information Science*. Contributor of articles and reviews to library journals. Editor, *Hoja Volante*, 1949-53.

WORK IN PROGRESS: Writing on the history of printing, especially in western Europe and America, on private press and amateur printers, and on problems of curatorship in rare book libraries and special collections; a study of book typography in the field of librarianship.

SIDELIGHTS: Archer has traveled widely in Europe, lecturing and doing research. He has a private library of 3,000 volumes, specializing in William Faulkner first editions and other work (300 items), history of private presses and private printing (1,000 items), modern literature, jazz music, and bibliography. His collection of American jazz records runs to 500 platters dating from 1932-1956.

* * *

ARDEN, John 1930-

PERSONAL: Born October 26, 1930, in Barnsley, Yorkshire, England; son of C. A. (a manager of a glass works) and A. E. (Layland) Arden; married Margaretta Ruth D'Arcy (an actress), 1957; children: four sons. *Education:* King's College, Cambridge, B.A., 1953; Edinburgh College of Architecture, diploma, 1955. *Address:* c/o Margaret Ramsey Ltd., 14a Goodwin Court, London W.C.2, England.

CAREER: Architectural assistant in London, England, 1955-57; playwright, 1957—. Visiting lecturer, New York University, 1967. *Military service:* British Army, Intelligence Corps, 1949-50. *Awards, honors:* British Broadcasting Corporation Northern Region prize for "The Life of Man"; *Encyclopaedia Britannica* prize, 1959, for *Serjeant Musgrave's Dance*; Bristol University fellowship in playwriting, 1959-60; *Evening Standard* (London) "most promising playwright" award, 1960; Trieste Festival prize, 1961, for "Soldier, Soldier"; Vernon Rice Award, 1966, for *Serjeant Musgrave's Dance*.

WRITINGS—Plays: "All Fall Down," produced in Edinburgh, 1955; "The Life of Man" (also see below), produced for radio, 1956; "The Waters of Babylon" (also see below), first produced in London at Royal Court Theatre, October 20, 1957, produced in Washington, D.C. at Washington Theatre Club, 1967; "When Is a Door Not a Door?" (also see below), first produced in London at Central School of Drama, 1958; "Live Like Pigs" (also see below), first produced at Royal Court Theatre, September 30, 1958, produced Off-Broadway at Actor's Playhouse, June 7, 1965; *Serjeant Musgrave's Dance: An Unhistorical Parable* (first produced at Royal Court Theatre, October 22, 1959; produced Off-Broadway at Theatre de Lys, March 8, 1966; revised version produced in London, 1972), Methuen, 1960, Grove, 1962; "A Christmas Play," first produced in Brent Knoll, England, 1960, produced in New York, N.Y., 1970, as *The Business of Good Government: A Christmas Play* and published under that title by Methuen, 1963, Grove, 1967; (with wife, Margaretta D'Arcy) "The Happy Haven" (also see below), first produced in Bristol, England at Old Vic Theatre, 1960, produced in New York, N.Y., 1967; "Soldier, Soldier" (also see below), produced in London for television, 1960; "Wet Fish" (also see below), produced in London for television, 1961; *Ironhand* (an adaptation of Goethe's *Goetz von Bertlichen*; first produced in Bristol at Old Vic Theatre, 1963), Methuen, 1965, Grove, 1967; *The Workhouse Donkey* (first produced at Chichester Festival Theatre, 1963; first play by a living British dramatist to be performed there), Methuen, 1964, Grove, 1967; *Three Plays: The Waters of Babylon, Live Like Pigs, The Happy Haven*, Penguin, 1964, Grove, 1966.

Armstrong's Last Goodnight: An Exercise in Diplomacy (first produced in Glasgow, Scotland at Citizen's Theatre, May, 1964; produced in Boston, 1966), Methuen, 1965, Grove, 1967; (with Margaret D'Arcy) *Ars Longa, Vita Brevis* (produced in London, 1964), Cassell, 1965; *Left-Handed Liberty* (commissioned by the City of London to celebrate the 750th anniversary of the sealing of the Magna Carta; first produced in London at Mermaid Theatre, June, 1965), Methuen, 1965, Grove, 1966; "Play Without Words," produced in Glasgow, Scotland, 1965; (with Margaretta D'Arcy) "Friday's Hiding" (also see below), first produced in Edinburgh, 1966; (with Margaretta D'Arcy) *The Royal Pardon: Or, The Soldier Who Became an Actor* (first produced in Beaford, England, 1966), Methuen, 1966; *Soldier, Soldier and Other Plays* (includes "Wet Fish," "Soldier, Soldier," "When Is a Door Not a Door?" "Friday's Hiding"), Methuen, 1967; "The True History of Squire Jonathan and His Unfortunate Treasure" (also see below), first produced in London, 1968; (with Margaretta D'Arcy) *The Hero Rises Up: A Romantic Melodrama* (musical; first produced in London, 1968), Methuen, 1969; (with Margaretta D'Arcy and others) "Harold Muggins Is a Martyr," produced in London, 1968; "The Bagman: Or, The Impromptu of Muswell Hill" (also see below), produced for radio, 1970; *Two Autobiographical Plays: The True History of Squire Jonathan and His Unfortunate Treasure, and The Bagman: Or, The Impromptu of Muswell Hill*, Methuen, 1971; (with Margaretta D'Arcy) "The Ballygombeen Bequest," first produced in Belfast, Northern Ireland, 1972; (with Margaretta D'Arcy) *The Island of the Mighty* (produced in London at Aldwych Theatre, December 5, 1972), Methuen, 1973.

Also author of libretti adaptations: Alban Berg, "Woyzeck" (based on play by Georg Buechner; music by Berg), produced in London, 1964; Joseph Sonnleithner and Friedrich Treitschke, "Fidelio" (music by Beethoven), produced in London, 1965; Charles Ramuz, "The Soldier's Tale" (music by Igor Stravinsky), produced in Bath, England, 1968.

Plays included in anthologies: *New English Dramatists*, Penguin, Volume III, 1961, Volume IV, 1962; *Scripts 9* [New York], 1972.

SIDELIGHTS: Speaking of British dramatists since 1956, John Russell Taylor writes: "One of the most strikingly independent of these writers, and, if one may venture to prophesy from work to date, one of those most likely still to be writing major plays in ten or twenty years' time, is John Arden." He is, writes Taylor, "probably more clearly, intellectually aware of what he is doing in his plays than virtually any other dramatist writing in Britain today: if he writes a nativity play it is in the light of his studies of medieval mysteries and miracle plays; if he incorporates a ballad in a dramatic scene its function is governed to some extent by his thought about the ballad tradition and ballad imagery.... [He has] continued to shatter any preconceptions we might have about what to expect from him almost before they have formed in our minds, disregarding entirely the fashion for the theatre of the Absurd, ... writing period drama at a time when everyone else was preoccupied with the contemporary scene, and gnomic comedy-dramas littered with ballads and rhymed dialogue set squarely in the present at a time when everyone else seemed ... to be looking to the past.... Arden is a genuine original, ... [and his plays are] unmistakably the product of one exceptional mind."

V. S. Pritchett believes that the basis of Arden's art, "from *Serjeant Musgrave* on, has been imaginative criticism. He is very little didactic. He is deeply concerned, not with politics, nor even history, but with government as a mystery, a work of nature, struggling for life among the weeds of violence and the simple brutalities and hypocrisies of self-interest. And this concern takes him to the exposed, raw, ragged aspects of people who, against their will, have the chance of being clothed with the beginnings of civilisation." Taylor considers Arden to be the most amoral British playwright writing today. Arden's "attitude to his creations is quite uncommitted; this means that, for instance, he does not defend the amorality of one group of characters nor, on the other hand, does he condemn it—they are individuals, and there are reasons, valid reasons, why they live as they do, even if they are displaced persons in the modern world.... He does not even seek to generalize from them...." He neither provides answers to moral dilemmas nor espouses causes. In an introduction to *Serjeant Musgrave's Dance* he states that this play is not simply a plea for pacifism: "Complete pacifism is a very hard doctrine: and if this play appears to advocate it with perhaps some timidity, it is probably because I am naturally a timid man—and also because I know that if I am hit I very easily hit back: and I do not care to preach too confidently what I am not sure I can practise." Taylor believes that behind Arden's works "there seems to be brooding one basic principle: not exactly the obvious one that today there are no causes—that would be altogether too facile, and in any case just not true—but that there are too many.... [And] only the naive can suppose that any two people who are, say, pacifists (to choose a nice, convenient label) will believe the same things for the same reasons."

Katherine J. Worth notes that Arden "writes in the tradition of all those playwrights who ... have been haunted by the achievement of the Irish in combining poetry and realism.... Arden explores the dramatic and poetic potentialities in the dialects of ordinary working-class people as well as in traditionally exotic sources, like the speech of gipsies. He evolves a rough, highly coloured, figurative language, based on a curious amalgam of northern dialects." His first play, "The Life of Man," adumbrated his mature style, namely what Taylor calls "the unpredictable alternation of racy, idiomatic prose and quite highly wrought formal verse, the extensive use of traditional song and ballad, and ... [the] interest in the bold, free, nomadic

life of the 'sturdy beggar' which was later to bear spectacular fruit in *Live Like Pigs*."

Critical opinion was sharply divided when *Serjeant Musgrave's Dance*, probably his best-known play, was first performed. Alan Pryce-Jones wrote that there were critics "hating it outright, others (like myself) having strong reserves about it, and a few delighting in it wholeheartedly...." Philip Hope-Wallace wrote: "Even now, at curtain-fall, some of its import escapes me, but for the best part of three hours it has worked on my curiosity and often put that ill-definable theatrical spell on my imagination. I think it is something short of a great play. But wild horses wouldn't have dragged me from my seat before the end." Arden, attempting to dispel some of the puzzlement, wrote: "This is not a nihilistic play. This is not (except perhaps unconsciously) a symbolist play. Nor does it advocate bloody revolution. I have endeavoured to write about the violence that is so evident in the world, and to do so through a story that is partly one of wish-fulfillment. I think that many of us must at some time have felt an overpowering urge to match some particularly outrageous piece of violence with an even greater and more outrageous retaliation. Musgrave tries to do this: and the fact that the sympathies of the play are clearly with him in his original horror, and then turn against him and his intended remedy, seems to have bewildered many people." Ronald Bryden believes that if the play fails, "it's failure on a scale no one else has come near in our generation."

Seeking to illuminate the complexity of this artist, Bryden draws a parallel between Arden and Thomas Hardy. Both, he says, "started life as architects; in their writing, both opt for fabrication rather than confession. Both were provincials born, who, submitting superficially to offical metropolitan culture, became highly literary, slightly old-fashioned stylists, handling words self-consciously but, sometimes, with a knotty lyricism better than grace. At their worst, there's something neo-Gothic and Gilbert Scottish about both of them.... Yet they share a massiveness which makes most of their contemporaries seem light-weight. Beneath their acquired literariness, they put down roots to a primitive strength which forces you to compare them with the classics: Hardy with Aeschylus, Arden (as Irving Wardle recently urged) with Aristophanes. Despite his failure to produce one unflawed major work, to bear comparison with Hardy is no small thing. Beneath the somewhat glacial, invented language, Arden fishes as Hardy did ponds like the one Ted Hughes's pike haunted, deep as England."

BIOGRAPHICAL/CRITICAL SOURCES: John Russell Taylor, *Anger and After*, Methuen, 1962; *Contemporary Theatre*, Stratford-Upon-Avon Studies 4, Edward Arnold, 1962; William A. Armstrong, general editor, *Experimental Drama*, G. Bell & Sons, 1963; George Wellworth, *The Theater of Protest and Paradox*, New York University Press, 1964; Walter Lowenfels, editor, *The Playwrights Speak*, Delacorte, 1967; Frederick Lumley, *New Trends in 20th Century Drama: A Survey Since Ibsen and Shaw*, Oxford University Press, 1967.†

*   *   *

ARMSTRONG, Anne(tte) 1924-

PERSONAL: Born September 3, 1924, in New Jersey; daughter of Thomas Laurence (a civil servant) and Amanda (Gutheil) Armstrong; married Henning von Royk-Lewinski, 1951 (divorced, 1954); children: Victoria-Luise (deceased). *Education:* Montclair State College, A.B., 1944; Columbia University, A.M., 1947, Ph.D., 1960. *Politics:* Republican. *Religion:* Lutheran. *Home:* 111 West Passaic Ave., Rutherford, N.J. *Office:* Department of Political Science, Herbert H. Lehman College of the City University of New York, Bronx, N.Y. 10468.

CAREER: U.S. Military Government, Berlin and Munich, Germany, international analyst, 1947-48; Fairleigh Dickinson University, Rutherford, N.J., 1952-64, began as instructor, became assistant professor of political science; Herbert H. Lehman College of the City University of New York, Bronx, N.Y., assistant professor, 1964-73, associate professor of political science, 1973—. *Military service:* U.S. Air Force (WAF), Continental Air Command, intelligence officer, 1950-51; became second lieutenant. *Member:* American Political Science Association, American Historical Association, American Society of International Law, Women's National Republican Club (member of board of governors of New York chapter).

WRITINGS: Unconditional Surrender: The Impact of the Casablanca Policy on World War II, Rutgers University Press, 1961; *Attentat* (title means "Assassination"), Molden Verlag, 1965; *Berliners: Both Sides of the Wall,* Rutgers University Press, 1973.

WORK IN PROGRESS: Liberation German Style, a study of women in public life in West Germany, for Rutgers University Press.

SIDELIGHTS: Ms. Armstrong lived abroad for a total of five years, chiefly in Germany; she speaks fluent German and French. *Avocational interests:* Dancing (ballet), the theater, writing fiction.

* * *

ARMSTRONG, Gerry (Breen) 1929-

PERSONAL: Born October 28, 1929, in Detroit, Mich.; daughter of Edward Patrick (a realtor) and Leona (Griese) Breen; married George D. Armstrong, Jr. (an illustrator), April 24, 1954; children: Rebecca Lee, Jennifer Ann. *Religion:* Roman Catholic. *Home:* 1535 Lake Ave., Wilmette, Ill. 60091.

CAREER: Folk singer and folk song collector. Performer with husband, George D. Armstrong, Jr. and daughters, at folk festivals, including English Folk Song and Dance Society Festival, Stratford-on-Avon, England, 1954, at concerts, and on radio and television. Recording artist with husband on long-play albums for Folkways and Folk-Legacy labels.

WRITINGS—All illustrated by husband, George D. Armstrong, Jr. and published by Whitman: *The Magic Bagpipe,* 1964; *The Boat on the Hill,* 1967; *The Fairy Thorn,* 1969.

* * *

ARMSTRONG, William A(lexander) 1912-
(Alexander Hazelton)

PERSONAL: Born March 1, 1912, in Edinburgh, Scotland; son of William and Catherine (Bain) Armstrong; married Elizabeth Burns. *Education:* University of Grenoble, student, 1932-33; University of Edinburgh, M.A. (honors), 1934; University of London, B.A. (honors), 1948. *Religion:* Presbyterian. *Home:* 56 Jackson St., Penicuik, Midlothian, Scotland. *Agent:* A. M. Heath & Co. Ltd., 35 Dover St., London, W.1, England.

CAREER: Assistant at Moffat Academy, 1935-40; senior

assistant at Daniel Stewart's College, 1946-54; principal teacher of modern languages at North Berwick High School, 1955-64; headmaster of Penicuik Senior Secondary School, Penicuik, Midlothian, Scotland, 1964—. *Military service:* British Army, 26th Guards Brigade, 1940-46; became staff captain. *Member:* Crime Writers' Association, P.E.N.

WRITINGS: (Under pseudonym Alexander Hazelton) *A Tale of Two Islands,* Cassell, 1958; *The Armstrong Borderland,* McQueen & Son, 1960; (under pseudonym Alexander Hazelton) *Escape Into Danger,* Panther Books, 1960.

WORK IN PROGRESS: A historical novel based on the Buccleuch clearance of the smaller clans in Liddlesdale in the seventeenth century.†

* * *

ARNDT, Walter W(erner) 1916-

PERSONAL: Surname is pronounced like "aren't"; born May 4, 1916, in Constantinople, Turkey; became U.S. citizen, 1955; son of Fritz Georg (a university professor) and Julia (Heimann) Arndt; married Miriam Bach (an instructor in French), January 6, 1945; children: Robert M., David J., Prudence J., Corinne C. *Education:* Oxford University, Diploma in Economics and Political Science, 1936; University of Warsaw, graduate student, 1939; Robert College, Istanbul, Turkey, B.S., 1943; University of North Carolina, Ph.D., 1956; other study at University of Michigan, 1953, Harvard University, 1956-57. *Religion:* Society of Friends. *Home:* 38 Maple St., Hanover, N.H. 03755.

CAREER: U.S. Office of Strategic Services, intelligence officer, 1943-44; U.S. Office of War Information, assistant to director, Istanbul, Turkey, 1944-45; Robert College, Istanbul, instructor in mechanical engineering, 1945-48; assistant to director, United Nations International Refugee Organization, Istanbul, and Istanbul correspondent for *Economist,* London, England, 1947-49; Guilford College, Greensboro, N.C., instructor, later assistant professor of classics and modern languages, 1950-56; University of North Carolina, Chapel Hill, assistant professor, 1957-62, associate professor, 1962-66, professor of Russian, 1966—, chairman of department, 1966-70. University of Munster, Fulbright research professor, 1961-62; visiting professor, University of Colorado, 1965.

MEMBER: American Association of Teachers of Slavic and East European Languages (vice-president, 1964-66), Modern Language Association of America, Linguistic Society of America, American Association for the Advancement of Slavic Studies, American Association of Teachers of German, National Slavic Honor Society (vice-president, 1964-65), South Atlantic Modern Language Association (chairman of Slavic section, 1959, 1963), Southern Conference on Slavic Studies (vice-president, 1964; president, 1965). *Awards, honors:* Ford Foundation fellowships, University of Michigan, 1952, Harvard University, 1956-57; Bollingen Poetry Translation Prize ($2,500) for *Eugene Onegin,* 1963; American Philosophical Society research grant, 1967.

WRITINGS: (Translator, and author of introduction and notes) Alexander Pushkin, *Eugene Onegin: A New Translation in the Onegin Stanza,* Dutton, 1963; (with Lewis Levine) *Grundzuege moderner Sprachbeschreibung,* Max Niemeyer, 1965; (editor with P. W. Brosman and others) *Studies in Historical Linguistics in Honor of George Lane,* University of North Carolina Press, 1967; (translator) Wilhelm Busch, *Balduin Bählamm: Der verhinderte Dichter,*

S. Mohn (Guetersloh), 1967; (translator) Aleksandr Pushkin, *Pushkin Threefold: Narrative, Lyric, Polemic, and Ribald Verse*, Dutton, 1972. Contributor of verse translations from the Russian to *Russian Review* and *Slavic Review*, and articles to *Word*, *Shakespeare Quarterly*, other journals.

WORK IN PROGRESS: Alexander Pushkin: The Gypsies and Selected Poems, first verse translations done in the metric form of the originals; other verse translations, including works of Wilhelm Busch; research in dialect geography, bilingualism, comparative literature, and structural grammar.

SIDELIGHTS: Arndt speaks German, Russian, Polish, French, Turkish; reads minor Slavic languages and other Germanic and Romance languages.

*   *   *

ARNSTEIN, Walter L(eonard)   1930-

PERSONAL: Second syllable of surname rhymes with "fine"; born May 14, 1930, in Stuttgart, Germany; became U.S. citizen, 1944; son of Richard (a wholesale dealer in textiles) and Charlotte (Heymann) Arnstein; married Charlotte Culver Sutphen (a teacher of piano), June 8, 1952; children: Sylvia, Peter. *Education:* City College (now City College of the City University of New York), B.S. in Social Science, 1951; Columbia University, M.A., 1954; University of London, graduate study, 1956-57; Northwestern University, Ph.D., 1961. *Politics:* Independent Democrat. *Home:* 1506 Maplecrest Dr., Champaign, Ill. 61820. *Office:* Department of History, 309 Gregory Hall, University of Illinois, Urbana, Ill. 61801.

CAREER: Roosevelt University, Chicago, Ill., assistant professor, 1957-62, associate professor, 1962-66, professor of history and acting dean of graduate division, 1966-67; University of Illinois, Urbana, professor of history, 1968—. Northwestern University, Evanston, Ill., visiting associate professor of history, 1963-64; visiting lecturer or professor at City College (now City College of the City University of New York), New York, N.Y., summers, 1954, 1955, University of Illinois, summer, 1964, University of Chicago, spring, 1965. *Military service:* U.S. Army, 1951-53; served in Korea. *Member:* American Historical Association, Historical Association (England), Royal History Society (fellow), Conference on British Studies (executive committee member, 1971—), American Association of University Professors, Midwest Conference on British Studies, Phi Beta Kappa, Phi Alpha Theta. *Awards, honors:* Fulbright scholarship in England, 1956-57; Roosevelt University faculty research fellowship, 1962; American Council of Learned Societies fellowship, 1967-68.

WRITINGS: The Bradlaugh Case: A Study in Late Victorian Opinion and Politics, Clarendon Press, 1965; *Britain Yesterday and Today, 1830 to the Present*, Heath, 1966, 2nd edition, 1971. Contributor to *Journal of the History of Ideas*, *Victorian Studies*, *Irish Historical Studies*, *Business and Society*, and to newspapers. Advisory board member, *Victorian Studies*, 1966—.†

*   *   *

ARROW, Kenneth J.   1921-

PERSONAL: Born August 23, 1921, in New York, N.Y.; son of Harry I. and Lillian (Greenberg) Arrow; married Selma Schweitzer (a social worker), August 31, 1947; children: David Michael, Andrew Seth. *Education:* College of the City of New York (now City College of the City University of New York), B.S., 1940; Columbia University, M.A., 1941, Ph.D., 1951. *Politics:* Democrat. *Religion:* Jewish. *Home:* 6 Walnut Ave., Cambridge, Mass. 02140. *Office:* Department of Economics, Harvard University, Room 401, 1737 Cambridge St., Cambridge, Mass. 02138.

CAREER: University of Chicago, Chicago, Ill., Cowles Commission for Research in Economics, research associate, 1947-49, assistant professor of economics, 1948-49; Stanford University, Stanford, Calif., acting assistant professor, 1949-50, associate professor, 1950-53, professor of economics and statistics, 1953-68, executive head of department of economics, 1953-56; Harvard University, Cambridge, Mass., professor of economics, 1968—. Consultant, Rand Corp., 1948—; economist, U.S. Council of Economic Advisers, 1962-63; guest professor, Institute for Advanced Studies, Vienna, 1964, 1970. *Military service:* U.S. Army Air Forces, weather officer, 1942-46; became captain.

MEMBER: National Academy of Sciences, American Academy of Arts and Sciences (fellow), Econometric Society (fellow; vice-president, 1955; president, 1956), Institute of Mathematical Statistics (fellow), American Statistical Association (fellow), American Economic Association (president, 1973), Institute of Management Sciences (president, 1963; chairman of council, 1964), American Philosophical Society, Phi Beta Kappa. *Awards, honors:* Fellow, Social Science Research Council, Europe, 1952, and Center for Advanced Study in the Behavioral Sciences, 1956-57; John Bates Clark medal, American Economic Association, 1957; overseas research fellow, Churchill College, Cambridge, 1963, 1964, 1970, and 1973; Nobel Memorial Prize in economic science (co-recipient, John R. Hicks), 1972, for pioneering contributions to general economic equilibrium theory and welfare theory; Guggenheim fellow, 1972-73; LL.D., University of Chicago, 1967; Doctor of Social and Economic Sciences, University of Vienna, 1971; LL.D., City University of New York, 1972; S.D., Columbia University, 1973.

WRITINGS: Social Choice and Individual Values, Wiley, 1951, 2nd edition, Yale University Press, 1970; (with S. Karlin and H. Scarf) *Studies in the Mathematical Theory of Inventory and Production*, Stanford University Press, 1958; (with L. Hurwicz and H. Uzawa) *Studies in Linear and Non-Linear Programming*, Stanford University Press, 1958; (with M. Hoffenberg) *A Time Series Analysis of Interindustry Demands*, North-Holland Publishing, 1959; (editor with Karlin and P. Suppes, and contributor) *Mathematical Methods in the Social Sciences, 1959*, Stanford University Press, 1960; (editor with Karlin and Scarf, and contributor) *Studies in Applied Probability and Management Science*, Stanford University Press, 1962; *Aspects of the Theory of Risk-Bearing*, Academic Bookstore (Helsinki), 1965; (with M. Kurz) *Public Investment, the Rate of Return and Optimal Fiscal Policy*, Johns Hopkins Press, 1970; *Essays in the Theory of Risk-Bearing*, North-Holland, 1970, Markham, 1971; (with F. H. Hahn) *General Competitive Analysis*, Holden-Day, 1971; *The Limits of Organization*, Norton, 1974.

Contributor: T. C. Koopmans, editor, *Activity Analysis of Production and Allocation*, Wiley, 1951; D. Lerner and H. D. Lasswell, editors, *The Policy Sciences*, Stanford University Press, 1951; R. W. Pfouts, editor, *Essays in Economics and Econometrics*, University of North Carolina Press, 1960; *The Rate and Direction of Inventive Activity: Economic and Social Factors*, Princeton University Press, 1962; S. Koch, editor, *Psychology: A Study of a Science*,

McGraw, 1963; C. P. Bonini, R. K. Jaedicke, and H. M. Wagner, editors, *Management Controls: New Directions in Basic Research*, McGraw, 1964. Contributor of lesser sections to other books and contributor to *Proceedings* of two Berkeley Symposiums on Mathematical Statistics and Probability. About seventy of his articles have appeared in economic and management journals.

WORK IN PROGRESS: Articles on the economics of information; with L. Hurwicz, *Studies in Resource Allocation Processes.*

SIDELIGHTS: Arrow is the third American to receive the Nobel Prize in economic science since it was established in 1969. In addition to his contributions to general economic equilibrium theory and welfare theory, Professor Arrow was also cited by the Swedish Academy of Science for his contributions to growth theory and decision theory. One of Arrow's major achievements is his "Impossibility Theorem," by means of which he uses fairly elementary mathematics of a kind never before applied to such a question to show that there is not, and in principle cannot be, any perfect form of government.

* * *

ARY, Sheila M(ary Littleboy) 1929-
(Sheila M. Littleboy)

PERSONAL: Born December 19, 1929, in Winscombe, Somerset, England; moved to U.S., July, 1964; daughter of Gerald (a teacher) and Gwendolen (Richardson) Littleboy; married Donald Eugene Ary, December 21, 1957; children: Richard Clinton, Eleanor Grace, Rachel Margaret. *Education:* St. Hilda's College, Oxford, B.A., 1952, M.A., 1955. *Religion:* Society of Friends. *Home:* 526 Russell Rd., DeKalb, Ill. 60115.

CAREER: Oxford University, Fielding Herbarium, Oxford, England, acting curator, 1952-56; Commonwealth Bureau of Plant Breeding and Genetics, Cambridge, England, abstractor, 1956-58. *Member:* Oxford University Scientific Club (secretary, 1949; president, 1950).

WRITINGS: (Under name Sheila M. Littleboy) *A Book of Wild Flowers*, illustrated by Elsa Felsko, Cassirer, 1956; (with Mary Gregory) *The Oxford Book of Wild Flowers*, illustrated by Barbara E. Nicholson, Oxford University Press, 1960, revised edition, 1970. Revised botanical entries for second printing of *Oxford Junior Encyclopedia.*†

* * *

ASCHERSON, Neal 1932-

PERSONAL: Born October 5, 1932, in Edinburgh, Scotland; son of Stephen Romer (a sailor) and Evelyn (Gilbertson) Ascherson; married Corinna Adam (now a journalist), November 20, 1958; children: Marina, Isobel. *Education:* King's College, Cambridge, degree (with distinction), 1955. *Politics:* Socialist. *Home:* Flat 3, Campden Hill Mansions, Edge St., London W.8, England. *Office:* *Observer*, 160 Queen Victoria St., London E.C.4, England.

CAREER: East African Institute of Social Research, Kampala, East Africa, researcher, 1955-56; journalist with *Guardian*, 1956-58, *Scotsman*, 1958-59; *Observer*, London, England, journalist, 1960—. Member of Islington Labour Party. *Military service:* Royal Marines; served in Malaya. *Member:* Society of Antiquaries of Scotland (fellow).

WRITINGS: *The King Incorporated*, Allen & Unwin, 1963, Doubleday, 1964. Contributor to *New Statesman, New York Review of Books*, and other periodicals.

WORK IN PROGRESS: West German Ostopolitik.

SIDELIGHTS: Ascherson speaks French, German, Polish.

* * *

ASCHMANN, Helen Tann

PERSONAL: Born in Kansas City, Mo.; daughter of Thomas George (a tinsmith) and Eleanor (Mahoney) Tann; married Charles Aschmann (a wholesale lumber dealer); children: Charles, Jr., Eleanor (Mrs. Randolph Turner). *Education:* Attended Illinois Institute of Technology, two years, and Northwestern University, one year. *Politics:* Republican. *Religion:* Episcopalian and Theosophist. *Home:* 901 East North St., Itasca, Ill. *Agent:* Max Siegel, 154 East Erie St., Chicago, Ill. 60611,

CAREER: Former secretary in various fields and staff member of trade journal and of newspapers; Northwestern University, Medill School of Journalism, teacher of creative writing, 1946-53. Speaker at writers' conferences and speaker (in humorous vein) for clubs and other groups. *Member:* Society of Midland Authors, Children's Reading Round Table of Chicago, Sigma Kappa. *Awards, honors:* Dodd, Mead Librarian and Teacher Prize Competition Award, 1962, for *Connie Bell, M.D.*

WRITINGS: Connie Bell, M.D. (teen-age book), Dodd, 1963. Writer of one-act plays for amateur, church, and school productions, published by *Progressive Farmer* and Eldridge Publishing. Contributor of light verse, articles, and short stories to newspapers and magazines.†

* * *

ASHLEY, Leonard R. N. 1929-

PERSONAL: Born December 5, 1929, in Miami, Fla.; son of Leonard Saville (a lawyer) and Anne Constance (Nelligan) Ashley. *Education:* McGill University, B.A. (first class honors), 1949, M.A., 1950; Princeton University, A.M., 1953, Ph.D., 1956. *Religion:* Episcopalian. *Home:* 44 Butler Pl., Brooklyn, N.Y. *Office:* Brooklyn College of the City University of New York, Brooklyn, N.Y.

CAREER: University of Utah, Salt Lake City, instructor in English, 1953-55; University of Rochester, Rochester, N.Y., instructor in English, 1958-60; New School for Social Research, New York, N.Y., lecturer, 1960-63; Brooklyn College of the City University of New York, Brooklyn, N.Y., assistant professor of English, 1960—. *Military service:* Royal Canadian Air Force, 1955-58; became flying officer. *Member:* International Society for General Semantics, Modern Language Association of America, National Council of Teachers of English, American Name Society, College English Association.

WRITINGS: (Contributor) F. F. Liu, *A Military History of Modern China*, Princeton University Press, 1956; (contributor) E. P. J. Corbett, *Classical Rhetoric for the Modern Student*, Oxford University Press, 1965; *Colley Cibber*, Twayne, 1965; *George Peele*, Twayne, 1966; (editor) *Nineteenth-Century British Drama: An Anthology of Representative Plays*, Scott, 1967; (editor with Stuart Astor) *British Short Stories: Classics and Criticism*, Prentice-Hall, 1967; (editor) *Other Peoples Lives: Thirty-Four Short Stories*, Houghton, 1970. Author of squadron histories, Royal Canadian Air Force. Poetry anthologized in *National Poetry Anthology*. Contributor of poetry to *Western Humanities Review, Carleton Miscellany, ETC, Evidence, December*, and to other little magazines; contributor of articles to learned journals and popular magazines, and of articles on military history to *Roundel* and *Air University Quarterly Review*.

WORK IN PROGRESS: Shakespeare's History Plays, for Twayne; a rhetoric handbook, for Prentice-Hall; *Animal Crackers*, a book of children's verse; *Words as Weapons*, the military uses of propaganda; an edition of the memoirs of Charles Kean; an anthology of criticism; three anthologies of the short story, for Prentice-Hall.†

*   *   *

ASHMORE, Harry S(cott)   1916-

PERSONAL: Born July 28, 1916, in Greenville, S.C.; son of William Green (a merchant) and Elizabeth (Scott) Ashmore; married Barbara Edith Laier, June 2, 1940; children: Anne Rogers. *Education:* Clemson College, B.S., 1937; Harvard University, Nieman Fellow, 1941-42. *Politics:* Democrat. *Address:* P.O. Box 4068, Santa Barbara, Calif.

CAREER: Reporter for newspapers in Greenville, S.C., 1937-40; *Charlotte News*, Charlotte, N.C., political writer, 1940-41, associate editor, 1945-47, editor, 1947; *Arkansas Gazette*, Little Rock, editorial page editor, 1947, executive editor, 1948-59; Fund for the Republic, Inc., Center for the Study of Democratic Institutions, Santa Barbara, Calif., chairman of executive committee, 1960-68, president, 1968—; *Encyclopaedia Britannica*, Chicago, Ill., editor-in-chief, 1960-63, consultant, 1963—. Assistant, Adlai Stevenson's presidential campaign committee, 1955-56. Director of Fund for the Republic, Inc. and Committee for an Effective Congress; vice-chairman, National Advisory Council, American Civil Liberties Union; trustee, Miles College. Member, Aspen Institute for Humanistic Studies. *Military service:* U.S. Army, infantry officer, 1942-45; became lieutenant colonel; received Bronze Star and two oak leaf clusters.

MEMBER: American Society of Newspaper Editors (former director), Authors League of America, Overseas Press Club, Century Association, and The Players (all New York); National Press Club (Washington, D.C.), Tavern Club (Chicago). *Awards, honors:* Pulitzer Prize for editorial writing (in *Arkansas Gazette*), 1958; Sidney Hillman Foundation Award for editorial writing, 1958; LL.D., Oberlin College, 1958, Grinnell College, 1961, University of Arkansas, 1972; senior fellow in Communications, Duke University, 1973-74.

WRITINGS: The Negro and the Schools, University of North Carolina Press, 1954; *An Epitaph for Dixie*, Norton, 1958; *The Other Side of Jordan*, Norton, 1960; *The Man in the Middle*, University of Missouri Press, 1966; (with William C. Baggs) *Mission to Hanoi*, Putnam, 1968; *Fear in the Air: Broadcasting and the First Amendment*, Norton, 1973. Contributor to magazines.

*   *   *

ASHWORTH, Wilfred   1912-

PERSONAL: Born September 10, 1912, in Heywood, Lancashire, England; son of George (a Congregational minister) and Mary Emma (Manock) Ashworth; married Ethel Ellen Wright, April 9, 1938; children: Michael John, David Trevor, Rosemary Jane. *Education:* University of Manchester, B.Sc., 1934; University College, University of London, Diploma in Librarianship, 1935. *Home:* 39 Melfort Rd., Newport, Monmouthshire, England. *Office:* ICI Fibres Ltd., Pontypool, Monmouthshire, England.

CAREER: Imperial Smelting Corp., Avonmouth, Bristol, England, librarian and information officer, 1936-45; British Cast Iron Research Association, Alvechurch, Worcestershire, England, librarian and information officer, 1945-48; ICI Fibres, Ltd. (formerly British Nylon Spinners Ltd.), Pontypool, Monmouthshire, England, librarian and information officer, 1948—. *Member:* Aslib (formerly Association of Special Libraries and Information Bureaux; chairman of council, 1961, 1962), Library Association (fellow; council, 1961—; chairman of special libraries committee, 1963, 1964), Royal Photographic Society (associate).

WRITINGS: (Editor and contributor) *Handbook of Special Librarianship and Information Work*, Aslib, 1955, 3rd edition, 1967. Contributor of articles and reviews to professional journals. Library adviser, *Technical Book Review*.

AVOCATIONAL INTERESTS: Information retrieval, photography.†

*   *   *

ATWATER, C(onstance) Elizabeth (Sullivan)   1923-

PERSONAL: Born September 18, 1923, in Chewelah, Wash.; daughter of Charles Lee (a salesman) and Mabel Ovid (Smith) Sullivan; married Vernon Eugene Atwater; children: Tyrone, Pamela, Shyrle, Vernon, Jr. *Education:* Attended Goddard Professional School, Kent School of Baton, Watson School of Dance, and Cornish Teachers Training School. *Religion:* Lutheran. *Address:* P.O. Box 7161, Burbank, Calif.

CAREER: Teacher of ballet, tap, and baton in U.S. Air Forces Special Services program at bases in Riverside, Calif., 1952-54, Bentwaters, England, 1955-58, Altus, Okla., 1963-64; teacher of ballet, tap, and baton at youth centers in Tachikawa and Yakota, Japan, 1959-63; baton director, District Recreation and Park Department, Simi, Calif., 1964—. *Member:* U.S. Twirling Association.

WRITINGS: Baton Twirling: The Fundamentals of an Art and Skill, Tuttle, 1965; *Sword-Spinning Manual*, Kraskin, 1967; *Tap Dancing: Techniques, Routines, Terminology*, Tuttle, 1971.

WORK IN PROGRESS: Baton-Twirlers Parade Manual; *Sword Spinning: A New Creative Field for an Ancient Art*; *Drill Team Manual*; two novels and a children's story.

SIDELIGHTS: Mrs. Atwater introduced baton twirling in Japan, and started training of groups that eventually performed in the 1964 Olympic ceremonies.

*   *   *

AUGSBURGER, Myron S.   1929-

PERSONAL: Born August 20, 1929, in Elida, Ohio; son of Clarence A. (a farmer) and Estella (Shenk) Augsburger; married Esther Kniss, November 28, 1950; children: John Myron, Michael David, Marcia Louise. *Education:* Eastern Mennonite College, A.B., 1955, Th.B., 1958; Goshen College, B.D., 1959; Union Theological Seminary, Richmond, Va., Th.M., 1961, Th.D., 1964. *Home:* 1539 Hillcrest, Parkview, Harrisonburg, Va. 22801. *Office:* Eastern Mennonite College, Harrisonburg, Va. 22801.

CAREER: Minister of Mennonite Church. Inter-Church Evangelism, Inc., Harrisonburg, Va., evangelist, 1956—; Eastern Mennonite College, Harrisonburg, Va., professor of theology, 1962-65, president, 1965—. Mennonite Board of Education, member. *Member:* Association for Higher

Education, Evangelical Theological Association, Council for the Advancement of Small Colleges.

WRITINGS: Called to Maturity, Herald, 1960; *Quench Not the Spirit*, Herald, 1962; *Plus Living*, Zondervan, 1963; *Invitation to Discipleship*, Herald, 1964; *Principles of Biblical Interpretation*, Herald, 1967; *Pilgrim Aflame*, Herald, 1967; *Faith for a Secular World*, Word Books, 1968; *The Broken Chalice*, Herald, 1971; *The Expanded Life: The Sermon on the Mount for Today*, Abingdon, 1972.

* * *

AUSTIN, James C(layton) 1923-

PERSONAL: Born November 27, 1923, in Kansas City, Mo.; son of William McKinley (an automobile dealer) and Leone (Weaver) Austin; married Lenke Hricisak, September 2, 1945; children: Eric Eugene, Bruce William. *Education:* Kent State University, student, 1940-42; Western Reserve University, B.A., 1944, M.A., 1945, Ph.D., 1952. *Home:* 111 Westridge Rd., Collinsville, Ill. *Office:* Department of English, Southern Illinois University, Edwardsville, Ill.

CAREER: High school teacher in Batavia, Ohio, 1945-46; instructor in English at University of Nebraska, Lincoln, 1946-48, Waynesburg College, Waynesburg, Pa., 1950-51, Ohio University, Athens, 1951-54; Yankton College, Yankton, S.D., professor of English and chairman of department, 1954-60; Southern Illinois University, Edwardsville Campus, professor of English, 1960—, acting head of Humanities Division, 1963-64. Fulbright lecturer in Philippine Islands, 1957-58, and in England, 1965-66. American specialist for U.S. State Department in Romania, 1966. Exchange professor in France, 1972-73. *Military service:* U.S. Army Enlisted Reserve Corps, 1942-43. *Member:* Modern Language Association of America, American Studies Association, American Association of University Professors, Midcontinent American Studies Association, Illinois Historical Society, Association Francaise d'Etudes Americaines, Popular Culture Association, Society for the Study of Midwestern Literature, Western Literature Association, St. Louis Westerners.

WRITINGS: Fields of the Atlantic Monthly, Letters to an Editor, 1861-1870, Huntington Library, 1953; *Artemus Ward*, Twayne, 1964; *Petroleum V. Nasby*, Twayne, 1965; *Bill Arp*, Twayne, 1970; (editor) *Popular Literature in America*, Bowling Green University Popular Press, 1972.

Librettist with F. A. McClain: "Snack Shop" (short opera), produced and privately published, 1957; "The Princess and the Frog" (short opera), produced and privately published, 1958; "Dakota Dakota Dakota" (full-length musical), produced, 1961; "Shangri-Lost" (short opera), produced, 1962.

Contributor of articles to *New England Quarterly, Yale University Library Gazette, American Literary Realism, Papers on Language and Literature, American Studies*, and other journals; regular contributor, *Abstracts of English Studies*, 1959—.

WORK IN PROGRESS: The Progress of American Humor in France; An Anthology of Popular Literature; articles.

AVOCATIONAL INTERESTS: Trombonist in Old Guys Jazz Band; cartooning.

* * *

AUTRY, Ewart (Arthur) 1900-

PERSONAL: Born January 15, 1900, in Hickory Flat,

Miss.; son of James Arthur (a Baptist minister) and Mary Almarinda (Hudspeth) Autry; married second wife, Lola Mae Lineberry (her husband's secretary and photographer), February 21, 1941; children: (first marriage) Ewart Ronald, Ruth Evelyn (deceased), James Arthur; (second marriage) Jerry Duane (deceased), Lanny Lemuel, Martha Lynn. *Education:* Student, University of Mississippi, 1918, Mississippi College, 1919, and Blue Mountain College, 1920. *Home:* Whippoorwill Valley, Hickory Flat, Miss. 38633. *Agent:* Lurton Blassingame, 10 East 43rd St., New York, N.Y. 10017.

CAREER: Baptist minister. School teacher, principal, and superintendent, 1918-28; pastor of rural churches in Mississippi, 1921-28; Central Avenue Church (now Southern Avenue Church), Memphis, Tenn., pastor, 1928-41; pastor of rural churches in Mississippi, 1941—, holding pastorate at Pine Grove, 1943—, Bay Springs, 1944-67. Benton County Baptist Association, moderator, 1950-51, 1956-60, 1964-65, 1971-73; Baptist Convention Board, member, 1963-68. *Member:* Benton County Sportsmen's Club (president, 1955-56), Whippoorwill Valley Men's Club (president, 1963-65). *Awards, honors:* Dodd, Mead Librarian and Teacher Prize for *Ghost Hound of Thunder Valley*, 1964; named rural minister of the year by Emory University and *Progressive Farmer*, 1964.

WRITINGS: (With A. Roy Beasley) *In Prison—And Visited Me*, Eerdmans, 1952; *Ghost Hound of Thunder Valley*, Dodd, 1965; (with wife, Lola M. Autry) *Bible Puppet Plays*, Baker Book, 1972.

Contributor to anthologies: *Teen-Age Tales*, Heath, 1958; *Good Old Days*, Harper, 1960; *Teen-Age Tales*, Heath, 1962; *The Guideposts Trilogy*, Guideposts Associates, 1962; *Twenty Short Stories You'll Remember*, Progressive Farmer, 1964; *Light from Above*, Broadman, 1968; *Human Listening*, Bobbs-Merrill, 1972. Has sold more than a million words to more than one hundred different publications, including a series of fourteen stories, "Tales of Whippoorwill Valley," in *Bluebook*, 1950-52, other stories and articles in *Reader's Digest, Sports Afield, Parents' Magazine, Field and Stream, Better Homes and Gardens, Country Gentlemen, Guideposts*, and *Ford Times*.

WORK IN PROGRESS: A semi-autobiography, *Don't Look Back, Mama*.

SIDELIGHTS: Autry believes that "we are not, basically, a generation of smut consumers," and that clean fiction will be read—especially in the outdoor field. He is vitally interested in young people and in all forms of nature, outdoor life, and conservation.

BIOGRAPHICAL/CRITICAL SOURCES: Bluebook, September, 1950; *Home Life*, May, 1963; *Memphis Press-Scimitar*, Memphis, Tenn., May 7, 1965; *Tupelo Daily Journal*, August 21, 1972.

* * *

AVERY, Peter 1923-

PERSONAL: Born May 15, 1923, in Derby, England; son of Ernest William Richard (a mariner) and Edity Amy (Bartlam) Avery. *Education:* Attended University of Liverpool, 1941-42; London School of Oriental and African Studies, University of London, B.A. (honors), 1949. *Politics:* Liberal. *Religion:* "Once Roman Catholic, now again Church of England." *Home and office:* King's College, Cambridge, England.

CAREER: Anglo-Iranian Oil Co., training officer, 1949-51;

Bagdad College, Bagdad, Iraq, lecturer in English, 1951-55; personal assistant to the general manager of an Iranian company, 1955-57; Cambridge University, Cambridge, England, university lecturer in Persian, 1957—, and fellow of King's College, 1964—. *Military service:* Royal Indian Navy, 1942-47. *Member:* Royal Institute of International Affairs, Royal Asiatic Society, Royal Central Asian Society, Iran Society, Chatham House (fellow), Reform Club (all London).

WRITINGS: (Translator with John Heath-Stubbs) Hafiz, *Thirty Poems*, Murray, 1952; *Modern Iran*, Praeger, 1965. Also editor of Persian readers. Scripts for British Broadcasting Corp. Contributor to *Muslim World*, *Times Literary Supplement*, and other publications. Editorial secretary, *Cambridge History of Iran*.

WORK IN PROGRESS: Translating Farid al-Din Attar's *Mantiq ut-Tair*; a social history of the Middle East since 1800, for Praeger; a history of Persian literature for *Handbuch der Orientalistik*.

SIDELIGHTS: Avery told *CA*: "Chief interests are, apart from Persian literature and the Persian and Arabic languages, history, books, antique furniture, the English countryside, the sea and ships."†

*   *   *

AVERY, Robert Sterling 1917-

PERSONAL: Born December 25, 1917, in Pittsfield, Ohio; son of Winfield Scott (an accountant) and Amanda (Schlobohm) Avery; married Betty Bear, June 19, 1941; children: Sharon, Michael, Suzanne. *Education:* Baldwin-Wallace College, A.B. (magna cum laude), 1939; Northwestern University, M.A., 1940, Ph.D., 1951. *Religion:* Presbyterian. *Office:* University of Tennessee, Knoxville, Tenn.

CAREER: Tennessee Valley Authority, Knoxville, Tenn., member of personnel staff, 1941-47; University of Tennessee, Knoxville, associate professor, 1947-52, professor of political science, 1952—, associate director of Bureau of Public Administration, 1947-60, chief of missions to Bolivia, 1955-57, and to Panama, 1958-60, assistant vice-president for academic affairs, 1963-67. Member of U.S. Operations Mission to Panama (on leave from university), 1952-54; consultant to government of Guatemala, 1958, to government of Nicaragua, 1960, 1961; chairman of advisory council, Tennessee Municipal Technical Advisory Service, 1961-63; member, Alliance for Progress evaluation team to Ecuador, summer, 1961; consultant for the Organization of American States at Public Administration Conference in Brazil, 1963; member, Regional Committee on Critical Languages and World Area Studies, Southern Regional Education Board, 1963-67; consultant to U.S. AID Mission to Panama, January, 1965; director of the Peace Corps in Brazil, 1967-70. *Military service:* U.S. Army, 1943-45. *Member:* Panamanian Society for Public Administration (honorary member), Southern Political Science Association (member of executive council, 1961-64), Association for Latin American Studies (member of Midwest council), National Education Association, Phi Kappa Phi, Pi Kappa Delta, Pi Sigma Alpha. *Awards, honors:* Honorary professor of public administration, Universidad de San Andres, La Paz, Bolivia, 1957; Alumni Merit Award, Baldwin-Wallace College, 1964.

WRITINGS: Experiment in Management, University of Tennessee Press, 1954; (contributor) *National Organization for the Conduct of Economic Development Programs*, International Institute of Administrative Sciences (Brussels), 1954; (contributor) *Ecuador's Participation in the Alliance for Progress: A Study of Problems and Possibilities in a Program for Social and Economic Development*, International Cooperation Administration, 1961; (with Lee S. Greene) *Government in Tennessee*, University of Tennessee Press, 1962, 2nd edition, 1966. Contributor to *International Review of Administrative Sciences*. Associate editor, *Journal of Politics*, 1954-56.

*   *   *

AWA, Eme Onuoha 1921-

PERSONAL: Born December 15, 1921, in Nigeria; married Paulina Kempi Kosiba (a secretary and typist), December 12, 1957; children: Uzoma, Eme J., Gabriel Nwachukwu. *Education:* Lincoln University, Pennsylvania, B.A., 1951; New York University, M.A., 1952, Ph.D., 1955. *Religion:* Christian. *Office:* Department of Political Science, University of Nigeria, Nsukka, Nigeria.

CAREER: Federal Public Service of Nigeria, Lagos, assistant secretary, 1956-57; University of Lagos, Yaba, Nigeria, lecturer in political science, beginning 1957, now at University of Nigeria, Nsukka, Nigeria. *Member:* African Political Science Association, African Association for Public Administration and Management, Nigerian Political Science Association, Nigerian Society for Public Administration. *Awards, honors:* Founder's Day Merit Award, New York University, 1955.

WRITINGS: (With Richard S. Sklar) *The Voting Behaviour and Attitudes of Eastern Nigerians*, Ofomatas Press (Aba, Nigeria), 1961; (co-author) *Africa: Dynamics of Change*, Ibadan University Press, 1963; *Federal Government in Nigeria*, University of California Press, 1964.

WORK IN PROGRESS: Issues in Federalism, for publication by Ethiope Publishing (Benin, Nigeria).

AVOCATIONAL INTERESTS: Farming.

*   *   *

AYLMER, G(erald) E(dward) 1926-

PERSONAL: Surname is pronounced *Ale*-mer; born April 30, 1926, in England; married wife, Ursula (a part-time author), 1955; children: Bartholomew, Emma. *Education:* Balliol College, Oxford, B.A. and M.A., 1950, D.Phil., 1955. Princeton University, graduate study, 1950-51. *Office:* Department of History, University of York, Heslington, York YOL 5DD, England.

CAREER: Oxford University, Balliol College, Oxford, England, junior, research fellow, 1951-54; University of Manchester, Manchester, England, assistant lecturer, 1954-57, lecturer in history, 1957-62; University of York, York, England, 1962—, now professor of history and chairman of department. *Military service:* British Navy, 1944-47. *Member:* Historical Association, Past and Present Society, Economic History Society.

WRITINGS: The King's Servants: The Civil Service of Charles I, 1625-1642, Columbia University Press, 1961; (editor) *The Diary of William Lawrence*, Toucan Press, 1961; *The Struggle for the Constitution, 1603-1689*, Mentor Books, 1963; (editor) *The Interregnum, 1646-1660*, Macmillan, 1972; *The State's Servants: The Civil Service of the English Republic, 1649-1660*, Routledge & Kegan Paul, 1973; *The Levellers in the English Revolution*, Thames & Hudson, in press. Contributor of articles and book reviews to scholarly journals, weeklies, and newspapers. Member of editorial board, *History of Parliament*.

WORK IN PROGRESS: Research in sixteenth- through nineteenth-century British history, and the history of bureaucracy.

* * *

BABB, Howard S. 1924-

PERSONAL: Born May 14, 1924, in Portland, Me.; son of Hugh Webster (a professor) and Persis (Conant) Babb; married Corinna Meyer, February 14, 1952; children: Stephen. Education: Kenyon College, B.A., 1948; Harvard University, M.A., 1949, Ph.D., 1955. Home: 2507 Via Marina, Newport Beach, Calif. 92660. Office: Department of English and Comparative Literature, University of California, Irvine, Calif. 92664.

CAREER: Kenyon College, Gambier, Ohio, instructor in English, 1951-52; Ohio State University, Columbus, instructor, 1954-56, assistant professor, 1956-62, associate professor of English, 1962-65; University of California, Irvine, associate professor, 1965-67, professor of English, 1967—, chairman of department, 1969-72. Military service: U.S. Naval Reserve, 1943-46; became lieutenant junior grade. Member: Modern Language Association of America, American Association of University Professors.

WRITINGS: Jane Austen's Novels: The Fabric of Dialogue, Ohio State University Press, 1962, Shoe String, 1967; The Novels of William Golding, Ohio State University Press, 1970; (editor) Essays in Stylistic Analysis, Harcourt, 1972.

* * *

BABB, Sanora 1907-

PERSONAL: Born April 21, 1907, in Leavenworth, Kan.; daughter of Walter Lacy and Jennie (Parks) Babb; married James Wong Howe (a motion picture photography director), September 16, 1949. Education: Attended University of Kansas and Garden City (Kan.) Junior College. Politics: Democrat. Residence: Hollywood, Calif. Agent: McIntosh & Otis, Inc., 18 East 41st St., New York, N.Y. 10017.

CAREER: Free-lance writer. Worked on small town newspapers and a farm magazine, 1925-28; co-editor of literary magazines, Clipper, 1940-41, and California Quarterly, 1951-53, both published in Los Angeles, Calif.; University of California Extension, Los Angeles, instructor in short story, 1958-59. Member: Authors League of America, National Wildlife Federation, Humane Society. Awards, honors: Five Arts Award for story, "The Vine by Root Embraced."

WRITINGS: The Lost Traveler (novel), Reynal, 1958; An Owl on Every Post (a memoir), Saturday Review Press, 1970.

Short stories included in U.S. Stories, 1949; Best American Short Stories, edited by Martha Foley, Houghton, 1950; Best American Short Stories, edited by Foley and David Burnett, Houghton, 1960; Anatomy of Readings, 1965. Poetry included in Zero anthology and Borestone Mountain Poetry Awards 1967, edited by Lionel Stevenson and others, Pacific Books, 1967. Contributor to The Writer's Handbook. Contributor of short stories to Saturday Evening Post, Redbook, Seventeen, Ellery Queen's Mystery Magazine, Woman's Journal (London) and Homes and Gardens (London), and of stories and poetry to literary journals, including Antioch Review, Southwest Review, Northwest Review, Prairie Schooner, and Dalhousie Review. Poetry included in Outdoor World.

WORK IN PROGRESS: A novel; short stories.

SIDELIGHTS: Sanora Babb has lived in Europe and Mexico and traveled over much of the world. Avocational interests: The American Indian (history, customs, beliefs, and our treatment), conservation of wild life, natural nutrition, art, books, music, human beings, ghosts, earth, space, and "all of life, including the varieties of consciousness."

* * *

BABCOCK, Robert J(oseph) 1928-

PERSONAL: Born 1928, in Lynbrook, N.Y.; son of David H. and Doretta (Kreckman) Babcock; married Jean MacLeod, 1951. Education: State University of New York College at Oswego, B.S., 1949; New York University, M.A., 1955; Cornell University, Ed.D., 1963. Home: 257 Syracuse Ave., Oswego, N.Y. Office: State University of New York College at Oswego, Oswego, N.Y.

CAREER: Hagerstown (Md.) Board of Education, industrial arts teacher, 1949-50; Great Neck (N.Y.) public schools, elementary industrial arts consultant, 1950-57; State University of New York College at Oswego, 1957—, now associate professor of elementary education industrial arts. Member: National Education Association (life), American Council on Industrial Arts Teacher Education, New York State Teachers Association (president, 1956), Epsilon Pi Tau.

WRITINGS: (Co-author) Industrial Arts for Grades K-6, Bruce, 1959. Contributor to Yearbook of American and Council on Industrial Arts Teacher Education.†

* * *

BACK, Kurt W(olfgang) 1919-

PERSONAL: Surname originally Baeck; born October 17, 1919, in Vienna, Austria; son of Paul L. and Thehla F. Baeck; married Edith Bierharst, May 15, 1949; children: Allan. Education: New York University, B.S., 1940; University of California, Los Angeles, M.A., 1941; Massachusetts Institute of Technology, Ph.D., 1949. Home: 2735 McDowell St., Durham, N.C. 27703. Office: Sociology Department, Duke University, Durham, N.C. 27706.

CAREER: U.S. Bureau of the Census, Washington, D.C., social science analyst, 1949-51; Columbia University, Bureau of Applied Social Research, New York, N.Y., research associate, 1951-53; University of Puerto Rico, Rio Piedras, research associate, 1953-56; University of North Carolina, Chapel Hill, research associate professor, 1956-59; Duke University, 1959—, began as associate professor, now professor of sociology and psychology. Military service: U.S. Army, 1943-46; became sergeant.

WRITINGS: (With L. Festinger and S. Schachter) Social Pressures in Informal Groups, Harper, 1950; (with R. Hill and J. M. Stycos) The Family and Population Control, University of North Carolina Press, 1959; (with J. M. Stycos) The Survey under Unusual Conditions, Human Organization (Ithaca), 1959; Slums, Projects and People, Duke University Press, 1962; (with J. M. Stycos) The Control of Human Fertility in Jamaica, Cornell University Press, 1964; (with Thomas Pettigrew) Sociology in the Desegregation Process, [New York], 1967; (with Alan Kerckhoff) The June Bug, Appleton, 1968; Beyond Words: The Story of Sensitivity and the Encounter Movement, Russell Sage, 1972.

WORK IN PROGRESS: Logical System for Social Science, for Prentice-Hall.†

BACKSTROM, Charles H(erbert) 1926-

PERSONAL: Born October 5, 1926, in Valley City, N.D.; son of Carl H. (a state employment supervisor) and Helen (Stroud) Backstrom; married Barbara Meyer, August 25, 1957; children: Paul Meyer, Anne Elizabeth, Brian Dean, Claudia Joan. Education: Moorhead State College, B.S. and B.A., 1949; University of Wisconsin, M.A., 1953, Ph.D., 1956. Politics: Democrat. Religion: Methodist. Home: 70 Arthur Ave., S.E., Minneapolis, Minn. 55414. Office: 1414 Social Science Building, University of Minnesota, Minneapolis, Minn. 55455.

CAREER: Eastern Michigan University, Ypsilanti, assistant professor, 1955-59; University of Minnesota, Minneapolis, assistant professor, 1959-63, associate professor of political science, 1963—. Minnesota Council for Education in Politics, director, 1959—; Minnesota Governor's Reapportionment Commission, member, 1964; Citizens League of Minneapolis and Hennepin County, member. Military service: U.S. Army, Infantry, 1944-47; became second lieutenant. U.S. Army Reserve, 1947-63; became captain. Member: American Political Science Association, American Association of University Professors, Midwest Conference of Political Scientists. Awards, honors: Congressional fellowship from American Political Science Association, 1957; National Center for Education in Politics fellowship, 1965.

WRITINGS: (With Gerald D. Hursh) Survey Research, Northwestern University Press, 1963; (with Ronald F. Stinnett) Recount, National Document Publishers, 1964.

WORK IN PROGRESS: Studies of attitudes on metropolitan affairs, of campaign techniques, and of government organization for mental health.†

* * *

BAER, Jean L.

PERSONAL: Born in Chicago, Ill.; daughter of Fred Eugene and Helen (Roth) Baer; married Herbert Fensterheim, 1968. Education: Cornell University, B.A. Politics: Democrat. Home: 151 East 37th St., New York, N.Y. Agent: Anita Diamant, 51 East 42nd St., New York, N.Y. 10016. Office: Seventeen, 320 Park Ave., New York, N.Y.

CAREER: Seventeen, New York, N.Y., senior editor and director of public relations, 1953-70, special projects director, 1970—. Member: Overseas Press Club, American Women in Radio and Television, New York Newspaper Women's Club, Woman Pays Club (New York).

WRITINGS: Follow Me!, Macmillan, 1965; The Single Girl Goes to Town, Macmillan, 1968; The Second Wife, Doubleday, 1972.

WORK IN PROGRESS: A book for McKay, with husband.

SIDELIGHTS: Reviewer Juliet Woodbury observed that Ms. Baer's advice to single women is "mature, encouraging, and free of the opportunistic qualities" found in other books on this subject. Avocational interests: Travel, the theater, and collecting antiques.

* * *

BAGGALEY, Andrew R(obert) 1923-

PERSONAL: Born December 1, 1923, in Cleveland, Ohio; son of Walter (an engineer) and Jean (Brown) Baggaley; married Arlene Aberle, September 3, 1949; children: Philip, Paula. Education: Harvard University, A.B., 1947, Ed.M.,

1949; University of Chicago, Ph.D., 1952. Politics: Independent. Home: 38 Woodcroft Rd., Havertown, Pa. 19083. Office: Department of Education, University of Pennsylvania, 3700 Walnut St., Philadelphia, Pa. 19174.

CAREER: University of Illinois, Urbana, research associate, 1952-54; University of Wisconsin, Milwaukee, assistant professor, 1954-58, associate professor of psychology, 1958-61; Temple University, Philadelphia, Pa., associate professor, 1961-64, professor of psychology, 1964-66, research director of Counseling Center; University of Pennsylvania, Philadelphia, professor of education, 1966—. Member: American Psychological Association, Psychometric Society, Eastern Psychological Association, Pennsylvania Psychological Association.

WRITINGS: Intermediate Correlational Methods, Wiley, 1964; Mathematics for Introductory Statistics: A Programmed Review, Wiley, 1969. Contributor of about thirty articles to psychological and political science journals.

* * *

BAILEY, Frederick George 1924-

PERSONAL: Born February 24, 1924, in Liverpool, England. Education: Oxford University, B.A., 1948, B.Litt., 1950; University of Manchester, Ph.D., 1954. Office: University of Sussex, Falmer, Brighton, England.

CAREER: University of London, London, England, reader in Asian anthropology, 1960-63; University of Sussex, Brighton, England, professor of anthropology, 1964—. Military service: British Army, 1943-46. Awards, honors: S. C. Roy Gold Medal from Asiatic Society, 1961.

WRITINGS: Caste and the Economic Frontier, Manchester University Press, 1957; Tribe Caste and Nation: A Study of Political Activity and Political Change in Highland Orissa, Humanities, 1960; Politics and Social Change: Orissa in 1959, California University Press, 1963; Stratagems and Spoils: A Social Anthropology of Politics, Schocken, 1969; (editor) Gifts and Poisons: The Politics of Reputation, Schocken, 1971.

WORK IN PROGRESS: A study of village politics in India; research into the politics of small groups.

SIDELIGHTS: Did field research in India, 1952-54, 1955, and 1959.†

* * *

BAILEY, Helen Miller 1909-

PERSONAL: Born March 13, 1909, in Modesto, Calif.; daughter of Guy H. (a farmer) and Maud (Piggott) Miller; married Henry Morle Bailey (a teacher), June 18, 1932; children: (adopted) Bruce M., Theodore R., Donald Lee. Education: University of California, Berkeley, A.B., 1929, M.A., 1930; University of Southern California, Ph.D., 1934. Politics: Democrat. Religion: Protestant. Home and office: 1026 Bradshawe, Monterey Park, Calif. 91754.

CAREER: Teacher in Los Angeles, Calif., schools and junior colleges, 1934-74; East Los Angeles College, Los Angeles, chairman of department of social sciences, 1952-74. Attended Fulbright summer seminar in Brazil, 1964. Member of Youth Opportunities Board, 1962-63, and of Los Angeles County Commission on Human Relations; trustee of East Los Angeles-Belvedere Area Coordinating Council, 1948—, Eastside Boys' Club, 1952-57, Cleland House of Neighborly Service, 1955-57, Eastern Area Welfare Planning Council of Los Angeles Community Fund,

1956—. Treasurer, Scholarship Fund for Students of Mexican Ancestry in Los Angeles County, 1958—; chairman, East Los Angeles Brotherhood Observance, 1959—. Volunteer social worker among students of Mexican descent for more than forty years.

MEMBER: Phi Beta Kappa, Phi Alpha Theta. *Awards, honors:* Community awards from Mexican-American civic societies, 1947, 1962, 1964; Los Angeles County Conference on Human Relations Public Service Award, 1956; Jewish War Veterans Human Relations Award for service to young people of minority backgrounds, 1963; at her retirement, 1974, a scholarship fund was raised in her name.

WRITINGS: (With Harriet Brown) *Our Latin American Neighbors*, Houghton, 1945, 3rd edition, 1956; (with E. L. Lazare) *Your American Government*, Longmans, Green, 1950, 2nd edition, 1956; *Santa Cruz of the Etla Hills*, University of Florida Press, 1958; (with A. P. Nasatir) *Latin America, the Development of Its Civilization*, Prentice-Hall, 1960, 3rd edition, 1973; *Forty American Biographies*, Harcourt, 1964; (with Frank Cruz) *The Latin Americans, Past, Present and Future*, Houghton, 1970; (with Maria Grijalva) *Fifteen Famous Latin Americans*, Prentice-Hall, 1972.

* * *

BAINBRIDGE, John 1913-

PERSONAL: Born March 12, 1913, in Monticello, Minn.; son of William Dean (a broker) and Bess (Lakin) Bainbridge; married Dorothy Hazlewood (an artist), June 2, 1936; children: Jonathan, Janet. *Education:* Northwestern University, B.S., 1935. *Home:* 15 Eaton Sq., London S.W.1, England. *Agent:* Robert Lescher, 155 East 71 St., New York, N.Y. 10021. *Office: New Yorker*, 25 West 43rd St., New York, N.Y. 10036.

CAREER: New Yorker, New York, N.Y., member of editorial staff, 1938—, with writing including a number of "Profiles," and, more recently, articles from Europe, where he has been living, 1963—. *Member:* Authors Guild, Coffee House.

WRITINGS: Little Wonder, or The Reader's Digest and How It Grew, Reynal, 1946; *The Wonderful World of Toots Shor*, Houghton, 1951; *Biography of an Idea*, Doubleday, 1952; *Garbo*, Doubleday, 1955; *The Super-Americans*, Doubleday, 1961; *Like a Homesick Angel*, Houghton, 1964; *Another Way of Living*, Holt, 1969.

AVOCATIONAL INTERESTS: Travel, painting, gardening.

* * *

BAIRD, Jesse Hays 1889-

PERSONAL: Born April 27, 1889, in Clintonville, Pa.; son of John M. (a farmer) and Mary Grace (Hovis) Baird; married Susanna Bradstad, July 4, 1917 (died March 15, 1951); children: Paul, James, Arthur, Mary (Mrs. James Carlsen), Margaret. *Education:* Grove City College, student, 1908-11; College of Wooster, A.B., 1912; McCormick Theological Seminary, B.D., 1917. *Politics:* Independent. *Home:* The Lakehurst, 1569 Jackson St., Oakland, Calif.

CAREER: Ordained minister, Presbyterian Church in the U.S.A., 1917; pastor in Rexburg and St. Anthony, Idaho, 1917-19; associate pastor in Youngstown, Ohio, 1919-20; pastor in Boise, Idaho, 1920-26, Pomona, Calif., 1926-28, Salt Lake City, Utah, 1928-31, and Oakland, Calif., 1931-37; San Francisco Theological Seminary, San Anselmo,

Calif., president and professor of English Bible, 1937-58, now president emeritus. Moderator of Presbyterian Synod of Idaho, 1925, of Synod of Utah, 1931; moderator of Presbyterian Church in the U.S.A., 1948-49, former representative on Presbyterian World Alliance, and former chairman of Theological Council. *Member:* Phi Beta Kappa. *Awards, honors:* D.D., Grove City College, 1918, College of Wooster, 1928, Parsons College, 1948; LL.D., Occidental College, 1941.

WRITINGS: God's Law of Life, Caxton, 1931; *The San Anselmo Story*, Lantern Press (California), 1963; *They Who Are Called Christians*, Westminster, 1965; *That Amazing Galilean*, Lantern Press, 1969; *Land of the Pilgrims' Pride*, John Knox, 1973. Also author of *Pioneers in the Christian Quest*, 1936; *Church Membership and the Church*, 1936; *Great Christian Leaders*, 1938; *Christians Everyday*, 1941; *Today*, 1947. Contributor of chapters to several books.

AVOCATIONAL INTERESTS: Natural science, American history, art, and music.

* * *

BAIRD, William (Robb) 1924-

PERSONAL: Born February 27, 1924, in Santa Cruz, Calif.; son of William Robb (a minister) and Martha (Watson) Baird; married Shirley Bauman (a teacher), June 21, 1946; children: Elisabeth Gay, Eric Robb. *Education:* Northwest Christian College, B.Th., 1946; University of Oregon, B.A., 1947; Yale University, B.D., 1950, M.A., 1952, Ph.D., 1955. *Politics:* Democrat. *Office:* Brite Divinity School, Texas Christian University, Fort Worth, Tex.

CAREER: Minister of Christian (Disciples of Christ) churches in Brownsville and Fall Creek, Ore., 1944-47, and of Baptist church in Yalesville, Conn., 1950-51; Phillips University, Enid, Okla., associate prof., New Testament and church history, 1952-56; Lexington Theological Seminary, Lexington, Ky., professor of New Testament, 1956-67; Texas Christian University, Fort Worth, Tex., professor of New Testament, 1967—. *Member:* Society of Biblical Literature, Association of Disciples for Theological Discussion, Studiorum Novi Testamenti Societas, Phi Beta Kappa. *Awards, honors:* American Association of Theological Schools faculty fellowship, University of Marburg, 1962-63.

WRITINGS: Paul's Message and Mission, Abingdon, 1960; *The Corinthian Church—A Biblical Approach to Urban Culture*, Abingdon, 1964; (contributor) C. M. Laymon, editor, *Interpreter's One-Volume Commentary on the Bible*, Abingdon, 1972. Contributor to theological journals.

WORK IN PROGRESS: A book on recent New Testament theology.

SIDELIGHTS: Baird is competent in ancient Greek, German, ancient Hebrew, French, Latin, and Aramaic. *Avocational interests:* Photography, music (violin).

* * *

BAKER, Margaret 1890-

PERSONAL: Born April 8, 1890, in Langley Green, Oldbury, Birmingham, England; daughter of Harry (a head chemist) and Mary (Eccles) Baker. *Education:* Privately educated. *Politics:* Liberal. *Religion:* Society of Friends. *Home:* Tarver's Orchard, Sutton-under-Brailes, near Banbury, Oxfordshire, England.

CAREER: Writer of books for children, most of them illustrated (largely in silhouette) by her sister, Mary Baker. National British Women's Total Abstinence Union, honorary superintendent of local and county work, 1910-28; lecturer throughout England on total abstinence, prior to 1939. *Member:* Society of Authors.

WRITINGS: The Black Cats and the Tinker's Wife, Duffield & Co., 1923; *The Dog, the Brownie and the Bramble-Patch,* Duffield & Co., 1924; *The Little Girl Who Curtsied to the Owl,* Duffield & Co., 1925; *Pedlar's Ware,* Duffield & Co., 1925; *Four Times Once Upon a Time,* Duffield & Co., 1926; *The Lost Merbaby,* Duffield & Co., 1927; *The Pixies and the Silver Crown,* Duffield & Co., 1927; *The Story of St. Paul,* Oxford University Press, 1927, revised edition published as *St. Paul,* 1947; *The Water Elf and the Miller's Child,* Duffield & Co., 1928; *Tomson's Hallowe'en,* Duffield & Co., 1929.

Favorite Fables, Oxford University Press, 1930; *Noddy Goes A-Plowing,* Duffield & Co., 1930; *Peacock Eggs,* Basil Blackwell, 1931, Duffield & Green, 1932; *Cat's-Cradles for His Majesty,* Duffield & Green, 1933; *Patsy and the Leprechauns,* Basil Blackwell, 1932, Duffield & Green, 1933; *The Button Who Had a Sense of Humour,* Basil Blackwell, 1933, Artists and Writers Guild, 1935; *Pollie Who Did as She Was Told,* Dodd, 1934; *Nick and the Diccon,* Oxford University Press, 1935; *Three for an Acorn,* Dodd, 1935; *A Wife for the Mayor of Buncastle,* Basil Blackwell, 1935; *What Does It Matter?, and Other Tales,* R. J. James, 1935; *Diccon, the Pedlar,* Basil Blackwell, 1936; *Victoria Josephine,* Dodd, 1936 (published in England as *The Roaming Doll,* Basil Blackwell, 1936); *Tales of All the World,* Oxford University Press, 1936; *A Matter of Time,* Basil Blackwell, 1937; *Mrs. Bobbity's Crust,* Dodd, 1937; *The Very Little Dragon, and Other Stories,* Oxford University Press, 1938; *The Witch's Broom, and Other Stories,* Oxford University Press, 1938; *Dunderpate,* Dodd, 1938; *Fifteen Tales for Lively Children,* University of London Press, 1938, Dodd, 1939; *The Margaret and Mary Baker Story Book,* Laurie, 1939; *The Puppy Called Spinach,* Dodd, 1939.

Lady Arabella's Birthday Party, Dodd, 1940; *The Bakers' Big Book,* Dodd, 1941; *Tinker, Tailor and Other Nonsense Tales,* University of London Press, 1941, Dodd, 1942; *The Wishing-Nut Tree,* Basil Blackwell, 1942; *The Weathercock, and Other Stories,* University of London Press, 1943; *The Nightingale,* Shakespeare Head Press, 1944; *The Wind's Adopted Daughter, and Other Stories,* University of London Press, 1944; *Trotters,* Basil Blackwell, 1946; *The Men of Peace,* Friends Peace Committee, 1947; *Seven Times Once Upon a Time,* Carwal, 1948; *A Book of Happy Tales,* University of London Press, 1948.

The Wishing Well, and Other Stories, University of London Press, 1955; *The Key of Rose Cottage,* Collins, 1964; *Juby,* Hutchinson, 1970.

Writer of books and booklets for World Women's Christian Temperance Union, National British Women's Total Abstinence Union, and Temperance Collegiate Association, including *Here's Health to You!,* 1927, 7th revised edition, 1937, *Fit as a Fiddle,* 1937, *The Joy of Living,* 1940, *Temperance Tales to Tell with a Blackboard,* 1952, and "Plain Tales Series." Contributor of stories to British Broadcasting Corp. "Children's Hour."

Editor and illustrator of children's page in *White Ribbon* (periodical of British Women's Total Abstinence Union), 1923-62, and of a monthly leaflet for Hope Union, 1940-61. Also editor of country books for Aubrey Seymour, 1968-72.

SIDELIGHTS: Miss Baker told *CA,* "My work is almost all for children. . . . My only visit to the U.S.A. was at the age of five! I used to be very fond of mountain climbing—not rock-climbing. Holidays are always spent in wild, picturesque country—English lakes, west coasts of Ireland and Scotland, the Hebrides, etc." *Avocational interests:* "A keen gardener, even at eighty-four, and active in local affairs."

*   *   *

BAKER, Margaret J(oyce)   1918-

PERSONAL: Born May 21, 1918, in Reading, Berkshire, England; daughter of Alfred Cosier Slaney (a sales manager) and Irene Wentworth (Aveline) Baker. *Education:* Attended King's College, University of London, 1936-37. *Home and office:* Prickets Old Cleeve, Minehead, Somerset, England. *Agent:* Curtis Brown Ltd., 1 Craven Hill, London W2 3EW, England; and Curtis Brown, 60 East 56th St., New York, N.Y. 10022.

CAREER: Author of children's books, 1948—. Church Army, driver of mobile canteen, World War II. *Member:* Society of Authors. *Awards, honors:* Second prize for short story, *Child Life,* 1945; *Homer the Tortoise* was an honor book in *New York Herald Tribune* Children's Spring Book Festival, 1950; *Castaway Christmas* was a runner-up for Carnegie Medal of Library Association (British), 1963.

WRITINGS: Nonsense Said the Tortoise, Brockhampton Press, 1949, published as *Homer the Tortoise,* Whittlesey House, 1950; *Four Farthings and a Thimble,* Longmans, Green, 1950; *A Castle and Sixpence,* Longmans, Green, 1951; *Benbow and the Angels,* Longmans, Green, 1952; *The Family That Grew and Grew,* Whittlesey House, 1952; *Homer Sees the Queen,* Whittlesey House, 1953; *Lions in the Potting Shed,* Brockhampton Press, 1954, published as *Lions in the Woodshed,* Whittlesey House, 1955; *Ann Sewell and Black Beauty,* Harrap, 1956, Longmans, Green, 1957; *Acorns and Aerials,* Brockhampton Press, 1956; *The Bright High Flyer,* Longmans, Green, 1957; *Homer Goes to Stratford,* Prentice-Hall, 1958; *The Magic Seashell,* Harrap, 1959, Holt, 1960.

The Birds of the Thimblepins, Harrap, 1960; *Homer in Orbit,* Brockhampton Press, 1961; *The Cats of Honeytown,* Harrap, 1962; *Away Went Galloper,* Methuen, 1962, Encyclopaedia Britannica, 1964; *Castaway Christmas,* Methuen, 1963, Farrar, Straus, 1964; *Cut Off from Crumpets,* Methuen, 1964; *The Shoe Shop Bears,* Harrap, 1964, Farrar, Straus, 1965; *Homer Goes West,* Brockhampton Press, 1965; *Hannibal and the Bears,* Harrap, 1965, Farrar, Straus, 1966; *Porterhouse Major,* Prentice-Hall, 1967; *Bears Back in Business,* Farrar, Straus, 1967; *Hi-Jinks Joins the Bears,* Harrap, 1968, Farrar, Straus, 1969; *Home From the Hill,* Methuen, 1968, Farrar, Straus, 1969.

Teabag and the Bears, Harrap, 1970; *Snails' Pace,* Dent, 1970; *The Last Straw,* Methuen, 1971; *Boots and the Ginger Beans,* Harrap, 1972; *The Sand Bird,* Thomas Nelson, 1973; *Prickets Way,* Methuen, 1973; *Lock Stock & Barrel,* Methuen, 1974.

Short story collections: *Treasure Trove,* 1952, *The Young Magicians,* 1954, *The Wonderful Wellington Boots,* 1955, *Into the Castle,* 1962 (all published by Brockhampton Press).

Contributor of short stories to *Christian Science Monitor, Story Parade, Jack and Jill,* and *Child Life.*

WORK IN PROGRESS: Hopscotch and the Bears.

SIDELIGHTS: Ms. Baker told *CA*: "My interests mostly centre round the countryside, particularly Somerset and North Devon. I used to live in a house which was once an inn close to Exmoor. Now I live in a bungalow near the sea. I am interested in gardening, motoring, antiques, the Brontes, the history of children's books, tortoises and Pekingese dogs who come into my books, walking, swimming, house decorating. I think humanism and realism are the two qualities I strive for when writing for children. I like to write two kinds of books—magic books for younger children and family adventure stories for children from 10 to 13."

Two of her books, *A Castle and Sixpence* and *Benbow and the Angels* were serialized on British Broadcasting Corp. television programs; ten of them have appeared in translations.

BIOGRAPHICAL/CRITICAL SOURCES: Margery Fisher, *Intent on Reading*, Brockhampton Press, 1961; Naomi Lewis, *The Best Children's Books of 1963*, Hamish Hamilton, 1964.

* * *

BAKER, Richard M., Jr. 1924-

PERSONAL: Born February 13, 1924, in Worcester, Mass.; son of Richard M. (a tax specialist) and Theodora (Cooper) Baker; married Jean McAllaster, November 15, 1947; children: Virginia, Dan, Laura Jean, Eleanor, Sally Ann. *Education:* Bowdoin College, B.A., 1946. *Politics:* Independent. *Home and office:* 88 Ivie Rd., Cape Elizabeth, Me. 04107. *Agent:* James Oliver Brown, James Brown Associates, Inc., 22 East 60th St., New York, N.Y. 10022.

CAREER: Public accountant, Portland, Me., 1946-58; began writing after being confined to home with multiple sclerosis in 1957. *Military service:* U.S. Army, 1943. *Member:* Authors Guild.

WRITINGS: The Revolt of Zengo Takakuwa, Farrar, Straus, 1962.

BIOGRAPHICAL/CRITICAL SOURCES: Gerald Gross, *Editors on Editing*, Grosset, 1962.†

* * *

BALEY, James A. 1918-

PERSONAL: Born March 30, 1918, in Cleveland, Ohio; son of James (a toolmaker and draftsman) and Mary (Prohaska) Baley; married Estelle Domino, April 29, 1945; children: James M., Timothy J., Gary E., D. Scott, Brian C. *Education:* University of Illinois, B.S., 1946, M.S., 1948; Ohio State University, Ph.D., 1952. *Politics:* Democrat. *Home:* R.D. 1, Browns Rd., Storrs, Conn. *Office:* U-110, University of Connecticut, Storrs, Conn.

CAREER: Duke University, Durham, N.C., instructor in physical education, 1947-49; Ohio Wesleyan University, Delaware, assistant professor of physical education, 1950-54; State University of New York College at Corland, associate professor of physical education, 1954-57; University of Southern Mississippi, Hattiesburg, professor and head of health department, 1957-60; University of Connecticut, Storrs, instructor, 1960-61, assistant professor of physical education, 1961—. American National Red Cross, state vice-chairman of funds, Connecticut, 1964-65. *Military service:* U.S. Army Air Forces, 1941-45; became staff sergeant. *Member:* American Association for Health, Physical Education and Recreation (fellow), American College of

Sports Medicine, National College Physical Education Association, Connecticut Association for Health, Physical Education and Recreation, Phi Epsilon Kappa.

WRITINGS: (Contributor) *The Complete Book of Gymnastics*, Prentice-Hall, 1960; *Gymnastics in the Schools*, Allyn & Bacon, 1965; *Handbook of Gymnastics in the Schools*, Allyn & Bacon, 1974. Contributor of sixty articles to professional journals.

WORK IN PROGRESS: Studies on the effects of isometric exercises upon selected measures of physical fitness and upon selected anthropometric measures.†

* * *

BALLARD, (Willis) Todhunter 1903-
(W. T. Ballard, Willis T. Ballard; pseudonyms, Brian Agar, P. D. Ballard, Parker Bonner, Sam Bowie, Nick Carter, Hunter D'Allard, Brian Fox, Harrison Hunt, John Hunter, Neil MacNeil, Clint Reno, John Shepherd, Jack Slade, Clay Turner)

PERSONAL: Born December 13, 1903, in Cleveland, Ohio; son of Fredrick Wayne (an engineer) and Cordelia (Todhunter) Ballard; married Phoebe Dwiggins (a writer), February 5, 1936; children: Wayne. *Education:* Wilmington College, B.S., 1926. *Residence:* Canada Lake, N.Y., and Mt. Dora, Fla. *Agent:* August Lenniger, Lenniger Literary Agency, 437 Fifth Ave., New York, N.Y. 10016; H. M. Swanson, 8523 Sunset Blvd., Los Angeles, Calif. 90069.

CAREER: Professional writer, 1927—. F. W. Ballard & Co., Cleveland, Ohio, engineer, 1926-28; employed by various magazines, newspapers, and film studios, 1929-34; Wright Paterson Field, Ohio, member of production control staff in Maintenance Division, 1942-45. *Member:* Western Writers of America (past vice-president), Writers Guild of America West. *Awards, honors:* Spur Award for best historical novel, Western Writers of America, 1965, for *Gold in California*.

WRITINGS: Two Edged Vengeance, Macmillan, 1951; *Incident at Sun Mountain*, Houghton, 1952; *West of Quarantine*, Houghton, 1953; *High Iron*, Houghton, 1954; *Guns for the Lawless*, Popular Library, 1956; (with James Charles Lynch) *Showdown*, Popular Library, 1957; *Trailtown Marshal*, Popular Library, 1957; *Roundup*, Popular Library, 1957; *Saddle Tramp*, Popular Library, 1958; *Trouble on the Massacre*, Popular Library, 1959; *Trigger Trail*, Popular Library, 1960; *Blizzard Range*, Popular Library, 1960; *Gunman from Texas*, Popular Library, 1960; *Rawhide Gunman*, Popular Library, 1960; *The Long Trail Back*, Doubleday, 1960; *The Night Riders*, Doubleday, 1961; *Gopher Gold*, Doubleday, 1962; *Westward the Monitors Roar*, Doubleday, 1963; *Gold in California*, Doubleday, 1965; (with wife, Phoebe Ballard) *The Man Who Stole a University*, Doubleday, 1967; *The Californian*, Doubleday, 1971; *Nowhere Left to Run*, 1972; *Outlaw Brand*, Avon, 1972; *Loco and the Wolf*, Doubleday, 1973.

(Editor) *A Western Bonanza: Eight Short Novels of the West*, Doubleday, 1969.

Under name W. T. Ballard: *Say Yes to Murder*, Putnam, 1942; *Dealing Out Death*, McKay, 1948; *Murder Can't Stop*, McKay, 1948; *Walk in Fear*, Gold Medal Books, 1952; *Chance Elson*, Pocket Books, 1958; *Fury in the Heart*, Monarch Books, 1959; *Pretty Miss Murder*, Pocket Books, 1961; *The Seven Sisters*, Pocket Books, 1962; *Three for the Money*, Pocket Books, 1963; *Murder Las Vegas Style*, Tower, 1967.

Under name Willis T. Ballard: *The Package Deal*, Appleton, 1957.

Under pseudonym Brian Agar: *Have Love, Will Share*, Monarch Books, 1961; *Land of Promise*, Universal Publishing & Distributing, 1967.

Under pseudonym P. D. Ballard: *Age of the Junkman*, Gold Medal Books, 1963; *End of a Millionaire*, Gold Medal Books, 1964; *Brothers in Blood*, Gold Medal Books, 1972; *The Death Brokers*, Gold Medal Books, 1973.

Under pseudonym Parker Bonner: *Superstition Range*, Popular Library, 1952; *Outlaw Brand*, Popular Library, 1954; *Tough in the Saddle*, Monarch Books, 1964; *Modoc Indian Wars*, Monarch Books, 1965; *Plunder Canyon*, Avon, 1967; *The Man from Yuma*, Berkley Publishing, 1967; *The Town Tamer*, Paperback Library, 1968; *Applegate's Gold*, Avon, 1969; *Borders to Cross*, Paperback Library, 1969; *Look to Your Guns*, Paperback Library, 1969.

Under pseudonym Sam Bowie: *Thunderhead Range*, Monarch Books, 1959; *Chisum*, Ace Books, 1970; *Train Robbers*, Ace Books, 1973.

Under pseudonym Nick Carter: *The Kremlin File*, Universal Publishing & Distributing, 1973.

Under pseudonym Hunter D'Allard: *The Long Sword*, Avon, 1962.

Under pseudonym Brian Fox; all published by Universal Publishing & Distributing: *A Dollar to Die For*, 1968; *The Wild Bunch*, 1969; *Sabata*, 1970; *The Outlaw Trail*, 1972; *Unholy Angel*, 1972; *Return of Sabata*, 1972.

Under pseudonym Harrison Hunt: *Murder Picks the Jury*, Curl, 1947.

Under pseudonym John Hunter: *West of Justice*, Ballantine, 1954; *Ride the Wind South*, Pocket Books, 1957; *Badlands Buccaneer*, Pocket Books, 1959; *Marshal from Deadwood*, Pocket Books, 1960; *Desperation Valley*, Macmillan, 1964; *Duke*, Paperback Library, 1965; *Death in the Mountain*, Ballantine, 1969; *Lost Valley*, Ballantine, 1971; *Hell Hole*, Ballantine, 1971; *The Burning Land*, Ballantine, 1973; *Gambler's Gun*, Ballantine, 1973; *The Higraders*, Ballantine, 1974.

Under pseudonym Neil MacNeil; all published by Gold Medal Books: *Death Takes an Option*, 1958; *Third on a Seesaw*, 1959; *Two Guns for Hire*, 1959; *The Death Ridge*, 1960; *Hot Dam*, 1960; *Mexican Slay Ride*, 1962; *The Spy Catchers*, 1965.

Under pseudonym Clint Reno: *Sun Mountain Slaughter*, Fawcett, 1974; *Sierra Massacre*, Fawcett, in press.

Under pseudonym John Shepherd: *Lights, Action, Murder*, Belmont Books, 1962.

Under pseudonym Jack Slade: *Bandito*, Tower, 1968; *Lassiter*, Tower, 1968; *The Man from Cheyenne*, Tower, 1968, reissued as *Lassiter: The Man from Cheyenne*, Belmont-Tower, 1973; *The Man from Yuma*, Tower, 1968.

Under pseudonym Clay Turner: *Give a Man a Gun*, Paperback Library, 1971; *Go West Ben Gold*, Paperback Library, in press; *Gold Goes to the Mountain*, Paperback Library, in press.

Writer of about fifty motion picture and television scripts, including "The Outcast," Republic Pictures, 1954. Contributor of over one thousand stories to magazines, 1930—, including *Saturday Evening Post*, *Esquire*, *This Week*, *Collier's*, *Liberty*, and *McCall's*.

WORK IN PROGRESS: Trouble Range, under pseudonym John Hunter, for Ballantine; *This Range is Mine* (tentative title), under name Todhunter Ballard, for Doubleday.

SIDELIGHTS: Ballard told *CA* that all his books, "no matter what name they carry, are collaborations with Phoebe Ballard." *Two Edged Vengeance* and a short story, "Red Horizon" (published in *Esquire*), were adapted as the film "The Outcast," 1954; film rights to *Applegate's Gold* were sold to Solar Productions in 1969. *Avocational interests:* Western history, metals, oil deposits, mining, fishing, travel.

*   *   *

BALLINGER, Louise Bowen   1909-

PERSONAL: Born February 9, 1909, in Palmyra, N.J.; daughter of Russell H. and Louise (Rudduck) Bowen; married Raymond A. Ballinger (an advertising designer, and director of department of graphic art, Philadelphia College of Art). *Education:* Barnes Foundation, student for two years; Philadelphia College of Art, B.F.A., 1951; University of Pennsylvania, M.S., 1961. *Home:* 334 South Camac St., Philadelphia, Pa. *Office:* 321 South Iseminger St., Philadelphia, Pa.

CAREER: Pennsylvania Academy of Fine Arts, Philadelphia, curator of schools, 1943-48; Philadelphia College of Art, Philadelphia, Pa., 1948-62, began as assistant director in department of art education, became director; University of Pennsylvania, Philadelphia, lecturer on education, Graduate School of Education, 1962—. *Member:* National Art Education Association (conference design coordinator, 1965), American Education Association (design coordinator), National Committee on Art Education, National Education Association, Eastern Arts Association (member of council; former secretary), Pennsylvania Academy of Fine Arts, Pennsylvania State Educators Association, Philadelphia Art Teachers Association, Philadelphia Art Alliance, Philadelphia Museum of Art.

WRITINGS: (With Thomas F. Vroman) *Design Sources and Resources*, Reinhold, 1965; *Perspective: Space and Design*, Van Nostrand, 1969; (with husband, Raymond A. Ballinger) *Sign, Symbol and Form*, Van Nostrand, 1972.

WORK IN PROGRESS: Other books in an art education series.

AVOCATIONAL INTERESTS: Silver work, drawing, painting, little theater work.†

*   *   *

BALSLEY, Irol Whitmore   1912-

PERSONAL: Born August 22, 1912, in Venus, Neb.; daughter of Sylvanus B. and Nanna (Carson) Whitmore; married Howard L. Balsley (a professor), August 24, 1947. *Education:* Wayne State College, Wayne, Neb., B.A., 1933; University of Tennessee, M.S., 1940; Indiana University, Ed.D., 1952. *Office:* Texas Tech University, Lubbock, Tex.

CAREER: High school teacher in Nebraska, 1934-37; South-Western Publishing Co., Cincinnati, Ohio, editorial assistant, 1940-41; Tennessee Valley Authority, head of office training section, 1941-42; Indiana University, Bloomington, assistant professor of business education, 1942-49; University of Utah, Salt Lake City, lecturer, 1949-50; Russell Sage College, Troy, N.Y., lecturer, 1953-54; Louisiana Polytechnic Institute (now Louisiana Tech University),

Ruston, professor of office administration, 1954-65, head of department, 1963-65; Texas Tech University, Lubbock, professor of education, 1965—, chairman of business teacher education program, 1973—. Visiting summer professor at Michigan State University, 1954, Indiana University, 1955, 1960. *Member:* National Collegiate Association for Secretaries (president, 1962-66), National Business Education Association (vice-president, research division, 1965-67, president, 1967-69), Administrative Management Society, Mountain-Plains Business Education Association, Delta Pi Epsilon, Pi Lambda Theta, Beta Gamma Sigma, Sigma Tau Delta, Alpha Psi Omega, Pi Omega Pi.

WRITINGS: (With S. J. Wanous) *Shorthand Transcription Studies,* 4th edition, South-Western Publishing, 1968; (with Jerry W. Robinson) *Integrated Secretarial Studies,* South-Western Publishing, 1964; *Current Transcription Studies,* Division of Research, Louisiana Polytechnic Institute, 1964; (with others) *Homestyle Baking,* Dorrance, 1973; *Century 21 Shorthand,* Collegiate Series, Volume I, (with Hoskinson) Volume II, South-Western, in press.

* * *

BAMBERGER, Bernard J(acob) 1904-

PERSONAL: Born May 30, 1904, in Baltimore, Md.; son of William B. (an attorney) and Gussie (Erlanger) Bamberger; married Ethel R. Kraus, June 14, 1932; children: Henry, David. *Education:* Johns Hopkins University, A.B., 1923; Hebrew Union College, Cincinnati, Ohio, Rabbi, 1926, D.D., 1929. *Politics:* Independent. *Home:* 225 West 86th St., New York, N.Y. 10024. *Office:* Temple Shaaray Tefila, 250 East 79th St., New York, N.Y. 10021.

CAREER: Temple Israel, Lafayette, Ind., rabbi, 1926-29; Congregation Beth Emeth, Albany, N.Y., rabbi, 1929-44; Temple Shaaray Tefila, New York, N.Y., rabbi, 1944-70, rabbi emeritus, 1970—. President of Synagogue Council of America, 1950-51, Central Conference of American Rabbis, 1959-61, and World Union for Progressive Judaism, 1970-72. *Member:* American Academy for Jewish Research, Society of Biblical Literature and Exegesis. *Awards, honors:* D.H.L., Hebrew Union College, Cincinnati, Ohio, 1950.

WRITINGS: Proselytism in the Talmudic Period, Hebrew Union College Press, 1939, second edition, Ktav, 1968; (editor) *Reform Judaism,* Hebrew Union College Press, 1949; *Fallen Angels,* Jewish Publication Society, 1952; *The Bible: A Modern Jewish Approach,* Hillel Little Books, 1955; *The Story of Judaism,* Union of American Hebrew, 1957; (member of editorial committee; new American Jewish translation of the Bible) Jewish Publication Society, *The Torah,* 1963; *The Five Megillot,* 1969; *Jonah,* 1969; *Isaiah,* 1973; *Jeremiah,* 1974; (editor) Jacob Z. Leuterbach, *Studies in Jewish Law, Custom, and Folklore,* Ktav, 1970. Contributor of articles, reviews, and sermons to scholarly and popular periodicals.

WORK IN PROGRESS: Further work on American Jewish translation of Bible; research in Talmudic Judaism and in contemporary religious problems.

SIDELIGHTS: Rabbi Bamberger is competent in French, German, Hebrew, and Aramaic, and has some ability in Latin, Greek, and Italian.

* * *

BANDER, Edward J. 1923-

PERSONAL: Born August 10, 1923, in Boston, Mass.; son of Abraham (a tailor) and Ida (Lendman) Bander; married Frances Waite, March 22, 1952; children: Lida, David, Steven. *Education:* Boston University, A.B., 1949, LL.B., 1951; Simmons College, M.S. in L.S., 1955. *Politics:* Democrat. *Religion:* Jewish. *Home:* 5601 Riverdale Ave., New York, N.Y. 10471. *Office:* 40 Washington Sq. West, New York, N.Y. 10012.

CAREER: Attorney, Boston, Mass., 1951-52; Cuyahoga County, Ohio, researcher in juvenile court, 1952-53; Harvard University, Cambridge, Mass., assistant reference librarian in Law School, 1953-54; U.S. Court of Appeals, Boston, Mass., librarian, 1955-60; New York University, New York, N.Y., assistant professor, 1960-72, associate professor of law, 1972—. *Military service:* U.S. Navy, 1942-46. *Member:* American Association of Law Libraries, New England Law Librarians (president, 1959), Law Library Association of Greater New York (president, 1963-64).

WRITINGS: (Editor) *Mr. Dooley on the Choice of Law,* Michie, 1963; *Law Dictionary of Practical Definitions,* Oceana, 1966; *Justice Holmes, Ex Cathedra,* Michie, 1967; (editor) *Turmoil on the Campus,* H. W. Wilson, 1970; (editor with Julius J. Marke) *Commercial Law: A Guide to Information Sources,* Gale, 1970; *How to Change Your Name and the Law of Names,* H. W. Wilson, 1974. Contributor of articles on Finley Peter Dunne's "Mr. Dooley," on the novel and law, and on Shakespeare, to journals.

WORK IN PROGRESS: The Corporation in American Society for publication by H. W. Wilson; a biography of Finley Peter Dunne, for Twayne.

* * *

BANDURA, Albert 1925-

PERSONAL: Born December 4, 1925, in Mundare, Alberta, Canada; son of Joseph and Jessie (Berazanski) Bandura; married Virginia B. Varnes; children: Mary, Carol. *Education:* University of British Columbia, B.A., 1949; University of Iowa, M.A., 1951, Ph.D., 1952. *Home:* 820 San Francisco Ct., Stanford, Calif. *Office:* Department of Psychology, Stanford University, Stanford, Calif.

CAREER: Stanford University, Stanford, Calif., 1953—, began as instructor, now professor of psychology. Fellow, Center for Advanced Study in the Behavioral Sciences, 1969-70. *Member:* American Psychological Association (president, 1974), Society for Research in Child Development. *Awards, honors:* Guggenheim Fellowship, 1972.

WRITINGS: (With R. H. Walters) *Adolescent Aggression,* Ronald, 1959; (with Walters) *Social Learning and Personality Development,* Holt, 1963; *Principles of Behavior Modification,* Holt, 1969; (editor) *Psychological Modeling: Conflicting Theories,* Aldine, 1971; *Aggression: A Social Learning Analysis,* Prentice-Hall, 1973.

WORK IN PROGRESS: Research in social learning theory.

* * *

BARACK, Nathan A. 1913-

PERSONAL: Born July 2, 1913, in Ukraine, Russia; son of Phillip (a businessman) and Etta (Cohen) Barack; married Lillian Astrachan, February 15, 1942; children: Sylvia, Judie, Sara. *Education:* Lewis Institute, B.A., 1934; Hebrew Theological College, Chicago, Ill., Rabbi, 1936; Jewish Theological Seminary of America, D.H.L., 1959. *Home:* 2623 North Tenth St., Sheboygan, Wis.

CAREER: Congregation Beth El, Sheboygan, Wis., rabbi, 1949—. School for Christian Workers, instructor, 1960-63. *Member:* Rabbinical Assembly of America, Jewish Chaplains Association, Association for Mental Health (board member), Kiwanis Club.

WRITINGS: Tale of a Wonderful Ladder, Bloch, 1943; *Faith for Fallibles*, Bloch, 1952; *Mount Moriah View*, Bloch, 1956; *A History of the Sabbath*, Jonathan David, 1965; *The Jewish Way to Life*, Jonathan David, 1974. Contributor of articles to periodicals.

*   *   *

BARBE, Walter Burke 1926-

PERSONAL: Born October 30, 1926, in Miami, Fla.; son of Victor Elza and Edith (Burris) Barbe; married Marilyn Wood (a high school guidance counselor), February 7, 1967; children: Frederick W. *Education:* Northwestern University, B.S., 1949, M.A., 1950, Ph.D., 1953. *Politics:* Democrat. *Religion:* Presbyterian. *Home:* R.D. 1, Narrowsburg, N.Y. 12764. *Office: Highlights For Children*, 803 Church St., Honesdale, Pa.

CAREER: Baylor University, Waco, Tex., instructor in psychology, 1950; Kent State University, Kent, Ohio, assistant professor of elementary education and director of reading clinic, 1950-52; University of Chattanooga, Chattanooga, Tenn., professor of education and director of Junior League Reading Center, 1953-60; Kent State University, professor of education and head of special education department, 1960-64; *Highlights for Children*, Honesdale, Pa., editor, 1964—. Adjunct professor, University of Pittsburg, 1964, Ohio State University, 1973—. Editor, Zaner-Bloser, Inc. *Military service:* U.S. Army, 1944-46. *Member:* Council for Exceptional Children, American Psychological Association (fellow), National Association for Gifted Children (president, 1958-60), National Education Association, The Association for the Gifted (president, 1967), International Reading Association, Council of State Directors of Programs for Gifted, Phi Delta, Kappa Delta Pi, Psi Chi, Lookout Mountain Fairyland Club, Honesdale Golf Club, Rotary. *Awards, honors:* Psi Chi research award, 1953.

WRITINGS: Directory of Reading Clinics, University of Chattanooga Press, 1955; (with Dorothy Hinman) *We Build Our Words*, Bookman Associates, 1957; (editor with others) *Teen-Age Tales*, Heath, 1957; (editor with Thomas M. Stephens) *Educating Tomorrow's Leaders*, Ohio State Department of Education, 1961; *Educator's Guide to Personalized Reading Instruction*, Prentice-Hall, 1961; *The Exceptional Child*, Center for Applied Research in Education, 1963; (editor) *Teaching Reading: Selected Materials*, Oxford University Press, 1965; (editor) *Psychology and Education of the Gifted: Selected Readings*, Appleton, 1965; (compiler) *Creative Writing Activities*, Highlights for Children, 1965; (editor with Edward C. Frierson) *Educating Children With Learning Disabilities: Selected Readings*, Appleton, 1967; (editor) Annette Wynne and others, *Children Around the World*, Highlights for Children, 1968; (editor) *Searchlights on Literature* (basic reading program series), Harper, 1969; (editor) *Sports Handbook*, Highlights for Children, 1970. Contributor of more than one hundred articles to educational and psychological journals.

WORK IN PROGRESS: A series, *Creative Growth With Handwriting*.

BARBER, James David 1930-

PERSONAL: Born July 31, 1930, in Charleston, W.Va.; son of Daniel Newman (a physician) and Edith Margaret (Naismith) Barber; married Ann Goodridge Sale (a research assistant), December 27, 1951; children: Sara Naismith, Jane Lewis. *Education:* University of Chicago, B.A., 1950, M.A., 1955; Yale University, Ph.D., 1960. *Home:* 3088 Colony Rd., Apt. E, Durham, N.C. 27705. *Office:* Department of Political Science, Duke University, Durham, N.C. 27706.

CAREER: Stetson University, De Land, Fla., assistant professor of political science, 1955-57; Yale University, New Haven, Conn., assistant professor, 1961-65, associate professor of political science, 1965-72, director of graduate studies in political science, 1965-67, director, Office for Advanced Political Studies, 1967-68; Duke University, Durham, N.C., professor of political science, and chairman of department, 1970—. Research associate at University of Chicago Industrial Relations Center, 1951-53, 1955; guest scholar at Brookings Institution, 1964-65. Director, Harvard-Yale-Columbia Intensive Summer Studies Program, 1966-67. Member of Wallingford (Conn.) Charter Commission, 1959-61, Board of Finance, 1960-61, and Connecticut Commission on Municipal Employees, 1963-64. *Military service:* U.S. Army, Counter-Intelligence Corps, 1953-55; became sergeant. *Member:* American Political Science Association, American Association of University Professors. *Awards, honors:* National Science Foundation fellow, 1961-63; fellow, Center for Advanced Study in Behavioral Sciences, 1968-69.

WRITINGS: (With R. E. Lane and F. I. Greenstein) *An Introduction to Political Analysis*, Prentice-Hall, 1962; (compiler) *Political Leadership in American Government*, Little, Brown, 1964; (editor) Alan Barth, *Heritage of Liberty*, Part II, McGraw, 1964; *The Lawmakers: Recruitment and Adaptation to Legislative Life*, Yale University Press, 1965; *Power in Committees: An Experiment in the Governmental Process*, Rand McNally, 1966; *Citizen Politics: An Introduction to Political Behavior*, Markham, 1969, 2nd edition, 1972; (compiler) *Readings in Citizen Politics: Studies of Political Behavior*, Markham, 1969, 2nd edition, published as *Power to the Citizen: Introductory Readings*, 1972; *The Presidential Character: Predicting Performance in the White House*, Prentice-Hall, 1972; (editor) *Choosing the President*, Prentice-Hall, 1974. Editor of series, for Harcourt, 1970—. Contributor to professional journals. Chairman of editorial board, *Political Science*, 1969-71.†

*   *   *

BARCHILON, Jacques 1923-

PERSONAL: Born April 8, 1923, in Casablanca, Morocco; naturalized U.S. citizen, 1957; son of Jaime Ohana and Perla Barchilon; married Helen Redman, 1960. *Education:* Received Baccalauréat de Philosophie in Tangiers, Morocco, 1946; University of Rochester, B.A., 1950; Harvard University, M.A., 1951, Ph.D., 1956. *Home:* 638 Pleasant St., Boulder, Colo. *Office:* French Department, University of Colorado, Boulder, Colo.

CAREER: Smith College, Northampton, Mass., instructor, 1955-56; Brown University, Providence, R.I., instructor, 1955-59; University of Colorado, Boulder, assistant professor, 1959-64, associate professor of French literature, 1964—. *Military service:* Free French Forces, 1943-45, serving in England and France. *Member:* Modern Language Association of America, American Association of

Teachers of French, Association Internationale des Etudes Francaises, Modern Humanities Research Association, Societe d'Etudes du Dix-septieme Siecle. *Awards, honors:* Research grants from the University of Colorado, and from American Philosophical Society.

WRITINGS: Perrault's Tales of Mother Goose: A Critical Edition of the 1695 Dedication Manuscript, Pierpont Morgan Library, 1956; (editor, with Henry Pettit) *The Authentic Mother Goose Fairy Tales and Nursery Rhymes,* A. Swallow, 1960. Contributor of articles to French and American journals.

WORK IN PROGRESS: A book, *The Art of the Fairy Tale.*

SIDELIGHTS: Barchilon reports that he is doing research specifically on the fairy tale as an art form. In French literature, his special field is the seventeenth century. His third scholarly interest is comparative literature. *Avocational interests:* Reading, writing, camping, and gardening.†

* * *

BARDOS, Marie (Dupuis) 1935-

PERSONAL: Born March 2, 1935, in Lafayette, La.; daughter of Rudolph (a businessman) and Beatrice (Parkerson) Dupuis; married Thomas Bardos (a lawyer), October 29, 1955; children: Paul. *Education:* Radcliffe College, B.A. (magna cum laude), 1956. *Home:* 116 Pinehurst Ave., Apartment C32, New York, N.Y. 10033. *Agent:* Diarmuid Russell, Russell & Volkening, Inc., 551 Fifth Ave., New York, N.Y. 10017.

CAREER: Educational Advisory Center, Boston, Mass., secretary, 1956-57. Writer. *Member:* Phi Beta Kappa. *Awards, honors:* Doubleday-Columbia University fellowship for *Night Light.*

WRITINGS: Night Light (novel), Doubleday, 1964. Short stories have appeared in *Audience* and *Liberal Context.*

WORK IN PROGRESS: A novel involving research in various aspects of the history of Christianity.

SIDELIGHTS: Marie Bardos told *CA* that her competence in French is "more Louisiana Acadian than Parisian." *Avocational interests:* Music.†

* * *

BARITZ, Loren 1928-

PERSONAL: Born December 26, 1928, in Chicago, Ill.; son of Joseph H. and Helen (Garland) Baritz; married Phyllis Handelsman, December 26, 1948; children: Anthony, Joseph. *Education:* Roosevelt University, B.A., 1953; University of Wisconsin, M.S., 1953, Ph.D., 1956. *Home:* 122 South Main Ave., Albany, N.Y. 12208.

CAREER: Wesleyan University, Middletown, Conn., assistant professor of history, 1956-62; Roosevelt University, Chicago, Ill., associate professor of history, 1962-63; University of Rochester, Rochester, N.Y., associate professor of history and chairman of department, 1963-69; State University of New York at Albany, professor of history, 1969-71; Empire State College of the State University of New York, Saratoga Springs, executive vice-president, 1971—. Visiting lecturer, University of Wisconsin, 1959-60. *Member:* American Historical Association, American Association of University Professors. *Awards, honors:* Social Science Research Council grant-in-aid, 1961; American Council of Learned Societies grant-in-aid, 1963.

WRITINGS: Servants of Power: A History of the Use of Social Science in American Industry, Wesleyan University Press, 1961; *City on a Hill: A History of Ideas and Myths in America,* Wiley, 1964; *Sources of the American Mind,* two volumes, Wiley, 1965; *The Culture of the Twenties,* Bobbs-Merrill, 1969; (editor) *The American Left: Radical Political Thought in the Twentieth Century,* Basic Books, 1971. Contributor to *American Historical Review.*

* * *

BARKER, A(rthur) J(ames) 1918-

PERSONAL: Born September 20, 1918, in Yorkshire, England; son of John Robert Marlow and Caroline Frances (Roe) Barker; married Dorothy Jeanna Hirst (marriage dissolved, 1968); married Alexandra Franziska Roderbourg, 1969; children: (first marriage) Timothy Marlow. *Education:* Attended Staff College, Quetta, India, 1944; Royal Military College of Science, 1948-50. *Politics:* Conservative. *Religion:* Humanist. *Address:* c/o Westminster Bank Ltd., Beverley, Yorkshire, England; United Service Club, Pall Mall, London S.W. 1, England. *Agent:* Peter Janson-Smith Ltd., 31 Newington Green, London N 169 PU, England.

CAREER: Career officer in British Army, 1936-58; commissioned in East Yorkshire Regiment; served as Infantry officer in Africa, 1940-41, Burma, 1942-44, and Malaya, 1952-54, as staff officer in Burma-India, 1945-46, Palestine and Egypt, 1947, and Malaya, 1956-58, and in other posts in northwestern Europe; retired with rank of lieutenant colonel, 1958; United Kingdom Atomic Energy Authority, London, England, administrator and editor of scientific reports, 1959-68; writer, 1968—. *Member:* Royal Society of Arts (fellow), P.E.N., Authors Guild, Royal United Service Institution, Society for Army Historical Research, British Atlantic Committee (associate). *Awards, honors:* NATO research fellowship, 1968.

WRITINGS: Principles of Small Arms, Gale & Polden, 1952; *The March on Delhi,* Faber, 1963; *Suez: The Seven Day War,* Praeger, 1964; *Eritrea 1941,* Faber, 1966; *The Bastard War: The Mesopotamian Campaign of 1914-1918,* Dial, 1967 (published in England as *The Neglected War: Mesopotamia, 1914-1918,* Faber, 1967); *Townshend of Kut: A Biography of Major-General Sir Charles Townshend,* Cassell, 1967; *The Civilizing Mission: A History of the Italo-Ethiopian War of 1935-1936,* Dial, 1968; *German Infantry Weapons of World War II,* Arco, 1969; *The Vainglorious War: 1854-56,* Weidenfeld & Nicolson, 1970, published in America as *The War Against Russia: 1854-1856,* Holt, 1971; *Pearl Harbor,* Ballantine, 1969; *British and American Infantry Weapons of World War II,* Arco, 1969, revised edition, Leventhal, 1973.

(With John Walter) *Russian Infantry Weapons of World War II,* Arco, 1971; *The East Yorkshire Regiment,* Leo Cooper, 1971; *Midway: The Turning Point,* Ballantine, 1971; *The Suicide Weapon,* Ballantine, 1971; *The Rape of Ethiopia, 1936,* Ballantine, 1971; *Fortune Favours the Brave,* Leo Cooper, 1973; *Behind Barbed Wire,* Batsford, 1974; *The October War: Yom Kippur, 1973,* Ballantine, 1974; *The Redcoats Are Coming,* Saxon, in press.

Juvenile: *Weapons and Armour,* Paul Hamlyn, 1974; *Famous Military Battles,* Paul Hamlyn, 1974. Contributor to *Royal United Service Institutional Journal, Army Quarterly,* and other military journals.

SIDELIGHTS: Commenting on *The Bastard War* in *The New York Times Book Review,* Cyril Falls wrote, "... Barker's thorough study of the four-year struggle between the British and the Turks during World War I for the control of the Persian Gulf and the rich oil fields of Mesopotamia is the best that has appeared since F. J. Moberly's official history of that campaign.'' *Avocational interests:* Travel, talk (philosophizing and arguments), games and sports (in accordance with age and service), and Cavalier King Charles spaniels.

* * *

BARKER, Charles M., Jr. 1926-

PERSONAL: Born February 5, 1926, in Los Angeles, Calif.; married; children: three. *Education:* University of California, Berkeley, B.A., 1950, M.A., 1959. *Home:* 7062 Broadway Ter., Oakland, Calif. 94611.

CAREER: Oakland, Calif., public schools, teacher of mathematics, 1954-74, consultant, 1974—. *Military service:* U.S. Army and U.S. Air Force. *Member:* National Council of Teachers of Mathematics, California Teachers Association, Metric Association, Phi Delta Kappa.

WRITINGS: (With H. Curran) *The ''New'' Math*, Fearon, 1964, revised edition published as *The ''New'' Maths*, Arlington Books, 1965; *Problems in New Math*, Fearon, 1966.

WORK IN PROGRESS: Metrication.

* * *

BARKER, T(heodore Cardwell) 1923-

PERSONAL: Born July 19, 1923, in Manchester, England; son of Norman Humphrey (an electrical engineer) and Louie (Cardwell) Barker; married Judith Pierce (an opera singer), August 2, 1955. *Education:* Jesus College, Oxford, M.A., 1948; University of Manchester, Ph.D., 1951. *Home:* Minsen Dane, Brogdale Rd., Faversham, Kent, England. *Office:* University of Kent at Canterbury, Westgate House, Canterbury, England.

CAREER: University of Aberdeen, Aberdeen, Scotland, research fellow in economic history, 1952-53; University of London, London School of Economics and Political Science, London, England, lecturer in economic history, 1953-64; University of Kent at Canterbury, Canterbury, England, professor of economic history, 1964—. *Member:* Royal Historical Society (fellow), Economic History Society (secretary).

WRITINGS: (With J. R. Harris) *A Merseyside Town in the Industrial Revolution*, Liverpool University Press, 1954; *The Girdlers' Company: A Second History*, Girdlers' Company, 1957; *Pilkington Brothers and the Glass Industry*, Allen & Unwin, 1960; (with Michael Robbins) *A History of London Transport*, Volume I, Allen & Unwin, 1964; (editor with John C. McKenzie and John Yudkin, *Our Changing Fare: Two Hundred Years of British Food Habits*, MacGibbon & Kee, 1966.

WORK IN PROGRESS: A History of London Transport, Volume II; a textbook on British economic history since 1700.†

* * *

BARNES, Sam(uel) G(ill) 1913-

PERSONAL: Born August 5, 1913, in Kansas City, Mo.; son of Welden Fairbanks and Mary (Gill) Barnes; married Ruth Adams Royal, 1947; children: David, Peter, Stephen, Andrew. *Education:* Oklahoma Agricultural and Mechanical College (now Oklahoma State University), B.S., 1936;

University of North Carolina, M.A., 1946, Ph.D., 1953. *Politics:* Republican. *Religion:* Methodist. *Home:* Penick Lane, Chapel Hill, N.C. *Agent:* Dorothy Markinko, McIntosh & Otis, Inc., 18 East 41st St., New York, N.Y. 10017.

CAREER: Instructor in English at Virginia Military Institute, Lexington, 1939-41, 1946-50, Washington and Lee University, Lexington, 1946-47; University of North Carolina, Chapel Hill, lecturer, 1953-56, assistant professor, 1956-65, associate professor of English, 1965—, head wrestling coach, 1937—. *Military service:* U.S. Navy, 1941-45.

WRITINGS: Learning Composition Skill by Means of Controlled-Source Books, Odyssey, 1962; *Ready, Wrestle!*, Farrar, Strauss, 1965.

WORK IN PROGRESS: Juvenile books on sports, particularly wrestling.†

* * *

BARNET, Richard J.

PERSONAL: Son of Carl J. and Margaret (Block) Barnet; married Ann Birnbaum, 1953; children: Juliana Elisabeth, Michael. *Education:* Harvard University, A.B., 1952, L.L.B., 1954. *Home:* 5409 Duvall St., Washington, D.C. 20016.

CAREER: Admitted to bar, 1954; Choate, Hall and Stewart (law firm), Boston, Mass., attorney, 1958-60; Harvard University, Cambridge, Mass., research fellow, 1960-1961; with U.S. Arms Control and Disarmament Agency, Washington, D.C.; co-founder and co-director, Institute for Policy Studies. Consultant to Department of Defense. *Military service:* U.S. Army, 1954-57; became first lieutenant.

WRITINGS: Who Wants Disarmament?, Beacon, 1960; (editor with Richard A. Falk) *Security in Disarmament*, Princeton University Press, 1965; (with Marcus G. Raskin) *After Twenty Years: The Decline of NATO and the Search for a New Policy in Europe*, Vintage, 1966; *Intervention and Revolution: The United States in the Third World*, World Publishing, 1968; *The Economy of Death*, Atheneum, 1969; (contributor) Richard B. Gray, editor, *International Security Systems: Concepts and Models of World Order*, F. E. Peacock, 1969; (with Raskin) *An American Manifesto: What's Wrong with America and What We Can Do About It*, New American Library, 1970; *Can the United States Promote Foreign Development?*, Overseas Development Council, 1971; (with Ralph Stavins and Raskin) *Washington Plans an Aggressive War*, Vintage, 1971; *Roots of War*, Atheneum, 1972; (with Ronald E. Muller) *Global Reach: The Power of the Multinational Corporation*, Simon & Schuster, 1974. Contributor to *Commonweal* and to law journals.

SIDELIGHTS: Reviewing *Intervention and Revolution*, Ronald Steel describes it as a ''brilliantly argued and devastatingly detailed study.'' He notes: ''One of the great virtues of Barnet's splendid book is that it offers a devastating examination of the bureaucratic mentality that has led the United States on the path of intervention and counter-revolution.... [it is] an absorbing and revealing document of the highest utility, one that is likely to become a case-book for a new generation of Americans who are questioning the traditional explanations of the cold war and are rejecting the concept of an American guardianship over the world.... Barnet has produced a work of crucial importance in the growing debate over the use and limitations of American power.'' Tristram Coffin suggests that *Interven-*

tion and Revolution "may well become one of those two or three [books] in a generation that move the mountain of history."†

* * *

BARNETT, Correlli (Douglas) 1927-

PERSONAL: Born June 28, 1927, in Norbury, Surrey, England; son of Douglas Alfred and Kathleen Mabel (Nichols) Barnett; married Ruth Murby (a private secretary), December 30, 1950; children: Clare, Hilary. *Education:* Exeter College, Oxford, B.A. (second class honors), 1951, M.A., 1955. *Home:* Catbridge House, East Carleton, Norwich, Norfolk, England. *Agents:* David Higham Associates Ltd., 76 Dean St., London W. 1, England; and Harold Ober Associates, Inc., 40 East 49th St., New York, N.Y. 10017.

CAREER: Author. Employed in industry, advertising, and public relations in London, 1952-63; free-lance military historian, 1963—. Chairman, Literature Panel, Eastern Arts Association, 1972. *Military service:* British Army, 1945-48; became sergeant. *Member:* Royal Society of Literature (fellow), Institute for Strategic Studies, Royal United Service Institute for Defence Studies, Savage Club (London). *Awards, honors:* Heinemann Award, Royal Society of Literature, 1970, for *Britain and Her Army.*

WRITINGS: The Hump Organisation, Wingate, 1957; *The Desert Generals*, Kimber & Co., 1960, Viking, 1961; *The Swordbearers*, Eyre & Spottiswoode, 1963, Morrow, 1964; (contributor) G. A. Panichas, editor, *Promise of Greatness*, Cassell, 1969; (contributor) Rupert Wilkinson, editor, *Governing Elites*, Oxford University Press, 1969; *Britain and Her Army, 1509-1970: A Military, Political and Social Study*, Morrow, 1970; *The Collapse of British Power*, Morrow, 1972. Co-author and historical consultant for British Broadcasting Corp. television series, "The Great War," "The Lost Peace, 1918-1933," and "The Commanders."

WORK IN PROGRESS: A biography of John Churchill, First Duke of Marlborough.

SIDELIGHTS: The *Times Literary Supplement* called *Britain and Her Army* "a work of considerable authority, full of shrewd observations, thought-provoking comparisons . . ., and controversial themes. . . ." *Avocational interests:* Landscape gardening, architecture, interior decoration, music, the theatre; eating, drinking, and lazing; moletrapping. "Principal likes: all things elegant, whether writing, thought, design, or manners. Principal dislikes: Bores, especially solemn bores. Jargon. Muzak. Bad behaviour."

* * *

BARNETT, S(amuel) A(nthony) 1915-

PERSONAL: Born July 16, 1915, in Middlesex, England. *Education:* Oxford University, student, 1934-37. *Office:* Department of Zoology, Australian National University, Canberra, A.C.T. 2600, Australia.

CAREER: Ministry of Agriculture, head of pest control research unit, 1946-50; University of Glasgow, Glasgow, Scotland, senior lecturer in zoology, 1951-71; Australian National University, Canberra, Australia, professor and head of zoology department, 1971—.

WRITINGS: The Human Species: A Biology of Man, Norton, 1950, 5th revised edition, Harper, 1971; (editor and contributor) *A Century of Darwin*, Harvard University Press, 1958; *The Rat: A Study in Behavior*, Aldine, 1963

(published in England as *A Study in Behavior: Principles of Ethology and Behavioral Physiology, Displayed Mainly in the Rat*, Methuen, 1963), 2nd revised edition, University of Chicago Press, 1975; *Instinct and Intelligence: Behavior of Animals and Man*, Prentice-Hall, 1967, revised edition, Penguin, 1970; (editor) *Ethology and Development*, Heinemann Medical, 1973; (contributor) Ashley Montagu, editor, *Man and Aggression*, 2nd edition (Barnett was not associated with first edition), Oxford University Press, 1973. Contributor to *New Statesman*, *New Society*, and other publications.

* * *

BARNHART, Clarence L(ewis) 1900-

PERSONAL: Born December 30, 1900, near Plattsburg, Mo.; son of Franklin Chester and Frances (Eliot) Barnhart; married Frances Knox, February 21, 1931; children: Robert K., David K. *Education:* University of Chicago, Ph.B., 1930, graduate study, 1934-37. *Home:* 19 Ridge Rd., Bronxville, N.Y. 10708. *Office:* Clarence L. Barnhart, Reference Books, Box 359, Bronxville, N.Y. 10708.

CAREER: Scott, Foresman & Co., Chicago, Ill., editor, 1929-45; Random House, New York, N.Y., editor, 1945-48; Clarence L. Barnhart, Inc. (reference books), Bronxville, N.Y., editor and owner, 1948—. Editor, U.S. War Department, 1943. Honorary research associate, Institute of Psychological Research, Columbia University, 1945-46. *Member:* Modern Language Association of America, Linguistic Society of America, American Name Society, American Dialect Society, American Association for the Advancement of Science, National Council of Teachers of English, Phi Beta Kappa, University Club; Century Association, Authors' Club (both London). *Awards, honors:* U.S. War Department Certificate of Appreciation, 1946, for *Dictionary of United States Army Terms.*

*WRITINGS—*Editor, except where indicated: *Thorndike Century Junior Dictionary*, Scott, 1935, revised edition, with E. L. Thorndike, published as *Thorndike-Barnhart Junior Dictionary*, Scott, 1952, 7th edition, 1968; *Thorndike Century Senior Dictionary*, Scott, 1941; *Dictionary of United States Army Terms*, U.S. Government Printing Office, 1943; *Thorndike Century Beginning Dictionary*, Scott, 1945; *American College Dictionary*, Random House, 1948.

Thorndike-Barnhart Comprehensive Desk Dictionary, Doubleday, 1951; *Thorndike-Barnhart Handy Pocket Dictionary*, Permabooks, 1951, revised edition, 1952; *American College Encyclopedic Dictionary*, Spenser Press (Chicago), 1952; *Thorndike-Barnhart Beginning Dictionary*, Scott, 1952, 7th edition, 1972; *Thorndike-Barnhart High School Dictionary*, Scott, 1952, 5th edition, 1968; (with William D. Halsey) *New Century Cyclopedia of Names*, 3 volumes, Appleton, 1954; *New Century Handbook of English Literature*, Appleton, 1956, revised edition, 1967; *Thorndike-Barnhart Concise Dictionary*, Scott, 1956; *Thorndike-Barnhart Advanced Junior Dictionary*, Scott, 1957, 4th edition, 1968; (author with Leonard Bloomfield) *Let's Read: A Linguistic Approach*, Wayne State University Press, 1961; (co-author) *Let's Read*, privately printed, volumes 1-3, 1963, volumes 4-6, 1964, volumes 7-8, 1965, volume 9, 1966, workbook, 1-4, 1964-65, handbook, 1971; *World Book Encyclopedia Dictionary*, Field Enterprises Educational Corp., 1963, published as *World Book Dictionary*, 1967; *Let's Look at the ABC's*, volumes 1-9, privately printed, 1963-66; *Barnhart Dictionary of New English Since 1963*, Harper, 1973. Contributor to professional journals, including *Teachers College Record* and *American Speech.*

WORK IN PROGRESS: A book, *Language of the Sixties*.

* * *

BARNOUW, Erik 1908-

PERSONAL: Born June 23, 1908, in The Hague, Netherlands; son of Adriaan J. (a teacher) and Ann (Midgley) Barnouw; married Dorothy Beach, June 3, 1939; children: Jeffrey, Susanna, Karen. *Education:* Princeton University, A.B., 1929; University of Vienna, studied at Reinhardt Seminar, 1930. *Home:* 39 Claremont Ave., New York, N.Y. 10027. *Agent:* Harold Ober Associates, 40 East 49th St., New York, N.Y. 10017. *Office:* Columbia University, New York, N.Y. 10027.

CAREER: During early career, worked as broadcasting program director and writer for advertising agencies; Columbia Broadcasting System, New York, N.Y., writer and editor, 1939-40; National Broadcasting Co., New York, N.Y., editor of Script Division, 1942-44; U.S. War Department, Washington, D.C., supervisor of education unit, Armed Forces Radio Service, 1944-45; Columbia University, New York, N.Y., 1946—, became professor of dramatic arts, and editor, Center for Mass Communication of Columbia University Press, now professor emeritus of dramatic arts. Television and radio adapter for Theatre Guild, 1954-61. Consultant on communication, U.S. Public Health Service, 1947-50; producer of "Freedom to Read," Columbia University Bicentennial film, 1954. International Film Seminars, Inc., president, 1960-67.

MEMBER: Writers Guild of America (national chairman, 1957-59), Authors League of America (secretary, 1949-53), International Film Seminars (president, 1960-67), Society of American Historians, Society for Cinema Studies, National Academy of Television Arts and Sciences (member, board of governors, New York, 1958-61), American Civil Liberties Union (member, television-radio panel, 1946-73), Public Affairs Committee (member of board, 1961-65). *Awards, honors:* George Foster Peabody Award for achievement in radio or television, 1944, for National Broadcasting Co. radio series, "Words at War"; Ohio State Institute for Education by Radio award, for best single program, 1944, for "Conspiracy of Silence"; "Freedom to Read" was Edinburgh Film Festival selection, 1954; Gavel Award of American Bar Association and Sylvania Television Award for best noncommercial television series, 1959, for "Decision: The Constitution in Action"; Fulbright grant, 1961-62, for research in India on use of mass media; Guggenheim Fellowship, 1969; Bancroft Prize, 1971, for *The Image Empire*; George Polk Award, 1971, for *A History of Broadcasting in the United States*; Silver Dragon award of Cracow Film Festival, 1972, for "Fable-Safe"; John D. Rockefeller III Fund Fellowship, 1972.

WRITINGS: Handbook of Radio Writing, Little, 1939; (editor) *Radio Drama in Action*, Rinehart, 1945; *Mass Communication: Television, Radio, Film, Press*, Rinehart, 1956; *The Television Writer*, Hill & Wang, 1962; (with S. Krishnaswamy) *Indian Film*, Columbia University Press, 1963; *A History of Broadcasting in the United States*, Oxford University Press, Volume I: *A Tower in Babel*, 1966, Volume II: *The Golden Web*, 1968, Volume III: *The Image Empire*, 1970; *Documentary: A History of the Non-Fiction Film*, Oxford University Press, in press.

Films: (Writer and producer, in consultation with Herbert Wechsler) "Decision: The Constitution in Action," a series of seven films, Center for Mass Communication and National Educational Television, 1957-59; (writer) "Memento," Center for Mass Communication, 1968; (writer and director) "Fable-Safe," Center for Mass Communication, 1971.

Television—Adaptor; all for U.S. Steel Hour: Patterson Greene, "Papa Is All," Roger Eddy, "The Women of Hadley," Henrik Ibsen, "Hedda Gabler."

Author of radio documentary, "The Conspiracy of Silence," produced by ABC, 1948. Author, with Joshua Logan, of Princeton University Triangle Club musical, "Zuider Zee," 1928.

SIDELIGHTS: In 1928 Barnouw helped organize the University Players of Princeton University, an intercollegiate summer theatre group that included Joshua Logan, Henry Fonda, Margaret Sullavan, James Stewart and others.

Barnouw speaks Dutch, and during World War II broadcast occasional news commentaries to The Netherlands for Voice of America. His book, *Mass Communication*, has been translated into Arabic, Chinese, and Indonesian. In preparation for, *Documentary: A History of the Non-Fiction Film*, Barnouw spent eight months visiting film archives and studios in twenty countries.

* * *

BARNSLEY, Alan Gabriel 1916-
(Gabriel Fielding)

PERSONAL: Born March 25, 1916, in Hexham, Northumberland, England; son of George (a clergyman, Church of England) and Katherine (a playwright; maiden name Fielding-Smith) Barnsley; married Edwina Eleanora Cook (a secretary), October 31, 1943; children: Michael, Jonathan, Simon, Felicity, Gabriel (daughter), Anna Swan (ward). *Education:* Trinity College, Dublin, B.A., 1940; St. George's Hospital, London, England, licentiate, 1943; M.R.C.S., L.R.C.P. *Politics:* Left-wing Conservative. *Religion:* Roman Catholic convert, 1952. *Home:* 945 Monroe St., Pullman, Wash. *Office:* Department of English, Washington State University, Pullman, Wash. 99163.

CAREER: Physician in general practice, Maidstone, Kent, England, beginning, 1948; Washington State University, Pullman, author-in-residence, 1966-67, professor of English, 1967—. Part-time medical officer, Her Majesty's Prison, Maidstone, 1952-64. *Military service:* Royal Army Medical Corps, 1943-46; became captain. *Awards, honors:* W. H. Smith Award for "most important contribution to English literature, 1962-63," for *The Birthday King*; Gold Medal of St. Thomas More Association, 1964; D.Litt., Gonzaga University, 1967.

WRITINGS—All under pseudonym Gabriel Fielding, except as indicated: (Under name Alan Gabriel Barnsley) *The Frog Prince, and Other Poems*, Hand and Flower Press, 1952; *Brotherly Love* (novel), Hutchinson, 1954, Morrow, 1961; *Twenty-Eight Poems*, Hand and Flower Press, 1955; *In the Time of Greenbloom* (novel), Hutchinson, 1956, Morrow, 1957; *Eight Days* (novel), Morrow, 1958; *Through Streets Broad and Narrow* (novel), Morrow, 1960; *The Birthday King* (novel), Hutchinson, 1962, Morrow, 1963; *Gentlemen in Their Season*, Morrow, 1966; *New Queens for Old: A Novella and Nine Stories*, Hutchinson, 1972. Contributor to *Harper's*, *Listener*, and *The Critic* (Chicago). Regular broadcaster for the British Broadcasting Corp.

WORK IN PROGRESS: A novel, *Conversations in the Dark*; a film treatment of the Pharaoh Akhnaten and his

Queen Nefertiti, for an Anglo-Egyptian epic; a book of essays and criticism, for Heinemann.

SIDELIGHTS: Barnsley's *The Birthday King* has assured him a prominent position among contemporary novelists. Although he always wanted to write, he turned without enthusiasm to the study of medicine, and did not publish a book before the age of 36. He told Roy Newquist in *Counterpoint* (Rand McNally, 1964): "Medicine, to me, was the sentence I had to fulfill in order to be free to write.... By the time I emerged from medicine I had more or less succeeded in convincing myself that I was a doctor. I honestly didn't think the other dream, the vision of being a writer, could come true." He believes the function of the writer is first to entertain, then to instruct ("One of the loveliest things about this is when you say or feel, 'Ah, I, too, knew this. I knew it without knowing it, but now I know it.' "), and finally, to ask wise questions.

The Birthday King, which deals with Nazi-Jewish relationships, began to evolve early in his life. As a child just after the First World War he used to play "Germans and English," and for a long time believed "that if a man could become monstrous he would be a monster in German form." As he grew older "it became a private obsession not to incriminate the Germans for what they had obviously done, but, from my own sense of humanity, to explain and resolve it."

Barnsley believes the novel form is currently in decline largely because too many people believe they can write. "I know writers who are working on their sixth [novel], numerically, but who are still writing their first. They're subjective novels, full of boredom, frustration, sexual fantasy." He favors the novelist who is "obsessed" with what he has to say, in the manner of James Joyce, Dostoevski, Tolstoy, and Dickens.

He is reportedly descended on his mother's side from the eighteenth-century novelist, Henry Fielding.

BIOGRAPHICAL/CRITICAL SOURCES: Manchester Guardian, June 19, 1956; *Time*, May 23, 1960; *Saturday Review*, June 4, 1960, March 9, 1963; *Critic* (Chicago), December, 1960, January, 1961, April, 1963; *New Statesman*, October 12, 1962; *Times Literary Supplement*, October 12, 1962; *New York Times Book Review*, April 14, 1963; *New Yorker*, May 18, 1963; *Newsweek*, May 20, 1963; *Counterpoint*, compiled by Roy Newquist, Rand McNally, 1964.†

* * *

BARR, O(rlando) Sydney 1919-

PERSONAL: Born April 3, 1919, in Haverhill, Mass.; son of Orlando Sydney (a musician) and Alice Imogene (Haas) Barr; married Marylin Worth Lytle, November 6, 1942; children: Margaret Worth, Joyce Manley, Mark Sydney. *Education:* Yale University, B.A., 1942, Ph.D., 1958; Berkeley Divinity School, New Haven, Conn., S.T.B. (magna cum laude), 1948. *Politics:* Independent. *Home and office:* General Theological Seminary, 175 Ninth Ave., New York, N.Y. 10011.

CAREER: Episcopal clergyman; curate of church in New Britain, Conn., and vicar in Newington, Conn., 1947-50, rector protem of church in Branford, Conn., 1951-52; General Theological Seminary, New York, N.Y., 1952—, began as visiting lecturer, now professor of New Testament. Summer supply rector of church in Newcastle, Me., 1956-61. *Military service:* U.S. Army Air Forces, 1942-45;

served with 14th Air Force in China. *Member:* Society of Biblical Literature, Studiorum Novi Testamenti Societas, Chaplaincy Guild of Scholars of the Episcopal Church, University Seminar of Columbia University (associate).

WRITINGS: (Contributor) *Viewpoints*, edited by Coburn and Pittenger, Seabury, 1959; *From the Apostles' Faith to the Apostles' Creed*, Oxford University Press, 1964; *The Christian New Morality: A Biblical Study of Situation Ethics*, Oxford University Press, 1969. Contributor to *Encyclopedia Americana*. Also contributor of articles to *Witness*, *Anglican Theological Review*, and reviews to *Religion in Life* and *Journal of Biblical Literature*. Member of editorial board, *Witness*.

WORK IN PROGRESS: A study of the concept of "mission" in the New Testament; research for future publication on special Johannine studies, ethics of the New Testament, and credal origins in the tradition of the earliest church.

SIDELIGHTS: Barr has competence in French, German, Greek, Latin, Hebrew, and Aramaic. *Avocational interests:* Sports (especially tennis and baseball), hiking.

* * *

BARRES, Oliver 1921-

PERSONAL: Born July 31, 1921, in Bethlehem, Pa.; son of Oliver Morgan and Matilda Mary (Ritter) Barres; married Marjorie Jane Catchpole, March 21, 1946; children: Margaret, Mary, Catherine, Clare, John, William. *Education:* Yale University, B.A., 1943; Lehigh University, M.A., 1951; Yale University Divinity School, B.D., 1951. *Religion:* Roman Catholic.

CAREER: First Congregational Church, East Windsor, Conn., minister, 1951-55; Manhattanville College, Purchase, N.Y., instructor in European history, 1956-59; Society for the Propagation of the Fatih, New York, N.Y., staff member, 1959—. *Wartime service:* American Field Service Ambulance Corps, serving in Africa and Italy, 1943-45. *Member:* Third Order of St. Francis.

WRITINGS: One Shepherd, One Flock, Sheed, 1956; *World Mission Windows*, Alba, 1963. Contributor to *America*, *Catholic World*, *Saturday Review*, and other periodicals.

WORK IN PROGRESS: "Catholic Missions" for Harper's *Encyclopedia of Modern Christian Missions*.†

* * *

BARRETT, Donald N(eil) 1920-

PERSONAL: Born October 27, 1920, in Norfolk, Va.; son of Edward C. and Loretta C. (McNeil) Barrett; married Marion M. Moody, November 22, 1948; children: Edward, Mary, Brian, Loretta, Virginia. *Education:* Attended Georgetown University, 1938-42; St. Louis University, A.B., 1945, Ph.L., 1946; Catholic University of America, graduate study, 1947; University of Pennsylvania, M.A., 1951, graduate study, 1955. *Home:* 1021 North Brookfield St., South Bend, Ind.

CAREER: LaSalle College, Philadelphia, Pa., instructor, later assistant professor, 1948-55; University of Notre Dame, Notre Dame, Ind., assistant professor of sociology, 1955—. *Member:* American Sociological Association, American Population Association, American Catholic Sociological Society.

WRITINGS: (Editor) *Values in America*, University of

Notre Dame Press, 1961; (editor) *The Problem of Population*, University of Notre Dame Press, Volume I: *Moral and Theological Considerations*, 1964. Contributor to *Sociological Analysis* and other journals.

WORK IN PROGRESS: A book, *Criminological Theories*, for Prentice-Hall; contributions to forthcoming book by research staff of the Study of Catholic Education; a study of family and fertility counseling in England on a research grant from the Population Council.

SIDELIGHTS: Barrett is competent in French, and knows some German.†

*   *   *

BARRETT, William   1913-

PERSONAL: Born December 30, 1913, in New York, N.Y., son of John Patrick (an engineer) and Delia (Connolly) Barrett. *Education:* City College (now City College of the City University of New York), A.B., 1933; Columbia University, A.M., Ph.D., 1938. *Office:* New York University, New York, N.Y. 10003.

CAREER: Partisan Review, New York, N.Y., editor, 1945-53; New York University, New York, professor of philosophy, 1950—. *Member:* American Philosophical Association, Authors Guild of the Authors League of America, Phi Beta Kappa. *Awards, honors:* Rockefeller Foundation fellow, 1946-47.

WRITINGS: (Editor with D. T. Suzuki) *Zen Buddhism*, Doubleday, 1956; *Irrational Man*, Doubleday, 1958; (editor with Henry D. Aiken) *Philosophy in the 20th Century*, 4 volumes, Random House, 1962, published in 3 volumes, Harper, 1971; *What is Existentialism?*, Grove, 1964; (with Daniel Yankelovich) *Ego and Instinct: The Psychoanalytic View of Human Nature*, Random House, 1970; *Time of Need: Forms of Imagination in the Twentieth Century*, Harper, 1972. Literary reviewer for *Atlantic Monthly*, 1960—, columnist, "Reader's Choice," *Atlantic Monthly*, 1961—.

WORK IN PROGRESS: A study of Marcel Proust; a general study of the philosophic themes in modern literature and art.

SIDELIGHTS: Barrett is competent in French, German, and Italian, and has slight knowledge of Russian. *Avocational interests:* Painting ("but find little time for it these days").†

*   *   *

BARRY, Colman J.   1921-

PERSONAL: Born May 29, 1921, in Lake City, Minn.; son of John (a federal employee) and Frances (O'Brien) Barry. *Education:* St. John's University, Collegeville, Minn., B.A., 1942; Catholic University of America, M.A., 1950, Ph.D., 1953. *Home:* St. John's University, Collegeville, Minn.

CAREER: Roman Catholic priest, member of Order of Saint Benedict. St. John's University, Collegeville, Minn., professor of history, 1953-64, president, 1964—. Summer professor of history, Catholic University of America, Washington, D.C., and San Raphael (Calif.) extension, 1956-64; visiting professor, Divinity School, Yale University, 1973; dean of Religious Studies, Catholic University of America, Washington, D.C., 1974. Has served as secretary of American Benedictine Academy. *Awards, honors:* Penfield fellowship for historical research in Europe, 1950.

WRITINGS: The Catholic University of America, Volume IV, Catholic University of America Press, 1950; *The Catholic Church and German Americans*, Bruce, 1952; *Worship and Work* (centennial history of St. John's Abbey and University, Collegeville, Minn.), St. John's Abbey, 1956; *Catholic Minnesota*, Catholic Aid Association (St. Paul), 1958; *Readings in Church History*, three volumes, Newman, 1959-65; *American Nuncio: Cardinal Aloysius Muench*, St. John's University Press, 1969; *Upon These Rocks: Catholics in the Bahamas*, St. John's University Press, 1973. Contributor to published symposia on American, regional, and religious history. Editor of "Benedictine Studies" series and of *American Bendictine Review*, 1959-64.

*   *   *

BARTELS, Robert   1913-

PERSONAL: Born January 28, 1913, in Wheeling, W.Va.; son of William Frederick and Ida Mae (Schafer) Bartels. *Education:* Carnegie Institute of Technology, student, 1930-31; The Ohio State University, B.S., 1935, Ph.D., 1941; Northwestern University, M.B.A., 1936. *Religion:* Christian Science. *Home:* 1631 Roxbury Rd., B-8, Columbus, Ohio 43212. *Office:* Ohio State University, 1775 South College Rd., Columbus, Ohio 43210.

CAREER: University of Washington, Seattle, assistant professor, 1938-41; self-employed real estate developer in Washington, D.C., 1945-46; Ohio State University, Columbus, 1946—, professor of business organization, 1955—. Fulbright lecturer and researcher at University of Salonica, 1954-55; visiting professor, University of Southern California, 1961; cultural exchange lecturer, University of Moscow, 1963. Teacher at University of Iowa and University of Colorado. Lecturer in Greece, India, Ceylon, Japan, and Soviet Union. *Military service:* U.S. Naval Reserve, 1942-45; became lieutenant junior grade. *Member:* American Marketing Association (president of Central Ohio Chapter), Academy for International Business.

WRITINGS: The Miracles of Credit, Ohio Consumer Loan Association, 1958; (contribuor) E. J. Kelly and W. Lazier, editors, *Managerial Marketing: Perspectives and Viewpoints*, Irwin, 1958, revised edition, 1962; (contributor) *Marketing: A Maturing Discipline*, American Marketing Association, 1961; *Business Ethics—Compliance or Conviction*, University of Southern California Press, 1961; *The Development of Marketing Thought*, Irwin, 1962; (editor with P. M. Holmes and others) *Readings in Marketing*, C. E. Merrill, 1963; (editor) *Ethics in Business*, Ohio State University Bureau of Business Research, 1963; (editor) *Comparative Marketing: Wholesaling in Fifteen Countries*, Irwin, 1963; (contributor) George Schwartz, editor, *Science in Marketing*, Wiley, 1965; (contributor and subject editor) *Lincoln Library*, 25th edition, Frontier Press, 1961. Also contributor to marketing journals.

AVOCATIONAL INTERESTS: The performing arts, water-color painting.

*   *   *

BARWICK, Steven   1921-

PERSONAL: Born March 2, 1921, in Lincoln, Neb.; son of Leonard H. and Cynthia (Johnson) Barwick. *Education:* Coe College, B.A. and B.Mus., 1942; Eastman School of Music, M.Mus., 1943; Harvard University, M.A., 1944, Ph.D., 1949; private study of piano at Juilliard School of Music, Conservatoire de Paris, and under Claudio Arrau in

New York, and other teachers in America and London. *Home:* 709 West Elm, Carbondale, Ill. *Office:* Southern Illinois University, Carbondale, Ill.

CAREER: Traveled in Mexico and Central America under John Knowles Paine traveling fellowship from Harvard University, 1945-47; Blue Mountain College, Blue Mountain, Miss., head of department of music, 1948-49; University of Pittsburgh, Pittsburgh, Pa., assistant professor of music, 1949-51; Western Kentucky State College, Bowling Green, associate professor of music, 1951-55; Southern Illinois University, Carbondale, associate professor, 1955-58, professor of music, 1958—. Violist with Cedar Rapids Symphony, 1937-42; pianist on European concert tours, 1956, 1961. *Member:* Music Teachers National Association, American Musicological Society, American Association of University Professors, Phi Mu Alpha Sinfonia, Pi Kappa Lambda. *Awards, honors:* Doctor of Fine Arts, Coe College, 1969.

WRITINGS: (Contributor) *Essays on Music, A Garland Wreathed in Honor of A. T. Davison*, Harvard University Press, 1955; *The Franco Codex of the Cathedral of Mexico*, Southern Illinois University Press, 1965. Collector and transcriber of "Motets from Mexican Archives" (series of choruses), translated and edited by Hugh Ross and Robert Hines, Peer International, 1951-59.

WORK IN PROGRESS: Preparing two Mexico City choirbooks of 1718, editions of manuscripts of seventeenth-century music from the Cathedral of Mexico.

*   *   *

BARZINI, Luigi 1908-

PERSONAL: Born December 21, 1908, in Milan, Italy; son of Luigi (a journalist) and Mantica (Pesavento) Barzini; married (second wife) Paola Gadola, September 12, 1949; children: (first marriage) Ludovica, Benedetta, (second marriage) Luigi, Andrea, Francesca. *Education:* Columbia University, B.Litt., 1930. *Politics:* Partito Liberale Italiano. *Religion:* Catholic. *Home:* 1055 Via Cassia, Tomba di Nerone, Rome, Italy.

CAREER: Corriere della Sera, Milan, Italy, special writer, 1931-40, 1954-61; *Il Globo*, Rome, Italy, editor and publisher, 1944-47. Elected member of Italian parliament, 1958, re-elected, 1963, and 1968.

WRITINGS: Americans Are Alone in the World, Random, 1953; *Mosca Mosca*, Mondadori, 1961; *The Italians*, Atheneum, 1964; *From Caesar to the Mafia* (essays), Library Press, 1971. Also author of play, "I Disarmati," produced in Rome, 1957. Contributor to *Encounter, Harper's, Preuves, Der Monat, New York Review of Books, Life*, and other magazines.

WORK IN PROGRESS: Several books; articles for Italian and American magazines; a play.

SIDELIGHTS: Barzini's book, *The Italians*, has been adapted for television and was presented as a CBS News special. He also served as narrator for another special for that network on the frescoes salvaged from the Florence flood in 1966.

*   *   *

BATES, J(ames) Leonard 1919-

PERSONAL: Born May 6, 1919, in Birmingham, Ala.; son of Howard Edward (in lumber sales) and Mattie (Gammel) Bates; married Dorothy Pettit, August 9, 1942; children: Daniel Leonard, Alan Jefferson. *Education:* Wake Forest College, B.A., 1941; University of North Carolina, M.A., 1946, Ph.D., 1952. *Home:* 505 West Nevada, Urbana, Ill. *Office:* 316 Gregory Hall, University of Illinois, Urbana, Ill.

CAREER: University of North Carolina, Chapel Hill, instructor in social sciences, 1946-47; University of Maryland, instructor in history, 1947-54; University of Illinois, Urbana, assistant professor, 1954-59, associate professor, 1959-66, professor of history, 1966—. *Military service:* U.S. Navy, 1942-45; became lieutenant. *Member:* American Historical Association, American Association of University Professors, Organization of American Historians. Southern Historical Association, Champaign County Historical Society, Phi Beta Kappa.

WRITINGS: The Origins of Teapot Dome: Progressives, Parties, and Petroleum, 1909-1921, University of Illinois Press, 1963; (editor) *Tom Walsh in Dakota Territory: Personal Correspondence of Senator Thomas J. Walsh and Elinor C. McClements*, University of Illinois Press, 1966. Contributor to historical journals.

WORK IN PROGRESS: A biography of Senator Thomas J. Walsh of Montana; *Opening the Twentieth Century*, an interpretive volume for publication by McGraw.; writing on conservation of natural resources, and on social and political questions of the late nineteenth- and twentieth-centuries.

*   *   *

BATTAN, Louis J(oseph) 1923-

PERSONAL: Born February 9, 1923, in New York, N.Y.; son of Anibale and Louise (Webber) Battan; married Jeannette A. Waitches (a sculptor), June 8, 1952; children: Suzette, Paul. *Education:* College of the City of New York (now City College of the City University of New York), student, 1941-43; New York University, B.S., 1946; graduate study at Harvard University and Massachusetts Institute of Technology, 1944; University of Chicago, M.S., 1949, Ph.D., 1953. *Religion:* Catholic. *Home:* 5141 East Rosewood Ave., Tucson, Ariz. 85711. *Office:* Institute of Atmospheric Physics, University of Arizona, Tucson, Ariz. 85721.

CAREER: U.S. Weather Bureau, research meteorologist, 1947-51; University of Chicago, Chicago, Ill., research meteorologist, 1951-58; University of Arizona, Tucson, professor of atmospheric sciences, 1958—, associate director, then director of Institute of Atmospheric Physics, 1958—. Consultant to U.S. Weather Bureau, U.S. Air Force, U.S. Army, National Science Foundation, and National Institutes of Health. *Military service:* U.S. Army Air Forces, 1944-46. U.S. Air Force Reserve, 1946-52; became captain. *Member:* American Meteorological Society (fellow; president, 1966-67; councilor, 1959-61, 1968-69), American Geophysical Union (fellow; vice-president, meteorology section, 1972-73), Royal Meteorological Society, Arizona Academy of Sciences, American Association of Science Writers, Sigma Xi. *Awards, honors:* American Meteorological Society Meisinger Award, 1962, and Brooks Award, 1971, for research accomplishments.

WRITINGS: Radar Meteorology, University of Chicago Press, 1959; *The Nature of Violent Storms*, Anchor Books, 1961; *Radar Observes the Weather*, Anchor Books, 1962; *Cloud Physics and Cloud Seeding*, Anchor Books, 1962; *The Thunderstorm*, New American Library, 1963; (with C. W. Wolfe, R. H. Fleming, G. S. Hawkins, and H. Skornik)

Earth and Space Science, Heath, 1966, 2nd edition, 1971; *The Unclean Sky*, Doubleday Anchor, 1966; *Harvesting the Clouds*, Doubleday, 1969; *Radar Observation of the Atmosphere*, University of Chicago Press, 1973; *Weather*, Prentice-Hall, 1974. Contributor to encyclopedias and to scientific and technical journals. Associate editor, *Journal of Atmospheric Sciences*.

WORK IN PROGRESS: Research in atmospheric sciences.

SIDELIGHTS: Battan told *CA*: I feel strongly that the public is entitled to know what scientists are doing. [Writing] books and articles in non-technical language is one way to bring this about.

* * *

BATTEN, Thomas Reginald 1904-

PERSONAL: Born November 30, 1904, in London, England; married Madge Gill, January 27, 1956. *Education:* St. John's College, Oxford, B.A. (first class honors), 1926, Diploma in Education, 1927, M.A., 1937; University of London, Ph.D., 1962. *Home:* Tawh Cottage, Windyridge Close, London S.W.19 5HB, England.

CAREER: Nigeria Department of Education, 1927-43, began as history teacher in a secondary school, became superintendent of education; Makerere College, Kampala, Uganda, vice-principal and head of social studies department, 1943-49; University of London, Institute of Education, London, England, senior lecturer in community development, 1943-62, reader in community development studies, 1962-72. Community development and training consultant, 1972—.

WRITINGS: Handbook on the Teaching of History and Geography in Nigeria, Church Missionary Society Bookshop (Nigeria), 1933, and six subsequent editions; *Koyawar Labarin Kasa de Tarihi*, Church Missionary Society Bookshop (Nigeria), 1934; *Tropical Africa in World History* (four-year course for African schools), Oxford University Press, 1939, 5th edition, 1966; *The British Empire and the Modern World*, Oxford University Press, 1941; *Africa Past and Present*, Oxford University Press, 1943, 5th edition, 1963; *Thoughts on African Citizenship*, Oxford University Press, 1944, 2nd edition, 1955; *Problems of African Development* (two volumes), Oxford University Press, 1947-48, 3rd edition, 1960.

Communities and Their Development, Oxford University Press, 1957; (with G. A. Goodban and Chien Ching-Lien) *China in World History*, four books, Oxford University Press, 1958-61; *School and Community in the Tropics*, Oxford University Press, 1959; (with A. G. Dickson) *Voluntary Action and Social Progress*, British Council, 1959; *Training for Community Development: A Critical Study of Method*, Oxford University Press, 1962; *The Human Factor in Community Work*, Oxford University Press, 1965; *The Non-Directive Approach in Group and Community Work*, Oxford University Press, 1967; *The Human Factor in Youth Work*, Oxford University Press, 1970. Contributor of some thirty articles on community development topics to sociological and other journals.

WORK IN PROGRESS: Applications of the non-directive approach in the field of development; *Development and People*, completion expected 1976.

SIDELIGHTS: Communities and Their Development has been translated into Spanish, Italian, Bengali, Hindi, Oriyya, Assamese, Hebrew, Sinhali, Tamil, Korean, Persian and Kannada.

BATTENHOUSE, Roy W(esley) 1912-

PERSONAL: Born April 9, 1912, in Nevinville, Iowa; son of Henry Martin (an educator) and Sarah (Krill) Battenhouse; married Marian Gaber, February 2, 1952; children: Anna Marie. *Education:* Albion College, A.B., 1933; Yale University, B.D., 1936, Ph.D., 1938. *Home:* 1216 East Second St., Bloomington, Ind.

CAREER: Ordained priest of Protestant Episcopal Church, 1942—. Ohio State University, Columbus, instructor in English, 1938-40; Vanderbilt University, Nashville, Tenn., assistant professor, then associate professor of church history, 1940-46; Episcopal Theological School, Cambridge, Mass., associate professor of church history, 1946-49; Indiana University, Bloomington, associate professor, 1950-56, professor of English, 1956—. Acting rector in Franklin, Tenn., 1942-46; substitute rector in Chattanooga, Tenn., 1949-50. *Member:* Modern Language Association of America, Society for Religion in Higher Education, Shakespeare Society of America, Renaissance Society of America. *Awards, honors:* Ford Faculty Fellow, 1954-55; Guggenheim Fellow, 1958-59; Litt.D. from Ripon College, 1964, and St. Michael's College, 1974.

WRITINGS: Marlowe's Tamburlaine: A Study in Renaissance Moral Philosophy, Vanderbilt University Press, 1941; (editor and contributor) *A Companion to the Study of St. Augustine*, Oxford University Press, 1955; *Shakespearean Tragedy: Its Art and Its Christian Premises*, Indiana University Press, 1969. Contributor to academic journals and to various collections of essays, especially on the subjects of Shakespeare and other Elizabethan authors. Editorial consultant, *Shakespeare Studies*.

WORK IN PROGRESS: Shakespeare's Sense of English History.

* * *

BATTESTIN, Martin C(arey) 1930-

PERSONAL: Born March 25, 1930, in New York, N.Y.; son of Martin August (an advertising man) and Marion (Kirkland) Battestin; married Ruthe Rootes (a research scholar and real estate agent), June 14, 1963; children: David, Catherine. *Education:* Princeton University, B.A., 1952, Ph.D., 1958. *Home:* 115 Bollingwood Rd., Charlottesville, Va. *Office:* Department of English, University of Virginia, Charlottesville, Va.

CAREER: Wesleyan University, Middletown, Conn., instructor, 1956-58, assistant professor of English, 1958-61; University of Virginia, Charlottesville, assistant professor, 1961-63, associate professor, 1963-67, professor of English, 1967—. Associate, Center for Advanced Studies, University of Virginia, 1970-71, 1974, 1975, and Clare Hall, Cambridge University, 1972. *Member:* Modern Language Association of America, South Atlantic Modern Language Association, American Society for Eighteenth-Century Studies, Academy of Literary Studies. *Awards, honors:* American Council of Learned Societies fellow, 1960-61, 1972; Guggenheim fellow, 1964-65; honorary research fellow, University College, London, 1970-71; senior fellow, Council of the Humanities, Princeton University, 1971.

WRITINGS: The Moral Basis of Fielding's Art: A Study of Joseph Andrews, Wesleyan University Press, 1959; (editor) Henry Fielding, *Joseph Andrews* [and] *Shamela*, Houghton, 1961; (editor and author of introduction) Fielding, *Joseph Andrews*, Wesleyan University Press, 1967; (editor) *Twentieth Century Interpretations of Tom Jones: A*

Collection of Critical Essays, Prentice-Hall, 1968; (editor) Fielding, *Tom Jones*, Wesleyan University Press, 1974; *The Providence of Wit: Aspects of Form in Augustan Literature and the Arts*, Clarendon Press, Oxford, 1974. Contributor to journals. Advisory editor, *Eighteenth-Century Studies*, *Studies in the Novel*, *Studies in English Literature*.

WORK IN PROGRESS: A critical edition of *Tom Jones*, for Houghton; an annotated textual edition of Fielding's *Amelia*, publication by Clarendon Press and Wesleyan University Press expected in 1977.

* * *

BATTISTA, O(rlando) A(loysius) 1917-

PERSONAL: Born June 20, 1917, in Cornwall, Ontario, Canada; son of James Liberato (a stonemason) and Carmella (Infante) Battista; married Helen Keffer, August 25, 1945; children: William K., Elizabeth Ann. *Education:* McGill University, B.Sc. (first class honors), 1940. *Home:* Landell, 3725 Fox Hollow, Fort Worth, Tex. 76109.

CAREER: American Viscose Corp., Marcus Hook, Pa., research chemist, later assistant director of corporate research, 1940-63; F.M.C. Corp., Research Center, Princeton, N.J., manager of interdisciplinary research, 1963-65, assistant director of central research department, 1965-71; Avicon, Inc., Fort Worth, Tex., vice-president of science and technology, 1971-74; Research Services Corp., Fort Worth, Tex., chairman of the board and president, 1974—. Inventor or co-inventor of more than 450 U.S. and foreign patent items; discoverer of avicel microcrystalline cellulose, a noncaloric food ingredient used to engineer caloric content levels of conventional foods. *Member:* American Chemical Society (chairman of cellulose chemistry division, 1959-60), American Association for the Advancement of Science, American Institute of Chemists (fellow), National Association of Science Writers, American Medical Writers Association, Chemists Club. *Awards, honors:* Sc.D., St. Vincent College, 1955; honor award, New Jersey chapter, American Institute of Chemists, 1965; Chemical Pioneer award, American Institute of Chemists, 1969; James T. Grady award, American Chemical Society, 1973.

WRITINGS: How to Enjoy Work and Get More Fun Out of Life, Prentice-Hall, 1957; *God's World and You*, Bruce, 1957; *Fundamentals of High Polymers* (college textbook), Reinhold, 1958; *The Challenge of Chemistry*, Holt, 1959; *Commonscience in Everyday Life*, Bruce, 1960; *The Power to Influence People*, Prentice-Hall, 1960; *Mental Drugs . . . Chemistry's Challenge to Psychotherapy*, Chilton, 1960; *Toward the Conquest of Cancer*, Chilton, 1961; (editor) *Synthetic Fibers in Papermaking*, Wiley, 1964; *A Dictionary of Quotoons*, Reader-Services Co., 1966; *Childish Questions*, Research Services Corp., 1973; *Microcrystal Polymer Science*, McGraw, 1974.

Author of syndicated features, "Quotoons" and "Jest Around the Home." Contributor of more than 750 science and medical articles to national magazines.

WORK IN PROGRESS: Encyclopedia of Fantastic Facts, and *Management of Research for Profit*.

BIOGRAPHICAL/CRITICAL SOURCES: Peter Wyden, *The Overweight Society*, Morrow, 1964; *Chemist*, September, 1965.

* * *

BATTLES, Ford Lewis 1915-

PERSONAL: Born January 15, 1915, in Erie, Pa.; son of Ford Lewis (a banker) and Lucy (Stewart) Battles; married Marion Ruth Davis (a teacher of piano), January 20, 1945; children: Nancy Marion, Emily Stewart. *Education:* West Virginia University, A.B., 1936; Tufts University, M.A., 1938; Oxford University, Rhodes Scholar, 1938-40; Hartford Seminary Foundation, Ph.D., 1950. *Politics:* Independent. *Religion:* Congregationalist. *Home:* 94 Sherman St., Hartford, Conn. *Office:* Hartford Seminary Foundation, 55 Elizabeth St., Hartford, Conn.

CAREER: West Virginia University, Morgantown, instructor, 1940-41, associate professor of English, 1945-48; Hartford Seminary Foundation, Hartford, Conn., professor of church history, 1950—, acting academic dean, 1961-62. *Military service:* U.S. Army Air Forces, 1941-45; director of Airfield Intelligence-Joint Topography Sub-Committee and Joint Army-Navy Intelligence Studies Publishing Board, 1944-45; became major. *Member:* American Historical Association, American Society of Church History, Connecticut Historical Society, Phi Beta Kappa. *Awards, honors:* Guggenheim fellowship, 1962-63.

WRITINGS: (Translator) *John Wyclif and Erasmus*, Westminster, 1953; (translator) John Calvin, *Institutes of the Christian Religion*, 2 volumes, Westminster, 1960; (with Goodwin B. Beach) *Locutionum Cotidianarum Glossarium: A Guide to Latin Conversation*, Hartford Seminary Press, 1961, 3rd edition, 1967; (contributor) Gervase E. Duffield, editor, *John Calvin*, Sutton Courteney Press, 1966; *An Analysis of the Institutes of the Christian Religion of John Calvin*, Hartford Seminary Press, 1966; *New Light on Calvin's Institutes*, Hartford Seminary Press, 1966; (translator and author of introduction with Andre M. Hugo) *Calvin's Commentary on Seneca's De Clementia*, E. J. Brill, 1969; (editor and translator) John Calvin, *Institution of the Christian Religion*, Pittsburgh Theological Seminary, 1969; (editor) *The Piety of John Calvin*, Pittsburgh Theological Seminary, 1969; (compiler with Edward J. Furcha) *The Piety of Caspar Schwenckfeld*, Pittsburgh Theological Seminary, 1969. Also author of introduction to "A Computerized Concordance to Instituto Christianae Religionis" (microfilm), published by Pittsburgh Theological Seminary, 1972. Contributor to *American Oxonian*, *Religion and Life*, *Church History*, and other journals.†

* * *

BATY, Wayne 1925-

PERSONAL: Born November 20, 1925, in Marshfield, Mo.; son of John Cyrus and Mary (Atchley) Baty; married Maxine Ragsdale, 1947; children: Benson Lee, Keeman Todd. *Education:* Southwest Missouri State College, Springfield, B.S.; Northwestern University, M.A.; University of Southern California, Ph.D. *Office:* Department of Administrative Services, Arizona State University, Tempe, Ariz.

CAREER: High school instructor, Lebanon, Mo., 1951-55; assistant professor of business communications at University of Southern California, Los Angeles, 1956-57, 1959-62, at Emporia State Teachers College, Emporia, Kan., 1958-59; Arizona State University, Tempe, 1962—, began as associate professor, now professor of administrative services. *Military service:* U.S. Army, Infantry; received Bronze Star, Purple Heart with oak leaf cluster, two battle stars. *Member:* American Business Communication Association, Pi Omega Pi, Delta Pi Epsilon, Beta Gamma Sigma, Phi Kappa Phi.

WRITINGS: (With William C. Himstreet) *Business Com-*

munications, Wadsworth, 1961, 4th edition, 1973; (contributor) *College Typewriting*, Pitman, 1960; *Business Communications and Typewriting*, Wadsworth, 1962; (contributor) *Modern Business Communication*, Pitman, 1962; *English for Business*, Wadsworth, 1966.

*   *   *

BAUER, Wolfgang L(eander) 1930-

PERSONAL: Born February 23, 1930, in Halle, Germany; son of Hans (a university professor) and Eugenie (Kerschbaumer) Bauer; married Ingeborg Kosel, March 18, 1955; children: Michael, Nicola. *Education:* University of Munich, Ph.D. *Home:* Antwerpener Strasse 16, Muenchen, West Germany.

CAREER: University of Munich, Munich, West Germany, assistant professor of Chinese, 1958-62; University of Heidelberg, Heidelberg, Germany, professor of Chinese, 1962-65; University of Munich, professor of Chinese, 1966—. Visiting professor at University of Michigan, 1961, 1968, and 1969, and at University of Washington, Seattle, 1962. *Member:* Association for Asian Studies, Deutsche Gesellschaft fuer Ostasien Kunde, Deutsche Morgenlandische Gesellschaft.

WRITINGS: Der chinesische Personenname, O. Harrassowitz, 1959; *Tsch'un-Tsch'iu, in mandschurischer Ubersetzung*, Steiner, 1959; *Western Literature and Translation Work in Communist China*, Metzner (Frankfurt), 1964; (compiler with Herbert Franke) *Die goldene Truhe: Chinesische Novellen aus zwei Jahrtausenden*, Deutscher Taschenbuch (Munich), 1966, translation by Christopher Levenson published in England as *The Golden Casket: Chinese Novellas of Two Millennia*, Penguin, 1967; *Chinas Vergangenheit als Trauma und Vorbild*, W. Kohlhammer, 1968; *China und die Hoffnung auf Glueck: Paradiese, Utopien, Idealvorstellungen*, C. Hanser, 1971; (editor and author of introduction) Richard Wilhelm, *Botschafter zweier Welten*, Diederichs, 1973; *Das Bild in der weissage Literatur Chinas*, [Munich], 1973. Contributor to *Propylaen Weltgeschichte*, Volume XI, 1965.

WORK IN PROGRESS: Writing on the history of Chinese autobiography and modern Chinese personal names.

SIDELIGHTS: Bauer has traveled in the Far East, 1962, 1964-65, 1972, 1974. *Avocational interests:* Painting, chess.

*   *   *

BAUM, Daniel (Jay) 1934-

PERSONAL: Born November 24, 1934, in Cincinnati, Ohio; son of Millard M. (a factory worker) and Ida (Friedman) Baum; married Harriet Brav (an artist), December 24, 1957; children: Aaron Edward, Miriam Brav. *Education:* University of Cincinnati, B.A., 1956, LL.B., 1958; New York University, LL.M., 1959, J.S.D., 1960. *Religion:* Jewish. *Home:* 1 Sutcliffe Dr., Toronto, Ontario, Canada. *Office:* Osgoode Hall School, York University, 4700 Keele St., Downsview, Ontario, Canada.

CAREER: Cincinnati Enquirer, Cincinnati, Ohio, reporter, 1953-56; U.S. Federal Trade Commission, Washington, D.C., trial attorney, 1960-62; Indiana University, Indianapolis Campus, professor of law, 1962-68; York University, Downsview, Ontario, professor of law and administrative studies, 1968—. Arbitrator, Indiana Department of Labor. Member of Federal Mediation and Conciliation Service; member of National Labor Panel, American Arbitration Association; member of labor panel, Ontario Labor Arbi-

tration Commission. Member of Department of Communications (Canada). Regent of Canadian Institute of Financial Planning. Consultant to National Law Reform Commission (Canada). *Member:* American Bar Association.

WRITINGS: The Robinson-Patman Act: Summary and Comment, Syracuse University Press, 1964; (with Ned B. Stiles) *The Silent Partners: Institutional Investors and Corporate Control*, Syracuse University Press, 1965; *Toward a Free Housing Market*, University of Miami Press, 1969; *The Investment Function of Canadian Financial Institutions*, Praeger, 1972; *Canadian Banks in the Commonwealth Caribbean*, Praeger, 1973; *The Welfare Family*, Praeger, 1974; *The Final Plateau: The Betrayal of Our Older Citizens*, Burns & MacEachern, 1974. Contributor to law reviews. Editor-in-chief of *Administrative Law Review* (American Bar Association), and *Transportation Law Journal* (U.S. Motor Carriers Association).

WORK IN PROGRESS: A study on youth.

*   *   *

BAUMBACH, Jonathan 1933-

PERSONAL: Born July 5, 1933; son of Harold M. (an artist) and Ida (Zackheim) Baumbach; married Elinor Berkman, September 10, 1956 (divorced, 1967); married Georgia Brown, June 10, 1969; children: (first marriage) David, Nina; (second marriage) Noah. *Education:* Brooklyn College, A.B., 1955; Columbia University, M.F.A., 1956; Stanford University, Ph.D., 1961. *Home:* 307 Sterling Pl., Brooklyn, N.Y. 11258. *Agent:* Candide Donadio, 111 West 57th St., New York, N.Y.

CAREER: Stanford University, Stanford, Calif., instructor in English, 1958-60; Ohio State University, Columbus, assistant professor of English, 1961-64; New York University, New York, N.Y., assistant professor of English, 1964-66; Brooklyn College of the City University of New York, Brooklyn, N.Y., professor of English, 1966—. *Military service:* U.S. Army, 1956-58. *Awards, honors:* Young Writers Award, *New Republic*, 1958; Yaddo fellowship, summers, 1963, 1964, 1965; National Endowment of Arts fellowship, 1969.

WRITINGS: The Landscape of Nightmare: Studies in the Contemporary American Novel, New York University Press, 1965; *A Man to Conjure With* (novel), Random, 1965; *What Comes Next*, Harper, 1968; (editor) *Writers as Teachers/Teachers as Writers*, Holt, 1970; *Reruns* (novel), Fiction Collective, 1974. Also author of play, "The One-Eyed Man is King," first produced at Theater East, New York, 1956. Contributor to *Kenyon Review, Saturday Review, Esquire, Partisan Review, New York Times Book Review, TriQuarterly*, and other periodicals.

WORK IN PROGRESS: A novel, *Love Scenes*; a book on nine film directors.

SIDELIGHTS: "The novel's principal conceit is that against the background of the war in Vietnam and the violence of our cities we are all potential criminals, deeply implicated in a wave of inhuman brutality. We are all, in short, guilty," explained Henry S. Resnick, in a review of *What Comes Next*. He added, however, that the overall effect was self-righteously gloomy, "a moral sledgehammer," and, concurring with Thomas Glynn, exceedingly tedious.

On the other hand, Bernard McCabe, like certain other reviewers, considered this same book convincing and "freshly and fiercely done out." C. D. B. Bryan wrote:

"Baumbach's writing . . . is finely chiseled, keen and tough; his images are violent and garish. . . . Its chief value lies in its portrayal of the madness, the disturbing, menacing atmosphere that is now so much a part of our cities."

BIOGRAPHICAL/CRITICAL SOURCES: Kenyon Review, January, 1966.

* * *

BAUMGARD, Herbert Mark 1920-

PERSONAL: Born August 3, 1920, in Norfolk, Va.; son of Samuel E. (a tailor) and Sarah (Segal) Baumgard; married Selma Geller (a choir director), June 20, 1948; children: Jonathan, Shirah, Daniel. *Education:* University of Virginia, B.S., 1941, law student, 1941-42; Hebrew Union College-Jewish Institute of Religion, New York, N.Y., M.H.L. and Rabbi, 1950, D.H.L., 1962; Columbia University, graduate study, 1950-55. *Home:* 7290 Southwest 113th St., Miami, Fla.

CAREER: Rabbi, 1950—. Hebrew Union School of Education, New York, N.Y., instructor, 1953-55; Union of American Hebrew Congregations, Miami, Fla., director, 1956-60; Temple Beth Am, South Miami, Fla., rabbi, 1956—. Chairman of committee on synagogue music, 1964-65; Central Conference of American Rabbis, vice-president of Southeast region, Anti-Defamation League; member of executive board of American Jewish Committee, Miami. Member of Dade County Community Relations board. *Military service:* U.S. Army, 1942-46; became staff sergeant. *Member:* Society of Biblical Literature and Exegesis, Greater Miami Rabbinical Association (president, 1964-65).

WRITINGS: Judaism and Prayer, Union of American Hebrew, 1964; (contributor) *Sermonettes for Young People*, Bloch, 1964; *Currents and Trends in Contemporary Jewish Thought*, Ktav, 1965. Author of pamphlets.

WORK IN PROGRESS: Preparing doctoral thesis, "The Word 'Tob' in Old Testament Times," for publication.

* * *

BAUMOL, William J(ack) 1922-

PERSONAL: Born February 26, 1922, in New York, N.Y.; son of Solomon (a bookbinder) and Lillian (Itzkowitz) Baumol; married Hilda Missel, December 27, 1941; children: Ellen Frances, Daniel Aaron. *Education:* City College of New York (now City College of the City University of New York), B.S.S., 1942; London School of Economics and Political Science, Ph.D., 1949. *Home:* 61 Jefferson Rd., Princeton, N.J. 08540. *Office:* Department of Economics, Princeton University, Princeton, N.J. 08540.

CAREER: With U.S. Department of Agriculture, Washington, D.C., 1942-43, 1946; London School of Economics and Political Science, London, England, assistant lecturer in economics, 1947-49; Princeton University, Princeton, N.J., assistant professor, 1949-52, associate professor, 1952-54, professor of economics, 1954—, joint appointment, New York University, 1972—. Consultant to Mathematica, Inc. Member of board of editors, Harcourt, Brace, Jovanovich. *Military service:* U.S. Army, 1943-46. *Member:* American Economic Association (vice-president, 1966-67), Econometric Society (fellow; member of council, 1960-61), Institute of Management Sciences, American Association of University Professors. *Awards, honors:* Guggenheim fellow, 1957-58; Ford faculty fellowship, 1965-66; Dr. of Laws, Rider College, 1965; Dr. of Economics, Stockholm

School of Economics, 1971; also received degrees from Knox College and University of Basel; honorary fellow, London School of Economics and Political Science.

WRITINGS: Welfare Economics and the Theory of the State, Harvard University Press, 1951, 2nd edition, 1965; *Economic Dynamics*, Macmillan, 1952, 3rd edition, 1970; (with L. V. Chandler) *Economic Processes and Policies*, Harper, 1954; *Business Behavior, Value and Growth*, Macmillan, 1959, revised edition, Harcourt, 1967; *Economic Theory and Operations Analysis*, Prentice-Hall, 1961, 3rd edition, 1972; (editor with Klaus Knorr) *What Price Economic Growth?*, Prentice-Hall, 1962; *The Stock Market and Economic Efficiency*, Fordham University Press, 1965; (with W. G. Bowen) *Performing Arts—the Economic Dilemma: A Study of Problems Common to Theater, Opera, Music, and Dance*, Twentieth Century Fund, 1966; (editor) E. M. Lerner and W. T. Carleton, *A Theory of Financial Analysis*, Harcourt, 1966; (editor) E. Shapiro, *Macroeconomic Analysis*, Harcourt, 1966; (editor with S. M. Goldfeld) *Precursors in Mathematical Economics: An Anthology*, London School of Economics, 1968; *Portfolio Theory: The Selection of Asset Combinations*, McCaleb-Seiler, 1970. Member of boards of editors, *Quarterly Journal of Economics, American Economic Review*, and *Journal of Economic Literature*.

WORK IN PROGRESS: A book with W. G. Oates, *Economics and the Quality of Life.*

* * *

BAXTER, Maurice Glen 1920-

PERSONAL: Born September 22, 1920, in Augusta, Ill.; son of Sterling R. and Anna (Walsh) Baxter; married Cynthia Lewis, January 6, 1951; children: Kent, Hugh. *Education:* University of Illinois, B.A., 1941, M.A., 1942, Ph.D., 1948. *Religion:* Presbyterian. *Home:* 501 Arbutus, Bloomington, Ind. *Office:* Department of History, Indiana University, Bloomington, Ind.

CAREER: Indiana University, Bloomington, 1948—, began as instructor, associate professor of history, 1959—. *Military service:* U.S. Navy, 1942-46. *Member:* American Historical Association.

WRITINGS: Orville H. Browning, Indiana University Press, 1957; (with Robert Ferrell and John E. Wiltz) *The Teaching of American History in High Schools*, Indiana University Press, 1964; *Daniel Webster and the Supreme Court*, University of Massachusetts Press, 1966; *The Steamboat Monopoly: Gibbons v. Ogden, 1824*, Knopf, 1972.

WORK IN PROGRESS: A book, *Daniel Webster: A Biography.*†

* * *

BAYLEY, David H(ume) 1933-

PERSONAL: Born March 26, 1933, in New York, N.Y.; son of Francis C. (a professor) and Constance (Zeigler) Bayley; married Chris Ellis, August 23, 1957; children: Jennifer R., Tracy Lynn. *Education:* Denison University, B.A., 1955; Oxford University, M.A., 1957; Princeton University, Ph.D., 1961. *Home:* 2153 South St. Paul St., Denver, Colo. *Office:* Graduate School of International Studies, University of Denver, Denver, Colo. 80210.

CAREER: University of Wisconsin, Milwaukee, assistant professor of political science, 1960-61; University of Denver, Graduate School of International Studies, Denver,

Colo., assistant professor, 1961-65, associate professor, 1965-69, professor of international studies, 1969—. Staff consultant, National Commission on the Causes and Prevention of Violence, 1968. *Member:* American Political Science Association, Association for Asian Studies, Phi Beta Kappa. *Awards, honors:* Fulbright scholar at Oxford University, 1955-57; senior research fellowship to New Delhi, American Institute of Indian Studies, 1963-64; National Science Foundation grant, 1972-74.

WRITINGS: Preventive Detention in India, Mukhopadhyay (Calcutta), 1962; *Public Liberties in the New States*, Rand McNally, 1964; (with Harold Mendelsohn) *Minorities and the Police*, Free Press, 1969; *The Police and Political Development in India*, Princeton University Press, 1969. Contributor to *Pacific Affairs*, *World Politics*, *Indian Journal of Public Administration*, and other political science journals.

WORK IN PROGRESS: A comparative study of Japanese and American police.

* * *

BAYLISS, John Clifford 1919-
(John Clifford)

PERSONAL: Born October 4, 1919, in Wotton-under-edge, Gloucestershire, England; son of Alfred Edward Macduff (an author and teacher) and Doris Isabel (Herrick) Bayliss; married Amalia Fleischerova (died, 1966); children: Clare Yvonne. *Education:* St. Catharine's College, Cambridge, B.A. (honors), 1940, M.A., 1944. *Politics:* "Civil servants are allowed none!" *Home:* 9 Thames Village, Hartington Rd., Chiswick, London W. 4, England. *Office:* British Council, London, England.

CAREER: Colonial Office, London, England, assistant principal, 1946-49; Macmillan & Co. (publishers), London, England, editor, 1949-52; Northern Rhodesia and Nyasaland Publications Bureau, Lusaka, Northern Rhodesia, senior editorial officer, 1952-59; Central Office of Information, London, England, principal information officer, 1959-73; British Council, director of low-priced book department, 1973—. Publishers reader. *Military service:* Royal Air Force, 1942-46; became acting flight lieutenant. *Member:* National Book League, Paternosters, Institute of Professional Civil Servants, R.A.F. Club. *Awards, honors:* Young Writers Bursary from Authors' Society (chiefly on basis of wartime poetry), 1948, Order of the British Empire, 1971.

WRITINGS: (Editor with Alex Comfort) *New Road 1943*, Grey Walls Press, 1943; (editor with Comfort) *New Road 1944*, Grey Walls Press, 1944; *The White Knight* (poetry), Fortune Press, 1944; (with Derek Stanford) *A Romantic Miscellany* (poetry), Fortune Press, 1945; (under pseudonym John Clifford) *Atlantis Adventure* (boys' book), Lutterworth, 1958; (compiler) *Exploits in Africa*, Hamish Hamilton, 1962, New York Graphic Society, 1964; (compiler) *Solo*, Hamish Hamilton, 1966.

Anthologies compiled with father, A. E. M. Bayliss: *The Way of Adventure*, Macmillan, 1951; *They Went to Sea*, Heinemann, 1954; *Science in Fiction*, University of London Press, 1957. Reviewer for journals and radio.

WORK IN PROGRESS: Poems for *Orbis* and the Hub Press.

SIDELIGHTS: Bayliss visited India, Pakistan, Ceylon, and Indonesia in 1951, Ghana, Nigeria, and Sierra Leone in 1964, and Jamaica, Trinidad, Barbados, and St. Lucia in 1974, in connection with Books Scheme.

BAYLOR, Robert 1925-

PERSONAL: Born December 7, 1925, in Danville, Pa.; son of Arthur (a steel mill rigger) and Bert (Morrison) Baylor; married Mary Schultz (a medical secretary), 1947. *Education:* Bloomsburg State College, B.S. in Ed., 1950; Columbia University, A.M., 1951. *Home:* 246 East Arrow Hwy., Claremont, Calif. 91712. *Agent:* Martha Winston, Curtis Brown Ltd., 575 Madison Ave., New York, N.Y. 10022.

CAREER: Mount San Antonio College, Walnut, Calif., instructor in English, 1955—. *Military service:* U.S. Navy, 1943-46. *Member:* Authors Guild, California Teachers Association.

WRITINGS: To Sting the Child (novel), Bobbs, 1964; *Detail and Pattern: Essays for Composition*, McGraw, 1969, revised edition, 1972; (with James Moore) *In the Presence of this Continent: American Themes and Ideas*, Holt, 1971; *Fine Frenzy: Enduring Themes in Poetry*, McGraw, 1972.

* * *

BAYS, Gwendolyn McKee

PERSONAL: Born in Atlanta, Ga.; daughter of Oran Miles and Mary (Peek) McKee; married Robert Alexander Bays (a professor of Spanish and German); children: Robert A., Jr., Geoffrey Alan. *Education:* Agnes Scott College, B.A.; Emory University, M.A.; Yale University, Ph.D. *Home:* 88 Payne St., Clarion, Pa. *Office:* Department of Foreign Languages, Clarion State College, Clarion, Pa.

CAREER: University of Maryland, Overseas Program, instructor in French, Heidelberg, Germany, 1954; Yale University, New Haven, Conn., research associate, 1957-58; Antioch College, Yellow Springs, Ohio, associate professor of French and German, 1958-62; Clarion State College, Clarion, Pa., associate professor of French and German, 1962—. Public lecturer on European schools. *Member:* Modern Language Association of America, American Association of Teachers of French, American Association of University Professors, Phi Beta Kappa. *Awards, honors:* Fulbright scholarship to Sorbonne, University of Paris; Ford Foundation award for *The Orphic Vision*.

WRITINGS: The Orphic Vision: Seer Poets from Novalis to Rimbaud, University of Nebraska Press, 1964. Contributor to language journals.

WORK IN PROGRESS: A book on modern French novelists; writing on Proust.

SIDELIGHTS: Mrs. Bays speaks French and German, competent in Latin, reads Spanish.

* * *

BEACH, Dale S. 1923-

PERSONAL: Born August 7, 1923, in Buffalo, N.Y.; son of Elmer J. and Octavia E. (Wahl) Beach; married Shirley Ann Wheeler, June 17, 1950; children: Jeffrey D., Eric A. *Education:* Cornell University, B.S., 1948, M.S., 1952. *Office:* School of Management, Rensselaer Polytechnic Institute, Troy, N.Y.

CAREER: Cornell University, Ithaca, N.Y., instructor in industrial engineering, 1950-52; Lehigh University, Bethlehem, Pa., assistant professor of industrial engineering, 1952-54; Rensselaer Polytechnic Institute, School of Management, Troy, N.Y., 1954—, began as associate professor, now professor of management. Member of Labor Arbitration Panel of American Arbitration Association, and member of Mediation and Fact Finding Panel, New York State Public Employment Relations Board. Consultant to New York Telephone Co., 1956-60, 1962, and Star Textile and Research, Inc., 1963—. *Member:* Society for the Advancement of Management (president, Hudson Valley chapter, 1968-69), Industrial Relations Research Association, American Association of University Professors (chapter president, 1964-65), Academy of Management, Sierra Club.

WRITINGS: Personnel: The Management of People at Work, Macmillan, 1965, 2nd edition, 1970; (editor) *Managing People at Work: Readings in Personnel*, Macmillan, 1971. Contributor to *Personnel, Advanced Management*, and *Journal of Industrial Engineering*.

WORK IN PROGRESS: Research in organizational behavior in the construction industry.

*   *   *

BEACH, Earl F(rancis) 1912-

PERSONAL: Born March 13, 1912, in Chicago, Ill.; son of Albert and Florence (Krafft) Beach; married Katharine MacAdam, 1938; children: Elizabeth, Charles. *Education:* Queen's University, Kingston, Ontario, B.A. (honors), 1934; Harvard University, A.M., 1936, Ph.D., 1938. *Home:* 508 Victoria Ave., Westmount, Quebec, Canada. *Office:* McGill University, 1020 Pine Ave., Montreal, Quebec, Canada.

CAREER: McGill University, Montreal, Quebec, director of School of Commerce, 1940-46, professor of economics, 1946—, chairman of department of economics and political science, 1951-54. Chairman, Social Science Research Council of Canada, 1958-60. *Member:* Canadian Political Science Association, Royal Economic Society, American Economic Association, American Statistical Association, Econometric Society. *Awards, honors:* Guggenheim fellow, 1949-50; Canada Council fellow, 1969-70.

WRITINGS: Economic Models, John Wiley, 1957; (editor with J. C. Weldon) *Papers of the Canadian Political Science Association*, University of Toronto Press, 1962.

SIDELIGHTS: Economic Models has been translated into Spanish and Japanese.

*   *   *

BEAMISH, Annie O'Meara de Vic 1883-
(Noel de Vic Beamish)

PERSONAL: Born April 30, 1883, in Dublin, Ireland; daughter of Frank John (a military chaplain) and Annie S. (Greenfield) de Vic. *Education:* Educated at home by tutors and governesses. *Politics:* Conservative. *Religion:* Church of England. *Residence:* Cannes, France. *Agent:* John Farquharson Ltd., 15 Red Lion Sq., London W.C. 1, England.

CAREER: Novelist. Founder and director of language schools in various parts of Europe. *Member:* Club Gastronomie (Paris; honorary).

WRITINGS—All under pseudonym Noel de Vic Beamish: *Tweet*, Jenkins, 1925; *Miss Perfection*, Hutchinson, 1932; *Beatrice in Babel*, Hutchinson, 1933; *Cocktail*, Hutchinson, 1934; *The King's Missal*, Jenkins, 1934; *Fair Fat Lady*, Nicholson & Watson, 1937; *The Grafting of the Rose*, McGraw, 1954.

All published by R. Hale: *Shadows of Splendour*, 1955; *Lady Beyond the Walls*, 1956; *Sword of Love*, 1959; *Quest of Love*, 1960; *Tudor Girl*, 1960; *The Blooming of the Rose*, 1962; *Venetian Lady*, 1962; *The Wayward Wench*, 1963; *The Peerless Popinjay*, 1964; *The King's Bastard*, 1966; *The Prince Ordains*, 1966; *A Royal Scandal*, 1966; *For the Honour of a Queen*, 1967; *The King's Sister*, 1967; *The Adorable Ninon de Lenclos*, 1968; *The Queen's Jester*, 1969; *The Unfortunate Queen Matilda*, 1971.

During World War I contributed articles on Venice, Milan, and Rome to *Liverpool Gazette* and other newspapers; more recently contributor to *Wine Gazette*.

AVOCATIONAL INTERESTS: Dogs and dog breeding.†

*   *   *

BEARD, Peter H. 1938-

PERSONAL: Born January 22, 1938, in New York, N.Y.; son of Anson McCook and Rosanne (Hoar) Beard. *Education:* Attended Felsted College, Essex, England, 1956-57, Yale University, 1957-61. *Politics:* None. *Religion:* None. *Home:* c/o Mill, 1860 Broadway, New York, N.Y.

CAREER: Works for Tsavo National Park, Kenya, East Africa. Has photography contract with Conde Nast Publications, Inc. (magazine publisher).

WRITINGS: The End of the Game, Viking, 1965; (editor) *Longing for Darkness: Kamate's Tales From Out of Africa*, Harcourt, 1975.

WORK IN PROGRESS: A book on Mt. Kenya.

SIDELIGHTS: Beard did a feature film, "Hallelujah the Hills," 1963, directed by Adolphus Mekas; he exhibited some of his art work in the Jerome Hill Collection in St. Paul, Minn., 1965. Beard has traveled to Madagascar and to various parts of Africa, including South Africa.

BIOGRAPHICAL/CRITICAL SOURCES: Saturday Evening Post, January and February, 1962; *Time*, November 13, 1963; *Quick* (Germany), spring, 1964; *Adam* (Paris), November, 1964; *Twen* (Germany), March, 1965; *Du Atlantis* (Germany), March, 1965.†

*   *   *

BEATY, Janice J(anowski) 1930-

PERSONAL: Surname is pronounced *Bait*-ey; born January 31, 1930, in Elmira, N.Y.; daughter of Henry A. (a pipefitter) and Marjorie (Finch) Janowski; married James B. Beaty (a teacher), October 5, 1957 (deceased); children: William James, Bruce Henry, David Charles. *Education:* State University of New York College at Geneseo, B.S., 1952; Cornell University, Ph.D. candidate, 1955; Elmira College, M.S., 1969. *Home:* 546 Esty St., Elmira, N.Y. 14904.

CAREER: Former teacher; writer for young people. Elmira College, Elmira, New York, instructor and assistant to Dean of Continuing Education in Human Services. *Member:* National Education Association (life member).

WRITINGS: Plants in His Pack: A Life of Edward Palmer, Adventurous Botanist and Collector, Pantheon, 1964; *Seeker of Seaways: A Life of Matthew Fontaine Maury, Pioneer Oceanographer*, Pantheon, 1966; *Discovering Guam*, Faith Book Store (Agana, Guam), 1967; *Guam Today and Yesterday*, Tuttle, 1968; *Nufu and the Turkeyfish*, Pantheon, 1969. Contributor of articles, largely on natural history subjects, to *Pacific Discovery, Desert Magazine, Highlights for Children, Guam Times Weekly*, and other periodicals.

BEAUMONT, Cyril William 1891-

PERSONAL: Born November 1, 1891, in London, England; son of Frederick John (a mechanical and electrical engineer) and Mary Adelaide (Balchin) Beaumont; married Alice Mari Beha, December 10, 1914. *Education:* Educated privately and at school in England. *Religion:* Church of England. *Home:* 68 Bedford Court Mansions, Bedford Ave., London W.C. 1, England.

CAREER: Antiquarian bookseller, London, England, 1910-65; Beaumont Press, London, founder and publisher, 1917-65; editor of *Dance Journal*, London, 1924-70; writer on the theater and dance. Ballet critic, *Dancing World*, 1921-24, and *Sunday Times*, 1950-59. President, London Archives of the Dance (now part of Victoria and Albert Museum).

MEMBER: Royal Society of Literature (fellow), Royal Society of Arts (fellow), Imperial Society of Teachers of Dancing (honorary fellow; chairman of Cecchetti Society branch, 1924—; chairman of Imperial Society, 1958-70), Critics Circle (president, 1957). *Awards, honors:* Gold Medal of Institute Historique et Heraldique de France, 1934; Officier d'Academie, 1934; Renaissance Francaise Gold Medal, 1938; Chevalier de la Legion d'Honneur, 1950; Imperial Award of Imperial Society of Teachers of Dancing, 1961; Queen Elizabeth II Coronation Award of Royal Academy of Dancing, 1962; Officer, Order of the British Empire, 1962; Knight Officer, Order of Merit (Italy), 1962.

WRITINGS—All published by Beaumont, except as indicated: *The Art of Lydia Lopokova*, 1920; *The Art of Lubov Tchernicheva*, 1921; (with Stanislas Idzikowski) *A Manual of the Theory and Practice of Classical Theatrical Dancing (Cecchetti Method)*, 1922, new edition, 1961; *The Mysterious Toyshop, a Fairy Tale*, 1924; *A Burmese pwe at Wembley; Some Impressions of Burmese Dancing*, 1924; *The Art of Stanislas Idzikowski*, 1926; *The Strange Adventures of a Toy Soldier* (juvenile), 1926; *The History of Harlequin*, 1926, reprinted, Benjamin Blom, 1967; *The Wonderful Journey* (juvenile), 1927; *The First Score: An Account of the Foundation and Development of the Beaumont Press*, 1927; *Sea Magic* (juvenile), John Lane, 1928; (compiler) *A Bibliography of Dancing*, Dancing Times, 1929, reissued, Benjamin Blom, 1963; *Enrico Cecchetti; a Memoir*, 1929.

Toys (rhymes for children), 1930; (with Margaret Craske) *The Theory and Practice of Allegro in Classical Ballet (Cecchetti Method)*, 1930; *A History of Ballet in Russia (1613-1881)*, 1930; *Fanny Elssler (1810-1884)*, 1931; (compiler) *A French-English Dictionary of Technical Terms Used in Classical Ballet*, 1931, 13th edition, 1959, reprint of earlier edition, 1966; *Flash-back: Memories of My Youth*, 1931; *A Primer of Classical Ballet for Children (Cecchetti Method)*, 1933, revised edition, 1961; *A Second Primer of Classical Ballet for Children*, 1935, revised edition, 1960; *Michel Fokine and His Ballets*, 1935, 2nd edition, 1945; *Design for the Ballet*, Studio Publications (New York), 1937, revised edition, Studio (London), 1939 (also see below); *The Complete Book of Ballets; a Guide to the Principal Ballets of the Nineteenth and Twentieth Centuries*, Putnam, 1937, revised edition, 1949, *Supplement*, 1942; (with Sacheverell Sitwell) *The Romantic Ballet in Lithographs of the Time*, Faber, 1938; *Puppets and the Puppet Stage*, Studio Publications, 1938, reprinted, Finch Press, 1973; *Five Centuries of Ballet Design*, Studio Publications, 1939 (also see below).

The Diaghilev Ballet in London: A Personal Record, Put-

nam, 1940, 3rd edition, A & C. Black, 1951; *A Third Primer of Classical Ballet for Children*, 1941, revised edition, 1967; *The Ballet Called Giselle*, 1944, revised edition, 1945, reprinted, Dance Horizons, 1970; (author of introduction) *Leslie Hurry: Settings and Costumes for Sadler's Wells Ballets*, Faber, 1946; *The Sleeping Beauty: The Sadler's Wells Ballet*, 1946; *The Sadler's Wells Ballet, a Detailed Account of Works in the Permanent Repertory*, 1946, revised and enlarged edition, 1947; *Ballet Design: Past and Present* (includes revisions of *Five Centuries of Ballet* and *Design for the Ballet*), Studio Publications (New York), 1946; *The Swan Lake*, 1948; *Dancers Under My Lens*, 1949.

Antonio: Impressions of the Spanish Dancer, A. & C. Black, 1952; *The Ballet Called Swan Lake*, 1952; *Ballets of Today* (2nd supplement to *Complete Book of Ballets*), Putnam, 1954; *Ballets, Past and Present* (3rd supplement to *Complete Book of Ballets*), Putnam, 1955, Dufour, 1964; *Puppets and Puppetry*, Studio Publications, 1958.

Also author of "Impressions of the Russian Ballet," a series of twelve booklets, 1918-21, and of "Essays on Dancing and Dancers," a series of ten booklets, 1932-48.

Editor: (With M. T. H. Sadler) *New Paths*, 1918; Valerian Svetlov, *Thamar Karsavina*, translated from the Russian by H. de Vere Beauclerk and Nadia Evrenov, 1922; Vladimir Polunin, *The Continental Method of Scene Painting*, 1927; (and author of preface) Gregorio Lambranzi, *New and Curious School of Theatrical Dancing*, translated from the German by Derra de Moroda, 1928; Zelia Raye, *Rational Limbering*, 1929; George D. Taylor, *Some Traditional Scottish Dances*, 1929; Derra de Moroda, *The Csardas and Sor Tanc*, 1929; Rikuhei Umemoto, *Some Classical Dances of Japan*, 1935; Margaret Craske and Derra de Moroda, *The Theory and Practice of Advanced Allegro in Classical Ballet*, 1956, revised edition, 1971; (and author of preface) Istvan Barlanghi, *Mime Training and Exercises*, 1959; *A Bibliography of the Dance Collection of Doris Niles and Serge Leslie*, Part I, 1966, Part II, 1968, Part III, 1974; D. I. Leshkov, *Marius Petipa*, 1971.

Translator from the French: Francis de Miomandre, *Vaslav Nijinsky*, 1913; Angelo Constantini, *The Birth, Life and Death of Scaramouch*, 1924; Thoinot Arbeau, *Orchesography*, 1925, reprinted, Dance Horizons, 1965; Andre Levinson, *Marie Taglioni*, Beaumont, 1930; Jean G. Noverre, *Letters on Dancing and Ballets*, 1930; Philippe Rameau, *Dancing-Master*, 1931; Theophile Gautier, *Romantic Ballet*, 1932; (and compiler) *A Miscellany for Dancers*, 1934; Serge Lifar, *Ballet, Traditional to Modern*, Putnam, 1938.

WORK IN PROGRESS: Bookseller at the Ballet, an account of his life and activities in bookselling, publishing, and writing, and to include *The Diaghilev Ballet in London*.

BIOGRAPHICAL/CRITICAL SOURCES: Cyril William Beaumont, *Flash-back: Memories of My Youth*, Beaumont, 1931; *Dance Magazine*, October, 1953; *Dance and Dancers*, December, 1961; *Dancing Times*, November, 1972.

*   *   *

BECHERVAISE, John Mayston 1910-

PERSONAL: Born May 11, 1910, in Melbourne, Victoria, Australia; son of Herbert Walter and Lilian (Mayston) Bechervaise; married Lorna Fearn-Wannan, January 3, 1935; children: Elizabeth (Mrs. Hubert Ward), Judith (Mrs. Ranald McCowan), William, Anne. *Education:* Attended

Royal Melbourne Institute of Technology, 1924-26; Melbourne Teachers College, T.T.C., 1930; attended Courtauld Institute of Art, University of London, 1937-42. *Home:* 185 Roslyn Rd., Belmont, Victoria, Australia.

CAREER: Geelong College, Geelong, Victoria, Australia, first Warden of House of Guilds, 1935-36; St. George's School, Harpenden, Hertfordshire, England, master of lower school, 1937-45; *Walkabout* (geographical journal), Melbourne, Australia, co-editor, 1949-53; Geelong Grammar School, Geelong, Victoria, Australia, director of studies, 1957-73; full-time writer, 1973—. Leader of Australian National Antarctic Research (wintering) Expeditions, 1953-54, 1955-56, 1959-60, and of other expeditions in Southwest Pacific area, Central America, Nepal, and central Australia. Australian observer on U.S. Antarctic expeditions Deep Freeze and High Jump, 1966. Lecturer and television broadcaster for Australian Broadcasting Commission; lecturer on Australian work in Antarctica on U.S. tours, 1961, 1966, 1973, and in Europe, 1966, 1973.

MEMBER: Royal Society of Arts (fellow), Royal Geographical Society (fellow), Australian College of Education, International P.E.N. (Victoria center), Fellowship of Australian Writers, Antarctic Club, Anare Club (former president), Climbers' Club and Fell and Rock Climbing Club (both Great Britain), Savage Club (Melbourne). *Awards, honors:* Queen's Polar Medal in Silver, 1957; Order of British Empire, 1960; John Lewis Gold Medal of Royal Geographical Society (South Australia), 1965; Weickhardt Award for Australian Literature, 1968.

WRITINGS: Barwon and Barrabools (poems), privately printed, 1947; (with Philip Law) *Anare: Australia's Antarctic Outposts*, Oxford University Press, 1958; *Antarctica*, Oxford University Press, 1959; *The Far South*, Angus & Robertson, 1961; *Blizzard and Fire*, Angus & Robertson, 1963; *Australia: World of Difference*, Rigby, 1967; *Mountaineering*, Oxford University Press, 1971. Author of "Sketchbook Series," published by Rigby, including *Ballarat and the Western Goldfields*, 1970; *Bendigo and the Eastern Goldfields*, 1970; *The Blue Mountains*, 1971; *The Grampians*, 1971; *Old Melbourne Hotels*, 1973. Also author of *Australia and Antarctica* and *Australian Mountains and Rivers*, two volumes in the "Around Australia" series published by Doubleday.

Short stories anthologized in *Treasury of Australian Humour*, *Treasury of Australian Wildlife*, and *Walkabout's Australia*. Contributor to *Encyclopaedia Britannica*, *Australian Encyclopaedia*, *Meanjin*, *Southerly*, *Age*, *Modern Reading*, *Reader's Digest* (Australia), and other magazines and journals.

WORK IN PROGRESS: Toka-Desina, a novel set in the future; a collection of short stories with common theme of "old houses"; *Walking in the Himalayas*; and further volumes in Rigby's "Sketchbook" series.

AVOCATIONAL INTERESTS: Art history, mountaineering.

* * *

BECKER, Manning H. 1922-

PERSONAL: Born March 2, 1922, in Emerald, Neb.; son of Christian A. and Doris (Lohmeier) Becker; married Lois Legard, September 29, 1944; children: David Manning, Ann Christine. *Education:* Oregon State University, B.S., 1947, M.S., 1948. *Religion:* Lutheran. *Home:* 3050 Northwest Lynnwood Circle, Corvallis, Ore. 97330.

CAREER: Oregon State University, Corvallis, 1948—, now professor of farm management. *Military service:* U.S. Army, Field Artillery, 1943-46; became captain. *Member:* American Farm Economics Association, American Society of Farm Managers and Rural Appraisers, Western Farm Economics Association, Oregon Society of Farm Managers and Rural Appraisers (secretary-treasurer), Corvallis Chamber of Commerce, Elks. *Awards, honors:* Award from Western Farm Economics Association for outstanding extension program in agricultural economics, 1959; Oregon State University, School of Agriculture, outstanding teacher award, 1966-67.

WRITINGS: (With Emery N. Castle) *Farm Business Management*, Macmillan, 1962, 2nd edition (with Castle and Frederick J. Smith), 1972. Contributor to *Professional Farm Management Manual*, of American Society of Farm Managers and Rural Appraisers, 1972.

* * *

BECKER, Samuel L(eo) 1923-

PERSONAL: Born January 5, 1923, in Quincy, Ill.; son of Nathan (a cobbler) and Ruth (Dicker) Becker; married Ruth Salzmann, June 13, 1953; children: Judith Ann, Harold Craig, Anne Louise. *Education:* University of Iowa, student, 1940-42, 1946-47, B.A., 1947, M.A., 1949, Ph.D., 1953; Columbia University, postdoctoral study, 1958-59. *Politics:* Democrat. *Religion:* Jewish. *Home:* 521 West Park Rd., Iowa City, Iowa 52240.

CAREER: Announcer, director, and free-lance actor at various radio stations prior to 1949; University of Wyoming, Laramie, director of radio, 1949-50; University of Iowa, Iowa City, instructor in television, radio, and speech, 1950-55, assistant professor, 1955-56, professor of communications and director of Division of Television, Radio and Film, 1956—. Media research consultant, U.S. Office of Education, 1960—; Fulbright professor, University of Nottingham, 1963-64. *Military service:* U.S. Army, Infantry, 1942-45; became battalion sergeant major; received Bronze Star. *Member:* Speech Communication Association (president, 1974), International Communication Association, National Association of Educational Broadcasters (former member of board of directors), Central States Speech Association, American Association of University Professors, Retarded Childrens Association, American Civil Liberties Union. *Awards, honors:* Fund for Adult Education mass media fellowship at Columbia University, 1958-59.

WRITINGS: (With H. Clay Harshbarger) *Television: Techniques for Planning and Performance*, Holt, 1958; (with Oscar G. Brockett and Donald C. Bryant) *A Bibliographical Guide to Research in Speech and Dramatic Art*, Scott, Foresman, 1963; (with A. Craig Baird and Franklin Knower) *General Speech Communication*, McGraw, 1971; (with Baird and Knower) *Essentials of General Speech Communication*, McGraw, 1973.

Contributor: Wilbur Schramm, editor, *The Impact of Educational Television*, University of Illinois Press, 1960; Sidney Kraus, editor, *The Great Debates*, University of Indiana Press, 1962; R. E. Nebergall, editor, *Dimensions of Rhetorical Scholarship*, University of Oklahoma Press, 1963; Ronald Reid, editor, *An Introduction to the Field of Speech*, Scott, Foresman, 1965; Philip Emmert and William D. Brooks, editors, *Methods of Research in Communication*, Houghton, 1970; Lloyd F. Bitzer and Edwin Black, editors, *The Prospect of Rhetoric*, Prentice-Hall, 1971.

Also author of monographs. Contributor to journals. Editor, *Speech Monographs*, 1969-71.

WORK IN PROGRESS: A book-length manuscript on mass communication processes.

* * *

BEDDALL-SMITH, Charles John 1916-

PERSONAL: Born December 11, 1916, in Hitchin, Hertfordshire, England; son of John Beddall (an analytical chemist) and Marian Kate Isobel Grellet Smith; married Monica Letitia Surtees, October 10, 1945. *Education:* Attended Felsted School, 1927-34. *Politics:* Conservative. *Religion:* Church of England. *Home:* 303 Rugby Rd., Binley Woods, Coventry, Warwickshire, England.

CAREER: Humber Ltd., Coventry, England, technical writer, 1948-59; Bristol Siddeley Engines Ltd., Industrial Division, Ansty, near Coventry, England, technical writer, 1959—. Free-lance writer. *Member:* Institute of the Motor Industry.

WRITINGS: Humber Cars: A Practical Guide to Maintenance and Repair Covering Models from 1946, Pearson, 1961; *The Hillman Minx and Husky (Side Valve Models)*, Odhams, 1963; *Hillman Minx: Series I to V and Super Minx*, Arco, 1964; *Hillman Imp and Singer Chamois*, Pearson, 1965; *Hillman Cars: A Practical Guide to Maintenance and Repair Covering All Models from 1948 including Minx, Husky, and Super Minx and Imp*, 2nd edition, Pearson, 1966.†

* * *

BEDSOLE, Adolph 1914-

PERSONAL: Born June 16, 1914; son of Barney S. (a farmer) and Delah (Phillips) Bedsole; married Lillie Marlyn Kirkland, June 4, 1934; children: Norma Jean (Mrs. Brian Reaves), Angeline (Mrs. Prichard Cutshaw), Wanda (Mrs. Jerry Strickland). *Education:* Howard College, B.A., 1937. *Home:* 212 Center Ave., Panama City, Fla. 32401.

CAREER: Southern Baptist minister; pastor of church in Panama City, Fla., 1942—.

WRITINGS: The Pastor in Profile, Baker Book, 1958; *Sermon Outlines on the Family and the Home*, Baker Book, 1959; *The Supreme Court Decision on Bible Reading and Prayer*, Baker Book, 1964; *Parson to Parson*, Baker Book, 1964; *My God, My God, Why . . . ?*, Baker Book, 1965; *Sermon Outlines on the Family and Home*, Baker Book, 1968.

* * *

BEEK, Martin(us) A(drianus) 1909-

PERSONAL: Surname is pronounced *Bake*; born June 25, 1909, in Ommen, Netherlands; son of Klaas Jan (a tax officer) and Betsy (Schotsman) Beek; married J. Christina Reeser, August 18, 1934; children: Klaas Jan, Leonie W., Johanna C., Martinus A. *Education:* University of Leyden, D.Th., 1935; also studied at the Universities of Leyden, Leipzig, and Tuebingen. *Religion:* Dutch Reformed. *Home:* Banstraat 62, Amsterdam, Netherlands. *Office:* Theologisch Instituut, Kloveniers Burgwal 99, Amsterdam, The Netherlands.

CAREER: Minister of Dutch Reformed Church, 1934-46; University of Amsterdam, Amsterdam, The Netherlands, professor of Old Testament exegesis and Hebrew literature, 1946—. *Member:* Hollandsche Maatschappij der We-

tenschappen, Teylers Godgeleerd Genootschap, P.E.N., Rotary International.

WRITINGS: Das Danielbuch, sein historischer Hintergrund und sein literarische Entwicklung: Versuch eines Beitrages zur Loesung des Problems, J. Ginsberg (Leiden), 1935; *Het boek Daniel: Een godsdienstige waardering op grond van zijn oorspronkelijke bedoeling*, De Tijdstroom, 1942; *Aan Babylons stromen: Hoofdmomenten uit de cultuurgeschiedenis van Mesopotamie in het Oud-Testamentische tijdvak*, Kosmos, 1950, 3rd edition, 1955; (with J. M. de Jong) *Bijbelse knooppunten*, D. A. Daamen, 1952; (with others) *Maskerspel, voor Dr. W. Leendertz*, Moussault, 1955; *Geschiedenis van Israel: Van Abraham tot Bar Kochba*, W. de Haan, 1957, translation by Arnold J. Pomerans published as *Concise History of Israel: From Abraham to the Bar Cochba Rebellion*, Harper, 1963; *Atlas van het tweestromenland: Overzicht over geschiedenis en beschaving van Mesopotamie van de steentijd tot de val van Babylon*, Elsevier, 1960, translation by D. R. Welsh published as *Atlas of Mesopotamia: A Survey of the History and Civilisation of Mesopotamia from the Stone Age to the Fall of Babylon*, Nelson, 1962; *Israel: Land, volk, cultuur*, Wereldvenster, 1962, 4th edition, 1967.

(Editor with A. van den Born and J. L. Koole) Michael Avi-Yonah and Emil G. Kraeling, *De Bijbel in zijn wereld: Een beeld van de wereld en de tijd waarin de Bijbel ontstond* (title means "Our Living Bible"), J. J. Tijl, 1963; (author of preface) *Israel: Traditie en vernieuwing*, published for Genootschap Nederland-Israel, 1964; (with J. Sperna Weiland) *Martin Buber*, Wereldvenster, 1964, 2nd edition, 1967, translation published as *Martin Buber: Personalist and Prophet*, Newman, 1968; (with C. J. Bleeker, W. F. Golterman, and others) *Een bundel essays over hermeneutische regels en hun toepassing in de theologie*, Van Gennep, 1967; *Wegen en voetsporen van het Oude Testament*, 6th edition, Wereldvenster, 1970, translation of earlier edition by Arnold J. Pomerans published as *A Journey Through the Old Testament*, Harper, 1959; (with others) *The Witness of Tradition: Papers of the Joint British-Dutch Old Testament Conference*, E. J. Brill, 1970.

WORK IN PROGRESS: Exegesis of the Old Testament; *Judaism and Christianity*.

SIDELIGHTS: Beek speaks German, French, English, and modern Hebrew.†

* * *

BEER, Eloise C. S. 1903-
(Lisl Beer, Lisl Drake)

PERSONAL: Born December 8, 1903, in Philadelphia, Pa.; daughter of Leonard Owen (a silk manufacturer) and Eva J. (Crowell) Smith; married Sanel Beer (a retired physician), July 31, 1942. *Education:* Baldwin School, student, 1921-23; Wellesley College, B.A., 1926; other courses at University of London, University of California, Yale University, and University of Miami, Coral Gables, Fla. *Politics:* Republican. *Religion:* Unitarian Universalist. *Home:* 12300 Old Cutler Rd., Miami, Fla. 33156.

CAREER: Rivermont Hospital, Miami, Fla., manager, 1942-47; University of Miami, Coral Gables, Fla., instructor in drama department, 1947-49; free-lance writer and professional artist, with work exhibited at one-woman shows in New York, Boston, and Miami. *Member:* American Artists Professional League, Puppeteers of America, National League of American Pen Women, Artists Equity Association, Florida Artists Group, Blue Dome Art Fellowship (Miami; president, 1963-64; vice-president, 1964-65), Miami Art League, Dramatists Guild, Miami Opera Guild (life).

WRITINGS—Under name Lisl Beer: (Self-illustrated) *Stones for Bread* (poetry), Humphries, 1950; *This, My Island* (novel), Humphries, 1963. Variously author, translator, or adapter, "Silver Series of Puppet Play," Humphries, 1964-65. Contributor of short stories and travel articles to magazines, under pseudonym Lisl Drake.

WORK IN PROGRESS: A mystery, *Murder in Lagner*; a novel, *The Last Tango.*

SIDELIGHTS: Mrs. Beer is competent in German, French, Spanish, and knows some Italian. *Avocational interests:* Puppetry, drama, photography, music, and world travel (Europe, including iron curtain countries, east Africa, Tanzania, Rhodesia, Zambia, Uganda, South Africa, Morocco, Canada, Alaska, Mexico, Guatemala, Panama and the Caribbean).

* * *

BEERS, Henry Putney 1907-

PERSONAL: Born May 7, 1907, in Scranton, Pa.; son of Harry D. (a salesman) and Emma Grace (Putney) Beers; married Alice Winfrey Tharpe (a retired teacher); children: Beverly Anne, Judith Hope (Mrs. Peter D. Trelogan), Janet M. (Mrs. Felix Bendann III), Marion Drane (Mrs. Robert M. Fitzgerald). *Education:* Lafayette College, B.S., 1930; University of Pennsylvania, M.A., 1931, Ph.D., 1935. *Religion:* Methodist. *Home:* 2372 North Quincy St., Arlington, Va. 22207.

CAREER: Work Projects Administration, Survey of Federal Archives, Washington, D.C., research assistant, Historical Records Survey, 1936-38; National Archives, Washington, D.C., archivist, 1938-43, historian, 1943-44; U.S. Department of State, Washington, D.C., foreign relations historian, 1946-50; National Archives, assistant editor of "Territorial Papers of United States," 1950-58, finding aids specialist, 1958-68. *Military service:* U.S. Navy, 1944-46. *Member:* Society of American Archivists. *Awards, honors:* Waldo Gifford Leland Prize of Society of American Archivists, 1963, for *Guide to Federal Archives Relating to the Civil War*, and 1969, for *Guide to the Archives of the Government of the Confederate States of America*; meritorious service award and commendable service award from the General Services Administration for the foregoing publications.

WRITINGS: The Western Military Frontier, 1815-1846, privately printed, 1935; *Bibliographies in American History: Guide to Materials for Research*, Wilson, 1938, 2nd edition, 1942, reprinted, Octagon Books, 1973; *The French in North America: A Bibliographical Guide to French Archives, Reproductions, and Research Missions*, Louisiana State University Press, 1957; (with Kenneth W. Munden) *Guide to Federal Archives Relating to the Civil War*, U.S. Government Printing Office, 1962; *The French and British in the Old Northwest: A Bibliographical Guide to Archive and Manuscript Sources*, Wayne State University Press, 1964; *Guide to the Archives of the Government of the Confederate States of America*, U.S. Government Printing Office, 1968.

WORK IN PROGRESS: Bibliographies in American History: Guide to Materials for Research, Supplement, 1942-1973, completion expected about 1976.

BEHM, William H(erman), Jr. 1922-

PERSONAL: Surname rhymes with "same"; born December 18, 1922, in Ceylon, Minn.; son of William Herman and Sena (Hoebben) Behm; married Laurel Heiden, November 16, 1948; children: Kristi Lee, Kim Alan, Janis Laureen. *Education:* Drake University, B.F.A., 1949; University of Iowa, M.F.A., 1951. *Religion:* Lutheran (Missouri Synod). *Home:* 1306 Merle Hay Rd., Des Moines, Iowa 50311. *Office:* Bill Behm Art, 820 Locust, Des Moines, Iowa 50309.

CAREER: Free-lance commercial artist, Des Moines, Iowa. Exhibitor at one-man shows in St. Louis, Mo., 1953, and Des Moines, Iowa, 1955, 1958. Instructor, Des Moines Art Center. Juror at art shows; chairman of Life of Christ Art Show, 1955—. *Military service:* U.S. Army, 1942-45; became technical sergeant. *Member:* Lutheran Society of Music, Worship and Arts, Iowa Art Directors and Artists Association. *Awards, honors:* Iowa Annual Purchase Prize, 1954; first and second awards in oil and watercolors, Iowa State Fair, 1954, 1955, 1956; Purchase Award, Life of Christ competition, 1956; Purchase Award through Meltzer Gallery, New York, N.Y., 1957, for U.S. Embassy collection; and other prizes.

WRITINGS: Little Lambs, Concordia, 1960; *The Night Jesus Was Born*, Concordia, 1964. Contributor of editorial and spot cartoons to *Lutheran Reporter*, 1965, and to other periodicals.

WORK IN PROGRESS: Two books for children, *People I Know* and *Mardi Gras*; spot cartoons for high school and college periodicals.†

* * *

BEIK, Paul H(arold) 1915-

PERSONAL: Born January 23, 1915, in Olivet, Mich.; son of Arthur Kennedy (a professor) and Katie Isabel (Larson) Beik; married Doris Humphrey (a librarian), September 1, 1939; children: William Humphrey, Stephen Wright. *Education:* Union College and University, Schenectady, N.Y., A.B., 1935; State University of New York at Albany, M.A., 1938; Columbia University, M.A., 1939, Ph.D., 1943, postdoctoral study at Russian Institute, 1952. *Home:* 603 Ogden Ave., Swarthmore, Pa. 19081.

CAREER: Teacher of social studies, Delmar, N.Y., 1935-38; Columbia University, New York, N.Y., instructor in history, 1941-45; Swarthmore College, Swarthmore, Pa., assistant professor, 1945-50, associate professor, 1950-57, professor of history, 1957-68, Centenial Professor of History, 1968—. *Member:* American Historical Association, Society for French Historical Studies, Phi Beta Kappa. *Awards, honors:* Guggenheim fellowship to France, 1948-49; Fund for Advancement of Education faculty fellowship, 1952-53; Fulbright research fellowship to Paris, 1968-69.

WRITINGS: A Judgment of the Old Regime, Columbia University Press, 1944; *The French Revolution Seen from the Right*, American Philosophical Society, 1956; (with Laurence Lafore) *Modern Europe: A History Since 1500*, Holt, 1959; *Louis Philippe and the July Monarchy*, Van Nostrand, 1965; (editor) *The French Revolution*, Harper, 1970.

* * *

BELAIR, Richard L. 1934-

PERSONAL: Born June 11, 1934, in Central Falls, R.I.; son of Leo A. (a machinist) and Eva (Berard) Belair; married Pauline Lariviere, November 28, 1959; children: Alex. *Education:* Assumption College, Worcester, Mass., A.B., 1960; Worcester State College, M.Ed., 1968; University of Connecticut, C.A.G.S. in media production, 1974. *Religion:* Catholic. *Home:* 7 Meadowbrook Rd., Auburn, Mass. 01501. *Agent:* Curtis Brown Ltd., 60 East 56th St., New York, N.Y. 10022.

CAREER: High school teacher of English, Auburn, Mass., 1961—. *Military service:* U.S. Army, 1953-56. *Member:* Catholic Playwrights Circle.

WRITINGS: Road Less Traveled, Doubleday, 1965. Author of full-length play, "Praying-Mantis."

WORK IN PROGRESS: A movie script in high school setting.

*   *   *

BELGUM, David 1922-

PERSONAL: Born December 22, 1922, in Glenwood, Minn.; son of Anton H. and Selma (Johnshoy) Belgum; married Katherine Geigenmueller, August 8, 1953; children: Karl, Kurt, Kirsten. *Education:* University of Minnesota, B.A., 1944; Northwestern Lutheran Theological Seminary, B.D., 1946; Boston University, Ph.D., 1952. *Home:* 7538 Grand Ave. S., Minneapolis, Minn. *Office:* Northwestern Lutheran Theological Seminary, 100 East 22nd St., Minneapolis, Minn.

CAREER: Ordained to Lutheran ministry, 1946; assistant pastor in Minneapolis, Minn., 1946-47; pastor in Boston, Mass., 1947-52; Ypsilanti State Hospital, Ypsilanti, Mich., child therapist, 1952-53; Wittenberg University, Springfield, Ohio, assistant professor, 1953-55; Northwestern Lutheran Theological Seminary, Minneapolis, Minn., began as associate professor, became professor of pastoral counseling. Chaplain supervisor, Institute of Pastoral Care. *Member:* American Psychological Association.

WRITINGS: Clinical Training for Pastoral Care, Westminster, 1956; *His Death and Ours*, Augsburg, 1958; *Why Did It Happen to Me?*, Augsburg, 1960; *The Church and Its Ministry*, Prentice-Hall, 1963; *Guilt: Where Religion and Psychology Meet*, Prentice-Hall, 1963; *Church Camp Counselor's Manual*, Lutheran Church Press, 1964; *The Cross and the Creed*, Augsburg, 1966; *The Church and Sex Education*, Lutheran Church Press, 1967; (editor) *Religion and Medicine: Essays on Meaning, Values, and Health*, Iowa State University Press, 1967; *Why Marry? Since You Don't Need a License to Love*, Augsburg, 1972; *Alone, Alone, All, All Alone*, Concordia, 1972; *Engagement*, Concordia, 1972.†

*   *   *

BELITT, Ben 1911-

PERSONAL: Born May 2, 1911, in New York, N.Y.; son of Lewis (a teacher) and Ida (Lewitt) Belitt. *Education:* University of Virginia, B.A., 1932, M.A., 1934, Ph.D. candidate, 1934-36. *Office:* Department of English, Bennington College, Bennington, Vt. 05201.

CAREER: The Nation, New York, N.Y., assistant literary editor, 1936-37; Bennington College, Bennington, Vt., professor of literature, 1938—. Editor-scenarist for U.S. Photographic Centre, Department of Historical Films, 1945. *Military service:* U.S. Army, 1943-44. *Member:* Phi Beta Kappa. *Awards, honors:* Shelley Memorial Award for Poetry, 1936; Guggenheim fellowship in poetry, 1946; Oscar Blumenthal Award for Poetry, 1956; Union League Civic

and Arts Foundation Prize for Poetry, 1958; Brandeis University Creative Arts Award in Poetry, 1962; National Institute of Arts and Letters Award in Poetry, 1965; National Book Award candidate in poetry, 1965; National Book Award in Translation candidate, 1966; National Endowment for the Arts grant, 1967-68.

WRITINGS: The Five-Fold Mesh (poems), Knopf, 1938; *Four Poems by Rimbaud: The Problem of Translation*, Alan Swallow, 1947; *Wilderness Stair* (poems), Grove, 1955; *The Enemy of Joy: New and Selected Poems*, University of Chicago Press, 1964; (contributor) Howard Nemerov, editor, *Poets on Poetry*, Basic Books, 1965; *Nowhere but Light* (poems), University of Chicago Press, 1970.

Translator: (And editor) F. Garcia Lorca, *Poet in New York*, Grove, 1955; (and editor) Pablo Neruda, *Selected Poems of Pablo Neruda*, Grove, 1961; (and editor) Antonio Machado, *Juan de Mairena*, University of California Press, 1963; (and editor) Rafael Alberti, *Selected Poems of Rafael Alberti*, University of California Press, 1965; (and contributor) Jorge Guillen, *Cantico*, edited by N. T. Di-Giovanni, Little, Brown, 1965; Neruda, *Poems from the Canto General*, Racolin, 1968; (with Alastair Reid, and editor) Neruda, *A New Decade: Poems 1958-1967*, Grove, 1969; (and editor) Neruda, *New Poems: 1968-1970*, Grove, 1972; (and editor) Neruda, *Splendor and Death of Joaquin Murieta* (play), Farrar, Straus, 1972; Alberti, *A la pintura*, Universal Limited Art Editions, 1972; (and contributor) N. T. DiGiovanni, editor, *Jorge Luis Borges: Selected Poems*, Delacorte, 1972; (and editor) Neruda, *Five Decades: Poems 1925-1970*, Grove, 1974.

Also author of a prose journal, "School of the Soldier," published in *Quarterly Review of Literature*, 1949. Contributor of prose and poetry to *Poetry, Virginia Quarterly Review, Nation, Southern Review, New Republic, Sewanee Review, New Yorker, Harper's Bazaar, Harper's, Partisan Review*, and other periodicals. GALLEY 45—5671-14

WORK IN PROGRESS: Further translations of contemporary Spanish poetry in South America, Mexico, and Spain; a selection of poems, *The Invisible Edge: New Poems, 1970-1975*; a volume of collected essays, completion expected in 1975.

SIDELIGHTS: Wallace Fowlie in *Poetry* writes of the collection, *The Enemy Joy*: "A study of these poems would lead one to the very heart of the poetic process. The tension in them is almost too tight. At first view, the poetry will seem solemn and majestic, but it is permeated with volatile flashes. . . . His book testifies to the responsibility of a man in the presence of his language." John Malcolm Brinnin writes "Belitt is one of the few poets whose care for the language is as great as his self-concern. . . . He writes with an unabashed sense of the grandeur and theatricality of the English tongue. . . . One reads Belitt with the delight in the fact that, even today, depths of feeling and the reports of a caustic eye are not necessarily presented in basic English or words of four letters." May Swenson, in *The Nation*, remarks that Belitt's language "is pared of excess and metaphors and sculptures; scrupulous detail is less sought after than an effective whole with apocalyptic and psychological reverberations." And according to Richard Eberhart: "In reading the best poems of Ben Belitt, one is passed through a screen of artistry into the open air of mature, deep, universal significance. . . . He has pointed his finger to the depths of the heart."

In *Reflexions on Poetry and Poetics*, Howard Nemerov

comments on Belitt's poetic style, "Belitt receives the world more exclusively by the ear than most; he writes by a kind of radar, and a relevant sound, by the rules of his procedures, is assumed to be a relevant sense; as though the one response would naturally evoke the other.... This reliance on how things sound ... makes possible his characteristic combination of great elaboration with great intensity ... a menacing intensity...." Noting another trait of the poet's style, Nemerov writes, "More than any other poet writing in English, more than Mr. Ransom or Miss Moore, Belitt plays that dangerous game of the *mot juste*, the specialized name kept for the one occasion...."

"The meaning of the poem," according to Nemerov, "is gained not from reading through it so much as from reading around in it, and from listening to recurrences and obsessive preoccupations in a series of poems. This kind of writing suggests something that may perhaps be true of all poetry, though less apparent in most, that the body of a poet's work supplies the attentive reader with a grammar and a lexicon which he must elicit in order to read beautifully.... By reason of the musical, echoing, inter-allusive mode of its composition, wherever you touch [Belitt's poetry], some relevance appears, like answers to like, an imitation not quite exact enlarges the area of apprehended relations and one's sense of their fluent order."

Belitt told *CA* that he has a long-standing interest in modern dance, in the relation of poetry to dance (four dances in the Martha Graham Repertory are based in part on the poems in *The Enemy Joy*), and in the motion picture and motion picture photography. Belitt knows French, Spanish, Italian, and Russian. He has traveled abroad in Spain, Sicily, Italy, and France, and spends his annual winter recesses in Cuernavaca, Mexico.

BIOGRAPHICAL/CRITICAL SOURCES: New York Times, October 16, 1938; *New York Herald Tribune*, October 30, 1938; George K. Anderson and Eda L. Walton, *This Generation*, Scott, Foresman, 1949; *Nation*, June 11, 1955; *New York Times Book Review*, October 25, 1964; *Midway* (Chicago), February, 1965; *Poetry*, February, 1965; *Voyages* (Ben Belitt issue), fall, 1967; Howard Nemerov, *Reflexions on Poetry and Poetics*, Rutgers University Press, 1972; *Salmagundi*, December, 1972, spring-summer, 1973; *Sewanee Review*, autumn, 1973.

* * *

BELL, Gertrude (Wood)   1911-

PERSONAL: Born January 28, 1911, in Liberty, Mo.; daughter of William Edward and Myrtle (Griffith) Bell. *Education:* William Jewell College, A.B., 1933. *Home:* 30 South Fairview, Liberty, Mo. 64068. *Agent:* Ruth Cantor, 156 Fifth Ave., New York, N.Y. 10017.

CAREER: Freelance fiction writer, 1954—. *Member:* National League of American Pen Women, Missouri Historical Society, Missouri Writers Guild, Clay County Museum Association. *Awards, honors:* Missouri Writers Guild award, 1963, for juvenile short story; Midwest section of National League of American Pen Women award, 1963, for teen-age short story; awards from Missouri Writers Guild and National League of American Pen Women, both 1965, for *Posse of Two*.

WRITINGS: Posse of Two, Criterion, 1964; *Roundabout Road*, Independence Press, 1972; *First Crop*, Independence Press, 1973; *A Ladder for Silvanus*, Independence Press, in press. Contributor of short stories to periodicals.

WORK IN PROGRESS: Where Runs the River, for publication by Independence Press; *Sand, Silver, and a Mule Named Mike*, fiction for 10-14 year-old readers.

SIDELIGHTS: "I grew up with the sort of yarn I enjoy spinning," writes Gertrude Bell. Historical fiction is her means of documenting local landmarks.

* * *

BELLAN, Ruben C.   1918-

PERSONAL: Born October 2, 1918, in Winnipeg, Manitoba, Canada; son of Hyman and Lily (Kolovson) Bellan; married Ruth Lercher, June 1, 1947; children: Paul, Susan, Lorne. *Education:* University of Manitoba, B.A., 1938; University of Toronto, M.A., 1941; Columbia University, Ph.D., 1958. *Religion:* Hebrew. *Home:* 628 Niagara, Winnipeg, Manitoba, Canada. *Office:* University of Manitoba, Winnipeg, Manitoba, Canada.

CAREER: University of Manitoba, Winnipeg, 1946—, associate professor of economics. *Military service:* Royal Canadian Air Force, 1941-45; became flying officer. *Member:* Canadian Institute of International Affairs, John Howard Society of Manitoba (president).

WRITINGS: Principles of Economics and the Canadian Economy, McGraw, 1960, 4th edition, 1972; *Fundamentals of Economics*, McGraw, 1962; *The Evolving City*, Pitman, 1971.

WORK IN PROGRESS: A study of the nature and extent of unemployment in Greater Winnipeg in 1964, and the public policy measures that would have served to prevent it.†

* * *

BENCE-JONES, Mark   1930-

PERSONAL: Born May 29, 1930, in London, England; son of Philip (an engineer and landowner) and Victoria May (Thomas) Bence-Jones; married Gillian Enid Pretyman (a poet), 1965; children: one son, one daughter. *Education:* Attended Pembroke College, Cambridge, 1949-52; Royal Agricultural College, B.A., 1952, M.R.A.C., 1954, M.A., 1958. *Politics:* Conservative. *Religion:* Roman Catholic. *Home:* Glenville Park, County Cork, Ireland. *Agent:* Anthony Sheil Associates Ltd., 52 Floral St., London, England WC29DE.

CAREER: Engaged in farming and estate management in Ireland, as well as writing. *Member:* Irish Georgian Society, Kildare Street Club (Dublin).

WRITINGS—Novels: All a Nonsense, P. Davies, 1957; *Paradise Escaped*, P. Davies, 1958; *Nothing in the City*, Sidgwick & Jackson, 1965; *The Remarkable Irish*, McKay, 1966; *Palaces of the Raj*, Allen & Unwin, 1973; *Clive of India*, Constable, 1974.

Author of introduction: *Burke's Landed Gentry of Ireland*, 1958; *Burke's Landed Gentry of Great Britain*, Volume I, 1965, Volume II, 1969, Volume III, 1972; *Burke's Peerage*, 1970.

Contributor to *Burke's Guide to the Royal Family*, 1973; contributor of humorous and satirical articles, and articles on art, architecture, and travel, to magazines and newspapers, including *Holiday*, *Vogue*, *Country Life*, *Tatler*, *Sunday Graphic*, *Nottingham Observer*, and *Irish Times*.

WORK IN PROGRESS: Assisting in production of *Burke's Irish Family Records*.

BENEDICT, Stewart H(urd) 1924-

PERSONAL: Born December 27, 1924, in Mineola, N.Y.; son of Chauncey Lester (an insurance agent) and Elsie (Stewart) Benedict. *Education:* Drew University, A.B. (summa cum laude), 1944; Johns Hopkins University, M.A., 1945; New York University, graduate study, 1946-49, 1961-64. *Politics:* Democrat. *Home:* Apartment 4-A, 27 Washington Sq. N., New York, N.Y. 10011.

CAREER: New York University, University College, Bronx, N.Y., instructor in German, 1946-49; Michigan College of Mining and Technology (now Michigan Technological University), Houghton, assistant professor of humanities, 1951-54, 1955-61; Jersey City State College, Jersey City, N.J., assistant professor of English, 1961-64; Rutgers, The State University, New Brunswick, N.J., lecturer, 1965; City College of the City University of New York, New York, N.Y., lecturer, 1965-66. Free-lance writer, 1964—. Secretary, Houghton County (Mich.) Democratic Committee, 1956-60. *Member:* New York Critics Drama Desk, The Newspaper Guild, American Civil Liberties Union.

WRITINGS: (Contributor) Jerome Weiss, editor, *An English Teacher's Reader*, Odyssey, 1962; (contributor) Webb Ellis, *A Teacher's Guide to Selected Literary Works*, Dell, 1965; *A Teacher's Guide to Senior High School Literature*, Dell, 1966; *A Teacher's Guide to Modern Drama*, Dell, 1967; *A Teacher's Guide to Poetry*, Dell, 1969; *Making a Difference*, Heath, 1971; *A Teacher's Guide to Contemporary Teenage Fiction*, Dell, 1973; *A Teacher's Guide to "Jonathan Livingston Seagull,"* Avon, 1973; *A Teacher's Guide to "The Faraway Lurs,"* Avon, 1973; *A Teacher's Guide to "Fireweed,"* Avon, 1973.

Plays: *One Day in the Life of Ivy Dennison* (produced Off-Off-Broadway by the New York Theater Ensemble, July 16, 1971), Samuel French, 1969; *Bad Guy* (produced Off-Off-Broadway at the Playbox Studio, December, 1970), Breakthrough Press, 1972.

Editor: *Tales of Terror and Suspense*, Dell, 1963; (with John B. Opdycke) *Harper's English Grammar*, revised edition, Harper, 1966; *The Crime-Solvers*, Dell, 1966; *Famous American Speeches*, Dell, 1967; *Backlash*, Popular Library, 1970; *Your Own Thing and "Twelfth Night,"* Dell, 1970; *Seven Great Modern Short Novel Masterpieces*, Popular Library, 1970.

Contributor of play and book reviews and a weekly column to *Jersey Journal*, 1964-70. Contributor of articles to literary and scholarly magazines, including *South Atlantic Quarterly*, *CEA Critic*, and *Claremont Quarterly*.

WORK IN PROGRESS: A novel about police work and political corruption in an urban New Jersey area.

SIDELIGHTS: Benedict speaks, reads, and writes French, reads and writes German, reads Latin, and knows some Greek. *Avocational interests:* Seeing New York plays, and reading.

*   *   *

BENEDIKT, Michael 1935-

PERSONAL: Born May 26, 1935, in New York, N.Y.; son of John (an engineer) and Helen (Davis) Benedikt; married Marianne Sabados (a librarian), August 2, 1962. *Education:* New York University, B.A., 1956; Columbia University, M.A., 1961. *Home:* 315 West 98th St., New York, N.Y. 10025. *Agent:* Georges Borchardt, Inc., 145 East 52nd St., New York, N.Y. 10022.

CAREER: Horizon Press, Inc., New York, N.Y., editor, 1959-62; free-lance writer and editor, 1962—; Bennington College, Bennington, Vt., instructor in English, 1967-68; Sarah Lawrence College, Bronxville, N.Y., instructor in English, 1968-73; Hampshire College, Amherst, Mass., associate professor of English, 1973—. Judge of Lamont competition in poetry, 1970-72, and National Book Award in Translation, 1973. *Military service:* U.S. Army, active duty, 1958-59. U.S. Army Reserve, 1955-66; became sergeant. *Member:* College de Pataphysique, Modern Language Association of America, P.E.N. *Awards, honors:* Guggenheim grant in poetry, 1968; Bess Hokin Prize, 1968, for best group of poems in *Poetry*; National Endowment for the Arts Prize, 1970, for poem "The Wings of the Nose."

WRITINGS—Poems: *The Body*, Wesleyan University Press, 1968; *Sky*, Wesleyan University Press, 1970; *Mole Notes*, Wesleyan University Press, 1971.

Editor and contributor of translations: (With George E. Wellwarth) *Modern French Theatre*, Dutton, 1964; (with Wellwarth) *Post-War German Theatre*, Dutton, 1967; (with Wellwarth) *Modern Spanish Theatre*, Dutton, 1968; *Twenty-Two Poems of Robert Desnos*, Kayak Press, 1972; *The Poetry of Surrealism*, Little, Brown, in press.

Editor: *Theatre Experiment*, Doubleday, 1967; (and translator) *Ring around the World: Poems of Jean L'Anselme*, Swallow Press, 1968.

Contributor of translations: *Medieval Age*, Dell, 1963.

Poetry is represented in over fifteen anthologies, including *The Young American Poets*, edited by Paul Carroll, Follett, 1969; *The Modern Poets*, edited by J. M. Brinnin and Bill Read, McGraw, 1970; *Contemporary American Poetry*, edited by Donald Hall, Penguin, 1972; *The Major Young Poets*, edited by Al Lee, World Publishing, 1972. Contributor of criticism to collections, including *Minimal Art*, edited by Gregory Battcock, Dutton, 1968; *Jean-Luc Godard*, edited by Toby Mussman, Dutton, 1968; *The Grand Eccentrics*, edited by T. B. Hess and John Ashbery, Collier, 1971; *The New Music*, edited by Gregory Battcock, Dutton, in press.

Contributor of plays and poems to literary periodicals, including *Poetry*, *New American Review*, *Partisan Review*, and *American Poetry Review*. Associate editor, *Art News*, 1963-72; New York correspondent, *Art International*, 1965-67; poetry editor, *Paris Review*, 1974—.

WORK IN PROGRESS: *Surrealism: Prose*, for Little, Brown, and *The Prose Poem*, for Dell, completion of both expected in 1975; research in twentieth-century theater, art, and poetry in prose and verse.

SIDELIGHTS: "Benedikt might be a cubist or surrealist painter," notes a *Time* reviewer, "continually inspecting, distorting and re-creating the skyline of human existence. The method is often deliberately and delightfully nonsensical." Most of the poems in *The Body*, writes Jean Farley, "move and sport and have their being in the surrealist mode. Some of them even gaze forth with a rather mild version of the Cheshire grin of Dada." She further notes that Benedikt prefers, very often, "that free exchange and interchange, the dance of things-in-the-mind," to statement of ideas. Timothy Baland finds that the poems in *The Body* "are not often moving. Instead, there is dissonance in them, aside-like remarks. The images come out of a fantastic geometry, the thoughts tilted to meet at jazzy angles. Preposterous lines float gaily off into space."

BIOGRAPHICAL/CRITICAL SOURCES: Carolyn Riley, editor, *Contemporary Literary Criticism*, Volume IV, Gale, 1975.

* * *

BENEZRA, Barbara (Beardsley) 1921-

PERSONAL: Born April 2, 1921, in Woodman, Colo.; daughter of Earl (a dentist) and Alice (a teacher; maiden name, Smith) Beardsley; married Leo L. Benezra (a chemist); children: Heather Lee, Paul Louis, Judith Ann, David Allen. *Education:* San Francisco State College (now University), student, 1939-40; University of California, Berkeley, student, General Secondary Certificate, 1944; University of the Pacific, A.B., 1943; San Jose State College (now University of California), Librarian Degree, 1960. *Home:* 7170 Hawthorn Dr., Mentor, Ohio 44060.

CAREER: Elementary school librarian in Sunnyvale, Calif., 1960-67, and in Eastlake, Ohio, 1967—. *Member:* American Library Association, National Education Association, Ohio State Library Association.

WRITINGS: Gold Dust and Petticoats, Bobbs-Merrill, 1964; *Nuggets in My Pocket*, Bobbs-Merrill, 1966; *Fire Dragon*, Abelard, 1970. Contributor to library journals.

WORK IN PROGRESS: Peggy Moran, a sequel to *Gold Dust and Petticoats* and *Nuggets in My Pocket*.

SIDELIGHTS: Mrs. Benezra is also a practicing Scientologist and Dianetic Auditor.

* * *

BENNETT, Geoffrey (Martin) 1909-
(Sea-Lion)

PERSONAL: Born June 7, 1909, in England; son of Martin Gilbert (a rear admiral, Royal Navy) and Esme Geraldine (Hicks) Bennett; married Rosemary Alys Bechervaise, July 29, 1932; children: Rodney Martin Dumaresq, Richard Hugh Hamilton Geoffrey. *Education:* Attended Royal Naval College, Dartmouth, 1923-26, Royal Naval College, Greenwich, 1929-30. *Religion:* Church of England. *Home:* Stage Coach Cottage, 57 Broad St., Ludlow, Shropshire, England. *Agent:* Curtis Brown Ltd., 1 Craven Hill, London W2, England.

CAREER: Royal Navy, 1923-58, becoming commander, 1945, captain, 1953; lord mayor's esquire, London, England, 1958-60; secretary to lord mayor of Westminster, London, England, 1960-74. Served with Royal Navy as signal officer of cruiser squadron, 1940, signal officer in South Atlantic and Mediterranean stations, 1940-45, in Admiralty posts, 1945-46, 1951-53, as captain of H.M.S. "St. Brides' Bay," 1948, naval attache in Moscow, Warsaw, and Helsinki, 1953-55. Visiting lecturer, University of New Brunswick, 1973. *Member:* Royal Historical Society (fellow), Royal United Services, Institute for Defence Studies, Naval Records Society. *Awards, honors*—Military: Distinguished Service Cross, 1943; Order of Orange Nassau, 1972. Civilian: Gold Medal and Trench-Gascoigne Prize of Royal United Service Institution, 1935, 1941, 1942.

WRITINGS: By Human Error, Seeley Service, 1961; *Coronel and the Falklands*, Macmillan, 1962; *Cowan's War*, Collins, 1964; *The Battle of Jutland*, Dufour, 1964; *Charlie B.: A Biography of Admiral Lord Beresford*, Dawnay, 1968; *Naval Battles of the First World War*, Scribners, 1969; (contributor) Peter Kemp, editor, *A History of the Royal Navy*, Barker, 1969; *Nelson the Commander*, Scribners, 1972; *Battle of the River Plate*, Ian Allen, 1972; *Loss of the "Prince of Wales" and "Repulse"*, Ian Allen, 1973.

Novels under pseudonym Sea-Lion: *Phantom Fleet*, Collins, 1946; *Sink Me the Ship*, Collins, 1947; *Sea of Troubles*, Collins, 1947; *Cargo for Crooks*, Collins, 1948; *When Danger Threatens*, Collins, 1949; *This Creeping Evil*, Hutchinson, 1950; *The Invisible Ships*, Hutchinson, 1950; *The Quest of John Clare*, Hutchinson, 1951; *Pirate Destroyer*, Hutchinson, 1951; *The Diamond Rock*, Hutchinson, 1952; *Secret Weapon*, Hutchinson, 1952; *Meet Desmond Drake*, Hutchinson, 1952; *Wrecked on the Goodwins*, Hutchinson, 1953; *Damn Desmond Drake!*, Hutchinson, 1953; *Falkland Islands Mystery*, Hutchinson, 1954; *The Stolen Cipher*, Hutchinson, 1955; *Desmond Drake Goes West*, Hutchinson, 1956; *Detective Tiger Ransome*, Hutchinson, 1957; *Death in Russian Habit*, Long, 1958; *Operation Fireball*, Long, 1959; *Missing Submarine*, Warne, 1960; *Down Among the Dead Men*, Long, 1961; *Death in the Dog Watches*, Long, 1962.

Radio plays: "The Phantom Fleet"; "The Fair Quaker of Deal"; "The Quest of John Clare"; other radio plays for adults and several for children, produced by British Broadcasting Corp. Occasional contributor to *History Today*, *Proceedings of U.S. Naval Institute*, *Journal of Royal United Services*, *International History Magazine*, and others.

WORK IN PROGRESS: Naval Battles of the Second World War.

SIDELIGHTS: Of *Nelson the Commander*, Austin Wheatley has written in the *Detroit News*: "'Nelson the Commander' is a superb book by a retired Royal Navy captain. . . . It is an achievement to produce a work that the professional experts cannot fault but that is also an absorbing story for those who have never set foot even on a minesweeper. . . . Geoffrey Bennett comes well qualified to write Nelson's biography."

AVOCATIONAL INTERESTS: History, especially of the Royal Navy, from 1750 onwards.

* * *

BENNETT, Penelope Agnes 1938-

PERSONAL: Born September 22, 1938, in London, England; daughter of Christopher Dillon (British Navy) and Margaret (Slack) Bennett. *Education:* Attended Steiner School, University of Leeds. *Politics:* Liberal. *Home:* 41 Sydney St., Chelsea, London S.W. 3, England.

CAREER: Writer, potter.

WRITINGS: (With Lina M. Slack) *Rock Engravings from Driekops Eiland*, Centaur Press, 1962. Short stories anthologized in *Pick of Today's Short Stories, 10-11*, edited by John Pudney, McClelland, 1960; *Winter's Tales, 12*, edited by A. D. MacLean, Macmillan (London), 1966, St. Martin's, 1967; *Winter's Tales, 13*, edited by MacLean, Macmillan (London), 1967, St. Martin's, 1968. Author of a pamphlet of poetry; contributor of short stories, poems, and reviews to periodicals, including *Atlantic Monthly*, *Mademoiselle*, *New Mexico Quarterly*, *New English Review*, *John O'London's*, and *Shenandoah*; has also written for the British Broadcasting Corporation.

WORK IN PROGRESS: A book on Egypt, tentatively titled *Love Letters to Egypt*.

SIDELIGHTS: Miss Bennett is competent in German and Italian. *Avocational interests:* Pottery, gardening.

BENNETT, Robert A(ndrew)   1927-

PERSONAL: Born May 31, 1927, in Albert Lea, Minn.; son of Glenn Kelling (a tailor) and Agnes (Dyrdal) Bennett; married Bonita June Dudley, September 4, 1949; children: Nancy Jo, Robert Kelling, Ronald Dudley. *Education:* University of California, Los Angeles, A.B., 1949; University of Minnesota, B.S., 1951, M.A., 1953; Florida State University, Ed.D., 1964. *Residence:* San Diego, Calif.

CAREER: Minneapolis (Minn.) public schools, teacher of English, 1951-57, curriculum consultant, 1958-61, 1962-63; University School, Tallahassee, Fla., teacher of English, 1957-58; Florida State University, Tallahassee, instructor in English education, 1961-62; San Diego (Calif.) city schools, specialist in language arts, 1963—. U.S. Office of Education, chairman of Conference of Supervisors of English, 1964; Educational Testing Service, member of committees to revise national teacher examination in English and the College Entrance Examination Board examination in English. *Member:* National Council of Teachers of English (member of commission on the English curriculum, 1962—, commission director, 1965—), Phi Delta Kappa.

WRITINGS: (Editor) *Mirrors*, Scholastic Book Service, 1960; (compiler with Verda Evans and Edward J. Gordon) *Types of Literature*, Ginn, 1967, new edition, 1970. Contributor of articles to English and education journals.

WORK IN PROGRESS: A book on use of dictionaries in elementary school; a book on junior high school literature; research in programmed instruction, linguistic approach to beginning reading, and compensatory education.†

*   *   *

BENNETT, W(illiam) R(obert)   1921-

PERSONAL: Born July 11, 1921, in Durban, South Africa; son of Charles Henry (a managing director) and Daisy Violet (Walters) Bennett; married; children: Cheryl June, Adam William Charles. *Education:* Attended high school in Queensland, Australia. *Politics:* Liberal. *Religion:* Church of England. *Home:* 94 Solar St., Coorparoo, Brisbane, Queensland, Australia. *Agent:* Curtis Brown Ltd., 13 King Street, Covent Garden, London WC2E 8HU England.

CAREER: Royal Australian Air Force, fighter pilot in Europe, 1941-45, spending six months of that time as prisoner of war after his Spitfire was shot down; Bennett Chain Co. Pty. Ltd., Brisbane, Queensland, Australia, director, 1945-50; Royal Australian Air Force, jet pilot, 1950-59 (flew two hundred missions in Korea); left service to become full-time writer, 1959—. *Member:* Society of Australian Authors. *Awards, honors—*Military: Distinguished Flying Cross and bar (Britain); Distinguished Flying Cross and Air Medal with four oak leaf clusters (United States).

*WRITINGS—*All published by Horwitz, except as noted: *Mig Meat*, 1960; *The Squadron Leader*, 1960; *The Red Parallel*, 1960; *Edge of Hell*, 1960; *Men with a Mission*, 1961; *Wingman*, 1961; *Flaps and Jetwash*, 1961; *Hurricane Pilot*, 1961; *Ranger Flight*, 1962; *Savage Sky*, 1962; *Night Intruder*, 1962; *Target Turin*, 1962; *Angry Eagles*, 1962; *Spitfire Attack*, 1962; *Suicide Sortie*, 1963; *War Wings*, 1963; *High Conflict*, 1963; *Fighter Pilot*, 1964; *Bandits Above*, 1964; *Nightfighter*, 1964; *Angels Zero*, 1965; *Top Cover*, 1965; *The Proud Eagles*, 1965; *Wings Over Malta*, 1965; *Fighter/Bomber*, 1965; *Skybolt*, 1965.

The Devil's Angels, 1966; *High Fury*, 1966; *Flak Alley, War Birds*, 1966; *Flames in the Sky*, 1967; *The Man from Checkmate*, R. Hale, 1971; *Dossier on a Mantis*, R. Hale,

1972. Contributor of about two hundred short stories and articles to periodicals in Australia and New Zealand.

WORK IN PROGRESS: A novel.

SIDELIGHTS: Bennett's books have been translated into French, Belgian, Danish, German, Swedish, Finnish, and Norwegian. Bennett says that he speaks a smattering of German, French, and Japanese.

BIOGRAPHICAL/CRITICAL SOURCES: Frank Johnson, *R.A.A.F. Over Europe*, Eyre & Spottiswoode, 1946; John Herington, *Air Power Over Europe*, Canberra Australian War Memorial, 1963.

*   *   *

BENSON, Stephana Vere   1909-

PERSONAL: Born February 10, 1909, in Bromley, Kent, England; daughter of Sir Frank and Lady Stephana Rose (Pooley) Benson; married H. T. Hillier (a clergyman; deceased); married William Wynne Taylor (a retired captain, British Army), October 27, 1958; children: (first marriage) Fay Vere Harvey Hillier (Mrs. David Anthony Wright). *Education:* Privately at home. *Religion:* Christian. *Home:* Fairbourne, 9 Great Austins, Farnham, Surrey, England.

CAREER: Writer and artist. Founder and honorary secretary of Bird-Lovers' League. *Member:* British Trust for Ornithology, Wild Fowl Trust, Royal Society for Protection of Birds (fellow), British Ornithologists' Club, British Ornithologists' Union, Devon and Cornwall Bird-Watching and Preservation Societies.

*WRITINGS—*All published by Warne: *The Observer's Book of Birds*, 1937; *The Greatest of These*, 1938; *The Child's Own Book of Prayers and Hymns*, 1940; *Birds at Sight* (self-illustrated), 1943; *Spotting British Birds* (self-illustrated), 1951; *Birds of Lebanon and the Jordan Area* (self-illustrated), Warne for International Council for Bird Preservation, 1970, 2nd edition in Arabic, translated by A. Tibi, 1974.

WORK IN PROGRESS: A book on God's dimension for man, completion expected in 1976.

SIDELIGHTS: Miss Benson has been studying the birds of Lebanon for eight years. She is attempting, with the Arabic revision of her book, to introduce into Middle Eastern places of learning, an awareness of the urgent need for conservation. She hopes to found in Lebanon an organization like the Bird-Lovers' League, which has fifty thousand members.

*   *   *

BENSTED-SMITH, Richard (Brian)   1929-

PERSONAL: Born July 20, 1929, son of William Francis and Katharine Ethel (Thomson) Bensted-Smith; married Patricia Fender, April 15, 1961; children: Nicholas Michael. *Education:* Cambridge University, B.A., 1952. *Religion:* Church of England.

CAREER: Motor, London, England, member of editorial staff, 1952-60, editor, 1962-67. Free-lance journalist, 1960-61. *Member:* Royal Automobile Club.

WRITINGS: Turn Left for Tangier, Temple Press Books, 1959; *Rally Manual*, Motor Racing Publications, 1961; *Racing Cars in Colour*, Batsford, 1962. Contributor to *Atlantic*, *Car and Driver*, *Auto-Visie*, and *Road and Track*.

BENTLEY, Janice Babb 1933-
(Janice B. Babb)

PERSONAL: Born January 13, 1933, in Philadelphia, Pa.; daughter of John William and Janice (Whittier) Babb; married Charles A. Bentley, September 10, 1966. *Education:* University of Illinois, A.B., 1954, M.S., 1956. *Politics:* Republican. *Home:* 1825 North Lincoln Plaza, Chicago, Ill. 60614. *Office:* CNA Financial Corp., CNA Plaza, Chicago, Ill. 60685.

CAREER: National Association of Real Estate Boards, Chicago, Ill., librarian, 1956-59, director, department of information, 1960-63; CNA Financial Corp. (formerly Continental National American Group), Chicago, Ill., librarian, 1963—. *Member:* American Association of Law Libraries, American Documentation Institute (secretary-treasurer of Chicago chapter, 1963), Special Libraries Association (chairman of planning, building and housing section, 1962-63; vice-chairman of social science division, 1964-65; chairman of social science division, 1965-66; president, Illinois chapter, 1967-68; chairman, insurance division, 1974-75).

WRITINGS—Under name Janice B. Babb: (With Beverly F. Dordick) *Real Estate Information Sources*, Gale, 1963; (with Dordick) *Real Estate Appraisal Bibliography*, American Institute of Real Estate Appraisers, 1964.

* * *

BENZ, Ernst (Wilhelm) 1907-

PERSONAL: Born November 17, 1907, in Friedrichshafen, Germany; son of Ernst (an engineer) and Lina Bofinger) Benz; married Dr. Brigitte von Boxberger, October 16, 1950; children: Sebastian, Balthasar, Stefan. *Education:* University of Tuebingen, Dr. phil., 1929; University of Berlin, Lic. theol., 1931; also attended University of Rome. *Religion:* Evangelical. *Home:* Lutherstrasse 7a, Marburg (Lahn), Hessen, Germany. *Office:* ·Philipps-Universitaet Marburg, Theological Faculty, Marburg (Lahn), Germany.

CAREER: University of Halle-Wittenberg, Halle, Germany, docent, 1932-35; Philipps-Universitaet Marburg, Marburg (Lahn), Germany, professor extraordinarius of church history, 1935-37, professor ordinarius, 1937—. Academy of Sciences and Literature, Mainz, Germany, member, 1949—; Doshisha University, Kyoto, Japan, guest professor, 1957-58; Academy Septentrionale, Paris, France, member, 1958—; Harvard Divinity School, Cambridge, Mass., guest professor, spring, 1960. Member of German UNESCO Commission, 1963—. *Member:* American Academy of Arts and Sciences (foreign-honorary). *Awards, honors:* Doctor of Theology, University of Marburg, 1948, Institut Orthodoxe St. Serge, Paris, 1961.

WRITINGS: Das Todesproblem in der Stoa, Kohlhammer, 1929; *Marius Victorinus und die Entwicklung der abendlaendischen Willensmetaphysik*, Kohlhammer, 1932; *Ecclesia Spiritualis: Die Geschichtsanschauung und Kirchenidee der franziskanischen Reformation*, 1934, reprinted, Wissenschaftliche Buchgesellschaft, 1964; *Der vollkommene Mensch nach Jacob Boehme*, Kohlhammer, 1937; *Nietzsches Ideen zur Geschichte des Christentums*, Kohlhammer, 1938; *Leibniz und Peter der Grosse*, de Gruyter, 1947; *Emanuel Swedenborg: Naturforscher und Seher*, Hermann Rinn, 1948, 2nd edition, two volumes, Swedenborg-verlag, 1969; *Swedenborg in Deutschland*, Klostermann, 1948; *Wittenberg und Byzanz*, Elwert, 1949, 2nd edition, W. Fink, 1971; *Die Ost-Kirche und die russische Christenheit*, 1949.

Die abendlaendische Sendung der oestlich-orthodoxen Kirche, Steiner-Verlag, 1950; *Indische Einfluesse auf die fruehchristliche Theologie*, Steiner-Verlag, 1951; *Paulus als Visionaer*, Steiner-Verlag, 1952; *Bischofsamt und apostolische Sukzession*, Evangelische Verlagswerk, 1953; *Die Ostkirche im Lichte der protestantischen Geschichtsschreibung von der Reformation*, Karl Alber, 1953; *Augustins Lehre von der Kirche*, Steiner-Verlag, 1954; *Schelling, Werden und Wirken seines Denkens*, Rhein-Verlag, 1955; *Schellings theologische Geistesahnen*, Steiner-Verlag, 1955; *Geist und Leben der Ostkirche*, Rowohlt, 1957, translation by Richard and Clara Winston published as *The Eastern Orthodox Church: Its Thought and Life*, Anchor Books, 1963, 2nd German edition, W. Fink, 1971; *Die christliche Kabbala*, Rhein-Verlag, 1958; *Der Prophet Jacob Boehme*, Steiner-Verlag, 1959; *Die Bedeutung der griechischorthodoxen Kirche fuer das Abendland*, Steiner-Verlag, 1959.

Ideen zu einer Theologie der Religionsgeschichte, Steiner-Verlag, 1960; *Kirchengeschichte in oekumenischer Sicht*, E. J. Brill, 1961; *Zen in europaeischer Sicht*, O. W. Barth-Verlag, 1962; (with Hans Thurn and Constantin Floros) *Das Buch der heiligen Gesaenge der Ostkirche*, Furche-Verlag, 1962; *Die protestantische Thebais*, Steiner-Verlag, 1963; *Asiatische Begegnungen*, E. Diederichs-Verlag, 1963; *Buddhas Wiederkehr und die Zukunft Asiens*, Nymphenburger Verlagshandlung, 1963, translation by Richard and Clara Winston published as *Buddhism or Communism: Which Holds the Future of Asia?*, Doubleday, 1965; *Patriarchen und Einsiedler*, E. Diederichs-Verlag, 1964; *Schoepfungsglaube und Endzeiterwartung*, Nymphenburger Verlagshandlung, 1965; translation by Heinz G. Frank published as *Evolution and Christian Hope*, Doubleday, 1966; *Die Vision: Erfahrungsformen und Bilderwelt*, Ernst Klett-Verlag, 1969.

Der Heilige Geist in Amerika, E. Diederichs-Verlag, 1970; *Neue Religionen*, Ernst Klett-Verlag, 1971; *Das Recht auf Faulheit*, Ernst Klett-Verlag, 1974.

Editor: (with Heinz Renkewitz) *Zinzendorf-Gedenkbuch*, Evangelisches Verlagswerk, 1951; (with L. A. Zander) *Evangelisches und orthodoxes Christentum in Begegnung und Auseinandersetzung*, Agentur des Rauhen Hauses, 1952; *Russische Heiligenlegenden*, Verlag Die Waage, 1953; *Adam, Der Muthus vom Urmenschen*, O. W. Barth-Verlag, 1955.

(With Minoru Nambara) *Das Christentum und die nichtchristlichen Hochreligionen*, E. J. Brill, 1960; *Der Uebermensch*, Rhein-Verlag, 1961; *Messianische Kirken, Sekten und Bewegungen im heutigen Afrika*, E. J. Brill, 1965; (and author of introduction) Ernesto Buonaiuti, *Die exkommunizierte Kirche*, Rhein-Verlag, 1966.

Contributor: Mircea Eliade and J. M. Kitagawa, editors, *The History of Religions: Essays in Methodology*, University of Chicago Press, 1959; Gerald H. Anderson, editor, *The Theology of the Christian Mission*, McGraw, 1961.

WORK IN PROGRESS: Research on the encounter of Christianity with non-Christian religions, history of Christian mysticism, and Eastern Orthodox Church and its ecumenical relations.

SIDELIGHTS: "Benz is interested in the history of nature and the future of man," commented *The Christian Century*, and "uses the telescope to search for the history of salvation in the history of the evolution of life in the cosmos.... Beginning with the earliest Christian era, [he] traces [in *Evolution and Christian Hope*] the process by which the initial radical eschatological expectation has changed under the impact of disappointment.''

Benz has traveled in Russia, the Balkans, Turkey, Greece, India, Pakistan, Ceylon, Burma, Thailand, the Philippines, Japan, Hong Kong, and Latin America.

BIOGRAPHICAL/CRITICAL SOURCES: Gerhard Mueller and Winfried Zeller, editors, *Glaube, Geist, Geschichte: Festschrift fuer Ernst Benz zum 60*, E. J. Brill, 1967.

*   *   *

BENZIGER, James   1914-

PERSONAL: Born March 31, 1914, in New York, N.Y.; son of George Joseph and Helen (Brown) Benziger; married Patricia Rey (a teacher), January 10, 1944; children: Bradford, Kathrine, Vincent. *Education:* Princeton University, B.A., 1936, Ph.D., 1941. *Politics:* Democrat. *Religion:* Episcopalian. *Home:* 404 West Walnut St., Carbondale, Ill. *Office:* Southern Illinois University, Carbondale, Ill.

CAREER: Employed by *New York Journal of Commerce*, New York, N.Y., 1936-37; Northwestern University, Evanston, Ill., instructor in English, 1940-41; New York University, New York, N.Y., member of faculty, 1946; Carleton College, Northfield, Minn., assistant and associate professor, 1946-50; Southern Illinois University, Carbondale, 1950—, began as associate professor, became professor of English. *Military service:* U.S. Army Air Forces, 1941-45; became captain. *Member:* Modern Language Association of America.

WRITINGS: Images of Eternity: Studies in the Poetry of Religious Vision from Wordsworth to T. S. Eliot, Southern Illinois University Press, 1962.

AVOCATIONAL INTERESTS: Gardening, hiking, reading who-done-its.†

*   *   *

BERESFORD, Maurice Warwick   1920-

PERSONAL: Born February 6, 1920, in Sutton, Coldfield, Warwickshire, England; son of Harry Bertram (a clerk) and Nora Elizabeth (Jefferies) Beresford. *Education:* Jesus College, Cambridge, B.A., 1941, M.A., 1945. *Politics:* Socialist. *Home:* 10 Holt Close, Leeds 16, Yorkshire, England. *Office:* University of Leeds, Leeds, England.

CAREER: University of Leeds, Leeds, England, lecturer in economic history, 1948-55, reader, 1955-59, professor of economic history, 1959—, dean, 1958-60, chairman of School of Economic Studies, 1965-68 and 1971-72, chairman of faculty board, 1968-70. Adult Education Centre, Rugby, warden, 1943-48; Yorkshire Citizens Advice Bureau Committee, chairman, 1962—; Yorkshire Dales National Park Committee, 1964-71; Leeds Probation Committee member, 1972—.

WRITINGS: The Leeds Chamber of Commerce, E. J. Arnold, 1951; *The Lost Villages of England*, Lutterworth, 1956; *History on the Ground*, Lutterworth, 1957, revised edition, 1971; (with J. K. S. St. Joseph) *Medieval England: An Aerial Survey*, Cambridge University Press, 1958; (editor with G. R. Jones) *Leeds and Its Region*, British Association for the Advancement of Science, 1967; *New Towns of the Middle Ages: Town Plantation in England, Wales, and Gascony*, Praeger, 1967; (editor with John Hurst) *Deserted Medieval Villages: Studies*, Lutterworth, 1971; St.

Martin's, 1972; (with H. P. Finberg) *English Medieval Boroughs: A Hand-List*, Rowman & Littlefield, 1973. Contributor to economics and history journals.

AVOCATIONAL INTERESTS: The cinema as a serious art, music, walking, travel, theatre, maps.†

*   *   *

BERG, Irwin August   1913-

PERSONAL: Born October 9, 1913, in Chicago, Ill.; son of Bertil Sigfried and Clara (Anderson) Berg; married Sylvia Maria Taipale, March 4, 1939; children: Karen Astrid (Mrs. Albert Kirby). *Education:* Knox College, A.B. (cum laude), 1936; University of Michigan, A.M., 1940, Ph.D., 1942. *Religion:* Lutheran. *Home:* 853 Dubois Dr., Baton Rouge, La. 70808. *Office:* Department of Psychology, Louisiana State University, Baton Rouge, La. 70803.

CAREER: American Board of Examiners in Professional Psychology, diplomate in counseling psychology, Western Electric Co., Chicago, Ill., personnel counselor, 1936-39; University of Illinois, Urbana, assistant professor of psychology, 1942-47; Pomona College, Claremont, Calif., associate professor of psychology, 1947-48; Northwestern University, Evanston, Ill., associate professor of psychology, 1948-55; Louisiana State University, Baton Rouge, professor of psychology, 1955—, chairman of department of psychology, 1955-66, dean of College of Arts and Sciences, 1965—. *Member:* American Psychological Association (fellow in clinical counseling, and in teaching of psychology), Southeastern Psychological Association (president, 1962-63), Southwestern Psychological Association (president, 1963-64), Phi Beta Kappa, Sigma Xi.

WRITINGS: (With L. A. Pennington) *Introduction to Clinical Psychology*, Ronald, 3rd edition, 1966; (editor with B. M. Bass) *Objective Approaches to Personality Assessment*, Van Nostrand, 1959; (editor with Bass) *Symposium on Conformity and Deviation*, Harper, 1961; (editor) *Response Set in Personality Assessment*, Aldine, 1967; (contributor) T. S. Krawiec, editor, *The Psychologists*, Oxford University Press, 1972. Editor, *Counseling News and Views*, 1950, and *Newsletter of Illinois Psychological Association*, 1950; column editor, *Journal of Counseling Psychology*, 1960-67.

*   *   *

BERG, Stephen   1934-

PERSONAL: Born August 2, 1934, in Philadelphia, Pa.; son of Harry Sidney (a businessman) and Hilda (Wachansky) Berg; married Millie Lane, August 26, 1959; children: Clair, Margot. *Education:* Attended University of Pennsylvania, three years, Boston University, one year, and University of Indiana, School of Letters, one summer; State University of Iowa, B.A., 1959. *Office:* Philadelphia College of Art, Philadelphia, Pa.

CAREER: Temple University, Philadelphia, Pa., instructor in English, beginning 1963; now teaching at Philadelphia College of Art, Philadelphia, Pa. *Awards, honors:* Frank O'Hara Poetry Prize, 1970.

WRITINGS: Berg-Goodman-Mezey, New Ventures Press (London), 1957; *Bearing Weapons* (poems), Cummington Press, 1963; (contributor of translations) *Cantico: A Selection*, by Jorge Guillen, Atlantic-Little, Brown, 1965; (editor with Robert Mezey; contributor) *Naked Poetry: Recent American Poetry in Open Forms*, Bobbs-Merrill, 1969; *The*

Queen's Triangle: A Romance, Cummington Press, 1970; *The Daughters: Poems*, Bobbs-Merrill, 1971; (compiler and contributor) *Between People: A Reader for Open Learning*, Scott, Foresman, 1972; (translator) Miklos Radnoti, *Clouded Sky*, Harper, 1972; *Nothing in the World: Versions of Aztec Poetry*, Grossman, 1972; (compiler with S. J. Marks) *About Women: An Anthology of Contemporary Fiction, Poetry, and Essays*, Fawcett, 1973. Contributor of poetry to *Paris Review, Yale Review, Poetry, Prairie Schooner, Chicago Review, Mademoiselle* and *New Yorker*. Poetry editor, *Saturday Evening Post*, 1961-62.

WORK IN PROGRESS: A second book of poems, an anthology of free verse, a long poem, and *Caros*, translations from Spanish poetry.

SIDELIGHTS: Berg writes: "Interested in most aspects of literature and philosophy. [Took] 2000 mile bike trip through Maritime Provinces when I was 15. Read a great deal. Translate Spanish, South American, and Mexican poetry."

BIOGRAPHICAL/CRITICAL SOURCES: Poetry, December, 1958.†

* * *

BERGE, Carol

PERSONAL: Surname pronounced Ber-*jhay*; born in New York, N.Y.; children: Peter. *Education:* Attended New York University, and New School for Social Research. *Address:* Thomas Jefferson College, Allendale, Mich. 49401.

CAREER: Editorial assistant and secretary with Simon & Schuster, *Forbes* magazine, and Hart Publishing Co., New York, N.Y., with Green-Brodie Advertising Agency, New York, N.Y., Pendray & Co. (public relations), New York, N.Y., assistant to the president; full-time writer, 1959—. Co-founder of a New York poetry group. *Member:* P.E.N., Authors Guild, Authors League, Coordinating Council of Literary Magazines (member of New York State Council Committee, 1972, 1974), National Society of Literature and the Arts, Committee of Small Magazine Editors and Publishers (member of board of directors, 1971-73), American Civil Liberties Union, National Organization for Women. *Awards, honors:* New York State Council on the Arts, Creative Artists Public Service Grant in fiction, for *Acts of Love*; MacDowell Colony, fellow, 1971, 1973, 1974.

WRITINGS—Poetry: *The Vulnerable Island*, Renegade Press, 1964; *Lumina*, Renegade Press, 1965; *Poems Made of Skin*, Weed/Flower Press, 1965; *Circles As In the Eye*, Desert Review Press, 1966; *The Chambers*, Aylesford Review Press, 1967; *An American Romance*, Black Sparrow Press, 1969; *From A Soft Angle: Poems About Women*, Bobbs-Merrill, 1971.

Prose: *The Vancouver Report*, Vector Press, 1964; *A Chronograph of the Poets*, Interim Press, 1965; *The Unfolding*, Part I, Theo Press, 1969; *A Couple Called Moebius* (stories and novellas), Bobbs-Merrill, 1972; *Acts of Love: An American Novel*, Bobbs-Merrill, 1973.

Contributor to *Four Young Lady Poets*, Totem/Corinth, 1962; *Erotic Poetry: Classical to Contemporary*, edited by William Cole, Random House, 1963; *Of Poetry and Power: Poems Occasioned by the Presidency and by the Death of John F. Kennedy*, edited by Paul Schwaber and Erwin A. Glikes, Basic Books, 1964; *Kulchur Anthology of Poetry*, Kulchur Magazine, 1966. Poetry represented in other anthologies including *Poems from the Third World*, Double-

day, 1972; *House of Good Porportions*, Simon & Schuster, 1973. Contributor to *Beautitude East, Nation, Genesis West, Nomad, Mica, Poems From Deux Magots, Seventh St. Quarterly, Origin, Recall, El Corno Emplumado, F—You: A Magazine of the Arts, Teekkari B.* (Finland), *Judson Review, Siempre!* (Mexico), *Outburst, Midwest, Beloit Poetry Journal, Aylesford Review* (England), *Insect Trust Gazette, Imago, Yowl, Fluxus, Joglars, Sum, Blue Beat, Poetry* (Chicago), *Grist, Dream Sheet, Tish* (Canada), *Some/Thing, East Village Other, Village Voice, Chelsea, Partisan Review, Film Culture, Aphra, Sunbury, 13th Moon*, and other publications.

Editor, *New York Poets' Section*, Volume 63, (University of Waterloo), 1965-66; editor, *Center* (a magazine for innovative poets), 1971—.

WORK IN PROGRESS: Visual Purple, poetry; *Slander and Gossip*, short stories and novellas; two novels: *In Motion*, and *Arch of Desire*.

SIDELIGHTS: Ms. Berge writes: "I am interested in people and in their environments. Prose as a medium is easily as interesting to me as poetry, and is much more difficult. I enjoy challenge: it causes growth. Writing is part of life, not vice versa. When reviewing a book or the work of a filmmaker or such, I'm interested in sharing my excitement with the reader. The best audience is composed of students. Second-best is an audience of non-writers. Communication is vital to change.

"For me, the most interesting writers who've worked in the prose medium have been Lady Murasaki, Tolstoi (and not because I am half Russian), D. H. Lawrence, Isak Dinesen. I admire Nadine Gordimer and Shirley Jackson among the modern women, and Hubert Selby Jr., Fielding Dawson, LeRoi Jones, and John Cage, of the men. The only poet who has equalled the scope of any good novelist in dealing with the human as an entity existing in a time/space continuum is Charles Olson. Poetry seems a beautiful and too-precious art which has for me led directly to prose: the wideness of the life experience." She adds: "My all-time poet people are Browning, Dylan Thomas, LeRoi Jones, Charles Olson, Chaucer, Ginsberg, Shakespeare, Han Shan: who open doors."

Ms. Berge has given readings at many universities and colleges including Long Island University, University of New Mexico, University of British Columbia, Highlands University, San Francisco State College (now University), University of California, Redlands University, and has also read in cafes and on radio programs in New York, Washington, D.C., and Mexico.

BIOGRAPHICAL/CRITICAL SOURCES: Teekkari B (Finland), spring, 1963; *Seawanhaka* (Long Island University), March, 1964; *Times Literary Supplement*, August 6, 1964; *New York World Telegram and Sun*, November 20, 1964.

* * *

BERGER, H. Jean 1924-

PERSONAL: Born April 24, 1924, in Broken Bow, Neb.; daughter of Stuart A. and Eglantine (Bolles) Berger. *Education:* State University of New York College at Buffalo, B.S., 1945; New York University, M.A., 1949, Ed.D., 1958. *Home:* 30 Huyler Ct., Setauket, N.Y.

CAREER: Teacher at schools in Springville, N.Y., 1946-48, and Bay Shore, N.Y., 1948-50; State University of New York College at Cortland, associate professor of physical education, 1950-58; New York University, New York, N.Y., associate professor of education, 1958-66; Three Village Schools, Setauket, N.Y., coordinator of girls' secondary physical education, 1966—. *Member:* American Association for Health, Physical Education and Recreation, (National Education Association), National Association for Physical Education of College Women, Eastern Association for Physical Education of College Women, New York Association for Health, Physical Education, and Recreation, Association for Women in Physical Education in New York State, Order of the Eastern Star.

WRITINGS: (Compiler) *Inspirational Poetry for Youth and Camp Groups*, Burgess, 1958; *Program Activities for Camps*, Burgess, 1961, revised edition, 1966.

AVOCATIONAL INTERESTS: Travel, camping, photography, sailing, and cone craft.

*   *   *

BERGER, Marjorie Sue 1916-

PERSONAL: Born January 4, 1916, in Chicago, Ill.; daughter of Henry A. and Dorothy (Cole) Berger. *Education:* University of Chicago, B.A., 1941; The American University, graduate study, 1943-44; Massachusetts Institute of Technology, special study, summer, 1961. *Home:* 400 East Randolph, Chicago, Ill., 60601. *Office:* American Society of Planning Officials, 1313 East 60th St., Chicago 37, Ill.

CAREER: U.S. Office of Price Administration, economist in Foreign Information Branch, Washington, D.C., 1942-44, economist in Office of Economic Adviser, Washington, D.C., 1944-45; price economist in Chicago, Ill., 1946; American Society of Planning Officials, Chicago, Ill., assistant to director, 1947-53, assistant director, 1953-65, associate director, 1965-74, special projects, 1974—. *Member:* International Federation for Housing and Planning (secretary of U.S. committee, 1957-60; advisory committee, World Congress, 1960, and 1968; international film competition jury, 1964; U.S. member of council, 1970—); American Association of Junior Colleges, Task Force on Public Service Career Education, 1970-71.

WRITINGS: (Co-author) *British Wartime Price Administration*, Office of Price Administration, 1942; (co-author) *Effect of the War on the British Retail Trade*, Office of Price Administration, 1943; *Opportunities in City Planning*, Vocational Guidance Manuals, 1961; (contributor) W. M. Arnold, editor, *Career Opportunities: Community Service and Related Specialists*, Doubleday, 1970. Editor, American Society of Planning Officials, annual conference proceedings, 1948-55, and monthly newsletter, 1950-68.

WORK IN PROGRESS: Editing a volume of selected editorials, speeches, and research papers of the late Dennis O'Harron, executive director of American Society of Planning Officials.

*   *   *

BERGSON, Abram 1914-

PERSONAL: Born April 21, 1914, in Baltimore, Md.; son of Isaac and Sophie (Rabinovich) Burk; married Rita S. Macht, November 5, 1939; children: Judith, Emily, Lucy. *Education:* Johns Hopkins University, A.B., 1933; Harvard University, Ph.D., 1940. *Home:* 334 Marsh St., Belmont, Mass. 02178. *Office:* Harvard University, Cambridge 38, Mass.

CAREER: Harvard University, Cambridge, Mass., in-

structor in economics, 1937-38, 1939-40; University of Texas, Austin, assistant professor of economics, 1940-42; U.S. government, Washington, D.C., economist with various agencies, including Russian section, U.S. Office of Strategic Services, 1942-46; Columbia University, New York, N.Y., associate professor, 1946-50, professor of economics, 1950-56; Harvard University, professor of economics, 1956—, director of Russian Research Center, 1964-68. Member of American delegation, Moscow Reparations Conference, 1945; chairman, Social Science Research Council and American Council of Learned Societies Joint Committee on Slavic Studies, 1960-62; member of board of directors, Social Science Research Council, 1962—; consultant, RAND Corp., 1948—. *Member:* Econometric Society (fellow), American Academy of Arts and Sciences (fellow), American Philosophical Society, Harvard Club (New York).

WRITINGS: The Structure of Soviet Wages, Harvard University Press, 1944; (editor) *Soviet Economic Growth*, Row, Peterson, 1953; *Real National Income of Soviet Russia Since 1928*, Harvard University Press, 1961; (editor with Simon S. Kuznets) *Economic Trends in the Soviet Union*, Harvard University Press, 1963; *Economics of Soviet Planning*, Yale University Press, 1964.

*   *   *

BERKHOFER, Robert Frederick, Jr. 1931-

PERSONAL: Born November 20, 1931, in Teaneck, N.J.; son of Robert F. and Elsa (Techow) Berkhofer; married Genevieve Zito (a teacher), June 9, 1962. *Education:* State University of New York at Albany, B.A., 1953; Cornell University, M.A., 1955, Ph.D., 1960. *Home:* 13 Westbury Ct., Ann Arbor, Mich. 48105. *Office:* Department of History, University of Michigan, Ann Arbor, Mich. 48104.

CAREER: U.S. Department of Justice, Washington, D.C., research analyst, 1955-56; Ohio State University, Columbus, instructor, 1959-60; University of Minnesota, Minneapolis, instructor, 1960-62, assistant professor, 1962-65, associate professor of American history, 1965-69; University of Wisconsin, Madison, professor of American history, 1969-73; University of Michigan, Ann Arbor, professor of American history, 1973—. *Member:* American Historical Association, American Studies Association, Organization of American Historians. *Awards, honors:* McKnight Foundation Prize for *Salvation and the Savage*; senior fellow, National Endowment for the Humanities, 1973-74.

WRITINGS: Salvation and the Savage: An Analysis of Protestant Missions and American Indian Response, 1787-1862, University of Kentucky Press, 1965; *A Behavioral Approach to Historical Analysis*, Free Press, 1969; (editor) *The American Revolution*, Little, Brown, 1971.

WORK IN PROGRESS: Three books: on the idea of the Indian and native American history, on the search for structure in American history, and on the evolution of American society.

*   *   *

BERLYNE, D(aniel) E(llis) 1924-

PERSONAL: Born April 25, 1924, in Salford, England; son of Mark and Cissie (Spurgin) Berlyne; married Hilde Strauss, 1953; children: Judith, Deborah, Naomi. *Education:* Cambridge University, B.A., 1947, M.A., 1949; Yale University, Ph.D., 1953. *Home:* 25 Clarendon Ave.; Toronto, Ontario M4V 1H8, Canada. *Office:* Psychology

Department, University of Toronto, Toronto, Ontario M5S 1A1, Canada.

CAREER: University of St. Andrews, St. Andrews, Scotland, lecturer in psychology, 1948-52; University of Aberdeen, Aberdeen, Scotland, 1953-57, began as lecturer, became senior lecturer in psychology, 1953-57; University of California, Berkeley, visiting associate professor of psychology, 1957-58; University of Geneva, Geneva, Switzerland, member-resident of Centre International d'Epistemologie Genetique, 1958-59; National Institute of Mental Health, Washington, D.C., visiting scientist, Laboratory of Psychology, 1959-60; Boston University, Boston, Mass., associate professor of psychology, 1960-62; University of Toronto, Toronto, Ontario, 1962—, began as associate professor, currently professor of psychology. University of Vermont, visiting summer professor, 1952, 1954. *Military service:* British Army, Intelligence Corps, 1943-46; served in North Africa, Corsica, Italy, and Malta.

MEMBER: British Psychological Society (fellow), American Psychological Association (fellow), Canadian Psychological Association (fellow), Royal Society of Canada (fellow), American Association for the Advancement of Science, International Association of Empirical Aesthetics, Interamerican Society of Psychology, Experimental Psychology Society, Psychonomic Society, Sigma Xi. *Awards, honors:* Center for Advanced Study in the Behavioral Sciences fellow, 1956-57.

WRITINGS: Conflict, Arousal and Curiosity, McGraw, 1960; (with Jean Piaget) *Theorie du Comportement et Operations*, Presses Universitaires de France, 1960; *Structure and Direction in Thinking*, Wiley, 1965; *Aesthetics and Psychobiology*, Appleton, 1971; (editor with K. B. Madsen) *Pleasure, Reward Preference*, Academic Press, 1973; (editor) *Studies in the New Experimental Aesthetics*, V. H. Winston, 1974. Contributor to psychology journals in Britain, Canada, and United States.

* * *

BERMAN, Ronald 1930-

PERSONAL: Born December 15, 1930, in New York, N.Y.; son of Herman and Jean (Wolfson) Berman; married Barbara Barr, August 29, 1953; children: Andrew, Julia, Katherine. *Education:* Harvard University, A.B., 1952; Yale University, M.A., 1957, Ph.D., 1959. *Residence:* Washington, D.C. *Office:* Office of the Chairman, The National Endowment for the Humanities, Washington, D.C. 20506.

CAREER: Columbia University, New York, N.Y., instructor, 1959-61, assistant professor of English, 1961-62; Kenyon College, Gambier, Ohio, associate professor of English, 1962-65; University of California, San Diego, associate professor, 1965-68, professor of English, 1968-71; National Endowment for the Humanities, Washington, D.C., chairman, 1971—. *Military service:* U.S. Naval Reserve, Intelligence, 1952-56; became lieutenant. *Awards, honors:* H.H.D. from George Washington University, 1974, LL.D. from St. Anselm's College, 1974, L.H.D. from Hebrew Union College, 1974.

WRITINGS: Henry King and the Seventeenth Century, Oxford University Press, 1964; *A Reader's Guide to Shakespeare's Plays*, Scott, Foresman, 1965; *Henry V: A Collection of Critical Essays*, Prentice-Hall, 1968; *America in the Sixties*, Free Press, 1968. Contributor to *Shakespeare Quarterly, Sewanee Review, Moderna Sprak, Symposium*, and other literary reviews. Editorial associate, *Kenyon Review*.

SIDELIGHTS: In Jeffrey Hart's opinion, *America in the Sixties* "is an ambitious undertaking, but a successful one. Berman sets out to describe and evaluate the cultural-intellectual life of the decade, or at least the first eight years of it. With great skill, and with abundant and expert quotation, Berman manages an astonishing range of material.... His own stand is skeptical and critical, and he acknowledges a good point when it is made, whether by Left or Right.... I think an ethical position does underlie it all [and] Berman's own prose has a mordant concentration and irony that give a distinctive voice to his criticism, and is itself an instrument of judgment."

* * *

BERNARD, Oliver 1925-

PERSONAL: Surname is pronounced Ber-*nard*; born December 6, 1925, in Chalfont St. Peter, Buckinghamshire, England; son of Oliver Percy (an architect) and Edith Dora (Hodges) Bernard; married Jacqueline Guise (a dancer), October 12, 1959; children: Jonathan, Emma, Katharine. *Education:* Goldsmiths' College, University of London, B.A., 1953. *Home:* The Walnut Tree, Banham, Norwich, Norfolk, England.

CAREER: Drawing office assistant, 1941-42; book packer, 1942-43; seasonal farm worker, 1948-54; teacher of English in France and Corsica, 1948-50, 1954-55; advertising copywriter, 1958-64; Eye Grammar School, Eye, Suffolk, England, senior English master, 1964—. *Military service:* Royal Air Force, 1943-47; became leading aircraftsman. *Awards, honors:* Copywriting awards, 1959, 1961, and 1962, two from World's Press News and one from *New Statesman*.

WRITINGS: Country Matters and Other Poems, Putnam, 1960; (translator, editor, and author of introduction) *Rimbaud*, Penguin, 1962; (translator, and author of introduction) *Apollinaire: Selection Poems*, Penguin, 1965. Contributor of poems to *Poetry* (Chicago), *Botteghe Oscure, Encounter, Gemini, Listener, Times Literary Supplement*, and other publications.

SIDELIGHTS: Bernard told *CA* that he found advertising writing he did (for steel and steel products and engineering firms) "less dishonest than most other kinds, engineers being harder to deceive than the general public—on their own ground, at any rate."†

* * *

BERNSTEIN, Jeremy 1929-

PERSONAL: Born December 31, 1929, in Rochester, N.Y.; son of Philip Sidney (a rabbi) and Sophy (Rubin) Bernstein. *Education:* Harvard University, B.A., 1951, M.A., 1953, Ph.D., 1955. *Office:* Department of Physics, Stevens Institute of Technology, Hoboken, N.J. 07030.

CAREER: Research associate, Harvard University, 1955-57, Institute for Advanced Study, 1957-60, National Science Foundation and Brookhaven National Laboratory, 1960-62; New York University, New York, N.Y., associate professor of physics, 1962-67; Stevens Institute of Technology, Hoboken, N.J., faculty member of physics department, 1967—. *New Yorker*, New York, staff member, 1962—. Consultant to RAND Corp. and General Atomic Co. *Member:* American Physical Society, French Alpine Club, American Alpine Club. *Awards, honors:* Westinghouse Prize for science writing, 1964.

WRITINGS: The Analytical Engine: Computers, Past,

Present, and Future, Random House, 1964; *Ascent: Of the Invention of Mountain Climbing and Its Practice*, Random House, 1965; *A Comprehensible World: On Modern Science and Its Origins*, Random House, 1967; *Elementary Particles and Their Currents*, W. H. Freeman, 1968; *The Elusive Neutrino*, Division of Technical Information, U.S. Atomic Energy Commission, 1969; *The Wildest Dreams of Kew: A Profile of Nepal*, Simon & Schuster, 1970; *Einstein*, Viking, 1973. Contributor to *New Yorker*.

WORK IN PROGRESS: A series of articles and a book about Chamonix Valley and its climbing guides.

SIDELIGHTS: Bernstein spends three months a year abroad, usually in Switzerland, doing research in physics, climbing mountains and speaking French with the natives.†

* * *

BERRIGAN, Philip Francis 1923-

PERSONAL: Born October 5, 1923, in Two Harbors, Minn.; son of Thomas William (a labor official) and Freda (Fromhart) Berrigan; married Elizabeth McAlister, 1969. *Education:* College of the Holy Cross A.B., 1950; Loyola University, New Orleans, La., B.S., 1960; Xavier University, New Orleans, La., M.A., 1963. *Politics:* Independent (usually Democrat). *Home:* 1933 Park Ave., Baltimore, Md. 21217.

CAREER: Roman Catholic priest, member of St. Joseph's Society of the Sacred Heart (S.S.J.); ordained, 1955. Assistant pastor in Washington, D.C., 1955-56; parochial high school counselor, New Orleans, La., 1956-63; St. Joseph's Society of the Sacred Heart, New York, N.Y., director of promotion, 1963-64; Epiphany College, Newburgh, N.Y., instructor in English, for a period beginning in 1964. Active in anti-war movement, 1962—; frequent lecturer on Indochina, world hunger, the arms race, and Biblical perspectives on nonviolence; also involved in organizing small communities of nonviolent resistance to aspects of American militarism. *Military service:* U.S. Army, Artillery and Infantry, 1943-46; served in three European campaigns; became second lieutenant. *Member:* Catholic Peace Fellowship (co-founder; co-chairman).

WRITINGS: No More Strangers (essays), Macmillan, 1965; (contributor) John O'connor, editor, *American Catholic Exodus*, Corpus Books, 1968; *A Punishment for Peace*, Macmillan, 1969; *Prison Journals of a Priest Revolutionary*, compiled and edited by Vincent McGee, introduction by Daniel Berrigan, Holt, 1970; *Widen the Prison Gates*, Simon & Schuster, 1973. Contributor of articles to *Commonweal, Jubilee, Catholic Worker, Interracial Review*, and other publications.

SIDELIGHTS: Berrigan was indicted and convicted four times by federal and state authorities for his anti-war activities, and served a total of thirty-nine months in federal prisons as a result. Berrigan told *CA* that his work "centers currently on Biblical nonviolence as a measure of sanity, resistance to the State and survival."

BIOGRAPHICAL/CRITICAL SOURCES: New Yorker, March 14, 1970; Francine du Plessix Gray, *Divine Disobedience: Profiles in Catholic Radicalism*, Hamish Hamilton, 1970, Vintage, 1971.

* * *

BERRY, Brian J(oe) L(obley) 1934-

PERSONAL: Born February 16, 1934, in Sedgley, Staffordshire, England; naturalized U.S. citizen; son of Joe (an engineer) and Alice (Lobley) Berry; married Janet Shapley, September 6, 1958; children: Duncan, Carol, Diane. *Education:* University College, University of London, B.Sc. (first class honors), 1955; University of Washington, Seattle, M.A., 1956, Ph.D., 1958. *Home address:* P.O. Box 190, Park Forest, Ill. 60466. *Office:* Department of Geography, University of Chicago, 5828 University Ave., Chicago, Ill. 60637.

CAREER: University of Washington, Seattle, instructor in civil engineering and geography, 1957-58; University of Chicago, Chicago, Ill., assistant professor, 1958-62, associate professor, 1962-65, professor of geography, 1965-72, Irving B. Harris Professor of Urban Geography, 1972—. Consultant: City of Chicago, 1961-65; Northeastern Illinois Planning Commission, 1963-65; Canada Land Inventory, 1964; Metropolitan Toronto Planning Board, 1964-65; U.S. Department of Agriculture, 1965-66; U.S. Bureau of Public Roads, 1965-66; Ford Foundation, Metropolitan Planning Organization, Calcutta, India, 1962; Economic Development Administration, 1966-70; World Bank, 1970-74.

MEMBER: International Geographical Union, National Academy of Sciences—Social Science Research Council, American Geographical Society, American Statistical Association, Association of American Geographers (secretary and treasurer of West Lakes division, 1960-61; division chairman, 1961-62), Econometric Society, Institute of British Geographers, Royal Statistical Society, Regional Science Association, National Academy of Engineering, International Federation of Housing and Planning, International Sociological Association, National Science Foundation, Maconochie Foundation (honorary member), Sigma Xi, Lambda Alpha. *Awards, honors:* Association of American Geographers participation fellowship to XIXth International Geographical Congress, 1960; Social Science Research Council auxiliary research award, 1962; Association of American Geographers' award for meritorious contributions to the field of geography, 1968.

WRITINGS: (With W. L. Garrison and others) *Studies of Highway Development and Geographic Change*, University of Washington Press, 1959; (with others) *Commercial Structure and Commercial Blight: Retail Patterns and Processes in the City of Chicago*, Department of Geography, University of Chicago, 1963; *The Science of Geography*, National Academy of Sciences—National Research Council, 1965; (with Ranajit Dhar and others) *Essays on Commodity Flows and the Spatial Structure of the Indian Economy*, Department of Geography, University of Chicago, 1966; *Geography of Market Centers and Retail Distribution*, Prentice-Hall, 1967; (editor with Jack Meltzer) *Goals for Urban America*, Prentice-Hall, 1967; (compiler with Duane F. Marble) *Spatial Analysis: A Reader in Statistical Geography*, Prentice-Hall, 1968; (with Sandra J. Parsons and Rutherford H. Platt) *The Impact of Urban Renewal on Small Business: The Hyde Park-Kenwood Case*, Center for Urban Studies, University of Chicago, 1968; (with others) *A Strategic Approach to Urban Research and Development*, National Academy of Sciences—National Research Council, 1969.

(Editor with Frank E. Horton) *Geographic Perspectives on Urban Systems*, Prentice-Hall, 1970; (editor with K. B. Smith) *City Classification Handbook: Methods and Applications*, Wiley Interscience, 1972; *The Human Consequences of Urbanisation: Divergent Paths in the Urban Experience of the Twentieth Century*, St. Martin's, 1973; *Growth Centers in the American Urban System*, Ballinger, 1973, Volume I: *Community Development and Regional*

Growth in the Sixties and Seventies, Volume II: *Working Materials on the U.S. Urban Hierarchy and on Growth Center Characteristics Organized by Economic Regions*; (with Frank E. Horton) *Urban Environmental Management: Planning for Pollution Control*, Prentice-Hall, 1974; *Land Use, Urban Form and Environmental Quality*, University of Chicago, 1974; *Towards an Understanding of Metropolitan America*, National Academy of Sciences, 1974; *The Geography of Economic Systems*, Prentice-Hall, 1974.

Contributor: H. M. Mayer and C. F. Kohn, editors, *Readings in Urban Geography*, University of Chicago Press, 1959; Norton Ginsburg, *Atlas of Economic Development*, University of Chicago Press, 1961; Forest R. Pitts, editor, *Urban Systems and Economic Development*, School of Business Administration, University of Oregon, 1962; J. R. P. Friedmann and William Alonso, editors, *Regional Development and Planning*, Massachusetts Institute of Technology, 1964; P. M. Hauser and L. F. Schore, editors, *The Study of Urbanization*, Wiley, 1965; R. S. Thomas, *Areas of Economic Stress in Canada*, Queen's University, 1965.

Author of reports and studies for government agencies and of research papers. Contributor to *International Encyclopedia of the Social Sciences*; also contributor of articles and reviews to professional journals.

* * *

BERRY, Lloyd E(ason) 1935-

PERSONAL: Born August 1, 1935, in Houston, Tex.; son of Joel H. (a lawyer and banker) and Fay (Eason) Berry; married Elizabeth Moncrief Perry, December 28, 1955 (divorced, 1971); married Lynn Elizabeth Umstead, 1973; children: (first marriage) Susan Antoinette, Lloyd Eason, Jr., Sharon Louise. *Education:* Baylor University, student, 1953-56; University of North Carolina, B.A., 1957, M.A., 1958; Cambridge University, Ph.D., 1960. *Religion:* Baptist. *Home:* 913 Randy Lane, Columbia, Mo. 65201. *Office:* 202 Jesse Hall, University of Missouri-Columbia, Columbia, Mo. 65201.

CAREER: University of Illinois, Urbana, assistant professor, 1960-63, associate professor, 1963-66, professor of English, 1966-72, assistant chancellor, 1969-72; University of Missouri-Columbia, professor of English, 1972—, dean of graduate school and director of research, 1972—. Member of board of directors: University of Illinois YMCA, 1964-72, Camp Howard, 1965-67, National Academy for the Dance, 1967—, United Community Council of Champaign, 1969-72, Champaign Chamber of Commerce, 1971-72; associate member, Center for Advanced Study, University of Illinois, 1968-69; trustee, Carle Hospital Foundation, 1969—.

MEMBER: Modern Language Association of America, Modern Humanities Research Association, Renaissance English Text Society (member of executive council, 1965-73), Renaissance Society of America (member of advisory council, 1969-71, 1973—), Central Renaissance Conference (member of executive committee, 1969-70, 1973—), Bibliographical Society of America, Milton Society (member of executive committee, 1964-68), Cambridge Bibliographical Society (secretary for United States and Canada, 1960—), Association of Marshall Scholars (member of executive council, 1967—; secretary general, 1971—), Marshall Scholarships Commission (commissioner, 1970—), Urban League, Champaign-Urbana Civic Symphony Association, Phi Kappa Phi. *Awards, honors:* Carnegie Scholar, 1957-58; Marshall Scholar, 1958-60; University of Illinois faculty fellow, 1962; American Philosophical Society grant-in-aid, 1963, 1965; Folger Library fellow, 1965; Huntington Library fellow, 1966; John Simon Guggenheim fellow, 1966-67.

WRITINGS: A Bibliography of Studies in Metaphysical Poetry, 1939-1960, University of Wisconsin Press, 1964.

Editor: *The English Works of Giles Fletcher, the Elder*, University of Wisconsin Press, 1964; John Stubb, *Gaping Gulf: With Letters and Other Relevant Documents*, University Press of Virginia, 1968; (with Robert O. Crummey) *Rude and Barbarous Kingdom: Russia in the Accounts of Sixteenth-Century English Voyagers*, University of Wisconsin Press, 1968; (and author of introduction) *The Geneva Bible: A Facsimile Edition of the 1560 Edition*, University of Wisconsin Press, 1969; (co-editor) *The Dramatic Works of George Chapman*, University of Illinois Press, 1970.

Contributor of articles and notes to learned journals.

WORK IN PROGRESS: A critical edition of the complete works of Sir Thomas Elyot; the life and letters of Sir William Davison.

SIDELIGHTS: Rude and Barbarous Kingdom "is a most welcome compilation," according to the *Virginia Quarterly Review*, for the travelers' accounts "demonstrate the importance of Muscovite Russia to England . . . the English viewed this 'oriental' country as a bridge to the wealth of Asia and the Americas. . . . This book is carefully edited and of considerable scholarly value." *Avocational interests:* Sports, especially golf and tennis.

* * *

BERTIN, Leonard M. 1918-

PERSONAL: Born August 20, 1918, in London, England; son of Reginald B. (a clergyman) and Ethel (Chadwick) Bertin; married Eleonora Ferraris, July 5, 1947; children: Oliver Joseph Brackstone, Johanna Ethel Mary. *Education:* Attended Forest School, London, England, 1928-37; Selwyn College, Cambridge, B.A., 1953, M.A., 1956. *Religion:* Anglican. *Home:* 65 Hazelton Ave., Toronto 5, Ontario, Canada. *Office:* Simcoe Hall, University of Toronto, Toronto 5, Ontario, Canada.

CAREER: Daily Telegraph, London, England, reporter and foreign correspondent, 1946-48, science correspondent, 1949-57; *Financial Post*, Toronto, Ontario, science editor, 1957-59; *Toronto Daily Star, Star Weekly*, and *Canadian Weekly*, Toronto, science editor, 1959-64; University of Toronto, Toronto, science editor, Information Services, 1964—. Broadcaster on radio and television. Canadian Broadcasting Corp., technical consultant; Minister of Education's Museum of Science and Technology Committee, member. *Military service:* Royal Artillery, active duty, 1939-46; became honorary captain. *Member:* National Association of Science Writers, American Institute of Aeronautics and Astronautics.

WRITINGS: Atom Harvest, Secker & Warburg, 1955; *Boys' Book of Scientific Wonders and Inventions*, Burke Publishing Co., 1957; *Boys' Book of Engineering Wonders of the World*, Burke Publishing Co., 1957; *Target 2067: Canada's Second Century*, Macmillan, 1968. Contributor to *Encyclopaedia Britannica, Times, Saturday Review, Chatelaine, Discovery*, and other British, American, Canadian, French, German, and Italian periodicals. Consulting editor and chairman of advisory board, *Canadian Nuclear Technology*, 1960—.

WORK IN PROGRESS: A crime story.

SIDELIGHTS: Bertin is competent in French, Italian, Hindustani; he has traveled five continents, attended atomic and thermonuclear tests, and conferences on science, engineering, space, and mental health subjects. *Avocational interests:* Riding, swimming, squash, shooting, handy work.†

* * *

BERTRAM, (George) Colin (Lawder) 1911-

PERSONAL: Born April 27, 1911, in Worcester, England; son of Francis George Lawder (a civil servant) and Mabel (Smith) Bertram; married Kate Ricardo (a zoologist and college president), September 28, 1939; children: Mark, Brian, Roger, William. *Education:* St. John's College, Cambridge, M.A., 1937, Ph.D., 1939. *Religion:* Church of England. *Home:* Linton House, Linton, Cambridgeshire, England. *Agent:* John Farquharson Ltd., 15 Red Lion Sq., London W.C.1, England. *Office:* St. John's College, Cambridge, England.

CAREER: British Graham and Land Expedition, Antarctica, biologist, 1934-37; Palestine government, chief fisheries officer, 1940-44; Middle East Supply Centre, Cairo, fisheries adviser, 1944-45; Scott Polar Research Institute, Cambridge, England, director, 1949-56; Eugenics Society, London, England, general secretary, 1957-64; St. John's College, Cambridge University, Cambridge, England, 1945—, fellow, tutor, and senior tutor. Chairman, Marie Stopes Memorial Foundation, 1960-71. *Member:* Royal Geographical Society (honorary secretary), Fauna Preservation Society (member of council). *Awards, honors:* Polar Medal, 1939 Murchison Award of Royal Geographical Society, 1957.

WRITINGS: Arctic and Antarctic: The Technique of Polar Travel, Heffer, 1939; *Arctic and Antarctic: A Perspective of the Polar Regions,* Heffer, 1958; *Adam's Brood: Hopes and Fears of a Biologist,* P. Davies, 1959; *In Search of Mermaids: The Manatees of Guiana,* P. Davies, 1962, Crowell, 1964. Author of scientific papers, mainly zoological.

WORK IN PROGRESS: Zoological research on Sirenians; a book on pigeon buildings world-wide.

SIDELIGHTS: Bertram has traveled and worked on all seven continents, including arctic and antarctic regions.

* * *

BESSINGER, Jess B(alsor), Jr. 1921-

PERSONAL: Born September 25, 1921, in Detroit, Mich.; son of Jess Balsor and Elaine (Brown) Bessinger; married Elizabeth Lieber DuVally, July 12, 1956; children: Anthony DuVally, Jess Balsor III. *Education:* Rice Institute (now Rice University), B.A., 1943; Harvard University, M.A., 1947, Ph.D., 1952. *Home:* 393 Indian Ave., Middletown, R.I. 02840. *Office:* Department of English, New York University, Washington Sq., New York, N.Y. 10003.

CAREER: University of London, London, England, teaching associate in English, 1951-52; Brown University, Providence, R.I., assistant professor of English, 1952-56; University of Toronto, Toronto, Ontario, 1956-62, began as associate professor, became professor of English; New York University, New York, N.Y., professor of English, 1963—. *Military service:* U.S. Army, Military Intelligence, 1943-45; became technical sergeant. U.S. Army Reserve, 1948-53; became first lieutenant. *Member:* Mediaeval Academy of America, Modern Language Association of America. *Awards, honors:* Fulbright scholarship, 1951-53; Canada Council fellowship; Guggenheim fellowship.

WRITINGS: A Short Dictionary of Anglo-Saxon Poetry, University of Toronto Press, 1960; (editor with S. M. Parrish) *Proceedings of a Literary Data Processing Conference,* International Business Machines, 1964; (editor with Robert P. Creed) *Franciplegius: Medieval and Linguistic Studies in Honor of Francis P. Magoun, Jr.,* New York University Press, 1965; *A Concordance to Beowulf,* Cornell University Press, 1967. Author with A. D. Van Nostrand of "A Prospect of Literature," Ford Foundation series for educational television. Contributor of articles and reviews to learned periodicals.

WORK IN PROGRESS: A Computer Concordance to the Anglo-Saxon Poetic Records, completion expected in 1975.

* * *

BESTER, Alfred 1913-

PERSONAL: Born December 18, 1913, in New York, N.Y.; son of James J. (a shoe merchant) and Belle (Silverman) Bester; married Rolly Goulko (an advertising executive), September 16, 1936. *Education:* University of Pennsylvania, B.A., 1935. *Politics:* "Emotional liberal." *Religion:* Jew. *Home:* Red Hill Farm, Box 153, Ottsville, Pa. 18942. *Agent:* Lurton Blassingame, 60 East 42nd St., New York, N.Y. 10017.

CAREER: Full-time professional writer.

WRITINGS: Who He?, Dial, 1953; *The Demolished Man,* Shasta Press, 1953; *The Stars My Destination,* New American Library, 1957; *Starburst,* New American Library, 1958; *The Dark Side of the Earth,* New American Library, 1964. Writer of television scripts. Contributor to *Holiday, Show, Venture, Rogue.*

WORK IN PROGRESS: "My entire life is work in progress."

SIDELIGHTS: Bester told *CA:* "The greatest mistake of the twentieth century has been the exposure of artists' private lives to civilians. Civilians can't understand artists, and professional artists have no need to have other professionals' private lives described to them."

* * *

BESTIC, Alan Kent 1922-

PERSONAL: Born July 11, 1922, in London, England; son of Albert Arthur (a journalist, author, and master mariner) and Queenie (Kent) Bestic; married Patricia Geraghty, August 28, 1944; children: Paul, Penny, Richard, Amanda, Patrick. *Education:* Attended Irish schools. *Politics:* Socialist. *Home:* 173 York Rd., Woking, Surrey, England.

CAREER: Irish Times, Dublin, Ireland, reporter, 1940-44; *Irish Press,* Dublin, reporter, 1944-46, foreign correspondent, 1946-48; *People,* London, England, staff representative in Ireland, 1948-53, feature writer in London, 1953-57; feature writer in London for *Evening Standard,* 1957-58, and *Daily Herald,* 1958-60; free-lance writer, 1960—.

WRITINGS: The Girl Outside, Barrie & Rockliff, 1959; (with Richard Carlish) *King of Clubs,* Elek, 1962; *The Amorous Prawn* (novel adapted from play by Anthony Kimmins), Elek, 1963; (with Rudolf Vrba) *I Cannot Forgive,* Sidgwick & Jackson, 1963, Grove, 1964; *Turn Me On, Man,* Library 33, 1966, Award Books, 1968; (with Gary Sobers) *King Cricket,* Pelham Books, 1967; *The*

Importance of Being Irish, Morrow, 1969; *Praise the Lord and Pass the Contribution*, Taplinger, 1971; *Sex and the Singular English*, Taplinger, 1972. Contributor to numerous newspapers and magazines.

SIDELIGHTS: Bestic has covered most of Europe and the United States on writing assignments, as well as Siam, Malaya, and the Congo. He also covers a wide range of topics in his books. Reviewer Benedict Kiely recalled knowing Bestic when he "had the reputation of being the most alert young Irish journalist of his time." He added that wide experience and mature judgment resulted in "a lively and informative book [*The Importance of Being Irish*] that touches on everything from exports and economic progress ... to frog-jumping competitions in County Clare."

To reviewer Frank L. Ryan, "The importance of being Irish today lies in the Irishman's realization that, while there is an Irish nation with its unique characteristics, there is an Irish inter-nation the success of which depends to a great extent on the characteristics which are not solely Irish but belong to the family of man." He feels that while Bestic's surface intent is to contrast the Irish image of ethnic jokes, "Mother Machree," leprechauns, and the like, with Irish reality, his book's more vital purpose is to present modern Ireland with its progress and its difficulties in attempting "to take its place in the family of nations."

Praise the Lord and Pass the Contribution, Bestic's cross-country tour of American religionists as big-businessmen, was considered amusing and informative, although not well-balanced. Alan Seaburg pointed out that Bestic's compilation of American Churches is incomplete, because he ignores traditional churches to concentrate on the revivalists ... and on the sects." The *Times Literary Supplement* notes that he included "some Christians in the United States who are trying to tackle the problems of race and poverty ... admirable examples of the combination of faith and works, but appearing rather out of place wedged between his chapters on the religious mass-media con-men" and various sects.

"*Turn Me On Man* is a horror story," said *The Times Literary Supplement*, adding: "that addiction to any drug should be discouraged by the strongest methods possible ... is the conclusion reached by Alan Bestic, who presses it home by giving a collection of real case histories, which read like a series of headlines from the daily press."

*   *   *

BETTENSON, Henry (Scowcroft) 1908-

PERSONAL: Born October 5, 1908, in Bolton, Lancashire, England; son of Reginald (a clerk in Holy Orders) and Edith (Scowcroft) Bettenson; married, February 23, 1935; children: Matthew, Josephine Bettenson Ryan. *Education:* University of Bristol, B.A., 1931; Cuddesdon College, theological study, 1932-33; Oriel College, Oxford, B.A., 1938, M.A., 1942. *Home:* Purleigh Rectory, Chelmsford, Essex, England.

CAREER: Church of England, assistant priest in London, England, 1933-35, in Oxford, England, 1935-38, rector at Swerford, Oxfordshire, England, 1938-40; assistant master and chaplain at Wellingborough School, Northampshire, England, 1940-44; King's School, Canterbury, England, 1944-45, and Charterhouse School, Godalming, England, beginning, 1945; Purleigh Rectory, Essex, England, rector, 1969—. *Member:* Mind Association, Royal Institute of Philosophy.

WRITINGS: (Editor) *Documents of the Christian Church*, Oxford University Press, 1942, 2nd edition, 1963; (editor and translator) *The Early Christian Fathers*, Oxford University Press, 1956; (editor and translator) *The Later Christian Fathers*, Oxford University Press, 1970; (translator) Saint Aurelius Augustinus, *Concerning the City of God Against the Pagans*, Penguin Books, 1972. Contributor to theology and philosophy journals.†

*   *   *

BETTS, Doris (Waugh) 1932-

PERSONAL: Born June 4, 1932, in Statesville, N.C.; daughter of William Elmore and Mary Ellen (Freeze) Waugh; married Lowry Matthews Betts (an attorney), July 5, 1952; children: Doris LewEllyn, David Lowry, Erskine Moore II. *Education:* Attended University of North Carolina at Greensboro, 1950-53, University of North Carolina at Chapel Hill, 1954. *Politics:* Democrat. *Address:* P.O. Box 142, Sanford, N.C. 27330. *Office:* Department of English, University of North Carolina, Chapel Hill, N.C. 27514. *Agent:* Timothy Seldes, Russell & Volkening, Inc., 551 Fifth Ave., New York, N.Y. 10017.

CAREER: Has been a store clerk, secretary, and office manager; member of editorial staff of *Sanford Daily Herald*, Sanford, N.C., 1956-57, *North Carolina Democrat*, Raleigh, N.C., 1960-62; editor of *Sanford News Leader* (weekly), Sanford, N.C., 1962; University of North Carolina, Chapel Hill, N.C., member of faculty, department of English, 1966—, director of Freshman-Sophomore English, 1972—, associate professor of English, 1974—. Visiting lecturer in creative writing, Duke University, spring, 1971. Member of North Carolina Tercentenary Commission, 1961-62; board member, North Carolina Committee for Continuing Education in the Humanities, 1972—; staff member, Indiana University Summer Writers Conference, 1970-74, and Squaw Valley Writers Conference, 1974. *Awards, honors:* *Mademoiselle* College Fiction Contest, winner, 1953; Putnam-University of North Carolina $2,000 Fiction Award, 1954, for *The Gentle Insurrection*; Sir Walter Raleigh Award for Fiction, Historical Book Club of North Carolina, 1957, for *Tall Houses in Winter*, and 1965, for *The Scarlet Thread*. Guggenheim fellowship in fiction, 1958-59; National Book award finalist, 1974, for *Beasts of the Southern Wild*; University of North Carolina, Tanner award, 1973, for excellence in undergraduate teaching.

WRITINGS: *The Gentle Insurrection* (story collection), Putnam, 1954; *Tall Houses in Winter* (novel), Putnam, 1957; *The Scarlet Thread* (novel), Harper, 1964; *The Astronomer and Other Stories*, Harper, 1966; *The River to Pickle Beach* (novel), Harper, 1972; *Beasts of the Southern Wild and Other Stories*, Harper, 1973.

Short stories, originally published in *Redbook*, *Rebel*, *Woman's Day*, *Mademoiselle*, *Cosmopolitan*, *Ms.*, and literary reviews, have been anthologized in *Best American Short Stories*, *North Carolina in the Short Story*, *A New Southern Reader*, *Young Writers at Work*, *Red Clay Reader*, *Best Little Magazine Fiction*, *Archetypes in the Short Story*, *Red Clay Anthology*, and other collections. Contributor of articles and poems to literary magazines and journals.

WORK IN PROGRESS: A story collection; a novel about a cross-country kidnapping; a college rhetoric text.

SIDELIGHTS: Manuscripts and papers are being assembled by Boston University Libraries for the Doris Betts Collection. *Avocational interests:* Reading, camping, natural history, wilderness trips, birds.

BIOGRAPHICAL/CRITICAL SOURCES: Carolyn Riley, editor, *Contemporary Literary Criticism*, Volume III, Gale, 1975.

* * *

BEVAN, Bryan 1913-

PERSONAL: Born March 14, 1913, in London, England; son of Edmund Henry and Joan (Norton) Bevan. *Education:* Studied at Jesus College, Cambridge, 1932-35. *Politics:* Conservative. *Home:* 7 Bunsen Rd., Twickenham, Middlesex, England.

CAREER: British Embassy, Rio de Janeiro, Brazil, attache, 1938. *Member:* Society of Authors, St. James Club.

WRITINGS: The Real Francis Bacon, Centaur Press, 1960; *I Was James the Second's Queen*, Heinemann, 1963; *King James the Third of England*, R. Hale, 1967; *Nell Gwyn: Vivacious Mistress of Charles II*, R. Hale, 1969; *The Great Seamen of Elizabeth I*, R. Hale, 1971; *Charles the Second's French Mistress*, R. Hale, 1972; *James Duke of Monmouth*, R. Hale, 1973; *Marlborough the Man*, in press. Writer of British Broadcasting feature, "Trial of the Earl of Essex." Contributor to *Contemporary Review*, *Country Life*, and other periodicals.

SIDELIGHTS: Library Journal describes *Nell Gwyn: Vivacious Mistress of Charles II* as an "engaging biography" in which Bevan "uses Nell as a mirror of the times, reflecting the social, political, religious, and intellectual attitudes of the Restoration period." Bevan is competent in Italian and knows some Portuguese and French. *Avocational interests:* Travel.

* * *

BEVAN, Jack 1920-

PERSONAL: Born January 18, 1920, in Blackpool, England; son of Edwin James and Beatrice N. (Greaves) Bevan; married Katie O'Neill (a teacher) on March 27, 1962; children: Franco, Katie-Jane. *Education:* Cambridge University, M.A. (honors in English), 1943. *Home:* 9 Old Hill, Tettenhall, Wolverhampton, England. *Office:* General Studies Department, Wolverhampton College of Education, Wolverhampton, England.

CAREER: Nonington College, Kent, England, head of English and drama department, 1953-61; Liverpool College of Art, Liverpool, England, senior lecturer in liberal studies department, 1961-67; Wolverhampton College of Education, Wolverhampton, England, head of general studies department, 1967—. *Military service:* British Army, Royal Artillery, 1940-46. *Member:* P.E.N.

WRITINGS: Dragons' Teeth (poetry), Guild Press, 1957; *Brief Candles* (poetry), Outposts Publications, 1961; *Verse Translations of Salvatore Quasimodo*, Penguin, 1965; *My Sad Pharaohs* (poems), Routledge & Kegan Paul, 1968; (contributor) *Quasimodo e la Critica*, Mondadori, 1969; *Debit and Credit: Verse Translations of Salvatore Quasimodo*, Anvil Press, 1972. Poems broadcast on British Broadcasting Corp. "Third Programme," 1963-70. Contributor of verse and criticism to *Times Literary Supplement*, *English*, *New Opinion*, *New Voice*, *Minnesota Review*, *Southern Review*, *Listener*, *Stand*, *London Magazine*, and other periodicals.

WORK IN PROGRESS: Preparing a book of his own verse; translations of Italian poet Giuliano Dego's book *Solo L'ironia*.

SIDELIGHTS: Bevan has lived in Iceland and Italy, and traveled widely in Europe.

* * *

BEVINGTON, Helen 1906-

PERSONAL: Born April 2, 1906, in Afton, N.Y.; daughter of Charles Wesley (a preacher) and Elizabeth (Raymond) Smith; married Merle M. Bevington (a professor of English), June 1, 1928 (deceased); children: David M., Philip R. *Education:* University of Chicago, Ph.B., 1926; Columbia University, M.A., 1928. *Home:* 4428 Guess Rd., Durham, N.C. 27705. *Office:* Department of English, Duke University, Durham, N.C.

CAREER: Journal of Biological Chemistry, assistant editor, 1928; Bedford Academy, Brooklyn, N.Y., teacher, 1929-31; New York University, New York, N.Y., librarian, 1936-42; Duke University, Durham, N.C., associate professor, 1943-70, professor of English, 1970—. *Member:* American Association of University Professors, Modern Language Association of America, Phi Beta Kappa. *Awards, honors:* Roanoke-Chowan award for poetry, 1956, for *A Change of Sky*, and 1962, for *When Found, Make a Verse Of*; North Carolina Award for Literature, 1973.

WRITINGS: Dr. Johnson's Waterfall, and Other Poems, Houghton, 1946; *Nineteen Million Elephants, and Other Poems*, Houghton, 1950; *A Change of Sky, and Other Poems*, Houghton, 1956; *When Found, Make a Verse Of* (poems and prose), Simon & Schuster, 1961; *Charley Smith's Girl* (autobiography), Simon & Schuster, 1965; *A Book and a Love Affair* (autobiography), Harcourt, 1968; *The House Was Quiet and the World Was Calm* (autobiography), Harcourt, 1971; *Beautiful Lofty People* (literary essays), Harcourt, 1974. Contributor to *New Yorker*, *Atlantic*, *Saturday Review*, *New York Times Book Review*, and *American Scholar*.

SIDELIGHTS: Mrs. Bevington is primarily a writer of light verse. She writes: "Having a bad memory, I write mostly for notation, to use agreeable words and keep track of pleasures."

BIOGRAPHICAL/CRITICAL SOURCES: New York Times Book Review, June 6, 1965; *Atlantic*, July, 1965; *Book Week*, July 4, 1965; *Virginia Quarterly Review*, autumn 1965.

* * *

BEYER, Audrey White 1916-

PERSONAL: Born November 12, 1916, in Portland, Me.; daughter of William Joseph and Hermon (Brand) White; married Walter Archer Beyer (a teacher of mathematics), July 20, 1940; children: Henry G. II, Edmund Brand. *Education:* Westbrook Junior College (now Westbrook College), diploma, 1937; University of Maine, A.B., 1939, graduate study; Northeastern University, graduate study. *Politics:* Independent (registered Republican). *Religion:* Episcopalian. *Home:* Belfield Rd., Cape Elizabeth, Me.

CAREER: Teacher of English at Westbrook Junior College (now Westbrook College), Portland, Me., 1939-43, Milton Academy Girls' School, Milton, Mass., 1956, and Waynflete Summer School, 1957-59; Northeastern University, Boston, Mass., instructor in English, 1967-72; Milton Academy Boys' School, Milton, Mass., teacher of composition, 1973-74; private tutor in English. *Member:* Maine Historical Society. *Awards, honors:* Jack and Jill Award, 1958; Westbrook College Award for Alumnae Achievement, 1960.

WRITINGS: Capture at Sea (juvenile), Knopf, 1959; *The Sapphire Pendant*, Knopf, 1961; *Katharine Leslie*, Knopf, 1963; *Dark Venture*, Knopf, 1968.

WORK IN PROGRESS: A story for young adults based on nineteenth-century New England history.

SIDELIGHTS: Capture at Sea ran as a serial in *Jack and Jill*. *Avocational interests:* Reading, walking.

* * *

BIBBY, Cyril 1914-

PERSONAL: Born May 1, 1914, in Liverpool, England; son of William (a chemical worker) and Elizabeth Jane (Dolman) Bibby; married Frances Hirst (a teacher of handicapped children), August 15, 1936; children: Peter Conrad, John Michael, Helen Elisabeth, Gillian Margaret. *Education:* Queens' College, Cambridge, B.A., 1935, M.A., 1939; University of Liverpool, M.Sc., 1940; University of London, Ph.D., 1955. *Politics:* Socialist. *Religion:* Agnostic. *Home:* 246 Cottingham Rd., Hull, England. *Office:* College of Education, Cottingham, Rd., Hull, England.

CAREER: Oulton School, Liverpool, England, sixth form physics and chemistry master, 1935-38; Chesterfield School, Derbyshire, England, senior biology master, 1938-40; British Social Hygiene Council and Central Council for Health Education, London, England, education officer, 1941-46; College of S. Mark and S. John, London, England, principal lecturer in biology, and coordinator of sciences, 1946-59; Kingston upon Hull College of Education, Hull, England, principal, 1959—. Visiting professor at University of Illinois; lecturer at other U.S. universities and colleges. Co-organizer of Union Internationale des Organismes Familaux, 1946, and World Congress on Population, 1948. Member of executive, National Foundation for Educational Research; member of universities and colleges committee, Schools Broadcasting Council of United Kingdom. Producer of film-strips; broadcaster on British Broadcasting Corp. radio and television. *Member:* Royal Society of Arts (fellow), Eugenics Society (fellow), Linnean Society (fellow). *Awards, honors:* Silver Medal of Royal Society of Arts.

WRITINGS: The Evolution of Man and His Culture, Gollancz, 1938; *Heredity, Eugenics and Social Progress*, Gollancz, 1939; *Simple Experiments in Biology*, Heinemann, 1943; *Sex Education: A Guide for Parents, Teachers and Youth Leaders*, Macmillan, 1944; *How Life Is Handed On*, Nelson, 1946, Emerson, 1947; *Health Readers for Juniors*, Macmillan, 1948-50; *An Active Human Biology*, Heinemann, 1950; *Health Education: A Guide to Principles and Practice*, Heinemann, 1952; (with I. T. Morison) *The Human Body*, Penguin, 1955, revised edition published as *Your Body and How It Works*, McGraw, 1969; *Education in Racial and Intergroup Relations*, UNESCO, 1957; *Race, Prejudice and Education*, Heinemann, 1959, Praeger, 1967; *T. H. Huxley: Scientist, Humanist and Educator* (Book-of-the-Month Club selection), C. A. Watts, 1959, Horizon Press, 1960.

(Contributor) Albert Ellis, editor, *Encyclopedia of Sexual Behavior*, Hawthorn Press, 1961; (editor) *The First Fifty Years*, Hull College of Education, 1963; (contributor) Paul Nash and others, editors, *The Educated Man: Studies in the History of Educational Thought*, Wiley, 1965; *The Essence of T. H. Huxley*, Macmillan, 1967; *Biology of Mankind*, Heinemann, 1968; (contributor) A. J. Ayer, editor, *The Humanist Outlook*, Barrie & Rockliff, 1968; (contributor) Hermann Roehrs, editor, *Friedenspaedagogik*, Akademische Verlagsgesellschaft, 1970; *Scientist Extraordinary: T. H. Huxley*, St. Martin's, 1972 (published in England as *Scientist Extraordinary: The Life and Scientific Works of T. H. Huxley*, Pergamon, 1972); (editor) *T. H. Huxley on Education*, Cambridge University Press, 1973.

Contributor to proceedings and of over fifty articles to *Nature, Twentieth Century, Common Ground, Evidence, Victorian Studies, Research Review, Horizons, Child Care Quarterly Review, Better Health*, and others. Former joint editor of *Biology and Human Affairs, Health Education Journal*, and *Family*; member of editorial board, *Aspects of Education*.

WORK IN PROGRESS: Research on the cultural potential of scientific education; historical and literary study of limerick and verse-form; own cantos of verse.

* * *

BIGGLE, Lloyd, Jr. 1923-

PERSONAL: Born April 17, 1923, in Waterloo, Iowa; son of Lloyd B. (an electrician) and Ethel (Cruthers) Biggle; married Hedwig T. Janiszewski (a teacher of violin), June 21, 1947; children: Donna Helene, Kenneth Lloyd. *Education:* Wayne University (now Wayne State University), A.B. (with high distinction), 1947; University of Michigan, M.M., 1948, Ph.D., 1953. *Home:* 569 Dubie St., Ypsilanti, Mich.

CAREER: University of Michigan, Ann Arbor, teacher of music literature and history, 1948-51; self-employed, 1951—. Science fiction and mystery writer. *Military service:* U.S. Army, 102nd Infantry Division, World War II; became sergeant; received Purple Heart with oak leaf cluster.

WRITINGS—Novels, except as indicated: *The Angry Espers*, Ace Books, 1961; *All the Colors of Darkness*, Doubleday, 1963; *The Fury Out of Time*, Doubleday, 1965; *Watchers of the Dark*, Doubleday, 1966; *The Rule of the Door* (short stories), Doubleday, 1967; *The Still, Small Voice of Trumpets*, Doubleday, 1968; *The World Menders*, Doubleday, 1971; *The Light That Never Was*, Doubleday, 1972; *The Metallic Muse* (short stories), Doubleday, 1972; (editor) *Nebula Award Stories Seven*, Harper, 1973; *Monument*, Doubleday, 1974. Stories anthologized in science fiction and mystery story collections. Contributor of more than fifty stories to magazines.

WORK IN PROGRESS: A book, *This Darkening Universe*, for Doubleday; a third novel in the Jan Darzek series that includes *All the Colors of Darkness* and *Watchers of the Dark*.

SIDELIGHTS: Biggle often draws on his musical background for story themes, particularly for short stories. His novels and stories have been translated into at least a dozen languages, including Russian and Yugoslavian.

* * *

BIGGS-DAVISON, John (Alec) 1918-

PERSONAL: Born June 7, 1918, in Boscombe, Bournemouth, England; son of John Norman (a major, Royal Artillery) and Sara (Wright) Biggs-Davison; married Pamela Hodder-Williams, November 27, 1948; children: Elizabeth, Thomas, Sara, Henry, Helena. *Education:* Attended Clifton College, 1932-37; Magdalen College, Oxford, M.A. *Politics:* Conservative. *Religion:* Roman Catholic. *Home:* 35 Hereford Sq., London S.W. 7, England. *Office:* House of Commons, Westminster, London S.W. 1, England.

CAREER: Entered Indian Civil Service, 1942; forward liaison officer on Arakan Frontier, 1943-44; assistant commissioner and magistrate in the Punjab, 1945; various posts, including deputy commissioner and commandant of Border Military Police, Dera Ghazi Khan, 1945-47; entered politics in England, 1948; secretary of British Conservative delegation to Council of Europe, 1952, 1953; Conservative member of Parliament, 1955, independent Conservative, 1957-58. Vice-president, Pan-European Union. *Military service:* Royal Marines, 1939-42; became lieutenant. *Member:* Pakistan Society (co-founder), Monday Club (chairman).

WRITINGS: George Wyndham: A Study in Toryism, Hodder & Stoughton, 1951; *Tory Lives*, Putnam, 1952; *The Uncertain Ally, 1917-1957*, Johnson Publications, 1957; *The Walls of Europe*, Johnson Publications, 1962; *The Hand is Red*, Johnson Publications, 1974. Contributor of articles to *The Times* (London), *Daily Telegraph* (London), *Royal Central Asian Journal*, *Courier* (London), *Twentieth Century*, *Contemporary Review*, *New Commonwealth*, *Time and Tide*, *Quarterly*, *Tablet*, and *Catholic Herald*. Author of various political pamphlets, including *Portuguese Guinea*, Congo-Africa Publications, 1970.

*   *   *

BILINSKY, Yaroslav 1932-

PERSONAL: Born February 26, 1932, in Lusk, Ukrainian Soviet Socialist Republic; came to United States in 1951; son of Peter (an accountant) and Natalia (Balabay) Bilinsky; married Wira Rusaniwskyj (a chemist), February 18, 1962; children: Peter Yaroslav, Sophia Vera Yaroslava, Nadia Yaroslava, Mark Paul Yaroslav. *Education:* Harvard University, A.B. (magna cum laude), 1954, graduate study, 1956-57; Princeton University, Ph.D., 1958. *Religion:* Ukrainian Orthodox. *Home:* 2 Mimosa Dr., Newark, Del. 19711.

CAREER: Rutgers University, Douglass College, New Brunswick, N.J., instructor in political science, 1958-61; University of Delaware, Newark, assistant professor, 1961-65, associate professor, 1965-69, professor of political science, 1969—. *Member:* American Political Science Association, American Association for the Advancement of Slavic Studies, Ukrainian Academy of Arts and Sciences in the U.S., Phi Beta Kappa.

WRITINGS: Perspectives on Soviet Youth, East European Student and Youth Service, 1960; *The Second Soviet Republic: The Ukraine after World War II*, Rutgers University Press, 1964; *Changes in the Central Committee, Communist Party of the Soviet Union, 1961-66*, Social Science Foundation and Graduate School of International Studies, University of Denver, 1967; (contributor) Erich Goldhagen, editor, *Ethnic Minorities in the Soviet Union*, Praeger, 1968; (contributor) John W. Strong, editor, *The Soviet Union Under Brezhnev and Kosygin*, Van Nostrand, 1971; (contributor) Arvids Ziedonis, Jr., Rein Taagepera, and Mardi Valgemae, editors, *Problems of Mininations: Baltic Perspectives*, Association for the Advancement of Baltic Studies, 1973. Contributor to *Jahrbuecher fuer Geschichte Osteuropas*, and to *Comparative Education Review*, *Problems of Communism*, *Revue de l'Occident Musulman et de la Mediteranee*, *Slavic Review*, *Soviet Studies*, *Ukranian Quarterly*, and other professional journals.

WORK IN PROGRESS: A book on Franco-Tunisian relations after 1956.

SIDELIGHTS: Bilinsky reads and speaks, with varying degrees of fluency, Russian, Polish, Ukranian, German, and French.

*   *   *

BILL, Valentine T.

PERSONAL: Born in Pavlovsk, Russia; daughter of Porfiry G. and Valentina (Dubiagsky) Tschebotarioff; married Edward C. Bill, 1941; children: Sonia. *Education:* University of Berlin, Ph.D., 1936. *Home:* 26 Alexander St., Princeton, N.J. *Office:* Pyne Administration Building, Princeton University, Princeton, N.J.

CAREER: Institute for Advanced Study, Princeton, N.J., research assistant, 1939-44; Princeton University, Princeton, N.J., lecturer in Russian, 1946—. *Member:* American Association of Teachers of Slavic and East European Languages, Pretty Brook Tennis Club.

WRITINGS: The Forgotten Class—The Russian Bourgeoisie, Praeger, 1959; *The Russian People—A Reader on Their History and Culture*, University of Chicago Press, 1959, 2nd edition, 1965; (with Ludmilla Turkevich) *Russian Readers*, five volumes, Van Nostrand, 1961-62; *Introduction to Russian Syntax*, Holt, 1972.

AVOCATIONAL INTERESTS: Tennis.

*   *   *

BILLETT, Roy O(ren) 1891-

PERSONAL: Born June 17, 1891, in Martel, Ohio; son of Edward Elmore and Ida Lenora (Earley) Billett; married Edna Mae Cunningham, September 14, 1912; children: Evelyn Margaret (Mrs. John P. Cochrane). *Education:* Attended business college, 1917, and Bowling Green State Normal School (now Bowling Green State University), 1918; Ohio State University, B.Sc. in Ed., 1923, M.A., 1927, Ph.D., 1929. *Home:* 5921 Northeast 15th Ave., Fort Lauderdale, Fla. 33308.

CAREER: Teacher, principal, and county superintendent of schools in Ohio, 1912-28; Ohio State University, Columbus, instructor, 1929; U.S. Office of Education, Washington, D.C., specialist in school administration, 1930-32; Illinois State Normal University (now Illinois State University), Normal, associate professor of secondary education, 1932-33; Boston University, Boston, Mass., associate professor of education, 1934-35, professor, 1935-57, chairman of department of education, Graduate School, 1944-57; professor emeritus, 1957—. Professorial lecturer at The American University, 1930-32, George Washington University, 1931-32, Harvard University, 1933-34, University of British Columbia, 1946, 1951, University of Southern California, 1948, Duke University, 1955, University of Florida, 1959, Florida State University, 1960. *Member:* American Educational Research Association, American Association of University Professors, Phi Delta Kappa, Boston Authors Club. *Awards, honors:* Ed.D., Rhode Island College.

WRITINGS: The Administration and Supervision of Homogeneous Grouping, Ohio State University Press, 1930; *Provisions for Individual Differences, Marking and Promotion* (monograph), National Survey of Secondary Education, U.S. Government Printing Office, 1933; *Supervision of Instruction* (monograph), National Survey of Secondary Education, U.S. Government Printing Office, 1933; *Fundamentals of Secondary-School Teaching*, Houghton, 1940; *A Survey of the Public Schools of Harford County,*

Maryland, Harford County Board of Education, 1946; *Growing Up*, Heath, 1951, 2nd edition with teacher's manual, 1958; *Preparing Theses and Other Typed Manuscripts*, Littlefield, 1959; *Billett-Starr Youth Problems Inventory*, junior level, senior level, and manual, Harcourt, 1961; *Teaching in Junior and Senior High Schools*, W. C. Brown, 1963; *Improving the Secondary School Curriculum*, Atherton Press, 1970. Contributor to education journals.†

* * *

BINGHAM, Madeleine 1912-
(Julia Mannering)

PERSONAL: Born February 1, 1912, in London, England; daughter of Clement Mary and Charlotte (Collins) Ebel; married John Michael Ward Bingham (seventh baron of Clanmorris; a writer of crime stories), July 28, 1934; children: Simon, Charlotte (Mrs. Terence Brady). *Education:* Educated in private schools in England and Belgium. *Religion:* Roman Catholic. *Home:* 24 Abingdon Villas, London W. 8, England. *Agent:* London Management, 235 Regent St., London W. 1, England.

CAREER: Author and playwright.

WRITINGS: (Under pseudonym Julia Mannering) *The Passionate Poet*, Museum Press, 1952; *Look to the Rose*, Museum Press, 1953; *Cheapest in the End*, Dodd, 1963; *Mary, Queen of Scots*, A. S. Barnes, 1969; *Scotland Under Mary Stuart: An Account of Everyday Life*, Allen & Unwin, 1971, St. Martin's, 1973; *Sheridan: The Tracks of a Comet*, St. Martin's, 1972.

Plays produced include *The Man from the Ministry* (three-act comedy), Samuel French, 1947, "In the Red," and "The Real McCoy." Contributor of short stories to *Harper's*, *Vanity Fair*, and other magazines.

WORK IN PROGRESS: Peers and Plebs, a biography of two families.

SIDELIGHTS: Madeleine Bingham told *CA:* "I can speak good French and what my husband calls 'dog German.' I have an ambition to translate French plays as I think most translations seen on the English stage miss the spirit of the originals. I think you need French blood to understand the *sous-entendu*." *Avocational interests:* The theater, cooking, and traveling.

* * *

BIOT, Francois 1923-

PERSONAL: Born 1923, in Lyons, France; son of Rene (a doctor of medicine) and Mathilde (Delcour) Biot. *Education:* Attended Lycee Ampere, Lyons, France. Ecole Superieure Dominicaine de Theologie, lecteur en theologie, 1951. *Office:* Ecole Superieure Dominicaine de Theologie, Eveux sur l'Arbresle, Lyon, France.

CAREER: Ecole Superieure Dominicaine de Theologie, Lyons, France, professeur de theologie dogmatique. Member of Centre d'Etudes Oecumeniques St. Irenee, Lyons, France; Episcopal adviser to Vatican II Ecumenical Council.

WRITINGS: Communautes protestantes, Fleurus, 1961, translation by W. J. Kerrigan, published as *The Rise of Protestant Monasticism*, Helicon, 1963; *Evangelische ordensgemeinschaften*, Matthias-Gruenewald, 1962; *De la polemique au dialogue*, two volumes, Editions du Cerf, 1963; *En route vers l'unite*, Bibliotheque de l'Homme d'Action, 1965; *Les Eveques contre*

l'imperialisme de l'argent, Temoignage chretien, 1968; *Theologie du politique: Foi et politique, elements de reflexion*, Editions universitaires, 1972. Member of directing committee, *Temoignage Chretien*. Contributor of numerous articles to *Istina*, *Lumiere et Vie*, and other periodicals.†

* * *

BIRCH, Anthony H(arold) 1924-

PERSONAL: Born February 17, 1924, in Ventnor, Isle of Wight, England; son of Frederick Harold (an Army officer) and Rosalind (Noblett) Birch; married Dorothy Overton, January 7, 1953; children: Peter Anthony, Tanya Dorothy. *Education:* University College, Nottingham, B.Sc. (Econ.), 1945; London School of Economics and Political Science, graduate study, 1945-46, Ph.D., 1951. *Office:* The University, Exeter, Devon, England.

CAREER: Board of Trade, London, England, assistant principal, 1945-47; University of Manchester, Manchester, England, 1947-61, started as assistant lecturer, became senior lecturer in government; University of Hull, Hull, England, professor of political studies, 1961-70; University of Exeter, Exeter, England, professor of political science, 1970—. Consultant to the government of Western Nigeria, 1956-58. *Member:* International Political Science Association (member of executive committee, 1973—), United Kingdom Political Studies Association (chairman, 1972-75). *Awards, honors:* Commonwealth fellow, Harvard University and University of Chicago, 1951-52.

WRITINGS: Federalism, Finance and Social Legislation in Canada, Australia, and the United States, Oxford University Press, 1955; *Small-Town Politics*, Oxford University Press, 1959; *Representative and Responsible Government: An Essay on the British Constitution*, Allen & Unwin, 1964; *The British System of Government*, Praeger, 1967; *Representation*, Pall Mall, 1971, Praeger, 1972. Contributor of articles to *Political Studies*, *British Journal of Political Science*, *Parliamentary Affairs*, *British Journal of Sociology*, and *International Social Science Journal*.

WORK IN PROGRESS: A study of political integration and disintegration in the British Isles; a study of types of explanation in political science.

SIDELIGHTS: Birch has traveled extensively in North America, Africa, Europe, and Southeast Asia. *Avocational interests:* Sailing.

* * *

BIRD, Anthony (Cole) 1917-

PERSONAL: Born April 26, 1917, in London, England; son of Percy Hyde and Marjorie (Benson) Bird; married second wife, Barbara Mary Hunter, October 27, 1961; children: (first marriage) Janet Penelope (Mrs. D. B. Tubbs), Amanda Judith. *Education:* Educated in English private and preparatory schools. *Politics:* "An old-fashioned Whig of the sort now branded as reactionary, who thinks all politicians stink anyway." *Home:* Chevertons, Potbridge, Odiham, Hampshire, England.

CAREER: Factory and garage hand and other unskilled labor, 1932-36; Guildhall Library, London, England, junior assistant, 1936-38; antique dealer, part-time chauffeur, 1938-39; co-owner of fleet of Rolls Royce for-hire cars, 1946-48; antique dealer and horologist, 1949-65. International Business Machines (United Kingdom), part-time employee, 1956-58. *Military service:* British Army, 1939-45.

Member: Antiquarian Horological Society, Veteran Car Club, Vintage Sports Car Club.

WRITINGS: The Motor Car 1765-1914, Batsford, 1961; *Veteran Cars in Colour*, Batsford, 1962; *Gottlieb Daimler: Inventor of the Motor Engine*, Barker, 1962, Soccer, 1964; *English Furniture for the Private Collector*, Batsford, 1962; (with F. W. Hutton-Scott) *Veteran Motor Car Pocket Book*, Batsford, 1963; *Early Victorian Furniture*, Hamish Hamilton, 1964; (with Ian Hallows) *The Rolls-Royce Motor Car*, Batsford, 1964, Crown, 1965, 3rd edition, Crown, 1973; (with Francis Hutton-Stott) *A History of the Lanchester Motor Cars*, Cassell, 1965; *The Damnable Duke of Cumberland: A Character Study and Vindication of Ernest Augustus, Duke of Cumberland and King of Hanover, 1771-1851*, Barrie & Rockliff, 1966; *The Empress Alexandra*, Albany Press, 1968; *Roads and Vehicles*, Longmans, 1969; (with Lord Montagu of Beaulieu) *Steam Cars: 1770-1970*, Cassell, 1971; *An Illustrated Guide to House Clocks*, Arco, 1973 (published in England as *English House Clocks: 1650-1850*, David & Charles, 1973); *Travellers by Road*, Hugh Evelyn, in press; *Mid-Victorian Masterpiece: An Account of the Crystal Palace Building from the Structural Engineering Point of View*, Cassell, in press.

SIDELIGHTS: Bird on literary agents—"Why pay a chap 10% to make bad blood between author and publisher?" On vocational and avocational interests—"Where, pray, does the difference lie? One of my interests is to try to avoid such woolly thinking. Another is to live long enough to be the last man in England who has never been in an aeroplane."

*   *   *

BIRD, Will R.   1891-

PERSONAL: Born May 11, 1891, in East Mapleton, Nova Scotia, Canada; son of Stephen and Augusta Caroline (Bird) Bird; married Ethel May Sutton, June 18, 1919; children: Stephen Stanley (killed in action, 1944); Betty Caroline (Mrs. I. M. Murray). *Education:* Attended schools in Nova Scotia, Canada. *Religion:* United Church of Canada. *Home:* 963 Marlborough Ave., Halifax, Nova Scotia, Canada.

CAREER: Free-lance writer, 1928-34; Province of Nova Scotia, Halifax, assistant director of travel bureau, 1947, chairman of Historic Sites Advisory Council, 1948-66. *Military service:* Royal Highlanders of Canada, 1916-19; served overseas two years; received Military Medal for action at Mons, Belgium. *Member:* Canadian Authors Association (national president, 1949; Maritimes vice-president, 1947-48; Nova Scotia president, 1945-46; life member), Canadian Legion, St. George's Society (president, Halifax, 1957), Nova Scotia Historical Society (life member), Haliburton Club (fellow), Rough Necks (oil drillers), Toastmasters International (honorary member). *Awards, honors:* Litt.D. from Mount Allison University; Ryerson Fiction Award, 1945, for *Here Stays Good Yorkshire*, and 1947, for *Judgment Glen*; University of Alberta, National Award in Letters, 1965; Coronation Medal; Canada Centennial Medal.

WRITINGS: A Century at Chignecto, Ryerson, 1926; *Private Timothy Fergus Clancy*, Graphic Press, 1927; *And We Go On*, privately printed, 1927; *The Communication Trench*, privately printed, 1928; *Maid of the Marshes*, Perrault Publishing, 1931; *Thirteen Years After*, Maclean, 1932; *Here Stays Good Yorkshire*, Ryerson, 1945; *Sunrise for Peter*, Ryerson, 1946; *Judgment Glen*, Ryerson, 1947; *The Passionate Pilgrim*, Ryerson, 1949.

This is Nova Scotia, Ryerson, 1950; *So Much to Record*, Ryerson, 1951; *To Love and to Cherish*, Ryerson, 1953; *No Retreating Footsteps*, Kentville, 1954; *The Two Jacks*, Ryerson, 1954; *Done at Grand Pre*, Ryerson, 1955; *The Shy Yorkshireman*, Ryerson, 1955; *Off-Trail in Nova Scotia*, Ryerson, 1956; (editor) *Atlantic Anthology*, McClelland & Stewart, 1958; *These Are the Maritimes*, Ryerson, 1959; *Tristam's Salvation*, Ryerson, 1960; *Despite the Distance*, Ryerson, 1961; *The North Shore Regiment*, Brunswick Press, 1962; *Ghosts Have Warm Hands*, Clarke, Irwin, 1968; *An Earl Must Have a Wife*, Clarke, Irwin, 1969; *Angel Cove*, Macmillan, 1972.

Contributor of more than five hundred short stories to Canadian, American, British, and Australian periodicals.

WORK IN PROGRESS: A book on J. F. W. DesBarres, author of *Atlantic Neptune*, first governor of Cape Breton Island, and governor of Prince Edward Island.

SIDELIGHTS: Bird's short stories have appeared in eight translations; eleven of them currently are used in textbooks. In 1931 he spent five months covering all the World War I battlefields in which Canadians had served, with the resulting series running in eighteen consecutive issues of *Maclean's Magazine*, the most coverage ever given to one subject by the Canadian publication. That same year Bird wrote a booklet, "Vimy Ridge," printed in both French and English; more than half a million copies were sold to visitors at the battlefield.

*   *   *

BIRLEY, Julia (Davies)   1928-

PERSONAL: Born May 13, 1928, in London, England; daughter of David Davies (a national insurance commissioner) and Margaret (Kennedy) Davies; married J. L. T. Birley (now a medical doctor), September 11, 1954; children: Margaret, Humphrey, Ellen, Rosalind. *Education:* Lady Margaret Hall, Oxford, student, 1946-50, honors degree in classics. *Politics:* Liberal. *Religion:* Church of England. *Home:* 6 Mount Adon Park, London S.E. 22, England. *Agent:* Curtis Brown Ltd., 13 King St., London W.C. 2, England.

CAREER: Classics teacher in London and Beaconsfield, England, 1950-54.

WRITINGS—Novels: The Children on the Shore, Hamish Hamilton, 1958; *The Time of the Cuckoo*, Bles, 1960; *When You Were There*, Bles, 1963; *A Serpent's Egg*, Bles, 1966. Contributor of articles and short stories to periodicals.

WORK IN PROGRESS: A novel.†

*   *   *

BIRREN, Faber   1900-
(Gregor Lang, Martin Lang)

PERSONAL: Born September 21, 1900, in Chicago, Ill.; son of Joseph P. and Crescentia (Lang) Birren; married Wanda Martin, April 25, 1934; children: Zoe (Mrs. William H. Kirby), Fay (Mrs. John Koedel, Jr.). *Education:* Attended Art Institute of Chicago, 1918-20, and University of Chicago, 1920-21. *Home:* 77 Prospect St., Stamford, Conn. 06902. *Office:* 184 Bedford St., Stamford, Conn. 06901.

CAREER: Self-employed color consultant, 1934—, currently with headquarters in Stamford, Conn., and affiliated office in Montreal, Quebec. Developer of manuals of color practice for U.S. Navy, U.S. Army, and U.S. Coast

Guard. *Member:* Optical Society of America, American Institute of Architects, American Society for Photobiology. *Awards, honors:* M.S. from Arnold College, 1941.

WRITINGS—Non-fiction: *Color in Vision*, C. V. Ritter, 1928; *Color Dimensions*, Crimson Press, 1934; *The Printer's Art of Color*, Crimson Press, 1935; *Color in Modern Packaging*, Crimson Press, 1935; *Functional Color*, Crimson Press, 1937; *The Wonderful Wonders of Red-Yellow-Blue* (juvenile), McFarlane, Warde, McFarlane, 1937; *Monument to Color*, McFarlane, Warde, McFarlane, 1938.

(Under pseudonym Martin Lang) *Character Analysis Through Color*, Crimson Press, 1940; *The Story of Color*, Crimson Press, 1941; *Selling with Color*, McGraw, 1945; *Color Psychology and Color Therapy*, McGraw, 1950, revised edition, University Books, 1961; *Your Color and Your Self*, Prang Co., 1952; *New Horizons in Color*, Reinhold, 1955; *Selling Color to People*, University Books, 1956.

Creative Color, Reinhold, 1961; *Color, Form and Space*, Reinhold, 1961; *Color in Your World*, Collier, 1962; *Color: A Survey in Words and Pictures*, University Books, 1963; *Color for Interiors*, Whitney Library of Design, 1963; (author of notes and commentary) Moses Harris, *The Natural System of Colours*, Whitney Library of Design, 1963; *History of Color in Painting: With New Principles of Color Expression*, Van Nostrand, 1965; (author of introduction) Thomas Sully, *Hints to Young Painters*, Reinhold, 1965; *Principles of Color*, Van Nostrand, 1969; *Light, Color, and Environment*, Van Nostrand, 1969.

Editor: Edwin D. Babbitt, *The Principles of Light and Color*, University Books, 1967; Michel E. Chevreul, *The Principles of Harmony*, Reinhold, 1967; *The Color Primer: A Basic Treatise on the Color System of Wilhelm Ostwald*, Van Nostrand, 1969; *A Grammar of Color: A Basic Treatise on the Color System of Albert H. Munsell*, Van Nostrand, 1969; Johannes Itten, *The Elements of Color*, Van Nostrand, 1970.

Fiction: (Under pseudonym Gregor Lang) *Terra*, Philosophical Library, 1953; (under pseudonym Gregor Lang) *The Unconsidered*, Citadel, 1955; *Make Mine Love*, Fell, 1958.

Contributor of more than 250 articles to trade and scientific magazines.

WORK IN PROGRESS: Color Perception in Art, for Van Nostrand.

* * *

BISHOP, George W(esley), Jr. 1910-

PERSONAL: Born January 13, 1910, in New York, N.Y.; son of George Wesley and Anna (Farrington) Bishop; married Helen Young, December 22, 1942; children: Georgelen Elizabeth Kuhn, George III. *Education:* College of William and Mary, A.B., 1935; New York University, M.B.A., 1955, Ph.D., 1959. *Politics:* Democrat. *Religion:* Protestant Episcopal. *Home:* 120 Ridge Dr., DeKalb, Ill. 60115.

CAREER: Began business career with Union Carbide Co., New York, N.Y., 1935-36; U.S. Gypsum Co., New York, N.Y., sales correspondent, 1936-39, sales representative, 1940-42; Merrill Lynch, Pierce, Fenner & Smith, Inc., Providence, R.I., account executive, 1947-50, portfolio analyst, New York, N.Y., 1954-59; University of Tennessee, Knoxville, assistant professor, 1959-60, associate professor of finance, 1960-64, professor, 1964-65; Northern Illi-

nois University, DeKalb, professor of finance and chairman of department, 1965—. Research fellow, Yale University, 1970-71. *Military service:* U.S. Naval Reserve, active duty, 1942-46, 1950-54; became captain. *Member:* American Finance Association, American Economic Association, Economic History Association, Pi Kappa Alpha, Delta Sigma Pi, Omicron Delta Kappa, Beta Gamma Sigma.

WRITINGS: Charles H. Dow and the Dow Theory, Appleton, 1960; (editor) *Charles H. Dow: Economist*, Dow Jones Books, 1967. Contributor to *Encyclopaedia Britannica, Collier's Encyclopedia, Financial Analysts Journal, Business History Review, Wall Street Journal*, and *National Observer*.

WORK IN PROGRESS: Additional research on the writings of Charles H. Dow.

* * *

BISHOP, Leonard 1922-

PERSONAL: Born October 17, 1922, in New York, N.Y.; son of Edward and Essie (Milembach) Bishop; married Linda Allen, August 12, 1955; children: Matthew, Michael. *Education:* Attended public schools in New York, N.Y., but dropped out before completing high school. *Home:* 1608 Felton St., San Francisco, Calif. *Agent:* Harold D. Cohen, 580 Fifth Ave., New York, N.Y.

CAREER: Prior to 1950, traveled throughout the country, working as draftsman, prizefighter, teacher, actor, flagpole painter, salesman, carpenter, waiter, short-order cook, construction worker, and lecturer; full-time writer, 1950—. Has taught creative writing at Columbia University, New York University, Windham College, and University of California Extension.

WRITINGS: Down All Your Streets, Dial, 1952; *Days of My Love*, Dial, 1953; *Creep Into Thy Narrow Bed*, Dial, 1954; *The Butchers*, Dial, 1956; *The Angry Time*, Fell, 1960; *Make My Bed in Hell*, Gold Medal Books, 1960; *The Desire Years*, Gold Medal Books, 1962; *Against Heaven's Hand*, Random House, 1963. Contributor to magazines, including *Esquire* and *New World Writing*.

WORK IN PROGRESS: A biography of Louis R. Lurie.

SIDELIGHTS: Blanche Gelfant compared Bishop's work to James T. Farrell's ''ecological novel of manners that reveals the . . . intimate insider's knowledge of an everyday way of life.'' Bishop's novels, like Farrell's, employ the episodic structure and ''alternating point-of-view characters. . . . [The] characters are created mainly through their speech, whether it is their outer dialogue or the interior dialogue in terms of which their thoughts and emotions are expressed and the outer scene realized.'' There is now a Leonard Bishop Collection at Boston University.

BIOGRAPHICAL/CRITICAL SOURCES: The American City Novel, by Blanche Gelfant, University of Oklahoma Press, 1954; *Man in Modern Fiction*, by Edmund Fuller, Random House, 1958; *Book Week*, November 17, 1963.†

* * *

BISHOP, Robert Lee 1931-

PERSONAL: Born August 17, 1931, in Mt. Healthy, Ohio; son of Chester Lee (a minister) and Nova (McGuire) Bishop; married Nadean Hawkins (a college teacher), April 19, 1952; children: Anita, Gail, James, Susan. *Education:* Oklahoma Baptist University, B.S., 1952; Southern Baptist

Theological Seminary, M.R.E., 1956, D.R.E., 1960; post-doctoral study at University of Oklahoma, 1963; University of Wisconsin, Ph.D., 1966. *Politics:* Democrat. *Religion:* Baptist. *Home:* 1516 Morton, Ann Arbor, Mich. 48104.

CAREER: Worked for printing company in Kansas City, Mo., 1946-48, newspaper in Shawnee, Okla., 1950-52, an oil company, 1952, and in church posts, 1955-57; Southern Baptist Theological Seminary, Louisville, Ky., instructor in writing, 1957-58; Oklahoma Baptist University, Shawnee, instructor, 1958-60, assistant professor of journalism, 1960-63, director of public relations, 1962-63; University of Michigan, Ann Arbor, assistant professor, 1965-70, associate professor of journalism, 1970—. Copy editor, *Detroit Free Press*, 1966. *Military service:* U.S. Navy, 1952-54; became commander. *Member:* Public Relations Society of America (fellow), Association for Education in Journalism, American College Public Relations Association, American Association of University Professors, American Alumni Council, Sigma Delta Chi.

WRITINGS: (Contributor and co-editor) *Principles of Advertising*, Pitman, 1963; (contributor) *Modern Journalism*, Pitman, 1963; *A Book Study of the Bible*, two volumes, Broadman, 1964; *Basic News Writing*, privately printed, 1972. Author of film scripts, "Education for the Space Age," for National Science Foundation, and "So You Want to Go to College," for Oklahoma Baptist University. Contributor to journals.

WORK IN PROGRESS: A book, *Economics, Politics, and Information: Mass Media Systems of Western Europe*; further work on economics of the mass media, computer-assisted instruction, and international communications.

*   *   *

BITTEL, Lester Robert   1918-

PERSONAL: Surname rhymes with "little"; born December 9, 1918, in East Orange, N.J.; son of William Frederick (a tradesman) and Helen (Korte) Bittel; married Edythe Gilbert Hulett (now a schoolteacher), November 1, 1947. *Education:* Lehigh University, B.S. in Industrial Engineering, 1940. *Politics:* Republican. *Religion:* Unitarian Universalist. *Home:* 52 Wilson Ave., Riverdale, N.J. 07457. *Office:* McGraw-Hill Book Co., Inc., 330 West 42nd St., New York, N.Y. 10036.

CAREER: Leeds & Northrup Co., Philadelphia, Pa., field engineer, 1940-46; Western Electric Co., Kearny, N.J., industrial engineer, 1947; Koppers Co., Inc., plant superintendent at Kearny, N.J., 1947-52, training director at Pittsburgh, Pa., 1952-54; McGraw-Hill Book Co., Inc., New York, editor, *Factory* (business paper), 1954—. Technical adviser for six films on supervisory problems produced by McGraw. Member of public information committee, National Safety Council, 1959—, and of industrial board, national board of Young Men's Christian Association, 1965; vice-president of board of trustees of Chilton Memorial Hospital, 1960—. *Military service:* U.S. Army Air Forces, 1942-46; became first lieutenant.

MEMBER: American Society of Mechanical Engineers (executive committee, 1963—), American Production and Inventory Control Society (advisory board, 1960—), American Society of Training Directors (chairman, 1962). *Awards, honors:* Jesse Neale Award of Merit, American Business Press, 1957, 1959, 1960, 1961.

WRITINGS: (With Melden and Rice) *Practical Automation*, McGraw, 1956; *What Every Supervisor Should Know*,

McGraw, 1959, 3rd edition, 1974; *Management by Exception*, McGraw, 1964; (with Robert Craig) *Training and Development Handbook*, McGraw, 1967; *The Nine Master Keys of Management*, McGraw, 1972.†

*   *   *

BLACK, Kenneth, Jr.   1925-

PERSONAL: Born January 30, 1925, in Norfolk, Va.; son of Kenneth (a contractor) and Margaret (Wolf) Black; married Mabel Folger, September 20, 1948; children: Kenneth III, Kathryn Anne. *Education:* University of North Carolina, A.B., 1948, M.S., 1951; University of Pennsylvania, Ph.D., 1953. *Religion:* Catholic. *Home:* 1762 Nancy Creek Bluff, N.W., Atlanta, Ga. 30327. *Office:* Georgia State University, University Plaza, Atlanta, Ga. 30303.

CAREER: Colonial Insurance Agency, Chapel Hill, N.C., partner, 1946-50; chartered property casualty underwriter, 1955, chartered life underwriter, 1956; Georgia State University, Atlanta, 1953—, Regents' Professor of Insurance, 1959—, chairman of department, 1953-69, dean of School of Business Administration, 1969—. Management consultant. Executive director and trustee of Educational Foundation, Inc., and Harold T. Dillon Foundation, Inc., Atlanta, Ga.; member of board of directors of North American Reinsurance Corp., North American Reassurance Co., and US-LIFE Corp., all of New York, N.Y., Cousins Properties, Inc. and Computone Systems, Inc. of Atlanta, Ga.; trustee of the Griffith Foundation for Insurance Education, Ohio State University. *Military service:* U.S. Navy, 1944-46.

MEMBER: Society of Chartered Property and Casualty Underwriters (past president, Georgia chapter; past regional vice-president), American Society of Insurance Management (past president, Atlanta chapter), American Risk and Insurance Association (president, 1964), American Society of Chartered Life Underwriters, Phi Beta Kappa, Beta Gamma Sigma. *Awards, honors:* Paul Speicher Award, 1958.

WRITINGS: Group Annuities, Irwin, 1955; (with S. S. Huebner) *Property Insurance*, 4th edition, Appleton, 1957; (with Huebner) *Life Insurance*, 5th edition, Appleton, 1958, 8th edition, 1972; (with G. Hugh Russell) *Human Behavior*, American College of Life Underwriters, 1962; (with Russell) *Human Behavior and Life Insurance*, Prentice-Hall, 1963; (contributor) *Life Insurance Handbook*, 2nd edition, Irwin, 1964, 3rd edition, 1973; (with Russell) *Human Behavior and Property and Liability Insurance*, Prentice-Hall, 1964; (with Jack C. Keir and Sterling Surrey) *Cases in Life Insurance*, Irwin, 1965; (with Huebner and others) *Property and Liability Insurance*, Appleton, 1968; (with Russell) *Human Behavior in Business*, Appleton, 1972. Contributor to *Encyclopedia Americana*.

Editor of insurance series for Prentice-Hall. Editor of *Journal of American Society of Chartered Life Underwriters*.

WORK IN PROGRESS: Revising *Life Insurance*, completion expected in 1975.

*   *   *

BLACKSTOCK, Paul W(illiam)   1913-

PERSONAL: Born March 19, 1913, in Humboldt, Iowa; son of William Ernest (a minister) and Mabel Edith (Entwhistle) Blackstock; married Isabel Gagian, November 27, 1942 (divorced, 1953); married Marie Chandler, August 27,

1960; children: two stepdaughters. *Education:* University of Colorado, B.A. (magna cum laude), 1935; graduate study at University of Utah and University of Colorado, 1935-37; Institut de phonetique, University of Paris, diplome, 1939; American University, M.S., 1951, Ph.D., 1954. *Office:* Department of Government and International Studies, University of South Carolina, Columbia, S.C. 29208.

CAREER: High school teacher in Milford, Utah, 1938-39, and Salt Lake City, Utah, 1940-42; U.S. Army, civilian specialist, with posts as chief research analyst and intelligence specialist for western Europe and North Africa, Army Intelligence Group, General Staff, 1945-51, and psychological warfare specialist for western Europe, Soviet Union, and Soviet satellite countries, Office of the Chief of Psychological Warfare, 1951-60; University of South Carolina, Columbia, associate professor of international relations, 1960—. Lecturer on political warfare at George Washington University, Johns Hopkins University, School of Advanced International Studies, and U.S. Department of State, Foreign Service Institute during period 1951-60. Consultant to Special Operations Research Office, U.S. Department of Defense, 1960—. *Military service:* U.S. Army, 1942-45. *Member:* Authors League, Phi Beta Kappa, American Alpine Club. *Awards, honors:* Commendation for intelligence research, Assistant Secretary of War, 1947.

WRITINGS: (With Bert F. Hoselitz, editor and author of critical notes) *The Russian Menace to Europe* (collection of suppressed political works of Marx and Engels), Free Press of Glencoe, 1952; (contributor) William E. Daugherty and Morris Janowitz, editors, *Psychological Warfare Casebook*, Johns Hopkins Press, 1958; (translator and author of introduction) Alexander Solzhenitsyn, *We Never Make Mistakes* (two short novels), University of South Carolina Press, 1963, revised edition, 1971; *The Strategy of Subversion: Manipulating the Politics of Other Nations*, Quadrangle, 1964; *Agents of Deceit*, Quadrangle, 1966; *The Secret Road to World War II: Soviet versus Western Intelligence, 1921-1939*, Quadrangle, 1971; *The CIA and the Intelligence Community*, Forum, 1974; (editor with Frank Schaf) *Intelligence, Espionage, and Covert Political Operations*, Gale, in press.

Writer of classified reports on intelligence studies, 1946-51. Contributor of articles on intelligence and world affairs to *Worldview* and *Baltimore Sun*, and on mountaineering to *Summit* and *Amerika Illustrated* (U.S. Information Agency).

WORK IN PROGRESS: Articles on intelligence, world affairs, and mountaineering.

SIDELIGHTS: Blackstock is competent in French, German, Spanish, Russian, Italian, and Latin.

Reviewing *The Secret Road to World War II*, John L. Earl noted that the book "delve[s] into previously little-known areas of intelligence and counter-intelligence between the world wars.... [Blackstock's] research is detailed and exhaustive considering the difficulty of acquiring sources in such an area.... [He] has shown that when one deals with the subsurfaces of intelligence services, truth is indeed stranger than fiction." *Avocational interests:* Mountain climbing, skiing, tennis, music (plays piano), literature.

*   *   *

BLACKWOOD, George D(ouglas)   1919-

PERSONAL; Born September 27, 1919, in Saskatoon, Saskatchewan, Canada; son of Robert (an architect) and Sarah (MacDougall) Blackwood; married Ethel Youngquist, August 27, 1950; children: Kristine, Douglas Ian. *Education:* Flint Junior College (now Flint Community Junior College), Flint, Mich., A.A., 1940; University of Chicago, A.B., 1942, A.M., 1947, Ph.D., 1951. *Politics:* Democrat. *Religion:* Lutheran. *Home:* 96 Columbia Rd., Arlington, Mass.

CAREER: Boston University, Boston, Mass., instructor, 1949-52, assistant professor, 1952-57, associate professor, 1957-63, professor of political economy, 1963—. Member of Massachusetts Civil War Centennial Commission, Massachusetts Board of Library Commissioners, and Massachusetts Board of Regional Community Colleges. *Military service:* U.S. Army, 1942-46; became staff sergeant. *Member:* American Historical Association, American Political Science Association, New England Political Science Association, Organization of American Historians.

WRITINGS: (With Murray B. Levin) *The Alienated Voter*, Holt, Rinehart & Winston, 1960; (with Levin) *The Compleat Politician*, Bobbs-Merrill, 1962; (with Andrew Gyorgy) *Ideologies in World Affairs*, Blaisdell, 1967. Contributor to *South Atlantic Quarterly*, *Mississippi Valley Historical Review*, *Nation*, and *New Leader*.

WORK IN PROGRESS: A study of the basic political history of Massachusetts; an analysis of direct action and political action among American Negroes.†

*   *   *

BLAIR, Calvin Patton   1924-

PERSONAL: Born November 25, 1924, in Orange, Tex.; son of Thomas David and Mary Jane (Patton) Blair; married Eleanor Ruth Davis, 1946; children: Bonnie Jane, Lisa Jill. *Education:* University of Texas, B.A., 1949, M.A., 1953, Ph.D., 1957; National University of Mexico, graduate study, 1950. *Home:* 2115 West 12th St., Austin, Tex. 78703. *Office:* Department of Marketing Administration, University of Texas, Austin, Tex. 78712.

CAREER: University of Texas, Austin, instructor, 1953-56, assistant professor, 1956-59, associate professor, 1959-63, professor of international trade and resources, 1963—, research associate, Bureau of Business Research, 1958-61, assistant dean, College of Business Administration, 1958-59. Visiting professor at Universidad de Nuevo Leon, Monterrey, Mexico, 1959-60, Instituto Tecnologico, Monterrey, Mexico, summer, 1963, Harvard University, Graduate School of Business Administration, 1964, Centro de Estudios Monetarios Latinoamericanos, Mexico City, at intervals, 1965-73, and National University of Mexico, 1969 and 1970; lecturer in Latin American under U.S. State Department specialist grant, 1963 and 1972; consultant, Arthur D. Little, Inc., 1962-67. *Military service:* U.S. Navy, 1943-46. *Member:* American Economic Association, Latin American Studies Association, Phi Beta Kappa, Sigma Delta Pi. *Awards, honors:* International Educational Exchange professor grantee to Mexico, 1959-60.

WRITINGS: Fluctuations in United States Imports from Brazil, Colombia, Chile, and Mexico, 1919-1954, Bureau of Business Research, University of Texas, 1959; (with Robert H. Ryan) *Big Spring Texas: A Study of Economic Potential*, Bureau of Business Research, University of Texas, 1959; *Economic Growth Projections for the Dallas, Forth Worth, and Houston Trading Areas*, Bureau of Business Research, University of Texas, 1961.

Contributor: Raymond Vernon, editor, *Public Policy and Private Enterprise in Mexico*, Harvard University Press, 1964; William F. Glueck, editor, *Hemisphere West: el Futuro*, Bureau of Business Research, University of Texas, 1968; Richard N. Adams, editor, *Responsibilities of the Foreign Scholar to the Local Scholarly Community: Studies of U.S. Research in Guatemala, Chile, and Paraguay*, Education and World Affairs and Latin American Studies Association (New York), 1969; Stanley R. Ross, editor, *Latin America in Transition: Problems in Training and Research*, State University of New York Press, 1970.

Contributor to *Encyclopedia of Latin America*, and to periodicals, including *Texas Business Review, Current History*, and *Armas y Letras* (Mexico). Editor of series, "Studies in Latin American Business," published by Bureau of Business Research, University of Texas, 1970—.

WORK IN PROGRESS: Research on Mexican economic policy, 1970-76; foreign investment in Latin America; United States direct investment in Mexico.

*   *   *

BLAIR, John G(eorge)   1934-

PERSONAL: Born December 3, 1934, in Brooklyn, N.Y.; son of Howard Allen (an engineer) and Edith (Chabot) Blair; married Karin Latham, April 1, 1961; children: Ann. *Education:* Brown University, B.A., 1956, Ph.D., 1962; Columbia University, M.A., 1957. *Office:* Faculty of Letters, University of Geneva, Geneva, Switzerland.

CAREER: Rhode Island School of Design, Providence, instructor in English, 1958-62; Oakland University, Rochester, Mich., 1962-70, began as assistant professor, became professor of English, University of Geneva, Geneva, Switzerland, professeur extraordinaire, 1970-72, professeur ordinaire of American literature and civilization, 1972—. *Member:* Modern Language Association of America, American Association of University Professors, American Studies Associations of America and Europe, Phi Beta Kappa.

WRITINGS: The Poetic Art of W. H. Auden, Princeton University Press, 1965. Contributor to *American Quarterly, Shenandoah, Bulletin of the Faculty of Letters of Strasbourg* (France), *American Transcendental Quarterly*.

WORK IN PROGRESS: Investigations in American Romanticism and American studies; the figure of the confidence man in modern fiction.

*   *   *

BLALOCK, Hubert Morse, Jr.   1926-

PERSONAL: Born August 23, 1926, in Baltimore, Md.; son of Hubert Morse and Dorothy (Welsh) Blalock; married Ann Bonar, 1951; children: Susan Lynn, Kathleen Ann. *Education:* Dartmouth College, A.B., 1949; Brown University, M.A., 1953; University of North Carolina, Ph.D., 1954. *Home:* 18425 17th Ave. N.W., Seattle, Wash. *Office:* Department of Sociology, University of Washington, Seattle, Wash.

CAREER: University of Michigan, Ann Arbor, instructor, 1954-57, assistant professor of sociology, 1957-61; Yale University, New Haven, Conn., associate professor of sociology, 1961-64; University of North Carolina, Chapel Hill, professor of sociology, 1964-71; University of Washington, Seattle, professor of sociology, 1971—. *Military service:* U.S. Navy, 1944-46. *Member:* American Statistical Association (member of council), American Sociological Association (member of council).

WRITINGS: Social Statistics, McGraw, 1960, 2nd edition, 1972; *Causal Inferences in Nonexperimental Research*, University of North Carolina Press, 1964; *Toward a Theory of Minority-Group Relations*, Wiley, 1967; (editor with A. B. Blalock) *Methodology in Social Research*, McGraw, 1968; *Theory Construction: From Verbal to Mathematical Formulations*, Prentice-Hall, 1969; *An Introduction to Social Research*, Prentice-Hall, 1970; (editor) *Causal Models in the Social Sciences*, Aldine-Atherton, 1971. Contributor to professional journals. Associate editor, *American Sociological Review, American Journal of Sociology, Journal of the American Statistical Association*.

*   *   *

BLANCHARD, Carroll Henry, Jr.   1928-

PERSONAL: Born October 14, 1928; son of Carroll Henry and Alice (O'Brien) Blanchard. *Education:* Boston University, B.S. in Ed.; M.S. in Ed., 1957. *Residence:* Albany, N.Y.

CAREER: State University of New York at Albany, 1957—, now associate professor. Consultant to Kurlin Graphic Aids. *Military service:* U.S. Army, 1951-54; served in Korea; became first lieutenant; received Bronze Star.

WRITINGS: Korean War Bibliography and Maps of Korea, Korean Conflict Research Foundation, 1964.

WORK IN PROGRESS: An Atlas of the War in Korea, in five volumes; Volume I, *Of Rivers and Retreat*, Volume II, *Of the Pusan Perimeter*, Volume III, *Of Daring and Decision*, Volume IV, *Of Courage and Caution*, Volume V, *Of Patience, Prisoners, and Peace*.

*   *   *

BLANKENSHIP, A(lbert) B.   1914-

PERSONAL: Born August 21, 1914, in Lancaster, Pa.; son of Walter D. and Winifred (Breneman) Blankenship; married Janet Simpson; children: Patricia Ann (Mrs. Joseph Lurie), Walter V., Donn R. *Education:* Franklin and Marshall College, A.B., 1935; University of Oregon, A.M., 1936; Columbia University, Ph.D., 1940. *Home:* 8 Bacon Hill Rd., Pleasantville, N.Y.

CAREER: Research director of business firms, 1939-44; National Analysts, Inc., Philadelphia, Pa., managing director, 1944-48; A. B. Blankenship & Associates, Philadelphia, Pa., president, 1948-51; Stewart, Dougall & Associates, New York, N.Y., senior research associate, 1951-52; Young & Rubicam, Inc., New York, research manager, 1952-55; Ted Bates & Co., Inc., New York, vice-president and research director, 1955-56; Blankenship, Gruneau Research Ltd., Toronto, Ontario, executive vice-president, 1956-61; Canadian Fact Ltd., Toronto, vice-president, 1961-62; Carter Products (proprietaries, toiletries), New York, director of market research, 1962—. Temple University, Philadelphia, 1944-51, started as lecturer, became associate professor of marketing; New York University, New York, adjunct professor of marketing, 1954-56. Diplomate in industrial psychology, American Board of Examiners in Professional Psychology. Former trustee, Village of North Tarrytown, N.Y.

MEMBER: American Psychological Association (fellow), American Marketing Association, Market Research Council, Council of Marketing Research Directors, National Industrial Conference Board, Sigma Xi. *Awards, honors:* Rockefeller Foundation Fellow, 1940-41.

WRITINGS: Consumer and Opinion Research, Harper, 1943; (editor) *How to Conduct Consumer and Opinion Research*, Harper, 1946; (with M. S. Heidingsfield) *Market and Marketing Analysis*, Henry Holt, 1947; (with M. S. Heidingsfield) *Marketing*, Barnes & Noble, 1953, 2nd edition, revised and enlarged, 1968; (with J. B. Doyle) *Marketing Research Management*, American Management Association, 1965. Member of board of editors, *Journal of Marketing*.†

* * *

BLAU, Joshua
(Yehoshua Blau)

PERSONAL: Given name is spelled variously Joshua and Yehoshua; born September 22, 1919, in Cluj, Rumania; son of Dr. Paul (a journalist) and Simah (Gruenfeld) Blau; married Shulamith Haviv (a teacher), June, 1945; children: Mordechai, Yael. *Education:* University of Vienna, student, 1937-38; Hebrew University of Jerusalem, M.A., 1942, Ph.D., 1950. *Religion:* Jewish. *Home:* 15 Palmakh, Jerusalem, Israel.

CAREER: Teacher at secondary schools in Tel Aviv, Israel, 1942-47, and at seminary in Jerusalem, Israel, 1946-55; Hebrew University of Jerusalem, Jerusalem, Israel, 1952—, began as teacher, now M. Schloessinger Professor of Arabic Language and Literature; University of Tel Aviv, Tel Aviv, Israel, 1962—, began as assistant professor, now professor of Hebrew and Semitic linguistics. Visiting professor, University of California at Berkeley, 1967-68, 1974-75. *Member:* Hebrew Language Academy, Israel Academy of Sciences and Humanities.

WRITINGS: (With E. F. Burak) *ha-Lashon ha-'aravit ha-ma'asit* (title means "The Practical Teaching of Arabic"), Kiryath Sepher (Jerusalem), 1952; *Dikduk 'ivri shitati* (title means "Methodical Hebrew Grammar"), Hebrew Institute for Teaching by Correspondence in Israel (Jerusalem), 1954; (editor with Samuel E. Loewenstamm) *Otsar Leshon ha-Mikra* (title means "Thesaurus of the Language of the Bible"), Bible Concordance Press (Jerusalem), 1957 ff.; (editor) *Moses ben Maimon Responsa*, Volumes I-III, Mekize Niroslamim (Jerusalem), 1957-61; *Syntax des palaestinensischen Bauern-dialektes von Bir-Zet*, Verlag fuer Orientkunde, Vorndran (Walldorf-Hessen), 1960; *Dikduk ha-'aravit-ha-yehudit* (title means "A Grammar of Mediaeval Judaeo-Arabic"), Magnes Press (Jerusalem), 1961; *The Emergence and Linguistic Background of Judaeo-Arabic: A Study of the Origins of Middle Arabic*, Oxford University Press, 1965; *Yesodot ha-tahbir* (title means "Foundations of Syntax"), Hebrew Institute for Teaching by Correspondence in Israel, 1966; *A Grammar of Christian Arabic*, Volumes 267, 276, 279, Corpus Scriptorum Christianorum Orientalium (Louvain), 1966-67; *Pseudo-Corrections in Some Semitic Languages*, Israel Academy of Sciences and Humanites (Jerusalem), 1970; *Torat ha-hegeh veha-tsurot* (title means "Phonology and Morphology of Biblical Hebrew"), Hakibbutz Hameuchad (Tel Aviv), 1972-73. Contributor to journals.

WORK IN PROGRESS: A Grammar of Biblical Hebrew, publication by Porta Linguarum Orientalium.

BIOGRAPHICAL/CRITICAL SOURCES: Orbis (Louvain), Volume VII, 1958, Volume IX, 1960.

* * *

BLEDSOE, Thomas (Alexander)   1914-

PERSONAL: Born September 17, 1914, in Charleston, W. Va.; son of Thomas Alexander and Walker (Bradford) Bledsoe; married Bozenka Skrinar, May 14, 1964; children: (previous marriage) Elizabeth Page, Jane Byrd, Mary Walker, Elizabeth Carter, Margaret Randolph, Ann Alexander, Thomas Alexander IV; (stepchildren) Sonja Suzanne Huff, Charles Remmele Huff. *Education:* University of Louisville, A.B., 1937; University of Illinois, A.M., 1938. *Home:* 635 Connecticut St., San Francisco, Calif. 94107. *Agent:* Alex Jackinson, 11 West 42nd St., New York, N.Y. 10036.

CAREER: University of Illinois, Urbana, instructor in English, 1938-43; Rinehart & Co., New York, N.Y., editor, college department, 1946-54; Alfred A. Knopf, Inc., New York, editor, college department, 1954-56; Beacon Press, Inc., Boston, Mass., director and editor-in-chief, 1956-58; Arlington Books, Cambridge, Mass., president and editor-in-chief, 1958-59; Council for Basic Education, Washington, D.C., executive director, 1959-61; American Printing House for the Blind, Louisville, Ky., textbook consultant, 1962-63; Macmillan Co., New York, senior editor, 1963-64; Chandler Publishing Co., San Francisco, Calif., director of elementary and high school division, 1964-65. *Military service:* U.S. Naval Reserve, 1943-45; became lieutenant. *Member:* Authors League of America. *Awards, honors:* H.H.D., University of Louisville, 1959.

WRITINGS: (With Robert J. Geist) *Current Prose*, Rinehart, 1953; (editor, and author of critical and historical introduction) Hamlin Garland, *Main Travelled Roads*, Rinehart, 1954; *Dear Uncle Bramwell* (novel), A. Swallow, 1963; *Jane Austen: Pride and Prejudice* (study guide), Barnes & Noble, 1966; *Great Expectations [by] Charles Dickens*, Barnes & Noble, 1966; *Meanwhile Back at the Henhouse* (novel), A. Swallow, 1966; *Or We'll All Hang Separately: The Highlander Idea*, Beacon Press, 1969; (translator) Rodolfo Usigli, *Two Plays: Crown of Light and One of These Days*, Illinois University Press, 1971. Contributor of short stories, articles, and reviews to periodicals, including *Western Review, Trace, Accent, Anvil*, and *CEA Critic*.

WORK IN PROGRESS: Several novels.

SIDELIGHTS: Bledsoe describes his novels (he has six more written or in the works) as "off-beat" and adds candidly that he has had more split decisions from publishers about them "than Bobo Olsen."

"My research is into the human interior, my effort [is] to keep writing novels that interpret the condition of modern man. That high-sounding phrase means that I am interested in people in the *now* in which they exist. To make both come alive is a rough job, almost as tough as trying to get the results published."

His viewpoint after almost twenty years as a professional editor: "I've settled on educational publishing because here I can introduce a lot of subversive (and important) ideas in books that will make money, or can, and might actually teach kids something important.... I am personally bitten by the bug of doing something that I consider important to make a living, but I am much impressed for the case for doing exactly the opposite. What I know for certain is that there is no middle ground between the two, for the writer at least. That ambivalence has been the fate of most of the many ad-men I have known, the majority of them aspiring writers at the bar at lunch.

"The years I have spent in publishing and my own experiences as a writer have left me both cynical and determined about the chances of a writer who follows no party line, neither square nor hip ... and my advice to any young writer is that if you are good enough in your own terms, publication depends on a combination of energy and luck. ...

"The serious writer's task ... is to enforce his art and his view of life on people who don't have the imagination to conceive it themselves. He has to believe in himself, start with the knowledge that he has nine strikes against him and be willing to erect a corpus that finally cannot be ignored. In short, he has to work.

"My chief avocations are music, sports, and books. But this doesn't get said in proper perspective. My single avocation is the marvelous, ribald, delicate, wonderful joy of life, and out of this all my writing comes as anyone's must."†

*   *   *

BLEICH, Alan R.   1913-

PERSONAL: Born September 26, 1913, in Brooklyn, N.Y.; son of Max (a dress designer) and Anna (Greenberg) Bleich; married Vera Schwartz (an interior decorator), May 27, 1936; children: Herbert, William, Laurie. *Education:* New York University, B.A., 1934; Royal College of Edinburgh, M.D., 1940. *Home:* 34 West 11th St., New York, N.Y. 10011. *Agent:* Paul R. Reynolds, Inc., 599 Fifth Ave., New York, N.Y. 10017.

CAREER: Diplomate, American Board of Radiology, Bellevue Hospital, New York, N.Y., resident in radiology, 1949; Central Nassau Medical Group, Hempstead, N.Y., now medical director. Associate professor, New York Medical College, New York, N.Y. *Military service:* U.S. Army Air Forces, flight surgeon, 1942-46; became major; received Soldier's Medal. *Member:* North American Radiological Society, American Medical Association, American College of Radiology, New York Roentgen Society, New York County Medical Society.

WRITINGS: The Story of X-Rays from Roentgen to Isotopes, Dover, 1962; *Your Career in Medicine*, Messner, 1964. Contributor to medical periodicals.

*   *   *

BLENCH, J(ohn) W(heatley)   1926-

PERSONAL: Born July 17, 1926, in Berwick upon Tweed, Northumberland, England; son of John (a businessman) and Frances (Fisackerly) Blench. *Education:* St. John's College, Cambridge, B.A., 1949, M.A., 1954, Ph.D., 1956. *Politics:* Conservative ("progressive traditionalism"). *Office:* University of Durham, Newcastle upon Tyne, England.

CAREER: University of Aberdeen, Aberdeen, Scotland, lecturer in English, 1956-65; University of Durham, Newcastle upon Tyne, England, lecturer in English, 1965—. Scottish Episcopal Church, lay reader of Diocese of Aberdeen and Orkney, 1963-65, and lay member of Provincial Synod. *Military service:* Royal Navy, 1945-47; became lieutenant. *Member:* Gregorian Association, United University Club (London).

WRITINGS: Preaching in England in the Late Fifteenth and Sixteenth Centuries, Barnes & Noble, 1964. Contributor to learned journals.

WORK IN PROGRESS: Studies in late nineteenth- and early twentieth-century fiction.

SIDELIGHTS: Blench said: "I believe very much in the civilizing value of a literary education, but like T. S. Eliot, I do not think that literature should be regarded as in some way a substitute for religion." He is competent in French, reads Latin and ancient Greek, has working knowledge of Italian and German. *Avocational interests:* Sports, motoring, the theater (especially Shakespeare and Elizabethan drama), music (Bach, Wagner, folksongs, and military bands), travel in western Europe.†

*   *   *

BLODGETT, Harold William   1900-

PERSONAL: Born March 24, 1900, in Corning, N.Y.; son of Arba Martin and Minnie (Alderman) Blodgett; married Dorothy Briggs, August 21, 1924; children: Millicent Blodgett Seely, William (deceased), Geoffrey. *Education:* Cornell University, A.B., 1921, A.M., 1923, Ph.D., 1929. *Politics:* Independent. *Religion:* Protestant. *Home:* 1086 Gillespie St., Schenectady, N.Y. 12308.

CAREER: Cornell University, Ithaca, N.Y., instructor in English, 1921-23; *Buffalo Courier*, Buffalo, N.Y., reporter, 1923-24; University of Illinois, Urbana, instructor in English, 1924-26; Keuka College, Keuka Park, N.Y., assistant professor of English, 1926-28, head of department of English, 1934-36; Dartmouth College, Hanover, N.H., assistant professor of English, 1929-34; Union College, Schenectady, N.Y., 1936-65, professor of English and chairman of department, then Thomas Lamont Professor of English Literature, 1965, professor emeritus, 1965—. Fulbright lecturer at University of Leiden, 1952-53, University of Teheran, 1958-59, University of Bombay, 1965-66; summer lecturer at University of Pennsylvania, New York University, Duke University, Salzburg Seminar in American Studies, 1953, Warsaw, Poland, 1959; visiting professor, University of New Mexico, 1966-67. *Military service:* U.S. Navy, 1918.

MEMBER: American Studies Association (president, New York chapter, 1962), College English Association (president, New York chapter, 1954), Modern Language Association of America, American Association of University Professors, Iran-America Society, Schenectady County Historical Association, Phi Kappa Phi, Sigma Upsilon. *Awards, honors:* Guggenheim fellow, 1955-56.

WRITINGS: Walt Whitman in England, Cornell University Press, 1934; *Samson Occom: The Biography of an Indian Preacher*, Dartmouth College Publications, 1935.

(Contributor) Robert E. Spiller and others, editors, *Literary History of the United States*, Macmillian, 1948.

Editor: *The Story Survey*, Lippincott, 1939, revised edition, 1953; (with Burges Johnson) *Readings for Our Time*, two volumes, Ginn, 1942, revised edition, 1948-49; (with Spiller) *The Roots of National Culture*, Macmillan, 1949; *The Best of Whitman*, Ronald, 1953; Walt Whitman, *1855-56 Notebook*, Southern Illinois University Press, 1959; (with Sculley Bradley) Whitman, *Leaves of Grass*, New York University Press, 1965, critical edition, Norton, 1973, variorum edition, New York University Press, 1974.

*   *   *

BLOESCH, Donald G.   1928-

PERSONAL: Born May 3, 1928, in Bremen, Ind.; son of Herbert P. (a minister) and Adele (Silberman) Bloesch; married November, 1962, wife's maiden name Jackson. *Education:* Elmhurst College, B.A., 1950; Chicago Theological Seminary, B.D., 1953; University of Chicago,

Ph.D., 1956; Oxford University, postdoctoral study, 1956-57. *Politics:* Independent. *Home:* 2126 University Ave., Dubuque, Iowa.

CAREER: Ordained minister of Evangelical and Reformed Church (now United Church of Christ), 1953; pastor, 1953-56; University of Dubuque Theological Seminary, Dubuque, Iowa, professor of theology, 1958. *Member:* American Theological Association. *Awards, honors:* World Council of Churches fellowship, Oxford University, 1956-57; Sealantic fellowship for study in Germany, 1963-64.

WRITINGS: Centers of Christian Renewal, United Church, 1964; *The Christian Life and Salvation,* Eerdmans, 1967; *The Christian Witness in a Secular Age: An Evaluation of Nine Contemporary Theologians,* Augsburg, 1968; *The Crisis of Piety: Essays Towards a Theology of the Christian Life,* Eerdmans, 1968; (with Jordan Aumann and others) *Christian Spirituality East and West,* Priory, 1968; *The Reform of the Church,* Eerdmans, 1970; *The Ground of Certainty: Toward an Evangelical Theology of Revelation,* Eerdmans, 1971; (editor and author of introduction) *Servants of Christ: Deaconesses in Renewal,* Bethany Fellowship, 1971; *The Evangelical Renaissance,* Eerdmans, 1973; *Wellsprings of Renewal: Promise in Christian Communal Life,* Eerdmans, in press. Contributor to *Theology and Life, Christian Century, Pulpit,* and *Interpretation.*

WORK IN PROGRESS: A manuscript on the doctrine of salvation.†

* * *

BLOOM, Gordon F. 1918-

PERSONAL: Born November 11, 1918, in Buffalo, N.Y.; son of Hyman A. and Mina Bloom; married Marjorie Winer (a teacher), June 27, 1948; children: Barbara, Martha, Nancy. *Education:* University of Buffalo, B.A. (summa cum laude), 1939; Harvard University, M.A. and M.P.A., 1941, Ph.D., 1946, LL.B. and J.D. (cum laude), 1948. *Religion:* Jewish. *Home:* 160 Dartmouth St., West Newton, Mass. 02165.

CAREER: Office of Price Administration, Washington, D.C., economist, 1941-42; Foley, Hoag & Eliot (law firm), Boston, Mass., lawyer, 1948-53; Elm Farm Foods Co. (retail food chain), Boston, Mass., vice president of operations, 1953-60, president and general manager, 1960-67; Marathon Realty Corp., president and director, 1967—; Metropolitan Markets, Inc., president, 1967—. Chairman of board of directors, National Association of Food Chains, 1964-66; treasurer and director, Riteway Department Stores, Ltd., Canada, 1964-66; senior lecturer at Sloan School of Management, Massachusetts Institute of Technology, 1968—; panel member, White House Conference on Food, Nutrition, and Health, 1969-70; member, Food Retailing Advisory Commission, Office of Emergency Preparedness, Executive Office of the President, 1969—. Trustee and member of board of investment, Newton Savings Bank, 1969; member of planning board, City of Newton, 1970—; member of Governor's Emergency Commission on Food, 1973-74; director, Tyco Laboratories, Inc., and Miralin Company. Director of Junior Achievement, Inc.; trustee of Combined Jewish Philanthropies; vice-chairman, Boston College Development Fund. *Military service:* U.S. Navy, 1942-46; became lieutenant commander. *Member:* American Marketing Association, Industrial Relations Research Association, Phi Beta Kappa.

WRITINGS: (With Herbert R. Northrup) *Economics of Labor Relations,* Irwin, 1954, 7th edition, 1973; (with Northrup) *Government and Labor,* Irwin, 1963; (with Northrup and Richard L. Rowan) *Readings in Labor Economics,* Irwin, 1963; *Productivity in the Food Industry: Problems and Potential,* M.I.T. Press, 1972; (with F. Marion Fletcher) *The Negro in the Supermarket Industry,* University of Pennsylvania Press, 1972; (with Fletcher and Charles Perry) *The Negro in Retail Trade: A Study of Racial Policies in the Department Store, Drugstore and Supermarket Industries,* University of Pennsylvania Press, 1972; (contributor) John Mayer, editor, *U.S. Nutrition Policies in the Seventies,* W. H. Freeman, 1972. Contributor of articles to professional journals.

WORK IN PROGRESS: A book on the social responsibility of corporations.

* * *

BLOOM, Harold 1930-

PERSONAL: Born July 11, 1930, in New York, N.Y.; son of William and Paula (Lev) Bloom; married Jeanne Gould, 1958; children: Daniel, David. *Education:* Cornell University, B.A., 1951; Yale University, Ph.D., 1955. *Religion:* Jewish. *Office:* Department of English, Yale University, New Haven, Conn.

CAREER: Yale University, New Haven, Conn., instructor, 1955-60, assistant professor, 1960-63, associate professor, 1963-65, professor of English, 1965-74, DeVane Professor of the Humanities, 1974—. *Member:* Modern Language Association of America. *Awards, honors:* John Addison Porter Prize, Yale University, 1956, for *Shelley's Mythmaking;* Guggenheim fellowship, 1962-63; Melville Cane Award, Poetry Society of America, 1971, for *Yeats;* National Book Awards juror, 1973; Doctor of Humane Letters, Boston College, 1973.

WRITINGS: Shelley's Mythmaking, Yale University Press, 1959; *The Visionary Company: A Reading of English Romantic Poetry,* Doubleday, 1961, revised edition, Cornell University Press, 1971; *Blake's Apocalypse,* Doubleday, 1963, reprinted, Cornell University Press, 1970; *Yeats,* Oxford University Press, 1970; *The Ringers in the Tower: Studies in Romantic Tradition,* University of Chicago Press, 1971; *The Anxiety of Influence: A Theory of Poetry,* Oxford University Press, 1973; *Kabbalah and Criticism,* Oxford University Press, 1974.

Editor, except as indicated: *English Romantic Poetry,* Doubleday, 1961, two-volume revised edition, Anchor Books, 1963; (with John Hollander) *The Wind and the Rain,* Doubleday, 1961; *Literary Criticism of John Ruskin,* Anchor Books, 1965; (author of commentary) D. V. Erdman, editor, *The Poetry and Prose of William Blake,* Doubleday, 1965; (with Frederick W. Hilles) *From Sensibility to Romanticism: Essays Presented to Frederick A. Pottle,* Oxford University Press, 1965, reprinted, 1970; Percy Bysshe Shelley, *Selected Poetry,* New American Library, 1966.

Walter Horatio Pater, *Marius the Epicurean: His Sensations and Ideas,* New American Library, 1970; (compiler) *Romanticism and Consciousness: Essays in Criticism,* Norton, 1970; Samuel Taylor Coleridge, *Selected Poetry,* New American Library, 1972; *The Romantic Tradition in American Literature,* thirty-three volumes, Arno, 1972; (with Lionel Trilling) *Romantic Prose and Poetry,* Oxford University Press, 1973; (with Trilling) *Victorian Prose and Poetry,* Oxford University Press, 1973; (with Frank Kermode, Hollander and others) *Oxford Anthology of English Literature*, two volumes, Oxford University Press, 1973.

WORK IN PROGRESS: The Native Strain: American Romanticism, and *The Covering Cherub, or Poetic Influence.*

SIDELIGHTS: In Allen Grossman's opinion, "Professor Harold Bloom's large book on Yeats is, I think, the best thing going on the subject. His exegetical seriousness makes him the most lucid of hostile witnesses." John Hollander said: "Anyone studying or teaching modern poetry will be using this book for decades. And Yeats aside, anyone interested in sophisticated treatments of the relation of art to life will need to start again with its opening chapters."

*   *   *

BLOOM, Lynn Marie Zimmerman   1934-

PERSONAL: Born July 11, 1934, in Ann Arbor, Mich.; daughter of Oswald Theodore (a professor of chemical engineering) and Mildred (Kisling) Zimmerman; married Martin Bloom (a social psychologist), July 11, 1958; children: Bard, Laird. *Education:* University of Michigan, B.A., 1956, M.A., 1957, Ph.D., 1963; Ohio State University, graduate study, 1957-58. *Politics:* Liberal. *Home:* 96 Arundel Place, Clayton, Mo. 63105.

CAREER: Western Reserve University (now Case Western Reserve University), Cleveland, Ohio, lecturer in English, 1962-63, instructor, 1963-65, associate in English, 1965-67; full-time writer, 1967-70; Butler University, Indianapolis, Ind., assistant professor, 1970-73, associate professor of English, 1973-74. Member, Heights Citizens for Human Rights, 1964-67; member of Host Family Committee, Cleveland Council on World Affairs, 1965-67; advisor to Indiana Commission on the Humanities project on Indiana racial history, 1973-74; judge of National Council of Teachers of English national high school writing contests, 1973, 1974. *Member:* Modern Language Association of America, National Council of Teachers of English, American Association of University Professors, College Conference on Composition and Communication (meeting section chairman, 1973), Popular Culture Association (meeting section chairman, 1973), Midwest Modern Language Association, Indiana College English Association, Indiana Civil Liberties Union, Non-Partisans for Better Schools (Indianapolis), Phi Beta Kappa, Phi Kappa Phi, Alpha Lambda Delta. *Awards, honors: Mademoiselle* College Board Contest national award for fiction, 1955; Butler University Outstanding Educator, 1972-73, 1973-74; Butler University Faculty Fellowship, 1974.

WRITINGS: (Editor with Francis L. Utley and Arthur F. Kinney) *Bear, Man, and God: Seven Approaches to William Faulkner's "The Bear,"* Random House, 1964, revised edition, 1971; (editor with Kinney and Kenneth W. Kuiper) *Symposium*, Houghton, 1969; (editor with Kinney and Kuiper) *Symposium on Love*, Houghton, 1970; *Doctor Spock: Biography of a Conservative Radical*, Bobbs-Merrill, 1972. Regular contributor to *Abstracts of English Studies*, 1961-68. Articles on biography, world literature, and the teaching and learning of writing (several with husband, Martin Bloom) have been published in scholarly journals. Contributor of poetry and reviews to magazines and journals.

WORK IN PROGRESS: A book *Re-Creations of Creators: The Uses of Imaginative Writings in Literary Biographies*; an authorized biography of Indianapolis Mayor Richard G. Lugar; a book on biographies and autobiographies of women; editing a diary kept throughout World War II by Natalie Crouter, an American civilian captive in a Japanese internment camp in the Philippines, *Courage is 'Grace under Pressure.'*

AVOCATIONAL INTERESTS: Gourmet cooking, swimming and travel.

*   *   *

BLUESTONE, Max   1926-

PERSONAL: Born June 30, 1926, in New York, N.Y.; son of Samuel and Rebecca (Blum) Bluestone; married Joanne Baxter, Sept. 23, 1950; children: Scott, Rebecca, Daniel, Deborah. *Education:* College of the Holy Cross, Bachelor of Naval Science, 1946; Harvard University, A.M., 1952, Ph.D., 1959. *Home:* 17 Oxford Rd., Newton Center, Mass. 02159. *Office:* Department of English, University of Massachusetts at Boston, 100 Arlington St., Boston, Mass. 02116.

CAREER: Haverford College, Haverford, Pa., instructor, 1955-57; Eastern Pennsylvania Psychiatric Institute, part-time instructor, 1956-57; Babson Institute, Babson Park, Mass., associate professor and chairman, department of humanities, 1957-62; Harvard University, Graduate School of Education, Cambridge, Mass., lecturer in education, 1962-65; University of Massachusetts at Boston, associate professor of English, 1965—. *Military service:* U.S. Naval Reserve, 1943-47; became ensign. *Member:* Modern Language Association of America, Shakespeare Association, Renaissance Society of America, College English Association, Conference on College Composition and Communication, English Institute, National Council of Teachers of English, American Association of University Professors.

WRITINGS: (Editor with Norman C. Rabkin) *Shakespeare's Contemporaries: Modern Studies in English Renaissance Drama* (anthology), Prentice-Hall, 1961, 2nd edition, 1970; *From Story to Stage: The Dramatic Adaptation of Prose Fiction in the Period of Shakespeare and His Contemporaries*, Humanities, 1974. Author of manual on expository writing. Contributor to *Drama Survey, Essays in Criticism, Western Humanities Review*, and other scholarly journals.

SIDELIGHTS: Bluestone has a knowledge of French, German, and Latin.†

*   *   *

BLUHM, William T(heodore)   1923-

PERSONAL: Born October 13, 1923, in Newark, N.J.; son of Frederick Theodore and Charlotte (Walz) Bluhm; married Eleanor Kearns, April 22, 1950; children: Catherine Elizabeth, Susanna Marie, Andrew Edward Frederick. *Education:* Brown University, B.A., 1948; Fletcher School of Law and Diplomacy, M.A., 1949; University of Chicago, Ph.D., 1957. *Home:* 589 Bending Bough Dr., Webster, N.Y. 14580. *Office:* Harkness Hall, University of Rochester, Rochester, N.Y. 14627.

CAREER: University of Rochester, Rochester, N.Y., instructor in government, 1952-53; Brown University, Providence, R.I., instructor in government, 1953-57; University of Rochester, assistant professor, 1957-63, associate professor, 1963-67, professor of political science, 1967—. Secretary of Wedge, Inc., 1968—. *Military service:* U.S. Army,

Signal Corps, 1943-46; became technical sergeant; received Bronze Star. *Member:* American Political Science Association, American Association for Legal and Political Philosophy, American Association of University Professors, New York State Political Science Association (president, 1971-72), Rochester Association for the United Nations (board of directors, 1964-68), Phi Beta Kappa, Sigma Nu. *Awards, honors:* Fulbright grant, 1965-66.

WRITINGS: Theories of the Political Systems: Classics of Political Thought and Modern Political Analysis, Prentice-Hall, 1965, 2nd edition, 1971; *Building an Austrian Nation: The Political Integration of a Western State*, Yale University Press, 1973; *Ideologies and Attitudes: Modern Political Culture*, Prentice-Hall, 1974. Contributor to *Encyclopedia of Philosophy* and to political science journals.

SIDELIGHTS: Blum told *CA*: "I am an admirer of the Realist school of political philosophy exemplified in the writings of Hans Morgenthau and Reinhold Niebuhr. My own political philosophy is greatly influenced by these two writers." Bluhm reads, writes, and speaks German and French fluently.†

*   *   *

BLUM, Fred 1932-

PERSONAL: Born November 27, 1932, in New York, N.Y.; son of Henry and Jennie (Cohen) Blum; married Beula Eisenstadt (an educator). *Education:* Oberlin College, B.M., 1954; Ohio University, M.F.A., 1955; University of Iowa, Ph.D., 1959; Catholic University, M.S. L.S., 1968. *Politics:* Democrat. *Religion:* Jewish. *Office:* Office of the Director, Eastern Michigan University Library, Ypsilanti, Mich. 48197.

CAREER: With New York Public Library, New York, N.Y., 1959; Library of Congress, Washington, D.C., reference librarian in Music Division, 1961-66, editor in Union Catalog Division, 1966-67; Catholic University Libraries, Washington D.C., head of special services department, 1967-71, head of technical services department, 1971-74; Eastern Michigan University, Ypsilanti, Mich., director of library and Center of Educational Resources, 1974—. Exchange teacher in Germany, 1960-61. *Member:* American Library Association (representative to American National Standards Institute, 1972-74), Music Library Association (chairman, Audiovisual and Microform Committee), American Society for Information Science, Michigan Library Association, District of Columbia Library Association, Beta Phi Mu. *Awards, honors:* Exchange student, Germany, 1959-60.

WRITINGS: Music Monographs in Series: A Bibliography of Numbered Monograph Series in the Field of Music Current since 1945, Scarecrow, 1964; *Jean Sibelius: An International Bibliography on the Occasion of the Centennial Celebrations, 1965*, Information Service, Inc., 1965. Contributor of reviews and articles to *Catholic Library World*, *Civil War History*, *Current Musicology*, *Journal of the American Society for Information Science*, *Microcosm*, and other publications.

*   *   *

BLUM, Richard H(osmer Adams) 1927-

PERSONAL: Born October 7, 1927, in Fort Wayne, Ind.; son of Hosmer Louie (an engineer) and Imogene Ruth (Hartshorn Heino) Blum; married Eva Maria Spitz (a psychologist), July 6, 1957; stepchildren: Mary Elizabeth Ship-

pee, John Shippee. *Education:* San Jose State College (now California State University, San Jose), A.B. (magna cum laude), 1948; Stanford University, Ph.D., 1951. *Politics:* Democrat. *Religion:* Unitarian. *Address:* P.O. Box 4012, Woodside, Calif. 94062.

CAREER: Stanford Research Institute, Stanford, Calif., research associate, 1953-56; California Medical Association, Medical Review and Advisory Board, research director, 1956-58; San Mateo (Calif.) County Mental Health Services, acting research director, 1959-61; University of California, School of Criminology, Berkeley, lecturer, 1962-64; Stanford University, Stanford, Calif., director of Joint Program in Drugs, Crime, and Community Studies, and consulting professor of psychology, 1964—. Consultant to police departments; member of San Mateo County Democratic Central Committee, 1954-60. *Military service:* U.S. Army, served in Korea, 1951-53. *Member:* International Society of Criminology, American Criminological Association, American Psychological Association, American Sociological Association, American Public Health Association, Royal Society of Health, American Archaeological Institute, Sigma Xi.

WRITINGS: Management of the Doctor-Patient Relationship, McGraw, 1960; (with J. Ezekiel) *Clinical Records for Mental Health Services*, C. C Thomas, 1962; (editor and contributor) *Police Selection* (foreword by Earl Warren) C. C Thomas, 1964; *A Commonsense Guide to Doctors, Hospitals and Medical Care*, Macmillan, 1964; (with others) *Utopiates: A Study of the Use and Users of LSD 25*, Atherton, 1964; (with wife, Eva Blum) *Health and Healing in Rural Greece*, Stanford University Press, 1965; (with Eva Blum) *Alcoholism: Modern Psychological Approaches to Treatment*, Jossey-Bass, 1967; (with associates) *Society and Drugs*, Jossey-Bass, 1969; (with associates) *Students and Drugs*, Jossey-Bass, 1969.

(With Eva Blum) *The Dangerous Hour: The Lore of Crisis and Mystery in Rural Greece* (foreword by Prince Peter of Greece), Scribner, 1970; *Deceivers and Deceived: Observations on Confidence Men and Their Victims, Informants and Their Quarry, Political and Industrial Spies and Ordinary Citizens*, C. C Thomas, 1972; (with associates) *Horatio Alger's Children: Role of the Family in the Origin and Prevention of Drug Risk*, Jossey-Bass, 1972; (with associates) *The Dream Sellers: Perspectives on Drug Dealers*, Jossey-Bass, 1972; *Surveillance and Espionage in a Free Society*, Praeger, 1972; (with associates) *Drug Dealers—Taking Action: Options for International Response*, Jossey-Bass, 1973; (editor with D. Bovet and J. Moore) *Controlling Drugs: International Handbook for Psychoactive Drug Classification*, Jossey-Bass, 1974.

Fiction: *Death and Festivals* (novel), R. Hale, 1968; *The Late Lieutenant Dessin and Other Stories*, M. Jones, 1968.

Contributor of articles to scientific journals, and of short stories and poetry to magazines.

*   *   *

BLUM, Virgil C(larence) 1913-

PERSONAL: Born March 27, 1913, in Defiance, Iowa; son of John Peter (a farmer) and Elizabeth (Rushenberg) Blum. *Education:* St. Louis University, A.B., 1938, M.A., 1945, Ph.D., 1954; University of Chicago, graduate study, 1950-51. *Home:* 1131 West Wisconsin Ave., Milwaukee, Wis. 53233. *Office:* Department of Political Science, Marquette University, Milwaukee, Wis. 53233.

CAREER: Roman Catholic priest, member of Society of Jesus; Campion High School, Prairie du Chien, Wis., instructor in history, mathematics, and Latin, 1941-44; Creighton University, Omaha, Neb., instructor, 1953-54, assistant professor of political science, 1954-56; Marquette University, Milwaukee, Wis., associate professor, 1958-61, professor of political science, 1961—, chairman of political science department, 1961-65. Lecturer on freedom of choice in education. Citizens for Educational Freedom, member of board of trustees, 1963—, chairman, 1972—. Member: American Political Science Association, Midwest Political Science Association, Catholic League for Religious and Civil Rights (president, 1973—), Pi Gamma Mu.

WRITINGS: Freedom of Choice in Education, Macmillan, 1958, revised edition, Paulist Press, 1963; (contributor) Bower Aly, editor, Government and Education: A Complete Discussion and Debate, Artcraft, 1961; (contributor) Federal Aid and Catholic Schools, Helicon, 1964; Freedom in Education, Doubleday, 1965; Education: Freedom and Competition, Argus, 1967; Catholic Education: Survival or Demise, Argus, 1969; (contributor) D. D. McGarry and Leo Ward, editors, Educational Freedom, Bruce, 1969; (contributor) Russell Shaw and Richard J. Hurley, editors, Trends and Issues in Catholic Education, Citation, 1969; Catholic Parents—Political Eunuchs, Media and Materials, 1972; (contributor) George R. La Noue, editor, Educational Vouchers: Concepts and Controversies, Teachers College Press, 1972.

WORK IN PROGRESS: Choice in Education as a Function of Wealth; Constitutionality of Education Tax Credits; and research in freedom in education versus state monopoly in education.

SIDELIGHTS: Blum is competent in German and has traveled through Germany as a guest of the West German government.

* * *

BLUNT, Wilfrid (Jasper Walter) 1901-

PERSONAL: Born July 19, 1901, in Ham, Surrey, England; son of Arthur Stanley Vaughan (a clergyman) and Hilda (Master) Blunt. Education: Attended Marlborough College, 1915-20, and Worcester College, Oxford, 1920-21; Royal College of Art, London, England, A.R.C.A., 1923. Agent: Curtis Brown Ltd., 1 Craven Hill, London W.2, England. Office: Watts Gallery, Compton, Guildford, Surrey, England.

CAREER: Haileybury College, Hertfordshire, England, art master, 1923-38; Eton College, Windsor, England, drawing master, 1938-59; Watts Gallery, Compton, Guildford, England, curator, 1959—. Member: Linnean Society (fellow). Awards, honors: Veitch Gold Medal for The Art of Botanical Illustration.

WRITINGS: The Haileybury Buildings, privately printed, 1936; Desert Hawk, Methuen, 1947; The Art of Botanical Illustration, Collins, 1950, Scribner, 1951; Tulipomania, Penguin, 1950; Black Sunrise: The Life and Times of Mulai Ismail, Emperor of Morocco, Methuen, 1951; Sweet Roman Hand: Five Hundred Years of Italic Cursive Script, J. Barrie, 1952; Japanese Colour Prints, Faber, 1952; Georg Dionysius Ehret, Traylen, 1953; Pietro's Pilgrimage, J. Barrie, 1953; Sebastiano, J. Barrie, 1956; (with Sacheverell Sitwell and Patrick Synge) Great Flower Books, 1700-1900, Collins, 1956; A Persian Spring, Dufour, 1957; (with James Russell) Old Garden Roses, New York Graphic Society, 1957; Lady Muriel, Methuen, 1962; Of

Flowers and a Village, Hamish Hamilton, 1963; Cockerell, Hamish Hamilton, 1964, Knopf, 1965; Omar: A Fantasy for Animal Lovers, Chapman & Hall, 1966; Isfahan: Pearl of Persia, Elek, 1966; John Christie of Glyndebourne, Bles, 1968; The Dream King: Ludwig II of Bavaria, Hamish Hamilton, 1970; The Compleat Naturalist: A Life of Linnaeus, Collins, 1971; The Golden Road to Samarkand, Hamish Hamilton, 1973; On Wings of Song, Hamish Hamilton, 1974. Contributor of articles to journals.

SIDELIGHTS: Martin Levin, writing in The New York Times Book Review, called Omar "a delicious satire." He further commented, "Mr. Blunt has gone through the looking glass to create a beautifully modulated put-on of animal lovers and other types."

Noting the "excellent text" of Isfahan, The Times Literary Supplement wrote, "In his witty, graceful account of this unique city [Blunt] has done an inestimable service to all who will visit it in the future."

In its review of The Compleat Naturalist, Time observed, "Wilfrid Blunt's richly decorated biography admirably illustrates how Linnaeus' single-mindedness and plodding devotion to stamens and pistils laid the foundation of modern botany."

AVOCATIONAL INTERESTS: Singing, travel.

* * *

BOAK, (Charles) Denis 1932-

PERSONAL: Born August 25, 1932, in Hazel Grove, England; son of Arthur Tyson (a schoolmaster) and Nora (Jenkinson) Boak; married Estelle Christi Bok (a librarian), March 8, 1966. Education: Attended Manchester Grammar School, Manchester, England, 1943-50; Clare College, Cambridge, B.A., 1954, M.A., 1958, Ph.D., 1961; Sorbonne, University of Paris, graduate study, 1954-55, 1956-57. Office: Department of Romance Studies, University of Calgary, Alberta, Canada.

CAREER: University of Hong Kong, Hong Kong, lecturer in modern languages, 1961-65, head of department of modern languages, 1964-65; University of Hull, Hull, England, senior lecturer in modern French literature, 1966-69; University of Calgary, Calgary, Alberta, professor of French, 1969—. Military service: British Army, Royal Artillery, 1950-51. Member: Society of Authors, Association Internationale des Etudes Francaises, Society for French Studies.

WRITINGS: Roger Martin du Gard, Clarendon Press, 1963; Andre Malraux, Clarendon Press, 1968; Jules Romains, Twayne, 1974. Contributor to Encyclopedia of World Biography, Revue des Letters Modernes, Critical Bibliography of Twentieth Century French Literature.

WORK IN PROGRESS: A book on pessimism in nineteenth century French literature.

SIDELIGHTS: Boak lived for some time in France, Spain, Italy, Germany, Austria, and Switzerland, and has traveled widely in western Europe and the Far East. He speaks French, German, Spanish, Italian, some Chinese. Avocational interests: Swimming, skiing, walking, talking, eating, drinking, reading, listening to music.

* * *

BOARMAN, Patrick M(adigan) 1922-

PERSONAL: Born April 23, 1922, in Buffalo, N.Y.; son of Marcus Daly (a lawyer) and Virginia (Madigan) Boarman;

married Katrin Schumacher, December 12, 1953; children: Thomas, Christopher, Jesse, Barbara. *Education:* Fordham University, A.B., 1943; Columbia University, M.S. in Journalism, 1946; University of Geneva, Ph.D., 1965; also studied at University of Amsterdam, 1949-50, University of Michigan, 1958, University of Virginia, 1965. *Office:* Center for International Business, Pepperdine University, 333 South Flower St., Los Angeles, Calif. 90017.

CAREER: Columbia Broadcasting System, correspondent in Geneva, Switzerland, 1947-48; John Carroll University, Cleveland, Ohio, assistant professor of economics, 1948-49; National Catholic Welfare Conference, director of Office of Cultural Affairs, Bonn, Germany, 1951-55; University of Wisconsin—Milwaukee, assistant professor of economics, 1956-62; Bucknell University, Lewisburg, Pa., associate professor of economics, 1962-67; Republican Conference, House of Representatives, U.S. Congress, Washington, D.C., director of research, 1967-68; Pepperdine University, Center for International Business, Los Angeles, Calif., director of research, 1972—. Consultant, General Electric, 1964-65, American Telephone and Telegraph, 1969, and U.S. Secretary of the Treasury, 1970-71. *Military service:* U.S. Army, 1943. *Member:* American Economic Association, National Association of Business Economists, Royal Economic Society. *Awards, honors:* Fulbright fellow at University of Amsterdam, 1949-50; Distinguished Service Cross of Order of Merit, West German Federal Republic, 1956.

WRITINGS: (Editor) *Der Christ und die soziale Marktwirtschaft*, Kohlhammer (Stuttgart), 1955; (translator) Wilhelm Roepke, *Economics of the Free Society*, Regnery, 1963; *Union Monopolies and Antitrust Restraints*, Labor Policy Association, 1963; *Germany's Economic Dilemma—Inflation and the Balance of Payments*, Yale University Press, 1964; *The World's Money*, Bucknell University, 1965; (editor) *The Economy of South Vietnam: A New Beginning*, Center for International Business, 1973; (editor) *Trade with China*, Praeger, 1974. Contributor to *Modern Age*, *Challenge*, *Wall Street Journal*, and other journals and newspapers.

WORK IN PROGRESS: Research on international economic policy, on the theory and practice of the gold standard, and on capitalism and Christianity; a book on multinational firms and governments; a book on world monetary disorder.

*   *   *

BOECKMAN, Charles 1920-

PERSONAL: Surname is pronounced Beckman; born November 9, 1920, in San Antonio, Tex.; son of Charles Otto (a salesman) and Elizabeth (Kiesewetter) von Boeckman; married Patricia Ellen Kennelly (a teacher), July 25, 1965. *Education:* Attended Texas Lutheran College, 1938-39, and New School for Social Research, 1958. *Religion:* Lutheran. *Home:* 322 Del Mar, Corpus Christi, Tex. 78404. *Agent:* Lenniger Literary Agency, 437 Fifth Ave., New York, N.Y. 10016.

CAREER: Copywriter and advertising account executive in Corpus Christi, Tex., 1947-51; full-time author, 1951—. Teacher of creative writing, Del Mar College, 1955—; instructor in writers' workshops at University of Houston and for Abiline Writers' Guild. *Member:* Corpus Christi Press Club, Corpus Christi Musicians Association.

WRITINGS: *Maverick Brand*, Bouregy, 1961; *Unsolved Riddles of the Ages*, Criterion, 1965; *Our Regional Indus-*

tries, Criterion, 1966; *Cool, Hot and Blue*, Luce, 1968; *And the Beat Goes On*, Luce, 1972. Author of television plays for "Alfred Hitchcock Presents" and "Celebrity Playhouse." Contributor of short stories to magazines, including *Mystery Magazine*; about one thousand stories published since 1940.

WORK IN PROGRESS: A suspense novel.

SIDELIGHTS: In his review of *Cool, Hot and Blue* in *Book World*, Will Leonard noted, "Boeckman . . . tells it like it was and is. He radiates affection for jazz and jazzmen. . . . He tells the history and development of the succeeding fads with remarkable clarity. . . . This is a good enough compendium to interest many an adult."

Boeckman's papers and correspondence are now on file in the library at the University of Oregon. He speaks Spanish and some German.

AVOCATIONAL INTERESTS: Travel, jazz music (plays clarinet and saxophone), and photography.

*   *   *

BOEHM, Eric H. 1918-

PERSONAL: Born July 15, 1918, in Hof, Germany; became U.S. citizen; son of Karl and Bertha (Oppenheimer) Boehm; married Inge Pauli, June 5, 1948; children: Ronald James, Steven David. *Education:* College of Wooster, B.A., 1940; Fletcher School of Law and Diplomacy, M.A., 1942; Yale University, Ph.D., 1951. *Home:* 800 East Micheltorena St., Santa Barbara, Calif. *Office:* ABC-Clio, Inc., P.O. Box 4397, Santa Barbara, Calif. 93103.

CAREER: U.S. Military Government, Berlin, Germany, member of press scrutiny board, 1946-47; U.S. Government, analyst in Vienna, Austria, and at other posts, 1951-58; ABC-Clio, Inc., Santa Barbara, Calif., publisher, 1960—. President, International Academy at Santa Barbara, 1961—; member of advisory board, Summer School of World Affairs, 1963, and of Brooks Foundation. Consultant on bibliography, computer use, and information systems, 1963—. Board member, California Institute of International Studies. *Military service:* U.S. Army Air Forces, 1942-46; became first lieutenant. *Member:* American Society for Information Sciences, American History Association, American Library Association, American Political Science Association, American Studies Association, Western History Association (board member), Western Slavic Association (board member), California Library Association, United Nations Association (member of board of directors, Santa Barbara), Rotary, Phi Beta Kappa. *Awards, honors:* Grants from American Council of Learned Societies, Carnegie Endowment, and U.S. Department of State; Litt.D., Wooster College, 1973.

WRITINGS: (Editor) *We Survived: Fourteen Histories of the Hidden and Hunted of Nazi Germany*, Yale University Press, 1949, reprinted with a new epilogue, Clio Press, 1966; (contributor) William E. Daugherty and Morris Janowitz, *A Psychological Warfare Casebook*, Johns Hopkins Press, 1958; (editor with Lalit Adolphus) *Historical Periodicals: An Annotated World List of Historical and Related Serial Publications*, Clio Press, 1961; *Bibliographies on International Relations and World Affairs: An Annotated Directory*, Clio Press, 1965; *Blueprint for Bibliography: A System for the Social Sciences and Humanities*, Clio Press, 1965; *The Cue System for Bibliography and Indexing*, Clio Press, 1967; (contributor) Dagmar H. Perman, editor, *Bibliography and the Historian*, Clio Press, 1968; (contributor)

Lyman H. Legters, editor, *Russia: Essays in History and Literature*, Humanities, 1972. Editor, *Historical Abstracts*, 1955—; editor, *America: History and Life, a Guide to Periodical Literature*, 1964—; member of editorial board, *Computer Studies*, 1967—. Contributor to journals.

* * *

BOGGESS, Louise Bradford 1912-

PERSONAL: Surname is pronounced *Bog*-gess, with hard g's; born March 28, 1912, in Sweetwater, Tex.; daughter of Giles Edward (a banker and rancher) and Hattie (Corbett) Bradford; married William Fannin Boggess, Jr. (an investigator, U.S. Immigration and Naturalization Service), June 1, 1946; children: Patricia Anne, William Fannin III. *Education:* University of Texas, B.A., 1933, M.A., 1934, graduate study, summers, 1935-39. *Politics:* Democrat. *Religion:* Episcopalian. *Home:* 4016 Martin Dr., San Mateo, Calif. 94403. *Agent:* Curtis Brown Ltd., 575 Madison Ave., New York, N.Y. 10022.

CAREER: Junior high school teacher in Dallas, Tex., 1937-39; high school teacher in Wichita Falls, Tex., 1941-46; Texas College of Arts and Industry (now Texas A. & I. University), Kingsville, instructor in history and government, 1946-47; *Kingsville Record*, Kingsville, Tex., women's editor, 1947-51; College of San Mateo, San Mateo, Calif., instructor in professional writing, 1955—. Staff member of writers conferences and workshops. *Member:* American Association of University Women (president of Kingsville chapter, 1948), Authors Guild, National Early American Glass Club, California Writers Club (past president), Burlingame Writers Club (past president), Scribblers Club, Phi Beta Kappa, Phi Lambda Theta, Phi Sigma Alpha.

WRITINGS: Fiction Techniques That Sell, Prentice-Hall, 1964; *Writing Articles That Sell*, Prentice-Hall, 1965; *Writing Fillers That Sell*, Funk, 1967; *Journey to Citizenship*, Funk, 1968; *Your Social Security Benefits*, Funk, 1969. Writer of short stories and articles. Regular columnist, "Over Coffee Cups," *Kingsville Record*, 1951-61. Contributor and columnist for antique magazines.

WORK IN PROGRESS: Two juvenile books, *Wedding Customs* and *Creating with Words*; a career book, *Deadline for Danger*; *Collecting American Cut Glass*.

SIDELIGHTS: Mrs. Boggess teaches professional writing by television for the College of San Mateo, the only such course offered in the United States. She also teaches a television course in antique glass and conducts one-woman workshops in glass.

* * *

BOGGS, Wade Hamilton, Jr. 1916-

PERSONAL: Born June 19, 1916, in Shawnee, Okla.; son of Wade Hamilton (a Presbyterian minister) and Louise (Sheldon) Boggs; married Florence Louise McLeod, August 28, 1941; children: Wade Hamilton III, Peter McLeod. *Education:* Davidson College, A.B., 1937; Union Theological Seminary, Richmond, Va., B.D., 1942, Th.M., 1943, Th.D., 1948; University of Richmond, M.A., 1944. *Home:* 1208 Palmyra Ave., Richmond, Va. *Office:* Presbyterian School of Christian Education, 1205 Palmyra Ave., Richmond, Va.

CAREER: Davidson College, Davidson, N.C., secretary of Young Men's Christian Association, 1937-39; Presbyterian Church in the U.S.A., ordained minister, 1942;

pastor in Buchanan, Va., 1943-44; Queens College, Charlotte, N.C., chairman of department of philosophy and religion, 1944-48; Presbyterian School of Christian Education, Richmond, Va., professor of Bible and theology, 1948—.

WRITINGS: Faith Healing and the Christian Faith, John Knox, 1956; *All Ye Who Labor*, John Knox, 1961. Contributor to religious journals.

* * *

BOLINGER, Dwight 1907-

PERSONAL: Born August 18, 1907, in Topeka, Kan.; son of Arthur Joel (a judge) and Gertrude (Ott) Bolinger; married Louise Schrynemakers, July 1, 1934; children: Bruce Clyde, Ann Celeste. *Education:* Washburn Municipal University of Topeka (now Washburn University of Topeka), A.B., 1930; University of Kansas, M.A., 1932; University of Wisconsin, Ph.D., 1936. *Home:* 2718 Ramona St., Palo Alto, Calif. 94306.

CAREER: Washburn University of Topeka, Topeka, Kan., associate professor of Spanish, 1937-44; University of Southern California, Los Angeles, 1944-60, began as assistant professor, became professor of Spanish; University of Colorado, Boulder, professor of Spanish, 1960-63; Harvard University, Cambridge, Mass., professor of Romance languages and literatures, 1963-73. Visiting professor, University of Michigan, summer, 1956. *Member:* Modern Language Association of America, Linguistic Society of America (president, 1972), American Association of Teachers of Spanish and Portuguese (president, 1960), American Dialect Society, American Association of University Professors, American Civil Liberties Union, American Name Society, Asociacion de Linguistica y Filologia de America Latina, Phonetic Society of Japan, International Linguistic Association. *Awards, honors:* Sterling Fellow in linguistics at Yale University, 1943-44; research fellow in speech at Haskins Laboratories, 1956-57; honorary D.Litt., Washburn University of Topeka, 1964; Center for Advanced Study in the Behavioral Sciences, fellow, 1969-70; American Academy of Arts and Sciences, fellow, 1973.

WRITINGS: Intensive Spanish, Russell, 1948; *Spanish Review Grammar*, Henry Holt, 1956; *Interrogative Structures of American English*, American Dialect Society, 1957; (with J. D. Bowen, A. M. Brady, E. F. Haden, L. Poston, and N. P. Sachs) *Modern Spanish*, Harcourt, 1960, 2nd edition, 1966; *Forms of English: Accent, Morpheme, Order*, Harvard University Press, 1965; *Aspects of Language*, Harcourt, 1968; *The Phrasal Verb in English*, Harvard University Press, 1971; *Degree Words*, Mouton & Co., 1972. Contributor to linguistics journals. Associate editor, *Hispania*, 1960-64; member of advisory board, *American Speech*, 1965-66.

WORK IN PROGRESS: Second edition of *Aspects of Language*, completion expected in 1975.

SIDELIGHTS: Bolinger told *CA* his "main hope is to make linguistics intelligible and interesting to as wide an audience as possible; to interpret today's linguistic formalism in ordinary language, and to encourage more data-oriented research as a test and counterbalance for formalisms. I have always been impressed by the tremendous reach of language, and depressed by efforts to confine it by defining it too narrowly."

BIOGRAPHICAL/CRITICAL SOURCES: "General Linguistics in the Works of Dwight L. Bolinger," *Voprosy Tazkoznanija* (Moscow), spring, 1964.

BOND, Donald F(rederic) 1898-

PERSONAL: Born November 27, 1898, in Frankfort, Ind.; son of J. Fred and Laura Almeda (Norris) Bond; married Judith Strohm, September 1, 1927; children: James F., Deborah (Mrs. Robert D. Falk). *Education:* University of Chicago, Ph.B., 1922, M.A., 1923, Ph.D., 1934. *Religion:* Episcopalian. *Home:* 501 Balra Dr., El Cerrito, Calif. 94530.

CAREER: Washington University, St. Louis, Mo., instructor, 1923, assistant professor of English, 1924-28; University of Chicago, Chicago, Ill., instructor, 1930-40, assistant professor, 1940-47, associate professor, 1947-52, professor of English, 1952-66, William H. Colvin Research Professor, 1961-62, professor emeritus, 1966—. Visiting professor, Northern Illinois University, 1969-71. *Member:* Modern Language Association of America, Modern Humanities Research Association, International Association of University Professors of English, Phi Beta Kappa, Lambda Chi Alpha. *Awards, honors:* Guggenheim fellow, 1958-59, 1966-67.

WRITINGS: (With G. R. Haves) *A Critical Bibliography of French Literature*, Volume IV, *The Eighteenth Century*, Syracuse University Press, 1951; *Reference Guide to English Studies*, University of Chicago Press, 1962, 2nd edition, 1971; (editor) Joseph Addison and Richard Steele, *The Spectator*, five volumes, Clarendon Press, 1965; *The Age of Dryden*, Appleton, 1970; (editor) *Critical Essays from "The Spectator"*, Oxford University Press, 1970. Contributor to *Encyclopedia Britannica* and to professional journals. Member of editorial board, *Modern Philology*, 1952-59, editor, 1959-66.

WORK IN PROGRESS: A critical edition of Steele's *The Tatler*.

*   *   *

BONGARTZ, Roy 1924-

PERSONAL: Born December 8, 1924, in Providence, R.I.; son of Royal B. (a salesman) and Emma (Asplund) Bongartz; married Cecilia Leigh (an editor), June, 1955; children: Joe. *Education:* University of Paris, Diploma, 1948; University of Grenoble, graduate study, 1948-49; Miami University, Oxford, Ohio, M.A., 1951; Mexico City College, graduate study, 1951-52. *Residence:* Foster, R.I. *Agent:* Cyrilly Abels, 119 West 57th St., New York, N.Y. 10019.

CAREER: U.S. Armed Forces, Europe, education adviser, 1952-55; Rockland County *Journal-News*, Nyack, N.Y., reporter, 1957-58; *New Yorker*, New York, N.Y., editorial staff member, 1958-60; free-lance writer, 1960—. *Military service:* U.S. Army, 1943-46. *Awards, honors:* Mary Roberts Rinehart Foundation award, 1960, for novel in progress.

WRITINGS: Twelve Chases on West Ninety-Ninth Street (short stories), Houghton, 1965; "The Applicant" (play), produced at Tower Theatre, London, 1961. Contributor of stories to *New Yorker, Saturday Evening Post, Horizon*, and *Transatlantic Review*. Fiction editor of *Points* (literary magazine), Paris, France, 1947-50, and *Quixote* (literary magazine), London, England, 1954-58; travel writer, *New York Times*, 1970—.

WORK IN PROGRESS: A novel about expatriate New Yorkers in country New England; a book on unique communities in the United States.

SIDELIGHTS: Bongartz lived in France for eight years. *Avocational interests:* Collecting jazz records, canoeing.

BONINI, Charles P(ius) 1933-

PERSONAL: Born November 22, 1933, in Ridgway, Pa.; son of Louis A. (a merchant) and Margaret (Murphy) Bonini; married Cissie Rafferty, August 30, 1958; children: Julia, Charles, Barbara, Sheila. *Education:* College of the Holy Cross, A.B., 1955; Carnegie Institute of Technology, M.S., 1957, Ph.D., 1962. *Religion:* Roman Catholic. *Home:* 1582 Ardenwood Dr., San Jose, Calif.

CAREER: Stanford University, Graduate School of Business, Palo Alto, Calif., 1959—, now associate professor of business statistics. *Member:* American Statistical Association, Institute of Management Sciences. *Awards, honors:* Ford Foundation Dissertation Prize, 1962, for *Simulation of Information and Decision Systems in the Firm.*

WRITINGS: (With William Spurr) *Workbook in Business and Economic Statistics*, Irwin, 1961; *Simulation of Information and Decision Systems in the Firm*, Prentice-Hall, 1963; (editor with R. Jaedicke and H. Wagner) *Management Controls: New Directions in Basic Research*, McGraw, 1964; (with H. Bierman, L. Fouraker, R. Jaedicke) *Quantitative Analysis for Business Decisions*, Irwin, 1965, 4th edition, 1973; (with William Spurr) *Statistical Analysis for Business Decisions*, Irwin, 1967, revised edition, 1973.

WORK IN PROGRESS: A book on the simulation of organizational behavior; research on management of research and development.†

*   *   *

BOOTH, Charles Orrell 1918-

PERSONAL: Born April 18, 1918, in Cheshire, England; son of Fred Bradshaw (a genealogist) and Bessie (Gould) Booth; married Mary Bowie Cairns, November 3, 1945; children: Gillian Frances. *Education:* Attended King's School, Cheshire, England, 1929-36. *Politics:* Conservative. *Religion:* Church of England. *Home:* 33 Tavistock Rd., Cambridge, England.

CAREER: Cambridge University, Cambridge, England, researcher in unit of insect physiology, 1946-63; free-lance consultant and writer, 1963—. Anasoil Ltd., director; Maxicrop Ltd., research consultant; *Garden News*, scientific adviser. *Military service:* British Army, 1939-45; served in Italy and North Africa; mentioned in dispatches.

WRITINGS: An Encyclopaedia of Annual and Biennial Garden Plants, Faber, 1957. Contributor of research papers to scientific journals, and of articles (mainly series) on aspects of applied science of interest to gardeners, commercial growers, and farmers, to journals.

WORK IN PROGRESS: Studies on the importance of malaria and other endemic diseases in determining historical development, and on the rat as a laboratory animal and its association with man; also writing on rare annuals, diseases of garden plants, and soil subjects.†

*   *   *

BORCHARD, Ruth (Berendsohn) 1910-
(Anne Medley)

PERSONAL: Born February 16, 1910, in Hamburg, Germany; daughter of Robert L. and Alma (Ellermann) Berendsohn; married Kurt Borchard (a shipowner); children: Katherine Borchard Hallgarten, Joanna Borchard Yehiel, Richard, Lucy. *Education:* Attended Lichtwarkschule, Hamburg, Germany, and University of Wisconsin; University of Hamburg, Ph.D., 1937. *Politics:* Labour. *Home:* 37 Cumberland Terrace, London N.W.I., England.

CAREER: London School of Economics and Political Science, University of London, London, England, assistant to F. A. Hayek, 1941-44. *Member:* British Federation of University Women, P.E.N. (England), Contemporary Art Society, British Dowsers.

WRITINGS: John Stuart Mill: The Man, C. A. Watts, 1957, Humanities, 1959; *Children of the Old House* (juvenile), Lutterworth, 1961, Doubleday, 1963; *Donkeys of Rogador* (juvenile), Dial, 1967.

Under pseudonym Anne Medley: *Your First Baby*, Faber, 1943, Transatlantic, 1944; *Minnie, or The Innocent Sinners: A Fairy Tale of the Present Day* (novel), Phoenix House, 1967, published as *Minnie*, Morrow, 1968.

WORK IN PROGRESS: Articles on the neurophysiology of extrasensory perception; manuscript, "Natural E.S.P. and P.S.I. Effects"; research on harmonics (cosmic pattern) according to Dr. Hans Kayser; manuscript, "Light of the Esoteric Hebrew Tradition on the Bible."

SIDELIGHTS: Mrs. Borchard's books have appeared in six countries. *Avocational interests:* Collecting contemporary self-portraits, dowsing, and propagating old roses.

*   *   *

BORKO, Harold 1922-

PERSONAL: Born February 4, 1922, in New York, N.Y.; son of George and Hilda (Karpel) Borko; married Hannah Levin, June 22, 1947; children: Hilda, Martin. *Education:* City College (now City College of the City University of New York), student, 1939-41; University of California, Los Angeles, A.B., 1948; University of Southern California, M.A., 1949, Ph.D., 1952. *Home:* 11507 National Blvd., Los Angeles, Calif. 90064.

CAREER: U.S. Army, 1942-46, 1950-56, became captain; System Development Corp., Santa Monica, Calif., research leader, 1956-67; University of California, Los Angeles, lecturer in psychology, professor, Graduate School of Library and Information Science, 1967—. *Member:* American Society for Information Science (president, 1966; formerly American Documentation Institute), American Psychological Association (fellow), Association for Computing Machinery, Scientific Research Society of America, American Association of Library Schools.

WRITINGS—Editor: *Computer Application in the Behavioral Sciences*, Prentice-Hall, 1962; *Automated Language Processing*, Wiley, 1966; *Computers and the Problems of Society*, American Federation of Information Processing Societies, 1972; *Targets for Research in Library Education*, American Library Association, 1973. Contributor of articles and reviews to professional journals. U.S. editor, *International Journal of Information Storage*; book review editor, *Journal of Educational Data Processing*.

WORK IN PROGRESS: Abstracting Concepts and Methods, and *Indexing Concepts and Methods*, both for Academic Press, completion of both expected in 1975.

*   *   *

BORNEMANN, Alfred H. 1908-

PERSONAL: Born November 30, 1908, in New York, N.Y.; son of Ernest A. (a printer) and Carrie (Wolters) Bornemann; married Bertha Kohl, August 20, 1938; children: Alfred Richard. *Education:* New York University, B.A. (cum laude), 1933, M.A., 1937, Ph.D., 1941; Industrial College of the Armed Forces, certificate (with honors), 1963. *Home:* 151 Engle St., Englewood, N.J.

CAREER: Accountant in New York, N.Y., 1933-40; Rutgers The State University, New Brunswick, N.J., instructor in economics, 1941-44; Boston University, Boston, Mass., assistant professor of economics, 1945-46; Long Island University, Brooklyn, N.Y., assistant professor of economics, 1946-48; Muhlenberg College, Allentown, Pa., associate professor of economics, 1948-50; Florida State University, Tallahassee, associate professor of finance, 1950-51; Norwich University, Northfield, Vt., professor and head of department of economics and business administration, 1951-58; St. Francis College, Brooklyn, N.Y., chairman of economics department, 1958-60; Long Island University, C. W. Post College, Greenvale, N.Y., professor of economics and business administration, 1960-68; City University of New York, Hunter College, member of faculty, 1967—. Visiting lecturer, New York University, 1944-45.

MEMBER: American Economic Association, American Accounting Association, American Finance Association, American Marketing Association, American Association of University Professors, Academy of Management, Business History Conference, Alpha Kappa Psi (chairman, national expansion committee, 1956-62; district director, 1953-67; acting regional director, 1962; chairman, history committee, 1965-66), Omicron Delta Epsilon, Pi Gamma Mu, Vermont Historical Society. *Awards, honors:* Silver Distinguished Service Award from Alpha Kappa Psi.

WRITINGS: J. Laurence Laughlin: Chapters in the Career of an Economist, American Council on Public Affairs, 1940; *Fundamentals of Industrial Management*, Bruce, 1963; *Essentials of Purchasing*, Grid, 1974. Contributor to *Dictionary of American Biography*. Author of brochures and of some fifty articles and reviews for professional periodicals.

WORK IN PROGRESS: Full Employement and Society; Turning Points in American Government.

*   *   *

BOSCO, Antoinette (Oppedisano) 1928-

PERSONAL: Born September 18, 1928, in Rome, N.Y.; daughter of Joseph S. (a meat dealer) and Mary (Sgambellone) Oppedisano; married Peter Paul Bosco (a language instructor), June 7, 1948; children: Sterling (adopted), Paul, John, Mary, Margaret, Francis, Peter. *Education:* College of St. Rose, B.A., 1950; additional study at St. Lawrence University, Middlebury College, Syracuse University, and Siena College. *Religion:* Roman Catholic. *Home:* 12 Einstein Pl., Smithtown, Long Island, N.Y.

CAREER: Cape Vincent (N.Y.) Central School District, high school teacher, 1948-49; Albany (N.Y.) public schools, adult education teacher of creative writing, 1954-56; *Long Island Catholic*, Rockville Center, N.Y., woman's editor, 1962—. *Member:* Delta Epsilon Sigma.

WRITINGS: Charles John Seghers, Pioneer in Alaska, Kenedy, 1960; *Joseph the Huron*, Kenedy, 1961; *Marriage Encounter: The Rediscovery of Love*, Abbey Press, 1972. Contributor of about two hundred articles and stories to *Family Weekly, Calling All Girls, Columbia, Family Digest, Writers' Digest, Your Life, Marriage, Your New Baby, Highlights for Children*, and other periodicals.†

*   *   *

BOSKOFF, Alvin 1924-

PERSONAL: Born August 28, 1924, in Brooklyn, N.Y.;

son of Benjamin (a salesman) and Pauline (Lazaroff) Boskoff; married Priscilla W. Sutherland, July 19, 1950; children: Katharine Julia, Andrew Daniel, Alexander Julian. *Education:* City College (now City College of the City University of New York), B.S.S., 1945; Columbia University, M.A., 1948; University of North Carolina, Ph.D., 1950. *Religion:* Unitarian. *Home:* 1802 Ridgewood Dr., N.E., Atlanta, Ga. 30307. *Office:* Emory University, Atlanta, Ga. 30322.

CAREER: University of Illinois, Urbana, instructor in sociology, 1950-51; Drake University, Des Moines, Iowa, assistant professor of sociology, 1951-54; College of William and Mary, Norfolk, Va., associate professor and head of department of sociology, 1955-58; Emory University, Atlanta, Ga., professor of sociology, 1958—. Member of the board of directors, Family Service Society of Atlanta. *Military service:* U.S. Army, 1946-47. *Member:* American Sociological Association, Southern Sociological Society, Phi Beta Kappa, Alpha Kappa Delta.

WRITINGS: (Editor with Howard Becker) *Modern Sociological Theory*, Dryden Press, 1957; *Sociology of Urban Regions*, Appleton, 1962, 2nd edition, 1970; (with Harmon Zeigler) *Voting Patterns in a Local Election*, Lippincott, 1964; (editor with Werner Cahnman) *Sociology and History*, Free Press of Glencoe, 1964; *Theory in American Sociology*, Crowell, 1969; *The Mosaic of Sociological Theory*, Crowell, 1972; (with John Doby and William Pendleton) *Sociology: The Study of Man in Adaptation*, Heath, 1973. Contributor to sociological journals. Associate editor, *American Sociological Review*.

WORK IN PROGRESS: Studies on social mobility and family relations, style of life, the role of intellectuals in innovation in our time, and comparative urbanism and quality of life.

* * *

BOSQUET, Alain 1919-
(Anatole Bisque)

PERSONAL: Born March 28, 1919, in Odessa, Russia; grew up in Brussels, Belgium; became citizen of the United States, 1943; son of Alexander and Berthe (Turiansky) Bisk; married Norma Caplan (with foreign service), January 9, 1954. *Education:* Attended University of Brussels, 1938-40, University of Montpellier, 1940; Sorbonne, University of Paris, M.A., 1951. *Home:* 32 rue de Laborde, Paris 8e, France.

CAREER: Founded, with Yvan Goll, the bilingual poetry magazine, *Hemispheres*, New York, N.Y., 1942; was assistant editor of *The Voice of France*, the first Gaullist paper in the United States, 1942-43; served with Allied Control Council, Berlin, Germany, 1945-51, and then with the Department of State; columnist for *Combat*, Paris, France, 1953—, critic for the French National Broadcasting Office, 1956—; literary director for Editions Calmann-Levy, Paris, 1956-72; columnist for *Le Monde*, Paris, 1961—; literary critic for Radio-Canada, Paris, 1961—; editor-in-chief, *La Cote des Peintres*, 1963—. Professor of French literature, Brandeis University, 1958-59; professor of American literature, University of Lyons, 1959-60. *Military service:* French Army, 1940; U.S. Army, 1942-45; received Bronze Star. *Member:* Academie d'Alsace, Academy of Political Science (Brazil). *Awards, honors:* Prix Guillaume Apollinaire, 1952, for *Langue morte*; Prix Sainte-Beuve, 1957, for *Premier testament*; Prix Max Jacob, 1959, for *Deuxieme testament*; Prix Femina Vacaresco, Prix Broquette-Gonin of the French Academy, and Jungmann Foundation Prize, 1962, all for *Verbe et Vertige*; Prix Interallie, 1965, for *La Confession mexicaine*; Grand Prix de Poesie of the French Academy, 1967, for *Quartre testaments et autre poemes*.

WRITINGS: Walt Whitman (essays), Gallimard, 1959; *Hiquily* (essays), Galerie-editions du Dragon, 1960; *Verbe et vertige* (essays on contemporary poetry), Hachette, 1961, new edition, 1963; (author of introduction) *Max Ernst: Oeuvre sculpte*, 1913-1961, [Paris], 1961; *Entretiens avec Salvador Dali*, Pierre Belfond, 1966, translation by Joachim Neugroschel published as *Conversations with Dali*, Dutton, 1969; *La Peinture de Dorothea Tanning*, J. J. Pauvert, 1966; *Middle West*, Editions Recontre, 1967; *Injustice*, La Table Ronde, 1969; *Les Americains sont-ils adultes?*, Hachette, 1969; (author of preface) *Cathelin, 11 mai-20 juin 1971*, Galerie de Paris, 1971; *Roger Caillois*, Seghers, 1971; *Chicago: Oignon sauvage*, Bernard Grasset, 1971; *Alechinsky*, Musee de Poche, 1971; *Pense contre soi*, Galanis, 1972; *Monsieur Vaudeville*, Bernard Grasset, 1973; *En Compagnie de Marcel Arland*, Gallimard, 1973.

Poetry: *L'Image impardonnable*, Hemispheres, 1942; *Syncopes*, Hemispheres, 1943; *La Vie est clandestine*, Correa, 1945; *A la memoire de ma planete*, Sagittaire, 1948; *Syncopes: Seconde version*, Seghers, 1951; *Langue morte* (another version of *L'image impardonnable* and *Syncopes*), Sagittaire, 1951; *Quel royaume oublie?*, Mercure de France, 1955; (with Charles Le Quintrec and Robert Sabatier) *Trois poetes*, Seghers, 1956; *Premier testament*, Gallimard, 1957; *Micromacro*, Galerie Parnass (Wuppertal, Germany), 1957; *Danse mon sang*, Falaize, 1959; *Paroles peintes*, Galerie Diderot, 1959; *Deuxieme testament*, Gallimard, 1959; *Cosmiques*, Robert Atteln (Wuelfrath, Germany); *Maitre objet*, Gallimard, 1962; *Lettre a un genou*, Lacouriere et Frelaut, 1963; (in English) *Selected Poems*, translated by Samuel Beckett, Charles Guenther, and Edouard Roditi, New Directions, 1963; *Alain Bosquet* (collection of poems), edited by Charles Le Quintrec, Seghers, 1964; *J'Ecrirai ce poeme*, Blaeschke Verlag, 1965; *Quatre testaments et autre poemes*, Gallimard, 1967; *Cent notes pour une solitude*, Gallimard, 1970; *Notes pour un amour*, Gallimard, 1972.

Novels: *La Grande eclipse*, Gallimard, 1952; *Ni singe ni Dieu*, La Table Ronde, 1953; *Le Mecreant*, La Table Ronde, 1960; *Un Besoin de malheur*, Bernard Grasset, 1963; *Les Petites eternites*, Bernard Grasset, 1964; *La Confession mexicaine*, Bernard Grasset, 1965; *Les Tigres de papier*, Bernard Grasset, 1968; *L'Amour a deux tetes*, Bernard Grasset, 1970.

Editor: (Under name Anatole Bisque) *Anthologie de poemes inedits de Belgique*, Pylone (Brussels), 1940; Alex Saint-Leger Leger, *Saint-John Perse*, Seghers, 1953, 10th edition, 1971; (with Pierre Seghers) *Les Poemes de l'annee*, Seghers, annually, 1955-59, 1967-68; *Anthologie de la poesie americaine*, Stock, 1956; *Les Vingt meilleures nouvelles francaises*, Seghers, 1956, new edition, 1964; *Les Vingt meilleures nouvelles americaines*, Seghers, 1957; *Emily Dickinson*, Seghers, 1957; *Les Americains*, R. Delpire, 1958; *Pierre Emmanuel*, Seghers, 1959, 3rd edition, 1971; *Trente-cinq jeunes poetes americains*, Gallimard, 1960; *Les Vingt meilleures nouvelles russes*, Seghers, 1960; *La Poesie canadienne*, Seghers, 1962, published as *Poesie du Quebec*, 1968, revised edition published as *La Poesie canadienne contemporaine de langue francaise*, 1966; *Robert Coffin*, Seghers, 1965; *Robert Goffin*, Seghers, 1966; *Anthologie de la poesie roumaine*, Editions du Seuil,

1968; *Anthologie de la poesie francaise de Villon a Rimbaud*, Presses de la Renaissance, 1968; *Adieu a la lune*, Calmann-Levy, 1969.

Translator: Bertolt Brecht, *Chansons et poemes*, Seghers, 1952; Merrill Moore, *Moi et autres poemes fugitifs*, Caracteres, 1956; Carl Sandburg, *Le Peuple, oui*, Seghers, 1956; Conrad Aiken, *Preludes*, Seghers, 1957; (with Zoran Michitch) Vasko Popa, *Rends-moi mes chiffons*, Seghers, 1959; Alston Anderson, *Le Tombeur*, Calmann-Levy, 1964; James Laughlin, *Certaines choses naturelles*, Seghers, 1964; Vasko Popa, *Le Ciel secondaire*, Gallimard, 1970.

Also author of *Venez venez L'absence est une volupte*, 1967, and *La Terre ecrit la terre*, 1967.

Contributor to numerous journals, including *Nouvelle Revue Francaise*.

WORK IN PROGRESS: Translating the collected poems of Lawrence Durrell into French.

SIDELIGHTS: Bosquet has written: "The need to define the essential relationship of man with the world that surrounds him . . . is an important phenomenon of our time. It is not the only one; it is accompanied by another, the need to give back to the cosmos a place which . . . was snatched away from it at the time when man appeared to be the unchallenged monarch of his planet. Since Hiroshima . . . our disappearance as an animal species is incontrovertible. Our collective suicide, through a simple miscalculation or an act of banditism, is not impossible. As a result . . . we feel bonds of solidarity, not so much with our fellow men as with our shrunken habitat and with what it was before we put in an appearance. Something impels us to love plants (after all they may, perhaps, survive us); stones (after all they may survive plants); the sun (but of course it will survive both plant and stone)."

Claude Vigee maintains that Bosquet's poetic position is "founded upon a perpetual paradox. In *Le Defi du Crital*, an unpublished text (1952), Bosquet asks himself "Why write?" And his answer: "Because tomorrow at dawn we shall all be pulverised. Unable to save anything whatsoever, unanxious to save anything, already crossed out of time, swallowed up by space, I at least throw this challenge at myself: to write a few lines which translate the serenity, the humanism, the tolerance of which neither my skin nor my blood is still capable. . . . He who speaks of prestige speaks of responsibility. . . . I want my poetry to be dense, difficult, revised, postponed until tomorrow: form—i.e. the trouble I took to write, to hesitate, to erase, to modify—constitutes the safest defense I could oppose to a murderous today. . . . Poetry: a faith which feeds on analyses. Poetry: a scepticism which does not accept the far too easy solution consisting in the denial of all solutions. Poetry: a ruthless discipline imposed on the most complete chaos. . . . Perfection, you are my guillotine, and you save me. . . . To be total, such is the law which replaces the former password: to be new."

Wallace Fowlie believes that *Verbe et vertige* is "one of the most penetrating analyses of modern poetry." In this work Bosquet maintains that the poet is mastered by the poem rather than mastering it. "The poem writes the poet," says Bosquet.

BIOGRAPHICAL/CRITICAL SOURCES—In French: Jacques Bour, *Les Poetes de la vie*, Correa, 1945; Jean Rousselot, *Les Nouveaux poetes francais*, Seghers, 1959; *L'Express*, September 20, 1962; *Nouvelle Revue Francaise*, December, 1962; Charles Le Quintrec, editor, *Alain Bosquet*, Seghers, 1964.

In English: *Poetry*, September, 1952, August, 1964; Francis J. Carmody, *French Poetry Since 1940*, [Berkeley], 1954; *New World Writing: Ten French Poets*, 1957; *Partisan Review*, winter, 1958; Georges Borchardt, *New French Writing*, Grove, 1961; *Books Abroad*, 1961; *Times of India*, December, 1963.†

* * *

BOSWORTH, Clifford Edmund 1928-

PERSONAL: Born December 29, 1928, in Sheffield, England; son of Clifford (a civil servant) and Gladys (Gregory) Bosworth; married Annette Ellen Todd, September 19, 1957; children: Felicity Ann, Caroline Mary. *Education:* St. John's College, Oxford, student, 1949-52 (first class honors in modern history, 1952); University of Edinburgh, (first class honors in Oriental langues, 1956), Ph.D., 1961. *Religion:* Anglican. *Home:* 144 North St., St. Andrews, Fife, Scotland. *Office:* Department of Oriental Languages, University of St. Andrews, Fife, Scotland.

CAREER: Department of Agriculture for Scotland, Edinburgh, Scotland, assistant principal, 1952-54; University of St. Andrews, St. Andrews, Scotland, lecturer in Arabic, 1956—. *Military service:* British Army, 1947-49. *Member:* Royal Asiatic Society of Great Britain and Ireland.

WRITINGS: The Ghaznavids: Their Empire of Afghanistan and Eastern Iran, 994-1040, Edinburgh University Press, 1963; *The Islamic Dynasties: A Chronological and Genealogical Handbook*, University Press, 1967; (editor) V. V. Bartol'd, *Turkestan Down to the Mongol Invasion*, 3rd edition, Luzac, 1968; *Sistan Under the Arabs: From the Islamic Conquest to the Rise of the Saffarids*, IsMEO (Rome), 1968; (editor) Hudud al-Alam, *"The Regions of the World": A Persian Geography*, 2nd edition, Luzac, 1970; (editor) *Iran and Islam*, Edinburgh University Press, 1971. Contributor to *Cambridge History of Iran*, Volume V, Cambridge University Press. Contributor of articles on Islamic history and literature to journals in United States, England, Germany, Netherlands, France, Pakistan.

WORK IN PROGRESS: Translator, and author of introduction and commentary for *Ath-Tha'alibi's Book of Curious and Entertaining Information*.

SIDELIGHTS: Bosworth is competent in Persian and Turkish in addition to language taught.†

* * *

BOWDEN, Edwin T(urner) 1924-

PERSONAL: Born June 5, 1924, in Milledgeville, Ga.; son of Edwin T. and Allie (Myrick) Bowden; married, 1948; children: Elisabeth, Susan, Edwin Eric, James, Margaret. *Education:* Harvard University, B.A., 1948; Yale University, Ph.D., 1952. *Office:* Department of English, University of Texas, Austin, Tex. 78712.

CAREER: Yale University, New Haven, Conn., instructor in English, 1952-56; University of Texas, Austin, 1956—, became professor of English. Visiting professor, University of New Mexico, summer, 1965. *Military service:* U.S. Army Air Forces, 1943-46. *Member:* Modern Language Association of America, Texas Institute of Letters. *Awards, honors:* Fulbright scholar, Cambridge University, 1949-50.

WRITINGS: The Themes of Henry James, Yale University Press, 1956; *An Introduction to Prose Style*, Rinehart, 1956; *The Dungeon of the Heart*, Macmillan, 1961; (editor) *The Satiric Poems of John Trumbull*, University of Texas

Press, 1962; (editor) Washington Irving, *A History of New York*, Twayne, 1964; *James Thurber: A Bibliography*, Ohio State University Press, 1969. Co-editor of *Texas Studies in Literature and Language*, 1967—.

WORK IN PROGRESS: Textual editing of the nationwide edition of *The Complete Works of Washington Irving*.

* * *

BOWEN, Elbert Russell 1918-

PERSONAL: Born June 21, 1918, in Lynn, Ind.; son of Carl William and Ruth (Russell) Bowen; married Glenna Louise White, 1941; children: Glenna Ruth, Bonnie Louise, Jennifer Beth. *Education:* DePauw University, A.B., 1941; University of Denver, M.A., 1946; University of Missouri, Ph.D., 1950. *Home:* 609 Crescent Dr., Mount Pleasant, Mich. *Office:* Central Michigan University, Mount Pleasant, Mich.

CAREER: University of Missouri, Columbia, instructor in speech, 1946-50; Central Michigan University, Mount Pleasant, associate professor, 1950-54, professor of speech and drama, 1954—. *Military service:* U.S. Army, 1942-45; became staff sergeant. *Member:* Speech Association of America, Central States Speech Association, Michigan Speech Association, Beta Theta Pi.

WRITINGS: (With Otis J. Aggertt) *Communicative Reading*, Macmillan, 1956, 3rd edition, 1972; *Theatrical Entertainments in Rural Missouri before the Civil War*, University of Missouri Press, 1959. Contributor to speech and psychiatric journals.

WORK IN PROGRESS: Research and articles in oral interpretation of literature and readers theatre.

* * *

BOWLES, Frank H(amilton) 1907-

PERSONAL: Born November 20, 1907, in Taihoku, Japan; son of Frank Carroll and Sarah (Siceloff) Bowles; married Frances Porcher, April 22, 1939; children: Francis Porcher, Courtney Callaway, Mason Banks. *Education:* Central College, student; Columbia University, A.B., 1928, M.A., 1930. *Politics:* Democrat. *Religion:* Episcopalian. *Home:* 113 Anderson Ave., Demarest, N.J. 07627. *Office:* Ford Foundation, 477 Madison Ave., New York, N.Y. 10022.

CAREER: Columbia University, New York, N.Y., director of university admissions, 1934-48; College Entrance Examination Board, New York, N.Y., president, 1948-63; director, International Study of University Admissions (UNESCO-International Association of Universities), Paris, France, 1960-62 (on leave from CEEB); Ford Foundation, New York N.Y., director of education program, 1963-66, advisor to president, Ford Foundation in International Education, 1966—. Fund for Advancement of Education, vice-president, 1964-67, president, 1967—, Fund for Adult Education, president, 1965—. Fulbright National Selection Committee, member, 1949-51; University of Puerto Rico, consultant, 1946-56; Middle States Association of Colleges and Secondary Schools, secretary, commission on institutions of higher education, 1934-47, chairman, 1947-50, honorary member, 1950—; U.S. Military Academy, member of board of visitors, 1958-61; trustee, Institute of International Education, 1962-63. *Military service:* U.S. Naval Reserve, on active duty, 1942-45; now commander. *Member:* Council on Foreign Relations, Century Club, University Club (all New York), Cosmos Club (Washington D.C.), and Englewood Field Club (Engle-

wood, N.J.). *Awards, honors:* Honorary degrees from Wagner College, Providence College, Dickinson College, Pratt Institute, Long Island University, Manhattan College, Manhattanville College, Juniata College, Bates College.

WRITINGS: How to Get into College, Dutton, 1958, 4th revised edition, 1968; (with Richard Pearson) *Admission to College*, College Entrance Examination Board, 1962; *The Refounding of the College Board*, 1948-1963, College Entrance Examination Board, 1967; (with Frank A. DeCosta) *Between Two Worlds: A Profile of Negro Higher Education*, McGraw, 1971. *Access to Higher Education*, UNESCO, Volume I, 1963, Volume II, 1965.†

* * *

BOYD, Harper W(hite), Jr. 1917-

PERSONAL: Born September 14, 1917, in Tampa, Fla.; son of Harper White and Julia Dade (Dabney) Boyd; married second wife, Helge Huneke, 1974; children: (first marriage) Lucinda Brewer. *Education:* Beloit College, B.A., 1938; Northwestern University, M.B.A., 1941, Ph.D., 1952. *Politics:* Democrat. *Religion:* Congregationalist. *Home:* 705 Putnam St., Fayetteville, Ark. 72701. *Office:* College of Business Administration, University of Arkansas, Fayetteville, Ark. 72701.

CAREER: Chicago Tribune, Chicago, Ill., manager of field research, 1946-48; Market Research Corp. of America, research director, 1948-52; Northwestern University, Evanston, Ill., associate professor, 1952-57, professor of marketing, 1957-63, member of Institute for Management, 1955-63, director of Graduate Division of School of Business, 1958-63; Stanford University, Stanford, Calif., professor of marketing, 1963-67, Sebastian S. Kresge Professor of Marketing, 1967-73, director of International Center for the Advancement of Management Education, and director of Continuing Education, Graduate School of Business, 1970-73; University of Arkansas, Fayetteville, distinguished professor of business administration, 1974—. Member of advisory committee, U.S. Department of Agriculture, 1959-62; member of board of directors, National Asbestos Co., 1959-65; project director, Executive Management Program, Egypt, 1960-61; consultant, Management Development Institute, Egypt, 1960-64; director, Bureau of Commercial Research, London, England, 1961-64; external examiner, University of Ghana, 1964—; member of Australian Institute for Management, 1965—; visiting professor, Fontainebleau, France, 1970; consultant, U.S. Price Commission, 1972-73; participant in numerous executive management development programs in United States and abroad. *Military service:* U.S. Naval Reserve, 1942-46; became lieutenant commander. *Member:* American Marketing Association (president, Chicago chapter, 1951-52; member of national board of directors, 1953-55), American Association of University Professors, Phi Beta Kappa, Beta Gamma Sigma. *Awards, honors:* Distinguished service citation, Beloit College, 1963; Marketing Educator of the Year, Sales and Marketing Executives International, 1967.

WRITINGS: (With Ralph Westfall) *Marketing Research: Text and Cases*, Irwin, 1956, 3rd edition, 1972; (with Westfall) *Cases in Marketing Management*, Irwin, 1961; (with others) *Channels of Distribution for Consumer Goods in U.A.R.*, National Institute of Management Development (Cairo), 1962; (with Abdel-Aziz el Sherbini) *Marketing Research as an Aid to Egyptian Management*, National

Institute of Management Development (Cairo), 1962; (with el Sherbini and Ahmed Fouad Sherif) *The Need for Marketing in U.A.R.*, National Institute of Management Development (Cairo), 1962; (with S. H. Britt) *Marketing Management and Administrative Action*, McGraw, 1963, 3rd edition, 1973; (with Westfall and Richard Clewett) *Cases in Marketing Strategy*, Irwin, 1958, revised edition, 1964; (with Westfall and Vernon Fryburger) *Cases in Advertising Management*, McGraw, 1964; (with Sidney J. Levy) *Promotion: A Behavioral View*, Prentice-Hall, 1967; *Channels of Distribution*, International Correspondence Schools (Scranton), 1968; (with William F. Massey) *Marketing Management*, Harcourt, 1972.

Monographs: (With Westfall) *An Evaluation of Continuous Consumer Panels as a Source of Marketing Information*, American Marketing Association, 1960; *Advertising Procedures and Practices of Agricultural Commodity Promotional Groups*, U.S. Department of Agriculture, 1962.

Contributor: Thomas McNichols, *Policy Making and Executive Action*, 2nd edition, McGraw, 1963; Robert Bartels, editor, *Comparative Marketing*, Irwin, 1963; Lee Adler, editor, *Plotting Marketing Strategy: A New Orientation*, Simon & Schuster, 1967; Victor P. Buell and Carl Heyel, editors, *Handbook of Modern Marketing*, McGraw, 1970.

Editor: (With Westfall and Clewett) *Contemporary American Marketing*, Irwin, 1957, revised edition, 1962; (with Joseph Newman) *Advertising Management: Selected Readings*, Irwin, 1965; (with others) *Marketing Management: Cases from the Emerging Countries*, Addison-Wesley, 1966; (with others) *Casos en "Marketing,"* Addison-Wesley, 1967; (with others) *Marketing Management with Special Reference to Southeast Asia*, Asia Publishing House (New Delhi), 1967; (with Robert T. Davis) *Readings in Sales Management*, Irwin, 1970; (with Davis) *Marketing Management Casebook*, Irwin, 1971.

Also editor of *The Marketing Revolution*, proceedings of the 37th National Conference of the American Marketing Association, 1955. General editor, *Lecturas Escogidas en "Marketing,"* Addison-Wesley, 1967. Member of editorial board, *Journal of Marketing*, 1959-70. Contributor to journals, including *Harvard Business Review*, *Public Opinion Quarterly*, *Journal of Marketing*, *Sales Management*, and *Business Horizons*.

WORK IN PROGRESS: Books on basic marketing and on channels of distribution.

*   *   *

BOYD, Robert S.   1928-

PERSONAL: Born January 11, 1928, in Chicago, Ill.; son of Alden W. (a businessman and government employee) and Mary A. (Skinner) Boyd; married Gloria L. Paulsen, December 31, 1949; children: Peter, Susan, Andrew, Timothy. *Education:* Harvard University, B.A., 1949. *Politics:* Independent. *Religion:* Episcopalian. *Home:* 5410 Mohican Rd., Washington, D.C. 20016. *Office:* Knight Newspapers, 1195 National Press Building, Washington, D.C.

CAREER: U.S. Department of State, Washington, D.C., member of staff, 1950-53; reporter on newspapers in Lafayette, La., 1953-54, and Benton Harbor, Mich., 1954-57; Knight Newspapers, reporter for *Detroit Free Press*, Detroit, Mich., 1957-60, Washington correspondent for Knight chain, 1960—. *Military service:* U.S. Army, 1946-47. *Member:* National Press Club, White House Correspondents Association, Gridiron Club, Federal City Club.

Awards, honors: Pulitzer Prize for National Reporting, 1973 (shared with Clark Hoyt).

WRITINGS: (With David Kraslow) *A Certain Evil*, Little, Brown, 1965.

*   *   *

BOYER, William W., (Jr.)   1923-

PERSONAL: Born December 10, 1923, in Verona, Pa.; son of William Walter and Helen (Kelly) Boyer; married Barbara W. Massey, September 7, 1946; children: Jeffrey, David, Suzanne, Rebecca. *Education:* College of Wooster, B.A., 1947; University of Wisconsin, M.A., Ph.D., 1952. *Religion:* Unitarian Universalist. *Home:* 1145 Wightman St., Pittsburgh, Pa. *Office:* Department of Political Science, University of Pittsburgh, Pittsburgh, Pa.

CAREER: Governor of Wisconsin, Madison, administrative assistant and press secretary, 1954-55; University of Pittsburgh, Pittsburgh, Pa., 1955—, became associate professor of political science. University of the Panjab, Lahore, Pakistan, professor-adviser, department of public administration, 1962-64. U.S. Department of State, specialist lecturer on American public affairs on world tour, 1960. *Military service:* U.S. Army Air Forces, 1943-46; became sergeant. *Member:* American Political Science Association, American Society for Public Administration, United World Federalists, American Association of University Professors (chapter president).

WRITINGS: (With Ernest R. Bartley) *Municipal Zoning: Florida Law and Practice*, University of Florida Press, 1950; *Bureaucracy on Trial: Policy Making by Government Agencies*, Bobbs, 1964; (editor) *Issues 1968*, University Press of Kansas, 1968. Contributor to political science journals and law reviews.

WORK IN PROGRESS: A study of education as it relates to national development in Pakistan.

SIDELIGHTS: Boyer is competent in French, Spanish, and Urdu.†

*   *   *

BOYLE, Harry Joseph   1915-

PERSONAL: Born October 7, 1915, in St. Augustine, Ontario, Canada; son of William Augustine (a farmer and merchant) and Mary Adeline (Leddy) Boyle; married Marion L. McCaffery (a teacher), January, 1937; children: Patricia, Michael. *Education:* Attended St. Jerome's College, Kitchener, Ontario, Canada. *Politics:* Liberal. *Religion:* Roman Catholic. *Home:* 174 Melrose Ave., Toronto 12, Ontario, Canada. *Agent:* Canadian Writers & Speakers, 44 Douglas Crescent, Toronto 5, Ontario, Canada. *Office:* Canadian Broadcasting Corp., 354 Jarvis St., Toronto, Ontario, Canada.

CAREER: Worked for Radio Station CKNX, Wingham, Ontario, 1936-41, and *Beacon-Herald*, Stratford, Ontario, 1941-42; Canadian Broadcasting Corp., Toronto, Ontario, farm broadcaster, 1942-43, supervisor, farm broadcasts, 1943-45, program director of Trans-Canada Network, 1946-52, regional program director, radio and television, 1952-55, supervisor of radio features, 1955—, executive producer of television, 1963—. *Toronto Telegram*, weekly columnist, 1956—. *Member:* Canadian Authors Association, Authors League. *Awards, honors:* Stephen Leacock Medal for Humour for *Homebrew and Patches*, 1963.

WRITINGS: Mostly in Clover (collection of columns),

Clarke, Irwin, 1961, Dutton, 1965; *Homebrew and Patches* (collection of columns), Clarke, Irwin, 1963, Dutton, 1964; *A Summer Burning* (novel), Doubleday, 1964; *God and the Methodists*, Doubleday, 1965; *With a Pinch of Sin* (autobiography), Doubleday, 1966; *The Great Canadian Novel*, Doubleday, 1972. Author of play, "The Inheritance," produced in Canada, and of several hundred radio plays. Contributor of articles and stories with rural and farm background to periodicals.

WORK IN PROGRESS: A novel; a book of essays.

BIOGRAPHICAL/CRITICAL SOURCES: Toronto Telegram, April 11, 1964.†

*   *   *

BOYLE, Kay 1903-

PERSONAL: Born February 19, 1903, in St. Paul, Minn.; daughter of Howard Peyton and Katherine (Evans) Boyle; married Richard Brault, 1923 (divorced); married Laurence Vail, 1931 (divorced, 1943); married Baron Joseph von Franckenstein (died, 1963); children: (first marriage) Sharon; (second marriage) Apple-Joan, Kathe, Clover; (third marriage) Faith, Ian Savin. *Education:* Studied violin at Cincinnati Conservatory of Music, two years and studied architecture at Ohio Mechanics' Institute. *Politics:* Democrat. *Religion:* None. *Agent:* Armitage Watkins, A. Watkins, Inc., 77 Park Ave., New York, N.Y. 10017.

CAREER: Novelist, short story writer, and poet; lived in England, Austria, and France for almost twenty years prior to 1941, and in Germany following World War II; taught night school course in writing, Nyack, N.Y., 1941-43; served as secretary to a fashion writer; worked on *Broom* (magazine); *New Yorker*, New York, N.Y., foreign correspondent, 1946-53; San Francisco State College (now San Francisco State University), San Francisco, Calif., member of English faculty, 1963—. Member of workshop in the short story, New School for Social Research, 1962; director of writers' conference, Wagner College, 1964; lecturer at other colleges and universities.

MEMBER: National Institute of Arts and Letters. *Awards, honors:* Guggenheim fellowships, 1934 and 1961; O. Henry Memorial Award for best short story of the year, 1934, for "The White Horses of Vienna," and 1941, for "Defeat"; Wesleyan University, Middletown, Conn., fellow, 1963; Radcliffe Institute for Independent Study, fellow, 1965.

WRITINGS: Wedding Day, and Other Stories, H. Smith, 1930; *Plagued by the Nightingale* (novel), H. Smith, 1931, new edition, Southern Illinois University Press, 1966; *Year before Last* (novel), H. Smith, 1932, new edition, Southern Illinois University Press, 1969; *Gentlemen, I Address You Privately* (novel), H. Smith, 1933; *The First Lover, and Other Stories*, Random, 1933; *My Next Bride* (novel), Harcourt, 1934; *Death of a Man* (novel), Harcourt, 1936; (editor with Laurence Vail and Nina Conarain, and contributor) *365 Days* (story collection), Harcourt, 1936; *The White Horses of Vienna, and Other Stories*, Harcourt, 1936; *Monday Night* (novel), Harcourt, 1938; *A Glad Day* (poems), New Directions, 1938; *The Youngest Camel* (allegory for children), Little, Brown, 1939, revised edition, Harper, 1959.

The Crazy Hunter (three short novels, "The Crazy Hunter," "The Bridegroom's Body," "Big Fiddle"), Harcourt, 1940; *Primer for Combat* (novel), Simon and Schuster, 1942; *Avalanche* (novel), Simon & Schuster, 1944; *American Citizen* (poem), Simon & Schuster, 1944; *A Frenchman Must Die* (novel), Simon & Schuster, 1946; *Thirty Stories*, Simon & Schuster, 1946; *1939* (novel), Simon & Schuster, 1948; *His Human Majesty* (novel), Whittlesey House, 1949.

The Smoking Mountain (story collection), McGraw, 1951; *The Seagull on the Step* (novel), Knopf, 1955; *Three Short Novels* ("The Crazy Hunter," "The Bridegroom's Body," "Decision"), Beacon, 1958.

Generation without Farewell (novel), Knopf, 1960; *Collected Poems*, Knopf, 1962; (author of foreword) Herbert Kubly, *At Large*, Gollancz, 1963, Doubleday, 1964; *Nothing Ever Breaks Except the Heart* (stories), Doubleday, 1966; *Pinky, the Cat Who Liked to Sleep* (juvenile), Crowell-Collier, 1966; (editor and author of introduction) *The Autobiography of Emanuel Carnevali*, Horizon Press, 1967; *Pinky in Persia* (juvenile), Crowell-Collier, 1968; (with Robert McAlmon) *Being Geniuses Together* (memoirs), Doubleday, 1968.

Testament for My Students (poems), Doubleday, 1970; *The Long Walk at San Francisco State* (essays), Grove, 1970; *The Underground Woman* (novel), Doubleday, 1974.

Translator from the French: Joseph Delteil, *Don Juan*, H. Smith, 1931; Raymond Radiguet, *Devil in the Flesh*, H. Smith, 1932.

Ghost writer of two other novels; author of a pamphlet on the Nazi regime in Germany, published by American Jewish Committee, 1962. Contributor to *New Yorker, Harper's, Saturday Evening Post, Nation, Harper's Bazaar, Reader's Digest, American Mercury, Poetry, Broom, transition.*

WORK IN PROGRESS: A history of German women (researched at Radcliffe Institute for Independent Study), for Doubleday.

SIDELIGHTS: Miss Boyle's renown rests principally on the strength of her masterful short stories which are intellectually scrupulous, and at times experimental. Robert E. Knoll writes: "If her stories are more difficult than much popular fiction, this difficulty is due to their frequent omission of transitions and their minimizing of exposition. They pay readers the compliment of assuming that they too have minds which may participate in experience. The stories are, in their way, lyrics, even as [her] poems are. Both succeed because of the intensity of a single moment of passion, because they isolate a spot in time." David Daiches adds: " . . . [The stories] are far from being merely 'on the spot' reporting. . . . Their object is not to describe either horror or heroism, but to explore the core of human meaning in these desperate situations." Most of her 'desperate situations' involve human beings struggling with love, dreams, and with themselves. Her theme "is nearly always the perennial human need for love," writes Richard C. Carpenter; "her design is woven from the many forms the frustration and misdirection of love may take."

Miss Boyle "always wrote." She once told a *Newsweek* reporter: "My sister and I had the idea that you made books for your family—for birthdays and for Christmas. I don't know where we got it. But I still have some of those old books around that I made when I was ten." As for her later published works, she believes *Monday Night* is her best.

"The Many Ways of Heaven," a short story, was adapted for television by Nicholas E. Baehr and presented by the Theatre Guild on April 17, 1963. Another short story, "The Ballet of Central Park," was adapted and filmed as a short subject in 1972.

AVOCATIONAL INTERESTS: Riding horses and climbing mountains.

BIOGRAPHICAL/CRITICAL SOURCES: Nation, December 24, 1930; *New Republic*, April 22, 1931, July 13, 1932; *Bookman*, June, 1932; *Saturday Review of Literature*, April 9, 1949; *English Journal*, November, 1953; *Newsweek*, January 25, 1960; Herbert Gold, *Stories of Modern America*, St. Martin's, 1961; *Prairie Schooner*, summer, 1963; *Critique*, winter, 1964-1965; Carolyn Riley, editor, *Contemporary Literary Criticism*, Volume I, Gale, 1973.

*   *   *

BOYLE, Robert (Richard)   1915-

PERSONAL: Born June 13, 1915; son of Thomas J. (a railroad conductor) and Agnes (McHugh) Boyle. *Education:* University of Illinois, A.B., 1938; St. Louis University, Ph.L., 1945, M.A., 1947, S.T.L., 1951; Yale University, Ph.D., 1955. *Politics:* Democrat. *Home and office:* 1404 West Wisconsin, Milwaukee, Wis. 53233.

CAREER: Entered Society of Jesus (Jesuits), 1939, ordained priest, 1950. Regis High School, Denver, Colo., teacher, 1945-47; Regis College, Denver, 1955-68, became professor of English, chairman of department of English, and Chairman of Division of Humanities; Marquette University, Milwaukee, Wis., visiting professor of English, 1968-69; Kent State University, Kent, Ohio, visiting professor of English, 1969-70; Marquette University, professor of English, 1970—. *Member:* Modern Language Association of America, Dante Society, Hopkins Society, James Joyce Association.

WRITINGS: Metaphor in Hopkins, University of North Carolina Press, 1961; *Regis College English Handbook* (articles on teaching of English), Regis College Press, 1962; (contributor) Michael Begnal and Fritz Senn, editors, *A Conceptual Guide to "Finnegans Wake"*, Pennsylvania State University Press, 1974; (contributor) Thomas F. Staley, editor, *Ulysses: Fifty Years*, Indiana University Press, 1974. Contributor of articles, mostly on literary topics, to *Victorian Poetry*, *Contemporary Literature*, *America*, *Catholic Mind*, and other periodicals.

WORK IN PROGRESS: Studies on Joyce as a Catholic artist, on the nature of literature, and on Shakespeare and St. Paul.

SIDELIGHTS: Boyle considers his most important original work to be his theory of metaphor, a critical method applied to the poetry of Gerard Manley Hopkins, in *Metaphor in Hopkins*.

*   *   *

BRACE, Gerald Warner   1901-

PERSONAL: Born September 23, 1901, in Islip, N.Y.; son of Charles Loring and Louise (Warner) Brace; married Huldah Laird, December 3, 1927; children: Charles Loring, Gerald Warner, Barbara B. (Mrs. Richard Gotshalk). *Education:* Amherst College, B.A., 1922; Harvard University, M.A., 1924, Ph.D., 1930. *Home:* 123 Pinehurst Rd., Belmont, Mass. 02178. *Agent:* McIntosh & Otis, Inc., 18 East 41st St., New York, N.Y. 10017. *Office:* Boston University, Boston, Mass.

CAREER: Williams College, Williamstown, Mass., instructor in English, 1924-26; Harvard University and Radcliffe College, Cambridge, Mass., instructor and tutor in English, 1927-30; Dartmouth College, Hanover, N.H., instructor in English, 1930-34; Mount Holyoke College,

South Hadley, Mass., 1934-39, began as instructor, became assistant professor of English, 1934-39; Boston University, Boston, Mass., professor of English, 1939-71, professor emeritus, 1971—. *Member:* American Association of University Professors, Phi Beta Kappa. *Awards, honors:* D.Litt. from Massachusetts Southeast Technical Institute, 1965, Amherst College, 1969, University of Maine, 1972.

WRITINGS: The Islands, Putnam, 1936; *The Wayward Pilgrims*, Putnam, 1938; *Light on a Mountain*, Putnam, 1941; *The Garretson Chronicle*, Norton, 1947; *A Summer's Tale*, Norton, 1950; *The Spire*, Norton, 1952; *Bell's Landing*, Norton, 1955; *The World of Carrick's Cove*, Norton, 1957; *The Age of the Novel*, Boston University Press, 1957; *Winter Solstice*, Norton, 1960; *The Wind's Will*, Norton, 1964; (self-illustrated) *Between Wind and Water*, Norton, 1966; *The Department*, Norton, 1968; *The Stuff of Fiction*, Norton, 1969. Author of essays and reviews.

SIDELIGHTS: Of *The Department*, Carlos Baker has written in the *New York Times Book Review*: "Academia is a special world containing special people. Having lived in it through most of his adult life, Gerald Warner Brace knows it like a book, and this latest of his books is about it. It is his 11th novel, and resembles all its predecessors in being low-keyed, beautifully put together, very well written, and thoroughly engaging. In the spate of academic novels that we have had in the past 20 years, 'The Department' is among the wisest and best."

*   *   *

BRACEY, Howard E(dwin)   1905-

PERSONAL: Born October 8, 1905, in Bristol, England; married Gladys Fooks, 1931; children: two. *Education:* University of London, B.Sc., 1938, M.Sc., 1943, Ph.D., 1947. *Home:* Fieldings, 56 Farleigh Rd., Backwell, Bristol, England. *Office:* University of Bristol, Bristol, England.

CAREER: London County Council, London, England, schoolmaster, 1926-38; Royal Air Force Educational Service, education officer, 1938-46; University of Bristol, Bristol, England, research fellow in rural sociology, 1946—. Visiting professor, Louisiana State University, 1963-64. *Member:* European Society for Rural Sociology (member of council and executive committee, 1959—), World Committee for Rural Sociology (member of council, 1964—).

WRITINGS: Social Provision in Rural Wiltshire, Methuen, 1952; *English Rural Life*, Routledge & Kegan Paul, 1959; *Industry and the Countryside*, Faber, 1963; *Neighbours: Subdivision Life in England and the United States*, Louisiana State University Press, 1964, published in England as, *Neighbors: On New Estates and Subdivisions in England and U.S.A.*, Routledge and Kegan Paul, 1964; *In Retirement: Pensioners in Great Britain and the United States*, Routledge and Kegan Paul, 1966, Louisiana State University Press, 1967; *People and the Countryside*, foreword by H. R. H. Duke of Edinburgh, Routledge and Kegan Paul, 1970. Contributor to geographical and sociological journals. English editor, *Sociologia Ruralis* (journal of European Society for Rural Sociology).†

*   *   *

BRADBROOK, Muriel Clara   1909-

PERSONAL: Born April 27, 1909, in England; daughter of Samuel (a superintendent in His Majesty's waterguard) and Annie (Harvey) Bradbrook. *Education:* Girton College, Cambridge, B.A., 1930, M.A. and Ph.D., 1933, Litt.D.,

1955. *Religion:* Church of England. *Home:* Girton College, Cambridge, England.

CAREER: Cambridge University, Cambridge, England, research fellow of Girton College, 1932-35, staff fellow, 1936-62, university lecturer, 1945-62, reader, 1962-65, professor of English, 1965—, vice-principal, 1961-66, principal of Girton College, 1968—. Principal officer of Industries and Manufactures Departments two and three, Board of Trade, London, 1941-45; in residence, Folger Shakespeare Library, Washington, D.C., and Huntington Library, California, 1958-59; trustee, Shakespeare's Birthplace, 1967. Visiting professor, University of California at Santa Cruz, 1966, Kuwait University, 1969. *Member:* Royal Society of Arts (fellow), Royal Society of Literature (fellow), Norwegian Academy of Arts and Sciences. *Awards, honors:* Harness prize, 1931, for *Elizabethan Stage Conditions*; Allen scholar, Cambridge University, 1935; Litt.D., University of Liverpool, 1964, University of Sussex, 1972, University of London, 1973; LL.D., Smith College, 1965.

WRITINGS: Elizabethan Stage Conditions: A Study of Their Place in the Interpretation of Shakespeare's Plays, Cambridge University Press, 1932, reprinted, 1968; *Themes and Conventions of Elizabethan Tragedy*, Cambridge University Press, 1934, reprinted, 1966; *The School of Night: A Study in the Literary Relationships of Sir Walter Raleigh*, Cambridge University Press, 1936, Russell, 1965; (with M. G. Lloyd Thomas) *Andrew Marvell*, Cambridge University Press, 1940; *Joseph Conrad: Poland's English Genius*, Cambridge University Press, 1941, Russell, 1965; *Ibsen the Norwegian: A Revaluation*, Chatto & Windus, 1946, revised edition, Shoe String, 1966.

T. S. Eliot, Longmans, Green, 1950, revised edition, 1968; *Shakespeare and Elizabethan Poetry: A Study of His Earlier Work in Relation to the Poetry of the Time*, Chatto & Windus, 1951, Oxford University Press, 1952; (compiler) *The Queen's Garland: Verses Made by Her Subjects for Elizabeth I, Now Collected in Honour of Her Majesty Queen Elizabeth II*, Oxford University Press, 1953; *The Growth and Structure of Elizabethan Comedy*, Chatto & Windus, 1955, Humanities, 1956; *Sir Thomas Malory*, Longmans, Green, 1958, 2nd edition, 1967.

The Rise of the Common Player: A Study of Actor and Society in Shakespeare's England, Harvard University Press, 1962; *Sir Thomas Malory* (with *Geoffrey Chaucer* by Nevill Coghill), University of Nebraska Press, 1964; *English Dramatic Form: A History of Its Development*, Barnes & Noble, 1965; *T. S. Eliot* (with *W. H. Auden* by Richard Hoggart and *Dylan Thomas* by G. S. Fraser), University of Nebraska Press, 1965; *Shakespeare's Primitive Art*, British Academy, 1965; *The Tragic Pageant of Timon of Athens: An Inaugural Lecture*, Cambridge University Press, 1966; *That Infidel Place: A Short History of Girton College, 1869-1969*, Chatto & Windus, 1969; *Shakespeare the Craftsman*, Barnes & Noble, 1969.

(Contributor) *Tributes in Prose and Verse to Shotaro Oshima, President of the Yeats Society of Japan*, Hokuseido Press (Tokyo), 1970; *T. S. Eliot: The Making of "The Waste Land,"* Longmans, Green, 1972, British Book Center, 1973; *Literature in Action: Studies in Continental and Commonwealth Society*, Barnes & Noble, 1972; *Malcolm Lowry: His Art and Early Life*, Cambridge University Press, 1974.

Contributor of articles and reviews to *Sunday Telegraph* (London), *New Statesman*, *Modern Language Review*, and other periodicals and newspapers.

SIDELIGHTS: In his review of *Shakespeare the Craftsman*, Frank Kermode commented, "Muriel Bradbrook . . . has always had in mind the need for a more immediate dissemination of the learning necessary to good common reading. She has produced over the years a large body of writing, learned but accessible and occasionally adventurous, in the Elizabethan and Shakespearian fields."

Miss Bradbrook toured the Far East in 1964 in conjunction with the observance of Shakespeare's Fourth Centenary.

* * *

BRADBURY, Bianca 1908-

PERSONAL: Born December 4, 1908, in Mystic, Conn.; daughter of Thomas Wheeler (a purchasing agent) and Blanche (Keigwin) Ryley; married Harry Burdette Bradbury (an attorney), August 14, 1930; children: William Wyatt, Michael Ryley. *Education:* Connecticut College for Women, B.A., 1930. *Politics:* Democratic. *Home:* Merryall, New Milford, Conn. *Agent:* McIntosh & Otis, Inc., 18 East 41st St., New York, N.Y. 10017.

CAREER: Author, writing primarily for children and young adults. New Milford (Conn.) Board of Education, member, 1953-63; trustee, New Milford Library, 1965—.

WRITINGS: Half the Music (poetry), Fine Editions, 1944; *The Curious Wine* (novel), Beechhurst, 1949.

Juvenile books: *Muggins*, Houghton, 1943; *The Antique Cat* (Junior Literary Guild selection), Winston, 1946; *One Kitten Too Many*, Houghton, 1951; *Tough Guy*, Houghton, 1952; *Mutt*, Houghton, 1954; *Mike's Island*, Putnam, 1958; *Jim and His Monkey*, Houghton, 1958; *Happy Acres*, Steck, 1959; *A Flood in Still River*, Dial, 1960; *The Circus Punk*, Macrae, 1963; *Two on an Island*, Houghton, 1965; *Sam and the Colonels*, Macrae, 1966; *The Three Keys*, Houghton, 1967; *Dogs and More Dogs*, Houghton, 1968; *Andy's Mountain*, Houghton, 1969; *The Loner*, Houghton, 1970.

Young adult novels: *Say Hello, Candy*, Coward, 1960; *The Amethyst Summer* (Junior Literary Guild selection), Washburn, 1962; *Goodness and Mercy Jenkins*, Washburn, 1963; *Shoes in September*, Washburn, 1963; *Laughter in Our House*, Washburn, 1963; *Flight into Spring* (Junior Literary Guild Selection), Washburn, 1965; *Laurie*, Washburn, 1965; *Lots of Love, Lucinda*, Washburn, 1966 (published in England as *Lucinda*, MacDonald, 1969); *The Undergrounders*, Washburn, 1966; *The Blue Year*, Washburn, 1967; *Red Sky at Night*, Washburn, 1968; *To a Different Tune*, Washburn, 1968; *Girl in the Middle*, Washburn, 1969; *Nancy and Her Johnny-O*, Washburn, 1970; *The New Penny*, Houghton, 1971; *Those Traver Kids*, Houghton, 1972.

WORK IN PROGRESS: A young adult novel, tentatively titled *Laurie*; a second young adult novel, *My Pretty Girl*, for Houghton; a juvenile book, *Boy on the Run*.

AVOCATIONAL INTERESTS: Jazz, sports cars, travel, numismatics, animal welfare, and gardening.

* * *

BRADBURY, Parnell 1904-

PERSONAL: Born January 19, 1904, in London, England; son of Frederick Stephen (a dentist) and Kate (Lynn) Bradbury; married Elsie Betty Faiers, January, 1940; children: Farel, Bridget Bradbury Duckenfield, Andrea, Deryn, Brita. *Education:* Attended English schools until fourteen.

CAREER: Osteopath in private practice, 1947—. Lecturer, Societe de Recherches Osteopathique; co-founder, John Paterson Trust for Independent Research. *Member:* Osteopathic Association of Great Britain, British Naturopathic and Osteopath Association, P.E.N., Society of Authors.

WRITINGS: The Tree Was Quiet, Crabtree Press, 1947; *Healing by Hand*, Harvill, 1957; *The Mechanics of Healing*, Peter Owen, 1967; *Adventures In Healing*, Spearman, 1970. Also author, with Philip King, of *My Blessed Aunt*, 1961.

Plays: *Johnny Get Your Gun*, Samuel French, 1942; *The Marzipan Prince* (juvenile; collection), Harrap, 1943; *Calling All Kings* (juvenile; collection), Harrap, 1944; *Off the Camden Road*, H. F. W. Deane, 1949; *A Man of No Experience*, H. F. W. Deane, 1949; *The Islands*, H. F. W. Deane, 1950; *The Judgement of Harris*, H. F. W. Deane, 1951; *The Come Back*, H. F. W. Deane, 1955; *The Fallen Angel*, H. F. W. Deane, 1957. Author of other plays produced in London club theaters, of radio plays for British Broadcasting Corp., and a television play, "The Great Game," produced on Netherlands and Belgium networks, 1962.

SIDELIGHTS: Bradbury, who went to sea with fishing fleets when he had to leave school, is largely self-educated. He won a prize for a short story at eighteen, and says he really is more interested in writing, lecturing, and educational work than in his osteopathic practice. Bradbury told *CA:* "... I have been suspect for turning the theatre into a platform. I consider that the theatre should be all things to all men and that a play is a play when it stimulates and provokes no less than when it simply entertains. My play about criminal abortion, 'Angry Dust,' captured a world press."

*   *   *

BRADFORD, Leland P(owers) 1905-

PERSONAL: Born July, 1905, in Chicago, Ill.; son of Theron Draper (a salesman) and Ivy (Powers) Bradford; married Martha Irene De Maeyer, October 12, 1933; children: David Lee. *Education:* University of Illinois, A.B., 1930, A.M., 1935, Ph.D., 1939. *Address:* Box 548, Pinehurst, N.C.

CAREER: University of Illinois, Urbana, instructor in education psychology, 1936-42; U.S. government, chief of training for Works Progress Administration, Ill., 1939-43, for U.S. Immigration and Naturalization Service, Washington, D.C., 1943-44, and for Federal Security Agency, Washington, D.C., 1944-45; National Education Association, Washington, D.C., director of Division of Adult Education, 1946-62, director of National Training Laboratories, 1947-67, National Training Laboratories, Institute of Applied Behavioral Science, executive director, 1967-69, president, 1969-70; consultant on organizational development, 1970—; diplomate in industrial psychology, American Board of Professional Psychology, 1970. Coordinator of research and training, Adult Education Association, 1951; member of U.S. Technical Assistance Team to Austria, 1954; delegate to UNESCO and other international conferences in Europe and Canada, 1955-60; member of National Committee on Study Awards, Fund for Adult Education, 1952-54, of National Screening Committee for Fulbright Awards, 1952-56; trustee, Lesley College, 1965—.

MEMBER: American Psychological Association (fellow), National Education Association, Society for the Psychological Study of Social Issues, New York Academy of Science, Kenwood Country Club (Bethesda, Md.), Pinehurst Club (Pinehurst, N.C.), Country Club of North Carolina. *Awards, honors:* Fellow, Ford Foundation, 1952-53; honored by Federation of Community Councils of Philadelphia, 1954, and National Association of Public School Adult Educators, 1959; American Association of Training and Development award, 1969; first distinguished fellow, National Training Laboratories, 1970; L.H.D., Boston University, 1968, Lesley College, 1973.

WRITINGS: (With Jack Gibb and Kenneth Benne) *T-Group Theory and Laboratory Method: Innovation in Re-Education*, Wiley, 1964; (contributor) A. J. Morrow, *The Failure of Success*, American Marketing Association, 1972; *History of the National Training Laboratories*, National Training Laboratories Institute, 1974; (with Benne, Gibb, and Ronald Lippitt) *Laboratory Method of Learning and Changing*, Learning Resources Corp., 1974. Contributor of articles to magazines and journals in field of adult education, training, and group dynamics. Editor, *Adult Education Bulletin*, 1942-50.

*   *   *

BRADLEY, David G. 1916-

PERSONAL: Born September 1, 1916, in Portland, Ore.; son of Rowland Hill and Edith (Gilbert) Bradley; married Gail Soules, March 19, 1940; children: Katherine Ann. *Education:* University of Southern California, A.B., 1938; Drew Theological Seminary, student, 1938-39; Garrett Theological Seminary, B.D., 1942; Northwestern University, M.A., 1942; Yale University, Ph.D., 1947; School of Oriental and African Studies, University of London, postdoctoral study, 1955-56. *Politics:* Democrat. *Home:* 2507 Sevier St., Durham, N.C. 27705. *Office:* Duke University, Durham, N.C.

CAREER: Ordained Methodist minister, 1941. Western Maryland College, Westminster, assistant professor of religion, 1946-49; Duke University, Durham, N.C., professor of religion, 1949—. *Member:* American Society for the Study of Religion, American Academy of Religion (president of southern section, 1963-64), American Association of University Professors, Association for Asian Studies.

WRITINGS: A Guide to the World's Religions, Prentice-Hall, 1963; *Circles of Faith*, Abingdon, 1965. Contributor of articles and reviews to periodicals.

WORK IN PROGRESS: The Scriptures of Asia (introduction and anthology).

SIDELIGHTS: Bradley is competent in German, reads French, has knowledge of Semitic languages and Greek, and slight knowledge of Sanskrit.

*   *   *

BRADY, Frank 1924-

PERSONAL: Born November 3, 1924, in Brookline, Mass.; son of Francis Anthony and Alma (Ranger) Brady. *Education:* Dartmouth College, B.A. (magna cum laude), 1948; Yale University, Ph.D., 1952. *Office:* Ph.D. Program in English, City University of New York, 33 West 42nd St., New York, N.Y. 10036.

CAREER: Yale University, New Haven, Conn., instructor, 1951-56, Morse fellow, 1955-56, assistant professor of English, 1956-60; Dartmouth College, Hanover, N.H., associate professor of English, 1960-63; Pennsylvania State University, University Park, professor of English, 1963-67; City University of New York, Graduate School, and

Hunter College, New York, N.Y., professor of English, 1967—. Associate fellow, Calhoun College, Yale University. *Military service:* U.S. Army, Quartermaster Corps, 1943-46; became first lieutenant. *Member:* Modern Language Association of America, American Association of University Professors, Phi Beta Kappa, Johnsonians (New York). *Awards, honors:* Guggenheim fellow, 1965-66.

WRITINGS: (Editor with F. A. Pottle) *Boswell on the Grand Tour: Italy, Corsica, and France*, McGraw, 1955; (editor with Pottle) *Boswell in Search of a Wife*, McGraw, 1956; (editor with Martin Price) *English Prose and Poetry: 1660-1800*, Holt, 1961; *Boswell's Political Career*, Yale University Press, 1965; (contributor) F. W. Hilles and Harold Bloom, editors, *From Sensibility to Romanticism: Essays Presented to Frederick A. Pottle*, Oxford University Press, 1965; (editor with John Palmer and Martin Price) *Literary Theory and Structure*, Yale University Press, 1973. Contributor to *Studies in English Literature, Eighteenth-Century Studies*, and *Bulletin of the New York Public Library*.

WORK IN PROGRESS: Collaborating with F. A. Pottle on second book of two-volume biography of James Boswell.

*   *   *

BRADY, John Paul 1928-

PERSONAL: Born June 23, 1928, in Boston, Mass.; son of James Henry (an engineer) and Evelyn Louise (Rice) Brady; married second wife, Christeen Nelson, March 22, 1963; children: (first marriage) James Palmer, June Pamela; (step-children) Pamela Eros, David Duncan. *Education:* Boston University, A.B., 1951, M.D., 1955. *Politics:* Democrat. *Home:* 428 South 47th St., Philadelphia, Pa. 19143. *Office:* Hospital of University of Pennsylvania, Philadelphia, Pa. 19104.

CAREER: Indiana University School of Medicine, Indianapolis, assistant professor of psychiatry, 1959-64; University of Pennsylvania, School of Medicine, Philadelphia, associate professor of psychiatry, 1964—. *Member:* American Psychiatric Association, Psychiatric Research Society, Interamerican Society of Psychology, Society for Clinical and Experimental Hypnosis, Society of Biological Psychiatry, Royal-Medico-Psychological Association. *Awards, honors:* Career Development Award from U.S. Public Health Service for research in psychiatry.

WRITINGS: (With J. I. Nurnberger and C. B. Ferster) *An Introduction to the Science of Human Behavior*, Appleton, 1963; (with E. E. Levitt and J. Persky) *Hypnotic Induction of Anxiety*, C. C Thomas, 1964; *Classics of American Psychiatry*, Green, 1974.

Contributor: *Recent Advances in Biological Psychiatry*, edited by J. Wortis, volume III, Grune & Stratton, 1961, volume V, Plenum, 1963, volume VI, Plenum, 1964; *Hypnosis in Modern Medicine*, edited by J. M. Schneck, 3rd edition, C. C Thomas, 1963. Contributor of some fifty articles to scientific journals.

WORK IN PROGRESS: Full-time research in the uses of conditioning in psychiatry and in the physiological aspects of hypnosis, either of which may result in a book.†

*   *   *

BRAIN, Joseph J. 1920-

PERSONAL: Born February 3, 1920, in New York, N.Y.; son of Louis (a used-furniture dealer) and Anna (Rabin-owitz) Brain; married Evelyn Swidler, December, 1944; children: Ellen Carol, Janet Ruth. *Education:* City College (now City College of the City University of New York), B.S.S., 1950, M.A.Ed., 1951; New York University, graduate study. *Home:* 5 Metropolitan Oval, Bronx, New York, N.Y. 10462.

CAREER: New York (N.Y.) Board of Education, 1951—, social studies teacher, 1951-55, teacher of mentally defective children, 1952-53, coordinator of junior high reading curriculum committee, 1955-57, teacher-in-charge of adult English and citizenship classes, 1957-58, teacher of remedial reading, 1959-62, now an associate in zoning (in charge of school zoning in borough of the Bronx), coordinator of the Elementary Free Choice Transfer Program, 1969—. Technical director of English classes for educated foreign-born adults, New York Junior League, 1957—; remedial reading consultant, New York Foundling Hospital, 1958-62; director of Summer English Program for Nightingale-Bauford School, New York, N.Y., 1973—. *Military service:* U.S. Army Air Forces, 1942-46. *Member:* National Education Association (vice-president, New York City unit), National Association of Public School Adult Educators, American Association for the United Nations, American Political Items Collectors, Kappa Delta Pi (secretary), Phi Alpha Theta.

WRITINGS: (Contributor) *Teaching World Affairs in American Schools: A Case Book*, edited by Samuel Everett and Christian O. Arndt, Harper, 1956; (editor) *Resource Materials in Civic Education for Adult Elementary Classes*, Board of Education of New York City, 1959; (coordinator) *Reading, Grades 7, 8, 9; A Teacher's Guide to Curriculum Planning*, Board of Education of New York City, 1959; *Blue Book of Spelling*, Regents Publishing Co., 1960; *Blue Book of Grammar and Composition*, Regents Publishing Co., 1963; *Blue Book of Poetry and Prose*, Regents Publishing Co., 1967; (with Galdys E. Alesi) *Resource Manual for Teachers of Non-English Speaking Adults*, American Immigration and Citizenship Conference, 1968, 4th revised edition, 1974; (contributor) *An Innovative Approach to Ethnic Studies*, Office of Instructional Services, Board of Education of New York City, 1970; *Teacher's Guide to the Cambridge Pre-GED Program*, Cambridge Book Co., 1972. Contributor to *TESOL Quarterly* and *Adult Leadership*.

WORK IN PROGRESS: Research in use of the telephone as a means of teaching English to foreign-born adults; research on the use of choral reading for teaching English as a second language.

SIDELIGHTS: Brain is competent in Yiddish, German, French, and Spanish. *Avocational interests:* Collecting presidential campaign buttons.

*   *   *

BRAMMER, Lawrence M(artin) 1922-

PERSONAL: Born August 20, 1922, in Minnesota; son of Martin G. and Edna L. Brammer; married Marian Sholin; children; Karin, Kristen. *Education:* St. Cloud State College, B.S., 1943; Stanford University, M.A., 1948, Ph.D., 1950. *Home:* 7714 56th Pl. N.E., Seattle, Wash. 98115. *Office:* Miller Hall, University of Washington, Seattle, Wash. 98195.

CAREER: Diplomate, American Board of Examiners in Professional Psychology. Sacramento State College, Sacramento, Calif., assistant professor, 1950-52, associate professor of psychology, and associate dean, 1952-64; University of Washington, Seattle, professor of educational psychology, 1964—. Fulbright lecturer, University of Tehran, 1960-61, 1964. *Military service:* U.S. Army, 1942-46; became first lieutenant. *Member:* American Psychological Association (fellow), American Personnel and Guidance Association, Sigma Xi, Phi Delta Kappa.

WRITINGS: Dynamics of the Counseling Process, McGraw, 1952; (with Henry A. Bamman) *How to Study Successfully*, Pacific Books, 1959, revised edition, 1969; (with Everett L. Shostrom) *Therapeutic Psychology*, Prentice-Hall, 1960, 2nd edition, 1968; *The Helping Relationship*, Prentice-Hall, 1973.

*   *   *

BRANCA, Albert A.   1916-

PERSONAL: Born November 13, 1916, in Montclair, N.J.; son of Pasquale and Grace (Lanzillotti) Branca; married Mona Faye Riley (coordinator of publications, International Reading Association), March 14, 1942; children: John C., Phillip A. *Education:* University of North Carolina, A.B., 1940, Ph.D., 1953. *Home:* 21 Georgian Circle, Newark, Del.

CAREER: U.S. Veterans Administration Hospital, Fayetteville, N.C., chief clinical psychologist, 1953-57; University of Delaware, Newark, assistant professor, 1957-61, associate professor of psychology, 1961—. *Military service:* U.S. Army, Medical Department, 1942-46; became captain. *Member:* American Psychological Association, Eastern Psychological Association, Sigma Xi.

WRITINGS: Psychology, the Science of Behavior, Allyn & Bacon, 1964.

WORK IN PROGRESS: A textbook in the psychology of adjustment.

*   *   *

BRANCH, Edgar Marquess   1913-

PERSONAL: Born March 21, 1913, in Chicago, Ill.; son of Raymond Sydney (a publisher) and Marian (Marquess) Branch; married Mary Josephine Emerson, April 29, 1939; children: Sydney Elizabeth (Mrs. James A. Diez), Robert Marquess, Marian Emerson. *Education:* University College, London, student, 1932-33; Beloit College, A.B., 1934; Brown University, graduate study, 1934-35; University of Chicago, M.A., 1938; University of Iowa, Ph.D., 1941. *Politics:* Democrat. *Religion:* Episcopalian. *Home:* 4810 Bonham Rd., Oxford, Ohio 45056. *Office:* Department of English, Upham Hall, Miami University, Oxford, Ohio.

CAREER: Miami University, Oxford, Ohio, instructor, 1941-43, assistant professor, 1943-49, associate professor, 1949-57, professor, 1957-64, research professor of English, 1964—, chairman of English department, 1959-64. Visiting associate professor, University of Missouri, 1949. *Member:* National Council of Teachers of English, Modern Language Association of America, American Studies Association (member of executive board for Ohio-Indiana, 1961-62), English Association of Ohio (member of executive board, 1959-60), College English Association of Ohio, Phi Beta Kappa, Beta Theta Pi. *Awards, honors:* Summer fellow, American Council of Learned Societies, 1969; senior fellow, National Endowment for the Humanities, 1971-72, for edition of Mark Twain's *Early Tales and Sketches*.

WRITINGS: (Editor) *Mark Twain's Letters in the Muscatine Journal* (monograph), Mark Twain Association of America, 1942; *The Literary Apprenticeship of Mark Twain*, University of Illinois Press, 1950; *A Bibliography of James T. Farrell's Writings, 1921-1957*, University of Pennsylvania Press, 1959; *James T. Farrell*, University of Minnesota Press, 1963; (contributor) *Essays on Determinism in American Literature*, Kent State University Press, 1964; (editor) *Clemens of the "Call,"* University of California Press, 1969; (author of introduction) Mark Twain, *Adventures of Huckleberry Finn*, edited by James K. Bowen and Richard VanDerBeets, Scott, Foresman, 1970; *James T. Farrell*, Twayne, 1971; (with Frederick Anderson) *The Great Landslide Case*, Friends of the Bancroft Library, 1972; (contributor) Charles C. Walcutt, editor, *Seven Novelists in the American Naturalist Tradition: An Introduction*, University of Minnesota Press, 1974; (editor) *Mark Twain's Early Tales and Sketches*, four volumes in Iowa-California edition of *The Works of Mark Twain*, University of California Press, in press. Contributor to *American Book Collector, American Literature, American Quarterly, College English, PMLA, University of Kansas City Review*, and other journals in field.

WORK IN PROGRESS: Mark Twain: From Hannibal to Hartford, a study of Twain's early life; *James T. Farrell: A Biography*.

AVOCATIONAL INTERESTS: Tennis, golf, gardening, and camping with his family.

*   *   *

BRAND, Carl F(remont)   1892-

PERSONAL: Born October 8, 1892, in Greenfield, Ind.; son of Charles Samuel (a glassblower) and Jessie (Davis) Brand; married Nan Surface, September 12, 1930; children: Charles Macy, Robert Alan, Donald Edwin. *Education:* Indiana University, A.B., 1915, A.M., 1916; Harvard University, A.M., 1918, Ph.D., 1923. *Home:* 433 Gerona Rd., Stanford, Calif. 94305.

CAREER: Instructor in history at Smith College, Northampton, Mass., 1919-20, University of Michigan, Ann Arbor, 1921-24; Stanford Universtiy, Stanford, Calif., assistant professor, 1924-30, associate professor, 1930-40, professor of history, 1940-58, professor emeritus, 1958—. Visiting professor of history, University of California, Los Angeles, 1964-65. *Member:* American Historical Association (secretary-treasurer of Pacific Coast branch, 1928-34; branch vice-president, 1948; branch president, 1949), Pacific Coast Conference of British Studies (president, 1960-61), Phi Beta Kappa.

WRITINGS: British Labour's Rise to Power: Eight Studies, Stanford University Press, 1941; *The British Labour Party: A Short History*, Stanford University Press, 1964, revised edition, Hoover Institution, 1974. Author of "The Know Nothing Party in Indiana," published serially by *Indiana Magazine of History*, and of articles and reviews in history journals and *South Atlantic Quarterly*.

WORK IN PROGRESS: Additional chapters in *The British Labour Party: A Short History*, to include the Wilson government.

*   *   *

BRAND, Charles Peter   1923-

PERSONAL: Born February 7, 1923, in Cambridge, England; son of Charles Frank and Dorothy Lois Brand; married Gunvor Hellgren; children: Jane, Anne, Catharine, Simon. *Education:* Trinity Hall, Cambridge, M.A., 1948, Ph.D., 1951. *Religion:* Church of England. *Home:* 21 Succoth Park, Edinburgh 12, Scotland.

CAREER: Cambridge University, Cambridge, England, university lecturer in Italian, 1952-66; University of Edinburgh, professor of Italian, 1966—.

WRITINGS: Italy and the English Romantics, Cambridge University Press, 1957; (editor with K. Foster and U. Limentani) *Italian Studies*, W. Heffer, 1962; *Torquato Tasso*, Cambridge University Press, 1965. Contributor to *The Mind of Dante*, U. Limentani, editor, Cambridge University Press. Contributor to *Cambridge Italian Dictionary*, *Italian Studies Presented to E. R. Vincent*, and to *Italian Studies* and other language journals. General editor, *Modern Language Review*, 1971—.

WORK IN PROGRESS: A linguistic and stylistic study of Torquato Tasso, including production of word-indices by computer; a study of Ariosto's *Orlando Furioso*.†

* * *

BRAND, Jeanne L(aurel) 1919-

PERSONAL: Born October 12, 1919, in New York, N.Y.; daughter of Paul LeClair and Maude Eaton (MacLean) Brand. *Education:* St. Lawrence University, Canton, N.Y., B.A. (magna cum laude), 1941; University of Rochester, M.A., 1942; graduate study at Radcliffe College, 1942-43; Columbia University 1947-49; University of London, Ph.D., 1953; Washington School of Psychiatry, postdoctoral study, 1957-60. *Politics:* Democrat. *Office:* International Programs Division, National Library of Medicine, Bethesda, Md. 20014.

CAREER: U.S. Mission to the United Nations, documents officer, 1946-49; National Foundation for Infantile Paralysis, New York, N.Y., associate historian, 1953-56; Carnegie Corp., New York, N.Y., research assistant to the president, 1956; National Institutes of Health, Bethesda, Md., medical research programs specialist, National Institute of Mental Health, 1956-60, executive secretary, History of Medicine Study Section, 1960-62, scientist administrator (social sciences), National Institute of Mental Health, 1960-67; National Library of Medicine, chief of international programs division, 1967—. *Military service:* U.S. Navy Women's Reserve (WAVES), 1943-46; became lieutenant junior grade.

MEMBER: American Association for the History of Medicine (member of council, 1964-67), American Historical Association, Conference on British Studies, World Federation for Mental Health, Assembly of Scientists (National Institute of Mental Health—National Institute of Neurological Diseases and Blindness; secretary, 1962-63), Washington Society for the History of Medicine (vice-president, 1963-64; member of executive committee, 1965-66; president, 67-68). *Awards, honors:* Fulbright scholar, University of London, 1949-50, and Leverhulme scholar, 1950-52.

WRITINGS: Private Support for Mental Health, U.S. Government Printing Office, 1961; *Doctors and the State: The British Medical Profession and Government Action for Public Health, 1870-1912*, Johns Hopkins Press, 1965; (editor with George Mora) *Psychiatry and Its History: Methodological Problems in Research*, C. C Thomas, 1970. Contributor to *Journal of the History of Behavioral Sciences* and history of medicine periodicals.

WORK IN PROGRESS: Research in the development of social medicine, 1900 to the present, and in the concepts of psychosomatic medicine at the beginning of the twentieth century.

BRANDENBURG, Frank R(alph) 1926-

PERSONAL: Born July 8, 1926, in Fairbault, Minn.; son of Franklin B. (a businessman) and Rose (Carlson) Brandenburg; married Rachel Griffin, March 23, 1958; children: Joan. *Education:* University of California, B.A., 1950; University of Pennsylvania, M.A., 1951, Ph.D., 1955. *Office:* Committee for Economic Development, 1000 Connecticut Ave., Washington, D.C.

CAREER: University of Mexico, Mexico City, professor, 1957-62; University of the Americas, Mexico City, Mexico, chairman and professor of economics, 1957-62; National Planning Association, Washington, D.C., director of Latin American program, 1962-63; The American University, School for International Service, Washington, D.C., professor of economics, 1963—; Committee for Economic Development, New York, N.Y., and Washington, D.C., staff member, 1964—. Consultant to business and government groups. *Military service:* U.S. Navy, 1944-46. *Member:* Pi Sigma Alpha, Phi Alpha Theta, Delta Sigma Pi, Delta Phi Epsilon.

WRITINGS: The Making of Modern Mexico, Prentice-Hall, 1964; *The Development of Latin American Private Enterprise*, National Planning Association, 1964. Contributor to *Inter-American Economic Affairs*, *Mexico This Month*, *World Affairs*, *Orbus*.

WORK IN PROGRESS: Writing on Alliance for Progress, U.S. foreign economic policy, and comparative economic and political systems.

SIDELIGHTS: Brandenburg speaks Spanish, Portuguese. *Avocational interests:* Golf, bridge, yachting.†

* * *

BRANDT, Alvin G. 1922-

PERSONAL: Born January 3, 1922, in Union City, N.J.; son of Henry W. and Mabel (Webb) Brandt; married Josephine Baldessari, October 21, 1950; children: Andrew, Elizabeth. *Education:* Educated in New Jersey public schools. *Politics:* Democrat. *Religion:* Episcopalian. *Home:* 33 Columbia St., Wharton, N.J. 07885.

CAREER: American National Theatre and Academy, New York, N.Y., staff member, writer, and correspondent, 1947-49; American Guild of Variety Artists, New York, N.Y., 1949-69, auditions coordinator, 1957-59, editor of *AGVA News*, 1957-66, executive head of minutes, meetings, and elections department, 1952-69; Dover General Hospital, Dover, N.J., personnel director, 1969-72, outpatient accounts manager, 1972—. Actor, singer, and director with The Giles Players, Two-by-Four Playshop, and St. John's Chancel Players. *Military service:* U.S. Army, Infantry, 1942-46; served in Pacific; became technical sergeant. *Member:* Episcopal Actors Guild.

WRITINGS: Drama Handbook for Churches, Seabury, 1964. Contributor of articles, editorials, and book reviews to *AGVA News*, 1957-66, and of editorials to *The Churchcaster*, 1965—. Also contributor of occasional articles to trade publications.

WORK IN PROGRESS: Chancel plays, musical revue material.

SIDELIGHTS: Brandt has written music, lyrics, and skits for non-professional musical revues.

* * *

BRANDT, Rex(ford Elson) 1914-

PERSONAL: Born September 12, 1914, in San Diego,

Calif.; son of Alfred O. and Ellen Dale (Woodward) Brandt; married Joan Malloch Irving (an artist), June 22, 1938; children: Joan Dale Brandt Scarboro, Shelley Nora Brandt Walker. *Education:* Riverside Junior College (now Riverside City College), graduate, 1934; University of California, Berkeley, B.A., 1936; graduate study at Stanford University, 1938, and University of Redlands, 1939. *Home:* 405 Goldenrod, Corona del Mar, Calif.; and Point Pond, Shaw Island, Wash. (summer).

CAREER: Artist, specializing in water colors, and working at studio in Corona del Mar, Calif., 1944—. First portfolio of paintings appeared in *Fortune*, 1937; first major exhibit held in Los Angeles County Museum, 1939; exhibitor in invitational shows in Washington, D.C., New York, Denver, Los Angeles, and in other cities across the country; paintings included in museum and public collections. Teacher of art at Riverside College Art Center, 1937-43, University of Vermont, 1940, University of Southern California, 1941, and at other colleges, art institutes, and workshops, 1941—; director of Brandt Painting Workshop (formerly Rex Brandt Summer School of Paintings), 1955-62. Chief designer, South Coast Co. (shipbuilders), 1941-44.

MEMBER: National Academy of Design, American Watercolor Society, Foundation of Western Art, California Water Color Society (former president), San Francisco Art Association, San Diego Fine Arts Society, Riverside Fine Arts Guild (former president), Philadelphia Water Color Club; honorary member of nine other art associations. *Awards, honors:* More than sixty awards in art shows, primarily for water colors (several for oils and prints).

WRITINGS: Watercolor with Rex Brandt, Press of Rex Brandt School, 1949; *Watercolor Technique in Fifteen Lessons*, Press of Rex Brandt School, 1950, 6th edition, Van Nostrand, 1963; *Watercolor Landscape in Fifteen Lessons*, Press of Rex Brandt School, 1953; *The Composition of Landscape Painting*, Press of Rex Brandt School, 1959; *Watercolor Landscape*, Van Nostrand, 1963; *The Artist's Sketchbook and Its Uses*, Van Nostrand, 1966; *San Diego, Land of the Sundown Sea*, Copley Press, 1969; (with Jerome Muller) *Rex Brandt*, Brandt Painting Workshop, 1972; *The Winning Ways of Watercolor*, Van Nostrand, 1973.

Contributor of articles and/or color reproductions: Norman Kent, *Seascapes and Landscapes in Watercolor*, Watson, 1956; Ernest W. Watson, *Composition in Landscape and Still Life*, Watson, 1959; Cynthia Lindsay, *The Natives Are Restless*, Lippincott, 1960. Also contributor to *Watercolor Painting*, by Walter Foster.

Color films: "Watercolor Method"; "Watercolor Landscape"; "Oil Painting Method"; "Graphic Elements of Landscape," expanded and re-released as "Rex Brandt Paints the Big Sur," 1971; "Watercolor and Printer's Ink"; "George Post." Work has been reproduced in *Life, Westways, Ford Times*, and other periodicals.

WORK IN PROGRESS: Rex Brandt's West Coast: An Artist's Sketchbook, completion expected in 1975.

SIDELIGHTS: Two of Brandt's books are correlated with films; the text is in pictures and the illustrations are in words.

*   *   *

BRAUN, Theodore E. D. 1933-

PERSONAL: Born April 18, 1933, in Brooklyn, N.Y.; son of Leopold (a clerk) and Genevieve (Gersitz) Braun; mar-

ried Anne Wildman (a college teacher), September, 1965. *Education:* St. John's University, Jamaica, N.Y., B.A. (cum laude), 1955; University of California, Berkeley, M.A., 1961, Ph.D., 1965. *Office:* French Department, University of Wisconsin—Milwaukee, Milwaukee, Wis.

CAREER: Bishop Loughlin High School, Brooklyn, N.Y., teacher of French and English, 1954-55; Lycee Emile-Loubet, Valence, Drome, France, assistant d'anglais, 1955-56; University of California, French assistant, 1958-63; University of Wisconsin, Milwaukee, assistant professor of French, 1964—. Humes Foundation, Inc., New York, N.Y., director of Holiday Farm (camp for underprivileged children of the New York City area), 1958—. *Military service:* U.S. Army, 1956-58; served in Germany. *Member:* Modern Language Association of America, American Association of Teachers of French, Central States Modern Language Association.

WRITINGS: (With Paul Barrette) *First French*, Scott, 1964; *Le Franc de Pompignon: Sa vie, ses oeuvres, ses rapports avec Voltaire*, Lettres Modernes (Paris), 1972.

WORK IN PROGRESS: Articles on French literature of the eighteenth century.

SIDELIGHTS: Braun reads Spanish and Italian.†

*   *   *

BRAUNTHAL, Gerard 1923-

PERSONAL: Born December 27, 1923, in Gera, Germany; became U.S. citizen; son of Alfred (an economist) and Hilde (Elkan) Braunthal; married Sabina F. Diamond, September 30, 1950; children: Peter, Stephen. *Education:* Queens College (now City University of New York, Queens College), Flushing, N.Y., B.A., 1947; University of Michigan, M.A., 1948; Columbia University, Ph.D., 1953. *Home:* 161 Red Gate Lane, Amherst, Mass.

CAREER: National Bureau of Economic Research, New York, N.Y., research assistant, 1953-54; University of Massachusetts, Amherst, instructor, 1954-57, assistant professor, 1957-62, associate professor, 1962-67, professor of political science, 1967—. Visiting lecturer, Mt. Holyoke College, 1957-58, Columbia University, summer, 1968, University of Freiburg, fall, 1970. *Military service:* U.S. Army, 1943-46; became technical sergeant. *Member:* American Political Science Association. *Awards, honors:* Fulbright grants, 1959-60, 1965-66.

WRITINGS: The Federation of German Industry in Politics, Cornell University Press, 1965; (contributor) James Christoph and Bernard Brown, editors, *Cases in Comparative Politics*, Little, Brown, 1965, 2nd edition, 1969; *The West German Legislative Process: A Case Study of Two Transportation Bills*, Cornell University Press, 1972. Contributor to scholarly journals.

WORK IN PROGRESS: Labor and Politics in Weimar Germany: The Socialist Trade Unions.

*   *   *

BRAY, Douglas W. 1918-

PERSONAL: Born November 7, 1918, in Springfield, Mass.; son of Marvin J. (a salesman) and Lena E. (Brown) Bray; married Lois Jacobi, September 24, 1945; children: Gerald, Christopher. *Education:* American International College, B.A., 1940; Clark University, M.A., 1941; Yale University, Ph.D., 1948. *Religion:* Episcopalian. *Office:* American Telephone & Telegraph Co., 195 Broadway, New York, N.Y. 10007.

CAREER: Princeton University, Princeton, N.J., research associate, 1948-50; Columbia University, New York, N.Y., research associate, 1950-55; American Telephone & Telegraph Co., New York, N.Y., director of personnel research, 1956—. President, East Meadow (N.Y.) Public Library Board, 1955-56. *Member:* American Psychological Association, Duke Ellington Jazz Society (founder and past president).

WRITINGS: (With Eli Ginzberg) *The Uneducated*, Columbia University Press, 1953; *Issues in the Study of Talent*, Columbia University Press, 1954; (with Ginzberg and others) *Patterns of Performance*, Columbia University Press, 1959; (with Richard J. Campbell and Donald L. Grant) *Formative Years in Business: A Long-Term AT&T Study of Managerial Lives*, Wiley, 1974.

*　*　*

BREACH, Robert Walter 1927-

PERSONAL: Born September 19, 1927, in Devizes, Wiltshire, England; son of Jack and Gladys (Witchell) Breach; married Susan Ruth Boughton, August 27, 1955; children: John Frederick, Robert Michael, William David. *Education:* University of Bristol, B.A. (honors), 1948, Postgraduate Certificate of Education, 1951. *Religion:* Church of England. *Home:* St. George's, Ivy Rock, Tidenham, Chepstow, Monmouthshire, England. *Office:* City of Cardiff, College of Education, Cyncoed, Cardiff, Wales.

CAREER: St. George's School, Harpenden, Hertfordshire, England, senior history master, 1954-59; Chepstow Grammar School, Monmouthshire, Wales, senior history master, 1959-64; College of Education, Cyncoed, Cardiff, Wales, lecturer in history, 1964—. Chepstow Round Table, vice-chairman, 1964-65.

WRITINGS: (Editor) *Documents and Descriptions in European History: 1815-1939*, Oxford University Press, 1964; (editor) *Documents and Descriptions in World History: 1914-1965*, Oxford University Press, 1964; (editor) *Documents and Descriptions: The World Since 1914*, Oxford University Press, 1966; *A History of Our Times: Britain, 1900-1964*, Pergamon Press, 1968; (compiler and editor) *British Economy and Society, 1870-1970: Documents, Descriptions, Statistics*, Oxford University Press, 1972.†

*　*　*

BREATHETT, George 1925-

PERSONAL: Born November 11, 1925; son of Granville (a businessman) and Mable (Edouards) Breathett; married Florence Simpson, August 21, 1954; children: Lisa, Mellisandre, Granville, Alex. *Education:* Tennessee Agricultural and Industrial State University, B.S., 1948; University of Michigan, A.M., 1950; University of Iowa, Ph.D., 1954. *Politics:* Independent. *Religion:* Catholic. *Home:* 1901 Finley St., Greensboro, N.C. *Office:* Bennett College, Greensboro, N.C.

CAREER: Bennett College, Greensboro, N.C., associate professor, 1953-60, professor of history, 1960—, chairman of Division of Social Sciences, 1964—. Tuskegee Institute, coordinator of summer programs, 1959—. *Military service:* U.S. Army, 1944-46; became master sergeant. *Member:* American Historical Association, American Association of University Professors, Southern Historical Association, Pi Gamma Mu, Phi Alpha Theta, Alpha Kappa Mu, Sigma Rho Sigma, Alpha Pi Alpha, Knights of Columbus.

WRITINGS: (With E. R. Edmonds) *A Social Studies Handbook*, Tuskegee Institute Press, 1959. Contributor to *Historian*, *Phylon*, several other journals.

WORK IN PROGRESS: Church and State in Colonial Haiti.

SIDELIGHTS: Breathett speaks, reads, and writes French.†

*　*　*

BRECHER, Edward M(oritz) 1911-

PERSONAL: Born July 20, 1911, in Minneapolis, Minn.; son of Hans (a salesman) and Rhodessa (Roston) Brecher; married Ruth Ernestine Cook (a free-lance writer), December 27, 1941 (died October, 1966); children: William Earl, John Samuel, Jeremy Hans. *Education:* University of Wisconsin, student, 1928-30; Swarthmore College, B.A. (with highest honors), 1932; University of Minnesota, M.A., 1934; Brown University, postgraduate study, 1934-35. *Home and office:* Yelping Hill, West Cornwall, Conn.

CAREER: U.S. Senate Committee on Interstate Commerce, Washington, D.C., research supervisor, 1938-41; U.S. Federal Communications Commission, Washington, D.C., assistant to chairman, 1941-46; *Consumer Reports*, New York, N.Y., associate editor, 1947-51; United Nations Technical Assistance Administration, New York, N.Y., editor, 1951-52; free-lance writer in collaboration with wife, Ruth E. Brecher, 1952-66; free-lance writer, 1966—. Justice of the peace, Cornwall, Conn. *Member:* Society of Magazine Writers, National Association of Science Writers, Society for the Scientific Study of Sex (fellow). *Awards and honors*—All jointly with Ruth E. Brecher: Albert Lasker Medical Journalism Award for "We Can Save More Babies," in *Saturday Evening Post*, 1962; Russell L. Cecil Award of Arthritis and Rheumatism Foundation for "New Clues to the Arthritis Mystery," in *Family Circle*, 1962; grant from Philip M. Stern Family Fund for study of integration, segregation, and discrimination problems, 1962 (report published in *Harper's*, 1963).

WRITINGS: (With wife, Ruth E. Brecher) *Medical and Hospital Benefit Plans*, Prentice-Hall, 1961; (with R. E. Brecher and others) *Consumers Union Report on Smoking and the Public Interest*, Simon & Schuster, 1963; (editor with R. E. Brecher) *An Analysis of Human Sexual Response*, Little, Brown, 1966; (with R. E. Brecher) *The Rays: A History of Radiology*, Williams & Wilkins, 1969; *The Sex Researchers*, Little, Brown, 1969; *Licit and Illicit Drugs: The Consumers Union Report*, Little, Brown, 1972. Co-author with wife of two Public Affairs pamphlets and of some two hundred articles on medical, scientific, economic, and sociological subjects in *Good Housekeeping, Reader's Digest, Saturday Evening Post, Harper's, Parents' Magazine, Redbook, Consumer Reports*, and other national magazines.

*　*　*

BRECK, Allen duPont 1914-

PERSONAL: Born May 21, 1914, in Denver, Colo,; son of Chesney Yales (an engineer) and Isabelle E. (Lee) Breck; married Alice Wolfe, September 7, 1944; children: Anne Rose Breck Peterson. *Education:* University of Denver, A.B., 1936; University of Colorado, M.A., 1939, Ph.D., 1950. *Politics:* Republican. *Religion:* Episcopalian. *Home:* 2060 South St. Paul, Denver Colo. 80210. *Office:* Department of History, University of Denver, Denver, Colo. 80210.

CAREER: Denver (Colo.) public schools, instructor in social studies, 1936-42, 1946; University of Denver, Denver, Colo., 1946—, professor of history, 1960—, chairman of department, 1960—. Member of Colorado Governor's Commission on Educational Standards, 1960-63; vice-chairman, Colorado State Commission on Social Studies, 1963—; member of American Council on Education Commission on the College Student. Historiographer, Episcopal Diocese of Colorado. Lecturer, member of national advisory board, and chairman of regional selection committee of Danforth Foundation Associate Program. Lecturer, Phi Beta Kappa Associates, 1960—. *Military service:* U.S. Army, Field Artillery, 1942-46. *Member:* American Historical Association Mediaeval Academy of America, Renaissance Society of America, Royal Historical Society of Great Britain (fellow), Western History Association, Rocky Mountain Social Science Association (president, 1963-64), Rocky Mountain Medieval and Renaissance Association (president, 1970—), English-Speaking Union of the United States (vice-chairman, Denver branch, 1963-64), Phi Beta Kappa (president, Denver chapter, 1963-64), Omicron Delta Kappa, Lambda Chi Alpha, Phi Alpha Theta. *Awards, honors:* L.H.D., University of Denver, 1973.

WRITINGS: A Centennial History of the Jews of Colorado, 1859-1959, Hirschfeld, 1960; *Johannis Wyclyf, Tractatus de Trinitate*, University of Colorado Press, 1962; *The Episcopal Church in Colorado, 1860-1960*, Big Mountain Press, 1964; *William Gray Evans, Western Executive, 1855-1924*, University of Denver Press, 1964; *John Evans of Denver: Portrait of a Twentieth Century Banker*, Pruett, 1973. Author of articles and short monographs. Editor, "The West in American History" series and "Studies in History" series of University of Denver.

WORK IN PROGRESS: History Teaching in Theory and Practice, Clergy and Churches on the Western Frontier, and *John Wyclyf, Tractatus de Tempore*, completion of all expected in 1975.

SIDELIGHTS: Breck told *CA* that he is concerned for the moral and intellectual dimension of historical study.

*   *   *

BRENNAN, Maynard J. 1921-

PERSONAL: Born February 24, 1921, in St. Marys, Pa.; son of Alfred P. and Julia (Caskey) Brennan; married L. Carole Zippie, August 28, 1970; children: Joel Adam. *Education:* St. Vincent College, B.A., 1944, M.A. in Philosophy, 1946; University of Wisconsin, M.A. in English, 1948; University of Michigan, Ph.D., 1953. *Politics:* Democrat. *Religion:* Roman Catholic. *Home and office:* 511 Rosslyn Ave., Springdale, Pa. 15144.

CAREER: Ordained Roman Catholic priest, 1947. St. Vincent College, Latrobe, Pa., chairman of English department, 1955-63, chaplain, 1958-62, president of college 1963-68; Monmouth College, West Long Branch, N.J., professor, 1970-72; University of Pittsburgh, Pittsburgh, Pa., Associate Director of Development, 1973—. *Member:* Modern Language Association of America, National Conference of College Teachers of English, American Benedictine Academy, Phi Kappa Phi, Delta Epsilon Sigma.

WRITINGS: Compact Handbook of College Composition, Heath, 1964, 2nd edition, 1972. Columnist, *Our Sunday Visitor*; contributor to *Modern Language Quarterly*. Editor, *Catholic Accent*.

BRENNAN, Michael Joseph, Jr. 1928-

PERSONAL: Born August 29, 1928, in Chicago, Ill.; son of Michael Joseph (a laborer) and Nora (McHugh) Brennan; married Isabel Thomas, December 4, 1954; children: Mark Etienne, Moira Sioban, Keelin Marta. *Education:* DePaul University, B.S., 1952; University of Chicago, M.A., 1954, Ph.D., 1956. *Politics:* Liberal. *Home:* 44 Oriole Ave., Providence, R.I. 02906. *Office:* Brown University, Providence, R.I. 02912.

CAREER: Brown University, Providence, R.I., instructor, 1956-57, assistant professor, 1957-60, associate professor, 1960-64, professor of economics, 1964—, dean of graduate school, 1966—. Trustee, Lincoln School (Providence, R.I.), 1968, member of executive committee, 1970; Executive secretary, Howard Foundation, 1968; consultant, U.S. Office of Education, 1968-70; director, Providence Child Guidance Clinic, 1969-72; director, Graduate Record Examination Board, 1969-72; consultant, National Endowment on Humanities, 1970-71; member of advance board, Danforth Foundation, 1971; president, New England Conference on Graduate Education, 1973. *Military service:* U.S. Army, 1946-48; became technical sergeant. *Member:* American Economic Association, Econometric Society, Association of Graduate Schools (secretary-treasurer, 1970—), Council of Graduate Schools in U.S., New England Council of Graduate Schools (member of executive board, 1972). *Awards, honors:* Ford Foundation faculty research fellow.

WRITINGS: Preface to Econometrics, South-Western Publishing, 1960, 3rd edition, 1973; (editor and co-author) *Patterns of Market Behavior*, Brown University Press, 1965; *Theory of Economic Statics*, Prentice-Hall, 1965, 2nd edition, 1970; (with Mark B. Schupack) *The Economics of Age*, Norton, 1967; (with Thomas J. Hailstones) *Economics: An Analysis of Principles and Policies*, South-Western Publishing, 1970. Contributor to economics, statistical, and banking journals.

WORK IN PROGRESS: A book on the dynamics of higher education.

SIDELIGHTS: Brennan told *CA* that he has a "committment to higher education." He speaks and writes French, and reads German. *Avocational interests:* Travel, music, and hiking.

*   *   *

BRENNAN, Niall 1918-

PERSONAL: Born February 3, 1918, in Melbourne, Victoria, Australia; son of Frank (a member of Australian Parliament) and Sheila (O'Donnell) Brennan; married Elaine Bourchier, August 29, 1951; children: Christopher, Peter, Sally, Rosemary, Angela, Gabriel, Catriona, Patrick. *Education:* Educated at Christian Brothers schools in Melbourne, Victoria, Australia, and at University of Melbourne. *Religion:* Catholic. *Home:* Kingajanik, Gladysdale, Victoria, Australia.

CAREER: Free-lance writer; Council of Adult Education, Melbourne, Victoria, Australia, lecturer, 1945—. Minister of War Organisation of Industry, 1940; minister of information and Radio Australia, 1940-45. Director, University of Melbourne Union Theatre, 1955. Managing director, Sheed & Ward Pty. Ltd., 1967-71. Executive secretary, Good Neighbor Club of Victoria, 1973—. *Member:* Royal Geographic Society (fellow), Catholic Evidence Guild (master, 1960).

WRITINGS: The Ballad of a Government Man, Hawthorne Press, 1944; *Debating Clubs in Schools*, Whitcombe & Tombs, 1946; *The Making of a Moron*, Sheed, 1953; *A Hoax Called Jones*, Sheed, 1962; *Dr. Mannix*, Rigby, 1964; *John Wren, Gambler: His Life and Times*, Hill of Content (Melbourne), 1971; *Men and War: The Challenge to Youth*, Hawthorn Press, 1972; *A History of Nunawading*, Hawthorn Press, 1972; *Chronicles of Dandenong*, Hawthorn Press, 1973. Also author of *Ode to an Asiatic*, 1946, *Indoctrination and Education*, 1972, *The Politics of Catholics*, 1973, and *Village School*, 1973. Critic, and author of numerous television and radio scripts for British Broadcasting Corp., Australian Broadcasting Commission, and Radio Australia.

WORK IN PROGRESS: Novels and poetry.

AVOCATIONAL INTERESTS: Exploration, skiing, surfing, riding, walking, and mountaineering.

* * *

BREUNIG, Jerome Edward 1917-

PERSONAL: Born September 30, 1917, in Fond du Lac, Wis.; son of Anton Michael (a Chicago & Northwestern Railroad car repairer) and Mathilda (Kraus) Breunig. *Education:* St. Louis University, B.A., 1940, Ph.L., 1942, M.A., 1943; St. Mary's Theologate, St. Marys, Kan., S.T.L., 1950. *Home:* 1131 West Wisconsin Ave., Milwaukee, Wis. 53233. *Office:* Engineering School, Marquette University, 1515 West Wisconsin Ave., Milwaukee, Wis. 53233.

CAREER: Roman Catholic priest, member of Society of Jesus. St. Mary's Theologate, St. Marys, Kan., editor of *Review for Religious* and teacher of ascetical theology, 1950-53; St. Louis University, St. Louis, Mo., teacher of English, 1953-55; Wisconsin Province Education Association (Jesuit), Milwaukee, Wis., founder and editor of *Jesuit Blackrobe*, 1955-58; Marquette University, Milwaukee, Wis., teacher of English, Jesuit counselor in College of Engineering, and chaplain of Schroeder Hall, 1959—. Sogang College, Seoul, Korea, visiting teacher of English, 1963. Temporary chaplain at Fort Riley, Kan., 1950-53. Conductor of retreats throughout Midwest.

MEMBER: Amici Thomae Mori (Friends of Thomas More), Modern Language Association of America, Association of English Teachers of Greater Milwaukee. *Awards, honors:* Midwest Books Competition Award, 1964, for *Have You Had Your Rice Today?*

WRITINGS: Have You Had Your Rice Today?, Loyola University Press (Chicago), 1964. Contributor to *Columbia*, *America*, *Catholic Mind*, *Catholic School Journal*, and to other journals. Managing editor of *Jesuit Bulletin*, 1946-48.

WORK IN PROGRESS: A short story; continued research on Korea.

SIDELIGHTS: Breunig knows German, Latin, and some French; he has studied Greek, Hebrew, and Korean. *Have You Had Your Rice Today?*, a book on Korea, began as an accident, he says, prompted by response to letters he wrote from Korea.†

* * *

BRICHANT, Colette Dubois 1926-

PERSONAL: Born July 9, 1926, in Noisy le Sec, France; naturalized U.S. citizen; daughter of Henri and Suzanne (Aubourg) Dubois; married Andrew Brichant, September 8, 1955; children: Stephen. *Education:* University of Paris, Baccalaureat (B.A.), 1945, Licence es Lettres (M.A.), 1947, Diplome d'Etudes Superieures, 1948, Doctorat, 1953. *Home:* 3232 Glendon Ave., Los Angeles, Calif. 90034.

CAREER: Colleges Modernes de la Ville de Paris, Paris, France, teacher of English, 1945-49; instructor in French at Indiana University, Bloomington, 1949-50, Russell Sage College, Troy, N.Y., 1950-54, Middlebury College, Middlebury, Vt., 1954-57; University of California, Los Angeles, lecturer in French, 1957—. Instructor, Peace Corps Program, 1963-65. *Member:* Modern Language Association of America. *Awards, honors:* Fulbright scholar, 1949; Ford Foundation grant.

WRITINGS: Charles de Gaulle: Artiste de l'action, McGraw, 1968; *French Grammar: The Key to Reading*, Prentice-Hall, 1969; *La France au cours des ages*, McGraw, 1973.

Editor: *Perspectives sur la civilisation francaise*, American Book Co., Volume I: *Tableaux d'histoire*, 1964, Volume II: *L'Heritage culturel*, 1964, Volume III: *La France au travail*, 1965, Volume IV: *Arts de France*, 1965; *French for the Sciences*, Prentice-Hall, 1968; *French for the Social Sciences*, Prentice Hall, 1968; *French for the Humanities*, Prentice-Hall, 1968.

WORK IN PROGRESS: Publications on French civilization and history of agriculture.

SIDELIGHTS: Mrs. Brichant is fluent in French and English, has competence in Spanish and Italian, and knows some German and Russian.

* * *

BRICK, Michael 1922-

PERSONAL: Born March 27, 1922, in Brooklyn, N.Y.; son of Abraham (an insurance agent) and Anna (Petrushka) Brick; married Barbara L. Rosen, June 19, 1949; children: Barrett Lee. *Education:* Brooklyn College, B.A., 1941; University of Pittsburgh, M.Litt., 1948; Columbia University, M.A., 1950, Ph.D., 1963. *Religion:* Hebrew. *Home:* 520 West 122nd St., New York, N.Y. 10027.

CAREER: Journalist on *PM*, *New York Star*, and *Compass*, in New York, N.Y., during 1946-51; Orange County Community College, Middletown, N.Y., teacher of history and chairman of department, 1952-58; Dutchess Community College, Poughkeepsie, N.Y., dean of the college, 1958-60; Columbia University, Teachers College, New York, N.Y., instructor, 1960-63, associate professor of higher education, 1963—. *Military service:* U.S. Army, 1943-46; became staff sergeant. *Member:* American Historical Association, American Association of Junior Colleges, Association for Higher Education, American Association of University Professors, Phi Delta Kappa, Kappa Delta Phi.

WRITINGS: Forum and Focus for the Junior College Movement—The American Association of Junior Colleges, Teachers College, Bureau of Publications, Columbia University, 1964; (with Earl J. McGrath) *Innovation in Liberal Arts Colleges*, Teachers College Press, 1969.

WORK IN PROGRESS: One book on F. A. P. Barnard, one on the faculty role in governance in community colleges.

SIDELIGHTS: Brick is competent in French and German.†

BRIDWELL, Norman 1928-

PERSONAL: Born February 15, 1928, in Kokomo, Ind.; son of Vern Ray (a factory foreman) and Mary Leona (Koontz) Bridwell; married Norma Howard (an artist), June 13, 1958; children: Emily Elizabeth, Timothy Howard. *Education:* Attended John Herron Art Institute, Indianapolis, Ind., 1945-49, and Cooper Union Art School, New York, N.Y., 1953-54. *Politics:* Independent. *Religion:* Unitarian. *Home address:* Box 869, High St., Edgartown, Mass. 02539.

CAREER: Started as messenger for a lettering company, New York, N.Y.; Raxon Fabrics Co., New York, N.Y., artist-designer, 1951-53; H. D. Rose Co. (filmstrips), New York, N.Y., artist, 1953-56; free-lance commercial artist, New York, N.Y., 1956-70.

WRITINGS—All self-illustrated; all published by Scholastic Book Services except as indicated: *Clifford the Big Red Dog*, 1962; *Zany Zoo*, 1963; *Bird in the Hat*, 1964; *Clifford Gets a Job*, 1965; *The Witch Next Door*, 1965; *Clifford Takes a Trip*, 1966; *Clifford's Halloween*, 1966; *A Tiny Family*, 1968; *The Country Cat*, 1969; *What Do They Do When It Rains?*, 1969; *Clifford's Tricks*, 1969.

How to Care for Your Monster, 1970; *The Witch's Christmas*, 1970; *Monster Jokes and Riddles*, 1972; *Clifford the Small Red Puppy*, 1972; *The Witch's Vacation*, 1973; *The Dog Frog Book*, Xerox Education Division, 1973; *Merton the Monkey Mouse*, Xerox Education Division, 1973; *Clifford's Riddles*, 1974; *Monster Holidays*, 1974.

SIDELIGHTS: Bridwell has prepared slides of children's stories for "Show 'n Tell" projectors, and has designed record jackets for children's records. *Avocational interests:* Photography, history, and music.

* * *

BRISTER, C(ommodore) W(ebster) 1926-

PERSONAL: Born January 15, 1926, in Pineville, La.; son of Commodore W. and Elaine (Holmes) Brister; married Gloria Nugent (a public school teacher), March 28, 1946; children: Mark Allen. *Education:* Louisiana College, B.A., 1947; Louisiana State University, graduate study, 1948-49; New Orleans Baptist Theological Seminary, B.D., 1952; Southwestern Baptist Theological Seminary, Th.D., 1957; postdoctoral study at Union Theological Seminary, New York, N.Y., and Princeton Theological Seminary, 1962-63. *Home:* 3533 Wooten Dr., Fort Worth, Tex. 76133.

CAREER: Ordained Baptist minister, 1949. Pastor, Halton Road Baptist Church, Fort Worth, Tex., 1954-57; Southwestern Baptist Theological Seminary, Fort Worth, Tex., professor of pastoral ministry, 1957—. President, South Baptist Conference on Counseling and Guidance, 1967-68; guest lecturer, Round-the-World Study Tour, 1968; member of board of directors, Fort Worth Easter Seal Society, 1969-72; supervisor, Pastoral Care Center, Texas Christian University, 1969-72. *Wartime service:* U.S. Maritime Service, World War II; warrant officer. *Member:* American Association of Theological Schools (fellow), Association of Seminary Professors in the Practical Fields.

WRITINGS: Pastoral Care in the Church, Harper, 1964; *People Who Care*, Broadman Press, 1967; *Dealing With Doubt*, Broadman Press, 1970; *It's Tough Growing Up*, Broadman Press, 1971. Contributor to books and professional periodicals. Guest editor, *Pastoral Psychology*, 1971.

WORK IN PROGRESS: Rays of Hope, a book of devotions, for Harper; *A Sheaf of Pastoral Letters*, for Harper.

AVOCATIONAL INTERESTS: Fishing, tenting, and gardening.†

* * *

BRISTER, Richard 1915-
(Will O. Grove, C. L. Lewin, George Richmond)

PERSONAL: Born January 21, 1915, in New Britain, Pa.; son of Frederick Elmer (a doctor of medicine) and Edna (Richmond) Brister; married Lydia Catharine Lewin, September 7, 1943; children: Barbara. *Education:* Dartmouth College, B.A., 1936. *Politics:* Republican. *Religion:* Presbyterian. *Home:* 2122 Wayne Ave., Abington, Pa.

CAREER: Liggett & Myers, Philadelphia, Pa., tobacco salesman, 1936-38; Pennsylvania Department of Public Assistance, Norristown, investigator, 1938-41; free-lance writer for magazines, 1945-50; Pennsylvania State Liquor Store, Willow Grove, manager, 1950—. *Military service:* U.S. Coast Guard, 1941-45. *Member:* Western Writers of America.

WRITINGS: The Kansan, Avon, 1954; *Sentinel Peak*, Ace Books, 1954; *Renegade Brand*, Gold Medal Books, 1956, Avon, 1973; *The Wolf Streak*, Avon, 1958; *Law Killer*, Avon, 1959; *Matheson*, R. Hale, 1965; *Cat Eyes*, Avon, 1973; *Shootout at Sentinel*, Avon, 1973. A short story was anthologized in *Best Stories from Liberty Magazine*, 1949. Contributor of some four hundred sport, detective, and western stories and novelettes to pulp magazines, 1939-50, some under pseudonyms.

WORK IN PROGRESS: A contemporary novel with a baseball background, tentatively titled *The Winners*.

SIDELIGHTS: Brister has specialized until now in westerns, "because a good western sells indefinitely . . . and the writer is rewarded, eventually, to the degree that he has succeeded in entertaining his readers." His westerns, all published by Avon, are regularly reissued. The pole vault record that he set as an undergraduate stood at Dartmouth for twenty-four years; now he golfs in the eighties.

* * *

BROCKETT, Oscar Gross 1923-

PERSONAL: Born March 18, 1923, in Hartsville, Tenn.; son of Oscar Hill (a farmer) and Minnie (Gross) Brockett; married Lenyth Spenker, September 4, 1951; children: Francesca Lane. *Education:* George Peabody College for Teachers, B.A., 1947; Stanford University, M.A., 1949, Ph.D., 1953. *Politics:* Democrat. *Religion:* Episcopalian. *Home:* 2210 Woodstock Pl., Bloomington, Ind. 47401. *Office:* University Theatre, Indiana University, Bloomington, Ind. 47401.

CAREER: University of Kentucky, Lexington, instructor in English, 1949-50; Stetson University, DeLand, Fla., assistant professor of drama, 1952-56; University of Iowa, Iowa City, 1956-63, began as assistant professor, became associate professor of drama; Indiana University, Bloomington, professor of theatre, 1963—. Visiting professor, University of Southern California, 1959, University of Illinois, 1963. *Military service:* U.S. Naval Reserve, 1943-46; commanding officer of a landing craft, infantry; became lieutenant junior grade. *Member:* American Theatre Association (vice-president for program, 1973-75), American Society for Theatre Research (member of executive committee, 1970-73), Speech Association of America (member of administrative council, 1966-69), International Society for Theatre Research, Modern Language Association of

America, Central States Speech Association. *Awards, honors:* Fulbright grant to England, 1963-64; Guggenheim fellowship, 1970-71; fellow, American Theatre Association, 1971.

WRITINGS: (With S. L. Becker and D. C. Bryant) *A Bibliographical Guide to Research in Speech and Dramatic Art*, Scott, Foresman, 1963; *The Theatre: An Introduction*, Holt, 1964, 3rd edition, 1974; (contributor) *Classical Drama and Its Influence*, Methuen, 1965; (with Lenyth Brockett) *Plays for the Theatre*, Holt, 1967, 2nd edition, 1974; *History of the Theatre*, Allyn and Bacon, 1968, 2nd edition, 1974; *Perspectives on Contemporary Theatre*, Louisiana State University Press, 1971; (editor and contributor) *Studies in Theatre and Drama*, Mouton, 1972; (with Robert R. Findlay) *Century of Innovation: A History of European and American Theatre and Drama since 1870*, Prentice-Hall, 1973. Contributor to *Encyclopaedia Britannica*, *Encyclopedia Americana*, and *World Book Encyclopedia*; also contributor to *Educational Theatre Journal*, *Shakespeare Quarterly*, *Tulane Drama Review*, *Modern Philology*, *Theatre Research*, and other professional journals. Editor, *Educational Theatre Journal*, 1960-63; consulting editor, Prentice-Hall series in theatre and drama.

SIDELIGHTS: Brockett is competent in French.

* * *

BRODERICK, Dorothy M. 1929-

PERSONAL: Born June 23, 1929, in Bridgeport, Conn. *Education:* New Haven College (now Southern Connecticut College), B.S., 1953; Columbia University, M.S. in L.S., 1956, D.L.S., 1971. *Home:* Shad Bay, Nova Scotia, Canada. *Office:* School of Library Service, Dalhousie University, Halifax, Nova Scotia, Canada.

CAREER: St. John's University, Jamaica, N.Y., assistant professor of children's literature, 1958-60; New York State Library, Albany, public library children's consultant, 1960-62; Western Reserve University (now Case Western Reserve University), Cleveland, Ohio, School of Library Science, associate professor of children's literature, 1963-69; University of Wisconsin, Madison, visiting lecturer in children's and young adult literature, 1969-71; Dalhousie University, Halifax, Nova Scotia, associate professor of children's and young adult literature, 1972—. *Member:* American Library Association (member of Newbery-Caldecott Awards committee, 1962; councilor, 1965-68), Canadian Library Association.

WRITINGS: Leete's Island Adventure, Prentice-Hall, 1962; *Training a Companion Dog*, Prentice-Hall, 1965; *Introduction to Children's Work in Public Libraries*, Wilson, 1965; *Hank*, Harper, 1966; (with May Hill Arbuthnot) *Time for Stories of the Past and Present*, Scott, Foresman, 1968; (with Arbuthnot) *Time for Biography*, Scott, Foresman, 1969; *Image of the Black in Children's Fiction*, Bowker, 1973.

WORK IN PROGRESS: A revision of *Introduction to Children's Work in Public Libraries*.

SIDELIGHTS: Ms. Broderick told *CA:* "My major motivation in directing my professional and writing energies toward work with youth comes from a sense of commitment to the idea that how we are raised as children influences how we behave as adults." Initially, this view took her into the Civil Rights Movement, but she has become an "ardent feminist working toward human liberation." *Avo-*

cational interests: Bridge; Doberman Pinscher, Heidi; cat, Billy; "and anything that helps people be human beings."

* * *

BRODY, Jules 1928-

PERSONAL: Born March 6, 1928, in New York, N.Y.; son of Harry (a business executive) and Ida (Josephson) Brody; married Roxane Offner, July 26, 1953; children: Rachel, David, Jonathan. *Education:* Cornell University, B.A., 1948; Columbia University, M.A., 1949, Ph.D., 1956. *Home:* 62 Trenor Dr., New Rochelle, N.Y. 10804. *Office:* Queens College, Flushing, N.Y. 11367.

CAREER: Columbia University, New York, N.Y., lecturer in French, 1950-53, instructor, 1953-56, assistant professor, 1956-59, associate professor, 1959-63; University of Rochester, Rochester, N.Y., professor of French and chairman of department of foreign and comparative literature, 1963-68; Queens College of the City University of New York, Flushing, professor of French and dean of faculty, 1968—. United Jewish Welfare Fund, Rochester, N.Y., member of Speakers Bureau; Hillel School, Rochester, N.Y., trustee. *Member:* Modern Language Association of America, Society for French Studies (Oxford), American Association of Teachers of French, Societe D'Etudes du XVII Siecle (Paris), Phi Beta Kappa. *Awards, honors:* Fulbright research grant to Paris, 1961-62; Guggenheim Fellow, 1961-62; recipient of L'Ordre des Palmes Academiques, France, 1968.

WRITINGS: Boileau and Longinus, Droz, 1958; (editor with N. Edelman and D. C. Cabeen) *Critical Bibliography of French Literature*, Volume III, *The 17th Century*, Syracuse University Press, 1961; (editor) *French Classicism: A Critical Miscellany*, Prentice-Hall, 1965.

WORK IN PROGRESS: The Classical Temper: Studies in Seventeenth-Century French Literature.

SIDELIGHTS: Brody speaks French, Italian, Spanish, German, Latin, and Greek. *Avocational interests:* Playing banjo and guitar, cabinetmaking.†

* * *

BROEG, Bob 1918-

PERSONAL: Surname rhymes with "vague"; born March 18, 1918, in St. Louis, Mo.; son of Robert M. (a bread salesman) and Alice (Wiley) Broeg; married Dorothy Carr, June 19, 1943. *Education:* University of Missouri, B.J., 1941. *Home:* Apartment 702, 30 Plaza Sq., St. Louis, Mo. 63103. *Office: St. Louis Post-Dispatch*, St. Louis, Mo. 63101.

CAREER: Reporter for Associated Press in Jefferson City, Mo., 1941, and Boston, Mass., 1942; *St. Louis Post-Dispatch*, St. Louis, Mo., sports writer, 1945-58, sports editor, 1958—. Seminar lecturer, American Press Institute, Columbia University. District director, Football Foundation and Hall of Fame; member of board of directors, Missouri Sports Hall of Fame, University of Missouri. *Military service:* U.S. Marine Corps, 1942-45; became technical sergeant. *Member:* Baseball Writers Association of America (president, 1958), Football Writers Association of America, Basketball Writers Association, St. Louis Press Club, Sigma Phi Epsilon, Omicron Delta Kappa, Kappa Tau Alpha, Sigma Delta Chi. *Awards, honors:* Sportswriter of the Year Award, Knute Rockne Club, 1964; numerous other sportswriting awards.

WRITINGS: (With Bob Burrill) *Don't Bring That Up!*, A.

S. Barnes, 1946; *Stan Musial: The Man's Own Story*, Doubleday, 1964; *Super Stars of Baseball*, Spink & Son, 1971; *Mizzou: A Tale of Tiger Football*, Stroud, 1974. Contributor to *Saturday Evening Post, Sporting News,* and *Sport.*

* * *

BROER, Marion Ruth 1910-

PERSONAL: Born December 10, 1910, in Toledo, Ohio; daughter of William Frederick and Ethel (Griffin) Broer. *Education:* Bradford Junior College, student, 1928-30; University of Wisconsin, B.S., 1933, M.S., 1936; New York University, Ph.D., 1954. *Home:* 16599 Caminto Vecinos #8, San Diego, Calif. 92128.

CAREER: Instructor in physical education at Newcomb College, Tulane University, New Orleans, La., 1933-35, University of Colorado, Boulder, 1936-37, University of Wisconsin, Madison, 1937-39, Bradford Junior College, Bradford, Mass., 1939-41, Smith College, Northampton, Mass., 1941-43; American Red Cross Services to the Armed Forces, recreation and club director in India, 1943-45; University of Washington, Seattle, assistant professor, 1948-54, associate professor, 1954-60, professor of physical education, 1960-73, professor emeritus, 1973—. Medina Children's Service, Seattle, treasurer, 1959-61, secretary, 1961-62, president, 1965-66. *Member:* American Association for Health, Physical Education and Recreation (vice-president for Northwest district, 1958-60; district president, 1962-63), National Association for Physical Education of College Women (vice-president, 1959-61; president, 1967-69), American Academy of Physical Education, Western Society for Physical Education of College Women (member of executive board, 1956-58; honorary member, 1973—), Alpha Chi Omega, Phi Kappa Phi, Pi Lambda Theta.

WRITINGS: (Contributor) *Measuring Achievement in Physical Education*, Saunders, 1938; *Individual Sports for Women*, Saunders, 1943; *Marching Handbook*, University of Washington Press, 1956, 5th edition, 1971; *Efficiency of Human Movement*, Saunders, 1960, 3rd edition, 1973; *Patterns of Muscular Activity in Selected Sport Skills*, C. C Thomas, 1966; *Laboratory Experiences Exploring Efficiency of Human Movement*, Saunders, 1973. Contributor to professional journals. Past associate editor, *Journal of Health and Physical Education* and *Research Quarterly;* chairman of editorial committee, National Association for Physical Education of College Women, 1952-57.

* * *

BROMBERT, Victor H. 1923-

PERSONAL: Born November 11, 1923; married Beth Archer (a translator), June 18, 1950; children: Lauren, Marc. *Education:* Yale University, B.A., 1948, M.A., 1949, Ph.D., 1952; University of Rome, graduate study, 1950-51. *Home:* 115 West Park Ave., New Haven, Conn. *Office:* 317 William Harkness Hall, Yale University, New Haven, Conn.

CAREER: Yale University, New Haven, Conn., instructor, 1951-55, assistant professor, 1955-58, associate professor, 1958-62, professor of French, 1962—, Benjamin Barge Professor of Romance Languages, 1969—, chairman of Romance languages department, 1964—. *Military service:* U.S. Army, Military Intelligence, 1943-45. *Member:* Modern Language Association of America, American Association of Teachers of French, Association Internationale des Etudes Francaises, Societe des Etudes Romantiques,

Elizabethan Club. *Awards, honors:* Fulbright fellow, 1950-51; Guggenheim fellow, 1954-55, and 1970; grantee, American Council of Learned Societies, 1967; senior fellow, National Endowment for the Humanities, 1973-74.

WRITINGS: The Criticism of T. S. Eliot, Yale University Press, 1949; *Stendhal et la voie oblique*, Presses Universitaires de France, 1954; *The Intellectual Hero: Studies in the French Novel*, Lippincott, 1961; (editor) *Stendhal: A Collection of Critical Essays*, Prentice-Hall, 1962; *The Novels of Flaubert: A Study of Themes and Techniques*, Princeton Univeristy Press, 1966; *Stendhal: Fiction and the Themes of Freedom*, Random House, 1968; (editor) *The Hero in Literature*, Fawcett, 1969; *Flaubert par lui-meme*, Editions du Seuil, new edition, 1971. Contributor to *Romantic Review, Partisan Review, Literature Moderne, Revue des Sciences Humaines, Aurea Parma*, and other journals, and to *New York Times Book Review.*

WORK IN PROGRESS: A study of the Romantic imagination; a work on Victor Hugo.

SIDELIGHTS: Germaine Bree wrote in reviewing *The Novels of Flaubert:* "Mr. Brombert's understanding of Flaubert is characteristically generous, humanly imaginative and his book is rich in insights ... The over-all development is vivid, sparkling and convicingly brings to light a Flaubert many have sensed beneath the limited bourgeois 'hermit of Croisset'..."

Commenting on *Stendhal: Fiction and the Themes of Freedom*, Martin Lebowitz noted: "Brombert's work ... is extremely well-written, combining an extensive knowledge of literature and an acutely contextual historical sense essential to an understanding of Stendhal. Brombert is certainly one of our ablest academic critics—academic in the sense of being knowledgeable, lucid, profound, and intellectual."

* * *

BROMKE, Adam 1928-

PERSONAL: Born July 11, 1928, in Warsaw, Poland; son of Waclaw (a civil engineer) and Romualda (Beckmann) Bromke; married Alina Kosmider, July 7, 1958; children: Adam Robert, Alexander, Richard. *Education:* University of St. Andrews, M.A., 1950; University of Montreal, Ph.D., 1953; McGill University, Ph.D., 1964. *Home:* 1821 Walkley Rd., Ottawa ON K1H 6X9, Canada. *Office:* Carleton University, Ottawa, Ontario, Canada.

CAREER: University of Montreal, Montreal, Quebec, lecturer, 1953-54; Free Europe Committee, New York, N.Y., editor-in-chief, Polish Overseas Project, 1955-56; McGill University, Montreal, Quebec, lecturer, 1957-60; Harvard University, Cambridge, Mass., research fellow, 1960-62; Carleton University, Ottawa, Ontario, associate professor of political science and chairman of Soviet and East European studies program, 1962-66, professor of political science and chairman of department, 1968-71; Canadian Council, senior fellow, 1967-68. *Military service:* Polish underground, 1943-44. Polish Forces under British Command, 1945-47; became officer in commission. *Member:* American Council of Learned Societies (member of joint committee in Eastern Europe), Canadian Association of Slavists (president, 1968), Le Cercle Universitaire (Ottawa).

WRITINGS: Labour Relations Board in Ontario, Industrial Relations Centre, McGill University, 1961; (editor) *The Communist States at the Crossroads*, Praeger, 1965; *Poland's Politics: Political Idealism versus Political Real-*

ism, Harvard University Press, 1967; (editor with Philip E. Uren) *The Communist States and the West*, Praeger, 1967; (editor with Teresa Rakowska-Harmstone) *The Communist States in Disarray, 1965-1971*, University of Minnesota Press, 1972; (editor with John W. Strong) *Gierek's Poland*, Praeger, 1973. Managing editor, Canadian *Slavic Papers*, 1963-66.†

* * *

BRONFENBRENNER, Martin 1914-

PERSONAL: Surname is accented on first syllable; born December 2, 1914, in Pittsburgh, Pa.; son of Jacques Jacob; and Martha (Ornstein) Bronfenbrenner; married Teruko Okuaki, November 13, 1951; children: Kenneth, June. *Education:* Washington University, St. Louis, Mo., A.B., 1934; University of Chicago, Ph.D., 1939; University of Colorado, Certificate in Japanese, 1944. *Home:* 2915 Friendship Rd., Durham, N.C. 22705.

CAREER: Roosevelt University, Chicago, Ill., instructor, 1938-40, associate professor of economics, 1946-47; U.S. Treasury Department, Washington, D.C., economics, 1940-41, 1942-43; Federal Reserve Bank, Chicago, Ill., financial economist, 1941-42, 1946-47; University of Wisconsin, Madison, associate professor, 1947-54, professor of economics, 1954-57; Michigan State University, East Lansing, professor of economics, 1957-58; University of Minnesota, Minneapolis, professor of economics, 1959-62; Carnegie Institute of Technology (now Carnegie-Mellon University), Pittsburgh, Pa., professor of economics, 1962-71, chairman of economics department, 1966-71; Duke University, Durham, N.C., Kenan Professor of Economics, 1971—. Fiscal economist, SCAP, Tokyo, Japan, 1949-50; economist, UN Economics Commission for Asia and Far East, Bangkok, Thailand, 1952; Fulbright lecturer, Japan, 1962-63; visiting fellow, Behavioral Sciences Center, Stanford, Calif., 1966-67. *Military service:* U.S. Naval Reserve, 1943-46. *Member:* American Economic Association, American Statistical Association, American Association for Asian Studies, Econometric Society, American Association of University Professors, Phi Beta Kappa.

WRITINGS: Academic Encounter, Free Press of Glencoe, 1961; (editor with W. W. Lockwood) *The State and Economic Enterprise in Japan*, Princeton University Press, 1965; (editor) *Is the Business Cycle Obsolete?*, Wiley-Interscience, 1969; *Income Distribution Theory*, Aldine, 1971; *Tomioka Stories: From the Japanese Occupation*, Exposition Press, 1975. Articles in professional journals in United States and abroad include a number on Japanese academic and educational problems. Editor, *American Economic Review*, 1961-64.

SIDELIGHTS: Bronfenbrenner has visited Japan seven times since 1945, combining economics with interest in studies in Japanese area.†

* * *

BROOK, David 1932-

PERSONAL: Born April 1, 1932, in Brooklyn, N.Y.; son of Nathan Harry (a teacher) and Pearl (Efros) Brook. *Education:* Johns Hopkins University, B.A., 1954; Columbia University, M.A., 1955, Ph.D., 1961. *Home:* 135 Hawthorne St., Brooklyn, N.Y. 11225.

CAREER: St. John's University, Brooklyn, N.Y., instructor in political science, 1961-63; Rutgers University, New Brunswick, N.J., lecturer, in the rank of assistant professor, 1963-64, lecturer in political science, 1964-67; City University of New York, assistant professor of political science, 1964-67; Jersey City State College, Jersey City, New Jersey, assistant professor, 1967-69, associate professor, 1969-72, professor of political science and chairman of department, 1972—. Associate director of summer seminar, Institute of World Affairs, 1967; member of Seminar on Problems of Peace, Columbia University, 1972—. Consultant to Dodd, Mead & Co., Inc. *Member:* American Society of International Law, American Political Science Association, American Association of University Professors, Middle States Council of Social Studies. *Awards, honors:* Wilton Park fellow, England, 1972.

WRITINGS: The U.N. and the China Dilemma, Vantage, 1956; *Preface to Peace: The United Nations and the Arab-Israel Armistice System*, Public Affairs, 1964; (editor) *Search for Peace: Readings in International Relations*, Dodd, 1970. Contributor to *Journal of East Asiatic Studies* and other professional journals. Associate editor, Middle States Council of Social Studies, *Annual Proceeding and Bulletin*, 1968-70, and director of publications, 1970-71.

BIOGRAPHICAL/CRITICAL SOURCES: Journal of International Affairs, American Journal of International Law, July, 1957, March, 1957; *International Affairs*, April 8, 1957.

* * *

BROOKE-ROSE, Christine

PERSONAL: Born in Geneva, Switzerland; married Jerzy Peterkiewicz (a writer and university lecturer). *Education:* Somerville College, Oxford, B.A., 1949, M.A., 1953; University College, London, Ph.D., 1954. *Residence:* Paris, France. *Address:* c/o Hamish Hamilton, 90 Great Russell St., London W.C. 1, England.

CAREER: Novelist, critic, and university lecturer. *Awards, honors:* Society of Authors Travelling Prize, 1965, for *Out;* James Tait Black Prize, 1966, for *Such;* Arts Council Translation Prize, 1969, for *In the Labyrinth.*

WRITINGS: The Languages of Love, Secker & Warburg, 1957; *The Sycamore Tree*, Secker & Warburg, 1958, Norton, 1959; *A Grammar of Metaphor* (criticism), Secker & Warburg, 1958, 2nd edition, 1970; (translator) Juan Goytisolo, *Children of Chaos*, MacGibbon, 1959; *The Dear Deceit*, Secker & Warburg, 1960, Doubleday, 1961; *The Middlemen*, Secker & Warburg, 1961; (translator) Alfred Sauvy, *Fertility and Survival: Population Problems from Malthus to Mao Tse Tung*, Macmillan, 1962; *Out* (novel), M. Joseph, 1964; *Such* (novel), M. Joseph, 1965; (translator) Alain Robbe-Grillet, *In the Labyrinth*, Calder & Boyars, 1968; *Between* (novel), M. Joseph, 1968; *Go When You See The Green Man Walking* (collection of short stories), M. Joseph, 1969; *A ZBC of Ezra Pound* (criticism), California University Press, 1971; *Thru* (fiction), Hamish Hamilton, 1975; *A Structuralist Analysis of Pound's Usura Canto*, Mouton & Co., in press. Author of radio plays. Contributor of short stories, critical essays, and reviews to *London Magazine, Observer, Spectator, Modern Fiction Studies, Sunday Times, Times Literary Supplement, Revue des Lettres Modernes, Quarterly Review of Literature, New Statesman*, and other periodicals.

SIDELIGHTS: Ms. Brooke-Rose speaks French, German, Spanish, Italian, and a little Polish. *Avocational interests:* Travel, people.

BROOKS, John 1920-
(John Nixon Brooks)

PERSONAL: Born December 5, 1920, in New York, N.Y.; son of John Nixon and Bessie (Lyon) Brooks; married Rae Everitt; children: Carolyn, John Alexander. *Education:* Princeton University, A.B., 1942. *Home:* 41 Barrow St., New York, N.Y. 10014. *Agent:* Harold Ober Associates, Inc., 40 East 49th St., New York, N.Y. 10017.

CAREER: Full-time writer, 1945—. Contributing editor, *Time*, 1945-47; regular contributor to *New Yorker*, 1949—. *Member:* Authors Guild (treasurer, 1964-69; vice-president, 1969—). *Awards, honors:* Loeb Magazine Award, 1964, and 1968, for articles in *New Yorker*.

WRITINGS—All under name John Nixon Brooks; novels: *The Big Wheel*, Harper, 1949; *A Pride of Lions*, Harper, 1954; *The Man Who Broke Things*, Harper, 1958.

Nonfiction: *The Seven Fat Years: Chronicles of Wall Street*, Harper, 1958; *The Fate of the Edsel and Other Business Adventures*, Harper, 1963; *The Great Leap: The Past Twenty-Five Years in America*, Harper, 1966; *Business Adventures: Twelve Classic Tales from the Worlds of Wall Street and the Modern American Corporation*, Weybright, 1969; *Once in Golconda: A True Drama of Wall Street, 1920-1938*, Harper, 1969; *The Go-Go Years*, Weybright, 1973; *The Autobiography of American Business*, Doubleday, 1974.

Editor: (And contributor) *The One and the Many: The Individual in the Modern World*, Harper, 1962. Contributor of articles and reviews to national magazines.

WORK IN PROGRESS: A social and economic history of the telephone, publication by Harper expected in 1976.

SIDELIGHTS: Brooks has been praised for both his novelistic skill and his ability to present a readable factual report. Charles Poore reported: "He uses his novelist's gifts of characterization, lucid narrative, and suspense with considerable felicity." Martin Mayer wrote, "Fun is fun, and *Once in Golconda* will occupy an evening more entertainingly and doubtless more profitably than anything television is likely to offer." And Robert J. Landry commented on the same work: "A vastly instructive book, carefully researched, redeemed from muckraking by compassion and scholarship." Some of Brooks' material originally appeared in *The New Yorker*.

* * *

BROOKS, (Frank) Leonard 1911-

PERSONAL: Born November 7, 1911, in London, England; son of Herbert Henry (an accountant) and Ellen (Barnard) Brooks; married Reva Silverman (a photographer), October 18, 1935. *Education:* Attended public schools in Toronto and North Bay, Ontario, Canada; studied briefly at Ontario College of Art. *Home:* Calle de la Quinta, Col. Guadiana, San Miguel de Allende, Guanajuato, Mexico.

CAREER: Professional artist. Traveled and painted in England, France, and Spain, 1933-34; taught art in Toronto, Ontario, 1936-43 and 1946-47; went to Mexico in 1947 to devote full time to painting and has since spent part of every year there. Work exhibited in many major cities in United States and Canada, and in Barcelona, London, and Mexico City; paintings in collections of National Gallery in Ottawa, Art Gallery of Toronto, and in city, university, and private collections in United States and elsewhere. Occasional guest art instructor at Ohio University, University of British Columbia, Wells College, and at art schools. *Military service:* Royal Canadian Naval Volunteer Reserve, official war artist, 1943-46; became lieutenant.

WRITINGS—All published by Reinhold: *Watercolor: A Challenge*, 1957; *Oil Painting: Traditional and New*, 1959, revised edition, 1971; *Casein Painting*, 1961; *Wash Drawing*, 1961; *Painting and Understanding Abstract Art*, 1964; *Painter's Workshop*, 1969; *Watercolor and Aqueous Media*, in press.

AVOCATIONAL INTERESTS: Chamber music (plays violin and viola).

* * *

BROOKS, Paul 1909-

PERSONAL: Born February 16, 1909, in New York, N.Y.; son of Ernest (an architect) and Jeanne (Marion) Brooks; married Susan Anderson Moller, June 24, 1931; children: Elizabeth Sweetser (Mrs. John W. Harris), Douglas (deceased), Samuel Jameson, Susan (Mrs. John D. Morris), Kate. *Education:* Harvard University, A.B. (cum laude), 1931. *Home:* Silver Hill Rd., Lincoln, Mass. *Office:* Houghton Mifflin Co., 2 Park St., Boston, Mass.

CAREER: Entire career has been spent with publisher, Houghton Mifflin Co., Boston, Mass.; began as editorial reader, 1931, subsequently assistant editor, then managing editor; editor-in-chief and director of company, 1943-67, vice-president, 1967-69. Chief of book section, U.S. Office of War Information, 1945. Trustee, Trustees for Conservation; member of national council, Nature Conservancy. *Member:* American Academy of Arts and Sciences (fellow), Massachusetts Audubon Society (director, 1943-47), Signet Associates (president, 1964-65), Phi Beta Kappa, St. Botolph Club, Tavern Club, Saturday Club, Examiner Club (Boston), Century Association (New York). *Awards, honors:* John Burroughs Medal of American Museum of Natural History, and the Sarah Chapman Francis Medal of the Garden Club of America, both for *Roadless Area*, 1965; H.L.D. from University of Massachusetts, 1973.

WRITINGS: *Roadless Area*, Knopf, 1964; *The Pursuit of Wilderness*, Houghton, 1971; *The House of Life: Rachel Carson at Work*, Houghton, 1973. Contributor to *Atlantic Monthly*, *Harper's*, *Horizon*, and other magazines. Contributing editor, *Audubon Magazine*.

SIDELIGHTS: Paul Brooks was the editor of Rachel Carson's *Silent Spring*, which he acknowledges "as one of those rare books that change the course of history." *The House of Life: Rachel Carson at Work* is based on her papers and published work.

Paul Brooks' book *The Pursuit of Wilderness* "is beautiful for two reasons: the sheer lyricism of much of the prose and more pragmatically, the fact that national concern for environment is catching on. . . . Even if your're not an ardent conservationist, or even a lukewarm one, reading this book will leave you considerably enriched," wrote F. J. MacEntee.

* * *

BROOM, Leonard 1911-

PERSONAL: Born November 8, 1911, in Boston, Mass.; married Gretchan Noel Cooke, August 31, 1940; children: Karl Cooke, Dorothy Howard (Mrs. Russell Kent Darroch). *Education:* Boston University, B.S., 1933, A.M., 1934; Duke University, Ph.D., 1937. *Office:* Department of Sociology, Institute of Advanced Studies, Australian National University, Canberra ACT 2600, Australia.

CAREER: Instructor in sociology at Clemson College, Clemson, S.C., 1937-38, Kent State University, Kent, Ohio, 1938-41; University of California, Los Angeles, assistant professor, 1941-48, associate professor, 1948-53, professor of anthropology and sociology, 1953-59, chairman of department of anthropology and sociology, 1952-57; University of Texas, Austin, professor of sociology, 1957-63, chairman of department, 1959-66, vice-president, 1962-63, Ashbel Smith Professor of Sociology, 1963-71. Visiting professor, Australian National University, 1964-65, 1969-70, professor, 1971—. *Member:* American Sociological Association (fellow), American Anthropological Association (fellow), Royal Anthropological Institute (fellow), Population Association of America, Australian Academy of Social Sciences, Sociological Research Association, International Institute of Differing Civilization, Pacific Sociological Association (president, 1951). *Awards, honors:* Fulbright research fellow, British West Indies, 1950-51; faculty fellow, Fund for Advancement of Education, 1953-54; Guggenheim fellow, 1958; honorary fellow, Australian National University, 1958; fellow, Center For Advanced Study in the Behavioral Sciences, 1962-63; D.Sc., Boston University, 1973.

WRITINGS: (With Ruth Riemer) *Removal and Return: The Socio-economic Effects of the War on Japanese Americans*, University of California Press, 1949; (with Frank J. Speck) *Cherokee Dance and Drama*, University of California Press, 1951; (with Philip Selznick) *Sociology: A Text with Adapted Readings*, Row, Peterson & Co., 1955, 5th edition, Harper, 1973; *A Controlled Attitude-Tension Survey*, University of California Press, 1956; (with John I. Kitsuse) *The Managed Casualty: The Japanese-American Family in World War II*, University of California Press, 1956; (with Norval D. Glenn) *Transformation of the Negro American*, Harper, 1965, 2nd edition, 1967; (with P. Selznick) *Principles of Sociology*, Harper, 1970; (with F. Lancaster Jones) *A Blanket a Year*, Australian National University Press, 1973. Editor, Chandler Publishing Company's publications in sociology and anthropology. Contributor to professional journals. Editor, *American Sociological Review*, 1955-57.†

*   *   *

BROOMSNODDER, B(radley) MacKinley 1940-

PERSONAL: Born April 1, 1940, in Pittsborough, N.D.; son of MacKinley (a silkworm breeder) and Bertha (Pansy) Broomsnodder; married Drucilla Farnsworthy (a ballet dancer), April 1, 1962; children: Bradley MacKinley, Jr. *Education:* Attended public schools in Pittsborough, N.D. *Religion:* Universalist. *Home:* 800 Ironwood Dr., #319, Rochester, Mich. 48063.

CAREER: Worked as assistant silk collector in father's silkworm factory, Pittsborough, N.D., 1957-60; wrote, illustrated, and edited own newspaper, *Pittsborough Weekly Sentinel* (now defunct), Pittsborough, N.D., 1958-61. Worked part-time as assistant to the manager of the shell collection, Pittsborough Museum of Natural History, Pittsborough, N.D., 1958-61. Consultant and full-time writer, 1961—.

WRITINGS: The Art of Shell Collection and Classification, Peabody, 1961; *Humbert and Hubert: A Tale of Two Silkworms* (juvenile), Peabody, 1961; *Oneness: The Reality of the Psychedelic Soul*, privately printed, 1962; *The Soul and the Silkworm* (a fantasy), privately printed, 1963; *Perhaps to Dream: An Inspiration*, privately printed, 1965;

Shell We Dance?: Shell Collecting for All Ages, Peabody, 1968; *The Silkworm Breeder's Handbook*, Pittsborough Museum of Natural History, 1970; *Conqueror Worm: The Story of Silk through the Ages*, Pittsborough Museum of Natural History, 1973.

AVOCATIONAL INTERESTS: Shell collecting, soul-painting, doodling.

*   *   *

BROSTOWIN, Patrick Ronald 1931-

PERSONAL: Surname is pronounced *Brost*-o-win, first syllable rhymes with "cost"; born January 27, 1931, in Brooklyn, N.Y.; son of George and Matilda (Schwint) Brostowin; married Marie S. Milazzo, April, 1952; children: Annemarie, Patrick T., James, Peter, Terry (son), William, Robert. *Education:* St. John's University, Jamaica, N.Y., B.A., 1951; New York University, M.A., 1953, Ph.D., 1969. *Home:* 356 East Rd., Garden City, N.Y.

CAREER: Teacher of English at parochial high school in Brooklyn, N.Y., 1951-53, and public high school in Levittown, N.Y., 1953-61; Nassau Community College, Garden City, N.Y., associate professor of English, 1961—. Speaker and co-leader of discussion, National Broadcasting Co. radio program, "Extra Curricula." *Member:* Modern Language Association of America, National Council of Teachers of English, New York State Association of Junior Colleges.

WRITINGS: (Editor with John Cadden) *Science and Literature: A Reader*, Heath, 1964. Has done a series of educational filmstrips on English literature for Eye Gate Productions.

WORK IN PROGRESS: A history of the influence of science on American literature.†

*   *   *

BROWN, Allen 1926-

PERSONAL: Born February 23, 1926, in Omaha, Neb.; son of Henry A. (a businessman) and Gerturde (Carter) Brown. *Education:* Morningside College, B.A. (cum laude), 1949. *Politics:* Independent Republican. *Home:* Rio Tigris 30-c, Mexico City, Mexico. *Agent:* The Sterling Lord Agency, 75 East 55th St., New York, N.Y. 10022.

CAREER: Reporter in Council Bluffs, Iowa, 1950-53, on *Des Moines Register and Tribune*, Des Moines, Iowa, 1953-56, *San Francisco Examiner*, San Francisco, Calif., 1956; reporter and columnist, *San Francisco Chronicle*, San Francisco, Calif., 1956-60; full-time free-lance writer, 1960—.

WRITINGS: (With Edward Teller) *The Legacy of Hiroshima*, Doubleday, 1962; *Golden Gate: Biography of a Bridge*, Doubleday, 1965. Contributor to *Saturday Evening Post, Reader's Digest, This Week, Catholic Digest, Escapade, New York Times Magazine.*

WORK IN PROGRESS: A novel.

SIDELIGHTS: Brown told *CA:* "Interested . . . [in] the creative personality and.... the problems of minorities ranging from the U.S. Negro to the U.S. homosexual. Have competence in Spanish and am studying growth of the middle class in Mexico."†

*   *   *

BROWN, B(essie) Katherine (Taylor) 1917-

PERSONAL: Born October 3, 1917, in Olympia, Wash.;

daughter of Guy Raymond (a farmer) and Agnes Emily (Giles) Taylor; married Robert E. Brown (a professor of history), May 11, 1937. *Education:* University of Washington, Seattle, B.A., 1946; Michigan State University, M.A., 1952. *Home:* 2070 Lagoon Dr., Okemos, Mich. 48864.

CAREER: Free-lance writer and researcher. *Member:* Phi Beta Kappa.

WRITINGS: (With husband, Robert E. Brown) *Virginia, 1705-1786: Democracy or Aristocracy?*, Michigan State University Press, 1964. Contributor of articles and reviews to historical journals.

WORK IN PROGRESS: A book, tentatively titled *Primogeniture and Entail in Colonial America*.

*   *   *

BROWN, Blanche R. (Levine) 1915-

PERSONAL: Born April 12, 1915, in Boston, Mass.; daughter of Samuel (a businessman) and Bertha (Nanes) Levine; married Milton W. Brown, July 15, 1938. *Education:* Wayne (now Wayne State) University, student, 1932-34; New York University, B.F.A., 1936, M.A., 1938, Ph.D., 1967. *Politics:* Independent. *Religion:* Atheist. *Home:* 15 West 70th St., New York, N.Y. 10023. *Office:* Department of Fine Arts, New York University, Washington Sq. E., New York, N.Y. 10003.

CAREER: Art historian. Metropolitan Museum of Art, New York, N.Y., lecturer, 1942-65; New York University, associate professor, 1966-73, professor of art, 1973—. Former instructor at Vassar College and Hunter College. *Member:* College Art Association, Archaeological Institute of America.

WRITINGS: Ptolemaic Paintings and Mosaics, Archaeological Institute of America, 1957; *Five Cities*, Doubleday, 1964; *Anticlassicism in Greek Sculpture of the Fourth Century B.C.*, Archaeological Institute of America, 1973. Contributor of articles and reviews to scholarly journals.

WORK IN PROGRESS: A study of the painted stelai of Demetrias; research in Hellenistic art; second edition of *Five Cities*.

SIDELIGHTS: Mrs. Brown reads German, French, Italian, and ancient Greek for research. *Five Cities* is an art guide to Athens, Rome, Florence, Paris, and London.

*   *   *

BROWN, David 1916-

PERSONAL: Born July 28, 1916, in New York, N.Y.; son of Edward Fisher and Lillian (Baren) Brown; married Helen Gurley (an author and editor), September 25, 1959; children: Bruce LeGacy. *Education:* Stanford University, A.B., 1936; Columbia University, M.A., 1937. *Home:* 605 Park Ave., New York, N.Y. 10021. *Office:* Zanuck-Brown Co., 445 Park Ave., New York, N.Y. 10022.

CAREER: Fairchild Publications, New York, N.Y., night editor and assistant drama critic, 1937-39; Milk Research Council, New York, N.Y., editorial director, 1939-40; Street & Smith Publications, New York, N.Y., associate editor, 1940-43; *Liberty*, New York, N.Y., 1943-49, successively associate editor, executive editor, and editor-in-chief; *Cosmopolitan*, New York, N.Y., 1949-52, associate editor, then managing editor; 20th Century-Fox Film Corp., Beverly Hills, Calif., 1952-63, successively story editor, head of scenario department, executive in charge of story operations; New American Library of World Litera-

ture, Inc., New York, N.Y., editorial vice-president, 1963-64; 20th Century-Fox Film Corp., New York, N.Y., executive vice-president in charge of creative operations, member of board of directors, and other posts, 1964-70; executive vice-president in charge of creative operations and member of board of directors, Warner Brothers Pictures, 1971-72; Zanuck-Brown Co. (independent film producers), New York, N.Y., director and partner, 1972—. Judge, Benjamin Franklin Magazine Awards, 1955-58. *Military service:* U.S. Army, Quartermaster Corps and Military Intelligence, 1943-45; became first lieutenant. *Member:* Academy of Motion Picture Arts and Sciences, Producers Guild of America (trustee and member of executive committee), American Film Institute (Washington, D.C.), National Press Club, Overseas Press Club.

WRITINGS: (Contributor) *Journalists in Action*, Channel Press (Manhasset, N.Y.), 1963; (editor) *I Can Tell It Now*, Dutton, 1964; (editor with W. Richard Bruner) *How I Got That Story*, Dutton, 1967. Contributor of short stories and articles to *Collier's, Saturday Review, American, Harper's, Reader's Digest, Saturday Evening Post, American Mercury*, and other magazines.

*   *   *

BROWN, David Grant 1936-

PERSONAL: Born February 19, 1936, in Chicago, Ill.; son of Wendell Jacob (an attorney) and Margaret (James) Brown; married Eleanor Ann Rosene, August 16, 1958; children: Alison, Dirk. *Education:* Denison University, A.B. (with honors), 1958; Princeton University, M.A., 1960, Ph.D., 1961. *Home:* 6 Robin Ct., Oxford, Ohio.

CAREER: University of North Carolina, Chapel Hill, assistant professor of economics, 1961-64, associate professor, 1964-67; Drake University, Des Moines, Iowa, provost and vice president for academic affairs, 1967-70; Miami University, Oxford, Ohio, provost and executive vice president for academic affairs, 1970—. American Council on Education-Ford Foundation administrative intern, University of Minnesota, 1966-67. *Member:* American Economic Association, Industrial Relations Research Association, American Association of University Professors. *Awards, honors:* Tanner Award for excellence in teaching; research grants from National Science Foundation and U.S. Department of Labor.

WRITINGS: The Market for College Teachers, University of North Carolina Press, 1965; *The Mobile Professors*, American Council on Education, 1967.

*   *   *

BROWN, Dee (Alexander) 1908-

PERSONAL: Born February 28, 1908, in Louisiana; son of Daniel Alexander and Lula (Crawford) Brown; married Sara Baird Stroud, 1934; children: James Mitchell, Linda. *Education:* Arkansas State Teachers College, student; George Washington University, B.S. in L.S., 1937; University of Illinois, M.S., 1952.

CAREER: Started as a printer, then switched to journalism, and later to library work; U.S. Department of Agriculture, Washington, D.C., library assistant, 1934-42; U.S. War Department, Washington, D.C., technical librarian, 1945-48; University of Illinois, Urbana, librarian of agriculture, 1948-72. Author. *Military service:* U.S. Army, 1942-45. *Member:* American Library Association, Western Writers of America, Organization of American Historians.

WRITINGS: Wave High the Banner (novel based on life of Davy Crockett), Macrae Smith, 1942; (with Martin F. Schmitt) *Fighting Indians of the West*, Scribner, 1948.

Trial Driving Days, Scribner, 1952; *Grierson's Raid*, University of Illinois Press, 1954; (with Schmitt) *The Settlers' West*, Scribner, 1955; *Yellowhorse* (novel), Houghton, 1956; *The Gentle Tamers: Women of the Old Wild West*, Putnam, 1958; *Cavalry Scout* (novel), Permabooks, 1958; *The Bold Cavaliers: Morgan's Second Kentucky Cavalry Raiders*, Lippincott, 1959.

They Went Thataway (satirical novel), Putnam, 1960; (editor) *Pawnee, Blackfoot and Cheyenne*, Scribner, 1961; *Fort Phil Kearny: An American Saga*, Putnam, 1962; *The Galvanized Yankees*, University of Illinois Press, 1963; *Showdown at Little Big Horn*, Putnam, 1964; *The Girl from Fort Wicked* (novel), Doubleday, 1964; *The Year of the Century*, Scribner, 1966; *Action at Beecher Island*, Doubleday, 1967.

Bury My Heart at Wounded Knee, Holt, 1971; *The Westerners*, Holt, 1974.

Editor, *Agricultural History*, 1956-58.

SIDELIGHTS: Bury My Heart at Wounded Knee, Dee Brown's best seller, was included in *Time* magazine's Selection of the Year's Best Books. All of his books, even *They Went Thataway*, which has a modern setting, are rooted in the American frontier—an interest spiked in his youth by a grandmother who remembered the California gold rush, had driven ox wagons, and could recall the Civil War in detail.

*   *   *

BROWN, Joe David   1915-

PERSONAL: Born May 12, 1915, in Birmingham, Ala.; son of William Samuel (a newspaper publisher) and Lucille (Lokey) Brown; married Mildred Harbour, October 24, 1935 (divorced, 1943); married Frances O'Reilly, June 30, 1945; children: Joe David, Jr., Tedd H., Gilbreth. *Education:* Attended University of Alabama. *Politics:* Independent. *Religion:* Protestant. *Agent:* Curtis Brown Ltd., 60 East 56th St., New York, N.Y. 10022.

CAREER: Worked on newspapers in Alabama and Missouri, 1935-39; *New York Daily News*, New York, N.Y., feature writer, 1939-46; *Time* and *Life*, New York, N.Y., foreign correspondent in New Delhi, Paris, London, Moscow, 1949-57; free-lance writer, 1957—. *Military service:* U.S. Army, parachutist with 517th Combat Team, 1942-45; became second lieutenant; received battlefield commission, Purple Heart, and Croix de Guerre with palm (France).

WRITINGS—Novels: Stars in My Crown, Morrow, 1946 (also author of film adaptation, produced by Metro-Goldwyn-Mayer, 1949); *The Freeholder*, Morrow, 1949; *Kings Go Forth*, Morrow, 1956; *Glimpse of a Stranger*, Morrow, 1968; *Addie Pray* (Literary Guild selection), Simon & Schuster, 1971, published as *Paper Moon*, New American Library, 1972.

Nonfiction: (With the editors of *Life*) *India*, Time-Life, 1961, revised edition, 1969.

Editor—All published by Time-Life: *The Hippies*, 1967; *Can Christianity Survive?*, 1967; *Sex in the 60's*, 1967.

Short stories anthologized in *Best Post Stories, Literature in America*, and *This Is Your War*. Contributor of short stories and articles to most national magazines, including *Saturday Evening Post, Sports Illustrated*, and *Colliers*.

WORK IN PROGRESS: A novel for Simon & Schuster.

SIDELIGHTS: Kings Go Forth was made into a motion picture by United Artists in 1958; *Addie Pray* was made into a motion picture titled *Paper Moon* by Paramount in 1973.

Reviewing *Addie Pray* in *Time*, Martha Duffy observed, "Brown has a special feeling for the Depression-era South . . . [and] for the likes of his protagonist. . . . Addie's speech . . . is vulgar, pungent country talk, which adds greatly to the book's easygoing charm. . . . the book is a long tall, oldtime tale. But as Addie might put it, in the right hands that kind of yarn has a lot of prance left."

AVOCATIONAL INTERESTS: Hunting and fishing.

*   *   *

BROWN, John J.   1916-
(Boris Sherashevski)

PERSONAL: Born April 28, 1916, in Penhold, Alberta, Canada; son of John H. (a merchant) and Estella I. (White) Brown; married Barbara Tarbox (a psychologist), September 4, 1941; children: Christopher, Alan, Lawrence. *Education:* University of Toronto, B.A. (honors), 1939; Yale University, M.A., 1941, Ph.D., 1943. *Politics:* "Small-'l' liberal." *Religion:* Quaker. *Home:* 19 Blvd. de Suisse, Monte Carlo, Monaco. *Agent:* Matie Molinaro, 25 Douglas Crescent, Toronto, Ontario, Canada. *Office:* Institute for Entrepreneurial History, MacLennan Library, McGill University, Montreal, Quebec, Canada.

CAREER: Cornell University, Ithaca, N.Y., instructor in English, 1943-44; Research Enterprises Ltd., Toronto, Ontario, technical editor, 1944-46; Aluminium Ltd., Montreal, Quebec, financial writer, 1948-57; Industrial Automation Ltd. (management consultants), Montreal, president, 1957—; McGill University, Montreal, research fellow in history and director of Institute for Entrepreneurial History, 1964—. Director, Electronic Associates Ltd., Toronto; trustee, Ontario Centennial Project of Center for Science and Technology. *Member:* Society for History of Technology, Yale Club of Montreal, University Club, Royal St. Lawrence Yacht Club, Montreal Athletic Club, Monte Carlo Country Club.

WRITINGS: Investment Value Tables, privately printed (Montreal), 1955; *Start with $100: Common Sense Investing*, Longmans, Green (Toronto), 1960, Putnam, 1962; *The Intelligent Investor's Guide to Real Estate*, Putnam, 1964; *Life Insurance—Benefit or Fraud?*, Longmans, Green (Toronto), 1964, revised edition, 1972; *Ideas in Exile: A History of Canadian Invention*, McClelland, 1967; *The Inventors: Great Ideas in Canadian Enterprise*, McClelland, 1967. Contributor of more than one hundred articles to learned and popular journals.

WORK IN PROGRESS: A Primer of Expropriation, with case studies, completion expected in 1976; *My Life In Court*, 1976.

AVOCATIONAL INTERESTS: Sports cars, sailing (planing centerboarders), and squash.

BIOGRAPHICAL/CRITICAL SOURCES: Fortune, November, 1946; *Toronto Telegram*, June 18, 1964; *Maclean's Magazine*, July, 1964.

*   *   *

BROWN, Kenneth H.   1936-

PERSONAL: Born March 9, 1936, in Brooklyn, N.Y.; son of Kenneth F. (a policeman) and Helen (Bella) Brown;

married Tamara V. Boettcher (a jockey), August 22, 1970. *Education:* Attended Columbia University. *Politics:* "Freedom to be productive; understanding through communication." *Religion:* "Happiness through constant struggle." *Address:* 150 74th St., Brooklyn, N.Y. 11209. *Agent:* Ellen Neuwald, 905 West End Ave., New York, N.Y. 10025.

CAREER: Mail clerk with a newspaper, 1951-54; bank clerk on Wall Street, 1960; bartender, waiter, cigarette salesman, service captain in New York, N.Y. and Miami, Fla., 1958-63; Living Theatre, New York, N.Y., resident playwright, 1963-67; private tutor in New Haven, Conn., 1966-69; Yale University, New Haven, Conn., resident playwright with Yale School of Drama, 1966-69; Hunter College of the City University of New York, New York, N.Y., visiting lecturer in theatre, 1969-70; University of Iowa, Iowa City, associate professor in theatre, 1971; playwright, poet, and novelist. *Military service:* U.S. Marine Corps, 1954-57. *Member:* Actors Studio (playwright's unit), New Dramatists, Writers Guild. *Awards, honors:* Venice Film Festival Gold Medal, 1964; Rockefeller fellowship, 1965; ABC-Yale fellowship, 1966, 1967; Guggenheim fellowship, 1966-67; Rockefeller grant, 1967; National Endowment for the Arts grant, 1973; Creative Artists Public Service Program Award, 1974.

WRITINGS—Plays: *The Brig* (produced in New York, N.Y. at Living Theatre, 1963), Methuen, 1964, Hill & Wang, 1965; "Devices," first produced in New York, N.Y., at Actors Studio, 1964, produced Off-Off Broadway at Judson Poet's Theatre, 1965; "The Happy Bar," produced in New York, N.Y., 1967; "The Cretan Bull," produced on Off-Off Broadway at Gotham Art Theatre, 1967; "Blake's Design," produced in New Haven, Conn., by Yale Drama School, 1968; "Nightlife in the Locking Ring," produced in New York, N.Y. at Lincoln Center, December, 1968; "The Green Room," produced in Iowa City, Iowa, at University of Iowa, 1971; *Night Light* (first produced by Hartford Stage Co., January, 1973), Samuel French, 1973. Also author of play, "Three Dreams From Dell's Couch."

Author of novel, *The Narrows*, Dial, 1970.

Screenplays: "The Brig," 1964; "Devices," 1967.

WORK IN PROGRESS: "The Dinosaurs," an original screenplay.

SIDELIGHTS: Brown wrote: "My first play, *The Brig*, was written as an exercise in 1960 when I was experimenting with the combining of Meyerhold's Constructivist theory and Artaud's Theatre of Cruelty. Meyerhold stated that the theatre was, at best, a frivolous spectacle because stage settings were built around the action of the play. He suggested that the design be made before the play was written so that the actors would experience some of the limitations of space that we are forced to accept in life.... Artaud, on the other hand, said, 'Without an element of cruelty at the root of every spectacle, the theatre is not possible. In our present state of degeneration, it is through the skin that metaphysics must be made to re-enter our minds.' There are very few people who have seen my play who would not admit that it got under their skins.

"My second play, 'The Green Room,' was a further step in this direction. I gave the form some elements of fantasy and satire, and used a civilian rather than military situation.

"My third play, 'Three Dreams From Dell's Couch,' was an investigation of three common and distinct points of view in middle-class America. It deals specifically with the lives of three men: a bartender and ex-marine, a professional student, and a philosophical scientist.

"My fourth play, 'Devices,' was my first one-act play, and it deals with the problems of a career woman and how she solves them." The *Village Voice* called the production "intricate and provocative.... What occurs upon the stage is low-key to the point of neutrality."

"My fifth play, 'The Happy Bar,' is by far the best thing I have written. It deals with life in a brothel in post-war Japan and examines the relationships and situations of American servicemen and Japanese prostitutes.... I feel as though good use will finally be made of one of the dead hulks along the great white way. It is a huge play that is more aptly described as a theatrical event, and it may bring some justification to the great facilities of the Broadway stage for the first time in many years if it is realized."

Brown believes that the theatre "is a reflection of its society. As our society is politically and religiously false, economically avaricious, and essentially evil, its theatre is the theatre of evil. Its artists are the artists of deceit.

"My theatre is the theatre of God. My God is Love, Truth, and Beauty, three words that continue the same ideal. Love is the nature of all things as they are related to themselves and to each other.... Art is a noble effort to illustrate Truth. My theatre is the theatre of Art. Those of us who have some understanding of the nature of God are the Artists of my theatre."

"The Brig," was filmed by Jonas Mekas.

A collection of Brown's manuscripts has been established at the New York Public Library.

BIOGRAPHICAL/CRITICAL SOURCES: Tulane Drama Review, March, 1964; Frederick Lumley, *New Trends in 20th Century Drama: A Survey Since Ibsen and Shaw*, Oxford University Press, 1967; *Wisconsin Studies*, summer, 1967.

*   *   *

BROWN, M(ary) L(oretta) T(herese)

PERSONAL: Born in New York, N.Y.; daughter of John J. (a publisher, printer, and inventor) and Caecilia (Reynolds) Brown. *Education:* Attended Columbia University. *Politics:* Republican. *Religion:* Roman Catholic. *Home:* 1025 Park Ave., New York, N.Y. 10028.

CAREER: Lever Brothers, New York, N.Y., 1946-54, becoming publicity and public relations director for Harriet Hubbard Ayer products, then creative coordinator for Lux products; Hill and Knowlton, Inc., New York, N.Y., account executive and public relations director for Coca-Cola Co., 1954-60, director of women's activities, 1960-67, vice-president, 1967—. *Awards, honors:* Mayor's Gold Key to the City of New York, 1965, for contributions to civic programs; Woman of the Month, *Sign*, 1967; St. Thomas More Award of the Oriel Society, 1969, for *The Gift*; Dame of the Military Order of the Collar of St. Agatha, 1972; Lady of the Holy Sepulchre, conferred by Pope Paul VI, 1972.

WRITINGS: Angela in Public Relations (teen-age book), Dodd, 1965; *The Gift* (juvenile), Dimension Books, 1968; *Gems for the Taking* (nonfiction), Macmillan, 1971. Contributor of short stories and poetry to magazines and newspapers. Former writer of syndicated newspaper column on beauty.

WORK IN PROGRESS: A play on sixteenth-century Spain; a mystery novel.

SIDELIGHTS: Miss Brown is the only American woman to be named a Dame of the ancient dynastic Order of the Collar of St. Agatha. She speaks Spanish and French. *Avocational interests:* Gem mining for precious stones, collecting antique portrait miniatures.

* * *

BROWN, Pamela Beatrice 1924-

PERSONAL: Born December 31, 1924, in Colchester, Essex, England; daughter of Frederick Leonard and Sepha (Sale) Brown; married Donald Masters, June 24, 1949 (died, 1963); children: Verity Madeleine, Juliet Maxine Sepha. *Education:* Attended county schools in England and Royal Academy of Dramatic Art. *Home:* Casa Moreno, Pollensa, Mallorca.

CAREER: Worked in theatre, films and broadcasting before 1950; British Broadcasting Corp., London, England, producer, 1950-55; Scottish Television, Glasgow, Scotland, producer, 1956-57; Granada Television, London and Manchester, England, producer, 1958-63. Author, 1940—. *Member:* National Book League, Arts Theatre Club.

WRITINGS:—All novels for young people: *The Swish of the Curtain*, Thomas Nelson, 1941, Winston, 1943, revised edition, Brockhampton Press, 1971; *Maddy Alone*, Thomas Nelson, 1945, Hutchinson Library Service, 1972; *Golden Pavements*, Thomas Nelson, 1947; *Blue Door Venture*, Thomas Nelson, 1949, Hutchinson Library Service, 1972.

To Be a Ballerina and Other Stories, Thomas Nelson, 1950; *Family Playbill*, Thomas Nelson, 1951, published as *Family Troupe*, Harcourt, 1953; *The Television Twins*, Thomas Nelson, 1952; *Harlequin Corner*, Thomas Nelson, 1953, Meredith, 1969; *The Windmill Family*, Thomas Nelson, 1954, Crowell, 1955; *Louisa*, Crowell, 1955; *Maddy Again*, Thomas Nelson, 1956; *The Bridesmaids*, Brockhampton Press, 1956, McKay, 1957; *Backstage Portrait*, Thomas Nelson, 1957; *Showboat Summer*, Brockhampton Press, 1957; *Understudy*, Thomas Nelson, 1958; *First House*, Thomas Nelson, 1959; *As Far as Singapore*, Brockhampton Press, 1959, Taplinger, 1961.

The Other Side of the Street, Brockhampton Press, 1965, Follett, 1967; *The Girl Who Ran Away*, Brockhampton Press, 1968.

A Little Universe, Brockhampton Press, 1970; *Summer Is a Festival*, Brockhampton Press, 1972; *Looking After Libbey*, Brockhampton Press, 1974.

SIDELIGHTS: The Chicago Tribune Book World wrote of *The Other Side of the Street*, "The vital, gritty quality and the sturdy realism that many English books for children possess, but which often are lacking in their American counterparts, are found in good measure in this excellent story."

Mrs. Brown has become fluent in Spanish since emigrating to Mallorca in 1965 to concentrate on writing. She hopes to be able to translate one of her own books into Spanish. Her books have been translated into the major European languages and Japanese.

* * *

BROWN, Robert McAfee 1920-
(St. Hereticus)

PERSONAL: Born May 28, 1920, in Carthage, Ill.; son of George William and Ruth (McAfee) Brown; married Sydney Thomson, June 21, 1944; children: Peter, Mark, Alison, Thomas. *Education:* Amherst College, B.A., 1943; Union Theological Seminary, New York, N.Y., B.D., 1945; Mansfield College, Oxford, graduate study, 1949-50; Columbia Unversity, Ph.D., 1951; St. Mary's College, University of St. Andrews, postdoctoral study, 1959-60. *Home:* 837 Cedro Way, Stanford, Calif. 94305. *Office:* Humanities Special Programs, Stanford University, Stanford, Calif.

CAREER: Ordained minister, Presbyterian Church, 1944. Amherst College, Amherst, Mass., assistant chaplain, 1946-48; Macalester College, St. Paul, Minn., professor of religion and chairman of department, 1951-53; Union Theological Seminary, New York, N.Y., professor of theology, 1953-62; Stanford University, Stanford, Calif., professor of religion, 1962—. *Military service:* U.S. Navy, 1945-46; lieutenant junior grade, chaplain's corps. *Member:* American Theological Society, Society for Theological Discussion, Phi Beta Kappa. *Awards, honors:* D.D., Amherst College, 1958, Pacific School of Religion, 1967; Litt.D., University of San Francisco, 1964; L.H.D., Lewis and Clark College, 1964, St. Louis University, 1966, St. Mary's College, 1968; LL.D., Loyola University, University of Notre Dame, and Boston College, all in 1965.

WRITINGS: P.T. Forsyth: Prophet for Today, Westminster, 1952; *The Bible Speaks to You*, Westminster, 1955; *The Significance of the Church*, Westminster, 1956; (with Gustave Weigel) *An American Dialogue*, Doubleday, 1960; (translator) Suzanne de Dietrich, *God's Unfolding Purpose*, Westminster, 1960; *The Spirit of Protestantism*, Oxford University Press, 1961; (editor with David Scott) *The Challenge to Reunion*, McGraw, 1963; (translator and author of introduction) Georges Casalis, *Portrait of Karl Barth*, Doubleday, 1963; *The Collected Writings of St. Hereticus*, Westminster, 1964; *Observer in Rome: A Protestant Reports on the Vatican Council*, Doubleday, 1964; (with Abraham Heschel and Michael Novak) *Vietnam: Crisis of Conscience*, Association Press, 1967; *The Ecumenical Revolution*, Doubleday, 1967; (translator) Andre Dumas, *Dietrich Bonhoeffer: Theologian of Reality*, Macmillan, 1971; *The Pseudonyms of God*, Westminster, 1972; *Frontiers for the Church Today*, Oxford University Press, 1973; *Religion and Violence*, Westminster, 1973; *Is Faith Obsolete?*, Westminster, 1974.

Contributor: F. Ernest Johnson, editor, *Patterns of Faith in America Today*, Harper, 1957; Philip Scharper, editor, *American Catholics: A Protestant-Jewish View*, Sheed, 1959; J. A. O'Brien, editor, *Steps to Christian Unity*, Doubleday, 1965; L. J. Swidler, editor, *Scripture and Ecumenism*, Duquesne University Press, 1965; D. T. Jenkins, editor, *The Scope of Theology*, World Publishing, 1965; M. E. Marty and D. G. Peerman, editors, *Handbook of Christian Theologians*, World Publishing, 1965; W. M. Abbott, editor, *Documents of Vatican II*, Association Press, 1966; Bernard Murchland, editor, *The Meaning of the Death of God*, Random House, 1967; L. J. Swidler, editor, *Ecumenism: The Spirit and Worship*, Duquesne University Press, 1967; Patrick Granfield, editor, *Theologians at Work*, Macmillan, 1967; John O'Connor, editor, *American Catholic Exodus*, Corpus, 1968; H. J. Mooney and T. F. Staley, editors, *The Shapeless God*, University of Pittsburgh Press, 1968; Donald R. Cutler, editor, *The Religious Situation: 1968*, Beacon, 1968; C. F. Mooney, editor, *The Presence and Absence of God*, Fordham University Press,

1969; C. E. Curran, editor, *Contraception: Authority and Dissent*, Herder & Herder, 1969.

E. L. Long, Jr. and R. T. Handy, editors, *Theology and Church in Times of Change*, Westminster, 1970; J. Andrews, editor, *Paul VI: Critical Appraisals*, Bruce, 1970; William V. Casey and Philip Nobile, editors, *The Berrigans*, Praeger, 1971; Huston Smith and others, *Great Religions of the World*, National Geographic Society, 1971; Alan Geyer and Dean Peerman, *Theological Crossings*, Eerdmans, 1971; *Military Chaplains*, American Report Press, 1972; David Kennedy, editor, *The American People in the Age of Kennedy*, Pendulum Press, new edition, 1973; Norbert O. Schedler, editor, *Philosophy of Religion: Contemporary Perspectives*, Macmillan, 1974.

Author of introduction: Karl Barth and Johannes Hamel, *How to Serve God in a Marxist Land*, Association Press, 1959; F. W. Foerster, *The Jews*, Farrar, Straus, 1962.

General editor, "Layman's Theological Library," twelve volumes, Westminster, 1956-58. Member of editorial board of *Christianity and Crisis, Journal of Ecumenical Studies*, and *Theology Today*.

SIDELIGHTS: The Collected Writings of St. Hereticus consists of a selection from columns Brown contributed under that pseudonym to *Christianity and Crisis*. Lester G. McAllister called *The Ecumenical Revolution* "a definitive study of the ecumenical movement in its modern form to the present hopes for ultimate Christian unity." Cecil Northcott noted "the book is written with a freshness and a freedom that eschew the customary ecumenical jargon."

Already prominent in the ecumenical movement, Brown became one of the leading figures in the movement against the Vietnam War. *Avocational interests:* Carpentry.

*   *   *

BROWN, Roger William 1925-

PERSONAL: Born April 14, 1925, in Detroit, Mich.; son of Frank Herbert and Muriel Louise (Graham) Brown. *Education:* University of Michigan, A.B., 1948, Ph.D., 1952. *Home:* 100 Memorial Dr., Cambridge, Mass. 02142. *Office:* 1270 William James, Harvard University, Cambridge, Mass.

CAREER: Harvard University, Cambridge, Mass., assistant professor of psychology, 1952-57; Massachusetts Institute of Technology, Cambridge, associate professor of psychology, 1957-61, professor of social psychology, 1961-62; Harvard University, professor of social psychology, 1962—, chairman of department of social relations, 1967-70. National Institutes of Health, chairman of Behavioral Science Study Section, 1961-63. *Military service:* U.S. Naval Reserve; became ensign. *Member:* American Psychological Association (president of division of personality and social psychology, 1965-66), Linguistic Society of America, American Academy of Arts and Sciences, National Academy of Sciences, Eastern Psychological Association (president, 1971-72), New England Psychological Association (president, 1965-66). *Awards, honors:* M.A., Harvard University, 1962; D.Univ., University of York (England).

WRITINGS: Words and Things, Free Press of Glencoe, 1958; (with E. Galanter, E. Hess, and G. Mandler) *New Directions in Psychology*, Holt, 1962; (editor with Ursula Bellugi) *The Acquisition of Language*, Society for Research in Child Development, 1964; *Social Psychology*, Free Press, 1965; (editor) *Cognition and the Development of Language*, Wiley, 1970; (compiler with Albert Gilman and others) *Psycholinguistics: Selected Papers*, Free Press, 1970; *A First Language: The Early Stages*, Harvard University Press, 1973.†

*   *   *

BROWN, Truesdell S(parhawk) 1906-

PERSONAL: Born March 21, 1906, in Philadelphia, Pa.; son of Carleton (an educator) and Emily (Truesdell) Brown; married Ruth Edgar; children: Priscilla (Mrs. Arthur P. Collins), Edgar N., Truesdell S., Jr. *Education:* Haverford College, student, 1922-23; Harvard University, A.B., 1928, A.M., 1929; University of Innsbruck, graduate study, 1932-33; Columbia University, Ph.D., 1947. *Politicis:* Democrat. *Religion:* Unitarian Universalist. *Home:* 3816 Rambla Orienta, Malibu, Calif. 90265. *Office:* History Department, University of California, Los Angeles, Calif. 90024.

CAREER: University of Colorado, Boulder, instructor in ancient history, 1929-32, 1933-37; University of Texas, Austin, 1940-47, instructor, later assistant professor of ancient history; University of California, Los Angeles, lecturer, 1947-48, assistant professor, 1948-51, associate professor, 1951-56, professor of ancient history, 1956-73, chairman of history department, 1959-62, professor emeritus, 1973—. *Member:* American Historical Association, International Platform Association. *Awards, honors:* Fulbright research fellow in Greece, 1950; Guggenheim fellow in England, 1954-55.

WRITINGS: Onesicritus: A Study in Hellenistic Historiography, University of California Press, 1949; *Timaeus of Tauromenium*, University of California Press, 1958; (editor and translator) *Ancient Greece* (documentary), Free Press, 1965; (contributor) L. W. Spitz and R. W. Lyman, editors, *Major Crises in Western Civilization*, Harcourt, Volume I: *The Greeks to 1660*, 1965; (editor with W. Kendrick Pritchett) *California Studies in Classical Antiquity*, University of California Press, Volume I, 1968, Volume II, 1969, Volume III, 1970; *The Greek Historians*, Heath, 1973.

WORK IN PROGRESS: Research in the intellectual background of Herodotus, eventually leading to a book-length study; examination of the fragments of Xanthus of Lydia.

SIDELIGHTS: Brown reads Latin, Greek, modern Greek, French, German, Italian, and Dutch. He speaks French and German ("badly").

*   *   *

BROWN, Virginia Sharpe 1916-
(Ginny Brown)

PERSONAL: Born September 13, 1916, in La Habra, Calif.; daughter of Harold Henry (a farmer) and Gertrude (Old) Sharpe; married Phil Brown (an actor-producer); children: Robin K., Jed. *Education:* University of California, Los Angeles, student, 1935-1936; Stanford University, B.A., 1938, graduate student, 1939. *Home:* Mayflower II, Chiswick Mall, London W.4, England. *Agent:* Hope Leresche, 11 Jubilee Pl., London S.W.3, England.

WRITINGS: (Under name Ginny Brown) *Swans at My Window*, Heinemann, 1959. Contributor to *Woman's Illustrated, Daily Express* (London), *Review* (Belgrade, Yugoslavia).

AVOCATIONAL INTERESTS: Jewelry, landscape painting.

BIOGRAPHICAL/CRITICAL SOURCES: Sketch, May 18, 1955; *Sunday Express* (London), November 6, 1960.

BROWNING, (Grayson) Douglas 1929-

PERSONAL: Born March 7, 1929, in Seminole, Okla.; son of Grayson Douglas and Dorothea (Cook) Browning; married Susan Gilman, June 2, 1953; children: Tony, Luke, Lauren. Education: University of Texas, B.A., 1954, M.A., 1955, Ph.D., 1958. Politics: Democrat. Office: Department of Philosophy, University of Texas, Austin, Tex. 78712.

CAREER: University of Miami, Coral Gables, Fla., instructor, 1958, assistant professor, 1958-63, associate professor, 1963-68, professor of philosophy, 1968-71; University of Texas, Austin, professor of philosophy, 1971—, chairman of philosophy department, 1972—. Visiting instructor, University of Miami, summers, 1963, 1964; visiting professor, University of Texas, Austin, 1969-70, 1970-71. Military service: U.S. Air Force, 1948-52; became sergeant. Member: American Philosophical Association, American Association of University Professors, Southern Society for Philosophy and Psychology (secretary, 1966-69; president, 1972-73), Southwestern Philosophical Society, Florida Philosophical Society (secretary-treasurer, 1964-66; president, 1967).

WRITINGS: Act and Agent: An Essay in Philosophical Anthropology, University of Miami Press, 1964; (editor) Philosophers of Process, Random House, 1965; Poems and Visions, Threefools Press, 1968. Contributor to Review of Metaphysics, Dialogue, Francisan Studies, Australasian Journal of Philosophy, The Philosophical Quarterly, Methodos, Southern Journal of Philosophy, Southwestern Journal of Philosophy, Personalist, Philosophy and Phenomenological Research, and other philosophy journals.

WORK IN PROGRESS: The Problem of Man, a work in philosophical anthropology; Reference and Reality: An Essay on the Foundations of Ontology.

SIDELIGHTS: Browning has reading competence in German, French, and Spanish, and speaking competence in Spanish.

* * *

BRUCE, Ben F., Jr. 1920-

PERSONAL: Born July 29, 1920, in Bloomington, Ind.; son of Ben F. (a railroad employee) and Arie (Nilson) Bruce; married Marie Chambers, July 20, 1941; children: Terri Jayne, Suzann, Joseph Paul. Education: Indiana University, B.S., 1948, M.S., 1950. Religion: Protestant. Home and office: Route 10, Box 544, Bloomington, Ind. 47401.

CAREER: Indiana University, Bloomington, 1956—, now supervisor of men's physical education program. Member of Bloomington Welfare Board. Military service: U.S. Army, 1940-45. Member: American Association for Health, Physical Education and Recreation, Phi Delta Kappa.

WRITINGS: Beginning Golf, Wadsworth, 1961.

* * *

BRUGGINK, Donald J. 1929-

PERSONAL: Born June 30, 1929, in Kalamazoo, Mich.; son of Dirk John and Gertrude A. (Hyink) Bruggink; married Erma H. Van Roekel, August 13, 1953; children: Donald Ian, John Gerrit. Education: Central College, Pella, Iowa, B.A. (cum laude), 1951; Western Theological Seminary, Holland, Mich., B.D., 1954; University of Edin-

burgh, Ph.D., 1956. Politics: Independent. Home: 880 South Shore Dr., Holland, Mich. 49423. Office: Western Theological Seminary, Holland, Mich. 49423.

CAREER: Clergyman of Reformed Church in America. Minister in New York, N.Y., 1957-62; New Brunswick Theological Seminary, New Brunswick, N.J., lecturer in systematic theology, 1960; Western Theological Seminary, Holland, Mich., visiting professor of systematic theology, 1962-63, assistant professor of historical theology, 1963-66, James A. H. Cornell Professor of historical theology, 1966—. Theological consultant to churches and architectural firms. Reformed Church of America, member of board of education, 1959-65, theological commission, 1960-65, and committee on liturgy, 1966—. Trustee, Hope College, 1959-65. Member: American Society of Church History, American Historical Association, American Society for Church Architecture (member of board of directors), Guild of Religious Architecture (honorary member), Michigan Society of Architects (honorary member), Dutch-American Historical Commission (president).

WRITINGS: (Editor and contributor) Guilt, Grace and Gratitude, Eerdmans, 1964; (with Carl H. Droppers) Christ and Architecture: Building Presbyterian Reformed Churches, Eerdmans, 1965; (contributor) Harish D. Merchant, editor, Encounter with Books: A Guide to Christian Reading, Inter-Varsity Press, 1970; (with Droppers) When Faith Takes Form, Eerdmans, 1971. General editor of historical series of Reformed Church in America, 1968—. Contributor to religious periodicals, including Your Church and Faith and Form.

WORK IN PROGRESS: Iconography for an Anaconic Faith: The Images and Symbols of the Early Church; Multi-Service Churches, for Eerdmans.

SIDELIGHTS: Bruggink told CA, "A long interest in architecture, rather dormant during doctoral studies, was revived while traveling on the Continent in 1956, when it became apparent that the churches of the various branches of Christendom spoke through their architecture with theological precision—an experience quite new to someone acquainted only with the theologically heterogeneous architecture of the Presbyterian/Reformed churches of America. Research for Christ and Architecture took my co-author and myself back to the Continent for on-the-spot research, and photographs to illustrate our book. While it was feared that reaction to such a subject might remain at best academic—there is, after all, no work published in English which deals specifically with the theological implications of architecture for Presbyterian/Reformed churches—these fears were totally unfounded."

Bruggink was awarded honorary memberships in the Guild of Religious Architecture and the Michigan Society of Architects for Christ and Architecture.

AVOCATIONAL INTERESTS: Photography and music.

* * *

BRUTON, Eric Moore

PERSONAL: Married Anne Valerie Britton (an author and reviewer). Home: White House, Widmer End, Buckinghamshire, England. Agent: Elaine Greene Ltd., 31 Newington Green, London, N.1., England.

CAREER: Former director of riding school. Freeman of City of London. Writer, publisher, jeweller, teacher. Visiting lecturer, Sir John Cass College, London; founder and director of Diamond Boutique Ltd., and of Things and

Ideas Ltd. *Military service:* Royal Air Force, engineer officer, 1940-46. *Member:* Gemmological Association of Great Britain (fellow), British Horological Institute (fellow), Worshipful Company of Clockmakers (liveryman), Worshipful Company of Turners (liveryman).

WRITINGS—Fiction; all published by T. V. Boardman, except as indicated: *Death in Ten Point Bold*, Jenkins, 1957, *Die Darling Die*, 1959, *Violent Brothers*, 1960, *The Hold Out*, 1961, *King Diamond*, 1961, *The Devil's Pawn*, 1962, *The Laughing Policeman*, 1963, *The Finsbury Mob*, 1964, *The Smithfield Slayer*, 1965, *The Wicket Saint*, 1965, *The Firebug*, 1967.

Nonfiction: *True Book About Clocks*, Muller, 1957; *True Book About Diamonds*, Muller, 1961; *Automation*, Muller, 1961, 2nd edition, English Language Society, 1964; *Dictionary of Clocks and Watches*, Arco Publications, 1962, Archer House, 1963; *The Longcase Clock*, Arco Publications, 1964, Praeger, 1967; *Clocks and Watches 1400-1900*, Praeger, 1967; *Clocks and Watches*, Paul Hamlyn, 1968; *Diamonds*, N.A.G. Press, 1970, Chilton, 1971; *Antique Clocks and Clock Collecting*, Paul Hamlyn, 1974.

Contributor of articles on engineering and antiquarian subjects to periodicals. Currently publisher of *Retail Jeweller* (incorporating *Gemmologist*, *Goldsmiths Journal*, and *Horological Review*). Editor of *Travel, Goldsmiths Journal, Horological Journal, Gemmologist, Industrial Diamond Review*, and other publications.

WORK IN PROGRESS: The World of Clocks (tentative title), for Thomas Nelson.

AVOCATIONAL INTERESTS: Foreign travel to visit gem mining areas and to see ancient clocks; gardening; "learning about off-beat subjects."

* * *

BRYANT, Beth Elaine 1936-

PERSONAL: Born December 3, 1936, in New York, N.Y.; daughter of Lloyd Thurston (a minister) and Dorothy Elizabeth (Richards) Bryant; married John Godwin (an author), August 25, 1969. *Education:* Barrington College, student, 1954-56. *Home:* 1335 Washington St., San Francisco, Calif. 94109.

CAREER: Traveled through United States, Mexico, and Canada as magazine writer and folk-singer, 1956-63; freelance writer and editor in New York, N.Y., 1963—. Production editor of *Crafts Guide*, 1963; editor of *Manhattan Shopper*, 1964.

WRITINGS: Broadside Ballads for Christmastyde, Hansen, 1963; *The Inside Guide to Greenwich Village*, Oak Publications, 1964, revised edition published as *The New Inside Guide to Greenwich Village*, 1965; *Washington, D.C. on $5 a Day*, Frommer, 1965, revised editions published as *Washington, D.C. on $5 and $10 a Day*, 1969—; *The Dollarwise Guide to California*, Frommer, 1965, revised edition published as *Arthur Frommer's Dollar-Wise Guide to California*, 1968; *The Dollarwise Guide to Washington, D.C.*, Frommer, 1965; *Europe on $5 and $10 a Day*, Frommer, revised editions, 1965-71; *Ireland on $5 a Day*, Frommer, 1967, subsequent editions published as *Ireland on $5 and $10 a Day*; (with John Wilcock) *The 1968-69 Edition of the West Coast on $5 and $10 a Day*, Frommer, 1968, revised editions, 1969, 1970; *Israel on $5 and $10 a Day*, Frommer, revised edition, 1969; (with Wilcock) *TWA's Budget Guide to Paris*, Frommer/Pasmantier, 1970; (with Wilcock) *TWA's Getaway Guide to San Francisco*, Frommer/Pasmantier, 1971, revised edition, 1974; (with Wilcock) *TWA's Getaway Guide to Dublin/Shannon, Ireland*, Frommer/Pasmantier, 1974; *New Zealand and Australia on $10 a Day*, Frommer, in press. Contributor of articles on travel and folk music to *Sing Out, Folk Music, Folk World, Mademoiselle, Cosmopolitan, Cara*, and *Ireland of the Welcomes*. Editor, *The Inside Guide to Greenwich Village* (quarterly), 1963-64.

BIOGRAPHICAL/CRITICAL SOURCES: Mademoiselle, September, 1964.

* * *

BRYANT, Donald C(ross) 1905-

PERSONAL: Born September 17, 1905, in New York, N.Y.; son of William A. (a businessman) and Rebecca L. (Cross) Bryant; married Mary Osborne, June 25, 1932. *Education:* Cornell University, B.A., 1927, M.A., 1930, Ph.D., 1937. *Home:* 903 Highwood St., Iowa City, Iowa 52240. *Office:* 231 Jessup Hall, Iowa City, Iowa 52242.

CAREER: High school teacher in Ardsley, N.Y., 1927-29; State College for Teachers, Albany, N.Y., instructor, 1929-37; Washington University, St. Louis, Mo., assistant professor, 1937-43, associate professor, 1943-48, professor of English, 1948-58, professor of speech and English, 1950-58, director of Division of Speech, 1948-58, chairman of English department, 1956-58; University of Iowa, Iowa City, professor of speech, 1958-73, research professor (in England), 1962, Carver Professor, 1972-73, professor emeritus, 1973—. Visiting professor, University of Colorado, summer, 1939-41, University of Southern California, 1956, University of Washington, 1969; visiting scholar, University Center Virginia, 1971; Distinguished Lecturer in Speech, Louisiana State University, 1972. *Member:* Modern Language Association of America, Speech Communication Association (second vice-president, 1968; first vice-president, 1969; president, 1970), American Association of University Professors, Phi Beta Kappa, Delta Sigma Rho, Phi Kappa Phi. *Awards, honors:* Distinguished Service Award, Speech Communication Association, 1972.

WRITINGS: Edmund Burke and His Literary Friends, Washington University Studies, 1939; (editor) *Papers in Rhetoric*, [St. Louis], 1940; (co-editor and contributor) *Studies in Speech and Drama*, Cornell University Press, 1944; (with Karl R. Wallace) *Fundamentals of Public Speaking*, Appleton, 1947, 5th revised edition, 1974; (with Wallace) *Oral Communication*, Appleton, 1948, 4th revised edition, 1974; (editor with Marie Hockmuth and W. N. Brigance) *A History and Criticism of American Public Address*, Volume III, Longmans, Green, 1955; (editor) *The Rhetorical Idiom*, Cornell University Press, 1958; (with Oscar G. Brocket and Samuel L. Becker) *A Bibliographic Guide to Research in Speech and Dramatic Art*, Scott, Foresman, 1963; (editor and contributor) *Essays in Rhetoric and Poetic*, University of Iowa Press, 1965; (editor and contributor) *An Historical Anthology of Select British Speeches*, Ronald, 1967; (editor) *Ancient Greek and Roman Rhetoricians*, Artcraft Press, 1968; *Rhetorical Dimensions in Criticism*, Louisiana State University Press, 1973. Contributor of about forty articles to journals. Editor, *Quarterly Journal of Speech*, 1957-59.

* * *

BRYANT, Katherine Cliffton 1912-
(Katherine Potter Cliffton)

PERSONAL: Born February 2, 1912, in Blunt, S.D.;

daughter of William Swim and Mary (Congdon) Potter; married Bacon L. Cliffton (an oral surgeon), December 26, 1936 (divorced); married William C. Bryant, April 12, 1969; children: (first marriage) James Potter Cliffton. *Education:* University of South Dakota, A.B. (cum laude), 1932; University of Southern California, M.S. in Ed., 1964. *Politics:* Republican. *Home:* 241 South St. Andrews Pl., Los Angeles, Calif.

CAREER: Argosy Pictures, Los Angeles, Calif., story editor and research director, 1945-50; Woodbury College, Los Angeles, Calif., 1954—, began as instructor, became professor of government, former chairman of department of English and dean of women; John Ford Productions, Los Angeles, Calif., story and research consultant, 1955-72. Lecturer on current literature and business communications. *Member:* National Society of Colonial Dames of the XVII Century, Daughters of the American Revolution, Phi Beta Kappa, Alpha Phi, Theta Alpha Phi, Desert Shelter for Animals (founder; secretary-treasurer), Golden State Humane Society (member of board of directors).

WRITINGS: (Under name Katherine Potter Cliffton; with Ralph S. Handy) *Business English in Practice*, 3rd edition, Pitman, 1963; (under name Katherine Cliffton Bryant) *Business Writing*, Science Research Associates, 1970. Author of film script, "Motua."

* * *

BRYCE, Murray D(avidson) 1917-

PERSONAL: Born September 25, 1917, in Keeler, Saskatchewan, Canada; son of David Henry and Evelyn (Morgan) Bryce; married Frances A. Mjolsness, 1945 (divorced, 1971); children: Karen Lorraine, Lisa Kathryn. *Education:* University of British Columbia, B.A. (first class honors), 1949; American University, M.A., 1956. *Home:* 2075 Comox St., Apt. 2103, Vancouver, British Columbia, Canada. *Office:* Canadian Projects Ltd., Penthouse, 355 Burrard St., Vancouver, British Columbia, Canada.

CAREER: Public Administration Service, Chicago, Ill., field staff member, 1949-51; International Bank for Reconstruction and Development, Washington, D.C., operations officer, 1951-57; Robert Nathan Associates, Rangoon, Burma, economic adviser, 1957-59; Arthur D. Little, Inc., Cambridge, Mass., senior development economist, 1959-64; Project International, Inc., president, 1964-72; Canadian Projects Ltd., president, 1967—. Mission chief, Industrial Development Mission to Cuba, 1959, Peru, 1960, Argentina, 1961, and Nigeria, 1962; United Nations consultant, Korea, 1965; economic adviser, Pahang, Malaysia, 1971-72. Guest lecturer at Institute on Development Programming, Johns Hopkins University, 1959-61, with A. D. Little, Inc., 1966-70, at University of Libya, 1968, and at International Development Center, Japan, 1972. *Military service:* Royal Canadian Air Force, 1940-45; became flying officer. *Member:* Society for International Development (council member, 1961-62; past president, Canadian division), American Economic Association.

WRITINGS: Industrial Development: A Guide for Accelerating Economic Growth, McGraw, 1960; *Policies and Methods for Industrial Development*, McGraw, 1965.

* * *

BUCHANAN, A(lbert) Russell 1906-

PERSONAL: Born March 6, 1906, in Ness City, Kan.; son of Albert Martin (a Presbyterian minister) and Lida (King) Buchanan; married Mary Ethel O'Keefe, July 2, 1933; children: Barbara McCaleb, Joanne Millard. *Education:* Stanford University, A.B., 1927, M.A., 1928, Ph.D., 1935. *Home:* 3411 Calle Noguera, Santa Barbara, Calif. *Office:* Department of History, University of California, Santa Barbara, Calif.

CAREER: Stanford University, Palo Alto, Calif., assistant reference librarian and instructor in history, 1928-38; University of California, Santa Barbara, assistant professor, 1938-40, associate professor, 1940-42, professor of history, 1946-73, professor emeritus, 1973—. Acting dean of men, 1940-42, vice-chancellor of academic affairs, 1960-71. Visiting summer instructor at University of New Mexico, 1938. *Military service:* U.S. Naval Reserve, 1942-46; became lieutenant. *Member:* American Historical Association (Pacific Coast branch), Organization of American Historians, Phi Alpha Theta.

WRITINGS: (Editor) *The Navy's Air War: A Mission Completed*, Harper, 1946; *David S. Terry: Dueling Judge*, Huntington Library, 1956; *The United States in World War II*, two volumes, Harper, 1963; (editor) *The United States and World War II: Military and Diplomatic Documents*, University of South Carolina Press, 1972. Contributor of articles to *American Historical Review, Pacific Historical Review*, and other professional journals.

* * *

BUECHNER, (Carl) Frederick 1926-

PERSONAL: Born July 11, 1926, in New York, N.Y.; son of Carl Frederick and Katherine (Kuhn) Buechner; married Judith F. Merck, April 7, 1956; children: Katherine, Dinah, Sharman. *Education:* Princeton University, A.B., 1948; Union Theological Seminary, B.D., 1958. *Agent:* Lucy Kroll Agency, 119 West 57th St., New York, N.Y. 10019.

CAREER: Lawrenceville School, Lawrenceville, N.J., teacher of English, 1948-53; East Harlem Protestant Parish, New York, N.Y., head of employment clinic, 1954-58; ordained Presbyterian minister, 1958; Phillips Exeter Academy, Exeter, N.H., chairman of department of religion, 1958-60, minister, 1960-67; itinerant preacher and teacher, and writer, 1967—. Instructor, New York University, summers, 1953, 1954; William Belden Nobel lecturer, Harvard University, 1969; Russell lecturer, Tufts University, 1971. Trustee, Barlow School, 1965-71. *Military service:* U.S. Army, 1944-46. *Member:* National Council of Churches, Council for Religion in Independent Schools (regional chairman, 1959-63), Foundation for Arts, Religion, and Culture, Presbytery of Northern New England, P.E.N., Author's Guild, Century Association. *Awards, honors:* O. Henry Memorial Award, 1955, for "The Tiger"; Richard and Hinda Rosenthal Award, 1959, for *The Return of Ansel Gibbs*.

WRITINGS—Novels; all published by Atheneum, except as indicated: *A Long Day's Dying*, Knopf, 1950; *The Seasons' Difference*, Knopf, 1953; *The Return of Ansel Gibbs*, Knopf, 1958; *The Final Beast*, 1965; *The Entrance to Porlock*, 1970; *Lion Country*, 1971; *Open Heart*, 1972; *Love Feast*, 1974.

Non-fiction: *The Magnificent Defeat*, Seabury, 1966; *The Hungering Dark*, Seabury, 1969; *The Alphabet of Grace*, Seabury, 1970; *Wishful Thinking: A Theological ABC*, Harper, 1973; *The Faces of Jesus*, Simon & Schuster, 1974.

SIDELIGHTS: "There is a quality of distinction about Frederich Buechner's writing," said A. C. Spectorsky, "which might best be compared to the gleam of hand-polished old silver—as opposed to the chromium gloss of much of the 'sophisticated' writing being done today." Wrote Frances Burnette: "The style is subtle and polished and, against a background of cadenced and muted prose, the characters stand out in brilliant color. Although it drags a little in spots and is rather self-consciously a work of art, this is a quietly absorbing, timely, and thoughtful novel." The book to which they referred was *The Return of Ansel Gibbs*, and Simon Raven mentioned "descriptive writing of such brilliance that it will strike new fire into the most blase novel-reader. . . ."

Buechner's non-fiction elicited this sort of comment from William MacKaye: "The sermon and the spiritual meditation have become of late a decidely unfashionable literary genre. . . . The publication of *The Hungering Dark* leads me to wonder whether the disappearance of the literate clergyman is not at least part of that cause. Frederick Buechner writes a rich and imaged prose that puts to shame what is heard from the average pulpit or published in the average religious journal. . . . If you can bear to be led into the places of silence, Frederick Buechner is a worthy educator."

BIOGRAPHICAL/CRITICAL SOURCES: John W. Aldridge, *After the Lost Generation*, McGraw, 1951; Carolyn Riley, editor, *Contemporary Literary Criticism*, Gale, Volume II, 1974, Volume IV, 1975.

*   *   *

BUGLASS, Leslie J. 1917-

PERSONAL: Born January 3, 1917, in Easington, County Durham, England; came to United States in 1949; son of John (a railway worker) and Annie (Parker) Buglass; married Mary S. Galley, November 30, 1950; children: Margaret S. *Education:* Educated in England. *Politics:* Democrat. *Religion:* Episcopalian. *Home:* 140 Downey Dr., Tenafly, N.J. *Office:* Johnson & Higgins, 95 Wall St., New York, N.Y.

CAREER: Johnson & Higgins (insurance brokers and average adjusters), New York, N.Y., 1950—, now vice-president in charge of average adjusting department. *Military service:* British Army, World War II. *Member:* Association of Average Adjusters of the United States, Maritime Law Association of the United States.

WRITINGS: General Average and Marine Insurance in the United States, Witherby, 1955; *General Average and the York/Antwerp Rules, 1950*, Cornell Maritime, 1959; *Marine Insurance Claims*, Cornell Maritime, 1963; *Marine Insurance and General Average in the United States: An Average Adjusters Viewpoint*, Cornell Maritime, 1973; *General Average and the York/Antwerp Rules, 1974*, Cornell Maritime, in press.

*   *   *

BULMER, Henry Kenneth 1921-
(Kenneth Bulmer, Ernest Corley, Arthur Frazier, Adam Hardy, Philip Kent, Karl Maras; Kenneth Johns, a joint pseudonym)

PERSONAL: Born January 14, 1921, in London, England; son of Walter Ernest (a chemist) and Hilda Louise (Corley) Bulmer; married Pamela Kathleen Buckmaster, March 7, 1953; children: Deborah Louise, Lucy-Ellen, Kenneth

Laurence. *Education:* Attended schools in London, England, until fifteen. *Religion:* Congregational. *Home:* 19 Orchard Way, Horsmonden, Kent TN1Z 8LA, England. *Agent:* Scott Meredith, 44 Great Russell St., London W.C.1, England; and E. J. Carnell, 17 Burwash Rd., Plumstead, London S.E. 18, England.

CAREER: Representative of paper merchandising and office equipment firms in England, 1947-54; full-time professional writer, 1954—. *Military service:* British Army, Royal Corps of Signals, 1941-46. *Member:* Airship Association, Science Fiction Writers Association, British Science Fiction Association (honorary life member), Science Fiction Foundation (vice-president), Horsmondon Players, (secretary, 1964-72).

WRITINGS—Under name Kenneth Bulmer: *Encounter in Space*, Hamilton & Co., 1952; *Space Treason*, Hamilton & Co., 1952; (with A. V. Clarke) *Cybernetic Controller*, Hamilton & Co., 1952; (with Clarke) *Space Salvage*, Hamilton & Co., 1953; *The Stars Are Ours*, Hamilton & Co., 1953; *Galactic Intrigue*, Hamilton & Co., 1953; *Empire of Chaos*, Hamilton & Co., 1953; *World Aflame*, Hamilton & Co., 1954; *Challenge*, Curtis Warren, 1954; *City Under the Sea*, Ace Books, 1957; *The Secret of Zi*, Ace Books, 1958 (published in England as *The Patient Dark*, R. Hale, 1969); *The Changeling Worlds*, Ace Books, 1959.

The Earth Gods Are Coming, Ace Books, 1960 (published in England as *Of Earth Foretold*, Brown, Watson, 1961); *No Man's World*, Ace Books, 1961 (published in England as *Earth's Long Shadow*, Brown, Watson, 1962); *Beyond the Silver Sky*, Ace Books, 1961; *The Fatal Fire*, Brown, Watson, 1962; *The Wind of Liberty*, Brown, Watson, 1962; *Defiance*, Brown, Watson, 1963; *The Wizard of Starship Poseidon*, Ace Books, 1963; *The Million Year Hunt*, Ace Books, 1964; *Demon's World*, Ace Books, 1964 (published in England as *The Demons*, Compact Books, 1965); *Land Beyond the Map*, Ace Books, 1965; *Behold the Stars*, Ace Books, 1965; *Worlds for the Taking*, Ace Books, 1966; *To Outrun Doomsday*, Ace Books, 1967; *The Key to Irunium*, Ace Books, 1967; *The Doomsday Men*, Doubleday, 1968; *The Key to Venudine*, Ace Books, 1968; *Cycle of Nemesis*, Ace Books, 1968; *The Wizards of Senchuria*, Ace Books, 1969; *The Star Venturers*, Ace Books, 1969; *Kandar*, Paperback Library, 1969.

Blazon, Curtis Books, 1970 (published in England as *Quench the Burning Stars*, R. Hale, 1970); *The Ships of Durostorum*, Ace Books, 1970; *The Ulcer Culture*, Macdonald, 1970; *Star Trove*, R. Hale, 1970; *Swords of the Barbarians*, New English Library, 1970; *The Insane City*, Curtis Books, 1971; *The Hunters of Jundagai*, Ace Books, 1971; *The Electric Sword-Swallowers*, Ace Books, 1971; *The Chariots of Ra*, Ace Books, 1972; *On the Symb-Socket Circuit*, Ace Books, 1972; *Pretenders*, New English Library, 1972; *Roller Coaster World*, Ace Books, 1972; (editor) *New Writings in Science Fiction #22*, Sidgwick & Jackson, 1973; (editor) *New Writings in Science Fiction #23*, Sidgwick & Jackson, 1973; (editor) *New Writings in Science Fiction #24*, Sidgwick & Jackson, 1974; (editor) *New Writings in Science Fiction #25*, Sidgwick & Jackson, in press.

Under pseudonym Ernest Corley: *White-Out*, Jarrolds, 1960.

Under pseudonym Arthur Frazier; all published by New English Library: *Oath of Blood*, 1973; *The King's Death*, 1973; *A Light in the West*, 1973; *Viking Slaughter*, 1974; *A Flame in the Fens*, 1974.

Under pseudonym Adam Hardy; all published by New English Library: *The Press Gang*, 1972; *Prize Money*, 1972; *Siege*, 1973; *Treasure*, 1973; *Powder Monkey*, 1973; *Blood for Breakfast*, 1973; *Court Martial*, 1974; *Battle Smoke*, 1974; *Cut and Thrust*, 1974.

Under pseudonym Philip Kent: *Mission to the Stars*, Pearson, 1953; *Vassals of Venus*, Pearson, 1953; *Slaves of the Spectrum*, Pearson, 1954; *Home Is the Martian*, Pearson, 1954.

Under pseudonym Karl Maras: *Zhorani*, Comyns, 1954; *Peril from Space*, Comyns, 1954.

With John Newman, under joint pseudonym Kenneth Johns: *The True Book about Space Travel*, Muller, 1960, revised edition, 1965.

WORK IN PROGRESS: Further books under pseudonym Adam Hardy; research into the relevance and updated presentation of Heroic Fantasy; *Project Viking*; history of the British Empire; mythology as applied to archaeology; the future of the airship; Napoleon.

SIDELIGHTS: Most of the Bulmer books published since 1954 have appeared in German editions, a number in the Italian and the Scandinavian languages.

* * *

BURGESS, M(argaret) Elaine

PERSONAL: Daughter of Halsey William (a businessman and rancher) and Emma E. (Layman) Burgess. *Education:* Washington State University, B.A., 1948, M.A., 1949; University of North Carolina, Ph.D., 1960. *Religion:* Congregational. *Office:* Department of Sociology and Anthropology, University of North Carolina at Greensboro, Greensboro, N.C.

CAREER: Student personnel work at University of Hawaii, Honolulu, 1950-52, at University of Connecticut, Storrs, 1952-56; University of North Carolina, Chapel Hill, assistant instructor and research assistant, 1956-60, associate of Institute for Research in Social Science, 1960-64; University of North Carolina at Greensboro, assistant professor, 1960-64, associate professor, 1964—. *Member:* American Sociological Association, American Association of University Professors, Southern Sociological Society, New York Academy of Science, Phi Kappa Phi, Kappa Kappa Gamma, Alpha Kappa Delta, Pi Sigma Alpha, Mortar Board. *Awards, honors:* Grant from Greensboro Research Council, University of North Carolina, for research on Negro class mobility.

WRITINGS: Negro Leadership in a Southern City, University of North Carolina Press, 1962; (with Daniel O. Price) *An American Dependency Challenge*, American Public Welfare Association, 1963; (contributor) *Change and Continuity in the South*, edited by John C. McKinney and Edgar T. Thompson, Duke University Press, 1965. Contributor of articles and review to *American Journal of Orthopsychiatry*, *Social Forces*, and other periodicals.

WORK IN PROGRESS: Research with Daniel O. Price on development of measuring tools for variables relating to characteristics of lower-class dependent family structure, under a grant from Division of Research and Statistics, Social Security Administration.†

* * *

BURKE, Fred G(eorge) 1926-

PERSONAL: Born January 1, 1926, in Collins, N.Y.; son of Fred F. and Sophie (Blesy) Burke; married Daphne Ruttenbur, September 17, 1949; children: Rebecca, Frederick, Daniel, Adam. *Education:* University of Utah, student, 1949-50; Williams College, B.A., 1953; Princeton University, M.A., 1955, Ph.D., 1958; Oxford University, postgraduate study, 1955-56. *Politics:* Democrat. *Home:* 32 Seaview Ave., Cranston, R.I. 02905. *Office:* 199 Promenade St., Providence, R.I. 02908.

CAREER: Ohio Wesleyan University, Delaware, 1957-60, started as assistant professor, became associate professor of political science and director of Institute of Politics; Syracuse University, Maxwell Graduate School, associate professor, 1960-64, professor of political science and director of East African Studies, 1964-68; State University of New York, Buffalo, dean of international studies; State of Rhode Island, Providence, commissioner of education, 1971—. Member of Delaware City Council, 1958-60; chairman, Ohio Citizenship Clearing House. *Military service:* Served with USAAF, World War II; USAK, Korean War. *Member:* American Political Science Association, African Studies Association, American Society of Public Administration (chairman, CAG). *Awards, honors:* J. Kimborough Owen Award from American Political Science Association, 1958; Ford Foundation fellow; Social Science Research Council fellow.

WRITINGS: Africa's Quest for Order, Prentice-Hall, 1964; *Local Government and Politics in Uganda*, Syracuse University Press, 1964; *Tanganyika: Preplanning*, Syracuse University Press, 1965; (editor with Stanley Diamond) *The Transformation of East Africa*, Basic Books, 1967; *Sub-Saharan Africa*, Harcourt, 1968; (compiler and editor) *Africa: Selected Readings*, Houghton, 1969.†

* * *

BURKE, James Lee 1936-

PERSONAL: Born December 5, 1936, in Houston, Tex.; son of James Lee (a natural gas engineer) and Francis (Benbow) Burke; married Pearl Pai, January 22, 1960; children: James, Andre, Pamala. *Education:* University of Southwest Louisiana, student, 1955-57; University of Missouri, B.A., 1959, M.A., 1960. *Politics:* Jeffersonian Democrat. *Religion:* "On the edge of Catholicism." *Home:* Lexington Rd., Winchester, Ky. *Agent:* Kurt Hellmer, 52 Vanderbilt Ave., New York, N.Y. 10017.

CAREER: Variously surveyor, English instructor, newspaper reporter, and social worker; instructor with U.S. Forest Service, at Frenchburg, Ky., Job Corps Conservation Center, 1966—.

WRITINGS: Half of Paradise (novel), Houghton, 1965; *To the Bright and Shining Sun* (novel), Scribner, 1970; *Lay Down My Sword and Shield* (novel), Crowell, 1971.

WORK IN PROGRESS: Two novels, *A Rose Petal in June* and *The Evening's Fire*.

AVOCATIONAL INTERESTS: Baseball, fishing, and "picking on my six-string."†

* * *

BURKHART, Charles 1924-

PERSONAL: Born September 13, 1924, in Macon, Mo.; son of Edgar C. M. (a civil engineer) and Eva (Wilson) Burkhart. *Education:* Cornell University, A.B., 1948, A.M., 1949; Lincoln College, Oxford, postgraduate study, 1949-51; University of Maryland, Ph.D., 1958. *Home:* 332 West Hortter St., Philadelphia, Pa. 19119. *Office:* Department of English, Temple University, Philadelphia, Pa. 19122.

CAREER: Temple University, Philadelphia, Pa., instructor, 1956-60, assistant professor, 1961-63, associate professor of English, 1964—. *Military service:* U.S. Naval Intelligence, 1943-46; became ensign. *Member:* Modern Language Association of America, American Association of University Professors, Phi Beta Kappa. *Awards, honors:* Fulbright scholar, 1949-51.

WRITINGS: (Editor with Georgianne Trask) *Storytellers and Their Art*, Anchor Books, 1963; *I. Compton-Burnett*, Gollancz, 1965; (author of introduction) Ivy Compton-Burnett, *Dolores*, Blackwood, 1971; (editor) *The Art of I. Compton-Burnett: A Collection of Critical Essays*, Gollancz, 1972; *Charlotte Bronte: A Psychosexual Study of Her Novels*, Gollancz, 1973; *Ada Leverson*, Twayne, 1973. Contributor to critical journals.

WORK IN PROGRESS: A book on James Joyce's characters.†

* * *

BURLAND, Brian Berkeley   1931-

PERSONAL: Born April 23, 1931, in Bermuda; son of Gordon Hamilton (a yacht builder) and Honor Alice Croydon (Gosling) Burland; married Edwina Ann Trentham, July 7, 1962; children: Susan, Anne, William, Benjamin. *Education:* Attended University of Western Ontario. *Home:* Book Hill Rd., Essex, Conn. 06426. *Agent:* Georges Borchardt, 145 East 52nd St., New York, N.Y. 10022, and Hilary Rubinstein, A. P. Watt & Son, 26-28 Bedford Row, London W.C. 1, England.

CAREER: Company director of family business in Bermuda, 1951-55; now full-time professional writer. Teacher of seminars on his own novels at Washington and Lee University, Southern Seminary, and American School, London. *Wartime service:* British Merchant Marine, 1944.

WRITINGS—Novels: *A Fall from Aloft*, Barrie & Rockliff, 1968, Random House, 1969; *A Few Flowers for St. George*, Barrie & Rockliff, 1970; *Undertow*, Barrie & Rockliff, 1971; *The Sailor and the Fox*, Farrar, Straus, 1973; *Surprise*, Harper, 1974.

Juveniles: *St. Nicholas and the Tub*, Holiday, 1964; *Willie and the Whoozie*, Allen & Unwin, in press.

Assistant editor, *Bermudian*, 1960-62.

WORK IN PROGRESS: Three novels, two plays, short stories, and three children's books.

SIDELIGHTS: Burland told *CA*: "*A Fall from Aloft* and *A Few Flowers for St. George* are required reading at many universities in the United States, Great Britain, Canada, and Holland. Just before his death, Dr. Mark Van Doren nominated *A Fall from Aloft* for an award for excellence to the American Academy of Arts and Letters."

Jeanne Cavallini called *A Fall from Aloft* "a probing study of adolescence that will be compared with *Lord of the Flies* and *A High Wind in Jamaica*...." In her review of the book Janice Elliott noted, "Brian Burland is one of the very few writers who has written so well about children and childhood that comparisons are pointless.... Burland's writing is tautly poetic and he knows how to peg allegory to the ground with realism. On one level *A Fall from Aloft* is a fast, well-told story. On another it is one of the best studies of puberty I have ever read."

An option on the movie rights to *The Sailor and the Fox* is held by QM Productions.

BURNE, Kevin G.   1925-

PERSONAL: Born May 22, 1925, in Los Angeles, Calif.; married Jane Kingsbury, December 17, 1956; children: Laurel, Brian, Jeffry, Gregory. *Education:* Pepperdine College, student, 1946-48; University of California, Los Angeles, A.B., 1950; University of Southern California, M.S., 1955, and M.A., 1959. *Religion:* Protestant. *Home:* 7316 Wilson Ct., Buena Park, Calif.

CAREER: Long Beach City College (now California State University, Long Beach), Long Beach, Calif., instructor in English, 1956—. Macmillan Co., consulting editor; Dickenson Publishing Co., advisory editor and series editor. *Military service:* U.S. Navy, 1943-46. *Member:* American Association of University Professors, California Junior College Association (vice-president, and member of board of directors for Southwest region), California Junior College Faculty Association.

WRITINGS: (With Edward Jones, Jr., and Robert Wylder) *Functional English for Writers*, Scott, 1964; (with Jones and Wylder) *RX: Remedies for Writing*, Lippincott, 1964; (with Jones and Wylder) *Limits and Latitudes*, Lippincott, 1964.

WORK IN PROGRESS: Editing, in collaboration with Robert Wylder, a series of books for freshman composition and a series for introductory literature courses; a series of remedial English books at college level, for Macmillan.†

* * *

BURNETT, Hallie Southgate

PERSONAL: Born in St. Louis, Mo.; daughter of John McKnight (a consulting engineer) and Elizabeth (Baker) Southgate; married Whit Burnett (an author and editor), 1942 (deceased); children: John Southgate, Whitney Ann Stevens. *Politics:* Independent. *Religion:* Episcopal. *Residence:* 174 Huckleberry Hill Rd., Wilton, Conn. 06897.

CAREER: Story (magazine), New York, N.Y., co-editor, 1942-70; editor of Story Press books published by Lippincott, Dutton, and others, 1942-45; Sarah Lawrence College, Bronxville, N.Y., associate professor of literature and creative writing, 1960-64. Book-of-the-Month Club, reader, 1957-59; Prentice-Hall, Inc., senior editor, 1959-60; *Yankee* (magazine), fiction editor, 1959-60. Conductor of fiction workshop at New York City Writer's Conference, Wagner College, 1955-60; instructor in short story writing at Hunter College (now of the City University of New York), 1959-61; lecturer on creative writing at University of Cincinnati, University of Missouri, and other universities and colleges. *Member:* Authors Guild, American Association of University Professors, Women's National Book Association, P.E.N. (director, 1951-71), College English Association, New York Junior League Woman Pays Club, Overseas Press, Old York (N.Y.C.). *Awards, honors:* O. Henry Award (third prize), for "Eighteenth Summer," 1942.

WRITINGS: (Editor, with husband, Whit Burnett) *Story: The Fiction of the Forties*, Dutton, 1950; (editor) *The Fiction of a Generation*, two volumes, McGibbon & Kee; *A Woman in Possession* (novel), Dutton, 1951; (editor with W. Burnett) *Story*, Volumes I-IV, McKay, 1951-54; *This Heart, This Hunter* (novel), Henry Holt, 1953; *The Brain Pickers* (novel), Messner, 1957; (with W. Burnett) *The Modern Short Story in the Making*, Hawthorn, 1964; (editor with W. Burnett) *Story Jubilee: Thirty-three Years of Story*, Doubleday, 1965; *The Watch on the Wall*, Morrow, 1965; *The Boarders in the Rue Madame: Nine Gallic*

Tales, Morrow, 1966; (editor) *Story: The Yearbook of Discovery*, Four Winds Press, 1968; *The Daughter-in-law Cookbook*, Hewitt House, 1969; *The Millionaire's Cookbook*, Pyramid Publications, 1973. Contributing editor, *Junior League Magazine*, 1937-42. Other editorial posts with *Reader's Digest*, *Book Club*, and *Yankee Magazine*. Contributor of book reviews to *New York Times*, *Saturday Review*, *Book of the Month*. Contributor of articles and short stories to various magazines.

WORK IN PROGRESS: Two novels, *The French Experiment* and *An Ear to Aphrodite*; a book with Dr. S. Rosner on *Second Marriage*.

SIDELIGHTS: Mrs. Burnett told *CA*: "Have only one recurring problem: what to put on a passport as occupation. Have tried editor, novelist, short story writer, college professor, and housewife. Have finally settled for the latter, as nobody is very impressed anyway.

"I write hard, look soft, think clear, talk vague, and generally wish I had the exterior of somebody else, preferably thinner. I prefer young people to old, old books to new (although I find young talent the most exciting thing in the world), and I hope I never die—at least until I have made a hundred more trips to Europe and at least one around the world."

* * *

BURNHAM, Alan 1913-

PERSONAL: Born February 10, 1913, in Englewood, N.J.; son of Enoch Lewis and Cora (Sellers) Burnham; married Frances Berking; children: Roderick Hotchkiss, Cora Lewis. *Education:* Harvard University, B.S., 1936; Columbia University, B.Arch., 1940. *Politics:* Democrat. *Religion:* Unitarian Universalist. *Home:* 65 Fairfield Rd., Greenwich, Conn.

CAREER: Architect in New York, N.Y., with Ebasco Services, Inc., 1952-60, Burns & Roe, Inc., 1960-62, and Shanley & Sturges, 1962—. Instructor, New School for Social Research; director, American Architectural Archive. *Member:* American Institute of Architects (fellow), Society of Architectural Historians (past chapter president), New York Society of Architects, New York Historical Society, Municipal Art Society of New York (chairman of committee on historic landmarks, 1955-60; director, 1962—), National Trust for Historic Preservation (councillor of historic property at Lyndhurst), Century Association, Harvard Club. *Awards, honors:* Award of merit, American Association for State and Local History, for *New York Landmarks*.

WRITINGS: (Editor) *New York Landmarks*, Wesleyan University Press, 1963. Contributor to *Dictionary of American Biography*, *Scribner's Dictionary of History*, and to periodicals, including *Architectural Record* and *Architectural Forum*.

WORK IN PROGRESS: A history of ornament in the United States; research on Richard Morris Hunt, a nineteenth-century architect, and on the dwelling in greater New York.

* * *

BURNS, Arthur F(rank) 1904-

PERSONAL: Born April 27, 1904, in Stanislau, Austria (now in Ukrainian Soviet Socialist Republic); son of Nathan and Sarah (Juran) Burns; married Helen Bernstein, January 25, 1930; children: David, Joseph. *Education:* Columbia University, A.B. and A.M., 1925, Ph.D., 1934. *Home:* 2510 Virginia Ave. N.W., Washington, D.C. 20037. *Office:* Federal Reserve Board, Washington, D.C. 20551.

CAREER: Rutgers College, The State University of New Jersey (now Rutgers—The State University), New Brunswick, instructor, 1927-30, assistant professor, 1930-33, associate professor, 1933-43, professor of economics, 1943-44; Columbia University, New York, N.Y., visiting lecturer, 1941-42, visiting professor, 1942-44, professor, 1944-59, John Bates Clark Professor of economics, 1959-69, emeritus professor, 1969—; counsellor to the President, 1969-70; chairman, board of governors of Federal Reserve System, 1970—; alternate governor, International Monetary Fund, 1973—. National Bureau of Economic Research, New York, N.Y., research associate, 1930-31, member of research staff, 1933-69, director of research, 1945-53, member of board of directors, 1945—, president, 1957-69, chairman, 1967-68, honorary chairman, 1969—. Visiting professor and lecturer at various universities. Chairman of President's Council of Economic Advisors, 1953-56, of President's Advisory Board on Economic Growth and Stability, 1953-56, and of Cabinet Committee on Small Business, 1956; member of Advisory Council on Social Security Financing, 1957-58, of Temporary State Commission on Economic Expansion, New York, 1959-60, of President's Advisory Committee on Labor-Management Policy, 1961-66, and of Governor's Committee on Minimum Wage, New York, 1964; consultant to U.S. Treasury, National Security Council, Department of Defense, and other departments and agencies of the federal government.

MEMBER: American Economic Association (president, 1959; distinguished fellow), American Statistical Association (fellow), Academy of Political Science (member of board of directors, 1957-68; president, 1962-68), Econometric Society (fellow), American Academy of Arts and Sciences (fellow), American Philosophical Society, Council on Foreign Relations, Institut de Science Economique Appliquee (correspondent), Pilgrims Society, Cosmos Club (Washington, D.C.), Century Association and Men's Faculty Club of Columbia University (both New York). *Awards, honors:* Alexander Hamilton Medal, Columbia University, 1969; Distinguished Public Service Award, Tax Foundation, Inc., 1969; Mugungwha Decoration, Korean Government, 1970; *Finance* Magazine's Star of Achievement, 1971; fellow, Jewish Theological Seminary of America, 1971; honorary degrees from twenty-two universities and colleges, including University of Chicago, Rikkyo University (Tokyo), University of Pennsylvania, Dartmouth College and Columbia University.

WRITINGS: Production Trends in the United States Since 1870, National Bureau of Economic Research, 1934; (with W. C. Mitchell) *Measuring Business Cycles*, National Bureau of Economic Research, 1946; *Economic Research and the Keynesian Thinking of Our Times*, National Bureau of Economic Research, 1946; *Frontiers of Economic Knowledge*, National Bureau of Economic Research, 1954; *Prosperity Without Inflation*, Fordham University Press, 1958; *The Management of Prosperity*, Columbia University Press, 1966; (with P. A. Samuelson) *Full Employment, Guideposts, and Economic Stability*, American Enterprise Institute, 1967; (with Jacob K. Javits and Charles J. Hitch) *The Defense Sector and the American Economy*, New York University Press, 1968; *The Business Cycle in a Changing World*, National Bureau of Economic Research, 1969.

SIDELIGHTS: "Burns, a formidable figure in his own right," commented Robert Lekchman, "is the first professional economist to attain the summit of the mysterious realm of central banking ... as Chairman of the Board of Governors of the Federal Reserve System, a job having great actual and still larger symbolic consequence." Lekchman also pointed out that *The Business Cycle in a Changing World*, a collection of essays written between 1957 and 1969, gives us "the opportunity to enter his frame of thought." That approach, Albert L. Kraus tells us, is that of a political economist, but not a polemicist. He quotes Burns: "' ... professional economists should stick to their knitting ... economic counseling and political advocacy could get in one another's way, and ... economists should not devote their precious time to do what politicians—who at least then were not in short supply—can do better.'" Kraus adds, "The knitting, as Mr. Burns sees it, is what this book is about."

* * *

BUSCH, Niven 1903-

PERSONAL: Born April 26, 1903, in New York, N.Y.; son of Briton Niven and Christine (Fairchild) Busch; married Teresa Wright, 1942 (divorced, 1952); married Carmencita Baker, March 14, 1956; children: Peter, Tony, Niven Terence, Mary, Joseph, Nicholas and Eliza (twins). *Education:* Attended Princeton University, 1922-24. *Politics:* Republican. *Religion:* Episcopalian. *Home:* 3055 Pacific Ave., San Francisco, Calif. *Agent:* Ashley-Steiner-Famous Artists, Inc., 555 Madison Ave., New York, N.Y. 10022.

CAREER: Associate editor of *Time* and *New Yorker*, 1927-31; full-time author and film writer, 1931—, working mainly at office in San Francisco, Calif. Operator of fruit and cattle ranch, Hollister, Calif. *Member:* Authors League of America, Academy of Motion Picture Arts and Sciences; Press Club and Union League Club (both San Francisco). *Awards, honors:* Nominated for Academy of Motion Picture Arts and Sciences Award (Oscar) for best original screen play, "In Old Chicago," 1937.

WRITINGS: 21 Americans, Doubleday, 1930, reprinted, Books for Libraries Press, 1970; *Carrington Incident* (novel), Morrow, 1939; *Duel in the Sun* (novel), Morrow, 1944; *They Dream of Home* (novel), Appleton, 1944; *Day of the Conquerors,* Harper, 1946; *The Furies* (novel), Dial, 1948; *The Hate Merchant* (novel), Simon and Schuster, 1952; *The Actor* (novel), Simon and Schuster, 1954; *California Street* (novel), Simon and Schuster, 1957; *The San Franciscans* (novel), Simon and Schuster, 1961; *The Gentleman From California*, Simon and Schuster, 1965; *The Takeover* (novel), Simon and Schuster, 1973.

Screenplays: "In Old Chicago," 1937; "Duel in the Sun"; "Pursued," 1946; "The Capture," 1946; "Distant Drums," 1951; "Man from the Alamo," 1952; "The Moonlighter," 1953; "The Treasure of Pancho Villa," 1955; "Galveston," 1956; "California Street," 1959; and about twenty others.

Contributor to *Life, New Yorker, Harper's*, and most other leading national magazines.

WORK IN PROGRESS: An original screenplay for Embassy Pictures.

AVOCATIONAL INTERESTS: Golf, fishing, riding, and shooting.†

BUSHELL, Raymond 1910-

PERSONAL: Surname is pronounced Bu-*shell;* born December 30, 1910, in New York, N.Y.; son of Harry (a merchant) and Estelle (Spellman) Bushell; married Frances Numano (a partner in an art gallery), April 18, 1952. *Education:* University of Virginia, student, 1927-29; St. Laurence University, LL.B., 1934, LL.M., 1935. *Home:* 3-43, 5-Chome, Minami Azabu, Minato-ku, Tokyo, Japan. *Office:* Bushell, Shimeall, & Asahina Law Office, Sumitomo Building, Marunouchi, Tokyo, 100 Japan.

CAREER: Admitted to bar of New York State, 1935; U.S. Merchant Marine, Sea-Air Rescue Service, 1943-46; U.S. Army, I Corps, Kyoto, Japan, civilian legal assistance officer, 1946-47; private practice of law, Tokyo, Japan, 1948—, currently partner, Bushell, Shimeall & Asahina. *Member:* International Lawyers Association, Tokyo Bar Association.

WRITINGS: (Adapter) *The Netsuke Handbook of Ueda Reikichi*, Tuttle, 1963; *The Wonderful World of Netsuke*, Tuttle, 1965; *Collectors' Netsuke*, Weatherhill, 1971; *Introduction to Netsuke*, Tuttle, 1971. Contributor to *Collectors Encyclopedia of Antiques, Arts of Asia*, and *Orientations*.

WORK IN PROGRESS: A study of netsuke, Japanese lacquer (especially inro), and Chinese jade carvings.

* * *

BUSKE, Morris Roger 1912-

PERSONAL: Born April 24, 1912, in Cadott, Wis.; son of Henry Walter and Ada Frances (Budge) Buske; married Dorothy Hohler, June 26, 1937; children: Dorothy Lynn (Mrs. R. R. Graybill), Carol Frances. *Education:* River Falls State Teacher's College (now University of Wisconsin-River Falls), B.E., 1934; University of Wisconsin, Ph.M., 1937, graduate study, 1938-40; Columbia University, graduate study, 1964-65. *Politics:* Independent. *Religion:* Protestant. *Home:* 831 North Grove Ave., Oak Park, Ill. 60302.

CAREER: Oak Park and River Forest High School, Oak Park, Ill., history teacher, 1940—. Denoyer-Geppert Co., Chicago, Ill., member of editorial board. *Member:* National Council for the Social Studies, Organization of American Historians, Illinois Education Association, Illinois Council for the Social Studies, West Suburban Council for the Social Studies, National Education Association. *Awards, honors:* Coe fellowship, Stanford University, 1961; John Hay fellowship in the humanities, Columbia University, 1964-65.

WRITINGS: (With A. Wesley Roehm and others) *The Record of Mankind* (based on *World Civilization*, by Hutton Webster and Edgar Bruce Wesley), Heath, 1949, 4th edition, 1970; (editor with Roehm and William H. McNeill) *The World: Its History in Maps*, Denoyer-Geppert, 1963, adaptation published as *The World: Its History in Cartovues*, Denoyer-Geppert, 1966. Also author of "Learning Guides" in American history, economics, and sociology for LaSalle University Extension; author of *Problems in American Democracy* for U.S. Armed Forces Institute. Editor with McNeill and Roehm of Denoyer-Geppert "World History Wall Map" series; editor of "American History Filmstrips" for Davco Publishing.

* * *

BUTLER, Albert 1923-

PERSONAL: Born December 15, 1923, in Phillipsburg,

Kan.; son of Albert Frederick (a farmer) and Clara (Pettey) Butler; married Joan Norene Lincoln, August 23, 1951; children: Janice Norene, Debra Ann. *Education:* Attended business college in Nampa, Idaho. *Politics:* Republican. *Religion:* Congregational. *Home:* 12 Jackson, Boise, Idaho 83705. *Agent:* Lambert Wilson Associates, 8 East Tenth St., New York, N.Y. 10003. *Office:* KTVB-TV, 709 Idaho St., Boise, Idaho.

CAREER: Reporter for newspapers in Payette, Idaho, 1950, John Day, Ore., 1951; KGEM, Boise, Idaho, radio writer, 1952-56; KTVB-TV, Boise, Idaho, television writer, 1956—. *Military service:* U.S. Army, 1943-46.

WRITINGS: Reporter for the Sentinel, Abelard, 1961; *Fast Flows the River,* Abelard, 1963; *Out From Tombstone,* Arcadia House, 1966.†

*   *   *

BUTLER, E(dward) H(arry)   1913-

PERSONAL: Born May 28, 1913, in Peterborough, England. *Education:* Attended English schools. *Home:* 24 Victor Court, Hornchurch, Essex, England.

CAREER: Peterborough Advertiser, Peterborough, England, junior reporter, 1927-35; *Kettering Evening Telegraph,* Kettering, England, reporter, 1935-39; Press Association, London, England, reporter, 1947-60, deputy night news editor, 1960-68, night news editor, 1968—. Shorthand advisor, National Council for the Training of Journalists; producer of documentary films on art for George Rowney & Co. Ltd. *Military service:* Royal Army Service Corps, 1939-45; became warrant officer. *Member:* Incorporated Phonographic Society (life fellow), New York State Shorthand Reporters' Association (honorary life member), Pennsylvania Shorthand Reporters' Association (honorary life member), Teeline Shorthand Association.

WRITINGS: The Story of British Shorthand, Pitman, 1951; *An Introduction to Journalism,* Allen & Unwin, 1955; (contributor) E.D. Smith, editor, *High Speed Shorthand Round the World,* Pitman, 1961; *A Journalist's Guide to Pitman's Shorthand,* Pitman, 1967; (editor) *Graded Shorthand Reading for Journalists,* Pitman, 1969; *Basic Teeline Self-Taught,* Heinemann Educational Books, 1974. Contributor to shorthand magazines and amateur cinema publications.

WORK IN PROGRESS: Shorthand textbooks in the Teeline system for Heinemann.

*   *   *

BUTLER, Joseph Thomas   1932-

PERSONAL: Born January 25, 1932, in Winchester, Va.; son of Joseph Kaspar (a salesman) and Sara (Thomas) Butler. *Education:* University of Maryland, B.S., 1954; Ohio University, M.A., 1955; University of Delaware, M.A., 1957. *Home:* 635 S. Broadway, Tarrytown, N.Y. 10591.

CAREER: Sleepy Hollow Restorations, Tarrytown, N.Y., curator, 1957—. Adjunct associate professor of architecture, Columbia University, 1970—. Advisory member of Special Acquisitions Committee of Bowdoin College Museum of Art; member of advisory boards of several historic sites on the East coast and of Victorian Society in America. *Member:* National Arts Club (member of board of governers).

WRITINGS: Sunnyside, Washington Irving's Home,

Sleepy Hollow Restorations, 1962, 3rd edition, 1974; *American Antiques 1800-1900: A Collector's History and Guide,* Odyssey, 1965; (contributor) Helena Hayward, editor, *World Furniture,* Paul Hamlyn, 1965; *Candleholders in America, 1650-1900,* Crown, 1967; *The Family Collections at Van Cortlandt Manor,* Sleepy Hollow Restorations, 1967; (with W. D. Garrett et al) *The Arts in America: The 19th Century,* Scribner, 1969; *American Furniture,* Triune, 1973; (contributor) Phoebe Phillips, editor, *The Collectors' Encyclopedia of Antiques,* Crown, 1973. Also author of *Boscabel and Its Builder,* 1974. Contributor to *Encyclopaedia Britannica, Encyclopedia Americana, Encyclopedia of World Biography,* and to *Antiques, Connoisseur,* and *House Beautiful.* American editor, *Connoisseur,* 1967—.

*   *   *

BUTOW, Robert J. C.   1924-

PERSONAL: Born March 19, 1924, in San Mateo, Calif.; son of Frederick W. C. and Louise (Gut) Butow; married Irene Ruth Elkeles, June 14, 1950 (divorced); children: Stephanie Cecile. *Education:* Stanford University, A.B. (magna cum laude), 1947, A.M., 1948, Ph.D., 1953. *Office:* Foreign Area Studies, Thomson Hall, DR-05, University of Washington, Seattle, Wash. 98195.

CAREER: Princeton University, Princeton, N.J., instructor, 1954-59, assistant professor of history, 1959-60; University of Washington, Seattle, associate professor, 1960-66, professor of history, 1966—. Member of Institute for Advanced Study, 1962-63. *Military service:* U.S. Army, 1943-46; became first lieutenant. *Member:* Society for Historians of American Foreign Relations, American Committee on the History of the Second World War. *Awards, honors:* Rotary International fellowship, Tokyo, 1951-52; Center of International Studies postdoctoral research fellowship, Princeton University, 1953-54; Social Science Research Council fellowship and Rockefeller Foundation fellowship for research in Japan, 1956-57; Guggenheim fellowship, 1965-66.

WRITINGS: Japan's Decision to Surrender, Stanford University Press, 1954; *Tojo and the Coming of the War,* Princeton University Press, 1961, reprinted, Stanford University Press, 1969; *The John Doe Associates: Backdoor Diplomacy for Peace, 1941,* Stanford University Press, 1974. Contributor to professional periodicals.

WORK IN PROGRESS: Continuing research on various aspects of Japanese-American relations and on the diplomatic history of World War II.

SIDELIGHTS: Butow's books have been translated into Japanese.

*   *   *

BUTTS, R. Freeman   1910-

PERSONAL: Born May 14, 1910, in Springfield, Ill.; son of R. Freeman and Cornelia Ann (Paddock) Butts; married Florence Randolph, May 30, 1936; children: Stephen Jay, Ann Randolph (Mrs. David Griffiths). *Education:* University of Wisconsin, A.B. (honors), 1931, A.M., 1932, Ph.D., 1935. *Home:* 39 Neptune Avenue, Madison, Conn. 06443. *Office:* Teachers College, Columbia University, 525 West 120th St., New York, N.Y. 10027.

CAREER: Columbia University, Teachers College, New York, N.Y., instructor, 1936-38, assistant professor, 1938-41, associate professor, 1941-47, professor of education, 1947—, William F. Russell Professor in the Foundations of

Education, 1958—, director of International Studies, 1960-64, associate dean for International Studies, 1964—. Visiting professor, University of Wisconsin, 1949. Consultant on education, Holt, Reinhart and Winston, 1950—; chief of Teachers College Educational Mission to India, 1959; director of Teachers for East Africa Project at Teachers College, 1961-63, and Nigeria Peace Corps Training Program, 1962-63; senior specialist, East-West Center, University of Hawaii, 1965. Member of advanced placement committee, College Entrance Examination Board, 1963—, and of advisory committee on educational planning, Council on Higher Education in the American Republics (CHEAR), 1964—; consultant, Bureau of Research, U.S. Office of Education, 1965—; member of Committee on Education and Human Resource Development, Education and World Affairs, 1964-68; member of advisory committee, Center for Mass Communications, Columbia University Press, 1969-72. Consultant to many education organizations both national and international. Lecturer.

MEMBER: American Historical Association, American Educational Research Association, American Studies Association, American Association of University Professors, National Education Association (chairman, committee on international relations, 1965-66), History of Education Society, John Dewey Society, International Council on Education for Teaching, Philosophy of Education Society, National Society for the Study of Education, Comparative Education Society (board; president, 1964-65), American Academy of Political and Social Science, Center for the Study of Democratic Institutions, International Studies Association, Social Science Education Consortium, Cleveland, Kappa Delta Pi. *Awards, honors:* Fulbright award for research with Australian Council for Educational Research, Melbourne, 1954; Carnegie travel grant to Africa and Asia, 1961-62. Annual R. Freeman Butts Lecture Series was established by American Educational Studies Association, 1974.

WRITINGS: The College Charts Its Course, McGraw, 1939; *A Cultural History of Education,* McGraw, 1947; *The American Tradition in Religion and Education,* Beacon, 1950; (co-author) *A History of Education in American Culture,* Holt, 1953; *Assumptions Underlying Australian Education,* Bureau of Publications, Teachers College, Columbia University, 1955; *A Cultural History of Western Education,* McGraw, 1955; *American Education in International Development,* Harper, 1963; (editor with W. Roy Niblett) *Universities Facing the Future: An International Perspective,* Jossey-Bass, 1972; *The Education of the West: A Formative Chapter in the History of Civilization,* McGraw, 1973; *Public Education: Revolution to Reform,* Holt, 1975.

Contributor: John Guy Fowlkes, editor, *Higher Education for American Society,* University of Wisconsin Press, 1949; George Z. F. Bereday and Luigi Volpicelli editors, *Public Education in America: A New Interpretation of Purpose and Practice,* Harper, 1958; Kenneth F. Roulding compiler, *What Is the Nature of Man? Images of Man in Our American Culture,* Christian Education Press, 1959; Brand Blanshard editor, *Education in the Age of Science,* Basic Books, 1959; Philip H. Phenix editor, *Philosophies of Education,* Wiley, 1961; *Education for National Development,* American Association of Colleges for Teacher Education, 1964; *Frontiers of Educational Thought,* Indiana University Press, 1964; *The African University and National Development,* Institute for Education in Africa, Teachers College, Columbia University, 1964; John W. Hanson and

Cole S. Brembeck editors, *Education and the Development of Nations,* Holt, 1966; Kahil I. Gezi and James E. Myers, *Teaching in American Culture,* Holt, 1968; Bereday editor, *Essays on World Education: The Crisis of Supply and Demand,* Oxford University Press, 1969; Margaret Gillet and John A. Laska editors, *Foundations Studies in Education: Justifications and New Directions,* Scarecrow Press, 1973; James A. Perkins editor, *Higher Education: Crisis and Support, An International Perspective,* International Council for Educational Development, 1974.

Contributor to yearbooks, *Higher Education,* World Book Co., 1959, and *The United States and International Education,* University of Chicago Press, 1969. Contributor to *Encyclopedia Britannica, World Book Encyclopedia,* and to education journals.

Chairman of editorial board, *The World Year Book of Education,* 1963-74; member of advisory board, *Educational Studies,* 1969—; member of editorial board, *Educational Forum,* 1971-74.

*   *   *

BYATT, A(ntonia) S(usan Drabble)   1936-

PERSONAL: Born August 24, 1936, in Sheffield, England; daughter of John Frederick (a judge) and Kathleen Marie (Bloor) Drabble; married Ian Charles Rayner Byatt (an economist), July 4, 1959; children: Antonia, Charles. *Education:* Newnham College, Cambridge, B.A. (first class honors), 1957; graduate study at Bryn Mawr College, 1957-58, and Somerville College, Oxford, 1958-59. *Politics:* Radical. *Home and office:* 33 Ridgmount Gardens, London, W.C. 1, England. *Agent:* A. D. Peters, 10 Buckingham St., Adelphi, London, W.C. 2, England.

CAREER: Part-time teacher of literature at University of London, and Central School of Arts and Crafts, London, England, 1964—. *Awards, honors:* English-Speaking Union fellowship, 1957-58.

WRITINGS: Shadow of a Sun (novel), Harcourt, 1964; *Degrees of Freedom: The Novels of Iris Murdock,* Barnes, 1965; *The Game* (novel), Chatto & Windus, 1967, Scribner, 1968; *Wordsworth and Coleridge in Their Time,* Nelson, 1970, Crane, Russak, 1973.

SIDELIGHTS: Mrs. Byatt told *CA:* "I had always intended to be a university teacher, and have in my possession an unfinished thesis on seventeenth-century religious allegory, which was interrupted by marriage, children, and writing a novel. Can speak French, some German, less Italian."†

*   *   *

BYRNES, Thomas Edmund   1911-

PERSONAL: Born June 4, 1911, in Chicago, Ill.; son of Thomas Stephen (a salesman) and Mary Loretta (Duffey) Byrnes; married Virginia Howell, December 18, 1937; children: Christopher, David, Virginia (Mrs. Jerry Jones), Danielle, Margaret, Daniel, Thomas, Mary Johanna, Gael, Jamie, Monica, Brendan. *Education:* Loyola University, Chicago, Ill., A.B., 1934. *Religion:* Catholic. *Home and office:* 8105 Bull Valley Rd., Woodstock, Ill. *Agent:* Maurice Crain, Inc., 18 East 41st St., New York, N.Y. 10017.

CAREER: Chicago Daily News, Chicago, Ill., feature writer, 1936-44; now full-time professional writer. *Member:* Midland Authors, Woodstock Fine Arts Association.

WRITINGS: The Inevitable Hour (one-act play), Samuel French, 1939; *All My Darlings* (family autobiography), Crowell, 1955, play version (three-act), Samuel French, 1964.

Writer of television play, "The Christmas Chimes," produced by Columbia Broadcasting System, 1963, 1964. Scriptwriter for motion pictures and live shows for industrial clients. Contributor of children's verses to *McCall's*.

WORK IN PROGRESS: Two short juvenile books; a book of children's verse; a musical drama on the life of Mother Cabrini.

SIDELIGHTS: Byrnes told *CA:* "I especially like to write for and about children. My chief interest, aside from my writing, is encouraging my own children (twelve) to develop their imaginations, whether the work at hand be an oil painting, a Christmas playlet, or a bridge of building blocks. . . . In a day when it seems to be a parental duty to cram the lives of our young with organized activity, it is well to reflect that great scientists, as well as great artists, are essentially creative men, who at some point in their lives, had nowhere to look but into themselves, and nothing to depend on but their own imaginings."

Byrnes family autobiography, *All My Darlings*, has gone into French and German editions.†

*   *   *

CAGE, John (Milton, Jr.) 1912-

PERSONAL: Born September 5, 1912, in Los Angeles, Calif.; son of John M. and Lucretia (Harvey) Cage; married Xenia Andreyevna Kashevarcff, June 7, 1935 (divorced 1945). *Education:* Pomona College, student, 1928-30; studied music and composition privately with Richard Buhlig, Adolph Weiss, Henry Cowell, and Arnold Schoenberg. *Residence:* Stony Point, N.Y. *Address:* 107 Bank St., New York, N.Y. 10014.

CAREER: Before beginning musical career worked as dishwasher in Carmel, Calif., and as wall washer in Brooklyn, 1933-34, and as free-lance library researcher, 1934-35; at one time privately taught composition; pianist and lecturer; Cornish School, Seattle Wash., accompanist and teacher, 1936-38; School of Design, Chicago, Ill., faculty member,1941-42; Merce Cunningham and Dance Co., New York, N.Y., musical director, 1944-66; University of Cincinnati, Cincinnati, Ohio, composer in residence, 1967—. Member of summer faculty, Mills College, 1938-39, Black Mountain College, 1950-52; teacher of composition, New School for Social Research, 1955-60; Center for Advanced Studies fellow, Wesleyan University, 1960-61; research professor and associate, Center for Advanced Studies, University of Illinois, 1967-69. Invented "prepared" piano, 1938. Directed concert of percussion music sponsored by Music of Modern Art and League Composers, 1943. Organized group of musicians and engineers for recording music directly on magnetic tape, 1951. Art director for Jack Lenor Larson (textile company), circa 1956-57.

MEMBER: American Society of Composers, Authors and Publishers, American Federation of Musicians, Foundation for Contemporary Performance Arts, Cunningham Dance Foundation (past president and member of board of directors), New York Mycological Society (founding honorary member). *Awards, honors:* Guggenheim fellowship, 1949, for "extending the boundaries of musical art"; Woodstock Art Film Festival First Prize, 1951, for the score of *Works*

of Calder; award for contributions to amateur mycology, 1964, from sub-committee on fungi of People-to-People Program; Thorne Music Fund grantee, 1967-69.

WRITINGS: (With Kathleen Hoover) *Virgil Thomson: His Life and Music*, Yoseloff, 1959, Books for Libraries, 1970; *Silence: Selected Lectures and Writings*, Wesleyan University Press, 1961, revised edition, 1973; *Diary: How to Improve the World (You Will Only Make Matters Worse) Continued, Part 3* (an exerpt from *A Year from Monday*), Something Else Press, 1967; *A Year from Monday: New Lectures and Writings*, Wesleyan University Press, 1967; (with Alison Knowles) *Notations*, Something Else Press, 1969; (contributor) Robert Fillison, *Teaching and Learning as Performing Arts*, Wittenhorn, 1970; (contributor with others) Ihab Hassan, editor, *Liberations: New Essays on the Humanities in Revolution*, Wesleyan University Press, 1971; *M: Writings '67-'72*, Wesleyan University Press, 1973. Also author with Lois Long and Alexander H. Smith of *Mushroom Book*.

Musical Compositions—all published by Henmar Press: *Construction in Metal*, 1939; *Amores*, 1943; *Dance*, 1944; *Sonatas and Interludes*, 1946-48; *The Seasons*, 1947; *Imaginary Landscape No. 4*, 1951; *Imaginary Landscape No. 5*, 1952; *4'33"*, 1952; *William Mix*, 1952; *Music of Changes*, 1952; *Music for Carillon No. 2*, 1954; *34'46.766*, 1954; *Winter Music*, 1957; *Fontana Mix*, 1958; *Aria*, 1958; *Theatre Piece*, 1960; *Atlas Eclipticalis* (with or without *Winter Music*), 1961-62; *The Shape of Time*, 1962; *Rozart Mix*, 1965; *How to Pass, Kick, Fall, and Run*, 1967; *HPSCHD*, 1967-69; *Cheap Imitations*, 1972. Also composer of numerous other works for piano and harpsichord, prepared piano, voice, solo and chamber music instrumentals, percussion and electronic devices, audio-visual effects, and orchestra and chamber orchestra; all published by Henmar Press.

Contributor to museum catalogues and periodicals. Co-editor, *New Music*, 1943-54.

SIDELIGHTS: The controversy concerning John Cage's music has existed for years. "In 1937," writes Virgil Thomson, "thirty years before this work [*HPSCHD*, composed for seven harpsichords, 52 tape machines, 59 power amplifiers, 59 loud speakers, and 208 computer-generated tapes, 1967-69] was started, Cage has proclaimed his credo regarding the future of music: 'I believe that the use of noise to make music will continue and increase until we reach a music produced through the aid of electrical instruments which will make available for musical purposes any and all sounds that can be heard' . . . Cage, however, when he began to compose in 1933, was virtually alone in following out the futurist noise principle as a career." While Thomson acknowledges Cage's "inventor's ingenuity", he also comments "But Cage's aim with music . . . has long been clearly destructive." Earlier in the article he explains that Cage's "ultimate aim was to produce a homogenized chaos that would carry no program, no plot, no reminders of the history of beauty, and no personal statement . . . to save music from itself by removing its narcotic qualities and its personalized pretentiousness, as well as all identifiable structure and rhetoric." Richard Kostelanetz describes Cage's compositions of "chance" as "aleatoric methods of composition, where patterns developed by accidental means could be translated into musical notation . . . Cage undertakes such procedures precisely to divorce the final piece from his conscious desires. He calls it 'indeterminate' or 'unintentional' music."

As for his popular aclaim, Kostelanetz said that "For many years Cage was excluded from the general run of musical activities and beneficient spoils; but now that his ideas have become more acceptable, his work is at least taken more seriously (although it is hardly universally approved). Whereas he once took diverse jobs, in the last few years he has been able to live as a musician."

As a musician, Cage has said, concerning his tastes: "If you want to know the truth of the matter, the music I prefer, even to my own and everything, is what we hear if we are just quiet." Kostelanetz explains: "Cage deduces that the most agreeable art is not only just like life; it is life." John Kobler quotes Cage: "Everything we do is music. Wherever we are, what we hear is mostly noise. When we ignore it, it disturbs us. When we listen to it, we find it fascinating."

Cage was commissioned by the Ballet Society to write *The Seasons*, 1947; by Donaueschinger Musiktage to write work for two prepared pianos, *34'46.766*, 1954; by Montreal Festivals Society to write work for full orchestra, *Atlas Eclipticalis*, 1961; by Serge Koussevitsky Music Foundation to write *Cheap Imitation* for full orchestra, 1972. Cage recorded *Fontana Mix* on magnetic tape for Studio di Fonologia, in Milan, Italy, 1958. Many of Cage's compositions have been recorded by various record companies.

BIOGRAPHICAL/CRITICAL SOURCES: Richard Kostelanetz, editor, *John Cage*, Praeger, 1970.

*   *   *

CAHILL, Robert S. 1933-

PERSONAL: Born May 1, 1933, in Clatskanie, Ore.; son of Robert C. and Lucia May (Stoddart) Cahill; married Amefie Agbayani, December 12, 1970; children: (former marriage) Christopher S. *Education:* Studied at Oregon State College, 1949-51, and College of the City of New York (now City College of the City University of New York), 1952-53; Reed College, student, 1951-52, B.A., 1954; University of Oregon, M.A., 1961, Ph.D., 1962. *Politics:* Democrat. *Home:* 2427 Palolo Ave., Honolulu, Hawaii 96816. *Office:* Department of Political Science, University of Hawaii, Honolulu, Hawaii 96822.

CAREER: University of Hawaii, Honolulu, professor of political science and chairman of department, 1962—. *Military service:* U.S. Army, 1954-56. *Member:* American Political Science Association, American Association of University Professors (president, University of Hawaii chapter). *Awards, honors:* Social Science Research Council research training fellowship, 1962.

WRITINGS: (Editor with Stephen P. Hencley) *The Politics of Education in the Local Community*, Interstate, 1964; (contributor) W. J. Gore and J. W. Dyson, editors, *The Making of Decisions*, Free Press, 1964.

WORK IN PROGRESS: Two books: *Sexuality and Social Power*; *Three Commentaries on Political Reality: Madness, Comedy, and Religion*.

*   *   *

CAIGER-SMITH, Alan 1930-

PERSONAL: Born February 8, 1930, in Buenos Aires, Argentina; son of Christopher and Helen (Massey) Caiger-Smith; married Anne-Marie Hulteus, December 27, 1956; children: Nicholas, Martin, Patrick, Daniel. *Education:* Attended Camberwell School of Art, 1948, King's College, Cambridge, 1949-53. *Home:* Shalford Farmhouse, Brimpton, Berkshire, England.

CAREER: Potter and ceramist, 1955—.

WRITINGS: English Medieval Mural Paintings, Clarendon Press, 1963; *Tin-Glaze Pottery in Europe and the Islamic World*, Faber, 1973.

*   *   *

CAIRNS, John C(ampbell) 1924-

PERSONAL: Born April 27, 1924, in Windsor, Ontario, Canada; son of William Garroway and Mabel (Campbell) Cairns. *Education:* University of Toronto, B.A., 1945, M.A., 1947; Cornell University, Ph.D., 1951. *Office:* Department of History, University of Toronto, Toronto, Ontario, Canada.

CAREER: University of Toronto, Toronto, Ontario, lecturer, 1952-58, assistant professor, 1958-62, associate professor, 1962-64, professor of history, 1964—. Visiting professor at Stanford University, 1968-69. *Military service:* Royal Canadian Air Force, 1943-44. *Member:* American Historical Association, Canadian Historical Association, Society for French Historical Studies, Canadian Society for the Abolition of the Death Penalty.

WRITINGS: (With B. Wilkinson and D. Fishwick) *The Foundations of the West*, Clarke, Irwin, 1963; (editor and author of introduction) *The Nineteenth Century*, Free Press of Glencoe, 1965; *France*, Prentice-Hall, 1965.

*   *   *

CALEF, Wesley (Carr) 1914-

PERSONAL: Born June 22, 1914, in Alma Center, Wis.; son of Ellis (a teacher) and Hazel (Carr) Calef; married Beulah L. Waller, 1941; children: George, Charles, Daniel. *Education:* University of Wisconsin, B.A., 1936; University of California, Los Angeles, M.S., 1944; University of Chicago, Ph.D., 1948. *Office:* Department of Geography, University of Chicago, Chicago, Ill.

CAREER: University of Chicago, Chicago, Ill., instructor, 1947-49, assistant professor, 1949-55, associate professor, 1955-58, professor of geography, 1958—. *Member:* American Association for the Advancement of Science, Association of American Geographers, National Council of Geographic Education.

WRITINGS: Private Grazing and Public Land, University of Chicago Press, 1960. Editor, "Geography Research Series," University of Chicago.†

*   *   *

CALL, Alice E(lizabeth) LaPlant 1914-

PERSONAL: Born July 18, 1914, in Chicago, Ill.; daughter of John F. (an insurance executive and Alice G. (Wright) LaPlant; divorced; children: Joan Elizabeth (Mrs. John L. Andrew). *Education:* University of Washington, Seattle, B.S., 1936; University of Colorado, M.Ed., 1950, graduate extension courses. *Politics:* Republican. *Religion:* Presbyterian. *Home:* 4061 East 11th Ave., Denver, Colo. 80220.

CAREER: Teacher in secondary schools in Denver, Colo., 1948—. Certified guidance counselor, state of Colorado, 1964. East High School, Denver, Colo., teacher of course in social problems, 1954-64, now counselor, teacher, and part-time staff member in guidance office. *Member:* National Education Association, National Council on Family Relations, American Personnel and Guidance Association, Colorado Education Association, Denver Classroom Teachers. *Awards, honors:* Graduate fellowship to Merrill-Palmer Institute, 1959-60.

WRITINGS: Toward Adulthood, Lippincott, 1964.

WORK IN PROGRESS: To Joan with Love, a mother's letters to her daughter from about age sixteen until marriage, touching on common adolescent problems and other facets of the mother-daughter relationship.

AVOCATIONAL INTERESTS: Golf, knitting, and sewing.†

* * *

CALLISTER, Frank 1916-

PERSONAL: Born July 9, 1916, in Douglas, Isle of Man; son of Joseph (a postman) and Agnes Annie (Clarke) Callister. *Education:* Didsbury College, Manchester, England, theological student, 1935-39, B.D. (London), 1939; University of Glasgow, M.A., 1946. *Politics:* "Relative to time and candidate." *Home:* 53 Longlands Rd., New Mills, Stockport, Cheshire, England. *Office:* Manchester Training College, Long Millgate, Manchester 3, England.

CAREER: Methodist minister in Scotland and in Yorkshire, England, 1939-56; schoolteacher in Staffordshire and Lancashire, England, 1956-62; Manchester Training College, Manchester, England, lecturer in divinity, 1962-64, senior lecturer, 1964—. *Member:* Institute of Christian Education, National Trust, Royal Automobile Club (associate member).

WRITINGS: Bible Plays for the Morning Assembly, Epworth, 1958; *The Vacant Throne*, Epworth, 1960; (with H. F. Matthews) *Living in the Kingdom*, Epworth, 1963; *One World Not Two: An Examination of Bible Wonders in the Old and New Testaments*, Religious Education Press, 1968. Occasional articles in *Guardian*, *Religion in Education*, *Times Educational Supplement*, *London Quarterly*, *Poetry Review*, other journals and newspapers in England.

SIDELIGHTS: Callister told *CA*: "I read French easily, Spanish and Italian with difficulty. I also have an acquaintance with Hebrew, Greek, and Latin." *Avocational interests:* Music, walking, appreciation of art, gardening.†

* * *

CALLOW, Philip Kenneth 1924-

PERSONAL: Born October 26, 1924, in Birmingham, England; son of Hubert Arthur (a clerk) and Beatrice May (Rady) Callow; married Irene Christian Watts, February, 1951; married second wife, Penelope Jane Newman, 1974; children: (first marriage) Fleur Alyse. *Education:* Attended Coventry Technical College, St. Luke's College. *Home:* Little Thatch, Hasselbury, Crewkerne, Somerset, England. *Agent:* John Johnson, 10 Suffield House, 79 Davies St., London W.1, England.

CAREER: Employed in England at earlier periods as apprentice, then toolmaker for Coventry Gauge and Tool Co., telephonist, civil servant with British Ministry of Works, clerk in Nottingham and Plymouth, and as autosetter with Tecalemit Ltd., Plymouth, England; novelist and poet, 1966—. *Member:* P.E.N. (London). *Awards, honors:* Two writers' fellowships; traveling scholarship, Society of Authors.

WRITINGS: The Hosanna Man (novel), J. Cape, 1956; *Common People* (novel), Heinemann, 1958; *Native Ground* (short stories), Heinemann, 1959; *A Pledge for the Earth* (novel), Heinemann, 1960; (contributor) *New Granada Plays*, Faber, 1961; *Turning Point* (poems), Heinemann, 1964; *Clipped Wings* (novel), Gibbs & Phillips, 1964; *The Real Life* (poems), Gibbs & Phillips, 1965; *In My Own Land*, Times Press, 1965; *Going to the Moon* (novel), MacGibbon & Kee, 1968; *The Bliss Body* (novel), MacGibbon & Kee, 1969; *Flesh of Morning* (novel), Bodley Head, 1971; *Bare Wires* (poems), Chatto & Windus, 1971; *Yours* (novel), Bodley Head, 1972; *Son and Lover* (biography of D. H. Lawrence), Bodley Head, in press; *Hanging On* (novel), Bodley Head, in press. Contributor to *New Statesman*, *Spectator*, *Tribune*, *Listener*.

SIDELIGHTS: Stephen Wall explains that Callow's trilogy, *Going to the Moon*, *The Bliss Body*, and *Flesh of Morning*, conveys its hero's "emerging experience of the adult world with an authenticity that is often aimed at but not often got across." Wall compares Callow to D. H. Lawrence and notes that the trilogy is "written in a prose which seems to move with a spontaneity so convincing that you feel it must be telling the truth, and which yet has eloquence and lyric intensity and fidelity to the idioms people actually use."

Manuscripts, work sheets, and proof copies of Callow's first four books are deposited in the University of Texas Library.

* * *

CAMERON, Mary Owen 1915-

PERSONAL: Born December 8, 1915; daughter of Bert T. and Jane (Congleton) Owen; married Kenneth Neill Cameron (a professor of English), April 26, 1946; children: Kathleen. *Education:* Indiana University, A.B., 1937, M.A., 1938, Ph.D., 1953. *Home:* 160 Riverside Dr., New York, N.Y., 10024. *Office:* Hunter College of the City University of New York, 695 Park Ave., New York, N.Y. 10021.

CAREER: Indiana University, Bloomington, instructor in sociology, 1940-46; Finch College, New York, N.Y., instructor in sociology, 1954-58; Hunter College of the City University of New York, professor of education, 1958—. *Member:* American Sociological Society, American Association of University Professors, Women's International League for Peace and Freedom, Eastern Sociological Society.

WRITINGS: The Booster and the Snitch, Free Press of Glencoe, 1964; (editor with Bernice Samalonis and Robert Roth) *School and Community: A Book of Readings*, W. C. Brown, 1965.†

* * *

CAMP, T(homas) Edward 1929-

PERSONAL: Born July 12, 1929, in Haynesville, La.; son of Charles Walter and Annie Laura (Brazzel) Camp; married Elizabeth Anne Sowar, September 4, 1952; children: Anne Winifred, Thomas David. *Education:* Centenary College, B.A., 1950; Vanderbilt University Divinity School, student, 1950-51; Louisiana State University, M.S. in L.S., 1953. *Politics:* Democrat. *Religion:* Protestant Episcopal. *Home:* South Carolina Ave., Sewanee, Tenn. 37375.

CAREER: Southern Methodist University, Perkins School of Theology, Dallas, Tex., circulation librarian, 1955-57; University of the South, School of Theology, Sewanee, Tenn., librarian, 1957—. Church organist. Sewanee Civic Association, member. *Military service:* U.S. Army, 1953-55. *Member:* American Library Association, American Theological Library Association (executive secretary, 1965—), American Guild of Organists, Southeastern Library Association, Tennessee Library Association, Beta Phi Mu.

WRITINGS: (With Ella V. Aldrich) *Using Theological Books and Libraries*, Prentice-Hall, 1963.†

*   *   *

CAMPBELL, Edward F(ay), Jr.   1932-

PERSONAL: Born January 5, 1932, in New Haven, Conn.; son of Edward Fay (a clergyman) and Edith (May) Campbell; married Phyllis Kletzien (a teacher), September 4, 1954; children: Thomas Edward, Sarah Ives. *Education:* Yale University, B.A. 1953; McCormick Theological Seminary, B.D., 1956; Johns Hopkins University, Ph.D., 1959. *Home:* 841 Chalmers Pl., Chicago, Ill. 60614. *Office:* McCormick Theological Seminary, 800 West Belden Ave., Chicago, Ill. 60614.

CAREER: Ordained minister, United Presbyterian Church, 1956; McCormick Theological Seminary, Chicago, Ill., instructor, 1958-59, assistant professor, 1959-62, associate professor, 1962-66, professor of Old Testament, 1966—. W. F. Albright Institute of Archaeological Research (formerly American School of Oriental Research in Jerusalem), acting director and annual professor, 1964-65, president, 1970-71, member of board of trustees, 1970—. Vice-president, American Schools of Oriental Research, 1967-70; Drew-McCormick Archaeological Expedition to Balata, Jordan, associate director, conducting excavations in summers of 1957, 1960, 1962, 1964, director, 1966, 1968; assistant director, Joint Expedition to Shechem, 1960—. *Member:* Society of Biblical Literature, Archaeological Institute of America, American Oriental Society, Chicago Society of Biblical Research (treasurer, 1960-63), Independent Voters of Chicago.

WRITINGS: (Contributor) George Ernest Wright, editor, *The Bible and the Ancient Near East: Essays in Honor of William Foxwell Albright*, Doubleday, 1961; *The Chronology of the Amarna Letters*, Johns Hopkins Press, 1964; (editor with David Noel Freedman) *The Biblical Archaeologist Reader*, volume 2, Doubleday-Anchor, 1964, volume 3, 1970; (contributor) Wright, editor, *Shechem: The Biography of a Biblical City*, McGraw, 1965. Editor, *Biblical Archaeologist*.

WORK IN PROGRESS: Contributing to Volume I and editing Volume IV of the final excavation report of the Drew-McCormick expedition to Balata; Volume VII, Ruth, of the *Anchor Bible*; I and II Samuel, in the series *Hermeneia*.

SIDELIGHTS: Mr. Campbell maintains a reading knowledge of the Akradian, Ugaritic, Aramaic, Hebrew, Greek, and Latin languages.

*   *   *

CAMPBELL, Rosemae Wells   1909-
(R. W. Campbell)

PERSONAL: Born May 4, 1909, in Brooklyn, N.Y.; daughter of Fullerton (an attorney) and Rose May (Lascell) Wells; married William Tod Campbell (an editor), August 12, 1932. *Education:* Elmira College, B.S., 1930; Brooklyn Public Library Training School, certificate, 1930; Colorado College, M.A., 1953. *Politics:* Republican. *Religion:* Congregational. *Home and office:* 802 Mira Dr., Colorado Springs, Colo. 80906.

CAREER: Worked for public libraries in New York area, 1931-37; Sperry Gyroscope Co., Garden City, N.Y., engi-

neering librarian, 1942-45; New Hampshire State Library, Concord, bookmobile librarian, 1945-46; American Management Association, New York, N.Y., assistant cataloger, 1946-47; Cheyenne Mountain Schools, Colorado Springs, Colo., librarian, 1952-58; Coburn Library, Colorado Springs, circulation librarian, 1958-59; Pioneers' Museum, Colorado Springs, lecturer, 1965-66; Colorado Springs School for Girls, librarian, 1965-69; Colorado College, Colorado Springs, special collections librarian, 1970—. Colorado College, visiting summer professor, 1955-63. Book selection consultant, Colorado State Library, 1962. First-aid instructor, American Red Cross, 1941-73, instructor-trainer, 1965-73. *Member:* Authors Guild, Colorado Library Association (state treasurer, 1955-57), Western History Association, Colorado State Historical Society, Historical Society of the Pikes Peak Region, League of Women Voters, Broadmoor Waltz Club.

WRITINGS: The Crystal River Valley: Jewel or Jinx?, Sage Books, 1966; (with W. M. Calvert) *Law in Action: An Introduction to the Courts of El Paso County*, El Paso County Bar Association Auxiliary, 1971; *From Trappers to Tourists: Fremont County, Colorado, 1830-1950*, Filter Press, 1972; *Meals on the Road*, Ritchie, 1974.

Juvenile: *Books and Beaux*, Westminster, 1958; (under name R. W. Campbell) *Tops and Gyroscopes* (nonfiction), Crowell, 1959; *The Split Rock Mystery*, Westminster, 1960; (under name R. W. Campbell) *Drag Doll*, Funk, 1962.

Contributor of articles and reviews to newspapers and magazines.

WORK IN PROGESSS: An adult biography.

SIDELIGHTS: Mrs. Campbell comments: "After I was engineering librarian at Sperry Gyroscope, I wanted to write down what I had learned about that fascinating device so that I wouldn't forget it when my work was concerned with other areas of interest. As bookmobile librarian, I found myself trying to explain gyroscopic principles to young readers who were interested in airplanes and found that it was difficult. I therefore decided to try to translate engineering formulae and jargon into English that could be understood by high school science students. . . .

"Cars were the consuming interest of the male students at Cheyenne Mountain High School. As I had been interested in automobiles, too, ever since World War II days when I drove ambulances and all sorts of other vehicles for the American Red Cross Motor Corps on a volunteer basis, I decided to write a car story. I wanted it not only to appeal to boys because of the hot rods, but, in addition, I wanted it to help them understand themselves as well. . . .

"A vacation spent in Redstone, Colorado, led to . . . *Crystal River Valley*. The widely held superstition that a jinx lay over this beautiful remote valley led me to seek out the story of the many millions of dollars that were spent there in the development of mines, quarries, and railroads, and why hardly a vestige remains even of what was once the largest marble finishing mill in the world where the stone for the Tomb of the Unknown Soldier and other famous monuments and buildings was quarried." *Avocational interests:* Recreational vehicle travel, photography, oil painting.

*   *   *

CANADAY, John E(dwin)   1907-
(Matthew Head)

PERSONAL: Born February 1, 1907, in Fort Scott, Kan.;

son of Franklin (a lawyer) and Agnes (Musson) Canaday; married Katherine Hoover, September 19, 1935; children: Rudd Hoover, John Harrington. *Education:* University of Texas, B.A., 1925; Yale University, M.A., 1932. *Office: New York Times*, 229 West 43rd St., New York, N.Y., 10036.

CAREER: Began career as a painter and art historian. University of Virginia, Charlottesville, teacher of art history, 1938-50; Newcomb College of Tulane University, New Orleans, La., head of school of art, 1950-52; Philadelphia Museum of Art, Philadelphia, Pa., chief of division of education, 1952-59; *New York Times*, New York, N.Y., art critic, 1959—. Member of mission to Belgian Congo, U.S. Board of Economic Warfare, 1943. *Military service:* U.S. Marine Corps, 1943-45; became first lieutenant. *Awards, honors:* Athenaeum Literary Award for *Mainstreams of Modern Art: David to Picasso*, 1959.

WRITINGS: Mainstreams of Modern Art: David to Picasso, Simon & Schuster, 1959; *Embattled Critic: Views on Modern Art*, Farrar, Straus & Cudahy, 1962; (with wife, Katherine H. Canaday) *Keys to Art*, Tudor, 1963 (published in England under title *Look; or, The Keys to Art*, Methuen, 1964); *The Lives of the Painters*, four volumes, Norton, 1969; *Culture Gulch: Notes on Art and Its Public in the 1960's*, Farrar, Straus, 1969; *Baroque Painters*, Norton, 1972; *Late Gothic to Renaissance Painters*, Norton, 1972; *Neoclassic to Post-Impressionist Painters*, Norton, 1972; (editor) *Western Painting Illustrated: Giotto to Cezanne*, Norton, 1972; *Artful Avocado*, Doubleday, 1973. Also author of "Metropolitan Seminars in Art," a series of portfolios, published by Metropolitan Museum of Art and distributed by Book-of-the-Month Club, 1957-58.

Under pseudonym Matthew Head—"Inner Sanctum" mysteries; all published by Simon & Schuster: *The Smell of Money*, 1943, *The Devil in the Bush*, 1945, *The Accomplice*, 1947, *The Cabinda Affair*, 1949, *The Congo Venus*, 1950, *Another Man's Life*, 1953, *Murder at the Flea Club*, 1955.

Contributor of articles to *Horizon, Art in America, Show*, and other magazines.

SIDELIGHTS: Dissatisfied with murder mysteries that told little about the murderer and the murderee, Canaday decided to write his own. He wrote the first, *The Smell of Money*, in three weeks, and told the *New Yorker:* "I didn't want to sign it with my own name, because I didn't know whether it would be a success, and if it wasn't a success I didn't want my name on it. . . . Also, I wanted to save my own name for writing about art, which I began doing later. I picked the name Matthew Head because I once knew a beautiful girl called Beverly Head and because I thought the combination of Matthew and Head looked faintly sinister."

BIOGRAPHICAL/CRITICAL SOURCES: "The Talk of the Town," *New Yorker*, January 4, 1964.

*   *   *

CANNAM, Peggie 1925-

PERSONAL: Born March 31, 1925, in Gloucester, England; daughter of Harry Gould and Gladys Mary (Winson) Cannam. *Education:* Attended schools in Gloucestershire and Surrey, England; College of All Saints, London, England, student, 1963-65. *Politics:* Conservative. *Religion:* Church of England. *Home:* 136 Estcourt Rd., Gloucester, England.

CAREER: In British Women's Land Army, 1944-47, then free-lance writer with sideline jobs as kennelmaid and factory worker; now completing teacher training. *Member:* Society of Authors, London Writers Circle.

WRITINGS: She Wanted a Pony, Museum Press, 1950; *Black Fury*, Lutterworth, 1953, Whittlesey House, 1956; *Riding for Ridge Abbey*, Lutterworth, 1955; *Hoof Beats*, Phoenix House, 1955; *Triple Bar*, Lutterworth, 1956; (with R. Sanders Leroy) *Three Great Horse Stories*, Whittlesey House, 1956; *Tawny Brush*, Lutterworth, 1957; *Musical Ride*, Lutterworth, 1958; *My Dog Echo*, Lutterworth, 1959; *Corn and Carrot Tops*, Epworth, 1960; *Riding*, Arco Publications, 1964.

WORK IN PROGRESS: A collection of verse plays for use in secondary schools.

SIDELIGHTS: Cannam went to Spain as a tutor to small boy, lived in Jersey (Channel Islands) for a few years, traveled on a cargo boat around West Africa, and hitchhiked in France. *Avocational interests:* Sketching, photography, riding, swimming, reading, and sun bathing (out of England).†

*   *   *

CANNING, Victor 1911-
(Alan Gould)

PERSONAL: Born June 16, 1911, in Plymouth, Denvonshire, England. *Home:* Riverside House, Alswear, South Molten, Devon, England. *Agent:* John Cushman Associates, 25 West 43rd St., New York, N.Y. and Curtis Brown Ltd., 1 Craven Hill, London W2 3EW, England.

CAREER: Author. *Military service:* Royal Artillery, 1939-45; became major. *Member:* Flyfisher's Club (London).

WRITINGS: Polycarp's Progress, Hodder & Stoughton, 1935; *Mr. Finchley's Holiday*, Reynal & Hitchock, 1935 (published in England under title *Mr. Finchley Discovers His England*, Hodder & Stoughton, 1941); *Everyman's England*, Hodder & Stoughton, 1936; *Fly Away*, Reynal & Hitchcock, 1936; *Matthew Silverman*, Hodder & Stoughton, 1937; *Mr. Finchely Goes to Paris*, Carrick & Evans, 1938; *Fountain Inn*, Hodder & Stoughton, 1939.

Mr. Finchley Takes the Road, Hodder & Stoughton, 1940; *Green Battlefield*, Hodder & Stoughton, 1944; *The Chasm*, M. S. Mill, 1947; *Panther's Moon*, M. S. Mill, 1948, abridged edition edited by John Webber, Chatto & Windus, 1964; *The Golden Salamander*, Morrow, 1949.

Bird of Prey, Morrow, 1950 (published in England under title *Venetian Bird*, Hodder & Stoughton, 1951); *A Forest of Eyes*, M. S. Mill, 1950; *The House of the Seven Flies*, Morrow, 1952; *The Man from the "Turkish Slave,"* Sloane, 1954; *A Handful of Silver*, Sloane, 1954 (also published as *Castle Minerva*, Sloane); *Twist of the Knife*, Sloane, 1955 (published in England under title *His Bones are Coral*, Hodder & Stoughton, 1955); *Burden of Proof*, Sloane, 1956 (published in England under title *Hidden Face*, Hodder & Stoughton, 1956); *The Manasco Road*, Sloane, 1957, published as *The Forbidden Road*, Permabooks, 1959; *The Dragon Tree*, Sloane, 1958; *Oasis Nine* (four short novels), Sloane, 1958 (published in England under title *Young Man on a Bicycle, and Other Stories*, Hodder & Stoughton, 1958).

The Burning Eye, Sloane, 1960; *A Delivery of Furies*, Sloane, 1961; *Black Flamingo*, Hodder & Stoughton, 1962, Sloane, 1963; *The Limbo Line*, Heinemann, 1963, Sloane, 1964; *The Scorpio Letters*, Sloane, 1964; *The Whip Hand*,

Morrow, 1965; *Doubled in Diamonds*, Heinemann, 1966, Morrow, 1967; *The Python Project*, Heinemann, 1967, Morrow, 1968; *The Melting Man*, Heinemann, 1968, Morrow, 1969; *Queen's Pawn*, Heinemann, 1969, Morrow, 1970.

The Great Affair (Collectors Editions Club selection), Heinemann, 1970, Morrow, 1971; *Firecrest*, Heinemann, 1971, Morrow, 1972; *The Runaways*, Heinemann, 1971, Morrow, 1972; *The Rainbird Pattern*, Heinemann, 1972, Morrow, 1973; *Flight of the Grey Goose*, Heinemann, 1972, Morrow, 1973; *The Finger of Saturn*, Heinemann, 1973, Morrow, 1974; *The Painted Tent*, Heinemann, 1973, Morrow, 1974; *The Mask of Memory*, Heinemann, 1974, Morrow, 1975.

Under pseudonym Alan Gould; all published by Hodder & Stoughton: *Two Men Fought*, 1936; *Mercy Lane*, 1936; *Sanctuary From the Dragon*, 1938; *Every Creature of God is Good*, 1939; *The Viaduct*, 1940; *Atlantic Company*, 1941.

Author of television and film scripts and short stories.

SIDELIGHTS: Canning speaks French and Italian. *Avocational interests:* Golf, travel, and fly fishing.

* * *

CANNON, Mark W(ilcox) 1928-

PERSONAL: Born August 29, 1928, in Salt Lake City, Utah; son of Joseph Jenne (an editor and church leader) and Ramona (Wilcox) Cannon; married Ruth Marian Dixon, December 28, 1956; children: Lucile, Mark, Kristen. *Education:* University of Utah, B.A., 1949; Harvard University, M.A., 1954, M.P.A., 1955, Ph.D., 1961. *Religion:* Church of Jesus Christ of Latter-Day Saints. *Home:* 8404 Martingale Dr., McLean, Va. 22101. *Office:* U.S. Supreme Court, 1 First St., N.E., Washington, D.C. 20543.

CAREER: Former Mormon missionary in Argentina; Brigham Young University, Provo, Utah, instructor, 1955; administrative assistant to Congressman Henry Aldous Dixon, Washington, D.C., 1955-60; Brigham Young University, associate professor of political science and chairman of department, 1961-64; Institute of Public Administration, N.Y., director of urban development project in Venezuela, 1964-65, director of international programs, 1965-68, director of institute, 1968-72, member of board of trustees, 1972—; administrative assistant to the Chief Justice of the U.S. Supreme Court, 1972—. Field representative for Senator Wallace F. Bennett, 1961-63; consultant, Foreign Area Fellowship Program (sponsored jointly by Social Science Research Council and American Council of Learned Societies), 1970-72; member of Inter-American Advisory Council, U.S. State Department, 1972-74. *Member:* National Academy of Public Administration, American Bar Association (Judicial Associates Program), American Political Science Association, American Society for Public Administration, International Studies Association (secretary, 1962-63), Western Political Science Association. *Awards, honors:* Western Political Science Association prize for outstanding work of scholarship on western government.

WRITINGS: (With R. Joseph Monsen) *The Makers of Public Policy: American Power Groups and Their Ideologies*, McGraw, 1965; (with Carlos Moran) *The Challenge of Urban Development in Valencia [Venezuela]: Administrative Aspects of Rapid Growth*, Foundation for Community Development and Municipal Improvement (Caracas),

1966; (with Lyle C. Fitch, Carwin Williams, and others) *Partnership for Progress: Atlanta-Fulton County Consolidation*, Institute of Public Administration, 1969; (with R. Scott Fosler and Robert Witherspoon) *Urban Government for Valencia*, Praeger, 1973; (contributor) Clarence E. Thurber and Lawrence S. Graham, editors, *Development Administration in Latin America*, Duke University Press, 1973. Contributor of articles to professional journals, including *Criminology, Judicature*, and *Public Administration Review*.

SIDELIGHTS: Cannon is fluent in Spanish. He lived in England three years, in Argentina two and one-half years, in Venezuela eighteen months, and in Mexico.

* * *

CAPLAN, Ralph 1925-

PERSONAL: Born January 4, 1925, in Sewickley, Pa.; son of Louis and Ruth (Hersch) Caplan; married Deborah Frank (a physical therapist), September 9, 1956; children: Aaron. *Education:* Attended Kiski Preparatory School; Earlham College, B.A., 1949; Indiana University, M.A., 1950.

CAREER: Wabash College, Crawfordsville, Ind., assistant professor of English, 1951-55; *Industrial Design* Magazine, New York, N.Y., editor, 1958-62. Project consultant to Commission on College Physics, International Business Machines, Columbia Broadcasting System, Taconic Foundation, Gotham Lighting, Burlington Industries, Chermayeff & Geismar, and State University of New York (Stony Brook). *Military service:* U.S. Marine Corps, 1942-46; became corporal.

WRITINGS: Say Yes!, Doubleday, 1965; (editor) *Design in America: Selected Work*, McGraw, 1969. Wrote monthly column, "Cross Section" in *Industrial Design*, 1962, weekly column, "Cross Fire" in *Quote*, 1963. Contributor to *Nation, New Yorker, Design* (England), *Consumer Reports, Canadian Art*, and other publications.

WORK IN PROGRESS: A novel, *The Path Through the Office*.

SIDELIGHTS: Caplan writes: "For one year of the second World War I toured the South Pacific as a comedian with a special services show. During my sophomore year in college I lived in a funeral home, answering phones and washing hearses in exchange for a room. At present I write in a gynecologist's office on the ground floor of the apartment building I live in. Is *this* what you mean by 'sidelights'?"†

* * *

CARDWELL, Guy A(dams) 1905-

PERSONAL: Born November 14, 1905, in Savannah, Ga.; son of Guy Adams and Ethel (Parmele) Cardwell; married Margaret Bullitt, December 21, 1935; children: Evelyn Bullitt, Margaret Randolph, Ethel Parmele (deceased), Lucy Adams. *Education:* University of North Carolina, A.B., 1926, Ph.D., 1936; Harvard University, A.M., 1932. *Politics:* Democrat. *Religion:* Episcopalian. *Address:* Box 163, Moose, Wyo. 83012; and 984 Memorial Dr., Cambridge, Mass. 02138.

CAREER: Wake Forest College, Wake Forest, N.C., 1936-38, began as instructor in English, became assistant professor; Tulane University of Louisiana, New Orleans, 1938-45, began as assistant professor, became professor of English, 1943-45; University of Maryland, College Park, professor of English and head of department, 1945-49; Washington University, St. Louis, Mo., professor of English 1949-68, professor emeritus, 1968—, head of department, 1949-56, 1959-63; State University of New York, Albany, professor of English, 1968-71. Fulbright professor, University of Vienna, 1951-52; visiting professor, University of Buenos Aires, 1957; Fulbright-Smith-Mundt professor, National University of Mexico, 1960-61. *Member:* Modern Language Association of America, Phi Beta Kappa. *Awards, honors:* General Education Board fellowship, 1934-35; American Council of Learned Societies faculty study fellowship, 1951; research fellow, Henry E. Huntington Library, 1954-55; $1,000 *American Literary Anthology* award, 1970; second prize, O. Henry award, 1971.

WRITINGS: (Editor) *The Uncollected Poems of Henry Timrod*, University of Georgia Press, 1942; (editor) *Readings from the Americas*, Ronald, 1947; *Der amerikanische Roman, 1850-1951*, translated by Josef Novotny, U.S. Information Service, 1953; *Twins of Genius*, Michigan State College Press, 1953; (editor and author of introduction) *Discussions of Mark Twain*, Heath, 1963; (author of introduction) Mark Twain, *Life on the Mississippi*, Dodd, 1968.

Short stories anthologized in *American Literary Anthology, Volume III*, edited by George Plimpton and Peter Ardery, Viking, 1970; and *Prize Stories 1971: The O. Henry Awards*, edited by William Abrahams, Doubleday, 1971. Contributor of essays, poems, and short stories to periodicals, including *Poetry, Saturday Review of Literature, Virginia Quarterly Review*; contributor of articles to professional journals.

WORK IN PROGRESS: Research on Mark Twain, George W. Cable, and topics in the literature of the Old South.

* * *

CAREW, John Mohun 1921-
(Tim Carew)

PERSONAL: Surname is pronounced Car-oo; born July 8, 1921, in Bury St. Edmunds, England; son of Peter Fitzwilliam (a soldier) and Joyce (Fortescue) Carew; married Barbara Shakespear, December 1, 1950; children: Nicholas John Stewart. *Education:* Marlborough College, student, 1934-38. *Religion:* Church of England. *Home:* Forge Cottage, Binfield, Berkshire, England. *Agent:* James Kinross, Sheill Associates Ltd., 6 Grafton St., London W. 1, England.

CAREER: Soldier, 1939-49, serving with Gurkha Rifles in India, Burma, Malaya, and Indonesia, and with Devon Regiment in Hong Kong and Malaya; awarded Military Cross and Burma Star. Feature writer in London, England, for *Sunday Express*, for *Soldier* (magazine), and for *Reville* (newspaper). *Member:* Press Club (London).

WRITINGS—All under name Tim Carew: *All This and a Medal Too*, Constable, 1954; *Evens the Field*, Constable, 1955; *Man for Man*, Constable, 1955; *Married Quarters*, Constable, 1956; *The Last Warrior*, Constable, 1958; *The Fall of Hong Kong*, Blond, 1960; *The Vanished Army*, William Kimber & Co., 1964; *Korea: The Commonwealth at War*, Cassell, 1967, published as *The Korean War: The Story of the Fighting Commonwealth Regiments*, Pan Books, 1970; *The Royal Norfolk Regiment: The Ninth Regiment of Foot*, Hamish Hamilton, 1967; *The Longest Retreat: The Burma Campaign, 1942*, Hamish Hamilton, 1969; *The Glorius Glosters*, Leo Cooper, 1970; *Hostages*

to Fortune, Hamish Hamilton, 1971. Author of screenplay, "Laughing in the Sunshine," 1954. Contributor to *Evening Standard, Evening News, Daily Mail, English Digest, Men Only, British Army Journal, Wide World*, and other periodicals.

SIDELIGHTS: Speaks French, Italian, Hindustani, Gurkhali.†

* * *

CAREY, James Charles 1915-

PERSONAL: Born April 1, 1915, in Bancroft, Neb.; son of Floyd L. (a farmer) and Leona (Graff) Carey; married Wenonah Moline, November 27, 1937; children: Steven, Wenonah, James. *Education:* Nebraska State Teachers College (now Wayne State College), B.A., 1937; University of Colorado, M.A., 1940, Ph.D., 1948; Universidad de San Marcos, Certificate, 1942. *Home:* 332 North 15th St., Manhattan, Kan. 66504. *Office:* History Department, Kansas State University, Manhattan, Kan. 66504.

CAREER: Colegio America del Callao, Callao, Peru, director, 1941-45; University of Colorado, Boulder, instructor in Latin American history, 1947-48; Kansas State University, Manhattan, associate professor, 1948-54, professor of history, 1954—. Member of the City Council, Callao, Peru, 1945. *Member:* American Association of University Professors (member of national council, 1953-56), American Historical Association, Phi Alpha Theta (member of national council, 1960-63), Kappa Delta Pi, Phi Kappa Phi.

WRITINGS: (Contributor) *Kansas: The First Century*, Lewis Historical Publishing, 1956; *Peru and the United States, 1900-1962*, University of Notre Dame Press, 1964; (contributor) Joseph Dunner, editor, *Handbook of World History*, Philosophical Library, 1967; (contributor) Robin Higham, editor, *Civil Wars in the Twentieth Century*, University Press of Kentucky, 1972. Contributor to historical journals.

WORK IN PROGRESS: Dan D. Casement, Last Viking of the Plains; The Revolution Comes to Yucatan, 1915-1924.

* * *

CAREY, Mother Marie Aimee 1931-

PERSONAL: Secular name, Dorothy Ann Carey; born February 20, 1931, in New York, N.Y.; daughter of Edward Vincent (a manufacturing executive) and Dorothy (Makahon) Carey. *Education:* College of New Rochelle, B.A., 1954; Catholic University of America, M.A., 1963. *Politics:* Independent. *Home and office:* Ursuline School, 1338 North Ave., New Rochelle, N.Y. 10804.

CAREER: Roman Catholic nun, entering order of Ursulines of the Roman Union, Beacon, N.Y., 1949; teacher at Catholic schools in New Rochelle, N.Y., 1953-54, Bethesda, Md., 1955-63; Ursuline School, New Rochelle, N.Y., teacher, 1964—. Also teacher of music and piano; organist. *Member:* National Catholic Education Association. *Awards, honors:* National winner of Scott, Foresman & Co. Primary Activities Contest for project to develop reading ability and research skills in young children, 1960.

WRITINGS: A Bibliography for Christian Formation in the Family, Paulist Press, 1964. Contributor of articles to *America, Catholic Layman, Catholic School Journal, Marriage*, and reviews to *Sponsa Regis* (now *Sisters Today*).

WORK IN PROGRESS: Ten playlets based on the liturgical year, for Abbey Press; series of articles on family religious customs, with possible compilation in book form.

SIDELIGHTS: Mother Carey is competent in French and Latin. She has traveled in the United States, Canada, Europe, and North Africa. Avocational interests: Psychology, philosophy, civil rights, art, books.†

* * *

CARGAS, Harry J. 1932-

PERSONAL: Born June 18, 1932, in Hamtramck, Michigan; son of James H. (a businessman) and Sophia (Kozlowski) Cargas; married Millie Rieder, August 24, 1957; children: Martin de Porres, Joachim James, Siena Catherine, Manon Theresa, Jacinta Teilhard, Sarita Jo. Education: Attended Aquinas College, 1955-56; University of Michigan, B.A., 1957, M.A., 1958; St. Louis University, Ph.D., 1968. Religion: Roman Catholic. Home: 127 Park Ave., Kirkwood, Mo. 63122

CAREER: St. David's School, New York, N.Y., English teacher and athletic director, 1958-61; Catholic Book Reporter, New York, N.Y., editor-in-chief, 1960-61; Montclair Academy, Montclair, N.J., instructor in English and athletic coach, 1962-63; Queen's Work, St. Louis, Mo., editor-in-chief, 1963-64; St. Louis University, St. Louis, Mo., instructor in English, 1963-69; Webster College, St. Louis, Mo., chairman of department of English, 1969—. Consulting editor to Catechetical Guild, National Council of Catholic Men, and National Catholic High School Reading Program. Staff editor, Simon & Schuster; free lance editor, Herder & Herder. Moderator and occasional producer of the television program, The Church Is You.

WRITINGS: I Lay Down My Life: Biography of Joyce Kilmer, Daughters of St. Paul, 1964; (editor) Graham Green, B. Herder, 1968; (editor with Thomas P. Neill) Renewing the Face of the Earth: Essays in Contemporary Church-World Relationships, Bruce, 1968; (editor) The Continuous Flame: Teilhard in the Great Traditions, B. Herder, 1969; (editor) Religious and Cultural Factors in Latin America, St. Louis University, 1970; (editor with Ed Erazmus) English As A Second Language: A Reader, W. C. Brown, 1970; (editor with Ann White) Death and Hope, Corpus Books, 1970; Daniel Berrigan and Contemporary Protest Poetry, College & University Press, 1972. General editor, Christian Critic Series, B. Herder. Contributor of articles and more than 500 book reviews to Jubilee, America, New York Times, Catholic World, Ave Maria and other publications; book columns in Way, Friar, Catholic Book Reporter and Catholic Library World.

WORK IN PROGRESS: Research on fatherhood in America; work on Thomas Merton.

* * *

CARLISLE, Henry (Coffin) 1926-

PERSONAL: Born September 14, 1926, in San Francisco, Calif.; son of Henry (a mining engineer) and Mary (Gorgas) Carlisle; married Olga Andreyev (an artist and writer), December 22, 1951; children: Michael Vadim. Education: Stanford University, B.A., 1950, M.A., 1953; University of Paris, student, 1948-49. Politics: Democrat. Home: South St., Washington, Conn. Agent: Phyllis Jackson, International Famous Agency, 1301 Avenue of the Americas, New York, N.Y. 10019.

CAREER: Alfred A. Knopf, Inc., New York, N.Y., trade editor, 1954-57; Rinehart & Co., New York, N.Y., trade editor, 1957-60; Purdy, Carlisle & Dodds, New York, N.Y., editor and publisher, 1960-61. Free-lance writer. Military service: U.S. Naval Reserve, 1944-46. Member: P.E.N. (freedom to write committee, vice-president, 1973—), University Club and The Century (both New York).

WRITINGS: (Editor) American Satire in Prose and Verse, Random House, 1962; Ilyitch Slept Here, Lippincott, 1965; The Contract, Bobbs-Merrill, 1968; (translator with wife, Olga Carlisle) Fyodor Dostoyevsky, The Idiot, New American Library, 1969; Voyage to the First of December, Putnam, 1972. Contributor of reviews to American Scholar and other periodicals.

WORK IN PROGRESS: Kind Men of This Land, a novel for Putnam.

SIDELIGHTS: "The Contract is expertly written as Carlisle has obvious style and wit," wrote David F. Sharp. Allen J. Hubin called the book, "a spicy creampuff from the Murder-Can-Be-Fun shelf in which the sublime confidence of octogenaria muzzles the frenetic machinations of youth."

* * *

CARLISLE, Olga Andreyev 1930-

PERSONAL: Born January 22, 1930; daughter of Vadim (a writer) and Olga (a painter; maiden name, Tchernoff) Andreyev; married Henry Carlisle (a writer), 1951; children: Michael Vadim. Education: Studied at Bard College, 1949-50, Sorbonne, University of Paris, 1951-52, Hunter College, 1956-57. Home: South St., Washington, Conn.

CAREER: Artist with shows in Paris, 1965, 1967, and San Francisco, 1974; writer.

WRITINGS: Voices in the Snow, Random House, 1963; (editor) Poets on Street Corners: Portraits of Fifteen Russian Poets, Random House, 1968; (translator with husband, Henry Carlisle) Fyodor Dostoyevsky, The Idiot, New American Library, 1969; (editor and translator with Rose Styron) Modern Russian Poetry, Viking, 1972. Contributor to Paris Review and Vogue.

WORK IN PROGRESS: Autobiographical work on childhood in Russian family in France under occupation, for Houghton.

SIDELIGHTS: Raymond A. Sokolov wrote of Poets on Street Corners: "Russian poets since the turn of the century have not been the darlings of a literary coterie but widely influential heroes involved in the 'flow of everyday life as it is symbolized by the street,' as Olga Carlisle puts it in her enormously useful anthology of modern Russian poetry.... During several trips to the Soviet Union, she has talked with writers, many of whom knew her father [the Russian poet, Vadim Andreyev]. In Voices in the Snow, she wrote affectingly about these rare encounters. And now, the same insider's approach ... is applied to the remarkable poets and poetry Russia has produced over the last 75 years."

* * *

CARLON, Patricia Bernardette

PERSONAL: Born in Wagga Wagga, New South Wales, Australia; daughter of Bernard and Beatrice (Broad) Carlon. Education: Attended schools in New South Wales, Australia.

CAREER: Writer of crime novels. *Awards, honors:* Commonwealth Literary fellowships, 1970, 1973.

WRITINGS—All published by Hodder & Stoughton, except as indicated: *Circle of Fear*, Ward, Lock, 1961; *Danger in the Dark*, Ward, Lock, 1962; *Who Are You, Linda Condrick?*, Ward, Lock, 1962; *Price of an Orphan*, 1964; *Crime of Silence*, 1965; *The Unquiet Night*, 1965; *The Running Woman*, 1966; *Betray Me If You Dare*, 1966; *See Nothing, Say Nothing*, 1967; *Hush, It's a Game*, 1967; *40 Pieces of Alloy*, 1968; *The Whispering Wall*, 1969; *The Souvenir*, 1970; *Death By Demonstration*, 1971.

* * *

CARLQUIST, Sherwin 1930-

PERSONAL: Born July 7, 1930, in Los Angeles, Calif.; son of Robert William Carlquist and Helen Carlquist Bauer (a writer). *Education:* University of California, Berkeley, B.A., 1952, Ph.D., 1955; Harvard University, postdoctoral study, 1955-56. *Home:* 4041 Olive Hill Dr., Claremont, Calif. 91711. *Office:* Rancho Santa Ana Botanic Garden, 1500 North College Ave., Claremont, Calif. 91711.

CAREER: Claremont Graduate School and University Center, Claremont, Calif., 1956—, now associate professor of botany. Consultant, California Research Corp. (subsidiary of Standard Oil Co.). Field work in Hawaiian Islands, 1953, 1958, 1960, 1964, in South Pacific and Southeast Asia, 1962-63, in African offshore islands, Australia, and South Pacific, 1967-68, and in South Africa, 1973. *Member:* Phi Beta Kappa, Sigma Xi.

WRITINGS: Comparative Plant Anatomy, Holt, 1961; (with mother, Helen Bauer) *Japanese Festivals*, Doubleday, 1965; *Island Life*, Doubleday, 1965; *Hawaii: A Natural History*, Doubleday, 1970; *Island Biology*, Columbia University Press, 1974; *Ecological Strategies of Xylem Evolution*, University of California Press, 1974. Contributor of some fifty-eight papers dealing chiefly with wood anatomy, pollen morphology, and the anatomy of island plants to journals, including *Brittonia, Pacific Science, American Journal of Botany, Tropical Woods, Madrono,* and *Aliso.*

WORK IN PROGRESS: Continuing research and papers on anatomy of plants of Hawaii and other Pacific islands, and on relationships between anatomy, taxonomy, and ecology.

SIDELIGHTS: Carlquist speaks and reads French and German; he speaks "passable" Japanese. *Avocational interests:* Japanese Noh plays, twentieth-century classical music.

* * *

CARMAN, William Y(oung) 1909-

PERSONAL: Born May 21, 1909, in Ottawa, Ontario, Canada; son of Frederick William (a civil servant) and K. Simms (Steed) Carman; married Consuelo Phyllis Romer; children: William John, Elizabeth Mary. *Education:* Richmond Art School, Surrey, England. *Religion:* Church of England. *Home:* 94 Mulgrave Rd., Sutton, Surrey, England.

CAREER: Free-lance research artist specializing in uniform of the British Army prior to 1950; Imperial War Museum, London, England, 1950-65, became keeper of department of exhibits; National Army Museum, Camberley and Chelsea, London, deputy director, 1965-74. Consultant on uniform to museums (including United States), and film companies. *Military service:* British Army, 1940-45. *Member:* Society of Antiquaries of London (fellow), Royal Historical Society (fellow), Society for Army Historical Research (council), Military Historical Society, British Model Soldier Society (former president).

WRITINGS: Uniform of the Navy, Past and Present, Forster, Groom, 1942; *Military History of Egypt*, R. Chindler, 1945; *A History of Firearms from Earliest Times to 1914*, Routledge & Kegan Paul, 1955; *British Military Uniforms from Contemporary Pictures*, Leonard Hill, 1957; *Indian Army Uniform (Cavalry)*, Leonard Hill, 1961; *British Military Uniforms*, Longacre Press, 1962; (editor) *Louis Napoleon on Artillery*, Shumway, 1967; *Head Dresses of the British Army: Cavalry*, Sutton, 1968; *Indian Army Uniforms: Infantry*, Morgan-Grampian, 1969; *Model Soldiers*, World Publishing, 1972; *Royal Artillery*, Osprey, 1973; *Glengarry Badges: Pre-1881*, Arms & Armorer Press, 1973; (co-author) *Badges and Insignia of the British Armed Services*, A. & C. Black, 1974. Contributor to *Encyclopaedia Britannica, World Book Encyclopedia, Oxford Junior Encyclopedia*, and to journals.

WORK IN PROGRESS: Research for further works on uniform and allied subjects.

AVOCATIONAL INTERESTS: Collector of books, prints, and uniforms.

* * *

CARNALL, Geoffrey 1927-

PERSONAL: Born February 1, 1927, in London, England; son of William Ewart (a clerk and publican) and Dorothea Kathleen (Smith) Carnall; married Elisabeth Murray, August 30, 1962; children: one son, two daughters. *Education:* Magdalen College, Oxford, B.A., 1948, M.A., 1952, B. Litt., 1953. *Politics:* Labour Party. *Religion:* Society of Friends. *Office:* Department of English Literature, University of Edinburgh, Edinburgh, Scotland.

CAREER: Baring Union Christian College, Batala, East Punjab, India, temporary lecturer in English, 1949; The Queen's University of Belfast, Belfast, Northern Ireland, lecturer in English, 1952-60; University of Edinburgh, Edinburgh, Scotland, lecturer in English literature, 1960-65, senior lecturer, 1965-69, reader, 1969—. Member of board of trustees, *Peace News*, London, England; Edinburgh Council for Nuclear Disarmament, vice-chairman, 1962-65, chairman, 1965-71; convener, Southeast Scotland Friends' Peace Committee, 1970—.

WRITINGS: Robert Southey and His Age: The Development of a Conservative Mind, Oxford University Press, 1960; *Robert Southey*, London House, 1964; *To Keep the Peace: The United Nations Peace Force*, Peace News, 1965. Occasional contributor of articles and reviews to *Victorian Studies, Modern Language Review, Essays in Criticism*, and other journals in field.

WORK IN PROGRESS: Completing the *Oxford History of English Literature*, Volume VIII, *The Mid-Eighteenth Century*, by John Butt.

SIDELIGHTS: Carnall finds Southey particularly illuminating for the study of the fear of social change (Carnall's specialized interest) because the development of his reactions to the events of the time is so fully documented.

* * *

CARPENTER, Peter 1922-

PERSONAL: Born March 8, 1922, in Germany; married

Dagmar Peetz (a marriage guidance counselor), August 4, 1949; children: David, Andrew, Anne. *Education:* St. Edmund Hall, Oxford, M.A., 1948, B.Litt., 1958. *Home:* 289 Hills Rd., Cambridge, England. *Office:* Institute of Education, Shaftesbury Rd., Cambridge, England.

CAREER: Outward Bound Sea School, Aberdovey, Wales, instructor, 1943-46; Thornbury Grammar School, Bristol, England, senior history master, 1948-53; Oxford University, department of education, Oxford, England, assistant tutor, 1953-56; Cambridge Institute of Education, Cambridge, England, secretary for courses and conferences, 1956—. Duke of Edinburgh's Award, honorary liaison officer, 1958—. Director of Studies in Education, Churchill College, Cambridge, 1970—. *Member:* Historical Association, Achilles Club.

WRITINGS: History for Fun, Hutchinson, 1954; *Geography for Fun*, Hutchinson, 1955; *Sport for Fun*, Hutchinson, 1959; (contributor) *A New Look at Adventure*, Educational Productions, 1960; *History Teaching: The Era Approach*, Cambridge University Press, 1964; (editor) *Challenge: The Duke of Edinburgh's Award in Action*, Ward, Lock, 1966; (contributor) *Bildung Als Wagnis Und Bewaehrung*, Quelle & Meyer, 1966; (contributor) *Kurt Hahn: A Life Span in Education and Politics*, Routledge & Kegan Paul, 1970. History adviser, "Picture Background Books," Ward, Lock, 1965-1967. Editor, *Cambridge Institute of Education Bulletin*, 1956-1970.

AVOCATIONAL INTERESTS: Music, sports.

*   *   *

CARPENTER, Richard C(oles) 1916-

PERSONAL: Born August 30, 1916, in Melrose, Mass.; son of Garfield (a police officer) and Grace (Thompson) Carpenter; married Ethel Agnew, June 3, 1945; children: Peter John, Andrew David. *Education:* Tufts University, B.A. (cum laude), 1938; Boston University, M.A., 1939, Ph.D., 1951. *Home:* 205 Ridge St., Bowling Green, Ohio 43402.

CAREER: Boston University, Boston, Mass., instructor in English, 1946-53; Bowling Green State University, Bowling Green, Ohio, assistant professor, 1953-59, associate professor, 1959-62, professor of English, 1962—. *Military service:* U.S. Army, 1942-46; became technical sergeant. *Member:* Modern Language Association of America, American Association of University Professors (chapter president, 1961-62).

WRITINGS: Thomas Hardy, Twayne, 1965; (contributor) Helmut E. Gerber and W. Eugene Davis, editors, *Thomas Hardy: An Annotated Secondary Bibliography of Writings About Him*, Northern Illinois University Press, 1972. Contributor of articles on fiction to *Critique, Nineteenth-Century Fiction, Modern Fiction Studies, James Joyce Review*, and other reviews.

WORK IN PROGRESS: Research on money-theme in the Victorian novel; book on I. A. Richards for Twayne, expected completion date, 1976; articles on Conrad and Hardy; a biography of Denmark Vesey and Jehudi Ashmun.

AVOCATIONAL INTERESTS: Reading in philosophy, anthropology, and mythology; sports, particularly tennis.

*   *   *

CARPOZI, George, Jr. 1920-

PERSONAL: Born November 25, 1920, in New York, N.Y.; son of George John (a restaurateur) and Julie (Camber) Carpozi; married Chrysanthe Haranis, June 26, 1949; children: Julie, Elaine, George III, Harriette, Chrysanthe. *Education:* Studied at New York University, 1940-43, 1946-47, Dartmouth College, 1943. *Home:* 710 Regent Dr., Westbury, N.Y. *Agent:* The Foley Agency, 34 East 38th St., New York, N.Y. 10016.

CAREER: New York Times, New York, N.Y., sports copy boy, 1946-47; Standard News Association, New York, N.Y., 1948-53, became assistant city editor; *Bronx Press Review*, Bronx, N.Y., assistant editor, 1949-53; *New York Journal-American*, New York, N.Y., 1953—, now chief assistant city editor. *Military service:* U.S. Marine Corps, 1943-46; served in Pacific; became staff sergeant. *Member:* New York City Newspaper Reporters Association. *Awards, honors:* New York City Newspaper Reporters Association Gold Typewriter Award for helping in the capture of city's "Mad Bomber"; Hearst Newspapers awards for writing achievement; New York City Uniformed Firemen's Association award for excellence in reporting; National Police Officers Association public service award.

WRITINGS: The Brigitte Bardot Story, Belmont Books, 1961; *Clark Gable*, Pyramid Books, 1961; *Let's Twist*, Pyramid Books, 1962; *Vince Edwards*, Belmont Books, 1962; (with Pierre J. Huss) *Red Spies in the UN*, Coward, 1965; *The Hidden Side of Jacqueline Kennedy*, Pyramid Books, 1967; *Red Spies in Washington*, Trident, 1968; *Three Mothers: Their Life Stories*, Macfadden, 1968; *The Gary Cooper Story*, Arlington House, 1970; *The Johnny Cash Story*, Pyramid Publications, 1970; *The John Wayne Story*, Arlington House, 1972; *Ordeal by Trial: The Alice Crimmins Case*, Walker & Co., 1972; (with Anne-Marie Stein) *Three Picassos Before Breakfast: The Story of an Art Forgers Wife*, Hawthorne Books, 1973. Contributor of some 250 stories to magazines, writing regularly for *Photoplay, TV-Radio Mirror, True Detective, Master Detective, Saga*, and *Pageant*, and occasionally for *Modern Screen, Startling Detective, Impact*, and others.

SIDELIGHTS: Carpozi averages roughly sixty stories a year for magazines; has written a number of exposes on insurance rackets, phony clinics, and police shakedowns for the *Journal-American*, and covered the burning of the carrier "Bennington," the sinking of the "Andrea Doria," and the Harlem riots of the summer of 1964. Besides helping in the capture of New York's "Mad Bomber," he uncloaked the British spy, Jack Kroger, as a former Bronx resident (real name, Morris "Unc" Cohen).

He was a long-distance runner for New York University and Dartmouth, ran on the NYU two-mile relay team that won the national championship in Madison Square Garden, 1943. *Avocational interests:* Work on own home (laid seven thousand bricks for a patio), gardening, astronomy, photography.

BIOGRAPHICAL/CRITICAL SOURCES: Editor and Publisher, June 18, 1960.†

*   *   *

CARR, Archie F(airly, Jr.) 1909-

PERSONAL: Born June 16, 1909, in Mobile, Ala.; son of Archibald Fairly (a minister) and Louise (Deaderick) Carr; married Marjorie Harris, January 1, 1937; children: Marjorie, Archie F. III, Stephen, Thomas, David. *Education:* University of Florida, B.S., 1933, M.S., 1934, Ph.D., 1937. *Office:* Department of Zoology, University of Florida, Gainesville, Fla.

CAREER: University of Florida, Gainesville, instructor, 1938-40, assistant professor, 1940-44, associate professor, 1945-49, professor of biological sciences, 1949—, graduate research professor of biology, 1959—. Harvard University, summer fellow, Museum of Comparative Zoology, 1937-43; Escuela Agricola Panamericana, Honduras, professor of biology, 1945-49; United Fruit Co., biologist, 1949; American Museum of Natural History, research associate, 1949—; Florida State Museum, associate, 1953—; Caribbean Conservation Corps., technical director, 1961. Principal investigator, National Science Foundation marine turtle migration project, 1955—; chairman of sea turtle survival service commission, International Union for Conservation of Nature. Member of three University of Florida-Harvard University expeditions to Mexico, 1939-41, and of other expeditions to Honduras, 1944, Mexico, 1951, Jamaica, 1951, Panama, Costa Rica, and Trinidad, 1953, Central America, 1955, Brazil, French West Africa, Portugal, and the Azores, 1956, South Africa, Argentina, and Chile, 1958.

MEMBER: American Society of Ichthyologists and Herpetologists, American Society of Naturalists, Smithsonian Associates (council member), Florida Academy of Science, Phi Beta Kappa, Sigma Xi. Awards, honors: Daniel Giraud Elliott Medal of National Academy of Sciences; O. Henry Memorial Award for short story, 1956; John Burroughs Medal of American Museum of Natural History for nature writing, 1957, for Windward Road; first annual research award, American Society of Naturalists; first annual Honors Medal, Florida Academy of Science, 1963; honorary consultant to World Wildlife Fund; World Wildlife Fund Gold Medal, 1973.

WRITINGS: Handbook of Turtles, Comstock Publishing Associates, 1952; High Jungles and Low, University of Florida Press, 1953; (with Coleman Goin) Guide to the Reptiles, Amphibians and Freshwater Fishes of Florida, University of Florida Press, 1955; The Windward Road, Knopf, 1956; Reptiles, Life Nature Library, 1963; Ulendo, Knopf, 1964; Land and Wildlife of Africa, Life Nature Library, 1964; So Excellent a Fishe: A Natural History of Sea Turtles, Natural History Press, 1967; The Everglades (American Wilderness Series), Time-Life, 1973. Writer of more than one hundred articles and papers on natural history subjects.

WORK IN PROGRESS: A book on Florida and research in the ecology and migrations of marine turtles.

*   *   *

CARR, Donald Eaton   1903-

PERSONAL: Born October 17, 1903, in Los Angeles, Calif.; son of Harry (a journalist) and Alice (Eaton) Carr; married Mildred Clarke, February 10, 1934; children: Michael E. Education: University of California, B.S. (summa cum laude), 1930. Politics: Republican. Religion: Catholic. Home: 1433 Shawnee, Bartlesville, Okla. 74003. Agent: Harold Ober Associates, Inc., 40 East 49th St., New York, N.Y. 10017.

CAREER: Portland Oregonian, reporter, 1922-26; Union Oil Co. of California, research chemist, 1930-38, research supervisor, 1938-40, research manager, 1940-47; Phillips Petroleum Co., Bartlesville, Okla., consultant, 1947, associate director of fuels and lubricants division, research department, 1948-50, deputy director of research, 1950-65; independent research consultant in various fields, 1962—. During World War II served on Petroleum Industry War

Council, Office of Scientific Research and Development, and with Navy (as civilian). Member: American Chemical Society, American Association for the Advancement of Science, Society of Automotive Engineers, American Rocket Society, Authors Guild, Air Force Association, Phi Beta Kappa, Sigma Xi, Elks. Awards, honors: Distinguished Service Award, Army Ordnance Association, 1943; Certificate of Achievement, U.S. Navy, 1945; Achievement Award, Petroleum Industry War Council, 1945; Oklahoma Writers nonfiction award, 1973, for The Forgotten Senses.

WRITINGS: (Contributor) A. M. Bass and H. P. Broida, editors, Formation and Trapping of Free Radicals, Academic Press, 1960; The Breath of Life: The Probelm of Poisoned Air, Norton, 1965; Death of the Sweet Waters, Norton, 1966; The Eternal Return, Doubleday, 1968; The Sexes, Doubleday, 1970; The Deadly Feast of Life, Doubleday, 1971; The Forgotten Senses, Doubleday, 1972. Contributor to Atlantic Monthly, Christian Science Monitor, Medical Economics, Saturday Review, Los Angeles Times, New York Times, and other magazines and newspapers.

WORK IN PROGRESS: In Search of Angels; research on the energy situation.

SIDELIGHTS: Carr speaks Spanish and has a reading knowledge of French and German. He also reads scientific Russian and has translated Russian articles on scientific subjects.

Most of Carr's books have been translated into German, French, Spanish, Italian, and Japanese.

*   *   *

CARR, William H(enry) A(lexander)   1924-

PERSONAL: Born November 25, 1924, in Albany, N.Y.; son of John J. (a printer) and Ruby (Sokol) Carr. Education: Attended Loyola University, Chicago, Ill., and University of Chicago. Home and office: Box E, River Edge, N.J. Agent: Sterling Lord, The Sterling Lord Agency, 75 East 55th St., New York, N.Y. 10022.

CAREER: Newsman for City News Bureau of Chicago, Chicago Sun, Chicago Times, and American Broadcasting Co., all Chicago, Ill., 1942-49; John Price Jones Co. (fund-raising counselors), New York, N.Y., public relations director for campaigns, 1949-52; United Community Defense Services (national federation of social agencies), New York, N.Y., associate director of public relations, 1952-55; New York Post, New York, N.Y., night city editor, 1955-64; now full-time free-lance writer. Breeder of standard schnauzers. Military service: U.S. Army Air Forces, 1943.

MEMBER: Authors League of America, Dog Writers Association of America, Aircraft Owners and Pilots Association, National Pilots Association, National Aeronautic Association, Kennel Club of Northern New Jersey. Awards, honors: Albert Schweitzer Medal and $500 award of Animal Welfare Institute for disclosures leading to more humane treatment of animals, 1961; Friends of American Writers Award ($1,000) for The du Ponts of Delaware, 1965.

WRITINGS: Beauty in the White House, Magnum, 1961; Those Fabulous Kennedy Women, Wisdom House, 1962; What is Jack Paar Really Like?, Lancer, 1962; Hollywood Tragedy, Lancer, 1962; JFK: An Informal Biography, Lancer, 1962, revised edition published as JFK: The Life and Death of a President, 1964; Medical Examiner, Lancer, 1963; *Basic Book of the Cat*, Scribner, 1963; *The du Ponts of Delaware*, Dodd, 1964; *The Emergence of Red China: The Story of the World's Third Great Power*, Lancer, 1967; *Perils, Named and Unnamed: The Story of the Insurance Company of North America*, McGraw, 1967. Monthly columnist, *Dog World*; contributor of articles on flying to other magazines.

WORK IN PROGRESS: Four books.

AVOCATIONAL INTERESTS: Humane activities; flying his Cessna 127 plane.†

* * *

CARRILLO, Lawrence W(ilbert) 1920-

PERSONAL: Born October 10, 1920, in Santa Rosa Calif.; son of Lawrence W. (a farmer) and Alma (McDaniel) Carrillo; married second wife, Elma Boyer Penn (a college professor), December 18, 1962; children: (first marriage) Lawrence, Linda, Robert, Cheri, Denise; (stepchildren) Charles I. Penn, Karen Bryer. *Education:* Santa Rosa Junior College, A.A., 1941; Oregon State College (now University) B.S. and M.S., 1949; Syracuse University, Ed.D., 1957. *Politics:* Democrat. *Office:* San Francisco State University, 1600 Holloway, San Francisco, Calif. 94132.

CAREER: Long Beach (Calif.) public schools, head teacher in reading clinics, 1951-53; Sonoma County Schools, Santa Rosa, Calif., supervisor of reading, 1953-57; San Francisco State University, San Francisco, Calif., professor of education, 1959—. Specialist in Elementary curriculum and materials, Monrovia, Liberia, 1964-66; reading consultant to schools and publishers. *Military service:* U.S. Army Air Forces, 1942-46; became sergeant; received two battle stars for service in Okinawa and Mariana Islands. *Member:* International Reading Association (international committee on publications, 1960-63), California Teachers Association, California State Employees Association, Kappa Delta Pi.

WRITINGS: (With William D. Sheldon) *College Reading Workbook*, Syracuse University Press, 1953; (with Helen F. Campbell) *Reader's Digest Reading Skill Builder*, Grade 6, Part 3, Reader's Digest Services, 1960; *Informal Reading Readiness Experiences*, Chandler Publishing, 1964, revised edition, Noble, 1971; (with Elizabeth N. Zumwalt) *Let's Look* (and teacher's guide), Chandler Publishing, 1964; (with Zumwalt) *Words to Read* (and teacher's guide), Chandler Publishing, 1964; (with Zumwalt) *Pictures to Read* (and teacher's guide), Chandler Publishing, 1964; *Writing Book I*, Liberian Information Service, 1965; (contributor) John Downing, editor, *The Second International Reading Symposium*, Cassell, 1967; (with Donald J. Bissett) *Looking Everywhere*, Noble, 1970; (contributor) Margaret M. Clark and Alastair Milne, editors, *Reading and Related Skills*, Ward, Lock, 1973.

Editor: *Landon Phonics Program Kit*, Chandler Publishing, 1967; *Handbook for Teaching Language Arts*, Intext, 1969; *Language Art: An Ideabook*, Intext, 1970. General editor, with Donald J. Bissett, of the Chandler Reading Program and associated materials, 1964-71, Chandler Publishing and Noble. Also editor of a series of programmed booklets for teaching reading, California Test Bureau, 1963-66.

Also writer of a reading course for Mendocino county (Calif.) schools, 1960, and of materials for administrators and supervisors of extension reading institutes, published by Science Research Associates, 1962-68. Contributor to *Reading in Action in the Sixties: Proceedings of the 1967 Summer Conference*, Western Washington State College, 1968. Also contributor of articles to *Journal of Educational Research, Journal of Educational Psychology, Journal of Reading, National Association of Remedial Teaching News, California Journal of Secondary Education, Elementary School Journal, Elementary English*, and *Instructor*.

* * *

CARROLL, John J(oseph) 1924-

PERSONAL: Born January 16, 1924, in Orange, N.J.; son of Benjamin Aloysius (an engineer) and Agnes (McCloskey) Carroll. *Education:* Woodstock College, S.T.L., 1956; Fordham University, M.A., 1958; Cornell University, Ph.D., 1962. *Home and office:* Ateneo de Manila, P.O. Box 154, Manila, Philippines.

CAREER: Roman Catholic priest of Society of Jesus; Ateneo de Manila, Manila, Philippines, instructor in sociology, 1949-52, assistant professor, 1962-63, associate professor, 1965—. Pontificia Universita Gregoriana, Rome, Italy, visiting professor of sociology, 1964-65. Institute of Social Order, Manila, Philippines, member of staff, 1962-63, 1965—. *Member:* American Sociological Association, Philippine Sociological Society, Philippine Statistical Association.

WRITINGS: (With others) *Provisional Paper on Changing Patterns of Social Structure in the Philippines, 1896-1963*, UNESCO Research Centre (Delhi), 1963 (new edition published in Philippines as *Changing Patterns of Social Structure in the Philippines, 1896-1963*, Ateneo de Manila University Press, 1968); *The Filipino Manufacturing Entrepreneur: Agent and Product of Change*, Cornell University Press, 1965; (with Salvador Parco) *Social Organization in a Crisis Situation: The Taal Disaster, a Research Report Submitted to the Asia Foundation*, Philippine Sociological Society, 1966; *The Philippines: The Church in an Unfinished Society*, Institute of Social Order (Manila), 1969; (with others) *Philippine Institutions*, Solidaridad Publishing House, 1970; (with Keith Ignatius) *Youth Ministry: Sunday, Monday, and Every Day*, Judson, 1972. Writer of research report on changing social patterns in the Philippines for UNESCO, 1963. Contributor to sociological and statistical journals in the Philippines.

WORK IN PROGRESS: Further research on social change in the Philippines, the entrepreneur and business leadership, social organization of business enterprise, industrial relations, and the Philippine labor movement.

SIDELIGHTS: Reads French, Italian, Spanish; speaks Italian.†

* * *

CARSON, John F. 1920-

PERSONAL: Born August 2, 1920, in Indianapolis, Ind.; son of Frederick P. Carson and Mary McKenzie Carson; married Beverly V. Carlisle, February 1, 1942; children: Jacqueline Ann (Mrs. William Phillips, Jr.), John, Bruce. *Education:* Butler University, B.S., 1948; Indiana University, M.S., 1954, Ph.D., 1972. *Politics:* Republican ("not beyond scratching"). *Religion:* Presbyterian. *Agent:* Dorothy Markinko, McIntosh & Otis, Inc., 18 East 41st St., New York, N.Y. 10017.

CAREER: Grassyfork Fisheries, Inc., Martinsville, Ind., biologist, 1948-49; Indianapolis Children's Museum, Indianapolis, Ind., naturalist, 1949-50; Martinsville (Ind.) High School, teacher of English and biology, 1950-56; Indiana Lumber and Builders' Supply Association, Indianapolis, Ind., magazine editor, educational coordinator, field representative, 1956-57; Gosport-Wayne Township (Ind.) School, principal, 1957-58; North Judson (Ind.) Consolidated Schools, high school principal, 1958-61; Taipei (Taiwan) American Schools, high school principal, 1961-64; Indiana University, Bloomington, graduate student, 1964-66; Central Michigan University, Mt. Pleasant, associate professor of secondary education, 1966—. North Judson (Ind.) Chamber of Commerce, president, 1961. *Military service:* U.S. Coast Guard Reserve, three years. *Member:* National Association of Secondary School Principals, Phi Delta Kappa.

WRITINGS: Floorburns, Farrar, Straus & Cudahy, 1957; *The 23rd Street Crusaders*, Farrar, Straus & Cudahy, 1958; *The Boys Who Vanished* (Junior Literary Guild selection), Duell, Sloane & Pearce, 1959; *The Coach Nobody Liked* (Junior Literary Guild selection), Farrar, Straus & Cudahy, 1960; *Hotshot*, Farrar, Straus & Cudahy, 1961; *The Mystery of the Missing Monkey*, Farrar, Straus, 1963; *Court Clown*, Farrar, Straus, 1963; *The Mystery of the Tarnished Trophy*, Farrar, Straus, 1964.

WORK IN PROGRESS: Writing on trends in the field of student teaching.

SIDELIGHTS: Has visited schools in Okinawa, Japan, the Philippines, Quemoy, and the Pescadores Islands, and twice participated in UNESCO-Chinese Ministry of Education projects.†

*   *   *

CARSTEN, Francis Ludwig   1911-

PERSONAL: Born June 25, 1911, in Berlin, Germany; son of Paul and Frida (Born) Carsten; married Ruth Moses, August 21, 1945; children: Oliver Michael, Colin Andrew, Janet Frances. *Education:* Attended University of Heidelberg, 1930-31, University of Berlin, 1931-33, University of Amsterdam, 1936-39; Oxford University, D.Phil, 1942, D.Litt., 1961. *Office:* University of London, London W.C.1, England.

CAREER: University of London, London, England, lecturer in history at Westfield College, 1947-61, Masaryk Professor of Central European History, 1961—. Krater Visiting Professor in European History, Stanford University. *Member:* British Academy (fellow, 1971).

WRITINGS: The Origins of Prussia, Oxford University Press, 1954, 2nd edition, 1968; *Princes and Parliaments in Germany*, Oxford University Press, 1959; (editor and contributor) *New Cambridge Modern History*, Volume V: *The Ascendancy of France, 1648-1688*, Cambridge University Press, 1961; *Reichswehr und Politik, 1918-1933*, Kiepenheuer & Witsch, 1964, revised English translation, *The Reichswehr and Politics, 1918-33*, Oxford University Press, 1966; *The Rise of Fascism*, University of California Press, 1967, revised edition, Methuen, 1970; (author of introduction) Walter Schmitthenner, editor, *The German Resistance to Hitler*, University of California Press, 1970; *Revolution in Central Europe 1918-1919*, University of California Press, 1972.

Also author of "Medieval Democracy in the Brandenburg Towns and Its Defeat in the Fifteenth Century" (Alexander prize essay), Transactions of the Royal Historical Society, London, 1943. Co-editor, *Slavonic and East Euro-*

pean Review. Contributor of articles to periodicals, including: *English Historical Review, History, Survey of British and Commonwealth Affairs*, and *Historische Zeitschrift.*

WORK IN PROGRESS: Fascist Movements in Austria.

SIDELIGHTS: Reviewing *The Nature of Fascism* in *The New York Review of Books*, James Joll observed, "This is a valuable historical introduction to the subject which . . . will stimulate discussion of a number of interesting questions about the nature of fascism and the reasons for its success in some countries and not in others, and it draws attention to the problem of distinguishing what in fascism is the result of earlier intellectual and political doctrines and what was produced by the immediate social and economic conditions of Europe in the 1920's."

AVOCATIONAL INTERESTS: Gardening, climbing, and swimming.

*   *   *

CARTER, Boyd (George)   1908-

PERSONAL: Born May 8, 1908, in Duffield, Va.; son of James David (a lawyer) and Viola L. (Fraley) Carter; first wife deceased; married Mary Eileen Barry, June 16, 1965. *Education:* William and Mary College, B.A., 1929; University of Toulouse, student, 1926-27; University of Illinois, M.A., 1933, Ph.D., 1937. *Home:* 1108 West Stewart Rd., Columbia, Mo. 65201. *Office:* 23 Arts and Science, University of Missouri, Columbia, Mo.

CAREER: Beaver High School, Bluefield, W. Va., teacher of French, 1929-31; University of Idaho, Boise, instructor in modern languages, 1937-38; University of Wyoming, Laramie, assistant professor of modern languages, 1938-39; Coe College, Cedar Rapids, Iowa, 1939-45, started as assistant professor, became professor and chairman of department of foreign languages; University of Nebraska, Lincoln, associate professor, 1945-59, and chairman of department of Romance languages, 1950-56; Southern Illinois University, Carbondale, professor of Romance languages and literature, 1959-67; University of Missouri, Columbia, professor of romance languages, 1967—. Lecturer, Mexico City, 1962, Managua, Nicaragua, 1967; advisory committee member, Massachusetts Council of Public Schools, 1959—. *Member:* Modern Language Association of America, American Association of Teachers of Spanish and Portuguese, American Association of Teachers of French (West Central chapter president, 1948-50), American Association of University Professors. *Awards, honors:* Palmes Academiques, 1956.

WRITINGS: (Co-author) *French Review Grammar*, Ronald, 1948, 2nd edition, 1956; (editor) *Those Devils in Baggy Pants*, Appleton, 1951; (co-author) *French for Children*, Johnsen Publishing, 1955; (co-author) *Spanish for Children*, Johnsen Publishing, 1955; (co-author) *German for Children*, Johnsen Publishing, 1956; *Manuel Gutierrez Najera: Estudio y Escritos Ineditos*, Andrea (Mexico), 1956; *Las Revistas Literarias de Hispanoamerica*, Andrea, 1959; *En Torno a Gutierrez Najera y las Letras Mexicanas del Siglo XIX*, Botas (Mexico), 1960; (editor with Frances Easter) Rosario Nunez, *Raiz India* (novela), Odyssey, 1961; (co-editor) *German Review Grammer*, Ronald, 1965; *La "Revista de America" de Ruben Dario y Ricardo Jaimes Freyre*, [Managua, Nicaragua], 1967; *Historia de la literatura hispanoamericana a traves de sus revistas*, Ediciones de Andrea, 1968; (editor with wife, Mary Eileen Carter) *Manuel Gutierrez Najera: Escritos ineditos de sabor satir-*

ico, "*Plato del dia*," University of Missouri Press, 1972. Contributor of more than eighty short stories, and of essays, poetry, and articles to some fifty periodicals in United States and abroad. Advisory editor, *Prairie Schooner*, 1949-59.

WORK IN PROGRESS: Fiction of Mexican Revolution; *The Maximilian Period*; a series of short stories called "Mid-Night Confessions," for *Mexican Life*; a study on Manuel Guiterrez Najera, for Twayne.

SIDELIGHTS: Fluent in French and Spanish; German adequate. *Avocational interests:* Gardening.

* * *

CARTER, Everett 1919-

PERSONAL: Born April 28, 1919, in New York, N.Y.; son of Ben and Myra Carter; married Cecile Doudna, June 27, 1940; children: Dale, Tim. *Education:* University of California, Los Angeles, A.B., 1939, M.A., 1943, Ph.D., 1947. *Home:* 734 Hawthorne Lane, Davis, Calif. *Office:* 202 Sproul Hall, University of California, Davis, Calif.

CAREER: Southern Counties and Southern California Gas Co., Los Angeles, writer and editor, 1939-42; Universal Pictures, Universal City, Los Angeles, Calif., writer, 1942-46; Claremont Men's College, Claremont, Calif., instructor, 1946-47, assistant professor of English, 1947-49; University of California, Berkeley, associate professor of English, 1949-57; University of California, Davis, associate professor, 1957-62, professor of English and vice-chancellor, 1962—, assistant to the president, 1961-62, dean of research, 1962-65, director, Centre d'Etudes de l'Universite de Californie a l' Universite de Bordeaux, 1970-72. Lecturer, University of Copenhagen. *Member:* Modern Language Association of America, American Society of Composers, Authors and Publishers. *Awards, honors:* Guggenheim fellow, 1952-53; Fulbright fellow, 1954-55; Commonwealth Gold Medal for nonfiction, 1955.

WRITINGS: Howells and the Age of Realism, Lippincott, 1954; (author of introduction) William Dean Howells, *The Rise of Silas Lapham*, Harper, 1958; (editor) Harold Frederic, *The Damnation of Theron Ware*, Harvard University Press, 1960. Contributor to *Dictionary of American Biography*, and to American and French literary journals.

WORK IN PROGRESS: Writing on the idea of progress in American literature.

* * *

CARTHY, Mother Mary Peter 1911-

PERSONAL: Born October 15, 1911, in New York, N.Y.; daughter of Patrick and Helen (Horsburg) Carthy. *Education:* College of New Rochelle, B.A., 1933; Columbia University, graduate student, 1934-36; Catholic University of America, M.A. in history, 1947, Ph.D., 1957; University of Notre Dame, M.A. in theology, 1962. *Home:* 1404 Hampshire West Ct., Silver Spring, Md. 20903. *Office:* University of Maryland, College Park, Md. 20742.

CAREER: Roman Catholic nun. Columbia University, Teachers College, New York, N.Y., assistant to business manager, 1933-37; College of New Rochelle, New Rochelle, N.Y., assistant registrar, 1941-49, dean, 1950-57, president, 1957-61; Catholic University of America, Washington, D.C., American church history editor for *New Catholic Encyclopedia*, 1962-66, professor of American church history, 1963-64; Corpus Instrumentorum, Inc., editor, 1966-67; University of Maryland, College Park, asso-

ciate professor and director of general education program, 1967-72, associate dean of undergraduate studies, 1972—. *Member:* American Catholic Historical Association.

WRITINGS: Old St. Patrick's, U.S. Catholic Historical Society, 1947; *English Influences on Early American Catholicism*, Catholic University of America Press, 1959; *Catholicism in English Speaking Lands*, Hawthorn, 1964. Contributor of book reviews to *Catholic Historical Review*.

WORK IN PROGRESS: History of Catholic Education in the U.S., for Hawthorn.†

* * *

CASADY, Donald Rex 1926-

PERSONAL: Born June 8, 1926, in Dean, Iowa; son of Benjamin Harrison and Hazel (Rachford) Casady; married Gwen Ellen Hoglan, 1958; children: Richard Mark, Martin Dean, Kevin Rex. *Education:* University of Iowa, B.S., 1950, M.A., 1955, Ph.D., 1959. *Address:* P.O. Box 6028, Coralville, Iowa. *Office:* Room 123, Field House, University of Iowa, Iowa City, Iowa.

CAREER: Atlanta Athletic Club, Atlanta, Ga., athletic director, 1950-51; Georgia Military Academy, College Park, physical education director, 1951-54; University of Iowa, Iowa City, instructor, 1955-59, assistant professor of physical education, 1960-64, associate professor, 1964—. *Military service:* U.S. Army Air Forces, 1944-46, U.S. Air Force Reserve, 1946—; now major. *Member:* American Association for Health, Physical Education and Recreation, College Physical Education Association, American Association of University Professors, American Association for the Advancement of Science, Phi Epsilon Kappa, Sigma Delta Psi.

WRITINGS: Beginning Bowling, Wadsworth, 1962, revised edition, 1968; (with Donald Mapes and Louis Alley) *Handbook of Physical Fitness Activities*, Macmillan, 1965; (with Frank Musker) *A Guide to Gymnastics*, Macmillan, 1968.

WORK IN PROGRESS: Handbook of Gymnastics, and *Physical Education Activities for Men*, both for Macmillan.

AVOCATIONAL INTERESTS: Handball, gardening.†

* * *

CASE, Lynn M(arshall) 1903-

PERSONAL: Born December 18, 1903, in Verona, N.Y.; son of Joseph Arthur (a government clerk) and Bertha (Page) Case; married Doris Adell Fellows, May 24, 1930; children: Beverly (Mrs. John W. Rorer), Ronald Marshall. *Education:* Hamilton College, A.B., 1925; Columbia University, graduate study, 1928; University of Pennsylvania, M.A., 1929, Ph.D., 1931. *Home:* 37 Rodmor Rd., Havertown, Pa. 19083. *Office:* Department of History, University of Pennsylvania, Philadelphia, Pa. 19174.

CAREER: Rice Institute (now Rice University), Houston, Tex., instructor, 1930-37; Louisiana State University, Baton Rouge, 1937-46, began as assistant professor, became associate professor of European history; University of Pennsylvania, Philadelphia, associate professor, 1946-55, professor of history, 1955-69, chairman of department, 1966-68. *Military service:* U.S. Army, General Staff Corps, 1942-46; became major; received Legion of Merit and Bronze Star. *Member:* American Historical Association (chairman of war documents committee, 1956-57), Society for French Historical Studies (president, 1955-56), Society for Italian Historical Studies, Societe d'Histoire moderne, Phi Beta Kappa. *Awards, honors:* Social Science Research Council grant, 1933, 1948; Beveridge Fund award of American Historical Association, 1934; American Philosophical Society award, 1956; Phi Alpha Theta prize, 1970, for *The United States and France*; Centre National des Recherches Scientifiques publication award, 1974, for *Edouard Thouvenel*; Doctoris honoris causa, Universite de Besancon.

WRITINGS: Franco-Italian Relations, 1860-1865, University of Pennsylvania Press, 1932, reprinted, AMS Press, 1971; *French Opinion on the United States and Mexico, 1861-1867*, Appleton, 1936, reprinted, Archon, 1969; (with C. E. Smith) *A Short History of Western Civilization*, Health, 1940, 2nd edition, 1948; *French Opinion on War and Diplomacy during the Second Empire*, University of Pennsylvania Press, 1954, reprinted, Octagon, 1972; (editor with D. H. Thomas) *Guide to the Diplomatic Archives of Western Europe*, University of Pennsylvania Press, 1958; (translator) Guillaume de Bertier de Sauvigny, *The Bourbon Restoration*, University of Pennsylvania Press, 1963; (with W. E. Spencer) *The United States and France: Civil War Diplomacy*, University of Pennsylvania Press, 1970; *Edouard Thouvenel et la diplomatie du Second Empire*, Editions Pedone (Paris), 1974.

Contributor to numerous professional journals. Editor of French articles section, *American Historical Review*, 1973—; member of editorial board, *Southwest Social Science Quarterly*, 1938-39.

WORK IN PROGRESS: With D. H. Thomas, a revised edition of *Guide to the Diplomatic Archives of Western Europe*.

SIDELIGHTS: Case told *CA*: "As a student I became convinced that history is as essential to human society as memory is to the individual man. Especially in present world crises we need to know the long stretch of diplomatic history. That is why I finally devoted myself to the writing and college teaching of diplomatic history. In recent years I have become very discouraged over the lack of knowledge of diplomatic experience by the average citizen whose will is decisive in a democracy and over the refusal of statesmen to heed the lessons of diplomatic history.

"In the earlier years of my career I had the erroneous notion that the common man had the instinct for right decisions in foreign affairs if it could be brought to bear on the decision makers. This was the motivation behind my undertaking my book on *French Opinion on War and Diplomacy during the Second Empire*. As an honest historian I had to come to the conclusion, however, that French opinion during the Second Empire was too ignorant and naive to be able to dictate a successful foreign policy. Then and now, when statesmen went contrary to opinion, they usually succeeded; when they followed public opinion, they usually failed. Democracies are sheep among wolves in a world system based on force instead of on orderly government."

Case has traveled extensively in western Europe and in the Near East. He knows French, Italian, Spanish, and German.

BIOGRAPHICAL/CRITICAL SOURCES: Nancy N. Barker and Marvin L. Brown, editors, *Diplomacy in an Age of Nationalism: Essays in Honor of Lynn Marshall Case*, Martinus Nijhoff (The Hague), 1971.

CASEWIT, Curtis 1922-

PERSONAL: Born March 21, 1922, in Mannheim, Germany; came to United States in 1948; divorced; children: Carla, Stephen, Niccolo. *Education:* Florence Language School, Florence, Italy, student, 1933-38; courses in journalism and writing at University of Denver and University of Colorado. *Home:* 355 Lowell, Denver, Colo. 80219.

CAREER: Book buyer in department store in Denver, Colo., 1959-64; free-lance writer. Denver Opportunity School, teacher of creative writing, 1961-62. Translator in German, French, and Italian. Consultant, *Writer's Digest*. *Military service:* British Army, interpreter, 1945-47; became sergeant. *Member:* National Writers Club, Colorado Authors League, Colorado Mountain Club, Mile Hi Writers (president, 1954—). *Awards, honors:* Mystery Writers of America Edgar Allan Poe Award ("Edgar"), 1956, for best book reviewing; *Writer's Digest* short story contest award, 1955; Dutton Award for article published in *Best Articles of 1964*.

WRITINGS: The Peacemakers (science fiction), Bouregy, 1960; *Ski Racing: Advice by the Experts*, Arco, 1963, second edition, 1969; *Adventure in Deepmore Cave*, Doubleday, 1965; *How to Get a Job Overseas*, Arco, 1965, revised edition, Arc Books, 1970; *Ski Fever: How to Master the Fastest-Growing Winter Sport*, Hawthorn Books, 1965; *United Air Lines Guide to Western Skiing*, Doubleday, 1967; (with Bob Beattie) *Bob Beattie's Learn to Ski*, Bantam, 1967; (with Richard Pownall) *Mountaineering Handbook: An Invitation to Climbing*, Lippincott, 1968; *Ski Racer*, Four Winds, 1968; *The Hiking-Climbing Handbook*, Hawthorn, 1969; *The Adventures of Snowshoe Thompson*, Putnam, 1970; *Skier's Handbook: Advice From the Experts*, Winchester, 1971; *Overseas Jobs: The Ten Best Countries*, Paperback Library, 1972; *A Guide to Western Skiing*, Chronicle Books, 1972; *Mountain Troopers! The Story of the Tenth Mountain Division*, Crowell, 1972; *Colorado*, Viking, 1973. Short stories and articles published in more than fifty newspapers and magazines (in seven countries), including *Saga, Argosy, Catholic Digest, Coronet, Overseas Weekly*, and *Science and Mechanics*.

WORK IN PROGRESS: Guide to Denver and Colorado; Freelance Writing: Advice by the Pros; Tennis.

* * *

CASEY, Thomas Francis 1923-

PERSONAL: Born May 17, 1923; son of Thomas F. and Josephine F. (Sullivan) Casey. *Education:* College of the Holy Cross, student, 1940-42; St. John's Seminary, Brighton, Mass., A.B., 1947; Pontifical Gregorian University, Rome, Italy, Doctor of Ecclesiastical History, 1956. *Home:* 459 Weld St., West Roxbury, Mass. *Office:* St. John's Seminary, Lake St., Brighton, Mass.

CAREER: Ordained Roman Catholic priest, 1947; parish assistant, 1947-53, 1956-58; St. John's Seminary, Brighton, Mass., professor of church history, 1958—. Lecturer in Japan, 1961. Chaplain, Melrose (Mass.) Police and Fire Departments, 1950-53. *Member:* North American College Alumni.

WRITINGS: The Sacred Congregation de Propaganda Fide and the Revision of the First Provincial Council of Baltimore, Gregorian University Press, 1957; *Pastoral Manual for New Priests*, Bruce, 1962; (with Leo Gainor) *Social Manual for Seminarians*, Bruce, 1963.†

CASHMAN, Paul Harrison 1924-

PERSONAL: Born June 30, 1924, in Des Moines, Iowa; son of Roy H. and Iva (McBeth) Cashman; married Veryl Ann, 1951; children: Todd, Timothy, Kay. *Education:* University of Minnesota, B.S.L., 1948, M.A., 1950, Ph.D., 1957. *Home:* 2333 Priscilla, St. Paul, Minn. *Office:* University of Minnesota, St. Paul, Minn.

CAREER: Hamline University, St. Paul, Minn., faculty member, 1950-53; University of Minnesota, St. Paul, faculty member, 1953—. *Military service:* U.S. Army Air Forces, 1943-45; became first lieutenant; received Air Medal. *Member:* Speech Association of America, National Society for the Study of Communication, Central States Speech Association, Danforth Associates.

WRITINGS: A Handbook for Beginning Debaters, Burgess, 1961. Consulting editor, *Central States Speech Journal.*

WORK IN PROGRESS: Two books *Listening in the Church Setting* and *Learning Through Listening.*†

*   *   *

CASKEY, John L. 1908-

PERSONAL: Born December 7, 1908, in Boston, Mass.; son of Lacey D. (a curator) and Elsie L. (Stern) Caskey; married second wife, Miriam Ervin, 1967. *Education:* Yale University, B.A., 1931; University of Cincinnati, Ph.D., 1939. *Home:* 622 Evanswood Pl., Cincinnati, Ohio 45220. *Office:* Department of the Classics, University of Cincinnati, Cincinnati, Ohio 45221.

CAREER: University of Cincinnati, Cincinnati, Ohio, member of staff excavations at Troy, 1932-38, instructor, 1939-42, assistant professor of classics, 1946-48; American School of Classical Studies at Athens, Athens, Greece, assistant director, 1948-49, director, 1949-59; University of Cincinnati, professor of classical archaeology, 1959—, head of department of classics, 1959-72, fellow of the Graduate School, 1961—. Director of excavations in Greece, at Heraion of Argos, 1949, Lerna, 1952-58, Eutresis, 1958, and Ceos, 1960—; vice-chairman of managing committee, American School of Classical Studies. *Military service:* U.S. Army, 1942-46; became lieutenant colonel; received Legion of Merit. U.S. Army Reserve, 1946-61.

MEMBER: Archaeological Institute of America, American Philological Association, Classical Association of Canada, Hellenic Society (England), German Archaeological Institute, Archaeological Society of Athens (honorary). *Awards, honors:* Royal Order of the Phoenix (Greece); named honorary citizen of Athens.

WRITINGS: (Contributor and editor with C. W. Blegen and others) *Troy: Excavations Conducted by the University of Cincinnati, 1932-38*, Volumes I-IV, Princeton University Press, 1950-58. Contributor and editor with others of supplementary monographs to *Troy*, 1950—. Contributor to *Cambridge Ancient History*. Contributor of classical and archaeological reports and articles to learned journals.

WORK IN PROGRESS: A definitive publication on excavations at Lerna, 1952-58, and Ceos, 1960-74.

*   *   *

CASPARY, Vera 1904-

PERSONAL: Born November 13, 1904, in Chicago, Ill.; daughter of Paul (a department store buyer) and Julia (Cohen) Caspary; married I. G. Goldsmith (a film producer), October 5, 1949 (deceased). *Education:* Educated in Chicago public schools. *Politics:* Independent Democrat. *Address:* Skadron, P.O. Box 1065, Studio City, Calif. 91604; c/o W. H. Allen & Co., 43 Essex St., London W.C.2, England; 1454 Blue Ridge Dr., Beverly Hills, Calif. *Agent:* Monica McCall, Inc., 667 Madison Ave., New York, N.Y. 10021

CAREER: Dance (magazine), New York, N.Y., editor, 1925-27; free-lance author of books, plays, and films. *Member:* Writers Guild of America (West), Authors Guild, Dramatists Guild. *Awards, honors:* Awards from Screen Writers Guild for "Letter to Three Wives" and "Les Girls."

WRITINGS: The White Girl, Sears, 1929; *Ladies and Gents*, Century, 1929; *Music in the Street*, Sears, 1930; *Thicker Than Water*, Liveright, 1932; *Laura*, Houghton, 1942; *Bedelia*, Houghton, 1944; *Stranger Than Truth*, Random House, 1946; *The Weeping and the Laughter*, Little, Brown, 1950; *Thelma*, Little, Brown, 1952; *The Husband*, Harper, 1957; *Evvie*, Harper, 1960; *A Chosen Sparrow*, Putnam, 1964; *The Man Who Loved His Wife*, Putnam, 1966; *The Rosecrest Cell*, Putnam, 1967; *Final Portrait*, W. H. Allen, 1971.

Plays: (with Winifred Lenihan) "Blind Mice"; (with George Sklar) "Laura"; "Wedding in Paris"; "Geraniums in My Window." Original screen scripts and adaptations include "Night of June 13," "Easy Living," "Bedelia," "Letter to Three Wives," "Three Husbands," "Les Girls," "Bachelor in Paradise," "The Young Bachelors," "Such Women are Dangerous," "Claudia and David," "I can get it for you Whole-Sale," "The Blue Gardenia," "Give a girl a Break," "Out of the Blue."

WORK IN PROGRESS: Sin of Omission, a novel.

AVOCATIONAL INTERESTS: Travel, theater, gardening, looking at things and people.†

*   *   *

CASRIEL, H(arold) Daniel 1924-

PERSONAL: Born March 1, 1924, in New York, N.Y.; son of Abe Lewis (a merchant) and Lillian (Stern) Casriel; married Olivia Corwin; children: Seth. *Education:* Attended Rutgers University, 1941-43, Iowa State College (now Iowa State University of Science and Technology), 1943-44, Indiana University, 1944-49; University of Cincinnati, M.D., 1949. *Home:* 47 East 51st St., New York, N.Y. 10022.

CAREER: Psychiatrist, 1953—. Daytop Village, Inc., Staten Island, N.Y., psychiatric director and medical superintendent, 1963-70; assistant professor, Temple Medical School, 1967-1970; member of board, Spruce Institute, 1967-70; visiting professor, New Jersey State Teachers College, 1969—; director, Casriel Institute, 1969—. Consultant to Probation Department, New York State Supreme Court, Second Judicial District; consultant on youth projects. *Military service:* U.S. Army, 1943-46, 1950-52; became captain. *Member:* American Society of Psychoanalytic Physicians (past president), American Medical Association, American Psychiatric Association, Association for the Advancement of Psychotherapy, Royal Society of Health, American Public Health Association, International Association of Social Psychiatry, National Association of Private Psychiatric Hospitals, American Society on Alcoholism, Pan American Medical Association, Medical Correctional Officers Association, New York County and State Medical Association.

WRITINGS: So Fair a House: The Story of Synanon, Prentice-Hall, 1963; *Daytop: Three Addicts and Their Cure*, Hill & Wang, 1971; *A Scream Away From Happiness*, Grosset, 1972.

Contributor: Jules Masserman, editor, *Current Psychiatric Therapies*, Volume 8, Grune, 1968; Herman W. Laud, *What You Can Do About Drugs and Your Child*, Hart Publishing, 1969; Laud, *How To Talk With Your Teenager About Drugs*, Readers Digest Services, 1970; Nathan Strauss, *Addicts and Drug Abusers: Current Approaches to the Problem*, Center for New York City Affairs, New School for Social Research, 1971; Robert Siroka, Ellen W. Siroka, and Gilbert Schloss, editors, *Sensitivity Training and Group Encounter: An Introduction*, Grosset, 1971; Leonard Blank, Gloria Gottsegen, and Monroe Gottsegen, editors, *Confrontation: Encounters in Self and Interpersonal Awareness*, Macmillan, 1971.

AVOCATIONAL INTERESTS: Music.

* * *

CASTELLANETA, Carlo 1930-

PERSONAL: Born February 8, 1930, in Milan, Italy; son of Michele and Teresa (Ruffini) Castellaneta; married Donatella Facchinetti, September 21, 1961. *Education:* Attended public high school. *Home:* Via Muratori 29, Milan, Italy. *Office:* C/o *Storia Illustrata*, Arnoldo Mondadori Editore, Via Bianca di Savoia 20, Milan, Italy.

CAREER: Journalist; currently works for *Storia Illustrata*, Milan, Italy.

*WRITINGS—*All novels, except as noted: *Viaggio col padre*, Mondadori, 1958, translation published as *Journey with Father*, MacDonald & Co., 1962; *Una lunga rabbia*, Feltrinelli, 1961; *Villa di delizia* (title means "Villa of Delights"), Rizzoli, 1965; *Gli incantesimi*, Rizzoli, 1968, translation by George Kay published as *Until the Next Enchantment*, Chatto & Windus, 1970; *La dolce compagna*, Rizzoli, 1970, translation published as *This Gentle Companion*, Chatto & Windus, 1971; *La Paloma*, Rizzoli, 1972; *Tante storie* (short stories), Rizzoli, 1973. Contributor of short stories to newspapers; writer and illustrator of reports from Senegal, Gibraltar, Spain, and Andorra, for *Le vie del mondo* and *Atlas Histoire*; translator of French-language poets, including Leopold Sedar Senghor. Author of script for motion picture "Pelle Viva," 1962.

WORK IN PROGRESS: A History of Milan.

SIDELIGHTS: In its review of *Until the Next Enchantment*, the *Observer* noted, "It is a novel of exceptional beauty, on a small scale but very successful. . . . The writing, veering between direct statement and Mollie Bloom meanderings, manages to capture the quintessence of Italy."

* * *

CASTOR, Grahame (Douglas) 1932-

PERSONAL: Born December 20, 1932, in Leicester, England. *Education:* Gonville and Caius College, Cambridge, B.A., 1954, Ph.D., 1962. *Office:* Cambridge University, Cambridge, England.

CAREER: University College of the West Indies, Jamaica, assistant lecturer, 1957-59, lecturer in French, 1959-61; University of Glasgow, Glasgow, Scotland, lecturer in French, 1961-63; Cambridge University, Cambridge, England, lecturer in French and fellow of Gonville and Caius

College, 1963—. *Military service:* British Army, 1954-56. *Member:* Modern Humanities Research Association, Society for French Studies, Association of University Teachers.

WRITINGS: Pleiade Poetics: A Study in 16th Century Thought and Terminology, Cambridge University Press, 1964. Contributor to *Modern Language Review*.

WORK IN PROGRESS: Further research in sixteenth-century French literature.†

* * *

CATE, William Burke 1924-

PERSONAL: Born March 25, 1924, in Itasca, Tex.; son of Emmett (a farmer) and Irene (Kincaid) Cate; married Janice Patterson, August 20, 1946; children: Lucy Margaret, Nancy Elizabeth, Michael Patterson, Sara Irene, Rebecca Kincaid. *Education:* Willamette University, B.A., 1945; Boston University, S.T.B., 1948, Ph.D., 1953. *Home:* 248 Southeast 44th St., Portland, Ore. *Office:* Greater Portland Council of Churches, 0245 Southwest Bancroft, Portland, Ore.

CAREER: Ordained Methodist minister, 1952; Interchurch Council of Greater New Bedford, New Bedford, Mass., executive secretary, 1953-58; Greater Portland Council of Churches, Portland, Ore., executive secretary, 1958—. *Member:* Association of Council Secretaries (chairman of study committee, 1961-62), Rotary International, Urban League, United Good Neighbors. *Awards, honors:* D.D. from Lewis and Clark College, 1964.

WRITINGS: (Contributor) *Institutionalism and Unity*, Association Press, 1963; (contributor) *Unity in Mid-Career*, Macmillan, 1963; *Ecumenical Scandal on Main Street*, Association Press, 1965. Also contributor to *Church and Unity in Pacific Northwest*, 1962.

WORK IN PROGRESS: Research on relationship of Protestant fundamentalism to the ecumenical movement.†

* * *

CATLIN, George E(dward) G(ordon) 1896-

PERSONAL: Born July 29, 1896, in Liverpool, England; son of George Edward (an Episcopal clergyman) and Edith K. (Orton) Catlin; married Vera Brittain (a writer), July 24, 1925 (died, 1970); married Delinda Tassi Gates, April 16, 1971; children: (first marriage) John E.J.B., Shirely V.T.B. Catlin Williams (member of Parliament). *Education:* New College, Oxford, B.A., 1920, M.A., 1924; Cornell University, Ph.D., 1924. *Politics:* Labour. *Religion:* Catholic. *Home:* 5 Wilton Pl., London SW1, England.

CAREER: Cornell University, Ithaca, N.Y., professor of politics, 1924-35, acting head of department, 1928; Yale University, New Haven, Conn., associate in quantitative political science, 1935-56; McGill University, Montreal, Quebec, Bronman Professor of Political Science and chairman of department, 1956-60, professor emeritus, 1960—; University of Washington, Seattle, Walker-Ames Lecturer and chairman of department, 1964. Special lecturer at Yale University, 1937, University of Calcutta, 1947, University of Peking, 1948, University of North Carolina, 1949 and 1957, University of Copenhagen, 1949, University of Heidelberg, 1949, University of California at Berkeley, 1953, and Royal Society of Arts, 1961; special advisor to Arthur Greenwood, 1930-41, Wendell Wilkie, 1940, Harold Wilson, 1964—; twice nominated to executive committee of British Labour Party; member of Institute for

Strategic Studies; co-founder and member of advisory council of American and British Commonwealth Association (now English-Speaking Union); drafter of International Declaration in Support of Independence of India, 1943; active in fostering of Atlantic Community. *Realist* (magazine), co-founder, with H. G. Wells, Arnold Bennett, and others, co-editor, 1929-30.

MEMBER: Royal Society of Literature (fellow), International Political Science Association, World Academy of Arts and Sciences (fellow; vice-president), Union Mondiale des Europeens (British president; international vice-president), Nouvelles Equipes Internationales (member of international executive committee), Anglo-German Association (vice-president), Instituto Estudios Politicos (Spain; honorary member), American Political Science Association, Canadian Political Science Association, British Political Studies Association, American Sociological Association, British Sociological Association. *Awards, honors:* Commander, Grand Cross, Order of Merit (Germany); medallist, Societe de l'Encouragement au Progres (France); knighted, 1970.

WRITINGS: Thomas Hobbes as Philosopher, Publicist, and Man of Letters: An Introduction, Basil Blackwell, 1922; *The Science and Method of Politics*, Knopf, 1927, Shoe String, 1968; (author of introduction) Mary Wollstonecraft, *Vindication*, Dent, 1928.

Study of the Principles of Politics: Being an Essay Toward Political Rationalization, Macmillan, 1930, Russell, 1967; *Liquor Control*, H. Holt, 1931; *Preface to Action*, Macmillan, 1934; (editor) *New Trends in Socialism*, Lovat Dickson & Thompson, 1935; (editor) *War and Democracy*, Routledge & Kegan Paul, 1938; (editor and author of introduction) E. Durkheim, *Rules of Sociological Method*, University of Chicago Press, 1938; *Anglo-Saxony and Its Tradition*, Macmillan, 1939 (published in England as *The Anglo-Saxon Tradition*, Routledge & Kegan Paul, 1939); *The Story of the Political Philosophers*, McGraw, 1939 (8th edition published in England as *A History of the Political Philosophers*, Unwin, 1950).

One Anglo-American Nation: The Foundation of Anglo-Saxony as Basis of World Federation, Macmillan, 1941; *The Unity of Europe*, C. & J. Temple, 1944; (compiler with others) *Above All Nations: An Anthology*, Gollancz, 1945, Harper, 1949; *In the Path of Mahatma Gandhi*, Macdonald, 1948, Regnery, 1950.

On Political Goals, St. Martins, 1957; *What Does the West Want? A Study of Political Goals*, Phoenix House, 1957; *The Atlantic Community*, Macmillan, 1959.

Systematic Politics: Elementa Politica et Sociologica, University of Toronto Press, 1962; *Political and Sociological Theory and Its Applications*, University of Michigan Press, 1964; *The Grandeur of England and the Atlantic Community*, Pergamon, 1966, published as *The Stronger Community*, Hawthorn, 1967; *The Atlantic Commonwealth*, Penguin, 1969.

For Gods Sake, Go! (autobiography), Colin Smythe, 1972; *Kissinger's Atlantic Charter*, Schenkman, 1975.

Also author of pamphlets and published lectures and addresses.

Editorial writer, *Yorkshire Post*, 1927-28; editor and special correspondent, *People and Freedom*.

*   *   *

CAVANAH, Frances 1899-

PERSONAL: Born September 26, 1899, in Princeton, Ind.; daughter of Rufus O. and Luella (Neale) Cavanah. *Education:* DePauw University, A.B., 1920. *Home:* 2501 East 104th Ave., Denver, Colo. 80233.

CAREER: Rand McNally & Co., Chicago, Ill., member of editorial staff, then associate editor of *Child Life*, 1923-38; Row, Peterson, Inc., Evanston, Ill., contributing writer, 1939-42; Field Enterprises, Inc., Chicago, Ill., biography editor of 1947 edition of *World Book Encyclopedia*, 1944-46, anthology editor of 1949 revision of *Childcraft*, 1947-48; Row, Peterson & Co., director of biographies, 1948-52; writer, editor of books for children. *Member:* Authors League, National Historical Society, Society of Midland Authors, Washington Children's Book Guild, Mortar Board, Theta Sigma Phi, Delta Delta Delta. *Awards, honors:* Theta Sigma Phi Headliner Award, 1941; DePauw University citation for meritorious achievement, 1952; Indiana University Writers' Conference citation for most distinguished children's book by a Hoosier author, 1960, for *Abe Lincoln Gets His Chance*.

WRITINGS: The Treasure of Belden Place, Laidlaw Brothers, 1928, new edition, 1938; *The Transfiguration of the Gifts* (pageant play), Womans Press, 1928; *Joy-Time* (children's play), Eldridge Publishing, 1929; *The Knight of the Funny Bone, and Other Plays for Children*, Baker's Plays, 1929; *Thanksgiving Wonders*, Eldridge Publishing, 1929.

Robin Hood's Enchanted Spring, and Other One-Act Plays for Children, Banner Play Bureau, 1930; *The Pine Tree's Blossoming: A Christmas Play*, Banner Play Bureau, 1930; *Children of America*, Thomas Rockwell, 1930; *Lil' Black Heliotrope: A One-Act Play for Girls*, Baker's Plays, 1932; *A Patriot in Hoops*, R. M. McBride, 1932; *Children of America*, Follett, 1935; *Children of the White House*, Rand McNally, 1936; *Boyhood Adventures of Our Presidents*, Rand McNally, 1938.

Famous Paintings: A Guide to the Masters, Whitman Publishing, 1941; *Marta Finds the Golden Door*, Grosset, 1941; *Louis of New Orleans*, David McKay, 1941; (compiler) *Told Under the Christmas Tree: A Collection of Christmas Stories, Poems and Legends*, Grosset, 1941, new edition published as *Favorite Christmas Stories: A Collection of Christmas Stories, Poems, and Legends*, 1949; *Pedro of Santa Fe*, David McKay, 1941; *Down the Santa Fe Trail*, Row, Peterson, 1942; (compiler and editor) *I Am an American: What We All Are Fighting For, A Handbook For Every American's Pledge to Win the Final Victory and the Peace That Shall Follow*, Whitman Publishing, 1942; (compiler with Ruth Cromer Weir) *Liberty Laughs: A Collection of the Best War Jokes and Cartoons*, Dell, 1943; (with Ruth Cromer Weir) *Private Pepper of Dogs for Defense*, Whitman & Co., 1943; *The Happy Giraffe*, Wilcox & Follett, 1944; *Our Country's Story* (Junior Literary Guild selection), Rand McNally, 1945, revised edition, 1962; (with Ruth Cromer Weir) *Private Pepper Comes Home*, A Whitman, 1945; *Benjy of Boston*, David McKay, 1946; *Sandy of San Francisco*, David McKay, 1946; (compiler with Ruth Cromer Weir) *A Treasury of Dog Stories*, Rand McNally, 1947; (with) *Our New Land*, Row, Peterson, 1948; *Our New Nation*, Row, Peterson, 1948.

(Compiler with Ruth Cromer Weir) *24 Horses: A Treasury of Stories*, Rand McNally, 1950; (editor with Lucille Pannell) *Holiday Roundup*, Macrae, 1950, revised edition, 1968; (compiler) *Prayers for Boys and Girls*, Whitman, 1950; *They Knew Abe Lincoln: A Boy in Indiana*, Rand

McNally, 1952; (editor) *We Came to America* Macrae, 1954; *Two Loves for Jenny Lind*, Macrae, 1956; *Pocahontas, A Little Indian Girl of Jamestown*, Rand McNally, 1957; (editor) *Family Reading Festival: Stories and Poems to Read Together*, Prentice-Hall, 1958; *They Lived in the White House*, Macrae, 1959; *Abe Lincoln Gets His Chance* (My Weekly Reader Book Club Selection) Rand McNally, 1959.

(Compiler) *Friends to Man: The Wonderful World of Animals*, Macrae, 1961; *Jenny Lind and Her Listening Cat*, Vanguard, 1961; *Adventure in Courage: The Story of Theodore Roosevelt*, Rand McNally, 1961; *The Busters: A Story of Paganini Smith and Two Canine Gentlemen*, Macrae, 1964; *Triumphant Adventure: The Story of Franklin Delano Roosevelt*, Rand McNally, 1964; (with Elizabeth L. Crandall) *Meet the Presidents*, Macrae, 1962, revised edition, 1965; *The Secret of Madame Doll: A Story of the American Revolution*, Vanguard, 1965; *Our Country's Freedom*, Rand McNally, 1966; (editor with Elizabeth Crandall) *Freedom Encyclopedia: American Liberties in the Making*, Rand McNally, 1968; *Jenny Lind's America* (Family Bookshelf selection), Chilton, 1969.

When Americans Came to New Orleans, Garrard, 1970; *We Wanted To Be Free: The Refugee's Own Stories, an Anthology*, Macrae, 1971; *Marta and the Nazis*, Scholastic Book Services, 1974.

Editor of "Real People" series, forty-eight titles, Row, Peterson & Co., 1948-53. Contributor to *This Week, Jack and Jill, Scholastic, Christian Science Monitor*, and to anthologies and school readers.

SIDELIGHTS: Several of Miss Cavanah's books have been recorded as Talking Books for the Blind, transcribed into Braille, and translated into other languages. *Avocational interests:* Theater.

BIOGRAPHICAL/CRITICAL SOURCES: Chicago Schools Journal, May-June, 1951; *Wilson Library Bulletin*, February, 1954; *Washington Post*, Washington, D.C., December 6, 1959.

* * *

CERVANTES, Lucius F. 1914-

PERSONAL: Born February 10, 1914, in St. Louis, Mo.; son of Augustine Aloysius and Victoria (Kussenberger) Cervantes. *Education:* St. Louis University, A.B., 1938, M.A. and Ph.L., 1941, S.T.L., 1947, Ph.D., 1952. *Home and office:* St. Louis University, St. Louis, Mo. 63103.

CAREER: Entered Society of Jesus (Jesuits), 1933, ordained priest, 1946. Regis College, Denver, Colo., director of department of sociology, 1951-58; St. Louis University, St. Louis, Mo., associate professor, 1959-62, professor of sociology and anthropology and director of Family Research Center, 1963—. International Sacred Heart Radio and Television Program, regular staff member, 1950—, broadcasting on major networks in United States; speaker on religious and sociological subjects at universities and institutes in United States and abroad; research assistant to mayor of St. Louis, 1955-66. Rocky Mountain Council on Family Relations, president, 1957-59; National Catholic Welfare Council, member of advisory board of Family Life Bureau, 1959—; Sir Thomas More Marriage and Family Clinic, Los Angeles, Calif., member of national advisory committee, 1961—; Marriage Counseling Foundation, St. Louis, Mo., adviser, 1961—.

MEMBER: Institut International de Sociologie, American

Sociological Association, American Catholic Sociological Society (executive council, 1959—), American Association for the Advancement of Science, Social Science Association, National Council on Family Relations, National Catholic Welfare Council, Academy of Religion and Mental Health, National Institute of Social and Behavioral Science, American Association of University Professors, National Committee on the Education of Migrant Children, Catholic Commission on Intellectual Affairs, Instituto de Estudios Politicos (corresponding member). *Awards, honors:* Ford Foundation fellowship, Harvard University, 1956; Book-of-the-Year Award from American Catholic Sociological Society, 1960; various research awards, largely to study family background and academic achievement in America, Europe, and Middle East.

WRITINGS: That You May Live, Guild Press, 1945; (contributor) *Social Theorists*, edited by C. S. Mihanovich, Bruce, 1952; (contributor) *Sanctity and Success in Marriage*, edited by Irving DeBlanc, National Catholic Welfare Council, 1956; (with Carle C. Zimmerman) *Marriage and the Family*, Regnery, 1956; (contributor) *God and the Family*, edited by Irving DeBlanc, National Catholic Welfare Council, 1958; *And God Made Man and Woman*, Regnery, 1959; (with Carle C. Zimmerman) *Successful American Families*, Pageant, 1960; *The Dropout: Causes and Cures*, University of Michigan Press, 1965; *A Better Education, A Better Job*, America Press, 1965. Contributor of articles and reviews to periodicals.†

* * *

CERYCH, Ladislav 1925-

PERSONAL: Surname pronounced *Chair*-ick; born September 24, 1925, in Trutnov, Czechoslovakia; son of Jiri and Marie (Barton) Cerych; married Vera Tomsova, March 29, 1952. *Education:* Attended Prague Polytechnicum, 1945-48; University of Geneva, licence in social sciences, 1950, Ph.D., 1965; attended College of Europe, 1950-51. *Home:* 42, rue des Marais, St. Germain en Laye, France 78. *Office:* International Institute for Educational Planning (UNESCO), rue Eugene Delacroix, Paris 16e, France.

CAREER: Radio Free Europe, Munich, Germany, editor, 1952-53; Ets B.E.T.A., Casablanca, Morocco, manager, 1954-56; College of Europe, Bruges, Belgium, assistant professor of sociology and political science, and chief of research; International Institute for Educational Planning (UNESCO), Paris, France, consultant in charge of training program, 1964—. *Member:* International Association of French Speaking Sociologists, Society for International Development.

WRITINGS: Europeens et Marocains: Sociologie d'une decolonisation, De Tempel, 1964; *Former les Hommes*, Plon, 1965, translation by Noel Lindsay and others published as *Problems of Aid to Education in Developing Countries*, Praeger, 1965; *The Integration of External Assistance with Educational Planning in Nigeria*, International Institute for Educational Planning, 1967; *L'Aide exterieure et la planification de l'education en Cote-d'Ivoire*, Institut international de planification de l'education, 1967.

Editor: Sciences Humaines et Integration Europeenne, Sythoff, 1960; *Universite Europeenne*, Sythoff, 1960; *The Atlantic Community: An Introductory Bibliography*, Sythoff, 1961; *Basic Values of the Atlantic Community*, Pall Mall, 1962.

WORK IN PROGRESS: Research on the social aspect of educational planning.

SIDELIGHTS: Cerych is fluent in English, French, German. He has traveled in Western Europe, Africa, India, Latin America, and the United States.

* * *

CHAFETZ, Morris E(dward) 1924-

PERSONAL: Born April 20, 1924, in Worcester, Mass.; son of Isaac and Rose (Handel) Chafetz; married Marion Donovan, September 2, 1946; children: Gary, Marc, Adam. *Education:* Tufts University, M.D., 1948. *Politics:* Independent. *Home:* 3129 Dumbarton St. N.W., Washington, D.C. 20007. *Office:* 5600 Fishers Lane, Rockville, Md. 20852.

CAREER: Harvard University Medical School, Cambridge, Mass., 1953-70, became assistant clinical professor of psychiatry; Massachusetts General Hospital, Boston, director of Alcohol Clinic, 1957-68, director of Acute Psychiatric Service, 1961-68, director of clinical psychiatric services, 1968-70; National Institute on Alcohol Abuse and Alcoholism of Department of Health, Education, and Welfare, Rockville, Md., director, 1971—. Consulting psychiatrist to Massachusetts Eye and Ear Infirmary, 1958-70; special consultant to National Institute of Mental Health, 1959-65; consultant to National Commission on Marihuana and Drug Abuse, 1971-72, and to Pan American Health Organization, 1972—. Member of subcommittee on alcoholism, Massachusetts Mental Health Planning Project, 1963, and of executive committee, Advisory Council on Massachusetts Mental Health, 1964-70. Lecturer throughout United States and in twenty-two countries of Asia, Africa, Middle East, and Europe. *Military service:* U.S. Public Health Service, senior assistant surgeon; on inactive reserve status. *Member:* American Psychiatric Association, Group for the Advancement of Psychiatry, American Association for the Advancement of Science, Sigma Xi.

WRITINGS: (With H. W. Demone, Jr.) *Alcoholism and Society*, Oxford University Press, 1962; (contributor) Raymond McCarthy, *Alcohol Education for Classroom and Community*, McGraw, 1964; *Liquor: The Servant of Man*, Little, 1965; (with others) *The Treatment of Alcoholism: A Study of Programs and Problems*, Joint Information Service of American Psychiatric Association and National Association for Mental Health, 1967; (editor with others) *Frontiers of Alcoholism*, Science House, 1970; (editor) *Proceedings, First and Second Annual Alcoholism Conferences of the National Institute on Alcohol Abuse and Alcoholism*, U.S. Government Printing Office, 1973. Contributor of more than eighty articles to professional journals.

AVOCATIONAL INTERESTS: Skiing.

* * *

CHAMBERLAIN, Narcisse 1924-

PERSONAL: Born June 17, 1924, in Paris, France; daughter of Samuel Vance (an artist, author, and photographer) and Narcissa (an author; maiden name, Gellatly) Chamberlain. *Education:* Bennington College, B.A., 1946. *Home:* 300 East 33rd St., New York, N.Y. 10016. *Office:* 105 Madison Ave., New York, N.Y. 10016.

CAREER: Time, New York, N.Y., researcher, 1950-52; *Newsweek*, researcher and reporter, Paris, France, 1952-53; *Gourmet*, New York, N.Y., assistant editor, 1954-56; Hastings House, Publishers, New York, N.Y., assistant editor, 1956-60; M. Barrows & Co., Inc. (affiliate of Wil-

liam Morrow and Co., Inc.), New York, N.Y., editor, 1960-65, vice-president and editor-in-chief, 1966-68; William Morrow and Co., Inc., New York, N.Y., senior editor, 1968—.

*WRITINGS—*All with parents, Samuel and Narcissa G. Chamberlain: *The Chamberlain Calendar of French Cooking*, Hastings, annually, 1955-63; *The Chamberlain Calendar of American Cooking*, Hastings, annually, 1956-59; *The Flavor of France*, two volumes, Hastings, 1959, 1964; *The Chamberlain Calendar of Italian Cooking*, Hastings, annually, 1960-63; *The Chamberlain Sampler of American Cooking*, Hastings, 1960; *The Chamberlain Calendar of French Menus*, Hastings, annually, 1964-65; *The Flavor of Italy*, Hastings, 1965; *French Menus for Parties*, Hastings House, 1968.

SIDELIGHTS: Narcisse Chamberlain is fluent in French.

* * *

CHAMBERLAIN, Neil Wolverton 1915-

PERSONAL: Born May 18, 1915, in Charlotte, N.C.; son of Henry Bryan and Elizabeth (Wolverton) Chamberlain; married Marian Kenosian (an executive secretary), June 27, 1942, (divorced June, 1967); married Harriet Feigenbaum, August 9, 1968. *Education:* Western Reserve University (now Case Western Reserve University), A.B., 1937, M.A., 1939; Ohio State University, Ph.D., 1942. *Home:* 39 Claremont Ave., New York, N.Y. 10027. *Office:* Department of Economics, Columbia University, New York, N.Y.

CAREER: Brookings Institution, Washington, D.C., research fellow, 1941-42; Yale University, New Haven, Conn., research director, Labor and Management Center, 1946-49, assistant professor of economics, 1947-49, associate professor, 1949-54; Columbia University, New York, N.Y., professor of economics, 1954-59; Yale University, professor of economics, 1959-67; Columbia University, professor of economics, 1967-69, Armand G. Erpf Professor of Modern Corporations, 1969—. Ford Foundation Program in Economic Development and Administration, director, 1957-60; Salzburg Seminar in American Studies, member of board of directors, 1957—. *Military service:* U.S. Naval Reserve, 1942-46; became lieutenant senior grade. *Member:* American Economic Association, Royal Economic Association, Industrial Relations Research Association (executive board member, 1955-58; president, 1967), Phi Beta Kappa.

WRITINGS: Collective Bargaining Procedures, American Council on Public Affairs, 1944; *The Union Challenge to Management Control*, Harper, 1948, reprinted, Shoe String, 1967; (co-editor) *Cases on Labor Relations*, Foundation Press, 1949; *Management in Motion*, Yale University Press, 1950; (with James W. Kuhn). *Collective Bargaining*, McGraw, 1951, 2nd edition, 1965; *Social Responsibility and Strikes*, Harper, 1953; (with J. M. Schilling) *The Impact of Strikes*, Harper, 1954; *A General Theory of Economic Process*, Harper, 1955; (editor with Frank Pierson and Theresa Wolfson) *A Decade of Industrial Relations Research*, Industrial Relations Research Association, 1958; *Labor*, McGraw, 1958; *Sourcebook on Labor*, McGraw, 1958, revised and abridged edition, with Richard Perlman, 1964.

The Firm: Micro-Economic Planning and Action, McGraw, 1962; *The West in a World Without War*, McGraw, 1963; *The Labor Sector: An Introduction to Labor in the American Economy*, McGraw, 1965, 2nd edition, 1971;

Private and Public Planning, McGraw, 1965; (editor) *Frontiers of Collective Bargaining*, Harper, 1967; *Enterprise and Environment: The Firm in Time and Place*, McGraw, 1968; (editor) *Contemporary Economic Issues*, Irwin, 1969, revised edition, 1973; *Beyond Malthus: Population and Power*, Basic Books, 1970; (compiler) *Business and the Cities: A Book of Relevant Readings*, Basic Books, 1970; *The Place of Business in America's Future: A Study in Social Values*, Basic Books, 1973; *The Limits of Corporate Responsibility*, Basic Books, 1974.

Member of editorial board, *American Economic Review*, 1957-59, *Management International*, 1960-70; consulting editor, Basic Books Inc.†

* * *

CHAMBERLAIN, Robert Lyall 1923-

PERSONAL: Born May 17, 1923, in Syracuse, N.Y.; son of Rudolph Wilson (a college teacher, newspaper editor, and writer) and Barbara (Watson) Chamberlain; married Roberta Simone (a college teacher), June 10, 1960; children: Anthony Lyall Alexander, Skye Simone (daughter). *Education:* Drew University, A.B., 1947; Syracuse University, M.A., 1950, Ph.D., 1956; Fritzwilliam House, Cambridge, graduate study, 1954-56. *Politics:* Moderate liberal. *Religion:* Episcopalian. *Home:* 61 Poplar Ridge, Grand Haven, Mich. *Office:* Grand Valley State College, College Landing, Allendale, Mich.

CAREER: Syracuse University, Syracuse, N.Y., 1947-56, began as tutor, became lecturer in English; instructor in English at Bowling Green State University, Bowling Green, Ohio, 1956-59, Russell Sage College, Troy, N.Y., 1959-61, University of Illinois, Urbana, 1961-63; Grand Valley State College, Allendale, Mich., associate professor of English, 1963—, chairman of department, 1963-65, chairman of Humanities Division, 1964—. Laval University, Quebec, summer teacher of English literature, 1959, 1960. *Military service:* U.S. Army Air Forces, 1943-45. *Member:* Modern Language Association of America, American Association of University Professors (vice-president, Russell Sage College branch, 1960-61), American Civil Liberties Union.

WRITINGS: (Editor with G. G. Winn) *Beacon Lights of Literature*, two volumes, Iroquois Press, 1952; *George Crabbe*, Twayne, 1965. Contributor to literary journals.

WORK IN PROGRESS: Articles on Crabbe, Hardy, Shelley, Godwin, and others.

AVOCATIONAL INTERESTS: Piano, drama, art films, and travel.†

* * *

CHAMBLISS, William J(ones) 1923-

PERSONAL: Born July 7, 1923, in Anderson, Mo.; son of William Jones and Emma (Baird) Chambliss, Jr.; married Mioko Eya, September 24, 1952; children: Paul William, Ann Eya, James Masao, Roger Baird. *Education:* University of Louisville, B.A., 1948; University of Michigan, M.A., 1954, Ph.D., 1963. *Home:* 149 Goodrich Ave., Lexington, Ky. 40503. *Office:* Department of History, University of Kentucky, Lexington, Ky. 40506.

CAREER: University of Kentucky, Lexington, instructor of East Asian history and Japanese, 1959-63, assistant professor, 1963-68, associate professor of East Asian history, 1968—. *Military service:* U.S. Army, 1943-47; became second lieutenant. *Member:* Association for Asian Studies.

Awards, honors: Fulbright Research Fellow, Tokyo, Japan, 1956-58; Fulbright-Hays Research Scholar and American Council of Learned Societies area study grant, Japan, 1966-67.

WRITINGS: (Translator) Ryosuke Ishii, *Japanese Legislation in the Meiji Era*, Pan-Pacific Press (Tokyo), 1958; *Chiaraijima Village: Land Tenure, Taxation, and Local Trade, 1818-1884*, University of Arizona Press, 1965.

* * *

CHAMPION, John E(lmer) 1922-

PERSONAL: Born May 11, 1922, in Chipley, Ga.; son of Jesse and Fannie Lou (Stripling) Champion; married Mary Lanier, June 4, 1955; children: Sally Lanier, John Elmer, Jr. *Education:* University of Georgia, B.B.A., 1942, M.B.A., 1949; Indiana University, graduate study, 1949-50; University of Michigan, Ph.D., 1960. *Politics:* Republican. *Religion:* Presbyterian. *Home:* 2214 Killarney Way, Tallahassee, Fla. 32303. *Office:* School of Business, Florida State University, Tallahassee, Fla.

CAREER: University of Georgia, Athens, assistant professor, 1948-54, associate professor of accounting, 1954-56; Florida State University, Tallahassee, associate professor, 1956-60, professor of accounting and assistant dean of School of Business, 1960-62, vice-president for administration, 1962-65, president, 1965-69, professor of accounting, 1969—. Certified Public Accountant in Georgia, 1952. Educational consultant to General Accounting Office, Washington, D.C., 1968—. Member of Governor's Commission on Quality Education, 1966-67. Member of boards of directors, Tallahassee Bank & Trust Co., Tallahassee Bank North, and Tallahassee Chamber of Commerce. *Military service:* U.S. Army, 1943-46; served in South Pacific; became captain; received Commendation Medal for outstanding services.

MEMBER: American Institute of Certified Public Accountants, American Accounting Association, Southeastern Accounting Association (chairman, 1959), Florida Institute of Certified Public Accountants, Tallahassee Chapter of Certified Public Accountants, Phi Beta Kappa (past president), Phi Kappa Phi, Beta Gamma Sigma (secretary), Beta Alpha Psi, Delta Sigma Pi, Alpha Phi Omega, Gold Key, Omicron Delta Kappa, Delta Kappa Gamma, Kappa Delta Pi, Rotary (member of board of directors, 1970-72; president, 1973-74). *Awards, honors:* Grand Cross of the Order of Vasco Nunez de Balboa (Panama), 1966; Outstanding Alumnus award, University of Georgia, School of Business, 1966.

WRITINGS: Effectiveness of Life Inventory in the Textile Industry, University of Michigan Press, 1960; (with Homer A. Black) *Accounting in Business Decisions*, Prentice-Hall, 1961, 2nd edition (with Black and Gene Brown), 1967, 3rd edition (with Black and U. Gibbes Miller), 1973.

* * *

CHAPIN, Ned 1927-

PERSONAL: Surname is pronounced *Chay*-pin; born August 8, 1927, in Port Gamble, Wash.; son of M. C. and Rose (Smallwood) Chapin; married June Roediger (a college teacher), June 12, 1954; children: Suzanne, Elaine. *Education:* Studied at Stanford University, 1945-46, San Jose State College, 1946-47; University of Chicago, M.B.A., 1949; Illinois Institute of Technology, Ph.D., 1959. *Home:* 1190 Bellair Way, Menlo Park, Calif. 94026.

CAREER: Lecturer at North Park College, Chicago, Ill., 1953-54, at Roosevelt University, Chicago, Ill., 1953-55; Illinois Institute of Technology, Chicago, Ill., instructor in business and economics, 1954-56; Stanford Research Institute, Menlo Park, Calif., systems analyst, 1956-61; San Francisco State College (now University), San Francisco, associate professor of finance, 1961-63; College of San Mateo, San Mateo, Calif., director of data processing, 1963-66. Self-employed data processing consultant, 1954—. *Military service:* U.S. Army, 1951-53; served in Europe. *Member:* American Management Association, Association for Computing Machinery, Association of Educational Data Systems, Data Processing Management Association, American Institute of Industrial Engineers, American Economic Association, Operations Research Society of America, Institute of Management Sciences, Scientific Research Society of America, California Educational Data Processing Association, New York Academy of Sciences, Delta Sigma Rho.

WRITINGS: An Introduction to Automatic Computers (with teacher's manual), Van Nostrand, 1955, 3rd edition, 1963, teacher's manual 2nd edition, 1964; *Programming Computers for Business Applications*, McGraw, 1961; *360 Programming in Assembly Language*, McGraw, 1968, 2nd edition published as *360/370 Programming in Assembly Language Workbook*, McGraw, 1969, *Computers: A Systems Approach*, Van Nostrand, 1971; *Flowcharts*, Auerbach, 1971. Contributor of articles to periodicals and proceedings; reviewer for *Computing Reviews* (publication of Association for Computing machinery).

WORK IN PROGRESS: Further research on computer data processing, systems, and programming.†

* * *

CHAPMAN, Kenneth G. 1927-

PERSONAL: Born June 13, 1927, in Orange, N.J.; son of Arthur Garner (an electrical engineer) and L. Elizabeth (Bennett) Chapman; married second wife, Astrid Gronneberg (a biochemist), August 1, 1958; children: (first marriage) Martin David, Mark Daniel. *Education:* University of Minnesota, B.S., 1949, M.A., 1952; University of Wisconsin, Ph.D., 1956. *Office:* Department of Germanic Languages, University of California, Los Angeles, Calif. 90024.

CAREER: University of Wisconsin, Madison, instructor, 1958-59; University of California, Los Angeles, assistant professor, 1959-64, associate professor, 1964-70, professor of Scandinavian languages and literature, 1970—. *Military service:* U.S. Naval Reserve, 1945-46. *Member:* Modern Language Association of America, Linguistic Society of America, Society for the Advancement of Scandinavian Languages.

WRITINGS: Norwegian-Icelandic Linguistic Relationships, Norwegian Universities Press, 1962; (with Einar Haugen) *Spoken Norwegian, Revised*, Holt, Rinehart & Winston, 1964; *Graded Readings and Exercises in Old Icelandic*, University of California Press, 1964; (translator), Tarjei Vesaas, *The Seed* [and] *Spring Night*, American Scandinavian Foundation, 1964, *The Seed*, published separately, Peter Owen, 1966; *Basic Norwegian Reader*, Holt, Rinehart & Winston, 1965; (associate editor) *Norwegian-English Dictionary*, University of Wisconsin Press, 1965; *Tarjei Vesaas*, Twayne, 1970.

WORK IN PROGRESS: Translations of prose and poetry from Norwegian, Icelandic and Swedish.

SIDELIGHTS: Chapman is fluent in Norwegian, Finnish, and Icelandic, and has a reading knowledge of Danish, Swedish, German, French, and Italian.

* * *

CHAPMAN-MORTIMER, William Charles 1907-
(Chapman Mortimer)

PERSONAL: Born May 15, 1907, in Glasgow, Scotland; son of William George and Martha Jane (McLelland) Chapman-Mortimer; married Frances Statler, 1934; married second wife, Ursula Merits (a physician), January 31, 1956; children: Helene Jane. *Education:* Educated privately, attended Glasgow School of Art, and studied in Paris. *Home:* Gisebo, 561 00 Huskvarna, Sweden. *Agent:* Rosica Colin, 4 Hereford Sq., London S.W. 7, England.

CAREER: Author. *Military service:* British Army, 1939-45; became major. *Awards, honors:* James Tait Black Memorial Prize for best novel published in United Kingdom, 1952, for *Father Goose.*

WRITINGS—All novels, except as noted; all under name Chapman Mortimer: *A Stranger on the Stair*, McGraw, 1950; *Father Goose*, Hart-Davis, 1951; *Young Men Waiting*, Cresset, 1952, Grove, 1954; *Mediterraneo*, Cresset, 1955; *Here in Spain* (nonfiction), Cresset, 1955; *Madrigal*, Cresset, 1960; (author of introduction) Bill Brandt, *Perspective of Nudes*, Bodley Head, 1961; *Amparo*, Weidenfeld & Nicholson, 1971. Contributor to *Botteghe Oscure.*

WORK IN PROGRESS: A novel.

* * *

CHAR, Rene (-Emile) 1907-

PERSONAL: Born June 14, 1907, in L'Isle-sur-Sorgue, Vaucluse, France; son of Emile (an industrialist) and Marie-Therese-Armande (Rouget) Char; married Georgette Goldstein, 1933. *Education:* Baccalaureate degree from Lycee d'Avignon; attended Ecole de Commerce a Marseille, 1925. *Religion:* No religious convictions. *Residence:* L'Isle-sur-Sorgue, Vaucluse 84, France.

CAREER: Poet. Sojourn in Tunisia, 1924; first went to Paris in 1929, where he met Louis Aragon, Paul Eluard, and Andre Breton; was a companion of the Surrealists, 1930-34, during the second period of the movement; in L'Isle-sur-Sorgue in 1940 the Vichy police searched his home, leading to his denunciation as a communist as a result of his Surrealist activities before the war; left Paris for the Alps; during the Resistance he was associated with the Armee Secrete, working for the Resistance in France and North Africa, using the name Capitaine, Alexandre. *Military service:* French Artillery, Nimes, 1927-28; served again, 1939-40, in Alsace. *Member:* Academie de Baviere (Germany), Modern Language Association of America (honorary fellow). *Awards, honors—Military:* Chevalier de la Legion d'Honneur; Medaille de la Resistance; Croix de Guerre; Prix des Critiques, 1966, for *Retour amont.*

WRITINGS: Les Cloches sur le coeur, Le Rouge et le noir, 1928; *Arsenal*, Meridiens (Nimes), 1929, new edition published as *De la Main a la main*, 1930; (with Andre Breton and Paul Eluard) *Ralentir travaux*, Editions Surrealistes, 1930, reprinted, J. Corti, 1968.

Le Tombeau des secrets, [Nimes], 1930; *Artine*, Editions Surrealistes, 1930, new edition published as *Artine et autres poemes*, Tchou, 1967; *L'Action de la justice est eteinte*, Editions Surrealistes, 1931; *Le Marteau sans maitre*, Editions Surrealistes, 1934 (also see below); *Dependance de l'adieu*, G.L.M., 1936; *Moulin premier*, G.L.M., 1936 (also see below); *Placard pour un chemin des ecoliers*, G.L.M., 1937 (also see below); *Dehors la nuit est gouvernee*, G.L.M., 1938 (also see below).

Seuls demeurent, Gallimard, 1945; *Le Marteau sans maitre* [and] *Moulin premier, 1927-1935*, J. Corti, 1945, reprinted, 1963; *Feuillets d'Hypnos* (war journal), Gallimard, 1946, translation by Cid Corman published as *Leaves of Hypnos*, Grossman, 1973; *Le Poeme pulverise*, Fontaine, 1947 (also see below); *Fureur et Mystere*, Gallimard, 1948, new edition, 1962; *Fete des arbres et du chasseur*, G.L.M., 1948; *Dehors la nuit est gouvernee* [and] *Placard pour un chemin des ecoliers*, G.L.M., 1949; *Claire: Theatre de verdure*, Gallimard, 1949; *Le Soleil des eaux*, etchings by Georges Braque, H. Matarasso, 1949, new edition, Gallimard, 1951.

Les Matinaux, Gallimard, 1950, new edition, 1962; *Art bref* [and] *Premieres alluvions*, G.L.M., 1950; *Quatre fascinants: La Minutieuse*, S.N. (Paris), 1951; *A une serenite crispee*, Gallimard, 1951; *Poemes*, wood-cuts by Nicolas de Stael, S.N., 1951; *La Paroi et la prairie*, G.L.M., 1952; *Lettera amorosa*, Gallimard, 1953, 2nd edition, 1962, lithographs by Braque, E. Engelberts (Geneva), 1963; *Arriere-histoire de "Poeme pulverise"* (the 19 texts of *Le Poeme pulverise* with the author's comments on each), lithographs by de Stael, J. Hugues, 1953, 2nd edition, 1972; *Choix de poemes*, Brigadas Liricas (Mendoza, Argentina), 1953; *Le Rempart de Brindilles*, etchings by Wilfredo Lam, L. Broder, 1953; *A la sante du serpent*, G.L.M., 1954; *Le Deuil des nevons*, etchings by Louis Fernandez, Le Cormier (Brussels), 1954; *Recherche de la base et du sommet* [and] *Pauvrete et privilege*, Gallimard, 1955, new edition, 1965; *Poemes des deux annees, 1953-1954*, G.L.M., 1955; *Chanson des etages*, P.A.B. (Ales), 1955.

La Bibliotheque est en feu, etchings by Braque, L. Broder, 1956 (also see below); *Hypnos Waking* (poems and prose), selected and translated by Jackson Mathews, with the collaboration of William Carlos Williams, Richard Wilbur, William Jay Smith, Barbara Howes, W. S. Merwin, and James Wright, Random House, 1956; *Pour nous, Rimbaud*, G.L.M., 1956; *En trente-trois morceaux* (aphorisms), G.L.M., 1956, reprinted, 1970; *Jeanne qu'on brula verte*, illustration by Braque, P.A.B., 1956; *La Bibliotheque est en feu, et autres poemes*, G.L.M., 1957; *L'Abominable homme des neiges*, Librairie L.D.F. (Cairo), 1957; *L'Une et l'autre*, P.A.B., 1957; *De moment en moment*, engravings by Joan Miro, P.A.B., 1957; *Les Compagnons dans le jardin*, engravings by Zao Wou-Ki, L. Broder, 1957; *Poemes et prose choisis*, Gallimard, 1957; *Elisabeth, petite fille*, Benoit, 1958; *Sur la poesie*, G.L.M., 1958, new edition, 1967; *Cinq poesies en hommage a Georges Braque*, lithographs by Braque, S.N. (Geneva), 1958; *L'Escalier de Flore*, engravings by Pablo Picasso, P.A.B., 1958; *La Faux relevee*, P.A.B., 1959; *Nous avons* (prose poem), engravings by Miro, L. Broder, 1959.

Pourquoi la journee vole, engraving by Picasso, P.A.B., 1960; *Le Rebanque*, P.A.B., 1960; *Anthologie*, G.L.M., 1960, new edition published as *Anthologie, 1934-1969*, 1970; *Les Dentelles de Montmirail*, P.A.B., 1960; *L'Allegresse*, engraving by Madeleine Grenier, P.A.B., 1960; (with Paul Eluard) *Deux poemes*, J. Hugues, 1960; *L'Inclemence lointaine*, engravings by Vieira da Silva, P. Beres, 1961; *L'Issue*, P.A.B., 1961; *La Montee de la nuit*, P.A.B., 1961; *La Parole en archipel*, Gallimard, 1962; *Deux Poemes*, engraving by da Silva, P.A.B., 1963; *Poemes et prose choisis*, Gallimard, 1963; *Impressions anciennes*, G.L.M.,

1964; *Commune presence*, Gallimard, 1964; *L'An 1964*, P.A.B., 1964; *L'Age cassant*, J. Corti, 1965; *Flux de l'aimant*, 2nd edition, G. P. Tarn (Veilhes), 1965; *La Provence, point Omega*, [Paris], 1965; (with Albert Camus) *La Posterite du soleil*, E. Engelberts, 1965; *Retour amont*, illustrations by Alberto Giacometti, G.L.M., 1966; *Le Terme epars*, Imprimerie Union, 1966; *Trois coups sous les arbres: Theatre saisonnier* (collection of six plays), Gallimard, 1967; *Dans la pluie giboyeuse*, Gallimard, 1968; (with Martin Heidegger) *L'Endurance de la pensee*, Plon, 1968; (with Andre Frenaud and Jean Tardieu) *Bazaine*, Maeght, 1968; *Le Chien de coeur*, G.L.M., 1969; *L'Effroi, la joie*, Au vent d'Arles (Saint-Paul), 1969.†

Le Nu perdu, Gallimard, 1971; *La Nuit talismanique*, A. Skira (Geneva), 1972.

Contributor: *Violette nozieres*, N. Flamel (Brussels), 1933; *Reves d'encre*, J. Corti, 1945; *Les Miroirs profonds*, Editions Pierre a Feu, 1947; *Cinq parmi d'autres*, Edtions de Minuit, 1947; *A Braque*, P.A.B., 1955; *Le Ruisseau de ble*, P.A.B., 1960; *Poetes, Peintres, Sculpteurs*, Maeght, 1960; *Un Jour entier*, P.A.B., 1960; *25 octobre 1961*, P.A.B., 1961; *13 mai 1962*, P.A.B., 1962; *20 avril 1963*, P.A.B., 1963.

Translator from the English language: Tiggie Ghika, *Le Bleu de l'aile*, Cahiers d'Art, 1948; Theodore Roethke, "Le Reveil," and "Les Orchidees," published in *Preuves*, June, 1959.

Author of numerous prefaces, forewords, introductions, and catalogs, and of Surrealism tracts (1930-34). Also author of numerous pamphlets and leaflets, some decorated with his own engravings. Contributor to *Le Revue nouvelle*, *Sagesse*, *La Revolution surrealiste*, *L'Impossible*, *Cahiers d'art*, *Les Lettres francaises*, *Les Quatre vents*, *Fontaine*, *Cahiers du sud*, *Combat*, *Mercure de France*, *Botteghe Oscure*, *Le Figaro litteraire*, *Le Journal des poetes*, *Temoins*, *Carrefour*, *Action*, *Realities secretes*, *Poetry* (Chicago), *Miscellaneous Man*, *Western Review*, *Quarterly Review of Literature*, *Chelsea*, *Tiger's Eye*, *Minnesota Review*, and other publications.

SIDELIGHTS: In 1952 France's most prominent novelist, the late Albert Camus, wrote: "I consider Rene Char to be our greatest living poet, and *Fureur et Mystere* to be the most astonishing product of French poetry since *Les Illuminations* and *Alcools*." Gabriel Bounoure notes a typical reaction to Char's work: "I remember when I first read Char's poetry I was drawn by its evident greatness, repelled by the asperities, the challenge, and the seismic violence of its inner meaning.... Nothing more salutary had appeared since Nietzsche. Cruel and devouring, this work, enclosing us like a single diamond, yet with all the sting of immense spaces of air.... Char's universe is the kingdom of the open air. No poetry is less enclosed." Camus called this poetry "strange and rigorous," emanating from "a poet of all time who speaks for our time in particular."

In the early thirties Char became involved with Surrealism, and though he broke with the movement shortly thereafter, the novelty of his imagery and his liberated imagination remain. He is his own master; Camus wrote: "No doubt he did take part in Surrealism, but rather as an ally than as an adherent, and just long enough to discover that he could walk alone with more conviction." Gaetan Picon adds: "... Char's work is great, in so far as it both confirms and transcends Surrealism, both fulfils and exposes the poetry of today, inherits the past and opens up the future."

Many of Char's poems are aphoristic—stabbing distillations

of language stripped to its core. Emile Snyder writes: "A poem by Rene Char is an act of violence within which serenity awaits the end of violence." The concentrated lucidity he attains is, in Char's words "the wound closest to the sun," and, he might have added, closest to the essence of poetry, so simple that it is most commonly considered difficult. Camus remarked that this poetry "carries daytime and night on the same impulse.... And so, when Char's poetry appears to be obscure, it is because a furious condensation of imagery, an intensification of light removes it from that degree of abstract transparency which we all too often demand only because it makes no demands on us."

"A poem," writes Char, "is the fulfilment of a desire which remains desire ... that instant when beauty, after keeping us waiting a long time, rises out of common things, passes across our radiant field, binds everything that can be bound, lights up everything that needs lighting in our bundle of shadows." His position is one of total involvement and his themes are great and often difficult. Rene Menard observes that "all the poetry of Char seems to me the writing of a presence who wishes himself just, at every instant in his relations with the world.... Char does not believe ... that man or his destiny are absurd. On the contrary, the circumstances of earth, if men would not ruin them by stupidity, blindness, or cruelty, would be a magnificent, an inexhaustible theater for them.... Man could be a great 'accompanist' of life. In order to understand and animate that alliance, he has at his disposal Poetry...." Char's concern is with human experience and with beauty amid struggle and chaos. He has said: "Nothing obsesses me but life." And, "In our darkness, there is no one place for beauty. The whole place is for beauty." Ralph J. Mills, Jr. notes Char's concern with the primacy of the poet: "In a world 'faced with the destroyed god,' as he believes, the solitary figure of the poet is transformed into the last priest, the final proprietor of value." Char believes that "to every collapse of the proofs, the poet replies with a salvo of futurity." And, though he calls himself a humanist, the meaning of the poem, James Wright observes, "is not to be found in a prose commentary. It is somewhow to be found in the lightning's weeping face."

His language, most frequently compared to fireworks, is "a contained violence," according to Picon, and bears "the tranquil solidity of a mine which the slightest nudge will detonate." He has "surprised the secret of atomic energy in language," identifying "poetry with the word." He seeks in language "cruel tools," and Picon believes this language is lethal, "possessing something of the feeling of weapons set beneath a glass case." Menard believes it to be a language "unique in present-day Letters. It is neither prose nor poem.... Char appears to me the first writer of that future in which, as Being is to be known directly without the cheats of myths and theologies, language will be truly, in the image of Heidegger, 'the house of Being' and will reflect its unity." When obscurity arises in Char's work, it is due, writes Wallace Fowlie, to his "seeking essentially to transcribe the subconscious." Beyond this, he seeks to transcribe with beauty, reinstating, writes Picon, "the language which all modern poetry from Rimbaud to Surrealism has constantly tended to disqualify," namely beautiful language. "Char demands not only that language be effective, but that it have beauty."

Char's philosophical master is Heraclitus whom he calls that "vision of a solar eagle" reconciling opposites. Char believes that "the poem is always married to someone," and the technique of his poetry can be expressed in the Heraclitian saying, "The Lord whose oracle is at Delphi neither expresses nor conceals, but indicates." "I am torn," writes Char, "by all the fragments there are." Yet his mind "can polarize the most neutral objects," writes Bounoure. His inspiration is ancient. Camus noted Char's right to "lay claim to the tragic optimism of pre-Socratic Greece. From Empedocles to Nietzsche, a secret had been passed on from summit to summit, an austere and rare tradition which Char has revived after prolonged eclipse.... What he has called 'Wisdom, her eyes filled with tears,' is brought to life again, on the very heights of our disasters."

BIOGRAPHICAL/CRITICAL SOURCES: Georges Mounin, *Avez-vous lu Char?*, Gallimard, 1946; Pierre Berger, *Rene Char*, Segher, 1951; *Western Review*, autumn, 1953; *Rene Char's Poetry*, Editions de Luca (Italy), 1956; Greta Rau, *Rene Char ou la Poesie accrue*, Corti, 1957; Wallace Fowlie, *A Guide to Contemporary French Literature*, Meridian Books, 1957; *The Fifties*, third issue, 1959; *Chicago Review*, autumn, 1961; P. A. Benoit, *Bibliographie des oeuvres de Rene Char de 1928 a 1963*, Demi-Jour, 1964; *Liberte*, July-August, 1968.

*   *   *

CHARHADI, Driss ben Hamed

PERSONAL: Surname pronounced "Sharadi" to rhyme with "body"; born circa 1938 (no record), in Er Rif area of Morocco; son of Si Mohammed Belgassim (a religious teacher) and Aicha (bent Chafaai) Charhadi; married Mina bent Mohammed Taieb, 1962; children: Fatima Zohra. *Religion:* Moslem. *Residence:* Barrio, Calif.; Tangiers, Morocco. *Agent:* Helen Strauss, William Morris Agency, 1740 Broadway, New York, N.Y.

CAREER: Houseboy and gardener.

WRITINGS: A Life Full of Holes (tape recorded and translated by Paul Bowles), Grove, 1964.

SIDELIGHTS: The *New Statesman* wrote of his book: "Whether it is truly fiction or arranged autobiography, this touching comedy is beautifully constructed. A deadpan Candide wanders in and out of jobs and prisons, commenting with quiet indignation on the fact that society will not admit that poverty is treated like crime." Charhadi, who is totally illiterate, recited his novel into a tape recorder. He has language competence in Moghrebi (a variety of Arabic) and Spanish. His book has been published in Dutch, French, Italian, Spanish, and English. He is currently in the United States to learn to read and write.

BIOGRAPHICAL/CRITICAL SOURCES: Times Literary Supplement, October 15, 1964; *New Statesman*, November 27, 1964; *New York Times Book Review*, January 3, 1965.†

*   *   *

CHARNY, Carmi 1925-
(T. Carmi)

PERSONAL: Born December 31, 1925, in Bronx, N.Y.; settled in Israel, 1947; son of Bernard and Anna (Aichenbaum) Charny; married Shoshana Heiman, 1951; married second wife, Tamara Rikman; children: Gad, Daniel. *Education:* Yeshiva University, B.A., 1946; graduate study at Columbia University, 1946, Sorbonne, 1946-47, Hebrew University, 1947, 1949-51. *Religion:* Jewish. *Home:* 10 Aminadav St., Jerusalem, Israel. *Agent:* Curtis Brown Ltd., 13 King St., Covent Garden, London W.C.2, England.

CAREER: Worked in children's homes in France, 1946; *Massa* (art and literature bi-weekly), Tel Aviv, Israel, co-editor, 1951-54; *Orot* (art and literature quarterly), Jerusalem, Israel, editor, 1955; Sifriat Hapoalim Publishers, Tel Aviv, co-editor of children's section, 1957-62; Am Oved Publishers, Tel Aviv, editor of children's section, 1963-70; *Ariel* (quarterly review of arts and letters), Jerusalem, editor, 1971-74. Ziskind Visiting Professor of Humanities, Brandeis University, 1970; associate professor, Institute for Arts and Communications, Tel Aviv University, 1973; visiting fellow, Oxford Centre for Post-Graduate Hebrew Studies, 1974-76. *Military service:* Israeli Army, 1948-49; became captain. *Member:* Writers Association of Israel, Acum, Ein Hod Artists Village. *Awards, honors:* Shlonsky Prize, 1958, for *The Last Sea*; National Translation Center commission, 1966, and fellowship, 1968; Lucius N. Littauer Foundation grant, 1969; Israel Matz Foundation grant, 1971; Brenner Prize for Literature, 1972, for *Selected Poems 1951-1969*; Prime Minister's Award for creative writing, 1973.

WRITINGS—Under pseudonym T. Carmi, in Hebrew; poems: *Mum vehalom* (title means "Blemish and Dream"), Mahbarot Lesifrut (Tel Aviv), 1951; *Eyn prahim shehorim* (title means "There are No Black Flowers"), Mahbarot Lesifrut, 1953; *Sheleg bi-Yrushalayim* (title means "Snow in Jerusalem"), Sifriat Poalim (Tel Aviv), 1955; *Hayam ha'aharon* (title means "The Last Sea"), Mahbarot Lesifrut, 1958; *Nehash hanehoshet*, Tarshish Books (Jerusalem), 1961, translation by Dom Moraes published as *The Brass Serpent*, Deutsch, 1964, Ohio University Press, 1965; *Ha'unicorn mistakel bamar'ah* (title means "The Unicorn Looks in the Mirror"), Tarshish Books, 1967.

Davar aher/Selected Poems, 1951-1969 (title means "Another Version . . ."), Am Oved (Tel Aviv), 1970; *Somebody Like You*, selection translated into English by Stephen Mitchell, Deutsch, 1971; *Hitnatslut hamehaber* (title means "Author's Apology"), Dvir (Tel Aviv), 1974.

Editor: (With Stanley Burnshaw and Ezra Spicehandler) *The Modern Hebrew Poem Itself*, Holt, 1965; *The Penguin Book of Hebrew Verse*, Penguin, in press.

Also translator into Hebrew of plays of Christopher Fry, Bertolt Brecht, Sophocles, William Shakespeare, Brendan Behan, John Osborne, Edward Albee, and others. Translations of his poems have appeared in *Encounter, Poetry, Midstream*, and other periodicals.

SIDELIGHTS: "Carmi is fascinated by the problem of the point at which tradition becomes inertia, or endurance becomes stubbornness," wrote Christopher Hicks, reviewing *The Brass Serpent*. James Dickey commented about that same book: "Though Mr. Carmi's work stems . . . from the Old Testament, he is no throwback to Biblical diction and Biblical rhetoric. He is modern without losing the sense of being rooted in human concerns that have lived in many generations of men before him. This gives his poems great depth as well as great continuity, and allows him to cherish and revel in his own individuality."

*   *   *

CHATELET, Albert 1928-

PERSONAL: Born June 27, 1928, in Lille, France; son of Albert (a mathematician) and Marguerite (Brey) Chatelet; married Lilian Lange (an art historian), March 25, 1961; children: Madeleine. *Education:* Ecole du Louvre, diplome d'etudes superieures; Faculte des Lettres de Paris, licencie es lettres, docteur es lettres. *Home:* 72 rue de Chemin de fer, Souffelweyersheim, 67460, France. *Office:* Palais universitaire, Strasbourg Cedex, 67084, France.

CAREER: Musee du Louvre, Paris, France, departement des peintures, charge de mission, 1951-55, assistant, 1955-59; Centre National de la Recherche Scientifique, Paris, France, attache, 1959-62; Musee des Beaux-Arts, Lille, France, directeur, 1962-69; Universite des Sciences humaines de Strasbourg, Strasbourg, France, professor of art history, 1969—. *Member:* International Association of Art Critics, Societe Nationale des Antiquaires de France, Societe d' Histoire de l'Art Francais.

WRITINGS: *Les Sources du XXe siecle* (includes slide films), three volumes, Publications Filmees d'Art et Histoire, 1961; *Impressionist Painting*, McGraw, 1962; (with Jacques Thuillier) *La Peinture francaise*, Skira, Volume I: *De Fouquet a Poussin*, 1963, translation by Stuart Gilbert published as *French Painting: From Fouquet to Poussin*, 1963, Volume II: *De Le Nain a Fragonard*, 1964, translation by James Emmons published as *French Painting: From Le Nain to Fragonard*, 1964; *Titien*, Nouvelles Editions Francaises, 1964. Contributor to several exposition catalogs and to periodicals in the field of art.

WORK IN PROGRESS: Research on painting in the northern Netherlands in the fifteenth century.

*   *   *

CH'EN, Jerome 1921-

PERSONAL: Born October 2, 1921, in Chengtu, China; son of K'o-ta (an office clerk) and Hui-chih (Ma) Ch'en; married Joan Marjorie Gold, April 6, 1950; children: Barbara, Rosemary. *Education:* Southwest Associated University, Kunming, China, B.A., 1943; Nankai Institute of Economics, M.A., 1945; University of London, Ph.D., 1956. *Home:* 70 Henconner Lane, Leeds 7, Yorkshire, England. *Office:* University of Leeds, Leeds, England.

CAREER: University of Leeds, Leeds, England, reader in Asian history, 1965—.

WRITINGS: (translator from the Chinese with Michael Bullock) *Poems of Solitude*, Abelard, 1960, 2nd edition, Tuttle, 1970; *Yuan Shih-k'ai*, Stanford University Press, 1961, 2nd edition, 1972 (published in England as *Yuan Shin-k'ai, 1859-1916: Brutus Assumes the Purple*, Allen & Unwin, 1961); *Mao and the Chinese Revolution* (with thirty-seven poems by Mao Tse-tung), Oxford University Press, 1967; (compiler) *Mao*, Prentice-Hall, 1969; (editor) *Mao Papers: Anthology and Bibliography*, Oxford University Press, 1970. Contributor of essays to *Twentieth Century, China Quarterly, T'oung Pao*, and other periodicals.

WORK IN PROGRESS: Mao Tse-tung's literary writings, for Twayne.†

*   *   *

CHENEVIX TRENCH, Charles Pocklington 1914-

PERSONAL: Born June 29, 1914, in Simla, India; son of Sir Richard (in Indian political service) and May (Pocklington) Chenevix Trench; married Mary Elizabeth Kirkbride, October 4, 1954; children: Lucy, Georgia. *Education:* Attended Winchester College, 1928-32, and Oxford University, 1932-35. *Home:* Abbot's Sharpham, Walton, Street, Somersetshire, England. *Agent:* Maurice Michael, 3-4 Fox Ct., London E.C. 1, England.

CAREER: Indian Army, officer in Hodson's Horse, 1935-47, becoming major serving in African and Italian campaigns; British Colonial Service, district commissioner in Kenya, 1948-63; Millfield School, Street, Somersetshire, England, teacher of history and English, 1964—. *Awards, honors*—Military: Military Cross, 1944.

WRITINGS: My Mother Told Me, W. Blackwood, 1956, Norton, 1958; *Portrait of a Patriot: A Biography of John Wilkes*, W. Blackwood, 1961; *The Royal Malady*, Harcourt, 1964; *The Desert's Dusty Face*, W. Blackwood, 1964, Morrow, 1966; *The Poacher and the Squire: A History of Poaching and Game Preservation in England*, Longmans, Green, 1967; *The Shooter and His Gun*, Farm Journals (London), 1969; *The Western Rising: An Account of the Rebellion of James Scott, Duke of Monmouth*, Longmans, Green, 1969; *The Fly-Fisher and His Rod*, Farm Journals, 1969; *A History of Horsemanship*, Doubleday, 1970; *A History of Marksmanship*, Follett, 1972; (contributor) *The Treasury of Horses*, Octopus Books, 1972; *George II*, Lane, 1973; *The History of Angling*, Follett, 1974. Contributor to *Blackwood's Magazine, History Today*, and *Geographical Magazine*.

WORK IN PROGRESS: A history of wildlife preservation and poaching.

AVOCATIONAL INTERESTS: Fox hunting, polo, fishing.†

* * *

CHENG, Chu-yuan 1927-

PERSONAL: Born April 8, 1927, in Kwangtung Province, China; naturalized U.S. citizen; son of Kwan-san and Hsu-tsing Cheng; married Hua Liang, August 15, 1964; children: Anita, Andrew. *Education:* National Chengchi University, Nanking, China, B.A., 1947; Georgetown University, M.A., 1962, Ph.D., 1964. *Office:* Department of Economics, Ball State University, Muncie, Ind. 47306.

CAREER: Seton Hall University, South Orange, N.J., research professor, 1960-64; University of Michigan, Ann Arbor, senior research economist, 1964-70; Lawrence University, Appleton, Wis., associate professor of economics, 1970-71; Ball State University, Muncie, Ind., associate professor, 1971-74, professor of economics and chairman of Asian Studies Committee, 1974—. Visiting research professor, George Washington University, 1963; consultant, National Science Foundation, 1966—. *Member:* American Economic Association, Association for Comparative Economic Studies, Association for Asian Studies, American Academy of Political and Social Sciences, Indiana Academy of Social Sciences.

WRITINGS: Income and Standard of Living in Mainland China, Union Research Institute (Hong Kong), Volume I, 1957, 2nd edition 1958, Volume II, 1957; *The People's Communes*, Union Press, 1959; *Communist China's Economy, 1949-1962: Structural Changes and Crisis*, Seton Hall University Press, 1963; *Economic Relations Between Peking and Moscow, 1949-63*, Praeger, 1964; *Scientific and Engineering Manpower in Communist China, 1949-1963*, National Science Foundation, 1966; *The Machine-Building Industry in Communist China*, Aldine, 1971; *Allocation of Fixed Capital Formation in China*, Center for Chinese Studies, University of Michigan, 1974.

Writings originally in Chinese, but having English translations: *Monetary Affairs of Communist China*, Union Press, 1954, 23rd edition, 1959; *The Chinese Market under Communist Control*, Union Press, 1955; *The Anshan Iron and Steel Industry in Communist China*, Union Press, 1955, 2nd edition, 1956.

Writings available in Chinese edition only: "The Forced Labor System of Communist China," Freedom Press (Hong Kong), 1952; "An Analysis of Financial and Economic Policies in Communist China," Freedom Press, 1952; "New Trends in Financial and Economic Policies in Communist China," two volumes, Freedom Press, 1953; "Financial and Economic Developments in Communist China During 1949-1954," New Cultural Institute (Hong Kong), 1954; "An Analysis of the First Five Year Plan in Communist China," Freedom Press, 1955; "Communist China: Its Situation and Prospect," Freedom Press, 1959.

Contributor: Myron E. Wegman, editor, *Public Health in the People's Republic of China*, Josiah Macy Jr. Foundation, 1973; William W. Whitson, editor, *American Opportunities for Doing Business In China in the 1970's*, Praeger, 1974; *Collected Documents of the Third Sino-American Conference on Mainland China*, Institute of International Relations, 1974. Contributor to *Encyclopaedia Britannica*, and to Chinese, Japanese, and English periodicals.

WORK IN PROGRESS: The Petroleum Industry in China, 1949-1985.

BIOGRAPHICAL/CRITICAL SOURCES: U.S. News and World Report, December 23, 1964.

* * *

CHERWINSKI, Joseph 1915-

PERSONAL: Born December 3, 1915, in Green Bay, Wis.; son of Louis (a farmer) and Josephine (Zmich) Cherwinski. *Education:* Attended public schools in Lansing, Mich. *Politics:* Democrat. *Home:* 1207 Walsh St., Lansing, Mich. 48912.

CAREER: Michigan State Library, Lansing, 1941—, began as page, currently member of reference staff. Poetry contest judge for Poetry Society of Texas and other groups. *Member:* Poetry Society of America, Poetry Society of Michigan. *Awards, honors:* Reynolds Lyric Award from *Lyric* (magazine), 1958; awards from *Kaleidograph* and Poetry Society of America.

WRITINGS—Poetry: No Blue Tomorrow, Kaleidograph Press, 1952; *A Land of Green: Poems for Youth*, Eerdmans, 1960; *Don Quixote with a Rake*, Humphries, 1964; *A Breath of Snow*, Branden Press, 1969. Poetry is represented in *The Diamond Anthology*, edited by Charles Angoff and others, A. S. Barnes, 1971. Editor, *Peninsula Poets* (quarterly of Poetry Society of Michigan), 1953—.

SIDELIGHTS: Cherwinski contributed a poem to the Official Highway Map of Michigan, 1972, to accompany a series of photographs on Michigan's scenic beauties.

BIOGRAPHICAL/CRITICAL SOURCES: New Michigan Verse, University of Michigan Press, 1940; *The Golden Year*, Poetry Society of America, 1960; *Michigan Poets*, Michigan Association of School Librarians, 1964.

* * *

CHESSMAN, G(eorge) Wallace 1919-

PERSONAL: Born March 1, 1919, in Ottawa, Ill.; son of George W. (a clergyman) and Olive (Grieves) Chessman; married Eleanor Osgood (a psychiatric social worker); children: Robert Osgood, Anne Grieves, Harriet Scott, Alexander Wallace. *Education:* Harvard University, B.A., 1941, Ph.D., 1951. *Politics:* Democrat. *Religion:* Baptist. *Home:* Briarwood Rd., Granville, Ohio. *Office:* Denison University, Granville, Ohio.

CAREER: Denison University, Granville, Ohio, instructor, 1950-51; U.S. Department of State, Washington, D.C., historian, 1951-53; Denison University, 1953—, became Alumni Professor of History, 1963. *Military service:* U.S. Coast Guard Reserve, active duty, 1943-46; now lieutenant commander, retired. *Member:* American Association of University Professors, Organization of American Historians, Ohio Historical Society.

WRITINGS: Denison: The Story of an Ohio College, Denison University Press, 1957; *Governor Theodore Roosevelt: The Albany Apprenticeship 1898-1900*, Harvard University Press, 1965; *Theodore Roosevelt and the Politics of Power*, Little, Brown, 1969.

WORK IN PROGRESS: A study of Newark, Ohio, 1880-1930.

SIDELIGHTS: Gerald W. Johnson wrote of *Theodore Roosevelt and the Politics of Power*: "The great merit of this study is the fact that the author, realizing and respecting his limitations of space, has restricted his attention to the Rooseveltian achievements that were solid, rather than spectacular. . . .The result is a book less amusing, but more informative, therefore far more worth the attention of contemporary readers."

* * *

CHI, Wen-shun 1910-

PERSONAL: Born March 17, 1910, in Hopei, China; son of Chung-te and Shih (Wang) Chi; married Ellen T. F. Hsiao, April 7, 1937; children: Josephine (Mrs. T. P. Lee), Francis, Franklin, Alice. *Education:* Tsing Hua University, B.A., 1932; University of Washington, M.A., 1955. *Home:* 1545 Douglas Dr., El Cerrito, Calif. *Office:* Center for Chinese Studies, University of California, Berkeley, Calif.

CAREER: Yi-Shih Pao (a Chinese metropolitan daily), Tientsin and Kunming, editor, 1933-42; U.S. Office of War Information, Kunming Branch, editor-in-chief, 1943-45; Committee for a Free Asia, San Francisco, Calif., radio editor and writer, 1951-53; taught Chinese at the University of Washington, Stanford University, and the Army Language School, Monterey, Calif., 1946-59; University of California, Berkeley, Calif., Center for Chinese Studies, research linguist, and member of the executive committee of the center, 1959—.

WRITINGS: (Editor) *Readings in Chinese Communist Documents*, University of California Press, 1963, 3rd edition, 1968; (editor) *Readings in Chinese Communist Ideology*, University of California Press, 1968; *Readings in the Chinese Communist Cultural Revolution*, University of California Press, 1971.

WORK IN PROGRESS: Chinese-English Dictionary for Communist Readings; Ideological Conflicts in Modern China, a book of intellectual history of modern Chinese thinkers.

* * *

CHMIELEWSKI, Edward 1928-

PERSONAL: Born July 19, 1928, in Albany, N.Y.; son of John J. (an insurance agent) and Rose (Nowicki) Chmielewski. *Education:* Union College and University, Schenectady, N.Y., B.A., 1948; Harvard University, M.A., 1950, Ph.D., 1957. *Office:* Department of History, University of Tennessee, Knoxville, Tenn. 37916.

CAREER: Carnegie Institute of Technology (now Carnegie-Mellon University), Pittsburgh, Pa., instructor in history, 1957-58; University of Florida, Gainsville, assistant professor, 1958-61; University of California, Santa Barbara, assistant professor of history, beginning 1961; now member of faculty at University of Tennessee, Knoxville. *Military service:* U.S. Army, Army Security Agency, 1954-56. *Member:* American Historical Association, American Association for the Advancement of Slavic Studies, Phi Beta Kappa.

WRITINGS: Tribune of the Slavophiles; Konstantin Aksakov, University of Florida Press, 1963; (contributor) *California Slavic Studies*, Volume III, 1964, Volume IV, 1965; *The Polish Question in the Russian State Duma*, University of Tennessee Press, 1970; (editor) *The Fall of the Russian Empire*, Wiley, 1973.

WORK IN PROGRESS: Peter Stolypin and the Constitutional Period of Russian History, 1905-17.

SIDELIGHTS: Chmielewski is competent in Russian, Polish, French, German.†

* * *

CHOPER, Jesse H(erbert) 1935-

PERSONAL: First syllable of surname rhymes with "show"; born September 19, 1935, in Wilkes-Barre, Pa.; son of Edward and Dorothy (Resnick) Choper; married Sonya Rae Schwartz, June 27, 1961; children: Marc Steven, Edward Nathaniel. *Education:* Wilkes College, B.S., 1957; University of Pennsylvania, LL.B., 1960. *Politics:* Democrat. *Religion:* Jewish. *Home:* 115 Alvarado Rd., Berkeley, Calif. 94705. *Office:* University of California Law School, Berkeley, Calif. 94720.

CAREER: Law clerk to Chief Justice Earl Warren of the U.S. Supreme Court, 1960-61; University of Minnesota Law School, Minneapolis, assistant professor, 1961-62, associate professor of law, 1962-65; University of California, Berkeley, professor of law, 1965—. Visiting professor, Catholic University, 1967, Harvard University, 1971-72. *Member:* Order of the Coif, American Law Institute. *Awards, honors:* L.H.D. from Wilkes College, 1967.

WRITINGS: (With W. B. Lockhart and Yale Kamisar) *Constitutional Rights and Liberties: Cases and Materials*, West, 1964, 3rd edition, 1970; (with Lockhart and Kamisar) *The American Constitution: Cases and Materials*, West, 1964, 3rd edition, 1970; (with Lockhart and Kamisar) *Constitutional Law Cases, Comments and Questions*, West, 1964, 3rd edition, 1970; (with A. H. Frey and C. R. Morris, Jr.) *Corporations: Cases and Materials*, Little, Brown, 1966. Contributor to *Minnesota Law Review, California Law Review, Journal of Legal Education, Catholic University Law Review, University of Pennsylvania Law Review.*

WORK IN PROGRESS: New editions of his books to be completed in 1975.

* * *

CHOW, Gregory C. 1929-

PERSONAL: Born December 25, 1929, in Macau, South China; came to United States, 1948, naturalized, 1963; son of Tin-Pong and Pauline (Law) Chow; married Paula Chen, August 27, 1955; Children: John Shan-yi, James Shan-chi, Jeanne S. *Education:* Cornell University, A.B., 1951; University of Chicago, A.M., 1952, Ph.D., 1955. *Home:* 30 Hardy Dr., Princeton, N.J. 08540.

CAREER: Massachusetts Institute of Technology, Cambridge, Mass., assistant professor, 1955-59; Cornell University, Ithaca, N.Y., associate professor, 1959-63; I.B.M. Research Center, Yorktown Heights, N.Y., manager of economic research, 1963-70; Princeton University, Princeton, N.J., professor and director of economic research program, 1970—. Visiting professor, Cornell University, 1964-65; adjunct professor, Columbia University, 1965-70; visiting professor, Harvard University, 1967, Rutgers University, 1969. *Member:* American Economic Association, American Statistical Association, Econometric Society (fellow), Academia Sinica (fellow), Institute of Mathematical Statistics.

WRITINGS: *Demand for Automobiles in the United States*, North-Holland, 1957; (co-author) *The Demand for Durable Goods*, University of Chicago Press, 1960. Also author of research reports. Member of board of editors, *American Economic Review*, 1970-72.†

*   *   *

CHRISTENSEN, David E(mun)   1921-

PERSONAL: Born February 17, 1921, in Ashland, Wis.; son of Emun P. (a Young Men's Christian Association secretary) and Carrie (Loken) Christensen; married Carol D. Bullis, February 16, 1946; children: Danley, Alan, Karen, Sharon. *Education:* Mankato State College, student, 1939-42, 1946; University of Chicago, M.A., 1948, Ph.D., 1956. *Religion:* Unitarian Universalist. *Home:* 908 Glenview Dr., Carbondale, Ill.

CAREER: Florida State University, Tallahassee, assistant professor, then associate professor of geography, 1948-62; Southern Illinois University, Carbondale, professor of geography and associate dean, College of Liberal Arts, 1962—. Visiting lecturer, University of Liverpool, 1964-65. *Military service:* U.S. Army Air Forces, 1942-46; became captain. *Member:* Association of American Geographers, National Council for Geographic Education, Institute of British Geographers, American Association of University Professors, American Association of Higher Education.

WRITINGS: *Agricultural Occupance in Transition: Lee and Sumter Countries, Georgia*, University of Chicago Press, 1956; (with H. F. Becker) *Florida Reference Atlas*, Dixie Printers (Tallahassee), 1961; *Urban Development*, Holt, Rinehart & Winston, 1963; (editor with Robert Alexander Harper) *The Mississippi-Ohio Confluence Area: A Geographic Interpretation of the Paducah 1:250,000 Topographic Map*, National Council for Geographic Education, Illinois State University, 1967. Author of syllabus-workbooks for televised geography course, *World of the Late 1960's*, 1967, and *World Systems: Economic and Ecological*, 1971. Contributor to geography journals.

WORK IN PROGRESS: An introductory college geography textbook; research in problems of development in technologically less-advanced areas.

AVOCATIONAL INTERESTS: Photography, travel.

*   *   *

CHRISTIANI, Dounia Bunis   1913-

PERSONAL: Born August 15, 1913, in Dubno, Russia; came to United States, 1921; daughter of James (a teacher) and Pearl (Bunis) Eisengardt; married Henning Oldenburg Christiani (a civil engineer), December 20, 1936 (deceased); children: Karin Anita (Mrs. Edwin Komisaruk), Hedda Marina, Erica Hope. *Education:* Hunter College, B.A.,

1934; Columbia University, M.A., 1956, Ph.D., 1963. *Home:* West Harwich, Mass.

CAREER: Film actress, 1934-36; stage designer in Southampton, N.Y., 1937; broadcaster with own radio program, New Haven, Conn., 1937; Mariaforbundet, Copenhagen, Denmark, teacher of English, 1938-39; University of Wisconsin–Eau Claire, 1964—, began as assistant professor, became professor of English, 1968. *Member:* Modern Language Association of America, Association of Wisconsin State University Faculties.

WRITINGS: *Scandinavian Elements of Finnegans Wake*, Northwestern University Press, 1965; (editor and translator from the Norwegian) Henrik Ibsen, *The Wild Duck*, Norton, 1968. Contributor to *Proceedings of Comparative Literature Symposium*, Texas Tech, and *James Joyce Quarterly*.

WORK IN PROGRESS: A play, *Adam Dreaming*, and a critical history of drama, *Drama and Society*.

*   *   *

CHRISTOPHER, John B.   1914-

PERSONAL: Born November 20, 1914, in Philadelphia, Pa.; son of John (an educator) and Gertrude (Barrett) Christopher; married Marjorie Gilles, December 21, 1957. *Education:* Haverford College, A.B., 1935; Harvard University, A.M., 1936, Ph.D., 1942. *Home:* 2105 Clover St., Rochester, N.Y. 14618. *Office:* Department of History, University of Rochester, Rochester, N.Y. 14627.

CAREER: Haverford College, Haverford, Pa., instructor, 1938; Duke University, Durham, N.C., instructor, 1941-42; U.S. Department of State, Washington, D.C., research analyst, 1945-46; University of Rochester, Rochester, N.Y., assistant professor, 1946-52, associate professor, 1952-65, professor of history, 1965—. Consultant on college proficiency examinations, New York State Education Department, 1964-66. *Military service:* U.S. Army, Office of Strategic Services, 1942-45; became first lieutenant. *Member:* American Historical Association, Middle East Institute, Middle East Studies Association, Society for French Historical Studies, American Association of University Professors, Rochester Association for United Nations (chairman of policy committee, 1957-58). *Awards, honors:* Fund for the Advancement of Education fellowship for study in Middle East, 1955-56.

WRITINGS: (Contributor) E. M. Earle, *Modern France*, Princeton University Press, 1950; (with Crane Brinton and R. L. Wolff) *A History of Civilization: Prehistory to 1715*, Prentice-Hall, 1955, 4th edition, 1971; (with Brinton and Wolff) *Modern Civilization*, Prentice-Hall, 1957, 3rd edition, 1973; *The Middle East: National Growing Pains*, Foreign Policy Association, 1961; (with Brinton and Wolff) *Civilization in the West*, Prentice-Hall, 1964, 3rd edition, 1973; *Lebanon: Yesterday and Today*, Holt, 1966; *The Islamic Tradition*, Harper, 1972. Contributor of reviews to *American Historical Review*.

WORK IN PROGRESS: *The United States and Turkey*, for Harvard University Press.

*   *   *

CHU, Daniel   1933-

PERSONAL: Born June 11, 1933, in Nanking, China; son of Shih-ming and Grace (Zia) Chu. *Education:* Brown University, A.B., 1955; Northwestern University, graduate study, 1956. *Politics:* Democrat ("most of the time").

Home: 303 West 106th St., New York, N.Y. 10025. *Office:* Scholastic Magazines, Inc., 50 West 44th St., New York, N.Y. 10036.

CAREER: Pawtucket Times, Pawtucket, R.I., reporter, 1956-59; Scholastic Magazines, Inc., New York, N.Y., senior associate editor, 1959—. *Military service:* U.S. Army Reserve, 1958-64, active duty, 1958, 1961-62. *Member:* American Newspaper Guild, Sigma Delta Chi, Brown University Club (New York).

WRITINGS: (with Elliott Skinner) *A Glorious Age in Africa*, Doubleday, 1965; (with Samuel Chu) *Passage to the Golden Gate: A History of the Chinese in America to 1910*, Doubleday, 1967; (editor) *America's Hall of Fame*, Scholastic Book Service, 1969. Scholastic Magazines, Inc., auto editor, 1965—.

SIDELIGHTS: Chu told *CA* "[I] traveled extensively in childhood. . . . Have retained a minimal knowledge of spoken Chinese. Actually, I don't find myself especially interesting. And if sometimes opinionated, I do my best not to foist my personal viewpoints on others—vital issues or not." *Avocational interests:* Reading, music, sailing (as a participant), most other sports (as a spectator), and automobiles.†

* * *

CHU, Louis H. 1915-

PERSONAL: Born October 1, 1915, in Toishan, China; married Kang Wong, 1940; children: May Jean, May Jane, May Joan, Pong Fay. *Education:* Upsala College, A.B., 1937; New York University, M.A., 1940; New School for Social Research, graduate study, 1950-52. *Home:* 88-12 190th St., Hollis, N.Y. *Office:* Hamilton Madison House, 50 Madison St., New York, N.Y.

CAREER: Radio Station WHOM, New York, N.Y., disc jockey, 1951-61; New York (N.Y.) Department of Welfare, director of day center, 1961—. Acme Co., New York, N.Y., owner, 1950—. Soo Yuen Benevolent Association, executive secretary, 1954—. *Military service:* U.S. Army, Signal Corps, 1943-45.

WRITINGS: Eat a Bowl of Tea, Lyle Stuart, 1961.†

* * *

CHURCH, Margaret 1920-

PERSONAL: Born April 8, 1920, in Boston, Mass.; daughter of Joseph William and Sophy (Phillips) Church. *Education:* Radcliffe College, A.B., 1941, Ph.D., 1944; Columbia University, A.M., 1942. *Religion:* Episcopalian. *Home:* 808 North, Road 400 W., West Lafayette, Ind. 47906.

CAREER: Instructor in English at Temple University, Philadelphia, Pa., 1944-46, and Duke University, Durham, N.C., 1946-53; Purdue University, Lafayette, Ind., assistant professor, 1953-61, associate professor, 1961-65, professor of English, 1965—. *Member:* Modern Language Association of America, American Association of University Professors.

WRITINGS: Time and Reality: Studies in Contemporary Fiction, University of North Carolina Press, 1963; *Don Quixote: The Knight of La Mancha*, New York University Press, 1971. Editor, *Modern Fiction Studies*.

WORK IN PROGRESS: Research on comparative trends in the continental novel.

AVOCATIONAL INTERESTS: Horses (owns a Tennessee walking horse), tennis, and other sports.

BIOGRAPHICAL/CRITICAL SOURCES: Purdue Exponent, October 9, 1965.

* * *

CLANCY, John Gregory 1922-

PERSONAL: Born July 4, 1922, in Portland, Me.; son of John Joseph (a laborer) and Ann (Conley) Clancy. *Education:* College of the Holy Cross, student, 1940-42; St. Mary's Seminary, Baltimore, Md., A.B. and S.T.L., 1947; Lateran University, Rome, Italy, J.C.D., 1950.

CAREER: Ordained Roman Catholic priest, Baltimore, Md., 1947; Chamberlain of Papal Household, with title of monsignor, 1953. Vatican Secretariat, Rome, Italy, adetto, 1950-53; Papal Legation, South Africa and Southern Rhodesia, first secretary, 1953-55; Institute for Studies in Social Cooperation, New York, N.Y., president, 1955-58; St. Joseph's College, North Windham, Me., chaplain and professor of theology, 1958-64; St. John's University, Jamaica, N.Y., professor of theology, 1964—. Lecturer at colleges and universities, with special interest in ecumenism. Former member of Maine Health Facilities Planning Council, Maine Mental Health Seminar, and Maine Commission on Civil Rights. *Awards, honors:* Gold Cross—Pro Ecclesia et Pontifice, 1955.

WRITINGS: Apostle for Our Time: The Life of Paul VI, Kenedy, 1963; (translator, compiler, and author of introduction) Paul VI, *Dialogues: Reflections on God and Man*, Trident, 1964; (editor and translator) Pope John XXIII, *An Invitation to Hope*, Simon & Schuster, 1967.

WORK IN PROGRESS: Textbooks in theology.†

* * *

CLANCY, Thomas H(anley) 1923-

PERSONAL: Born August 8, 1923, in Helena, Ark.; son of Thomas Horner (a dairy farmer) and Ruth (Lewis) Clancy. *Education:* Spring Hill College, A.B., 1948; Fordham University, M.A., 1951; Catholic University of Louvain, S.T.L. (cum laude), 1956; London School of Economics and Political Science, University of London, Ph.D., 1960. *Politics:* Democrat. *Home and office address:* Jesuit Provincial Residence, P.O. Box 6378, New Orleans, La. 70114.

CAREER: Entered Society of Jesus (Jesuits), 1942, ordained priest, 1955. Spring Hill College, Mobile, Ala., member of faculty, 1950-52; parish work in Cleveland, Ohio, and vicinity, 1956-57; Loyola University, New Orleans, La., professor of political science, 1960-70, vice-president, 1968-70; *America*, associate editor, 1970-71; Catholic Society for Religious and Literary Education, president, 1971—. Board member, Urban League of New Orleans, 1964-65. *Member:* American Political Science Association, Historical Society (London), Catholic Record Society, Southern Political Science Association. *Awards, honors:* Folger Library fellowship for political research, 1961; grant from Society for Religion in Higher Education for research on religious literature at Oxford University, 1965-66.

WRITINGS: Papist Pamphleteers: The Allen-Persons Party and the Political Thought of the Counter-Reformation in England, Loyola University Press (Chicago), 1964; *English Catholic Books: 1614-1700*, Loyola University Press, in press. Contributor to *New Catholic Encyclopedia*, and of more than thirty articles and reviews to *Social Order, America, Interracial Review, Thought, Nouvelle Revue Theologique, National Catholic Reporter*, and other journals. Assistant editor, *America*, summer, 1963.

WORK IN PROGRESS: Research in seventeenth-century English political theory with special attention to religious influences.

*   *   *

CLARK, Alan 1928-

PERSONAL: Born April 13, 1928, in London, England; son of Sir Kenneth McKenzie (an art authority and professor at Oxford University) and Lady Elizabeth (Martin) Clark; married Caroline Jane Beuttler, July 31, 1958; children: James Alasdair, Andrew McKenzie. Education: Christ Church, Oxford, B.A., 1949, M.A., 1950. Politics: Conservative. Religion: Anglican. Home: Manor House, Seend, Melksham, Wiltshire, England. Agent: Harold Matson Co., Inc., 30 Rockefeller Plaza, New York, N.Y. 10020.

CAREER: After Oxford, served in Royal Australian Air Force, 1950-54; writer on military subjects; Institute for Strategic Studies, London, England, member, 1963—; Governor, St. Thomas Hospital. Member: St. James Club (London).

WRITINGS: The Donkeys: A Study of the British Expeditionary Force in 1915, Morrow, 1961; The Fall of Crete, Morrow, 1962; Barbarossa—The Russian-German Conflict, 1941-45, Morrow, 1965; The Lion Heart, Morrow, 1969; Suicide of the Empires: the Battles on the Eastern Front, 1914-18, American Heritage Press, 1971; Aces High: The War in the Air Over the Western Front, Putnam, 1973. Contributor to Sunday Times, Spectator, History Today, and other journals and newspapers.

WORK IN PROGRESS: Current defense postures.

SIDELIGHTS: Clark speaks French, Russian, Italian, and is widely traveled. He went to Moscow with the British amatuer wrestling team in 1957.

*   *   *

CLARK, Charles Tallifero 1917-

PERSONAL: Born March 18, 1917, in Danville, Ill.; son of Charles A. and Kathryn Clark; married October, 1942; children: Charles A., Mary D., Robert S. Education: University of Texas, B.B.A., 1938, M.B.A., 1939, Ph.D., 1956. Office: Department of General Business, University of Texas, Austin, Tex.

CAREER: Chamber of Commerce, Austin, Tex., assistant manager, 1940-41; University of Texas, Austin, assistant dean of student life, 1946-48, director of classified personnel, 1948-59, system personnel adviser, Office of the Chancellor, 1959-61, associate professor of business statistics and research associate, Bureau of Business Research, 1961—. Consultant to Austin National Bank, Texas State Bank, and Texas Medical Association. Military service: U.S. Army Air Forces, 1941-46; became second lieutenant. Member: American Statistical Association, College and University Personnel Association (past president), Southwest Social Science Association, Austin Statistical Association.

WRITINGS: (With John R. Stockton) Introduction to Business and Economic Statistics, 4th edition, South-Western Publishing Co., 1971; (with L. L. Schkade) Statistical Analysis for Administrative Decisions, 2nd edition, South-Western Publishing Co., 1974. Contributor of articles and reviews to personnel and business journals.

CLARK, Eric 1911-

PERSONAL: Born June 22, 1911, in Belfast, Ulster, Northern Ireland; married Margaret Thompson McKee, August 4, 1947; children: Robin, Hilary. Education: Larkfield College, D.L.T.C., 1947; The Queens University of Belfast, Dip. Ed., 1960. Home: 22 Eastleigh Dr., Belfast 5, Northern Ireland.

CAREER: Galleon Press, Belfast, Northern Ireland, editor, 1949—. Contemporary painter, whose work has been exhibited in Europe and in the Indies. Military service: British Army, Royal Corps of Signals, 1940-46; received Burma Star. Member: British Society of Commerce (fellow), P.E.N., Ulster Academy.

WRITINGS: Morse, Galleon Press, 1941; Ulster Quizbook, three volumes, Galleon Press, 1944-48; Ulster Soccer Quiz, Galleon Press, 1947; Greenwood Anthology (poems), Muller, 1950; Sleeves Up, Galleon Press, 1950; Stark Passage, Galleon Press, 1950; Don a Green Battledress, Galleon Press, 1951; Laugh with Ulster, Galleon Press, 1955; The Troopship Was Bound for Bombay, Galleon Press, 1958; Learning to Paint, Galleon Press, 1965; Drills for Drawing, in press; Adventures in Oil Paint, in press. Writer of television scripts for British Broadcasting Corp. and other television services. Contributor of articles and poems to journals and newspapers. Editor, Ulster Weekend.

WORK IN PROGRESS: Jungle Adventures and Burma Green, both war stories; Water Color Experiments; Art for Art's Sake; and poems.†

*   *   *

CLARK, Frank J(ames) 1922-

PERSONAL: Born August 4, 1922, in Brooklyn, N.Y.; son of J. Franklin and Anna (Koch) Clark; married Betty Schulte, November 8, 1946; children: John, Donald. Education: New York University, B.A., 1953, further study, 1966-72; Columbia University, M.A., 1961; further study, Mannes College of Music, 1961-62; Electronic Computer Programming Institute, certificate, 1965; also attended State University of New York at New Paltz, Dutchess Community College, and Genessee Community College, 1966-70. Home: 205 Grandview Terr., Batavia, N.Y. 14020. Office address: Department of Data Processing, Box 718, Genessee Community College, College Rd., Batavia, N.Y.

CAREER: Trumpeter with Boston Pops Orchestra, Boston, Mass., 1953, Band of America, New York, N.Y., 1964-65, and Gershwin Orchestra, American Album of Famous Music Orchestra, and others; music teacher in public schools, Plainview, Long Island, N.Y., 1958-64; teacher of mathematics in other schools; Dutchess Community College, Poughkeepsie, N.Y., assistant professor of data processing, 1965-68; Genessee Community College, Batavia, N.Y., director of data processing and associate professor of data processing, 1968—. Programmer, International City Manager's Association, spring, 1967; designer of several city and county data processing systems. Military service: U.S. Navy, 1942-45; musician on U.S.S. "Iowa"; received twelve battle stars, Presidential Unit Citation. Member: New York State Association of Junior Colleges, American Technical Education Association, Authors Guild.

WRITINGS: (With Melvin Berger) Science and Music: From Tom-tom to Hi-fi, McGraw, 1961; (with Alan Vorwald) Computers: From Sand Table to Electronic Brain,

McGraw, 1961, 3rd edition, 1970; (with Berger) *Music in Perspective*, S. Fox, 1962; *Contemporary Studies for the Trumpet*, Adler, 1963; *Contemporary Math*, F. Watts, 1963; *Contemporary Math for Parents*, F. Watts, 1965; *Speed Math*, F. Watts, 1966.

Information Processing, Goodyear Publishing, 1970; *Introduction to PL/I Programming*, Allyn & Bacon, 1970, new edition, 1971; (with Robert L. Gray) *Accounting Programs and Business Systems: Case Studies*, Goodyear Publishing, 1971; *Business Systems and Data Processing Procedures*, Prentice-Hall, 1972; (with Joseph M. Whalen) *RPG I and RPG II Programming*, Addison-Wesley, 1974; *Mathematics for Data Processing*, Reston, 1974; *Data Recorder*, Reston, 1974. Also author of television scripts.

SIDELIGHTS: There is a collection of Clark's writings at the University of Mississippi.

* * *

CLARK, Gerald 1918-

PERSONAL: Born April 3, 1918, in Montreal, Quebec, Canada; son of Samuel (a fashion designer) and Polly (Fink) Clark; married Rosalie Arbess, September 16, 1954 (died, 1960); children: Bette. *Education:* McGill University, B.Sc., 1939. *Home:* 3 Westmount Square, Montreal H3Z 2S5, Quebec, Canada. *Agent:* Willis Kingsley Wing, 24 East 38th St., New York, N.Y. 10016. *Office: Montreal Star*, 245 St. James St., W., Montreal, Quebec, Canada.

CAREER: Journalist, 1940—. World War II correspondent from invasion of Normandy on, and one of seventeen correspondents representing world press at peace signing at Rheims; *Montreal Star*, Montreal, Quebec, New York correspondent, 1953-55, chief overseas correspondent with headquarters in London, England, 1955-60, associate editor, Montreal, 1960-69, editor, 1969—. *Awards, honors:* National Newspaper Award, Canada, for series of articles on the Soviet Union, 1954.

WRITINGS: Impatient Giant: Red China Today, McKay, 1959; *The Coming Explosion in Latin America*, McKay, 1963; *Canada: The Uneasy Neighbor*, McKay, 1965.

* * *

CLARK, James V(aughan) 1927-

PERSONAL: Born July 9, 1927, in Highland Park, Ill.; son of Robert Eliot and Ruth (Morris) Clark; married second wife, Frances Campbell (an elementary school principal), 1964; children: (previous marriage) Peter, David, Jennifer Ann, Sarah. *Education:* Northwestern University, student, 1947-50; Harvard University, M.B.A., 1956, D.B.A., 1958. *Home:* 400 Pioneer Dr., Glendale, Calif. 91203. *Office:* Graduate School of Business Administration, University of California, Los Angeles, Los Angeles, Calif.

CAREER: Harvard University, Cambridge, Mass., with Graduate School of Business Administration, 1958-61; University of California, Los Angeles, Graduate School of Business Administration, associate professor of business administration, 1961—. *Military service:* U.S. Maritime Service, 1944-46; served in Pacific theater; became warrent officer junior grade. *Member:* Society for Applied Anthropology (fellow), American Psychological Association, American Sociological Association, American Association for Humanistic Psychology.

WRITINGS: (With Lawrence and others) *Organizational Behavior and Administration*, Irwin-Dorsey, 1961; *Education for the Use of Behavioral Science*, Institute of Industrial Relations, University of California, Los Angeles, 1962. Contributor to psychology, behavioral science, and management journals.

WORK IN PROGRESS: Research on the therapeutic dimensions of sensitivity training groups in industry, education, and home.†

* * *

CLARK, John W(illiams) 1907-

PERSONAL: Born December 23, 1907, in Excelsior, Minn.; son of Harry Oscar (a salesman) and Gertrude (Williams) Clark; married Lucile Ann Bayer, September 6, 1930. *Education:* University of Minnesota, B.A., 1928, Ph.D., 1941; Harvard University, M.A., 1929. *Home:* 403 Oak Grove, Minneapolis, Minn. 55403.

CAREER: Rensselaer Polytechnic Institute, Troy, N.Y., instructor in English, 1929-30; University of Minnesota, Minneapolis, instructor, 1930-42, assistant professor, 1942-49, associate professor, 1949-53, professor of English, 1953-73, professor emeritus, 1973—, chairman of department, 1958-69. *Military service:* U.S. Army Air Forces, 1944-46; became sergeant. *Member:* Council on Basic Education, Society for the Preservation of the Book of Common Prayer, Phi Beta Kappa.

WRITINGS: (With Eric Partridge) *British and American English Since 1900*, Philosophical Library, 1951; (with Ernest Weekley) *The English Language*, Deutsch, 1952; (with Eric Partridge) *You Have a Point There*, Hamish Hamilton, 1953; (with G. H. Vallins) *Spelling*, Deutsch, 1954; *Early English: A Study of Old and Middle English*, Deutsch, 1957, 2nd edition, 1967; *The Language and Style of Anthony Trollope*, Deutsch, 1974.

WORK IN PROGRESS: A Reactionary Guide to English Usage, a book on word oddities.

* * *

CLARK, Laurence (Walter) 1914-

PERSONAL: Born May 16, 1914, in Maidstone, Kent, England; son of Henry Charles and Gladys (Friend) Clark; married Marion Pies, December 3, 1958; children: Oliver George, Barnaby Alan. *Education:* Peterhouse College, Cambridge, B.A., 1935, M.A., 1940. *Home and office:* 6 Temple Gardens, Moor Park, Rickmansworth, Hertfordshire, England.

CAREER: Free-lance journalist in London, England, 1935-39; free-lance writer, 1947—; Veracity Ventures Ltd., Rickmansworth, Hertfordshire, England, founder and director, 1964—. *Military service:* British Army, Infantry, 1940-46; served in India and Burma; brigade intelligence officer, local guerilla commander. *Member:* Society of Authors, and Special Forces Club (both London).

WRITINGS: Thirty Nine Preludes (poems), Villiers Publications, 1953; *Kingdom Come* (novel), Centaur Press, 1958; *More Than Moon* (novel), Centaur Press, 1961; *Murder of the Prime Minister* (novel), Veracity Ventures, 1965; (contributor) Michael Ivens and Reginald Dunstan, editors, *The Case for Capitalism*, Michael Joseph, 1967; *A Father of the Nation*, Veracity Ventures, 1968. Also author of *Interim Papers*, Veracity Ventures, 1964-74. Contributor to *Economist, Poetry London, Observer*, and to other journals and periodicals.

WORK IN PROGRESS: A book with tentative title, *Democracy Has Three Dimensions*, about development of democracy in its economic, cultural, and purely political aspects, on a world scale.

BIOGRAPHICAL/CRITICAL SOURCES: Twentieth Century, March, 1954.

*   *   *

CLARK, LaVerne Harrell   1929-

PERSONAL: Born June 6, 1929, in Smithville, Tex.; daughter of James Boyce (a railway engineer) and Belle (Bunte) Harrell; married L. D. Clark (a professor and writer), September 15, 1951. *Education:* Texas Woman's University, B.A., 1950; Columbia University, courses in creative writing, and graduate study, 1951-54; University of Arizona, M.A., 1962. *Home:* Route 4, Box 54, Tucson, Ariz. 85704. *Office:* Poetry Center, Department of English, University of Arizona, Tucson, Ariz.

CAREER: Fort Worth Press, Fort Worth, Tex., reporter and librarian, 1950-51; Columbia University Press, New York, N.Y., secretary, sales-advertising department, 1951-53; Episcopal Diocese of New York, New York, N.Y., secretary, promotion-news department, 1958-59; University of Arizona, executive secretary, Poetry Center, 1962—. *Member:* Theta Sigma Phi, Kappa Alpha Mu, Pi Lambda Theta.

WRITINGS: They Sang for Horses: A Study of the Impact of the Horse on Navajo and Apache Folklore, University of Arizona Press, 1966. Contributor to *The Western Folklore Conference: Selected Papers*, Utah State University Press, 1964, and to *Arizona and the West*, and *American Scandinavian Review*. Did photographic studies for book by husband, L. D. Clark, *Dark Night of the Body: D. H. Lawrence's "The Plumed Serpent"*, University of Texas Press, 1964.

SIDELIGHTS: Mrs. Clark began writing while an undergraduate at Texas Woman's University. She said: "I [began] writing about folklore when I collected the cures and beliefs of a Texas Negro community and presented papers on that subject for the student literary quarterly and at a Texas Folklore Society meeting." In 1960-61, she traveled in Mexico to make a photographic study for her husband's book on D. H. Lawrence. She has also made informal portraits of contemporary poets with whom she has become acquainted.

BIOGRAPHICAL/CRITICAL SOURCES: The Western Folklore Conference: Selected Papers, Monograph Series of the Utah State University Press, Volume XI, Number 3, June, 1964.†

*   *   *

CLARK, Leonard   1905-

PERSONAL: Born August 1, 1905, in St. Peter Port, Guernsey, Channel Islands; married Jane Callow, April 14, 1954; children: Robert Andrew, Mary Louise. *Education:* Normal College, Bangor, North Wales, Teacher's Certificate, 1930. *Religion:* Church of England. *Home:* 50 Cholmeley Crescent, Highgate, London N. 6, England.

CAREER: Teacher in Gloucestershire and London, 1921-28, 1930-36; Ministry of Education (now Department of Education and Science), Devonshire, Yorkshire, London, England, assistant inspector of schools, 1936-45, H.M. inspector of schools, 1945-70. Poet, author, and editor. Lecturer and broadcaster on poetry and education of children. Consultant on poetry for Seafarers' Education Service, 1940-54; member of literature panel of the Arts

Council of Great Britain, 1965-69; member of Westminster Diocesan Schools Commission, 1971; member of the executive council of the National Book League of Great Britain, 1970. *Wartime Service:* Devonshire Regiment of the Home Guard, 1940-43. *Member:* Order of British Empire, Royal Society of Literature (fellow), National Union of Teachers (life member), London Academy of Music and Dramatic Art (associate), Poetry Society of Great Britain, Guild of Freemen of City of London, Haberdashers' Company (liveryman), National Liberal Club, Highgate Literary Club, Marylebone Cricket Club. *Awards, honors:* Knight of St. Sylvester, 1970; joint first prize winner, *International Who's Who in Poetry*, 1972, for "The Coin."

WRITINGS: Poems, privately printed, 1925; (editor) *The Open Door: An Anthology of Verse for Children*, Mathews & Marrot, 1937; (editor) *The Magic Kingdom: An Anthology of Verse for Seniors*, Mathews & Marrot, 1937; *Poems*, Fortune Press, 1940; *Passage to the Pole*, Fortune Press, 1944; (editor) *The Kingdom of the Mind: Essays and Addresses by Albert Mansbridge, 1903-1937*, Dent, 1944; *Alfred Williams: His Life and Work*, Basil Blackwell, 1945, reprinted with new introduction, Augustus M. Kelley, 1969; *Rhandanim*, Salamander Press, 1945; *The Mirror and Other Poems* (introduction by Walter de la Mare), Wingate, 1948; *XII Poems*, City of Birmingham School of Printing, 1948.

English Morning and Other Poems (introduction by Edith Sitwell), Hutchinson, 1953; *Walter de la Mare: A Checklist*, National Book League and Cambridge University Press, 1956; *Sark Discovered*, Dent, 1956, revised edition, Dobson, 1971; (translator with Iris Allam) Edmund de Goncourt, *The Zemganno Brothers*, Redman, 1957; (editor) Andrew Young, *Prospect of a Poet*, Hart-Davis, 1957; (editor) *Quiet as Moss: 36 Poems by Andrew Young*, Hart-Davis, 1959.

(Editor) *Collected Poems of Andrew Young*, Hart-Davis, 1960; *Walter de la Mare: A Monograph*, Bodley Head, 1960; *Green Wood, A Gloucestershire Childhood* (autobiography), Parrish, 1962; (editor) *Drums and Trumpets* (anthology for the very young), Bodley Head, 1962, Dufour, 1963; *Daybreak* (poems for children), Hart-Davis, 1963; *Andrew Young*, British Council, 1963; (editor) *Selected Poems of John Clare*, E. J. Arnold, 1964; *When They Were Children* (biographies), Roy, 1964; (editor) *Common Ground* (poetry anthology for children), Faber, 1964; *Who Killed the Bears?*, Forest of Dean Newspapers (Cinderford), 1964; *A Fool in the Forest* (autobiography), Dobson, 1965; (editor) *All Things New* (anthology for children), Constable, 1965, Dufour, 1968; (editor) *The Poetry of Nature*, Hart-Davis, 1965; *The Year Round* (poems for children), Hart-Davis, 1965; *Fields and Territories* (poems), Turret Press, 1967; *Prospect of Highgate and Hampstead*, Highgate Press, 1967; (compiler and author of introduction) *Following the Sun: Poems by Children*, Odhams, 1967; *Good Company: Poems for Children*, Dobson, 1968; *Grateful Caliban* (autobiography), Dobson, 1968; (compiler) *Flutes and Cymbals: Poetry for the Young*, Bodley Head, 1968, Crowell, 1969; (editor with Giles de la Mare) *The Complete Poems of Walter de la Mare*, Faber, 1969; *Near and Far: Poems for Children*, Hamlyn, 1969; *Here and There: Poems for Children*, Hamlyn, 1969; (compiler) *Sound of Battle*, Pergamon, 1969; (author of introduction) Alfred Williams, *Life in a Railway Factory*, Augustus M. Kelley, 1969.

(Editor and author of introduction) *Poems by Children*, Studio Vista, 1970; *Walking with Trees, Alone*, Enitharmon

Press, 1970; (editor) *A Book of Narrative Poems*, Longman Group, 1970; *Every Voice*, Words Press, 1971; (compiler) *All Along, Down Along: A Book of Stories in Verse*, Longman Young Books, 1971; *Secret as Toads*, Chatto & Windus, 1972; *Singing in the Streets*, Dobson, 1972; (author of introduction) Edward Lowbury, *Green Magic*, Chatto & Windus, 1972; (compiler) *Poems of Ivor Gurney*, Chatto & Windus, 1973; *The Hearing Heart*, Enitharmon Press, 1973; (compiler) *Great and Familiar: The Heritage of English Poetry*, Fenrose, 1974; *The Broad Atlantic*, Dobson, 1974; *Mr. Pettigrew's Harvest Festival*, Thornhill Press, 1974; (editor) *Complete Poems of Andrew Young*, Secker & Warburg, 1974; *The Four Seasons*, Dobson, 1975; *The Tale of Prince Igor*, Dobson, 1975; *Mr. Pettigrew's Train*, Thornhill Press, 1975.

Also author of the "Robert Andrew" series, seven books, E.J. Arnold, 1965-66. Editor of "Longman's Poetry Library," 64 titles, 1966-70. Work represented in many anthologies, including *New Poems, 1960: A P.E.N. Anthology of Contemporary Poetry*, edited by C. V. Wedgwood, Hutchinson, 1961; *From Darkness to Light*, edited by Victor Gollancz, Gollancz, 1964; *New Poems, 1965: A P.E.N. anthology of Contemporary Poetry*, edited by Anthony Cronin and others, Hutchinson, 1966. Contributor of poems and articles to *Outposts, Poetry Review* (London), *Sunday Times* (London), *Anglo Welsh Review, Horn Book*, and numerous other magazines and journals.

WORK IN PROGRESS: A book on his experience as one of Her Majesty's Inspectors of Schools; the writing of poetry.

SIDELIGHTS: Clark has travelled in Germany, France, Malta, and Mauritius. *Avocational interests:* Children, gardening, walking, the countryside, reading, and book collecting.

*　　*　　*

CLARKE, Robin Harwood 1937-

PERSONAL: Born October 19, 1937, in Bedford, England; son of Leonard Harwood (a schoolmaster) and Dorothy (Hawkins) Clarke; married Janine Hill (an actress), February 8, 1962. *Education:* Cambridge University, B.A. (honors), 1960. *Home:* 8 Lambert St., London N.1, England. *Office:* Dorset House, Stamford St., London S.E.1, England.

CAREER: Encyclopaedia Britannica, London, England, scientific subeditor, 1960-61; *Discovery*, London England, assistant editor, 1961-63, editor, 1963-64; *Science Journal*, London, England, editor, 1964—. British Broadcasting Corp., Overseas Service, science writer and broadcaster. *Member:* Association of British Science writers (secretary).

WRITINGS: The Diversity of Man, Roy, 1964; (editor) Germaine and Arthur Beiser, *Story of Cosmic Rays*, Phoenix House, 1964; *We All Fall Down: The Prospect of Biological and Chemical Warfare*, Penguin, 1968; *The Silent Weapons: The Realities of Chemical and Biological Warfare*, McKay, 1968; *The Great Experiment: Science and Technology in the Second United Nations Development Decade*, United Nations, 1971; *The Science of War and Peace*, McGraw, 1972. Contributor of articles to *Daily Express Science Annual* and *Elizabethan*. Editor, "World of Science Library Series."

SIDELIGHTS: We All Fall Down has been translated into Spanish and German.†

CLEBSCH, William Anthony 1923-

PERSONAL: Born July 27, 1923, in Clarksville, Tenn.; son of Alfred (a warehouseman) and Julia (Wilee) Clebsch; married Betsy Birchfield, June 10, 1944; children: William Ernst, Sarah Elizabeth. *Education:* University of Tennessee, B.A., 1946; Virginia Theological Seminary, B.D., 1946, S.T.M., 1951; Union Theological Seminary, New York, N.Y., Th.D., 1957; Cambridge University, postdoctoral study, 1959-60. *Home:* 847 Mayfield Ave., Stanford, Calif. 94305. *Office:* Department of Religious Studies, Stanford University, Stanford, Calif.

CAREER: Michigan State University, East Lansing, lecturer in religion, 1947-49; Protestant Episcopal Theological Seminary in Virginia, Alexandria, assistant professor of church history, 1949-56; Episcopal Theological Seminary of the Southwest, Austin, Tex., professor of history, 1956-64; Stanford University, Stanford, Calif., associate professor of religion, 1964-67, professor of religious studies and humanities, 1967—, chairman of special programs in humanities, 1967-73, chairman of department of religious studies, 1973—. *Member:* American Society of Church History (president, 1973). *Awards, honors:* Faculty fellow, American Association of Theological Schools, 1959-60; research scholar, Huntington Library, 1961, 1964; senior fellow, National Endowment for the Humanities, 1971-72; visiting fellow in religious studies and associate fellow of Silliman College, Yale University, 1971-72.

WRITINGS: Contemporary Perspectives, National Lutheran Council, 1962; (editor) *Journals of the Episcopal Church in the Confederate States of America*, Church Historical Society, 1962; (with Charles R. Jaekle) *Pastoral Care in Historical Perspective*, Prentice-Hall, 1964; *England's Earliest Protestants, 1520-1535*, Yale University Press, 1964; *From Sacred to Profane: The Role of Religion in American History*, Harper, 1968; *American Religious Thought: A History*, University of Chicago Press, 1973.

WORK IN PROGRESS: A History of Christian Life-Styles, completion expected in 1976; *Varieties of Religious Personality*, 1977.

SIDELIGHTS: Reviewing *From Sacred to Profane* in *Commonweal*, James H. Smylie wrote, "Prof. Clebsch has a fertile mind and this volume fairly bursts with fresh ideas. . . . The basic thesis is clear and he has succeeded in carrying the conversation about the relation between religion and American life to another level."

*　　*　　*

CLEMENTS, E(llen) Catherine (Scott) 1920-

PERSONAL: Born November 29, 1920, in Church End, Finchley, Middlesex, England; daughter of Isaac James (an electrical engineer) and Naomi Ellen (White) Scott; married Albert Edward Clements (a teacher), September 13, 1941; children: Penelope Ann. *Education:* Attended schools in England. *Politics:* Liberal party. *Religion:* Methodist. *Home:* Birds' Haven, Willoughby Waterless, Leicestershire, England.

CAREER: Secretary to book exporter, 1938-39; outpatient almoner to an Outer London hospital receiving war casualties, 1939-43; worked in special section of British Foreign Office, 1943-45. *Member:* Women's Institute (branch secretary, eight years).

WRITINGS: Birds at My Door, Faber, 1963, Transatlantic, 1964. Contributor to *Leicester Mercury*.

WORK IN PROGRESS: Two books, *Birds of Character* and *Birds' Diseases and Hand Rearing*.

SIDELIGHTS: Mrs. Clements said, "[I] have a strong sympathetic understanding with animals of all sorts, and because of this am able to save many wild injured birds and hand-rear nestlings which are found ill and abandoned. Ninety per cent of all birds brought are cured and returned to the wild." *Avocational interests:* Gardening, knitting, basketry, leather glove making, rug making.

BIOGRAPHICAL/CRITICAL SOURCES: Leicester Mercury, May 28, 1964, April 6, 1971; Leicester Advertiser, January 18, 1963, January 15, 1965, April 11, 1969, September 11, 1970.

* * *

CLEMENTS, Ronald Ernest 1929-

PERSONAL: Born May 27, 1929, in South Woodford, London, England; son of Cyril George (in police work) and Elizabeth (Cook) Clements; married Valerie Suffield, March 19, 1955; children: Gillian Valerie, Marian Elizabeth. *Education:* Spurgeon's College, London, B.D. (second class honors), 1954; Cambridge University, B.A. (first class honors), 1956, M.A., 1960, B.D., 1969; University of Sheffield, Ph.D., 1961. *Politics:* Conservative. *Home:* 8 Brookfield Rd., Coton, Cambridge, CB3 7PT, England. *Office:* Fitzwilliam College, Cambridge University, Cambridge, CB3 ODG, England.

CAREER: Baptist minister in Sheffield, England, 1956-59, in Stratford on Avon, England, 1959-60; University of Edinburgh, Edinburgh, Scotland, assistant lecturer in Hebrew and Semitic languages, 1960-64, lecturer in Old Testament literature and theology, 1964-67; Cambridge University, Cambridge, England, fellow of Fitzwilliam College and lecturer in Old Testament, 1968—. *Military service:* Royal Air Force, 1947-49. *Member:* Society for Old Testament Study.

WRITINGS: Prophecy and Covenant, S.C.M. Press, 1965; God and Temple, Basil Blackwell, 1965; Abraham and David, S.C.M. Press, 1968; Prophecy and Tradition, Basil Blackwell, 1974.

WORK IN PROGRESS: A commentary on *Isaiah*, completion expected in 1977.

* * *

CLEMO, Reginald John 1916-
(Jack Clemo)

PERSONAL: Born March 11, 1916, in St. Austell, Cornwall, England; son of Reginald (a kiln laborer) and Eveline (Polmounter) Clemo; married Ruth Grace Peaty, in 1968. *Education:* Received elementary education in Trethosa Council School. *Politics:* "No fixed political allegiance." *Religion:* Evangelical Christian. *Home:* Goonamarris, St. Stephen's, St. Austell, Cornwall, England.

CAREER: Author and poet. *Member:* West Country Writers' Association (honorary). *Awards, honors:* Atlantic Award in Literature, University of Birmingham, for *Wilding Graft,* 1948; Arts Council Festival Poetry Prize for "The Wintry Priesthood," 1951; Civil List pension from Queen Elizabeth, 1961.

WRITINGS—Under name Jack Clemo: Wilding Graft (novel), Macmillan, 1948; Confession of a Rebel (autobiography), Chatto & Windus, 1949; The Clay Verge (poetry), Chatto & Windus, 1951; The Invading Gospel (theology), Bles, 1958; The Map of Clay (poetry), Methuen, 1961; Cactus on Carmel (poetry), Methuen, 1967; The Echoing Tip (poetry), Methuen, 1971. Twenty poems anthologized in *Penguin Modern Poets 6,* 1964. Contributor of occasional poems to London Magazine, Poetry Review, and other periodicals.

WORK IN PROGRESS: Poetry.

SIDELIGHTS: Clemo told *CA:* "Interests limited in recent years by attacks of blindness and partial deafness. I found most of my literary stimulus in theology, evangelism, and erotic mysticism. My early work was pervaded by a deep love for the Cornish clay landscape with its artificial mountains. Since my marriage the range of my work has broadened, many of my later poems being set in foreign countries. I had previously lived a lonely hermit life with a widowed mother."

BIOGRAPHICAL/CRITICAL SOURCES: Western Review, winter, 1956; London Magazine, October, 1960; Sunday Times Colour Supplement (London), August 19, 1962.

* * *

CLENDENIN, William R(itchie) 1917-

PERSONAL: Surname is accented on second syllable; born July 23, 1917, in Sparta, Ill.; son of Harry Orrin (a florist) and Mabel (Ritchie) Clendenin; married Virginia June Van Zandt (a piano teacher), June 14, 1941; children: William Ritchie, Jr. *Education:* University of Illinois, B.Mus., 1940; Union Theological Seminary, New York, N.Y., M.S.M., 1942; University of Iowa, Ph.D., 1952. *Religion:* Episcopal. *Home:* 460 South 44th St., Boulder, Colo. 80302.

CAREER: Trinity Church, Columbia, S.C., organist and choirmaster, 1942-44; Queens College, Charlotte, N.C., assistant professor of organ and theory, 1944-46; Iowa State University of Science and Technology, Ames, assistant professor and college organist, 1946-49; University of Colorado, Boulder, assistant professor of music, 1952-59, associate professor, 1959—, chairman of graduate studies in music. Organist and choirmaster, St. John's Church, Boulder, Colo. 1953-61. Lecturer on music, and organ recitalist. *Member:* American Musicological Society (chairman of Rocky Mountain chapter, 1956-58), American Guild of Organists (dean of Boulder chapter, 1956-57), Music Teachers National Association, Pi Kappa Lambda, Phi Mu Alpha, Alpha Kappa Lambda.

WRITINGS: (With Louis Trzcinski) Visual Aids in Western Music, 2nd edition, Pruett Press, 1960; Music: History and Theory, Doubleday, 1965; History of Music, Littlefield, 1974. Contributor to music journals; music and concert reviews for *Boulder Daily Camera,* 1953—.

SIDELIGHTS: Clendenin is competent in French and German.†

* * *

CLEPHANE, Irene (Amy)

PERSONAL: Born in Harringay, London, England; daughter of Peter H. F. (a schoolmaster) and Amy Jessie (Lavington) Clephane. *Education:* Educated privately at home and at The Regent Street Polytechnic, London, England. *Politics:* Labour. *Home and office:* 4 Fitzwarren Gardens, London N19 3TP, England.

CAREER: Daily Herald, London, England, editorial secretary, 1919-23; Queen, London, England, assistant editor, 1923-29; Graphic (weekly illustrated), London, England, art editor, 1929-35; Home and Country, London, England, editor, 1937-41; Amalgamated Press, London, England, associate editor of serial publication, "The History of the Second Great War," 1943-47, deputy head of encyclopedia department and executive editor of *New Universal Encyclopedia*, 1949-59; free-lance writer, editior, and translator. *Member:* Incorporated Society of Authors, Playwrights, and Composers, Translators' Association, Le Petit Club Francais.

WRITINGS: (With Alan Bott) *Our Mothers*, Gollancz, 1932; *Ourselves*, Lane, 1933; *Towards Sex Freedom*, Lane, 1935; (translator from the Dutch, with David Hallett) Johan Fabricius, *The Son of Marietta*, Gollancz, 1936; (translator from the Dutch, with Hallett) Marianne Philips, *A House in Vienna*, Dickson, 1963; (translator from the Dutch, with Hallett) Maurits Dekker, *Beggars' Revolt*, Doubleday, 1938; (translator from the French) Jean-Paul Sartre, *Words*, Hamish Hamilton, 1964; (translator from the French) Jean-Paul Sartre, *The Communists and Peace*, Hamish Hamilton, 1969; (translator from the French) Jean-Paul Sartre, *The Spectre of Stalin*, Hamish Hamilton, 1969; (translator from the French) Andre Malraux, *Fallen Oaks*, Hamish Hamilton, 1972.

Editor of translations and original works for publishers. Contributor to *New Universal Encyclopedia, Hutchinson's Twentieth-Century Encyclopedia*, and to newspapers and periodicals.

* * *

CLIFTON, Marguerite Ann 1925-

PERSONAL: Born July 17, 1925, in Santa Monica, Calif.; daughter of James and Bertha (Flossman) Clifton. *Education:* University of Redlands, B.A., 1946; University of Southern California, M.S., 1951; Stanford University, Ed.D., 1957. *Politics:* Democrat. *Religion:* Roman Catholic. *Office:* Purdue University, Lafayette, Ind.

CAREER: Teacher in secondary schools in California, 1946-51; San Francisco State College, San Francisco, Calif., instructor in physical education, 1951-55; Stanford University, Stanford, Calif., instructor in physical education, 1955-56; University of California, Los Angeles, assistant professor of physical education, 1956-64; Purdue University, Lafayette, Ind., professor and head of department of physical education for women, 1964—. *Member:* American Association for Health, Physical Education and Recreation (member of research council; vice-president, 1963-64), American College of Sports Medicine (fellow), National Association for Physical Education of College Women.

WRITINGS: (With Hope Smith) *Physical Education: Exploring Your Future*, Prentice-Hall, 1962; (with others) *Toward Excellence in College Teaching*, W. C. Brown, 1964. Contributor of research papers to *Research Quarterly* and *Perceptual and Motor Skills*.

WORK IN PROGRESS: The Theory and Principles of Human Movement, for Lea & Febiger.†

* * *

CLOUD, (Joseph) Fred (Jr.) 1925-

PERSONAL: Born April 6, 1925, in Dallas, Tex.; son of Joseph Fred and Dolia (Owens) Cloud; married second wife, Barbara Ann Dickerson, July 31, 1969. *Education:* Attended Little Rock University, 1940-42, Hendrix College, 1942-43; Vanderbilt University, B.A., 1944; Vanderbilt Divinity School, B.D., 1947; Scarritt College for Christian Workers, M.A., 1961. *Politics:* Democrat. *Office:* Human Relations Commission, Rm. 1107, Parkway Towers, Nashville, Tenn. 37219.

CAREER: Ordained Methodist minister, 1946; pastor of churches in Tennessee, 1946-47, 1948-53; Methodist Board of Education, Nashville, Tenn., editor of youth publications, 1953-65, editor of junior high school publications, 1966-67; Human Relations Commission, Nashville, Tenn., executive director, 1967—. Visiting professor, Vanderbilt Divinity School, 1954-55, Iliff School of Theology, summer, 1958, Scarritt College for Christian Workers, 1964-65, University of Oklahoma, 1974. Lecturer on writing, National Christian Writers Workshop, July, 1961, World Committee on Literacy and Christian Literature, Singapore, Sarawak, and Fiji, summer, 1963, World Council of Christian Education, Furigen, Switzerland, summer, 1964. President, Volunteer Assistance in the Community, 1974—.

MEMBER: National Association of Human Rights Workers (president, 1972-73), United Nations Association. *Awards, honors:* Freedoms Foundation awards for essay, 1960, and editorial, 1965; National Conference of Christians and Jews citation for editorials, 1965; Outstanding Alumnus Award, Little Rock University, 1965.

WRITINGS: Youth Guide on Southeast Asia, Friendship, 1956; *Youth and Home Missions*, Friendship, 1960; *In Step With Time*, Friendship, 1960; *God's Hand in Our Lives*, Tidings, 1964; *Writing Curriculum Materials for Christian Education*, World Council of Christian Education (London), 1964; *Youth Guide on Spanish Americans*, Friendship, 1964; (editor) *A Traveler's Prayerbook*, Upper Room, 1965; *Let's Be Reasonable About Race*, Graded Press, 1968; *Prayers for Reconciliation*, Upper Room, 1970. Contributor to *Christian Century, Journal of Intergroup Relations*, and various religious journals. Assistant editor, *Motive*, 1944-45, *Pastor*, 1947-48; editor, *Christian Action*, 1953-65.

WORK IN PROGRESS: Pushing Life: The Urban Ministry of Edgehill Church, about an inner city church's multifaceted program.

SIDELIGHTS: In 1963 Cloud traveled more that 28,000 miles in Southeast Asia and the South Pacific, in line with his interest in helping persons in emerging nations to develop indigenous literature. In 1973 he initiated a human rights training program for professionals in twelve Southern states. Currently he is organizing a clinical legal education program at Vanderbilt University.

* * *

CLOUGH, Rosa Trillo 1906-

PERSONAL: Born March 20, 1906, in New York, N.Y.; daughter of Salvatore (a musician) and Carmela Trillo; married Shephard B. Clough (a professor of history at Columbia University), June 6, 1926; children: Shephard Anthony, Peter Nelson. *Education:* Hunter College (now Hunter College of the City University of New York), B.A., 1926; Columbia University, M.A., 1934, Ph.D., 1941; additional study at Sorbonne, University of Paris, at University of Turin, University of Florence, University of Perugia, University of Rome, and University of Heidelberg. *Home:* 460 Riverside Dr., New York, N.Y. 10027.

CAREER: Hunter College (now Hunter College of the City University of New York), New York, N.Y., tutor, 1936-37, instructor, 1937-47, assistant professor of Romance languages, 1947-56; Finch College, New York, N.Y., professor of Italian, head of Italian department, and chairman of the department of modern languages, 1956-71. Lecturer throughout Italy for U.S. Information Service.

Member: Modern Language Association of America, American Association of Teachers of Italian, Mediaeval Academy of America, American Association of University Professors, Renaissance Society of America, Dante Society of America, Medieval Club of New York, Columbia University Seminar.

WRITINGS: Cenni geografici sull'Italia, Columbia University Press, 1940; *Looking Back at Futurism*, Cocce Press, 1942; *Carlotta e Amedeo*, Cocce Press, 1951; (with Maria Piccirilli) *Piccolo mondo autice*, Mondadori, 1957; (with Giovanni Getto and A. Enriques) *Thirty Beautiful Italian Short Stories*, Zanichelli, 1959; (with Teresa Petriccioli) *Si dice cosi: The New Italian Grammar*, Avio Press, 1962; *Futurism: The Story of an Art Movement, a New Appraisal*, Philosophical Library, 1961, 2nd edition, 1969. Contributor to literary journals in United States and Italy.

WORK IN PROGRESS: A new edition of *Futurism: A New Appraisal*, to be titled *Futurism: Past and Present, 1909-1972*.

SIDELIGHTS: Mrs. Clough is fluent in spoken and written Italian, French, and Spanish; she has knowledge of Latin and German. *Avocational interests:* Painting and art.

*   *   *

CLUTE, Morrel J.   1912-

PERSONAL: Born 1912, in Clare County, Mich.; son of Elmer C. and Pearl E. Clute; married Averyl O. Gaines; married Janet A. Wilson; children: Morrel G., Monte D., Kelley. *Education:* Central Michigan College (now University), B.S., 1939; Wayne State University, M.Ed., 1949, D.Ed., 1959. *Home:* Oxford, Mich. *Office:* Education Bldg., Wayne State University, Detroit, Mich.

CAREER: Teacher in rural schools in Clare County, Mich., 1934-37, in Clare (Mich.) public schools, 1937-42, and in Rochester (Mich.) public schools, 1942-54; Wayne State University, Detroit, Mich., 1954—, began as special instructor, now professor of educational leadership. Visiting professor, Western Washington State College, summer 1971. Consultant to Delinquency Study and Youth Development Project, Southern Illinois University, 1960-72, Nationwide Education Program in Corrections, and to Association of Schools of Allied Health Professon of Department of Health, Education and Welfare. Field director, American Red Cross, serving overseas with 10th Mountain Division, 1944-45. *Member:* Association for Supervision and Curriculum Development.

WRITINGS: (With Roland C. Faunce) *Teaching and Learning in the Junior High School*, Wadsworth, 1961.

Contributor: Glen Hass and Kimball Wiles, editors, *Readings in Curriculum*, Allyn and Bacon, 1965; Gordon Vars, editor, *Common Learnings, Core and Interdisciplinary Approaches*, Intext, 1969; Robert R. Leeper, editor, *Curricular Concerns in a Revolutionary Era*, Association for Supervision and Curriculum Development, 1971.

Also contributor to *Schools for the Middle Years*, published by Intext, and to *The Self-Contained Classroom* (monograph), published by the Association for Supervision and Curriculum Development. Contributor to professional journals.

*   *   *

COBLEY, John   1914-

PERSONAL: Born August 3, 1914, in Newcastle, New South Wales, Australia; son of Joseph Will and Ada Creagh (Robertson) Cobley; married Margaret Sandbrook, March 9, 1943; children: Jan, Susan, Margaret. *Education:* University of Sydney, M.B. and B.S., 1937. *Religion:* Church of England. *Home:* 34 Beatty St., Balgowlah, New South Wales, Australia. *Office:* 231 Macquarie St., Sydney, New South Wales, Australia.

CAREER: Physician practicing in Sydney, New South Wales, 1946—. *Military service:* Australian Imperial Forces, 1940-46; Commonwealth Military Forces, 1948-58; became lieutenant colonel. *Member:* Royal Australasian College of Physicians, Royal College of Physicians (London), Royal Australian Historical Society, Society of Australian Geneaologists.

WRITINGS: Sydney Cove 1788, Hodder & Stoughton, 1962; *Sydney Cove 1789-90*, Angus & Robertson, 1963; *The Convicts: A Study of a One in Twenty Sample*, Wentworth, 1964; *Sydney Cove 1791-92*, Angus & Robertson, 1965; (compiler) *The Crimes of the First Fleet Convicts*, Angus & Robertson, 1970.

WORK IN PROGRESS: A Register of First Fleet Convicts, in collaboration with A. J. Gray.†

*   *   *

COCCIOLI, Carlo   1920-

PERSONAL: Born May 15, 1920, in Leghorn, Italy; son of Attilio and Anna (Duranti) Coccioli. *Education:* University of Naples and University of Rome, Doctorate in colonial sciences. *Religion:* Roman Catholic. *Agent:* Georges Borchardt, 14 West 55th St., New York, N.Y. 10019.

CAREER: Author, primarily of novels, 1946—. *Military service:* Italian Army, officer; received Medaglia d'Argento al V.M. (star medal) for activities in anti-fascist Resistance. *Awards, honors:* Charles Veillon Prize, 1950, for *Il Giuoco*.

WRITINGS: Il Migliore d l'ultimo (novel), Vallecchi, 1946; *La Difficile speranza*, [Florence], 1947; *La Piccola valle di Dio* (novel), [Florence], 1948, translation by Campbell Nairne published as *The Little Valley of God*, Heineman, 1956, Simon & Schuster, 1957; *Il Cielo e la terra*, [Florence], 1950, translation by Frances Frenaye published as *Heaven and Earth*, Prentice-Hall, 1952; *Il Giuoco*, [Milan], 1950; *Le Bal des egares*, [Milan], 1951; *Fabrizio Lupo*, [Milan], 1952, translation by Bernard Frechtman published as *The Eye and the Heart*, Heinemann, 1960, *Fabrizio's Book*, Shorecrest, 1966; *L'Immagine e le stagioni*, [Florence], 1954; *La Ville et le sang* (novel), Flammarion, 1955, translation by Mary McLean published as *Daughter of the Town*, Heinemann, 1957; *Manuel, le Mexicain* (novel), Plon, 1956, translation by Hans Koningsberger published as *Manuel, the Mexican*, Simon & Schuster, 1958; *Journal*, Table Ronde (Paris), 1957; *Le Caillou blanc* (novel), Plon, 1958, translation by Elizabeth Sutherland and Vera Bleuer published as *The White Stone*, Simon & Schuster, 1960; *Un Suicide* (novel), Flammarion, 1959; *Florence que j'aime*, Editions Sun (Paris), 1959, translation published as *The Florence I Love*, Tudor, 1960; *Ambroise* (novel), Flammarion, 1961; *Soleil* (novel), Plon, 1961; *Il Giuoco; Nuovo teste*, Vallecchi, 1961; *Omeyotl: Diario messicano*, Vallecchi, 1962; *L'Aigle azteque est tombe* (novel), Plon, 1964; *L'erede di Montezuma*, Vallecchi, 1964; *Le corde dell'arpa*, Longanesi, 1967; *Le tourment de Dieu*, Fayard, 1971.

Author of play, "Los Fanatico." Regular contributor to *Corriere della Sera* (Milan) and *Siempre* (Mexico City).†

COEN, Rena Neumann 1925-

PERSONAL: Born February 22, 1925, in New York, N.Y.; daughter of Joshua H. (a professor) and Tamar (Mohl) Neumann; married Edward Coen (a professor of economics), June 26, 1949; children: Deborah, Joel, Ethan. *Education:* Barnard College, B.A., 1946; New York University, graduate study, 1946-47; Yale University, M.A., 1948, graduate study, 1948-49; Courtauld Institute, University of London, graduate study, 1949-50; University of Minnesota, Ph.D., 1969. *Politics:* Democrat. *Religion:* Jewish. *Home:* 1425 Flag Ave., S., Minneapolis, Minn. 55426.

CAREER: Minneapolis Institute of Arts, Minneapolis, Minn., research assistant and lecturer, 1961-66; St. Cloud State College, St. Cloud, Minn., assistant professor, 1969-72, associate professor of art history, 1973—. Docent, Jewish Museum, New York, summer, 1948. Organizer, Bicentennial Exhibition, University of Minnesota Gallery, 1974—. *Member:* American Association of University Professors, College Art Association of America, The Society for Religion in Higher Education (fellow), Minnesota Historical Society, Minneapolis Society of Fine Arts. *Awards, honors:* Danforth fellowship, 1966-69.

WRITINGS—All published by Lerner: *Kings and Queens in Art*, 1965; *American History in Art*, 1966; *Medicine in Art*, 1970; *The Old Testament in Art*, 1970; *The Black Man in Art*, 1970; *The Red Man in Art*, 1972. Contributor to art and histroical journals.

WORK IN PROGRESS: Research in nineteenth century American painting and its iconography.

SIDELIGHTS: Mrs. Coen has lived abroad for varying periods, including three years' residence in England, 1949-52.

* * *

COGGINS, Ross 1927-

PERSONAL: Born November 23, 1927; son of Robert William and Cecile (Sheppard) Coggins; married Doryce Lengefeld, August 12, 1948; children: Cathryn, Joanna. *Education:* Baylor University, B.A., 1948; Southwestern Baptist Theological Seminary, B.D., 1951. *Politics:* Democrat. *Home:* 6608 Jocelyn Hollow Rd., Nashville, Tenn. 37205. *Office:* Southern Baptist Convention, 460 James Robertson Parkway, Nashville, Tenn. 37219.

CAREER: Baptist General Convention of Texas, associate director of student work, 1953-55; Baptist missionary in Java, 1955-61; Southern Baptist Convention, Nashville, Tenn., director of communications, 1961—.

WRITINGS: Missions Today, Convention Press, 1962; *To Change the World*, Broadman, 1964; (editor) *The Gambling Menace*, Broadman, 1966; (with William Crook) *Seven Who Fought*, Word Books, 1971. Television scriptwriter. Contributor of articles to religious journals.

SIDELIGHTS: Coggins is fluent in Indonesian language.†

* * *

COGHILL, Nevill (Henry Kendall Aylmer) 1899-

PERSONAL: Born April 19, 1899, in England; son of Sir Egerton Bushe (a painter) and Hildegarde (Somerville) Coghill; married Elspeth Nora Harley (an author and translator); children: Carol (Mrs. Robert Martin). *Education:* Exeter College, Oxford, B.A., 1922, M.A., 1926. *Religion:* Church of England. *Home:* Savran House, Aylbur-ton, near Lydney, Gloucestershire, England. *Agent:* Innes Rose, John Farquharson Ltd., 15 Red Lion Sq., London W.C. 1, England.

CAREER: Oxford University, Oxford, England, fellow and tutor in English literature at Exeter College, 1925-57, Merton Professor of English Literature, 1957-66. Senior member of Oxford University Dramatic Society, 1934-66; founder of Oxford University Experimental Theatre Club, 1935; curator of Oxford University Theatre. Director and producer of plays by Milton, Shakespeare, Marlowe, and others, in Oxford and London, 1930—. *Military service:* British Army, Royal Field Artillery, 1918-19; served on Salonika front; became second lieutenant. *Member:* Royal Society of English Literature (fellow), Poetry Society (president, 1964-66), Travellers' Club. *Awards, honors:* D.Litt., Williams College, 1966; LL.D., St. Andrews College, 1971.

WRITINGS: The Poet Chaucer, Oxford University Press, 1949, 2nd edition, 1967; *Visions from Piers Plowman*, Phoenix House, 1949, Oxford University Press, 1970; *The Canterbury Tales* (in modern English), Penguin, 1951, revised edition, 1966; (editor, with C. Tolkien) Geoffrey Chaucer, *The Pardoner's Tale*, Harrap, 1958; (editor, with Tolkien) Chaucer, *The Nun's Priest's Tale*, Harrap, 1959; *Shakespeare's Professional Skills*, Cambridge University Press, 1964; (editor) Geoffrey Chaucer, *The Man of Law's Tale*, Harrap, 1969; *Geoffrey Chaucer*, Longmans, 1969; *The Tragedy of Romeo and Juliet*, Pan Books, 1971; (translator) Geoffrey Chaucer, *Troilus and Criseyde*, Penguin, 1971; *A Choice of Chaucer*, Faber, 1972. Also author with Martin Starkie of play, "Canterbury Tales" (first produced in London at Phoenix Theatre, 1968), and screenplay adaptation for film "Doctor Faustus," produced by Columbia, 1968.

WORK IN PROGRESS: Writing on Elizabethan drama and on twentieth-century drama, especially English.

AVOCATIONAL INTEREST: Music.†

* * *

COGSWELL, Coralie (Norris) 1930- (Coralie Howard)

PERSONAL: Born March 4, 1930, in Cleveland, Ohio; daughter of Wendell Webb (a professor of journalism) and Mildred (Winkler) Norris; married Robert E. Howard, January 19, 1950 (divorced, 1961); married Theodoe R. Cogswell (a professor of English and science fiction writer), December 17, 1964 (divorced, 1970); children: (first marriage) Madeline Karen, Lucy Dawn. *Education:* University of Chicago, Ph.B. (with honors), 1948; North Dakota State University, B.S., 1949; University of Arkansas, M.A., 1951. *Religion:* Cosmic Ecology. *Home:* Greengok, Route 1, Winslow, Ark. 72959.

CAREER: School librarian in Pinellas County, Fla., 1961-64, and Tunkhannock, Pa., 1966-68; Pennsylvania State University, Scranton, instructor in English, 1968-70.

WRITINGS—All under name Coralie Howard: (Compiler) *First Book of Short Verse*, F. Watts, 1964; (compiler) *Lyric Poems*, F. Watts, 1968; *What Do You Want to Know?*, Simon & Schuster, 1968.

WORK IN PROGRESS: 2142, a fantasy novel for older children.

SIDELIGHTS: Ms. Cogswell informed *CA*: "I try to keep in harmony with nature and the evolutionary changes humanity is undergoing now; living simply, working towards land trusts, barter, alternative forms of energy, and independence of destructive social traditions. I like to translate the symbols of science, art, and mystery into each other and to glimpse the universal language underlying them.''

* * *

COHEN, Albert Kircidel 1918-

PERSONAL: Born June 15, 1918, in Boston, Mass.; son of Morris and Clara (Scolnick) Cohen; married Natividad Manguerra, 1948. *Education:* Harvard University, B.A., 1939, Ph.D., 1951; Indiana University, M.A., 1949. *Home:* Route 1, Box 113, Mansfield Center, Conn. *Office:* Department of Sociology and Anthropology, University of Connecticut, Storrs, Conn. 06268.

CAREER: Indiana Boys School (correctional institution), Plainfield, Ind., director of orientation, 1942; Indiana University, Bloomington, 1947-65, began as instructor, became professor of sociology; University of Connecticut, Storrs, professor of sociology, 1965—. Visiting professor at University of California, Berkeley, 1960-61, University of California, Santa Cruz, 1968-69, and Institute of Criminology, Cambridge, England, 1972-73; fellow of Center for Advanced Study in the Behavioral Sciences, Stanford, Calif., 1961-62. *Military service:* U.S. Army, Chemical Warfare Service, 1942-46; became first lieutenant. *Member:* American Sociological Association, Society for the Study of Social Problems, Ohio Valley Sociological Association.

WRITINGS: Delinquent Boys: The Culture of the Gang, Free Press of Glencoe, 1955; (contributor) *Sociology Today,* edited by Robert K. Merton and others, Basic Books, 1959; (contributor) *Contemporary Social Problems,* edited by Merton and Robert Nisbet, Harcourt, 1961; *Deviance and Control,* Prentice-Hall, 1966; (contributor) Bernard Barber and Alex Inkeles, editors, *Stability and Social Change,* Little, Brown, 1971. Contributor of articles to journals and periodicals.

* * *

COHEN, John (Isaac) 1911-

PERSONAL: Born January 20, 1911, in England; son of Joseph (a merchant) and Rebecca (Kahn) Cohen; married second wife, Rosemarie Loss, July 20, 1955; children: (first marriage) Katherine, Geoffrey; (second marriage) Nicholas, Oliver, James. *Education:* University College, London, B.S., 1936, M.A., 1936, Ph.D., 1940. *Home:* 15 Didsbury Park, Manchester, England. *Agent:* Shaw Maclean, 2-10 St. John's Rd., London S.W.11 1QG, England. *Office:* Department of Psychology, University of Manchester, Manchester M13 9PL, England.

CAREER: British government, London, England, technical adviser to Offices of the War Cabinet, 1941-45, to Cabinet Office, 1945-48; University of Leeds, Leeds, England, lecturer in psychology, 1948-49; University of Jerusalem, Jerusalem, Israel, professor of psychology, 1949-51; University of London, Birkbeck College, London, England, lecturer in psychology, 1951-52; University of Manchester, Manchester, England, professor of psychology, 1952—. Member of interprofessional advisory committee, World Federation for Mental Health, 1949-52; consultant to UNESCO, 1948, 1950, 1962, and 1967. *Military service:* British Army, Royal Armoured Corps, 1941. *Member:* British Psychological Society (fellow), World Academy of Art and Science (fellow), International Association of Semiotics (member of executive committee), International Society for the Study of Time, Centre de Recherches de Psychologie Comparative (foreign member). *Awards, honors:* M.A. from University of Manchester.

WRITINGS: (Editor with Raymond B. Cattell) *Human Affairs,* Macmillan, 1937, Books for Libraries, 1970; (editor with Robert M. W. Travers) *Educating for Democracy,* Macmillan, 1939, Books for Libraries, 1970; *Human Nature, War and Society,* C. A. Watts, 1946; (with Mark Hansel) *Risk and Gambling,* Philosophical Library, 1956; (translator) H. E. Hammerschlag, *Hypnotism and Crime,* Rider & Co., 1956; *Humanistic Psychology,* Collier, 1958, 2nd edition, 1962; (translator) Geza Revesz, *The Human Hand,* Routledge & Kegan Paul, 1958.

Chance, Skill and Luck, Penguin, 1960; *Behaviour in Uncertainty and Its Social Implications,* Basic Books, 1964; (editor) *Readings in Psychology,* Allen & Unwin, 1964; *Human Robots in Myth and Science,* A. S. Barnes, 1966; *A New Introduction to Psychology,* Allen & Unwin, 1966; *Psychological Time in Health and Disease,* C. C Thomas, 1967; (editor) *Psychology: An Outline for the Intending Student,* Routledge & Kegan Paul, 1968; (with Barbara Preston) *Causes and Prevention of Road Accidents,* Faber, 1968; (with Ian Christensen) *Information and Choice,* Oliver & Boyd, 1970; *Elements of Child Psychology for Student Teachers,* Morten, 1970; *Homo Psychologicus,* Allen & Unwin, 1970; *Psychological Probability,* Allen & Unwin, 1972; *Everyman's Psychology,* Allen & Unwin, 1973.

Contributor to psychiatric, medical, psychological, and other scientific and learned journals. British editor, *Acta Psychologica,* and *Medikon.*

WORK IN PROGRESS: Experimental studies of psychological probability, risk-taking, search strategies and metaphor, subjective time, and cerebral dominance and laterality.

SIDELIGHTS: Cohen is interested in popular exposition of psychology and allied topics on television and radio, believing that this can be made ''both entertaining and dramatic.'' *Avocational interests:* Music.

* * *

COHEN, Kalman J(oseph) 1931-

PERSONAL: Born February 3, 1931, in Youngstown, Ohio; son of Abraham W. (a salesman) and Dorothy (Middleman) Cohen; married Joan C. Newman (an artist), June 6, 1956; children: Jonathan Stuart, Deborah Ann, Andrew Bruce. *Education:* Reed College, B.A., 1951; Oxford University, B.Litt, 1953; Cornell University, graduate study, 1953-54; Carnegie Institute of Technology, M.S., 1956, Ph.D., 1959. *Home:* 2312 Honeysuckle Ct., Chapel Hill, North Carolina 27514. *Office:* Graduate School of Business Administration, Duke University, Durham, North Carolina 27706.

CAREER: Carnegie-Mellon University, Pittsburgh, Pa., assistant professor, 1958-61, associate professor, 1961-66, professor of economics and industrial administration, 1966-72, acting head of department, 1962-63, department head, 1963-66, associate dean of graduate school, 1971-72; New York University, New York, N.Y., Distinguished Professor of Economics and Finance, 1972-74; Duke University, Durham, North Carolina, Distinguished Bank Research Professor, 1974—. Director of the Salomon Brothers Center for the Study of Financial Institutions, 1972-74. Consultant to both the management and the technical staffs of various financial institutions, industrial firms, trade associations, and government agencies, 1959—. *Member:* American Economic Association, American Finance Association, Econometric Society, Institute of Management

Sciences, Operations Research Society of America, Phi Beta Kappa, Sigma Xi, Phi Kappa Phi. *Awards, honors:* Rhodes scholar, Oxford University, 1951-53; Ford Foundation faculty research fellow, 1963-64; Robert Morris Associates research grant, 1964; National Science Foundation research grant, 1964-66; Federal Deposit Insurance Corporation research grant, 1967-68; Scaife Grant for the Improvement of Faculty, 1967-68.

WRITINGS: Computer Models of the Shoe, Leather, Hide Sequence, Prentice-Hall, 1960; (with Franco Modigliani) *The Role of Anticipations and Plans in Economic Behavior and Their Use in Economic Analysis and Forecasting*, Bureau of Economic and Business Research, University of Illinois, 1961; (with William R. Dill, Alfred A. Kuehn, and Peter R. Winters) *The Carnegie Tech Management Game: An Experiment in Business Education*, Irwin, 1964; (with Richard M. Cyert) *Theory of the Firm: Resource Allocation in a Market Economy*, Prentice-Hall, 1965; (editor with Frederick S. Hammer, and contributor) *Analytical Methods in Banking*, Irwin, 1966.

Contributor: Mary Jean Bowman, editor, *Expectations, Uncertainty, and Business Behavior*, Social Science Research Council, 1958; *Readings in Marketing*, South-Western, 1962; Harold Guetzkow, editor, *Simulation in Social Science: Readings*, Prentice-Hall, 1962; Richard M. Cyert and James G. March, editors, *Behavioral Theory of the Firm*, Prentice-Hall, 1963; Hiram C. Barksdale, editor, *Marketing in Progress: Patterns and Potentials*, Holt, 1964; James G. March, editor, *Handbook of Organizations*, Rand McNally, 1965; Nicholas A. Fattu and Stanley Elam, editors, *Simulation Models for Education*, Phi Delta Kappa, 1965; Martin K. Starr, editor, *Executive Readings in Management Science*, Macmillan, 1965; H. B. Maynard, editor-in-chief, *Handbook of Business Administration*, McGraw, 1967; Gerald J. Karaska and David F. Bramhall, editors, *Locational Analysis for Manufacturing*, M.I.T. Press, 1969; Walter Goldberg, editor, *Behavioral Approaches to Modern Management*, Gothenburg Studies in Business Administration, Volume II, 1970; Edwin J. Elton and Martin J. Cruber, editors, *Security Evaluation and Portfolio Analysis*, Prentice-Hall, 1972. Also contributor to published conference reports and to management, data processing, financial, and banking journals.

WORK IN PROGRESS: Normative research in banking, financial management and corporate strategy; empirical research on the financial markets.

*   *   *

COHEN, Sidney 1910-

PERSONAL: Born June 7, 1910, in New York, N.Y.; son of Adolph (a merchant) and Esther (Gordon) Cohen; married Ilse Annelouise Franke, September 2, 1934; children: Dorothy Elizabeth, Richard Sidney. *Education:* Columbia University, Ph.C., 1930; University of Bonn, M.D., 1938. *Politics:* Democrat. *Home:* 13020 Sky Valley Rd., Los Angeles, Calif. 90049. *Agent:* Laurence Pollinger Ltd., 18 Maddox St., London W.1, England.

CAREER: Physician, Wadsworth Veterans Administration Hospital, Los Angeles, Calif., chief of psychiatry service, 1960—. Clinical professor of medicine, University of California, Los Angeles. Consultant to National Institute of Drug Abuse. William Harvey Taylor Lecturer, American Therapeutic Society, 1964. Member of scientific advisory board, American Schizophrenia Foundation. *Military service:* U.S. Army, Medical Corps, 1941-46; became colonel; received Bronze Star, Distinguished Unit Citation, and Presidential Unit Citation.

MEMBER: Society of Biological Psychiatry, American Academy of Psychosomatics, International Society for Comprehensive Medicine, American Medical Association, California Medical Association, California Medical Research Association, Los Angeles County Medical Association.

WRITINGS: (With Remmen, Ditman, and Frantz) *Psychochemotherapy*, Western Medical, 1963; *The Beyond Within: The LSD Story*, Atheneum, 1964; *The Drug Dilemma*, McGraw, 1970. Contributor of 150 articles to medical journals, 1949—. Editor in chief, *Mind—Psychiatry in General Practice*; member of editorial staff, *Psychosomatics*.

WORK IN PROGRESS: Second edition, *The Drug Dilemma*, completion expected in 1976; further research in human psychopharmacology, particularly on the hallucinogenic drugs.

*   *   *

COKE, Van Deren 1921-

PERSONAL: Born July 4, 1921, in Lexington, Ky.; son of Sterling Dent (chairman of the board of a wholesale hardware firm) and Elizabeth (Van Deren) Coke; married Eleanor Barton (a librarian); children: Sterling Van Deren, Eleanor Browning. *Education:* Attended University of Kentucky, 1939-42, B.A., 1956; Indiana University, M.F.A., 1958; Harvard University, graduate student, summers, 1958-61; studied photography with Ansel Adams. *Home:* 1412 Las Lomas, N.E., Albuquerque, N.M. 87106. *Office:* Director, Art Museum, University of New Mexico, Albuquerque, N.M. 87131.

CAREER: Van Deren Hardware, sales manager, vice-president, and president, 1946-56; University of Florida, Gainesville, assistant professor of art, 1958-61; Arizona State University, Tempe, associate professor of art, 1961; University of New Mexico, Albuquerque, director of art museum, 1962—, chairman of art department, 1963-70. International Museum of Photography, Rochester, N.Y., deputy director, 1970-71, director, 1971-72. Chairman, Albuquerque Fine Arts Advisory Board. *Military service:* U.S. Naval Reserve, 1942-46; became lieutenant; received one Pacific battle and three European stars. *Member:* College Art Association of America, American Association of Museums, Society of Photographic Education, Western Association of Art Museums, George Eastman House Associates. *Awards, honors:* International awards from *Photography*, 1955, 1956, 1957, from *Modern Photography*, 1956, and *U.S. Camera*, 1957, 1958, 1960; first award ($1,000) in National Newspaper-Eastman Kodak Competition, 1956; *Art in America* new talent award, 1960.

WRITINGS: Taos and Santa Fe: The Artist's Environment, 1882-1942, University of New Mexico Press, 1963; *Kenneth M. Adams*, University of New Mexico Press, 1964; *Raymond Jonson*, University of New Mexico Press, 1964; *The Painter and the Photograph*, University of New Mexico Press, 1964; *Impressionism in America*, University of New Mexico Art Gallery, 1965; *The Drawings of Andrew Dasburg*, University of New Mexico Art Museum, 1966; *Marin in New Mexico, 1929-1930*, University of New Mexico Art Museum, 1968; *Young Photographers*, University of New Mexico Art Museum, 1969; *The Painter and the Photograph: From Delacroix to Warhol*, University of New Mexico Press, 1972; *Norfeldt the Painter*, University of New Mexico Press, 1972; *Photography in the Nineteenth Century*, Morgan & Morgan, 1974; (contributor and editor) *A Hundred Years of Photographic History: Essays in Honor of Beaumont Newhall*, University of New Mexico Press, 1974. Contributor to *Encyclopedia of Photography* and to art journals. Editor, *University of New Mexico Art Museum Bulletin* and *Aperture*.

SIDELIGHTS: Coke travels frequently in Europe and Mexico in connection with the study of art history.

*   *   *

COLAW, Emerson S. 1921-

PERSONAL: Born November 13, 1921, in Chanute, Kan.; son of Charles Benjamin and Emma (Powell) Colaw; married Jane Curry, August 26, 1942; children: Prudence, Deborah, Marcella, David. *Education:* University of Cincinnati, B.S., 1944; Drew Theological Seminary, B.D., 1946; Northwestern University, M.A., 1953; other study at Chicago Lutheran Seminary, 1953-57. *Home:* 3050 Observatory, Cincinnati, Ohio.

CAREER: Methodist minister, 1946—, now pastor of Hyde Park Community Methodist Church, Cincinnati, Ohio. Chairman of Ohio Conference Board of Evangelism, 1965; delegate to World Conference on Methodism, Oslo, Norway, 1961. Conductor of preaching missions in Great Britain and of tours to the Holy Land.

WRITINGS: My Call to Preach, Tidings, 1962; *The Way of the Master*, Abingdon, 1965; *Christ's Imperatives*, Beacon Hill Press of Kansas, 1969; *Beliefs of a United Methodist Christian*, Tidings, 1972. Contributor to *Christian Advocate, Pulpit*, other religious journals.

WORK IN PROGRESS: Things About Which I've Wondered.†

*   *   *

COLBECK, Maurice 1925-

PERSONAL: Born September 21, 1925, in Batley, Yorkshire, England; son of Norman Bradley and Mary Jane (Poole) Colbeck; married Brenda Barrowclough; children: Anne, Peter. *Education:* Attended schools in Batley, Yorkshire, England. *Home:* 164 Soothill Lane, Batley, Yorkshire, England. *Office:* Whitethorn Press Ltd., 33-35 Cross Green, Otley, Yorkshire, England.

CAREER: Worked as journalist on newspapers in Yorkshire, England, and as assistant editor for E. J. Arnold & Son Ltd. (publishers), prior to 1956; *Yorkshire Life* (monthly magazine), Leeds, Yorkshire, England, editor, 1956—. *Military service:* Royal Navy, 1943-46.

WRITINGS: Jungle Rivals, Schofield & Sims, 1953; *White God's Fury*, E. J. Arnold, 1953; *Four Against Crime*, E. J. Arnold, 1957; *Mosquitoes!* (children's biography of Sir Ronald Ross), Edinburgh House Press, 1964; *Sister Kenny of the Outback* (children's biography of Elizabeth Kenny), Edinburgh House Press, 1965; *How to be a Family Man* (humor), Muller, 1970. Contributor to *Collins Magazine* (now *Young Elizabethan*), *Writer, Daily Mirror*, and other periodicals and newspapers.

WORK IN PROGRESS: A topographical Book on Yorkshire.

*   *   *

COLE, Clifford A. 1915-

PERSONAL: Born November 16, 1915, in Lamoni, Iowa;

son of Fayette V. (a farmer) and Mabel (Adair) Cole; married H. Lucile Hartshorn (a teacher); children: Alethea Rae (Mrs. Justus Allen), Beverly, Lawrence. *Education:* Graceland College, A.A., 1942; Central Missouri State College, B.S. in Education, 1943; University of Missouri at Kansas City, M.A., 1957. *Home:* 800 East Manor Rd., Independence, Mo. 64050. *Office:* Reorganized Latter Day Saints Auditorium, Independence, Mo. 64051.

CAREER: Teacher of social sciences in public high schools in Iowa, 1943-47; Graceland College, Lamoni, Iowa, dean of students, 1951-53; Reorganized Church of Jesus Christ of Latter Day Saints, Independence, Mo., minister, 1947-51, 1953—, member of Council of Twelve, 1958—, council president, 1964—.

WRITINGS—All published by Herald House: *The Prophets Speak*, 1954, *Working Together in Our Families*, 1955, *Celebrating Together in Our Families*, 1955, *Faith for New Frontiers*, 1957, *The Revelation in Christ*, 1963. Contributor of articles to denominational publications.†

*   *   *

COLE, Dandridge MacFarlan 1921-

PERSONAL: Born February 19, 1921, in Sandusky, Ohio; son of Robert MacFarlan (a chemist) and Wertha (an astronomer; maiden name, Pendleton) Cole; married Charlotte Ellen Davis, June 17, 1949; children: Stephen Dandridge, Jency Ellen, Martha Aubrey, Thomas MacFarlan, Cathlin Davis, Mary Jane Cudmore. *Education:* Columbia University, medical student, 1942; Princeton University, A.B., 1943; University of Pennsylvania, M.A., 1949. *Politics:* Republican. *Religion:* Swedenborgian. *Home:* Huntingdon Valley, Pa. *Office:* Missile and Space Division, General Electric Co., Box 8555, Philadelphia, Pa.

CAREER: Science instructor at Academy of New Church 1945-46, and Phillips Exeter Academy, 1949-53; instructor in physics at University of Pennsylvania, Philadelphia, 1947-49; Martin Co., Baltimore, Md., and Denver, Colo., 1953-60, began as group and staff engineer, became senior advanced planning specialist; General Electric Co., Missile and Space Division, Philadelphia, Pa., space programs analyst, 1960—. Space commentator, WPEN, Philadelphia. Independently conceived nuclear pulse propulsion system, 1956; originator of concept of Macro Life as next step in evolution, 1957, and of Panama Theory (strategic areas in space could be excluded from United States use by unfriendly space powers). *Military service:* U.S. Army, paratrooper, 1943-45. *Member:* American Institute of Aeronautics and Astronautics (associate fellow), American Astronautical Society, British Interplanetary Society (fellow), American Rocket Society (president, Colorado section, 1959).

WRITINGS: (With I. M. Levitt) *Exploring the Secrets of Space*, Prentice-Hall, 1963; (with D. W. Cox) *Islands in Space: The Challenge of the Planetoids*, Chilton, 1964; (with R. Scarfo) *Beyond Tomorrow: The Next Fifty Years in Space*, Amherst Press, 1965. Contributor to *Journal of the Institute of Navigation, Jet Propulsion, Astronautics, Missiles and Rockets*. Writer of other papers on asteroids, interplanetary colonization, moon trips, and the Panama Theory.

WORK IN PROGRESS: Study of manned missions to the planetoids, "which should be undertaken in the 1970's with Apollo technology."

AVOCATIONAL INTERESTS: Camping (at sixteen

made an eighty-mile solo trip on foot across Sequoia National Park), trampolining, diving, and surfing.

BIOGRAPHICAL/CRITICAL SOURCES: Fortune, August, 1964.†

* * *

COLE, Edward C(yrus) 1904-

PERSONAL: Born March 26, 1904, in Pawtucket, R.I.; son of Washington Leverett (a merchant) and Fanny (Nicholson) Cole; married Alice Crawford (an interior designer), September 6, 1930; children: Ann Frances (Mrs. Ellsworth H. Wheeler, Jr.), James W. L. *Education:* Dartmouth College, A.B., 1926; Yale University, M.F.A., 1942. *Religion:* Episcopalian. *Home:* 17 Parker Pl., Branford, Conn. 06405. *Office:* School of Drama, Yale University, 1903-A Yale Station, New Haven, Conn. 06520.

CAREER: Yale University, New Haven, Conn., 1930—, became associate professor of drama, 1946, professor emeritus, 1971—, production manager and executive officer of School of Drama, 1959-65, acting dean of School of Drama, 1965-66, fellow of Timothy Dwight College, 1959—. Theater planning consultant, 1937—. Vice-president of New England Theatre Conference, 1951-53; civilian adviser on the theater, U.S. Army Special Services, 1953-54. *Member:* American Educational Theatre Association (director, 1954-61; president, 1958; fellow), American National Theatre and Academy (member of board of directors), National Council of the Arts in Education (member of board of directors, 1962—; fellow). *Awards, honors:* Theta Alpha Phi Award, 1958; American Educational Theatre Association Award of Merit, 1964; American College Theatre Festival Gold medal, 1972, Silver medal, 1973.

WRITINGS: Stage Manager's Manual, privately printed, 1930; (with Harold Burris-Meyer) *Scenery for the Theatre*, Little, Brown, 1938, revised edition, 1971; (with Burris-Meyer) *Theatres and Auditoriums*, Reinhold, 1949, 2nd edition, 1964, *Supplement*, R. E. Krieger, in press. Contributor to *Theatre Arts* and *Progressive Architecture*.

* * *

COLEBURT, J(ames) Russell 1920-

PERSONAL: Born September 2, 1920, in London, England; son of James Herbert and Gladys (Cooper) Coleburt. *Education:* Exeter College, Oxford, M.A., 1946. *Agent:* A. M. Heath & Co. Ltd., 35 Dover St., London W.1, England. *Office:* Worth School, Crawley, Sussex, England.

CAREER: Stonyhurst College, Lancashire, England, senior classics master, 1947-62; Worth School, Crawley, Sussex, England, senior classics master, 1962—. *Military service:* Royal Artillery, 1941-46; became lieutenant.

WRITINGS: An Introduction to Western Philosophy, Sheed, 1957; *The Search for Values*, Sheed, 1960. Contributor to *Downside Review*.

* * *

COLEMAN, D(onald) C(uthbert) 1920-

PERSONAL: Born January 21, 1920, in London, England; son of Hugh Augustus (a civil servant) and Marion (Cuthbert) Coleman; married Jessie Ann Matilda Child, February 5, 1954. *Education:* London School of Economics and Political Science, B.Sc. (first class honors), 1949, Ph.D., 1951. *Home:* Overhall, Cavendish, Suffolk, England. *Office:* Faculty of History, Cambridge University, West Rd., Cambridge, England.

CAREER: London School of Economics and political Science, London, England, lecturer in industrial history, 1951-58, reader, 1958-69, professor of economic history, 1969-71; Cambridge University, Cambridge, England, professor of economic history 1971—, fellow of Pembroke College, 1971. Visiting professor, Yale University, 1957-58. Lecturer in Great Britain, Scandinavia, and United States. *Military service:* British Army, Royal Artillery, 1940-46; became lieutenant. *Member:* Economic History Society (member of council, 1959—), Royal Historical Society, British Academy (fellow).

WRITINGS: (Contributor) M. W. Thomas, editor, *A Survey of English Economic History*, Blackie & Son, 1957, 3rd edition, 1967; *The British Paper Industry, 1495-1860*, Clarendon Press, 1958; (editor and author of introduction) Kurt Samuelsson, *Religion and Economic Action*, Heinemann, 1961; (contributor) *New Cambridge Modern History*, Volume V, Cambridge University Press, 1961; *Sir John Banks: Baronet and Businessman*, Clarendon Press, 1963; *Courtaulds: An Economic and Social History*, two volumes, Clarendon Press, 1969; *Revisions in Mercantilism*, Metheun, 1969; *Industry in Tudor and Stuart England*, Macmillan, in press. Contributor to economics and history journals.

WORK IN PROGRESS: Economy and Society in England, 1450-1750, publication by Oxford University Press expected in 1976; a third volume of *Courtaulds: An Economic and Social History*, publication by Clarendon Press expected about 1979.

SIDELIGHTS: Coleman speaks French, German, and Swedish.

* * *

COLEMAN, James S(amuel) 1926-

PERSONAL: Born May 12, 1926, in Bedford, Ind.; son of James Fox (a foreman) and Maurine (Lappin) Coleman; married Lucille Richey (divorced, 1973); children: Thomas, John, James. *Education:* Purdue University, B.S., 1949; Columbia University, Ph.D., 1955. *Office:* University of Chicago, Chicago, Ill. 60637.

CAREER: University of Chicago, Chicago, Ill., assistant professor of sociology, 1956-59; Johns Hopkins University, Baltimore, Md., associate professor, 1959-61, professor of sociology, 1961-73; University of Chicago, Chicago, Ill., professor of sociology, 1973—. *Military service:* U.S. Navy, 1944-46. *Member:* American Sociological Association, National Academy of Education, American Academy of Arts and Sciences, National Academy of Sciences. *Awards, honors:* Fellow, Center for the Advanced Study in the Behavioral Sciences, 1955-56; LL.D., Purdue University; Nicholas Murray Butler Award, Columbia University.

WRITINGS: (With S. M. Lipset and M. Tron) *Union Democracy*, Free Press of Glencoe, 1956; *Community Conflict*, Free Press of Glencoe, 1957; *The Adolescent Society*, Free Press of Glencoe, 1961; *Introduction to Mathematical Sociology*, Free Press of Glencoe, 1964; *Models of Change and Response Uncertainty*, Prentice-Hall, 1964; *Adolescents and the Schools*, Basic Books, 1965; (with others) *Equality of Educational Opportunity*, U.S. Department of Health, Education, and Welfare, 1966; (with Elihu Katz and Herbert Menzet) *Medical Innovation: A Diffusion Study*, Bobbs-Merrill, 1966; (with Amitari Elzioni and John Porter) *Macrosociology: Research and Theory*, Allyn & Bacon, 1970; (with Nancy Karweit) *Multilevel Information Systems in Education*, Rand Corp., 1970; *Resources for Social Change: Race in the United States*, Wiley, 1971; *The Mathematics of Collective Action*, Aldine, 1973; *Power and the Structure of Society*, Norton, 1973; (with others) *Youth: Transition to Adulthood*, University of Chicago Press, 1974.†

*   *   *

COLEMAN, Robert E(merson)   1928-

PERSONAL: Born April 4, 1928, in Dallas, Tex.; son of James Henry (a lawyer and realtor) and Helen (Hood) Coleman; married Marietta Emmons, June 3, 1951; children: Alathea Dawn, Angela Denise, James Russell. *Education:* Southwestern University, Georgetown, Tex., A.B., 1948; Asbury Theological Seminary, B.D., 1951; Princeton Theological Seminary, M.Th., 1952; University of Iowa, Ph.D., 1954; other study at Biblical Seminary in New York, 1951, and Union Theological Seminary, New York, N.Y., 1957. *Home:* 200 Asbury Dr., Wilmore, Ky. *Office:* Asbury Theological Seminary, Wilmore, Ky. 40390.

CAREER: Ordained deacon of Methodist Church in 1950, and elder, 1953; served churches in Indiana, New Jersey, and Iowa, 1949-55; Asbury Theological Seminary, Wilmore, Ky., McCreless Professor of Evangelism, 1955—. Evangelist throughout United States; speaker at church conventions, workshops, seminars, crusades, and revivals; has led ministers' conferences in Central and South America, 1966, 1973, and in Liberia, Ghana, and Zaire, 1972. Delegate to World Congress on Evangelism in Berlin, Germany, 1966, and International Congress on World Evangelism, Switzerland, 1974. President of Christian Outreach, Inc., 1960—; vice-president, Academy for Evangelism in Theological Education, 1973—. Advisory member of several national evangelistic associations. *Member:* Evangelical Theological Society, National Association of Evangelicals.

WRITINGS—All published by Department of Evangelism, Asbury Theological Seminary, except as indicated: *Introducing the Prayer Cell*, 1956, 6th edition, Christian Outreach, 1960; *Established by Word of God*, 1959, 13th edition, 1971; *Life in the Living Word*, 1961; *The Master Plan of Evangelism*, Christian Outreach, 1963, 2nd edition, Revell, 1964, edition in English for Indian readers, adapted by Herbert Bennett and edited by J. W. McMillan, published as *The Lord's Plan to Spread the Good News*, Evangelical Literature Service (Madras), 1968; *The Spirit and the Word*, 1965; *Dry Bones Can Live Again: Revival in the Local Church*, Revell, 1969; (editor) *One Divine Moment*, Revell, 1970; *Written in Blood: A Devotional Bible Study of the Blood of Christ*, Revell, 1971; *They Meet the Master*, Christian Outreach, 1973. Contributor to periodicals.

WORK IN PROGRESS: Continuing research in the evangelism of Jesus, the evangelism of the early church, and in ways of discipling men.

SIDELIGHTS: Coleman was the first professor of evangelism appointed by the Methodist Church. His books have sold over 1,600,000 copies in English editions, alone; presently there are also about one hundred foreign editions in forty languages. *Avocational interests:* Painting in oil, gardening, sports.

COLEMAN, Terry   1931-

PERSONAL: Born February 13, 1931, in Bournemouth, England; married Lesley Fox-Strangways-Vane; children: Tigre and Eleanor (daughters). *Education:* Studied at University of Exeter and University of London; LL.B., 1958. *Agent:* A. D. Peters, 10 Buckingham St., London WC2 England.

CAREER: University College, Cork, Ireland, Lyon lecturer in medieval law, 1959; former journalist on five English newspapers and onetime editor of *Savoir Faire* (women's magazine, now defunct); *Guardian* (formerly, *Manchester Guardian*), London, England, reporter, arts correspondent, and chief feature writer, 1961-74; *Daily Mail*, London, special writer, 1974—.

WRITINGS: The Railway Navvies (nonfiction), Hutchinson, 1965; *A Girl for the Afternoons* (novel), Elek, 1965; (with Lois Deacon) *Providence and Mr. Hardy* (biography of Thomas Hardy), Hutchinson, 1966; *The Only True History* (collected journalism), Hutchinson, 1969; *Going to America* (social history), Pantheon, 1972 (published in England as *Passage to America*, Hutchinson, 1972); *The Pantheretti* (poems), [London], 1972.

WORK IN PROGRESS: The Liner Was a Lady, a social history of the North Atlantic, for Allen Lane; editor and author of preface for the first English public edition of *The Poor Man and the Lady* (Thomas Hardy's unpublished first novel), for Hutchinson.

*   *   *

COLLINS, Barry E(merson)   1937-

PERSONAL: Born June 2, 1937, in Raleigh, N.C.; son of Emerson Rosco and Helen (Temple) Collins; married Doris Kraeling, May 1, 1964. *Education:* Cornell University, student, 1955-57; Northwestern University, B.S., 1959, M.S., 1960, Ph.D., 1963. *Office:* Department of Psychology, University of California, Los Angeles, Calif. 90024.

CAREER: Yale University, New Haven, Conn., assistant professor of psychology, 1963-66; University of California, Los Angeles, assistant professor, 1966-68, associate professor of psychology, 1968-71; Institute of Government and Public Affairs, acting associate director, 1970-71; University of Wisconsin, professor of sociology, 1971-72; University of California, Los Angeles, associate professor, 1972-73, professor of psychology, 1973—.

WRITINGS: (With Harold Guetzkow) *A Social Psychology of Group Processes for Decision-Making*, Wiley, 1964; (with Charles Kiesler and Norman Miller) *Attitude Change: A Critical Analysis of Theoretical Approaches*, Wiley, 1969; *Social Psychology: Social Influence, Attitude Change, Small Groups and Prejudice*, Addison-Wesley, 1970; (with Alan Gross and James Bryan) *An Introduction to Research in Social Psychology*, Wiley, 1972; (editor) *Public and Private Conformity: Competing Explanations by Improvisation, Cognitive Dissonance, and Attribution Theories*, Warner Modular Publications, 1973.

*   *   *

COLMAN, Hila

PERSONAL: Born in New York, N.Y.; daughter of Harris (a manufacturer) and Sarah (a designer; maiden name, Kinsberg) Crayder; married Louis Colman (a medical writer); children: Jonathan, James. *Education:* attended Radcliffe College, two years. *Politics:* Democrat. *Home:* Bridgewater, Conn.

CAREER: National War Relief Agency, New York, N.Y., publicity and promotion work, 1940-45; Labor Book Club, New York, N.Y., executive director, 1945-47; free-lance writer, 1949—. Member of Democratic Town Committee, Bridgewater; former member of Bridgewater Board of Education: *Awards, honors:* Child Study Association of America Children's Book Award for *Girl from Puerto Rico*, 1962.

WRITINGS—Youth books; all published by Morrow except as indicated: *The Big Step*, 1957; *Crown for Gina*, 1958; *Julie Builds Her Castle*, 1959; *Best Wedding Dress*, 1960; *Girl from Puerto Rico*, 1961; *Mrs. Darling's Daughter*, 1962; *Watch That Watch*, 1962; *Phoebe's First Campaign*, 1963; *Peter Brownstone House*, 1963; *Classmates by Request*, 1964; *Christmas Cruise*, 1965; *The Boy Who Couldn't Make Up His Mind*, Macmillan, 1965; *Bride at Eighteen*, 1966; *Car Crazy Girl*, 1967; *Mixed Marriage Daughter*, 1968; *Something Out of Nothing*, Weybright, 1968; *A Career in Medical Research*, World, 1968; *Beauty, Brains, and Glamour: A Career in Magazine Publishing*, World, 1968; *Claudia, Where Are You?*, 1969; *Making Movies: Student Films to Features*, World, 1969; *Andy's Landmark House*, Parent's Magazine Press, 1969; *The Happenings at North End School*, 1970; *End of the Game*, World, 1971; *Daughter of Discontent*, 1971; *City Planning: What Its All About—in the Planners Own Words*, World, 1971; *The Family and the Fugitive*, 1972; *Diary of a Frantic Kid Sister*, Crown, 1973; *Chicano Girl*, 1973; *Friends and Strangers on Location*, 1974.

With husband, Louis Colman: *Country Week-end Cookbook*, Barrows, 1961.

Adult stories and articles have appeared in *McCall's, Saturday Evening Post, Redbook* and *Today's Woman*; regular contributor to *Ingenue*.

WORK IN PROGRESS: Several books for young people.†

*   *   *

COLQUHOUN, Ithell 1906-

PERSONAL: Surname is pronounced Co-*houn*; born October 9, 1906, in Shillong, Assam, India; daughter of H.A.C., and Georgia (Manley) Colquhoun. *Education:* Slade School of Fine Art, University of London, Diploma in Fine Art, 1930. *Home:* Stone Cross Cottage, Paul, Penzance, England.

CAREER: Professional painter whose work has been shown in twenty one-woman exhibitions, and at other shows in England, Ireland, France, Belgium, Holland, and Germany. Lecturer-demonstrator on surrealist automatic processes on British Broadcasting Corp. television and at universities in England; poetry reader. *Member:* Women's International Art Club, Newlyn Society of Artists, West Country Writers' Association.

WRITINGS: *The Crying of the Wind: Ireland*, P. Owen, 1955; *The Living Stones: Cornwall*, P. Owen, 1957; *Goose of Hermogenes* (Gothic novel), P. Owen, 1961; *Grimoire of the Entangled Thicket* (poems and drawings), Ore Publications, 1973. Contributor to *Springtime Anthology*, and to *Time and Tide, Poetry Quarterly, Poetry Review*, other journals in England, France, Belgium, and United States. Translator of poetry and articles from the French.

WORK IN PROGRESS: *I Saw Water*, a novel; *Osmazone: Poems; Destination Limbo*, a novel; *MacGregor Mathers and the Golden Dawn*, for publication by Neville Spearman.

SIDELIGHTS: Miss Colquhoun speaks French, some Spanish and Greek. *Avocational interests:* Celtic culture, the occult, archaeology, and anthropology.

*   *   *

COMBS, (Elisha) Tram(mell, Jr.) 1924-

PERSONAL: Born September 25, 1924, in Riverview, Ala.; son of Elisha Trammell (a cotton mill superintendent) and LaFaye (Hunt) Combs. *Education:* Attended University of Washington, 1943-44; University of Chicago, certificate of professional competence in meteorology, 1945; University of California, A.B., 1948; work in electronics engineering at Harvard University and Massachusetts Institute of Technology. *Politics:* Individualist. *Religion:* Unaffiliated.

CAREER: Tidewater-Associated Oil Co., Avon, Calif., oil chemist, 1948-51; Island Studios, Inc. (photographic studio), owner-manager, 1951-52; Tram Combs, Books (bookshop specializing in middle and southern Americas), St. Thomas, Virgin Islands, owner-manager, beginning 1952. Trustee and a founder, Virgin Islands Museum, Inc., 1955-56. *Military service:* U.S. Army Air Forces, 1943-46; meteorologist; became second lieutenant. *Member:* American Association for the Advancement of Science, American Civil Liberties Union, Bibliographical Society of America, American Meteorological Society, Chinese Historical Society of America, Chattahoochee Valley Historical Society, Hakluyt Society, Bibliographical Society of the University of Virginia, San Francisco Poetry Center, Amigos de Calle del Cristo 255.

WRITINGS: *pilgrim's terrace: poems american west indian* (forewords by William Carlos Williams and Kenneth Rexroth), Editorial La Nueva Salamanca, 1957; *Saints Thomas' & Francis' cities songs o' Tram*, [St. Thomas], 1958; *Ceremonies in Mind: artists, boys, cats, lovers, judges, priests*, privately printed, 1959; *but never mind: poems etc. 1946-1950*, Golden Mountain Press, 1961; *Saint Thomas: poems*, Wesleyan University Press, 1965; *Briefs: poems*, Hillside Press, 1966. Regular contributor to *Bim* (Barbados, West Indies).

WORK IN PROGRESS: A history and bibliography of San Francisco Bay area poetry, 1941-1965, with Thomas Parkinson; a recording of folk songs on St. Thomas; a recording of poems of Tu Fu, with Chao Tzechiang, for Folkways Records.

SIDELIGHTS: Combs has travelled in Canada, Iceland, China, the Philippines, Cuba, North Africa, Mexico, northeast Caribbean, and every part of the United States. He has lived in India, Japan, and in the Virgin Islands since 1951. He told *CA* he is able in French, has some ability in Latin, German, and Spanish, and slight ability in Chinese, Japanese, Danish, and Dutch ("all languages here estimated primarily for reading ability," he says). He is professionally interested in science, general scholarship, social engineering, and bibliography.

In a review of *St. Thomas: poems*, Harriet Zinnes observed, "The remains of Combs's scientific interest lie in his detailed descriptions of nature. . . . He throws over his vision of things a lyric, even romantic interest so that the world seems like a supreme decoration. . . . Tram Combs . . . has his own voice, delicate, yet not fuzzy. . . . The effect his punctuation and lines have upon the page is one of his major preoccupations. . . . To set eyes upon his pages is to look at a kind of black and white dull op art. It has a dizzying effect. . . . The poet is using typography to imitate acutal speech inflections."

AVOCATIONAL INTERESTS: Swimming; fine food and drink; loving the arts, fine and applied.†

* * *

COMFORT, Iris Tracy

PERSONAL: Born in Racine, Wis.; daughter of A. T. and Iva Tracy; married James Dustin Comfort (an installation supervisor, Southern Bell Telephone Co.), April 19, 1941; children: Alain James. *Home:* Orlando, Fla. *Agent:* Larry Sternig, 2407 North 44th St., Milwaukee, Wis. 53210.

CAREER: One-time reporter for *St. Paul Dispatch*, St. Paul, Minn., member of public relations staff, Allis-Chalmers Manufacturing Co., Milwaukee, Wis., operator of own public relations agency in Milwaukee, Wis., and Chicago, Ill., and editor of Chicago edition of *Where* (entertainment magazine); free-lance writer, mainly for magazines and trade journals, 1945—. Member of Lay Curriculum Committee, Orange County, Florida, 1968—; owns and maintains Wildlife Sanctuary, Volusia County, Florida, 1969—. *Member:* National League of American Pen Women Audubon Society, Spiritual Frontiers.

WRITINGS: Earth Treasures: Rocks and Minerals, Prentice-Hall, 1964; *Let's Grow Things*, Rand McNally, 1968; *Rock Riddles*, Rand McNally, 1968; *Let's Read About Rocks*, Rand McNally, 1969; *Joey Tigertail*, Ginn. 1973. Contributor of fiction to *New York Daily News*, 1958-64, other stories and articles to *Parents' Magazine, Success, Charm, McCall's, Modern Industry, Wings, Seventeen, Building America, Industrial Relations, Etude, Children's Activities, Together, Better Homes & Gardens, The Instructor, Today's Catholic Teacher*, and other periodicals.

WORK IN PROGRESS: Research and writing on the Everglades, the Seminoles, the use and propagation of plants, specific psychic phenomena, caves, and fiction using researched backgrounds.

* * *

CONANT, James Bryant 1893-

PERSONAL: Born March 26, 1893, in Boston, Mass.; son of James Scott and Jennett Orr (Bryant) Conant; married Grace Thayer Richards, April 17, 1921; children; James Richards, Theodore Richards. *Education:* Harvard University, A.B., 1913, Ph.D., 1916. *Home:* 200 East 66th St., New York, N.Y.

CAREER: Harvard University, Cambridge, Mass., instructor 1916-17, assistant professor, 1919-25, associate professor, 1925-27, professor of chemistry, 1927-29, Sheldon Emory Professor of Organic Chemistry, 1929-33, president of university, 1933-53, president emeritus, 1953—; U.S. High Commissioner for Germany, 1953-55; U.S. Ambassador to Federal Republic of Germany, 1955-57; Carnegie Corp. of New York, director of Study of the American High School, 1957-59, of A Study of American Education, 1960-63; Ford Foundation, educational adviser in Berlin, Germany, 1963-65; writer and educational consultant in United States, 1965—. Deputy director of Office of Scientific Research and Development and chairman of National Defense Research Committee, 1941-46. Member of board of science directors, Rockefeller Institute, 1930-49, committee on scientific aids to learning, National Research Council, 1937-42, U.S. Education Policies Commission, 1941-46, 1947-50, general advisory committee of Atomic Energy Commission, 1947-52, President's Committee on Youth Employment, and national advisory council of Office of Economic Opportunity. *Military service:* U.S. Army, 1917-18.

MEMBER: American Academy of Arts and Sciences, American Association for the Advancement of Science, American Society of Biological Chemists, American Chemical Society, American Philosophical Association, Chemical Society (England; honorary), Royal Society of England, Royal Society of Edinburgh, Phi Beta Kappa, Sigma Xi, Alpha Chi Sigma; Tavern Club, Harvard Club (all Boston); Century Association, Chemists Club, University Club, and Harvard Club (all New York); Cosmos Club (Washington, D.C.), Athenaeum Club (London).

AWARDS, HONORS: Chandler Medal, Columbia University, 1932; Nicholas Medal of American Chemical Society, 1932; American Institute of Chemistry Medal, 1934; Priestley Medal, 1944; Commander, Legion of Honor (France); Commander, Order of the British Empire; U.S. Medal of Merit with oak leaf cluster, 1948; Woodrow Wilson Award, 1959; Medal of Freedom, 1963; Great Living American Award, 1965; Sylvanus Thayer Award, 1965; (with V. Bush and General Leslie R. Groves) Atomic Pioneer Award, 1970. Fifty honorary degrees from universities and colleges in eight countries, including New York University, Princeton University, Yale University, Oxford University, University of California, Cambridge University, University of Algiers, University of Toronto, McGill University, University of London, University of Michigan, Jewish Theological Seminary of America, University of Melbourne, University of Edinburgh, Columbia University, and Colgate University.

WRITINGS: (With Newton Henry Black) *Practical Chemistry*, Macmillan, 1920, revised edition, 1927; *Organic Chemistry*, Macmillan, 1928, revised edition (with Max Tishler), 1936.

Chemistry of Organic Compounds, Macmillan, 1933, 5th edition (with A. H. Blatt), 1959; (with others) *History and Traditions of Harvard College*, Harvard Crimson, 1934; (with Newton Henry Black) *New Practical Chemistry*, Macmillan, 1936, revised edition published as *New Practical Chemistry as Applied to Modern Life*, 1942; *Academical Patronage and Superintendence: An Historical Discussion of the Appointment of Professors in Universities*, Harvard University Graduate School of Education, 1938.

(With F. T. Spaulding) *Education for a Classless Society*, Harvard University Graduate School of Education, 1940; *Speaking as a Private Citizen*, Harvard University Press, 1941; *Our Fighting Faith: Five Addresses to College Students*, Harvard University Press, 1942, revised edition published as *Our Fighting Faith: Six Addresses to College Students*, 1944; *On Understanding Science: An Historical Approach*, Yale University Press, 1947; *Case Histories in Experimental Science*, Harvard University Press, 1948; *Education in a Divided World*, Harvard University Press, 1948; *The Growth of the Experimental Sciences: Progress Report on the Use of Case Method*, Harvard University Press, 1949.

(With A. H. Blatt) *Fundamentals of Organic Chemistry*, Macmillan, 1950; *Our Future in the Atomic Age*, Foreign Policy Association, 1951; *Science and Common Sense*, Yale University Press, 1951, revised edition, 1961; *Modern Science and Modern Man*, Columbia University Press, 1952; *Education and Liberty: The Role of Schools in a Modern Democracy*, Harvard University Press, 1953; *The Citadel of Learning*, Yale University Press, 1956; *The*

Identification and Education of the Academically Talented Student in the American Secondary School, National Education Association, 1958; *Germany and Freedom: A Personal Appraisal*, Harvard University Press, 1958; *The American High School Today*, McGraw, 1959; *The Child, the Parent, and the State*, Harvard University Press, 1959; *The Revolutionary Transformation of the American High School*, Harvard University Press, 1959.

Recommendation for Education in the Junior High School Years: A Memorandum to School Boards, Educational Testing Service, 1960; *Slums and Suburbs: A Commentary on Schools in Metropolitan Areas*, McGraw, 1961; *Trial and Error in the Improvement of Education*, Association for Supervision and Curriculum Development, 1961; *Thomas Jefferson and the Development of American Public Education*, University of California Press, 1962; *The Education of American Teachers*, McGraw, 1963, revised edition, 1964; *Shaping Educational Policy*, McGraw, 1964; *Two Modes of Thought: My Encounters with Science and Education*, Simon & Schuster, 1964; *Slums and Suburbs*, New American Library, 1964; *The Comprehensive High School* (sequel to *The American High School Today*), McGraw, 1967; *My Several Lives: Memoirs of a Social Inventor* (autobiography), Harper, 1970.

Editor: *Overthrow of the Phlogiston Theory: The Chemical Revolution of 1775-1789*, Harvard University Press, 1950; *Robert Boyle's Experiments in Pneumatics*, Harvard University Press, 1950; *Pasteur's Study of Fermentation*, Harvard University Press, 1952; *Pasteur's and Tyndall's Study of Spontaneous Generation*, Harvard University Press, 1953; (with L. K. Nash) *Harvard Case Histories in Experimental Science*, two volumes, Harvard University Press, 1957.

* * *

CONARD, Alfred Fletcher 1911-

PERSONAL: Born November 30, 1911, in Grinnell, Iowa; son of Henry S. and Letitia (Moon) Conard; married Georgia Murray; children: Joy Louise, Deborah Jane. *Education:* Grinnell College, A.B., 1932; University of Iowa, further study, 1932-34; University of Pennsylvania, LL.B., 1936; Columbia University, LL.M., 1939, Jur.Sc.D., 1942. *Politics:* Democrat. *Religion:* Quaker. *Home:* 16 Heatheridge, Ann Arbor, Mich. 48104. *Office:* Law School, University of Michigan, Ann Arbor, Mich. 48104.

CAREER: Admitted to Pennsylvania bar, 1937; Murdoch, Paxson, Kalish, and Green, Philadelphia, Pa., attorney, 1936-38; University of Kansas City, assistant professor of law, 1939-42, acting dean, 1941-42; Office of Price Administration, attorney, 1942-43; Office of Alien Property Custodian, attorney, 1945-46; University of Illinois, Urbana, 1946-54, began as associate professor, became professor of law; University of Michigan, Ann Arbor, professor of law, 1954—. *Military service:* U.S. Army, Office of Strategic Services, 1943-45; received Purple Heart and Chevalier de la Couronne (Belgium). *Member:* American Bar Association, American Judicature Society, Association of American Law Schools (executive committee, 1963-65; president, 1971), American Association of University Professors (chapter president, 1963-64), Rotary Club (Ann Arbor; director, 1962-64), International Academy of Corporate Law (associate member, 1970—), National Research Council.

WRITINGS: Cases on the Law of Business Organization, Foundation Press, 1950, 3rd edition (with R. L. Knauss) published as *Cases and Materials on the Law of Business Organization*, Foundation Press, 1965; (with others) *American Enterprise in the European Common Market; A Legal Profile*, Michigan Legal Publications, 1960; (with Morgan, Pratt, Volz, and Bombaugh) *Automobile Accident Costs and Payments: Studies in the Economics of Injury Reparation*, University of Michigan Press, 1964; (with Robert L. Knauss and Stanley Siegel) *Enterprise Organizations: Cases, Statutes and Analysis on Licensing, Employment, Agency, Partnerships, Associations, and Corporations*, Foundation Press, 1972. Editor-in-chief, *American Journal of Corporate Law*, 1968-71. Editorial advisory board chairman, "Contemporary Legal Education" series, Bobbs-Merrill. Contributor to legal journals.

* * *

CONARD, Joseph W. 1911-

PERSONAL: Born November 19, 1911, in Lansdowne, Pa.; son of Ralph W. and Rachel (Wickersham) Conard; married Florence Thomas, 1942; children: John Henry. *Education:* Grinnell College, B.A., 1935; University of California, Berkeley, M.A., 1943, Ph.D., 1956. *Home:* 217 North Swarthmore Ave., Swarthmore, Pa. *Office:* Swarthmore College, Swarthmore, Pa.

CAREER: American Friends Service Committee, executive in California, 1935-48; Swarthmore College, Swarthmore, Pa., 1950—, now professor of economics. Federal Reserve Bank of New York, economist, 1953-54; Commission on Money and Credit, New York, economist, 1959-60. *Member:* American Economic Association, American Association of University Professors.

WRITINGS: An Introduction to the Theory of Interest, University of California Press, 1960; *Inflation, Growth, and Employment*, Prentice-Hall, 1964; *The Behavior of Interest Rates*, Columbia University Press, 1966.

WORK IN PROGRESS: Causes and Consequences of Inflation, for Commission on Money and Credit.†

* * *

CONGDON, Kirby 1924-

PERSONAL: Born November 13, 1924, in West Chester, Pa.; son of William Ellsworth (a printer) and Ragna (Jorgenson) Congdon. *Education:* Columbia College, B.A., 1950; graduate study at Columbia University, 1951. *Residence:* Lives in Key West, Fla., Fire Island Pines, N.Y., and Old Mystic, Conn. *Agent:* McIntosh & Otis, Inc., 18 East 41st St., New York, N.Y. 10017.

CAREER: John Schaffner Literary Agency, New York, N.Y., secretary, 1954-58; *Collier's Encyclopedia*. New York, N.Y. editorial assistant, 1958-62. Now scavenger; also does odd jobs. *Military service:* U.S. Army, 1943-46. *Member:* American Motorcycle Association.

WRITINGS: Iron Ark, Interim Books, 1962; *A Century of Progress*, Interim Books, 1963; *Icarus in Aipotu*, Interim Books, 1963; *Hart Crane: A Conversation with Samuel Loveman*, J. Socin, 1964; *Juggernaut*, Interim Books, 1966; *Black Sun*, Pilot Press, 1973.

The Gravy Train: A One Act Play, Interim Press, 1963; (contributor) *3 One-Act Plays*, Hors Commerce Press, 1964. Also author of miscellaneous collections of poems and plays, 1962—. Author of introductions to volumes of avant-garde poetry.

Editor and publisher of Crank Books, distributed by Interim Books; editor or co-editor of Interim Books series. Editor of annual, *Magazine*, 1964, *Magazine Two*, 1965, and *Magazine Three*, 1966. Included in Walter Loewenfels project, "Jazz Poets," a recording and anthology. Contributor to other publications.

WORK IN PROGRESS: Locomotive and the Hobo, a work tracing the American individual; work on the attraction toward and repulsion to the machine, as evident in nineteenth- and twentieth-century poetry; a bibliography of the most important books of poetry in Western civilization; *Dream-Work*, a new collection of poems.

SIDELIGHTS: Congdon has been active in establishing, here and in England, a poetry milieu independent of commercial and academic publishing traditions.

BIOGRAPHICAL/CRITICAL SOURCES: Times Literary Supplement, August 6, 1964; *Writer's Forum 2*, fall, 1965.†

*　　*　　*

CONGER, John (Janeway)　1921-

PERSONAL: Born February 27, 1921, in New Brunswick, N.J.; son of John C. and Katharine (Janeway) Conger; married Mayo Trist Kline (a teacher), January 1, 1944; children: Steven Janeway, David Trist. *Education:* Amherst College, B.A. (magna cum laude), 1943; Yale University, M.S., 1947, Ph.D., 1949. *Home:* 130 South Birch, Denver, Colo.

CAREER: Indiana University, Indianapolis Campus, assistant professor of psychology, 1949-53; University of Colorado, School of Medicine, Denver, associate professor of psychology and head of division of clinical psychology, 1953-57, professor, 1957—, associate dean, 1961-63, vice-president for medical affairs, 1963-70, and dean, 1963-68. Consultant to Veterans Administration, 1953—, Division of Research Grants, National Institute of Mental Health, 1959-61, Community Services Branch, U.S. Public Health Service, 1959—, Health Facilities Branch, National Institutes of Health, 1964—, Division of Hospital and Medical Facilities, U.S. Public Health Service, 1964—. President's Committee for Traffic Safety, chairman of research committee, 1960-63; National Research Council, member of committee on road-user characteristics, Highway Research Board, 1960—. Colorado State Board of Psychologist Examiners, vice-chairman, 1961-64. *Military service:* U.S. Naval Reserve, on active duty, 1944-46, 1951-52; chief staff psychologist, U.S. Naval Academy, 1951-52; became lieutenant.

MEMBER: American Psychological Association (fellow), American Association of Medical Colleges, American Association for the Advancement of Science, Colorado Psychological Association, Rocky Mountain Psychological Association, Colorado Medical Society (honorary), Denver Medical Society (honorary), Phi Beta Kappa, Sigma Xi.

WRITINGS: (With P. H. Mussen and J. Kagan) *Child Development and Personality*, Harper, 1956, 3rd edition, 1969; (contributor) *Alcoholism: Theory, Problem, and Challenge*, Yale Alcohol Studies Press, 1956; (contributor) G. F. Reed, I. D. Alexander, and S. S. Tomkins, editors, *Psychopathology: A Source Book*, Harvard University Press, 1958; (with W. C. Miller) *Personality, Social Class and Juvenile Delinquency*, Wiley, 1966; (with Mussen and Kagan) *Readings in Child Development*, Harper, 2nd edition, 1970; *Adolescence and Youth Psychological Development in a Changing World*, Harper, 1973. Contributor to *The Encyclopedia of Mental Health*, 1963, and of more than twenty articles and reviews to medical, psychological, and highway safety journals.†

*　　*　　*

CONIL, Jean　1917-

PERSONAL: Born August 28, 1917, in Fontenay-le-Comte, France; son of Octave (a restaurateur) and Marie-Josephine (Gorriez) Conil; married October 10, 1942, wife is a nurse; children: Patricia, Christopher. *Education:* Attended Stanislas College, Paris, France. *Politics:* Socialist-Liberal. *Religion:* Spiritualist. *Home:* 282 Dollis Hill Lane, London N.W. 2, England. *Office:* Overseas Bankers Club, 7 Lothbury, London E.C. 2, England.

CAREER: Managing director, private catering firm, 1953—; Hurlingham Club, London, senior catering manager, 1961—; Overseas Bankers Club, London, general manager, 1963—. *Military service:* Served in British and French navies. *Member:* International Academy of Chefs (president), Cercle Epicurien (president), Academie Culinaire de France (corresponding). *Awards, honors:* Silver Medal, Berne Exhibition, 1950, and Gold Medal, London Exhibition, 1951, 1952, all for cookery.

WRITINGS: For Epicures Only, Laurie, 1953; *Haute Cuisine*, Faber, 1955; *The Home Cookery*, Methuen, 1956; *The Jean Conil Cookery Classes*, P. Owen, 1957; *The Gastronomic Tour de France*, Allen & Unwin, 1959; *The Epicurean Book*, Allen & Unwin, 1961. Contributor to *Epicurien* and *Sunday Times* (London).†

*　　*　　*

CONNOR, John Anthony　1930-
(Tony Connor)

PERSONAL: Born March 16, 1930, in Salford, Lancashire, England; son of John (a hotelier) and Dorothy Mabel (Richings) Connor; married Frances Foad (a speech therapist), July 22, 1961; children: Samuel McKeen, Stephan Simon. *Education:* University of Manchester, M.A. *Home:* 44 Brainerd Ave., Middletown, Conn. 06457.

CAREER: Textile designer in Manchester, Lancashire, England, 1944-60; Technical College, Bolton, Lancashire, England, lecturer in liberal studies, 1961-64; currently professor of literature at Wesleyan University, Middletown, Conn. Lecturer in drawing and painting at the Salford School of Art, Lancashire. *Military service:* British Army, 1948-50; trooper.

WRITINGS—All under the name Tony Connor; poems: *With Love Somehow*, Oxford University Press, 1962; (with Austin Clarke and Charles Tomlinson) *Lodgers*, Oxford University Press, 1965; *Kon In Springtime*, Oxford University Press, 1968; *In the Happy Valley*, Oxford University Press, 1971; *The Memoirs of Uncle Harry*, Oxford University Press, 1970; *Seven Last Poems*, Northern House, 1974.

Plays: *Billy's Wonderful Kettle*, Dennis Dobson, 1974: "The Last of the Feinsteins" (not published), 1974. Author of numerous scripts for television.

WORK IN PROGRESS: Poems and a children's play commissioned by Oxford Playhouse, England.

*　　*　　*

CONOVER, Hobart H.　1914-

PERSONAL: Born May 25, 1914, in Gloversville, N.Y.;

son of Earl A. (an electrical contractor) and Minnie (Hample) Conover; married Phebe Jane Carpenter. *Education:* Syracuse University, B.S., 1935, M.S., 1941, graduate study, 1943. *Home:* 71 Marlboro Rd., Delmar, N.Y. 12054. *Office:* New York State Department of Education, Albany, N.Y. 12224.

CAREER: High school teacher and vice-principal in Hermon and Weedsport, N.Y., 1935-43, 1946-49; American National Red Cross, field director, 1945-46; New York State Department of Education, Albany, supervisor of business education, 1950—. Husson College, Bangor, Me., professor of business education, four summers, 1946-63. *Military service:* U.S. Army, Anti-Aircraft Command, 1943-45. *Member:* American Vocational Association, National Association of Supervisors of Business Education, National Business Teachers Association, Eastern Business Teachers Association, Business Teachers Association of New York State (director), Phi Delta Kappa, Gamma Rho Tau, Beta Alpha Psi.

WRITINGS: (With C. A. Reed and R. E. Stearns) *Introduction to Business*, Allyn & Bacon, 1958; *Comprehensive Typewriting–First Course*, Allyn & Bacon, 1964; *Comprehensive Typewriting–Two Year Course*, Allyn & Bacon, 1964; *Comprehensive Typewriting for Colleges*, Allyn & Bacon, 1964. Contributor to business education periodicals.

WORK IN PROGRESS: Developing *General Business*, a textbook, with B. Bertha Wakin and Helene Zimmerman.

AVOCATIONAL INTERESTS: Playing piano and organ.

* * *

CONQUEST, (George) Robert (Acworth) 1917-
(J. E. M. Arden)

PERSONAL: Born July 15, 1917, in Malvern, England; son of R. Folger W. and Rosamund A. (Acworth) Conquest; married Joan Watkins, 1942 (divorced 1948); married Tatiana Mihailova, 1948 (divorced 1962); married Caroleen Macfarlane, April 4, 1964; children: (first marriage) John, Richard. *Education:* Attended University of Grenoble, 1935-36; Magdalen College, Oxford, B.A., 1939. *Home:* 4 York Mansions, Prince of Wales Drive, London S.W. 11, England. *Agent:* Scott Meredith Literary Agency, Inc., 580 Fifth Ave., New York, N.Y. 10036.

CAREER: H.M. Foreign Service, 1946-56, served in Sofia, Bulgaria, as first secretary, was member of United Kingdom delegation to United Nations; London School of Economics and Political Science, London, England, research fellow, 1956-58; State University of New York at Buffalo, visiting lecturer, 1959-60; *The Spectator*, London, England, literary editor, 1962-63; Columbia University, New York, N.Y., senior fellow, 1964-65. *Military service:* Oxfordshire and Buckinghamshire Light Infantry, 1939-46; awarded Order of the British Empire. *Member:* Authors Society, Science Fiction Writers of America, British Interplanetary Society, Travellers Club. *Awards, honors:* P.E.N. prize for long poem, 1945; Festival of Britain verse prize, 1951.

WRITINGS: (Editor with others) *New Poems: A P.E.N. Anthology*, Transatlantic, 1953; *A World of Difference* (novel), Ward, Lock, 1955, new edition, Ballantine, 1964; *Poems*, St. Martins, 1955; (editor) *New Lines*, St. Martins, 1956; (under pseudonym J.E.M. Arden) *Where Do Marxists Go From Here?*, Phoenix House, 1958; (editor) *Back to Life: Poems From Behind the Iron Curtain*, Hutchinson, 1958, St. Martins, 1960;

Common Sense About Russia, Macmillan, 1960; *Soviet Deportation of Nationalities*, St. Martins, 1960, revised edition published as *The Nation Killers: The Soviet Deportation of Nationalities*, Macmillan, 1970; (editor with Kingsley Amis) *Spectrum: A Science Fiction Anthology* (annual), Gollancz, 1961—, Harcourt, 1963—; *Power and Policy in the U.S.S.R.: The Study of Soviet Dynastics*, Macmillan, 1961, St. Martins, 1962, published as *Power and Policy in the U.S.S.R.: The Struggle for Stalin's Succession, 1945-60*, Harper, 1967; *Courage of Genius: The Pasternak Affair*, Collins, 1961, published as *The Pasternak Affair: Courage of Genius*, Lippincott, 1962; *Between Mars and Venus* (poems), St. Martins, 1962; *The Last Empire*, Ampersand Books, 1962; *The Future of Communism*, Today Publications, 1963; (editor) *New Lines 2*, Macmillan (London), 1963; *The Soviet Succession Problems*, 1964; *Marxism Today*, Ampersand Books, 1964; *Russia After Khrushchev*, Praeger, 1965; (with Kingsley Amis) *The Egyptologists* (novel), J. Cape, 1965, Random House, 1966.

Industrial Workers in the U.S.S.R., Praeger, 1967; *The Politics of Ideas in the U.S.S.R.*, Praeger, 1967; (editor) *Soviet Nationalities Policy in Practice*, Praeger, 1967; *Religion in the U.S.S.R.*, Praeger, 1968; *The Soviet Political System*, Praeger, 1968; *The Great Terror: Stalin's Purge of the Thirties*, Macmillan, 1968; (editor) *Justice and the Legal System in the U.S.S.R.*, Praeger, 1968; (editor) *The Soviet Police System*, Praeger, 1968; *Arias From a Love Opera, and Other Poems*, Macmillan, 1969; *Where Marx Went Wrong*, T. Stacey, 1970; *V. I. Lenin*, Viking, 1972.

WORK IN PROGRESS: A book of essays, *A Cool Look at Communism*; *The Abomination of Moab*, a book of literary essays; a novel and science fiction stories.

BIOGRAPHICAL/CRITICAL SOURCES: Spectator, June 2, 1961; *Times Literary Supplement*, June 9, 1961, December 14, 1962, October 14, 1965; *Nation*, August 12, 1961, August 11, 1962; *New Yorker*, August 19, 1961; *New Statesman*, November 24, 1961, May 18, 1962, October 15, 1965; *Commonweal*, June 8, 1962; *Yale Review*, October, 1962; *Saturday Review*, October 13, 1962; *New York Review of Books*, August 5, 1965; *Observer*, August 8, 1965, January 6, 1969; *Washington Post*, December 17, 1969.†

* * *

CONROY, Charles W. 1922-

PERSONAL: Born September 7, 1922, in Houston, Tex.; son of William Ernest and Lucille (Evans) Conroy; married Marjorie Lee McGlothlin (a high school teacher), 1947; children: Charles W., Jr., Janet Susanne. *Education:* Houston Junior College, A.A., 1942; University of Houston, B.S., 1947, M.S., 1948, M.L., 1949; also studied at Southwestern Louisiana University, Indiana State Teachers College (now Indiana State University), DePauw University, and State University of Iowa. *Religion:* Methodist. *Home:* 11911 Northwest Freeway, Houston, Tex. 77018. *Office:* Headquarters, U.S. Customs Service, 2100 K St. N.W., Washington, D.C.

CAREER: University of Houston, Houston, Tex., education counselor, 1946-48, assistant director of guidance, 1948-51; U.S. Air Force, Ellington Air Force Base, Tex., education adviser (as civilian), 1951-59; Civil Air Patrol, National Headquarters, Ellington Air Force Base, Tex., assistant director of Editorial and Curriculum Division, 1959-62, director, 1962-67, member of national Decorations and Awards Board and Scholarship Selection Committee;

U.S. Customs Service, Houston, Tex., regional training officer, 1967-69, public information officer, 1969-74, acting director of Public Information Division in Washington, D.C., 1974—. *Military service:* U.S. Navy, 1942-46. *Member:* Aerospace Education Association, National Aerospace Education Council, National Society for Programmed Instruction, Association of Aviation Psychologists, Civil Air Patrol. *Awards, honors:* Sustained Superior Performance awards, U.S. Air Force, 1962-63; superior performance awards, U.S. Customs Service, 1970, 1973.

WRITINGS—Instructional materials for schools and colleges: *Introduction to Aerospace*, Civil Air Patrol, 1963; *The Dawning Space Age*, Civil Air Patrol, 1963; *Aircraft Identification*, Civil Air Patrol, 1965; *Navigation and the Weather*, Civil Air Patrol, 1966. Author of instructor guides, workbooks, filmstrip scripts, and a filmograph script, "The Rebirth of Rocketry." Contributor to *Education, Hoosier Schoolmaster*, and other education journals.

WORK IN PROGRESS: Feature articles, news stories, fact sheets, information briefs, and public service announcements for radio and television.

* * *

CONSTANTIN, James A. 1922-

PERSONAL: Born June 15, 1922, in Tulsa, Okla.; son of Jules J. and Nelle (Alford) Constantin; married Wanda A. Moyer, May 18, 1941; children: Katherine (Mrs. Robert D. Beaird), James A., Jr., Jules J. II, Anne C. Keown. *Education:* University of Texas, B.B.A., 1943, M.B.A., 1944, Ph.D., 1950. *Home:* 929 West Lindsay, Norman, Okla. *Office:* Department of Marketing, Room 106, University of Oklahoma, Norman, Okla. 73069.

CAREER: University of Texas, Austin, instructor in business administration, 1946-47; University of Alabama, University, 1947-51, began as assistant professor, became associate professor of business administration, research associate of Bureau of Business Research, 1951-52; University of Washington, Seattle, associate professor of business administration, 1952-53; University of Oklahoma, Norman, professor of marketing and transportation, 1953-68, David Ross Boyd Professor of Marketing and Transportation, 1968—. *Member:* American Economic Association, Transportation Research Forum, American Society of Traffic and Transportation, Associated Traffic Clubs of America, Southwestern Social Science Association.

WRITINGS: Water Transportation: Foundation, Principles, and Practices, University of Alabama Press, 1950; (contributor) Kent Ruth, editor, *Oklahoma: A Guide to the Sooner State*, University of Oklahoma Press, 1957; (with William J. Hudson) *Motor Transportation*, Ronald, 1958; *Marketing Logistics*, Appleton, 1965; (with W. N. Peach) *Zimmermann's World Resources and Industries*, 3rd edition, Harper, 1972; (with Rodney E. Evans and Malcolm L. Morris) *Planning and Managing the Marketing Function*, Business Publications, in press.

Monographs: *The Characteristics of Motor Freight Movements in Oklahoma by General Commodity Carriers*, University of Oklahoma Research Institute (under grant from U.S. Small Business Administration), 1963; (with A. J. Kondonassis and Jim E. Reese) *An Economic Base Study of Lawton, Okla.*, University of Oklahoma Research Institute, 1963. Contributor to *Distribution Age, Southern Economic Journal, Terminal Operator*, other journals in field.

CONVERSE, Philip E. 1928-

PERSONAL: Born November 17, 1928, in Concord, N.H.; son of Ernest Luther (a minister) and Evelyn (Eaton) Converse; married Jean G. McDonnell, August 25, 1951; children: Peter Everett, Timothy McDonnell. *Education:* Denison University, B.A., 1949; University of Iowa, M.A. in English, 1950; University of Paris, graduate study, 1953-54; University of Michigan, M.A. in sociology, 1956, Ph.D., 1958. *Home:* 2564 Easy St., Ann Arbor, Mich. *Office:* Survey Research Center, University of Michigan, Ann Arbor, Mich.

CAREER: Fulbright research fellowship in France, 1959-60; University of Michigan, Ann Arbor, senior study director, Survey Research Center, 1960—, assistant professor of sociology, 1960-63, associate professor of sociology and political science, 1963-65, professor, 1965—. Lecturer in France, Norway, and Sweden; teacher at first UNESCO European Seminar, Cologne, Germany, 1964. *Military service:* U.S. Army, 1950-52. *Member:* American Sociological Association, American Political Science Association, American Association for Public Opinion Research, Phi Beta Kappa.

WRITINGS: (With Angus Campbell, Warren E. Miller, and Donald E. Stokes) *The American Voter*, Wiley, 1960; (with T. M. Newcomb and Ralph Turner) *Social Psychology*, Holt, Rinehart & Winston, 1965; *Some Priority Variables in Comparable Electoral Research*, University of Strathclyde (Glasgow), 1968; (with Milton J. Rosenberg) *Vietnam and the Silent Majority*, Harper, 1970; (editor with Angus Campbell) *The Meaning of Social Change*, Russell Sage, 1972; (with Henry Valen) *Velgere og politiske frontlinner*, Gyldendal (Oslo), 1972; Contributor of articles to journals of political science, sociology, and psychology.†

* * *

CONZE, Edward J. D. 1904-

PERSONAL: Born March 18, 1904, in London, England; son of Ernst (a judge) and Adele (Koettgen) Conze. *Education:* Studied at universities in Germany, 1923-28, University of Cologne, Ph.D., 1928. *Religion:* Buddhist. *Home:* Foxwell, Marston Rd., Sherborne, Dorset, England.

CAREER: Lecturer in psychology, philosophy, and comparative religion in extramural departments of universities of London, Oxford, and Southampton, 1934-60; University of Wisconsin, Madison, Distinguished Visiting Professor of Indian studies, 1963-64; Manchester College, Oxford, England, research fellow, 1964-65; University of Washington, Seattle, professor of Indic studies, 1965-68; University of Lancaster, Lancaster, England, visiting professor of comparative religions, 1968-69; Friedrich Wilhelm Universitaet, Bonn, Germany, visiting professor of Buddhist studies, 1969-70; University of California, Berkeley and Santa Barbara, visiting professor of religious studies, 1971-73; University of Lancaster, visiting professor of religious studies, 1973-75.

WRITINGS: Der Begriff der Metaphysik bei F. Suarez, F. Meiner (Leipzig), 1928; *Contradiction and Reality*, Wightman & Co., 1939.

Buddhism: Its Essence and Development, Cassirer, 1951, Torchbooks, 1959; (editor) *Buddhist Texts Through the Ages*, Cassirer, 1954, Torchbooks, 1964; (translator) *Abhisamayalankara*, Serie Orientale Roma VI, 1954; *Selected Sayings from the Perfection of Wisdom*, Buddhist Society (London), 1955; (translator from the Tibetan, and author of commentary) *The Buddha's Law Among the Birds*, Cassirer, 1956; *Buddhist Meditation*, Allen & Unwin, 1956, Torchbooks, 1969; (editor, translator, and author of introduction and glossary) *Vajracchedika Prajnaparamita*, Serie Orientale Roma XIII, 1957; *Buddhist Wisdom Books*, Allen & Unwin, 1958, Torchbooks, 1972; (translator) *Ashtasahasrika Prajnaparamita*, Asiatic Society (Calcutta), 1958; *Buddhist Scriptures*, Penguin, 1959.

The Prajnaparamita Literature, Mouton, 1960; *A Short History of Buddhism*, Chetana, 1960; (contributor) S. Yamagucchi, editor, *Buddhism and Culture: Dedicated to D. T. Suzuki in Commemoration of His Ninetieth Birthday*, [Kyoto], 1960; *The Large Sutra on Perfect Wisdom*, Part I, Luzac, 1961, Parts II and III, College Printing Co. (Madison, Wis.), 1964; (editor and translator) *The Gilgit Manuscript of the Ashtadasasahasrika Prajnaparamita* (Chapters 55-70), Serie Orientale Roma XXVI, 1962; *Buddhist Thought in India*, Allen & Unwin, 1962, Ann Arbor Paperbacks, 1967; (contributor) Guy Wint, editor, *Asia: A Handbook*, Praeger, 1966; *Materials for a Dictionary of the Prajnaparamita Literature*, Suzuki Research Foundation (Tokyo), 1967; *Thirty Years of Buddhist Studies*, University of South Carolina Press, 1968.

The Perfection of Wisdom in Eight Thousand Lines and Its Verse Summary, Four Seasons Foundation, 1973; (translator) The *Short Prajnaparamita Texts*, Rowman & Littlefield, 1974; (editor and translator) *The Gilgit Manuscript of the Ashtadasasahasrika Prajnaparamita* (Chapters 70-82), Serie Orientale Roma XLVI, 1974; *Further Buddhist Studies*, University of South Carolina Press, 1974. Author of prefatory notes and introductions to other publications.

Contributor to *The Concise Encyclopedia of Living Faiths*, *Encyclopedia of Buddhism*, and *Encyclopaedia Britannica*. Also contributor of more than ninety articles and about one hundred reviews to journals and newspapers, including *Middle Way*, *Guardian*, *Hibbert Journal*, *Aryan Path*, *Indo-Iranian Journal*, and *Philosophy East and West*.

WORK IN PROGRESS: A translation of *Saddharmapundarika*, publication by Oxford University Press expected in 1976.

* * *

COOK, Don(ald Paul) 1920-

PERSONAL: Born August 8, 1920, in Bridgeport, Conn.; son of Paul J. (a schoolteacher) and Nelle Brown (Reed) Cook; married Cherry Mitchell, October 31, 1943; children: Christopher, Jennifer, Adrienne, Deborah, Caron, Danielle, Dominique. *Education:* Attended schools in Pennsylvania. *Religion:* Protestant. *Home:* 4 Allee Jose Roland, L'Etang la Ville, France 78620. *Agent:* Brandt & Brandt, 101 Park Ave., New York, N.Y. 10017. *Office:* Los Angeles Times, 73 Ave. des Champs-Elysees, Paris, France 75008.

CAREER: Began newspaper work at eighteen; *New York Herald Tribune*, New York, N.Y., reporter, Washington bureau, 1943-45, foreign correspondent, London, 1945-49, Germany, 1949-52, roving European correspondent based in Paris, 1952-55, chief of London Bureau, 1956-60, chief European correspondent, 1960-65; *Los Angeles Times*, Los Angeles, Calif., Paris correspondent, 1965—. *Member:* Authors League of America, Anglo-American Press Association of Paris, Association of American Correspondents in London (former president), Garrick Club (London). *Awards, honors:* William the Silent Award for Journalism (The Netherlands), 1956; English-Speaking Union Award, 1958.

WRITINGS: Floodtide in Europe, Putnam, 1965. Contributor to *Saturday Evening Post, Reporter, Harper's, Look, Reader's Digest, Atlantic Monthly*, and *Encounter*.

SIDELIGHTS: Cook has traveled and reported extensively in Europe, Africa, and the Middle East.

* * *

COOK, Harold Reed 1902-

PERSONAL: Born December 7, 1902, in Quincy, Ill.; son of Alonzo Dell and Mary Lois (Reed) Cook; married Florence S. Hosie, August 12, 1926; children: Harold Dale, Addison Gilbert. *Education:* Attended Moody Bible Institute, 1923-26, Wheaton College, Wheaton, Ill.; 1927, John B. Stetson University, 1936-37, University of Florida, 1937; University of Southern California, A.B., 1942, M.A., 1943. *Relgion:* Protestant. *Home:* 611 East Willow Ave., Wheaton, Ill. 60187.

CAREER: Orinoco River Mission, Venezuela, missionary, 1928-37; Western Bible College, Bible Missionary Institute, Los Angeles, Calif., teacher, 1937-40, registrar, 1939-40, acting dean, 1939; Moody Bible Institute, Chicago, Ill., teacher, 1944-73, chairman of department of missions, 1963-69, 1972-73. Bible House of Los Angeles, member of board of directors and Spanish consultant, 1937-45; Spanish consultant and member of textbook committee for Moody Press. *Member:* Fellowship of Evangelical Professors of Missions, Committee to Assist Missionary Education Overseas, International African Institute, Midwest Fellowship of Professors of Missions, Phi Beta Kappa, Phi Alpha Theta, Phi Kappa Phi.

WRITINGS: Introduction to Christian Missions, Moody, 1954, revised edition, 1971; *Missionary Life and Work*, Moody, 1959; *A Strategy of Missions*, Moody, 1963; (contributor) Peter F. Gunther, editor, *The Fields at Home*, Moody, 1963; *Highlights of Christian Missions*, Moody, 1967; *Historic Patterns of Church Growth*, Moody, 1971; *Preparing Tomorrow's Missionaries*, American Association of Bible Colleges, 1972. Also writer of studygraph, "Missionary History," Moody, 1963. Missions editor, *Moody Monthly*, 1946-70.

WORK IN PROGRESS: Continued research and writing in field of missionary history since 1914; collaborating on a book about missions in Africa; revising *Missionary Life and Work*; translating a correspondence course into Spanish.

* * *

COOK, Olive Rambo 1892-

PERSONAL: Born August 26, 1892, in Avalon, Mo.; daughter of George W. (a farmer) and Effie M. (Green) Rambo; married Frank K. Cook, August 7, 1920 (deceased); children: George R. *Education:* Attended high school and business college in Chillicothe, Mo. *Politics:* Registered Republican but votes independently. *Religion:* Methodist. *Home and office:* 566 Oak St., Mountain View, Calif.

CAREER: City of Chillicothe, Mo., city clerk, 1921-23; State Training School for Girls, Chillicothe, teacher of arts and crafts, 1933-39; free-lance writer. *Member:* National League of American Pen Women.

WRITINGS: Coon Holler (Junior Literary Guild selection), Longmans, Green, 1958; *Serilda's Star* (juvenile; Catholic Book Club Selection), Longmans, Green, 1959; *Locket* (juvenile), McKay, 1963; *The Sign at Six Corners* (young adult; condensed version published as serial in *American Girl*), McKay, 1965; *The Magic of the Golden Gourd* (juvenile), Leswing Communications, 1971. Contributor of articles to adult periodicals, and short stories and series to juvenile magazines.

*   *   *

COOK, P(auline) Lesley 1922-

PERSONAL: Born December 28, 1922, in Cambridge, England; daughter of Leslie Eric and Phyllis E. G. (Wakelin) Cook. *Education:* Newnham College, Cambridge, B.A., 1947; studied at Cambridge University and University of Leeds, 1947-50, Ph.D. (Cambridge), 1950. *Home:* The Street, Kingston, near Lewes, Sussex, England.

CAREER: University of Exeter, Exeter, England, lecturer, 1951-53; Cambridge University, Cambridge, England, research officer, 1953-63, tutor, and later senior tutor, Newnham College, 1956-63; University of Sussex, Brighton, England, 1963—, began as senior lecturer, became reader in economics. Economic adviser to Restrictive Practices Court; member of board of governors, Cambridge United Hospitals, 1962-63; senior economic adviser, Ministry of Power, 1967-69; member of South Eastern Gas Board, 1969-72.

WRITINGS: (With Ruth Cohen) *Effects of Mergers*, Macmillan, 1958; *Railway Workshops: The Problems of Contraction*, Cambridge University Press, 1964.

*   *   *

COOKE, Bernard J. 1922-

PERSONAL: Born May 31, 1922, in Norway, Mich.; son of John Michael (a dentist) and Eleanor (Crevier) Cooke. *Education:* St. Louis University, A.B., 1944, M.A., 1946; St. Mary's College, St. Mary's Kan., S.T.L., 1953; Institut catholique de Paris, S.T.D., 1956.

CAREER: Entered Society of Jesus, 1939; ordained Roman Catholic priest, 1952, requested release from Society of Jesus, 1970; Marquette University, Milwaukee, Wis., professor and chairman of department of theology, 1958-70. National Liturgical Conference, member of board of directors. North Central Association of Colleges and Secondary Schools, consultant. *Military service:* U.S. Army, auxiliary chaplain, 1954-56. *Member:* Religious Education Association (national board of directors, 1963—), Society for the Scientific Study of Religion, Academy of Religion and Mental Health, Catholic Theological Society, Catholic Biblical Society of America, Society of Catholic College Teachers of Sacred Doctrine (president, 1960-62).

WRITINGS: Christian Sacraments and Christian Personality, Holt, 1965; *Formation of Faith*, Loyola University Press, 1965; *The Challenge of Vatican II*, Argus, 1966; *Christian Involvement*, Argus, 1966; *New Dimensions in Catholic Life*, Dimension Books, 1968; *The Spirit and Power of Christian Secularity*, University of Notre Dame, 1969; *The God of Space and Time*, Holt, 1969; *The Eucharist: Mystery of a Friendship*, Pflaum, 1969; *Beyond Trinity*, Marquette University Press, 1969; *Christian Community: Response to Reality*, Holt, 1970; *Toward a Future for Religious Education*, Pflaum, 1970.

Contributor: R. Pelton, editor, *The Church as the Body of Christ*, University of Notre Dame Press, 1963; Hofinger and Stone, editors, *Pastoral Catechetics*, Herder, 1964; R. Ryan, editor, *Contemporary New Testament Studies*, Li-

turgical Press, 1965; Keller and Armstrong, editors, *Apostolic Renewal in the Seminary*, Christopher, 1965. Contributor to religious and theological journals.

WORK IN PROGRESS: Research and preliminary work on books on the theology of priesthood, on imagination, and on American culture.†

*   *   *

COOKE, Gerald 1925-

PERSONAL: Born October 18, 1925, in Colorado Springs, Colo.; son of Alfred Bruce (a movie projectionist) and Frances E. (Cupples) Cooke; married Brigitte Maria Cossmann, September 6, 1947; children: David Bainton, Mark Julian, Johannes Christopher. *Education:* Colorado College, B.A. (magna cum laude), 1950; Yale Divinity School, B.D., 1952; Yale University, Ph.D., 1958. *Office:* Department of Religion, Bucknell University, Lewisburg, Pa.

CAREER: Ordained minister, United Church of Christ, 1954. Pastor in Middlefield, Conn. 1954-55; Oberlin College, Oberlin, Ohio, instructor, then assistant professor of religion, 1955-62; Bucknell University, Lewisburg, Pa., chaplain, 1962-63, assistant professor 1964-68, associate professor of religion, 1968—; chairman of department of religion, 1964-70. Staff member of archaeological expedition of University of Pennsylvania Museum, in El Jib, Jordan, summer, 1960. *Military service:* U.S. Coast Guard, 1943-46. *Member:* American Academy of Religion, Society for the Scientific Study of Religion, American Association of University Professors, Phi Beta Kappa. *Awards, honors:* American Institute of Indian Studies fellowship for study of contemporary aspects of Hinduism, in India, 1963-64; National Defense Education Act summer fellowship for study of Japanese, 1970; Fulbright-Hays research study award for study of Buddhism and modernization in Japan, 1970-71; National Endowment for the Humanites award for research in Japan, 1974.

WRITINGS: As Christians Face Rival Religions, Association Press, 1962. Author of pamphlet, *A Neo-Hindu Ashrama in South India*, C.I.S.R.S. (Bangalore, India), 1966. Contributor to *The Interpreter's Dictionary of the Bible*, Abingdon, 1962; editorial assistant, *The Oxford Atlas of the Bible*, Oxford University Press, 1962. Contributor of research articles to *Zeitschrift fuer die Altestamentliche Wissenschaft*, Journal of the American Academy of Religion, Japanese Journal of Religious Studies, of reviews and articles to *Christian Century, Journal of Biblical Literature*, other professional journals.

WORK IN PROGRESS: Research on Japanese Buddhism and modernization, including field study of two Shin temples and reformist measures in Otani Shin Shu.

*   *   *

COOKE, Greville (Vaughan Turner) 1894-

PERSONAL: Born July 14, 1894, in England; son of William Turner (chief clerk, Royal Courts of Justice) and Adeline Hannah (Johnson) Cooke. *Education:* Royal Academy of Music, A.R.A.M., 1913; Christ's College, Cambridge, B.A. and Mus.B., 1916, M.A., 1920; Ridley Hall, Cambridge, theology student. *Politics:* Conservative. *Home:* Waveney, 26 West Close, Middleton on Sea, West Sussex, England.

CAREER: Ordained in Church of England, 1918. Curate in Tavistock, 1918, Ealing, 1920; minor canon of St. Paul's Cathedral, 1920-21; vicar of Cransley, 1921-56; canon (non-residentiary) of Peterborough Cathedral, 1955-56, canon emeritus, 1956—; rector of Buxted, 1956-71. Professor, Royal Academy of Music, 1925-59; lecturer at London University, Royal Institution of Great Britain, League of Arts (England), and other organizations and societies: composer of more than sixty published works, including orchestral compositions, songs, choral works, anthems, instrumental pieces, and hymns. *Member:* Royal Academy of Music (fellow), Society of Antiquaries (fellow), Sussex Archaeological Society (council member).

WRITINGS: The Theory of Music, Benn, 1928; *Art and Reality*, Williams & Norgate, 1929; *Tonality and Expression*, William & Norgate, 1929; *Poems*, Basil Blackwell, 1933; *Cransley Broadcast Sermons*, Skeffington & Sons, 1933; *The Light of the World*, Hodder & Stoughton, 1949, Bobbs-Merrill, 1959; (contributor) *Hymns Ancient and Modern*, Oxford University Press, 1950; (contributor) *W. K. Stanton*, editor-in-chief, *B.B.C. Hymn Book*, Oxford University Press, 1951; *A Chronicle of Buxted*, Uckfield Press, 1960; *The Grand Design*, Faith Press, 1964; *Thus Saith the Lord: A Biblical Anthology*, Clark's (Haywards Heath, England), 1967; *Jenny Pluck Pears and Other Poems*, Clark's (Haywards Heath, England), 1972.

Also contributor to *Baptist Hymn Book*. Contributor of poems to *Cornhill Magazine, Cambridge Review, Royal Society of Arts Journal*, and other periodicals.

WORK IN PROGRESS: Writing on authorship of the Fourth Gospel and on modernism in the arts; a book on the Bible.

* * *

COOKSON, Catherine (McMullen) 1906-
(Catherine Marchant)

PERSONAL: Born June 20, 1906, in Tyne Dock, Durham, England; married Thomas H. Cookson (a schoolmaster), June 1, 1940. *Home:* Loreto, Saint Helens Park Rd., Hastings, Sussex, England. *Agent:* John Smith, Christy & Moore Ltd., 52 Floral St., Covent Garden, London W.C. 2, England.

CAREER: Author. Lecturer for women's groups and other organizations. *Member:* Women's Press Club (London).

WRITINGS—All published by MacDonald except as indicated: *Kate Hannigan*, 1950; *The Fifteen Streets*, 1952; *Colour Blind*, 1953; *A Grand Man*, 1954, Macmillan, 1955; *Maggie Rowan*, 1954; *Rooney*, 1957; *The Menagerie*, 1958; *Slinky Jane*, 1959; *Fenwick Houses*, 1960; *The Garment*, 1962; *The Blind Miller*, 1963; *Hannah Massey*, 1964; *The Long Corridor*, 1965; *Matty Doolin*, 1965.

The Unbaited Trap, MacDonald, 1966; *Katie Mulholland*, MacDonald, 1967; *Joe and the Gladiator*, MacDonald, 1968; *The Round Tower*, MacDonald, 1968; *The Glass Virgin*, Bobbs-Merrill, 1969, *The Nipper*, MacDonald, 1969, Bobbs-Merrill, 1970; *The Nice Bloke*, MacDonald, 1969; *Our Kate: An Autobiography*, MacDonald, 1969, Bobbs-Merrill, 1971; *The Invitation*, MacDonald, 1970; *Blue Baccy*, Bobbs-Merrill, 1971; *The Dwelling Place*, Bobbs-Merrill, 1972; *Feathers in the Fire*, Bobbs-Merrill, 1972; *Pure as the Lily*, Bobbs-Merrill, 1973; *The Mallen Girl*, Dutton, 1973; *The Mallen Streak*, Dutton, 1973; *The Mallen Lot*, Dutton, 1974; *Our John Willy*, Bobbs-Merrill, 1974.

"Mary Ann" series—All published by MacDonald: *The Lord and Mary Ann*, 1956, *The Devil and Mary Ann*, 1958, *Love and Mary Ann*, 1961, *Life and Mary Ann*, 1962, *Marriage and Mary Ann*, 1964; *Mary Ann and Bill*, 1967.

Under pseudonym Catherine Marchant—All published by MacDonald: *Heritage of Folly*, 1962, *The Fen Tiger*, 1963, *House of Men*, 1964.

SIDELIGHTS: Rooney and A Grand Man were made into films, the latter as "Jacqueline." All of the "Mary Ann" books have been published in Germany, where they have a large following, and in Holland and Italy. *Avocational interests:* Gardening, particularly cultivating a two-acre woodland plot; painting.

BIOGRAPHICAL/CRITICAL SOURCES: Books and Bookmen, June, 1969.†

* * *

COOLEY, John Kent 1927-

PERSONAL: Born November 25, 1927, in New York, N.Y.; son of John Landon and Ruth (Robinson) Cooley; married April 2, 1950 (divorced); married second wife in 1970; choldren: (first marriage) Katherine Anne; (second marriage) Alexander. *Education:* Attended University of Zurich, 1948-49, University of Vienna, 1951-53; Dartmouth College, A.B. (cum laude), 1952; graduate study, New School for Social Research, 1954, and Columbia University, 1964-65. *Office:* c/o *Christian Science Monitor*, Hotel St. George, Beirut, Lebanon.

CAREER: Began as reporter, 1948; free-lance foreign correspondent, 1949-57; civilian clerk, editor, and interpreter with U.S. military groups and Department of State in Austria, 1949-51, 1952-53; personnel clerk for civilian contractor, and editor of weekly newspaper for construction workers on U.S. air base, Ben Guerir, Morocco, 1953; editorial writer for *New York Herald Tribune*, 1954; U.S. Army Engineers (Mediterranean), Nouasseur, Morocco, 1955-57, civilian translator, then intelligence analyst and public information officer; *Christian Science Monitor*, Boston, Mass. special North Africa correspondent with assignments in other Mediterranean countries, 1958-64, staff correspondent based in Beirut, Lebanon, 1965—. Also freelance correspondent for *New York Herald Tribune* in central Europe, 1949-51, 1952-53, Morocco, 1953, for *Christian Science Monitor*, 1954-58, Radio Press International, 1957-60, *Observer* and Observer Foreign News Service, 1960-64, Canadian Broadcasting Corp., 1961-64, *Newsweek*, 1962-64, *New York Times*, 1964. *Military service:* U.S. Army, Signal Corps, cryptographer in Vienna, Austria, 1946-47. *Member:* Phi Beta Kappa. *Awards, honors:* Foreign correspondent fellowship, Council on Foreign Relations, 1964-65; citations from Overseas Press Club of America, 1967 and 1969, for best interpretive reporting of foreign affairs.

WRITINGS: Baal, Christ and Mohammed: Religion and Revolution in North Africa, Holt, 1965; *East Wind Over Africa: Red China's African Offensive*, Walker, 1965; *Green March, Black September: The Story of the Palestinian Arabs*, International Scholarly Book Services, 1973. Contributor to textbooks and encyclopedias; also contributor of articles on current affairs and literature and the arts to *Commonweal, Reporter, American Abroad* (Paris), *This Week, Wort und Wahrheit* (Vienna), *Books Abroad*, and *Musical Courier*.

WORK IN PROGRESS: A book on the Kurds and Kurdistan.

SIDELIGHTS: Cooley speaks French, German, Spanish, and Russian, and has reading competence in Arabic, Portuguese, and Italian. His report on Chinese Communism in Africa, *East Wind over Africa*, was termed by reviewers both objective and valuable. James Kritzeck wrote of *Baal, Christ, and Mohammed:* "For the first time in English, the history of civilization in North Africa is written here, by the distinguished correspondent of *The Christian Science Monitor*, with all the hard coin and delicate vision often missing in historians' work. ... Mr. Cooley's focus is sharply upon the cultural force of religion ... such a focus provides us with a uniquely illuminating method of ordering and understanding the masses of unwieldy facts which make up the long, checkered history of that region."

*   *   *

COOMBS, Douglas (Stafford)   1924-

PERSONAL: Born August 23, 1924, in London, England; son of Alexander John (in commerce) and Rosina (Stafford) Coombs; married Valerie Nyman, November 29, 1950; children: Rachel Amanda, Kenneth Alexander, Deborah Sally, Elizabeth Jessica. *Education:* University College, Southampton, England, student, 1942-43; University College, University of London, B.A. (honors), 1950, Ph.D., 1953. *Home:* 14 Brondesbury Ct., 235 Willesden Lane, London, N.W. 2, England. *Office:* British Council, 11 Portland Pl., London W. 2, England.

CAREER: University College of Ghana (now University of Ghana), Accra, lecturer in English and European history, 1952-60; British Council, assistant director in Ibadan, Nigeria, 1960-62, director of Overseas Students Centre, London, England, beginning 1963. *Military service:* Royal Air Force, 1943-47; became flight sergeant pilot.

WRITINGS: The Conduct of the Dutch: British Opinion and the Dutch Alliance During the War of the Spanish Succession, Nijhoff, 1958; *The Gold Coast, Britain and the Netherlands, 1850-72*, Oxford University Press, 1963. Contributor to professional journals.†

*   *   *

COOPER, Bruce M.   1925-

PERSONAL: Born September 6, 1925, in Shrewsbury, England; son of Frederick Joseph (a business executive) and Myrtle (Horey) Cooper; married Maud Helena Martennson, June 11, 1954; children: Kristina, Crispin, Joanna, Barbara, Susan. *Education:* Attended Ratcliffe College, Leicester, England; University of Edinburgh, M.A. (honors), 1952; Peterhouse, Cambridge, Certificate of Education, 1953. *Politics:* Liberal. *Religion:* Roman Catholic. *Home:* 15 Claude Ave., Middlesbrough, England.

CAREER: Workers' Educational Association, tutor and organizer in Suffolk, England, 1954-56; Hatfield College of Technology, Hatfield, England, lecturer in communication, 1956-61; Stockton Billingham Technical College, Billingham, England, head of department of liberal studies, 1961-65; Imperial Chemical Industries Ltd., agricultural division, management training executive, 1966—. Consultant to industry on report writing. Broadcaster on British Broadcasting Corp. programs, more recently as spokesman for Roman Catholic viewpoint on birth control and contraception issues. *Military service:* British Army, Royal Artillery, 1943-47; served in India, 1945-47.

WRITINGS: Writing Technical Reports, Penguin, 1964. Contributor to educational and industrial journals, and to *Spectator, Sunday Telegraph, Listener*, and *Times Educational Supplement*.

WORK IN PROGRESS: Writing the Project; compiling a series of essays by authorities in the field for *Modern Thought in Technical Education*.

AVOCATIONAL INTERESTS: Penal reform.†

*   *   *

COOPER, Michael (John)   1930-

PERSONAL: Born April 4, 1930, in London, England; son of A. B. (a publisher) and Dorothy (Morris) Cooper. *Education:* Attended Heythrop College, 1959-63, Oxford University, 1964—. *Home:* Campion Hall, Oxford University, Oxford England.

CAREER: Roman Catholic priest, member of Society of Jesus. Sophia University, Tokyo, Japan, faculty member.

WRITINGS: (Compiler and annotator) *They Came to Japan*, University of California Press, 1965; (editor) *Southern Barbarians: The First Europeans in Japan*, Kodansha, 1971; *This Island of Japon: Joao Rodrigues Account of 16th Century Japan*, Kodansha, 1973; *Rodriques the Interpreter: An Early Jesuit in Japan*, Weatherhill, 1974.†

*   *   *

COOPER, Wendy (Lowe)   1919-

PERSONAL: Born December 6, 1919, in Sutton Coldfield, Warwickshire, England; daughter of Walter Edward and Edith (Samworth) Lowe; married Alfred Hebert Jack (in electroplating business), November 14, 1942; children: Jacqueline Ann. *Education:* Sutton Grammar School. *Politics:* Liberal. *Religion:* Humanist. *Home:* 32 Vesey Rd., Sutton Coldfield, Warwickshire, England.

CAREER: Secretary for British Broadcasting Corp., and Aeronautical Inspection Directorate (during war); television and radio writer, interviewer, and panelist; free-lance journalist and author. *Member:* Society of Authors, Screenwriters Guild. *Awards, honors:* Hannen Swaffer Award for British Woman Journalist of the Year, 1966.

WRITINGS:—Children's books; all published by Brockhampton Press: *The Laughing Lady*, 1957; *Alibi Children*, 1958; *The Cat Strikes at Night*, 1959; *Disappearing Diamonds*, 1960.

Other: *Hair: Sex, Society, and Symbolism*, Stein & Day, 1971; *Is Your Menopause Really Necessary?*, Stein & Day, in press.

Also author of play, "The Burning Question," and of television and radio plays and serials for adults and children. Contributor of articles on social and medical subjects to *Telegraph Magazine, Observer Magazine, Guardian, Sunday Mirror, Good Housekeeping, Cosmopolitan, Nova, Homes and Gardens, Woman's Journal.*

SIDELIGHTS: Ms. Cooper told *CA:* "I am currently campaigning in print, on television, and radio for biological lib for the older woman in the form of hormone replacement therapy at menopause. Researching for this and the book involved visiting the United States in 1972 and 1974, with nationwide tours of medical centres." *Avocational interests:* Travel and people; "addicted to" sunbathing and surfing; "tennis, once played for Warwickshire and at Wimbledon, has given way to undistinguished golf."

*   *   *

COOPER, William W(ager)   1914-

PERSONAL: Born July 23, 1914, in Birmingham, Ala.; son of William W. and Rae (Rossman) Cooper; married Ruth Fay (an attorney), September 11, 1944. *Education:* University of Chicago, A.B., 1938; Columbia University, graduate study, 1940-42. *Home address:* Box 232, R.D. 2, Cheswick, Pa. 15024. *Office:* School of Urban and Public Affairs, Carnegie-Mellon University, Pittsburgh, Pa. 15213.

CAREER: Tennessee Valley Authority, Knoxville, assistant to the controller, 1938-40; U.S. Bureau of the Budget, Washington, D.C., senior economist, 1942-44; University of Chicago, Chicago, Ill., instructor in economics, 1944-46; U.S. Bureau of the Budget, principal economist, 1946, consultant, 1946-56; Carnegie-Mellon University (formerly Carnegie Institute of Technology), Pitsburgh, Pa., professor of economics and industrial administration, 1946-68, now dean, School of Urban and Public Affairs. Consultant to business firms and government agencies, including Economic Cooperation Administration, 1948-50.

MEMBER: American Accounting Association, American Economic Association, Institute of Management Sciences (president, 1953-54), American Statistical Association, Econometric Society (fellow), American Association for the Advancement of Science (fellow), Phi Beta Kappa, Pi Mu Epsilon, Beta Alpha Psi. *Awards, honors:* Ford Distinguished Research Professor, Carnegie Institute of Technology (now Carnegie-Mellon University), 1958-59; Ford Foundation faculty fellowship, 1962-63; D.Sc. from Ohio State University, 1970.

WRITINGS: (With Abraham Charnes and Alexander Henderson) *Introduction to Linear Programming*, Wiley, 1953; (with Charnes) *Management Models and Industrial Applications of Linear Programming*, two volumes, Wiley, 1961; (editor with H. J. Leavitt and M. Shelly, and contributor) *New Perspectives in Organization Research*, Wiley, 1964; (editor with others) *Studies in Budgeting*, North Holland, 1970; (with Charnes and R. J. Niehaus) *Studies in Manpower Planning*, U.S. Navy, 1973.

Contributor: P. M. Hauser and W. R. Leonard, editors, *Government Statistics for Business Use*, Wiley, 1946; Robert Herman, editor, *Theory of Traffic Flow*, Elsevier, 1961; R. W. Graves and Philip Wolfe, editors, *Recent Advances in Mathematical Programming*, McGraw, 1963; Charles P. Bonini and other editors, *Management Controls: New Directions in Basic Research*, McGraw, 1964. Also contributor to *A Dictionary for Accountants*, *Encyclopaedia Britannica*, other books, handbooks, conference proceedings, and journals, with published papers and articles exceeding one hundred ninety.

Member of editorial Board, *Management Science, Operations Research*, and *Naval Research Logistics Quarterly*; former assistant editor, *Accounting Review.*

WORK IN PROGRESS: General research in management sciences with public policy applications, operations research, and related topics.

*   *   *

COPLESTON, Federick Charles (John Paul) 1907-

PERSONAL: Born April 10, 1907, in Taunton, England; son of Frederick Selwyn (a judge) and Norah Margaret (Little) Copleston. *Education:* Oxford University, M.A., 1929; Pontifical Gregorian University, Rome, Italy, Ph.D. *Home and office:* 114 Mount St., London W1Y 6AH, England.

CAREER: Entered Roman Catholic order, Society of Jesus (Jesuit), 1930 (a Catholic convert, 1925), ordained priest, 1937. University of London, London, England, professor of history of philosophy, 1939-69, and principal, 1970-74, at Heythrop College (formerly located in Chipping Norton,

Oxfordshire, now part of University of London), professor of history of philosophy and dean of faculty of theology, 1972-74, professor emeritus, 1974—. Spent some parts of each year as professor of metaphysics in doctorate courses at Pontifical Gregorian University, 1952-68; lecturer, mainly for British Council, in nine European countries; visiting professor, University of Santa Clara, 1974-75. *Member:* Royal Institute of Philosophy, Aristotelian Society (London), British Academy (fellow).

WRITINGS: Friedrich Nietzsche: Philosopher of Culture, Burns, 1942, 2nd edition, Search Press, 1974; *Arthur Schopenhauer: Philosopher of Pessimism*, Burns, 1946; *A History of Philosophy:* Volume I: *Greece and Rome*, Newman, 1946; revised edition, Burns, 1951, Newman, 1959, Volume II: *Mediaeval Philosophy: Augustine to Scotus*, Newman, 1946, revised edition, 1962. Volume III: *Ockham to Suarez*, Newman, 1953, revised edition, 1962, Volume IV: *Descartes to Leibniz*, Newman, 1958, revised edition, 1962, Volume V: *Hobbes to Hume*, Newman, 1959, Volume VI: *Wolff to Kant*, Newman, 1960, Volume VII: *Fichte to Nietzsche*, Newman, 1963, Volume VIII: *Bentham to Russell*, Newman, 1966. Volume IX: *Maine de Biran to Sartre*, Search Press, 1974; *Medieval Philosophy*, Philosophical Library, 1952, revised and enlarged edition published as *A History of Medieval Philosophy*, Harper, 1972; *Aquinas*, Penguin, 1955; *Contemporary Philosophy: Studies of Logical Positivism and Existentialism*, Newman, 1956, 2nd edition, 1972; *Religion and Philosophy*, Macmillan, 1974.

Contributor: H. D. Lewis, editor, *Contemporary British Philosophy*, Macmillan, 1956; John Morris, editor, *From the Third Programme*, Nonesuch Library, 1956; Paul Edwards and Arthur Pap, editors, *A Modern Introduction to Philosophy*, Free Press of Glencoe, 1957; Maurice Cranston, editor, *Western Political Philosophers*, Bodley Head, 1964; Harmon Grisewood, editor, *Ideas and Beliefs of the Victorians*, Dutton, 1966; G. N. A. Vesey, editor, *Talk of God*, Macmillan, 1969; Warren E. Steinkraus, editor, *New Studies in Hegel's Philosophy*, Holt, 1971.

Three lectures published as booklets in London. Contributer to *Month, Dublin Review, Philosophy, Mind*, and other journals.

WORK IN PROGRESS: A History of Philosophy, Volume X, *Philosophy of the History of Philosophy.*

SIDELIGHTS: Copleston's books have been translated into Spanish, Japanese, French, and Italian. He speaks German and Italian, reads French and some Spanish. *Avocational interests:* Reading English and American thrillers and spy stories (but not detective stories).

*   *   *

COPPOCK, John (Oates) 1914-

PERSONAL: Born March 12, 1914, in Peru, Ind.; son of Donald Morton and Madge (Oates) Coppock; married Joan Inman, May 10, 1946; children: Michael, Paul, David. *Education:* Attended DePauw University, 1932-34, Hendrix College, 1935-37, Kalamazoo College, 1937-38, University of Arkansas, 1938; Columbia University, M.A., 1939; Cambridge University, postgraduate study, 1950-51. *Politics:* Democrat. *Religion:* Unaffiliated. *Home:* 1047 Ramona St., Palo Alto, Calif. *Office:* Food Research Institute, Stanford, Calif.

CAREER: Economist for United Nations Relief and Rehabilitation Administration in Athens, Greece, 1945-47, for

U.S. government (foreign aid programs) in Athens and in Washington, D.C., 1947-53; McGraw-Hill International Corp., correspondent in Paris, France, 1954-56; Robert Nathan Associates, government adviser in Rangoon, Burma, 1956-57; Twentieth Century Fund, researcher in economics in Geneva, Switzerland, and Washington, D.C., 1957-61; U.S. Department of State, Washington, D.C., economist, 1961-63; Food Research Institute, Stanford, Calif., researcher and writer, 1963—. *Military service:* U.S. Army, 1943-45; became master sergeant.

WRITINGS: (With Dewhurst and Yates) *Europe's Needs and Resources*, Twentieth Century, 1961; *North Atlantic Policy—The Agricultural Gap*, Twentieth Century, 1963; *Atlantic Agricultural Unity: Is it Possible?*, McGraw, 1966.†

*   *   *

CORBISHLEY, Thomas 1903-

PERSONAL: Surname is accented on first syllable; born May 30, 1903, in England; son of William and Catherine (Bamford) Corbishley. *Education:* Oxford University, B.A., 1930, M.A., 1933. *Religion:* Roman Catholic *Home and Office:* 114 Mount St., London W.1, England.

CAREER: Entered Society of Jesus, 1919, ordained priest, 1936. Campion Hall, Oxford University, Oxford, England, master, 1945-58; Farm Street Church, London, England, superior, 1958-66.

WRITINGS: Agnosticism, Catholic Truth Society, 1936; (translator from the German) *The Divine Majesty*, 1948, revised edition, 1971; *Roman Catholicism*, Hutchinson, 1950, reprinted, 1957; (contributor) *Catholic Commentary on Holy Scripture*, Nelson 1953; *Religion is Reasonable*, Burns & Oates, 1960; (translator from the Spanish) *The Spiritual Exercises of St. Ignatius*, Burns, 1963; *Ronald Knox the Priest*, Sheed, 1964; *Mary Ward in the Twentieth Century: The Life of Reverend Mother M. Cecilia Marshall*, St. George's Press, 1969; *The Spirituality of Teilhard de Chardin*, Collins, 1971; *One Body, One Spirit*, Faith Press, 1973. Contributor to *Klio, Month, Dublin Review, Journal of Roman Studies*, and other journals.

BIOGRAPHICAL/CRITICAL SOURCES: Christian Century, July 15, 1964.

*   *   *

CORDASCO, Francesco 1920-

PERSONAL: Born November 2, 1920, in West New York, N.J.; son of Giovanni and Carmela (Madorma) Cordasco; married Edna Vaughn, October 22, 1946; children: Michael, Carmela. *Education:* Columbia University, A.B., 1944; New York University, M.A., 1945, Ph.D., 1959; further study, University of Salamanca, 1946-48, and London School of Economics, 1952-53. *Home:* 6606 Jackson St., West New York, N.J. 07093. *Office:* Department of Education, Montclair State College, Upper Montclair, N.J. 07043.

CAREER: Long Island University, Brooklyn, N.Y., 1946-53, began as instructor, became associate professor of English; New Jersey Public Schools, teacher of English and social studies, 1953-63, assistant director of adult education, 1960-62, assistant principal, 1961-63; Montclair State College, Upper Montclair, N.J., associate professor of education, 1963-65; Jersey City State College, Jersey City, N.J., professor of education and assistant to the president, 1965-66; Montclair State College, professor of education,

1966—, assistant to the president, 1967-72. Adjunct professor, Fairleigh Dickinson University, 1953-58, Seton Hall University, 1958-63; visiting professor, City University of New York, various terms, 1959-73, New York University, summer, 1962, University of Puerto Rico, summer, 1969. Numerous consultancies, including Commonwealth of Puerto Rico, 1961-71, Consumers Union, 1969—, and U.S. Government committees; director or staff member of federally funded programs. Archdiocesan Board of Education, Newark, N.J., vice president, 1968-71, president 1971—. *Military service:* U.S. Army, 1941-43.

MEMBER: History of Education Society, National Education Association, National Society for the Study of Education, American Educational Research Association, Society for the Advancement of Education, American Association of University Professors, Bibliographical Society of America, Oxford Bibliographical Society, American Sociological Association (fellow), British Sociological Association (fellow). *Awards, honors:* Founder's Day award, New York University, 1959, for academic excellence; citation from Commonwealth of Puerto Rico, 1967; Brotherhood Award, National Conference of Christians and Jews (New Jersey Region), 1967.

WRITINGS: (With Elliott Gatner) *University Handbook for Research and Report Writing*, Edwards Bros., 1946, 15th edition published as *Research and Report Writing*, Barnes & Noble, 1974; (with Gatner) *Study Guides to English Literature*, two volumes, Lamb's Book Exchange, 1947; *A Junius Bibliography. With a Preliminary Essay on the Political Background, Text, and Identity: A Contribution to 18th Century Constitutional and Social History*, B. Franklin, 1949, revised edition, 1974.

(Author of introduction) *A Bibliography of Robert Watt, M.D.*, Kelleher, 1950, reprinted edition edited by Cordasco, Gale, 1968; *A Register of 18th Century Bibliographies and References*, B. Franklin, 1950, reprinted, Gale, 1968; (with Burt Franklin) *Adam Smith: A Bibliographical Checklist*, B. Franklin, 1950; (editor) *Letters of Tobias George Smollett*, Harvard University Press, 1950; (compiler with Kenneth W. Scott) *A Brief Shakespeare Bibliography for the Use of Students*, Phoenix Press, 1950; *The Bohn Libraries: A History and Checklist*, B. Franklin, 1951; (editor) *Works of Spinoza*, Dover, 1955.

Daniel Coit Gilman and the Protean Ph.D.: The Shaping of American Graduate Education, E. J. Brill, 1960, reprinted as *The Shaping of American Graduate Education: Daniel Coit Gilman and the Protean Ph.D.*, Rowman & Littlefield, 1973; *A Brief History of Education: A Handbook of Information on Greek, Roman, Medieval, Renaissance and Modern Educational Practice*, Littlefield, 1963, 2nd edition, 1970; (editor) *Educational Essays of Herbert Spencer*, Littlefield, 1963; (contributor) *American Portrait Gallery*, Dover, 1965; (compiler with Leonard Covello) *Educational Sociology: A Subject Index of Doctoral Dissertations Completed at American Universities, 1941-1963*, Scarecrow, 1965; (editor with F. N. Reister) *Readings in American Secondary Education: Reform and Challenge*, Selected Academic Readings, 1966; (editor with Covello) *The Social Background of the Italo-American School Child*, E. J. Brill, 1967, Rowman & Littlefield, 1972; (editor) *Jacob Riis Revisited: Poverty and the Slum in Another Era*, Doubleday, 1968; (editor with Eugene Bucchioni) *Puerto Rican Children in Mainland Schools: A Source Book for Teachers*, Scarecrow, 1968, revised edition published as *The Puerto Rican Community and Its Children on the Mainland: A Source Book for Teachers*, Social Workers, and Other Professionals, 1972; (author of introduction with others) Paul Monroe, *A Cyclopedia of Education*, five volumes, reprinted, Gale, 1968 (Cordasco was not associated with earlier editions); (author of introduction) Will Seymour Monroe, *Bibliography of Education*, reprinted, Gale, 1968 (Cordasco was not associated with earlier editions); (author of introduction) William Swan Sonnenscheim, *The Best Books*, six volumes, reprinted, Gale, 1969 (Cordasco was not associated with earlier editions); (editor with Maurie Hillson) *Education and the Urban Community: Schools and the Crisis of the Cities*, American Book Co., 1969; (with David Alloway) *The Agony of the Cities: Urban Problems in Contemporary America*, Montclair State College Press, 1969; (editor) Leonard Covello, *Teacher in the Urban Community*, Littlefield, 1969.

Eighteenth Century Bibliographies: Handlists of Critical Studies . . . (originally published separately as "Eighteenth Century Bibliographical Pamphlets" series, 1947-50), Scarecrow, 1970; (with Alloway) *Minorities in the American City: A Sociological Primer for Educators*, McKay, 1970; (compiler with Hillson and Henry Bullock) *The School in the Social Order: A Sociological Introduction to Educational Understanding*, International Textbook Co., 1970; (editor) Samuel Chester Parker, *A History of Elementary Education*, Littlefield & Adams, 1970; (editor) Robert Quick, *Educational Reformers*, Littlefield & Adams, 1970; (editor) Elmer Ellsworth Brown, *The Making of Our Middle Schools*, Rowman & Littlefield, 1970; *Teacher Education in the United States: A Guide for Foreign Students*, Institute for International Education, 1971; (with Eugene Bucchioni and Diego Castellanos) *Puerto Ricans on the United States Mainland: A Bibliography* . . . , Rowman & Littlefield, 1972; (with Salvatore LaGumina) *Italians in the United States: A Bibliography.* . . , Oriole Editions, 1972; (editor) Alice Crow, *Educational Psychology*, revised edition (Cordasco was not associated with earlier editions), Littlefield, 1972; (author of foreword) G. Stanley Hall and J. M. Mansfield, *Hints toward a Select and Descriptive Bibliography of Education*, reprinted, Gale, 1972 (Cordasco was not associated with earlier editions); (with Bucchioni) *The Puerto Rican Experience: A Sociological Sourcebook*, Rowman & Littlefield, 1973; *The Italian in America: A Bibliographical Guide*, B. Franklin, 1974; *The Italians: Social Backgrounds of an American Group*, Augustus M. Kelley, 1974; (editor) *Bibliography of Research Studies in Education, 1926-40*, four volumes, reprinted, Gale, in press (Cordasco was not associated with earlier editions).

Editor: *The Social History of Poverty: The Urban Experience*, fifteen volumes, Garrett Press, 1969-70; *The Children of Immigrants in Schools* (U.S. Commission on Immigration reports, 1911), five volumes, Scarecrow, 1970; *Annual Reports: 1867-1917*, 144 volumes, Rowman & Littlefield for U.S. Office of Education, 1970—.

Contributor of numerous articles and over 200 reviews to professional journals. Contributing editor, *Journal of Human Relations*, 1967-69.

*   *   *

CORRINGTON, John William 1932-

PERSONAL: Born October 28, 1932, in Memphis, Tenn; son of John Wesley (an insurance) and Viva (Shelley) Corrington; married Joyce Elaine Hooper (a chemistry professor), February 6, 1960; children: Shelley, John, Robert, Thomas. *Education:* Centenary College, B.A., 1956; Rice University, M.A., 1960; University of Sussex, D.Phil., 1964. *Politics:* Independent. *Religion:* Catholic. *Home address:* Route 1, Box 186, Covington, La. 70433. *Office:* Department of English, Loyola University, New Orleans, La. 70118.

CAREER: Spent about two years in Europe as foreign correspondent and lecturer in contemporary literature; Louisiana State University, Baton Rouge, instructor, 1960-65, assistant professor of English, 1965-66; Loyola University, New Orleans, La., associate professor of English, 1966—. Visiting professor of modern literature, University of California at Berkeley, 1968. *Awards, honors:* Charioteer Poetry Prize, 1967; National Endowment for the Arts Award, 1968, for short story "To Carthage Then I Came."

WRITINGS—Poetry: *Where We Are*, Charioteer Press, 1962; *The Anatomy of Love*, Roman Books, 1964; *Mr. Clean and Other Poems*, Amber House Press (San Francisco), 1964; *Lines to the South and Other Poems*, Louisiana State University Press, 1965. Poems represented in anthologies, including *Poets of Today*, edited by Walter Lowenfels, International Publishers, 1964; *19 Poetas de Hoy en los Estados Unidos*, edited by Miller Williams, Ministerio de Education Publica (Chile), 1966; *Black and White Culture in America*, University of Massachusetts Press, 1969; *"Mandala": Literature for Critical Analysis*, edited by W. L. Guerin and others, Harper, 1970; *Contemporary Poetry in America*, edited by Williams, Random House, 1973.

Fiction: *And Wait for the Night*, Putnam, 1964; *The Upper Hand*, Putnam, 1967; *The Lonesome Traveler and Other Stories*, Putnam, 1968; *The Bombardier*, Putnam, 1970.

Nonfiction: (Contributor) D. E. Stanford, editor, *Nine Essays in Modern Literature*, Louisiana State University Press, 1965; (editor with Miller Williams) *Southern Writing in the Sixties: Fiction*, Louisiana State University Press, 1966; (editor with Williams) *Southern Writing in the Sixties: Poetry*, Louisiana State University Press, 1967; (contributor) Clive Hart, editor, *James Joyce's "Dubliners": Critical Essays*, Viking, 1969; (contributor) *Etudes anglaises et nordamericaines*, University of Strausbourg, in press.

Screenplays—with wife, Joyce H. Corrington: "Von Richthofen and Brown," United Artists, 1970 (later released as "The Red Baron," 1971); "I Am Legend," Warner Brothers, 1971 (later released as "The Omega Man," 1971); "Box Car Bertha," American International Production, 1972.

Contributor of poetry, fiction, and criticism to *Kenyon Review, Massachusetts Review, Outsider, Georgia Review, James Joyce Quarterly, Southern Literary Journal, Dalhousie Review, Sewanee Review, Saturday Review*, and numerous other periodicals.

WORK IN PROGRESS: Three books of fiction, *The Disintegrator, Transactions/Under the Gun*, and *Under the Double Eagle*; a book of poetry, *The Prophet Remembered; R. S. Surtees: A Critical Study*, for Twayne; a screenplay, "Heart-Stopper," with his wife, Joyce H. Corrington.

SIDELIGHTS: Reviewing *The Lonesome Traveler and Other Stories*, Bruce Cook notes: "As with so many other Southern writers, a keen sense of history informs Mr. Corrington's work. . . . When Mr. Corrington is at his best . . . he has a sense of sureness with his characters and a plummeting drive in his narration that hardly a Southern writer since Faulkner can match." Echoing this assessment,

James P. Degman comments on the title story, "It is, in its way, as good or better than anything Faulkner ever wrote on the subject." *Avocational interests:* American history, sports, travel.

*   *   *

CORTY, Floyd L(ouis)   1916-

PERSONAL: Surname originally Corte; born March 26, 1916, in Central City, Pa.; son of Emanuel Louis (a miner) and Easter J. (Zandi) Corte; married Olivia Jo Miller, March 28, 1945; children: Jon Andrew, Marvin Floyd. *Education:* Pennsylvania State University, B.S., 1940, M.S., 1949; Cornell University, Ph.D., 1955. *Home:* 415 Bancroft Way, Baton Rouge, La. 70808. *Office:* Department of Agricultural Economics, Louisiana State University, Baton Rouge, La. 70803.

CAREER: Farm representative, then high school teacher in Pennsylvania, 1946-48; Pennsylvania State University, University Park, instructor in marketing, 1949-53; U.S. Department of Agriculture and Southeast Milk Marketing Committee, Starkville, Miss., cooperative agent, 1955-58; Louisiana State University, Baton Rouge, assistant professor, 1958-63, associate professor, 1963-65, professor of land economics, 1967—. Consultant to Secretary General, Ministry of Agriculture, Morocco, 1963; agricultural economist, USAID, Morocco, 1965-67; team leader and senior visiting professor, Agricultural College, Malaysia, 1970-71; consultant, Bureau of Planning, Tunisia, 1972. *Military service:* U.S. Army Air Forces, 1941-43; became technical sergeant. U.S. Army, 1943-45; became second lieutenant. U.S. Army Reserve, 1945-62; became major. *Member:* American Farm Economic Association, Southwest Social Science Association, Southeastern Land Economics Research Committee (chairman, 1963-64), American Legion (local adjutant, 1960-61; local commander, 1961-62).

WRITINGS: (Contributor and editor with A. L. Bertrand) *Land Tenure in the United States*, Louisiana State University Press, 1962; (with W. C. Havard, Jr.) *Rural-Urban Consolidation: The Merger of Governments in the Baton Rouge Area*, Louisiana State University Press, 1964; (with E. P. Roy and G. D. Sullivan) *Economics: Applications to Agriculture and Agribusiness*, Interstate, 1971; (with L. L. Pesson) *Institutional Development: The College of Agriculture in Malaysia*, Center for Agricultural Sciences and Rural Development, Louisiana State University, 1973. Also writer of Experiment Station bulletins.

SIDELIGHTS: Corty has working knowledge of French, Italian, Spanish, and Russian.

*   *   *

COSER, Rose Laub   1916-

PERSONAL: Born May 4, 1916, in Berlin, Germany; naturalized U.S. citizen; daughter of Elias and Rachel (Lachowsky) Laub; married Lewis A. Coser (a sociologist), August 12, 1942; children: Ellen, Steven. *Education:* Ecole Libre des Hautes Etudes, certified in philosophy, 1945; Columbia University, M.A., 1951, Ph.D., 1957. *Politics:* Socialist. *Home:* 52 Erland Rd., Stony Brook, N.Y. 11790. *Office:* Division of Social Science and Humanities, Health Sciences Center, State University of New York, Stony Brook, N.Y. 11790.

CAREER: Wellesley College, Wellesley, Mass., instructor, 1951-57, assistant professor of sociology, 1958-59; Harvard University, Medical School, Boston, Mass., assistant,

1959-64, associate in sociology, department of psychiatry, 1964-70; Northeastern University, Boston, Mass., associate professor of sociology, 1965-68; State University of New York at Stony Brook, professor of sociology, 1968—. Associate sociologist, McLean Hospital, 1958-69; visiting lecturer, Boston University, 1962-65; consultant, Children's Hospital, Boston, 1964-65. *Member:* American Sociological Association (chairperson of medical sociology section, 1973-74), Society for the Study of Social Problems (president, 1973-74), American Association for the Advancement of Science, Eastern Sociological Society. *Awards, honors:* National Institute of Mental Health grant, 1959-64.

WRITINGS: (Contributor) Richard H. Blum, *Hospitals and Patient Dissatisfaction*, California Medical Association, 1958; (contributor) Apple Dorian, editor, *Sociological Studies of Health and Sickness*, McGraw, 1960; *Life in the Ward*, Michigan State University Press, 1962; (contributor) Eliot Freidson, editor, *Studies in the Hospital*, Free Press of Glencoe, 1963; (editor and contributor) *The Family, Its Structure and Functions*, St. Martin's, 1964, revised edition, 1974; (editor) *Life Cycle and Achievement in America*, Harper, 1969. Contributor to *Hospital Digest Yearbook, Look, Hospital Administration*, and other journals in her field.

WORK IN PROGRESS: A research study on the training of psychiatrists.

*   *   *

COSS, Thurman L.   1926-

PERSONAL: Born April 26, 1926, in Beverly, Ohio; son of Ollie R. (a farmer) and Mary V. (Schob) Coss; married Barbara J. Parret, August 11, 1948; children: Carol, Anne, David, Robert. *Education:* University of Notre Dame, B.S., 1947; Oberlin College, M.A., 1949, B.D., 1951; Drew University, Ph.D., 1957. *Politics:* Democratic. *Home:* 1468 Van Buren, St. Paul, Minn. 55104. *Office:* Hamline University, St. Paul, Minn. 55101.

CAREER: Ordained Methodist minister, 1951; Hamline University, St. Paul, Minn., 1953—, became chairman of department of philosophy and religion. Lecturer to civic and church groups, and on educational television. United Theological Seminary, member of advisory council. *Military service:* U.S. Navy, 1944-46. *Member:* American Academy of Religion. *Awards, honors:* Fulbright grant to England.

WRITINGS: Secrets From the Caves: A Layman's Guide to the Dead Sea Scrolls, Abingdon, 1963. Contributor of reviews to religious journals.

AVOCATIONAL INTERESTS: Amateur radio (licensed "ham").†

*   *   *

COSTA, Albert Bernard   1929-

PERSONAL: Born August 14, 1929, in Hayward, Calif.; son of Albert Francis and Cynthia (Bernardo) Costa. *Education:* Saint Mary's College of California, B.S., 1952; Oregon State University, M.S., 1954; University of Wisconsin, Ph.D., 1960. *Politics:* Democrat. *Religion:* Roman Catholic. *Home:* 6109 Walnut, Pittsburgh, Pa. *Office:* Duquesne University, Pittsburgh, Pa.

CAREER: St. Mary's College of California, Moraga, assistant professor of chemistry, 1959-62; Duquesne University, Pittsburgh, Pa., assistant professor of history, 1963—.

Member: History of Science Society, American Association for the Advancement of Science, American Association of University Professors, Sigma Xi. *Awards, honors:* National Science Foundation grant, 1960, for history of science education project.

WRITINGS: Michel Eugene Chevreul: Pioneer of Organic Chemistry, State Historical Society of Wisconsin, 1962.

WORK IN PROGRESS: An essay, "The Cosmos and the Christian," for *The Christian Intellectual,* publication by Duquesne University Press.

SIDELIGHTS: Costa is competent in French and German. *Avocational interests:* Music (plays classical guitar), natural history and conservation.†

* * *

COTTER, Charles H(enry) 1919-

PERSONAL: Born January 21, 1919, in Hirwaun, Wales; son of William Henry and Eleanor (Evans) Cotter; married Lilian Palmer, December 27, 1941; children: Raymond, David, Stephen, Simon. *Education:* South West Essex Technical College, student, 1950-52; Birkbeck College, London, B.Sc. (special), 1957; University of Wales, M.Sc., 1968. *Home:* Middle Ground, Mill Rd., Lisvane, Cardiff, Wales. *Office:* Department of Maritime Studies, University of Wales Institute of Science and Technology, Cardiff, CF1 3NU, Wales.

CAREER: British Merchant Navy, executive officer, 1934-47; King Edward VII Nautical College, London, England, lecturer, 1948-53; Sir John Cass College, London, England, lecturer in navigation, 1953-62; Marine College, South Shields, England, senior lecturer in navigation, 1962-65; University of Wales Institute of Science and Technology, Cardiff, senior lecturer in department of maritime studies, 1965—. *Member:* Institute of Navigation, Royal Meteorological Society (fellow), Society for Nautical Research, South Shields Astronomical Society (chairman, 1962-65).

WRITINGS: The Elements of Navigation, Pitman, 1953; *The Principles and Practice of Radio Direction Finding,* Pitman, 1961; *The Master and His Ship,* Maritime Press, 1962; *The Apprentice and His Ship,* Maritime Press, 1963; *The Complete Coastal Navigator,* Hollis & Carter, 1964; *The Physical Geography of the Ocean,* Hollis & Carter, 1965; *The Astronomical and Mathematical Foundations of Geography,* Hollis & Carter, 1966; *A History of Nautical Astronomy,* Hollis & Carter 1968; *The Complete Nautical Astronomer,* Hollis & Carter, 1969; *The Atlantic Ocean,* Brown, Son, & Ferguson, 1974. Contributor to *Journal of the Institute of Navigation.*

WORK IN PROGRESS: A History of Nautical Astronomical Tables; A History of the Sailings.

AVOCATIONAL INTERESTS: Reading history.

* * *

COUGHLIN, Bernard J. 1922-

PERSONAL: Born December 7, 1922, in Galveston, Tex.; son of Eugene J. and Celeste M. (Ott) Coughlin. *Education:* St. Louis University, A.B., 1946, Ph.L., 1949, S.T.L., 1956; University of Southern California, M.S.W., 1959; Brandeis University, Ph.D., 1963. *Home:* 221 North Grand Blvd., St. Louis, Mo. 63103. *Office:* 3550 Lindell Blvd., St. Louis, Mo. 63103.

CAREER: Roman Catholic priest, member of Society of Jesus (Jesuits). St. Louis University, School of Social Ser-

vice, St. Louis, Mo., dean, 1962—. Social work consultant in Guatemala, San Salvador, Costa Rica, Honduras, and Panama, 1960, and at Universidad Catolica del Ecuador and Universidad San Marcos del Peru, 1963, Universidad Catolica de Chile, 1967, Universidad Caldas de Colombia, 1970, Universidad Javeriana and Universidad Bolivariana, both in Colombia, 1971. Member of board of directors, National Conference of Catholic Charities. *Member:* International Association of Schools of Social Work, International Conference of Social Work, National Association of Social Workers, National Conference on Social Welfare, Council on Social Work Education, Missouri Association for Social Welfare.

WRITINGS: Church and State in Social Welfare, Columbia University Press, 1965. Contributor of articles to magazines and professional journals.

SIDELIGHTS: Coughlin reads, writes, and speaks Spanish and Latin.

* * *

COUNTRYMAN, Vern 1917-

PERSONAL: Born May 13, 1917, in Roundup, Mont.; son of Alexander (a police officer) and Carrie (Harriman) Countryman; married Vera Pound, November 9, 1940; children: Kay, Debra. *Education:* University of Washington, Seattle, B.A., 1939, LL.B., 1942; Yale University, graduate law student, 1947-48. *Home:* 98 Adams St., Lexington, Mass.

CAREER: University of Washington Law School, Seattle, instructor, 1946-47; Yale University Law School, New Haven, Conn., assistant professor, then associate professor, 1947-55; Shea, Greenman and Gardner (law firm), Washington, D.C., attorney, 1955-59; University of New Mexico Law School, Albuquerque, dean, 1959-64; Harvard Law School, Cambridge, Mass., professor of law, 1964—. *Military service:* U.S. Army Air Forces, 1943-46. *Member:* American Bar Association, Washington State Bar Association, American Civil Liberties Union (national committee).

WRITINGS: (With James W. Moore) *Debtors' and Creditors' Rights: Cases and Materials,* Bender, 1951; *Un-American Activities in the State of Washington: The Work of the Canwell Committee,* Cornell University Press, 1951, reprinted, Johnson Reprint, 1967; *The States and Subversion,* Cornell University Press, 1952; (editor and author of biographical sketch) *Douglas of the Supreme Court: A Selection of His Opinions,* Doubleday, 1959; (editor) *Bankruptcy Act, 1963,* Little, Brown, 1964; *Cases and Materials on Debtor and Creditor,* Little, Brown, 1964; (editor) *Discrimination and the Law,* University of Chicago Press, 1965; (with Ted Finman) *The Lawyer in Modern Society,* Little, Brown, 1966; *Problems of Professional Responsibility Under the Uniform Commercial Code,* Joint Committee on Continuing Legal Education of the American Law Institute and the American Bar Association, 1969; (with Andrew L. Kaufman) *Commercial Law: Cases and Materials,* Little, Brown, 1971. Contributor to legal periodicals.

WORK IN PROGRESS: Acting as chief legal consultant, Brookings Institution's study on administration of the Bankruptcy Act.

* * *

COWEN, David L(aurence) 1909-

PERSONAL: Born September 1, 1909, in New York,

N.Y.; son of Meyer (a meat packer) and Mary (Goodstein) Cohen; married Mae Wisokolsky, January 24, 1934 (deceased); married Florence Weisberg, July 23, 1972; children: (first marriage) Bruce R. *Education:* Rutgers College, The State University of New Jersey (now Rutgers University), Litt.B., 1930, M.A., 1931. *Politics:* Independent. *Religion:* Hebrew. *Home:* 186 C Malden Lane, Rossmoor, N.J. 08831. *Office:* Rutgers University, New Brunswick, N.J. 08903.

CAREER: Rutgers University, New Brunswick, N.J., instructor in history, College of Pharmacy, 1933-44, assistant professor, University College, 1944-54, associate professor, 1954-60, professor of history, 1960—, chairman of department of history and political science, University College, 1945-65, chairman of department of history, 1965—, lecturer in College of Pharmacy, 1956—. Assistant chief reader and chief reader, Educational Testing Service, 1953-56; research associate, College of Physicians, Philadelphia, Pa., 1964-66; member, history of life sciences study section, National Institutes of Health, 1966-70; consultant, Medical Heritage Society, 1969—.

MEMBER: American Historical Association, American Institute of the History of Pharmacy (member of council, 1957-65; president, 1961-62; council chairman, 1971—), American Association for the History of Medicine (member of council 1967-70), International Academy of the History of Pharmacy (fellow), History of Science Society, American Association of University Professors (chapter vice-president, 1953-54, 1961-62), Internationale Gesellschaft fuer Geschichte der Pharmazie (member of council, 1969—), Deutsche Gesellschaft fuer Geschichte der Medizin, Gesellschaft fuer Wissenschaft Geschichte, British Society for the History of Pharmacy, New Jersey Academy of Science (vice-president, 1963-65), New Jersey Historical Society (fellow), New Jersey Pharmaceutical Association, Rho Chi, Alpha Zeta Omega.

AWARDS, HONORS: Lindback Award for distinguished teaching, 1961, and faculty research fellowships, 1962-63, 1964-65, 1972-73, all from Rutgers University; Kremers Award, American Institute of the History of Pharmacy, for distinguished writing; U.S. Public Health Service research grant, 1965-66; Ferchl Medal, Deutsche Gesellschaft fuer Geschichte der Pharmazie, 1972; Cestoni Medal, Academia Italiano di Storia della Farmacia, 1973; Rutgers Award, 1974.

WRITINGS: (With Roy A. Bowers) *The Rho Chi Society*, American Institute of the History of Pharmacy, 1955, 4th edition, Rho Chi Society, 1972; *America's Pre-Pharmacopoeial Literature*, American Institute of the History of Pharmacy, 1961; *Medicine and Health in New Jersey: A History*, Van Nostrand, 1964; *Medical Education: The Queen's-Rutgers Experience, 1792-1830*, The State University Bicentennial Commission, 1966; *The New Jersey Pharmaceutical Association, 1870-1970*, New Jersey Pharmaceutical Association, 1970. Contributor to *Nation, Medical History*, and professional journals. Book review editor, *Pharmacy in History*; member of editorial board, "Opera pharmaceutica raiorum" series.

WORK IN PROGRESS: The Impact of British Pharmacopoeial and Related Literature Abroad.

SIDELIGHTS: Cowen, who is competent in German, has done considerable research in Great Britain and Germany.

COWEN, Robert Churchill 1927-

PERSONAL: Born June 9, 1927, in Concord, N.H.; son of Levi Albert and Anna Louise (Shortsleve) Cowen; married Mary Shafer, 1955. *Education:* Massachusetts Institute of Technology, S.B., 1949, S.M., 1950. *Religion:* Christian Science Church. *Home:* 298 Holden Wood, Concord, Mass. *Office:* One Norway St., Boston, Mass. 02115.

CAREER: The Christian Science Monitor, Boston, Mass., natural science editor, 1950-72, feature editor, 1972—. American correspondent for *British Communications and Electronics* and *Electronics Weekly*. *Member:* American Meteorological Society, National Association of Science Writers, American Association for the Advancement of Science, Society of the Sigma Xi.

WRITINGS: Frontiers of the Sea, Doubleday, 1960.

*   *   *

COWIE, Evelyn E(lizabeth) 1924-

PERSONAL: Born September 17, 1924, in Peterborough, England; daughter of Robert (a civil servant) and Edith (Scott) Trafford; married Leonard Wallace Cowie (a clerk in holy orders), August 9, 1949; children: Alan Leonard. *Education:* University College, London, M.A., 1948. *Politics:* Conservative. *Religion:* Church of England. *Home:* 38 Stratton Rd., Merton Park, London S.W. 19, England.

CAREER: Goldsmiths' College, London, England, senior lecturer in history, 1957-65; King's College, University of London, lecturer in education, 1965—.

WRITINGS—Juvenile: *Breakfasts*, Jenkins, 1958; *Left-Overs*, Jenkins, 1959; *Man and Roads*, Hamish Hamilton, 1963; *Man and Shops*, Hamish Hamilton, 1964; *Homes*, Cassell, 1967; *The Land*, Cassell, 1967; *Towns*, Cassell, 1967; *Villages*, Cassell, 1967 *Industry*, Cassell, 1968; *Leisure*, Cassell, 1968; *Man and the Crusades*, Hamish Hamilton, 1969; *Transport*, Cassell, 1969.

Communication, Cassell, 1969; *Discovery*, Cassell, 1970; (with husband, Leonard W. Cowie) *Great Ideas in Education*, Pergamon General Books, 1971; *Education*, Methuen, 1973.

*   *   *

COWIE, Leonard W(allace) 1919-

PERSONAL: Born May 10, 1919, in Brighton, Sussex, England; son of Reginald George (a clerk in holy orders) and Ella Constance (Peerless) Cowie; married Evelyn Elizabeth Trafford (a writer and lecturer at a training college), August 9, 1949; children: Alan Leonard. *Education:* Pembroke College, Oxford, M.A., 1941; University of London, Ph.D., 1954. *Politics:* Conservative. *Home:* 38 Stratton Rd., Merton Park, London S.W. 19, England.

CAREER: Clergyman, Church of England. Assistant curate, High Wycombe, Buckinghamshire, England, and history master at Royal Grammar School, High Wycombe, 1943-45; College of St. Mark and St. John, Chelsea, London, England, principal lecturer in history, 1945-68; Whitelands College, Putney, London, England, senior lecturer in history, 1969—.

WRITINGS: Henry Newman: An American in London, 1708-43, S.P.C.K., 1956; *The True Book about the Bible*, Muller, 1959; *Seventeenth-Century Europe*, G. Bell, 1960, Ungar, 1964; *The New Outlook History*, Hamish Hamilton, Volume I: *English Social History to 1603*, 1961, Volume II: *English Social History, 1603 to Modern Times*,

1962, Volume III: *From Empire to Common wealth*, 1963, Volume IV: *Britain, 1837 to Modern Times*, 1963, Volume V: *British Social and Economic History from 1900*, 1965; *The March of the Cross*, McGraw, 1962; *Eighteenth-Century Europe*, G. Bell, 1963, Ungar, 1964; *English History, 55 B.C.-A.D. 1485*, Hamish Hamilton, 1964; *From the Peace of Paris to World War I: British History, 1763-1914*, Thomas Nelson, 1966; *Hanoverian England, 1714-1837*, Humanities, 1967; (editor) *Documents and Descriptions in European History, 1714-1815*, Oxford University Press, 1967; *Luther: Father of the Reformation*, Weidenfeld & Nicolson, 1968, published as *Martin Luther: Leader of the Reformation*, Praeger, 1969; *The Reformation*, John Day, 1968; *Europe, 1789-1939*, Thomas Nelson, 1969.

Industrial Evolution: 1750 to the Present Day, Thomas Nelson, 1970; *The Pilgrim Fathers*, Wayland, 1970, Putnam, 1972; *Plague and Fire: London, 1665-6*, Putnam, 1970; *The Reformation of the Sixteenth Century*, Putnam, 1970; *The Hamlyn History of the World in Colour*, Volume V, *The Age of Feudalism*, P. Hamlyn, 1971; *The Super-Powers*, Thomas Nelson, 1971; (with wife, Evelyn E. Cowie) *Great Ideas in Education*, Pergamon General Books, 1971; *The Black Death and the Peasants' Revolt*, Wayland, 1972; *The Trial and Execution of Charles I*, Putnam, 1972; *The Christian Calendar*, Weidenfeld & Nicolson, 1974.

*   *   *

COX, James M(elville)   1925-

PERSONAL: Born August 4, 1925, in Independence, Va.; son of Kyle Thomas and Elizabeth (Jordan) Cox; married wife, Marguerite, September 4, 1948; children: Karen, Marian, Julia, Ellen, David. *Education:* University of Michigan, B.A., 1948, M.A., 1949; Indiana University, Ph.D., 1955. *Office:* Dartmouth College, Hanover, N.H.

CAREER: Emory and Henry College, Emory, Va., assistant professor of English, 1950-52; Dartmouth College, Hanover, N.H., instructor, 1955-57; Indiana University, Bloomington, teacher, 1957-58, assistant professor, 1958-61, associate professor, 1961-63; Dartmouth College, associate professor, 1963-65, professor of English, 1965—, Avalon professor of humanities, 1970—. *Military service:* U.S. Navy, Submarine Service, 1943-46. *Member:* Modern Language Association of America, American Association of University Professors, Dante Society of America. *Awards, honors:* American Council of Learned Societies fellowship, 1960-61; fellow, School of Letters, Indiana University, 1960—; Danforth Harbison Award for Distinguished Teaching, 1969; Guggenheim fellowship, 1972-73.

WRITINGS: (With Alan M. Hollingsworth) *The Third Day at Gettysburg: Pickett's Charge*, Holt, 1959; (editor) *Twentieth Century Views: Robert Frost*, Prentice-Hall, 1962; *Mark Twain: The Fate of Humor*, Princeton University Press, 1966. Essays in *Sewanne Review, Kenyon Review, South Atlantic Quarterly, Virginia Quarterly Review*, and other literary periodicals.

WORK IN PROGRESS: Critical studies of Nathaniel Hawthorne's major writings, and of American autobiography.

*   *   *

COX, Martha Heasley   1919-

PERSONAL: Born February 26, 1919, in Calico Rock, Ark.; daughter of Jesse Richard (owner of an appliance and furniture store) and Lillian (Seay) Heasley; married Cecil Lester Cox (a teacher), December 21, 1946. *Education:* Arkansas College, Batesville, A.B., 1938; University of Arkansas, M.A., 1943, Ph.D., 1955; graduate study at University of Wisconsin, 1943, and University of Texas, 1953. *Home:* 787 East William St., San Jose, Calif. *Office:* English Department, San Jose State University, San Jose, Calif.

CAREER: Arkansas Polytechnic College, Russellville, assistant professor of English, 1943-48; Harding College, Searcy, Ark., assistant professor of English, 1948-53; University of Arkansas, Fayetteville, instructor in speech, 1953-54; San Jose State University, San Jose, associate professor of English, 1955—. *Member:* Modern Language Association of America, National Council of Teachers of English, Conference on College Composition and Communication, American Association of University Professors, American Association of University Women.

WRITINGS: Maxwell Anderson Bibliography, University of Virginia Bibliographical Society, 1958; (editor) *A Reading Approach to College Writing*, Chandler Publishing, 1959 (first four editions with Dorothy Foote), 8th edition, 1968; *Aids for Teaching a Reading Approach to College Writing*, Chandler Publishing, 1959 (first edition with Dorothy Foote), 7th edition, 1966; (editor) *Writing: Form, Process, Purpose*, Chandler Publishing, 1962; *Better Writing: With Student Papers for Analysis*, Chandler Publishing, 1964; *Image and Value: An Invitation to Literature*, Harcourt, 1966; (compiler) *Classic American Short Novels*, Chandler Publishing, 1969. Contributor to *Encyclopaedia of World Literature, Players'*, and professional periodicals.

WORK IN PROGRESS: A book, *Nelson Algren*, for Twayne.†

*   *   *

COX, Richard Howard   1925-

PERSONAL: Born March 3, 1925, in Hammond, Ind.; son of Roy Howard and Elsie (Schoenbaum) Cox; married Margaret Merle Deems, 1953. *Education:* Northwestern University, B.S., 1949, M.A., 1952; University of Lyon, graduate study, 1949-50; University of Chicago, Ph.D., 1955. *Home:* 261 Colgate Ave., Berkeley, Calif. *Office:* Department of Political Science, University of California, Berkeley, Calif.

CAREER: Harvard University, Cambridge, Mass., instructor in government, 1955-57; University of California, Berkeley, assistant professor of political science, 1957—. *Military service:* U.S. Army, 1943-46. *Member:* American Political Science Association, Phi Beta Kappa.

WRITINGS: Locke on War and Peace, Clarendon Press, 1960; (editor) *The State in International Relations*, Chandler Publishing, 1965; (editor) *Ideology, Politics, and Political Theory*, Wadsworth, 1969. Contributor to *William and Mary Quarterly, University of Chicago Law Review*, and political science journals.†

*   *   *

COXE, Louis (Osborne)   1918-

PERSONAL: Born 1918, in Manchester, N.H.; son of Charles Shearman and Helen (Osborne) Coxe; married Edith Winsor, 1946; children: Robert, Louis, Jr., Charles, Helen. *Education:* Princeton University, B.A., 1940. *Home address:* R.D. #2, Brunswick, Me. *Office:* Bowdoin College, Brunswick, Me.

CAREER: Bowdoin College, Pierce Professor of English; poet. *Military service:* United States Naval Reserve, 1942-46; became lieutenant. *Awards, honors: Sewanee Review* Fellow; Fulbright lecturer; Brandeis Award; Maine Humanities Award.

WRITINGS: The Sea Faring and Other Poems, Holt, 1947; (with Robert Chapman) *Billy Budd* (three-act play; based on novel by Herman Melville), Princeton University Press, 1951, reprinted, Hill & Wang, 1962; *The Second Man and Other Poems*, University of Minnesota Press, 1955; *The Wilderness and Other Poems*, University of Minnesota Press, 1958; *The Middle Passage*, University of Chicago Press, 1960; *Edwin Arlington Robinson*, University of Minnesota Press, 1962; (editor and author of introduction) *Chaucer*, Dell, 1963; *The Last Hero and Other Poems*, Vanderbilt University Press, 1965; *Nikal Seyn and Decoration Day: A Poem and A Play*, Vanderbilt University Press, 1966; *Edwin Arlington Robinson: The Life of Poetry*, Pegasus, 1969. Contributor to *Poetry, Sewanee Review, New Yorker, Nation, Hudson Review*, and other periodicals.

*   *   *

COX-GEORGE, Noah Arthur William   1915-

PERSONAL: Born June 15, 1915, in Degema, Nigeria; son of Noah Obedial Collingwood (a civil servant) and Rosabel Abigail Regina (Cox) George; married Rachel Ademike Biola Wright, August 5, 1933; children: Luba Bonita (daughter), Siegfried Amadeus Maynard, Beryl Effuah Zorah (daughter), Christabel Isadora Richenda. *Education:* London School of Economics and Political Science, B.Sc. (second class honors), 1946, M.Sc., 1951, Ph.D., 1954; Oxford University, graduate study, 1952-53. *Home and office:* Fourah Bay College-The University College of Sierra Leone, Freetown, Sierra Leone.

CAREER: Fourah Bay College-The University College of Sierra Leone, Freetown, lecturer-in-charge, department of economics, 1946-51, senior lecturer and dean of faculty of economic studies, 1955-61; University of Nigeria, Nsukka, professor and head of department of economics, 1961-64; Fourah Bay College-The University College of Sierra Leone, professor of political economy, 1965—, dean of faculty and head of department of economic and social studies, 1969—. Delhi University, Delhi, India, external examiner in economics in African Studies Programme. Government of Sierra Leone, chairman of Commission of Enquiry into Price Structure of Motor Vehicles, 1960-61, chairman of Price Control Advisory Board, 1957-61, and member of various government committees. Director, Trade, Monetary and Fiscal Division, Department of Economic Affairs of the United Nations, 1965-67; chief of Trade Policies Problem Section, United Nations Conference on Trade and Development, 1967-69; chairman, Sierra Leone Road Transport Corporation, 1969-73; chairman, National Committee on Africanization of Commerce and Industry (Sierra Leone), 1969-74; Phelps-Stokes visiting professor, African lecture program, 1973. *Member:* Royal Economic Society (England), Royal Commonwealth Society, Nigerian Economic Society (vice-president, 1962—), London School of Economics Society (life member), London House Club.

WRITINGS: Finance and Development in West Africa, Dobson, 1961, Humanities, 1962. Also author of *Studies in Finance and Development—The Gold Coast Experience 1914-1960*, Dobson. Writer of government publications and political pamphlets. Contributor to *West African Review, New Commonwealth*, other journals and newspapers.

WORK IN PROGRESS: An autobiography.

AVOCATIONAL INTERESTS: Political theory, shooting, and travel.

*   *   *

COYNE, Joseph E.   1918-
(William O. Berch)

PERSONAL: Born May 9, 1918, in Portland, Me.; son of Michael A. and Mary (Corcoran) Coyne; married Mary Ellen Thornton, June 25, 1949; children: Susan Marie, Joseph Patrick. *Education:* Attended Cheverus, the Jesuit Institute; later took special courses in writing. *Home:* 66 Cumberland Ave., Portland, Me. *Office: Portland Press Herald*, Portland, Me.

CAREER: Guy Gannett Publishing Co., Portland, Me., reporter, 1957; *Portland Press Herald-Evening Express*, Portland, Me., religious news editor, 1961—.

WRITINGS: The Threshing Floor (novel), Putnam, 1957; *House of Exile* (novel), Bruce, 1964. Contributor of short stories (some under pseudonym William O. Berch), and articles to periodicals.

WORK IN PROGRESS: The Tragedies and Last Days of the U.S. Presidents; a novel.

AVOCATIONAL INTERESTS: Travel, historical research, reading—chiefly mystery and biography.†

*   *   *

CRABB, Cecil V., Jr.   1924-

PERSONAL: Born July 18, 1924, in Clarksdale, Miss.; son of Cecil V. (a minister) and Mary (Dupree) Crabb; married Harriet Frierson, June 28, 1947; children: Cecil V. III, Cornelia Maguire. *Education:* Centre College of Kentucky, B.A., 1947; Vanderbilt University, M.A., 1948, graduate study, 1950-51; Johns Hopkins University, Ph.D., 1952. *Home:* 5295 Timber Cove, Baton Rouge, La. 70808. *Office:* 240 Stubbs Hall, Louisiana State University, Baton Rouge, La. 70803.

CAREER: Vassar College, Poughkeepsie, N.Y., 1952-68, began as instructor, became professor of political science; Louisiana State University, Baton Rouge, professor of political science, and chairman of department, 1968—. Lecturer, Salzburg Seminar in American Studies, 1960. *Military service:* U.S. Army, 1942-45; served in European theater. *Member:* American Political Science Association, New York State Political Science Association. *Awards, honors:* U.S. Department of State national intern, 1952.

WRITINGS: Bipartisan Foreign Policy: Myth or Reality, Harper, 1957; *American Foreign Policy in the Nuclear Age*, Harper, 1960, 3rd edition, 1972; (contributor) Peter Odegard, *The American Republic*, Harper, 1964; *The Elephants and the Grass: A Study of Non-Alignment*, Praeger, 1965. Contributor of articles and reviews to journals.

WORK IN PROGRESS: Policy-Makers and Critics: Conflicting Approaches to American Foreign Policy; Major Doctrines of American Foreign Policy.

*   *   *

CRAIG, Edward Anthony   1905-
(Edward Carrick)

PERSONAL: Born January 3, 1905, in London, England; son of Edward Gordon (a writer and stage producer) and Elena (Meo) Craig; married second wife, Mary Timewell,

September 10, 1960; children: (first marriage) John Edward, Helen Paula. *Education:* Studied art, the theater, and photography in Italy, 1917-26. *Home:* Cutlers Orchard, Bledlow, Aylesbury, Buckinghamshire HP17 9PA, England.

CAREER: Art director and designer for the films and theater, engraver and illustrator, and writer. In early career was a photographer and sub-editor of *The Mask*; art director in England for Welsh Pearson Film Co., 1928-29, Associated Talking Pictures, 1932-35, Criterion Films, 1937-39, and for Crown Film Unit, British Ministry of Information, 1939-46; executive art director for Independent Producers, London, England, 1947-49; designer for other film companies and for London stage productions. Founder (1928) and president of Grubb Group of modern English artists; executor of wood engravings and stage and film designs exhibited in London, Canadian, and American galleries; work purchased for the permanent collections of British Museum, Victoria and Albert Museum, Kupferstich Museum (Berlin), Metropolitan Museum of New York, and Yale University. Also discoverer and translator of numerous Italian documents on the history of the theater, founder and principal of first English film school, London, 1938. Lecturer on Renaissance and baroque theater architecture and stage decor and the films as an art. *Member:* Royal Society of Arts (fellow), Architectural Association, Society of Authors, Association of Cine Technicians, Society for Theatre Research.

WRITINGS: Gordon Craig, The Story of his Life, Gollancz, 1968; *Farbizio Carini Motta, Trattato sopra la Struttura de Teatri*, Il Polifilo, Milano, 1972.

Under pseudonym, Edward Carrick: (Contributor) E. Gordon Craig, *Nothing or the Bookplate*, Chatto & Windus, 1925; *Designing for Moving Pictures*, Studio Books, 1941, 2nd edition published as *Designing for Films*, 1950; (compiler with Gerry Bradley) *Meet ... the Common People*, Studio Books, 1942; *Art and Design in the British Film*, Dobson, 1948; (contributor) *Oxford Companion to the Theatre*, Oxford University Press, 1951.

Illustrator: Andre Maurois, *Voyage to the Island of the the Articoles*, Appleton, 1928; *The Poems and Verse of John Keats*, compiled by John Middleton Murry, King's Printers, 1929; *The Review of Revues*, edited by Charles B. Cochran, J. Cape, 1930; *The Georgics of Virgil*, translated by R. D. Blackmore, Dolphin, 1931; Edith Sitwell, *In Spring*, privately printed for Fytton Armstrong, 1931; Edmund Blunden, *In Summer*, privately printed for Fytton Armstrong, 1931; Herbert Palmer, *In Autumn*, privately printed for Fytton Armstrong, 1931; W. H. Davies, *In Winter*, privately printed for Fytton Armstrong, 1931; John Gawsworth (pseudonym for Fytton Armstrong), *Above the River*, Ulysses Bookshop, 1931; John Gawsworth, *Fifteen Poems, Three Friends*, Twyn Barlyn Press, 1931; E. Selsey (pseudonym for Edward James), *So Far So Glad*, Duckworth, 1934; William Shakespeare, *The Life of Henry V*, French, 1939. Film critic for *International Film Review*. Contributor of historical articles to *Mask, Architectural Record, Architectural Review, Penrose Annual, La Tribuna, Theatre Notebook*, and other publications.

WORK IN PROGRESS: Gaetano, a book about his grandfather, a Victorian painter; *The Magnificent Theatre*, concerning the baroque court spectacle in Italy; *Eye Witness Account of the Theatre*, an anthology of first-hand reports on theatrical performances through the ages; *Candle-Ends*, autobiographical sketches.

SIDELIGHTS: In reference to *Gordon Craig, The Story of his Life*, Stanley Young writes, "Edward Craig has, no doubt, turned over a library of memorabilia to give us fuller insight into the character of the man who displayed such sublime or exaggerated responses to life and theatre for nearly a century ... this present work ... stands forth unmistakably as the most honest and objective full-length portrait to date of Gordon Craig, whose lifelong cry seems above all else to have been 'Remember Me'."

BIOGRAPHICAL/CRITICAL SOURCES: Marguerite Steen, *A Pride of Terrys*, Longmans, Green, 1962; Edward Anthony Craig, *Gordon Craig, The Story of his Life*, Gollancz, 1968.

* * *

CRAMER, Clarence Henley 1905-

PERSONAL: Born June 23, 1905, in Eureka, Kan.; son of David H. (a minister) and Irma (Henley) Cramer; married Elizabeth Garman, December 30, 1949. *Education:* Ohio State University, A.B. and B.Sc. in Education, 1927; M.A., 1928, Ph.D., 1931. *Politics:* Democrat. *Religion:* Presbyterian. *Home:* 11424 Cedar Glen Pkwy., Cleveland, Ohio 44106.

CAREER: Southern Illinois University, Carbondale, associate professor of history, 1931-42; with National War Labor Board, 1943-44, United Nations Relief and Rehabilitation Administration, in Germany, 1944-47, International Refugee Organization, 1947-48; Case Western Reserve University, Cleveland, Ohio, professor of history, 1949—, associate, later acting dean of School of Business Administration, 1949-54, dean of Adelbert College, 1954-59. *Member:* American Historical Association, Organization of American Historians, Ohio Academy of History, Phi Beta Kappa, University Club and Skating Club (both Cleveland). *Awards, honors:* Fine Arts Awards in Literature, Woman's City Club of Cleveland, 1973.

WRITINGS: Royal Bob–The Life of Robert G. Ingersoll, Bobbs-Merrill, 1952; *Newton D. Baker, A Biography*, World Publishing, 1961; *Open Shelves and Open Minds: A History of the Cleveland Public Library*, Press of Case Western Reserve University, 1972; *American Enterprise: Free and Not So Free*, Little, Brown, 1972.

WORK IN PROGRESS: The sesquicentennial history of Case Western Reserve University.

* * *

CRANE, James G(ordon) 1927-
(Jim Crane)

PERSONAL: Born May 21, 1927, in Hartshorne, Okla.; son of Gordon T. and Naomi (Harrison) Crane; married Jeanette Forgie, June 23, 1951; children: Lise Margaret, Catherine Jean, James Carey. *Education:* Jackson Junior College, A.A., 1949; Albion College, A.B., 1951; University of Iowa, M.A., 1953; Michigan State University, M.F.A., 1961. *Religion:* Methodist. *Office:* Eckerd College, St. Petersburg, Fla.

CAREER: Wisconsin State College (now University), River Falls, art faculty, 1955-57, chairman of art department, 1958-62; St. Cloud State College, St. Cloud, Minn., art faculty, 1957-58; Eckerd College, St. Petersburg, 1962—, began as associate professor, now professor of art. Chairman, Collegium of Creative Arts, 1973-74, 1974-75. Painter and cartoonist. *Military service:* U.S. Army Air Forces, 1945-46. *Member:* American Association of University Professors. *Awards, honors:* Ford Foundation purchase award for painting; other exhibition awards, Albion College distinguished Alumni Award.

WRITINGS: (Under name Jim Crane) *What Other Time?* (cartoons), Source, 1953; (contributor) *Christianity and the Contemporary Arts*, Association Press, 1962; (under name Jim Crane) *On Edge* (cartoons), John Knox, 1965; *The Great Teaching Machine*, John Knox, 1966; *Inside Out*, Harper, 1967; *Parables*, John Knox, 1971.

Illustrator: *Bachelor of Divinity*, Associated Press, 1963; *The Worry and the Wonder of Being Human*, CLC Press, 1966; J. M. Bailey, *From Wrecks To Reconciliation*, Friendship Press, 1969; G. Freeman, *A Funny Thing Happened on the Way to Heaven*, Harper, 1969; *Rich Man Poor Man*, John Knox, 1972; T. R. Weber, *Foreign Policy is Your Business*, John Knox, 1972; G. A. Chauncey, *Decisions! Decisions!*, John Knox, 1972.

Contributor of cartoons to *Motive* and *Ave Marie*.

SIDELIGHTS: Crane told *CA:* "My cartoons are protest. I protest anything that dehumanizes people. When protest becomes an end in itself, I protest protest."

BIOGRAPHICAL/CRITICAL SOURCES: Motive, April, 1964.

*   *   *

CREDLE, Ellis   1902-

PERSONAL: Surname pronounced "Cradle"; born August 18, 1902, in North Carolina; daughter of Zach (a planter) and Bessie (Cooper) Credle, married Charles de Kay Townsend (a photographer, now retired); children: Richard Fraser Townsend. *Education:* Louisburg Junior College, graduate, 1922; attended Art Students League, New York, N.Y., New York School of Interior Decoration, 1925, and Beaux Arts Architectural Institute. *Home:* Apdo. 26 Zapopan, Jalisco, Mexico.

CAREER: Taught school in Blue Ridge Mountains for two years; held a variety of jobs, including that of salesgirl, librarian, guitarist, soap distributor, usher in Carnegie Hall, and governess; artist with American Museum and Brooklyn Children's Museum. Author and illustrator, mainly of books for children.

WRITINGS—Author and illustrator: *Down, Down the Mountain*, Nelson, 1934; *Pig-O-Wee*, Grosset, 1935; *Across the Cotton Patch*, Nelson, 1935; *Little Jeemes Henry*, Nelson, 1936; *Pepe and the Parrot*, Nelson, 1937; *The Goat That Went to School*, Grosset, 1940; *Here Comes the Show Boat*, Nelson, 1940; *Janie's Shoes*, Grosset, 1941; *Adventures of Tittletom*, Oxford University Press, 1949; *Big Doin's on Razor Back Ridge*, Nelson, 1956; *Little Fraid, Big Fraid*, Nelson 1964; *Monkey See, Monkey Do*, Nelson, 1968. Also, *Don't Wash My Ears*, Cadmus.

Author: *The Flop-Eared Hound*, Oxford University Press, 1938; *Johnny and His Mule*, Walck, 1946; *My Pet Peepelo*, Oxford University Press, 1948; *Tall Tales from the High Hills*, Nelson, 1957; *Little Pest Pico*, Nelson, 1969; *Mexico, Land of Hidden Treasure*, Nelson, 1971.

WORK IN PROGRESS: Two adult novels about plantation life in South Carolina, the first titled *Mist on the Marshes*.

SIDELIGHTS: The background of most of Ms. Credle's stories reflects her childhood on the North Carolina coast and her life in the Blue Ridge Mountains.

CREGER, Ralph (Clinton)   1914-

PERSONAL: Born October 30, 1914, in Monroe, Iowa; son of Walter Pearl and Nellie (Graves) Creger; married Barbara Jones, 1941; children: Carl Clinton, Jerry W. *Education:* Attended Central College, Pella, Iowa, 1933, and Ottawa University, Ottawa, Kan., 1934-35. *Religion:* Southern Baptist. *Home:* 14 Rosemont Dr., Little Rock, Ark. *Office:* Roch Island Railroad Passenger Station, Little Rock, Ark.

CAREER: Rock Island Railroad, 1936—, began as section laborer; later worked as telegrapher and dispatcher in Iowa, Missouri, Kansas, Nebraska, and Arkansas; chief dispatcher, Little Rock, Ark., 1955—. *Awards, honors:* Award from American Friendship Club for writings in field of human relations.

WRITINGS: (With son, Carl Creger) *This Is What We Found*, Lyle Stuart, 1961; (with Erwin McDonald) *Look Down the Lonesome Road*, Doubleday, 1964.

WORK IN PROGRESS: A book on the plight of American railroads.†

*   *   *

CREMER, Jan   1940-

PERSONAL: Born April 20, 1940, in Enschede, The Netherlands; son of Jan (reporter and war correspondent) and Rosza (Szomorkay-Wendl) Cremer; never married; children: Claudia Carmen, Cassidy Clinton, Clifford Caleb. *Educaton:* Studied at art academies in The Hague and Paris, 1958-60. *Politics:* "Non-interested." *Religion:* "Non-religious." *Home:* Chelsea Hotel, 222 West 23rd St., New York, N.Y. 10011. *Agent:* Sterling Lord Agency, 660 Madison Ave., New York, N.Y. 10021.

CAREER: Traveled for seven years, living in Algeria, Spain, Paris, and London, going as a sailor to Russia, Africa, and Arabia; has worked as reporter, publicity man, actor, stuntman, and film director; worked as pop singer in London and Holland; had his own radio program; author and painter; has been in America since spring, 1965, learning English, painting, writing, and negotiating to act in films. Director, Jan Cremer, Inc. (publicity and stunt company); co-owner of recording company and of beat teen-age magazine in London and Amsterdam.

WRITINGS: Ik Jan Cremer (autobiographical novel), De Bezige Bij (Amsterdam), 1964, translation by R E. Wyngaard and Alexander Trocchi published as *I Jan Cremer*, New American Library, 1965; *Ik Jan Cremer: Tweed Boek*, De Bezige Bij, 1965; *Made in U.S.A.*, A. W. Bruna & Zoons Uitgeversmij, 1969; *Toneel*, A. W. Bruna & Zoons Uitgeversmij, 1970. Contributor of short stories and articles to such publications as *Randstad*, *Podium*, and *Zero*.

WORK IN PROGRESS: English edition of *I Jan Cremer: Second Book*; writing *I Jan Cremer: Third Book*.

SIDELIGHTS: Books called Cremer's well-publicized novel, translated into 28 languages, the "Dirty Book of the Year." A more restrained reviewer in the *Manchester Guardian* wrote: "I'm not so sure that it's very shocking. I'd call it more disgusting, in a routine sort of way." Anthony Burgess considers it to be an "imaginative teenage autobiography on the Celine-Miller-Genet pattern, in which the youth of the author is presented, we presume, as sufficient excuse for a lack of style and genuine robustness—qualities not lacking in those three fine dirty masters."

"As a boy," reports the *Times Literary Supplement*, "Jan Cremer was an avid reader of lurid comic strips; later he admired Mickey Spillane, the Saint, and, of course, James Bond. His book (which could easily be made into a cartoon strip) reflects the dreams and occasional nightmares of a young man on the make in a world on the make."

Cremer writes any time and paints at night, currently doing "enormous canvases dedicated to non-representation and Bob Dylan," according to the *New York Times Book Review*. He has held about sixty exhibitions of his work in Europe, and is preparing a New York show. He told *CA* he will work in America "as a playwright and an actor."

BIOGRAPHICAL/CRITICAL SOURCES: Hij Jan Cremer, by Denis Arnolds, Walter Southoudt (Antwerp), 1965; *New York Times* (daily), November 1, 1965; *Best Sellers*, November 15, 1965; *Spectator*, December 3, 1965; *Observer*, December 5, 1965; *Newsweek*, December 20, 1965; *Books and Bookmen*, January, 1966; *Times Literary Supplement*, January 20, 1966.†

* * *

CRENNER, James 1938-

PERSONAL: Born February 10, 1938, in Pittsburgh, Pa.; son of James August and Mae (Connors) Crenner; married Catherine Lybarger, November 14, 1959 (divorced June, 1973); children: Christopher, Belle Mary, Timothy. *Education:* St. Vincent College, B.A., 1959; State University of Iowa (now University of Iowa), M.A., 1961, M.F.A., 1962, Ph.D., 1967. *Home:* 603 S. Main St., Geneva, New York.

CAREER: St. Vincent College, Latrobe, Pa., instructor in English, 1962-64; University of Iowa, Iowa City, graduate assistant in English, 1964-67; Hobart and William Smith Colleges, Geneva, N.Y., associate professor of English, 1967—. *Awards, honors:* Woodrow Wilson fellowship, 1959.

WRITINGS: The Aging Ghost (poems), Golden Quill Press, 1964.

WORK IN PROGRESS: A new collection of poems, projected title, *Yonder*.

* * *

CRESSEY, Donald R(ay) 1919-

PERSONAL: Born April 27, 1919, in Fergus Falls, Minn.; son of Raymond Wilbert (an electrician) and Myrtle (Prentiss) Cressey; married Elaine M. Smythe, December 16, 1943; children: Martha Jean, Ann Kathleen, Mary Dee. *Education:* Iowa State University of Technology and Science, B.S., 1943; Indiana University, Ph.D., 1950. *Politics:* Democrat. *Religion:* Unitarian. *Home:* 4310 Via Esperanza, Santa Barbara, Calif. *Office:* Department of Sociology, University of California, Santa Barbara, Calif.

CAREER: Illinois State Penitentiary, Joliet, sociologist, 1949; University of California, Los Angeles, 1949-61, started as instructor, professor of sociology, 1959-61, chairman of department of anthropology and sociology, 1957-58, acting dean of division of social science, 1960-61; University of California, Santa Barbara, professor of sociology, 1962—, dean of College of Letters and Science, 1962-67. Research associate at California Institution for Men, 1950-51, at U.S. Penitentiary, Terre Haute, Ind., 1951. Visiting professor at University of Chicago, 1955-56, Institute of Criminal Law and Criminology, Cambridge University, 1961-62, University of Oslo, 1965, University of Washington, 1968, University of Minnesota, 1969, Churchill College, Cambridge University, 1970-71, and Australian National University, 1973. *Military service:* U.S. Army Air Forces, 1943-46; received five battle stars and two Presidential Unit Citations.

MEMBER: American Sociological Association (member of national council, 1960-63; visiting scientist, 1963—), Pacific Sociological Association (vice-president, 1957-58; president, 1959-60; member of council, 1960-61), American Correctional Association. *Awards, honors:* Research grants from Russell Sage Foundation, 1955-56, Ford Foundation, 1960, American Council of Learned Societies, 1960, and Social Science Research Council; citation by Illinois Academy of Criminology, 1964, for contributions to research and the theory and practice of corrections; Edwin H. Sutherland Award, American Society of Criminology, 1968; Distinguished Alumni Service Award, Indiana University, 1974.

WRITINGS: With Other Peoples' Money: A Study in the Social Psychology of Embezzlement, Free Press of Glencoe, 1953; (with Edwin H. Sutherland) *Principles of Criminology*, Lippincott, 5th edition, 1955, 9th edition, 1974; (with Richard A. Cloward and others) *Theoretical Studies in Social Organization of the Prison*, Social Science Research Council, 1960; (editor) *The Prison: Studies in Institutional Organization and Change*, Holt, 1961; *Delinquency, Crime and Differential Association*, Nijhoff, 1964; *Theft of the Nation: The Structure and Operations of Organized Crime in America*, Harper, 1969; (with David A. Ward) *Delinquency, Crime and Social Process*, Harper, 1969, (editor and author of introduction) *Crime and Criminal Justice*, Quadrangle, 1971; *Criminal Organization: Its Elementary Forms*, Harper, 1972.

Contributor to books and to sociological, psychological, and legal journals. Chairman of editorial board, "Culture and Society Series," University of California Press, 1953-55, 1956-58; associate editor, *American Sociological Review*, 1953-56; advisory editor, *American Journal of Sociology*, 1959-62, of *Transactions: Social Science and the Community*, 1963-67, of *Social Problems*, 1970—.

WORK IN PROGRESS: A book on plea bargaining in American and foreign courts; a book on prison reform; research on social control of drunken driving in America and Europe.

SIDELIGHTS: Theft of the Nation: The Structure and Operations of Organized Crime in America has been widely acclaimed. Arthur Cooper describes it as "a terrifyingly engrossing and the most authoritative account yet of the crime syndicate that is operating as an invisible—and nearly invincible—government." Fred J. Cook defines "theft of the nation" as "the power to corrupt official life and to take over legitimate businesses" through "possession of such enormous resources, the wages of crime." He lauds the book as "probably the most thorough and explicit account we have of both the manner in which the criminal structure is organized and its awesome, pervasive power." Cressey speaks Norwegian, French, German.

* * *

CRETZMEYER, F(rancis) X(avier), Jr. 1913-

PERSONAL: Born January 7, 1913; son of Francis Xavier and Mary (Laughlin) Cretzmeyer; married December 28, 1939, wife's maiden name Cornwall; children: Mary Frances (Mrs. John Neimeyer), Catherine (Mrs. John McGarvey), Margaret, Francis Xavier III, John. *Educa-*

tion: University of Iowa, B.A., 1936, M.A., 1939. *Politics:* Democrat. *Religion:* Roman Catholic. *Home:* 3 Melrose Circle, Iowa City, Iowa. *Office:* University of Iowa, Iowa City, Iowa.

CAREER: University of Iowa, Iowa City, assistant professor and track coach, 1950—.

WRITINGS: Track and Field Athletics, Mosby, 1964.

* * *

CREWS, Judson (Campbell) 1917-

PERSONAL: Born June 30, 1917, in Waco, Tex.; son of Noah George (a nurseryman) and Tommie (Farmer) Crews; married Mildred Tolbert (a photographer), October 19, 1947; children: Anna Bush, Carole Judith. *Education:* Baylor University, A.B., 1941, M.A. (with honors in sociology-psychology), 1944, study in fine arts, 1946-47. *Politics:* None. *Religion:* None. *Home:* Este Es Rd., Taos, N.M. 87571.

CAREER: "Though definitely an earlier phase, I was involved in editing and publishing several of the avant garde magazines of the 30's, 40's and 50's. Ranging from *Vers Libre* which lasted over two years, to *Taos*, a deluxe magazine of the arts which was a one-shot deal. In addition to the two above, *Motive, The Flying Fish, Suck-Egg Mule, The Deer and Dachshund, Poetry Taos*, and *The Naked Ear* were my soul responsibility. I was more than slightly involved with *Crescendo*, edited by Scott Greer, and *Gale*, edited by Jay Waite." Formerly printer for Leeside Press, Waco, Tex., Wells Press, Taos, N.M., and El Crepulsculo de la Libertad, Taos, N.M. Publisher of Motive Press until it ceased operations. Bibliophilist with Motive Book Shop, Waco, Tex., 1938—; with Taos News Publishing Co., 1960—; instructor in sociology and psychology, Wharton County Junior College, Wharton, Tex. *Military service:* U.S. Army Medical Corps, 1942-44; became staff sergeant. *Member:* American Civil Liberties Union.

WRITINGS: Psalms for a Late Season, Inconograph Press (New Orleans), 1942; *The Southern Temper*, Motive Book Shop, 1946; *No is the Night*, privately printed (Taos, N.M.), 1949.

The Anatomy of Proserpine, [Ranches of Taos, N.M.], c. 1955; (with wife, Mildred Tolbert Crews and Wendell B. Anderson) *Patrocinio Barela: Taos Wood Carver*, Taos Recording & Publications, 1955, revised edition, 1962; *The Wrath Wrenched Splendor of Love Poems*, [Ranches of Taos, N.M.], c. 1956; *The Heart in Naked Hunger*, Motive Book Shop (Taos), c. 1958; *The Ogres Who Were His Henchmen*, Hearse Press (Eureka, Calif.), 1958.

Inwade to Briney Garth (nudes by Eric Gill), Este Es Press (Taos), 1960; *The Feel of Sun and Air Upon Her Body*, Hearse Press, 1960; (contributor) Fred Baver, compiler, *River*, River Spring (Memphis), 1960; *A Unicorn When Needs Be*, Este Es Press, 1963; *Hermes Past the Hour*, Este Es Press, 1963; *Selected Poems* (prints by Lester Czaban), Renegade Press (Cleveland), 1964; *You, Mark Anthony, Navigator Upon the Nile*, [Taos], c. 1965; *Angels Fall, They Are Towers*, Este Es Press, 1965; *The Stones of Kanorak*, American Poets Press (Santa Fe), 1966; (with Anderson and Cerise Farallon) *Three on a Match*, [Taos], 1966; (contributor) Robert L. Williams, compiler, *Mehy in His Carriage*, Summit Press (Austin), 1968. Also author of *A Sheaf of Christmas Verse*, Three Hands (Washington, D.C.), *Come Curse the Moon*, and *To Wed Beneath the Sun*. Work represented in anthologies, including *An Unin-*

hibited Treasury of Erotic Poetry, edited by Louis Untermeyer, Dial, 1963; *Poems Southwest*, edited by A.W. Stevens, Prescott College Press, 1968.

Contributor to *Poetry, Accent, Black Mountain Review, Circle, Departure, Death, Experiment, Evergreen Review, Golden Goose, Hearse, Merlin, Outsider, New Mexico Quarterly, Southwest Review, Massachusetts Review, Prairie Schooner, Phoenix, Points, Tiger's Eye, Voices, Wormwood Review*, and *Yugen*.

WORK IN PROGRESS: Crews said: "I continue with my poetry. And am especially engaged in work on a longer poem of autobiographical cast which will counter-point Eastern and Western attitudes toward the essentially physical basis of love. In addition I continue research on a prose work which might well develop into a definitive treatment on 'the question of genital beauty'. Also a critical work, probably book-length, relating Henry Miller's autobiographical Paris-novels to Anais Nin's *Cities of the Interior*. If the time ever comes when I can publish my first novel (now several years old, and characterized by Lepska Miller [Henry Miller's third wife] as 'stronger, in a sexual way, than *Tropic of Cancer*') I may turn back to writing fiction again."

SIDELIGHTS: Crews writes: "Unduly impressed by the unfortunate records of Yvor winters, John Crowe Ransom, and Paul Engle in the role of Poet as Professor, I made the hasty exit from academia at the age of thirty knowing that teaching would warp the poet's view of the world and dry up his soul. Reconsidering the question more recently, on the basis of the records of Charles Olson, Robert Creeley and Edward Dorn, I must concede that the position of Poet-Professor may after all constitute a marriage of true minds. The earlier poets may have died on the stem even if they had chosen to be hodcarriers."

"The poet especially must remain the 'rebel' in Camus' exemplary sense of the word. In this respect, the academic setting may offer a danger to the conformists and the administration stooges, but for the real poet it may also offer an opportunity."

Crews, however, continues to find his opportunities elsewhere. In 1963, Winfield Townley Scott wrote: "Judson Crews, the Taos poet, remains over the years pretty generally a 'little magazine' poet. He stays avant garde. This is not only not reprehensible but rather admirable. . . ."

Some of Crews's materials, including manuscripts and letters, are at University of California at Los Angeles library and Humanities Research Center, University of Texas.†

* * *

CRICHTON, James Dunlop 1907-

PERSONAL: Surname is pronounced *Cry*-ton; born June 18, 1907, in England; son of Rurik and Anna (Oaten) Crichton. *Education:* Educated at Oscott College, Birmingham, England, 1925-32. *Home:* 14 Priest Lane, Pershore, Worcestershire, England.

CAREER: Ordained Roman Catholic priest, 1932; parish priest; *Liturgy* (publication of Society of St. Gregory), Pershore, Worcestershire, England, editor, 1951-71; University of Birmingham, Institute of Liturgy and Architecture, Birmingham, England, member, 1964—. Visiting professor of liturgy, Lumen Vitae Centre, Brussels, Belgium, 1958, Catholic University of America, 1963; lecturer in liturgy, Catechetical Institute, Nelson, British Columbia, 1965. Member of Midland region religious advisory committee,

British Broadcasting Corp., 1948-54, 1964-68. *Awards, honors:* Honorary fellow, University of Birmingham.

WRITINGS: (Editor of British edition) J. A. Jungmann, *Handing on the Faith*, Burns, 1959; (contributor) G. Sloyan, editor, *Shaping the Christian Message*, Macmillan, 1959; *The Church's Worship*, Sheed, 1964; (contributor) L. Bright, editor, *The People of God*, Sheed (London), 1965; *Changes in the Liturgy*, Geoffrey Chapman, 1965; *The Parish in the Modern World*, Sheed (London), 1965; (contributor) *The Liturgy and the Future*, Alba, 1965; (editor) *The Mass and the People of God*, Burns & Oates, 1966; (contributor) P. Milner, editor, *The Ministry of the Word*, Burns & Oates, 1967; (contributor) J. Fitzsimons, editor, *Penance: Virtue and Sacrament*, Burns & Oates, 1969; *Christian Celebration: The Mass*, Geoffrey Chapman, 1971; *The Liturgy of Holy Week*, Goodliffe Neale, 1971; (contributor) J. G. Davies, editor, *A Dictionary of Liturgy and Worship*, S.C.M. Press, 1972; *Christian Celebration: The Sacraments*, Geoffrey Chapman, 1973; (contributor) F. L. Cross and E. A. Livingstone, editors, *Oxford Dictionary of the Christian Church*, Oxford University Press, 1974; *The Order of Penance*, Geoffrey Chapman, 1974. Regular contributor to the Catholic press and periodicals.

WORK IN PROGRESS: Christian Celebration: The Prayer of the Church.

* * *

CRIPPS, (Matthew) Anthony (Leonard) 1913-

PERSONAL: Born December 30, 1913, in London, England; son of Honorable Leonard Harrison (a shipowner) and Barbara (Joyce) Cripps; married Margaret Scott, June 21, 1941; children: Michael Leonard Seddon, Jeremy George Anthony, Richard James Nigel. *Education:* Attended Christ Church, Oxford, 1933-37. *Politics:* Democrat. *Religion:* Church of England. *Home:* Alton House, Felbridge, East Grinstead, Sussex, England. *Office:* 1 Harcourt Buildings, Temple, London, England.

CAREER: Barrister-at-law, Middle Temple, 1938; Queen's Counsel, 1958—; recorder of Nottingham, 1961-71. Chairman, Isle of Man Agriculture Marketing Commission, 1960-61; member, United Kingdom Agricultural Wages Board, 1964-67; member, U.K. Committee of Inquiry into Foot and Mouth Disease, 1968-69; member, U.K. Committee of Inquiry into Export of Live Animals for Slaughter, 1973-74. *Military service:* Royal Leicestershire Regiment, 1933-46, on active duty, 1939-46; served in Norway, Sweden, Finland, Iceland, North Africa, Italy, and Egypt, 1939-44, in Palestine and Syria, 1944-46; became lieutenant colonel; received Distinguished Service Order, 1943, Territorial Decoration, 1945. *Awards, honors:* Commander of the British Empire, 1972.

WRITINGS: Agriculture Act 1947, Butterworth & Co., 1947; *Agricultural Holdings Act 1948*, Butterworth & Co., 1948; (editor) *Cripps on Compensation*, 9th edition, Stevens and Sons, 1950. Contributor of articles on legal subjects to *Encyclopaedia Britannica*, and to *Observer* and *Times* (London).

WORK IN PROGRESS: Several aspects of law reform, especially women's rights.

* * *

CROCOMBE, Ronald G(ordon) 1929-

PERSONAL: Born October 8, 1929, in Auckland, New Zealand; son of George William (a farmer) and Helen (McLeod) Crocombe; married Marjorie Hosking (a writer), April 7, 1959; children: Taturoanui and Kevin (sons), Narida (daughter). *Education:* University of New Zealand, B.A., 1956; Australian National University, Ph.D., 1961. *Politics:* "No political affiliation." *Religion:* "No religion." *Office:* University of the South Pacific, Box 1168, Suva, Fiji.

CAREER: Administrative work in New Zealand's Pacific Island territories, 1950-58; social science research in the South Pacific for Australian National University, 1958-69; University of the South Pacific, Suva, Fiji, professor of pacific studies, 1969—.

WRITINGS: The Cook Islands, New Zealand Education Department, 1958; *Land Tenure in the Cook Islands*, Oxford University Press, 1964; (contributor) *A Select Annotated Bibliography on Land Tenure in the Territory of Papua and New Guinea*, Lands Department, Port Moresby, 1964; *Improving Land Tenure*, South Pacific Commission, 1968; (editor with wife, Marjorie Crocombe) *The Works of Ta'unga*, Australian National University Press, 1968; (editor) *Land Tenure in the Pacific*, Oxford University Press, 1971; *The Now South Pacific*, Australian National University Press, 1974. Contributor to journals.

WORK IN PROGRESS: Editing writings by Pacific Islands authors.

* * *

CROMIE, William J(oseph) 1930-

PERSONAL: Born March 12, 1930, in New York, N.Y.; son of Harry Joseph and Margaret (Terrifoy) Cromie; married Alicia M. Connors, December 28, 1958; children: Steven William. *Education:* Attended State University of New York Maritime College, 1951-53; Columbia University, B.S., 1956, graduate study in journalism, 1960-61. *Home:* 2344 Sunset Blvd., Houston, Tex. 77005. *Office:* World Book Encyclopedia Science Service, 820 Chronicle Building, Houston, Tex. 77002.

CAREER: U.S. Merchant Marine, 1945-50; Anaconda Mining Co., Butte, Mont., geologist, 1956; Arctic Institute of North America, member of International Geophysical Year Expedition to Antarctica, 1956-58; Columbia University, Lamont Geophysical Laboratory, research scientist on expeditions, 1958-60; Brown & Root, Inc., Houston Tex., public information director for project Mohole, 1962-63; with World Book Encyclopedia Science Service, Houston, Tex., 1963—. Archeological Research Foundation, geologist on 1964 Mount Arat Expedition. Columbia University Oral History Program, interviewer. *Military service:* U.S. Naval Reserve, 1948-53. *Member:* American Association for the Advancement of Science, International Oceanographic Foundation, Press Club of Houston.

WRITINGS: Earthquakes, Science Service and Doubleday, 1961; *Volcanos*, Science Service and Doubleday, 1962; *Exploring the Secrets of the Sea*, Prentice-Hall, 1962; *Why The Mohole: Adventures in Inner Space*, Little, Brown, 1964; *The Living World of the Sea*, Prentice-Hall, 1966; *Steven and the Green Turtle*, Harper, 1970; *Secrets of the Seas*, Readers Digest Association, 1971. Contributor to *Life's* "Nature Series," *Reader's Digest*, *Natural History*, *Science World*, *Science Digest*, *U.S. Naval Institute Proceedings*. Writer of by-line articles for International Science News Service.

SIDELIGHTS: Cromie's Geophysical Year activities included nine months at Little America, a four-month Ross

Ice Shelf traverse over previously unexplored regions, and an expedition to the Indian Ocean and Red Sea as chief officer and oceanographer aboard the three-masted research schooner, ''Vema,'' in 1958. He also served aboard Drifting Station Charlie, a research outpost on an ice floe in the Arctic Ocean in 1959. Mount Cromie in Antarctica is named in his honor.†

*   *   *

CROSBY, Harry H(erbert)   1919-

PERSONAL: Born April 18, 1919, in New England, N.D.; son of Guy L. and Eva L. (McClellan) Crosby; married Jean E. Boehner, 1943; children: Stephen, April, Jeffrey, Rebecca. *Education:* University of Iowa, B.A., 1941, M.A., 1947; Stanford University, Ph.D., 1953. *Politics:* Democrat. *Religion:* Episcopalian. *Home:* 48 Ruthven Rd., Newton, Mass. 02158. *Office:* College of Basic Studies, Boston University, 688 Boylston St., Boston, Mass. 02116.

CAREER: San Jose State College (now University), San Jose, Calif., instructor in rhetoric, 1947-49; University of Iowa, Iowa City, instructor, 1950-51, assistant professor of communication, 1951-58; Boston University, Boston, Mass., associate professor, 1958-59, professor and chairman of Division of Communication, 1959—. Director of studies, Pakistan Air Force College, and educational adviser to the commander in chief, Pakistan Air Force, 1960-62. Consultant to U.S. Air Force Academy, 1953-60. Member of Board of Aldermen, Newton, Mass., 1970-73. *Military service:* U.S. Army Air Forces, 1942-45; group navigator, 100th Group; became lieutenant colonel; received Distinguished Flying Cross and two oak-leaf clusters, Air Medal and four oak-leaf clusters, Bronze Star, seven battle stars, two unit citations, Croix de Guerre, and citations from British, Norwegian, and Pakistan governments.

MEMBER: National Council of Teachers of English, Modern Language Association of America, Conference on College Communication and Composition (director, 1953-55), Phi Eta Sigma. *Awards, honors:* Ford Foundation grant for experiment in instruction, 1957.

WRITINGS: Radio Navigation Systems, Collins Radio Co. (Cedar Rapids, Iowa), 1953; (co-author) *Communication Skills: An Experiment in Method,* University of Iowa Press, 1958; (editor with C. B. Strandness) *Language, Form and Idea,* McGraw, 1965; (compiler with George R. Bond) *The McLuhan Explosion: A Casebook on Marshall McLuhan and Understanding Media,* American Book Co., 1968; (with George F. Estey) *Just Rhetoric,* Harper, 1972; (with Estey) *College Writing: The Rhetorical Imperative,* Harper, 1972.

Scripts: ''Highway in the Sky'' (film), 1956; ''Operation Unlimited'' (television), 1957; ''The Great Diamond Fraud'' (television play), 1957.

Contributor to *American Heritage* and other journals and newspapers. Editor, *Splasher Six* (a World War II Air Force journal), *Iowa English Bulletin,* 1953-58.

WORK IN PROGRESS: The Third Best Bungalow, a novel set in Pakistan.

*   *   *

CROSBY, Sumner McK(night)   1909-

PERSONAL: Born July 29, 1909, in Minneapolis, Minn.; son of Franklin M. (a miller) and Harriet (McKnight) Crosby; married Sarah Rathbone Townsend, October 19, 1935; children: Sumner McKnight, Jr., William Fellowes, Frederick Townsend, Gerrit Lansing. *Education:* Yale University, B.A., 1932, Ph.D., 1937; Ecole des Chartes, Paris, France, graduate study, 1933-35. *Home:* Fairgrounds Rd., Woodbridge, Conn. 06525. *Office:* History of Art Department, Yale University, 56 High St., New Haven, Conn. 06520.

CAREER: Yale University, New Haven, Conn., instructor, 1936-41, assistant professor, 1941-47, associate professor, 1947-53, professor of history of art, 1953—, chairman of department, 1948-54, 1962-65, curator of medieval art, Yale University Art Gallery, 1946—, director of Audio-Visual Center, 1950-58, fellow of Berkeley College, 1938—. Director of excavations in Abbey Church of Saint Denis, France, summers, 1938-39, 1946-48, and 1968-71. Executive secretary of American Council of Learned Societies Committee for the Protection of Cultural Treasures in War Areas, 1943-45; special advisor to American Commission for the Protection and Salvage of Artistic and Historic Monuments in War Areas, 1944-45, and to Department of State on restitution of cultural materials, 1945. Phillips Academy, Andover, member of alumni council, 1950-52, of advisory committee on Addison Gallery, 1946—. International Center of Medieval Art, director, 1964—, president, 1967-70; member of advisory committee of the Cloisters, New York, 1971—.

MEMBER: College Art Association of America (director, 1939-45, 1947-52; president, 1940-44), American Federation of Arts (trustee, 1941-44, 1947-51), Mediaeval Academy of America (councillor, 1951—), Societe Nationale des Antiquaires de France (honorary correspondent); Century Association and Yale Club (both New York). *Awards, honors:* Guggenheim Fellow, 1948; Chevalier, Legion of Honor, 1950, for work on excavations of Abbey Church; D.F.A., Minneapolis College of Art and Design, 1968.

WRITINGS: The Abbey of St.-Denis, Volume I, Yale University Press, 1942; *L'Abbaye Royale de St.-Denis,* Paul Hartman, 1953; (editor, with others), Helen Gardner, *Art Through the Ages,* 4th edition, revised, Harcourt, 1959; *The Apostle Bas-relief at Saint-Denis,* Yale University Press, 1972. Contributor of editorials and articles to *College Art Journal,* 1940-44, other articles and reviews to *Listener* (London), *Studio* (London), *New York Times, Gazettes des Beaux Arts* (Paris), other journals, Member of editorial board, *Art Bulletin,* 1941—, *Speculum,* 1946-54.

WORK IN PROGRESS: A revision of Volume I of *The Abbey of St.-Denis,* and preparation of Volume II for press; editing *Corpus Vitrearum Medii Aevi.*

*   *   *

CROW, John A(rmstrong)   1906-

PERSONAL: Born December 18, 1906, in Wilmington, N.C.; son of George Davis (a banker) and Olive Lois (Armstrong) Crow; married Josephine Gorden (a teacher), August 19, 1956; children: John A., Jr., Diane Olivia. *Education:* University of North Carolina, A.B., 1927; Columbia University, M.A., 1930; University of Madrid, Doctor en filosofia y letras (with highest honors), 1933. *Politics:* Independent. *Religion:* Episcopalian. *Home:* 218 North Bundy Dr., Los Angeles, Calif. 90049. *Office:* Department of Spanish, University of California, Los Angeles, Calif. 90024.

CAREER: University of North Carolina, Chapel Hill, instructor in Spanish, 1927-28; Davidson College, Davidson, N.C., assistant professor of Spanish, 1928-29; New York

University, New York, N.Y., instructor in Spanish, 1929-37; University of California, Los Angeles, 1937—, began as instructor, professor of Spanish, 1950—, head of department of Spanish and Portuguese, 1949-54. *Member:* International Institute of Ibero-American Literature (cofounder; secretary, 1938-40; chairman of cultural exchange section, 1940—), American Association of Teachers of Spanish and Portuguese (vice-president, 1950-53), Modern Language Association of America, Authors League of America, Descendants of Knights of the Garter, Descendants of Signers of the Magna Carta, General Society of Mayflower Descendants, Phi Beta Kappa. *Awards, honors:* Named in American Library Association's "Best Books of the Year," 1946, for *The Epic of Latin America*; also named in *New York Times'* "Best Books of the Year," 1957, for *Mexico Today*.

WRITINGS: (Editor and author of introduction) *Cuentos hispanicos*, Holt, 1939; (editor and author of critique) Horacio Quiroga, *Los perseguidos y otros cuentos*, Biblioteca Rodo (Montevideo), 1940; *Spanish American Life* Holt, 1941; (co-author) *An Outline History of Spanish American Literature*, Appleton, 1942, revised edition, 1965; (editor and contributor) *Latin America*, Americana Corp., 1943; (editor and author of introduction) *Horacio Quiroga: sus mejores cuentos*, Editorial Cultura (Mexico), 1943; *Federico Garcia Lorca* (monograph), privately printed, 1946; (co-editor) *An Anthology of Spanish American Literature*, two volumes, Appleton, 1946; *The Epic of Latin America*, Doubleday, 1946, 3rd edition, 1971; (with G. D. Crow) *Panorama de las Americas*, Holt, 1949, revised edition, 1956.

California as a Place to Live, Scribner, 1953; *Spanish for Beginners*, Holt, 1953; *Mexico Today*, Harper, 1957, revised edition, 1959; (contributor of translations) Angel Flores, editor, *An Anthology of Spanish Poetry from Garcilaso to Garcia Lorca*, Doubleday, 1961; *Spanish American Life*, Holt, 1963; *Spain: The Root and the Flower*, Harper, 1963, revised edition, 1974; *Italy: A Journey through Time*, Harper, 1965; *Greece: The Magic Spring*, Harper, 1970.

Contributor to *Encyclopaedia Britannica, Encyclopedia Americana, Collier's Encyclopedia, World Book Encyclopedia*, and *Encyclopedia of Poetry and Poetica*. Contributor to journals and magazines. Collaborating editor, *Handbook of Latin American Studies*, Harvard University Press, 1950-51. Co-editor, *Journal Revista Iberoamericana*, 1938-42; collaborating editor, *Humanismo*, 1956-59.

SIDELIGHTS: Crow told CA, "Early in life I began to prefer the world of books to the world of people. The best minds are there, but personalities do not impose themselves; the best ideas are there, but no one attempts to ram them down your throat. In the world of books one learns to accept absolute responsibility and absolute freedom of choice."

Crow speaks French, in addition to Spanish, which he teaches. *Avocational interests:* Travel; has made numerous trips to Europe and Latin America.

* * *

CRUMP, Barry (John) 1935-

PERSONAL: Born May 16, 1935, in Auckland, New Zealand; son of Walter William (a farmer) and Lilly (Hendry) Crump; married Fleur Adcock (a librarian and poet), 1961 (separated). *Education:* Attended Otahuhu Technical College, Auckland, New Zealand. *Politics:* "Politically irre-

sponsible." *Religion:* Baha'i. *Address:* Box 5090, Auckland, New Zealand.

CAREER: Worked at more than seventy jobs since leaving school and has continued his wandering ways ("no fixed abode") since becoming a writer, 1960—. Experiences as a professional deer shooter, employed by the New Zealand Forest Service, 1951-56, led to his first book, *A Good Keen Man*, and professional crocodile hunting in Queensland, Australia, 1956-64, led to another book, *Gulf*; film actor in "Runaway," produced in New Zealand, 1964; radio reader of his own works, New Zealand. *Member:* P.E.N. *Awards, honors:* Hubert Church Award (P.E.N.) for prose, 1963, for *One of Us*.

WRITINGS—All published by A. H. & A. W. Reed, except as indicated: *A Good Keen Man*, 1960; *Hang On a Minute, Mate*, 1961; *One of Us*, 1962; *There and Back*, 1963; *Gulf*, 1964; *Scrapwaggon*, 1965; *The Odd Spot of Bother*, 1967; *Warm Beer and Other Stories*, 1969; *A Good Keen Girl*, 1970; *No Reference Intended*, 1971; *Bastards I Have Met: An ABC of Bastardry*, Crump Productions, 1971; *Fred*, Crump Productions, 1972; *The Best of Barry Crump*, Crump Productions, 1974. Contributor of short stories and articles to New Zealand and Australian periodicals.

SIDELIGHTS: Crump's first book was an instant success and has gone into twelve printings in five years; sales of that book and the three novels that followed it (featuring a Kiwi vagabond, Sam Cash) have passed the 200,000-mark. He says that he expects to write a "*good* (for me) book on human relationships" when he's about forty and claims that he is largely uneducated.

BIOGRAPHICAL/CRITICAL SOURCES: Ron Helmer, *Stag Party*, Whitcombe & Tombs, 1964.

* * *

CRUMRINE, N(orman) Ross II 1934-

PERSONAL: Born May 22, 1934, in Beaver, Pa.; son of Norman Ross (a physician) and Elizabeth (Seiple) Crumrine; married Lynne Scoggins (an anthropologist), August 29, 1959; children: Juli Maria. *Education:* Northwestern University, B.A., 1957; University of Washington, Seattle, graduate study, 1957-58; University of Arizona, M.A., 1962, graduate study, 1963; University of Chicago, graduate study, 1962-63. *Home:* 1747 Germain Ct., Hayward, Calif. *Office:* Geography-Anthropology Department, California State University at Hayward, Calif.

CAREER: California State University at Hayward, assistant professor of anthropology, 1965—. *Member:* American Anthropological Association, American Ethnological Society.

WRITINGS: The House Cross of the Mayo Indians of Sonora, Mexico: A Symbol in Ethnic Identity, University of Arizona Press, 1964. Also author of *The Mayo Indians of Sonora, Mexico: A People Who Refuse to Die*, University of Arizona Press.†

* * *

CUMMINGS, Milton C(urtis), Jr. 1933-

PERSONAL: Born April 23, 1933, in New Haven, Conn.; son of Milton Curtis (an adult education specialist) and Lela (Belt) Cummings; married Nancy Boucot (a medical research administrator), July 31, 1959; children: Christopher Ronald, Jonathan Benton, Susan Sturgis. *Education:* Swarthmore College, B.A., 1954; Oxford University,

B.Phil., 1956; Harvard University, Ph.D., 1960. *Home:* 2811 35th St. N.W., Washington, D.C. 20007.

CAREER: Brookings Institution, Washington, D.C., research assistant, 1959-61, research associate, 1961-64, senior staff member, 1964-65; Johns Hopkins University, Baltimore, Md., associate professor, 1965-68, professor of political science, 1968—, chairman of department, 1970-72. Case writer, Inter-university Case Program; consultant to National Broadcasting Co. on election news coverage. *Member:* American Political Science Association, International Political Science Association, Phi Beta Kappa. *Awards, honors:* Rhodes Scholar; Social Science Research Council fellowship; National Science Foundation fellowship.

WRITINGS: (With Peter B. Bart) *The Transfer of the Kansas Civil Service Department*, University of Alabama Press, 1956; (contributor) Robert L. Peabody and Nelson W. Polsby, editors, *New Perspectives on the House of Representatives*, Rand McNally, 1963; (with Franklin P. Kilpatrick and M. Kent Jennings) *The Image of the Federal Service*, Brookings, 1964; (with F. P. Kilpatrick and M. K. Jennings) *Source Book of a Study of Occupational Values and the Image of the Federal Service*, Brookings, 1964; (editor and contributor) *The National Elections of 1964*, Brookings, 1966; *Congressmen and the Electorate*, Free Press, 1966; (with David Wise) *Democracy Under Pressure: An Introduction to the American Political System*, Harcourt, 1971, 2nd edition, 1974. Contributor to *Encyclopedia Americana*, *Public Opinion Quarterly,* and *Public Administration Review.*

WORK IN PROGRESS: A study of the development of the seniority system in the United States Senate.

SIDELIGHTS: Virginia Quarterly Review describes *Congressmen and the Electorate* as an analysis of "all elections to the United States House of Representatives between 1920 and 1964" which "fills a large void, gives statistical underpinning to the impressionistic, but often accurate, findings of historians, and puts between two covers a mass of data not readily available otherwise."

*   *   *

CUNNINGHAM, Dale S(peers)   1932-

PERSONAL: Born May 27, 1932, in Elmira, N.Y.; son of Arthur G. and Aletha (Speers) Cunningham. *Education:* Hamilton College; A.B., 1954; graduate study at Sorbonne, University of Paris, 1954, and Johann Wolfgang Goethe-Universitat, 1954-55; Columbia University, A.M., 1959; graduate study at Bryn Mawr College, 1962-65, and at Princeton University. *Address:* Box 401, Main Office, Camden, N.J. 08101.

CAREER: Renssalaer Polytechnic Institute, Troy, N.Y., instructor in English and German, 1960-61; Rutgers University, Camden Campus, Camden, N.J., instructor in German, 1961-65; Smith, Kline & French Laboratories, Philadelphia, Pa., medical writer, 1965; Uniworld Languages, Philadelphia, Pa., translations director, 1965-73, president, 1973—. Editor, translator, and translations consultant. *Member:* Modern Language Association of America, American Translators Association (secretary, 1963-64; director, 1965-69; president, 1969-71), American Association of University Professors, Delaware Valley Translators Association (vice-chairman, 1962-63; chairman, 1963-64), P.E.N., Bund Deutscher Uebersetzer, Verband Deutscher Uebersetzer (honorary), Chambre Belge des Traducteurs (honorary). *Awards, honors:* Fulbright assistantship in Germany, 1954-55.

WRITINGS: Pioneers in Science, Sterling, 1962; *Picture Book of Music and Its Makers*, Sterling, 1963.

Translator and adapter: (With Margrete Cunningham) Walter Sperling, *How to Make Things out of Paper*, Sterling, 1961; (with Margrete Cunningham) Gerhard Gollwitzer, *The Joy of Drawing*, Sterling, 1961; Bruno Knobel, *Camping-Out Ideas and Activities*, Sterling, 1961; Gerhard Gollwitzer, *Abstract Art*, Sterling, 1962; Harald Doering, *A Bee is Born*, Sterling, 1962; (with Marianne Das) Dieter Krauter, *Experimenting with the Microscope*, Sterling, 1963; (with Ida H. Washington) Rudolf Dittrich, *Juggling*, Sterling, 1963; Rudolf Dittrich, *Tricks and Games for Children*, Sterling, 1964.

Contributor of articles, translations, and notes to learned journals, including *Meta*. Former contributing editor, *Babel.*

WORK IN PROGRESS: Die Welt von heute, an intermediate German reader, for Houghton; several translations; research in the history and theory of translation.

SIDELIGHTS: Cunningham is competent in German and French.

*   *   *

CURRY, Richard Orr   1931-

PERSONAL: Born January 26, 1931, in White Sulphur Springs, W.Va.; son of Ernest Chalmers and Ida Mitt (Atkinson) Curry; married Patricia Leist, April 6, 1953 (died April 15, 1967); married Patricia Del Rosario, February 11, 1968; children: (first marriage) Kimberly Therese, Andrea Rebecca, Jonathan Stuart. *Education:* Marshall University, B.A., 1952, M.A., 1956; University of Pennsylvania, Ph.D., 1961; Harvard University, postdoctoral fellow in Divinity School, 1965-66. *Office:* Department of History, University of Connecticut, Storrs, Conn. 06268.

CAREER: Morris Harvey College, Charleston, W.Va., instructor in history, 1959-60; Pennsylvania State University, University Park, instructor in history, 1960-62; University of Pittsburgh, Pittsburgh, Pa., visiting assistant professor of history, 1962-63; University of Connecticut, Storrs, assistant professor, 1963-66, associate professor, 1966-71, professor of history, 1971—. Participant in seminar on methods of historical analysis, University of Michigan, 1965; Haynes lecturer, Marshall University, 1974. *Military service:* U.S. Navy, 1952-54.

MEMBER: Organization of American Historians, Southern Historical Association, New England Historical Association, Society for Religion in Higher Education, Phi Alpha Theta, Sigma Delta Pi, Omicron Delta Kappa. *Awards, honors:* Annual Literary Award, Military Order of the Loyal Legion of the United States, 1958, for essay on abolitionism; summer research fellowship at West Virginia University Library, 1960 and 1962; grants-in-aid, University of Connecticut Research Foundation, 1964-74; grant-in-aid, American Association for State and Local History, 1964; postdoctoral cross-disciplinary fellowship, Society for Religion in Higher Education, 1965-66; grants-in-aid, National Science Foundation and Social Science Research Council, summer 1966; summer fellowship, National Endowment for the Humanities, 1967; grants-in-aid, American Philosophical Society, 1967 and 1970; Award of Merit, American Association for State and Local History, 1971, for *Radicalism, Racism, and Party Realignment: The Border States During Reconstruction.*

WRITINGS: A House Divided: A Study of Statehood Poli-

tics and the Copperhead Movement in West Virginia, University of Pittsburgh Press, 1964; (editor) The Abolitionists: Reformers or Fanatics?, Holt, 1965, 3rd edition, Dryden Press, 1974; (editor) Radicalism, Racism, and Party Realignment: The Border States During Reconstruction, Johns Hopkins Press, 1969; (with others) The Shaping of America, Holt, 1972; (with others) The Shaping of American Civilization, two volumes, Winston Press, 1972; (editor with Joanna D. Cowden) Slavery in America: Theodore Wild's American Slavery As It Is, F. E. Peacock, 1972; (editor with T. N. Brown) Conspiracy: The Fear of Subversion in American History, Holt, 1972. Contributor of numerous articles to historical journals, including Journal of Southern History, Civil War History, Mid-America, and Journal of Negro History.

WORK IN PROGRESS: A study of the secession crisis and a book of critical essays on the Civil War and Reconstruction.

* * *

CURTIN, Phillip D. 1922-

PERSONAL: Born May 22, 1922, in Philadelphia, Pa.; son of Ellsworth F. and Margaretta (Cope) Curtin; married Phyllis Smith, August, 1946 (divorced, 1956); married Anne Gilbert (a writer), September 14, 1957; children: Steven D., Charles G., Christopher C. Education: Swarthmore College, B.A., 1948; Harvard University, M.A., 1949, Ph.D., 1953. Politics: Democrat. Home: 3964 Plymouth Circle, Madison, Wis. 53705. Office: Bascom Hall, University of Wisconsin, Madison, Wis. 53706.

CAREER: Swarthmore College, Swarthmore, Pa., assistant professor of history, 1953-56; University of Wisconsin, Madison, 1956—, began as assistant professor, now professor of history. Wartime service: U.S. Merchant Marine, 1943-46. Member: American Historical Association, African Studies Association (member of board of directors 1962-64; president, 1970-71), Conference on British Studies. Awards, honors: J. L. Schuyler Prize for 1961-64, from American Historical Association, for Image of Africa.

WRITINGS: Two Jamaicas, Harvard University Press, 1955; The Image of Africa, University of Wisconsin Press, 1964; African History, Macmillan, 1964; (editor and contributor) Africa Remembered: Narratives by West Africans from the Era of the Slave Trade, University of Wisconsin Press, 1967; (with Michael Petrovich) The Human Achievement, Silver Burdett, 1967; The Atlantic Slave Trade, University of Wisconsin Press, 1970; The Islamic World, Silver Burdett, 1970; (with Paul Bohannan) Africa and Africans, 2nd edition (Curtin was not associated with first edition), Natural History Press, 1971; (editor) Imperialism, Harper & Row, 1971; Africa and the West, University of Wisconsin Press, 1972; Economic Change in Pre-Colonial Africa: Senegambia in the Era of the Slave Trade, University of Wisconsin Press, in press.

* * *

DAIN, Martin J. 1924-

PERSONAL: Born September 20, 1924, in Cambridge, Mass. Education: University of Miami, Coral Gables, Fla., B.A., 1948; University of Paris, graduate study, 1948-50. Politics: Independent Democrat. Religion: Atheist. Home: 16 Ford Rd., Carmel Valley, Calif. 93924.

CAREER: Free-lance magazine photographer, Paris, France, 1950-53; free-lance editorial photographer for mag-

azines, industry, and advertising, New York, N.Y., beginning 1953; Scope, New York, N.Y., editorial photographer, beginning 1959; now owner and operator of "Seals and Owl" (arts and crafts studio), Carmel, Calif. Military service: U.S. Army, 1943-46. Member: Association on American Indian Affairs, American Society of Magazine Photographers.

WRITINGS: (With William Stone) A Guide to American Sports Car Racing, Doubleday, 1960; Faulkner's County: Yoknapatawpha, Random House, 1964; (with Barry Robinson) On the Beat (juvenile), Harcourt, 1968.

* * *

DAIUTE, Robert James 1926-

PERSONAL: Surname is pronounced Die-you-tee; born December 27, 1926, in Braintree, Mass.; son of Carroll F. (an attorney) and Dorothy (Park) Daiute; married Eleanor Mae Stevens, June 6, 1953; children: Robert, Jr., Eleanor Maria. Education: Princeton University, A.B., 1951; University of Pennsylvania, M.B.A., 1954. Religion: Protestant. Home: 16 Camelia Ct., Lawrence Township, N.J. Office: Rider College, Lawrence Township, N.J.

CAREER: Johns-Manville, Waukegan, Ill., cost accountant, 1953-54; Norwich University, Northfield, Vt., instructor in business administration, 1955-57; Alfred University, Alfred, N.Y., assistant professor of business, 1957-60; Rider College, Trenton, N.J., assistant professor of business administration, 1960—. Military service: U.S. Navy, 1944-46. Member: Academy of Management, American Economic Association, Alpha Kappa Psi.

WRITINGS: Scientific Management and Human Relations, Holt, 1964; Land Use Data Sources for an Interstate Region, Pennsylvania Department of Commerce, 1966; Economic Highway Planning: Relating Economic Analysis to Sufficiency Rating, Chandler-Davis, 1970; (with Kenneth Gorman) Statistical Sampling of Book Readership at a College Library, U.S. Office of Education, Bureau of Research, 1970; (with Kenneth Gorman) Library Operations Research: Computer Programming of Circulation, Trans-Media Publishing, 1974.†

* * *

DALE, Ernest 1917-

PERSONAL: Born February 4, 1917, son of Eric and Matilda (Koebke) Dale; married Heddy Matthias; children: Dorian, Frank. Education: Cambridge University, B.A., 1939, M.A., 1943; Yale University, M.A., 1946, Ph.D., 1950. Home: 30 Berkeley Ave., Yonkers, N.Y. Office: 15 East 55th St., New York, N.Y. 10022.

CAREER: Yale University, New Haven, Conn., instructor in economics, 1944-47; Columbia University, New York, N.Y., 1946-54, began as instructor, became assistant professor of labor economics; Cornell University, Graduate School of Business and Public Admininstration, Ithaca, N.Y., associate professor of industrial economics, 1954-63; with University of Virginia, Charlottesville, 1963-65; University of Pennsylvania, Wharton School of Finance and Commerce, Philadelphia, Pa., visiting professor of industrial organization, 1965—. President of Ernest Dale Associates (management consultants); consultant on reorganization to companies in America and abroad. Member: American Economic Association, American Management Association, Academy of Management (fellow; president, 1968), Royal Economic Society, Authors

Guild, Yale Club. *Awards, honors:* McKinsey Prize, 1961; Newcomen Prize, 1962.

WRITINGS: Planning and Developing the Company Organization Structure, American Management Association, 1952; *The Great Organizers*, McGraw, 1960; (with L. F. Urwick) *Staff in Organization*, McGraw, 1960; *The Decision-Making Process in the Commercial Use of High-Speed Computers*, Graduate School of Business and Administration, Cornell University, 1964; *Management: Theory and Practice*, McGraw, 1965, 3rd edition, 1973; (editor) *Readings in Management: Landmarks and New Frontiers*, McGraw, 1965, 3rd edition, 1974; (with L. C. Michelon) *Modern Management Methods*, World Publishing, 1966; *Organization*, American Management Association, 1967. Contributor of articles to *Atlantic Monthly, New Statesman, New York Times Sunday Magazine, New Republic, American Economic Review,* and *Journal of Political Economy.*

AVOCATIONAL INTERESTS: Tennis, walking, and skiing.

*   *   *

DALE, John B. 1905-

PERSONAL: Born January 24, 1905, in Wilmington, Del.; son of John Francis and Carrie E. (Taylor) Dale; married Magdalene Larsen (a writer), November 19, 1927. *Education:* Attended University of Delaware, 1923-25, 1926-27, A.B., 1927; attended Sorbonne, University of Paris, 1925-26; Columbia University, M.A., 1931; additional study at Institut de Phonetique, University of Paris, 1938. *Politics:* Independent. *Religion:* Protestant. *Home and office:* 1008 South Gulph Rd., Gulph Mills, Conshohocken, Pa. 19428.

CAREER: Teacher of French, Ardmore, Pa., 1929-62; writer of French textbooks, 1935—. *Member:* American Association of Teachers of French, Plays and Players (Philadelphia). *Awards, honors:* Travel fellowship, French government, 1947.

WRITINGS—All with wife, Magdalene L. Dale: (Editor, and author of notes) *La Poudre aux yeux*, Heath, 1935; (editor, and author of notes) *Tales of Adventure and Romance*, Heath, 1939; (editor, and author of notes) *Des Pas sur la neige*, Heath, 1940; *Cours elementaire de francais*, Heath, 1949, 3rd edition, 1964; *Cours moyen de francais*, Heath, 1950, 3rd edition, 1964; *Lectures Francaises*, Heath, 1971.

WORK IN PROGRESS: With wife, Magdalene L. Dale, *Cours superieur de francais.*

AVOCATIONAL INTERESTS: Travel, art, music, and the theater.

BIOGRAPHICAL/CRITICAL SOURCES: Norristown Times Herald, Norristown, Pa., November 11, 1961.†

*   *   *

DALE, Magdalene L(arsen) 1904-

PERSONAL: Born June 6, 1904, in Mohall, N.D.; daughter of Birgir and Hilda (Johnson) Larsen; married John B. Dale (a writer), November 19, 1927. *Education:* Attended University of Montana, 1922-25, A.B., 1926; attended University of Paris, 1925-26; Johns Hopkins University, graduate study, 1926-27; Columbia University, M.A., 1931; Institut de Phonetique, Paris, advanced study, 1938. *Politics:* Independent. *Religion:* Protestant. *Home:* 1008 South Gulph Rd., Gulph Mills, Conshohocken, Pa. 19428.

CAREER: University of Delaware, Newark, assistant in French, 1926-27; high school teacher of French in Upper Darby, Pa., 1927-43, and in Germantown Friends School, Philadelphia, Pa., 1943-54; writer of French textbooks for secondary schools, in collaboration with husband.

WRITINGS—All with husband John B. Dale: (Editor, and author of notes and exercises) *La Poudre aux yeux*, Heath, 1935; (editor, and author of notes) *Tales of Adventure and Romance*, Heath, 1939; (editor, and author of notes and exercises) *Des Pas sur la Neige*, Heath, 1940; *Cours elementaire de francais*, Heath, 1949, 3rd edition, Heath, 1964; *Cours moyen de francais*, Heath, 1950, 3rd edition, Heath, 1964; *Lectures Francaise*, Heath, 1971.

AVOCATIONAL INTERESTS: Travel, art, music, and the theater.

BIOGRAPHICAL/CRITICAL SOURCES: Norristown Times Herald, Norristown, Pa., November 11, 1961.†

*   *   *

DALY, Lowrie John 1914-

PERSONAL: Born July 11, 1914, in Omaha, Neb. *Education:* St. Louis University, A.B., 1938, M.A., 1942; St. Mary's College, St. Marys Kan., S.T.L., 1947; University of Toronto, Ph.D. 1949. *Office:* St. Louis University, St. Louis, Mo.

CAREER: Roman Catholic priest, member of Society of Jesus (Jesuit). St. Louis University, St. Louis, Mo., instructor, 1949-50, assistant professor, 1955-58, associate professor, 1958-63; professor of history, 1963—, director of microfilm projects, 1954—. Proposed and directed microfilming of large sections of the Vatican Library's manuscript resources under grant from Supreme Council of the Knights of Columbus; 1951-57.

WRITINGS: The Medieval University, Sheed, 1961; *Political Theory of John Wyclif*, Loyola University Press, 1962; *Benedictine Monasticism*, Sheed, 1965; (with Sister Mary Virgene Daly) *Meditations for Educators*, Sheed, 1965. Contributor to historical, library, and educational journals. Editor, *Manuscripta* (research periodical).

SIDELIGHTS: The microfilming project at the Vatican Library, authorized by Pope Pius XII, has made available to American scholars more than twelve million pages of rare manuscript materials.

*   *   *

DALZEL JOB, P(atrick) 1913-
(Peter Dalzel)

PERSONAL: Born June 1, 1913, in London, England; son of Ernest (an army officer) and Ethel Elizabeth (Griffiths) Dalzel Job; married Bjorg Bangsund, June 26, 1945; children: Iain. *Education:* Attended Berkhamstead School, 1924-27, and Le Pont, Vaud, Switzerland, 1927-30. *Religion:* Episcopalian Church of Scotland. *Home:* Nead-an-Eoin, by Plockton, Ross-shire, Scotland.

CAREER: Schooner master, 1934-39; Royal Navy and Royal Canadian Navy, reserve officer on continuous duty, 1939-55, becoming lieutenant commander; teacher in Sussex, Yorkshire, Scotland, 1956-63. On Special Services Operations during World War II landed alone by motor-torpedo boat in Norway to photograph enemy ships, and worked with armed jeeps behind enemy lines in France and Germany; parachutist. Leader of Duke of Edinburg's Award Scheme for Boys in southwest Ross-shire. *Member:*

P.E.N. *Awards, honors:* Knight's Cross (first class) of Royal Norwegian Order of St. Olav.

WRITINGS: (Under pseudonym Peter Dalzel) *The Settlers*, Constable, 1957. Contributor to *Blackwood's Magazine, Countryman, Animals,* and to travel, Scottish, young peoples', poetry, sports, and sea periodicals.

WORKS IN PROGRESS: An account of a sailing voyage to Arctic Russia.

SIDELIGHTS: Dalzel Job speaks Norwegian, French, and some German. *Avocational interests:* Outdoor activities, wildlife, youth training.

BIOGRAPHICAL/CRITICAL SOURCES: Theodor Broch, *The Mountains Wait*, M. Joseph, 1943.†

*　　*　　*

DANBY, Miles William 1925-

PERSONAL: Born May 23, 1925, in Eastbourne, Sussex, England; son of William Alfred (an officer, British Army) and Winifred (Sturrock) Danby; married Ilse Scharlow, April 8, 1948; children: Josephine Rose, Claudia Joan. *Education:* University College, London, Certificate in Architecture, 1951; Architectural Association School of Architecture, London, England, A.A. and A.R.I.B.A., 1953. *Home:* 6 Collingwood Ter., Jesmond, Newcastle upon Tyne 2, England. *Office:* School of Architecture, University of Newcastle upon Tyne, Newcastle upon Tyne NE1 7RV, England.

CAREER: Practicing architect with firms in London, England, 1953-56; Charles Pike & Partners, London, England, senior architect, 1956-59; Kwame Nkrumah University of Science and Technology, Kumasi, Ghana, lecturer, 1959-63, head of department of architecture, 1963-65; University of Khartoum, Khartoum, Sudan, professor of architecture, and head of department, 1965-70; University of Newcastle upon Tyne, Newcastle upon Tyne, England, professor of architecture, and director of project office, 1970—. Consultant to Volta River Authority, Kumasi City Council, British Council; also consultant in Sudan. *Military services:* Royal Air Force, 1943-47; became flight lieutenant-navigator. *Member:* Architectural Association (London), Ghana Society of Architects.

WRITINGS: Grammar of Architectural Design, Oxford University Press, 1963; (contributor) Robert Chambers, editor, *Volta Resettlement Experience*, Praeger, 1970; (contributor) Paul Oliver, editor, *Shelter in Africa*, Barrie & Jenkins, 1971, Praeger, 1972.

WORK IN PROGRESS: Preparing a Spanish edition of *Grammar of Architectural Design*, for Editorial Diana-Mexico; research into low-cost housing and vernacular architecture of West Africa; preparing a volume on housing in developing countries, with Ian Beuton, for Wiley.

*　　*　　*

DANELSKI, David J. 1930-

PERSONAL: Born October 29, 1930, in Green Bay, Wis.; son of Peter Anthony (a factory worker) and Magdalen (Piontek) Danelski; married Jill Parmer, June 12, 1954; children: Christine, Catherine, David M., Ann, Rebecca. *Education:* St. Norbert College, student, 1948-50; DePaul University, L.L.B., 1953; Seattle University, B.A., 1955; University of Chicago, M.A., 1957, Ph.D., 1961. *Politics:* Democrat. *Home:* 1220 Mecklenburg Rd., Ithaca, N.Y. 14850. *Office:* Department of Government, Cornell University, Ithaca, N.Y. 14850.

CAREER: Attorney in private practice, Mount Vernon, Wash., 1955-56; American Bar Foundation, Chicago, Ill., research attorney, 1957-60; University of Illinois, Urbana, 1959-61, began as instructor, became assistant professor; University of Washington, Seattle, 1961-64, began as assistant professor, became associate professor; Yale University, New Haven, Conn., 1964-70, began as lecturer, became an associate professor of political science; Cornell University, Ithaca, N.Y., 1970—, began as professor of government, became Goldwin Smith Professor of Government and university ombudsman. Counsel, American Civil Liberties Union of Washington, 1963-64. Fulbright lecturer, Tokyo University, 1968-69. *Military service:* U.S. Naval Reserve, 1953-55; general court-martial trial and defense counsel; became lieutenant junior grade. *Member:* American Political Science Association. *Awards, honors:* Guggenheim fellowship, 1968-69; E. Harris Harbison Prize for Gifted Teaching from Danforth Foundation, 1970; fellow of Center for Advanced Study in the Behavioral Sciences, Stanford University, 1971-72.

WRITINGS: A Supreme Court Justice is Appointed, Random House, 1964; (editor with Glendon Schubert) *Comparative Judicial Behavior*, Oxford University Press, 1969; (contributor) Joel Grossman and Joseph Tanenhaus, editors, *Frontiers of Judicial Research*, Wiley, 1969; (contributor) S. Sidney Ulmer, *Political Decision-Making*, Van Nostrand, 1970; (contributor) Theodore Becker, editor, *Political Trials*, Bobbs-Merrill, 1971; (editor with Joseph Tulchin) *The Autobiographical Notes of Charles Evans Hughes*, Harvard University Press, 1973; (contributor) J. Roland Pennock and John Chapman, editors, *The Limits of Law*, Atherton, 1974. Contributor to *American Political Science Review, Yale Review*, and other professional journals.

WORK IN PROGRESS: A book, *Judicial Behavior*; a book on the U.S. Supreme Court, tentatively entitled *Decision-Making in the Supreme Court*; a book on the Japanese Supreme Court.

*　　*　　*

DANI, Ahmad Hasan 1920-

PERSONAL: Born June 20, 1920, in Basna, Raipur, Madhya Pradesh, India; son of Ghulam Nabi (a landlord) and Sharif (Begam) Dani; married Safiya Sultana, August 1, 1949; children: Fauziva Sultana (daughter), Anis Ahmad, Nawed Ahmad, and Junaid Ahmad (sons). *Education:* Nagpur University, B.A., 1942; Banaras Hindu University, M.A., 1944; Institute of Archaeology, London, Ph.D., 1955. *Religion:* Islam. *Home:* No. 298 Shalimar 8/3, Islamabad, Pakistan. *Office:* Dean, Faculty of Social Sciences, University of Islamabad, Pakistan.

CAREER: Government of India, assistant superintendent of Department of Archaeology, 1946-47; government of Pakistan, superintendent of Department of Archaeology, 1948-50; University of Dacca, Ramna, East Pakistan, reader in history and curator of Dacca Museum, 1960-62; University of Peshawar, Peshawar, West Pakistan, professor of archaeology and chairman of department, 1962-71; University of Islamabad, Islamabad, Pakistan, professor of history, 1972—. Research associate, University of London, School of Oriental and African Studies, 1958-59; Asian fellow, Australian National University, 1969. *Member:* Asiatic Society of Pakistan (fellow; secretary, 1951-53, 1955-58, 1960-61), Pakistan History Conference (president, 1961).

WRITINGS: Dacca: A Record of Its Changing Fortunes, privately printed, 1956, 2nd edition, 1962; Bibliography of the Muslim Inscriptions of Bengal, Asiatic Society of Pakistan, 1957; Prehistory and Protohistory of Eastern India, K. L. Mufchopadhyay, 1960; Muslim Architecture in Bengal, Asiatic Society of Pakistan; Indian Palaeography, Oxford University Press, 1963; Peshawar: The Historic City of the Frontier, Khyber Mail Press (Peshawar), 1969; Alberuni's Indica, University of Islamabad Press, 1973. Editor, Ancient Pakistan (bulletin of Department of Archaeology, University of Peshawar).

WORK IN PROGRESS: A book on the history of Pakistan.

SIDELIGHTS: Dani has a grounding in the Indo-European group of languages, with the main base being Sanskrit.

* * *

DANIEL, George Bernard, Jr. 1927-

Personal: Born May 17, 1927, in Franklin, Ga.; son of George B. (a farmer) and Corine (Adams) Daniel; married Elizabeth Rezner (a teacher at North Carolina Central University), August 23, 1958; children: Elizabeth, Thomas. Education: Attended University of Georgia, 1944-45, West Georgia College, 1946-47; Emory University, A.B., 1949, A.M., 1950; Sorbonne, University of Paris, Diplome de litterature contemporaine, 1953; University of North Carolina, Ph.D., 1959. Politics: Democrat. Religion: Methodist. Home: 2 Gooseneck Rd., Chapel Hill, N.C. Office: Department of Romance Languages, University of North Carolina, Chapel Hill, N.C.

CAREER: Berea College, Berea, Ky., instructor, 1950-53, assistant professor of French, 1953-55; University of North Carolina, Chapel Hill, instructor, 1957-60, assistant professor, 1960-63, associate professor, 1963-69, professor of French, 1969—. Military service: U.S. Navy, 1945-46. Member: American Association of Teachers of French (director of placement bureau, 1961-69), Modern Language Association of America, South Atlantic Modern Language Association, Hillsborough Historical Society, Alliance Francaise of Chapel Hill (president, 1965-67).

WRITINGS: (Editor with Jacques Hardre) Jean-Paul Sartre, Huis clos, Appleton, 1962; The Development of the Tragedie Nationale in France, 1580-1800, University of North Carolina Press, 1963; (editor with Hardre) Albert Camus, Le Malentendu, Macmillan, 1963; (editor) Jean Racine, Phedre [and] Britannicus, Dell, 1963; (editor with Robert Linker) Contes de plusieurs siecles, Odyssey, 1964; (editor) Renaissance and Other Studies, University of North Carolina Press, 1968; (editor) Moliere Studies, [Madrid], 1974. Contributor of articles on Proust, Corneille, Moliere, and Honore d'Urfe to journals in his field. Editor, Romance Notes.

WORK IN PROGRESS: A study of the works of Jean de la Fontaine, for Twayne.

* * *

DANIELS, John Clifford 1915-

PERSONAL: Born November 29, 1915, in Newcastle under Lyme, England; son of William Henry and Elizabeth (Scragg) Daniels; married Sylvia Genders, September 28, 1940 (deceased); children: John Sebastian, Stefan David. Education: University of Durham, B.Sc., M.Ed., Ph.D. Home: 16 Greendale Gardens, Aspley, Nottingham, England. Office: The University, Nottingham, England.

CAREER: Physics teacher in grammar schools in England, 1945-48; University of Nottingham, Institute of Education, Nottingham, England, 1948—, now senior tutor. Delegate to UNESCO conferences; lecturer in Germany. Military service: British Army, 1941-45. Associate of British Psychological Society.

WRITINGS: Handbook of Text Construction, Crosby Lockwood & Son, 1949; (with Hunter Diack) Royal Road Readers, Chatto & Windus, 1954; (with Diack) Progress in Reading, Institute of Education, University of Nottingham, 1956; (with Diack) Standard Reading Tests, Chatto & Windus, 1958; (with Diack) Progress in the Infant School, Institute of Education, University of Nottingham, 1960; (with Diack and E. C. Walcott) Your Child's Reading, 1963; (editor) Reading: Problems and Perspectives, United Kingdom Reading Association, 1970. Also author with Diack of Tommorow's Illiterates, edited by Walcott. Author of reading booklets. Contributor to Schoolmaster, Times Educational Supplement, Forward Trends, other journals.

WORK IN PROGRESS: Grouping in Schools, and Programmed Reading Instruction.†

* * *

DANILOV, Victor J(oseph) 1924-

PERSONAL: Born December 30, 1924, in Farrell, Pa.; son of Joseph M. and Ella (Tominovich) Danilov; married Carolyn A. Klockner, 1950; children: Duane, Denise, David. Education: Pennsylvania State University, B.A., 1945; Northwestern University, M.S., 1946; University of Colorado, Ed.D., 1964. Residence: Michigan City, Ind. 46360. Office: Museum of Science and Industry, 57th St. and Lake Shore Dr., Chicago, Ill. 60637.

CAREER: Worked for newspapers in Sharon, Pa., Youngstown, Ohio, and Pittsburgh, Pa., 1943-47; Chicago Daily News, Chicago, Ill., reporter, rewriteman, 1947-50; University of Colorado, Boulder, instructor in journalism, 1950-51; University of Kansas, Lawrence, assistant professor of journalism, 1951-53; Star, Kansas City, Mo., copyreader, 1953; Illinois Institute of Technology and Armour Research Foundation, Chicago, Ill., public relations manager, 1953-57; University of Colorado, director of public information and university relations, 1957-60; Profile Co., Boulder, Colo., president, 1960-62; Industrial Research, Beverly Shores, Ind., executive editor and executive vice-president, 1962-71; Museum of Science and Industry, Chicago, Ill., director and vice-president, 1971—.

WRITINGS: Public Affairs Reporting, Macmillan, 1955; (editor) Crucial Issues in Public Relations, Colorado Chapter of Public Relations Society of America, 1960; (editor) Corporate Research and Profitability, Industrial Research, 1966; (editor) Innovation and Profitability, Industrial Research, 1967; (editor) Research Decision-Making in New Product Development, Industrial Research, 1968; (editor) New Products–and Profits, Industrial Research, 1969; (editor) Applying Emerging Technologies, Industrial Research, 1970; (editor) Nuclear Power in the South, Southern Governors' Conference, 1970. Contributor of more than one hundred articles to professional journals.

* * *

DANKER, Frederick William 1920-

PERSONAL: Born July 12, 1920, in Frankenmuth, Mich.; son of William John and Wilhelmina (Classen) Danker;

married Lois R. Dreyer, June 2, 1948; children: Kathleen Lois, James Paul Frederick. *Education:* Concordia College, Milwaukee, Wis., student, 1936-40; Concordia Seminary, student, 1940-45, B.D., 1950; University of Chicago, Ph.D., 1963; attended Washington University, 1955-56. *Home and office;* 6928 Plateau Ave., St. Louis, Mo. 63139.

CAREER: Ordained Lutheran minister, 1945. Pastor of churches in Warrenville, Ill., 1946-47, and Merritt Township, Mich., 1948-54; Concordia Seminary, St. Louis, Mo., assistant professor, 1954-60, associate professor, 1960-68, professor of exegetical theology, New Testament, 1968-74; Seminex, St. Louis, Mo., professor of exegetical theology, 1974—. *Member:* American Philological Association, American Oriental Society, Archaeological Institute of America, Society of Biblical Literature, Lutheran Academy for Scholarship, Studiorum Novi Testamenti Societas.

WRITINGS: Multipurpose Tools for Bible Study, Concordia, 1960, 3rd revised edition, 1970; *The Kingdom in Action,* Concordia, 1965; *Jesus and the New Age According to St. Luke: A Commentary on the Third Gospel,* Clayton Publishing House, 1972.

WORK IN PROGRESS: Editing, with F. Wilbur Gingrich, a revision of Arndt-Gingrich, *A Greek-English Lexicon of the New Testament,* for publication by University of Chicago Press and Cambridge University Press.

* * *

DANKER, W(illiam) John 1914-

PERSONAL: Born June 19, 1914, in Willow Creek, Minn.; son of William Julius and Elmi (Classen) Danker; married Elizabeth Miller, June 16, 1942; children: Elizabeth Marie, William John, Deborah Jean. *Education:* Concordia College, Milwaukee, Wis., diploma (summa cum laude), 1933; Concordia Seminary, B.A., 1937; Wheaton College, Wheaton, Ill., M.A., 1948; University of Chicago Divinity School, graduate study, 1955-57. *Home:* 14 Seminary Ter., St. Louis, Mo. 63105.

CAREER: Ordained Lutheran minister, 1937; pastor of churches in Harvard, Ill., 1937-42, and West Chicago, Ill., 1942-48; Lutheran Church-Missouri Synod, founder and chairman of Japan Mission, 1948-56; Concordia Seminary, St. Louis, Mo., director of missionary training program, and professor of missions, 1956—. Wheatridge Foundation, member of board. Lutheran Church-Missouri Synod, adviser, Board of Missions. *Member:* Association of Professors of Missions, All-Lutheran Free Conference of Japan, Lutheran Literature Society of Japan (board member), Midwest Fellowship of Professors of Missions (president, 1963-64).

WRITINGS: Two Worlds or None, Concordia, 1964; (contributor) *Moving Frontiers,* Concordia, 1964; (contributor) *Toward a More Excellent Ministry,* Concordia, 1964; *Profit for the Lord: Economic Activities in Moravian Missions and the Basel Mission Trading Company,* Eerdmans, 1971; (co-editor) *The Future of the Christian World Mission,* Eerdmans, 1971; (with Kiyoko Matsuda) *More Than Healing: The Story of Kiyoko Matsuda,* Concordia, 1973. Editor, "Witnessing Church Series," Concordia, 1962—. Contributor to *Christian Century* and Lutheran periodicals.

WORK IN PROGRESS: Mission and Mammon, a study of the economic basis of the Christian world mission.

SIDELIGHTS: Danker is competent in German and Japanese. He has been around the world twice.†

d'ARCH SMITH, Timothy 1936-

PERSONAL: Born October 15, 1936, in Farnborough, England; son of Charles Harry and Ursula (Frankau) d'Arch Smith. *Education:* Attended Cheltenham College, Cheltenham, England, 1950-54. *Home:* 64a St. John's Wood High St., London N.W.8, England.

CAREER: Dealer in rare books and manuscripts, London, England, 1961—. *Military service:* British Army, Intelligence Corps, Russian translator, 1955-57. *Member:* Society of Psychical Research, Bibliographical Society, Arthur Machen Society.

WRITINGS: (Published anonymously) *English Private Presses, 1757-1961,* Times Bookshop, 1961; (published anonymously) *John Drinkwater: Catalogue of His First Editions,* Times Bookshop, 1962; *A Bibliography of the Works of Montague Summers,* Vane, 1964; *Love in Earnest: Some Notes on the Lives and Writings of English Uranian Poets from 1889 to 1930,* Routledge & Kegan Paul, 1970.

WORK IN PROGRESS: With Cecil Woolf, *A Bibliography of Aleister Crowley.*

* * *

DAS, Manmath Nath 1929-

PERSONAL: Born January 5, 1926, in Balasore, India; son of Madhu Sudan and Kadambini (Samal) Das; married Rajasri, 1944; children: Sanghamitra (daughter), Siddhartha (son). *Education:* Ravenshaw College, B.A. (honors), 1946; Allahabad University, M.A., 1948; University of London, Ph.D., 1956. *Home:* Sankhari, District Balasore, Orissa, India. *Office:* History Department, Utkal University, Bhubaneswar, Orissa, India.

CAREER: F. M. College, Balasore, India, lecturer, 1948-53; S.C.S. College, Puri, India, lecturer, 1953-54; Ravenshaw College, Cuttack, India, reader, 1957-59; School of Oriental and African Studies, University of London, London, England, research associate, 1960-61; Utkal University, Bhubaneswar, Orissa, India, professor and head of department, 1961—. Government of India, member of advisory board for archaeology. Member of Indian History Congress, Indian Council of World Affairs, and of advisory council of Institute of Historical Studies, Calcutta.

WRITINGS: Glimpses of Kalinga History, Century (Calcutta), 1949; *The Substance Behind India's New Constitution,* Orissa (Balasore), 1951; *Economic and Social Development of Modern India: 1848-56,* K. L. Mukhopadhyay, 1959; *Political Philosophy of Jawajarlal Nehru,* Day, 1961; *India Under Morley and Minto,* Hillary, 1964; *Keep the Story Secret,* Vidyapuri, 1968; *Laws Relating to Partition,* Eastern Law House (Calcutta), 1972. Contributor of research papers to journals.†

* * *

DAVID, Henry P. 1923-

PERSONAL: Born May 28, 1923, in Germany; now U.S. citizen; son of Ferdinand (a lawyer) and Ilse David; married Tema Seidman, March 28, 1953; children: Jonathan V., Gail Ann. *Education:* University of Cincinnati, B.A. (high honors in psychology), 1948, M.A., 1949; Columbia University, Ph.D., 1951. *Office:* Transnational Family Research Institute, American Institutes for Research, 8555 16th St., Silver Spring, Md. 20910.

CAREER: Diplomate in clinical psychology, American

Board of Examiners in Professional Psychology, 1956. Topeka State Hospital, Topeka, Kan., senior clinical psychologist, 1951-52; University of Pittsburgh School of Medicine, Pittsburgh, Pa., instructor in psychiatry department of Western Psychiatric Institute, 1952-55; Wayne State University, Detroit, Mich., assistant professor, and head of division of psychology at Lafayette Clinic, 1955-56; New Jersey State Department of Institutions and Agencies, Trenton, chief psychologist and psychology consultant, 1956-63; World Federation for Mental Health, Geneva, Switzerland, associate director, 1963-65; American Institutes for Research, Silver Spring, Md., associate director of International Research Institute, 1966-70, director of Transnational Family Research Institute, 1970—. Adjunct lecturer, Rutgers University, 1960-63; lecturer, Princeton University, 1962; associate clinical professor of psychology in department of psychiatry, University of Maryland School of Medicine, 1971—. Research advisor, Preterm Institute, 1971—; occasional consultant to World Health Organization, 1971—; consultant to American Psychiatric Association, 1973—. Secretary-treasurer, New Jersey Mental Health Research and Development Fund, 1958-63. *Military service:* U.S. Army Air Forces, 1943-46.

MEMBER: International Council of Psychologists (president, 1967-71, 1973—), International Association of Applied Psychology, International Union for Scientific Study of Population, International Association for Cross-Cultural Psychology, World Federation for Mental Health (member of executive board, 1968-73), Society for International Development, Inter-American Society for Psychology, American Psychological Association (fellow), American Association for the Advancement of Science, Population Association of America, Society for Projective Techniques, District of Columbia Psychological Association, Maryland Psychological Association, Phi Beta Kappa, Sigma Xi. *Awards, honors:* Ford Foundation travel grant to western Europe and Israel, 1957; Social Science Research Council travel grants to western Europe and South Africa, 1961; Human Ecology Fund grant for projects on international resources in clinical psychology and international trends in mental health, 1962.

WRITINGS: Family Planning and Abortion in the Socialist Countries of Central and Eastern Europe, Population Council (New York), 1970; (with Siegfried Katsch) *Sousa, verheissenes Land,* Sozial Forschungsstelle, University of Muenster, 1970; (contributor) L. Miller, editor, *Mental Health in Rapid Changing Society,* Jerusalem Academic Press, 1971; (contributor) C. F. Westoff and R. Parke, Jr., editors, *Demographic and Social Aspects of Population Growth,* U.S. Government Printing Office, 1972; (contributor) J. T. Fawcett, editor, *Psychological Perspectives on Population,* Basic Books, 1973; (contributor) H. J. Osofsky and J. D. Osofsky, editors, *The Abortion Experience: Psychological and Medical Impact,* Harper. 1973.

Editor: (With H. von Braclaen) *Perspectives in Personality Theory,* Basic Books, 1956; (with J. C. Brengelmann) *Perspectives in Personality Research,* Springer, 1960; *International Resources in Clinical Psychology,* McGraw, 1964; (with Leonard Blank) *Sourcebook for Training in Clinical Psychology,* Springer, 1964; *Population and Mental Health,* Springer, 1964; *International Trends in Mental Health,* McGraw, 1966; *Migration, Mental Health, and Community Services,* Joint Distribution Committee (Geneva), 1968; *Child Mental Health in International Perspective,* Harper, 1972.

Author or co-author of more than sixty papers published in scientific journals. Consultant, *Contemporary Psychology,* 1963—, *Progress in Clinical Psychology,* 1963—, *International Journal of Psychiatry,* 1965—, *The Professional Psychologist,* 1969—, *Journal of Psychiatric Nursing,* 1966—, *Community Mental Health Journal,* 1966—, and *Journal of Nervous and Mental Disease,* 1970—.

*   *   *

DAVIDSON, Paul 1930-

PERSONAL: Born October 23, 1930, in Brooklyn, N.Y.; son of Charles and Lillian (Janow) Davidson; married Louise Tattenbaum, 1952; children: Robert Alan, Diane Carol, Greg Stuart. *Education:* Brooklyn College (now Brooklyn College of the City University of New York), B.S., 1950; City College (now City College of the City University of New York), M.B.A., 1955; University of Pennsylvania, Ph.D., 1959. *Home:* 18 Turner Ct., Princeton, N.J. *Office:* Department of Economics, Rutgers University, New Brunswick, N.J.

CAREER: University of Pennsylvania, Philadelphia, instructor in economics, 1955-58; Rutgers University, New Brunswick, N.J., assistant professor of economics, 1958-60; Continental Oil Co., Houston, Tex., assistant director economics division, 1960-61; University of Pennsylvania, associate professor of economics, 1961-66; Rutgers University, New Brunswick, N.J., professor of economics and associate director of Bureau of Economic Research, 1966—. Visitng lecturer, University of Bristol, 1964-65; senior visiting lecturer, Cambridge University, 1970-71. *Military service:* U.S. Army, 1953-55. *Member:* American Economic Association, Econometric Society, National Association of Business Economists, Royal Economic Society, Epsilon Phi Alpha.

WRITINGS: Theories of Aggregate Income Distribution, Rutgers University Press, 1960; (with Eugene Smolensky) *Aggregate Supply and Demand Analysis,* Harper, 1964; (with C. J. Chiccetti and J. J. Seneca) *The Demand and Supply of Outdoor Recreation: An Econometric Study,* U.S. Department of Interior, 1968; *Money and the Real World,* Macmillan, 1972. Contributor to economic and public finance journals.

*   *   *

DAVIES, Alfred T(homas) 1930-

PERSONAL: Born February 5, 1930, in New York, N.Y.; son of Alfred Mervyn (a writer) and Monica (Borglum) Davies; married Wylene Young, June 11, 1955; children: Mervyn, Allyson. *Education:* Kenyon College, student, 1948-49; Davidson College, A.B., 1952; Princeton Theological School, B.D., 1955; Oxford University, Diploma in Theology, 1958. *Politics:* Democrat. *Home and office:* 3250 Leap Rd., Hilliard, Ohio.

CAREER: Ordained Presbyterian minister, 1955. Pastor, Northview Church, Columbus, Ohio, 1955-58, and in Hilliard, Ohio, 1959—.

WRITINGS: (Editor) *The Pulpit Speaks on Race,* Abingdon, 1965. Contributor to *Pulpit Digest, Monday Morning, Christian Century,* and *Survey.*†

*   *   *

DAVIES, (William Thomas) Pennar 1911-

PERSONAL: Born November 12, 1911, in Aberpennar, Wales; son of Joseph (a coal miner) and Edith Annie

(Moss) Davies; married Rosemarie Wolff (a German refugee), June 26, 1943; children: Meirion, Rhiannon (daughter), Geraint, Hywel, Owain. *Education:* University College of South Wales and Monmouthshire, University of Wales, B.A., 1932; Balliol College, Oxford, B. Litt., 1938; Mansfield College, Oxford, graduate study, 1940-43; Yale University, Ph.D., 1944. *Politics:* Plaid Cymru. *Religion:* Christian. *Home:* Llwyn Helyg, Ffynhonnau, Swansea, Wales. *Office:* Coleg Coffa, Ffynhonnau, Swansea, Wales.

CAREER: Minster Road Congregational Church, Cardiff, Wales, pastor, 1943-46; Bala-Bangor and University College, Bangor, Wales, professor of theology, 1946-50; Coleg Coffa (theological college), Swansea Wales, professor of church history, 1950—, principal, 1952—. Plain Cymru (Welsh Home Rule Party), candidate in general election, 1964. President, Free Church Council of Wales, 1963-69. *Member:* Welsh Academy.

WRITINGS: Cinio'r Cythraul (poems), Gee & Co., 1946; *Mansfield College*, Mansfield College, 1947; *Geiriau'r Iesu,* John Penry, 1951; *Y Ddau Gleddyf,* Brython Press, 1951; *Naw Wfft* (poems), Gee & Co., 1957; *Cudd fy Meiau* (diary), John Penry, 1957; *Anadl O'r Uchelder* (novel), John Penry, 1958; *John Penry,* Independent Press, 1961; *Yr Efrydd o Lyn Cynon* (poems), Llyfrau'r Dryw, 1961; *Rhwng Chwedl a Chredo,* University of Wales Press, 1966; *Caregl Nwyf* (stories), Llyfrau'r Dryw, 1967; *Meibion Darogan* (novel), Llyfrau'r Dryw, 1968; *Y Tlws Yn Y Lotws* (poems), Llyfrau'r Dryw, 1971; *Y Brenin in Alltud* (theology), Christopher Davies, 1974.

Editor and contributor; *Ap,* Plaid Cymru, 1945; *Look You,* Plaid Cymru, 1947; *Saunders Lewis,* Gee & Co., 1950; *Rhyddid ac Undeb,* Gomer, 1963; *Athrawon ac Annibynwyr,* John Penry, 1971. Contributor of studies to *Oxford Bibliographical Society Transactions,* 1939, and *Brycheiniog,* 1957; contributor to collections of poems, stories, studies, and essays in Welsh and English. Contributor to periodicals.

WORK IN PROGRESS: A volume of short stories; critical studies; a novel.

SIDELIGHTS: Davies said: "spent the years 1936-38 in the United States; there I met Haniel Long, with whom I remained friendly until he died. In 1939 I made an unsuccessful attempt to get Dylan Thomas and some other 'Anglo-Welsh' writers to take an interest in Wales as a living people rather than as a region providing them with romantic 'background.' In the early years of the Second World War I belonged to a small circle of writers sometimes called the 'Cadwgan' group, which rebelled against certain conventions and treated fleshly themes with zest...."

* * *

DAVIS, Arthur G. 1915-

PERSONAL: Born July 17, 1915, in New York, N.Y.; son of Henry L. (a court stenographer) and Margaret (Ryall) Davis; married Gisela Niemeier (a teacher), April 14, 1952; children: Arthur G., Paul C., Giselle Marie. *Education:* University of Notre Dame, B.A., 1939; St. John's University, Jamaica, N.Y., M.S., 1949. *Religion:* Roman Catholic. *Office:* St. John's University, Jamaica, N.Y.

CAREER: St. John's University, Jamaica, N.Y., assistant professor of English, 1949—. *Military service:* U.S. Army, 1942-46; became staff sergeant. *Member:* American Association of University Professors, Veterans of Foreign Wars.

WRITINGS: Hamlet and the Eternal Problem of Man, St. John's University Press, 1964; *The Royalty of Lear,* St. John's University Press, 1974.

WORK IN PROGRESS: Merry Jack Falstaff, Tentative title, completion expected in 1975.

* * *

DAVIS, Fred 1925-

PERSONAL: Born May 12, 1925, in New York, N.Y.; son of Samuel (a proprietor of a small business) and Bessie (Seltzer) Davis; married Marcella Zaleski (a university teacher), August 28, 1955; children: Philip M. *Education:* Brooklyn College (now Brooklyn College of the City University of New York), student, 1941-43; University of Chicago, M.A., 1951, Ph.D., 1958. *Politics:* Democrat. *Home:* 73A Cervantes Blvd., San Francisco, Calif. *Office:* School of Nursing, University of California Medical Center, San Francisco, Calif. 94143.

CAREER: U.S. Air Force, Human Relations Research Institute, Montgomery, Ala., project officer, 1951-53; University of Maryland, Psychiatric Institute, Baltimore, research associate, 1953-57; Jewish Family Service, New York, N.Y., associate research director, 1957-59; Association for the Aid of Crippled Children, New York, N.Y., research fellow, 1959-60; University of California, Medical Center, San Francisco, associate research sociologist, 1960-66, associate professor, 1966-68, professor, 1968—. *Military service:* U.S. Army, 1943-46; received Purple Heart and Bronze Star. *Member:* American Sociological Association (secretary-treasurer of section on social psychology, 1961-64), Society for the Study of Social Problems.

WRITINGS: Passage Through Crisis: Polio Victims and Their Families, Bobbs-Merrill, 1963; *The Nursing Profession,* Wiley, 1966; *Illness, Interaction, and the Self,* Wadsworth, 1972. Contributor to *American Journal of Sociology, Social Problems,* other sociology journals.

* * *

DAVIS, Kenneth S. 1912-

PERSONAL: Born September 29, 1912, in Salina, Kan.; son of Charles Deforest (a college professor) and Lydia (Ericson) Davis; married Florence Olenhouse (an artist and gift shop owner), February 19, 1938. *Education:* Kansas State University of Agriculture and Applied Science (now Kansas State University), B.S., 1934; University of Wisconsin, M.S., 1935. *Home:* Hubbardston Rd., Princeton, Mass. *Agent:* Paul R. Reynolds, Inc., 599 Fifth Ave., New York, N.Y. 10017.

CAREER: Topeka Daily Capital, Topeka, Kan., reporter, 1934; U.S. Soil Conservation Service, information specialist in La Crosse, Wis., Des Moines, Iowa, and Milwaukee, Wis., 1936-42; war correspondent in London and Normandy, 1945; New York University, New York, N.Y., instructor in journalism, 1945-47; U.S. Commission for UNESCO, public relations assistant to chairman, 1947-49; Kansas State University of Agriculture and Applied Science (now Kansas State University), Manhattan, part-time editor, 1949-51; full-time writer, 1951—. Consultant, Worcester Public Library, 1963—. *Awards, honors:* Friends of American Writers Award, 1943, for *In the Forests of the Night;* honorable mention, Thormod Monsen Award of Society of Midland Authors, 1960, for *The Hero;* Centennial Award for distinguished service, Kansas State

University, 1963; doctor of letters, Assumption College, 1968; Francis Parkman Prize, Society of American Historians, 1973, for *FDR: The Beckoning of Destiny*.

WRITINGS: In the Forests of the Night (novel), Houghton, 1943; *Soldier of Democracy: A Biography of Dwight Eisenhower*, Doubleday, 1945; *The Years of the Pilgrimage* (novel), Doubleday, 1948; *Morning in Kansas* (novel), Doubleday, 1952; *River on the Rampage* (nonfiction), Doubleday, 1953; *A Prophet in His Own Country: The Triumphs and Defeats of Adlai E. Stevenson*, Doubleday, 1957, expanded and updated edition published as *The Politics of Honor: A Biography of Adlai Stevenson*, Putnam, 1967; *The Hero: Charles A. Lindbergh and the American Dream*, Doubleday, 1959.

(With John A. Day) *Water, the Mirror of Science*, Anchor Books, 1961; *Experience of War: The United States in World War II*, Doubleday, 1965 (published in England as *The American Experience of War, 1939-1945*, Secker & Warburg, 1967); *The Cautionary Scientists*, Putnam, 1966; *Eisenhower: American Hero*, American Heritage Press, 1969; *FDR: The Beckoning of Destiny*, Putnam, 1972; (author of text) *The Eisenhower College Collection: The Paintings of Dwight D. Eisenhower*, Nash Publishing, 1973; *Invincible Summer: An Intimate Portrait of the Roosevelts*, Atheneum, 1974.

WORK IN PROGRESS: The second volume of the biography of Franklin D. Roosevelt, *FDR: The Years of Destiny*.

SIDELIGHTS: Alan Moorehead describes *The American Experience of War, 1939-1945* as a "splendid compendium of the total United States war effort from 1939 to 1945. . . . There can be few sources of first-hand experience which have not been traced, meticulously examined, connected up and thoughtfully integrated into this well-rounded work."

The Politics of Honor: A Biography of Adlai E. Stevenson has also been generally praised. Stuart Gerry Brown finds it "the fullest and most reliable study of Stevenson. It is a richly textured book based on documents, many interviews, and personal knowledge." There has, however, been some disagreement over Davis's approach in his biography. Herbert J. Spiro explains that "Mr. Davis, journalist, one-time speech writer for Governor Stevenson, and author of an Eisenhower biography is . . . detached from and critical of his subject." Eliot Fremont-Smith partially agrees, noting, "acute perceptions do shine through, and also criticism," but he qualifies his assessent of the work with the comments that it suffers "from love" and is "notably protective." Henrietta Buckmaster, however, views this aspect of the book more positively: "Mr. Davis writes in exhaustive and loving detail. His approach is touched with sentiment which is by no means unattractive."

*   *   *

DAVIS, Kingsley 1908-

PERSONAL: Born August 20, 1908, in Tuxedo, Tex.; son of Joseph Dier (a physician) and Winifred (Kingsley) Davis; married second wife, Judith Blake, November 4, 1954; children: (previous marriage) Jo Ann (Mrs. Charles Daily), Jefferson K.; (present marriage) Laura Isabelle. *Education:* University of Texas, A.B., 1930, M.A., 1932; Harvard University, M.A., 1933, Ph.D., 1936. *Home:* 7 Selbourne Dr., Piedmont, Calif. 94611. *Office:* University of California, 2234 Piedmont Ave., Berkeley, Calif. 94520.

CAREER: Smith College, Northampton, Mass., instructor in sociology, 1934-36; Clark University, Worcester, Mass., assistant professor of sociology, 1936-37; The Pennsylvania State University, University Park, associate professor of sociology and chairman of department, 1937-42; Princeton University, Princeton, N.J., associate professor of anthropology and sociology, 1942-48; Columbia University, New York, director of Bureau of Applied Social Research, 1949-55, professor of sociology, 1952-55; University of California, Berkeley, professor of sociology, 1955-71, Ford Professor of Sociology and Comparative Studies, 1971—, director of international population and urban research, 1957-71, chairman of department, 1961-63. Consultant on population studies, Conservation Foundation, 1951-54; vice-president of Population Reference Bureau, 1952-55, trustee, 1952—; U.S. representative, United Nations Population Commission, 1954-61. Member of National Committee on Marriage and Divorce Law, American Bar Association, 1950-53, of U.S. Ad Hoc Committee on the International Biological Program, 1963-64, and of Committee on the Sonic Boom, American Academy of Arts and Sciences, 1964-65; National Research Council, Behavioral Science Division, member, 1963—, chairman, 1966-68.

MEMBER: International Statistical Institute, International Union for the Scientific Study of Population, American Sociological Association (president, 1959), Sociological Research Association (president, 1960), Population Association of America (president, 1962-63), American Association for the Advancement of Science (fellow; vice-president and chairman of section K, 1963), American Academy of Arts and Sciences, American Statistical Association (fellow; council member, 1968-69), American Philosophical Society, National Academy of Sciences (council member, 1970-73), Inter-American Statistical Institute, American Eugenics Society, American Association of University Professors (council member, 1962-64), Regional Science Association. *Awards, honors:* Post-doctoral fellow, Social Science Research Council, 1940-41; fellow, Center for Advanced Study in the Behavioral Sciences, 1956-57; senior postdoctoral fellow, National Science Foundation, 1964-65.

WRITINGS: (Editor) *World Population in Transition*, American Academy of Political and Social Science, 1945; *Human Society*, Macmillan, 1949, reprinted, 1967; (editor with Marion J. Levy, Jr. and Harry C. Bredeneuer) *Modern American Society*, Henry Holt, 1949; *Population of India and Pakistan*, Princeton University Press, 1951; (editor) *A Crowding Hemisphere: Population Change in the Americas*, American Academy of Political and Social Science, 1958; (with others) *The World's Metropolitan Areas*, University of California Press, 1959.

(With Roy Turner, Richard L. Park, and Catherine Bauer Wurster) *India's Urban Future*, University of California Press, 1962; *World Urbanization, 1950-70*, Institute of International Studies, University of California, Volume I: *Basic Data for Cities, Countries, and Regions*, 1969, Volume II: *Analysis of Trends, Relationships, and Development*, 1972; (editor with Frederick Styles) *California's Twenty Million: Research Contributions to Population Policy*, Institute of International Studies, University of California, 1971; (compiler and author of introduction) *Cities: Their Origin, Growth, and Human Impact, Readings from Scientific American*, W. H. Freeman, 1973.

Also author of population studies and sociology papers. Contributor to professional journals.

SIDELIGHTS: Davis headed social science team sent by

Carnegie Corp. to ten countries in Africa and has made other social studies in India, Europe, and Latin America. He speaks Spanish and French, has some acquaintance with Russian, German, and Portuguese.

BIOGRAPHICAL/CRITICAL SOURCES: American Sociological Review, Volume XVIII, August, 1953; Charles P. and Zona K. Loomis, *Modern Social Theories: Selected American Writers*, Van Nostrand, 2nd edition, 1965.

* * *

DAVIS, Lois Carlile 1921-
(Lois Lamplugh)

PERSONAL: Surname is pronounced Lamploo; born June 9, 1921, in Barnstaple, Devonshire, England; daughter of Aubrey Penfound and Ruth (Lister) Lamplugh; married Lawrence Carlile Davis (a sales representative), September 24, 1955; children: Susan Ruth, Hugh Lawrence. *Education:* Educated privately in England. *Home:* Elmhurst, Crellow Lane, Stithians, near Truro, Cornwall, England. *Agent:* A.P. Watt & Son, Hastings House, Norfolk St., Strand, London W.C. 2, England.

CAREER: Formerly on editorial staff of Jonathan Cape Ltd., London, England; author of books for young people. Served in Auxiliary Territorial Service, World War II. *Member:* P.E.N., West Country Writers' Association.

WRITINGS—All juveniles except where indicated; under name Lois Lamplugh: *The Stream Way* (adult), Golden Galley Press, 1949; *The Pigeongram Puzzle*, J. Cape, 1955; *Nine Bright Shiners*, J. Cape, 1955; *Vagabonds' Castle*, J. Cape, 1957; *Rockets in the Dunes*, J. Cape, 1958; *The Sixpenny Runner*, J. Cape, 1960; *Midsummer Mountains*, J. Cape, 1961; *The Rifle House Friends*, Deutsch, 1965; *The Linhay on Hunter's Hill*, Deutsch, 1966; *The Fur Princess and the Fir Prince*, Dent, 1969.

WORK IN PROGRESS: Collecting material for a biography of W. N. P. Barbellion (Bruce Cummings); a book about living in Cornwall (as a newcomer to that section of England).

SIDELIGHTS: Mrs. Davis told *CA*: "It is possible that I became a writer simply because I happened to spend the first eighteen years of my life in or near the village of Georgeham [where] in the 1920's Henry Williamson was living—for part of the time in a cottage he rented from my grandmother. (He wrote most, if not all, of *Tarka the Otter* in that cottage)."

A country child, she still prefers country living, adding "for all that, I wrote my first children's books when I was living and working in London—perhaps a form of escape, since they were set in North Devon." She wrote a great deal of unpublished work, mainly novels and verse, in her teens, and had a book accepted for publication by Faber in 1942. It was an account of her experiences in the Auxiliary Territorial Service and the War Office withheld approval of publication on the grounds that it would discourage recruiting. The manuscript remains unpublished.

AVOCATIONAL INTERESTS: Listening to music, especially Italian opera, and travel in southern Europe.†

* * *

DAVIS, Maggie (Hill)

PERSONAL: Born in Norfolk, Va.; daughter of George Blair and Dorothy (Mason) Hill; children: four sons. *Edu-*cation: Attended schools in New York, N.Y. *Religion:* Episcopalian.

CAREER: Formerly radio and television script writer and producer, public relations agent, and newspaper feature writer; WAGA-TV, formerly assistant director of promotion; now full-time writer. Lecturer on writing at Emory University and University of Georgia. Visiting artist, International Cultural Center, Tunisia, 1965. Volunteer member of Georgia Governor's Committee to Improve Education, 1964. *Member:* Authors Guild, Theta Sigma Phi. *Awards, honors:* Award for fiction, Georgia Writers Association, 1964.

WRITINGS—Novels: *The Winter Serpent*, McGraw, 1958; *The Far Side of Home* (Literary Guild Selection), Macmillan, 1963; *Rommel's Gold*, Lippincott, 1971. Contributor of stories and articles to *Ladies' Home Journal*, *Holiday*, and *Georgia Review*.

WORK IN PROGRESS: A novel.†

* * *

DAWES, Neville 1926-

PERSONAL: Born June 16, 1926, in Warri, Nigeria; son of Levi Augustus (a teacher) and Laura (Mills) Dawes, *Education:* Attended Jamaica College, Kingston, 1938-44; Oriel College, Oxford, B.A., 1951, M.A., 1955. *Home:* School of Administration, P.O. Box 48, Achimota, Accra, Ghana. *Agent:* A. M. Heath & Co., Ltd., 35 Dover St., London W.1, England. *Office:* School of Administration, University of Ghana, Legon, Accra, Ghana.

CAREER: Calabar High School, Kingston, Jamaica, senior English master, 1953-55; Kumasi College of Technology, Kumasi, Ghana, lecturer in English, 1956-59; University of Ghana, School of Administration, Accra, lecturer in English, 1960—. University of Guiana, Georgetown, visiting professor of English and dean of Faculty of Arts, 1963-64. *Member:* Oxford Union.

WRITINGS: The Last Enchantment, MacGibbon & Kee, 1960, reprinted, Kraus Reprint Co., 1970. Contributor to British Broadcasting Corp. programs and literary magazines in Barbados and Jamaica.

WORK IN PROGRESS: A novel, *I Remember Lucien*; first part of an autobiography; research into analogues of Ashanti-Twi folk tale in the English-speaking Caribbean.†

* * *

DAY, James Wentworth 1899-

PERSONAL: Born April 21, 1899, in Exning, Suffolk, England; son of James Thomas (a landowner) and Martha Ethel (Staples) Day; married Marion Edith MacLean, November 9, 1943; children: Marion Clare Wentworth. *Education:* Educated at Newton College (now Blundell's School) and Cambridge University (extramural). *Politics:* Conservative. *Religion:* Church of England. *Home and office:* Ingatestone, Essex, England.

CAREER: British publicist, editor, journalist, and author. Publicity manager for *Daily Express*, London, England, 1923-24; onetime chairman and managing director of News Publicity Ltd., England; publicity adviser to Egyptian government, Newfoundland government, Anglo-Turk Relief Committee, British aviation firms, and, currently, to Animal Health Trust. Assistant editor of *Country Life*, 1925; editor of *Field*, 1930, *Saturday Review*, 1932-35, *Sporting and Dramatic News*, 1935-37, *East Anglia Life*, 1962-66;

was war correspondent for *London Daily Mail* and British Broadcasting Corp., in France, 1939-41, and with minesweepers; columnist for newspapers and magazines; broadcaster on British and Canadian networks. Official biographer of British royalty and others. Was a Conservative candidate for Parliament for Hornchurch Division of Essex in 1950 and 1951. *Military service:* Royal Fusiliers, 1917-19. *Member:* Institute of Journalists, Society of Authors, Royal Society of Arts (fellow), Wildfowlers' Association of Great Britain and Ireland (honorary life member), Essex Wildfowlers Association (founder), Farmers and Countryman's Association (founder), Farmers Club.

WRITINGS: The Lure of Speed, Hutchinson, 1929.

The Life of Sir Henry Segrave, Hutchinson, 1930; *Speed: The Life of Sir Malcolm Campbell*, Hutchinson, 1931; *My Greatest Adventure* (for Sir Malcolm Campbell), Hutchinson, 1932; *Kaye Don—The Man*, Hutchinson, 1934; *The Modern Fowler*, Longmans, Green, 1934, reprinted, British Book Centre, 1973; *A Falcon on St. Paul's*, Hutchinson, 1935; *King George V as a Sportsman*, Cassell, 1935; *Sporting Adventure*, Harrap, 1937; *The Dog in Sport*, Harrap, 1938; *Sport in Egypt*, Country Life, 1939.

Farming Adventure, Harrap, 1943; *Harvest Adventure*, Harrap, 1945; *A Horse, A Horse*, Moss, 1947; *Gamblers Gallery*, Background Books, 1948; *Wild Wings*, Blandford, 1948; *Coastal Adventure*, Harrap, 1949; *Inns of Sport*, Whitebread, 1949; *The Wisest Dogs in the World*, Longshaw, 1949.

Marshland Adventure, Harrap, 1950; *Broadland Adventure*, Country Life, 1951; *The New Yeoman of England*, Harrap, 1952; *Rural Revolution*, H. Ferguson, 1952; *Stoneleigh Abbey*, H. Ferguson, 1952; *The Modern Shooter*, Jenkins, 1953; *In Quest of the Inn*, Vaux, 1953; *Norwich and the Broads*, Batsford, 1953; *A History of the Fens*, Harrap, 1954; *Ghosts and Witches*, Batsford, 1954; *They Walk the Wild Places*, Blandford, 1956; *Poison on the Land*, Eyre & Spottiswoode, 1957; *The Angler's Pocket Book*, Evans, 1957; *The Dog Lover's Pocket Book*, Evans 1957; *Lady Houston—The Woman Who Won the War*, Wingate, 1958; *Newfoundland—The Fortress Isle*, Government of Newfoundland, 1958; *A Ghost-Hunter's Game Book*, Muller, 1958.

H.R.H. Princess Marina, Duchess of Kent, R. Hale, 1962, 2nd edition, 1969; *Portrait of the Broads*, R. Hale, 1967; *The Queen Mother's Family Story*, R. Hale, 1967; *In Search of Ghosts*, Muller, 1969; Taplinger, 1970.

Contributor to other books and series; editor, *Best Sporting Stories*. Former columnist, *London Daily Mail, Evening News* (London), and *Ford Times*. Contributor to *Daily Telegraph* (London), *Country Life*, and other national journals.

SIDELIGHTS: Day represented the late Lady Houston on the committee for the Houston/Mount Everest flight which set a world altitude record in April, 1933. Ten years later he set his own record for another mode of transportation—riding his horse, Master Robert II, some 1,355 miles in ten weeks, the longest ride on horseback made in England for more than 100 years. An outgrowth of the ride was the best-selling book, *Farming Adventure*, which described the transition from horse-powered farming to mechanical farming.

Day's collections include historical portraits, English stuffed birds (including extinct species), and the state papers of the first Earl of Strafford and other historical manuscripts of the period 1610-1642.

AVOCATIONAL INTERESTS: Shooting, fishing, hunting, natural history, dogs, reading, old furniture, vintage port and claret.†

* * *

DEATS, Paul (Kindred), Jr. 1918-

PERSONAL: Born October 1, 1918, in Graham, Tex.; son of Paul Kindred (a cattleman) and Agnes (Craig) Deats; married Ruth Zumbrunnen, September 10, 1941; children: Patricia Zee, Carolyn Kay, Frances Ann, Randall Kin. *Education:* Tarleton State College, A.A., 1937; Southern Methodist University, A.B., 1939; Union Theological Seminary, New York, N.Y., B.D., 1943; Boston University, Ph.D., 1954; other study at Garrett Biblical Institute, University of Texas, Harvard University, *Home:* 106 Berkeley St., West Newton, Mass. 02165. *Office:* Boston University School of Theology, 745 Commonwealth Ave., Boston, Mass. 02215.

CAREER: Ordained to ministry of Methodist Church, 1943. University of Texas, Austin, associate director of Wesley Foundation, 1942-51; Boston University, School of Theology, Boston, Mass., director of United Ministry. 1953-55, assistant professor, 1954-58, associate professor, 1958-63, professor of social ethics and religion in higher education, 1963—, chairman of theological and religious studies of Graduate School, 1969—. Member of General Commission on Church-Government Relations, 1965-68; National Council of Churches, member of executive committee, Commission on Higher Education; Massachusetts Council of Churches, chairman of department of social relations. Civil Liberties Union of Massachusetts, member of executive committee. *Member:* American Anthropological Association, American Sociological Society, Society for the Scientific Study of Religion, Association for Christian Ethics, Fellowship of Reconciliation (national council), American Association of University Professors. *Awards, honors:* American Association of Theological School fellowship for study of social responsibility in universities in West Africa and Middle East, 1961-62.

WRITINGS: (With P. Bertocci and others) *The Responsible Student*, Methodist Student Movement, 1957; (with H. E. Stotts) *Methodism and Society: Guidelines for Strategy*, Abingdon, 1962; *Social Change and Moral Values*, Methodist Board of Christian Social Concerns, 1963; (editor) *Toward a Discipline of Social Ethics: Essays in Honor of Walter Muelder*, Boston University Press, 1972.

WORK IN PROGRESS: Directing study center for Danforth Study of Campus Ministry; a study of introduction to social ethics in seminaries.†

* * *

de BLIJ, Harm J(an) 1935-

PERSONAL: Surname is pronounced *duh-Blay*; born October 9, 1935, in Schiedam, Netherlands; son of Hendrik and Nelly (Erwich) de Blij; married Katherine Powers (now a teacher), December 27, 1964. *Education:* University of the Witwatersrand, B.Sc., 1955; Northwestern University, M.A., 1957, Ph.D., 1959. *Home:* 1049 Cresenwood, East Lansing, Mich. *Office:* African Studies Center, Michigan State University, East Lansing, Mich.

CAREER: University of Natal, Pietermaritzburg, South

Africa, lecturer in geology and geography, 1959-60; Northwestern University, Evanston, Ill., assistant professor of geography, 1960-61; Michigan State University, East Lansing, assistant professor of geography, 1961-63; Northwestern University, associate professor of geography, 1963-64; Michigan State University, associate professor of geography and associate director of African Studies Center, 1964—. Sometime professional violinist. *Member:* Association of American Geographers, National Council for Geographic Education, American Committee on Africa, African Studies Association, Society for the Teaching of Geography (Africa), South African Association for the Advancement of Science, American Association of University Professors, Natal Scientific Society, Sigma Xi, Gamma Theta Upsilon.

WRITINGS: A Text and Apercu for Subsaharan Africa: A Lecture Series, Continuing Education Service, Michigan State University and WMSB Television, 1960; *Africa South*, Northwestern University Press, 1962; *Dar es Salaam*, Northwestern University Press, 1963; *A Geography of Subsaharan Africa*, Rand McNally, 1964; *Systematic Political Geography*, Wiley, 1967, 2nd edition, 1973; *Mombasa: An African City*, Northwestern University Press, 1968; *Geography: Regions & Concepts*, Wiley, 1971; *Essentials of Geography: Regions and Concepts*, Wiley, 1974; *Man Shapes the Earth: A Topical Geography*, Hamilton Publishing, 1974.

Textbooks (and guides) for televised series: *Subsaharan Africa*, 1963, *Political Geography*, 1964 (both published by Michigan State University Continuing Education Service).

WORK IN PROGRESS: Principles of Physical Geography.

SIDELIGHTS: Spent ten years in Africa, has continued research there at intervals since leaving; visited Soviet Union in 1964. Fluent in Afrikaans, Dutch, and German. A generalist by temperament, interested in the arts, and concerned with human dignity and peace.†

* * *

DECKERT, Alice Mae

PERSONAL; Born in Guernsey, Saskatchewan, Canada; daughter of David (a farmer) amd Mabel (Bowman) Deckert. *Education:* Attended Sakatchewan Teachers College and Goshen College; University of Alberta, B.Ed. *Religion:* Mennonite. *Residence:* Edmonton, Alberta, Canada.

CAREER: Formerly teacher in Newfoundland; teacher in La Crete and Edmonton, Alberta, 1964—. Secretary-treasurer, La Crete Library, 1965—.

WRITINGS: Prairie Pals, Herald, 1964. Contributor of short stories to Mennonite publications.

* * *

DeFALCO, Joseph Michael 1931-

PERSONAL: Born August 17, 1931, in Washington, Pa., son of Lawrence James and Mary Anna (Cicero) DeFalco; married Jessie Irene Mirialakis, February 14, 1952; children: Melissa Irene. *Education:* Washington and Jefferson College, B.A., 1956; University of Florida, M.A., 1958, Ph.D., 1961. *Home:* 1059 Redstone Rd., Washington, Pa. 15301. *Office:* Washington and Jefferson College, Washington, Pa. 15301.

CAREER: University of Florida, Gainesville, instructor in

English, 1960-61; Washington and Jefferson College, Washington, Pa., assistant professor, 1961-65, associate professor of English, 1965—. *Military service:* U.S. Army, 1948-51; received Unit Commendation. U.S. Army Reserve, 1953—; now captain. *Member:* Modern Language Association of America, American Association of University Professors, Phi Beta Kappa, Phi Kappa Phi. *Awards, honors:* American Council of Learned Societies grant, 1963.

WRITINGS: The Hero in Hemingway's Short Stories, University of Pittsburgh Press, 1963; (editor) Christopher Cranch, *Collected Poems, 1835-92*, Scholars Facsimilies & Reprints, 1971. Contributor to *Literature and Psychology*, and *Walt Whitman Review*. Member of bibliography staff, *Twentieth Century Literature*.

WORK IN PROGRESS: Investigation of the sublime in American literature of the late nineteenth and early twentieth centuries.†

* * *

de GAURY, Gerald 1897-

PERSONAL: Born April 1, 1897, in London, England. *Agent:* A.P. Watt & Son, 26 Bedford Row, London WC1 R.4 HL, England.

CAREER: British Army, regular officer, 1914-36; British political agent in Kuwait, 1936-39; first secretary, British Legation, Teheran, Iran, 1940-41; rejoined British army and served as special liaison officer for Arab countries, Minister of State's Office Cairo, Egypt, 1941-43; British Foreign Office, attached to visiting Arab rulers and dignitaries, London, England, 1944-45; Iraq government, Baghdad, organizer and first head of Departments of Publicity and Labour Welfare, 1946-49. Member of United Kingdom delegation to first United Nations conference. Director, Consolidated Holdings (Middle East) Ltd., 1950-55. *Member:* Anglo-Arab Association (former member of council), Anglo-Iraq Society (founder member), Travellers Club (London). *Awards, honors:* Military Cross, 1917; order of the Two Rivers of Iraq.

WRITINGS: (Co-author) *A Saudi Arabian Notebook*, S.A.E. (Cairo), 1943; *Arabia Phoenix* (travel), Harrap, 1946; *Arabian Journey* (Travel), Harrap, 1950; *Rulers of Mecca* (history), Harrap, 1951; *The New State of Israel*, Prager, 1952; *The Grand Captain: Gonzalode Cordoba* (biography), Longmans, Green, 1955; *Three Kings in Baghdad* (biographies), Hutchinson, 1961; *Faisal: King of Saudi Arabia* (biography), Barker, 1966; *Travelling Gent: The Life of Alexander King Lake, 1809-1891* (biography), Routledge, 1972. Contributor to *Spectator, London Magazine, Foreign Affairs* (United States), and other periodicals.

SIDELIGHTS: As part of his duties with the Foreign Office in London, de Gaury translated for King George VI when Arab heads of state visited Buckingham Palace. He also accompanied the Regent of Iraq on a tour of Europe's battlefields and on a state visit to the President of Turkey, 1945. de Gaury spent some time in Oman in 1955 and 1956, visited other Arab countries, 1964 and 1965.

* * *

De GENNARO, Angelo Anthony 1919-

PERSONAL: Born December 9, 1919, in Niagara Falls, N.Y.; son of Salvatore and Mary (Felicia) De Gennaro; married Ann Di Candito, 1958; children: Gina, Laura. *Education:* Nola College, Italy, B.A., 1939; University of

Naples, Ph.D., 1943; Columbia University, postdoctoral study, 1949-51. *Home:* 4493 Don Miguel Dr., Los Angeles, Calif. *Office:* Loyola University of Los Angeles, Los Angeles, Calif.

CAREER: Loyola University of Los Angeles, Los Angeles, Calif., instructor, 1951-53, assistant professor, 1953-56, associate professor, 1956-59, professor of Romance languages, 1959—. *Member:* American Association of Teachers of Italian, American Society for Aesthetics, American Association of University Professors.

WRITINGS: The Philosophy of Benedetto Croce: An Introduction, Philosophical Library, 1961; (editor) Benedetto Croce, *Essays on Marx and Russia,* Ungar, 1966. Contributor to *Italica, Hispania, Journal of Aesthetics and Art Criticism, Personalist, Kentucky Foreign Language Quarterly.*†

* * *

de GRAZIA, Alfred 1919-

PERSONAL: Born December 29, 1919, in Chicago, Ill.; son of Alfred Joseph (a musician) and Katherine (Lupo) de Grazia; married Bertha Jill Oppenheim, May 11, 1942 (divorced); married Nina Mavridis, December 21, 1972; children: (first marriage) Catherine (Mrs. Dante Matelli), Victoria, Jessica, Paul, John, Carl, Christopher. *Education:* University of Chicago, A.B., 1939, Ph.D., 1948; Columbia University, postgraduate study, 1940-41. *Home:* 16 Linden Lane, Princeton, N.J. *Office:* New York University, Washington Square, New York, N.Y. 10003.

CAREER: University of Minnesota, Minneapolis, assistant professor of political science, 1948-50; Brown University, Providence, R.I., associate professor of political science, 1950-52; Stanford University, Stanford, Calif., associate professor, 1952-57, executive officer of committee for research in the social sciences, 1952-55; New York University, New York, N.Y., professor of government and social theory, 1959—, director of research program in representative government, 1966—. Metron, Inc., New York, N.Y., president, 1958-65; Princeton Information Technology, Inc., board chairman, 1967-70. Member of U.S. delegation to UNESCO, 1960. Consultant to U.S. Operations Research Office, 1951-52; Republican Party National Committee, 1964; consultant at various times to Hoover Commission, Ford Foundation, National Science Foundation, U.S. Information Agency, and Twentieth Century Fund. Visiting lecturer, University of Rome, University of Bombay, University of Istanbul, and University of Gothenburg. *Military service:* U.S. Army, Psychological Warfare Branch, 1942-46; became captain; received Bronze Star.

MEMBER: American Political Science Association (executive council member, 1962-64), Mediterranean Social Science Research Council, Behavioral Research Council (board of councilors), International Political Science Association, American Federation of Scientists, American Association for Public Opinion Research.

WRITINGS: (Translator and author of introduction) Robert Michels, *First Lectures in Sociology,* University of Minnesota Press, 1949, new edition, Harper, 1965; *Public and Republic,* Knopf, 1951; *The Elements of Political Science,* Knopf, 1952, revised edition, Free Press, 1965, enlarged edition published as *Politics and Government: The Elements of Political Science,* two volumes, Colliers, 1962, revised edition, *Politics and Government: The Elements of Political Science,* two volumes, Free Press, 1965; *The Western Public, 1952 and Beyond,* Stanford University

Press, 1954; (editor) *Grass Roots Private Welfare,* New York University Press, 1957; *The American Way of Government,* Wiley, 1957.

(With Ted Gurr) *American Welfare,* New York University Press, 1961; *Public and Republic: Political Representation in America,* Knopf, 1961; (with Thomas Stevenson) *World Politics: A Study in International Relations,* Barnes & Noble, 1962, 2nd edition, 1966; *Apportionment and Representative Government,* Praeger, 1963, published as *Essay on Apportionment and Representative Government,* American Enterprise Institute for Public Policy Research, 1963; (editor with David Sohn) *Programs, Teachers, and Machines,* Bantam, 1964; (editor with Sohn) *Revolution in Teaching: New Theory, Technology, and Curricula,* Bantam, 1964; *Republic in Crisis: Congress Against the Executive Force,* Federal Legal Publications, 1965; *Political Behavior,* Free Press, 1965; *The Velikovsky Affair: The Welfare of Science and Scientism,* University Books, 1966; (editor and contributor) *Twelve Studies of the Organization of Congress,* American Enterprise Institute for Public Policy Research, 1966, published as *Congress: The First Branch, Twelve Studies of the Organization of Congress,* Doubleday, 1967; (with Arthur Schlisinger) *Congress and the Presidency: Their Role in Modern Times,* American Enterprise Institute for Public Policy Research, 1967; *Passage of the Year* (poems), Quiddity Press, 1967; (editor) *The Behavioral Sciences: Essays in Honor of George Lundberg,* Behavioral Research Council, 1968; (compiler with R. Eric Weise and John Appel) *Old Government, New People: Readings for the New Politics,* Scott, Foresman, 1971; *Politics for Better or Worse,* Scott, Foresman, 1973.

Also author of published political science papers. Contributor to professional journals. Designer of computerized Universal Reference System and co-editor of the system's annual yearbook. *American Behavioral Scientist,* founder, editor, 1957-66.†

* * *

DeJONG, Meindert 1906-

PERSONAL: Surname is pronounced *DeYoung;* born March 4, 1906, in Wierum, Netherlands; son of Raymond R. and Jennie (DeJong) DeJong; married Beatrice DeClaire. *Education:* Calvin College, A.B., 1928. *Politics:* Democrat. *Religion:* "Tentatively" Anglican. *Home:* 504 Lake Dr., Allegan, Mich. 49010.

CAREER: Full-time author of children's books since the 1930's. In his early years (when writing income had to be supplemented) he worked at odd jobs, ranging from tinner through janitor to grave digger—jobs "too menial and too briefly held (was inept) to remember them or their dates." *Military service:* U.S. Army Air Forces, World War II; served in China as historian with Chinese-American Wing of 14th Air Force; became sergeant.

AWARDS, HONORS: John Newbery Medal of American Library Association for most distinguished contribution to children's literature for *The Wheel on the School,* 1954, and Deutschen Kinderbuchpreis for German edition of same book, 1957; Children's Book Award of Child Study Association of America for *The House of Sixty Fathers,* 1956, and Deutschen Kinderbuchpreis for German edition of same book, 1959; Aurianne Award of American Library Association, given for book which tends to develop humane attitudes toward animal life, for *Along Came a Dog,* 1960; International Hans Christian Andersen Award (normally given for world's best single book of fiction for children) for his overall works for children and young people, 1962; National Book Award in Children's Literature for *Journey From Peppermint Street*, 1969; National Catholic Regina Award, 1972.

WRITINGS—All published by Harper, except as indicated: *The Big Goose and the Little White Duck*, 1938, new edition, 1963; *Dirk's Dog, Bello*, 1939; *The Cat that Walked a Week*, 1943; *Billy and the Unhappy Bull*, 1946; *Bible Days* (nonfiction), Fidler, 1948.

Good Luck Duck, 1950; *The Tower by the Sea*, 1950; *Smoke Above the Lane*, 1951; *Shadrach*, 1953; *Hurry Home, Candy*, 1953, new edition, 1965; *The Wheel on the School*, 1954; *The Little Cow and the Turtle*, 1955; *The House of Sixty Fathers*, 1956; *Along Came a Dog*, 1958; *The Mighty Ones*, 1959; *The Last Cat*, 1961; *Nobody Plays with a Cabbage*, 1962; *The Singing Hill*, 1962; *Far Out the Long Canal*, 1964; *Puppy Summer*, 1966; *Journey From Peppermint Street*, 1968.

A Horse Came Running, Macmillan, 1970; *The Easter Cat*, Macmillan, 1971; *The Almost All-White Rabbity Cat*, Macmillan, 1972.

WORK IN PROGRESS: Creek and Old Jack.

SIDELIGHTS: Horn Book published DeJong's Newbery and Hans Christian Andersen awards acceptance speeches, but outside of one article for *Author and Journalist* (on how to write for children) his work has been confined to books. DeJong shuns organizations and civic activities, lives with his wife, two collies, and two siamese cats. He enjoys occasional swimming, and good talk with other writers.

DeJong believes he must be the "runner-uppinest guy" in the history of the Newbery, since his books were second choice for that bronze medal three years—*Shadrach* and *Hurry Home, Candy* in 1954, *The House of Sixty Fathers* in 1957, and *Along Came a Dog* in 1959. *Along Came a Dog* also was a 1960 Honor Book in the bi-annual Hans Christian Andersen Award (which DeJong won the next time around). His books have been translated into twenty languages, and published in Europe, Australia, Japan, and South Africa.†

* * *

DeKOSTER, Lester Ronald 1915-

PERSONAL: Born April 21, 1915, in Zeeland, Mich.; son of Cornelius C. and Sarah (Cass) DeKoster; married Ruth Jane De Vries, June 6, 1941; children: Leslie Ann, Paul Ronald, Mark Edward, Stephen James. *Education:* Calvin College, A.B., 1937; University of Michigan, A.M. (philosophy), 1942, A.M. (library science), 1954, Ph.D., 1964. *Politics:* Democrat. *Religion:* Protestant. *Home:* 2800 Thornapple River Dr., S.E., Grand Rapids, Mich. 49506.

CAREER: Calvin College, Grand Rapids, Mich., instructor in speech, 1947-49, assistant professor, 1949-64, professor of speech, 1964—, librarian, 1951—; Calvin Theological Seminary, Grand Rapids, Mich., librarian 1951—. Kent County Democratic Party, delegate, 1955—, member of executive committee, 1957-63. *Military service:* U.S. Naval Reserve, 1943-45; became lieutenant junior grade. *Member:* Michigan Library Association, Associated Church Press, Evangelical Press Association.

WRITINGS: All Ye That Labor, Eerdmans, 1956; (editor) Phelps, *Speaking in Public*, Baker Book, 1958; *Communism and Christian Faith*, Eerdmans, 1962; *Vocabulary of Communism*, Eerdmans, 1964; *Christian and John Birch Society*, Eerdmans, 1966; *Citizen and John Birch Society*,

Eerdmans, 1967; *How to Read the Bible*, Baker, 1974. Contributor to *Christianity Today, Eternity,* and *Church Herald*. Editor, *The Banner*, 1969—.

WORK IN PROGRESS: The Church in the City.

SIDELIGHTS: DeKoster has reading knowledge of German, French, and talks Dutch. *Avocational interests:* Book-hunting, long talks, boating, and chess.

* * *

DELANEY, Edmund T. 1914-

PERSONAL: Born January 29, 1914, in Newark, N.J.; son of William F. (an attorney) and Viola (Kelly) Delaney; married Barbara Snow (former managing editor of *Antiques* magazine); children: Denise Christopher, Nicholson. *Education:* Princeton University, A.B., 1933; Harvard University, LL.B., 1936. *Religion:* Catholic. *Home:* 5 Gorham Rd., Chester, Conn. 06412. *Office:* Copp, Brenneman, Tighe, Koletsky, & Berall, 71 Main St., Essex, Conn. 06426.

CAREER: Admitted to the Bar of New York State, 1936, and to the Bar of Connecticut State, 1970; now partner in Copp, Brenneman, Tighe, Koletsky, & Berall (law firm), Essex, Conn. Member of board of directors of Oppenheimer Funds. *Military service:* U.S. Army, 1940-46; became lieutenant colonel; received Commendation Medal, French Resistance Medal. *Member:* Association of the Bar of the City of New York.

WRITINGS: New York's Turtle Bay, Old and New, Barre, 1965; *New York's Greenwich Village*, Barre, 1968; *The Connecticut Shore*, Barre, 1970. Contributor of articles on legal subjects to professional journals.

SIDELIGHTS: Delaney is competent in French and Spanish.

* * *

DELL, E(dward) T(homas), Jr. 1923-

PERSONAL: Born February 12, 1923; son of Edward Thomas and Virginia Prue (Hopper) Dell; married Carol Jane Carr (an editor), August 21, 1954; children: Chad Edward, Heather Salisbury, Sara Hilary. *Education:* Eastern Nazarene College, A.B., 1948, Th.B., 1949; Boston University, graduate study, 1949-53; Episcopal Theological School, Cambridge, Mass., M.Div., 1955. *Politics:* Liberal Republican. *Home:* 307 Dickinson Ave., Swarthmore, Pa. 19081. *Office: The Audio Amateur Magazine*, Box 30, Swarthmore, Pa. 19081.

CAREER: Teacher at Eastern Nazarene Academy, Wollaston, Mass., 1949-52, and at Mary Brooks Junior College, Boston, Mass., 1951-53; ordained priest of Protestant Episcopal Church, 1955; curate of church in Boston, Mass., 1955-57; priest in charge of church in Millis, Mass., 1957-61; *Episcopalian*, Philadelphia, Pa., book editor, 1960-61, associate editor, 1962-67, managing editor, 1967-73; *The Audio Amateur Magazine*, Swarthmore, Pa., founder, 1969—. *Member:* Interlocutors (monthly discussion group, Philadelphia).

WRITINGS: A Handbook for Church Weddings, Morehouse, 1964. Contributor of articles, mainly on English apologists C. S. Lewis, Dorothy Sayers, and Charles Williams, to periodicals.

WORK IN PROGRESS: A survey of C. S. Lewis and his work; an introductory book on small periodical publishing; a series of magazine articles for *Stereophile* and MBA corporation.

DELLOFF, Irving Arthur 1920-

PERSONAL: Born October 19, 1920; son of Max and Lillian (Woods) Delloff; married Beatrice Tolciss (a teacher), April 12, 1937, children: Stefan Tolciss. *Education:* Pace College, B.B.A., 1940; New York University, graduate study, 1940-43. *Home:* 5-18 Essex Pl., Fair Lawn, N.J.

CAREER: Presto Lock Co., Garfield, N.J., director of industrial engineering, 1943-69; Rutgers Unviersity, New Brunswick, N.J., instructor in management, Newark Campus, 1954—, executive director of motivation and training programs, 1969, lecturer at Institute of Management and Labor Relations, New Brunswick Campus, 1958—, management program coordinator, 1973. Course leader and speaker at management and labor organization institutes, including those of American Management Association and National Metal Trades Association; member of Labor Panel of American Arbitration Association. *Member:* American Institute of Industrial Engineers (director of professional relations, 1962), Society for Advancement of Management (fellow); Institute of Management Consultants, American National Standards Institute (secretary, terminology committee, 1969).

WRITINGS: (With John D. Staley) *Improving Individual Productivity*, American Management Association, 1963; (with Dr. William J. Jaffee) *Go to Arbitration*, American Management Association, 1967. Contributor to industrial and professional journals.

WORK IN PROGRESS: Two books, *Management Controls* and *Motivation–Financial and Non-Financial.*

AVOCATIONAL INTERESTS: The arts, gardening.

*   *   *

DEMPSTER, Derek David 1924-

PERSONAL: Born November 12, 1924, in Tangier, Morocco; son of Ernest James (a legal and treaty adviser) and Bess (Lee) Dempster; married Isolde Denham (an actress), February 26, 1951 (divorced); married Josephine Carole Newton, July 5, 1968; children: (first marriage) Tamara Ustinov (stepdaughter), *Education:* Pembroke College, Cambridge, B.A., 1949, M.A., 1956. *Religion:* Eclectic. *Home:* The Coach House, Upton House, Worth, Deal, Kent, England. *Agent:* Curtis Brown Ltd., 1 Craven Hill, London, W. 2, England.

CAREER: Reuters News Agency, London, England, subeditor and reporter, 1950; *Aeroplane* (magazine), London, England, writer on military aviation and test flights, 1950-52; *Daily Express*, London, England, aviation editor, 1952-54; British Overseas Airways Corp., London Airport, England, editor of aircrew magazine and BOAC News (weekly); 1955-59; self-employed aviation consultant, founder and director of Skylink Ltd., London, England, (publishers of *Skytrader International*), Economic Liaison Services Ltd., London, England (distribution and transport advisers), and Airport Publishing Co., Ltd., London, England; now president, Interface Publishing Consultants, Ltd. *Military service:* Royal Air Force, pilot, 1943-47. Royal Auxiliary Air Force, 1949-56; flight lieutenant. *Member:* Writer's Guild of Great Britain. *Awards, honors:* C. P. Robertson Memorial Trophy, 1961, for *The Narrow Margin*.

WRITINGS: (With Kenneth Gatland) *The Inhabited Universe*, McKay, 1957; *The Tale of the Comet*, Wingate, 1958, McKay, 1959; (with Derek Wood) *The Narrow Margin*, Hutchinson, 1961, McGraw, 1962, revised edition, Paperback Library, 1969. Wrote and appeared in own television series, British Broadcasting Corp., 1961; has done documentaries for Associated Television Ltd., and other television scripts. Contributor to journals and newspapers.

WORK IN PROGRESS: A novel, *I'll Meet You Half Way Back*, completion expected in 1975; regular television work.

*   *   *

DENG, William 1929-

PERSONAL: Born January 1, 1929, in Ameth, Tonj, Sudan; son of Nhial (a tribal deputy chief) and Ghai (Mangok) Deng; married Christine Ayen, May 12, 1956; children: Abraham Nhial, Francis, Elena Ghai. *Education:* University of Khartoum, Certificate in Public Administration and Law, 1955. *Politics:* Sudan African National Union (SANU).

CAREER: Assistant district commissioner and magistrate, Republic of the Sudan, 1954-61; resigned official post, 1961, to become secretary general of Sudan African National Union (political party), with special responsibilities in international and African affairs.

WRITINGS: (With Joseph Oduho) *The Problem of the Southern Sudan*, Oxford University Press, 1962.

SIDELIGHTS: Deng speaks English, French, and Arabic in addition to a number of African languages. He has traveled extensively in Europe, and visited America.†

*   *   *

DENIS, Michaela Holdsworth

PERSONAL: Born in London, England; daughter of Oliver Edwin Nicholas (an archaeologist) and Florence (Weatherhead-Hunt) Holdsworth; married Armand Georges Denis (a producer of television films and editor), November 23, 1948. *Education:* Studied in Paris, France. *Religion:* Agnostic. *Home and office:* P.O. Box 15033, Nairobi, Kenya, East Africa. *Agent:* M. D. (Literary Enterprises) Ltd., 23 Grafton St., London W.1, England.

CAREER: Author, and writer of television and film series. Member of executive committees of Kenya Family Planning Association, Nairobi Family Planning Association, Beauty Without Cruelty, Men of the Trees, Junior Society for the Prevention of Cruelty to Animals, Amani Home for the Aged, all Kenya; vice-president of International League Against Bull Fighting. *Member:* Society of Authors, P.E.N.

WRITINGS: Minnie the Mongoose, W. H. Allen; *Leopard in My Lap*, Messner, 1955; *Ride a Rhino*, W. H. Allen, 1959, Doubleday, 1960; *Maid of Money*, W. H. Allen, 1961; *Voice of the Lark*, W. H. Allen, 1964; *At Home with Michaela*, Hutchinson, 1965.

Writer of television shows produced in thirty countries. Occasional contributor to journals.

AVOCATIONAL INTERESTS: Psychic research, ethnography, physics, gardening, wildlife, and conservation of natural resources.†

*   *   *

DENISON, Barbara 1926-

PERSONAL: Born December 12, 1926, in Cleveland, Ohio; daughter of Adam Benjamin (a physician) and Ruth (McConnell) Denison. *Education:* Radcliffe College, B.A.,

1948; Western Reserve University (now Case Western Reserve University), M.A., 1949, M.S. in Library Science, 1965. *Home:* 12700 Shaker Blvd., Cleveland, Ohio 44120. *Office:* Cleveland Public Library, 325 Superior Ave., Cleveland, Ohio 44114.

CAREER: U.S. government, Washington, D.C., secretary, 1950-53; Case Western Reserve University, Cleveland, Ohio, School of Business, secretary to dean, 1953-55, School of Library Science, secretary to dean, 1955-56, research associate, 1956-60, administrative assistant to dean, 1960-65, research assistant, 1965-68, educational research activities manager, 1968-70; Cleveland Public Library, music librarian, 1970—. Special Libraries Association Special Classification Center (at School of Library Science, Case Western Reserve University), assistant curator, 1956-63, director, 1963-66; executive secretary of Training Program in Medical Librarianship, 1967-70; fiscal officer of Hope Inc., 1967-68. *Member:* English-Speaking Union (member of board of directors, Cleveland branch, 1959-66; national secretary, 1969—), Archeological Institute of America, National Trust for Historic Preservation, National Geographic Society, Mosart Society.

WRITINGS: (With Bertha R. Barden) *Special Libraries Association Loan Collection of Classification Schemes and Subject Heading Lists*, Special Libraries Association, 1959, revised edition, 1961; (with Doris C. Holladay) *Library Statistics of Colleges and Universities, 1959-60*, Part 2: *Analytic Report*, U.S. Government Printing Office, 1963; (with Nathan M. Cohen and Jessie C. Boehlert) *Library Science Dissertations, 1925-60; An Annotated Bibliography of Doctoral Studies*, U.S. Government Printing Office, 1963; (compiler) *Selected Materials in Classification*, Special Libraries Association, 1968. Contributor to *Encyclopedia Americana*, 1962, *United Educator Encyclopedia*, 1964. Managing editor, *Encyclopedia of Librarianship*, 1961-66.†

* * *

DENT, Colin 1921-

PERSONAL: Born April 26, 1921, in Droxford, Hampshire, England; son of Thomas William (a surveyor) and Gladys (Crouch) Dent; married Bess Smeeden, May 28, 1960. *Education:* Attended Southampton College of Art; College of Estate Management, London; University of Southampton A.R.I.C.S., 1952, F.R.I.C.S., 1966, M.Phil., 1973. *Home:* 28 Saxholm Way, Southampton, England.

CAREER: London County Council, London, England, quantity surveyor, 1949-56; British Admiralty, London, England, quantity surveyor, 1956-58; Portsmouth Corp., England, deputy chief quantity surveyor, 1958-61; Southampton College of Technology, Southampton, England, lecturer in quantity surveying, 1961—. Visiting lecturer at University of London, University of Southampton, Oxford College of Technology, and Trinity College, Dublin. *Member:* Royal Institution of Chartered Surveyors (examiner; member of research and development panel), Joint Consultative Committee of Architects and Quantity Surveyors (Southern region). *Awards, honors:* International Computers and Tabulators research fellow at Oxford University, 1965.

WRITINGS: *Quantity Surveying by Computer*, Oxford University Press, 1964; *Quantity Surveying: A Fully Metricated Text*, Oxford University Press, 1970; *Construction Cost Appraisal*, Godwin, 1974. Contributor to *Chartered Surveyor*.

WORK IN PROGRESS: *Elemental Cost Planning*, completion expected in 1976.

AVOCATIONAL INTERESTS: Sailing, golf, painting, and music.

* * *

de REGNIERS, Beatrice Schenk (Freedman) 1914-

PERSONAL: Surname is prounced de Rain-yay; born August 16, 1914, in Lafayette, Ind.; daughter of Harry and Sophie Freedman; married Francis de Regniers (an airline shipping manager), 1946. *Education:* University of Illinois, student, 1931-33; University of Chicago, Ph.B., 1935, graduate study, 1936-37; Winnetka Graduate Teachers College, M.Ed., 1941. *Office:* Scholastic Book Services, 50 West 44th St., New York, N.Y. 10036.

CAREER: American Heart Association, New York, N.Y., director of educational materials, 1949-61; Scholastic Book Services, New York, N.Y., editor of Lucky Book Club, 1961—. Author of juvenile books. *Member:* Loose-enders. *Awards, honors: Cats Cats Cats Cats Cats*, was a *New York Herald Tribune* Children's Spring Book Festival honor book, 1958; Boys' Clubs Junior Book Award, 1960, for *The Snow Party*; Indiana Authors Day awards, 1961, honorable mention for *The Shadow*; Brooklyn Art Books for Children citation, 1973, for *Red Riding Hood Retold in Verse for Boys and Girls to Read Themselves*.

WRITINGS: *The Giant Story*, Harper, 1953; *A Little House of Your Own*, Harcourt, 1954; *What Can You Do With a Shoe?*, Harper, 1955; *Was It a Good Trade?*, Harcourt, 1956; *A Child's Book of Dreams*, Harcourt, 1957; *Something Special*, Harcourt, 1958; *Cats Cats Cats Cats Cats*, Pantheon, 1958; *The Snow Party*, Pantheon, 1959; *What Happens Next?*, Macmillan, 1959; *The Shadow Book*, Harcourt, 1960; *Who Likes the Sun?*, Harcourt, 1961; (self-illustrated) *The Little Book*, Walck, 1961; *The Little Girl and Her Mother*, Vanguard, 1963; *May I Bring a Friend?*, Atheneum, 1964; *How Joe the Bear and Sam the Mouse Got Together*, Parents, 1965; *The Abraham Lincoln Joke Book*, Random House, 1965; *David and Goliath*, Viking, 1965; (with Marvin Bileck) *Penny*, Viking, 1966; *Circus*, Viking, 1966; *The Giant Book*, Atheneum, 1966; *The Day Everybody Cried*, Viking, 1967; *Willy O'-Dwyer Jumped in the Fire: Variations on a Folk Rhyme*, Atheneum, 1968; *Catch a Little Fox: Variations on a Folk Rhyme*, Seabury, 1970; (compiler with Eva Moore and Mary M. White) *Poems Children Will Sit Still For: A Selection For the Primary Grades*, Citation, 1969; *The Boy, the Rat, and the Butterfly*, Atheneum, 1971; *Red Riding Hood: Retold in Verse for Boys and Girls to Read Themselves*, Atheneum, 1972; *It Does Not Say Meow and Other Animal Riddle Rhymes*, Seabury, 1972. *The Enchanted Forest*, Atheneum, in press.

* * *

deRHAM, Edith 1933-

PERSONAL Born September 2, 1933, in New York, N.Y.; daughter of Henry Longfellow (an insurance broker) and Edith (Colby) deRham; married Peter Sutro, 1957; married second husband, Richard Coulson (a lawyer), September 9, 1960; children: (first marriage) Henry Sutro; (second marriage) Diana Coulson. *Education:* Vassar College, B.A., 1955. *Politics:* Republican. *Home:* 1040 Park Ave., New York, N.Y. 10028.

CAREER: American Theatre Wing, New York, N.Y.,

administrative secretary, 1956-57; Theater Guild, New York, N.Y., casting director, 1957-58; Kiernan & Co. (management consultants), New York, N.Y., office manager, 1958-60. Active in local Republican politics, Planned Parenthood League, and Police Athletic League.

WRITINGS: The Love Fraud: Why the Structure of the American Family is Changing and What Women Must Do to Make It Work (nonfiction), C. N. Potter, 1965, published as *The Love Fraud: A Direct Attack on the Staggering Waste of Education and Talent Among American Women*, Pegasus, 1965; *How Could She Do That? A Study of the Female Criminal*, C. N. Potter, 1969.

SIDELIGHTS: Ms. deRham is primarily an essayist (*The Love Fraud* is a study of the problems of educated American women). She lived and traveled in Europe for a year after college and still does considerable traveling in Mexico, Europe, and the Caribbean Islands. Her ambition is to become proficient in other literary forms. *Avocational interests:* Classical guitar.†

*   *   *

DERHAM, (Arthur) Morgan 1915-

PERSONAL: Born September 8, 1915, in Watford, Hertfordshire, England; son of Arthur (a fish farmer) and Lizzie (Woodley) Derham; married Muriel Joan Luetchford, October 5, 1940; children: Hugh Morgan, Ruth Christine. *Education:* Brockley Bible Institute, diploma; University of London, Certificate of Religious Knowledge. *Home:* The Manse, Chenies, Rickmansworth, Hertfordshire, England. *Office:* Scripture Union, 5 Wigmore St., London W.1, England.

CAREER: Metropolitan Police, London, England, police officer, 1934-38; Baptist minister in West Ham, London, England, and Barking, Essex, England, 1940-47; Scripture Union, London, England, editorial secretary, 1947—. Part-time Baptist minister, Chenies, Rickmansworth, Hertfordshire, England, 1953-65. Member, Council of Evangelical Alliance, London, England. *Wartime service:* Royal Observer Corps, 1940-44.

WRITINGS: On the Trail of the Windward, Children's Special Service Mission, 1947; *The Cruise of the Clipper*, Children's Special Service Mission, 1949; *No Darker Rooms*, Moody, 1950; *Why Be Different?*, Inter-Varsity Fellowship, 1951; *Shall These Things Be?*, Inter-Varsity Fellowship, 1953; *Bluewater Mere*, Children's Special Service Mission, 1955; *The Mature Christian*, Revell, 1962; *The Christian's Guide to Bible Study*, Revell, 1964. Contributor to religious periodicals in Great Britain and United States, Editor of Bible-reading material published by Scripture Union in London and Philadelphia; consulting editor, *Crusade* and *Pilgrim*.

WORK IN PROGRESS: A book, *The Christian's Guide to Love, Sex, and Marriage*, for Hodder & Stoughton.

SIDELIGHTS: Work with Scripture Union has taken Derham to Australasia, Asia, United States, Canada, several countries on the Continent.†

*   *   *

de ROMASZKAN, Gregor 1894-

PERSONAL: Born May 31, 1894, in Balatyna, Poland, of Austrian Citizenship; son of Peter (a gentleman farmer) and Kajetana (Merzowicz) de Romaszkan; married Elisabeth Everts, August 27, 1945. *Education:* Francisco Josephinum Academy, Modling, Austria, Student, 1911-14. *Politics:*

"Have never meddled with politics." *Religion:* Armenian-Catholic. *Home:* 153 Avenue Charles Pieur, Dammarie-les-Lys, Seine-et-Marne, France.

CAREER: Cavalry officer in three wars, and former riding instructor at the Cavalry School, Grudziadz, Poland. Served in Austrian Cavalry, 1914-18, as squadron leader in Polish Cavalry during Polish-Russian War, 1920, and with Polish forces in Poland and France, 1939-40; interned in Switzerland, 1940-45; resident of France, 1945—.

WRITINGS: Jezdziec i kon w rownowadze, privately printed, 1937; *Rieter und Pferd im Gleichgewicht*, Albert Mueller Verlag (Zurich), 1940, translation published as *Horse and Rider in Equilibrium*, Green, 1967; *Reiten lernen*, Albert Mueller Verlag, 1942, translation published as *Fundamentals of Riding*, Doubleday, 1964; *Pferde zureiten*, Albert Mueller Verlag, 1943; *Reitlehre in Bildern*, Verlag Sankt Georg (Dusseldorf), 1963, translation published as *Riding in Pictures*, Doubleday, 1965; *Das Olympische Viereck in Bildern*, Frackh'sche Verlagshandlung (Stuttgart), 1967, translation published as *The Olympic Dressage Test in Pictures*, Greene 1968; *Reitprobleme*, Erich Hoffmann Verlag (Heidenheim), 1967, translation published as *Riding Problems*, Greene, 1968; *Reiter, hast Du Keine Zwiefel?*, Erich Hoffman Verlag (Heidenheim), 1974. Contributor to riding periodicals in Germany, France, United States, England, and Switzerland.

SIDELIGHTS: de Romaszkan's books have been published in seven languages. He speaks German, French, and Russian.

*   *   *

DERRETT, J(ohn) Duncan M(artin) 1922-

PERSONAL: Surname is accented on second syllable; born August 30, 1922, in London, England; son of John West and Fay (Martin) Derrett; married Margaret Griffiths, September, 1950; children: Elizabeth, Paul, Christopher, Robin, Jonathan. *Education:* Jesus College, Oxford, B.A., 1945, M.A., 1947; School of Oriental and African Studies, London, Ph.D., 1949. *Home:* Chiltern House, Lee Common, Great Missenden, Buckinghamshire, England. *Office:* School of Oriental and African Studies, University of London, London WC1E 7HP, England.

CAREER: University of London, School of Oriental and African Studies, London, England, lecturer in Hindu law, 1949-56, reader in Oriental laws, 1956-65, professor of Oriental laws, 1965—. Tagore Professor of Law, University of Calcutta, 1953; visiting professor of Indian law, University of Chicago, spring, 1963; lecturer in Hindu law, Council of Legal Education, London, England, 1967—; visiting professor, University of Michigan, summer, 1970. *Military service:* British Army, 1942-45; served in India. *Member:* Royal Asiatic Society, Studiorum Novi Testamenti Societas, Gray's Inn. *Awards, honors:* D.C.L. from Jesus College, Oxford, 1966; LL.D. from School of Oriental and African Studies, London, 1971.

WRITINGS: The Hoysalas, Oxford University Press, 1957; *Hindu Law Past and Present*, A. Mukherjee (Calcutta), 1957; *Introduction to Modern Hindu Law*, Oxford University Press, 1963; (editor) *Studies in the Laws of Succession in Nigeria*, Oxford University Press, 1965; *Religion, Law and the State in India*, Faber & Faber, 1968; (editor and contributor) *Introduction to Legal Systems*, Praeger, 1968; *Critique of Modern Hindu Law*, Tripathi (Bombay, India), 1970; *Law in the New Testament*, Darton, 1970; (translator and editor) R. Lingat, *Classical Law of India*, University of California Press, 1973; *Jesus's Audience*, Darton, 1973; *Dharmasastra and Juridical Literature*, Harrassowitz (Wiesbaden), 1973; *Bharuci's Commentary on the Manusmrti*, two volumes (text and translation), Steiner Verlag, 1974. Contributor to journals and festschriften in England and abroad. Member of editorial board, *Zeitschrift fuer vergleichende Rechtweissenschaft* and *Kerala Law Times*.

WORK IN PROGRESS: Research studies in New Testament legal problems; research on Thomas More's *Utopia* and aspects of More's life; research with Graham Smith on early Indian legal procedure and juridical concepts.

* * *

DERWIN, Jordan 1931-

PERSONAL: Born September 15, 1931, in New York, N.Y.; son of Harry and Sadie (Baruch) Derwin; married Barbara Joan Concool, 1956 (divorced, 1970); married Joan Linda Wolfberg, 1973; children: (first marriage) Susan Lee, Moira Ellen. *Education:* New York University, B.S., 1953, LL.B., 1959. *Home:* 305 East 86th St., New York, N.Y. 10028. *Office:* 1775 Broadway, New York, N.Y. 10036.

CAREER: Duke University, School of Law, Durham, N.C., research associate, 1959-60; Brennan, London & Buttenwieser (attorneys), New York, N.Y., attorney, 1960-63; private law practice, 1963-72; New York City Off-Track Betting Corporation, general counsel, 1972-74; with General Instrument Corporation, 1974—. *Military service:* U.S. Naval Reserve, 1953-56; became lieutenant, junior grade; received Republic of Vietnam Presidential Unit Citation. *Member:* American Bar Association, New York State Bar Association, Association of the Bar of the City of New York, Phi Delta Phi.

WRITINGS: (With F. Hodge O'Neal) *Expulsion or Oppression of Business Associates: "Squeeze-Outs" in Small Enterprises*, Duke University Press, 1961; (contributor) T. G. Roady and W. R. Andersen, editors, *Selected Problems in the Law of Corporate Practice*, Vanderbilt University Press, 1960. Contributor of articles to law journals.

* * *

DESAI, Rashmi H(arilal) 1928-

PERSONAL: Born August 21, 1928, in Broach, India; son of Harilal G. (an estate manager) and Indumati (Desai) Desai. *Education:* University of Bombay, B.A., M.A., LL.B.; School of African and Oriental Studies, University of London, M.A., Ph.D., 1962. *Home:* 12 A Ratan Mansion, 2nd Khetwadi, Bombay 4, India. *Office:* East African Institute of Social Relations, P.O. Box 16022, Kampala, Uganda.

CAREER: Research under grant from Institute of Race Relations, London, England, 1960-62; East African Institute of Social Research, Kampala, Uganda, senior fellow, 1962-64; Makerere University College, University of East Africa, Kampala, Uganda, lecturer, 1964—.

WRITINGS: *Indian Immigrants in Britain*, Oxford University Press, 1963.†

* * *

De SUA, William Joseph 1930-

PERSONAL: Surname is pronounced Day *Sue*-ah; born August 13, 1930, in Monessen, Pa.; son of Joseph De Sua; married Marianne Garafalo, April 3, 1954; children: Justin

Michael. *Education:* University of Pittsburgh, B.A., 1952, M.Litt., 1955; University of Padova, graduate study, 1955-56; University of Michigan, Ph.D., 1963. *Home:* 1025 Huntington Dr., East Lansing, Mich. 48823. *Office:* Department of Romance Languages, Michigan State University, East Lansing, Mich. 48823.

CAREER: Tufts University, Medford, Mass., instructor in Italian and English, 1960-63; University of North Carolina, Chapel Hill, assistant professor of Italian and comparative literature, 1963-65, associate professor and chairman of comparative literature program, 1966-72; Michigan State University, professor and chairman of Department of Romance Languages, 1972—. *Military service:* U.S. Navy, 1952-54. *Member:* American Association of Teachers of Italian, Dante Society, Modern Language Association of America, American Comparative Literature Association. *Awards, honors:* Fulbright research grant to Italy, 1965-66; National Foundation for the Arts and the Humanities grant, 1967.

WRITINGS: Dante Into English: A Study of the Translation of the Divine Comedy in Britain and America, University of North Carolina Press, 1964; (editor with Gino Rizzo) *A Dante Symposium in Commemoration of the 700th Anniversary of the Poet's Birth (1265-1965)*, University of North Carolina Press, 1965. Contributor to *Columbia Dictionary of Modern European Literature*. Editor, "University of North Carolina Studies in Comparative Literature", 1966-72.

WORK IN PROGRESS: A Study of Italian poetry and poetics of the nineteenth and twentieth centuries.

* * *

DEUTSCH, Bernard Francis 1925-

PERSONAL: Surname is pronounced *Doytch*; born July 15, 1925, in St. Louis, Mo.; son of Anthony Bernard (an engineer) and Marie (Lueckerath) Deutsch. *Education:* Catholic University of America, Doctor of Canon Law, 1957; Lateran University, Rome, Italy, Doctor of Civil Law, 1959, special diploma in Roman law, 1961. *Politics:* "Subject to change without notice." *Home:* 1855 Madison, St. Louis, Mo. 63106. *Office:* Catholic University of America, Washington, D.C. 20017.

CAREER: Ordained Roman Catholic priest, 1951; St. Peter's Cathedral, Jefferson City, Mo., assistant pastor, 1951-54; Catholic University of America, Washington, D.C., instructor, 1959-62, assistant professor, 1962-65, associate professor of Roman law and history of juridic science, 1965—. Director, Missionary Flight Training Foundation, Catholic University of America, Riccobono Seminar of Roman Law (secretary-treasurer, 1959—).

WRITINGS: Jurisdiction of Pastors in the External Forum, Catholic University of America Press, 1957; *The Uniform Sales Act and the Roman Law of Sale*, Lateran University, 1959; *Our Lady of Ephesus*, Bruce, 1965. Associate editor, *Jurist*.

WORK IN PROGRESS: Research in constitutive elements of Jus Commune and in the Roman concept of Humanitas.

SIDELIGHTS: Deutsch speaks Spanish, Italian, and Latin. He reads French and German. *Avocational interests:* Skiing, tennis, skating, swimming, most sports.†

* * *

DEVAS, Nicolette (Macnamara) 1911-

PERSONAL: Born February 1, 1911, in London, England;

daughter of Francis and Mary (Majolier) Macnamara; married Anthony Devas (an artist; died, 1958); married Rupert Shephard (an artist), 1965; children: (first marriage) Emma (Lady Monson), Esmond, Prosper. *Education:* Studied in France for one year. *Home:* 68 Limerston St., London S.W. 10, England.

CAREER: British Museum, London, England, staff member in Bird Room of Natural History Museum, ten years. *Member:* Society of Authors, P.E.N.

WRITINGS: Bonfire (novel), Chatto & Windus, 1958; *Nighwatch* (novel), Harcourt, 1961; *Two Flamboyant Fathers* (autobiography), Collins, 1966; *Black Eggs* (novel), Collins, 1970; *Susannah's Nightingales*, Collins, in press.

SIDELIGHTS: Mrs. Devas's autobiography is set against a background of artists and literary figures—Augustus John (Mrs. Devas's "elected father"), W. B. Yeats, T. E. Lawrence, George Bernard Shaw, Virginia Woolf, and Dylan Thomas (a brother-in-law)—and the bohemian life style they lived.

Her book, *Nightwatch*, was serialized by the British Broadcasting Corp. and film rights to *Bonfire* were sold to a French producer.

* * *

DEVEREUX, Hilary   1919-

PERSONAL: Born November 12, 1919, in Gravesend, Kent, England; daughter of Charles Henry (a post office overseer) and Thilcah (Lyons) Devereux. *Education:* Battersea Polytechnic, Teacher's Certificate, 1941; University of London, Diploma in the Education of Handicapped Children, 1938. *Religion:* Church of England. *Home:* 38 Cross Lane East, Gravesend, Kent, England. *Office:* County Hall, Westminster Bridge, London S.E. 1, England.

CAREER: Teacher of housecraft in technical, secondary, special schools for handicapped children, and at Domestic Science Training College, Leicester, England, 1941-63; London County Council, London, England, inspector of housecraft, 1963—. *Member:* Association of Teachers of Domestic Subjects, Royal Society for Promotion of Health, National Association of Inspectors of Schools and Educational Organisers.

WRITINGS: Housecraft in the Education of Handicapped Children, Mills & Boon, 1963.

Contributor to *Teaching the Slow Learner in the Secondary School*, edited by M. F. Clough, Methuen and *Teaching the Slow Learner in the Special School*, edited by Clough, Methuen. Contributor to *Home Economics* and *Housecraft*.†

* * *

DEWAR, Mary (Williamson)   1921-

PERSONAL: Born February 13, 1921, in England; daughter of James and Louisa (Buckley) Williamson; married Michael J. S. Dewar (a professor of chemistry), June 3, 1944; children: Robert B. K., Charles E. Steuart. *Education:* Oxford University, B.A. (first class honors), 1942, M.A., 1952; University of London, Ph.D., 1956. *Home:* 6808 Mesa Dr., Austin, Tex. *Office:* University of Texas, Austin, Tex.

CAREER: University of Texas, Austin, research associate in Tudor history.

WRITINGS: Sir Thomas Smith: A Tudor Intellectual in Office, Athlone Press, 1964; (editor) *The Discourse of the Commonweal of This Realm of England* (attributed to Sir Thomas Smith), University Press of Virginia for the Folger Shakespeare Library, 1969.

WORK IN PROGRESS: A critical edition of the *De Republica Anglorum*.

* * *

DEWEY, Robert E(ugene)   1923-

PERSONAL: Born August 11, 1923, in Vermillion, S.D.; son of Ziba Norman and Mary (Eskelson) Dewey; married Mary Ellen Sim, 1943; children: Barbara Lynn, Christopher Sim. *Education:* University of Nebraska, B.A., 1943; Harvard University, M.A., 1947, Ph.D., 1949. *Religion:* Unitarian Universalist. *Home:* 441 Steinway Rd., Lincoln, Neb. *Office:* Department of Philosophy, University of Nebraska, Lincoln, Neb.

CAREER: University of Maryland, College Park, assistant professor of philosophy, 1949-52; Institute for Philosophical Research, San Francisco, Calif., research fellow, 1953-55; Mills College, Oakland, Calif., lecturer, 1955; Dartmouth College, Hanover, N.H., assistant professor of philosophy, 1955-58; University of Nebraska, Lincoln, associate professor, 1958-62, professor of philosophy, and chairman of department, 1962—. Goucher College, visiting lecturer, 1952. *Military service:* U.S. Army, Field Artillery, 1943-46; became first lieutenant; received two battle stars for Central Europe and Rhineland campaigns. *Member:* American Philosophical Association, American Association of University Professors, Mountain Plains Philosophical Conference, Phi Beta Kappa, Phi Sigma Tau.

WRITINGS: (Contributor) Mortimer J. Adler, editor, *The Idea of Freedom*, Doubleday, Volume I, 1958, Volume II, 1961; (with Francis Gramlich and Donald Loftsgordon) *Problems of Ethics*, Macmillan, 1961; (compiler with James Gould) *Freedom: Its History, Nature, and Varieties*, Macmillan, 1970. Contributor of articles to philosophical and educational journals.

WORK IN PROGRESS: A book on the philosophy of John Dewey.†

* * *

DEYERMOND, Alan D(avid)   1932-

PERSONAL: Born February 24, 1932, in Cairo, Egypt; son of Henry (a wholesaler) and Margaret (Lawson) Deyermond; married Ann Marie Bracken (a history teacher), March 30, 1957; children: Ruth Margaret. *Education:* Pembroke College, Oxford, B.A., 1953, M.A. and B.Litt., 1957. *Politics:* Liberal. *Religion:* Church of England. *Home:* 20 Lancaster Rd., St. Albans, Hertfordshire, England. *Office:* Westfield College, University of London, Hampstead, London NW3 7ST, England.

CAREER: Westfield College, University of London, London, England, assistant lecturer, 1955-58, lecturer, 1958-66, reader, 1966-69, professor of Spanish, 1969—, dean of faculty of arts, 1972-74. Visiting professor, University of Wisconsin, 1972. *Member:* Asociacion Internacional de Hispanistas, International Arthurian Society, Societe Rencesvals, Modern Humanities Research Association, Association of Hispanists of Great Britain (committee member, 1970-73), Hispanic Society of America (corresponding member, 1973), Anglo-Catalan Society (member of executive committee, 1964-70), Association of University Teachers (member of central council, 1957-62; local president, 1968-70), London Medieval Society (president, 1970-74).

WRITINGS: The Petrarchan Sources of La Celestina, Oxford University Press, 1961; *Epic Poetry and the Clergy: Studies on the Mocedades de Rodrigo*, Tamesis, 1969; *A Literary History of Spain*, Barnes & Noble, Volume I: *The Middle Ages*, 1971; *Apollonius of Tyre: Two Fifteenth Century Spanish Prose Romances*, University of Exeter Press, 1973; (with David Blamires and others) *Medieval Comic Tales*, D. S. Brewer, 1973; (editor) Felix Lecoy, *Recherches sur le Libro de buen amor de Juan Ruiz*, 2nd edition, Gregg, 1974. Contributor to *The Oxford Companion to the Theatre* and *Cassell's Encyclopedia of World Literature*; also contributor of articles, notes, and reviews to learned journals in Spanish and English. Joint general editor, *Critical Guides to Spanish Texts* and *Research Bibliographies and Checklists*; member of editorial committee of *Coleccion Tamesis* and *Romance Philology*.

WORK IN PROGRESS: Editions of *Libro de Apolonio*, for publication by Clasicos Castellanos; *Libro de Buen Amor* for Oxford University Press; and a critical bibliography of medieval Spanish literature for Grant & Cutler.

* * *

DIAMOND, Edwin 1925-

PERSONAL: Born June 18, 1925, in Chicago, Ill.; son of Louise Joseph (a journalist) and Jessie (Isaacson) Diamond; married Adelina Lust, December 5, 1948; children: Ellen, Franna, Louise. *Education:* University of Chicago, Ph.B., 1947, A.M., 1949. *Home:* 5 Prospect Lane, Sands Point, N.Y. *Office: New York Magazine*, 207 East 32nd St., New York, N.Y.

CAREER: City News Bureau and *Chicago Herald American*, Chicago, Ill., reporter, 1949-53; International News Service, Chicago, Ill., and Washington, D.C., science writer, 1953-57; *Newsweek*, New York, N.Y., science editor, 1958-62, senior editor, 1962-69; *New York Magazine*, New York, N.Y., contributing editor, 1970—. Lecturer, University of Chicago, 1949-53; consultant to National Educational Television, 1964-65; visiting lecturer in political science, Massachusetts Institute of Technology, 1970—; commentator, *Washington Post-Newsweek* Stations, Inc., 1970—; group study leader, Institute of Politics, Kennedy School of Government, Harvard University, 1974. *Military service:* U.S. Army, 1943-46, 1951-53; became first lieutenant; received Bronze Star Medal with oak leaf cluster. *Member:* National Association of Science Writers, National Press Club, Sands Point Bath and Tennis Club. *Awards, honors:* Page One Awards from Chicago and Washington Newspaper Guilds; Westinghouse-American Association for Advancement of Science science writer's award; and others.

WRITINGS: (Contributor) *Five Worlds of Our Lives*, Hammond, 1961; *The Science of Dreams*, Doubleday, 1962; *The Rise and Fall of the Space Age*, Doubleday, 1964; (contributor) *The Media and the Cities*, University of Chicago, 1966; (contributor) Alfred Balk and James Boylen, editors, *Our Troubled Press*, Little, Brown, 1971; (contributor) Michael Emery and Ted Smythe, editors, *Readings in Mass Communication: Concepts and Issues in the Mass Media*, W. C. Brown, 1974. Contributor to *New York Magazine, Columbia Journalism Review, New York Times Magazine, Saturday Review*, and other publications.

WORK IN PROGRESS: A study of television and presidential politics, for M.I.T. Press, tentatively entitled, *The Tin Kazoo*. Also continuing studies of television coverage of political news.

DICK, Kay 1915-

PERSONAL: Born July 29, 1915, in London, England. *Education:* Educated in English boarding schools, in Geneva, Switzerland, and at Lycee Francais, London, England. *Politics:* Radical. *Religion:* "Potential Roman Catholic convert." *Home:* 3 Essex Ct., Hampstead High St., London N.W. 3, England. *Agent:* David Higham Associated Ltd., 76 Dean St., London W.1, England; Harold Ober Associates, Inc., 40 East 49th St., New York, N.Y. 10017.

CAREER: For the first ten years of her career worked for publishing and bookselling firms in editorial, publicity, and production jobs; former editor of *Windmill*, published by Heinemann, and former assistant editor of *John O'-London's Weekly*; sometime publisher's reader and broadcaster; free-lance writer and novelist.

WRITINGS: (Compiler) *The Mandrake Root: An Anthology of Fantastic Tales*, Jarrolds, 1946; (compiler) *At the Close of Eve: An Anthology of New Curious Stories*, Jarrolds, 1947; *By the Lake* (novel), Heinemann, 1949; *Young Man* (novel), Heinemann, 1951; *An Affair of Love* (novel), Heinemann, 1953; *Solitaire* (novel), Heinemann, 1958; *Pierrot: An Investigation into the Commedia dell arte*, Hutchinson, 1960; *Sunday* (novel), Hutchinson, 1962; (editor) Edgar Allen Poe, *Bizarre and Arabesque: A New Anthology of Tales, Poems, and Prose*, Panther, 1967; *Ivy and Stevie: Ivy Compton-Burnett and Stevie Smith: Conversations and Reflections*, Duckworth, 1971; (compiler) *Writers at Work: The Paris Review Interviews*, Penguin, 1972. Author of plays, and of scripts for British Broadcasting Corp. Contributor to literary journals.

WORK IN PROGRESS: Suicide, a novel; *The Carlyle Marriage*, for M. Joseph and Coward.

SIDELIGHTS: Ms. Dick is bilingual in French and English. The University of Texas Library is acquiring her original manuscripts.†

* * *

DICKIE, John 1923-

PERSONAL: Born November 24, 1923, in Glasgow, Scotland; son of Hugh (a stock exchange dealer) and Euphemia Dickie; married Inez White, August 9, 1949; children: Lorna Kay, Nigel Hugh. *Education:* University of Glasgow, M.A. (honors), 1949. *Religion:* Presbyterian. *Home:* 4 Heathside, Esher, Surrey, England. *Office: Daily Mail*, Northcliffe House, London E.C. 4, England.

CAREER: Kemsley Newspapers, Sheffield, England, leader writer and reporter, 1949-53; Reuters News Agency, London, England, desk editor, 1953-55; *News Chronicle*, London, England, Commonwealth correspondent, 1955-59; *Daily Mail*, London, England, diplomatic correspondent, 1959—. Television and radio broadcaster. *Military service:* British Army, Royal Artillery, 1942-47; became major.

WRITINGS: The Uncommon Commoner (Sir Alec Douglas-Home), Praeger, 1964.

SIDELIGHTS: Dickie is competent in French and Italian. He has traveled as correspondent in Europe, Africa, and Asia, and covered all major international conferences of last five years in Moscow, New York, Paris, and Geneva.†

* * *

DICKINSON, Leon T. 1912-

PERSONAL: Born January 24, 1912, in Chicago, Ill.; son

of Frederick (a lawyer) and Lora (Townsend) Dickinson; married Margaret Stewart; married Carolyn Ford; children: Brian, Marjorie, Catherine. *Education:* Williams College, A.B., 1933; University of Chicago, M.A., 1934, Ph.D., 1945. *Politics:* Democrat. *Home:* 807 Crestland Ave., Columbia, Mo. 65201. *Office:* Arts and Science 214, University of Missouri, Columbia, Mo.

CAREER: Instructor at junior colleges and colleges, 1934-43, at University of Chicago, Chicago, Ill., 1943-46; University of Missouri, Columbia, assistant professor, 1946-56, associate professor, 1956-60, professor of English, 1960—. Fulbright lecturer in American literature in Netherlands, 1952-53, in Belgium, 1963-64, in France, 1971-72. *Member:* Modern Language Association of America, American Studies Association.

WRITINGS: (Editor with Donald Clark, Charles Hudson, and George Pace) *English Leterature: A College Anthology,* Macmillan, 1960; *A Guide to Literary Study,* Holt, 1960.

WORK IN PROGRESS: Editing Mark Twain's *Innocents Abroad* for "Manuscript Edition" of Mark Twain.

* * *

DICKSON, (Horatio Henry) Lovat 1902-

PERSONAL: Born June 30, 1902, in Victoria, Australia; son of Gordon Fraser and Josephine (Cunningham) Dickson; married Marguerite Brodie, December, 1934; children: Jonathan Alexander Brodie. *Education:* University of Alberta, B.A., 1927, M.A., 1929. *Home:* 21 Dale Ave., Toronto, Ontario, Canada. *Agent:* A. M. Heath, King William IV St., London, England.

CAREER: Worked in mines, dockyards, and farms in Canada before founding and editing a weekly newspaper in Alberta; University of Alberta, Edmonton, lecturer in English, 1927-29; *Fortnightly ReView,* London, England, associate editor, 1929-32; *Review of Reviews,* London, England, editor, 1930-32; Lovat Dickson Ltd. (publishers), London, England, managing editor, 1932-38, editor of *Lovat Dickson's Magazine,* 1934-37; Macmillan & Co. Ltd. (publishers), London, England, assistant general editor, 1938-41, director, 1941-64, retired, 1964. *Member:* Garrick Club.

WRITINGS: The Green Leaf, Lovat Dickson Ltd., 1938; *Half-Breed, the Story of Grey Owl,* P. Davies, 1938; *Out of the West Land,* Collins, 1944; *Richard Hillary,* St. Martin's, 1950; *The Ante Room* (Volume I of autobiography), Atheneum, 1960; *The House of Words* (Volume II of autobiography), Atheneum, 1962; *H. G. Wells: His Turbulent Life and Times,* Atheneum, 1969; *Wilderness Man,* Atheneum, 1974.

SIDELIGHTS: Dickson's biography of H. G. Wells was excellently received by critics. C. P. Snow commented in his review: "Mr. Dickson admires him rather more than he admits. Still, he has shown good equable sense throughout the biography, and it is beautifully written in the clear, positive English that lights up his own autobiographical works." Thomas Lask said of Dickson's work: ". . .he has been brilliantly successful in fixing on paper the propulsive, energetic, fertile, and imaginative character of Wells, the weaknesses in his moral nature, the play and force of his ideas, and the course of his life and popularity. His book will do what Well's own books evidently fail to do: send the reader back to the man and the works.

BIOGRAPHICAL/CRITICAL SOURCES: Lovat Dick-

son, *The Ante Room,* Atheneum, 1960; Dickson *The House of Words,* Atheneum, 1962.

* * *

DICKSON, Mora (Hope-Robertson) 1918-

PERSONAL: Born April 20, 1918, in Glasgow, Scotland; daughter of Laurence and Mora (Sloan) Hope-Robertson; married Alexander Graeme Dickson, August 30, 1951. *Education:* Edinburgh College of Art, Diploma of Art, 1941; Byam Shaw School of Drawing and Painting, London, England, Certificate, 1950. *Religion:* Christian. *Home:* 19 Blenheim Rd., London, W4, England.

CAREER: Writer and artist. Founder with husband of Community Service Volunteers and Voluntary Service Overseas, two organizations to guide volunteers in the sixteen to twenty-four age group.

WRITINGS: Baghdad and Beyond, Rand McNally, 1962; *New Nigerians,* Rand McNally, 1963; *A Season in Sarawak,* Rand McNally, 1964; *A World Elsewhere,* Rand McNally, 1965; *Israeli Interlude,* Dobson, 1965; *Count Us In,* Dobson, 1966; *Longhouse in Sarawak,* Gollancz, 1971; *Beloved Partner,* Gollancz, 1974.

SIDELIGHTS: Mrs. Dickson has lived and worked in Nigeria, Iraq, and Sarawak and has travelled extensively throughout Asia, the Pacific and the United States.

* * *

DICKSON, Peter George Muir 1929-

PERSONAL: Born April 26, 1929, in London, England; son of William Muir (a surgeon) and Regina Magdalene (Dowdall-Nicolls) Dickson; married Ariane Flore Faye, October 27, 1964. *Education:* Oxford University, B.A. (first class honors), 1950, M.A., 1954, D. Phil., 1962. *Politics:* Center. *Religion:* Church of England. *Home:* Field House, Iffley, Oxford, England. *Office:* St. Catherine's College, Oxford, England.

CAREER: Oxford University, Oxford, England, research fellow, Nuffield College, 1954-56, fellow and tutor in modern history, St. Catherine's College, 1960—.

WRITINGS: The Sun Insurance Office, 1710-1960, Oxford University Press, 1960; *The Financial Revolution in England: A Study in the Development of Public Credit, 1688-1756,* Macmillan, 1967; (contributor, with J. G. Sperling) J. S. Bromley, editor, *New Cambridge Modern History,* Volume VI: *The Rise of Great Britain and Russia, 1688-1715/25,* Cambridge University Press, 1970; (editor with Anne Whiteman and J. S. Bromley, and contributor) *Statesmen, Scholars, and Merchants: Essays in Eighteenth-Century History,* Oxford University Press, 1973.

WORK IN PROGRESS: Finance and Commerce under Maria Theresia: A Study of Economics and Government under Enlightened Absolutism, completion expected in 1976.

SIDELIGHTS: Dickson is competent, in varying degrees, in French, German, Dutch, Spanish, and Italian. *Avocational interests:* Swimming, tennis, walking.

* * *

DIEBOLD, William, Jr. 1918-

PERSONAL: Born March 23, 1918, in New York, N.Y.; son of William (a lawyer), and Rose (Theurer) Diebold; married second wife, Ruth Brody Corcoran (a librarian),

August 28, 1953; children: (first marriage) Barbara H. (Mrs. Thomas A. Wick), John B., Beatrice A., (second marriage) William J.; (stepchildren) David Corcoran, John Corcoran. *Education:* Swarthmore College, B.A., 1937; graduate study at Yale University and at London School of Economics and Political Science, London, 1937-39. *Home:* 204 North Broadway, Upper Nyack, N.Y. *Office:* Council on Foreign Relations, 58 East 68th St., New York, N.Y. 10021.

CAREER: Council on Foreign Relations, New York, N.Y., Rockefeller research fellow, 1939-40, research associate, War and Peace Studies, 1940-43; U.S. Department of State, Division of Commercial Policy, Washington, D.C., staff member, 1945-47; Council on Foreign Relations, director of economic studies, 1947-62, senior research fellow, 1962—. Diebold Group, Inc. (management consultants), New York, N.Y., director. U.S. Department of State, consultant, 1941-43. *Wartime service:* Office of Strategic Services, 1943-45, first as a civilian, later in U.S. Army; became sergeant. *Member:* American Economic Association, African Studies Association, Phi Beta Kappa.

WRITINGS: New Directions in Our Trade Policy, Council on Foreign Relations, 1941; *Trade and Payments in Western Europe: A Study in Economic Cooperation, 1947-51,* Harper, for Council on Foreign Relations, 1952; *The Schuman Plan: A Study in Economic Cooperation 1950-1959,* Praeger, for Council on Foreign Relations, 1959; *Dollars, Jobs, Trade, and Aid,* New York Foreign Policy Association, 1972; *The United States and the Industrial World: American Foreign Economic Policy in the Seventies,* Praeger, for Council on Foreign Relations, 1972. Writer of pamphlets, articles, and reviews.

WORK IN PROGRESS: Research in U.S. foreign economic policy.†

* * *

DIEZ DEL CORRAL, Luis 1911-

PERSONAL: Born July 5, 1911, in Logrono, Spain; son of Luis and Vicenta (Pedruzo) Diez del Corral; married Rosario de Garnica, July 3, 1942; children: Rosario, Isabel, Teresa, Luis. *Education:* University of Madrid, Lic. en Derecho; attended Universities of Berlin and Freiburg in Breisgau. *Religion:* Roman Catholic. *Home:* Jorge Juan 7, Madrid, Spain. *Office:* University of Madrid, San Bernardo 49, Madrid, Spain.

CAREER: Council of State, Madrid, Spain, lawyer, 1936—; University of Madrid, Madrid, Spain, professor of the history of political ideas, 1947—. *Member:* Sociedad de Estudios Clasicos, Sociedad de Ciencia Politica, Real Academia de Ciencias Morales y Politicas, Real Club de Puerta de Hierro. *Awards, honors:* Premio Nacional de Literatura, 1942, for *Mallorca.*

WRITINGS: (Translator) F. Hoelderlin, *El Archipielago,* Editora Nacional, 1942, 2nd edition, Revista de Occidente, 1971; *Mallorca,* Editorial Juventud, 1942 (published in English as *Majorca,* Norton, 1963); *El Liberalismo doctrinario,* Instituto de Estudios Politicos, 1945 2nd edition, 1964; *El Rapto de Europa,* Revista de Occidente, 1954 (published in English as *Rape of Europe,* Macmillan, 1959); *Ensayos sobre arte y sociedad,* Revista de Occidente, 1955; *De historia y politica,* Instituto de Estudio Politicos, 1956; *La Funcion del mito clasico en la literatura contemporanea,* Editorial Gredos, 1957; *Del Nuevo al Viejo Mundo,* Revista de Occidente, 1963; *La Mentalidad politica de Tocqueville con especial referencia a Pascal,* Madrid,

1965; *Valazquez y la monarquia catolica,* Madrid, 1968; *La desmitification de la Antiguedad clasica por los pensadores liberales, con especial referencia a Tocqueville,* Taurus, 1969; *Problemas actuales de la cultura superior,* Universidad de Valladolid, 1969.

SIDELIGHTS: Diez Del Corral has language competence in French, German, and English. His works have been translated into German, French, Dutch, Japanese, and Italian. *Avocational interests:* Art, travel.†

* * *

DILLEY, Frank B(rown) 1931-

PERSONAL: Born November 17, 1931, in Athens, Ohio; son of Frank Brown (a college administrator) and Geneva (Steiner) Dilley; married Jane Long, September 10, 1953; children: Frank Brian, Carol Jane, Kathryn Elizabeth. *Education:* Ohio University, A.B., 1952, M.A., 1953; Union Theological Seminary, New York, N.Y., B.D., 1955; Columbia University, Ph.D., 1962. *Politics:* Democrat. *Home:* 106 Tanglewood Lane, Newark, Del. 19711. *Office:* Department of Philosophy, University of Delaware, Newark, Del.

CAREER: Smith College, Northampton, Mass., 1957-62, began as instructor, became assistant professor of religion; Millikin University, Decatur, Ill., associate professor of philosophy and chairman of department, 1962-67; University of Delaware, Newark, Del., professor of philosophy and chairman of department, 1967—, associate provost, 1970-74. Member of board of advisors, Walden University, 1971—. *Military service:* U.S. Air Force Reserve, 1953-65. *Member:* American Academy of Religion, American Philosophical Association, Metaphysical Society of America. *Awards, honors:* American Council on Education academic administration internship, 1965-66.

WRITINGS: (Contributor) *Masterpieces of Christian Literature,* Harper, 1963; (contributor) *Philosophical Perplexities,* Holt, 1964; *Metaphysics and Religious Language,* Columbia University Press, 1964. Reviewer for *Religion in Life.* Contributor to philosophical and religious journals.

WORK IN PROGRESS: Two books, *What Should a Proof for God Be?,* and *The Interpretation of Religious Symbols.*

* * *

DILLINGHAM, William B(yron) 1930-

PERSONAL: Born March 7, 1930, in Atlanta, Ga.; son of Cornelius Howard and Emerald (Storey) Dillingham; married Elizabeth Joiner, July 3, 1952; children: Rebecca Lynn, Judith Ann, Paul Christopher. *Education:* Emory University, B.A., 1955, M.A., 1956; University of Pennsylvania, Ph.D., 1961. *Politics:* Democrat. *Religion:* Protestant. *Home:* 1416 Vistaleaf Dr., Decatur, Ga. 30038. *Office:* Department of English, Emory University, Atlanta, Ga. 30322.

CAREER: Emory University, Atlanta, Ga., instructor, 1956-62, assistant professor, 1962-66, associate professor, 1966-68, professor of English, 1968—. Fulbright visiting professor, American Institute, University of Oslo, Oslo, Norway, 1964-65. *Military service:* U.S. Army, 1950-52. *Member:* Modern Language Association of America, Melville Society, South Atlantic Modern Language Association.

WRITINGS: (Editor with Hennig Cohen) *Humor of the Old Southwest,* Houghton, 1964; (with Floyd C. Watkins and Edwin T. Martin) *Practical English Handbook*, Houghton, 1965, 4th edition, 1974; *Frank Norris: Instinct and Art*, University of Nebraska Press, 1969; *An Artist in the Rigging: The Early Work of Herman Melville*, University of Georgia Press, 1972. Contributor of numerous articles on American literature to periodicals.

WORK IN PROGRESS: A book on the short fiction of Herman Melville, completion expected in 1976.

*   *   *

DILLON, Merton L.   1924-

PERSONAL: Born April 4, 1924, in Addison, Mich.; son of Henry J. (a farmer) and Cecil (Sanford) Dillon. *Education:* Eastern Michigan University, B.A., 1945; University of Michigan, M.A., 1948, Ph.D., 1951. *Office:* Department of History, Ohio State University, Columbus, Ohio.

CAREER: New Mexico Military Institute, Roswell, assistant professor of history, 1951-56; Texas Technological College (now Texas Tech University), Lubbock, assistant professor, 1956-59, associate professor, 1959-63; professor of history, beginning 1963. Currently professor of history, Ohio State University, Columbus. Visiting instructor, Eastern Michigan University, 1951. *Member:* American Historical Association, American Association of University Professors, Organization of American Historians, Southern Historical Association.

WRITINGS: Elijah P. Lovejoy, Abolitionist Editor, University of Illinois Press, 1961; (with L. L. Graves and others) *A History of Lubbock*, West Texas Museum Association, 1962; *Benjamin Lundy and the Struggle for Negro Freedom*, University of Illinois Press, 1966; *The Abolitionists: The Growth of a Dissenting Minority*, Northern Illinois University Press, 1974. Contributor to *Journal of Southern History*. Member of board of editors, *Journal of Southern History*, 1960-64.

WORK IN PROGRESS: A biography, *Benjamin Lundy and the Struggle for Negro Equality in America*.†

*   *   *

DIMOND, Stanley E(llwood)   1905-

PERSONAL: Born September 9, 1905, in Aurora, Ill.; son of Herman C. (a businessman) and Grace (Lawrence) Dimond; married Helen Stewart, 1930 (died, 1934); married Ruth Bullis, March 30, 1937; children: Robert L., Paul R. *Education:* University of Michigan, A.B., 1927, M.A., 1929, Ph.D., 1942. *Religion:* Congregational. *Home:* 2012 Shadford Rd., Ann Arbor, Mich. 48104. *Office:* 3203 School of Education, University of Michigan, Ann Arbor, Mich. 48104.

CAREER: High school teacher of social studies in Monmouth, Ill., 1927-28, Detroit, Mich., 1929-37; Detroit (Mich.) public schools, supervisor of social studies, 1937-45; Wayne (now Wayne State) University, Detroit, Mich., associate professor, 1937-44, professor of education, 1944-46; director of Detroit Citizenship Education Study, 1945-50; University of Michigan, Ann Arbor, professor of education, 1950-72, professor emeritus, 1972—. *Member:* National Education Association, Association for Supervision and Curriculum Development, American Educational Research Association, National Council for the Social Studies (president, 1948), National Association of Secondary School Principals, Phi Beta Kappa, Phi Delta Kappa.

WRITINGS: Schools and Development of Good Citizens,

Wayne University Press, 1953; (with Elmer F. Pflieger) *Our American Government*, Lippincott, 1957, revised edition, 1973; (with Pflieger) *Civics for Citizens*, Lippincott, 1965, revised edition, 1970. Contributor to educational journals.

WORK IN PROGRESS: Revisions of *Our American Government* and *Civics for Citizens*.

AVOCATIONAL INTERESTS: Golf, bowling.

*   *   *

DINERMAN, Beatrice   1933-

PERSONAL: Born September 12, 1933, in Brooklyn, N.Y.; daughter of Simon (an automobile dealer) and Anna (Winitsky) Rytsis; married Norman Wartell (an engineer), November 9, 1963. *Education:* Hunter College (now Hunter College of the City University of New York), student, 1950-52; Brooklyn College (now Brooklyn College of the City University of New York), B.A. (cum laude), 1954; University of California, Los Angeles, M.P.A., 1957. *Politics:* Democrat. *Religion:* Jewish. *Home:* 15097 Encanto Dr., Sherman Oaks, Calif. *Office:* Comprehensive Health Planning Council of Los Angeles County, 1930 Wilshire Blvd., Los Angeles, Calif. 90057.

CAREER: University of California, Los Angeles, public administration analyst, Bureau of Governmental Research, 1956-62; Welfare Planning Council, Los Angeles, Calif., director of Ford Foundation project on decision-making process in public and private welfare agencies, 1962-65; Economic and Youth Opportunities Agency, Los Angeles, Calif., social science research analyst, 1965-66; University of California, Los Angeles, research associate in School of Public Health, 1966-67; University of Southern California, Los Angeles, consultant in School of Public Administration, 1967-68, research consultant for Regional Research Institute in Social Welfare, 1970-72; Comprehensive Health Planning Council of Los Angeles, Los Angeles, Calif, chief of research and information, 1972—. *Member:* Academy of Political Science, American Academy of Political and Social Science, American Political Science Association, American Society for Public Administration (secretary, Los Angeles chapter, 1957-60, and public administration correspondent, 1957—), National Civic League, Western Governmental Research Association, Public Personnel Association, Southern California Public Personnel Association, Southern California Political Science Association.

WRITINGS: Hospital Development and Communities, Bureau of Governmental Research, University of California, Los Angeles, 1961; (contributor) *Metropolitan Services: Studies of Allocation in a Federated Organization*, Bureau of Governmental Research, University of California, Los Angeles, 1961; (with Winston W. Crouch) *Southern California Metropolis*, University of California Press, 1963; *Priorities and the Decision-Making Process*, Research Department, Welfare Planning Council of Los Angeles, 1963; *The Dynamics of Priority Planning: A Study of Decision Making in Welfare*, Welfare Planning Council of Los Angeles, 1965; *Citizen Participation in the Model Cities Program*, Regional Research Institute in Social Welfare, University of Southern California, 1971. Contributor to professional journals in many fields.

SIDELIGHTS: Ms. Dinerman was the first woman to receive Master of Public Administration degree at University of California, Los Angeles.

BIOGRAPHICAL/CRITICAL SOURCES: Valley News, June 12, 1962.

DINGLE, Herbert 1890-

PERSONAL: Born August 2, 1890, in London, England; son of James Henry (a lecturer) and Emily Jane (Gorddard) Dingle; married Alice Law Westacott, December 7, 1918 (deceased); children: Peter. Education: Imperial College of Science and Technology, London, B.Sc. (first class honors), 1918, A.R.C.S. (first class honors), 1918, D.I.C., 1920, D.Sc., 1930. Home: 104 Downs Court Rd., Purley, Surrey, England.

CAREER: University of London, Imperial College of Science and Technology, London, England, 1918-46, began as lecturer, became professor of natural philosophy, University College, professor of history and philosophy of science, 1946-55, professor emeritus, 1955—. Member: International Astronomical Union, International Union for the History of Science (vice-president, 1953-56), British Society for the History of Science (president, 1955-57), Royal Astronomical Society (vice-president, 1938-39, 1942-44, 1948-50; president, 1951-53).

WRITINGS: Relativity for All, Methuen, 1922; Modern Astrophysics, Collins, 1924; (editor) Life and Work of Sir Norman Lockyer, Macmillan, 1929; Science and Human Experience, Williams & Norgate, 1931; Through Science to Philosophy, Oxford University Press, 1937; The Special Theory of Relativity, Methuen, 1940; Mechanical Physics, Nelson, 1941; Sub-Atomic Physics, Nelson, 1942; Science and Literary Criticism, Nelson, 1949; Practical Applications of Spectrum Analysis, Chapman & Hall, 1950; (editor) A Century of Science, Hutchinson, 1951; The Scientific Adventure, Pitman, 1952; The Sources of Eddington's Philosophy, Cambridge University Press, 1954; (with Viscount Samuel) A Threefold Cord, Allen & Unwin, 1961; (co-editor) Chemistry and Beyond, Wiley, 1964; Science at the Crossroads, Martin Brian & O'Keeffe, 1972; The Mind of Emily Brontë, Martin Brian & O'Keeffe, 1974.

Contributor: Splendour of the Heavens, 1923; The New World Order, 1932; The New Learning, 1933; Science Today, 1934. Also contributor to Encyclopaedia Britannica and to scientific and philosophy journals.

*　　*　　*

di ROCCAFERRERA FERRERO, Giuseppe M. 1912-

PERSONAL: Born July 20, 1912, in Turin, Italy; came to United States, 1957; son of Camillo Mario and Giuseppina (Mariano) di Roccaferrera Ferrero, married Luisa R. Bacchini, November 20, 1952; children: Fernanda, Maurizio. Education: Technical Institute of Turin, B.S., 1929; Technological and Industrial Institute, Turin, M.S., 1933; University of Turin, Ph.D. (summa cum laude), 1939. Home: 13 Brattle Rd., Syracuse, N.Y. 13203. Office: School of Management, Syracuse University, Syracuse, N.Y. 13210.

CAREER: Prior to coming to United States, owned and directed a consultant service for the mechanization of offices by computer systems, Milano, Italy, 1948-57; New York University, New York, N.Y., lecturer in management, 1957-58; University of Florida, Gainesville, associate professor of management, 1958-62; University of Pennsylvania, Philadelphia, associate professor of industry, 1962-65; Syracuse University, Syracuse, N.Y., professor of management science, 1965—. Associate of Consultants to Industry, Inc., New York, N.Y.; member of board of directors, Growth Research and Planning Institute of New York, 1972; member of scientific and management advisory

committee, Computer Systems Command of the U.S. Army, 1972. Military service: Italian Army, Artillery; became captain. Member: Operations Research Society of America, Institute of Management Science, American Association of University Professors, Alpha Kappa Psi, Beta Gamma Sigma, Rotary International.

WRITINGS: Le Richerche di Mercato, Spinardi (Turin), 1956; La Meccanizzazione nel Programma e nel Controllo della Produzione Industriale, Giuffre (Milan), 1957; Methods for Increasing the Effective Capacity of I.B.M. Punched Cards in Statistical and Accounting Applications, American Data Processing Publishing Co., 1962; Operations Research Models for Business and Industry, South-Western, 1964; Introduction to Linear Programming Processes, South-Western, 1967. Contributor of articles to specialized economics and business magazines.

WORK IN PROGRESS: Computer and Data Processing Techniques for Managerial Applications.

SIDELIGHTS: di Roccaferrera Ferrero is fluent in French and Spanish, as well as Italian.

*　　*　　*

DOBSON, Eric John 1913-

PERSONAL: Born August 16, 1913, in Sydney, Australia; son of John (an accountant) and Lottie Frances (Sippe) Dobson; married Francis Margaret Stinton, July 14, 1940; children: Jane Frances, Jeremy Thomas, John Charles. Education: University of Sydney, B.A., 1934; Oxford University, B.A. 1937, M.A., 1942, D.Phil., 1951. Home: 9 Davenant Rd., Oxford, England.

CAREER: University of Sydney, Sydney, Australia, tutor in English, 1934-35; University of Reading, Reading, England, lecturer in English. 1940-48; Oxford University, Oxford, England, lecturer in English at Jesus College and St. Edmund Hall, 1948-54, professorial fellow of Jesus College, 1954—, university reader in English language, 1954-64, university professor of English language, 1964—. Wartime service: British Intelligence Service, as civil servant, 1942-45. Member: British Academy (fellow), Philological Society (honorary treasurer, 1974—).

WRITINGS: English Pronunciation 1500-1700, Clarendon Press, 1957; (editor) Robert Robinson, The Phonetic Writings, Early English Text Society, 1957; (contributor) English and Medieval Studies Presented to J. R. R. Tolkien, Allen & Unwin, 1962; (editor) Ancrene Riwle (English text), Oxford University Press for the Early English Text Society, 1973. Contributor of articles and reviews to scholarly periodicals.

WORK IN PROGRESS: Books on newly discovered sources and origins of, Ancrene Wisse, for Clarendon Press; (with Frank Harrison) Medieval English Songs.

*　　*　　*

DOBSON, William A(rthur) C(harles) H(arvey) 1913-

PERSONAL: Born August 8, 1913, in London, England; son of William Archibald (an army officer) and Daisy Harriet (Hamblyn) Dobson; children: Guy St. Clair, Iain St. Clair. Education: Christ Church, Oxford, B.A. and M.A., 1946, D.Litt., 1964. Religion: Church of England. Home: Plaza 100, 100 Wellesley St. E., Toronto, Ontario, Canada. Office: 47 Queen's Park Crescent E., University of Toronto, Toronto, Ontario, Canada.

CAREER: University of Toronto, Toronto, Ontario, professor of Chinese, 1952—, head of department, 1952-64. Military service: British Army, 1940-46; became lieutenant colonel; received Order of Cloud and Banner (China).

WRITINGS—All published by University of Toronto Press, except as indicated: (Editor) Select List of Books on the Civilizations of the Orient, Oxford University Press, 1955; Late Archaic Chinese, 1959; Early Archaic Chinese, 1962; Mencius, 1963; Late Han Chinese, 1964; The Language of the Book of Songs, 1968; A Dictionary of the Chinese Particles, in press. Contributor of articles and reviews to learned journals.

WORK IN PROGRESS: The Tso Chuan: A Translation with Introduction and Notes; The Three Hundred Songs; The Poetry Classic of Ancient China.

* * *

DOCKSTADER, Frederick J. 1919-

PERSONAL: Born February 3, 1919, in Los Angeles, Calif.; son of Frederick and Dorothy (Wilson) Dockstader; married Alice Elizabeth Warren (an architect), December 25, 1952. Education: Arizona State College, B.A., 1940, M.A., 1941; Western Reserve University (now Case Western Reserve University), Ph.D., 1951. Home: 165 West 66th St., New York, N.Y. 10023. Office: Museum of the American Indian, Heye Foundation, Broadway at 155th St., New York, N.Y. 10032.

CAREER: Cranbrook Institute of Science, Bloomfield Hills, Mich., research associate, 1942-50, staff ethnologist, 1950-52; Dartmouth College, Hanover, N.H., faculty member and museum curator, 1952-55; Museum of the American Indian, Heye Foundation, New York, N.Y., associate director, 1955-60, director, 1960—. Practicing silversmith. U.S. Department of the Interior, Indian Arts and Crafts Board, commissioner, 1955-67, chairman, 1965-67. Adjunct professor, Columbia University, 1964-66. Member: Cranbrook Institute of Science (fellow), Rochester Museum of Arts and Sciences (fellow), American Anthropological Association (fellow), American Association of Museums, Society for American Archaeology, New York State Museum Association (treasurer), New York City Museums Council (former president), Cosmos Club (Washington, D.C.), Century Club (New York). Awards, honors: Lotos Club award, 1972.

WRITINGS: Kachina and the White Man, Cranbrook Institute of Science, 1954; (editor with Alice W. Dockstader) The American Indian in Graduate Studies: A Bibliography of Theses and Dissertations (1955-70), Museum of the American Indian, 1955, 2nd revised edition, 1974; Indian Art in America: The Arts and Crafts of the North American Indian, New York Graphic Society, 1962, 3rd revised edition, 1968; Indian Art in Middle America: Pre-Columbian and Contemporary Arts and Crafts of Mexico, Central America, and the Caribbean, New York Graphic Society, 1964; Indian Art in South America: Pre-Columbian and Contemporary Arts and Crafts, New York Graphic Society, 1967; (with Ferdinand Anton) Pre-Columbian Art and Later Indian Tribal Arts, Abrams, 1968; (with Lewis Krevolin) Naked Clay: Unadorned Pottery of the American Indian, Museum of the American Indian, 1972; (compiler) Books About Indians, 2nd revised edition, Museum of the American Indian, 1972; Indian Art of the Americas, Museum of the American Indian, 1973; Masterworks from the Museum of the American Indian, Heye Foundation, Metropolitan Museum of Art, 1973; Collecting American Indian Arts and Crafts, Crown, 1973.

WORK IN PROGRESS: A Hopi Kachina study; and other studies on American Indian languages and art.

SIDELIGHTS: Dr. Dockstader lived much of his early life on Navajo and Hopi reservations. He writes that his areas of interest cover all the Americas, and his "primary concern is the ability of aboriginal man to maintain his culture vis-a-vis encroaching Western civilization." He has traveled extensively, and knows Spanish, French, Portuguese, and several Amerindian tongues. Dockstader has been active in the designing and working of silver for most of his life, and taught the craft for many years in Michigan and New Hampshire. His work has been exhibited in a great many museums and has won prizes at the Cranbrook Art Academy, the Cleveland Institute of Art, and other exhibits of this nature.

* * *

DODGE, Richard Holmes 1926-

PERSONAL: Born May 22, 1926, in Lawrence, Mass.; son of Israel Rogers (a salesman) and Ann (McCarthy) Dodge; married Margaret Hangen, March 11, 1952; children: Ashley (daughter), Jason. Education: University of New Hampshire, B.A., 1951; University of California, Los Angeles, M.A., 1954, doctoral candidate. Politics: Democrat. Religion: Unitarian Universalist. Home: 1649 Wellesley Dr., Santa Monica, Calif.

CAREER: University of California, Los Angeles, instructor in English, 1955; Santa Monica City College, Santa Monica, Calif., professor of English, 1956—. Military service: U.S. Army, Infantry, 1944-46; 1951-53, served in Korean War, became first lieutenant. Member: American Federation of Teachers, National Council of Teachers of English, American Association of University Professors.

WRITINGS: How to Read and Write in College, Harper, Form 1, 1962, Form 2, 1964, Form 3, 1967, Form 4, 1969, Form 5, 1972; The Shorter Harper Handbook, Harper, 1965; The Shorter Harper Workbook (two forms), Harper, 1965; Divided We Stand, Canfield Press, 1970.

WORK IN PROGRESS: Writing a modern American rhetoric, completion expected in 1975; second series of How To Read and Write In College, Form 1, completion expected in 1976.

* * *

DOLL, Ronald C. 1913-

PERSONAL: Born March 14, 1913, in Mehoopany, Pa.; son of H. Stanley (a salesman) and Florence (Carpenter) Doll; married Ruth E. Paul, June 16, 1940; children: Cheryl R. Education: Columbia University, B.A., 1934, M.A., 1935, Ed.D., 1951. Religion: Presbyterian. Office: Richmond College of the City University of New York, 130 Stuyvesant Pl., Staten Island, N.Y. 10301.

CAREER: Dallas, Pa., and Cranford, N.J., Public Schools, teacher, counselor, acting principal, 1935-43; West Orange, N.J., Public Schools, administrative assistant and director of guidance, 1944-52; Columbia University, New York, N.Y., Citizenship Education Project, curriculum specialist, 1952-53; Montclair, N.J., Public Schools, director of instruction, 1953-57; New York University, New York, N.Y., professor of education, 1957-61; City University of New York, New York, N.Y., Hunter College, professor of education, 1961-67, Richmond College, dean of teacher education, 1967-68, professor of education, 1968—. Consultant to school systems, state departments of education, and publishers. *Member:* Association for Supervision and Curriculum Development, National Education Association, National Society for the Study of Education, American Educational Research Association, New York State Teachers' Association, Phi Delta Kappa, Kappa Delta Pi.

WRITINGS: (With others) *Organizing for Curriculum Improvement*, Horace Mann-Lincoln Institute of School Experimentation, Teachers College, Columbia University, 1953; (with T. C. Pollack and others) *The Art of Communicating* (textbook), Macmillan, 1955, 2nd edition, 1961; (contributor) B. M. Harris, editor, *Supervisory Behavior in Education*, Prentice-Hall, 1963; *Curriculum Improvement: Decision-Making and Process*, Allyn & Bacon, 1964, 2nd edition, 1970; (editor with R. S. Fleming) *Children Under Pressure: A Collection of Readings about Scholastic Pressure*, C. E. Merrill, 1966; (contributor) William Van Til, editor, *Curriculum: Quest for Relevance*, Houghton, 1971, 2nd edition, 1974; *Leadership to Improve Schools*, Charles A. Jones Publishing, 1972; (with Ruth C. Cook) *The Elementary School Curriculum*, Allyn & Bacon, 1972. Editor and contributor to yearbooks of the Association for Supervision of Curriculum Development; contributor to *Educational Leadership*.

WORK IN PROGRESS: The third edition of *Curriculum Improvement: Decision-Making and Process;* and a chapter for the 1976 yearbook of the National Society for the Study of Education.

AVOCATIONAL INTERESTS: Fishing, golf, history, and theology.

*   *   *

DONALDSON, Gordon 1913-

PERSONAL: Born April 13, 1913, in Edinburgh, Scotland; son of Magnus and Rachel (Swan) Donaldson. *Education:* University of Edinburgh, M.A., 1935, D.Litt., 1954; University of London, Ph.D., 1938. *Religion:* Episcopalian. *Home:* 24 East Hermitage Pl., Edinburgh 6, Scotland. *Office:* University of Edinburgh, William Robertson Building, Edinburgh 8, Scotland.

CAREER: H. M. General Register House, Edinburgh, Scotland, 1938-47; University of Edinburgh, Edinburgh, Scotland, lecturer in Scottish history and palaeography, 1947-55, reader, 1955-63, professor of Scottish history and palaeography, 1963—.

WRITINGS: The Making of the Scottish Prayer Book of 1637, Edinburgh University Press, 1954; *Shetland Life under Earl Patrick*, Oliver & Boyd, 1958; *Scotland: Church and Nation through Sixteen Centuries*, S.C.M. Press, 1960, 2nd edition, Scottish Academic Press, 1972; *The Scottish Reformation*, Cambridge University Press, 1960, 2nd edition, 1972; (with R. L. Mackie) *A Short History of Scotland*, Oliver & Boyd, 1962; *Scotland: James V to James VII*, Oliver & Boyd, 1965, Praeger, 1966; *The Scots Overseas*, R. Hale, 1966; *Northwards By Sea*, John Grant, 1966; *Scottish Kings*, Batsford, 1967, Wiley, 1967; *The First Trial of Mary, Queen of Scots*, Batsford, 1969, Stein & Day, 1970; *Scottish Historical Documents*, Barnes & Noble, 1970; (with Robert S. Morpeth) *Who's Who In Scottish History*, Barnes & Noble, 1973. Editor of texts for Scottish History Society, Scottish Record Society, and Stair Society.

DONAT, John (Annesley) 1933-

PERSONAL: Born September 12, 1933, in London, England; son of Robert (an actor) and Ella (Volsey) Donat. *Education:* Architectural Association School of Architecture, London, England, A.R.I.B.A. and A.A., 1956. *Home and office:* 5 Belsize Park Gardens, London, N.W.3, England.

CAREER: Architect, architectural photographer, and writer. *Member:* Architectural Association (associate), Royal Institute of British Architects.

WRITINGS: (Editor) *World Architecture* (annual review), Volume 1, Viking, 1964, Volume II, Viking, 1965, Volume III, 1966. Writer of documentary script, "The Rape of Utopia—Jam Tomorrow," and of television scripts for British Broadcasting Corp. "Monitor" program. Columnist, "Architectural Design," in *World News*; contributor of several illustrated articles to *Sunday Times*.

WORK IN PROGRESS: Documentaries for British Broadcasting Corp. television.

SIDELIGHTS: Donat told *CA*, "Most of what I do relates directly to the man-made world: architecture, planning, and the environment. My photographs (taken for architects and published by the technical press) probably prolong the incestuous myths created by the architects themselves, but *World Architecture* and especially scripts for television deliberately set out to break down the barriers between architects and the people they build for, with particular reference to the urban crisis, the population explosion, and the two-thirds of the world we have hardly begun to think about."†

*   *   *

DONER, Mary Frances 1893-

PERSONAL: Surname is pronounced to rhyme with "owner"; born July 29, 1893, in Port Huron, Mich.; daughter of James (a steamship line manager) and Mary Jane (O'Rourke) Doner. *Education:* Studied music at New City College (now City College of the City University of New York), and York University, privately, and journalism at Columbia University. *Religion:* Roman Catholic. *Home and office:* 210 North Lewis St., Ludington, Mich. 49431. *Agent:* Paul R. Reynolds, Inc., 599 Fifth Ave., New York, N.Y. 10017; (films) Annie Laurie Williams, Inc., 18 East 41st St., New York, N.Y. 10017.

CAREER: Dell Publishing Co., New York, N.Y., staff writer, 1924-32; *Herald-Traveller*, Boston, Mass., music reporter, 1928-31; magazine writer and novelist. Teacher of creative writing at Boston Center for Adult Education, 1943-45, and in Ludington, Mich.; lecturer at universities, libraries, book fairs, and writers' conferences; member of literary panel at Albion College, 1953, and University of Michigan Summer Writers' Conference, 1954. *Member:* Women's National Book Association, National League of Catholic Women, Pen and Brush Club (New York), Port Huron Library Association, Woman's Literary Club (Ludington, Mich.; honorary member), St. Clair Woman's Club (St. Clair, Mich.; honorary member).

WRITINGS—All published by Chelsea House, except as indicated: *The Dancer in the Shadow*, 1930; *The Dark Garden*, 1930; *The Lonely Heart*, 1930; *Fools' Heaven*, 1932; *Broken Melody*, 1932; *Forever More*, 1934; *Let's Burn Our Bridges*, Alfred H. King, 1935; *Child of Conflict*, 1936; *Gallant Traitor*, Penn Publishing, 1938; *Some Fell Among the Thorns*, Penn Publishing, 1939.

The Doctor's Party, Penn Publishing, 1940; *Chalice*, Penn Publishing, 1940; *Not By Bread Alone*, Doubleday, Doran, 1941; *Glass Mountain*, Doubleday, 1942; *O Distant Star!*, Doubleday, 1944; *Blue River*, Doubleday, 1946; *Ravenswood*, Doubleday, 1948; *Cloud of Arrows*, Doubleday, 1950; *The Host Rock*, Doubleday, 1952; *The Salvager* (biography), Ross & Haines, 1958.

The Shores of Home, Bouregy, 1961; *While the River Flows*, Bouregy, 1962; *The Wind and the Fog*, Bouregy, 1963; *Cleavenger vs. Castle: A Case of Breach of Promise and Seduction*, Dorrance, 1968; *Return a Stranger*, Bouregy, 1970; *Thine Is the Power*, Bouregy, 1972; *Not By Appointment*, Bouregy, 1973; *The Darker Star*, Bouregy, 1974. Also author of booklet, *Pere Marquette: Soldier of the Cross*, for Pere Marquette Society, 1969.

Contributor of nearly three hundred short stories and novelettes to pulp magazines in earlier years; later contributor to *Toronto Daily Star* and other Canadian newspapers, and to periodicals, including *Woman's Home Companion, Woman Today, Charm, Modern Priscilla, Chatelaine*.

WORK IN PROGRESS: A documentary for Albion College.

SIDELIGHTS: Ms. Doner's books generally are based in the Great Lakes area; a number of them have been transcribed into Braille, and *The Host Rock* was broadcast as a radio serial by American Broadcasting Co.

BIOGRAPHICAL/CRITICAL SOURCES: Harry R. Warfel, *American Novelists of Today*, American Book Co., 1951; *Michigan Authors*, Association of School Librarians of the Michigan Educational Association, 1960.

*   *   *

DONNELLY, Desmond L(ouis)   1920-

PERSONAL: Born October 16, 1920, in India; son of L. J. and Aimee (Tucker) Donnelly; married Rosemary Taggart, 1947; children: Elizabeth, Redmond and Rosamund (twins). *Education:* Attended Bembridge School, Isle of Wight. *Politics:* Conservative. *Home:* Dyfed, Roch, Haverfordwest, Pembrokeshire, Wales. *Agent:* Peter Janson-Smith Ltd., 2 Caxton St., London S.W.1, England.

CAREER: Town and Country Planning Association, editor of *Town and Country Planning*, 1946-49, director of association, 1948-50; Labour member of Parliament for Pembroke, 1950-68, Independent party member of Parliament, 1968-70. Joined Conservative party, 1971. Author. *Military service:* Royal Air Force, 1939-45; became flight lieutenant. *Member:* Travellers' Club, Pembrokeshire Country Club.

WRITINGS: The March Wind, Collins, 1959, Putnam, 1960; (with Alex Nove) *Trade with Communist Countries*, Deutsch, 1960; *David Brown's: The Story of a Family Business, 1860-1960*, Collins, 1960; *Struggle for the World*, St. Martins, 1965; *Gadarene '68: the Crimes Follies and Misfortunes of the Wilson Government*, Kimber, 1968; *The Nearing Storm*, Hutchinson, 1968. Contributor to leading journals in Britain.†

*   *   *

DONNELLY, Sister Gertrude Joseph   1920-

PERSONAL: Born July 29, 1920, in San Francisco, Calif.; daughter of Joseph Peter (a businessman) and Julia Agnes (O'Sullivan) Donnelly. *Education:* Dominican College, San Rafael, Calif., A.B., 1950; Catholic University of America, M.A., 1954, Ph.D., 1962; American Academy in Rome,

postdoctoral study, 1963. *Home:* St. Joseph College, Orange, Calif.

CAREER: Roman Catholic nun of Congregation of St. Joseph of Orange. St. Joseph College of Orange, Calif., chairman of department of Latin and Greek, 1962—. Summer professor at Catholic University of America, 1963, 1964, at California State College (now University), Fullerton, 1965. Active in leadership training in Young Christian Students' Movement and Christian Family Movement. *Member:* American Academy in Rome (fellow), Vergilian Society of America, Renaissance Society of America, Classical Association of the Pacific States. *Awards, honors:* Fulbright grant to American Academy in Rome, 1962, 1963; annual award for literary work, Council of Interamerican Student Relations, for Spanish edition of *How: Aids for Assistants in the Apostolate*, 1964.

WRITINGS: (Author of introduction and notes) St. Thomas More, *Responsio ad Lutherum*, Catholic University Press, 1962; *How: Aids for Assistants in the Apostolate*, Catholic Action Office, 1964; *Sister Apostle*, Fides, 1964. Contributor to *Classical Journal, New Catholic Encyclopedia*, and to Catholic periodicals.

WORK IN PROGRESS: Research on writings (Latin) of St. Thomas More and Erasmus.†

*   *   *

DONNER, Jorn   1933-

PERSONAL: Born February 5, 1933, in Helsinki, Finland; son of Kai and Greta (von Bonsdorff) Donner; married Inga-Britt Wik, 1954 (divorced, 1962); children Johan, Jakob. *Education:* Helsinki University, Mag. Phi., 1961. *Politics:* Left. *Home:* Svartmangatan 24, Stockholm C, Sweden; and Pohjoisranta 12, Helsinki, Finland. *Agent:* Ashley-Steiner-Famous Artists, Inc., 555 Madison Ave., New York 22, N.Y. *Office:* Northern Film Production Establishment, Vaduz, Liechtenstein.

CAREER: Dagens Nyheter, Stockholm, Sweden, literary critic, 1951—; AB Sandrew Film, Stockholm, Sweden, under contract as scriptwriter and feature film director, 1963—. Co-founder, Finnish Film Archive, Helsinki, Finland, 1957. *Member:* Union of Finnish Journalists, Union of Writers in Finland. *Awards, honors:* Venice Film festival, opera prima prize, 1963.

WRITINGS: Valsignade liv (short stories), Soderstrom & Co. (Helsinki), 1951; *Sla dej inte till ro*, Soderstrom & Co., 1952; *Brev*, Soderstrom & Co., 1954; *Jag, Erik Anders* (novel), Soderstrom & Co., 1955; *Bordet* (novel), Soderstrom & Co., 1957; *Rapport fran Berlin*, Albert Bonnier (Stockholm), 1958, published as *Report from Berlin*, Indiana University Press, 1961; *Berliini–arkea ja uhkaa*, Werner Soderstrom (Helsinki), 1958; *Helsingfors–Finlands ansikte*, Soderstrom & Co, 1960; *Djavulens ansikte* (monograph on Ingmar Bergman), Aldus Publishers (Stockholm), 1962, 2nd edition, 1965, published as *The Films of Ingmar Bergman*, Dover, 1972; *Rapport fran Donau* (travel book), Albert Bonnier, 1962; *The Personal Vision of Ingmar Berman*, Indiana University Press, 1964, reprinted by Books for Libraries Press, 1972; *Maailmankirja*, Otava, 1968; *Suomen Kuva Maailmalla*, Helsinki, 1969; *Sommarav Karlek och sorg*, Soderstrom & Co., 1971. Films (written and directed): "En sondag i september" (English title: "Sunday in September"), 1963; "Att alska" (English title: "To love"), 1964.

WORK IN PROGRESS: A book on Finland; a book about

the classics of the Swedish cinema; a novel; script and direction for film, "Adventure Starts Here," to be filmed in Helsinki; a book of the screenplays of the first three films.†

* * *

DOODY, Francis Stephen 1917-

PERSONAL: Born January 16, 1917, in Littleton, N.H.; son of Stephen A. and Ruth (Brooklins) Doody; married Marjorie Culver, June 5, 1943; children: John, Georgeanne, Carol. *Education:* Tufts University, A.B., 1938; Harvard University M.A., 1940, Ph.D., 1961. *Politics:* Independent. *Religion:* Roman Catholic. *Residence:* Pembroke, Mass. *Office:* Bureau of Business Research, Boston University, 685 Commonwealth Ave., Boston, Mass.

CAREER: Massachusetts Institute of Technology, Cambridge, assistant instructor in economics, 1940-42; Boston University, Boston, Mass., assistant professor, 1946-49, associate professor, 1950-59, director of Bureau of Business Research and professor of economics, 1960—. Visiting lecturer, Wellesley College, 1958. Industrial Relations Council of Metropolitan Boston, assistant director, 1946. Member, New England Council Research Advisory Committee, 1961—; member, Board of Economic Advisors to the Governor of Massachusetts, 1963-64. *Military service:* U.S. Navy, 1942-45; became lieutenant junior grade. *Member:* American Economic Association, Phi Beta Kappa.

WRITINGS: (Ediotr) *Readings in Labor Economics*, Addison-Wesley, 1950; (with Richard V. Clemence) *The Schumpeterian System*, Addison-Wesley, 1950, reprinted, Kelley, 1974. (With Richard V. Clemence and Stanley Wronski) *Modern Economics: A Secondary School Text*, Allyn & Bacon, 1964; *Introduction to the Use of Economics Indicators*, Random House, 1965. Contributor to journals. Editor, *Boston University Business Review*, 1956-59.

WORK IN PROGRESS: Studies in regional economics.

AVOCATIONAL INTERESTS: Jazz, golf, and antiques.†

* * *

DOOLEY, Arch R(ichard) 1925-

PERSONAL: Born February 1, 1925, in Oklahoma City, Okla.; son of A. E. (a businessman) and Grace Marie (Moore) Dooley; married Patricia Folts, September 5, 1953; children: Arch Richard, Jr., Christopher F. *Education:* Yale University, A.B., 1944; Harvard University, M.B.A., 1950, D.C.S., 1960. *Home:* 21 Summit Rd., Lexington, Mass. 02173. *Office:* Graduate School of Business Administration, Harvard University, Soldiers Field Road, Boston, Mass. 01263.

CAREER: Oklahoma City University, Oklahoma City, Okla., assistant professor, 1946-47; Harvard University, Graduate School of Business Administration, Cambridge, Mass., associate professor, 1952-53; University of North Carolina, School of Business Administration, Chapel Hill, assistant dean, 1950-54; Harvard University, Graduate School of Business Administration, associate professor, 1954-66, professor, 1966-69, Jesse Philips professor, 1969—. Instructor in advanced management programs conducted by Keio University, Tokyo, Japan, at University of Hawaii, University of Western Ontario, and Atlantic Summer School, Halifax, Nova Scotia. *Military service:* U.S. Naval Reserve, commissioned officer, 1944-46; *Member:* Academy of Management, Beta Theta Pi, Delta Sigma Phi (honorary).

WRITINGS: Business Management of Credit Bureaus, Bureau of Business Services and Research, University of North Carolina, 1953; (with R. E. McGarrah, J. L. McKenney, R. S. Rosenbloom, C. W. Skinner, and P. H. Thurston) *Casebooks in Production Management*, Wiley, 1964; *Basic Problems, Concepts, and Techniques*, 1964, revised edition, 1968, *Operations Planning and Control*, 1964, Production Operating Decisions in the Total Business Strategy, 1964, Wage Administration and Worker Productivity, 1964.

WORK IN PROGRESS: Studies in industrial relocation, critical path analytical techniques, manufacturing reliability, and personal values and business decisions.†

* * *

DOOLIN, Dennis James 1933-

PERSONAL: Born October 28, 1933, in Omaha, Neb.; son of Russell James (an accountant) and Sarah (Pickard) Doolin; married Maryann Lund, January 29, 1956; children: Maureen, David, Sarah. *Education:* University of San Francisco, B.S. (summa cum laude), 1958; Stanford University, M.A., 1960, Ph.D., 1964. *Politics:* Democrat. *Religion:* Presbyterian. *Home:* 4039 Freed Ave., San Jose, Calif. 95117. *Office:* Hoover Institution, Stanford University, Stanford, Calif. 94305.

CAREER: Stanford University, Stanford, Calif., assistant professor of political science, 1963-64, research associate, Hoover Institution, 1964—, research curator, East Asian collection, 1965—, lecturer in political science, Hoover Institution, 1965—. External examiner for advanced degrees, University of Hong Kong; consultant to American Institute for Research and to Stanford Studies of the Communist System. *Military service:* U.S. Navy, 1950-54; served in Korea, China, Japan; received five battle stars for Korean service. *Member:* American Political Science Association, Association for Asian Studies.

WRITINGS: Communist China: The Politics of Student Opposition, Hoover Institution, 1964; *Territorial Claims in the Sino-Soviet Conflict*, Hoover Institution, 1965; (editor) *Fifty Years of Chinese Philosophy: 1898-1948*, Praeger, 1965; (with Robert C. North) *The People's Republic of China*, Hoover Institution, 1966; (with Charles P. Ridley) *The Making of a Model Citizen in Communist China*, Hoover Institution Press, 1971; (with Ridley) *A Chinese-English Dictionary of Communist Chinese Terminology*, Hoover Institution Press, 1973. Contributor to political science journals published in London, Hong Kong, and Paris.

WORK IN PROGRESS: Chinese Communist Policies Toward the Chinese Intelligentsia.

SIDELIGHTS: Doolin speaks Chinese, Japanese, and Spanish. He spends part of each year in Asia on professional business. *Avocational interests:* Baseball.†

* * *

DORMAN, Michael 1932-

PERSONAL: Born October 9, 1932, in New York, N.Y.; son of Arthur A. (an auctioneer) and Hortense (Lowy) Dorman; married Jeanne O'Brien, June 25, 1955; children: Pamela Grace, Patricia Alice. *Education:* New York University, B.S. in Journalism, 1953; University of Houston, graduate study, 1954-55. *Politics:* Democrat. *Religion:* Presbyterian. *Home:* 7 Lauren Ave. South, Dix Hills, N.Y. *Agent:* McIntosh & Otis, Inc., 18 East 41st St., New York, N.Y. 10017.

CAREER: Reporter or department editor for Associated Press, Albany, N.Y., 1953, *Houston Press*, Houston, Tex., 1953-58, *Newsday*, Garden City, N.Y., 1959-64; Democratic Party, speech writer, 1964-65; full-time writer, 1965—. *Member:* American Newspaper Guild, Authors League, Authors Guild, Kappa Tau Alpha. *Awards, honors:* First prize in news story competition, Houston Press Club, for coverage of the Louisiana hurricane, 1957.

WRITINGS—All published by Delacorte, except as indicated: *We Shall Overcome*, 1964; *The Secret Service Story*, 1967; *The Second Man*, 1968; *King of the Courtroom*, 1969; *Under Twenty-One*, 1970; *Payoff*, David McKay, 1972; *The Making of a Slum*, 1972; *Confrontation: Politics and Protest*, 1974.

WORK IN PROGRESS: A book on dirty politics, for Delacorte.

SIDELIGHTS: Dorman told *CA:* "I am basically an investigative reporter, . . . have a passion for facts—as opposed to propaganda."

* * *

DOSTER, William C(lark) 1921-

PERSONAL: Born February 28, 1921, in Rochelle, Ga.; son of John P. (a farmer) and Lucy (Standard) Doster; married Jeanette Brazzeal, October 29, 1942; children: Sandra Jeanette Doster Lawson, Lucy Deborah. *Education:* Mercer University, A.B., 1942; University of Florida, M.A., 1948, Ph.D., 1955. *Politics:* Democrat. *Religion:* Baptist. *Home:* 593 Summerdale Ave., Glen Ellyn, Ill. 60137. *Office:* College of DuPage, Glen Ellyn, Ill. 60137.

CAREER: Ouachita Baptist College, Arkadelphia, Ark., chairman of English department, 1955-58; Oklahoma Baptist University, Shawnee, chairman of English department, 1958-60; Miami-Dade Junior College, Miami, Fla., chairman of Division of Communications, 1960-64, director of Division of Humanities, 1964-68; College of DuPage, Glen Ellyn, Ill., teacher of English, 1968—. Educational Testing Service, consultant, 1963-65. *Military service:* U.S. Army Air Forces, 1942-45; became staff sergeant; received Air Medal and Distinguished Flying Cross with oak leaf clusters. *Member:* Modern Language Association of America, National Council of Teachers of English, Conference on College Composition and Communication (executive committee, 1964-66).

WRITINGS: First Perspectives on Language, American Book Co., 1963, 2nd edition, 1968; (with Martha M. McDonough) *Poetry Is For People*, W.C. Brown, 1964; *Communications 101-102-201-202*, W.C. Brown, 1964; *Toward Better Writing*, W.C. Brown, 1965; *The Differing Eye*, Glencoe Press, 1970; (with others) *How to Take the Clep Test*, Barron's Educational Services, 1973.

* * *

DOUGLAS, J(ames) D(ixon) 1922-

PERSONAL: Born December 23, 1922, in Glasgow, Scotland; son of James Dickson (a shipyard laborer) and Margaret (Simpson) Douglas. *Education:* Attended University of Glasgow; University of St. Andrews, M.A., 1949, B.D., 1952; Hartford Theological Seminary (now Hartford Seminary Foundation), Hartford, Conn., S.T.M., 1954, Ph.D., 1955. *Home:* 2 Doocot Rd., St. Andrews, Scotland.

CAREER: Ordained to Presbyterian ministry, 1953. University of St. Andrews, St. Andrews, Scotland, lecturer in ecclesiastical history, 1955-56; Tyndale House, Cambridge,

England, librarian, 1958-61; *Christianity Today*, Washington D.C., editor-at-large, 1961—.

WRITINGS: (Editor) *The New Bible Dictionary*, Eerdmans, 1962; *Light in the North: The Story of the Scottish Covenanters*, Eerdmans, 1964; (editor) *Evangelism and Unity*, Marcham Manor Press, 1964; (editor) *The New International Dictionary of the Christian Church*, Zondervan, 1974. Contributor to *Encyclopedia International* and *Dictionary of Christian Ethics*; regular contributor to *Christianity Today*.

WORK IN PROGRESS: Biography of famous British lay evangelist, A. Lindsay Glegg, for Word Books.

* * *

DOVER, C(larence) J(oseph) 1919-

PERSONAL: Born October 6, 1919, in Memphis, Tenn.; son of Herbert and Gertrude (Thompson) Dover; married Dorothy J. Strain, June 16, 1943; children: Michael, Douglas, Deborah. *Education:* Kent State University B.A., 1948; Western Reserve University (now Case Western Reserve University), M.A., 1954; graduate study at University of Vienna and Mexico City College. *Home:* 253 Hillcrest Rd., Grosse Pointe Farms Mich. *Office:* Chrysler Corp., P.O. Box 1919, Detroit, Mich.

CAREER: United Nations Relief and Rehabilitation Administration, public relations director for central Europe, 1945-46; General Electric Co., manager of communication and community relations Cleveland, Ohio, 1948-53, consultant in New York, N.Y., 1954-62; Chrysler Corp., Detroit, Mich., manager of communication, 1962—. Consultant in employee communication, 1954-56, public affairs planning, 1957-59, and communication and group relations, 1958-62. *Military service:* U.S. Army, 1941-42. U.S. Army Air Forces, 1942-45; became captain. *Member:* International Council of Industrial Editors, National Society for the Study of Communication (president, 1965), Public Relations Society of America, American Academy of Political and Social Science, Sigma Delta Chi, Delta Tau Delta. *Awards, honors:* Citations from Freedoms Foundation, Kent State University, and American Public Relations Assocation.

WRITINGS: Effective Communication in Company Publications, Bureau of National Affairs, 1959; *Management Communication of Controversial Issues*, Bureau of National Affairs, 1965. Contributor of articles to *Nation's Business, Public Relations Journal* and other professional periodicals.†

* * *

DOWNEY, Harris

PERSONAL: Born in Baton Rouge, La.; son of Lawrence and Florence (Chiek) Downey. *Education:* Louisiana State University, B.A. and M.A.; New York University, graduate study. *Home:* 638 Staring Lane, Baton Rouge, La. 70808.

CAREER: Free-lance writer. *Awards, honors:* First prize, O. Henry Memorial Awards, for "The Hunters," 1951.

WRITINGS: Thunder in the Room, Macmillan, 1956; *The Key to My Prison*, Dell, 1964; *Carrie Dumain*, Regnery, 1966. Contributor of short stories to magazines.

* * *

DOYLE, Paul A. 1925-

PERSONAL: Born December 6, 1925, in Carbondale, Pa.;

son of Frank E. (a railroad worker) and Agatha (Kelly) Doyle; married Ann Keating, November 25, 1954 (died December 21, 1963); children: Paul, Edward, Robie. *Education:* University of Scranton, B.A., 1946; Fordham University, M.A., 1948, Ph.D., 1955. *Home:* 161 Park Ave., Williston Park, N.Y.

CAREER: Fordham University, New York, N.Y., 1948-60, began as instructor, became assistant professor of English; St. John's University, New York, N.Y., 1960-62, began as assistant professor, became associate professor of English; Nassau Community College, Garden City, N.Y., associate professor, 1962-65, professor of English, 1965—. *New York Times*, New York, N.Y., advertising adjustor, 1954-63. *Member:* National Council of Teachers of English, American Institute of the History of Pharmacy.

WRITINGS: (With Paul J. Centi) *Basic College Skills*, two volumes, Rinehart, 1959; (with Thomas Cahalan) *Modern American Drama*, Student Outlines Co., 1960; (editor with Grover Cronin) *Alexander Pope's Iliad: An Examination by William Melmoth*, Catholic University of America Press, 1960; (with Cahalan) *Modern British and Irish Drama*, Student Outlines Co., 1961; (with Cahalan) *Modern European Drama*, Student Outlines Co., 1962; *Gulliver's Travels: An Outline and a Commentary*, Student Outlines Co., 1962; (editor) *Readings in Pharmacy*, Wiley, 1962; *Goethe's Faust and the Sorrows of Young Werther: Outlines and Commentaries*, Student Outlines Co., 1963; *New American Novel*, Student Outlines Co., 1964; *Modern American Novel*, Student Outlines Co., 1964; *Shakespeare's Othello: An Outline and an Analysis*, Student Outlines Co., 1964; *Pearl S. Buck*, Twayne, 1965; (editor) *A Concordance of the Collected Poems of James Joyce*, Scarecrow, 1966; *Sean O'Faolain: A Critical Study*, Twayne, 1968; *Evelyn Waugh: A Critical Essay*, Eerdmans, 1969; *Liam O'Flaherty*, Twayne, 1971; *Paul Vincent Carroll*, Bucknell University Press, 1971; *Liam O'-Flaherty: An Annotated Bibliography*, Whitston, 1972; (editor) *Henry David Thoreau: Studies and Commentaries*, Fairleigh Dickinson University Press, 1972.

Poetry included in *National Poetry Anthology*, 1953-54, and 1959. Contributor of over thirty articles to journals (primarily pharmaceutical, bibliographical, and literary periodicals), and poetry to *Tablet, Irish World, Advocate*, and other publications. Sometime reviewer for *Choice*. Contributing editor, *Best Sellers*. Consultant, *National Education Association Journal*, 1963-64.

WORK IN PROGRESS: How to Read More Effectively, and a novel on the coal region of northeastern Pennsylvania.

SIDELIGHTS: Although Doyle feels that "there is much rich ore left to dig out on pharmacy research subjects," he does not plan to continue writing in this field (many of his magazine articles have dealt with pharmaceutical issues). "Writing in this area does not have a wide audience," he told *CA*, "and publication in this field is too often wrapped un with favoritism, rash judgments, petty jealousies, and the whims of the Establishment." He expects to "confine future writing and research to the areas of contemporary drama and fiction—both European and American." *Avocational interests:* Book collecting and hiking.†

*   *   *

DRABBLE, Margaret 1939-

PERSONAL: Born May 6, 1939, in Sheffield, England; daughter of John Frederick (a judge) and Marie (Bloor) Drabble; married Clive Walter Swift (an actor with Royal Shakespeare Company), June, 1960; children: Adam Richard George, Rebecca Margaret, Joseph. *Education:* Newnham College, Cambridge, B.A. (first class honors), 1960. *Home:* 70 Riversdale Rd., London N.5, England. *Agent:* A. D. Peters, 10 Buckingham St., London W.C.1, England.

CAREER: Writer. Member of Royal Shakespeare Company, one year. *Awards, honors:* John Llewelyn Rhys Memorial Award, 1966; James Tait Black Memorial Book Prize, 1968; E. M. Forster Award, 1973.

WRITINGS—Novels, except as indicated: *A Summer Bird-Cage*, Weidenfeld & Nicolson, 1963, Morrow, 1964; *The Garrick Year*, Weidenfeld & Nicolson, 1964, Morrow, 1965; *The Millstone*, Weidenfeld & Nicolson, 1965, Morrow, 1966, reissued with new introduction by Drabble and editorial material compiled by Michael Marland, Longman, 1970; *Wordsworth* (criticism), Evans Bros., 1966, Arco, 1969; *Jerusalem the Golden*, Morrow, 1967; *The Waterfall*, Knopf, 1969; *The Needle's Eye*, Knopf, 1972; (editor with B. S. Johnson) *London Consequences* (group novel), Greater London Arts Association, 1972; *Thank You All Very Much* (filmscript adaptation of *The Millstone*), New American Library, 1973; *Arnold Bennett* (biography), Knopf, 1974. Short fiction published in collections, including: *Winter's Tales 12*, edited by A. D. Maclean, Macmillan, 1966; *Winter's Tales 14*, edited by Kevin Crossley-Holland, Macmillan, 1968; *Penguin Modern Stories 3*, Penguin, 1969; *Winter's Tales 16*, edited by Maclean, Macmillan, 1970.

Author of play, "Bird of Paradise," produced in London, 1969. Author of screenplay, "Thank You All Very Much" (based on *The Millstone*), Columbia Pictures, 1969, released in Great Britain as "A Touch of Love." Writer of dialog, "Isadora," Universal, 1968, and of story for "A Roman Marriage," Winkast Productions. Author of television play, "Laura," produced by Granda Television, 1964. Contributor to British literary journals, and to *Punch* and *Vogue*.

BIOGRAPHICAL/CRITICAL SOURCES: Books and Bookmen, September, 1969; Carolyn Riley, editor, *Contemporary Literary Criticism*, Gale, Volume II, 1974, Volume III, 1975.†

*   *   *

DRAKE, Joan H(oward)

PERSONAL: Born in Wallasey, Cheshire, England; daughter of Sidney James (a bank manager) and Marjorie (Howard) Drake; married John Emry Davies (a veterinary surgeon), January 2, 1954. *Education:* Attended high schools and private schools in Wallasey and Liverpool, England. *Home:* Castle Rock, 46 Marine Dr., Barry, South Glamorganshire, South Wales.

CAREER: Writer of books and short stories for children, with first book published when she was sixteen. Lectures occasionally on writing for children. Became Justice of the Peace, 1970. *Member:* Society of Authors.

WRITINGS: The Story of Wimpy a Wump, Harrap, 1940; *More About Wimpy*, Harrap, 1941; *Wimpy on Holiday*, Harrap, 1946; *Wimpy Goes Abroad*, Harrap, 1954; *Jiggle Woggle Bus*, Brockhampton Press, 1957; *Mr. Grimpwinkle*, Brockhampton Press, 1958; *Mr. Grimpwinkle's Marrow*, Brockhampton Press, 1959; *Mr. Grimpwinkle, Priate Cook*, Brockhampton Press, 1960; *Mr. Grimpwinkle Buys a*

Bus, Brockhampton Press, 1961; *Mr. Grimpwinkle's Holiday*, Brockhampton Press, 1963; *Mr. Grimpwinkle's Visitor*, Brockhampton Press, 1964; *Jiggle Woggle Saves the Day*, Brockhampton Press, 1966; *Sally Seal's Summer*, Hutchinson, 1967; *James and Sally Again*, Hutchinson, 1970; *Mr. Bubbus and the Apple-Green Engine*, Brockhampton Press, 1971; *Miss Hendy's House*, Brockhampton Press, 1974. Contributor of stories to British Broadcasting Corp. "Children's Hour" and to youth magazines.

WORK IN PROGRESS: A sequel to *Mr. Bubbus and the Apple-Green Engine.*

AVOCATIONAL INTERESTS: Animals (dogs in particular), ballet, traditional jazz, serious music, cooking and entertaining, flowers and gardening, interior decorating, talking to children.

*   *   *

DRANE, James F.   1930-

PERSONAL: Born April 6, 1930, in Chester, Pa.; son of James F. and Ann (King) Drane. *Education:* Little Rock College, A.B., 1951; Gregorian University, Rome, Italy, M.Div., 1953; Middlebury College, M.A., 1961; University of Madrid, Ph.D., 1964; postdoctoral studies at Union Theological Seminary, Georgetown University, and Yale University. *Home:* 109 Skytop Rd., Edinboro, Pa. 16412. *Office:* Department of Philosophy, Edinboro State College, Edinboro, Pa.

CAREER: St. John's Seminary, Little Rock, Ark., teacher of philosophy and languages, 1956-67; University of Arkansas at Little Rock, Newman Chaplain and lecturer, 1964-67; Webster College, St. Louis, Mo., professor of theology, 1967-68; Edinboro State College, Edinboro, Pa., professor philosophy, 1969—. Has been engaged in ecumenical activities and work with Catholic Interracial Council, Little Rock, Ark. *Member:* American Catholic Philosophy Association.

WRITINGS: Pilgrimage to Utopia, Bruce, 1965; *Authority and Institution*, Bruce, 1969; *A New American Reformation*, Philosophical Library, 1973. Contributer to *Catholic World, America, Catholic Digest, Sign, Revista de Occidente* (Spain), and *Main Currents.*

WORK IN PROGRESS: A Philosophy of Man for Bussinessmen and *Freedom of Conscience.*

SIDELIGHTS: Drane speaks Latin, Spanish, French, Italian, and German.

*   *   *

DRAPER, Edgar   1926-

PERSONAL: Born February 5, 1926, in St. Louis, Mo.; son of Neal McLain (a physician) and Florence Mabel (Meyers) Draper; married Norma Jane Alexander, March 16, 1949; children: Susan Jane, Anne Meyers, Neal Edgar. *Education:* Washington University, St. Louis, Mo., A.B., 1946, M.D., 1953; Duke University Divinity School, student, 1946-47; Garrett Biblical Institute, B.D., 1949; Institute for Psychoanalysis, Chicago, Ill., graduate, 1966. *Home:* 3020 Provincial, Ann Arbor, Mich. 48104. *Office:* University Hospital, University of Michigan, 405 East Ann, Ann Arbor, Mich. 48104.

CAREER: Ordained elder, Methodist Church, 1951; served as student pastor in North Carolina and Illinois. Diplomate, American Board of Psychiatry and Neurology, 1961. U.S. Public Health Service, Washington, D.C.,

senior assistant surgeon, 1955-57; University of Chicago, Chicago, Ill., instructor, 1959-60, assistant professor, 1960-66, associate professor of psychiatry and co-director of psychiatry outpatient department, 1966-68; University of Michigan, Ann Arbor, professor and director of psychiatric resident education, 1968—, professor of postgraduate education, 1970—.

WRITINGS: (Co-author) *The Student Physician as Psychotherapist*, edited by Ralph Heine, University of Chicago Press, 1962; *Psychiatry and Pastoral Care*, Prentice-Hall, 1965; (with Granger Westberg) *Community Psychiatry and the Clergyman*, C. C Thomas, 1966; (contributor) E. Mansell Pattison, editor, *Clinical Psychiatry and Religion*, Little, Brown, 1968; (contributor) Paul H. Ornstein and Charles K. Hofling, editors, *Memos to Maury*, Henry Stratton, 1968; (contributor) Harvey H. Barten, editor, *Brief Therapies*, Behavioral Publications, 1971; (contributor) Paul Johnson, editor, *Healers of the Mind: Psychiatrists and Their Search for Faith*, Abingdon, 1972. Contributor of psychiatric articles to professional journals.

*   *   *

DRAPER, Theodore   1912-

PERSONAL: Born September 11, 1912, in Brooklyn, N.Y.; son of Samuel and Annie Draper; children: Roger. *Education:* Brooklyn College (now Brooklyn College of the City University of New York), B.S.S. *Home:* 35 Linwood Circle, Princeton, N.J. 08540.

CAREER: Writer; Stanford University, Stanford, Calif., research fellow at Hoover Institution on War, Revolution and Peace, 1963-74. Member of Institute for Advanced Study, Princeton, N.J., 1968-73.

WRITINGS: The Six Weeks' War, Viking, 1944; *The Roots of American Communism*, Viking, 1957; *American Communism and Soviet Russia*, Viking, 1960; *Castro's Revolution*, Praeger, 1962; *Castroism: Theory and Practice*, Praeger, 1965; *Abuse of Power*, Viking, 1967; *The Dominican Revolt: A Case Study in American Policy*, Commentary, 1968; *Israel and World Politics: Roots of the Third Arab-Israeli War*, Viking, 1968; *The Rediscovery of Black Nationalism*, Viking, 1970. Contributor to *New Leader, Reporter, Encounter, Commentary*, and other periodicals.

SIDELIGHTS: James Nelson Goodsell writes in reference to *The Dominican Revolt: A Case Study in American Policy:* "Its real value lies in its call for sober rethinking about an affair that evoked much passion at the time." Carl Gershman says of *The Rediscovery of Black Nationalism:* "In addition to providing us with an excellent history, he (Draper) probes the ambiguities and antinomies that have marked every black nationalist mode."

*   *   *

DRESNER, Hal   1937-

PERSONAL: Born June 4, 1937, in New York, N.Y.; son of Seymour H. (a hotel executive) and Syd (Frank) Dresner. *Education:* University of Florida, B.S., 1958. *Agent:* Scott Meredith Literary Agency, Inc., 580 Fifth Ave., New York, N.Y.

CAREER: Scott Meredith Literary Agency, New York, N.Y., editor, 1958; Kinloch Park Junior High School, Miami, Fla., teacher, 1959. Writer.

WRITINGS: The Man Who Wrote Dirty Books, Simon and Schuster, 1965. Also writer of filmscript, "The April

Fools'', 1968; and a film adaptation of *The Man Who Wrote Dirty Books*, 1968.

WORK IN PROGRESS: An untitled novel; an untitled screenplay, a "modern adventure-melodrama."

SIDELIGHTS: A *Newsweek* reviewer called Dresner's novel "an inversion of what used to be sneaked past customs—a funny, clean book carefully camouflaged to look dirty." The book appeared in two dust-jackets; the outer one was a plain brown wrapper stamped with the words "This is a plan brown wrapper." The inner jacket bore a picture of Dresner leaning against a table on which rested a large sculptured frog. Of the book itself (containing more than fifty pages only half filled with type), Phoebe Adams commented: "[The cast of characters] offers quite a variety of victims for satirical burlesque, and Mr. Dresner puts them all through a fine string of pratfalls. His best targets are the law, the FBI (don't ask me how they got in there), and the literary life. It would not be quite true to report that *The Man Who Wrote Dirty Books* contains no word capable of bringing the blush of shame to the cheek of modesty, but it is perfectly true that the thing is neither a dirty book nor about them." *Avocational interests:* Hunting.

BIOGRAPHICAL/CRITICAL SOURCES: Newsweek, February 22, 1965; *Saturday Review,* February 27, 1965; *Atlantic,* March, 1965.†

*   *   *

DREW, Fraser Bragg Robert   1913-

PERSONAL: Born June 23, 1913, in Randolph, Vt; son of George Albie and Hazel (Fraser) Drew. *Education:* University of Vermont, A.B. (magna cum laude), 1933; Duke University, A.M., 1935; Syracuse University, graduate study, 1939-41; State University of New York at Buffalo, Ph.D., 1952. *Religion:* Roman Catholic. *Home:* 119 Thurston Ave., Kenmore, N.Y. 14217. *Office:* State University of New York College at Buffalo, 1300 Elmwood Ave., Buffalo, N.Y. 14222.

CAREER: Green Mountain College, Poultney, Vt., instructor in Latin, 1936-39; United Aircraft Corp., Pratt & Whitney Aircraft Division, East Hartford, Conn., supervisor, Materials Division, 1941-45; State University of New York College at Buffalo, 1945—, started as instructor, professor of English, 1952—, distinguished teaching professor, 1973—, chairman of department of English, 1957-63; Member of committee on American literature, New York State Educational Department, 1962-63; member of advisory board, St. Patrick Scholarship Fund, Inc., 1967—. *Member:* Academy of American Poets, Poetry Society of America, American Committee for Irish Studies, Irish American Cultural Institute, College English Association Housman Society, County Kerry Historical Society, New York State Teachers Association, Phi Beta Kappa, Sigma Upsilon, Kappa Phi Kappa, Eta Sigma Phi, Lambda Iota, Sigma Tau Gamma. *Awards, honors:* John Henry Newman Honorary Award, 1952; State University of New York research fellowship, 1960, 1967; University of Vermont Distinguished Alumnus Award, 1968; Irishman of the Year Award, 1970.

WRITINGS: The Poet as House Guest: Unpublished Verse of A. E. Housman, Indiana University Press, 1961; *John Masefield's England: A Study of the National Themes in His Work,* Fairleigh Dickinson University Press, 1973. Contributor to *Papers of the Bibliographical Society of America* and of more than eighty articles to *Modern Language Notes, Western Humanities Review,*

Christian Science Monitor, Philological Quarterly, College English, Canadian Forum, Yale Library Gazette, Eire-Ireland, Ireland of the Welcomes, and other journals and reviews. Member of advisory board, *Dictionary of International Biography,* 1962—.

AVOCATIONAL INTERESTS: Collecting first editions of twentieth-century poets and novels (has complete collections of Ernest Hemingway and John Masefield, and an extensive library of work of Robinson Jerrers, Hart Crane, and modern Irish writers); travel, especially in Ireland.

*   *   *

DRINNON, Richard   1925-

PERSONAL: Born January 4, 1925, in Portland, Ore.; son of John Henry (a farmer) and Emma (Tweed) Drinnon; married Anna Maria Faulise, October 20, 1945; children: Donna Elizabeth, Jon Tweed. *Education:* Willamette University, B.A. (summa cum laude), 1950; University of Minnesota, M.A., 1951, Ph.D., 1957. *Politics:* Anarchist. *Home:* R.D.1, Milton, Pa. *Office:* Bucknell University, Lewisburg, Pa.

CAREER: University of Minnesota, Minneapolis, instructor in department of interdisciplinary studies, 1953, 1955-57; University of California, Berkeley, instructor, 1957-58, assistant professor of history, 1958-61; University of Leeds, Leeds, England, Bruern Fellow in American Studies, 1961-63; Hobart and William Smith Colleges, Geneva, N.Y., associate professor of history, 1964-66; Bucknell University, Lewisburg, Pa., professor of history and chairman of department 1966—. *Military service:* U.S. Naval Air Corps, aviation radioman, 1942-46. *Awards, honors:* Fulbright grant to Netherlands, 1953-54; Social Science Research Council faculty research fellowship, 1963-64.

WRITINGS: Rebel in Paradise: A Biography of Emma Goldman, University of Chicago Press, 1961; *White Savage: The Case of John Dunn Hunter,* Schocken, 1972; (editor and author of introduction) John D. Hunter, *Memoirs of a Captivity among the Indians of North America,* Schocken, 1973; (editor with wife, Anna M. Drinnon) *Nowhere at Home: Letters from Exile of Emma Goldman and Alexander Berkman,* Schocken, 1974. Contributor to *Nation, Psychoanalytic Review, Twentieth Century, Anarchy,* and *Massachusetts Review.*

WORK IN PROGRESS: Violent Delights: Patterns of American Killings and Hurtings, completion expected about 1984.

*   *   *

DROSSAART LULOFS, H(endrik) J(oan)   1906-

PERSONAL: Born April 22, 1906, in Amersfoort, Netherlands; son of Pieter Karel (a chemist) and Afina (van Linge) Drossaart Lulofs; married Abelia Albertine Tresling, April 11, 1952. *Education:* University of Leiden, Cand. Theol., 1930, Dr. Classical Philology, 1943. *Home:* Amsteldijk 31, Amsterdam, Netherlands.

CAREER: Teacher of classics and Hebrew at gymnasia in Netherlands, 1938-47; Gemeentelijk Lyceum, Emmen, Netherlands, teacher of classics and Hebrew, 1947-61; University of Leiden, Leiden, Netherlands, lecturer in Aristotelian studies, 1961-66; University of Amsterdam, Amsterdam, Netherlands, professor of ancient philosophy, 1966—. *Member:* Royal Netherlands Academy of Arts and Sciences, Society for Promotion of Hellenic Studies and

Royal Asiatic Society (both London), Oosters Genootschap (Leiden).

WRITINGS: (Editor) *Aristotelis De Somno et Vigilia*, Burgersdijk & Niermans, 1943; (translator) *Aristoteles: De insomniis et De divinatione per somnum*, Brill, 1947; (translator) Aeschylus, *De geboeide Prometheus*, Brill, 1953; (editor) *Aristotelis De Generatione Animalium*, Clarendon Press, 1965; (author of commentary) *Nicolaus Damascenus on the Philosophy of Aristotle*, Brill, 1965, revised edition, 1969; (editor) *De Generatione Animalium, translatio G. de Moerbeka: Aristoteles Latinus XVII*, two volumes, [Bruges], 1966; (editor with J. Brugman) *Aristotle, Generation of Animals, the Arabic Translation Commonly Ascribed to Yahya ibn al-Bitriq, De Goeje Stichting nr. XXIII*, [Leiden], 1971. Contributor to journals.

WORK IN PROGRESS: Fragments of *De Plantis* of Aristotle in Syriac, Arabic, Hebrew, and Latin.

SIDELIGHTS: Drossaart Lolufs is competent in English, French, German, Latin, Greek, classical Hebrew, classical Arabic, and classical Syriac. *Avocational interests:* Photography, music.

*   *   *

DRUMMOND, June   1923-

PERSONAL: Born November 15, 1923, in Durban, South Africa; daughter of John (a physician) and Florence (Green) Drummond. *Education:* University of Cape Town, B.A., 1944. *Politics:* Progressive Party of South Africa. *Religion:* Anglican. *Home:* 24a Miller Grove, Durban, South Africa.

CAREER: Journalist for *Woman's Weekly* and *Natal Mercury*, Durban, South Africa, 1946-48; secretary in London, England, 1948-50, with Durban Civic Orchestra, Durban, South Africa, 1950-53; Church Adoption Society, London, England, assistant secretary, 1954-60; full-time writer, Durban, South Africa, 1960—. Chairman of Durban adoption committee, Indian Child Welfare Society, 1963-74. Provincial candidate of Progressive Party in Durban, 1974. *Member:* Durban Writers Circle, Soroptimists International, Durban Country Club.

WRITINGS: The Black Unicorn, Gollancz, 1959; *Thursdays Child*, Gollancz 1961; *A Time to Speak*, Gollancz, 1962, World Publishing, 1963; *A Cage of Humming Birds*, Gollancz, 1964; *Welcome, Proud Lady*, Gollancz, 1964, Holt, 1968; *Cable Car*, Gollancz, 1965, Holt, 1967; *The Saboteurs*, Gollancz, 1967, Holt, 1969; *Murder on a Bad Trip*, Holt, 1968 (published in England as *The Gantry Episode*, Gollancz, 1968); *The People in Glass House*, Gollancz, 1969, Simon & Schuster, 1970; *Farewell Party*, Gollancz, 1971, Dodd, 1973; *Bang! Bang! You're Dead*, Gollancz, 1973; *The Boon Companions*, Gollancz, 1974.

WORK IN PROGRESS: A historical thriller set in Britain and South Africa.

SIDELIGHTS: June Drummond told *CA:* "[I am] unsure of competence in my own language, let alone others, but can read French. [I] like travel if it is not organized, and have visited a number of European countries in a highly disorganized way." *Avocational interests:* Skiing, reading, politics, playing "bad bridge," idling.

*   *   *

DRUMMOND, V(iolet) H(ilda)   1911-

PERSONAL: Born July, 1911, in London, England; daughter of David (an army officer) and Hilda Drummond; married Anthony Swetenham (a member of London Stock Exchange), December, 1948; children: Julian Pardoe. *Education:* Attended school in Eastbourne, England. *Politics:* Conservative. *Religion:* Church of England. *Home:* 24 Norfolk Rd., London N.W.8, England.

CAREER: V. H. Drummond Productions Ltd., London, England, chairman, 1960—, producing eighteen cartoon films for British Broadcasting Corp. "Children's Hour," 1963-64; author and illustrator of children's books. *Military service:* British Army, First Aid Nursing Yeomanry, 1938-42. *Member:* Society of Authors. *Awards, honors:* Kate Greenway Medal of Library Association (British), 1958, for most distinguished work in illustration of a children's book for *Mrs. Easter and the Storks.*

WRITINGS—All self-illustrated: *Phewtus the Squirrel*, Oxford University Press, 1939; *Mrs. Easter's Parasol*, Faber, 1944; *Miss Anna Truly*, Houghton, 1945; *Lady Talavera*, Faber, 1946; *Tidgies Innings*, Faber, 1947; *The Charming Taxicab*, Faber, 1947; *Mr. Finch's Pet Shop*, Walck, 1950; *Mrs. Easter and the Storks*, Faber, 1957; *Little Laura's Cat*, Faber, 1961; *Little Laura on the River*, Faber, 1961; *Little Laura and the Thief*, Nelson, 1962; *Little Laura's Best Friend*, Nelson, 1962; *Little Laura and the Lonely Ostrich*, Nelson, 1963; *The Flying Postman*, Walck, 1964; *Miss Anna Truly and the Christmas Lights*, Longman, Green, 1968; *Mrs. Easter and the Golden Bounder*, Faber, 1970; *Mrs. Easter's Christmas Flights*, Faber, 1972.

Illustrator: J.K. Stanford, *The Twelfth*, Faber, 1944; Lawrence Durrell, *Esprit de Corps*, Faber, 1957. Also illustrator of "Little Laura" cartoon series for television.

BIOGRAPHICAL/CRITICAL SOURCES: Horn Book, XXIV, Volume I; *Junior Bookshelf*, October, 1949.

*   *   *

DRUON, Maurice Samuel Roger Charles   1918-

PERSONAL: Born April 23, 1918, in Paris, France; married Madeline Marignac September 25, 1968. *Education:* Educated in Paris, France, at Lycee Michelet and Faculte des Lettres, Ecole des Sciences Politiques. *Home:* 73 rue de Varenne, Paris 7e, France. *Office:* c/o Institude France, 23 quaide Conti, Paris 6e, France. *Agent:* Andre Berheim, 55, avenue George V, Paris VIIIeme, France.

CAREER: Author. Minister of Cultural Affairs of France, 1973—. *Military service:* French Cavalry, officer, 1940; escaped from France through Spain, 1942, and served with Free French Forces in England, 1942-44. War correspondent, 1944-45. *Member:* French Academy, Societe des Gens de Lettres, Societe des Auteurs et Compositeurs Dramatiques, Societe des Auteurs Compositeurs et Editeurs de Musique, Savile Club (London). *Awards, honors:* Prix Goncourt for *Les Grandes Familles,* 1948; Monaco Literary Council Prize for the whole of his work, 1966; knight of the Legion of Honor.

WRITINGS—Novels: *La Derniere Brigade*, Julliard, 1946, revised edition, Societe des Editions, 1965 (English translation published as *The Last Detachment*, Hart-Davis, 1957); *Les Grandes Familles* (trilogy), Julliard, book 1: *Les Grandes Familles*, 1948, book 2: *La Chute des Corps*, 1950, book 3: *Rendez-vous aux enfers*, 1951 (one-volume English translation, *The Curtain Falls*, Scribner, 1959); *La Volupte d'Etre*, Julliard, 1954 (English translation, *The Film of Memory*, Scribner, 1955); *Les Rois Maudits* (historical novel series published in English under general title *The Accursed Kings*): *Le Roi de fer*, Del Duca, 1955 (English translation, *The Iron King*, Scribner, 1956), *La Reine Etranglee*, Del Duca, 1955 (English translation, *The Strangled Queen*, Scribner, 1956), *Les Poisons de la Couronne*, Del Duca, 1956 (English translation, *The Poisoned Crown*, Scribner, 1957), *La Loi des Males*, Del Duca, 1956 (English translation, *The Royal Succession*, Scribner, 1958), *La Louve de France*, Del Duca, 1959 (English translation, *The She-Wolf of France*, Scribner, 1960), *Le Lis et le Lion*, Del Duca, 1960 (English translation, *The Lily and the Lion*, Scribner, 1961).

Other books: *Lettres d'un Europeen* (essays), Julliard, 1944; *Remarques* (essays), Julliard, 1952; *Tistou les pouces verts* (juvenile), Del Duca, 1957, revised edition, Plon, 1968 (English translation, *Tistou of the Green Thumbs*, Scribner, 1958); *Alexandre le Dieu* (mythology), Del Duca, 1958 (English translation, *Alexander the God*, Scribner, 1961); *Des Seigneurs de la plaine a l'Hotel de Mondez* (short stories), Julliard, 1962 (English translation, *The Glass Coffin and Other Stories*, Scribner, 1963); *Les Memories de Zeus* (mythology), Volume I, Hachette, 1963, Volume II, 1965 (English translation, *The Memoirs of Zeus*, Volume I, Scribner, 1964); *Bernard Buffet* (essays), Hachette, 1964 (English translation, *Bernard Buffet*, October House, 1966); *Paris de Cesar a Saint Louis* (historical essay), Hachette, 1964 (English translation, *The History of Paris from Caesar to St. Louis*, Scribner, 1970); *Le Pouvoir* (maxims), Hachette, 1965; *Le Bonheur des uns*, Plon, 1967; *Ces Messieurs de Rothchild*, Editions P. Tinse, 1967; *L'Avenir en dessarroi*, Plon, 1968; (with Jaques Suffel) *Vezelay, Colline eternelle*, Union general d'editions, 1968; *Belles Histories de Chevaus*, Gautier-Languereau, 1968; *Alexander le Grand*, Plon, 1969; *Lettres d'un Europeen, 1943-70*, Plon, 1970; *Une Eglise quise tompe de siecle: responseset commentaires de Luc Baresta*, Plon, 1972.

Plays: *Theatre* (including "Megaree," produced, 1942, "Un Voyageur," 1954, "La Contessa," 1962), Julliard, 1962. Also writer with Joseph Kessel of "Le coup de Grace," a play produced, 1952, and "Le chant des Partisans," (the song of the French Resistance), with music by Anna Marly.

Film scripts: "Les Grandes Familles" (adaptation of his novel), 1958; "Le Baron de l'Ecluse" (adaptation of novel by Simenon), 1958 "Film of Memory" (adaptation of his novel), 1972. *Tistou of the Green Thumbs* was adapted for film in 1970.

Contributor to *La Nef*, *La Revue de Paris*, *Paris Match*, *Figaro Litteraire*, *Lettres Francaises*, *Nouvelles Litteraires*, *Marie Claire*, *Elle*.

SIDELIGHTS: Druon's books have been translated into twenty-four languages. He lived in Rome, 1947-48, and has spent considerable time there at other periods. He also has traveled in Czechoslovakia, Poland, Soviet Union, Turkey, and Greece. Druon is fluent in Italian and English.†

*　　*　　*

DUDLEY, Ernest 1908-
(Ernest Vivian Coltman)

PERSONAL: Surname originally Coltman-Allen; born July 23, 1908, in Dudley, Worcestershire, England; son of Frank (a physician) and Rose (Ambler) Coltman-Allen; married Jane Grahame (an actress), January 17, 1929; children: Susan. *Education:* Educated privately. *Religion:* Church of England. *Address:* 49 Hallam St., London W.1., England.

CAREER: British Broadcasting Corp., London, England, contract writer and broadcaster, mostly in crime fiction, criminological, and crime reporting fields, 1936—. Australian Broadcasting Co., Sydney, writer and broadcaster, 1948; feature writer under contract to national newspapers; lecturer on criminology. *Member:* Writers' Guild, Society of Authors, Our Society (crimes club).

WRITINGS: Mister Walker Wants to Know, Wright & Brown, 1940; *Meet Doctor Morelle*, John Long, 1944; *Adventures of Jimmy Strange* (short stories), John Long, 1945; *Menace for Doctor Morelle*, John Long, 1947; *Meet Doctor Morelle Again*, John Long, 1947; *Crocked Straight*, Hodder & Stoughton, 1948.

Dark Bureau, Hodder & Stoughton, 1950; *Dr. Morelle and the Drummer Girl*, Hodder & Stoughton, 1950; *Private Eye*, John Long, 1950; *Two-Face*, John Long, 1951; *Look Out for Lucifer!*, John Long, 1952; *Picaroon*, R. Hale, 1952, Bobbs-Merrill, 1953; *Bywaters and Mrs. Thompson*, Odhams, 1953; *Crooked Inn*, Hodder & Stoughton, 1953; *The Blind Beak*, R. Hale, 1955; *The Whistling Sands*, Hodder & Stoughton, 1956; *Callers for Dr. Morelle*, R. Hale, 1957; *Dr. Morelle Takes a Bow*, R. Hale, 1957; (with Jack Evans) *Confessions of a Special Agent*, R. Hale, 1957, published as *The Face of Death*, Morrow, 1958; *The Gilded Lily; The Life and Loves of the the Fabulous Lillie Langtry*, Odhams, 1958; *Leatherface*, R. Hale, 1958; *Mind of Dr. Morelle*, R. Hale, 1958; *Dr. Morelle at Midnight*, R. Hale, 1959; *Confess to Dr. Morelle*, R. Hale, 1959; *Alibi and Dr. Morelle*, R. Hale, 1959.

Dr. Morelle and the Doll, R. Hale, 1960; *Monsters of the Purple Twilight: The True Story of the Life and Death of the Zeppelins*, Harrap, 1960; *Nightmare for Dr. Morelle*, R. Hale, 1960; *The Scarlett Widow*, Muller, 1960; *To Love and Perish*, R. Hale, 1962; (under pseudonym Ernest Vivian Coltman) *Birds of the Storm*, Muller, 1963.

(With David Nockels) *Arthur*, Muller, 1970; *Rangi: Highland Rescue Dog*, Harvill Press, 1970; *An Elephant Called Slowly*, Collins, 1970; *Rufus: Story of a Fox*, Muller, 1971, published as *Rufus: The Remarkable True Story of a Tamed Fox*, Hart, 1972; *For Love of a Wild Thing*, Eriksson, 1974. Writer of film scripts. Story editor, Butcher's Films Distributor. Contributor of articles to periodicals, including *People*, *Daily Express*, *Evening News*.

AVOCATIONAL INTERESTS: Antiques, nineteenth-century art, ornithology.†

*　　*　　*

DUDLEY, Geoffrey A(rthur) 1917-

PERSONAL: Born January 8, 1917, in Grantham, Lincolnshire, England; son of Arthur Edwin and Ethel Florence (Bland) Dudley; married Eva Senescall, January 24, 1942; children: Susan Mary, Carol Frances Mary. *Education:* University of Nottingham, B.A., 1938. *Home:* 1 Thornton Dr., Handforth, Wilmslow, Cheshire SK9 3DA, England. *Office:* Psychology Publishing Co. Ltd., Psychology House, Marple, Cheshire SK6 6NE, England.

CAREER: Psychology Publishing Co. Ltd. (educational publishers), Marple, Cheshire, England, director of studies, 1942—. Director of *Successful Living* Magazine, 1952-68. *Military service:* British Army, Royal Artillery, gunner, 1939-41.

WRITINGS: Dreams: Their Meaning and Significance, Thorsons Publishers, 1956, published as *How to Understand Your Dreams*, Wilshire, 1957; (translator from the

French) Louis Frederic, *Yoga Asanas*, Thorsons Publishers, 1959; (translator from the German) Otto H. F. Buchinger, *About Fasting*, Thorsons Publishers, 1961; *The Right Way to Interpret Your Dreams*, Elliot Right Way Books, 1961; *Self-Help for Self-Mastery*, Fowler, 1962; *Your Personality and How to Use it*, Emerson, 1962; (editor) Hartrampf, *Vocabulary-Builder*, Psychology Publishing Co., 1963; *Rapid Reading*, Psychology Publishing Co., 1964; (contributor) *Course in Practical English*, Practical English Programme, 1965; *Use Your Imagination*, Thorsons Publishers, 1965.

Increase Your Learning Power, Thorsons Publishers, 1966; *Budget Accounts*, Lewis's, 1966; (editor) Bergen Evans, *Vocabulary Studies*, Psychology Publishing Co., 1967; (translator from the German) Maria Vogel, *Home Nursing*, Thorsons Publishers, 1967; (translator from the German) Lisa Mar, *Overweight Do's, Don'ts and Diet*, Thorsons Publishers, 1967; *Dreams: Their Mysteries Revealed*, Aquarian Press, 1969; (with Elizabeth Pugh) *How to Be a Good Talker*, Psychology Publishing Co., 1971; *How to Interpret Dreams Correctly*, A. N. Efstratiadis, 1973; (with Georg Fischhof) *Psychogenes Training*, Forum Verlag, 1974. Contributor to *International Journal of Sexology, Freethinker*, and *The Psychologist Magazine*.

WORK IN PROGRESS: Revised editions of *Your Personality and How to Use it* and *How to Be a Good Talker*.

SIDELIGHTS: Dudley is competent in French and German. *Avocational interests:* Cinema, philately, and home wine-making.

*   *   *

DUGMORE, Clifford W(illiam) 1909-

PERSONAL: Born May 9, 1909, in Birmingham, England; son of William Ernest (a clerk in holy orders) and Ethel (Westmore) Dugmore: married Ruth Mabel Prangley, August 23, 1938; children: Ruth Ismayne (Mrs. Edgar Richard Peters). *Education:* Exeter College, Oxford, B.A. (honors), 1932, M.A., 1935, B.D., 1940, D.D., 1957; Queen's College, Cambridge, B.A. (by incorporation), 1933, M.A., 1936. *Politics:* Conservative. *Home:* Thame Cottage, The Street, Puttenham, Surrey, England. *Office:* King's College, University of London, Strand, London W.C. 2, England.

CAREER: Ordained deacon, Church of England, 1935, priest, 1936; assistant curate, Formby, 1935-37; St. Deiniol's Library, Hawarden, sub-warden, 1937-38; Ingestrewith-Tixall, rector, 1938-43; Alleyn's College of God's Gift, Dulwich, chaplain, 1943-44; rector of Bredfield and director of religious education, Diocese of St. Edmundsbury and Ipswich, 1945-47; University of Manchester, Manchester, England, senior lecturer in ecclesiastical history, 1946-58; University of London, London, England, professor of ecclesiastical history, 1958—, member of senate and academic council, 1964-71. Hulsean Lecturer, Cambridge University, 1958-60; proctor in Convocation of Canterbury (general Synod), 1970—. Member of East Suffolk and West Suffolk County Council education committees, 1945-46.

MEMBER: Commission Internationale d'Histoire Ecclesiastique (president of British Sous Commission, 1952-62), Ecclesiastical History Society (president, 1963-64), Society for Old Testament Study, Studiorum Novi Testamenti Societas, Canterbury and York Society (council, 1960—).

WRITINGS: Eucharistic Doctrine in England from Hooker to Waterland, S.P.C.K., 1942; (editor) *The Interpretation of the Bible*, S.P.C.K., 1944, 2nd edition, 1946; *The Influence of the Synagogue Upon the Divine Office*, Oxford University Press, 1944, reprinted, Faith Press, 1964; *The Mass and the English Reformers*, Macmillan, 1958; *Ecclesiastical History No Soft Option*, S.P.C.K., 1959; (editor with C. Duggan) *Studies in Church History I*, Thomas Nelson, 1964; (editor with others) *Studies in Chruch History II*, Thomas Nelson, 1965; (with others) *Eucharistic Theology Then and Now*, S.P.C.K., 1968; (with others) *Man and His Gods*, Hamlyn, 1971. General editor of "Leaders of Religion" series, eight volumes published, Thomas Nelson, now published by A.&C. Black.

Contributor to *Chambers's Encyclopaedia*, 1950, *Wellkirchenlexikon*, 1960, *Studia Patristica IV*, 1961, *Neotestamentica et Patristica*, 1962, *The English Prayer Book*, 1963. Contributor to articles and reviews to *Times Educational Supplement*, theological journals, and periodicals. Editor of *Journal of Ecclesiastical History*, 1950—; British member of editorial board of *Novum Testamentum*, 1956—; advisory editor of *Chambers's Encyclopaedia*, 1960—.

WORK IN PROGRESS: The Doctrine of Grace in the English Reformers (Hulsean Lectures).

AVOCATIONAL INTERESTS: Motoring and philately.

*   *   *

DUHL, Leonard J. 1926-

PERSONAL: Born May 24, 1926, in New York, N.Y.; son of Louis (a dentist) and Rose (Josefsberg) Duhl; married Carola Meyer, May 24, 1951 (divorced); children: Pamela, Nina, David, Susan. *Education:* Columbia University, A.B., 1945; Albany Medical College, M.D., 1948; Washington Psychoanalytic Institute, postgraduate study, 1964. *Home:* 639 Cragmont, Berkeley, Calif. 94708. *Office:* University of California, Berkeley, Calif. 94720.

CAREER: Licensed physician in Maryland, New York, Massachusetts, California, and Washington, D.C.; certified fellow of Menniger Foundation, 1954, certified by American Board of Psychiatry and Neurology, 1956; Jewish Hospital, Brooklyn, N.Y., intern, 1948-49; Winter Veterans Administration Hospital, Topeka, Kan., resident in psychiatry, 1949-54; National Institute of Mental Health, Bethesda, Md., psychiatrist in professional services branch, 1954-66, chief of Office of Planning, 1964-66; U.S. Department of Housing and Urban Development, Washington, D.C., special assistant to secretary, 1966-68; University of California, Berkeley, professor of urban social policy and public health, 1968—. George Washington University, clinical instructor, 1958-61, assistant clinical professor, 1963-68; clinical professor at University of California's San Francisco Medical Center, 1969—; adjunct professor at Antioch College, 1970—. Visiting lecturer at colleges and universities, including Columbia University, Harvard University, Massachusetts Institute of Technology, University of Pennsylvania, University of Pittsburgh, Wayne State University, Webster College, Boston University, University of Southern California, University of California (Los Angeles), University of Michigan, and University of Connecticut. Fellow of Menninger Foundation School of Psychiatry, 1949-54; U.S. Public Health Service, member, 1951-53, medical director, 1954-72; senior assistant surgeon for California Public Health Service, 1951-53; co-director of documentation and evaluation of experimental schools programs for Berkeley Unified School District, 1971—.

Chairman of U.S. Department of Health, Education, and Welfare's subcommittee on cultural deprivation and poverty, 1963-65; member of California Council of Criminal Justice, Riots, and Disorders Task Force, 1969-70; member of science and technology advisory council of California Legislature, 1969—; member of board of directors of National Training Laboratories' Institute for Applied Behavioral Science, 1969—; chairman of board of technical and policy advisers of U.S. Health Corp., 1970—; member of Commission on the Year Two Thousand. Trustee of Park Forest College. Consultant to government offices, hospital, and businesses, including Man/Machine Interface Corp., President's Panel on Young Childhood Patterns, President's Commission on Civil Disorders, and House of Representatives Public Works Committee.

MEMBER: International Academy for Child Psychiatry and Allied Professions (assistant secretary general, 1962-66), American Psychiatric Association (fellow), American Orthopsychiatric Association (fellow; member of board of directors, 1964—), Academy of Psychoanalysis (fellow), American Association on Mental Deficiency (councilor, 1959-63), Group for the Advancement of Psychiatry, National Academy of Science (member of board on medicine, 1967—), American Association for the Advancement of Science (fellow), American Public Health Association (fellow), Society for Applied Anthropology (fellow), Royal Society of Medicine, Northern California Psychiatric Society, Delta Omega.

WRITINGS: Approaches to Research in Mental Retardation, Woods Schools, 1959; (author of preface) Richard W. Poston, *Democracy Speaks Many Tongues*, Harper, 1962; *The Urban Condition: People and Policy in the Metropolis*, Basic Books, 1963; *Urban America and the Planning of Mental Health Services: Symposium Number Ten*, Group for the Advancement of Psychiatry, 1964; (with R. L. Leopold) *Mental Health and Urban Social Policy*, Jossey-Bass, 1968; (author of foreword) Matthew Dumont, *The Absurd Healer*, Science House, 1968; (editor) *A Symposium on the Urban Crisis: Selections from the 1968 Department of Housing and Urban Development Summer Study in Urban Affairs*, Center for Planning and Development Research, University of California (Berkeley), 1969; (with Martin Meyerson, Chester Rapkin, and John Collins) *The City and the University*, St. Martin's, 1969.

Contributor: *Human Needs in the Changing City*, American Municipal Association, 1957; Paul David Cantor, editor, *Traumatic Medicine and Surgery for the Surgeon*, Volume VI, Butterworth, 1962; Lowdon Wingo, Jr., editor, *Cities and Space: The Future Use of Urban Land*, Johns Hopkins Press, 1963; Stephen Goldston, editor, *Concepts of Community Psychiatry: A Framework for Training*, U.S. Department of Health, Education, and Welfare, 1965; H.S. Becker, editor, *Social Problems: A Modern Approach*, Wiley, 1966; Stanford Anderson, editor, *Planning for Diversity and Choice*, MIT Press, 1968; *The Businessman and the City*, Graduate School of Business Administration, Harvard University, 1967; William Ryan, editor, *Distress in the City*, Press of Case Western Reserve University, 1967; William Gray, Nicholas Rizzo, and Frederick Duhl, editors, *General Systems Theory and Practice*, Little, Brown, 1969; *Man and His Urban Environment*, University of Cincinnati Press, 1970; Morton Levitt and Ben Rubenstein, editors, *The Mental Health Field*, Wayne State University Press, 1971.

Author of research bulletins and reports. Contributor to proceedings, annals, and archives. Contributor of nearly a hundred articles and reviews to medical and education journals, including *California Medicine, Journal of Applied Behavioral Science, Community Psychology, Urban and Social Change Review, American Journal of Psychiatry*, and *Mental Retardation*. Member of board of editors of *American Journal of Mental Deficiency*, 1957-60, *Trans-Action*, 1965—, and *Volunteer's Digest*, 1965—.

WORK IN PROGRESS: A book on social change.

* * *

DUIGNAN, Peter 1926-

PERSONAL: Surname is pronounced Deg-nan; born August 6, 1926, in San Francisco, Calif.; son of Peter James (a fireman) and Delia (Conway) Duignan; married Francis Helen Sharpe, August 13, 1949; children: one son, five daughters. *Education:* University of San Francisco, B.S. (cum laude), 1951; Stanford University, M.A., 1953, Ph.D., 1960. *Religion:* Roman Catholic. *Home:* 939 Casanueva, Stanford, Calif. *Office:* Hoover Institution, Stanford University, Stanford, Calif.

CAREER: Stanford University, Stanford, Calif., instructor in Western civilization, 1957-60, curator of African Collection, Hoover Institution, 1959—, research associate of Hoover Institution, 1960—, executive secretary of Hoover Institution, 1962-65, director of African program, 1965—. U.S. Army, 1944-46; served in South Pacific; received Combat Infantry Badge. *Member:* American Civil Liberties Union, National Association for the Advancement of Colored People, American Historical Association, American Political Science Association, African Studies Association, Bibliographical Society of America. *Awards, honors:* Ford Foundation Fellow in Africa, 1958-59; Rockefeller Foundation international fellowship, 1963-64; Guggenheim fellowship, 1973.

WRITINGS: (Co-author) *White Settlers in Tropical Africa*, Penguin, 1962; (contributor) Rogers and Frantz, editors, *Racial Themes in Southern Rhodesia*, Yale University Press, 1962; (with Clarence C. Clendenen) *The United States and the Slave Trade, 1619-1865*, Hoover Institution, 1963; (with Kenneth Glazier) *A Checklist of African Serials, Based on the Hoover Institution and Stanford University Libraries*, Hoover Institution, 1963; (co-author) *Americans in Africa: A Preliminary Guide to American Missionary Archives and Library Manuscript Collections on Africa*, Hoover Institution, 1963; (co-author) *Americans in Black Africa up to 1865*, Hoover Institution, 1964 (with C. C. Clendenen) *Americans in Africa: 1865-1900*, Stanford University, 1966; *Handbook of American Resources for African Studies*, Stanford University, 1967; (with Lewis Gann) *Burden of Empire: An Appraisal of Western Colonialism in Africa South of the Sahara*, Pall Mall, 1968; (compiler with Gann) *Colonialism in Africa, 1870-1960*, Cambridge University Press, 1969; (with Gann) *The History and Politics of Colonialism, 1914-1960*, Cambridge University Press, 1970. Contributor to *American Anthropologists, National Review, New Leader*, and to political science journals. Editor of *American and Canadian Publications on Africa* (annual), 1961—, of *Africana Newsletter* (quarterly), 1962-64, and of *African Studies Bulletin*, 1965—.

WORK IN PROGRESS: Co-director of four-volume study, *Imperialism in Africa;* co-author of *Guide to African Research;* writing *Handbook of American Resources for African Studies.†*

DUKER, Sam 1905-

PERSONAL: Born June 10, 1905, in Denver, Colo.; son of
Willem Frederick and Huibertine (Schuyten) Duker; married second wife, Laura Thompson (an anthropologist),
June 7, 1963; children: (prior marriage) Catherine (Mrs.
Everett Moran). Education: University of California, A.B.
and LL.B., 1928; Oklahoma State University of Agriculture and Applied Science, M.S., 1947; Columbia University, Ph.D., 1952. Politics: Republican. Home: 1530 Palisade Ave., Fort Lee, N.Y. 07024.

CAREER: Oklahoma State University of Agriculture and
Applied Science, Stillwater, assistant professor of psychology, 1947-50; Brooklyn College (now Brooklyn College of
the City University of New York), Brooklyn, N.Y., assistant professor, 1950-61, associate professor, 1961-65, professor of education, 1965-75. Member: American Psychological Association (fellow), National Education
Association.

WRITINGS: (With Thomas Nally) The Truth About Your
Child's Reading, Crown, 1956; Listening Bibliography,
Scarecrow, 1964, 2nd edition, 1968; Public Schools and
Religion: The Legal Context, Harper, 1965; (compiler) Lis-
tening: Readings, Scarecrow, Volume I, 1966, Volume II,
1971; Individualized Reading: An Annotated Bibliography,
Scarecrow, 1968; Individualized Reading: Readings, Scare-
crow, 1969; (compiler) Teaching Listening in the Elemen-
tary School: Readings, Scarecrow, 1971; Individualized
Reading, C.C Thomas, 1971; Individualized Instruction in
Mathematics, Scarecrow, 1972; Time-Compressed Speech:
An Anthology and Bibliography, three volumes, Scarecrow, 1974.

Contributor to more than 30 journals and several encyclopedias, mainly in the field of education. Editor, Journal of
Communication, 1967-69.

*   *   *

DUMPLETON, John Le F(evre) 1924-

PERSONAL: Born July 20, 1924, in St. Albans, Hertford-
shire, England; son of Cyril Walter and Louise (LeFevre)
Dumpleton; married Ruby C. Allen, April 16, 1945; chil-
dren: Timothy, Anthea. Education: Studied at Gaddesden
Training College, 1947-48, St. Albans School of Art, 1948-
50. Religion: Society of Friends (Quaker). Home: Higher
East Coombe House, Stockleigh Pomeroy, Credition,
Devonshire, England.

CAREER: Beaumont School, St. Albans, Hertfordshire,
England, head of art department, 1948-57; Spencer Primary
School, St. Albans, Hertfordshire, England, assistant master, 1957-62; Shelley School, Crediton, Devonshire, England, head of remedial department and senior house master, 1962—. Member of Hertfordshire Special
Constabulary, 1952-62, St. Albans Road Safety Council,
1957-62, Crediton Road Safety Committee, 1962—.
Member: Royal Society of Arts (fellow), National Union of
Teachers, Guild of Teachers of Backward Children, International Reading Association.

WRITINGS: The Art of Handwriting, Pitman, 1953;
Teach Yourself Handwriting, English Universities Press,
1954; Law and Order, A. & C. Black, 1963; Make Your
Own Booklet, A. & C. Black, 1965. Writer of filmstrip,
"The Development of Italic Handwriting," Dryad, 1952.

WORK IN PROGRESS: Cry Havoc! Disorder in 18th
Century London; The 'Queen's Peace,' Modern Law and
Order in Britain.†

DUNCAN, Otis Dudley 1921-

PERSONAL: Born December 2, 1921, in Nocona, Tex.;
son of Otis Durant and Ola (Johnson) Duncan; married
Beverly Davis (a writer), January 16, 1954. Education: Attended Oklahoma Agricultural and Mechanical College
(now Oklahoma State University), 1938-40; Louisiana State
University, B.A., 1941; University of Minnesota, M.A.,
1942; State University of Iowa, graduate study, 1943; University of Chicago, Ph.D., 1949. Office: Department of
Sociology, University of Arizona, Tucson, Ariz. 85721.

CAREER: Pennsylvania State College (now University),
University Park, assistant professor of sociology, 1948-50;
University of Wisconsin, Madison, assistant professor of
sociology, 1950-51; University of Chicago, Chicago, Ill.,
assistant professor of sociology, 1951-56, associate professor of human ecology, 1957-60, professor of human ecology, 1960-62, associate director of Population Research and
Training Center, 1953-56; University of Michigan, Ann
Arbor, professor of sociology, 1962-73, appointed Charles
Horton Cooley University Professor of Sociology, 1969,
associate director, Population Studies Center, 1962-67,
director, 1967-68; University of Arizona, Tucson, professor
of sociology, 1973—. Visiting professor, University of
Michigan, 1955, University of Southern California, 1960,
Institute for Advanced Studies (Vienna), 1973; visitor, Nuf-
field College of Oxford University, 1968. Member of
Human Ecology Study Section of National Institutes of
Health, 1959-62, and chairman of Advisory Committee for
the Coordination of Research on Social Indicators, 1972—.
Military service: U.S. Army, 1942-46.

MEMBER: International Union for the Scientific Study of
Population, Population Association of America (member of
board of directors, 1954-57; vice-president, 1965-66; presi-
dent, 1968-69), American Statistical Association (fellow),
American Sociological Association, American Academy of
Arts and Sciences (fellow), National Academy of Sciences,
American Philosophical Society, Society for the Study of
Social Biology (vice-president, 1969-71), Sociological Re-
search Association. Awards, honors: Sorokin Award for
American Sociological Association, 1968, for The Amer-
ican Occupational Structure.

WRITINGS: (With Albert J. Reiss, Jr.) Social Character-
istics of Urban and Rural Communities, 1950, Wiley, 1956;
(editor with Joseph J. Spengler) Population Theory and
Policy: Selected Readings, Free Press of Glencoe, 1956;
(editor with Spengler) Demographic Analysis: Selected
Readings, Free Press of Glencoe, 1956; (with wife, Beverly
Duncan) The Negro Population of Chicago, University of
Chicago Press, 1957; (editor with Philip M. Hauser, and
contributor) The Study of Population: An Inventory and
Appraisal, University of Chicago Press, 1959; (author of
foreword) G. Franklin Edwards, The Negro Professional
Class, Free Press of Glencoe, 1959.

(With W. Richard Scott, Stanley Lieberson, Hal H. Wins-
borough, and Beverly Duncan) Metropolis and Region,
Johns Hopkins Press, 1960; (translator with Harold W.
Pfautz) Maurice Halbwachs, Population and Society: Introduction to Social Morphology, Free Press of Glencoe,
1960; (with Ray P. Cuzzort and Beverly Duncan) Statistical Geography: Problems in Analyzing Areal Data, Free
Press of Glencoe, 1961; (with Reiss, Paul K. Hatt, and
Cecil C. North) Occupations and Social Status, Free Press
of Glencoe, 1961; (editor and author of introduction) William F. Ogburn, On Culture and Social Change: Selected
Writings, University of Chicago Press, 1964; (with Peter

M. Blau) *The American Occupational Structure*, Wiley, 1967; *Toward Social Reporting: Next Steps*, Russell Sage, 1969.

(With David L. Featherman and Beverly Duncan) *Socio-economic Background and Achievement*, Seminar Press, 1972; (editor with Arthur S. Goldberger, and contributor) *Structural Equation Models in the Social Sciences*, Seminar Press, 1973; (with Howard Schuman and Beverly Duncan) *Social Change in a Metropolitan Community*, Russell Sage, 1973; *Introduction to Structural Equation Models*, Academic Press, in press.

Contributor: Hatt and Reiss, editors, *A Reader in Urban Sociology*, Free Press of Glencoe, 1951; Hatt and Reiss, editors, *Cities and Society*, Free Press of Glencoe, 1957; D. V. Glass, editor, *Teaching of Social Sciences: Demography*, UNESCO, 1957; William Dobriner, editor, *The Suburban Community*, Putnam, 1958.

George A. Theodorson, editor, *Studies in Human Ecology*, Row, Peterson, 1961; Ernest W. Burgess and Donald J. Bogue, editors, *Contributions to Urban Sociology*, University of Chicago Press, 1964; R.E.L. Faris, editor, *Handbook of Modern Sociology*, Rand McNally, 1964; N. J. Smelser and S. M. Lipset, editors, *Social Structure and Social Mobility in Economic Development*, Aldine, 1966; Eleanor B. Sheldon and Wilbert E. Moore, editors, *Indicators of Social Change*, Russell Sage, 1968; D. P. Moynihan, editor, *On Understanding Poverty*, Basic Books, 1969.

H. M. Blalock, Jr., editor, *Causal Models in the Social Sciences*, Aldine-Atherton, 1971; Kenneth C. Land and Seymour Spilerman, editors, *Social Indicator Models*, Russell Sage, 1974.

Author of eleven monographs, most with Beverly Davis (now wife) for "Urban Analysis Series" of Chicago Community Inventory, University of Chicago, 1951-53; also author of government bulletins. Contributor to yearbook, *Sociological Methodology*, to proceedings, and to *Encyclopaedia Britannica*, *Collier's Encyclopedia*, and *Woerterbuch der Soziologie*; contributor of more than sixty articles on population, human ecology, and social stratification, and about fifty reviews to journals.

Associate editor, *American Sociological Review*, 1955-57; member of editorial board, *American Journal of Sociology*, 1955-61, *Journal of Human Ecology*, 1971—, and *Social Science Research*, 1971—; *Sociological Methodology*, advisory editor, 1969-70, member of editorial board, 1970-72; book review editor, *Social Biology*, 1969-71.

WORK IN PROGRESS: "Some Linear Models for Two-Wave, Two-Variable Panel Analysis, with One-Way Causation and Measurement Error," for *Mathematics and Sociology*, edited by H. M. Blalock; contributing German translations to *Korrelation und Kausalitaet*, edited by R. Ziegler and H. J. Hummell; and several other scientific papers.

*   *   *

DUNCAN, Pope A(lexander) 1920-

PERSONAL: Born September 8, 1920, in Glasgow, Ky.; son of Pope Alexander (a Baptist minister) and Mabelle (Roberts) Duncan; married Margaret Flexer, June 30, 1943; children: Mary Margaret, Annie Laurie, Katherine Maxwell. *Education:* University of Georgia, B.S., 1940, M.S., 1941; Southern Baptist Theological Seminary, Th.M., 1944, Th.D., 1947; also studied at Union Theological Seminary, New York, N.Y., University of Zurich, and Oxford University. *Politics:* Democrat. *Home and office:* Georgia Southern College, Statesboro, Ga. 30458.

CAREER: Baptist minister; pastor in Kentucky, 1942-45; Mercer University, Macon, Ga., director of religious activities, 1945-46, Roberts Professor of Church History, 1948-49; Stetson University, De Land, Fla., professor of religion, 1946-48, 1949-53; Southeastern Baptist Theological Seminary, Wake Forest, N.C., professor of church history, 1953-63; Brunswick College, Brunswick, Ga., dean, 1964; South Georgia College, Douglas, president, 1964-68; Georgia Southern College, Statesboro, vice-president, 1968-71, president, 1971—. Interim pastor in Florida, Virginia, North Carolina, and Georgia. Curator and secretary of Florida Baptist Historical Society. *Member:* American Historical Association, American Society of Church History, Phi Beta Kappa, Phi Kappa Phi, Pi Mu Epsilon, Phi Eta Sigma, Phi Delta Kappa, Omicron Delta Kappa, Rotary (Douglas and Statesboro, Ga.). *Awards, honors:* Carnegie grants, 1951, 1952; faculty fellowship, Southeastern Baptist Theological Seminary, 1960-61.

WRITINGS: (With O. LaFayette Walker) *Christianity and Western Thought*, privately printed, 1952; *Our Baptist Story*, Convention Press, 1958, revised edition, 1972; (contributor) *Baptist Advance*, Broadman, 1964; *The Pilgrimage of Christianity*, Broadman, 1965; *Hanserd Knollys: Seventeenth-Century Baptist*, Broadman, 1965; (contributor) G. H. Shriver, editor, *American Religious Heretics*, Abingdon, 1966. Area editor and contributor to *Encyclopedia of Southern Baptists*, Broadman, 1958. Contributor to Baptist periodicals.

SIDELIGHTS: Duncan is competent in German, slight ability in French and several ancient languages.

*   *   *

DUNCAN, W(illiam) Murdoch 1909-
(John Cassells, Neill Graham, Martin Locke, Peter Malloch, Lovat Marshall)

PERSONAL: Born November 18, 1909, in Glasgow, Scotland; son of William Kelly (an engineer) and Mary (Murdoch) Duncan; married Marion Hughes; children: Neil Murdoch, Rosemary Hughes. *Education:* Attended Windsor and Walkerville Collegiate Institutes; University of Glasgow, M.A. (honors in history), 1934. *Politics:* Conservative. *Religion:* Presbyterian. *Home:* Loup, Clachan, Tarbert, Argyll, Scotland. *Agent:* A. P. Watt & Son, 26/28 Bedford Row, London WC1R 4HL, England.

CAREER: Full-time writer of detective novels. *Military service:* British Army, 1940-41.

WRITINGS—All published by Melrose: *Doctor Deals with Murder*, 1944; *Death Wears a Silk Stocking*, 1945; *Mystery on the Clyde*, 1945; *Murder at Marks Caris*, 1945; *Death Beckons Quietly*, 1946; *Killer Keep*, 1946; *Straight Ahead for Danger*, 1946; *Tiled House Mystery*, 1947; *The Blackbird Sings of Murder*, 1948; *The Puppets of Father Bouvard*, 1948; *The Cult of the Queer People*, 1949.

The Brothers of Judgement, Melrose, 1950; *The Black Mitre*, Melrose, 1951; *The Company of Sinners*, Melrose, 1951; *The Blood Red Leaf*, Melrose, 1952; *Death Comes to Lady's Steps*, Melrose, 1952; *Deathmaster*, Hutchinson, 1954; *Death Stands Round the Corner*, Rich & Cowan, 1955; *Pennies for His Eyes*, Rich & Cowan, 1955; *Knife in the Night*, Rich & Cowan, 1955; *Murder Calls the Tune*, John Long, 1957; *The Joker Deals with Death*, John Long, 1958; *Murder Rings the Bell*, John Long, 1959; *The Murder Man*, John Long, 1959.

All published by John Long: *The Hooded Man*, 1960; *The Whispering Man*, 1960; *The House in Spite Street*, 1961; *The Nighthawk*, 1962; *Redfingers*, 1962; *The Crime Master*, 1963; *Meet the Dreamer*, 1963; *The Green Knight*, 1964; *The Hour of the Bishop*, 1964; *The House of Wailing Winds*, 1965; *Again the Dreamer*, 1965; *Presenting the Dreamer*, 1966; *Case for the Dreamer*, 1966; *The Council of Comforters*, 1967; *Problem for the Dreamer*, 1967; *Salute the Dreamer*, 1968; *The Dreamer Intervenes*, 1968; *Cord for a Killer*, 1969; *Challenge for the Dreamer*, 1969; *The Green Triangle*, 1969.

The Dreamer Deals with Murder, 1970; *The Whisperer*, 1970; *Detail for the Dreamer*, 1971; *The Breath of Murder*, 1971; *The Dreamer at Large*, 1972; *The Big Timer*, 1973; *Prey for the Dreamer*, 1974.

Under pseudonym John Cassells: *The Sons of the Morning*, Melrose, 1946; *The Bastion of the Damned*, Melrose, 1947; *The Master of the Dark*, Melrose, 1948; *Murder of Rothesay*, Melrose, 1949; *Castle of Sin*, Melrose, 1949.

The Mark of the Leech, Melrose, 1950; *The League of Nameless Men*, Melrose, 1950; *The Grey Ghost*, Melrose, 1951; *Exit Mr. Shane*, Melrose, 1952; *The Clue of the Purple Asters*, Melrose, 1952; *The Circle of Dust*, Melrose, 1952; *The Second Mrs. Locke*, Melrose, 1952; *The Rattler*, Melrose, 1952; *The Waters of Sadness*, Melrose, 1952; *Salute Inspector Flagg*, Muller, 1953; *Case for Inspector Flagg*, Muller, 1954; *Enter the Picaroon*, Muller, 1954; *Inspector Flagg and the Scarlet Skeleton*, Muller, 1955; *Beware, the Picaroon*, Muller, 1956; *Avenging Picaroon*, Muller, 1956; *Again, Inspector Flagg*, Muller, 1956; *Meet the Picaroon*, John Long, 1957; *Presenting Inspector Flagg*, Muller, 1957; *Case 29*, John Long, 1958; *The Engaging Picaroon*, John Long, 1958; *Enter Superintendent Flagg*, John Long, 1959; *The Enterprising Picaroon*, John Long, 1959.

Score for Superintendent Flagg, John Long, 1960; *Salute the Picaroon*, John Long, 1960; *Problem for Superintendent Flagg*, John Long, 1961; *The Brothers of Benevolence*, John Long, 1962; *The Picaroon Goes West*, John Long, 1962; *Prey for the Picaroon*, John Long, 1963; *The Council of the Rat*, John Long, 1963; *Blue Mask*, Hutchinson, 1964; *Challenge for the Picaroon*, John Long, 1964; *The Benevolent Picaroon*, John Long, 1964; *Greyface*, John Long, 1965; *Plunder for the Picaroon*, John Long, 1965; *Blackfingers*, John Long, 1966; *The Audacious Picaroon*, John Long, 1967; *The Room in Quiver Court*, John Long, 1967; *The Elusive Picaroon*, John Long, 1968; *Call for Superintendent Flagg*, John Long, 1968; *The Night of the Picaroon*, John Long, 1969; *The Double-Crosser*, John Long, 1969.

Quest for the Picaroon, John Long, 1970; *The Grafter*, John Long, 1970; *The Picaroon Collects*, John Long, 1970; *The Hatchet Man*, John Long, 1971; *Profit for the Picaroon*, John Long, 1972; *The Enforcer*, John Long, 1973; *The Picaroon Laughs Last*, John Long, 1973; *Killer's Rope*, John Long, 1974.

Under pseudonym Neill Graham: *Passport to Murder*, Melrose, 1949.

The Temple of Slumber, Melrose, 1950; *The Quest of Mr. Sandyman*, Jarrolds, 1951; *The Symbol of the Cat*, Melrose, 1952; *Again, Mr. Sandyman*, Jarrolds, 1952; *Murder Walks on Tiptoe*, Melrose, 1952; *Amazing Mr. Sandyman*, Jarrolds, 1952; *Salute Mr. Sandyman*, Jarrolds, 1955; *Play It Solo*, Jarrolds, 1955; *Murder Makes a Date*, Roy, 1955; *Say It With Murder*, Jarrolds, 1956; *You Can't Call It Murder*, Jarrolds, 1957; *Salute to Murder*, John Long, 1958; *Hit Me Hard*, John Long, 1958.

Killers Are on Velvet, John Long, 1960; *Murder is My Weakness*, John Long, 1961; *Murder on the Duchess*, John Long, 1961; *Make Mine Murder*, John Long, 1962; *Label It Murder*, John Long, 1963; *Graft Town*, John Long, 1963; *Murder Makes It Certain*, John Long, 1963; *Murder Made Easy*, John Long, 1964; *Murder of a Black Cat*, John Long, 1964; *Murder on My Hands*, John Long, 1965; *Murder's Always Final*, John Long, 1965; *Money for Murder*, John Long, 1966; *Murder on Demand*, John Long, 1966; *Murder Makes the News*, John Long, 1967; *Murder Has Been Done*, John Long, 1967; *Pay Off*, John Long, 1968; *Candidate for a Coffin*, John Long, 1968; *Death of a Canary*, John Long, 1969; *Murder Lies in Waiting*, John Long, 1969.

Blood on the Pavement, John Long, 1970; *One for the Book*, John Long, 1970; *A Matter of Murder*, John Long, 1971; *Murder, Double Murder*, John Long, 1971; *Frame-Up*, John Long, 1972; *Cop in a Tight Frame*, John Long, 1973; *Murder in a Dark Room*, John Long, 1973; *Assignment Murder*, John Long, 1974.

Under pseudonym Martin Locke: *The Vengeance of Mortimer Daly*, Ward, Lock, 1962.

Under pseudonym Peter Malloch; all published by John Long, except as indicated: *11:20 Glasgow Central*, Rich & Cowan, 1955; *Sweet Lady Death*, Rich & Cowan, 1956; *Death Tread Softly*, Rich & Cowan, 1957; *Walk In, Death*, Rich & Cowan, 1958; *Fly Away, Death*, 1958.

Hardiman's Landing, 1960; *Anchor Island*, 1962; *Blood Money*, 1962; *Break Through*, 1963; *Fugitive Road*, 1963; *Cop Lover*, 1964; *The Nicholas Snatch*, 1964; *The Sniper*, 1965; *Lady of No Compassion*, 1966; *The Big Steal*, 1966; *Murder of the Man Next Door*, 1966; *Die, My Beloved*, 1967; *Johnny Blood*, 1967; *Murder of a Student*, 1968; *Death Whispers Softly*, 1968; *Backwash*, 1969; *Blood on Pale Fingers*, 1969.

The Adjuster, 1970; *The Grab*, 1970; *The Slugger*, 1971; *Two with a Gun*, 1971; *Write-Off*, 1972; *Kickback*, 1973; *The Delinquents*, 1974.

Under pseudonym Lovat Marshall: *Sugar for the Lady*, Hurst & Blackett, 1955; *Sugar on the Carpet*, Hurst & Blackett, 1956; *Sugar Cuts the Corners*, Hurst & Blackett, 1957; *Sugar on the Target*, Hurst & Blackett, 1958.

Sugar on the Cuff, R. Hale, 1960; *Sugar on the Kill*, R. Hale, 1961; *Sugar on the Loose*, R. Hale, 1962; *Sugar on the Prowl*, R. Hale, 1962; *Murder in Triplicate*, R. Hale, 1963; *Murder Is the Reason*, R. Hale, 1964; *Ladies Can Be Dangerous*, R. Hale, 1964; *Death Strikes in Darkness*, R. Hale, 1965; *The Dead Are Silent*, R. Hale, 1966; *The Dead Are Dangerous*, R. Hale, 1966; *Murder of a Lady*, R. Hale, 1966; *Blood on the Blotter*, R. Hale, 1968; *Money Means Murder*, R. Hale, 1968; *Death Is For Ever*, R. Hale, 1969.

Murder's Out of Season, R. Hale, 1970; *Murder's Just for Cops*, R. Hale, 1971; *Death Casts a Shadow*, R. Hale, 1972; *Moment for Murder*, R. Hale, 1972; *Red Ice*, R. Hale, 1973; *Loose Lady Death*, R. Hale, 1973; *Date with Murder*, R. Hale, 1973; *Murder Town*, R. Hale, 1974.

Author of historical articles.

SIDELIGHTS: Duncan's books have been translated into German, French, Italian, Spanish, Norwegian, Dutch, Portuguese, and other languages.

DUNHAM, H(enry) Warren 1906-

PERSONAL: Born January 24, 1906, in Omaha, Neb.; son of Henry Warren and Elizabeth Marie (Cowan) Dunham; married Vera Sandomirsky (a professor of Slavic languages), November 1, 1942; children: Eugenie. *Education:* University of Omaha, student, 1924-26; University of Chicago, Ph.B., 1928, M.A., 1935, Ph.D., 1941. *Home:* 446 Fisher Rd., Grosse Pointe Farms, Mich. *Office:* Department of Psychiatry, School of Medicine, Wayne State University, Detroit, Mich. 48201.

CAREER: Vanderbilt University, Nashville, Tenn., instructor, 1940; Wayne University, (now Wayne State University), Detroit, Mich., instructor, 1940-42; U.S. Office of War Information, Washington, D.C., information research analyst, 1944-45; Wayne State University, Detroit, Mich., assistant professor, 1943-48, associate professor, 1948-54, professor of sociology, 1954-70, professor of sociological psychiatry, 1971—. Resident director, Michigan State Psychiatric Research Clinic, 1950; director of epidemiology laboratory, Lafayette Clinic, Detroit, Mich., 1959-64. Special lecturer, Howard University, 1944-45; visiting professor at Stanford University, summer, 1947, New York University, summer, 1948, Columbia University, 1970-71. Consultant, National Institute of Mental Health, 1949-53, member of review committee of Center for Epidemiological Studies, 1969-71. Speaker at International Congress on Social Psychiatry and International Congress of Psychotherapy, London, England, 1965.

MEMBER: American Sociological Association (chairman, section on social psychiatry, 1947), Michigan Academy of Science, Arts and Letters (chairman, sociology section, 1949), American Association of University Professors, Michigan Sociological Society (vice-president, 1943-44; executive committee, 1947-48; president, 1948-49), Ohio Valley Sociological Society (vice-president, 1946-47; president, 1949-50), Sigma Xi, Alpha Kappa Delta. *Awards, honors:* Leo M. Franklin Memorial Chair, Wayne State University, 1955-56; Fulbright scholar and lecturer at University of Amsterdam, 1956-57, and at University of Ain Shams, Cairo, U.A.R.; research grants from National Institute of Mental Health, 1959-62, Michigan State Department of Mental Health, 1964; Rema Lapouse Memorial Award, American Public Health Association, 1972.

WRITINGS: (With R.E.L. Faris) *Mental Disorders in Urban Areas*, University of Chicago Press, 1939; (with S. W. Waldfogel) *A Healthy Mind: It's Yours for the Doing*, Wayne State University Press, 1943; (contributor) O. J. Kaplan, editor, *Mental Disorders in Later Life*, Stanford University Press, 1945.

(With Francis E. Merrill, Arnold Rose and Paul W. Tappan) *Social Problems*, Knopf, 1950; *Crucial Issues in the Treatment and Control of Sexual Deviation*, Michigan State Department of Mental Health, 1951; (contributor) M. Caldwell and L. Foster, editors, *Analysis of Social Problems*, Stackpole, 1954; (editor) *The City in Mid-Century*, Wayne State University Press, 1957; *Sociological Theory and Mental Disorder*, Wayne State University Press, 1959; (with S. K. Weinberg) *The Culture of the State Mental Hospital*, Wayne State University Press, 1960; *Community and Schizophrenia: An Epidemiological Analysis* (monograph), Wayne State University Press, 1965; (contributor) Marshall Clinard, editor, *Anomie and Deviant Behavior*, Free Press, 1964; *Communities and Mental Health: Problems and Prospects*, Behavioral Publications, in press.

Contributor of articles to five books; more than eighty other articles and papers published in *Social Forces, Marriage and Family Living, International Journal of Social Psychiatry, Archives of General Psychiatry*, and in other sociology journals and conference reports.

* * *

DUNLOP, Agnes M. R.
(Elisabeth Kyle, Jan Ralston)

PERSONAL: Born in Ayr, Scotland; daughter of James (a lawyer) and Elizabeth (Riddell) Dunlop. *Education:* Educated privately. *Religion:* Presbyterian. *Home:* 10 Carrick Park, Ayr, Scotland. *Agent:* Brandt & Brandt, 101 Park Ave., New York, N.Y. 10017.

CAREER: Novelist, and author of books for children.

WRITINGS—Under pseudonym Elisabeth Kyle: *The Begonia Bed*, Bobbs-Merrill, 1934; *Orangefield*, Bobbs-Merrill, 1938; *The Mirrors of Versailles*, Constable, 1939.

Broken Glass, P. Davies, 1940; *The White Lady*, P. Davies, 1941; *Visitors from England*, P. Davies, 1941; *But We Are Exiles*, P. Davies, 1942; *Vanishing Island*, P. Davies, 1942, published as *Disappearing Island*, Houghton, 1944; *Behind the Waterfall*, P. Davies, 1943; *The Pleasure Dome*, P. Davies, 1943; *The Skaters' Waltz*, P. Davies, 1944; *Carp Country*, P. Davies, 1946; *Mally Lee*, Doubleday Crime Club, 1947; *The Mirrors of Castle Doone*, P. Davies, 1947, Houghton, 1949; *Holly Hotel*, Houghton, 1947; *Lost Karin*, P. Davies, 1947, Houghton, 1948; *West Wind*, P. Davies, 1948, Houghton, 1950; *A Man of Talent*, P. Davies, 1948.

A Little Fire, Appleton, 1950 (published in England as *Douce*, P. Davies, 1950); *The Provost's Jewel*, P. Davies, 1950, Houghton, 1951; *Lintowers*, P. Davies, 1951; *The Tontine Belle*, P. Davies, 1951; *The Captain's House*, P. Davies, 1952, Houghton, 1953; *Conor Sands*, P. Davies, 1952; *Forgotten as a Dream*, P. Davies, 1953; *Reiver's Road*, Thomas Nelson, 1953, American edition published as *On Lennox Moor*, 1954; *The House of the Pelican*, Thomas Nelson, 1954; *The Regent's Candlesticks*, P. Davies, 1954; *Carolina-House*, Thomas Nelson, 1955; *A Stillness in the Air*, P. Davies, 1956; *Maid of Orleans: The Story of Joan of Arc*, Thomas Nelson, 1957; *Queen of Scots: The Story of Mary Stuart*, Thomas Nelson, 1957; *Run to the Earth*, Thomas Nelson, 1957; *The Seven Sapphires*, Thomas Nelson, 1958; *The Money Cat*, Hamish Hamilton, 1958; *Oh, Say Can You See*, P. Davies, 1959; *The Other Miss Evans*, P. Davies, 1959.

Eagles' Nest, Thomas Nelson, 1961; *The Story of Grizel*, Thomas Nelson, 1961; *Girl with an Easil*, Evans Brothers, 1962; *Return to Alcazar*, P. Davies, 1962; *Portrait of Lisette*, Thomas Nelson, 1963; *Girl with a Pen*, Evans Brothers, 1963, published as *Girl with a Pen: Charlotte Bronte*, Holt, 1964; *Victoria: The Story of a Great Queen*, Thomas Nelson, 1964; *Girl with a Song: The Story of Jenny Lind*, Evans Brothers, 1964, published as *The Swedish Nightingale*, Holt, 1965; *Girl With a Destiny: The Story of Mary of Orange*, Evans Brothers, 1965; *The Boy Who Asked for More: The Early Life of Charles Dickens*, Evans Brothers, 1966; *Princess of Orange*, Holt, 1966; *Love is for the Living*, Holt, 1967; *High Season*, P. Davies, 1968; *Duet: The Story of Clara and Robert Schumann*, Holt, 1968; *Great Ambitions: A Story of the Early Years of Charles Dickens*, Holt, 1968; *Queen's Evidence*, P. Davies, 1969.

Song of the Waterfall: The Story of Edvard and Nina Grieg, Holt, 1970; *Mirror Dance*, P. Davies, 1970, Holt,

1971; *The Scent of Danger*, P. Davies, 1971, Holt, 1972; *The Silver Pineapple*, P. Davies, 1972; *The Stilt Walkers*, Heinemann, 1972.

Under pseudonym Jan Ralston: *Mystery of the Good Adventure*, Dodd, 1950.

WORK IN PROGRESS: A novel.

AVOCATIONAL INTERESTS: European travel, history, and art.†

*   *   *

DUNLOP, John Thomas   1914-

PERSONAL: Born July 5, 1914, in Placerville, Calif.; son of John Wallace and Antonia (Forni) Dunlop; married Dorothy Emily Webb, July 6, 1937; children: John Barrett, Beverly Claire, Thomas Frederick. *Education:* University of California, Berkeley, B.A., 1935, Ph.D., 1939. *Home:* 509 Pleasant St., Belmont, Mass 02178. *Office:* 226 Littauer Center, Harvard University, Cambridge, Mass. 02138.

CAREER: Stanford University, Stanford, Calif., acting instructor, 1936-37; Trinity College, Cambridge University, Cambridge, England, Social Science Research Council research fellow, 1937-38; Harvard University, Cambridge, Mass., instructor, 1938-44, associate professor, 1945-49, professor of economics, 1950—, chairman of department, 1961—, dean of faculty of arts and sciences, 1970-73. Consultant to U.S. Office of Economic Stabilization and Office of War Mobilization and Reconversion, 1945-47; member of Atomic Energy Labor Relations Panel, 1948-53; public member of Wage Stabilization Board, 1950-52, of Presidential Railroad Commission, of Missiles Sites Labor Commission, and of President's Committee on Equal Employment Opportunities; impartial chairman of joint administrative committee, Construction Industry Joint Conference, 1959-68; director, Cost of Living Council, 1973—. Arbitrator in labor-industry disputes. *Member:* American Academy of Arts and Sciences, American Philosophical Society. *Awards, honors:* Guggenheim fellowship, 1952-53.

WRITINGS: (Co-author) *Industrial Wage Rates, Labor Costs and Price Policies*, U.S. Government Printing Office, 1940; *Cost Behavior and Price Policy*, 1944; *Wage Determination Under Trade Unions*, Macmillan, 1944, 2nd edition, Kelley, 1950; (with James J. Healy) *Collective Bargaining: Principles and Cases*, Irwin, 1949, 2nd edition, 1953; (with Arthur D. Hill) *The Wage Adjustment Board*, Harvard University Press, 1950; (editor) *The Theory of Wage Determination*, Macmillan, 1957; *Industrial Relations Systems*, Henry Holt, 1958.

(With Clark Kerr, Frederick Harbison, and Charles Myers) *Industrialism and Industrial Man*, Harvard University Press, 1960; (editor) *Potentials of the American Economy*, Harvard University Press, 1961; (editor) *Economic Growth in the United States*, Louisiana State University Press, 1961; (editor) *Automation and Technological Change*, Prentice-Hall, 1962; (editor with V. P. Diatchenko) *Labor Productivity*, McGraw, 1964; *Wage Determination Under Trade Unions*, Kelley, 1966; (editor) *Frontiers of Collective Bargaining*, Harper, 1967; (editor) *Planning and Markets: Modern Trends in Various Economic Systems*, McGraw, 1969; (with Derek Curtis Bok) *Labor and the American Community*, Simon & Schuster, 1970; (with Charles Walker) *The Economy and Phase Four*, American Enterprise, 1973. Contributor to other books and to journals.

BIOGRAPHICAL/CRITICAL SOURCES: Engineering

News-Record, September 18, 1952; *House and Home*, April, 1960.†

*   *   *

DUNNE, John S(cribner)   1929-

PERSONAL: Born December 3, 1929, in Waco, Tex; son of John Scribner (an architect) and Dorothy (Vauhan) Dunne. *Education:* University of Notre Dame, A.B., 1951; Gregorian University, Rome, Italy, S.T.L., 1955, S.T.D., 1958. *Home and office:* 706 Park Ave., South Bend, Ind. 46616.

CAREER: Ordained to priesthood of Roman Catholic Church in Rome, Italy, 1954. University of Notre Dame, Notre Dame, Ind., instructor, 1957-61, assistant professor, 1961-65, associate professor, 1965-69, professor of theology, 1969—. Riggs Professor of Theology, Yale University, 1972-73. *Member:* Society for Religion in Higher Education, American Academy of Religion. *Awards, honors:* Rockefeller Foundation grant for theological research, 1960-61; Harbison Award for distinguished teaching, 1969.

WRITINGS: The City of the Gods, Macmillan, 1965; *A Search for God in Time and Memory*, Macmillan, 1969; *The Way of All the Earth*, Macmillan, 1972; *Time and Myth*, Doubleday, 1973. Contributor to *Review of Politics*, *Theological Studies*, and *Commonweal*. Advisory editor of *Review of Politics*.

SIDELIGHTS: Dunne told *CA*: "In my first book I study cultures in terms of their answers to death; in my second I study lives and the life story; in my third I study religions in their relation to the life story. In all of them I am looking for some kind of deeper life in man that can endure death and survive it."

Dunne has lived in Rome six years while studying theology, spending the summers during that period in the Tyrol, and in France, and England.

*   *   *

DURKEE, Mary C.   1921-

PERSONAL: Born December 4, 1921, in Warners, N.Y.; daughter of Fred and Ethel (Jones) Durkee. *Education:* Syracuse University, B.S., 1944, M.S., 1954, Ph.D., 1958. *Religion:* Episcopalian. *Home:* East Brickyard Rd., Warners, N.Y.

CAREER: Syracuse (N.Y.) public schools, teacher, 1944-53, principal, 1953-61, intermediate grade supervisor, 1961-70; Syracuse City School District, director of personnel, 1970—. Summer instructor at Syracuse University, Hobart College, University of Rochester, and University of Southern California. Trustee of Syracuse Chapter, Junior American Red Cross. *Member:* National Education Association, American Council on Education, International Reading Association, National Science Teachers Association, New York State Teachers Association, Syracuse Association of Administrators and Supervisors (president, 1959), Sigma XI (associate), Delta Kappa Gamma, Order of the Eastern Star.

WRITINGS: (With Walter Thurber) *Exploring Science*, Volumes I-VI, Allyn & Bacon, 1964.

*   *   *

DURR, William Kirtley   1924-

PERSONAL: Born February 5, 1924, in Independence, Ky.; son of Robert Kirtley and Viola (Klein) Durr; married

Shirley J. Melvin, 1950; children: John K., William R., James A. *Education:* Attended University of Cincinnati, 1942-43, Clemson College, 1943, University of Kentucky, 1946; Butler University, B.S., 1949, M.S., 1951; University of Illinois, Ed.D., 1955. *Home:* 5775 Green Road, Haslett, Mich. *Office:* Michigan State University, East Lansing, Mich.

CAREER: Teacher in Indianapolis (Ind.) public schools, 1949-51; grade school superintendent in St. Joseph, Ill., 1951-53; University of Illinois, Urbana, instructor in elementary curriculum, 1953-55; Michigan State University, East Lansing, assistant professor, 1955-57, associate professor, 1957-65, professor of education, 1965—. *Military service:* U.S. Army Air Forces, 1943-46; became first lieutenant; received Air Medal. *Member:* International Reading Association (president, 1973-74), National Association for Gifted Children (board of directors, 1961-64), Michigan Reading Association (treasurer, 1961-64; president, 1964-65), Michigan Congress of Parents and Teachers (member, board of directors, 1961-64).

WRITINGS: Gifted Student, Oxford University Press, 1964; (co-author) *Reading for Meaning,* 4th edition, Houghton, 1966; (collaborator) *Reading: A Program of Instruction for the Elementary School,* Houghton, 1966; (editor) *Reading Instruction: Dimensions and Issues,* Houghton, 1967; (with Paul McKee) *The Reading Skills Lab,* Houghton, 1968; (editor) *Reading Difficulties: Diagnosis, Correction, and Remediation,* International Reading Association, 1970; (co-author) *The Houghton Mifflin Readers,* Houghton, 1971, 2nd edition, 1974. Writer of booklets published by Bureau of Research, College of Education, Michigan State University, and by Garrard Press. Contributor to *Child and Family, Reading Teacher, Exceptional Children,* other education and reading journals.

*　　*　　*

DUTTON, Ralph (Stawell) 1898-

PERSONAL: Born August 25, 1898, in England; son of Henry John and Blanche (Cave) Dutton. *Education:* Attended Eton College and Christ Church, Oxford. *Politics:* Conservative. *Religion:* Church of England. *Home:* 95 North Eaton Sq., London S.W.1., England.

CAREER: With British Foreign Office, 1939-45; now member of Lloyd's London, 1928—. High sheriff of Hampshire, 1944-45. Member of executive committee of National Art Collections Fund, of historic buildings committee of National Trust, and of Historic Buildings Council; trustee of Wallace Collection. *Member:* Society of Antiquaries (fellow).

WRITINGS—All published by Batsford, except where otherwise noted: *The English Country House,* 1935; *The English Garden,* 1937; (with Lord Holden) *The Land of France,* 1939; *The English Interior,* 1948; *Wessex,* 1950; *The Age of Wren,* 1951; *London Homes,* Allen & Wingate, 1952; *Normandy and Britanny,* 1953; *The Victorian Home,* 1954; *The Chateaux of France,* 1957; *English Court Life,* 1963; *Hinton Ampner: A Hampshire Manor,* 1968; *Hampshire,* 1970.

SIDELIGHTS: Dutton is competent in French. *Avocational interests:* Collecting antiques, forestry, gardening, travel.

*　　*　　*

DUVOISIN, Roger Antoine 1904-

PERSONAL: Born August 28, 1904, in Geneva, Switzerland; became U.S. citizen, 1938; son of Jacques J. (an architect) and Judith (More) Duvoisin; married Louise Fatio (a writer of juvenile books), July 25, 1925; children: Roger, Jacques. *Education:* Attended College Moderne and Ecole des Arts et Metiers in Geneva, Switzerland. *Residence:* Gladstone, N.J.

CAREER: Manager of pottery, Ferney-Voltaire, France, and designer of scenery for Geneva Opera and other stage productions in Geneva, Switzerland, 1925-27; textile designer in Lyons and Paris, France, 1927, and in United States for Mallenson Silk Co., 1927-31; magazine and book advertising illustrator, New York, N.Y., 1929—; author and illustrator of children's books, 1932—. *Awards, honors:* Bronze Medal, Paris Exhibition of Potteries of Ferney, 1925; first prize, *New York Herald Tribune* Children's Spring Book Festival Award, for *They Put Out to Sea: The Story of the Map,* 1944; Caldecott Medal for best illustrated book for children for *White Snow, Bright Snow* (written by Alvin Tresselt), 1948; first prize for juvenile book, West German Republic, 1956; Society of Illustrators Award, 1961.

WRITINGS—Self-illustrated: *A Little Boy Was Drawing,* Scribner, 1932; *Donkey-Donkey,* Whitman, 1933, new edition, Grosset, 1940; *All Aboard,* Grosset, 1935; *And There Was America,* Knopf, 1938; *The Christmas Cake in Search of Its Owner,* American Artists Group, 1941; *The Three Sneezes, and Other Swiss Tales,* Knopf, 1941 (published in England under title *Fairy Tales from Switzerland,* Muller, 1958); *They Put Out to Sea: The Story of the Map,* Knopf, 1943, new edition, University of London Press, 1959; *The Christmas Whale,* Knopf, 1945; *Chanticleer, the Real Story of the Famous Rooster,* Grosset, 1947; *The Four Corners of the World,* Knopf, 1948.

Petunia, Knopf, 1950; *A for Ark,* Lothrop, 1952; *Petunia's Christmas,* Knopf, 1952; *Petunia Takes a Trip,* Knopf, 1953; *Petunia and the Song,* Knopf, 1953; *Easter Treat,* Knopf, 1954; *Two Lonely Ducks,* Knopf, 1955; *One Thousand Christmas Bears,* Knopf, 1955; *The House of Four Seasons,* Lothrop, 1956; *Petunia, Beware,* Knopf, 1958; *Day and Night,* Knopf, 1960; *Veronica,* Knopf, 1961; *The Happy Hunter,* Lothrop, 1961; *Our Veronica Goes to Petunia's Farm,* Knopf, 1962 (published in England under title *Vernonica Goes to Petunia's Farm,* Bodley Head, 1963); *Spring Snow,* Knopf, 1963; *Lonely Veronica,* Knopf, 1963; *Veronica's Smile,* Knopf, 1964; *Petunia, I Love You,* Knopf, 1965; *The Missing Milkman,* Knopf, 1967; *Donkey, Donkey,* Parent's Magazine Press, 1968; *What is Right for Tulip,* Knopf, 1969; *The Crocodile in the Tree,* Bodley Head, 1972, Knopf, 1973; *Jasmine,* Knopf, 1973; *See What I Am,* Lothrop, 1974.

Translator and illustrator of Aesopus, *Le Meunier, sons fils, et l'ane,* Whittlesey House, 1962. Illustrator of over one hundred children's books including two series of books written by wife, Louise Fatio, "The Happy Lion" series, 1954-61, and "Red-Bantam" series; illustrator of children's books by other writers.

Contributor to *New Yorker,* 1934—, and occasional contributor to juvenile and book magazines.

WORK IN PROGRESS: Research in European medieval folk tales.

SIDELIGHTS: American Institute of Graphic Arts has included Duvoisin-illustrated books on its list of the fifty best books of the year seventeen times since 1933, and the *New York Times* on its list of the ten best children's books four times since 1952. *Avocational interests:* Reading, music, gardening, painting, and travel abroad.

BIOGRAPHICAL/CRITICAL SOURCES: Horn Book, January, 1948, April, 1959; *Library Journal*, June 15, 1948; *American Artists*, December, 1949; *New York Herald Tribune Book Section*, November 16, 1952; *Elementary English*, November, 1956; *Publishers' Weekly*, March, 1961; *Books Are by People*, Citation Press, 1969.†

* * *

DYER, George J(ohn) 1927-

PERSONAL: Born November 3, 1927, in Chicago, Ill.; son of George Michael and Mae (DeLacy) Dyer. *Education:* St. Mary of the Lake Seminary, B.A., 1949, M.A., 1952, S.T.D. 1956. *Home:* St. Mary of the Lake Seminary, Mundelein, Ill.

CAREER: Ordained Roman Catholic priest; St. Mary of the Lake Seminary, Mundelein, Ill., professor of patristics, and librarian. *Member:* Catholic Theological Society, Catholic Library Association.

WRITINGS: Limbo: Unsettled Question, Sheed, 1964; (editor with C. E Curran) *Shared Responsibility in the Local Church*, Chicago, 1970. Editor, *Chicago Studies* (professional journal for priests).

WORK IN PROGRESS: An introduction to ancient Christian literature.†

* * *

DYER, John M(artin) 1920-

PERSONAL: Born February 27, 1920, in St. Louis, Mo.; son of George L. and Katharine (Dobson) Dyer; married Emily Ramsay Young, August 9, 1947; children: Katherine Young (Mrs. Jack T. Riley, Jr.), Susan Ramsay, Patricia-Ann Dobson, Theresa Mary, Carolyn Frances. *Education:* St. Louis University, A.B., 1941; University of Miami, Coral Gables, Fla., LL.B., 1951 (converted to J.D., 1967); University of Pennsylvania, M.B.A., 1953. *Religion:* Roman Catholic. *Home:* 7701 Southwest 52nd Court, Miami, Fla. 33130. *Office:* Marketing Department, University of Miami, Coral Gables, Fla.

CAREER: Admitted to Florida bar, 1951, and U.S. Supreme Court bar, 1966. Private practice of law in Florida, 1951—, former counsel with law firm of Brunstetter and Popper, South Miami, now counsel with law firm of Bittel, Langer, Blass, Miami, Florida. University of Miami, Coral Gables, Florida, assistant professor, 1952-55, associate professor, 1955-69, professor of marketing, 1969—. Staff director of sub-committee for Latin America, U.S. Senate Interstate and Foreign Commerce Committee; foreign trade consultant, U.S. Department of Commerce, 1960; visiting professor, University of Delaware, summers, 1969 and 1970; visiting lecturer at National University of Nicaragua. *Member:* American Foreign Law Association, American Marketing Association, Association for Education in International Business, American Arbitration Association, Florida Bar Association, Southern Marketing Association, El Centro de las Americas, Alpha Kappa Psi, Phi Alpha Delta, Coral Gables Country Club, Surf Club. *Awards, honors:* Pi Sigma Phi Award of Propellor Club of U.S. for achievement in foreign commerce; Thomas E. Flynn scholarship, 1971; Bacardi Grant, 1972-73.

WRITINGS: (Contributor) Frank M. Dunbaugh, *Marketing in Latin America*, Printers' Ink, 1960; *United States-Latin American Trade and Financial Relations*, University of Miami Press, 1961; *Export Financing*, University of Miami Press, 1963; (with F. C. Dyer) *Bureaucracy Verses*

Creativity: The Dilemma of Modern Leadership, University of Miami Press, 1965; *Guidelines to Operating in Latin America*, Academy of Arts and Sciences of the Americas, 1970; (with F. C. Dyer) *The Enjoyment of Management*, Dow-Jones-Irwin, 1971. Also author of published studies and contributor of articles to legal and business journals.

* * *

EARL, David M(agarey) 1911-

PERSONAL: Born October 23, 1911, in St. Joseph, Mo.; son of Edwin C. (a secretary, Young Men's Christian Association) and Barbara (Thurtell) Earl; married Jay N. Hill, June 19, 1933. *Education:* Oberlin College, A.B., 1933; Wayne State University, M.A., 1950; Columbia University, Certificate of East Asian Institute, 1952, Ph.D., 1957. *Religion:* Baha'i. *Home:* 2285 Cedar St., Holt, Mich. 48842. *Office address:* University of Maryland, G-1, EUSA, APO San Francisco 96301.

CAREER: Detroit Civil Service Commission, Detroit, Mich., personnel examiner, 1941-50; Meiji University, Tokyo, Japan, instructor in political science, 1952-54; Yamaguchi University, Yamaguchi, Japan, instructor in political science and English, 1954-56; University of Maryland, Overseas Program, instructor (in Japan, Korea, and Taiwan), 1957-63, assistant director for Korea, 1963—. National Spiritual Assembly of the Baha'is of the North East Asia, member, 1958-59, recording secretary, 1959-61, chairman, 1961-64; chairman of National Spiritual Assembly of the Baha'is of Korea, 1964. *Military service:* U.S. Navy, 1942-45. *Member:* Association for Asian Studies, Academy of Political Science, Asiatic Society of Japan, Royal Asiatic Society (Korea branch), Phi Beta Kappa.

WRITINGS: Emperor and Nation in Japan: Political Thinkers of the Tokugawa Period, University of Washington Press, 1964. Contributor to *Encyclopaedia Britannica* and to *Common Cause, Far Eastern Survey*, and other periodicals.

SIDELIGHTS: Earl lived in India from 1919-25, and has spent a total of eighteen years in Asia. He has reading knowledge of Esperanto, French, German, Japanese, and Spanish.†

* * *

EASTMAN, Joel Webb 1939-

PERSONAL: Born March 11, 1939, in Bridgton, Me.; son of Brooks (an urban development director) and Frances (Webb) Eastman; married Linda Joyce Bolton (a library clerk), June 16, 1962. *Education:* University of Maine, B.A., 1962, M.A., 1965; University of Florida, Ph.D., 1973. *Politics:* Democrat. *Religion:* Unitarian. *Office:* 325 Luther Bonney Hall, University of Maine at Portland-Gorham, Portland, Me. 04103.

CAREER: High school teacher of English in Glens Falls, N.Y., 1962-63; Appalachian State University, Boone, N.C., instructor in history, 1967-68; Harvard University, Cambridge, Mass., assistant editor, *Business History Review*, 1968-70; University of Maine at Portland-Gorham, assistant professor, 1970-75, associate professor of history, 1975—.

WRITINGS: The Maine Thing: Some of Our Best Friends Are Republicans (collection of political cartoons), Wheelwright, 1964. Contributor to *Florida Historical Quarterly*, and to *Encyclopedia of World Biography*, McGraw, 1972. Contributor of cartoons to *Portland Sunday Telegram*.†

EASTON, Robert (Olney) 1915-

PERSONAL: Born July 4, 1915; son of Robert Eastman (a business executive) and Ethel (Olney) Easton; married Jane Faust, September 24, 1940; children: Joan (Mrs. Gilbert W. Lentz), Katherine (Mrs. Armand Renga), Ellen (Mrs. Gregory W. Brumfiel), Jane. *Education:* Stanford University, student, 1933-34, graduate study, 1938-39; Harvard University, B.S., 1938; University of California at Santa Barbara, M.A., 1960. *Home:* 2222 Las Canoas Rd., Santa Barbara, Calif. 93105. *Agent:* Dorothy Olding, Harold Ober Associates, 40 E. 49th St., New York, N.Y. 10017.

CAREER: Grew up on a California cattle ranch; worked as a ranch hand, day laborer, and civil engineer; *Lampasas Dispatch*, Lampasas, Tex., co-publisher and editor, 1946-50; Radio Station KHIT, Lampasas, Tex., co-owner and manager, 1948-50; Santa Barbara City College, Santa Barbara, Calif., instructor in English, 1959-65; U.S. Naval Civil Engineering Laboratory, Port Hueneme, Calif., writing and publishing consultant, 1961-69; now a full-time writer. Co-chairman, Committee for Santa Barbara; trustee, Santa Barbara Museum of Natural History. *Military service:* U.S. Army, Field Artillery, Tank Destroyer Command, Infantry, 1942-46; became first lieutenant; received Combat Infantryman's Badge.

WRITINGS: The Happy Man, Viking, 1943; (with Mackenzie Brown) *Lord of Beasts*, University of Arizona Press, 1961; (with Jay Monoghan and others) *The Book of the American West*, Messner, 1963; *The Hearing*, McNally & Loftin, 1964; (with Dick Smith) *California Condor: Vanishing American*, McNally & Loftin, 1964.

(Editor) *Max Brand's Best Stories*, Dodd, 1967; (editor and author of introduction with Mackenzie Brown) Charles F. Lummis, *Bullying the Moqui*, Prescott College Press, 1968; *Max Brand: The Big Westerner*, University of Oklahoma Press, 1970; *Black Tide: The Santa Barbara Oil Spill and its Consequences* (introduction by Ross MacDonald), Delacorte, 1972. Works included in *Great Tales of the American West*, edited by Harry E. Maule, Modern Library, 1944; *Continent's End*, edited by Joseph Henry Jackson, McGraw, 1944; *Out West*, edited by Jack Schaefer, Houghton, 1955; *A Treasury of True*, edited by Charles N. Barnard, A. S. Barnes, 1956. Contributor of stories and articles to various magazines including *The Atlantic* and *New York Times Magazine*.

WORK IN PROGRESS: A novel of California.

AVOCATIONAL INTERESTS: The environment.

SIDELIGHTS: Robert Easton has edited a book of *Max Brand's Best Stories* and has written a biography of Max Brand's life. Max Brand is one of the many pseudonyms Frederick Faust used. Easton's interest in Max Brand goes beyond his literary works; Easton's wife, Jane, is the daughter of Frederick Faust.

In reference to *Max Brand: The Big Westerner*, David Dempsey quotes Easton: "'His actual setting was a never-never land,' Easton says. 'He used a minimum of actual circumstance' because 'he wanted to free his work from everyday reality.'" Dempsey continues: "Easton's biography supplies the 'everyday reality' with sympathy but without idolatry. Although other books have been written on Faust, none that I know of portrays so thoroughly the man behind the legend."

*   *   *

EAVES, James Clifton 1912-

PERSONAL: Born June 26, 1912, in Hillside, Ky.; son of John Ridley and Agnes (Williams) Eaves; married Mona Shinkle, August 20, 1938; children: James C., Jr., Mona Jane. *Education:* University of Kentucky, A.B., 1935, M.A., 1941; University of North Carolina, Ph.D., 1949. *Religion:* Baptist. *Home:* Hermits Holler, Route 11, Box 423, Morgantown, W.Va. 26505.

CAREER: University of Kentucky, Lexington, instructor in mathematics, 1942-43, 1946; University of North Carolina, Chapel Hill, instructor in mathematics, 1946-49; University of Alabama, Tuscaloosa, assistant professor of mathematics, 1949-50; Auburn University, Auburn, Ala., associate professor, 1950-51, research associate professor, 1951-52, professor of mathematics, 1953-54, research associate of Auburn Research Foundation, 1952-53; University of Kentucky, Lexington, professor of mathematics and astronomy, 1954-67, head of department, 1954-63; West Virginia University, Morgantown, Centennial Professor of Mathematics, 1967—. Director of Institute of Consultants in Mathematics, Statistics, and Patent Law, 1956—, of Kentucky Space Flight Program in Space Mathematics and Astronomy, 1959-63; consultant to International Business Machines, 1957-59, to National Aeronautics and Space Administration, 1964. Member, Kentucky Governor's Committee on Constitutional Revision, 1956-57. *Military service:* U.S. Naval Reserve, 1942-46; became lieutenant.

MEMBER: Mathematical Association of America (Kentucky section, president, 1956 and 1963, secretary-treasurer, 1960-66; Allegheny Mountain section, chairman, 1971-73), American Mathematical Society, American Association for the Advancement of Science (fellow), American Association of University Professors, Society for Industrial and Applied Mathematics, American Society for Engineering Education, Association for Higher Education, National Education Association, National Council of Teachers of Mathematics, International Congress of Mathematicians, Kentucky Academy of Science, Kentucky Association of Colleges and Secondary Schools (president of mathematics section, 1957 and 1964), Alabama Association of College Teachers of Mathematics (president, 1953-54), United Commerical Travelers (Lexington, Ky.; member of board, 1962—), Rotary, Kiwanis, Sigma Xi, Pi Mu Epsilon, Mu Alpha Theta, Phi Delta Kappa. *Awards, honors:* Fellow, American Association for the Advancement of Science, 1963.

WRITINGS: The ATRAP, U.S. Navy, 1944; *Antisubmarine Electronics*, U.S. Navy, 1945; (with others) *College Algebra*, Pitman, 1956; (with A. J. Robinson) *Introduction to Euclidean Geometry*, Addison-Wesley, 1956, 2nd edition, 1957; *The Kentucky Program for Large Classes*, University of Kentucky, 1958; (with Pignani) *Computer Programming*, University of Kentucky, 1959; (with William Parker) *Matrices*, Ronald, 1960; (with Pence) *Mathematics Honors Tests*, University of Kentucky, 1962.

General editor: *College Algebra with Basic Set Theory*, Pitman, 1963; *Who's Who of Calvary Business Men*, Hurst, 1964. Contributor to mathematics and science journals; contributor of popular articles on astronomy to magazines.

WORK IN PROGRESS: An Analysis of Problems for Electronic Computers, in collaboration with Pignani; *Mathematics for Business and Economics*; *An Index to Modern Algebra*; studies in higher dimensional matrices.

SIDELIGHTS: Eaves has invented a submarine tracking plotting board (ATRAP), an automatic clock set, and other devices. His interests include early computers, the theory and development of watch and clock mechanisms, the pattern markers' art, kites, and computer constructed songs and music.†

*   *   *

ECKERT, Allan W.   1931-

PERSONAL: Born January 30, 1931, in Buffalo, N.Y.; son of Edward Russell and ruth (Roth) Eckert; married Joan Dowling, May 14, 1955; children: Joseph Matthew. *Education:* Attended University of Dayton and Ohio State University. *Politics:* Uncommitted. *Religion:* Protestant. *Home and office:* 185 Sabal Lane, Englewood, Fla. 33533. *Agent:* Malcolm Reiss, Paul R. Reynolds, Inc., 599 Fifth Ave., New York, N.Y. 10017.

CAREER: Once worked as postman, private detective, fireman, plastics technician, cook, dishwasher, laundryman, salesman, chemist's assistant, trapper, commercial artist, draftsman, and at perhaps fifteen types of factory work and farming; *Dayton Journal-Herald*, Dayton, Ohio, at various times outdoor editor, nature editor, police reporter, columnist, feature writer, 1957-60; became a full-time free-lance magazine writer in 1960, and still does much magazine work. Writer's Digest, Inc., Cincinnati, Ohio, consultant; Dayton Museum of Natural History, Dayton, Ohio, board of trustees, 1964-65; founder and board chairman of Lemon Bay Conservancy; member of board of directors of Charlotte County (Florida) Civic Association. *Military service:* U.S. Air Force, 1948-52, became staff sergeant. *Member:* Outdoor Writers Association (board member, 1962—), Society of Magazine Writers, Authors Guild. *Awards, honors:* Ohioana Book Award, 1968; Best Book award from Friends of American Writers, 1968; Newbery-Caldecott Honor Book award from American Library Association, 1972.

WRITINGS—All published by Little, Brown, except as indicated: *The Writer's Digest Course in Article Writing*, Writer's Digest, 1962; *The Great Auk*, 1963; *The Silent Sky: The Incredible Extinction of the Passenger Pigeon*, 1965; *A Time of Terror: The Great Dayton Flood*, 1965; *Wild Season* (nature study), 1967; *The Frontiersman* (narrative), 1967; *Bayou Backwaters* (nature study), Doubleday, 1968; *The Crossbreed* (fictionalized nature study), 1968; *The Dreaming Tree* (novel), 1968; *The King Snake* (fictionalized nature study), 1968; *Blue Jacket: War Chief of the Shawnees*, 1969; *Wilderness Empire* (narrative), 1969; *The Conquerors* (narrative), 1970; *In Search of a Whale* (non-fiction), Doubleday, 1970; *Incident at Hawk's Hill* (novel), 1971; *The Court-Martial of Daniel Boone* (novel), 1973; *Tecumseh!* (play), 1974; (with Karl Karalus) *The Owls of North America: All The Species and Subspecies Described and Illustrated*, Doubleday, 1974, new edition, 1975.

Author of thirty-three television scripts for "Wild Kingdom" and a screenplay, "The Legend of Koo-Tan." Contributor of over 200 articles to magazines.

SIDELIGHTS: Eckert's narrative novels are an unusual combination of fact and fiction. James Goodsell explained: "For example, he leans heavily on dialogue to tell his story, making ample use of whatever historical conversation remains in archives but also adopting the practice of what he terms "hidden dialogue"—putting quotation marks around material not initially recorded as dialogue but reported as having been said or heard or thought after an event." Goodsell earier had called this: "An approach which in less skilled hands could prove objectionable, in his hands, however, this method not only is managed with restraint, but becomes an valuable tool for understanding the fascinating era. . . . His invention of dialogue hews closely to the speech of the era and appears generally honest to the characters of those quoted." Professional historians have reviewed Eckert's books rather critically in spite of his extensive research (seven years went into *The Frontiersman*) in his attemps to make history more interesting to the general reader.†

*   *   *

ECKERT, Ruth E(lizabeth)   1905-

PERSONAL: Born April 2, 1905, in Buffalo, N.Y.; daughter of Edward Lee and Elizabeth Margaret (Fix) Eckert; married Eric E. Paulson (a minister), April 2, 1941 (died, 1962); married John H. McComb (a minister), November 23, 1973. *Education:* University of Buffalo, A.B.. (cum laude), 1930, M.A., 1932; Harvard University, Ed.D., 1937. *Religion:* Lutheran. *Home:* 1624 East River Ter., Minneapolis, Minn.

CAREER: University of Buffalo, Buffalo, N.Y., research associate, 1932-36; American Council on Education, Washington, D.C., research adviser, 1937-38; University of Minnesota, Minneapolis, associate professor of education, 1938-45, professor of higher education, 1945-72, Regents' professor, 1973—, coordinator of educational research, 1940-50. Staff member, Joint Legislative Committee for Survey of New York City Public Colleges, 1943; chairman of committee on studies for higher educational needs of Minnesota Commission for Higher Education, 1945-49; member of National Advisory Committee on Presbyterian Colleges, 1952-56, and of advisory committees on research, U.S. Office of Education, 1956-58, and Educational Testing Service.

MEMBER: National Education Association (member of educational policies commission, 1956-60), American Educational Research Association, National Society for the Study of Education, National Society of College Teachers of Education (member of executive committee, 1951-56, 1963—; president, 1954-55), Association for Higher Education (member of executive committee, 1947-59, 1963—), American Association of University Professors, Phi Beta Kappa. *Awards, honors:* Litt. D. from Houghton College, 1962; Doctor of Humanities, Drake University, 1964.

WRITINGS: (With T. O. Marshall) *When Youth Leave School*, McGraw, 1938; *Outcomes of General Education*, University of Minnesota Press, 1943; (editor) *Higher Education in Minnesota*, Commission on Higher Education, 1950; (with R. J. Keller) *A University Looks at Its Program*, University of Minnesota Press, 1954; (with John E. Stecklein) *Job Motivations and Satisfactions of College Teachers*, U.S. Department of Health, Education, and Welfare, 1961; (with Howard Y. Williams) *College Faculty View Themselves and Their Jobs*, College of Education, University of Minnesota, 1972. Editor, *Studies in Higher Education, 1940-42*, 1941, 1943. Contributor of chapters to books, and articles to education journals.

*   *   *

ECKSTEIN, Otto   1927-

PERSONAL: Born August 1, 1927, in Ulm, Germany; married, 1954; two children. *Education:* Princeton University, A.B., 1951; Harvard University, A.M., 1952, Ph.D., 1955. *Office:* Department of Economics, Harvard University, Cambridge, Mass.

CAREER: Harvard University, Cambridge, Mass., instructor, 1955-57, assistant professor, 1957-60, associate professor, 1962-63, professor of economics, 1963—. Member of Council of Economic Advisers, 1964-66; president, Data Resources, Inc., 1969—. Director of study of employment, growth, and price levels, Joint Economic Committee, U.S. Congress, 1959-61. Military service: U.S. Army, 1946-47. Member: American Economic Association, Econometric Society. Awards, honors: Guggenheim fellow, 1960.

WRITINGS: Water Resource Development: The Economics of Project Evaluation, Harvard University Press, 1958; (with J. V. Krutilla) Multiple Purpose River Development: Studies in Applied Economic Analysis, Johns Hopkins Press, 1958; Trends in Public Expenditures in the Next Decade, Committee for Economic Development, 1959; (with others) Staff Report on Employment, Growth, and Price Levels, U.S. Government Printing Office, 1959; Public Finance: Budgets, Taxes, Fiscal Policy (textbook), Prentice-Hall, 1963, 3rd edition, 1973; (with others) Economic Policy in Our Time: An International Comparison, three volumes, North Holland Publishing Co., 1964. Author of articles on taxation, government expenditures, wages and prices, employment problems, economic development, forecasting, and econometric models.

*   *   *

EDDLEMAN, H(enry) Leo 1911-

PERSONAL: Born April 4, 1911, in Morgantown, Miss.; son of Richard Aaron (a minister), and Lucille (Power) Eddleman; married Sarah Fox, September 7, 1937; children: Sarah Enfield (Mrs. Donald Duvall), Evelyn Lucille (Mrs. John Gordinier). Education: Mississippi College, A.B., 1932; Southern Baptist Theological Seminary, Th.M., 1935, Ph.D., 1942. Home: 901 Capitol Towers, Nashville, Tenn. 37219.

CAREER: Southern Baptist Convention, ordained minister, 1931, missionary in Middle East, 1935-41; New Orleans Baptist Theological Seminary, New Orleans, La., teacher of Old Testament and Hebrew, 1941-42; pastor in Louisville, Ky., 1942-52; Southern Baptist Theological Seminary, Louisville, Ky., teacher of Old Testament and Hebrew, 1950, 1952-53; Georgetown College, Georgetown, Ky., president, 1954-59; New Orleans Baptist Theological Seminary, president, 1959-70; Baptist Sunday School Board, Nashville, Tenn., doctrinal reader, 1970—. Member: National Association of Professors of Hebrew of America, International Platform Association, American Association of Independent Colleges and Universities, Rotary. Awards, honors: D.D., Georgetown College, 1949.

WRITINGS: To Make Men Free, Broadman, 1954; The Teachings of Jesus (Matthew 5-7), Convention Press, 1955; Missionary Task of a Church, Convention Press, 1961; Mandelbaum Gate, Convention Press, 1963; (compiler) The Second Coming, Broadman, 1963; (editor) Last Things: A Symposium of Prophetic Messages, Zondervan, 1969.

SIDELIGHTS: Eddleman is competent in Arabic and Hebrew. Avocational interests: Tennis, Swimming, and fishing.†

*   *   *

EDMISTON, (Helen) Jean (Mary) 1913-

PERSONAL: Born August 9, 1913, in Southport, Lanca-

shire, England; daughter of John Francis (a physician) and Dorothy (Hawksley) Edmiston. Education: Attended Liverpool College, 1928-31; University of London, B.A., 1935. Home: 10 Russell St., Gravesend, Kent, England. Agent: John Johnson, 10 Suffield House, 79 Davies St., London W. 1, England. Office: Department of Statistics, University College, Gower St., London W.C. 1, England.

CAREER: British Broadcasting Corp., London, England, clerk and library assistant, 1938-42; University of London University College, London, England, librarian to departments of statistics and genetics, 1946—. Military service: Women's Royal Naval Service, 1942-45; became petty officer. Member: Society of Authors, P.E.N.

WRITINGS: The Winged Witnesses, Macdonald & Co., 1955; Venice of the Black Sea, Macdonald & Co., 1956; The Crystal-Gazers, Doubleday, 1957; Swan Song, Doubleday, 1960 (published in England as The Chinese Goose, Macdonald & Co., 1960); The Shake-up, Macdonald & Co., 1962.

WORK IN PROGRESS: A novel; translating Latin texts on rhythm and harmony.†

*   *   *

EDWARDS, Anthony David 1936-

PERSONAL: Born March 18, 1936, in London England; son of Donald Isaac and Enid (Bent) Edwards. Education: Oxford University, P.P.E. (honors), 1959. Politics: Liberal. Religion: Agnostic. Home: 2 Burghley Rd., London S.W.19, England. Office: Economist Intelligence Unit, 27 St. James's Pl., London S.W.1, England.

CAREER: Economist Intelligence Unit, London, England, member of staff, 1959—.

WRITINGS: Investment in the European Economic Community: A Study of Problems and Opportunities, Praeger, 1964; The Changing Sixth Form in the Twentieth Century, Routledge & Kegan Paul, 1970.

SIDELIGHTS: Edwards speaks French and German. Avocational interests: Music, architecture, skiing, climbing, golf, tennis, squash.†

*   *   *

EDWARDS, Henry (Harry) 1893-

PERSONAL: Born May 29, 1893, in London, England; son of Henry James (a printer) and Emma (Buist) Edwards; children: Felicity (Mrs. Paul Medland), Anthony Julian, Megan (Mrs. Victor Stone), Barbara (Mrs. Alan Pool), Education: Attended schools in London, England. Politics: Liberal. Home and office: Burrows Lea, Shere, Guildford, Surrey, England.

CAREER: Spiritual healer, 1934—, conducting healing missions in Britain, and in Greece, Holland, France, Switzerland, and Cyprus, and currently forming healers associations in Australia, New Zealand, Canada, and in southwest Africa. Director, Healer Publishing Co., Burrows Lea, Shere, Surrey, England, 1953-65. Patron of Guildford branch, Royal Society for the Prevention of Cruelty to Animals. Military service: Indian Reserve of Officers, 1917; became major. Member: National Federation of Spiritual Healers (president, 1955-65).

WRITINGS—All published by Spiritualist Press, London: The Mediumship of Jack Webber, 1945; The Mediumship of Arnold Clare, 1947; Psychic Healing, 1948; The Science of Spirit Healing, 1949; Guide to Spirit Healing, 1950; Evi-

dence for Spiritual Healing, 1952; *Born to Heal*, 1953; *The Truth about Spirit Healing*, 1958.

Spirit Healing, Jenkins, 1962; *The Power of Spirit Healing*, Jenkins, 1963.

All published by the Healer Publishing Company, Surrey, England: *The Healing Intelligence*, 1968; *Thirty Years a Spiritual Healer*, 1973; *A Guide to the Understanding and Practice of Spiritual Healing*, 1974.

*   *   *

EDWARDS, Iorwerth Eiddon Stephen   1909-

PERSONAL: Born July 21, 1909, in London, England; son of Edward and Ellen Jane (Higgs) Edwards; married Annie Elizabeth Lisle, 1938; children: Philip Reynold Lisle (deceased), Lucy Elizabeth Rosalind. *Education:* Gonville and Caius College, Cambridge, B.A., 1931, M.A., 1935. *Home:* Morden Lodge, Morden, Surrey, England.

CAREER: British Museum, department of Egyptian antiquities, London, England, assistant keeper, 1934-50, deputy keeper, 1950-55, keeper, 1955-74. British Foreign Office, attached to embassies in Cairo and Baghdad and to Secretariat in Jerusalem, 1942-45. Visiting professor, Brown University, Providence, R.I., 1953-54. *Member:* British Academy (fellow, 1962), Society of Antiquaries (fellow), Egypt Exploration Society (vice-president, 1962—), Athenaeum Club (London). *Awards, honors:* T. E. Peet Prize, University of Liverpool, 1947; Litt. D., Cambridge University, 1962; Commander of the Order of the British Empire, 1968; Companion of the Order of St. Michael and St. George, 1973.

WRITINGS: Hieroglyphic Texts in the British Museum, Volume VIII, British Museum, 1938; *The Pyramids of Egypt*, Penguin, 1949, revised edition, Pitman, 1961, new edition, Viking, 1972; (editor) *Hieratic Papyri in the British Museum*, two volumes, British Museum, 1960; (compiler with T. G. H. James and A. F. Shore) *A General Guide to the Egyptian Collection in the British Museum*, British Museum, 1964; (editor with others) *The Cambridge Ancient History*, third edition, Cambridge University Press, 1971; *Treasures of Tutankhamun*, Viking, 1972. Contributor to archeology and other scientific journals.

SIDELIGHTS: The Pyramids of Egypt has been translated into several languages, including Italian and German. *Avocational interests:* Gardening.

*   *   *

EDWARDS, Jane Campbell   1932-
   (Jane Campbell)

PERSONAL: Born March 31, 1932, in Miles City, Mont.; daughter of Christopher M. and Josephine (Gast) Campbell; married Richard B. Edwards (a department manager for a grocery chain), September 26, 1953; children: Linda, Richard, Andrew, Sheila, Patrick. *Education:* Attended schools in San Francisco, Calif. *Politics:* Democrat. *Religion:* Catholic. *Home:* 1531 Queenstown Ct., Sunnyvale, Calif.

CAREER: Writer for young people. Has worked for American Express and Thomas Cook travel agencies in San Francisco, Calif.

WRITINGS: What Happened to Amy? Lothrop, 1961; *Lab Secretary*, Bouregy, 1964; (under name Jane Campbell) *Carol Stevens, Newspaper Girl*, Bouregy, 1964; *The Houseboat Mystery*, Bouregy, 1965; (under name Jane Campbell) *Believe No Evil*, Bouregy, 1969; *Island Interlude*, Bouregy, 1969; (with Gilbert Martinez) *The Mexican American: His Life Across Four Centuries*, Houghton, 1973; (contributor) *The Taba Social Studies Southeast Asia Book*, Addison-Wesley, in press. Contributor of short stories to *Calling All Girls*.

WORK IN PROGRESS: Kilgaroom, a romantic novel of suspense.

AVOCATIONAL INTERESTS: Gardening, sports.

*   *   *

EDWARDS, Josephine Cunnington   1904-

PERSONAL: Born August 24, 1904, in Muncie, Ind.; daughter of David (a merchant) and Elizabeth (Gray) Cunnington; married Lowell A. Edwards (a minister; deceased); children: Robert E., Charles G. *Education:* Andrews University, B.A., 1944; Peabody College for Teachers, M.A., 1962; University of Southern California, graduate study. *Politics:* Republican. *Religion:* Seventh-day Adventist. *Office:* Laurelbrook School, Dayton, Tenn.

CAREER: Missionary, and principal of Malamulo Teacher Training College, Nyasaland (now Malawi), Africa, 1945-52; teacher of history and Spanish at high school in Ellijay, Ga., 1957-62; teacher of education at Oakwood College, Huntsville, Ala., 1963-64; Gem State Academy, Caldwell, Idaho, teacher of history, beginning, 1964; now teaching at Laurelbrook School, Dayton, Tenn. Traveling lecturer on Holy Land, Africa, Australia, New Zealand, Japan, Twaiwan, the Philippines, Hawaii, and Alaska.

WRITINGS: Loom o'Life, Pacific Press Publishing, 1933; *Bricks for Sale*, Review & Herald, 1937; *Enchanted Pillowcases*, Review & Herald, 1953; *Tales from Africa*, Southern Publishing, 1954; *Porch of the Old Witch*, 1957; *Reuben's Portion*, Southern Publishing, 1957; *Children Can Be Taught*, Southern Publishing, 1960; *I Saw Thee Philip*, Southern Publishing, 1961; *Unto a Knowledge of Truth*, Review & Herald, 1961; *These Commandments Are Mine*, Southern Publishing, c.1963; *Wings of Faith*, Southern Publishing, 1964; *In Your Steps: Manners for Children and the Power of Parental Example*, Review & Herald, 1965; *Kamwendo*, Southern Publishing, 1966; *Pioneers Together: A Biography of the Roy F. Cottrells*, Southern Publishing, 1967; *Sibande, and Other Stories*, Pacific Press Publishing Association, 1967; *Swift Arrow*, Pacific Press Publishing Association, 1967; *And I John Saw*, Southern Publishing, 1969; *A Light Shining in Cornwall*, Southern Publishing, 1969; *Secret in the Hayloft, and Other Stories*, Southern Publishing, c.1969; *Son of the Vikings*, Southern Publishing, 1973. Also author of *Lydia, A Seller of Purple*, 1960. Writer of three scripts for Ralph Edwards's radio-television show, "This is Your Life."

WORK IN PROGRESS: A book, *Life of Malinki*.

SIDELIGHTS: Josephine Edwards speaks Spanish and Cinyanja (a dialect of the Bantu language of Central Africa).

*   *   *

EDWARDS, Marvin L(ouis)   1915-

PERSONAL: Born January 5, 1915, in Kansas City, Mo.; son of E. C. (a retail businessman) and Lillie (Gladstone) Edwards; married Marga Schuhmann (a professor of German), June 26, 1951; children: Audray A. *Education:* Columbia University, B.S. (magna cum laude), 1949, A.M., 1950, Ph.D., 1959.

CAREER: Columbia University, New York, N.Y., lecturer in history, 1951-56; Beaver College, Glenside, Pa., assistant and associate professor, 1956-60, professor of history and government, and department chairman, 1960-64; Clarkson College of Technology, Potsdam, N.Y., professor of liberal studies, 1964—. *Military service:* U.S. Army, 1942-46, reserve, 1946—; current rank lieutenant colonel; awarded European Theater ribbon, five battle stars. *Member:* American Historical Association, Conference Group on Central European History, American Association of University Professors, Phi Alpha Theta.

WRITINGS: Stresemann and the Greater Germany, 1914-1918, Bookman Associates, 1963.

SIDELIGHTS: Edwards speaks German, French, and Spanish.†

* * *

EDWIN, Brother B. 1912-

PERSONAL: Secular name, Richard Arnandez; born January 14, 1912, in New Iberia, La.; son of Jules Gervais (a businessman) and Eugenie (Pellerin) Arnandez. *Education:* Manhattan College, B.A., 1935; University of Lille, Licence es Lettres, 1937. *Home:* 476 Via Aurelia, Rome, Italy.

CAREER: Roman Catholic religious, member of Congregation of Brothers of the Christian Schools. Teacher in schools operated by Christian Brothers; moderator of International Alumni Association, 1958-64; Congregation of Brothers of the Christian Schools, Rome, Italy, secretary general, 1955—.

WRITINGS: Points Worth Pondering, Bruce, 1961; *Brother E. Victor*, privately printed, 1963; *Retreat Conferences for Religious*, Bruce, 1964; *Examens for Retreat Time*, Bruce, 1964. Editor, *Bulletin des Ecoles Chretiennes* (Rome), 1957-60.

WORK IN PROGRESS: A biography of Aloys Grosde; articles for Catholic periodicals in Europe and America.

AVOCATIONAL INTERESTS: Music, archaeology, mathematical puzzles, swimming.†

* * *

EHLERS, Henry James 1907-

PERSONAL: Born March 4, 1907, in Council Bluffs, Iowa; son of Henry T. (a farmer) and Ann R. (McKinley) Ehlers; married Retta (a private teacher of music), December 23, 1939; children: Mary Ann Ehlers Waldo, Julia May Ehlers Quick. *Education:* Creighton University, Ph.B., 1928; University of Wisconsin, M.A., 1931; University of Pittsburgh, Ph.D., 1941. *Religion:* Methodist. *Home:* 1809 Woodland, Duluth, Minn. 55803.

CAREER: Junior high school teacher of music, Pittsburgh, Pa., 1935-41; State Teachers College, Plattsburgh, (now State University of New York College at Plattsburgh), associate professor of music, 1941-44; Eastern Oregon College, LaGrande, head of department of music, 1944-47; University of Minnesota, Duluth, assistant professor, 1947-49, associate professor, 1949-55, professor of philosophy, 1955—. *Member:* American Philosophical Association, Philosophy of Education Society, John Dewey Society, National Education Association, American Association of University Professors, American Civil Liberties Union, United World Federalists, Saturday Lunch Club (Duluth; president, 1950-52).

WRITINGS: (Editor) *Crucial Issues in Education: An Anthology*, Holt, 1955, 5th revised edition, 1973. Contributor to philosophy and education journals.

WORK IN PROGRESS: Studies in logic.

AVOCATIONAL INTERESTS: Music, gardening, and golf.

* * *

EICHNER, Alfred S. 1937-

PERSONAL: Surname is pronounced *Ike*-ner; born March 23, 1937, in Washington, D.C.; son of Nathan (a cab driver) and Gussie (Rimson) Eichner; married Barbara Aranov (a social worker), June 19, 1960; children: Matthew, James. *Education:* Columbia University, A.B., 1958, Ph.D., 1966. *Politics:* Independent Democrat (presently very independent). *Home:* 79 Everett St., Closter, N.J. 07624.

CAREER: Reporter, *Washington Evening Star*, Washington, D.C.; Columbia University, School of General Studies, New York, N.Y., assistant professor of economics, 1966-71; State University of New York College at Purchase, associate professor of economics, 1971—. Senior research associate of Conservation of Human Resources project, Columbia University, 1966—. *Member:* American Economic Association, Economic History Association. *Awards, honors:* Guggenheim fellow, 1971-72.

WRITINGS: (With Eli Ginzberg) *The Troublesome Presence: American Democracy and the Negro*, Free Press of Glencoe, 1964; (editor with Aaron W. Warner and Dean Morse) *The Impact of Science on Technology*, Columbia University Press, 1965; (contributor) Ginzberg, editor, *Manpower Strategy for the Metropolis*, Columbia University Press, 1968; *The Emergence of Oligopoly: Sugar Refining as a Case Study*, Johns Hopkins Press, 1969; *State Development Agencies and Employment Expansion*, Institute of Labor and Industrial Relations, University of Michigan—Wayne State University, 1970; (contributor) Robert L. Aronson, editor, *The Localization of Federal Manpower Planning*, New York State School of Industrial and Labor Relations, 1973; (contributor) Ginzberg, editor, *New York is Very Much Alive: A Manpower View*, McGraw, 1973. *The Megacorp and Oligopoly: Micro Foundations of Macro Foundations*, Cambridge University Press, 1975. Member of editorial board, *Business History Review*.

WORK IN PROGRESS: A short-run, disequilibrium macrodynamic model of the American economy; the development of better budgeting data for human resource programs; and an analysis of societal development based on systems and human resource theory.

* * *

EICHNER, James A. 1927-

PERSONAL: Born November 30, 1927, in Rochester, N.Y.; son of Perry C. (a salesman) and Katharine (Adams) Eichner; married Dorothy Wade, January 6, 1951; children: Katharine, Richard, Patricia. *Education:* Cornell University, B.A., 1949; Columbia University, graduate study, 1949-50; University of Richmond, LL.B., 1956. *Politics:* Independent. *Religion:* Episcopalian. *Home:* 702 Seneca Rd., Richmond, Va. 23226.

CAREER: Admitted to Virginia bar, 1956; assistant city attorney, Richmond, Va., 1956-65; Federal Reserve Bank of Richmond, Va., assistant counsel, 1965—. University of Richmond, Richmond, Va., instructor in business law at

University College, 1963-66, instructor in federal procedure, 1973. *Military service:* U.S. Navy, 1945-46. U.S. Naval Reserve, 1946-70; became lieutenant commander. *Member:* American Bar Association, Virginia Bar Association, Virginia Trial Lawyers' Association, Richmond Bar Association, Scribes.

WRITINGS—All published by F. Watts: *Law*, 1963; *First Book of Local Government*, 1964; *Thomas Jefferson: The Complete Man*, 1966; *Courts of Law: A First Book*, 1969; *First Book of the Cabinet of the United States*, 1969.

*   *   *

EIMER, D(ean) Robert   1927-

PERSONAL: Surname is pronounced *Eye*-mer; born April 16, 1927, in Lincoln, Ill.; son of Fred Herman (a mechanic) and Anna Rose (Feldman) Eimer. *Education:* University of Ottawa, B.A., 1948, B.Ph., 1950, B.Th., 1954; University of Notre Dame, M.A., 1956; other study at Catholic University of America and Marquette University. *Politics:* Independent. *Home:* St. Henry's Seminary, 5901 West Main St., Belleville, Ill. *Office:* Oblates of Mary Immaculate, 15 Montcalm Ct., St. Paul, Minn.

CAREER: Roman Catholic priest, member of Oblates of Mary Immaculate. St. Henry's Seminary, Belleville, Ill., professor of English and assistant sports director, 1954-56; Our Lady of the Ozarks College, Carthage, Mo., professor of English and director of athletics, 1956-64; St. Henry's Seminary, professor of English, 1964—. National Catholic Theatre Conference, member, 1962-64.

WRITINGS: Tilted Haloes, Bruce, 1964.

SIDELIGHTS: Father Eimer has this to say about his book: 'I had never intended to write a book for publication. *Tilted Haloes* began as an incentive for learning. I was looking for a way to get my students (seniors in high school and two years of college) interested in the whole process of creative writing. One day I came into class and told a group of seniors that we were going to write a book. The idea was that they would follow me through the whole process of creative writing—a process of thinking, of tedious and prolonged and exact research, of writing, revising, selecting, etc. Since I had the students for three straight years, I felt I could take them through the process step by step. Together, we did research, even during vacations. We had intended to publish, on our own, a group of anecdotes, but someone suggested that we write a publisher to see if he might be interested. Bruce Publishing Co. was interested and with their encouragement, seminal ideas were modified, original ideas were discarded, and a sprawling, rather ugly little literary baby became a much better looking adult.'' *Tilted Haloes* also stemmed from Father Eimer's inability to believe that "holy people are forbidding people or that Christ was a somber person.''

AVOCATIONAL INTERESTS: Mass communications, sports, drama.†

*   *   *

ELATH, Eliahu   1903-

PERSONAL: Born July 30, 1903, in Snowsk, Russia; son of Menahem (a businessman) and Rifka (Ripp) Epstein; married Zehava Zalel, September 14, 1930. *Education:* Hebrew University of Jerusalem, student, 1928-30; American University of Beirut, B.A., 1934. *Religion:* Jewish. *Home:* 17 Bialik St., Jerusalem, Israel.

CAREER: Jewish Agency for Palestine, member of political department, Jerusalem, Israel, 1934-45, director of political office, Washington, D.C., 1945-48; Ambassador of Israel to the United States, 1948-50; Minister of Israel, 1950-52; Ambassador of Israel to Court of St. James's, 1952-59; political adviser to Minister for Foreign Affairs, Israel, and director of Israel Institute of International Relations; President Emeritus, The Hebrew University of Jerusalem, Jerusalem, Israel, 1962-68. *Awards, honors:* Ph.D. from Brandeis University and Wayne State University.

WRITINGS: Bedouin, Their Life and Manners, Shtibel, 1932; *Trans-Jordan*, J.N.F., 1933; *Israel and Her Neighbours*, World Publishing, 1955; *The San Francisco Diary*, Dvir Publishing (Tel Aviv), 1971; *Britain's Routes to India*, Magnes Press, 1972; *Zionism and the Arabs*, Dvir Publishing, 1974.

WORK IN PROGRESS: Memoirs of an Ambassador to Washington and London.

*   *   *

ELIAS, C(laude) E(dward), Jr.   1924-

PERSONAL: Born December 15, 1924, in Rock Springs, Wyo.; son of Claude Edward (a banker) and Celeste (Ghainer) Elias; married Nancy Elizabeth Kale, June 5, 1961 (divorced, 1970); married Margaret Kubota, November 20, 1970; children: (first marriage) Celeste, Patricia Marie; (second marriage) Scott. *Education:* University of Wyoming, B.A., 1949, M.A., 1950; Indiana University, graduate study, 1950-51; University of California, Los Angeles, Ph.D., 1964. *Office:* Graduate School of Business Administration, University of Southern California, Los Angeles, Calif. 90007.

CAREER: Price economist, U.S. Office of Price Stabilization, 1951-53; trust investment analyst, Citizens National Bank, 1953-55; securities trader for Weeden & Co., 1955-58; University of California, Los Angeles, assistant professor of business administration, 1965-66; Arizona State University, Tempe, director of bureau of economic research, 1966-67; University of Southern California, Los Angeles, assistant professor of finance, 1967-69; Fresno State College (now University of California, Fresno), dean of School of Business, 1969-72; University of Southern California, Los Angeles, chairman of department of finance and business economics and associate dean for research and alternative education of Graduate School of Business Administration, 1972—. *Member:* Regional Science Association, Western Economics Association. *Awards, honors:* J. C. Nichols Award of Urban Land Institute, 1964.

WRITINGS: (Senior editor) *Metropolis: Values in Conflict*, Wadsworth, 1964 (contributor) *Essays in Urban Land Economics*, University of California, Los Angeles, Real Estate Research Program, 1966; *Arizona's Tax Structure and its Administration*, Arizona State University, 1967. Coauthor of other published reports on business and land surveys.

WORK IN PROGRESS: Research on real estate investment trusts and their relation to capital markets.

*   *   *

ELIAS, Taslim Olawale   1914-

PERSONAL: Born November 11, 1914, in Lagos, Nigeria; son of Momolesho and Ibidun (Balogun) Elias; married Ganiat Yetunde Fowosere (a lawyer), January 12, 1932; children: Olubunkola Gbolahan, Olusoji Adeola. *Education:* Igbobi College, Cambridge School Certificate, 1934;

University of London, B.A., 1944, LL.B. (honors), 1946, LL.M., 1947, Ph.D., 1949, LL.D. (first African to earn degree), 1963. *Home:* 20 Ozumba Mbadiwe, Victoria Island, Lagos, Nigeria. *Office:* Federal Ministry of Justice, Lagos, Nigeria.

CAREER: Government Audit Department, Lagos, Nigeria, assistant, 1934-35; Nigerian Railway, Lagos, Nigeria, with chief accountant's office, 1935-44; admitted to bar, 1947; University of Manchester, Manchester, England, Simon Senior Research Fellow, instructor in law and social anthropology, 1951-53; Queen Elizabeth House, University of Oxford, Oxford, England, Oppenheimer Research Fellow, 1954-60; University of Delhi, Delhi, India, visiting professor of political science, and concurrently lecturer in law, Universities of Bombay, Calcutta, Allahabad, and Aligar, 1956; University of London, London, England, governor of the School of Oriental and African studies, 1957-60; Nigerian Government, Lagos Federal Attorney-General, 1960—, Minister of Justice, 1960-66, Commissioner for Justice, 1967; University of Lagos, Lagos, Nigeria, professor of law and dean of faculty of law, 1966—. One of architects of Nigeria's constitution, 1958; member of International Law Commission of the United Nations, 1961—; frequent adviser on constitutional problems to governments and private groups. *Awards, honors:* Queen's Counsel, 1961; Commander of the Federal Republic (Nigeria), 1962; LL.D., University of Dakar, 1962.

WRITINGS: Nigerian Land Law and Custom, Routledge & Kegan Paul, 1951, 4th edition published as *Nigerian Land Law*, Sweet & Maxwell 1971; *Groundwork of Nigerian Law*, Routledge & Kegan Paul, 1954, second edition published as *The Nigerian Legal System*, 1963; *Nature of African Customary Law*, Manchester University Press, 1956, Humanities, 1962; *Government and Politics in Africa*, Asia Publishing House, 1961, second edition, 1963; *Ghana and Sierra Leone: Development of Their Laws and Constitutions*, Stevens, 1962; *British Colonial Law*, Stevens, 1962; *Nigeria: The Development of Its Law and Constitution*, Stevens, 1967; (editor) *The Prison System in Nigeria*, University of Lagos, 1969; (editor) *Nigerian Press Law*, Evans Brothers, 1969; *Africa and the Development of International Law*, Oceana, 1972; *The Modern Law of Treaties*, Oceana, 1974. Author of pamphlets on Nigerian law.

WORK IN PROGRESS: Law of International Institutions in Africa, and *The Nigerian Constitution*, for Cambridge University Press.

SIDELIGHTS: Elias is credited with the modernization and extensive revision of the laws of Nigeria to the extent that they are now commonly agreed to be the most original and up-to-date set of laws in Africa. He speaks Yoruba and English. *Avocational interests:* Table tennis, walking.†

*   *   *

ELIOVSON, Sima Benveniste 1919-

PERSONAL: Born November 1, 1919, in Cape Town, South Africa; daughter of Isaac Simon and Lena (Meyerowitz) Benveniste; married Ezra Eliovson, June 29, 1942 (died 1962); children: Robin David, Peter John, Stephen Andrew. *Education:* University of the Witwatersrand, B.A., 1939; Normal College, Johannesburg, teaching diploma, 1940. *Home:* 16 North Rd., Dunkeld West, Johannesburg, South Africa.

CAREER: Taught for two years prior to marriage; garden and travel writer. Frameworthy Publications, Ltd.,

director; independent consultant in garden planning and design. *Member:* Tree Society of Transvaal, Horticultural Society of Transvaal, Wild Flower Protection Society, Wild Life Society, Royal Horticultural Society (fellow), National Botanical Gardens (life member), Soroptomist Club, P.E.N., Botanical Society of South Africa (chairman, Transvaal branch).

WRITINGS: Little Umfaan (children's book), privately printed, 1949; *Flowering Shrubs and Trees for South African Gardens*, Howard Timmins (Cape Town), 1951, 6th edition, 1968; (author of text for book of photographs by husband, Ezra Eliovson) *South Africa, Land of Sunshine*, Howard Timmins, 1953; (author of text) Ezra Eliovson, *This Is Johannesburg, the Fabulous City*, Howard Timmins, 1956; *The Complete Gardening Book for Southern Africa*, Howard Timmins, 1960 6th edition, 1970; *South African Flowers for the Garden*, Howard Timmins, 1962; *Discovering South African Wild Flowers*, Howard Timmins, 1962; (author of text) Ezra Eliovson, *This Is South Africa*, Bailey, 1963, 2nd edition, 1969; (author of text) *Johannesburg, City of Gold*, Frameworthy Publications, 1965; *Proteas for Pleasure*, Howard Timmins, 1965, 2nd edition, 1967; *Bulbs for the Gardener*, Howard Timmins, 1967; *Gardening the Japanese Way*, Howard Timmins, 1970; *Namaqualand in Flower*, Macmillan, 1972.

WORK IN PROGRESS: A book on bulbs.

AVOCATIONAL INTERESTS: Painting, designing, playing the piano, all creative arts.†

*   *   *

ELLIOTT, Janice 1931-

PERSONAL: Born October 14, 1931, in Derby, England; daughter of Douglas John (an advertising executive) and Dorothy (Wilson) Elliott; married Robert Cooper (a public affairs adviser for an oil company), April 11, 1959; children: Alexander. *Education:* Oxford University, B.A. (honors), 1953. *Home:* Yew Tree Cottage, Partridge Green, Horsham, Sussex RH13 8EQ, England. *Agent:* Richard Scott Simon, Ltd., 36 Wellington St., London WC2E 7BD, England.

CAREER: Journalist, London, England, 1954-62, member of editorial staffs of *House and Garden, House Beautiful, Harper's Bazaar*, and *Sunday Times*; author, free-lance journalist, and critic, 1962—. *Member:* National Union of Journalists.

WRITINGS:—Novels: *Cave with Echoes*, Secker & Warburg, 1962; *The Somnambulists*, Secker & Warburg, 1964; *The Godmother*, Secker & Warburg, 1966, Holt, 1967; *The Buttercup Chain*, Secker & Warburg, 1967; *The Singing Head*, Secker & Warburg, 1968; *Angels Falling*, Knopf, 1969.

The Kindling, Knopf, 1970; *The Birthday Unicorn* (children's novel), Gollancz, 1970; *A State of Peace*, Knopf, 1971; *Private Life*, Hodder & Stoughton, 1972; *Alexander in the Land of Mog* (children's novel), Brockhampton Press, 1973.

Work is represented in anthologies, including *Winter's Tale*, edited by A. D. Maclean, Macmillan, 1966, *Good Talk*, edited by Derwent May, Gollancz, 1968; *Penguin Modern Stories 10*, edited by Judith Burnley Penguin, 1972, and *Techniques of Novel Writing*, edited by A. S. Burack, The Writer, 1973.

Regular book reviewer for *Sunday Telegraph*, 1969—. Contributor of short stories to *Harper's Bazaar, Transatlantic*

Review, *Nova*, and *Queen*, of articles to *Sunday Times*, *Twentieth Century*, and other newspapers and magazines, and of book reviews to *Sunday Times*, *Times*, *New York Times*, and *New Statesman*. Also has written for British Broadcasting Corporation, radio and television.

WORK IN PROGRESS: A novel, *Heaven on Earth*, for publication by Hodder & Stoughton.

SIDELIGHTS: Katherine Gauss Jackson writes in reference to Janice Elliott and *The Godmother*: "This is the first of her three novels to be published in this country (U.S.). May there be more. A very remarkable talent."

Referring to Elliott and *Angels Falling*, Janet Overmyer said: "She skillfully writes as one would weave a tapestry. Persons, character traits, and similar events surface, then disappear on the wrong side of the fabric only to surface again in a slightly different way. This device deepens and enriches the plot and ties disparate scenes together most effectively." Oscar A. Bouise quotes a passage from *Angels Falling* to describe his evaluation of Elliott's writing: ". . . one of our younger novelists, endowed with a crisp style and unusual perception. What she lacks in compassion she makes up for in sharpness of her vision."

Columbia Pictures filmed *The Buttercup Chain* in 1969.

AVOCATIONAL INTERESTS: Sailing.

* * *

ELLIS, C(uthbert) Hamilton   1909-

PERSONAL: Born June 9, 1909, in Merton, Surrey, England; son of Herbert Moates (a surveyor) and Jane Elizabeth (Hamilton) Ellis; married Olivia Sargent, 1933; children: Nicholas John. *Education:* Exeter College, Oxford, student, 1928-29; London School of Journalism, student, 1930. *Politics:* "Pagan." *Religion:* "Royalist." *Home:* Monk's Barn, Tilmore, Petersfield, Hampshire, England.

CAREER: Formerly on staff of several newspapers, including *Modern Transport* and *Daily Telegraph*, London, England (as leader-writer), and occasional writer for Eastern Region of British Railways; author and artist. *Military service:* British Army, Royal West Kent Regiment. *Member:* Royal Society of Arts (fellow), Victorian Society (fellow), Institution of Mechanical Engineers (associate), Historical Model Railway Society (vice-president), Transport Trust.

WRITINGS: Who Wrecked the Mail? (novel), Oxford University Press, 1944; *The Trains We Loved*, Allen & Unwin, 1947, Pan Books, 1971; *Dandy Hart* (novel), Gollancz, 1947, Macmillan, 1948; *Nineteenth-Century Railway Carriages in the British Isles from the Eighteen-Thirties to the Nineteen-Hundreds*, Modern Transport Publishing, 1949; *Some Classic Locomotives*, Allen & Unwin, 1949.

Four Main Lines, Allen & Unwin, 1950; *The Beauty of Old Trains*, Allen & Unwin, 1952; *The Midland Railway*, Ian Allan, 1953, Soccer, 1966; *British Railway History*, two volumes, Allen & Unwin, 1954-60; *The North British Railway*, Ian Allan, 1955; *A Picture History of Railways*, Hulton Educational Publications, 1955, Macmillan, 1956, revised edition, Peebles Press, 1974; *The South Western Railway*, Allen & Unwin, 1956; (self-illustrated) *Tractors and Trains* (juvenile), Allen & Unwin, 1957; *Famous Locomotives of the World*, Muller, 1957, 2nd edition, Soccer, 1963; *A Picture History of Ships*, Macmillan, 1957, new edition, Peebles Press, 1974; *Twenty Locomotive Men*, Ian Allan, 1958; (self-illustrated) *Rapidly Round the Bend* (satire), Parrish, 1959; *The Young George Stephenson*, Parrish, 1959.

The Beauty of Railways, Parrish, 1960; (editor) *British Trains of Yesteryear*, Soccer, 1960; *The London, Brighton and South Coast Railway*, Ian Allan, 1960; *The Flying Scotsman*, Allen & Unwin, 1962; *Model Railways, 1838-1939*, Allen & Unwin, 1963; (self-illustrated) *The Splendour of Steam*, Allen & Unwin, 1965, Hillary, 1966; *Railway Carriages in the British Isles, 1830-1914*, Allen & Unwin, 1965, Soccer, 1966; *Railway History*, Dutton, 1966; *The Pictorial Encyclopedia of Railways*, Hamlyn, 1966, Crown, 1968; (self-illustrated) *The Engines That Passed*, Allen & Unwin, 1968, Augustus M. Kelley, 1968.

London, Midland and Scottish: A Railway in Retrospect, Ian Allan, 1970; *The Lore of the Train*, Grosset, 1971; (author of captions) *King Steam: Railway Paintings and Drawings*, Times Newspapers, 1971; (translator from the German) Gustavo Reder, *Clockwork, Steam and Electric*, Ian Allan, 1972.

Contributor to British newspapers, railroad journals, and magazines; also contributor to broadcasting and television media.

WORK IN PROGRESS: A book on royal trains in continental Europe, Britain, the former British Empire, and Central and South America.

SIDELIGHTS: Ellis has had four one-man exhibitions in London. He told *CA* that he "paints with joy and success . . . speaks German and French, with smatterings of Italian, Hollands and Swedish . . . loves watching wild birds and beasts, and listening to music from Bach to Sibelius."

* * *

ELLIS, Mel(vin Richard)   1912-

PERSONAL: Born February 21, 1912, in Beaver Dam, Wis.; son of Fay Nathan (a businessman) and Paula (Minkes) Ellis; married, wife's name Gwendolyn; children: Sharon, Suzanne, Deborah, Dianne, Mary. *Education:* University of Notre Dame, B.A. in journalism. *Religion:* Catholic. *Home:* On-Little-Lakes, Big Bend, Wis. 53103. *Agent:* Larry Sternig, 2407 North 44th St., Milwaukee, Wis. 53210.

CAREER: Newspaperman in Sheboygan, Wis., and Rockford, Ill., 1935-40; *Milwaukee Journal*, Milwaukee, Wis., outdoors editor, 1947-63; *Field and Stream*, New York, N.Y., associate editor, 1958-70; Associated Press, syndicated columnist, 1972—. *Military service:* U.S. Air Force; became technical sergeant; received Legion of Merit, Distinguished Flying Cross, and five Air Medals. *Awards, honors:* Gordon MacQuarrie Award for conservation writing, 1961; Dorothy Canfield Fisher award, 1972, for *Flight of the White Wolf*; five time winner of "book of the year" award of Wisconsin Council of Writers; Audubon award, 1973; Sequoyah Children's Book Award, 1974, for *Flight of the White Wolf*.

WRITINGS: Good Fishing, Milwaukee Journal, 1956; *Notes from Little Lakes*, Milwaukee Journal, 1963; *Run, Rainey, Run*, Holt, 1967; *Sad Song of the Coyote*, Holt, 1967; *Ironhead*, Holt, 1968; *Softly Roars the Lion*, Holt, 1968; *Ghost Dog of Killicut*, Four Winds, 1969; *Wild Goose, Brother Goose*, Holt, 1969; *Flight of the White Wolf*, Holt, 1970; *The Wild Runners*, Holt, 1970; *When Lightning Strikes*, Four Winds, 1970; *Caribou Crossing*, Holt, 1971; *Hurry Up Harry Hanson*, Four Winds, 1972; *This Mysterious River*, Holt, 1972; *Peg Leg Pete*, Holt, 1973; *No Man for Murder*, Holt, 1973; *Sidewalk Indian*, Holt, 1974. Contributor of articles and fiction to thirty-four magazines including *National Geographic, Reader's Digest,* and *Liberty Magazine.*

SIDELIGHTS: Wild Goose, Brother Goose and *Flight of the White Wolf* were made into Walt Disney movies. *This Mysterious River* was a New York Times "outstanding book of the year". Ellis is a health buff and runs three miles daily.

* * *

ELLIS, Norman R. 1924-

PERSONAL: Born September 14, 1924, in Springville, Ala.; son of Olin D. (a contractor) and W. F. (Brock) Ellis; married Mattie K. Martin; children: David N., Emily K., Janet M., Ben E., Susan E. *Education:* Howard College, A.B., 1951; University of Alabama, M.A., 1953; Louisiana State University, Ph.D., 1956. *Home:* 12 Rollingwood, Tuscaloosa, Ala. *Office:* University of Alabama, University, Ala.

CAREER: State of Louisiana, Pineville, director of psychology, 1956-60; Peabody College, Nashville, Tenn., associate professor, became professor of psychology, 1960-64; University of Alabama, University, professor of psychology, 1964—. *Member:* American Psychological Association, American Association on Mental Deficiency, Sigma Xi.

WRITINGS: (Editor) *Handbook in Mental Deficiency,* McGraw, 1963. Contributor of some thirty-five articles to scientific periodicals. Editor of annual series, *International Review of Research in Mental Retardation,* Academic Press, 1966—.

WORK IN PROGRESS: Several research projects.

* * *

ELLISON, Herbert J(ay) 1929-

PERSONAL: Born October 3, 1929, in Portland, Ore.; son of Benjamin F. (a businessman) and Esther R. (Anderson) Ellison; married Alberta Moore, June 13, 1952; children: Valery, Pamela. *Education:* University of Washington, Seattle, B.A., 1951, M.A., 1952; University of London, Ph.D., 1955. *Home:* 12127 South East 15th, Bellevue, Wash. 98005. *Office:* Director, Institute for Comparative and Foreign Area Studies, University of Washington, Seattle, Wash. 98195.

CAREER: University of Washington, Seattle, instructor in history, 1955-56; University of Oklahoma, Norman, assistant professor of history, 1956-62; University of Kansas, Lawrence, associate professor of history and chairman of Slavic and Soviet area studies committee, 1962-65, professor of history and director of Language and Area Center for Slavic and Eastern European Studies, 1965-68; University of Washington, professor of history, 1968—, director, Division of International Programs, 1968-72, vice provost for educational development, 1969-72, director, Institute for Comparative and Foreign Area Studies, 1972—. *Member:* American Historical Association, American Association for the Advancement of Slavic Studies, American Association of University Professors. *Awards, honors:* Fulbright scholarship, University of London, 1953-55; study fellowship, University of Leningrad, 1963-64; Slavic and East European Studies grant, American Council of Learned Societies, 1966-67.

WRITINGS: History of Russia, Holt, 1964; (contributor) Lyman H. Legters, editor, *Russia; Essays in History and Literature,* E. J. Brill, 1972.

WORK IN PROGRESS: A biography of Stalin.

SIDELIGHTS: Ellison is fluent in Russian, and competent in German and French.

* * *

ELLISON, James E. 1927-
(Brother Flavius)

PERSONAL: Born March 28, 1927, in Covington, Ky.; son of Alois Harry (vice-president of a machine tool company) and Lyda (Keller) Ellison. *Education:* Studied at St. Joseph's Novitiate, Rolling Prairie, Ind., 1945-46, University of Notre Dame, 1946-47, Cardinal Stritch College, Milwaukee, Wis., 1968-69, St. Mary's College, Notre Dame, Ind., 1969; received high school teaching certificate from two Dioceses to teach mentally retarded children. *Home:* Columba Hall, Notre Dame, Ind. 46556.

CAREER: Member of the Brothers of Holy Cross (C.S.C.), 1945—, name in religion, Brother Flavius; University of Notre Dame, Notre Dame, Ind., civil service employee of university post office, 1947-58; director of community stores for the Brothers of Holy Cross at the university, 1958—; teacher of the retarded in Jefferson, Wis., 1968-69; Corvilla Home for the Retarded, South Bend, Ind., director, 1970—. Writer, mainly for young people. Teacher of religion at parishes in vicinity of Notre Dame, Ind.; conducts lectures on mental retardation.

WRITINGS—Under name Brother Flavius; all published by Dujarie Press: *St. Catherine of Alexandria: A Star in the East,* 1952; *St. Bridget: Miracle for the Bride,* 1953; *St. Francis de Sales: Proudly We Hail,* 1956; *St. John Bosco: Come on In,* 1959; *Captain John Barry: Father of the American Navy,* 1961; *St. Benedict: Melody in Their Hearts,* 1961; *Chief Justice Roger Taney: Pride of Our Nation,* 1961; *Story of St. Agnes of Assisi,* 1962; *Blessed Julie Brilliart: No Stranger in Paradise,* 1962; *General Casimir Pulaski: Father of the American Cavalry,* 1962; *Father Gabriel Richard: An Apostle in Michigan,* 1962; *St. Gaspar del Bufalo: Stepping Stones to Heaven,* 1964; *Blessed John Neumann: House on Logan Square,* 1964; *Story of John Barry,* 1965; *Story of St. Catherine of Alexandria,* 1965; *Listen With Your Heart,* 1966.

WORK IN PROGRESS: Jesus Is All Mine, a preparation for first communion for the retarded.

* * *

ELLISON, Reuben Young 1907-

PERSONAL: Born November 14, 1907, in Easley, S.C.; son of Columbus Jefferson (a farmer and florist) and Martha Lee (Robinson) Ellison; married Mary Rankin Beeson (an organist and pianist), September 3, 1946; children: David Richard. *Education:* The Citadel, B.A. (honors), 1928; University of North Carolina, M.A., 1932; Sorbonne, University of Paris, Diplome, 1938; University of Wisconsin, Ph.D., 1940. *Religion:* Congregationalist. *Home:* 9700 Southwest 60th Ct., Miami, Fla. 33156.

CAREER: Kentucky Military Institute, Lyndon, instructor in French and Spanish, 1928-31; Missouri Military Academy, Mexico, instructor in French, Spanish, and dramatic art, 1932-37; Washington and Lee University, Lexington, Va., instructor in French and Spanish, 1940-42; University of Miami, Coral Gables, Fla., 1946—, began as assistant professor, professor of French, 1952-73, professor emeritus, 1973—. *Military service:* U.S. Army, Signal Corps Intelligence, 1942-46; became lieutenant colonel; received four battle stars. *Member:* Modern Language Association of America, National Federation of Modern Language Teachers Association (member of executive committee, 1968-72), American Association of Teachers of French, (national vice-president and member of executive council, 1968-70; delegate to NFMLTA, 1968-72), American Association of University Professors, South Atlantic Modern Language Association, Pi Delta Phi, Pi Epsilon Delta. *Awards, honors:* Chevalier dans l'Ordre des Palmes Academiques, France, 1965.

WRITINGS: (Editor with Stowell C. Goding) *Seven French Plays for Study and Stage*, Odyssey, 1957; (editor with Stowell C. Goding) Eugene Ionesco, *Rhinoceros*, Holt, 1961; (with Albert Raffanel) *Profil de la France Nouvelle*, American Book Co., 1965, 2nd edition, Van Nostrand, 1970; (translator) Marcel Cohen, *A New Look at the French Language*, University of Miami Press, in press. Author of articles, short stories, and plays.

WORK IN PROGRESS: Research in the classical and contemporary French theater.

SIDELIGHTS: Ellison lived in France three years and has made three bicycle tours in France and one in southern England. *Avocational interests:* Photography—has some five hundred kodachrome slides, and his photographs were among those used to illustrate Andre Leveque's *Histoire de la civilisation francaise.*

* * *

ELSON, Ruth Miller 1917-

PERSONAL: Born March 4, 1917, in Scranton, Pa.; daughter of William Charles (a banker) and Margaret (Smithson) Miller; married Robert Elson (a photoengraver), January 31, 1953; children: Elizabeth Bransford. *Education:* Vassar College, A.B., 1939; Columbia University, M.A., 1940, Ph.D., 1952. *Politics:* Independent. *Home:* 100 La Salle St., Apartment 12 D, New York, N.Y. 10027.

CAREER: Vassar College, Poughkeepsie, N.Y., instructor in history, 1943-45; Hunter College, (now Hunter College of City University of New York), New York, N.Y., instructor in history, 1946-49; Rockford College, Rockford, Ill., assistant professor of history, 1949-51; Vassar College, instructor, 1951-53, assistant professor, 1953-58, associate professor of history, 1958-60; Finch College, New York, N.Y., member of faculty, 1962—. Member of University Seminar in American Civilization at Columbia University. *Member:* American Studies Association, American Historical Association, Phi Beta Kappa. *Awards, honors:* American Association of University Women fellowship, 1957-58; Vassar faculty fellow, 1957-58; National Endowment for the Humanities fellowship, 1974-75.

WRITINGS: Guardians of Tradition: American Schoolbooks of the Nineteenth Century, University of Nebraska Press, 1964. Contributor of articles and reviews to historical journals.

WORK IN PROGRESS: Study of social values in American best sellers since 1865.

AVOCATIONAL INTERESTS: Music, reading.

* * *

EMERSON, Everett Harvey 1925-

PERSONAL: Born February 16, 1925, in Malden, Mass.; son of Gordon Edward and Helen (Long) Emerson; married Katherine Terrell (a librarian); children: Stephen

McDonald. *Education:* Harvard University, A.B., 1948; Duke University, M.A., 1949; Louisiana State University, Ph.D., 1955. *Politics:* Liberal Democrat. *Religion:* Episcopalian. *Home:* Arnold Road, R.D. #2, Amherst, Mass. 01002. *Office:* Department of English, University of Massachusetts, Amherst, Mass. 01003.

CAREER: Western Carolina College, Cullowhee, N.C., instructor in English, 1949-51; Christchurch School, Christchurch, Va., master of English, 1951-52; Louisiana State University, Baton Rouge, instructor in English, 1952-55; Lehigh University, Bethlehem, Pa., instructor, later assistant professor of English, 1955-60; Florida Presbyterian College, St. Petersburg, associate professor, later professor of literature, 1960-65; University of Massachusetts, Amherst, associate professor, 1965-67, professor of English, 1967—, head of university honors program, 1967-71. *Military service:* U.S. Marine Corps, 1943-46; became second lieutenant. *Member:* Modern Language Association of America. *Awards, honors:* Robinson Award ($1,000), Lehigh University, 1959; senior fellow, Folger Shakespeare Library, 1971-72.

WRITINGS: John Cotton, Twayne, 1965; *English Puritanism from John Hooper to John Milton*, Duke University Press, 1968; *Captain John Smith*, Twayne, 1971; (editor) *Major Writers of Early American Literature*, University of Wisconsin Press, 1972. Contributor to *South Atlantic Quarterly, Church History, Seventeenth-Century News, Speculum*, other professional journals. Editor, *Early American Literature*.

WORK IN PROGRESS: Editing a collaborative literary history of the American Revolution.

AVOCATIONAL INTERESTS: Music, gardening, walking, and conversation.

* * *

EMME, Eugene M(orlock) 1919-

PERSONAL: Born November 3, 1919, in Evanston, Ill.; son of Earle Edward (a psychologist) and Ada (Morlock) Emme; married Ruth Rance, June 18, 1942; children: Sandra Jean, Stephen Rance, Stuart Morlock. *Education:* Morningside College, A.B., 1941; University of Iowa, M.A., 1946, Ph.D., 1949. *Religion:* Protestant. *Home:* 11308 Cloverhill Dr., Silver Spring, Md., 20902. *Office:* Headquarters, National Aeronautics and Space Administration, Washington, D.C. 20046.

CAREER: Civilian pilot prior to World War II and flight instructor for U.S. Army; University of Iowa, Iowa City, instructor in social studies at University High School, 1946-47, university instructor in history, 1947-48; Air University, Montgomery, Ala., assistant professor, 1949-50, associate professor, 1950-52, professor of international politics, 1952-57; U.S. Office of Civil and Defense Mobilization, Battle Creek, Mich., director of Operations Research project, 1958; National Aeronautics and Space Administration (NASA), Washington, D.C., historian, 1959—. Lecturer at military staff colleges and to academic groups. *Military service:* U.S. Navy, aviator, World War II. U.S. Air Force Reserve (inactive), now colonel.

MEMBER: International Academy of Astronautics, American Historical Association, Organization of American Historians, Society for the History of Technology (member of advisory board), American Academy of Political and Social Science, American Association for the Advancement of Science (fellow), Air Force Historical Foundation, American Military Institute, Air Force Association, British Interplanetary Society (fellow), National Space Club (founder and chairman of annual Robert H. Goddard Historical Essay Competition). *Awards, honors:* Commendation for Meritorious Civilian Service, U.S. Air Force, 1958; Apollo Award, NASA, 1969; alumni award, Morningside College, 1972.

WRITINGS: International Politics and National Air Power, Air University, 1950; *Hitler's Blitzbomber*, Air University, 1951; (editor) *The Impact of Air Power: National Security and World Politics*, Van Nostrand, 1959; *Aeronautics and Astronautics: An American Chronology of Science and Technology in the Exploration of Space, 1915-1960*, National Aeronautics and Space Administration, 1961, and editor of annual supplement, *Aeronautical and Astronautical Events*, 1961—; (editor) *The History of Rocket Technology*, Wayne State University Press, 1964; *A History of Space Flight*, Holt, 1965; (author of foreword) Shirley Thomas, *Men of Space*, Volume VII, Chilton, 1965; (contributor) Melvin Kranzberg and C. W. Pursell, editors, *Technology in Western Civilization*, two volumes, Oxford University Press, 1967. Contributor of articles and reviews to periodicals. Member of editorial board of *Aerospace Historian* and *Journal of the British Interplanetary Society*.

WORK IN PROGRESS: History of the National Aeronautics and Space Administration, The Impact of Space Exploration.

* * *

ENGEL, Bernard F. 1921-

PERSONAL: Born November 25, 1921, in Spokane, Wash.; son of I. L. (a dentist) and Katherine L. (McDonald) Engel; married Adele Say (a writer) December 23, 1946. *Education:* University of Oregon, student, 1939-42, B.A., 1946; Rutgers University, student, 1943-44; University of Chicago, M.A., 1949; University of California, Ph.D., 1956. *Home:* 6193 Captain's Way, East Lansing, Mich. *Office:* Department of American Thought and Language, Michigan State University, East Lansing, Mich.

CAREER: Started as newspaper reporter in Eugene, Ore., 1946-48; instructor in English at University of Idaho, Moscow, 1949-50, Oregon State College (now University), Corvallis, 1952-53, Sacramento State College, Sacramento, Calif., 1954-57; Consolidated Freightways, Oakland, Calif., clerk, 1953-54; Michigan State University, East Lansing, 1957—, began as assistant professor, now professor of American thought and language and chairman of the department, associate editor, *University College Quarterly*, 1958-62, editor, 1962-67. Fulbright lecturer in American literature, University of Argentina, 1963. *Military service:* U.S. Army, Infantry, 1942-45; served in European theater. *Member:* Modern Language Association of America, American Studies Association.

WRITINGS: (Editor and co-author) *History of the 413th Infantry*, Warren Lewis, 1946; *Marianne Moore*, Twayne, 1964; (editor) *The Achievement of Richard Eberhart*, Scott, Foresman, 1968; *Richard Eberhart*, Twayne, 1971. Contributor of articles on literary topics and on college teaching to academic journals.

SIDELIGHTS: Engel is competent in Spanish. *Avocational interests:* Reading modern American and English poetry.

ENGELS, John David 1931-

PERSONAL: Born January 19, 1931, in South Bend, Ind.; son of Norbert Anthony and Eleanore (Perry) Engels; married Gail Jochimsen, February 1, 1957; children: Jessica, David, John, Jr., Laura, Matthew. *Education:* University of Notre Dame, A.B., 1952; University College of Dublin, National University of Ireland, graduate study, 1955; University of Iowa, M.F.A., 1957. *Home:* Williston, Vt. *Office:* St. Michael's College, Winooski Park, Vt.

CAREER: St. Norbert College, West De Pere, Wis., instructor in English, 1957-62; St. Michael's College, Winooski Park, Vt., assistant professor 1962-70, professor of English, 1970—. Trustee, Vermont Council on the Arts. *Military service:* U.S. Navy, 1952-55; became lieutenant. *Awards, honors:* Bread Loaf scholarship in poetry, 1960.

WRITINGS: (With father, Norbert Engels) *Writing Techniques*, McKay, 1962; (with Norbert Engels) *Experience and Imagination*, McKay, 1965; *The Homer Mitchell Place* (poems), University of Pittsburgh Press, 1968; (editor) *The Merrill Guide to William Carlos Williams* C. E. Merrill, 1969; (editor) *The Merrill Checklist of William Carlos Williams*, C. E. Merrill, 1969; (editor) *The Merrill Studies in Paterson*, C. E. Merrill, 1971. Poems included in *Midland*, edited by Paul Engle, Random House, 1961, and *Poems Out of Wisconsin*, Wisconsin Fellowship of Poets, 1961. Contributor of poetry and reviews to *Poetry, Reporter, Prairie Schooner, Critic, Antioch Review, Poetry Northwest, Antaeus, Yale Review, Hudson Review, Chicago Review, Carleton Miscellany, Counter/Measures*, and other journals, 1958—.

WORK IN PROGRESS: A collection of poems, *Signals From the Safety Coffin*, publication by University of Pittsburgh Press expected in 1976; a third volume of poems.

SIDELIGHTS: In reference to Engels' first book of poems one reviewer said: "If his sense of mortality is often overwhelming, his rendering of that sense is sure and controlled. John Engels makes a good beginning here, sustained by belief in the darkness of his fear and doubt, sustained by his art in a world hungry, demanding, and disordered. *The Homer Mitchell Place* is a strong first book."

* * *

ENGGASS, Robert 1921-

PERSONAL: Surname sounds like *En*-gis; born December 20, 1921, in Detroit, Mich.; son of Clarence and Helen (Strasburger) Enggass; married Catherine Cavanaugh (a translator), June 27, 1949. *Education:* Harvard University, A.B., 1946; University of Michigan, M.A., 1950, Ph.D., 1955. *Politics:* Democrat. *Home:* 1503 Crescent Rd., Lawrence, Kan. 66044.

CAREER: Bryn Mawr College, Bryn Mawr, Pa., instructor in art history, 1955-56; Williams College, Williamstown, Mass., assistant professor of art history, 1956-57; University of Buffalo, Buffalo, N.Y., associate professor of art history, 1957-58; Pennsylvania State University, University Park, professor of art history, 1958-71; University of Kansas, Lawrence, professor of art history, 1971—. *Member:* College Art Association, Instituto di Studi Romani (Rome). *Awards, honors:* American Council of Learned Societies, grant-in-aid, 1958; Fulbright research scholar, Rome, 1963-64.

WRITINGS: The Painting of Baciccio, Pennsylvania State University Press, 1964; (author of foreword) Filippo Baldinucci, *The Life of Bernini*, Pennsylvania State University Press, 1964; (contributor) Frederick Cummings, editor, *Art in Italy, 1600-1750*, Detroit Institute of Arts, 1965; (author of foreword) G. B. Bellori, *The Lives of Annibale and Agostino Carracci*, Pennsylvania State University Press, 1967; (with Jonathan Brown) *Sources and Documents in the History of Art: Italy and Spain, 1600-1750*, Prentice-Hall, 1970. Contributor to *Burlington* (London), *Art Bulletin*, *Gazette des Beaux Arts* (Paris), *Paragone* (Florence), *Bollettino d'Arte* (Rome), and other art journals.

WORK IN PROGRESS: Catalogue raisonne of 18th century sculpture in Rome.

SIDELIGHTS: Enggass spends part of every year in Rome, where he keeps an apartment.

* * *

ENGLE, T(helburn) L(aRoy)   1901-

PERSONAL: Born September 28, 1901, in Indianapolis, Ind.; son of Frank Willard (a clerk) and Grace (Slider) Engle; married Eleanor A. Sawdon, August 17, 1933; children: Charles Frank, Robert Thelburn, John Thelburn, William Paul. *Education:* Butler University, A.B., 1922; Northwestern University, M.A., 1924; Indiana University, Ph.D., 1937; also studied at University of Chicago. *Politics:* Republican. *Religion:* Methodist. *Home:* 1025 Northlawn Dr., Fort Wayne, Ind. 46805. *Office:* Indiana University at Fort Wayne, 2101 Coliseum Blvd., East, Fort Wayne, Ind. 46805.

CAREER: High school teacher in Farmington, Ill., 1924-28, Michigan City, Ind., 1928-38; Indiana University at Fort Wayne, 1938-72, began as instructor, became professor of psychology, professor emeritus, 1972—. Former part-time psychologist at Fort Wayne State Hospital and Training Center. *Member:* American Psychological Association (former secretary-treasurer of division on teaching psychology), International Congress of Psychology, Midwestern Psychological Association, Indiana Association for Mental Health, Indiana Psychological Association, Fort Wayne Psychological Association (past president), Phi Delta Kappa, Phi Kappa Phi.

WRITINGS: Psychology: Its Principles and Applications, World Book, 1945, 6th edition with Louis Snellgrove, Harcourt, 1974; (contributor) John W. Ritchie, *Biology and Human Affairs*, new edition, World Book, 1948; *Workbook in Psychology*, World Book, 1951; (with Harold J. Mahoney) *Points for Decision*, World Book, 1957, revised edition, Harcourt, 1961; *Record of Activities and Experiments*, World Book, 1958, 4th edition, with Snellgrove, Harcourt, 1969; (contributor) Monroe G. Gottsegen and Gloria B. Gottsegen, editors, *Professional School Psychology*, Volume II, Grune, 1963; (with Leonard J. West and Ohmer Milton) *Record of Activities and Experiments with Programed Units*, Harcourt, 1964; (with Snellgrove) *Psychological Experiments and Experiences*, Harcourt, 1974; (contributor) Harwood Fisher, editor, *Developments in High School Psychology*, Behavioral Publications, 1974. Book review editor, *Behavioral and Social Science Teacher*. Author of *Engle Psychology Test*, published by World Book, 1952, and of manuals, tests, and supplements for teachers. Contributor of articles to *Encyclopedia International*, *Psychology 1973-74 Encyclopedia*, and to education and psychology periodicals.

WORK IN PROGRESS: The seventh edition of *Psychology: Its Principles and Applications*.

ENRICK, Norbert Lloyd   1920-

PERSONAL: Born April 11, 1920, in Berlin, Germany; son of Max M. (a medical doctor) and Elfe (Wilkiser) Enrick; married Mary Lynch, May 17, 1952; children: Ellen Marguerite, Robert Neal. *Education:* City College (now City College of the City University of New York), New York, N.Y., B.A., 1941; Columbia University, M.S., 1945, additional study, 1948-50; University of Virginia, Ph.D., 1963. *Home:* 1577 Morris Road, Kent, Ohio 44240. *Office:* Administrative Sciences Department, Kent State University, Kent, Ohio 44242.

CAREER: Werner Management Consultants, New York, N.Y., management consulting engineer, 1948-53; Institute of Textile Technology, Charlottesville, Va., director of operations research and computer laboratory, 1953-60; University of Virginia, Charlottesville, associate professor of management, 1960-65; Stevens Institute of Technology, Hoboken, N.J., professor of management science, 1965-66; Kent State University, Kent, Ohio, professor of administrative sciences, 1966—. Consultant to National Aeronautics and Space Administration and to business firms. *Member:* American Society for Quality Control (fellow), American Statistical Association (president, Virginia section, 1956-58), Operations Research Society of America, American Society for Testing and Materials, Fiber Society, Academy of Marketing Science, Scientific Society, Sigma Xi.

WRITINGS: Quality Control, Industrial Press, 1948, 6th edition, 1972; *Cases in Management Statistics*, Holt, 1963; *Management Control Manual*, Rayon Publishing, 1964; *Sales and Production Management Manual*, Wiley, 1964; *Management Operations Research*, Holt, 1965; *Management Planning*, McGraw, 1967; *Market & Sales Forecasting*, Intext, 1969; *Decision Oriented Statistics*, Mason & Lipscomb, 1970; *Statistical Functions*, Kent State University Press, 1970; *Effective Graphic Communication*, Mason & Lipscomb, 1972. Associate editor, *Journal of the Academy of Marketing Science*.

* * *

EPSTEIN, Leon D.   1919-

PERSONAL: Born May 29, 1919, in Milwaukee, Wis.; son of Harry A. (a businessman) and Anna (Lekachman) Epstein; married Shirley Galewitz, January 12, 1947. *Education:* University of Wisconsin, B.A., 1940, M.A., 1941; University of Chicago, Ph.D., 1948. *Home:* 2806 Ridge Rd., Madison, Wis. 53705. *Office:* Department of Political Science, University of Wisconsin, Madison, Wis. 53706.

CAREER: University of Oregon, Eugene, assistant professor of political science, 1947-48; University of Wisconsin, Madison, assistant professor, 1948-51, associate professor, 1951-54, professor of political science, 1954—, Bascom Professor of political science, 1974—, chairman of the department of political science, 1960-63, dean of the College of Letters and Science, 1965-69. *Military service:* U.S. Army, 1942-46; became captain. *Member:* American Association of University Professors, American Political Science Association (member of executive committee, 1963-64), Social Science Research Council (member of board of directors), Midwest Political Science Association (president, 1971-72), Phi Beta Kappa. *Awards, honors:* Ford Foundation grant, Rockefeller Foundation grant, Center for Advanced Study in the Behavioral Sciences, fellow, 1970-71.

WRITINGS: Britain: Uneasy Ally, University of Chicago

Press, 1954; *Politics in Wisconsin*, University of Wisconsin Press, 1958; *British Politics in the Suez Crisis*, University of Illinois Press, 1964; *Political Parties in Western Democracies*, Praeger, 1967; *Governing the University: The Campus and the Public Interest*, Jossey-Bass, 1974. Contributor to political science publications.

AVOCATIONAL INTERESTS: Tennis.

* * *

ERIKSSON, Marguerite A. 1911-

PERSONAL: Born December 3, 1911; daughter of August and Margaret (Kunkel) Eriksson. *Education:* Pennsylvania State University, B.A., 1938; graduate study at Sorbonne, University of Paris, 1954, and University of Grenoble, 1956; Western Reserve University (now Case Western Reserve University), M.A., 1960. *Religion:* Catholic. *Home:* 170 East Springettsbury Ave., York, Pa. 17403.

CAREER: York (Pa.) public schools, coordinator of French for elementary grades, 1952-73, French teacher at Pennsylvania Middle School, 1973—. Foreign language consultant, Ohio State Department of Education, 1960, 1961, and 1962. *Member:* Association for Childhood Education International, Modern Language Association of America (first vice-president of Pennsylvania section, 1964-66; section executive council, 1962-66), Delta Kappa Gamma. *Awards, honors:* Valley Forge Freedom Foundation award for classroom teachers, 1959.

WRITINGS: (With Ilse Forest and Ruth Mulhauser) *Foreign Languages in the Elementary School*, Prentice-Hall, 1964. Chairman of teachers' committee that wrote *Course of Study for the Teaching of French in the Elementary School*, first, second, and third-year manuals, published by York City School District, 1958-63.

SIDELIGHTS: In connection with York's People-to-People program, Miss Eriksson visited its French affiliate, the city of Arles, in 1954, 1956, and 1963, 1968, 1973. Under the Eriksson-initiated program, York offers a seven-year sequence of French study to public school pupils, in grades six through twelve.

* * *

ERNO, Richard B. 1923-

PERSONAL: Born May 11, 1923, in Boyne City, Mich.; son of Richard Gabriel and Edith (Stafford) Erno; married Edith Van Sickle, June 15, 1949; children: Deborah, Bruce, Richard, Christopher, Joanna, Janice. *Education:* Michigan State College of Agriculture and Applied Science (now Michigan State University), B.A., 1950; University of Denver, M.A., 1951; University of Minnesota, postgraduate study, 1951-53, Ph.D., 1961. *Home:* 1107 East Broadmor Dr., Tempe, Ariz. *Office:* Department of English, Arizona State University, Tempe, Ariz.

CAREER: Instructor in English at McCook Junior College, McCook, Neb., 1953-55, and George Washington University, Washington, D.C., 1955-57; Arizona State University, Tempe, instructor in English, 1957-58, assistant professor, 1958-62; Northern Montana College, Havre, associate professor and chairman of department of English, 1962-63; Arizona State University, associate professor, 1963-67, professor of English, 1967—. *Military service:* U.S. Army, Signal Corps, 1944-46. *Awards, honors:* Award from Friends of American Writers, 1966.

WRITINGS:—All published by Crown: *My Old Man*, 1955; *The Hunt*, 1959; *The Catwalk*, 1965; *Johnny Come Jingl-o*, 1967; *Billy Lightfoot*, 1969; *An Ultimate Retreat*, 1971. Contributor to *Saturday Evening Post*, *Collier's*, *Family Circle*, *Prairie Schooner*, and *Phoenix Point West*.

* * *

ERVIN, Theodore Robert 1928-

PERSONAL: Born May 12, 1928, in Lansing, Mich,; son of Grant D. (a toolmaker) and Queene (Munger) Ervin; married Yarda D. Anderson, September 11, 1948; children: Christine, Timothy. *Education:* Michigan State University, B.A., 1960, M.A., 1963. *Religion:* Protestant. *Home:* 1325 N. Fairview, Lansing, Mich. *Office:* Michigan Department of Health, 3500 North Logan, Lansing, Mich. 48914.

CAREER: Michigan Department of Public Health, Lansing, deputy director, 1956—. *Member:* Association of State and Territorial Directors of Local Health Services.

WRITINGS: Who Shall Rule?, Institute for Community Development, Michigan State University, Institute for Community Development, 1964. Editor, *Proceedings—1963 Conference of the Surgeon General, Public Health Service and Chief, Children's Bureau, with State and Territorial Health Officers*. Former editor *Michigan's Health* (journal of the Michigan Department of Health).

* * *

ESON, Morris E. 1921-

PERSONAL: Born April 18, 1921, in Montreal, Quebec, Canada; became U.S. citizen; married Joy Platt; children: four. *Education:* Illinois Institute of Technology, B.S., 1942; University of Chicago, M.A., 1944, Ph.D., 1951; Hebrew Theological College, Chicago, Ill., Rabbi, 1945. *Home:* 14 Holmes Dale St., Albany, N.Y.

CAREER: George Williams College, Chicago, Ill., instructor in psychology and director of student counseling program, 1948-51; State University of New York at Albany, 1951—, began as assistant professor, now professor of psychology, served as chairman of department. Certified psychologist, New York State. Consultant to Albany Child Guidance Center, Albany Medical Center, and to Language Research, Inc. Visiting professor, University of Haifa, Israel, 1970-71. *Military service:* U.S. Army, chaplain, 1945-47. *Member:* American Psychological Association (fellow), American Association for the Advancement of Science, National Society for the Study of Education. *Awards, honors:* Research grants from State University of New York Research Foundation, 1956, from State University of New York, 1963, 1964, 1965; Fulbright research scholar in Israel, 1957-58.

WRITINGS: Psychological Foundations of Education, Holt, 1964, 2nd edition, 1972. Contributor of articles and reviews to psychology journals.

* * *

ESTEP, W(illiam) R(oscoe), Jr. 1920-

PERSONAL: Surname is pronounced *Eas*-tep; born February 12, 1920, in Williamsburg, Ky.; son of William Roscoe and Rhoda Mae (Snyder) Estep; married Edna McDowell, December 23, 1942; children: William Merl, Rhoda Elaine, Mary McDowell, Lena Jane, Martin Andrew. *Education:* Berea College, B.A., 1942; Southern Baptist Theological Seminary, Th.M., 1945; Southwestern Baptist Theological Seminary, Th.D., 1951; La Escuela de Idiomas, Costa Rica, postdoctoral study, 1959. *Home:* Box 138, Rural Route 3, Fort Worth, Tex. *Office:* Box 22037, Fort Worth, Tex.

CAREER: Baptist minister. Los Angeles Baptist Seminary, Los Angeles, Calif., professor of church history, 1946-47; Union Baptist Seminary, Houston, Tex., professor of church history, 1951-53; Southwestern Baptist Theological Seminary, Fort Worth, Tex., professor of church history, 1954—. Pastor in Houston, Tex., 1951-54; teacher, Baylor University extension department, 1952-53; guest teacher, Seminario Bautista Internacional Teologico, Cali, Columbia, 1959-60; lecturer in Central and South America. *Member:* American Society of Church History, Southern Baptist Historical Society, Verein fuer Reformation-geschichte (Heidelberg, Germany), Delta Phi Alpha.

WRITINGS: La Fe de Los Apostoles, Editorial Verdad, 1962; *The Anabaptist Story*, Broadman, 1963; (contributor) *Baptist Advance*, Broadman, 1964; *Baptists and Christian Unity*, Broadman, 1966; *Columbia: Land of Conflict and Promise*, Convention Press, 1968. Contributor to *Encyclopedia of Southern Baptists.* Editor, *Southwestern Journal of Theology*, 1963-67.

SIDELIGHTS: Estep speaks Spanish and has reading knowledge of Greek, Hebrew, Latin, French, German, and Portuguese. *Avocational interests:* Photography, electronics, music, golf, fishing.

*   *   *

ESTHUS, Raymond Arthur   1925-

PERSONAL: Surname is pronounced Estus; born March 17, 1925, in Chicago, Ill.; son of Arthur Engen and Clara (Andersen) Esthus; married Gloria Dell Gilliam, August 27, 1955; children: Jan Elisabeth, Julie Roseanne. *Education:* Florida Southern College, A.B., 1948; Duke University, M.A., 1951, Ph.D., 1956. *Home:* 25 West Imperial Dr., Harahan, La. 70123. *Office:* Newcomb College, Tulane University, New Orleans, La. 70118.

CAREER: University of Houston, Houston, Tex., instructor in history, 1955-56, assistant professor, 1956-57; Tulane University, New Orleans, Louisiana, assistant professor, 1957-61, associate professor, 1961-66, professor of history, 1966—. *Military service:* U.S. Army, 1943-46; served in European Theater, 1944-46; became staff sergeant. *Member:* American Historical Association, Association for Asian Studies, Phi Beta Kappa.

WRITINGS: From Enmity to Alliance: U.S.—Australian Relations, 1931-1941, University of Washington Press, 1964; *Theodore Roosevelt and Japan*, University of Washington Press, 1966; *Theodore Roosevelt and the International Rivalries*, Ginn, 1970. Contributor to *Journal of Modern History* and *Mississippi Valley Historical Review.*

WORK IN PROGRESS: The Portsmouth Peace Conference.

*   *   *

ETTINGER, Robert C(hester) W(ilson)   1918-

PERSONAL: Born December 4, 1918, in Atlantic City, N.J.; son of Alfred and Rhea (Chaloff) Ettinger; married Elaine Mevis (a teacher), August 18, 1949; children: David A., Shelley B. *Education:* Wayne State University, B.S., 1950, M.S., 1951, M.A., 1953. *Home:* 24041 Stratford, Oak Park, Mich. 48237.

CAREER: Wayne State University, Detroit, Mich., physics teacher, 1953-63; Highland Park College, Highland Park, Mich., physics teacher, 1963—. *Military service:* U.S. Army, 1942-48; became first lieutenant; received Purple Heart. *Member:* American Association for the Advancement of Science, American Association of University Professors, American Association of Physics Teachers.

WRITINGS: The Prospect of Immortality, Doubleday, 1964; *Man into Superman*, St. Martin's Press, 1972; (contributor) Harry Harrison and Theodore J. Gordon, editors *Ahead of Time*, Doubleday, 1972. Contributor to *Esquire, The Christian Century, Ebony.*

WORK IN PROGRESS: Cryobiological research.

SIDELIGHTS: Ettinger has proposed, in his *Prospect of Immortality*, to quick-freeze the bodies of the dead and store them until medical techniques for revival are developed. *Life* noted that "the marvel is that Ettinger's proposals ... have struck such an instantaneous public nerve." Many have made provisions for quick-freezing in their wills, and twenty one people have been frozen to date. Cryonics Societies exist in several states and foreign countries.

BIOGRAPHICAL/CRITICAL SOURCES: Pageant, February, 1965; *Science and Mechanics*, May, 1965; *Life*, October 1, 1965; *Fact*, November-December, 1965.

*   *   *

EUNSON, Robert C(harles)   1912-

PERSONAL: Born July 23, 1912, in Billings, Mont.; son of Robert Strong and Jessie (Romaine) Eunson; married Katherine Rabogliatti, February 22, 1935; children: Eve (Mrs. Jackson Rannells), Dale (Mrs. Richardson Morse), Lisa. *Education:* Arizona State College (now University), A.B., 1936. *Politics:* Democrat. *Religion:* Episcopalian. *Home:* 7 Takeyacho, Azabu, Minato-ku, Tokyo, Japan. *Agent:* August Lenniger, Lenniger Literary Agency, 437 Fifth Ave., New York, N.Y. 10016.

CAREER: Associated Press, foreign correspondent, 1941—, now director of Asia Services, Tokyo, Japan. *Member:* Sigma Delta Chi, Foreign Correspondents Club of Tokyo (president, 1956). *Awards, honors:* LL.D., Arizona State College (now University), 1961.

WRITINGS: The Pearl King, Goldberg, 1955; *Mig Alley*, Ace Books, 1958; *Trial at Odawara*, Signet Books, 1963.†

*   *   *

EVANS, Gordon H(eyd)   1930-

PERSONAL: Born April 10, 1930, in New York, N.Y.; son of Dr. Charles H. and Eleanor Goodwin (Brown) Evans. *Education:* Columbia University, A.B., 1953, M.A., 1959. *Politics:* Independent. *Religion:* Protestant. *Address:* Box 174 A, R.F.D. 1, Hudson, N.Y. 12534.

CAREER: Hornblower & Weeks, New York, N.Y., stockbroker, 1954-55; Baker, Weeks & Co. (stockbrokers), New York, N.Y., security analyst, 1955; National Bureau for Economic Research, New York, N.Y., research assistant, 1955-56; General Electric Co., New York, N.Y., consultant, 1960; American Management Association, New York, N.Y., research associate, 1960-66; State University of New York, College at New Paltz, member of faculty of economics and political science department, 1966-73. *Member:* American Management Association.

WRITINGS: Managerial Job Descriptions in Manufacturing, American Management Association, 1964; (editor) *Sufferings in Africa: Captain Riley's Narrative*, C. N. Potter, 1965; *The Product Manager's Job*, American Management Association, 1965. Contributor of articles on national security and strategic studies, especially on Communist China, to *Bulletin of the Atomic Scientists*, *New Leader*, and *Current History*.

*   *   *

EVANS, I(drisyn) O(liver) 1894-

PERSONAL: Born November 11, 1894, in Bloemfontein, South Africa; son of Harry (a stationer) and Sara Winifred (a nurse; maiden name, Sutton) Evans; married Marie Elizabeth Mumford, March 6, 1937. *Education:* Attended schools in England. *Politics:* Socialist. *Religion:* Church of England. *Home:* 53 Waterer Gardens, Burgh Heath, Tadworth, Surrey KT20 5PD, England.

CAREER: British civil servant, 1912-56, executive officer in Ministry of Works at time of retirement; author and lecturer. *Military service:* British Army, 1914-19; served on Western Front. *Member:* Royal Geographical Society (fellow), Royal Geological Society of Cornwall, Geologists Association, Society of Authors, Society of Civil Service Authors, Societe Jules Verne.

WRITINGS: Woodcraft and World Service, Noel Douglas, 1930; *The Junior Outline of History* (adaptation of H.G. Wells book), Denis Archer, 1932, Appleton, 1933; *The World of Tomorrow*, Denis Archer, 1933; (editor) *An Upton Sinclair Anthology*, Laurie, 1934; (editor with Bernard Newman) *Anthology of Armageddon*, Denis Archer, 1935; *Cigarette Cards and How to Collect Them*, Jenkins, 1937.

Geology by the Wayside, Murby & Co., 1940; *Gadget City*, Warne, 1944; *The Heavens Declare*, Warne, 1949.

Strange Devices, Warne, 1950; *The Coming of a King*, Warne, 1950; (with Gordon Campbell) *The Book of Flags*, Oxford University Press, 1950, 7th edition, 1974; *The Observer's Book of Geology*, Warne, 1950, revised edition, 1971; *The Story of Early Times*, Newnes Educational Publishing Co., 1951; *Led by the Star*, Rylee, 1952; *Olympic Runner*, Hutchinson, 1955; (editor) *Jules Verne: Master of Science Fiction*, Sidgwick & Jackson, 1956; *The Story of Our World*, Hutchinson, 1957; *Discovering the Heavens*, Hutchinson, 1958; *The Observer's Book of Flags*, Warne, 1959, 4th edition, 1971; (editor) Lew Wallace, *Ben-Hur*, abridged edition, 1959.

(With Willis Hall) *They Found the World*, Warne, 1960; *Exploring the Earth*, Hutchinson, 1961; *The Boys' Book of the Rocks and Fossils*, Burke Publishing Co., 1961; (editor) *The Observer's Book of the Sea and Seashore*, Warne, 1962; *Inventors of the World*, Warne, 1962; *Engineers of the World*, Warne, 1963; *Jules Verne and His Work*, Arco, 1965; (editor) *Science Fiction Through the Ages*, Volume I, Panther Books, 1966; *Benefactors of the World* (juvenile), Warne, 1968.

(Editor) *Spy and Counter-spy: Bernard Newman's Story of the British Secret Service*, R. Hale, 1970; *Flags of the World*, Grosset, 1970; *Flags*, Hamlyn, 1970; *The Earth*, Hamlyn, 1971, revised edition, 1973; *Rocks, Minerals and Gemstones*, Hamlyn, 1972.

Editor and translator of numerous works by Jules Verne; editor and author of introduction for several works by Jack London. Contributor to *Field*, *Cycling*, and other outdoor and hobby journals.

WORK IN PROGRESS: Translating certain works of Jules Verne; revising books on flags.

SIDELIGHTS: Evans reads French (fluently), German, and Esperanto. *Avocational interests:* Science fiction (lifelong addict), geology, national and other flags.

*   *   *

EVANS, Joan 1893-

PERSONAL: Born June 22, 1893, in Hemel Hempstead, Hertfordshire, England; daughter of Sir John and Maria Millington (Lathbury) Evans. *Education:* Attended Berkhamsted Girls' School; St. Hugh's College, Oxford, B.Litt., 1917; University College, University of London, advanced study, 1921-24, D.Litt., 1930; Oxford University, D.Litt., 1932. *Home:* 72 Campden Hill Court, London W. 8, England.

CAREER: Author. St. Hugh's College, Oxford University, Oxford, England, librarian, 1917-22, member of council, 1922-58. Traveling fellow, Anglo-Swedish Society, 1922; Suzette Taylor Fellow, Lady Margaret Hall, Oxford, 1937-39; honorary fellow, St. Hugh's College, Oxford, 1936—, supernumerary fellow, 1951-58; external examiner in history of art, University of London, 1938-46; fellow, University College, London, 1950. Trustee, London Museum, 1951-66, British Museum, 1963-67; member of advisory committee, Victoria and Albert Museum, 1953-68.

MEMBER: Royal Historical Society (fellow), Royal Archaeological Institute (president, 1949-52; treasurer, 1958-62), Royal Society of Literature (fellow), Royal Institute of British Architects (associate), Society of Antiquaries of London (fellow; director, 1954-59; president, 1959-64), Friends of the National Libraries (member of executive committee, 1955-64), Mediaeval Academy of America (corresponding fellow and honorary research associate), Societe Nationale des Antiquaires de France (associate correspondent), Societe de l'histoire de l'art francais, Academie de Macon (honorary), Huguenot Society of London (honorary fellow), Bristol and Gloucester Archaeological Society (honorary member; editor and former president). *Awards, honors:* LL.D., University of Edinburgh, 1952; Litt.D., Cambridge University, 1956; Chevalier de la Legion d'Honneur.

WRITINGS: English Jewellery from the Fifth Century A.D. to 1800, Methuen, 1921; *Magical Jewels of the Middle Ages and the Renaissance, Particularly in England*, Clarendon Press, 1922; (with Paul Studer) *Anglo-Norman Lapidaries*, Champion (Paris), 1924; *Life in Mediaeval France*, Oxford University Press, 1925, third edition, Phaidon, 1969; *St. Joan of Orleans*, Oxford University Press, 1927; (translator and editor) Gutierre Diaz de Gamez, *The Unconquered Knight: A Chronicle of the Deeds of Don Pero Nino*, Harcourt, 1928.

Pattern: A Study of Ornament in Western Europe from 1180 to 1900, Clarendon Press, 1931; *Monastic Life at Cluny, 910-1157*, Oxford University Press, 1931, Archon Books, 1968; (compiler, and author of introduction) *English Posies and Posy Rings*, Oxford University Press, 1931; *Nature in Design: A Study of Naturalism in Decorative Art from the Bronze Age to the Renaissance*, Oxford University Press, 1933; (editor with Mary S. Serjeantson) *English Mediaeval Lapidaries*, Oxford University Press for Early English Text Society, 1933, reprinted, 1966; (indexer) Arthur John Evans, *The Palace of Minos*, Macmillan, 1936, Biblo & Tannen, 1964; (translator) Jean de Joinville, *History of St. Louis*, Oxford University Press, 1938; *The Romanesque Architecture of the Order of Cluny*, Cambridge University Press, 1938, AMS Press, 1971; *Taste and Temperament*, J. Cape, 1939; *Chateaubriand*, Macmillan, 1939.

Time and Chance: The Story of Arthur Evans and His Forbears, Longmans, Green, 1943; *The Pursuit of Happiness: The Story of Madame de Serilly, 1762-1799*, Longmans, Green, 1946; *The Unselfish Egoist*, Longmans, Green, 1947; *Oxford History of English Art*, Volume V: *Art in Medieval France, 987-1498*, Oxford University Press, 1948; *English Art, 1307-1461*, Clarendon Press, 1949.

Cluniac Art of the Romanesque Period, Cambridge University Press, 1950; *Style in Ornament*, Oxford University Press, 1950; (translator) Paul Michel, *Romanesque Wall Paintings in France*, Thames & Hudson, 1950; (translator) Emile Moe, *Illuminated Initials in Mediaeval Manuscripts*, Thames & Hudson, 1950; *Dress in Mediaeval France*, Clarendon Press, 1952; *A History of Jewellery, 1100-1870*, Pitman, 1953, 2nd edition, Boston Book & Art Shop, 1970; *John Ruskin*, Oxford University Press, 1954, Haskell House, 1970; *The Endless Web; John Dickinson & Co., Ltd., 1804-1954*, J. Cape, 1955; (editor) Charlotte Moberly and Eleanor Frances Jourdain, *An Adventure*, 5th edition, Coward, 1955; (editor) John Ruskin, *Diaries*, Clarendon Press, Volume I, 1956, Volume II, 1957, Volume III, 1958; *A History of the Society of Antiquaries*, Oxford University Press, 1956; (editor) John Ruskin, *The Lamp of Beauty*, Doubleday, 1959; *Madame Royale*, Museum Press, 1959.

Monastic Architecture in France from the Renaissance to the Revolution, Cambridge University Press, 1964; *Prelude and Fugue* (autobiography), Museum Press, 1964; *The Victorians*, Cambridge University Press, 1966; (editor) *The Flowering of the Middle Ages*, McGraw, 1966; *The Conways*, Museum Press, 1966; *Monastic Iconography in France from the Renaissance to the Revolution*, Cambridge University Press, 1970.

Contributor to archaeological periodicals.

AVOCATIONAL INTERESTS: Embroidery.

BIOGRAPHICAL/CRITICAL SOURCES: Joan Evans, *Prelude and Fugue*, Museum Press, 1964.

*   *   *

EVANS, Julia (Rendel)   1913-
(Polly Hobson)

PERSONAL: Born May 12, 1913, in Hindhead, England; daughter of Richard Meadows (an army colonel) and Julia Margaret (Marshall) Rendel; married Patrick Hutchinson Evans (a translator), April 4, 1946; children: Tom. *Education:* Oxford University, B.A. (second class honors), 1933. *Home:* Gloucester Lodge, Quarry Hills, St. Leonards-on-Sea, Sussex, England. *Agent:* Curtis Brown Ltd., 1 Craven Hill, London W2 3EW, England.

CAREER: Odd jobs, travel abroad, and study of art in London and Paris, 1933-39; writer. *Military service:* British Navy, Women's Reserve Naval Service, 1940-44; became second officer.

WRITINGS—All under pseudonym Polly Hobson: *Brought up in Bloomsbury*, Constable, 1959; *The Mystery House*, Benn, 1963, Lippincott, 1964; *Murder Won't Out*, Jenkins, 1964; *Titty's Dead*, Constable, 1968, published as *A Terrible Thing Has Happened to Miss Dupont*, McCall, 1970; *The Three Graces*, Constable, 1970. Contributor of short stories to *Women's Realm* (London).

WORK IN PROGRESS: A children's book.

SIDELIGHTS: Julia Evans speaks French and some German. *Avocational interests:* Painting, music, country living.†

EVANS, Robert Owen   1919-

PERSONAL: Born September 19, 1919, in Chicago, Ill.; son of Franklin B. (an investment banker) and Arline (Brown) Evans; married Margery Brooks; children: Robert Owen, Jr., Michele M., Douglas B. *Education:* University of Chicago, A.B., 1941; University of Florida, M.A., 1950, Ph.D., 1954; also studied at University of Heidelberg, 1939, Harvard University, 1950-51. *Religion:* Episcopalian. *Home:* 747 Zandale Dr., Lexington, Ky. *Office:* University of Kentucky, Lexington, Ky.

CAREER: University of Florida, Gainesville, instructor in English, 1952-54; University of Kentucky, Lexington, began 1954, associate professor, 1958-66, professor of English, 1966—, director of honors program, 1966—. Fulbright professor at University of Helsinki, 1957-58, University of the Saar, 1963-64; summer professor at Lincoln College, Oxford University, and director of University of Kentucky Summer School Abroad, England, 1963; lecturer at universities in Germany and Finland, 1963-64; visiting professor, University of Wisconsin at Madison, 1967, and American College, Paris, 1970-71. *Member:* International Association of Professors of English, International Comparative Literature Association, Modern Language Association of America, Shaw Society (London), Chamber Music Society of Central Kentucky, Phi Beta Kappa, Phi Kappa Phi.

WRITINGS: (With D. M. Crabb) *Norfolk Billy*, Comet, 1952; (editor) *Graham Greene: Certain Critical Considerations*, University Press of Kentucky, 1964; (co-editor) *The Papers of Morris Croll*, Princeton University Press, 1964; *The Osier Cage: Rhetorical Devices in Romeo and Juliet*, University Press of Kentucky, 1966; *Milton's Elisions*, University of Florida Press, 1966; (editor) Jeorge L. Borges, *Introduction to American Literature* (translated from Spanish by L. C. Keating), University Press of Kentucky, 1971; (editor) Borges, *Introduction to English Literature*, University Press of Kentucky, 1974. Contributing editor, *An Encyclopedia of Poetic and Rhetorical Terms*, Princeton University Press. Contributor of some thirty articles on English literary figures to scholarly journals.

WORK IN PROGRESS: Essays on William Golding.

SIDELIGHTS: Evans speaks German and French, and some Finnish, Russian, Spanish, and Italian.

*   *   *

EVANS, Robert P.   1918-

PERSONAL: Born February 21, 1918, in Baltimore, Md.; son of Rowland Hill and Bertha (Zipp) Evans; married Jeanette Gruner, June 5, 1942; children: Alyce, Bruce. *Education:* Wheaton College, Wheaton, Ill., B.A., 1939; Eastern Baptist Theological Seminary, Philadelphia, Pa., B.D., 1943. *Politics:* Conservative Republican. *Home:* 8 Avenue Charles de Gaulle, Le Pecq, Seine-et-Oise, France. *Office:* Greater Europe Mission, 214 North Hale St., Wheaton, Ill.

CAREER: Youth for Christ International, Chicago, exec. secretary, vice-pres., 1946-48; Greater Europe Mission, Paris, France, founder and European director, 1948—. President of European Bible Institute, Paris, France, 1952-54; part-time European director of Billy Graham Evangelistic Association. *Military service:* U.S. Navy, 1943-46; became lieutenant commander; received Commendation Ribbon, Purple Heart, European theater ribbon with five battle stars. *Member:* National Association of Evangelicals (Wheaton, Ill.), American Legion, Wheaton College

Alumni Club (Paris). *Awards, honors:* LL.D., Wheaton College, Wheaton Ill.

WRITINGS: Let Europe Hear: The Spiritual Plight of Europe, Moody, 1963; *Transformed Europeans*, Moody, 1963. Regular columnist for *Christian* (London), and *Mandate* (Chicago); regular contributor to other religious periodicals. Editor of *Together*.

WORK IN PROGRESS: Currently working on six books.

SIDELIGHTS: From his headquarters in Paris Evans has traveled about Europe almost constantly for sixteen years. He is fluent in French, and has working knowledge of several other languages.†

* * *

EVANSEN, Virginia Besaw 1921-

PERSONAL: Born March 23, 1921, in Havre, Mont.; daughter of Charles Burton and Selma (Peterson) Besaw; married Kenneth M. Evansen (an engineer), December 10, 1949; children: Virginia Ann, Patricia Merle, Nancy Marie. *Education:* University of Michigan, R.N., 1944. *Home:* Sunnyvale, Calif.

CAREER: One-time nurse. Sunnyvale (Calif.) Library Board, trustee, 1962-65, president, 1963-65. *Military service:* U.S. Army Nurse Corps, 1945-46; became second lieutenant. *Member:* National League of American Pen Women, Western History Association.

WRITINGS: Laura Reynolds M.D., Thomas Bouregy, 1963; *Nancy Kelsey*, McKay, 1965; *Sierra Summit*, McKay, 1967. Regular columnist for *Sunnyvale Daily Standard* and contributor to magazines.†

* * *

EVERETT, Peter W(illiam) 1924-

PERSONAL: Born April 7, 1924, in Bristol, Pa.; son of John Russell and Catherine (Mahan) Everett; married Virginia Muriel Huenger, December 19, 1947; children: Genevieve, John, Randall, James, Nancy. *Education:* University of Iowa, B.S., 1948, M.S., 1949, Ph.D., 1954. *Politics:* Republican. *Religion:* Methodist. *Home:* 2106 Great Oak Dr., Tallahassee, Fla. *Office:* Florida State University, Tallahassee, Fla.

CAREER: University of Iowa, Iowa City, instructor, 1949-52; high school teacher in Boone, N.C., 1952-55; Appalachian State Teachers College (now Appalachian State University), Boone, N.C., associate professor, 1955-57; Northern Illinois University, DeKalb, associate professor of physical education, 1957-59; Florida State University, Tallahassee, associate professor, 1959-64, professor of physical education, 1964—. *Military service:* U.S. Army, 1943-45; served in Europe; became sergeant. *Member:* American Association for Health, Physical Education and Recreation, National Foundation for Health, Physical Education and Recreation, College Physical Education Association, Florida Association for Health, Physical Education and Recreation, Phi Epsilon Kappa, Phi Delta Kappa.

WRITINGS: Beginning Tennis, Wadsworth, 1962; (contributor) *Physical Education Handbook*, W. C. Brown, 1963. Contributor to *Encyclopedia of Physical Education*, published by Research Council of American Association of Health, Physical Education and Recreation. Contributor to *Research Quarterly* and *Physical Educator*.

EVERY, George 1909-

PERSONAL: Born February 3, 1909, in Tipton, Devonshire, England; son of George (a clergyman) and Frances Rebecca (Branson) Every. *Education:* Attended University College of the South West (now University of Exeter), 1926-29; University of London, B.A., (external degree; first class honors in history), 1929; Kelham Theological College, student-tutor, 1929-32. *Home:* 7 Lenton Ave., The Park, Nottingham, England.

CAREER: Society of the Sacred Mission (Church of England), lay brother, 1933-73. Kelham Theological College, Kelham, Newark, England, lecturer in church history, 1934-72, also in comparative religion and liturgics, 1950-72, librarian, 1953-73; Oscott College, Sutton Coldfield, Birmingham, England, assistant lecturer, 1973—. Library consultant, visiting Kenya, Uganda, and Tanganyika for East African Association of Theological Colleges, 1963.

WRITINGS: (Contributor) K. Mackenzie, editor, *The Union of Christendom*, S.P.C.K., 1936; *Christian Discrimination*, S.P.C.K., 1940; (with S. L. Bethell and J. D. C. Pellow) *Selected Poems*, Staples Press, 1943; *The Byzantine Patriarchate*, S.P.C.K., 1947, 2nd edition, Allenson, 1962; *Poetry and Personal Responsibility*, S.C.M. Press, 1952; *The High Church Party, 1688-1718*, S.P.C.K., 1956; *Lamb to the Slaughter*, J. Clarke, 1957; *Light under a Door* (Christmas poems), Faith Press, 1958; *The Baptismal Sacrifice*, S.C.M. Press, 1959; *Basic Liturgy*, Faith Press, 1961; (contributor) A. H. Armstrong and E. J. B. Fry, editors, *Rediscovering Eastern Christendom*, Darton, Longman & Todd, 1963; *Misunderstandings between East and West*, John Knox, 1966; *Christian Mythology*, Paul Hamlyn, 1970. Contributor to *Encyclopaedia Britannica*; also contributor to *New English Weekly*, *Time and Tide*, *Theology*, *Heythrop Journal*, *The Tablet*, and other periodicals. Editor, *Eastern Churches Review*, 1968—.

WORK IN PROGRESS: Contributions to three symposia on religious matters.

* * *

EWING, John S(inclair) 1916

PERSONAL: Born July 10, 1916, in Taber, Alberta, Canada; son of George Edwin (a banker) and Lillian (Amos) Ewing; married Joan Eberle Rosencranz, November 29, 1947; children; Janet Alison, Eberle Ann, Amy Johanna. *Education:* Bishop's University, B.A., 1936; Harvard University, M.B.A., 1947, D.C.S., 1953. *Politics:* Independent. *Religion:* Agnostic. *Home:* 27811 Lupine Rd., Los Altos Hills, Calif.

CAREER: Graduate School of Business, Turin, Italy, professor of marketing, 1953-55; Administrative Staff College, Henley, England, member of directing staff, 1954-55; American Institute for Foreign Trade, Phoenix, Ariz., associate professor of marketing, 1955-56; Harbridge House (educational consultants), Boston, Mass., director of International Management Division, 1956-57; Stanford University, Stanford, Calif., associate professor of international business, 1957-59, 1960-65, director of Stanford Management Seminar in Ceylon and Australia, annually, 1961-63, senior industrial economist, Stanford Research Institute, 1965-69; University of Santa Clara, Santa Clara, Calif., professor of business administration, 1969—. Visiting consultant, W. D. Scott & Co., Sydney, Australia, 1959-60. *Military service:* Royal Canadian Army Service Corps, 1940-46; became captain. *Member:* American Marketing Association, Association for Education in International

Business (secretary, 1965), Society for International Development.

WRITINGS: (With Nancy P. Norton) *Broadlooms and Businessmen*, Harvard University Press, 1955; (with Frank Meissner) *International Business Management*, Wadsworth, 1964. Contributor to business and marketing periodicals.

WORK IN PROGRESS: With Joel Leidecker, *Influence of Community Activities on Management Effectiveness*; *Involvements for Retirement*.

SIDELIGHTS: Ewing is fluent in French and speaks some Spanish and Italian.

*   *   *

EZERA, Kalu 1925-

PERSONAL: Born November 12, 1925, in Ohafia, Eastern Nigeria; son of Uma and Enyidiya Ezera; married Onuma (an assistant librarian), April 5, 1958; children: Emeka, Nnamdi, Okorie, Uduma. *Education:* Lincoln University, Pennsylvania, B.A. (honors), 1953; Harvard University, M.A., 1955; Oxford University, D.Phil., 1957. *Home:* Asaga-Ohafia, Eastern Nigeria. *Office:* University of Nigeria, Nsukka, Nigeria.

CAREER: University of Nigeria, Nsukka, onetime senior lecturer and dean of Faculty of Social Studies; University College (now University of Ibadan), Ibadan, Nigeria, lecturer, 1957-60; University of Nigeria, associate professor of political science and acting head of department, 1963—, member of university council and senate. Nigeria Federal Parliament, member for Bende East, 1959—. *Member:* Inter-Parliamentary Union (chairman, Nigerian branch), Ohafia Union, Ohafia Field Club.

WRITINGS: Constitutional Developments in Nigeria, Cambridge University Press, 1960, 2nd edition, 1964; (co-author) *New Nations in a Divided World*, Praeger, 1963. Contributor to *Journal of Parliaments, Journal of Human Relations, Africa South Quarterly*, other journals.

WORK IN PROGRESS: A third edition of *Constitutional Developments in Nigeria.*†

*   *   *

FABER, Harold 1919-

PERSONAL: Born September 12, 1919, in New York, N.Y.; son of Charles and Anna (Glassman) Faber; married June 21, 1951; children: Alice, Marjorie. *Education:* City College (now of the City University of New York), B.S., 1940. *Home:* 50 High Ridge Ct., Pleasantville, N.Y. *Office: New York Times*, 229 West 43rd St., New York, N.Y.

CAREER: New York Times, New York, N.Y., reporter and war correspondent, 1940-52, day national news editor, 1952—. *Military service:* U.S. Army, 1942-46. *Awards, honors:* Purple Heart for war injuries received as correspondent in Korea, 1950-51.

WRITINGS: (Editor) *New York Times Election Handbook—1964*, McGraw, 1964; *George C. Marshall, Soldier and Statesman*, Farrar, Straus, 1964; (editor) *The Kennedy Years*, Viking, 1964; (editor) *The Road to the White House*, McGraw, 1965; (with Doris Faber) *American Heroes of the 20th Century*, Random House, 1967; *From Sea to Sea: The Growth of the United States*, Farrar, Straus, 1967; (editor) *New York Times Election Handbook—1968*, New American Library, 1968; (editor) *New York Times Guide for New Voters*, Quadrangle Books, 1972.†

FABER, John Henry 1918-

PERSONAL: Born February 13, 1918, in New York, N.Y.; son of John Martin and Jennie (Wacker) Faber; married Gertrud Jagode, October 26, 1964. *Education:* Attended University of Alabama, 1937-41. *Religion:* Lutheran. *Home:* 54 Crane Rd., Mountain Lakes, N.J. 07046. *Office:* Eastman Kodak Co., 343 State St., Rochester, N.Y. 14650.

CAREER: Alabama Ordnance Works, chief photographer, 1941-43; Bechtel-McCone-Parsons Corp., Birmingham Aircraft Modification Center, Birmingham, Ala., chief photographer, 1943-46; *Birmingham News* and television affiliate, WAFM-TV, Birmingham, Ala., photographic director, 1946-50; Eastman Kodak Co., Rochester, N.Y., photopress representative, 1950—. Free-lance photographer for national magazines. Faculty-associate, School of Modern Photography, 1970—. Has lectured on news photography at universities and associations, including Columbia University, University of Southern Ontario, Royal Photographic Society of Great Britain, United Arab Republic Press Photographers Association, and White House News Photographers Association. Advisor to curator of photography, Smithsonian Institution, 1960—. Member of board of directors, Photographic Administrators, Inc.

MEMBER: National Press Photographers Association (life member; regional vice-president, 1946-48; national secretary, 1948-50; historian, 1956—), Royal Photographic Society of Great Britain (associate), Society of American Historians, Kappa Alpha Mu (honorary life member), Explorers' Club. *Awards, honors:* Honorary Fellowship Awards from National Press Photographers Association, 1950, 1971; National Headliners Award from National Headliners Club, 1961, for *Great Moments in News Photography*; The President's Medal Award from National Press Photographers Association, 1961, for columns in *The National Press Photographer*, and 1967; Joseph A. Sprague Memorial Award from National Press Photographers Association, 1974.

WRITINGS: Industrial Photography, Trans World, 1948; (contributor) *The Complete Book of Press Photography*, National Press Photographers Association, 1950; *Great Moments in News Photography*, Nelson, 1960; (editor) *Humor in News Photography*, Nelson, 1961; *Travel Photography* (including color slides and tape cassette recordings), School of Modern Photography (New Jersey) , 1971. Contributor to *U.S. Camera, Life, Look, Time, Fortune, Saturday Evening Post, Collier's, Woman's Home Companion, Screen Guide, Popular Aviation, Popular Photography*, and other magazines. Technical editor, *Photographic Age*, 1946-48; regular columnist, "On the Record," *National Press Photographer* (magazine), 1956-64.

SIDELIGHTS: Faber's photographs were included in exhibitions at Eastman Kodak Grand Central Information Center, Photokina (Germany), and The Hague.

*   *   *

FAIR, Charles M. 1916-

PERSONAL: Born September 18, 1916, in New York, N.Y.; son of Charles Maitland and Gertrude (Bryan) Fair; married Mary Katherine Ruddy, February 2, 1952; children: Ellen Bryan, Kitty Healy, Charles M. *Education:* Yale University, student, 1935-36; University of California, Los Angeles, student, 1963-64. *Residence:* Shushan, N.Y. 12873. *Address:* 1426 Cambridge St., Cambridge, Mass. 02139.

CAREER: During World War II worked on the synthesis of an antimalarial drug in H.S. Polin Laboratories, New York, N.Y.; went to the Caribbean in 1946, and spent several years there as a banana-boat operator; later was with Hulick & Co., New York ship brokers, and with a division of Union Carbide Co., Carteret, N.J., which operated a tanker out of Texas City, Tex.; as professional jazz musician played piano and vibraphone nights, mainly around Lake George, N.Y., 1957-62, while learning the fundamentals of the nervous system; continued study in neurophysiology as Guggenheim fellow at University of California, Los Angeles, 1963-64, and fellow of Massachusetts Institute of Technology Neurosciences Research Program, Brookline, 1964-66; founded and served as officer of computer company in Cambridge, Mass.; full-time writer, 1972—. *Member:* American Association for the Advancement of Science (life member).

WRITINGS: The Physical Foundations of the Psyche, Wesleyan University Press, 1963; *The Dying Self*, Wesleyan University Press, 1969; *From the Jaws of Victory*, Simon & Schuster, 1971; *The New Nonsense*, Simon & Schuster, 1974. Article on jazz anthologized in *Modern Writing*, Avon, 1953. Contributor of other articles on jazz to *Arts Digest*, light verse to *New Yorker*, and a technical article to *Neurosciences Research Program Bulletin*; contributor of reviews to *Washington Post* and *Boston Herald-Traveler*.

SIDELIGHTS: Reviewer Erwin Knoll quotes Fair's description of *From the Jaws of Victory* as "a history of the character, causes and consequences of military stupidity from Crassus to Johnson and Westmoreland." Phil Casey also explains that the book is "all about military leaders who have done us in by, as he [Fair] says, 'snatching defeat from the jaws of victory.'" *The Dying Self* has been translated into German and *From the Jaws of Victory* has been translated into Italian. Fair told *CA:* "I speak colloquial Spanish, plain bad French; read both languages with ease and German with difficulty."

* * *

FAIRWEATHER, George W. 1921-

PERSONAL: Born February 1, 1921, in Dallas, Ore.; son of William and Vera Eleanor (Turner) Fairweather; married Betty J. Harper (a research clerk), February 12, 1944; children: James Steven, Robert Alan. *Education:* Iowa State College (now Iowa State University of Science and Technology), B.S., 1949; University of Illinois, M.S., 1951, Ph.D., 1953. *Home:* 1623 Fallen Leaf Lane, Los Altos, Calif.

CAREER: U.S. Veterans Administration Hospitals, co-director of research on psychological concomitants of tuberculosis, Houston, Tex., 1953-55, coordinator of psychological research, Perry Point, Md., 1955-57, chief of social-clinical psychology research and service unit, Palo Alto, Calif., 1957—. Stanford University, associate consulting professor of psychology. Certified psychologist, state of California. *Military service:* U.S. Army Air Forces, 1942-46; became first lieutenant. *Member:* American Psychological Association, Phi Kappa Phi.

WRITINGS: (Editor) *Social Psychology in Treating Mental Illness: An Experimental Approach*, Wiley, 1964; *Methods for Experimental Social Innovation*, Wiley, 1967; *Community Life for the Mentally Ill*, Aldine, 1969; *Social Change: The Challenge to Survival*, General Learning Press, 1972; *Creating Change in Mental Health Organiza-*

tions, Pergamon, 1974. With others, author of monograph, "Relative Effectiveness of Psychotherapeutic Programs," 1960. Contributor to psychological journals.†

* * *

FANE, Julian Charles 1927-

PERSONAL: Born May 25, 1927, in London, England; son of the Earl and Countess (nee Lister) of Westmoreland. *Education:* Attended Harrow School. *Home:* 32 Blenheim Terrace, London N.W.8, England.

CAREER: Novelist.

WRITINGS: Morning, John Murray, 1956; *A Letter*, John Murray, 1960; *Memoir in the Middle of the Journey*, Hamish Hamilton, 1971; *Gabriel Young*, Hamish Hamilton, 1973.

WORK IN PROGRESS: The Tug-of-War, publication by Hamish Hamilton expected in 1976.

* * *

FANGER, Donald (Lee) 1929-

PERSONAL: Born December 6, 1929, in Cleveland, Ohio; son of Max Leon and Rae (Bercu) Fanger; married Margot Taylor (a psychiatric social worker), June 18, 1955; children: Steffen, Ross, Katharine. *Education:* University of California, Los Angeles, student, 1947-50; University of California, Berkeley, B.A., 1951, M.A., 1953; Harvard University, Ph.D., 1962. *Home:* 74 Putnam St., West Newton, Mass. 02165. *Office:* Department of Slavic, Harvard University, Cambridge, Mass. 02138.

CAREER: Brown University, Providence, R.I., instructor, 1960-62, assistant professor, 1962-64, associate professor of Slavic and comparative literature, 1964-66; Stanford University, Stanford, Calif., associate professor of Slavic, 1966-68; Harvard University, Cambridge, Mass., professor of Slavic and comparative literature, 1968—. Visiting lecturer in Slavic and comparative literature, Harvard University, 1965-66. *Member:* Modern Language Association of America, American Comparative Literature Association, Phi Beta Kappa. *Awards, honors:* Exchange scholar at University of Leningrad, 1963.

WRITINGS: (Editor) V. Gippius, *Gogol*, Brown University Press, 1963; (editor) A. Slonismky, *Tekhika Komicheskogo u Gogolia*, Brown University Press, 1963; *Dostoevsky and Romantic Realism*, Harvard University Press, 1965; (editor) K. Leontiev, *Analiz, stil' i veianie*, Brown University Press, 1965. Contributor to *Survey, Comparative Literature, Nineteenth-Century Fiction, Slavic Review*, and other journals.

WORK IN PROGRESS: A book on Gogol and another on comic theory.

SIDELIGHTS: Reviewing *Dostoevsky and Romantic Realism*, Helen Muchnic says: "The most valuable aspect of Mr. Fanger's study is, to my mind, his insight into the special qualities of his writers and his ability to convey this insight in a telling, pithy way.... It is a mark of Mr. Fanger's good sense that, as he shows his romantic realists to be on the verge of symbolism, he does not succumb to the artificialities and extravagances that are prevalent in current 'symbolic' criticism. His views are well balanced and restrained, and always pertinent to the main interpretation and central argument." Fanger is competent in Russian, French, Spanish, German, and Latin.

FANT, Joseph Lewis III 1928-

PERSONAL: Born June 23, 1928, in Columbus, Miss.; son of Joseph Lewis, Jr., (a businessman) and Julia (Brazeale) Fant; married Carolyn Adeline Watkins, April 30, 1955; children: Carolyn Laura, Julia Lynn, Joseph Lewis IV. *Education:* Marion Institute, Associate in Science, 1947; U.S. Military Academy, B.S., 1951; University of Pennsylvania, A.M., 1960, currently Ph.D. candidate; graduate of U.S. Marine Corps Command and Staff College, and U.S. Army War College. *Religion:* Methodist. *Home:* 1209 North Second Ave., Columbus, Miss.

CAREER: U.S. Army, career officer, 1951—. U.S. Military Academy, West Point, assistant professor of English, 1960-64. *Member:* The National Society of Sons of the American Revolution. *Awards, honors*—Military: Legion of Merit with oak leaf cluster; Bronze Star with oak leaf cluster; Meritorious Service Medal with oak leaf cluster; Air Medal with oak leaf cluster; Commendation Medal.

WRITINGS: (Editor with Robert Ashley) *Faulkner at West Point*, Random House, 1964.

WORK IN PROGRESS: A book, *Gilbert Imlay: His Life and Works.*

*   *   *

FARB, Peter 1929-

PERSONAL: Born July 25, 1929, in New York, N.Y.; son of Solomon and Cecelia (Peters) Farb; married Oriole Horch (a museum director), February 27, 1953; children: Mark Daniel, Thomas Forest. *Education:* Vanderbilt University, B.A. (magna cum laude), 1950; Columbia University, graduate study, 1950-51. *Politics:* Independent. *Home:* 39 Pokeberry Ridge, Amherst, Mass. 01002.

CAREER: Argosy, New York, N.Y., feature editor, 1950-52. Free-lance writer and researcher in the science and natural history of North America, 1953—. Columbia Broadcasting System, New York, N.Y., editor-in-chief of Panorama (publishing project), 1960-61; Riverside Museum, New York, N.Y., curator of American Indian cultures, 1964-71; Yale University, New Haven, Conn., visiting lecturer, 1971-72, fellow, Calhoun College, 1971—. Consultant, Smithsonian Institution, 1966-71; judge, National Book Awards Committee, 1971. Member of board of directors, Allergy and Asthma Foundation of America, 1970-73. *Member:* American Association for the Advancement of Science (fellow), American Anthropological Association, Ecological Society of America, Society for American Archaeology, Society of American Historians (fellow), Society of Magazine Writers, New York Entomological Society (former secretary), P.E.N., Phi Beta Kappa, Omicron Delta Kappa.

WRITINGS: Living Earth, Harper, 1959; *The Story of Butterflies and Other Insects*, Harvey, 1959; *The Insect World*, Constable, 1960; *The Story of Dams*, Harvey, 1961; *The Forest*, Time Inc., 1961; (co-editor) *Prose by Professionals*, Doubleday, 1961; *The Insects*, Time, Inc., 1962; *The Story of Life*, Harvey, 1962; *Ecology*, Time, Inc., 1963, revised edition, 1970; *Face of North America: The Natural History of a Continent* (Book-of-the-Month Club selection), Harper, 1963, young reader's edition, 1964; *The Land and Wildlife of North America*, Time, Inc., 1964; (with John Hay) *The Atlantic Shore*, Harper, 1966; *The Land, Wildlife, and Peoples of the Bible*, Harper, 1967; *Man's Rise to Civilization as Shown by the Indians of North America from Primeval Times to the Coming of the Industrial State*, Dutton, 1968; *Yankee Doodle*, Simon & Schuster, 1970; *Word Play*, Knopf, 1974.

Editor, "North American Nature Series," Harper, 1964—. Columnist, *Better Homes and Gardens*, 1959-63, and contributor of science and nature articles to *Reader's Digest* and other national magazines. Member of editorial board, journal of New York Entomological Society.

WORK IN PROGRESS: A book on the evolution of man and his culture in North America.

SIDELIGHTS: President Kennedy presented *Face of North America* to the heads of one hundred foreign governments, and its author was hailed by Secretary of the Interior Stewart Udall in 1964 as "one of the finest conservation spokesmen of our period." Farb's books have been translated into a number of other languages and have set something of a sales record for works on natural history subjects by living writers.

BIOGRAPHICAL/CRITICAL SOURCES: Book of the Month, February, 1963.†

*   *   *

FARMER, Penelope 1939-

PERSONAL: Born June 14, 1939, in Westerham, Kent, England; daughter of Hugh Robert MacDonald and Penelope (Boothby) Farmer; married Michael John Mockridge (a lawyer), August 16, 1962; children: Clare Penelope, Thomas. *Education:* Attended private schools in England, 1945-56; St. Anne's College, Oxford, Degree in History (second-class honors), 1960; Bedford College, University of London, Diploma in Social Studies, 1962. *Politics:* "Leftwing." *Home:* 16 Park Rd., Richmond, Surrey, England. *Agent:* Deborah Owen, 78 Nawow St., London, E14, England.

CAREER: Teacher for London County Council Education Department, London, England, 1961-63; writer of juvenile fiction. *Member:* P.E.N., Society of Authors, Writers Action Group.

WRITINGS—All children's books: *The China People*, Hutchinson, 1960; *The Summer Birds*, Harcourt, 1962; *The Magic Stone*, Harcourt, 1964; *The Saturday Shillings*, Hamish Hamilton, 1965; *Emma in Winter*, Harcourt, 1966; *Charlotte Sometimes*, Harcourt, 1969; *A Castle of Bone*, Atheneum, 1972; *William and Mary*, Atheneum, 1974. Author of short stories and of television and radio scripts.

WORK IN PROGRESS: A novel; a myth collection; and much poetry.

AVOCATIONAL INTERESTS: Collecting early children's books; history of book design and illustration in general.

*   *   *

FARNSWORTH, E(dward) Allan 1928-

PERSONAL: Born June 30, 1928, in Providence, R.I.; son of Harrison E. (a physicist) and Gertrude (Romig) Farnsworth; married Patricia Ann Nordstrom (a biologist), May 30, 1952; children: Jeanne, Karen, Edward Allan, Jr., Pamela. *Education:* University of Michigan, B.S., 1948; Yale University, M.A., 1949; Columbia University, LL.B., 1952. *Religion:* Unitarian Universalist. *Home:* 201 Lincoln St., Englewood, N.J. 07631. *Office:* Columbia Law School, 435 West 116th St., New York, N.Y. 10027.

CAREER: Admitted to Bar of Washington, D.C., 1952, and Bar of State of New York, 1956; Columbia University,

New York, N.Y., assistant professor, 1953-56, associate professor, 1956-59, professor of law, 1959-70, Alfred McCormack Professor of Law, 1970—. Director, Association of American Law Schools Orientation Program in American Law, New York, N.Y., and Princeton, N.J., 1964—. Visiting professor at University of Istanbul, 1960, University of Dakar, 1964, Harvard Law School, 1970-71, and University of Chicago; faculty member, Salzburg Seminar in American Law, 1963, Columbia-Leyden-Amsterdam program in American Law, 1964, 1969, 1973; has done research in France. U.S. representative to United Nations Commission on International Trade Law, 1970—. Reporter, Restatement of Contracts (Second), 1971—. *Military service:* U.S. Air Force Reserve, active duty, 1952-53; became captain. *Member:* American Law Institute, American Bar Association, Association of the Bar of City of New York, Phi Beta Kappa, Phi Delta Phi.

WRITINGS: Introduction to the Legal System of the United States, Oceana, 1963; (with John Honnold) *Cases and Materials on Commercial Law,* Foundation Press, 1965, 2nd edition, 1968; (with William F. Young, Jr. and Harry W. Jones) *Cases and Materials on Contracts,* Foundation Press, 1965, 2nd edition, 1972; *Cases and Materials on Commercial Paper,* Foundation Press, 1968.

SIDELIGHTS: Farnsworth speaks French.

* * *

FARR, Diana Pullein-Thompson (Diana Pullein-Thompson)

PERSONAL: Born in Wimbledon, Surrey, England; daughter of Harold James (an army officer; later secretary to Headmasters' Conference) and Joanna (an author; maiden name, Cannan) Pullein-Thompson; married Dennis Larry Ashwell Farr (director of City of Birmingham Museums & Art Gallery), 1959; children: Benedict Edward, Joanna Helen. *Education:* Attended Wychwood School in England. *Religion:* Church of England. *Home:* Fernhill, 51 St. Bernard's Rd., Solihull, West Midlands, England.

CAREER: Began writing for children at the age of fourteen; supplemented income for a dozen years by breaking and schooling horses and teaching riding; later worked for a literary agent and occasionally as publishers' reader in England; Part-time editor, Faith Press, 1957-59. *Member:* P.E.N., Society of Authors, Children's Writers Group (founder member), Authors and Publishers Lending Right Association (committee member and delegate, 1959-65).

WRITINGS—Under name Diana Pullein-Thompson: *I Wanted a Pony,* Collins, 1946; *Three Ponies and Shannan,* Collins, 1947; *The Pennyfields,* Collins, 1949; *A Pony to School,* Collins, 1950; *A Pony for Sale,* Collins, 1951; *Horses at Home,* Collins, 1954; *Riding with the Lyntons,* Collins, 1956; *Riding for Children,* Foyle, 1956; *The Boy and the Donkey,* Criterion, 1958; *The Secret Dog,* Collins, 1959; *The Hidden River,* Hamish Hamilton, 1960; *The Boy Who Came to Stay,* Faith Press, 1960; *The Battle of Clapham Common,* Parrish, 1962; *Bindi Must Go,* Harrap, 1962; *The Hermit's Horse,* Collins, 1974; *Black Beauty's Clan,* Brockhampton Press, 1975. Contributor to *Daily Telegraph, Bookseller, Author, Library World, Young Elizabethan, Riding,* and other periodicals; has written for television.

WORK IN PROGRESS: A biography of Gilbert Cannan.

SIDELIGHTS: Several of Diana Pullein-Thompson Farr's books have had foreign editions.

FARRELL, Alan 1920-

PERSONAL: Born June 1, 1920, in Rainford, Lancashire, England; son of Joseph and Bridget (Donegan) Farrell; married Colette Einfalt, July 31, 1948; children: Margaret, Peter. *Education:* St. John's College, Oxford, M.A., 1948. *Home:* 29 Harvest Bank Rd., West Wickham, Kent BR4 9DL, England.

CAREER: Schoolmaster in England, 1949—, teaching English at Orpington Secondary School for Boys, Orpington, Kent, England, 1959—. *Military service:* British Army, 1940-43; Indian Army, Tenth Gurkha Rifles, 1943-46; became captain.

WRITINGS: Sir Winston Churchill, Faber, 1962, Putnam, 1964.

WORK IN PROGRESS: Chimp, a short novel for boys.

SIDELIGHTS: Farrell speaks French fluently.†

* * *

FARRELL, Melvin L(loyd) 1930-

PERSONAL: Born September 4, 1930, in St. Paul, Minn.; son of J. Lloyd and Barbara (Weber) Farrell. *Education:* Attended St. Edward's Minor Seminary, 1944-50; Catholic University of America, B.A., 1952, M.A., 1953, S.T.L., 1957; University of Washington, Seattle, M.A., 1956; Seattle University, summer education courses, 1957-62. *Home:* St. Edward's Seminary, Kenmore, Wash.

CAREER: Roman Catholic priest, member of the Society of St. Sulpice. St. Edward's Seminary, Kenmore, Wash., instructor in literature and religion, 1957-62, principal of high school department, 1962—.

WRITINGS: First Steps to the Priesthood, Bruce, 1960; *Getting to Know Christ,* Bruce, 1965. Composer of hymns for *People's Hymnal.* Contributor of series of articles to *Hi-Time* (Catholic weekly for high school students).†

* * *

FARRELLY, M(ark) John 1927-

PERSONAL: Born October 20, 1927, in St. Louis, Mo.; son of John Joseph and Cordelia (Gross) Farrelly. *Education:* Attended St. Louis University, 1944-47; Catholic University of America, A.B., 1950, S.T.L., 1954, M.A., 1957, S.T.D., 1962. *Home:* St. Anselm's Abbey, Washington, D.C. 20017.

CAREER: Entered Benedictine order, 1947; ordained Roman Catholic priest, 1955; St. Anselm's Abbey, Washington, D.C., teacher of doctrinal theology, beginning, 1956; now teacher at De Sales Hall School of Theology, Hyattaville, Md. *Member:* Catholic Theological Society of America, American Philosophical Association, American Academy of Religion.

WRITINGS: Predestination, Grace, and Free Will, Newman, 1964. Contributor to scholarly journals, including *Theological Studies, Thomist, American Benedictine Review, New Scholasticism,* and *American Ecclesiastical Review.*

WORK IN PROGRESS: A book with the working title, *Man's Religious Transcendence.*

* * *

FARWELL, Byron E. 1921-

PERSONAL: Born June 20, 1921, in Manchester, Iowa; son of E. L. and Nellie (Sheldon) Farwell; married Ruth

Saxby, December 15, 1941; children: Joyce, Byron, Lesley. *Education:* Attended Ohio State University, 1939-40, University of Chicago, 1946-49. *Home:* Les Courtils, Petit Saconnex, Geneva, Switzerland. *Agent:* Brandt & Brandt, 701 Park Ave., New York, N.Y. 10017.

CAREER: Chrysler International, Geneva, Switzerland, director of administration, 1965—. College du Leman, chairman of board of governors. *Military service:* U.S. Army, 1940-45, 1950-51; became captain. *Member:* Royal Society of Literature (fellow), Royal Geographical Society (fellow).

WRITINGS: Let's Take a Trip, Grosset, 1955; *The Man Who Presumed: A Biography of Henry M. Stanley,* Henry Holt, 1957, reprinted, Greenwood, 1974; *Burton: A Biography of Sir Richard F. Burton,* Holt, 1963; *Prisoners of the Mahdi,* Harper, 1967; *Queen Victoria's Little Wars,* Harper, 1972.

SIDELIGHTS: Farwell has lived in Europe and Africa for ten years, and traveled in more than ninety countries.†

* * *

FATOUROS, A(rghyrios) A. 1932-

PERSONAL: Born September 19, 1932, in Athens, Greece; son of Athanasios D. (a physician) and Eudocia (Sakalis) Fatouros; married Naomi Andree Feldman (a painter); children: Eudocia-Sophia, Athanasios. *Education:* National University of Athens, Diploma, 1955; Columbia University, M.C.L., 1956. LL.M., 1957, J.S.D., 1962. *Religion:* Greek Orthodox. *Office:* School of Law, Indiana University, Bloomington, Ind. 47405.

CAREER: University of Western Ontario, London, Ontario, lecturer and assistant professor, Faculty of Law, 1960-63; University of Chicago Law School, Chicago, Ill., visiting assistant professor, 1963-64; Indiana University School of Law, Bloomington, assistant professor, 1964-66, associate professor, 1966-68, professor, 1968—. *Member:* Hellenic Institute of International and Foreign Law (Athens), International Law Association (American branch), American Society of International Law, Society for International Development, Canadian Institute of International Affairs.

WRITINGS: Government Guarantees to Foreign Investors, Columbia University Press, 1962; (with R. N. Kelson) *Canada's Overseas Aid,* Canadian Institute of International Affairs, 1964; *Nomika Provlimata Prostasias kai Proselkyseos Xenon Idiotikon Ependyseon,* Center of Planning and Economic Research (Athens), 1965. Contributor to legal journals and symposia. Member of board of editors, *Current Law and Social Problems,* 1960-63.

WORK IN PROGRESS: Research in comparative and international legal aspects of economic development.

* * *

FAX, Elton Clay 1909-

PERSONAL: Born October 9, 1909, in Baltimore, Md.; son of Mark Oakland (a clerk) and Willie Estelle (Smith) Fax; wife deceased; children: Betty Louise (Mrs. James Evans). *Education:* Attended Syracuse University. *Religion:* Protestant. *Home:* 51-29 30th Ave., Woodside, N.Y.

CAREER: Illustrator, with work exhibited at National Gallery of Art and Corcoran Gallery of Art, Washington, D.C.; also illustrator of books; chalk-talk lecturer in high schools under management of School Assembly Service of Chicago, Ill., and Rochester, N.Y. U.S. Department of State specialist in South America and Caribbean, 1955, in East Africa, 1964; representative of American Society of African Culture on tour of Nigeria, 1963. *Member:* Authors Guild of America, International Platform Association.

WRITINGS: (Self-illustrated) *West Africa Vignettes,* American Society of African Culture, 1960, englarged edition, 1963; *Contemporary Black Leaders,* Dodd, 1970; *Seventeen Black Artists,* Dodd, 1971; *Garvey: The Story of a Pioneer Black Nationalist,* Dodd, 1972; *Through Black Eyes,* Dodd, 1974. Contributor to *Harlem, U.S.A.* Illustrator of other books.

SIDELIGHTS: Fax lived in Mexico for more than two years and is active in programs of international educational exchange. Fax has also traveled in U.S.S.R. as guest of Soviet Writers Union and Afro-Asian Writers.

* * *

FAY, Leo (Charles) 1920-

PERSONAL: Born February 27, 1920, in St. Paul, Minn.; son of Leo and Marie (Miller) Fay; married Jean Schwantes, 1943; children: Dan, Wendie, Jon. *Education:* University of Minnesota, B.S., 1942, M.A., 1947, Ph.D., 1948. *Home:* Inverness Woods Rd., Route 3, Bloomington, Ind. *Office:* Indiana University, Bloomington, Ind.

CAREER: State University of New York College at Cortland (formerly Courtland State Teachers College), professor of education, 1948-52; Indiana University, Bloomington, associate professor, 1952-56, professor of education, 1956—. *Military service:* U.S. Army, 1943-46; became staff sergeant. *Member:* International Reading Association, National Council of Teachers of English, American Educational Research Association, National Conference on Research in English, National Society for the Study of Education, Indiana State Teachers Association, Phi Delta Kappa.

WRITINGS: Meeting New Friends, Lyons & Carnahan, 1962; *Days of Adventure,* Lyons & Carnahan, 1962; *Stories to Remember,* Lyons & Carnahan, 1962; (with Carl Bernard Smith) *Getting People to Read: Volunteer Programs That Work,* Delacorte, 1973. Senior author, "Curriculum Enrichment Series," eight books, Lyons & Carnahan, 1965, and "Young America Basic Reading Program," sixteen books, Rand McNally, 1974. Educational consultant for David-Stewart "Nature Adventure" series. Author of bulletins on reading for education groups, and contributor to professional journals.

* * *

FAZAKERLEY, George Raymond 1921-

PERSONAL: Born June 25, 1921, in Liverpool, England; son of Ernest George and Gladys (Sharp) Fazakerley; married Elsie Ann Jones, June 25, 1946; children: Alan John, Sally Ann. *Education:* Attended schools in Liverpool, England. *Religion:* Christian. *Home and office:* 32 Myers Rd. W., Great Crosby, Liverpool L23 ORU, England. *Agent:* Hughes Massie Ltd., 18 Southampton Pl., London W.C. 1, England.

CAREER: Customs clerk in fruit trade, Liverpool, England, 1936-40; office manager and accountant for fruit importer, Liverpool, England, 1946-56; full-time writer, 1956—, with brief emergency posts "when particularly penniless." *Military service:* British Army, and later East African Intelligence, 1940-46; served in Africa, Ceylon,

Burma, and India; became sergeant. *Member:* British Display Society, Society of Authors.

WRITINGS: Shadow in Saffron (novel), Thames & Hudson, 1953; *Kongoni* (novel), Thames & Hudson, 1955; *Teach Yourself Window Display*, English Universities Press, 1958; *A Stranger Here* (novel), Macdonald & Co., 1959; *Teach Yourself Modern Interior Display*, English Universities Press, 1966. Contributor of illustrated articles to several dozen trade journals.

WORK IN PROGRESS: Research in Sumerian history and mythology for a novel, provisionally titled *The Dying of the Light.*

AVOCATIONAL INTERESTS: Beethoven, Brahms, modern art, archaeology, history, astronomy; other interests range from do-it-yourself house renovation to tape recordings.

BIOGRAPHICAL/CRITICAL SOURCES: The Good Education of Youth, University of Pennsylvania Press, 1956.†

* * *

FEERICK, John David 1936-

PERSONAL: Born July 12, 1936, in New York, N.Y.; son of John Joseph (a transit dispatcher) and Mary (Boyle) Feerick; married Emalie Platt, August 25, 1962; children: Maureen, Margaret, Jean, Rosemary, John. *Education:* Fordham University, B.S. (honors), 1958, LL.B. (honors), 1961. *Religion:* Roman Catholic. *Home:* 41 Highridge Rd., Mount Kisco, N.Y. 10549. *Office:* Skadden, Arps, Slate, Meagher & Flom, 919 Third Ave., New York, N.Y. 10022.

CAREER: Skadden Arps, Slate, Meagher & Flom (law firm), New York, N.Y., partner. Adviser on presidential succession, Committee on Economic Development, 1964. *Military service:* U.S. Army Reserve, Judge Advocate General's Corps, 1962-68; active duty, 1962. *Member:* American Bar Association, New York State Bar Association, Association of the Bar of the City of New York.

WRITINGS: From Failing Hands: The Story of Presidential Succession, Fordham University Press, 1965; *The Vice-Presidents of the United States*, F. Watts, 1967. Contributor to legal journals. Editor-in-chief, *Fordham Law Review*, 1960-61.

WORK IN PROGRESS: A book on the Twenty-fifth Amendment.

* * *

FEIED, Frederick (James) 1925-

PERSONAL: Surname is pronounced *Fee*-ed; born March 2, 1925, in Highland Park, Mich.; son of James and Helen (Kotlarek) Feied; married Barbara Asbury Bowen, November 26, 1949; children: (previous marriage) Shawn, Lonnie, (current marriage) Craig, Clinton, Nicole, Malcolm. *Education:* University of Denver, B.A., 1948; Columbia University, M.A., 1961, candidate for Ph.D. *Politics:* Independent. *Office:* Michigan State University, East Lansing, Mich.

CAREER: Sometime assistant editor, *National Union Farmer* and *Colorado Labor Advocate*, and editor for Olympic Press (publishers of weekly newspapers in northern California); Golden Gate College (now University), San Francisco, Calif., instructor, 1954-56, assistant professor of English, 1956-58; San Francisco Conservatory of Music, San Francisco, Calif., associate professor of English, 1958-60, professor, 1960-63; Michigan State University, East Lansing, instructor in American thought and language, 1963—. *Member:* Modern Language Association of America, American Studies Association (secretary-treasurer, North California chapter, 1961-63), American Association of University Professors, Philological Association of the Pacific Coast, Phi Beta Kappa.

WRITINGS: No Pie in the Sky, Citadel, 1964. Contributor of reviews to *San Francisco Chronicle*, other writing to *San Francisco Review* and *Landscape.*

WORK IN PROGRESS: An elaboration of *No Pie in the Sky*, with added chapters on such as Bret Harte, Stephen Crane, John Steinbeck, Nelson Algren, and others; a play, "Fleas"; a novel, *A Game of Losers.*†

* * *

FEIN, Leonard J. 1934-

PERSONAL: Born July 1, 1934, in Brooklyn, N.Y.; son of Isaac M. (a teacher) and Clara (Wertheim) Fein; married Zelda Kleiman; children: Rachel Fein Shulamith, Naomi, Jessica. *Education:* University of Chicago, A.B., 1955, M.A., 1958; Michigan State University, Ph.D., 1962. *Religion:* Jewish. *Residence:* Brookline, Mass.

CAREER: Massachusetts Institute of Technology, Cambridge, assistant professor, 1962-67, associate professor of political science, 1967-70, associate director and director of research, Massachusetts Institute of Technology-Harvard University Joint Center for Urban Studies, 1968-70; Brandeis University, Waltham, Mass., professor of politics and social policy, 1970—, Klutznick Family Professor in Contemporary Jewish Studies, 1973—, director of Benjamin S. Hornstein Program in Jewish Communal Service, 1970-73. *Member:* American Political Science Association.

WRITINGS: (Editor) *American Democracy: Essay on Image and Realities*, Holt, 1964; *Politics in Israel*, Little, Brown, 1967; *Israel: Politics and People*, Little, Brown, 1968; *The Ecology of Public Schools: An Inquiry into Community Control*, Pegasus, 1971. Contributor to professional journals, including *American Political Science Review, Journal of Jewish Social Studies*, and *Journalism Quarterly.*

SIDELIGHTS: Reviewing *Israel: Politics and People*, Ernest Stock says: "Fein's account achieves a rare level of interest and readability; above all by having something genuinely new to say, it brilliantly clears the hurdle of banality on which so many books on Israel have stumbled." Fein is competent in Hebrew.

* * *

FEINGOLD, S. Norman 1914-

PERSONAL: Born February 2, 1914, in Worcester, Mass.; son of William and Aida (Salit) Feingold; married Marie Goodman (a rehabilitation counselor), March 24, 1947; children: Elizabeth Anne, Margaret Ellen, Deborah Carol, Marilyn Nancy. *Education:* Indiana University, A.B., 1937; Clark University, M.A., 1940; Boston University, Ed.D., 1948. *Religion:* Jewish. *Home:* 9707 Singleton Dr., Bethesda, Md. *Office:* B'nai B'rith Career and Counseling Services, 1640 Rhode Island Ave., N.W., Washington, D.C. 20036.

CAREER: Associated Jewish Philanthropies, Boston, Mass., director of vocational service, 1941-43; Jewish Vocational Service of Greater Boston (Mass.), executive director, 1946-58, executive director of Work Adjustment

Center, 1956-58; B'nai B'rith Career and Counseling Services (formerly B'nai B'rith Vocational Service), Washington, D.C., national director, 1958—. U.S. Department of Health, Education, and Welfare, consultant, 1963—. Part-time instructor and special lecturer, Boston University, 1953-58. Member of Massachusetts Committee on Employment of Aging, 1953-57, of President's Committee on Employment of the Handicapped (currently). *Military service:* U.S. Army, 1943-46; served in Asiatic-Pacific and European theaters; became first lieutenant. *Member:* American Board on Counseling Services (former vice-president), National Vocational Guidance Association (trustee), Gerontological Society (fellow), American Association for the Advancement of Science, American Personnel and Guidance Association (president, 1974-75), American Psychological Association, National Rehabilitation Association, Maryland Psychological Association. *Awards, honors:* Citations from B'nai B'rith and Commonwealth of Massachusetts Division of the Blind; honorary doctorate, Edward Waters College.

WRITINGS: Scholarships, Fellowships and Loans, four editions, Bellman, Publishing, 1949, 4th edition, 1973; (with Harold List) *Opportunities in Unusual Occupations,* Science Research Associates, 1952; *How to Choose That Career,* Bellman, 1954; (with H. List) *How to Get That Part-Time Job,* Arco, 1958; (with Alfred Jospe) *College Guide for Jewish Youth,* B'nai B'rith Vocational Service, 1963, revised edition, 1969; *How About College Financing? A Guide for Parents of College-Bound Students,* revised edition, American Personnel and Guidance Association, 1964; (editor) *The College and Career Plans of Jewish High School Youth,* B'nai B'rith Vocational Service, 1964; *A Career Conference for Your Community,* B'nai B'rith Vocational Service, 1964; (editor) *Prep School Guide For Jewish Youth,* B'nai B'rith Career and Counseling Services, 1966; (with Sol Swerdloff) *Occupations and Careers,* Webster, 1969; (editor) *The Vocational Expert in the Social Security Disability Program,* C. C Thomas, 1969; (with others) *The College Handbook,* College Entrance Examination Board, 1969; *A Counselor's Handbook,* Carroll Press, 1972; *Scholarships, fellowships and loans,* Bellman Publishing, 1972.

Editor, *Counselor's Information Service,* B'nai B'rith Career and Counseling Services 1958—. Contributor of more than seventy-five articles to *Performance, Cerebral Palsy Review, Occupational Outlook Quarterly,* and other journals related to his field.

AVOCATIONAL INTERESTS: Photography, travel.

* * *

FEINSILVER, Alexander 1910-

PERSONAL: Born January 18, 1910, in Tel-Aviv, Palestine (now Israel); son of Morris and Rachel (Schulman) Feinsilver; married Lillian Mermin, 1946; children: David, Ruth. *Education:* Western Reserve (now Case Western Reserve), University, A.B., 1931; Hebrew Union College, Cincinnati, Ohio, B.H., 1935, Rabbi, 1937; American Foundation of Religion and Psychiatry, certificate in marriage counseling, 1967. *Home:* 510 McCartney St., Easton, Pa.

CAREER: Rabbi of congregations in Paducah, Ky., 1937-41, and Sacramento, Calif., 1941-46; Hillel Foundation director at University of Georgia, Athens, 1946-47, University of Connecticut, Storrs, 1947-50, and Purdue University, Lafayette, Ind., 1950-55; Temple Covenant of Peace,

Easton, Pa., rabbi, 1955-73. Hillel counselor, Lafayette College, Easton, Pa., 1955-73; staff counselor, American Foundation of Religion and Psychiatry, 1967; staff lecturer, Pastoral Institute of the Lehigh Valley, 1969-70. Board member, Visiting Nurse Association. *Member:* Central Conference of American Rabbis, American Association of Marriage and Family Counselors. *Awards, honors:* D.D., Hebrew Union College-Jewish Institute of Religion, 1962.

WRITINGS: In Search of Religious Maturity, Antioch Press, 1960; *Aspects of Jewish Belief,* Ktav, 1973. Contributor to *Commentary, Hebrew Union College Monthly, National Jewish Monthly,* and other periodicals.

AVOCATIONAL INTERESTS: Music (plays violin).

* * *

FELL, Joseph P(hineas) III 1931-

PERSONAL: Born May 22, 1931, in Troy, N.Y.; son of Joseph Phineas, Jr. (a business executive) and Mabel (Hunt) Fell; married Cynthia Ross (a teaching assistant in English), June 12, 1958; children: John Whittum, Caroline. *Education:* Williams College, B.A., 1953; Union Theological Seminary, New York, N.Y., graduate study, 1953-54; Columbia University, M.A., 1960, Ph.D., 1963. *Politics:* Democrat. *Home:* 315 Stein Lane, Lewisburg, Pa. 17837. *Office:* Department of Philosophy, Bucknell University, Lewisburg, Pa. 17837.

CAREER: Pennsylvania State University, University Park, instructor, 1962-63; Bucknell University, Lewisburg, Pa., assistant professor, 1963-67, associate professor, 1967-71, professor of philosophy, 1971—. *Military service:* U.S. Army, 1954-56. *Member:* American Philosophical Association, Society for Phenomenology and Existential Philosophy, Phi Beta Kappa (honorary). *Awards, honors:* Clarke F. Ansley Award of Columbia University Press, 1963, for manuscript of *Emotion in the Thought of Sartre;* Bucknell University summer fellowship, 1965, 1967; National Endowment for the Humanities, fellowship, 1969-70; Lindback Award, 1969.

WRITINGS: Emotion in the Thought of Sartre, Columbia University Press, 1965. Contributor to *Bucknell Review, Psychoanalytic Review, Philosophical Quarterly, School and Society, Journal of British Society for Phenomenology, Review of Metaphysics.*

WORK IN PROGRESS: Comparative study of the philosophies of Martin Heidegger and Jean-Paul Sartre.

SIDELIGHTS: Fell is competent in Greek, Latin, French, and German. *Avocational interests:* Music, literature (especially D. H. Lawrence).

* * *

FENLON, Paul Edward 1921-

PERSONAL: Born June 17, 1921, in Haverhill, Mass.; son of Edward J. and Hannah (Maxwell) Fenlon; married Barbara E. Noyes, May 15, 1942; children: Dorothy M. (Mrs. Larry A. Nagode), Robert, Barbara A. *Education:* College of the Holy Cross, B.S. in B.A., 1942; University of Illinois, A.B., 1947; University of Florida, M.A., 1951, Ph.D., 1955. *Office:* American Association of University Professors, 1785 Massachusetts Ave., N.W., Washington, D.C. 20036.

CAREER: Rollins College, Winter Park, Fla., assistant professor, 1946-51; University of Florida, Gainesville, instructor, 1951-55; College of the Holy Cross, Worcester,

Mass., associate professor of economics, 1955-60; Colorado State University, Fort Collins, professor of business and economics, 1960-65; American Association of University Professors, Washington, D.C., staff associate, 1965—. *Military service:* U.S. Army, 1942-46; received Bronze Star. U.S. Army Reserve, 1951-62; became major. *Member:* American Economic Association, American Finance Association, American Association of University Professors (president, Colorado conference, 1962-64), Catholic Economic Association.

WRITINGS: Financial Management Decisions: Case Problems, Allyn & Bacon, 1964; *Investment Decisions: A Casebook,* Grid, Inc., 1972. Contributor of articles to *Florida Historical Quarterly* and *Review of Social Economy.*†

* * *

FERGUSON, Charles W. 1901-
(Hilton Gregory)

PERSONAL: Born August 23, 1901, in Quanah, Tex.; son of Charles Nathaniel Newton (a minister) and Hannah (Wright) Ferguson; married Victoria Wallace, June 28, 1923 (divorced); children: Charles Wallace, Hugh McGinnis. *Education:* Southern Methodist University, B.A., 1923; additional study at Union Theological Seminary, New York, N.Y., 1925-26, and New School for Social Research, 1925-26. *Home:* Apple Tree Hill, Mount Kisco, N.Y. 10549. *Agent:* Paul R. Reynolds Inc., 599 Fifth Ave., New York, N.Y. 10017.

CAREER: Methodist minister, 1923-25; associate editor of *Bookman,* 1925-27; George H. Doran (later Doubleday, Doran & Co.), New York, N.Y., editor of religious books, 1925-30; Ray Long & Richard R. Smith, Inc. (publishers), New York, N.Y., secretary, 1930-32; Round Table Press, New York, N.Y., president, 1932-34; *Reader's Digest,* Pleasantville, N.Y., associate editor, 1934-42, senior editor, 1942-68. Cultural relations officer, U.S. Embassy, London, England, 1946. Visiting lecturer, University of Texas, 1969; visiting professor, Southern Methodist University, 1972. Member of National Council of Boy Scouts of America. *Awards, honors:* Litt.D., Hillsdale College, 1948, and Southern Methodist University, 1966; Christopher Award, 1958, for *Naked to Mine Enemies.*

WRITINGS: The Confusion of Tongues: A Review of Modern Isms, Doran, 1927; *Pigskin* (novel), Doubleday, Doran, 1928; *Fifty Mission Brothers: A Panorama of American Lodges and Clubs,* Farrar & Rinehart, 1937; *A Little Democracy Is a Dangerous Thing,* Association Press, 1948; *Naked to Mine Enemies: The Life of Cardinal Wolsey,* Little, Brown, 1958; *Say it with Words,* Knopf, 1959; *Getting to Know the U.S.A.,* Coward, 1963; *The Abecedarian Book,* Little, Brown, 1964; *The Male Attitude,* Little, Brown, 1966; *A is for Advent,* Little, Brown, 1968; *Organizing to Beat the Devil: Methodists and the Making of America,* Doubleday, 1971; *I, the Witness,* Little, Brown, 1975.

Writer of reviews and gossip for *Bookman.* Contributor of articles, sometimes under pseudonym Hilton Gregory, to Christian Century, Harper's, American Mercury, and other publications. Contributor of satirical verse to *Saturday Review,* and reviews to *New York Times Book Review.* Adapted *Naked to Mine Enemies* for a play produced at Dallas Theater Center, 1960.

WORK IN PROGRESS: An autobiography dealing with ideas entertained, rather than persons encountered, during the first 75 years of the century, completion expected in 1976; *The Horse You Could Hold in Your Hand,* a children's book.

SIDELIGHTS: Ferguson told *CA:* "I got out my first magazine when I was 12 years old in Abilene, Texas. It was done on a typewriter and had a circulation of one, but no magazine ever had a more avid readership." At Southern Methodist University, he worked as editor of the *Semi-Weekly Campus,* in which capacity, he admits, "I was more esteemed for my zest than for my precision. One professor said I spent most of my time as an undergraduate advising the administration on matters of policy." During his years with *Reader's Digest,* Ferguson frequently enjoyed testing out "self-improvement articles." He remembers an associate's description of him as "a walking art-of-living article—always trying to get the most out of such themes as 'Obey That Impulse' and 'Vacation Every Day.'"

"I live alone," Ferguson continued, "and, not caring much about sleep, am able to get a lot of work done at night. And when I sleep, it is the hardest work I do."

Reviewing *A Is for Advent,* Mary Reed Newland observed: "[It] says so many new things about words associated with religion, their history and meanings, that it is hard to put it down. It is written so that both children and adults will enjoy it ... and his fresh insights into old ideas make the book more than simply entertainment." Ferguson's "social and intellectual history of American Methodism," *Organizing to Beat the Devil,* was called "a real Methodist Western," by Bishop Gerald Kennedy. "It captures the movement and the practicality and the excitement of the Methodist Church in a marvelous way."

* * *

FERGUSON, John Henry 1907-

PERSONAL: Born August 22, 1907, in Lexington, Neb.; son of Leonard Calvin and Dicie Shirley (Sipes) Ferguson; married Ruth Arvilla Benton, June 10, 1930; children: Milton O., Richard B., David J., Rachel A. Rider. *Education:* Nebraska Central College, A.B., 1929; University of Pennsylvania, M.A., 1932, Ph.D., 1937. *Politics:* Democrat. *Religion:* Society of Friends. *Home:* 555 West Ridge Ave., State College, Pa. 16801. *Office:* 211 West Beaver Ave., State College, Pa. 16801.

CAREER: High school teacher and principal in Monroe, Neb., 1929-30; Friends Neighborhood Guild, Philadelphia, Pa., director of boys' work, 1930-34; Pennsylvania State University, University Park, instructor, 1934-37, assistant professor, 1937-41, associate professor, 1941-47, professor of political science, 1947-66, professor emeritus, 1966—, head of department, 1947-48, 1963-65, director of Social Science Research Center, 1953-55, director of Institute of Public Administration, 1959-65. Dean of School of Politics, New School for Social Research, New York, N.Y., 1948-49. Office of Governor of Pennsylvania, director of program evaluation, 1955-56, secretary of administration, 1956-59, budget secretary, 1957-59. American Friends Service Committee, administrative assistant, 1944-45, member of executive board, 1950-56, 1957-60. Director of Civilian Public Service Camp, Gatlinburg, Tenn., 1943-44. President and senior associate, Better Government Associates, Inc., 1967—. Visiting professor and lecturer, University of Pennsylvania, 1965—.

MEMBER: American Political Science Association (member of executive council, 1951-53), American Society for Public Administration, American Association of University Professors, Pennsylvania Political Science and Public Administration Association (president, 1958-60).

WRITINGS: American Diplomacy and the Boer War, University of Pennsylvania Press, 1939; (with D. E. McHenry) *The American System of Government*, McGraw, 1947, 12th edition, 1973; (with McHenry) *The American Federal Government*, McGraw, 1947, 12th edition, 1973; (with Charles F. LeeDecker) *Municipally Owned Waterworks in Pennsylvania*, Institute of Local Government, Pennsylvania State College, 1948; (with D. E. McHenry) *Elements of American Government*, McGraw, 1950, 9th edition, 1970; (with LeeDecker) *Municipally Owned Electric Plants in Pennsylvania*, Institute of Local Government, Pennsylvania State College, 1951; (with McHenry and E. B. Fincher) *American Government Today*, McGraw, 1951; (with David E. Cowell) *The Minor Courts in Pennsylvania*, Pennsylvania State University Institute of Public Administration, 1962.

*   *   *

FERM, Robert Livingston   1931-

PERSONAL: Born January 2, 1931, in Wooster, Ohio; son of Vergilius T.A. (a professor) and Nellie A. (Nelson) Ferm; married Flournoy Kinney, June 28, 1952; children: Eric Livingston, Alison Flournoy. *Education:* College of Wooster, B.A., 1952; Yale University Divinity School, B.D., 1955, M.A., 1956, Ph.D., 1958. *Home:* 248 West Seventh St., Claremont, Calif.; (summer) Payment Lake, Mercer, Wis. *Office:* Department of Religion, Pomona College, Claremont, Calif.

CAREER: United Presbyterian Church in the U.S.A., ordained minister, 1955. Pomona College, Claremont, Calif., instructor, later assistant professor of religion, 1958-63, John Knox McLean Associate Professor of Religion, and chairman of department, 1963—; Claremont Graduate School and University Center, Claremont, Calif., associate professor of religion, 1963—. Middlebury College, Middlebury, Vt., visiting associate professor of religion, 1964-65. *Member:* American Studies Association, American Society of Church History, American Academy of Religion. *Awards, honors:* Haynes Foundation fellowship, 1961.

WRITINGS: (Contributor) *Masterpieces in Christian Literature*, edited by Frank Magill, Harper, 1963; (editor) *Readings in the History of Christian Thought*, Holt, 1964; (compiler, editor, and author of introduction) *Issues in American Protestantism: A Documentary History From the Puritans to the Present*, Anchor Books, 1969. Contributor to *Church History*, other journals on religion and education.†

*   *   *

FERNEA, Elizabeth Warnock   1927-

PERSONAL: Surname is pronounced *Fur*-nee-ah; born October 21, 1927, in Milwaukee, Wis.; daughter of David Wallace (a chemist) and Elizabeth (Meshynsky) Warnock; married Robert Alan Fernea (a social anthropologist), June 8, 1956; children: Laura Ann, David Karim, Laila Catherine. *Education:* Reed College, B.A., 1949; Mount Holyoke College, graduate study, 1949-50. *Politics:* Democrat. *Religion:* Roman Catholic. *Home:* 3 Clinton St., Cambridge, Mass. *Agent:* A. Watkins, Inc., 77 Park Ave., New York, N.Y. 10016.

CAREER: Reed College, Portland, Ore., director of public relations, 1950-54; University of Chicago, Chicago, Ill., admissions counselor and promotion assistant, 1954-56; U.S. Information Agency, contract reporter and writer in Baghdad, Iraq, 1956-58; University of Chicago, member of public relations staff, 1958-59; now free-lance editor and writer.

WRITINGS: Guests of the Sheik, Doubleday, 1965, published as *Guests of the Sheik: An Ethnography of an Iraqui Village*, 1969; *A View of the Nile*, Doubleday, 1970. Contributor of free-lance articles and features to *Christian Science Monitor* and other newspapers.

WORK IN PROGRESS: Nubian Adventure, a juvenile; several articles.

SIDELIGHTS: Elizabeth Fernea told *CA:* "*Guests of the Sheik* grew out of the two years spent with my husband in a small village in Iraq (while he did anthropological field research). Since then we have spent almost all of the last six years in the Middle East, principally in Egypt." She speaks Arabic and French.†

*   *   *

FERRE, Frederick   1933-

PERSONAL: Accent in surname is on last syllable, as in "cafe"; born March 23, 1933, in Boston, Mass.; son of Nels F.S. (a theologian) and Katharine (Pond) Ferre; married Marie Booth, June 8, 1954; children: Katharine Marie. *Education:* Boston University, A.B. (summa cum laude), 1954; Vanderbilt University, M.A., 1955; University of St. Andrews, Ph.D., 1959. *Politics:* Democrat. *Home:* 111 South College St., Carlisle, Pa.

CAREER: Vanderbilt University, Nashville, Tenn., assistant professor of philosophy, 1958-59; Mount Holyoke College, South Hadley, Mass., assistant professor of religion, 1959-62; Dickinson College, Carlisle, Pa., associate professor, 1962-67, Charles A. Daus Professor of Philosophy, 1967—. Visiting professor and fellow of Graduate Council for the Humanities, Southern Methodist University, 1964-65; Eli Lilly visiting professor of science, theology and human values, Purdue University, 1974-75. *Member:* American Philosophical Association, Metaphysical Society of America, Society for Religion in Higher Education, Philosophy of Science Association, American Theological Society, American Association of University Professors (member of National Council, 1973-76).

WRITINGS: Language, Logic and God, Harper, 1961; (with Kent Bendall) *Exploring the Logic of Faith*, Association Press, 1962; (editor) *Paley's Natural Theology*, Bobbs-Merrill, 1963; *Basic Modern Philosophy of Religion*, Scribner, 1967; (editor and author of revised translation and introduction) Auguste Comte, *Introduction to Positive Philosophy*, Bobbs-Merrill, 1970.

Contributor: Frank N. Magill, editor, *Masterpieces of Christian Literature*, Volume II, Salem Press, 1963; William A. Beardslee, editor, *America and the Future of Theology*, Westminster Press, 1967; Perry LeFevre, editor, *Philosophical Resources for Christian Thought*, Abingdon, 1968; Ian G. Barbour, editor, *Science and Religion: New Perspective on the Dialogue*, Harper, 1968; Jerry A. Gill, editor, *Philosophy and Religion: Some Contemporary Perspectives*, Burgess, 1968; Dallas M. High, editor, *New Essays on Religious Language*, Oxford University Press, 1969; Barbour, editor, *Earth Might Be Fair: Reflections on Ethics, Religion and Ecology*, Prentice-Hall, 1972. Contributor to *The Encyclopedia of Philosophy*, and *Dictionary of the History of Ideas*.

FERRELL, Robert W(illingham) 1913-

PERSONAL: Born December 17, 1913, in Albany, Ga.; son of Ralph H. (an attorney) and Belle (Willingham) Ferrell; married Mary Jane Call, June 16, 1937; children: Maribel (Mrs. Eugene Sharkoff), Robert, Jr., Patricia. *Education:* University of Richmond, B.A., 1934; Harvard University, LL.B., 1937, advanced management study, 1948. *Politics:* Republican. *Religion:* Presbyterian. *Home:* 4405 Lancelot Rd., Toledo, Ohio.

CAREER: General Electric Co., 1937-59, variously corporate attorney, legal counsel, manager of employee and community relations, salesman, and marketing specialist; Owens-Illinois, Toledo, Ohio, director of marketing development, 1959-64. *Member:* American Management Association, American Marketing Association, New York Bar Association.

WRITINGS: Customer-Oriented Planning, American Management Association, 1964; *Managing Opportunity*, American Management Association, 1972.†

* * *

FERRY, David (Russell) 1924-

PERSONAL: Born March 5, 1924, in Orange, N.J., son of Robert Edward (an executive) and Elsie (Russell) Ferry; married Anne Elizabeth Davidson (a college teacher), March 22, 1958; children: Stephen Edward, Elizabeth Emma. *Education:* Amherst College, B.A., 1948; Harvard University, M.A., 1949, Ph.D., 1955. *Politics:* Democrat. *Home:* 8 Ellery St., Cambridge, Mass. *Office:* Department of English, Wellesley College, Wellesley, Mass.

CAREER: Wellesley College, Wellesley, Mass., instructor, 1952-55, assistant professor, 1955-61, associate professor, 1961-67, professor of English, 1967—, Sophie Chautal Hart professor, 1971—. Member, Democratic Ward Committee, Cambridge, Mass. *Military service:* U.S. Army Air Forces, 1943-46; became sergeant.

WRITINGS: (Editor) *The Laurel Wordsworth*, Dell, 1959; *The Limits of Mortality: An Essay on Wordsworth's Major Poems*, Wesleyan University Press, 1959; *On the Way to the Island* (poems), Wesleyan University Press, 1960; (editor with others) *British Literature*, 3rd edition (Ferry was not associated with earlier editions), Heath, 1974. Contributor to literary periodicals.

WORK IN PROGRESS: More poems; essays on modern poetry and Romantic poetry.

* * *

FESSENKO, Tatiana (Sviatenko) 1915-

PERSONAL: Born November 20, 1915, in Kiev, Russia (now Ukrainian Soviet Socialist Republic); came to United States in 1950 as a displaced person; daughter of Paul and Natalie Sviatenko; married Andrew V. Fessenko (a Library of Congress employee), September, 1, 1941. *Education:* Attended University of Kiev, 1932-36, graduate study, 1939-41. *Religion:* Greek Orthodox. *Home:* 3016 Q St., S.E., Washington, D.C. 20020.

CAREER: Academy of Sciences of the Ukrainian Soviet Socialist Republic, Kiev, junior research specialist, Institute of Linguistics, 1934-36; State Publishing House of Biological and Medical Literature, Kiev, Ukrainian Soviet Socialist Republic, literary editor, 1936-39; University of Kiev, Kiev, assistant professor of English, 1939-41; International Refugee Organization, Munich, Germany, secretary to field supervisor, 1947-50; Library of Congress, Washington, D.C., cataloger, 1951-63; Radio Liberty Committee, Inc., New York, N.Y., script writer, 1964. Researcher and bibliographer of bibliographic project on Ethiopia, Eritrea, and Somaliland, Hoover Institution on War, Peace and Revolution, 1967-69.

WRITINGS: (With husband, Andrew V. Fessenko) *First Steps; a Manual of English for Ukrainians*, privately printed, 1947, 2nd edition, 1950; (with A. V. Fessenko) *Russkii yazuk pri Sovetkh* (title means "The Russian Language Under the Soviets"), Rausen, 1955; *Eighteenth-Century Russian Publications in the Library of Congress* (catalog), Library of Congress, 1961; *Povest' krivykh let* (title means "The Ragged Years"), Novoye Russkoye Slovo, 1963; *Glazami turista*, (title means "As Seen by a Tourist"), Victor Kamkin Book Store, 1966; (editor and compiler) *Sodruzhestro* (title means "Concord"; an anthology of 75 Russian emigre poets), Victor Kamkin Book Store, 1966. Regular columnist, *Novoye Russkoye Slovo* (Russian-language newspaper published in New York); contributor to *Novyi Zhurnal* (Russian-language quarterly published in New York) and to *Sovremennik* (Russian-language journal published in Toronto, Ontario).

WORK IN PROGRESS: A collection of critical essays on Russian literature abroad.

SIDELIGHTS: Mrs. Fessenko is fluent in English, Russian, and Ukrainian; speaks good German, and fair French. *Avocational interests:* Travel and folk art.

* * *

FETLER, Andrew 1925-

PERSONAL: Born July 24, 1925, in Riga, Latvia (now Latvian Soviet Socialist Republic); son of Basil A. (a Protestant minister) and Barbara (Kovalevskaya) Malof-Fetler; married Carol McMahon, August 29, 1960; children: (former marriage) James; (present marriage) Jonathan. *Education:* Attended University of Chicago, 1946-48, DePaul University, 1949-50, University of California, Los Angeles, 1951-52; Loyola University, Chicago, Ill., B.S., 1959; University of Iowa, M.F.A., 1964. *Agent:* Russell & Volkening, Inc., 551 Fifth Ave., New York, N.Y. 10017. *Office:* Department of English, University of Massachusetts, Amherst, Mass.

CAREER: University of Massachusetts, Amherst, 1964—, began as assistant professor, currently associate professor of English. *Military service:* U.S. Army, 1944-46. *Awards, honors:* Coolbrith Poetry Award, 1952; Atlantic "First Award, 1962; Iowa Industries fellowship in creative writing, 1962-63; University of Massachusetts faculty growth grant, 1965; Northwest Review Fiction Award, 1972.

WRITINGS: The Travelers, Houghton, 1965. Contributor of short stories to popular magazines and literary quarterlies.

SIDELIGHTS: Felter speaks Russian and German.

* * *

FICKETT, Harold L., Jr. 1918-

PERSONAL: Born March 15, 1918, in Tucson, Ariz.; son of Harold L. (a pastor) and Gertrude (McCrary) Fickett; married Mary Frances Dorsey, June 4, 1940; children: Mary, Ruth, Harold L. III. *Education:* Baylor University, A.B., 1938; Southern Baptist Theological Seminary, Th.M., 1941; Eastern Baptist Theological Seminary, Th.M., 1947, Th.D., 1948, postdoctoral study, 1948-49.

Home: 14815 Leadwell St., Van Nuys, Calif. *Office:* First Baptist Church of Van Nuys, Van Nuys, Calif.

CAREER: Baptist minister; minister in Coatesville, Pa., 1947-50, Pomona, Calif., 1950-54, Boston, Mass., 1954-59; First Baptist Church of Van Nuys, Calif., pastor, 1959—. Visiting professor of homiletics at California Baptist Theological Seminary, 1952-53, Fuller Theological Seminary, 1963. Member of Ministers Council, American Baptist Convention, 1947—; trustee of Eastern Baptist Theological Seminary, 1954—, Eastern Baptist College, 1954—, and California Baptist Theological Seminary, 1959—. Member of Van Nuys Chamber of Commerce and board of directors of Bethlehem Star Parade, Van Nuys. *Military service:* U.S. Navy, chaplain, 1943-50; became lieutenant commander. *Member:* National Association of Evangelicals (president of Van Nuys chapter, 1963-65). *Awards, honors:* Freedoms Foundation award, 1964, for sermon, "Lest We Forget."

WRITINGS: Profiles in Clay, Cowman, 1963; *A Layman's Guide to Baptist Beliefs,* Cowman, 1963; *James: Faith that Works,* Regal Books, 1972; *Hope for Your Church,* Regal Books, 1972; *Peter's Principles,* Regal Books, 1974.

*   *   *

FIELD, Edward 1924-

PERSONAL: Born June 7, 1924, in Brooklyn, N.Y. *Education:* Attended New York University. *Mailing address:* Box 72, Village P.O., New York, N.Y. 10014.

CAREER: Began writing poetry while in the Army; lived in Europe a year and a half; returned to United States where he worked in a warehouse, in art reproduction, as a machinist, and as a clerk-typist; acted with amateur groups, studied with Vera Soloviova of the Moscow Art Theatre, and was leading man in summer theatre; has done narrations for film documentaries; writer. *Military service:* U.S. Army Air Forces, 1942-46; became 2nd lieutenant. *Awards, honors:* Lamant Poetry Selection, 1962, for *Stand Up, Friend, With Me;* Guggenheim fellowship, 1963.

WRITINGS: Stand Up, Friend, With Me (poems), Grove, 1963; *Variety Photoplays* (poems), Grove, 1967; *Eskimo Songs and Stories,* Delacorte, 1974. Contributor to *Botteghe Oscure.*

SIDELIGHTS: Chad Walsh wrote of *Variety Photoplays;* "Mr Field seems to be . . . deeply involved in the human drama, and this makes a difference in his subject and tone. Like a kind of secular pilgrim he travels light in order to go farther and see more. He pays a price for his poetic asceticism. There are many effects unattainable because he has denied himself the tools that would make them possible. But his gain is a kind of lean, stripped-down power and ability to speak the direct words of a common humanity. Somehow his book is bigger than the total of its poems." Stanley Moss commented that "his best poems . . . tell beautiful and believable stories of the indestructibility of the human spirit, at a time when most of human energies and resources are perversely wasted or destroyed."

*   *   *

FIELDER, Mildred (Craig) 1913-

PERSONAL: Born January 14, 1913, in Quinn, S.D.; daughter of William (a farmer) and Edna Verna (Edzards) Craig; married Ronald George Fielder (engineer for Homestake Mining Co.), September 17, 1932; children: Robert Allan, John Ronald. *Education:* Attended Huron College,

1929-31, University of Colorado, 1946. *Politics:* Republican. *Religion:* Presbyterian. *Home:* 2525 Bay Vista Lane, Los Osos, Calif. 93401.

CAREER: Rapid City Daily Journal, Rapid City, S.D., society editor, 1930-31; free-lance writer, 1951—. *Member:* Society of American Historians, National League of American Pen Women (national Historian, 1962-64), Western Writers of America, South Dakota State Historical Society, South Dakota Poetry Society (regional vice-president, 1950-65), P.E.O. Sisterhood, Lawrence County Historical Society. *Awards honors:* More than 390 prizes for writing, 26 of them awards on national level from General Federation of Women's Clubs, National League of American Pen Women, and poetry societies.

WRITINGS: Wandering Foot in the West, Humphries, 1955; *Railroads of the Black Hills,* limited edition, South Dakota Historical Society, 1960, Superior, 1964, 3rd edition, Bonanza Books, 1972; *The Edzards Family and Related Lines,* privately printed, 1965; *Wild Bill and Deadwood,* Superior, 1965, 2nd edition, Bonanza Books, 1969; *The Treasure of Homestake Gold,* North Plains Press, 1972; *A Guide to Black Hills Ghost Mines,* North Plains Press, 1972; *The Chinese in the Black Hills,* Bonanza Trails Publishers, 1972; (editor and author of chapter introductions) Carl Leedy, *Black Hills Pioneer Stories,* Bonanza Trails Publishers, 1973; *Potato Creek Johnny,* Bonanza Trails Publishers, 1973; *Hiking Trails in the Black Hills,* North Plains Press, 1973; *Preacher Smith of Deadwood,* Bonanza Trails Publishers, 1974; *The Legend of Lame Johnny Creek,* Bonanza Trails Publishers, 1974; *Poker Alice,* Bonanza Trails Publishers, 1974; *Wild Bill Hickok: Gun Man,* Bonanza Trails Publishers, 1974; *Theodore Roosevelt in Dakota Territory,* Bonanza Trails Publishers, 1974; *Deadwood Dick and the Dime Novels,* Bonanza Trails Publishers, 1974.

Poetry included in *Anthology of American Poetry,* Royal, 1962, *Yearbook of Modern Poetry,* Young Publications, 1971, and eight other collections; contributor of articles and poetry to periodicals; book review editor, *The Pen Woman,* 1972-74.

BIOGRAPHICAL/CRITICAL SOURCES: Lead Daily Call, Lead, S.D., May 17, 1958; *The Pen Woman,* March, 1962.

*   *   *

FIELDING, William J(ohn) 1886-

PERSONAL: Born April 10, 1886, in Wharton, N.J.; son of William and Mary (Mitchell) Fielding; married Elizabeth Beale, June 30, 1910 (deceased); married third wife, Mary B. Cameron, August 29, 1942; children: (first marriage) Elsie (deceased), John Carbis. *Education:* Educated in public schools and with private teachers. *Politics:* Independent. *Religion:* Ethical Culture Movement. *Home:* 1393 Long Beach Rd., Rockville Centre, Long Island, N.Y. 11570.

CAREER: Tiffany & Co., New York, N.Y., executive secretary, 1909-63. Louis Comfort Tiffany Foundation, New York, N.Y., secretary-treasurer, 1942-68, trustee, 1946-68, honorary trustee, 1968—. Thomas Paine Foundation, New York, N.Y., president, beginning 1960. Editor of *Newark Leader,* Newark, N.J., 1915-18; literary editor of *New Jersey Leader,* 1919-22; editor of *Know Thyself,* 1923-24; dramatic editor of *Golden Rule,* 1925-27, and *Sketch Book,* 1927-32. *Member:* Authors League of America, Freethinkers of America, National Council on Family Relations, American Social Health Association, American Humanist Association, Institut Litteraire et Artistique de France, American Birth Control League, American Civil Liberties Union, American Ethical Union, Euthanasia Society of America, Society of American Graphic Artists, Society for Constructive Birth Control and Racial Progress (London), Pi Gamma Mu. *Awards, honors:* Humanist of the year Award from Humanist Society of Greater New York, 1971.

WRITINGS: Pebbles From Parnassus (verse), Badger & Co., 1917; *Sanity in Sex*, Dodd, 1920; *The Caveman Within Us*, Dutton, 1922; *Health and Self-Mastery*, Lothrop, 1923, published as *Self-Mastery Through Psychoanalysis*, Avon, 1952; *Sex and the Love-Life*, Dodd, 1927, revised edition, Dodd, 1959; (contributor) V. F. Calverton and S. D. Schmalhausen, editors, *Sex in Civilization*, Macauley, 1928; *Love and the Sex Emotions*, Dodd, 1932; *The Shackles of the Supernatural*, Haldeman-Julius, 1938, revised edition, Vantage Press, 1969; *Strange Customs of Courtship and Marriage*, Garden City, 1942, new edition with illustrations, Hart Publishing, 1966; *Strange Superstitions and Magical Practices*, Doubleday, 1945; (author of introduction) Wilhelm Stekel, *How to Understand Your Dreams*, Avon, 1951; *Autosuggestion You Can Use*, Academy of Applied Mental Sciences, 1960; *All the Lives I Have Lived* (autobiography), Dorrance, 1971.

Author of thirty "Little Blue Books," published by Haldeman-Julius, 1921-32; *Boccaccio: Lover and Chronicler of Love; Woman's Sexual Life; Man's Sexual Life; The Child's Sexual Life; Homosexual Life; Woman: The Eternal Primitive; Woman: The Warrior; Woman: The Criminal; Sex Symbolism; The Determination of Sex; Sexual Obessions of Saints and Mystics; Facts About the Art of Love; What Every Boy Should Know; What Every Young Man Should Know; What Every Young Woman Should Know; What Every Married Man Should Know; What Every Married Woman Should Know; What the Woman Past Forty Should Know; Auto-suggestion: How It Works; Autosuggestion and Health; Psychoanalysis: The Key to Behavior; Unconscious Love Elements in Psychoanalysis; The Puzzle of Personality; The Cause and Nature of Genius; The Nature of Our Instincts and Emotions; How the Sun's Rays Give Health and Beauty; The Marvels and Oddities of Sunlight; Rejuvenation;* (with Louis Reiss) *Teeth and Mouth Hygiene; Dual and Multiple Personality.*

SIDELIGHTS: Fielding's *Sex and the Love-Life* sold over a million copies and his "Little Blue Books" have had an aggregate circulation of over six million.

BIOGRAPHICAL/CRITICAL SOURCES: New Yorker, March 29, 1952.

* * *

FIELDS, Wilbert J. 1917-

PERSONAL: Born March 24, 1917, in Reedsburg, Wis.; son of James Joseph and Anna (Pohlmann) Fields; married Janet Doll, September 13, 1942; children: Ann (Mrs. Albert Trost), Lois, Miriam. *Education:* Studied at Concordia College, Milwaukee, Wis., Concordia Seminary, and Oberlin College; Iowa State University, M.S., 1956. *Home:* 114 East Woodbine, Kirkwood, Mo. 63122. *Office:* 500 North Broadway, St. Louis, Mo. 63102.

CAREER: Lutheran clergyman. Pastor of churches in St. Louis, Mo., 1941-43, and Oberlin, Ohio, 1943-50; Memorial Lutheran Church, Ames, Iowa, pastor, 1950-70; Lutheran

Church, Missouri Synod, St. Louis, Mo., executive secretary of department of campus ministry, 1970—. *Member:* Psi Chi, Alpha Lambda Phi. *Awards, honors:* D.D. from Concordia Seminary.

WRITINGS: (With others) *Meditations for College Students*, Concordia, 1961; *Unity in Marriage*, Concordia, 1962; *Communion with Christ*, Concordia, 1964. Editor of "Concordia Sex Education" series, 6 volumes, published by Concordia.

* * *

FIESER, Max (Eugene) 1930-

PERSONAL: Born December 29, 1930, in Wichita, Kan.; son of Fredrick George (a produce wholesaler) and Myrtle Pearl (Schroeder) Fieser; married Rosemary Leanore Sleeth, July 3, 1951; children: Stephen Eugene, Fredrick George II. *Education:* Washington State University, student, 1947-49; University of Wichita, B.A., 1955; University of Oregon, M.A., 1957, Ph.D., 1961. *Home:* 5233 Minerva Ave., Sacramento, Calif. *Office:* Department of Economics, California State University, Sacramento, Calif. 95819.

CAREER: Midwest Research Institute, Kansas City, Mo., associate economist, 1958; Arizona State University, Tempe, assistant professor of economics, 1958-60; University of Oregon, Eugene, instructor in economics, 1961-62; Central Intelligence Agency, Washington, D.C., economist, 1961-62; George Washington University, Washington, D.C., lecturer in economics, 1961-63; Board of Governors of the Federal Reserve System, Washington, D.C., economist, 1962-63; University of California, Davis, lecturer in economics, 1963-64; California State University, Sacramento, assistant professor of economics, 1963—. Senate Fact-Finding Committee on Revenue and Taxation, California Legislature, consultant, 1963—. *Military service:* U.S. Army, 1949-53; became sergeant. *Member:* American Economic Association, National Tax Association, Western Economic Association, Regional Science Association, Association of Artus.

WRITINGS: Economic Policy and War Potential, Public Affairs, 1964. Contributor to professional journals.

WORK IN PROGRESS: Broad-based study of local-government revenues and expenditures, with a consideration of the burden distribution from local property taxes; a study of the behavior of international capital during periods of stress.

SIDELIGHTS: Fieser is competent in Russian. He holds a general class amateur radio license.†

* * *

FIFIELD, William 1916-

PERSONAL: Born April 5, 1916, in Chicago, Ill.; son of Lawrence Wendell (a Congregational minister) and Juanita (Sloan) Fifield; married Donna Hamilton (formerly an actress); children: John Lawrence, Donna Lee and Brian Robert (twins). *Education:* Whitman College, A.B. (magna cum laude), 1937. *Politics:* None. *Religion:* None. *Home:* Mas du Rouge, St.-Remy de Provence, B.D.R., France. *Agent:* Brandt & Brandt, 101 Park Ave., New York, N.Y. 10017.

CAREER: Began radio work while an undergraduate and returned to it (and later television) as an announcer, writer, actor, producer-director, for CBS and NBC, in Chicago, New York, and Hollywood at various short intervals, 1937-

60; left radio originally to freelance as a short story writer, living and traveling abroad most of the time since 1940; onetime bullfighter; novelist, 1957—. *Member:* Phi Beta Kappa. *Awards, honors:* O. Henry Memorial Award for "Fishermen of Patzcuaro"; Huntington Hartford Foundation Award for creative writing.

WRITINGS: The Devil's Marchioness (novel), Dial, 1957; *The Sign of Taurus* (novel), Holt, 1960; *Matadora* (novel),Weidenfield & Nicolson, 1960; (with Alexis Lichine) *Encyclopaedia of Wines and Spirits*, Knopf, 1967. Author of more than one hundred short stories, appearing in *Harper's, Story, American Mercury, Paris Review, Show, Liberty, Yale Review, Tomorrow, Argosy, Town*, and other magazines, with some anthologized in *Best American Short Stories* and *Fiction of the Forties*. Writer of some 130 radio and television plays.

WORK IN PROGRESS: A tetralogy on the Florentine Renaissance period, the first volume titled *Bull Borgia*.

SIDELIGHTS: The much-traveled Fifield prefers not to be called an expatriate. "I'm an outlander," he says, "just as Lawrence Durrell is." Born in Chicago, raised in Seattle, he has lived abroad intermittently for some 25 years, settling in Mexico, Haiti, Martinique, Austria, London, Portugal, Spain, Florence, the Italian Riviera, Paris, and Provence. His activities and interests have included a spell as an amateur bullfighter, and a continuing concern with psychic phenomena, including the crystal ball, hypnotism, the seance, and clairvoyance.

When he is writing, he begins working at 4 a.m. and writes for about ten hours at a stretch, composing directly onto a typewriter at the rate of 80 or 90 words per minute. He is interested in achieving a new novel-form, one which "will keep it within readable length without loss of breadth or depth."

The *Times Literary Supplement* called *The Sign of Taurus* "a most accomplished novel." This novel took ten years to write, though he says he has written other (unpublished) novels in as little as three weeks.

He speaks and writes French, Italian, Spanish, and German (and speaks English with an overlay of many other languages, according to one interviewer).

BIOGRAPHICAL/CRITICAL SOURCES: Atlantic, July 1957; *New Statesman*, January 25, 1958; *Times Literary Supplement*, February 7, 1958, May 22, 1959; *New York Times Book Review*, May 8, 1960, May 29, 1960; *Chicago Daily News*, May 14, 1960; *New York Herald Tribune Book Review*, June 5, 1960; *Kansas City Star*, June 28, 1960.†

*　　　　*　　　　*

FINE, William Michael 1924-

PERSONAL: Born July 1, 1924, in New York, N.Y.; son of Joseph G. (a business executive) and Susan (Moss) Fine; married Patricia Purdy, August 22, 1946; married Susan Payson, December 2, 1967; children: (first marriage) William, Douglas Michael, Timothy James. *Education:* Attended Kenyon College. *Politics:* Independent. *Religion:* Protestant. *Home:* 42 Dan's Highway, New Canaan, Conn. *Agent:* Ashley Famous Agency, Inc., 1301 Avenue of the Americas, New York, N.Y. 100 19. *Office:* Bonwit Teller, 721 Fifth Ave., New York, N.Y. 10022.

CAREER: General manager of community newspaper chain, Westchester, N.Y., 1946-47, and publisher of two community papers, 1948-50; McCall Corp., fashion adver-

tising manager, *McCall's*, 1950-54, West Coast general manager, 1954-56; Hearst Corp., New York, N.Y., publisher of *Bride & Home*, 1955, executive editor of *Good Housekeeping*, 1957; Reach-McClinton Advertising Agency, New York, N.Y., vice-president and director of marketing, 1958-60; Hearst Corp., publisher of *Harper's Bazaar*, 1960-69, and vice-president of Hearst Magazines, 1961-69, publishing director of *Town and Country*, 1964—; Bonwit Teller, New York, N.Y., president, 1969—. Director of National Magazine Co. Ltd., Greenway Productions, and 20th Century-Fox. Member of town board, Weston, Conn., 1953-54. *Military service:* U.S. Army, Infantry, World War II; received Bronze Star. *Member:* Irish American Council of Industry and Culture, Overseas Press Club, Delta Tau Delta, Darien Country Club, Williams Club, Fifth Avenue Club.

WRITINGS: (Co-editor) *History of the 45th Infantry Division*, 1946; *That Day With God*, McGraw, 1965. Contributor to *Look, McCalls, Ladies Home Journal, Show, Printers' Ink*, and other magazines.

WORK IN PROGRESS: Short stories.

*　　　　*　　　　*

FINER, Leslie 1921-

PERSONAL: Born December 10, 1921, in London, England; son of Charles (a trader) and Ray (Topper) Finer; married Elsa Verghi (an actress), November 2, 1954. *Education:* Studied at London School of Economics and Political Science, London, 1940-42. *Home:* 5 Moschonission St., Athens, Greece 814.

CAREER: Ministry of War Transport, England, administrative officer, 1942-47; *Evening Standard*, London, England, staff writer, 1947-54; became correspondent in Greece for British Broadcasting Corp., *Observer, Financial Times, Sun*, and *Daily Mirror*, all London, England. *Member:* Foreign Correspondents Association of Greece.

WRITINGS: Passport to Greece, Longmans, Green, 1964, Doubleday, 1965; (translator) Costas Takis, *Third Wedding*, Red Dust Press, 1971; (translator with Mario Rinvolucri) Sotiris Spatharis, *Behind the White Screen*, Red Dust Press, 1974.

WORK IN PROGRESS: A play.

SIDELIGHTS: Finer speaks Greek and French fluently, German and Italian adequately. *Avocational interests:* Music, theater.†

*　　　　*　　　　*

FINGESTEN, Peter 1916-

PERSONAL: Surname is pronounced Fin-*ges*-ten, hard g; born March 20, 1916, in Berlin, Germany; came to United States, 1939, became citizen, 1943; son of Michel (a painter) and Bianca (Schiek) Fingesten; married Faye Simons, May 7, 1943; children: Alexandra. *Education:* Fine Arts College of Berlin, Diploma, 1934, M.A., 1935; additional study at Pennsylvania Academy of Fine Arts, 1940-43, and Asia Institute, New York, N.Y., 1949-51. *Religion:* Quaker. *Home:* 339 East 18th St., New York, N.Y. 10003.

CAREER: Artist, sculptor, and writer, 1935—. Manhattan College, New York, N.Y., teacher of art, 1946-50; Pace University, New York, N.Y., 1950—, became associate professor of art, 1960—, and chairman of department, 1965—. Sculpture exhibited in one-man shows in the United States and Europe (Berlin, Milan, and Paris). Radio and television lecturer on art in New York, N.Y., 1972—. *Military service:* U.S. Army, Technical Intelligence, 1943-45. *Member:* College Art Association of America, American Society for Aesthetics, American Association of University Professors. *Awards, honors:* L. C. Tiffany Foundation award for creative work, 1948; outstanding teacher award from Pace University, 1968.

WRITINGS: East Is East, Muhlenberg Press, 1956; *Fact Book of Art History*, Collier, 1963; *The Eclipse of Symbolism*, University of South Carolina Press, 1970. Contributor of numerous essays and reviews to national and international art magazines.

* * *

FINKEL, Lawrence S. 1925-

PERSONAL: Born September 18, 1925, in New York, N.Y.; son of Jack S. and Anne (Moskowitz) Finkel; married Elaine Powers, June 29, 1948; children: Janet, Robert. *Education:* City University of New York, B.S., 1949; Columbia University, M.A., 1950, and graduate study. *Religion:* Jewish. *Home:* 22 Trinity Ave., Spring Valley, N.Y. *Office:* 40 Cedar St., Dobbs Ferry, N.Y.

CAREER: New York City (N.Y.) Board of Education, 1949—, began as teacher, became assistant principal, later administrative assistant; City College of the City University of New York, New York, N.Y., 1959—, began as lecturer, became associate professor. Owner-director of Blue Hill Day Camp, Rockland County, N.Y. Educational consultant to Oceana Publications, Inc. *Military service:* U.S. Army, Infantry, 1943-46; served in Europe; became technical sergeant. *Member:* National Education Association, American Association of School Administrators, American Association for Health, Physical Education and Recreation, National Association for Supervision and Curriculum Development (member of board of directors), New York State Association for Supervision and Curriculum Development (treasurer, 1962-63; second vice-president, 1964; first vice-president, 1965; president, 1967), New York Society for Experimental Study of Education, Phi Delta Kappa.

WRITINGS: (With Ruth Krawitz) *How to Study*, Oceana, 1964; (editor with Krawitz) Diane Gess, *Its Really Up to You: You and Smoking*, Random House, 1973; *Learning English as a Second Language*, six volumes, Oceana, 1973. Contributor to *New Book of Knowledge*.

WORK IN PROGRESS: Beginning series of reading texts.

SIDELIGHTS: Finkel is fluent in French. *Avocational interests:* Reading, outdoor sports (worked way through college as lifeguard and instructor in horseback riding).

* * *

FINKELSTEIN, Louis 1895-

PERSONAL: Born June 14, 1895, in Cincinnati, Ohio; son of Simon J. (a rabbi) and Hannah (Brager) Finkelstein; married Carmel Bentwich, March 5, 1922; children: Hadassah Nita (Mrs. Philip J. Davis), Ezra Michael, Faith (Mrs. H. Jacob Katzenstein). *Education:* City College (now City College of the City University of New York), A.B., 1915; Columbia University, Ph.D., 1918; Jewish Theological Seminary of America, Rabbi and M.H.L., 1919. *Office:* Jewish Theological Seminary of America, 3080 Broadway, New York, N.Y. 10027.

CAREER: Congregation Kehilath Israel, New York, N.Y., rabbi, 1919-31; Jewish Theological Seminary of America, New York, N.Y., instructor in Talmud, 1920-24, Solomon Schechter Lecturer in Theology, 1924-30, professor of theology, 1931—, assistant to president, 1934-37, provost, 1937-40, president, 1940-51, chancellor, 1951-1972, chancellor emeritus, 1972—. Ingersoll lecturer, Harvard University, 1943-44. Religious adviser to President of United States, 1940-45. *Member:* Rabbinical Assembly of America (president, 1928-30), American Academy of Jewish Research (fellow; member of executive committee; president), Jewish Academy of Arts and Sciences (fellow), American Academy of Arts and Sciences (fellow), Conference on Science, Philosophy and Religion (president, 1940—), Phi Beta Kappa. *Awards, honors:* Phi Epsilon Pi National Service Award, 1952; S.T.D., Columbia University; Litt.D., Boston University; L.H.D., Dropsie College, Hebrew Union College, Woodstock College; LL.D., Temple University, Fordham University, Southeastern Massachusetts Technological Institute, Manhattan College; D.D., Yale University; D.S.T., New York University.

WRITINGS: Jewish Self-Government in the Middle Ages, Jewish Theological Society, 1924, 2nd edition, Philip Feldheim, 1964; (editor) *Kimchi's Commentary on Isaiah*, Columbia University Press, 1926; (editor) *Sifre on Deuteronomy*, Jewish Publication Society, Volume I, 1936, Volume II, 1937; *Akiba—Scholar, Saint, Martyr*, Covici Friede, 1936; *The Pharisees, The Sociological Background of Their Faith*, Jewish Publication Society, 1938; *Beliefs and Practices of Judaism*, Devin, 1941, revised edition, 1945; (with others) *Religions of Democracy*, Devin, 1941; (with others) *Faith for Today*, Doubleday, 1941; (editor) *American Spiritual Autobiographies*, Harper, 1948; *The Pharisees and the Men of the Great Synagogue*, Jewish Theological Seminary, 1950; (editor) *Saadia Gaon Abot of Rabbi Nathan*, Jewish Theological Seminary, 1950; (editor) *Thirteen Americans*, Harper, 1953; *Sifra, or Torat Kohanim According to Codex Assermani LXVI*, Jewish Theological Seminary, 1956; (editor) *The Jews: Their History, Culture and Religion*, three volumes, Harper, 1949, 3rd edition published in two volumes, Harper, 1960; *New Light from the Prophets*, Valentine, Mitchell, 1969; *Social Responsibility in the Age of Revolution*, Jewish Theological Seminary, 1971; *Pharisaism in the Making* (selected essays), Ktav, 1972.

Co-editor, *Science, Philosophy and Religion Annual Symposia*, 1942—. Member of editorial board, *Universal Jewish Encyclopedia*. Contributor to Jewish and other religious journals.

* * *

FINLAY, Matthew Henderson 1916-

PERSONAL: Born December 28, 1916, in Frankton, New Zealand; son of Benjamin Matthew and Stella (Grigg) Finlay; married Gladys Maynel Greening, April 14, 1945; children: Robert Wallace, Graeme John, Naomi Maynel. *Home:* 59 Hillsborough Rd., Auckland 4, New Zealand.

CAREER: Christian missionary in Singapore, Malaysia, working particularly among Muslims, beginning 1946; currently New Zealand secretary for Scripture Gift Mission, London, England.

WRITINGS: By Launch to Indonesian Isles, Pickering & Inglis, 1954; *Twelve Indonesian Adventures*, Pickering & Inglis, 1960; *The Arrows of the Almighty* (devotional book), Moody, 1963; *The Lim Family of Singapore*, Pickering & Inglis, 1965. Writer of booklets published in English and foreign languages.

SIDELIGHTS: Finlay's first two books are accounts of missionary work in the Rhio Archipelago, Indonesia. His booklets for Muslims have been translated into Turkish, Urdu, Hindi, Kannarese, Indonesian, Arabic, Persian, and Malayalam.

* * *

FINN, Reginald Patrick Arthur Welldon   1900-
(R. Welldon Finn, Rex Welldon Finn)

PERSONAL: Born March 14, 1900, in Sandbach, Cheshire, England; son of Sidney Wallace (a schoolmaster) and Amy Laura (Chapman) Finn; married Phyllis Ward, April 20, 1926; children: Seumas Vidal. *Education:* Attended Rossall School, Fleetwood, Lancashire, England, 1915-20, and Peterhouse, Cambridge, 1922-23. *Politics:* Independent. *Religion:* Roman Catholic. *Home:* Tigeen, Old Parsonage Way, Frinton-on-Sea, Essex, England. *Agent:* David Higham Associates Ltd., 76 Dean St., London W. 1, England.

CAREER: Christophers Ltd. (publishers), London, England, assistant, 1924-27; Alfred A. Knopf, Inc. (publishers), London, England, manager, 1927-29; William Heinemann Ltd. (publishers), London, England, manager, 1929-46; Macdonald & Co. Ltd. (publishers), London, England, manager, 1947-51; free-lance editor, 1951-55; University College, University of London, London, England, research post, 1955-58, 1964—; also editor for printing and publishing firm. *Military service:* Royal Air Force, 1941-45; became squadron leader.

WRITINGS: Wiltshire, Allen & Unwin, 1930; (editor) John Galsworthy, *Galsworthy Octave*, Heinemann, 1932; *Do You Want a Dog?* Country Life, 1933; *The Pups I Bought*, Country Life, 1933; *Man and His Conquest of England*, Heinemann, 1936; *The English Heritage*, Heinemann, 1937, Reynal & Hitchcock, 1938, revised edition, Macdonald & Co., 1948; *Scottish Heritage*, Heinemann, 1938; (with A. J. W. Hill) *And So Was England Born*, Heinemann, 1939; *Introducing Ireland*, Museum Press, 1955; *The Domesday Inquest and the Making of the Domesday Book*, Longmans, Green, 1961; *An Introduction to the Domesday Book*, Barnes & Noble, 1963; *Domesday Studies: The Liber Exoniensis*, Archon Books, 1963; (with H. C. Darby) *The Domesday Geography of South-West England*, Cambridge University Press, 1968; *Domesday Studies: The Eastern Countries*, Longmans, Green, 1968; *The Norman Conquest and Its Effect on the Economy*, Longmans, Green, 1971; *The Making and the Limitations of the Yorkshire Domesday*, St. Anthony's Press, 1972.†

* * *

FISCH, Gerald G(rant)   1922-

PERSONAL: Born April 19, 1922, in Toronto, Ontario, Canada; son of Arthur Fisch; married Jean Eleanor White, June 20, 1953; children: Susan Eleanor, Michael Gerald, Emily Elizabeth. *Education:* McGill University, B.Sc., 1944; Massachusetts Institute of Technology, S.B., 1950. *Religion:* United Church of Canada. *Office:* P. S. Ross & Partners, Place Ville Marie, Montreal, Quebec, Canada.

CAREER: Bruce Payne Associated and Canada Ltd. (management consulting firm), New York, N.Y., vice-president, 1955-57; P. S. & Partners (management consultants), Montreal, Quebec, managing partner, 1958—. Touche, Ross, Bailey & Smart (chartered accountants), principal and director of management services, Montreal, Quebec, and chairmen of international management consulting committee.

MEMBER: Engineering Institute of Canada, Society of Industrial and Cost Accountants of Canada, American Management Association, Canadian Association of Management Consultants (secretary, 1964-65), Society for Advancement of Management, Corporation of Professional Engineers of Quebec, Association of Professional Engineers of the Province of Ontario, Montreal Board of Trade, Board of Trade of Metropolitan Toronto, Canadian Club, University Club (Montreal and New York); Saint James' Club and Royal St. Lawrence Yacht Club (both Montreal); Stamford Yacht Club (Stamford, Conn.).

WRITINGS: Organization for Profit: Management for the Age of Technology, McGraw, 1964. Contributor to *Harvard Business Review* and other periodicals.

SIDELIGHTS: Fisch speaks French. *Avocational interests:* Sailing and skiing.†

* * *

FISCHMAN, Leonard L(ipman)   1919-

PERSONAL: Born January 23, 1919, in Brooklyn, N.Y.; married Evelyn R. Kay (an economist), April 18, 1958. *Education:* New York University, A.B., 1937; The American University, M.A., 1939. *Home:* 520 22nd St. N.W., Washington, D.C. 20037. *Office:* Resources for the Future, Inc., 1755 Massachusetts Ave. N.W., Washington, D.C. 20036.

CAREER: U.S. Bureau of the Census, Washington, D.C., assistant operation head, population and housing division, 1940-41; United Nations Relief and Rehabilitation Administration, Italy Mission, Rome, chief of statistics and special studies branch, 1946-47; U.S. Department of Commerce, Office of International Trade, Washington, D.C., economist and acting chief of Mediterranean Section, 1948-50; U.S. Bureau of Mines, Washington, D.C., international and business economist, 1950-53; Puerto Rico Economic Development Administration, San Juan, economic consultant, 1953-58; Economic Associates, Washington, D.C., economic consultant and director, 1958-74; Resources for the Future, Inc., Washington, D.C., senior research associate, 1973—. *Military service:* U.S. Army, 1941-46; served in Italy; became warrant officer junior grade.

MEMBER: American Economic Association, American Statistical Association, American Association for the Advancement of Science (fellow), National Association of Business Economists, Association for Evolutionary Economics, National Planning Association, American Academy of Political and Social Science, Society for International Development, Washington Planning and Housing Association, International Club (Washington, D.C.), National Economists Club.

WRITINGS: (Editor) *Minerals Yearbook*, U.S. Bureau of Mines, 1950; (with Hans H. Landsberg and Joseph L. Fisher) *Resources in America's Future*, Johns Hopkins Press, 1963; (with others) *The Economic Potential of the Mineral and Botanical Resources of the U.S. Continental Shelf and Slope*, National Technical Information Service, 1968; (contributor) Ronald G. Ridker, editor, *Population, Resources, and the Environment*, U.S. Government Printing Office, 1972.

SIDELIGHTS: Fischman speaks Spanish; he reads Spanish, French, Italian.

FISH, Robert L.   1912-
(Robert L. Pike)

PERSONAL: Born August 21, 1912, in Cleveland, Ohio; son of David and Sarah (Osserman) Fish; married Mamie Kates, December 26, 1935; children: Ruth (Mrs. David Stillson), Catherine Ann. *Education:* Case Institute of Technology (now Case Western Reserve University), B.S., 1933. *Politics:* Independent. *Religion:* Jewish. *Home:* 143 Sterling Rd., Trumbull, Conn. 06611. *Agent:* Robert Mills, 156 East 52nd St., New York, N.Y. 10022.

CAREER: Consulting engineer to the plastics industry. Consulting engineer to plastics industry in Brazil, 1952-62. *Member:* Society of Plastics Engineers, Mystery Writers of America, Authors Guild, Crime Club of England. *Awards, honors:* Edgar Allan Poe Award from Mystery Writers of America, 1962, for *The Fugitive*, 1963, for *Isle of the Snakes*, and for short story, "Moonlight Gardner."

WRITINGS: The Fugitive, Simon & Schuster, 1962; *Isle of the Snakes*, Simon & Schuster, 1963; (completed from notes of Jack London) *Assassination Bureau*, McGraw, 1963; (under pseudonym Robert L. Pike) *Mute Witness*, Doubleday, 1963; *Shrunken Head*, Simon & Schuster, 1963; (under pseudonym Robert L. Pike) *The Quarry*, Doubleday, 1964; *Brazilian Sleigh Ride*, Simon & Schuster, 1965; *The Diamond Bubble*, Simon & Schuster, 1965; (under pseudonym Robert L. Pike) *The Police Blotter*, Doubleday, 1965; *The Incredible Schlock Homes*, Simon & Schuster, 1966; *Always Kill a Stranger*, Putnam, 1967; *The Hochmann Miniatures*, New American Library, 1967; *The Murder League*, Simon & Schuster, 1968; *The Bridge that Went Nowhere*, Putnam, 1968; (editor and author of foreword) *With Malice Toward All: An Anthology of Mystery Stories*, Putnam, 1968; *The Xavier Affair*, Putnam, 1969.

Whirligig, New American Library, 1970; (under pseudonym Robert L. Pike) *Reardon*, 1970; *Rub-A-Dub-Dub*, Simon & Schuster, 1971, published as *Death Cuts the Deck*, Ace Books, 1972; *The Green Hill Treasure*, Putnam, 1971; *The Tricks of the Trade*, Putnam, 1972; (under pseudonym Robert L. Pike) *The Gremlin's Grampa*, Doubleday, 1972; (with Henry Rothblatt) *A Handy Death*, Simon & Schuster, 1973; *The Wager*, Putnam, 1974; (under pseudonym Robert L. Pike) *Bank Job*, Doubleday, 1974; *Trouble in Paradise*, Doubleday, 1974. Also author, with Bob Thomas, of *Weekend 33*, Doubleday. Author, with Arthur Marx, of play "The Chic Life," produced in Westport, Conn., at Westport Country Playhouse, June 30, 1969. Contributor of short stories to *Ellery Queen's Mystery Magazine, Saint, Argosy,* and *Fantasy and Science Fiction.*

SIDELIGHTS: Martha Liddy describes *Whirligig* as "a light, zestful mystery filled with international intrigue.... Frolicsome characters in a series of dashing settings, daring deeds and happy endings." Fish wrote on the subject of formulating plots for novels that "writers get their ideas from various sources, and it is impossible to set down any rigid rules for unearthing plots. My own favorite method ... is to dream up some inexplicable occurrence. For example: A man is murdered for a package which contains nothing but a dead coral snake.... Now, having established the illogical nature of the situation, the idea is to proceed to explain it in a manner that not only defends the logic of the seemingly illogical situation, but proves it to be inevitable. Out of the explanation, a book evolves."

The motion picture "Bullitt," Warner Brothers Studio-Seven Arts Productions Ltd., 1968, was based on *Mute Witness*; *The Assassination Bureau* was made into a motion picture with the same title, Paramount Pictures Corp., 1969. Fish speaks Spanish and Portuguese; he lived abroad for a total of twelve years in Brazil, Argentina, England, Spain, and other countries.

*   *   *

FISHER, Ernest Arthur   1887-

PERSONAL: Born April 4, 1887, in Oxford, England; son of Walter John (an organ builder) and Emily Jane (Manning) Fisher; married Amy Bertha Phillips, August 14, 1915; children: Hilary Joan (Mrs. Albert Leonard Tanner). *Education:* Balliol College, Oxford, B.A. (first class honors in chemistry), 1911, M.A., 1914, B.Sc., 1919; University of London, D.Sc., 1928. *Home:* The Cottage, Akeley near Buckingham, England.

CAREER: University of London, Wye College, London, England, assistant lecturer in chemistry, 1911-14; Rothamsted Experimental Station, Harpenden, England, physical chemist, 1919-20; University of Leeds, Leeds, England, lecturer in textile chemistry, 1920-24; Research Association of British Flour Millers, St. Albans, England, director, 1924-39; Board of Trade, London, England, principal, 1941-49. Consultant to Albright and Wilson (chemical manufacturers), 1939-40; director of Wyndham & Phillips Ltd. (pipe manufacturers), 1949-54. *Military service:* British Army, Royal Garrison Artillery, 1915-19; became lieutenant. *Member:* Royal Institute of Chemistry (former fellow), Institute of Physics (former fellow), British Association for the Advancement of Science (member of general committee), Royal Institute of Philosophy, Buckinghamshire Architectural and Archaeological Society.

WRITINGS: Flour Quality: Its Nature and Control, National Joint Industrial Council for the Flour Milling Industry, 1935; (with C. R. Jones) *The Wheats of Commerce*, two volumes, National Joint Industrial Council for the Flour Milling Industry, 1938; *An Introduction to Anglo-Saxon Architecture and Sculpture*, Faber, 1959; *The Greater Anglo-Saxon Churches: An Architectural Historical Study*, Faber, 1962; *Anglo-Saxon Towers: An Architectural Historical Study*, David & Charles, 1969; *The Saxon Churches of Sussex*, David & Charles, 1970. Author of about forty research papers published in agriculture, chemistry, and textile journals.

*   *   *

FISHER, Laura Harrison   1934-

PERSONAL: Born May 11, 1934, in Malad, Idaho; daughter of Parry Dredge (a farmer) and Laura (Wells) Harrison; married Roger D. Fisher (a college professor), December 19, 1955 (died March 6, 1972); married Gerhard R. Herbst (a college professor), January 1, 1974; children: (first marriage) Cari, Paul Roger, Eric Don, Scott. *Education:* Brigham Young University, B.A., 1956; University of Wyoming, M.A., 1973. *Religion:* Church of Jesus Christ of Latter-day Saints. *Home:* 168 Corthell Rd., Laramie, Wyo. 82070.

CAREER: Librarian, having worked in both public and school libraries for children; University of Wyoming, Laramie, now librarian at University School and Educational Center. *Member:* American Library Association, National Education Association, Wyoming Education Association, Kappa Delta Pi.

WRITINGS—Children's books: Amy and the Sorrel

Summer, Holt, 1964; *You Were the Princess Last Time!*, Holt, 1965; *Never Try Nathaniel*, Holt, 1968; *Charlie Dick*, Holt, 1972. Author of short stories for children. Contributor to professional journals.

SIDELIGHTS: Laura Fisher told *CA:* "Always interested in writing, I discovered an exciting field when looking for books for my own children. Much of the background and setting for my books I have taken from my own experiences . . . in rural communities in Utah, Idaho, and Wyoming."

* * *

FISHER, Miriam Louise (Scharfe) 1939-

PERSONAL: Born March 26, 1939, in Indianapolis, Ind.; daughter of Robert Frederick (a machinist) and Pauline (Daum) Scharfe; married Richard A. Fisher (a pharmacist), December 23, 1961; children: Christine Jo, Rebecca Anne. *Education:* Butler University, B.S., 1961. *Religion:* Baptist. *Home:* 5058 West 15th St., Indianapolis, Ind.

CAREER: Elementary teacher in Indianapolis, Ind., public schools, 1961-62. *Member:* Phi Kappa Phi, Mortar Board.

WRITINGS: Pamela Goes to School, Seale, 1962.

* * *

FISHER, Walter R. 1931-

PERSONAL: Born January 4, 1931, in Honolulu, Hawaii; son of Stephen G. (a writer) and Emily Fisher; married Shirley Hawkins, November 27, 1952; children: Beverly Joann, Roxanne. *Education:* San Diego State College (now San Diego State University), B.A., 1956, M.A., 1957; University of Iowa, Ph.D., 1960. *Office:* University of Southern California, Los Angeles, Calif.

CAREER: Boyden School, San Diego, Calif., teacher of speech, English, and history, 1956-57; University of Iowa, Iowa City, teacher of communication skills, 1957-60; California State College at Los Angeles (now California State University, Los Angeles), teacher of speech, 1960-65; University of Southern California, Los Angeles, assistant professor, 1965-66, associate professor, 1966-71, professor of speech, 1971—. *Military service:* U.S. Marine Corps, 1948-52. U.S. Air Force Reserve, 1956-61; became first lieutenant. *Member:* International Communication Association, American Forensic Association, Speech Communication Association, The Rhetoric Society, American Association of University Professors, Western Speech Communication Association.

WRITINGS: (Editor with Richard Dean Burns) *Armament and Disarmament: The Continuing Dispute*, Wadsworth, 1964; (contributor) G. R. Miller and T. R. Nilsen, editors, *Perspectives on Argumentation: A Book of Essays*, Scott, Foresman, 1966; (editor with James H. McBath) *British Public Addresses, 1828-1960*, Houghton, 1971. Contributor to five speech journals.

WORK IN PROGRESS: A book, *Rhetoric: A Tradition in Transition*, for Michigan State University Press.

* * *

FISKE, Roger E(lwyn) 1910-

PERSONAL: Born September 11, 1910, in Surbiton, Surrey, England; son of William Elwyn (a schoolmaster) and Helen (Ramsay) Fiske; married Elizabeth Sadler, July 17, 1939; children: Catherine, Alison, Veronica, John, Sarah. *Education:* Oxford University, B.A. (honors in English), 1932, D.Mus., 1937; Royal College of Music, London, England, A.R.C.M., 1935. *Politics:* Liberal. *Religion:* Church of England. *Home:* Kitty Crag, Ambleside, Cumbria, England.

CAREER: Schoolmaster in East Grinstead, England, 1932-39; British Broadcasting Corp., London, England, sound engineer, 1939-46, producer of educational broadcasts, 1946-53, producer in music department, 1953-59; *Gramophone*, London, England, critic, 1955—. Composer of children's music for British Broadcasting Corp. radio and television, of chamber music and songs for adult performance. Member, Arts Council Music Panel, 1960-64. *Member:* Royal Music Association, Incorporated Society of Musicians.

WRITINGS: Beethoven's Last Quartets, Oxford University Press, 1940; *Listening to Music*, Harrap, 1952; *Ballet Music*, Harrap, 1958; (with J.P.B. Dobbs) *Oxford School Music Books*, eight books, Oxford University Press, 1954-61; *Score Reading*, four volumes, Oxford University Press, 1958-64; (with others) *Shakespeare in Music*, Macmillan, 1964; *Beethoven's Concertos and Overtures*, British Broadcasting Corporation, 1970; *English Theatre Music in the Eighteenth Century*, Oxford University Press, 1973. General editor, Eulenburg Miniature Scores, 1969. Contributor to Pelican books, *Chamber Music* and *Choral Music* and to "Musica Britannica" series. Music editor, *Opera da Camera*, 1967—.

WORK IN PROGRESS: A book about Scotland's influence on music in London and on the continent.

AVOCATIONAL INTERESTS: Walking in England's Lake District.

* * *

FITCH, Lyle C(raig) 1913-

PERSONAL: Born May 22, 1913, in Merriman, Neb.; son of Fred B. and Frances (Logsdon) Fitch; married Violet Vaughn, September 4, 1937; children: Devin, Linda (Mrs. Peter Andrews). *Education:* Nebraska State Teachers College (now Chadron State Teachers College), B.S., 1935; University of Nebraska, M.A., 1937; Columbia University, Ph.D., 1942. *Religion:* Protestant. *Home:* 121 Red Hill Rd., Princeton, N.J. 08540. *Office:* Institute of Public Administration, 55 West 44th St., New York, N.Y. 10021.

CAREER: Wesleyan University, Middletown, Conn., assistant professor, 1946-50; Mayor's Committee on Management Survey, New York, N.Y., staff, 1950-52; Columbia University, New York, N.Y., associate professor of economics, 1953-54; City of New York, N.Y., senior management consultant, fiscal and economic research, Division of Administration, 1954-56, deputy city administrator, 1957-60, city administrator, 1961; Institute of Public Administration, New York, N.Y., president, 1961—. Consultant to U.S. government agencies, including U.S. Department of Commerce, 1961, to governments or government agencies in Nigeria, Peru, Venezuela, and India, to United Nations, 1964, and to Committee for Economic Development. Member of Advisory Commission on Intergovernmental Relations. *Member:* American Political Science Association, American Society for Public Administration, Institut International de Finances Publiques, Tax Institute of America.

WRITINGS: (Editor with Horace Taylor) *Planning for Jobs*, Blakiston, 1946; *Taxing Municipal Bond Income*, University of California, 1950; (with Haig and Shoup) *The*

Financial Problem of the City of New York, 1952; (with Shoup and others) *The Fiscal System of Venezuela*, Johns Hopkins Press, 1958; *Urban Transportation and Public Policy*, Chandler Publishing, 1964; (editor with Annmarie Hauck Walsh) *Agenda for a City: Issues Confronting New York*, Sage, 1970. Contributor to *Encyclopaedia Britannica* and to journals.

SIDELIGHTS: Fitch reads Spanish and German. As United Nations consultant he traveled to Yugoslavia, Sweden, Poland, and Soviet Russia in 1964; he also has traveled in Africa, South America, and India on consultant work.†

* * *

FITZELL, John 1922-

PERSONAL: Born March 22, 1922, in New York, N.Y.; son of Henry John (an investment banker) and Catherine (Cooley) Fitzell; married Ilse Pracht; children: Dorrit Elisabeth, Edward George; Ilse Dunn, William Dunn (stepchildren). *Education:* Princeton University, B.A., 1949, A.M., 1953, Ph.D., 1954. *Politics:* Republican. *Religion:* Protestant. *Home:* 46 Ridgeview Rd., Jamesburg, N.J.

CAREER: With U.S. Information Service, Austria, 1945-47; Peddie School, Hightstown, N.J., master of German and Latin, 1949-52; Princeton University, Princeton, N.J., instructor in German, 1952-54; Williams College, Williamstown, Mass., instructor in German, 1954-57; Rutgers, The State University, New Brunswick, N.J., assistant professor, 1957-62, associate professor of German literature, 1962—. *Military service:* U.S. Army, 26th Division, 1942-45; received Bronze Star Medal, five battle stars. *Member:* Modern Language Association of America, American Association of Teachers of German (vice-president, New Jersey chapter, 1961-63), Wilhelm Busch Society (Hanover, Germany).

WRITINGS: The Hermit in German Literature from Goethe to Eichendorff, University of North Carolina Press, 1961. Contributor to *German Quarterly, Die Deutsche Lyrik*, and *Lyrica Germanica*.

WORK IN PROGRESS: A study on Wilhelm Busch; translations of German poems, with essays; writing on folklore in poetry.

AVOCATIONAL INTERESTS: Opera; playing banjo and classical guitar.

* * *

FITZHARDINGE, Joan Margaret 1912-
(Joan Phipson)

PERSONAL: Born November 16, 1912, in Warrawee, New South Wales, Australia; married Colin Hardinge Fitzhardinge; children: one son, one daughter. *Education:* Frensham School, Mittagong, New South Wales, Australia. *Home:* Wongalong, Mandurama, New South Wales 2792, Australia. *Agent:* A. P. Watt & Son, 10 Norfolk St., Strand, London W.C.2, England.

CAREER: Author of children's books. *Member:* Australian Society of Authors. *Awards, honors:* Children's Book Council of Australia Book of the Year Award for *Good Luck to the Rider*, 1953, and *The Family Conspiracy*, 1963; Boys' Clubs of America Junior Book Award for *The Boundary Riders*, 1963; *New York Herald Tribune* Children's Spring Book Festival Award for *The Family Conspiracy*, 1964.

WRITINGS—All under pseudonym Joan Phipson: *Good Luck to the Rider*, Angus & Robertson, 1952, Harcourt, 1968; *Six and Silver*, Angus & Robertson, 1954; *It Happened One Summer*, Angus & Robertson, 1957; *The Boundary Riders*, Harcourt, 1962; *The Family Conspiracy*, Harcourt, 1962; *Threat to the Barkers*, Harcourt; 1963; *Birkin*, Lothian, 1965, Harcourt, 1966; *A Lamb in the Family*, Hamish Hamilton, 1966; *The Crew of the Merlin*, Constable, published as *Cross Currents*, Harcourt, 1967; *Peter and Butch*, Harcourt, 1969; *The Haunted Night*, Harcourt, 1970; *Bass and Billy Martin*, Macmillan of Australia, 1972; *The Way Home*, Atheneum, 1973; *Horse with Eight Hands*, Atheneum, 1974; *Polly's Tiger*, Dutton, 1974.†

* * *

FITZSIMONS, M(athew) A(nthony) 1912-

PERSONAL: Born July 1, 1912, in New York, N.Y.; son of Andrew (a watchman) and Helen (Murray) Fitzsimons; married Frances M. Schlosser, September 8, 1937; children: Robert B., Carol Ann Fitzsimons Baker, Gerald Aidan (deceased), David M. *Education:* Columbia University, B.A., 1934, M.A., 1938; Oriel College, Oxford, B.A., 1937; University of Chicago, Ph.D., 1947. *Home:* 3109 McKinley, South Bend, Ind. 46615. *Office:* Department of History, University of Notre Dame, Notre Dame, Ind. 46556.

CAREER: University of Notre Dame, Notre Dame, Ind., 1937—, began as instructor, became professor of history, 1955—. *Member:* American Historical Association, Catholic Commission on Intellectual and Cultural Affairs, Midwest Conference on British Historical Studies, Phi Beta Kappa.

WRITINGS: (With James Corbett) *Christianity and Civilization*, Sadlier, 1947; *Foreign Policy of British Labour Government, 1945-51*, University of Notre Dame Press, 1953; (editor with Waldemar Gurian) *The Catholic Church and World Affairs*, University of Notre Dame Press, 1954; (editor with Charles E. Nowell and Alfred G. Pundt) *The Development of Historiography*, Stackpole, 1955; (editor with Stephen D. Kertesz) *Diplomacy in a Changing World*, University of Notre Dame Press, 1959; (editor with Kertesz) *What America Stands For*, University of Notre Dame Press, 1959; (editor with Frank O'Malley and Thomas T. McAvoy) *The Image of Man: A Review of Politics Reader*, University of Notre Dame Press, 1959; *Empire by Treaty*, University of Notre Dame Press, 1964; (editor) *The Catholic Church Today: Western Europe*, University of Notre Dame Press, 1969. Publications director of Notre Dame Committee on International Relations, 1951-59; editor, *Review of Politics*, 1955-74.

WORK IN PROGRESS: Two books, *World History—World Cultures*, and *Man, Time, the Past, and History*; a study of eighteen great historians; studies in modern British history.

SIDELIGHTS: Fitzsimons has a reading knowledge of French, German, Spanish, and Latin.

* * *

FIXLER, Michael 1927-

PERSONAL: Born August 14, 1927, in Kisvarda, Hungary; son of Solomon (a rabbi) and Gizella (Stern) Fixler; married, 1949; children: David N., Jonathan Claude, Jessica Ann. *Education:* University of Wisconsin, A.B., 1948; Oxford University, B.A., 1954, M.A., 1959; University of

Chicago, Ph.D., 1961. *Home:* 55 Fletcher St., Winchester, Mass.

CAREER: Northwestern University, Evanston, Ill., instructor in English, 1957-61; Tufts University, Medford, Mass., assistant professor, 1961-64, associate professor, 1964-68, professor of English, 1968—. Visiting scholar, Divinity School of Harvard University, 1967. *Member:* Modern Language Association of America, Renaissance Society of America, Milton Society. *Awards, honors:* Danforth Foundation grant, 1959-60; American Council of Learned Societies grant-in-aid, 1965; Cross-Disciplinary Award from Society for Religion in Higher Education, 1967.

WRITINGS: Milton and the Kingdoms of God, Northwestern University Press, 1964; (contributor) Irving Maun, editor, *Critical Views of Isaac Bashevis Singer*, New York University Press, 1969; (contributor) Thomas Kranidas, editor, *New Essays on Paradise Lost*, University of California Press, 1969; (editor) *The Mentor Bible: A Literary Abridgement of The King James Version of the Old and New Testament*, New American Library, 1973. Staff writer, *American People's Encyclopedia*, 1957. Contributor to *The Milton Encyclopedia*, 1974; contributor to *Commentary, Kenyon Review*, and *Milton Studies*. Poetry editor, *Chicago Review*, 1955-56, member of editorial board, *Milton Studies*, 1969—.

WORK IN PROGRESS: A book, *The Cryptic Muse: Studies in Milton's Symbolic Structures.*

SIDELIGHTS: Fixler is competent in French, German, and Hebrew. *Avocational interests:* Anthropology, art.

*   *   *

FLANAGAN, Joseph David Stanislaus   1903- (Father M. Raymond)

PERSONAL: Born November 29, 1903, in Roxbury, Mass.; son of Patrick John and Mary Brigid (Meaney) Flanagan. *Education:* Studied at St. Stanislaus Seminary, 1920-22, St. Andrew Normal, 1922-24, Weston College, 1924-27, St. Mary's College, St. Mary's, Kan., 1934; Boston College, A.B. and A.M.; Gregorian University, Rome, Italy, S.T.L. *Home:* Abbey of Gethsemani, Trappist, Ky.

CAREER: Entered Roman Catholic order, Society of Jesus (Jesuits), 1920, ordained to priesthood, 1933; became member of Order of Cistercians of the Strict Observance (Trappist monk), 1936, now censor of books for order. College of the Holy Cross, Worcester, Mass., assistant dean of men and professor of rhetoric, 1927-35, professor of theology, 1935-36, director of debate and public speaking, 1928-30; Gethsemani College, Trappist, Ky., professor of canon law, 1952-54.

WRITINGS: The Man Who Got Even with God, Bruce, 1941; *The Family that Overtook Christ*, Kenedy, 1942; *Three Religious Rebels*, Kenedy, 1944; *Burnt Out Incense*, Kenedy, 1949; *Trappists, the Reds and You*, Gethsemani Press, 1949.

All published by Bruce: *God Goes to Murderer's Row*, 1951; *A New Way of the Cross*, 1952; *The Less Traveled Road*, 1953; *Love Does Such Things*, 1955; *God, A Woman, and the Way*, 1955; *These Women Walked with God*, 1956; *You*, 1957; *This is Your To-morrow and Today*, 1959.

Now!, Bruce, 1961; *Your Hour*, Bruce, 1962; *This Is Love*, Bruce, 1963; *The Mysteries in Your Life*, Bruce, 1965;

Relax and Rejoice, Culligan, 1968; *The Man for this Moment*, Alba House, 1971.

Author of more than twenty booklets (largely aimed at secular readers), published by Gethsemani Press, 1939-46.

*   *   *

FLANNERY, Edward H(ugh)   1912-

PERSONAL: Born August 20, 1912, in Providence, R.I.; son of John (a policeman) and Elizabeth (Mulvey) Flannery. *Education:* St. Charles College, Catonsville, Md., student, 1929-31; Seminaire St. Sulpice, Paris, France, A.B., 1935, S.T.L., 1936; Catholic University of America, advanced study, 1936-37. *Politics:* Independent. *Home:* 175 Dean St., Providence, R.I. 02903.

CAREER: Ordained Roman Catholic priest, 1937. *Providence Visitor*, Providence, R.I., editor, 1958—. St. Margaret's Home, Providence, R.I., chaplain. Seton Hall University, staff member of Judaeo-Christian Institute, Newark, N.J., 1950—. Rhode Island Association for Mental Health, member of board of directors, 1961—.

WRITINGS: (Translator) Maritain, *Essay on Christian Philosophy*, Philosophical Library, 1955; (translator) Mauriac, *Words of Faith*, Philosophical Library, 1956; *The Anguish of the Jews*, Macmillan, 1965. Contributor to *Bridge* (yearbook of Judaeo-Christian Studies).

WORK IN PROGRESS: A book on psychology and religion.

SIDELIGHTS: Flannery speaks French, Latin, and German.†

*   *   *

FLETCHER, Colin   1922-

PERSONAL: Born March 14, 1922, in Cardiff, Wales; became United States citizen, 1974; son of Herbert Reginald and Margaret Elizabeth (Williams) Fletcher; married twice (both marriages ending in divorce). *Education:* Attended West Buckland School, North Devon, England, 1934-39. *Residence:* Carmel Valley, Calif. *Agent:* Carl D. Brandt, Brandt and Brandt, 101 Park Ave., New York, N.Y. 10017.

CAREER: Emigrated to Kenya in 1947, working first as a manufacturer's representative in Nairobi, then as a manager of a hotel in Kitale, 1947-48; farmed near Nakuru, Kenya, 1948-52, turned road builder on a tea estate near Inyanga, Southern Rodesia, 1952-53; returned to England briefly before crossing the Atlantic as a herdsman for a planeload of cattle; prospected and helped lay out roads for a mining company in Western Canada during the summers, 1953-56, and spent the winter writing; moved to California where he was head janitor at Polyclinic Hospital in San Francisco, 1957-58, and a department store Santa Claus; full-time writer, 1958—. *Military service:* Royal Marines, commandos, 1940-47; became captain. *Member:* Wilderness Society, National Audubon Society, Sierra Club, Nature Conservancy, Common Cause, Friends of the Earth, East African Wild Life Society, Save the Redwoods League, Planning and Conservation League, Zero Population Growth, Environmental Defense Fund, Friends of the Sea Otter.

WRITINGS: The Thousand-Mile Summer—in Desert and High Sierra, Howell-North, 1964; *The Man Who Walked Through Time*, Knopf, 1968; *The Complete Walker: The Joys and Techniques of Hiking and Backpacking*, Knopf,

1969, revised edition published as *The New Complete Walker*, 1974; *The Winds of Mara*, Knopf, 1973. Contributor to *Reader's Digest, Field and Stream*, and other magazines in the United States, Canada, Britain, and Africa.

WORK IN PROGRESS: Research on the identity and life of a man who once lived in a remote cave in the Nevada desert; a book on short wilderness walks.

SIDELIGHTS: Fletcher, describing himself as a "semi-professional bum," made a trip from London to Vancouver, in 1953, on a fare of $10, hitch-hiking from New York (where he ended his duties as a cattle-tender) to Toronto, and driving a new car west. In 1958, he made a six-month thousand-mile walk from Mexico to Oregon, and in 1963, a two-month solitary foot trip through the Grand Canyon.

Fletcher says that his current thinking, and his writing on the Grand Canyon in particular, are influenced by modern evolutionary writings, such as Pierre Teilhard de Chardin's *Phenomenon of Man*. He speaks Swahili.

* * *

FLEXNER, Stuart Berg 1928-
(Adam Fletcher, Steve Mees, Collier Santee)

PERSONAL: Born March 22, 1928, in Jacksonville, Ill.; son of David and Gertrude (Berg) Flexner; married Mimi Bogan (divorced). *Education:* University of Louisville, A.B., 1948, M.A., 1949; Cornell University, three years postgraduate study. *Politics:* Democrat. *Religion:* Jewish. *Agent:* William Morris Agency, 1740 Broadway, New York, N.Y. 10019. *Office:* Random House, Inc., 501 Madison Ave., New York, N.Y. 10022.

CAREER: Cornell University, Ithaca, N.Y., instructor, 1949-52; editor, mainly for Macmillan Co. (publishers), New York, N.Y., 1954-58; bookseller, editor, and publisher, Mexico City, Mexico, 1960-64; Random House, Inc. (publishers), New York, N.Y., editor, 1964—. Lexicographer. *Member:* Modern Language Association of America, American Dialect Society, American Civil Liberties Union, Americans for Democratic Action, Congress on Racial Equality.

WRITINGS: (Editor with Harold Wentworth) *Dictionary of American Slang*, Crowell, 1960, revised edition, 1967; (editor) *The Random House Dictionary of the English Language*, school edition, Random House, 1970; *How to Increase your Word Power*, Reader's Digest Association, 1971. Contributor of short stories, poetry, and articles to magazines.

WORK IN PROGRESS: Two novels.

SIDELIGHTS: Flexner is fluent in Spanish; has a lexicographer's knowledge of German, Anglo-Saxon, and other languages.†

* * *

FLORA, Joseph Martin 1934-

PERSONAL: Born February 9, 1934, in Toledo, Ohio; son of Raymond Dwight (a factory worker) and Frances (Ricica) Flora; married Glenda Christine Lape (a correspondence instructor), January 30, 1959; children: Ronald James, Stephen Ray. *Education:* University of Michigan, B.A., 1956, M.A., 1957, Ph.D., 1962; University of California, Berkeley, summer study, 1957. *Home:* 84 Wesley Dr., Chapel Hill, N.C. 27514. *Office:* Department of English, University of North Carolina, Chapel Hill, N.C. 27515.

CAREER: University of Michigan, Ann Arbor, instructor in English, 1961-62; University of North Carolina, Chapel Hill, instructor, 1962-64, assistant professor of English, 1964—. Duke University-University of North Carolina Cooperative Program in Humanities, assistant to chairman. *Member:* Modern Language Association of America, American Association of University Professors, South Atlantic Modern Language Association, Phi Beta Kappa.

WRITINGS: Vardis Fisher, Twayne, 1965; *William Ernest Henley*, Twayne, 1970. Contributor to *American Book Collector*.†

* * *

FLUMIANI, Carlo M(aria) 1911-

PERSONAL: Born August 15, 1911, in Trieste, Italy; son of Aurelio and Irma Flumiani; married Cristina Capprelli, 1937; children: Victor, Leo. *Education:* University of Milan, Ph.D., 1934; London School of Economics and Political Science, University of London, postdoctoral study, 1936. *Religion:* Roman Catholic. *Home:* 22 Western Ave., Gloucester, Mass.

CAREER: Harvard University fellow in France, 1938; University of Santa Clara, Santa Clara, Calif., assistant professor of political science and head of department, 1946-53; St. Joseph's College, Albuquerque, N.M., dean of School of Business Administration, 1953-56; Boston College, Chestnut Hill, Mass., associate professor of finance, 1956—. Institute for Economic and Financial Research, director. Originator of cylinder theory for investment measurement. *Member:* American Economic Association.

WRITINGS—All published by Library of Wall Street except as indicated: *The Cylinder Theory*, 1961, 2nd revised edition, 1967; *The Warning Signals*, 1963; *How to Read the Wall Street Journal for Pleasure and for Profit*, 1964; *The Technical Wall Street Encyclopedia*, 1964; *Stock Market Charting for Fun and Profit*, 1965; *The Stock Market Trading Secrets of the Late Jesse Livermore*, 1965; *Teenager's Guide to the Stock Market*, 1965; *The Wall Street Diet and Reducing Guidebook*, 1965; *The Wall Street Cook Book*, 1966; *Stock Market Games People Play to Win*, 1967; *Young People Introduction to the World of Wall Street*, 1967; *How to Develop the Creative Powers of Your Imagination*, Library of Science, 1967; *I was a Teenage Bankrupt, and How I Recouped My Loses and Made a Fortune in the Stock Market*, 1968; *How to Make a Fortune in a Bear Market*, American Classical College Press, 1972.

WORK IN PROGRESS: The Laws of History and the Will of Men, a philosophical approach to history.

SIDELIGHTS: Flumiani believes that "all human events and the course of history have a divine origin and a divine goal."†

* * *

FON EISEN, Anthony T. 1917-

PERSONAL: Born May 20, 1917, in Avon, Conn.; married Marjorie Domick, October 15, 1951; children: Michael, David. *Politics:* "Unhappy but hopeful conservatist." *Religion:* Theist. *Home:* 97 Westphal St., West Hartford, Conn.

CAREER: G. C. Heublein, Inc. (food and liquor manufacturer), Hartford, Conn., product analyst, 1945—.

WRITINGS—All juveniles: *Storm, Dog of Newfoundland*,

Scribner, 1948; *The Prince of Omeya*, World Publishing, 1964; *Bond of the Fire*, World Publishing, 1965; *The Magnificent Mongrel*, World Publishing Co., 1970. Also writer of short stories.

SIDELIGHTS: Fon Eisen told *CA:* "I am a middle-aged moralist—old enough to draw lessons from experience, and young enough, I hope, to communicate enthusiasm and conviction to youth. My only excuse is that my moralizing will be disguised in fast-moving, exciting teen-age stories."†

*   *   *

FONSECA, Aloysius Joseph   1915-

PERSONAL: Born January 16, 1915, in Karachi, India; son of Alex (a printer) and Mary (Raymond) Fonseca. *Education:* University of Madras, M.A.; Economische Hogeschool, Ph.D.; Gregorian University, Rome, Italy, L. Th. and L. Ph. *Office:* Indian Social Institute, South Extension II, D-25-1, New Delhi 16, India.

CAREER: Roman Catholic priest, member of Society of Jesus (Jesuits). Professor of industrial relations in several Jesuit colleges in India. Indian Social Institute, New Delhi, India, editor of *Social Action* (monthly). *Member:* Indian Economic Association.

WRITINGS: The Citizen and the State, 3rd edition, Indian Institute of Social Order, 1955; *A Textbook of Civics and Indian Administration*, Orient Longmans, 1961; *Wage Determination and Organized Labour in India*, Oxford University Press, 1964; (editor) *Trade and Development*, Indian Social Institute, 1968; (editor) *Challenge of Poverty in India*, Vikas Publications, 1971. Contributor to *Economic Weekly* and other journals.†

*   *   *

FONTANA, Vincent James   1923-

PERSONAL: Born November 19, 1923, in New York, N.Y.; son of John G. and Pauline (Shortino) Fontana. *Education:* Long Island College of Medicine, M.D., 1947; New York University, graduate study in allergy, 1951-52. *Home:* 87-57 96th St., Woodhaven, N.Y.

CAREER: New York Foundling Hospital, New York, N.Y., medical director, 1959—; St. Vincent's Hospital and Medical Center of New York, New York, N.Y., director of pediatrics, 1962—; private practice of pediatrics in New York, 1962—. Clinical professor of pediatrics, New York University Medical Center College of Medicine, 1954; director of pediatric allergy, Bellevue Hospital, 1959. Consultant, St. Alban's Naval Hospital and St. Mary's Hospital. *Military service:* U.S. Navy, Medical Corps, 1952-54; received Surgeon General Citation. *Member:* American Academy of Pediatrics (fellow), American Academy of Allergy (fellow), American Federation for Clinical Research, American Medical Association, Pan-American Medical Society, Harvey Society, New York Academy of Medicine (fellow), New York Allergy Society, New York County Medical Society. *Awards, honors:* Knight of Malta; Knight of Holy Sepulcher; Joey Award from Childrens' Asthma Research Institute.

WRITINGS: (Contributor) Frederic Speer, editor, *The Allergic Child*, Hoeber Medical Division, Harper, 1963; (contributor) Michael G. Wohl and Robert S. Goodhart, editors, *Modern Nutrition in Health and Disease*, Lea & Febiger, 1964; *The Maltreated Child: The Maltreatment Syndrome in Children*, C. C Thomas, 1964, 2nd edition,

1971; *Practical Management of the Allergic Child*, Appleton, 1969; *Somewhere a Child is Crying: Maltreatment—Causes and Prevention*, Macmillan, 1973; *A Parents' Guide to Child Safety*, Crowell, 1973. Contributor to annals; contributor of about thirty articles on allergies, asthma, pediatrics, and child-abuse to medical journals.

*   *   *

FORBES-BOYD, Eric   1897-

PERSONAL: Born August 29, 1897, in Addlestone, Surrey, England; son of Franklin Forbes (an army officer) and Alice Adeline (Cobb) Boyd; married Aileen Isabel Jamieson (an education assistant with the Independent Broadcasting Authority), July 28, 1940. *Education:* Privately educated in England. *Home:* 11 Lloyd Sq., London W.C.1, England.

CAREER: Writer. Lecturer on Greece in Middle Ages. *Military service:* British Army, 1916-18, 1940-45; became captain.

WRITINGS: House of Whipplestaff (novel), Hodder & Stoughton, 1925; *Merlin Hold* (novel), Jarrolds, 1927; (editor) Benjamin Disraeli, *Selections from the Novels*, Grey Walls Press, 1948; *A Stranger in These Parts* (novel), Skeffington & Sons, 1952; *The General in Retreat* (novel), Centaur Press, 1960; *In Crusader Greece* (travel book; with photographs by wife, Aileen Forbes-Boyd), Norton, 1964; *Aegean Quest* (travel book; with photographs by A. Forbes-Boyd), Norton, 1970.

Plays: "XO.3," produced in London, 1926; "Knight Errant," produced in London, 1928; *Mariposa Bung* (produced at Children's Theatre, London, 1929), Samuel French, 1929; *The Deuce* (produced at Children's Theatre, London, 1930), Samuel French, 1951; *The Seventeenth Highwayman* (produced at Children's Theatre, London, 1930), Samuel French, 1951; "Blood Royal," produced in London, 1932; "He Loves Me Not," produced in London, 1940; "Inactive Service," produced in the provinces, 1943.

Regular monthly contributor and reviewer for *Christian Science Monitor* for many years; compiler of general knowledge feature, "Do You Know?" for *Sunday Times* (London). Contributor to *Country Life*.

WORK IN PROGRESS: A novel evoking the Homeric world; a children's book; a third travel book on medieval monuments in Greek islands.

SIDELIGHTS: Forbes-Boyd told *CA:* "my chief interest lies in Greece, in the classical and Homeric Periods, and also in the Franco-Venetian Period in which I have specialized. My wife and I have made frequent visits to Greece, traveling all over central Greece, the Peloponnesus and the islands. My novels are novels of humor, with a touch of fantasy; and my plays are light comedy." His play "Knight Errant" was filmed as "The Girl in the Night."

BIOGRAPHICAL SOURCES: Christian Science Monitor, January 25, 1955.

*   *   *

FORMAN, Charles William   1916-

PERSONAL: Born December 2, 1916, in Gwalior, India; son of Henry (a missionary in India) and Sarah (Taylor) Forman; married Janice Mitchell, 1944; children: David, Sarah, Harriet. *Education:* Ohio State University, B.A. and M.A., 1938; University of Wisconsin, Ph.D., 1941; Union Theological Seminary, New York, N.Y., B.D.,

1944, S.T.M., 1947. *Home:* Downs Rd., Bethany, New Haven, Conn. 06525. *Office:* Yale Divinity School, 409 Prospect St., New Haven, Conn.

CAREER: Ordained Presbyterian minister, 1944. North India United Theological College, Saharanpur, Uttar Pradesh, teacher of church history, 1945-50; National Council of Churches, New York, N.Y., executive, 1951-53; Yale University Divinity School, New Haven, Conn., 1953—, now professor of missions. Chairman of Theological Education Fund Committee, World Council of Churches, 1965-70; United Presbyterian Church, member of Commission on Ecumenical Mission and Relations, 1963-66, chairman, 1966-69; chairman, Foundation for Theological Education in Southeast Asia, 1970—. Member of Board of Education, Bethany, Conn., 1958-67. *Member:* Association of Professors of Missions.

WRITINGS: A Christian's Handbook on Communism, National Council of Churches, 1953; *A Faith for the Nations*, Westminster, 1958; *Nation and the Kingdom*, Friendship, 1964; (editor) *Christianity in the Non-Western World*, Prentice-Hall, 1967.

* * *

FORSTER, Arnold 1912-

PERSONAL: Born June 25, 1912, in New York, N.Y.; son of Hyman L. and Dorothy (Turits) Fastenberg; married May Kasner, September 29, 1940; children: Stuart W., Jane E. *Education:* St. Johns College, LL.B., 1935. *Religion:* Jewish. *Home:* 79 Wykagyl Ter., New Rochelle, N.Y. *Office:* Anti-Defamation League of B'nai B'rith, 315 Lexington Ave., New York, N.Y.

CAREER: General counsel for Anti-Defamation League of B'nai B'rith, New York, N.Y., 1940—, and International Council of B'nai B'rith, 1960—. Justice, New York State police, 1954-57. Member of New Rochelle (N.Y.) Board of Education, 1962-65.

WRITINGS: Anti-Semitism in the United States, privately printed, 1947; *A Measure of Freedom*, Doubleday, 1950; (with Benjamin R. Epstein) *The Troublemakers*, Doubleday, 1952; (with Epstein) *Cross-Currents*, Doubleday, 1956; (with Epstein) *Some of My Best Friends....*, Farrar, Straus, (with Epstein) *Danger on the Right*, Random House, 1964; (with Epstein) *Report on the John Birch Society*, Vintage Books, 1966; (with Epstein) *The Radical Right*, Random House, 1967; *Report from Israel*, Anti-Defamation League of B'nai B'rith (New York), 1970; (with Epstein) *The New Anti-Semitism*, McGraw, 1974.

* * *

FORSTMAN, H(enry) Jackson 1929-

PERSONAL: Born June 15, 1929, in Montgomery, Ala.; son of Joseph Carl (a grocer) and Kate (Kelley) Forstman; married Shirley Cronk, June 3, 1950; children: David, Valerie, Paul. *Education:* Phillips University, A.B., 1949; Union Theological Seminary, New York, N.Y., B.D., 1956, Th.D., 1959. *Politics:* Democrat. *Home:* 3913 Kimpalong, Nashville, Tenn. 37205. *Office:* Vanderbilt University, Nashville, Tenn. 37203.

CAREER: Ordained minister, Disciples of Christ, 1952. Randolph-Macon Woman's College, Lynchburg, Va., assistant professor of religion, 1958-60; Stanford University, Stanford, Calif., assistant professor of religion, 1960-64; Vanderbilt University Divinity School, Nashville, Tenn., associate professor, 1964-68, professor of religion, 1968—,

chairman of graduate department of religion, 1969-72, acting dean of Divinity School, 1970-71. *Member:* American Society of Church History, American Academy of Religion, American Association of University Professors, Society for Religion in Higher Education, Association of Disciples for Theological Discussion. *Awards, honors:* Fulbright research fellow, Germany, 1973-74.

WRITINGS: Word and Spirit: Calvin's Doctrine of Biblical Authority, Stanford University Press, 1962; *Christian Faith and the Church*, Bethany, 1965. Contributor to *Encounter, Interpretation*, and religious periodicals.

WORK IN PROGRESS: A study of Romanticism and the origins of Protestant liberal theology.†

* * *

FOSS, Phillip Oliver

PERSONAL: Born in Maxbass, N.D.; son of Oliver Olson and Petra (Elton) Foss; married Dorothy Hansen, May 31, 1941; children: Phyliss Foss Stoner, Coral, Phillip, Jr., Thorvald. *Education:* University of Washington, Seattle, B.A., 1947; University of Oregon, M.S., 1953, Ph.D., 1956. *Home:* 3019 Moore Lane, Fort Collins, Colo. 80521. *Office:* Department of Political Science, Colorado State University, Fort Collins, Colo. 80521.

CAREER: University of Oregon, Eugene, instructor in political science, 1956-57; San Francisco State College (now San Francisco State University), San Francisco, Calif., assistant professor, 1957-61, associate professor of political science, 1961-62; Colorado State University, Fort Collins, associate professor, 1962-64, professor of political science, 1964—, chairman of department, 1964-72. *Military service:* U.S. Army Air Forces, 1942-46. U.S. Air Force, 1951-53; became lieutenant colonel. *Member:* American Society for Public Administration, American Political Science Association, Western Political Science Association (president, 1972-73), Pi Sigma Alpha. *Awards, honors:* Harris T. Guard Distinguished Service Award, Colorado State University, 1970.

WRITINGS: Politics and Grass, University of Washington Press, 1960; *Battle of Soldier Creek*, University of Alabama Press, 1961; *Reorganization in the California Highway Patrol*, University of Alabama Press, 1962; *Federal Agencies and Outdoor Recreation*, U.S. Government Printing Office, 1962; (editor) *Public Land Policy*, Colorado Associated University Press, 1969; (with Duane W. Hill) *Politics and Policies*, Wadsworth, 1970; *Recreation*, Van Nostrand, 1971; (editor) *Politics and Ecology*, Wadsworth, 1972; (editor) *Outdoor Recreation and Environmental Quality*, Colorado State University Press, 1973; (editor) *Environment and Colorado*, Colorado State University Press, 1974. Contributor to professional journals, including *Natural Resources Journal.* Member of editorial board, *Western Political Quarterly*, 1963-66.

* * *

FOUSTE, E(thel) Bonita Rutledge 1926-

PERSONAL: Surname is pronounced *Faust;* born January 20, 1926, in Costa Mesa, Calif.; daughter of Elmer Elwood (a carpenter) and Doris (Keck) Rutledge; married Dale V. Fouste, October 24, 1943; children: James Edward, Teresa Nanette. *Education:* Attended La Sierra College, 1942-43, Riverside College, 1946-47, Pomona College, 1947; Long Beach State College (now California State University, Long Beach), A.B., 1954, graduate study, 1955; University of California, Los Angeles, graduate study, 1964—. *Politics:* Republican. *Residence:* Garden Grove, Calif. 92641.

CAREER: Douglas Aircraft Corp., Long Beach, Calif., chemist, 1954-55; high school teacher of mathematics in Orange, Calif., 1955-56; free-lance writer and substitute teacher, 1956—.

WRITINGS: Adventure Westward, Concordia, 1964. Contributor of articles and short stories to juvenile magazines.

WORK IN PROGRESS: A children's mystery, *Pathway to Peril*; working on M.A. in anthropology, with intention of using field work on the Mayas as basis for a book for young people.†

*   *   *

FOWLER, Alastair (David Shaw)   1930-

PERSONAL: Born August 17, 1930, in Glasgow, Scotland; son of David (a civil servant) and Maggie (Shaw) Fowler; married Jenny Catherine Simpson (a social worker), December 23, 1950; children: Alison, David. *Education:* Attended University of Glasgow, 1947-49; University of Edinburgh, M.A. (first class honours), 1952; Pembroke College, Oxford, M.A., 1955, D.Phil., 1957. *Politics:* Labour party. *Agent:* Christopher Busby, 27 Southampton St., Strand, London, W.C.2, England. *Office:* Department of English, David Hume Tower, George Square, University of Edinburgh, Edinburgh, Scotland.

CAREER: Oxford University, Queen's College, Oxford, England, junior research fellow, 1955-59; University of Wales, University College of Swansea, Swansea, lecturer in Renaissance literature, 1959-61; Oxford University, Brasenose College, fellow and tutor in English, 1962-71; University of Edinburgh, Edinburgh, Scotland, Regius Professor of Rhetoric and English Literature, 1972—. Visiting instructor, Indiana University, 1957-58; visiting professor, University of Virginia, 1969. Member, Institute of Advanced Study, Princeton, N.J., 1966. *Awards, honors:* D.Litt., Oxford University, 1972.

WRITINGS: (Translator, and author of notes and commentary) Richard Wills, *De re poetica*, Luttrell Reprint Society, 1958; *Spenser and the Numbers of Time*, Barnes & Noble, 1964; (editor) C. S. Lewis, *Spenser's Images of Life*, Cambridge University Press, 1967; (editor with John Carey) John Milton, *The Poems of John Milton*, Longmans, Green, 1968; *Triumphal Forms: Structural Patterns in Elizabethan Poetry*, Cambridge University Press, 1970; (editor) *Silent Poetry: Essays in Numerological Analysis*, Barnes & Noble, 1970; (compiler with Ian Christopher Butler) *Topics in Criticism: An Ordered Set of Positions in Literary Theory*, Longman, 1971; *Seventeen* (poems), Sycamore Press (Oxford, England), 1971; (editor) John Milton, *Paradise Lost*, Longman, 1971. General editor of Longman Annotated Anthologies. Contributor to literary journals.

*   *   *

FOX, Alan John

PERSONAL: Born in Birmingham, England; son of Alan Leslie (a civil servant) and Gladys (Johnson) Fox; married Mary Valerie Hawkings, August 17, 1960; children: Ruth Margaret, Stephen Alan Arthur. *Education:* St. John's College, Cambridge, B.A. (second class honors), 1956, M.A., 1960. *Politics:* Conservative. *Religion:* Christian. *Home:* 11 Lynn Grove, Gorleston-on-Sea, Great Yarmouth, Norfolk, England. *Office:* College of Further Education, Lichfield Rd., Great Yarmouth, England.

CAREER: Methodist Secondary School, Uzuakoli, Nigeria, senior history master, 1956-60; British Council, assistant representative in Nyasaland (now Malawi), 1960-64; College of Further Education, Great Yarmouth, England, tutor and librarian, 1964—. Nyasaland Council of Social Service, chairman, 1963-64.

WRITINGS: (Editor) *Uzuakoli: A Short History*, Oxford University Press, 1964.†

*   *   *

FOX, David J(oseph)   1927-

PERSONAL: Born January 24, 1927, in New York, N.Y.; son of Allen (a butcher) and Sophie (Cohen) Fox; married Louise Weiss (a psychology professor), November 24, 1960; children: Amy Elizabeth, Mara Rebecca, Heather Anne, Erica Leigh. *Education:* City College (now City College of the City University of New York), B.S. in S.S., 1949, M.A., 1950; Columbia University, Ph.D., 1955. *Home:* 139 Schraalenburgh Rd., Haworth, N.J. 07641. *Office:* City College of the City University of New York, Convent Ave., New York, N.Y. 10031.

CAREER: New York (N.Y.) Board of Education, research associate, Puerto Rican Study, 1953-56; City College of the City University of New York, New York, N.Y., 1956—, began as instructor, became professor of educational research, 1965—. Visiting assistant professor, Columbia University, 1956-61. Consultant, Hunter College, New Psychoanalytic Study and Research, 1962—. Executive officer, Institute for Educational Studies and Development. *Military service:* U.S. Navy, 1945-46. *Member:* American Psychological Association, American Educational Research Association, National Education Association, National Society for the Study of Education, American Association for the Advancement of Science, Eastern Psychological Association, Phi Beta Kappa, Sigma Xi, Phi Alpha Theta, Kappa Delta Pi.

WRITINGS: (Contributor) Rubenstein and Haberstroh, editors, *Some Theories of Organization*, Irwin, 1960; *Fundamentals of Research in Nursing*, Appleton, 1966, 2nd edition, 1970; (editor with Ruth L. Kelly) *The Research Process in Nursing*, Appleton, 1967; *The Research Process in Education*, Holt, 1969; (with Anne Steinmann) *The Male Dilemma: How to Survive the Sexual Revolution*, Jason Aronson, 1974.

Co-author of monographs for Human Resources Research Institute, Maxwell Field, Ala., *Evaluation of Staff Action in the Decision-Making*, and *Instructor's Manual for Evaluating Written Decisions: The OPS Method*, both 1953. Author of eight reports for New York City Board of Education, including, with S. M. Goodman, *Who Are Puerto Ricans in New York City Public Schools?*, 1956; author of more than ten research reports for Institute of Research and Service in Nursing Education, Teachers College, Columbia University, including, with Lorraine K. Diamond and Nadia Jacobowsky, *Career Decisions and Professional Expectations of Nursing Students*, 1961, and, with Diamond and Ruth C. Walsh, *Satisfying and Stressful Situations in Basic Programs in Nursing Education*, 1965. Joint author of a test of ability to understand spoken English. Contributor of more than fifteen articles to nursing and psychology journals.

WORK IN PROGRESS: A book on child development with his wife, Louise Fox.

AVOCATIONAL INTERESTS: Art, collecting antiques.

FOX, Robert Barlow 1930-

PERSONAL: Born December 11, 1930, in Ogden, Utah; son of Orland J. (a businessman) and Laura (Sanders) Fox; married Kathleen Reed, June 7, 1958; children: Trilby, Matt. *Education:* Brigham Young University, B.S., 1957, M.S., 1959; other courses at University of Utah, 1958-64, and Utah State University, 1960. *Politics:* Republican. *Religion:* Church of Jesus Christ of Latter-day Saints. *Home:* 302 East 550 North, Bountiful, Utah. *Agent:* W. J. Bern, 149 High Park Ave., Toronto 9, Canada.

CAREER: Morman missionary among Maoris of New Zealand, 1950-53; Utah State Industrial School, Ogden, caseworker, 1958-59; Weber County School District, Ogden, Utah, counselor, 1960-63; Utah State Industrial School, Salt Lake City, parole officer, 1963-64; Granite School District, Salt Lake City, Utah, high school counselor, 1964—. *Military service:* U.S. Navy, 1949-50. U.S. Army, 1953-55. *Member:* American Personnel and Guidance Association, National Education Association, Utah School Counselors Association, Utah Education Association. *Awards, honors:* Freedoms Foundation awards, 1961, 1965.

WRITINGS—All published by Deseret: *Pray Without Ceasing*, 1961; (editor) *Courage to Live*, 1962; (compiler) *Our Freedom, Our Liberty*, 1964; (compiler) *The Many Faces of Love*, 1964; (compiler) *Take My Hand*, 1965. Contributor of poetry, essays, and articles to magazines.

WORK IN PROGRESS: Adam Seeley and the Devil (novel); *Wild Oats* (novel); *To Devine a Delinquent* (nonfiction); *Little Injun* (juvenile); research on delinquency and school dropouts.

AVOCATIONAL INTERESTS: Woodcarving.†

*   *   *

FRAENKEL, Heinrich 1897-
(Assiac)

PERSONAL: Born September 28, 1897, in Germany; son of Benno and Alwine (Taendler) Fraenkel; married Gretel Levy-Ries, February 1, 1936; children: Peter, Michael. *Education:* Studied at University of Berlin and University of Frankfurt. *Politics:* Labour Party (British). *Religion:* Agnostic. *Home:* Christopher Cottage, Thaxted, Essex, England. *Agent:* John and Charlotte Wolpers Literary Agency, 3 Regent Sq., Bloomsbury, London W.C. 1, England.

CAREER: Began as journalist with film trade publications in Berlin, Germany, in mid-twenties; became publicity chief for Central European Film Distribution, joint unit of Paramount, Metro-Goldwyn-Mayer, and First National Pictures (a post that also required conducting beauty contests); wrote screenplays, going to Hollywood as a film writer in 1929, and continued writing for films when he returned to Germany in 1932; became involved in politics ("although not on party lines"), found himself on Nazi blacklist after an article considered "atrocity propaganda" appeared in *Variety* while he was its Berlin correspondent; left Germany to avoid arrest the night of the Reichstag fire in February, 1933; lived in Paris briefly, then in London, where he wrote more screenplays and published the first of his books on Germany; intended to live in Germany after the war, but trips there on writing assignments for the *New Statesman* (London), 1945-50, were disillusioning, and he became a British citizen in 1950; chess columnist of *New Statesman* under pseudonym, Assiac, 1949—, and frequent contributor of articles, usually on German affairs. Also lecturer in England and Germany. *Member:* Society of Authors (London), Authors' Club.

WRITINGS: The German People versus Hitler, Allen & Unwin, 1940; *Help Us Germans to Beat the Nazis*, Gollancz, 1941; *Vansittart's Gift for Goebbels: A German Exile's Answer to Black Record*, Fabian Society (London), 1941; *The Other Germany*, Transatlantic Book Service (New York), 1942; (with Richard Acland) *The Winning of the Peace*, Gollancz, 1942; (editor) *Germany's Road to Democracy*, Lindsay Drummond, 1942; *A Nation Divided*, Hutchinson, 1949; *The Boy Between*, Wingate, 1955; *Unsterblicher Film*, Kindler, Volume I, 1956, Volume II, 1958; *Farewell to Germany* (autobiographical), B. Hanison, 1959.

With Roger Manvell: *Doctor Goebbels: His Life and Death*, Simon & Schuster, 1960, revised edition published as *Dr. Goebbels*, New English Library, 1968; *Goering*, Simon & Schuster, 1962 (published in England as *Hermann Goering*, Heinemann, 1962); *The Man Who Tried to Kill Hitler*, Coward, 1964 (published in England as *The July Plot: The Attempt in 1944 on Hitler's Life and the Men Behind It*, Bodley Head, 1964); *Himmler*, Putnam, 1965 (published in England as *Heinrich Himmler*, Heinemann, 1965); *The Incomparable Crime: Mass Extermination in the Twentieth Century: the Legacy of Guilt*, Putnam, 1967; *The Canaris Conspiracy: The Secret Resistance to Hitler in the German Army*, McKay, 1969.

S.S. and Gestapo: Rule by Terror, Macdonald & Co., 1970, Ballantine, 1973; *The German Cinema*, Praeger, 1971; *Hess: A Biography*, MacGibbon and Kee, 1971; *Inside Adolf Hitler*, Pinnacle Books, 1973; *The Hundred Days to Hitler*, St. Martin's, 1974 (published in England as *Seizure of Power: One Hundred Days to Hitler*, Dent, 1974).

Translator: (With Constantine Fitzgibbon) L. C. Moyzisch, *Operation Cicero*, Coward, 1950; (with Diana Pyke) Hans Fritzsche, *Sword in the Scales*, Wingate, 1953; Jacques Hannak, *Emanuel Lasker: The Life of a Chess Master*, Simon & Schuster, 1960.

Under pseudonym Assiac: *The Pleasures of Chess*, Simon & Schuster, 1952 (published in England as *Adventure in Chess*, Turnstile Press, 1952); *The Delights of Chess*, MacGibbon & Kee, 1960, A. S. Barnes, 1961, 2nd edition, Dover, 1973.

WORK IN PROGRESS: A greatly augmented edition in English of *Unsterblicher Film*, Volume I, on silent films.

SIDELIGHTS: Political interests prior to World War II prompted Fraenkel's attempts to mediate ("somewhat naively") between Social Democrats and Communists-in-Exile, and to wander off to Spain on a self-appointed and quixotic mission during its Civil War. In England he stirred a controversy with a Fabian tract, *Vansittart's Gift for Goebbels. Farewell to Germany*, also published in German, explained his decision to become a British citizen.

His "labours [with Manvell] on the history of the Nazi era are now assuming Homeric proportions," noted Arthur Swinson, adding that "they have been able to give the most comprehensive account of the Canaris affair that I have come across, and their narrative has magnificent sweep and force." The *Times Literary Supplement* pointed out that the authors used quantities of previously unpublished material, including Gestapo records and evidence from survivors and Nazi officials, presenting "a competent and admirably-written account, historical journalism of the best kind, which will be a valuable contribution to the definitive study of this subject ... weaving ... meticulously accurate detail into a narrative of breadth.''

All of Fraenkel's various kinds of books have been widely translated.

*   *   *

FRANCIS, Helen Dannefer   1915-

PERSONAL: Born January 2, 1915, in Cuba, Kan.; daughter of Edward Rhule (a postmaster) and Lily Ann (Nutter) Dannefer; married Lowell Alexander Francis (a college teacher and athletic coach), June 3, 1935; children: Michael Jackson, John Alexander. *Education:* Fort Hays Kansas State College, A.B. in English and B.S. in Education, 1935. *Politics:* Republican. *Home:* 401 Walnut St., Hays, Kan.

CAREER: Fort Hays Kansas State College, Hays, journalism instructor and news service director, 1947-53; author, primarily of sports books for juvenile and teenage readers, 1953—. Member of board of directors, Hays Public Library, 1948-56, Hays Arts Council, 1966-72; chairman, Hays Council on Human Relations, 1964-65; member of board and public relations chairman, Community Day Care, Inc. (Hays, Kan.); member-at-large, Kansas Advisory Council on Civil Rights, 1965—. News consultant, High Plains Mental Health Clinic, 1964-65; member of advisory panel, Kansas Arts Council, 1966—. *Member:* National Association for the Advancement of Colored People, Hays League of Women Voters, Phi Kappa Phi. *Awards, honors:* $100 Bobbs-Merrill fellowship in adult fiction, Indiana University Writers' Conference, 1961, for manuscript of *Big Swat*; Alumni Achievement Award, Fort Hays Kansas State College, 1972.

WRITINGS: (With Floyd B. Streeter) *The Phantom Steer*, Pellegrini & Cudahy, 1953; *Double Reverse*, Doubleday, 1958; *Football Flash*, Hastings, 1961; *Basketball Bones*, Hastings, 1962; *Martha Norton and Operation Fitness U.S.A.*, Hastings, 1963; *Big Swat*, Follett, 1963. Contributor of feature articles to newspapers and periodicals.

WORK IN PROGRESS: Two adult books, *Operation Goat Gland—The Story of Dr. John R. Brinkley*, and a personal experience story, *I'm the Postmaster's Daughter, But the Males Don't Bother Me*; a book, *Jerry Wills Runs Around the World.*

BIOGRAPHICAL/CRITICAL SOURCES: Magazine of the Midlands, September 20, 1964; *Kansas Library Bulletin*, September, 1964.

*   *   *

FRANCOIS, William E.   1924-

PERSONAL: Born March 11, 1924, in Chicago, Ill.; son of William and Thelma (Aslaksen) Francois; married Irene W. Garratt, July 17, 1944; children: Louise A. *Education:* Northwestern University, B.S. and M.S. in journalism, 1951; Ohio State University, Ph.D., 1967. *Home:* 1320 62nd St., Des Moines, Iowa 50311. *Office:* Journalism School, Drake University, Des Moines, Iowa.

CAREER: Courier-Times, New Castle, Ind., reporter, 1951; *Iowa State Journal*, Pocatello, reporter and farm editor, 1952-54; *Journal Herald*, Dayton, Ohio, assistant city editor, 1954-58; Marshall University, Huntington, W.Va., assistant professor, 1958-65, associate professor, 1965-67, professor of journalism and department head, 1967-69, Drake University, Des Moines, Iowa, professor of journal-

ism, 1969—. *Military service:* U.S. Army, 1942-45. U.S. Army Reserve, 1963-72. *Member:* Sigma Delta Chi. *Awards, honors:* Benedum Foundation grant, 1963; Kappa Tau Alpha Distinctive Service Award, 1971.

WRITINGS: Automation: Industrialization Comes of Age, Collier, 1964. Author of column, ''Law and the Writer,'' published in *Writer's Digest*. Contributor of over one hundred articles to magazines, 1961—.

WORK IN PROGRESS: Two textbooks.

BIOGRAPHICAL/CRITICAL SOURCES: Augusta (Charleston, W.Va.), February, 1965.

*   *   *

FRANK, Robert Worth, Jr.   1914-

PERSONAL: Born April 8, 1914, in Logansport, Ind; son of Robert Worth (a teacher and clergyman) and Grace (Haun) Frank; married Gladys M. Loeb, May 11, 1940; children: Linnie Wright, Elizabeth Ann. *Education:* Wabash College, B.A., 1934; Columbia University, M.A., 1939; Yale University, Ph.D., 1948. *Home:* 749 West Hamilton Ave., State College, Pa. 16801. *Office:* Department of English, Pennsylvania State University, University Park, Pa. 16802.

CAREER: Instructor in English at Lafayette College, Easton, Pa., 1937-39, University of Rochester, Rochester, N.Y., 1940-42, Princeton University, Princeton, N.J., 1942-44, Northwestern University, Evanston, Ill., 1944-48; Illinois Institute of Technology, Chicago, assistant professor, 1948-54, associate professor of English, 1954-58; Pennsylvania State University, University Park, professor of English, 1958—. Visiting fellow, Clare Hall, Cambridge University, 1972-73. *Member:* Modern Language Association of America, Modern Humanities Research Association, International Association of Professors of English, Mediaeval Academy of America, Phi Beta Kappa. *Awards, honors:* American Council of Learned Societies faculty study fellowships, 1951-52, 1960-61; Fund for the Advancement of Education faculty fellowship, 1955-56; Guggenheim fellowship, 1970-71.

WRITINGS: Piers Plowman and the Scheme of Salvation, Yale University Press, 1957; (editor with Harrison T. Meserole) *The Critical Question*, Allyn & Bacon, 1963; (editor with Meserole) *The Responsible Man: The Insights of the Humanities*, Doubleday, 1965; *Chaucer and ''The Legend of Good Women''*, Harvard University Press, 1973.

WORK IN PROGRESS: Pathos in the Late English Middle Ages, an edition of ''Miracles of the Virgin.''

AVOCATIONAL INTERESTS: Medieval art history, jazz.

*   *   *

FRANKLIN, Alexander (John)   1921-

PERSONAL: Born July 13, 1921, in Stratford on Avon, Warwickshire, England; son of William Ewart (an accountant) and Constance Helen (Taylor) Franklin; married Pamela Mary Hardy, February 19, 1944; children: Anabel Mary Elizabeth, John Hilary, Freda Jancis Margaret. *Education:* Eastbourne Training College, student, 1947-48; Central School of Speech and Drama, London, England, L.R.A.M. and International Phonetics Certificate. *Home:* 20 Priory St., Lewes, Sussex BN 7 1HH, England.

CAREER: South-West Essex Technical College, London, England, lecturer in speech training and English, 1949-57;

Furzedown College of Education, London, England, lecturer in speech and drama, 1957-64, senior lecturer in speech and drama, 1964-70; Inner London Education Authority, Educational Television Service, scriptwriter and editor, 1970—. Part-time lecturer, Royal Academy of Dramatic Art, 1956; examiner for Cambridge University, University of London, and Greater London Council; British Council lecturer in Northern Nigeria, 1964. Lecturer and poetry reader in England, 1949—. *Military service:* Royal Naval Volunteer Reserve, 1940-46; became lieutenant. *Member:* Society of Teachers of Speech and Drama (council, 1953-56), Guild of Drama Adjudicators, Society of Authors, Society of Sussex Downsmen, Friends of Lewes Society, Nicholas Yonge Society.

WRITINGS: Choral Verse, Oliver & Boyd, 1962; *Seven Miracle Plays*, Oxford University Press, 1963; (with wife, Pamela Franklin) *Ways*, Oliver & Boyd, 1973. Writer of radio and television scripts; director of "Choral Verse," a recording issued in 1962; compiler, with F. Palmer, of "Looking Around" for Rickitt Encyclopedia of Slides, 1969. Contributor of articles and book reviews to *Use of English, Speech and Drama, Good Housekeeping, Times* (London).

AVOCATIONAL INTERESTS: Walking on Sussex Downs, music, and photography.

* * *

FRANKLIN, Edward Herbert 1930-

PERSONAL: Born September 23, 1930, in Santa Rosa, Calif.; son of Johan Herbert (a club manager) and Arlie (Ford) Franklin; married Susanne Reeves, July 10, 1955. *Education:* San Francisco State College, A.B., 1955. *Home:* 1901 Marin Ave., Berkeley, Calif. 94707.

CAREER: Standard Oil Co. of California, San Francisco, 1955-63, became head of central personnel record section; University of California, Berkeley, writer and editor working on a 1968 centennial celebration encyclopedia, 1965—. *Military service:* U.S. Marine Corps Reserve, 1951-53; became sergeant; received two battle stars for Korean service, and Purple Heart. *Member:* American Civil Liberties Union. *Awards, honors:* James D. Phelan Award for Literature 1960, for draft of *It's Cold in Pongo-ni*; honorable mention, Joseph Henry Jackson Award of San Francisco Foundation, for portion of a novel entitled "The Love Monitor," 1962.

WRITINGS: It's Cold in Pongo-ni (novel), Vanguard, 1965. Contributor of short stories to *Sapien, Focus-Midwest, Transatlantic Review, Nexus*, and *Dust*.

WORK IN PROGRESS: Two Novels, *The Love Monitor* and *The Monkey Tree.*†

* * *

FRANKS, Cyril Maurice 1923-

PERSONAL: Born July 26, 1923, in Neath, Wales; now U.S. citizen; son of Harry (an accountant) and Cecelia (Zeiler) Franks; married Violet Greenberg (a psychologist); children: Steven, Sharon. *Education:* University of Wales, B.Sc., 1943; University of London, diploma in education, 1946, diploma in educational psychology, 1949, diploma in clinical abnormal psychology, 1951, Ph.D., 1954; University of Minnesota, M.A., 1952. *Politics:* Usually Democrat. *Religion:* Jewish. *Home:* 315 Prospect Ave., Princeton, N.J. 08540. *Office:* Psychological Clinic, Rutgers University, New Brunswick, N.Y. 08903.

CAREER: His Master's Voice, Hayes, Middlesex, England, junior research engineer, 1943-46; London Nautical School, London, England, instructor, 1946-49; University of London, Institute of Psychiatry (Maudsley Hospital), London, England, intern, 1950-51, lecturer in psychology, 1954-57; New Jersey Neuro-Psychiatric Institute, Princeton, director of psychology service and research center, 1957-70; Rutgers University, New Brunswick, N.J., professor of psychology, and director of Psychological Clinic, 1970—. Research assistant, University of Minnesota, Institute of Child Welfare, 1951-52. Consultant to Veterans Administration; also managerial consultant in executive selection, and lecturer, Seton Hall University, College of Medicine, department of psychiatry. Lecturer on scientific subjects in Europe, North Africa, West Indies, United States, Canada, and Eastern Europe.

MEMBER: Association for Advancement of Behavior Therapy (president; 1966-67), International Association of Applied Psychology, World Federation for Mental Health, Interamerican Society of Psychology, American Psychological Association (fellow), Society for Psychophysiological Research, British Psychological Society (England; fellow), British Association for the Advancement of Science, Pavlovian Society of America, Eastern Psychological Association, New Jersey Psychological Association (executive committee, 1965-68). *Awards, honors:* Eastern Psychiatric Research Association Prize, 1958; grants from National Institute of Mental Health and U.S. Public Health Service for research on effects of alcohol as related to personality, 1959-61, and for establishing a training program, 1961-66.

WRITINGS: (Associate editor) *Abstracts of Psychiatry for the General Practitioner*, 1958; (editor) *Conditioning Techniques in Clinical Practice and Research*, Springer, 1964; *Behavior Therapy: Appraisal and Status*, McGraw, 1969.

Contributor: H. P. David and H. von Bracken, editors, *Perspectives in Personality Theory*, Basic, 1957; R. Staveley, editor, *Guide to Unpublished Research Material*, Library Association (London), 1957; H. J. Eysenck, editor, *Handbook of Abnormal Psychology*, Pitman, 1960; H. J. Eysenck, editor, *Behavior Therapy and the Neuroses*, Pergamon, 1960; J. C. Sarason, editor, *Contemporary Research in Personality*, Van Nostrand, 1961; A. C. Quay, editor, *Research in Psychopathology*, Van Nostrand, 1962; J. Wolpe, A. Salter, and J. Reyna, editors, *The Conditioning Therapies*, Holt, 1966. Contributor of articles to *Nature, Motor Skills*, and to psychology and psychiatry journals in United States, England, France, Germany, U.S.S.R., and other countries.

Editor, *Advances in Behavior Therapy*, 1967-70; editor-in-chief, *Behavior Therapy*, 1970—; editor, *Annual Review of Behavior Therapy: Theory and Practice*, 1973-74.

WORK IN PROGRESS: Developing methods of diagnosing and modifying abnormal behavior by techniques based on conditioning and learning theory as opposed to those of Freud; basic research into effects of drugs and individual personality differences upon perception, conditioning, learning, personality.

AVOCATIONAL INTERESTS: Elizabethan and Restoration theater, and wines.

* * *

FRASER, Stewart Erskine 1929-

PERSONAL: Born January 7, 1929, in Tientsin, China;

children: five. *Education:* University of Melbourne, B.C., 1951, B.Ed., 1959; Oxford University, B.A., 1955, M.A., 1959; Stanford University, M.A. in Ed., 1956; University of Colorado, Ed.D., 1961; University of London, Ph.D., 1970. *Office:* International Center, George Peabody College for Teachers, Nashville, Tenn.

CAREER: Research officer, Australia Department of Defense, 1950-55; Englehart High School, Ontario, Canada, teacher of social studies, 1955-56; research officer, Australia Department of Defense, 1956-57; University of Melbourne, Australia; senior tutor in political science, 1958-60; Harvard University, Cambridge, Mass., assistant director of international office, 1961-62; George Peabody College for Teachers, Nashville Tenn., professor of international and comparative education, 1962—, director of International Center, 1963—. *Member:* National Education Association, National Association for Foreign Students Affairs, Comparative Education Society, Phi Delta Kappa, Kappa Delta Pi.

WRITINGS: (Editor) *Jullien's Plan for Comparative Education, 1816-1817,* Teachers College Press, 1964; (editor) *Chinese Communist Education: Records of the First Decade,* Vanderbilt University Press, 1965; *Pacific Lands and Antarctica,* Prentice-Hall, 1965; (editor) *Governmental Policy and International Education,* Wiley, 1965; (co-editor) (editor) Birdsey Northrop *The Evils of a Foreign Education; or Birdsey Northrop on Education Abroad, 1873,* Peabody International Center, 1966; *Research in International Education, 1966-67,* Institute of International Education, 1967; (compiler and editor with William W. Brickman) *A History of International and Comparative Education: Nineteenth Century Documents,* Scott, Foresman, 1968; (with Bragi S. Josephson) *Education In Iceland,* Peabody International Center, 1968; (editor and compiler) *American Education in Foreign Perspectives: Twentieth Century Essays,* Wiley, 1969; (editor) *International Education: Understandings and Misunderstandings,* Peabody International Center, 1969; (editor and compiler) *Education and Communism in China: An Anthology of Commentary and Documents,* International Studies Group (Hong Kong), 1969; *A Study on North Korean Education Under Communism Since 1945,* two volumes, Peabody International Center, 1969.

(Editor) *Ludvig Holberg's Memoirs: A Danish Eighteenth Century Contribution to International Understanding,* two volumes, E. J. Brill, 1970; *British Commentary on American Education: A Select and Annotated Bibliography, the Nineteenth and Twentieth Centuries,* London University Institute of Education, 1970; *Sex, Schools and Society: International Perspectives,* Aurora Publishers, 1972; (with Hsu Kuang-ung) *Chinese Education and Society: A Bibliographic Guide; the Cultural Revolution and Its Aftermath,* International Arts and Sciences Press, 1972; (with others) *North Korean Education and Society: A Select and Partially Annotated Bibliography Pertaining to the Democratic People's Republic of Korea,* London University Institute of Education, 1972; (with Barbara J. Fraser) *Scandinavian Education: A Bibliography of English-Language Materials,* International Arts and Science Press, 1973; *A Glimpse of China Through Poster Art,* Aurora Publishers, 1973; (co-author) *Taxonomical Guide to International Educational Objectives,* Phi Delta Kappa, 1973.

FRAZER, Winifred (Loesch) Dusenbury 1916-
(Winifred Loesch Dusenbury)

PERSONAL: Born January 30, 1916, in Chicago, Ill.; daughter of Richards Llewellyn and Margaret (Johnson) Loesch; married second husband, Percy Warner Frazer, 1967; children: (first marriage) John, Richard, David. *Education:* University of Wisconsin, B.S., 1937; University of Maine, M.S., 1940; University of Minnesota, student, 1941-45; University of Florida, Ph.D., 1956. *Home:* 1007 North West 14th Ave., Gainesville, Fla. *Office:* Box 19, Anderson Hall, University of Florida, Gainesville, Fla.

CAREER: University of Florida, Gainesville, assistant professor, 1955-62, associate professor, 1962-70, professor of English, 1970—. *Member:* Modern Language Association of America, National Council of Teachers of English, American Association of University Professors, College English Association, South Atlantic Modern Language Association, Florida Council of Teachers of English (secretary, 1960-61), League of Women Voters of Gainesville (resource chairman, 1953-55), Zeta Phi Eta (faculty advisor on University of Florida campus), Gamma Phi Beta.

WRITINGS—All published by University of Florida Press: (Under name Winifred Loesch Dusenbury) *The Theme of Loneliness in Modern American Drama,* 1960; *Love as Death in The Iceman Cometh,* 1967; *E. G. and E. G. O.: Emma Goldman and The Iceman Cometh,* 1974. Contributor of articles to *Modern Drama, Players Magazine, Shakespeare Quarterly,* and *American Literature,* and short fiction to other periodicals.

WORK IN PROGRESS: A study of mythology in modern American drama: Eugene O'Neill and the American Dream.

*   *   *

FREDERICKS, Pierce Griffin 1920-

PERSONAL: Born April 8, 1920, in Reading, Pa.; son of John E. (an engineer) and Helen (Scott) Fredericks; married Joan Bundy (an editor), 1962; children: Devon S., Stacey. *Education:* Williams College, B.A., 1941. *Home:* 392 Central Park West, New York, N.Y. *Agent:* McIntosh, McKee & Dodds, 30 East 60th St., New York, N.Y. 10022.

CAREER: New York Times, New York, N.Y., assistant to Sunday editor. *Military service:* U.S. Navy, 1942-45; became lieutenant. *Member:* Phi Beta Kappa.

WRITINGS: The People's Choice, Dodd, 1955; *The Great Adventure,* Dutton, 1960; (with Leonard Stern) *All Around New York,* Putnam, 1961; *The Civil War as They Knew It,* Bantam, 1962; *The Yanks are Coming,* Bantam, 1964; *The Sepoy and the Cossack,* World Publishing, 1971.†

*   *   *

FREE, Lloyd A. 1908-

PERSONAL: Born September 29, 1908, in San Jose, Calif; son of Arthur M. (a lawyer) and Mabel C. (Boscow) Free; married Elsbeth Studer, February 11, 1946; children: Peter, Kathleen, Christine, Andrew. *Education:* Princeton University, B.S., 1930; Yenching University, graduate study, 1930-31; George Washington University, law student, 1931-33; Stanford University, LL.B. (later converted to J.D.), 1934. *Home:* 5703 Warwick Pl., Chevy Chase, Md. 20015. *Office:* Institute for International Social Research, 1740 Massachusetts Ave., N.W., Washington, D.C. 20036

CAREER: Lawyer in private practice, Los Angeles, Calif., 1934-37; Princeton University, Princeton, N.J., lecturer in social psychology, 1939-40, editor of *Public Opinion Quarterly*, 1939-40, 1946-47; UNESCO, senior counselor in charge of mass communications, London and Paris, 1946-47; U.S. Department of State, Washington, D.C., various posts, 1947-50; American Embassy, Rome, Italy, counselor, 1950-53; Institute for International Social Research, Washington, D.C., director, 1953—. Consultant to President Dwight D. Eisenhower, 1955, to U.S. Information Agency, 1955—. *Military service:* U.S. Army, 1942-46; served as assistant military attache in Switzerland; became captain; received Army Commendation Ribbon. *Member:* World Association for Public Opinion Research, Council on Foreign Relations.

WRITINGS—All published by the Institute for International Social Research, except as noted: *Six Allies and a Neutral*, Free Press of Glencoe, 1959; *The Dynamics of Philippine Politics*, 1960; *Attitudes of the Cuban People Toward the Castro Regime*, 1960; *Some International Implications of the Political Psychology of Brazilians*, 1961; *Attitudes, Hopes and Fears of the Dominican People*, 1962; *Attitudes, Hopes and Fears of Nigerians*, 1964; *Italy: Dependent Ally or Independent Partner?*, 1965; *The Political Beliefs of Americans*, Rutgers University Press, 1967; *State of the Nation*, Universe Books, 1973.

WORK IN PROGRESS: The International Attitudes of Americans.

SIDELIGHTS: Free is competent in French and German and speaks some Italian. *Avocational interests:* Reading, music, gardening.

* * *

FREEDGOOD, Lillian (Fischel) 1911-

PERSONAL: Born October 28, 1911, in New York, N.Y.; daughter of Samuel (a shoe factory foreman) and Flora (Sohn) Fischel; married Morton Freedgood (a writer), April 23, 1937; children: Laura. *Education:* Pratt Institute, Certificate of Fine Arts, 1931; also studied at Art Student's League and Florence Cane School of Art.

CAREER: Warner Bros. (motion picture producers), artist, 1931-36; free-lance art work, including book and magazine illustrations for Harcourt, Brace and World, Inc., Behrman House, Farrar, Straus and Co., *Woman's Day*, and *Harper's*, 1936-44; Silvermine Guild, Norwalk, Conn., instructor in art workshop, 1955-60; Norwalk Jewish Center, Norwalk, Conn., adult education instructor in oil painting, 1962—. Exhibitor in one-man show at Silvermine Guild, 1959, and in national and international shows. *Member:* Silvermine Guild of Artists, Print Council (New York).

WRITINGS: Great Artists of America, Crowell, 1963; *An Enduring Image: American Painting From 1665*, Crowell, 1970. Contributor to *Gifted Child Quarterly.*†

* * *

FREELAND, John Maxwell 1920-

PERSONAL: Born July 11, 1920, in Launceston, Tasmania, Australia; son of John Douglas (a banker) and Mary Grant (Waterhouse) Freeland; married Kathleen Elizabeth Horton, September 25, 1944; children: Anthony Peter, Robyn Gay (daughter), Michael John. *Education:* University of Melbourne, B.Arch., 1951, Diploma in Town and Regional Planning, 1954, M.Arch., 1957. *Home:* 29 Allard Ave., Roseville Chase, New South Wales, Australia 2069.

Office: P.O. Box 1, Kensington, New South Wales, Australia.

CAREER: Practicing architect, 1951-57; Royal Melbourne Technical College, Melbourne, Australia, senior lecturer, and deputy head of the School of Architecture and Building, 1955-57; University of New South Wales, Kensington, Australia, associate professor, 1957-60, professor of architecture, 1960—, chairman of the department of architecture, 1960—, acting dean of the faculty of architecture, 1962-64. Consulting architect to private parties and finance companies, 1957—. Member of Architectural Draftsmen's Certificate Course Advisory Committee, Department of Technical Education, 1964—; member of council, University of New South Wales, 1962-64, 1973; National Trust of Australia (New South Wales), councilor, 1969—, chairman of Historic Buildings Committee, 1970—; honorary associate, University of Sydney, 1969—; member of Preservation Committee, Sydney City Council, 1970—; director, Old Tote Limited, 1970—; member of Architecture, Building and Quantity Surveying Course Assestment Committee, Advanced Education Board, 1971—; fellow of Basser College. *Military service:* Royal Australian Air Force, pilot, 1940-44; became squadron leader; received Distinguished Flying Cross. *Member:* Society of Architectural Historians (Great Britain and United States), Australian Society of Authors, Royal Australian Historical Society, Royal Australian Institute of Architects (life fellow; councillor, 1960-64), Royal Society of Arts (fellow), Art Gallery Society of New South Wales, Australian Historical Association, Civic Design Society. *Awards, honors:* M. Arch., 1971, and D.Litt., 1972 from University of New South Wales.

WRITINGS: Melbourne Churches, 1836-1851, Melbourne University press, 1963; *The Australian Pub*, Melbourne University Press, 1966; *Architecture In Australia: A History*, Cheshire, 1968; *Rude Timber Buildings in Australia*, Thames & Hudson, 1969; (contributor) Australian Council of National Trusts, *Historic Homesteads of Australia*, Cassell, 1969; *Architect Extraordinary: The Life and Work of John Horbury Hunt, 1838-1904*, Cassell, 1971; *The Making of a Profession*, Angus & Robertson, 1971; (contributor) Amos Rapoport, editor, *Australia as Human Setting: Approaches to the Designed Environment*, Verry, 1973. Contributor to *Australia's Heritage, A Dictionary of World History*, and *The New Australian Encyclopedia*.

Contributor of articles to *Architecture in Australia, Royal Australian Historical Society Journal and Proceedings, Architectural Review, Hemisphere, Bulletin, The Australian* and *Sydney Morning Herald*.

WORK IN PROGRESS: Life and Work of Sir John Sulman.

AVOCATIONAL INTERESTS: Theater, films, music of all sorts, comparative religions, archaeology, history, and poor children.

* * *

FREEMAN, G(raydon) L(a Verne) 1904-
(Larry Freeman; pseudonyms, James H. Thompson, Serry Wood)

PERSONAL. Born August 30, 1904, in LaGrange, Ohio; son of Glenn Simeon (a salesman) and Lena (Goodman) Freeman; married Ruth Lazeare Sunderlin (business manager of Century House), June 22, 1929; children: James Lazeare, John Crosby, Peter Sunderlin. *Education:* State

University of New York College of Education at Cortland (now State University of New York College at Cortland), B.E., 1923; Syracuse University, B.S., 1925; Cornell University, M.A., 1927, Ph.D., 1929. *Religion:* Protestant. *Home and office:* American Life Foundation, Watkins Glen, N.Y.

CAREER: High school principal in Marathon, N.Y., 1926-27; Yale University, New Haven, Conn., National Research Foundation Fellow, 1930-31; Northwestern University, Evanston, Ill., 1932-45, began as instructor, became professor of psychology and director of Psychophysiology Laboratory, director of general education at University College, 1937-42; Century House Publishers, Watkins Glen, N.Y., president, 1949-69. Director of retirement research for U.S. Public Health Service at Western Reserve University 1955-57; executive director of American Life Foundation (non-profit organization advising corporations on retirement problems). Visiting professor, New School for Social Research, 1949. Executive development consultant to U.S. Small Business Administration, U.S. Air Force, and private industry. Public lecturer on tour, 1952-53. Visiting fellow at various times, Medical Research Council, applied Medical Psychology Unit, Cambridge University, and University of London, 1962-70. *Military service:* U.S. Naval Reserve, director of naval officer procurement and service school selections, 1942-45; became commander. *Member:* American Psychological Association (fellow of group on maturity and old age). *Awards, honors:* Social Science Research fellow, 1939; Guggenheim fellow, 1945-46; Cambridge University fellow, 1961-62.

WRITINGS—All published by Century House, except as indicated: *The Role of Context in Associative Formation*, Cornell University Press, 1930; (with wife, Ruth Freeman) *The Child's First Picture Book*, Northwestern University Press, 1933; (with R. Freeman) *The Child and His Picture Book*, Northwestern University Press, 1933; *Introduction to Physiological Psychology*, Ronald, 1934, revised edition published as *Physiological Psychology*, Van Nostrand, 1948; *Diurnal Variations in Performance and Energy Expenditure*, Northwestern University Press, 1935; *Syllabus-Manual in Systematic Experimental Psychology*, two volumes, Northwestern Student Co-op Association, 1937.

(With R. Freeman) *Cavalcade of Toys*, 1942; (under name Larry Freeman) *Light on Old Lamps*, 1944, expanded edition published as *New Light on Old Lamps*, 1968; (under name Larry Freeman) *One Collector's Luck*, 1946; (with Edith Stern) *Mastering Your Nerves*, Harper & Brothers, 1946; (under pseudonym James H. Thompson) *Bitter Bottles*, 1947, reissued as *The Medicine Showman*, 1957; (with Jane Beaumont) *Early American Plated Silver*, 1947; *The Energetics of Human Behavior*, Cornell University Press, 1948; *How to Price Antiques*, 1948; *Nursery Americana*, 1948; *Majolica*, 1949; *The Merry Old Mobiles*, 1949.

(With E. K. Taylor) *How to Pick Leaders*, Funk, 1950; *Self-Management for Management Men*, Funk, 1950; (with R. Freeman) *Antique Furniture Handbook*, 1950; *Motivation and Morale in Industry*, Cornell University Press, 1951; *The Melodies Linger On*, 1951; (compiler) *Historical Prints of American Cities*, 1952; (with R. Freeman) *American Dolls*, 1952; (under pseudonym Serry Wood) *Hand Painted China*, 1953; *Ironstone China*, 1954; (with R. Freeman) *O Promise Me: An Album of Wedding Memories*, 1954; *The Country Store*, 1955; *Iridescent Glass*, 1956, enlarged edition, 1964; (under pseudonym Serry Wood) *The Old Apothecary Shop*, 1956; *Period Furniture*,

1956; *Federal and Empire Furniture*, 1956; *Vocation and Avocation*, 1958; *The Primitive Painter*, 1959.

Stills (in old penny banks), 1960; (with J. M. Flagg) *Celebrity-Artist*, 1960; *How to Restore Antiques*, 1960; (editor) Minnie Kamm, *The Kamm-Wood Encyclopedia of Antique Pattern Glass*, 1961; (editor) *Currier & Ives Pictorial History of American Battle Scenes*, 1961; (with R. Freeman) *Yesterday's Toys*, 1962; *The Hope Paintings* (limited edition), 1962; *Grand Old American Bottles*, 1964; *How to Buy and Sell Old Books*, 1964; *Fountains of Youth—How Never to Retire*, 1964; (under name Larry Freeman) *Big Top Circus Days*, 1964; (contributor) Jack Burton, *The Blue Book of Tin Pan Alley*, 1965; (under name Larry Freeman) *Victorian Silver*, 1967; (contributor) Jack Burton, *The Blue Book of Broadway Musicals*, 1969; (compiler, under name Larry Freeman) *Victorian Posters*, 1969.

(Editor, under name Larry Freeman) *Yesterdays Games*, 1970; (editor, under pseudonym Serry Wood) Rita Wellman, *Victoria Royal*, American Life Foundation, 1970; (under name Larry Freeman) *Louis Prang: Color Lithographer*, 1971; *Self-Fulfillment and Aging*, American Life Foundation, 1973.

Author of "Next Horizons," a series of bulletins on retirement planning. Contributor to psychological journals. Editor, *The American Life Collector's Annual*, American Life Foundation, 1962—.

WORK IN PROGRESS: Psychology and Psychologists, a fifty-year study from the inside.

*   *   *

FREEMAN, Harrop A(rthur)   1907-

PERSONAL: Born December 7, 1907, in Elyria, Ohio; son of Glen S. and Lena (Goodman) Freeman; married Ruth St. John (a writer); children: Norman. *Education:* Cornell University, A.B., 1929, LL.B., 1930, J.S.D. 1945. *Politics:* Democratic-liberal. *Religion:* Quaker *Home:* 103 Needham Pl., Ithaca, N.Y. *Office:* Myron Taylor Hall, Cornell, University, Ithaca, N.Y.

CAREER: Admitted to bar of New York State, 1930 partner in law firms, Niagara Falls, N.Y., 1930-41; Pacific Research Bureau, Philadelphia, Pa., executive director 1941-50; College of William and Mary, Williamsburg, Va. professor of law, 1942-45; Cornell University, Ithaca N.Y., professor of law, 1945—. Fellow-consultant, Center for the Study of Democratic Institutions, 1965-70. *Member:* American Bar Association, Phi Beta Kappa, Order of Coif.

WRITINGS: Peace Is the Victory, Harper, 1944; *Road to Peace*, Pacific Research Bureau, 1946; (with Norman D Freeman) *Tax Practice Deskbook*, Little, Brown, 1960 Gorham-Lamont, 1973; *Dear Mr. President: An Open Letter on Foreign Policy*, Sargeant, 1961; *Legal Interviewing and Counseling*, West, 1964; *Counseling: A Bibliography*, Scarecrow, 1964; (with wife, Ruth Freeman) *Counseling in the United States*, Oceana, 1967; (with Henry Weihofen) *Clinical Law Training*, West, 1972.

WORK IN PROGRESS: On Amnesty, Law for the Poor, and *Federal Tax Reform*.

*   *   *

FREEMAN, John Crosby   1941-
(Hugh Guthrie, Crosby McDowell)

PERSONAL: Born June 9, 1941, in Elmira, N.Y.; son of

Graydon Laverne (a writer) and Ruth (Sunderlin) Freeman (also a writer); married Judith Ann Schoot (a curator), September 5, 1964. *Education:* Harpur College (now State University of New York at Binghamton), B.A., 1962; University of Delaware, graduate study, 1962-64, M.A., 1965; Cornell University, Ph.D. candidate, 1966—. *Home:* Old Irelandville, Watkins Glen, N.Y. 14891. *Office:* American Life Foundation, Watkins Glen, N.Y. 14891.

CAREER: Yorker Yankee Village Museum, Library and Preservation Projects, Watkins Glen, N.Y., director, 1964-65, summer director, 1966—; University of Victoria, Victoria, British Columbia, instructor in art history and University Museum curator, winter months, 1967—. *Member:* Society of Architectural Historians, College Art Association. *Awards, honors:* Fellow at Winterthur Museum, 1962-64; Decorative Arts Book Award of American Life Foundation, 1966.

WRITINGS: (Compiler) *The People's Choice: Ford, Chevrolet, and Plymouth Battle for the Popular Car Market of the 1920's*, Century House, 1959; (editor) *Francis B. Carpenter's Six Months at the White House with Lincoln*, Century House, 1961; (compiler) *Prints Pertaining to America*, Walpole Society, 1964; (editor and contributor) *The American Life: A Collector's Annual*, University of Victoria, 1964; *The Forgotten Rebel: Gustav Stickley and His Craftsman Mission Furniture*, Century House, 1966; *Blue-Decorated Stoneware of New York State*, Century House, 1966; (editor) *Mission and Art Nouveau*, Century House, 1966; (editor) *A. J. Downing's Cottage Residences*, American Life Foundation, 1967; (co-editor) *Studies in Architectural History*, University of Victoria, 1968; (compiler) *Furniture for the Victorian Home*, American Life Foundation, 1968; *Late Victorian Decor from Eastlake's Gothic to Cook's House Beautiful*, American Life Foundation, 1968. (Pseudonyms used for magazine articles.)

WORK IN PROGRESS: American Art Pottery; The Picture Poster; Annotated Bibliography of Books on North American Architecture, Landscape Gardening, and City Planning, to 1915.†

* * *

FREIHOFER, Lois Diane 1933-
(Lois Barth)

PERSONAL: Surname is pronounced *Fry-hawfer;* born January 6, 1933, in Bellows Falls, Vt.; daughter of George Theodore and Mathilde Emma (Girardin) Freihofer. *Education:* Attended schools in Gageville and Bellows Falls, Vt. *Politics:* Republican. *Religion:* Lutheran. *Home:* School St., Westminster, Vt. 05158.

CAREER: Edwards & Bigelow (law firm), Bellows Falls, Vt., secretary, 1950-51; Robertson Paper Co., Inc., Bellows Falls, Vt., executive secretary, 1951—.

WRITINGS: (Under pseudonym Lois Barth) *Run from the River*, Bouregy, 1965; *Dark Labyrinth*, Lenox Press, 1971; *Epitaph for a Teddy Bear*, Lenox Press, 1973.

WORK IN PROGRESS: Said the Spider to the Fly, Scent of Lilac, To Never Say Good-bye, a romance, and an autobiography.

* * *

FREMANTLE, Anne 1910-

PERSONAL: Born June 15, 1910, in Tresserve, Savoie, France; came to United States, 1940, naturalized, 1947; daughter of Frederick (a privy councillor, Sheriff of London, and a director of Bank of England) and Clara (Grant Duff) Huth Jackson; married Christopher Fremantle, November 12, 1930; children: Adam, Richard, Hugh. *Education:* Lady Margaret Hall, Oxford, B.A., 1930, M.A., 1932; graduate of London School of Economics and Political Science. *Politics:* Democrat in United States, Labour in England. *Religion:* Baptized in Church of England; became a Muslim at the age of nine, converted by British author, Marmaduke Pickthall; converted to Catholicism, 1943. *Home:* 252 East 78th St., New York 21, N.Y.

CAREER: Worked for *London Mercury*, 1931; writer for *Manchester Guardian* and *London Times*, 1932-35; stood as unsuccessful Labour Party candidate in general election against Sir Alfred Duff Cooper, 1935; drove ambulance for London County Council for a few months during early years of World War II; broadcaster in German and French for joint broadcasting section of British Broadcasting Corporation; British Embassy, Washington, D.C., research assistant in Indian section, 1942-45; Catholic Book Club, New York, N.Y., editor, 1947-65. Lecturer, Fordham University, 1948-51; part-time editor at United Nations, 1950-61; had own program on NBC, 1961-62; senior history fellow, Wesleyan University, 1966; visiting professor, New York University, 1970-72. Writer and lecturer; frequent guest on radio and television. National Book Award judge, 1972. *Member:* American P.E.N. (vice-president, 1973-74), English Speaking Union, Authors League, Authors Guild of America—East, Societe Asiatique (France), Cosmopolitan Club (New York). *Awards, honors:* Christopher Award for *A Treasury of Early Christianity;* LL.D., St. Mary's College, 1958, Western College for Women, 1962; fellow, Pennsylvania State University, 1971.

WRITINGS: Poems, Swan Press, 1931; *George Eliot*, Duckworth, 1933, reissued, Haskell House, 1972; *Loyal Enemy: The Life of Marmaduke Pickthall*, Hutchinson, 1938; *Come to Dust*, Putnam, 1941; *James and Joan*, Holt, 1948, reissued, Curtis Books, 1972; *Desert Calling*, Holt, 1949 (published in England as *Desert Calling: The Life of Charles de Foucauld*, [Catholic Book Club selection], Hollis & Carter, 1950); (with Bryan Holme) *Europe: A Journey With Pictures*, Studio Publications, 1954; *The Age of Belief: The Medieval Philosophers*, Houghton, 1955, reissued, Books for Libraries, 1970; *By Grace of Love*, Macmillan, 1957; *This Little Band of Prophets: The British Fabians*, Macmillan, 1960; *Holiday in Europe*, Viking, 1963; *The Protestant Mystics*, Little, 1964; *The Island of Cats*, Astor-Honor, 1964; (with editors of Time-Life Books) *The Age of Faith*, Time, 1965; *Pilgrimage to People*, McKay, 1968; *Three-Cornered Heart*, Viking, 1970; *A Primer of Linguistics*, St. Martin's, 1974.

Editor: Frederick H. Jackson, *Sicily*, 4th edition, Methuen, 1935; *The Wynne Diaries, 1789-1820*, Oxford University Press, 1936, 1937, 1939, published in one volume, Oxford University Press, 1952; *The Commonweal Reader*, Harper, 1949; *The Greatest Bible Stories: A Catholic Anthology From World Literature*, Stephen Daye Press, 1951, abridged edition, Image Books, 1957; *Mothers: A Catholic Treasury of Great Stories*, Stephen Daye Press, 1951; *Christian Conversation: Catholic Thought for Every Day of the Year*, Stephen Daye Press, 1953; *A Treasury of Early Christianity*, Viking, 1953; George Macdonald, *Visionary Novels: Lilith [and] Phantastes*, Noonday, 1954; *Christmas is Here: A Catholic Selection of Stories and Poems*, Stephen Daye Press, 1955; *The Papal Encyclicals in Their Historical Context*, Putnam, 1956; *Robert Hugh Benson, Oddsfish!*, Kenedy, 1957; *Mao Tse-tung: An Anthology of His Writings*, New American Library, 1962, revised edition, 1971; *The Social Teachings of the Church*, New American Library, 1963; *Communism: Basic Writings*, New American Library, 1970; Caroline Lamb, *Glenarvon*, Curtis Books, 1973.

Translator: Wilhelm Schamoni, *Face of the Saints*, Pantheon, 1947; (with husband Christopher Fremantle) Omer Englebert, *Lives of the Saints*, McKay, 1951; (with Christopher Fremantle) Maurice Zermatten, *Fountain of Arethusa*, Doubleday, 1960; (with Christopher Fremantle) Anne Denieul-Cormier, *A Time of Glory: The Renaissance in France, 1488-1559*, Doubleday, 1967; Jean Guitton, *The Pope Speaks*, Meredith, 1968.

Author of introduction: Andre Maurois, *The Maurois Reader*, Didier, 1949; Feodor Dostoevski, *The Grand Inquisitor*, Ungar, 1956; Frederick C. Giffin, *Woman as Revolutionary*, New American Library, 1964; *How to Read a Dirty Book*, Franciscan Press, 1966.

Also regular reviewer, *Times Literary Supplement*, 1930-40. Contributor to *New Statesman, Sphere, New York Herald Tribune, New York Times, New Yorker, Town and Country, Mademoiselle, Vogue, Harper's Bazaar, Catholic World, Psychoanalytical Quarterly*, and other publications. A founder of *A.D.*; associate editor of *Commonweal*, 1950-57.

WORK IN PROGRESS: A Matter of Choice, a study of twelve men of six nationalities, who chose opposite sides in World War II (for example, French admirals D'Argenlieu, a Gaulliste, and Auphan, a Petainiste), for Viking.

SIDELIGHTS: "An Englishwoman of aristocratic background," wrote reviewer Constantine Fitzgibbon, "for many years now a resident of the United States and Mexico, a devout Roman Catholic with strongly liberal views, Anne Fremantle is almost a walking example of ecumenicism, and [*Pilgrimage to People*] is filled with the spirit of Pope John and of Vatican II. . . . Not only does she recognize the virtues of the other Christian faiths but is immediately responsive to the high spirituality of all great religions. . . . [She] writes of her meetings with . . . men and women who . . . have devoted their lives to the struggle for human decency. . . . [She is] 'liberal' in the old-fashioned, English sense. . . . "

Three-Cornered Heart, Mrs. Fremantle's biography of her mother and herself, evoked the following comments from Eugenie Bolger: "Without disturbing the tranquility, even the sweetness, of her memoirs, she reveals the uglier aspects of life in a large Victorian household. Peeling off the gentle nostalgia that wraps the past, she is nevertheless careful to preserve it; nostalgia is not disposed of, but rather set aside. This enables Mrs. Fremantle to see everything in both an objective and subjective light, to record the most painful memories with a certain affection."

Both mother and daughter grew up in homes frequented by the most distinguished persons of their times. For her mother, there were, among other friends, Gladstone, Disraeli, Matthew Arnold, Robert Browning, Thackeray, Karl Marx, Cardinal Newman, and Charles Darwin; for the author, W. B. Yeats, Sidney and Beatrice Webb (the latter a great aunt), Ramsay MacDonald, and Bertrand Russell. In fact, reviewer Thomas Lask complained that in "such a roster of names . . . they tend to run together and cancel one another out."

BIOGRAPHICAL/CRITICAL SOURCES: New York Times Book Review, March 6, 1960, May 17, 1964; *Times Literary Supplement*, July 29, 1960, November 19, 1964; *New Statesman*, November 10, 1961.

*   *   *

FREUDENBERGER, Herman 1922-

PERSONAL: Born April 14, 1922, in Eberbach, Germany; son of Alfred (a merchant) and Frieda (Gruenebaum) Freudenberger; married Paulette Gross, June 17, 1951; children: Joseph, Alfred Carl. *Education:* Columbia University, B.S., 1950, M.A., 1951, Ph.D., 1957. *Office:* Tulane University, New Orleans, La. 70118.

CAREER: School of Insurance, New York, N.Y., lecturer, 1955-56; Rutgers University, New Brunswick, N.J., lecturer, 1958-59; Brooklyn College (now Brooklyn College of the City University of New York), Brooklyn, N.Y. instructor in history, 1956-58, 1959-60; Montana State University, Missoula, assistant professor of history, 1960-62; Tulane University of Louisiana, New Orleans, associate professor, 1962-66, professor of economic history, 1966—, chairman of the department of economics, 1966-70. Research in Czechoslovakia, 1964-65; Fulbright lecturer in Austria, 1973-74. *Military service:* U.S. Army, 1942-46; became technician third grade (sergeant). *Member:* American Historical Association, American Economic Association, Economic History Association, Gesellschaft fuer Sozial und Wirtschaftsgeschichte.

WRITINGS: The Waldstein Woolen Mill: Noble Entrepreneurship in Eighteenth-Century Bohemia, Baker Library, Harvard School of Business Administration, 1963; (contributor) Wolfram Fischer, compiler, *Wirtschafts-und sozialgeschichtliche Probleme der fruehen Industrialisierung*, Colloquium Verlag, 1968. Contributor to *Journal of Central European Affairs, Kyklos, Journal of Economic History*, and *Business History Review, Explorations in Economic History*, and *Technology and Culture*.

WORK IN PROGRESS: Innovation und Regionale Industrialisierung; The Industrialization of a Central European City; "The Working Year"; "Health, Work and Leisure Before the Industrial Revolution"; *Aristocracy in Industry*; and *The Transfer of Technology From England to Austria*.

*   *   *

FREUND, John E(rnst) 1921-

PERSONAL: Born August 6, 1921, in Berlin, Germany; married Maxine I. Henville, August 26, 1949; children: Douglas Eric, John E., Jr. *Education:* University of California, Los Angeles, B.A., 1943, M.A., 1944; University of Pittsburgh, Ph.D., 1952. *Home:* 7035 North 69th Pl., Scottsdale, Ariz.

CAREER: Alfred University, Alfred, N.Y., 1946-54, started as assistant professor, became professor of mathematics; Virginia Polytechnic Institute and State University, Blacksburg, professor of statistics, 1954-57; Arizona State University, Tempe, professor of mathematics, 1957—. *Member:* American Statistical Association (fellow; member of board, 1965-67), American Association for the Advancement of Science (fellow), Institute of Mathematical Statistics, Mathematics Association of America, Industrial Mathematics Society, National Council of Teachers of Mathematics, Arizona Academy of Science.

WRITINGS: Modern Elementary Statistics, Prentice-Hall, 1952, 4th edition, 1973; *A Modern Introduction to*

Mathematics, Prentice-Hall, 1956; (with F. J. Williams) *Modern Business Statistics*, Prentice-Hall, 1958, 2nd edition published as *Freund and Williams' Modern Business Statistics*, revised by Benjamin Perles and Charles Sullivan, 1969; (translator from the German with M. Reichenbach) H. Reichenbach, *Philosophy of Time and Space*, Dover, 1958; (with I. Miller and P. Livermore) *Manual of Experimental Statistics*, Prentice-Hall, 1960; *Mathematical Statistics*, Prentice-Hall, 1962, 2nd edition, 1965; (translator from the German) E. Burger, *Introduction to the Theory of Games*, Prentice-Hall, 1963 (with Williams) *Elementary Business Statistics: The Modern Approach*, Prentice-Hall, 1964, 2nd edition, 1972; (with I. Miller) *Probability and Statistics for Engineers*, Prentice-Hall, 1965; (translator from the French) E. Borel, *Introduction to the Theory of Probability*, Prentice-Hall, 1965; (with Williams) *Dictionary/Outline of Basic Statistics*, McGraw, 1966; *College Mathematics With Business Applications*, Prentice-Hall, 1969; *Statistics: A First Course*, Prentice-Hall, 1970; *Introduction to Probability*, Dickenson, 1973; (with Perles) *Business Statistics: A First Course*, Prentice-Hall, 1974.

* * *

FREUND, Philip 1909-

PERSONAL: Born February 5, 1909, in Vancouver, British Columbia, Canada; son of Henry and Gussie (Robinson) Freund. *Education:* Cornell University, B.A., 1929, M.A., 1932. *Home:* 1025 Fifth Ave., New York, N.Y. 10028. *Agent:* Bertha Klausner, International Literary Agency, Inc., 71 Park Ave., New York, N.Y. 10016.

CAREER: City University of New York, New York, N.Y., lecturer at Film Institute at City College, 1945—, lecturer in English at Hunter College, 1946—; Fordham University, New York, N.Y., 1957—, began as adjunct assistant professor, now professor of communication arts. Taught at Cornell University, 1946, and University of British Columbia, 1948-50. Former Consultant to Secretary of the Army, Anti-Defamation League of B'nai B'rith, and Young America Films. *Military service:* U.S. Army, 1941-45. *Member:* Sigma Delta Chi, New Dramatists Committee. *Awards, honors:* Bureau of New Plays fellowship, 1937.

WRITINGS: The Merry Communist (fantasy), Pilgrim House, 1934; (author of critical preface) Kimi Gengo, *To One Who Mourns at the Death of the Emperor*, Pilgrim House, 1934; *The Snow and Other Stories*, Pilgrim House, 1935; *Book of Kings* (first novel in trilogy; also see below), Pilgrim House, 1937; *The Evening Heron* (novel), Pilgrim House, 1937; *Dreams of Youth* (novel), Pilgrim House, 1938.

The Dark Shore (novel), Washburn, 1941; *The Young Greek and the Creole* (stories), Pilgrim House, 1944; *Three Exotic Tales*, Pilgrim House, 1945; *Edward Zoltan* (second novel in trilogy; also see below), Beechhurst Press, 1946; *How to Become a Literary Critic*, Beechhurst Press, 1947, reissued as *The Art of Reading the Novel*, Collier, 1965; *Stephanie's Son* (third novel in trilogy; also see below), Beechhurst Press, 1947; *Easter Island* (novel), Beechhurst Press, 1947; *The Zoltans* (trilogy; includes *Book of Kings, Edward Zoltan*, and *Stephanie's Son*), Beechhurst Press, 1948; *A Man of Taste and Other Stories*, Beechhurst Press, 1949.

Private Speech (poetry), W. H. Allen, 1951, Pilgrim House, 1952; *Saturnalia and the Nomads* (first novel in trilogy; also see below), Secker & Warburg, 1956; *The Rooftop and Eurasia* (second novel in trilogy; also see below), Secker & Warburg, 1957; *How the World Began* (third novel in trilogy; also see below), Secker & Warburg, 1958; *The Volcano God* (trilogy; includes *Saturnalia and the Nomads, The Rooftop and Eurasia*, and *How the World Began*), British Book Center, 1959; (editor and author of critical preface) Otto Rand, *The Myth of the Birth of the Hero and Other Essays*, Vintage Press, 1959.

The Beholder: Seven Tales of Sebastian Romm, W. H. Allen, 1961, British Book Center, 1962; *The Devious Ways* (stories), W. H. Allen, 1962, London House, 1963; *Myths of Creation* (belles lettres), W. H. Allen, 1964, Washington Square Press, 1966; (author of critical preface) Joseph Conrad, *Lord Jim*, Collier, 1965; *The Spymaster* (stories), W. H. Allen, 1965, Washburn, 1966; *The Young Artists* (stories), W. H. Allen, 1966.

Searching, W. H. Allen, 1972.

Plays: "Black Velvet" published in *Cornell Plays*, Samuel French, 1932; *Mario's Well* (one-act), Samuel French, 1940; *Prince Hamlet* (one-act, fourteen scenes), Bookman Associates, 1953; *Three Off-Broadway Plays* (includes "The Fire Bringers," "The Peons," produced Off-Broadway at the Brander Matthews Theatre, and "The Brooding Angel," produced Off-Broadway at the Key Theatre), Pitman, 1968; *Three Poetic Plays* (includes "Flame and Cedar," "Jocasta," and "The Bacchae"), W. H. Allen, 1970; *More Off-Broadway Plays*, W. H. Allen, 1974. Also author of "Simon, Simon," published in *One Act Play Magazine*, 1935.

Writer of television scripts for "Kraft Theater, "Chrysler Theater, " "General Electric Theater," "Jane Wyman Theater," "Matinee Theater," and others. Writer of over twenty-five documentary films. Also contributor of stories and articles to magazines and journals.

* * *

FREWER, Glyn 1931-

PERSONAL: Born September 4, 1931, in Oxford, England; son of Louis (superintendent of Rhodes House Library, Oxford) and Dorothy (Poulter) Frewer; married Lorna F. Townsend (a teacher of piano and violin), August 11, 1956; children: Neil, Sean, Claire. *Education:* St. Catherine's College, Oxford, B.A. (honors), 1955, M.A., 1959. *Home:* Wychwood, 20 Stanstead Rd., Caterham, Surrey, England. *Agent:* Bolt & Watson Ltd., 8 Storey's Gate, London S.W.1, England. *Office:* Masius, Wynne-Williams & D'Arcy MacManus, 2 St. James's Sq., London S.W.1, England.

CAREER: British Council, student officer in Oxford, England, 1955; Spottiswoode Ltd. (advertising agency), London, England, trainee copywriter, 1955-57; Masius, Wynne-Williams & D'Arcy MacManus (advertising agency), London, England, 1961—, creative controller, 1965—. *Military service:* Royal Army Ordnance Corps, 1950-52. *Member:* Society of Authors.

WRITINGS: Adventure in Forgotten Valley (Junior Literary Guild selection), Faber, 1962, Putnam, 1964; *Adventure in the Barren Lands* (juvenile), Faber, 1964, Putnam, 1966; *The Last of the Wispies* (juvenile), Faber, 1965; *The Token of Elkin* (juvenile), Heinemann, 1970; *Crossroad*, Heinemann, 1970; *The Square Peg*, Heinemann, 1972. Radio play, "The Hitch-hikers," produced by British Broadcasting Corp., 1957.

WORK IN PROGRESS: A story for Heinemann's "Guided Readers" series.

SIDELIGHTS: Frewer has traveled "by thumb" over 17,000 miles through twelve European countries. He later wrote about these trips for his school magazine, an activity which, he believes, gave him his start as a writer.

BIOGRAPHICAL/CRITICAL SOURCES: Caterham Times, June 6, 1972.

*   *   *

FRICK, George F(rederick)   1925-

PERSONAL: Born May 20, 1925, in Estherville, Iowa; son of George and Hertha (Spies) Frick; married Phyllis McConnell, August 12, 1950; children: Margaret, Karl, Elizabeth. *Education:* St. Olaf College, B.A., 1949; University of California, Berkeley, M.A., 1951; University of Illinois, Ph.D., 1957. *Politics:* Republican. *Religion:* Episcopalian. *Home:* 101 Ritter Lane, Newark, Del. *Office:* University of Delaware, Newark, Del.

CAREER: University of Illinois, Urbana, instructor in history, 1956-57; Rutgers University, New Brunswick, N.J., instructor in history, 1957-60; Library Company of Philadelphia, Philadelphia, Pa., fellow, 1959-60; University of Delaware, Newark, assistant professor, 1960-64, associate professor of history, 1964—. *Military service:* U.S. Army Air Forces, 1943-46. *Member:* American Historical Association, Organization of American Historians, Historical Society of Delaware.

WRITINGS: (With R. P. Stearns) *Mark Catesby: The Colonial Audubon,* University of Illinois Press, 1961. Contributor to journals.

WORK IN PROGRESS: Book on the life of Peter Collinson.†

*   *   *

FRICKE, Cedric V.   1928-

PERSONAL: Born March 18, 1928, in Millburg, Mich.; son of William P. and Gladys (Kral) Fricke; married Janet Hoenshel, June 10, 1955; children: William Neff, Karl Wilmer. *Education:* University of Michigan, B.S.E., 1949, M.B.A., 1950, Ph.D., 1959. *Home:* 18158 Westover, Southfield Mich. 48706. *Office:* University of Michigan, Dearborn Campus, 4901 Evergreen, Dearborn, Mich. 48128.

CAREER: General Motors Corp., Detroit, Mich., statistician, 1950-55; University of Michigan, Ann Arbor, research associate, 1955-57; Wayne State University, Detroit, Mich., instructor in economics, 1957-59, assistant professor, 1959-60; University of Michigan, Dearborn Campus, assistant professor, 1960-63, associate professor 1963-67, professor of business administration, 1967—. Member of Michigan Economic Stabilization Task Group. *Military service:* U.S. Army, Chemical Corps, 1950-52. *Member:* National Association of Business Economicists, American Economic Association, American Finance Association, American Statistical Association (Detroit president, 1965).

WRITINGS: The Variable Annuity, Bureau of Business Research, University of Michigan, 1959; (with T. Gies and M. Seger) *Consumer Finance Companies in Michigan,* Bureau of Business Research, University of Michigan, 1961; (with P. W. McCracken and J. C. T. Mao) *Consumer Installment Credit and Public Policy,* Bureau of Business Research, University of Michigan, 1965.

FRIEDEN, Bernard J.   1930-

PERSONAL: Born August, 1930, in New York, N.Y.; son of George and Jean (Harris) Frieden; married Elaine Leibowitz (a sociologist), November 23, 1958. *Education:* Cornell University, B.A., 1951; Pennsylvania State University, M.A., 1953; Massachusetts Institute of Technology, M.C.P., 1957, Ph.D., 1962. *Office:* Joint Center for Urban Studies of the Massachusetts Institute of Technology and Harvard University, 53 Church St., Cambridge, Mass. 02138.

CAREER: Massachusetts Institute of Technology, Cambridge, instructor, 1959-60, assistant professor, 1961-65, associate professor of city planning, 1965-69, professor of urban studies, 1969—. director of Joint Center for Urban Studies of the Massachusetts Institute of Technology and Harvard University, 1971—. Consultant to: Agency for International Development (study of housing in Mexico City), 1964, Advisory Commission on Intergovernmental Relations, 1965, Department of Housing and Urban Development, 1966-68, U.S. Commission on Civil Rights, 1967, 1971, National Institute of Mental Health, 1968-70, Urban Coalition, 1969-70, Urban Institute 1969, 1971, and U.S. Congress, House Subcommittee on Housing, 1970-71. Member, Task Force on the Organization of Social Services, U.S. Department of Health, Education and Welfare, 1968, member, President-Elect Nixon's Task Force on Urban Problems, 1968, member, White House Task Force on Model Cities, 1969. *Military service:* U.S. Army, 1952-54; served in Germany. *Member:* Phi Beta Kappa. *Awards, honors:* Research fellow, Massachusetts Institute of Technology-Harvard Joint Center for Urban Studies, 1960-61.

WRITINGS: (With Melvin F. Levine) *Report on Metropolitan Problems,* Americans for Democratic Action, 1957; *The Future of Old Neighborhoods,* M.I.T. Press, 1964; (contributor) *Social Structure and Human Problems in the Boston Metropolitan Area,* Massachusetts Institute of Technology-Harvard Joint Center for Urban Studies, 1965; *Metropolitan America: Challenge to Federalism,* Advisory Commission on Intergovernmental Relations, 1966; (editor with Robert Morris) *Urban Planning and Social Policy,* Basic Books, 1968; (editor with William W. Nash) *Shaping an Urban Future: Essays in Memory of Catherine Bauer Wurster,* M.I.T. Press, 1969; (contributor) James Q. Wilson, editor, *The Metropolitan Enigma: Inquiries Into the Nature and Dimensions of America's Urban Crisis,* Doubleday, 1970; (contributor) Samuel H. Beer and Richard E. Barringer, editors, *The State and The Poor,* Winthrop, 1970; (contributor) Robert Morris, editor, *Encyclopedia of Social Work,* two volumes, National Association of Social Workers, 1971; (with Daniel W. Fessler and Dale Rogers Marshall) *The Governance of Metropolitan Regions: Minority Perspectives,* Johns Hopkins Press, 1972. Contributor of articles to *Journal of the American Institute of Planners, Trans-action,* and *Town Planning Review.* Editor, *Journal of the American Institute of Town Planners,* 1962-65.

*   *   *

FRIEDERICH, Werner P(aul)   1905-

PERSONAL: Surname is pronounced *Free*-der-ick; born June 2, 1905, in Thun, Switzerland; came to United States, 1927, became citizen, 1937; son of Robert and Katherine (Reusser) Friederich; married Molly I. Heuberger, December 27, 1935 (died, 1958); married Iris Isabel Wilcock (a lecturer at University of North Carolina), February 12, 1960; children: (first marriage) Nicolette. *Education:* Attended University of Bern, 1924-25, 1929-31, Swiss State Diploma; Sorbonne, University of Paris, student, 1925-27; Harvard University, M.A., 1929, Ph.D., 1932. *Politics:* Liberal Republican. *Religion:* Zwinglian. *Home:* 698 Gimghoul Rd., Chapel Hill, N.C. *Office:* University of North Carolina, Chapel Hill, N.C.

CAREER: University of North Carolina, Chapel Hill, 1935—, professor of German and comparative literature, 1948-70, chairman of curriculum of comparative literature, 1956-67, Kenan Professor, 1959-70, professor emeritus, 1970—. Fulbright professor to Australia, 1955, 1964; visiting professor at University of Bern, 1938, University of Zurich, 1960; visiting summer professor at University of Hawaii, 1959, University of California, Berkeley, 1962, University of Colorado, 1963, Duke University, 1966-68, and University of Southern California, 1968. Lecturer in India, 1959, Germany and Austria, 1960, and Japan, 1964.

MEMBER: American Comparative Literature Association (president, 1959-62), International Comparative Literature Association (president, 1958-61), Modern Language Association of America (founder of comparative literature section, 1947, chairman, 1948), Modern Humanities Research Association (executive committee, 1959-64). *Awards, honors:* Grants from Carnegie Foundation, Ford Foundation, and UNESCO.

WRITINGS: Spiritualismus und Sensualismus in der englischen Barocklyrik, Braumueller (Vienna), 1932; *Werden und Wachsen der USA in 300 Jahren*, Francke (Berne), 1939; *History of German Literature*, Barnes & Noble, 1949; *Dante's Fame Abroad, 1350-1850*, Storia e Letteratura (Rome), 1950; *Bibliography of Comparative Literature*, University of North Carolina Press, 1950; *Outline of Comparative Literature from Dante to O'Neill*, University of North Carolina Press, 1954; *Australia in Western Imaginative Prose Writings, 1600-1960*, University of North Carolina Press, 1967; *The Challenge of Comparative Literature, and Other Addresses*, University of North Carolina Press, 1970.

Editor, "University of North Carolina Studies in Comparative Literature," 1950-66, and *Yearbook of Comparative and General Literature*, 1952-59; associate editor, *Comparative Literature*, 1949-72; member of editorial board, *Revue de Litterature comparee.*†

* * *

FRIEDLAND, William H. 1923-

PERSONAL: Born May 27, 1923, in New York, N.Y.; married; two children. *Education:* Wayne State University, B.A., 1956, M.A., 1957; University of California, Berkeley, Ph.D., 1963. *Office:* Stevenson College, University of California, Santa Cruz, Calif. 95064.

CAREER: Did miscellaneous automobile assembly and machine work with Hudson Motor Car Co. and Ford Motor Co., Detroit, Mich., 1942-49; Michigan CIO Council, assistant education director, 1949-51; United Automobile Workers, research and engineering, international representative, 1951-53; New York State School of Industrial and Labor Relations at Cornell University, Ithaca, N.Y., 1961, assistant professor, 1961-64, associate professor, 1964-69; University of California, Santa Cruz, professor of Community studies and sociology, 1969—. *Member:* American Sociological Association.

WRITINGS: (Editor with Carl G. Rosberg) *African Socialism*, Stanford University Press, 1964; *Unions, Labor and Industrial Relations in Africa: An Annotated Bibliography*, Center for International Studies, Cornell University, 1965; *Vuta Kamba: The Development of Trade Unions in Tanganyika*, Hoover Institution Press, 1969; (with Irving Louis Horowitz) *The Knowledge Factory: Student Power and Academic Politics in America*, Aldine, 1970; (with Dorothy Nelkin) *Migrant: Agricultural Workers in America's Northeast*, Holt, 1971.

* * *

FRIEDMAN, Lawrence Meir 1930-

PERSONAL: Born April 2, 1930, in Chicago, Ill.; son of I. M. and Ethel (Shapiro) Friedman; married Leah Feigenbaum, March 27, 1955; children: Jane, Amy. *Education:* University of Chicago, A.B., 1948, J.D., 1951, M.LL., 1953. *Home:* 724 Frenchman's Rd., Stanford, Calif. 94305.

CAREER: D'Ancona, Pflaum, Wyatt & Riskind (law firm), Chicago, Ill., associate, 1955-57; St. Louis University Law School, St. Louis, Mo., 1957-61, began as assistant professor, became associate professor; University of Wisconsin Law School, Madison, 1961-68, began as associate professor of law, now professor; Stanford University, Stanford, Calif., professor of law, 1968—. David Stouffer Memorial lecturer, Rutgers University Law School, 1969. *Military service:* U.S. Army, 1953-54; became sergeant.

WRITINGS: Contract Law in America, University of Wisconsin Press, 1965; *Government and Slum Housing: A Century of Frustration*, Rand McNally, 1968; (with Stewart Macaulay) *Law and the Behavioral Sciences*, Bobbs, 1969; *A History of American Law*, Simon & Schuster, 1973. Contributor to legal periodicals.

SIDELIGHTS: Friedman is competent, in varying degrees, in German, French, Hebrew, Russian. *Avocational interests:* Music, literature, history, Bible studies.†

* * *

FRIEDMAN, Maurice Stanley 1921-

PERSONAL: Born December 29, 1921, in Tulsa, Okla.; son of Samuel Herman and Fanny (Smirin) Friedman; married Eugenia Chifos, January 17, 1947; children: David Michael, Dvora Lisa. *Education:* Harvard University, S.B. (magna cum laude), 1942; Ohio State University, M.A., 1947; University of Chicago, Ph.D., 1950. *Politics:* Liberal. *Religion:* Jewish. *Home:* 1801 Sea View Ave., Del Mar, Calif. 92014. *Agent:* Georges Borchardt, 145 East 52nd St., New York, N.Y. 10022. *Office:* Department of Religious Studies, San Diego State University, San Diego, Calif.

CAREER: Ohio State University, Columbus, instructor in philosophy, 1950-51; Sarah Lawrence College, Bronxville, N.Y., professor of philosophy, literature, and religion, 1951-65; Manhattanville College of the Sacred Heart, Purchase, N.Y., professor of philosophy, 1966-67; Temple University, Philadelphia, Pa., professor of religion and director of doctoral programs in religion, literature, and psychology, 1967-73; San Diego State University, Calif., visiting distinguished professor, 1972, professor of religious studies, philosophy, and comparative literature, 1973—. Member of faculty of New School for Social Research, 1954-66, Washington School of Psychiatry, 1956-59, Pendle Hill Center for Study, 1959, 1964-65, 1967-73, and California School of Professional Psychology, 1973—. Assistant professor of religion, Columbia University, summer,

1955 and 1956; visiting professor, Hebrew Union College, 1956-57; guest lecturer, William Alanson White Institute of Psychiatry, Psychoanalysis, and Psychology, 1958-60; seminar leader, Esalen Institute, 1965—; visiting professor, Union Theological Seminary, summer, 1965 and 1967; visiting lecturer, Vassar College, 1967. Chairman of American Friends of Ichud (Jewish-Arab rapproachement), 1955-58.

MEMBER: American Philosophical Association, Metaphysical Society of America, Religious Education Association (member of executive committee of national conferences, 1957, 1962), Conference on Jewish Philosophy (treasurer, 1961—), Association for Existential Psychology and Psychiatry (council member), American Academy of Religion, Association for Humanistic Psychology, Fellowship of Reconciliation, Jewish Peace Fellowship, Phi Beta Kappa. *Awards, honors:* Littauer Foundation fellowship, 1960, for work on *Problematic Rebel*; LL.D., University of Vermont, 1961.

WRITINGS: Martin Buber: The Life of Dialogue, University of Chicago Press, 1955, 2nd edition, 1960; *Problematic Rebel: An Image of Modern Man*, Random House, 1963, revised edition published as *Problematic Rebel: Melville, Dostoievsky, Kafka, Camus*, University of Chicago Press, 1970; (editor with Paul A. Schilpp); *Martin Buber in Philosophen*, W. Kohlhammer, 1963, (translation published as *The Philosophy of Martin Buber*, Open Court, 1967; (editor, author of introduction and conclusion) *The Worlds of Existentialism: A Critical Reader*, Random House, 1964; *To Deny Our Nothingness: Contemporary Images of Man*, Delacorte, 1967, 2nd edition, 1968; *Touchstones of Reality: Existential Trust and the Community of Peace*, Dutton, 1972; (with T. Patrick Burke and Samuel Laeuchli) *Searching in the Syntax of Things: Experiments in the Study of Religion*, Fortress, 1972; *The Hidden Human Image*, Delacorte, 1974; *Martin Buber: A Critical Biography*, Dutton, 1975.

Editor, translator, and author of introduction of works of Martin Buber: *Hasidism and Modern Man*, Horizon, 1958; *The Origin and Meaning of Hasidism*, Horizon, 1960; *Pointing the Way*, Torchbooks, 1963; *Daniel: Dialogues of Realization*, Holt, 1964; *The Knowledge of Man*, Harper, 1965; *A Believing Humanism: My Testament*, Simon & Schuster, 1968; *Martin Buber and the Theater*, Funk, 1969.

Translator of works of Martin Buber: *The Tales of Rabbi Nachman*, Horizon, 1956; *Eclipse of God*, Torchbooks, 1957; *The Legend of the Baal-shem*, Harper, 1957.

Also author of pamphlets and studies; contributor of articles to journals; member of editorial committee, Religious Education Association, 1956—; member of editorial board of *Judaism, Journal of Existentialism, Review of Existential Psychology and Psychiatry*, and *Religious Education*.

SIDELIGHTS: Friedman is competent in German and French, and has some knowledge of Hebrew but still is studying the language in order to read the literature of Hasidism as well as the Hebrew Bible in the original. *Avocational interests:* Piano, literature, photography, working with clay.

*   *   *

FRIEND, Robert 1913-

PERSONAL: Born November 25, 1913, in Brooklyn, N.Y.; son of Charles (a sewing machine operator) and Lilly (Halperin) Friend. *Education:* Brooklyn College (now Brooklyn College of the City of New York), B.A., 1934;

Harvard University, M.A., 1947; additional study at Cambridge University, 1954-55; Hebrew University, Ph.D., 1970. *Home:* 13 Jabotinsky St., Jerusalem, Israel.

CAREER: Taught English in Puerto Rico, 1937-38 and 1940, and in Panama, 1942-46; has taught or studied in France, Germany, and England; Hebrew University, Jerusalem, Israel, 1951—, began as lecturer, now senior lecturer in English literature. *Awards, honors:* Jeannette Sewell Davis Prize, *Poetry* magazine, 1940.

WRITINGS: Shadow on the Sun (poems), Decker, 1941; (with Harold Schimmel and Dennis Silk) *Now*, Ah'shav Publishers (Jerusalem), 1964; *Salt Gifts* (poems), Charioteer Press, 1964; *The Practice of Absence* (poems), Beth Shalom Press (Jerusalem), 1971; *Selected Poems*, Lyrebird Press (London), in press. Poems have appeared in *Poetry, Atlantic, Adam, Saturday Review, Partisan Review, New Republic, Quarterly Review of Literature, London Magazine, Epoch, Prairie Schooner, New York Times Book Review, Jerusalem Post, New Yorker, Beloit Poetry Journal, Furioso*, and other publications. Has translated poems from French, Spanish, German, Hebrew, and Yiddish.

WORK IN PROGRESS: Friend is translating the poems of Leah Goldberg, Gabriel Preil and Dan Pagis from Hebrew into English for *Modern Poetry in Translation* (London), and is translating other works of Leah Goldberg.

SIDELIGHTS: Friend has visited Guatemala, Mexico, Columbia, Italy, Greece and Holland, in addition to the countries mentioned above.

*   *   *

FRYKLUND, Verne C(harles) 1896-

PERSONAL: Born January 4, 1896, in Prentice, Wis.; son of Olaf John and Hannah (Pearson) Fryklund; married Adah Agnes Smythe, 1919 (died 1951); married Laurel Minor Colton, December 19, 1955; children: (first marriage) Verne C., Jr., John Richard. *Education:* Stout Institute (now University of Wisconsin—Stout), student 1914-16; Colorado College of Education (now University of Northern Colorado), A.B., 1923; University of Missouri, M.A., 1927; University of Minnesota, Ph.D., 1933. *Home and office:* 4007 Calle Mayo, San Clemente, Calif. 92672.

CAREER: Teacher in public schools in Arizona, Michigan, Colorado, and Texas, 1916-22; Nebraska State Teachers College, Kearney, instructor in industrial education and head of department, 1922-30; University of Minnesota, Minneapolis, instructor, later assistant professor, 1930-37, associate professor of industrial education, 1941-42; supervisor in Detroit public schools and associate professor of vocational education at Wayne University (now Wayne State), Detroit, Mich., 1937-41; Stout Institute (now University of Wisconsin—Stout), Menomonie, Wis., president, 1945-61. Visiting summer professor at six colleges and universities. Educational consultant in Japan for Secretary of Defense, 1948; consultant, Ford Motor Co. Industrial Arts Awards, 1950-60, U.S. Department of Defense Committee on Education for Armed Forces, 1959-62. *Military service:* U.S. Army, Field Artillery, 1916-17; became sergeant. U.S. Army, served with Armored Force, Air Corps, Office of Air Surgeon, and Personnel Distribution Command, 1942-45; became lieutenant colonel; received Legion of Merit. U.S. Army Reserve, 1946-54; now colonel (retired). *Awards, honors:* Outstanding Achievement Award, University of Minnesota, 1953; Ship's Man of the Year Award, American Industrial Arts Association, 1961; Outstanding Achievement Award, University of Wisconsin—Stout, 1972.

MEMBER: American Association for the Advancement of Science (fellow), American Vocational Association (life member), National Education Association, American Education Research Association, American Association of Teacher Educators in Vocational Education (president, 1940), American Industrial Arts Association (chairman, accreditation committee), American Council on Industrial Arts Teacher Education, American Association of Colleges for Teacher Education (regional planning commmittee), North Central Association of Colleges and Secondary Schools Commission for Colleges, Mississippi Valley Industrial Arts Conference (chairman, 1941-61), Michigan Industrial Education Society (life member), Wisconsin Vocational Association, Wisconsin Education Association, Phi Delta Kappa, Epsilon Pi Tau (honorary), Mu Sigma Pi (honorary), Iota Lambda Sigma (honorary), Masons, Loyal Order of Moose, Rotary, American Legion.

WRITINGS: (With R. W. Selvidge) *Principles of Trade and Industrial Teaching*, Manual Arts Press, 1930, revised edition, 1946; (with A. J. LaBerge) *General Shop Woodworking*, McKnight & McKnight, 1936, 7th edition, 1972; (editor) *Household Mechanics* (course of study), Detroit Public Schools, 1938, 2nd edition, 1940; (with F. R. Kepler) *General Drafting*, McKnight & McKnight, 1939, 4th edition, 1969; (editor) *General Drafting, Intermediate Grades* (course of study), Detroit Public Schools, 1939; (with others) *Analysis of General Machine Shop*, Detroit Public Schools, 1939; (editor) *Patternmaking* (course of study), Detroit Public Schools, 1939; (editor) *General Woodworking* (course of study), Detroit Public Schools, 1939.

(With others) *Analysis of Activities in Household Mechanics*, Detroit Public Schools, 1940; *Industrial Arts Teacher Education in the United States*, McKnight & McKnight, 1940; (with others) *Handbook for Directed Teaching in Industrial Education*, Wayne University Press, 1940; *Combat Tank Repair and Maintenance* (analysis), Rock Island Arsenal, U.S. Army, 1941; *Repair and Overhaul of Light Tanks*, Books I-II, Chief of Ordnance, U.S. Army, 1942; *Trade and Job Analysis*, Bruce, 1942, 2nd revised edition published as *Analysis Technique for Instructors*, 1956, new revised edition published as *Occupational Analysis*, 1970; (editor) *Teaching Techniques in the Armored Force School*, Armored School (Fort Knox), 1942; (with C. H. Sechrest) *Materials Construction*, Bruce, 1943.

Author and editor of bulletins and yearbooks, including nine military training bulletins. Contributor of more than seventy articles, mainly on aspects of industrial arts and vocational education, to journals.

WORK IN PROGRESS: Revisions of his books.

SIDELIGHTS: Fryklund's writings have been translated into Russian, Japanese, Chinese, Spanish, Persian, Greek, Hebrew, and Turkish. He has traveled in sixty-three countries, and speaks Swedish.

* * *

FUERER-HAIMENDORF, Christoph von 1909-

PERSONAL: Born July 27, 1909, in Vienna, Austria; now British subject; son of Rudolf (a civil servant) and Ida (Kurzbauer) von Fuerer-Haimendorf; married Elizabeth Barnardo (a bibliographer), 1938; children: Nicholas. *Education:* University of Vienna, Ph.D., 1931; London School of Economics and Political Science, postdoctoral research, 1935-36. *Religion:* Roman Catholic. *Home:* 32 Clarendon Rd., London W.11, England. *Office:* School of Oriental and African Studies, University of London, London, W.C.1, England.

CAREER: University of Vienna, Vienna, Austria, research assistant, 1931-36, lecturer, 1937-38; Indian Government, External Affairs Department, special officer in Subansiri and assistant political officer, Balipara Frontier Tract, 1944-45; Osmania University, Hyderabad, India, professor of anthropology, 1945-49, and adviser to government for tribes and backward classes; School of Oriental and African Studies, University of London, London, England, reader in anthropology, 1949-51, professor of Asian anthropology, 1951—. Anthropological field work in India, 1936-37, 1939-49, 1953, 1962, 1970, in Nepal, 1953-54, 1957-58, 1962, 1966, 1972, 1974, and Ceylon, 1960. *Member:* Royal Anthropological Institute, Royal Geographical Society, Austrian Academy of Sciences (corresponding member). *Awards, honors:* Rockefeller fellow, 1935-37; Rivers Memorial Medal of Royal Anthropological Institute, 1949.

WRITINGS: *The Naked Nagas*, Methuen, 1939; *The Chenchus*, Macmillan, 1943; *The Reddis of the Bison Hills*, Macmillan, 1945; *Tribal Hyderabad: Four Reports*, Revenue Department, Hyderabad Government, 1945; *Ethnographic Notes on the Tribes of the Subansiri Region*, Assam Government, 1947; *The Raj Gonds of Adilabad*, Macmillan, 1948; *Himalayan Barbary*, J. Murray, 1956; *The Apa Tanis and Their Neighbours: A Primitive Civilization of the Eastern Himalayas*, Free Press of Glencoe, 1962; *The Sherpas of Nepal: Buddhist Highlanders*, University of California Press, 1964; (editor and contributor) *Caste and Kin in Nepal, India, and Ceylon: Anthropological Studies in Hindu-Buddhist Contact Zones*, Asia Publishing, 1966; *Morals and Merit: A Study of Values and Social Controls in South Asian Societies*, University of Chicago Press, 1967; *The Konyak Nagas: An Indian Frontier Tribe*, Holt, 1969; (editor) *Contributions to the Anthropology of Nepal*, Philips & Aris, 1974; *Himalayan Traders*, J. Murray, 1975.

Contributor: *Custom is Kind* (essays presented to R. R. Marett), Hutchinson, 1936; D. Westerman, editor, *Die heutigen Naturvolker im Kampf und Ausgleich mit der neuen Zeit*, F. Enke, 1939; F. M. Schnitger, *Forgotten Kingdoms in Sumatra*, Brill (Leiden), 1939; *Essays in Anthropology Presented to Sarat Chandra Roy*, Maxwell & Co. (Lucknow), 1942; (author of appendix) *Census of India 1941*, Volume XXI, 1945; (author of foreword) Stephen Fuchs, *The Children of Hari*, Herold (Vienna), 1950; (author of foreword) S. C. Dube, *The Kamar*, Universal Publishers (Lucknow), 1951; *Historia Mundi*, Volume II, 1953; (author of foreword) Elizabeth von Fuerer-Haimendorf, *An Anthropological Bibliography of South Asia*, Mouton (Paris), 1958-70; *Mount Everest: Formation, Population and Exploration of the Mount Everest Region*, Oxford University Press, 1963; C. Maloney, editor, *South Asia: Seven Community Profiles*, Holt, 1974.

Contributor to *Yearbook of Anthropology*, 1955, and to the *Proceedings* of the 37th Indian Science Congress. Also contributor of about thirty articles to professional journals.

WORK IN PROGRESS: Research on the anthropology of Nepal.

SIDELIGHTS: Fuerer-Haimendorf is competent in French and moderately competent in Latin, Greek, Gondi, Hindi, Assamese, and Nepali. *Avocational interests:* Music.

* * *

FUKEI, Gladys Arlene (Harper) 1920-

PERSONAL: Surname is pronounced to rhyme with "lei";

born November 18, 1920, in Frankfort, Kan.; daughter of Harry T. and Edna (Warnica) Harper; married Budd S. Fukei (a newspaperman), May 1, 1954; children: Sumiye Josephine. *Education:* University of Washington, Seattle, B.A., 1957, Master of Librarianship, 1963. *Home:* 5267 12th N.E., Seattle, Wash. 98105.

CAREER: South Mercer Junior High School, Mercer Island, Wash., librarian, 1963—. *Member:* American Library Association, National Education Association, Washington Library Association, Washington Education Association, Washington State School Librarians Association.

WRITINGS: East to Freedom, Westminster, 1964. Contributor to *Pacific Citizen, Sunset, U.S. Lady, Link.*

SIDELIGHTS: East to Freedom was the result of personal observation of Communist occupation of China. Has knowledge of spoken Chinese.

AVOCATIONAL INTERESTS: Oriental cookery.†

*   *   *

FUKUTAKE, Tadashi   1917-

PERSONAL: Born February 12, 1917, in Okayama, Japan; son of Tatsue and Kaoru Fukutake; married Yoshiko Hasegawa, January, 1943; children: Hisayo and Kyoko (daughters). *Education:* Tokyo Imperial University (now University of Tokyo), student, 1937-40, graduate student, 1940-42, Ph.D., 1962. *Home:* 6-31-20 Daita, Setagaya-ku, Tokyo, Japan. *Office:* University of Tokyo, 1 Motofuji-cho, Bunkyo-ku, Tokyo, Japan.

CAREER: University of Tokyo, Japan, assistant, 1942-48, assistant professor, 1948-56, associate professor, 1956-60, professor of sociology, 1960—. *Member:* Japan Sociological Society (secretary-general, 1952-60; vice-president, 1962-66; president, 1968-70), Science Council of Japan. *Awards, honors:* Mainichi Publication Prize for *Sekai Noson no Tabi* ("Travel Reports on Foreign Villages"), 1963.

WRITINGS: Chugoku Noson Shakai no Kozo (title means "The Structure of the Chinese Rural Society"), Taigado, 1946, revised and enlarged edition, Yuhikaku, 1953; *Chugoku Sonraku no Shakai Seikatsu* (title means "Social Life in Chinese Village"), Kobundo, 1947; *Shakaigaku no Gendaiteki Kadai* (title means "Current Problems of Sociology"), Nihonhyoronsha, 1948, 2nd edition, University of Tokyo Press, 1953; *Nihon Noson no Shakaiteki Seikaku* (title means "The Social Character of the Japanese Rural Village"), University of Tokyo Press, 1949; *Shakai Kagaku to Kachi Handan* (title means "Social Science and Freedom-from-Value Judgement"), Shunjusha, 1949.

(With Rokuro Hidaka) *Shakaigaku: Shakai to Bunka no Kiso Riron* (title means "Sociology: Basic Theories on Society and Culture"), Kobunsha, 1952; *Shakaigaku no Kihon Mondai* (title means "Fundamental Problems of Sociology"), University of Tokyo Press, 1952, enlarged edition, 1957; *Nihon no Noson Shakai* (title means "Rural Society in Japan"), University of Tokyo Press, 1953; (with Tetsundo Tsukamoto) *Nihon Nomin no Shakaiteki Seikaku* (title means "The Social Character of Japanese Farmers"), Yuhikaku, 1954; *Shakai Chosa* (title means "Social Research"), Iwanami Shoten, 1958; *Nihon Sonraku no Shakai Kozo* (title means "The Social Structure of the Japanese Village"), University of Tokyo Press, 1959.

Sekai Noson no Tabi (title means "Travel Reports on Foreign Villages"), University of Tokyo Press, 1962; *Man and Society in Japan*, University of Tokyo Press, 1962; (contributor) *Japanese Culture: Its Development and Characteristics*, edited by R. J. Smith and R. K. Beardsley, Aldine, 1962; (contributor) *Public Administration Problems of New and Rapidly Growing Towns in Asia*, United Nations, 1962; *Nihon Noson Shakai Ron*, University of Tokyo Press, 1964, translation by Ronald P. Dore, published as *Japanese Rural Society*, Oxford University Press, 1967; (with Tsutomu Ouchi and Chie Nakane) *The Socio-Economic Structure of the Indian Village*, Institute of Asian Economic Affairs, 1964; *Asian Rural Society: China, India, Japan*, University of Washington Press, 1967; *Nihon Noson no Shakaimondai* (title means "Social Problems of the Japanese Rural Village"), University of Tokyo Press, 1967; *Shakaigaku no Hoho to Kadai* (title means "Methods and Problems of Sociology"), University of Tokyo Press, 1969; *Gendai Nihon Shakairon*, English edition published as *Contemporary Japanese Society*, University of Tokyo Press, 1974; (editor with K. Morioka) *Sociology and Social Development in Asia: Proceedings of the Symposium*, University of Tokyo Press, 1974.

Author of four other community studies (in English) published by Mainichi Newspapers in its "Population Problems" series, and by the Japanese National Commission for UNESCO. Contributor to *Orient/West* and *Sociologia Ruralis*.

*   *   *

FULLER, Wayne E(dison)   1919-

PERSONAL: Born April 13, 1919, in Henderson, Colo.; son of William Edgar (a rural mail carrier) and Dora (Foster) Fuller; married Wilma Jean Bryan, February 12, 1944; children: Jamie Louise, Douglas, Bryan. *Education:* University of Colorado, B.A., 1941; University of Denver, M.A., 1949; University of California, Berkeley, Ph.D., 1954. *Politics:* Democrat. *Religion:* Presbyterian. *Home:* 309 Benedict Dr., El Paso, Tex. *Office:* Department of History, University of Texas, El Paso, Tex.

CAREER: Rock County Historical Society, Janesville, Wis., director, 1954-55; University of Texas at El Paso, assistant professor, 1955-57, associate professor, 1957-63, professor of history, 1963—, president of the board of directors of United Christian Campus Fellowship. *Military service:* U.S. Army, 1942-48; became captain; wounded in Normandy, 1944; received Purple Heart. *Member:* American Historical Association, Organization of American Historians, Agricultural History Society, American Association of University Professors, Southern Historical Association, Western History Association. *Awards, honors:* Southern Fellowship award for research, 1960.

WRITINGS: RFD: The Changing Face of Rural America, Indiana University Press, 1964; *The American Mail: Enlarger of the Common Life*, University of Chicago Press, 1972. Contributor to historical journals.

WORK IN PROGRESS: American Country Schools; Country Life.

*   *   *

GABRIEL, Ralph Henry   1890-

PERSONAL: Born April 29, 1890, in Reading, N.Y.; son of Cleveland (a farmer) and Alta (Monroe) Gabriel; married Christine Davis, August 18, 1917; children: Robert Todd, John Cleveland, Susan (Mrs. Keith Cunliffe). *Education:* Yale University, B.A., 1913, M.A., 1915, Ph.D., 1919. *Politics:* Independent. *Religion:* Congregationalist. *Home:* 3440 38th St. N.W., Washington, D.C. 20016.

CAREER: Yale University, New Haven, Conn., 1915-58, associate professor, 1925-28, professor of history, 1928-58, fellow of Trumbull College, 1933—; American University, School of International Service, Washington, D.C., professor of American civilization, 1958-64. Member of faculty, U.S. War Department School of Military Government, 1943-46; Pitt Professor of American History and Institutions, Cambridge University, 1951-52; visiting professor at other universities in America, Australia, and Tokyo, 1933-65. UNESCO, member of U.S. delegation to Paris Conference, 1958, member of U.S. National Committee, 1959-63. *Military service:* U.S. Army, Infantry, 1917-18.

MEMBER: American Historical Association, American Studies Association (president, 1953-58), New Haven Colony Historical Society (president, 195'58), Massachusetts Historical Society, Phi Beta Kappa, Sigma Xi, Beta Theta Phi, Cosmos Club (Washington, D.C.), Graduate Club (New Haven). *Awards, honors:* M.A. from Cambridge University, 1952; Litt.D. from Bucknell University, 1952, Williams College, 1958; L.H.D. from Colgate University, 1963.

WRITINGS: (With Dumas Malone and Frederick J. Manning) *An Outline of U.S. History* (for use at Yale College), Yale University Press, 1921; *The Evolution of Long Island*, Yale University Press, 1921, revised edition, I. J. Friedman, 1960; (with Arthur B. Darling) *The Yale Course of Home Study* (based on *The Chronicles of America*), Yale University Press, 1924; *Toilers of Land and Sea*, Yale University Press, 1926; *The Lure of the Frontier: A Story of Race Conflict*, Yale University Press, 1929; (with Mabel B. Casner) *Exploring American History*, Harcourt, 1931; *American Democracy in the World Crisis*, Periwinkle Press, 1940; *The Course of American Democratic Thought: An Intellectual History Since 1815*, Ronald, 1940, 2nd edition, 1956; *Elias Boudinot, Cherokee, and His America*, University of Oklahoma Press, 1941; *Main Currents in American History*, Appleton, 1942.

(With Casner) *The Story of American Democracy*, Harcourt, 1950, 3rd edition, 1955; *Religion and Learning at Yale: The Church of Christ in the College and University, 1757-1957*, Yale University Press, 1958; *Traditional Values in American Life*, prepared for the U.S. National Commission for UNESCO, ca. 1960; (with Casner) *Story of the American Nation*, Harcourt, 1962; (with Leonard Wood) *America: It's People and Values*, Harcourt, 1971, 2nd edition, 1975; *American Values, Continuity and Change*, Greenwood Press, 1974.

Editor: C. R. Brown, C. Dinsmore, and others, *Christianity and Modern Thought*, Yale University Press, 1924; (with others) Michel Guillaume St. Jean de Crevecoeur, *Sketches of Eighteenth Century America: More Letters From an American Farmer*, Yale University Press, 1925; "The Pageant of America," Volumes 3, 6, and 7, Yale University Press, 1925-29; Sarah E. Royce, *Frontier Lady: Recollections of the Gold Rush and Early California*, Yale University Press, 1932; (with H. R. Warfel and S. T. Williams) *The American Mind*, two volumes, American Book Co., 1947; *The Federalist: Hamilton, Madison and Jay on the Constitution*, Liberal Arts Press, 1954. General editor, Library of Congress series in American civilization.

AVOCATIONAL INTERESTS: Photography.

BIOGRAPHICAL SOURCES: Robert A. Skotheim, "The Writing of American Histories of Ideas: Two Traditions in the XXth Century," *Journal of the History of Ideas*, April-June, 1964.

GADDIS, Vincent H. 1913-

PERSONAL: Born December 28, 1913; son of Tilden H. (a minister) and Alice M. (Smith) Gaddis; married Margaret Paine Rea (a free-lance writer), July 14, 1947. *Education:* Attended Olivet College Academy, Olivet, Ill., 1937-38, Olivet College, 1939. *Politics:* Independent. *Home and office:* Route 3, Box 437, Escondido, Calif. 92025. *Agent:* Jay Garon-Brooke Associates, Inc., 415 Central Park W., 17-D, New York, N.Y. 10025.

CAREER: Newspaper reporter, then writer-editor for radio station, Warsaw, Ind., 1947-52; *Elkhart Truth* (daily newspaper), Elkhart, Ind., feature writer, 1952-59; public relations writer for Studebaker-Packard Corp. and Mercedes-Benz Sales, Inc., both South Bend, Ind., 1959-61; free-lance writer, 1962—. Semi-professional magician. *Member:* International Brotherhood of Magicians, National Investigations Committee on Aerial Phenomena, Authors Guild, American Society for Psychic Research, International Fortean Organization (honorary chairman), Society for Investigation of the Unexplained, Parapsychology Foundation, Aerial Phenomena Research Organization.

WRITINGS: *Winona Lake: A Memory and a Vision*, Berne Witness Co., 1949; *Invisible Horizons: True Mysteries of the Sea*, Chilton, 1965; *Mysterious Fires and Lights*, McKay, 1967; *Wide World of Magic*, Criterion, 1967; (with wife, Margaret Gaddis) *Strange World of Animals and Pets*, Regnery, 1970; (with Margaret Gaddis) *Curious World of Twins*, Hawthorn, 1972; *Courage in Crisis*, Hawthorn, 1973. Contributor of more than two hundred articles to sixty magazines, including *Coronet*, *Pageant*, *American Mercury*, *Travel*, and *True*.

WORK IN PROGRESS: *Amerindian Lore*, additional works on mysterious psychical and physical phenomena.

* * *

GAEBELEIN, Frank E(ly) 1899-

PERSONAL: Surname is pronounced *Gay*-ba-line; born March 31, 1899, in Mount Vernon, N.Y.; son of Arno Clemens (a clergyman and author) and Emma Fredericka (Grimm) Gaebelein; married Dorothy Laura Medd, December 8, 1923; children: Dorothy Laura (Mrs. Clyde R. Hampton), Donn Medd, Gretchen Elizabeth (Mrs. Philip G. Hull). *Education:* New York University, A.B., 1920; Harvard University, A.M., 1921. *Politics:* Independent. *Home:* 3816 Lorcom Lane, Arlington, Va. 22207.

CAREER: Stony Brook School, Stony Brook, N.Y., organizer, 1921, headmaster, 1922-63, headmaster emeritus, 1963-66; *Christianity Today*, Washington, D.C., co-editor, 1963—. Reformed Episcopal Church, ordained deacon, 1940, presbyter, 1941—; guest preacher at colleges and universities and lecturer at theological seminaries; director of faculty of summer seminar on faith and learning, Wheaton College, Wheaton, Ill., 1969-72. Chairman of board, Evangelical Books, Inc. Former chairman, Council for Religion in Independent Schools; former president, American Tract Society. Pianist; has appeared with orchestra and in recital and on national radio broadcasts. *Military service:* U.S. Army, Infantry, 1918; became second lieutenant.

MEMBER: Headmasters Association, American Academy of Religion, Evangelical Theological Society, Phi Beta Kappa, Kappa Sigma, American Alpine Club, Alpine Club of Canada Harvard Club of New York, Cosmos Club (Washington, D.C.). *Awards, honors:* Litt. D., Wheaton

College, Wheaton, Ill., 1931; D.D., Reformed Episcopal Theological Seminary, 1951; LL.D., Houghton College, 1960.

WRITINGS: Down Through the Ages, Macmillan, 1924; *A Brief Survey of Scripture*, Our Hope, 1929; *Exploring the Bible*, Harper, 1929, 3rd revised edition, Van Kampden, 1950; *The Hollow Queen* (fiction), Christopher, 1933; *Philemon, the Gospel of Emancipation*, Our Hope, 1939; *Looking Unto Him*, Zondervan, 1941, new edition, 1961; *The Christian Use of the Bible*, Moody, 1946; *The Servant and the Dove*, Our Hope, 1946; *Christian Education in a Democracy*, Oxford University Press, 1951; (editor) Samuel Rutherford, *Letters*, Moody, 1951; *The Pattern of God's Truth*, Oxford University Press, 1954; *The Practical Epistle of James*, Channel Press, 1955; *The Story of the Scofield Reference Bible 1909-1959*, Oxford University Press, 1959; (editor with Earl G. Harrison Jr. and William L. Swing), *Education for Decision*, Seabury, 1963; (editor and author of introduction) *A Christianity Today Reader*, Meredith, 1966; *A Varied Harvest*, Eerdmans, 1967; *Four Minor Prophets*, Moody, 1970; *From Day to Day*, Canon, 1974.

Writer of booklets, brochures, and articles on biblical subjects and on Christian education. Former publisher, *Our Hope*; former associate editor, later consulting editor, *Eternity*; general editor, *The Expositor's Bible Commentary*, 1971—; vice-chairman of Oxford University Press committee on revision of *Scofield Reference Bible*.

WORK IN PROGRESS: Books on biblical and educational subjects.

AVOCATIONAL INTERESTS: Mountaineering, music.

*   *   *

GAGE, William W(hitney)   1925-

PERSONAL: Born February 8, 1925, in Corning, N.Y.; son of Henry Phelps (a physicist) and Luella (Cowan) Gage. *Education:* Cornell University, A.B., 1950, A.M., 1952, Ph.D., 1958; summer study at University of Michigan, 1951, 1958, Indiana University, 1953, University of Chicago, 1955. *Politics:* Republican. *Religion:* Episcopalian. *Home:* 10 Trafalgar St., Rochester, N.Y. 14619. *Office:* Center for Applied Linguistics, 1755 Massachusetts Ave., N.W., Washington, D.C. 20036.

CAREER: Cornell University, Ithaca, N.Y., research associate, 1951-55; Center for Applied Linguistics, Washington, D.C., project linguist, 1959-61, research linguist, 1961—. Consultant to Defense Language Institute. *Military service:* U.S. Naval Reserve, active duty, 1943-46, 1951. *Member:* Linguistic Society of America, Modern Language Association of America, American Anthropological Association, American Indian Ethnohistoric Conference, Canadian Linguistic Association, Phi Beta Kappa, Phi Kappa Phi, Anthropological Society of Washington, Linguistic Circle of New York, Washington Linguistic Club.

WRITINGS: (With H. Merill Jackson) *Verb Constructions in Vietnamese*, Department of Far Eastern Studies, Cornell University, 1953; (with others) *Tieng Anh cho Nguoi Viet* (title means "Speakers of Vietnamese"), American Council of Learned Societies, 1955; (with Jacob Ornstein) *The ABC's of Languages and Linguistics*, Chilton, C. 1964; (with Birgit A. Blass) *A Provisional Survey of Materials for the Study of Neglected Languages*, Center for Applied Linguistics, 1969; *English for Speakers of Vietnamese*, Spoken Language Services, 1971.

WORK IN PROGRESS: The Sounds of English and Russian; *The Grammatical Structures of English and Russian*; *Handbook of Information about the Vietnamese Language.*†

*   *   *

GAINES, Pierce Welch   1905-

PERSONAL: Born August 13, 1905, in New Haven, Conn.; son of John Marshall (an efficiency expert) and Cornelia (Welch) Gaines; married Carolyn Fliess, July 28, 1934; children: Julie L. (Mrs. Clifton A. Phalen), Carolyn M. (Mrs. Samuel A. Roberson), Pierce, Jr. *Education:* Yale University, A.B., 1927; Harvard University, LL.B., 1931. *Politics:* Republican. *Religion:* Episcopalian. *Home:* 1614 Bronson Rd., Fairfield, Conn.

CAREER: Allan R. Campbell (law firm), New York, N.Y., attorney, 1932-34; U.S. Reconstruction Finance Corp., New York, N.Y., attorney, 1935-36; Curtis & Stoddard (law firm), Bridgeport, Conn., partner, 1936-40; Davis Polk Wardwell Sunderland & Kiendl, New York, N.Y., attorney, 1940-42, 1945-46; American Telephone and Telegraph Co., New York, N.Y., attorney, 1947-68. U.S. Department of the Navy, Bureau of Aeronautics, Washington, D.C., assistant counsel, later counsel, 1942-45. Trustee, Yale Library Associates, 1962—; Fairfield Country Day School, trustee, 1952-63, secretary of the board, 1953-58; director, Fairfield Community Chest, 1961-62; vice-president, Fairfield Historical Society, 1971—.

MEMBER: American Antiquarian Society, Bibliographical Society of America, Bibliographical Society of University of Virginia, Connecticut Historical Society, New York Historical Society, Acorn Club (Connecticut). *Awards, honors:* Distinguished Civilian Service Award, U.S. Navy, 1945.

WRITINGS: Political Works of Concealed Authorship During the Administrations of Washington, Adams and Jefferson, 1789-1809, Yale University Library, 1959, third edition, revised and enlarged, published as *Political Works of Concealed Authorship Relating to the United States, 1789-1810*, Shoe String, 1972; (editor) *The Journal of William Stebbins*, Acorn Club, 1968; *William Cobbett and the United States, 1792-1835: A Bibliography with Notes and Extracts*, American Antiquarian Society, 1971. Contributor of articles to *American Antiquarian Society Proceedings* and *Yale University Library Gazette*.

AVOCATIONAL INTERESTS: Collecting political Americana for period 1789-1810.

*   *   *

GALANTE, Pierre   1909-

PERSONAL: Born November 22, 1909, in Nice, France; son of Antoine and Anne (Sicart) Galante; married Olivia de Havilland (an actress), April 2, 1955; children: Gisele. *Education:* University of Paris, law student, two years. *Religion:* Roman Catholic. *Home:* 3 Rue Benouville, Paris 16, France. *Agent:* Mrs. Carlton Cole, Waldorf Towers, New York, N.Y. *Office: Paris Match*, 51 Rue Pierre Charron, Paris 8e, France.

CAREER: Paris Match, Paris, France, journalist, 1949—, now secretary general. *Wartime service:* Member of French Resistance, 1940-45; received Legion of Honor. *Member:* Sacem (French authors association).

WRITINGS: Lew hommes bleus au Maroc, Barraud Disney, 1956; *Algerie sous mensonge*, Paris Match, 1960; *Ja-*

pon, archipel des hommes, Paris Match, 1961; (with Jack Miller) *The Berlin Wall*, Doubleday, 1965; *The General*, Random House, 1968; *Malraux*, Cowles, 1971; *Madamoiselle Chanel*, Regnery, 1973. Author of two film scripts.

WORK IN PROGRESS: A book about the Corsican Connection.

SIDELIGHTS: Competent in English and Italian.

* * *

GALLAGHER, Robert E(mmett) 1922-

PERSONAL: Born July 28, 1922, in Chicago, Ill.; son of Peter Joseph (an engineer) and Frances (Kelly) Gallagher. *Education:* DePaul University, A.B., 1947; Northwestern University, M.A., 1950, Ph.D., 1957.

CAREER: University of Illinois, Chicago, associate professor of English, 1960-64. *Military service:* U.S. Navy, 1943-46; became lieutenant junior grade. *Member:* Hakluyt Society, Society for Nautical Research, Society for History of Discoveries, Modern Language Association of America.

WRITINGS: (Editor) *Byron's Journal of His Circumnavigation, 1764-66*, Cambridge University Press, 1964.

WORK IN PROGRESS: A book, *Shipwreck of the Wager.*†

* * *

GALLERY, Daniel V. 1901-
(Dan Gallery)

PERSONAL: Born July 10, 1901, in Chicago, Ill.; son of Daniel Vincent (a lawyer) and Mary (Onahan) Gallery; married Vera Lee Dunn (an artist), August 9, 1929; children: James J., Daniel V., Beatrice Constance (Mrs. W. R. Moyer). *Education:* Attended U.S. Naval Academy at Annapolis and U.S. Navy Postgraduate School. *Religion:* Roman Catholic. *Home:* R.F.D. 1, 3042 Fox Mill Rd., Oakton, Va. *Agent:* Harold Matson Co., Inc., 30 Rockefeller Plaza, New York, N.Y. 10020.

CAREER: U.S. Navy, 1917-60; naval aviator, 1926-60; retired as rear admiral, 1960. Little League baseball commissioner in Latin America, 1957-60. *Awards, honors:* Navy Distinguished Service Medal; Presidential Unit Citation; Commander, Order of the British Empire (military).

WRITINGS—All novels, except as noted: *Clear the Decks*, Morrow, 1951; *Twenty Million Tons Under the Sea*, Regnery, 1956; *Now Hear This*, Norton, 1965; *Eight Bells and All's Well*, Norton, 1965; *Stand By-y-y to Start Engines*, Norton, 1966; *The Brink*, Doubleday, 1968; *Cap'n Fatso*, Norton, 1969; *Pueblo Incident* (nonfiction), Doubleday, 1970; *Away Boarders*, Norton, 1971. Writer of motion picture and television scripts on naval subjects. Author of more than forty articles and short stories published in national magazines since 1945, with twenty in the *Saturday Evening Post*, others in *Esquire, Collier's, Reader's Digest, Coronet, Sports Illustrated, Argosy, Adventure, Nation's Business*, and *What's New*. All fiction appears under the name Dan Gallery.

SIDELIGHTS: Gallery commanded the Task Group of the Atlantic fleet which, on June 4, 1944, off French West Africa, boarded and seized the German Submarine U-505. This was the first enemy warship captured by the U.S. Navy in 129 years and the only German U-boat ever taken in such a manner. Gallery told *CA*: "U-505 is now hauled out of the water and parked alongside the Museum of Science and Industry in Chicago." The novels *Clear the*

Decks and *Twenty Million Tons Under the Sea* have been published in several translations. *Avocational interests:* Baseball, cartooning, West Indian steel bands.

* * *

GALLIN, Sister Mary Alice 1921-

PERSONAL: Born December 30, 1921, in New York, N.Y.; daughter of William L. H. (a contractor) and Alice T. (Monteith) Gallin. *Education:* College of New Rochelle, A.B., 1942; Fordham University, A.M., 1944; Catholic University of America, Ph.D., 1955. *Home and office:* College of New Rochelle, New Rochelle, N.Y.

CAREER: Roman Catholic nun. College of New Rochelle, New Rochelle, N.Y., associate professor of history, 1950-67, professor of history, 1967—, acting dean, 1955-57, chairman of department of history, 1957-63, 1968-71, director of public relations, 1961-63, director of students, 1963-67. *Member:* American Historical Association, American Catholic Historical Association (member of executive council, 1963-66), American Association of University Professors.

WRITINGS: German Resistance to Hitler, Catholic University Press, 1955, 2nd edition, 1961. Contributor of biographical articles to *The New Catholic Encyclopedia*.

WORK IN PROGRESS: A book on German universities on the eve of Nazism.

* * *

GALLOWAY, Margaret C(ecilia) 1915-

PERSONAL: Born June 13, 1915, in Rochester, Kent, England; daughter of Vance Ewart and Cecilia (Day) Galloway. *Education:* Royal College of Music, London, England, A.R.C.M., 1936. *Home:* Half Acre, R.R.1, Orangeville, Ontario L9W 2Y8, Canada; and 53 Periwinkle Park, Sanibel Island, Fla. 33957.

CAREER: Teacher of music at schools in Kent, England 1936-39, in East Ham, London, England, 1941-48; Redland Training College, Bristol, England, lecturer in music, 1948-61; University of Bristol, Institute of Education, taught courses for teachers, 1951-61; teacher at international courses in music in Switzerland, France, and Belgium, 1957-61; Scarborough Board of Education, Scarborough, Ontario, music supervisor, 1961-67; University of Toronto, Institute of Child Study, Toronto, Ontario, member of staff in music education, 1967-74. Instructor in courses for teachers, University of Minnesota, 1963, 1964, University of Toronto, and University of Manitoba. Co-founder of company, Educational Musical Instruments, 1962. *Awards, honors:* Award of Excellence in Canada Design Program, 1967.

WRITINGS: Making and Playing Bamboo Pipes, Dryad, 1958; *Young Canada Music Book*, Thomas Nelson, 1967. Contributor to music journals.

WORK IN PROGRESS: Work with adults and children in creative music and expansion of counsciousness.

* * *

GALLUP, George (Horace) 1901-

PERSONAL: Born November 18, 1901, in Jefferson, Iowa; son of George Henry (a farmer and dealer in farm and ranch lands) and Nettie (Davenport) Gallup; married Ophelia Smith Miller, December 27, 1925; children: Alec Miller, George H. III, Julia Gallup Laughlin. *Education:*

University of Iowa, B.A., 1923, Ph.D., 1928. *Residence:* Great Rd., Princeton, N.J. *Office:* American Institute of Public Opinion, 53 Bank St., Princeton, N.J.

CAREER: University of Iowa, Iowa City, teacher of journalism and psychology, 1923-29; Drake University, Des Moines, Iowa, head of department of journalism, 1929-31; Northwestern University, Evanston, Ill., professor of journalism and advertising, 1931-32; Young & Rubicum Advertising Agency, New York, N.Y., director of research, 1932-47, vice-president, 1937-47; Columbia University, New York, N.Y., professor of journalism, 1933-37; American Institute of Public Opinion (attitude research), New York, N.Y., and Princeton, N.J., founder, 1935, director, 1935—; Audience Research Institute, founder, 1939, president, 1939—. Chairman of the board of Gallup Organization, Inc., Princeton, N.J.; chairman emeritus, of Gallup & Robinson, Inc. (advertising and market research), Princeton, N.J. President of International Association of Public Opinion Institutes, 1947—. President of National Municipal League, 1953-56, and chairman of All-America Cities Award Committee. Founder of Quill & Scroll (high school journalism honorary society) and chairman of the board of trustees.

MEMBER: American Association of Public Opinion Research (president, 1954-55), American Association of Advertising Agencies, American Marketing Association, American Political Science Association, American Psychological Association (associate member), National Press Club (Washington), Sigma Xi, Sigma Alpha Epsilon, Sigma Delta Chi.

AWARDS, HONORS: Distinguished Achievement Award, Syracuse University, 1950; Honor Award, University of Missouri, 1958; elected to Hall of Fame in Distribution, 1962; Distinguished Citizen Award, National Municipal League, 1962; Advertising Gold Medal, *Printers' Ink*, 1964; Parlin Award, American Marketing Association, 1965; Christopher Columbus International Prize, 1968. LL.D. from Northwestern University, Drake University, Boston University, Chattanooga University, and University of Iowa; D.Sc. from Tufts University; L.H.D. from Colgate University; D.C.L. from Rider College.

WRITINGS: (With Saul F. Rae) *The Pulse of Democracy: The Public Opinion Poll and How It Works*, Simon & Schuster, 1940; *A Guidebook to Public Opinion Polls*, Princeton University Press, 1944; *Birthday Biography*, Strode Press, 1952; *Secrets of Long Life*, Bernard Geis, 1960; *The Miracle Ahead*, Harper, 1964; *A Survey of the Public's Attitudes Toward the Public Schools*, Gallup International, 1969; *How the Nation Views the Public Schools: A Study of the Public Schools of the United States*, Gallup International, 1969; *A Guidebook for Parents of Children in the First Year of School*, Institute for Development of Educational Activities, 1970; *The Gallup Poll: Public Opinion*, 1935-1971, Random House, 1972. Editor of *Gallup Political Almanac*. Contributor of articles on public opinion to national magazines.

SIDELIGHTS: Gallup is most clearly identified in the national (and international) mind with the Gallup Poll, which scored its first major success by correctly predicting the election of Franklin D. Roosevelt in 1936. However, some years earlier at the University of Iowa, Gallup developed a method, still widely used, for measuring reader interest in the news, features, and advertising of newspapers and magazines, as well as a method for measuring radio audience response, developed in 1938.

The British Institute of Public Opinion was founded by Gallup shortly after the American, and other public opinion affiliates of the Gallup Organization have been formed in twenty-six foreign countries since 1937.

BIOGRAPHICAL/CRITICAL SOURCES: New Yorker, March 2, 1940.†

*   *   *

GALVIN, Thomas J(ohn) 1932-

PERSONAL: Born December 30, 1932, in Arlington, Mass.; son of Thomas J. and Elizabeth (Rossiter) Galvin; married Marie Schumb, November 24, 1956; children: Siobhan Marie. *Education:* Columbia University, A.B. (distinction in English), 1954; Simmons College, S.M. in L.S., 1956; Case Western Reserve University, Ph.D., 1973. *Home:* 30 Winter St., Braintree, Mass. 02185. *Office:* School of Library Science, Simmons College, Boston, Mass. 02115.

CAREER: Boston University Libraries, Boston, Mass., reference librarian, 1954-56; Abbot Public Library, Marblehead, Mass., chief librarian, 1956-59; Simmons College, Boston, School of Library Science, Mass., lecturer, 1957-62, assistant director of Library, 1959-62, director of students and assistant professor, 1962-73, associate director and professor of library science, 1973—. Library consultant to Massachusetts Board of Regional Community Colleges, Massachusetts State College at Salem, Vermont Technical College, Nevins Memorial Library, Methuen, Mass., 1973, and Lesley College, Cambridge, Mass., 1974; library advisor to Pierce College, Athens, Greece. Member of international advisory committee, *World Book Dictionary*; member of advisory editorial board, Pierian Press, 1969—. Life Trustee, Thayer Public Library, Braintree, Mass. *Member:* American Library Association (member of council, 1964-66, 1969-72), Association of American Library Schools, New England Library Association, Massachusetts Library Association (treasurer, 1959-62), American Association of University Professors, Phi Beta Kappa. *Awards, honors:* Isadore G. Mudge Citation, American Library Association, 1972.

WRITINGS: Problems in Reference Service: Case Studies in Method and Policy, Bowker, 1965; *Current Problems in Reference Service*, Bowker, 1971; *The Case Method in Library Education and In-Service Training*, Scarecrow, 1973. Editor of series, "Problem-Centered Approaches to Librarianship," for Bowker. Contributor of articles and reviews to library journals.

*   *   *

GAMBS, John S(ake) 1899-

PERSONAL: Surname rhymes with "lambs"; born May 14, 1899, in Guatemala; came to United States, 1903, became U.S. citizen, 1904; son of Gustave Adolphe (a civil servant) and Caroline (Herrmann) Gambs; married Alice Chase, July 7, 1938; children: Louise Martha, John Frederick. *Education:* George Washington University, A.B., 1920, M.A., 1924; Columbia University, Ph.D., 1932. *Home:* 81 College St., Clinton, N.Y. 13323.

CAREER: High School teacher in Washington, D.C., 1924-29; Columbia University, New York, N.Y., associate in social science, 1933-38; International Labour Organization, Geneva, Switzerland, member of permanent U.S. delegation and substitute U.S. member of governing body, 1938-40; Louisiana State University, Baton Rouge, associate professor of social science, 1940-42; National War Labor Board, Washington, D.C., staff mediation officer, 1942-44; U.S. Department of Labor, Washington, D.C., international labor adviser, 1944-46; Hamilton College, Clinton, N.Y., professor of economics, 1946-55, Leavenworth professor, 1955-67, chairman of department, 1954-67. Consultant, U.S. Wage Stabilization Board, 1951. *Member:* American Economic Association, Association for Evolutionary Economics (president, 1967; member of board of directors), New York State Economic Association (president, 1957-58).

WRITINGS: Decline of I.W.W., Columbia University Press, 1932; *Beyond Supply and Demand*, Columbia University Press, 1946; *Man, Money and Goods*, Columbia University Press, 1952; (with Sidney Wertimer) *Economics and Man*, Irwin, 1959; *The Quintessence of Galbraith*, Twayne, in press. Contributor of articles and reviews to professional and popular periodicals.

SIDELIGHTS: Gambs speaks French.

* * *

GANLEY, Albert Charles 1918-

PERSONAL: Born March 14, 1918, in Glens Falls, N.Y.; son of Albert Charles and Verna Adelaide (Holland) Ganley; married Barbara Ellen Thrope, August 11, 1951; children: David Charles, Michael John, Barbara Ellen. *Education:* Williams College, B.A., 1939; Cornell University, M.A., 1940; Columbia University, further graduate study, 1946. *Home:* 10 Elliot St., Exeter, New Hampshire.

CAREER: Williams College, Williamstown, Mass., instructor in history, 1946-47; Manhasset (N.Y.) High School, social studies teacher, 1947-63; Phillips Exeter Academy, Exeter, N.H., instructor in history, 1964—, chairman of history department, 1969-74. *Member:* American Historical Association, National Council for Social Studies, Organization of American Historians, Phi Beta Kappa, Phi Delta Kappa. *Awards, honors:* John Hay Fellow, Harvard University, 1959-60.

WRITINGS: The Progressive Movement: Traditional Reform, Macmillan, 1964.

WORK IN PROGRESS: Law and Disorder: Boston, 1767-1770.

* * *

GARB, Solomon 1920-

PERSONAL: Born October 19, 1920, in New York, N.Y.; son of Gerson and Fanny (Smith) Garb; married Hildreth Rose; children James, Gordon, Richard. *Education:* Cornell University, A.B., 1940, M.D., 1943. *Office:* University of Missouri Medical School, Columbia, Mo.

CAREER: Cornell University Medical College, New York, N.Y., instructor, later assistant professor of clinical pharmacology, 1950-57; Albany Medical College, Albany, N.Y., associate professor of pharmacology, 1957-61; University of Missouri Medical School, Columbia, associate professor of pharmacology, 1961—, currently working full time on cancer research. Consultant to American Medical Association Council on Drugs. Vice-chairman of Civil Defense advisory committee, Boone County, Mo., and member of Columbia Civil Defense advisory committee. *Military service:* U.S. Army, Medical Corps, 1944-46; became captain.

MEMBER: American Medical Association, American College of Clinical Pharmacology (fellow), American Association for the Advancement of Science, Society for Experimental Biology and Medicine, American Society for Pharmacology and Experimental Therapeutics, Association of Hospital Directors of Medical Education, American Federation for Clinical Research, New York Academy of Sciences, Missouri Medical Society, Boone County Medical Society. *Awards, honors:* Polk Prize for research, Cornell University Medical College, 1943; Henry M. Moses Prize for research, Montefiore Hospital (New York), 1949; senior research fellowship, U.S. Public Health Service, 1957, and career research development award, 1962; research fellowships from New York Heart Association, 1949, and American Heart Association, 1953.

WRITINGS: Laboratory Tests in Common Use, Springer, 1956, 5th edition, 1971; *Essentials of Therapeutic Nutrition*, Springer, 1958; (with Betty J. Crim) *Pharmacology and Patient Care*, Springer, 1962, 2nd edition, 1966, 3rd edition, with Garf Thomas, 1970; (with Evelyn Eng) *Disaster Handbook*, Springer, 1964, 2nd edition, 1969; *Cure for Cancer: A National Goal*, Springer, 1968; *Clinical Guide to Undesirable Drug Interactions and Interferences*, Springer, 1971, revised edition published as *Undesirable Drug Interactions*, 1974. Also author of *The Physician in Civil Defense*, c.1961. Contributor to *World Book Encyclopedia* and contributor of more than fifty articles to medical journals.

WORK IN PROGRESS: A book on drug advertising and its effects on the public; a book on moondoggling.†

* * *

GARDNER, (Robert) Brian 1931-

PERSONAL: Born June 28, 1931, in Selsdon, England; son of Robert and Florence (Watson) Gardner; married Jean Walsh; children: Stuart Murrow, Neil, Melanie. *Education:* Trinity College, University of Dublin, M.A., 1953. *Residence:* London, England. *Agent:* Brandt & Brandt, 101 Park Ave., New York, N.Y. 10017.

CAREER: Free-lance writer. *Military service:* British Army, 1954-56.

WRITINGS: The Big Push, Morrow, 1963; *On to Kilimanjaro*, Maccrae Smith, 1964; *The Year That Changed the World*, Coward, 1964; *Up the Line to Death* (anthology), Methuen, 1964; *Allenby*, Coward, 1965; *The War Poets, 1939-1945*, Methuen, 1966; *Mafeking: A Victorian Legend*, Harcourt, 1967; *The Quest for Timbuctoo*, Harcourt, 1968; *The Lion's Cage*, Barker, 1969; *Rhodes and the Siege of Kimberly*, Barker, 1969; *Churchill In Power: As Seen By His Contemporaries* (non-fiction), Houghton, 1970; *The African Dream* (history), Putnam, 1970; *The East India Company*, McCalls, 1972; *The Public Schools*, Hamish Hamilton, 1973. Contributor to magazines and newspapers in England.

SIDELIGHTS: In reference to *Mafeking*, a reviewer for *The Virginian Quarterly Review* said: "Gardner is fair and honest, sympathetic and iconoclastic; the book is well-written, with a journalist's flair and a historian's accuracy." Ambrose Agius wrote of *The Quest for Timbuctoo* that "It is to the merit of Brian Gardner that he has assimilated the often unsatisfactory sources of information, explored unpublished material, and woven all of it into an engrossing story of mounting excitement, as the race for Timbuctoo proceeds." Concerning *The African Dream*, Harold Lancour stated that "Gardner, an English popular historian, has found a remarkably productive formula for his well-researched British histories and biographies. His style is refreshingly unpedantic; he writes with candor and wit, and has a sharp eye for the amusing. . . . Interesting and readable, and recommended for both general and special collections.''

The Big Push was published in French, and *The Year That Changed the World* in French, Dutch, Swedish, Finnish, and German.

* * *

GARDNER, E(dward) Clinton 1920-

PERSONAL: Born August 17, 1920, in Columbia, Tenn.; son of Carl C. (a teacher) and Sarah (Berry) Gardner; married Ruth Cohen, June 9, 1948; children: Edward, Marilyn, Arnold. *Education:* Vanderbilt University, A.B., 1942; Yale University, B.D., 1945, Ph.D., 1952. *Home:* 2504 Tanglewood Rd., Decatur, Ga. 30033. *Office:* Candler School of Theology, Emory University, Atlanta, Ga. 30322.

CAREER: Methodist pastor in New York, 1944-45, and Connecticut, 1948-49; North Carolina State College (now University) Raleigh, assistant professor of philosophy and religion, 1949-54; Emory University, Candler School of Theology, Atlanta, Ga., assistant professor of Christian ethics, 1954-58, associate professor, 1958-61, professor, 1961—. Member of board of trustees of Urban Training Organization of Atlanta. *Military service:* U.S. Army, chaplain, 1945-46. *Member:* American Society of Christian Ethics (president, 1961-62), Institute of Society, Ethics, and Life Sciences (associate member), American Association of University Professors, Atlanta Theological Association (member of board of governors). Phi Beta Kappa, Theta Phi. *Awards, honors:* American Association of Theological Schools faculty fellowship, 1962-63.

WRITINGS: Biblical Faith and Social Ethics, Harper, 1960; *The Church as a Prophetic Community*, Westminster Press, 1967; (contributor) John Macquarrie, editor, *Storm Over Ethics*, United Church Press, 1967; (contributor) Gibson Winter, editor, *Social Ethics: Issues in Ethics and Society*, Harper, 1968; (contributor) William Pinson, Jr. and Clyde Fant, Jr., editors, *Contemporary Christian Trends*, Word Books, 1972; (contributor) J. Philip Wogaman, editor, *The Population Crisis and Moral Responsibility*, Public Affairs Press, 1973.

Contributor to *Dictionary of Christian Ethics, Encyclopedia of World Methodism*, and to theological and denominational journals.

* * *

GARDNER, Nancy Bruff 1915-
(Nancy Bruff)

PERSONAL: Born November 15, 1915, in Fairfield County, Connecticut; daughter of Austin J. (a broker) and Alice (Birdsall) Bruff; married Edwin Thurston Clarke, March 11, 1937 (died, 1962); married Esmond B. Gardner (a banker), July 20, 1963; children: (first marriage) Thurston B., Penelope. *Education:* Attended Sorbonne, University of Paris. *Home:* 150 East 72nd St., New York, N.Y. *Agent:* Lerniger Literary Agency, 437 Fifth Ave., New York, N.Y.

CAREER: Novelist and poet.

WRITINGS—All under name Nancy Bruff: *The Manatee*, Dutton, 1945; *My Talon in Your Heart* (poems), Dutton, 1946; *Cider from Eden*, Dutton, 1947; *Beloved Women*,

Messner, 1949 (published in England as *Love is Not Love*, Laurie, 1950); *The Fig Tree*, Obolensky, 1965; *The Country Club*, Bartholomew House, 1969; *Mooncussers* (novel) Dell, in press.

WORK IN PROGRESS: Two novels, *A Subtle and Violent Plan* and *Mr. Beel*; a suspense novel, *Shark Island*; *500 Poems*; two plays.

* * *

GARDNER, Ralph D(avid) 1923-

PERSONAL: Born April 16, 1923, in New York, N.Y.; son of Benjamin and Myra (Berman) Gardner; married Nellie Jaglom, April 9, 1952; children: Ralph D., Jr., John Jaglom, Peter Jaglom, James Jaglom. *Education:* Attended New York University, 1939-42, Colorado State College, 1943. *Home:* 135 Central Park West, New York, N.Y. 10023. *Office:* Ralph D. Gardner Advertising, 745 Fifth Ave., New York, N.Y. 10022.

CAREER: New York Times, New York, N.Y., 1942-55, began as copyboy, started International Edition, Paris, France, 1949, bureau manager for Germany and Austria, Frankfurt, Germany, 1950-55; Ralph D. Gardner Advertising, New York, N.Y., president, 1955—. Member of board, Fresh Air Council; gives lectures on nineteenth century American literature. *Military service:* U.S. Army, 1943-46; served as newswriter in Europe. *Member:* Overseas Press Club of America, Bibliographical Society of America, Manuscript Society, Brandeis University Bibliophiles (honorary), Syracuse University Library Associates (honorary), Friends of Princeton University Library, Frankfurt Press Club, The Lambs, Grand Street Boys Association, Alpha Epsilon Pi. *Awards, honors:* Horatio Alger Society of America Prize for Literature for *Horatio Alger; or, The American Hero Era*, 1964, and for *Road to Success: The Bibliography of the Works of Horatio Alger*, 1972.

WRITINGS: Horatio Alger; or, The American Hero Era, Wayside Press, 1964; *Road to Success: Bibliography of the Works of Horatio Alger*, Wayside Press, 1971; (author of introduction) Horatio Alger, *Silas Snobden's Office Boy*, reprint edition, Doubleday, 1973; (author of introduction) Horatio Alger, *Cast Upon the Breakers*, reprint edition, Doubleday, 1974. Contributor of articles and reviews on military subjects, foreign travel, and nineteenth-century American literature and bibliography to newspapers and magazines, including *New York Times Book Review* and *Chicago Daily News*.

WORK IN PROGRESS: A novel, completion expected in 1977.

SIDELIGHTS: Gardner says he wrote the biography of Horatio Alger to set the record straight on a writer who "had meager literary quality, but was, nevertheless, America's most influential and all-time best-selling author." *Road to Success* contains the most complete bibliography of Horatio Alger's novels, articles, short stories, and poems. Gardner speaks French and German, travels abroad regularly, and collects nineteenth-century American first editions and manuscripts.

* * *

GARDNER, Riley W(etherell) 1921-

PERSONAL: Born October 31, 1921, in Ree Heights, S.D.; son of Hugh H. and Ruth (Speicher) Gardner; married Ruth Janssen, 1950; children: Helen, Mark. *Educa-*

tion: Yankton College, B.A., 1945; University of Kansas, Ph.D., 1952. *Home:* 207 South Broadmoor, Topeka, Kan. *Office:* Menninger Foundation, Box 829, Topeka, Kan.

CAREER: Menninger Foundation, Topeka, Kan., research assistant, 1951, resident in psychology, 1951-52, assistant psychologist, 1952-53, associate psychologist, 1953-62, director of Cognition Project, 1957—, senior psychologist, 1962—. *Military service:* U.S. Army, two years; became staff sergeant. *Member:* American Psychological Association, Interamerican Society of Psychology, Kansas Psychological Association (chairman of Science Fair committee, 1959-61; president, 1965-66), Topeka Psychological Association.

WRITINGS: (Senior author) *Cognitive Control: A Study of Individual Consistencies in Cognitive Behavior*, International Universities, 1959; (senior author) *Personality Organization in Cognitive Controls and Intellectual Abilities*, International Universities, 1960; (with Alice E. Moriarty) *Personality Development at Preadolescence: Explorations of Structure Formation*, University of Washington Press, 1968. Author of monographs and contributor to psychology and sociology books and journals in United States, Britain, Japan, Mexico, and India.

WORK IN PROGRESS: Reports on the Menninger Foundation study of twins and their parents; reports on studies of deprived children; and studies of personality in relation to vocational interest and creativity.

BIOGRAPHICAL/CRITICAL SOURCES: Kansas City Star, June 12, 1960; *Topeka State Journal*, February 13, 1962, and March 6, 1962.

* * *

GARRISON, R. Benjamin 1926-

PERSONAL: Born February 26, 1926, in Kokomo, Ind.; son of Claude and Eilene (Kendall) Garrison; married Elizabeth Martin, December 28, 1947; children: Richard Benjamin II, Thomas Martin, Barbara Elizabeth. *Education:* DePauw University, A.B., 1947; Drew University, B.D., 1950, M.A., 1955. *Office:* Wesley Methodist Church, 1203 West Green, Urbana, Ill.

CAREER: Ordained Methodist minister, 1950. Served Bishop Janes Methodist Church, Basking Ridge, N.J., 1951-57; First Methodist Church, Bloomington, Ind., 1957-61; Wesley Methodist Church, Urbana, Ill., senior minister, 1961—; University of Illinois, Urbana, director of Wesley Foundation, 1961—. Delegate to Methodist conferences in London, Dallas, St. Louis, Denver, and Atlanta, 1966-72; undertook church-sponsored mission to Peru, 1973. Associate member, United Church of Christ, Fifield, Wis. Senior research fellow at Wesley House, Cambridge University, 1969; visiting lecturer, University of Illinois, 1973-74; guest lecturer at Drew University, Indiana University, and Southwestern University. Member of board of trustees, Drew University; member of Urbana Board of Education. Charter chairman, Bloomington (Ind.) Housing Authority. *Military service:* U.S. Army, 1945-46. *Member:* American Civil Liberties Union, Hymn Society of America. *Awards, honors:* D.D., MacMurray College, 1963.

WRITINGS: Portrait of the Church—Warts and All, Abingdon, 1964; (contributor) G. Paul Butler, editor, *Best Sermons*, Volume IX, Van Nostrand, 1964; *The Decalogue in a New Key: Sermons Based on the Ten Commandments*, Wesley Methodist Church (Urbana, Ill.),

1966; *Creeds in Collision*, Abingdon, 1967; (with Ernest J. Fiedler) *The Sacraments: An Experiment in Ecumenical Honesty*, Abingdon, 1969; *Worldly Holiness*, Abingdon, 1971. Contributor to *Collier's Encyclopedia*. Writer of articles and book reviews for *American Jewish Post and Opinion*, *Indiana Catholic*, *Motive*, *Pulpit Digest*, *Christian Advocate*, *Christian Century*, and *Religion in Life*.

AVOCATIONAL INTERESTS: Fishing and reading.

* * *

GARSTANG, James Gordon 1927-
(Jack Garstang)

PERSONAL: Born August 26, 1927, in Preston, England; son of James (a civil servant) and Edith (Nicholson) Garstang; married Jean McNeil, September 30, 1955; children: Jacqueline, Jennifer. *Education:* Attended Loughborough College of Physical Education, 1947-50; University of Nottingham, Diploma of Physical Education and Teaching Certificate. *Religion:* Church of England. *Home:* 62, route de Chene, Geneva, Switzerland. *Agent:* Peter Janson-Smith, 2 Caxton St., London S.W. 1, England. *Office:* International School of Geneva, Geneva, Switzerland.

CAREER: The Polytechnic, London, England, assistant organizer of physical education and social activities, 1958-61; International School of Geneva, Geneva, Switzerland, director of physical education, 1961—; University of Geneva, Geneva, Switzerland, gymnastic and swimming coach, 1962—. *Weekly Tribune*, Geneva, Switzerland, sports editor, 1963—. International judge for swimming, diving, and gymnastics.

WRITINGS: Basketball the Modern Way, Souvenir Press, 1961, Sterling, 1962, revised edition, 1967; (with Joseph Edmundson) *Activities on P.E. Apparatus*, Oldbourne, 1962; *Swimming, Step by Step*, Museum Press, 1962; *Coaching for Swimming*, Museum Press, 1963; *Coaching for Gymnastics*, Museum Press, 1964; *Physical Education for Teachers, Coaches and Students*, Pergamon, 1965; *Skiing*, International Publications Service, 1968. Feature writer on physical education for *Teacher*; contributor of other articles on sports and recreation to journals in England.

SIDELIGHTS: Garstang's writings have occasionally appeared under the name Jack Garstang.†

* * *

GARSTEIN, Oskar Bernhard 1924-

PERSONAL: Born November 12, 1924, in Peking, China; son of Norwegian nationals; married Karen-Eline Ebbing (a college professor), April 2, 1955. *Education:* University of Oslo, D. Theol., 1954, D. Phil., 1965. *Religion:* Lutheran. *Home:* 30 Viggo Hansteens vei, Oslo 3, Norway.

CAREER: Aars & Voss College, Oslo, Norway, professor of history, 1954-69; Cathedral College, Oslo, Norway, professor of history, 1969—. Athena Center, Aliquippa, Pa., professor, 1969—. Visiting professor, University of Wisconsin, 1968-69. *Member:* Norwegian Society of Historical Research, Society of Norwegian Ecclesiastical History, Carl Johan Society.

WRITINGS: Cort Aslaksson. Studier over dansk-norsk universitets-og laerdomshistorie, Lutherstiftelsen, 1953; *Rome and the Counter-Reformation in Scandinavia Until the Establishment of the S. Congregatio de Propaganda Fide in 1622*, Volume I (1539-83), Universitetsforlaget, 1963. Also author of *Fra Ostens og Vestens Kirker*, Oslo,

1968; and *Epistolarium Commercium P. Laurentii Nicolai Norvegi, S. J.*, Oslo, 1975. Contributor to historical and theological periodicals in western Europe.

WORK IN PROGRESS: Rome and the Counter-Reformation in Scandinavia, Volume II, covering 1583-1622, completion expected in 1976; gathering material for an extension of the series, covering 1622-54.

SIDELIGHTS: Garstein is competent in English, has reading knowledge of German, French, Italian, Greek, Hebrew, and Latin.

*   *   *

GARVIN, Paul L(ucian)   1919-

PERSONAL: Born August 28, 1919, in Vienna, Austria; son of Jacques and Barbara (Schwarcz) Goldberger; married Madeleine Mathiot (a linguistic scientist), July 31, 1960; children: (previous marriage) Deborah. *Education:* Ecole Libre des Hautes Etudes, New York, N.Y., Licence-es-lettres, 1945; Indiana University, Ph.D., 1947. *Home:* 449 Skyeway Rd., Los Angeles, Calif. 90049. *Office:* Bunker-Ramo Corp., 8433 Fallbrook Ave., Canoga Park, Calif. 91304.

CAREER: University of Oklahoma, Norman, assistant professor of anthropology, 1949-51; Georgetown University, Washington, D.C., associate professor of linguistics, 1952-60; Thompson Ramo Wooldridge, Inc., Canoga Park, Calif., senior staff member, Computer Division, 1960-64; Bunker-Ramo Corp., Canoga Park, Calif., manager of language analysis and translation, 1964—; University of Southern California, Los Angeles, adjunct professor of linguistics, 1965—. *Member:* Linguistic Society of America (former member of executive committee), Association for Machine Translation and Computational Linguistics (president-elect, 1966), American Anthropological Association (fellow).

WRITINGS: (Translator) Giorgio Papasogli, *Saint Ignatius Loyola*, Society of Saint Paul, 1959; (editor) *Natural Language and the Computer*, McGraw, 1963; (translator) Jean Baptiste de Saint Jure and Claude de la Columbiere, *The Secret of Peace and Happiness*, Society of Saint Paul, 1961; (editor) *Soviet and East European Linguistics*, Mouton, 1963; *On Linguistic Method*, Mouton, 1964 2nd revised edition, 1972; (editor and translator) *A Prague School Reader in Esthetics, Literary Structure and Style*, Georgetown University Press, 1964; (editor and translator) *The Life and Sayings of Saint Catherine of Genoa*, Alba House, 1964; (editor with Bernard Spolsky) *Computation in Linguistics: A Case Book*, Indiana University Press, 1966; (with Jocelyn Brewer and Madelaine Mathiot) *Predication-Typing: A Pilot Study in Semantic Analysis*, Waverly, 1967; (editor) *Method and Theory in Linguistics*, Mouton, 1970; (editor) *Cognition: a Multiple View*, Spartan, 1970; *On Machine Translation*, Humanities, 1972. Writer of more than fifty professional papers and reviews.

SIDELIGHTS: Garvin and his associates at Bunker-Ramo, a research firm, explore machine translation of languages under grants from the Air Force and the National Science Foundation.

Garvin speaks, reads, and writes seven languages fluently—French, German, Spanish, Czech, Hungarian, Russia, and Swedish.†

*   *   *

GASPER, Louis   1911-

PERSONAL: Born February 10, 1911, in Lorain, Ohio;

son of Daniel and Matilda (Cinders) Gasper; married Nellie Kremer (an accountant and accounting instructor), March 27, 1943. *Education:* Bowling Green State University, B.A. (cum laude) and B.S. in Ed. (cum laude), 1947, M.A., 1949; Findlay College, B.D., 1954; Western Reserve University (now Case Western Reserve University), Ph.D., 1958; University of Southern California, Adv. M.Ed., 1962; Winebrenner Theological Seminary, M.Div., 1968. *Home:* 313 West Andrix St., Monterey Park, Calif. 91754. *Office:* 6201 Winnetka Ave., Woodland Hills, Calif. 91364.

CAREER: National Tube Co., Lorain, Ohio, steelworker, 1929-38; minister, American Baptist Convention, 1939-57, United Church of Christ, 1962—. High school teacher in Fostoria, Ohio, 1945-47; Florence State College (now Florence State University), Florence, Ala., associate professor of sociology, 1957-58; Los Angeles, Calif., schools, social studies teacher, 1958-61; Los Angeles Pacific College, Los Angeles, Calif., associate professor of sociology and director of teacher education, 1961-63; Los Angeles Pierce College, Woodland Hills, Calif., assistant professor, 1963-67, associate professor, 1967-70, professor of philosophy and sociology, 1970—, chairman of department of philosophy, sociology, and education, 1967—. Assistant professor of sociology, Humbolt State College (now California State University, Humbolt), part-time, 1959-60; San Fernando Valley State College (now California State University, Northridge), part-time, 1964-67; instructor in sociology, East Los Angeles College, Extension, 1960—; part-time associate professor of sociology, California State College (now California State University), Los Angeles campus, 1968-70, Long Beach campus, 1971—; licensed marriage, family, and child counselor, 1963—. Summer lecturer in Russian history, Bluffton College, 1949. *Member:* American Historical Association, American Sociological Association, American Association of Marriage and Family Counselors, American Studies Association, Medical Correctional Association, American Society for Criminology, Society for the Study of Social Problems, Pacific Sociological Association, Group Psychotherapy Association of Southern California, California State Marriage Counseling Association, Phi Kappa Phi.

WRITINGS: Introduction to Sociology, Academic Readings, 1962; *The Fundamentalist Movement*, Humanities, 1963; *Fundamentals of Sociology*, McCutchan, 1966, 2nd edition, 1969; (compiler) *Vital Social Problems*, McCutchan, 1968; (contributor) Arthur Goddard, editor, *Harry Elmer Barnes: Learned Crusader*, Ralph Myles Publisher, 1968. Contributor to professional journals.

WORK IN PROGRESS: A syllabus for acupuncture trainees.

*   *   *

GATES, Robbins L(adew)   1922-

PERSONAL: Born May 24, 1922, in Martinsville, Va.; son of William Benjamin (an educator) and Fanny Robbins (Ladew) Gates; married Caroline Murray, April 15, 1950; children: Martha Robbins, Catherine MacGregor. *Education:* Washington and Lee University, B.A., 1948; Columbia University, A.M., 1955, Ph.D., 1962. *Politics:* Democrat. *Religion:* Episcopalian. *Home:* 1011 Hawthorne Lane, Waynesboro, Va. 22980. *Office:* Mary Baldwin College, Staunton, Va. 24401.

CAREER: Trinity College, Hartford, Conn., instructor in government, 1956-59; Fairfax Hall, Waynesboro, Va., academic dean, 1959-65; Mary Baldwin College, Staunton,

Va., assistant professor of political science, 1965—. Fishburne-Hudgins Educational Foundation, trustee; Fairfax Hall, Inc., director; Virginia Museum of Fine Arts, president of Waynesboro chapter, 1963-64. *Military service:* U.S. Army Air Forces, 1943-46; became sergeant. *Member:* American Political Science Association, American Academy of Political and Social Science, American Association of University Professors, American Civil Liberties Union, Pi Gamma Mu, Waynesboro Rotary Club, Waynesboro Country Club.

WRITINGS: The Making of Massive Resistance: Virginia's Politics of Public School Desegregation, 1954-1956, University of North Carolina Press, 1964.

WORK IN PROGRESS: Research in politics of extremism and social ethics.

SIDELIGHTS: Gates told *CA:* "I am intent on teaching, talking, writing (and whatever else may offer itself) regarding the absolute necessity for honest communication and compromise in all phases of the political and social process. The noisy minorities on the right and left extreme will fail to effect great damage only if sober and conscientious persons in the 'great middle' accept the obligation of vocal and time-consuming leadership...."†

* * *

GATTEY, Charles Neilson 1921-

PERSONAL: Born September 3, 1921, in London, England; son of Francis William (a physician) and Victoria (Neilson) Gattey. *Education:* Studied at University of London. *Home:* Savage Club, 86 St. James's St., London S.W.1, England.

CAREER: Playwright; lecturer on variety of subjects, including the theater and the occult, to women's organizations in Britain. *Member:* Savage Club. *Awards, honors:* Winner, Hampstead Festival of Britain Playwrighting Competition, with "The King Who Got His Feet Wet," presented at Everyman Theatre, London.

WRITINGS—Three-act plays: The White Falcon, H. F. W. Deane & Sons, 1951; *The Eleventh Hour,* H. F. W. Deane & Sons, 1952; *A Spell of Virtue,* Quekett, 1956; *Man in a Million,* Quekett, 1957; *By a Hand Unknown,* Quekett, 1958; *True Love—or the Bloomer,* Evans, 1962; *The Colour of Anger,* H. F. W. Deane & Sons, 1963.

One-act plays: *Mrs. Griggs Loses Her Bed,* H. F. W. Deane & Sons, 1956; *The Cloak of Courage,* Evans, 1958; *The Landlady's Brother,* Samuel French, 1959; *Fair Cops,* H. F. W. Deane & Sons, 1965.

Nonfiction: *The Bloomer Girls* (social history), Coward, 1968; *Gauguin's Astonishing Grandmother: A Biography of Flora Tristan,* Femina Books, 1970; *The King Who Could Not Stay the Tide* (biography), Epworth Press, 1971; *A Bird of Curious Plumage* (biography), Constable, 1971; *The Incredible Mrs. Van der Elst* (biography), Frewin, 1973.

Other plays produced, several on tour: "The Birth of Elizabeth"; "Queen of a Thousand Dresses"; "Tidings of Canute"; "Farewell Pots and Pans"; "Mightier Than the Sword"; "Queen's Night"; "The Birth of the Bloomer"; "Mrs. Adam and Eve"; "In the Maze"; "Treasure from France"; "The Enemy of Time"; "The King Who Got His Feet Wet."

Writer of radio plays produced in Britain, in four countries on the Continent, and in Canada, Australia, and South Africa; author of original story on which the film, "The Love Lottery" (Earling Studios) was based; author and adapter of "The White Falcon" for British Broadcasting Corp. television, 1956. Contributor to *Saturday Book* (periodical).

WORK IN PROGRESS: A biography of Henry Frederick, Duke of Cumberland, tentatively entitled *The Duke Who Caused the Royal Marriage Act.*

SIDELIGHTS: Gattey has lived in France and speaks French fluently.

* * *

GAUER, Harold 1914-

PERSONAL: Born August 29, 1914, in Milwaukee, Wis.; son of John Nicholas (an engineer) and Vernie (Raczkowski) Gauer; married Alice A. Bedard, February 9, 1957. *Home:* 3462 North Downer Ave., Milwaukee, Wis. 53211. *Agent:* Larry Sternig, 2407 North 44th St., Milwaukee, Wis. 53210. *Office:* CARE Inc., 125 East Wells St., Milwaukee, Wis. 53202.

CAREER: National Youth Administration, Washington, D.C., social science analyst, 1942-43; Security Mutual Life Insurance Co., Milwaukee, Wis., administrative assistant, 1944-48; Cooperative for American Relief Everywhere, Inc. (CARE), Midwest regional director, Milwaukee, Wis., 1948—; MEDICO, executive director of Midwest office, Milwaukee, Wis., 1961—. Manager, Milwaukee Pops Orchestra, 1957-58. *Awards, honors:* Civic Service Award, National Fraternal Order of Eagles, 1958.

WRITINGS: How to Win in Politics, Humphries, 1947, revised edition, 1964.

WORK IN PROGRESS: The Office Seekers, an examination of candidates and campaigns for public office; novels, *Rotten Reiley's Loose Connection, The World Conspiracy Against Casey Utecht, Bury Me Not,* and *The Dreadful Past.*†

* * *

GAULD, Charles A(nderson) 1911-

PERSONAL: Surname rhymes with "auld," as in "Auld Lang Syne"; born August 12, 1911, in Portland, Ore.; son of Charles (a businessman) and Elizabeth (Anderson) Gauld. *Education:* Stanford University, A.B., 1932, Ph.D., 1964; University of Washington, Seattle, M.A., 1935; University of California, Berkeley, graduate student, 1935-37. *Politics:* Democrat. *Religion:* Quaker. *Home:* 7803 Kendall Dr., Miami, Fla. 33156.

CAREER: U.S. Library of Congress, Washington, D.C., specialist on official publications of Latin America, 1938-41; Foreign Broadcast Intelligence, Washington, D.C., editorial assistant, 1941-42; Office of Inter-American Affairs, Washington, D.C., assistant editor, 1942-45; Stanford University, Stanford, Calif., lecturer in Hispanic-American studies and assistant editor of *Hispanic American Report,* 1955-58, 1962-63; Inter-American University, San German, Puerto Rico, assistant professor of Latin American history, geography, and government, 1958-61; free-lance writer in Brazil, 1946-50, 1952-54, 1965. Miami-Dade Junior College, Miami, Fla., associate professor of history and geography, 1966—. *Member:* Southeastern Council of Latin American Studies, Society of Florida Geographers, Historical Association of Southern Florida, Council for International Visitors, Tropical Audubon Society. *Awards, honors:* Research grants, 1953, 1965.

WRITINGS: The Last Titan: Percival Farquhar, American Entrepreneur in Latin America, Institute of Hispanic Studies, Stanford University, 1964.

WORK IN PROGRESS: Blacks in Florida History and Development, completion expected in 1975.

* * *

GAVETT, Thomas W(illiam)   1932-

PERSONAL: Born January 16, 1932, in Milwaukee, Wis.; son of Harold Stetson and Verona (Reinhold) Gavett; married Patricia Dummer, August 21, 1954; children: Geoffrey, Stephen, Christopher. *Education:* University of Wisconsin, B.B.A., 1953, M.S., 1954, Ph.D., 1957. *Politics:* Democrat. *Religion:* Unitarian Universalist. *Home:* 513 Springlock Rd., Silver Spring, Md. 20904. *Office:* Bureau of Labor Statistics, U.S. Department of Labor, Washington, D.C. 20212.

CAREER: Marquette University, Milwaukee, Wis., part-time lecturer, 1956-57; West Virginia University, Morgantown, assistant professor, 1957-61, associate professor of economics, 1961-66, director of Institute of Industrial Relations, 1958-66; U.S. Department of Labor, Bureau of Labor Statistics, assistant commissioner, 1967-71, deputy commissioner, 1971—. Chairman, West Virginia Human Rights Commission, 1961-66. *Member:* American Economic Association, Industrial Relations Research Association.

WRITINGS: The Development of the Labor Movement in Milwaukee, University of Wisconsin Press, 1965. Writer of reports on West Virginia employment and wages, published by Bureau of Business Research, West Virginia University; author of articles on prices, wages, and youth unemployment, published by Bureau of Labor Statistics, U.S. Department of Labor.

* * *

GAY, Peter (Jack)   1923-

PERSONAL: Born June 20, 1923, in Berlin, Germany; came to United States in 1941, naturalized in 1946; son of Morris Peter and Helga (Kohnke) Gay; married Ruth Slotkin (a writer), May 30, 1959; children: Sarah, Sophie, Elizabeth. *Education:* University of Denver, A.B., 1946; Columbia University, M.A., 1947, Ph.D., 1951. *Politics:* Democrat. *Religion:* Atheist. *Home:* 13 Tulip Tree Lane, Woodbridge, Conn. 06525. *Office:* Hall of Graduate Studies, Yale University, New Haven, Conn. 06520.

CAREER: Columbia University, New York, N.Y., 1947-70, began as instructor in government, professor of history, 1962-70; Yale University, New Haven, Conn., professor of history, 1969—, Durfee Professor of history, 1970—. *Member:* American Council of Learned Societies (fellow), Center for Advanced Study in the Behavioral Sciences (fellow), American Historical Association, French Historical Association, Phi Beta Kappa. *Awards, honors:* Alfred Hodder, Jr. Fellow, Princeton University, 1955-56; Frederic G. Melcher Book Award, 1967, for *The Enlightenment*; National Book Award, 1967, for *The Enlightenment*; Ralph Waldo Emerson Award Phi Beta Kappa, 1969; Doctorate of Humane Letters, 1970; Overseas fellow, Churchill College, Cambridge, 1970-71.

WRITINGS: The Dilemma of Democratic Socialism: Eduard Bernstein's Challenge to Marx, Columbia University Press, 1952; (translator and editor) Ernst Cassirer, *The Question of Jean Jacques Rousseau*, Columbia University

Press, 1954; *Voltaire's Politics: The Poet as Realist*, Princeton University Press, 1959; (translator and editor) Voltaire, *Philosophical Dictionary*, Basic Books, 1962; (translator and editor) Voltaire, *Candide*, St. Martin's, 1963; *The Party of Humanity: Essays in the French Enlightenment*, Knopf, 1964; (editor and author of introduction) John Locke, *John Locke on Education*, Columbia University Press, 1964; (with editors of Time-Life books) *Age of Enlightenment*, Time, 1966; *A Loss of Mastery: Puritan Historians in Colonial America*, University of California Press, 1966; *The Enlightenment: An Interpretation*, Knopf, Volume I: *The Rise of Modern Paganism*, 1966, Volume II: *The Science of Freedom*, 1969; *Weimer Culture: The Outsider as Insider*, Harper, 1968; (compiler) *Deism: An Anthology*, Van Nostrand, 1968; *The Bridge of Criticism: Dialogues Among Lucian, Erasmus and Voltaire on the Enlightenment*, Harper, 1970; (author of introduction) Karl Dietrich Bracher, *The German Dictatorship: The Origins, Structure, and Effects of National Socialism*, Praeger, 1971; (author of introduction) translated by Felice Harcourt, *Memoirs of Madame de la Tour du Pin*, McCall, 1971; (editor with John Arthur Garraty) *Columbia History of the World*, Harper, 1972; (editor with Garraty) *A History of the World*, Harper, 1972; (editor with Gerald J. Cavanaugh) *Historians at Work*, Harper, Volume I: *Herodotus to Froissart*, 1972, Volume II: *Valla to Gibbon*, 1972; (editor) *Eighteenth Century Studies*, University Press of New England, 1972; (with Robert K. Webb) *Modern Europe*, Harper, 1973; *Style in History*, Basic Books, 1974. Contributor of articles to *The New Republic*.

WORK IN PROGRESS: A book, *Three Variations on the Theme of Cause: Manet, Gropius, Mondrian*.

SIDELIGHTS: In reference to *The Enlightenment*, a *Times Literary Supplement* reviewer wrote: "This book is such an important contribution to Enlightenment commentary that merely kind words would be an unkindness.... For a very long time to come the Enlightenment researcher will have to reckon with Professor Gay's two books, a monument of humane scholarship." A reviewer for the *Antioch Review* said: "Dr. Gay is the rarest of scholars. He is a brilliant writer; he is stuffed with facts, for he has unquestionably read everything, knows everything ... it is a pleasure to share a scholar's knowledge." Also, J. H. Plumb commented that Gay's book is "... one of the most impressive feats of scholarship of the sixties. For the work, as a whole, I have the most profound admiration. It will be a long time before it is surpassed."

Other reviewers also raved about Gay's *Weimer Culture*. For example, Kurt P. Tauber exclaimed that "It has been a long time since this reviewer spent a more enjoyable and rewarding evening than when he revisited the intellectual and artistic Germany of the twenties in the company of so urbane, scintillating, and expert guide as Peter Gay." To reiterate, Peter Jacobsohn stated that "Although Peter Gay presents his study as an essay, it is more: a brief historical introduction to a seminal epoch, and a work exhibiting such easy mastery of its materials, subtlety of exposition and elegance of style that it can only have sprung from a passionate absorption in the subject and an almost sensuous delight in writing about it."

Gay is fluent in French and German, "rudimentary" knowledge of Italian and fair knowledge of Latin.

AVOCATIONAL INTERESTS: Visiting art galleries.

GEARY, Douglas 1931-

PERSONAL: Born February 21, 1931, in Brentwood, Essex, England; son of Charles Henry (an engineer) and Winifred (Davies) Geary; married Mary Neamonitakis, October 9, 1954; children: Christopher Douglas, Richard Charles. Education: University of London, B.A., 1951. Politics: Liberal. Religion: Church of England. Home: 1 Netherleigh Park, Kings Cross Lane, South Nutfield, near Redhill, Surrey, England.

CAREER: Royal Air Force, 1950-55, becoming flight lieutenant; personnel posts with Ford Motor Co., England, 1955-57, and Rockware Glass Ltd., England, 1957-60; Hallmark Cards Ltd., England, personnel manager, 1960-63; Rank Organization Ltd., England, personnel manager, 1963—. Liberal candidate for Romford in general elections, 1959 and 1964; councilor, Hayes and Harlington Urban District Council. Church of England, lay reader, Chelmsford Diocese. Member: Institute of Personnel Management, Royal Society of Arts (fellow), Society of Antiquaries of Scotland (fellow).

WRITINGS: The Latin Letters of Lady Jane Grey, Stockwell, 1951; Sir Thomas Wyatt the Younger, Forte, 1954; The Songs and Sonnets of the Earl of Surrey, Forbes Robertson, 1957; The Poetry of the Sixteenth Century, Forte, 1960. Contributor to magazines.

WORK IN PROGRESS: A revision of The Songs and Sonnets of the Earl of Surrey; editing a new edition of The Hoods and Degrees of the World's Universities and Colleges; a life of Edward I.

AVOCATIONAL INTERESTS: Motoring and owning specialist cars, collecting rare books and fine bindings, the occult.†

*   *   *

GEHMAN, Henry Snyder 1888-

PERSONAL: Born June 1, 1888, in Lancaster County, Pa.; son of Christian Eberly and Amanda Minerva (Snyder) Gehman; married Bertha Lausch, 1917; children: Elizabeth (Mrs. Samuel E. Kidd), Henry Nevin. Education: Franklin and Marshall College, A.B., 1909, A.M., 1911; University of Pennsylvania, Ph.D., 1913; Philadelphia Divinity School, S.T.B., 1926, S.T.D., 1927. Home and office: 24 Hawthorne Ave., Princeton, N.J.

CAREER: Minister, United Presbyterian Church in the U.S.A. Organizer and pastor of Tabor Reformed Church, Philadelphia, Pa., 1917-21; Princeton University, Princeton, N.J., lecturer in Semitic languages, 1929-59; Princeton Theological Seminary, Princeton, N.J., professor of Old Testament literature, 1931-58, chairman of department of biblical studies, 1942-58, professor emeritus, 1958—. Visiting professor at Dropsie College, 1943, Presbyterian theological seminaries in Brazil, 1955, Facultad Luterana de Teologia, Buenos Aires, Argentina, 1957, 1959, 1961, Columbia Theological Seminary, Decatur, Ga., 1960, Lancaster Theological Seminary, 1961, Lutheran Theological Seminary, Philadelphia, 1962-63, and Gurukul Lutheran Theological College and Research Institute, Madras, India, 1964; commissioner to General Assembly of the Presbyterian Church in the U.S.A., 1943.

MEMBER: American Oriental Society, Society of Biblical Literature and Exegesis, Archaeological Institute of America, Pennsylvania German Folklore Society (president, 1947-48), Symposium of Ministers (Princeton, N.J.), Phi Beta Kappa, Philadelphia Classical Club, Philadelphia Oriental Club (president, 1929-30, 1946-47). Awards, honors: Litt.D. from Franklin and Marshall College, 1947; Guggenheim fellow, 1954; first recipient of Ring of the Faculty and diploma for contributions to theology in Latin America, from Facultad Luterana de Teologia, Buenos Aires, 1961.

WRITINGS: The Interpreters of Foreign Languages Among the Ancients, University of Pennsylvania, 1914; The Peta-Vatthu, Pali Text Society, 1942; (editor) Westminster Dictionary of the Bible, Westminster Press, 1944, new edition, published as New Westminster Dictionary of the Bible, 1970; (editor-in-chief of Old Testament section) Westminster Study Edition of Holy Bible, Westminster Press, 1948.

Special editor of etymologies for Webster's New International Dictionary, 1934; consulting editor for Spanish translation of the Bible (Mexico City); editor of commentary on Books of Kings, "International Critical Commentary" series, T. and T. Clark, 1951. Contributor of articles to theological and other learned journals in United States and abroad. Member editorial council of Journal of Biblical Literature and Theology Today.

*   *   *

GEIGER, Louis G. 1913-

PERSONAL: Born March 21, 1913, in Boonville, Mo.; son of George V. (a farmer) and Dorothea (Hoflander) Geiger; married Helen Margery Watson, December 20, 1946; children: Mark Watson. Education: Elmhurst College, student, 1929-30; Central Missouri State College, B.S., 1934; University of Missouri, M.A., 1940, Ph.D., 1948. Politics: Independent. Home: 111 Lynn Ave., Ames, Iowa 50010. Office: 609 Ross Hall, Iowa State University of Science and Technology, Ames, Iowa 50010.

CAREER: University of North Dakota, Grand Forks, 1946-60, began as assistant professor, became professor of history; Colorado College, Colorado Springs, professor of history, and chairman of department, 1960-70; Arizona State University, Tempe, visiting professor, 1970-71; Iowa State University of Science and Technology, Ames, professor of history and chairman of department, 1972—. Fulbright lecturer in American civilization, University of Helsinki, 1954-55; visiting professor at University of Missouri, 1960, Jadavpur University, 1963-64, and Miami University, 1967. Military service: U.S. Army, 1942-46, Fifth Army historian, 1944-45.

MEMBER: American Historical Association, Agricultural History Society, Southern Historical Association, Organization of American Historians, Rocky Mountain Social Science Association, North Dakota Social Science Association (founder; president, 1959-60), Saturday Club (Calcutta), Rotary Club. Awards, honors: Fellow, Fund for Advancement of Education, 1953-54; Ford Foundation research award, 1962; Social Science Research Council award, 1963.

WRITINGS: "Fifth Army History," Volume IX, From Apennines to Alps, U.S. Government Printing Office, 1948; Joseph W. Folk of Missouri, University of Missouri Press, 1953; University of Northern Plains, University of North Dakota Press, 1958; Higher Education in a Maturing Democracy, University of Nebraska Press, 1963; (contributor) Herbert Shapiro, editor, The Muckrakers and American Society, Heath, 1968; Voluntary Accreditation: A History of the North Central Association, North Central Association (Chicago), 1970. Contributor of articles and reviews to historical journals.

WORK IN PROGRESS: Research for a book, *The Unwanted Presidents.*

* * *

GEIRINGER, Karl 1899-

PERSONAL: Born April 26, 1899, in Vienna, Austria; married Irene Steckel (a writer); children: Martin Frederick, George Karl. *Education:* Studied at University of Berlin and at conservatories in Berlin and Vienna; University of Vienna, Ph.D., 1923. *Religion:* Methodist. *Home:* 1823 Mira Vista Ave., Santa Barbara, Calif. *Office:* Department of Music, University of California, Santa Barbara, Calif.

CAREER: Gesellschaft der Musik Freunde, Vienna, Austria, custodian of archives in instrument collection, 1930-38; lived in London, England, 1938-40; Boston University, Boston, Mass., professor of music, 1941-62; University of California, Santa Barbara, professor of music, 1962—. Arranger of orchestral works. *Member:* International Musicological Society, American Musicological Society (president, 1955-56), American Academy of Arts and Sciences (fellow). *Awards, honors:* Guggenheim Fellow, 1957-58; Bollinger Fellow, 1948-53; American Philosophical Society grant, 1943, 1950, 1954.

WRITINGS: Johannes Brahms, Leben unt Schaffen eines Deutschen Meister, Rohrer, Wien, 1935 (English translation, *Brahms, His Life and Works,* Oxford University Press, 1937, 2nd edition, 1947, Anchor Books, 1961); *Musical Instruments,* Oxford University Press, 1945; *Haydn, A Creative Life in Music,* Norton, 1946, 2nd edition (with wife Irene Geiringer), Anchor books, 1963; (with I. Geiringer) *The Bach Family,* Oxford University Press, 1954; *Music of the Bach Family,* Harvard University Press, 1955.

Johann Sebastian Bach: The Culmination of an Era, Oxford University Press, 1966; (with I. Geiringer) *Johann Sebastian Bach,* Allen & Unwin, 1967; *Hayden: A Creative Life in Music,* University of California Press, 1968; (editor and author of preface) *Hayden: Symphony Number Three in E-Flat Major,* Norton, 1974. Has done about 200 studies, primarily on musical instruments and eighteenth-century music.

Arranger of a collection of piano works published, 1935, and of published orchestral works. Editor of more than one hundred previously un-edited compositions from the seventeenth and eighteenth centuries.

SIDELIGHTS: Geiringer's books have been translated (and published) in eight languages, including Japanese, Dutch, and Swedish.†

* * *

GEISEL, Theodor Seuss 1904-
(Dr. Seuss, Theo LeSieg)

PERSONAL: Surname is pronounced *Guy*-zel; born March 2, 1904, in Springfield, Mass.; son of Theodor Robert (superintendent of Springfield, Mass., public park system) and Henrietta (Seuss) Geisel; married Helen Palmer (an author, and vice-president of Beginner Books), November 29, 1927 (died, October, 1967); married second wife, Audrey Stone Diamond, August 6, 1968. *Education:* Dartmouth College, A.B., 1925; graduate study at Lincoln College, Oxford, 1925-26, Sorbonne, University of Paris,

1926. *Residence:* La Jolla, Calif. *Agent:* Phyllis Jackson, International Famous Agency, Inc., 555 Madison Ave., New York, N.Y. 10022. *Office:* Random House, Inc., 457 Madison Ave., New York, N.Y. 10022.

CAREER: Author, illustrator, and creator of nonsense creatures, 1927—, best known in field of children's books as Dr. Seuss; president of Beginner Books, Random House, Inc., New York, N.Y., 1957—. Originally intended to teach, but upon his return from Europe in 1927, became instead a humorist and cartoonist for *Judge, Vanity Fair, Liberty, Life* (humor periodical), and other national magazines of the day; advertising illustrator, turning out among other campaigns, "Quick Henry, the Flit!" series for Standard Oil of New Jersey, 1928-41; editorial cartoonist for *PM,* New York, N.Y., 1940-42; propaganda publicist for War Production Board, Treasury Department, and other government agencies, 1940-42; later screen artist and writer for Hollywood studios and producer of animated cartoons for television; *Life* correspondent in Japan, 1954. Trustee of La Jolla (Calif.) Town Council, 1956—. *Military service:* U.S. Army, Signal Corps, Information and Education Division, 1943-46; became lieutenant colonel; received Legion of Merit.

MEMBER: Authors League of America, American Society of Composers, Authors and Publishers, Sigma Phi Epsilon. *Awards, honors:* D.H.L., Dartmouth College, 1956, American International College, 1968; Academy Awards made to documentary short, "Hitler Lives," 1946, to documentary feature, "Design for Death," 1947, and to animated cartoon, "Gerald McBoing-Boing," 1951; awards made to animated television programs include Peabody Awards, 1971, for "How the Grinch Stole Christmas" and "Horton Hears a Who," and Critics' Award and Silver Medal, both 1972, for "The Lorax."

WRITINGS—Author and illustrator under pseudonym Dr. Seuss; all juvenile books except where otherwise noted: *And to Think That I Saw It on Mulberry Street,* Vanguard, 1937; *The 500 Hats of Bartholomew Cubbins,* Vanguard, 1938; *The Seven Lady Godivas* (adult), Random House, 1939; *The King's Stilts,* Random House, 1939.

Horton Hatches the Egg, Random House, 1940; *McElligot's Pool,* Random House, 1947; *Thidwick, the Big-Hearted Moose,* Random House, 1949; *Bartholomew and the Oobleck,* Random House, 1949.

If I Ran the Zoo, Random House, 1950; *Scrambled Eggs Super!,* Random House, 1953; *Horton Hears a Who,* Random House, 1954; *On Beyond Zebra,* Random House, 1955; *If I Ran the Circus,* Random House, 1956; *The Cat in the Hat,* Houghton, 1957, bilingual, French, and English edition, published as *La Chat au Chapeau,* Random House, 1967; *How the Grinch Stole Christmas,* Random House, 1957; *The Cat in the Hat Comes Back,* Beginner Books, 1958; *Yertle, the Turtle, and Other Stories,* Random House, 1958; *Happy Birthday to You!,* Random House, 1959.

One Fish, Two Fish, Red Fish, Blue Fish, Beginner Books, 1960; *Green Eggs and Ham,* Beginner Books, 1960; *The Sneetches and Other Stories,* Random House, 1961; *Dr. Seuss's Sleep Book,* Random House, 1962; *Hop on Pop,* Beginner Books, 1963; *Dr. Seuss's ABC,* Beginner Books, 1963; (with Philip D. Eastman) *The Cat in the Hat Dictionary, by the Cat Himself,* Beginner Books, 1964, bilingual, Spanish and English edition, published as *El Gato Ensombrerado,* Random House, 1967; *Fox in Socks Knox in Box,* Beginner Books, 1965; *I Had Trouble in Getting to*

Solla Sollew, Random House, 1965; *The Cat in the Hat Songbook*, Random House, 1967; *Dr. Seuss' Lost World Revisited* (adult), Award Books, 1967; *The Foot Book*, Random House, 1968; *I Can Lick 30 Tigers Today and Other Stories*, Random House, 1969; *My Book About Me*, Beginner Books, 1969.

I Can Draw It Myself, Beginner Books, 1970; *Mr. Brown Can Moo! Can You?*, Random House, 1970; *The Lorax*, Random House, 1971; *Marvin K. Mooney, Will You Please Go Now!*, Beginner Books, 1972; *Did I Ever Tell You How Lucky You Are?*, Random House, 1973; *The Shape of Me and Other Stuff*, Beginner Books, 1973; *There's a Wocket in My Pocket!*, Beginner Books, 1974; *Great Day for Up*, Beginner Books, 1974.

Under pseudonym Theo LeSieg: *Ten Apples Up on Top*, Beginner Books, 1961; *I Wish That I Had Duck Feet*, Beginner Books, 1965; *Come Over to My House*, Beginner Books, 1966; *The Eye Book*, Random House, 1968; *I Can Write-by Me, Myself*, Random House, 1971; *In a People House*, Random House, 1972; *The Many Mice of Mr. Brice*, Beginner Books, 1973; *Wacky Wednesday*, Beginner Books, 1974.

Illustrator: *Boners*, Viking, 1931; *More Boners*, Viking, 1931.

Screenplays: "Your Job in Germany," written for U.S. Army, and later released by Warner Brothers as "Hitler Lives"; (with wife Helen P. Geisel) "Design for Death," RKO Pictures; "Gerald McBoing-Boing" (animated cartoon); "The 5000 Fingers of Dr. T." (a musical). Also author of an unpublished novel.

SIDELIGHTS: Geisel is considered to be a "genius pure and simple." Currently Random House's best-selling author, he began a revolution in young children's readers which had been until his time largely variations on the "Dick and Jane" series. Geisel originated absurd and floppy animals ("they are all people, sort of," he says), gave them names such as Yuzz-a-ma-Tuzz, invented new words and what one critic called "a facile sort of knock-about word play," or what he himself has termed "logical insanity." Not since the days of Edward Lear have children's books provided such sprightly fare. (His books, he confides, "have a secret following among adults, but they have to read me when no one is watching.")

Discussing his work habits, Geisel has said: "I have no set pattern of working. Sometimes a doodled sketch contains a character I think is worth developing; sometimes a doodled couplet of verse suggests a dramatic situation. When I get a character who appeals to me . . . I introduce him to another character and see what happens. When two characters get into conflict, the plot takes care of itself."

He has no children of his own. "You have 'em, I'll amuse 'em," he has said. A *New Yorker* profile describes him as "shy, tense, and serious-minded," meticulous about every detail of his own books and those he edits. His Beginner Books and pre-beginner books seek to interest the very young in actual reading. With tongue in cheek he once remarked that perhaps one day he may initiate prenatal reading "by inventing a two-hundred-and-fifty-word pill that expectant mothers can swallow."

And to Think That I Saw It on Mulberry Street, his first book, has been read and dramatized on radio many times, and a set of variations for orchestra, based on the book, was composed by Deems Taylor and performed at Carnegie Hall in 1943. Some of his books have been recorded by RCA Victor. Animated cartoons based on the books *How the Grinch Stole Christmas, Horton Hears a Who, The Cat in the Hat*, and *The Loraz* have been presented on CBS-TV.

Original drawings and manuscripts of most of Geisel's books are in the Special Collections Division of University of California at Los Angeles library.

AVOCATIONAL INTERESTS: Rocks.

BIOGRAPHICAL/CRITICAL SOURCES: New York Times Book Review, November 16, 1952, May 11, 1958, and November 11, 1962; *Life*, May 24, 1954; *Saturday Evening Post*, July 6, 1957, October 23, 1965; *Education Magazine*, February, 1958; *Eduation Summary*, March 5, 1958; *Parents' Magazine*, November, 1960; *Good House-keeping*, December, 1960; *New Yorker* (profile), December 17, 1960; *Junior Bookshelf*, December, 1963; *Christian Science Monitor*, January 29, 1964; *Los Angeles Times*, January 5, 1964; *McCall's*, November, 1964; *Coronet*, December, 1964; *Woman's Day*, September, 1965; *New Statesman*, November 3, 1967; *New York Times*, October 17, 1968; *Variety*, December 18, 1967; Lee Bennett Hopkins, *Books Are By People*, Citation Press, 1969; *Washington Post*, November 15, 1971; *Newsweek*, February 21, 1972; *Reader's Digest*, April, 1972.

* * *

GELATT, Roland 1920-

PERSONAL: Born July 24, 1920, in Kansas City, Mo.; son of Arthur Alvin (a business executive) and Leah (Kaufman) Gelatt; married Esther Frishkoff (an editor and writer), May 26, 1948; children: Timothy A. *Education:* Attended University of Chicago, 1937-39; Swarthmore College, B.A., 1941. *Home:* 155 East 76th St., New York, N.Y. 10021. *Office: Saturday Review-World*, 488 Madison Ave., New York, N.Y. 10022.

CAREER: Associate editor, *Musical Digest*, 1946-47; *Saturday Review*, New York, N.Y., feature editor, 1948-54; *High Fidelity*, Great Barrington, Mass., music editor, 1954-58, editor-in-chief, 1958-67, editor and associate publisher, 1967-68; *Saturday Review*, managing editor, 1969-71; *World Magazine*, New York, N.Y., international editor, 1972-73; *Saturday Review-World*, New York, N.Y., international editor, 1973—. *Military service:* U.S. Navy, 1942-46; became lieutenant junior grade.

WRITINGS: Music Makers: Some Outstanding Musical Performers of Our Day, Knopf, 1952; *The Fabulous Phonograph: From Edison to Stereo*, Lippincott, 1955, revised edition, Appleton, 1965. Contributor to *New York Times Book Review, House and Garden, Playboy*, and other magazines.†

* * *

GELBER, Lionel (Morris) 1907-

PERSONAL: Born September 13, 1907, in Toronto, Ontario, Canada; son of Louis (a businessman) and Sara (Morris) Gelber. *Education:* University of Toronto, B.A., 1930; Balliol College, Oxford, B.Litt., 1933. *Office:* c/o Gelber Bros. Ltd., 203 Richmond St. W., Toronto, Ontario, Canada.

CAREER: Free-lance writer, London, England, 1934-38; University of Toronto, Toronto, Ontario, lecturer in international affairs, 1941-43; free-lance writer, New York, N.Y., 1945-60; special assistant to Prime Minister of Canada, Ottawa, Ontario, 1960-61; free-lance writer, London,

England, 1961—. Visiting summer lecturer at University of Saskatchewan, 1939, and University of Alberta, 1941. *Military service:* Royal Canadian Air Force, 1943-45; became flight lieutenant. *Member:* Canadian Institute of International Affairs, International Institute of Strategic Studies and St. James' Club (both London). *Awards, honors:* Rhodes Scholar, Balliol College, Oxford University, 1930-33.

WRITINGS: The Rise of Anglo-American Friendship: A Study in World Politics, 1898-1906, Oxford University Press, 1938, published with a new preface, Archon Books, 1966; *Peace by Power: The Plain Man's Guide to the Key Issue of the War and of the Post-War World*, Oxford University Press, 1942; *Reprieve from War: A Manual for Realists*, Macmillan, 1950; *The American Anarchy: Democracy in an Era of Bigness*, Abelard-Schuman, 1953; *America in Britain's Place: The Leadership of the West and Anglo-American Unity*, Praeger, 1961; *The Alliance of Necessity: Britain's Crisis, the New Europe and American Interests*, Stein & Day, 1966; (contributor) Harry G. Johnson, editor, *New Trade Strategy for the World Economy*, University of Toronto Press, 1969; (contributor) Paul Streeten and Hugh Corbet, editors, *Commonwealth Policy in a Global Context*, University of Toronto Press, 1971; (contributor) Douglas Evans, editor, *Destiny or Delusion: Britain and the Common Market*, Gollancz, 1971. Author of six pamphlets, and articles in American and British periodicals, including *Spectator*.

*   *   *

GELLHORN, Walter 1906-

PERSONAL: Born September 18, 1906, in St. Louis, Mo.; son of George and Edna (Fischel) Gellhorn; married Kitty Minus, 1932; children: Ellis, Gay. *Education:* Amherst College, A.B., 1927; Columbia University, LL.B., 1931. *Home:* 54 Morningside Dr., New York, N.Y. 10025. *Office:* Law School, Columbia University, 435 West 116th St., New York, N.Y. 10027.

CAREER: Office of U.S. Supreme Court Justice Harlan F. Stone, Washington, D.C., law secretary, 1931; admitted to New York bar, 1932; U.S. Department of Justice, Washington, D.C., employed in Office of Solicitor General, 1932-33; Columbia University, New York, N.Y., member of law faculty, 1933—, of political science faculty, 1937—, Betts Professor of Law, 1957-1973, university professor, 1973—. Member of New York State Public Works Advisory Board, 1935; regional attorney, U.S. Social Security Board, 1936-38; director, Attorney General's Committee on Administrative Procedure, 1939-41; director of research, New York Law Society, 1941; assistant general counsel and regional attorney, Office of Price Administration, 1942-43; special assistant to Secretary of the Interior, 1943-44; National War Labor Board, second region, vice-chairman, 1944-45, chairman, 1945.

MEMBER: Association of American Law Schools (president, 1963), American Philosophical Society, American Academy of Arts and Sciences (fellow), Alpha Delta Phi (president, 1955-58), Phi Beta Kappa, Phi Delta Phi. *Awards, honors:* Co-recipient, Henderson Memorial Prize, 1946, for work as director of Attorney General's Committee on Administrative Procedure during its study of federal administration; Goldsmith Prize, 1951, for *Security, Loyalty and Science*; Hillman Award, 1957, for *Individual Freedom and Government Restraints*, L.H.D., Amherst College, 1952; LL.D., University of Pennsylvania, 1963,

University of Akron, 1967, Boston University, 1970, L'Universite Catholique de Louvain (Belgium), 1972, and Rutgers University, 1973.

WRITINGS: Federal Administrative Proceedings, Johns Hopkins University Press, 1941; *Security, Loyalty, and Science*, Cornell University Press, 1950; (co-author) *The States and Subversion*, Cornell University Press, 1952; *Children and Families in the Courts*, Dodd, 1954; *Individual Freedom and Governmental Restraints*, Louisiana State University Press, 1956; (co-author) *The Freedom to Read*, Bowker, 1957; *Administrative Law—Cases and Comments*, Foundation, 1940, 6th edition, 1974; *American Rights*, Macmillan, 1960; *Kihonteki Jinken*, Yuhikaku, 1960; (with Louis Lauer) *Administration of the New York Workmen's Compensation*, School of Law, New York University, 1961; *Ombudsmen and Others: Citizens' Protectors in Nine Countries*, Harvard University Press, 1966; *When Americans Complain: Governmental Grievance Procedures*, Harvard University Press, 1966; *A Proposal in Legislative Form: To Create the Office of Ombudsman*, School of Law, Columbia University, 1967; (with R. Kent Greenawalt) *The Sectarian College and the Public Purse: Fordham—A Case Study*, Oceana, 1970. Member of editorial board, American Scholar, 1951-55.

*   *   *

GENET, Jean 1910-

PERSONAL: Born December 19, 1910, in Paris, France; never knew his parents; was abandoned by his mother, Gabrielle Genet, to the Assistance Publique, and was raised by a family of peasants; at the age of ten, after having been caught stealing, he was placed in a reformatory at Mettray; after escaping from the reformatory he joined the French Foreign Legion, under a false name, and subsequently deserted; was a beggar, thief, and homosexual prostitute ("For a time I loved stealing, but prostitution appealed more to my easygoing ways," he said.); was thrown out of five countries and spent time in thirteen jails before he was thirty-five; escaped a life sentence through the intervention of such prominent French intellectuals as Jean-Paul Sartre and Jean Cocteau. He gives this explanation for his criminal life: "Abandoned by my family, I found it natural to aggravate this fact by the love of males, and that love by stealing, and stealing by crime, or the complicity with crime. Thus I decisively repudiated a world that had repudiated me."

AWARDS, HONORS: Village Voice Off-Broadway (Obie) Awards, 1960, for "The Balcony," and 1961, for "The Blacks."

WRITINGS: Notre-Dame-des-Fleurs (novel), dated from Fresnes prison, 1942, limited edition, L'Arbalete, 1943, revised edition published by Gallimard (Paris), 1951, translation by Bernard Frechtman published as *Our Lady of the Flowers*, Morihien (Paris), 1949, published with introduction by Jean-Paul Sartre, Grove, 1963; *Miracle de la rose* (prose-poem), dated from La Sante and Tourelles prisons, 1943, privately printed by Arbalete, 1946, 2nd edition, Arbalete, 1956, translation by Frechtman published as *Miracle of the Rose*, Blond, 1965, Grove, 1966; *Chants secrets* (poems), privately printed (Lyons), 1944; *Querelle de Brest*, privately printed, 1947, translation by Gregory Streatham published as *Querelle of Brest*, Blond, 1966; *Pompes funebres*, privately printed, c. 1947, revised edition, 1948, translation by Frechtman published as *Funeral Rites*, Grove, 1969; *Poemes*, privately printed by Arbalete,

1948, 2nd edition, Arbalete, 1962; *Journal du voleur*, Gallimard, 1949, translation by Frechtman published as *The Thief's Journal*, foreword by Sartre, Olympia Press, 1954, Grove, 1964; *Haute surveillance* (play; first performed at Theatre des Mathurins, February, 1949; produced in New York at Theatre East, October 9, 1958), Gallimard, 1949, translation by Frechtman published as *Deathwatch: A Play*, Faber, 1961 (also see below); *L'enfant criminel et 'Adame Miroir*, Morihien, 1949.

Les beaux gars, [Paris], 1951; *Les Bonnes* (play; first performed in Paris, April 17, 1947; produced in New York at Tempo Playhouse, May 6, 1955), Pauvert, 1954, translation by Frechtman published as *The Maids*, introduction by Sartre, Grove, 1954, augmented French edition published as *Les Bonnes et comment jouer Les Bonnes*, M. Barbezat, 1963 (also see below); *The Maids*, [*and*] *Deathwatch*, two plays in one volume, translation by Frechtman, introduction by Sartre, Grove, 1954, revised edition, 1962; *Le Balcon* (play; first produced in London at London Arts Theatre Club, April 22, 1957; produced in New York at Circle in the Square, March 3, 1960), with lithographs by Alberto Giacometti, Arbalete, 1956, translation by Frechtman published as *The Balcony*, Faber, 1957, Grove, 1958, revised edition, Grove, 1960; *Les Negres: Clownerie* (play; first produced at Theatre de Lutece, October 28, 1959; produced in New York at St. Mark's Playhouse, May 4, 1961), M. Barbezat, 1958, 3rd edition, with photographs, M. Barbezat, 1963, translation by Frechtman published as *The Blacks: A Clown Show*, Grove, 1960.

Les Paravents (play; first produced in West Berlin at Schlosspark Theatre, May 19, 1961; produced in Brooklyn, N.Y., at Brooklyn Academy of Music, November, 1971), M. Barbezat, 1961, translation by Frechtman published as *The Screens*, Grove, 1962; *Lettres a Roger Blin*, Gallimard, 1966, translation by Richard Seaver published as *Letters to Roger Blin: Reflections on the Theater*, Grove, 1969; *May Day Speech* (delivered in 1970 at Yale University), with description by Allen Ginsberg, City Lights, 1970.

Omnibus volumes: *Oeuvres completes* (Volume I: "Saint Genet: Comedien et martyr," by Jean-Paul Sartre; Volume II: "Notre-Dame-des-Fleurs," "Le Condamne a mort," "Miracle de la rose," and "Un Chant d'amour"; Volume III: "Pompes funebres," "Le Pecheur du suquet," and "Querelle de Brest"; Volume IV: "Les Bonnes," "Le Balcon," and "Haute Surveillance"), Gallimard, 1951—, four volumes (with Volume IV containing additional works, "L'Etrange Mot d'....," "Ce qui est reste d'un Rembrant dechire en petits carres," "Comment jouer Les Bonnes," and "Comment jouer Le Balcon"), French & European Publications, 1951-53; *L'Atelier d'Alberto Giacometti; Les Bonnes, suivi d'une lettre; L'Enfant criminel; Le Funambule*, Arbalete, 1958.

Work is represented in anthologies, including *Seven Plays of the Modern Theatre*, edited by Harold Clurman, Grove, 1962. Author of scenario, "Mademoiselle," Woodfall Films, 1966. Contributor to *Esquire*.

SIDELIGHTS: Genet's frankly amoral books, which include accounts of homosexuality, theft, murder, and sordidness in general, have been the objects of attacks by moralists and book censors, and of adulation from the avantgarde. Foremost among the latter is Jean-Paul Sartre who first discussed his canonization (in *Saint Genet*), arguing that if sainthood consists of a life of humility, coming from the acceptance of evil and sin as the human condition, then

there is a comparison to be made between Genet and St. Teresa of Avila. Genet's face, staring back from dust jackets and magazines, may be indicative of his spiritual state. It bears a look that Bell Gale Chevigny calls "at once abject, crushed, begging crumbs of attention, and utterly superior, inacessible."

His early books were written in prison on brown paper intended for the construction of paper bags. Sartre reports that a turnkey once burned Genet's manuscript of *Our Lady of the Flowers* only to have Genet begin again. The early books are mainly erotic fantasies. ("My books are not novels because none of my characters makes decisions on his own," he told Sartre.) *Our Lady* is permeated with a daydream quality, which, according to the *Times Literary Supplement*, "gives the book its peculiar tone and, by so doing, distinguishes it most clearly from the works of commercial pornography with which it has been confused in the past."

It is less pornography than poetry. Genet writes: "My life must be a legend, in other words, legible, and the reading of it must give birth to a certain new emotion which I call poetry." The poetic quality of his writings is perhaps the most valuable aspect for most readers. Genet once called his language "the very language used by the mystics of all religions to speak of their gods and their mysteries."

However, he uses this religious language and ritual to portray a world where evil is the greatest good, a position he originally adopted as a deliberate affront to the society which repudiated him. "I want to sing murder," he writes, "for I love murderers. To sing it plainly. Without pretending, for example, that I want to be redeemed through it, though I do yearn for redemption. I would like to kill." As the *Times Literary Supplement* carefully pointed out, "This is his view of the world, and he sees no reason why other people should either condemn or imitate him." "Genet ... shows us just how far a writer can go on the path of rebellion and in the deliberate creation of evil. He thereby, with Sade, adds a totally new dimension to the literary experience of the West."

"Genet's point," writes Alfred Chester in *Commentary*, "is not to make us laugh, but to rub our noses in his offensive roses...." What he has to say holds little appeal for most readers. In 1949, Eleanor Clark could write that "There has been an air around his name here as of some perverse perfume, too strong for general consumption." At the present time his books are readily available in bookshops and even through an American book club. There still remains a good deal of uncertainty concerning the value placed on his work. Eric Keown in *Punch* writes: "Whether Genet's work should be put in the dust-bin or on the top shelf of one's library must be a personal decision. It qualifies amply for either." Christopher Ricks is more critical: "It may be (though I doubt it) that convincing claims for Genet's greatness can be made." Eleanor Clark, however, has high praise, calling him "one of the most gifted French prose writers of this generation, and the only one to have created a world nearly comparable in compulsion if not in scope to that of Proust or Celine." "[He is] the one writer of the time who has most extended the [novel] form—and extended it not at all to bursting, or down another dead end excpet as any achievement is that, but only by a natural infusion of genius, or life." He is at least unique. Peter S. Beagle writes: "I don't believe that Genet is a genius, or even a great writer, but his is a completely individual voice, and that has never been a small recommendation." The late Louis-Ferdinand Celine once remarked: "There are only two real writers among living Frenchmen: Genet and I."

Since 1949 Genet has written solely for the theater, a progression, as Martin Esslin notes, from the subjective form of poetic expression to one of the most objective forms. A reviewer in the *Atlantic* wrote: "Only in his plays, where the ritual of the theater and the requirements of dramatic structure compel him to escape from his narcissism, has Genet been able to give fullest expression to his remarkable talent in works of almost classical form."

Genet does not intend to write entertaining plays, or even plays having social significance, philosophic argument, clear plots, or fixed and coherent characters. Rather the plays are what Sartre calls "whirligigs of being and appearance, of the imaginary and the real," in effect, the projections of private myth through the use of ritual, symbols, and illusions. "In Genet's plays," Sartre writes, "every character must play the role of a character who plays a role." Even Genet cannot be certain of the identity of his characters: "My characters are all masks. How do you expect me to tell you whether they are true or false? I no longer know myself."

Genet's theater is essentially one of revolt. Leonard Cabell Pronko writes: "His revolt is not only against ordered society, it is against life itself, a life which refuses man the satisfactions of an absolute purity. Diving into the inverted world of dark and evil, Genet adopts an essentially religious attitude, attempting to reach the absolute through his inverted religion. His theater is a Mass celebrating that religion." Genet says, "Theatrically speaking, I know of nothing more effective than the elevation."

His play *The Blacks* has had a recent long run in America—more than three years at St. Mark's Playhouse in New York. It is written for an all-Negro cast and intended to be performed before a white audience. Genet has given these instructions to the players:"... if, which is unlikely, it is ever performed before a black audience, then a white person, male or female, should be invited every evening.... A spotlight should be focused on this symbolic white throughout the performance." On stage, the masked Negro characters are preparing for the ritual murder of a white woman. At one point a character declares an attitude that is analogous to Genet's own: "We have masked our faces in order to live the loathsome lives they have ordered.... We are what they would have us be." And, though Genet on the surface seems to deal with a contemporary issue, Robert Hatch observes that "there is not a trace of goodwill in Genet, and the question of whether society is to be integrated or segregated is to him a matter of perfect indifference. It would still be society, and he would still be outside it."

He may still be an outsider, but he is now, reportedly, "quite the lion of the Paris salons," says Hatch, "and I'm told the hostesses are wont to put a piece of silver, or some charming bric-a-brac, temptingly within his reach: there is always the chance of enjoying the glory of being robbed by so distinguished a guest."

Selections from his works have been recorded on Caedmon Records, including a reading by Genet, in French, from *The Thief's Journal. The Balcony* was filmed by Continental, 1963. Genet created the film, "Un Chant d'amour," which, upon being shown in New York early in 1964, led to police action, including the closing of the theater, seizure of the film, and arrests of the people responsible for the program; the charges were eventually dropped.

BIOGRAPHICAL/CRITICAL SOURCES—Books: Jean Paul, Sartre, *Saint Genet: Comedien et martyr*, Gallimard, 1952, translation by Bernard Frechtman published as *Saint Genet: Actor and Martyr*, Baziller, 1963; Martin Esslin, *The Theatre of the Absurd*, Anchor Books, 1961; Leonard Cabell Pronko, *Avant Garde: The Experimental Theater in France*, University of California Press, 1962; D. I. Grossvogel, *Four Playwrights and a Postscript*, Cornell University Press, 1962; J. H. McMahon, *The Imagination of Jean Genet*, Yale University Press, 1964; Richard Kostelanetz, editor, *On Contemporary Literature*, Avon, 1964; George Wellwarth, *Theatre of Protest and Paradox*, New York University Press, 1964; Tom F. Driver, *Jean Genet*, Columbia University Press, 1966, Richard N. Coe, *The Vision of Jean Genet*, Grove, 1968; Philip Thody, *Jean Genet: A Study of His Novels and Plays*, Hamish Hamilton, 1968, Stein & Day, 1969; Carolyn Riley, editor, *Contemporary Literary Criticism*, Gale, Volume I, 1973, Volume II, 1974.

Articles: *Figaro litteraire*, March 26, 1949, October 15, 1951; *Partisan Review*, April, 1949; *Horizon*, November 29, 1964; *New Statesman*, January 10, 1964; *New Yorker*, January 16, 1965; *Village Voice*, March 18, 1965; *Times Literary Supplement*, April 8, 1965; *Holiday*, June, 1965; *Kenyon Review*, March, 1967; *Drama Review*, fall, 1969.*†

*   *   *

GENTRY, Byron B. 1913-

PERSONAL: Born October 20, 1913, in Coulee, Wash.; son of James J. and Evelena (Burk) Gentry; married Ruth Genevieve Jensen, 1949; children: Kathleen Marie, Sharon Christine. *Education:* University of Southern California, A.B., 1936; Southwestern University, LL.B., 1941. *Politics:* Republican. *Religion:* Episcopalian. *Home:* 730 Huerta Verde Rd., Glendora, Calif.

CAREER: Pittsburgh Steelers, Pittsburgh, Pa., professional football player, 1937-40; deputy sheriff, Los Angeles County, Calif., 1939-42, 1946-47; admitted to California bar, 1947; city prosecutor, Pasadena, Calif., 1948-62, 1963—; Veterans of Foreign Wars, national commander, 1962-63. Member, California State Veterans Board, 1957—; member of board, American Gold Star Mothers Home Corp. Former president of Pasadena Committee for Education for Alcholism and Pasadena Committee for Narcotics Education; member of Los Angeles County Committee on the Aging and Los Angeles Veterans Service Center. *Military service:* U.S. Army Air Forces, 1942-46; became captain; received Presidential Citation, six battle stars for European campaigns, Belgian Fourragere, Combat Cross (France). U.S. Army Reserve, 1946-54.

MEMBER: California State Bar Association, Veterans of Foreign Wars of the U.S.A., Phi Kappa Tau, Phi Alpha Delta, Lions Club (Pasadena). *Awards, honors:* Named member of United Press All-American Professional Football Team, 1938; Distinguished Service Award of Veterans of Foreign Wars of the U.S.A. (twice), for work as district commander; Freedoms Foundation outstanding service award, 1963.

WRITINGS: Voices of the Airways (poetry), Naylor, 1962; *The Way the Ball Bounces* (prose), Naylor, 1963. Contributor to magazines.

WORK IN PROGRESS: Within My Heart, poetry.†

*   *   *

GEORGE, Alexander Lawrence 1920-

PERSONAL: Born May 31, 1920, in Chicago, Ill.; son of

John and Mary (Sargis) George; married Juliette Lombard (a researcher and writer), April 20, 1948; children: Lee, Mary. *Education:* University of Chicago, A.M., 1942, Ph.D., 1958. *Home:* 218 South Medio Dr., Los Angeles, Calif. *Office:* RAND Corp., 1700 Main St., Santa Monica, Calif.

CAREER: U.S. government, Washington, D.C., analyst, Federal Broadcast Intelligence Service and Federal Communications Commission, 1942-44, political analyst, Office of Strategic Services, 1944-45; Office of Military Government for Germany (U.S.), deputy chief of research branch, Information Control Division, 1945-47; RAND Corp., Santa Monica, Calif., senior staff member, 1948—. Lecturer at University of Chicago, 1950, American University, 1952-56. *Member:* Phi Beta Kappa. *Awards, honors:* Rockefeller Foundation fellow, 1942; fellow, Center for Advanced Study in the Behavioral Sciences, 1956-57; Foundations' Fund research grant to study the application of psychoanalytic theory to biographical research, 1960.

WRITINGS: (With wife, Juliette L. George) *Woodrow Wilson and Colonel House: A Personality Study*, Dover, 1956; *Propaganda Analysis: A Study of Inferences Made from Nazi Propaganda in World War II*, Row, Peterson & Co., 1959; *The Chinese Communist Army in Action: The korean War and Its Aftermath*, Columbia University Press, 1967; *The "Operational Code": A Neglected Approach to the Study of Political Leaders and Decision-Making*, Rand Corp., 1967; (with David K. Hall and William E. Simons) *The Limits of Coercive Diplomacy: Laos, Cuba, Vietnam*, Little, Brown, 1971; (with others) *Deterrence in American Foreign Policy: Theory and Practice*, Columbia University Press, 1974. Contributor to *World Politics, Public Opinion Quarterly*, and *American Political Science Review*.†

*   *   *

GEORGE, Claude Swanson, Jr. 1920-

PERSONAL: Born June 4, 1920, in Danville, Va.; son of Claude Swanson and Myrtle Ann (Dillard) George; married Eleanor Anthony, December 22, 1960. *Education:* University of North Carolina, B.S., 1942, M.S., 1951; University of Iowa, Ph.D., 1953. *Politics:* Democrat. *Religion:* Methodist. *Home:* Coker Dr., Chapel Hill, N.C. 27514. *Office:* School of Business Administration, University of North Carolina, Chapel Hill, N.C. 27514.

CAREER: Western Electric Co., Burlington, N.C., management staff, 1946-50; University of Iowa, Iowa City, instructor, 1951-53; University of Texas, Austin, associate professor of management, 1953-54; University of North Carolina, Chapel Hill, professor of industrial management, 1954—, associate dean of School of Business Administration, 1959—. *Military service:* U.S. Army, 1943-46. *Member:* Academy of Management (fellow), American Institute of Management, Society for Advancement of Management, Southern Management Association (past president), Phi Beta Kappa, Beta Gamma Sigma, Sigma Iota Epsilon, Order of Artus.

WRITINGS: Management in Industry, Prentice-Hall, 1959, 2nd edition, 1964; *History of Management Thought*, Prentice-Hall, 1968, 2nd edition, 1972; *Management for Business and Industry*, Prentice-Hall, 1970. Contributor to journals.

*   *   *

GEORGIOU, Constantine 1927-

PERSONAL: Born April 2, 1927, in Calcutta, India; son of Anthony (an industrialist) and Harichlia (Dangas) Georgiou. *Education:* Early education in India and others countries; Columbia Union College, B.A., 1952; University of Maryland, M. Ed., 1954; New York University, Ed.D., 1964. *Home:* 1 Washington Square Village, New York, N.Y. 10012.

CAREER: New York University, New York, N.Y., professor of children's literature, 1961—. Author of books for children. *Member:* National Council of Teachers of English, American Association of University Professors, Kappa Delta Pi.

WRITINGS: Wait and See, Harvey, 1962; *The Little Red Hen and the Gingerbread Boy*, American Book Co., 1963; *Ham and Astrochimp*, American Book Co., 1963; *The Elephant's Funny Way*, American Book Co., 1963; *The Monkey and the Alligator: Who Was the Strongest?*, American Book Co., 1963; *Whitey and Whiskers and Food*, Harvey House, 1964; *Escape From Moscow*, American Book Co. 1964; *The Clock*, Harvey House, 1967; *Proserpina: The Duck That Came to School*, Harvey House, 1968; *Children and Their Literature*, Prentice-Hall, 1969; *Rani-Queen of the Jungle*, Prentice-Hall, 1970; *The Nest*, Harvey House, 1972.

SIDELIGHTS: Georgiou started seeing the world in early childhood, accompanying his parents (of Greek descent) to various countries where his father had business interests. He visits Greece often, "especially since I enjoy the classical heritage." *Avocational interests:* Music, Byzantine art.†

*   *   *

GERBER, Merrill Joan 1938-

PERSONAL: Born March 15, 1938, in Brooklyn, N.Y.; daughter of William (an antique dealer) and Jessie (Sorblum) Gerber; married Joseph Spiro (a college teacher), June 23, 1960; children: Becky Ann, Joanna Emily, Susanna Willa. *Education:* University of Miami, student, 1955; University of Florida, B.A., 1959; graduate study at Brandeis University, 1959-60. *Religion:* Jewish. *Agent:* Cyrilly Abels, 119 W. 57th St., New York, N.Y. 10019.

AWARDS, HONORS: Stanford University creative writing fellowship, 1962-63.

WRITINGS: Stop Here, My Friend (short stories), Houghton, 1965; *An Antique Man* (novel), Houghton, 1967; *Now Molly Knows*, Arbor House, 1974. Contributor of short stories to *Mademoiselle, New Yorker, Redbook, Sewanee Review, McCall's, Ladies' Home Journal, Woman's Day* and *Family Circle*. Also has contributed articles on writing fiction to *The Writer* and *Writer's Digest*.

WORK IN PROGRESS: A novel and a collection of short stories.

SIDELIGHTS: Ms. Gerber has published more short stories in *Redbook* than any other contributor.

*   *   *

GERBOTH, Walter W. 1925-

PERSONAL: Born February 27, 1925, in New York, N.Y.; son of Walter W. and Florence (Lindeke) Gerboth; married Janice Lake, March 9, 1950; children: Christopher, Alix, Owen. *Education:* Queens College, Flushing, N.Y., B.A., 1950; Columbia University, M.S., 1953. *Office:* Department of Music, Brooklyn College, Brooklyn, N.Y.

CAREER: Brooklyn College, Brooklyn, N.Y., teacher and

librarian of music, 1956—. Director of musical projects, New York State Department of Education, summer, 1963. *Member:* American Musicological Society, Music Library Association (chairman, New York chapter, 1959-61; president, 1970-1971), Society for Asian Music, Society for Ethnomusicology, American Association of University Professors, American Society of Indexers.

WRITINGS: English Madrigals and Ayres, Arranged for Recorder Ensemble, Hargail Music Press, 1959; (with Harold Prucha) *Primer for the Bass Recorder*, Hargail Music Press, 1960; *A Selected Bibliography of Books, Pamphlets and Articles About African Music*, New York State Department of Education, 1963; *Music of East and Southeast Asia: A Selected Bibliography of Books, Pamphlets, Articles and Recordings*, New York State Department of Education, 1963; *Music of the Fifteenth Century, Arranged for Recorders*, Hargail Music Press, 1963; (editor with Robert L. Sanders, Robert Starer, and Frances Steiner) *An Introduction to Music: Selected Readings*, Norton, 1964, revised edition, 1969; (contributor) *Studies in Renaissance and Medieval Music*, Norton, 1965; *An Index to Musical Festschriften and Some Similar Publications*, Norton, 1969. Chairman of publication committee of Music Library Association, 1960—.

WORK IN PROGRESS: Music bibliographies; studies on the comic element in music, and the use of the computer in music bibliography.

*　　*　　*

GERDTS, William H. 1929-

PERSONAL: Born January 18, 1929, in New York, N.Y.; son of William H. (a business executive) and Suzanne (Zonowick) Gerdts; divorced; children: Jeffrey. *Education:* Amherst College, B.A., 1949; Harvard University, M.A., 1950, graduate study, 1950-53. *Office:* Newark Museum, 43 Washington St., Newark, N.J.

CAREER: Norfolk Museum of Arts and Sciences, Norfolk, Va., curator, 1943-54; Newark Museum, Newark, N.J., curator of painting and sculpture, 1954—. Lecturer on American art at colleges and museums throughout the country; teacher of adult education courses related to art. *Member:* Phi Beta Kappa.

WRITINGS: Drawings of Joseph Stella, Rabin & Krueger Gallery (Newark, N.J.), 1962; *Painting and Sculpture in New Jersey*, Van Nostrand, 1964; (with Russell Burke) *Still-Life Painting*, Praeger, 1971; *American Neo-Classic Sculpture: The Marble Resurrection*, Viking, 1973; *The Great American Nude: A History in Art*, Praeger, 1974. Also author of art exhibition catalogs for museums in New Jersey, New York, Maryland, and California. Contributor to *Antiques, Art Quarterly*, and to New Jersey Historical Society and Newark Museum publications.

WORK IN PROGRESS: A book on the life and art of Henry Inman.

SIDELIGHTS: Gerdts speaks French and German, is studying Egyptian hieroglyphics and Arabic. He visits Europe annually to study art collections and monuments.†

*　　*　　*

GERRING, Ray H. 1926-

PERSONAL: Born June 11, 1926, in Seattle, Wash.; son of Harry and Svea (Larson) Gerring; married June Paylor, October 22, 1948; children: Lynne, Dale, Richard. *Education:* Attended Burnley School of Art and Design, Seattle,

Wash., 1946-49, and Seattle University, 1961; University of Washington, Seattle, B.A., 1964. *Home:* 5928 South Carver St., Seattle, Wash.

CAREER: F. E. Baker & Associates (advertising), Seattle, Wash., staff artist, 1949-51; Penman Neil Advertising, Seattle, Wash., art director, 1951-54; Studio Art (advertising art service), Seattle, Wash., partner and art director-artist, 1954-60; free-lance commercial artist in Seattle, Wash., 1960-62; Metropolitan Press (printers), Seattle, Wash., art director and graphic designer, 1962-64; Seattle (Wash.) public schools, high school teacher of art, 1964—. Instructor in commercial art, Cornish School of Allied Arts, Seattle, Wash. *Military service:* U.S. Army Air Forces, 1944-46. *Member:* Puget Sound Group of Northwest Painters (president, 1960), Seattle Art Studio Association (president, 1961), Seattle Art Directors Society.

WRITINGS: (With Henry Petterson) *Exploring With Paint*, Reinhold, 1964.

WORK IN PROGRESS: Developing ideas for several books about art education, with Henry Petterson.†

*　　*　　*

GERTZ, Elmer 1906-

PERSONAL: Born September 14, 1906, in Chicago, Ill.; son of Morris (a merchant) and Grace (Grossman) Gertz; married Ceretta Samuels, August 16, 1931 (died, 1958); married Mamie Laitchin Friedman, June 21, 1959; children: (first marriage) Theodore Gerson, Margery Ann (Mrs. Henry R. Hechtman); (stepson) Jack M. Friedman. *Education:* University of Chicago, Ph.D., 1928, J.D., 1930. *Politics:* Independent Democrat. *Religion:* Jewish. *Home:* 6249 North Albany Ave., Chicago, Ill. 60659. *Office:* 120 South La Salle St., Chicago, Ill. 60603.

CAREER: Admitted to Illinois bar, 1930; McInerney, Epstein, and Arvey (law firm), Chicago, Ill., associate, 1930-41; attorney in private practice in Chicago, 1941-73; Gertz & Giampietro (law firm), Chicago, partner, 1973—. Active in civic and community activities in Chicago for more than four decades, serving as president of Public Housing Association, 1943-49, legislative chairman of Mayor's Emergency Housing Committee, 1946-48, member of Mayor's Housing Action Committee, 1949-51; president of Greater Chicago Council of the American Jewish Congress, 1959-63, and president of Adult Education Council of Greater Chicago, 1965-69; delegate, Illinois Constitutional Convention, 1969; professor, John Marshall Law School, 1970—; member of board of trustees, Bellefaire and City of Hope; member of board of directors, Jackson Park Hospital.

MEMBER: American Bar Association, American Judicature Society, Federal Bar Association, Illinois State Bar Association, Chicago Bar Association (chairman of legal education committee), First Amendment Lawyers Association, Appellate Lawyers Association, Decalogue Society of Lawyers (president, 1954-55), Civil War Round Table of Chicago (a founder; president, 1952-53; honorary life member), Society of Midland Authors, Friends of Literature, Shaw Society of Chicago (founder; president, 1956-61), Chicago Literary Club, Cliff Dwellers (Chicago), City Club (Chicago), Caxton Club. *Awards, honors:* Decalogue Society of Lawyers Award of Merit, 1949; citations from Illinois Division of American Civil Liberties Union, 1963, from University of Chicago Alumni Association, for public service, and from Roosevelt University, Society of Midland Authors, American Jewish Congress, and Chicago Council Against Discrimination; State of Israel's Prime Minister's Medal, 1972.

WRITINGS: (With A. I. Tobin) *Frank Harris: A Study in Black and White*, Mendelsohn, 1931, reprinted, Haskell, 1970; *The People vs. the Chicago Tribune*, Union for Democratic Action, 1942; *American Ghettos*, American Jewish Congress, 1946; (contributor) *Henry Miller and the Critics*, Southern Illinois University Press, 1963; *A Handful of Clients*, Follett, 1965; *Books and Their Right to Live*, University of Kansas Library, 1965; *Moment of Madness: The People vs. Jack Ruby*, Follett, 1968; (author of preface) Earl R. Hutchison, *Tropic of Cancer on Trial*, Grove, 1968; (contributor) David G. Clark and Hutchison, *Mass Media and the Law: Freedom and Restraint*, Wiley, 1970; *For the First Hours of Tomorrow: The New Illinois Bill of Rights*, University of Illinois Press, 1972; (contributor) Alan S. Gratch and Virginia H. Ubik, *Ballots for Change: New Suffrage and Amending Articles for Illinois*, University of Illinois Press, 1974; *To Life*, McGraw, 1974.

Writer of radio plays, including "Mrs. Bixby Gets a Letter," 1942, and "Second Inaugural." Contributor to *Encyclopaedia Britannica*, *Junior Britannica*, *Encyclopedia Judaica*, *American People's Encyclopedia*, *Nation*, *Progressive*, *Public Opinion Quarterly*, *American Mercury*, *Journal of the Illinois State Historical Society*, other magazines, and to newspapers.

WORK IN PROGRESS: Editing a collection of short stories by Frank Harris; a history of the 6th Illinois Constitutional Convention, with Joseph Pisciotta; several juveniles.

SIDELIGHTS: "I instinctively am attracted to the unusual, bizarre, the unpopular. This has led to my interest in such persons as Frank Harris, George Sylvester Viereck, Henry Miller. I believe in freedom to err."

Gertz represented Nathan Leopold in his successful bid for parole from a life sentence in 1957-58, includes Leopold among the clients who have become his friends. Another is Henry Miller who was his client during the Illinois litigation over *Tropic of Cancer*.

Gertz helped set aside the death sentence for Jack Ruby, the convicted killer of President John F. Kennedy's assassin, Lee Harvey Oswald. He also filed amicus briefs in all of the capital punishment cases leading to the Supreme Court's declaration of the unconstitutionality of the death sentence.

* * *

GERVASI, Frank H(enry) 1908-

PERSONAL: Born February 5, 1908, in Baltimore, Md.; son of Eugene Leone (a mechanic) and Teresa (Guarnera) Gervasi; separated; children: Sean David, Eugene Michael. *Education:* Attended Drexel Institute of Technology, 1927-28, University of Pennsylvania, 1928-30. *Politics:* Independent liberal. *Religion:* Christian. *Residence:* New York, N.Y. *Agent:* (Books) Scott Meredith, Inc., 580 Fifth Ave., New York, N.Y. 10036; (lectures) JWB Lecture Bureau, 15 East 26th St., New York, N.Y. 10010.

CAREER: Reporter for *Philadelphia Record*, Philadelphia, Pa., 1929-30, Associated Press, New York, N.Y., 1930-34; Hearst Newspapers, Madrid correspondent, 1934-35; London correspondent, 1935; International News Service, chief of Rome bureau, 1935-39; *Collier's*, roving war correspondent, 1939-45, associate editor, 1939-49; U.S. Department of State, chief of information for Marshall Plan, Rome, Italy, 1950-52; *New York Post*, foreign correspondent based in Rome, Italy, with column, "Dateline Your World," syndicated by Worldwide Press Service, 1954-57;

Motion Picture Export Association, New York, N.Y., director of Mediterranean area, Rome, Italy, 1957-60; Fairbanks-Whitney Corp., vice-president of European operations, 1960-61; consultant and speechwriter on staff of Governor Nelson Rockefeller, New York, N.Y., 1961-63; full-time professional writer, 1963—. Lecturer on international affairs. *Members:* American Academy of Social and Political Science, Author's League, Writers Guild East, P.E.N., Overseas Press Club (New York).

WRITINGS: War Has Seven Faces, Doubleday, 1942; *But Soldiers Wondered Why*, Doubleday, 1943; *To Whom Palestine?*, Appleton, 1945; *Big Government*, Whittlesey House, 1949; *The Real Rockefeller*, Atheneum, 1964; *The Case for Israel*, foreword by Abba Eban, Viking Press, 1967; *Adolf Hitler: A Biography*, Hawthorn, 1973; *Thunder Over the Mediterranean*, McKay, 1975.

Writer and narrator of eight half-hour television films, American Broadcasting Co., 1953-54, and of "Zero Hour in Greece," Columbia Broadcasting System "Twentieth Century" program.

Contributor to national magazines, including *Business Week, Atlantic Monthly, Reporter, Cosmopolitan*, and *Show*.

WORK IN PROGRESS: A biography of Guiseppi Garibaldi, completion expected in 1977 and *A Matter of Identity*, a personal history.

SIDELIGHTS: Gervasi is fluent in Italian, Spanish, and French.

* * *

GHISELIN, Brewster 1903-

PERSONAL: Surname is pronounced *Geez*-lyn; born June 13, 1903, in Webster Groves, Mo.; son of Horace and Eleanor (Weeks) Ghiselin; married Olive Franks, June 7, 1929; children: Jon Brewster, Michael Tenant. *Education:* University of California, Los Angeles, A.B., 1927, Berkeley, M.A., 1928. *Office:* University of Utah, Salt Lake City, Utah 84112.

CAREER: University of Utah, Salt Lake City, instructor in English, 1929-31; University of California, Berkeley, assistant in English, 1931-33; University of Utah, instructor, 1934-38, lecturer, 1938-39, assistant professor, 1939-46, associate professor, 1946-50, professor of English, 1950-71, professor emeritus, 1971—. Director of writers conference, University of Utah, 1947-66. *Member:* Modern Language Association of America, Phi Beta Kappa (honorary), Phi Kappa Phi. *Awards, honors:* Ford Foundation fellowship, 1952-53; award from National Institute of Arts and Letters, 1970; Blumenthal-Leviton-Blonder prize from *Poetry* (magazine), 1973.

WRITINGS: Against the Circle (poems), Dutton, 1946; (editor) *The Creative Process: A Symposium*, University of California Press, 1952; *Writing*, American Association of University Women, 1959; *The Nets* (poems), Dutton, 1965; *The Country of the Minotaur* (poems), University of Utah Press, 1970.

Contributor: Calvin W. Taylor and Frank Barron, editors, *Scientific Curiosity: Its Recognition and Development*, Wiley, 1963; Taylor, editor, *Widening Horizons in Creativity*, Wiley, 1964; Peter K. Garrett, editor, *Twentieth Century Interpretations of Dubliners*, Prentice-Hall, 1968; Robert Scholes and A. Walton Litz, editors, *James Joyce's Dubliners*, Viking, 1969; Morris Beja, editor, *Dubliners and Portrait of the Artist as a Young Man*, Macmillan

(London), 1973; M. E. Bradford, editor, *The Form Discovered: Essays on the Achievement of Andrew Lytle*, University & College Press of Mississippi, 1973. Contributor to periodicals, including *Quarterly Review of Literature*, *Georgia Review*, and *Michigan Quarterly Review*.

WORK IN PROGRESS: Research in the creative process; an article on D. H. Lawrence.

SIDELIGHTS: Henry Taylor notes of *Country of the Minotaur* that Ghiselin's "control over poetic texture can make quite ordinary words sound fresh and forceful." Taylor finds the love poems in this collection "admirable for their grave gaiety" and cites the poems "Sea" and "The Wheel" as "two superb long lyrical meditations."

*   *   *

GIBBONS, Stella   1902-

PERSONAL: Born January 5, 1902, in London, England; daughter of Telford Charles (a doctor) and Maud (Williams) Gibbons; married Allan Bourne Webb, April 1, 1933 (died, 1959); children: Laura Caroline (Mrs. J. C. Richardson). *Education:* Attended North London Collegiate School for Girls and University College, University of London. *Religion:* Church of England. *Home:* 19 Oakeshott Ave., London N. 6, England. *Agent:* Curtis Brown Ltd., 13 King St., London W.C. 1, England.

CAREER: Worked for the British United Press as a cable decoder; held various jobs for ten years, including that of drama and literature critic, special reporter, and fashion writer. Poet, novelist, and short story writer. *Member:* Royal Society of Literature (fellow, 1950—). *Awards, honors:* Femina Vie Heureuse Prize, 1933, for *Cold Comfort Farm*.

WRITINGS—All published by Longmans, Green, except as indicated: *The Mountain Beast* (poems), 1930; *Cold Comfort Farm*, 1932, Bassett, 1934; *The Untidy Gnome* (children's book), 1935; *Enbury Heath*, 1935; *Miss Linsey and Pa*, 1936; *Roaring Tower* (short stories), 1937; *Nightingale Wood*, 1938; *My American*, 1939.

Christmas at Cold Comfort Farm (short stories), 1940; *The Rich House*, 1941; *Ticky*, 1943; *The Bachelor*, 1944; *Westwood*, 1946; *Conference at Cold Comfort Farm* (short stories), 1949; *The Matchmaker*, 1949.

Collected Poems, 1950; *The Swiss Summer*, 1951; *The Priestess* (poems), circa 1951; *The Lowland Venus* (poems), circa, 1952; *Fort of the Bear*, 1953; *Beside the Pearly Water*, Nevill, 1954.

All published by Hodder & Stoughton: *The Shadow of a Sorcerer*, 1955; *Here Be Dragons*, 1956; *White Sand and Gray Sand*, 1958; *A Pink Front Door*, 1959; *The Weather at Tregulla*, 1962; *The Wolves Were in the Sledge*, 1964; *The Charmers*, 1965; *Starlight*, 1967; *The Snow Woman*, 1969; *The Woods in Winter*, 1970.

Poems anthologized in: *Twentieth Century Poetry*, Chatto & Windus, 1929; *Best Poems of 1930*, and 1931, 1933, 1935 editions, J. Cape; *Mercury Book of Verse*, Macmillan, 1931; *Younger Poets of Today*, Secker & Warburg, 1932; *The Pattern of Courtesy*, Dent, 1934; *Neo-Georgian Poetry*, Richards Press, 1937; *An Anthology of Modern Poetry*, Nelson, 1939; *The Quiet Spirit*, Oxford University Press, 1946; *All Day Long*, Oxford University Press, 1954; *Albermarle Book of Modern Verse*, J. Murray, 1961; *The Birds and the Beasts Were Three*, World Publishing, 1963; *Birthday Poetry*, Hamish Hamilton, 1963.

Extracts from *Cold Comfort Farm* anthologized in: *Modern Humor*, J. Dent, 1940; *The English Scene*, Batsford, 1941; *Phoenix Book of Wit and Humor*, Phoenix House, 1949; *Laughter in a Damp Climate*, Jenkins, 1963; and in a collection published in Germany.

Contributor to *Punch*, *Tatler*, and other magazines.

WORK IN PROGRESS: A volume of poems, to be published (if possible) posthumously.

*   *   *

GIBBY, Robert Gwyn   1916-

PERSONAL: Born June 28, 1916; son of William James and Ann (Jones) Gibby; married Catherine Ellen Reber, June 12, 1937; children: Robert G., Jr., Carole Jeanne (Mrs. A. James Anderson). *Education:* Ohio State University, B.A., 1939, M.A., 1942; University of Michigan, Ph.D., 1949. *Home:* 8023 Lake Shore Dr., Bon Air, Va. 23235. *Office:* Drs. Gibby and Gibby, Jr., Ltd., 207 West Franklin St., Richmond, Va. 23220.

CAREER: Michigan State Reformatory, Lansing, chief psychologist, 1942-46; U.S. Veterans Administration, chief psychologist at hospitals in Detroit, Mich., Marion, Ind., and Richmond, Va., 1946-72; director, Drs. Gibby and Gibby, Jr., Ltd., Richmond, Va., 1972—; director, psychology service of Tucker Hospital, Inc., Richmond, Va., 1972—. Associate professor of psychology, Purdue University, and Richmond Professional Institute, beginning 1959; professor of psychology, Virginia Commonwealth University, 1958-71; lecturer in psychology at University of Richmond, and Michigan State University. Has done research on the heart rates in manual flights, and consultant on sensory deprivation, both for National Aeronautics and Space Administration (NASA). *Member:* International Psychological Association, Inter-American Psychological Association, Virginia Psychological Association, Richmond Psychological Association, Phi Delta Kappa, Sigma Xi.

WRITINGS—With Max Hutt: *Patterns of Abnormal Behavior*, Allyn & Bacon, 1957; *The Child: Growth and Development*, Allyn & Bacon, 1958; *The Mentally Retarded Child*, Allyn & Bacon, 1958, 3rd edition, in press; *The Child: Development and Adjustment*, Allyn & Bacon, 1959; *An Atlas for the Hutt Adaptation of the Bender-Gestalt Test*, Grune & Stratton, 1970.

(Contributor) Gardner Murphy and Wayne Holtzman, editors, *Psychology: The Science of Interpersonal Behavior*, Harper, 1966. Author of more than forty-five research papers; author of newspaper column, "Your Emotional Balance." Contributor to research journals.

WORK IN PROGRESS: The third edition of *The Mentally Retarded Child*; research on aversive conditioning, and biofeedback as treatment.

*   *   *

GILBERT, Douglas L.   1925-

PERSONAL: Born June 28, 1925, in LaVeta, Colo.; son of Paul (a forest ranger) and M. Louise (Baehr) Gilbert; married Dorothy C. Waggoner (a dietitian), May 1, 1949; children: Becky, Ronald. *Education:* Colorado State University, B.S. (magna cum laude), 1950, M.S., 1951; University of Michigan, Ph.D., 1962. *Politics:* Republican. *Religion:* Methodist. *Home:* 1205 Ellis, Fort Collins, Colo. 80521. *Office:* Colorado State University, Fort Collins, Colo. 80522.

CAREER: Colorado Game and Fish Department, biologist, 1951-52, public relations officer, 1953-55; Colorado State University, Fort Collins, temporary instructor of wildlife management, 1952-53; Montana State University (now University of Montana), Missoula, assistant professor of forestry, 1955-56; Colorado State University, assistant professor of wildlife management, 1956-62, associate professor, 1962-66, professor of wildlife biology and chairman of department, 1966-69; Cornell University, Ithaca, N.Y., professor of wildlife science, and extension director of department of natural resources, 1969-71; Colorado State University, professor of wildlife biology, and assistant dean of college of forestry and natural resources, 1971—. Visiting professor, Cornell University, 1967-68; visiting lecturer at Cornell University, Florida State University, State University of New York College of Environmental Science and Forestry, Texas A & M University, University of Wisconsin, New Mexico Game and Fish Department, North Carolina State Forest Service, U.S. Forest Service, U.S. National Park Service, and U.S. Soil Conservation Service. Assistant director or director, National Science Foundation Institutes in Ecology for College and High School Teachers, summers, 1960-63, 1965-66, 1969. Member, evaluation and reorganization team of Tennessee Game and Fish Commission, 1973.

MEMBER: Wildlife Society (honorary life member), National Wildlife Federation, Wildlife Disease Association, American Association for the Advancement of Science (fellow), American Institute of Biological Sciences, Outdoor Writers Association of America, Public Relations Society of America, Colorado Wildlife Federation (honorary life member), Sigma Xi, Xi Sigma Pi, Phi Kappa Phi, Beta Beta Beta. *Awards, honors:* Conservation Education Award, Wildlife Society, 1965, for *Public Relations in Natural Resources Management*; American Motors Conservation Award for Professionals, 1972; Outstanding Educators of America award, 1972.

WRITINGS: Public Relations in Natural Resources Management, Burgess, 1964; (with Dwight R. Smith) *Field Wildlife Studies in Colorado*, College of Forestry and Natural Resources, Colorado State University, 1967; *Natural Resources and Public Relations*, Wildlife Society, 1971; (contributor) Richard D. Teague, editor, *A Manual of Wildlife Conservation*, Wildlife Society, 1971; (editor) *Forestry and Natural Resources Professions*, College of Forestry and Natural Resources, Colorado State University, 1973; (author of foreword) Aaron N. Moen, *Wildlife Ecology*, W. H. Freeman, 1973. Author of reports and bulletins for Colorado Game and Fish Department; also author of two manuals on wildlife, and editor of handbook on forestry for Colorado State University. Contributor of articles to journals in his field, including *Journal of Wildlife Management, Journal of Forestry*, and *Colorado Outdoors.* Member of editorial board, *Journal of Wildlife Management.*

WORK IN PROGRESS: A book, *Big Game Management.*

*   *   *

GILLESE, John Patrick   1920-
(Dale O'Hara, John A. Starr)

PERSONAL: Surname is pronounced Gill-lease; born 1920, in Omagh, County Tyrone, Ireland; son of Francis and Ellen (Sharkey) Gillese; married Thelma Elizabeth Ashby, October 8, 1947; children: Patrick Tyrone, John Timothy, Mary-Ann, Eileen Elizabeth, Kevin Eardley, Thelma Virginia. *Education:* Attended high school in Rochfort Bridge, Alberta, Canada, and continued education through correspondence courses with University of Alberta and other institutions. *Religion:* Roman Catholic. *Home and office:* 10450 144th St., Edmonton, Alberta, Canada.

CAREER: Free-lance writer all of adult life except for several years as a trapper in the Canadian bush country and three years as editor of an Alberta weekly newspaper; director of literary arts for the province of Alberta, 1971—. *Member:* Canadian Authors Association (national executive board; president, Edmonton branch). *Awards, honors:* Fiction Award (first place) of Catholic Press Association, 1954, for short story, "Bushwacker's Christmas."

WRITINGS: (Associate editor) *Alberta Golden Jubilee Anthology*, McClelland & Stewart, 1955; *Kirby's Gander*, Ryerson, 1957. Short stories anthologized in *All Manner of Men*, edited by Riley Hughes, *Stories to Read Again*, Brunswick Press, *Golden Spurs*, Holt, Rinehart & Winston, and *Teen-Age Tales*, Book C, Heath. Author of more than five thousand short stories, serials, and feature stories appearing in more than one hundred Canadian, American, British, French, Danish, and German magazines and newspapers, including *American Weekly, Collier's, Field and Stream, Ideal, Sign, Writer's Digest, Star Weekly, Chambers's Journal, My Weekly, Der Feurreiter.* Also writer of television documentaries.

SIDELIGHTS: Gillese sold his first article in 1938, at the age of eighteen, his first fiction in 1939. He specializes in wildlife fiction and most of his foreign sales are made in that category; his own favorites are stories of the Alberta bushland. *Kirby's Gander* first appeared as a serial in *Country Gentlemen*, was later made into a film, "Wings of Chance," in Canada, and distributed by Universal-International in the United States. He also organized the first creative writing division of a provincial government in Canada, with outstanding success and international recognition.

*   *   *

GILLIATT, Penelope (Ann Douglass)   1932-

PERSONAL: Born March 25, 1932, in London, England; daughter of Cyril (a barrister) and Mary (Douglass) Conner; married Roger William Gilliatt (a professor), December, 1954 (divorced); married John Osborne (a playwright), May 25, 1963 (divorced); children: (second marriage) Nolan Kate. *Education:* Attended Bennington College, 1948. *Politics:* Socialist. *Agent:* David Higham Associates Ltd., 76 Dean St., London W.1, England. *Office: New Yorker*, 25 West 43rd St., New York, N.Y. 10036.

CAREER: Has worked at Institute of Pacific Relations, New York, N.Y., and for magazines in London, England, including *Vogue*, where she became feature editor; *Observer*, London, England, film critic, 1961-64, drama critic, 1964-67; *New Yorker*, New York, N.Y., guest film critic, summer, 1967, regular film critic, six months a year, 1968—. *Awards, honors:* Prizes for best screenplay from National Society of Film Critics and New York Film Critics, both 1971, and from Writer's Guild of Britain, 1972, all for "Sunday Bloody Sunday"; American Academy of Arts and Letters award for literature, 1972.

WRITINGS: One by One (novel), Atheneum, 1965; *What's It Like Out? And Other Stories* (short fiction; all except one selection previously published in *New Yorker*),

Secker & Warburg, 1968, published as *Come Back if It Doesn't Get Better*, Random House, 1969; *A State of Change* (novel), Secker & Warburg, 1967, Random House, 1968; *Sunday Bloody Sunday* (script of film released by United Artists, 1971), Viking, 1972; *Nobody's Business* (short stories previously published in *New Yorker*), Viking, 1972; *Unholy Fools: Wits, Comics, Disturbers of the Peace*, Viking, 1973. Short fiction anthologized in *Penguin Modern Stories*, 1971. Author of feature film script and scripts for television specials. Contributor to *Transatlantic Review*, *New Statesman*, *Spectator*, *Encounter*, *Guardian*, *Partisan Review*, *Nation*, and *Harper's*.

SIDELIGHTS: Anthony Burgess, in a review of *One By One*, wrote: "There is a pretty wit ... and a total absence of that bitchiness which disfigures so much of the work of our established women novelists." *One By One*," the Times Literary Supplement wrote, "does not quite gell into an effective novel. But the passion and intelligence which produced it are far too rare and ambitious for one to wish that it had been written in any other way or to forget the impression it leaves."

In *Nobody's Business*, notes Joseph Kanon, Miss Gilliatt's writing exhibits an irony that "is fine-edged, rich, and funny—a species of literary humor rare in contemporary writing. And though her style is often intentionally oblique, it is not superficial. The writing seems to float above its subject, then focus on a situation like a high-intensity beam. She is a master of the revealing detail, the overhead snatch of restaurant conversation.... [She has] an intuitive feel for the density of relationships, the almost impossible confusion and variety of life."

Miss Gilliatt has traveled since the end of the war. She is especially interested in the arts in Poland and Czechoslovakia. She spent two months in 1964 in India.

BIOGRAPHICAL/CRITICAL SOURCES: New York Times Book Review, April 25, 1965; *Observer*, April 25, 1965; *Times Literary Supplement*, April 29, 1965; *Spectator*, April 30, 1965; *New Statesman*, April 30, 1965; *Books and Bookmen*, May, 1965; *Book Week*, July 18, 1965; Carolyn Riley, editor, *Contemporary Literary Criticism*, Volume I, Gale, 1973.†

*   *   *

GILLISPIE, Charles C(oulston)   1918-

PERSONAL: Born August 6, 1918, in Harrisburg, Pa.; son of Raymond Livingston and Virginia Lambert (Coulston) Gillispie; married Emily Ramsdell Clapp, January 29, 1949. *Education:* Wesleyan University, A.B., 1940, M.A., 1942; Massachusetts Institute of Technology, graduate study, 1940-41; Harvard University, Ph.D., 1949. *Home:* 3 Morgan Pl., Princeton, N.J. 08540. *Office:* Princeton University, Princeton, N.J.

CAREER: Princeton University, Princeton, N.J., instructor, 1947-50, assistant professor, 1950-56, associate professor, 1956-59, professor of history of science, 1959-67, Shelby Cullom Davis professor of European history, 1967-73, Dayton-Stockton professor of history, 1973—, chairman of department of history, 1971-73. A. J. Balfour professor of history of science, Weizmann Institute, Israel, 1972. *Military service:* U.S. Army, Chemical Warfare Service, 1942-45; became captain. *Member:* History of Science Society (council, 1952-55, 1959-60; vice-president, 1960-64, president, 1964-66,) American Academy of Arts and Sciences, Academie Internationale d'Histoire des Science (vice-president, 1965-68), American Philosophical Society, Sigma Xi,

Phi Beta Kappa. *Awards, honors:* American Council of Learned Societies fellow, 1951-52; Guggenheim fellow, 1954-55, 1970-71; National Science Foundation fellow, 1958-59, 1962-63; Center for Advanced Study in Behavioral Sciences, 1970-71; D.Sc., Wesleyan University, 1971.

WRITINGS: Genesis and Geology, Harper, 1959; (editor) *A Diderot Pictorial Encyclopedia of Trades and Industry*, two volumes, Dover, 1959; *The Edge of Objectivity; An Essay in the History of Scientific Ideas*, Princeton University Press, 1960; *Lazare Carnot Savant*, Princeton University Press, 1971. Editor-in-chief of *Dictionary of Scientific Biography*.

*   *   *

GILLON, Diana (Pleasance Case)   1915-

PERSONAL: Born September 1, 1915, in London, England; daughter of Thomas Henry Towler and Evelyn Beatrice (White) Case; married Meir Selig Gillon, 1937; children: Evelyn Zvi Raanan (son), Richard Benedict, Dikla Lalage (daughter). *Education:* University of London, Diploma in Librarianship, 1935. *Home and office:* 30 Ravenscroft Park, Barnet, Hertfordshire, England.

CAREER: Archivist with Imperial Chemical Industries, 1935-38; film critic and member of editorial staff, *Palestine Post*, 1941-47; film critic, Palestine Broadcasting Service, 1944-45; free-lance journalist and author, writing in collaboration with husband. *Member:* Society of Authors.

*WRITINGS—*All with husband, Meir Gillon: *Vanquish the Angel*, Constable, 1955, Day, 1956; *The Unsleep*, Barrie & Rockliff, 1961, Ballantine, 1962; *The Sand and the Stars: A Short History of the Jewish People*, Lothrop, 1971. Contributor of features, book reviews, and some forty short stories to *New York Times Magazine*, *New York Herald Tribune*, *Philadelphia Inquirer*, *Toronto Star Weekly*, *New Liberty*, *Weekend*, *Farmers' Advocate*, *Guardian*, *New Statesman*, *Observer*, *Daily Telegraph*, and other periodicals and newspapers. Writer of radio scripts for British Broadcasting Corp., and some columns in *Tatler* and *Punch*.

WORK IN PROGRESS: A novel.

SIDELIGHTS: Mrs. Gillon's short stories have been translated into six languages. *Avocational interests:* Music, bridge, walking, motoring, travel, and politics.

*   *   *

GILLON, Meir Selig   1907-

PERSONAL: Born August 11, 1907, in Sibiu, Transylvania; son of Josef Hirsch and Sara (Weinberger) Goldstein; married Diana Case, 1937; children: Evelyn Zvi Raanan (son), Richard Benedict, Dikla Lalage (daughter). *Education:* University College, London, LL.B. *Home and office:* 30 Ravenscroft Park, Barnet, Hertfordshire, England.

CAREER: Government of Palestine, civil servant, 1941-46; with British Broadcasting Corp., England, 1949-50. Free-lance journalist and author, in collaboration with wife. *Member:* Society of Authors, Muswell Hill Bridge Club (London).

*WRITINGS—*All with wife, Diana Gillon: *Vanquish the Angel*, Constable, 1955, Day, 1956; *The Unsleep*, Barrie & Rockliff, 1961, Ballantine, 1962; *The Sand and the Stars: The Story of the Jewish People*, Lothrop, 1971. Contributor of features, book reviews, and some forty short stories to

New York Times Magazine, *New York Herald Tribune*, *Philadelphia Inquirer*, *Toronto Star Weekly*, *New Liberty*, *Weekend*, *Farmers' Advocate*, *Guardian*, *New Statesman*, *Observer*, *Daily Telegraph*, and other periodicals and newspapers. Has written radio talks for British Broadcasting Corp., and some columns in *Tatler* and *Punch*.

WORK IN PROGRESS: A novel.

SIDELIGHTS: Gillon's short stories have been translated into six languages. *Avocational interests:* Music, bridge, motoring, travel, and politics.

* * *

GIMBUTAS, Marija (Alseika) 1921-

PERSONAL: Surname is pronounced *Gim*-boo-tas; born January 23, 1921, in Vilnius, Lithuania; daughter of Danielius (a historian and physician) and Veronika (a physician; maiden name, Janulaitis) Alseika; married Jurgis Gimbutas (an engineer), July 12, 1941 (divorced, 1964); children: Danute, Zivile, Rasa-Julie. *Education:* Attended University of Vilnius, 1938-42, University of Vienna, 1944; University of Tuebingen, Ph.D., 1946. *Home:* 21434 West Entrada Rd., Topanga, Calif. *Office:* 5288 Bunche Hall, University of California, Los Angeles, Calif.

CAREER: Harvard University, Cambridge, Mass., 1950-63, began as research fellow, lecturer, 1962-63; University of California, Los Angeles, professor of European archaeology, 1964—, curator of Cultural History Museum, 1966—. Fellow of Center for Advanced Study in the Behavioral Sciences, 1961-62, and Netherlands Institute for Advanced Study in the Humanities and Social Sciences, 1973-74. *Member:* American Institute of Archaeology, Association of Field Archaeology, Association of Baltic Studies, Author's Guild. *Awards, honors:* Grants from Bollingen Foundation, 1955, National Science Foundation, 1956-60, 1968-69, 1973-74, National Endowment for the Humanities, 1967, Smithsonian Institution, 1967-70, Samuel Kress Foundation, 1967-74, Wenner-Gren Foundation, 1969; *Los Angeles Times* Woman of the Year, 1968.

WRITINGS: Die Bestattung in Litauen in der vorgeschichtlichen Zeit, Siebeck & Mohr, 1946; *The Prehistory of Eastern Europe*, Peabody Museum, Harvard University, 1956; *Ancient Symbolism in Lithuanian Folk Art*, American Folklore Society, 1958; *The Balts*, Praeger, 1963; *The Bronze Age Cultures of Central and Eastern Europe*, Mouton (The Hague), 1965; *The Slavs*, Praeger, 1971; *Gods and Goddesses of Old Europe, 7000-3500 B.C.: Myths, Legends, and Cult Images*, University of California Press, 1974. Contributor to *Encyclopaedia Britannica*, *Lietuviu Enciklopedija*, *Fischer Weltgeschichte*; and *Archaeology*, *The Journal of Indo-European Studies*, *The Journal of Field Archaeology*, *American Anthropologist*, *Proceedings of the Prehistoric Society* (London), and other journals.

WORK IN PROGRESS: Old Europe; *Baltic and Slavic Mythology*; *Concepts, Designs, and Script of Old Europe, 6500-3500 B.C.*; and excavation reports.

SIDELIGHTS: Mrs. Gimbutas is competent in German, Polish, and Russian, and has visited much of Europe on study trips. She has conducted neolithic archaeological excavations in Yugoslavia and Greece.

* * *

GINGRICH, Arnold 1903-

PERSONAL: Born December 5, 1903, in Grand Rapids, Mich.; son of John Hembling and Clara (Speare) Gingrich; married Helen Mary Rowe, October 24, 1924 (died March 22, 1955); married Jane Kendall, November 13, 1955; children: (first marriage) Rowe Wakefield, John Arnold, Michael Gregory. *Education:* University of Michigan, A.B., 1925. *Home:* 605 East Saddle River Rd., Ridgewood, N.J. 07450. *Agent:* Dorothy Olding, Harold Ober Associates Inc., 40 East 49 St., New York, N.Y. 10017. *Office:* Esquire, Inc., 488 Madison Ave., New York, N.Y. 10022.

CAREER: Began career as an advertising copywriter, 1925; *Apparel Arts*, Chicago, Ill., editor, 1931-45; Esquire, Inc., Chicago, Ill., vice-president and editor of *Esquire*, 1933-45, editor of *Coronet*, 1936-45, European editor of *Esquire* and *Coronet*, 1945-49; Cowles Magazines, Inc., New York, N.Y., vice-president and general manager of *Flair*, 1949-51; Esquire, Inc., New York, N.Y., senior vice-president and publisher of *Esquire*, 1952—. *Member:* Phi Beta Kappa, Phi Sigma Kappa, Overseas Press Club, Authors Guild.

WRITINGS: Cast Down the Laurel, Knopf, 1935; *The Well-Tempered Angler*, Knopf, 1965; *Toys of a Lifetime*, Knopf (autobiography), 1966; *Business and the Arts*, Ericksson, 1969; *A Thousand Mornings of Music*, Crown, 1970; *Nothing But People: The Early Days at Esquire*, Crown, 1971; *The Joys of Trout*, Crown, 1973. Member of editorial board, *Writer*.

* * *

GINSBERG, Louis 1895-

PERSONAL: Born October 1, 1895, in Newark, N.J.; son of Peter G. (a cigar store owner) and Rebecca (Schectman) Ginsberg; married Naomi Levy, December 18, 1920 (deceased); married Edith Cohen (an office manager), March 26, 1950; children: (first marriage) Eugene, Allen. *Education:* Rutgers University, B.A., 1918; Columbia University, M.A., 1924. *Home:* 416 East 34th St., Paterson 4, N.J.

CAREER: Central High School, Paterson, N.J., English teacher, 1921-61; Rutgers University College, Paterson Center, N.J., English instructor, 1950—. Former vice-president of Paterson Library Board. *Member:* Poetry Society of America (formerly on executive board).

WRITINGS—All poetry: The Attic of the Past, Small, Maynard, 1920; *The Everlasting Minute*, Liveright, 1937; *Morning in Spring and Other Poems*, Morrow, 1970. His poems have appeared in more than 90 anthologies, including Untermeyer's *Modern American Poetry*, Harcourt, 1919, revised edition, 1962, and Thomas Moult's *Best Poems* (of 1935 and 1936). Contributor to *Atlantic Monthly*, *American Scholar*, *Saturday Review*, *Poetry*, *New Mexico Quarterly*, *Ladies' Home Journal*, *Saturday Evening Post*, *McCall's*, *Good Housekeeping*, *Evergreen Review*, *Plumed Horn* (Mexico), *New Statesman*, *Times Literary Supplement*, *New Yorker*, *Minnesota Review*, *Commonweal*, *Beloit Poetry Journal*, *Fiddlehead*, and other publications. He has contributed puns to various publications such as *Reader's Digest* and *Try and Stop Me*.

WORK IN PROGRESS: A fourth book of poems.

SIDELIGHTS: Ginsberg has lectured on poetry and has read his poems at various college campuses throughout the country. He tells his students and his audiences that one value of poetry is that "poets express better and more clearly the feelings of most of us who cannot articulate such thoughts. When one has bottled up feelings, poetry helps release these feelings by helping the reader to say 'That's just how I felt.'" He adds: "Poetry reveals the glory of the commonplace, makes permanent [the] beauty that is fleeting, intensifies our emotional life, and snares the significance of things." Ginsberg gives joint poetry readings with his son, Allen, at colleges in the United States and abroad.

*   *   *

GINSBURGH, Robert N(eville) 1923-

PERSONAL: Born November 19, 1923, at Fort Sill, Okla.; son of A. Robert (a brigadier general, U.S. Army Air Forces) and Elsie (Pinney) Ginsburgh; married Gail H. Whitehead Winslow (a stockbroker), April 4, 1959; children: (previous marriage) Robert, Charles; (present marriage) Carolyn, Anne; stepchildren: Alan Winslow, William Winslow. Education: Harvard University, student, 1940-41, M.P.A., 1947, M.A., 1948, Ph.D., 1949; U.S. Military Academy, B.S., 1944; attended Air War College, 1961; National War College, graduate, 1963. Home: 5500 Newington Rd., Washington, D.C. 20016. Office: Policy Planning Council, Department of State, Washington, D.C.

CAREER: U.S. Army and U.S. Air Force, career service, 1944—, with current rank of major general. Assignments include assistant professor of social sciences, U.S. Military Academy, West Point, N.Y., 1948-51, plans officer, Allied Air Forces, Southern Europe, Naples, Italy, 1955-58, assistant executive, Office of Chief of Staff, U.S. Air Force, Washington, D.C., 1959-62, member of Policy Planning Council, Department of State, Washington, D.C., 1964-66, senior staff member, National Security Council, 1966-69, Air University, Maxwell, Ala., commander of Aerospace Studies Institute, 1969-71, chief of Air Force history, 1971-72, director of Air Force Information, 1972—. Council on Foreign Relations, New York, N.Y., research associate, 1963-64. Awards, honors: Silver Star, Purple Heart, and Army Commendation, all for World War II service.

WRITINGS: (Editor) Principles of Insurance, Military Service Publishing Co., 1949; (contributor) Lincoln Stone, and Harvey, Economics of National Security, Prentice-Hall, 1950; U.S. Military Strategy in the Sixties, Norton, 1965. Also author of U.S. Military Strategy in the Seventies, 1970, and The Nixon Doctrine and Military Strategy, 1971. Contributor to U.S. News and World Report, Foreign Affairs, and military publications.†

*   *   *

GIOVANNITTI, Len 1920-

PERSONAL: Surname is pronounced Joe-van-knee-tee; born April 16, 1920, in New York, N.Y.; son of Arturo and Carrie (Zaikaner) Giovannitti; married Sara Steinberg, August 28, 1943; children: David, Nina. Education: St. John's University, Jamaica, N.Y., B.A., 1942. Home: 239 Central Park West, New York, N.Y. 10024. Office: National Broadcasting Co., 30 Rockefeller Plaza, New York, N.Y.

CAREER: Writer and producer of television documentaries; with National Broadcasting Co., New York, N.Y., 1962—. Military service: U.S. Army Air Forces, 1943-45; became first lieutenant. Member: Writers Guild of America, East, Authors Guild. Awards, honors: American Library Association Liberty and Justice Book Award in creative literature, 1958, for The Prisoners of Combine D; Lasker Medical Foundation Award for NBC White Paper, "The American Alcoholic."

WRITINGS: The Prisoners of Combine D, Henry Holt, 1957; (with Fred Freed) The Decision to Drop the Bomb (nonfiction), Coward, 1965; The Man Who Won the Medal of Honor (novel), Random House, 1973.

Writer-producer of NBC White Papers, "The Decision of Japan to Surrender," "The American Alcoholic," "LBJ: The Hill Country," "The Energy Crisis," "In White Collar America," "The Energy Crisis: American Solutions, Part I and II," "Organized Crime in America"; writer of television documentaries, "Walking Hard," produced by American Broadcasting Co., and "San Francisco Detective," National Broadcasting Co.

*   *   *

GLAD, Donald 1915-

PERSONAL: Born April 23, 1915, in Salt Lake City, Utah; son of Andrew A. (a tailor) and Ada (Davison) Glad; married second wife, Virginia Markey Brown (a psychologist), January 13, 1952; children: Virginia Lynn Brown Wask, Dawn Glad Lundquist, Toni Ann Glad Saunders, Sue Ellyn, Roger Bruce. Education: University of Utah, B.A. and M.A. in Psychology, 1942; Stanford University, Ph.D., 1946. Home: Lake Quivira, Kansas City, Kan.

CAREER: San Jose State College (now California State University, San Jose), assistant professor of psychology, 1946-47; University of Colorado Medical School, Denver, assistant professor of psychology, 1948-57; San Jose State College (now California State University, San Jose), assistant professor of psychology, 1956-57; University of Denver, Denver, Colo., associate professor of psychology, 1957-59; Greater Kansas City Mental Health Foundation, Kansas City, Mo., director of psychology, 1959—; University of Missouri Medical Center, Kansas City, professor of psychiatry, 1964—. Diplomate, American Board of Examiners in Professional Psychology. University of Kansas Medical School, clinical professor of psychology, 1962; Kansas State University, visiting professor of psychology, 1963—. Member: American Psychological Association (fellow), American Orthopsychiatric Association (fellow), American Group Psychotherapy Association, Sigma Xi.

WRITINGS: Operational Values in Psychotherapy, Oxford University Press, 1959; (with wife, Virginia B. Glad) Interpersonality Synopsis, Libra, 1963. Contributor to Personnel Administration, and to psychology and medical journals.

WORK IN PROGRESS: A monograph on organizational mental health; a test manual, The Emotional Projection Test; research for a book on community mental health gatekeepers.†

*   *   *

GLASSCO, John 1909-
(Miles Underwood)

PERSONAL: Born December 15, 1909, in Montreal, Quebec, Canada; son of Archibald P.S. (a bursar) and Beatrice (Rawlings) Glassco; married Elma von Colmar, September 10, 1963. Education: Attended Bishop's College School, Lennoxville, Quebec, 1923-24, Lower Canada College, Montreal, Quebec, 1924-25, McGill University, 1925-28. Politics: Liberal. Religion: Church of England. Residence: Foster, Quebec, Canada.

CAREER: Admittedly a wastrel, 1928-48; councillor, Village of Foster, Quebec, Canada, 1948-52, mayor, 1952-54. Founder of Foster Horse Show, 1951, honorary chairman, 1964. Writer. Member: League of Canadian Poets. Awards, *honors:* Borestone Mountain Poetry Award, 1955, 1958; Quebec Provincial Prize for Best Work in English literature, 1960-62; Canada Council senior fellowship, 1965.

WRITINGS: Conan's Fig (poem), transition (Paris), 1928; *Contes en crinoline*, Gaucher (Paris), 1930; *The Deficit Made Flesh* (poems), McClelland & Stewart, 1958; (with Aubrey Beardsley) *Under thd Hill*, Olympia Press, 1959; (under pseudonym Miles Underwood) *The English Governess*, Olympia Press, 1960; (translator) *The Journal of Saint-Denys/Garneau*, McClelland & Stewart, 1962; *A Point of Sky* (poems), Oxford University Press, 1964; (editor) *English Poetry in Quebec* (proceedings of the Foster Poetry Conference), McGill University Press, 1964; *Memoirs of Montparnasse*, Oxford University Press, 1970; (editor and author of introduction) *The Poetry of French Canada in Translation*, Oxford University Press, 1970; *Selected Poems*, Oxford University Press, 1971; *Montreal*, D C Books, 1974. Contributor to *Canadian Forum, McGill Fortnightly Review, Queen's Quarterly, Tamarack Review*, and other journals.

WORK IN PROGRESS: Poems and satires; translating the *Poesies Completes* of Saint-Denys-Garneau; a book, *The Art of Pornography*.

BIOGRAPHICAL/CRITICAL SOURCES: Canadian Forum, July, 1965; *University of Toronto Quarterly*, July, 1965; *Canadian Literature*, autumn, 1965; Carl F. Klinck, editor, *Canadian Literature in English*, University of Toronto Press, 1965.†

* * *

GLASSMAN, Michael 1899-

PERSONAL: Born October 12, 1899, in Kiev, Russia; son of Meyer Joseph (a factory worker) and Frieda Leah (Kaganowsky) Glassman; married Miriam Frantz (a teacher), August 24, 1935; children: Rhoda, Judith. *Education:* City College (now City College of the City University of New York), B.A., 1923, M.S., 1932; New York University, Jur.D., 1926. *Politics:* Independent liberal. *Religion:* Jewish. *Home:* 2666 Emory Drive East, West Palm Beach, Fla. 33406.

CAREER: New York (N.Y.) Board of Education, beginning, 1925; high school teacher of history and civics, 1925-44; chairman of department of social studies, Samuel J. Tilden High School, Brooklyn, 1944-55; principal of Benjamin Franklin Junior High School, Bronx, 1955-60; principal of Parsons Junior High School, Flushing, beginning, 1960. Instructor in political science, Brooklyn College (now Brooklyn College of the City University of New York), 1944-49; adjunct assistant professor of education, Pace College, 1970-73. Admitted to New York bar, 1927, but has used legal background mainly as an adjunct to teaching. Manuscript reader and textbook revisions editor, Barron's Educational Series, Inc.; educational consultant, *New York Herald Tribune. Member:* Junior High School Principals Association, Association of Secondary School Principals, New York Teachers Guild (member of executive board, 1938-44), American Civil Liberties Union, National Association for the Advancement of Colored People.

WRITINGS: New York State: Its History and Its Constitution, Barron's, 1949, revised edition published as *New York State (and New York City) Geography, History and Government*, 1964; *Pollution of the Environment: Can We Survive?*, Globe Book, 1974. Author or co-author of six books of answers to high school examinations in American history, citizenship education, world geography, and world history, published by Barron's, 1949—. Compiler of "History in the Making Test," for *New York Herald Tribune*, 1965.

WORK IN PROGRESS: Mass Media In a Time of Crisis, a textbook.

SIDELIGHTS: Glassman is fluent in Yiddish and Hebrew, has a speaking knowledge of German, and reading knowledge of Latin and Spanish. *Avocational interests:* Music, drawing and painting, travel.

* * *

GLATTHORN, Allan A. 1924-

PERSONAL: Born September 5, 1924, in Philadelphia, Pa.; son of Louis (a cabinet finisher) and Anna (Girvan) Glatthorn; married Ruth Kirk, July 4, 1947; children: Carolyn, Dale, Laura and Louise (twins), Gwen. *Education:* Temple University, A.B., 1947, M.Ed., 1949, D.Ed., 1960; additional study at University of Pennsylvania and University of Chicago. *Religion:* Quaker. *Home:* 739 Crescent Ave., Glenside, Pa.

CAREER: Abington (Pa.) High School, teacher, 1947-62, coordinator of instruction, 1962-63, principal, North Campus, 1963—. Abington public schools, coordinator of language arts, 1955-63; Pennsylvania State University, Ogontz Center, administrator of evening technical school, 1956-58; Abington Adult School, director, 1959-63. College Entrance Examination Board, reader for English tests, 1959—; National Council of Teachers of English Achievement Award, judge, 1959—. Consultant in language arts and teaching the gifted. *Military service:* U.S. Army, Infantry, 1944-46; combat rifleman in Europe. *Member:* National Council of Teachers of English, National Association of Secondary School Principals, National Education Association, Pennsylvania State Education Association. *Awards, honors:* John Hay fellowship at University of Chicago, 1961-62.

WRITINGS: (With Carl J. Manone) *A Program for the Gifted Student in the Abington Senior High School*, [Abington], 1961; (editor with Clifton Fadiman) *Five American Adventures* (eighth grade literature book), Harcourt, 1963; (with Manone) *The Next Five Years* (on college admissions), Interstate, 1965; (with Harold Fleming) *Composition: Models and Exercises*, two books, Grades 10, 11, Harcourt, 1965; (consultant and contributor) *English Grammar and Composition*, three books, Grades 9-11, Harcourt, 1965 (compiler with Fleming) *Models for Composition*, 2 volumes, Harcourt, 1967-68; (with Charles W. Kreidler and Ernest J. Heiman) *The Dynamics of Language*, Heath, 1971—. Author of handbooks and school district publications. Weekly columnist, *Jenkintown Times Chronicle*, 1956-57. Contributor to educational journals and to *Friends Journal.*

WORK IN PROGRESS: Tenth grade literature textbook, for Harcourt.

AVOCATIONAL INTERESTS: Collecting books (has five thousand volumes, specializing in Mark Twain and Robert Frost first editions, and commentaries on the Book of Job), reading, theater-going, riding motor scooter.†

* * *

GLATZER, Nahum Norbert 1903-

PERSONAL: Born March 25, 1903, in Lemberg, Austria (now in Union of Soviet Socialist Republics); son of Daniel (a businessman) and Rose (Gottlieb) Glatzer; married Anne

Stiebel (a teacher); children: Daniel Franz, Judith Eve Wechsler. *Education:* University of Frankfurt, Ph.D., 1931. *Religion:* Jewish. *Office:* Boston University, Boston, Mass.

CAREER: University of Frankfurt, Frankfurt am Main, Germany, lecturer in Jewish philosophy, 1932-33; Bet Sefer Reali, Haifa, Palestine, instructor in Bible, 1933-37; The College of Jewish Studies (now Spertus College of Judaica), Chicago, Ill., instructor in Bible, 1938-43; Hebrew Teachers College (now Hebrew College), Boston, Mass., professor of Talmud, 1943-47; Yeshiva University, New York, N.Y., professor of history, 1948-50; Brandeis University, Waltham, Mass., professor of Jewish history, 1950-73, chairman of department of Near Eastern and Judaic Studies, 1957-69; Boston University, Mass., professor of religion, 1973—. Schocken Books, Inc., New York, N.Y., editor, 1945—. Seminar associate, Columbia University, 1960-63; visiting professor, University of California, Los Angeles, 1967, 1974. *Member:* American Academy for Jewish Research (fellow), Leo Baeck Institute (member of board of directors; fellow), Jewish Publication Society, American Society for the Study of Religion. *Awards, honors:* Guggenheim Fellow, 1959-60; Dr. honoris causa, Brandeis University, 1973; B'nai B'rith Prize for Literary Excellence, 1973.

WRITINGS: Untersuchungen zur Geschichtslehre der Tannaiten, Schocken Verlag (Berlin), 1933; *Geschichte der talmudischen Zeit*, Schocken Verlag, 1937; *Kizur toldoth Yisrael*, Beth Sefer Reali Press (Haifa), 1947; *Hillel the Elder: The Emergence of Classical Judaism*, B'nai B'rith Hillel Foundations, 1956, revised edition, Schocken, 1966; *Anfaenge des Judentums: Eine Einfuehrung*, G. Mohn (Guetersloh), 1966.

Editor—Except as indicated: (Compiler with Ludwig Strauss) *Sendung und Schicksal: Aus dem Schrifttum des nachbiblischen Judentums*, Schocken Verlag, 1931, published as *Sendung und Schicksal des Judentums*, Hegner, 1969; (compiler) *Gespraeche der Weisen: Aus talmudisch—midraschischen Texten*, Schocken Verlag, 1935; (compiler) Mosche ben Maimon, *Moses Maimonides: Ein systematischer Querschnitt durch sein Werk*, Schocken Verlag, 1935.

Flavius Josephus, *Jerusalem and Rome: The Writings of Josephus*, Meridian Books, 1940; (and translator) Moses ben Maimon, *Maimonides Said: An Anthology*, Jewish Book Club (New York), 1941; *In Time and Eternity: A Jewish Reader*, Schocken, 1946, 2nd revised edition, 1961; *The Language of Faith: Selected Jewish Prayers*, Schocken, 1947, 2nd revised edition published as *Language of Faith: A Selection From the Most Expressive Jewish Prayers*, 1967; Samuel J. Agnon, *Days of Awe*, Schocken, 1948; *Hammer on the Rock: A Short Midrash Reader*, Schocken, 1948.

S. D. Goldschmidt, *Passover Haggadah: Introduction and Commentary*, Schocken, 1953, revised edition, 1969; *Franz Rosenzweig: His Life and Thought*, Farrar, Straus, 1953, revised edition, Schocken, 1961; Franz Rosenzweig, *Understanding the Sick and the Healthy*, Noonday, 1954; Rosenzweig, *On Jewish Learning*, Schocken, 1955, revised edition, 1965; *Leopold and Adelheid Zunz: An Account in Letters, 1815-1885*, East & West Library, for Leo Baeck Institute, 1958; *Frants Rozentsvaig*, [Tel-Aviv], 1959.

The Rest is Commentary: A Source Book of Judaic Antiquity (also see below), Beacon Press, 1961; Franz Kafka, *Parables and Paradoxes*, Schocken, 1961; (and abridger)

Emil Schuerer, *A History of the Jewish People in the Time of Jesus*, Schocken, 1961, revised edition, 1963; (and author of introduction) *Faith and Knowledge: The Jew in the Medieval World* (also see below), Beacon Press, 1963; *Leopold Zunz: Jude-Deutscher-Europaeer*, J. C. B. Mohr, (Tuebingen), 1964; (and author of introduction) *The Dynamics of Emancipation: The Jew in the Modern Age* (also see below), Beacon Press, 1965; Martin Buber, *The Way of Response*, Schocken, 1966; Martin Buber, *On Judaism*, Schocken, 1967; Martin Buber, *On the Bible*, Schocken, 1969; (compiler) *The Dimensions of Job: A Study and Selected Readings*, Schocken, 1969; (compiler and author of introduction) *The Judaic Tradition*, includes revisions of *The Rest is Commentary*, *Faith and Knowledge*, *The Dynamics of Emancipation*, Beacon Press, 1969.

Agnon, *Twenty-One Stories*, Schocken, 1970; Flavius Josephus, *The Second Jewish Commonwealth*, Schocken, 1970; Kafka, *The Complete Stories*, Schocken, 1971; Philo Judaeus, *The Essential Philo*, Schocken, 1971.

Contributor: *Aus unbekannten Schriften*, Lambert Schneider (Heidelberg), 1928; *Paul Lazarus Gedenkbuch*, [Jerusalem], 1951; *Der Friede: Idee und Verwirklichung* (Leschnitzer Festschrift), [Heidelberg], 1951; *Ale Ayyin* (Schocken Festschrift), [Jerusalem], 1952; *The Scrolls and the New Testament*, Harper, 1957; *Between East and West*, [London], 1958; *Yuval Shay* (Agnon Jubilee Volume), Ramat Gan, 1958; *Hokmat Yisrael be-Maarav Europa*, Ogen, 1958; *Zion in Jewish Literature*, Herzl, 1961; *Politische Ordnung und menschlichte Existenz* (Voegelin Festschrift), [Munich], 1962; P. A. Schilpp and M. Friedman, editors, *Martin Buber*, [Germany], 1963, translation published as *The Philosophy of Martin Buber*, Open Court, 1965; *Great Jewish Thinkers of the Twentieth Century*, B'nai B'rith, 1963; *Hugo Hahn Jubilee Volume*, Habonim, 1963; *Brandeis Judaica Texts and Studies*, Volume II-III, Harvard University Press, 1964; Arthur A. Cohen, editor, *Arguments and Doctrines: A Reader of Jewish Thinking in the Aftermath of the Holocaust*, Harper, 1970.

Other: (Author of foreword) Flavius Josephus, *The Great Roman-Jewish War*, Harper, 1960; (author of introduction to 2nd edition of German translation) Robert T. Herford, *The Pharisees*, Macmillan, 1924, published as *Die Pharisaeer*, 2nd edition, [Cologne], 1961; (author of foreword) J. M. Guyau, *The Non-Religion of the Future*, 2nd edition, Schocken, 1962.

Also contributor to *Encyclopaedia Britannica*, *Jewish Book Annual*, *Grolier Encyclopedia*, *Encyclopaedia Judaica*, and to journals in Germany, United States, and Israel. Member of editorial board of Jewish Publication Society; contributing editor, *Judaism*, and *Bitzaron* (Hebrew monthly).

WORK IN PROGRESS: I am a Memory Come Alive, a documentary biography of Kafka.

BIOGRAPHICAL/CRITICAL SOURCES: A. Altmann, "Nahum N. Glatzer: The Man and His Work," *Judaism*, Volume XII, number 2, 1963.

*   *   *

GLIDEWELL, John Calvin 1919-

PERSONAL: Born November 5, 1919, in Okolona, Miss.; son of Henry Clay and Jessie Kate Glidewell; married Frances Reed, 1941; children: Pamela, Janis. *Education:* University of Chicago, A.M., 1949, Ph.D., 1953. *Home:* 1403 Berry Lane, Flossmoor, Ill. 60422. *Office:* Department of Education, University of Chicago, Chicago, Ill. 60637.

CAREER: University of Chicago, Chicago, Ill., project director, Human Dynamics Laboratory, 1948-49; Meridian (Miss.) public schools, director, psychological services, 1949-51; National Education Association, Washington, D.C., National Training Laboratories, adjunct staff member, 1950—; U.S. Air Force, Maxwell Air Force Base, Ala., Human Resources Research Institute, project director, 1951-53; St. Louis County Health Department, Clayton, Mo., director of research and development, 1953-67; Washington University, St. Louis, Mo., director of training program for social science research in community mental health, Social Science Institute, 1958-66, associate professor of social psychology, department of sociology and anthropology, 1963-65, associate professor of educational psychology, Graduate Institute of Education, 1965-67; University of Chicago, professor of education and behavioral science, 1967—, chairman of educational psychology faculty, 1970-73. Washington University Medical School, St. Louis, Mo., research assistant in medical psychology, 1954-58, research instructor in medical psychology, 1958-64, research assistant professor of medical psychology, 1964-67. Lecturer in public health at Washington University School of Nursing, St. Louis University School of Nursing, and Marilac College, 1957-65. *Military service:* U.S. Army, 1942-46; became captain. U.S. Air Force Reserve, 1946-50; active duty, 1950-52; now major (retired).

MEMBER: International Association of Applied Social Scientists (member of board of directors, 1970-73), American Psychological Association (fellow), American Sociological Association (fellow), National Training Laboratories Association (fellow), American Public Health Association (fellow; Mental Health Section, secretary, 1964-66, chairman, 1968), Society for the Psychological Study of Social Issues (fellow), Illinois Psychological Association, Sigma Xi.

WRITINGS: (Contributor) *Leadership Training for Community Health Promotion,* U.S. Public Health Service, 1957; (contributor) Dorothy Stock and H. A. Thelen, *Emotional Dynamics and Group Culture,* New York University Press, 1958; (editor and contributor) *Parental Attitudes and Child Behavior,* C. C Thomas, 1961; (contributor) W. G. Bennis, K. D. Benne, and R. Chin, editors, *Planning of Change,* Holt, 1961; (contributor) Mildred B. Kantor, editor, *Mobility and Mental Health,* C. C Thomas, 1965; (contributor) M. L. Hoffman and L. W. Hoffman, editors, *Review of Child Development Research,* Russell Sage, 1966; (contributor) E. M. Bower and W. G. Hollister, editors, *Behavioral Science Frontiers in Education,* Wiley, 1967; (contributor) R. Williams and L. Ozarin, editors, *Community Mental Health: An International Perspective,* Jossey-Bass, 1967; (contributor) E. L. Cowan, E. A. Garner, and M. Zax, editors, *Emergent Approaches to Mental Health Problems,* Appleton, 1967; (with Martha Brown and others) *Nurses, Patients, and Social Systems,* University of Missouri Press, 1968; (contributor) J. W. Carter, editor, *Research Contributions from Psychology to Community Mental Health,* Behavioral Publications, 1968; (contributor) L. M. Roberts, N. S. Greenfield, and M. H. Miller, editors, *Comprehensive Mental Health: The Challenge of Evaluation,* University of Wisconsin Press, 1968; (contributor) S. B. Sells, editor, *The Definition and Measurement of Mental Health,* U.S. Public Health Service, 1968; (contributor) J. G. Howells, editor, *Modern Perspectives in International Child Psychiatry,* Oliver & Boyd, 1969; (contributor) A. J. Bindman and A. D. Spiegel, editors, *Perspectives in Community Mental Health,* Aldine, 1969;

Choice Points: The Emotional Problems of Living With People, M.I.T. Press, 1970; (contributor) S. Golann and C. Eisdorfer, editors, *Handbook of Community Mental Health,* Appleton, 1972.

Contributor to psychiatric, public health, educational, and sociological journals. Associate editor, *Adult Leadership,* 1958-62; special issue editor, *Journal of Social Issues,* 1959.

*   *   *

GLIKES, Erwin 1937-

PERSONAL: Born June 30, 1937, in Heide, Belgium; came to United States in 1942, naturalized in 1947; son of Morris I. and Gella (Lubowski) Glikes; married Toni Marlene Brown (a teacher), June 24, 1959; children: Michael Joseph, Lela Maeve. *Education:* Columbia University, A.B., 1959, graduate study, 1960-62. *Home:* 23 Overlook Rd., Hastings-on-Hudson, N.Y. 10706. *Office:* 10 East 53rd St., New York, N.Y. 10022.

CAREER: Columbia University, Columbia College, New York, N.Y., lecturer in English and comparative literature, 1960-62; Basic Books, Inc. (publishers), free-lance editor, 1963-65; Columbia University, assistant dean of Columbia College, 1965-69; Basic Books, 1969—, executive vice-president, 1971-72, president and publisher, 1972—. Consultant, National Endowment for the Humanities, 1971—. *Member:* Phi Beta Kappa. *Awards, honors:* Deutscher Verein Essay Prize, 1959; Woodrow Wilson fellow, 1959-60; dankstipendiat, University of Tuebingen (Germany), 1962-63.

WRITINGS: (Editor and author of introduction with Paul Schwaber) *Of Poetry and Power: Poems Occasioned by the Presidency and by the Death of John F. Kennedy,* Basic Books, 1964. One of the founding editors of *The Second Coming,* a national literary review, 1960-64.

WORK IN PROGRESS: A biographical and critical study of Samuel Taylor Coleridge.

SIDELIGHTS: Gilkes's major field of interest is English and German literature of the nineteenth century, especially the relations between literature, critical theory, and politics and political theory.†

*   *   *

GLOVER, (David) Tony "Harp Dog" 1939-

PERSONAL: Surname sounds like "lover"; he publishes under several variations of name listed above; born October 7, 1939, in Minneapolis, Minn.; son of Harold E. and Margaret (Hauser) Glover; married Karin (a dancer), April 3, 1961 (divorced October, 1971) "Things change". *Education:* Attended high school in Minneapolis. *Address:* Box 3689, Loring Station, Minneapolis, Minn. 55403.

CAREER: "Worked several years as offset pressman in mail advertising firm. Left to record and play gigs with Dave Ray and John Koerner; five albums on Electra label; appearances at Newport and Philadelphia folk festivals, etc. Somewhere near the end of the 60's, spent a year and a half as an all night DJ playing Moondog, Miles Davis, and Sonny Boy Williamson records and answering a lot of bizarre phone calls. Went to New York City on vacation, didn't come back for two years. In New York City, did mostly freelance music writing. Moved back to Minneapolis, tired of guerilla warfare necessary when going to the deli after dark. At present, writing mostly record reviews, working in a funky band called 'Nine Below Zero', and doing some reunion recording and concerts with Koerner and Ray." *Awards, honors:* "Won an overnight traveling case in talent show at a bar once."

WRITINGS: (Editor) Ron McElderry, *The Little Black Songbook*, Little Sandy Review Press, 1960; (with Ted Sheilds) *That Ain't Quite What I Meant, Babe* (cartoons), "printed by Glover after hours at shop where he worked," 1963; *Mad Coast 1* (poems), privately printed ("since each page of every copy was created individually, this was produced only in a severely limited edition"), 1964; (under name Tony "Little Sun" Glover I) *Blues Harp: An Instruction Method for Playing the Blues Harmonica*, Oak, 1965 (under name Tony Glover, with Paul Nelson) *The Festival Songbook*, Amsco Music Publishing, 1972; *Blues Harp Songbook*, Oak Publications, 1975. Has also published *Big Joe Blues*, a section of an autobiographical novel.

Other writings: Liner notes for "Get Together," by Sonny Terry, 1965, "Country Blues," by John Hammond, 1965, and for "Blues Harp" (to accompany the book), "Tribute" (to Sonny Boy Williamson), radio script, 1965. Contributor to *Little Sandy Review*, *Music Journal*, *Sing Out!*, *Folk Scene*, *Region*, *Twin Citian*, *Hullabaloo*, *Eye*, *Circus*, *Rock*, *Crawdaddy*, *Rolling Stone*, and *Cream*.

WORK IN PROGRESS: "*Rambling Blues*, an autobiographical novel which I have alternately tried to write/not write, depending on how much my memories kept me more interested than my present."

SIDELIGHTS: "My major areas of interest are making music (blues, Indian, and electronic music). In writing about music I only write about what interests me and arouses my enthusiasm—which explains why I've only done one or two negative reviews—and also why, of late, my writing is slacking off some—it's pretty boring out there. Besides, I'd rather write and play music right now than write *about* it.

"In my writing, I'm interested in finding the spaces that nobody speaks of because they're too personal—but everybody needs to know that others feel as well. In my early life I was greatly influenced by Edgar Allen Poe, ... later I discovered that I was born 90 years (almost to the hour) after his death, and wonder if perhaps I'm not a reincarnation of his spirit—a feeling deepened by a visit to his house in Philadelphia. ...

"Wrote many gloomy Orson Welles-like vignettes in midnight hours, and wandered in AM alleys looking for something. Was a juvenile delinquent for a few years, ran with a minor gang, but quit because their society and concepts were as stifling as the ones they were rebelling against. At the age of 16 I succeeded in staying drunk for a month and a half, but I don't have that much time or money nowadays.

"Somewhere along there found blues music of people like Sonny Boy Williamson, Muddy Waters, Jimmy Reed, Little Walter etc., and got hung in learning how to play it on harp (harmonica). Had an R&B band for half a year.... Fell into the 'folk-music' scene, played with various singer-guitarists until I met my current partner, Dave Ray—have worked on and off with him ever since.... At the moment, my main interest is in survival—mine (and hopefully the planets). Good luck to us all."

BIOGRAPHICAL/CRITICAL SOURCES: Ivory Tower (University of Minnesota), June 1, 1964; *Sing Out*, July, 1964; *Little Sandy Review*, Number 30, fall, 1964; *Twin Citian*, November, 1965; *The Face of Folk Music*, Citadel Press, 1968; *Insider*, September, 1971.

GODSEY, John Drew 1922-

PERSONAL: Born October 10, 1922, in Bristol, Tenn.; son of William C. (a dairy company executive) and Mary Lynn (Corns) Godsey; married Emalee Caldwell, June 26, 1943; children: Emalee Lynn, John Drew, Jr., Suzanne, Gretchen. *Education:* Virginia Polytechnic Institute, B.S., 1947; Drew University, B.D., 1953; University of Basel, D.Theol., 1960. *Religion:* Methodist. *Home:* 8306 Bryant Drive, Bethesda, Md. 20034. *Office:* Wesley Theological Seminary, 4400 Massachusetts Ave. N.W., Washington, D.C. 20016.

CAREER: Worked in industry, 1947-50; ordained Methodist minister, 1953; Drew University Theological School, Madison, N.J., assistant dean, and instructor in systematic theology, 1956-59, assistant professor, 1959-64, associate professor, 1964-66, professor of systematic theology, 1966-68; Wesley Theological Seminary, Washington, D.C., professor of systematic theology, 1968—, dean of systematic theology, 1968-71. *Member:* American Theological Society, American Association of University Professors, Omicron Delta Kappa, Phi Kappa Phi, Alpha Zeta. *Awards, honors:* Fulbright research scholar, University of Goettingen, 1964-65.

WRITINGS: The Theology of Dietrich Bonhoeffer, Westminster, 1960; (editor) *Karl Barth's Table Talk*, John Knox, 1963; (contributor) F. N. Magill, editor, *Masterpieces of Christian Literature in Summary Form*, Salem Press, 1963; *Preface to Bonhoeffer: The Man and Two of His Shorter Works*, Fortress, 1965; (editor) Karl Barth, *How I Changed My Mind*, John Knox, 1966; (contributor) Gerald H. Anderson, editor, *Christian Mission in Theological Perspective*, Abingdon, 1967; (contributor) Peter Vorkink II, editor, *Bonhoeffer in a World Come of Age*, Fortune Press, 1968; *The Promise of H. Richard Niebuhr*, Lippincott, 1970. Contributor of articles to theological and other journals.

*   *   *

GOETHALS, George W. 1920-

PERSONAL: Born August 19, 1920, in Boston, Mass.; married Natalie Nowell; children: seven. *Education:* Harvard University, A.B., 1943, Ed.D., 1953. *Home:* 100 Russell Ave., Watertown, Mass. 02172. *Office:* William James Hall, Harvard University, 33 Kirkland St., Cambridge, Mass.

CAREER: Sarah Lawrence College, Bronxville, N.Y., member of faculty of psychology department and director of teacher training, 1952-56; Harvard University, Cambridge, Mass., lecturer in education, 1956-60, lecturer in social relations, 1960—, assistant dean, Harvard College, 1964-68, chairman of department of social relations, 1970-72, consultant in Psychology, Harvard University Health Services, 1974—, chairman of board of tutors and advisors, department of psychology and social relations, 1974—. *Military service:* U.S. Army Air Forces, 1944-46; became sergeant. *Member:* American Psychological Association (fellow), American Sociological Association (fellow), Massachusetts Mental Health Association (member of board of directors), Phi Delta Kappa.

WRITINGS: (With Wesley Allensmith) *The Role of Schools in Mental Health*, Basic Books, 1962; (editor with Leon Bramson) *War*, Basic Books, 1964; (with Dennis Klos) *Experiencing Youth: First-Person Accounts of the Adolescent Experience*, Little, Brown, 1970; (contributor) J. Henslin, editor, *The Sociology of Sex: A Book of Read-*

ings, Appleton, 1971. Contributor of articles to professional journals.

* * *

GOHDES, Clarence Louis Frank 1901-

PERSONAL: Surname is pronounced *Go*-dess; born July 2, 1901, in San Antonio, Tex.; son of Conrad and Clara (Heiser) Gohdes; married Celestine Marie Beamer, June 3, 1938; children: Eleanor Clara, Dorothy Mary. *Education:* Capital University, A.B., 1921; Ohio State University, M.A., 1922; Harvard University, M.A., 1928; Columbia University, Ph.D., 1931. *Home:* 2737 Circle Dr., Durham, N.C.

CAREER: Southern Methodist University, Dallas, Tex., assistant professor of English, 1926-27; New York University, New York, N.Y., instructor in English, 1929-30; Duke University, Durham, N.C., 1930-71, began as assistant professor of English, James B. Duke Professor of English, 1961-71, professor emeritus, 1971—. Visiting professor at Harvard University, Columbia University, University of Pennsylvania, University of Utah, University of California, and Bowling Green State University. *Member:* Modern Language Association of America, American Historical Association, Phi Beta Kappa, Phi Gamma Mu, Theta Alpha Phi. *Awards, honors:* Guggenheim fellow, 1962.

WRITINGS: The Periodicals of American Transcendentalism, Duke University Press, 1931; (editor with Paul Franklin Baum) William Michael Rossetti, *Letters Concerning Whitman, Blake and Shelley to Anne Gilchrist and Her Son, Herbert Gilchrist*, Duke University Press, 1934; *American Literature in Nineteenth-Century England*, Columbia University Press, 1944, 2nd edition, Southern Illinois University Press, 1963; (editor with Rollo G. Silver) *Faint Clews and Indirections; Manuscripts of Walt Whitman and His Family*, Duke University Press, 1949; (contributor) A. H. Quinn, editor, *Literature of the American People*, Appleton, 1951; (editor with James D. Hart) *America's Literature*, Dryden Press, 1955; *Bibliographical Guide to the Study of Literature of the U.S.A.*, Duke University Press, 1959, 3rd edition, 1970.

Contributor of articles to scholarly periodicals. Chairman of board of editors, Duke University Press. Managing editor, *American Literature*, 1931-54, editor-in-chief, 1954-69.

* * *

GOLDBERG, Louis 1908-

PERSONAL: Born February 22, 1908, in Melbourne, Victoria, Australia; son of Philip (a tailor) and Mary (Cohen) Goldberg; married Myrtle H. Silverman, January 11, 1938 (deceased); married Jean M. Nethercote, March 23, 1972; children: (first marriage) Loretta J. *Education:* University of Melbourne, B.Com., 1930, M.Com., 1938, B.A., 1948. *Home:* 5 Kemsley Ct., Hawthorn 3123, Victoria, Australia.

CAREER: Accountant in public, industrial, and government positions in Australia, 1930-45; University of Melbourne, Parkville, Victoria, Australia, lecturer, 1946-49, senior lecturer, 1949-57, associate professor of accounting, 1957-58, G. L. Wood Professor of Accounting, 1958-73. Visiting professor, City College (now City College of the City University of New York), 1963, University of Florida, 1970. *Member:* Australian Society of Accountants (divisional councillor, 1958-65), Chartered Institute of Secretaries, Australasian Institute of Cost Accountants, Economic

Society of Australia and New Zealand, Royal Economic Society, American Accounting Association, Australasian Association of University Teachers of Accounting (president, 1962), Australian and New Zealand Association for the Advancement of Science, Australian Academy of Social Sciences. *Awards, honors:* Rockefeller Foundation traveling fellow to United States and Great Britain, 1955; Fulbright travel grant, 1963; Litt.D., University of Melbourne, 1967.

WRITINGS: A Philosophy of Accounting, Accountants Publishing Co. (Melbourne), 1939, 6th edition published as *An Outline of Accounting*, Law Book Co. (Sydney), 1973; (with V. R. Hill) *Elements of Accounting*, Accountants Publishing Co. (Melbourne), 1947, 5th edition, Law Book Co. (Melbourne), 1966, 3rd edition with amendments, Melbourne University Press, 1968; (with others) *Intermediate Accounting*, edited by A. A. Fitzgerald, Butterworth & Co. (Sydney), 1948, 2nd edition published as *Accounting Stage I*, 1954, 3rd edition published as *Fitzgerald's Accounting*, 1960; *Concepts of Depreciation*, Law Book Co. (Sydney), 1960; *An Inquiry into the Nature of Accounting*, American Accounting Association, 1965; (editor with Raymond J. Chambers and R. L. Mathews) *The Accounting Frontier: In Honour of Sir Alexander Fitzgerald*, F. W. Cheshire, 1966. Also editor of 1967 edition of book published originally as *Intermediate Accounting*. Contributor to *Economic Record* and to accounting journals.

* * *

GOLDFARB, Nathan 1913-

PERSONAL: Born April 28, 1913, in New York, N.Y.; son of Samuel (a retailer) and Pessie (Feldman) Goldfarb; married Evelyn Richman, March 17, 1935; children: Louis, Aaron, Johanna. *Education:* New York University, B.A., 1934, M.A., 1936, Ph.D., 1955. *Home:* 29-14 139th St., Flushing, N.Y. 11354. *Office:* Hofstra University, Fulton Ave., Hempstead, N.Y.

CAREER: U.S. Federal Security Agency, Baltimore, Md., statistician, 1937-51; Forbes Publishing, New York, N.Y., director of research, 1953-55; Hofstra University, Hempstead, N.Y., member of statistics faculty, 1955—, director of computer center, 1955-72; Ittleson Center for Research in Childhood Schizophrenia, New York, N.Y., statistician, 1962—. *Member:* Association for Computing Machinery, American Statistical Association, New York Academy of Sciences.

WRITINGS: An Introduction to Longitudinal Statistics Analysis, Free Press, 1960; (editor with William K. Kaiser) *Gantt Charts and Statistical Quality Control*, Hofstra University, 1964. Developed and edited a collection of computer programs, *HUNT-Hofstra University Non-Parametric Tests*, IBM Data Processing, Program Information Department, 1965. Contributor of articles on growth of schizophrenic children to periodicals.

* * *

GOLDSMITH, Arthur (A., Jr.) 1926-

PERSONAL: Born July 7, 1926, in Merrimac, Mass.; son of Arthur (an aviator) and Daisy (Bishop) Goldsmith; married Carolyn Milford, September, 1950; children: Arthur, James, Susan, Amy. *Education:* Attended University of New Hampshire, 1946-47; Northwestern University, B.S. in Journalism, 1951, M.S., 1951. *Residence:* Wilton, Conn.

CAREER: Popular Photography, New York, N.Y., executive editor, 1951-60; *This Week*, New York, N.Y., picture editor, 1960-62; Famous Photographers School, Westport, Conn., editor and head of instruction, 1962—. *Military service:* U.S. Navy, 1944-46. *Member:* Photographic Administrators, Overseas Press Club, Sigma Delta Chi, Kappa Tau Alpha.

WRITINGS: How to Take Better Pictures, Bobbs-Merill, 1955; revised edition, Arco, 1964; *Seeing Beyond the Obvious*, Famous Photographers School, 1965; (with Alfred Eisenstaedt) *The Eye of Eisenstaedt*, Viking, 1969; *The Photography Game: What It Is and How to Play It*, Viking, 1971. Edited textbooks for Famous Photographers School course, 1964. Contributor to *Encyclopedia of Photography, Photography Annual*, and to magazines.

WORK IN PROGRESS: Books on photography.

AVOCATIONAL INTERESTS: World War II history; painting and skiing.†

* * *

GOLDSTEIN, Leo S. 1924-

PERSONAL: Born November 25, 1924, in New York, N.Y.; son of Max (a chef) and Irene (Berger) Goldstein; married Francis L. King, June 17, 1951; children: Susan Jan. *Education:* Queens College (now Queens College of the City University of New York), B.A., 1949; Columbia University, M.A., 1950, Ph.D., 1957. *Office:* New York Medical College, Flower-Fifth Ave. Hospitals, 106 St. and Fifth Ave., New York, N.Y. 10029.

CAREER: Columbia University, New York, N.Y., research associate, 1950-56; Cornell University School of Medicine, New York, N.Y., resident fellow in medicine, 1957-61; Center for Programed Instruction, New York, N.Y., research director, 1961-63; Institute for Developmental Studies, New York, N.Y., senior research associate, 1963—. *Military service:* U.S. Army Air Forces, 1943-46. *Member:* American Psychological Association, American Association for the Advancement of Science, National Society for Programed Instruction, National Council on Measurement in Education, New York Academy of Sciences.

WRITINGS: (With Lassar G. Gotkin) *Descriptive Statistics: A Programmed Textbook*, Wiley, Volume I, 1964, Volume II, 1965; (contributor) M. Miles, editor, *Innovation in Education*, Bureau of Publications, Teachers College, Columbia University, 1964. Writer of Center for Programed Instruction research reports. Contributor to *Biometrics, Merrill-Palmer Quarterly*, and *Journal of Programed Instruction*.

WORK IN PROGRESS: Directing the evaluation of a research study dealing with an enriched program for socially disadvantaged children of pre-school and primary ages.†

* * *

GOLDSTEIN, William Isaac 1932-
(Rex Lode)

PERSONAL: Born July 10, 1932, in Troy, N.Y.; son of Max (a tailor) and Florence (Tamea) Goldstein; married Barbara Lipp, 1955; married second wife, Fiora D'-Agonadi, 1960; married third wife, Marjorie Morninglory, 1964; children: (first marriage) Adam, Damon. *Education:* Columbia University, B.S., 1955; University of Chicago, graduate study, 1956. *Religion:* Jewish. *Home:* 21 Hillway, San Francisco, Calif. 94117. *Agent:* Sindell Agency, 449 South Beverly Dr., Beverly Hills, Calif. *Office:* P.O. Box 2473, San Francisco, Calif. 94126.

WRITINGS: (Under pseudonym Rex Lode, with Boyd Boylan) *The Third Eye of America*, Lyle Stuart, 1963. Author of filmscript, "The Great Big Fat Train Robbery," Claudel Productions, 1964.

WORK IN PROGRESS: Three books, *The Sexual Propeller, The All New Uncle Tom's Cabin*, and *The Fingers of Dr. Pibe*; a translation of *Wonnebald Gozo, Als Leben und Dichten* from the German: a filmscript, "The Prix and Bollix Caper."

SIDELIGHTS: Goldstein is doing "independent philosophical investigation into relaxation and related phenomena." *Avocational interests:* Surf fishing, race-car driving, dancing.†

* * *

GOLLAN, Robin 1917-

PERSONAL: Born December 8, 1917, in New South Wales, Australia; son of William Ernest (a farmer) and Jane (McLean) Gollan; married Daphne Morris, May 10, 1941 (divorced, 1966); married Anne Ayrton, 1970; children: (first marriage) John K., Katherine. *Education:* University of Sydney, B.A., 1939, M.A., 1948; University of London, Ph.D., 1951. *Residence:* Canberra, Australian Capital Territory, Australia.

CAREER: Australian National University, Canberra, Australian Capital Territory, 1953—, now professorial fellow in history. *Military service:* Royal Australian Air Force, 1942-45; became flight lieutenant.

WRITINGS: Radical and Working Class Politics, Melbourne University Press, 1960; *The Coalminers of New South Wales*, Melbourne University Press, 1962; *The Commonwealth Bank of Australia, Origins and Early History*, Australian National University Press, 1968; *Revolutionaries and Reformists: Communism and the Australian Labour Movement, 1920-55*, Australian National University Press, 1975.

* * *

GOLLER, Celia (Fremlin) 1914-
(Celia Fremlin)

PERSONAL: Born June 20, 1914, in London, England; daughter of Heaver Stuart (a bacteriologist) and Margaret (Addiscott) Fremlin; married Elia Goller (a schoolteacher), July 6, 1942; children: Nicholas, Geraldine, Sylvia. *Education:* Somerville College, Oxford, B.A. (in classics) and B.Litt. (in philosophy), 1937. *Politics:* "Disagree with all of them." *Religion:* "Ditto." *Home:* 50 South Hill Park, London N.W. 3, England.

CAREER: Writer. *Awards, honors:* Edgar Allen Poe Award ("Edgar") of Mystery Writers of America for best mystery novel of 1959, *The Hours Before Dawn*.

WRITINGS—Under name Celia Fremlin: *The Seven Chars of Chelsea*, Methuen, 1939; *The Hours Before Dawn*, Lippincott, 1959; *Uncle Paul*, Lippincott, 1960; *Wait for the Wedding*, Lippincott, 1961 (published in England as *Seven Lean Years*, Gollancz, 1961); *The Trouble Makers*, Lippincott, 1963; *The Jealous One*, Lippincott, 1965; *Prisoner's Base*, Lippincott, 1967; *Possession*, Lippincott, 1969; *Don't Go to Sleep in the Dark* (short stories), Lippincott, 1970; *Appointment with Yesterday*, Lippincott, 1972; *By Honor Haunted* (short stories), Lippincott, 1974.

AVOCATIONAL INTERESTS: Ancient languages, teenagers, parent-child problems, and educational experiments.

GOLZ, R(einhardt) Lud 1936-

PERSONAL: Born September 16, 1936, in Vancouver, British Columbia, Canada; son of Robert (an ornamental ironworker) and Olga (Witzke) Golz; married Muriel Jane Erickson, August 8, 1959; children: Gregory Lud, Debra Lyn, Tamra Lee, Jeffrey Lon. *Education:* Moody Bible Institute, diploma, 1959; Wheaton College, B.A., 1961. *Home:* 13968 Chillicothe Rd., Novelty, Ohio 44072.

CAREER: Minister of Independent Evangelical Church. Pastor in Elmhurst, Ill., 1958-63; Wheaton Academy, West Chicago, Ill., instructor in Bible, 1963-64; Pleasant Hill Community Church, Wheaton, Ill., pastor, 1964-72; Riverview Church, Novelty, Ohio, pastor, 1972—.

WRITINGS: Walking as He Walked, Moody, 1963; *Hindrances and Helps to Christian Living,* Moody, 1964, revised edition published as *Living It,* Good News Publishers, 1971; *A Practical Guide to Profitable Bible Reading,* Personal Press, 1971.

WORK IN PROGRESS: A devotional book, *Daily Food for Your Heart,* completion expected in 1975.

*   *   *

GONZALEZ, Arturo F., Jr. 1928-

PERSONAL: Born June 5, 1928, in New York, N.Y.; son of Arturo F. and Katherine (Phippen) Gonzalez; married Gloria Garvin (also a writer), October 3, 1964; children: (previous marriage) Martha, Peter, Ann. *Education:* Brown University, A.B., 1952. *Politics:* Independent. *Religion:* Agnostic. *Home:* One Princess Gate, Flat 4, London W. 7, England. *Agent:* Malcolm Reiss, Paul R. Reynolds, Inc., 599 Fifth Ave., New York, N.Y. 10017.

CAREER: Time, Inc., New York, N.Y., 1952-57, began as trainee copywriter, later merchandising manager, worked on *Time, Life, Fortune,* and *Reader's Digest,* 1957-61, foreign correspondent, Hong Kong, 1961-63; Time-Life International, sales promotion manager, 1963—. *Military service:* U.S. Navy, 1946-48. *Member:* Society of Magazine Writers, Society of American Travel Writers, P.E.N., Education Writers Association, Overseas Press Club (New York), Foreign Correspondents Club (Hong Kong), Brown University Club of New York (member of board of governors).

WRITINGS: (Contributor) *Live Them Again,* Simon & Schuster, 1953; (contributor) *Prose by Professionals,* Doubleday, 1959; *Eugene H. Nickerson: Statesman of a New Society,* Heinemann, 1964; (contributor) Marvin Weisbord, editor, *Treasury of Tips for Writers,* Writer's Digest, 1965. Writer of more than six hundred articles for magazines and newspapers, including *Reporter, Saturday Review, Ladies' Home Journal, New York Times,* and *Redbook.*

SIDELIGHTS: Writing assignments have taken Gonzalez around the world four times; his coverage includes the war in Vietnam. *Avocational interests:* Flying, sailing, photography.†

*   *   *

GOOCH, Brison D(owling) 1925-

PERSONAL: Born March 1, 1925, in Bar Harbor, Me.; son of Austin MacLellan (a carpenter) and Clara (Dowling) Gooch; married Dorothy Gale, August 21, 1951; children: Linda, David. *Education:* Miami University, Oxford, Ohio, B.A., 1949; University of Wisconsin, M.A., 1950, Ph.D., 1955. *Office:* History Department, University of Oklahoma, Norman, Okla.

CAREER: Culver Military Academy, Culver, Ind., instructor, 1951-52; Massachusetts Institute of Technology, Cambridge, instructor, later assistant professor of history, 1954-56, 1957-60; University of Oklahoma, Norman, associate professor of history, 1960—. Visiting instructor at Yale University, 1956-57; visiting summer professor at University of Maine, 1961, at University of Nebraska, 1960, 1963. *Military service:* U.S. Army, 1945-47. *Member:* American Historical Association, Society for French Historical Studies. *Awards, honors:* Fulbright research scholar in Belgium, 1963-64.

WRITINGS: The New Bonapartist Generals and the Crimean War, Nijhoff, 1963; *Belgium and the February Revolution,* Nijhoff, 1963; (editor and author of introduction) *Napoleon III: Man of Destiny,* Holt, 1963; (editor) *Interpreting European History,* two volumes, Dorsey, 1967; *The Reign of Napoleon III,* Rand McNally, 1969; (editor and author of introduction) *The Origins of the Crimean War,* Heath, 1969; (editor) *Interpreting Western Civilization,* two volumes, Dorsey, 1969; *Europe in the Nineteenth Century,* Macmillan, 1970; (editor and author of introduction) *Napoleonic Ideas,* William Gannon, 1970. Contributor of articles to historical periodicals.

WORK IN PROGRESS: Articles on various phases of Belgian colonial interest during the reign of Leopold I.†

*   *   *

GOOD, Lawrence R. 1924-

PERSONAL: Born November 6, 1924, in Omaha, Neb.; son of Everett H. (a farmer) and Virginia (Lowe) Good; married Marrillie Cochran, September 13, 1954; children: Jeffrey L., James C., Carolyn J. *Education:* Studied at Nebraska State Teachers College, Peru, 1943, University of Idaho, 1945, Architectural Association, London, England, 1946; Kansas State University of Agriculture and Applied Science (now Kansas State University), B.Ar., 1953; University of Kansas, M.Ar., 1963. *Religion:* Protestant. *Home:* 1652 Hillcrest Rd., Lawrence, Kan.

CAREER: Lawrence R. Good and Associates (architects), Lawrence, Kan., practice of architecture. President, Environmental Research Foundation, 1964—; member of research advisory panel, American Institute of Architects, 1971-72; member of National Research Council, National Academy of Sciences, 1972-74. *Military service:* U.S. Army. *Member:* American Institute of Architects, Tau Sigma Delta.

WRITINGS: (Editor with others) *Therapy by Design,* C. C Thomas, 1965, (with Rajendra K. Srivastava) *Patterns of Group Interaction in Three Architecturally Different Psychiatric Treatment Environments,* Environmental Research Foundation, 1968; (with Srivastava) *St. Margaret's Park Public Housing Project: An Environmental and Behavioral Profile,* Environmental Research Foundation, 1969.

WORK IN PROGRESS: (With Sherman E. Anderson) *Design for Innovative Mental Health Care Facility in a Wisconsin Community.*

*   *   *

GOODNOW, Henry F(rank) 1917-

PERSONAL: Born December 13, 1917; son of H. Frank (in furniture manufacturing business) and Miriam (Ward) Goodnow; married Anne Denney, June 1, 1948; children: David Henry. *Education:* Amherst College, B.A., 1939; University of Chicago, M.A., 1941; Columbia University,

Ph.D., 1960. *Politics:* Democrat. *Religion:* Protestant. *Home:* 855 12th St., Boulder, Colo. 80302. *Office:* Department of Political Science, University of Colorado, Boulder, Colo. 80304.

CAREER: Before World War II worked in Washington, D.C., for Federal Housing Administration and War Production Board; assistant to city manager, Pontiac, Mich., 1946-48; city manager, Keene, N.H., 1948-51; planning consultant, state of New Hampshire, Durham, 1952; University of Pennsylvania, Philadelphia, supervisor of municipal assistance, Fels Institute of Local and State Government, 1953-54, public administration adviser on Pakistan Project, 1954-57; Yale University, New Haven, Conn., research assistant and writer, Human Relations Area Files, 1957-58; University of Colorado, Boulder, assistant professor of political science, 1958—. Boulder City Planning Board, member, 1962-64, chairman, 1964. *Military service:* U.S. Army, Adjutant General's Department, 1942-46; became staff sergeant. *Member:* International City Managers Association, American Political Science Association, American Society for Public Administration.

WRITINGS: *The Civil Service of Pakistan: Bureaucracy in a New Nation*, 1964; (with others) *Pakistan*, Human Relations Area File Press, 1964; *The Civil Service of Pakistan: Bureaucracy in a New Nation*, Yale University Press, 1964. Occasional contributor to journals.

WORK IN PROGRESS: A study of problems of development in emerging nations; comparative studies in municipal administration.

AVOCATIONAL INTERESTS: Mountain hiking, swimming, skiing.†

*   *   *

GOODNOW, Jacqueline (Jarrett) 1924-

PERSONAL: Born November 25, 1924, in Toowoomba, Queensland, Australia; became U.S. citizen in 1957; daughter of George Bellingen and Florence (Bickley) Jarrett; married Robert E. Goodnow, October 30, 1951; children: Christopher, Katherine. *Education:* University of Sydney, B.A., 1944; Radcliffe College, Ph.D., 1951. *Home:* 5113 Wissioming Rd., Washington, D.C. 20016. *Office:* George Washington University, Washington, D.C. 20006.

CAREER: University of Sydney, Sydney, Australia, lecturer, 1944-48; U.S. Army, civilian research psychologist, Munich, Germany, 1951-53; Harvard University, Cambridge, Mass., lecturer and research associate, 1953-55; Walter Reed Army Institute of Research. Washington, D.C., research psychologist, 1955-59; George Washington University, Washington, D.C., assistant research professor of psychology, 1961—. Consultant, University of Hong Kong, 1959-61. *Member:* American Psychological Association, Phi Beta Kappa. *Awards, honors:* Woolley traveling scholar, University of Sydney, 1949-51.

WRITINGS: (with Jerome S. Bruner and others) *A Study of Thinking*, Wiley, 1956. Contributor to psychology journals.

WORK IN PROGRESS: Research on development of reasoning.†

*   *   *

GOOLD-ADAMS, Richard 1916-

PERSONAL: Born January 24, 1916, in Brisbane, Australia; son of Sir Hamilton John (in government service) and Elsie (Riordon) Goold-Adams; married Deenagh Blennerhassett (an author), March 31, 1939. *Education:* Attended Winchester College, 1929-33; New College, Oxford, M.A., 1937. *Home:* 25 Porchester Pl., London, W.2, England; and Highfield House, Binley, Andover, Hampshire, England.

CAREER: *Economist*, London, England, 1947-55, became assistant editor; radio and television commentator on international affairs, 1956-61; Institute for Strategic Studies, London, England, vice-chairman, 1958-63, chairman, 1963—. Director of six companies. British Atlantic Committee, chairman, 1959-62, vice-president, 1963—. Governor, Atlantic Institute in Paris, 1962-71. *Military service:* British Army, 1939-46; served in Italy and Middle East; became major. *Member:* National Institute of Industrial Psychology (London; councilor, 1956-70), Atlantic Institute (Paris; governor), Royal Institute of International Affairs (London; councilor, 1957—), Society for Nautreal Research (councilor, 1970—).

WRITINGS: *Middle East Journey*, J. Murray, 1947; *John Foster Dulles: A Reappraisal*, Appleton, 1963 (published in England under title *The Time of Power: A Reappraisal of John Foster Dulles*, Weidenfeld & Nicolson, 1962). Also author of *South Africa Today and Tomorrow*, 1936; author of pamphlets on atomic war and the nuclear age. Special contributor for several years to *Sunday Times* (London); contributor to other newspapers.

SIDELIGHTS: Goold-Adams' journeys have spanned much of the world, including Africa, Middle East, Australia, Malaya, United States, Canada (many visits), the Soviet Union as far as Lake Baikal in Siberia, most other European countries. *Avocational interests:* Photography, travelling.†

*   *   *

GORDH, George (Rudolph) 1912-

PERSONAL: Born May 18, 1912, in St. Paul, Minn.; son of Arvid (a professor and minister) and Agnes (Ostergren) Gordh; married Gwen Reed (a teacher), June 2, 1943; children: George, Jr., Robert, William, Gwendolyn. *Education:* Macalester College, A.B., 1931; University of Minnesota, A.M., 1935; Southern Baptist Theological Seminary, Th.M., 1936; University of Chicago, Ph.D., 1941. *Politics:* Democrat. *Home:* 815 Chester Ave., N.W., Roanoke, Va. *Office:* Hollins College, Roanoke, Va.

CAREER: Methodist minister. Mercer University, Macon, Ga., associate professor of philosophy, 1941-45; University of Chicago, Chicago, Ill., assistant professor of historical theology, 1945-51; Hollins College, Roanoke, Va., professor of religion, 1951—, chaplain, 1951-58, chairman of Division of the Humanities, 1963—. Preacher and lecturer at churches, colleges, and universities. *Member:* Southern Society for Philosophy of Religion.

WRITINGS: *Christian Faith and its Cultural Expression*, Prentice-Hall, 1962. Contributor to religious periodicals.

WORK IN PROGRESS: Research into the relationship between Christianity and contemporary culture.

SIDELIGHTS: Gordh is competent in German, Swedish, and Greek. *Avocational interests:* Church architecture.†

*   *   *

GORDIS, Robert 1908-

PERSONAL: Born February 6, 1908, in Brooklyn, N.Y.;

son of Hyman and Lizzie (Engel) Gordis; married Fannie Jacobson, February 5, 1928; children: Enoch, Leon, David. *Education:* Yeshiva University, diploma, 1923; City College (now City College of the City University of New York), B.A. (cum laude), 1926; Dropsie College, Ph.D., 1929; Jewish Theological Seminary of America, Rabbi (with distinction), 1932. *Home:* 153 Beach 133rd St., Belle Harbor, Long Island, N.Y. *Office:* Jewish Theological Seminary of America, 3080 Broadway, New York, N.Y.

CAREER: Temple Beth-El, Rockaway Park, N.Y., rabbi, 1931—; Jewish Theological Seminary of America, New York, N.Y., professor of Bible, 1937-67; Temple University, Philadelphia, Pa., professor of religion, 1967-74; Jewish Theological Seminary of America, professor of the philosophies of religion, 1974—. Adjunct professor of religion, Columbia University, 1948-57; visiting professor of Old Testament, Union Theological Seminary, 1953-54; teacher at Jewish institutions. Rabbinical Assembly of America, member of executive council, 1935, president, 1944-46; president, Synagogue Council of America, 1948-49. Member of national advisory committee on freedom and religious affairs, National Conference of Christians and Jews. Consultant, Fund for the Republic Center for the Study of Democratic Institutions. Member of board of directors, Villanova University Institute of Church and State. Member of national council, Boy Scouts of America. Public lecturer on contemporary American issues, the status and problems of religion, and on Jewish life and culture. *Awards, honors:* D.D. from Jewish Theological Seminary of America.

WRITINGS: The Biblical Text in the Making, Dropsie College Press, 1937, augmented edition, Ktav, 1971; *The Jew Faces a New World*, Behrman, 1941; *The Wisdom of Ecclesiastes*, Jewish Publication Society, 1945; *Conservative Judaism—An American Philosophy*, Behrman, 1945; *Koheleth: The Man and His World*, Bloch, 1955, 3rd revised edition, Schocken, 1968; *Judaism for the Modern Age*, Farrar, Straus, 1957; *A Faith for Moderns*, Bloch, 1960; *The Song of Songs*, Jewish Theological Seminary Press, 1961; *The Root and the Branch: Judaism and the Free Society*, University of Chicago Press, 1962; *The Book of God and Man: A Study of Job*, University of Chicago Press, 1965; *Sex and the Family in the Jewish Tradition*, Burning Bush Press, 1967; (editor) *Encounters with Job*, Department of Religion, Temple University, 1969. Contributor to the Judaism Pamphlet Series, B'nai B'rith, Youth Organization and to journals and magazines in United States, Israel, and Great Britain.

Associate editor, *Universal Jewish Encyclopedia*; contributing editor, *Menorah Journal, Reconstructionist, Conservative Judaism, Jewish Forum*; founder, and member of board of editors, *Judaism*; member of publications committee, Jewish Publication Society.

WORK IN PROGRESS: Commentary on Job and Song of Songs and Lamentations.

* * *

GOSHAY, Robert C. 1931-

PERSONAL: Born July 12, 1931, in Los Angeles, Calif.; son of Donald C. and Mary M. (Knox) Goshay; married Nancy Jane Lindblad, August 31, 1957; children: Mark, Jeffrey, Eric, Jennifer. *Education:* University of California, Los Angeles, B.S., 1957; University of Pennsylvania, Ph.D., 1961. *Home:* 875 Regal Rd., Berkeley, Calif. 94708.

CAREER: University of California, Berkeley, 1960—,

member of department of business administration. *Military service:* U.S. Navy, 1951-55. *Member:* American Education Association, American Finance Association, American Risk Association.

WRITINGS: Corporate Self Insurance and Risk Retention Plans, Irwin, 1964; *Information Technology in the Insurance Industry*, Irwin, 1964. Contributor to professional journals.

WORK IN PROGRESS: Research in insurance taxation, financial analysis of insurers, and medical care financing.†

* * *

GOSSETT, Thomas F. 1916-

PERSONAL: Born July 13, 1916; son of Rufus Albert and Fern (White) Gossett; married Louise May Young (a teacher), March 18, 1950. *Education:* Southern Methodist University, B.A., 1946, M.A., 1948; University of Minnesota, Ph.D., 1953. *Politics:* Democrat. *Religion:* Presbyterian. *Home:* 417 Belknap Pl., San Antonio 12, Tex.

CAREER: U.S. government civil service, Washington, D.C., and Bermuda, 1941-43; Southern Methodist University, Dallas, Tex., instructor in English, 1946-48; University of Minnesota, Minneapolis, instructor in English, 1949-52; Louisiana State University, Baton Rouge, instructor in English, 1953-54; Wesleyan College, Macon, Ga., associate professor, 1954-57, professor of English, 1957-59; Trinity University, San Antonio, Tex., associate professor of English, 1959-64, professor, 1964—. *Military service:* U.S. Army Air Forces, 1943-46. *Member:* Modern Language Association of America, American Studies Association, American Association of University Professors, Texas Institute of Letters, Phi Beta Kappa. *Awards, honors:* Grants from American Council of Learned Societies, Duke University Visiting Scholar Fund, Southern Fellowships Fund, and Trinity University; Ralph Waldo Emerson Book Award, 1964, for *Race*; Theta Sigma Phi Book Award, 1964.

WRITINGS: Race: The History of an Idea in America, Southern Methodist University Press, 1963, revised edition, 1965.

WORK IN PROGRESS: A book on attitudes toward war and warfare in American thought in the twentieth century.

BIOGRAPHICAL SOURCES: Time, March 13, 1964; *Journal of Southern History*, August, 1964.†

* * *

GOTLIEB, Phyllis Fay (Bloom) 1926-

PERSONAL: Born May 25, 1926, in Toronto, Ontario, Canada; daughter of Leo (a theater manager) and Mary (Kates) Bloom; married Calvin Gotlieb (a professor of Computer Science, University of Toronto), June 12, 1949; children: Leo, Margaret, Jane. *Education:* University of Toronto, B.A., 1948, M.A., 1950. *Religion:* Jewish. *Home:* 29 Ridgevale Dr., Toronto M6A 1K9 Ontario, Canada.

CAREER: Writer.

WRITINGS: Within the Zodiac (poetry), McClelland & Stewart, 1964; *Sunburst* (science fiction novel), Gold Medal Books, 1964; *Why Should I Have All The Grief?* (novel), Macmillan, 1969; *Ordinary, Moving* (poems), Oxford University Press, 1969; *Doctor Umlaut's Earthly Kingdom* (poems), Calliope Press, 1974. Poems anthologized in *Canadian Writers*, edited by Guy Sylvestre, Brandon Conron, and Carl F. Klinck, Ryerson Press, 1964;

How Do I Love Thee: Sixty Poets of Canada (and Quebec) Select and Introduce Their Favourite Poems from Their Own Work, edited by John Robert Colombo, M. G. Hurtig, 1970. Contributor of poems to *Tamarack Review* and *Canadian Forum*, *Queen's Quarterly*, and science fiction stories to *Amazing*, *Fantastic*, and *If*.

*   *   *

GOTTEHRER, Barry H.   1935-

PERSONAL: Born January 25, 1935, in New York, N.Y.; son of Arthur (an executive of crude rubber firm) and Hilda (Klein) Gottehrer; married Judith Loeffler, January 19, 1958 (divorced, 1967); married Patricia Cox, September 7, 1973; children: (first marriage) Andrea, Gregg. *Education:* Brown University, B.A., 1956; Columbia University, M.S. in journalism, 1957. *Politics:* Independent. *Home:* 50 West 70th St., New York, N.Y. 10023. *Agent:* Donald Mac-Campbell, Inc., 12 East 41st St., New York, N.Y. 10017. *Office:* Madison Square Garden Corp., 2 Penn Plaza, New York, N.Y.

CAREER: Started with *New Bedford Standard Times*, New Bedford, Mass., 1958-59; *Sport*, New York, N.Y., associate editor, 1959-60; *Newsweek*, New York, N.Y., sports editor, later press editor, 1960-64; *New York Herald Tribune*, New York, N.Y., editor, "New York City in Crisis" series, 1964-65; assistant to Mayor John Lindsay, New York, N.Y., 1966-71; Columbia University, New York, N.Y., lecturer in journalism, 1970—; Madison Square Garden Corp., New York, N.Y., senior vice-president, 1971—. *Military service:* U.S. Army, 1957-58. *Member:* Magazine Sports Writers Association (president, 1963). *Awards, honors:* New York Reporters Association golden typewriter award, 1965, for "New York City in Crisis" series; James Wright Brown Award from Deadline Club (New York), 1965; Ralph Jonas Award from Long Island University, 1965; Bronze Medal from Citizens Budget Commission of New York City, 1966; George Polk Memorial Award from Long Island University, 1966.

WRITINGS: Football Stars of 1963, Pyramid Books, 1963, and subsequent editions for 1964, 1965; *The Giants of New York*, Putnam, 1963; *Basketball Stars of 1965*, Pyramid Books, 1964; (editor) *New York City in Crisis*, McKay, 1965. Contributor of more than seventy articles to national magazines.

WORK IN PROGRESS: A history of the National Football League championship game, for Putnam; *The High and Low Life of Professional Golf*, for World Publishing.

BIOGRAPHICAL / CRITICAL SOURCES: *Time*, March 26, 1965.†

*   *   *

GOTTSCHALK, Louis (Reichenthal)   1899-

PERSONAL: Born February 21, 1899, in Brooklyn, N.Y.; son of Morris Frank and Anna (Krystall) Gottschalk; married Laura Riding (a writer), 1920 (divorced, 1925); married Fruma Kasdan (an associate professor, University of Chicago), December 16, 1930; children: (second marriage) Alexander, Paul. *Education:* Cornell University, A.B., 1919, A.M., 1920, Ph.D., 1921. *Home:* 5551 University Ave., Chicago, Ill. 60637. *Office:* 1126 East 59th St., Chicago, Ill. 60637.

CAREER: University of Illinois, Urbana, instructor in history, 1921-22; University of Louisville, Louisville, Ky., assistant professor, 1923-25, associate professor of history,

1925-27; University of Chicago, Chicago, Ill., associate professor, 1927-35, professor of history, 1935-59, department chairman, 1937-42, Swift Distinguished Service Professor, 1959-64, professor emeritus, 1964—. Visiting professor, University of Illinois, Chicago Circle, 1966-74. B'nai B'rith Hillel Commission, chairman, 1963-69, honorary chairman, 1969—. Consultant, U.S. Army Air Forces, 1943-44. *Military service:* U.S. Naval Reserve, 1918. *Member:* American Historical Association (president, 1953), Conference on Jewish Relations, American Friends of Lafayette, American Philosophical Society, American Academy of Arts and Sciences, Societe d'Histoire Moderne, American Council of Learned Societies (vice-chairman, 1965), Social Science Research Council, American Society for Eighteenth-Century Studies (president, 1971), Phi Beta Kappa, Zeta Beta Tau, Quadrangle Club. *Awards, honors:* Guggenheim fellowship, 1928-29, 1954-55; Anciens Combattants de France, medal of merit, 1938; Princeton Bicentennial Medal, 1946; Newberry Library fellow, 1946; James H. Hyde prize, 1948; University of Louisville Sesquicentennial Award, 1948, and LL.D., 1970; Legion d'Honneur, 1953; Center for Advanced Studies in the Behavioral Sciences, fellow, 1957-58; D.Litt., Augustana College, 1954; Dr. honoris causa, University of Toulouse, 1957; D.H.L., Hebrew Union College, 1963.

WRITINGS: Jean Paul Marat: Study in Radicalism, Greenberg, 1927, revised edition, University of Chicago Press, 1967; *Era of the French Revolution*, Houghton, 1929; *Lafayette Comes to America*, University of Chicago Press, 1935; *Lafayette Joins the American Army*, University of Chicago Press, 1937; *Lady-In-Waiting: The Romance of Lafayette and Aglae de Hunolstein*, Johns Hopkins Press, 1939; *Lafayette and the Close of the American Revolution*, University of Chicago Press, 1942; (editor) *Letters of Lafayette to Washington, 1777-1799*, privately printed, 1944; (with others) *The Use of Personal Documents in History, Anthropology, and Sociology*, Social Science Research Council, 1945; *The Place of the American Revolution in the Causal Pattern of the French Revolution: An Address at the Seventeenth Annual Meeting of the American Friends of Lafayette*, American Friends of Lafayette, 1948.

Lafayette Between the American and the French Revolution, University of Chicago Press, 1950; *Understanding History: A Primer of Historical Method*, Knopf, 1950; (with D. F. Lach) *Europe and the Modern World*, Scott, Foresman, Volume I: *The Rise of Modern Europe*, Volume II: *The Transformation of Modern Europe*, 1951-54, last eleven chapters of Volume II published as *Europe and the Modern World Since 1870*, 1954; (editor) *Generalization in the Writing of History: A Report to the Committee on Historical Analysis, Social Science Research Council*, University of Chicago Press, 1963; (author and editor) *UNESCO History of Mankind*, Allen & Unwin, Volume IV, 1969; (with Margaret Maddox) *Lafayette in the French Revolution: Through the October Days*, University of Chicago Press, 1969; (with Maddox) *Lafayette in the French Revolution: From the October Days Through the Federation*, University of Chicago Press, 1973; (with Lach and S. A. Bill) *Toward the French Revolution: Europe and America in the Eighteenth Century World*, Scribner, 1973.

Assistant editor, *Journal of Modern History*, 1929-43, acting editor, 1943-45.

WORK IN PROGRESS: Lafayette in the French Revolution: From July, 1790 to August, 1792, for University of

Chicago Press; *Reflections on Revolution*, a collection of autobiographical anecdotes.

SIDELIGHTS: Of *Lafayette in the French Revolution: Through the October Days*, Leo Gershoy has written in the *Saturday Review*: "[The authors] cannot be charged with taking the ritual of academic scholarship lightly. The research is masterly; the narration impressive. Conscientiously discharging their responsibilities, the authors do not shrink from leaving the highways to follow smaller side paths. Now and then the larger scene is blurred, but this is no doubt inevitable and unavoidable, for the authors refuse to be rushed. The reader can settle down comfortably for a leisurely and enjoyable journey."

BIOGRAPHICAL/CRITICAL SOURCES: Richard Herr and H. T. Parker, editors, *Ideas in History: Essays Presented to Louis Gottschalk by His Former Students*, Duke University Press, 1965.

*   *   *

GOUGH, John W(iedhofft) 1900-

PERSONAL: Born February 23, 1900, in Penarth, Glamorganshire, Wales; son of John Henry and Anne (Wiedhofft) Gough; married Margaret Christian Rintoul, 1926 (died, 1939); married Margaret Johnston Maclagan, 1941; children: (first marriage) David Johm, Anne Catherine Gough Mulgan, Margaret Penelope. *Education:* Attended Clifton College; Merton College, Oxford, B.A., 1922, M.A., 1926. *Home:* 28 Hill Top Rd., Oxford, England.

CAREER: University of Bristol, Bristol, England, lecturer, 1923-32; Oxford University, Oriel College, Oxford, England, fellow and tutor, 1932-67, treasurer, 1941-51, librarian, 1951-67, vice-provost, 1954-56. Visiting lecturer, Western Reserve University (now Case Western Reserve University), 1929-30. *Military service:* British Army, 1918-19; became second lieutenant. *Member:* Royal Historical Society (fellow). *Awards, honors:* Honorary D.Litt., Merton College, Oxford University, 1965.

WRITINGS: The Mines of Mendip, Clarendon Press, 1930, 2nd revised edition, David & Charles, 1967; *Mendip Mining Laws and Forest Bounds*, Somerset Record Society, 1931; *The Superlative Prodigall*, Arrowsmith, 1932; *The Social Contract*, Clarendon Press, 1936, 2nd revised edition, 1957; (editor) *John Locke: Social Treatise of Government and a Letter Concerning Toleration*, Blackwell's Political Texts, 1946, 3rd revised edition, 1966; *John Locke's Political Philosophy*, Clarendon Press, 1950, 2nd revised edition, 1973; *Fundamental Law in English Constitutional History*, Clarendon Press, 1955, 2nd revised edition, 1971; *Sir Hugh Myddelton: Entrepreneur and Engineer*, Clarendon Press, 1964; (editor with Raymond Klibansky, translator and author of introduction) *John Locke, Epistola de Toleantia: A Letter on Toleration*, Clarendon Press, 1968; *The Rise of the Entrepreneur*, Batsford, 1969, Schocken, 1970. Contributor of articles and reviews to journals.

*   *   *

GOULDNER, Alvin Ward 1920-

PERSONAL: Born July 29, 1920, in New York, N.Y.; son of Louis and Estelle (Fetbrandt) Gouldner; married second wife Janet Walker, February, 1967; children: Richard, Alan, Andrew, Alessandra. *Education:* City College (now City College of the City University of New York), B.B.A., 1941; Columbia University, M.A., 1945, Ph.D., 1953. *Of-fice:* Sociologisch Instituut, University of Amsterdam, Korte Spinhuissteeg 3, Amsterdam, Netherlands.

CAREER: American Jewish Committee, New York, N.Y., resident sociologist, 1945-47; State University of New York College at Buffalo, assistant professor of sociology, 1947-51; Standard Oil Co. of New Jersey, New York, N.Y., consulting sociologist, 1951-52; Antioch College, Yellow Springs, Ohio, associate professor of sociology, 1952-54; University of Illinois, Urbana, associate professor, later professor of sociology, 1954-59; Washington University, St. Louis, Mo., professor of sociology, 1959-64, Max Weber Professor of Social Theory, 1967—; visiting professor at Free University, Berlin, Germany, 1965, School of Economics, Stockholm, Sweden, 1965; Hebrew University, Jerusalem, Israel, 1966, Warsaw University, Poland, 1966; University of Amsterdam, Netherlands, professor of sociology, 1972—. Consulting editor, Penguin Books (London), 1969. *Member:* American Sociological Association (member of council), Society for the Study of Social Problems (former president), Society for the Psychological Study of Social Issues, Sociological Research Association. *Awards, honors:* Social Science Research Council awards and fellowships; Fellow of the Center for Advanced Study in the Behavioral Sciences, Stanford University, 1961-62.

WRITINGS: (Editor) *Studies in Leadership*, Harper, 1950; *Patterns of Industrial Bureaucracy*, Free Press of Glencoe, 1954; *Wildcat Strike*, Antioch, 1954; (editor) Emile Durkheim, *Socialism and Saint-Simon*, Antioch, 1958; (with Richard Peterson) *Notes on Technology and the Moral Order*, Bobbs-Merrill, 1962; (with H. P. Gouldner) *Modern Sociology*, Harcourt, 1963; *Enter Plato: Classical Greece and the Origins of Social Theory*, Basic Books, 1965, part I published as *The Hellenic World: A Sociological Analysis*, Harper, 1969; *The Coming Crisis of Western Sociology*, Basic Books, 1970; (editor with S. M. Miller) *Applied Sociology: Opportunities and Problems*, Free Press, 1965; *For Sociology: Renewal and Critique in Sociology Today*, Basic Books, 1973. Editor, Bobbs-Merrill reprint series in sociology, 1960—.

Founder and editor-in-chief, *Trans-Action*, 1963-66; editor-in-chief, *New Critics Press*, St. Louis, 1969—; co-founder and editor, *Theory and Society*, Amsterdam, 1973—. Also associate editor of *Social Problems*, *Sociological Abstracts*, and *Journal of the History of the Behavioral Sciences*.

*   *   *

GOVORCHIN, Gerald Gilbert 1912-

PERSONAL: Born August 29, 1912, in Mali Iz, Yugoslavia; naturalized U.S. citizen; son of Christ and Lucy (Marelic) Govorchin; married Lillian Poludniak; children: Rexford Elliott, Cherilyn Regina. *Education:* University of Southern California, A.B., 1940; University of Chicago, M.A., 1942; Northwestern University, Ph.D., 1946. *Home:* 8540 South West 48th St., Miami, Fla. 33155. *Office:* University of Miami, Coral Gables, Fla. 33124.

CAREER: University of Miami, Coral Gables, Fla., member of history dept., 1946—. *Member:* American Historical Association, American Association for the Advancement of Slavic Studies, Association for South Slavic Studies (vice-president, 1974-75), National Geographic Society, American Association of University Professors, Southern Conference on Slavic Studies (president, 1973-74), Southern Historical Association, Florida Conference of College Teachers of History, Phi Beta Kappa, Phi Alpha Theta, Phi Kappa Phi.

WRITINGS: The Gray Falcon in the United States, Public Affairs Press, 1949; *Americans from Yugoslavia*, University of Florida Press, 1961. Contributor of articles and reviews to professional journals.

*   *   *

GOWAN, John Curtis   1912-

PERSONAL: Born May 21, 1912, in Boston, Mass.; son of Isaiah Harry J. (a businessman) and Edythe (Chute) Gowan; married Priscilla Buckwell, 1934; married second wife, May Seagoe, 1953; married third wife, Jane Thompson, 1958; children: (first marriage) John A., Anne M. (Mrs. Larry Curry). *Education:* Harvard University, A.B., 1933, Ed.M., 1935; University of California, Los Angeles, Ed.D., 1952. *Politics:* Democrat. *Home:* 9030 Darby St., Northridge, Calif. 91324.

CAREER: Registrar at private school in New Hampshire, 1935-41; Culver Military Academy, Culver, Ind., counselor, 1941-52; Los Angeles State College (now California State University at Los Angeles), assistant professor, 1953-58; San Fernando Valley State College (now California State University at Northridge), School of Education, associate professor, 1958-60, professor and chairman of department of guidance, 1960—. Fulbright lecturer, University of Singapore, 1962-63; visiting professor, University of Canterbury, New Zealand, 1970. *Member:* American Psychological Association (fellow), American Educational Research Association, Council for Exceptional Children (president), National Association for Gifted Children, American Personnel and Guidance Association, Phi Delta Kappa.

WRITINGS: Annotated Bibliography of Writings on Gifted Children, National Education Association, 1961; (with George D. Demos) *The Education and Guidance of the Ablest*, C. C Thomas, 1964; *Annotated Bibliography on Creativity and Giftedness*, San Fernando State Valley State College Foundation, 1965; (editor with others) *The Guidance of Exceptional Children*, McKay, 1965, revised edition, 1972; (editor with Demos) *The Disadvantaged and Potential Dropout*, C. C Thomas, 1966; (with Demos and E. Paul Torrance) *Creativity: Its Educational Implications*, Wiley, 1967; (with C. B. Bruch) *The Academically Talented Student and Guidance*, Houghton, 1971; (with Torrance) *Educating the Ablest*, Peacock, 1971; *The Development of the Creative Individual*, Knapp, 1972; *The Guidance and Measurement of Intelligence, Development and Creativity*, privately printed, 1972; *The Development of the Psychedelic Individual*, privately printed, 1972. Editor, *The Gifted Child Quarterly*.

WORK IN PROGRESS: A book, *Trance, Art and Creativity*.

*   *   *

GRACZA, Margaret Young   1928-

PERSONAL: Surname is pronounced *Grah*-suh; born April 16, 1928, in St. Paul, Minn.; daughter of Harold Curtice (a janitor-engineer) and Amanda (Garvick) Young; married Rezsoe Miklos Gracza (a research engineer), October 27, 1959; children: Susan, Edward. *Education:* Macalester College, B.A., 1950; Danish Graduate School for Foreign Students, Copenhagen, Fulbright scholar, 1952-53. *Religion:* Episcopalian. *Home:* 3944 14th Ave. S., Minneapolis, Minn. 55407.

CAREER: International Institute (community service or-

ganization), St. Paul, Minn., activities director, 1950-52; St. Paul (Minn.) public schools, high school teacher of English and art, 1954-56; Minneapolis Institute of Arts, Minneapolis, Minn., staff member in education department, 1956-62, 1964—. Lecturer on art; artist, working in water colors and ceramics.

WRITINGS: The Ship and The Sea in Art, Lerner, 1964; (translator from the Danish) Grete Janus Hertz, *Hi, Daddy, Here I Am*, Lerner, 1964; *The Bird in Art*, Lerner, 1966; (with husband Rezsoe Gracza) *The Hungarians in America*, Lerner, 1969; *Art: Looking Forward to a Career*, Dillon, 1971. Writer of twelve radio scripts for children's program on art for University of Minnesota educational station, KUOM, 1959-61.†

*   *   *

GRAEBNER, Norman A.   1915-

PERSONAL: Born October 19, 1915, in Kingman, Kan.; son of Rudolph W. (a minister) and Helen (Brauer) Graebner; married Laura Baum, August 30, 1941; children: Harriet, Norman Brooks, Emily. *Education:* Milwaukee State Teachers College (now University of Wisconsin at Milwaukee), B.S., 1939; University of Oklahoma, M.A., 1940; University of Chicago, Ph.D., 1949. *Religion:* Lutheran. *Home:* 1501 South Hillcrest St., Urbana, Ill. *Office:* Department of History, University of Illinois, Champaign, Ill.

CAREER: Oklahoma College for Women, Chickasha, assistant professor, 1942-43, 1946-47; Iowa State University, Ames, 1948-56, began as assistant professor, became professor of history; University of Illinois, Champaign, professor of history, 1956—. Visiting associate professor, Stanford University, 1952-53; Commonwealth Fund lecturer, University of London, 1958; Fulbright lecturer, University of Queensland, 1963. Radio broadcaster from classroom, 1958-59, and of weekly program, "Background of the News," WBBM, Chicago, Ill., 1958-60. *Military service:* U.S. Army, Ordnance, 1943-46; became first lieutenant; received Commendation Ribbon for establishing first school for American soldiers in Japan, 1946.

MEMBER: American Historical Association, American Association of University Professors, Organization of American Historians, Southern Historical Association, Illinois State Historical Society, Phi Alpha Theta. *Awards, honors:* Outstanding teacher award, University of Illinois, 1962.

WRITINGS: Empire on the Pacific, Ronald, 1955; *The New Isolationism*, Ronald, 1956; *Cold War Diplomacy, 1945-1960*, Van Nostrand, 1962; *Ideas and Diplomacy*, Oxford University Press, 1964; (with others) *A History of the United States*, two volumes, McGraw, 1970; *A History of the American People*, McGraw, 1970; *Recent United States History*, Ronald, 1972.

Editor: *The Enduring Lincoln*, University of Illinois Press, 1959; *Politics and the Crisis of 1860*, University of Illinois Press, 1961; *An Uncertain Tradition: American Secretaries of State in the Twentieth Century*, McGraw, 1961; *The Cold War: Ideological Conflict or Power Struggle?*, Heath, 1963; *Manifest Destiny*, Bobbs-Merrill, 1968.

Contributor: *Lincoln for the Ages*, Doubleday, 1960; *Lincoln Images*, Augustana College Library, 1960; *Why the North Won the Civil War*, Louisiana State University Press, 1960; *America's Ten Greatest Presidents*, Rand McNally, 1961; *Contemporary Civilization*, Scott, Foresman, 1961; *The Unity of Western Europe*, Washington State University Press, 1964. Contributor to *Collier's Encyclopedia Yearbook*.

Contributor of some sixty articles to periodicals. Contributing editor, *Current History*.

WORK IN PROGRESS: Several volumes on American foreign policy, one dealing with the period of the 1840's and 1850's, others dealing with the period since World War II.

* * *

GRAHAM, A(lexander) John 1930-

PERSONAL: Born March 9, 1930, in Lowestoft, England; son of Godfrey Michael (a naturalist) and Edith (Meek) Graham; married Jenny Fitter, July 6, 1963; children: William Richard, Oliver James. *Education:* King's College, Cambridge, B.A. (first class honors), 1952, Ph.D., 1957. *Office:* Department of History, University of Manchester, Manchester M13 9PL, England.

CAREER: University of London, Bedford College, London, England, assistant lecturer in classics, 1955-57; University of Manchester, Manchester, England, assistant lecturer, 1957-59, lecturer, 1959-70, senior lecturer in history, 1970—. Member, British School at Athens. *Military service:* British Army, 1948-49. *Member:* Classical Association (secretary of Manchester branch, 1959-62), Hellenic Society (member of council, 1960-63, 1974—), Inland Waterways Association.

WRITINGS: Colony and Mother City in Ancient Greece, Barnes & Noble, 1964, revised edition, 1971; (co-editor) V. L. Ehrenberg, *Polis und Imperium*, Artemis Press, 1965; (contributor) Hildegard Temporini, editor, *Aufstieg und Niedergang der roemischen Welt*, de Gruyter, 1972; (contributor) M. R. D. Foot, editor, *War and Society: Essays in Honor and Memory of John Western*, Paul Elek, 1973. Contributor of articles to *Historia, Journal of Hellenic Studies, Journal of Roman Studies, Annual of the British School at Athens*, and other periodicals.

WORK IN PROGRESS: Studies in early Greek history and epigraphy; research in the Severan period of Roman history; aspects of ancient beekeeping.

SIDELIGHTS: Graham is competent in Latin, classical and modern Greek, and the major modern European languages. *Avocational interests:* Archaeology, especially Greek and Roman, including excavation; canoeing, cricket, photography, and travel in Mediterranean countries.

* * *

GRALAPP, Leland Wilson 1921-

PERSONAL: Surname is pronounced *Gray*-lap; born May 5, 1921, in La Grande, Ore.; son of Arnold Leland and Iva (Wilson) Gralapp; married Joan Royal, August 6, 1948; children: Laura, Arthur. *Education:* University of Oregon, B.S., 1943; University of Iowa, M.F.A., 1948, Ph.D., 1953. *Politics:* Democrat. *Home:* 5190 Sonoma Hwy., Santa Rosa, Calif., *Agent:* McIntosh, McKee & Dodds, 30 East 60th St., New York, N.Y. 10022. *Office:* Sonoma State College, Rohnart Park, Calif.

CAREER: University of Iowa, Iowa City, instructor in art history, 1950-53; Colorado College, Colorado Springs, assistant professor of art, 1953-57, associate professor, 1957-58; University of California, Santa Barbara, visiting assistant professor of art history, 1958-61, assistant professor, 1961-64; Sonoma State College, Rohnhart Park, Calif., as-

sociate professor of art, 1964—. Colorado Springs Fine Arts Center School, curriculum coordinator,1956-58; University of California, Los Angeles, adviser on Balinese art, Institute of Ethnomusicology, 1960-63. Colorado Springs Adult Education Council, member, 1955-58. Exhibitor of intaglio prints in major shows in United States, and in traveling exhibitions in Europe and South America. *Military service:* U.S. Naval Reserve, 1943-46; became lieutenant junior grade; received seven battle stars for Pacific campaigns.

MEMBER: College Art Association, American Association of University Professors, American-Indonesian Society, Southern California Art Historians Association, Oregon Printmakers, Iowa Archaeological Society. *Awards, honors:* Purchase Prize, Los Angeles Printmakers Society, 1965.

WRITINGS: Balinese Painting, A. Swallow for Taylor Museum (Colorado Springs, Colo.); *Boom!* (satirical novel), Dutton, 1965.

WORK IN PROGRESS: Another satirical novel, tentatively titled *Loser's Circle*; experimenting with applications of the process camera in intaglio printmaking.†

* * *

GRASS, Guenter (Wilhelm) 1927-

PERSONAL: Born October 16, 1927, in the Free City of Danzig; married Anna Margareta (a professional dancer), 1954, children: Franz and Raoul (twins), Laura. *Education:* the *New York Times Book Review* reports: "When he heard his history professor recite the catalogues of wars and battles and the calendar of national holidays, he quit school in disgust and never bothered to have his education officially certified." Later, he received training as a stone mason and sculptor; attended Kunstakademie, Duesseldorf, Germany; attended Berlin Academy of Fine Arts, 1953-55. *Politics:* Social Democrat. *Religion:* Roman Catholic. *Home:* 13 Niedstrasse, Berlin-Grunewald 41, West Germany.

CAREER: Former farm laborer in the Rhineland; worked in potash mine near Hildesheim, Germany; black marketeer; as an apprentice stonecutter during the late forties, chiseled tombstones for firms in Duesseldorf; worked as a drummer and washboard accompanist with a jazz band; moved to Paris in 1956 while working on his first novel. Speech-writer for Willy Brandt, while mayor of West Berlin. Visited the United States in 1964 and 1965, giving lectures and readings at Harvard, Yale, Smith College, and at Goethe House and Poetry Center of YM and YWHA, New York, N.Y.; writer-in-residence at Columbia University, 1966. *Military service:* German Army, World War II; aide with the Luftwaffe; prisoner of war in Marienbad. *Member:* Akademie der Kuenste (Berlin), Deutscher PEN, Zentrum der Bundesrepublik, Verband Deutscher Schriftsteller, American Academy of Arts and Sciences, Gruppe 47. *Awards, honors:* Lyrikpreis, Sueddeutscher Rundfunk, 1955; prize of Gruppe 47, 1958; literary prize from the Association of German Critics, 1960; *The Tin Drum* was selected by a French jury as the best foreign-language book of 1962; a plaster bust of Grass was placed in the Regensburger Ruhmestempel Walhalla, 1963; Georg Buechner Preis, 1965; Theodor Heuss Preis, 1969; *Local Anaesthetic* was selected as one of 1970's ten best books by *Time*.

WRITINGS: Die Vorzuege der Windhuehner (poems, prose, and drawings), Luchterhand, 1956, 3rd edition, 1967; (author of text) *O Susanna: Ein Jazzbilderbuch: Blues, Bal-*

laden, Spirituals, Jazz, Kiepenheuer & Witsch, 1959; *Die Blechtrommel* (novel), Luchterhand, 1959, translation by Ralph Manheim published as *The Tin Drum*, Vintage Books, 1962.

Gleisdreieck (poems and drawings), Luchterhand, 1960; *Katz und Maus* (novel), Luchterhand, 1961, German reader edition, edited by Edgar Lohner, Blaisdell, 1969, translation by Manheim published as *Cat and Mouse*, Harcourt, 1963; *Die Ballerina*, Friedenauer Presse, 1963, 3rd edition, 1969; *Hundejahre* (novel), Luchterhand, 1963, translation by Manheim published as *Dog Years*, Harcourt, 1965; *Rede ueber das Selbstverstaendliche* (speech), Luchterhand, 1965; (illustrator) Ingeborg Buchmann, *Ein Ort fuer Zufaelle*, Wagenbach, 1965; *Dich singe ich, Demokratie* (addresses, essays, and lectures), Luchterhand, 1965, Volume I: *Es steht zur Wahl*, Volume II: *Loblied auf Willy*, Volume III: *Was ist des Deutschen Vaterland*, Volume IV: *Karl Schiller: Politik in dieser Gesellschaft*, Volume V: *Ich klage an*, Volume VI: *Des Kaisers neue Kleider*, 2nd edition, in one volume, 1965; *Selected Poems*, in German with translations by Michael Hamburger and Christopher Middleton, Harcourt, 1966; *Ausgefragt* (poems and drawings), Luchterhand, 1967, translation by Hamburger published as *New Poems*, Harcourt, 1968; *Der Fall Axel C. Springer am Beispiel Arnold Zweig: Eine Rede, ihr Anlass, und die Folgen*, Voltaire Verlag, 1967; *Ueber das Selbstverstaendliche: Reden, Aufsaetze, offene Briefe, Kommentare*, Luchterhand, 1968, revised and supplemented edition published as *Ueber das Selbstverstaendliche: Politische Schriften*, Deutscher Taschenbuch-Verlag, 1969, selections from first edition, translated by Manheim, published as *Speak Out: Speeches, Open Letters, Commentaries*, Harcourt, 1969; *Briefe ueber die Grenze: Versuch eines Ost-West-Dialogs* [by] Guenter Grass [and] Pavel Kohout (letters), C. Wegner, 1968; *Ueber meinen Lehrer Doeblin und andere Vortraege*, Literarische Collequium Berlin, 1968; *Guenter Grass: Ausgewaehlte Texte, Abbildungen, Faksimiles, Bio-Bibliographie*, edited by Theodor Wieser, Luchterhand, 1968, also published as *Portraet und Poesie*, 1968; *Kunst oder Pornographie?*, J. F. Lehmann, 1969; *Poems of Guenter Grass*, translated by Michael Hamburger and Christopher Middleton, Penguin, 1969; *Oerlich betaeubt* (novel), Luchterhand, 1969, translation by Manheim published as *Local Anaesthetic*, Harcourt, 1970; *Die Schweinekopfsuelze*, Merlin-Verlag, 1969.

Originalgraphik (poem with illustrations), limited edition, Argelander, 1970; *Gesammelte Gedichte* (collected poems), Luchterhand, 1971; *Aus dem Tagebuch einer Schnecke*, Luchterhand, 1972, translation by Manheim published as *From the Diary of a Snail*, Harcourt, 1973; *Inmarypreise*, translated by Christopher Middleton, Harcourt, 1974.

Plays: *Hochwasser: Ein Stueck in zwei Akten* (two act), Suhrkamp, 1963, 4th edition, 1968; *Onkel, Onkel* (four acts), Wagenbach, 1965; *Die Plebejer proben den Aufstand: Ein deutsches Trauerspiel* (first produced in West Berlin at Schiller Theatre, January 15, 1966), Luchterhand, 1966, translation by Ralph Manheim published as *The Plebeians Rehearse the Uprising: A German Tragedy* (produced in Kingston, R.I. by Theatre Company of Boston, February, 1968), Harcourt, 1966; "The World of Guenter Grass," adapted by Dennis Rosa, produced in New York at Pocket Theatre, April 26, 1966; *Four Plays* (includes "Flood," "Mister, Mister," "Only Ten Minutes to Buffalo," and "The Wicked Cooks"), Harcourt, 1967; *Hochwasser and Noch Zehn Minuten bis Buffalo*, edited by A. Leslie Will-

son, Appleton, 1967; "The Wicked Cooks," translated by Willson, produced in New York at Orpheum Theatre, January 23, 1967; "Davor" (first produced in West Berlin at Schiller Theatre, February 16, 1969; translation by Willson and Manheim produced as "Uptight" in Washington, D.C. at Kreeger Theatre, March 22, 1972) published as *Davor: Ein Stuck in Dreizehn Szenen*, Harcourt, 1974, translation published as *Max: A Play*, Harcourt, 1972; *Theater-spiele* (includes "Hochwasser," "Onkel, Onkel," "Die Plebejer proben den Aufstand," and "Davor"), Luchterhand, 1970. Other plays include "Goldmaeulchen" and "Zwei und dreizig Zaehne."

Wrote screenplay for film adaptation of *Cat and Mouse*, released in Germany, 1967. Work represented in anthologies, including *Deutsche Literatur seit 1945 in Einzeldorstellunger*, edited by Dietrich Weber, Kroener, 1968. "Oertlich betaeubt," LP recording of selected readings by the author, Deutsche Grammophon Gesellschaft, 1971.

SIDELIGHTS: The Tin Drum is generally regarded as the first major literary work to be published in Germany in the past 30 years. The *New York Times Book Review* wrote: "With a single book, the lackluster reputation of contemporary German letters has improved everywhere. Not since the days of Thomas Mann has a German writer captured such an international audience." Fred Grunfeld in *The Reporter* called the novel "brilliant and hilarious," and noted that "Grass harks back to that superb and, except for Kafka, still forgotten group of expressionist writers who accounted for the flowering of German literature during the 1920's and early 1930's. . . ."

The Tin Drum evokes the Nazi era with astonishing candor. George Steiner wrote: "It is the power of that bawling voice to drown the siren-song of smooth oblivion, to make the Germans—as no writer did before—face up to their monstrous past." "A former member of the Hitler Youth, Grass has had the nerve, the indispensable tactlessness to evoke the past. By force of his macabre, often obscene wit, he has rubbed the noses of his readers in the great filth, in the vomit of their time. Like no other writer, he has mocked and subverted the bland oblivion, the self-acquittal which underlie Germany's material resurgence." Grass is by no means a timid spokesman for the anti-Adenauer intellectuals. "He stomps," says Steiner, "like a boisterous giant through a literature often marked by slim volumes of whispered lyricism. The energy of his devices, the scale on which he works, are fantastic. He suggests an action painter wrestling, dancing across a huge canvas, then rolling himself in the paint in a final logic of design."

Abroad, he is the most widely read modern German author. In Germany he is both lauded and attacked. J. P. Bauke writes: "He was denied prizes and given prizes, denounced as a national disgrace and praised as the voice of conscience asserting itself against the soothing lullabies of oblivion. Above all, he was read and continues to be read."

In Germany, however, some 35 attempts have been made, mainly by right-wing groups, to ban his books as pornographic and blasphemous. The books are contraband east of the Berlin Wall. In 1961 he was expelled from the premises while promoting literary freedom at the fifth German writers congress in East Berlin. A staunch supporter of the *Spandauer Volksblatt* (one of the few truly independent newspapers, he believes), he has even sold copies on the streets of Berlin.

He is considered to be today's answer to the Renaissance

Man, at once novelist, poet, dramatist, sculptor, and graphic artist (he designs his own book jackets, and his work has been exhibited at Goethe House, New York). He is a careful craftsman, respectful of facts and of the meanings words carry, yet at the same time something of a revolutionary. Wrote Steiner: "It is as if Grass had taken the German dictionary by the throat and was trying to throttle the falsehood and cant out of the old words, trying to cleanse them with laughter and impropriety so as to make them new."

Grass is considered "non-literary" because, says Steiner, "he handles literary conventions with the unworried naivete of an artisan." His free-wheeling style leaves him open to critical attacks. Steiner, for example, believes that he is "nearly always too long; nearly always too loud. The raucous brutalities which he satirizes infect his own art." Grass appears to be undisturbed by such criticism; he considers himself primarily a storyteller, rather than an artist, and while he remains impressed by the ability of critics to find symbolism in his works, he has this comment: "So many of them look for symbols and allegories and deeper meanings, but sometimes I write of potato peels and mean potato peels."

Grass's novels are generally written in three drafts, the first from memory, the second substantiated by research, the third a final revision. He acknowledges the influence of Herman Melville, John Dos Passos, Marcel Proust, Jean Paul Richter, and Laurence Sterne, among others.

BIOGRAPHICAL/CRITICAL SOURCES: Time, January 4, 1963; Virginia Quarterly Review, spring, 1963; America, March 9, 1963; Reporter, March 14, 1963; Saturday Review, August 10, 1963; Guardian (Manchester, England), January 16, 1964; Commentary, May, 1964; New York Times Book Review, May 31, 1964; New York Times, May 19, 1965, July 11, 1965; Atlantic, June, 1965; New York Review of Books, June 3, 1965; Life, June 4, 1965 Carolyn Riley, editor, Contemporary Literary Criticism, Gale, Volume I, 1973, Volume II, 1974, Volume IV, 1975.†

* * *

GRAVES, John (Alexander III) 1920-

PERSONAL: Born August 6, 1920, in Fort Worth, Tex.; son of John Alexander and Nancy (Kay) Graves; married Jane Cole, 1958; children: Helen, Sally. Education: Rice University, B.A., 1942; Columbia University, M.A., 1948. Office: Texas Christian University, Fort Worth, Tex.

CAREER: University of Texas, Austin, instructor in English, 1948-50; free-lance writer in United States and abroad, 1951-58; Texas Christian University, Fort Worth, adjunct professor of English, 1958—. Military service: U.S. Marine Corps, 1941-45; became captain; received Purple Heart. Member: Audubon Society, Texas Institute of Letters, Phi Beta Kappa. Awards, honors: Collins Award of Texas Institute of Letters, 1961, for Goodbye to a River.

WRITINGS: Goodbye to a River, Knopf, 1960; (with Robert Boyle and others) The Water Hustlers, Sierra Club, 1971, revised edition, 1973; (with others) Growing Up in Texas, Encino Press, 1972; The Last Running, Encino Press, 1974; Hard Scrabble, Knopf, 1974. Contributor to magazines, 1947—; short stories included in Prize Stories: The O'Henry Awards, 1955 and 1962, and Best American Short Stories, 1960.

AVOCATIONAL INTERESTS: Natural history, the outdoors.†

GRAY, James 1899-

PERSONAL: Born June 30, 1899, in Minneapolis, Minn.; son of James and Grace (Farrington) Gray; married Sophie Stryker, 1923 (deceased); married Elizabeth Bishop, December 15, 1952; children: (first marriage) James, Jr., Richard Alan, Gabriella Perin (Mrs. Jeremy Richard Azrael; deceased). Education: University of Minnesota, A.B., 1920. Politics: Democrat. Religion: Unitarian Universalist. Home: 163 Cedarwood Rd., Stamford, Conn. 06903.

CAREER: St. Paul Dispatch-Pioneer Press, St. Paul, Minn., critic and columnist, 1920-46; Chicago Daily News, Chicago, Ill., literary editor, 1946-48; University of Minnesota, Minneapolis, member of English faculty, 1948-57. Awards, honors: Litt.D. from Hamline University, 1944.

WRITINGS: The Penciled Frown, Scribner, 1925; Shoulder the Sky, Putnam, 1935; Wake and Remember, Macmillan, 1936; Wings of Great Desire, Macmillan, 1938; The Illinois, Farrar & Rinehart, 1940; Vagabond Path, Macmillan, 1941; Pine, Stream and Prairie: Wisconsin and Minnesota Profile, Knopf, 1944; On Second Thought (critical essays), University of Minnesota Press, 1946; The University of Minnesota, 1851-1951, University of Minnesota Press, 1951; (with May Brodbeck and Walter Metzer) American Non-Fiction, 1900-1950, Regnery, 1952; Business Without Boundary: The Story of General Mills, University of Minnesota Press, 1953; Education for Nursing, University of Minnesota Press, 1960; Edna St. Vincent Millay, University of Minnesota Press, 1967; John Steinbeck, University of Minnesota Press, 1971.

Plays: "Husbands for Three"; "Gentle Empire"; "Claudius and Gertrude"; "Once in My Pride"; "In Such a Night." Contributor of book reviews to New York Times, New York Herald Tribune, and Saturday Review.

* * *

GRAY, Robert Mack 1922-

PERSONAL: Born April 27, 1922, in Farmington, Utah; son of Lee P. and Lillian (Backman) Gray; married Helen Hale, January 5, 1946; children: Michael, Linda Low, Robert, Jr., Susan, Steven. Education: University of Utah, B.A. and M.A., 1949; University of Chicago, Ph.D., 1954. Home: 3454 Cummings Rd., Salt Lake City, Utah.

CAREER: New Mexico Highlands University, Las Vegas, assistant professor of sociology, 1952-54; University of Utah, Salt Lake City, associate professor of sociology and preventive medicine, 1954—. Military service: U.S. Naval Reserve, 1943-44. Member: American Sociological Association.

WRITINGS: The Older Person in the Church, Eerdmans, 1962.†

* * *

GRAY, William Bittle 1891-
(Captain Bill Gray)

PERSONAL: Born 1891 in Lima, Pa.; son of William Smith and Annie (Bittle) Gray; married Sarah Githens, 1921. Home: 2451 Burkell Ave., Miami, Fla. 33129. Office: Seaquarium, Virginia Key, Miami, Fla.

CAREER: Left school at sixteen to work as a fisherman off the New Jersey coast. His continuing interest in fish led him to Florida, where he eventually began collecting live specimens for the salt water aquarium he built on his own pier. Since 1955, he has been director of collections and exhibits of the Miami Seaquarium, Miami Beach, Fla. He has also directed several expeditions into the Pacific for scientific and museum purposes, including the Leon Mandel Expedition sponsored by Field Museum, Chicago, and the George Vanderbilt Expedition, sponsored by the Academy of Natural Sciences, Philadelphia. *Military service:* U.S. Coast Guard, five years. *Member:* Explorers Club (New York), Surf Club and LaGorce Country Club (both Miami).

WRITINGS: Creatures of the Sea, Funk, 1960; *Porpoise Tales*, A. S. Barnes, 1964; *Fish Tales and Ocean Oddballs*, A. S. Barnes, 1970. Short stories in magazines.

SIDELIGHTS: Gray has been responsible for catching Miami Seaquarium's 10,000 sea creatures. A number of newly-identified fish have been named for him. Interests are centered on biology and natural history.†

*   *   *

GRAYSON, Cecil   1920-

PERSONAL: Born February 5, 1920, in Batley, Yorkshire, England; son of John Micklethwaite and Dora (Hartley) Grayson; married Margaret Parry Jordan, March 17, 1947; children: Celia Elisabeth, Catherine Ann, Julia Mary, Robin John. *Education:* St. Edmund Hall, Oxford, M.A., 1947. *Home:* 11 Norham Rd., Oxford, England.

CAREER: Oxford University, Oxford, England, lecturer in Italian, 1948-57, Serena Professor of Italian Studies, 1958—, fellow of Magdalen College, 1958—. *Military service:* British Army, 1940-45; became major. *Member:* Accademia della Crusca (Florence), Accademia Letteraria dell'Arcadia (Rome), Accademia delle Scienze (Bologna), Commissione per i Testi di Lingua (Bologna), Accademia Nazionale dei Lincei (Rome).

WRITINGS: Opuscoli Inediti di L. B. Alberti, Olschki, 1945; (editor with Carlo Dionisotti) *Early Italian Texts*, Basil Blackwell, 1949; *L. B. Alberti and the Tempio Malatestiano*, Pierpont Morgan Library, 1957; (translator) Roberto Ridolfi, *The Life of Girolamo Savonarola*, Knopf, 1958; *V. Calmeta: Prose e Lettere*, Testi di Lingua (Bologna), 1959; *L. B. Alberti: Opere Volgari*, Laterza, Volume I, 1960, Volume II, 1966, Volume III, 1973; (translator) Ridolfi, *The Life of Machiavelli*, University of Chicago Press, 1963; (editor) L. B. Alberti, *La Prima Grammatica del Volgare*, Testi di Lingua, 1964; (translator) Francesco Guicciardini, *History of Italy in the Renaissance*, Pocket Books, 1964; (translator) Guicciardini, *History of Florence*, Pocket Books, 1964; (editor) Guicciardini, *Selected Writings*, Oxford University Press, 1965; (translator) Ridolfi, *Life of Francesco Guicciardini*, Routledge, 1967; (translator) Alberti, *On Painting and on Sculpture*, Phaidon Press, 1972; *Cinque Saggi Su Dante*, Patron (Bologna), 1972. Contributor to learned journals in England, Italy, Germany, and United States. Editor, Italian Studies.

WORK IN PROGRESS: Annotated edition of L. B. Alberti's *Della pittura*, and a survey of Italian literary history.

*   *   *

GREEN, David Bronte   1910-

PERSONAL: Born April 20, 1910, in Surrey, England; son of Francis Herbert (a wine merchant and common councilor) and Mary Helena (Carr) Green; married Joyce Margaret Westrup, July 2, 1938; children: Roger Swithin. *Education:* Attended Bishop's Stortford College. *Politics:*

Conservative. *Religion:* Church of England. *Home:* Church Hanborough, Oxford, England. *Agent:* Richard Scott Simon Ltd., 36 Wellington St., London W.C. 2, England.

CAREER: With *Punch*, London, England, 1936-65; retired to write full time, 1965—. Director, Greens Ltd. (wine merchants), London, England. *Member:* Society of Antiquaries (fellow).

WRITINGS: In the Wood (children's stories), Acorn, 1946; *Country Neighbours*, Blandford, 1948; *Blenheim Palace*, Country Life, 1951; *Gardener to Queen Anne*, Oxford University Press, 1956; *Sir Winston Churchill at Blenheim Palace*, Alden Press, 1959; *Grinling Gibbons, Carver and Statuary*, Country Life, 1964; *Sarah Duchess of Marlborough*, Scribner, 1967; *Queen Anne*, Scribner, 1970. Writer of official guidebooks to Blenheim Palace. Regular contributor to *Country Life*.

WORK IN PROGRESS: An account of the battle of Blenheim.

SIDELIGHTS: Reviewing *Sarah Duchess of Marlborough*, J. P. Kenyon says: "David Green's biography of this difficult woman could not be bettered. He is witty, but never cynical, plainly in favor of the Duchess, but never sentimental about her or willing to accept her at her own valuation; and he contrives to hold our interest through endless pages of wrangling about nothing. He is working in the shadow of Sir Winston Churchill, whose massive biography of the Duke of Marlborough also dealt very thoroughly with his wife, but he sustains the inevitable comparison with ease."

Green told *CA:* "Specially fond of France, the French, and their cooking. Dote on Gertrude Stein, Robert Frost, and Emily Dickinson." *Avocational interests:* Ornithology, and seventeenth- and eighteenth-century architecture.

*   *   *

GREEN, Edward   1920-

PERSONAL: Born February 28, 1920, in New York, N.Y.; son of Harry (a teacher) and Sadie (Wildfeuer) Green; married Evelyn Gershenhorn, October 20, 1946; children: Roslyn, Mark, Jonathan, David. *Education:* Kent State University, student, 1937-39; Ohio State University, student, 1939-40; University of Pennsylvania, B.A., 1949, A.M., 1950, Ph.D., 1959. *Home:* 808 Cornell Rd., Ypsilanti, Mich.

CAREER: Mount Holyoke College, South Hadley, Mass., instructor in sociology, 1950-51; Beaver College, Glenside, Pa., 1951-62, started as assistant professor, became professor of sociology; University of South Florida, Tampa, professor of sociology, 1962-63; Eastern Michigan University, professor of sociology, 1963—, chairman of department, 1968—. *Military service:* U.S. Marine Corps, 1941-46. *Member:* American Sociological Association, International Society of Criminology, American Society of Criminology. *Awards, honors:* Social Science Research Council grants, 1961, 1963, and 1965; Meyer Research Institute for Law Research, grant, 1967-68; U.S. Department of Health, Education, and Welfare, grant, 1971-72.

WRITINGS: Judicial Attitudes in Sentencing, Macmillan, 1961. Contributor to *Journal of Criminal Law, Criminology and Police Science* and *American Journal of Correction*.

WORK IN PROGRESS: Studies in the social psychology of judicial activity.†

GREEN, Gerald 1922-

PERSONAL: Born April 8, 1922, in Brooklyn, N.Y.; son of Samuel (a doctor) and Anna Ruth (Matzkin) Greenberg; married Marie Pomposelli, November 9, 1950; children: Nancy, Theodore, David. *Education:* Columbia University, A.B., 1942, M.S. (journalism), 1947. *Politics:* Democrat. *Religion:* Jewish. *Residence:* Stamford, Conn. *Agent:* Scott Meredith Literary Agency, Inc., 580 Fifth Ave., New York, N.Y. 10036.

CAREER: International News Service, New York, N.Y., editor, 1947-50; National Broadcasting Co. Television News, New York, N.Y., producer and writer, 1950—, with programs including "Today," "Wide Wide World," "Chet Huntley Reporting," and a number of documentaries. Columbia University, John Jay associate. *Military service:* U.S. Army, Ordnance, 1942-46; served with Armed Forces Network in Germany; became sergeant. *Member:* Authors League of America, Writers Guild of America—East, P.E.N., Phi Beta Kappa. *Awards, honors:* Alumni Award, Columbia University School of Journalism, 1957.

WRITINGS: (With L. Klingman) *His Majesty O'Keefe*, Scribner, 1948; *The Sword and the Sun*, Scribner, 1950; *The Last Angry Man*, Scribner, 1957; *The Lotus Eaters*, Scribner, 1959; *The Heartless Light*, Scribner, 1961; *The Portofino PTA*, Scribner, 1962; *The Legion of Noble Christians; or, The Sweeney Survey*, Trident, 1965; (with Drew Pearson) *The Senator*, Doubleday, 1968; *To Brooklyn With Love* (Book of the Month Club selection), Trident, 1968; *The Artists of Terezin*, Hawthorn, 1969; *Faking It; or, The Wrong Hungarian*, Trident, 1971; *The Stones of Zion: A Novelist's Journal in Israel*, Hawthorn, 1971; *Blockbuster*, Doubleday, 1972; *Tourist*, Doubleday, 1973. Wrote screenplay based on *The Last Angry Man* for picture with the same title, released in 1958.

SIDELIGHTS: Green speaks and reads French and Italian. He lived in Italy, 1959-60 and currently is living in France.†

* * *

GREEN, Harold P(aul) 1922-

PERSONAL: Born February 23, 1922, in Wilkes-Barre, Pa.; married Pauline Goldstein, March 1, 1946; children: Nancy Jo, Philip D., Ellen F. *Education:* University of Chicago, A.B., 1942, J.D., 1948. *Politics:* Democrat. *Office:* 600 New Hampshire Ave. N.W., Washington, D.C. 20006.

CAREER: Admitted to bar of Illinois, 1949, District of Columbia, 1954, Maryland, 1960. Fried, Frank, Harris, Shriver & Kampelman (law firm), Washington, D.C., partner, 1961—; George Washington University, National Law Center, Washington, D.C., professor, 1964—. *Military service:* U.S. Army, 1943-46; became technical sergeant. *Member:* American Bar Association, Federal Bar Association, District of Columbia Bar Association. *Awards, honors:* Order of the Coif.

WRITINGS: (With Alan Rosenthal) *Government of the Atom: The Integration of Powers*, Atherton, 1963. Contributor of articles on government security problems and legal aspects of atomic energy to law reviews and science journals.

WORK IN PROGRESS: Research on the relationships between law, government, science, and technology.

GREEN, Joseph F(ranklin), Jr. 1924-

PERSONAL: Born 1924, in Waco, Tex.; son of Joseph F. and Nell (Kilby) Green; married Mary Jane Stowell, 1949; children: Mary Lynn, Carol Ann. *Education:* Texas Wesleyan College, B.S., 1947; Southwestern Baptist Theological Seminary, B.D., 1949, Th.D., 1961; Baylor University, M.A. (with honor), 1951. *Home:* 419 Barrywood Dr., Nashville, Tenn. 37211. *Office:* Broadman Press, 127 Ninth Ave. N., Nashville, Tenn. 37234.

CAREER: Ordained Baptist minister, 1942; pastor in Thorndale, Tex., 1951-52, Alamosa, Colo., 1952-54; Baylor University, Waco, Tex., instructor in religion, 1952; Broadman Press, Nashville, Tenn., general book editor, 1954-65, editor of specialized books, 1965-70, supervisor, books section, 1970—. *Military service:* U.S. Army, 1943-46.

WRITINGS: *Faith to Grow On*, Broadman, 1960; (with Janie Green) *God Wants You*, Convention, 1966; (with Edmond D. Keith) *Know Your Hymns No. 2*, Convention, 1966; *Biblical Foundations for Church Music*, Convention, 1967; *The Heart of the Gospel*, Broadman, 1968; *The Bible's Secret of Full Happiness*, Broadman, 1970. Contributor to Baptist journals.

WORK IN PROGRESS: Articles for journals.

* * *

GREEN, Leslie Claude 1920-

PERSONAL: Born November 6, 1920, in London, England; son of Willie and Raie (Goldberg) Green; married Lilian Denise Meyer, September 1, 1945; children: Anne Roslyn. *Education:* University College, London, LL.B. (first class honors), 1941. *Home:* 7911 119 St., Edmonton, Alberta, Canada. *Office:* Department of Political Science, University of Alberta, Edmonton, Alberta, Canada.

CAREER: University of London, University College, London, England, lecturer in international law and relations, 1949-60; University of Singapore, Singapore, Malaysia, professor of international law, 1960-65, director of Institute of Advanced Legal Studies, dean of Faculty of Law; University of Alberta, Edmonton, professor of political science, 1965-69, University professor, 1969—. Academic in residence, Legal Division, Department of Foreign Affairs, Canada, 1974-75; visiting professor at universities in Australia, Europe, India, Ethiopia, Israel, Canada, Latin America, and United States. *Military service:* British Army, 1941-46; Japanese translator and military prosecutor, General Headquarters, India, and deputy assistant adjutant general; became major. *Member:* International Law Association, International Commission of Jurists, Canadian Institute of International Affairs, Society of International and Comparative Law, London Institute of World Affairs (secretary, 1947-60), American Society of International Law. *Awards, honors:* Grotius Medal, 1956.

WRITINGS: (Editor) *Chen's International Law of Recognition*, Stevens & Sons, 1951; *International Law Through the Cases*, Praeger, 1951, 2nd edition, 1959. Contributor of articles to legal and other journals. Assistant editor of "Library of World Affairs," and *Year Book of World Affairs*, 1947-60.

WORK IN PROGRESS: *Problems of Asylum*; *Terrorism, Human Rights and Military Law*.

SIDELIGHTS: Competent in French; reads German, Italian, and Spanish.

GREEN, Maurice R(ichard)   1922-

PERSONAL: Born October 28, 1922; son of Solomon (a pharmacist) and Anna Teresa (Zawadska) Green; married Amelia Heilbron; children: Melissa Ann, Suzanne Elizabeth, Constance Amelia. *Education:* Northwestern University, B.S., 1942, B.M., 1945, M.D., 1946. *Religion:* Unitarian Universalist. *Home:* 162 East 80th St., New York, N.Y. 10021. *Agent:* Mary Yost Associates, 141 East 55th St., New York, N.Y. 10022. *Office:* William Alanson White Institute, 20 West 64th St., New York, N.Y.

CAREER: William Alanson White Institute, New York, N.Y., associate faculty, 1955—, clinical supervisor, 1962—, training psychoanalyst, 1964—. Bellevue Hospital, New York, N.Y., assistant attending physician, 1962—; New York University, New York, N.Y., clinical assistant professor, 1965—. Bleuler Psychotherapy Center, consultant supervisor. Spring Lake Ranch, trustee. *Military service:* U.S. Army, Medical Corps, 1946-48; chief neuropsychiatrist, 221st Hospital Ship; became captain; received two citations.

MEMBER: American Psychiatric Association (fellow), Academy of Psychoanalysis (fellow), American Association for the Advancement of Science (fellow), American Orthopsychiatric Association, American Medical Association, World Federation for Mental Health, New York State Medical Society, New York Academy of Sciences, New York Council for Child Psychiatry, Medical Society of the County of New York, William Alanson White Psychoanalytic Society, Phi Beta Kappa.

WRITINGS: (With Edward S. Tauber) *Prelogical Experience*, Basic Books, 1959; (contributor) *Cry for Help*, McGraw, 1961; (contributor) *Psychosomatic Obstetrics, Gynecology and Endocrinology*, edited by William S. Kroger, C. C Thomas, 1962; (editor) *Interpersonal Psychoanalysis*, Basic Books, 1964. Contributor to *American Handbook of Psychiatry*, and to *Military Surgeon, Pediatrics, Psychiatric Quarterly*, and other medical journals.

WORK IN PROGRESS: Prelogical Experience and Dreaming—Interpretation and Clinical Use; other writing on social psychiatry and child psychiatry.†

*   *   *

GREENBERG, Moshe   1928-

PERSONAL: Born July 10, 1928, in Philadelphia, Pa.; son of Simon (a rabbi) and Betty (Davis) Greenberg; married Evelyn Gelber, June 21, 1949; children: Joel, Raphael, Ethan. *Education:* University of Pennsylvania, A.B., 1949, Ph.D., 1954; Jewish Theological Seminary of America, Master of Hebrew Literature, 1954. *Religion:* Jewish. *Home:* 29 Mitudela St., Jerusalem, Israel.

CAREER: University of Pennsylvania, Philadelphia, assistant professor of Hebrew, 1954-65, A. M. Ellis Professor of Hebrew and Semitic Languages and Literatures, 1965-70; Hebrew University of Jerusalem, Jerusalem, Israel, professor of Bible, 1970—. *Member:* American Oriental Society, Society of Biblical Literature, Biblical Colloquium.

WRITINGS: The Hab-piru, American Oriental Society, 1955, 2nd edition, 1962; (abridger and translator) Jecheskel Kaufmann, *The Religion of Israel*, University of Chicago Press, 1960, revised edition, 1963; *Introduction to Hebrew*, Prentice-Hall, 1964; *Understanding Exodus, part 1*, Behrman House, 1969. Member of Bible translation committee of the Jewish Publication Society of America, 1966—.

WORK IN PROGRESS: Writing introduction and commentary, and translating Ezekiel for Anchor Bible (Doubleday).

*   *   *

GREENBURG, Dan   1936-

PERSONAL: Born June 20, 1936, in Chicago, Ill.; son of Samuel (an artist) and Leah (Rozalsky) Greenburg; married Nora Ephron (a journalist), April 9, 1967. *Education:* University of Illinois, B.F.A., 1958; University of California at Los Angeles, M.A., 1960. *Politics:* Democrat. *Religion:* Jewish. *Home and office:* 346 East 19th St., New York, N.Y. 10003. *Agent:* Ann Elmo Agency, Inc., 545 Fifth Ave., New York, N.Y. 10017; and Sam Gelfman, General Artists Corp., 640 Fifth Ave., New York, N.Y. 10017.

CAREER: Lansdale Co. (advertising agency), Los Angeles, Calif., copywriter, 1960-61; Carson/Roberts (advertising agency), Los Angeles, Calif., copywriter, 1961-62; *Eros* Magazine, New York, N.Y., managing editor, 1962-63; Papert, Koenig, Lois (advertising agency), New York, N.Y., copywriter, 1963-65; full-time writer, 1965—. *Member:* Authors Guild, Authors League. *Awards, honors:* Playboy Magazine prize for best humorous piece published in 1964, for condensation of *How To Be a Jewish Mother*; Advertising Writers Association of New York Silver Key Awards, 1964 and 1972.

WRITINGS: How To Be a Jewish Mother, Price/Stern/Sloan, 1964; *Kiss My Firm But Pliant Lips*, Grossman Publishers, 1965; (with Marcia Jacobs) *How to Make Yourself Miserable: Another Vital Training Manual*, Random House, 1966; *Chewsday: A Sex Novel*, Stein & Day, 1968; *Jumbo the Boy and Arnold The Elephant* (children's book), Bobbs-Merrill, 1969; *Philly* (novel), Simon & Schuster, 1969; *Porno-Graphics: The Shame of Our Art Museums* (humor), Random House, 1969; *Scoring: A Sexual Memoir*, Doubleday, 1972.

Plays: "How To Be a Jewish Mother" (adapted from his book), first produced in New York at Hudson Theatre, December 28, 1967; "Arf" and "The Great Airplane Snatch" (both one-act), first produced in New York at Stage 73 Theatre, May 27, 1969; (contributor with others) Kenneth Tynan, compiler, *Oh! Calcutta!* (first produced in New York at Eden Theatre, June 18, 1969), Grove, 1969.

Also author of screenplays, "Live a Little, Love a Little" (adapted from *Kiss My Firm But Pliant Lips*), "Chewsday," "Philly," "California Safari," and "I Could Never Have Sex With Any Man Who Has So Little Regard for My Husband."

Work represented in many anthologies, including *Twentieth Century Parody: American and British, Twelfth Anniversary Playboy Reader*, and *Esquire's World of Humor*. Contributor to *Playboy, Esquire, Monocle*, and *Eros*.

WORK IN PROGRESS: A play; a novel; and a screenplay.

SIDELIGHTS: Has traveled to Israel and Europe, 1954 and 1962. Speaks French and Hebrew haltingly.

BIOGRAPHICAL/CRITICAL SOURCES: Playboy, February, 1965.†

*   *   *

GREENE, Gael

PERSONAL: Born in Detroit, Mich.; daughter of Nathaniel Robert and Saralee (Gilbert) Greene. *Education:*

University of Michigan, B.A., 1956. *Agent:* Don Congdon, Harold Matson Co., Inc., 22 East 40th Street, New York, N.Y. 10016.

CAREER: United Press International, New York, N.Y., reporter, 1956-57; *New York Post*, New York, N.Y., reporter, 1957-61; free-lance writer, 1961—. *Awards, honors:* New York Newspaper Women's award for best feature writing, 1958; *Mademoiselle* Merit Award as young woman of the year in journalism, 1959.

WRITINGS: Don't Come Back Without It, Simon & Schuster, 1960; *Sex and the College Girl*, Delacorte, 1964; *Bite: A New York Restaurant Strategy*, Norton, 1972. Contributor to *McCall's, Cosmopolitan, Saturday Evening Post, Ladies' Home Journal, Mademoiselle.* Contributing editor (restaurant critic), *New York Magazine*, 1969—.

*　　*　　*

GREENE, Graham 1904-

PERSONAL: Born October 2, 1904, in Berkhamsted, Hertfordshire, England; son of Charles Henry (headmaster of Berkhamstead School) and Marion Raymond (Greene) Greene; married Vivien Dayrell Browning, 1927; children: one son, one daughter. *Education:* Attended Berkhamstead School; attended Balliol College, Oxford, 1922-25. *Religion:* Catholic convert, 1926. *Home address:* 9 Bow St., London W.C. 2, England.

CAREER: Times, London, England, sub-editor, 1926-30; film critic for *Night and Day* during the thirties; *Spectator*, London, England, film critic, 1935-39, literary editor, 1940-41; with Foreign Office in Africa, 1941-44; Eyre & Spottiswoode Ltd. (publishers), London, England, director, 1944-48; Indo-China correspondent for *New Republic*, 1954; Bodley Head (publishers), London, England, director, 1958-68. *Awards, honors:* Hawthornden Prize, 1940, for *The Labyrinthine Ways (The Power and the Glory)*; James Tait Black Memorial Prize, 1949, for *The Heart of the Matter*; Catholic Literary Award, 1952, for *The End of the Affair*; Boys' Clubs of America Junior Book Award, 1955, for *The Little Horse Bus*; Pietzak Award (Poland), 1960; Litt.D., Cambridge University, 1962; Balliol College, Oxford, honorary fellow, 1963; Royal Society of Literature Prize; Companion of Honour, 1966; D.Litt., University of Edinburgh, 1967; Legion d'Honneur, chevalier, 1969.

WRITINGS—Fiction, except as indicated: *Babbling April* (poems), Basil Blackwell, 1925; *The Man Within*, Doubleday, 1929; *The Name of Action*, Heinemann, 1930, Doubleday, 1931; *Rumour at Nightfall*, Heinemann, 1931, Doubleday, 1932; *Orient Express*, Doubleday, 1932 (published in England as *Stamboul Train*, Heinemann, 1932); *It's a Battlefield*, Doubleday, 1934, reissued with new introduction by author, Heinemann & Bodley Head, 1970; *Basement Room, and Other Stories*, Cresset, 1935 ("Basement Room" revised and entitled "The Fallen Idol" published in *The Third Man* [and] *The Fallen Idol*, Heinemann, 1950); *England Made Me*, Doubleday, 1935, reissued as *The Shipwrecked*, Viking, 1953, reissued under original title with new introduction by author, Heinemann & Bodley Head, 1970; *The Bear Fell Free*, Grayson & Grayson, 1935; *Journey Without Maps* (travel), Doubleday, 1936, 2nd edition, Viking, 1961; *This Gun for Hire*, Doubleday, 1936 (published in England as *A Gun for Sale*, Heinemann, 1936); *Brighton Rock*, Viking, 1938, reissued with new introduction by author, Heinemann & Bodley Head, 1970; *The Confidential Agent*, Viking, 1939, reissued with new introduction by author, Heinemann & Bodley Head, 1971; *Another Mexico*, Viking, 1939 (published in England as *The Lawless Roads*, Longmans, Green, 1939).

The Labyrinthine Ways, Viking, 1940 (published in England as *The Power and the Glory*, Heinemann, 1940), reissued under British title, Viking, 1946, reissued under British title with new introduction by author, Heinemann & Bodley Head, 1971; *British Dramatists* (nonfiction), Collins, 1942; *The Ministry of Fear*, Viking, 1943; *Nineteen Stories*, Heinemann, 1947, Viking, 1949, later published with some substitutions and additions as *Twenty-one Stories*, Heinemann, 1955, Viking, 1962; *The Heart of the Matter*, Viking, 1948, reissued with new introduction by author, Heinemann & Bodley Head, 1971; *The Third Man*, Viking, 1950; *The Lost Childhood, and Other Essays*, Eyre & Spottiswoode, 1951, Viking, 1952; *The End of the Affair*, Viking, 1951; *The Living Room* (play in two acts), Heinemann, 1953, Viking, 1957; *The Quiet American*, Heinemann, 1955, Viking, 1956; *Loser Takes All*, Heinemann, 1955, Viking, 1957; *The Potting Shed* (play in three acts; first produced, 1957), Viking, 1957; *Our Man in Havana*, Viking, 1958, reissued with new introduction by author, Heinemann & Bodley Head, 1970; *The Complaisant Lover* (play; first produced, 1959), Heinemann, 1959, Viking, 1961; *A Visit to Moran* (short story), Heinemann, 1959.

A Burnt-Out Case, Viking, 1961; *In Search of a Character: Two African Journals*, Bodley Head, 1961, Viking, 1962; *Introductions to Three Novels*, Norstedt (Stockholm), 1962; *The Destructors, and Other Stories*, Eihosha Ltd. (Japan), 1962; *A Sense of Reality*, Viking, 1963; *Carving a Statue* (play in two acts; first produced, 1968), Bodley Head, 1964; *The Comedians*, Viking, 1966; (with Dorothy Craigie) *Victorian Detective Fiction: A Catalogue of the Collection*, Bodley Head, 1966; *May We Borrow Your Husband? And Other Comedies of the Sexual Life*, Viking, 1967; (with Carol Reed) *The Third Man: A Film* (annotated filmscript), Simon & Schuster, 1968; *Travels With My Aunt*, Viking, 1969; *Collected Essays*, Viking, 1969; (author of introduction) Al Burt and Bernard Diederich, *Papa Doc*, McGraw, 1969; *A Sort of Life* (autobiography), Simon & Schuster, 1971; *Graham Greene on Film: Collected Film Criticism, 1935-1940*, Simon & Schuster, 1972 (published in England as *The Pleasure Dome*, Secker & Warburg, 1972); *The Portable Graham Greene*, includes *The Heart of the Matter*, with a new chapter, *The Third Man*, sections from eight other novels, six short stories, nine critical essays, and ten public statements, Viking, 1972; *The Honorary Consul*, Simon & Schuster, 1973; *Collected Stories*, Viking, 1973.

Omnibus volumes: *3: This Gun for Hire; The Confidential Agent; The Ministry of Fear*, Viking, 1952, reissued as *Three by Graham Greene: This Gun for Hire; Confidential Agent; The Ministry of Fear*, 1958; *Three Plays*, Mercury Books, 1961; *The Travel Books: Journey Without Maps* [and] *The Lawless Roads*, Heinemann, 1963; *Triple Pursuit: A Graham Greene Omnibus*, includes *This Gun for Hire, The Third Man, Our Man in Havana*, Viking, 1971.

Juvenile books: *This Little Fire Engine*, Parrish, 1950 published as *The Little Red Fire Engine*, Lee & Shepard, 1952; *The Little Horse Bus*, Parrish, 1952, Lothrop, Lee & Shepard, 1954; *The Little Steamroller*, Lothrop, Lee & Shepard, 1955; *The Little Train*, Parrish, 1957, Lothrop, Lee & Shepard, 1958.

Editor: *The Old School* (essays), J. Cape, 1934; H. H. Munro, *The Best of Saki*, 2nd edition, Lane, 1952; (with borther, Hugh Greene) *The Spy's Bedside Book*, British Book Service, 1957; (author of introduction) Marjorie Bowen, *The Viper of Milan*, Bodley Head, 1960; *The Bodly Head Ford Madox Ford*, Volumes I and II, Bodley Head, 1962.

Contributor: *24 Short Stories*, Cresset, 1939; *Alfred Hitchcock's Fireside Book of Suspense*, Simon & Schuster, 1947; *Why Do I Write?*, Percival Marshall, 1948. Contributor to *Esquire*, *Commonweal*, *Spectator*, *Playboy*, *Saturday Evening Post*, *New Statesman*, *Atlantic*, *London Mercury*, *New Republic*, *America*, *Life*, and other publications.

SIDELIGHTS: To open a novel by Graham Greene is to risk an encounter with "a faint smell of sulphur." Evil is everywhere, evil wins; innocence is suspect. Arthur Calder-Marshall believes "it is this conviction of evil which gives to [Greene's] work its intensity. The prose, carefully free from direct comment, is vivid with comment metaphors, which build up the atmosphere of horror, disgust, evil, terror, loneliness." His characters live "on the border between love and hate, good and evil, heaven and hell," writes Francis L. Kunkel. A. A. DeVitis notes that Greene's characters are "the seedy, the unlikable, the unhappy—those in whom he feels the strange power of God." He has taken innate evil for his background, and, according to Sean O'Faolain, "lives vicariously the broken lives of the betrayed ones of the earth."

In Greene's novels the only way out of this morass of evil is faith in God and in divine mercy. Much has been made of Greene, the Catholic novelist. But he is no theologian. Calder-Marshall writes: "What the philosophy is, it is impossible to extract from the novels; because it *is* the novels." Greene himself says: "I would claim not to be a writer of Catholic novels, but a writer who in four or five books took characters with Catholic ideas for his material. Nonetheless for years—particularly after *The Heart of the Matter*—I found myself hunted by people who wanted help with spiritual problems that I was incapable of giving. Not a few of these were priests themselves." In a letter to Elizabeth Bowen and V. S. Pritchett he wrote: "I belong to a group, the Catholic Church, which would present me with grave problems as a writer were I not saved by my disloyalty. If my conscience were as acute as M. Mauriac's showed itself to be in his essay *God and Mammon*, I could not write a line." More recently he told *Life* magazine: "I'm not a religious man, though it interests me. Of all my books only four are about Catholicism. Religion is important, as atomic science is.

Included among his works are a number of entertainments or thrillers which many of his readers believe to be his finest books. He likes to write these because he says they "vent my penchant for melodrama." Critics believe the entertainments were originally a response to the spirit of the thirties. Morton Dauwen Zabel notes that "since the social and political conditions of the age had . . . reverted to primitive forms of violence, brutality, and anarchy he found his purpose matched in the events of the historic moment. For that moment the thriller was an obvious and logical imaginative medium, and Greene proceeded to raise it to a skill and artistry few other writers of the period, and none in English, had arrived at." His entertainments are based on contemporary life and on the daily newspapers. "I am journalistically minded," he says. "And I want to see the dead body, and not just read about it." However, unlike the ordinary thriller-writer, "Greene uses the detective

story to dramatize a moral problem of far-reaching significance," writes Kunkel. The result is what Zabel calls "collaboration between realism and spritiuality." In 1941 Charles A. Brady wrote: "Only Graham Greene, among contemporary melodramatists, fights the battle of Augustine in the mantle of Buchan and Conrad and Dostoievski."

Walter Allen believes Greene "has learnt much of his narrative art from Stevenson [a distant relative] and Conrad but not less from the film. . . . He shares with Auden a common symbolism of frontiers, spies and betrayal; and his prose, at any rate in individual phrases and images, is the nearest equivalent we have to Auden's verse." Greene thinks the writers having most effect on him were Ford Madox Ford, Joseph Conrad, and Henry James, who was his idol. But to say James influenced him is "a bit absurd," he told *Life*. "Like saying a mountain influenced a mouse." After the publication of *The Power and the Glory*, his own favorite among his books, Zabel wrote: "[Greene's] skill already puts him in the descent of the modern masters—James, Conrad, Joyce—in whom judgment and imagination achieved their richest combination, as well as in the company of the few living novelists—Mauriac, Malraux, Hemingway, Faulkner—in whom their standard survives."

Of *The Honorary Consul* a *Times Literary Supplement* reviewer wrote: "*The Honorary Consul* belongs with the successes. It is in the familiar mainstream of Greene's work, a melodramatic novel with more than melodramatic meaning, a mixture of violent action and religious speculation that is simply what Greene does best. It is not new, in the sense of a formal departure from customary methods (as *Travels With My Aunt* was new), but neither is it simply more of the same: it establishes the idea of "the great Church beyond our time and place," it develops the theme of love beyond earlier expressions, and it deals elaborately with the concept of Fatherhood. It is wiser and less angry about politics than *The Quiet American* was. In all these ways the new novel extends and clarifies our understanding of Greene's imagined world, not only the world of this book, but the whole canon. For the later work of a major artist is always a further explanation of the earlier work, a new survey of old territories. So this story of a priest and a policeman will affect the way we read *The Power and the Glory*, and this sexual betrayal will touch *The End of the Affair* and *The Heart of the Matter* and *The Comedians*. Its appearance is an important event in the world of Greene, which is our world, too."

In 1970, film rights were purchased for "May We Borrow Your Husband?," and, in 1971, *The End of the Affair* was filmed for television.

Screenplays based on his books and stories: "Orient Express," 1934; "This Gun for Hire," 1942; "The Ministry of Fear," 1944; "The Confidential Agent," 1945; "The Smugglers," 1948; "Brighton Rock," 1948; "The Fallen Idol," screenplay by Greene, 1949; "The Third Man," screenplay by Greene, 1950; "The Heart of the Matter," 1954; "The End of the Affair," 1955; "Loser Takes All," 1957; "The Quiet American," 1958; "Across the Bridge," 1958; "Our Man in Havana," screenplay by Greene, 1960; "The Power and the Glory," 1962; "The Comedians," screenplay by Greene, 1967; "The Living Room," 1969; "The Shipwrecked," 1970; "Travels with My Aunt," 1973; "England Made Me," 1973; "A Burned-Out Case," 1973.

BIOGRAPHICAL/CRITICAL SOURCES: America, January 25, 1941; *Living Writers*, Sylvan Press, 1947; Henry Reed, *The Novel Since 1939*, Longmans, Green,

1947; Paul Rostenne, *Graham Greene: Temoin des temps tragiques*, Julliard, 1949; Kenneth Allott and Miriam Farris, *The Art of Graham Greene*, Hamish Hamilton, 1951, Russell & Russell, 1965; P. H. Newby, *The Novel: 1945-1950*, Longmans, Green, 1951; Orville Prescott, *In My Opinion*, Bobbs-Merrill, 1952; Francois Mauriac, *Great Men*, Rockliff, 1952; Maire-Beatrice Mesnet, *Graham Greene and the Heart of the Matter*, Cresset, 1954; Francis Wyndham, *Graham Greene*, Longmans, Green, 1955; Sean O'Faolain, *The Vanishing Hero*, Atlantic Monthly Press, 1956; Morton Dauwen Zabel, *Craft and Character in Modern Fiction*, Viking, 1957; John Atkins, *Graham Greene*, Roy, 1958; William R. Mueller, *The Prophetic Voice in Modern Fiction*, Association Press, 1959; Francis L. Kunkel, *The Labyrinthine Ways of Graham Greene*, Sheed, 1959; Frank Kermode, *Puzzles and Epiphanies*, Chilmark, 1962; R. O. Evans, editor, *Graham Greene: Some Critical Considerations*, University of Kentucky Press, 1963; Philip Stratford, *Faith and Fiction*, University of Notre Dame Press, 1964; L. A. DeVitis, *Graham Greene*, Twayne, 1964; Walter Allen, *The Modern Novel*, Dutton, 1965; *New York Times Book Review*, January 23, 1966; *Times Literary Supplement*, January 27, 1966; *Life*, February 4, 1966; *New York Review of Books*, March 3, 1966; David Lodge, *Graham Greene*, Columbia University Press, 1966; Carolyn Riley, editor, *Contemporary Literary Criticism,* Gale, Volume I, 1973, Volume III, 1975.

*   *   *

GREENE, Harris (Carl)   1921-

PERSONAL: Born October 22, 1921, in Waltham, Mass.; son of Benjamin and Sara (Krongard) Greene; married Charlotte Wolk, October 5, 1943; children: Sharon Elizabeth (Mrs. Anthony Erdmann), Deborah Ann. *Education:* Boston University, B.S., 1943; Lehigh University, graduate study, 1943-44; George Washington University, graduate study, 1950-51. *Home:* 3671 North Harrison St., Arlington, Va. 22207.

CAREER: Boston Herald Traveler, Boston, Mass., researcher and reporter, 1942-43; U.S. Department of State, 1950—, vice-consul in Genoa and Rome, Italy, 1950-51, embassy attache in Athens, Greece, 1964-68, first secretary of embassy in Berne, Switzerland, 1969-73. *Military service:* U.S. Army, 1943-46. *Member:* Authors Guild. *Awards, honors:* Macdowell Colony fellowship, 1966, 1971.

WRITINGS: The 'Mozart' Leaves at Nine, Doubleday, 1960; *The Flags at Doney*, Doubleday, 1964; *The Thieves of Tumbutu*, Doubleday, 1968; *Cancelled Accounts*, Doubleday, 1973.

WORK IN PROGRESS: Another book.

*   *   *

GREENE, Lee S(eifert)   1905-

PERSONAL: Born May 31, 1905, in Esbon, Kan.; son of Eugene C. and Margaret (Cline) Greene; married Dorothy Kuersteiner, December 24, 1932; children: Harriet Greene Hitch, Robert Everist. *Education:* University of Kansas, B.M., 1927, A.B., 1930; University of Leipzig, graduate study, 1930-31; University of Wisconsin, M.A., 1932, Ph.D., 1934; also studied at Brookings Institution, 1933-34 and University of Michigan, 1935. *Home:* 1410 Tugaloo Drive, Knoxville, Tenn. *Office:* University of Tennessee, Department of Political Science, Knoxville, Tenn.

CAREER: University of Kansas, Lawrence, instructor in music, 1926-30; University of Wisconsin, Madison, instructor in political science, 1934-36; Tennessee Valley Authority, Knoxville, research associate, supervisor of public administration, 1936-37, 1938-41, University of Tennessee, Knoxville, lecturer, 1937, assistant professor, 1938-39, associate professor, 1939-45, professor of political science, 1945-64, distinguished service professor, 1964—, acting head of department, 1942-46, head of department, 1946-71, director, Bureau of Public Administration, 1945-71. Visiting professor, University of Alabama, University of Georgia, University of California at Los Angeles, Syracuse University, and Duke University. Executive director, Community Services Commission, Nashville, Tenn., 1951-52, and Harris County Home Rule Commission, Houston, Tex., 1956-57; executive secretary, Knoxville-Knox County Metropolitan Charter Commission, Nashville, Tenn., 1957-59; Civil Service Board, Knoxville, member, 1941-47, chairman, 1945-47; member, Southern Regional Education Board, 1952-53; member, Foreign Operations Administration, 1954; chairman of research committee, Tennessee Constitutional Convention, 1953; public panel member or labor arbitrator for National War Labor Board, National Wage Stabilization Board, U.S. Conciliation Service, Federal Mediation and Conciliation Service. *Member:* American Political Science Association (member of council, 1951-53), National Institute of Public Affairs (member of board of trustees, 1961-71), Southern Political Science Association (president, 1957-58), National Municipal League, Phi Beta Kappa, Phi Kappa Phi, Pi Kappa Lambda, Beta Theta Pi, Phi Mu Alpha, Masons.

WRITINGS: (With V. H. Brown and Evan A. Iverson) *Rescued Earth: The Public Administration of Natural Resources in Tennessee*, University of Tennessee Press, 1948; (editor with D. R. deV. Williamson) *Five Years of British Labour, 1945-50*, Kallman, 1950; *Resources and Policy*, Kallman, 1951; (with D. R. Grant) *A Future for Nashville*, Community Services Commission, 1952; (with Grant) *Metropolitan Harris County*, Home Rule Commission, 1957; (with R. S. Avery) *Government in Tennessee*, University of Tennessee Press, 1962, 3rd edition, 1975; (with George S. Parthemos) *American Government: Policies and Functions*, Scribners, 1967; (with Grant and Malcolm E. Jewell) *The States and the Metropolis*, University of Alabama Press, 1968; (with Parthemos and Thomas R. Dye) *American Government: Theory, Structure and Process*, Wadsworth, 1969, 2nd edition, Duxbury Press, 1972; (contributor) William C. Havard, editor, *The Changing Politics of the South*, Louisiana State University Press, 1972. Contributor to professional journals, both in this country and abroad. Associate editor, *Journal of Politics*, 1949-52, editor, 1953-57; special issue editor of *Annals* of the American Academy of Political and Social Science, 1962, 1964.

WORK IN PROGRESS: A study of politics in Tennessee, publication expected in 1976, and a political and administrative biography of Frank Goad Clement, 1977, both by University of Tennessee Press.

*   *   *

GREENE, William C.   1933-

PERSONAL: Born June 5, 1933, in Natick, Mass.; son of Whitney E. and Maud (Larsson) Greene; married Davis Crane, November 27, 1954; children: William, Jr., Bruce Boardman, Josephine Boardman, Winnie, Amy Larson. *Education:* Princeton University, B.A., 1954; Babson Institute, M.B.A., 1956; Harvard University, postgraduate study, 1957. *Politics:* Republican. *Religion:* Protestant. *Home:* Meadowbrook Rd., Dover, Mass. *Office:* Greene & Vecchi, 572 Washington St., Wellesley, Mass.

CAREER: Certified Public accountant, 1962—; McCann & Greene, Boston, Mass., partner, 1965-66; Greene & Vecchi, Wellesley, Mass., founder and partner, 1966—. Secretary, Dover School Committee, 1964—; member, Dover Town Republican Committee, 1964—. *Member:* American Institute of Certified Public Accountants, Charles River Watershed Association (treasurer), Massachusetts Society of Certified Public Accountants.

WRITINGS: Case Problems in Managerial Accounting, Holt, 1964. Contributor to professional journals. Associate editor and manager, *CPA Review*.

WORK IN PROGRESS: Text and Cases in Auditing; a "workshop in management of small business."

* * *

GREENHUT, Melvin L. 1921-

PERSONAL: Born March 10, 1921, in New York, N.Y.; son of Ab S. and Lillian (Frudman) Greenhut; married Elmara Griffith, March 24, 1944; children: Peggy, Pamela, John, Patricia. *Education:* Hofstra College, A.B. (cum laude), 1940; Washington University, St. Louis, Mo., M.A., 1947, Ph.D., 1951. *Religion:* Lutheran. *Home:* 2917 Lasswade Dr., Tallahassee, Fla.

CAREER: Auburn University, Auburn, Ala., assistant professor of economics, 1948-52; Mississippi State College, Starkeville, associate professor of economics, 1952-53; Rollins College, Winter Park, Fla., professor of business and economics, 1953-57; Florida State University, Tallahassee, professor of economics, 1957-59; University of Richmond, Richmond, Va., associate dean, School of Business, 1959-62; Florida State University, professor of economics, 1962-66; Texas A.&M. University, College Station, professor of economics and head of department, 1966-69, distinguished professor 1969—. Visiting professor, Michigan State University, 1963, University of Cape Town, 1971, University of Mannheim, University of Karlsruhe, and University of Muenster, 1972; consultant to Florida Development Commission, Southern Council of State Government, Atlantic Telephone & Telegraph, and other firms. U.S. Chamber of Commerce, member of Economic Policy Committee and Economic Advisory Council, 1961-62; Richmond Chamber of Commerce, member of Industrial Development Committee, 1962. *Military service:* U.S. Army, 1942-46. U.S. Army Reserve, 1946—; now major. *Member:* American Economic Association, Institute of Management Science, Southern Economic Association (executive committee, 1961-63), Regional Science Association.

WRITINGS: Plant Location in Theory and Practice, University of North Carolina Press, 1956; *Full Employment, Inflation and Common Stock*, Public Affairs, 1961; (with Frank Jackson) *Intermediate Income and Growth Theory*, Prentice-Hall, 1961; (with Marshall Colberg) *Factors in the Location of Florida Industry*, Florida State University Studies, 1962; *Microeconomics and the Space Economy*, Scott, 1963; (editor with Tate Whitman) *Essays on Southern Economic Development*, University of North Carolina Press, 1964; *A Theory of the Firm in Economic Space*, Appleton, 1970. Member of publications committee, Institute of Management Science, 1956-59.

WORK IN PROGRESS: Research on relations between linear programming and economic theory.†

GREENOUGH, William Croan 1914-

PERSONAL: Born July 27, 1914, in Indianapolis, Ind.; son of Walter S. and Katharine (Croan) Greenough; married Doris Decker, 1941; children: David William, Walter Croan, Martha Alice. *Education:* Indiana University, A.B., 1938; Harvard University, A.M., 1938, Ph.D., 1949. *Home:* 870 United Nations Plaza, New York, N.Y. 10017. *Office:* Teachers Insurance & Annuity Association, 730 Third Ave., New York, N.Y. 10017.

CAREER: Indiana University, Bloomington, assistant to dean and instructor in School of Business, 1937-38, assistant to president, 1938-40, personnel director, 1940-41; Teachers Insurance and Annuity Association of America, New York, N.Y., assistant to president, 1941-43, 1946-48, vice-president, 1948-55, executive vice-president, 1955-57, president, 1957-62, trustee, 1955—; Teachers Insurance & Annuity Association, College Retirement Equities Fund, New York, N.Y., vice-president, 1952-55, executive vice-president, 1955-57, president, 1957-62, trustee, 1954—, chairman and president, 1963-67, chairman and chief executive officer, 1967—. Member of executive committees of National Council on the Aging, 1955-64, of commission on faculty and staff benefits, Association of American Colleges, 1958-64, of joint committee of the Retired Professors Registry, 1958-63, of National Civil Service League, 1959-63, of commission on students and faculty, 1964-66; Civil Service Reform Association, chairman of executive committee, 1957-59, president, 1959-63. Trustee of Bennington College (and chairman of finance committee), 1955-62, of Foundation Library Center, 1961-67, of Indiana University Foundation, 1964—, of Russell Sage Foundation, 1967—, of Aspen Institute for Humanistic Studies, 1970—; member of board of directors of New York Stock Exchange, 1972—. *Military service:* U.S. Navy, 1943-45; became lieutenant; received Bronze Star.

MEMBER: American Economic Association, American Finance Association, American Pension Conference, American Risk and Insurance Association, Life Office Management Association (associate member), American Association of University Professors, Phi Beta Kappa, Phi Kappa Psi, Sigma Delta Chi; Century Association and Harvard Club (both New York). *Awards, honors:* Distinguished Alumni Service Award, Indiana University, 1960; Elizur Wright Award for contribution to insurance literature, 1961, for *A New Approach to Retirement Income*; L.L.D., Indiana University, 1965.

WRITINGS: College Retirement and Insurance Plans, Columbia University Press, 1948; *A New Approach to Retirement Income*, Teachers Insurance and Annuity Association, 1951; (editor) Rainard B. Robbins, *Pension Planning in the United States*, Teachers Insurance and Annuity Association, 1952; (with Francis P. King) *Retirement and Insurance Plans in American Colleges*, Columbia University Press, 1959; (with King) *Benefit Plans in American Colleges*, Columbia University Press, 1969. Contributor of articles on pensions and social security to periodicals.

WORK IN PROGRESS: A book, with King, *Private Pensions and Public Policy*.

* * *

GREEN-WANSTALL, Kenneth 1918-
(Ken Wanstall)

PERSONAL: Born June 13, 1918, in Leeds, England; son of Ambrose Clerk and Winifred (Green) Green-Wanstall;

married Florence Elizabeth Baker, July 30, 1938; children: John Martin. *Education:* Privately educated in England; also attended Eastbourne College. *Politics:* Conservative. *Religion:* Church of England. *Home:* Oaklea, Kingswear, Devonshire, England.

CAREER: Straits Times, Singapore, news editor for twenty-five years; now director of Torbay and Westcountry News and Pictures Ltd. (news agency), Brixham, Devonshire, England. Correspondent during World War II. *Member:* National Union of Journalists, Press Club (London), Royal Yachting Association, Brixham Yacht Club.

WRITINGS: (With David Roxan under name Ken Wanstall) *Jackdaw of Linz*, Cassell, 1964, published as *The Rape of Art: The Story of Hitler's Plunder of Great Masterpieces of Europe*, Coward, 1965. Contributor to British Broadcasting Corp. television program, "Tonight."

WORK IN PROGRESS: A book on the Singapore underworld.

AVOCATIONAL INTERESTS: Politics, yachting.†

* * *

GREET, T(homas) Y(oung) 1923-

PERSONAL: Born April 4, 1923, in Atlanta, Ga.; son of Loui and Jewel (Hooks) Greet. *Education:* Duke University, A.B., 1947; University of North Carolina, M.A., 1950; University of Wisconsin, graduate study, 1956-60. *Politics:* Democrat. *Home:* 306 North Main St., Lexington, Va. *Office:* English Department, Virginia Military Institute, Lexington, Va.

CAREER: Davidson College, Davidson, N.C., teacher of English, 1947-49; West Virginia University, Morgantown, teacher of English, 1950-55; bartender in Madison, Wis., and Chicago, Ill., 1957-60; University of North Carolina, Chapel Hill, instructor in English, 1960-63; Virginia Military Institute, Lexington, assistant professor of English, 1963—. Self-employed editorial consultant on fiction manuscripts. *Military service:* U.S. Army, Ordnance, 1942-45. *Member:* Modern Language Association of America.

WRITINGS: (Contributor) Hoffman and Vickery, *William Faulkner: Three Decades of Criticism*, Michigan State University Press, 1960; (editor with Charles Edge and John M. Munro) *Worlds of Fiction*, Houghton, 1964; (contributor) Linda Welsheimer Wagner, *William Faulkner: Four Decades of Criticism*, Michigan State University Press, 1973. Contributor to literary journals.

* * *

GREGG, Richard A(lexander) 1927-

PERSONAL: Born August 22, 1927, in Paris, France; son of Alan (a doctor) and Eleanor (Barrows) Gregg; married Francoise Bouriez (a teacher), June 5, 1953; children: Jonathan Alan. *Education:* Harvard University, A.B. (cum laude), 1951, M.A., 1952; Columbia University, Ph.D., 1962. *Politics:* Democrat. *Home:* 64 Boardman Rd., Poughkeepsie, N.Y. 12603.

CAREER: Amherst College, Amherst, Mass., instructor in Russian language, 1957-58; Brown University, Providence, R.I., instructor in Russian language and literature, 1959-60; Columbia University, New York, N.Y., instructor, 1960-62, assistant professor, 1962-65, associate professor, of Russian language and literature, 1965-69; Vassar College, Poughkeepsie, N.Y., professor of Russian language and literature, and chairman of department, 1969—. *Military*

service: U.S. Army Air Forces, 1946-47. *Member:* Modern Language Association of America, American Association for the Advancement of Slavic Studies. *Awards, honors:* Ford Foundation fellowship, 1956-57; U.S. Government fellow in Leningrad, 1958-59; Guggenheim fellowship for research in Europe, 1965-66.

WRITINGS: Theodore Tiutchev: The Evolution of a Poet, Columbia University Press, 1965. Contributor to *Harper's* and professional journals.

WORK IN PROGRESS: Research for a book on the Russian poet, N. A. Nekrasov (1821-77); a book on Alexander Pushkin (1799-1837).

* * *

GREGOR, Rex H. 1922-

PERSONAL: Born August 20, 1922, in Elgin, Minn.; son of Harold K. and Lotta (Johnson) Gregor; married Arlene Haugerud, 1949; children: Thomas, Sandra, Debra, John, Cheryl. *Education:* Studied at Ursinus College, 1944-45, University of Minnesota, 1945-48. *Politics:* Republican. *Religion:* Congregational. *Home:* 1015 15th St., N.E., Rochester, Minn. *Office:* Kahler Center Building, Rochester, Minn.

CAREER: Kahler Corp. Hospitals, Rochester, Minn., assistant administrator, 1948-54; Rochester Methodist Hospital, Rochester, Minn., director of purchases, 1954—; Josten's, Owatonna, Minn., director of medical services, 1964—. *Member:* Upper Midwest Association of Hospital Purchasing Agents, Rochester Chamber of Commerce, Kiwanis International. *Military service:* U.S. Navy and U.S. Marine Corps, 1942-45; received Silver Star.

WRITINGS: (With H. C. Mickey) *Procurement and Materials Management for Hospitals*, C. C Thomas, 1960. Writer of about twenty-five published papers and articles on purchasing and other hospital administration topics.

WORK IN PROGRESS: A historical novel.†

* * *

GRENE, Marjorie (Glicksman) 1910-

PERSONAL: Born December 13, 1910, in Milwaukee, Wis.; daughter of Harry (a professor of English) and Edna (Kerngood) Glicksman; divorced; children: Ruth, Nicholas. *Education:* Wellesley College, B.A., 1931; graduate study at University of Freiburg, 1931-32, at University of Heidelberg, 1932-33; Radcliffe College, M.A., 1934, Ph.D., 1935. *Home:* 835 F St., Davis, Calif. *Office:* Department of Philosophy, University of California, Davis, Calif.

CAREER: University of Chicago, Chicago, Ill., instructor in philosophy, 1937-44; University of Manchester, Manchester, England, research assistant, 1957-58; University of Leeds, Leeds, England, research fellow in education, 1958-59, lecturer in philosophy, 1959-60; The Queen's University of Belfast, Belfast, Northern Ireland, lecturer in philosophy, 1960-65; University of California, Davis, professor of philosophy, 1965—, faculty research lecturer, 1971. *Member:* American Philosophical Association (president of Pacific Division, 1971-72). *Awards, honors:* Alice Freeman Palmer Fellow, Wellesley College, 1935-36; Lucy Martin Donnelloy Fellow, Bryn Mawr College, 1960-61.

WRITINGS: (Editor with T. V. Smith) *From Descartes to Kant*, University of Chicago Press, 1940; *Dreadful Freedom, a Critique of Existentialism*, University of Chicago Press, 1948, published as *Introduction to Existentialism*,

University of Chicago Press, 1959; *Heidegger*, Hillary, 1957; *A Portrait of Aristotle*, University of Chicago Press, 1963; *The Knower and the Known*, Basic Books, 1969; *Approaches to a Philosophical Biology*, Basic Books, 1971; *Sartre*, F. Watts, 1973; (editor) *Spinoza*, Doubleday, 1973; *The Understanding of Nature: Essays in the Philosophy of Biology*, Reidel, in press. Contributor of articles and reviews to philosophy journals.

WORK IN PROGRESS: A book, *In and Out of Europe: Essays in Continental Philosophy*.

*　　*　　*

GREW, Raymond 1930-

PERSONAL: Born October 28, 1930, in San Jose, Calif.; son of David (a writer) and Claire (Kuykendall) Grew; married Daphne Merriam, August 16, 1952; children: Philip, Sarah, Douglas. *Education:* Harvard University, A.B., 1951, A.M., 1952, Ph.D., 1957. *Home:* 187 Barton Dr., Ann Arbor, Mich. *Office:* Department of History, University of Michigan, Ann Arbor, Mich.

CAREER: Brandeis University, Waltham, Mass., instructor in history, 1957-58; Princeton University, Princeton, N.J., instructor, 1958-59; assistant professor, 1959-64, Rollins Preceptor, 1961-64; University of Michigan, Ann Arbor, associate professor, 1964-69, professor of history, 1969—, director of Center for Western European Studies, 1969-71. *Member:* American Historical Association (secretary of Modern European section, 1973—), Society for French Historical Studies, Society for Italian Historical Studies (member of advisory committee, 1963-66), Council for European Studies (chairman, 1969). *Awards, honors:* Fulbright fellowship to Italy, 1954-55; first annual prize of Society for Italian Historical Studies, 1959; Chester Higby Prize of American Historical Association, 1962, for article in *Journal of Modern History*; American Philosophical Society grant, 1962-63; Unita d'Italia Prize from Italian government for *A Sterner Plan for Italian Unity: The Italian National Society in the Risorgimento*; Guggenheim fellowship, 1968.

WRITINGS: A Sterner Plan for Italian Unity: The Italian National Society in the Risorgimento, Princeton University Press, 1963; *The Western Experience*, Knopf, 1974.

WORK IN PROGRESS: Research in modern social history; in the role of the Church in the process of industrialization in France, Italy, and Spain, 1815-1870; and in social change and French education.

SIDELIGHTS: Grew speaks French, Italian, and Spanish, and reads German. *Avocational interests:* Travel with family in western Europe, hiking, and photography.

*　　*　　*

GRIFFEN, (James) Jeff(erds) 1923-

PERSONAL: Born October 11, 1923, in White Plains, N.Y.; son of Chauncey B. (a real estate man) and Florence (Hustis) Griffen. *Education:* Hamilton College, B.A., 1947; other courses at Columbia University and New York University, 1948-50. *Religion:* Unitarian Universalist. *Home:* 1131 North St., White Plains, N.Y. 10601. *Agent:* Jules Fields, 505 Fifth Ave., New York, N.Y.

CAREER: Before becoming a full-time free-lance writer in 1955, worked as a typewriter salesman, department store buyer, construction worker in Turkey, and newspaper reporter. Field trial judge (bird dogs). *Military service:* U.S. Army, French interpreter, 1943-46. *Member:* New York

State Bird Dog Association, Tennessee Walking Horse Breeders and Owners Association, Jockey Hollow Field Trial Club. *Awards, honors:* Dog Writers Association of America Award for best dog book of the year, for *The Hunting Dogs of America*, 1964.

WRITINGS: The Book of Horses and Horsemanship, Prentice-Hall, 1963; *The Hunting Dogs of America*, Doubleday, 1964; *The Pony Book*, Doubleday, 1966; *The Poodle Book*, Doubleday, 1968; *Puppy Owner's Handbook*, Puppy Palace Enterprises, 1968, revised edition, Sterling, 1970. Contributor to *American Field*.

WORK IN PROGRESS: A novel on Turkey.

SIDELIGHTS: Griffen speaks fluent French, and some Turkish and Italian.†

*　　*　　*

GRIFFITH, Ernest S(tacey) 1896-

PERSONAL: Born November 28, 1896, in Utica, N.Y.; son of George and Elizabeth (Stacey) Griffith; married Margaret Dyckman Davenport, June 8, 1929; children: Margaret (Mrs. George Earley), Alison (Mrs. Leonard B. Tennyson), Lawrence S. C., Julia (Mrs. David Abernethy), Stephen L. *Education:* Hamilton College, B.A., 1917; Oxford University, D.Phil., 1925. *Politics:* Republican. *Religion:* Methodist. *Home:* 1941 Parkside Dr., N.W., Washington, D.C. 20012. *Office:* School of International Service, American University, Ward Circle, Washington, D.C.

CAREER: Princeton University, Princeton, N.J., preceptor in economics, 1920-21; Liverpool University Settlement, Liverpool, England, warden, 1923-28; Syracuse University, Syracuse, N.Y., associate professor of political science, 1928-29, professor of comparative government and dean of Lower Division, 1930-35; American University, Washington, D.C., professor of political science and dean of Graduate School, 1935-40; Library of Congress, Washington, D.C., director of Legislative Reference Service, 1940-58; American University, dean of School of International Service, 1958-65. Visiting professor, Harvard University, 1929-30; Fulbright lecturer, Oxford University, 1951-52; Stokes lecturer, New York University, 1951; visiting lecturer at other universities in United States, England, Japan, and Norway. Member-at-large of Board of Missions and Church Extension, Methodist Church, 1947-51; vice-president of Department of International Affairs, National Council of Churches, 1955-59; delegate to New Delhi, World Council of Churches, 1961; member of American National Commission, UNESCO, 1963. *Military service:* U.S. Navy, 1918.

MEMBER: National Academy of Economics and Political Science (president, 1958-62), American Political Science Association (chairman of research committee, 1942-47; vice-president, 1958-59), American Society for Public Administration, Wilderness Society (treasurer, 1938-52, 1958-72), Phi Beta Kappa, Delta Upsilon, Phi Kappa Phi. *Awards, honors:* Rhodes Scholar, 1917; D.Litt., West Virginia Wesleyan College, 1957; L.H.D., Hamilton College, 1958; named layman of the year, National Capitol Area, by Federation of churches, 1958.

WRITINGS: The Modern Development of City Government in the United Kingdom and the United States, two volumes, Oxford University Press, 1927, reprinted, McGrath, 1973; *Current Municipal Problems*, Houghton, 1933; *History of American City Government*, Volume I:

The Colonial Period, Oxford University Press, 1938, reprinted, Da Capo Press, 1972, Volume III: *The Conspicuous Failure, 1870-1900*, Praeger, 1973, Volume IV: *The Progressive Years and Their Aftermath, 1900-1920*, Praeger, 1973; *The Impasse of Democracy*, Harrison-Hilton Books, 1939; *The Modern Government in Action*, Columbia University Press, 1942; (editor and contributor) *Research in Political Science*, University of North Carolina Press, 1948, reprinted, Kennikat, 1969; *Congress: Its Contemporary Role*, New York University Press, 1951, 5th edition, in press; *The American System of Government*, Praeger, 1954, 4th edition, 1965; (editor with Kenton Kilmer) *The Congressional Anthology*, 1955, revised edition, 1958.

Contributor: R. V. Peel and J. S. Roucek, editors, *Introduction to Politics*, Crowell, 1941; Pierce Butler, editor, *Reference Function of the Library*, University of Chicago Press, 1943; John Francis Timmons and William G. Murray, editors, *Land Problems and Politics*, Iowa State College Press, 1950; *Legislative-Executive Relationships in the Government of the United States*, U.S. Department of Agriculture, Graduate School, 1954; Henry Jarret, editor, *Perspectives on Conservation*, Johns Hopkins Press, 1958; S. D. Kertesz, editor, *American Diplomacy in a New Era*, University of Notre Dame, 1961; C. J. Friedrich, editor, *The Public Interest*, Atherton, 1962.

Also contributor of about twenty articles to political science journals and to *American City*, *Taxbits*, *Special Libraries*, *Living Wilderness*, and *Outdoor America*.

WORK IN PROGRESS: Volume II of the series, *History of American City Government*; 5th British edition of *The American System of Government*.

SIDELIGHTS: The American System of Government has been published in Italian, German, Arabic, Korean, Greek, Burmese, Hindi, Bengali, and other languages. *Avocational interests:* Mountain climbing, square dancing, and hiking.

* * *

GRIFFITHS, A(lan) Bede 1906-

PERSONAL: Born December 17, 1906, in Walton on Thames, England; son of Walter and Lilian (Day) Griffiths. *Education:* Magdalen College, Oxford, B.A., 1929. *Home:* Kurisumala Ashram, Vaghamon, Kottayam, Kerala, India.

CAREER: Catholic (Benedictine) monk; Prinknash Abbey, Gloucester, England, monk, 1933-55; Kurisumala Ashram, Vaghamon, India, sub-prior, 1958—. *Awards, honors:* Gold Medal of Catholic Art Association (United States) for ecumenical work, N.M., 1963.

WRITINGS: The Golden String (autobiography), Harvill Press, 1954, Kenedy, 1955; *Christian Ashram: Essays Towards a Hindu-Christian Dialogue*, Darton, Longman & Todd, 1966, published as *Christ in India: Essays Towards a Hindu-Christian Dialogue*, Scribner, 1967; *Vedanta and Christian Faith*, Uttarkhand Press, 1968, 2nd revised edition, Dawn Horse Press, 1973. Contributor to *Commonweal*, *Jubilee*, *Blackfriars*, *Catholic Herald*, and other journals.

WORK IN PROGRESS: Hindu Search for God.

SIDELIGHTS: Languages include Sanskrit and Syriac; Griffiths' work in fostering ecumenical relations between Christians and Hindus in India has involved a deep study of Hindu traditions, especially the mystical traditions, requiring a knowledge of Sanskrit; the Ashram belongs to the Syrian Rite of the Catholic Church and Syriac is used in prayers at the monastery.

BIOGRAPHICAL/CRITICAL SOURCES: Agnes de la Gorce, *Convertis du XXieme siecle*, [Brussels].

* * *

GRIGG, Charles M(eade) 1918-

PERSONAL: Born November 1, 1918, in Richmond, Va.; son of Joseph Warren (an accountant) and Nellie Archer (Chockley) Grigg; married Virginia Elizabeth Caffee (now a librarian), August 24, 1947; children: Meade, John, Joseph, Ruth. *Education:* College of William and Mary, B.S., 1947; University of North Carolina, M.A., 1950, Ph.D., 1952. *Politics:* Democrat. *Religion:* Presbyterian. *Home:* 2500 Harriman Circle, Tallahassee, Fla. 32302. *Office:* Florida State University, Tallahassee, Leon, Fla.

CAREER: Brown University, Providence, R.I., assistant professor of sociology, 1952-54; Florida State University, Tallahassee, associate professor, 1955-60, professor of sociology, 1960—, director of Institute for Social Research, 1955—, associate dean of arts and sciences, 1966—. Consultant to State of Florida Alcoholic Rehabilitation Program, to State of Florida Committee on Research and Education, and to Florida Tuberculosis and Health Association. Presbyterian Christian Action Council, Synod of Florida, member. *Military service:* U.S. Army Air Forces, 1941-46; became captain. *Member:* American Sociological Association, Population Association of America, New York Academy of Science, Southern Sociological Association (executive committee), Alpha Kappa Delta.

WRITINGS: (With Lewis M. Killian) *Racial Crisis in America: Leadership in Conflict*, Prentice-Hall, 1964; *Graduate Education*, Center for Applied Research in Education, 1965; *Recruitment to Graduate Study: College Senior's Plans for Postgraduate Education and Their Implementation the Year After Commencement*, Southern Regional Education Board, 1965; *Vocational Rehabilitation of Disabled Public Assistance Clients: An Evaluation of Fourteen Research and Demonstration Projects*, Institute for Social Research, 1969; (with Alphonse Holtman and Patricia Martin) *Vocational Rehabilitation for the Disadvantaged: An Economic and Sociological Evaluation*, Lexington Books, 1970. Also author, co-author, and editor of Florida sociological studies. Contributor of articles to professional journals.

WORK IN PROGRESS: A study of the impact of the space program in a seven-county area; a study on community and bi-racial committee activities; a book on graduate education.†

* * *

GRIMAL, Pierre Antoine 1912-

PERSONAL: Born November 21, 1912, in Paris, France; son of Henri and Marguerite (Rouquie) Grimal; married Benevieve Borel, April 18, 1945; children: Francois, Antoine, Nicolas, Benoite. *Education:* Attended College de Barbezieux, College de Fontainebleau, Lycee Louis-le-Grand, Ecole Normale Superieure (Paris), Ecole Francaise de Rome. *Religion:* Roman Catholic. *Home:* 30 rue des Fonds, Jouy-en-Josas, Yrelines, France.

CAREER: Lycee de Rennes, Rennes, France, professeur, 1938-41; Universite de Caen, Caen, France, professeur, Faculte des Lettres, 1941-45; Universite de Bordeaux, Bordeaux, France, professeur, Faculte des Lettres, 1945-52; Universite de Paris, Paris, France, professeur, Faculte des Lettres et Sciences Humaines, 1952—.

WRITINGS: Les Jardins romains a la fin de la republique et aux deux premiers siecles de l'empire: Essai sur le naturalisme romain, de Boccard, 1943, 2nd edition, Presses universitaires de France, 1969; *Seneque: Sa Vie, son oeuvre, avec un expose de sa philosophie*, Presses universitaires de France, 1948, 3rd edition, 1966; *Dictionnaire de la mythologie grecque et romaine*, Presses universitaires de France, 1951, 4th edition, 1969; *Le Siecle des Scipions: Rome et l'hellenisme au temps de guerres puniques*, Aubier, 1953; *Les Intentions de Properce et la composition du livre IV des "Elegies,"* Latomus, 1953; *La Vie a Rome dans L'antiquite*, Presses universitaires de France, 1953, 3rd edition, 1960; *La Mythologie grecque*, Presses universitaires de France, 1953, 6th edition, 1968; *Les Villes romaines*, Presses universitaires de France, 1954, 4th edition, 1971; *Le Siecle d'Auguste*, Presses universitaires de France, 1955, 4th edition, 1968; (author of introduction and text) *Dans les pas des Cesars* (photographic essay), Hachette, 1955, translation by Lucy Norton published as *Rome of the Caesars*, Phaidon, 1956; *Tibulle: Elegies deliennes*, Centre de documentation universitaire (Paris), 1956; *Contes et legendes du temps d'Alexandre*, Nathan, 1958, translation by Barbara Whelpton published as *Stories of Alexander the Great*, World Publishing, 1966; *Horace*, Editions du seuil, 1958.

La Civilisation romaine, Arthaud, 1960, translation by W. S. Maguinness published as *The Civilization of Rome*, Simon & Schuster, 1963; *A la recherche de l'Italie antique*, Hachette, 1961, translation by P. D. Cummings published as *In Search of Ancient Italy*, Hill & Wang, 1964; *Contes et legendes de Babylone et de Perse*, Nathan, 1962, translation by Barbara Whelpton published as *Stories from Babylon and Persia*, Burke Publishing, 1964, World Publishing, 1965; *Nous partons pour Rome*, Presses universitaires de France, 1962; *L'Amour a Rome*, Hachette, 1963, translation by Arthur Train, Jr., published as *Love in Ancient Rome*, Crown, 1967; *L'Art des jardins*, Presses universitaires de France, 1964; *Horace: Art poetique, commentaire et etude*, Centre de documentation universitaire, 1964; *La Litterature latine*, Presses universitaires de France, 1965; (author of text) *La Mythologie et les dieux*, Nathan, 1966; *L'Explication latine en classes terminales: Litterature et pensee romaines*, Nathan, 1967; *Rome devant Cesar: Memoires de T. Pomponius Atticus*, Larousse, 1967; *Etudes de chronologie ciceronienne*, Les Belles Lettres, 1967; *Essai sur l'art poetique d'Horace*, Societe d'Edition de Dictionnaires et Encyclopedies, 1968; (with Jerome Catcopino) *Jules Cesar*, 5th edition (Grimal was not associated with earlier editions), Presses universitaires de France, 1968; *Guide de l'etudiant latiniste*, Presses universitaires de France, 1971; (with Eckart Peterich) *Goetter und Helden: Die klassischen Mythen und Sagen der Griechen, Roemer, und Germanen*, Walter, 1971; *Seneca*, Wissenschaftliche Buchgesellschaft, in press.

Editor: Seneca, *De Constantia Sapientis*, Les Belles Lettres, 1953; Voltaire, *Candide, l'ingenu* [and] *L'homme aux quarante ecus*, A. Colin, 1957; (with others) *Dictionnaire des biographies*, Presses universitaires de France, 1958; Joachim Du Bellay, *Les Regrets, suivis des Antiquites de Rome*, A. Colin, 1958; (and author of introduction) Seneca, *De brevitate vitae*, Presses universitaires de France, 1959, 2nd edition, 1966; Rabelais, *Pantagruel*, A. Colin, 1959; Voltaire, *Zadig, Micromegas, et autres contes*, A. Colin, 1961; (and author of introduction) Montesquieu, *Lettres persanes*, A Colin, 1961; Rabelais, *Le Tiers Livre*, A. Colin, 1962; *Mythologies des montagnes, des forets, et des iles*, Larousse, 1963; *Mythologies de la Mediterranee au Gange: Prehistoire, Egypte, Sumer, Babylone, Hittites, Semites, Grece, Rome, Perse, Inde* (also see below), Larousse, 1963; Voltaire, *La Princesse de Babylone, et autres contes*, A. Colin, 1963; Apuleius Madaurensis, *Apulei Metamorphoseis, IV 28- VI 24: Le Conte d'Amour et Psyche*, Presses universitaires de France, 1963; *Larousse World Mythology* (includes *Mythologies de la Mediterranee au Grange*), translated by Patricia Beardsworth, Putnam, 1965; (and contributor) *Der Hellenismus und der Aufstieg Roms*, Fischer Buecherei, 1965, translation from the German and French by A. M. Sheridan Smith and Carla Wartenburg published as *Hellenism and the Rise of Rome*, Weidenfeld & Nicolson, 1968, American edition, translated by A. M. Sheridan Smith, Dial, 1969; Seneca, *Phaedra*, Presses universitaires de France, 1965; *Der Aufbau des Roemischen Reiches*, Fischer Buecherei, 1966; Petronius Arbiter, *Le Satiricon*, Gallimard, 1972.

Translator and editor: Sextus Julius Frontinus, *Les Aqueducs de la ville de Rome*, Les Belles Lettres, 1944, 2nd edition, 1961; (and author of introduction) *Romans, Grecs, et Latins*, Gallimard, 1958; (and author of introduction) Cornelius Tacitus, *Oeuvres choisies*, Le Club du Meilleur Livre (Paris), 1959; Plautus and Terence, *Oeuvres completes*, Gallimard, 1971.

Also author of studies and published lectures on Seneca. Editor of "Histoire mondiale de la femme," published by Nouvelle librairie de France, 1965-67.

WORK IN PROGRESS: The French edition of *Seneca*.

*   *   *

GRIMAULT, Berthe   1940-

PERSONAL: Born April 13, 1940, in Jassay per Lezay, Deux-Sevres, France; daughter of Henri and Eva (Bonneau) Grimault; married Robert Portier, October 22, 1960 (separated, 1964); children: Jean-Michel, Jean. *Education:* Attended The Grove Seal (near Sevenoaks, Kent, England), 1957-58. *Agent:* Odette Arnaud, 11 rue de Teheran, Paris VIII, France.

CAREER: Full-time writer.

WRITINGS: Beau Clown, Julliard, 1956, translation by Diana Athill, Rinehart, 1957; *Tuer son enfant*, Julliard, 1957, translation by Lucianne Hill published as *Blood on the Straw*, Fleet Publications, 1959; Lucianne Hill, translator, *Berthe in Paradise*, W. H. Allen, 1960.

WORK IN PROGRESS: Le Pipeau bleu, Pan cartouche, and *Le Berger du desert.*†

*   *   *

GRIMM, Harold J(ohn)   1901-

PERSONAL: Born August 16, 1901, in Saginaw, Mich.; son of Henry Frederick and Ella (Lepien) Grimm; married Thelma Rickey, 1931; children: Jane (Mrs. Harvey S. Minton). *Education:* Capital University, A.B., 1924; Evangelical Lutheran Theological Seminary, diploma, 1927; Ohio State University, A.M., 1928, Ph.D., 1932; graduate study at University of Leipzig, 1929-30, University of Hamburg, summer, 1930. *Religion:* Lutheran. *Home:* 76 North Stanwood Rd., Columbus, Ohio 43209. *Office:* Department of History, Ohio State University, Columbus, Ohio 43210.

CAREER: Capital University, Columbus, Ohio, instructor, 1925-29, assistant professor, 1930-33, associate professor,

1933-36, professor of history and chairman of department, 1936-37; Ohio State University, Columbus, assistant professor, 1937-42, associate professor, 1942-47, professor of history, 1947-54; Indiana University, Bloomington, professor of history and chairman of department, 1954-58; Ohio State University, professor of history, 1958-68, Regents professor of history, 1968-72, professor emeritus, 1972—, chairman of department of history, 1958-66. Fulbright fellow and visiting professor, University of Freiburg, Germany, 1954; summer professor at West Virginia University, San Diego State College (now University), University of Texas.

MEMBER: American Historical Association, American Society of Church History (president, 1961), American Society for Reformation Research (past president), Foundation for Reformation Research (vice-president), Hansischer Geschichtsverein (Germany), Royal Historical Society (Great Britain; fellow), Royal Society of Arts (Great Britain; fellow), American Association of University Professors, Ohio State University Faculty Club, Rotary Club (Columbus).

WRITINGS: Luther as a Preacher, Lutheran Book Concern, 1929; (with F. J. Tschan and J. D. Squires) *Western Civilization*, two volumes, Lippincott, 1942; *The Reformation Era: 1500-1650*, Macmillan, 1954; (editor) Martin Luther, *Works*, volume 31, Muhlenberg Press, 1957; (with G. Forell and T. Hoelty-Nickel) *Luther and Culture*, Luther College Press, 1960; *The Social History of the Reformation*; Ohio State University Press, 1972. *Archiv Fuer Reformationsgeschichte*, U.S. editor, 1950-62, member of editorial board, 1962—.

* * *

GRINDELL, Robert M(aclean) 1933-

PERSONAL: Born January 30, 1933, in San Juan, Puerto Rico; son of Horace Maclean (a bank official) and Ruth (Elliott) Grindell; married Anne Pettit, June 6, 1959; children: Michael Maclean, Jennifer Anne. *Education:* Harvard University, A.B. (magna cum laude), 1956; New York University, M.A., 1964. *Politics:* Liberal. *Home:* 1615 East Third St., Tucson, Ariz. 85716.

CAREER: Scott Meredith Literary Agency, Inc., New York, N.Y., editor, 1957-60; New York University, New York, N.Y., instructor in English, 1960-64; University of Arizona, Tucson, instructor in English, 1964—. *Member:* Modern Language Association of America, National Council of Teachers of English, National Association of Foreign Student Advisers.

WRITINGS: (Editor with Leonard R. Marelli and Harvey Nadler) *American Readings: Selections and Exercises for Vocabulary Development*, McGraw, 1964.

SIDELIGHTS: Grindell is competent in French and Spanish.†

* * *

GRINSTEIN, Alexander 1918-

PERSONAL: Born August 21, 1918, in Russia; son of Mark (a physician) and Esther (a physician; maiden name, Alpert) Grinstein; married Adele Brotslaw (a child psychologist), September 27, 1941; children: David Robert, Richard Leonard. *Education:* University of Buffalo, B.A., 1938, M.D., 1942. *Home:* 31510 Bellvine Trail, Birmingham, Mich. 48010.

CAREER: Psychoanalyst in private practice, Birmingham,

Mich. Training and supervising analyst, Michigan Psychoanalytic Institute. *Member:* American Psychiatric Association, International Psycho-Analytic Association, American Psychoanalytic Association (fellow; member of board on professional standards, 1966-72), Michigan Association for Psychoanalysis (vice-president, 1959-61; president, 1961-62, 1972-74), Sigma Xi.

WRITINGS: (With Editha Sterba) *Understanding Your Family*, Random House, 1957; *The Index of Psychoanalytic Writings*, International Universities, Volume I, 1956, Volume II, 1957, Volume III, 1958, Volume IV, 1958, Volume V, 1960, Volume VI, 1964, Volume VII, 1964, Volume VIII, 1965, Volume IX, 1965. Contributor to professional journals.

WORK IN PROGRESS: Sigmund Freud's Dreams.

AVOCATIONAL INTERESTS: Photography, playing violin, horseback riding.

* * *

GRISEZ, Germain G. 1929-

PERSONAL: Surname is pronounced Gree-zay; born September 30, 1929, in University Heights, Ohio; son of William J. and Mary C. (Lindesmith) Grisez; married Jeannette Eunice Selby, June 9, 1951; children: Thomas, James, Joseph, Paul. *Education:* John Carroll University, B.A. (magna cum laude), 1951; Dominican College of St. Thomas Aquinas, River Forest, Ill., M.A. and Ph.L. (summa cum laude), 1951; University of Chicago, Ph.D., 1959. *Politics:* Independent. *Religion:* Catholic. *Office:* Campion College, University of Regina, Regina, Saskatchewan S4S OA2, Canada.

CAREER: Georgetown University, Washington, D.C., 1957-72, became professor of philosophy; University of Regina, Campion College, Regina, Saskatchewan, professor of philosophy, 1972—. Lecturer at University of Virginia, 1960-61; special assistant, Archdiocese of Washington, D.C., 1968-70. *Member:* American Philosophical Association, Metaphysical Society of America, American Catholic Philosophical Association. *Awards, honors:* Lilly post-doctoral fellowship in religion, 1963-64; Medora A. Feehan grant, 1967, 1971, 1973; Pro Ecclesia et Pontifice Medal, 1972.

WRITINGS: Contraception and the Natural Law, Bruce, 1965; *Abortion: The Myths, the Realities, and the Arguments*, Corpus Publications, 1971; (with Russell Shaw) *Beyond the New Morality: The Responsibilities of Freedom*, University of Notre Dame Press, 1974; *Beyond the New Theism: A Philosophy of Religion*, University of Notre Dame Press, in press. Contributor to *Natural Law Forum* and to other philosophical and theological journals.

WORK IN PROGRESS: Ethical theory, including theory of human action, and fundamental moral theology.

* * *

GROSS, Bertram M(yron) 1912-

PERSONAL: Born December 25, 1912, in Philadelphia, Pa.; son of Samuel and Regina Gross; married Nora Faine, September 4, 1938; children: David, Larry, Samuel, Theodore. *Education:* University of Pennsylvania, B.A., 1933, M.A., 1935. *Home:* 170 West End Ave., New York, N.Y. *Office:* Urban Affairs Department, Hunter College of the City University of New York, New York, N.Y.

CAREER: U.S. government posts, Washington, D.C.,

1938-53, including research and hearings director, Senate Committee on Small Business, 1942-43, staff director, Senate Military Affairs Subcommittee on War Contracts, 1943-44, economic adviser, Senate Banking and Currency Committee, 1945-46, executive secretary, Council of Economic Advisers to the President, 1946-51, chairman of National Capital Regional Planning Council, 1952-53; government of Israel, Jerusalem, economic adviser, 1953-56; Hebrew University of Jerusalem, external lecturer, 1955-56, visiting professor of administration, 1956-60; Syracuse University, Maxwell School of Citizenship and Public Affairs, Syracuse, N.Y., professor of administration, 1960-68; Wayne State University, Detroit, Mich., director of Urban Studies Center, 1968-69; Hunter College of the City University of New York, New York, N.Y., Distinguished Professor of Urban Affairs, 1970—. Consultant to United Nations Korean Reconstruction Administration, 1952-53, El Al (Israel national airlines), 1956-57, 1959, Ford Foundation and Indian Institute of Public Administration, 1961, Secretary of Department of Health, Education, and Welfare, 1966-67. Visiting professor at University of California, Berkeley, 1962, Harvard University, 1962-63. Member, then vice-chairman, of Arlington County Planning Commission, 1950-52.

MEMBER: American Political Science Association (chairman, committee on political parties), American Society for Public Administration. *Awards, honors:* Woodrow Wilson Foundation Award (given for best book of the year in the field of government and democracy), 1953, for *The Legislative Struggle;* Center for Advanced Study in the Behavioral Sciences fellowship, 1961-62; Social Science Research Council, faculty research fellow, 1961-62; Mosher award for best article in 1971, for "Planning in an Era of Social Revolution."

WRITINGS: The Home That Jack's Building, (marionette play; produced at Philadelphia Federal Theatre), U.S. Housing Authority, 1939; (with others) *Toward a More Responsible Two-Party System,* Rinehart, 1950; *The Legislative Struggle: A Study in Social Combat,* McGraw, 1953; (contributor) Richard W. Taylor, editor, *Life, Language, Law: Essays in Honor of Arthur E. Bentley,* Antioch Press, 1957; (contributor) Lewis A. Dexter and David M. White, editors, *People, Society and Mass Communications,* Free Press of Glencoe, 1964; (contributor) Jesse Burkhead, *Public School Finance: Economics and Politics,* Syracuse University Press, 1964; *The Managing of Organizations: The Administrative Struggle,* two volumes, Free Press of Glencoe, 1964, condensed edition published in one volume as *Organizations and Their Managing,* Free Press, 1968; *The State of the Nation: Systems Accounting,* Tavistock Press, 1966; *The Administration of Economic Development Planning: Principles and Fallacies* (booklet), United Nations, 1966.

Editor: *Action under Planning: The Guidance of Economic Development,* McGraw, 1967; *A Great Society?,* Basic Books, 1968; *Social Intelligence for America's Future: Explorations in Societal Problems,* Allyn & Bacon, 1969; (with Herman Mertins) *Symposium on Changing Styles of Planning in Post-Industrial America,* American Society for Public Administration, 1971.

Also author of *Mutsre ha-minhal,* 1964, and *Planning against Poverty: Guided Development in Poor Nations,* 1965. Editor of "National Planning Series" published by Syracuse University, 1965-68. Contributor to *Encyclopedia of the Social Sciences,* and to *American Political Science Review, Challenge, Public Administration,* and *Social*

Policy. Special editor of *The Annals,* American Academy of Political and Social Science, 1967 and 1970.

WORK IN PROGRESS: Two books, *Friendly Fascism: The Logic of American Capitalism* and *What Is To Be Done?*

*   *   *

GROSS, Carl H. 1911-

PERSONAL: Born December 31, 1911, in Salem, Ore.; married Margaret L. Ulm. *Education:* University of Oregon, B.A., 1933, M.A. 1935; The Ohio State University, Ph.D., 1939. *Religion:* Lutheran. *Home:* 644 Grove St., East Lansing, Mich.

CAREER: Michigan State University, East Lansing, member of department of education. *Member:* History of Education Society (director, 1962-65), Philosophy of Education Society, Comparative Education Society, National Education Association, National Society of College Teachers of Education, Michigan Education Association, Phi Kappa Phi, Phi Delta Kappa. *Awards, honors:* Distinguished Faculty Award, Michigan State University.

WRITINGS: (With Wronski and Hanson) *School and Society,* Heath, 1962; (editor with Charles C. Chandler) *History of American Education through Readings,* Heath, 1965; (editor) *College Teachers Look at Teaching,* American Association of Colleges for Teacher Education, 1965; (editor) *Higher Education in Canada,* Michigan State University, 1968; *Sokagakkai and Education,* Institute for International Studies, Michigan State University, 1970. Contributor to *History of Education Journal* and other journals in education field.

SIDELIGHTS: Gross is competent in German. *Avocational interests:* Fishing, golf, bridge.†

*   *   *

GROSS, Harvey S. 1922-

PERSONAL: Born March 6, 1922, in Cleveland, Ohio; son of Jack and Sadie (Gross) Gross; married Virginia La Rue (a teacher), June 25, 1949; children: Joseph Warren, Daniel La Rue. *Education:* University of California, Los Angeles, B.A., 1947, M.A., 1949; University of Michigan, Ph.D., 1955. *Home:* 2298 Waterman Way, Costa Mesa, Calif. 92664.

CAREER: Hofstra College, Hempstead, N.Y., instructor in English, 1954-57; University of Denver (Colo.), 1957-65, started as assistant professor, became professor of English; University of California, Irvine, associate professor of English, 1965—. *Military service:* U.S. Army Air Forces, 1942-45; became staff sergeant. *Member:* Modern Language Association of America, National Council of Teachers of English, Michigan Academy of Science, Arts, and Letters. *Awards, honors:* Fulbright award to Austria, 1951-52; Avery and Jule Hopwood Award in creative writing, University of Michigan, 1953; Folger Library fellow, 1964; American Council of Learned Societies fellow, 1965-67.

WRITINGS: Sound and Form in Modern Poetry, University of Michigan Press, 1964; (editor) *The Structure of Verse: Modern Essays on Prosody,* Fawcett, 1966; *Plans for an Orderly Apocalypse and Other Poems,* University of Michigan Press, 1968; *The Contrived Corridor: History and Fatality in Modern Literature,* University of Michigan Press, 1971. Contributor to *Centennial Review, Commentary, Prairie Schooner,* and other journals.

WORK IN PROGRESS: The Elizabethan Art-Song, for University of Michigan Press; a book on modern literature and the idea of history, undertaken under American Council of Learned Societies fellowship.†

* * *

GROSS, Martin (Arnold) 1934-

PERSONAL: Born June 23, 1934, in New York, N.Y. Education: Hunter College, B.A., 1956. Home: 39A Gramercy Park North, New York, N.Y. 10010.

CAREER: Advertising copywriter.

WRITINGS: Feature Writer's Passport to the Travel Market, Gross, 1959; (with Ted Sennett) Are You Sure You're Kosher?, Paul S. Eriksson, 1964; The Nostalgia Quiz Book, Arlington House, 1969.†

* * *

GROSSHOLTZ, Jean 1929-

PERSONAL: Born April 17, 1929, in McKean, Pa.; daughter of Theodore George and Hazel (Kerns) Grossholtz. Education: Pennsylvania State University, B.A., 1956; University of Denver, M.A., 1957; Massachusetts Institute of Technology, Ph.D., 1961. Office: Department of Political Science, Mount Holyoke College, South Hadley, Mass. 01075.

CAREER: U.S. Army, Women's Army Corps, 1949-53; Mount Holyoke College, South Hadley, Mass., member of department of political science, 1961—. Member: American Political Science Association, Association for Asian Studies, American Association of University Professors, New England Political Science Association. Awards, honors: Fulbright fellow in Philippine Islands, 1959-60; National Science Foundation fellowship in Malaysia, 1965-66.

WRITINGS: Politics in the Philippines: A Country Study, Little, Brown, 1964.

WORK IN PROGRESS: Comparative Political Development in Malaysia and the Philippines.

* * *

GROSSKURTH, Phyllis 1924-

PERSONAL: Born March 16, 1924, in Toronto, Ontario, Canada; daughter of Milton Palmer (an actuary) and Winifred (Owen) Langstaff; married Robert A. Grosskurth (now a naval commander); children: Christopher, Brian, Ann. Education: University of Toronto, B.A., 1946; University of Ottawa, M.A., 1960; University of London, Ph.D., 1962. Home: 131 Roxborough St. East, Toronto, Ontario, Canada. Office: Department of English, University College, University of Toronto, Toronto, Ontario, Canada.

CAREER: Carleton University, Ottawa, Ontario, Canada, lecturer, 1964-65; University of Toronto, Toronto, Ontario, Canada, assistant professor of English, 1965—. Awards, honors: Governor General's Literary Award for nonfiction and University of Columbia Medal for Biography, both for his biography of John Addington Symonds, 1965.

WRITINGS: John Addington Symonds: A Biography, Longmans, Green, 1964, published as The Woeful Victorian, Holt, 1965; Notes on Browning's Works, [Toronto], 1967; Leslie Stephen, Longmans, Green for National Book League and British Council, 1968; Gabrielle Roy, edited by William French, Forum House, 1969. Contributor to English Studies and other journals in field.†

GROVER, David H(ubert) 1925-

PERSONAL: Born June 12, 1925, in Port Richmond, N.Y.; son of Martin C. and Bertha (Tilton) Grover; married Marilyn Barnett, January 28, 1950; children: Gretchen, Jill, Jeffrey, Rebecca. Education: Colorado State University, B.S., 1949; U.S. Merchant Marine Academy, B.S., 1950; University of Colorado, M.A., 1951; University of Oregon, Ph.D., 1961. Politics: Republican. Religion: Episcopalian. Home: 677 Rio Vista Dr., Napa, Calif. Office: California Postsecondary Education Commission, Sacramento, Calif.

CAREER: Instructor at Auburn University, Auburn, Ala., 1951-52, University of South Dakota, Vermillion, 1952-53, Boise High School, Boise, Idaho, 1953-57; Oregon State University, Corvallis, assistant professor of speech, 1957-64; Colorado State University, Fort Collins, assistant professor of speech, 1964-67; University of Wyoming, Laramie, associate professor of speech and chairman of department, 1967-69; Idaho Office of Higher Education, Boise, associate director, 1969-72; California Maritime Academy, Vallejo, academic dean, 1972-74; California Postsecondary Education Commission, Sacramento, higher education specialist, 1974—. Operations analyst, Standard Oil Co. of California, 1957. Military service: U.S. Merchant Marine, 1943-46; U.S. Navy, 1946-47. U.S. Naval Reserve, 1947—; now commander. Member: Speech Association of America, Western Speech Association (public address councilor, 1965-66; second vice-president, 1966-67), Idaho Historical Society. Awards, honors: Marion F. McClain Award of University of Oregon for best work on Pacific Northwest history, 1962, for manuscript of Debaters and Dynamiters; research grants from Oregon State University, 1958-59, 1962-63, and from Colorado State University, 1966-67.

WRITINGS: Debaters and Dynamiters: The Story of the Haywood Trial, Oregon State University Press, 1964; Diamondfield Jack: A Study in Frontier Justice, University of Nevada Press, 1968; (editor) Landmarks in Western Oratory, Graduate School, University of Wyoming, 1968. Contributor to speech and history journals.

WORK IN PROGRESS: September Snow, a novel of a contemporary May-September relationship.

* * *

GROVES, Reg(inald) 1908-

PERSONAL: Born April 16, 1908, in England; son of Percy Reginald and Dora (Canler) Groves; married Daisy Cox, February 15, 1931; children: Jennifer Ann, Frances Clare. Education: Attended school in London, England. Politics: Socialist. Religion: Church of England. Home: 7 Heathfield Rd., London S.W. 18, England.

CAREER: Writer and journalist; lecturer in history, English literature, and international affairs for London County Council and Workers' Educational Association. Member: National Union of Journalists, Society for the Study of Labour History, Association of Cine and Television Technicians.

WRITINGS: But We Shall Rise Again: A Narrative History of Chartism, Secker & Warburg, 1938; Jesse James, Pendulum, 1946; The Mystery of Victor Grayson, Pendulum Press, 1946; Rebels Oak, Red Flag Fellowship, 1949; Sharpen the Sickle, Porcupine Press, 1949; (with Philip Lindsay) The Peasants Revolt of 1381, Hutchinson, 1950; Conrad Noel and the Thaxted Movement, Merlin Press, 1967; The Catholic Crusade, 1918-1936, Archive

Press, 1970; *Seed Time and Harvest*, Merlin Press, 1972; *The Balham Group*, Pluto Press, 1974.

Also author of *Trades Councils*, 1935, *East End Crisis*, 1936, and *Arms and the Unions*, 1937, all published by the Socialist League. Editor of *World Film News*, 1936-38, *Cine Technician*, 1950-56.

WORK IN PROGRESS: The Breaking of the Left: A Study of Socialism in the Thirties, completion expected in 1975.

AVOCATIONAL INTERESTS: Football, cricket, public affairs.

* * *

GRUEN, Victor D(avid) 1903-

PERSONAL: Born July 18, 1903, in Vienna, Austria; came to United States in 1938, naturalized in 1943; son of Adolf (a lawyer) and Elizabeth (Levy) Gruenbaum; married Lazette Van Houten, September 28, 1951 (deceased); married Kemija Salihefendic, February 28, 1963; children: (prior marriage) Michael Stephen, Margaret. *Education:* Attended Federal Academy of Fine Arts, Vienna, Austria, and Technological Institute, Vienna. *Home:* 315 North Beverly Glen, Los Angeles, Calif. *Address:* 1040 Goldeggasse 7, Vienna, Austria.

CAREER: Building supervisor and engineer for architectural firms in Vienna, Austria, 1923-32; private architectural practice in Vienna, Austria, 1932-38, in New York, N.Y. (with later branches in Los Angeles, Calif., and Chicago, Ill.), 1938-48; Victor Gruen Associates (architects, engineers, and planners), Los Angeles, Calif., principal, 1948-68; Victor Gruen Center for Environmental Planning, Los Angeles, and Zentrum fuer Umweltplanung, Vienna, Austria, founder and president, 1968—. Registered architect in twenty-odd states and District of Columbia. Projects include urban redevelopment programs, shopping centers, and business buildings from coast to coast, among them Northland, Eastland, and Westland regional shopping centers, Detroit, Mich., Southdale regional shopping centers, Minneapolis, Minn., city planning developments in Fort Worth, Tex., and redevelopment plans for Fresno, Calif., Rochester, N.Y., and Paterson, N.J. Former director of Citizens Housing and Planning Council of New York; member of Mrs. Lyndon Baines Johnson's White House Committee for a More Beautiful Capital. Member of executive committee, People to People, Inc.

MEMBER: American Institute of Architects (fellow), American Institute of Planners, National Association of Housing and Redevelopment Officials, Urban Land Institute, Authors Guild, Architectural League of New York, Michigan Society of Architects, and a number of other professional organizations; Lambda Alpha. *Awards, honors:* American Institute of Architects awards include Award of Merit for Northland Shopping Center, 1954; named Architect of the People, Rice University, 1964; prize for the Architecture of the city of Vienna, 1972.

WRITINGS: How to Live with Your Architect, Store Modernization Institute, 1949; (with Larry Smith) *Shopping Towns U.S.A.*, Reinhold, 1959; *The Heart of Our Cities*, Simon & Schuster, 1964; *Centers for the Urban Environment: Survival of the Cities*, Van Nostrand, 1973. Contributor to magazines and professional journals.

WORK IN PROGRESS: Environmental Planning.

SIDELIGHTS: Exhibits of Northland and Eastland centers were shown at American Institute of Architects Cen-

tennial Exhibit, National Gallery of Art, Washington, D.C.; other exhibits in Mexico City, 1952, Lausanne, Switzerland, 1959, Moscow, 1959. Gruen now resides in Europe.

BIOGRAPHICAL/CRITICAL SOURCES: Fortune, January, 1962.

* * *

GUINN, Paul (Spencer, Jr.) 1928-

PERSONAL: Born October 30, 1928, in The Hague, Netherlands; son of Paul (a foreign service officer) and J. Caroline (Westhoven) Guinn. *Education:* Swarthmore College, B.A., 1950; Harvard University, M.A., 1951, Ph.D., 1962; also attended University of Paris, 1948-49, and King's College, University of London, 1958-61. *Office:* Department of History, Red Jacket Quadrangle, Amherst Campus, State University of New York at Buffalo.

CAREER: Library of Congress, Washington, D.C., analyst, Legislative Reference Service, 1955-56; instructor in history, Simmons College, Boston, Mass., 1956-57, University of Maryland Overseas Program, England, 1959; Institute for Defense Analyses, Arlington, Va., member of research staff, 1961-67; State University of New York at Buffalo, Buffalo, N.Y., associate professor of history, 1967—. Associate professorial lecturer, George Washington University, Washington, D.C., 1965. *Military service:* U.S. Air Force, 1952-55; instructor in history at Air University, 1953-54, writer and editor in Historical Division, 1953-55, at Maxwell Air Force Base, Ala. *Member:* American Historical Association, American Political Science Association, Conference on British Studies. *Awards, honors:* George Louis Beer Prize, American Historical Association, 1965, for *British Strategy and Politics, 1914-1918.*

WRITINGS: British Strategy and Politics, 1914-1918, Clarendon Press, 1965; (contributor) Robin Higham, editor, *A Guide to the Sources of British Military History*, University of California Press, 1971. Contributor of reviews to periodicals.

* * *

GULLICK, John M(ichael) 1916-

PERSONAL: Born February 6, 1916, in Bristol, England; son of Lionel Oliver and Isobel (Douthwaite) Gullick; married Pamela Whitley, July 20, 1946; children: Sheila, William. *Education:* Christ's College, Cambridge, M.A., 1939; London School of Economics and Political Science, Diploma in Anthropology, 1953. *Office:* E. F. Turner & Sons, 12 Bedford Row, London WC1R 4DN, England.

CAREER: British Colonial Service, administrative officer in Malaya, 1945-57; director of British companies owning Malayan plantations, London, England, 1957-62; practicing lawyer, London, England, 1963—, currently with E. F. Turner & Sons. *Military service:* British Army, 1940-46; became lieutenant colonel. *Member:* Royal Anthropological Institute (fellow), Royal Asiatic Society (fellow).

WRITINGS: Indigenous Political Systems of Western Malaya, Humanities, 1958; *Malaya*, Praeger, 1963, 3rd edition, revised and enlarged, published as *Malaysia*, 1969. Author of monographs. Contributor to *Journal of Royal Asiatic Society*.

SIDELIGHTS: Gullick speaks Malay and French.

GULLIFORD, Ronald 1920-

PERSONAL: Born December 8, 1920, in Manchester, England; son of Frederick George (a blacksmith) and Lily (Latchem) Gulliford; married Alison Barbara Dawe, May 26, 1950 (died, 1971); children: Stephen Peter, Martin Christopher, Frances Susan, Anthea Mary. Education: University of London, B.A. (honors), 1944; University of Birmingham, Diploma in Educational Psychology, 1949. Politics: Labour. Religion: Humanist. Home: 53 Billesley Lane, Moseley, Birmingham, England. Office: University of Birmingham, Edgbaston, Birmingham, England.

CAREER: Teaching posts in England, 1941-48; Bolton Education Committee, Bolton, Lancashire, England, educational psychologist, 1949-51; University of Birmingham, Birmingham, England, psychologist in department of child study, 1951-54, tutor in diploma course for teachers of educationally subnormal children, department of education, 1954—. Member: British Psychological Society, Association for Special Education (president, 1962-64), British Association for Early Childhood Education (chairman, Birmingham branch, 1964—).

WRITINGS: (With A. E. Tansley) The Education of Slow Learning Children, Routledge & Kegan Paul, 1960; Backwardness and Educational Failure, National Foundation for Educational Research, 1970; Special Educational Needs, Routledge & Kegan Paul, 1971; Teaching Materials for Disadvantaged Children, Schools Council, 1974. Honorary editor of Special Education, 1966—.

WORK IN PROGRESS: Studies in the language and thinking of educationally subnormal children.

AVOCATIONAL INTERESTS: Playing the piano, listening to music, gardening, walking.

*   *   *

GUNDREY, Elizabeth 1924-

PERSONAL: Born November 6, 1924, in London, England; daughter of Victor Gareth and Mabel (Carey) Gundrey. Education: University of London, B.A. (honors in history), 1946. Politics: Conservative. Religion: Protestant. Home: 10 Regents Park Rd., London N.W. 1, England.

CAREER: Formerly feature writer for News Chronicle, and home editor of House and Garden and Housewife; Shopper's Guide, London, England, editor until 1963; self-employed consultant on consumer needs, London, England, 1963—. National Economic Committee for the Distributive Trades, special member. Active in social work with ex-convicts and elderly women. Member: Society of Authors, National Union of Journalists.

WRITINGS: Your Money's Worth, Penguin, 1962; At Your Service, Penguin, 1954; A Foot in Your Door, Muller, 1965; Value for Money, Hodder & Stroughton, 1966; Jobs for Mothers, Hodder & Stroughton, 1967; (with Jean Carper) Stay Alive! How to Prevent Accidents in the Home, MacGibbon & Kee, 1967; (editor) The Book of Egg Cookery, Spectator Publications, 1969; (editor) Martin Mayhew and Cherille Mayhew, Fun With Art, Scroll Press, 1973. Regular contributor to Guardian, Sunday Times, Daily Mail, Daily Mirror, and other newspapers in England, and to British Broadcasting Corp. programs.†

*   *   *

GUNN, William Harrison 1934-
(Bill Gunn)

PERSONAL: Born July 15, 1934, in Philadelphia, Pa.; son of William Harrison and Louise (Alexander) Gunn. Education: Attended public schools in Philadelphia, Pa. Politics: Democrat. Home: New York, N.Y. Agent: Bertha Case, 42 West 53rd St., New York, N.Y.

CAREER: Actor on stage, television, and in films, 1955—. Military service: U.S. Navy.

WRITINGS—Under name Bill Gunn: All the Rest Have Died (novel), Delacorte, 1964. "Marcus in the High Grass" (play; produced by Theatre Guild, 1959); "Johnnas" (play; produced in New York at Chelsea Theatre, Summer, 1968).

Filmscripts: (With Ronald Ribman) "The Angel Levine" (adaptation of a novel by Bernard Malamud); "The Landlord" (adaptation of a novel by Kristin Hunter); "Don't the Moon Look Lonesome" (adaptation of a novel by Don Asher).

WORK IN PROGRESS: A novel, The Death Game; four plays, "The Celebration," "The Owlight," "That's Gustavo," "Jonnas."

SIDELIGHTS: After turning out a few plays, Gunn wrote a novel "because I thought I had something to say which had to be said without the help of the producers, the star, the directors, and the 11:30 cocktail.... It has been an exciting and revealing experience for me to write this book about a man (an American Negro) ... who did not make the mistake of living and dying for a cause that for him would have been a secondary passion" (Library Journal, October 1, 1964).

BIOGRAPHICAL SOURCES: Philadelphia Inquirer, October 25, 1964; Philadelphia Bulletin, October 27, 1964; Variety, November 4, 1964.†

*   *   *

GUNTHER, Max 1927-

PERSONAL: Born June 28, 1927, in Hendon, England; son of Frank Henry (a banker) and Edith Malshinger Gunther; married Dorothy Eckberg, July 5, 1952; children: Robert, Katherine, Margaret. Education: Princeton University, B.A., 1949. Politics: Independent. Religion: Protestant. Home: 36 Beechwood Lane, Ridgefield, Conn.

CAREER: Business Week, New York, N.Y., rewrite desk, 1951-55; Time, New York, N.Y., contributing editor, 1955-56; free-lance writer, 1956—. Military service: U.S. Army, 1950-51.

WRITINGS: (With Richard and Katherine Gordon) Split-Level Trap, Bernard Geis Associates, 1961; The Weekenders, Lippincott, 1964; Writing the Modern Magazine Article, Writer, Inc., 1966, revised edition, 1973; Wall Street and Witchcraft, Geis, 1970; The Very, Very Rich and How They Got That Way, Playboy Press, 1972; (editor) Instant Millionaires, Playboy Press, 1973; Writing and Selling a Nonfiction Book, Writer, Inc., 1973; Virility 8, Playboy Press, in press. Regular contributor of articles to TV Guide; also contributor to Reader's Digest, Good Housekeeping, McCall's, Playboy, New York Times, and True.

SIDELIGHTS: Gunther writes: "[I am] more likely to call myself a free-lance reporter than a Writer with a capital W. I deliberately avoid specializing, will accept assignment on any subject that sounds interesting.... You don't get rich in this odd business, but for sheer variety and fascination it's probably the best profession in the world. I usually write from 6 a.m. to noon, take the rest of the day off. Spend spare time ambling around my acre of Connecticut woods, swimming, playing banjo, singing in church choir."

GUPTA, Sulekh Chandra 1928-

PERSONAL: Born August 25, 1928, in Ghaziabad, Uttar Pradesh, India; the son of Ram (a businessman) and Chameli (Devile) Gupta; married Gargi (a lecturer in translation, department of Hindi, University of Delhi), October 19, 1952; children: Smiti Tanya (daughter), Anu Shekhar and Chara Shekhar (sons). *Education:* Allahabad University, M.A., 1949; University of Delhi, Ph.D., 1961. *Religion:* Hindu. *Home:* F 2-7, Model Town, Delhi 9, India. *Office:* Agricultural Economics Research Centre, University of Delhi, Delhi 7, India.

CAREER: University of Delhi, Delhi, India, researcher and teacher of agricultural economics, 1955—, deputy director of Agricultural Economics Research Centre, 1960—. Government of India, member of Study Team on Fair Price Shops and of Agricultural Economics and Marketing Committee of Indian Council of Agricultural Research. *Member:* Indian Society of Agricultural Economics, Royal Economic Society (England; fellow), Indian Economic Association, American Farm Economic Association, Agricultural Economics Society (England), International Agricultural Economists Conference.

WRITINGS: Decline of Agricultural Prices, University of Delhi Press, 1956; (with P. K. Mukherjee) *A Pilot Survey of Fourteen Villages in Uttar Pradesh and Punjab*, Asia Publishing House, 1959; *An Economic Survey of Shamaspur Village*, Asia Publishing House, 1959; (contributor) *Agricultural Labour in India*, edited by V. K. R. V. Rao, Asia Publishing House, 1962; *Agrarian Relations and Early British Rule in India*, Asia Publishing House, 1963; (contributor) *Readings in Indian Economic History*, edited by B. N. Ganguli, Asia Publishing House, 1964; (with A. Majid) *Producer's Response to Changes in Prices and Marketing Policies*, Asia Publishing House, 1965; *Freedom From Foreign Food*, Blitz National Forum, 1965; *India's Agrarian Structure: A Study in Evolution*, Mainstream, 1966. Contributor to journals. Member of editorial board, *Enquiry* (Delhi).

WORK IN PROGRESS: Research projects on capital formation in Indian agriculture, on the extent of commercialization and monetization in the Indian rural economy, and on village social accounts in the Indian rural economy.†

* * *

GUTHRIE, Donald 1916-

PERSONAL: Born February 21, 1916, in Ipswich, England; son of Malcolm (an engineer) and Maud (Lindenboom) Guthrie; married Mary Freeman, March 2, 1946; children: Eleanor, Alistair, Rosalyn, Anthony, Adrian. *Education:* London Bible College, B.D. (honors), 1949; London University, M.Th., 1951, Ph.D., 1961. *Religion:* Christian.

CAREER: Worked as an accountant, 1932-46; London Bible College, London, England, senior lecturer in New Testament, 1949—. *Member:* Studiorum Novi Testamenti Societas.

WRITINGS: The Pastoral Epistles and the Mind of Paul, Tyndale Press, 1956; *The Epistle to the Hebrews in Recent Thought*, London Bible College, 1956; *The Pastoral Epistles*, Tyndale Press, 1957; *New Testament Introduction* Volume I: *The Pauline Epistles*, Tyndale, 1961, 2nd edition, Inter-Varsity, 1964; Volume II: *Hebrews to Revelation*, Tyndale, 1962, 2nd edition, Inter-Varsity, 1964; Volume III: *Gospel and Acts*, Inter-Varsity, 1965; *New Testament Introduction*, one volume, 3rd revised edition, Tyndale, 1970; *Epistles from Prison*, Abingdon, 1964; (editor) *Galatians*, Nelson, 1969; (editor with J. A. Moyer) *The New Bible Commentary*, 3rd revised edition, Eerdmans, 1970; *A Shorter Life of Christ*, Zondervan, 1970; *Jesus the Messiah: An Illustrated Life of Christ*, Zondervan, 1972. Articles in theological publications. Contributor to encyclopedias.

WORK IN PROGRESS: Book on the practice of pseudepigraphy, 200 B.C.-200 A.D., for Tyndale Press.

AVOCATIONAL INTERESTS: Music, photography, motoring.†

* * *

GUTHRIE, Harvey Henry, Jr. 1924-

PERSONAL: Born October 31, 1924, in Santa Paula, Calif.; son of Harvey Henry and Emma (Aubrey) Guthrie; married Doris Peyton, December 29, 1945; children: Lawrence, Lynn, Stephen, Andrew. *Education:* Missouri Valley College, B.A., 1945; studied at Union Theological Seminary, New York, 1944-46; General Theological Seminary, S.T.B., 1948, S.T.M., 1953, Th.D., 1958. *Politics:* Democrat. *Home:* 4 Berkeley St., Cambridge, Mass. 02138. *Office:* Episcopal Theological School, Cambridge, Mass. 02138.

CAREER: Ordained to Episcopal Ministry, 1947; St. Martha's Church, White Plains, N.Y., vicar, 1947-50; General Theological Seminary, New York, N.Y., tutor and instructor, 1950-58; Episcopal Theological School, Cambridge, Mass., assistant professor, 1958-64, professor of Old Testament, 1964—, associate dean, 1967-69, dean, 1969—. Visiting lecturer, Columbia University, 1955-56; research fellow, Yale University, 1965; visiting professor, Andover-Newton Theological School, 1966-67. *Member:* Society of Biblical Literature and Exegesis, American Oriental Society, National Association of Biblical Instructors, American Schools of Oriental Research. *Awards, honors:* American Association of Theological Schools Faculty fellowship, 1961-62.

WRITINGS: God and History in the Old Testament, Seabury, 1960; *Israel's Sacred Songs*, Seabury, 1966. Contributor of book reviews and articles to theological publications in this country and abroad.

SIDELIGHTS: Guthrie did private study and research at University of Gottingen, Germany, 1961-62.

* * *

GUTTERIDGE, William F(rank) 1919-

PERSONAL: Born September 21, 1919, in Beddington, Surrey, England; son of Frank Leonard (a local government official) and Norah (Tighe) Gutteridge; married Margaret Parker, July 5, 1944; children: Susan, Jane, Judith. *Education:* Oxford University, B.A., 1948, diploma in education, 1949, M.A., 1953. *Home:* 26 St. Mark's Rd., Leamington Spa, Warwickshire, England. *Office:* Office of Director of Complementary Studies, University of Aston, Gosta Green, Birmingham B4 7ET, England.

CAREER: Royal Military Academy, Sandhurst, England, senior lecturer in modern subjects, 1949-63; Lanchester Polytechnic, Coventry, England, head of department of languages and social science (modern studies), 1963-71. Council of National Academic Awards, chairman of combined studies board, 1971—, and politics panel, 1974—;

secretary, Pugwash Group for Scientists in World Affairs, 1966—. *Military service:* British Army, 1939-45; became major; served in India-Burma Theater; received Order of the British Empire. *Member:* Royal Institute of International Affairs, Institute for Strategic Studies, Institute of Race Relations, African Studies Association of Great Britain. *Awards, honors:* Nuffield Foundation traveling fellowship in Africa, 1960-61.

WRITINGS: Armed Forces in New States, Oxford University Press, 1962; (with Neville Brown) *The African Military Balance*, Institute for Strategic Studies, 1964; *Military Institutions and Power in New States*, Praeger, 1965; *The Military in African Politics*, Methuen, 1969; (with Richard Booth) *Armed Forces of African States*, Institute for Strategic Studies, 1970; *The Coming Confrontation in Southern Africa*, Institute for the Study of Conflict, 1971; *Military Regimes in Africa: Six Case Studies*, Methuen, 1974. Contributor to *Parliamentary Affairs*, *British Army Review*, *Western Political Quarterly*, and other journals.

* * *

GUZIE, Tad W(alter) 1934-

PERSONAL: Born August 27, 1934, in Milwaukee, Wis.; son of Walter T. and Kathryn (Janke) Guzie. *Education:* Saint Louis University, A.B. (summa cum laude), 1958, M.A., 1959; studied at Catholic University of Louvain, and Saint Louis University, 1962-66, received S.T.L., 1967; Cambridge University, Ph.D., 1970. *Office:* Department of Theology, Marquette University, Milwaukee, Wis. 53233.

CAREER: Member of Society of Jesus; ordained Roman Catholic priest, 1965. Creighton Preparatory School, Omaha, Neb., instructor in Latin, Greek, and English literature, 1959-62; Marquette University, Milwaukee, Wis., assistant professor of theology, 1970—.

WRITINGS: Analogy of Learning, Sheed, 1960; *For Adult Catholics Only*, Bruce, 1967; *Jesus and the Eucharist*, Paulist, 1974; *What a Modern Catholic Believes about Confession*, Thomas More, 1974; *What a Modern Catholic Believes about Salvation*, Thomas More, in press. Contributor of articles to theological journals and Catholic periodicals.

WORK IN PROGRESS: Studies in psychology and religious symbolism.

* * *

GUZZWELL, John 1930-

PERSONAL: Born June 22, 1930, in Southampton, England; son of John (a marine engineer) and Maria (Boltman) Guzzwell; married Maureen Samways, April 19, 1960; children: James and John (twins). *Education:* Attended St. George's Preparatory School, Jersey, Channel Islands; received remainder of education in prison camp in Germany during World War II (a period covering two-and one-half years). *Home:* 2 Normandy Close, Sway, Hampshire, England.

CAREER: Served five-year apprenticeship as a joiner, then became a woodworker and cabinetmaker in South Africa, chiefly in the building industry; worked for short periods in yacht yards in Canada and Australia; sailed solo around the world in a twenty-foot boat, covering 33,000 miles during a four-year period; now a self-employed boat builder in England. *Member:* Slocum Society (life), Ocean Cruising Club. *Awards, honors:* Royal Cruising Club Seamanship Medal, 1957; Slocum Society Award, 1959; Cruising Club of America Blue Water Medal, 1959.

WRITINGS: "Trekka" Round the World, Adlard Coles, 1963. Contributor of articles to *Sea Spray* (New Zealand yachting magazine), 1956-59.

WORK IN PROGRESS: Building a forty-five foot yacht for own use, expecting to write on this project and future voyaging with boat.

AVOCATIONAL INTERESTS: Outdoor life.

BIOGRAPHICAL/CRITICAL SOURCES: Miles Smeeton, *Once is Enough*, Hart-Davis, 1959.†

* * *

GWYN, W(illiam) B(rent) 1927-

PERSONAL: Born October 10, 1927, in Baltimore, Md.; son of Lawrence Sangston and Deborah (Tingle) Gwyn; married Ann Stewart MacDougall, July 14, 1956; children: Hugh Tingle, Bruce Alexander. *Education:* University of Virginia, B.A. (honors), 1950, M.A., 1952, graduate study, 1952-54; University of London, Ph.D., 1956. *Politics:* Democrat. *Home:* 8011 Jeannette St., New Orleans, La. *Office:* Department of Political Science, Tulane University, New Orleans, La.

CAREER: University of Tennessee, Knoxville, assistant professor of political science, 1956-57; Bucknell University, Lewisburg, Pa., assistant professor of political science, 1957-63; Tulane University of Louisiana, New Orleans, associate professor, 1963-69, professor of political science, 1969—. *Military service:* U.S. Army, 1945-47. *Member:* American Political Science Association, International Commission for History of Representative and Parliamentary Institutions, Phi Beta Kappa.

WRITINGS: Democracy and the Cost of Politics in Britain, Athlone Press, 1962; *The Meaning of the Separation of Powers*, Tulane Studies in Political Science, 1965; (contributor) Stanley V. Anderson, editor, *Ombudsmen for American Government?*, Prentice-Hall, 1968. Contributor of articles to political science journals.

WORK IN PROGRESS: Research on the institutionalization of the British parliamentary commission for administration.

* * *

GYLDENVAND, Lily M. 1917-

PERSONAL: Born May 26, 1917, in LaMoure, N.D.; daughter of Ole C. (a merchant) and Karen G. (Myhr) Gyldenvand. *Education:* Concordia College, Moorhead, Minn., B.A., 1939. *Religion:* Lutheran. *Home:* 2088 Fry St., St. Paul, Minn. 55113.

CAREER: Secretary for Department of Christian Education, Evangelical Lutheran Church, Minneapolis, Minn., 1939-41, and Commodity Credit Corporation, U.S. Department of Agriculture, Minneapolis, Minn., 1941-52; The American Lutheran Church, Minneapolis, Minn., administrative and editorial assistant, 1953-60; American Lutheran Church Women, Minneapolis, Minn., editor of *Scope* (magazine), 1960—. *Member:* Associated Church Press, Lutheran Daughters of Reformation (international president, 1948-54), Lutheran Editors and Managers Association,

WRITINGS—All published by Augsburg: *Beyond All Doubt*, 1949; *What Am I Saying?*, 1952; *Of All Things*, 1956; *So You're Only Human*, 1957; *What Am I Praying?*, 1964; *Call Her Blessed: Every Woman Who Discovers the Gifts of God*, 1967; *Invitation to Joy*, 1969.

Co-author of study manuals for American Lutheran Church

Women, 1964, 1965. Writer of tracts, radio scripts, and magazine articles. Editor of *Yearbook of the Evangelical Lutheran Church*, 1953-60, and editorial assistant for *Annual Report of Evangelical Lutheran Church*, 1953-60.

BIOGRAPHICAL SOURCES: Minneapolis Sunday Tribune, December 27, 1964.

*   *   *

HAAG, Jessie Helen 1917-

PERSONAL: Born April 7, 1917, in Reading, Pa.; daughter of Charles Milton and Helen Annie (Sell) Haag. *Education:* Temple University, B.S., 1939, M.Ed., 1943, Ed.D., 1950. *Office:* Belmont Hall 222, University of Texas, Austin, Tex. 78712.

CAREER: Lansdale (Pa.) public schools, teacher of health education and health coordinator-supervisor, 1939-46; Lebanon Valley College, Annville, Pa., chairman of college health education, 1946-47; Pennsylvania State College, West Chester, instructor in health education, 1947-50; University of Texas, Austin, assistant professor, 1950-56, associate professor, 1956-57, professor of physical and health education, 1967—.

MEMBER: American Association for Health, Physical Education and Recreation (fellow; member of executive council, School Health Division; member of Southern District board of director, 1961-64), American Association for the Advancement of Science (fellow; member of research council), American College Health Association (Southwest section president, 1957), Royal Society of Health (fellow), American Public Health Association (fellow), American School Health Association (fellow), International Congress for Health Education of the Public, American Association of University Professors, Texas Classroom Teachers Association, Texas Association for Health, Physical Education and Recreation, Pi Lambda Theta, Delta Psi Kappa. *Awards, honors:* International Congress for Health Education of the Public award, 1959; Texas Association for Health, Physical Education and Recreation Honor Award, 1962; Southern District, American Association for Health, Physical Education, and Recreation Honor Award, 1970.

WRITINGS: School Health Program (college text), Holt, 1958, 3rd edition, Lea & Febiger, 1972; *Physiology* (intermediate text), Steck, 1959; *School Health Practices in the United States*, American Association for Health, Physical Education and Recreation, 1961; *Health Education for Young Adults* (high school text), and teacher's manual, Steck, 1965; *Focusing On Health* (high school text with teacher's manual and tests), Steck, 1973; *Toward Sexual Maturity*, Steck, 1973; *Tests for Focusing on Health*, Steck, 1973.

Author, co-author, and editor of publications for Texas Education Agency. Contributor of articles to professional journals. Member of Editorial board: *American Journal of Public Health, Research Quarterly*, and *TAHPER Journal*.

*   *   *

HABGOOD, John Stapylton 1927-

PERSONAL: Born June 23, 1927, in Buckinghamshire, England; son of Arthur Henry (a medical doctor) and Vera (Chetwynd-Stapylton) Habgood; married Rosalie Mary Anne Boston, June 7, 1961; children: Laura Caroline, Francis John. *Education:* King's College, Cambridge, B.A., 1948, theological study, 1953-54. *Politics:* Various. *Home:* St. John's Rectory, Jedburgh, Roxburghshire, Scotland.

CAREER: Cambridge University, Cambridge, England, university demonstrator in pharmacology, 1950-52, fellow, King's College, 1952-55; ordained priest, Church of England, 1954; curate in Kensington, London, England, 1954-56; Westcott House (theological college), Cambridge, England, vice-principal, 1956-62; St. John's Episcopal Church, Jedburgh, Scotland, rector, 1962—. Select preacher, Cambridge University, 1959; lecturer in ethics, Edinburgh Theological College. Examining chaplain to Bishop of Worcester and Bishop of Edinburgh.

WRITINGS: (Contributor) *Soundings*, edited by A. R. Vidler, Cambridge University Press, 1962; *Religion and Science*, Mills & Boon, 1964 (published as *Truths in Tension*, Holt, 1965); *A Biologist Looks at Life*, S.P.C.K., 1965. Book reviewer for numerous journals. Contributor to *Journal of Physiology, Theology*, and other periodicals.

WORK IN PROGRESS: Scientific and Christian Mythology.†

*   *   *

HACH, Clarence Woodrow 1917-

PERSONAL: Born February 5, 1917, in Clutier, Iowa; son of James and Frieda (Dose) Hach. *Education:* Iowa State Teachers College (now University of Northern Iowa), A.B., 1937; University of Iowa, A.M., 1939; postgraduate study at University of Wisconsin, 1941, University of Minnesota, 1953, and Columbia University, 1954. *Politics:* Democrat. *Religion:* Lutheran. *Home:* 9425 Ridgeway Ave., Evanston, Ill. *Office:* Evanston Township High School, 1600 Dodge Ave., Evanston, Ill.

CAREER: High school teacher in Crystal Lake and Davenport, Iowa, 1937-44; Stephens College, Columbia, Mo., teacher of English and journalism, 1944-45; Evanston Township High School, Evanston, Ill., teacher of English and journalism, 1945—, English Department chairman, 1954-69, supervisor of English, 1969—. *Member:* National Education Association, National Council of Teachers of English, Journalism Education Association (president, 1951-53), Illinois Association of Teachers of English, Illinois Association of Teachers of Journalism, Chicago Press Club. *Awards, honors:* Teacher of the Year, Illinois Association of Teachers of Journalism, 1947; Ford Foundation fellowship, 1953-54; Pioneer Award, National Scholastic Press Association, 1970.

WRITINGS: (With Martha Gray) *English for Today*, Lippincott, 1950, revised edition, 1955; (with E. E. English) *Scholastic Journalism*, Iowa State University Press, 1950, 5th edition, 1972; (with Wallace Stegner and others) *Modern Composition*, six books, Holt, 2nd edition, 1968. Contributor to *English Journal, Education Digest*, and *Scholastic Editor*.

*   *   *

HACKER, Rose (Goldbloom) 1906-

PERSONAL: Born March 3, 1906, in London, England; daughter of Abraham (a clothing manufacturer) and Rebecca (Silverstone) Goldbloom; married Mark Gould Hacker, November 9, 1930; children: Lawrence, Michael. *Education:* Attended The Polytechnic, London, England. *Politics:* Labour. *Religion:* Jewish. *Home:* 9 Highgate West Hill, London, England.

CAREER: Volunteer social worker, marriage counselor, and family life educator. London County Council Children's Committee (children's homes), member for northeast district, 1948-67; Friern Hospital Management Committee, member, 1950-62; National Hospital for Nervous Diseases, member of board of governors, 1962—. *Member:* National Marriage Guidance Council, National Association for Mental Health, Greater London Council, London Council for Social Service, London Marriage Guidance Council.

WRITINGS: Telling the Teenagers, Deutsch, 1957; *The Opposite Sex,* Pan Books, 1960; *You and Your Daughter,* New English Library, 1964; (contributor) Boyd Crouch, editor, *Overcoming Learning Difficulties,* Verry, 1972. Contributor to *Sex Education Perspective,* published by National Marriage Guidance Council; contributor of series of articles to *Woman's Own.*

SIDELIGHTS: Mrs. Hacker speaks French and German. *Avocational interests:* Travel.

* * *

HACKETT, Cecil Arthur 1908-

PERSONAL: Born January 19, 1908, in Birmingham, England; son of Henry (an engineer) and Alice (Setchell) Hackett; married Mary Hazel Armstrong (a journalist), January 26, 1942. *Education:* Attended University of Birmingham; Emmanuel College, Cambridge (scholar and prizeman), B.A., 1931, M.A., 1934; Universite de Paris, Docteur de l'Universite, 1938. *Home:* Shawford Close, Shawford, Winchester, England.

CAREER: Lycee Louis-le-Grand, Paris, France, assistant d'Anglais, 1934-36; Borough Road College, Isleworth, England, lecturer in French and English, 1936-39; British Council, Paris, France, education officer, 1945-46; University of Glasgow, Glasgow, Scotland, lecturer in French, 1947-52; University of Southampton, Southampton, England, professor of French and head of department of French language and literature, 1952-70, now professor emeritus. Visiting professor, Brown University, 1962-63, Dalhousie University, 1967-68, and University of Western Australia, 1972. *Military service:* British Army, 1939-45; served in France, Italy, and North Africa; became major; designated Commandeur de l'Ordre du Nichan-Iftikhar. Alliance Francaise (president, Southampton branch, 1954-58), Society of Authors, Southampton Modern Languages Society (president, 1961-65). *Awards, honors:* Chevalier de la Legion d'Honneur (for literary work), 1958.

WRITINGS: Le Lyrisme de Rimbaud, Nizet, 1938; *Rimbaud l'enfant,* Corti, 1948; (compiler) *Anthology of Modern French Poetry,* Macmillan, 1952, 3rd revised edition, Blackwell, 1970; *Rimbaud,* Bowes, 1957; *Autour de Rimbaud,* Editions Klincksieck, 1967; (compiler) *New French Poetry: An Anthology,* Blackwell, 1972.

WORK IN PROGRESS: A book on modern French prose; studies on Rimbaud.

AVOCATIONAL INTERESTS: Travel, photography, painting.

* * *

HACKFORTH-JONES, (Frank) Gilbert 1900-

PERSONAL: Born May 14, 1900, in Arkley, Hertfordshire, England; married, 1923; one child. *Education:* Attended Royal Naval Colleges at Osborne and Dartmouth, 1914-17. *Religion:* Church of England. *Address:* c/o Lloyds Bank, Lymington, Hampshire, England.

CAREER: Formerly with Royal Navy, retiring as commander; writer on sea-going subjects, especially life in the British Navy and sailing. *Member:* Royal Naval Sailing Association.

WRITINGS—All published by Hodder & Stoughton, except as indicated: *No Less Renowned,* W. Blackwood, 1939.

Submarine Flotilla, 1940; *Rough Passage,* 1941; *One-One-One: Stories of the Navy,* 1942, published as *Torpedo!: Stories of the Royal Navy,* Morrow, 1943; *Submarine Alone: A Story of H. M. S. Steadfast,* 1943; *Price Was High,* 1946; *Sixteen Bells: Stories of the Royal Navy in Peace and War,* 1946; *Dangerous Trade: A Novel of the Submarine Branch,* 1946; *Greatest Fool,* 1948; *Questing Hound,* 1948; *Come Sailing,* Batchworth Press, 1948; *Sweethearts and Wives,* 1949.

Worst Enemy: Portrait of a Harassed Naval Officer, 1950; *Green Sailors,* 1951; *Green Sailors in the South Seas,* 1951; *Green Sailors on Holiday,* 1952; *Green Sailors, Ahoy! Or, Wanted A Crew,* 1953; *The Sole Survivor,* 1953; *Green Sailors Beware!,* 1954; *Fish Out of Water,* 1954; *True Book About Submarines,* Muller, 1955; *Green Sailors and Blue Water,* 1955; *Green Sailors and Fair Winds,* 1956; *Death of an Admiral,* 1956; *Green Sailors to Gibralter,* 1957; *Life in the Navy Today: A Youngman's Guide to All Branches of the Royal Navy,* Cassell, 1957; *Green Sailors in the Caribbean,* 1958; *Hurricane Harbour, Pre-View of a Victor,* 1958.

Green Sailors in the Galapagos, 1960; *Life on the Ocean Wave: A Chapter in the Life of a Naval Officer* (novel), 1960; *The Boys' Book of Sailing,* Roy, 1961 (published in England as *Sailing,* Burke Publishing Co., 1964); *Crack of Doom,* 1961; *I Am the Captain* (novel), 1963; *Danger Below,* 1963; *One Man's Wars* (novel), 1964; *Warrior's Playtime* (novel), 1965; *Fight to a Finish* (novel), 1966; *The Stern Chase* (novel), 1967; (contributor) John Welcome, editor, *Best Secret Service Stories,* Faber, 1967; *Storm in Harbor* (novel), 1968; *Yellow Peril* (novel), 1969.

Chinese Poison (novel), 1970; (contributor) *Tales of the Sea,* W. Blackwood, 1970; *Security Risk* (novel), 1971; *All Stations to Malta* (novel), 1972; *An Explosive Situation* (novel), 1973; *Second in Command* (novel), 1974.

Author of radio plays, television series, and filmscripts.

WORK IN PROGRESS: A novel, *No Bloodshed.*

* * *

HADFIELD, Ellis Charles Raymond 1909-
(Charles Hadfield; E. C. R. Hadfield; pseudonym, Charles Alexander)

PERSONAL: Born August 5, 1909, in Pietersburg, South Africa; son of Alexander Charles and Marion Francis (Fulford) Hadfield; married Alice Mary Smyth (now a part-time writer), October 20, 1945; children: Laura (stepdaughter); Alexander, John, Caroline. *Education:* Attended Blundell's School and St. Edmund Hall, Oxford. *Religion:* Society of Friends. *Home and office:* 21 Randolph Road, London W9 1AN, England. *Agent:* David Higham Associates Ltd., 5-8 Lower John St., Golden Square, London W1R 3PE, England.

CAREER: Oxford University Press, London, England, editor, 1936-38, chief editor of juvenile books, 1938-39, 1945-46; Central Office of Information, London, England, director of publications, 1946-48, overseas controller, 1948-62. Director of David & Charles (publishers), 1960-64. Councillor, Paddington Borough Council, 1924-35; part-time member, British Waterways Board, 1962-66. *Member:* Railway and Canal Historical Society (president, 1960-63), Newcomen Society. *Awards, honors:* Companion of Order of St. Michael and St. George, 1954.

WRITINGS—Under name Charles Hadfield: (with John Norris) *Waterways to Stratford*, David & Charles, 1962, 2nd edition, 1968; *Canals of the World*, Basil Blackwell, 1964; *The Canals of the West Midlands*, David & Charles, 1966, 2nd edition, Augustus M. Kelley, 1969; *The Canals of the East Midlands*, David & Charles, 1966, 2nd edition, 1970; *Canals and Waterways*, Raleigh press, 1966; (with wife, Alice Mary Hadfield) *The Cotswolds*, Batsford, 1966; *The Canals of South West England*, David & Charles, 1967, Augustus M. Kelley, 1968; *Atmospheric Railways: A Victorian Venture in Silent Speed*, David & Charles, 1967; (with Michael Streat) *Holiday Cruising on Inland Waterways*, David & Charles, 1968, 2nd edition, 1971; *The Canal Age*, David & Charles, 1968, Praeger, 1969; *The Canals of North West England*, David & Charles, 1970; *The Canals of Yorkshire and North East England*, David & Charles, 1972-73.

Under name E. C. R. Hadfield: *Civilian Fire Fighter*, English Universities Press, 1941; (with James E. MacColl) *Pilot Guide to Political London*, Pilot Press, 1945; (with MacColl) *British Local Government*, Hutchinson's University Library, 1948.

Under name Ellis Charles Raymond: (editor) *Book of Sea Verse*, Oxford University Press, 1940; (compiler) *Book of Animal Verse*, Oxford University Press, circa 1943; (with Frank Eyre) *English Rivers and Canals*, Collins, 1945; *British Canals: An Illustrated History*, Phoenix House, 1950, 4th edition, Augustus M. Kelley, 1969; *The Canals of Southern England*, Phoenix House, 1955, augmented excerpts published as *The Canals of South and Southeast England*, Augustus M. Kelley, 1967; *Introducing Canals: A Guide to British Waterways Today*, Benn, 1955; *The Canals of South Wales and the Border*, University of Wales Press, 1960, 2nd edition, David & Charles in conjunction with University of Wales Press, 1967.

Under pseudonym Charles Alexander: *The Church's Year*, Oxford University Press, 1950.

Children's books—under name Ellis Charles Raymond Hadfield: (with C. H. Ellis) *Young Collector's Handbook*, Oxford University Press, 1940; (with Alexander D'Agapeyeff) *Maps*, Oxford University Press, 1942, 2nd edition, 1950; *Fire Service To-day*, Oxford University Press, 1944, 2nd edition, 1953.

Contributor of articles on canals to journals. *Editor,* Quaker Monthly, 1963-69.

*   *   *

HAGEN, Elizabeth Pauline   1915-

PERSONAL: Born December 2, 1915, in Maryland; daughter of Charles Frederick and Kathryn (Bernard) Hagen. *Education:* Western Maryland College, A.B., 1936; Columbia University, M.A., 1948, Ph.D., 1952. *Home:* 525 East 86th St., New York, N.Y. *Office:* Teachers College, Columbia University, 525 West 120th St., New York, N.Y. 10027.

CAREER: High school science teacher in Elkton, Md., 1936-43, and Haverstraw, N.Y., 1946-47; Board of High Education, New York, N.Y., lecturer, 1949-50; Columbia University, Teachers College, New York, N.Y., research associate and instructor, 1950-56, associate professor, 1956-

72, professor of education, and associate dean for program development, 1972—. Visiting professor, University of Puerto Rico, 1958. Consultant, Central Institute of Education, Delhi, India. *Military service:* U.S. Naval Reserve (WAVES), 1943-46; became lieutenant. *Member:* American Psychological Association, American Association for the Advancement of Science, American Educational Research Association, National Education Association, Sigma Xi, Pi Lambda Theta.

WRITINGS: (With Robert L. Thorndike) *10,000 Careers*, Wiley, 1959; (with Thorndike) *Measurement and Evaluation in Psychology and Education*, Wiley, 1961. Contributor of articles to U.S. military service research reports and bulletins, and to professional journals.

*   *   *

HALE, Oron James   1902-

PERSONAL: Born July 29, 1902, in Goldendale, Wash.; son of William Robert (a farmer) and Frances I. (Putnam) Hale; married Annette F. Van Winkle, August 7, 1929 (died August, 1968); married Virginia Smith Zehmer, July, 1970. *Education:* University of Washington, Seattle, B.A., 1925; University of Pennsylvania, M.A., 1928, Ph.D., 1930. *Politics:* Democrat. *Religion:* Presbyterian. *Home:* 1867 Winston Rd., Charlottesville, Va. *Office:* Department of History, University of Virginia, Charlottesville, Va.

CAREER: University of Pennsylvania, Philadelphia, instructor in history, 1926-28; University of Virginia, Charlottesville, assistant professor, 1929-38, associate professor, 1938-46, professor of European history, 1946-72, professor emeritus, 1972—, chairman of department, 1955-62. U.S. High Commission for Germany, commissioner for Bavaria, 1950-52. Member of Institute for Advanced Study, Princeton, N.J., 1963-64. Visiting summer professor at Duke University, University of Missouri, University of North Carolina, and Harvard University. *Military service:* U.S. Army Reserve, 1946-60; on active duty with General Staff, 1942-46; became colonel; received Commendation Ribbon.

MEMBER: American Historical Association (chairman of committee on war documents, 1957-62; chairman of conference group for central European history, 1962-63), Society of American Historians, Southern Historical Association, Phi Beta Kappa, Colonnade Club. *Awards, honors:* Social Science Research Council fellowship in London and Berlin, 1932-33; George Louis Beer Prize of American Historical Association, 1931, for *Germany and the Diplomatic Revolution, 1904-1906*; Litt.D. from Hampden-Sydney College, 1958; Outstanding Civilian Award from U.S. Department of the Army, 1964; Commander's Cross, Order of Merit, Federal Republic of Germany, 1969.

WRITINGS: Germany and the Diplomatic Revolution, 1904-1906, University of Pennsylvania Press, 1930; *Publicity and Diplomacy, 1890-1914*, Appleton, 1940; *The Captive Press in the Third Reich*, Princeton University Press, 1964; *The Great Illusion, 1900-1914*, Harper, 1971. Contributor to *Virginia Quarterly Review*, *South Atlantic Quarterly*, *Journal of Modern History*, other historical and military journals.

SIDELIGHTS: Hale speaks and writes German and has reading knowledge of French, Spanish, and Italian. *Avocational interests:* Hunting, golf, reading military history.

*   *   *

HALEY, Joseph E.   1915-

PERSONAL: Born February 26, 1915, in Sewickley, Pa.;

son of Bartholomew Ignatius (a railroad movement director) and Margaret (Hegner) Haley. *Education:* Carnegie Institute of Technology (now Carnegie-Mellon University), student, 1932-33; University of Notre Dame, A.B. (magna cum laude), 1937; Catholic University of America, M.A., 1950. *Politics:* "Generally Democratic." *Home and office:* University of Portland, Portland, Ore. 97203.

CAREER: Roman Catholic priest, member of Congregation of Holy Cross, University of Notre Dame, Notre Dame, Ind., assistant professor of theology, 1946-60; University of Portland, Portland, Ore., assistant professor of theology, 1960-71, director of international programs, 1971—. Active in Portland Ecumenical Conference and in lay mission work. *Member:* National Catholic Social Action Conference, Society of Catholic College Teachers of Sacred Doctrine, Mental Health Association of Oregon, Portland Urban League (member of board of directors), Knights of Columbus.

WRITINGS: Accent on Purity: Guide for Sex Education, Fides, 1948, revised edition, 1957; (editor) *Apostolic Sanctity in the World,* University of Notre Dame Press, 1957; (editor) *The Sister in America Today,* Fides, 1965; *New Directions in Religious Life, and Mental Health and Religion,* University of Portland Press, 1965; (contributor) William C. Beir, editor, *Woman in Modern Life,* Fordham University Press, 1968. Contributor to *Encyclopaedia Britannica.* Editor of *Proceedings of Sisters' Institute of Spirituality,* University of Notre Dame Press, 1953, 1954, 1957-60.

* * *

HALL, Calvin (Springer) 1909-

PERSONAL: Born January 18, 1909, in Seattle, Wash.; son of Calvin Springer and Dovre (Johnson) Hall; married Irene Sanborn (a teacher), November 10, 1932; children: Dovre Pamela. *Education:* Attended University of Washington, Seattle; University of California, Berkeley, A.B., 1930, Ph.D., 1933. *Home and office:* 3525 Crystal View Court, Miami, Fla. 33133.

CAREER: University of California, Berkeley, instructor in psychology, 1933-34; University of Oregon, Eugene, assistant professor of psychology, 1934-37; Western Reserve University, Cleveland, Ohio, associate professor of psychology, 1937-40, professor, 1940-57, chairman of department of psychology, 1937-57; Syracuse University, Syracuse, N.Y., professor and executive officer, department of psychology, 1957-59; University of Miami, Coral Gables, Fla., visiting professor of psychology, 1959-60; University of Nijmegen, Nijmegen, Netherlands, Fulbright professor, 1960-61; Institute of Dream Research, Miami, Fla., director, 1961—. *Member:* American Psychological Association.

WRITINGS: The Meaning of Dreams, Harper, 1953; *A Primer of Freudian Psychology,* World Publishing, 1954; (with Gardner Lindzey) *Theories of Personality,* Wiley, 1957, 2nd edition, 1970; *Psychology,* Howard Allen, 1960; (with VandeCastle) *The Content Analysis of Dreams,* Appleton, 1966; (with Richard E. Lind) *Dreams, Life, and Literature: A Study of Franz Kafka,* University of North Carolina Press, 1970; (with Alan P. Bell) *The Personality of a Child Molester,* Aldine, 1971; (with Vernon J. Nordby) *A Primer of Jungian Psychology,* Taplinger, 1973; (with V. J. Nordby) *A Guide to Psychologists and their Concepts,* Freeman, 1974. Contributor of chapters to *Handbook of Experimental Psychology, Handbook of Social Psychology, Comparative Psychology, You and Marriage,* and *Read-*

ings in Child Development. Also contributor to psychological journals.

WORK IN PROGRESS: Essays on Freudian psychology.†

* * *

HALL, D(onald) J(ohn) 1903-

PERSONAL: Born August 3, 1903, in Oxford, England; son of Herbert Henry and Ada (Grainger) Hall; married Isabel Compton, February 23, 1928; children: Christopher, Sarah Hall van Niekerk. *Education:* Corpus Christi College, Cambridge, B.A., 1923, and M.A. *Politics:* "A plague on all their houses." *Religion:* Christian. *Home:* Porth-y-Castell, Portmeirion, Penrhyndeudraeth, Merioneth, Wales. *Agent:* A. P. Watt & Son, Norfolk St., Strand, London W.C. 2, England.

CAREER: Lawyer in London, England, 1925-28, and solicitor of Supreme Court, 1927; author, 1932—. Served with British Foreign Office in London, England, and Washington, D.C., 1939-46. Diplomatic adviser to British Broadcasting Corp., 1946-47. *Member:* P.E.N.

WRITINGS: Enchanted Sand (travel), Methuen, 1932, Morrow, 1933; *Romanian Furrow* (travel), Methuen, 1933; *No Retreat* (novel), Harrap, 1936; *Perilous Sanctuary* (novel), Macmillan, 1937; *This Other Eden* (novel), Harrap, 1938; *The Phoenix-Flower* (epic poem), Falcon Publishing Co., 1953; *The Seeming Truth* (novel), Falcon Publishing Co., 1954; *Eagle Argent* (travel), Methuen, 1956; *The Crowd is Silent* (novel), Dent, 1961; *The Ring of Words* (autobiographical career book), Educational Explorers, 1965; *Mediaeval English Pilgrimage,* Routledge & Kegan Paul, 1965; *Journey Into Morning* (poems), Chatto & Windus, 1972, Wesleyan University Press, 1973; *The Trinity Brothers,* Stockwell, 1973. Also writer of broadcasting scripts and articles.

WORK IN PROGRESS: Vachek, a novel.

SIDELIGHTS: Hall said: "I have lived with Indians in New Mexico and with peasants in Romania; I have traveled all over the place and enjoyed it all. But I have most pleasure in my grandchildren, my children and my wife. This takes up a lot of my time so that I miss important things which might possibly be useful to me, but for which I don't give a hoot. For the rest, I like gardening and searching for a nice wild place where I can be quiet. I read, write, and avoid arithmetic." His novel, *Perilous Sanctuary,* was published in four countries.

* * *

HALL, Elvajean 1910-

PERSONAL: Born May 30, 1910, in Hamilton, Ill.; daughter of Nelson (a clergyman) and Nellie Jean (Hyer) Hall. *Education:* Oberlin College, A.B., 1930; University of Wisconsin, graduate study, 1931-32; Columbia University, M.L.S., 1941. *Politics:* Independent Republican. *Religion:* Protestant. *Home:* 233 Commonwealth Ave., Boston, Mass. 02116. *Office:* Division of Instruction, 88 Chestnut St., West Newton, Mass. 02161.

CAREER: Milwaukee University School, Milwaukee, Wis., teacher and librarian, 1937-42; Jackson (Mich.) public schools, school library supervisor, 1942-44; Stephens College, Columbia Mo., head librarian, 1944-46; Newton (Mass.) public schools, supervisor of School Library Services, 1946—. Library consultant, Chung Chi College, The Chinese University of Hong Kong, 1962-63; visiting lecturer, University College, Dublin, summers, 1967-69. *Member:* Authors Guild, National League of American Pen Women (president, Boston chapter, 1970-72), Women's National Book Association (president, Boston chapter, 1957-59; national secretary, 1959-61), Boston Authors Club (member of board, 1973—), Delta Kappa Gamma, Kappa Delta.

WRITINGS: Books to Build On, Bowker, 1954, 2nd edition, 1957; *Land and People of Argentina*, Lippincott, 1960, 2nd edition, 1972; *Pilgrim Stories*, Rand McNally, 1961; *Land and People of Norway*, Lippincott, 1963, 2nd edition, 1973; *Pilgrim Neighbors*, Rand McNally, 1964; *The Volga: Lifeline of Russia*, Rand McNally, 1965; *Land and People of Czechoslovakia*, Lippincott, 1966; *Hong Kong*, Rand McNally, 1967; *The Psalms*, Watts, 1968; (with Calvin L. Criner) *Picture Map of Eastern Europe*, Lippincott, 1968; *The Proverbs*, Watts, 1970; (with R. J. Houlehen) *Battle for Sales*, Lippincott, 1973; *Careers in Marketing and Distribution*, Lothrop, 1974. Contributor of articles to educational and library journals, cartoons and reviews to library journals.

WORK IN PROGRESS: A series on the great cities of the world, and a study of American colonial and nineteenth century history.

SIDELIGHTS: Ms. Hall enjoys freighter travel, researching for books, and taking colored films to use in her lectures to school and community groups. She has visited every continent at least once. Hobbies include bicycle riding and cartooning.

*   *   *

HALL, Michael Garibaldi 1926-

PERSONAL: Born January 8, 1926, in Princeton, N.J.; son of Walter P. and Margaret (Nixon) Hall; married Jean Ellen Kirkpatrick, 1952; children: Michael G. K., Katherine Margaret. *Education:* Princeton University, A.B. (magna cum laude), 1949; Johns Hopkins University, Ph.D., 1956. *Home:* 1902 San Gabriel St., Austin, Tex. *Office:* Department of History, University of Texas, Austin, Tex.

CAREER: Institute of Early American History and Culture, Williamsburg, Va., fellow, 1956-59; University of Texas, Austin, assistant professor of history, 1959-63, associate professor, 1963—. *Wartime service:* American Field Service, volunteer, 1944-45.

WRITINGS: Edward Randolph and the American Colonies, 1676-1703, Institute of Early American History, 1960; (editor with L. H. Leder and M. G. Kammen) *The Glorious Revolution in America: Documents on the Colonial Crisis of 1689*, University of North Carolina Press, 1964; (editor with D. D. VanTassel) *Science and Society in the United States*, Dorsey, 1966.†

*   *   *

HALL, Robert A(nderson), Jr. 1911-

PERSONAL: Born April 4, 1911, in Raleigh, N.C.; son of Robert Anderson (a chemist) and Lolabel (House) Hall; married Frances Adkins (a social worker), August 31, 1936; children: Philip Adkins, Diana Katherine (Mrs. William C. Goodall), Caroline A. *Education:* Princeton University, A.B., 1931; University of Rome, Dottore in Lettere, 1934; University of Chicago, A.M., 1935. *Politics:* Independent. *Religion:* Congregational. *Home:* 308 Cayuga Heights Rd., Ithaca, N.Y. 14850. *Office:* Division of Modern Languages, Cornell University, Ithaca, N.Y. 14850.

CAREER: University of Puerto Rico, Rio Piedras, assistant professor of modern languages, 1937-39; Princeton University, Princeton, N.J., instructor in modern languages, 1939-40; Brown University, Providence, R.I., instructor, 1940-42, assistant professor of Italian, 1942-46; Cornell University, Ithaca, N.Y., associate professor, 1946-50, professor of linguistics, 1950—, director English program in Rome, 1966-67. Yale University, New Haven, Conn., visiting assistant professor of international administration, 1943-44; University of Rome, Rome, Italy, Fulbright lecturer in linguistics, 1950-51, 1957-58. Linguistica, Ithaca, N.Y., owner and publisher, 1950—. *Member:* Linguistic Society of America (vice-president, 1961), American Association of Teachers of Italian (first vice-president, 1945), Modern Language Association of America, American Dialect Society, American Anthropological Association. *Awards, honors:* Guggenheim Fellow, 1954, 1970.

WRITINGS: An Analytical Grammar of the Hungarian Language, Linguistic Society of America, 1938; *Bibliography of Italian Linguistics*, Linguistic Society of America, 1941; *The Italian Questions della Lingua*, University of North Carolina Press, 1942; *Melanesian Pidgin Phrase-Book*, Linguistic Society of America, 1942; *Melanesian Pidgin English: Grammar, Texts, Vocabulary*, Linguistic Society of America, 1943; *Hungarian Grammar*, Linguistic Society of America, 1944; (with F. Denoeu) *Spoken French*, Heath, 1944; (with M. Reno and V. Cioffari) *Spoken Portuguese*, Heath, 1945; *Spoken and Written French*, Heath, 1947; *Descriptive Italian Grammar*, Linguistic Society of American and Cornell University Press, 1948; *Structural Sketch No. 1: French*, Linguistic Society of America, 1948.

Leave Your Language Alone!, Linguistica, 1950; *Short History of Italian Literature*, Linguistica, 1951; *Haitian Creole: Grammar, Texts, Vocabulary*, American Anthropological Association, 1953; *Hands Off Pidgin English!*, Pacific Publications, 1955; *Vest-Pocket Italian Dictionary*, Random, 1956; *Bibliografia della linguistica italiana*, Sansoni, 1958; *Italian for Modern Living*, Linguistica, 1959.

(Editor) *Italian Stories*, Bantam, 1960; *Sound and Spelling in English*, Chilton, 1961; *Applied Linguistics: Italian*, Heath, 1961; *Cultural Symbolism in Literature*, Linguistica, 1963; *Basic Conversational Italian*, Holt, 1963; *Idealism in Romance Linguistics*, Cornell University Press, 1963; *Introductory Linguistics*, Chilton, 1964; *New Ways to Learn a Foreign Language*, Bantam, 1966; *Pidgin and Creole Languages*, Cornell University Press, 1966, *Antonio Fogazzaro e la crisi dell'Italia moderna, sagglo d'interpretazione letterario-morale*, Linguistica, 1967; *An Essay on Language*, Chilton, 1968; *Essentials of English Phrase-and Clause Structure in Diagrams*, Center for Curriculum Development, 1969; *La Struttura dell'italiano*, A. Armando, 1971; *The Comic Style of P. G. Wodehouse*, Shoe String, 1974.

Contributor of more than three hundred articles and book reviews to linguistic and literary journals.

WORK IN PROGRESS: A monograph, *Wagner's Ring—eine kulturelle Deutung*; *Comparative Romance Grammar*.

SIDELIGHTS: Hall's chief languages (of competency) are Italian, French, German, Spanish, Melanesian Pidgin English. *Avocational interests:* Choral singing, record-collecting, railroads.†

HALLAM, J(ohn) Harvey 1917-

PERSONAL: Born January 27, 1917, in London, England; married Elaine Roberts, March 28, 1940; children: Caroline. Education: University of London, B.A. (honors in geography), 1939, graduate study, 1939-40. Religion: Church of England. Home: 191 Green Lane, Norbury, London S.W. 16, England.

CAREER: Raynes Park Grammar School, geography master, 1946-50; Mitcham Grammar School for Boys, Surrey, England, sixth form master and head of geography department, 1950—. Military service: Royal Air Force, 1940-46; became flight sergeant. Member: Geographical Association, Incorporated Association of Assistant Masters.

WRITINGS: Australia: The Fight Against Drought, Common Ground, 1948; The Murray Darling Basin, Common Ground, 1949; The Problem of the Tropics, Common Ground, 1949; Tasmania, Common Ground, 1950; Mediterranean Australia, Common Ground, 1953; A Visual Geography of Australia, Evans, 1958. Contributor to Kingsway Encyclopedia.†

* * *

HALLIE, Philip P. 1922-

PERSONAL: Born May 4, 1922, in Chicago, Ill.; son of William and Nettie (Leibowitz) Hallie; married Doris Ann Gabrielle, September 19, 1954; children: Michelena Louise, Louis Gabriel. Education: Grinnell College, B.A., 1946; Harvard University, M.A., 1948, Ph.D., 1951; Oxford University, B.Litt., 1950. Home: 79 Lawn Ave., Middletown, Conn. Office: Wesleyan University, Box N, Wesleyan Station, Middletown, Conn.

CAREER: Vanderbilt University, Nashville, Tenn., assistant professor, 1952-56, associate professor, 1956-59, professor, 1959-62; Wesleyan University, Middletown, Conn., Griffin Professor of Philosophy and Humanities, 1962—. Member of national screening board, Fulbright graduate scholarships to Britain; represented United States at International Congress of Philosophy, Mysore, India, 1959. Military service: U.S. Army, Field Artillery, 1944-45; received three battle stars. Member: American Philosophical Association, Mind Association, American Association of University Professors, Phi Beta Kappa. Awards, honors: Midwest Poetry Conference Prize, 1946; Fulbright scholarship, 1948-50; Guggenheim fellow, 1958-59; senior fellow, Center for Advanced Study, 1961-62; M.A., Wesleyan University, 1965; American Council of Learned Societies fellow, 1966-67; D.Litt., Grinnell College.

WRITINGS: Maine de Biran: Reform of Empiricism, Harvard University Press, 1959; (editor) Scepticism, Man, and God, Wesleyan University Press, 1965; The Scar of Montaigne, Wesleyan University Press, 1967; The Paradox of Cruelty, Wesleyan University Press, 1967. Contributor to Encyclopedia of Philosophy and to philosophy journals. Member of editorial board, American Scholar, 1964-66.

WORK IN PROGRESS: Good and Evil in the Nazi Concentration Camps, completion expected in 1976.

SIDELIGHTS: Hallie writes: "I am going back to writing poetry, to capturing in the direct language of picture-discourse feelings and ideas that elude plain talk and analytical philosophizing; in fact, more and more I find that everything really importantly human has been said in literary language, and said better and more profoundly in literature—I am becoming obsessed with the humane uses of literature. Also I've discovered what Aristotle knew thousands of years ago, that walking and thinking stimulate, enrich each other, and make the intellectual life vigorous, profound, powerfully epigrammatic or concise, and joyous.

"All of my professional career in philosophy has been spent trying to make room for personal judgment, thinking that does not purport to have the universal cogency of a science, but is not merely idiosyncratic or private either. I believe that dogmatists in philosophy are deluded if they think they can convince all 'right-thinking' men; and I believe the self-expressionist, subjective emotion-mongers in philosophy have too little faith in the common sense of men. In short, I think philosophy can grow and communicate and do more worthwhile work in the world if it sets its sights somewhat lower than dogmatism, somewhat higher than scepticism or emotivistic existentialism; I think it can do a great deal if it becomes frankly personal and commonsensical.

"To implement and flesh out this belief I have worked at length on the thought of Montaigne, who first, to my knowledge, proposed signature or personal philosophizing; and I am studying the style of all philosophers who had some suspicion that they were not laying down The Law given them by God or Universal Reason. I wish to use such a mode of philosophizing for understanding good and evil in history and literature."

* * *

HALLIGAN, Nicholas 1917-

PERSONAL: Born December 3, 1917, in Fall River, Mass.; son of Francis Joseph and Anna (Conners) Halligan. Education: Providence College, Providence, R.I., student, 1934-36; College of St. Thomas Aquinas, River Forest, Ill., A.B., 1940; College of the Immaculate Conception, Washington, D.C., S.T.L., 1944; University of St. Thomas Aquinas, Rome, Italy, S.T.D., 1948. Home: St. Stephen's College, Dover, Mass. 02030. Agent: Michael Glazier, 11 East 87th St., New York, N.Y. 10028.

CAREER: Roman Catholic priest, member of Order of Preachers (Dominicans); St. Joseph's Priory, Somerset, Ohio, professor of history of philosophy, 1944-46; College of the Immaculate Conception, Washington, D.C., professor of pastoral theology, 1948-59, master of studies, 1948-57; Stephen's College, Dover, Mass., professor of philosophy of religion, 1959—. Member: Canon Law Society of America. Awards, honors: Master of Sacred Theology, 1963.

WRITINGS: The Problem of Authorities in the Summa Theologiae, College of the Immaculate Conception Press, 1949; The Administration of the Sacraments, Alba, 1963; The Ministry of the Celebration of the Sacraments, Alba, 1973; Sacraments of Initiation and Union: Baptism, Confirmation, Eucharist, Alba, 1973. Contributor to Catholic theological journals. Former editor of Thomist.

WORK IN PROGRESS: A book on pastoral justice.†

* * *

HALLMAN, Ralph J(efferson) 1911-

PERSONAL: Born December 28, 1911, in Scurry County, Tex.; son of A. L. (a farmer) and Lizzie May (Beights) Hallman. Education: Rice University, B.A., 1934, M.A., 1936; University of California, Los Angeles, graduate study, 1936-38; Claremont Graduate School, Ph.D., 1964. Home: 357 North Chester Ave., Pasadena, Calif. 91106.

Office: Pasadena City College, 1570 East Colorado Blvd., Pasadena, Calif. 91106.

CAREER: Pasadena City College, Pasadena, Calif., associate professor of philosophy, chairman of social science department, 1955—. Claremont Graduate School, visiting lecturer, 1961-63. Pasadena Tuesday Evening Forum, director; Pasadena Art Museum, member of education committee. *Military service:* U.S. Army, Artillery, 1942-46; served in European theater with Second Armored Division; became captain; received Bronze Star, Belgian Fourragere, Presidential Unit Citation. *Member:* American Society for Aesthetics, American Philosophy of Education Society, American Association of University Professors, Pasadena Education Association (past president), Phi Beta Kappa, Phi Delta Kappa.

WRITINGS: Psychology of Literature, Philosophical Library, 1961. Contributor of a dozen articles to professional journals.

SIDELIGHTS: Hallman lived in India for one year and has traveled in Europe, Southeast Asia, and the Middle East.†

*   *   *

HALLOWELL, John H(amilton)   1913-

PERSONAL: Born August 19, 1913, in Spokane, Wash.; son of Harold Atlee and Anna Blanche (Williams) Hallowell; married Sally Rubin, 1941; children: Carol (Mrs. Thomas Dana Hill), John, Jr., Katherine. *Education:* Harvard University, A.B. (cum laude), 1935; Duke University, M.A., 1937; Princeton University, Ph.D., 1939. *Politics:* Democrat. *Religion:* Episcopalian. *Home:* 2709 Augusta Dr., Durham, N.C. *Office:* Duke University, Durham, N.C.

CAREER: Instructor in political science at Princeton University, Princeton, N.J., 1937-38, University of California, Los Angeles, 1939-42; Duke University, Durham, N.C., 1942—, began as assistant professor, became professor of political science, 1950—, chairman of department of political science, 1964-71, director of Lilly Endowment Research Program in Christianity and Politics. Visiting professor at other American universities; Walgreen Foundation lecturer, University of Chicago, 1952; Fulbright professor at University of Munich, 1955-56. *Member:* American Political Science Association (council, 1961-63), Southern Political Science Association (vice-president, 1954-55; president, 1963-64). *Awards, honors:* Guggenheim Fellow in Germany, 1955-56; Litt.D., College of the Holy Cross, 1963.

WRITINGS: The Decline of Liberalism as an Ideology, University of California Press, 1943; *Main Currents in Modern Political Thought,* Holt, 1950; *The Moral Foundation of Democracy,* University of Chicago Press, 1954; (editor) *Development: For What?,* Duke University Press, 1964.

Contributor to *Encyclopaedia Britannica,* and to journals, including *Journal of Politics, South Atlantic Quarterly, American Political Science Review,* and *Zeitschrift fuer Politik.*

SIDELIGHTS: Hallowell told *CA* that he considers *Main Currents,* in which he evaluates modern political thought from the perspective of classical-Christian thought, his most important book. He believes that "it is the loss of the experience of transcendence that accounts for the trouble in which Western civilization finds itself."†

HAMILTON, B(ertram) L(awson) St. John   1914-

PERSONAL: Born November 17, 1914, in Port Maria, Jamaica; son of William Gottlieb (an engineer) and Anne Roberta (Lawson) Hamilton; children: Norman Wellesley, Faith Angela. *Education:* Mico College, Jamaica, Teacher Training Certificates, 1934; University of the South-West, Exeter, England, B.A., 1950; New York University, M.P.A., 1959. *Office:* 20 Old Hope Rd., Kingston 5, Jamaica.

CAREER: Teacher in Jamaica, 1935-44, 1951; field officer, Jamaica Social Welfare Commission, 1944-50; held various government posts in Kingston, Jamaica, including chief education officer, Ministry of Education, 1952-56, permanent secretary to Prime Minister and Ministry of Defense, 1962-63, secretary-manager of National Water Authority, 1963-64, and permanent secretary, Ministry of Labour, 1964-65; private consultant on industrial relations and management, Kingston, Jamaica, 1965—. Consultant in education to British Honduras, 1953; leader of British Caribbean delegation to UNESCO Conference, New Delhi, India, 1956; Jamaican representative to Commonwealth Defence Conference in England, 1963; diplomatic attache, Jamaican High Commission to Canada, 1964. Consultant and member of advisory groups on public administration and civic service.

MEMBER: Jamaica Civil Service Association (president, 1960-62), American Society for Public Administration, New York University Alumni Club (president of Kingston chapter, 1962-64, 1965), Steward Jockey Club of Jamaica, Kingston Cricket Club. *Awards, honors:* Jamaica Independence Medal from government of Jamaica, 1962; Order of the British Empire for distinguished public service, 1964.

WRITINGS: Problems of Administration in an Emergent Nation: A Case Study of Jamaica, Praeger, 1965.

AVOCATIONAL INTERESTS: Conversation, bridge, traveling for "cultural sampling."†

*   *   *

HAMILTON, Holman   1910-

PERSONAL: Born May 30, 1910, in Fort Wayne, Ind.; son of Allen (a physician) and Helen (Knight) Hamilton; married Suzanne Bowerfield, October 7, 1939; children: Susan. *Education:* Williams College, A.B., 1932; University of Kentucky, Ph.D., 1954. *Politics:* Democrat. *Home:* 220 Barrow Rd., Lexington, Ky. *Office:* University of Kentucky, Lexington, Ky.

CAREER: Fort Wayne Journal-Gazette, Fort Wayne, Ind., reporter, 1932-34, editorial writer, 1935-42, 1947-50; University of Kentucky, Lexington, assistant professor, 1954-57, associate professor, 1957-65, professor of history, 1965—, distinguished professor, College of Arts and Sciences, 1972. Fulbright professor, University of Chile, 1966. Trustee, Lincoln Memorial University, 1956-63. *Military service:* U.S. Army, 1942-46; became major. *Member:* American Historical Association, Society of American Historians, Organization of American Historians, Southern Historical Association (member of executive council), Kentucky Civil War Round Table (vice-president, 1963-64; president, 1964—), Indiana Historical Society, Kentucky Historical Society. *Awards, honors:* Guggenheim fellow, 1946; Pelzer Award of Mississippi Valley Historical Association, 1954; LH.D., Franklin College, 1966; LL.D., Lincoln Memorial University, 1973.

WRITINGS: Zachary Taylor: Soldier of the Republic,

Bobbs-Merrill, 1941; *Zachary Taylor; Soldier in the White House*, Bobbs-Merrill, 1951; *White House Images and Realities*, University of Florida Press, 1958; (with Carl N. Degler and others) *The Democratic Experience*, Scott, Foresman, 1963, 3rd edition, revised, 1973; *Prologue to Conflict*, University Press of Kentucky, 1964; (editor with Claude Gernade Bowers) *Indianapolis in the Gay Nineties*, Indiana Historical Society, 1964; (editor) *Three American Frontiers*, University Press of Kentucky, 1968; (contributor) Arthur M. Schlesinger, editor, *History of American Presidential Elections*, Chelsea, 1971; (contributor) Edward T. James and Janet W. James, editors, *Notable American Women*, Harvard University Press, 1971. Contributor to *Dictionary of American History*, 1940, and to *Major Crises in American History*, 1962. Also contributor of articles and reviews to historical journals.

WORK IN PROGRESS: A study of Claude G. Bowers (1878-1958) and his times.

* * *

HAMILTON, Howard Devon 1920-

PERSONAL: Born December 18, 1920, in Greenfield, Ind.; son of Brooks S. (a farmer) and Irene (Poer) Hamilton; married Leavitta, September 15, 1947; children: Anna, Felicity, Sarah, Lynne. *Education:* Purdue University, B.S., 1942; Syracuse University, graduate study, 1942-43; University of Illinois, Ph.D., 1950. *Politics:* Independent. *Religion:* Quaker. *Home:* 814 South 34th St., Terre Haute, Ind.

CAREER: University of Illinois, Urbana, instructor in political science, 1946-50; Albion College, Albion, Mich., professor of political science, 1950-51; State of Michigan, research director, 1951-55; Indiana State College, Terre Haute, professor of political science, 1955—. *Member:* American Political Science Association, American Society for Public Administration, Pi Gamma Mu, Kappa Delta Pi.

WRITINGS: Federal Grants in Aid in Michigan, Michigan Department of Administration, 1953; (editor) *Political Institutions*, Houghton, 1963; (editor) *Legislative Apportionment: Key to Power*, Harper, 1964; (editor) *Reapportioning Legistatures: A Consideration of Criteria and Computers*, Merrill, 1966. Contributor of articles to *New Leader, Public Finance*, and to economics and sociology journals.†

* * *

HAMILTON, Ronald 1909-

PERSONAL: Born July 30, 1909, in Leeds, Yorkshire, England; son of George Claude (an engineer) and Jane (Ingham) Hamilton; married Jean Grant Brook, April 19, 1958; children: Ian, David, and Charles Brook (stepsons). *Education:* Attended Winchester College, 1923-28; Magdalene College, Cambridge, B.A., 1932, M.A., 1935. *Politics:* Conservative. *Religion:* Church of England. *Home:* Cherry Orchard Cottage, Broad Campden, Gloucestershire, England.

CAREER: Winchester College, Winchester, England, history, French, and German master, 1933-39, 1946-69. *Military service:* Territorial Army, 1933-56; active service in France, Iraq, Persia, India, and Burma, 1939-45; became colonel; received Order of British Empire (military). *Member:* United Oxford and Cambridge University Club.

WRITINGS: Frederick the Great, Heffer, 1936; (with Colin Badcock) *Pendlebury and the Plaster Saints*, P. & G.

Wells, 1959; (editor and contributor) *Budge Firth: A Memoir and Some Sermons*, P. & G. Wells, 1960; *A Visitor's History of Britain*, Houghton, 1964 (published in England as *Now I Remember: A Holiday History of Britain*, Chatto & Windus, 1964); *A Holiday History of France*, Chatto & Windus, 1971; *Summer Pilgrimage*, Wells, 1973; *A Holiday History of Scotland*, Chatto & Windus, in press. Contributor to *Times* (London) and military periodicals.

SIDELIGHTS: Speaks French and German fluently; holds rating of first class military interpreter in French. In addition to war travels, has been in United States and Africa. *Avocational interests:* Drama.

* * *

HAMMERMAN, Donald R. 1925-

PERSONAL: Born February 10, 1925, in Boston, Mass.; son of Morris and Neva (Smith) Hammerman; married Betty Jane Johnson, August 21, 1948; children: Michael. *Education:* Maryland State Teachers College, Towson, B.S. in Ed., 1948; University of Maryland, M.Ed., 1951; The Pennsylvania State University, Ed.D., 1961. *Religion:* Methodist. *Address:* Box 299, Oregon, Ill. 61061. *Office:* Northern Illinois University, Lorado Taft Field Campus, Oregon, Ill. 61061.

CAREER: Teacher in public schools of Montgomery County, Md., 1948-51, Battle Creek, Mich., 1951-54; Northern Illinois University, Lorado Taft Field Campus, Oregon, assistant director of department of outdoor teacher education, 1954-65, director and chairman, 1965—. *Military service:* U.S. Army, 1943. *Member:* Outdoor Education Association, American Association for Health, Physical Education, and Recreation, American Association of University Professors, Association for Higher Education, Phi Delta Kappa. *Awards, honors:* Howard C. Bell Award, 1966.

WRITINGS: (Editor and compiler) *Outdoor Education* (teacher handbook), Northern Illinois University Press, 1957; (with William Hammerman) *Teaching in the Outdoors*, Burgess, 1964, 2nd edition, 1973; (with Hammerman) *Outdoor Education: A Book of Readings*, Burgess, 1968, 2nd edition, 1973. Filmscripts: "Education Moves Outdoors," 1956; "Teacher Education in the Out-of-Doors," 1958. Contributor of more than thirty articles to *Camping*, and to education journals. Editor, *Lorado Taft Newsletter*, 1954-62, *Newsletter of the Illinois State Advisory Council on Outdoor Education*, 1963-64. Compiler, *Illinois Journal of Education* issue on outdoor education, December, 1964, September, 1967.

AVOCATIONAL INTERESTS: Skiing, sailing, chess; all areas of natural science, especially geology and birding.

* * *

HAMMES, John A(nthony) 1924-

PERSONAL: Surname is accented on first syllable; born November 1, 1924, in Sault Sainte Marie, Mich.; son of Roman Burchart (a career officer in U.S. Navy) and Daisy (Martin) Hammes; married Dorothy Janelle Perkins, February 22, 1964; children: John, Paul, Penny. *Education:* Duquesne University, B.A., 1948; Catholic University of America, M.A., 1950; The Pennsylvania State University, Ph.D., 1953; also studied at College of Charleston, University of South Carolina, and Columbia University. *Religion:* Roman Catholic. *Home:* 235 Davis Estates Rd., Athens, Ga. 30601. *Office:* Department of Psychology, University of Georgia, Athens, Ga. 30601.

CAREER: U.S. Army, Human Resources Research Office, Fort Benning, Ga., research associate, 1953-56; University of Georgia, Athens, assistant professor, 1956-62, associate professor of psychology, 1962-68, director of Civil Defense Research, 1962-68, professor of psychology, 1968-72, head of psychology department, 1969—. *Military service:* U.S. Navy, 1943-46. *Member:* American Psychological Association, Mariological Society, John Henry Cardinal Newman Honorary Society, Sigma Xi, Psi Chi.

WRITINGS: To Help You Say the Rosary Better, St. Anthony, 1962; *To Help You Follow the Way of the Cross*, Bruce, 1963; *Humanistic Psychology: A Christian Interpretation*, Grune, 1971. Contributor of articles to psychological and theological journals. Also has produced twelve volumes of military research reports, 1962-68.

WORK IN PROGRESS: More publications in area of humanistic psychology and values.

*   *   *

HAMMOND, Edwin Hughes 1919-

PERSONAL: Born January 8, 1919, in Ann Arbor, Mich.; son of Harry Emmons (a professor of physics) and Elizabeth (Huddle) Hammond; married Elizabeth Mills, December 28, 1940; children: Janet Elizabeth (Mrs. John Weigel), Richard Edwin, Lawrence Alan. *Education:* University of Missouri, A.B. (with distinction), 1939; University of Wisconsin, M.A., 1940; University of California, Berkeley, Ph.D., 1951. *Politics:* Democrat. *Home:* 7901 Corteland Dr., Knoxville, Tenn. 37919.

CAREER: U.S. Office of Strategic Services, Washington, D.C., geographer, 1942; University of California, Berkeley, lecturer in geography, 1946-48; University of Nebraska, Lincoln, instructor in geography, 1948-49; University of Wisconsin, Madison, instructor, 1949-51, assistant professor, 1951-55, associate professor of geography, 1955-64; Syracuse University, Syracuse, N.Y., professor of physical geography, 1964-70. *Military service:* U.S. Naval Reserve, aerological officer, 1942-46; became lieutenant; received Air Medal. *Member:* Association of American Geographers (member of national council, 1967-70), American Geographical Society, American Association of University Professors, American Association for the Advancement of Science, Phi Beta Kappa, Sigma Xi. *Awards, honors:* Award for meritorious contribution to the field of geography, Association of American Geographers, 1968.

WRITINGS: A Geomorphic Study of the Cape Region of Baja California, University of California Publications in Geography, 1954; (with V. C. Finch, G. T. Trewartha, and A. H. Robinson) *Elements of Geography*, 4th edition (Hammond was not associated with earlier editions), McGraw, 1957, 5th edition, 1967 (portion of 4th edition published separately as *Physical Elements of Geography*, McGraw, 1957, 5th edition, 1967); *Procedures in the Descriptive Analysis of Terrain*, U.S. Office of Naval Research Projects, 1958; (with Trewartha and Robinson) *Fundamentals of Physical Geography*, McGraw, 1961, 2nd edition, 1968. Contributor of articles and reviews to professional periodicals. Member of editorial board, *Annals of the Association of American Geographers*, 1955-58, review editor, 1969-71.

WORK IN PROGRESS: Research in general physical geography, mapping of land-surface form, valley development in carbonate rocks, and problems of scale in geographical research.

HAMMOND, N(icholas) G(eoffrey) L(empriere) 1907-

PERSONAL: Born November 15, 1907, in Bristol, England; son of James Vavasor and Dorothy (May) Hammond; married Margaret Townley, December 15, 1938; children: Caroline, John, Helen, Nicholas, Catherine. *Education:* Attended Caius College, Cambridge, student, 1926-29. *Home:* 3 Belvoir Ter., Trumpington Rd., Cambridge, England.

CAREER: Cambridge University, Clare College, Cambridge, England, fellow, 1930-36, university lecturer in classics, 1936-39, junior proctor, 1939, senior tutor, 1947-54; Clifton College, Bristol, England, headmaster, 1954-62; University of Bristol, Bristol, England, professor of Greek, 1962-73, pro-vice-chancellor, 1964-66. *Military service:* British Army, 1939-45; served in Crete, Syria, and as member of Allied Military Mission in Greece, 1943-44; became lieutenant colonel; received Distinguished Service Order and Royal Hellenic Order of the Phoenix (Greece), mentioned in dispatches twice. *Awards, honors:* Fellow of the British Empire, 1968; Commander, Order of the British Empire, 1974.

WRITINGS: John Edwin Sandys, Cambridge University Press, 1933; *A History of Greece*, Oxford University Press, 1959, 2nd edition, 1967; *Epirus*, Oxford University Press, 1967; (editor with Howard H. Scullard) *The Oxford Classical Dictionary*, 2nd edition, Clarendon Press, 1970; *A History of Macedonia*, Volume I, Oxford University Press, 1973; *Studies in Greek History*, Oxford University Press, 1973. Co-editor, *Cambridge Ancient History*, Volumes I and II, 1970-74. Contributor to *Encyclopaedia Britannica*. Contributor of articles to *Historia*, *Journal of Hellenic Studies*, and other classical journals.

WORK IN PROGRESS: Two books, *The Classical Age of Greece*, for Weidenfeld & Nicholson, and Volume II of *A History of Macedonia*, for Oxford University Press.

SIDELIGHTS: Hammond is fluent in Albanian and modern Greek.

*   *   *

HAMPSCH, George H(arold) 1927-

PERSONAL: Born July 2, 1927, in Nashville, Tenn.; son of Oswald Harold (an insurance executive) and Elisabeth (Gore) Hampsch; married Harriet Robinson, February 9, 1957; children: Kathleen, Timothy, Robert, James, Brian, Maureen. *Education:* Student at Gustavus Adolphus College, 1945, Iowa State University, 1945-46, and University of Kansas, 1946; Loyola University, Chicago, Ill., B.S.C., 1949; DePaul University, M.A., 1959; University of Notre Dame, Ph.D., 1963. *Religion:* Roman Catholic. *Home:* 11 Chamberlain Parkway, Worcester, Mass. 01602. *Office:* Department of Philosophy, College of the Holy Cross, Worcester, Mass. 01610.

CAREER: Trappist monk at New Melleray Abbey, Dubuque, Iowa, 1949-56; Automatic Electric Co., Northlake, Ill., assistant credit manager, 1956-57; high school instructor in Oak Park, Ill., 1957-59; John Carroll University, University Heights, Ohio, assistant professor, 1961-65, associate professor of philosophy, 1965-70; College of the Holy Cross, Worcester, Mass., professor of philosophy, 1970—. Member of executive committee, Moreland Community Association, Shaker Heights, Ohio, 1965-66. *Military service:* U.S. Navy, aviation cadet, 1945-46. *Member:* American Philosophical Association, Society for the Philosophical Study of Marxism (chairman of Eastern division, 1974—), Metaphysical Society of America, American Institute of Marxist Studies, American Society for the Study of the German Democratic Republic, Conference Group on German Politics, American Association of University Professors (president of College of the Holy Cross chapter, 1973-74). *Awards, honors:* John Carroll University faculty fellowship, 1965; College of the Holy Cross faculty fellowship, 1973.

WRITINGS: The Theory of Communism, Philosophical Library, 1965; (contributor) Herbert Aptheker, editor, *Marxism and Christianity*, Humanities, 1968; (contributor) John Somerville and Howard L. Parsons, editors, *Dialogues on the Philosophy of Marxism*, Greenwood Press, 1974; (contributor) Bernard W. Eissenstat, editor, *The Soviet Union: The Seventies and Beyond*, Heath, 1974. Contributor of articles to scholarly journals.

WORK IN PROGRESS: Editing a book, *Revolutionary Worldview*; research in the loss of religious reflex in second and third generation Soviets, the question of detente, and the Sino-Soviet conflict.

SIDELIGHTS: Hampsch has traveled in the Soviet Union, Poland, Hungary, Czechoslovakia, Bulgaria, and the German Democratic Republic to study and observe attitudes toward religion and detente.

*   *   *

HAND, Thomas A(lypius)   1915-

PERSONAL: Born July 16, 1915, in County Louth, Ireland; son of Edward Matthew and Mary (Downes) Hand. *Education:* Attended schools in County Louth and Dublin, Ireland; studied at Gregorian University, Rome, Italy, 1932-41. *Home:* St. Augustine's, Washington St., Cork, Ireland.

CAREER: Entered Roman Catholic order of St. Augustine, in Ireland, 1931, ordained priest, 1939; preacher at missions and retreats in Ireland, 1942—, with exception of three years in London, England.

WRITINGS: The Rule of St. Augustine, M. H. Gill, 1956; *St. Augustine on Prayer*, M. H. Gill, 1963.

WORK IN PROGRESS: Rewriting *The Rule of St. Augustine*; *Book of Meditations*, based on writings of Augustine; a comprehensive work, *The Life of Augustine*, expected to take at least five years.

SIDELIGHTS: Calling himself a part-time writer, Father Hand writes: "Am very interested in preaching; believe that no other means of communication will ever take its place. Writing is just an extension of the spoken word. Believe that the Church is reaching backwards to St. Augustine's day for renewal of its spirit."†

*   *   *

HANEY, Thomas K.   1936-

PERSONAL: Born June 27, 1936, in Butte, Mont.; son of Thomas Henry (a miner) and Kathleen (Reilly) Haney; married Constance Niemeyer, September 6, 1958; children: Mark William, Lisa Kay. *Education:* University of Montana, B.A., 1958, LL.B., 1961. *Home:* 1723 35th Ave., San Francisco, Calif.

CAREER: Practicing attorney in San Francisco, Calif., 1963—. *Military service:* U.S. Army, 1961-63; became captain. *Member:* American Bar Association, American Trial Lawyers Association, Montana Bar Association, State Bar of California.

WRITINGS: An Introduction to Debate, Ginn, 1964.

WORK IN PROGRESS: A novel.†

*   *   *

HANFORD, Lloyd D(avid)   1901-

PERSONAL: Born June 29, 1901, in San Francisco, Calif.; son of Albert J. (a merchant) and Blanche (Coblentz) Hirschfeld; married Elise Phillips, February 11, 1926. *Education:* University of California, Berkeley, A.B. *Office:* 47 Kearny St., San Francisco, Calif. 94108.

CAREER: Realtor; president, Property Management Company; consultant, San Francisco Redevelopment Agency for South of Market; former chairman of San Francisco Citizens Participation Committee for Urban Renewal. *Military service:* U.S. Army, Chemical Corps, 1940-42; became captain. *Member:* National Association of Real Estate Boards (member of board of directors, 1959—), Institute of Real Estate Management (president, 1958), National Institute of Real Estate Brokers, American Society of Real Estate Counsellors, California Real Estate Association (member of board of directors, 1958-64), San Francisco Real Estate Board (president, 1954), San Francisco Chamber of Commerce, San Francisco Building Owners and Managers Association, Lambda Alpha.

WRITINGS: (Co-author) *Investment Properties*, University of California Press, 1952; (co-author) *The Management Office–How to Operate It*, Institute of Real Estate Management, 1957; *Development and Management of Investment Property*, Institute of Real Estate Management, 1964, 3rd edition published as *Analysis and Management of Investment Property*, 1970; *Investing in Real Estate*, Institute of Real Estate Management, 1966; *The Real Estate Dollar*, Institute of Real Estate Management, 1969. Contributor to *Journal of Property Management* and to appraisal journals.

AVOCATIONAL INTERESTS: Fishing (both stream and deep sea) in Canada, California, Hawaii, Florida.

*   *   *

HANLE, Dorothea Zack   1917-

PERSONAL: Born November 29, 1917, in Philadelphia, Pa.; daughter of Richard Albert (a realtor) and Theresa (Gressmann) Zachariae; married Frank L. Hanle (a realtor), October 15, 1941; children: Jennifer Leigh, Alan Randolph. *Education:* Attended Wilson College, Chambersburg, Pa., 1933-36; Barnard College, A.B., 1937. *Office:* Dell Publishing Co., Inc., 750 Third Ave., New York, N.Y. 10017.

CAREER: Buchanan & Co., New York, N.Y., advertising research, 1937; *Mademoiselle*, New York, N.Y., college editor, 1938-42; *Everywoman's*, New York, N.Y., editor-in-chief, 1952-58; Dell Publishing Co., Inc., New York, N.Y., women's special projects editor, 1959—. *Member:* American Society of Magazine Editors, National Home Fashions League, Fashion Group.

WRITINGS: (With Martin Herz) *The Golden Ladle* (juvenile), Ziff-Davis Publishing Co., 1944; *The Hairdo Handbook: A Complete Guide to Hair Beauty*, Doubleday, 1964; (with Kirk Cameron) *The Surfer's Handbook*, Dell, 1968; *Cooking With Flowers: Wherein an Age-Old Art is Revived*, Price, Stern, 1971; *Cooking Wild Game*, Liveright, 1974.†

HANNA, Lavone Agnes 1896-

PERSONAL: Born October 8, 1896, in Clay Center, Kan.; daughter of George William (a banker) and Mary Alice (Gillespie) Hanna. *Education:* Lindenwood College, A.A., 1916; University of Wisconsin, B.A., 1919; University of Chicago, M.A., 1927; Stanford University, Ed.D., 1943. *Politics:* Republican. *Religion:* Presbyterian. *Home:* 15 Berenda Way, Menlo Park, Calif.

CAREER: History teacher in Bartlesville, Okla., 1923-31, Tulsa, Okla., 1931-39; Stanford University, Stanford, Calif., research associate and assistant professor of education, 1939-44; Long Beach (Calif.) public schools, curriculum director, 1944-47; San Francisco State College (now University), San Francisco, Calif., professor of education, 1947-61, professor emeritus, 1961—. Visiting professor, American University of Beirut, 1957-58; lecturer at Mills College, 1947-51; summer professor at University of Chicago and Claremont Graduate School, 1946-53. *Member:* National Council for Social Studies, Association for Supervision and Curriculum Development (executive committee, 1957-60), National Conference of Christians and Jews (member of educational commission), Phi Beta Kappa, Phi Lambda Theta, Delta Kappa Gamma.

WRITINGS: (With G. Potter and N. Hagaman) *Unit Teaching in Elementary Schools*, Holt, 1955, 3rd edition (with G. Potter and R. Reynolds) published as *Dynamic Elementary Social Studies: Unit Teaching*, 1973; *Facing Life's Problems*, Rand McNally, 1955; (with I. J. Quillen) *Education for Social Competence*, Scott, 1948, revised edition, 1961; *Challenge for a Free People*, Rand McNally, 1964.

Contributor: *Evaluation of Modern Education*, Appleton, 1942; *Organizing Elementary School for Living and Learning*, Association for Supervision and Curriculum Development, 1947; *Growing Up in an Anxious Age*, Association for Supervision and Curriculum Development, 1952; *What Are the Sources of the Curriculum?*, Association for Supervision and Curriculum Development, 1962; *Social Studies in Elementary Schools*, National Council for the Social Studies, 1962; *To Nurture Humaneness*, Association for Curriculum Development, 1970. Contributor to educational journals.

*   *   *

HANSEN, Kenneth H(arvey) 1917-

PERSONAL: Born September 4, 1917, in Jamestown, N.D.; son of Harvey Chester (a professor) and Bessie (MacDonald) Hansen; married Mary Alice Larson, June 25, 1939; children: John R., Henry R., Christopher S. *Education:* University of Oklahoma, B.A., 1938, Ed.M., 1940; University of Missouri, Ph.D., 1949. *Politics:* Democrat. *Religion:* Presbyterian. *Home:* 1201 Angels Camp Dr., Carson City, Nev. 89701. *Office:* Office of State Superintendent of Public Instruction, Department of Education, Carson City, Nev. 89701.

CAREER: High school English and music teacher in Oklahoma, 1939-40; Westminster College, Fulton, Mo., associate professor of English, 1946-49; Western State College of Colorado, Gunnison, professor of education, 1949-65, chairman of Division of Education and Pyschology, 1952-58, director of School of Education, 1958-65; director, National Education Association Development Project, 1965-67, and Program Development of Education Commission of the States, 1967-68; Washington State University, Pullman, professor of education administration, 1968-72; Department of Education, Carson City, Nev., state superintendent of public instruction, 1972—. Summer instructor or professor at University of Oklahoma, Johns Hopkins University; lecturer at University of Southern California, 1959. Speaker, consultant, and workshop leader for public school systems, educational foundations, and other organizations. *Member:* Philosophy of Education Society (fellow), American Association of School Administrators, National Education Association, Phi Beta Kappa, Phi Delta Kappa, Kappa Delta Pi.

WRITINGS: Public Education in American Society, Prentice-Hall, 1956, 2nd edition, 1963; (with Peter P. Mickelson) *Elementary School Administration*, McGraw, 1957; *High School Teaching*, Prentice-Hall, 1957; *Philosophy for American Education*, Prentice-Hall, 1960. Writer of pamphlets on education. Frequent contributor to magazines.

WORK IN PROGRESS: A manuscript on pluralism in American education and education administration.

SIDELIGHTS: Hansen headed educational survey teams in various countries of Africa, 1964, 1966-68, visiting schools in which the U.S. Department of State has an interest. *Avocational interests:* Fishing.

*   *   *

HANSON, E(ugene) Kenneth 1930-

PERSONAL: Born June 2, 1930, in Le Mars, Iowa; son of Odin Hartman (a carpenter) and Edith (Johnson) Hanson; married Dorothy Janssen (a secretary), November 13, 1949; children: Luther Eugene, Cynthia Dawn. *Education:* Attended Wartburg College, 1948-49; Westmar College, B.A., 1953; Luther Theological Seminary, B.Th., 1957; advanced study at University of Iowa, 1961-63, Claremont Graduate School, 1963—. *Home:* 374 Omaha Court, Claremont, Calif. *Office:* First Lutheran Church, 395 San Bernardino Ave., Pomona, Calif.

CAREER: Lutheran minister. Pastor in Linn Grove, Iowa, 1957-60, Iowa City, Iowa, 1960-63; First Lutheran Church, Pomona, Calif., pastor, 1963—.

WRITINGS: Little Star, Augsburg, 1960; *The Savior's Suffering*, Augsburg, 1964.

WORK IN PROGRESS: The Critical Approach to the Bible: An Introduction.†

*   *   *

HAPGOOD, David 1926-

PERSONAL: Born October 30, 1926, in Petersham, Mass.; son of Norman (an editor) and Elizabeth (Reynolds) Hapgood; married Janice Terhune (a teacher), July 25, 1955; children: Bruce and David Van Ness (stepsons). *Education:* Swarthmore College, A.B., 1947. *Home:* 110 Bleecker St., New York, N.Y. 10012. *Agent:* John Cushman, 24 East 38th St., New York, N.Y.

CAREER: Worked in book publishing and as free-lance translator prior to 1953; *Trentonian*, Trenton, N.J., reporter, 1953-57; *New York Times*, New York, N.Y., writer-editor, Sunday edition, 1957-61; Peace Corps, consultant, writer, and evaluator, 1964-67; New York University, New York, Center for International Studies, fellow, 1967-69. Princeton Association for Human Rights, public relations chairman. *Member:* Society for International Development. *Awards, honors:* Institute of Current World Affairs travel-study grant, 1961-63.

WRITINGS: The Purge That Failed: Tammany v. Powell,

McGraw, 1960; (editor) *Policies for Promoting Agricultural Development*, Center for International Studies, Massachusetts Institute of Technology, 1965; *Africa*, Ginn, 1965; *Africa: From Independence to Tomorrow*, Atheneum, 1965; (with M. F. Millikan) *No Easy Harvest*, Little, Brown, 1968; (with Meridian Bennett) *Agents of Change: A Close Look at the Peace Corps*, Little, Brown, 1968; *Diplomaism*, D. W. Brown, 1971; *The Screwing of the Average Man*, Doubleday, 1974. Editor, *Development*, published by International Studies. Contributor to *Harper's, Nation, Reporter, Book Week, Current History*, other journals.

SIDELIGHTS: Hapgood spent several years in France and traveled in Africa, 1961-63.†

* * *

HAQ, Mahbub ul 1934-

PERSONAL: Haq rhymes with "luck"; born February 22, 1934, in Jammu, Kashmir; son of Mohammad Abdul (an educator) and Inayat (Begum) Aziz; married Khadija Khanam (an economist), October 7, 1960; children: Toneema Mahbub (daughter). *Education:* Government College, Lahore, Pakistan, B.A. (honors), 1953; King's College, Cambridge, M.A., 1955; Yale University, Ph.D., 1957; Harvard University, research associate, 1960-61. *Politics:* Liberal. *Religion:* Islam. *Home:* 6-C Garden Rd., Karachi, West Pakistan. *Office:* Joint Chief Economist, Planning Commission, Karachi, West Pakistan.

CAREER: In government service, Karachi, Pakistan, 1957—, currently joint chief economist, Planning Commission, President's Secretariat. United Nations Economic Commission for Asia and Far East, consultant. Lecturer on economic subjects. *Member:* Pakistan Economic Association (executive committee). *Awards, honors:* Tamgh-e-Pakistan, a civic award from the government of Pakistan; Pakistan Writers Guild literary prize (for best book) for *The Strategy of Economic Planning*.

WRITINGS: (With wife, Khadija Khanam) *Deficit Financing in Pakistan, 1951-1960*, Institute of Development Economics (Karachi), 1961; *The Strategy of Economic Planning: A Case Study of Pakistan*, Oxford University Press, 1963; *Structural Change in Asia: India and Pakistan*, (New York), 1970, *Islam in Secular India*, Verry, 1974. Contributor to United Nations publications on programming techniques and to Organization for Economic Co-operation and Development report on planning strategy.

WORK IN PROGRESS: A comparative analysis of planning techniques in Communist China, Egypt, India, and Pakistan; a long-term planning framework for Pakistan.

SIDELIGHTS: Haq speaks English, Urdu, Punjabi, and some French and Arabic. He has traveled extensively all over the world, including Communist China in 1964.†

* * *

HARBERGER, Arnold C. 1924-

PERSONAL: Born July 27, 1924, in Newark, N.J.; son of Ferdinand C. (an accountant) and Martha (Bucher) Harberger; married Ana Valjalo, March 15, 1958; children: Paul, Carl. *Education:* Johns Hopkins University, student, 1941-43; University of Chicago, M.A., 1947, Ph.D., 1950. *Office:* Department of Economics, University of Chicago, Chicago, Ill.

CAREER: Johns Hopkins University, Baltimore, Md., assistant professor of political economy, 1949-53; University of Chicago, Chicago, Ill., associate professor, 1953-59, professor of economics, 1959—, chairman of department, 1964—. Economist, International Monetary Fund, 1950; member of research advisory committee, National Academy of Sciences, Office of Scientific Personnel, 1961-65; Economist, Massachusetts Institute of Technology Center for International Studies and Indian Planning Commission (New Delhi), 1961-62. Visiting professor at Harvard University, 1971, and Princeton University, 1973-74. Consultant to Committee for Economic Development, 1955, U.S. Department of Agriculture, 1955, U.S. Treasury Department, 1962—, U.S. Department of State, 1963—, International Bank for Reconstruction and Development, 1963—, U.S. Department of Commerce, 1965. *Military service:* U.S. Army, 1943-46. *Member:* American Economic Association (member, executive committee), Econometric Society (fellow), American Academy of Arts and Sciences (fellow), Phi Beta Kappa. *Awards, honors:* Social Science Research Council faculty research fellow, 1951-53, 1954-55; Guggenheim fellow in England, 1958; Ford Foundation faculty research fellow, 1967-68.

WRITINGS: (Editor, and author of introduction) *The Demand for Durable Goods*, University of Chicago Press, 1960; *Project Evaluation*, Rand McNally, 1973; *Taxation and Welfare*, Little, Brown, 1974.

Contributor: *Resources For Freedom*, U.S. Government Printing Office, 1952; *Federal Tax Policy for Economic Growth and Stability*, 1955; *Federal Expenditure Policy for Economic Growth and Stability*, Government Printing Office, 1957; Roy G. Francis, editor, *The Population Ahead*, University of Minnesota Press, 1958; Carl F. Christ and others, editors, *Measurement in Economics*, Stanford University Press, 1963; Werner Baer and Isaac Kerstenetsky, editors, *Inflation and Growth in Latin America*, Irwin, 1964; Paul N. Rosenstein-Rodan, editor, *Pricing and Fiscal Policies*, M.I.T. Press, 1964; *The Role of Direct and Indirect Taxes in the Federal Revenue System*, Princeton University Press, 1964; Charles A. Anderson and Mary J. Bowman, editors, *Education and Economic Development*, Aldine, 1965.

Contributor of more than twenty articles to economics journals. Member of board of editors, *American Economic Review*, 1959-61.

* * *

HARDMAN, Richards Lynden 1924-
(Bronson Howitzer)

PERSONAL: Born November 8, 1924, in Seattle, Wash.; son of Lynden Leonard and Eugenia (Purple) Hardman; married Kathleen Keifer (a writer); children: Christopher Lynden, Regan Lynden (daughter). *Education:* University of Washington, Seattle, B.A., 1949; University of California, Los Angeles, M.A., 1951. *Religion:* Unitarian Universalist. *Home:* 13211 Valleyheart Dr., Sherman Oaks, Calif.

CAREER: Paramount Pictures, Hollywood, Calif., associate producer, 1952-57; Columbia Pictures, Hollywood, Calif., film producer, 1959-60; full-time professional writer, 1960—.

WRITINGS: No Other Harvest, Doubleday, 1962; *The Chaplain's Raid*, Coward, 1965; *The Virgin War*, M. Joseph, 1965; *Fifteen Flags*, Little, Brown, 1968. Author of television scripts and several motion pictures.

WORK IN PROGRESS: A novel.†

HARDY, John Edward 1922-

PERSONAL: Born April 3, 1922, in Baton Rouge, La.; son of Roger B. (an accountant) and Mary (McCoy) Hardy; married Marie Earle Elam (a public school music teacher), December 30, 1942; children: Margot (Mrs. Edward V. Minczeski, Jr.), Leonore, Catherine, Laura, Anne, Eve. Education: Louisiana State University, B.A., 1944; University of Iowa, M.A., 1946; Johns Hopkins University, Ph.D., 1956. Politics: Independent Liberal. Religion: Roman Catholic. Home: 412 North Humphrey Ave., Oak Park, Ill. 60302. Office: Department of English, University of Illinois-Chicago Circle, Chicago, Ill. 60680.

CAREER: Instructor in English at University of Detroit, Detroit, Mich., 1945-46, Yale University, New Haven, Conn., 1946-48, University of Oklahoma, Norman, 1948-52; Johns Hopkins University, Baltimore, Md., instructor in English writing, 1952-54; University of Notre Dame, Notre Dame, Ind., professor of English, 1964-66; University of South Alabama, Mobile, professor and chairman of department of English, 1966-69; University of Colorado, Boulder, professor of English, 1969-70, University of Missouri, St. Louis, professor and chairman of department of English, 1970-72; University of Illinois, Chicago Circle, professor of English and co-ordinator of graduate studies, 1972—. Fulbright professor of American literature, University of Munich, Munich, Germany, 1959-61. Member: Modern Language Association of America, American Association of University Professors, Phi Beta Kappa. Awards, honors: Ford Faculty fellowship, 1952-53; Sewanee Review fellowship in poetry, 1954.

WRITINGS: (With Cleanth Brooks) Poems of Mr. John Milton, Harcourt, 1951; Certain Poems, Macmillan, 1958; The Curious Frame, University of Notre Dame Press, 1962; Man in the Modern Novel, University of Washington Press, 1964; (editor) The Modern Talent, Holt, 1964; (editor with Seymour Lee Gross) Images of the Negro in American Literature, University of Chicago Press, 1966; Katherine Anne Porter, Ungar, 1973. Contributor of poetry, essays, and reviews to Sewanee Review, Yale Review, Poetry, and other literary periodicals.

WORK IN PROGRESS: A novel; a second volume of poetry; a critical study of D. H. Lawrence.

SIDELIGHTS: "Despite relatively small output, think of myself as primarily a poet.... Southerner by heritage, liberal by temperament, but shun 'in groups' of all kinds—literary, academic, political, religious, ethnic. Husband and father to a family of musicians."†

*   *   *

HARINGTON, Donald 1935-

PERSONAL: Born December 22, 1935, in Little Rock, Ark.; son of Conrad Fred and Jimmie (Walker) Harington; married Nita Harrison, July 20, 1957; children: Jennifer, Calico, Katy. Education: University of Arkansas, B.A., 1956, M.F.A., 1958; Boston University, M.A., 1959; graduate study, Harvard University, 1959-60. Home address: RFD 3, Putney, Vt. 05346. Office: Windham College, Putney, Vt. 05346.

CAREER: Bennett College, Millbrook, N.Y., instructor in art history, 1960-62; Windham College, Putney, Vt., associate professor of art history, 1964—. Awards, honors: Rockefeller Foundation fellowship, 1966-67.

WRITINGS: The Cherry Pit, Random House, 1965; The Lightning Bug, Delacorte, 1970; Some Other Place. The Right Place, Little, Brown, 1972.

HARKNESS, Bruce 1923-

PERSONAL: Born April 16, 1923, in Beaver Dam, Wis.; son of Reuben E. E. (a professor) and Ruth (Thomas) Harkness; married Leslie F. Whitsit, April 24, 1943; children: Stephen, Marguerite, Laura, Jonathan, Michael. Education: Attended Kalamazoo College, 1940-42, Swarthmore College, 1942-43; University of Chicago, M.A., 1948, Ph.D., 1950. Politics: Democrat. Home: 1295 Lake Martin Dr., Kent, Ohio 44240. Office: Department of English, Kent State University, Kent, Ohio.

CAREER: University of Illinois, Urbana, 1950-63, started as instructor, became professor of English and director of graduate studies; Southern Illinois University, Carbondale, professor of English and chairman of department, 1963-64; University of Illinois, professor of English and associate dean, 1964-66; Kent State University, Kent, Ohio, dean of arts and sciences, 1966—. Military service: U.S. Army Air Forces, 1943-45. Member: Modern Language Association of America, National Council of Teachers of English (advisory committee for study of undergraduate English programs), Bibliographical Society of London, Bibliographical Society of Virginia.

WRITINGS—Editor: (With R. A. Gettmann) A Book of Stories (with Teacher's Manual), Rinehart, 1955; Joseph Conrad, Heart of Darkness and the Critics, Wadsworth, 1960; Conrad, Secret Sharer and the Critics, Wadsworth, 1962. Member of advisory board, College English, 1964-70.

WORK IN PROGRESS: A book on Conrad, for Houghton.†

*   *   *

HARLOW, W(illiam) M. 1900-

PERSONAL: Born December 18, 1900, in Somers, Conn.; son of William B. (a teacher) and Gertrude (Morehouse) Harlow; married Alma Malcomb, May 28, 1926; children: Charles M. (deceased). Education: State University College of Forestry at Syracuse University (now State University of New York College of Environmental Science and Forestry), B.S., 1925, M.S., 1926, Ph.D., 1928. Religion: Protestant. Home: 1568 Westmoreland Ave., Syracuse, N.Y. 13210. Office: State University of New York College of Environmental Science and Forestry, Syracuse, N.Y. 13210.

CAREER: State University of New York College of Environmental Science and Forestry, Syracuse, 1928-1965, began as instructor, became professor of wood technology, 1949, film producer and teacher, 1956-65, professor emeritus, 1965—. Producer and photographer of films on nature subjects, 1952—. Instructor and consultant in camping, and director of various summer camps, 1921—. Member: Society of American Foresters, Sigma Xi. Awards, honors: Golden Reel Award of Film Council of America and Dick Byrd Trophy of Photographic Society of America, 1954, for "Insect Catchers of the Bog Jungle"; Golden Reel Award, 1955, for "Tree Portraits"; Blue Ribbon Award of American Film Festival and Bucranio d'Argento Prize of Venice International Festival, 1958, for "Rhythmic Motions of Growing Plants"; Golden Eagle Award of Committee on International Non-Theatrical Events, 1964, for "How Pine Trees Reproduce"; American Film Festival certificates for ten other films; Hedley S. Dimock award of American Camping Association, 1974, for outstanding contributions to camping and outdoor recreation.

WRITINGS: (With E. S. Harrar) Textbook of Dendrology,

McGraw, 1937, 5th edition, 1968; (contributor) L. E. Wise, editor, *Wood Chemistry*, Reinhold, 1944, 2nd edition, 1952; *The Chemical Softening of Wood for Microtome Sectioning*, New York State College of Forestry, 1944; *Poisonivy and Poisonsumac*, New York State College of Forestry, 1945, 3rd edition, 1949; *Trees of the Eastern and Central United States and Canada*, Dover, 1957; *Fruit Key and Twig Key to Trees and Shrubs*, Dover, 1959; *Patterns of Life: The Unseen World of Plants*, Harper, 1966; *Inside Wood: Masterpiece of Nature*, American Forestry Association, 1970. Contributor of more than twenty papers on the microchemistry of the cell walls of wood to scientific publications.

Films for State University of New York College of Environmental Science and Forestry: "Time-lapse Studies of Growing Trees," 1952; "Tree Portraits," 1955; "New Horizons for Wood," 1958; "From Wood Fibers to Paper," 1958; "The Challenge of Forestry in New York State," 1960; "Wood Decay by Fungi," 1961; "Forestry College," 1962; (with Fay Welch) "Introduction to Forest Adventuring," 1963; (with Christen Skaar) "The Mechanism of Moisture Movement in Wood," produced under National Science Foundation grant, 1963; (with Gerald R. Stairs) "Tree Improvement and Genetics," 1965; "Wood: Masterpiece of Creation," 1966.

Films for Encyclopaedia Britannica Educational Corp.: "Flowers at Work," 1956; "Seed Dispersal," 1956; "Growth of Seeds," 1957; "Learning About Flowers," 1957; "What Plants Need for Growth," 1958; "Learning About Leaves," 1958; "Rhythmic Motions of Growing Plants" (distributed as "Plant Motions"), 1958; "Seed Germination," 1960; "Fungi," 1960; "Learning About Seeds," 1961; "How Pine Trees Reproduce," 1963.

Other films: "The Story of Wood in the Northeast," 1953; "Insect Catchers of the Bog Jungle," 1954; "Ocean Tides," 1954; "River: An Allegory," 1961; "Lake Louise: Cloudland," 1964; "Exploring with the Time-Lapse Camera," 1968; "Trees: How to Know Them." Contributor to Walt Disney's "Secrets of Life," and Warner Brothers', "The Animal World."

WORK IN PROGRESS: A book distilling the experiences of fifty years in leadership training in camping and outdoor recreation.

SIDELIGHTS: The Harlow-Harrar book on dendrology is the standard text on the subject in sixty colleges. *Trees of the Eastern and Central United States and Canada* has sold more than 100,000 copies. Certain of Harlow's films, or portions of them, have been broadcast on all the major commercial and educational television networks in the United States as well as on the British Broadcasting Corp.

Harlow has camped in or traveled through most of the forest regions of the United States and Canada.

* * *

HARNACK, R(obert) Victor 1927-

PERSONAL: Born July 29, 1927, in Milan, Italy; became U.S. citizen; son of Harold Henry and Anna (Peshak) Harnack; married Martha Jane Beebe, June 6, 1948; children: Douglas Hall, Harold James. *Education:* Attended Westmar College, 1946-47; State College of Iowa, B.A., 1950; University of Oklahoma, M.A., 1951; Northwestern University, Ph.D., 1954. *Politics:* Democrat. *Religion:* Methodist. *Home:* 1737 South Brookview, Palatine, Ill. *Office:* University of Illinois, Box 4348, Chicago, Ill. 60680.

CAREER: University of Oklahoma, Norman, instructor in speech, 1951-52; University of Colorado, Boulder, assistant professor of speech, 1954-60, associate professor, 1960-64; University of Illinois, Chicago Campus, professor and head of department of speech and theater, 1964—. Educational consultant to North American Air Defense Command, 1955—, and to Colorado Democratic Party, 1960-64. Boulder (Colo.) Opera Association, onetime director and performer. *Military service:* U.S. Navy, 1945-46. *Member:* Speech Association of America, National Society for the Study of Communication, American Association of University Professors, Central States Speech\Association, Illinois Speech Association, Delta Sigma Rho, Tau Kappa Alpha.

WRITINGS: (With Thorrel Fest) *Group Discussion: Theory and Technique*, Appleton, 1964. Contributor to six speech journals.

WORK IN PROGRESS: A major work dealing with communication theory; research in the relationship between personality variables and discussion group participation.

AVOCATIONAL INTERESTS: Music.†

* * *

HARPER, Robert J(ohnston) C(raig) 1927-

PERSONAL: Born March 29, 1927, in Greenock, Scotland; son of Abram Craig and Anne (Berryman) Harper; married Margaret E. Kirk, December 18, 1953; children: Paul, Alan, David, Michael. *Education:* University of St. Andrews, M.A., 1951; University of Edinburgh, M.A. (honors), 1953, Ph.D., 1964. *Home:* 7175 Maureen Crescent, Burnaby, British Columbia, Canada. *Office:* Simon Fraser University, Burnaby, British Columbia, Canada.

CAREER: University of Alberta, Edmonton, Alberta, Canada, associate professor of psychology, 1954-65; Simon Fraser University, Burnaby, British Columbia, professor of psychology, 1965—. *Military service:* Royal Air Force, 1945-48, Royal Air Force Volunteer Reserves, 1949-54.

WRITINGS: (Editor with C. C. Anderson, C. M. Christensen, and S. M. Hunka) *The Cognitive Processes—Readings*, Prentice-Hall, 1964. Author of play, "The Rockall Affair," produced by Canadian Broadcasting Corp., 1957.

WORK IN PROGRESS: Cognitive Development.

AVOCATIONAL INTERESTS: Rock collecting, fishing.†

* * *

HARRIS, Charles H(ouston) III 1937-

PERSONAL: Born February 6, 1937, in Chihuahua, Mexico; son of Charles Houston II (a surgeon) and Elvira (Hernandez) Harris; married Betty McGrew, June 17, 1961; children: Charles Jeffrey, John Anthony, Stanley Neville. *Education:* University of Texas, B.A., 1959, M.A., 1962, Ph.D., 1968. *Politics:* Republican. *Religion:* Methodist. *Home:* 1003 Avondale Dr., Las Cruces, N.M. 88001. *Office:* Department of History, New Mexico State University, Las Cruces, N.M. 88001.

CAREER: New Mexico State University, Las Cruces, N.M., member of faculty. *Military service:* U.S. Army, 1961-63; became first lieutenant. *Member:* American Historical Association, Phi Beta Kappa, Phi Alpha Theta. *Awards, honors:* Social Science Research Council grant, 1965 (declined); Fulbright-Hays award for research in Mexico, 1965; National Endowment for the Humanities research grant, 1970.

WRITINGS: The Sanchez Navarros: A Socioeconomic Study of a Coahuilan Latifundio, 1846-1853, Loyola University Press (Chicago), 1964.

WORK IN PROGRESS: A book, *A Mexican Empire: The Latifundio of the Sanchez Navarro Family, 1765-1867*, for University of Texas Press.

SIDELIGHTS: Harris is fluent in Spanish (his mother was a Mexican and he has spent summers in Mexico since childhood).

* * *

HARRIS, Dale B(enner) 1914-

PERSONAL: Born June 28, 1914, in Elkhart, Ind.; son of Ward Manning (a mechanic) and Lillian (Benner) Harris; married Elizabeth Saltmarsh (a writer and parent-educator), July 17, 1935; children: Ruthann E., James S., David B., Geoffrey M. *Education:* DePauw University, A.B. (with high distinction), 1935; University of Minnesota, M.A., 1937, Ph.D., 1941. *Politics:* Independent. *Religion:* Protestant. *Home:* 317 Ridge Ave., State College, Pa. 16801. *Office:* Department of Psychology, 511 Moore Building, Pennsylvania State University, University Park, Pa. 16802.

CAREER: Minnesota State Training School for Boys, educational director, 1936-38; University of Minnesota, Institute of Child Welfare, Minneapolis, instructor, 1939-42, assistant professor, 1942-46, associate professor, 1946-48, professor, 1948-59, director, 1954-59; Pennsylvania State University, University Park, professor of psychology, 1959—, chairman of department, 1963—. White House Conference on Children and Youth, representative of American Psychological Association, 1950, staff consultant, 1960. Member of advisory committee on young workers, U.S. Department of Labor, 1955-59, of research advisory committee, Commonwealth of Pennsylvania Mental Health Research Foundation, and of advisory committee on psychological resources, Office of Pennsylvania Commissioner of Mental Health. Member of board, Pennsylvania Mental Health Association, 1970—. *Military service:* U.S. Marine Corps Reserve, 1944-50; became captain.

MEMBER: American Psychological Association (fellow; secretary of division on childhood and adolescence, 1949-52, president of division, 1955-56); American Association for the Advancement of Science (chairman of executive committee of psychology committee, 1972), Society for Research in Child Development (secretary, 1957-61; representative to governing council of American Association for the Advancement of Science, 1961-67), National Society for the Study of Education, National Council on Family Life, American Statistical Association, American Educational Research Association, American Association of University Professors, Midwestern Psychological Association, Phi Beta Kappa, Sigma Xi, Psi Chi, Phi Delta Kappa.

WRITINGS: (Editor) *The Concept of Development*, University of Minnesota Press, 1957; (with Marion L. Faegre and John E. Anderson) *Child Care and Training*, 8th edition, University of Minnesota Press, 1958; *Children's Drawings as Measures of Intellectual Maturity*, Harcourt, 1963. Contributor to professional journals. Member of editorial committee, *Annual Review of Psychology*, 1956-62.

WORK IN PROGRESS: Studies of children's fantasies, and children's literature.

* * *

HARRIS, Irving David 1914-

PERSONAL: Born October 18, 1914, in Minneapolis,

Minn.; son of Charles and Sarah (Bazelon) Harris; married Tobie Zion, July 25, 1949; children: Daniel, Lisa. *Education:* University of Chicago, B.S., 1935; Rush Medical College, M.D., 1939. *Politics:* Independent. *Religion:* Jewish. *Home:* 4828 South Kimbark Ave., Chicago, Ill. *Office:* 737 North Michigan Ave., Chicago, Ill.

CAREER: Private practice of psychoanalysis, Chicago, Ill., 1946—. Research consultant to the Institute for Juvenile Research, Chicago, Ill., 1960—. *Military service:* U.S. Army, 1942-46; became major. *Member:* American Psychiatric Association, American Psychoanalytic Association, Academy of Psychoanalysis.

WRITINGS: Normal Children and Mothers, Free Press of Glencoe, 1959; *Emotional Blocks to Learning*, Free Press of Glencoe, 1961; *The Promised Seed*, Free Press of Glencoe, 1964.

WORK IN PROGRESS: Research on the relationship of early family experience to later political and social attitudes.†

* * *

HARRIS, Louis 1921-

PERSONAL: Born January 6, 1921, in New Haven, Conn.; son of Harry (a realtor) and Frances (Smith) Harris; married Florence Yard, 1943; children: Susan, Peter, Richard. *Education:* University of North Carolina, A.B., 1942. *Office:* 1270 Avenue of the Americas, New York, N.Y. 10020.

CAREER: Louis Harris & Associates, Inc. (marketing and public opinion research), New York, N.Y., president, 1956—. Faculty associate at Columbia University, New York, N.Y., ten years. Syndicated newspaper columnist, columnist for *Newsweek*. Consultant to CBS News on political and public affairs research and developer of Vote Profile Analysis (VPA), an analytical tool for election reporting. Director, *Time*-Harris Poll, 1969—, and *Life* poll, 1969—. Trustee of Riverdale Country School. *Military service:* U.S. Navy. *Member:* American Sociological Association, American Association for Public Opinion Research (director), American Statistical Association, American Management Association, American Marketing Association, American Political Science Association.

WRITINGS: Is There a Republican Majority?, Harper, 1954; (with William Brink) *The Negro Revolution in America*, Simon & Schuster, 1964; (with William A. Brink) *Black and White: A Study of U.S. Racial Attitudes Today*, Simon & Schuster, 1967; (with Bert E. Swanson) *Black-Jewish Relations in New York City: The Anguish of Change*, Praeger, 1970; *Confidence and Concern: Citizen's View of American Government*, Regal, 1974. Contributor to *Saturday Review, Public Opinion Quarterly, New York Times Magazine, Collier's*, other periodicals.

SIDELIGHTS: Harris probably is most widely known in connection with President Kennedy's 1960 primary and election campaign, although his firm has done research in more than two hundred other campaigns. As a newspaper and magazine columnist he reports what people are thinking about current news events.

BIOGRAPHICAL SOURCES: Newsweek (cover story), October 1, 1962; *New York Times*, April 1, 1963; *True*, November, 1964; *New York Post*, a series, week of November 9, 1964.†

HARRISON, James 1937-
(Jim Harrison)

PERSONAL: Born December 11, 1937, in Grayling, Mich.; son of Winfield Sprague (an agriculturist) and Norma (Wahlgren) Harrison; married Linda King, October, 1960; children: Jamie Louise, Anna Severin. *Education:* Michigan State University, B.A., 1960, M.A., 1964. *Religion:* "Zennist." *Residence:* Lake Leelanau, Mich. 49653.

CAREER: Poet, novelist, and journalist. *Awards, honors:* National Endowment for the Arts grant, 1968-69; Guggenheim fellowship, 1969-70; two awards from National Literary Anthology.

WRITINGS—Under name Jim Harrison, except as indicated: *Plain Song* (poems), Norton, 1965; *Locations* (poems), Norton, 1968; *Outlyer and Ghazals* (poems), Simon & Schuster, 1971; *Wolf: A False Memoir* (novel), Simon & Schuster, 1971; (under name James Harrison) *A Good Day to Die* (novel), Simon & Schuster, 1973; *Letters to Yesenin* (poems), Sumac Press, 1973. Work represented in anthologies, including *Out of the War Shadow*, War Resisters League (New York), 1967; *Lyric Poems*, edited by Coralie Howard, F. Watts, 1968; *Thirty-One New American Poets*, edited by Ron Schreiber, Hill & Wang, 1969; *Contemporary American Poetry*, edited by A. Poulin, Jr., Houghton, 1971. Contributor to journals and newspapers, including *Poetry, Tri-Quarterly Review, Stony Brook Journal, Sumac, Partisan Review*, and *New York Times*.

WORK IN PROGRESS: A novel; poems; a screenplay.

SIDELIGHTS: Reviewing *Plain Song*, George Quasha wrote that "one feels drawn to speak of Jim Harrison's poetry as 'new' and of his extraordinary first book, 'Plain Song,' as an important event in American poetry. His work hardly ever seems derivative but it can call to our minds in a fresh and strange way the virtues of some of the best modern poetry. Thus more than any recent poet I know, he manages a clear and simple self-abandon to the rude force alive in nature; he captures the regenerative empathy of self-discovery outside the self."

Talking to Eric Siegel of *Detroit Magazine*, Harrison stated that he decided at age twelve to be a writer because of a "very romantic conviction that that was an attractive way to live. Middle class life seemed to me then to be very remote and boring and meaningless. . . . It still does." Harrison continued: "As a writer . . . you begin to find out it wasn't given to people to be good at many things. You have to be devoted to art as a single cause. You have to be possessed by it." On writing poetry, Harrison noted: "I get a super-exhilarated sense of verbal humor. . . . My mind begins to play with things. It's sort of like I'm super-alive." When he is not writing, Harrison often turns to fishing, which he described as "very therapeutic. . . . Most writers go batty because of the problem of what to do when they're not writing. It's very stabilizing to be able to stand in a river. . . . When you're a writer at a university, you're a freak, sort of a town clown. I feel much less isolated from people here than at a university." Harrison owns nine acres of land which he does not farm.

BIOGRAPHICAL/CRITICAL SOURCES: Detroit Free Press, April 16, 1972.

*   *   *

HARRISON, S(ydney) Gerald 1924-

PERSONAL: Born April 21, 1924, in Harrogate, Yorkshire, England; son of Herbert and Annie Elizabeth (Blamey) Harrison; married Janet Scott, April 6, 1946; children: Susan, David Scott. *Education:* University of Leeds, B.Sc., 1949. *Home:* 8 Queen Wood Close, Cardiff, Glamorganshire, Wales.

CAREER: Royal Botanic Gardens, Kew, Richmond, Surrey, England, botanist and assistant keeper, 1949-62; National Museum of Wales, Cardiff, keeper of botany, 1962—. *Military service:* Indian Army, Rajputana Rifles, 1944-47. *Member:* Royal Horticultural Society, Royal Forestry Society, International Association for Plant Taxonomy, British Bryological Society, Botanical Society of the British Isles, British Pteridological Society, Cardiff Naturalists Society, Linnean Society (London).

WRITINGS: (Contributor) Sidney Locket, *Clinical Toxicology: The Clinical Diagnosis and Treatment of Poisoning*, Mosby, 1957; *Garden Shrubs and Trees*, Eyre & Spottiswoode, 1960; (author of revision) Albert B. Jackson and William Dallimore, *A Handbook of Coniferae and Ginkgoaceae*, 4th revised edition, E. J. Arnold, 1966; (with others) *Oxford Book of Food Plants*, Oxford University Press, 1969; (author of revision) Harold A. Hyde and Arthur E. Wade, *Welsh Ferns*, 5th revised and expanded edition, National Museum of Wales, 1969. Contributor to professional journals.

WORK IN PROGRESS: Research in flora of Wales and Welsh National Herbarium collections.

AVOCATIONAL INTERESTS: Gardening, swimming.

*   *   *

HARRISON CHURCH, Ronald James 1915-

PERSONAL: Born July 26, 1915, in Wimbledon, England; son of James Walter (a schoolmaster) and Jessie May (Fennymore) Church; married Dorothy Violet Harrison (a biology teacher), August 2, 1944; children: Julia Rosalind, Christopher Julian. *Education:* University of London, London School of Economics and Political Science, B.S., 1936, Ph.D., 1943, Institute of Education, diploma in education, 1939; attended University of Paris. *Home:* 8 Mannicotts, Welwyn Garden City, Hertfordshire, England. *Office:* London School of Economics and Political Science, London W.C.2, England.

CAREER: University of London, London School of Economics and Political Science, London, England, assistant lecturer, 1944-47, lecturer, 1947-58, reader, 1958-64, professor of geography, 1964—. Visiting professor at University of Wisconsin, 1956, Indiana University, 1965, and Universities of Tel Aviv and Haifa, 1972-73. Lecturer at Universities of Chicago, Minnesota, Kansas, Kansas City, Cincinnati, and Syracuse University, and at universities in Brazil, France, Belgium, and Germany. Lecturer and broadcaster in French in France and for the French and African services of British Broadcasting Corp. *Member:* Royal Geographical Society, Institute of British Geographers, Geographical Association, African Studies Association of the United Kingdom. *Awards, honors:* Back Award from Royal Geographical Society, 1957, for contributions to the economic geography of West Africa.

WRITINGS: Modern Colonization, Hutchinson, 1951; *West Africa*, Longmans, Green, 1957, Wiley, 1959, 7th edition, 1974; *Environment and Policies in West Africa*, Van Nostrand, 1963, revised edition, 1974; (with J. I. Clarke, P. J. H. Clarke, and H. J. R. Henderson) *Africa and the Islands*, Wiley, 1964, 3rd edition, Longmans, Green, 1971, Wiley, 1972; (with Peter Hall, G. R. P. Lawrence, W. R.

Mead, and Alice Mutton) *An Advanced Geography of Northern and Western Europe*, Hulton Educational Publications, 1967, 2nd edition, 1973; *Looking at France*, Lippincott, 1970, 2nd edition, 1974. Contributor to *Africa South of the Sahara*; also contributor to *Encyclopaedia Britannica*, and *Chambers's Encyclopaedia*. Contributor to professional journals.

SIDELIGHTS: Harrison Church has visited several times every country in West Africa except Portuguese Guinea, and traveled in many other African countries, as well as in Europe, Asia, and the Americas.

*   *   *

HARROD, Leonard Montague 1905-

PERSONAL: Born May 21, 1905, in Horsham, Sussex, England; married Florence Janetta Fincham; children: Sydney Montague, Zillah Janetta. *Education:* Studied librarianship privately and at University of London; Library Association, diploma (honors), 1937. *Politics:* "Not aligned to any party." *Religion:* Methodist. *Home:* 41 Milton Rd., Harpenden, Hertfordshire, England.

CAREER: Various library posts in England prior to 1940; Islington Public Libraries, Islington, England, chief librarian and curator, 1940-54; National Library, Singapore, director, 1954-60; North-Western Polytechnic, London, England, senior lecturer in charge of course for overseas librarians, 1961-70. British Standards Institution, member of committees on alphabetic arrangement, preparation of indexes, and documentation. *Member:* Library Association (fellow; member of council, 1954), Society of Authors, Society of Indexers (member of council, 1955—). *Awards, honors:* Wheatley medal, 1973, for outstanding book index.

WRITINGS: Lending Library Methods, Grafton & Co., 1933; *The Librarians' Glossary: Terms Used in Librarianship and the Bookcrafts*, Grafton & Co., 1938, 3rd edition published as *The Librarians' Glossary . . . and Reference Book*, Deutsch, 1971; *The Libraries of Greater London*, G. Bell, 1951; *Library Work with Children*, Deutsch, 1969. Contributor to *Library Association Record*, *Times Educational Supplement*, *Municipal Journal*, and other periodicals. Honorary editor, *Indexer*, 1964—.

WORK IN PROGRESS: A revision of the third edition of *The Librarians' Glossary . . . and Reference Book.*

*   *   *

HART, Carolyn Gimpel 1936-

PERSONAL: Born August 25, 1936, in Oklahoma City, Okla.; daughter of Roy William (an organ builder) and Doris (Akin) Gimpel; married Philip Donnell Hart (an attorney), June 10, 1958; children: Philip Donnell, Jr., Sarah Ann. *Education:* University of Oklahoma, B.A., 1958. *Religion:* Protestant. *Home:* 1705 Drakestone, Oklahoma City, Okla.

MEMBER: Phi Beta Kappa, Theta Sigma Phi, Kappa Tau Alpha. *Awards, honors:* Dodd, Mead-*Calling All Girls* Prize, 1964, for *The Secret of the Cellars.*

WRITINGS—All for young people, except as indicated: *The Secret of the Cellars*, Dodd, 1964; *Dangerous Summer*, Fair Winds, 1968; *Rendezvous in Vera Cruz*, M. Evans, 1970; *No Easy Answers*, M. Evans, 1970; *Danger: High Explosives!*, M. Evans, 1972; *Flee From the Past*, (adult Gothic mystery), Bantam, 1975.

HART, Jim Allee 1914-

PERSONAL: Born April 9, 1914, in Crowell, Tex.; son of Aaron S. and Carrie (Allee) Hart; married La Rue Hardin, 1948. *Education:* Tarleton State College, student, 1929-31; Texas Technological College (now Texas Tech University), B.A., 1934, M.A., 1936; University of Missouri, Ph.D., 1959. *Home:* 202 Orchard Dr., Carbondale, Ill. *Office:* School of Journalism, Southern Illinois University, Carbondale, Ill.

CAREER: High school teacher in Crane, Tex., 1935-40; Tarleton State College, Stephenville, Tex., associate professor of journalism and director of information, 1946-54; Mississippi State College for Women, Columbus, assistant professor of journalism and news editor, 1954-55; Northern Illinois University, DeKalb, instructor in journalism, 1955-57; Ohio University, Athens, associate professor of journalism, 1959-65; Southern Illinois University, Carbondale, professor of journalism, 1965—. Former stringer (sports) for *Fort Worth Star-Telegram* and *Dallas Morning News*. *Military service:* U.S. Army, 1942-45, became lieutenant; received Bronze Star, Purple Heart, and Middle Eastern Campaign Medal with three Bronze Stars; Texas National Guard, 1947-50, captain. *Member:* American Association for Education in Journalism, American Association of University Professors, National Educational Association, Sigma Delta Chi, Kappa Tau Alpha.

WRITINGS: A History of the St. Louis Globe-Democrat, University of Missouri Press, 1961; *Views on the News: The Developing Editorial Syndrome*, Southern Illinois University Press, 1970. Contributor of more than fifty articles to periodicals.

AVOCATIONAL INTERESTS: Bridge, golf.

*   *   *

HART, V(orhis) Donn 1918-

PERSONAL: Born February 15, 1918, in Syracuse N.Y.; son of Manton Edgar and Iva (Vorhis) Hart; married Harriett Colegrove (a folklorist), July, 1954; children: Susan Elizabeth. *Education:* University of California, Berkeley, A.B., 1941; Harvard University, M.A., 1942; Syracuse University, D.S.Sc., 1954. *Politics:* Democrat. *Religion:* Protestant. *Home:* 430 Hillcrest Dr., DeKalb, Ill. 60115. *Office:* Center for Southeast Asian Studies, Northern Illinois University, DeKalb, Ill. 60115.

CAREER: University of Denver, Denver, Colo., assistant professor of anthropology, 1951-54; University of the Philippines, Diliman, Rizal, Smith-Mundt Visiting Professor of Anthropology, 1956-57; Yale University, New Haven, Conn., research associate in Southeast Asia program, 1957-58; Syracuse University, Syracuse, N.Y., associate professor of anthropology, 1958-71; Northern Illinois University, DeKalb, Center for Southeast Asia Studies, 1971—. Consultant to Peace Corps, Washington, D.C., and New York State Education Department. *Military service:* U.S. Army Air Forces, 1941-46; became staff sergeant. *Member:* American Anthropological Association, American Folklore Association, Committee on Research Materials on Southeast Asia (chairman), Association for Asian Studies, Asia Society. *Awards, honors:* Three Fulbright research fellowships to the Philippines, 1950-51, 1954-55, 1964-65.

WRITINGS: (With H. E. Wilson) *The Philippines*, American Book Co., 1946; *Riddles in Filipino Folklore: An Anthropological Analysis*, Syracuse University Press, 1964; (with Anuman Radadhon and Richard Coughlin) *Southeast*

Asia Birth Customs: Three Studies in Human Reproduction, Human Relations Area Files, Yale University, 1965; *Bisayan Filipino and Malayan Humoral Pathology: Folk Medicine and Ethnohistory in Southeast Asia*, Ithaca, N.Y., 1969. Contributor to *Encyclopaedia Britannica* and *Encyclopedia Americana*. Also contributor of articles to *Western Folklore, American Journal of Folklore, Pacific Affairs*.

SIDELIGHTS: Hart has traveled extensively in Europe, Mexico, and Asia, particularly Southeast Asia, 1950, 1957, 1965.

*   *   *

HARTMAN, David N. 1921-

PERSONAL: Born October 11, 1921, in Chicago, Ill.; son of David Nathaniel and Annette (Vana) Hartman; married Lucile R. Brandt, November 24, 1945; children: David, Daniel, Mark, Philip. *Education:* Roosevelt University, B.A., 1954; University of Chicago, M.A., 1957. *Home:* 940 West 19th St., Santa Ana, Calif. 92706.

CAREER: Santa Ana College, Santa Ana, Calif., teacher of political science, and chairman of division of social sciences, 1963-68. Democratic candidate for U.S. Congress, 1970, and California State Assembly, 1974. *Military service:* U.S. Navy, air cadet, 1944-45. *Member:* American Political Science Association, Association of American Geographers, United Nations Association (president of Orange County chapter, 1965), Santa Ana College Faculty Association (president, 1964-65).

WRITINGS: California and Man, W. C. Brown, 1964, 3rd edition, Pierce Publishers, 1972; *California and the Nation*, Appleton, 1971; *American Election Manual*, Pierce Publishers, 1974.

*   *   *

HARVEY, John F(rederick) 1921-

PERSONAL: Born August 21, 1921, in Maryville, Mo.; son of Abraham Frederick and Lois Ernestine (Glenn) Harvey; married Velda Harrison, April 16, 1954; children: Marshall Leland, Bruce Talbott. *Education:* Dartmouth College, A.B., 1943; University of Illinois, B.S. in Library Science, 1944; University of Chicago, Ph.D., 1949. *Religion:* Methodist. *Home:* 290 Lewis Rd., Springfield, Pa. *Office:* Graduate School of Library Science, Drexel Institute of Technology, Philadelphia, Pa. 19104.

CAREER: John Crerar Library, Chicago, Ill., assistant cataloger, 1944-45, assistant medical reference librarian, 1945-47; University of Chicago Library, Chicago, Ill., administrative assistant, 1949-50; Parsons College, Fairfield, Iowa, librarian and professor of library science, 1950-53; State College, Pittsburg, Kan., head librarian, chairman of department of library science, professor, 1953-58; Drexel Institute of Technology, Philadelphia, Pa., director of libraries, 1958-62, graduate school of library science, dean and professor, 1958—. Library consultant for Lipservice, 1965—. Pennsylvania director National Library Week, 1960-62. *Military service:* U.S. Army, 1942-43. *Member:* American Library Association (statistics committee, 1953-55, executive board, junior members round table, 1955-56, joint committee on Librarianship as a Career, chairman, 1955-58, Library Periodicals Round Table, chairman, 1955-56, audio-visual committee, 1956-58, council member, 1957-61, resolutions committee, chairman, 1962-63), American Association of University Professors, American Chemical Society (chemical literature section), American Documentation Institute (executive council, 1962-64, advisory board, chairman, 1962-64, student membership committee chairman, 1966), American Personnel and Guidance Association, American Translators Association, Archons of Colophon (New York), Association of American Library Schools (curriculum committee, chairman, 1959-60), Association of College and Research Libraries (audio-visual committee, chairman, 1955-58, board of directors, 1957-61, research committee, university libraries section, 1958-62, constitution committee, chairman, 1959-61), Medical Library Association (conference publicity director, 1965), Special Libraries Association, Melvil Dui Association (New York), Pennsylvania Library Association (president, 1964-65), Dartmouth Club (Philadelphia), Phi Kappa Phi, Philibiblon Club (Philadelphia). *Awards, honors:* Library Binding Institute Silver Book Award, 1965.

WRITINGS: Action Manual for Library Recruiters (monograph), Joint Committee on Library Work as a Career, 1956; *The Librarian's Career: A Study of Mobility*, University of Rochester Press, for Association of College and Research Libraries, 1957; (compiler with Phillips Temple) *A Directory of Library Periodicals in the Continental United States*, State College Library (Pittsburg, Kan.), 1957; (contributor) *Bowker Library Annual*, 1963. Contributor to *Encyclopedia Americana*, 1963, and *American Educator Encyclopedia*, United Educators, in press. Editor, *Drexel Library School Series*, 1960—; Monthly Recruitment Series, *Library Journal*, 1962; *Drexel Information Science Series*, Spartan Press, 1964—.†

*   *   *

HARWOOD, Pearl Augusta (Bragdon) 1903-

PERSONAL: Born December 21, 1903, in Grafton, Mass.; daughter of Clifford Sawyer (a school superintendent) and Helen (Woodside) Bragdon; married Lester E. Harwood (a life insurance underwriter), 1933. *Education:* Mount Holyoke College, A.B.; Boston University, M.Ed.; San Jose State College (now California State University), library training. *Religion:* Protestant. *Home:* 909 La Fiesta Court, San Marcos, Calif. 92069.

CAREER: San Jose (Calif.) Unified School District, home teacher, 1948-54; Las Lomitas (Calif.) School District, elementary librarian at Atherton, 1955-57; public library work with children in Alameda and Ventura counties, and Los Gatos, Calif., 1955, and 1958-62; Vista (Calif.) School District, home teacher, 1963—. Occasional worker in psychological and nursery school fields.

WRITINGS—All children's books; all published by Lerner: *The Widdles*, 1966.

"Mr. Bumba" series: *Mr. Bumba's New Home*, 1964; *. . . Plants a Garden*, 1964; *. . . Keeps House*, 1964; *. . . and the Orange Grove*, 1964; *. . . New Job*, 1964; *. . . Has a Party*, 1964; *. . . Draws a Kitten*, 1966; *. . . Four-Legged Company*, 1966; *. . . Rides a Bicycle*, 1966; *. . . Tuesday Club*, 1966.

"Mrs. Moon" series; all published in 1967: *Mrs. Moon's Story Hour*; *. . . and Her Friends*; *. . . Polliwogs*; *. . . Picnic*; *. . . Goes Shopping*; *. . . Harbor Trip*; *. . . Rescue*; *. . . and the Dark Stairs*; *. . . Takes a Drive*; *. . . Cement Hat*.

"Mr. and Mrs. Bumba" series; all published in 1971: *A Long Vacation for Mr. and Mrs. Bumba*; *The Rummage Sale and . . .*; *A Special Guest for . . .*; *The Make-It Room of* . . . ; *A Thief Visits* . . . ; *A Happy Halloween for* . . . ; *New Year's Day with* . . . ; *The Carnival with* . . . ; *Climbing a Mountain with* . . . ; *The Very Big Problem of* . . . .

*   *   *

HASSALL, William Owen   1912-

PERSONAL: Born August 4, 1912, in York, England; son of Owen (a lieutenant colonel, British Army) and Bessie Frances (Cory) Hassall; married Averil Grafton Beaves (an artist, teacher, and lecturer), July 24, 1936; children: Timothy Richard Cory, Mark William Cory, Cory Frances (Mrs. Rodney Lyons), Tom Grafton. *Education:* Corpus Christi College, Oxford, M.A. (first class honors), 1938, D.Phil., 1941. *Home:* Manor House, Wheatley, Oxford, England.

CAREER: Librarian to the Earl of Leicester, Holkham, Norfolk, England, 1937; Oxford University, Bodleian Library, Oxford, England, assistant librarian, 1938—. Former external examiner for various teacher training colleges in Great Britain; lecturer on medieval manuscripts. Member of local history committee, Oxfordshire Rural Community Council. *Military service:* British Army, Royal Artillery, 1942-46; assigned to Ministry of Economic Warfare during most of service. *Member:* Society of Antiquaries (fellow, 1942), Oxfordshire Record Society (honorary secretary).

WRITINGS: An Italian Bibliography, Association of Special Libraries and Information Bureaux, 1946; *Cartulary of St. Mary Clerkenwell*, Royal Historical Society, 1949; *The Library Catalogue of Chief Justice Coke*, Yale University Law Library, 1950; *The Holkham Bible Picture Book*, Dropmore Press, 1953; *Wheatley Records, 956-1956*, Oxfordshire Record Society, 1956; *They Saw It Happen*, Volume I (to 1485), Basil Blackwell, 1957; *Who's Who in History*, Volume I (to 1485), Basil Blackwell, 1960; (editor with wife, Averil B. Hassall) *The Douce Apocalypse*, Faber, 1961; *How They Lived*, Volume I (to 1485), Basil Blackwell, 1962; *Medieval England: As Viewed by Contemporaries*, Harper, 1965; *Index of Persons in Oxfordshire Deeds Acquired by the Bodleian Library*, Oxfordshire Record Society, 1966; *History Through Surnames*, Pergamon, 1967; *The Holkham Library Illuminations and Illustrations From the Library of the Earl of Leicester*, privately printed, 1970. Editor of filmstrips for Bodleian Library and Educational Productions. Contributor of articles on medieval manuscripts at Holkham to *Connoisseur*. Former member of editorial committee, *Archives*.

WORK IN PROGRESS: In collaboration with his wife, a book on the treasures of the Bodleian Library, for Gordon Fraser, completion expected in 1975; and studies of Holkham.

SIDELIGHTS: Hassall is competent in Latin, Greek, French, and German, reads Russian and Italian. He is interested in the maintenance of Wheatley Manor House, last restored in 1601 by the uncle of Mary Powell, first wife of John Milton.

*   *   *

HATHAWAY, Lulu (Bailey)   1903-

PERSONAL: Born January 24, 1903, in Royal Leamington Spa, England; daughter of William Edwin (a career soldier in British Army) and Edith May (Leach) Bailey; married B. Bailey Hathaway (a clergyman), December 21, 1925; children: Edwin, Phoebe (Mrs. Charles Marshall Foster), F.

Randel. *Education:* University of Leeds, B.Sc., 1924; University of Rochester, A.M., 1926; Syracuse University, M.S.in L.S., 1961. *Politics:* Democrat. *Religion:* Lutheran. *Residence:* Cape Coral, Fla.

CAREER: New York State Council of Churches, director of children's work, 1948-53; National Council of American Baptist Women, vice-president, 1953-57; Edmeston Central School, Edmeston, N.Y., librarian, 1957-59; Fabius Central School, Fabius, N.Y., director of library service, 1959-64; Edison Junior College, Fort Myers, Fla., librarian, 1964-69. *Member:* American Library Association, Beta Phi Mu.

WRITINGS: Bible Friends and Friends Today, American Baptist Publication Society, 1957; *Westward the Church*, American Baptist Publication Society, 1962; *Primary Guide on India*, Friendship, 1963; *The Boy Who Couldn't Talk*, Friendship, 1964; *They Lived Their Love*, Friendship, 1965; *Especially Rosita*, Friendship, 1967; *Partners*, Judson, 1970.

SIDELIGHTS: Mrs. Hathaway lived in the Congo for three years during the 1920's. She is competent in French and Lingala.

*   *   *

HAWES, Evelyn (Johnson)

PERSONAL: Born in Colville, Wash.; daughter of W. Lon (a lawyer, judge, and lieutenant governor) and Iva (Dickey) Johnson; married Nat H. Hawes (an executive of J. C. Penney Co.), July 25, 1937; children: Linda Clever. *Education:* Attended Washington State University, 1933-34; University of Washington, graduate, 1936, graduate study, 1937; further graduate study University of Cincinnati, 1948-49; Purdue University, 1950-51; State University of New York at Buffalo, 1957-58. *Politics:* Moderate. *Religion:* Congregationalist. *Home:* 10550 North East 29th, Apt. D, Bellevue, Wash. 98004. *Agent:* Ann Elmo Agency, Inc., 52 Vanderbilt, New York, N.Y. 10017.

CAREER: University of Washington, Seattle, member of public relations department, 1941-43, faculty of speech department, 1943-47; University of Cincinnati, Cincinnati, Ohio, teacher of world literature, 1950-51; teacher of creative writing in adult education classes, Buffalo, N.Y., 1956, Amhurst, N.Y., 1957-64; State University of New York at Buffalo, member of faculty of continuing education, 1971-72. Lecturer for Music and Art Foundation Speaker's Forum, Seattle, Wash., 1938-41. Volunteer worker in speech therapy and writing at Veterans Administration hospitals, and for service organizations.

MEMBER: National Association of Public School Adult Educators, National League of American Pen Women (president, Western New York branch, 1964-66; national vice-president, 1972-74), American Association of University Women, Edward J. Meyer Memorial Hospital Auxiliary (Buffalo), Chi Omega. *Awards, honors:* Third Prize in national fiction contest, *Tomorrow* (magazine); Founder's Medal for distinction in writing, Western New York branch of National League of American Pen Women, 1955; National League of American Pen Women, Best Published Novel Award, 1968, for *A Madras-Type Jacket*; Award of Achievement, Buffalo and Erie County Historical Society, 1970 and 1973.

WRITINGS: Proud Vision: The History of The Buffalo General Hospital: The First Hundred Years, Crowell, 1964; *The Happy Land* (fiction), Harcourt, 1965; *A*

Madras-Type Jacket (fiction), Harcourt, 1967; *Six Nights a Week* (fiction), Harcourt, 1971. Contributor of short stories and articles to periodicals, including *Parents' Magazine*, *Saturday Evening Post*, *Ladies' Home Journal*, *Tomorrow*, *Family Circle*, *Writer*.

WORK IN PROGRESS: Country Lawyer, a nonfiction book; *Vagabond Prince*, a fictionalized story of a nineteenth-century American rover; a play, "The Happy Land."

BIOGRAPHICAL/CRITICAL SOURCES: Writer, September, 1954.

*   *   *

HAWTON, Hector   1901-
(Virginia Curzon)

PERSONAL: Born February 7, 1901, in Plymouth, Devonshire, England; son of James and Harriet (Goddard) Hawton; married second wife, Mary Bishop, 1958; children (previous marriage) two sons. *Education:* Attended Plymouth College, Plymouth, England. *Home:* 53 Palace Rd., London N.8, England. *Agent:* International Literary Management, 2 Ellis St., Sloane St., London S.W. 1, England.

CAREER: Western Morning News, reporter, 1919-23; National Press Agency, parliamentary correspondent, 1923-27; *Empire News*, subeditor, 1927-29; free-lance writer, 1929-39; with Rationalist Press Association Ltd., London, England, 1946-49, managing director, 1952-71. Former editor of *Humanist* (monthly) and *Rationalist* (annual). Author. Director of Pemberton Publishing Co. Ltd. and N. I. Thompson Press Ltd. *Military service:* Royal Air Force, Intelligence, 1940-45; served at Bomber Command Headquarters; became flight lieutenant; mentioned in dispatches. *Member:* National Liberal Club.

WRITINGS: Tides of Enchantment, Jenkins, 1931; *Eternal Masculine*, Jenkins, 1932; *Forty Love*, Hurst & Blackett, 1932; *Chasing the Moon*, Collins, 1934; *Husbands Are Human*, Collins, 1935; *Men Must Love*; *A Romantic Novel*, Collins, 1935; *Spare Time Wife*, Collins, 1935; *Escape with Me*, Collins, 1936.

Why Be Moral?, C. A. Watts, 1940; *The Flight from Reality*, C. A. Watts, 1941; *Will Religion Survive?*, C. A. Watts, 1942; *The Men Who Fly*, Nelson, 1944; *Night Bombing*, Nelson, 1944; *Murder at H.Q.*, Ward, Lock, 1945; *Murder Most Foul*, Ward, Lock, 1946; *Unnatural Causes*, Ward, Lock, 1947; *Case of the Crazy Atom*, Ward, Lock, 1948; *Men Without Gods*, C. A. Watts, 1948; *Murder by Mathematics*, Ward, Lock, 1948; *Deadly Nightcap*, Ward, Lock, 1949; *Philosophy for Pleasure*, Philosophical Library, 1949.

Nine Singing Apes, Ward, Lock, 1950; *The Thinkers Handbook: A Guide to Religious Controversy*, C. A. Watts, 1950; *Tower of Darkness*, Hodder & Stoughton, 1950, Roy Publishers, 1951; *Blue-Eyed Buddha*, Hodder & Stoughton, 1951; *Operation Superman*, Ward, Lock, 1951; *Black Emperor*, Hodder & Stoughton, 1952; *Death of a Witch*, Ward, Lock, 1952; *The Feast of Unreason*, C. A. Watts, 1952; *Lost Valley*, Hodder & Stoughton, 1953; *Rope for the Judge*, Ward, Lock, 1954; *Skeleton in the Cupboard*, Ward, Lock, 1955; (editor with others) *Reason in Action*, C. A. Watts, 1956; *Green Scorpion*, Ward, Lock, 1957; *The Humanist Revolution*, Pemberton Publishing Co., 1963; *Controversy: The Humanist/Christian Encounter*, Pemberton, Publishing Co., 1971.

Under pseudonym Virginia Curzon: *Sweet Rebel*, Harrap, 1935; *The Virgin of the Forest*, Harrap, 1935.†

HAY, Denys   1915-

PERSONAL: Born August 29, 1915, in Newcastle upon Tyne, England; son of William King (a clergyman) and Janet (Waugh) Hay; married Sarah Gwyneth Morely, 1937; children: one son, two daughters. *Education:* Balliol College, Oxford, B.A. and M.A. *Home:* 31 Fountainhall Rd., Edinburgh 9, Scotland. *Office:* History Department, The University, Edinburgh 8, Scotland.

CAREER: University of Southampton, Southampton, England, assistant lecturer, 1939-40; Cabinet Office, London, England, war historian, 1943-45; University of Edinburgh, Edinburgh, Scotland, lecturer, 1945-54, professor of medieval history, 1954—. Visiting professor, Cornell University, 1963. Italian lecturer, British Academy, 1959; Wiles Lecturer, The Queen's University of Belfast, 1960; senior fellow, Newberry Library, Chicago, 1966; Birkbeck lecturer, Trinity College, Cambridge, 1971. *Military service:* Royal Army Service Corps, 1940-43; became lieutenant. *Member:* Royal Historical Society (literary director, 1956-58), Historical Association (president, 1967-70), British Academy (fellow), Renaissance Society of America.

WRITINGS: (Editor) Vergil, *Anglica Historia*, Royal Historical Society, 1950; *Polydore Vergil*, Clarendon Press, 1952; *From Roman Empire to Renaissance Europe*, Methuen, 1953, revised edition published as *The Medieval Centuries*, 1964, Harper, 1965; (editor) R. K. Hannay, *Letters of James V.*, H.M.S.O., 1954; *Europe: The Emergence of an Idea*, Edinburgh University Press, 1957; *Italian Renaissance in Its Historical Background*, Cambridge University Press, 1961; *The Renaissance Debate*, Holt, 1965; *Europe in the Fourteenth and Fifteenth Centuries*, Holt, 1966; (editor) Nicolai Rubinstein and others, *The Age of the Renaissance: The Turning Point of Modern History*, McGraw, 1967; (editor and translator) Pope Pius, II, *De gestis concilli Basilunsis commentariorum*, Clarendon Press, (Oxford) 1967. Editor, *English Historical Review*, 1958-65.

WORK IN PROGRESS: Renaissance history.

*   *   *

HAYAKAWA, S(amuel) I(chiye)   1906-

PERSONAL: Born July 18, 1906, in Vancouver, British Columbia; son of Ichiro (an import-export merchant) and Tora (Isono) Hayakawa; married Margedant Peters, May 29, 1937; children: Alan, Mark, Wynne. *Education:* University of Manitoba, B.A., 1927; McGill University, M.A., 1928; University of Wisconsin, Ph.D., 1935. *Politics:* Republican. *Address:* Box 100, Mill Valley, Calif. 94941. *Office:* San Francisco State University, San Francisco, Calif. 94132.

CAREER: University of Wisconsin, Madison, assistant instructor in English, 1930-36, instructor in English in English Extension Division, 1936-39; Armour Institute (now Illinois Institute of Technology), Chicago, Ill., instructor, 1939-40, assistant professor, 1940-42, associate professor of English, 1942-47; University of Chicago, Chicago, Ill., lecturer in University College, 1950-55; San Francisco State College (now San Francisco State University), San Francisco, Calif., professor of English, 1955-68, acting president, 1968-69, president, 1969-72, president emeritus, 1972—. Claude Bernard Lecturer at Institute of Experimental Medicine and Surgery, University of Montreal, 1959; Alfred P. Sloan Visiting Professor, Menninger School of Psychiatry, 1961. *Member:* International Society for General Semantics (president, 1949-50), American Association for the Advancement of Science (fellow), American Psychological Association (fellow), American Sociological Association, American Anthropological Association, Modern Language Association of America, American Dialect Society, National Council of Teachers of English, Society for the Psychological Study of Social Issues, Institute of Jazz Studies (director), Press and Union League (San Francisco), Pannonia Athletic Club. *Awards, honors:* D.F.A., California College of Arts and Crafts, 1956; Claude Bernard Medal for Experimental Medicine and Surgery, University of Montreal, 1959; Litt.D., Grinnell College, 1967; L.H.D., Pepperdine University, 1972; LL.D., The Citadel, 1972.

WRITINGS: (Editor with Howard Mumford Jones) *Oliver Wendell Holmes: Representative Selections*, American Book Co., 1939; *Language in Action* (Book-of-the-Month Club selection), Harcourt, 1941; (with Basil H. Pillard) *Language in Thought and Action* (based on *Language in Action*), Harcourt, 1949, 2nd edition, 1964; (contributor) *Middle English Dictionary*, University of Michigan Press, 1952; (editor) *Language, Meaning, and Maturity: Selections from "ETC: A Review of General Semantics,"* 1943-53, Harper, 1954; (editor) *Our Language and Our World: Selections from "ETC: A Review of General Semantics,"* 1953-58, Harper, 1959, reprinted, Books for Libraries, 1971; *Symbol, Status, and Personality*, Harcourt, 1963; (editor) *Funk & Wagnalls Modern Guide to Synonyms and Related Words*, Funk, 1968 (new edition published in England as *Cassell's Modern Guide to Synonyms and Related Words*, Cassells, 1971); *Modern Guide to Synonyms and Related Words*, Verlag Darmstaedter Blatter Schwartz, 1969; *Quotations from Chairman S. I. Hayakawa*, [San Francisco], 1969; (editor with William Dresser) *Dimensions of Meaning*, Bobbs-Merrill, 1970.

Contributor to *New Republic, Harper's, Poetry, Sewanee Review*, and other periodicals. Columnist for *Defender* (Chicago), 1942-47; founder and editor, *ETC: A Review of General Semantics*, 1943—.

SIDELIGHTS: P. T. Kimball, speaking of *Symbol, Status, and Personality*, said "[Hayakawa] makes the reader stop and think. That, perhaps, is the most constructive step of all in the quest for more effective communication. . . ." C. M. Brown noted that "Hayakawa's observation is sharp, his style lively, and his wit diverting."

Perhaps Hayakawa's greatest contribution to modern letters is his periodical, *ETC*. Of *Our Language and Our World*, an *ETC* anthology, a *Kirkus* reviewer wrote: "This provocative book . . . endeavors to apply semantics, the science of meanings and communication, to the problems of present-day life. . . . Of highly specialized and limited appeal, [it] is not for the average layman, but professors and serious students of semantics and world conditions should welcome it. . . ."

AVOCATIONAL INTERESTS: Fishing, collecting jazz records, African and Chinese art, fencing.

BIOGRAPHICAL/CRITICAL SOURCES: Virginia Kirkus Service, February 15, 1959; *Chicago Sunday Tribune*, April 19, 1959; *San Francisco Chronicle*, April 26, 1959; *New York Herald Tribune Book Review*, May 24, 1959; *Book Week*, November 3, 1963; *Newsweek*, December 2, 1963.

* * *

HAYCRAFT, Molly Costain 1911-

PERSONAL: Born December 6, 1911, in Toronto, Ontario, Canada; daughter of Thomas B. (a writer) and Ida (Spragge) Costain; married Howard Haycraft (chairman of board of publishing firm and author), October 9, 1942. *Education:* Attended Ogontz School for Girls. *Residence:* Hightstown, N.J. *Agent:* Curtis Brown, 60 East 56th St., New York, N.Y. 10022.

CAREER: Otto K. Liveright (literary agent), New York, N.Y., assistant, 1935-37; *Saturday Review of Literature*, New York, N.Y., secretary to Amy Loveman, 1937-39; Curtis Brown Ltd. (literary agents), New York, N.Y., assistant in magazine department, 1939-42. Author. Mercantile Library Association, director, 1960-68, secretary, 1965-68.

WRITINGS: Queen Victoria, Messner, 1956; *First Lady of the Theatre: Sarah Siddons*, Messner, 1958; *Too Near the Throne*, Lippincott, 1959; *The Reluctant Queen*, Lippincott, 1962; *The Lady Royal*, Lippincott, 1964; *My Lord Brother, the Lionheart*, Lippincott, 1968; *The King's Daughters*, Lippincott, 1971; *Countess Carrots*, Lippincott, 1973.

WORK IN PROGRESS: A novel about the daughter of Henry III of England; *Royal Lovers*, a novel about King Alexander III and Queen Margaret of Scotland.

SIDELIGHTS: Mrs. Haycraft researches her books on trips abroad, mainly in England.

* * *

HAZARD, Patrick D. 1927-

PERSONAL: Born February 8, 1927, in Battle Creek, Mich.; son of Harry Edward (a realtor) and May (Fitzpatrick) Hazard; married Mary Elizabeth Schneider (a college teacher), December 30, 1950 (divorced, 1970); children: Michael, Catherine, Timothy. *Education:* University of Detroit, Ph.B., 1949; Western Reserve University, (now Case Western Reserve University) M.A., 1952, Ph.D., 1957. *Home:* 8 Longford St., Philadelphia, Pa. 19136. *Office:* Beaver College, Glenside, Pa.

CAREER: Taught at East Lansing High School, East Lansing, Mich., 1952-55; Trenton State College, Trenton, N.J., assistant professor of English, 1956-57; University of Pennsylvania, Philadelphia, assistant professor, 1957-61; University of Hawaii, Honolulu, associate professor of English, 1961-62; Beaver College, Glenside, Pa., professor, and chairman of English Department, 1962-69; founded Centre for Internationalizing English, 1972. *Military service:* U.S. Naval Reserve, 1944-46. *Member:* Modern Language Association of America, American Studies Association, National Council of Teachers of English. *Awards, honors:* Carnegie Foundation postdoctoral fellowship, 1957-59.

WRITINGS: (With Mary E. Hazard) *Language and Literacy Today*, Science Research Associates, 1964; *Dolphin Guide to Hawaii*, Dolphin Books, 1965; *TV as Art: Some Essays in Criticism*, Appleton, 1966.

WORK IN PROGRESS: Three books, *Internationalizing English: A Primer*; *Putting on Poetry Fairs: A Community Handbook*; and *Eden as Eldorado*.

* * *

HEAD, Timothy E. 1934-

PERSONAL: Born July 2, 1934; son of Louis E. and Ruth (Mitchell) Head; married February 18, 1960; children: Jennifer Kamuela. *Education:* Long Beach City College,

A.A., 1954; Long Beach State College (now California State College at Long Beach), B.A. and M.A., 1960; University of Hawaii, M.A., 1963. *Address:* Box 631, Kehei, Maui, Hawaii.

CAREER: Long Beach Press Telegram, Long Beach, Calif., part-time reporter, 1956-60; University of Hawaii, Honolulu, research fellow at East-West Center, 1963; Meiji Gakuin University, Tokyo, Japan, instructor in English, 1964-65; Zama American High School, Tokyo, Japan, instructor in history, 1965—. *Military service:* U.S. Army, 1955-56. *Member:* Travel Writers Society of America.

WRITINGS: Going Native in Hawaii: A Poor Man's Guide to Paradise, Tuttle, 1965.

WORK IN PROGRESS: The Bonin Islands: A History, Hirohito: His Life and His Job, Kamakura: A Historical Guide.†

* * *

HEATH, Robert W. 1931-

PERSONAL: Born March 30, 1931, in Lafayette, Ind.; son of Donald Leroy and Zula (Whicker) Heath; married Marjorie E. Funk, November 22, 1950; children: James, Paul, John, Scott. *Education:* Purdue University, B.S., 1954, M.S., 1955, Ph.D., 1957. *Politics:* Independent. *Office:* Educational Testing Service, 1947 Center St., Berkeley 4, Calif.

CAREER: Purdue University, Lafayette, Ind., assistant director, Division of Educational Reference, 1955-58; University of Arizona, Tucson, research psychologist, 1958-61; Educational Testing Service, Princeton, N.J., head of special studies section, 1961-63, director of research at western office, Berkeley, Calif., 1963—.

WRITINGS: (With N. M. Downie) *Basic Statistical Methods*, Harper, 1959, 4th edition, 1974; (editor) *New Curricula*, Harper, 1964 (with Landers Roy and Delores Mack) *Evaluation of an E.P.D.A. Institute: Teachers for Multicultural Education*, Stanford Center for Research and Development in Teaching, 1970. Contributor of articles to professional journals.

WORK IN PROGRESS: Research in testing, curriculum, and statistics.†

* * *

HEATH-STUBBS, John (Francis Alexander) 1918-

PERSONAL: Born July 9, 1918, in London, England; son of Francis and Edith (a professional pianist; maiden name Marr) Heath-Stubbs. *Education:* Queen's College, Oxford, B.A. (first class honours), 1943, M.A., 1972. *Politics:* Philosophical Tory. *Religion:* Church of England. *Home:* 35 Sutherland Place, London W. 2, England. *Agent:* David Higham Associates, 5-8 Lower John St., London W. 1, England.

CAREER: Hall School, Hampstead, England, English master, 1945; *Hutchinson's Illustrated Encyclopedia*, editorial assistant, 1945-46; Leeds University, Leeds, England, Gregory Fellow in Poetry, 1953-55; University of Alexandria, Alexandria, Egypt, visiting professor of English, 1955-58; University of Michigan, Ann Arbor, visiting professor of English, 1960-61; part-time lecturer in English, College of St. Mark and St. John, Chelsea, London, England, until 1973. *Member:* Royal Society of Literature (fellow). *Awards, honors:* Arts Council of Great Britian

Award, 1965, for *Selected Poems*; Queen's Gold Medal for Poetry, 1973.

WRITINGS—Poetry: *Wounded Thammuz*, Routledge & Kegan Paul, 1942; *Beauty and the Beast*, Routledge & Kegan Paul, 1943; *The Divided Ways*, Routledge & Kegan Paul, 1946; *The Swarming of the Bees*, Eyre & Spottiswoode, 1950; *A Charm Against the Toothache*, Methuen, 1954; *The Triumph of the Muse*, Oxford University Press, 1958; *The Blue-Fly in His Head*, Oxford University Press, 1962; *Selected Poems*, Oxford University Press, 1965; *Satires & Epigrams*, Turrett Books, 1968; *Artorius, Book One*, Wittenborn, 1970; (with Stephen Spender and F. T. Prince) *Penguin Modern Poets No. 20*, Penguin, 1972; *Indifferent Weather*, Ian McKelvie, 1974.

Plays: *Helen in Egypt*, Oxford University Press, 1959.

Translations: *Poems From Giacomo Leopardi*, J. Lehmann, 1947; *Aphrodite's Garland*, Crescendo Press, 1952; (with Peter Avery) Hafiz of Shiraz, *Thirty Poems*, J. Murray, 1955; *Selected Prose & Poetry of Giacomo Leopardi*, Oxford University Press, 1966; Alfred Victor Vigny, *The Horn*, Keepsake Press, 1969.

Criticism: *The Darkling Plain* (study of Victorian romantic poetry), Eyre & Spottiswoode, 1950, reprinted, Folcroft Press, 1970; *Charles Williams*, Longmans, Green (for the British Council), 1955; (contributor) Bruce Alvin King, editor, *Dryden's Mind and Art*, Oliver & Boyd, 1969; *The Ode*, Clarendon Press, 1969; *The Verse Satire*, Clarendon Press, 1969; *The Pastoral*, Clarendon Press, 1969.

Editor: *Selected Poems of Shelley*, Falcon Press, 1947; *Selected Poems of Tennyson*, Falcon Press, 1947; *Selected Poems of Swift*, Falcon Press, 1947; (with David Wright) *The Forsaken Garden*, J. Lehmann, 1950; *Images of Tomorrow*, S. C. M. Press, 1953; (with Wright) *The Faber Book of Twentieth Century Verse*, Faber, 1954, revised edition, 1965; *Selected Poems of Alexander Pope*, Heinemann, 1964.

Contributor to *Times Literary Supplement, Time and Tide, Spectator, New English Weekly, New English Review, Occult Observer, Poetry Quarterly, Poetry London, Modern Churchman's Journal, Cairo Review of English Studies, New Republic, Aquarius, Tablet, Frontier*, and other periodicals.

WORK IN PROGRESS: Translating Omar Khayyam with Peter Avery; 2nd revision of *The Faber Book of Twentieth Century Verse* with David Wright; preparing a collection of modern Egyptian folk poetry, in collaboration with Shafik Megally.

SIDELIGHTS: "John Heath-Stubbs," writes John Press, "is a curiously anachronistic figure in post-war England: a neo-Romantic with a keen satirical wit, a scholar who frequents Soho, a Christian haunted by guilt, remorse, and a fear of damnation. His affinities are with certain members of the Rhymers' Club, those friends and acquaintances of W. B. Yeats who met at the Cheshire Cheese in the eighteen-nineties. . . ." Heath-Stubbs's poetry makes use of myth and of history-as-myth. Thomas Blackburn comments that he also takes care "to discipline his language by some ironic twist or dry, casual word, and so bring it to heel in the present day."

BIOGRAPHICAL/CRITICAL SOURCES: Thomas Blackburn, *The Price of an Eye*, Morrow, 1961; John Wain, *Sprightly Running*, St. Martin's, 1962; John Press, *Rule and Energy*, Oxford University Press, 1963.

HEER, David MacAlpine 1930-

PERSONAL: Surname is pronounced Hare; born April 15, 1930, in Chapel Hill, N.C.; son of Clarence and Jean (MacAlpine) Heer; married Nancy Whittier, June 29, 1957; children: Douglas MacAlpine (deceased), Laura Page, Catherine Reid. *Education:* Harvard University, A.B. (magna cum laude), 1950, A.M., 1954, Ph.D., 1958. *Politics:* Democrat. *Religion:* Unitarian Universalist. *Home:* 10251 Monte Mar Drive, Los Angeles, Calif. 90064. *Office:* Population Research Laboratory, University of Southern California, Los Angeles, Calif. 90007.

CAREER: U.S. Bureau of the Census, Washington, D.C., statistician, 1957-61; University of California, Berkeley, lecturer in sociology, 1961-64; Harvard University, School of Public Health, Boston, Mass., assistant professor of biostatistics and demography, 1964-68, associate professor of demography, 1968-72; University of Southern California, Los Angeles, professor of sociology, 1972—. *Member:* Population Association of America, American Sociological Association, International Union for the Scientific Study of Population, National Council on Family Relations.

WRITINGS: After Nuclear Attack: A Demographic Inquiry, Praeger, 1965; *Society and Population*, Prentice-Hall, 1968, revised edition, 1975; (compiler) *Readings on Population*, Prentice-Hall, 1968; (editor) *Social Statistics and the City*, Harvard-M.I.T. Joint Center for Urban Studies, 1968. Associate editor, *Journal of Marriage and the Family*; editorial consultant, *Demography*; member of editorial board, *Human Ecology*.

SIDELGHTS: Heer speaks Russian, Spanish and French.

*   *   *

HEFLEY, James C(arl) 1930-

PERSONAL: Born June 2, 1930, in Chillicothe, Ohio; son of Fred J. (a merchant) and Hester (Foster) Hefley; married Martha S. Smedley; children: Cynthia Joy, Cecilia Faith, Cheryl Grace. *Education:* Arkansas Polytechnic College, student, 1944-47; Ouachita Baptist College, B.A., 1950; New Orleans Baptist Theological Seminary, B.D., 1953, and graduate study. *Home:* 117 West Hintz Road, Arlington Heights, Ill. 60004.

CAREER: Baptist minister, ordained, 1948. Pastor of Baptist churches in New Orleans, La., 1953-58; David C. Cook Publishing Co. (religious publications), Elgin, Ill., editor, 1961-64; full-time free-lance writer specializing in religious field, 1964—. *Member:* American Scientific Affiliation. *Awards, honors:* Feature-writing awards from Evangelical Press Association, 1966, 1971.

WRITINGS—All published by Zondervan, except as indicated: *Heroes of the Faith*, Moody, 1963; *Get the Facts*, Broadman, 1963; *Scientists Who Believe*, David C. Cook, 1963; *Living Miracles*, 1964; *Play Ball: True Stories of Faith in Action*, 1964; *Sports Alive*, 1965; *The Will to Win*, 1966; *Adventurers With God*, 1967; *Peril by Choice*, 1968; *Intrigue in Santo Domingo*, Word Books, 1968; *Businessman Who Believe*, David C. Cook, 1968; (compiler) *Sourcebook of Humor*, 1968; (with Phil Regan) *Phil Regan*, 1968; (editor) Steve Sloan, *Calling Life's Signals*, 1968; *By Life or by Death*, 1969; (with Don Schinnick) *Always a Winner*, 1969; *What's So Great About the Bible?*, David C. Cook, 1969.

Lift Off!, 1970; *God Goes to High School*, Word Books, 1970; (with Stephen Harris) *My Anchor Held*, Revell, 1970; (editor) A. D. Dennison, *Shock It To Me, Doctor*, 1970;

The Cross and the Scalpel, Word Books, 1971; *Dictionary of Illustrations*, 1971; *Thinkables*, Revell, 1971; *Aaron Saenz: Mexico's Revolutionary Capitalist*, Word Books, 1971; *Sex, Sense, and Nonsense*, David C. Cook, 1971; *Space Twins on the Moon* (fiction), Standard, 1971; *A Prejudiced Protestant Takes Another Look at the Catholic Church*, Revell, 1971; (with wife, Marti Hefley) *Dawn Over Amazonia*, Word Books, 1971; *Be a Man*, Scripture Press, 1971; *Miracles in Mexico*, Moody, 1972; *Move Out*, Scripture Press, 1972; *God on the Gridiron*, 1972; *Why Drink?*, Scripture Press, 1973; *Sourcebook of Bible Words*, 1973; (with Marti Hefley) *Christ in Bangladesh*, Harper, 1973; *The New Jews*, Tyndale, 1974; (with Marti Hefley) *God's Tribesman*, Lippincott, 1974; (with Marti Hefley) *Where in the World Are the Jews Today?*, Scripture Press, 1974; (with Marti Hefley) *No Time for Tombstones*, Tyndale, 1974; (with Marti Hefley) *Cameron Townsend*, Word Books, in press; *Sacred Cows Make Good Hamburgers*, Regal Books, in press.

One-time director and script writer for "Transformed," weekly Christian dramatic radio program on twenty southern stations. Contributor to *Today's Health*, *Chicago Tribune Magazine*, and various religious magazines.

WORK IN PROGRESS: A study of spiritual renewal among Watergate figures and elected officials in Washington, D.C.

SIDELIGHTS: Hefley has traveled extensively in Latin America, with additional travel to Asia, Europe and the Middle East. His book, *Living Miracles*, was selected for the White House Library by the Christian Booksellers Association. Hefley has served as a speaker and lecturer for the Christian Writer's Institute and Judson College Writer's Workshop. He also taught journalism at Judson College.

BIOGRAPHICAL/CRITICAL SOURCES: Sunday Digest, January 10, 1971; *Bookstore Journal*, February, 1970.

*   *   *

HEILIGER, Edward Martin 1909-

PERSONAL: Born December 14, 1909, in Rockford, Ill.; son of Edward Martin (an insurance agent) and Hazel (Hicks) Heiliger; married Beatrice Kelley, July 16, 1937; children: Mary. *Education:* University of the Pacific, A.B., 1933; University of Denver, B.S. in L.S., 1935, M.A., 1941. *Religion:* Methodist. *Home:* 694 Northeast 36th St., Boca Raton, Fla. 33432. *Office:* Florida Atlantic University, Boca Raton, Fla. 33432.

CAREER: Detroit (Mich.) Public Library, junior assistant, 1935-37; Wayne State University, Detroit, Mich., assistant librarian, 1937-43; American Library Association, Chicago, Ill., director of American Library of Nicaragua at Managua, 1944-46; Rockefeller Foundation, New York, N.Y., founder of School of Librarianship at University of Chile, Santiago, and adviser to the university's Central Library, 1946-48; U.S. Department of State, director of overseas libraries management project, 1949, and director of Benjamin Franklin Library, Mexico Distrito Federal, 1950-53; New York State Library, Watertown, associate librarian, 1953-55; University of Illinois, Chicago Campus, director of library, 1955-63; Florida Atlantic University, Boca Raton, director of library, 1963—. Visiting professor of library science at University of Chile, National University of Mexico, and Syracuse University. U.S. delegate to UNESCO Conference on Scientific Documentation, Lima, Peru, 1962. Member of Chilean National Scholarship Commission, 1946-48, of Mexican-American Cultural Commission, 1951-52, of board of Adult Education Council of Greater Chicago, 1956-64, and of advisory committee, Library of Congress Automation Study, 1961-64. *Member:* American Library Association, Special Libraries Association, American Documentation Institute, Southeastern Library Association, Florida Library Association.

WRITINGS: (With Luis Arce) *Catalogacion y clasificacion*, Universidad de Chile, 1946; (translator) William Stetson Merrill, *Codigo para clasificadores*, Editorial Kapelusz, 1958; (with Schultheiss and Culbertson) *Advanced Data Processing in the University Library*, Scarecrow, 1962; (with Paul B. Henderson, Jr.) *Library Automation*, McGraw, 1971. Contributor of articles and reviews to professional journals. Associate editor of *Illinois Libraries*, 1956-63.†

*   *   *

HEILMAN, Robert Bechtold 1906-

PERSONAL: Born July 18, 1906, in Philadelphia, Pa.; son of Edgar James (a clergyman) and Mary (Bechtold) Heilman; married Ruth Champlin, July 31, 1935; children: Champlin. *Education:* Lafayette College, A.B., 1927; Tufts University, graduate student, 1927-28; Ohio State University, M.A., 1930; Harvard University, M.A., 1931, Ph.D., 1935. *Religion:* Lutheran. *Home:* 4554 45th Ave., N.E., Seattle, Wash. 98105. *Office:* Department of English, University of Washington, Seattle, Wash. 98105.

CAREER: University of Maine, Orono, instructor in English, 1930-33, 1934-35; Louisiana State University, Baton Rouge, instructor, 1935-36, assistant professor, 1936-42, associate professor, 1942-46, professor of English, 1946-48; University of Washington, Seattle, professor of English, 1948—, chairman of department, 1948-71. *Member:* International Association of University Professors of English, Modern Language Association of America (member of national executive council, 1966-69), National Council of Teachers of English, (distinguished lecturer, 1968), American Association of University Professors (member of national executive council, 1962-65), Shakespeare Association of America, Philological Association of Pacific Coast (president, 1958), Phi Beta Kappa (Senator, 1967; member of executive committee, 1973—). *Awards, honors:* Arizona *Quarterly* Essay Prize, 1956, for an essay on *Othello; Explicator* Award (for criticism), 1957, for *Magic in the Web: Action and Language in Othello;* Huntington Library grant, 1959; Longview Award, 1960, for essay in *Texas Quarterly*; Guggenheim fellowship, 1964-65; Senior Fellow of National Endowment for the Humanites, 1971-72; D. Litt., Lafayette College, 1967; LL.D., Grinnell College, 1971; L.H.D., Kenyon College, 1973.

WRITINGS: America in English Fiction 1760-1800, Louisiana State University Press, 1937; *This Great Stage: Image and Structure in King Lear*, Louisiana State University Press, 1948; *Magic in the Web: Action and Language in Othello*, University Press of Kentucky, 1956; *Tragedy and Melodrama: Versions of Experience*, University of Washington Press, 1968; *The Iceman, the Arsonist, and the Troubled Agent: Tragedy and Melodrama on the Modern Stage*, University of Washington Press, 1973; *The Ghost on the Ramparts and other Essays in the Humanities*, University of Georgia Press, 1973. Also author of *The Charliad (verse), 1973.*

Editor, and author of critical introduction: Jonathan Swift,

Gulliver's Travels, Modern Library, 1950, revised edition, 1969; Jonathan Swift, *A Tale of a Tub* and *The Battle of the Books*, Modern Library, 1950; *An Anthology of English Drama Before Shakespeare*, Rinehart, 1952; Joseph Conrad, *Lord Jim*, Rinehart, 1957; Thomas Hardy, *The Mayor of Casterbridge*, Riverside, 1962; George Eliot, *Silas Marner*, Riverside, 1962; William Shakespeare, *Cymbeline*, Pelican, 1964; Euripides, *Alcestis*, Chandler, 1965; Thomas Hardy, *Jude the Obscure*, Harper, 1966; William Shakespeare, *The Taming of the Shrew*, Signet, 1966; Thomas Hardy, *Tess of the D'Urbervilles*, Bantam, 1971.

Editor: *Aspects of Democracy*, Louisiana State University Press, 1941; *Aspects of a World at War*, Louisiana State University Press, 1943; (with Cleanth Brooks) *Understanding Drama* (textbook), Henry Holt, 1945, enlarged edition, 1948; *Modern Short Stories: A Critical Anthology* (textbook), Harcourt, 1950.

Contributor: T. A. Kirby and N. M. Caffee, editors, *Studies for W. A. Read*, Louisiana State University Press, 1941; Louis Rubin and Robert Jacobs, editors, *Southern Renascence*, Johns Hopkins Press, 1953; Robert Rathburn and Martin Steinman, editors, *From Jane Austen to Joseph Conrad*, University of Minnesota Press, 1958; James G. McManaway, editor, *Shakespeare 400*, Holt, 1964; Edward A. Bloom, editor, *Shakespeare 1564-1964*, Brown University Press, 1965; Gerald W. Chapman, editor, *Essays on Shakespeare*, Princeton University Press, 1966; Kenneth Muir, editor, *Shakespeare Survey 19*, Cambridge University Press, 1966; Kirby and W. Olive, editors, *Essays in Honor of E. L. Marilla*, Louisiana State University Press, 1970; David Madden, editor, *American Dreams, American Nightmares*, Southern Illinois University Press, 1970; Brom Weber, *Sense and Sensibility in 20th Century Writings*, Southern Illinois University Press, 1970; John Halperin, editor, *The Theory of the Novel: New Essays*, Oxford University Press, 1974. Contributor to *English Institute Annual* published by Columbia University Press, 1949, and *The Range of English: NCTE 1968 Distinguished Lectures*, published by the National Council of Teachers of English, 1968. Also contributor of essays and reviews to various journals.

Member of editorial board, *Poetry Northwest*, 1962—, *Studies in the Novel*, 1966—, *Shakespeare Studies*, 1966—, *Modern Language Quarterly*, 1973—, *Sewanee Review*, 1974—. Regular reviewer for Phi Beta Kappa *Key Reporter*, 1959—.

WORK IN PROGRESS: A book length study of comedy.

AVOCATIONAL INTERESTS: Watching football games, and doing chores at a hideaway shack on a high bank overlooking Puget Sound.

*   *   *

HEIMLER, Eugene 1922-

PERSONAL: Born March 27, 1922, in Szombathely, Hungary; son of Ernest (an attorney) and Maria (Lax) Heimler; first wife killed at Auschwitz; married Livia Salgo, November 30, 1946; children: (second marriage) George Ernest, Susan Maria. *Education:* Academy of Social Science, Budapest, Hungary, Diploma in Social Science, 1947; University of Manchester, Diploma in Psychiatric Social Work, 1953; also studied at University of London. *Religion:* Jewish. *Agent:* Curtis Brown Ltd., 575 Madison Ave., New York, N.Y. 10022. *Office:* Hounslow Project, Glampton Rd., Hounslow, Middlesex, England.

CAREER: Prisoner in German concentration camps during World War II; returned to Hungary after the war and worked as journalist (while studying) until he went to England in 1947; trained as psychiatric social worker at Bexley Mental Hospital, Kent, England; psychiatric social worker for Middlesex County Council, London, England, 1953-60, psychiatric social work organizer for Middlesex County Council, 1960-65; Hounslow Project (community care), Hounslow, England, director, 1965—. Consultant to U.S. government, and speaker on mental health as it relates to the unemployed, on U.S. tour, early 1964; director of community care course, University of London, 1960—. *Member:* British Association of Psychiatric Social Workers; other social work organizations in Britain.

WRITINGS: Eternal Dawn (poems; Hungary), 1939; *Confession to the World* (poems; Hungary), 1943; *Night of the Mist* (experiences in Nazi concentration camps), Vanguard, 1960; *A Link in the Chain* (experiences under Communist regime in Hungary), Bodley Head, 1962; *Prison,* Horizon, 1964; (editor) *Resistance Against Tyranny: A Symposium,* Routledge & Kegan Paul, 1966, Praeger, 1967; *Mental Illness and Social Work,* Penguin, 1967, *Survival in Society,* Halstead, 1975. Contributor to newspapers and to professional journals.

WORK IN PROGRESS: The Hendon Experiment, dealing with his 1954 experiment with forty-one individuals unable to get and hold a job (half were returned to productive permanent work through psychiatric social work counseling).†

*   *   *

HEITLER, Walter (Heinrich)   1904-

PERSONAL: Born January 2, 1904, in Karlsruhe, Germany; son of Adolf (a professor) and Ottilie (Rudolf) Heitler; married Kathleen Nicholson, March, 1942; children: Eric. *Education:* Attended University of Berlin, 1921-22; University of Munich, Ph.D., 1926. *Office:* University of Zurich, Zurich, Switzerland.

CAREER: University of Goettingen, Goettingen, Germany, privatdocent for theoretical physics, 1929-33; University of Bristol, Bristol, England, research fellow, 1933-41; Dublin Institute for Advanced Science, Dublin, Ireland, professor of theoretical physics, 1941-45, director of School of Theoretical Physics, 1945-49; University of Zurich, Zurich, Switzerland, professor of theoretical physics, 1949—. *Member:* Royal Society (London; fellow), Royal Irish Academy, Academy of Science (Uppsala), Akademie Leopoldina (Halle), Akademie der Wissenschaften und der Literatur (Mainz). *Awards, honors:* Max Planck Medal; Marcel Benoist prize; D.Sc., National University of Ireland; Dr. rer. nat., University of Goettingen; Dr. phil., University of Uppsala.

WRITINGS: Quantum Theory of Radiation, Oxford University Press, 1936, 3rd edition, 1954; *Elementary Wave Mechanics,* Oxford University Press, 1945, 2nd edition, 1956; *Der Mensch und die Naturwissenchaftliche Erkenntnis,* Vieweg, 1961, published as *Man and Science,* Basic Books, 1963, 4th edition, 1966; *Naturphilosophische Streifzuege,* Vieweg, 1970; *Die Natur und das Goettliche,* Klett & Balmer, 1974.

BIOGRAPHICAL/CRITICAL SOURCES: Helvetiea Physica Acta (Basel), December 22, 1964.

HELLER, Erich   1911-

PERSONAL: Born March 27, 1911, in Komotau, Bohemia (now Czechoslovakia); became British citizen in 1947. *Education:* Charles University, Prague, Czechoslovakia, D. Jur. (with distinction), 1935; Cambridge University, Ph.D., 1948. *Office:* Department of German, Northwestern University, Evanston, Ill. 60201.

CAREER: University of London, London School of Economics and Political Science, London, England, assistant lecturer in German, 1943-45; Cambridge University, Peterhouse College, Cambridge, England, lecturer in German and director of studies in modern languages, 1945-48; University of Wales, University College, Swansea, professor of German, 1948-60, Northwestern University, Evanston, Ill., professor of German, 1960-66, professor of the humanities, 1966-68, Avalon professor of the humanities, 1968—. Ziskind Visiting Professor at Brandeis University, 1957-58; visiting professor at University of Heidelberg, spring, 1963; Carnegie visiting professor of humanities at Massachusetts Institute of Technology, fall, 1963. Visiting lecturer at Universities in Germany, 1947-48, at Harvard University, Yale University, Brown University, and other American universities, 1953-54; 1957-58. *Member:* German Academy for Language and Literature, Bavarian Academy of Fine Arts, P.E.N. (Germany and Austria), American Academy of Arts and Sciences.

WRITINGS: Die Flucht aus dem zwanzigsten Jahrhundert (essay), Saturn Verlag, 1938; *The Disinherited Mind* (essays), Bowes, 1952, Farrar, Straus, 1957, 2nd edition, Meridian, 1959; *The Hazard of Modern Poetry,* Bowes, 1953; *The Ironic German, a Study of Thomas Mann,* Little, Brown, 1958; *Studien zur Modernen Literator,* Suhrkamp Verlag, 1963; *Nietzsche–Drei Essays,* Suhrkamp Verlag, 1964; *The Artist's Journey into the Interior and Other Essays,* Random House, 1965; *Franz Kafka,* Heimeran (Munich), 1969, Viking, 1974; *Essays Uber Goethe,* Insel Verlag, 1970; (editor with Juergen Born and author of introduction) Franz Kafka, *Letters to Felice,* Shocken, 1973.

Author of introductions to the Everyman's Library *Thomas Mann* and to the German edition of *Works of Ludwig Wittgenstein,* Suhrkamp Verlag, 1960. Contributor to three volumes of *Jahresring* (an annual survey of contemporary German literature and art), Deutsche Verlags-Anstalt, 1956-59, to *New Cambridge Modern History,* Volume X, 1960. Also contributor of essays on German writers and philosophers to *Cambridge Journal, Times Literary Supplement* (London), *Sewanee Review, Forum, Der Monat, Merkur,* and other journals.

SIDELIGHTS: Heller adapted and translated three of his books, *The Disinherited Mind, The Ironic German,* and *The Artist's Journey into the Interior* for publication in Germany.

*   *   *

HELLMAN, Lillian (Florence)   1906-

PERSONAL: Born June 20, 1906, in New Orleans, La.; daughter of Max Bernard (a businessman) and Julia (Newhouse) Hellman; married Arthur Kober (a writer), December 30, 1925 (divorced, 1932). *Education:* Attended New York University, 1922-24, Columbia University, 1924. *Politics:* Liberal. *Home:* 630 Park Ave., New York, N.Y. 10021; and Vineyard Haven, Mass. 02568. *Agent:* Harold Matson, 22 East 40th St., New York, N.Y. 10016.

CAREER: Playwright and author. Manuscript reader for Horace Liveright, Inc. (publisher), New York, N.Y., 1924-25; theatrical playreader in New York, 1927-30; scenario reader for Metro-Goldwyn-Mayer, Hollywood, Calif., 1930-31; returned to New York, 1932, working as part-time playreader for producer Herman Shulman. Has taught or conducted seminars in literature and writing at Yale University, 1966, and at Massachusetts Institute of Technology and Harvard University. *Member:* American Academy of Arts and Letters, American Academy of Arts and Sciences (fellow), Dramatists Guild (member of council), American Federation of Television and Radio Artists.

AWARDS, HONORS: New York Drama Critics Circle Award, 1941, for *Watch on the Rhine*, and 1960, for *Toys in the Attic*; Academy Award nominations for screenplays, "The Little Foxes," 1941, and "The North Star," 1943; M.A. from Tufts University, 1950; Brandeis University Creative Arts Medal in Theater, 1960-61; LL.D. from Wheaton College, 1961, Douglass College of Rutgers University, 1963, Brandeis University, 1965, and from Yale University, Smith College, and New York University, all 1974; Gold Medal for drama from National Institute of Arts and Letters, 1964; National Book Award in Arts and Letters, 1969, for *An Unfinished Woman*, and nomination, 1974, for *Pentimento*.

WRITINGS—Plays: *The Children's Hour* (three-act; first produced in New York, N.Y., at Maxine Elliott's Theatre, November 20, 1934), Knopf, 1934, acting edition, Dramatists Play Service, 1953; *Days to Come* (three-act; first produced in New York at Vanderbilt Theatre, December 15, 1936), Knopf, 1936; *The Little Foxes* (three-act; first produced in New York at National Theatre, February 15, 1939), Random House, 1939, acting edition, Dramatists Play Service, 1942.

Watch on the Rhine (three-act; first produced in New York at Martin Beck Theatre, April 1, 1941), Random House, 1941, limited edition with foreword by Dorothy Parker, privately printed, 1942, acting edition, Dramatists Play Service, 1944; *The Searching Wind* (two-act; first produced in New York at Fulton Theatre, April 12, 1944), Viking, 1944; *Another Part of the Forest* (three-act; first produced at Fulton Theatre, November 20, 1946), Viking, 1947.

The Autumn Garden (three act; first produced in New York at Coronet Theatre, March 7, 1951), Little, Brown, 1951, acting edition, revised, Dramatists Play Service, 1952; *Toys in the Attic* (three-act; first produced in New York at Hudson Theatre, February 25, 1960), Random House, 1960, acting edition, Samuel French, 1960.

Play adaptations: *Montserrat* (two-act; based on the novel by Emmanuel Robles; first produced in New York at Fulton Theatre, October 29, 1949), Dramatists Play Service, 1950; *The Lark* (based on a play by Jean Anouilh; first produced in New York at Longacre Theatre, November 17, 1955), Random House, 1956, acting edition, Dramatists Play Service, 1957; (author of book) *Candide: A Comic Operetta Based on Voltaire's Satire* (music by Leonard Bernstien; first produced in New York at Martin Beck Theatre, December 1, 1956), Random House, 1957; *My Mother, My Father, and Me* (two-act; based on Burt Blechman's novel, *How Much?*; first produced in New York at Plymouth Theatre, April 6, 1963), Random House, 1963.

Omnibus volumes: *Four Plays* (contains "The Children's Hour," "Days to Come," "The Little Foxes," and "Watch on the Rhine"), Random House, 1942; *Six Plays* (contains "Another Part of the Forest," "The Autumn Garden," "The Children's Hour," "Days to Come," "The Little Foxes," and "Watch on the Rhine"), Modern Library, 1960; *Collected Plays*, Little, Brown, 1972.

Memoirs: *An Unfinished Woman*, Little, Brown, 1969; *Pentimento: A Book of Portraits*, Little, Brown, 1974.

Editor: Anton Chekhov, *Selected Letters*, Farrar, Straus, 1955; (and author of introduction) Dashiell Hammett, *The Big Knockover* (selected stories and short novels), Random House, 1966 (published in England as *The Dashiell Hammett Story Omnibus*, Cassell, 1966).

Screenplays; all adaptations, except as noted: (With Mordaunt Shairp) "Dark Angel," United Artists, 1935; "These Three" (based on "The Children's Hour"), United Artists, 1936; "Dead End," United Artists, 1937; "The Little Foxes," RKO, 1941; *The North Star* (original work; released by RKO, 1943, later released to television under title "Armored Attack"), published by Viking, 1943; "The Searching Wind," Paramount, 1946; "The Chase," Columbia, 1966).

Work is represented in anthologies, including: *Twenty Best Plays of the Modern American Theatre, 1930-1939*, edited by John Gassner, Crown, 1939; *Contemporary Drama: Eleven Plays*, edited by E. Bradlee Watson and Benfield Pressey, Scribner, 1956; *Four Contemporary American Plays*, compiled by Bennet Cerf, Vintage, 1961; *Famous American Plays of the 1950's*, edited by Lee Strasberg, Dell, 1962; *The Modern Theatre*, edited by Robert W. Corrigan, Macmillan, 1964; *A Treasury of the Theatre: Modern Drama from Oscar Wilde to Eugene Ionesco*, edited by Gassner, Simon & Schuster, 1967; *Twelve American Plays, 1920-1960*, edited by Richard Corbin, Scribner, 1969.

Author, with Louis Kronenberger, of unproduced play, "Dear Queen," during early 1930's; contributor of lyrics to "Leonard Bernstein's Theatre Songs," 1965; contributor of sketches to "Broadway Revue," produced in New York, 1968. Contributor to *Comet* (Paris), *Collier's, New York Times, Travel and Leisure*, and other publications. Book reviewer for *New York Herald Tribune*, 1925-28.

SIDELIGHTS: Considered by many critics to be the best craftsman in the American theater and the country's leading woman playwright, Miss Hellman is known for her perceptive characterizations and the precision of her language. Harold Clurman once wrote: "The author is just with her characters; she sees them with a certain smiling asperity, an astringent, almost cruel, clarity. Miss Hellman refuses to be 'metaphysical,' poetic or soft. She will not embrace her people; she does not believe they deserve her (or our) love. Love is present only through the ache of its absence." Allan Lewis estimates that "Hellman's dark world of those who triumph through a calculated disregard of moral values is as grim and full of pain as in the most extreme theatre of the absurd. Her dramas differ in that they are portraits of people and not of abstract symbols. Events are causative, and the individual the product of his environment."

Commenting on "Autumn Garden," John Mason Brown found "the same instinctive awareness of the theater's needs that have always animated her writing"—an awareness which, by Miss Hellman's own admission, does not include any great amount of affection. She has called the theater a "tight, unbending, unfluid, meager . . . second-rate form." She once commented on her alienation from contemporary theater: "I have a sense of sadness about my not understanding the theater any more.... The only time I've felt happy and excited about the theater in many years is when I've seen or read some of Beckett. Then I've been at home.''

With the publication of the first volume of Miss Hellman's memoirs, *An Unfinished Woman*, V.S. Pritchett notes that although "she says she wanted to be a novelist or story writer and could not bring it off . . . she can write a brilliant memoir, and it was the theater that taught her to break it up into short, strong scenes and to present herself with remarkable directness." Another critic notes that her writing "possesses charm and forbearance, it is highly civilized, and it is written in a prose style so sparkling that every sentence is a delight." Commenting on the sequel volume, *Pentimento*, Eliot Fremont-Smith notes that Miss Hellman "has developed a way to do autobiography perfectly suited to her special strengths, and has written a totally absorbing and marvelous book that is, in its coherence and control and electric passion, a masterpiece on the order of her very best plays."

Miss Hellman staged "Another Part of the Forest" in 1946, and directed "Montserrat" in 1949.

Marc Blitzstein adapted "The Little Foxes" as an opera, "Regina," in 1949. "Another Part of the Forest" was filmed by Universal in 1948, and "Toys in the Attic" was adapted for film by United Artists, 1963. Television adaptations were made of "Montserrat,', 1971, and "The Lark," produced for Hallmark Hall of Fame.

AVOCATIONAL INTERESTS: Reading (especially Donne and Blake), fishing, swimming, cooking.

BIOGRAPHICAL/CRITICAL SOURCES: Nation, December 26, 1936; *New Republic*, March 26, 1951; W. David Sievers, *Freud on Broadway*, Hermitage, 1955; *New York Herald Tribune*, March 6, 1960; Allan Lewis, *American Plays and Playwrights of the Contemporary Theatre*, Crown, 1965; Jean Gould, *Modern American Playwrights*, Dodd, 1966; Carolyn Riley, editor, *Contemporary Literary Criticism*, Gale, Volume II, 1974, Volume IV, 1975.

* * *

HELLMUTH, Jerome 1911-

PERSONAL: Born February 13, 1911, in Chicago, Ill.; son of Joseph and Jenny (Sowinski) Hellmuth; married Elane Summers (a dance instructor), January 15, 1941; children: Karen (Mrs. Paul West Rickenbacker), Jana, Thane (died, 1972), Darien. *Education:* Notre Dame University, student, 1930-31; Loyola University, Chicago, Ill., Ph.B., 1934; Graduate Teachers College, Winnetka, Ill., M.Ed., 1938; other study at University of Chicago, 1934-35, 1940-41, New York University, 1945-47. *Address:* Route 8, Box 8167, Bainbridge Island, Wash. 98110. *Office Address:* Bucklin Hill School, P.O. Box 10356, Bainbridge Island, Wash. 98110.

CAREER: Elisabeth Irwin High School of the Little Red School House, New York, N.Y., assistant director and guidance director, 1942-58; practicing lay analyst, New York, N.Y., 1950-58; Special Child Publications (non-profit publishers), Seattle, Wash., editor and co-publisher, 1962-70; Seattle Seguin School (for children with learning disorders), Seattle, Wash., director, 1963-73; Bucklin Hill School (for mentally handicapped adolescents), Bainbridge Island, Wash., director, 1970—. Art therapist, Youth Service Center (juvenile court detention facility), Seattle, Wash.; executive director, Northwest Summer Conference

on the Special Child (held intermittently at University of Washington).

WRITINGS: (Editor) *The Special Child: Diagnosis, Treatment, Habilitation*, Special Child, 1962; (editor) *The Special Child in Century 21*, Special Child, 1964; *A Wolf in the Family*, New American Library, 1965; (editor) *Learning Disorders*, Special Child, Volume I, 1965, Volume II, 1966, Volume III, 1968; (editor) *Educational Therapy*, Special Child, Volume I, 1966, Volume II, 1968; (editor) *Disadvantaged Child*, Brunner, Volume I: *Disadvantaged Child*, 1967, Volume II: *Head Start and Early Intervention*, 1969, Volume III: *Compensatory Education: A National Debate*, 1970; (editor) *Exceptional Infant*, two volumes, Special Child, 1967-68, Volume I published as *The Normal Infant*, Brunner, 1970, Volume II published as *Abnormalities*, Brunner, 1971; (editor) *Cognitive Studies*, Brunner, Volume I, 1970, Volume II: *Deficits in Cognition*, 1971.

Also editor of *Special Disorders*. Contributor to *Saturday Evening Post*.

WORK IN PROGRESS: Additional volumes for *The Disadvantaged Child* and *The Exceptional Infant*.

SIDELIGHTS: Art work done under Hellmuth's direction by delinquents at Seattle's Youth Service Center has been exhibited across the country. *The Special Child* and *The Special Child in Century 21* are used by Teachers College, Columbia University, in special education courses.

* * *

HELMSTADTER, Gerald C. 1925-

PERSONAL: Born November 28, 1925, in West Point, Neb.; son of Carl William (a professor) and Freda (Coonley) Helmstadter; married Eleanor J. Lemmer, June 30, 1951; married Ronda A. Moffet, August 9, 1974; children: (first marriage) Lynda, Pamela. *Education:* Iowa State University of Science and Technology, B.Sc., 1949, M.Sc., 1950; University of Minnesota, Ph.D., 1954. *Politics:* Democrat. *Religion:* Unitarian Universalist. *Home:* 515 East Dunbar Dr., Number 8, Tempe, Ariz. 85282. *Office:* Arizona State University, Tempe, Ariz. 85281.

CAREER: Educational Testing Service, Princeton, N.J., research associate, 1954-56; Colorado State University, Fort Collins, assistant professor of psychology and head of psychometric services, 1956-59; Arizona State University, Tempe, associate professor, 1959-65, professor of educational psychology, 1965—, director of testing services, 1965—. *Military service:* U.S. Army, 1943-46. *Member:* American Educational Research Association, American Psychological Association, American Statistical Association, National Council for Measurement in Education, Psychometric Society, Sigma Xi.

WRITINGS: Principles of Psychological Measurement, Appleton, 1964; *Research Concepts in Human Behavior*, Appleton, 1971. Contributor to professional journals.

WORK IN PROGRESS: Statistical Logic and Methods in the Behavioral Sciences, publication by Brooks-Cole expected in 1976.

* * *

HEMPHILL, George 1922-

PERSONAL: Born May 15, 1922, in Chicago, Ill.; son of George Boyd (a traffic clerk) and Clara (Jacobs) Hemphill; married Margaret Allison, August 30, 1949; children: Christopher, Lowry, Clara, Thomas. *Education:* Kenyon College, A.B., 1947; University of Minnesota, M.A., 1948, Ph.D., 1954. *Politics:* Republican. *Religion:* Episcopalian. *Home:* Old Canterbury Rd., Hampton, Conn. 06247. *Office:* Department of English, University of Connecticut, Storrs, Conn. 06268.

CAREER: University of Connecticut, Storrs, instructor, 1954-60, assistant professor, 1960-65, associate professor, 1965-69, professor of English, 1969—. University of Hamburg, Hamburg, Germany, Fulbright lecturer, 1956-57. *Military service:* U.S. Army, 1942-46. *Member:* Modern Language Association of America.

WRITINGS: (Contributor) John K. M. McCaffery, editor, *Ernest Hemingway: The Man and his Work*, World Publishing, 1950; (editor) *Discussions of Poetry: Rhythm and Sound*, Heath, 1961; *Allen Tate*, University of Minnesota Press, 1964; (contributor) H. T. Swedenberg, Jr., editor, *Essential Articles for the Study of John Dryden*, Archon Books, 1966; (contributor) Leonard Unger, editor, *Seven Modern American Poets*, University of Minnesota Press, 1967; *A Mathematical Grammar of English*, Mouton, 1973.

WORK IN PROGRESS: A book, *Theory of Linguistic Signs.*

* * *

HENDERSON, Richard 1924-

PERSONAL: Born October 20, 1924, in Baltimore, Md.; son of William Lynn (a judge) and Vera (Price) Henderson; married Sarah E. Symington (a schoolteacher), June 28, 1947; children: Richard Cameron, Sarah Livingston. *Education:* Johns Hopkins University, B.F.A., 1951. *Politics:* Democrat. *Religion:* Episcopal. *Home and office:* Gibson Island, Maryland.

CAREER: Formed partnership art studio, Henderson-Atherton Studio, 1951, in Baltimore; began free-lance work, 1953; now self-employed writer and illustrator. *Military service:* U.S. Army Air Forces, Air-Sea Rescue Service, 1943-46. *Member:* American Boat and Yacht Council, North American Yacht Racing Union, Author's Guild, Slocum Society, Cruising Club of America, Delta Phi, Baltimore Watercolor Club, Windjammers Club, Gibson Island Yacht Squadron, Chesapeake Yacht Racing Association.

WRITINGS: First Sail for Skipper, Reilly & Lee, 1960; *Hand, Reef, and Steer*, Reilly & Lee, 1965; (editor) William A. Andrews, *Dangerous Voyages of Captain William Andrews*, Abercrombie & Fitch, 1966; (with B. S. Dunbar) *Sail and Power: A Manual of Seamanship for the U.S. Naval Academy*, Naval Institute Press, 1967; *The Racing-Cruiser*, Reilly & Lee, 1970; *Sea Sense*, International Marine Publishing Co., 1972; *The Cruiser's Compendium*, Regnery, 1973; *The Singlehander's*, International Marine Publishing Co., in press.

AVOCATIONAL INTERESTS: Boats, sailing, playing the piano, jazz music, water color painting, and doing murals in various media.

* * *

HENDRICK, George 1929-

PERSONAL: Born March 30, 1929, in Stephenville, Tex.; son of Hoyt (a rancher) and Bessie Lea (Sears) Hendrick; married Willene Lowery, January 23, 1955. *Education:* Texas Christian University, B.A., 1948, M.A., 1950; University of Texas, Ph.D., 1954. *Office:* Department of En-

glish, University of Illinois at Urbana-Champaign, Urbana, Ill. 61810.

CAREER: Southwest Texas State College, San Marcos, member of English department faculty, 1954-56; University of Colorado, Boulder, member of English department faculty, 1956-60; Johann Wolfgang Goethe-Universitat (University of Frankfurt), Frankfurt am Main, West Germany, professor of American literature and culture, co-director of English seminar, and director of Amerika-Institut. University of Illinois at Urbana-Champaign, Urbana, visiting professor 1964-65, currently professor and head of department of English. *Member:* Modern Language Association of America, Modern Humanities Research Association, American Studies Association.

WRITINGS: (With Donna Gerstenberger) *Directory of Periodicals Publishing Articles in English and American Language and Literature*, A. Swallow, 1959, 3rd edition, 1970. (Editor) *1785 Bhagavad-Gita*, translated by Charles Wilkins, Scholars' Facsimiles, 1959; (with Gerstenberger) *The American Novel: A Checklist of Twentieth Century Criticism*, A. Swallow, 1960; *Katherine Anne Porter*, Twayne, 1965; *Mazo de la Roche*, Twayne, 1970. Editor, *Abstracts of English Studies.*

WORK IN PROGRESS: American Literary Manuscripts in Continental Libraries.†

* * *

HENDRIKSEN, Eldon Sende 1917-

PERSONAL: Born October 20, 1917, in Alhambra, Calif.; son of Henry A. and Margot (Sende) Hendriksen; married E. Kathleen Podmore, October 18, 1942; children; Margot, Dan. *Education:* University of California, Berkeley, B.S., 1941, M.B.A., 1947, Ph.D., 1957. *Home:* 100 Southeast Derby St., Pullman, Wash. 99163. *Office:* College of Economics and Business, Washington State University, Pullman, Wash.

CAREER: Haskins & Sells (certified public accountants), San Francisco, Calif., staff accountant, 1951-53; University of Idaho, Moscow, assistant professor of accounting, 1953-55; Washington State University, Pullman, 1955—, now professor of business administration. Visiting professor of accounting, University of Illinois, 1970-71. *Military service:* U.S. Naval Reserve, 1941-45; became lieutenant. *Member:* American Accounting Association (vice-president, 1969-70), American Economic Association, American Institute of Certified Public Accountants.

WRITINGS: (Co-editor) *Readings in Current Economics*, Irwin, 1958, revised edition, 1961; *Price-Level Adjustments of Financial Statements: An Evaluation and Case Study of Two Public Utility Firms*, Washington State University Press, 1961; *Accounting Theory*, Irwin, 1965, revised edition, 1970; (editor with Bruce P. Budge) *Contemporary Accounting Theory*, Dickenson, 1974. Editor of *Accounting Review*, 1970-72. Contributor of articles to *Accounting Review, National Tax Journal*, and *International Journal of Accounting Education and Research.*

* * *

HENFREY, Colin (Vere Fleetwood) 1941-

PERSONAL: Born June 16, 1941, in Nairobi, Kenya; son of L. O. (a lieutenant colonel) and E. V. F. (Turner) Henfrey; married June Gollop, July 25, 1964. *Education:* New College, Oxford, B.A., 1964; Cornell University, research fellow, 1964-65. *Politics:* Socialist. *Religion:* Agnostic. *Home:* Whin Holt, Fleet, Hampshire, England.

CAREER: Writer, and student of anthropology. *Awards, honors:* Harkness fellowship, 1964-65.

WRITINGS: The Gentle People: A Journey Among the Indian Tribes of Guiana, Hutchinson, 1964, published as *Through Indian Eyes: A Journey Among the Indian Tribes of Guiana*, Holt, 1965; *Manscapes: An American Journey*, Deutsch, 1973. Contributor to British Broadcasting Corp. programs and to magazines and periodicals.

WORK IN PROGRESS: Research on the sociological aspects of modernization in Latin America; short stories.†

*   *   *

HENNESSY, Bernard C.   1924-

PERSONAL: Born November 2, 1924, in Oneida, N.Y.; son of Francis B. (a farmer) and Frances S. (Schaller) Hennessy; married Erna A. Roberts (a teacher), January 27, 1947; children: Michael, Steven, Heidi. *Education:* John Carroll University, student, 1942-43; Syracuse University, A.B., 1948, A.M., 1949; London School of Economics and Political Science, graduate study, 1953-54; University of Wisconsin, Ph.D., 1955. *Politics:* Democrat. *Home:* 22149 Main St., Hayward, Calif. 94541. *Office:* Department of Political Science, California State University, Hayward, Calif. 94542.

CAREER: University of Arizona, Tucson, instructor, 1954-55, assistant professor, 1955-59, associate professor of government, 1959-61; New York University, School of Law, New York, N.Y., professor of politics, 1961-66; Pennsylvania State University, University Park, chairman of department of political science, 1966-71; California State University, Hayward, professor and chairman of department of political science, 1971—. Director, National Center for Education in Politics, New York, N.Y., 1961-69. *Military service:* U.S. Navy, 1943-46. *Member:* American Political Science Association, Western Political Science Association (council member, 1959-61). *Awards, honors:* Ford Foundation fellow at Center for International Studies, Massachusetts Institute of Technology, 1956-57; Democratic National Committee faculty fellow, Washington, D.C., 1959-60.

WRITINGS: Dollars for Democrats 1959, McGraw, 1960; (with Cornelius P. Cotter) *Politics Without Power*, Atherton, 1964; *Public Opinion*, Wadsworth, 1965, 2nd edition, 1970; *Political Internships: Theory, Practice, Evaluation*, Pennsylvania State University Press, 1970. Contributor to political science journals.

WORK IN PROGRESS: Research on political parties.

*   *   *

HENREY, Madeleine   1906-
(Mrs. Robert Henrey; Robert Henrey, pseudonym)

PERSONAL: Born August 13, 1906, in Paris, France; daughter of Emile (a bricklayer) and Mathilde (a seamstress and worker of fine lace; maiden name, Bernhard) Gal; married Robert Selby Henrey (a journalist), December 1, 1929; children: Robert John Edward. *Education:* Attended school in Paris, France, and Convent of the Sacred Heart, London, England. *Home:* Villers-sur-Mer, Calvados I4 640, France.

CAREER: Left France with her widowed mother to live in England at the age of fourteen, later working as a secretary, shop girl, manicurist, and columnist for *London Evening News*; in the 1930's the author and her husband bought a farm in Normandy, France, where they have spent most of the time since (except for the war years) and where the "Madeleine" books were written. *Member:* Women's Press Club (London).

WRITINGS—Under pseudonym Robert Henrey; all published by Dent, except as indicated: *A Farm in Normandy* (also see below), 1941; *A Journey to Gibraltar*, 1943; *A Village in Piccadilly*, 1943; *The Incredible City*, 1944; *The Foolish Decade*, 1945; *The King of Brentford*, P. Davies, 1946; *The Seige of London*, 1946; *The Return to the Farm* (also see below), P. Davies, 1947; *London*, 1948, Dutton, 1949; *A Film Star in Belgrave Square*, P. Davies, 1948; *A Farm in Normandy* [and] *The Return to the Farm*, 1952.

Under name Mrs. Robert Henrey; all published by Dent, except as indicated: *A Journey to Vienna*, 1950; *Matilda and the Chickens*, 1950; *The Little Madeleine*, 1951, published as *The Little Madeleine: The Autobiography of a Young Girl in Montmartre*, Dutton, 1953; *Paloma*, 1951, Dutton, 1955; *Madeleine Grown Up*, 1952, published as *Madeleine Grown Up: The Autobiography of a French Girl*, Dutton, 1953; *An Exile in Soho*, 1952; *Madeleine's Journal*, 1953; *Madeleine, Young Wife: The Autobiography of a French Girl*, Dutton, 1954 (published in England as *Madeleine, Young Wife*, 1960); *A Month in Paris*, 1954; *Milou's Daughter, Madeleine: A Sentimental Journey to the South of France*, Dutton, 1955 (published in England as *Milou's Daughter*, 1955); *Bloomsbury Fair*, 1955; *This Feminine World*, 1956; *A Daughter for a Fortnight*, 1957; *The Virgin of Aldermanbury: Rebirth of the City of London*, 1958; *Mistress of Myself*, 1959; *The Dream Makers*, 1961; *Spring in a Soho Street*, 1962; *Her April Days*, 1963; *Wednesday at Four*, 1964; *Winter Wild*, 1966; *London Under Fire, 1940-1945*, 1969; *She Who Pays*, 1969; *Julia: Reminiscences of a Year in Madeleine's Life as a London Shop Girl*, 1971; *A Girl at Twenty: Six Months in the Life of the Young Madeleine*, 1974.

SIDELIGHTS: In order to form a consecutive narrative, Mrs. Henrey suggests that certain of her books be read in the following order: *The Little Madeleine, An Exile in Soho, Julia, A Girl at Twenty, Madeleine Grown Up, Madeleine Young Wife, London Under Fire, 1940-1945, Her April Days, Wednesday at Four, She Who Pays.* Mrs. Henrey, whose books have sold nearly a million copies, divides her time between town and country—gardening, sewing, knitting, and reading.

*   *   *

HENRY, Carl F(erdinand) H(oward)   1913-

PERSONAL: Born January 22, 1913, in New York, N.Y.; son of Karl F. E. and Johanna (Vaethroeder) Henry; married Helga Bender, August 17, 1940; children: Paul Brentwood, Carol Jennifer. *Education:* Wheaton College, Wheaton, Ill., B.A., 1938, M.A., 1940; Northern Baptist Theological Seminary, B.D., 1941, Th.D., 1942; Boston University, Ph.D., 1949; postdoctoral study at Loyola University, Chicago, Ill., 1941, Indiana University, 1944, New College, University of Edinburgh, 1953, and Cambridge University, 1968. *Home:* 3824 North 37th St., Arlington, Va. 22207.

CAREER: Before 1940, editor of weekly newspapers in Smithtown and Port Jefferson, N.Y., and correspondent for *New York Times, New York Herald Tribune*, and *Chicago Tribune*; ordained Baptist minister, 1941; Northern Baptist Theological Seminary, Chicago, Ill., assistant professor, 1940-42, professor and chairman of department of philosophy of religion, 1942-47; Fuller Theological Seminary, Pasadena, Calif., professor of theology and Christian philosophy, 1947-56; *Christianity Today*, Washington, D.C., editor, 1956-68, editor-at-large, 1968—; Eastern Baptist Theological Seminary, Philadelphia, Pa., visiting professor, 1969-70, professor of theology, 1970-71, professor-at-large, 1971-74; World Vision, Monrovia, Calif., lecturer-at-large, 1974—. Preacher throughout United States and Canada, with World Vision party in Burma, Thailand, Malaya, and the Philippines, 1959, in Colombia, 1960, in India and Ceylon, 1968, in Korea and Singapore, 1974; preacher with Billy Graham in Germany and Switzerland, 1960; co-chairman of Rose Bowl Sunrise Service, 1948-56; broadcaster on radio and television, including daily program, KPOL, Los Angeles, 1952-53. Chairman of World Congress on Evangelism, Berlin, 1966; program chairman of Jerusalem Conference on Biblical Prophecy, 1971; program chairman of Conference on Christianity and the Counterculture, 1971; president of board of directors of Institute for Advanced Christian Studies, 1971-73.

MEMBER: American Philosophical Society, American Theological Society, Evangelical Theological Society (president, 1969-70), Society of Biblical Literature, National Association of Biblical Instructors, Mind Association, American Association for the Advancement of Science, American Society of Church History, American Schools of Oriental Research, American Society for Christian Social Ethics, Victoria Institute (Great Britain), Cosmos Club (Washington D.C.). *Awards, honors:* Freedoms Foundation Medal for article, "Christianity and the American Heritage"; D.Litt., Seattle Pacific College, 1959, Wheaton College, 1968; L.H.D., Houghton College, 1973.

WRITINGS: A Doorway to Heaven, Zondervan, 1941; *Successful Church Publicity*, Zondervan, 1942; *Remaking the Modern Mind*, Eerdmans, 1948; *The Uneasy Conscience of Modern Fundamentalism*, Eerdmans, 1948; *Giving a Reason for Our Hope*, W. A. Wilde, 1949; *The Protestant Dilemma*, Eerdmans, 1949; *Note on the Doctrine of God*, W. A. Wilde, 1949; *Fifty Years of Protestant Theology*, W. A. Wilde, 1950; *The Drift of Western Thought*, Eerdmans, 1951; *Personal Idealism and Strong's Theology*, Van Kampen, 1951; *Glimpses of a Sacred Land*, W. A. Wilde, 1953; *Christian Personal Ethics*, Eerdmans, 1957; *Evangelical Responsibility in Contemporary Theology*, Eerdmans, 1957; *Aspects of Christian Social Ethics*, Eerdmans, 1964; *Frontiers in Modern Theology*, Moody, 1966; *The God Who Shows Himself*, Word Books, 1966; *Evangelicals at the Brink of Crisis*, Word Books, 1967; *Faith at the Frontiers*, Moody, 1969; *A Plea for Evangelical Demonstration*, Baker Book, 1971; *New Strides of Faith*, Moody, 1972.

Editor: *Contemporary Evangelical Thought*, Channel, 1957; *Revelation and the Bible: Contemporary Evangelical Thought*, Baker Book, 1959, 3rd edition, 1967; *The Biblical Expositor*, Holman, 1960; (consulting) *Baker's Dictionary of Theology*, Baker Book, 1960; *Basic Christian Doctrines*, Holt, 1962; *Christian Faith and Modern Theology*, Meredith, 1964; *Jesus of Nazareth: Saviour and Lord*, Eerdmans, 1966; (with W. Stanley Mooneyham) *One Race, One Gospel, One Task*, two volumes, World Wide Publications, 1967; *Fundamentals of the Faith*, Zondervan, 1969; *Baker's Dictionary of Christian Ethics*, Baker Book, 1973. Literary editor of *United Evangelical Action*, 1945-52.

WORK IN PROGRESS: A work in three volumes, Volumes I and II: *The God Who Speaks and Shows*, Volume III: *The God Who Stands, Stoops, and Stays*, completion expected in 1978.

SIDELIGHTS: Henry has traveled more than 800,000 miles by air and three times around the world on his religious missions.

BIOGRAPHICAL/CRITICAL SOURCES: Time, July 13, 1962.

* * *

HEPBURN, Ronald W(illiam) 1927-

PERSONAL: Born March 16, 1927, in Aberdeen, Scotland; son of William George (a motor engineer) and Grace (Fraser) Hepburn; married Agnes Forbes Anderson, July 16, 1953; children: David William, Antony Ronald. *Education:* University of Aberdeen, M.A., 1951, Ph.D., 1955. *Office:* Department of Philosophy, University of Edinburgh, David Hume Tower, George Sq., Edinburgh, Scotland.

CAREER: University of Aberdeen, Aberdeen, Scotland, lecturer in moral philosophy, 1955-60; University of Nottingham, Nottingham, England, professor of philosophy, and head of department, 1960-64; University of Edinburgh, Edinburgh, Scotland, professor of philosophy, 1964—. Visiting associate professor at New York University, 1959-60. *Military service:* British Army, 1944-48; became lieutenant. *Member:* British Society of Aesthetics, Aristotelian Society.

WRITINGS: (Contributor) *New Essays in Philosophical Theology*, S.C.M. Press, 1955; (with S. Toulmin and A. MacIntyre) *Metaphysical Beliefs*, S.C.M. Press, 1957, 2nd edition, 1970; *Christianity and Paradox: Critical Studies in Twentieth-Century Theology*, C. A. Watts, 1958.

Contributor: *Objections to Humanism*, Constable, 1963; *Collected Papers on Aesthetics*, Blackwell, 1965; *Christian Ethics and Contemporary Philosophy*, S.C.M. Press, 1966; *British Analytical Philosophy*, Routledge & Kegan Paul, 1966; *Hobbs and Rousseau*, 1972; *Education and the Development of Reason*, Routledge & Kegan Paul, 1972. Contributor to *The Encyclopedia of Philosophy* and *A Concise Encyclopedia of Philosophy and Philosophers*. Contributor of articles to aesthetic and philosophic journals.†

* * *

HESBURGH, Theodore M(artin) 1917-

PERSONAL: Born May 25, 1917, in Syracuse, N.Y.; son of Theodore Bernard and Anne (Murphy) Hesburgh. *Education:* University of Notre Dame, student, 1934-37; Gregorian University, Rome, Italy, Ph.B., 1939; Catholic University of America, S.T.D., 1945. *Politics:* Independent. *Home:* Corby Hall, Notre Dame, Ind. *Office:* University of Notre Dame, Ind.

CAREER: Entered Roman Catholic order, Congregation of the Holy Cross at Notre Dame, Ind., 1934, ordained priest, 1943; National Training School for Boys, Washington, D.C., chaplain, 1943-44; University of Notre Dame, Notre Dame, Ind., assistant professor of religion, 1945-47, head of department, 1948-49, executive vice-president of university, 1949-52, president, 1952—. Permanent Vatican City representative to International Atomic Energy Agency. Trustee of Rockefeller Foundation and Carnegie Foundation for the Advancement of Teaching; director of American Council on Education, Institute of International Education, Midwestern Universities Research Association, Woodrow Wilson National Fellowship Corp., Nutrition Foundation, Freedoms Foundation, and Educational Services, Inc. of Massachusetts Institute of Technology.

Member of U.S. Commission on Civil Rights, U.S. Advisory Commission on International Educational, and Cultural Affairs, and of National Science Board; president, International Federation of Catholic Universities.

MEMBER: Association of American Colleges (president, 1961), National Students Association (advisory board), National Confederation of Catholic College Students (advisory board). *Awards, honors:* Honorary degrees from Princeton University, Columbia University, Brandeis University, Indiana University, Dartmouth College, Rhode Island College, Villanova University, Bradley University, LeMoyne College, St. Benedict's College, Catholic University of Santiago, Chile, Northwestern University, and Lafayette College; received Medal of Freedom, 1964; Meiklejohn Award, American Association of University Professors, 1970; Charles Evans Hughes Award, National Conference of Christians and Jews, 1970; American Liberties Medallion, American Jewish Committee, 1971.

WRITINGS—All published by University of Notre Dame Press: *Thoughts for Our Times*, 1962; *More Thoughts for Our Times*, 1965; *Still More Thoughts for Our Times*, 1966; *Thoughts IV*, 1968; *Thoughts V*, 1969; *Patterns for Lifelong Learning*, Jossey-Bass, 1973; *The Humane Millennium: A Challenge for the Year 2000*, Yale University Press, 1974. *Theology of Catholic Action*, Ave Maria Press, 1945; *God and the World of Men*, 1950, 2nd edition, 1960; *Patterns for Educational Growth*, 1958.

SIDELIGHTS: Speaks Latin, Italian, French, and Spanish.

BIOGRAPHICAL SOURCES: Look, October 24, 1961; *Time* (cover story), February 9, 1962; *Catholic Digest*, May, 1962.†

* * *

HESKETT, J. L. 1933-

PERSONAL: Born May 8, 1933, in Cedar Falls, Iowa; son of Gail Stewart (a farmer) and Leone (Stein) Heskett; married Marilyn Louise Taylor (a teacher); children: Sarah Louise. *Education:* Iowa State Teachers College, A.B., 1954; Stanford University, M.B.A., 1958; Ph.D., 1960. *Home:* 5246 Riverside Dr., Columbus 20, Ohio.

CAREER: Ohio State University, Columbus, assistant professor, 1960-63, associate professor, 1963-65, professor of business organization, 1965-69; Harvard Graduate School of Business Administration, professor of business logistics, 1969—. Consultant to industry. *Military service:* U.S. Army, 1954-56. *Member:* American Society of Traffic and Transportation, Society of Logistics and Engineers, American Marketing Association, Transportation Research Forum (board of trustees).

WRITINGS: (With Gayton E. Germane and Nicholas A. Glaskowsky, Jr.) *Highway Transportation Management*, McGraw, 1963; (with Robert M. Ivie and N. A. Glaskowsky, Jr.) *Business Logistics*, Ronald, 1964, 2nd edition, 1973. Contributor to marketing and transportation journals. Member of board of editors, *Journal of Marketing Research*.

WORK IN PROGRESS: Editing a book of papers given at Fourth West Coast Logistics Forum and the 1964 meeting of the National Defense Transportation Association; researching several external management problems and also the impact of geographic pricing practices on logistics costs.†

HETHMON, Robert H(enry) 1925-

PERSONAL: Born October 19, 1925, in Paducah, Ky.; son of Robert Henry (a salesman) and Ruth (Hummel) Hethmon; married Charlotte B. Fortune, July 19, 1952; children: Michael M., Mark A., Thomas A. *Education:* University of Tennessee, B.A., 1946; Cornell University, M.A., 1948; Stanford University, Ph.D., 1955. *Home:* 18676 Fairweather St., Saugus, Calif. 91351. *Office:* Department of Theater Arts, University of California, Los Angeles, Calif. 90024.

CAREER: University of Colorado, Boulder, instructor, 1948-51; University of California, Riverside, instructor, 1955-56; University of Wisconsin, Madison, assistant professor, 1956-62; University of California, Los Angeles, assistant professor, 1963-66, associate professor, 1966—. *Military service:* U.S. Army, 1951-53. *Awards, honors:* Fulbright fellowship to England, 1953-54.

WRITINGS: (Editor) *Strasberg at the Actors Studio*, Viking, 1965. Contributor to *Tulane Drama Review*, *Drama Survey*, *Drama Critique*, and *New Mexico Quarterly*.

WORK IN PROGRESS: Two books, *Group Theater*, and *Habimah Theater*.

* * *

HEWES, Henry 1917-

PERSONAL: Born April 9, 1917, in Boston, Mass.; son of Henry Fox (a physician) and Margaret (Warman) Hewes; married Jane Fowle (an editor), August 21, 1945; children: Henry, Tucker, Havelock. *Education:* Studied at Harvard University, 1935-39. Carnegie Institute of Technology, 1940-41; Columbia University, B.S., 1949. *Home:* 1326 Madison Ave., New York, N.Y. 10028. *Agent:* Audrey Wood, Ashley-Steiner-Famous Artists, Inc., 555 Madison Ave., New York, N.Y. 10022.

CAREER: New York Times, New York, N.Y., 1949-51, started as copy boy, became news assistant and staff writer; *Saturday Review*, New York, N.Y., drama editor, 1952-53, drama critic, 1954-73, Saturday Review/World, drama critic, 1973—. President, New York Drama Critics Circle, 1971-73. Greater New York Chapter of American National Theatre and Academy, executive director, 1953-57, inaugurating Matinee Theatre Series; Board of Standards and Planning for the Living Theatre, 1956-66. Lecturer on drama at Sarah Lawrence College, 1955-56, on playwriting at Columbia University, 1956-57, and at New School for Social Research, 1972—. Sometime play director, including an experimental version of "Hamlet." Member of Vernon Rice Awards, Committee, 1954—, Lolo D'Annunzio Award Committee, 1961—, Margo Jones Committee, 1963—, member of board of directors of American Theatre Wing, 1972—. *Military service:* U.S. Army Air Forces, 1941-45; became technical sergeant. *Member:* Drama Critics Circle, Drama Desk.

WRITINGS—Editor: *Famous Plays of the 1940's*, Dell, 1959; *The Best Plays of 1961-62*, Dodd, 1962, and subsequent editions, 1963, 1964; *Famous American Plays of the 1940's*, Dell, 1967. Adapter of the French play, "La Belle Adventure," for London production, "Accounting for Love," 1954. Contributor to *Encyclopaedia Britannica, Encyclopaedia Britannica Yearbook*; also contributor to *Theatre Arts, World Theatre*.

WORK IN PROGRESS: Adapting Swedish play, "My Love Is Like a Rose," for a Broadway Production; *100 Great Plays*, for Macfadden.†

HEWITT, Barnard (Wolcott) 1906-

PERSONAL: Born December 23, 1906, in North Tonawanda, N.Y.; son of Charles Edward (a newspaper editor and publisher) and Ruth (Barnard) Hewitt; married Rose Lancaster (a high school teacher), August 2, 1932; children: Diana (Mrs. Alan F. Neidle). *Education:* Cornell University, B.A., 1928, M.A., 1929, Ph.D., 1934. *Religion:* Unitarian Universalist. *Home:* 2205 Brett Dr., Champaign, Ill. *Office:* Department of Theatre, University of Illinois, 4-122 Kannert Center, Urbana, Ill.

CAREER: University of Colorado, Boulder, instructor in English and director of theatre, 1930-31; Montana State University, Missoula, instructor and director of theatre, 1932-34, assistant professor of English, 1934-36; Brooklyn College (now Brooklyn College of the City University of New York) Brooklyn, N.Y., instructor, 1936-40, assistant professor of speech, 1940-48; University of Illinois, Champaign-Urbana, professor of speech and theatre, 1948—, associate director of University Theatre, 1948-67, chairman of department of theatre, 1967—. *Member:* American Educational Theatre Association (president, 1953), American National Theatre and Academy (member of board of directors, 1953-56), American Society for Theatre Research, Theatre Library Association, British Society for Theatre Research. *Awards, honors:* Guggenheim fellow, 1962; Eaves Senior Award for achievement in university theatre, 1962; Theta Alpha Phi Medallion of Honor, 1973.

WRITINGS: Art and Craft of Play Production, Lippincott, 1940; (with J. F. Foster and M. S. Wolle) *Play Production, Theory and Practice*, Lippincott, 1952; (editor) *The Renaissance Stage: Serlio, Sabbattini, Furttenbach*, University of Miami Press, 1958; *Theatre U.S.A. 1668-1957*, McGraw, 1959; (editor) Adolphe Appia, *The Work of Living Art*, University of Miami Press, 1960; (editor) Apia, *Music and the Art of the Theatre*, University of Miami Press, 1962; *History of the Theatre from 1800 to the Present*, Random House, 1970. Contributor of articles on American theatre to *Encyclopaedia Britannica*. Founding editor, *Educational Theatre Journal*, 1949-51; contributing editor, *Tulane Drama Review*, 1958-62.

WORK IN PROGRESS: A study of the career of Stephen Price, who managed the Park Theatre in New York from 1808-40, and the Drury Lane Theatre in London from 1826-30.

*   *   *

HEWITT, H(erbert) J(ames) 1890-

PERSONAL: Born March 11, 1890, in Birmingham, England; married Margaret Morag Black, 1918 (deceased); children: John, David. *Education:* University of London, B.A., 1911, Ph.D., 1926; University of Liverpool, M.A., 1917. *Religion:* Church of England. *Home:* 61 St. Stephens Rd., Saltash, Cornwall, England.

CAREER: Saltash Grammar School, Saltash, Cornwall, England, headmaster, 1927-52. Member of Cornwall Education Committee, 1945-62; president of Plymouth Athenaeum, 1958-61. *Military service:* British Army Medical Corps, 1917-19.

WRITINGS: Medieval Cheshire, Manchester University Press, 1929; *The Black Prince's Expedition of 1355-57*, Manchester University Press, 1958; *The Organisation of War Under Edward III: Civilian Aspects*, Manchester University Press, 1966; *Cheshire Under the Three Edwards*, Cheshire Community Council, 1967; *The Building of Railways in Cheshire Down to 1860*, E. J. Morten, 1972.

AVOCATIONAL INTERESTS: French and English history, architecture, and language.

*   *   *

HEXTER, J(ack) H. 1910-

PERSONAL: Born May 25, 1910, in Memphis, Tenn.; son of Milton J. and Alma (Marks) Hexter; married Ruth Mullin, March 29, 1942; children: Christopher, Eleanor, Anne (Mrs. Max Green), Richard. *Education:* University of Cincinnati, B.A., 1931; Harvard University, M.A., 1933, Ph.D., 1937. *Home:* 455 Orange St., New Haven, Conn. 06511. *Office:* Department of History, Yale University, New Haven, Conn. 06520.

CAREER: Instructor at University of Cincinnati, Cincinnati, Ohio, 1936, Harvard University, Cambridge, Mass., 1937, and Massachusetts Institute of Technology, Cambridge, 1938; Queens College (now Queens College of the City University of New York), New York, N.Y., 1939-57, began as instructor, became associate professor of history; Washington University, St. Louis, Mo., professor of history, 1957-64, chairman of department of history, 1957-60; Yale University, New Haven, Conn., professor of history, 1964-67, Charles J. Stille Professor of History, 1967—, director of Yale Center for Parliamentary History, 1965—. Director of humanities, Washington University, 1973; trustee of Danforth Foundation, 1973—. *Military service:* U.S. Army, 1942-45. *Member:* American Academy of Arts and Sciences, American Historical Association, Economic History Association, Economic History Society (Great Britain), Conference on British Studies (president, 1973-75). *Awards, honors:* Guggengein fellowships, 1942 and 1947; Social Science research grants, 1947 and 1971; Yaddo fellowship, summer, 1949; Fulbright fellowships, 1950 and 1959-60; Ford Foundation fellowship, 1953-54; Litt.D., Brown University, 1964; fellow of Center for Advanced Study in Behavioral Science, 1966-67.

WRITINGS: The Reign of King Pym, Harvard University Press, 1941; *More's Utopia: The Biography of an Idea*, Princeton University Press, 1952; *Reappraisals in History*, Northwestern University Press, 1961; (editor with Edward Surtz) *The Complete Works of Thomas More*, Volume IV: *Utopia*, Yale University Press, 1965; *The Judaeo-Christian Tradition*, Harper, 1966; (editor with others) *The Traditions of the Western World*, Rand McNally, 1967; (with Richard Pipes and Anthony Molho) *Europe Since 1500*, Harper, 1971; *The History Primer*, Basic Books, 1971; *Doing History*, Indiana University Press, 1971; *The Vision of Politics on the Eve of the Reformation*, Basic Books, 1973. Member of editorial board of *Journal of Modern History*, *Journal of British Studies*, 1961—, and *Journal of the History of Ideas*, 1964—.

WORK IN PROGRESS: History of Western Civilization.

*   *   *

HIGBEE, Edward (Counselman) 1910-

PERSONAL: Born December 29, 1910, in New York, N.Y.; son of R. B. and Celia (Walker) Higbee. *Education:* University of Wisconsin, M.A., 1938; Johns Hopkins University, Ph.D., 1949. *Home:* Mooresfield Farm, Kingston, R.I.

CAREER: U.S. Department of Agriculture, soil conservationist, 1939-41, agronomist, then senior agronomist, 1941-47; Johns Hopkins University, Baltimore, Md., assistant professor of geography and research associate, 1948-49;

Clark University, Worcester, Mass., professor of geography, 1950-57; University of Delaware, Newark, professor of geography and agriculture economics, 1957-60; University of Rhode Island, Kingston, professor of geography, 1960—. Visiting associate professor, Yale University, 1950. Director of research on America's public environment, Twentieth Century Fund; consultant to Brookings Institution and to agricultural ministries in Central and South America. *Member:* American Geographical Society, Soil Science Society of America, American Association for the Advancement of Science, Sigma Xi, Phi Kappa Phi.

WRITINGS: American Oasis: The Land and Its Uses, Knopf, 1957; *American Agriculture: Geography, Resources, Conservation*, Wiley, 1958; *The Squeeze: Cities Without Space*, Morrow, 1960; *Farms and Farmers in an Urban Age*, Twentieth Century, 1963; *A Question of Priorities*, Morrow, 1970.

SIDELIGHTS: Higbee has studied agriculture and urbanism and conducted field surveys in America, Europe, Latin America, and Japan.

*   *   *

HIGGINS, A(ngus) J(ohn) B(rockhurst) 1911-

PERSONAL: Born November 5, 1911, in Narberth, Wales; married Celia Miller, December 27, 1939; children: Ruth. *Education:* University College of Wales, Aberystwyth, B.A. (first class honors), 1934, M.A., 1937; University of Manchester, B.D., 1939, Ph.D., 1945, D.D., 1965. *Home:* Cwm., North Rd., Lampeter, Cardiganshire, Wales. *Office:* Department of Theology, St. David's University College, University of Wales, Lampeter, Cardiganshire, Wales.

CAREER: Priest, Church of England. University of London, New College, London, England, lecturer in New Testament and Biblical theology, 1946-52; University of Leeds, Leeds, England, lecturer in New Testament, 1953-61, senior lecturer, 1961-1966, reader, 1966-70; University of Wales, St. David's University College, Lampeter, professor of theology, 1970—. Visiting professor in New Testament studies, Trinity College, Toronto, Ontario, 1958-59. Honorary assistant priest, St. Margaret's Church, Ilkley, Yorkshire, England, 1957-70. *Member:* Society for Old Testament Study, Studiorum Novi Testamenti Societas, Society of Biblical Literature.

WRITINGS: The Christian Significance of the Old Testament, Independent Press, 1949; *The Reliability of the Gospels*, Independent Press, 1952; *The Lord's Supper in the New Testament*, S.C.M. Press, 1952; (editor) O. Cullmann, *The Early Church*, S.C.M. Press, 1956; (editor) *New Testament Essays: Studies in Memory of T. W. Manson*, Manchester University Press, 1959; *The Historicity of the Fourth Gospel*, Lutterworth, 1960; *Jesus and the Son of Man*, Lutterworth, 1964; *Menschensohn-Studien*, Kohlhammer, 1965; *The Tradition about Jesus*, Oliver & Boyd, 1969; (contributor) E. E. Ellis and M. Wilcox, editors, *Neotestamentica et Semitica*, T. & T. Clark, 1969; (contributor) W. Gasgus and R. P. Martin, editors, *Apostolic History and the Gospel*, Paternoster, 1970. Contributor to *Biblisch-Historisches Handwoerterbuch*, 1962—; also contributor to theology journals.

WORK IN PROGRESS: Material for the international Greek New Testament project; *The Earliest Christology.*

SIDELIGHTS: Higgins is competent in Hebrew, Syriac, Arabic, Latin, Greek, French, German, and Italian. *Avocational interests:* Music, astronomy.

BIOGRAPHICAL/CRITICAL SOURCES: New Testament Abstracts, Volume VI, number 2, 1962.

*   *   *

HIGGINS, Richard C(arter) 1938-
(Dick Higgins)

PERSONAL: Born March 15, 1938, in Cambridge, England; son of Carter Chapin Higgins (a steel manufacturer) and Katharine (Bigelow) Higgins Doman; married Alison Knowles (a silk screen technician and artist), May 30, 1960 (divorced, 1970); children: Hannah and Jessie (twins). *Education:* Attended Yale University, 1955-57; studied music with John Cage, Henry Cowell, and others, 1957-59; Columbia University B.S., 1960; Manhattan School of Printing, C.P.O. certificate, 1961. *Politics:* Progressive Republican. *Address:* P.O. Box 26, West Glover, Vt. 05875.

CAREER: Zaccar Offset (printers), New York, N.Y., cameraman, 1963; Book Press, New York, N.Y., technician, and in production, 1963-64; Russell & Russell (publisher), in production, beginning 1964; The Something Else Press, New York, N.Y., founder, designer, and U.S. manager, 1964—; California Institute of the Arts, Valencia, instructor in publishing, 1970-71; Unpublished Editions, West Glover, Vt., founder, 1973—. *Member:* Film Makers' Co-op, New York Audio-Visual Society (co-founder; vice-president), Broadway Opera Company.

WRITINGS: What Are Legends (essay), Bern Porter, 1960; *Jefferson's Birthday* (plays) and *Postface* (essay), Something Else, 1964; *A Book About Love and War and Death, Canto One* (also see below), Something Else, 1965; *Towards the 1970's*, Abyss Publications, 1969; *foew&ombwhnw: A Grammar of the Mind and a Phenomenology of Love and a Science of the Arts as Seen by a Stalker of the Wild Mushroom*, Something Else, 1969; *A Book About Love and War and Death, Cantos Two and Three* (also see below), Nova Broadcast Express, 1969; (with Wolf Vostell) *Pop Architektur*, Droste (Dusseldorf), 1969, translation published as *Fantastic Architecture*, Something Else, 1971; *Die fabelhafte Getraume von Taifun-Willi*, Relection Press (Stuttgart), 1969, Abyss Publications, 1970; *Computers for the Arts*, Abyss Publications, 1970; *amigo*, Unpublished Editions, 1972; *A Book About Love and War and Death* (cantos 1-3), Something Else, 1972; *The Ladder to the Moon*, Unpublished Editions, 1973; *for eugene in germany*, Unpublished Editions, 1973.

Poetry represented in many anthologies, including *The Young American Writers*, edited by Richard Kostelanetz, Funk, 1967; *Concrete Poetry: A World View*, edited by Mary Ellen Solt, Indiana University Press, 1968; *Breakthrough Fictioneers*, edited by Kostelanetz, Something Else, 1973. Wrote "Stacked Deck," first electronic opera, with music by Richard Maxfield, 1958. Creator of graphics and "multiples," "postcards and miniatures," and "sound poems," as well as films. Contributor to journals and periodicals. U.S. editor of *Fluxus*, beginning 1961, *De-collage*, 1962—; editor, *Something Else Review*, 1964—.

SIDELIGHTS: Higgins considers himself primarily a playwright. He was involved in the founding of the "Happenings" Movement, 1959, and the Fluxus Festivals, 1962-64, which introduced much of the "happenings" art form to Europe.

HILL, Clifford S. 1927-

PERSONAL: Born June 23, 1927, in London, England; son of Horace William (a London telephone manager) and Miriam (Cooper) Hill; married Monica Ford, August 10, 1957; children: Jennifer, Alison. *Education:* Paton Theological College, Nottingham, England, student, 1949-52; University of London, B.D., 1960; London School of Economics and Political Science, University of London, M.A., 1964. *Home:* 96 Downhills Park Rd., Tottenham, London N. 17, England. *Office:* Institute of Race Relations, 36 Jermyn St., London S.W. 1, England.

CAREER: Congregational minister. British government, electronics research scientist on radar and guided missiles, 1943-49; Harlesden Congregational Church, London, England, minister, 1952-57; High Cross Congregational Church, Tottenham, London, England, minister, 1957—. Broadcaster on race relations; A. R. Television, London, adviser on race relations, 1963. *Military service:* British Army, research with Royal Electrical and Mechanical Engineers, 1947-49. *Member:* Institute of Race Relations, Philosophical Society of Great Britain, Convocation of the University of London.

WRITINGS: Black and White in Harmony, Hodder & Stoughton, 1958; *West Indian Migrants and the London Churches*, Oxford University Press, 1963; *How Colour Prejudiced Is Britain?*, Gollancz, 1965; (editor) *Race: A Christian Symposium*, Gollancz, 1968; *Immigration and Integration: A Study of the Settlement of Coloured Minorities in Britain*, Pergamon, 1969; *Black Churches: West Indian & African Sects in Britain*, British Council of Churches, 1971. Weekly religious columnist, *Willesden Chronicle*, 1953-57. Contributor of articles on religion and sociology to newspapers and periodicals.

WORK IN PROGRESS: Dishonest to God, a book about paganism in Britain; *Family and Marriage Customs Among West Indians in Britain*.

SIDELIGHTS: Hill has done considerable traveling in the West Indies, took a leading part in organizing West Indian immigrants after the Notting Hill riots in London.†

*   *   *

HILL, Donna (Marie)

PERSONAL: Born in Salt Lake City, Utah; daughter of Clarence Henry (a U.S. Customs official) and Emma (Wirthlin) Hill. *Education:* Phillips Gallery Art School, Washington, 1940-43; George Washington University, A.B., 1948; Columbia University, M.S. in L.S., 1952. *Religion:* Church of Jesus Christ of Latter-Day Saints. *Agent:* Muriel Fuller, P.O. Box 193, Grand Central Station, New York, N.Y. 10017.

CAREER: U.S. Department of State, code clerk in Washington, D.C., 1944-49, at U.S. Embassy, Paris, France, 1949-51; New York (N.Y.) Public Library, librarian, 1952-59; part-time librarian at New York area colleges, and freelance writer and illustrator, 1959-60; City University of New York, New York, N.Y., assistant to librarian at City College Library, 1962-63, assistant to librarian at Hunter College Library, 1964-67, instructor, Hunter College, 1970—. Painter, with work exhibited in several Paris shows, and in U.S. Information Services exhibition touring Europe, 1950-51. *Member:* American Recorder Society (national secretary, 1959-61), National Educational Association, Library Association of the City University of

New York, Phi Beta Kappa, Kappa Delta, Pi Gamma Mu. *Awards, honors:* Maurice Fromkes painting scholarship to international workshop, Segovia, Spain, summer, 1953; research fellowship to Huntington Library, summer, 1970.

WRITINGS: (Self-illustrated) *Not One More Day* (juvenile), Viking, 1957; (illustrator) Janet Konkle, *The Sea Cart*, Abingdon, 1961; *Catch a Brass Canary* (novel), Lippincott, 1965; (editor with Doris De Montreville) *The Third Book of Junior Authors*, Wilson, 1972; *The Picture File in School and Teachers College Library: A Manual and a Subject Heading List*, Shoe String, 1975. Editor-in-chief, *American Recorder*, 1962-63.

WORK IN PROGRESS: A biography of Joseph Smith, for Doubleday, completion expected in 1976; a novel about a handicapped adolescent in New York.

AVOCATIONAL INTERESTS: Travel, playing the recorder.

BIOGRAPHICAL/CRITICAL SOURCES: Look, August 29, 1950; *Art d'Aujourd'hui*, October, 1950; *Angelos of Kappa Delta*, May, 1957, March, 1965.

*   *   *

HILL, Thomas English 1909-

PERSONAL: Born February 12, 1909, in Gadsden, Ala; son of William Edwin (a minister) and Zaida Dumond (English) Hill; married Sara Prather Armfield (a teacher of mathematics and physics at Northrop Collegiate School), August 14, 1933; children: Sara Prather, Thomas English, Jr., Mary Armfield (Mrs. David Lewis Porter). *Education:* Davidson College, A.B., 1929; Union Theological Seminary, Richmond, Va., B.D., 1932; University of Tuebingen, graduate study, 1933; University of Edinburgh, Ph.D., 1937; University of Richmond, M.A., 1939; Oxford University, postdoctoral study, 1959. *Politics:* Democrat. *Home:* 412 Brandywine Rd., Chapel Hill, N.C. 27514.

CAREER: Ordained Presbyterian minister, 1933. University of Georgia, Atlanta, instructor in Greek in Evening Division, 1934-36; College Park Presbyterian Church, College Park, Ga., pastor, 1934-38: King College, Bristol, Tennessee, professor of Bible and philosophy, 1938-40; Southwestern College, Memphis, Tenn., professor of Bible, 1940-46; Macalester College, St. Paul, Minn., associate professor, 1946-47, professor of philosophy, 1947-62, Bloedel Professor, 1962-74, department chairman, 1964-74. *Member:* American Philosophical Association, Minnesota Philosophical Association, (president, 1963), Phi Beta Kappa, Omnicron Delta Kappa. *Awards, honors:* Rockefeller Foundation research fellow at Harvard University, 1944-46; Ford Foundation fellowship, 1952-53; Thomas Jefferson Award from Macalester College, 1968.

WRITINGS: Contemporary Ethical Theories, Macmillan, 1950; *Ethics in Theory and Practice*, Crowell, 1956; *Contemporary Theories of Knowledge*, Ronald, 1961; *The Concept of Meaning*, Humanites, 1971.

WORK IN PROGRESS: Value Concepts, an inquiry into the major concepts employed in making value judgments.

*   *   *

HILLIS, Charles Richard 1913-
(Dick Hillis)

PERSONAL: Born February 13, 1913, in Victoria, British Columbia, Canada; son of Harry M. and Frances (Harger) Hillis; married Margaret Humphrey, April 8, 1938; children: John, Margaret (Mrs. Jack Pageler), Nancy (Mrs. David Lundsgaard), Stephen, Jennifer, Brian. *Education:* Bible Institute of Los Angeles, graduate, 1932; Dallas Theological Seminary, student, 1942-43. *Home:* 101 Miramonte Ave., Palo Alto, Calif. *Office:* Overseas Crusades, Inc., 3033 Scott Blvd., Santa Clara, Calif. 95050.

CAREER: Missionary in China, 1933-49, in Formosa, 1950-60; Overseas Crusades, Inc., Palo Alto, Calif., general director and founder, 1950—. Member of board of directors of World Gospel Crusades, Steer, Inc., Missionary Supply Lines, and Preaching Print, Inc. *Awards, honors:* Honorary doctorate, Biola College, 1956.

WRITINGS—Under name Dick Hillis: *Shall We Forfeit Formosa?*, Zondervan, 1954; *Dare We Recognize Red China?*, Zondervan, 1956; *Are the Heathen Really Lost?*, Moody, 1961; *Unlock the Heavens*, Moody, 1963; *Inhale the Incense*, Fabrizio, 1964; *Strange Gods*, Moody, 1965; *Born to Climb*, Word Books, 1967; *China Assignment*, [Taiwan], 1967; *Sayings of Mao, of Jesus*, Regal Books, 1972; *Not Made for Quitting*, Dimension Books, 1973; *Listen to the Spirit*, Baker Book, 1973; *Is There Really Only One Way?*, Vision House, 1974. Contributor of articles to periodicals. Editor of *Cable.*

WORK IN PROGRESS: What Is a Missionary?

SIDELIGHTS: Hillis is competent in Mandarin language. He has made many missionary journeys to South America and the Far East.

*   *   *

HILTON, Thomas Leonard   1924-

PERSONAL: Born June 7, 1924; son of William (a paper company executive) and Florence (Rogers) Hilton; married Alice Robertson, June 18, 1949; children: Robert, William, Thomas. *Education:* Massachusetts Institute of Technology, B.S., 1949, part-time graduate study, 1949-52; Harvard University, Ph.D., 1956. *Religion:* Unitarian. *Home:* Deerfield, R.D.1, Stockton, N.J. 08559. *Office:* Educational Testing Service, Princeton, N.J.

CAREER: Massachusetts Institute of Technology, Cambridge, assistant to dean, later assistant dean of students, 1949-52; Harvard University, Cambridge, Mass., director of teacher education research project, 1955-56; Carnegie Institute of Technology, Pittsburgh, Pa., assistant professor of psychology and education, 1956-62, director of teacher education, 1961-62; Educational Testing Service, Princeton, N.J., senior research psychologist, 1962. *Military service:* U.S. Air Force, B-29 Pilot in Pacific theater, 1943-46; became first lieutenant. *Member:* American Psychological Association, American Educational Research Association.

WRITINGS: (Contributor) Beverly von Haller Gilmer and others, editors, *Industrial Psychology*, McGraw, 1961, 2nd edition, 1966; (with William R. Dill and W. R. Reitman) *The New Managers*, Prentice-Hall, 1962. Contributor to professional journals.

*   *   *

HINDLE, Brooke   1918-

PERSONAL: Born September 28, 1918, in Drexel Hill, Pa; son of Howard Brooke and Marion (Manchester) Hindle; married Helen Morris, August 21, 1943; children: Margaret Joan (Mrs. Robert M. Hazen), Donald Morris. *Education:* Massachusetts Institute of Technology, student, 1936-38; Brown University, A.B., (magna cum laude), 1940; University of Pennsylvania, M.A., 1942, Ph.D., 1949. *Home:* 5114 Dalecarlia Dr., Washington D.C. 20016. *Office:* National Museum of History and Technology, Smithsonian Institution, Washington, D.C. 20560.

CAREER: Institute of Early American History and Culture, Williamsburg, Va., research associate, 1948-50; New York University, New York, N.Y., associate professor, 1950-61, professor of history, 1961-74, chairman of department, University College, 1965-67, dean of University College, 1967-69, head of university department of history, beginning, 1970; Smithsonian Institution, National Museum of History and Technology, Washington, D.C., director, 1974—. Lecturer in history at College of William and Mary, 1948-50, Northwestern University, summer, 1950; National Defense Education Act (NDEA) lecturer, North Carolina State University, summer, 1967. Killian Visiting Professor, Massachusetts Institute of Technology, 1971-72. Columbia University Seminar on Early American History and Culture, member, 1967—, member of steering committee, 1971—. Eleutherian Mills-Hagley Foundation, senior resident scholar, 1969-70, member of advisory committee, 1971—. Council member, Institute of Early American History and Culture, 1964-67. Consultant, Smithsonian Institution, 1957. Member of board of directors, George Sarton Memorial Foundation, 1958-64. Member of fellowship committee, Macy Foundation. *Military service:* U.S. Navy, radar maintenance officer, 1942-45; became lieutenant; received Pacific Theater Ribbon with seven stars, Philippine Liberation Ribbon with one star, Navy Unit Commendation.

MEMBER: International Academy of the History of Science, American Historical Association, Society of American Historians, Organization of American Historians, American Antiquarian Society, American Studies Association (joint program coordinator, 1963-65), American Association for the Advancement of Science (fellow), History of Science Society (member of council, 1955-58, 1962-65; secretary, 1958-60), Society for the History of Technology (member of advisory council, 1965-70; member of executive council, 1970—), Society for Industrial Archeology, Phi Beta Kappa. *Awards, honors:* National Science Foundation grant, 1959; American Philosophical Society grant, 1961; Guggenheim fellowship, 1964-65.

WRITINGS: The Pursuit of Science in Revolutionary America, University of North Carolina Press, 1956; *David Rittenhouse*, Princeton University Press, 1964; *Technology in Early America*, University of North Carolina Press, 1966; (contributor) Harold Trevor Colbourn, editor, *The Colonial Experience: Readings in Early American History*, Houghton, 1966; (contributor) *Early Scientific Books in Schaffer Library, Union College*, [Schenectady], 1971. Contributor to *Dictionary of Scientific Biography*, 1970—, *Dictionary of Notable American Women*, 1971, and *Encyclopedia of American History*. Contributor of articles and reviews to professional journals, including *American Historical Review, Canadian Historical Review, Isis*, and *New England Quarterly*. Member of board of editors, *William and Mary Quarterly*, 1964—.

WORK IN PROGRESS: A study of American fairs to 1876.

*   *   *

HINE, Sesyle Joslin   1929-
(Sesyle Joslin; pseudonyms, Josephine Gibson, G. B. Kirtland)

PERSONAL: Born August 30, 1929, in Providence, R.I.;

daughter of Harry and Cara (Selinger) Joslin; married Al Hine (a writer), August 21, 1950; children: Victoria, Alexandra, Julia. *Education:* Attended School of Organic Education, Fairhope, Ala., 1945-46, University of Miami, Coral Gables, Fla., 1946-47, Goddard College, 1947-48, and Antioch College, 1948-49. *Home:* Old Mill Rd., New Milford, Conn.

CAREER: Holiday, Philadelphia, Pa. editorial assistant, 1948-49; Westminster Press, Philadelphia, Pa., assistant editor, 1949-51; *Country Gentleman,* Philadelphia, Pa., book columnist, 1949-51. Free-lance writer. Production assistant on film, "Lord of the Flies," in Puerto Rico, 1961. Goddard College, trustee, 1949-54.

WRITINGS: All under name Sesyle Joslin: *What Do You Say, Dear?,* Scott, 1958; *Brave Baby Elephant,* Harcourt, 1960; *What Do You Do, Dear?,* Scott, 1961; *Baby Elephant's Trunk,* Harcourt, 1961; *There Is a Dragon in My Bed,* Harcourt, 1961; *Senor Baby Elephant, The Pirate,* Harcourt, 1962; *Baby Elephant and the Secret Wishes,* Harcourt, 1962; *Dear Dragon,* Harcourt, 1962; *Baby Elephant Goes to China,* Harcourt, 1963; *Baby Elephant's Baby Book,* Harcourt, 1964; *La Petite Famille,* Harcourt, 1964; *Spaghetti for Breakfast,* Harcourt, 1965; *Please Share That Peanut!,* Harcourt, 1965; *There is a Bull on My Balcony,* Harcourt, 1966; *Pinkety, Pinkety: A Practical Guide to Wishing,* Harcourt, 1966; *La Fiesta,* Harcourt, 1967; *The Night They Stole the Alphabet,* Harcourt, 1968; *Doctor George Owl,* Houghton, 1970; *The Spy Lady and the Muffin Man,* Harcourt, 1971; *Last Summer's Smugglers,* Harcourt, 1973.

With Al Hine, under pseudonym Josephine Gibson: *Is There a Mouse in the House?,* Macmillan, 1965.

With Al Hine, under pseudonym G. B. Kirtland: *One Day in Ancient Rome,* Harcourt, 1961; *One Day in Elizabethan England,* Harcourt, 1962; *One Day in Aztec Mexico,* Harcourt, 1963.†

* * *

HINSHAW, Cecil E(ugene) 1911-

PERSONAL: Born April 12, 1911; son of Verlin Chauncy (a farmer) and Florence (McLaughlin) Hinshaw; married Pauline Smith, August 16, 1932; children: Robert E., Eleanor Hinshaw Mullendore, Elizabeth Ann Baxter, Esther Mae. *Education:* Friends University, B.A., 1934; Iliff School of Theology, Th.M., Th.D., 1938; Harvard University, postdoctoral study, 1938-39. *Religion:* Society of Friends. *Residence:* Allenspark, Colo. 80510.

CAREER: Friends University, Wichita, Kan., professor of religion and philosophy, 1940-43; William Penn College, Oskaloosa, Iowa, president, 1944-49; free-lance lecturer and writer, 1949-56; American Friends Service Committee, North Central Regional Office, Des Moines, Iowa, staff member, 1956-64, executive secretary, 1964-71. Visiting lecturer at Pendle Hill, Wallingford, Pa., 1954, 1956. *Member:* Friends Historical Association.

WRITINGS: Toward Political Responsibility, Pendle Hill, 1954; *Nonviolent Resistance,* Pendle Hill, 1956; *Apology for Perfection,* Pendle Hill, 1964.

* * *

HIRSCH, Walter 1919-

PERSONAL: Born May 12, 1919, in Stuttgart, Germany; came to United States, 1933, naturalized, 1940; son of Eugene and Fanny (Wormser) Hirsch; married Lotte E. Land-

man, January 26, 1946; children: Martin D., Judit M., Janet D., Daniel R. *Education:* Queens College, (now Queens College of the City University of New York), A.B., 1941; graduate study at University of Connecticut, 1941-42, Columbia University, 1946-47; Northwestern University, M.A., 1954, Ph.D., 1957. *Politics:* Democrat. *Religion:* Jewish. *Home:* 514 Dodge St., West Lafayette, Ind. *Office:* Department of Sociology, Purdue University, West Lafayette, Ind.

CAREER: Purdue University, Lafayette, Ind., 1947—, began as assistant professor, now professor of sociology. Lecturer, Indiana University Extension Center, 1954-55. Member of board, Greater Lafayette Federated Jewish Charities, 1958—. *Military service:* U.S. Army, 1942-45; received Bronze Star and three battle stars. *Member:* American Sociological Association (fellow), American Association for the Advancement of Science, American Civil Liberties Union, American Association of University Professors, Ohio Valley Sociological Association.

WRITINGS: (Editor with Bernard Barber) *The Sociology of Science,* Free Press of Glencoe, 1962; (editor with George Zollschan) *Explorations in Social Change,* Houghton, 1964; *Scientists in American Society,* Random House, 1968; (with Zollschan) *Social Change,* Schenkman, 1974. Contributor to *Bulletin of the Atomic Scientists* and sociological journals.

WORK IN PROGRESS: Research on the sociology of science, the sociology of book reviews, and science in Nazi Germany.

* * *

HIRSCHMEIER, Johannes 1921-

PERSONAL: Born October 28, 1921, in Germany; son of Karl (a farmer) and Thekla (Obornik) Hirschmeier. *Education:* St. Augustin Seminary, Bonn, Germany, B.A., 1951; Catholic University of America, graduate study, 1954-55; Harvard University, M.A., 1957, Ph.D., 1960. *Home and office:* Nanzan University, 1 Nanzancho, Show-ku, Nagoya, Japan.

CAREER: Roman Catholic priest, member of Society of the Divine Word. Nanzan University, Showa-ku, Nagoya, Japan, 1960—, began as associate professor, became professor of economics, president, 1972—.

WRITINGS: The Origin of Entrepreneurship in Meiji Japan, Harvard University Press, 1964; (with T. Yui) *The Development of Japanese Business, 1600-1973,* Allen & Unwin, 1974.

WORK IN PROGRESS: A book, *Problems of Japanese Business History.*

* * *

HIRST, Wilma E(llis) 1914-

PERSONAL: Born July 6, 1914, in Shenandoah, Iowa; daughter of James Harrison and Lena Lucinda (Donahue) Ellis; married Clyde Henry Hirst, February 27, 1935; children: Donna Jean (Mrs. Alan Robert Goss). *Education:* University of Wyoming, M.A., 1951; Colorado State College, Ed.D., 1954. *Religion:* Presbyterian. *Home:* 3458 Green Valley Rd., Cheyenne, Wyo. 82001. *Office:* School District 1, School Administration Building, Cheyenne, Wyo. 82001.

CAREER: Kearney State Teachers College, Kearney, Neb., director or Laboratory School and professor of education, 1954-56; School District 1, Cheyenne, Wyo., co-ordinator of guidance, and school psychologist, 1957-66, director of research and special projects, 1966—. Investigator, U.S. Department of Health, Education, and Welfare, 1965-69. Summer lecturer at University of Southern California, University of Oklahoma, University of Nebraska, University of Wyoming, and University of Omaha. *Member:* International Council of Psychologists, American Association of University Professors, National Education Association (life member), American Psychological Association, Association for the Gifted, American Personnel and Guidance Association, Wyoming Psychological Association (president, 1962-63), Psi Chi, Kappa Delta Pi, Pi Lambda Theta, Alpha Delta Kappa.

WRITINGS: Know Your School Psychologist, Grune, 1963.†

*   *   *

HITCHIN, Martin Mewburn   1917-
(Martin Mewburn)

PERSONAL: Born July 19, 1917, in Stockport, Cheshire, England; son of Percy David (a law agent) and Amy Gladys (Mewburn) Hitchin; married Muriel Mary Britten (a social worker). *Education:* Attended St. Paul's School, 1934-37, University of Paris, 1938. *Politics:* Liberal. *Religion:* Agnostic. *Home:* Peachum's Cottage, 8 Malvern Terrace, London N.1, England; and Old Post Cottage, Sidlesham, Sussex, England.

CAREER: Writer. *Military service:* Royal Hampshires, second battalion, 1940-42; British Army, Intelligence Corps, 1943-46. *Member:* Society of Authors.

WRITINGS—Under pseudonym Martin Mewburn: *The Garden*, Hogarth, 1952; *I Was a Stranger*, Hogarth, 1955. Contributor to *Lilliput*

WORK IN PROGRESS: Two novels, *The Square Circle*, and *There's No Telling*.

SIDELIGHTS: Hitchin told *CA* that "the sexual relationship in all its ramifications, ie. emotional, physical and intellectual, in that order of importance, is my principal interest, and the subject matter of all my novels. I am interested in drama as well as the novel, but to a lesser extent. I know France, Germany, Italy, Belgium and Holland, have lived in East Africa and have travelled round the continent of Africa by sea."

*   *   *

HOAG, Edwin   1926-

PERSONAL: Born 1926, in New York, N.Y.; married Joy Marie Landry; children: four. *Education:* Florida Southern College, earned B.S. in Journalism. *Politics:* Democratic. *Religion:* Catholic. *Home:* 134 Colonial Parkway N., Yonkers, N.Y. *Agent:* Lurton Blassingame, 10 East 43rd St., New York, N.Y. 10017.

CAREER: City editor of *Lakeland Ledger*, Lakeland, Fla., 1951-52, and *Wilmington Star*, Wilmington, N.C., 1952-53; *New Orleans States-Item*, New Orleans, La., rewriteman, columnist, and feature writer, 1953-58; Paul Martin & Associates (public relations), New Orleans, La., staff, 1958-61; Tulane University of Louisiana, New Orleans, education and science writer for university news service, 1961-63, medical news editor, 1963-65; *Computing Report* (IBM), editor, 1965—. Science News Seminar for Southern Newspaper Editors, co-director, 1961. Free-lance writer. *Member:* National Association of Science Writers, Authors

League, New Orleans Press Club (charter member). *Awards, honors:* Distinguished achievement award of American College Public Relations Association for "Dimension Education," a weekly educational column, 1963.

WRITINGS: (Contributor) *Mission to Mankind*, Random, 1963; *American Houses*, Lippincott, 1964; *Roads of Man*, Putnam, 1966; *American Cities: Their Historical and Social Development*, Lippincott, 1969. Contributor to *American Mercury, Coronet, Pageant, Boys' Life, Family Circle, Catholic Digest, Today's Family, Woman's Day, Family Digest* and other national magazines.

WORK IN PROGRESS: A book on the history of roads; research on U.S. history, 1870-1900, the history of sulphur mining in the United States.†

*   *   *

HOANG Van Chi   1915-

PERSONAL: Born October 1, 1915, in Thanh-hoa, North Vietnam; came to United States in 1965; son of Hoang Van Thu and (Le) Thi Lieu; married Le Hang Phan, June 20, 1940; children: Hoang Viet Dung, Hoang Ngoc Anh, Hoang Minh Tho. *Education:* University of Hanoi, P.C.B. (physics, chemistry, biology), 1938; Hanoi Faculty of Medicine, medical studies, 1938-40. *Home:* 12653 Hemming Lane, Bowie, Md.

CAREER: Papeteries de l'Indochine, Tongking, Indochina, chemist, 1941-42; Co-operatives of Papermakers, Hanoi, Vietnam, chemist, 1942-45; National Mint, Hanoi, Vietnam, director, 1945-46; National Paper Factory, North Vietnam, director, 1947-49; South Vietnam Ministry of Information, Saigon, chief of cultural service, 1955-56; free-lance writer, 1956-59; Government of South Vietnam, vice-consul in New Delhi, India, 1959-60; full-time writer in Paris, France, 1960-65; member of staff, Voice of America, 1965-69, Agency for International Development, 1969—. *Awards, honors:* Citation by Ho Chi Minh, 1948, for building a hydroelectric station during Resistance War (against the French).

WRITINGS: The Fate of the Last Viets, Hoa Mai, 1956; *The New Class in North Vietnam*, Cong Dan, 1958; *From Colonialism to Communism: A Case History of North Vietnam*, Praeger, 1963. Author of other books published in Vietnamese. Contributor of articles to Saigon newspapers and to *China Quarterly* and *Peace News* (London).

WORK IN PROGRESS: A book, *An Ideology of Peace*, completion expected in 1977.

SIDELIGHTS: Most of Hoang's writing has dealt with experiences under communism in North Vietnam and in China. Feeling that it was impossible to write objectively under the Ngo Dinh Diem regime in South Vietnam, Hoang sought a diplomatic post as the only way to get abroad, abandoned it after a year and went to Europe. *From Colonialism to Communism: A Case History of North Vietnam* has been translated into twelve languages.

*   *   *

HOBBS, Charles R(ene)   1931-

PERSONAL: Born February 13, 1931, in Logan, Utah; son of Milo Purnell and Bertha (Skidmore) Hobbs; married Nola Davis, March 16, 1956; children: Christine, Charles Mark, Janice. *Education:* Brigham Young University, B.A., 1956, M.A., 1958; Columbia University, Ed.D., 1970. *Home:* 1842 Beaumont Circle, Salt Lake City, Utah 84121. *Office:* Department of Teacher Development, 50 East North Temple, Salt Lake City, Utah 84150.

CAREER: Church of Jesus Christ of Latter-Day Saints, missionary in Netherlands, 1951-53; Latter-Day Saints Seminaries, teacher of religious education, Lehi, Utah, 1956-57, seminary principal, Malad, Idaho, 1958-60, seminary coordinator for southern Utah, Cedar City, 1961-64, seminary district coordinator for Salt Lake Valley, Salt Lake City, Utah, 1964-66, and member of general curriculum advisory committee for religious education of students of high school age, director, Latter-Day Saints institute, Columbia University, New York, 1966-69, director, Center for Teacher Training, Latter-Day Saints Institute of Religion, Utah State University, Logan, 1969-70, executive secretary, Church Teacher Development Program, Salt Lake City, Utah, 1970-72, associate director, Church Teacher Development Program, 1972—. Brigham Young University, field lecturer on teaching methods, traveling throughout the United States and Canada.

WRITINGS: Teaching with New Techniques, Deseret, 1964; *The Power of Teaching with New Techniques,* Deseret, 1972. Contributor to *Instructor, Improvement Era, New Era,* and *Brigham Young University Studies.*

WORK IN PROGRESS: Three books, *Great Teacher Power, Great Father and Mother Teachers,* and *The Principle of Accessibility.*

SIDELIGHTS: Hobbs is fluent in Dutch. *Avocational interests:* Painting landscapes in oils, classical music, public speaking, skiing, gardening.

*   *   *

HOBLEY, Leonard Frank 1903-

PERSONAL: Born January 19, 1903, in London, England; son of Edgar Frank (a printer and bookseller) and Lucy (Robson) Hobley; married Edith May Cheverall, March 28, 1932; children: Diana (Mrs. Brian Atkinson), Elisabeth. *Education:* Goldsmiths' College, London, B.A., 1924. *Home:* 45 Orchard Gardens, Hove 4, Sussex, England.

CAREER: Schoolmaster in Brighton, England, 1924-63. Friends' Adult Educational Centre, Brighton, vice-chairman, 1958—. Member of committee, Community Centres Association of Brighton; also active in Workers' Educational Association. *Member:* Society of Authors, National Union of Teachers, Historical Association.

WRITINGS: (With Peter Leyden) *The Story Path to Reading,* Blackie & Son, 1952; *Early Explorers,* Methuen, 1954; *Opening Africa,* Methuen, 1955; *Exploring America,* Methuen, 1955; *Exploring the Pacific,* Methuen, 1957; *City in Peril* (juvenile), Ginn, 1958; *Roman and Briton?* (juvenile), Ginn, 1959; *Friends Divided* (juvenile), Ginn, 1959.

Britain's Place in the World (history), four books, Oliver & Boyd, 1960; (with G. R. Davis) *How to Use an Atlas,* Blackie & Son, 1962; *Living and Working: A Social and Economic History of England and Wales from 1760 to 1960,* Oxford University Press, 1964; *Geography Through Maps,* Blackie & Son, 1965; *Active Geography,* Gibson, 1965; *The Fire Service,* Allman & Son, 1968; *The Story of the Police,* Allman & Son, 1969; *The Trade Union Story,* Blackie & Son, 1969.

Working Class and Democratic Movements, Blackie & Son, 1970; *Introducing Earth,* nine books, Macmillan, 1970-71; *The First World War,* Blackie & Son, 1971; *The Second World War,* Blackie & Son, 1971; *The Town Councillor,* Allman & Son, 1972; *The Farmer,* Allman & Son, 1972; *The Monarchy,* Batsford, 1972; *Customs and Excise Men,* Allman & Son, 1974; *Ancient Greece,* Evans Broth-

ers, 1974; *Knowing British History,* three books: *The Stuarts, The Eighteenth Century,* and *The Nineteenth Century,* Evans Brothers, 1974.

AVOCATIONAL INTERESTS: Adult education, gardening, tennis.

*   *   *

HODGES, C(yril) Walter 1909-

PERSONAL: Born March 18, 1909, in Beckenham, Kent, England; son of Cyril James (an advertising manager) and Mary Margaret (Finch) Hodges; married Margaret Becker, April 9, 1936; children: Nicholas Adam, Crispin James. *Education:* Goldsmiths' College, London, art student, 1925-28. *Home:* 15 Hill Rise, Bishopstone, Seaford, Sussex, England.

CAREER: Free-lance illustrator, designer, and artist. Work includes mural paintings in Chartered Insurance Institute and United Kingdom Provident Institution, exhibitions (designed) for Lloyds of London and United Kingdom Provident Institution, and stage scenery and costumes for Everyman Theatre and Mermaid Theatre, London; illustrator of more than seventy children's books; magazine and advertising illustrator; art director, writer for Encyclopaedia Britannica Films, Chicago, 1958-61. *Military service:* British Army, 1940-46; became captain; mentioned in dispatches. *Member:* Society of Industrial Artists (fellow), International P.E.N., Society of Authors (England). *Awards, honors:* Kate Greenaway Medal of Library Association (England) for the most distinguished work in the illustration of children's books, 1965, for *Shakespeare's Theatre.*

WRITINGS—Self-illustrated, all for young people, except as indicated: *Columbus Sails,* Coward, 1939; *Sky High,* Coward, 1947 (published in England as *The Flying House,* Benn, 1947); *Shakespeare and the Players,* Benn, 1948, Coward, 1949; *The Globe Restored* (adult), Benn, 1953, Coward, 1954, 2nd edition, 1968; *The Namesake,* Coward, 1964 (published in England as *The Namesake: A Story of King Alfred,* Bell, 1964); *Shakespeare's Theatre,* Coward, 1964; *The Norman Conquest,* Coward, 1966; *Magna Carta,* Coward, 1966; *The Marsh King,* Coward, 1967; *The Spanish Armada,* Coward, 1967; *The Overland Launch,* Bell, 1969, Coward, 1970; *The Puritan Revolution,* Coward, 1972; *Shakespeare's Second Globe* (adult), Oxford University Press, 1973; *Playhouse Tales,* Coward, 1974.

Illustrator: Gerald W. Bullett, *The Happy Mariners,* Dent, 1935; Robert A. Foster-Melliar, *My Garden by the Sea,* Bell, 1936; G. B. Harrison, *New Tales from Shakespeare,* Nelson, 1938; Harrison, *More New Tales from Shakespeare,* Nelson, 1939.

Edith N. Bland, *Story of the Treasure Seekers,* new edition, Coward, 1948; Johann Wyss, *Swiss Family Robinson,* Oxford University Press, 1949.

Rosemary Sutcliff, *Chronicles of Robin Hood,* Oxford University Press, 1950; Sutcliff, *Brother Dusty-Feet,* Oxford University Press, 1952; Rhoda D. Power, *Redcap Runs Away,* J. Cape, 1952, Houghton, 1954; Sutcliff, *Eagle of the Ninth,* Oxford University Press, 1954; Mark Twain, *The Adventures of Huckleberry Finn,* Dutton, 1955; Twain, *The Adventures of Tom Sawyer,* Dutton, 1955; Ian Serraillier, *Silver Sword,* J. Cape, 1956, Criterion, 1959; Sutcliff, *Shield Ring,* Oxford University Press, 1956; Alexander Dumas, *The Three Musketeers,* World Publishing, 1957; Rose Dobbs, *Once-Upon-a-Time Story Book,* Random House, 1958.

Ruth Manning-Sanders, *Red Indian Folk and Fairy Tales*, Oxford University Press, 1960; Robert Graves, *The Siege and Fall of Troy*, Doubleday, 1962; Alfred Leo Duggan, *Growing Up With the Norman Conquest*, Faber, 1965, Pantheon, 1966.

Author of articles on Shakespearean theater in specialist periodicals.

WORK IN PROGRESS: Two picture books, *The Emperor's Elephant* and *The Industrial Revolution*; further series of *Playhouse Tales*.

SIDELIGHTS: Hodges is an authority on the structure of Elizabethan playhouses. He speaks French, travels considerably in Europe, and has visited the United States several times. *Avocational interests:* Music (listening), books, theater, films, photography.

*　　*　　*

HODGETTS, J(ohn) E(dwin) 1917-

PERSONAL: Born May 28, 1917, in Omemee, Ontario, Canada; son of Alfred Clark (a bank manager) and Mary Elsie (Birnie) Hodgetts; married Ruth Woodger, June 26, 1943; children: Edwin C., P. Geoffrey, E. Anne. *Education:* University of Toronto, B.A., 1939, M.A., 1940; University of Chicago, Ph.D., 1946. *Religion:* United Church of Canada. *Home:* R.R. Newtonville, Toronto, Ontario, Canada. *Office:* University of Toronto, Toronto, Ontario, Canada.

CAREER: University of Toronto, Toronto, Ontario, lecturer in political science, 1943-45; Queen's University, Kingston, Ontario, lecturer, 1945-47, assistant professor 1947-50, associate professor, 1950-57, professor of political science, 1957-65, Hardy Professor of Political Science, 1961-65, head of department, 1963-65; University of Toronto, professor of political science, 1965—, principal, Victoria College, 1967-70, president, Victoria University, 1970-72. Research director, Royal Commission on Government Organization, 1960-62. *Member:* International Political Science Association, Canadian Political Science Association (vice-president, 1958; president, 1972), Institute of Public Administration of Canada, Royal Society of Canada (fellow). *Awards, honors:* Rhodes scholar, 1939; University of Western Ontario Medal, 1957, for best scholarly article published in Canada ("The Civil Service and Policy Formation").

WRITINGS: Pioneer Public Service: An Administrative History of the United Canadas, University of Toronto Press, 1956; (author of revision with Corry) James A. Corry, *Democratic Government and Politics*, University of Toronto Press, 3rd edition, revised, 1959, Oxford University Press, 1960; (with David C. Corbett) *Canadian Public Administration: A Book of Readings*, Macmillan (Canada), 1960; *Administering the Atom for Peace*, Atherton, 1964; (with others) *The Biography of an Institution: A History of the Civil Service Commission of Canada, 1907-1967*, McGill-Queen's University Press, 1972; *The Canadian Public Service: A Physiology of Government, 1867-1970*, University of Toronto Press, 1972. Contributor to periodicals in Canada, Britain, and the United States. Editor of *Queen's Quarterly*, 1956-58.

WORK IN PROGRESS: A book, *Provincial Governments as Employers*, with O. P. Dwivedi.

*　　*　　*

HODGSON, Richard Sargeant 1924-

PERSONAL: Surname is pronounced *Hod*-son; born October 18, 1924, in Breckenridge, Minn.; son of Lorin Baird (a dentist) and Ruth (Sargeant) Hodgson; married Lois Hogan, January 19, 1952; children: Susan Eleanor, Steven Sargeant, Scott Richard, Lisa Ruth. *Education:* North Dakota State School of Science, A.A., 1949; studied at Gustavus Adolphus College, 1943-44, Western Michigan University, 1944, Northwestern University, 1947-48. *Religion:* Presbyterian. *Home:* 1441 Johnny's Way, Route 3, West Chester, Pa. 19380.

CAREER: Billboard Publishing Co., Chicago, Ill., associate editor, *Billboard* and *Vend*, 1947-48; *Tide* (magazine), Chicago, Ill., associate editor, 1948-49; North Dakota State School of Science, Wahpeton, director of public relations, 1949-50; Advertising Publications, Inc., Chicago, Ill., executive editor of *Advertising Requirements* and *Industrial Marketing*, 1952-59; American Marketing Services, Inc. (publishers), Boston, Mass., president, 1960-61; R. R. Donnelley & Sons Co., Chicago, Ill., advertising and sales promotion manager, 1962-65, director of Creative Graphics Division, 1965-72; The Franklin Mint, Franklin Center, Pa., creative director, 1972, vice-president, 1973—, managing director of Gallery of American Art, 1973—. Former instructor in journalism and advertising at North Dakota State School of Science, and in magazine layout and editing at University of Chicago; lecturer at Northwestern University and University of Wisconsin. *Military service:* U.S. Marine Corps, active duty, 1942-47, 1950-52; combat correspondent in North China, and radio and television chief during four atomic bomb tests. U.S. Marine Corps Reserve, 1952-67; became lieutenant colonel.

MEMBER: Sales Promotion Executives Association (now Marketing Communications Executives International; member of board of directors, 1958—; president of Boston chapter, 1961, of Chicago chapter, 1964), Direct Mail Advertising Association (member of board of directors, 1963—), Marine Corps Reserve Officers Association, Marine Corps Combat Correspondents Association, Mail Advertising Club of Chicago (president, 1959), Chicago Federated Advertising Club, Chicago Business Paper Publishers Association. *Awards, honors:* Jesse H. Neale Editorial Achievement Award, Associated Business Publications, 1959, for outstanding business journalism; Dartnell Gold Medal Award, 1963, for business letter writing; Sales Promotion Executive-of-the-Year from Chicago Chapter, Sales Promotion Executive Association; Marketing Communicator-of-the-Year from Marketing Communications Executives International; other awards, including Gold Mailbox of Direct Mail Advertising Association.

WRITINGS: (With H. Jay Bullen) *How to Use a Tape Recorder*, Hastings, 1957; *Direct Mail Showmanship*, American Marketing Services, 1961; *How to Promote Meeting Attendance*, American Marketing Services, 1961; *Direct Mail and Mail Order Handbook*, Dartnell, 1964, 2nd edition, 1974; (editor) *In Quiet Ways* (biography of George M. Mead), Mead Corporation, 1970; *America the Beautiful*, The Franklin Mint Gallery of American Art, 1974. Contributor of more than a hundred articles to consumer and business magazines.

WORK IN PROGRESS: Three books, *Great Promotions of the Twentieth Century*, *Showmanship for Profit* and *Encyclopedia of Promotion Ideas*.

AVOCATIONAL INTERESTS: Photography, and operation of private press.

HODNETT, Edward 1901-

PERSONAL: Born October 15, 1901, in Sag Harbor, N.Y.; son of John Richard and Mary (Radigan) Hodnett; married Jessie Patrick, 1923; children: Grey. *Education:* Columbia University, A.B., 1922, Ph.D., 1935. *Address:* c/o Trust Department, Chemical Bank, Midland, Mich.

CAREER: Columbia University, New York, N.Y., teacher of English, 1922-40, advisory editor, Columbia University Press, 1936-42, editor of *Columbia University Quarterly*, 1940-41; University of Newark (now part of Rutgers University), Newark, N.J., professor of English and dean of College of Arts and Sciences, 1940-42; Houghton Mifflin Co., Boston, Mass., editor, 1945-46; University of Massachusetts, Amherst, vice-president 1946-48; Fenn College (now Cleveland State University), Cleveland, Ohio, president, 1948-51; Ohio University, Athens, professor of English, 1951-57; Dow Corning Corp., Midland, Mich., director of public relations, 1957-66. *Military service:* U.S. Navy, 1942-45; became lieutenant commander. *Member:* The Bibliographical Society (London), Beta Theta Pi.

WRITINGS: (Editor) Jonathan Swift, *A Tale of a Tub*, Columbia University Press, 1930; *Plain English*, Ronald, 1935; *English Woodcuts, 1480-1535*, Oxford University Press, 1935, reprinted with additions and corrections, Bibliographical Society, 1973; *The Art of Problem Solving*, Harper, 1955; *Industry-College Relations*, World Publishing, 1955; *Poems to Read Aloud*, Norton, 1957, revised edition, 1967; *The Art of Working with People*, Harper, 1959; *Which College for You?*, Harper, 1960; *So You Want to Go into Industry*, Harper, 1960; *The Cultivated Mind*, Harper, 1963; *Effective Presentations: How to Present Facts, Figures, and Ideas Successfully*, Parker Publishing, 1967; *Marcus Gheeraets the Elder of Bruges, London, and Antwerp*, Haentjens Dekker & Gumbert, 1971; *Aesop in England*, Shakespeare Studies Monographs, 1974. Contributor to *Book Collector*.

WORK IN PROGRESS: Modern English Book Illustrators; Francis Barlow and his Predecessors.

* * *

HOENIGSWALD, Henry M(ax) 1915-

PERSONAL: Born April 17, 1915, in Breslau, Germany; son of Richard and Gertrud (Grunwald) Hoenigswald; married Gabriele L. Schoepflich (a university lecturer), December 26, 1944; children: Frances Gertrude, Susan Ann. *Education:* Attended University of Munich, 1932-33, University of Zurich, 1933-34, University of Padua, 1934-36; University of Florence, D.Litt., 1936, Perfezionamento, 1937. *Home:* 908 Westdale Ave., Swarthmore, Pa. 19081. *Office:* 619 Williams Hall, University of Pennsylvania, Philadelphia, Pa. 19174.

CAREER: Yale University, New Haven, Conn., lecturer and research assistant, 1932-42, instructor, 1944-45; Hartford Seminary Foundation, New Haven, Conn., lecturer and instructor, 1941-42, 1945-46; Hunter College (now Hunter College of the City University of New York) New York, N.Y., lecturer, 1942-43, 1946; University of Pennsylvania, Philadelphia, lecturer in Hindustani, U.S. Army Specialized Training Program, 1943-44; with U.S. Department of State, Washington, D.C., 1946-47; University of Texas, Austin, associate professor of classical languages, 1947-48; University of Pennsylvania, associate professor, 1948-49, professor of linguistics, 1959—, chairman of department, 1963-70. Deccan College, Poona, India, senior linguist, 1955. Visiting professor at University of Michigan, Georgetown University, Princeton University, Yale University, and others. Hermann Collitz Professor of the Linguistic Society of America, 1955. Fulbright lecturer, Kiel, 1968.

MEMBER: American Philosophical Society, Linguistic Society of America (president, 1958), American Oriental Society (president, 1966-67), American Philological Association, Archaeological Institute of America, American Association of University Professors, Philological Society (London), Linguistic Society of India, Societas Linguistica Europaea, International Linguistic Association, Classical Association of Atlantic States, Oriental Club of Philadelphia. *Awards, honors:* Fellow, American Council of Learned Societies, 1942-43, 1944-45, Guggenheim Foundation, 1950, Newberry Library, 1958, National Science Foundation, 1962, Center for Advanced Study in the Behavioral Sciences, 1962, 1963.

WRITINGS: Spoken Hindustani, I and II, Henry Holt, 1946, 1947; *Language Change and Linguistic Reconstruction*, University of Chicago Press, 1960; (editor with George Cardona and Alfred Senn) *Indo-European and Indo-Europeans*, University of Pennsylvania Press, 1970; (editor with T. A. Sebeok and R. E. Longacre, and contributor) *Diachronic, Areal, and Typological Linguistics*, Mouton & Co., 1973, Humanities, in press; *Studies in Formal Historical Linguistics*, Reidel, 1973. Contributor to journals in his field. *Journal of the American Oriental Society* and "American Oriental Series," associate editor, 1952-54, editor, 1954-58.

WORK IN PROGRESS: Historical Linguistics, History of Linguistics, and *Italic and Etruscan Epigraphy.*

* * *

HOFFER, Charles R(ussell) 1929-

PERSONAL: Surname rhymes with "offer"; born December 12, 1929, in Lansing, Mich.; son of Charles Russell (a college professor) and Luella (Holmes) Hoffer; married Marjorie Latham (a teacher and musician), November 27, 1953; children: Charles Allan, Martha Clarice. *Education:* Michigan State College (now University) of Agriculture and Applied Science, B.M., 1951, Ph.D., 1955; Eastman School of Music, M.M., 1952. *Religion:* Presbyterian. *Home:* 869 Oakbrook Lane, University City, Mo. 63132.

CAREER: Grand Ledge (Mich.) public schools, music teacher, 1953-56; State University of New York College at Buffalo, associate professor of music, 1956-59; Clayton (Mo.) School District, director of music, 1959—. Spirit of St. Louis Fund, member of board, 1962-63; Young Audiences, Inc. (St. Louis chapter), member of board, 1959-65; Community Music School of St. Louis, member of board, 1965—; director, Mark Twain Summer Institute, 1965—. *Member:* National Conference of Music Educators, National Education Association, Missouri State Teachers Association, St. Louis Suburban Music Educators (president, 1963-64).

WRITINGS: Teaching Music in the Secondary Schools, Wadsworth, 1964, revised edition, 1974; (with wife, Marjorie L. Hoffer) *Scored for the Understanding of Music*, Wordsworth, 1969; (with Donald K. Anderson) *Performing Music With Understanding* (with teacher's edition), Wordsworth, 1971. Contributor to music and music education journals and *St. Louis Post-Dispatch*. Instrumental consultant to Follett's basal music series, 1965—.†

HOFFER, Eric 1902-

PERSONAL: Born July 25, 1902, in New York, N.Y.; son of Knut (a cabinet-maker) and Elsa (Goebel) Hoffer. *Education:* Self-educated. *Home:* 440 Davis Ct., San Francisco, Calif. 94111.

CAREER: Worked in a box factory in Los Angeles, Calif., for three years in the early twenties; was a migratory field laborer, a gold miner near Nevada City, Calif., and a dishwasher in a construction camp near Los Angeles, among other jobs; longshoreman on Pacific Coast, for the most part in San Francisco, 1943-66; author. Senior research professor, holding weekly seminars, University of California at Berkeley (Hoffer rejected an offer of full professorship). Member of San Francisco Art Commission. *Member:* International Longshoremen's and Warehousemen's Union. *Awards, honors:* Commonwealth Club of California Gold Medal, 1952, for *The True Believer*.

WRITINGS: The True Believer, Harper, 1951, issued with new introduction, Time, Inc., 1963; *The Passionate State of Mind*, Harper, 1955; *The Ordeal of Change*, Harper, 1963; *The Temper of Our Time*, Harper, 1967; (author of epilog) James M. Burns, editor, *To Heal and to Build: The Programs of President Lyndon B. Johnson*, McGraw, 1968; *Working and Thinking on the Waterfront: A Journal, June 1958-May 1959*, Harper, 1969; *First Things, Last Things*, Harper, 1971; *Reflections on the Human Condition*, Harper, 1973. Epigrams published weekly in San Francisco *Examiner*.

SIDELIGHTS: Hoffer writes of his early life: "I was practically blind up to the age of fifteen. When my eyesight came back I was seized with an enormous hunger for the printed word. I read indiscriminately everything within reach—English and German.... I knew several things: One, that I didn't want to work in a factory; two, that I couldn't stand being dependent on the good graces of a boss; three, that I was going to stay poor; four, that I had to get out of New York. Logic told me that California was the poor man's country."

In the West he secured library cards in a dozen towns and did his writing "in railroad yards while waiting for a freight, in the fields while waiting for a truck, and at noon after lunch." He continued to read avidly, pursuing his studies alone. He told Margaret Anderson that his first book was written "in complete intellectual isolation. I have not discussed one idea with any human being...."

The True Believer, a remarkable book that, for its brilliance and cold logic, has been favorably compared with Machiavelli's *The Prince*, is an analysis of the revivalist phase of mass movements. In his introduction Hoffer writes that the true believer is a "man of fanatical faith who is ready to sacrifice his life for a holy cause...." The true believer is a frustrated man who seeks for hope in a collective vision. A mass movement, according to Hoffer, "offers substitutes either for the whole self or for the elements which make life bearable; ... [and] it does not seem to make any difference who it is that is seized with a wild hope—whether it be an enthusiastic intellectual, a land-hungry farmer, a get-rich-quick speculator, a sober merchant or industrialist, a plain workingman or a noble lord; ... they all proceed recklessly with the present, wreck it if necessary, and create a new world."

In a review of *The True Believer*, Neil Martin noted that Hoffer "is not a scholar in the common sense. But he is a student of extraordinary perception and insight. The range of his reading and research is vast, amazing." A *New Yorker* critic wrote that the book "owes its distinction as a piece of writing to the fact that Hoffer is a born generalizer, with a mind that inclines to the wry epigram and the icy aphorism as naturally as did that of the Duc de La Rochefoucauld."

A *Newsweek* reviewer wrote of *The Ordeal of Change*: "It is not a book full of happy notions and pleasing prospects; it is a book which is stimulating despite its burden of dismay." While Hoffer's pessimistic view of man is frequently noted, Eugene Burdick believes there is "a great deal of optimism in his view of individual capacity for growth. [Hoffer] feels, for example, that with only the slightest effort he was able to make a large number of migratory farm workers appreciate Montaigne.... [During one winter], when he was snowed in, he read again and again a copy of Montaigne's *Essays*.... By spring ... he had read it through six times and came out of the spring thaw and down into the agricultural valleys a firm apostle of Montaigne." The prospectors' moral and personal problems were clarified by consulting Montaigne. Hoffer believes there are men who are "still quoting Montaigne in the valleys of California."

BIOGRAPHICAL/CRITICAL SOURCES: New York Times Book Review, March 18, 1951, April 1, 1956; *New Yorker*, April 7, 1951, April 28, 1951, May 21, 1955; *Christian Science Monitor*, April 26, 1951; *New York Herald Tribune Book Review*, May 27, 1951; *New Republic*, December 10, 1951; *Christian Century*, June 29, 1955; *Reporter*, February 21, 1957; *Newsweek*, March 18, 1963; *Atlantic*, April, 1963; *Harper's*, April, 1963; *Nation*, April 20, 1963; *Critic*, June, 1963; *National Review*, June 18, 1963; *New Yorker*, January 7, 1967; Calvin Tomkins, *Eric Hoffer: An American Odyssey*, Dutton, 1968.†

*   *   *

HOFFMAN, George W(alter) 1914-

PERSONAL: Born June 19, 1914, in Vienna, Austria; came to United States in 1939, naturalized U.S. citizen in 1943; son of W(ilhelm) Albert (a publisher) and Hedwig (Weihs) Hoffman; married Viola Smith (a travel consultant), September 30, 1944; children: Jeane (Mrs. Hugh Pendery), Suzanne, Alan Michael. *Education:* Studied at University of Vienna, 1934-36, Harvard University, 1946-47, and at American University; University of Michigan, Ph.D., 1950. *Home:* 3516 Highland View Dr., Austin, Tex. 78731. *Office:* Department of Geography, University of Texas, Austin, Tex. 78712.

CAREER: Wirtschaftlicher Beobachter, Vienna, Austria, assistant editor, 1935-38; Indiana University, Bloomington, instructor in geography, 1947-48; University of Texas at Austin, assistant professor, 1949-53, associate professor, 1953-60, professor of geography, 1961—. Fulbright lecturer at University of Munich, 1961-62, 1972, and at University of Heidelberg, 1972; visiting lecturer at universities in America and Europe, including Yugoslavia, Poland, and Rumania. Consultant, F. A. Brockhaus (publishers), Weisbaden, Germany, 1964-69; member of committee on Eastern Europe, American Council of Learned Societies, 1965-71; member of joint committee of Social Science Research Council and American Council of Learned Societies, 1970-72. *Military service:* U.S. Army, 1942-45; assigned to Research and Analysis Branch, Office of Strategic Services.

MEMBER: Association of American Geographers (chairman of committee on Eastern Europe, 1973—), National Council for Geographic Education, American Association for the Advancement of Science, American Geographical Society, Royal Geographic Society (London; fellow), Osterreichische Geographische Gesellschaft and Wiener Geographische Gesellschaft (both Vienna), Suedosteuropa Institute and Suedosteuropa Gesellschaft (both Munich), Serbian Geographical Society (Yugoslavia; honorary member), Southwest Social Science Association, Southwest Slavic Conference (president, 1964-65), American Association of University Professors (secretary-treasurer of University of Texas chapter, 1969-70), Texas Council of Geography Teachers (president, 1954-55; member of board of directors, 1955-58), Texas Association of College Teachers (president of Austin chapter, 1969-72), Austin Committee on Foreign Relations (executive secretary, 1954—), Phi Kappa Alpha.

AWARDS, HONORS: Fellowship from Ford Foundation Fund for the Advancement of Education, 1952-53; *Journal of Geography* Prize, 1953 and 1958, for best political geography contribution in a period of five years; International Relations Award from St. Mary's University of San Antonio, 1962; grants from Social Science Research Council, 1953 and 1957, from American Philosophical Society, 1957, 1962, and 1969, from Twentieth Century Fund, 1958-61, for research project on Yugoslavia, from National Science Foundation, 1964-67, 1968-69, and from American Council of Learned Societies, 1970 and 1972.

WRITINGS: (Editor and contributor) *A Geography of Europe*, Ronald, 1953, 3rd edition, 1969; (with wife, Viola Hoffman) *Switzerland*, Fideler, 1955, 7th edition, 1973; (contributor) G. E. Pearcy, editor, *World Political Geography*, 2nd edition (Hoffman was not associated with earlier edition), Crowell, 1957; (with Viola Hoffman) *Austria*, Fideler, 1958, 6th edition, 1973; (contributor) Norman J. G. Pounds, editor, *Geographical Essays on Eastern Europe*, Indiana University Press, 1961; (with F. W. Neal) *Yugoslavia and the New Communism*, Twentieth Century, 1962; *The Balkans in Transition*, Van Nostrand, 1963; (editor with others, and contributor) *Eastern Europe: Essays in Geographical Problems*, Methuen, 1971; *Regional Development Strategy in Southeast Europe*, Praeger, 1972.

Co-editor of Searchlight Books, published by Van Nostrand, 1961—. Contributor of articles to *Journal of Geography, Geographic Review, Slavic Review, Economic Geography, Wirtschafts geographie* (Germany), *Geographical Studies* (London), and other professional journals; contributor to numerous encyclopedias. Editor of conference proceedings; member of board of advisers and consultants, *Funk & Wagnalls Encyclopedia*, 1958-61; editorial advisor, Standard Educational Corp., 1966—, Frederick A. Praeger, Inc., 1968-72. Member of board of editors, *The East European Quarterly*, 1969—.

WORK IN PROGRESS: Social and Economic Changes in Europe, East/West linkages.

SIDELIGHTS: Hoffman speaks German and French and reads Serbo-Croatian. *Avocational interests:* Photography, travel, and stamp collecting.

* * *

HOFFMAN, L. Richard 1930-

PERSONAL: Born June 6, 1930; married Roslyn Braverman; children: Cynthia, Karen, Elizabeth, Valerie. *Education:* Queens College, Flushing, N.Y., B.S., 1952; University of Michigan, M.A., 1953, Ph.D., 1957. *Home:* 3731 Aspen St., Flossmoor, Ill. 60422. *Office:* Graduate School of Business, University of Chicago, Chicago, Ill. 60637.

CAREER: University of Michigan, Ann Arbor, associate research psychologist, 1957-59, lecturer, instructor 1958-60, assistant professor, 1960-62, associate professor, 1962-65; University of Chicago, Graduate School of Business, Chicago, Ill., professor of psychology, 1965—. *Member:* American Psychological Association (fellow), Eastern Psychological Association, Midwestern Psychological Association, Society for Applied Anthropology, Sigma Xi.

WRITINGS: (With F. C. Mann) *Automation and the Worker: Social Change in Power Plants*, Holt, 1960; *Are People Really Important in Business?*, University of Chicago, 1968. Contributor of some twenty articles to technical and professional publications.†

* * *

HOFFMAN, Lois Wladis 1929-

PERSONAL: Born March 25, 1929, in Elmira, N.Y.; daughter of Gustave and Etta (Wladis) Wladis; married Martin L. Hoffman (a psychologist), June 24, 1951; children: Amy Gabrielle, Jill Adrienne. *Education:* University of Buffalo, B.A., 1951; Purdue University, M.S., 1953; University of Michigan, Ph.D., 1958. *Home:* 1307 Baldwin Ave., Ann Arbor, Mich.

CAREER: Purdue University, Lafayette, Ind., research fellow in sociology, 1951-53; University of Michigan, Ann Arbor, Flint Metropolitan Research Fellow in Sociology, 1954-55, research assistant, Research Center for Group Dynamics, 1955-56, research associate, 1956-60; Society for Research in Child Development, Ann Arbor, Mich., co-editor of *Review of Child Development Research*, 1962-67; University of Michigan, lecturer, 1967-72, associate professor of psychology, 1972—. Consultant to Michigan Youth Commission's White House Conference Program, 1958-59, to Psychological Clinic, University of Michigan, 1959-60, to Office of Economic Opportunity, 1967-70. *Member:* American Psychological Association, Society for the Psychological Study of Social Issues, Society for Research in Child Development.

WRITINGS: (Contributor) P. Mussen, editor, *Handbook of Research Methods in Child Development*, Wiley, 1960; (author and editor with F. I. Nye) *The Employed Mother in America*, Rand McNally, 1963; (editor with husband, M. L. Hoffman) *Review of Child Development Research*, Russell Sage, Volume I, 1964, Volume II, 1966; (with F. I. Nye) *The Working Mother and the Family*, Jossey-Bass, 1975; (with M. Mednick and S. Tangri) *Women and Achievement*, Holt, 1975. Contributor to *Developmental Psychology, Journal of Social Issues, Child Development*, and other journals in her field.

* * *

HOFFMANN, Charles G. 1921-

PERSONAL: Born August 8, 1921, in Port Washington, Wis.; son of Henry William and Celia (Goldammer) Hoffmann; married Anastasia Carlos (an art teacher), April 28, 1945. *Education:* University of Wisconsin, Ph.B., 1944, Ph.D., 1952; University of Iowa, M.A., 1947. *Home:* 43 Little Rest Rd., Kingston, R.I. *Office:* University of Rhode Island, Kingston, R.I.

CAREER: University of Rhode Island, Kingston, instructor, 1952-55, assistant professor, 1955-58, associate professor, 1958-64, professor of English, 1964—. *Member:* Modern Language Association of America, American Association of University Professors. *Awards, honors:* University of Rhode Island summer fellowship, 1964, to do a series of studies on the manuscript revisions of Ford Madox Ford's novels.

WRITINGS: The Short Novels of Henry James, Bookman Associates, 1957; *Joyce Cary: The Comedy of Freedom*, University of Pittsburgh Press, 1964; *Ford Maddox Ford*, Twayne, 1967. Contributor of literary essays to *South Atlantic Quarterly, Personalist, Modern Fiction Studies*, and half a dozen other journals in that field.

WORK IN PROGRESS: Research for a series of studies on the multiple novel by such authors as Lawrence Durrell, C. P. Snow, and Anthony Powell.†

*　　*　　*

HOFFMANN, Stanley   1928-

PERSONAL: Born November 27, 1928, in Vienna, Austria; came to United States, 1955, became citizen, 1960; married Inge Schneier, October 6, 1963. *Education:* Institut d'Etudes Politiques, Paris, France, diplome, 1948; Paris Law School, doctorate, 1953.

CAREER: Harvard University, Cambridge, Mass., instructor, 1955-57, assistant professor, 1957-59, associate professor, 1959-63, professor, 1963—, Center for International Affairs, research associate, 1961-71, faculty member, 1971—, chairman, West European studies, 1969—. *Military service:* French Army, 1953-55. *Member:* American Academy of Arts and Sciences, American Political Science Association, American Society of International Law, Institut International de Philosophie Politique, Council on Foreign Relations. *Awards, honors:* Carnegie Prize, 1955, for *Organisations Internationales et pouvoirs politiques des Etats.*

WRITINGS: Organisations Internationales et pouvoirs politiques des Etats, Colin, 1954; *Le mouvement Poujade*, Colin, 1956; (editor) *Contemporary Theory in International Relations*, Prentice-Hall, 1960; (co-author) *In Search of France*, Harvard University Press, 1963; *The State of War*, Praeger, 1965; *Gulliver's Troubles: Or the Setting of American Foreign Policy*, McGraw, 1968; (editor) *Conditions of World Order*, Houghton, 1968; (editor with Karl Deutsch) *Relevance of International Law*, Anchor Books, 1971; *Decline or Renewal?*, Viking, 1974; *Solomon's Temple*, Viking, 1974.

WORK IN PROGRESS: A book on U.S. foreign policy, for McGraw.

SIDELIGHTS: Hoffmann is fluent in French and German.

BIOGRAPHICAL/CRITICAL SOURCES: Carolyn Riley, editor, *Contemporary Literary Criticism*, Volume IV, Gale, 1975.

*　　*　　*

HOGAN, Bernice Harris   1929-

PERSONAL: Born January 24, 1929, in Philadelphia, Pa.; daughter of Robert H. (a salesman) and Lily (Garrison) Harris; married Donald Thomas Hogan (a minister), June 30, 1951; children: Carol Louise, Robert Lawrence, Susan Lynn. *Education:* Ursinus College, student, 1947-49; Bethany College, Bethany, W.Va., A.B., 1951; graduate study, Western Illinois University, 1968-72, Kearney State College, 1974. *Religion:* Disciples of Christ. *Home:* 1014 East 33rd St., Kearney, Neb. 68847.

CAREER: Teacher at Abingdon Grade School, Abingdon, Ill., seven years; writer. Japan International Christian Uni-

versity, member of women's planning committee, 1963—; Illinois Disciples of Christ, district chairman of children's work, 1964-65, district chairman, 1965-66. *Member:* Illinois Christian Women's Fellowship, Phi Mu, Abingdon Delphian Club.

WRITINGS—All published by Abingdon, except as indicated: *Abingdon Party Parade*, 1954; *Abingdon Shower Parade*, 1957; *Pre-School Party Parade*, 1958; *More from Your Class Meetings*, 1959; *Now I Lay Me Down to Wonder* (children's book), 1961; *Grains of Sand* (devotional), 1961; *Deborah* (children's book), 1964; *Listen for a Rainbow!* (devotional), Revell, 1965; *Party Planner*, Revell, 1967; *A Small Green Tree and a Square Brick Church* (children's book), 1967; *Fun Party Games*, Revell, 1969.

*　　*　　*

HOHENBERG, John   1906-

PERSONAL: Born February 17, 1906, in New York, N.Y.; son of Louis and Jettchen (Scheuermann) Hohenberg; married Dorothy Lannuier, October 16, 1928. *Education:* University of Washington, Seattle, student, 1922-24; Columbia University, B.Litt., 1927; University of Vienna, graduate study, 1928. *Home:* 90 Morningside Dr., New York, N.Y. 10027; and Aquebogue, N.Y. *Office:* 702 Journalism, Columbia University, New York, N.Y. 10027.

CAREER: Reporter for newspapers in Seattle, Wash., and New York, N.Y., 1923-25; foreign correspondent for United Press and *New York Evening Post*, 1927-28; *New York Post*, New York, N.Y., assistant city editor, 1928-33; *New York Journal-American*, New York, N.Y., political writer and military affairs editor, 1933-42; *New York Post*, United Nations correspondent, 1946-50; Columbia University, New York, N.Y., lecturer in English, 1948, associate in journalism, 1949-50, professor of journalism, 1950—. Special consultant, Office of the Secretary of the U.S. Air Force, 1953-63; secretary of advisory board on the Pulitzer Prizes, 1954—; American specialist traveling in Asia, U.S. State Department, 1963-64; senior specialist, East-West Center, 1967; member of Japanese-American Assembly in Japan, 1967; visiting professor, Chinese University of Hong Kong, 1970-71. *Military service:* U.S. Army, 1943-45. *Member:* Council on Foreign Relations, Overseas Press Club, Columbia Journalism Alumni (president, 1954), Sigma Delta Chi. *Awards, honors:* Pulitzer traveling scholar, 1927-28; visiting fellow, Council on Foreign Relations, 1964-65; Distinguished Service award for journalism research, Sigma Delta Chi, 1964 and 1967; Knight Foundation in Europe grant, 1968-69; Ford Foundation in Asia grant, 1970-71; L.H.D., Wilkes College, 1971.

WRITINGS: The Pulitzer Prize Story, Columbia University Press, 1959; *The Professional Journalist*, Holt, 1960, 3rd edition, 1973; *Foreign Correspondence: The Great Reporters and Their Times*, Columbia University Press, 1964; *The New Front Page*, Columbia University Press, 1965; *Between Two Worlds: Policy, Press, and Public Opinion in Asian-American Relations*, Praeger, for the Council on Foreign Relations, 1967; *The News Media: A Journalist Looks at his Profession*, Holt, 1968; *Free Press/Free People: The Best Cause*, Columbia University Press, 1971; *New Era in the Pacific*, Simon & Schuster, 1973; *A History of the Pulitzer Prizes*, Columbia University Press, 1975.

*　　*　　*

HOLLANDER, Robert   1933-

PERSONAL: Born July 31, 1933, in New York, N.Y.; son

of Robert B. (a stockbroker) and Laurene (McGookey) Hollander; married Jean Abrams (a teacher), April 23, 1964. *Education:* Princeton University, A.B., 1955; Columbia University, Ph.D., 1962.

CAREER: Columbia University, New York, N.Y., instructor in English, 1958-62; Princeton University, Princeton, N.J., assistant professor of European literature, 1962—. *Member:* American Association of University Professors, Cannon Club (Princeton, N.J.).

WRITINGS: (Translator) Andre Malraux, *The Temptation of the West*, Vintage Books, 1961; (compiler) *A Poetry Reader*, American Book Co., 1963; (compiler with Sidney E. Lind) *Literature in English: Stories, Poems, and Plays*; American Book Co., 1966; (with Lind) *The Art of the Story: An Introduction*, American Book Co., 1968; *Allegory in Dante's Commedia*, Princeton University Press, 1969. Contributor of poetry to *Kenyon Review, Second Coming, Georgia Review*, other literary journals.

WORK IN PROGRESS: Studies in *The Divine Comedy.*

SIDELIGHTS: Hollander is competent in French and Italian, knows some German, Russian, Spanish, and Latin.†

*   *   *

HOLLANDER, Sophie Smith   1911-

PERSONAL: Born January 26, 1911, in New York, N.Y.; daughter of Isaac (an insurance agent) and Manya (Boretz) Smith; married A. Gerson Hollander (a physician), September 8, 1942; children: Rina (Mrs. David F. Humphers), Robert J., Edith C., Jonathan A. *Education:* Hunter College (now of the City University of New York), B.A., 1931; Columbia University, M.A., 1932. *Address:* V.A. Center, Martinsburg, W.Va.

CAREER: Free-lance journalist and writer while traveling in Middle East, 1934-36, 1937-38; McKinley Adult School, Berkeley, Calif., teacher of English, 1952-65; Merritt College, Oakland, Calif., teacher of English as a second language, 1965. Also has taught at Berkeley Evening School. Member of California Council on Adult Education and publications director of Berkeley-Albany chapter, 1955-56.

WRITINGS: Impressions of the American, California Book, 1960; *Impressions of The United States*, Holt, 1965.

WORK IN PROGRESS: Book of Common Errors in Usage, classification of broken English by grammar, word order, and idioms.†

*   *   *

HOLLINGSHEAD, August deBelmont   1907-

PERSONAL: Born April 15, 1907, in Lyman, Wyo.; son of William Thomas (a stock breeder) and Daisy (Rollins) Hollingshead; married Carol E. Dempsey, November 4, 1931; children: Anne Marie (Mrs. Gary English Hanna), Ellen Mae (Mrs. Russell Wade Steele). *Education:* University of California, Berkeley, B.A., 1931, M.A., 1933; University of Nebraska, Ph.D., 1935. *Politics:* Republican. *Religion:* Episcopalian. *Home:* Enoch Dr., Woodbridge, Conn. *Office:* Yale University, 1965 Yale Station, New Haven, Conn.

CAREER: Instructor in sociology at University of Iowa, Iowa City, 1935, University of Alabama, University, 1935-36; Indiana University, Bloomington, instructor, 1936-39, assistant professor, 1939-41, associate professor of sociology, 1946-47; Yale University, New Haven, Conn., associate professor, 1947-52, professor of sociology, 1952—,

Sumner Professor of Sociology, 1963—, chairman of department, 1959-65. Visiting summer professor at University of Southern California, 1946-51; visiting professor at University of Chicago, 1948, University of London, 1957-58. U.S. Public Health Service, consultant to Surgeon General, 1950—. National Association for Retarded Children, member of research board, 1960—. *Military service:* U.S. Army Air Forces, 1943-45; became first lieutenant; received General Commendation.

MEMBER: American Sociological Association (executive council, 1953-54; vice-president, 1957), Eastern Sociological Association (executive committee, 1952-55; vice-president, 1957; president, 1959), American Association of University Professors, Sigma Xi, Alpha Kappa Delta (president, 1947-50). *Awards, honors:* Social Science Research Council postdoctoral fellow, 1941-42; senior Fulbright scholar, United Kingdom, 1957-58; McKeever Award of American Sociological Association.

WRITINGS: Personnel of Human Ecology, Barnes & Noble, 1938; *Elmtown's Youth*, Wiley, 1949; (with Fredrick C. Redlich) *Social Class and Mental Illness*, Wiley, 1958; (with Lloyd H. Rogler) *Trapped*, Wiley, 1965; (contributor) H. Rodman, editor, *Marriage, Family, and Society*, Random House, 1965; (contributor) L. Bernstein and C. Burris, editors, *Contributions of the Social Sciences to Psychotherapy*, Thomas, 1967; (with R. S. Duff) *Sickness and Society*, Harper, 1968; (contributor) E. Norbeck, editor, *The Study of Personality*, Holt, 1968; (contributor) A. McC. Lee, editor, *Principles of Sociology*, Barnes & Noble, 1969; (contributor) E. D. Wittkower, editor, *Social Psychiatry*, McGill University Press, 1968; (contributor) D. O. Arnold, editor, *The Sociology of Subcultures*, Glendessary Press, 1970; (contributor) G. H. Morris, editor, *The Mentally Ill and the Right to Treatment*, Thomas, 1971. Contributor to journals in field.

WORK IN PROGRESS: A book with Raymond S. Duff, *Human Group in Patient Care*, a study of medical and surgical patients in a large New England medical center.

AVOCATIONAL INTERESTS: Travel and plant breeding.†

*   *   *

HOLLINGSWORTH, J(oseph) Rogers   1932-

PERSONAL: Born July 26, 1932, in Anniston, Ala.; son of Efford Lawrence and Pearl (Rogers) Hollingsworth; married Ellen Bywaters, September 5, 1957. *Education:* Emory University, B.A., 1954, M.A., 1955; University of Chicago, Ph.D., 1960. *Home:* 5814 Cable Ave., Madison, Wis.

CAREER: University of Chicago, Chicago, Ill., instructor in social science, 1957-59; University of Illinois, Urbana, assistant professor of history, 1960-64; University of Wisconsin, Madison, associate professor of history, 1964—. *Member:* American Sociological Association, American Historical Association. *Awards, honors:* Andrew Mellon postdoctoral fellowship, 1962-63; John Spencer Bassett Memorial Prize, 1964.

WRITINGS: American Democracy: A Documentary Record, Crowell, Volume I, 1961, Volume II, 1962; *The Whirligig of Politics*, University of Chicago Press, 1963; (compiler) *American Expansion in the Late Nineteenth Century: Colonialist or Anticolonialist?*, Holt, 1968; (compiler) *Nation and State Building in America: Comparative Historical Perspectives*, Little, Brown, 1971.

WORK IN PROGRESS: A book on the history of American political parties.†

*   *   *

HOLLOM, Philip Arthur Dominic   1912-

PERSONAL: Born June 9, 1912, in Bickley, Kent, England; son of Arthur and Kate Louisa (Robinson) Hollom; married Nancy Jenefer Bell, October 4, 1947; children: Diana Elizabeth, Mark Richard, Peter Michael. Education: Attended King's School, Bruton, England. Religion: Church of England. Home: Crastock Cottage, Crastock, Woking, England.

CAREER: John Batt and Co. Ltd. (exporters), London, England, secretary and director, 1946-60; Bowmaker Ltd. (financial agents), London, England, secretary, 1960—. Military service: Royal Air Force, pilot, 1940-46; became flight lieutenant. Member: Association of Certified and Corporate Accountants. Awards, honors: Leverhulme research award to study birds in the Middle East, 1955.

WRITINGS: Trapping Methods for Bird Ringers, British Trust for Ornithology, 1950; Popular Handbook of British Birds, Witherby, 1952, 5th edition, 1971; (with Roger Tory Peterson and Guy Mountfort) Field Guide to the Birds of Britain and Europe, Houghton, 1954, 3rd edition, 1974; Popular Handbook of Rarer British Birds, Witherby, 1960. Joint editor, 1951-71, and contributor, British Birds (monthly journal).

SIDELIGHTS: Hollom has made bird watching trips in most European countries, including Bulgaria and Rumania. He has also traveled in Turkey, Syria, Lebanon, Jordan, Iran, North and Central America, North Africa, and the Caribbean.

*   *   *

HOLLOWAY, Robert J.   1921-

PERSONAL: Born September 13, 1921, in Walker, Iowa; son of John Theron and Mabel Marie (Condon) Holloway; married Lois Anita Ita, January 13, 1945; children: Steven Robert, Ann Louise, Bruce Ita. Education: University of Iowa, B.S.C., 1943; Stanford University, M.B.A., 1948, Ph.D., 1952. Religion: Congregational. Home: 1576 Vincent St., St. Paul, Minn.

CAREER: University of Minnesota, Minneapolis, 1950—, professor of marketing, 1957—, chairman of department of business administration, 1957-59. Military service: U.S. Army, 1944-46; became first lieutenant. Member: American Marketing Association (vice-president, 1960; president, 1967-68), Twin Cities Association of Purchasing Agents. Awards, honors: Ford Foundation faculty research grants, 1961-62, 1964-65.

WRITINGS: The Development of the Russian Iron and Steel Industry, Stanford University Press, 1952; A City is More Than People, University of Minnesota Press, 1954; (editor with H. M. Smith) The Effect on Minnesota of a Liberalization of U.S. Foreign Trade Policy, University of Minnesota Press, 1956; Marketing Research and Market Planning for the Small Manufacturer, University of Minnesota Press; (with E. H. Lewis and R. S. Hancock) Growth of the Marketing Concept in Manufacturing Companies, University of Minnesota Press, 1964; (with Hancock) The Environment of Marketing Behavior, Wiley, 1964, 2nd edition, 1973. Contributor to marketing and business journals in the United States and the Philippines.

WORK IN PROGRESS: Business and Society, Demarketing, Business and the Physical Environment.

HOLT, Lee E(lbert)   1912-

PERSONAL: Born March 23, 1912, in Ann Arbor, Mich.; son of Lee Cone (a chemist) and Daisy (Benoliel) Holt; married Margaret Goddard (an art teacher), August 12, 1939; children: Geoffrey Lincoln, Alison. Education: Studied in Germany, 1927-28; Swarthmore College, B.A. (with high honors), 1934; studied in England, 1934-35; Columbia University, M.A., 1936; University of Wisconsin, Ph.D., 1940. Politics: Democrat. Religion: Unitarian Universalist. Home: 40 Northumberland St., Springfield, Mass. 01109. Office: American International College, Springfield Mass. 01109.

CAREER: Indiana University, Bloomington, instructor in English, 1940-42; Union College, Schenectady, N.Y., instructor in English, 1942-43; Williams College, Williamstown, Mass., instructor in physics, 1943-45; U.S. Navy Underwater Sound Laboratory, New London, Conn., technical editor, 1945-47; American International College, Springfield, Mass., 1947—, now professor of English, acting head of department of German, 1954-57. Visiting professor, University of Massachusetts, 1956-57. Broadcaster on eighty educational television programs on English fundamentals and introduction to literature, Springfield, Mass. Member: College English Association (director, New England division, 1957-60, 1961-64; national director, 1960-63), Modern Language Association of America, American Association of University Professors, Springfield Library Association (life member), Phi Beta Kappa.

WRITINGS: (Co-editor) H. C. Goddard, The Meaning of Shakespeare, University of Chicago Press, 1951; Samuel Butler, Twayne, 1964. Author of classified research reports for U.S. Navy Underwater Sound Laboratory, 1945-57. Also author of booklet on tradition and innovation in university adult education, published by Center for the Study of Liberal Education for Adults, 1954. Contributor of articles and reports to Saturday Review, and to literary, historical, and other learned journals. Managing editor of CEA Critic (publication of College English Association), 1950-57.

AVOCATIONAL INTERESTS: Mountain climbing, photography, hi-fi.

*   *   *

HOLTON, Gerald (James)   1922-

PERSONAL: Born May 23, 1922, in Berlin, Germany; became U.S. citizen, 1945; son of Emanuel (an attorney) and Regina (Rossmann) Holton; married Nina Rossfort (a sculptor), September 12, 1947; children: Thomas, Stephan. Education: Wesleyan University, Middletown, Conn., B.A., 1941, M.A., 1942; Brown University, graduate study, 1942-43; Harvard University, M.A., 1946, Ph.D., 1948. Home: 14 Trotting Horse Dr., Lexington, Mass. 02173. Office: 358 Jefferson Physical Laboratory, Harvard University, Cambridge, Mass. 01238.

CAREER: Harvard University, Cambridge, Mass., instructor, 1947-49, assistant professor, 1949-54, associate professor, 1954-59, professor of physics, 1959—. Member of staff, Officers' Radar Course, Harvard University, 1943-45. Exchange professor, Leningrad University, spring, 1962. George Sarton Memorial Lecturer, 1962. National Science Foundation, member of advisory panel for history and philosophy of science, 1963-65, member of advisory committee on ethical and human values impact of science, 1973—. Visiting member, Institute for Advanced Study, Princeton, N.J., 1964, 1967; member, International Scientific Advisory Council of Royaumont Centre, Paris, 1973—. Trustee, Boston Museum of Science, 1965-67, and Van Leer Jerusalem Foundation, 1969-74.

MEMBER: American Physical Society (fellow), American Institute of Physics (chairman of committee on history and philosophy of physics, 1960-73; member of board of governors, 1969—; member of executive committee, 1972—), American Association of Physics Teachers (member of national commission on college physics, 1960-64), American Academy of Arts and Sciences (fellow; editor, 1957-63), American Association for the Advancement of Science (fellow; vice-president of section on history and philosophy of science, 1961-62; member of council, 1962-73; member of board of directors, 1967-71), National Academy of Science (member of committee on communication with scholars in the People's Republic of China), Federation of American Scientists (member of council, 1963-65, 1968-71), Academie Internationale d'Histoire des Sciences, Phi Beta Kappa, Sigmi Xi. Awards, honors: National Science Foundation faculty fellow in Paris, 1960-61; Outstanding Achievement Citation, Wesleyan University Convocation in Honor of Scholarship, 1961; Distinguished Service Citation, American Association of Physics Teachers, 1962; Doctor of Science, Grinnell College, 1967; Robert A. Millikan Award and Medal, 1967.

WRITINGS: Introduction to Concepts and Theories of Physical Science, Addison-Wesley, 1952, 2nd edition, 1973; (with Duane H. D. Roller) Foundations of Modern Physical Science, Addison-Wesley, 1958; (editor) Science and the Modern Mind, Beacon, 1958; (editor with Stephen R. Graubard) Excellence and Leadership in a Democracy, Columbia University Press, 1962; (member of editorial committee) Collected Papers on Experimental Physics of P. W. Bridgman, Harvard University Press, 1964; (editor) Science and Culture, Houghton, 1965; (with others) The Project Physics Course, Holt, 1970; (editor) The Twentieth Century Sciences: Studies in the Biography of Ideas, Norton, 1972; Thematic Origins of Scientific Thought, Harvard University Press, 1973. Editor, Daedalus (quarterly of American Academy of Arts and Sciences), 1958-61. Member of editorial board, Daedalus, Synthese, Minerva, Graduate Journal (University of Texas), Archives for the History of Exact Sciences, Historical Studies in the Physical Sciences, and Source Book in History of Science, published by Harvard University Press.

WORK IN PROGRESS: Experimental Physics at High Pressures, and History of Physics.

*   *   *

HOLZER, Hans   1920-

PERSONAL: Born January 26, 1920, in Vienna, Austria; son of Leo (a businessman) and Martha (Stransky) Holzer; married Countess Catherine de Buxhoeveden, September 29, 1962; children: Nadine Joan, Alexandra. Education: Attended University of Vienna and Columbia University; College of Applied Science, M.A. Politics: Liberal. Religion: Episcopalian. Home: 140 Riverside Dr., New York, N.Y. 10024.

CAREER: Author and parapsychologist, known as "The Ghost Hunter"; has appeared as guest expert on extrasensory perception, ghosts, and haunted houses on Mike Wallace, Betty Furness, Steve Allen, Johnny Carson, and Art Linkletter shows, and on other radio and television programs; produced documentary films and radio series on ESP, 1964-65, 1972; editor-in-chief of EPS News Syndicate, New York, N.Y., 1948-53, and columnist for Psychic News; writer-producer of musical revues staged Off-Broadway, writer of night club acts, and composer-lyricist of recorded songs; parapsychlogoist and research director, New York Committee for the Investigation of Paranormal Occurences; research director, American Society for the Occult Sciences; professor of parapsychology, New York Institute of Technology; fellow, College of Psychic Studies; visiting instructor, La Verne College, 1972. Member: American Federation of Television and Radio Artists, Screen Actors Guild, Writers Guild of America, American Society of Composers, Authors and Publishers, American Guild of Authors and Composers, Archeological Institute of America (fellow), French Numismatic Society (corresponding member), Austrian Numismatic Society (corresponding member), New York Historical Society, Kit Kat Club (vice-president). Awards, honors: Grant from Parapsychology Foundation for investigation of haunted houses in New York, 1960-61.

WRITINGS: Ghost Hunter, Bobbs-Merrill, 1963; Ghosts I've Met, Bobbs-Merrill, 1965; Collector's Guidebook to Coins: How and Why to Collect, Stories Behind Famous, Valuable Coins of the World, All American Denominations, Maco, 1965; Yankee Ghosts, Bobbs-Merrill, 1966; The Lively Ghosts of Ireland, Bobbs-Merrill, 1967; ESP and You, Hawthorn, 1968; Ghosts of the Golden West, Bobbs-Merrill, 1968; Predictions: Fact or Fallacy, Hawthorn, 1968; Psychic Investigators, Hawthorn, 1968; Star in the East, Harper, 1968; Life After Death: The Challenge and the Evidence, Bobbs-Merrill, 1969; Psychic Photography: Threshold of a New Science, McGraw, 1969; The Truth About Witchcraft, Doubleday, 1969; Window to the Past: Exploring History Through ESP, Doubleday, 1969.

Born Again, Doubleday, 1970; Gothic Ghosts, Bobbs-Merrill, 1970; The Zodiac Affairs, Universal Publishing, 1970; The Psychic World of Bishop Pike, Crown, 1970; Charismatics: How to Make Things Happen, Coward, 1971; Psycho-ecstasy: How to Awaken the Secret Powers of Your Inner Self, Nash Publishing, 1971; The Ghosts That Walk in Washington, Doubleday, 1971; The Prophets Speak: What the Leading Psychics Say About the World of Tomorrow, Bobbs-Merrill, 1971; Hans Holzer's Haunted Houses: A Pictorial Register of the World's Most Interesting Ghost Houses, Crown, 1972; The Handbook of Parapsychology, Nash, 1972; Phantoms of Dixie, Bobbs-Merrill, 1972; The New Pagans, Doubleday, 1972; The Habsburg Curse, Doubleday, 1973; The Power of Hypnosis: How Mind-to-Mind Communication Works, Bobbs-Merrill, 1973; The Witchcraft Report, Ace Books, 1973; The Vegetarian Way of Life, Pyramid, 1973; Red Chindvit Conspiracy, Universal Publishing, 1973; Possessed!, Fawcett, 1973; Beyond Medicine: The Facts About Unorthodox and Psychic Healing, Regnery, 1973; The Alchemy Deception, Universal Publishing, 1973; Haunted Hollywood, Bobbs-Merrill, 1974; Patterns of Destiny: A Primer on Reincarnation, Nash Publishing, 1974; The Unicorn, Universal Publishing, 1974; The Aquarian Age, Bobbs-Merrill, 1974.

Also author of revues and stage productions, including "Hotel Excelsior," 1956; "A La Carte," 1958; "Adam and Evenings," 1963. Contributor to Cosmopolitan, Mademoiselle, Exploring the Unknown, London Mystery Magazine, and others. Drama and music critic, Sporting Review, 1949-60; theatre columnist, Dance, 1952-55.

HOMBERGER, Conrad P. 1900-

PERSONAL: Born October 12, 1900, in Germany; son of Paul (a judge) and Pauline (Schulmann) Homberger; married Ann Mary Rasberger, May, 1931. *Education:* Studied at University of Munich and University of Erlangen, 1919-24, Ph.D., 1924; additional study at Harvard University, 1942-43, Columbia University, 1945-48. *Office:* Polytechnic Institute of Brooklyn, 333 Jay St., Brooklyn, N.Y. 11201.

CAREER: Lawyer in Munich, Germany, 1927-36; Polytechnic Institute of Brooklyn, Brooklyn, N.Y., 1948—, started as instructor, professor of modern languages, 1963—. *Member:* Linguistic Society of America, Modern Language Association of America, American Association of Teachers of German.

WRITINGS: (With John Ebelke) *Foundation Course in German*, Heath, 1958, revised edition, 1964; (translator into German) Edward Sapir, *Die Sprache (Language)*, Max Hueber (Munich), 1961; (with Rechtschaffen) *Phonetic English-German, German-English Dictionary*, Monarch Books, 1964; (with Rechtschaffen and Bobetski) *Literatur fuer den Deutschunterricht*, American Book Co., Book I, 1964, Book 2, 1965; (with Rechtschaffen) *Kurze Deutsche Grammatik*, American Book Co., 1965; (editor) Erich Kaestner and Frank Wedekind, *Ein Abend in den Muenchner Kammerspielen* (German reader for colleges), Scribner, 1965; *Rueckschau und Fortschritt: A Continuation Course in German*, Heath, 1969; (compiler with Rechtschaffen) *German for Research: Humanities and Social Sciences*, Random House, 1973. Contributor to *German Quarterly, Educational Theory, Modern Language Journal*, and other journals.

WORK IN PROGRESS: Advanced Course in German, for Heath.

SIDELIGHTS: In addition to German, Homberger is competent in Latin, Italian, Spanish and French. *Avocational interests:* Reading in history, philosophy, government, and science.†

* * *

HOMER, William Innes 1929-

PERSONAL: Born November 8, 1929, in Merion, Pa.; son of Austin (an executive) and Evelyn Homer; married Virginia Keller, August 14, 1954. *Education:* Princeton University, A.B., 1951; New York University, graduate student, 1952-53; Harvard University, M.A., 1954, Ph.D., 1961. *Home:* 15 Dickinson Lane, Wilmington, Del. 19807. *Office:* Department of Art History, University of Delaware, Newark, Del. 19711.

CAREER: Princeton University, Princeton, N.J., instructor in department of art and archaeology, 1955-59, lecturer, 1959-61, assistant professor, 1961-64; Cornell University, Ithaca, N.Y., associate professor of history of art, 1965-66; University of Delaware, Newark, professor of art history and chairman of department, 1966—, professor of Winterthur Program in Early American Culture, 1966—. Member of corporation, Museum of Art, Ogunquit, Me., 1958—, of advisory committee, American Studies Institute of Lincoln University, 1967—, of exhibition committee of Delaware Art Museum, 1968—; chairman of overseas screening committee of Fulbright-Hays Fellowship Awards, 1971—.

MEMBER: American Studies Association, Royal Society of Arts (fellow), College Art Association of America, Society of Architectural Historians, American Society for Aesthetics, History of Science Society, Athenaeum (Philadelphia), Historical Society of Princeton, Wilmington Society of Fine Arts, Princeton Club (New York). *Awards, honors:* Council of the Humanities fellowship, Princeton University, 1962-63; American Council of Learned Societies fellowship, 1964-65; Guggenheim fellowship, 1972-73; Princeton University, visiting fellow, 1972-73.

WRITINGS: Georges Seurat: Port-en-Bessin, Minneapolis Institute of Arts, 1957; *A Catalogue of the Ceramic Sculpture of Carl Walters*, Museum of Art of Ogunquit, 1958; *Books on American Art, 1607-1900: A Selected Bibliography*, Special Program in American Civilization, Princeton University, 1963; *Seurat and the Science of Painting*, M.I.T. Press, 1964, 2nd edition, 1971; (with Violet Organ) *Robert Henri and His Circle*, Cornell University Press, 1969. Contributor to *Encyclopedia of World Art*, and to *Art Quarterly, Burlington Magazine, Connoisseur, Art in America*, and other art journals. Member of editorial board, *America Art Journal*, 1970—.

WORK IN PROGRESS: Research and writing on American painting, 1890-1920, and on the Neo-Impressionist movement in French painting.†

* * *

HONEY, P(atrick) J(ames) 1922-

PERSONAL: Born December 16, 1922, in Navan, County Meath, Eire; son of Michael W. and C. Edith (Clarke) Honey; married Frances Mary Knox Watson, July 28, 1945; children: Michael Peter, Fiona Mary, Alison Frances. *Education:* Studied at Birkbeck College, University of London, 1940-41, University College, University of London, 1946-49, B.A. (honors), 1949. *Politics:* Unaffiliated. *Home:* 43 Royston Park Rd., Hatch End, Middlesex, England.

CAREER: School of Oriental and African Studies, University of London, London, England, lecturer in Vietnamese language and institutions, 1949—, reader in Vietnamese studies, 1964; British Broadcasting Corp., Asian Service, London, England, supervisor of Vietnamese program, 1951—. *Military service:* Royal Navy, 1941-46; became lieutenant. *Member:* Royal Asiatic Society (fellow), Philological Society.

WRITINGS: Lich-Su Viet-Nam, Truong Dai Hoc, 1957; *Historians of South East Asia*, edited by D. G. E. Hall, Oxford University Press, 1958; *Politics in South and South East Asia*, edited by S. Rose, Macmillan, 1963; (editor) *North Vietnam Today*, Praeger, 1963; *Communism in North Vietnam*, Massachusetts Institute of Technology Press, 1963; *Genesis of a Tragedy: The Historical Background to the Vietnam War*, Benn, 1968; *North Vietnam and Its Neighbours*, Institute for the Study of Conflict, 1971; *Vietnam: If the Communists Won*, American Friends of Vietnam, 1971. Writer of television documentaries, "The Quiet War," and "Watch on the Mekong." Contributor to *China News Analysis, China Quarterly, Soviet Survey, Encounter, Pacific Affairs*, and other journals.

WORK IN PROGRESS: A Modern History of Vietnam, other writing on developments in North and South Vietnam.

AVOCATIONAL INTERESTS: Classical archaeology, travel (has visited most parts of the world with the exception of the Soviet Union and South America).†

HONNOLD, John Otis, Jr. 1915-

PERSONAL: Born December 5, 1915, in Kansas, Ill.; son of John Otis and Louretta (Wright) Honnold; married Annamarie Kunz, June 26, 1939; children: Carol (Mrs. Vinton Deming), Heidi (Mrs. David Spencer), Edward E. Education: University of Illinois, A.B., 1936; Harvard University, LL.B., 1949, converted to J.D. Politics: Democrat. Religion: Society of Friends. Home: Braxmar Drive South, Harrison, N.Y. 10528. Office: United Nations, Room 3464A, New York, N.Y. 10017.

CAREER: Wright, Gordon, Zachry & Parlin, New York, N.Y., attorney, 1939-41; U.S. Securities and Exchange Commission, Washington, D.C., attorney, 1941; U.S. Office of Price Administration, Washington, D.C., chief of court review, 1942-46; University of Pennsylvania, Philadelphia, assistant professor, 1946-49, associate professor, 1949-52, professor of constitutional law, sales, and sales financing, 1952-69; United Nations, New York, N.Y., Office of Legal Affairs, secretary of Commission on International Trade Law, 1969-74, chief of International Trade Law Branch, 1969—. Salzburg Seminar in American Studies, chairman 1963, 1966, and faculty member, 1960. Member, U.S. delegation and drafting committee, Diplomatic Conference on Uniform Law for International Sales, The Hague, 1964. Member: American Bar Association, Societe de Legislation Comparee, American Friends Service Committee, (member of board and executive committee, 1967-69), Phi Beta Kappa, Phi Kappa Phi. Awards, honors: Fulbright research scholar, University of Paris, 1957-58; Guggenheim fellow, 1958.

WRITINGS: (Editor) Sales and Sales Financing—Cases and Materials, Foundation Press, 1954, 3rd edition, 1968; (editor with Edward L. Barrett, Jr. and Paul W. Bruton) Constitutional Law, Cases and Materials, Foundation Press, 1959, 3rd edition, 1968; (editor) The Life of the Law: Readings on the Growth of Legal Institutions, Free Press of Glencoe, 1964; (with Allan Farnsworth) Commercial Law, Cases and Materials, Foundation Press, 1965, 2nd edition, 1968; Unification of the Law Governing International Sales of Goods, Librairie Dalloz (Paris), 1966.

WORK IN PROGRESS: A general book on constitutional law.

* * *

HOOFNAGLE, Keith Lundy 1941-

PERSONAL: Born June 20, 1941, in Bremerton, Wash.; son of John Raymond (a businessman) and Alice M. (Murdach) Hoofnagle. Education: Studied at Everett Junior College, 1959-60, Burnley School of Professional Art, 1960, and Washington State University, part-time, 1960-65. Home: Siskin Farm Rt. 1 Box 95, Harpers Ferry, W.Va. 25425. Agent: Vinson Brown, 8339 West Dry Creek Rd., Healdsburg, Calif.

CAREER: U.S. Department of the Interior, National Park Service, park ranger and exhibit planner; freelance graphic designer and illustrator. Member: Delta Phi Delta. Awards, honors: Award of Distinctive Merit for achievement in graphic arts, Advertising and Sales Association of Spokane, 1962.

WRITINGS: The Story of Linda Lookout (self-illustrated), Naturegraph, 1965; Park Ranger!, Yellowstone Library and Museum Association, 1971.

WORK IN PROGRESS: Booklet on National Park areas in the Southwest and children's picture books.

AVOCATIONAL INTERESTS: Film-making, animation, painting, natural sciences and nature study, conservation and ecology.

* * *

HOOVER, Edgar M. 1907-

PERSONAL: Born February 22, 1907, in Boise, Idaho; son of Edgar M. and Mary Jane (Redfield) Hoover; married Mary Frances Wolfe (now a social worker), January 31, 1934; children: William G., Peter R. Education: Harvard University, A.M., 1928, Ph.D., 1932. Home: 15331 Bohlman Rd., Saratoga, Calif. 95070.

CAREER: Harvard University, Cambridge, Mass., instructor and tutor in economics, 1934-36; University of Michigan, Ann Arbor, 1936-47, began as assistant professor of economics, became professor; U.S. government, Washington, D.C., served with National Resources Planning Board and Office of Price Administration, 1942, as member of staff of President's Council of Economic Advisers, 1947-52, as member of Board of National Estimates, Central Intelligence Agency, 1952-54; Princeton University, Princeton, N.J., economist, Office of Population Research, 1954-56; Harvard University, Cambridge, Mass., visiting professor of economics, 1957-59; University of Pittsburgh, Pittsburgh, Pa., distinguished service professor of economics, 1959-72, distinguished service professor emeritus, 1972—, director of Center for Regional Economic Studies, 1962-65. Military service: U.S. Navy, assigned to Research and Analysis Branch, Office of Strategic Services, 1943-46; served in Europe, 1945; became lieutenant.

MEMBER: American Economic Association, Population Association of America, Regional Science Association (president, 1962), Cosmos Club (Washington, D.C.), Phi Beta Kappa. Awards, honors: Henry Russel Award, University of Michigan, 1940.

WRITINGS: Location Theory and the Shoe and Leather Industries, Harvard University Press, 1937, reprinted, Johnson Reprint, 1968; The Economic Effects of the St. Lawrence Power Project, U.S. Government Printing Office, 1941; (co-author) Industrial Location and National Resources, National Resources Planning Board, 1942; Economia Geografica, Fondo de Cultura Economica, 1943, published as The Location of Economic Activity, McGraw, 1948.

(With Ansley J. Coale) Population Growth and Economic Development in Low-Income Countries, Princeton University Press, 1958; (with Raymond Vernon) Anatomy of a Metropolis, Harvard University Press, 1959; (with Barbara R. Berman and Benjamin Chinitz) Projection of a Metropolis, Harvard University Press, 1960; (co-author and study director) Economic Study of the Pittsburgh Region, Volume I, Region in Transition, Volume II, Portrait of a Region, Volume III, Region with a Future, University of Pittsburgh Press, for Pittsburgh Regional Planning Association, 1964; The Evolving Form and Organization of the Metropolis, Center for Regional Economic Studies, University of Pittsburgh, 1967; An Introduction to Regional Economics, Knopf, 1971.

Contributor: The Growth of the American Economy, edited by Harold F. Williamson, Prentice-Hall, 1944, 2nd edition, 1951; Problems in the Study of Economic Growth, National Bureau of Economic Research, 1949; American Economic History, edited by Seymour E. Harris, McGraw, 1960; Taxes and Economic Growth in Michigan, edited by Paul W. McCracken, Upjohn, 1960; Planning and the Urban

Community, edited by Harvey Perloff, Carnegie Institute of Technology and University of Pittsburgh Press, 1961; *Design of Regional Accounts*, edited by Werner Hochwald, Johns Hopkins Press, 1961; *Men Without Work*, edited by Stanley Lebergott, Prentice-Hall, 1964.

Contributor to published conference reports. Also contributor of about twenty-five articles and book reviews to economic, business, and statistical journals.

WORK IN PROGRESS: Projects in regional economics and economics of population.

SIDELIGHTS: The Location of Economic Activity was published in Mexico, France, and Poland. Hoover has various degrees of competence in French, Spanish, German, and Polish.

*   *   *

HOPE, Quentin M(anning)   1923-

PERSONAL: Born January 25, 1923, in Stamford, Conn.; son of Frank R. and Blanche (Lovett) Hope; married Nathalie Weaver, May 22, 1944; children: Kenneth, Geoffrey, Persis. *Education:* Harvard University, B.A., 1942, M.A. 1946; Columbia University, Ph.D., 1956. *Home:* 910 South Highland, Bloomington, Ind. *Office:* Department of French and Italian, Indiana University, Bloomington, Ind.

CAREER: High school teacher of French, 1946-51; Wesleyan University, Middletown, Conn., instructor in French, 1953-56; Indiana University, Bloomington, assistant professor, 1956-61, associate professor of French, 1961—. Served with American Field Service in North Africa, Italy, and France, 1943-45. *Member:* Modern Language Association of America, American Association of Teachers of French, American Association of University Professors. *Awards, honors:* Fulbright fellowship, 1962-63.

WRITINGS: Saint-Evremond; The "Honnete Homme" as Critic, Indiana University Press, 1962; *Spoken French in Review*, Macmillan, 1963; *Reading French for Comprehension*, Macmillan, 1965. Contributor of articles and reviews to *French Review, Romanic Review, Esprit createur*, and other journals.

WORK IN PROGRESS: The Imagery of Snow in European Literature.

*   *   *

HOPE SIMPSON, Jacynth   1930-

PERSONAL: Born November 10, 1930, in Birmingham, England; daughter of Frank and Mabelle (Brooks) Cureton; married Dermot Hope Simpson (a headmaster), August 3, 1955; children: Elinor. *Education:* University of Lausanne, student, 1949; Oxford University, M.A. and Diploma of Education, 1953. *Religion:* Church of England. *Home:* The Red House, Hartley Rd., Plymouth, England.

CAREER: Teacher of senior English at Bournemouth School for Girls, Bournemouth, Hampshire, England, 1953-54, at Croham Hurst School, Croydon, Surrey, England, 1954-57; examiner for Cambridge and Oxford General Certificates of Education, 1957-58; author, 1958—.

WRITINGS—Novels: *The Bishop of Kenelminster*, Putnam, 1961; *The Bishop's Picture*, Putnam, 1962; *The Unravished Bride*, Putnam, 1963.

Children's books—All published by Hamish Hamilton, except as indicated: *Anne, Young Swimmer*, Constable, 1959, *The Stranger in the Train*, 1960, *Young Netball Player*, Constable, 1961, *The Great Fire*, 1961, *Danger on

the Line, 1962, *The Man Who Came Back*, 1962, *The Ice Fair*, 1963, *The Ninepenney*, 1964, *The Witch's Cave*, 1964, (editor) *Hamish Hamilton Book of Myths and Legends*, 1963, *The Edge of the World*, 1965, Coward, 1966; (editor) *A Cavalcade of Witches*, 1966, Walck, 1967; (editor) *The Hamish Hamilton Book of Witches*, 1966; *The Unknown Island*, 1968, Coward, 1969; *The Curse of the Dragon's Gold: European Myths and Legends*, Doubleday, 1969; *Elizabeth I*, 1971; (compiler) *Tales in School: An Anthology of Boarding-School Life*, 1971.

WORK IN PROGRESS: A novel for older children, *The Butterfly Man.*

AVOCATIONAL INTERESTS: Foreign travel, especially with reference to art and architecture.†

*   *   *

HORAN, James David   1914-

PERSONAL: Born July 27, 1914, in New York, N.Y.; son of Eugene (a newspaperman) and Elizabeth (Schaub) Horan; married Gertrude Dorrity, September 4, 1938; children: Patricia, Brian Boru, Gary, James C. *Education:* Drake College, New Jersey, student, two years. *Politics:* Independent. *Religion:* Catholic. *Home:* 27 Woods Rd., Groat Notch, Little Falls, N.J. 07424.

CAREER: New York Journal-American, New York, N.Y., 1930-66, assistant city editor, 1936, war correspondent, 1942-45, special events editor, 1955, assistant managing editor, 1961, Sunday editor, 1964. Novelist and historian. Co-producer of television series, "Turnpike"; story editor and technical adviser and scriptwriter, "The D.A.'s Man"; story editor of television series, "The Black Cat"; commentator, "Armstrong-Circle Theatre Hour" show, "Assignment, Teen-age Junkie."

MEMBER: Western Writers of America, New York Civil War Round Table (president, 1956-57), New York City Reporters Association, Westerners (co-founder, New York Corral; sheriff, 1952-53). *Awards, honors:* Edgar Allan Poe Award ("Edgar") of Mystery Writers of America, 1957; Westerners, New York Posse Buffalo Award, 1960, for *The Great American West*, and 1970, for *The Life and Art of Charles Schreyvogel*; special award, New Jersey Association of Teachers of English, 1960, 1962; Western Heritage Award, 1961; New York Reporters Association Gold Typewriter Award, 1961; American Newspaper Guild Page One Citation, 1961.

WRITINGS: (Editor with Gerold Frank) *Out in the Boondocks: Marines in Action in the Pacific, 21 U.S. Marines Tell Their Stories*, Putnam, 1943; (editor with Frank) *U.S.S. Seawolf: Submarine Raider in the Pacific* (as told by J. M. Eckbert), Putnam, 1945; *Action Tonight: The Story of the Destroyer O'Bannon in the Pacific*, Putnam, 1945; *Desperate Men: Revelations from the Sealed Pinkerton File*, Putnam, 1949, revised edition, Doubleday, 1962.

(With Howard Swiggett) *The Pinkerton Story*, Putnam, 1951; *Desperate Women*, Putnam, 1952; *King's Rebel* (novel), Crown, 1953; *Confederate Agent: A Discovery in History*, Crown, 1954; (with Paul Sann) *Pictorial History of the Wild West*, Crown, 1954, new edition, Spring Books, 1961; *Mathew Brady: Historian with a Camera*, Crown, 1955, 11th revised edition, 1974; *Across the Cimarron*, Crown, 1956; (with Harold R. Danforth) *The D.A.'s Man*, Crown, 1957; *Seek Out and Destroy* (novel), Crown, 1958;

The Wild Bunch, New American Library, 1958, revised edition, 1970; *The Great American West: A Pictorial History from Coronado to the Last Frontier*, Crown, 1959; *The Mob's Man*, Crown, 1959.

(With H. R. Danforth) *Big City Crimes*, Permabooks, 1960; (editor) James Iredell Waddell, *C.S.S. Shenandoah*, Crown, 1960; *The Shadow Catcher* (novel), Crown, 1961; *The Desperate Years: A Pictorial History of the Thirties*, Crown, 1962; *The Seat of Power* (novel), Crown, 1965; *Timothy O'Sullivan: American's Forgotten Photographer*, Doubleday, 1966; *The Right Image* (novel) Crown, 1967; *The Pinkerton's: The Detective Dynasty that Made History*, Crown, 1967.

The Life and Art of Charles Schreyvogel, Crown, 1970; *The Blue Messiah* (novel), Crown, 1971; *The Mc-Kenney–Hall Portrait Gallery of American Indians*, Crown, 1972; (editor with wife, Gertrude Horan), *Gunner's Mate: The Autobiography of J. B. Stuart*, Crown, 1975; *Face and Voice of America's Wild, Wild West*, Crown, 1975; *The Disenchanted Seven*, Crown, in press.

WORK IN PROGRESS: A series of books about the Western frontier of which *Face and Voice of America's Wild, Wild West* is the first.

SIDELIGHTS: The Pinkerton's was sold to the RME group to be produced as a television series.

* * *

HORDERN, William (Edward) 1920-

PERSONAL: Born September 8, 1920, in Dundurn, Saskatchewan, Canada; son of Paul Sylvester and Ethyl (Davis) Hordern; married Marjorie E. Joyce, January 28, 1944; children: Richard, Joyce, Davis. *Education:* University of Saskatchewan, B.A., 1941; St. Andrew's College, Saskatoon, Saskatchewan, Canada, B.D., 1945; Union Theological Seminary, New York, N.Y., S.T.M., 1946, Th.D., 1951. *Politics:* Independent. *Home:* 2 Morton Pl., Saskatoon, Saskatchewan, Canada.

CAREER: Ordained minister, United Church of Canada, 1945. Pastor, St. John's Lutheran Church, Richmond Hill, N.Y., 1945-49; Union Theological Seminary, New York, N.Y., instructor in religion, 1946-48; Swarthmore College, Swarthmore, Pa., associate professor of religion, 1949-57; Garrett Biblical Institute, Evanston, Ill., professor of religion, 1949-57; Garrett Biblical Institute, Evanston, Ill., professor of systematic theology, 1957-60, Henry Pfeiffer Professor, 1960-66; Lutheran Theological Seminary, Saskatoon, Saskatchewan, president, 1966—. Assistant pastor, Trinity Lutheran Church, Skokie, Ill., 1960-66. Crozer Theological Seminary, Chester, Pa., visiting professor. Broadcaster on thirteen-week television series, "The Teachings of Jesus," WTTW, Chicago, Ill. *Member:* American Theological Society, American Academy of Religion (president, 1966).

WRITINGS: Christianity, Communism and History, Abingdon, 1954; *A Layman's Guide to Protestant Theology*, Macmillan, 1955, revised edition, 1968; *The Case for a New Reformation Theology*, Westminster, 1959; *Speaking of God*, Macmillan, 1964; (editor) *New Directions in Theology Today*, Westminster Press, Volume I: *Introduction to Theology Today*, 1966. Contributor of articles to some thirty periodicals.†

* * *

HORGAN, Paul 1903-

PERSONAL: Born August 1, 1903, in Buffalo, N.Y.; son of Edward Daniel and Rose Marie (Rohr) Horgan. *Education:* Attended New Mexico Military Institute, 1920-23. *Religion:* Roman Catholic. *Office:* Wesleyan University, Middletown, Conn.

CAREER: Author and novelist. Eastman Theatre, Rochester, N.Y., production staff, 1923-26; New Mexico Military Institute, Roswell, librarian, 1926-42, assistant to president, 1947-49; Wesleyan University, Middletown, Conn., fellow of Center for Advanced Studies, 1959, 1961, director of center, 1962-67, adjunct professor of English, 1967-71, professor emeritus and author in residence, 1971—. Member of board of managers, School of American Research; president of board of directors, Roswell Museum, 1948-55; chairman of board of directors, Santa Fe Opera, 1958-71; member of board of directors, Roswell Public Library, 1958-62; lay trustee, St. Joseph's College, West Hartford, Conn., 1964-68; member of advisory board, J. S. Guggenheim Foundation, 1961-67; Book-of-the-Month Club, member of board of judges, 1969-72, associate, 1972—; Saybrook College of Yale University, Hoyt Fellow, 1965, associate fellow, 1966; Aspen Institute for Humanistic Studies, scholar in residence, 1968, 1971, 1973, fellow, 1973—; visiting lecturer, University of Iowa, 1946, Yale University, 1969. *Military service:* U.S. Army, 1942-46; became lieutenant colonel; temporary active duty with U.S. Department of the Army general staff, 1952; received Legion of Merit.

MEMBER: National Institute of Arts and Letters, American Catholic Historical Association (president, 1960), National Council of the Humanities, Phi Beta Kappa, Athenaeum Club (London), Century Club, and University Club (New York), Army-Navy Club and Cosmos Club (Washington, D.C.). *Awards, honors:* Harper Prize Novel Award ($7,500), 1933, for *The Fault of Angels*; Guggenheim fellowship, 1945, 1959; Pulitzer Prize in history, Bancroft Prize of Columbia University, both for *Great River: The Rio Grande in North American History*, 1955; Campion Award for eminent service to Catholic letters, 1957; created Knight of St. Gregory, 1957. Litt.D. from Wesleyan University, 1956, Southern Methodist University, 1957, University of Notre Dame, 1958, Boston College, 1958, New Mexico State University, 1961, College of the Holy Cross, 1962, University of New Mexico, 1963, Fairfield University, 1964; D.H.L. from Canisius College, 1960, Georgetown University, 1963, Lincoln College, 1968, Loyola College, Baltimore, 1968, D'Youville College, 1968, St. Bonaventure University, 1970, La Salle University, 1971, Catholic University of America, 1973.

WRITINGS: Men of Arms, McKay, 1931; *The Fault of Angels*, Harper, 1933; *No Quarter Given*, Harper, 1935; *From the Royal City of the Holy Faith of St. Francis of Assisi*, Rydal, 1936; *Main Line West* (also see below), Harper, 1936; *Return of the Weed* (short stories), Harper, 1936 (published in England as *Lingering Walls*, Constable, 1936); *A Lamp on the Plains*, Harper, 1937; (editor with Maurice G. Fulton) *New Mexico's Own Chronicle*, Upshaw, 1937; *Far from Cibola* (also see below), Harper, 1938; *The Habit of Empire*, Rydal, 1938.

Figures in a Landscape, Harper, 1940; (author of biographical introduction) *Diary and Letters of Josiah Gregg*, University of Oklahoma Press, Volume I, 1941, Volume II, 1943; *The Common Heart* (also see below), Harper, 1942; (in collaboration with editors of *Look* magazine) *Look at America: The Southwest*, Houghton, 1947.

The Devil in the Desert, Longmans, Green, 1952; *One Red*

Rose for Christmas, Longmans, Green, 1952; Great River: The Rio Grande in North American History, two volumes, Rinehart, 1954; Humble Powers (three novelettes) Macmillan (London), 1954, Image Books, 1956; The Saintmaker's Christmas Eve, Farrar, Straus, 1955; The Centuries of Santa Fe, Dutton, 1956; Rome Eternal, Farrar, Straus, 1959.

A Distant Trumpet, Farrar, Straus, 1960; Citizen of New Salem, Farrar, Straus, 1961 (published in England as Abraham Lincoln, Citizen of New Salem, Macmillan, 1961); Mountain Standard Time (includes Main Line West, Far from Cibola, The Common Heart), Farrar, Straus, 1962; Conquistadors in North American History, Farrar, Straus, 1963 (published in England as Conquistadors in North America, Macmillan, 1963); Toby and the Nighttime, Farrar, Straus, 1963; Things as They Are, Farrar, Straus, 1964; Peter Hurd: A Portrait Sketch from Life, Amon G. Carter Museum-University of Texas Press, 1965; Songs After Lincoln, Farrar, Straus, 1965; Memories of the Future, Farrar, Straus, 1966; The Peach Stone: Stories from Four Decades, Farrar, Straus, 1967; Everything to Live For (novel), Farrar, Straus, 1968.

The Heroic Triad, Holt, 1970; Whitewater (novel; selection of Book-of-the Month Club, Literary Guild, Reader's Digest Condensed Book Club), Farrar, Straus, 1970; (editor and author of introduction and commentary) Maurice Baring Restored, Farrar, Straus, 1970; Encounters with Stravinsky: A Personal Record, Farrar, Straus, 1971; Approaches to Writing, Farrar, Straus, 1973.

Librettist, A Tree on the Plains, an American opera with music by Ernst Bacon, 1942. Also author of play, "Yours, A. Lincoln," 1942. Contributor of fiction and nonfiction to periodicals.

SIDELIGHTS: In assessing the body of Horgan's work, Lawrence Clark Powell wrote: "To be read in his own time should be reward enough for any writer. The rest is vanity. One's ultimate reputation is a mystery. 'My books are a lottery ticket,' Stendahl said in 1844, 'and the drawing won't occur for a hundred years.' What good was it to him that his ticket came up a winner in our time? ... It is useless to speculate on which books of Paul Horgan's will be read the longest. Perhaps it will be the river history and the biography of the archbishop, for the substance, the passion, the faith, and the sheer depth of them. He holds a goodly share of tickets in Stendahl's lottery of fame, and who among us will be present at the drawing in 2067?"

A one-act dramatization of the novel, One Red Rose for Christmas, by Sister Mary Olive O'Connell was published, by Longmans, Green, as One Red Rose, in 1954; an adaptation was produced for television in 1958. The novel, Things As They Are, was filmed in 1970.

A wing of the Roswell Museum and the library of the New Mexico Military Institute have been named for Horgan.

*   *   *

HORN, (John) Stephen 1931-

PERSONAL: Born May 31, 1931, in Gilroy, Calif.; son of John Stephen (a geologist) and Isabelle (McCaffrey) Horn; married Nini Moore, September 4, 1954; children: Marcia Karen, John Stephen. Education: Stanford University, A.B. (with great distinction in political science), 1953, Ph.D., 1958; Harvard University, M.P.A., 1955. Politics: Republican. Home: 3944 Pine Avenue, Long Beach, Calif. 90807. Office: California State University, 6101 East Seventh St., Long Beach, Calif. 90840.

CAREER: Congressional Fellow of American Political Science Association, Washington, D.C., 1958-59; administrative assistant to Secretary of Labor James P. Mitchell, Washington, D.C., 1959-60; legislative assistant to U.S. Senator Thomas H. Kuchel, Washington, D.C., 1960-66; Brookings Institution, Washington, D.C., member of senior staff of governmental studies, 1966-69; American University, Washington, D.C., dean of graduate studies and research, 1969-70; California State University, Long Beach, president, 1970—. Vice-chairman, U.S. Commission on Civil Rights, 1969—. Military service: U.S. Army, Strategic Intelligence Reserve, 1954-62. Member: American Political Science Association, Western Governmental Research Association, American Society for Public Administration, Phi Beta Kappa, Pi Sigma Alpha.

WRITINGS: The Cabinet and Congress, Columbia University Press, 1960; Unused Power: The Work of the Senate Committee on Appropriations, Brookings Institution, 1970.

WORK IN PROGRESS: The Memorable Campaign: Hiram Johnson and the 1910 Campaign for the Governorship of California, and Congressional Ethics.

*   *   *

HORN, Thomas D 1918-

PERSONAL: Born June 26, 1918. Education: University of Iowa, B.A., 1940, M.A., 1946, Ph.D., 1947; Cambridge University, graduate study, 1945. Home: 5302 Ridge Oak Dr., Austin, Tex. 78731. Office: University of Texas, Austin, Tex. 78712.

CAREER: Elementary school teacher in Denver, Colo., 1940-42, and River Forest, Ill., 1942-43; Iowa State Teachers College (now University of Northern Iowa), Cedar Falls, principal of campus elementary school and assistant professor, 1947-51; University of Texas, College of Education, Austin, associate professor in department of curriculum and instruction, 1951-59, professor, 1959—, chairman of department, 1962-73. Summer visiting professor at University of Pittsburgh, 1949, Harvard University, 1959, and University of Michigan, 1963. Military service: U.S. Army, 78th Infantry Division, 1943-46; served in European theater; received three battle stars.

MEMBER: International Reading Association, American Educational Research Association, Association for Student Teaching (president, 1957-58), National Conference on Research in English (president, 1958-59), National Council of Teachers of English, National Education Association (life), National Society for the Study of Education, Phi Delta Kappa, Phi Kappa Phi.

WRITINGS: (Co-editor) Spelling Instruction: A Curriculum-Wide Approach, University of Texas Press, 1954; (with Martha Zivley) Helps for Writing Your Thesis, Hemphill, 1955, revised edition, 1956; (co-author) Around the Bend, Holt, 1961; (co-author) Above the Clouds, Holt, 1961; (co-author) Through the Years, Holt, 1961; (with Dorothy J. Ebert) Books for the Partially Sighted Child, National Council of Teachers of English, 1965; (editor) Reading for the Disadvantaged: Problems of Linguistically Different Learners, Harcourt, 1970, (editor) Research Bases for Oral Language Instruction, National Council of Teachers of English, 1971.

"Spelling We Use Workbooks": Co-author of two books and consultant for five in first series of seven books, grades 2-8, Lippincott, 1955; co-author of seven books in second series, Lippincott, 1959, and of seven books in revised series, 1960. Contributor to *Encyclopedia of Educational Research*, Macmillan, 1969, and to educational journals. Editorial chairman for research bulletins of the National Conference on Research in English, 1966 and 1971. Educational Collaborator on "Spelling for Beginners" (film), issued by Coronet Films, 1952.

* * *

HOROWITZ, David (Joel)   1939-

PERSONAL: Born January 10, 1939, in New York, N.Y.; married Elissa Krauthamer, June 14, 1959; children: Jonathan, Sarah. *Education:* Columbia University, A.B., 1959; University of California, Berkeley, M.A., 1961, graduate study, 1962; London School of Economics and Political Science, University of London, graduate study, 1964—.

CAREER: Bertrand Russell Peace Foundation, London, England, director of research and publications; *Ramparts* (magazine), Berkeley, California, editor, 1968—.

WRITINGS: Student, Ballantine, 1962; *Shakespeare: An Existential View*, Hill & Wang, 1965; *The Free World Colossus*, Hill & Wang, 1965, revised edition, 1971 (published in England as *From Yalta to Vietnam: American Foreign Policy in the Cold War*, Penguin, 1967); *Hemispheres North and South: Economic Disparity Among Nations*, Johns Hopkins University Press, 1966; (editor) *Containment and Revolution*, Beacon Press, 1967 (published in England as *Containment and Revolution: Western Policy Towards Social Revolution, 1917 to Vietnam*, Blond, 1967); (compiler) *Marx and Modern Economics*, Monthly Review Press, 1968; *Empire and Revolution: A Radical Interpretation of Contemporary History*, Random House, 1969 (published in England as *Imperialism and Revolution*, Allen Lane, 1969); (editor) *Corporations and the Cold War*, Monthly Review Press, 1970; (editor) *Issac Deutscher: The Man and His Work*, Macdonald & Co., 1971; (compiler) *Radical Sociology: An Introduction*, Canfield Press, 1971; (compiler with Michael Lerner and Craig Pyes; contributor) *Counterculture and Revolution*, Random House, 1972; *The Enigma of Economic Growth: A Case Study of Israel*, Praeger, 1972; *The Fate of Midas and Other Essays*, Ramparts Press, 1973. Contributor to *Nation* and *Studies on the Left.*†

* * *

HORSEMAN, Elaine Hall   1925-

PERSONAL: Born November 23, 1925, in Lichfield, Staffordshire, England; daughter of Harold (a vicar choral) and Olive E. (Bowey) Hall; married Leslie A. Horseman (a computer applications engineer), 1950; children: Stephen Thomas, Christopher Michael. *Education:* Studied at University of Birmingham; qualified as teacher, 1944. *Religion:* Church of England. *Home:* 49 Cheriton Pl., Westbury on Trym, Bristol, England.

CAREER: Primary schoolteacher in England, 1944-62.

WRITINGS: Hubble's Bubble (juvenile), Norton, 1964; *The Hubbles' Treasure Hunt*, Chatto & Windus, 1965, Norton, 1966; *The Hubbles and the Robot*, Chatto & Windus, 1968.

WORK IN PROGRESS: Another book in "Hubble" series to be titled *The Winter Magic* or *The Flower of Winter.*

AVOCATIONAL INTERESTS: Reading, gardening, walking, and camping.

HOSKINS, William George   1908-

PERSONAL: Born May 22, 1908, in Exeter, Devonshire, England; son of William George and Alice Beatrice (Dymond) Hoskins; married Frances Jackson, February 4, 1933; children: William Dommett, Susan Mary. *Education:* Studied at University College, Exeter (now University of Exeter), 1925-30, B.Sc., 1927, M.Sc., 1929, and Ph.D., 1938 (all London); Oxford University, M.A., 1951. *Politics:* Liberal. *Religion:* Church of England. *Home:* 2 Lyndhurst Rd., Exeter, Devonshire, England.

CAREER: University College, Leicester, England (now University of Leicester), lecturer, 1931-41, 1946-48, reader in English local history, 1948-51; Oxford University, Oxford, England, reader in economic history, 1952-65; University of Leicester, Hatton Professor of English History, 1965-68, professor emeritus, 1968—. Board of Trade, London, England, temporary civil servant, 1941-45. Royal Commission on Common Land, member, 1955-58; British Ministry of Housing, member of Advisory Committee on Buildings of Special Architectural and Historic Interest, 1955-64. Member of Leicester County Council, 1946-51, of Devon County Council, 1955-65, of Exeter City Council, 1963-65. Reviewer for "Listener," British Broadcasting Corp., and broadcaster on other programs. *Member:* Leicestershire Archaeological and Historical Society (vice-president, 1952), Dartmoor Preservation Association (president, 1962—), British Agricultural History Society (president, 1972—), British Academy (fellow). *Awards, honors:* Leverhulme research fellowship, 1961-63; Leverhulme emeritus fellowship, 1970-71; Commander of the British Empire, 1971.

WRITINGS: Industry, Trade and People in Exeter 1688-1800, Manchester University Press, 1935, 2nd edition, 1968; *The Heritage of Leicestershire*, Backus, 1946; *Midland England: A Survey of the Country Between the Chilterns and the Trent*, Batsford, 1949; *Rutland*, City of Leicester, 1949.

Essays in Leicestershire History, Liverpool University Press, 1950; *Chilterns to Black Country*, Collins, 1951; *East Midlands and the Peak*, Collins, 1951; (with H. P. R. Finberg) *Devonshire Studies*, J. Cape, 1952; *Devon*, Collins, 1954; *The Making of the English Landscape*, Hodder & Stoughton, 1955; *Leicestershire: An Illustrated Essay on the History of the Landscape*, Hodder & Stoughton, 1957; (editor, and author of introduction) *Exeter in the Seventeenth Century: Tax and Rate Assessments*, Devonshire Press, 1957; *The Midland Peasant: The Economic and Social History of a Leicestershire Village*, Macmillan (London), 1957, St. Martins, 1965; *Local History in England*, Longmans, Green, 1959, 2nd edition, 1972; *Devon and Its People*, Wheaton & Co., 1959, Augustus M. Kelley, 1968; *The Westward Expansion of Wessex*, Leicester University Press, 1960; *Two Thousand Years in Exeter*, Townsend, 1960; (with L. Dudley Stamp) *The Common Lands of England and Wales*, Collins, 1963; *Rutland*, Faber, 1963; *Provincial England: Essays in Social and Economic History*, St. Martins, 1963; *The Shilling Guides*, four books, Shell-Mex, 1963-64; *Old Devon*, David & Charles, 1966, Augustus M. Kelley, 1968; *Fieldwork in Local History*, Faber, 1967; *The Human Geography of the South West*, Seale-Hayne Agricultural College, 1968; *Leicestershire*, Faber, 1970; (editor and author of introduction) *Exeter Militia List, 1803*, Chicester, Phillimore for the Devon and Cornwall Record Society, 1972.

Editor, *Victoria County History of Leicestershire*, 1948-55.

WORK IN PROGRESS: Social and Economic History of England in the 16th Century, and *The English Village.*

AVOCATIONAL INTERESTS: Parochial explorations all over England, drinking with friends.†

*   *   *

HOSMER, Charles B(ridgham), Jr. 1932-

PERSONAL: Born February 23, 1932, in Naples, Italy; son of Charles Bridgham (a diplomat) and Faye (Durham) Hosmer; married Jeralyn Prugh (a museum curator), December 27, 1955; children: Kathryn, Jonathan Prescott. *Education:* Principia College, B.A., 1953; Columbia University, M.A., 1956, Ph.D., 1961. *Politics:* Independent. *Religion:* Christian Science. *Home and office:* Principia College, Elsah, Ill. 62028.

CAREER: Junior high school teacher of social studies, South Huntington, N.Y., 1956-59; Principia College, Elsah, Ill., research, 1959-60, Jay P. Walker Professor of History, 1961—. *Military service:* U.S. Army, Signal Corps, 1953-55; served in Germany. *Member:* American Historical Association, National Trust for Historic Preservation, Organization of American Historians, Society for the Preservation of New England Antiquities, Eastern National Park and Monuments Association, St. Louis Landmarks, Missouri Historical Society.

WRITINGS: Presence of the Past: A History of the Preservation Movement in the United States Before Williamsburg, Putnam, 1965; (contributor) C. L. Lord, editor, *Keepers of the Past,* University of North Carolina Press, 1965; (with Paul Williams) *Elsah: A Historical Guidebook,* Historic Elsah (Elsah, Ill.), 1967; (contributor) *Historic Preservation Today,* University of Virginia, 1967. Contributor to the publications of American Jewish Historical Society.

WORK IN PROGRESS: Research in preservation movement in United States, 1926-49.

SIDELIGHTS: Hosmer has traveled in Europe, collecting material on the history of preservation work in Britain, France, and Spain. He is interested in American historic sites as teaching aids, and in American architecture. He reads French and Spanish.†

*   *   *

HOUGHTON, George William 1905-

PERSONAL: Born September 9, 1905, in Perth, Scotland; son of Herbert Frodsham and Christina (Duff) Houghton; married Krithia Staughton, June, 1948; children: Donald Richard John. *Education:* Studies in Paris, France, at Sorbonne, University of Paris, and at Ecoles des Beaux Arts. *Home:* Coneygar House, Bridport, Dorsetshire, DT6 3BA, England.

CAREER: With *London Daily Mail,* 1926-36; with George Newnes Ltd. (periodicals publisher), London, England, beginning, 1936, group manager, 1946-63. Author and cartoonist. *Military service:* Royal Air Force, 1940-46; group captain on staff of deputy commander, Supreme Headquarters, Allied Expeditionary Force; received Order of British Empire (military); mentioned in dispatches.

WRITINGS—All self-illustrated: *The Adventures of a Gadabout, Grave and Gay,* Selwyn & Blount, 1936; *Parade of Violence,* Selwyn & Blount, 1936; *They Flew Through Sand,* Jarrolds, 1942; *Between the Red Lines,* Newnes, 1949; *Confessions of a Golf Addict,* Museum Press, 1952, Soccer, 1957; *More Confessions of a Golf Addict,* Museum Press, 1954; *Golf Addict Visits U.S.A.,* Museum Press, 1955; *Golf Addicts through the Ages,* Museum Press, 1956, Soccer, 1957; *The Truth about Golf Addicts,* Soccer, 1957; *An Addict's Guide to British Golf,* S. Paul, 1959.

Golf Addicts on Parade, Country Life, 1960; *Golf on My Pillow,* S. Paul, 1960; *Portrait of a Golf Addict,* Country Life, 1960; *I Am a Golf Widow,* Country Life, 1961; *Addict in Bunkerland,* with an introduction by Bob Hope, Country Life, 1962; *Blast Your Horn!,* S. Paul, 1962; *Golf Addict Strikes Again,* Country Life, 1963; (compiler) *Golfer's Treasury,* Newnes, 1964; *The Secret Diary of a Golf Addict's Caddie,* Country Life, 1964; *Golf Addict Among the Irish,* Country Life, 1965; *The Full Confessions of a Golf Addict,* Pelham, 1966; *Golf Addict Goes East,* Country Life, 1967; *Golfers in Orbit,* Pelham, 1969; *Golf Addicts Galore,* Country Life, 1968; *Golf Addict Invades Wales,* Pelham, 1969; *How to be a Golf Addict,* Pelham, 1971; *Golf with a Whippy Shaft,* A. S. Barnes, 1971. Also author of *Believe It or Not—That's Golf,* and *Golf Addict in Goucholand.*

Other: (Translator from the French) *Siege of Bir Hakim: An Account of the Fighting Which Took Place Between May and June 11, 1942,* Schindler, 1943; *They Flew Through Sand: A Play in Three Acts about the Royal Air Force in the Western Desert,* C. H. Fox, 1944; *The Penny Spenders* (personal narrative), Arlington, 1966. Also author of television plays "They Flew Through Sand," and "Motive." Writer of radio scripts, stories, and articles. Creator of "Calendar for Golf Addicts" (a cartoon turn-over calendar), Country Life, annually, 1952-64, Collins, annually, 1964—.

SIDELIGHTS: Sales of Houghton's golf humor books reached 600,000 copies in January, 1974. They have been translated into many languages, including Japanese, and have been sold all over the world.

*   *   *

HOUSTON, James M(ackintosh) 1922-

PERSONAL: Born November 21, 1922, in Edinburgh, Scotland; son of James (a missionary) and Ethel (Watson) Houston; married Margaret Davidson, March 20, 1953; children: Christopher, Lydele, Claire, Penelope. *Education:* University of Edinburgh, M.A. (first class honors), 1944; Oxford University, B.Sc., 1947, D.Phil, 1948. *Religion:* Christian. *Home:* 17 Third Acre Rise, Oxford, England. *Office:* School of Geography, Mansfield Rd., Oxford, England.

CAREER: Oxford University, Oxford, England, departmental demonstrator, 1947-49, university lecturer, 1949—, Hertford College, fellow and bursar, 1964—. Lay preacher. Clyde Valley Regional Planning Advisory Committee, Glasgow, Scotland, geographer, 1944-45. *Member:* Royal Geographical Society, American Geographical Society, Institute of British Geographers.

WRITINGS: A Social Geography of Europe, Duckworth, 1953, revised edition, Praeger, 1963; *The Western Mediterranean World,* Longmans, Green, 1964, Praeger, 1967; (editor) *Urbanization and Its Problems,* Barnes & Noble, 1968. Contributor to *Encyclopaedia Britannica* and to town planning and geographical journals.

WORK IN PROGRESS: A book on landscape and culture and another on land use studies in Ecuador and Colombia.

SIDELIGHTS: Competent in Spanish and French; travels have been centered on the western Mediterranean and western European countries, North and South America, and North Africa.†

* * *

HOUTART, Francois 1925-

PERSONAL: Born March 4, 1925, in Brussels, Belgium; son of Paul (a businessman) and Gudule (Carton de Wiart) Houtart. Education: University of Louvain, License in Political and Social Sciences, 1952; University of Chicago, graduate study, 1952-53; L'Institut Superieur International d'Urbanisme applique, Brussels, Belgium, diploma, 1954. Home: Herestraat 51, B-3000, Louvain, Belgium. Office: FERES, Vlamingenstraat 116, B-3000, Louvain, Belgium.

CAREER: Roman Catholic priest. Centre de Recherches Socio-Religieuses, Brussels, Belgium, director, 1955; International Conference of Religious Sociology, Brussels, Belgium, general secretary, 1956; University of Louvain, Louvain, Belgium, professor of sociology, 1959; Federation Internationale des Institutions Catholiques des Recherches Sociales et Socio-Religieuses (FERES), Louvain, general secretary, 1964—. Military service: Belgium Secret Army; received Croix de Guerre. Member: American Sociological Association, Belgium-Vietnam Association (chairman).

WRITINGS: Aspects sociologiques du catholicisme americain: Vie urbain et institutions religieuses, Editions Ouvrieres, 1957.

(Editor) Leandor Tormo, Historia de la iglesia en America Latina, FERES (Madrid), 1962; (with Michael Cepede) Nourrir les hommes, Editions du Cercle d'Education Populaire, 1963; The Latin American Church and the Council, FERES (Friborg, Switzerland), 1963; Sociologie et pastorale, Edition Fleurus, 1963, translation by Malachy Carroll published as Sociology and Pastoral Care, Franciscan Herald Press, 1965; L'Eglise et le monde: Vatican II, Editions du Cerf, 1964; The Challenge to Change: The Church Confronts the Future, edited by Mary Anne Chouteau, Sheed, 1964; (with others) Bilan du monde, volumes I-II, 2nd edition, Casterman, 1964; El cambio social en America Latina, FERES (Brussels), 1964; (with Emile Pin) L'Eglise a l'heure de l'Amerique latine, Casterman, 1965, translation by Gilbert Barth published as The Church and the Latin American Revolution, Sheed, 1965; (with Vincente O. Vetrano) Hacia una teologia del desarrollo, algunas reflexiones, Latinoamerica Libros (Buenos Aries), 1967; L'Etat et l'Eglise en Belgique, Cercle d'Education Populaire, 1967; The Eleventh Hour: Explosion of a Church, edited by Mary Anne Chouteau, introduction by Harvey Cox, Sheed, 1968; (with Jean Remy) Milieu urbain et communaute chretienne, Mame (Tours), 1968; (with Remy) Eglise et societe en mutation, Mame, 1969.

(With Remy) Sacerdoce, autorite et innovation dans l'Eglise, Mame, 1970; (with Andre Rousseau) The Church and Revolution, translation by Violet Nevile, Orbis, 1971; (editor with Genevieve Lemercinier) Les Juifs dans la catechese: Etude sur la transmission des codes religieux, Les Editions "Vie Ouvriere" (Brussels), 1972; Religion and Ideology: Sri Lanks, Hansa, 1974. Contributor to Belgian, French, Dutch, German, Spanish, and American publications.

WORK IN PROGRESS: Sociological research in Asia.

SIDELIGHTS: Houtart is competent in Spanish, Portuguese, English, Polish and Japanese. He also is conversant in Ceylonese, Indian, and some South American dialects.

HOWARD, A(rthur) E(llsworth) Dick 1933-

PERSONAL: Born July 5, 1933; son of Thomas Landon (a pharmacist and businessman) and Marie (Dick) Howard. Education: University of Richmond, B.A., 1954; Oxford University, B.A. (honors), 1960, M.A., 1965; University of Virginia, LL.B., 1961. Politics: Democrat. Religion: Episcopalian. Home: 627 Park St., Charlottesville, Va. 22901. Office: School of Law, University of Virginia, Charlottesville, Va. 22901.

CAREER: Admitted to District of Columbia bar, 1961; Covington & Burlington (law firm), Washington, D.C., associate, 1961-62; law clerk to U.S. Supreme Court Justice Hugo Black, Washington, D.C., 1962-64; University of Virginia, Charlottesville, associate professor, 1964-67, professor of law, 1967—, associate dean, 1967-69, director of graduate program, 1972—. Lecturer, Army Judge Advocate General's School. Counsel, General Assembly of Virginia, 1969-70. Vice-chairman, Magna Carta Commission of Virginia, 1964-65. Executive director, Virginia Commission on Constitutional Revision, 1968-69. Member of executive committee, Virginia Bicentennial Committee; member of committee on natural resources and environment, Virginia State Chamber of Commerce. Member of advisory board, John Marshall House, Richmond, Va; member of council, Tayloe Murphy Institute. Member of board, University Press of Virginia. Virginia secretary, Rhodes Scholarship Trust. Military service: U.S. Army 1954-56; became first lieutenant. Member: American, and District of Columbia bar associations, Virginia State Bar Association (vice-president, 1970-71), University of Richmond Alumni Council (member of executive council), Civic League of Charlottesville-Albemarle (member of board of directors), Phi Beta Kappa, Order of the Coif, Omicron Delta Kappa, Tau Kappa Alpha, Pi Sigma Alpha, Phi Alpha Theta, Phi Alpha Delta, Scabbard and Blade. Awards, honors: Rhodes scholar; sesquicentennial fellow, University of Virginia, 1970; Woodrow Wilson fellow, Smithsonian Institution, 1974.

WRITINGS: Magna Carta: Text and Commentary, University Press of Virginia, 1964; (editor) Magna Carta Commission Essays, University Press of Virginia, 1965; (editor) The Virginia Lawyer, Virginia State Bar Association, 1966, revised edition, 1970; The Road from Runnymede: Magna Carta and Constitutionalism in America, University Press of Virginia, 1968; (editor) Jamestown Essays on Regeneration, University Press of Virginia, 1969; (with Grosenick, Barnes, and Mashaw) Virginia's Urban Corridor, Center for the Study of Science, Technology, and Public Policy (Charlottesville, Va.), 1970; (author of introduction) George W. Jennings, editor, Virginia Government, Virginia State Chamber of Commerce, 1971; (with Tom Finchem) Virginia Votes for a New Constitution, [Roanoke, Va.], 1973; Commentaries on the Constitution of Virginia, two volumes, University Press of Virginia, 1974. Also contributor to The Constitution of Virginia: Report of the Commission on Constitutional Revision, 1969. Contributor to legal journals and other professional periodicals, including Michigan Law Review, Virginia Law Review, American Bar Association Journal, and Commonwealth; contributor of articles to newspapers, including Richmond News Leader. Member of board of editors, American Oxonian.

WORK IN PROGRESS: A book on the Nixon Court, and a book on Mr. Justice Hugo Black, both for Oxford University Press.

HOWARD, Bion B. 1912-

PERSONAL: Born October 28, 1912, in Paris, France; son of American nationals, Bion B. and Lucile (Jones) Howard; married Lita Dickerson, December 24, 1940; children: Bion Dickerson, Julia. *Education:* University of Chicago, Ph.B., 1933; Northwestern University, M.B.A., 1940, Ph.D., 1950. *Home:* 2745 Lawndale Ave., Evanston, Ill. 60201.

CAREER: Montgomery Ward & Co., Chicago, assistant buyer, 1933-36; U.S. Office of Price Administration, Washington, D.C., economist, 1942-46; Northwestern University, School of Business, Evanston, Ill., lecturer, 1947-50, assistant professor, 1950-51, associate professor, 1951-56, professor of finance, 1956—, Nathan and Mary Sharp Professor of Finance, 1961—, chairman of department, 1956-59. Assistant director and division economist, Consumer Durable Goods Division, U.S. Office of Price Stabilization, 1951. Visiting professor at Stanford University, 1954-55, University of Virginia, 1971-72, and University of Cape Town, 1973. Chartered financial analyst. Director of United Wirecraft, Inc., and Consumer Display Co.

MEMBER: American Finance Association (director, 1959-60; president, 1962), American Risk and Insurance Association, Financial Management Association, Investment Analyst Society of Chicago, Public Utilities Security Club of Chicago, University Club of Chicago, Phi Beta Kappa, Beta Gamma Sigma.

WRITINGS: (With Miller Upton) *Introduction to Business Finance*, McGraw, 1953; (with Sidney L. Jones) *Managerial Problems in Finance*, McGraw, 1964; (with Peter O. Dietz) *A Study of the Financial Significance of Profit Sharing*, Council of Profit Sharing Industries, 1974. Contributor to professional journals.

* * *

HOWARD, James A(rch) 1922-
(Laine Fisher)

PERSONAL: Born May 8, 1922, in Delavan, Ill.; son of Arch Clark (a contractor) and Claudine (Boyd) Howard; married second wife, Nancy C. Thompson, 1966; children: one. *Education:* Heidelberg College, Tiffin, Ohio, A.B., 1948; Columbia University, M.A., 1949; University of California, Los Angeles, Ph.D., 1957. *Residence:* Fallbrook, Calif. *Agent:* James M. Fox, Roberto Dr., Palm Springs, Calif.

CAREER: Alabama Polytechnic Institute (now Auburn University), Auburn, Ala., instructor, 1949-51; Los Angeles Psychiatric Service, Los Angeles, Calif., U.S. Public Health Service fellow, 1956-57; Los Angeles State College (now California State University at Los Angeles), lecturer in creative writing, 1956-57; Office of Vocational Rehabilitation, Long Beach, Calif., research director, 1957-60; Southwestern Mental Health Center, Luverne, Minn., clinical psychologist, 1961-65; in private practice as clinical and consulting psychologist, Luverne, Minn., 1961-65, in San Diego, Calif., 1965—; Mesa Vista Hospital, San Diego, Calif., clinical psychologist, 1965—; San Diego State University, San Diego, Calif., lecturer, 1966-72. Author of mystery fiction. Dean for administrative affairs, California School of Professional Psychology, 1972. *Military service:* U.S. Army Air Forces, 1942-43.

MEMBER: American Psychological Association, National Rehabilitation Association, Mystery Writers of America, Minnesota Psychological Association, California Psychological Association. *Awards, honors:* Tuberculosis and Health Association Merit Award, 1960; Community Rehabilitation Industries Merit Award, 1960.

WRITINGS: I Like It Tough, Popular Library, 1955; *I'll Get You Yet*, Popular Library, 1956; *Blow Out My Torch*, Popular Library, 1956; *Die on Easy Street*, Popular Library, 1957; *Murder Takes a Wife*, Dutton, 1958; *Murder in Mind*, Dutton, 1959; (under pseudonym Laine Fisher) *Fare Prey*, Ace Books, 1959; *Bullet Proof Martyr*, Dutton, 1961; *The Ego Mill: 5 Cases in Clinical Psychology*, Cowles, 1971; *The Flesh-Colored Cage*, Hawthorn, in press. Author of television plays for "Alfred Hitchcock Presents." Contributor of short stories to mystery magazines.

AVOCATIONAL INTERESTS: Private flying, avocado and citrus ranching, woodworking and construction, design and "gadgeteering."

* * *

HOWARD, Lowell B(ennett) 1925-

PERSONAL: Born February 12, 1925, in New Boston, Ohio; son of James Arland (a railway brakeman) and Imogene (Sullivan) Howard; married Jeanetta Turner, June 16, 1947; children: Lowell Bennett, Jr., Brent Turner, Rebecca Ann. *Education:* Bowling Green State University, A.B., 1947; Ohio State University, LL.B., 1949, M.A., 1954, J.D., 1969. *Politics:* Democrat. *Religion:* Methodist. *Home:* 68 Briarwood Dr., Athens, Ohio 45701. *Office:* Courthouse, Athens, Ohio 45701.

CAREER: Attorney-at-law in Wellston, Ohio, 1950-51, 1954-57, a senior partner in law firm of Howard and Gilliland, 1956-57; Ohio University, Athens, assistant professor, 1955-59, associate professor, 1959-65, professor of business law, 1965-71; Athens County, Ohio, judge of common pleas court, 1971—. City solicitor, Wellston, Ohio, 1954-56; legal consultant, city of Athens, Ohio, 1955-71; secretary, Athens Zoning Board of Appeals, 1963-66. *Military service:* U.S. Naval Reserve, World War II and Korean War; became captain. *Member:* American Bar Association, American Business Law Association, American Association of University Professors, Ohio State Bar Association, Athens County Bar Association. *Awards, honors:* Outstanding Judicial Service Award from Ohio Supreme Court, 1972, 1973.

WRITINGS: Business Law: An Introduction, Barron's, 1965. Contributor to *American Business Law Journal*, *American Bar Association Journal*, and other legal journals.

* * *

HOWARTH, David 1912-

PERSONAL: Born July 18, 1912, in London, England; son of Osbert J. R. and Eleanor (Paget) Howarth; married Nanette Smith; children: Clare, Virginia, Stephen, Joanna. *Education:* Cambridge University, B.A., 1933. *Home:* Blackboys, Sussex, England. *Agent:* Curtis Brown Ltd., 60 East 56th St., New York, N.Y. 10022.

CAREER: Baird Television Co., London, England, researcher, 1933-34; British Broadcasting Corp., London, England, assistant talks editor, 1934-40, war correspondent, 1939-40; free-lance-writer. *Military service:* Royal Naval Volunteer Reserve, World War II; became lieutenant commander.

WRITINGS: The Shetland Bus, Nelson, 1951, published as *Across to Norway*, Sloane, 1952; *Thieves' Hole*, Rinehart, 1954; *We Die Alone*, Macmillan, 1955; *Sledge Patrol*, Macmillan, 1958; *D-Day*, McGraw, 1959; *The Shadow of the Dam*, Macmillan, 1961; (editor) Ngawang Lobsang Yishey Tenzing Gyatso, *My Land and My People: The Autobiography of His Holiness the Dalai Lama*, Weidenfeld & Nicolson, 1962; *The Desert King: Ibn Saud and His Arabia*, McGraw, 1964; (contributor) *Three Great Escape Stories from the Second World War*, Collins, 1965; *Panama: Four Hundred Years of Dreams and Cruelty*, McGraw, 1966 (published in England as *The Golden Isthmus*, Collins, 1966); *Waterloo: Day of Battle*, Atheneum, 1968 (published in England as *A Near Run Thing: The Day of Waterloo*, Collins, 1968); *Trafalgar: The Nelson Touch*, Atheneum, 1969; (editor) *Great Escapes*, David White, 1969; *Sovereign of the Seas: The Story of British Sea Power*, Collins, 1974. Writer of serials and articles appearing in *Saturday Evening Post, Harper's* and in British periodicals.

SIDELIGHTS: Christopher Hibbert describes *Waterloo: Day of Battle* as "vivid and moving as well as being beautifully produced and illustrated. It is not a book with any pretense to scholarship; it tells us little about either the historical background to Napoleon's last campaign or even about its conduct, and it adds nothing new to our knowledge of the battle that ended it. But what it does do, with highly accomplished artistry, is to present an authentic picture of what a day's fighting in Wellington's army was really like." As Kellow Chesney notes, "This time the battle is seen more from the worm's-eye viewpoint of the slogging combatants, less from the chessboard perspectives of their commanders than usual."

Reviewing *Trafalgar: The Nelson Touch*, Eric Forbes-Boyd explains, "Not only does Mr. Howarth tell the great story with power and vividness, but to some degree he puts it in a fresh perspective, and he does justice where too often justice has been wanting."

* * *

HOWIE, Carl G(ordon) 1920-

PERSONAL: Born August 28, 1920, in Lancaster County, S.C.; son of Thomas Eldridge (a builder) and Mary (Ross) Howie; married Jean Lewis, May 26, 1947; children: Gordon, Lewis, Anna. *Education:* Lees McRae College, A.A., 1938; Davidson College, B.A., 1941; Union Theological Seminary, Richmond, Va., B.D., 1944, Th.M., 1947; Johns Hopkins University, Ph.D., 1949. *Home:* 1 Sixth Ave., San Francisco, Calif. 94118.

CAREER: Ordained Presbyterian minister, 1944; minister in Baltimore, Md., 1947-49, Lynchburg, Va., 1949-52, Washington, D.C., 1952-56; Calvary Presbyterian Church, San Francisco, Calif., minister, 1956—. The American University, Washington, D.C., lecturer, 1955-56. General Assembly of United Presbyterian Church in the U.S.A., member of General Commission on Chaplains and Service Personnel; Presbytery of San Francisco, former moderator; San Francisco Council of Churches, president. United Crusade of San Francisco Bay Area, member of executive committee; American National Red Cross, director of Golden Gate District chapter; Presbyterian Medical Center, San Francisco, trustee. *Military service:* U.S. Navy, chaplain, 1944-46.

MEMBER: National Association of Biblical Instructors, Society of Biblical Literature, Press Club, Union League Club, and Rotary Club (all San Francisco). *Awards, honors:* LL.D., Lincoln University, San Francisco, 1958.

WRITINGS: The Date and Composition of Ezekiel, Westminster, 1950; *The Dead Sea Scrolls and the Living Church*, John Knox, 1958; *God in the Eternal Present*, John Knox, 1959; *Layman's Commentary on Ezekiel and Daniel*, John Knox, 1961; *The Creative Era Between the Testaments*, John Knox, 1965; *The Old Testament Story*, Harper, 1965. Contributor to *Bulletin of American School of Oriental Research* and religion journals.†

* * *

HOYE, Anna Scott 1915-

PERSONAL: Born March 31, 1915, in Louisa, Va. *Education:* Lynchburg College, B.S., 1936; University of Wisconsin, M.S., 1939, Ph.D., 1962; Duke University, postgraduate study, 1960-61. *Home:* Deltaville, Va. *Office:* Mary Washington College, Fredericksburg, Va.

CAREER: Principal of elementary school, Thelma, Va., 1936-37; University of North Carolina, Woman's College, Greensboro, instructor, 1939-41; University of Virginia, Mary Washington College, Fredericksburg, assistant professor of physical education, 1941-44, associate professor of physical education, 1951-59, associate professor of biology, 1962—. *Military service:* U.S. Army, Women's Army Corps (WAC), 1944-46; became second lieutenant. *Member:* Sigma Delta Epsilon.

WRITINGS: Fundamentals of Movement: A Study Guide for Students and Teachers, National Press, 1961. Contributor to *Journal of Applied Physiology*.†

* * *

HUBBELL, Richard Whittaker 1914-

PERSONAL: Born September 13, 1914, in Mount Vernon, N.Y.; son of Rowland Southworth and Hildegarde (Whittaker) Hubbell; married Kyra Deakin, May 31, 1941 (died, 1965); married June Cortelyou, 1965. *Education:* Wesleyan University, Middletown, Conn., B.A., 1936; Columbia University, graduate study, 1936-38. *Home:* 360 First Ave., New York, N.Y. 10010. *Agent:* Nannine Joseph, 200 West 54th St., New York, N.Y. 10019. *Office:* World Wide Information Services, 660 First Ave., New York, N.Y. 10016.

CAREER: Affiliated with radio station WQXR, New York, N.Y., 1937-39; Columbia Broadcasting System-Television, New York, N.Y., news director, 1939-43; Crosley Broadcasting Corp., Cincinnati, Ohio, production manager, 1944-47; U.S. Department of State, New York, N.Y., television officer, 1951-53; Easton Express, Easton, Pa., assistant to president, 1953-54; sales executive at DuMont Television, N.Y., 1954-55; International News Service, New York, N.Y., sales executive, 1957-58; World Wide Information Services (news agency), New York, N.Y., president, 1958—.

WRITINGS: 4000 Years of Television, Putnam, 1942; *Television Programming and Production*, Rinehart, 1945, 3rd edition, 1956. Contributor to magazines.

* * *

HUBERMAN, Edward 1910-

PERSONAL: Surname is pronounced *Hugh*-bur-man; born January 30, 1910, in Newark, N.J.; son of Joseph and Fanny (Kramer) Huberman; married Elizabeth Duncan Lyle (a college professor), September 17, 1939; children: Joel Anthony, Jamie Lyle, Vincent Michael, Joan Laurie. *Education:* Harvard University, A.B., 1929; Rutgers University, A.M., 1930; Sorbonne, University of Paris, graduate student, 1931-32; Duke University, Ph.D., 1934. *Home:* 33 Hickory Dr., Maplewood, N.J. 07040. *Office:* Rutgers University, 360 High St., Newark, N.J. 07102.

CAREER: Former teacher at Essex Junior College, Newark, N.J., and U.S. Department of Agriculture Graduate School, Washington, D.C.; Rutgers University, Newark Campus, N.J., 1947—, professor of English, 1960—. Visiting professor, Adelphi University, 1960-61, New York University, Graduate School, 1961-62; Fulbright professor of American literature, University of Innsbruck, 1963-64, Alaska Methodist University, 1966. Radio and television lecturer. Advisor to American delegation, First Inter-American Indian Congress, Patzcuaro, Mexico, 1940. Trustee, Maplewood-South Orange Adult School, 1961-67. President, Consumers' Cooperative Association of the Oranges, 1950-52.

MEMBER: College English Association (regional president, 1960-62; national director and director of bureau of appointments, 1961-70; national treasurer, 1965-67; national president, 1970-71), Modern Language Association of America (chairman, faculty exchange, 1958), Renaissance Society of America, Shakespeare Association of America, Malone Society, American Association of University Professors (chapter president, 1959-60), Sigma Delta Pi.

WRITINGS: Indian Stamps, Simon & Schuster, 1957; (editor with Robert R. Raymo) *Angles of Vision,* Houghton, 1962; (editor with wife, Elizabeth Huberman) *Fifty Great Essays,* Bantam, 1964; (editor with Elizabeth Huberman) *Great British Short Stories,* Bantam, 1968; (editor with Elizabeth Huberman) *War: An Anthology,* Washington Square Press, 1969; (editor with Elizabeth Huberman) *Fifty Great European Short Stories,* Bantam, 1971. Contributor to magazines and journals, among them *Books Abroad, Indian Education, Critic, CEA Forum, Transactions of the Bibliographical Society, Story Parade,* and *Consumer's Guide.*

Translator: Antoniorrobles, *Tales of Living Playthings,* Modern Age, 1938; Antoniorrobles, *Merry Tales From Spain,* Winston, 1939; (with Elizabeth Huberman) Antoniorrobles, *The Refugee Centaur,* Twayne, 1952. Also translator with Elizabeth Huberman of Calderon's "Life Is a Dream," published in *Spanish Drama,* edited by Angel Flores, Bantam, 1962.

WORK IN PROGRESS: New translations from Spanish and Mexican drama; studies in Shakespeare, Joyce, and Irish literature.

SIDELIGHTS: Huberman speaks Spanish, German, French, and Italian.

* * *

HUBERMAN, Elizabeth Duncan Lyle 1915-

PERSONAL: Surname is pronounced *Hugh*-bur-man; born November 30, 1915, in Gloucester, Mass.; daughter of James Macfarlane (in insurance) and Laura (Lorentzen) Lyle; married Edward Huberman (a professor of English), September 17, 1939; children: Joel Anthony, Jamie Lyle, Vincent Michael, Joan Laurie. *Education:* Bryn Mawr College, A.B. (summa cum laude), 1937; New York University, A.M., 1963, Ph.D., 1969. *Home:* 33 Hickory Dr., Maplewood, N.J. 07040. *Office:* Department of English, Kean College of New Jersey, Union, N.J.

CAREER: Fairleigh Dickinson University, Madison, N.J., part-time instructor in English, 1961-63; University of In-

nsbruck, Innsbruck, Austria, instructor in English, 1963-64; Upsala College, East Orange, N.J., lecturer in English, 1964-67; Kean College of New Jersey, Union, assistant professor, 1968-69, associate professor, 1969-73, professor of English, and chairman of department, 1973—. Secretary, Women's Trade Union League. Chairman, William Roy Smith Memorial Committee. *Member:* Modern Language Association of America, College English Association. *Awards, honors:* Bryn Mawr traveling fellowship.

WRITINGS: (Translator with husband, Edward Huberman) Antoniorrobles, *The Refugee Centaur,* Twayne, 1952; *Historia del Movimiento Obrero Mexicano,* Problemas Agricolas, 1959; (editor with Edward Huberman) *Fifty Great Essays,* Bantam, 1964; (editor with Edward Huberman) *Great British Short Stories,* Bantam, 1968; (editor with Edward Huberman) *War: An Anthology,* Washington Square Press, 1969; (editor with Edward Huberman) *Fifty Great European Short Stories,* Bantam, 1971; *The Poetry of Edwin Muir,* Oxford University Press, 1971. Also translator with Edward Huberman of Calderon's "Life Is a Dream," published in *Spanish Drama,* edited by Angel Flores, Bantam, 1962. Contributor to *Story Parade, Baby Talk, American Junior Red Cross Journal, Publications of the Modern Language Association of America,* and other periodicals.

WORK IN PROGRESS: Studies of Muir, Yeats, Pound, and other twentieth-century poets.

SIDELIGHTS: Elizabeth Huberman speaks French, Spanish, and German.

* * *

HUBKA, Betty (Josephine Morgan) 1924-

PERSONAL: First syllable of surname rhymes with "tub"; born July 25, 1924, in Portland, Ore.; daughter of Joseph Cooksey (a building contractor) and Maybelle (Moulder) Morgan; married Miles William Hubka (now manager of industrial development, Tucson Chamber of Commerce), June 28, 1944; children: Rebecca, Cheryl, Kevin. *Education:* Texas Technological College, B.S. in Home Economics, 1941, M.Ed., 1955; other courses at University of Arizona. *Religion:* Methodist. *Home:* Tucson, Ariz. 85704.

CAREER: Elementary teacher in public schools in Texas, 1945-46, 1954-55; Amphitheater public schools, Tucson, Ariz., first grade teacher, 1963—.

WRITINGS—Juveniles: Bernie, Steck, 1962; *Octavius,* Steck, 1963; *Stubborn as a Mule,* Steck, 1967; *Where is the Bear?,* Golden Press, 1967. Contributor of stories to *Jack and Jill, Highlights for Children,* and *Wee Wisdom,* and articles to *Arizona Teacher.*

WORK IN PROGRESS: Two children's books with graded vocabularies, *Kachinas of the Pueblos* and a collection of Southwest Indian legends; testing and measuring, curriculum content, and other phases of the education of academically talented children.†

* * *

HUDSON, R(obert) Lofton 1910-

PERSONAL: Born August 5, 1910, in Watertown, Tenn.; son of Robert Sidney (a farmer) and Laura (Vantrease) Hudson; married Jessie Thompson (a schoolteacher), January 2, 1933; children: Patricia. *Education:* George Peabody College for Teachers, B.S., 1936, Ph.D., 1946; Southern Baptist Theological Seminary, Th.B., 1938; Vanderbilt University, M.A., 1940; summer student at University of Denver, Yale University, and Menninger School of Psychiatry. *Politics:* Democrat. *Home:* 310 West 49th St., Kansas City, Mo. 64112. *Office:* Midwest Christian Counseling Center, 605 West 47th St., Kansas City, Mo. 64112.

CAREER: Ordained Baptist minister, 1932; pastor of Baptist churches in Tennessee, 1932-46, and Shawnee, Okla., 1946-50; Central Baptist Seminary, Kansas City, Kan., instructor in pastoral counseling, 1950-54; Wornall Road Baptist Church, Kansas City, Mo., pastor, 1950-57; Midwest Christian Counseling Center, Kansas City, Mo., founder and director, 1957—. Oklahoma Baptist University, special lecturer in English, 1946-48; Missouri State College Extension, lecturer on adolescent psychology. Formerly conductor of Kansas City radio program, "Counselor's Corner." Member of board of Council on Alcoholism of Greater Kansas City and Service Corp. for Senior Citizens.

MEMBER: International Platform Association, American Psychological Association, American Association of Pastoral Counselors, American Association of Marriage Counselors, National Council on Family Relations, National Academy of Religion and Mental Health, Christian Association for Psychological Studies, American Society of Clinical Hypnosis, Society of Clinical and Experimental Hypnosis, Institute of Pastoral Care, Regional Health and Welfare Council, Phi Delta Kappa, Kappa Delta Pi. *Awards, honors:* Distinguished Alumnus award from George Peabody College for Teachers, 1971.

WRITINGS: The Religion of a Sound Mind, Broadman, 1949; *The Religion of a Mature Person*, Broadman, 1952; *Taproots for Tall Souls*, Broadman, 1954; *Growing a Christian Personality*, Broadman, 1955; *For Our Age of Anxiety*, Broadman, 1956; *Sir, I Have a Problem*, Crowell, 1959; *Marital Counseling*, Prentice-Hall, 1963; *Love and Marriage*, Fremerman-Papin, 1964; *The Religion of a Happy Home*, Pittcraft, 1965; *Home Is the Place*, Broadman, 1967; *Grace Is Not a Blue Eyed Blond*, Word Books, 1968; *Persons In Crisis*, Broadman, 1969; *Helping Each Other Be Human*, Word Books, 1970; *Til Divorce Do Us Part: A Christian Looks At Divorce*, Nelson, 1973. Author of syndicated radio program "Love and Marriage." Contributor to Baptist periodicals.

WORK IN PROGRESS: A study on the traveling man's family.

BIOGRAPHICAL SOURCES: Life, August 20, 1956; *Kansas City Star*, May 20, 1962.†

*   *   *

HUEGLI, A(lbert) G(eorge)   1913-

PERSONAL: Surname is pronounced to rhyme with "frugally"; born June 7, 1913, in Detroit, Mich.; son of Albert G. (a physician) and Lydia (Reif) Huegli; married Rae Merritt (an interior decorator), January 2, 1941; children: Karen (Mrs. Robert A. Buethe, Jr.), Jon Merritt. *Education:* Concordia Seminary, St. Louis, Mo., B.D., 1936; University of Michigan, M.A., 1937; Wayne University (now Wayne State University), A.B., 1938; Northwestern University, Ph.D., 1944. *Politics:* Independent. *Home:* 1401 Linwood St., Valparaiso, Ind. *Office:* Office of the President, Valparaiso University, Valparaiso, Ind.

CAREER: Ordained Lutheran minister, 1944. St. John's College, Winfield, Kan., assistant professor of history and government, 1938-40; Concordia Teachers College, River Forest, Ill., professor of history and government, 1940-61,

dean, 1944-61; Valparaiso University, Valparaiso, Ind., professor of government and vice-president for academic affairs, 1961-68, acting president, 1968, president, 1968—. Northwestern University, visiting lecturer in government, 1944-55; North Central Association of Colleges and Secondary Schools, examiner and consultant, 1961—; Village of Oak Park, Ill., trustee, 1957-61; member of board of higher education and vice-president of Lutheran Academy for Scholarship of Lutheran Church Missouri Synod, 1964-69. *Member:* Associated Independent Colleges and Universities (Indiana vice-president, 1972—), National Education Association, American Political Science Association, Lutheran Education Association, Associated Colleges of Indiana (vice-president, 1972—). *Awards, honors:* LL.D., Concordia Teachers College, (River Forest, Ill.).

WRITINGS: (With R. B. Posey) *Government for Americans*, Harper, 1953, 3rd edition, 1963; *The Big Change and Its Challenge to the Church*, Concordia, 1957; (editor) *Church and State Under God*, Concordia, 1964; (contributor) A. J. Buehner, editor, *Operation Theology: The Layman and Current Religions Developments*, Lutheran Academy for Scholarship, 1968.

WORK IN PROGRESS: A paperback on the citizen in the modern state.†

*   *   *

HUFF, Robert   1924-

PERSONAL: Born April 3, 1924, in Evanston, Ill.; son of Robert E. (a dentist) and Elaine (Fontaine) Huff; married Sally Ann Sener, March, 1959; children: Ursula, Michele, Dylan. *Education:* Wayne (now Wayne State) University, A.B., 1949, A.M., 1952. *Home:* 2820 Eldridge, Bellingham, Wash. *Office:* English Department, Western Washington State College, Bellingham, Wash.

CAREER: Wayne University, Detroit, Mich., graduate assistant part-time instructor in humanities, and counselor for the College of Liberal Arts, 1950-52; instructor in English, 1957-58; University of Oregon, Eugene, instructor in English, 1952-53; Fresno State College, Fresno, Calif., instructor in English, 1953-55; Oregon State College, Corvallis, instructor in English, 1955-57, 1958-60; University of Delaware, Newark, assistant professor, and poet-in-residence, 1960-64; Western Washington State College, Bellingham, assistant professor of English, 1964—. *Military service:* U.S. Army Air Forces, 1943-46. *Awards, honors:* Indiana University School of Letters Fellowship, 1957; Bread Loaf Writers' Conference fellowship, 1961; MacDowell Colony fellowship, 1963.

WRITINGS: Colonel Johnson's Ride, and Other Poems, Wayne State University Press, 1959; *Poems*, Portland (Ore.) Art Museum, 1959; *The Course: One, Two, Three, Now!* (poems), Wayne State University, 1966; (with Kenneth Erickson) *Activism in the Secondary Schools: Analysis and Recommendations*, University of Oregon, 1969; *The Ventriloquist* (poems), Swallow Press, 1973.

Work represented in many anthologies, including *The Contemporary American Poets*, edited by Mark Strand, World, 1969, *The Realities of Literature*, edited by R. F. Dietrich, Blaisdell, 1970, and *Contemporary Poetry in America*, edited by Miller Williams, Random House, 1973.

Contributor of poetry to *Harper's, Poetry, Atlantic Monthly, Voices, Saturday Review, Northwest Review, Prairie Schooner, New York Herald Tribune, Paris Review, Poetry Northwest, College English, Mademoiselle*,

Kenyon Review, Mad River Review, American Weave, Arts & Society, and to other publications.

WORK IN PROGRESS: Poems.

SIDELIGHTS: Huff says that for his poetical training he is grateful "to the shores of Lake Michigan near Saugatuck, Michigan, and to the forests of the Northwest." *Avocational interests:* Hunting and fishing, "both of which are rapidly becoming sitting by the sea."

*   *   *

HUFFERT, Anton M. 1912-

PERSONAL: Born February 22, 1912, in Mertisoara, Rumania; son of Joseph Frank and Elizabeth (Frank) Huffert; married E. Barbara Stahl, June 16, 1956; children: Robert, Elaine, Susan, Anthony. *Education:* City College (now of the City University of New York), B.A., 1933, M.S., 1935, post-graduate study, 1938-40; New York University, Ph.D., 1951; other study at University of Bern, 1933-34, Columbia University, 1940, Northwestern University, 1944, Texas A & M University, 1944. *Home:* 4 Earl St., Westbury, Long Island, N.Y. *Office:* Department of German and General Linguistics, Adelphi University, Garden City, Long Island, N.Y.

CAREER: City College (now of the City University of New York), New York, N.Y., evening instructor in German, 1936-38; high school teacher of German and social studies, Ozone Park, N.Y., 1938-42; civilian translator in New York, N.Y., for U.S. Office of Censorship, 1942-43, U.S. Army Air Forces, 1946; Rutgers University, Douglass College, New Brunswick, N.J., instructor in German, 1946-50; Queens College (now of the City University of New York), Flushing, N.Y., instructor in English, 1950-51; St. John's Preparatory School, Brooklyn, N.Y., teacher of German, 1951-52; Adelphi University, Garden City, Long Island, N.Y., 1952—, now associate professor of German. *Military service:* U.S. Navy, 1943-45. *Member:* American Association of Teachers of German, Modern Language Association of America, American Association of University Professors, Thoreau Society, Freies Deutsches Hochstift. *Awards, honors:* Research awards from Adelphi University to study influence of Leibniz on Goethe's thought, 1960, 1962.

WRITINGS: Basic Facts of German Grammar, Collier, 1963. Contributor of articles on four German writers to *European Authors*, Wilson, 1964. Reviewer (and consultant) for *Choice: Books for College Libraries*.

WORK IN PROGRESS: Further research on influence of Leibniz on Goethe's thought for a book tentatively titled *Goethe and Leibniz*.

SIDELIGHTS: Huffert lived for periods in former Austria-Hungary, in Rumania, and in Switzerland and did research in libraries of West Germany, East Germany, and Austria in 1960. He has knowledge of French, Latin, and Italian, in addition to fluency in German. *Avocational interests:* American Southwest and its scenery, geography, and geology; international affairs, reading, swimming, tennis, skiing, ice skating, and hiking.†

*   *   *

HUGHES, (John) Cledwyn 1920-

PERSONAL: Born May 21, 1920, in Llansantffraid, Montgomeryshire, Wales; son of John Watkin (a gentleman farmer) and Janet (Bynner) Hughes; married Alyna Jones-Davies, 1947; children: Janet, Rebecca. *Education:* Uni-

versity of Liverpool, registered pharmacist with pharmaceutical chemist diploma, 1945. *Home and office:* The Crescent, Arthog, Merionethshire, Wales.

CAREER: Hospital pharmacist at Liverpool Cancer Hospital, Liverpool, England, and Maelor General Hospital, Wrexham, Wales, 1945-47; full-time writer, 1947—. *Member:* Pharmaceutical Society of Great Britain. *Awards, honors:* Short story awards, *New York Herald Tribune*.

WRITINGS: He Dared Not Look Behind, Wyn, 1947 (published in England as *The Inn Closes for Christmas*, Pilot Press, 1947); *The Different Drummer* [and] *The Inn Closes for Christmas*, Pilot Press, 1947; *Wennon*, Pilot Press, 1948; *Civil Strangers*, Phoenix House, 1949; *Wanderer in Wales*, Phoenix House, 1949; *After the Holiday*, Phoenix House, 1950; *The Northern Marches*, R. Hale, 1951; *Poaching Down the Dee*, R. Hale, 1953; *Gold and the Moonspray*, Heinemann, 1953; *West with the Tinkers*, Odhams, 1954; *Royal Wales*, Roy, 1957; *House in the Cornfield*, Laurie, 1957; *Leonard Cheshire, V.C.*, Roy, 1961; *The King Who Lived on Jelly*, Routledge & Kegan Paul, 1961; *Making an Orchard*, St. Martins, 1962; *Ponies for Children*, Routledge & Kegan Paul, 1962; *La Jambe du Cain*, Gallimard, 1963; *Portrait of Snowdonia*, R. Hale, 1967; *The Colour Book of Wales*, Batsford, 1973.

Writer of radio and television scripts for British Broadcasting Corp. Short stories anthologized in *Best World Short Stories, New York Herald Tribune Prize Stories Awards*, and other collections.

WORK IN PROGRESS: The Pirate Mountain, and *The Wise Old Men on the Blue Hill*, books for children; *Story from the Dead*, a suspense novel; *Roads Again*, a novel; *Let's Go to Wales*, a travel book; *Windmill and Twelve Cherry Trees*, a collection of short stories; *The Welsh in the United States of America*; "Golden Mountains," a play.

SIDELIGHTS: Hughes told *CA:* "Fond of country life and travel. Theatre addict. Orderly by nature, avoid all public platforms, gentle with enemies but have motto on desk about 'nice guys finish last.'" Hughes' short stories have been translated into many languages and transcribed into Braille.

*   *   *

HUGHES, Helen (Gintz) 1928-

PERSONAL: Born October 1, 1928, in Prague, Czechoslovakia; daughter of Charles (a business executive) and Elsa (Cohen) Gintz; children: John Charles, Mark Andrew. *Education:* University of Melbourne, B.A. (honors), 1949, M.A. (honors), 1951; London School of Economics and Political Science, University of London, Ph.D., 1954. *Address:* Australian National University, Canberra, Australia.

CAREER: Economics and statistical researcher in Melbourne, Victoria, Australia, 1956-58; University of New South Wales, Sydney, Australia, lecturer in economics, 1959-60; University of Queensland, Brisbane, Australia, senior lecturer in economics, 1961-63; Australian National University, Canberra, Australian Capital Territory, senior research fellow in economics, 1963—.

WRITINGS: The Australian Iron and Steel Industry, 1848-1962, Melbourne University Press, 1964; (with M. Gough, B. J. McFarland, and G. Palmer) *Queensland: Industrial Enigma*, Melbourne University Press, 1964; (with Ozzie Simmons) *Work and Mental Illness*, Wiley, 1965; *The Zoopie Zats*, Horwitz, 1969, Platt & Munk,

1971; (editor with You-Poh Seng) *Investment and Industrialisation in Singapore*, University of Wisconsin Press, 1969; *Problems of Food Processing Industries in Developing Countries*, International Bank for Reconstruction and Development, 1969. Contributor to economic and economic history journals.†

* * *

HUGHES, James Quentin 1920-

PERSONAL: Born February 28, 1920, in Liverpool, England; son of James Stanley (an estate agent) and Marjorie (Edwards) Hughes; married Margaret Evans, April 27, 1947; children: Ceridwen Ann, Deborah Sian. *Education:* University of Liverpool, Bachelor of Architecture (with honors), 1945, Diploma in Civic Design, 1948; University of Leeds, Ph.D., 1954. *Home:* Loma Linda, Criccieth, Gwynedd, North Wales. *Office:* School of Architecture, University of Liverpool, Liverpool, England.

CAREER: A practicing architect, 1948—. University of Leeds, School of Architecture, Leeds, England, senior lecturer, 1950-56; University of Liverpool, School of Architecture, Liverpool, England, lecturer and studio instructor, 1954-61, senior lecturer, 1961—, reader, 1972—, sub-dean, 1964. Professor of architecture, and dean of faculty of engineering, Royal University of Malta, 1968. Chairman, Chester Civic Trust. *Military service:* British Army, Second Special Air Service Regiment, 1940-45; became captain; received Military Cross and bar. *Member:* Royal Institute of British Architects, Royal Society of Arts (fellow), Royal Historical Society (fellow).

WRITINGS: The Buildings of Malta During the Period of the Knights of St. John of Jerusalem, 1530-1795, Tiranti, 1956; (with Norbert Lynton) *Renaissance Architecture*, Longmans, Green, 1962; *Seaport–Architecture and Townscape of Liverpool*, Lund, Humphries, 1964; *Fortress–Architecture and Military History in Malta*, Lund, Humphries, 1966; *Liverpool*, Studio Vista, 1970; *Military Architecture*, Evelyn, 1974.

* * *

HULL, William (Doyle) 1918-

PERSONAL: Born April 13, 1918, in Westminster, S.C.; son of William Doyle (a salesman) and Mayme (Miller) Hull. *Education:* Furman University, B.A., 1938; University of Virginia, M.A., 1940, Ph.D., 1941. *Home:* 5 First Ave., Merrick, Long Island, N.Y. 11566. *Office:* Hofstra University, California Ave., Hempstead, N.Y. 11550.

CAREER: Howard College, Birmingham, Ala., instructor, 1941-42; North Carolina State College, Raleigh, instructor, 1946; Hofstra University, Hempstead, N.Y., 1946—began as instructor, became professor of English, 1963. Fulbright professor of American Literature, University of Ceylon, 1955-56, Patna University, 1959-60. *Military service:* U.S. Army Air Forces, 1942-46; service in India; became staff sergeant. *Member:* Society for Pre-Columbian Art, Phi Beta Kappa Alumni Association. *Awards, honors:* Shell assistance grant for *The Other Side of Silence.*

*WRITINGS—*All poetry: *Saul at Endor*, Brigant Press, 1954; *Selected Poems: 1942-52*, Brigant Press, 1954; *Dandy Brown*, Experiment Press, 1959; *The Catullus of William Hull*, Calcutta Writers Workshop Press, 1960; *The Other Side of Silence*, Swallowtree Press, 1964; *The Mastery of Love*, Swallowtree Press, 1967; *Collected Poems: 1942-1968*, Calcutta Writers Workshop Press, 1969; *Visions of*

Handy Hopper, Calcutta Writers Workshop Press, Book I: *Flood*, 1970, Book II: *Churn*, 1971, Book III: *Park*, 1972, Book IV: *Post*, 1973, Book V: *Hinge*, 1974. Author of play, "Journey Into Night"; wrote libretto for opera, "Fall Into Fire." Contributor to *Sewanee Review, Beloit Poetry Journal, Approach, Accent, Chicago Review, New Letters, Experiment, New Mexico Quarterly*, and *Bard Review.*

WORK IN PROGRESS: The last five books of Handy Hopper, completion expected in 1979.

SIDELIGHTS: Hull is interested in Western and Eastern literature, music, and the arts; Indian and hermetic metaphysics; American folklore. He knows French, Italian, German, Latin. He told *CA:* "I am trying to make an American mythology; I think poets should make poetry, not write about it."

Chad Walsh calls Hull "a poet who intrigues me, baffles me, and sometimes maddens me." Referring to the mixture of public and private mythology in Hull's poems, Walsh says Hull is "stubbornly out of fashion: his poetry is obscure, replete with hidden allusions, more akin to Eliot and Pound than to the chastened clarity of the newer poetic generations. His language has a whirling splendor to it, flinging linguistic sparks into the dark air. He is never dull."

BIOGRAPHICAL/CRITICAL SOURCES: Sewanee Review, spring, 1960; *Thought* (India), April 30, 1960; *Saturday Review*, January 2, 1965.

* * *

HULME, William E(dward) 1920-

PERSONAL: Surname rhymes with "fume"; born January 25, 1920, in Youngstown, Ohio; son of William and Carrie (Schanz) Hulme; married Lucy Combs, January 26, 1946; children: Sally, Dale, Polly, Marcia, Lance. *Education:* Capital University, B.S., 1942; The Evangelical Lutheran Seminary, B.D., 1945; Boston University, Ph.D., 1947. *Politics:* Independent. *Home:* 1720 West Eldridge, St. Paul, Minn. 55113.

CAREER: Lutheran minister, 1946—. Pastor in Columbus, Ohio, 1946-49; Wartburg College, Waverly, Iowa, chaplain and professor of religion, 1949-55; Wartburg Theological Seminary, Dubuque, Iowa, professor of pastoral care, 1955-66; affiliated with Luther Theological Seminary, St. Paul, Minn., 1966—. Lutheran tutor, Mansfield College, Oxford University, 1958-59. Visiting professor of religion and personality, Divinity School, University of Chicago, 1964.

WRITINGS: Face Your Life with Confidence, Prentice-Hall, 1953; *How to Start Counseling*, Abingdon, 1955; *Counseling and Theology*, Fortress, 1956; *God, Sex and Youth*, Prentice-Hall, 1959; *Pastoral Care of Families*, Abingdon, 1962; *Living with Myself*, Prentice-Hall, 1964; *Youth Looks at Sex*, Nelson, 1965; *Building a Christian Marriage*, Prentice-Hall, 1965; *Your Pastor's Problems*, Doubleday, 1966; *The Dynamics of Sanctification*, Augsburg, 1966; *Dialogue in Despair*, Abingdon, 1968; *Pastoral Care Comes of Age*, Abingdon, 1970; *Am I Losing My Faith?*, Fortress, 1971; *When I Don't Like Myself*, Nelson, 1972; *When Two Become One*, Augsburg, 1972; *Two Ways of Caring*, Augsburg, 1973.

AVOCATIONAL INTERESTS: Family camping.

* * *

HUMPHREYVILLE, Theresa R. 1918-

PERSONAL: Born January 28, 1918, in New Philadelphia,

Ohio; daughter of Charles K. (a printer) and Dana (Orr) Humphreyville. *Education:* Ohio State University, B.Sc., 1940; New York University, M.Sc., 1941; Columbia University, Ed.D., 1953. *Home:* 64 Delamere Rd., Williamsville, N.Y. *Office:* State University of New York College at Buffalo, 1300 Elmwood Ave., Buffalo, N.Y.

CAREER: Registered psychologist, New York State. Johns-Manville Corp., New York, N.Y., personnel employee, 1941-46; New York State College of Home Economics at Cornell (now College of Human Ecology), Ithaca, professor in the counseling service, 1946-68; State University of New York College at Buffalo, now professor of human development. *Member:* American Psychological Association, New York State Association of Deans and Guidance Personnel.

WRITINGS: Futures for Home Economists, Prentice-Hall, 1963.

* * *

HUNKER, Henry L. 1924-

PERSONAL: Born November 14, 1924, in Wilkinsburg, Pa.; son of Frederick (a streetcar operator) and Dorothy (Schirra) Hunker; married M. Beth Sterner, August 1, 1945; children: Frederick, Kurt Christian, David Burd, Erich James. *Education:* University of Pittsburgh, B.A., 1945, M.A., 1948; Ohio State University, Ph.D., 1953. *Religion:* Christian. *Home:* 88 West Royal Forest Blvd., Columbus, Ohio 43214. *Office:* Department of Geography, Ohio State University, 1775 South College Rd., Columbus, Ohio 43210.

CAREER: Michigan State College of Agriculture and Applied Science (now Michigan State University), East Lansing, instructor, 1948-49; Ohio State University, Columbus, 1953—, began as research associate in geography, professor of geography, 1964—, assistant dean, College of Commerce and Administration, 1966-68, director, Center for Community and Regional Analysis, 1968-70. Fulbright lecturer at University of Queensland, 1957; visiting professor at Wayne State University, summer, 1958, and Miami University, Oxford, Ohio, 1960. Consultant to Battelle Memorial Institute, Educational Testing Consultants, Ohio Department of Natural Resources, and to private industry.

MEMBER: Association of American Geographers (chairman of East Lakes division, 1956-57), Ohio Academy of Science (fellow; membership vice-president of geography section, 1958), Alpha Kappa Delta. *Awards, honors:* Grants from National Science Foundation, 1961, and Ohio State University Development Fund; Battelle Memorial Institute fellow, 1972-73.

WRITINGS: (Contributor of maps and drawings) Alfred J. Wright, *United States and Canada* (textbook), 2nd edition, Appleton, 1956; *Industrial Evolution of Columbus, Ohio*, Bureau of Business Research, Ohio State University, 1958; *Ohio*, Doubleday, 1960; (with Alfred J. Wright) *Factors of Industrial Location in Ohio*, Bureau of Business Research, Ohio State University, 1963; (editor) Erich W. Zimmermann, *Introduction to World Resources*, Harper, 1964; *Industrial Development: Concepts and Principles*, Lexington Press, 1974. Contributor to *Encyclopaedia Britannica, Collier's Encyclopedia, Lincoln Library*, and *Book of Knowledge;* contributor of abstracts, reviews, and articles to professional journals. Editor, *East Lakes Geographer*, 1963—.

HUNT, Chester L. 1912-

PERSONAL: Born July 24, 1912, in Duluth, Minn.; son of Ray E. and Ada (Bash) Hunt; married Maxine Cole, August 28, 1942; children: Joanna, Leigh Rae (daughters). *Education:* Nebraska Wesleyan University, A.B., 1934; Washington University, St. Louis, Mo., M.A., 1937; University of Nebraska, Ph.D., 1948. *Politics:* Democrat. *Religion:* Disciples of Christ. *Home:* 2248 Crest Dr., Kalamazoo, Mich.

CAREER: Social caseworker, St. Louis, Mo., 1934-37; Nebraska State Teachers College (now Chadron State College), Chadron, Neb., assistant professor of sociology, 1939-41; Western Michigan University, Kalamazoo, 1948—, now professor of sociology. President, Kalamazoo Human Relations Council, 1955-57; member, Oakwood Board of Education. *Member:* Association for Asian Studies, Michigan Sociological Society (president, 1964-65), Philippine Sociological Society.

WRITINGS: Sociology in the Philippine Setting, Alemas, 1954, revised edition, 1963; (editor with Socorro Espiritu) *Community Development: Readings on the Philippines*, Garcia, 1964; (with Paul Horton) *Sociology*, McGraw, 1964, 3rd edition, 1972; *Social Aspects of Economic Development*, McGraw, 1966; (with Lewis Walker) *Ethnic Dynamics: Patterns of Intergroup Relations in Various Societies*, Dorsey, 1974. Contributor of articles to sociological journals.

* * *

HUNT, Douglas 1918-

PERSONAL: Born November 6, 1918, in Newark, N.J.; son of Melvin M. (a physician) and Ruth (Ashworth) Hunt; married Eleanor (Kari) Babcock (an artist), July 3, 1940; children: Karen. *Education:* Rutgers State University, B.S. in Mechanical Engineering, 1939. *Home:* 60 Joyce Kilmer Ave., New Brunswick, N.J.

CAREER: Engineer in chemical industry, New Jersey, 1941-62. Rutgers University, New Brunswick, N.J., extension lecturer in engineering, 1941-63. *Member:* Phi Beta Kappa, Tau Beta Pi.

WRITINGS: (With wife, Kari Hunt) *Pantomime—The Silent Theater*, Atheneum, 1964; *Exploring the Occult*, Arthur Barker, 1964, Ballantine, 1965, revised edition published as *A Handbook on the Occult*, Arthur Barker, 1967; (with Kari Hunt) *The Art of Magic*, Atheneum, 1967. Did photographic illustrations for his wife's book, *Masks and Mask Makers*, Abingdon, 1961.

WORK IN PROGRESS: A book on magic, completion expected in 1975; research with wife for book on Egypt "to make ancient Egyptians seem livelier than they appear in tomb-oriented books"; an engineering book for non-engineers.

AVOCATIONAL INTERESTS: Sleight-of-hand magic, photography, travel, and "fighting ignorance, especially my own."†

* * *

HUNT, Florine E(lizabeth) 1928-

PERSONAL: Born August 11, 1928, in Richmond, Va.; daughter of Alfred Carl (a carpenter) and Elva (Blacklidge) Hunt. *Education:* College of William and Mary, B.S., 1949; Western Reserve University (now Case Western Reserve University), graduate study, 1949-50; Rutgers University,

M.S. in L.S. 1955. *Politics:* Republican. *Religion:* Episcopalian. *Home:* 56 Oak Lane, Trenton, N.J. 18618. *Office:* Public Service Electric and Gas Co., 80 Park Pl., Newark, N.J. 07101.

CAREER: Social Service Bureau, Norfolk, Va., child welfare caseworker, 1950-52; Free Public Library, Trenton, N.J., junior librarian, 1952-55; Public Service Electric and Gas Company, Newark, N.J., junior assistant librarian, 1955-59, senior assistant librarian, 1959, librarian, 1959—. *Member:* Special Libraries Association (treasurer, New Jersey chapter, 1958-60; director of chapter, 1960-62; chairman, Public Utilities Division, 1973-74), National Association for the Advancement of Colored People (N.A.A.C.P.), Trenton Council on Human Relations.

WRITINGS: Public Utilities Information Sources, Gale, 1965.

* * *

HUNT, Todd T. 1938-

PERSONAL: Born June 19, 1938, in St. Paul, Minn.; son of Eldred Milo (a horticulturist) and Ruth (Bengtson) Hunt; married Karli Jo Webber (an editorial writer), April 15, 1962. *Education:* University of Minnesota, B.A., 1960; Ohio State University, M.A., 1967. *Home:* 6 Brookside Ave., New Brunswick, N.J. 08901. *Office:* Department of Journalism, Rutgers University, New Brunswick, N.J. 08903.

CAREER: Rome Daily American, Rome, Italy, reporter and night editor, 1960-61; *St. Paul Dispatch*, St. Paul, Minn., copyreader, 1961; Ohio State University, Columbus, instructor in journalism, 1965-68; Rutgers University, New Brunswick, N.J., associate professor of communication, 1968—. *Military Service:* U.S. Navy Supply Corps Reserve, active service, 1962-65; became lieutenant. *Member:* Authors Guild, Authors League, Association for Education in Journalism, Sigma Delta Chi. *Awards, honors:* George Washington Honor Medal of Freedoms Foundation, 1965, for essay.

WRITINGS: Anastasia Schultz, Doubleday, 1960; *The Ship with the Flat Tire*, Doubleday, 1964; (with Phil Bengtson) *Packer Dynasty*, Doubleday, 1969; *Reviewing for the Mass Media*, Chilton, 1972. Contributor to *Catholic Digest, Kiwanis, McCalls, Atlantic Monthly, Travel*, and *New York Times*.

BIOGRAPHICAL/CRITICAL SOURCES: Providence (R.I.) Sunday Journal, October 11, 1964.

* * *

HUNTER, John M(erlin) 1921-

PERSONAL: Born December 1, 1921, in Champaign, Ill.; son of Merlin H. (a teacher) and Evangeline (Groves) Hunter; married Kathryn Einbecker, June 5, 1948; children: Judith Lynn, Cynthia Leigh, Virginia Ann. *Education:* Swarthmore College, student, 1939-40; University of Illinois, B.S., 1943, M.S., 1947; Harvard University, M.A., 1949, Ph.D., 1951. *Politics:* Independent. *Religion:* Protestant. *Home:* 632 Baldwin Ct., East Lansing, Mich. 48823. *Office:* Department of Economics, Michigan State University, East Lansing, Mich. 48823.

CAREER: Tufts College, Medford, Mass., instructor in economics, 1949-50; Michigan State University, East Lansing, 1950—, started as assistant professor, professor of economics, 1958—, economist for university's advisory group to Vietnam, 1955-56, acting head of department of economics, 1957-58. University of the Andes, Bogota, Colombia, director of Center for Economic Studies, 1958-60; National University of Cordoba, Cordoba, Argentina, adviser to Institute of Economics and Finance and Ford Foundation program specialist, 1962-64. *Military service:* U.S. Army, Infantry, active duty 1943-47; now captain (retired).

WRITINGS: (With R. W. Lindholm and John Balles) *Money and Banking*, Norton, 1955; *Emerging Colombia*, Public Affairs, 1962; *Economic Aspects of Higher Education in Brazil*, Latin American Studies Center, Michigan State University, 1971.†

* * *

HUNTER, Kristin (Eggleston) 1931-

PERSONAL: Born September 12, 1931, in Philadelphia, Pa.; daughter of George Lorenzo and Mabel (Manigault) Eggleston; married John I. Lattany, June 22, 1968. *Education:* University of Pennsylvania, B.S. in Ed., 1951. *Home:* 1233 Pine St., Philadelphia 7, Pa. *Agent:* Harold Matson Co., Inc., 22 East 40th St., New York, N.Y. 10016.

CAREER: Pittsburgh Courier, Philadelphia (Pa.) edition, columnist and feature writer, 1946-52; copywriter for Lavenson Bureau of Advertising, Philadelphia, Pa., 1952-59, Wermen & Schorr, Inc., Philadelphia, 1962-63; City of Philadelphia, Philadelphia, Pa., information officer, 1963-64, 1965-66, free-lance writer, 1964—; Temple University, Philadelphia, Pa., director of comprehensive health services, 1971—. Instructor in creative writing, University of Pennsylvania, 1972-73. *Member:* Philadelphia Art Alliance, University of Pennsylvania Alumnae Association (director, 1970-73). *Awards, honors:* Fund for the Republic prize for television documentary, "Minority of One," 1955; John Hay Whitney "opportunity" fellowship, 1959-60; Philadelphia Athenaeum award, 1964; National Council on Interracial Books for Children award, 1968, for *The Soul Brothers and Sister Lou*; Sigma Delta Chi reporting award, 1968; Mass Media Brotherhood Award from National Conference of Christians and Jews, 1969, for *The Soul Brothers and Sister Lou*; Book World Children's Spring Festival, first prize, 1973.

WRITINGS—All published by Scribner: *God Bless the Child* (novel), 1964; *The Landlord* (novel), 1966; *The Soul Brothers and Sister Lou* (novel), 1968; *Boss Cat*, 1971; *Guests in the Promised Land: Stories*, 1973; *The Survivors*, 1975.

Wrote television documentary "Minority of One," produced by Columbia Broadcasting System, 1955. Contributor to *Philadelphia Magazine*.

SIDELIGHTS: Kristin Hunter's novel *The Landlord* was filmed by United Artists, released in 1970. *God Bless the Child* has been translated into German.†

* * *

HUNTER, Sam 1923-

PERSONAL: Born January 5, 1923, in Springfield, Mass.; son of Morris and Lottie (Sherman) Hunter; married Edys Merrill, July 22, 1954; children: Emily, Alexa. *Education:* Williams College (now University), A.B., 1943; University of Florence, Certificate of Studies, 1951. *Home:* 451 West End Ave., New York, N.Y. 10024. *Office:* McCormick Hall, Princeton University, Princeton, N.J. 08540.

CAREER: New York Times, New York, N.Y., art critic, 1947-49; Harry N. Abrams, Inc. (publisher of art books),

New York, N.Y., editor, 1952-53; *Arts* (magazine), New York, N.Y., editor, 1953-54; University of California, Los Angeles, associate professor, 1955-56; Museum of Modern Art, New York, N.Y., curator, 1956-58; Minneapolis Institute of Arts, Minneapolis, Minn., chief curator and acting director, 1958-60; Brandeis University, Waltham, Mass., director of Rose Art Museum and associate professor of fine arts, 1960-65; Jewish Museum, New York, N.Y., director, 1965-68; Princeton University, Princeton, N.J., professor of art and archeology, 1969—. Director, American Art, Century 21 exhibition at Seattle World's Fair, 1962; International Art juror at Thirty-Second Venice Biennale, 1964; visiting professor, Cornell University, 1967-69; lecturer, New School for Social Research, 1967-68; director of studies in visual arts, Massachusetts Board of Higher Education, 1968-69; critic's choice program director of New York State Council of the Arts, 1968-69; Regent's Professor and visiting critic, University of California, Riverside, 1968; visiting critic, State University of New York, 1968-69; vice-president and editor-in-chief, Harry N. Abrams, Inc., 1971-72. *Military service:* U.S. Navy, 1943-46; became lieutenant junior grade, received five battle stars. *Member:* College Art Association, Phi Beta Kappa. *Awards, honors:* Guggenheim fellowship, 1971-72.

WRITINGS: Henri de Toulouse-Lautrec, Abrams, 1953; *Raoul Dufy,* Abrams, 1953; *Jackson Pollock,* New York Museum of Modern Art, 1956; *Modern French Painting, 1855-1956,* Dell, 1956, 2nd edition, 1964; *Picasso: Cubism to the Present,* Abrams, 1957; *Mondrian,* Abrams, 1958; (editor) *Modern American Painting and Sculpture,* Dell, 1959; (editor) *European Art Today,* [Minneapolis], 1959, *Joan Miro: His Graphic Work,* Abrams, 1959; (co-author) *Art Since 1945,* Abrams, 1959; *Hans Hofmann,* Abrams, 1963; *James Brooks,* Praeger for Whitney Museum of American Art, 1963; (with others) *New Art Around the World: Painting and Sculpture,* Abrams, 1966; *Larry Rivers,* Abrams, 1970, 2nd edition with supplement, 1971; *La pittura americana del dopoguerra,* Fabbri, 1970; *Rivers,* Abrams, 1972; *American Art of the Twentieth Century,* Abrams, 1972; *Chryssa,* Abrams, 1974; (with John Jacobus) *American Art of the Twentieth Century* (textbook), Prentice-Hall, 1974. Also author and compiler of museum and special exhibition catalogues.

WORK IN PROGRESS: A revision of *Art Since 1945;* and *History of 19th Century Painting and Sculpture,* for publication by Abrams.

SIDELIGHTS: Hunter speaks Italian and French. *Avocational interests:* Golf, tennis.

*   *   *

HUNTER, William A(lbert) 1908-

PERSONAL: Born September 24, 1908, in Kinsman, Ohio; son of James LeRoy and Elizabeth Jane (Lee) Hunter; married Ada Harriet Amelia Short, June 7, 1947; children: Charles Edward. *Education:* Thiel College, student, 1927; Allegheny College, B.A., 1933; University of California, Berkeley, M.A., 1935; Duke University, graduate study, 1937. *Home:* R.D. 5, Mechanicsburg, Pa. *Office:* Pennsylvania Historical and Museum Commission, Harrisburg, Pa.

CAREER: Teacher in Sharpsville, Pa., 1927-28, 1936-45; Westinghouse Electric and Manufacturing Co., Sharon, Pa., transformer assembler, 1929-30, production clerk, 1944-46; Pennsylvania Historical and Museum Commission, Harrisburg, assistant historian, 1946-48, senior archivist, 1948-56, associate historian, 1956-61, chief of research

and publications, 1961—. *Member:* American Indian Ethnohistoric Conference, Society for Pennsylvania Archaeology, Pennsylvania Historical Association, Historical Society of Western Pennsylvania, Cumberland County Historical Society (director, 1962—), Harrisburg Scottish Society (president, 1958-59), Phi Beta Kappa. *Awards, honors:* American Association for State and Local History Award of Merit, 1961, for *Forts on the Pennsylvania Frontier, 1753-58.*

WRITINGS: (Contributor) John Witthoft and W. Fred Kinsey III, editors, *Susquehannock Miscellany,* Pennsylvania Historical and Museum Commission, 1959; *Forts on the Pennsylvania Frontier, 1753-58,* Pennsylvania Historical and Museum Commission, 1960; (with Sanford W. Higginbotham and Donald H. Kent) *Pennsylvania and the Civil War: A Handbook,* Pennsylvania Historical and Museum Commission, 1961; *Archibald Loudon: Pioneer Historian,* Cumberland County Historical Society, 1962; *Peter Chartier: Knave of the Wild Frontier,* Cumberland County Historical Society, 1973; (contributor) Herbert C. Kraft, editor, *A Delaware Indian Symposium,* Pennsylvania Historical and Museum Commission, 1974; (contributor) Bruce G. Trigger, editor, *Handbook of North American Indians,* Smithsonian Institution, in press. Writer of booklets published by Pennsylvania Historical and Museum Commission, and by Cumberland County Historical Society. Contributor to *Dictionary of Canadian Biography, Ethnohistory,* and to Pennsylvania historical and archaeological journals.

WORK IN PROGRESS: Forts on the Pennsylvania Frontier, covering the period after 1758; research in the field of seventeenth-century and eighteenth-century Indian and frontier history.

SIDELIGHTS: William Hunter has some knowledge (mostly reading) of German, French, and Gaelic.

BIOGRAPHICAL/CRITICAL SOURCES: Pittsburgh Press, January 1, 1961.

*   *   *

HURD, Edith (Thacher) 1910-
(Juniper Sage, a joint pseudonym)

PERSONAL: Born September 14, 1910, in Kansas City, Mo.; daughter of Hamilton John and Edith (Gilman) Thacher; married Clement Hurd (an artist and illustrator), June 24, 1939; children: John Thacher. *Education:* Radcliffe College, A.B., 1933; Bank Street College of Education, additional study, 1934. *Politics:* Democrat. *Home:* 80 Mountain Lane, Mill Valley, Calif. 94941. *Agent:* Marilyn Marlow, Curtis Brown Ltd., 60 East 56th St., New York, N.Y. 10022.

CAREER: Taught four years at the Dalton School, New York, N.Y.; U.S. Office of War Information, San Francisco, Calif., news analyst, 1942-45; author of books for children.

WRITINGS: Hurry, Hurry, W. R. Scott, 1938, published as *Hurry Hurry: A Story of What Happened to a Hurrier,* 1947, enlarged edition published as *Hurry Hurry,* Harper, 1960; *Engine, Engine, No. 9,* Lothrop, 1940; *Sky High,* Lothrop, 1941; *The Annie Moran,* Lothrop, 1942; *Speedy, the Hook and Ladder Truck,* Lothrop, 1942; *The Wreck of the Wild Wave,* Oxford University Press, 1942; *Jerry, the Jeep,* Lothrop, 1945; *Benny, the Bulldozer,* Lothrop, 1947, special edition, E. M. Hale, 1956; *Toughy and His Trailer Truck,* Lothrop, 1948; *The Galleon from Manila,* Oxford University Press, 1949; *Willy's Farm,* Lothrop, 1949.

Caboose, Lothrop, 1950; *Old Silversides*, Lothrop, 1951; *Mr. Shortsleeves' Great Big Store*, Simon & Schuster, 1952; *The Devil's Tail*, Doubleday, 1954; *Mary's Scary House*, Sterling, 1956; *Windy and the Willow Whistle*, Sterling, 1956; *Fox in a Box*, Doubleday, 1957; *It's Snowing*, Sterling, 1957; *The Faraway Christmas*, Lothrop, 1958; *Last One Home Is a Green Pig*, Harper, 1959.

The Golden Hind, Crowell, 1960; *Sandpipers*, Crowell, 1961; *Stop, Stop*, Harper, 1961; *Christmas Eve*, Harper, 1962; *Come and Have Fun*, Harper, 1962; *No Funny Business*, Harper, 1962; *Starfish*, Crowell, 1962; *Follow Tomas*, Dial, 1963; *Sailers, Whalers and Steamers*, Lane, 1964; *The So-So Cat*, Harper, 1965; *Johnny Lion's Book*, Harper, 1965; *The Day the Sun Danced*, Harper, 1965; *Who Will Be Mine?*, Golden Gate, 1966; *What Whale? Where?*, Harper, 1966; *Rain and the Valley*, Coward, 1968; *The Blue Heron Tree*, Viking, 1968; *This Is the Forest*, Coward, 1969.

Come With Me to Nursery School, Coward, 1970; *The White Horse*, Harper, 1970; *Johnny Lion's Bad Day*, Harper, 1970; *Catfish*, Viking, 1970; *Wilson's World*, Harper, 1971 (published in England as *Wilkie's World*, Faber, 1973); *The Mother Beaver*, Little, Brown, 1971; *The Mother Deer*, Little, Brown, 1972; *Johnny Lion's Rubber Boots*, Harper, 1972; *The Mother Whale*, Little, Brown, 1973; *The Mother Owl*, Little, Brown, 1974; *Catfish and the Kidnapped Cat*, Harper, 1974.

With husband, Clement Hurd: *St. George's Day in Williamsburg*, Colonial Williamsburg, 1952; *Somebody's House*, Lothrop, 1953; *Nino and His Fish*, Lothrop, 1954; *The Cat From Telegraph Hill*, Lothrop, 1955; *Mr. Charlie's Chicken House*, Lippincott, 1955; *Mr. Charlie's Gas Station*, Lippincott, 1956; *Johnny Littlejohn*, Lothrop, 1957; *Mr. Charlie's Camping Trip*, Lippincott, 1957; *Mr. Charlie, the Fireman's Friend*, Lippincott, 1958; *Mr. Charlie's Pet Shop*, Lippincott, 1959; *Mr. Charlie's Farm*, Lippincott, 1960; (with Thacher Hurd) *Little Dog, Dreaming*, Harper, 1967.

With Margaret Wise Brown: *Five Little Firemen*, Simon & Schuster, 1948; *Two Little Miners*, Simon & Schuster, 1949; *The Little Fat Policeman*, Simon & Schuster, 1950.

With Margaret Wise Brown, under joint pseudonym Juniper Sage: *The Man in the Manhole and the Fix-it Men*, W. R. Scott, 1946.

SIDELIGHTS: Edith Hurd's husband, Clement Hurd, has illustrated more than thirty of her books.

* * *

HURLBUTT, Robert H(arris) III 1924-

PERSONAL: Born February 13, 1924, in Springfield, Mo.; son of Robert Harris, Jr. (a printer) and Nora (Staley) Hurlbutt; married Laura M. Mutz, September 15, 1944; children: Robert H. IV, Elizabeth B., Jane H. *Education:* Drury College, A.B., 1946; University of Michigan, M.A. (philosophy), 1948; University of California, Berkeley, M.A. (history), 1951, Ph.D. (philosophy), 1953. *Home:* 2955 Stratford, Lincoln, Neb. 68502. *Office:* Department of Philosophy, University of Nebraska, Lincoln, Neb. 68508.

CAREER: University of Arizona, Tucson, 1952-62, began as instructor, became associate professor of philosophy; University of Nebraska, Lincoln, 1962—, began as associate professor, now professor of philosophy. University of California, Berkeley, visiting assistant professor, 1954-55. *Military service:* U.S. Naval Reserve, 1943-46; became

lieutenant junior grade. *Member:* American Philosophical Association, American Society for Aesthetics, Mountain Plains Philosophical Association.

WRITINGS: Hume, Newton, and the Design Argument, University of Nebraska Press, 1965. Contributor to professional journals.

WORK IN PROGRESS: The Philosophy of History, Modern Ethical Skepticism; and studies in aesthetics.

AVOCATIONAL INTERESTS: Painting, music, playing the piano.†

* * *

HURLEY, Jane (Hezel) 1928-

PERSONAL: Born August 11, 1928, in Chicago, Ill.; daughter of Gustave William (a business executive) and Ellen (Munro) Hezel; married William James Hurley, Jr. (a professor at Illinois Teachers College), July 10, 1954; children: Ellen Maureen, Jane Ann, William James III, Michael Sean, Patrick Vincent, Matthew John. *Education:* DePaul University, Ph.B., 1950, M.A., 1952; graduate courses at DePaul University, Chicago Teachers College, and University of Illinois, 1954-64. *Religion:* Roman Catholic. *Home:* 8346 North Waukegan Rd., Niles, Ill. 60648.

CAREER: Chicago (Ill.) Board of Education, elementary teacher, 1950-62; Loyola University, Chicago, Ill., lecturer in education, 1962; Chicago Board of Education, teacher-librarian, 1965.

WRITINGS: (With husband, William James Hurley, Jr.) *Dan Frontier Goes to Congress*, Benefic, 1964; (with Doris Haynes) *Afro-Americans, Then and Now*, Benefic, 1969.†

* * *

HUTCHENS, Eleanor Newman 1919-

PERSONAL: Born October 9, 1919, in Huntsville, Ala.; daughter of Morton McAllister (a merchant) and Susie (Newman) Hutchens. *Education:* Agnes Scott College, B.A., 1940; University of Pennsylvania, M.A., 1944, Ph.D., 1957; summer study at New York University, 1947, Oxford University, 1950, and University of Birmingham (England), 1960. *Politics:* Independent. *Religion:* Episcopalian. *Home:* 300 Williams Ave., S.E., Huntsville, Ala. 35801. *Office:* University of Alabama, P.O. Box 1247, Huntsville, Ala. 35801.

CAREER: Agnes Scott College, Decatur, Ga., director of publicity, 1940-43; *Huntsville Times*, Huntsville, Ala., assistant editor, 1944-47; Agnes Scott College, director of publicity and alumnae affairs and editor of *Alumnae Quarterly*, 1947-54; University of Alabama, Huntsville, assistant professor of English, 1957-61; Agnes Scott College, associate professor of English, 1961-67; University of Alabama, professor of English, 1967—. Director, Huntsville Land Co., and West Huntsville Land Co., 1966—; president, Huntsville Hotel Co., 1968—. Trustee of Randolph School, Huntsville, Ala., 1959-70, and Agnes Scott College, 1962-64. *Member:* Modern Language Association of America, American Society for Eighteenth-Century Studies, Agnes Scott Alumnae Association (president, 1960-62), Phi Beta Kappa, Mortar Board, Phi Kappa Phi.

WRITINGS: Irony in Tom Jones, University of Alabama Press, 1965; *Writing to be Read*, Prentice-Hall, 1969. Contributor to literary journals. Editor, *Mortar Board Quarterly*, 1945-50.

* * *

HUTCHINSON, Robert 1924-

PERSONAL: Born April 11, 1924, in Hutchinson, Kan.;

son of Orie Lowell (a wholesale grocer) and Lennie Ann (Baker) Hutchinson. *Education:* University of Kansas, A.B., 1947; Middlebury College, M.A., 1950; Columbia University, and Union Theological Seminary, Ph.D. candidate, 1947-50, 1952-53. *Politics:* Democrat. *Religion:* Protestant. *Home:* 1437 First Ave., New York, N.Y. 10021. *Agent:* Harold Matson Co., 22 East 40th St., New York, N.Y. 10016. *Office:* Dover Publications, Inc., 180 Varick St., New York, N.Y. 10014.

CAREER: Mount Hermon School, Mount Hermon, Mass., instructor in English, 1950-51; Alabama College, Montevallo, assistant professor of philosophy and religion, 1951-52; McGraw-Hill Book Co., Inc., New York, N.Y., assistant editor, 1954-58; City College of New York (now City College of the City University of New York), New York, N.Y., instructor in English, 1962-63; Dover Publications, Inc., New York, N.Y., editor, 1960—. *Military Service:* U.S. Army Air Forces, meteorologist, 1943-46; became 1st lieutenant. *Member:* Summerfield Scholars, Society for Religion in Higher Education, Phi Beta Kappa. *Awards, honors:* Crowell Short Story Award, 1947; Elinor Frost Poetry Scholarship, Bread Loaf School of English, 1956; Eugene F. Saxton Fellowship (Harper & Brothers), 1959-60; Bernard de Voto Fellowship for Prose, Bread Loaf Writers Conference, 1963.

WRITINGS: The Kitchen Dance (poems), A. Swallow, 1955; (editor) *The Humorous World of Jerome K. Jerome,* Dover, 1962; (editor) Finley Peter Dunne, *Mr. Dooley on Ivrything and Ivrybody,* Dover, 1963; (editor) *Poems of Anne Bradstreet,* Dover, 1969; (editor) *Poems of George Santayana,* Dover, 1970; *Standing Still While Traffic Moved About Me* (poems), Eakins, 1971.

Author of introduction: Franklin P. Adams, *The Melancholy Lute,* Dover, 1962; *1800 Woodcuts of Thomas Bewick and His School,* Dover, 1962; William Rimmer, *Art Anatomy,* Dover, revised edition, 1962; *Joe Miller's Jests, or the Wits Vade Mecum,* Dover, 1963; *Dictionary of American Portraits,* Dover, 1966.

Poems represented in anthology, *The New Yorker Book of Poems,* Viking, 1969.

Contributor of poems and short stories to *Saturday Review, Poetry, Quarterly Review of Literature, Atlantic, Harper's, Southwest Review, Springtime Two, Springtime Three* (London), *American Scholar, Accent, New Yorker, Epoch,* and other periodicals.

WORK IN PROGRESS: Poetry; a novel under option to Atlantic-Little.

SIDELIGHTS: Hutchinson told *CA:* "My early work, as exemplified in *The Kitchen Dance,* was largely an exploration of childhood experiences; my more recent poems seem to me to be concerned with the shapes of history, and with the necessities and purposes of art. The work, essentially lyric, usually centers about a person or specific human situation."

Stanley Kunitz said that "Robert Hutchinson stands at the opposite pole from the 'public' poet. He is not to be found gossiping on the terrace or declaiming from a balcony.... Many of his poems are evocations of childhood, the world in which he seems to be most at home, and of which he writes with affecting pathos and nostalgia." John Dillon Husband believes that "there is a freshness and vitality in this turning to roots, to childhood evocations. As Mr. Hutchinson's work indicates, it is not the prompting of a sad nostalgia, but the tapping of a resource that freshens

perception and image, offers an unalienable point of vantage and a strength of its own kind. It keeps the ruthlessness as well as the freshness of its taproot.... His imagery is highly selective, his structural metaphor is disciplined to a fine balance of its components. He works in a subdued vein, a limited orbit prosodically, but this, like chamber music, offers its own satisfaction."

Kunitz finds the poems of adult experience to be less sharply realized and sees Hutchinson's future as dependent on his ability to "come out of the kitchen and get his hooks into the immediate world." But he suggests that Hutchinson "has intellectual powers and a gift for synthesis that he does not usually put to the test." Husband, in an overview, sees Hutchinson as influential to the modern school of poetry: "Contemporary poetry seems to me to be gathering toward a new direction, and Robert Hutchinson suggests a shape and promise of that direction."

In a letter to Hutchinson, Mark Van Doren wrote of *Standing Still While Traffic Moved About Me:* "I liked the whole book, and particularly, very particularly, 'Street' on page 37, to name no other poem, though I could name many. 'Street' is bewitched and bewitching—cockeyed, in fact, and I truly love it."

Hutchinson has given numerous poetry readings and has worked in residence at Yaddo, 1956 and 1958, and at the MacDowell Colony, 1957 and 1959. His poems have been read for radio by Edward Field, Kimon Friar, and Robert Glauber. His short story, "Drug Store: Sunday Noon," was adapted for television by Horton Foote and presented, with Helen Hayes in the leading role, on *"Omnibus,"* December, 1956.

BIOGRAPHICAL/CRITICAL SOURCES: New Mexico Quarterly, summer, 1954; *Poetry,* Jane, 1956, *Saturday Review,* February 2, 1957; *Kansas City Times,* March 17, 1965.

*   *   *

HUTT, Maurice George 1928-

PERSONAL: Born September 22, 1928, in Rugby, England; son of Robert (principal of Stratford on Avon College of Further Education) and Marie (Laguiller) Hutt; married Rosemary Orton, July, 1953; children: Paul Edward, Nicholas John, Michael Anthony, Tonie Ann, Peter Louis. *Education:* Jesus College, Oxford, B.A. 1951, M.A., 1955. *Office:* University of Sussex, Brighton BN19QN, England.

CAREER: University of Leeds, Leeds, England, lecturer in modern history, 1952-61; University of Sussex, Brighton, England, lecturer, 1961-63, reader in history, 1963—, on leave as Leverhulme fellow, 1964-65. Visiting professor, Cornell University, 1955-56.

WRITINGS: (Contributor) D. Daiches, *The Idea of a New University,* Deutsch, 1964; *Napoleon,* Oxford University Press, 1965; (contributor) J. Cruickshank, *French Literature and its Background,* Volume 4, Oxford University Press, 1969; (editor) *Napoleon,* Prentice-Hall, 1972. Contributor to English, Canadian, and French historical reviews.

WORK IN PROGRESS: Research on the counterrevolution in western France in the late eighteenth century.

*   *   *

HUXLEY, Laura Archera

PERSONAL: Born in Turin, Italy; came to United States

in 1937; daughter of Fede (Bellini) Archera and Mr. Archera; married Aldous Huxley (a philosopher, novelist, and critic), 1956 (died,1963). *Education* Studied violin in Berlin, Paris, and United States; attended Curtis Institute, Philadelphia, Pa.; also attended drama school. *Home:* 6233 Mulholland Hwy., Hollywood, Calif. 90068.

CAREER: Formerly a concert violinist; after the outbreak of war, was a partner in the production of documentary films, a partner in a poodle-breeding concern, and a film cutter for a major Hollywood motion picture studio.

WRITINGS: You Are Not the Target, Farrar, Straus, 1963; *This Timeless Moment: A Personal View of Aldous Huxley,* Farrar, Strauss, 1968.

WORK IN PROGRESS: Between Heaven and Earth.

SIDELIGHTS: Mrs. Huxley writes: "A succession of explorations and discoveries; that's what my life has been. The world of my childhood was the formal family-centered world typical of Italian life. My first voyage of discovery took me from this restricted world into another—equally restricted—the world of the professional virtuoso.

"The outbreak of World War II found me at the Curtis Institute in Philadelphia. I decided to return to Italy, but travel was difficult and dangerous.... I found that I was an enemy alien.... The walls of my closed universe began to crumble, and I suddenly realized that there were other things in life beside the violin—other ideals beside those of artistic integrity and technical perfection.... I decided, finally and irrevocably, to give up my career as a concert violinist.

"The event that finally launched me upon the most extended expedition into the unknown was the critical illness of one of my closest friends. She was being treated by first-rate specialists; but, if they confined themselves to orthodox medical methods, could even first-rate specialists save my friend and, having saved her, bring her back to a full and fruitful life? I had my doubts. Specialization, and I knew this well from my own experience with the violin, had to be supplemented by generalization.

"The interrelatedness of life and sickness had to be looked at from every angle, attacked on every front.... What was there to know, I found myself wondering, about constitutional differences? ... How much does the mind influence the body—and the body the mind? What about suggestion—and autosuggestion—and animal magnetism? What about Coue and New Thought, hydrotherapy and fast? How are we being conditioned—and how can we be deconditioned? ...

"After my marriage to Aldous Huxley, the learning process was still accelerated. He had started from the theoretical end of the spectrum of knowledge and had travelled mainly in the world of philosophy and literature. I had set out from the limited world of the virtuoso, and my voyage of discovery had been in the realms of empirical practice of day by day trial and error. But, by entirely different roads, we have reached the same conclusion: that is, that 'nothing short of everything is enough.' This is the idea underlying the Recipes for Living and Loving in *You Are Not the Target.*"

Of *This Timeless Moment,* Philip Toynbee writes: "[Laura Huxley] shows us the greatness of Huxley as a man more clearly than he ever quite showed it in his own writing. I don't mean, of course, that the wife is a better writer than the husband was: she is not. But she has taken the best possible advantage of her unique position. She has been able to look at her husband from very close at hand but also from that infinite distance which always separates one human being from another. In spite of its minor failings *This Timeless Moment* is a lucid, persuasive, intimate and loving portrait of a great man." A segment of an autobiographical novel Huxley was writing at the time of his death is included in *This Timeless Moment.*

BIOGRAPHICAL/CRITICAL SOURCES: New Statesman, April 17, 1964.

* * *

HUXTABLE, (William) John (Fairchild) 1912-

PERSONAL: Born July 25, 1912, in England; son of John (a minister) and Florence (Watts) Huxtable; married Joan Lorimer Snow, September 6, 1939; children: Janet (Mrs. Christopher Mellor), Peter John, Felicity Joan. *Education:* University of Bristol, B.A.; Oxford University, M.A.; D.D. (Aberdeen and Lambeth). *Politics:* Conservative. *Home:* 10 Gerard Rd., Harrow, Middlesex, England. *Office:* 86 Tavistock Place, London, WC1H 9RT, England.

CAREER: Congregational minister in Newton Abbot, Devonshire, England, 1937-42, in Palmers Green, London, England, 1942-54; University of London, New College, London, England, principal, 1953-64; Congregational Union of England and Wales, chairman, 1962-63, secretary general with headquarters in London, 1964-66; Congregational Church in England and Wales, minister secretary, 1966-72; United Reformed Church, joint general secretary and clerk of the General Assembly, 1972—, moderator, 1972-73. Member of Joint Committee of the Translation of the Bible, 1947—. Maynard Chapman Lecturer at Westfield College, University of London, 1960.

WRITINGS: The Ministry, Independent Press, 1943; (editor with others) *A Book of Public Worshop,* Independent Press, 1948, 2nd edition, Oxford University Press, 1949; *The Faith That Is in Us,* Independent Press, 1953; *The Promise of the Father,* Independent Press, 1959; *Like a Strange People,* London Missionary Society, 1961; *The Christian Doctrine of God,* Independent Press, 1961; *Church and State in Education,* Religious Education Press, 1962; *The Tradition of Our Fathers,* Independent Press, 1962; *The Bible Says,* Knox Press, 1962; (editor) *Revelation Old and New,* Independent Press, 1962; (contributor) Nuttall & Chadwick, editors, *From Uniformity to Unity,* S.P.C.K., 1962; (contributor) H. H. Rowley, editor, *A Companion to the Bible,* T. & T. Clark, 1964; *The Preacher's Integrity,* Epworth, 1964; *Christian Unity: Some of the Issues,* Independent Press, 1966.

Also author of *Preaching the Law,* 1964. Editor of *John Owen's True Nature of a Gospel Church.* Contributor to symposia and to religious periodicals.

SIDELIGHTS: Huxtable wrote: "I am a country man, marooned in London; my chief hobby is escaping from London." Huxtable is competent in French, knows some Italian, and a little German.

* * *

HYAMS, Barry 1911-

PERSONAL: Born April 7, 1911; son of Phineas and Fanny (Gold) Hyams; married second wife, Helen Baron (an actress), May 18, 1956; children: (first marriage) Nessa, Peter; (second marriage) Danna. *Office:* Repertory Theater of Lincoln Center, 150 West 65th St., New York, N.Y. 10023.

CAREER: National Play Bureau, New York, N.Y., editor, 1935-37; director of publicity and production associate to S. Hurok (impresario), New York, N.Y., 1937-50; Repertory Theater of Lincoln Center, New York, N.Y., director of public relations, 1962—. Producer of plays, "Endgame," "The Bald Soprano," and "Ulysses in Nighttown"; associate producer of Medea," with Judith Anderson in lead, "Member of the Wedding," with Ethel Waters and Julie Harris, and "Time of the Cuckoo," with Shirley Booth. American Examiner, New York, N.Y., theater columnist, 1963—. Military service: U.S. Navy, 1944-45.

WRITINGS: (Editor) Theatre, Volume I, Playbill, 1964, Volume II, Hill & Wang, 1965. Writer of plays for Columbia Broadcasting System Television and American Broadcasting Co.-Paramount. Contributor of articles to New York Times, New York Herald Tribune, Theatre Arts, Coronet, Reconstructionist, Playbill, and New York State Community Theatre Journal.†

*   *   *

HYMES, Dell H(athaway) 1927-

PERSONAL: Born June 7, 1927, in Portland, Ore; son of Howard Hathaway and Dorothy (Bowman) Hymes; married Virginia Margaret Dosch, 1954; children: Robert Paul (stepson), Alison Bowman, Kenneth Dell. Education: Reed College, B.A., 1950; Indiana University, M.A., 1953, Ph.D., 1955. Home: 439 South 44th St., Philadelphia, Pa. 19104. Office: Department of Folklore, University of Pennsylvania, Philadelphia, Pa. 19104.

CAREER: Harvard University, Cambridge, Mass., instructor in social anthropology, 1955-57, assistant professor, 1957-59, assistant professor of social anthropology and linguistics, 1959-60; University of California, Berkeley, associate professor, 1960-64, professor of anthropology, 1964-65; University of Pennsylvania, Philadelphia, professor of anthropology, 1965-71, professor of folklore and linguistics, 1972—. Consultant, Merriam-Webster Co., 1957. Military service: U.S. Army, 1945-47; served in Pacific Theater; became staff sergeant. Member: American Anthropological Association (fellow), Linguistic Society of America, American Folklore Society (president, 1973-74), American Ethnological Society, Phi Beta Kappa, Sigma Xi. Awards, honors: Fellow, Center for Advanced Study in the Behavioral Sciences, 1957-58; Guggenheim fellow, 1969; National Endowment for the Humanities, senior fellow, 1972-73.

WRITINGS—Editor: Language, Society and Culture: An Anthropological Reader, Harper, 1964; The Use of Computers in Anthropology, Humanities, 1965; Studies in Southwestern Ethnolinguistics, Mouton, 1967; Pidginization and Creolization of Languages, Cambridge, 1971; Reinventing Anthropology, Pantheon, 1973; Foundations in Sociolinguistics, University of Pennsylvania Press,1974. Associate editor, American Anthropologist, Daedalus, and International Journal of American Linguistics; editor, Language and Society.

WORK IN PROGRESS: Various aspects of anthropological study of language.

AVOCATIONAL INTERESTS: Tennis, music, poetry.

*   *   *

IBRAHIM, Ibrahim Abdelkader 1923-

PERSONAL: Born December 29, 1923, in Cairo, Egypt; son of Abdelkader and Quadriah (Ali) Ibrahim. Education: Cairo School of Social Work, diploma, 1946; American University at Cairo, B.A., 1951; University of Chicago, M.A., 1955; Princeton University, Ph.D., 1957. Home: 46 Chemin Sarasin, 1218 Grand-Saconnex, Geneva, Switzerland. Office: International Labour Office, Case Postale 500, 1211 Geneva 22, Switzerland.

CAREER: Department of Labour, Cairo, Egypt, senior inspector, 1946-57; Inter-University Study of Labour Problems in Economic Development, Cairo, Egypt, and Princeton University, Princeton, N.J., research associate, 1952-54; National Planning Commission, and Committee on High-Level Manpower, Cairo, Egypt, manpower expert, March-November 1957; International Labour Office, Geneva, Switzerland, with labour management relations programme, 1957-60, with technical assistance programme, 1960-62, with technical assistance program of field office for the Near and Middle East in Istanbul, 1962-65, with management development programme, Geneva, 1965—.

WRITINGS: (With F. H. Harbison) Human Resources for Egyptian Enterprise, McGraw, 1958.

AVOCATIONAL INTERESTS: Skiing.†

*   *   *

IGO, John N., Jr. 1927-

PERSONAL: Born May 29, 1927, in San Antonio, Tex.; son of John N. and Anna (Woller) Igo. Education: Trinity University, B.A., 1948, M.A., 1952. Politics: Democrat. Religion: Catholic. Home: 12505 Woller Rd., San Antonio, Tex. 78228. Office: Department of English, San Antonio College, San Antonio, Tex. 78284.

CAREER: Trinity University, San Antonio, Tex., instructor in English and acquisitions librarian, 1952-53; San Antonio College, San Antonio, Tex., 1953—, began as associate professor, now professor of English. Currently serving as chairman of parish board, Our Lady of Guadalupe Church, Helotes, Tex. Member: Modern Language Association of America, Conference of College Teachers of English, Texas Folklore Society, Esperanto Association of North America. Awards, honors: National Society of Arts and Letters, National Literature Award, 1954, for poem, "The Third Temptation of St. John"; Southwest Writer's Conference, Chapbook Publication Award, 1962; Piper Foundation, Piper Professor of 1974.

WRITINGS: God of Gardens (poems), American Weave Press, 1962; (editor) Yanaguana, privately printed by Flotsam Press, 1963; A Chamber Faust (poems), Wake-Brook House, 1964; Igo on Poetry (lectures), privately printed by Grace Philippi, 1965; The Tempted Monk (poems), Hors Commerce Press, 1967; No Harbor, Else (poems), Et Cetera Press, 1972; Golgotha (poem), Et Cetera, 1973. Staff reviewer for Choice magazine, 1964—. Contributor to Poet Lore, Quixote, and Laurel Review.

WORK IN PROGRESS: A Calendar of Fausts, an annotated calendar of treatments of the Faust theme in several arts, for the Bulletin of the New York Public Library.

AVOCATIONAL INTERESTS: Spanish survivals in the Southwest; Mexican literature; pre-Columbian literature; the 1890s; commedia dell'arte; myth.

*   *   *

IKERMAN, Ruth C. (Percival) 1910-

PERSONAL: Born September 4, 1910, in Redlands, Calif;

daughter of Clarence C. (a merchant) and Sophie (Doll) Percival; married Lawrence Howser Ikerman, January 12, 1947. *Education:* University of Redlands, B.A., 1931. *Religion:* Protestant. *Office:* 11 Panorama Drive, Redlands, Calif. 92373.

CAREER: Formerly did secretarial work for youth secretary in Southern California Baptist Convention, for superintendent of schools, Redlands, Calif., and for sales manager of a citrus fruit products firm, Redlands; owner with husband of a paint store, Redlands, Calif., 1955-72; writer of religious articles and books. *Member:* National League of American Pen Women, Cosmos Club (Redlands), Fellows of the University of Redlands. *Awards, honors:* Three George Washington Medals from Freedoms Foundation for magazine articles on American heritage.

WRITINGS:—All published by Abingdon: *Devotional Programs for Every Month*, 1956; *Devotional Programs for the Changing Seasons*, 1958; *Devotional Programs About People and Places*, 1960; *Cooking by Heart*, 1962; *The Disciplined Heart*, 1964; *Prayers of a Homemaker*, 1966; *Devotional Thoughts From the Holy Land*, 1968; *Golden Words for Every Day*, 1969; *Calendar of Faith and Flowers*, 1970; *Meditations for Bird Lovers*, 1972; *On Morning Trails*, 1974. Writer of religious pamphlets published by Abingdon. Contributor of articles to periodicals, and book reviews to *Los Angeles Times* "Family Books" column.

* * *

ILLINGWORTH, Neil 1934-

PERSONAL: Born January 5, 1934, in Bradford, Yorkshire, England; son of Hubert George and Mabel Lucy (Harland) Illingworth; married Trixie Noeline McGowan (an art teacher), November 14, 1958; children: Mark. *Education:* Educated in England. *Home:* 16 Combes Rd., Remuera, Auckland, New Zealand. *Office:* Editorial Department, *New Zealand Herald*, P.O. Box 32, Auckland, New Zealand.

CAREER: Bay of Plenty Times, Tauranga, New Zealand, reporter, 1951-52; *New Zealand Herald*, Auckland, New Zealand, cable sub-editor, 1952-64, cable editor, 1964—. Publicity Associates Ltd., Auckland, New Zealand, governing director, 1963—. *Member:* Auckland Press Club, Auckland University Car Club.

WRITINGS: Fighting Fins: Big Game Fishing in New Zealand Waters, A. H. & A. W. Reed, 1961; (with Brian Clifford) *Voyage of the Golden Lotus*, A. H. & A. W. Reed, 1962, DeGraff, 1963; (with Rex Forrester) *Hunter for Hire*, A. H. & A. W. Reed, 1965; *Jobbing Along* (biography ghost-written for Esther Julian), Whitcombe & Thombs, 1965; (with Forrester) *Hunting in New Zealand*, A. H. & A. W. Reed, 1967.

WORK IN PROGRESS: A biography of a woman sheepshearer.

AVOCATIONAL INTERESTS: Trout fishing, motor racing, jazz, and reading contemporary literature.†

* * *

IMMEL, Mary Blair 1930-

PERSONAL: Born December 8, 1930, in Wichita, Kan; daughter of Clinton C. and Hope (de Vore) Blair; married Daniel M. Immel (a minister), September 7, 1950; children Daniel C., Michael, Douglas. *Education:* Chapman College, B.A., 1952; Purdue University, M.A., 1967. *Religion:* Disciples of Christ. *Home:* 1600 East 8th St., Chico, Calif. 95926.

CAREER: Former primary teacher and substitute teacher; Tippecanoe County Historical Association and Museums, Lafayette, Ind., former assistant director. *Awards, honors:* Indiana University Writers' Conference scholarship for short story; Indiana University, Hoosier Authors Award for *Two Way Street*.

WRITINGS: Men of God, Christian Board of Publication, 1958; *Two Way Street* (teen-age novel), Bethany, 1965; *Call Up the Thunder* (young adult novel), Bethany 1967. Writer of church school curriculum materials. Contributor of more than one hundred poems, articles, and stories to religious and secular periodicals.

WORK IN PROGRESS: Historical novel for children entitled *River of Wind*, historical novel for adults, and a book on family celebrations.

AVOCATIONAL INTERESTS: Mrs. Immel enjoys travel and has visited forty states and fourteen countries. She also enjoys sketching, painting, gardening, and genealogy.

* * *

INGLIS, R(obert) M(orton) G(all) 1910-

PERSONAL: Born February 6, 1910, in Edinburgh, Scotland; son of James Gall and Charlotte (Kinmont) Inglis; married Vera Evelyn Murray Johnstone, July 2, 1943; children: Evelyn, Jean. *Education:* Attended Edinburgh Academy, 1920-28. *Home:* 19 Dalrymple Crescent, Edinburgh 9, Scotland. *Office:* Gall & Inglis, 12 Newington Rd., Edinburgh 9, Scotland.

CAREER: Gall & Inglis (publishers), Edinburgh, 1932—, senior partner, 1939—, managing director of Gall & Inglis (Reckoners), Ltd., 1964—. Church of Scotland, lay reader. *Military service:* British Army, 1943-46; became sergeant. *Member:* British Astronomical Association (president, 1971-73), Edinburgh Astronomical Society, Scottish Mountaineering Club (librarian, 1960; vice-president, 1971-73).

WRITINGS—All published by Gall and Inglis except as indicated: *Northern and Southern Constellations and How to Find Them*, 1940; *The Presto Decimals of an Hour, and Minutes Calculator*, 1943; *The Swift Specific Gravity Reckoner*, 1948; (with James Gall Inglis) *The Express Foreign Exchange Reckoner*, 1948; *The 'long range' 40-hour Wages Reckoner*, 1949; (with J. G. Inglis) *The "Express" Profit on Cost and Percentage on Returns Reckoner*, 1949; (with J. G. Inglis) *British Weights Expressed in lbs. and kilos*, 1949; (with J. G. Inglis) *Easy Guide to the Constellations*, revised edition, 1949; *Popular Star Atlas*, 1950, second edition published as *A New Popular Star Atlas*, 1958; *The 'Presto' Purchase Tax Reckoner*, 1950; (general editor) Sir Hugh T. Munro, *Munro's Tables of the 3000-Feet Mountains of Scotland*, 1953; *The Swift Every Farthing Reckoner*, 1954; *The Presto Grosses and Dozens into Units Reckoner*, 1954; *The "Express" Salary, Monthly Wages and Per Hour Wages Reckoner*, 1955; *The 'Presto' Pounds and Ounces Pricing Card*, 1955; *The "Express" Sterling to Dollars Reckoner for American and Canadian Dollars*, 1955; *Decimal Equivalents Reckoner*, 1955; *The Presto Decimals of an Hour and Minutes Calculator*, 1956; (with Harry Robert Gall Inglis) *Hill Path Contours of the Chief Mountain Passes in Scotland*, 1963; *The "Express" Universal Decimal Coinage Reckoner*, 1964; (editor) *A Star Atlas and Reference Handbook*, 1910, 15th edition, Sky Publishing Corp., 1964; *The 'Ideal' Decimal Coinage Reckoner*, 1966; *The "Express" Dollars Exchange Reckoner*, 1968; *The "Express" Decimals of a Penny Reckoner*, 1970; (with J. G. Inglis) *Foreign Exchange Reckoner:*

British to Foreign, Foreign to British, 1971; (with A. P. Norton and others) *Norton's Star Atlas*, 1973. Also revisor and contributor to many other "ready reckoners" published by Gall & Inglis. Editor of "Guidebooks" series for Scottish Mountaineering Club, 1946-59.

* * *

IRVING, David (John Cawdell) 1938-

PERSONAL: Born March 24, 1938, in Hutton, Essex, England; son of John James Cawdell (a commander, Royal Navy) and Beryl Irene (Newington) Irving; married Maria Pilar Stuyck Roma, January 31, 1962; children: Josephine Victoria, Maria Pilar, Paloma, Beatrice. *Education:* Attended Imperial College of Science and Technology, London, 1956-59, and University College, London, 1960-61. *Politics:* Right-wing Conservative. *Home:* 81 Duke St., Grosvenor Square, London W.1, England. *Office:* 25 Elgin Mansions, London W.9, England.

CAREER: Writer, 1961—. Spent one year working in a German steel mill to perfect his knowledge of German.

WRITINGS: Und Deutschlands Stadte Starben Nicht, Schweizer Druck und Verlagshaus AG, 1963; *The Destruction of Dresden*, Kimber, 1963; *The Mare's Nest*, Kimber, 1964; *The Virus House*, Kimber, 1967, published as *The German Atomic Bomb: The History of Nuclear Research in Nazi Germany*, Simon & Schuster, 1968; *Accident—The Death of General Sikorski*, Kimber, 1967; *The Destruction of Convoy PQ.17*, Cassell, 1968; *Breach of Security*, Kimber, 1968; *The Rise and Fall of the Luftwaffe*, Weidenfeld & Nicholson, 1974; *The Eighty-Nine Months*, Viking, 1975. Author of two long series in *Neue Illustrierte* (Cologne), and of articles in *Sunday Telegraph* (London), *Evening Standard* (London) *Jewish Chronicle,* and other periodicals. Editor, *Anglo-German Review,* 1960-63.

WORK IN PROGRESS: A formal history of the Hungarian uprising of 1956, based on original records from both sides of the Iron Curtain, publication by Hodder & Stoughton in 1976.

SIDELIGHTS: Irving travels extensively in Europe, on both sides of the Iron Curtain, each year. He speaks fluent German and Spanish, can converse in French, and reads Russian and Latin. He writes: "I believe that it is the knowledge of a major foreign language that helps make one's books interesting to the reader, as he can expect your research to be based not merely on a scrapbook of other people's existing researches in your own language."

Alleging that *The Destruction of Convoy PQ.17* suggested he had disobeyed orders and was "careless, incompetent . . . and indifferent to the fate of the merchant ships and their crews," Captain John E. Broome, Retired, commander of the naval escort in World War II, sued Irving and his publisher. The High Court ordered payment to Broome of $96,000 in damages.

BIOGRAPHICAL/CRITICAL SOURCES: Phoenix, Summer, 1960; *Paris Match,* June 1, 1963; *Der Spiegel,* June 19, 1963; *Sunday Times* supplement (London), September 6, 1970.

* * *

ISAACS, Stan 1929-

PERSONAL: Born April 22, 1929, in Brooklyn, N.Y.; son of Abe (a cab driver) and Lillian (Lax) Isaacs; married Natalie Bobrove (a social worker), December 20, 1953; children: Nancy, Annie, Ellen. *Education:* Brooklyn College, B.A., 1950. *Agent:* The Sterling Lord Agency, 75 East 55th St., New York, N.Y. 10022. *Office:* Newsday, Garden City, Long Island, N.Y.

CAREER: Newsday, Garden City, N.Y., sports columnist, 1954—. *Awards, honors:* National Headliners Award for sports columns, 1961.

WRITINGS: Careers and Opportunities in Sports, Dutton, 1964; *Jim Brown: The Golden Year 1964,* Prentice-Hall, 1970. Stories anthologized in *Best Sports Stories of the Year,* Dutton, each year annually, 1960-65.

WORK IN PROGRESS: Biography of Walter Plinge; and *The Dincin Saga.*

SIDELIGHTS: Isaacs told *CA* he is a "self-styled national arbiter of ice cream excellence, . . . admirer of Heywood Broun, . . . collector of theatrical playbills, . . . moving force in drive to 'Bring Back Postal Telegraph,' . . . a chipmunk fancier. I like these sports best: marathon running, baseball, horse racing, track and field, and fun and frolic in any spontaneous form on an athletic field and elsewhere."†

* * *

ISHERWOOD, Christopher (William Bradshaw) 1904-

PERSONAL: Born August 26, 1904, in High Lane, Cheshire, England; came to United States, 1939, naturalized in 1946; son of Francis Edward (a military officer) and Kathleen (Machell-Smith) Isherwood. *Education:* Attended Repton School, 1919-22, Corpus Christi College, Cambridge, 1924-25; King's College, University of London, medical student, 1928-29. *Politics:* Democrat. *Religion:* Vedantist. *Home:* 145 Adelaide Dr., Santa Monica, Calif. 90402.

CAREER: Writer, 1926—; worked as a secretary to Andre Mangeot, the French violinist, and his Music Society String Quartet, London, England, 1926-27; private tutor in London, 1926-27; went to Berlin, Germany, in 1929 to visit W. H. Auden, and stayed, on and off, for four years; taught English in Berlin, 1930-33; traveled throughout Europe, 1933-37; did film script work for Gaumont-British; went to China with Auden, 1938; dialogue writer for Metro-Goldwyn-Mayer, Hollywood, Calif., 1940; worked with American Friends Service Committee, Haverford, Pa., in a hostel for Central European refugees, 1941-42; resident student of Vedanta Society of Southern California, Hollywood, and co-editor with Swami Prabhavananda of Society's magazine, *Vedanta and the West,* 1943-45; traveled in South America, 1947-48; guest professor at Los Angeles State College (now California State University, Los Angeles), and at University of California, Santa Barbara, 1959-62; Regents Professor at University of California, Los Angeles, 1965, and University of California, Riverside, 1966. *Member:* National Institute of Arts and Letters, American Civil Liberties Union, Wider Quaker Fellowship, Screenwriters Guild.

WRITINGS: All the Conspirators (novel), J. Cape, 1928, new edition, 1957, New Directions, 1958; *The Memorial: Portrait of a Family* (novel), Hogarth, 1932, New Directions, 1946; (with W. H. Auden) *Dog Beneath the Skin, or Where is Francis?* (three-act play), Random House, 1935; *The Last of Mr. Norris,* Morrow, 1935 (published in England as *Mr. Norris Changes Trains,* Hogarth, 1935); (with Auden) *The Ascent of F6* (play), Random House, 1937, 2nd edition, Faber, 1957; *Sally Bowles,* Hogarth, 1937; *Lions and Shadows: An Education in the Twenties* (autobiography), Hogarth, 1938, New Directions, 1947; *Goodbye to Berlin* (narratives), Random House, 1939; (with Auden) *Journey to War*, Random House, 1939; (with Auden) *A Melodrama in Three Acts: On the Frontier*, Faber, 1938, published in America as *On the Frontier: A Melodrama in Three Acts*, Random House, 1939.

Prater Violet (novel), Random House, 1945; (editor) *Vedanta for the Western World*, Marcel Rodd, 1945, published as *Vedanta and the West*, Harper, 1951; *The Berlin Stories* (contains *The Last of Mr. Norris* and *Goodbye to Berlin*), J. Laughlin, 1946, New Directions, 1963; *The Condor and the Cows: A South American Travel Diary*, Random House, 1949; (editor) *Vedanta for Modern Man*, Harper, 1951; *The World in the Evening* (novel), Random House, 1954; (editor) *Great English Short Stories*, Dell, 1957.

Down There on a Visit (novel), Simon & Schuster, 1962; *An Approach to Vedanta*, Vedanta Press, 1963; *A Single Man* (novel), Simon & Schuster, 1964; *Ramakrishna and His Disciples* (biography), Simon & Schuster, 1965; *Exhumations: Stories, Articles, Verses*, Simon & Schuster, 1966; *A Meeting by the River* (novel), Simon & Schuster, 1967; *Kathleen and Frank* (biography), Simon & Schuster, 1971.

Translator: Bertolt Brecht, *Penny for the Poor*, Hale, 1937; (with Swami Prabhavananda) *Bhagavad-Gita*, Rodd, 1944, published as *The Song of God: Bhagavad-Gita*, Harper, 1951, 3rd edition, Vedanta Press, 1965; (and editor, with Prabhavananda) Sankara, *Crest-Jewel of Discrimination*, Vedanta Press, 1947; Charles Baudelaire, *Intimate Journals*, Rodd, 1947; (and editor with Prabhavananda) *How to Know God* (Patanjali's *Yoga Aphorisms*), Harper, 1953; (translator of verse sections) Brecht, *Threepenny Novel*, Grove, 1956.

Play adaptations: "The Adventures of the Black Girl in Her Search for God" (based on a George Bernard Shaw novella), first produced in Los Angeles at Mark Taper Forum, March, 1969; "The Legend of Silent Night" (television special; adapted from a story by Paul Gallico), broadcast by ABC, 1969; (with Don Bachardy) "A Meeting by the River" (based on Isherwood's novel), first produced in Los Angeles at Mark Taper Forum, 1972.

Film scripts: (Author of scenario and dialogue with Margaret Kennedy) "Little Friend," Gaumont-British, 1934; (contributor) "A Woman's Face," MGM, 1941; (with Robert Thoeren) "Rage in Heaven" (based on novel by James Hilton), MGM, 1941; (contributor) "Forever and a Day," RKO, 1943; (with Ladislas Fodor) "The Great Sinner," Loew's, 1949; "Diane," MGM, 1955; (with Terry Southern) "The Loved One" (based on the novel by Evelyn Waugh), Filmways, 1965; (with Don Magner and Tony Richardson) "The Sailor from Gibraltar" (based on novel by Marguerite Duras), Woodfall, 1967. Also author, with Lesser Samuels, of original story for "Adventure in Baltimore," RKO, 1949.

Contributor to periodicals, including *Harper's Bazaar* and *Vogue*.

SIDELIGHTS: "Christopher Isherwood," writes W. J. Tuner, "may not be a great writer . . . but at least he is a real writer and not a pretentious bore. . . ." Through what David Daiches calls "quietly savage dead-pan observation" he unfolds his social comedies. As a student of the deformities of society he is, according to Frank Kermode, "farcical about desperate matters," and concentrates on those aspects that are amusing, "almost as if what mattered was their intrinsic comic value." His unique view of the comic in art, a theory of "High Camp," is explained by a character in *The World in the Evening:* "True High Camp always has an underlying seriousness. You can't camp about something you don't take seriously. You're not making fun of it; you're making fun out of it. You're expressing what's basically serious to you in terms of fun and artifice and elegance. Baroque art is largely camp about religion. The Ballet is camp about love. . . . It's terribly hard to define. You have to meditate on it and feel it intuitively, like Lao-Tze's *Tao.*"

"I believe in being a serious comic writer," Isherwood once said. "To me, everything is described in those terms. Not in the terms of the unredeemably tragic view of life, but at the same time, not in terms of screwballism. Nor in terms of saying, 'Oh, it's all lovely in the garden.' I think the full horror of life must be depicted, but in the end there should be a comedy which is beyond both comedy and tragedy. The thing Gerald Heard calls 'metacomedy.' . . . All I aspire to is to have something of this touch of 'metacomedy.' To give some description of life as it is lived now, and of what it has been like for me, personally, to have been alive."

The Berlin Stories was adapted by John Van Druten as a play entitled, "I Am a Camera"; it was produced in 1951, and published by Random House in 1952. "I Am a Camera" and *The Berlin Stories* were adapted by Joe Masteroff, John Kander, and Fred Ebb for the Broadway musical, "Cabaret," first produced in November, 1966. The screenplay for the movie version of "Cabaret" written by Jay Presson Allen was based on Isherwood's book, and released by Allied Artists in 1972.

AVOCATIONAL INTERESTS: "I was a born film fan."

BIOGRAPHICAL/CRITICAL SOURCES: Gilbert Phelps, editor, *Living Writers*, Transatlantic, 1947; Frank Kermode, *Puzzles and Epiphanies*, Chilmark, 1962; *New York Review of Books*, August 20, 1964; *New York Times Book Review*, August 30, 1964; *Times Literary Supplement*, September 10, 1964; Roy Newquist, *Conversations*, Rand McNally, 1967; Carolyn G. Heilbrun, *Christopher Isherwood*, Columbia University Press, 1970; Alan Wilde, *Christopher Isherwood*, Twayne, 1971; Carolyn Riley, editor, *Contemporary Literary Criticism*, Volume I, Gale, 1973; *Paris Review*, spring, 1974.

*   *   *

JACKSON, Dorothy Virginia Steinhauer 1924-

PERSONAL: Born September 27, 1924, in Brooklyn, N.Y.; daughter of Rudolph John and Emma A. (Iber) Steinhauer. *Education:* Attended Cooper Union three years; other study at Brooklyn College and Columbia University. *Politics:* Variable. *Religion:* Lutheran. *Agent:* Patricia Schartle, McIntosh & Otis, Inc., 18 East 41st St., New York, N.Y. 10017.

CAREER: Writer. *Member:* Authors Guild.

WRITINGS—Novels: *Bold Venture* (young adult), Lippincott, 1952; *Rising Star* (young adult), Lippincott, 1955; *Walk with Peril* (adult historical), Putnam, 1959.

Some short stories have been anthologized in high school textbooks.

WORK IN PROGRESS: An adult historical novel set in Italian Renaissance period; a contemporary young adult novel.

SIDELIGHTS: Ms. Jackson is competent in Spanish, with

reading knowledge of French and German. *Avocational interests:* Horses, ballet, outdoors, and people.†

* * *

JACKSON, Esther Merle 1922-

PERSONAL: Born September 3, 1922, in Pine Bluff, Ark.; daughter of Napoleon F. (a teacher) and Ruth (Atkinson) Jackson. *Education:* Hampton Institute, B.S., 1942; Ohio State University, M.A., 1946, Ph.D., 1958. *Office:* Department of Theatre and Drama, University of Wisconsin, Madison, Wis.

CAREER: Agricultural, Mechanical and Normal College (now University of Arkansas), Pine Bluff, Ark., instructor in English, 1942-44; Hampton Institute, Hampton, Va., assistant professor of speech and drama, 1946-49; Clark College, Atlanta, Ga., director of theater, 1949-56; Agricultural and Technical College of North Carolina (now North Carolina Agricultural and Technical State University), Greensboro, professor of English, 1958-59; Clark College, professor and chairman of department of speech and drama, 1961-64; New York Shakespeare Festival, New York, N.Y., assistant to producer, 1963, director of education, 1965-66; Free University of Berlin, John F. Kennedy Institute of American Studies, Berlin, Germany, Fulbright lecturer, 1967-68; University of Wisconsin, Madison, professor, 1969—. Theatre specialist, U.S. Office of Education, 1964.

MEMBER: American Educational Theatre Association (vice-president for research, 1972-74), American Society for Theatre Research (member of executive committee, 1974-77), Speech Association of America, Modern Language Association of America, International Federation for Theatre Research, American Association of University Professors, Phi Beta Kappa. *Awards, honors:* John Hay Whitney opportunity fellowship, 1956-57; Fulbright senior research fellowship for theater studies in United Kingdom, 1960-61; Alumni Award, Hampton Institute, 1962; Guggenheim fellow, 1968-69.

WRITINGS: The Broken World of Tennessee Williams, University of Wisconsin Press, 1965; (contributor) Alan Downer, editor, *The American Theatre Today*, Basic Books, 1967; (contributor) John M. Reilly, editor, *Twentieth Century Interpretations of "Invisible Man,"* Prentice-Hall, 1970; (contributor) Louis Finkelstein, editor, *Social Responsibility in an Age of Revolution*, Herbert H. Lehman Institute of Ethics, Jewish Theological Seminary of America, 1971; (contributor) Walter Meserve, editor, *Studies in "Death of a Salesman,"* C. E. Merrill, 1972; (contributor) Hans Itschert, editor, *Das amerikanische Drama von den Anfaengen bis zur Gegenwart*, Wissenschaftliche Buchgesellschaft (Darmstadt), 1973. Writer of introduction to four recordings in Crown's "Living Shakespeare Series." Contributor to *Revue d'Histoire du Theatre*, speech, language, and drama journals.

WORK IN PROGRESS: Study of form in American drama.

* * *

JACKSON, John Archer 1929-

PERSONAL: Born October 19, 1929, in Cheltenham, England; son of Vivian Archer (an army officer) and Dorothea (Gartside-Spaight) Jackson; married Wendy Tuke, November 27, 1954; children: Shona, Rory, Patrick, Rebecca. *Education:* Hiram College, B.A., 1951; University of Chi-

cago, graduate study, 1951-52; London School of Economics and Political Science, M.A., 1958. *Office:* Department of Social Studies, Queen's University, Belfast, Northern Ireland.

CAREER: University of Liverpool, Liverpool, England, research worker in sociology, 1957-59; University of Sheffield, Sheffield, England, lecturer in sociology, 1959-64; University of East Anglia, Norwich, England, senior lecturer, 1964-68, reader in sociology, 1968-70; Queen's University, Belfast, Northern Ireland, professor of social theory and institutions, 1970—. Visiting assistant professor of sociology, Hiram College, 1963. *Member:* Royal Association of Science Studies, British Sociological Association, Association of University Teachers, British Association of American Studies, Sociological Association of Ireland.

WRITINGS: The Irish in Britain, Western Reserve University Press, 1963; *Report of the Skibbereen Social Survey*, Human Science Committee of the Irish National Productivity Committee, 1967.

Editor—All published by Cambridge University Press: *Social Stratification*, 1968; *Migration*, 1969; *Professions and Professionalization*, 1970; *Role*, 1971.

WORK IN PROGRESS: Occupational mobility in Ireland.

* * *

JACKSON, W(illiam) Turrentine 1915-

PERSONAL: Born April 5, 1915, in Ruston, La.; son of Brice Hughes and Luther (Turrentine) Jackson; married Barbara Kone, November 28, 1942. *Education:* Texas Western College, B.A., 1935; University of Texas, M.A., 1936, Ph.D., 1940. *Politics:* Democrat *Religion:* Methodist. *Home:* 702 Miller Dr., Davis, Calif. *Office:* 715 Sproul Hall, University of California, Davis, Calif. 95616.

CAREER: University of California, Los Angeles, instructor in history, 1940-41; Iowa State College (now Iowa State University of Science and Technology), Ames, 1941-48, started as instructor, became associate professor of history; University of Chicago, Chicago, Ill., assistant professor of American history, 1947-51; University of California, Davis, assistant professor, 1951-53, associate professor, 1953-56, professor of American history, 1956—, chairman of history department, 1959-60. Fulton Foundation Lecturer, University of Nevada, 1964; seminar director, National Endowment for the Humanities, 1969-70, Rockefeller Foundation, 1970-71; Walter Prescott Webb Lecturer, University of Texas, 1975; member of Committee for Preservation of Historical Sites of the National Park Service; member of California Governor's History Commission. *Military service:* U.S. Naval Reserve, 1942-43; became ensign.

MEMBER: American Historical Association, American Association of University Professors, Western History Association, Organization of American Historians, California Historical Society, Society for Southern California History. *Awards, honors:* Fulbright research fellow in United Kingdom, 1949-50; American History Award of Pacific Coast branch of American Historical Association, 1952, for *Wagon Roads West*, which also was named among the Fifty Books of the Year by American Institute of Graphic Arts; Rockefeller Foundation fellowship at Huntington Library, 1953; Award of Merit of American Association for State and Local History, 1956, for *When Grass Was King*, and 1964, for *Treasure Hill*; Guggenheim fellowship, 1957-58 and 1965; Institute of Humanities

Award from University of California, 1971-72; Huntington Library fellowship, summer, 1972; Distinguished Teaching Award from Academic Senate of University of California, Davis, 1973-74. Grants from American Philosophical Society, 1955, American History Research Center, 1955-56, Social Science Research Council, 1956, National Science Foundation, 1970-72, American Council of Learned Societies, 1972.

WRITINGS: Wagon Roads West, University of California Press, 1952; *When Grass Was King*, University of Colorado Press, 1956; *Treasure Hill*, University of Arizona Press, 1963; *Twenty Years on the Pacific Slope*, Yale University Press, 1965; *The Enterprising Scot: American Investors in the American West After 1873*, University of Edinburgh Press, 1968; (editor and author of introduction) Adolphus Windeler, *The California Gold Rush Diary of a German Sailor*, Howell-North Books, 1969; (contributor) Ray A. Billington, editor, *People of the Plains and Mountains*, Greenwood Press, 1973. Also author or co-author of five monographs for "Environmental Quality Series," published by the Institute of Governmental Affairs. Contributor of articles to professional periodicals. Member of editorial committee, "History Series" of the University of California Press, 1960-61; member of board of editors of *Pacific Historical Review*, 1961-64, 1967-70, and *Southern California Quarterly*, 1962—; editorial consultant for *Arizona and the West*, 1968-73, and *Journal of San Diego History*, 1971.

* * *

JACOB, Charles E. 1931-

PERSONAL: Born June 5, 1931, in Detroit, Mich; son of Charles Henry (a pattern maker) and Thelma (Church) Jacob; married Gale Sypher, December 23, 1961; children: Charles Whitney, Andrew Wylie, John Church. *Education:* University of Michigan, B.A., 1953, M.A., 1954; Cornell University, Ph.D., 1961. *Politics:* Democrat. *Religion:* Protestant. *Home:* 525 Hancock St., Middlesex, N.J. 08846.

CAREER: Vassar College, Poughkeepsie, N.Y., assistant professor of political science, 1960-67; Rutgers University, New Brunswick, N.J., associate professor of political science, 1967-74, chairman of department of political science, 1974—. *Military service:* U.S. Army, 1954-56. *Member:* American Political Science Association, American Association of University Professors.

WRITINGS: Policy and Bureaucracy, Van Nostrand, 1966; *Leadership in the New Deal: The Administrative Challenge*, Prentice-Hall, 1967; (with Gerald M. Pomper and others) *The Performance of American Government: Checks and Minuses*, Free Press, 1972. Contributor to *World Book Encyclopedia*.

* * *

JACOBS, Frank 1929-

PERSONAL: Born May 30, 1929, in Lincoln, Neb.; son of David (a businessman) and Miriam (Frosh) Jacobs; married Barbara Stellman, September 1, 1964; children: Alexander. *Education:* University of Nebraska, B.A., 1951. *Home:* 164 West 79th St., New York, N.Y. 10024. *Agent:* Ann Elmo Agency, 52 Vanderbilt Ave., New York, N.Y. 10017.

CAREER: Freelance writer, 1957—. *Military service:* U.S. Army, correspondent and editor for *Pacific Stars and Stripes*, 1952-54.

WRITINGS: (With Sy Reit) *Canvas Confidential*, Dial, 1963; (with Alfred Gescheidt) *30 Ways to Stop Smoking*, Pocket Books, 1964; *The Highly Unlikely Celebrity Cookbook*, New American Library, 1964; *Alvin Steadfast on Vernacular Island*, Dial, 1965; *Mad For Better or Verse*, New American Library, 1968; *Sing Along With Mad*, New American Library, 1970; *The Mad World of William M. Gaines*, Lyle Stuart, 1972; (with Rickard) *Mad About Sports*, Paperback Library, 1972; *Mad's Talking Stamps*, Paperback Library, 1974. Contributor of articles to *Mad, Playboy, Oui,* and *Punch*.

* * *

JACOBS, Herbert A. 1903-

PERSONAL: Born April 8, 1903, in Milwaukee, Wis.; son of Herbert Henry (a minister and social worker) and Marybelle (Austin) Jacobs; married Katherine Wescott, February 17, 1934; children: Susan, Elizabeth, William. *Education:* Harvard University, B.S., 1926; studied at Sorbonne, University of Paris, and at College de France, 1926-27. *Home:* 1001 Euclid Ave., Berkeley, Calif. 94708. *Office:* Journalism Department, University of California, Berkeley, Calif.

CAREER: Wisconsin Anti-Tuberculosis Association, Milwaukee, publicity writer, 1927-30; *Milwaukee Journal*, Milwaukee, Wis., reporter, 1931-36; *Capital Times*, Madison, Wis., reporter, 1936-62, columnist, 1948-62; University of California, Berkeley, member of journalism faculty, 1962-71, extension instructor, 1972—. Part-time lecturer, University of Wisconsin, 1948-62. *Member:* American Newspaper Guild, American Association for Education in Journalism.

WRITINGS: We Chose the Country, Harper, 1948; *A Practical Guide for the Beginning Farmer*, Harper, 1951; *Practical Publicity: A Handbook for Public and Private Workers*, McGraw, 1964; *Frank Lloyd Wright: America's Greatest Architect*, Harcourt, 1965; (contributor) *Our Troubled Press: Ten Years of the Columbia Journalism Review*, Little, Brown, 1971. Writer of University of Wisconsin correspondence course, "The Community Newspaper." Editor of *Try and Stump Me!* (yearbook), Capital Times, 1949, and a centennial book about Middleton, Wis.

AVOCATIONAL INTERESTS: Sailing (began when he was past sixty), writing light verse.

* * *

JACOBS, Paul 1918-

PERSONAL: Born August 24, 1918, in New York, N.Y.; son of Julius (a businessman) and Tecla (Schmidt) Jacobs; married Ruth Rosenfield (a lawyer), January 1, 1939. *Education:* Attended public schools, New York, N.Y. *Politics:* Socialist Party. *Religion:* Jewish. *Home and office:* 2500 Filbert St., San Francisco, Calif. *Agent:* Cyrilly Abels, 597 Fifth Ave., New York, N.Y. 10017.

CAREER: Described self to *CA* as "professional revolutionist, 1935-40, attempting to overcome U.S. government by force and violence"; union representative and intergroup relations worker, 1940—; Center for Study of Democratic Institutions, Santa Barbara, Calif., staff director, 1956-69. University of California, Berkeley, research associate, 1962-72. Consultant to Peace Corps and to War on Poverty Program. Member of San Francisco Economic Opportunities Council, National Association for the Advancement of Colored People, Student Non-Violent Coordinating Committee. *Military service:* U.S. Army Air Forces, 1943-46; became sergeant. *Member:* Concordia Club, Tattoo Club of America. *Awards, honors:* Sigma Delta Chi National Public Service Journalism Award for article exposing Atomic Energy Commission activities in Nevada, 1958.

WRITINGS: (With Frank Pinner and Phillip Selznick) *Old Age and Political Behavior*, University of California Press, 1959; (with Michael Harrington) *Labor in a Free Society*, University of California Press, 1961; *State of the Unions*, Atheneum, 1963; *Is Curly Jewish?*, Atheneum, 1965; (with Saul Landau) *The New Radicals: A Report With Documents*, Random House, 1966; *Dialogue on Poverty*, Bobbs-Merrill, 1967; *Prelude to Riot: A View of Urban America From the Bottom*, Random House, 1968; *Between the Rock and the Hard Place*, Random House, 1970; (with Landau and Eve Pell) *To Serve the Devil*, two volumes, Random House, 1971. Contributor to *Atlantic Monthly, Harper's, Commentary, Commonweal, Dissent, New Politics, Reporter, Economist, New America, Playboy*, and to anthologies.

WORK IN PROGRESS: Unemployment as a Way of Life; a book analyzing the impact of the cold war on American life.

AVOCATIONAL INTERESTS: Cooking.†

*   *   *

JACOBS, Wilbur R(ipley)   1918-

PERSONAL: Born June 30, 1918, in Chicago, Ill.; son of Walter Ripley (a businessman) and Nona I. (Deutsch) Jacobs; married Josephine Kingsbury, August 19, 1951; children: Shirley Elizabeth, Catherine Elaine. *Education:* University of California, Los Angeles, A.B., 1940, A.M. (honors), 1941, Ph.D., 1947; Johns Hopkins University, graduate study, 1946. *Office:* Department of History, University of California, Santa Barbara, Calif. 93106.

CAREER: Stanford University, Stanford, Calif., instructor in history, 1947-49; University of California, Santa Barbara, instructor, 1949-50, assistant professor, 1950-55, associate professor, 1955-60, professor of history, 1960—, chairman of department, 1957-60, chairman of faculty, 1958-59, academic assistant to the president, 1964-65. Visiting professor at Indiana University, University of California, Los Angeles; Fulbright visiting professor, Australian National University, 1969. *Military service:* U.S. Army Air Forces, 1941-45. *Member:* American Historical Association (Pacific Coast branch), Western History Association, Organization of American Historians. *Awards, honors:* Rockefeller Foundation research grant, 1949; prize from Pacific Coast branch of American Historical Association, 1950, for *Diplomacy and Indian Gifts*; American Philosophical Society research grant, 1956; Huntington Library grant, 1970.

WRITINGS: Diplomacy and Indian Gifts: Anglo-French Rivalry on the Ohio and Northwest Frontiers, 1748-63, Stanford University Press, 1950, published as *Wilderness Politics and Indian Gifts: The Northern Colonial Frontier, 1748-63*, University of Nebraska Press, 1966; (with John Caughey and Joe Frantz) *Turner, Bolton and Webb: Three Historians of the Frontier*, University of Washington Press, 1965; *The Historical World of Frederick Jackson Turner, With Selections from his Correspondence*, Yale University Press, 1968; *Dispossessing the American Indian: Indians and Whites on the Colonial Frontier*, Scribner, 1972.

Editor: *Indians of the Southern Colonial Frontier: The Edmund Atkin Report and Plan of 1755*, University of South Carolina Press, 1954; *Letters of Francis Parkman*, two volumes, University of Oklahoma Press, 1960; *Frederick Jackson Turner's Legacy: Unpublished Writings in American History*, Huntington Library, 1965, published as *America's Great Frontiers and Sections*, University of Nebraska, 1969; (and compiler) *The Paxton Riots and the Frontier Theory*, Rand McNally, 1967; Edmond Atkin, *The Appalachian Indian Frontier* University of Nebraska Press, 1967; (and compiler) *Benjamin Franklin: Statesman-Philosopher or Materialist?*, Holt, 1971.

Contributor of articles on early American and frontier history and historiography to *Encyclopaedia Britannica, American Historical Review, American Quarterly, Los Angeles Times, American West, Saturday Review*, and other publications.

WORK IN PROGRESS: Environment and History: The Prelude to the American Revolution.

*   *   *

JACOBSEN, Lyle E.   1929-

PERSONAL: Born August 26, 1929, in Carroll County, Iowa; son of Theodore R. and Edith (Ninemires) Jacobsen. *Education:* Dana College, B.S., 1947; University of Nebraska, M.A., 1955; University of Illinois, Ph.D., 1957. *Office:* Stanford University, Stanford, Calif.

CAREER: Certified public accountant. Stanford University, Stanford, Calif., 1957—, assistant professor, 1957-60, associate professor of accounting, 1960—. Escuela de Administracion de Negocios Para Graduados, Lima, Peru, professor, 1964-65. *Military service:* U.S. Army, Finance Corps, 1952-54; became sergeant. *Member:* American Accounting Association, American Institute of Certified Public Accountants, National Accounting Association, California Society of Certified Public Accountants.

WRITINGS: (With Morton Backer) *Cost Accounting: A Managerial Approach*, McGraw, 1964. Contributor to professional journals.

WORK IN PROGRESS: A section for *Handbook of Modern Accounting Theory*, for Prentice-Hall; research in managerial accounting, international accounting.†

*   *   *

JAFFE, Gabriel Vivian   1923-

PERSONAL: Born May 12, 1923, in Nottingham, England; son of Henry (a physician) and Miriam (Woolf) Jaffe; married Colleen Corteel (a secretary), September 1, 1964. *Education:* Attended Clifton College; University of London and St. Thomas's Hospital Medical School, M.B., B.S., 1946, M.R.C.S., L.R.C.P. *Home:* 7 Alum Chine Rd., Bournemouth, England. *Agent:* John Farquharson Ltd., 15 Red Lion Sq., London W.C. 1, England. *Office:* 141 Harley St., London W. 1, England.

CAREER: Physician in private practice, London, England, 1950—. Part-time ship's surgeon aboard "Queen Mary," "Queen Elizabeth," and "Queen Elizabeth II," 1955—; medical editor, Mayflower Books Ltd. and Dell Publishing Co. Divisional surgeon, St. John Ambulance Brigade. *Military service:* Royal Navy, surgeon, 1947-49; became surgeon lieutenant. *Member:* British Medical Association, College of General Practitioners, Bournemouth and Poole Medical Society, Poole Harbour Yacht Club, West Hants Lawn Tennis Club, Dorset County Council, Bournemouth Borough Council.

WRITINGS: The Life Pill: A New Approach to Family Planning, Consul Books, 1961; *Design for Loving*, Mayflower Books, 1965; *Promiscuity*, Mayflower Books, 1965. Medical correspondent, *Bournemouth Evening Echo*; contributor to *British Medical Journal, Lancet, Financial Times, Practitioner, Health Horizon, Times* (London), and to other journals and newspapers.

WORK IN PROGRESS: Babies by Choice, Surgeon at Sea, Say 99.

*   *   *

JAMES, Edgar C. 1933-

PERSONAL: Born January 6, 1933, in Bryn Mawr, Pa.; son of Edgar J. and Dorothy (Cutler) James; married Barbara Gill, July 21, 1956; children: Sharon Louise, Brenda Kathleen. *Education:* Wheaton College, Wheaton, Ill., A.B., 1955; Dallas Theological Seminary, Th.M., 1959, Th.D., 1962. *Home:* 1460 Blanchard Ct., Wheaton, Ill. 60187. *Office:* Moody Bible Institute, Chicago, Ill. 60610.

CAREER: Ordained nondenominational minister. Calvary Bible College, Kansas City, Mo., professor and chairman of Division of Bible and Theology, beginning 1961, director of graduate division, beginning 1965; Southwest Bible Church, chairman of board of Christian education, beginning 1965; Bible-Centered Ministries, president, beginning 1965; Moody Bible Institute, Chicago, Ill., professor, 1973—. *Member:* Evangelical Theological Society. *Awards, honors:* A.S., Texas Institute of Technology.

WRITINGS: Romans in Outline, Calvary Press, 1963; *II Corinthians—Keys to Triumphant Living*, Moody, 1964; *The Epistles of Peter—Practical Advice for the Last Days*, Moody, 1964; *Romans—Amazing Grace*, Moody, 1971. Contributor of articles to theological publications.

*   *   *

JAMES, (William) Louis (Gabriel)

PERSONAL: Born in Shrewsbury, England; son of Henry Gerard (a clergyman) and Grace (Dunham) James; married Jill Alison Hemmings, July 29, 1961; children: Nicola, Michele. *Education:* Jesus College, Oxford, A.M. and D.Phil., both 1961. *Politics:* Liberal. *Religion:* Christian. *Home and office:* Department of English, University of the West Indies, Kingston 7, Jamaica.

CAREER: University of Hull, Hull, Yorkshire, England, staff tutor in English, 1958-63; University of the West Indies, Kingston, Jamaica, lecturer in English, 1963—.

WRITINGS: Fiction for the Working Man, Oxford University Press, 1963; (editor and author of introduction) *The Islands in Between: Essays on West Indian Literature*, Oxford University Press, 1968. Author of television scripts on Victorian popular culture for British broadcasts. Contributor to *Encyclopaedia Britannica* and to journals.

WORK IN PROGRESS: Research for standard biography and criticism of G. W. M. Reynolds; research into the visual aspects of Victorian fiction; a monograph on African literature for publication by Department of Adult Education, University of Hull.

AVOCATIONAL INTERESTS: Conjuring, judo, and sleeping.†

*   *   *

JANDA, Kenneth (Frank) 1935-

PERSONAL: Born November 14, 1935; son of John Frank (an electronic technician) and Bessie L. (Ringl) Janda; married Ann Mozolak, September 2, 1961. *Education:* Illinois State Normal University (now Illinois State University), B.S., 1957; Indiana University, Ph.D., 1961. *Home:* 2341 Pioneer Rd., Evanston, Ill. 60201.

CAREER: Northwestern University, Evanston, Ill., assistant professor, 1961-66, associate professor, 1966-69, professor of political science, 1969—, chairman of department, 1973-74. *Member:* American Political Science Association, Midwest Conference of Political Scientists. *Awards, honors: Cumulative Index to the American Political Science Review* was selected as one of the outstanding reference books of 1964 by American Library Association.

WRITINGS: (Editor) *Cumulative Index to the American Political Science Review, Volumes 1-57; 1906-1963*, Northwestern University Press, 1964; *Data Processing: Applications to Political Research*, Northwestern University Press, 1965; *Information Retrieval: Applications in Political Science*, Bobbs-Merrill, 1968.

WORK IN PROGRESS: Long-range research project on comparative study of political parties throughout the world.

*   *   *

JANIS, J(ack) Harold 1910-

PERSONAL: Born May 23, 1910, in New York, N.Y.; son of Joseph and Sophie (Aron) Janis; married Frieda Aron, June 19, 1938; children: Paul Henry, Stephen Lee. *Education:* New York University, B.S., 1932, M.A., 1942. *Home:* 2824 Morris Ave., New York, N.Y. 10068. *Office:* New York University, Washington Sq., New York, N.Y. 10003.

CAREER: New York University, New York, N.Y., instructor, 1934-42, assistant professor, 1942-46, associate professor, 1946-50, professor of business writing, 1950—, chairman of department of business writing and speaking, 1963-67. Consultant to Manufacturers Hanover Trust Co., New York, N.Y.; former consultant to City of New York and other banks and business firms. *Member:* American Business Communication Association (formerly American Business Writing Association; president, 1949-50), International Communication Association, New York University Faculty Club (acting president, 1963-64).

WRITINGS: (With E. J. Kilduff and G. B. Hotchkiss) *Handbook of Business English*, Harper, 1945; (with Kilduff and Hotchkiss) *Advanced Business Correspondence*, Harper, 1947; *Knowing and Using Words*, Appleton, 1948; *50 Years of Education for Business*, New York University Press, 1950; (with Kilduff and A. E. Manville) *Practice in Business Writing*, Harper, 1952; (with Kilduff and H. R. Dressner) *Business Writing*, Barnes & Noble, 1956, 2nd edition, 1972; (editor) *Business Communication Reader*, Harper, 1958; *Writing and Communicating in Business*, Macmillan, 1964, 2nd edition, 1973; *The Business Research Paper: A Manual of Style*, Hobbs, Dorman, 1967; (with Margaret Thompson) *New Standard Reference for Secretaries and Administrative Assistants*, Macmillan, 1972.

Assistant editor, *American Business Writing Association Bulletin*, 1947-49; editor, *Better Letters* (biweekly bulletin of Manufacturers Hanover Trust Co.); contributing editor, *Journal of Communication*, 1962-65. Contributor to *Reader's Digest, Nation's Business*, and *Journal of Business Communication*.

WORK IN PROGRESS: College Writing.

JANNER, Greville Ewan 1928-
(Ewan Mitchell)

PERSONAL: Born July 11, 1928, in Cardiff, South Wales; son of Lord Barnett (a solicitor, former member of parliament) and Lady Elsie (Cohen) Janner; married Myra Louise Sheink, July 6, 1955; children: Daniel Joseph Mitchell, Marion Juliette, Laura Naomi. *Education:* Trinity Hall, Cambridge, M.A., 1952; Harvard University, graduate study in law, 1952-53. *Politics:* Labour. *Religion:* Jewish. *Home:* 2 Linnell Dr., London N.W.11, England. *Agent:* Winant Towers Ltd., 14 Cliffords Inn, London E.C.4, England. *Office:* 1 Garden Ct., Temple, London E.C.4, England.

CAREER: Admitted to bar, 1954; Member of Parliament for Leicester West, 1970—; Queen's Council, 1971—. Vice-president of Board of Deputies of British Jews and of Association for British Youth. Director of the *Jewish Chronicle*. *Military service:* British Army, 1946-48; became sergeant. *Member:* British Academy of Forensic Science, Howard League for Penal Reform, Association for Scientific Treatment of Delinquency, National Union of Journalists (England), Society of Labour Lawyers, Fabian Society.

WRITINGS—All under pseudonym Ewan Mitchell: *The Businessman's Lawyer and Legal Lexicon*, Business Publications, 1962, 2nd edition, 1965, portion published as *The Businessman's Legal Lexicon*, Business Books, 1970; *Farming and the Law*, Farming Press, 1962; *The Lawyer and His World*, Gollancz, 1963; *All You Need to Know About the Law*, New English Library, 1963; *The Retailer's Lawyer*, Business Publications, 1963; *Motorists—Know Your Law*, Newnes, 1964; *The Personnel Manager's Lawyer and Employer's Guide to the Law*, Business Publications, 1964, 2nd edition, 1967; *Your Office and the Law*, Business Publications, 1964; *You and the Law: A Guide for Young People*, Parrish, 1964; *Your Factory and the Law*, Business Publications, 1966, 2nd edition, Business Books, 1969; *The Sales Executive's Lawyer and Businessman's Guide to the Laws of Buying and Selling*, Business Publications, 1966; *Your Property and the Law and Investor's Legal Guide*, Business Publications, 1967; *The Businessman's Guide to Speech-Making and to the Laws and Conduct of Meetings*, Business Books, 1968; *The Director's Lawyer and Company Secretary's Legal Guide*, Business Books, 1968, 2nd edition, 1972; *Coping With Crime*, Business Books, 1969.

The Executive's Guide to Successful Speechmaking, Vertex Books, 1970; *Letters of the Law: The Businessman's Encyclopedia of Draft Letters With Legal Implications*, Business Books, 1970; *The Businessman's Guide to Letter-Writing and to the Law on Letters*, Business Books, 1970; *The Employer's Lawyer*, Business Books, 1971; *The Business and Professional Man's Lawyer*, Business Books, 1971; *The Businessman's Guide to Travel and to Profits Abroad*, Business Books, 1971; *Letters of Industrial Law: The Executive's Practical Guide to the Industrial Relations Act*, Business Books; 1972; *The Businessman's Guide to Commercial Conduct and the Law*, Business Books, 1972.

Contributor of regular columns to *Daily Mail*, *Building Design*, *Pulse*, *Estates Times*, and of articles to other journals.

SIDELIGHTS: Janner knows French, Spanish, Hebrew, Yiddish, German, Italian, and is learning Russian.

JANOWITZ, Morris 1919-

PERSONAL: Born October 22, 1919; son of Samuel (a businessman) and Rose (Meyers) Janowitz; married Gayle A. Shulenberger (a university lecturer and remedial reading and educational consultant), December 22, 1951; children: Rebecca, Naomi. *Education:* New York University, A.B. (cum laude), 1941; University of Chicago, Ph.D., 1948. *Politics:* Democratic. *Home:* 1357 East 55th Pl., Chicago, Ill. 60637. *Office:* Department of Sociology, University of Chicago, Chicago, Ill. 60637.

CAREER: U.S. Department of Justice, Washington, D.C., senior propaganda analyst, 1941-43; University of Chicago, Chicago, Ill., instructor, 1947-48, assistant professor of sociology, 1948-51; University of Michigan, Ann Arbor, assistant professor, 1951-53, associate professor, 1953-57, professor of sociology, 1957-61; University of Chicago, Ford Foundation visiting professor, Graduate School of Business, 1961-62, professor of sociology and director of Center for Social Organization Studies, 1962—, chairman of department of sociology, 1961-72. Member of U.S. government bodies, 1948—, including External Research Division, U.S. Information Agency, 1956-57, National Institute of Mental Health, 1960-62, steering committee, National Conference of Education of the "Difficult Thirty Per Cent," 1963—. Consultant to President Truman's Commission on Civil Rights, 1947, to Committee on Armed Services, U.S. Senate, 1961—. Member of Committee on National Policy, Social Science Research Council, 1960—. Fulbright research professor, University of Frankfurt, 1954-55; Cambridge University, Pitt professor, 1972-73, Distinguished Professor, 1973. *Military service:* U.S. Army, chief Wehrmacht morale analyst, Supreme Headquarters, Allied Expeditionary Force, 1943-45; received Bronze Star and Purple Heart.

MEMBER: American Sociological Association (council member, 1962—; vice-president, 1970-71), American Academy of Arts and Sciences (fellow), American Political Science Association, American Association for Public Opinion Research, World Association for Public Opinion Research (co-chairman of World Conference, 1955), Committee on International Order (chairman, 1963—), Society for Social Research (president, 1948-49), International Sociological Association, Society for the Study of Social Problems (member of executive committee, 1963—), Phi Beta Kappa. *Awards, honors:* Social Science Research Council demobilization fellow, 1946-47; Center for the Study of Behavioral Sciences fellow, 1958-59.

WRITINGS: (With Bruno Bettelheim) *The Dynamics of Prejudice*, Harper, 1950; *The Community Press in an Urban Setting*, Free Press of Glencoe, 1952, 2nd edition, University of Chicago Press, 1967; (with Dwaine Marvick) *Campaign Pressures and Democratic Consent: An Interpretation of the 1952 Election*, Institute for Public Administration, University of Michigan, 1956, 2nd edition, Quadrangle, 1964; (with Deil Wright and William Delany) *Public Administration and the Public-Perspectives Toward Government in a Metropolitan Community*, Institute for Public Administration, University of Michigan, 1958; *Sociology and the Military Establishment*, Russell Sage, 1959, revised edition, 1965.

The Professional Soldier, Free Press of Glencoe, 1960; (with Robert Vinter) *The Comparative Study of Juvenile Correctional Institutions: A Research Report*, University of Michigan Press, 1961; (with others) *A Study of the Military Retired Pay System and Certain Related Subjects: A*

Report to the Committee on Armed Services, United States Senate, U.S. Government Printing Office, 1961; (with Bettelheim) *Social Change and Prejudice*, Free Press of Glencoe, 1964; *The Military in the Political Development of New Nations*, University of Chicago Press, 1964; *Judaism of the Next Generation: A Survey of Religious Education*, Rostrum, 1969; *Institution Building in Urban Education*, Russell Sage, 1969; *Political Conflict: Essays in Political Sociology*, Quadrangle, 1970.

Editor: (With Bernard Berelson) *Reader in Public Opinion and Communication*, Free Press of Glencoe, 1950, 2nd edition, Free Press, 1966; (with Heinz Eulau and Samuel Eldersveld) *Political Behavior*, Free Press of Glencoe, 1956; *Psychological Warfare: A Case Book*, Johns Hopkins Press, 1958; *Community Political Systems: International Yearbook of Political Behavior Research*, Volume I, Free Press of Glencoe, 1961; *Armed Forces and Society in Western Europe*, Librairie Plon (Paris), 1965; *The New Military: Changing Patterns of Organization*, Russell Sage, 1964; (with Jacques van Doorn) *On Military Intervention*, Rotterdam University Press, 1971; (with van Doorn) *On Military Ideology*, Rotterdam University Press, 1971.

Contributor: *Propaganda in War and Crisis*, Stewart, 1951; *Readings in Social Psychology*, Henry Holt, 1952; A. Reiss and P. Hatt, editors, *Reader in Urban Sociology*, Free Press of Glencoe, 1951; Daniel Aaron, editor, *America in Crisis*, Knopf, 1952; Robert K. Merton and Robert Nisbet, editors, *Contemporary Social Problems*, Harcourt, 1961.

General editor of "Heritage of Sociology" series published by University of Chicago Press, 1964—. Also author of social and military studies. Contributor of articles to *Public Opinion Quarterly*, *American Psychologist*, *Communications*, *Current Anthropology*, and other social science and sociology periodicals.

Associate editor of *American Sociological Review*, 1958-61, and of *Journal of Conflict Resolution*; member of editorial advisory board, *Journalism Quarterly*; member of editorial board, *American Journal of Sociology*, 1962—; member of executive committee, *International Encyclopedia of the Social Sciences*, 1961-62.

*   *   *

JANSSEN, Lawrence H(arm)   1921-

PERSONAL: Born October 2, 1921, in Corwith, Iowa; son of Harm Henry (a farmer and building maintenance engineer) and Katherine (Lawrence) Janssen; married Beverly Boynton, May 30, 1943; children: Laurel Lynn, Carolyn Ruth. *Education:* University of Wisconsin, B.A., 1944; Colgate Rochester Divinity School, B.D., 1946. *Home:* 210 South Main St., New Lisbon, Wis. 53950.

CAREER: Ordained Baptist minister, 1946; minister of churches in Berlin, Wis., 1946-49, Warrens, Wis., 1949-54; American Baptist Home Mission Societies, Valley Forge, Pa., field representative of juvenile protection, 1954-57, field director of juvenile protection, 1957-59, field director of church and community studies, 1959-63, associate in urban program, 1963—. Associate director, Church Strategy Program, 1964—.

WRITINGS: A Look Inside Your Church and Community (self-study manual), American Baptist Home Mission Societies, 1962; (contributor) *Leaven*, American Baptist Home Mission Societies, 1962; *These Cities Glorious*, Friendship, 1963. Contributor to religious publications.†

JAQUES, Elliott   1917-

PERSONAL: Surname is pronounced *Jacks*; born January 18, 1917, in Toronto, Ontario, Canada. *Education:* University of Toronto, B.A., 1936, M.A., 1937; Johns Hopkins University, M.D., 1940; Harvard University, Ph.D., 1942. *Home:* 30 Ennismore Gardens Mews, London S.W. 7, England. *Office:* Brunel University, Uxbridge, Middlesex, England.

CAREER: Tavistock Institute of Human Relations, London, England, founder member, senior project officer, 1946-51, director of Glacier Project (industrial social research), 1952; qualified as psychoanalyst, British Psycho-Analytical Society, 1951; private practice as psychoanalyst and as industrial social consultant, London, England, 1952—; Brunel University, London, England, professor, and director of Institute of Organization and Social Studies, 1965—. Honorary secretary, Melanie Klein Trust. *Military service:* Royal Canadian Army, Medical Corps, 1941-45; became major. *Member:* British Medical Association, British Psycho-Analytical Society (honorary scientific secretary, 1961-64; member of council), Royal College of Psychiatry (founder fellow).

WRITINGS: The Changing Culture of a Factory, Dryden Press, 1951; (contributor) M. Klein and others, editors, *New Directions in Psycho-Analysis*, Tavistock Publications, 1955, Basic Books, 1956; *Measurement of Responsibility: A Study of Work, Payment and Individual Capacity*, Harvard University Press, 1956; (contributor) J. D. Sutherland, editor, *Psycho-Analysis and Contemporary Thought*, Hogarth, 1958; *Equitable Payment: A General Theory of Work, Differential Payment, and Individual Progress*, Wiley, 1961; (with Wilfred Brown) *Product Analysis Pricing*, Basic Books, 1965; *Time-Span Handbook*, Basic Books, 1965; (with W. Brown) *Glacier Project Papers*, Basic Books, 1965; *Work, Creativity, and Social Justice*, International Universities Press, 1970. Contributor of some thirty articles to periodicals.

WORK IN PROGRESS: Glacier Project, and reorganization of the National Health Service.

*   *   *

JARMAIN, W. Edwin   1938-

PERSONAL: Born May 25, 1938, in London, Ontario, Canada; son of Edwin Roper and Ruth (Secord) Jarmain; married Patricia Carroll, February 29, 1964. *Education:* Massachusetts Institute of Technology, S.B. and S.M. in Electrical Engineering, 1962; S.M. in Industrial Management, 1964. *Home:* 412 Russell Hill Rd., Toronto M4V 2V2, Ontario, Canada. *Office:* Canadian Cablesystems Ltd., Suite 1110, 120 Adelaide St. West, Toronto, Ontario, Canada.

CAREER: McKinsey & Co., Inc. (management consultants), New York, N.Y., associate, 1964-66; with Jarmain Teleservices Ltd., 1966—, appointed president, 1971; Canadian Cablesystems Ltd., Toronto, Ontario, executive vice-president, 1974—. Visiting lecturer, University of Western Ontario, 1967; Canadian Cable Television Association, director, 1968-73, chairman, 1970-72; member of board of governors, Ryerson Polytechnical Institute, 1972-73; chairman of Broadbands Communications Networks Ltd., 1972—; director of Ontario Development Corporation, 1973—. *Member:* Institute of Electrical and Electronics Engineers, Association of Professional Engineers (Ontario), Sigma Xi.

WRITINGS: (Editor) *Problems in Industrial Dynamics*, M.I.T. Press, 1963.

* * *

JARVIS, Jennifer M(ary) 1935-

PERSONAL: Born January 2, 1935, in Plymouth, England; married john Gibson (a medical doctor), April 2, 1964. *Education:* University College of Exeter, B.A. (London), 1956; Institute of Psychiatry, London, England, Diploma of Abnormal Psychology, 1957; attended St. Thomas's Hospital Medical School, London, England. *Home:* 132 Coulsdon Rd., Caterham, Surrey, England.

CAREER: St. Lawrence's Hospital, Caterham, Surrey, England, senior psychologist, 1957-63. *Member:* British Psychological Society, Royal Medico-Psychological Association (associate), Royal Society of Medicine (fellow).

WRITINGS: (With John Gibson) *Psychology for Nurses*, Blackwell Scientific Publications, 1961, 3rd edition, 1971.†

* * *

JAYNE, Sears 1920-

PERSONAL: Born August 11, 1920, in Phoenix, Ariz.; son of A. S. (an attorney) and Beatrice (Bodge) Jayne; married Mae Cooper, December 28, 1941; children: Lynn, Emily, Elizabeth. *Education.* University of Missouri, B.A., 1941, M.A., 1942; Yale University, Ph.D., 1948. *Home:* 205 Grotto Ave., Providence, R.I. *Office:* Brown University, Providence, R.I. 02912.

CAREER: University of Missouri, Columbia, instructor in English, 1941-42; University of California, Berkeley, assistant professor of English, 1948-56; University of Virginia, Charlottesville, associate professor of English, 1956-59; Claremont Graduate School, Claremont, Calif., Arensberg Visiting Professor, 1959-60; Pomona College, Claremont, Calif., professor of English, 1960-63; Queens College of the City University of New York, Flushing, N.Y., professor of English, 1963-69; Brown University, Providence, R.I., professor of English, 1969—. *Military service:* U.S. Naval Reserve, 1943-45. *Member:* Modern Language Association of America, Renaissance Society of America, Phi Beta Kappa. *Awards, honors:* Fulbright Research fellowship in England; American Council of Learned Societies fellowship in Italy; Guggenheim fellow; fellow of Harvard Research Center, Florence, Italy.

WRITINGS: (Translator) M. Ficino, *Commentary on Plato's Symposium*, University of Missouri Press, 1944; (with F. R. Johnson) *Library of John, Lord Lumley*, British Museum, 1956; *Library Catalogues of English Renaissance*, University of California Press, 1956; *John Colet and Marsilio Ficino*, Oxford University Press, 1963. Contributor of articles and reviews to periodicals.

* * *

JEFFERS, Jo (Johnson) 1931-

PERSONAL: Born April 28, 1931, in New Ulm, Minn.; daughter of Norman L. and Geraldine (Scofield) Johnson; divorced. *Education:* Attended University of Nottingham, 1951-52, University of New Mexico, 1953; Stanford University, B.A., 1954. *Politics:* Republican. *Religion:* Episcopalian. *Residence:* Pinetop, Ariz.

CAREER: Writer.

WRITINGS: Ranch Wife, Doubleday, 1964. Contributor of articles to *Arizona Highways, Writer.*

WORK IN PROGRESS: A novel entitled *The Bond*, a history of Indian traders entitled, *The Traders* and *The Ross Santee Sketchbook* for Northland Press.

* * *

JEFKINS, Frank William 1920-

PERSONAL: Born June 27, 1920, in Norbury, Croydon, Surrey, England; son of Frederick and Edith Rhoda (Harmer) Jefkins; married Frances Kee, September 13, 1952; children: John Malcolm, Valerie Edith. *Education:* London University, BSc., B.A. Also studied through Open University. *Religion:* Church of England. *Home and office:* 84 Ballards Way, South Croydon, Surrey, England.

CAREER: Llandudno Publicity Association, Llandudno, Wales, publicity manager, 1949-51; Advertising Association, London, England, assistant general secretary, 1951-52; Amalgamated Press Ltd., London, England, copywriter, 1953-54; Odhams Press Ltd., London, England, group executive, 1954-58; George Newnes Ltd., London, England, senior copywriter-executive, 1958-59; Rentokil Group Ltd., London, England, public relations officer, 1959-63; Scientific Public Relations Ltd., London, England, general manager, 1963-68; Frank Jefkins School of Public Relations, Surrey, England, principal, 1968—. Lecturer on various communications subjects at The Polytechnic, London, College for Distributive Trades, and Croydon Technical College, 1951-58, 1963—. *Member:* Advertising Association, Society of Members of the Advertising Association (member of executive committee), Institute of Public Relations (honorary director of studies), Institute of Marketing and Sales Management, Association of Industrial Editors.

WRITINGS: Copywriting and Its Presentation, Crosby Lockwood, 1958; *Wanted on Holiday* (novel), Hodder & Stoughton, 1960; *Public Relations in World Marketing*, Crosby Lockwood, 1966; *Press Relations Practice*, Intertext, 1968; *Planned Public Relations*, Intertext, 1969; *Advertising Today*, Intertext, 1971; *Advertising Made Simple*, W. H. Allen, 1973; *Dictionary of Marketing and Communication*, Intertext, 1973; *Marketing and PR Media Planning*, Pergamon, 1974; *Advertisement Writing*, Macdonald & Evans, 1975. Contributor to advertising and public relations journals. Author of courses on advertising and public relations for various correspondence schools. Former editor, *Rentokil Review*, and *Rentokil International.*

AVOCATIONAL INTERESTS: Travel and motor touring, rose growing, photography, philately, and historical research.

* * *

JELLICOE, Geoffrey Alan 1900-

PERSONAL: Born August 10, 1900, in London, England; son of George Edward (a publisher) and Florence (Waylett) Jellicoe; married Ursula Pares, November 7, 1936. *Education:* Attended Cheltenham College, 1915-18, and Architectural Association School of Architecture, 1918-22. *Office:* Jellicoe & Coleridge, 12 Gower St., London W.C. 1, England.

CAREER: Architect, town planner, and landscape architect, now senior partner of Jellicoe & Coleridge (architects), London, England. Architectural Association School of Architecture, London, England, principal, 1939-41. Architectural consultant to Northern Rhodesian government, 1947-52; British Council lecturer in Latin America on English landscape and town planning, 1963. Member of Royal

Fine Arts Commission and Royal Parks Commission. *Member:* Royal Institute of British Architects (fellow), Town Planning Institute, Institute of Landscape Architects (past president), International Federation of Landscape Architects (honorary life president), Athenaeum Club (London). *Awards, honors:* Commander, Order of the British Empire, 1961.

WRITINGS: (With J. C. Shepherd) *Native Gardens of the Renaissance*, Benn, 1925, 2nd edition, 1954; *Austrian Baroque Gardens*, Benn, 1932; *Studies in Landscape Design*, Oxford University Press, Volume I, 1960, Volume II, 1965, Volume III, 1970; *Motopia*, 1961; (with J. C. Shepherd) *Italian Gardens of the Renaissance*, Architectural Book Publishing Co., 1966; (with Susan Jellicoe) *Modern Private Gardens*, Abelard-Schuman, 1968; (with Susan Jellicoe) *Water: The Use of Water in Landscape Architecture*, St. Martin's Press, 1971.†

*   *   *

JELLINEK, Paul 1897-

PERSONAL: Born October 31, 1897, in Vienna, Austria; son of Heinrich (a doctor of medicine) and Gisela (Mohr) Jellinek; married Lisa Fuerth, October 12, 1924; children: Franz J., Josef S. J. *Education:* University of Vienna, Dr.phil., 1922. *Home:* Anna Paulownalaan 28, Amersfoort, The Netherlands.

CAREER: Calderara & Bankmann, Vienna, Austria, cosmetic chemist, perfumer, and soapmaker, 1922-28; Haarmann & Reimer, Holzminden, Germany, chief perfumer, 1928-38; chemist-perfumer in Amersfoort, The Netherlands, 1938—. *Military service:* Austrian Army, 1915-18. *Member:* Nederlandse Vereniging voor Cosmetische Chemie, Parfumeure, Kosmetiker und Seifensieder Oesterreichs (president, 1924-28), American Society of Perfumers (honorary).

WRITINGS: Praktikum des modernen Parfumeurs, Huethig Verlag, 1949, second edition, 1960 (published in English as *The Practice of Modern Perfumery*, Leonard Hill, 1954); *Die psychologischen Grundlagen der Parfumerie* (title means "The Psychological Foundations of Perfumery") Huethig Verlag, 1951, 3rd edition, 1973. Contributor to periodicals in the field of perfumery.

SIDELIGHTS: Jellinek states that he is the first perfumer to stress the importance of the psychology of perfume and cosmetics in his books and in the papers which he has delivered in many countries. Has made business and study voyages to France, England, United States, Japan, and Scandinavia. Speaks and writes German, Dutch, and English.

*   *   *

JENKINS, Clive 1926-

PERSONAL: Born May 2, 1926, in Port Talbot, Glamorganshire, Wales; married Moira McGregor Maguire; children: Bronwen, Gareth. *Education:* Attended schools in Port Talbot. *Politics:* Socialist. *Home:* 16 St. Marks Crescent, London N.W.1, England.

CAREER: Employed in early years as alloy worker, metallurgist, chemist, and tin-plate works manager; Association of Supervisory Staffs, Executives, and Technicians, London, England, assistant divisional officer in Birmingham, England, 1946, national negotiator, 1950-56, deputy general secretary, 1956-61, general secretary, 1961-68; Association of Scientific, Technical and Managerial Staffs joint general secretary, 1968-70, general secretary, 1970—, parliamentary committee secretary. Councillor, St. Pancras Metropolitan Borough, 1950. Has appeared regularly on radio and television.

WRITINGS: Power at the Top: The Labour Party and the Public Corporations, MacGibbon & Kee, 1959; *Power Behind the Screen: Ownership, Control and Motivation in Commercial Television*, MacGibbon & Kee, 1961; (wit Jim Mortimer) *British Unions Today*, Pergamon, 1965; *Tiger in a White Collar*, Penguin, 1965; (with Mortimer) *The Kind of Laws the Unions Ought to Want*, Pergamon, 1968. Editor, *Trade Union Affairs.* Author of pamphlets. Contributor to various magazines.

WORK IN PROGRESS: Two books, *The Rise of the White Collar Worker*, for Pitman, and a handbook on collective bargaining, for Routledge.

*   *   *

JENKINS, James J(erome) 1923-

PERSONAL: Born July 29, 1923, in St. Louis, Mo.; son of Joe Elmer Ellsworth (an efficiency expert) and Frances (Reynolds) Jenkins; married Geraldine Schoech, August 11, 1946; children: Richard, Robert, Christopher, Lynn. *Education:* University of Chicago, B.S., 1944; William Jewell College, A.B., 1947; University of Minnesota, M.A., 1948, Ph.D., 1950. *Politics:* Democrat. *Religion:* Episcopal. *Home:* 2252 Folwell St., St. Paul, Minn. 55108. *Office:* Department of Psychology, University of Minnesota, Minneapolis, Minn. 55455.

CAREER: University of Minnesota, Minneapolis, instructor, 1948-51, assistant professor, 1951-56, associate professor, 1956-59, professor of psychology, 1959—, director, Center for Research in Human Learning, 1966-73. Minneapolis Veterans Administration Hospital, consultant to Aphasia Clinic, 1956-67. *Military service:* U.S. Army Air Forces, Air Weather Service, 1942-46; became first lieutenant. *Member:* American Association for the Advancement of Science (fellow), American Psychological Association (fellow; president, division 3, 1973), Midwestern Psychological Association (member of council, 1965-68; president, 1968), Minnesota Psychological Association (member of executive committee, 1952-55), Society of Experimental Psychologists (chairman, 1973). *Awards, honors:* Fellow, Center for Advanced Study in the Behavioral Sciences, 1958-59, 1964-65.

WRITINGS: (Editor with Donald G. Paterson) *Studies in Individual Differences: The Search for Intelligence*, Appleton, 1961; (with David S. Palermo) *Word Association Norms: Fourth Grade through College*, University of Minnesota Press, 1964; (with Hildred Schuell and Edward Jimenez-Pabon) *Aphasia in Adults: Diagnosis, Prognosis and Treatment*, Hoeber Medical Division, Harper, 1964, revised edition (with Jimenez-Pabon, Robert E. Shaw and Joyce W. Sefer) published as *Schuell's Aphasia in Adults*, 1974; (editor with David L. Horton) *The Perception of Language*, Bobbs-Merrill, 1971; (with William N. Dember) *General Psychology: Modeling Behavior and Experience*, Prentice-Hall, 1970; (with Robert M. Stutz and Dember) *Exploring Behavior and Experience*, Prentice-Hall, 1971. Editor of Prentice-Hall "Experimental Psychology" series.

WORK IN PROGRESS: A book on contextualism as an approach to cognitive psychology, for Prentice-Hall.

JOHNSON, Christopher 1931-
(Louis McIntosh)

PERSONAL: Born June 12, 1931, in London, England; son of Donald McIntosh (a publisher) and Christiane (Coussaert) Johnson; married Anne Robbins, January 4, 1958; children: James, Caroline, Victoria, Elizabeth. *Education:* Magdalen College, Oxford, demy, 1950-54 (first class honors in philosophy, politics, and economics), 1953. *Home:* 39 Wood Lane, London N6, England. *Office: Financial Times,* 10 Cannon St., London E.C. 4, England.

CAREER: Times Educational Supplement, London, England, editorial assistant, 1954-57; *The Times,* London, England, assistant to foreign news editor, 1957-59, foreign sub-editor, 1958-59, assistant Paris correspondent, 1959-60; *Financial Times,* London, England, diplomatic correspondent in Paris, France, 1960-63, diplomatic correspondent, 1963-65, foreign editor, 1965-67, managing editor, 1967-70, managing director, business enterprises division, 1970—, main board director, 1973—. *Military service:* British Army, 1949-50; became captain.

WRITINGS: (Under pseudonym Louis McIntosh) *Oxford Folly,* Johnson Publications, 1955; *Firms and Their Exports,* Political and Economic Planning, 1964. Contributor to *Mind, Crossbow,* and *Journal of Common Market Studies.*

SIDELIGHTS: Johnson is competent in French, German, Italian, Spanish, Russian, modern and ancient Greek, and Latin.

*   *   *

JOHNSON, David 1927-

PERSONAL: Born August 26, 1927, in Meir, Stoke on Trent, England; son of Robert Arthur and Winifred (Stewart) Johnson. *Education:* Attended Repton School, 1941-45, and Royal Military Academy at Sandhurst, 1946. *Home:* 26 Molyneux St., London W.1, England.

CAREER: Writer. *Military service:* British Army, Infantry, 1945, 1946-48; became lieutenant.

WRITINGS: Sabre General, Hodder & Stoughton, 1959 (published in America as *The Proud Canaries,* Sloane, 1960); *Promanade in Champagne,* Hodder & Stoughton, 1960, Sloane, 1961; *Lanterns in Gascony,* Sidgwick & Jackson, 1964; *A Candle in Aragon: A Fragment of Reconquista,* Jenkins, 1969.

Compiler: *Clive of India: A Collection of Contemporary Documents,* Cape, 1968; *The Monmouth Rebellion and the Bloody Assizes: A Collection of Contemporary Documents,* Cape, 1968; *The Tower of London: A Collection of Documents,* Cape, 1968; *Marlborough: A Collection of Contemporary Documents,* Cape, 1969; *Elizabeth Fry and Prison Reform: A Collection of Contemporary Documents,* Jackdaw, 1969; *Alfred the Great,* Grossman, 1969; *The Anglo-Boer War: A Collection of Contemporary Documents,* Cape, 1969; *The American Revolution,* Grossman, 1970; *Clipper Ships and the Cutty Sark,* Grossman, 1971; *London's Peelers and the British Police,* Grossman, 1971; *The Civil War,* Grossman, 1971; *Eighteenth Century,* Oxford University Press, 1972.

AVOCATIONAL INTERESTS: History, riding, travel.†

*   *   *

JOHNSON, Elmer Hubert 1917-

PERSONAL: Born April 10, 1917, in Racine, Wis.; son of Elmer D. and Lucy (Hinderholtz) Johnson; married Carol Holmes (a craft shop director), 1943; children: Joy Marjorie, Jill Catherine. *Education:* University of Wisconsin, B.A., 1946, M.A., 1948, Ph.D., 1950. *Office:* Center for the Study of Crime, Delinquency, and Corrections, Southern Illinois University, Carbondale, Ill.

CAREER: Racine Journal Times, Racine, Wis., teletype copy editor, 1934-40; North Carolina State University at Raleigh, 1949-66, began as assistant professor, professor of sociology, 1962-66; Southern Illinois University, Carbondale, professor at Center for the Study of Crime, Delinquency, and Corrections, 1966—. Assistant director, North Carolina Prison Department, Raleigh, 1958-60. Consultant to North Carolina Department of Public Welfare, 1951-52, North Carolina Prison Department and Board of Paroles, 1956-57. *Military service:* U.S. Army Air Forces, 1941-46; became captain. U.S. Air Force Reserve, 1946—; now colonel. *Member:* International Association of Criminology, American Sociological Association, American Correctional Association, American Society of Criminology, National Council on Crime and Delinquency, Society for the Study of Social Problems, Southern Sociological Society, Midwest Sociological Society.

WRITINGS: Crime, Correction, and Society, Dorsey, 1964, 3rd edition, 1974; *Social Problems of Urban Man,* Dorsey, 1973. Contributor to professional journals.

WORK IN PROGRESS: Research on the implications of community-based corrections.

*   *   *

JOHNSON, Harold L. 1924-

PERSONAL: Born April 5, 1924, in Sioux City, Iowa; son of Lloyd L. and Elizabeth (Kromstroh) Johnson; married Catherine C. Swan, June 1, 1948; children: Elizabeth, Suzanne, Bruce. *Education:* Southern Methodist University, student, 1941-43, 1945-46; University of Texas, B.B.A., 1947, M.B.A., 1948, Ph.D., 1952; Carnegie Institute of Technology, Ford Foundation postdoctoral fellow, 1960-61. *Religion:* United Church of Christ. *Home:* 2026 North Akin Dr., N.E., Atlanta, Ga. 30329. *Office:* Department of Economics, Emory University, Atlanta, Ga. 30322.

CAREER: Texas Legislative Council, Austin, research assistant, 1950; Georgia State College (now Georgia State University), Atlanta, assistant professor, later associate professor of economics, 1951-57; Emory University, Atlanta, Ga., associate professor, 1957-64, professor of economics, 1964—. *Military service:* U.S. Army Air Forces, 1943-45; became second lieutenant; received Air Medal with two oak leaf clusters. *Member:* American Economic Association, American Association of University Professors (chapter president, 1954), Southern Economic Association, Beta Gamma Sigma.

WRITINGS: Piggyback Transportation: An Economic Analysis, Bureau of Business Research, Georgia State College, 1954; *The Christian as a Businessman,* Association Press, 1964; *Business in Contemporary Society: Framework and Issues,* Wadsworth, 1971. Contributor to *Harvard Business Review, Annals* of American Academy of Political and Social Science, economic journals.

WORK IN PROGRESS: Research on the economics of health care delivery and on social audit of business.

*   *   *

JOHNSON, Johnni 1922-

PERSONAL: Born September 12, 1922, in Huntington,

W.Va.; daughter of Charles Edwin and Elizabeth (Troxell) Johnson. *Education:* Georgetown College, Georgetown, Ky., A.B., 1945; Woman's Missionary Union Training School (now part of Southern Baptist Theological Seminary), M.R.E., 1951. *Religion:* Baptist. *Home:* 3607 Brook Rd., Richmond, Va. 23227. *Office:* Foreign Mission Board, Southern Baptist Convention, Box 6597, Richmond, Va. 23230.

CAREER: Baptist Student, assistant editor, 1948-50; missionary in Japan, 1951-53; Southern Baptist Convention, Foreign Mission Board, assistant in division of visual education, 1954—.

WRITINGS: As Others See Us, Broadman, 1953; *Missionary Assignment*, Convention Press, 1959; *What Do Missionaries Do?*, Broadman, 1964.

WORK IN PROGRESS: A study of changes in the missionary vocation; a study of mission as related to church in evangelical context.†

*   *   *

JOHNSON, Paul E(manuel) 1898-

PERSONAL: Born February 19, 1898, in Niantic, Conn.; son of John Edward and Martha (Cadwallader) Johnson; married Evelyn Grant, June 2, 1922; children: Lois Kathay (Mrs. George A. Cummings), Mona Margaret (Mrs. William R. Valentine). *Education:* Cornell College, Mount Vernon, Iowa, A.B., 1920; University of Chicago, A.M., 1921; Boston University, S.T.B., 1923, Ph.D., 1928. *Home:* 213 Lakeside Dr., Centerville, Mass. 02632. *Office:* 3808 North Meridian St., Indianapolis, Ind.

CAREER: Ordained minister of Methodist Church. Hamline University, St. Paul, Minn., associate professor of philosophy, 1928-36; Morningside College, Sioux City, Iowa, professor of philosophy and religion and dean, 1936-41; Boston University School of Theology, professor of the psychology of religion, 1941-57, Danielsen Professor of Psychology and Pastoral Counseling, 1957-63, professor emeritus, 1963—; Indianapolis Pastoral Care and Counseling Center, Indianapolis, Ind., visiting professor of pastoral care, 1966-71, director, 1965-68. Visiting professor in Japan in Kwansei Gakuin, Aoyama Gakuin, and Tokyo Union Theological Seminary, 1963-64. Lecturer at Duke University, Garrett Theological Seminary, University of Southern California, and Pacific School of Religion.

MEMBER: American Association of Pastoral Counselors, American Philosophical Association, American Psychological Association, Institute of Pastoral Care, National Council of Churches of Christ in the U.S.A., American Society of Group Psychotherapy and Psychodrama, American Protestant Hospital Association, Massachusetts Council of Churches, Phi Beta Kappa. *Awards, honors:* D.D., Cornell College, 1939.

WRITINGS: Who Are You?, Abingdon, 1937; *Psychology of Religion*, Abingdon, 1945, revised edition, 1959; *Christian Love*, Abingdon, 1951; *Psychology of Pastoral Care*, Abingdon, 1953; *Personality and Religion*, Abingdon, 1957; (contributor) J. Masserman and J. L. Moreno, editors, *Progress in Psychotherapy*, volume five, Grune, 1960; (contributor) J. L. Moreno, editor, *Code of Ethics for Group Psychotherapy and Psychodrama*, Beacon House, 1962; *Person and Counselor*, Abingdon, 1967; *The Middle Years*, Fortress Press, 1971; (with Lowell Colston) *Personality and Christian Faith*, Abingdon, 1972; (editor) *Healer of the Mind: A Psychiatrist and His Faith*, Abingdon, 1972; *Dynamic Interpersonalism for Ministry*, Abingdon, 1973.

Contributor to religious periodicals and to philosophical and psychological journals.

*   *   *

JOHNSON, Philip A(rthur) 1915-

PERSONAL: Born August 3, 1915, in Chicago, Ill.; son of P. Arthur (a clergyman) and Edna (Peterson) Johnson; married Cecile Ryden (an artist), June 21, 1941; children: Pamela Cecile, Stevan Philip. *Education:* Augustana College, Rock Island, Ill., A.B., 1937; Augustana Theological Seminary, B.D., 1941; University of Chicago, theological studies, 1958-59. *Home:* 63 Church Lane, Scarsdale, N.Y. *Office:* National Lutheran Council, 50 Madison Ave., New York, N.Y. 10010.

CAREER: Lutheran clergyman; pastor of churches in Riverside, Calif., 1941-49, and Chicago, Ill., 1949-58; National Lutheran Council, New York, N.Y., executive secretary, Division of Public Relations, 1958—. Lutheran Service Commission, service pastor in Riverside (Calif.) military area, 1942-46. Member of board of directors of Contemporary Christian Art, Inc., New York, N.Y., and Wagner College; former trustee of Augustana College, Rock Island, Ill., and Augustana Hospital, Chicago, Ill. *Member:* Public Relations Society of America, National Religious Public Relations Council (board of governors, 1963—; president of New York chapter, 1963-65). *Awards, honors:* Human Relations Award from City of Chicago, 1956, and similar awards from Chicago Urban League and National Conference of Christians and Jews; honorary D.D. from Augustana Seminary, 1960.

WRITINGS: (Editor) *Telling the Good News*, Concordia, 1962; *Call Me Neighbor, Call Me Friend*, Doubleday, 1965; *The Epistles to Titus and Philemon: A Study Manual*, Baker Book House, 1966. Writer of "The Light of the World," script for Lutheran exhibit at New York World's Fair. Editorial columnist, *National Lutheran* (monthly). Also contributor to other religious periodicals.

WORK IN PROGRESS: Research for a book on Christian-Jewish relations.

AVOCATIONAL INTERESTS: Sailing, skiing, mountain climbing (has climbed the Matterhorn, Grand Teton, and Whitney).

BIOGRAPHICAL/CRITICAL SOURCES: "The Furious and the Godly," *Christian Century*, Volume LXXII, Number 7, 1955.†

*   *   *

JOHNSTON, Charles (Hepburn) 1912-

PERSONAL: Born March 11, 1912, in London, England; son of Ernest and Emma (Hepburn) Johnston; married Princess Natasha Bagration, 1944. *Education:* Attended Balliol College, Oxford. *Home:* 32 Kingston House South, London S.W.7, England.

CAREER: Entered British Diplomatic Service, 1936; served in Tokyo, Cairo, Madrid, and Bonn, 1939-55, ambassador to Jordan, 1956-60; governor and commander in chief of Aden, 1960-63; deputy undersecretary, Foreign Office, London, England, 1963-65; high commissioner in Australia, 1965-71; chairman of Thames Estuary Development Co., 1971—, and Maplin Development Co., 1971—; director of Australian Estates Ltd., 1971—. *Member:* St. James' Club, White's Club. *Awards, honors:* Companion of St. Michael and St. George, 1953; Knight Commander of St. Michael and St. George, 1959; Knight of Order of St.

John of Jerusalem, 1961; Knight Grand Cross of St. Michael and St. George, 1971.

WRITINGS: The View from Steamer Point, Praeger, 1965; *Mo and Other Originals*, Hamish Hamilton, 1971; *The Brink of Jordan*, Hamish Hamilton, 1972.

* * *

JOHNSTON, Fran(ces Jonsson) 1925-

PERSONAL: Born September 25, 1925, in Santa Monica, Calif.; daughter of Carl Rudolf (a customs officer) and Lillian W. (Tregillus) Jonsson; married Rodney W. Johnston (a missionary youth director), August 18, 1950; children: David Lawrence, Pamela Joanne, Daniel Charles, Gerald Philip. *Education:* Hong Kong University, student, 1941; Wheaton College, Wheaton, Ill., B.A., 1949, M.A., 1951. *Home:* Villa Bellevue-Bon Air, Route de Limonest, 69370 St. Didier-Au-Mt-D'or, France.

CAREER: Missionary (with husband) in Paris and Lyon, France, 1953—, serving under Evangelical Alliance Missions and as representative of Young Life Campaign, which is based in Colorado Springs, Colo.

WRITINGS: Rendez-vous with Paris, Moody, 1964; (contributor) Don W. Hillis, editor, *For More Than a Diamond*, Moody, 1966; *More Oceans to Cross*, Moody, 1967; (contributor) Don W. Hillis, editor, *Taller For God*, Moody, 1969; *Please Don't Strike That Match*, Zondervan, 1970.

WORK IN PROGRESS: Revision of book manuscript, *Doctor, You've Got to be Kidding!*; a children's book, *My Name is Felix*.

SIDELIGHTS: Mrs. Johnston lived in Hong Kong from 1937-45, spending the last four years under the Japanese Occupation. She is of Swedish descent on the paternal side and Chinese-English on the maternal (her grandmother was Cantonese). Mrs. Johnston speaks both Cantonese and French, and the four Johnston children are bilingual in English and French.

* * *

JOHNSTON, Leonard 1920-

PERSONAL: Born March 11, 1920, in County Durham, England. *Education:* Attended Ushaw College, Durham, England, 1932-45, University of Louvain, 1947-50, Biblical Institute, Rome, Italy, 1950-51. *Religion:* Roman Catholic. *Address:* Mary Ward College of Education, Keyworth, Nottingham, England.

CAREER: Ushaw College, Durham, England, lecturer in Biblical studies, 1951-66; Mary Ward College of Education, Keyworth, England, lecturer in religious studies, 1967—.

WRITINGS: (Translator) F. Van Steenbergen, *Aristotle in the West*, Nauwelaerts, 1955; *Witnesses to God*, Sheed, 1960; (with Aiden Pickering) *Before Our Lord*, Darton, 1962; (editor with Pickering) *A Harmony of the Gospels in the Knox Translation*, Sheed, 1963; *A History of Israel*, Sheed, 1963; *Teaching the Faith*, Sheed, 1973. Contributor to religious journals.

WORK IN PROGRESS: Old Testament editor of new edition of a *Catholic Commentary on Holy Scripture*, for Nelson.

* * *

JOHNSTON, Ronald 1926-

PERSONAL: Born May 11, 1926, in Edinburgh, Scotland; son of William (a school headmaster) and Susanna (Hay) Johnston; married Margaret Rae, June 16, 1955; children: Paul, Claire, Alan. *Education:* Leith Nautical College, Edinburgh, Scotland, Master Mariner, 1956. *Home and office:* Waverly House, Queen's Crescent, Edinburgh EH9 2BB, Scotland.

CAREER: British Merchant Navy, 1942-47, becoming third officer; Manufacturers Life Insurance of Canada, branch secretary, Glasgow, Scotland, and consultant, 1947-51; Socony Mobil Oil Co., marine transport service, 1952-58, becoming chief officer; Anglo-Dutch Cigar Co. Ltd. (importers), London, England, salesman, then general manager, 1959-63, part-time importers agent, 1963-65; full-time author, with occasional consulting work on communications, sales training, and public relations, 1965—. *Member:* Society of Authors, Scottish Arts Council, Scottish P.E.N. (vice-president), Chartered Insurance Institute (associate).

WRITINGS: Disaster at Dungeness, Collins, 1964, published as *Collision Ahead*, Doubleday, 1965; *Danger at Bravo Key*, Doubleday, 1965 (published in England as *Red Sky in the Morning*, Collins, 1965); *The Stowaway*, Harcourt, 1966; *The Wrecking of Offshore Five*, Collins, 1967, Harcourt, 1968; *The Angry Ocean*, Collins, 1968, Harcourt, 1969; *The Black Camels*, Harcourt, 1969; *Paradise Smith*, Harcourt, 1972; *The Eye of the Needle*, Harcourt, 1975.

WORK IN PROGRESS: A ninth novel; a stage play.

SIDELIGHTS: Johnston told *CA*: "Interested in the sea and ships, wine and food, but most of all in people.... When not thinking or writing, I talk and listen. Mix lethally dry Martinis and cook rather well.... The biggest hurdle I had to overcome in becoming a novelist was having been taught English in a British school."

A Ronald Johnston Collection (manuscripts, notes, letters, and biographical material) has been established at Boston University, Mugar Memorial Library.

* * *

JOHNSTON, Thomas E. 1931-

PERSONAL: Born June 19, 1931, in Kansas City, Mo.; son of Thomas E. and Evelyn G. (Enlow) Johnston. *Education:* University of Michigan, A.B., 1957, M.A., 1960; University of Valencia, diploma, 1960; University of Edinburgh, diploma, 1963. *Home:* 803 C St., Silver City, N.M. *Agent:* A. Watkins, Inc., 77 Park Ave., New York, N.Y. 10016.

CAREER: Albion College, Albion, Mich., instructor in English, 1960-61; Wisconsin State College and Institute of Technology, Platteville, instructor in English and Spanish, 1961-63; Eastern New Mexico University, Portales, assistant professor of English, 1963-65; Western New Mexico University, Silver City, lecturer in English, 1965—. *Member:* American Association of University Professors. *Awards, honors:* Wisconsin State College research grant, 1962; Avery and Jule Hopwood Award in creative writing, University of Michigan, 1963.

WRITINGS: Freud and Political Thought, Citadel, 1965. Editor of *El Portal* (a little literary magazine), 1963—.

WORK IN PROGRESS: Hemingway in Spain, and a novel dealing with North Americans in Mexico.

AVOCATIONAL INTERESTS: Travel and social psychology.†

JONAS, Arthur 1930-

PERSONAL: Born June 27, 1930, in New York, N.Y.; son of Jerome (a teacher) and Lillian (Newfield) Jonas. Education: Allegheny College, B.A., 1952; New York University, M.A., 1956, Ed.D., 1960. Religion: Jewish. Home: 59 Roseland Ave., Caldwell, N.J. Office: Wilson School, West Caldwell, N.J.

CAREER: Windward School, White Plains, N.Y., teacher, 1953-54, 1955-57; Heathcote School, Scarsdale, N.Y., teacher, 1957-62; Wilson School, West Caldwell, N.J., principal, 1962—. Summer instructor at New York University, Newark State College, and Bank Street College of Education. Military service: U.S. Army, Field Artillery, 1954-55. Member: National Education Association, American Association of School Administrators, Association for Supervision and Curriculum Development, Association for Childhood Education International, Association for Student Teaching, Mathematics Teachers Association, New Jersey Education Association, Essex County Principals Association.

WRITINGS: New Ways in Math, Prentice-Hall, 1962; Archimedes and His Wonderful Discoveries, Prentice-Hall, 1963; More New Ways in Math, Prentice-Hall, 1964; (with L. E. Raths, A. Rothstein, and Selma Wassermann) Teaching for Thinking, C. E. Merrill, 1965.

WORK IN PROGRESS: Children's books in various areas of science.

AVOCATIONAL INTERESTS: Music in general.†

*   *   *

JONES, Charles W(illiams) 1905-

PERSONAL: Born September 23, 1905, in Lincoln, Neb.; son of Charles Williams (a school administrator) and Grace (Cook) Jones; married Sarah Bosworth, June 30, 1928; children: Frances (Mrs. Donald Lammers), Charles Bosworth (deceased), Lawrence Wager, Gregory Hunt. Education: Oberlin College, B.A., 1926; Cornell University, M.A., 1930, Ph.D., 1932. Home: 766 Spruce St., Berkeley, Calif. 94707. Office: University of California, Berkeley, Calif. 94720.

CAREER: Allyn & Bacon, Inc. (educational publishers), Boston, Mass., field representative, 1926-29; Oberlin College, Oberlin, Ohio, instructor in English, 1932-35; Cornell University, Ithaca, N.Y., 1936-54, began as instructor, professor of English, 1948-54, director of summer sessions, 1944-48, dean of Graduate School, 1948-54; University of California, Berkeley, professor of English, 1954—, research professor in humanities, 1964-65. Awards, honors: American Council of Learned Societies research fellow, 1935-36; Guggenheim fellow, 1939-40, 1945-46; D.Litt., Oberlin College, 1952.

WRITINGS: Bedae Pseudepigrapha, Cornell University Press, 1939; (with Tressider and Shubert) Writing and Speaking, Ronald, 1943; The Library Paper, Thrift Press, 1943; Bedae Opera de Temporibus, Mediaeval Academy of America, 1943; Saints' Lives and Chronicles in Early England, Cornell University Press, 1947; Medieval Literature in Translation, Longmans, Green, 1950; The St. Nicholas Liturgy, University of California Press, 1963; Bedae in Genesim Commentarium, Corpus Christianorum, 1967; The Directives of Adalhard of Corbie, University of California Press, in press; Bedae Opera Didascalica, two volumes, Corpus Christianorum, in press.

Contributor to Encyclopaedia Britannica, Dictionary of World Literature, Encyclopedia of Poetry and Poetics, and to professional journals. Member of board of editors, Viator: Medieval and Renaissance Studies.

WORK IN PROGRESS: History of Western Christian Literature to A.D. 1050; The Biography of a Myth (about St. Nicholas); a third book, with W. Hom and R. Crocker, Modularity in Carolingian Aesthetics.

*   *   *

JONES, E(lbert) Winston 1911-

PERSONAL: Born July 6, 1911, in Karuizawa, Japan; son of James Ira (a missionary) and Bertha (Masden) Jones; married Lillian A. Monroe, February 20, 1937. Education: Indiana University, A.B., 1933; Boston University, graduate study, 1933-34; Garrett Theological Seminary, B.D., 1936; Northwestern University, M.A., 1937, Ph.D., 1950; Iliff School of Theology, Th.D., 1947. Home: Bolton Rd., Harvard, Mass. Office: Speech Department, Boston University, 232 Bay State Rd., Boston, Mass. 02215.

CAREER: Minister of Methodist churches in Illinois and Ohio, 1936-48; Boston University, Boston, Mass., assistant professor, 1950-56, associate professor, 1956-61, professor of speech, 1961—, chairman of department, 1956-73.

WRITINGS: Preaching and the Dramatic Arts, Macmillan, 1948; A Guide to Effective Speech, Longmans, Green, 1961.

*   *   *

JONES, Edward H(arral), Jr. 1922-

PERSONAL: Born July 10, 1922, in Alexandria, Va.; son of Edward Harral (a U.S. naval officer) and Thais (Yarowshoff) Jones; married Margaret Stigaard (a teacher), December 26, 1963; children: Leslie C., Edward III, Gregory S. Education: Attended University of Miami, 1941, Georgia Institute of Technology, 1942; University of Southern California, A.B., M.A., 1952. Office: El Camino College, El Camino College, Calif.

CAREER: El Camino College, El Camino College, Calif., member of English faculty, 1956-73, dean of Humanities Division, 1973—. Military service: U.S. Navy. Member: American Association of University Professors.

WRITINGS: (With K. G. Burne and Robert L. Wylder) Functional English for Writers, Scott, 1964, revised edition, 1969; (with Burne and Wylder) Remedies for Writers, Lippincott, 1964; (with Burne and Wylder) Limits and Latitudes, Lippincott, 1965; Outlines of Literature, Macmillan, 1968; (with wife, Margaret Jones) Arts and Crafts of the Mexican People, Ward Ritchie Press, 1971; (with Margaret Jones) Ancient Cities of Mexico, Ward Ritchie Press, 1974. Co-editor, Blue Guitar (magazine of poetry and criticism).

WORK IN PROGRESS: A book on Mexico.

AVOCATIONAL INTERESTS: Ancient and modern art, archaeology, and Mexico.

*   *   *

JONES, Everett L(ee) 1915-

PERSONAL: Born March 29, 1915, in Huron, S.D.; son of Henry Lee (a minister) and Edna (Fitch) Jones; married Mary Ayer Boyden (a physical therapist), December 26, 1940; children: Pamet A. (Mrs. Michael Tigar), Samuel L. Education: Antioch College, B.A., 1938; Lehigh University, M.A., 1941; University of California, Los Angeles, graduate study, 1947-50. Agent: Willis Kingsley Wing, 24

East 38th St., New York, N.Y. 10016. *Office:* University of California, Los Angeles, Calif.

CAREER: University of California, Los Angeles, 1948—, now supervisor of instruction in English.

WRITINGS: An Approach to College Reading, Henry Holt, 1953, alternate edition, 1955; (with Clarence Greenwood) *An Approach to College Writing*, Henry Holt, 1956, Form 2, Henry Holt, 1957, Form 3 (sole author), Henry Holt, 1959; (editor with Mark Schorer and Philip Durham) *The Harbrace College Reader*, Harcourt, 1959, 4th edition, 1972; (editor with Philip Durham) *Readings in Science and Engineering*, Holt, 1961; *A New Approach to College Reading*, Holt, 1964; (with Durham) *The Negro Cowboys*, Dodd, 1965; (with Durham) *The West: From Fact to Myth*, Los Angeles, 1967; (compiler with Durham) *The Frontier in American Literature*, Odyssey, 1969. Contributor to *American West, Pacific Historical Review*, other journals.

AVOCATIONAL INTERESTS: Hiking, fishing, and skiing in the Sierra Nevada Mountains.

*　　*　　*

JONES, Frank E(dward) 1917-

PERSONAL: Born October 28, 1917, in Montreal, Quebec, Canada; son of Richard Thomas and Victoria (Hughes) Jones; married Jean McEachran, 1946; children: David McEachran, Dilys Lemire. *Education:* McGill University, B.A., 1949, M.A., 1950; Harvard University, Ph.D., 1954. *Home:* 19 Brentwood Dr., Dundas, Ontario, Canada. *Office:* Department of Sociology, McMaster University, Hamilton, Ontario, Canada.

CAREER: Department of Citizenship and Immigration, Ottawa, Ontario, research director, 1953-55; McMaster University, Hamilton, Ontario, assistant professor, 1955-58, associate professor, 1958-64, professor of sociology, 1964—, department chairman, 1958-64, 1965—. Visiting fellow, Australian National University, 1961 and 1971; visiting professor, McGill University, 1966-67. *Military service:* Royal Canadian Navy, 1940-45; became petty officer. *Member:* Canadian Political Science Association, American Sociological Association.

WRITINGS: An Introduction to Sociology, Canadian Broadcasting Corp., 1961; (co-editor) *Canadian Society: Sociological Perspectives*, Free Press of Glencoe, 1961, 3rd edition, Macmillan, 1971.

Author of seven scripts for sociology series, Canadian Broadcasting Co. radio, 1961, and a television film, "Courtship and Marriage," produced by National Film Board of Canada, 1961. Contributor to *Social Forces, Public Opinion Quarterly, Canadian Journal of Economics and Political Science, British Journal of Sociology, Canadian Review of Sociology and Anthropology, Australian and New Zealand Journal of Sociology.*

WORK IN PROGRESS: Social origins in the professions; occupational mobility.

AVOCATIONAL INTERESTS: Literature, the theater, music.

*　　*　　*

JONES, George Fenwick 1916-

PERSONAL: Born April 3, 1916, in Savannah, Ga.; son of George Noble (an attorney) and Frances (Meldrim) Jones; married Joyce Cromer (a teacher), February 10, 1951; children: Jocelyn Fenwick, Andrew Berrien. *Education:* Emory University, B.A., 1938; University of Heidelberg, student, 1936-37; Oxford University, M.A., 1943; Columbia University, Ph.D., 1950. *Politics:* Democrat. *Religion:* Episcopalian. *Home:* 3931 Cloverhill Rd., Baltimore, Md.

CAREER: Princeton University, Princeton, N.J., assistant professor of modern languages, 1950-59, Ellsworth Preceptor, 1950-55; Goucher College, Towson, Md., associate professor of German, 1959-62; University of Maryland, College Park, professor of German, 1962—. Visiting professor at Johns Hopkins University, Catholic University of America, and University of Munich. *Military service:* U.S. Marine Corps Reserve, 1936-60, became lieutenant colonel; active duty, 1940-46, served in Pacific campaigns. *Member:* Modern Language Association of America, Mediaeval Academy of America, American Association of Teachers of German, Society of the Cincinnati, Goethe Society, Phi Beta Kappa. *Awards, honors:* Rhodes scholar.

WRITINGS: Wittenwiler's Ring and Colkelbie Sow, University of North Carolina Press, 1956; *Honor in German Literature*, University of North Carolina Press, 1959; *The Ethos of the Song of Roland*, Johns Hopkins Press, 1963; (editor) Henry Newman, *Salzburger Letterbooks*, University of Georgia Press, 1966; *Walther von der Vogelweide*, Twayne, 1968; (editor; also translator with Marie Hahn of Volume III) Samuel Urlsperger, compiler, *Detailed Reports on the Salzburger Emigrants Who Settled in America*, University of Georgia Press, Volume I: *1733-34*, 1968, Volume II: *1734-35*, 1969, Volume III: *1736*, 1972; *Spaetes Mittelalter*, Francke (Munich), 1971; (editor with Ann Demaitre) *La Chanson de Roland*, Prentice-Hall, 1971; *Oswald von Wolkenstein*, Twayne, 1972; (editor with Hans Mueck and Ulrich Mueller) *Verskonkordanz zu den Liedern Oswald von Wolkenstein*, Kuemmerle (Goeppingen), 1973. Contributor of more than fifty articles, dealing mainly with literature of medieval Germany and France, to scholarly journals.

WORK IN PROGRESS: Verse concordances to *El Libro de Buen Amor* by Juan Ruiz, and to the songs of the Monk of Salzburg.

*　　*　　*

JONES, Madison (Percy, Jr.) 1925-

PERSONAL: Born March 21, 1925, in Nashville, Tenn.; son of Madison Percy and Mary Temple (Webber) Jones; married Shailah McEvilley, February 5, 1951; children: Carroll, Madison III, Ellen, Michael, Andrew. *Education:* Vanderbilt University, A.B., 1949; University of Florida, A.M., 1951, graduate study, 1951-53. *Home:* 800 Kuderna Acres, Auburn, Ala. 36830. *Agent:* Elizabeth McKee, McIntosh, McKee & Dodds, 30 East 60th St., New York, N.Y. 10022. *Office:* Auburn University, Auburn, Ala.

CAREER: Sometime farmer and horse trainer; instructor in English at Miami University, Oxford, Ohio, 1952-55, 56-57, at University of Tennessee, Knoxville, 1955-56; Auburn University, Auburn, Ala., writer-in-residence, 1956—. *Military service:* U.S. Army, Corps of Military Police, 1944-45; served in Korea. *Member:* P.E.N., South Atlantic Modern Language Association. *Awards, honors:* Sewanee Review fellowship, 1954; Alabama Library Association Award, 1967; Rockefeller Foundation fellowship, 1968; Guggenheim fellowship, 1973.

WRITINGS—Novels: The Innocent, Harcourt, 1957; *Forest of the Night*, Harcourt, 1960; *A Buried Land*, Viking, 1963; *An Exile*, Viking, 1967, published as *I Walk the*

Line, Popular Library, 1970; *A Cry of Absence*, Crown, 1971; *Innocent*, Popular Library, 1971. Short story, "Dog Days," appeared in Martha Foley's *Best American Short Stories, 1953*; contributor of short stories to *Perspective* and *Sewanee Review*.

WORK IN PROGRESS: A novel.

SIDELIGHTS: An Exile has been translated into Japanese and has also been adapted for film under the title "I Walk the Line," 1970. *Avocational Interests:* Hunting, fishing, and sculpturing.

BIOGRAPHICAL/CRITICAL SOURCES: Carolyn Riley, editor, *Contemporary Literary Criticism*, Volume IV, Gale, 1975.†

* * *

JONES, Willis Knapp 1895-

PERSONAL: Born November 27, 1895, in Beacon, N.Y.; son of Plato Tydvil (a minister) and Louise (Knapp) Jones; married Polly Mae Replogle, July 10, 1921; children: Anita Lou (Mrs. Norman Francis), Robert Knapp. *Education:* Hamilton College, A.B., 1917; The Pennsylvania State University, M.A., 1922; University of Chicago, Ph.D., 1927. *Home:* 320 East Vine, Oxford, Ohio. 45056.

CAREER: Taught in Santiago, Chile, 1917-19, Montevideo, Uruguay, 1919-20; The Pennsylvania State University, University Park, instructor in Spanish, 1920-23; Miami University, Oxford, Ohio, associate professor, 1923-28, professor of Romance languages, 1928-63, professor emeritus, 1963—. U.S. Department of Education delegate to University of Chile Summer School, 1937; instructor at American University of Shrivenham, England, 1945, and at University of Guayaquil, Ecuador, 1946-47. Lecturer on Latin American drama and culture. *Member:* American Association of Teachers of Spanish and Portuguese (president, 1941), Casa de Cultura Ecuatoriana. *Awards, honors:* Order of Eloy Alfaro, 1953.

WRITINGS: (With H. C. Fenn) *Songs from Hypnia*, Osborne, 1915; (with Huntsman) *Teachers' Handbook: Pioneers*, Osborne, 1917; (editor with Paul Fancher) *A Book of Hamilton Verse*, Dodge, 1917.

The Hammon Twins, Century Co., 1926; (editor with H. H. Arnold) Palacio Valdes, *Marta y Maria*, Heath, 1928.

(Editor with Daniel DaCruz) *Five Spanish Plays*, Macmillan, 1930; (editor with DaCruz) Conde de las Navas, *Procurador Yerbabuena*, Century Co., 1931; *Mejores Cuentos de Pardo Bazan*, Doubleday, Doran, 1931; *Storm Before Sunset*, Row, Peterson & Co., 1931; *Spiced Wine*, Row, Peterson & Co., 1931; (editor) Luis De Oteyza, *Diablo blanco*, Macmillan, 1932; (with Van Tassell) *Miami Prognosis Test in Spanish*, Miami University Press, 1933; *Plays of the Dons*, Tardy, 1934; *A Knight in Spain*, Row, Peterson & Co., 1934; (translator) *Spanish One Act Plays in English*, Tardy, 1934, revised edition, Barron's, 1965; *How to Study Spanish*, Tardy, 1935; (editor) Agustin Moreto y Cavana, *Desden con el desden*, Henry Holt, 1935; *Calendar of Latin American Anniversaries*, Tardy, 1935; *Calendar of Spanish Anniversaries*, Tardy, 1935; (editor, with Harry J. Russell) Ramon de Navarrete, *Mujer misteriosa*, Tardy, 1936; (with Edmund Villela de Trzaska) *Teatro por medias horas*, Tardy, 1936.

(With Miriam Hanson) *Hispanoamericanos*, Henry Holt, 1941, 2nd edition published as *Spanish American Readings*, 1946; (with Glenn Barr) *Un verano en Mexico*, Heath, 1942; (with Barr) *Resumen gramatical*, Heath, 1942; *High-lights of Ibero-America*, Thrift, 1942, 2nd edition, 1955; *Highlights of Spain*, Thrift, 1942, 2nd edition, 1954; *Selective Bibliography for Spanish Teachers*, Thrift, 1942; *Latin American Writers in English Translation: A Bibliography*, Pan American Union, 1944, revised edition, Blaine Ethridge, 1972; *Short Plays of the Southern Americas*, Stanford University, 1944; *Hi Neighbor!*, Row, Peterson & Co., 1944; *El drama de las Americas*, University of Guayaquil, 1946; *Amor y vino*, Casa de Cultura, 1946; (with Demetrio Aguilera Malta) *Blue Blood: A Comedy in Three Acts*, Pan American Union, 1948; (editor) *Cuentos del Alto Peru*, Heath, 1947; *El teatro en el Ecuador*, Biblioteca minima, 1947; (editor with Barr) Horacio Quiroga, *Anaconda*, Heath, 1948; *Graded Spanish Reader*, Alternate Books 1-6, Heath, 1949.

(With Glenn Barr) *Our Friends in South America*, Macmillan, 1950; (with Aguilera Malta) *Dos Comedias faciles*, Houghton, 1950; *Latin American Drama in English Translation*, Pan American Union, 1950; *El tio de Carlos*, Henry Holt, 1950; (with Juan Castellano) *Spanish Through Speech*, Scribner, 1951; (editor) A. Rigoberto Moock, *Rigoberto*, Heath, 1954; (editor with Robert Woempner) *Teatro facil*, American Book Co., 1956; *Breve historia del teatro latinoamericano*, Studium, 1956; (editor) *Antologia de teatro hispanoamericano*, Studium, 1958.

(Translator) *Representative Plays of Florencio Sanchez*, Pan American Union, 1961; (editor) *Spanish American Literature in Translation: A Selection of Prose, Poetry and Drama Since 1888*, Ungar, 1963; (editor with Odette Scott) Olga Pineda, *El cuchillo de piedra*, Appleton, 1964; *Dialogos en castellano*, J. Weston Walch, 1964; *Behind Spanish American Footlights*, University of Texas Press, 1966; (editor) *Spanish American Literature in Translation: A Selection of Prose, Poetry and Drama Before 1888*, Ungar, 1966; *Mastering Spanish*, J. Weston Walch, 1966; (translator) Aguilera Malta, *Manuela*, Southern Illinois University Press, 1967.

(Translator) *Men and Angels: Three South American Comedies in Translation*, Southern Illinois University Press, 1970; *The Literatures of the World in English Translation: Spanish America*, Ungar, 1970; *Life in Latin America*, J. Weston Walch, 1966; (with Anita Francis) *Teaching Written English*, J. Weston Walch, 1974; (with Francis) *Our Changing Language*, J. Weston Walch, 1974.

Musical works with Joseph W. Clokey include: *Our American Cousin* (operetta), published, 1931; *The Nightingale* (operetta), Birchard, 1934; twenty-one songs published by Fischer, and five nocturnes published by Birchard. Also librettist, *Arrullo*, with music by Xavier Branda, published in Buenos Aires.

Contributor of more than seven hundred articles to popular magazines, 1920—, and of many other articles to encyclopedias and literary and language journals. Contributing editor and author of several hundred reviews, *Books Abroad*.

AVOCATIONAL INTERESTS: Photography.

* * *

JOOST, Nicholas (Teynac) 1916-

PERSONAL: Born May 28, 1916, in Jacksonville, Fla.; son of Nicholas Teynac (a businessman) and Margaret (Wrigley) Joost; married Laura A. Reed (a reference librarian), May 25, 1943; children: Anna, Mary Eliza, Nicholas. *Education:* Georgetown University, B.S.S., 1938; University of North Carolina, M.A., 1939, Ph.D., 1947. *Religion:* Roman Catholic. *Residence:* Alton, Ill.

CAREER: Northwestern University, Evanston, Ill., instructor, 1947-49; Loyola University, Chicago, Ill., assistant professor, 1949-54; Assumption College, Worcester, Mass., associate professor, 1954-58; Southern Illinois University, Edwardsville Campus, Alton, professor English, 1958—, head of Humanities Division, 1960-63. Editorial consultant to Bollingen Foundation, 1954—; Fulbright lecturer, University of Nijmegen, 1963-64; judge of quarterly poetry contest, Hospitalized Veterans Writing Project, 1954—; member of board of commissioners of Hayner District Library, 1969—; Lewis and Clark Library, member of board of directors, 1971, president, 1973. Military service: U.S. Army Air Forces, 1942-45; became technical sergeant.

MEMBER: Modern Language Association of America, American Studies Association (president of Midcontinent branch, 1965-66), Catholic Renascence Society, William Clark Society, St. Louis Westerners, Delta Epsilon Sigma (national president, 1957-58). Awards, honors: Bollingen Foundation grant, Worcester Art Museum, 1957-58; faculty award, Southern Illinois University, 1960; Service Award, Delta Epsilon Sigma, 1963; Chicago Book Clinic Award, 1964, for Scofield Thayer and "The Dial"; Chapelbrook Foundation grant, 1970-71; faculty award for excellence in scholarship, Southern Illinois University, 1972.

WRITINGS: (Contributor) H. C. Gardiner, editor, Fifty Years of the American Novel, Scribner, 1951; (contributor) R. P. Bond, editor, Studies in the Early English Periodical, University of North Carolina Press, 1957; Scofield Thayer and "The Dial", Southern Illinois University Press, 1964; (editor with John Champlin) Papers on the Art and Age of Geoffrey Chaucer, Southern Illinois University, 1967; (contributor) B. W. Patterson and A. B. Strauss, editors, Essays in English Literature of the Classical Period, University of North Carolina Press, 1967; Years of Transition: "The Dial," 1912-20, Barre, 1967; Ernest Hemingway and the Little Magazines: The Paris Years, Barre, 1968; (with Alvin Sullivan) D. H. Lawrence and "The Dial", Southern Illinois University Press, 1970; (contributor) J. F. McDermott, editor, Travelers on the Western Frontier, Southern Illinois University Press, 1970; (compiler with Sullivan) "The Dial": Two Author Indexes, Libraries, Southern Illinois University, 1971. Also editor and contributor, Toward the Modern, 1972.

Poetry, member of editorial staff, 1951-54, acting editor, 1953-54; editor, Delta Epsilon Sigma Bulletin, 1958-63; editor, Papers on English Language and Literature, Southern Illinois University, 1965-73.

WORK IN PROGRESS: An index to Papers on Language and Literature, 1965-74.

SIDELIGHTS: Joost reads French and Dutch and has some speaking competence in both languages. Avocational interests: Collecting Oriental porcelain, and early American silver, prints, and drawings.

BIOGRAPHICAL/CRITICAL SOURCES: Southern Alumnus, January, 1965.

*   *   *

JORDAN, William S(tone), Jr.   1917-

PERSONAL: Born September 28, 1917, in Fayetteville, N.C.; son of William Stone (a physician) and Louise Manning (Huske) Jordan; married Marion Elizabeth Anderson, May 17, 1947; children William S. III, Marion Anderson. Education: University of North Carolina, A.B., 1938; Har-

vard University, M.D., 1942. Religion: Episcopalian. Home: 1775 Mooreland Dr., Lexington, Ky. 40502. Office: School of Medicine, University of Kentucky, Lexington, Ky.

CAREER: Boston City Hospital, Boston, Mass., intern, 1942-43, resident, 1946-47; Western Reserve University (now Case Western Reserve University), School of Medicine, Cleveland, Ohio, 1947-58, started as teaching fellow, associate professor of preventive medicine and assistant professor of medicine, 1954-58; University of Virginia, Charlottesville, professor of preventive medicine and chairman of department, 1958-67; University of Kentucky, Lexington, dean of College of Medicine, and professor of community medicine, 1967—. Office of the U.S. Surgeon General, consultant, 1956—; Armed Forces Epidemiological Board, director of Commission on Acute Respiratory Diseases, 1959—; National Institutes of Health, chairman of Panel on Respiratory and Related Viruses, 1960-64, member of Board for Virus Reference Reagents, 1962-64; National Board of Medical Examiners, chairman of Public Health and Preventive Medicine Test Committee, 1962-65. Military service: U.S. Navy, medical officer, 1943-46; became lieutenant senior grade.

MEMBER: Association of American Physicians, American Federation for Clinical Research, American Epidemiological Society, American Public Health Association, American Thoracic Society, Infectious Disease Society of America, Central Society for Clinical Research, Phi Beta Kappa, Sigma Xi, Alpha Omega Alpha, Alpha Tau Omega. Awards, honors: Markle scholar in medical sciences, 1953-58.

WRITINGS: (With George F. Badger and John H. Dingle) Illness in the Home, Western Reserve University Press, 1964. Member of editorial board, American Review of Respiratory Diseases, 1962-65. Contributor of papers to medical journals.

WORK IN PROGRESS: Research on etiology and epidemiology of acute respiratory illnesses, particularly rhinoviruses.†

*   *   *

JOSEPH, Alexander   1907-

PERSONAL: Born May 17, 1907, in Paris, France; son of Isaac (a designer) and Katherine (Liebovitch) Joseph; married Sally Sandler, December 25, 1929; children: Richard E., Janet L., Ellen C. Education: City College (now City College of the City University of New York), B.S., 1929, M.S., 1931; New York University, Ed.D., 1941. Religion: Hebrew. Home: 42 Colonial Dr., Mahopac, N.Y. 10541. Office: John Jay College of Criminal Justice, City University of New York, 445 West 59th St., New York, N.Y.

CAREER: High school physics instructor, 1939-57; Harvard University, Cambridge, Mass., instructor, 1959-60; City University of New York, New York, N.Y., professor of physics and head of department at Bronx Community College, 1960-64, professor and director of Forensic Science Laboratories, John Jay College of Criminal Justice, 1965—, director of National Science Foundation Institute in Physics at City College, 1961-64. Lecturer, New York University, 1940, 1947-53, 1955-57, 1960—; professor, University of Connecticut, summer, 1958. Principal investigator, survey of crime labs in the United States, for U.S. Department of Justice, 1960-67; attached to Scotland Yard Laboratory, 1969-1970; consultant for crime study programs and establishment of crime labs in various states.

Member of Physical Science Study Committee, Massachusetts Institute of Technology, 1957-60; physics consultant to UNESCO, 1961-62; consultant to State University of New York, *Science World*, American Petroleum Institute, and U.S. Air Force. Designer of U.S. exhibit. "Alpha Particle Tracks," at Seattle World's Fair. *Military service:* U.S. Army Air Forces, 1943-46, 1953; became major; received Legion of Merit, Conspicuous Service Cross, French Air Force Honoraire Badge, Reserve Commendation Medal, French Medal of Liberation. *Member:* American Academy of Forensic Science (fellow), American Association of Physics Teachers, National Science Teachers Association (life member), American Association of University Professors, National Science Physics Institute, Physics Club of New York, American Legion. *Awards, honors:* Geneva Film Festival award for "Diffusion Cloud Chamber," 1959; Medaille d'Aeronautique.

WRITINGS: (With others) "Smithsonian Scientific Series," Volume XIII, Smithsonian Institution, 1937; (with F. B. Carroll) *Science for New Yorkers*, six volumes, Winston, 1939; (with others) *Science of Pre-Flight*, Macmillan, 1942; *Fundamentals of Machines*, Scribner, 1943; *Rockets Into Space*, Science Research Associates, 1955; (with Evelyn Morholt and others) *Teaching High School Science*, Harcourt, 1958, 2nd edition published as *A Sourcebook for the Biological Sciences*, 1966.

(With Irene D. Jaworski) *Atomic Energy: The Story of Nuclear Science*, Harcourt, 1961; (with others) *Teaching High School Science: A Sourcebook for the Physical Sciences*, Harcourt, 1961; (with Elizabeth B. Hone and others) *Teaching Elementary Science: A Sourcebook for Elementary Science*, Harcourt, 1962, 2nd edition, 1971; *Supplementary Physics Handbook*, State University of New York Science Education Department, 1964; (reviser) Don Herbert, *Mr. Wizard's Science Secrets*, new edition, Hawthorn, 1965; (with Daniel J. Leahy) *Programmed Physics*, five parts, Wiley, 1965-67; (with others) *Physics for Engineering Technology*, Wiley, 1966.

Author of filmscripts, "Ionization of Gases," "Diffusion Cloud Chamber," "Electric Lives of Force," and "Mass of Electrons," all for Massachusetts Institute of Technology; author of ten filmscripts and thirty television scripts for Westinghouse Research Laboratory; also translator of manuals for French Air Force.

*　　*　　*

JOY, Donald Marvin 1928-

PERSONAL: Born August 20, 1928, in Dodge City, Kan.; son of Marvin Earl (a farmer) and Marie (Royer) Joy; married Robbie Bowles (a teacher), July 15, 1948; children: John Marvin, Michael Charles. *Education:* Greenville College, A.B., 1949; Asbury Theological Seminary, B.D., 1954; Southern Methodist University, M.A., 1960; Indiana University, Ph.D., 1969. *Home:* 600 North Lexington Ave., Wilmore, Ky. *Office:* Asbury Theological Seminary, Wilmore, Ky. 40390.

CAREER: Free Methodist minister. Minneola (Kan.) public schools, teacher and director of choral music, 1949-52; pastor of churches in Ensign, Kan., 1950-52, Rockwall, Tex., 1954-58; Light and Life Press, Winona Lake, Ind., executive editor of Sunday school literature, 1960-72; Asbury Theological Seminary, Wilmore, Ky., associate professor of Christian education, 1971—. *Member:* National Society for the Study of Education, Phi Delta Kappa.

WRITINGS: (With others) *Let's Teach*, Light and Life

Press, 1961; *The Holy Spirit and You*, Abingdon, 1965; *Meaningful Learning in the Church*, Light and Life Press, 1969. Executive editor of *Arnold's Commentary*, Light and Life Press, 1966-72, and of "Aldersgate Biblical Series."

*　　*　　*

JUDSON, John 1930-

PERSONAL: Born September 9, 1930, in Stratford, Conn.; son of Irving John (a motel proprietor) and Edna (Hewitt) Judson; married Joanne Carol Aker, October 30, 1959; children: William Nicholas, Lisa Ann, Gary James, Sara Lea. *Education:* Colby College, A.B., 1958; attended University of Maine, 1962-63; State University of Iowa, M.F.A., 1965. *Office:* Department of English, Wisconsin State University, LaCrosse, Wisconsin.

CAREER: Semi-professional baseball player in Maine and Iowa; worked in research and development for Norden-Ketay Corporation and for Laboratory for Electronics (atomic bombing systems and missile systems), in Connecticut and Massachusetts; high school teacher in Iowa and Maine; graduate assistant in rhetoric, University of Iowa, Iowa City; Wisconsin State University, LaCrosse, assistant professor of English, 1965—. *Military service:* U.S. Air Force, 1951-55; became airman first class; received Korean medal.

WRITINGS: (With John Stevens Wade) *Two From Where It Snows*, Northeast, 1964; *Surreal Songs*, Juniper, 1968, revised edition, 1969; *Within Seasons*, Colby College, 1968; *Interview With Kathleen Wiegner*, Center for Contemporary Poetry, 1970; *Interview With John Woods*, Center for Contemporary Poetry, 1970; (compiler) *Voyages to the Inland Sea: Essays and Poems*, Center for Contemporary Poetry, 1971; *Finding Words in Winter*, Elizabeth Press, 1973. Contributor of poems to *Massachusetts Review, Choice, Coastlines, New York Times, Literary Review*, and other periodicals. Poetry editor, *Northeast*, 1967—.

WORK IN PROGRESS: A book of poems; a novel.

SIDELIGHTS: Judson has traveled in Mexico, Canada, Japan, Korea, and the United States.†

*　　*　　*

JURJI, Edward J. 1907-

PERSONAL: Born March 27, 1907, in Latakia, Syria; came to United States, 1933; naturalized, 1947; son of Jabara and Mary (Jureidini) Jurji; married Nahia Khuri, August 20, 1932 (died, 1957); married Ruth Guinter, November 27, 1958; children: (first marriage) Layla (Mrs. Willard Oxtoby), E. David. *Education:* American University of Beirut, B.A., 1928; Princeton University, M.A., 1934, Ph.D., 1936; Princeton Theological Seminary, B.D., 1942. *Home and office:* Princeton Theological Seminary, 89 Castle Howard Ct., Princeton, N.J. 08540.

CAREER: Teacher for Ministry of Education, Iraq, 1928-30, and at American School for Boys, Baghdad, Iraq, 1930-33; Institute for Advanced Study, Princeton, N.J., member, 1936-38; ordained to Presbyterian ministry, 1942; Princeton Theological Seminary, Princeton, N.J., 1939—, lecturer in Arabic, 1942-45, associate professor of Islamic and comparative religion, 1946-54, professor of comparative religion, 1954-63, professor of the history of religions, 1963—. Visiting summer professor at State University of New York College at Oneonta, 1947-49, Garrett Theological Seminary, 1947, Pacific School of Religion, 1955, Union Theological Seminary, New York, N.Y., 1958, Iliff

School of Theology, 1959. Chairman of World Religion Forum, 1963; director of Edward F. Gallahue Conference on Interfaith and Intercultural Communication.

MEMBER: American Society for the Study of Religion, Congress of International Association of the Historians of Religion, American Association of University Professors. *Awards, honors:* Fulbright senior scholar in India, 1960.

WRITINGS: Illumination in Islamic Mysticism, Princeton University Press, 1938; (editor) *The Great Religions of the Modern World*, Princeton University Press, 1947; (co-author) *Tarikh el Arab*, three volumes, Al-Kashshaf (Beirut), 1952; *Christian Interpretation of Religion*, Macmillan, 1952; *The Middle East: Its Religion and Culture*, Westminster, 1956; (editor) *The Ecumenical Era in Church and Society*, Macmillan, 1959; *The Phenomenology of Religion*, Westminster, 1963; (editor) *Religious Pluralism and World Community*, R. J. Brill, 1969; (contributor) *Great Religions of the World*, National Geographic Society, 1971.

Contributor of articles on Islam, Arabia, and religion to professional journals. Contributor and consultant, *Funk & Wagnalls New Encyclopedia*; member of consultant staff, *Dictionary of the English Language* published by Random House. Associate editor, *Moslem World*, 1943—; book review editor, *Princeton Seminary Bulletin*, 1945—.

WORK IN PROGRESS: Research in history of religions, particularly investigations of Islamic morphology and sprituality, and an appraisal of the phenomena of mysticism.

* * *

JUSTER, Norton 1929-

PERSONAL: Born June 2, 1929, in New York, N.Y.; son of Samuel H. (an architect) and Minnie (Silberman) Juster; married Jeanne Ray (a book designer), August 15, 1964. *Education:* University of Pennsylvania, B. of Arch., 1952; University of Liverpool, graduate study, 1952-53. *Address:* R.F.D., Charlemont, Mass. 01339. *Agent:* The Sterling Lord Agency, 75 East 55th St., New York, N.Y. 10022.

CAREER: Juster & Gugliotta, New York, N.Y., architect, 1960-68; Pratt Institute, Brooklyn, N.Y., instructor in interior design, 1960-70; Norton Juster Architect, Brooklyn, N.Y. and Charlemont, Mass., 1969—. Adjunct professor of design, Hampshire College, 1970—. *Military service:* U.S. Naval Reserve, Civil Engineer Corps, active duty, 1954-57. *Awards, honors:* George G. Stone Center for Children's Books Seventh Recognition of Merit, 1971.

WRITINGS: The Phantom Tollbooth, Random House, 1961; *The Dot and the Line*, Random House, 1963; *Alberic the Wise*, Pantheon, 1965; *Stark Naked*, Random House, 1970.

SIDELIGHTS: An animated full length feature of "The Phantom Tollbooth" was released by M-G-M, 1970.

BIOGRAPHICAL/CRITICAL SOURCES: Time, March 22, 1971.†

* * *

KAGY, Frederick D(avid) 1917-

PERSONAL: Born November 20, 1917, in Chicago, Ill.; son of Joseph R. (a dentist) and Viola (Schroeder) Kagy; married Bernice Olson, 1943; children: Suzanne, Fred, Jr., Peter, Barbara. *Education:* Northern Illinois University, B.S., 1948; Colorado State College (now University of Northern Colorado), Greeley, M.A., 1953; University of Wyoming, Ed.D., 1959. *Home:* 23 Ethell Parkway, Normal, Ill. *Office:* Illinois State University, Normal, Ill.

CAREER: Civilian instructor at U.S. Army Air Forces technical schools, 1941-43; worked for printers and lithographers, Chicago, Ill., and area, 1946-48; high school graphic arts teacher, Maywood, Ill., 1948-53; Colorado State College (now University of Northern Colorado), Greeley, 1953-65, became professor of industrial arts, 1959; Illinois State University, Normal, associate professor, 1965-69, professor of industrial technology, 1969—. *Military service:* U.S. Army Air Forces, 1943-46. *Member:* International Graphic Arts Education Association, American Vocational Association, American Industrial Arts Association, National Association of Industrial Teacher Educators, American Council of Industrial Arts Teacher Education, International Association of Printing House Craftsmen, Masons, Kappa Delta Pi, Phi Delta Kappa, Epsilon Pi Tau, Illinois Education Association, Illinois Vocational Association, Elks.

WRITINGS: Graphic Arts, Goodheart, 1961. Contributor to periodicals. Editor, *Colorado Industrial Arts Newsletter*, 1959-61.

AVOCATIONAL INTERESTS: Photography, golf.

* * *

KANDEL, Denise Bystryn 1933-

PERSONAL: Born February 27, 1933, in Paris, France; daughter of Iser I. (an engineer) and Sara Bystryn; married Eric R. Kandel (a physician), June 10, 1956; children: Paul Iser, Michelle. *Education:* Bryn Mawr College, B.A. (magna cum laude), 1952; Columbia University, M.A., 1953, Ph.D., 1960. *Home:* 9 Sigma Place, Riverdale, N.Y. 10471. *Office:* Biometrics Research, 722 West 168th St., New York, N.Y. 10032.

CAREER: National Institute of Mental Health, Bethesda, Md., social science analyst, 1959-60; Harvard University, research associate in department of psychiatry of Medical School, Boston, Mass., 1960-62; research associate in Laboratory of Human Development, Cambridge, Mass., beginning, 1964; presently with Biometrics Research, New York, N.Y. *Member:* American Sociological Association, Eastern Sociological Association.

WRITINGS: (With Richard H. Williams) *Psychiatric Rehabilitation: Some Problems of Research*, Atherton, 1964; (with Gerald Lesser) *Youth in Two Worlds*, Jossey-Bass, 1972; (contributor) Matthew B. Miles and others, editors, *Readings in the Social Psychology of Education*, Allyn & Bacon, 1970; (contributor) R. F Purnell, editor, *Adolescents in the American High School*, Holt, 1970; (contributor) M. B. Sussman and B. E. Cogswell, editors, *Cross-National Family Research*, E. K. Brill, 1972. Contributor to psychology and sociology journals.

WORK IN PROGRESS: Longitudinal study of parental and peer influences on adolescent illegal drug use.

* * *

KAPLAN, Abraham 1918-

PERSONAL: Born June 11, 1918, in Odessa, Union of Soviet Socialist Republics; came to United States in 1923, became U.S. citizen, 1930; Israeli citizen, 1972; son of Joseph J. (a rabbi) and Chava (Lerner) Kaplan; married Iona Judith Wax (a child psychologist), November 17, 1939; children: Karen E. Diskin, Jessica Aryia. *Education:* College of St. Thomas, St. Paul, Minn., B.A., 1937; University of Chicago, graduate study, 1937-40; University of California, Los Angeles, Ph.D., 1942. *Politics:* Democrat. *Religion:*

Jewish. *Home:* 51 Ruth St., Mount Carmel, Haifa, Israel. *Office:* University of Haifa, Mount Carmel, Haifa, Israel.

CAREER: New York University, New York, N.Y., instructor in philosophy, 1940-45; University of California, Los Angeles, assistant professor, 1946-49, associate professor, 1949-52, professor of philosophy, 1952-63, chairman of department, 1952-65; University of Michigan, Ann Arbor, professor of philosophy, 1962-72; University of Haifa, Mount Carmel, Haifa, Israel, professor of philosophy, 1972—, dean of faculty of social sciences, 1972—. Consultant to RAND Corp., 1952-64; faculty, Brandeis Institute, 1954-62; visiting professor at University of Cincinnati, Harvard University, Columbia University, University of Hawaii, University of Southern California, Oregon State University, and Hebrew University; adjunct professor, Union Graduate School, Antioch College. Director, Fifth East-West Philosophers' Conference; member, academic advisory board, RAND Graduate Institute for Policy Sciences; fellow, Center for Advanced Study in the Behavioral Sciences, 1960-61; fellow, Center for Advanced Studies, Wesleyan University, 1962-63; visiting fellow, Western Behavorial Sciences Institute, 1966; Adolf Meyer Lecturer, American Psychiatric Association; delegate to World Congress for Soviet Jewry and White House Conference on Youth.

MEMBER: American Philosophical Association (president of Pacific Division, 1947-58), Academy of Psychoanalysis, International Association of Applied Scientists (charter member), Institute of Social and Behavioral Pathology, Association for Jewish Philosophy, American Society for Aesthetics, Association for Legal and Political Philosophy. *Awards, honors:* Guggenheim fellow, 1945-46; Rockefeller fellow, 1957-58. Honorary degrees from University of Judaism and Hebrew Union College (now Hebrew Union College-Jewish Institute of Religion).

WRITINGS: (With H. D. Laswell) *Power and Society*, Yale University Press, 1960; *New World of Philosophy*, Random House, 1962; *American Ethics and Public Policy*, Oxford University Press, 1963; *The Conduct of Inquiry*, Chandler, 1964; (editor) *Individuality and the New Society*, University of Washington Press, 1970; *Love and Death*, University of Michigan Press, 1973. Member of editorial board, *Inquiry, Journal of Applied Behavioral Science, Journal of Humanistic Psychology.*

WORK IN PROGRESS: A book, *The Pursuit of Wisdom.*

SIDELIGHTS: Kaplan has traveled and studied in Israel, India and Japan.

BIOGRAPHICAL/CRITICAL SOURCES: Newsweek, August 21, 1961; *National Observer*, July 20, 1964.

* * *

KAPLAN, Philip 1916-

PERSONAL: Born January 8, 1916, in New York, N.Y.; son of Morris and Mirriam (Berman) Kaplan; married Esther Geller, June 24, 1951; children: Joan, Robert D. *Education:* City College (now City College of the City University of New York), B.S., 1935, M.S., 1936.

CAREER: Mathematics teacher in New York (N.Y.) high schools, 1936-42; New York (N.Y.), Port of Embarkation, Control and Planning Division, statistician, 1942-46; R. H. Macy Co., New York, N.Y., inventory controller, 1946-54; S. Klein Department Stores, Inc., New York, N.Y., assistant to treasurer and assistant to chairman of board, 1954-68; industrial security consultant, 1968-72; motion picture

producer, 1972—. *Military service:* U.S. Army Air Forces, 1942-44; became lieutenant.

WRITINGS: Posers (Eighty Delightful Hurdles for Reasonably Agile Minds), Harper, 1963; *More Posers (Eighty Intriguing New Hurdles for Reasonably Agile Minds)*, Harper, 1964; *Puzzle Me This*, Harper, 1968. Contributor of "posers" to *This Week, Harper's, San Francisco Chronicle*, and other periodicals.

WORK IN PROGRESS: A book of puzzles somewhat similar to double-crostics.

* * *

KAPLAN, Robert B. 1928-

PERSONAL: Born September 20, 1928; son of E. B. (a physician) and Natalie (Iretzky) Kaplan; married Audrey A. Lien, April 21, 1951; children: Robin Ann, Lisa, Robert Allen. *Education:* Willamette University, A.B., 1952; University of Southern California, M.A., 1957, Ph.D., 1963. *Office:* University of Southern California, University Park, Los Angeles, Calif. 90007.

CAREER: University of Oregon, Eugene, instructor in English, 1957-60; University of Southern California, Los Angeles, instructor in English Communication Program for Foreign Students, 1961-62, coordinator of program, 1962-63, director of program, 1966-73, assistant professor of English, 1963-65, associate professor of English and linguistics, 1965-73, professor of applied linguistics, 1973—, chairman of department of linguistics, 1967-69. *Military service:* U.S. Army, 1953-55; served in Japan and Korea. *Member:* American Anthropological Association, American Association for the Advancement of Science, American Council of Teachers of Foreign Languages, National Council of Teachers of English, Conference on College Composition and Communication, National Association for Foreign Student Affairs, American Association of University Professors, Teachers of English as a Second Language, Teachers of English to Speakers of Other Languages, English-Speaking Union, Canadian Council of Teachers of English, Royal Anthropological Institute of Great Britain and Ireland (fellow).

WRITINGS: Reading and Rhetoric, Odyssey, 1963; *Teachers Guide to Transformational Grammar*, English Language Services, 1968; *Learning English Through Typewriting*, English Language Services, 1969; (contributor) *Preparing the EFL Teacher: A Projection for the Seventies*, Center for Curriculum Development, 1970; (contributor) Harold B. Allen, editor, *Teaching English as a Second Language: A Book of Readings*, McGraw-Hill, 2nd edition, 1972; (contributor) Kenneth Croft, editor, *Readings on English as a Second Language for Teachers and Teacher-Trainees*, Winthrop, 1972; (contributor) William B. Brickman and Stanley Lehrer, editors, *Education and the Many Faces of the Disadvantaged: Cultural and Historical Perspectives*, Wiley, 1972. Contributor to speech and linguistic journals.

WORK IN PROGRESS: Research projects in English as a second language, in English-as-a-second-language teaching, and in applied linguistics.

SIDELIGHTS: Kaplan is "reasonably proficient" in Russian and French. *Avocational interests:* Collecting conchological specimens, weapons, and rare books; writing poetry ("largely unpublished").

KARIEL, Henry S. 1924-

PERSONAL: Born July 7, 1924, in Plauen, Germany; came to United States in 1937. *Education:* University of Washington, Seattle, B.A., 1948; University of Zurich, graduate study, 1949; Stanford University, M.A., 1950; University of California, Berkeley, Ph.D., 1954. *Home:* 3811 Tantalus Dr., Honolulu, Hawaii 96822. *Office:* Political Science Department, University of Hawaii, Honolulu, Hawaii.

CAREER: Harvard University, Cambridge, Mass., instructor in government, 1955-58; Bennington College, Bennington, Vt., professor of political science, 1959-64; University of Hawaii, Honolulu, professor of political science, 1964—. *Member:* American Political Science Association, Caucus for a New Political Science, Phi Beta Kappa. *Awards, honors:* Rockefeller Foundation grant, 1954-55.

WRITINGS: The Decline of American Pluralism, Stanford University Press, 1961; *In Search of Authority*, Free Press of Glencoe, 1964; *Sources in Twentieth-Century Political Thought*, Free Press of Glencoe, 1964; *The Promise of Politics*, Prentice-Hall, 1966; *Open Systems: Arenas for Public Action*, Peacock, 1968; (editor) *Frontiers of Democratic Appearances*, Random House, 1970; (editor and compiler) *The Political Order*, Basic Books, 1971; *Saving Appearances*, Duxbury Press, 1972.

WORK IN PROGRESS: "Beyond Liberalism, Where Relations Grow."

*   *   *

KARNEY, Beulah Mullen

PERSONAL: Born in Oakland, Calif.; daughter of William (a clergyman) and Anna Christian (Hepp) Mullen; married William J. Powers (in automobile business), May 8, 1948; children: (previous marriage) Ann Helena (Mrs. Robert K. Elliott). *Education:* Occidental College, B.A.; University of Southern California, Secondary School Certificate; graduate study at National University of Mexico. *Residence:* Carmel Valley, Calif.

CAREER: Midland Broadcasting Co., Kansas City, Mo., writer-broadcaster, 1935-40; Ewell-Thurber (advertising agency), Chicago, Ill., copywriter, 1941-44; ghost writer for George Rector, 1941-44; Radio Station WENR, Chicago, Ill., writer-commentator, 1941-54; Gordon Best Advertising Agency, Chicago, Ill., copywriter, 1944-46; American Broadcasting Co., Chicago, Ill., writer-commentator, 1944-50; WENR-TV and WBKB-TV, Chicago, Ill., writer-commentator, 1949-54; free-lance writer, 1960—. Women's editor, *Liberty*, 1945-48. *Member:* Authors Guild, American Federation of Television and Radio Artists, American Women in Radio and Television, Women's Advertising Club, Arabian Horse Association of Northern California, Monterey History and Art Association. *Awards, honors:* Zenith Award for outstanding work in field of television, 1954.

WRITINGS: Wild Imp (Junior Literary Guild selection), Day, 1960; *Keepers of the Bell*, Day, 1961; *The Listening One*, Day, 1962. Contributor to magazines. Author of scripts for "Magazine of the Air," "Woman Today," and "Beulah Karney Show."

AVOCATIONAL INTERESTS: Horses; reading philosophy; home arts and crafts; foreign travel.

BIOGRAPHICAL/CRITICAL SOURCES: Chicago Tribune, May 14, 1961; *Instructor*, June, 1961.

KARPIN, Fred L(eon) 1913-

PERSONAL: Born March 17, 1913, in New York, N.Y.; son of Solomon and Clara (Jabrow) Karpin; married Nettie Cantor (an assistant to a hotel manager), September 26, 1944; children: Carolyn, Rita. *Education:* Brooklyn College (now Brooklyn College of the City University of New York), B.S., 1934. *Religion:* Jewish. *Home and office:* 9814 Cottrell Ter., Silver Spring, Md.

CAREER: U.S. government, statistician and economist, 1934-42, 1946-49; free-lance economist, 1950-62; now writer and lecturer on contract bridge. *Military service:* U.S. Army Air Forces, 1943-45. *Member:* American Contract Bridge League.

WRITINGS: The Point Count System, Kaufman Press, 1948; *Contract Bridge: The Play of the Cards*, Bridge Quarterly, 1958; *Psychological Strategy in Contract Bridge*, Harper, 1960; *How to Play (and Misplay) Slam Contracts*, Harper, 1962; *Strategy at Trick One*, Dell, 1964; (with Norman Kay and Sidney Siloder) *The Complete Book of Duplicate Bridge*, Putnam, 1965; *The Finesse*, Prentice-Hall, 1972; *The Art of Card Reading*, Harper, 1973.

*   *   *

KASTENBAUM, Robert (Jay) 1932-

PERSONAL: Born August 8, 1932, in New York, N.Y.; son of Sam and Anne (Einson) Kastenbaum; married Barbara Elizabeth Brown, January 18, 1958; children: David Samuel. *Education:* East Los Angeles College, A.A., 1952; Long Beach State College (now California State University, Long Beach), B.A., 1954; University of Southern California, Ph.D., 1959. *Home:* 66 Green St., Ashland, Mass. 01721. *Office:* Cushing Hospital, Framingham, Mass. 01721.

CAREER: Worked way through high school and college as newspaperman, including editorship of community weeklies; Cushing Hospital (Commonwealth of Massachusetts geriatric institution), Framingham, director of psychological research, 1961—, currently co-principal investigator of U.S. Public Health Service mental health project (at the hospital) on training for work with the aged and dying. Clark University, Worcester, Mass., lecturer in psychology, 1960—. *Member:* American Psychological Association, Gerontological Society, Massachusetts Psychological Association (fellow; member of board of professional affairs), New York Academy of Sciences, Boston Society for Gerontological Psychiatry.

WRITINGS: (Contributor) H. Feifel, *The Meaning of Death*, McGraw, 1959; (editor and contributor) *New Thoughts on Old Age*, Springer, 1964; (editor and contributor) *Contributions to the Psycho-biology of Aging*, Springer, 1965; (with Avery D. Weisman) *The Psychological Autopsy*, Community Mental Health, 1968; (with Ruth Aisenberg) *The Psychology of Death*, Springer, 1972; (compiler with D. P. Kent) *Research Planning and Action for the Elderly*, Behavioral Publications, 1972. Editor of, and contributor to special edition of *Journal of Social Issues* devoted to "Old Age as a Social Issue," 1966; contributor of about twenty articles to psychology and gerontology journals, and to *Journal of Human Relations* and *Genetic Psychology Monographs*.

WORK IN PROGRESS: With Eugenia S. Shere, *Crisis and Transformation: A Psychological Inquiry*, and *Theories of Human Aging*. Current research in the psychology of time and in the effects of drugs on cognition and mood of elderly patients; current and long-range activity is the formulation and testing of a theory of human behavior and experience with special relevance to the understanding of maturity and old age.

SIDELIGHTS: Led to psychology by interest in philosophy; now pursuing "experimental philosophy in the field of psychology," and concentrating on time, love, aging, and death, subjects on which "rather little scientific investigation of a meaningful sort has been done . . . so my work is exploratory rather than conclusive or definitive." *Avocational interests:* Writing plays and poetry.

BIOGRAPHICAL/CRITICAL SOURCES: Newsweek, April 6, 1970.†

*   *   *

KATKOV, Norman 1918-

PERSONAL: Born July 26, 1918, in Russia; son of Hyman and Milia (Radovolsky) Kateekoffsky; married Betty Nelson, August 20, 1951; children: Richard Hyman, William Nelson. *Education:* University of Minnesota, B.A., 1940. *Home:* 129 North Woodburn Dr., Los Angeles, Calif. 90049. *Agent:* Harold Matson Co., Inc., 22 East 40th St., New York, N.Y. 10016.

CAREER: Professional writer. *Military service:* U.S. Army.

WRITINGS: Eagle At My Eyes, Doubleday, 1948; *A Little Sleep, A Little Slumber,* Doubleday, 1949; *The Fabulous Fanny* (about Fanny Brice), Knopf, 1953; *Eric Mattson,* Doubleday, 1964; *With These Hands,* Simon & Schuster, 1974.

Author of motion picture script, "It Happened to Jane." Writer of television scripts for "Ben Casey," "Slattery's People," "The Virginian," "Hawaiian Eye," "Studio One," "Kraft Theatre," "Rawhide," "Fireside Theatre," and a dozen other network shows.

Contributor of short stories, novelettes, serials, and articles to national magazine, including *Collier's, Saturday Evening Post, Cosmopolitan, Good Housekeeping, Reader's Digest, Ladies' Home Journal, American, Esquire, McCall's, Holiday,* and *Today's Woman.* Also contributor to newspapers and Sunday supplements.

*   *   *

KATZ, Menke 1906-
(Elchik Hiat)

PERSONAL: Born June 7, 1906, in Michalishek, Lithuania; came to United States, 1920; son of Heershe David (an operator of ice and coal business) and Badane (Gubersky) Katz; married Chaske Bliacher, 1926; married second wife, Ruth Feldman (a teacher), July 30, 1950; children: (first marriage) Troim Handler, Noah (deceased); (second marriage) Heershe David. *Education:* Attended Columbia University, 1924-26, University of Southern California, 1926-27, and Brooklyn College (now Brooklyn College of the City University of New York), 1946-48. *Home:* 1321 55th St., Brooklyn, N.Y. 11219. *Office address:* Blythebourne Station, P.O. Box 51, Brooklyn, N.Y. 11219.

CAREER: Teacher of Jewish studies in New York, N.Y., 1947-54, 1956-59, in Philadelphia, Pa., 1945-46, simultaneously in Washington, D.C., and Baltimore, Md., 1946-47, in Safad, Israel, 1954-56, 1959-60, on Long Island, N.Y., 1960-65, in Jackson Heights, N.Y., 1966—; *Bitter-*

root (poetry quarterly), Brooklyn, N.Y., editor-in-chief, 1962—. *Awards, honors:* Stephen Vincent Benet Award for poetry, 1970 and 1974.

WRITINGS—Poetry, in Yiddish: *Drei Shwester* (title means "Three Sisters"), [Milwaukee], 1932; *Der Mentch in Togn* (title means "Dawning Man"), [New York], 1935; *Brenendik Shtetl* (title means "Burning Village"), [New York], 1938; *Es Hut dos Vort Mine Bubeh Moina* (title means "My Grandmother Myrna Speaks"), [New York], 1939; *Tsu Dertsayln een Fraydn* (title means "A Story to Be Told in Happier Days"), [New York], 1941; *Der Pusheter Cholem* (title means "The Simple Dream"), [New York], 1947; *Inmitn Tog* (title means "Midday"), [New York], 1954.

Poetry, in English: *Land of Manna,* Windfall Press, 1965; *Rockrose,* Smith-Horizon Press, 1970; *Burning Village,* Smith-Horizon Press, 1970.

Translated the Hebrew writings of Rashi into English and Yiddish. Contributor, occasionally under pseudonym Elchik Hiat, to *Atlantic, Bitterroot, New York Times, Sewanee Review, Thought* (India), *Epos, Canadian Poetry, New York Herald Tribune, Commentary, South and West, Chicago Jewish Forum, Prairie Schooner,* and others. Poetry editor, *Meer,* 1944-47.

WORK IN PROGRESS: Two Friends, a book of poems with Harry Smith.

SIDELIGHTS: As the editor of *Bitterroot,* Katz has sought poetry that he calls "just, genuine and beautiful," and has for the most part eschewed the verse of those he considers "ultra 'modernists' with little or no talent," and those who rhyme their lines. Though he concedes that a rhymed poem can be great, he writes: "It is about time to leave the rhyme (where it belongs) in the nursery, forever and ever. The rhymeless poem may free the poet to create work of greater vision rich with the melody, rhythm, harmony of his own talent." He decidedly prefers a "tongue . . . unpolished as a wound," that allows him to "ride a word—free and rimeless as a tempest." "I am a Yiddish poet," he writes, "a doomed troubadour." His poems, however, are touched with what Evelyn Thorne calls "a blend of two elements, . . . by the fairy-tale quality of the old European villages, and they are alive with the shock and wonder of the modern city. . . ." Sanford Sternlich considers *Land of Manna* to be "a wedding feast" written by a "rogue fiddler."

Though his first seven books appeared in Yiddish, Katz began writing poems in English for local newspapers at the age of fifteen. Many of the poems in *Land of Manna* were written in Israel, 1959-60. His poems have been translated into Japanese, French, Hebrew, Italian, Korean, Lithuanian, Polish, Czech, Shona (an African dialect), Kannada (a Hindu dialect), and other languages.

BIOGRAPHICAL/CRITICAL SOURCES: Piggot Banner (Arkansas), March 12, 1965; *Poet Lore,* autumn, 1965; *South and West,* winter, 1966.

*   *   *

KAUFFMAN, Henry J. 1908-

PERSONAL: Born November 14, 1908, in York, Pa.; son of David C. and Anna (Sloat) Kauffman; married Elizabeth Zoe Toomer (an art instructor), July 19, 1938. *Education:* Millersville State College, B.S., 1932; University of Pennsylvania, M.S., 1937; studied silversmithing and design at Philadelphia Museum School of Art and under Baron Fleming, the court silversmith to King of Sweden. *Religion:* Protestant. *Home:* 1704 Millersville Pike, Lancaster, Pa. 17603.

CAREER: Millersville State College, Millersville, Pa., 1942—, now professor of industrial arts education. Craftsman, working in silver and other mediums, with work (silver bowl) exhibited at Metropolitan Museum in New York. Member of board of Rock Ford Foundation. *Member:* American Association of University Professors, Pennsylvania State Education Association, Pewter Collectors Club of America, Historical Society of Pennsylvania, Philadelphia Art Alliance, Lancaster Torch Club.

WRITINGS: Pennsylvania Dutch American Folk Art, Studio Books, 1946, revised edition, Dover, 1964; *Early American Copper, Brass and Tin*, Medill McBride Co., 1950; *Early American Gunsmiths, 1650-1850*, Stackpole, 1952; *The Pennsylvania-Kentuck Rifle*, Stackpole, 1960; *Early American Iron Ware: Cast and Wrought*, Tuttle, 1966; *American Copper and Bass*, T. Nelson, 1968; *The Colonial Silversmith: His Techniques and His Products*, T. Nelson, 1969; *The American Pewterer: His Techniques and His Products*, T. Nelson, 1970; *The American Fireplace: Chimneys, Mantlepieces, Fireplaces and Accessories*, T. Nelson, 1972; *American Axes: A Survey of Their Development and Their Makers*, S. Greene Press, 1972; *Andirons and Other Fireplace Accessories*, Nelson, 1974. Contributor of articles to *Antiques, Parents' Magazine, Country Gentleman*, and *School Shop*.

WORK IN PROGRESS: A study of eighteenth-century technology.

* * *

KAUFMAN, Bel

PERSONAL: Born in Berlin, Germany; raised in Russia; came to United States at age of twelve; daughter of Michael J. (a physician) and Lola (a writer; maiden name Rabinowitz) Kaufman; divorced; children: Jonathan Goldstine, Thea Goldstine. *Education:* Hunter College (now Hunter College of the City University of New York), B.A. (magna cum laude); Columbia University, M.A. (highest honors). *Home:* 1020 Park Ave., New York, N.Y. 10028. *Agent:* McIntosh & Otis, Inc., 18 East 41st St., New York, N.Y. 10017.

CAREER: Taught in New York, N.Y., high schools for twenty years; New School for Social Research, New York, N.Y., instructor in English, 1964; Borough of Manhattan Community College, New York, N.Y., assistant professor of English, 1964—. Lecturer; member, Advisory Commission of Performing Arts. *Member:* Authors League, P.E.N. (member of executive board), Dramatists Guild, Phi Beta Kappa, English Graduate Union (Columbia). *Awards, honors:* Plaques from Anti-Defamation League and from United Jewish Appeal; Doctor of Letters, Nasson College, 1965; Paperback of the Year award for fiction, National Bestsellers Institute, 1966, for *Up the Down Staircase*; named to Hall of Fame, Hunter College of the City University of New York, 1973.

WRITINGS: Up the Down Staircase (novel; Book-of-the-Month Club selection), Prentice-Hall, 1965. Author of lyrics for musicals. Contributor to *Esquire, Collier's, Saturday Review*, and other publications.

WORK IN PROGRESS: Book and lyrics for a musical; another novel.

SIDELIGHTS: Time called *Up the Down Staircase*

"easily the most popular novel about U.S. public schools in history." It sold 1,500,000 copies its first month in paperback, and was filmed by Warner Bros. in 1967.

While Bel Kaufman may have been surprised at the phenomenal success of her novel, she might well have considered it simply a family tradition. In her family, she has said, "Everyone breathes, everyone writes," and she had published a poem by the age of seven. Her mother, the daughter of famed Yiddish author Sholom Aleichem, wrote over 2000 short stories which are still popular among Russian-speaking people.

Ms. Kaufman told *CA* she enjoys travel, bicycling, and doodling, and that her only athletic skill is climbing ropes. She commented: "[My] best motivation for writing: guilt (deadlines, time pressures). Am passionate about teaching."

BIOGRAPHICAL/CRITICAL SOURCES: Book Week, February 7, 1965; *Time*, February 12, 1965; *New York Times Book Review*, February 14, 1965; *Saturday Review*, March 20, 1965; *Reporter*, May 6, 1965; *Commonweal*, May 14, 1965; *National Review*, June 1, 1965.

* * *

KAUFMAN, Gordon Dester 1925-

PERSONAL: Born June 22, 1925, in Newton, Kan.; son of Edmund George (a professor) and Hazel (Dester) Kaufman; married Dorothy Wedel, June 11, 1947; children: David W., Gretchen E., Anne L., Edmund G. *Education:* Bethel College, North Newton, Kan., A.B. (with highest distinction), 1947; Northwestern University, M.A., 1948; Yale University, B.D. (magna cum laude), 1951, Ph.D., 1955. *Home:* 4 Thoreau Rd., Lexington, Mass. 02173. *Office:* Harvard Divinity School, 45 Francis Ave., Cambridge, Mass. 02138.

CAREER: Ordained minister, Mennonite Church, 1953; Pomona College, Claremont, Calif., 1953-58; Vanderbilt Divinity School, Nashville, Tenn., 1958-63; Harvard Divinity School, Cambridge, Mass., professor of theology, 1963—. *Wartime service:* Civilian Public Service (conscientious objector), 1943-46. *Member:* Metaphysical Society of America, American Association of University Professors, American Philosophical Association, Society for Religion in Higher Education. *Awards, honors:* Fulbright scholar, 1961-62; Guggenheim fellow, 1969-70.

WRITINGS: Relativism, Knowledge and Faith, University of Chicago Press, 1960; *The Context of Decision*, Abingdon, 1961; *Systematic Theology: A Historicist Perspective*, Scribner, 1968; (contributor) Herbert W. Richardson and Donald Cutler, editors, *Transcendence*, Beacon, 1971; *God the Problem*, Harvard University Press, 1972.

* * *

KAUFMAN, William I(rving) 1922-

PERSONAL: Born June 8, 1922, in New York, N.Y.; married Rosamond (a writer), December 15, 1946; children: Iva Anne, Lazarus Seley. *Education:* Attended Wake Forest College, 1940-41, Leland Powers School of Radio and Theatre Technique, 1946-47. *Religion:* Hebrew. *Home and office:* 1361 Madison Ave., New York, N.Y. 10028.

CAREER: With National Broadcasting Co. Television, New York, N.Y., 1947-63, now free-lance writer and consultant. Veterans Hospital Radio and Television Guild, member of board of directors. *Military service:* U.S. Army, 1941-46. *Member:* Lamb's Club.

WRITINGS: (With Robert Colodzini) *Your Career in Television*, Merlin Press, 1950; (editor) *Best Television Plays of the Year*, Harcourt, annually, 1950—; *How to Direct for Television*, Hastings House, 1955; *How to Announce for Radio and Television*, Hastings House, 1955; *Cooking With Experts*, Random House, 1955.

(With Sister Mary Ursula Cooper) *The Art of Creole Cookery*, Doubleday, 1962; (with Sheridan Garth) *Cook's Pocket Travel Guide to Europe*, Pocket Books, 1963; (with Sarawathi Lakshaman) *The Art of India's Cookery*, Doubleday, 1964; *The Coffee Cookbook*, Doubleday, 1964; *The Nut Cookbook*, Doubleday, 1964; *The Sugar-Free Cookbook*, Doubleday, 1964; *The Wonderful World of Cooking*, Dell, 1964—, Volume I: *Far East, Near East*, Volume II: *Italy, France and Spain*, Volume III: *Northern Europe and British Isles*, Volume IV: *Caribbean and Latin America*; *The I Love Peanut Butter Cookbook*, Doubleday, 1965; *1001 Top Jobs for High School Graduates*, Bantam, 1965; *Cooking in a Castle: La Cuisine dans un Chateau*, Holt, 1965; *The Catholic Cookbook: Traditional Feast and Fast Day Recipies*, Citadel, 1965; *The Sugar-Free Cookbook of Family Favorites*, Doubleday, 1965.

The Tea Cookbook, Doubleday, 1966; *The Hot Dog Cookbook*, Doubleday, 1966; *The "I Love Garlic" Cookbook*, Doubleday, 1967; *The Cottage Cheese Cookbook*, Doubleday, 1967; *The Art of Caserole Cookery*, Doubleday, 1967; *The Apple Cookbook*, 1967; *Appetizers and Canapes*, Doubleday, 1968; *The Fish and Shellfish Cookbook*, Doubleday, 1968; *The Chocolate Cookbook*, Doubleday, 1968; *Cooking With Bread*, Corinthian Editions, 1969; *Desserts Flambe*, Centaur, 1969; *The Easy Can Opener Cookbook*, Hewitt House, 1969; *Eggs Exotique*, Centaur, 1969; *Fish Cookery*, Centaur, 1969; *The New Blender Cookbook*, Pyramid, 1969; *Oriental Cookery*, Centaur, 1969; *Potages*, Centaur, 1969; *Tear off a Pound: The No-Counting Calories, No-Keeping Score Diet*, Corinthian Editions, 1969; *Plain and Fancy Cookie Cookbook*, Pyramid, 1969; (editor) *Recipies from the Caribbean and Latin America*, Dell, 1969; *The Apple Cookbook*, Pyramid, 1969; *Plain and Fancy Chicken Cookbook*, Pyramid, 1969; *Plain and Fancy Hamburger Cookbook*, Pyramid, 1969.

Pancakes, Crepes, and Waffles, Pyramid, 1972; *Brand Name Guide to Calories and Carbohydrates*, Pyramid, 1973; *Calorie Counter for Six Quick Weight Loss Diets*, Pyramid, 1973; *Calorie Guide to Brand Names*, Pyramid, 1973; *Champagne*, Viking, 1973; *Natural Foods and Health Foods Calorie Counter*, Pyramid, 1973; *The New Low Carbohydrate Diet*, Pyramid, 1973; *Three-Hundred Sixty-five Meatless Main Dish Meals*, Doubleday, 1974.

* * *

KAUFMANN, R(alph) James 1924-

PERSONAL: Born August 2, 1924, in Grand Forks, N.D.; son of Ralph Jennings (a professor) and Mary (Allyn) Kaufmann; married Ruth Hackett, June 30, 1944; children: James, Margaret, Mary and Sarah (twins). *Education:* Grinnell College, B.A., 1947; Princeton University, M.A., 1949, Ph.D., 1953. *Politics:* Democrat. *Home:* 1516 Forest Trail, Austin, Tex. 78703.

CAREER: Princeton University, Princeton, N.J., instructor in English, 1949-53; Wesleyan University, Middletown, Conn., assistant professor of English, 1953-55; University of Rochester, Rochester, N.Y., assistant professor of English, 1955-60, associate professor, 1960-63, professor, 1963-64, professor of history and English, 1964-69, asso-

ciate dean of College of Arts and Science, 1961-63, University of Texas, Austin, professor, 1969-73, Stiles professor of humanities and comparative literature, 1973—, associate dean of college of humanities, 1971-73. Associate director, Center for Contemporary Culture, Birmingham, England. *Military service:* U.S. Naval Reserve, 1942-46; became lieutenant junior grade. *Member:* Modern Language Association of America, English Institute (member of executive committee, 1963-64), Phi Beta Kappa. *Awards, honors:* Woodrow Wilson fellow, 1947-48; Fulbright fellow, 1950-51; fellow, Folger Shakespeare Library, 1961; Guggenheim fellow, 1964-65; University of Rochester Curtis Prize for Excellence in Teaching, 1964; Danforth Foundation, Harbison Award for Distinguished Teaching, 1968.

WRITINGS: *Richard Brome: Caroline Playwright*, Columbia University Press, 1961; (editor) *Elizabethan Drama: Modern Essays in Criticism*, Oxford University Press, 1961; (editor) John Dryden, *All for Love*, Chandler Publishing, 1963; (editor) *Bernard Shaw: A Collection of Critical Essays*, Prentice-Hall, 1965; *Symposium: Literature and the Academy*, Grinnell College, 1966; (with John D. Maguire) *Campus Dialogue: Humanism and Christianity*, Chatham College, 1966. Contributor of articles and essays to *Nation, Modern Language Review, Tulane Drama Review*, and other periodicals. Associate editor, *Critical Quarterly*.

WORK IN PROGRESS: *Intellectual London Between the Wars.*†

* * *

KAUFMANN, William W. 1918-

PERSONAL: Born November 10, 1918, in New York, N.Y.; son of Charles Barnard (a businessman) and Nettie (Cramer) Kaufmann; married Julia T. Alexander, February 23, 1962. *Education:* Yale University, B.A., 1939, M.A., 1947, Ph.D., 1948. *Office:* 14N-226, Massachusetts Institute of Technology, Cambridge, Mass. 02139.

CAREER: Yale University, New Haven, Conn., instructor in international relations, 1948-51; Princeton University, Princeton, N.J., assistant professor of history, 1951-56; RAND Corp., Santa Monica, Calif., member of social science department, 1956-60, head of department, 1960-61; Massachusetts Institute of Technology, Cambridge, professor of political science, 1961—. Visiting professor of government, Yale University, 1959-60; visiting senior fellow, Brookings Institution, 1969-70. Consultant to Office of the Secretary of Defense, National Security Council, Office of Management and Budget, RAND Corp., Hudson Institute, and Center for Naval Analyses. *Military service:* U.S. Army Air Forces, 1941-45; became first lieutenant. *Member:* Council on Foreign Relations, Phi Beta Kappa. *Awards, honors:* Guggenheim fellow; Department of Defense Distinguished Public Service Medal; Central Intelligence Agency Medal of Merit.

WRITINGS: *British Policy and the Independence of Latin America*, Yale University Press, 1951; (editor with others, and contributor) *Military Policy and National Security*, Princeton University Press, 1956; *The McNamara Strategy*, Harper, 1964; (contributor) Charles L. Schultze and others, *Setting National Priorities: The 1971 Budget*, Brookings Institution, 1971. Managing editor, *World Politics*, 1953-56.

WORK IN PROGRESS: Research on U.S. defense policies.

KAVANAUGH, James J(oseph) 1929-

PERSONAL: Born September 17, 1929, in Kalamazoo, Mich.; son of Frank P. (a salesman) and Hazel Ann (Wendell) Kavanaugh; married Patricia Jean Walden (a nurse) December, 1967. *Education:* St. Mary's Seminary, Norwood, Ohio, B.A., 1950; graduate study, University of Michigan, 1958-60, Catholic University of America, 1964-65, and Howard University, 1964—.

CAREER: Ordained Roman Catholic priest, 1954, resigned priesthood, 1967. High school religion teacher at St. Mary Cathedral, Lansing, Mich., 1954-57, St. John Vianney, Flint, Mich., 1957-62, Sacred Heart, Flint, Mich., 1962-63; Flint Intercollegiate Newman Club, Flint, Mich., chaplain, 1958-64; Catholic University of America, Washington, D.C., taught at nursing school, 1961-63, instructor in theology, 1964. Marriage counselor, Human Resources Institute, JaHolla, Calif. Visiting professor of religious studies, University of Alberta.

WRITINGS: There's Two of You, Newman, 1964; *Man in Search of God*, Paulist Press, 1967; *A Modern Priest Looks at His Outdated Church*, Trident, 1967; *The Struggle of the Unbeliever*, Trident, 1968; *The Birth of God*, Trident, 1969; *The Crooked Angel*, Nash, 1970; *There Are Men Too Gentle to Live Among Wolves* (poems), Nash, 1971; *Will You Be My Friend?*, Nash, 1971; (with Everett L. Shostrom) *Between Man and Woman*, Nash, 1971; *Faces in the City* (poems), Nash, 1972; *Celebrate The Sun*, Nash, 1973; *The Poetry of James Kavanaugh* (collected), Nash, 1974. Contributor of articles to periodicals.

SIDELIGHTS: Kavanaugh speaks and reads German, French, Spanish, Latin; has professional knowledge of ancient Greek.†

*   *   *

KAY, Barbara Ann 1929-

PERSONAL: Born March 2, 1929, in Suffern, N.Y.; daughter of James W. (an executive) and Florence I. (Scott) Kay. *Education:* Ohio State University, B.Sc., 1955, M.A., 1956. *Office:* Department of Sociology, University of Massachusetts, Amherst, Mass.

CAREER: Wittenberg University, Springfield, Ohio, instructor in sociology, 1958-59; Northern Illinois University, De Kalb, assistant professor of sociology, 1961-63; University of Massachusetts, Amherst, assistant professor of sociology, 1963—. *Member:* American Sociological Association, American Society of Criminology, American Correctional Association, American Association of University Professors, Eastern Sociological Society, Midwest Sociological Society, Ohio Valley Sociological Society, Alpha Kappa Delta. *Awards, honors:* Research fellowships, National Institute of Health, 1960-61, 1962.

WRITINGS: (Editor with Clyde B. Vedder) *Probation and Parole: Test and Readings*, C. C Thomas, 1963, revised edition, 1970; (editor with Vedder) *Penology: A Realistic Approach*, C. C Thomas, 1964. Contributor of articles to *American Sociological Review, Police, Criminologica*, and other professional periodicals.

WORK IN PROGRESS: Research comparing female felony offenders with male criminals, and cross-cultural comparison of women offenders.†

*   *   *

KAY, Ernest 1915-
(George Ludlow, Alan Random)

PERSONAL: Born June 21, 1915, in Darwen, Lancashire, England; son of Harold (a mill manager) and Florence (Woodall) Kay; married Marjorie Peover (a journalist), August 11, 1942; children: John Michael, Richard Andrew, Belinda Jean. *Politics:* Labour. *Religion:* Quaker. *Home:* 68 Wildwood Rd., London N.W. 11, England. *Agent:* David Higham Associates Ltd., 76 Dean St., London W. 1, England. *Office: Time and Tide*, 40-43 Chancery Lane, London W.C. 2, England.

CAREER: Journalist, 1933—. *Evening News*, London, England, managing editor, 1955-58; *John O'London's* (weekly), London, England, editor, 1959-62; *Time and Tide* (news magazine), London, England, managing editor, 1962—. *Member:* Community of European Writers, Guild of British Newspaper Editors.

WRITINGS: Great Men of Yorkshire, Bodley Head, 1956; *Isles of Flowers: The Story of the Isles of Scilly*, Redman, 1956, 2nd edition, 1963; *Pragmatic Premier: An Intimate Portrait of Harold Wilson*, Frewin, 1967; (compiler) *The Wit of Harold Wilson*, Frewin, 1967; (editor) *The Two Thousand Women of Achievement*, Dartmouth, 1969; (editor) *Dictionary of Latin American and Caribbean Biography*, 2nd edition, Melrose Press, 1971; (editor) *Dictionary of Scandinavian Biography*, Melrose Press, 1972. Contributor of articles to newpapers and magazines.

WORK IN PROGRESS: A humorous book, *A Limey in Manhattan*, and a biography of George Frederick Handel.†

*   *   *

KAYE, Geraldine Hughesdon 1925-

PERSONAL: Born January 14, 1925, in Watford, Hertfordshire, England; daughter of Gerald (a surveyor) and Dorothy (White) Hughesdon; married Barrington L. B. Kaye (a lecturer and writer), April 16, 1948; children: Miranda Jane, Jennifer Sarah, Matthew Edward. *Education:* London School of Economics and Political Science, London, B.Sc. (second class honors), 1949. *Home:* 9 Abingdon Mansions, Abingdon Rd., London W. 8, England. *Agent:* A. M. Heath & Co. Ltd., 35 Dover St., London W. 1, England.

CAREER: Teacher at secondary school in Singapore, 1952-54, and at Mitford Colmer School, London, England, 1962-64. *Military service:* Women's Royal Naval Service, 1943-46.

WRITINGS—Juveniles: The Boy Who Wanted to Go Fishing, Methuen, 1960; *Kwasi Goes to Town*, Abelard, 1962 (also published as *Great Day in Ghana*, Abelard, 1962); *Kofi and the Eagle*, Methuen, 1963; *Koto and the Lagoon*, Deutsch, 1966; *The Raffle Pony*, Brockhampton, 1966; *Chik and the Bottle-House*, Nelson, 1966; *Tail of the Siamese Cat*, Nelson, 1966; *Koto and the Lagoon*, Funk & Wagnalls, 1967; *Yaa Goes South*, Oxford University Press, 1967; *The Sea Monkey: A Picture Story From Malaysia*, World, 1968; *Runaway Boy*, Heineman, 1971; *Nowhere to Stop*, Brockhampton Press, 1972. Author of a number of school readers for use in Africa, all published by Oxford University Press. Writer of children's programs for British Broadcasting Corp. and Radio Malaya.

SIDELIGHTS: Geraldine Kaye formerly lived in Africa and Malaya and writes about children of those countries.†

*   *   *

KEAST, William R(ea) 1914-

PERSONAL: Born November 1, 1914, in Malta, Ill.; son of Perce Marwood and Helen Gertrude (Dusher) Keast; married Mary Alice Hart, August 21, 1938; children: Sara

Hart, Stephen Calhoon, Emily Wrightsman. *Education:* University of Chicago, B.A., 1936, Ph.D., 1947. *Home:* 806 Rosedale Ter., Austin, Tex. 78704. *Office:* Humanities Research Center, University of Texas at Austin, Austin, Tex. 78172.

CAREER: University of Chicago, Chicago, Ill., instructor, 1938-47, assistant professor of English, 1947-51, secretary of department, 1949-51; Cornell University, Ithaca, N.Y., associate professor, 1951-57, professor of English, and department chairman, 1957-62, dean of College of Arts and Sciences, 1962-63, vice-president for academic affairs, 1963-65; Wayne State University, Detroit, Mich., president, 1965-71; National Commission on Tenure, Washington, D.C., director, 1971-72; University of Texas at Austin, chairman of English department, and director of Center for Higher Education, 1972-74, director of Humanities Research Center Special Collections, 1974—. Member, State Capitol Restoration Advisory Committee, Citizens Committee for Equal Opportunity, Metropolitan Fund (member of board of trustees, and member of executive committee, 1965-71). *Military service:* U.S. Army, 1941-46; became major. *Member:* American Academy of Political and Social Science, Johnsonians, Modern Language Association of America, Phi Beta Kappa, Grolier Club, Detroit Club, Detroit Athletic Club, University Club (Detroit). *Awards, honors:* Rockefeller postwar fellow in humanities, 1946-47; Fund for the Advancement of Education faculty fellow, 1955-56; Guggenheim fellow, 1958-59.

WRITINGS: (With R. R. Palmer and B. I. Wiley) *Procurement and Training of Ground Combat Troops*, U.S. Government Printing Office, 1948; (with Ronald S. Crane and others) *Critics and Criticism, Ancient and Modern*, University of Chicago Press, 1952; (editor with Robert E. Streeter) *The Province of Prose*, Harper, 1956, 2nd edition, 1959; (editor) *Seventeenth-Century English Poetry*, Oxford University Press, 1962. Member of editorial committee of Yale edition of "The Works of Samuel Johnson."

* * *

KEATING, Edward M. 1925-

PERSONAL: Born April 17, 1925, in New York, N.Y.; son of George Thomas and Harriet (Martin) Keating; married Helen English, September 14, 1947; children: Michael, Karen, Stephen, Mary Melissa, Katherine Ann. *Education:* Stanford University, A.B., 1948, LL.B., 1950. *Religion:* Catholic. *Home:* 54 Rosewood Dr., Atherton, Calif. *Office:* *Ramparts*, 1182 Chestnut St., Menlo Park, Calif.

CAREER: Private practice of law, 1950-54; University of Santa Clara, Santa Clara, Calif., instructor in English, 1959; *Ramparts* (magazine), Menlo Park, Calif., publisher and editor-in-chief, 1960—. *Military service:* U.S. Naval Reserve, 1943-45.

WRITINGS: The Scandal of Silence, Random House, 1965; *Free Huey!: The True Story of the Trial of Huey P. Newton for Murder*, Ramparts, 1971. Contributor to *Cosmopolitan* and *Book Week*.

BIOGRAPHICAL/CRITICAL SOURCES: Roy Newquist, *Conversations*, Rand McNally, 1967, pp. 194-203.†

* * *

KEETON, George Williams 1902-

PERSONAL: Born May 22, 1902, in Sheffield, Yorkshire, England; son of John William (a businessman) and Mary Emma (Williams) Keeton; married Gladys Calthorpe, 1924; married second wife, Kathleen Marian Williard, December 18, 1947; children: (first marriage) Peter Cecil Calthorpe, Michael George Williams. *Education:* Studied at Gonville and Caius College, Cambridge, and Gray's Inn; B.A., 1923, LL.B. (first class honors), 1923; M.A. and LL.M., 1927, LL.D., 1931. *Home:* Picts Close, Picts Lane, Princess Risborough, Buckinghamshire, England. *Office:* Brunel University, Kingston Lane, Uxbridge, Middlesex, England.

CAREER: University of Hong Kong, Hong Kong, reader in law and politics, 1924-27; called to bar, London, England, 1928; University of Manchester, Manchester, England, senior lecturer in law, 1928-31; University of London, University College, London, England, reader in English law, 1931-37, professor of law, and head of department, 1937-69, dean of Faculty of Laws, 1939-54, vice-provost, 1966-69. Brunel University, Uxbridge, Middlesex, England, associate professor of English law, 1969—. Professor of English law, University of Notre Dame, 1969-71; Distinguished Visiting Professor, University of Miami, 1972-73. President and treasurer, London Institute of World Affairs, 1945—. Lecturer in United States on two tours. *Member:* British Academy (fellow), Society of Public Teachers of Law (president, 1962). *Awards, honors:* LL.D., University of Sheffield, 1967, and University of Hong Kong, 1972; Leverhulme fellow, 1971.

WRITINGS: The Development of Extraterritoriality in China, 2 volumes, Longmans, Green, 1928; *The Austrian Theories of Law and Sovereignty*, Methuen, 1929; *Shakespeare and His Legal Problems*, A. & C. Black, 1930; *The Elementary Principles of Jurisprudence*, A. & C. Black, 1930, 2nd edition, Pitman, 1969; *The Problem of the Moscow Trial*, A. & C. Black, 1933; *The Law of Trusts: A Statement of the Rules of Law and Equity Applicable to Trusts of Real and Personal Property*, Pitman, 1934, 9th edition, 1968; *An Introduction to Equity*, Pitman, 1938, 6th edition, 1965; *The Speedy Return* (novel), G. Bell, 1938; *National Sovereignty and International Order: An Essay upon the International Community and International Order*, Peace Book Co., 1939; (with Georg Schwarzenberger) *Making International Law Work*, Peace Book Co., 1939, 2nd edition, Stevens & Sons, 1946, Garland Publishing, 1972.

Mutiny in the Caribbean (boy's novel), G. Bell, 1940; *The Case for an International University* (booklet), Watts & Co., 1941; (with Rudolf Schlesinger) *Russia and Her Western Neighbours*, J. Cape, 1942; *China, the Far East and the Future*, J. Cape, 1943, 2nd edition, Stevens, 1949; (editor) *The Path to Peace: A Debate*, Pitman, 1945; (editor with Schwarzenberger) *Jeremy Bentham and the Law: A Symposium*, Stevens, 1948, Greenwood Press, 1970; *Extraterritoriality in International and Comparative Law*, Recueil Sirey, 1949; *A Liberal Attorney General*, Nisbet, 1949; *The Soccer Club Secretary*, Naldrett Press, 1951; *The Passing of Parliament*, Benn, 1952, 2nd edition, 1954; (editor) *The Trial of Gustave Rau, Otto Monsson, and Willem Smith: The 'Veronica' Trial*, Hodge & Co., 1952; (editor) *The United Kingdom: The Development of Its Laws and Constitutions*, Volume I, Stevens, 1955; *Social Change in the Law of Trusts* (also see below), Pitman, 1958, Greenwood Press, 1974; *Trial for Treason*, Macdonald & Co., 1959; (editor) *Cases on Equity and Trusts*, Pitman, 1959.

(Editor) *Williams on Executors and Administrators*, 14th edition, Stevens, 1960; *Trial by Tribunal: A Study of the Development and Functioning of the Tribunal of Inquiry*,

Museum Press, 1960; *Guilty But Insane*, Macdonald & Co., 1961; *The Modern Law of Charities*, Pitman, 1962, 2nd edition (with Lionel A. Sheridan), Faculty of Law, The Queen's University of Belfast, 1971; (editor with Schwarzenberger) *English Law and the Common Market*, Stevens, 1963; *The Investment and Taxation of Trust Funds* (also see below), Pitman, 1964; *Lord Chancellor Jeffreys and the Stuart Cause*, Macdonald & Co., 1965; *The Norman Conquest and the Common Law*, Barnes & Noble, 1966; *Shakespeare's Legal and Political Background*, Pitman, 1967, Barnes & Noble, 1968; (with Sheridan) *Equity*, Pitman, 1969; *Government in Action in the United Kingdom*, Barnes & Noble, 1970; *Modern Developments in the Law of Trusts* (based on *Social Change in the Law of Trusts* and *The Investment and Taxation of Trust Funds*), Faculty of Law, The Queen's University of Belfast, 1971; *The Football Revolution: A Study of the Changing Pattern of Association Football*, David & Charles, 1972; *English Law: The Judicial Contribution*, David & Charles, 1974.

Editor, *Cambridge Review*, 1924; general editor, *The Laws and Constitutions of the Commonwealth*; joint editor, *Anglo-American Law Review*, and *Current Legal Problems*, 1948—. Contributor to *Law Quarterly Review*, *Current Legal Problems*, to other legal journals, and to popular magazines.

WORK IN PROGRESS: Research in the development of the Law of Trusts in the Commonwealth.

BIOGRAPHICAL/CRITICAL SOURCES: R. H. Code Holland and Georg Schwarzenberger, editors, *Law, Justice and Equity: Essays in Tribute to G. W. Keeton*, Oceana, 1967.

*   *   *

KEHOE, Constance (DeMuzio)   1933-

PERSONAL: Born July 25, 1933, in Malden, Mass.; daughter of Hector P. and Elizabeth (Antico) DeMuzio; married William F. Kehoe (a lawyer), September 12, 1959; children: John William. *Education:* Mount Holyoke College, A.B., 1955; Yale University, M.A., 1956; Middlebury College, M.A., 1959; Trinity College, University of Dublin, graduate study, 1959-60. *Home:* 13 Rock Glen Rd., Medford, Mass. 02155. *Office:* 39 Pilgrim Rd., Boston, Mass. 02115.

CAREER: Wheelock College, Boston, Mass., associate professor of English, 1960—. Free-lance photographer, exhibiting and publishing black and white prints and color slides; lecturer on travel and literature.

WRITINGS: (Author with husband, William F. Kehoe, and photographer) *Enjoying Ireland*, Devin, 1966.†

*   *   *

KEHOE, William F.   1933-

PERSONAL: Born December 3, 1933, in Stoneham, Mass.; son of William A. and Josephine A. (Crowley) Kehoe; married Constance DeMuzio (an associate professor of English), September 12, 1959; children: John William, Kathleen Emily. *Education:* Dartmouth College, A.B. (summa cum laude), 1955; Yale University, M.A., 1956; Trinity College, Dublin, Fulbright Scholar, 1959-60; Harvard University, LL.B., 1963. *Home:* 13 Rock Glen Rd., Medford, Mass. 02155. *Office:* 82 Devonshire St., Boston, Mass. 02109.

CAREER: Middlebury College, Middlebury, Vt., instructor in English, 1956-57; admitted to Massachusetts

bar, 1963; Gaston Snow and Ely Bartlett, Boston, Mass., lawyer, 1963—. *Military service:* U.S. Army, Intelligence, 1957-59. *Member:* Phi Beta Kappa.

WRITINGS: (With wife, Constance D. Kehoe) *Enjoying Ireland*, Devin, 1966.

*   *   *

KEISER, Norman F(red)   1930-

PERSONAL: Born March 20, 1930, in Scranton, Pa.; son of Fred H. and Isabel (Browning) Keiser; married Nancy Jean Unger (a teacher), August 7, 1952 (divorced, 1971); children: Cindy, Bruce. *Education:* Bloomsburg State College, B.S., 1950; University of Scranton, M.A., 1951; Syracuse University, Ph.D., 1954. *Home:* 15400 Hume Dr., Saratoga, Calif. *Office:* California State University, San Jose, Calif.

CAREER: Syracuse University, Syracuse, N.Y., assistant instructor, 1952-53; State Teachers College at Brockport (now State University of New York College at Brockport), instructor, 1953-54; Michigan State University, East Lansing, instructor, 1954-56; State University of New York College at Oswego, professor, 1956-61; California State University, San Jose, associate professor, 1961-64, professor of economics, 1964—, chairman of department, 1964-69. *Member:* American Economic Association, Royal Economic Society, Western Economics Association.

WRITINGS: Introductory Economics, Wiley, 1961; *Macroeconomics, Fiscal Policy, and Economic Growth*, Wiley, 1964; *Economics: Analysis and Policy*, Wiley, 1965; *Readings in Macroeconomics: Theory, Evidence and Policy*, Prentice-Hall, 1970; *Macroeconomics: Problems and a Survey of Theory*, Random House, 1971; *Macroeconomics*, Random House, 1971. Contributor to professional journals and Congressional committee publications.

*   *   *

KELLEY, Eugene J(ohn)   1922-

PERSONAL: Born July 8, 1922, in New York, N.Y.; son of Eugene L. and Agnes (Meskill) Kelley; married Dorothy Mildred Kane, August 3, 1946; children: Sharon Agnes. *Education:* University of Connecticut, B.S., 1944; Boston University, M.Ed., 1948, M.B.A., 1949; New York University, Ph.D., 1955. *Home:* 468 Sierra Lane, State College, Pa. 16801. *Office:* 234 Boucke, Pennsylvania State University, University Park, Pa. 16802.

CAREER: Salesman, 1945-47; Babson Institute of Business Administration, Babson Park, Mass., instructor, 1947-49; Clark University, Worcester, Mass., 1949-56, became associate professor and director of Division of Business Administration; Michigan State University, East Lansing, assistant professor, later associate professor of marketing, 1957-59; New York University, Graduate School of Business Administration, New York, N.Y., professor of marketing, and associate dean, 1959-63; Pennsylvania State University, University Park, research professor of business administration, 1963—. Harvard University, visiting lecturer at Business School, 1956-57. Atlantic Bank of New York, director. Marketing consultant. *Military service:* U.S. Army Air Forces, 1942-43. *Member:* American Marketing Association, Academy of Management, American Association of University Professors.

WRITINGS: Location of Controlled Regional Shopping Centers, Eno Foundation, 1956; (with W. Lazer) *Managerial Marketing: Perspectives and Viewpoints*, Irwin, 1958,

3rd edition, 1967; (with R. Simonds and R. Ball) *Business Administration: Problems and Functions*, with instructor's manual, Allyn & Bacon, 1962; (contributor) S. J. Shaw and C. McF. Gittinger, *Marketing in Business Management*, Macmillan, 1963; (editor) *Marketing Management: An Annotated Bibliography*, American Marketing Association, 1963; (contributor) *Marketing in Action: Readings*, Wadsworth, 1963; (contributor) George Schwartz, editor, *Marketing Science*, Wiley, 1965; *Marketing: Strategy and Functions*, Prentice-Hall, 1965; *Marketing Planning and Competitive Strategy*, Prentice-Hall, 1972; (with W. Lazer) *Social Marketing: Perspectives and Viewpoints*, Irwin, 1973.

General editor of Prentice-Hall's "Foundations of Marketing" series, and author of Volume I, *Marketing: Strategy and Functions*, 1965. The other ten books in the series are to follow, 1965-66. Editor, *Journal of Marketing*, 1967—.

WORK IN PROGRESS: Work on marketing planning; on science, technology, and marketing; and on the role of marketing in economic growth.†

*   *   *

KELLEY, Stanley, Jr. 1926-

PERSONAL: Born December 7, 1926, in Detroit, Kan.; son of Stanley and Stella (Marts) Kelley. *Education:* University of Kansas, A.B., 1949, M.A., 1951; University of Rome, graduate study, 1953-54; Johns Hopkins University, Ph.D., 1955. *Home:* 120 Prospect Ave., Princeton, N.J. *Office:* Department of Politics, Princeton University, Princeton, N.J.

CAREER: Brookings Institution, Washington, D.C., research assistant, 1956-57; Princeton University, Princeton, N.J., assistant professor of political science, 1957-62, associate professor of political science, 1962—. Visiting assistant professor, Johns Hopkins University, 1959. *Military service:* U.S. Army, 1945-47. *Member:* American Political Science Association.

WRITINGS: Professional Public Relations and Political Power, Johns Hopkins Press, 1956; *Political Campaigning*, Brookings, 1960; (with Paul T. Davis and others) *Presidential Election and Transition 1960-61*, Brookings, 1961. Contributor to *Journal of Politics, Law and Contemporary Problems, Antioch Review*, and *Public Opinion Quarterly*.

WORK IN PROGRESS: Studies of voter registration, the relationship of the Presidency to the American party system, political campaign strategies, party politics.†

*   *   *

KELLNER, Esther (Esther Cooper)

PERSONAL: Born in Henry County, Ind.; daughter of John Allen (a salesman) and Franke Anna (Cox) Armacost; married Wynn Ralph Cooper, September 17, 1927 (deceased); married Lee Kellner (a salesman), November 8, 1942; children: (first marriage) Jamie Lee (daughter).

CAREER: Public speaker; volunteer worker in state mental hospital, and with Civil Defense; has taught writers' workshops at college level. *Member:* Beta Sigma Phi, Kentucky Colonel. *Awards, honors:* Indiana University Novel Award, 1956, for *The Promise*; two awards from Indiana University "for distinguished fiction"; Woman of Achievement Award from Business and Professional Women.

WRITINGS: The Promise (story of Sarah), Westminster,

1956; *Mary of Nazareth*, Appleton, 1958; *The Wife of Pilate*, Appleton, 1959; *Background of the Old Testament*, Doubleday, 1963; *Out of the Woods* (nonfiction), Doubleday, 1964; (with Clarence Lewis) *Cry to the Hills*, Doubleday, 1966; *The Devil and Aunt Serena*, Bobbs-Merrill, 1968; *Moonshine: Its History and Folklore*, Bobbs-Merrill, 1971; *Animals Come to My House*, Putnam, 1974. Writer of radio scripts, and of filmstrips for Cathedral Films, Hollywood, Calif. Contributor of stories, articles, and poems to adult and juvenile magazines, and features and columns to newspapers; also has done children's activity material.

SIDELIGHTS: Esther Kellner speaks Spanish competently and some French. *Avocational interests:* Shooting (not hunting), outdoor activities, cooking, travel.

*   *   *

KELLY, Averill Alison 1913-

PERSONAL: Born October 17, 1913, in Liverpool, England; daughter of Sir Robert Ernest (a surgeon) and Averill Edith Irma (McDougall) Kelly. *Education:* Lady Margaret Hall, Oxford, M.A. (honors), 1940; also studied at Liverpool City College of Art. *Home:* Flat 8, 34 Phillimore Gardens, Kensington, London W. 8, England.

CAREER: British Ministry of Home Security, camouflage expert, 1940-45; lecturer for Oxford University and London University extramural departments, for City Literary Institute, London, England, and for Design Centre, London. *Member:* Association of Tutors in Adult Education, Wedgwood Society, English Ceramic Society, Furniture History Society, Society of Architectural Historians.

WRITINGS: Pottery, Educational Supply Association, 1961; *The Story of Wedgwood*, Faber, 1962, Viking, 1963, revised edition, Faber, 1974; *Decorative Wedgwood in Architecture and Furniture*, Country Life, 1965; *The Book of English Fireplaces*, Country Life, 1968; *Wedgwood Ware*, Ward, Lock, 1970; *Coade Stone*, Faber, in press. Writer of scripts for British Broadcasting Corp. "Looking at Things" series, and for experimental television series, "Using Our Eyes." Contributor of articles on eighteenth-century design to *Country Life*.

SIDELIGHTS: Averill Kelly told *CA* that she is a "keen student of English architectural and furniture history." She is fluent in French, and moderately competent in Italian.

*   *   *

KELLY, John M., Jr. 1919-

PERSONAL: Born March 3, 1919, in San Francisco, Calif.; son of John Melville (an artist) and Katherine (a sculptress; maiden name, Harland) Kelly; married Marion Anderson (an anthropologist), October 3, 1943; children: Colleen, Kathleen. *Education:* Julliard School of Music, B.S., 1950; graduate study at San Diego State University. *Home:* 4117 Black Point Rd., Honolulu, Hawaii 96815.

CAREER: Hockaday School, Dallas, Tex., choral director, 1950-51; Palama Settlement, Honolulu, Hawaii, director of music school, 1951-59; First Methodist Church, Honolulu, Hawaii, choral director, 1951-57; Honolulu Community Chorus, Honolulu, Hawaii, founder, conductor, 1953-60; Gleemen of Honolulu, Honolulu, Hawaii, conductor, 1962—. Inter Island Surf Shop, Honolulu, general manager, 1965; Emergency Committee to Save Our Surf, Honolulu, chairman; holder of patents for hydroplane surfboard. Active in world peace and disarmament organizations. *Military service:* U.S. Naval Reserve, 1940-45;

became chief warrant bo's'n; received Navy and Marine Corps Medal for volunteer work in hazardous duty.

WRITINGS: Folk Songs Hawaii Sings, Tuttle, 1962; *Surf and Sea*, A. S. Barnes, 1965; *Chang-gu, the Korean Drum*, Leeds Music Corp., 1965; *Folk Music Festival in Hawaii*, Boston Music Co., 1965. Contributor of occasional articles on music, surf sports, and world peace to periodicals.

WORK IN PROGRESS: Drums and Rhythms of Asia and the Pacific, for Leeds Music Corp.

AVOCATIONAL INTERESTS: Surfing (for thirty-five years).†

*   *   *

KELLY, Tim   1935-

PERSONAL: Born October 2, 1935, in Saugus, Mass.; son of Francis Seymour and Mary-Edna (Furey) Kelley. *Education:* Emerson College, B.A., 1956, M.A., 1957; Yale University, graduate study, 1966. *Home and office:* 8730 Lookout Mountain Ave., Hollywood, Calif. 90046.

CAREER: Full-time screenwriter and playwright. *Member:* Writers Guild of America (West), Dramatists Guild, Authors League of America. *Awards, honors:* American Broadcasting Co. fellow, 1965-66; University of Chicago, Sergel Drama Prize, 1973, for "Yankee Clipper."

WRITINGS: Ride of Fury (novel), Ace Books, 1964.

Plays: "Road Show," first produced in Martha's Vineyard, Mass., 1957; "O'Rourke's House," first produced by National Broadcasting Co. "Matinee Theatre," 1958; *Widow's Walk* (first produced in Scottsdale, Ariz., at Stagebrush Theatre, 1959), Harper, 1963; *Not Far from the Giaconda Tree* (one-act; first produced at Stagebrush Theatre, 1961), Pioneer Press (Cody, Wyo.), 1965; *The Burning Man* (first produced at Stagebrush Theatre, 1962), Samuel French, 1962; "A Darker Flower," first produced Off-Broadway at Pocket Theatre, 1963; "The Trunk and All That Jazz," first produced in Boston at Image Theatre, 1963; "The Floor Is Bright with Toys" (comedy), first produced in Phoenix, Ariz., at Arizona Repertory Theatre, 1963; "Song of the Dove," first produced at Stagebrush Theatre, 1964; "Murder on Ice," first produced at Stagebrush Theatre, 1964; "The Natives Are Restless" (long one-act), first produced in Seattle, Wash., at Theatre Northwest, 1965; "Welcome to the Casa," first produced in Fairfield, Conn., at Meadowbrook Playhouse, 1965; "Late Blooming Flowers," first produced in Los Angeles at Ivar Theatre, 1968; *Last of Sherlock Holmes*, Baker's Plays, 1969; *Yankee Doodle* (musical), Performance Publishing, 1972; (stage adapter) Mary Shelley, *Frankenstein*, Samuel French, 1974; *The Remarkable Susan*, Dramatists Play Service, 1974; *Virtue Victorious*, Dramatic Publishing, 1974; *Reunion on Gallows Hill*, Pioneer Drama Service, 1974.

Also author of plays, "Two Fools Who Gained a Measure of Wisdom," 1968; "The Silk Shirt," 1970; "Second Best Bed," 1970; "West of Pecos," 1971; "Merry Murders at Montmarie," 1972; "Creeps by Night," 1973; "M*A*S*H" (stage adaptation), 1973; "The Gift of Giving," 1973.

Filmscripts: "Cry of the Banshee"; "The Brothers O'Toole"; "Sugar Hill"; "Bogash"; "Get Fisk."

Contributor of articles and drama criticism to journals.

WORK IN PROGRESS: Belle and Blue Duck, novel based on the exploits of two legendary western figures.

SIDELIGHTS: Kelly speaks Spanish.

BIOGRAPHICAL/CRITICAL SOURCES: Arizonian, January 30, 1964.

*   *   *

KELLY, William Leo   1924-

PERSONAL: Born November 11, 1924, in Baltimore, Md.; son of William Leo and Agnes Veronica (Higgins) Kelly. *Education:* Loyola University, Chicago, A.B., 1947, M.A., 1952; Woodstock College, S.T.L., 1956; University of Mainz, Ph.D., 1960; U.S. Air Force Hospital, Wiesbaden, West Germany, certificate of internship in clinical psychology, 1961. *Home:* Georgetown University, Washington, D.C. 20007. *Office:* Psychological Services Bureau, Georgetown University, Washington, D.C. 20007.

CAREER: Ordained Roman Catholic priest, member of Society of Jesus, 1955. Georgetown Preparatory School, Garrett Park, Md., variously teacher of Latin, Greek, French, Spanish, English, and religion, 1947-52; Georgetown University, Washington, D.C., clinical psychologist and associate professor of philosophy and psychology, 1961—, psychological consultant to Center for Population Research, 1963. *Member:* American Psychological Association, Societe Internationale pour l'Etude des Symboles, Jesuit Philosophical Association, American Catholic Psychological Association, American College Health Association, American Personnel and Guidance Association, District of Columbia Psychological Association.

WRITINGS: Youth Before God, Newman, 1958, *Die Neuscholastiche und die Empirische Psychologie*, Hain (West Germany), 1960; *Women Before God*, Newman, 1961; *Men Before God*, Newman, 1963; (contributor) Robert Harvnak, editor, *Contemporary Thought and the Spiritual Exercises of St. Ignatius*, Loyola University Press, 1963; (editor with Andrew Tallon) *Readings in the Philosophy of Man*, McGraw-Hill, 1967, 2nd edition, 1972. Writer of television program, "Crises Through the Decades," and director of "Psychology and Philosophy of Freedom," on WRC-TV, Washington, D.C. Contributor of reviews and articles to psychological journals.

WORK IN PROGRESS: Philosophy and the Science of Man, Psychodiagnostics through Symbolism—the Kahn Test of Symbolic Arrangement, The Philosophy and Psychology of Alienation, and pilot studies on the so-called "bio-rhythmns" and on social and academic achievement; a research project on ophthalmographic diagnostics data and personality traits; research on personality assessment formats; research on factor of conceptualization and symbolization of college students.

SIDELIGHTS: Kelly has lived (as a non-tourist) in Germany, France, and Spain. He is competent in Latin, Greek, French, Spanish, and German.†

*   *   *

KELMAN, Herbert C(hanoch)   1927-

PERSONAL: Born March 18, 1927, in Vienna, Austria; became American citizen, 1950; son of Leo and Lea (Pomeranz) Kelman; married Rose Brousman (a social worker), August 23, 1953. *Education:* Brooklyn College (now Brooklyn College of the City University of New York), B.A., 1947; Seminary College of Jewish Studies, New York, N.Y., B.H.L., 1947; Yale University, M.S., 1949, Ph.D., 1951. *Politics:* Independent. *Religion:* Jewish. *Home:* 984 Memorial Dr., Cambridge, Mass. *Office:* Department of Psychology and Social Relations, Harvard University, Cambridge, Mass. 02138.

CAREER: Johns Hopkins University, Baltimore, Md., Social Science Research Council research fellow, 1951-52, U.S. Public Health Service research fellow, 1952-54; Center for Advanced Study in the Behavioral Sciences, Stanford, Calif., fellow, 1954-55, and 1967; National Institute of Mental Health, Bethesda, Md., research psychologist, 1955-57; Harvard University, Cambridge, Mass., lecturer on social psychology, 1957-62; Oslo Institute for Social Research, Oslo, Norway, U.S. Public Health Service special research fellow, 1960-61; University of Michigan, Ann Arbor, professor of psychology and research psychologist, Center for Research in Conflict Resolution, 1962-69; Harvard University, Cambridge, Mass., Richard Clarke Cabot Professor of Social Ethics, 1968—. Congress of Racial Equality, field representative, 1954-60; War Resisters League, member of national advisory committee.

MEMBER: American Psychological Association (president, Division of Personality and Social Psychology, 1970-71), Society for the Psychological Study of Social Issues (president, 1964-65), American Sociological Association, International Studies Association (vice-president, 1972-73), Interamerican Society of Psychology. *Awards, honors:* Socio-psychological prize of American Association for the Advancement of Science, 1956; Battele Seatle Research Center, fellow, 1972-73; Kurt Lewin Memorial Award of the Society for the Psychological Study of Social Illness, 1973.

WRITINGS: (Editor and contributor) *International Behavior: A Social-Psychological Analysis*, Holt, 1965; *A Time to Speak: On Human Values and Social Research*, Jossey-Bass, 1968; (co-author) *Cross-National Encounters: The Personal Impact of an Exchange Program for Broadcasters*, Jossey-Bass, 1970. Contributor to social-psychological and political journals. Member of editorial committee, *Journal of Personality and Social Psychology*, *Human Relations*, *Journal of Applied Behavioral Science*, *Journal of Conflict Resolution*, *Journal of Social Issues*, *Psychiatry*, *Sociometry*.

WORK IN PROGRESS: A book on social influence and personal belief; research on legitimate authority and personal responsibility to be reported in a book; joint books on attitude-discrepant behavior and/or the ethics of social intervention.

SIDELIGHTS: Kelman travels extensively in connection with research on international conflict resolution.

*   *   *

KENDALL, Robert 1934-

PERSONAL: Born June 26, 1934; son of William Austin and Valla Eunice (Bentley) Kendall. *Education:* Attended Emanuel Missionary College, Berrien Springs, Mich., 1952, La Sierra College, 1953-54, University of Southern California, 1956; Los Angeles State College (now California State University), B.A., 1959, and graduate study; University of California, Los Angeles, graduate study. *Office:* Ned Brown & Associates, 315 South Beverly Dr., Beverly Hills, Calif.

CAREER: Actor and writer. Made film debut at thirteen as elephant boy in "Song of Scheherazade," 1947, other motion picture appearances in "Casbah" (Universal International), 1949, "Benny Goodman Story," 1953, "The Ten Commandments," 1956, "Women of Pitcairn," 1958, "Guns Don't Argue," 1959, "Ma Barker's Killer Brood," 1960, and "Boy from Thailand," 1961. Television appearances on "Ford Hour," "Twentieth Century-Fox Hour,"

"Gangbusters" series, "Casablanca" series. Lecturer on juvenile delinquency at more than one hundred churches in forty cities, using Gospel Films picture, "Betrayed," in which he plays the lead. *Member:* Screen Actors Guild, Writers Guild, Young Men's Christian Association, Desert Highlands Club.

WRITINGS: White Teacher in a Black School, Devin, 1964; *The Girl From Panama*, Venice Poetry (Beverly Hills), 1973.

WORK IN PROGRESS: A screenplay for Dimitrios Films, "Summer in Spoleto"; *Psychic World of Lotte Von Strahl*.

*   *   *

KENNEDY, J(ames) Hardee 1915-

PERSONAL: Born June 12, 1915, in Quitman, Miss.; son of James Robert (a teacher and farmer) and Henrietta Maria (Hardee) Kennedy; married Mary Virginia Gamble, August 2, 1942; children: Virginia Jeannine. *Education:* Mississippi College, A.B., 1939; New Orleans Baptist Theological Seminary, Th.M., 1944, Th.D., 1947; Union Theological Seminary, New York, N.Y., postdoctoral study, 1955; Yale University Divinity School, research fellow, 1955-56. *Politics:* Republican. *Religion:* Baptist. *Home:* 4139 Seminary Pl., New Orleans, La. 70126.

CAREER: New Orleans Baptist Theological Seminary, New Orleans, La., assistant professor, 1947-49, associate professor, 1949-54, professor of Old Testament interpretation and Hebrew, 1954—, chairman of graduate committee, 1953-59, dean of School of Theology, 1959-68, dean of academic affairs, 1972—. Trustee, Union Baptist Theological Seminary, New Orleans, La., 1964—. *Member:* American Academy of Religion, National Association of Professors of Hebrew.

WRITINGS: Studies in the Book of Jonah, Broadman, 1956; *The Commission of Moses and the Christian Calling*, Eerdmans, 1964; (contributor) Clifton J. Allen and others, editors, *Broadman Bible Commentary*, Broadman, Volume II, 1970, Volume VII, 1972; (contributor) Hobbs and Paschall, editors, *The Teacher's Bible Commentary*, Broadman, 1972. Writer of syllabi on biblical topics. Contributor to encyclopedias; also contributor of articles and reviews to religious journals.

WORK IN PROGRESS: A book, *Studies in Old Testament Theology*.

AVOCATIONAL INTERESTS: Gardening, hunting.

*   *   *

KENNEDY, Michael 1926-

PERSONAL: Born February 19, 1926, in Manchester, England; son of Hew Gilbert and Marion Florence (Sinclair) Kennedy; married Eslyn May Durdle, May 16, 1947. *Education:* Attended Berkhamsted School, 1939-41. *Politics:* Conservative. *Religion:* Church of England. *Home:* 3 Moorwood Dr., Sale, Cheshire, England.

CAREER: Daily Telegraph, London, England, member of editorial staff, Manchester office, 1941—, northern music critic, 1951—, northern editor, 1960—. Royal Manchester College of Music, member of council, honorary member, 1971. *Military service:* Royal Navy, 1943-46. *Member:* Institute of Journalists (fellow), National Union of Journalists, Lancashire County Cricket Club.

WRITINGS: The Halle Tradition: A Century of Music,

Manchester University Press, 1960; *The Works of Ralph Vaughan Williams*, Oxford University Press, 1964; *Portrait of Elgar*, Oxford University Press, 1968; *Portrait of Manchester*, R. Hale, 1970; *Elgar Orchestral Works*, BBC Publications, 1970; *History of Royal Manchester College of Music*, Manchester University Press, 1971; *Barbirolli: Conductor Laureate*, MacGibbon & Kee, 1971; (editor) *Autobiography of Charles Halle*, Dent, 1974. Contributor to *Musical Times*, *Listener*, and *Halle Magazine*.

WORK IN PROGRESS: A book, *Richard Strauss*, for Dent.

SIDELIGHTS: Reviewing *Portrait of Elgar*, D. C. Goddard notes that it is a "brilliant biography." He further explains: "Mr. Kennedy succeeds superbly, displacing the flabby legend of Elgar as an Edwardian musical blimp with a convincing portrait of a complex, lonely man of great gifts whose music . . . has never quite achieved the place it deserves. Of the year's literary output, it [*Portrait of Elgar*] belongs in the 10 per cent that deserves to be read."

*   *   *

KENNICK, W(illiam) E(lmer)   1923-

PERSONAL: Born May 28, 1923, in Lebanon, Ill.; son of Samuel Arthur and Dorothy (Campbell) Kennick; married Anna Perkins Howes, June 25, 1949; children: Christopher Campbell, Justin Howes, Sylvia Bowditch. *Education:* Oberlin College, A.B., 1945; Cornell University, Ph.D., 1952. *Politics:* Independent. *Home:* 96 Northampton Rd., Amherst, Mass.

CAREER: Instructor in philosophy at Oberlin College, Oberlin, Ohio, 1947-48, Boston University, Boston, Mass., 1950-51; Oberlin College, assistant professor of philosophy, 1951-56; Amherst College, Amherst, Mass., associate professor, 1956-62, professor of philosophy, 1962—. *Military service:* U.S. Army, Medical Corps, 1946-47. *Member:* American Philosophical Association, Phi Beta Kappa. *Awards, honors:* M.A., Amherst College, 1962.

WRITINGS: (Editor and contributor) *Art and Philosophy: Readings in Aesthetics*, St. Martin's, 1964; (editor with Morris Lazerowitz) *Metaphysics: Readings and Reappraisals*, Prentice-Hall, 1965.

WORK IN PROGRESS: The Development of Western Philosophy, for Macmillan.

AVOCATIONAL INTERESTS: Painting.

*   *   *

KENYON, Ley   1913-

PERSONAL: Born May 28, 1913, in London, England; son of Arnold Kingsley (a company director) and Margaret (Jolly) Kenyon. *Education:* Attended Central School of Arts and Crafts, London, England, 1931-34. *Home:* 37 Cranley Gardens, London S.W.7, England.

CAREER: Artist, with war drawings in collection of Imperial War Museum; professional aqualung diver and underwater photographer, participating in British Research Divers' Expedition to the Red Sea, 1965. Commonwealth lecturer for J. Y. Cousteau (of the French Navy) Group, showing films made by Cousteau and himself, in England, continental Europe, the United States, Africa, and Near and Far East. *Military service:* Royal Canadian Air Force, 1940-45; became squadron gunnery leader; awarded Distinguished Flying Cross. *Member:* Chelsea Arts Club, British Sub-Aqua Club. *Awards, honors:* Winston Churchill fel-

lowship, 1970, for conservation film, "Aldabra—Island in Peril."

WRITINGS: Pocket Guide to the Undersea World, Collins, 1957; *Tauch Mit!*, Albert Muller, 1958; *Discovering the Undersea World*, Sterling, 1962; *Aqualung Diving*, Allen & Unwin, 1971.

SIDELIGHTS: An authority on aqualung diving, Kenyon was invited to Buckingham Palace in 1960 to teach the Duke of Edinburgh to dive.

*   *   *

KENYON, Michael   1931-

PERSONAL: Born June 26, 1931, in Huddersfield, Yorkshire, England; son of George (an engineer) and Madeleine (Roberts) Kenyon; married Catherine Bury, June 3, 1961; children: Lucy Jane, Kate Madeleine, Polly. *Education:* Oxford University, B.A. and M.A., 1954; Duke University, graduate student, 1954-55. *Home:* 40 Bowerdean St., London SW6, England.

CAREER: Reporter on *Bristol Evening Post*, Bristol, England, 1955-58, *News Chronicle*, London, England, 1958-60, *Guardian*, London, England, 1960-64; University of Illinois, Urbana, visiting lecturer in journalism, 1964-66; full-time professional writer, living in Jersey, the Channel Islands, Great Britain, 1966-72, and London, England, 1972—. *Military service:* Royal Air Force, pilot officer, 1949-51.

WRITINGS: Green Grass (novel), Macmillan (London), 1970.

All mystery novels: *You May Die in Ireland*, Morrow, 1965; *The Trouble with Series Three*, Morrow, 1967 (published in England as *The Whole Hog*, Collins, 1967); *Out of Season*, Collins, 1969; *The 100,000 Welcomes*, Coward, 1971; *The Shooting of Dan McGrew*, Collins, 1972; *A Sorry State*, McKay, 1974; *Mr. Big*, Collins, in press.

WORK IN PROGRESS: A children's mystery novel; an adult mystery novel; articles for *Gourmet*.

SIDELIGHTS: Reviewing *The Trouble With Series Three*, Anthony Boucher described Kenyon as "bright, perceptive and enlightening when he is simply writing about love, or about the academic world, or about America as viewed by a visiting swine nutritionist from Leeds." Maurice Prior notes in regard to *Out of Season*, "Michael Kenyon's style is diffuse without being pretentious or utterly bombastic." *Avocational interests:* Peace and quiet.

BIOGRAPHICAL/CRITICAL SOURCES: Observer, July 11, 1965; *Manchester Guardian*, July 22, 1965; *Spectator*, July 23, 1965; *New York Times Book Review*, August 1, 1965; *Books and Bookmen*, September, 1965; *Times Literary Supplement*, September 2, 1965; *Book Week*, September 12, 1965; *Publishers Weekly*, April 29, 1974.

*   *   *

KESSEL, Lipmann   1914-
(Daniel Paul)

PERSONAL: Born December 19, 1914, in Pretoria, South Africa; son of David and Gertrude (Girdisky) Kessel; married Mary Grace Oughton (a secretary), 1949; children: David, Paul. *Education:* Attended University of the Witwatersrand; St. Mary's Hospital School, University of London, M.R.C.S. and L.R.C.P., 1938, F.R.C.S. (England), 1947. *Home:* 48 Platts Lane, London N.W. 3, England.

CAREER: Senior registered orthopedist in London, 1947-53; clinical orthopedic surgeon, London, England, 1954—. *Military service:* Royal Army Medical Corps, 1941-46; became major; received Order of the British Empire and Military Cross. *Member:* British Orthopaedic Association (fellow), British Medical Association, Royal Society of Medicine (fellow), Society for Cultural Relations with U.S.S.R. (chairman).

WRITINGS: (With J. St. John Paul) *Surgeon at Arms*, Heinemann, 1958; (contributor) K. Lewis *Diagnostic Radiology*, 1964. Contributor of some forty scientific and technical articles to learned journals.

WORK IN PROGRESS: A chapter, "The Shoulder Joint" for *British Clinical Surgery*, for Butterworth & Co.†

* * *

KEY, Theodore 1912-
(Ted Key)

PERSONAL: Born August 25, 1912, in Fresno, Calif.; son of Simon Leon (a businessman) and Fanny (Kahn) Key; married Anne Elizabeth Wilkinson, September 30, 1937; children: Stephen, David, Peter. *Education:* University of California, Berkeley, A.B., 1933. *Religion:* Jewish. *Home and office:* 1694 Glenhardie Rd., Wayne, Pa.

CAREER: Cartoonist and writer, best known as creator of "Hazel," appearing in *Saturday Evening Post*, 1943—. Also cartoonist and writer for *New Yorker*, *Look*, *This Week*, *Jack and Jill*, and other magazines; writer of radio scripts for National Broadcasting Co. and Columbia Broadcasting System programs. *Military service:* U.S. Army, Signal Corps, 1944-46; became master sergeant. *Member:* National Cartoonists Society, Players Club.

WRITINGS—All under name Ted Key; all published by Dutton, except as indicated: *Hazel*, 1946; *Here's Hazel*, 1949; *Many Happy Returns*, 1951; *If You Like Hazel*, 1952; *So'm I*, 1954; *Hazel Rides Again*, 1955; *Fasten Your Seat Belts*, 1956; *Phyllis*, 1957; *All Hazel*, 1958; *The Hazel Jubilee*, 1959; *The Biggest Dog in the World*, 1960; *Hazel Time*, 1962; *Life with Hazel*, 1965; *Ted Key's Diz and Liz*, Wonder Books, 1966; *Squirrels in the Feeding Station: Ted Key's Suburban Survival Kit*, 1967; *Hazel Power*, Curtis, 1971; *Right On Hazel*, Curtis, 1972; *Ms Hazel*, Curtis, 1972. Also author of screenplay, "Showdown at Ulcer Gulch," and of a radio play, "The Clinic," anthologized in *Best Broadcasts of 1939-40*.

WORK IN PROGRESS: Hazel Superstar.

SIDELIGHTS: A film, "Million Dollar Duck," based on a story by Key, was made by Walt Disney Productions in 1972; two others, "Gus" and "Nessie Come Home," are also to be filmed.

* * *

KHERA, S(ucha) S(ingh) 1903-

PERSONAL: Born April 3, 1903, in Ipoh, Malaysia; son of M. S. Khera; married Esme Mohini, 1947; children: Ranjit (son), Venita Poppy (daughter). *Education:* University of London, LL.B. (with honors). *Home:* Casa Veneto, 10 Palam Marg, New Delhi 57, India; and 8 St. James's Chambers, Ryder St., London S.W.1, England.

CAREER: Government of India, New Delhi, 1927-65, serving as district officer, 1927-41, director of industries, 1941, director general of war supply, 1942-46, divisional commissioner and development land reforms commis-

sioner, 1947-54, secretary to government, 1956-62, cabinet secretary, 1962-65. One-time chairman of Hindustan Steel Ltd., National Coal Development Corp. Ltd., Heavy Electricals Ltd., Neyveli Lignite Corp. Ltd., Hindustan Aeronautics Ltd., Oil and Natural Gas Commission, and Scientific Advisory Committee to the Cabinet; now chairman of Management and Administrative Research Council, and Institute of Public Enterprise. Member, Board of Governors of Greycoat Foundation (England), Project Planning Committee of Bradford University (England), and Atomic Energy Commission. Professor emeritus, Osmania University.

WRITINGS: The Heavy Electrical Project—A Case Study, LIPA, 1962; *Government in Business*, Asia Publishing House, 1963; *District Administration in India*, Asia Publishing House, 1964; *Management and Control in Public Enterprise*, Asia Publishing House, 1964; *India's Defence Problem*, Orient Longmans (India), 1967; *The Central Executive*, Orient Longmans, 1974. Contributor of articles to periodicals.

WORK IN PROGRESS: Research on Indo-Soviet economic collaboration, Indian planning, administration science, and on oil and the turquoise goddess Cho-Oyu.

SIDELIGHTS: Khera is competent in French, English, and Malay. *Avocational interests:* Mountaineering, western classical music and ballet, travel.

* * *

KIELL, Norman 1916-

PERSONAL: Surname is pronounced Keel; born May 11, 1916, in Newark, N.J.; son of Louis and Anna T. Kiell; married Adele Israel, November 14, 1948; children: Jonathan, Matthew. *Education:* University of Michigan, B.A., 1939, M.A., 1947, Ed.D., 1949. *Politics:* Democrat. *Religion:* Jewish. *Home:* 2114 Seneca Dr. S., Merrick, N.Y. *Office:* Brooklyn College of the City University of New York, Bedford Ave., Brooklyn, N.Y. 11210.

CAREER: Brooklyn College of the City University of New York, Brooklyn, N.Y., 1950—, began as professor, department of student services, 1950—. Member of board of directors, South Shore Child Guidance Clinic, 1959-61. *Military service:* U.S. Army Air Forces, 1943-46. *Member:* American Psychological Association, New York State Psychological Association.

WRITINGS: The Adolescent Through Fiction: A Psychological Approach, International Universities, 1959; (editor) *Psychoanalysis, Psychology and Literature: A Bibliography*, University of Wisconsin Press, 1963; (editor) *Psychological Studies of Famous Americans*, Twayne, 1964; (editor) *The Universal Experience of Adolescence*, International Universities, 1964, 2nd edition, University of London Press, 1969; (editor) *Psychiatry and Psychology in the Visual Arts and Aesthetics: A Bibliography*, University of Wisconsin Press, 1965; (compiler) *The Psychodynamics of American Jewish Life: An Anthology*, Twayne, 1967; (editor) *The Psychology of Obesity: Dynamics and Treatment*, C. C Thomas, 1973.

SIDELIGHTS: Kiell resided in India, 1944-46, and in Copenhagen, Denmark, 1962-63.

* * *

KILBY, Clyde Samuel 1902-

PERSONAL: Born September 26, 1902, in Johnson City, Tenn.; son of James L. (a carpenter) and Sophronia C.

(Miller) Kilby; married Martha Harris, June 11, 1930. *Education:* University of Arkansas, B.A., 1929; University of Minnesota, M.A., 1931; New York University, Ph.D., 1938. *Religion:* Presbyterian. *Home:* 620 North Washington St., Wheaton, Ill. *Office:* Wheaton College, Wheaton, Ill.

CAREER: John Brown College (now University), Siloam Springs, Ark., dean, 1931-33; University of Arkansas, Fayetteville, extension instructor, 1934-35; Wheaton College, Wheaton, Ill., assistant dean of students and instructor, 1935-38, associate professor, 1938-45, professor of English, 1945—, chairman of department, 1951-66, curator, C. S. Lewis Collection, 1973—. *Member:* Modern Language Association of America, Near East Archeological Society (vice-president, 1958), Conference on Christianity and Literature (president, 1956-59), Johnsonian Circle, Lambda Iota Tau (international executive secretary, 1958-60). *Awards, honors:* Alumni grant, Wheaton College, 1948-49; Senior Teacher of the Year Award, Wheaton College, 1964; Illinois Author of the Year, Illinois Association of Teachers of English, 1973.

WRITINGS: Poetry and Life, Odyssey, 1953; *Minority of One,* Eerdmans, 1959; *Christianity and Aesthetics,* Inter-Varsity, 1961; *The Christian World of C. S. Lewis,* Eerdmans, 1964; (editor) *A Mind Awake: An Anthology of C. S. Lewis,* Harcourt, 1967; (editor) C. S. Lewis, *Letters to an American Lady,* Eerdmans, 1967; (contributor) M. R. Hillegas, editor, *Shadows of Imagination,* Southern Illinois University Press, 1969; (contributor) Carolyn Keefe, editor, *C. S. Lewis, Speaker and Teacher,* Zondervan, 1971; (with Douglas Gilbert) *C. S. Lewis: Images of his World,* Eerdmans, 1973. Book reviewer, *New York Herald-Tribune,* three years; contributor of articles to *Explicator, Studies in Philology, Word Study, Christianity Today,* and *Illinois State Historical Journal.* Contributing editor, *Christianity Today;* consulting editor, *His.*

WORK IN PROGRESS: Purposive Beauty, a manuscript dealing with the Christian aspects of aesthetics.

*   *   *

KIMBLE, David   1921-

PERSONAL: Born May 12, 1921, in Horam, England; married Helen Rankin (a Foreign Office economist), August, 1949; children: Jane, Judy, Jenny, Joy. *Education:* University of Reading, B.A., 1943; University of London, Ph.D., 1961. *Home:* Freshfields, Cookham, Berkshire, England. *Office:* University of Botswana, Lesotho and Swaziland, P.O. Roma, Maseru, Lesotho.

CAREER: Oxford University, Oxford, England, staff tutor in Berkshire, England, 1946-48, and resident tutor in Gold Coast, 1948-49; University of Ghana, Accra, director of extramural studies, 1949-62; University of East Africa University College, Dar es Salaam, Tanzania, professor of political science and director of Institute of Public Administration, 1962-68; Centre africain de formation et de recherche administratives pour le developpement, Tangier, Morocco, director of research, 1968-70; University of Botswana, Lesotho and Swaziland, Lesotho, professor of government and administration, and head of department, 1971—. *Military service:* Royal Navy Volunteer Reserve, 1943-45. *Awards, honors:* Order of the British Empire, 1962, for services to education in Ghana.

WRITINGS: The Machinery of Self-Government, Penguin, 1955; *A Political History of Ghana,* Volume I: *The Rise of Nationalism in the Gold Coast, 1850-1928,* Clar-

endon Press, 1963. Editor with wife, Helen Kimble, of ''Penguin African Series,'' 1955-60, and of *Journal of Modern African Studies,* 1963—.

WORK IN PROGRESS: Volume II of *A Political History of Ghana,* a book on the governments and politics of East Africa.

*   *   *

KINDER, James S.   1895-

PERSONAL: Born October 19, 1895, in Millersville, Mo.; son of Robert F. and Emily (Runnels) Kinder; married Mary Clare Lett, September 11, 1919 (deceased). *Education:* University College of Wales, Aberystwyth, student, 1919; Southeast Missouri State College (now University), B.S., 1920; University of Missouri, graduate study, 1922; Columbia University, A.M., 1923, Ph.D., 1934. *Office:* San Diego State University, San Diego, Calif. 92115.

CAREER: High school teacher in Missouri and Utah; Chatham College, Pittsburgh, Pa., 1923-52, professor of education, head of department, and director of film service, 1938-52; San Diego State University, San Diego, Calif., professor of education and coordinator of audiovisual services, beginning 1953, professor emeritus, 1968—. Summer visiting professor at University of Wyoming, University of Pittsburgh, Michigan State University, Pennsylvania State University, Geneva College, and University of Virginia. Assistant coordinator of Engineering Science Management War Training Program for western Pennsylvania, World War II. *Military service:* U.S. Army, American Expeditionary Forces, 1917-18. *Member:* Phi Delta Kappa.

WRITINGS: (With C. W. Odell) *Educational Tests for Use in Institutions of Higher Learning,* University of Illinois, 1930; *The Internal Administration of the Liberal Arts College,* Teachers College, 1934; (contributor) Joseph S. Roucek, editor, *Sociological Foundations of Education,* Crowell, 1942; *Audio-Visual Materials and Techniques,* American Book Co., 1950, revised edition, 1959; (with F. Dean McClusky) *The Audio-Visual Reader,* W. C. Brown, 1954; (with M. D. Alcorn and J. R. Schunert) *Better Teaching in Secretarial Schools,* Holt, 1964, revised edition, 1971; *Using Audio-Visual Materials in Education,* American Book Co., 1965; *Using Instructional Media,* Van Nostrand, 1973.

Producer with Dana Gibson of educational films, ''Mimeographing Techniques'' and ''Ditto Techniques.'' Contributor of articles and reviews to some two dozen magazines.

WORK IN PROGRESS: Travel articles for magazines.

AVOCATIONAL INTERESTS: Travel and photography.

*   *   *

KINES, Thomas Alvin   1922-
(Tom Kines)

PERSONAL: Born August 3, 1922, in Canada; son of Alvin Thomas (a postmaster) and Ethel (McNeill) Kines; married Mavis Jean Lauder (a schoolteacher), October 23, 1943; children: Donna Roberta, Wendy Lynn. *Education:* University of Manitoba, student, 1940-42; studied music and singing privately. *Politics:* Liberal (''with a small l''). *Religion:* United Church of Canada. *Home:* 2036 Leslie Ave., Ottawa, Ontario K1H 5M2, Canada .

CAREER; Royal Canadian Legion, 1946—, began in rehabilitation work, director of administration at national headquarters, Ottawa, Ontario, 1958—. Singer and musician, appearing professionally and semi-professionally since his early teens; has presented folk song concerts throughout Canada and at New York's Town Hall, 1962; founding member of Tudor Singers of Ottawa, soloist at five Mariposa Folk Festivals, and soloist with operatic and choral societies; broadcasts include weekly program, "Song Pedlar," Canadian Broadcasting Corp., 1959-68, three television series, and guest appearances on Canadian and American networks; recording artist for Elektra, Folkways, and RCA Victor albums. President, Ottawa Music Festival Association, 1960-61; vice-president, Federation of Canadian Music Festivals, 1961; CARE Canada, national director, 1966—. Chairman, National Miles for Millions Committee, 1969-72; executive member, Canadian Council for International Cooperation, 1970-73. *Military service:* Royal Canadian Navy, 1942-45; served in North Atlantic and Mediterranean; became lieutenant commander. *Member:* Guild of Canadian Folk Artists (honorary life member), American Federation of Musicians, Association of Canadian Television and Radio Artists.

WRITINGS: (Under name Tom Kines) *Songs from Shakespeare's Plays: Popular Songs of Shakespeare's Time*, Oak Press, 1965. Also author with Robert Fleming of "The Prairie Sailor," a folk cantata.

WORK IN PROGRESS: A book of songs of the Ottawa Valley, also "Merry Ballads of Robert Burns."

* * *

KING, Adele Cockshoot 1932-

PERSONAL: Born July 28, 1932, in Omaha, Neb.; daughter of Ralph Waldo (a lawyer) and Thera (Brown) Cockshoot; married Bruce A. King (a university lecturer), December 28, 1955. *Education:* University of Iowa, B.A., 1954; Sorbonne, University of Paris, graduate study, 1954-55; University of Leeds, M.A., 1960. *Home:* University of Ibadan, Ibadan, Nigeria.

CAREER: St. Luke's School and Allen-Stevenson School, New York, N.Y., teacher of French, 1960-61; University of Alberta, Calgary, Alberta, instructor in French, 1961-62; University of Ibadan, Ibadan, Nigeria, lecturer in French, 1962—. *Member:* Phi Beta Kappa.

WRITINGS: Albert Camus, Grove, 1964 (published in Scotland as *Camus*, Oliver & Boyd, 1964), published as *Camus*, Barnes & Noble, 1965; *Proust*, Oliver & Boyd, 1968. Contributor of articles to *PMLA* and *Le Musee Vivant*.

WORK IN PROGRESS: Additional research on Albert Camus; research for a book on the work of Paul Nizan.

AVOCATIONAL INTERESTS: Cooking, travel, and Nigerian art.†

* * *

KING, Donald B. 1913-

PERSONAL: Born September 3, 1913, in Bristol, Conn.; son of John (a milkman) and Kathryn (Jones) King; married Louise F. Dupraz, June 10, 1938; children: Judith, John, Peter, Jeremy, Robert, Kathryn. *Education:* Dartmouth College, B.A. (cum laude), 1935; Harvard University, Society of Fellows, 1939-41; Princeton University, Ph.D., 1940. *Religion:* Roman Catholic. *Home:* 2080 West Vista Cir., DePere, Wis. 45115. *Office:* St. Norbert College, DePere, Wis.

CAREER: Dartmouth College, Hanover, N.H., instructor

in classics, 1938-39; Pennsylvania State University, University Park, assistant professor of English, 1941-43; Beloit College, Beloit, Wis., professor of classics and history, 1946-51; College of Mount St. Joseph-on-the-Ohio, Mount St. Joseph, Ohio, chairman of Division of Humanities, 1951-67; St. Norbert College, DePere, Wis., dean of college, 1967—. North Central Association of Colleges and Secondary Schools, examiner and consultant, 1959—, commissioner, 1968-72;. Consultant in classical rhetoric to Institute of Curriculum Development, University of Nebraska, 1962. *Military service:* U.S. Navy, Naval Air Force, 1943-46. *Member:* American Association of University Professors, Classical Association of the Midwest and South, Ohio Classical Association.

WRITINGS: (Translator with H. David Rix) Erasmus, *On Copia of Words and Ideas*, Marquette University Press, 1963. Contributor to *America*, *Ave Maria*, *Catholic Mind*, *Catholic World*, and to classical journals.

WORK IN PROGRESS: Studies in the history of rhetoric.

* * *

KING, Francis P(aul) 1922-

PERSONAL: Born May 5, 1922, in Medford, Ore.; son of George Patrick and Ruth (Voruz) King. *Education:* Southern Oregon College, A.A., 1941; University of Oregon, B.S., 1942; Stanford University, M.A., 1948, Ph.D., 1953; Institut d'Etudes Politiques, Paris, France, certificate, 1952. *Home:* 225 East 74th St., New York, N.Y. 10021; and Carter Road, Pleasant Valley, N.Y. 12569. *Office:* TIAA-CREF, 730 Third Ave., New York, N.Y. 10017.

CAREER: Teachers Insurance and Annuity Association, New York, N.Y., 1953—, research officer, 1955-69, senior research officer, 1969—; College Retirement Equities Fund, New York, N.Y., research officer, 1955—. Board chairman, Tuition Exchange, Inc., Williamstown, Mass. *Military service:* U.S. Army Air Forces, 1943-46; became first lieutenant. *Member:* American Pension Conference, American Gerontological Society, Association for Institutional Research, Phi Beta Kappa. *Awards, honors:* Fulbright research grant for France, 1951.

WRITINGS: Financing the College Education of Faculty Children, Henry Holt, 1954; (with W. C. Greenough) *Retirement and Insurance Plans in American Colleges*, Columbia University Press, 1959; (with Mark H. Ingraham) *The Outer Fringe*, University of Wisconsin Press, 1965; (with Ingraham) *Mirror of Brass*, University of Wisconsin Press, 1968; (with Greenough) *Benefit Plans in American Colleges*, Columbia University Press, 1969; *Benefit Plans in Junior Colleges*, American Association of Junior Colleges, 1971.

WORK IN PROGRESS: With W. C. Greenough, a study of private pension plans and issues of public policy, under a grant from the Ford Foundation.

* * *

KING, K. DeWayne (Dewey) 1925-

PERSONAL: Born October 1, 1925, in Cando, N.D.; son of Abram R. (a plant foreman) and Vaughn (Owens) King; married Margaret Tiedeck, March 3, 1956; children: Douglas DeWayne, Everett Bruce. *Education:* University of North Dakota, B.S., 1950, M.S., 1966; Michigan State University, graduate study, 1952-53. *Politics:* Republican. *Religion:* Protestant. *Home:* 23 W. 261 Foxcroft Drive,

Glen Ellyn, Ill. *Office:* Athletic Department, Wheaton College, Wheaton, Ill. 60187.

CAREER: Assistant football coach at University of North Dakota, Grand Forks, 1949-50, Canton (Ohio) public schools, 1950-52, Michigan State University, East Lansing, 1952-54, University of Pennsylvania, Philadelphia, 1954-59, and Rutgers University, New Brunswick, N.J., 1959-67; Fellowship of Christian Athletes, North Central regional director, 1968; California State University, San Jose, football defensive coordinator, 1969, head football coach, 1970-72; Wheaton College, Wheaton, Ill., head football coach, 1973—. *Member:* American Football Coaches Association, Fellowship of Christian Athletes.

WRITINGS: Jericho—A Modern System of Pass Defense, Prentice-Hall, 1963. Author of ''Quarterbacking in Football,'' in *American Football Coaches Manual,* summer edition, 1962.

WORK IN PROGRESS: Gathering material for a book about total team defense in football.

* * *

KING, Larry L. 1929-

PERSONAL: Born January 1, 1929, in Putnam, Tex.; son of Clyde Clayton (a farmer and blacksmith) and Cora Lee (Clark) King; married second wife, Rosemarie Coumarias (a photographer), February 20, 1965; children: (first marriage) Cheryl Ann, Kerri Lee, Bradley Clayton. *Education:* Attended Texas Technological College (now Texas Tech University), 1948-50. *Politics:* Liberal-Internationalist-Democrat. *Home:* 110 Sixth St., S.W., Apartment 510, Washington, D.C.

CAREER: Newspaper reporter in Hobbs, N.M., 1949, and Midland, Tex., 1950-51, Odessa, Tex., 1952-54; Radio Station KCRS, Midland, Tex., news director, 1951-52; administrative assistant to U.S. Congressmen J. T. Rutherford, Washington, D.C., 1955-62, and James Wright, 1962-64; *Capitol Hill* (magazine), Washington, D.C., editor, 1965. *Texas Observer,* Washington correspondent. Member of Kennedy-Johnson campaign team, traveling in Southwest, 1960. *Military service:* U.S. Army, Signal Corps, writer, 1945-48; became staff sergeant.

WRITINGS: The One-Eyed Man (novel; Literary Guild selection), New American Library, 1966; *... And Other Dirty Stories,* World, 1968; *Confessions of a White Racist,* Viking, 1971; *The Old Man and Lesser Mortals,* Viking, 1974. Author of television scripts for National Educational Television Network. Contributor of articles to *New Times, Harper's, Progressive, Nation, True, Sports Illustrated,* and *Esquire.*

WORK IN PROGRESS: A novel and research for a book on Franklin D. Roosevelt as a politican; magazine articles.

BIOGRAPHICAL/CRITICAL SOURCES: New York Times Book Review, November 3, 1968; *Life,* June 11, 1971.†

* * *

KING, Louise W(ooster)

PERSONAL: Born in New York, N.Y.; daughter of David W. and Evelyn (Trapnell) King. *Education:* Bennington College, student, 1956-58; New School for Social Research, B.A., 1961. *Home:* Apartment 615, 5 West Eighth St., New York, N.Y. 10011.

WRITINGS: The Day We Were Mostly Butterflies, M.

Joseph, 1963, Doubleday, 1964; *The Velocipede Handicap,* M. Joseph, 1965; *The Rochemer Hag,* Doubleday, 1967; *The Ghosts of Umbrage,* Doubleday, 1974.

WORK IN PROGRESS: A novel, *The House Without a Number.*

* * *

KINGSBURY, John M(erriam) 1928-

PERSONAL: Born July 4, 1928, in Boston, Mass. *Education:* University of Massachusetts, B.S., 1950; Harvard University, M.A., 1952, Ph.D., 1954. *Office:* 202 Plant Science Building, Cornell University, Ithaca, N.Y. 14850.

CAREER: Brandeis University, Waltham, Mass., laboratory instructor in biology, 1952-54; New York State College of Agriculture and Life Science, Cornell University, Ithaca, assistant professor, 1954-60, associate professor, 1960-70, professor of botany, 1970—. Marine Biology Laboratories, Woods Hole, Mass., instructor, 1958-62, special lecturer, 1963—; New York State Veterinary College, Cornell University, Ithaca, lecturer in phytotoxicology, 1963—. Founder and director, Shoals Marine Laboratory, 1966—. *Member:* American College of Veterinary Toxicologists (fellow). *Awards, honors:* National Science Foundation fellow, 1957.

WRITINGS: Poisonous Plants of the United States and Canada, Prentice-Hall, 1964; *Deadly Harvest: Common Poisonous Plants,* Holt, 1965; *Seaweeds of Cape Cod and the Islands,* Chatham-Viking, 1969; *The Rocky Shore,* Chatham-Viking, 1970. Contributor to *Collier's Encyclopedia,* 1970, and to *Funk & Wagnalls New Encyclopedia,* 1972.

* * *

KIRBY, E(dward) Stuart 1909-

PERSONAL: Born December, 1909, in Yokohama, Japan; son of Charles Edward and Edith (Wakeling) Kirby; married Ruth Isaacs, 1943; children: Rowan Judith, Miriam Hazel, Laurence Arnold. *Education:* Ecole Superieure de Commerce, Neuchatel, Switzerland, student, 1926-28; London School of Economics and Political Science, B.Sc., 1933, Ph.D., 1938; Stanford University, graduate study, 1933-34. *Office:* Asian Institute of Technology, Bangkok, Thailand.

CAREER: International Institute of Agriculture, Rome, Italy, economist, 1934-35; Fukushima Kosho and Tohoku Imperial University, Japan, professor of economics, 1935-39; University of Hong Kong, British Crown Colony, professor of economics and head of department of economics and political science, 1948-65; University of Aston, Birmingham, England, professor of economics, 1965-72, professor of international economics, 1972-74; Asian Institute of Technology, Bangkok, Thailand, professor of economics, 1975—. Japan Society of Hong Kong, chairman; Hong Kong Management Association, member of general policy committee; Federation of Hong Kong Industries, member. *Military service:* Indian Army, 1940-46; became lieutenant colonel. *Member:* Royal Economic Society, Royal Central Asian Society.

WRITINGS: Essay on Japanese Culture, UNESCO, 1950; *Introduction to the Economic History of China,* Macmillan, 1953; (editor) *Contemporary China,* five volumes, Oxford University Press, 1956-63; *Economic Development in East Asia,* Allen & Unwin, 1968; *The Soviet Far East,* Macmillan, 1971. Also editor of *Hong Kong Economic Papers,* Oxford University Press, 1958-65.

KIRK, Richard (Edmund) 1931-
(Jeffrey Church)

PERSONAL: Born November 28, 1931, in Olney, Ill.; son of Charles Edmund (a high school teacher) and Arva (a high school teacher; maiden name, Ricker) Kirk; married Phyllis Wishard (juvenile editor, David-Stewart Publishing Co.), February 2, 1957; children: Kevin Edmund, Kathleen Ann. Education: Attended Indiana University, 1954-55, and University of Illinois, 1956-57. Politics: Independent. Home: 1001 Lawndale Dr., Greenwood, Ind. 46142. Office: David-Stewart Publishing Co., 3600 Washington Blvd., Indianapolis, Ind. 46205.

CAREER: Bobbs-Merrill Co., Inc., Indianapolis, Ind., assistant editor, 1957-59; Mayflower Transit Co., Indianapolis, Ind., correspondent, 1959-61; David-Stewart Publishing Co., Indianapolis, Ind., managing editor, 1961—. Military service: U.S. Air Force, 1950-53.

WRITINGS: (With Clara Lee Tanner) Our Indian Heritage—Arts That Live Today, Follett, 1961; (under pseudonym Jeffrey Church, with Willis Peterson) Nature's Lumberjack, Follett, 1961; Birds in Flight, Follett, 1962; The Lightning and the Rainbow, Follett, 1962; (under pseudonym Jeffrey Church, with Lewis Wayne Walker) The Desert Water Hole, Follett, 1962; (with Ethel Rosenberg) Living Indiana History: Heartland of America, David-Stewart, 1965. Contributor of short stories and articles to periodicals. Editor, "Curriculum Enrichment Series."

WORK IN PROGRESS: A juvenile novel—a futuristic tale about two boys.

SIDELIGHTS: Kirk speaks, reads, and writes French "feebly." Avocational interests: Reading, chess, music, golf, a fishing trip in the north every summer. "Although I've written largely on nature subjects, I never watch birds unless they watch me first."†

*   *   *

KIRK, Ruth (Kratz) 1925-

PERSONAL: Born May 7, 1925, in Los Angeles, Calif.; daughter of Reginald P. (an engineer) and Esther (a physician; maiden name, Cumberland) Kratz; married Louis G. Kirk (a National Park Service naturalist), September 3, 1945; children: Bruce, Wayne. Education: Attended Occidental College two years. Home: Port Angeles, Wash. Office: Peninsula College, Port Angeles, Wash.

CAREER: Peninsula College, Port Angeles, Wash., instructor in photography, 1963—. Writer and natural historian.

WRITINGS: (With Ansel Adams and Nancy Newhall) Death Valley, Five Associates (San Francisco), 1954; Exploring Death Valley, Stanford University Press, 1956, 2nd edition, 1965; The Olympic Seashore, Olympic Natural History Association, 1962; Exploring the Olympic Peninsula, University of Washington Press, 1964; Sigemi, A Japanese Village Girl (juvenile), Harcourt, 1965; The Olympics Rain Forest, University of Washington Press, 1966; Japan: Crossroads of East and West (juvenile), Nelson, 1966; David, Young Chief of the Quileutes: An American Indian Today, Harcourt, 1967; Exploring Mount Ranier, University of Washingto Press, 1968; Laura of Mexico, Singer, 1969; The Oldest Man in America: An Adventure in Archaeology, Harcourt, 1970; Desert Life, Natural History Press, 1970; Yellowstone: The First National Park, Atheneum, 1974; (with R. D. Daugherty) Hunters of the Whale: Adventures in Northwest Coast Archaeology, Morrow,

1974; (with Archie Satterfield) California Coast and Desert, Graphic Arts Center, 1974.

SIDELIGHTS: The author and her husband traveled in England, Scotland, and Wales in 1963, and in Southeast Asia and Japan in 1964, as advisers on national park development for the International Commission on National Parks. They have lived at ranger stations from the Mexican border to the Canadian, in such varied areas as Death Valley, Calif., Organ Pipe Cactus, Ariz., Olympic National Park, Wash., and the Badlands of North Dakota.

BIOGRAPHICAL SOURCES: Occidental College Alumnus, January, 1965.†

*   *   *

KIRK-GREENE, Christopher Walter Edward 1926-

PERSONAL: Born July 19, 1926, in Tunbridge Wells, Kent, England; son of Leslie (a civil engineer) and Helen (Millard) Kirk-Greene. Education: Christ Church, Oxford, 1945-48, M.A., 1952. Address: Eastbourne College, Eastbourne, Sussex, England.

CAREER: Lycee Bertholet, Annecy, France, assistant in English, 1948-49; Eastbourne College, Eastbourne, Sussex, England, modern languages master (French and German), 1949—, head of modern languages department, 1962—. Member: Modern Languages Association, East India, Sports and Public Schools Club (London).

WRITINGS: An Advanced French Vocabulary, Methuen, 1958; Sixty Modern French Unseens, Longmans, Green, 1963; Les Mots-Amis et les faux-amis, Methuen, 1968; Lisez! Regardez! Repondez!, Basil Blackwell, 1973; A First Book of French Idioms, Basil Blackwell, 1973; Lectures modernes, Basil Blackwell, in press.

AVOCATIONAL INTERESTS: Travel, and sports.

*   *   *

KIRSCH, Arthur C(lifford) 1932-

PERSONAL: Born August 22, 1932, in New York, N.Y.; son of Louis (an engineer) and Janet (Halperin) Kirsch. Education: Cornell University, B.A., 1953; Oxford University, B.Litt., 1955; Princeton University, Ph.D., 1961. Office: Department of English, University of Virginia, Charlottesville, Va.

CAREER: Princeton University, Princeton, N.J., instructor in English, 1960-63, became assistant professor; currently professor of English, University of Virginia, Charlottsville. Military service: U.S. Army, Quartermaster Corps, 1955-57; became first lieutenant. Member: Modern Language Association of America, Phi Beta Kappa. Awards, honors: Fulbright fellow, 1953-55; Princeton bicentennial preceptor, 1964-66.

WRITINGS: Dryden's Heroic Drama, Princeton University Press, 1965; (editor with Alan S. Downer) The Restoration, Dell, 1965; (editor) Literary Criticism of John Dryden, University of Nebraska Press, 1967; Jacobean Dramatic Perspectives, University Press of Virginia, 1972. Contributor to professional journals.

WORK IN PROGRESS: Research for a book on seventeenth-century tragedy and tragicomedy; an edition of Dryden's criticism, for University of Nebraska Press.†

*   *   *

KLAFS, Carl E. 1911-

PERSONAL: Surname is pronounced Kloffs; born August

29, 1911, in Chicago, Ill.; son of Ernest C. (a teacher) and Bertha A. (Sputh) Klafs; married Jean Louise Welty (an interior decorator), December 1, 1934; children: Cynthia Ann Klafs Weber, Keith Lance. *Education:* Normal College, American Gymnastic Union, B.P.E., 1933; Indiana University, B.S., 1941; Montana State University (now University of Montana), M.A., 1950; University of Southern California, Ph.D., 1956. *Politics:* Republican. *Religion:* Protestant. *Home:* 439 El Modena Ave., Newport Beach, Calif. 92660. *Office:* California State University, Long Beach, Calif.

CAREER: Elementary school teacher, 1935-56; secondary school teacher, 1936-45; various administrative positions in elementary, secondary, and junior high schools, 1945-56; Normal College, American Gymnastic Union, Indianapolis, Ind., instructor in physical education, 1932-35; Occidental College, Los Angeles, Calif., assistant professor of health and physical education, 1950-54; California State University, Long Beach, 1956—, now professor of physical education. Visiting lecturer at Montana State University (now University of Montana), 1948, 1949, and Occidental College, 1949, 1950. *Member:* American College of Sports Medicine (fellow; chairman of national convention), Southwest America College of Sports Medicine (president), Phi Epsilon Kappa (former national vice-president), Delta Epsilon, Phi Kappa Phi. *Awards, honors:* Phi Epsilon Kappa Hall of Fame; Outstanding Professor Award, California State University, Long Beach, 1969.

WRITINGS: (With Daniel Arnheim) *Modern Principles of Athletic Training*, Mosby, 1963, 3rd edition, 1973; (with M. J. Lyon) *The Female Athlete*, Mosby, 1973. Also author of *Test-Manual for Athletic Injury Instructors.* Also author of several Montana State education manuals.

WORK IN PROGRESS: Writing on aspects of health as related to athletes.

SIDELIGHTS: Klafs visited twenty-two universities and colleges and various laboratories on a year-long world trip that started in May, 1965. He also visited fourteen university laboratories in Europe during the fall of 1973.

*   *   *

KLEIMAN, Robert   1918-

PERSONAL: Born October 1, 1918, in New York, N.Y.; son of Louis and Rose (Newman) Kleiman. *Education:* University of Michigan, A.B., 1939. *Home:* 390 West End Ave., New York, N.Y. 10024. *Agent:* Julian Bach, Jr., 3 East 48th St., New York, N.Y. 10017. *Office: New York Times*, 229 West 43rd St., New York, N.Y. 10036.

CAREER: Washington Post, Washington, D.C., reporter, 1939-40; *New York Journal of Commerce*, New York, N.Y., White House correspondent, 1941; U.S. Office of War Information, Washington, D.C., White House correspondent, Voice of America, 1942, chief of psychological warfare teams, 1943-45; *U.S. News and World Report*, Washington, D.C., associate editor, 1945-48, roving correspondent, Moscow and east Europe, 1947, correspondent and chief of bureau, Germany, 1948-51, correspondent and chief of bureau, Paris, 1951-62; Columbia Broadcasting System News, New York, N.Y., correspondent and chief of bureau, Paris, 1962-63; *New York Times*, New York, N.Y., member of editorial board, 1963—. Research associate, International Institute for Strategic Studies, London, 1972-73. *Member:* American Academy of Arts and Sciences, Authors Guild, Council on Foreign Relations, Confrerie des Chevaliers du Tastevin, International Institute

for Strategic Studies (London), Overseas Press Club, Overseas Writers (Washington, D.C.), Century Association, Sigma Delta Chi, Phi Beta Kappa. *Awards, honors:* Alicia Patterson Foundation Fellowship Award, 1972-73.

WRITINGS: (Contributor) A. Settel, editor, *This is Germany*, Sloane, 1950; *Atlantic Crisis: American Diplomacy Confronts a Resurgent Europe*, Norton, 1964; (contributor) *NATO In Quest of Cohesion*, Praeger, 1965. Contributor to *Reader's Digest, New York Times Magazine*, and *New York Times Book Review.*

*   *   *

KLEIN, Frederic Shriver   1904-

PERSONAL: Born October 22, 1904, in York, Pa.; son of Harry Martin John (a professor of history) and Winifred (Shriver) Klein; married Florence Haenle (a musician), June 7, 1932; married second wife, Gloria Whitney (a musician), June 30, 1972; children: (first marriage) Joan Haenle (Mrs. Richard K. Weidman), Frederic Ferree. *Education:* Franklin and Marshall College, A.B., 1923; Columbia University, M.A., 1927. *Home:* 1050 Maple Ave., Lancaster, Pa. 17603. *Office:* Franklin and Marshall College, Lancaster, Pa.

CAREER: New York University, New York, N.Y., instructor in history at Washington Square College, 1927-28; Franklin and Marshall College, Lancaster, Pa., 1928—, began as instructor, professor of history, 1946—. Director, Students Foreign Travel Service, 1932-38; consultant, Civil Aeronautics Authority, 1942-44; president, National Association of Colleges and Universities in Civilian Pilot Training, 1942-45; director of public relations, James Buchanan Foundation, 1946-54; president, Lancaster Symphony Orchestra, 1947-48; president, Union Mills Homestead Foundation, Inc., 1964-65. *Wartime service:* Civil Air Patrol, commander of Squadron 304, with rank of major, 1941-46. *Member:* Maryland Historical Society, Pennsylvania Historical Association, Lancaster Rotary Club. *Awards, honors:* Alumni Medal, Franklin and Marshall College, 1965.

WRITINGS: The Spiritual and Educational Background of Franklin and Marshall College, Franklin and Marshall College Press, 1939; *Lancaster County, 1841-1941*, Lancaster County National Bank (Lancaster, Pa.), 1941; *Just South of Gettysburg*, Newman, 1963; (with Charles X. Carlson) *Old Lancaster*, Early America Series, 1964; (editor with John Howard Carrell) Henry Kyd Douglas, *The Douglas Diary: Student Days at Franklin and Marshall College 1856-58*, Franklin and Marshall College Press, 1973. Contributor to *Civil War Times Illustrated, American Heritage* and historical journals.

AVOCATIONAL INTERESTS: Music, early Americana, and preservation of historic sites and materials.

*   *   *

KLEIN, H(erbert) Arthur

PERSONAL: Married Mina Cooper; children: Laura, David. *Education:* Stanford University, A.B.; Occidental College, M.A.; graduate study at Columbia University, University of California, Los Angeles, University of Berlin, Handelshochschule, Berlin. *Residence:* Malibu, Calif.

CAREER: Writer (has done newspaper work, publicity, copywriting, feature writing). Council member, Malibu Township. *Member:* Authors League of America, National Association of Science Writers, American Civil Liberties

Union, Friends of the University of California at Los Angeles Library, Los Angeles County Museum of Art, Phi Beta Kappa.

WRITINGS—All published by Lippincott, except where noted: (Editor and author of commentary) *Graphic Worlds of Peter Bruegel the Elder*, Dover, 1963; *Masers and Lasers*, 1963; *Surfing*, 1965; *Bioluminescence*, 1965; *Fuel Cells: An Introduction to Electrochemistry*, 1966; *Holography, With an Introduction to the Optics of Diffraction, Interference, and Phase Differences*, 1970; *The New Gravitation: Key to Incredible Energies*, 1971; *Surf-Riding*, 1972; *The World of Measurements: Everyone's Guide to Masterpieces, Mysteries, and Muddles of Metrology*, Simon & Schuster, 1974.

With wife, Mina C. Klein: (Editors and contributors) *Surf's Up! An Anthology of Surfing*, Bobbs-Merrill, 1966; *Great Structures of the World*, World Publishing, 1968; *Peter Bruegel the Elder: Artist of Abundance*, Macmillan, 1968; *Temple Beyond Time: The Story of the Site of King Solomon's Temple*, Van Nostrand, 1970; *Israel, Land of the Jews: A Survey of Forty-Three Centuries*, Bobbs-Merrill, 1972; *Kaethe Kollwitz: Life in Art*, Holt, 1972; *The Kremlin: Citadel of History*, Macmillan, 1973; (editors) B. Traven, *The Kidnapped Saint and Other Stories*, Lawrence Hill, 1974.

Translator—With Mina C. Klein and others, and editor and annotator: Wilhelm Busch, *Hypocritical Helena, Plus a Plenty of Other Pleasures* (verse), Dover, 1962; Wilhelm Busch, *Max and Moritz, With Many More Mischief Makers More or Less Human or Approximately Animal* (verse), Dover, 1962.

Writer and producer of sound film, "Bruegel's Seven Deadly Sins," 1963. Contributor of German prose and poetry translations to periodicals.

WORK IN PROGRESS: Sex and the Swastika, with Mina C. Klein, a broad survey of male-female and family relationships and policies in Germany, 1933-45, completion expected 1976.

SIDELIGHTS: Klein has travelled widely in Europe. *Avocational interests:* Swimming, surfing, diving, foreign travel, music, and pictorial art (especially graphic art).

* * *

KLEIN, Woody 1929-

PERSONAL: Born December 17, 1929; son of Albert M. Klein; married Audry Lehman, February 4, 1962; children: Wendy Lehman. *Education:* Dartmouth College, B.A., 1951; Columbia University, M.S. in Journalism, 1952.

CAREER: Reporter for *Mount Vernon Daily Argus*, Mount Vernon, N.Y., 1954, and *Washington Post and Times Herald*, Washington, D.C., 1954-56; American Broadcasting Co., New York, N.Y., news writer, 1956; *New York World-Telegram and Sun*, New York, N.Y., reporter, 1956-65. City official in New York City, 1965-69, in the area of housing and development. Currently at IBM. Instructor in journalism at New York University, 1960—, and New School for Social Research, 1965. Consultant to "David Brinkley's Journal," National Broadcasting Co. Television, 1961, and to Office of Economic Opportunity on New York anti-poverty programs, 1965—. Moderator and panel member on radio and television programs on municipal affairs, housing, and civil rights. *Military service:* U.S. Army, public information officer, 1952-54; became first lieutenant.

MEMBER: Newspaper Guild and Newspaper Reporters Association (both New York), Sigma Delta Chi, Kappa Tau Alpha. *Awards, honors:* Page One Award of Newspaper Guild of New York for series, "I Lived in a Slum," 1960; Alumni Award, Graduate School of Journalism, Columbia University, 1962; other awards from Newspaper Reporters Association for series on Puerto Rican migration to New York, 1961, National Conference of Christians and Jews, 1965.

WRITINGS: Let in the Sun, Macmillan, 1964; *Lindsay's Promise: The Dream That Failed: A Personal Account*, Macmillan, 1970. Contributor to *Nation* and *Pageant*.†

* * *

KLING, Simcha 1922-

PERSONAL: Born January 27, 1922; son of Eli (a real estate agent) and Anna (Niman) Kling; married Edith Leeman, June 15, 1947; children: Elana, Adina, Reena. *Education:* University of Cincinnati, B.A., 1943; Columbia University, M.A., 1947; Jewish Theological Seminary of America, M.H.L., 1948, D.H.L., 1958. *Politics:* Democrat. *Home:* 2240 Millvale, Louisville, Ky. *Office:* Adath Jeshurun, 2401 Woodbourne Ave., Louisville, Ky.

CAREER: B'nai Amoona, St. Louis, Mo., assistant rabbi, education director, 1948-51; Beth David, Greensboro, N.C., rabbi, 1951-65; Adath Jeshurun, Louisville, Ky., rabbi, 1965—. *Member:* Rabbinical Assembly of America, American-Israel Public Affairs Committee, American Jewish Historical Society, North Carolina Association of Rabbis (president, 1956-58), B'nai B'rith, Louisville Board of Rabbis (president, 1971).

WRITINGS: Nachum Sokolow: Servant of His People, Herzl, 1960; *Menahem Ussishkin: The Mighty Warrior*, David, 1965; (compiler) *A Sense of Duty*, Department of Adult Jewish Education, B'nai B'rith, 1969; *Joseph Klausner*, Yoseloff, 1970. Contributor of biographical studies, essays, and translations to *Reconstructionist*, *Jewish Spectator*, other Jewish periodicals. Contributor to *Herzl Yearbook*.

* * *

KLOS, Frank W(illiam), Jr. 1924-

PERSONAL: Surname is pronounced to rhyme with "loss"; born July 20, 1924, in Wheeling, W. Va.; son of Frank William (a traffic manager) and Irma (Bayha) Klos; married Sarah Eleanor Wolfe, May 24, 1946; children: Kathryn Louise, Eric Gilbert, Beverly Anne, Thomas Andrew. *Education:* Gettysburg College, A.B., 1946; Lutheran Theological Seminary, Gettysburg, Pa., B.D., 1949, S.T.M., 1961; Temple University, M.Ed., 1969, doctoral studies, 1970—. *Politics:* Republican. *Home:* 84 Oreland Pl., Oreland, Pa. 19075. *Office:* Board of Parish Education, 2900 Queen Lane, Philadelphia, Pa. 19129.

CAREER: Ordained Lutheran minister, 1949; pastor at Martinsburg, W. Va., 1949-55; Lutheran Church in America, Division for Parish Services, field secretary, 1955-58, audiovisuals editor, 1958-60, editor of school of religion and catechetical materials, 1960-70, senior editor, 1970—. *Military service:* U.S. Army, 1943-45.

WRITINGS: (With Dale S. Bringman) *Prayer and the Devotional Life*, Lutheran Church Press, 1964; (with Marbury Anderson) *I Believe in Jesus Christ*, Lutheran Church Press, 1965; (with Robert Herhold) *Guidelines for Choosing a Career*, Lutheran Church Press, 1965; (with

Ralph D. Heim) *Four Pictures of Christ*, Lutheran Church Press, 1965; *Confirmation and First Communion: A Study Book*, Fortress Press, 1968; *A Companion for Reading and Understanding the Good News*, Fortress Press, 1972. Writer of scripts for three filmstrips on religious subjects and of three folk songs for youth hymnals. Contributor of cartoons to *Resource* and *Lutheran*.

WORK IN PROGRESS: A book on prayer.

AVOCATIONAL INTERESTS: The Civil War era, art, and Indian lore.

*   *   *

KNAPP, Bettina (Liebowitz)

PERSONAL: Born in New York, N.Y.; daughter of David and Emily (Gresser) Liebowitz; married Russell S. Knapp (a lawyer); children: Albert, Charles. *Education:* Barnard College, B.A., 1947; Columbia University, M.A., 1949, Ph.D., 1955; also studied at Sorbonne, University of Paris. *Residence:* New York, N.Y. *Agent:* McIntosh & Otis, Inc., 18 East 41st St., New York, N.Y. 10017. *Office:* Hunter College of the City University of New York, 68th St. and Park Ave., New York, N.Y.

CAREER: Columbia University, New York, N.Y., lecturer, 1952-61; Hunter College of the City University of New York, New York, N.Y., assistant professor of French, 1961—.

WRITINGS: Louis Jouvet: Man of the Theatre, Columbia University Press, 1957; (co-author) *That Was Yvette*, Holt, 1964; *Louise Labe*, Lettres Modernes, 1964; *Cymbalum Mundi*, Twayne, 1965; *Aristide Bruant: A Biography*, Nouvelles Editions Debresse, 1968; *Jean Genet: A Critical Study*, Twayne, 1968; *Antonin Artaud: Man of Vision*, David Lewis, 1969; *Jean Cocteau: A Critical Study*, Twayne, 1970; *Jean Racine: Mythos and Renewal in Modern Theatre*, University of Alabama Press, 1971; *Georges Duhamel: A Critical Study*, Twayne, 1972; *Celine: Man of Hate*, University of Alabama Press, 1974; *Off-Stage Voices*, Whitston Press, 1974.

Contributor of articles on the French theater to *Columbia Encyclopedia* and *Grolier Encyclopedia*, and to periodicals, including *Tulane Drama Review*, *Yale French Studies*, *Horizon*, *French Review*, *Show*, *Today's Speech*, *First Stage*, *French News*, *Revue d'Histoire du Theatre*, and *Modern Drama*.

*   *   *

KNEESE, Allen V(ictor)   1930-

PERSONAL: Born April 5, 1930; married, 1956. *Education:* Southwest Texas State College, B.S., 1951; University of Colorado, M.A., 1952; University of Indiana, Ph.D., 1956. *Home:* 4244 South 35th St., Arlington, Va.

CAREER: University of New Mexico, Albuquerque, assistant professor of economics, 1956-58; Federal Reserve Bank of Kansas City, Kansas City, Mo., industrial economist, 1958-60; Resources for the Future, Washington, D.C., research associate and director of water program, 1961—. Stanford University, Stanford, Calif., associate professor of economics, 1963. *Member:* American Economic Association.

WRITINGS: Water Resources Development and Use, Federal Reserve Bank of Kansas City, 1959; *Water Pollution: Economic Aspects*, Resources for the Future, 1962; (co-author) *A Water Quality Program for the Delaware Basin*, Delaware River Basin Commission, 1964; *The Economics of Water Quality Management*, Johns Hopkins Press, 1964; (co-author) *Problems and Opportunities in Managing Environmental Quality*, Resources for the Future, 1965; (with O. C. Herfindahl) *Quality of the Environment: An Economic Approach to Some Problems Using Land, Water, and Air*, Resources for the Future, 1965; *Water Pollution: Economic Aspects and Research Needs*, Resources for the Future, 1968; *The Economics of Regional Water Management*, Johns Hopkins Press, 1968; (with B. T. Bower) *Managing Water Quality: Economics, Technology, Institutions*, Johns Hopkins Press, 1968.

(With R. U. Ayres and R. C. d'Arge) *Economics and the Environment: A Materials Balance Approach*, Johns Hopkins Press, 1970; (with Peter Bohm) *The Economics of Environment*, Macmillan (London), 1971; (editor) *Managing the Environment: International Economic Cooperation for Pollution Control*, Praeger, 1971; (editor) *Environmental Quality Analysis: Theory and Method in the Social Sciences*, Johns Hopkins Press, 1972; *Controlling Air and Water Pollution: Economic Incentives Versus Regulation*, Brookings, 1974. Co-editor, *Water Resources Research Journal*. Contributor to other professional journals.†

*   *   *

KNICKERBOCKER, Charles H(errick)   1922-

PERSONAL: Born April 18, 1922, in Syracuse, N.Y.; son of William Skinkle and Frances (Cutler) Knickerbocker; married Julia Cheyney, July 1, 1944 (divorced March 17, 1969); married Gretchen W. Buendia, October 10, 1969 (divorced November 18, 1971); married Charlotte Erma Woodworth, December 19, 1971; children: (first marriage) Edward Ripley, Wendy, Barbara. *Education:* University of the South, B.S., 1943; University of Pennsylvania, M.D., 1946. *Politics:* Republican. *Religion:* Episcopal. *Residence:* Salisbury Cove, Me. *Agent:* Bill Berger Associates, Inc., 535 East 72nd St., New York, N.Y. 10021. *Office address:* P.O. Box 47, Bar Harbor, Me. 04609.

CAREER: Physician specializing in practice of internal medicine, Bar Harbor, Me., 1953—. Mount Desert Hospital, Bar Harbor, Me., member of medical staff, director of Heart-Lung Unit, chief of medical service, and utilization review officer; Hancock County (Me.) medical examiner, 1953-61. *Military service:* U.S. Army, 1943-45; attached to Surgeon General's Office, 1951-53, became captain. *Member:* American Medical Association, American Society of Internal Medicine, Authors Guild, Maine Medical Society, Hancock County Medical Society (secretary, 1948-51; president, 1958), Phi Beta Kappa.

WRITINGS—Novels: *The Boy Came Back*, Wyn, 1951; *Juniper Island*, Random House, 1958; *The Dynasty*, Doubleday, 1962; *Summer Doctor*, Doubleday, 1963; *The Hospital War* (novel), Doubleday, 1966.

Nonfiction: *Hide and Seek*, Doubleday, 1968; *The Minister's Daughter* (nonfiction), Dorrance, 1974.

Contributor to *Adventure*, *Maclean's Magazine*, *Bluebook*, *General Practitioner*, *Medical Economics*, *Reader's Digest*, and *True*.

WORK IN PROGRESS: Biography of Franklin Pierce.

*   *   *

KNIGHT, G(eorge) Wilson   1897-

PERSONAL: Born September 19, 1897, in Sutton, Surrey, England; son of George and Caroline Louisa (Jackson)

Knight. *Education:* Attended Dulwich College; St. Edmund Hall, Oxford, B.A., 1923, M.A., 1931. *Home:* Caroline House, Streatham Rise, Exeter, Devonshire, England.

CAREER: Master at Seaford House, Littlehampton, England, 1920, St. Peter's School, Seaford, England, 1921, Hawtreys School, Westgate on Sea, England, 1923-25; Dean Close School, Cheltenham, England, 1925-31; University of Toronto, Trinity College, Toronto, Ontario, Chancellors' Professor of English, 1931-40; Stowe School, Buckinghamshire, England, assistant master, 1941-46; University of Leeds, Leeds, England, reader in English literature, 1946-55, professor of English literature, 1955-62, professor emeritus, 1962—. Visiting lecturer at University College of West Indies, 1951, University of Cape Town, 1952, University of Chicago, 1963, Stratford (Ontario) Festival Seminars, 1963 and 1967. Byron Foundation Lecturer at University of Nottingham, 1953; Clark Lecturer at Trinity College, Cambridge, 1962. Shakespearian actor and producer, under name Wilson Knight, at Hart House Theatre, Toronto, 1931-40, Westminster Theatre, London, 1941, University of Leeds, 1946-60. *Military service:* Royal Engineers, Signal Service, 1916-20. *Member:* Royal Society of Literature (fellow), Spiritualist Association of Great Britain. *Awards, honors:* Fellow of St. Edmund Hall, Oxford, 1966; D.Litt., University of Sheffield, 1967, University of Exeter, 1968; Commander, Order of the British Empire, 1968.

WRITINGS: Myth and Miracle, Burrows & Co., 1929; *The Wheel of Fire: Interpretation of Shakespeare's Tragedy*, Oxford University Press, 1930, 6th edition, introduction by T. S. Eliot, World Publishing, 1964; *The Imperial Theme: Further Interpretations of Shakespeare's Tragedies Including the Roman Plays*, Oxford University Press, 1931, 3rd edition, Methuen, 1958; *The Shakespearian Tempest, with a Chart of Shakespeare's Dramatic Universe*, Oxford University Press, 1932, 3rd edition, Methuen, 1960; *The Christian Renaissance: With Interpretations of Dante, Shakespeare, and Goethe, and New Discussions of Oscar Wilde and the Gospel of Thomas*, Macmillan, 1933, revised edition, Methuen, 1962; *Principles of Shakespearian Production*, Macmillan, 1936, enlarged edition published as *Shakespearian Production*, Northwestern University Press, 1964; *Atlantic Crossing* (autobiography), Dent, 1936; *The Burning Oracle*, Oxford University Press, 1939, revised edition published as *Poets of Action*, Methuen, 1967; *This Sceptred Isle: Shakespeare's Message for England at War*, Macmillan, 1940; *The Starlit Dome: Studies in the Poetry of Vision*, Oxford University Press, 1941; *Chariot of Wrath*, Faber, 1942; *The Olive and the Sword: A Study of England's Shakespeare*, Oxford University Press, 1944; *The Dynasty of Stowe*, Fortune Press, 1945; *Hiroshima*, Dakers, 1946; *The Crown of Life: Essays in Interpretation of Shakespeare's Final Plays*, Oxford University Press, 1947; *Christ and Nietzsche*, Staples Press, 1948.

Lord Byron: Christian Virtues, Routledge & Kegan Paul, 1952, Oxford University Press, 1953; *The Last of the Incas* (play), privately printed, 1954; *Laureate of Peace: On the Genius of Alexander Pope*, Routledge & Kegan Paul, 1954, Oxford University Press, 1955, reissued as *The Poetry of Pope: Laureate of Peace*, Barnes & Noble, 1965; *The Mutual Flame: On Shakespeare's Sonnets and The Phoenix and the Turtle*, Methuen, 1955; *Lord Byron's Marriage*, Macmillan, 1957; *The Sovereign Flower*, Macmillan, 1958; (contributor) G. Handley-Taylor, editor, *John Masefield, O.M.*, Cranbrook Tower Press, 1960; *The Golden Labyrinth*, Norton, 1962; *Ibsen*, Oliver & Boyd, 1962, published as *Henrik Ibsen*, Grove Press, 1963; *The Saturnian Quest*, Barnes & Noble, 1964; *Byron and Shakespeare*, Barnes & Noble, 1966; *Shakespeare and Religion*, Barnes & Noble, 1967; (editor and author of introduction) W. F. Jackson Knight, *Elysion*, Barnes & Noble, 1970; *Neglected Power*, Routledge & Kegan Paul, 1971.

Tape recordings: "Shakespeare's Rhetoric," "Byron's Rhetoric," "Shakespeare and the English Language," distributed by Jeffrey Norton.

Contributor to *Times Literary Supplement* (London), *Review of English Studies*, *Contemporary Review*, and other periodicals.

* * *

KNIGHT, James A. 1918-

PERSONAL: Born October 20, 1918, in St. George, S.C.; son of Thomas S. and Carolyn Knight; married Sally Templeman; children: Steven Allen. *Education:* Wofford College, A.B., 1941; Duke University Divinity School, B.D., 1944; Vanderbilt University, M.D., 1952; Tulane University, M.P.H., 1962. *Office:* School of Medicine, Tulane University, New Orleans, La. 70112.

CAREER: Ordained minister of Methodist church, 1944; Grady Memorial Hospital, Atlanta, Ga., intern, 1952-53; Duke University Hospital, Durham, N.C., assistant resident in pediatrics, 1953-54; Tulane University Service of Charity Hospital, New Orleans, La., resident in psychiatry, 1955-57, chief resident, 1958; Baylor University College of Medicine, Houston, Tex., instructor, 1958, assistant professor, 1959-61, associate professor of psychiatry, 1961, assistant dean, 1960-61; Tulane University School of Medicine, New Orleans, La., associate professor of psychiatry, 1961-63; Union Theological Seminary, New York, N.Y., Harkness Professor of Psychiatry and Religion, 1963-64; Tulane University School of Medicine, New Orleans, La., associate dean, and professor of psychiatry, 1964—. Licensed to practice medicine in Tennessee, Florida, Louisiana, Texas, and New York; certified in psychiatry, American Board of Psychiatry and Neurology, 1960. *Military service:* U.S. Navy, chaplain, 1944-46.

MEMBER: Academy of Psychoanalysis, Institute of Religion and Health, American Psychiatric Association, Group for the Advancement of Psychiatry, Phi Beta Kappa. *Awards, honors:* Travel fellowship with World Health Organization, 1961.

WRITINGS: (Contributor) Harold I. Lief and others, editors, *The Psychological Basis of Medical Practice*, Hoeber Medical Division, Harper, 1963; *A Psychiatrist Looks at Religion and Health*, Abingdon, 1964; (with W. E. Davis) *Manual for the Comprehensive Community Mental Health Clinic*, C. C Thomas, 1964; (with Margaretta Bowers, Edgar Jackson, and Lawrence LeShan) *Counseling the Dying*, Nelson, 1964; *Allergy and Human Emotions*, C. C Thomas, 1967; (editor with Ralph Slovenko) *Motivations in Play, Games, and Sports*, C. C Thomas, 1967; *For Love of Money: Human Behavior and Money*, Lippincott, 1968; *Conscience and Guilt*, Appleton, 1969; *Medical Student: Doctor in the Making*, Appleton, 1973.

Contributor of more than fifty articles to psychiatric and other medical journals and to *Pastoral Psychology*. Member of editorial board, *Annals of Allergy*.

KNIGHT, Paul Emerson 1925-

PERSONAL: Born August 3, 1925, in North Adams, Mass.; son of Harold Carlton and Ruth (Emerson) Knight; married Thelma Isabel Ward, January 31, 1953; children: Harold Ward, Paula. *Education:* Harvard University, B.A. (honors), 1950. *Residence:* Jaffrey, N.H. *Office:* Drug Enforcement Administration, American Embassy, Paris, APO N.Y. 09777.

CAREER: U.S. Treasury Department, Bureau of Narcotics agent, 1950-62, serving abroad, 1952-62; Pan American Airways, regional security officer with headquarters in Beirut, Lebanon, 1962; U.S. Treasury Department, Bureau of Narcotics, special agent in charge in Beirut, 1965; U.S. Justice Department, Bureau of Narcotics and Dangerous Drugs, Washington, D.C., staff member, 1968-70, special agent in charge in Kabul, Afghanistan, 1970-72, Drug Enforcement Administration, regional director in Paris, 1972—. *Military service:* U.S. Army, 1943-46; became platoon sergeant; received Presidential Unit Citation, Combat Infantry Badge, Purple Heart, Bronze Star, Silver Star. U.S. Army Reserve, commissioned, 1951. *Member:* Harvard Club of Lebanon, St. George's Club (Beirut).

WRITINGS: (With Alan M. Richardson) *The Scope and Limitation of Industrial Security*, C. C Thomas, 1963.

SIDELIGHTS: Knight speaks French, German, Italian, and "limping" Arabic. *Avocational interests:* Reading, especially literary criticism; photography, motor cars, music.

* * *

KNIGHT, R(oy) C(lement) 1907-

PERSONAL: Born April 10, 1907, in Bournemouth, Hampshire, England; son of Clement George (a company director) and Alice Mabel (Atlee) Knight; married Ena Mary Stanbury, December 30, 1933; children: Andrew James. *Education:* Oriel College, Oxford, B.A., 1931, M.A., 1946; Sorbonne, University of Paris, Docteur-es-Lettres, 1950. *Politics:* "Slightly left of centre." *Religion:* Church in Wales. *Home:* 2 Greenfield Ter., Skelty, Swansea, Glamorganshire, Wales.

CAREER: University of Birmingham, Birmingham, England, assistant lecturer, 1933-36, lecturer, 1936-48, senior lecturer in French, 1948-50; University College of Swansea, University of Wales, professor of French, 1950-74, head of department of Romance studies, 1964-74. Visiting professor, University of Nigeria, Nsukka, six terms in period 1965-66. *Member:* Society for French Studies (Great Britain; president, 1962-64), Association of University Professors of French (Great Britain; chairman, 1971-73), Academie of Nimes (France; corresponding member). *Awards, honors:* Chevalier des Palmes Academiques (France), 1958; la Legion d'honneur, Chevalier, 1960, Officier, 1968.

WRITINGS: (Editor) Racine, *Phedre*, Manchester University Press, 1943; (with J. Milner) *The French You Want*, Pitman, 1947; *Racine et la Grece*, Boivin, 1951; (with F. W. A. George) *Advice to the Student of French*, Basil Blackwell, 1955; (editor) Corneille, *Nicomede*, University of London Press, 1960; (editor and contributor) *Racine*, Macmillian, 1969; (editor) Racine, *Phedre* (verse translation), University of Texas Press, 1971. Contributor of articles and book reviews to journals in England and France.

WORK IN PROGRESS: With H. T. Barnwell, a critical edition of Racine's *Andromaque*, text of 1668.

SIDELIGHTS: Knight is fluent in French, reads Italian

and German "if strictly necessary," and has some knowledge of Greek and Latin.

* * *

KNOEPFLE, John 1923-

PERSONAL: Born February 2, 1923, in Cincinnati, Ohio; son of Rudolph (a salesman) and Catherine (Brickley) Knoepfle; married Margaret Godfrey Sower, December 26, 1956; children: John Simeon, Mary Catherine, David Edmund. *Education:* Xavier University, Cincinnati, Ohio, Ph.B., 1947, M.A., 1949; graduate study, St. Louis University. *Politics:* Democrat. *Religion:* Catholic. *Office:* English Department, St. Louis University, St. Louis, Mo.

CAREER: WCET (educational television), Cincinnati, Ohio, producer-director, 1953-55; Ohio State University, Columbus, assistant instructor, 1956-57; Southern Illinois University, East St. Louis, lecturer 1957-61; St. Louis University High School, St. Louis, Mo., lecturer in English, 1961-62; Maryville College of the Sacred Heart, St. Louis, Mo., assistant professor of English, beginning, 1962; St. Louis University, St. Louis, Mo., currently writer-in-residence. *Military service:* U.S. Navy, 1942-46; became lieutenant junior grade; received Purple Heart. *Member:* Modern Language Association, American Studies Association.

WRITINGS: (Translator, with James Wright and Robert Bly) *Twenty Poems of Cesar Vallejo*, Sixties Press, 1961; *Rivers Into Islands*, University of Chicago Press, 1965; *Affair of Culture and Other Poems*, Juniper, 1969; *After Gray Days and Other Poems*, Crabgrass Press, 1969; *Songs for Gail Guidry's Guitar*, New Rivers Press, 1969.

The Intricate Land, New Rivers Press, 1970; (translator with Robert Bly) *Neruda and Vallejo: Selected Poems*, Beacon Press, 1971; *Dogs and Cats and Things Like That: Poems*, McGraw, 1971; *The Ten-Fifteen Community Poems*, Back Door, 1971; *Our Street Feels Good: Poems for Children*, McGraw, 1972. Anthologized in *Poets at the Gate*, 1964, and *Voyages to the Inland Sea*, 1971.

BIOGRAPHICAL/CRITICAL SOURCES: The Minnesota Review, Vol. 8, No. 3, 1968.†

* * *

KNOEPFLMACHER, U(lrich) C(amillus) 1931-

PERSONAL: Born June 26, 1931, in Munich, Germany; son of George A. (a civil engineer) and Hilde (Weiss) Knoepflmacher; married Cecilia Mandzuch, June 11, 1959; children: Julie, Paul, Daniel. *Education:* University of California, Berkeley, A.B., 1955, M.A., 1957; Princeton University, Ph.D., 1961. *Religion:* Jewish. *Home:* 1623 Walnut St., Berkeley, Calif. 94709. *Office:* Department of English, University of California, Berkeley, Calif. 94720.

CAREER: University of California, Berkeley, instructor, 1961-62, assistant professor, 1962-66, associate professor, 1966-69, professor of English Literature, 1969—, assistant dean of the College of Letters and Sciences, 1967-71. *Member:* Modern Language Association of America, National Council of Teachers of English. *Awards, honors:* American Council of Learned Societies research stipend, 1965; Guggenheim fellowship, 1969-70; National Endowment for the Humanities, senior fellow, 1972-73.

WRITINGS: Religious Humanism and the Victorian Novel: George Eliot, Walter Pater, and Samuel Butler, Princeton University Press, 1965, 2nd edition, 1970; *George Eliot's Early Novels: The Limits of Realism*, University of California Press, 1968; *Laughter and Despair: Readings in Ten Novels of the Victorian Era*, University of California Press, 2nd edition, 1973. Contributor to *Modern Fiction Studies, English Literature in Transition, Victorian Poetry*, and other journals.

WORK IN PROGRESS: A study of George Eliot as a philosophical novelist; a critical introduction to the Victorian novel.

SIDELIGHTS: Knoepflmacher lived in Bolivia for twelve years and attended high school there. He reads French and Italian. *Avocational interests:* Painting and sculpture, and Latin America.†

* * *

KNOX, Henry M(acdonald) 1916-

PERSONAL: Born November 26, 1916, in Edinburgh, Scotland; son of Robert McLaren (a minister) and Jane Eleanor (Church) Knox; married Marian Starkie, April 13, 1945; children: Christina Mary, Simon Douglas. *Education:* Attended George Watson's College, 1928-34; University of Edinburgh, M.A., 1938, M.Ed., 1940, Ph.D., 1949. *Religion:* Presbyterian. *Home:* 69 Maryville Park, Belfast BT9 6LQ, Northern Ireland. *Office:* The Queen's University, Belfast BT7 1NN, Northern Ireland.

CAREER: University College of Hull, Hull, England, lecturer in education, 1946-49; University of St. Andrews, St. Andrews, Scotland, lecturer in education, 1949-51; The Queen's University of Belfast, Belfast, Northern Ireland, professor of education, 1951—. Examiner in education, University of Aberdeen, 1954-57, University of Leeds, 1959-61 and 1972-74, University of Sheffield and University of Glasgow, 1963-66, National University of Ireland, 1968-70, University of Wales, 1972-75, and other universities. Member of Advisory Council on Education for Northern Ireland, 1955-58 and 1962-64. *Military service:* British Army, 1940-46; served in Burma; became captain.

WRITINGS: 250 Years of Scottish Education, Oliver & Boyd, 1953; *John Dury's Reformed School*, Liverpool University Press, 1958; *Introduction to Educational Method*, Oldbourne, 1961; (contributor) W. Schultze, editor, *Schools in Europe*, Deutches Institut fuer Pedagogische Forschung (Frankfurt), 1969. Contributor to *Times Educational Supplement* and to education journals.

* * *

KNOX, John 1900-

PERSONAL: Born December 30, 1900, in Frankfort, Ky.; son of Absalom (a minister) and Emma (Mann) Knox; married Lois Adelaide Bolles, June 14, 1930; children: John, Jr., Hamilton Bolles. *Education:* Randolph-Macon College, A.B., 1919; Emory University, B.D., 1925; University of Chicago, Ph.D., 1935. *Home:* 41 Medford Leas, Medford, N.J. 08055.

CAREER: Ordained Methodist minister, Winchester, Va., 1924; ordained Episcopal minister, 1962. Minister of parishes in Baltimore Conference of Methodist Episcopal Church, 1919-21, 1923-24, 1927, 1929; Emory University, Atlanta, Ga., assistant professor of Bible, 1924-27; Fisk University, Nashville, Tenn., minister, 1929-36; Hartford Theological Seminary (now Hartford Seminary Foundation), Hartford, Conn., associate professor of New Testament, 1938-39; University of Chicago, Chicago, Ill., associate professor of homiletics, 1939-42, professor of New Testament and homiletics, 1942-43; Union Theological Seminary, New York, N.Y., Baldwin Professor of Sacred Literature, 1943-66, professor emeritus, 1966—, director of studies, 1944-57; Episcopal Theological Seminary of the Southwest, Austin, Tex., professor of New Testament, 1966-71, professor emeritus, 1971—. Cambridge University, visiting lecturer, 1952-53; Harvard University, Noble Lecturer, 1946-47, and Ingersoll Lecturer, 1960; also lecturer at Yale University, University of Virginia, and other universities, 1944—.

MEMBER: American Theological Society (president, 1961), National Council on Religion in Higher Education (fellow), Society of Biblical Literature (president, 1963), Phi Beta Kappa. *Awards, honors:* Litt.D., Randolph-Macon College, 1948; S.T.D., Emory University, 1956, General Theological Seminary, 1964, Berkeley Theological Seminary, 1967; D.D., Philadelphia Divinity School and University of Glasgow, 1963.

WRITINGS: He Whom a Dream Hath Possessed, Harper, 1932; *Philemon Among the Letters of Paul*, University of Chicago Press, 1935, revised edition, Abingdon, 1958; *The Man Christ Jesus*, Willett, Clark & Co., 1941; (editor) *Religion and the Present Crisis*, University of Chicago Press, 1942; *Marcion and the New Testament*, University of Chicago Press, 1942; *Christ the Lord*, Willett, Clark & Co., 1945; *The Fourth Gospel and the Later Epistles*, Abingdon, 1945; *On the Meaning of Christ*, Scribner, 1947.

Chapters in a Life of Paul, Abingdon, 1950; *The Early Church and the Coming Great Church*, Abingdon, 1955; *The Integrity of Preaching*, Abingdon, 1956; *The Death of Christ*, Abingdon, 1958; *Jesus: Lord and Christ*, Harper, 1958; *Christ and the Hope of Glory*, Abingdon, 1960; *The Ethics of Jesus in the Teachings of the Church*, Abingdon, 1961; *Life in Christ Jesus*, Seabury, 1961; *The Church and the Reality of Christ*, Harper, 1962; *Myth and Truth*, University Press of Virginia, 1964; *Humanity and Divinity of Christ*, Cambridge University Press, 1967; *Limits of Unbelief*, Collins, 1970.

Contributor: H. P. Van Dusen, editor, *The Christian Answer*, Scribner, 1945; George F. Thomas, editor, *The Vitality of the Christian Tradition*, Harper, 1945; K. S. Latourette, editor, *The Gospel, The Church, and the World*, Harper, 1946; S. E. Johnson, editor, *The Joy of Study*, Macmillan, 1951; G. Paul Butler, editor, *Best Sermons*, McGraw, 1955; H. R. Niebuhr and D. D. Williams, editors, *The Ministry in Historical Perspectives*, Harper, 1956; H. G. May and B. M. Metzger, editors, *The Oxford Annotated Bible*, Oxford University Press, 1962; R. A. Norris, Jr., editor, *Lux in Lumine*, Seabury Press, 1966; L. E. Keck and J. L. Martyn, editors, *Studies in Luke-Acts*, 1966; S. F. Bayne, Jr., editor, *Theological Freedom and Social Responsibility*, Seabury Press, 1970.

Managing editor, *Christendom*, and editorial staff member of *Christian Century*, 1936-38; editor, *Journal of Religion*, 1939-43; associate editor of *The Interpreter's Bible*, twelve volumes, 1947-57, and *The Interpreter's Dictionary of the Bible*, four volumes, 1955-62.

* * *

KOBLER, Arthur L(eon) 1920-

PERSONAL: Born May 18, 1920, in New York, N.Y.; son of Harry and Lillie (Temple) Kobler; married Virginia Lee White (now an artist), March 28, 1947; children: Sarah Temple. *Education:* City College (now City College of the City University of New York), B.B.A., 1941; Columbia University, M.A., 1946; University of Kansas, Ph.D.,

1952. *Politics:* Liberal left. *Religion:* None. *Home:* 17890 40th Ave. N.E., Seattle, Wash. 98155. *Office:* 4731 12th Ave. N.E., Seattle, Wash. 98105.

CAREER: Winter Veterans Administration Hospital, Topeka, Kan., clinical psychology intern, 1946-50; Pinel Foundation, Seattle, Wash., chief clinical psychologist, 1951-54, research director, 1954-58; Ryther Child Center, Seattle, Wash., research director, 1958-61; private practice of psychotherapy, Seattle, Wash., 1961—; University of Washington, Seattle, associate professor of electrical engineering research, 1961-65, professor of clinical psychology, 1971—. Consultant to Seattle Crisis Clinic, 1964-67. *Military service:* U.S. Coast Guard Reserve, 1942-45; became lieutenant junior grade.

MEMBER: American Psychological Association, Society for the Psychological Study of Social Issues, American Civil Liberties Union (Washington state branch; member of board of directors, 1957-64; board secretary, 1961-63 and 1964; board president, 1967-68; national board member, 1970—), Western Psychological Association. *Awards, honors:* National Institute of Mental Health grants, 1956, 1959.

WRITINGS: (With Ezra Stotland) *The End of Hope: A Social-Clinical Study of Suicide*, Free Press of Glencoe, 1964; (with Ezra Stotland) *Life and Death of a Mental Hospital*, University of Washington Press, 1965. Contributor to *Science* and other journals.

*   *   *

KODANDA RAO, Pandurangi 1889-

PERSONAL: Born December 25, 1889, in Vishakhapatnam, Andhra State, India; married Mary Louise Campbell (a teacher and a lecturer in India, Canada, and United States), 1937. *Education:* Madras University, B.A. (honors), 1915, M.A. (honors), 1917; Yale University seminar on race relations, 1934-35. *Home:* Aloha, 26 Sir Krishna Rao Rd., Basavangudi, Bangalore 4, India.

CAREER: Mysore University, Central College, Bangalore, India, lecturer in botany, 1915-21; private secretary to V. S. Srinivasa Sastri (member of Indian Council of State and agent general of Indian government in South Africa), 1922-32; made world tour to investigate conditions of Indians, 1935-37; member of government (national and state) commissions and committees in India, including deputation to Malaya, 1946, Mysore Education Reforms Committee, 1952-53, Prohibition Enquiry Committee, 1955. Lecturer at universities in India, throughout Canada, 1935-36, 1946, in United States, 1936, 1947, and in Australia, New Zealand, and China. Member of Seminar-Conference on Education in the Pacific Countries, 1936, and of Conference on Race Relations in World Perspective, 1954. Member of senate, academic council, and executive council of Nagpur University, 1939-42, of senate and executive council, 1948. *Member:* Indian Council of World Affairs, (former vice-president, New Delhi; president of Bangalore branch; now president, Forum of International Affairs, Bangalore). *Awards, honors:* Carnegie Scholar at Yale University; Watumull Memorial Prize, 1964, for *The Rt. Hon. V. S. Srinivasa Sastri*.

WRITINGS: Malabar Tenancy Problems, Servants of India Society (Madras), 1926; *East versus West: Denial of Contrast*, Allen & Unwin, 1939; *Culture Conflicts: Cause and Cure*, Padna Publications, 1946; *Technical Education and Industrial Development in America—Some Aspects*, Government Press (Nagpur), 1948; *The Rt. Hon. V. S.*

Srinivasa Sastri—A Political Biography, Asia Publishing House, 1963; *Foreign Friends of India's Freedom*, P. T. I. Book (Bangalore), 1973. Contributor to *Current History* and to periodicals in India. Former editor, *Servant of India* (chief publication of Servants of India Society).

SIDELIGHTS: Kodanda Rao assisted Mahatma Gandhi in inauguration of the Anti-Untouchability Campaign from Yervada Prison in 1932, and Gandhi later wrote of him: "He is a moderate in politics and an ardent social reformer, holding advanced views on many social problems."

*   *   *

KOEHLER, Alan (Robert) 1928-

PERSONAL: Surname is pronounced *Kay*-ler; born July 1, 1928, in Easton, Pa.; son of Kenneth Brown and Helen (Wolbach) Koehler. *Education:* Columbia University, B.A., 1949. *Politics:* Republican. *Home:* 215 East 68th St., New York, N.Y. 10021. *Agent:* Robert Lescher, Brandt & Brandt, 101 Park Ave., New York, N.Y. 10017. *Office:* Ted Bates & Co., 666 Fifth Ave., New York, N.Y. 10019.

CAREER: Gimbels, New York, N.Y., assistant to advertising director, 1949-54; Bernice Fitz-Gibbon, Inc. (advertising), New York, N.Y., vice-president, 1954-58; Norman, Craig & Kummel (advertising), New York, N.Y., vice-president and copy chief, 1958-61; Ted Bates & Co. (advertising), New York, N.Y., senior writer, beginning 1961. *Military service:* U.S. Army, 1950-52; became sergeant. *Member:* Phi Beta Kappa.

WRITINGS: The Madison Avenue Cook Book, for people who can't cook and don't want other people to know it, Holt, 1962; *The Madison Avenue Speech Book, for people who are scared to make a speech and don't want to show it*, McGraw, 1964. Contributor of non-fiction to slick magazines.

SIDELIGHTS: Koehler has made fifteen trips abroad, traveled around the world. Says he strives to make writings (non-fiction) "both amusing and useful, not just one or the other. No published fiction, but coming up."†

*   *   *

KOLENDA, Konstantin 1923-

PERSONAL: Born May 17, 1923, in Poland; son of Theodore (a lawyer) and Helena (Nishtok) Kolenda; married Pauline Moller (a professor), June 9, 1962; children: Helena, Christopher. *Education:* Rice Institute (now Rice University), B.A., 1950; Cornell University, Ph.D., 1953. *Home:* 2515 Glenhaven, Houston, Tex. 77025. *Office:* Rice University, Houston, Tex. 77001.

CAREER: Rice University, Houston, Tex., assistant professor, 1953-58, associate professor, 1958-65, professor of philosophy, 1965—, department chairman, 1968—. *Member:* American Philosophical Association, Southwestern Philosophical Society (president, 1965), Phi Beta Kappa (chapter president, 1960-61). *Awards, honors:* Fulbright grant at University of Heidelberg, 1959-60.

WRITINGS: (Translator, and author of introduction) Arthur Schopenhauer, *Essay on the Freedom of the Will*, Liberal Arts Press, 1960; *The Freedom of Reason*, Principia Press of Trinity University, 1964; (editor) *Insight into Vision*, Trinity University Press, 1965; *In Defense of Practical Reason: A Study and an Application of Arthur Murphy's Theory*, Rice University, 1969; *Ethics for the Young*, Tourmaline Press, 1972; *Philosophy's Journey*, Addison-Wesley, 1974. Contributor to professional journals.

WORK IN PROGRESS: Religion for today, thoughts on the meaning of life.

* * *

KOLLER, Marvin Robert 1919-

PERSONAL: Born February 24, 1919, in Cleveland, Ohio; son of Julius George (a store manager) and Margaret (Spitz) Koller; married Pauline Steinfeld, January 27, 1945; children: Robert Lee. *Education:* Kent State University, B.S., 1940; Ohio State University, M.A., 1947, Ph.D., 1950. *Home:* 230 Trudy Ave., Munroe Falls, Ohio 44262.

CAREER: Kent State University, Kent, Ohio, instructor, then assistant professor, 1949-53, associate professor, 1953-61, professor of sociology, 1961—. Visiting professor, World Campus Afloat, spring, 1970, and summer, 1973. *Military service:* U.S. Army, 1941-45. *Member:* American Sociological Association, Gerontological Society, National Council on Family Relations, World Future Society, American Association of University Professors, Pi Gamma Mu, Alpha Kappa Delta, Kappa Delta Pi, Alpha Psi Omega, Delta Tau Kappa.

WRITINGS: (With Oscar W. Ritchie) *Sociology of Childhood*, Appleton, 1964; *Modern Sociology* (high school textbook), Holt, 1965, 3rd edition, 1974; (contributor) Joseph S. Roucek, editor, *The Teaching of History*, Philosophical Library, 1967; *Social Gerontology*, Random House, 1968; *Families: A Multigenerational Approach*, McGraw, 1974. Contributor to sociological, geriatric, and educational journals. Associate editor, *Teaching Sociology*.

AVOCATIONAL INTERESTS: Marionette productions, camping, hiking, biking, leather carving.

* * *

KONNYU, Leslie 1914-

PERSONAL: Born February 28, 1914, in Tamasi, Hungary; son of Joseph and Mary (Polhamer) Konnyu; married Elizabeth Gelencser (a finance officer), January 18, 1936; children: Ernest, Joseph, Gabriella (Mrs. Joseph Heiser). *Education:* Elementary Teachers' Training College, Baja, Hungary, diploma, 1936; Secondary Teachers' Training College, Szeged, Hungary, diploma, 1944; St. Louis Music and Arts College, Bachelor of Music Education, 1954; St. Louis University, M.A., 1965. *Home:* 5410 Kerth Rd., St. Louis, Mo. 63128.

CAREER: Literature and history teacher in Jaszbereny, Hungary, 1940-44; director of refugee school in Ampfhwang, Austria, 1945-49; church organist in Jefferson City, Mo., 1950-51; Washington University, School of Medicine, St. Louis, Mo., laboratory technician, 1951-55; Aeronautical Chart and Information Service, St. Louis, Mo., cartographer, 1955-73. Director of American Hungarian Welfare Committee, 1956—; founder of Friends of Hungarian Culture, 1959. *Member:* P.E.N. International, Missouri Historical Society, Missouri State Historical Society, St. Louis Writers Guild, St. Louis Poetry Center. *Awards, honors:* Distinguished Community Service Award from Mid-American Jubilee, St. Louis, Mo., 1956.

WRITINGS—In Hungarian: *Tavaszi uton* (title means "On the Road of the Spring"), privately printed (Tamasi, Hungary), 1934; *Sikoltas a pusztan* (title means "Screaming on the Prairie"), Szegedi Ujnemzedek (Szeged, Hungary), 1935; *Koltogeto almaim ravatalanal* (title means "Calls on the Bier of My Dreams"), privately printed (Tamasi), 1938; *Karacsonyi legenda* (title means "Christmas Legend"), Kokai (Budapest), 1939; *Vissza!* (title means "Back"), Tolnai (Budapest), 1940; *Magyar Bokreta* (title means "Magyar Bouquet"), Cooperative of Hungarian Teachers (Jaszbereny, Hungary), Volume I, 1940, Volume II, 1941, Volume III, 1942; *Utszeli fak* (title means "Trees on the Highway"), Berzy (Budapest), 1943; *Tavaszi Dal* (title means "Song of the Spring"), Nepszeru Regenytar (Budapest), 1944; *Ausztriai Magyar Anthologia* (title means "Hungarian Anthology in Austria"), Hungarian Boy Scout Association in Exile (Salzburg, Austria), 1948; *Koratavasztol oszirozsakig* (title means "From Early Spring to Aster-Time"), privately printed (St. Louis, Mo.), 1959; *Az amerikai magyar irodalom tortenete* (title means "A History of American-Hungarian Literature"), Cooperative of American-Hungarian Writers (St. Louis), 1961; *Kezdodik elolrol* (title means "Starts from the Beginning"), American Hungarian Review (St. Louis), 1965; *Egy kolto visszanez* (title means "A Poet Looks Back"), American Hungarian Review, 1966; *Idegenben* (title means "In Foreign Land"), American Hungarian Review, 1967; *Osszegyujtott versek* (title means "Collected Poems"), American Hungarian Review, 1969; *Europai Naplo* (title means "European Diary"), American Hungarian Review, 1969; *A terkep rovid tortenete* (title means "A Short History of Maps"), American Hungarian Review, 1970; *A gyava ferfi* (title means "A Yellow Man"), American Hungarian Review, 1973.

In German: *Gedichte von Oesterreich* (title means "Austrian Poems"), Amerikanisch Ungarischer Verlag (Koeln, Germany), 1965.

In French: *J'Accuse mon epogue* (title means "I Accuse My Age"), American Hungarian Review, 1972.

In English: *Bond of Beauty*, privately printed, 1959; *Against the River*, European Heritage, 1961; *A History of American-Hungarian Literature*, Cooperative of American-Hungarian Writers, 1962; *Eagles of Two Continents*, American Hungarian Review, 1963; *Modern Magyar Literature*, American Hungarian Review, 1964; *John Xantus: Hungarian Geographer in America*, American Hungarian Publishing (Koeln, Germany), 1965; (editor) *Historical Highlights of Cartography*, U.S. Air Force Cartographer School (St. Louis), 1965; *Hungarians in the U.S.A.*, American Hungarian Review, 1967; *Revisiting St. Louis*, American Hungarian Review, 1973. Editor of *American Hungarian Review*.

BIOGRAPHICAL/CRITICAL SOURCES: *St. Louis Globe Democrat*, April 26, 1961; *St. Louis Post-Dispatch*, October 26, 1971.

* * *

KOPPITZ, Elizabeth M(unsterberg) 1919-

PERSONAL: Born February 9, 1919, in Berlin, Germany; daughter of Oskar and Helen F. (Rice) Munsterberg; married Werner Koppitz (a research psychologist), June 14, 1955. *Education:* George Peabody College for Teachers, B.A., 1951; Ohio State University, M.A., 1952, Ph.D., 1955. *Home:* R.F.D. 1, Box 200, Mount Kisco, N.Y. *Office:* Board of Cooperative Educational Services, Yorktown Heights, N.Y.

CAREER: East Boston Social Center Council, Boston, Mass., arts and crafts instructor, 1942-45; Fisk University Social Center, Nashville, Tenn., head resident, 1945-50; Juvenile Diagnostic Center, Columbus, Ohio, psychologist, 1955; Children's Mental Health Center, Columbus, Ohio, psychologist, 1956-58; Endicott (N.Y.) public schools, psychologist, 1959; Board of Cooperative Educational Services, Yorktown Heights, N.Y., school psychologist, 1961—. *Member:* American Psychological Association, National Education Association, Westchester Association of School Psychologists.

WRITINGS: The Bender Gestalt Test with Human Figure Drawing Test (manual), Ohio Department of Education, 1962; *The Bender Gestalt Test for Young Children*, Grune, 1964; *Psychological Evaluation of Children's Human Figure Drawings*, Grune, 1968; *Children with Learning Disabilities: A Five Year Follow-Up Study*, Grune, 1971. Contributor to psychology periodicals.

WORK IN PROGRESS: Research on projective tests for young children.

AVOCATIONAL INTERESTS: Gardening, art, stamp-collecting, and travel.

* * *

KORNAI, J(anos) 1928-

PERSONAL: Born January 21, 1928, in Budapest, Hungary. *Education:* University of Budapest, C.Sc., 1956, Dr. Oec., 1961. *Office:* Computing Center of the Hungarian Academy of Sciences, Uri utca 53, Budapest I, Hungary.

CAREER: Hungarian Academy of Sciences, Institute for Economics, Budapest, Hungary, research officer, 1955-58; Institute for Textile Industry, Budapest, Hungary, head of economic research department, 1958-62; Hungarian Academy of Sciences, Computing Center, head of department for the mathematical model of the economy, beginning 1963. *Member:* Econometric Society, Hungarian Association for Economics (member of council of department for mathematical economics), Hungarian Academy of Sciences (member of committee for economics).

WRITINGS: A gazdasagi vezetes tulzott kozpontositasa, Kozgazdasagi es Jogi Konyvkiado, 1957, translation by John Knapp published as *Overcentralization in Economic Administration*, Oxford University Press, 1959; *A nyerese-gerdekeltseg matematikai vizsagalata* (title means "Mathematical Investigation of Profit-Sharing"), Kozgazdasagi es Jogi Konyvkiado, 1959; *A beruhaszasok matematikai programozasa* (title means "Mathematical Programming of Investment")' Kozgazdasagi es Jogi Konyvkiado, 1962; *Mathematical Planning of Structural Decisions*, translated from the original Hungarian by Josef Hatvany and Pal Morvay, Publishing House of the Hungarian Academy of Sciences, 1967; *Multi-level Programming: A First Report on the Model and on the Experiences of the Experimental Computations*, Institute for Economic Planning (Budapest), 1968; *Anti-equilibrium*, North-Holland Publishing Co., 1971; *Rush Versus Harmonic Growth*, North-Holland Publishing Co., 1972.†

* * *

KOSTELANETZ, Richard C(ory) 1940-

PERSONAL: Born May 14, 1940, in New York, N.Y.; son of Boris (a lawyer) and Ethel (Cory) Kostelanetz. *Education:* Brown University, A.B. (with honors), 1962; King's College, London, graduate study, 1964-65; Columbia University, M.A., 1966. *Politics:* Registered Democrat. *Residence:* New York, N.Y. *Office:* 80 Pine St., 38th floor, New York, N.Y. 10005.

CAREER: Author, critic, poet, lecturer. BBC-TV, London, England, producer-interviewer of television show, "New Release," 1965-66; City University of New York, New York, N.Y., program associate in thematic studies at John Jay College, 1972-73; gives public readings of his poetry and fiction, also illuminated demonstrations at colleges and universities, including New York University, Cooper Union, Barnard College, and others. *Member:* P.E.N., Phi Beta Kappa. *Awards, honors:* Woodrow Wilson fellowship, 1962-63; Fulbright fellowship, 1964-65; Pulitzer fellowship in critical writing, 1965-66; Guggenheim fellowship, 1967.

WRITINGS: Music of Today (booklet), Time-Life Records, 1967; *The Theatre of Mixed Means*, Dial, 1968; *Master Minds: Portraits of Contemporary American Artists and Intellectuals*, Macmillan, 1969; *Visual Language*, Assembling Press, 1970; *In the Beginning*, Abyss Publications, 1972; *Accounting* (booklet), Amodulo (Brescia, Italy), 1972; *The End of Intelligent Writing*, Sheed, 1974; *I Articulations/Short Fictions*, Kulchur Foundation, 1974; *Recyclings: A Literary Autobiography*, Assembling Press, 1974; *Metamorphosis in the Arts*, Abrams, in press.

Editor and author of introduction, except as indicated: *On Contemporary Literature*, Avon, 1964, revised edition, 1969; (and contributor) *The New American Arts*, Horizon, 1965; *Twelve from the Sixties*, Dell, 1967; *The Young American Writers: Fiction, Poetry, Drama, and Criticism*, Funk, 1967; *Beyond Left and Right*, Morrow, 1968; *Piccola anthologia della nuova poesia americana* (booklet), Nuova Presenza-Editrice Magenta, 1968; *Imaged Words & Worded Images*, Outerbridge & Dienstfrey, 1970; *Possibilities of Poetry*, Dell, 1970; *Moholy-Nagy*, Praeger, 1970; *John Cage*, Praeger, 1970; *Social Speculations: Visions for Our Time*, Morrow, 1971; *Breakthroughs in Fiction*, Something Else Press, 1971; *Human Alternatives*, Morrow, 1971; *Future's Fictions*, Panache, 1971; *In Youth*, Ballantine, 1972; *Seeing Through Shuck*, Ballantine, 1972; *Breakthrough Fictioneers*, Something Else Press, 1973; *The Edge of Adaptation*, Prentice-Hall, 1973; *Essaying Essays*, Something Else Press, 1974.

Also author of poster and post-card collections; co-founder and co-editor of annual book-length periodical, *Assembling*, 1970—.

Poetry and fiction represented in anthologies, including: *The Young American Poets*, edited by Paul Carroll, Follet, 1968; *Once Again*, edited by J. F. Bory, New Directions, 1968; *Experiments in Prose*, edited by Eugene Wildman, Swallow Press, 1969; *Being Born and Growing Older*, edited by B. T. G. Vance, Van Nostrand, 1971; *Sports Poems*, edited by Rozanne Lundson and P. K. Ebert, Dell, 1971; *This Book Is a Movie*, edited by J. G. Bowles and Tony Russell, Delta Books, 1971; *Art Work, No Commercial Value*, edited by Bowles, Grossman, 1972; *New American Poetry*, edited by Richard Monaco, McGraw, 1973.

Contributor of essays, poems, and fiction to *Partisan Review, Commonweal, New York Times Book Review, National Review, Ramparts, Listener, Harper's, New York, Twentieth Century, Hudson Review, Esquire, Tri-Quarterly, Holiday, Chicago Review, Panache, Chelsea Review, High Fidelity, Yale Review, Humanist, Les Temps Modernes, Village Voice, Kenyon Review, Sewanee Review, Approaches, Penumbra, Unmuzzled Ox, Nuova Presenza, Les Lettres Nouvelles*, and other periodicals throughout the western world.

Contributing editor, *Arts in Society*, 1970—, *San Francisco Book Review*, 1971, *Lotta Poetica* (Italy), 1971—, *Humanist*, 1972—.

WORK IN PROGRESS: Illuminations, a third book of visual poetry; *Constructions*, a short fiction collection; a history of post-World War II American thought; an essay on contemporary experimental writing; *Numbers: Poems & Stories*; *Manhattan: A Graphic Essay*; *Twenties in the Sixties*, a collection of critical essays.

SIDELIGHTS: Kostelanetz told *CA*: "I have recently been putting my visual poems on to silk-screens and canvas. I work at something nearly all the time. My favorite pastime is swimming."

* * *

KOTT, Jan 1914-

PERSONAL: Born October 27, 1914, in Warsaw, Poland; son of Maurycy (a clerk) and Kazimiera (Wertenstein) Kott; married Lidia Steinhaus, June 17, 1939; children: Teresa Lidia, Michal Hugo. *Education:* Attended University of Warsaw, University of Paris, University of Lodz; earned Ph.D.. *Home:* Aleja Roz 6, Warsaw, Poland.

CAREER: University of Warsaw, Warsaw, Poland, professor of history of Polish literature, 1953—. Visiting professor, Yale University, 1966-67, 1968-69; University of California, Berkeley, 1967-68; State University of New York, Stony Brook, 1969—. *Member:* P.E.N. (Polish section), Modern Language Association of America (honorary). *Awards, honors:* State prize in literature, 1951, 1955; Herder Award, Vienna, 1964; Guggenheim Fellowship, 1972-73.

WRITINGS: Mitologia i realizm (title means "Mythology and Realism"), Czytelnik (Warsaw), 1946; *Szkola klasykow* (title means "School of Classics"), Czytelnik, 1949; *Iak wam sie podoba* (title means "As You Like It"), PIW (Warsaw), 1955; *Postep i glupstwo* (title means "Progress and Folly"), PIW, 1956; *Szkice o Szekspirze*, PIW, 1961 (English translation by Boleslaw Taborski published as *Shakespeare Our Contemporary*, Doubleday, 1964), revised edition, preface by Peter Brook, 1967; (editor with Jerzy Jackl) *Teatr Narodowy: 1765-1794*, Panstwowy Instytut Wydawniczy, 1967; *Theatre Notebook 1947-1967*, Doubleday, 1968; *The Eating of the Gods: An Interpretation of Greek Tragedy*, Random House, 1973.

BIOGRAPHICAL/CRITICAL SOURCES: New York Review of Books, September 24, 1964.†

* * *

KOTZ, Samuel 1930-

PERSONAL: Born August 28, 1930, in Harbin, China; son of Boris and Guta (Kahana) Kotz; married Rosalyn Greenwald (a teacher), August 6, 1963; children: Tamar Ann. *Education:* The Hebrew University of Jerusalem, M.Sc., 1956; Cornell University, Ph.D., 1960. *Religion:* Jewish. *Home:* 1618 Griffin St., Philadelphia, Pa. 19111. *Office:* Temple University, Philadelphia, Pa.

CAREER: Bar Ilan University, Ramat Gan, Israel, lecturer in mathematics, 1960-62; University of North Carolina, Chapel Hill, research associate in mathematics and statistics, 1962-63; University of Toronto, Toronto, Ontario, senior research fellow, 1963-64, associate professor of industrial engineering, 1964-67; Temple University, Philadelphia, Pa., professor of mathematics, 1967—. *Military service:* Israeli Air Force, 1950-52. *Member:* American Mathematical Society, American Statistical Association (fellow), Institute of Mathematical Statistics, Canadian Society of Operational Research, London Mathematical Society.

WRITINGS: (With Wassily Hoeffding) *Russian-English Dictionary of Statistical Terms and Expressions and Russian Reader in Statistics*, University of North Carolina Press, 1964; *Russian-English Dictionary in Cybernetical Sciences and Russian Reader in Cybernetics*, Academic Press, 1966; *Recent Results in Information Theory*, Barnes & Noble, 1966; (with Norman L. Johnson) *Distributions in Statistics*, Volume I: *Discrete Distributions*, Houghton, 1969, Volumes II and III: *Continuous Univariate Distributions*, Houghton, 1970, Volume IV: *Continuous Multivariate Distributions*, Wiley, 1972. Contributor to *Survey*, *American Statistician*, and other journals in field. Associate editor, *Journal of the American Statistical Association*.

SIDELIGHTS: Kotz speaks Russian, Polish, and Hebrew.

* * *

KRADITOR, Aileen S. 1928-

PERSONAL: Born April 12, 1928, in Brooklyn, N.Y.; daughter of Abraham (an attorney and certified public accountant) and Henrietta L. Kraditor. *Education:* Syracuse University, student, 1945-47; Brooklyn College (now Brooklyn College of the City University of New York), B.A., 1950; Columbia University, M.A., 1951, Ph.D., 1962. *Office:* History Department, Boston University, Boston, Mass. 02215.

CAREER: Rhode Island College, Providence, instructor in history, 1962-63, assistant professor, 1963-67; Sir George Williams University, Montreal, Quebec, visiting professor, 1968-69; Boston University, Boston, Mass., professor of history, 1973—. *Member:* American Historical Association, American Studies Association, Organization of American Historians.

WRITINGS: The Ideas of the Woman Suffrage Movement 1890-1920, Columbia University Press, 1965; (editor) *Up from the Pedestal: Selected Writings in the History of American Feminism*, Quadrangle, 1968; *Means and Ends in American Abolitionism: Garrison and his Critics on Strategy and Tactics, 1834-1850*, Pantheon, 1969.

WORK IN PROGRESS: A book on American radical movements, 1880-1920, *Dilemmas of the Vangard*, publication by Pantheon expected in 1977.

* * *

KRAUS, Richard Gordon 1923-

PERSONAL: Born October 21, 1923, in New York, N.Y.; son of David (an attorney) and Ethel (Gordon) Kraus; married Anne Ripley (a ceramist), June 3, 1950; children: Lisa, Andrew. *Education:* City College (now City College of the City University of New York), B.A., 1942; Columbia University, M.A., Ed.D. *Home:* 4 Summit Ave., Ardsley, N.Y. *Office:* Teachers College, Columbia University, New York, N.Y. 10027.

CAREER: Editor of children's magazines for Fawcett Publications and Parents Institute, 1943-48; part-time recreation leader or dance teacher for Young Women's Christian Association, community recreation departments, hospitals, and schools, beginning 1943; with Columbia University, Teachers College, New York, N.Y., beginning 1951. Director of dance and recreation workshops in many states. *Member:* American Association for Health, Physical Education and Recreation (chairman of commission on research and evaluation; head of recreation division, Eastern district).

WRITINGS: Square Dances of Today, Ronald, 1950; *Recreation Leader's Handbook*, McGraw, 1955; *Play Activities of Boys and Girls*, McGraw, 1957; *Family Book of*

Games, McGraw, 1960; (with Dave Garroway) *Fun on Wheels*, McGraw, 1960; *Folk Dancing: A Teacher's Guide*, Macmillan, 1962; *Recreation and the Schools*, Macmillan, 1964; (with Lola Sadlo) *Beginning Social Dance*, Wadsworth, 1964; *A Pocket Guide of Folk and Square Dances and Singing Games for the Elementary School*, Prentice-Hall, 1966; *Recreation Today: Program Planning and Leadership*, Appleton, 1966; *Public Recreation and the Negro: A Study of Participation and Administrative Practices*, Center for Urban Educations, 1968; *History of the Dance in Art and Education*, Prentice-Hall, 1969; (with William Wiegand) *Students Choice*, Merrill, 1970; *Recreation and Leisure in Modern Society*, Appleton, 1971; (with Joseph E. Curtis) *Creative Administration in Recreation and Parks*, Mosby, 1973; *Therapeutic Recreation Service: Principles and Practices*, Saunders, 1973; *Yesterday's Children: A Longitudinal Study of Children from Kindergarten into the Adult Years*, Wiley, 1973.†

*   *   *

KREIG, Margaret B. (Baltzell) 1922-
(Peggy Craig)

PERSONAL: Surname is pronounced Craig; born January 11, 1922, in Chicago, Ill.; daughter of Walter T. and Gladys (Ramsey) Baltzell; married Albert A. Kreig (a purchasing manager), April 28, 1945; children: Raymond A., Andrew T., Lawrence A. *Education:* Attended University of Illinois, Urbana, 1940-42, and 1948, University of Chicago, 1944-45, and Northwestern University, 1949-50. *Home and office:* 20 West 77th St., New York, N.Y. 10024.

CAREER: Free-lance writer, specializing in science, medicine, mystery, and fiction. Fashion model in Chicago, Ill., for a period prior to 1950; public relations consultant to pharmaceutical and other manufacturing firms, 1956-59; *Parents' Magazine*, New York, N.Y., staff writer and an associate editor, 1959-61. *Military service:* U.S. Marine Corps Women's Reserve, 1943. *Member:* American Association for the Advancement of Science, American Society of Pharmacognosy, Society of Woman Geographers, Canadian Authors Association, National Association of Science Writers, Society of Magazine Writers, American Medical Writers Association, Mystery Writers of America (president of Midwest chapter, 1950-51), Overseas Press Club of America, Horticultural Society of New York, New Jersey Audubon Society. *Awards, honors:* Award for excellence in reporting advances in natural product research from Drug, Chemical and Allied Trades Association, Inc., 1964; Alpha Zeta Omega Award, 1965.

WRITINGS: Green Medicine: The Search for Plants That Heal, Rand McNally, 1964; *Black-market Medicine*, Prentice-Hall, 1967; *The Healing Herbs*, McKay, 1973. Ghost writer of other books. Contributor of more than seventy articles and stories to *This Week, Reader's Digest, Mademoiselle, Good Housekeeping, Better Homes and Gardens, Saint Mystery Magazine*, and other periodicals.

WORK IN PROGRESS: Several books dealing with various aspects of drugs, their use and abuse; pharmaceutical research, here and abroad, particularly in the field of natural products.

SIDELIGHTS: Margaret Kreig has accompanied scientific expeditions to South and Central America, including the Amazon Basin, and to remote areas in Mexico. *Avocational interests:* Collecting very old children's books; experimenting with exotic recipes; the theater.

BIOGRAPHICAL/CRITICAL SOURCES: "The Green World," *National Business Woman*, June, 1964.†

*   *   *

KREISMAN, Leonard T(heodore) 1925-

PERSONAL: Born July 30, 1925, in New York, N.Y.; son of Morris and Lottie (Parnes) Kreisman; married Ruth Mirner, November, 1965. *Education:* New York University, B.S., 1947, Ph.D., 1955; Harvard University, A.M.T., 1948. *Home:* 320 Central Park West, New York, N.Y. 10025.

CAREER: New York University, New York, N.Y., instructor in education, 1949-53; U.S. Army, educational adviser (civilian), Korea and Okinawa, 1953-55; Educational Testing Service, Princeton, N.J., test specialist, 1955-56; State University of New York College at Plattsburgh, Plattsburgh, N.Y., 1956-63, started as visiting assistant professor, became associate professor, 1958; New York State Education Department, Albany, administrator, 1963-65, consultant, 1965-66, chief of Bureau of Special College Programs, 1966-67; State University of New York College at Oneonta, director of institutional research, 1967-68; City College of the City University of New York, New York, director of College Discovery Program, 1968-70; Staten Island Community College of the City University of New York, Staten Island, N.Y., professor and dean of administration, 1970—. University of Dacca, Fulbright lecturer, 1962-63. *Military service:* U.S. Army, 1943-45; received Purple Heart. *Member:* National Council for the Social Studies, Organization of American Historians, American Association of University Professors, Kappa Delta Pi, Phi Delta Kappa.

WRITINGS: The Consumer in Society, Odyssey, 1964.

*   *   *

KRESH, Paul 1919-

PERSONAL: Born December 3, 1919, in New York, N.Y.; son of Samuel and Jean (Finesilver) Kresh. *Education:* Columbia University, student, 1936-38; City College (now City College of the City University of New York), B.A., 1940. *Politics:* Independent liberal. *Religion:* Jewish. *Home:* 2 Charlton St., New York, N.Y. 10014. *Office:* United Jewish Appeal of Greater New York, 220 West 58th St., New York, N.Y. 10019.

CAREER: Radio Station WNYC, New York, N.Y., scriptwriter, 1939-41; National Jewish Welfare Board, New York, N.Y., staff publicity writer, 1941-46; Nathan C. Belth Associates, New York, N.Y., account executive, 1946-48; American ORT (Organization for Rehabilitation Through Training) Federation, New York, N.Y., publicity director, 1948-49; United Jewish Appeal, New York, N.Y., assistant national public relations director and motion picture coordinator, 1949-59; Union of American Hebrew Congregations, New York, N.Y., public relations director and editor of *American Judaism*, 1959-67; Spoken Arts, Inc., New Rochelle, N.Y., vice-president, 1967-70; Caedmon Records, New York, N.Y., recording director and projects editor, 1970-71; United Jewish Appeal of Greater New York, New York, N.Y., public relations director, 1971—. *Member:* National Academy of Recording Arts and Sciences, Writers Guild of America, American Jewish Public Relations Society. *Awards, honors:* Radio award, Ohio State University, 1940 and 1941, for "Adventures in Music" and 1965, for "Adventures in Judaism"; Golden Eagle, Committee on International Non-Theatrical

Events, 1965, for film, "The Day the Doors Closed"; Faith and Freedom Award in Broadcasting, 1968; Silver Award, International Television and Film Festival of New York, 1972, for film, "The Jewish Year in Review."

WRITINGS: (With Stephen M. Young) Tales Out of Congress, Lippincott, 1964; (editor) An American Judaism Reader, Abelard, 1965; The Power of the Unknown Citizen, Lippincott, 1969.

Writer for eighteen films produced in Hollywood and Israel for United Jewish Appeal, of opera libretto, "The Marble Faun," and of film script, "The Day the Doors Closed." Writer and director of Columbia Broadcasting System series, "Adventures in Judaism," 1965, and of WQXR series, "The Jewish World," 1974.

Monthly columnist, Words Only and American Record Guide, 1959-63. Contributing editor and critic, Hi Fi-Stereo Review, 1963—; book reviewer, Saturday Review, 1967—; record reviewer, New York Times, 1974—. Also editor of "The Spoken Arts Treasury of 100 Modern American Poets Reading Their Poems," 1969.

SIDELIGHTS: Kresh told CA: "I am motivated more by literary aspirations than lust for profit and am writing nonfiction to be able to afford a luxury of time to devote to fiction, poetry, plays." He speaks French, Italian, and Spanish, with diminishing degrees of competence. Avocational interests: Music, photography, tropical fish.

* * *

KREYCHE, Robert J. 1920-

PERSONAL: Born August 26, 1920, in Racine, Wis.; son of Harold Joseph and Henreitta (Oteman) Kreyche; married Julianne Mangold, May 8, 1948 (died May, 1969); married Dolores Ann Pritchard, January 16, 1971; children: (first marriage) Michael K., Thomas H., John A., Catharine A., Andrew J. Education: Catholic University of America, B.A., 1942, M.A., 1943, graduate study, 1944; University of Ottawa, Ph.D., 1952. Politics: Democrat. Religion: Roman Catholic. Home: 2441 North Grannen Rd., Tucson, Ariz. 85705. Office: Department of Philosophy, University of Arizona, Tucson, Arizona 85721.

CAREER: Loyola University, Chicago, Ill., member of faculty, 1947-57; St. Joseph's College, Renssaeler, Ind., member of faculty, 1957-62; Rockhurst College, Kansas City, Mo., professor of philosophy, 1962-65; University of Arizona, Tucson, professor of philosophy, 1965—. Founder and president of Thomas More Institute. Member: American Philosophical Association, Metaphysical Society of America, American Catholic Philosophical Association (president, 1967-68), Delta Epsilon Sigma (honorary).

WRITINGS: First Philosophy: An Introductory Text in Metaphysics, Holt, 1959; Logic for Undergraduates, Dryden Press, 1954, revised edition, Holt, 1961; God and Contemporary Man, Bruce, 1965; God and Reality, Holt, 1965; The Betrayal of Wisdom and the Challenge to Philosophy Today, Alba House, 1972; The Making of A Saint, Alba House, 1973. Contributor to professional journals.

WORK IN PROGRESS: Preliminary research on the art of critical thinking, attempting to integrate the use of logical thinking with contemporary social criticism; a study of democracy and the common good, or the role of reason in administration of policies of the modern democratic state.†

* * *

KRISPYN, Egbert 1930-

PERSONAL: Born June 14, 1930, in Haarlem, Netherlands; came to United States in 1961, naturalized in 1970; son of Pieter Johan and Henriette L. (Lams) Krispyn; married Joan Willings, February 20, 1957; children: Hugo Joost. Education: University of Melbourne, B.A. (honors), 1957, M.A., 1958; University of Pennsylvania, Ph.D., 1963. Home: Route 2, Box 113A, Comer, Ga. 30629. Office: University of Georgia, Athens, Ga. 30601.

CAREER: Commercial employee for International Trading Co., Europe, Singapore, Thailand, Indonesia, 1948-51; variously office clerk, high school teacher, and proofreader for newspaper, Melbourne, Australia, 1952-56; University of Pennsylvania, Philadelphia, lecturer, 1961-63, assistant professor, 1964-66, associate professor of German and Netherlandic, 1966-68; University of Florida, Gainesville, assistant professor, 1963-64, professor and chairman of German and Russian departments, 1968-72; University of Georgia, Athens, professor of German and Netherlandic, 1972—. Member: Modern Language Association of America, American Association of Teachers of German, Modern Humanities Research Association, Nederlandse Vereniging van Leraren in de Levende Talen, Internationale Vereinigung fuer germanische Sprach-und Literaturwissenschaft. Awards, honors: Alexander von Humboldt Foundation stipend, 1960-61, research grant, 1965.

WRITINGS: Style and Society in German Literary Expression, University of Florida Press, 1964; Georg Heym: A Reluctant Rebel, University of Florida Press, 1968; Guenter Eich, Twayne, 1971; (compiler) Modern Stories From Holland and Flanders: An Anthology, Twayne, 1973. Contributor to professional journals and yearbooks in Belgium, Brazil, England, Germany, Netherlands, New Zealand, and United States.

Advisory editor, Dimensions, 1968—; co-editor, Germanic Notes, 1970—; editor of Netherlandic section, Twayne World Authors Series, 1966—, and Library of Netherlandic Literature, Twayne, 1970—.†

* * *

KROEGER, Arthur 1908-

PERSONAL: Surname is pronounced Crager; born September 15, 1908, in Fullerton, Calif.; son of William (an orchardist) and Katherine (Oefinger) Kroeger; married Julia Rose, August 4, 1937; children: Mary Katherine (Mrs. John Dudley Porter). Education: Stanford University, A.B., 1931, M.B.A., 1933. Home: 1750 Bay Laurel Dr., Menlo Park, Calif. Office: Graduate School of Business, Stanford University, Stanford, Calif.

CAREER: Manning's, Inc., San Francisco, Calif., resident manager, 1933-40; University of Idaho, Moscow, assistant professor of marketing, 1940-42; U.S. Office of Price Administration, Boise, Idaho, assistant state price officer, 1942-43; Stanford University, Graduate School of Business, Stanford, Calif., 1946—, professor of marketing, 1953—. Consultant to Sunset (magazine). Military service: U.S. Navy, 1943-46; became lieutenant commander. Member: American Marketing Association, American Academy of Advertising (regional dean, 1961-64), Peninsula Advertising Club (director, 1962-65), Stanford Faculty Club (president, 1964-65), University Club of Palo Alto, Phi Beta Kappa, Alpha Delta Sigma. Awards, honors: Silver Medal Advertising Award, Printers' Ink, 1965.

WRITINGS: (With Charles J. Dirksen) Advertising Principles and Problems, Irwin, 1960, 4th edition, 1973; (with Dirksen and Laurence Lockley) Readings in Marketing, Irwin, 1963, revised edition, 1968; (co-author) The American Association of Collegiate Schools of Business, 1916-66, Irwin, 1966; (with Lockley and Dirksen) Cases in Marketing, 4th edition (Kroeger was not associated with earlier editions), Allyn & Bacon, 1971. Contributor to Journal of Marketing, Journal of Retailing, and Western Advertising.

* * *

KRONINGER, Robert H(enry)   1923-

PERSONAL: Surname is pronounced Crow-nin-jer; born October 29, 1923, in Whittier, Calif.; son of Henry J. (a petroleum explorer) and Marilla (Driggs) Kroninger; married Robin A. Clark; children: four. Education: University of California, Berkeley, A.B., 1944, B.S., 1945, LL.B. (later converted to J.D.), 1948. Politics: Democrat. Religion: Methodist. Office: Superior Court, Court House, Oakland, Calif.

CAREER: U.S. War Department, Oakland, Calif., civilian psychologist, 1944-45; Supreme Court of California, San Francisco, law clerk, 1948-50; private practice of law, Oakland, Calif., 1950-59; Alameda County, Calif., judge, 1959-63; State of California, superior court judge, 1963—. Military service: U.S. Army Air Forces, 1942-43.

WRITINGS: (Co-author) Civil Procedure before Trial, University of California Press, 1959; Sarah and the Senator, Howell-North, 1964; (co-author) Civil Procedure after Trial, University of California Press, 1965. Contributor of legal articles and book reviews to journals.

WORK IN PROGRESS: A novel.

* * *

KUH, Katharine W.   1904-

PERSONAL: Surname is pronounced coo; born July 15, 1904, in St. Louis, Mo.; daughter of Morris and Olga (Weiner) Woolf; divorced. Education: Vassar College, B.A., 1925; University of Chicago, M.A. in Fine Arts, 1929. Home: 140 East 83rd St., New York, N.Y. 10028. Office: Saturday Review/World, 488 Madison Ave., New York, N.Y. 10022.

CAREER: Katharine Kuh Gallery (specializing in modern art), Chicago, Ill., director, 1936-43; Art Institute of Chicago, Chicago, Ill., editor of Quarterly, 1946-53, curator of modern painting and sculpture, 1953-57, curator of painting and sculpture, 1957-59, also curator of Gallery of Art Interpretation; Saturday Review, New York, N.Y., art editor, 1959—. Visiting professor of art, University School of Fine Arts, San Miguel, Mexico, 1938-40. Made special survey of Indian totemic carvings in Alaska for U.S. Office of Indian Affairs, 1946. Lecturer on art throughout United States and Canada, 1950—. Consultant, Southern Illinois University, 1964-68; director of art program, First National Bank of Chicago, 1958—.

WRITINGS: Art Has Many Faces, Harper, 1951; Leger, University of Illinois Press, 1953; The Artist's Voice, Harper, 1962; Break-Up: The Core of Modern Art, New York Graphic Society, 1965; The Open Eye, Harper, 1971.

* * *

KUP, Alexander Peter   1924-

PERSONAL: Born March 26, 1924, in Ryde, Isle of Wight, England; son of Robert Laurence (a company director) and Dorothy (Woodhead) Kup; married Philippa Warwick, February 14, 1958; children: Alexander Timothy Neville, Katherine. Education: University of St. Andrews, M.A.,

1948, Ph.D., 1952. Office: Department of History, Fourah Bay College—The University College of Sierra Leone, P.O. Box 87, Freetown, Sierra Leone, Africa.

CAREER: H.M. General Register House, Edinburgh, Scotland, assistant keeper of manuscripts, 1951-53; assistant archivist to Archbishop of York, York, England, 1953-54; Fourah Bay College—The University College of Sierra Leone, Freetown, professor of modern history, beginning 1954. Sierra Leone Museum, vice-chairman; Sierra Leone Monuments and Relics Commission, member.

WRITINGS: (With P. Gouldesborough) Printed Sources of Scottish History, British Records Association, 1954; A History of Sierra Leone 1400-1787, Cambridge University Press, 1961; The Story of Sierra Leone, Cambridge University Press, 1964; (editor) Adam Afzelius, Sierra Leone Journal 1795-1796, Uppsala Institute (Africa), 1967. Editor, Sierra Leone Studies, 1954-61. Contributor to Man, West African Review, other journals in Africa and Portugal.†

* * *

KURATH, Gertrude Prokosch   1903-

PERSONAL: Born August 19, 1903, in Chicago, Ill.; daughter of Eduard (a philologist) and Mathilde (a pianist; maiden name, Dapprich) Prokosch; married Hans Kurath (a professor of English), June 10, 1930; children: Ellen, Edward. Education: Attended University of Texas, 1917-19, University of Chicago, 1919-20; Bryn Mawr College, B.A., 1922, M.A., 1928; Yale University School of Drama, graduate study, 1929-30. Politics: Democrat ("vaguely"). Religion: Animist. Home: 1125 Spring St., Ann Arbor, Mich. 48103. Office: Dance Research Center, Ann Arbor, Mich.

CAREER: Professional dancer under name of Tula, and teacher of dancing, 1922-46; researcher and writer on dance ethnology and musicology of American and Mexican Indians, 1946—. Teacher of dance at Community Music School, Providence, R.I., 1935-40, for Brown University Extension, Providence, R.I., 1936-45; Creative Dance Guild of Rhode Island, Providence, director, 1937-46; New York State Museum, Albany, research associate, 1952; National Museum of Canada, Ottawa, Ontario, field employee, 1962—; Dance Research Center, Ann Arbor, Mich., founder-director, 1962—. Consultant, National Folk Music Festival Association.

MEMBER: American Folklore Society (member of council), Society for Ethnomusicology (member of council), Sociedad Mexicana de Anthropologia, Michigan Academy of Science, Arts, and Letters, Michigan Folklore Society (president, 1954-56), Women's Research Club (University of Michigan). Awards, honors: National Federation of Music Clubs Program Prize, 1945; Viking Fund fellow, 1949; Michigan Academy of Science, Arts, and Letters research grants, 1953, 1954, 1956; Wenner-Gren Foundation grants, 1957-58, 1960-61, 1963, 1964-65, 1970-73.

WRITINGS: (With Samuel Marti) Dances of Anahuac, Aldine, 1964; Iroquois Music & Dance: Ceremonial Arts of Two Seneca Longhouses, U.S. Government Printing Office, 1964; (contributor) June Helm MacNeish, Dogrib Hand Game, Queen's Printer, 1966; Michigan Indian Festivals, Ann Arbor Publishers, 1966; Dance and Song Rituals of Six Nations Reserve, Queen's Printer, 1968; Music and Dance of the Tewa Pueblos, Museum of New Mexico Press, 1970. Editor of music collection, Radiant Call, Ann Arbor Publishers, 1973. Author or co-author of Bureau of American Ethnology bulletins on Iroquois music and dance. Editor, "Songs and Dances of Great Lakes Indians," Ethnic Folkways album, 1956.

Contributor to *Dictionary of Folklore* (six hundred entries), *Encyclopedia Americana*, *Encyclopaedia Britannica*, and other encyclopedias. Contributor of about one hundred articles and sixty reviews to journals, including *Journal of American Folklore* and *American Anthropologist*. Dance editor, *Ethnomusicology*, 1953—; critic, *Ann Arbor News*, 1961—; editor of *Michigan Folklore Society Newsletter*.

WORK IN PROGRESS: Manuscripts on native songs and dances and hymnody of Michigan Indians, on music and dance of the Blue Water Reserves in Ontario, on Yaqui Indian fiestas in Mexico, and on rock 'n' roll.

SIDELIGHTS: Speaks German, French, and Spanish, reads Portuguese, and has some knowledge of the Aztec, Ottawa, and Tewa Indian languages. *Avocational interests:* Playing piano and guitar, outdoor sports, photography.

BIOGRAPHICAL/CRITICAL SOURCES: Ethnomusicology, Volume III, September, 1959; *Current Anthropology*, Volume I, number 3, May, 1960.

* * *

KURTZ, Paul 1925-

PERSONAL: Born December 21, 1925, in Newark, N.J.; son of Martin and Sara (Lasser) Kurtz; married Claudine C. Vial (a teacher), October 6, 1960; children: Valerie, Patricia, Jonathan. *Education:* New York University, B.A., 1948; Columbia Universtiy, M.A., 1949, Ph.D., 1952. *Home:* 660 Lebrun Rd., Eggertsville, N.Y. 14226. *Office:* Department of Philosophy, State University of New York College at Buffalo, 4244 Ridge Lea Rd., Amherst, N.Y. 14226.

CAREER: Queens College (now Queens College of the City University of New York), Flushing, N.Y., instructor in philosophy, 1950-52; Trinity College, Hartford, Conn., instructor, 1952-55, assistant professor, 1955-58, associate professor of philosophy, 1958-59; Vassar College, Poughkeepsie, N.Y., associate professor of philosophy, 1960-61; Union College, Schenectady, N.Y., associate professor, 1961-64, professor of philosophy, 1964-65; State University of New York College at Buffalo, Buffalo, N.Y., professor of philosophy, 1965—. Visiting lecturer, New School for Social Research, 1960-65; visiting professor, University of Besancon, 1965; chairman of Council on International Studies and World Affairs; trustee of Behavioral Research Council. *Military service:* U.S. Army, 1944-46; became technical sergeant. *Member:* American Philosophical Association, Aristotelian Society, American Humanist Association (director), United World Federalists (president of Schenectady branch, 1965-66), Charles Peirce Society, American Association of University Professors. *Awards, honors:* Behavioral Research Council fellowship, 1962-63; French Government fellow, 1965; Humanist fellow; Danforth fellow; Ford Foundation grant.

WRITINGS: The Problems of Value Theory, Eagle, 1952; (with Rollo Handy) *A Current Appraisal of the Behavioral Sciences*, Behavioral Research Council, 1963; *Decision and the Condition of Man*, University of Washington Press, 1965; (author of introduction) *Humanist Manifestos One and Two*, Prometheus Books, 1973; *The Fullness of Life*, Horizon, 1974.

Editor: (With Gilbert Varet) *International Directory of Philosophy and Philosophers*, Humanities, 1965; *Classics in the History of Thought*, Macmillan, Volume I: *American Thought Before 1900: A Sourcebook from Puritanism to Darwinism*, 1965, Volume II: *American Philosophy in the Twentieth Century: A Sourcebook from Pragmatism to Philosophical Analysis*, 1966; *Sidney Hook and the Contemporary World: Essays on the Pragmatic Intelligence*, John Day, 1968; *Moral Problems in Contemporary Society: Essays in Humanistic Ethics*, Prentice-Hall, 1969, 2nd edition, Prometheus Books, 1973; (with Svetozar Stojanovic) *Tolerance and Revolution*, Philosophical Society of Serbia, 1970, Prometheus Books, 1972; *Language and Human Nature: A French-American Philosopher's Dialogue*, Warren H. Green, 1971; *Definitions of Humanism*, Prometheus Books, 1971, reissued as *The Humanist Alternative*, 1973; (with Albert Dondeyne) *A Catholic/Humanist Dialogue*, Prometheus Books, 1972; (with Sidney Hook and Miro Todorovich) *The Idea of a Modern University*, Prometheus Books, 1974.

Member of U.S. board of directors, *Bibliography of Philosophy and Philosophers*, 1958-71; *The Humanist*, member of editorial board, 1964-67, editor, 1967—. Contributor to *Encyclopedia Americana*; contributor of over 300 reviews, articles, and abstracts to *American Behavioral Scientist*, *Dissent*, *Journal of Religion*, *Antioch Review*, *Social Studies*, and other magazines and journals.

SIDELIGHTS: Kurtz is moderator of the television series, "The Humanist Alternative."

* * *

KUTZ, LeRoy M. 1922-

PERSONAL: Born May 1, 1922, in Philadelphia, Pa.; son of LeRoy M. (a merchant) and Clara (Kulp) Kutz; married, 1943; children: Leroy M. III, Rebecca. *Education:* Franklin and Marshall College, A.B., 1943; Lancaster Theological Seminary, B.D., 1945. *Politics:* Republican. *Home:* 3455 Gratiot Ave., Port Huron, Mich.

CAREER: Ordained minister of United Church of Christ, 1945; St. John's Church, Columbus, Ohio, pastor, 1963-73; First Congregational Church, Port Huron, Mich., senior minister, 1973—.

WRITINGS: (With wife, Marie Kutz) *The Chancel: Why—What—How*, United Church of Christ, 1960. Contributor to *Christian Century* and other religious periodicals.

* * *

LACY, Creighton (Boutelle) 1919-

PERSONAL: Born May 31, 1919, in Kuling, China; son of George Carleton and Harriet (Boutelle) Lacy; married Frances Thompson, June 20, 1944; children: Linda Marie. *Education:* Swarthmore College, B.A. (summa cum laude), 1941; Yale University, B.D. (magna cum laude), 1944, Ph.D., 1953. *Politics:* Democrat. *Home:* 2714 Dogwood Rd., Durham, N.C. 27705. *Office:* Room 8, Divinity School, Duke University, Durham, N.C. 27706.

CAREER: Ordained Methodist minister, 1944; pastor in New Haven, Conn., 1944-46; University of Nanking, Nanking, China, teacher of philosophy and ethics, 1947-49; Fukien Union Theological College, Foochow, China, teacher of theology and ethics, 1949-51; pastor in Waterbury, Conn., 1951-53; Duke University, Durham, N.C., assistant professor of missions and social ethics, 1953-56, associate professor, 1956-64, professor of world Christianity, 1964—. Chairman, Methodist Regional Personnel Committee, 1956-64; chairman of the board of directors,

United Campus Christian Ministry of North Carolina College, 1964-65; Danforth visiting professor of philosophy, International Christian University, Tokyo, Japan, 1973-74. *Member:* Society for Religion in Higher Education, Association of Professors of Missions (vice-president, 1962-64; president, 1964-66), American Society of Missiology, Phi Beta Kappa. *Awards, honors:* American Association of Theological Schools Faculty fellowship, 1959-60; Fulbright Research scholarship in India, 1966-67.

WRITINGS: Is China a Democracy?, Day, 1943; *Christian Community*, Association Press, 1944; *Adam, Where Art Thou?*, Methodist Board of Missions, 1956; *Christian Responsibility for the United States and the New Nations*, Methodist Board of Social Concerns, 1964; *The Conscience of India*, Holt, 1965; (editor) *Christianity Amid Rising Men and Nations*, Association Press, 1965; *Frank Mason North: His Social and Ecumenical Mission*, Abingdon, 1967; *Adult Guide on Understanding China*, Friendship Press, 1970; *Indian Insights: Public Issues in Private Perspective*, Orient Longman (New Delhi), 1972. Contributor to *Weltkirchenlexicon*, 1960, and *Grolier's Encyclopedia*; also contributor to political and theological journals. Editor of *Duke Divinity School Review*, 1960-66.

*   *   *

LAFORE, Laurence Davis   1917-

PERSONAL: Born September 15, 1917, in Narberth, Pa.; son of John Armand and Anne Francis (Shearer) Lafore. *Education:* Swarthmore College, B.A. (highest honors), 1938; Fletcher School of Law and Diplomacy, M.A., 1939, Ph.D., 1950. *Religion:* Episcopalian. *Home:* 9 Parsons St., Iowa City, Iowa 52240. *Office:* Department of History, University of Iowa, Iowa City, Iowa.

CAREER: Trinity College, Hartford, Conn., instructor in history, 1940-42; U.S. Department of State, posts in Washington, D.C., 1942-43, Office of War Information, London, 1943, Supreme Headquarters, Psychological Warfare Division, London, 1944; assistant press attache, U.S. Embassy, Paris, 1944-46; Swarthmore College, Swarthmore, Pa., assistant professor, 1946-51, associate professor, 1951-59, professor of history, 1959-69; University of Iowa, Iowa City, professor of history, 1969—. Consultant of Higher Education, Pennsylvania Department of Public Instruction, 1956-57; visiting fellow, Johns Hopkins University, 1962; visiting professor, University of Iowa, 1967-68; Wright Memorial lecturer, Shippensburg State College, 1970. *Member:* Conference on British Studies, American Historical Association, Author's Guild, National Trust for Historic Preservation, National Pilot's Association, Pennsylvania Historical Society, Pennsylvania Horticultural Society, Alliance Francaise de Phildadelphia, Franklin Inn of Philadelphia, Phi Beta Kappa, Delta Upsilon. *Awards, honors:* Leary's Literary Award, 1962, for *Learner's Permit*; Philadelphia Athenaeum Prize, 1965.

WRITINGS: Press and Diplomacy in Liberated France, privately printed, 1950; (with Paul Beik) *Modern Europe*, Holt, 1960; *Learner's Permit* (novel), Doubleday, 1962 (published in England as *The Pride of the Parthenon*, Gollancz, 1963); *The Devil's Chapel* (novel), Doubleday, 1964; *The Long Fuse: An Interpretation of the Origins of World War I*, Lippincott, 1965; (with Sarah Lippincott) *Philadelphia: The Unexpected City*, Doubleday, 1965; *Stephen's Bridge* (novel), Doubleday, 1968; *Nine Seven Juliet* (novel), Doubleday, 1969; *The End of Glory: An Interpretation of the Origins of World War II*, Lippincott, 1970;

Days of Emperor and Clown, Doubleday, 1973. Contributor to *Harper's, Reader's Digest, Il Ponte, L'Ecran*, and other periodicals.

AVOCATIONAL INTERESTS: Gardening, cooking, cabinetry, flying, travel.

*   *   *

LAHUE, Kalton C.   1934-

PERSONAL: Surname is pronounced *Lay*-hue; born October 4, 1934, in Richford, Vt., son of Kenneth Kail (a contractor) and Florence (Anderson) Lahue; married; children: two. *Education:* University of Vermont, B.S., 1959; San Jose State College (now California State University), M.A., 1967. *Politics:* Republican. *Religion:* Protestant. *Home:* 612 E. Santa Anita, Burbank, Calif.

CAREER: American history teacher in Vermont public schools, 1959-64; Johnson State College, Johnson, Vt., audio-visual director, 1960-61; now free-lance writer. Research assistant for Blackhawk Films, Davenport, Iowa, 1964-74. *Military service:* U.S. Army, 1953-55; sergeant.

WRITINGS: Continued Next Week, University of Oklahoma Press, 1964; *The World of Laughter*, University of Oklahoma Press, 1966; *Kops and Custards*, University of Oklahoma Press, 1968; *Bound and Gagged*, A. S. Barnes, 1968.

Collecting Classic Films, Amphoto, 1970; *Clown Princes and Court Jesters*, A. S. Barnes, 1970; *Winners of the West*, A. S. Barnes, 1970; *Dreams For Sale*, A. S. Barnes, 1971; *Ladies in Distress*, A. S. Barnes, 1971; *Mack Sennett's Keystone*, A. S. Barnes, 1971; *Collecting Vintage Cameras*, Amphoto, 1972; *Glass, Brass, and Chrome*, University of Oklahoma Press, 1972; *Riders of the Range*, A. S. Barnes, 1973; *Motion Picture Pioneer*, A. S. Barnes, 1973; *Petersen's Guide to Pocket Cameras*, Petersen, 1973; *Petersen's Guide to Architectural Photography*, Petersen, 1973. Contributing editor to *Petersen's Photographic Magazine*.

AVOCATIONAL INTERESTS: Collecting films and other memorabilia of the motion picture.

*   *   *

LAIRD, Charlton G(rant)   1901-

PERSONAL: Born March 16, 1901, in Nashua, Iowa; son of John Grant (a businessman) and Elizabeth (Richardson) Laird; married Helen P. Gent, June 2, 1945; children: Nancy (Mrs. Robert Harms). *Education:* University of Iowa, B.A., 1925, M.A., 1927; Columbia University, graduate study, 1928-31; Stanford University, Ph.D., 1941; Yale University, postdoctoral fellow, 1944-45. *Home:* 1450 Mallory Lane, Reno, Nev. *Office:* Department of English, University of Nevada, Reno, Nev.

CAREER: Des Moines Register and Tribune, Des Moines, Iowa, editor, 1926; Drake University, Des Moines, Ia., instructor in journalism, 1926-28; University of Idaho, Pocatello, 1932-42, started as instructor in English, became associate professor; Purdue University, West Lafayette, Ind., assistant professor of English, 1942-43; University of Nevada, Reno, professor of English, 1943—. Visiting professor at University of Oregon, 1955-56; visiting summer professor at Columbia University, Portland State College (now Portland State University), and other schools. Consultant, World Publishing Co. Member of Nevada Governor's Board on Alcoholism and Nevada State Committee for Mental Health; former president,

Washoe County Council on Alcoholism. *Member:* Modern Language Association of America, American Dialect Society, American Names Society, Mediaeval Academy of America, National Council of Teachers of English (curriculum commission, 1946-62; executive committee, college section, 1956-59), American Association of University Professors (national council, 1964-67).

WRITINGS: Laird's Promptory: A Dictionary of Synonyms, Antonyms, and Specific Equivalents, Henry Holt, 1948; *Thunder on the River* (novel), Little, Brown, 1949; *A Writer's Handbook,* Ginn, 1964, published as *Handbook for English Language and Composition,* high school edition, 1964; *And Gladly Teche: Notes on Instructing the Natives in the Native Tongue,* Prentice-Hall, 1970; *Language in America,* World Publishing, 1970; *You and Your Language,* Prentice-Hall, 1973.

(Editor) *The World Through Literature,* Appleton, 1951; *West of the River* (novel), Little, Brown, 1953; (with Robert M. Gorrell) *Modern English Handbook,* Prentice-Hall, 1953, 5th edition, 1972; *The Miracle of Language,* World Publishing, 1953; (with wife, Helene Laird) *The Tree of Language,* World Publishing, 1957; (with R. M. Gorrell) *Modern English Workbook,* Prentice-Hall, 1957, 2nd edition, 1963; *Thinking About Language,* Holt, 1959; *Webster's New World Thesaurus,* World Publishing, 1971.

(Editor with R. M. Gorrell) *English as Language,* Harcourt, 1961; (with R. M. Gorrell) *A Course in Modern English,* Prentice-Hall, 1963; (with R. M. Gorrell and Ray Pflug) *A Basic Course in Modern English,* Prentice-Hall, 1963; *A Handbook for Writing,* Ginn, 1964; *Pickett at Gettysburg,* Ginn, 1965; *Modern English Reader,* Prentice-Hall, 1970; *Reading's About Language,* Harcourt, 1971.

Contributor and consultant to *Middle English Dictionary* and to *Webster's New World Dictionary of the American Language.* Contributor to popular, professional, and scholarly periodicals, including *PMLA, Saturday Review, Modern Language Review* (England), *English Studies* (Netherlands), *Speculum, American Literature.* Member of editorial board of *College English, Names, American Speech,* and University of Nevada Press. General editor, Ginn Casebook Series.

WORK IN PROGRESS: General editor, *A Guide for General and Comparative Literature,* sponsored by National Council of Teachers of English and American Library Association; *The Five Grammars of English,* for Prentice Hall; *Language in America* (working title), for World Publishing; *Which Seed Will Grow,* a book on the role of ideas; a new edition of *Laird's Promptory.*

SIDELIGHTS: Laird spent a year in Europe collating manuscripts, 1930-31, a sabbatical in England and Spain, collecting material for *Language in America,* 1963. Laird writes that "long ago I planned a number of novels, two of which were published and more of which are in some sort of draft in the file, but I seem to keep turning away from partly conceived people to intriguing ideas.... I have some acquaintance with Old English, Middle English, Old French, Old Norse, Latin, French, Spanish, and German, although I am fluent in none of them."†

* * *

LAL, P. 1929-

PERSONAL: Born August 28, 1929, in Kapurthala, Punjab, India; son of Parmeshwar (a businessman) and Jagdish (Devi) Lal; married Shyamasree Nag (a teacher), January 31, 1955; children: Ananda, Srimati. *Education:* St. Xavier's College, Calcutta, India, B.A., 1950; Calcutta University, M.A., 1952. *Religion:* Hindu. *Home:* 162/92 Lake Gardens, Calcutta 45, Bengal, India.

CAREER: St. Xavier's College, Calcutta, India, 1953—, began as lecturer, became professor of English. Writers Workshop, Calcutta, secretary, 1958—.

WRITINGS—All published by Writers Workshop (Calcutta), except as indicated: *The Art of the Essay,* Atma Ram, 1950; (editor with Raghavendra Rao) *Modern Indo-Anglican Poetry,* Kavita, 1958; *The Parrot's Death and Other Poems,* 1959, 3rd edition, 1968; *Love's The First* (poems), 1962; (editor) *T. S. Eliot: Homage from India,* 1965; *"Change!" They Said: New Poems,* 1966; (compiler and editor) *The First Workshop Story Anthology,* 1967; *Draupadi & Jayadratha & Other Poems,* 1967; (compiler) *Some Sanskrit Poems,* 1967; *The Annotated Mahabharata Bibliography,* 1967; *Creations and Transcreations,* Dialogue (Calcutta), 1968; *The Concept of an Indian Literature: Six Essays,* 1968; (compiler and editor) *Modern Indian Poetry in English,* 1969; *Yakshi from Didarganj: Poems,* 1969; (compiler) Manmohan Ghose, *Selected Poems,* 1969; *Transcreations: Two Essays,* Inter-Culture, 1973.

Translator—All published by Writers Workshop (Calcutta), except as indicated: Rehbar, *Premchand: His Mind and Art,* Atma Ram, 1952; (with Jai Ratan) Premchand, *Godan,* Jaico, 1956; (and editor) *Great Sanskrit Plays,* New Directions, 1964; Rgveda Vedas, *The Golden Womb of the Sun,* 1965; Bhagavadgita Mahabharata, *The Bhagavad Gita,* 1965; *Sanskrit Love Lyrics,* 1966; Dhammapada, *The Dhammadpada,* Farrar, Straus, 1967; Adi-Granth, *The Jap-ji: Fourteen Religious Songs,* 1967; Upanishads, *The Isa Upanisad,* 1968; Mahabharata, *The Mahabharata,* fifty-two volumes, 1968-73; Mahendra Vikrama Varma, King of Kanshi, *The Farce of the Drunk Monk,* 1968; Adi-Granth, *More Songs from the Jap-ji,* 1969: Subhash Mukherjee, *Selected Poems of Subhas Mukhopadyay,* Satyabrata Pal, 1969; Upanishads, *The Avyakta Upanisad,* 1969; Upanishads, *The Mahanarayana Upanisad,* 1971.

Editor with Alfred Schenkman, *Orient Review and Literary Digest,* 1954-58; editor, *Writers Workshop Miscellany,* 1958—.†

* * *

LAMONT, Corliss 1902-

PERSONAL: Born March, 28, 1902, in Englewood, N.J.; son of Thomas William and Florence (Corliss) Lamont; married Margaret E. Irish, 1928; married second wife, Helen Boyden (an economist), August 3, 1962; children: (first marriage) Margaret H. (Mrs. J. David Heap), Florence P. (Mrs. Ralph Antonides), Hayes C., Anne S. *Education:* Harvard University, A.B. (magna cum laude), 1924; New College, Oxford, graduate study, 1924-25; Columbia University, Ph.D., 1932. *Politics:* Independent. *Home and office:* 315 West 106th St., New York, N.Y. 10025.

CAREER: Writer. Instructor in philosophy at Columbia University, New York, N.Y., 1928-32, at New School for Social Research, New York, N.Y., 1940-42; lecturer on contemporary Russian civilization at Cornell University, Ithaca, N.Y., 1943; conductor of social studies workshop on Soviet Russia at Harvard University, Graduate School of Education, Cambridge, Mass., 1944, lecturer, Columbia

University, School of General Studies, seminar associate, 1971—. Candidate for U.S. Senate, American Labor Party, 1952, Independent Socialist Party, 1958. Chairman of Congress of American-Soviet Friendship, 1942, National Council of American-Soviet Friendship, 1943-46; indicted for contempt of Congress (McCarthy hearings), 1953, but dismissal of indictment upheld by U.S. Appeals Court, 1956; co-founder of Bill of Rights Fund, 1954, chairman, 1954-69; chairman of National Emergency Civil Liberties Committee, 1963—; vice-president, Poetry Society of America, 1973—.

MEMBER: American Philosophical Association, American Humanist Association, Academy of Political Science, American Civil Liberties Union (member of board, 1932-54), National Association for the Advancement of Colored People, United Nations Association of the U.S.A., Columbia Faculty Club, Harvard Club of New York City, Clan Lamont Society (Scotland), Phi Beta Kappa. *Awards, honors:* New York City Teachers Union Annual Award, 1955.

WRITINGS: Issues of Immortality: A Study in Implications, Henry Holt, 1932; (with Margaret Lamont) *Russia Day by Day: A Travel Diary*, Covici, Friede, 1933; *The Illusion of Immortality*, Putnam, 1935, 4th edition, revised, Ungar, 1965; *You Might Like Socialism: A Way of Life for Modern Man*, Modern Age Books, 1939; *Soviet Russia versus Nazi Germany: A Study in Contrasts*, American Council on Soviet Relations, 1941; *Soviet Russia and the Post-war World*, National Council of American-Soviet Friendship, 1943; *The Peoples of the Soviet Union*, Harcourt, 1946; *Humanism as a Philosophy*, Philosophical Library, 1949, reissued under title *The Philosophy of Humanism*, Philosophical Library, 1957, 5th edition, revised, Ungar, 1965.

The Independent Mind: Essays of a Humanist Philosopher, Horizon, 1951; *Soviet Civilization*, Philosophical Library, 1952, 2nd edition, 1955; *Freedom Is as Freedom Does: Civil Liberties Today*, Horizon, 1956; *The Crime Against Cuba*, Basic Pamphlets, 1961; *The Enduring Impact of George Santayana*, Basic Pamphlets, 1964; *Freedom of Choice Affirmed*, Horizon, 1967; *Remembering John Masefield*, Fairleigh Dickinson University Press, 1971; *Lovers Credo*, Barnes, 1972; *Voice in the Wilderness*, Prometheus, 1974.

Editor: *Man Answers Death: An Anthology of Poetry*, Putnam, 1936, 2nd enlarged edition, Philosophical Library, 1952; (with Mary Redmer) James T. Farrell and others, *Dialogue on John Dewey*, Horizon, 1959; (with Mary Redmer) James Gutmann and others, *Dialogue on George Santayana*, Horizon, 1959; *Albert Rhys Williams, Sept. 28, 1883-Feb. 27, 1962, in Memoriam*, Horizon, 1962; Thomas Lamont and others, *The Thomas Lamont Family*, Horizon, 1962; (author of introduction) *The Trial of Elizabeth Gurley, Flynn by the American Civil Liberties Union*, Horizon, 1968; *The Thomas Lamonts in America*, Barnes, 1971.

Also author of "Basic Pamphlet" series on contemporary issues, 1957—, including *My Trip Around the World*, 1960, and *My First Sixty Years*, 1962; *How To Be Happy—Though Married*, 1973.

SIDELIGHTS: Lamont has traveled extensively throughout the United States and the world, taking in all the countries of Western Europe except Spain. He has made several visits to the Soviet Union and has also visited India, Thailand, Hong Kong, and Japan. Lamont toured several countries in South America including Chile, where he studied the new Socialist regime and skied in the Andes. *Avocational interests:* Tennis, skiing, hiking, and the movies.

*   *   *

LAMPMAN, Evelyn Sibley   1907-
(Lynn Bronson)

PERSONAL: Born April 18, 1907, in Dallas, Ore.; daughter of Joseph E. and Harriet (Bronson) Sibley; married Herbert Sheldon Lampman, May 12, 1934 (died June, 1943); children: Linda Sibley Lampman McIsaac, Anne Hathaway Lampman Knutson. *Education:* Oregon State University, B.S., 1929. *Religion:* Episcopalian. *Home:* 3300 West Rosemont, West Linn, Ore. 97068.

CAREER: Radio Station KEX, Portland Ore., continuity writer, 1929-34, continuity chief, 1937-45; Radio Station KGW, Portland, Ore., educational director, 1945-52; full-time writer of children's books, 1952—. *Member:* Delta Delta Delta. *Awards, honors:* Award from Committee on Art of Democratic Living for *Treasure Mountain*, 1949; Dorothy Canfield Fisher Memorial Children's Book Award, 1962, for *City Under the Back Steps*; Western Writers of America Spur Award, 1970, for *Cayuse Courage*.

WRITINGS—Juveniles; all published by Doubleday, except as indicated: *Crazy Creek*, 1948; *Treasure Mountain*, 1949; *The Bounces of Cynthiann'*, 1950; *Elder Brother*, 1951; *Captain Apple's Ghost*, 1952; *Tree Wagon*, 1953; *Witch Doctor's Son*, 1954; *The Shy Stegosaurus of Cricket Creek*, 1955; *Navaho Sister*, 1956; *Rusty's Space Ship*, 1957; *Rock Hounds*, 1958; *Special Year*, 1959; *City Under the Back Steps*, 1960; *Princess of Fort Vancouver*, 1962; *Shy Stegosaurus at Indian Springs*, 1962; *The Tilted Sombrero*, 1966; *Half-Breed*, 1967; *The Bandit of Mok Hill*, 1970; *Cayuse Courage*, Harcourt, 1970; *Once Upon Little Big Horn*, Crowell, 1971; *The Year of Small Shadow*, Harcourt, 1971; *Go Up on The Road*, Atheneum, 1972; *Rattlesnake Cave*, Atheneum, 1974.

Under pseudonym Lynn Bronson: *Timberland Adventure*, Lippincott, 1950; *Coyote Kid*, Lippincott, 1951; *Rogue's Valley*, Lippincott, 1952; *The Runaway*, Lippincott, 1953; *Darcy's Harvest*, Doubleday, 1956; *Popular Girl*, Doubleday, 1957; *Mrs. Updaisy*, Doubleday, 1963; *Temple of the Sun*, Doubleday, 1964; *Wheels West*, Doubleday, 1965.†

*   *   *

LANCE, Derek (Paul)   1932-

PERSONAL: Born October 1, 1932, in Norwich, Norfolk, England; son of Joseph Bertram (a shopkeeper) and Florence Mary (Hunt) Lance. *Education:* Queens' College, Cambridge, M.A., 1957, Certificate of Education, 1958. *Religion:* Catholic. *Home:* Flat 1, Greenhill Ct., 70 Greenhill Rd., Moseley, Birmingham 13, England. *Office:* St. Thomas Aquinas School, Wychall Lane, Kings Norton, Birmingham, England.

CAREER: Becket School, Nottingham, England, head of history department, 1958-65; St. Thomas Aquinas Grammar School, Birmingham, England, deputy headmaster, 1965—. Borstal Institution (for delinquents), part-time religious instructor, 1964-65. Cheshire Homes, Nottingham, member of committee. *Military service:* British Army, Intelligence Corps, 1952-54; became sergeant. *Member:* Catholic Teachers Association (president, Nottingham branch, 1963), Catholic Colleges Conference, Historical Association, Newman Association (vice-president, Nottingham branch, 1964).

WRITINGS: Teaching Salvation History, Paulist Press, 1964 (published in England under title *Till Christ Be Formed*, Darton, Longman & Todd, 1964), also published as *Teaching the History of Salvation*, Paulist Press, 1964; *A Christian View of Life*, Living Parish, 1965; *Eleven-Sixteen: A Complete Course for Religious Education at the Secondary School Level*, Darton, Longman & Todd, 1967. Consulting editor "Where We Stand" series, Paulist Press (American edition called "Insight Series," Harcourt). Co-editor, *Living Parish*.

SIDELIGHTS: Lance speaks French and Italian. *Avocational interests:* Social work among delinquents and youth, music (classical and light), camping.†

* * *

LANCE, Leslie

PERSONAL: Born in Great Yarmouth, England; married I. M. Mossop. *Residence:* Dartmouth, Devon, England. *Agent:* S. Walker Literary Agency, 199 Hampermill Lane, Watford, Hertfordshire, England.

CAREER: Novelist; farmer.

WRITINGS: No Other Eve, Hodder & Stoughton, 1939; *Take a Chance*, Hodder & Stoughton, 1940; *Dark Stranger*, Lowe, 1946; *Man of the Family*, Hurst & Blackett, 1954; *Sisters in Love*, Ward, Lock, 1960; *Spun By the Moon*, Ward, Lock, 1960; *A Summer's Grace*, Ward, Lock, 1961; *Spreading Sails*, Ward, Lock, 1963; *Springtime for Sally*, Ward, Lock, 1962; *The Young Curmudgeon*, Ward, Lock, 1964; *Bright Winter*, Ward, Lock, 1965; *I'll Ride Beside You*, Ward, Lock, 1965; *No Summer Beauty*, R. Hale, 1967; *Return to King's Mere*, R. Hale, 1967; *Nurse in the Woods*, R. Hale, 1969; *Nurse on the Moors*, R. Hale, 1970; *Nurse Verena at Weirwater*, R. Hale, 1970; *No Laggard in Love*, R. Hale, 1971; *The House in the Woods*, Ace Books, 1973; *New Lord Winbridge*, R. Hale, 1973; *Now I Can Forget*, R. Hale, 1973; *Bride of Emersham*, Pyramid Publications, 1974. Also writer of serials for Fleetway Press and others.†

* * *

LAND, Myrick (Ebben) 1922-

PERSONAL: Born February 25, 1922, in Shreveport, La.; son of James Arthur and Mary Edna (Fancher) Land; married Barbara Neblett, 1949; children: Robert Arthur, Jacquelyn Myrick. *Education:* University of California, Los Angeles, B.A., 1945; Columbia University, M.S. in Journalism, 1946. *Agent:* Nannine Joseph, 200 West 54th St., New York, N.Y. 10019.

CAREER: American National Red Cross, Washington, D.C., director of information in Europe and North Africa, 1949-52; Scholastic Magazines, New York, N.Y., editor, 1952-55; *This Week*, New York, N.Y., assistant editor, 1955-59; *Look*, New York, N.Y., senior editor, beginning 1959; now teacher of journalism, University of Queensland, Brisbane, Australia. *Military service:* U.S. Army Air Forces, 1942-43. *Member:* Columbia Journalism Alumni (president, 1963-65). *Awards, honors:* Pulitzer traveling fellowship, 1946-47.

WRITINGS: Search the Dark Woods (novel), Funk, 1955, published as *The Search*, Dell, 1959; *The Fine Art of Literary Mayhem*, Holt, 1963; *Quicksand*, Harper, 1969.

Juvenile books with wife, Barbara Land: *Jungle Oil*, Coward, 1957; *The Changing South*, Coward, 1959; *The Quest of Isaac Newton*, Doubleday, 1961.

Contributor of some two hundred articles to *Look*, *This Week*, *New York Times Magazine*, *Cosmopolitan*, *Script*, *Coronet*, *Toronto Star*, and other periodicals and newspapers.

AVOCATIONAL INTERESTS: Painting.

* * *

LANDRY, Hilton (James) 1924-

PERSONAL: Born July 27, 1924, in Waltham, Mass.; son of Alexander and Winifred (Boudreau) Landry; married Ruth Hall (deceased); married Elaine Morris, December 24, 1961; children: Sutton George, Douglas Ivor, Philip Alexander, John Matthew. *Education:* Harvard University, B.A., 1950, M.A., 1951, Ph.D., 1958. *Politics:* Democrat. *Religion:* Protestant. *Home:* 609 D St., Davis, Calif. 95616. *Office:* Department of English, University of California, Davis, Calif. 95616.

CAREER: University of California, Davis, instructor in English, 1958-60, assistant professor, 1960—. *Military service:* U.S. Army, 1944-46. *Member:* Modern Language Association of America, Society for Religion in Higher Education (fellow), Philological Association of the Pacific Coast, Phi Beta Kappa.

WRITINGS: (Editor) *Magistri Terrarum: A Selection of Old and Rare Books, 1497-1798*, University of California Library, 1962; *Interpretations in Shakespeare's Sonnets*, University of California Press, 1963; *New Essays on Shakespeare's Sonnets*, AMS Press, 1971; (with Maurice Kramer) *A Concordance to the Poems of Hart Crane*, Scarecrow Press, 1973.

WORK IN PROGRESS: The Faith of Valor, an interpretation of Shakespeare's "Troilus and Cressida."†

* * *

LANDSTROM, Bjorn O(lof) 1917-

PERSONAL: Born April 21, 1917, in Kuopio, Finland; son of Artur August (a building engineer) and Ester (Aberg) Landstrom; married Else Gronros, July 16, 1939; children: Kristina, Olof. *Education:* Attended Svenska Normallyceet, Helsinki, Finland, 1928-35. *Religion:* Lutheran. *Home:* Danska Backarna 4, Saltsjobaden, Sweden.

CAREER: Author and artist. Taucher Advertising, Inc., Helsinki, Finland, advertising artist and art director, 1949-50; Mainosgraafikkojen Koulu (commercial art school), Helsinki, Finland, director, 1955-58. Paintings exhibited at four one-man shows in Helsinki, 1941-48, in Canada, 1963, and in Lisbon, 1964; illustrator of more than two hundred book jackets; designer of twenty settings for theaters in Finland and Sweden. Producer of several television shows on ships and geography for Finnish and Swedish television. *Military service:* Finnish Army, interpreter, and frontier correspondent and artist, Finnish-Russian War, 1939-44; became lieutenant.

MEMBER: Mainosgraafikot (Association of Advertising Artists; chairman, 1953-59), Nordiska Tecknare (Scandinavian Artists; chairman, 1961-63), Svenska Forfattar Foreningen, Society for Nautical Research, Hakluyt Society, Geographical Society (Sweden), Ethnographical Society (Sweden), Royal Swedish Yacht Club, Travellers Club (Stockholm).

WRITINGS: Agatan 8 (novel), Holger Schildt, 1942; *Regina och Gullkronan*, Holger Schildt, 1951; *Skeppet Flaskan*, Holger Schildt, 1952; *Havel Utan Ande* (novel about Magellan), Holger Schildt, 1953; *Vagen till Vinland* (novel about Leif Eriksson), Holger Schildt, 1954; *Skeppet*, Forum (Sweden), 1961 (translation published as *The Ship*, Doubleday [Toronto], 1961, Allen & Unwin, 1962); *Vagen till Indien*, Forum (Sweden), 1964 (translation published as *The Quest For India*, Doubleday, 1964), also published as *Bold Voyages and Great Explorers: The Quest for India*, Doubleday, 1973; *Columbus: Historien om amiralen over oceanen Don Cristobal Colon*, Forum, 1966, translation by Michael Phillips and Hugh B. Stubbs, published as *Columbus: The Story of Don Cristobal Colon, Admiral of the Ocean*, Macmillan, 1967; *Sailing Ships*, Doubleday, 1969; *Ships of the Pharaohs*, Doubleday, 1970; *Egyptian Ship Building*, Doubleday, 1970. Writer of Comedy, "Vem ar Du?" 1944.

SIDELIGHTS: Landstrom writes in Swedish and speaks Swedish in his home; also speaks Finnish, German and English. *Skeppet* has been published in twelve countries, *Vagen till Indien* in ten. *Avocational interests:* Ships, the sea, and "voyages of discovery" (has traveled to Africa, Arabia, India, Malaysia, Philippines, Hong Kong, United States, Europe, West Indies).†

*   *   *

LANE, Anthony 1916-

PERSONAL: Born February 7, 1916, in Minneapolis, Minn.; son of Marlboro Willis (a salesman) and Marjorie (Sorby) Lane; married Dorothy Marie Peterson, March 14, 1944; children: Christopher Willis and Kimberly Blythe (sons). *Education:* Studied at Minneapolis School of Arts, 1935-37. *Religion:* "Golden rule—sort of my own brand." *Home:* 2 Westwood Circle, Minnetonka 26, Minn. *Agent:* Howard Segal, 3333 Decatur Lane, St. Louis Park 26, Minn. *Office:* Anthony Lane Studios, 2701 Wayzata Blvd., Minneapolis 26, Minn.

CAREER: Started out as merchant seaman, then went into show business, working in films, stage productions, and stock; Anthony Lane Studios (producers of motion pictures and stills for government, business, and television), Minneapolis, Minn., president, 1939—. Former panelist on television program, "Sportsman's Round Table," Minneapolis. Formerly, director of Viking College. *Military service:* U.S. Navy, Photographic Division, 1941-45; served in South Pacific, 1941-42; became chief petty officer. *Member:* Minneapolis Motion Picture Producers Association (former president; treasurer), Minneapolis Christmas Tree Producers Association, Masons.

WRITINGS: How to Become a Model, Denison, 1964. Contributor of articles to outdoor publications.

WORK IN PROGRESS: How to Be Happy Though Alive; Your Outdoor Camera; a book on skiing, past, present, and future.†

*   *   *

LANE, Mary Beauchamp 1911-

PERSONAL: Born March 7, 1911, in Edwardsburg, Mich.; daughter of Hugh Dunning (a farmer) and Bea (Scott) Beauchamp; married Howard A. Lane, February 28, 1958 (deceased). *Education:* Northeast Missouri State Teachers College, B.A., 1930; Northwestern University, M.A., 1945; New York University, Ed.D., 1950. *Politics:* Democrat. *Home:* 75 Ashbury Terrace, San Francisco, Calif. 94117. *Office:* California State University, San Francisco, 1600 Holloway, San Francisco, Calif.

CAREER: Teacher in La Plata and Webster Groves, Mo.; Minneapolis (Minn.) public schools, curriculum consultant, 1945-48; New York University, New York, N.Y., instructor in elementary education and member of staff, Center for Human Relations Studies, 1951-58; University of California, Berkeley, instructor in educational psychology (part time), 1958-59; California State University, San Francisco, began as instructor, 1962, became professor of education. Director of summer workshops at University of Florida, 1951, University of Kansas City, 1956-59. Director, Cross Cultural Family Center. Consultant in early childhood education, group dynamics, and human relations. *Member:* Association for Supervision and Curriculum Development, Association for Childhood Education International, National Association for Young Children, American Civil Liberties Union, YWCA.

WRITINGS: (With husband, Howard A. Lane) *Human Relations in Teaching*, Prentice-Hall, 1956; (with H. A. Lane) *Understanding Human Development*, Prentice-Hall, 1959; (editor) H. A. Lane, *On Educating Human Beings* (essays), Follett, 1964. Also author of report on nurseries in cross cultural education. Contributor to education journals.

AVOCATIONAL INTERESTS: Outdoor living, gardening, camping, and travel.

*   *   *

LANE, Thomas A. 1906-

PERSONAL: Born November 19, 1906, in Revere, Mass.; son of Thomas A. and Julia (Fitzpatrick) Lane; married Jean Margaret Gee, June 3, 1933; children: Julia Ann Lane Rasmussen, Thomas Cleveland. *Education:* U.S. Military Academy, B.S., 1928; Massachusetts Institute of Technology, B.Sc. in C.E., 1932; graduate of Engineer School, Fort Belvoir, Va., and National War College. *Office:* 6157 Kellogg Dr., McLean, Va.

CAREER: U.S. Army, Corps of Engineers, regular officer, 1928-62, retiring as major general; *St. Louis Globe Democrat*, St. Louis, Mo., columnist, 1962-72, syndicated columnist, 1964—. Executive director, Institute for Human Progress, Inc., 1962-64; trustee, president, and chief executive officer, Americans for Constitutional Action, 1965-68. *Member:* American Society of Civil Engineers (fellow), Washington Society of Engineers (honorary). *Awards, honors*—Military: Distinguished Service Medal with oak leaf cluster.

WRITINGS: The Leadership of President Kennedy, Caxton, 1964; *The War for the World*, Viewpoint Books, 1968; *Cry Peace: The Kennedy Years*, Twin Circle, 1969; *America on Trial: The War for Vietnam*, Arlington House, 1971. Editor-in-chief, *Strategic Review*.

*   *   *

LANGLEY, Noel 1911-

PERSONAL: Born December 25, 1911, in Durban, South Africa; became U.S. citizen, 1961; married Naomi Mary Legate, 1937 (divorced, 1954); married Pamela Deeming, 1959; children: (first marriage) three sons, two daughters. *Education:* University of Natal, B.A.

CAREER: Author, playwright, and writer-director of films produced in Britain and United States. *Military service:* Canadian Navy, 1943-45; became lieutenant. *Member:*

Writers Guild of America, West. *Awards, honors:* Donaldson Award (shared with Robert Morley) for "Edward My Son," produced in New York, 1948.

WRITINGS: Cage Me a Peacock, Barker, 1935, Morrow, 1937; *There's a Porpoise Behind Us*, Barker, 1936, published as *So Unlike the English*, Morrow, 1937; *Tale of the Land of Green Ginger*, Morrow, 1938; *Hocus Pocus*, Methuen, 1941; *The Music of the Heart*, Barker, 1946; *The Cabbage Patch*, Barker, 1947; *Nymph in Clover*, Barker, 1948; *The True and Pathetic Story of Desbarollda the Waltzing Mouse*, Drummond, 1948; *The Inconstant Moon*, Barker, 1949; (with Hazel Pynegar) *Somebody's Rocking My Dreamboat*, Barker, 1949; *Tales of Mystery and Revenge*, Barker, 1950; (with H. Pynegar) *Cuckoo in the Dell*, Barker, 1951; *The Rift in the Lute*, Coward, 1951; *Where Did Everybody Go?*, Barker, 1960; *The Loner*, Triton, 1967; *Edgar Cayce on Reincarnation*, edited by Hugh Lynn Cayce, Hawthorn, 1968; *A Dream of Dragonflies*, Macmillan, 1970.

Plays: *Three Plays: Form of Three Echoes, For Ever, Friendly Relations* (*Form of Three Echoes* first produced in New York at Cort Theatre, November, 1939), Miles, 1936, *Form of Three Echoes* published separately, French, 1940; (with Robert Morley) *Edward My Son* (first produced in New York at Martin Beck Theatre, September, 1948), French, 1948; "The Burning Bush" (adaptation), first produced in New York at Erwin Piscator Dramatic Workshop, December, 1949; *An Elegance of Rebels: A Play in Three Acts*, Barker, 1960.

Other plays: "Queer Cargo," 1934; "No Regrets," 1937; "Little Lambs Eat Ivy," 1947; "Cage Me a Peacock" (adaptation of own book), 1948; "Married Alive," 1952.

Screenplays: "Maytime," 1936; "The Wizard of Oz," 1946; "They Made Me A Fugitive," 1946; "Cardboard Cavalier," 1948; "Adam and Evalyn," 1948; (with W. Somerset Maugham and R. C. Sherriff) "Trio," 1950; "Tom Brown's School Days," 1950; "Scrooge," 1951; "Ivanhoe," 1952; "Pickwick Papers," 1952; "Knights of the Round Table," 1953; "Prisoner of Zenda," 1953; "Our Girl Friday," 1954; "Trilby and Svengali," 1954; "Vagabond King," 1954; "The Adventures of Sadie," 1955; "The Search for Bridey Murphy," 1957.

* * *

LANGWILL, Lyndesay Graham 1897-

PERSONAL: Born March 19, 1897, in Edinburgh, Scotland; son of Archibald (a chartered accountant) and Jessie (Leishman) Langwill; married Freda Mary Wilson, April 22, 1922; children: Peter (killed in Naval Air Service, 1943), Winifred Joyce (Mrs. Charles Rasch). *Education:* Attended University of Edinburgh, 1915-16. *Religion:* Presbyterian. *Home:* 7 Dick Pl., Edinburgh 9, Scotland.

CAREER: Chartered accountant, Edinburgh, Scotland, 1921—. World Federation for Protection of Animals, president of council, 1958-62; Scottish Society for Prevention of Cruelty to Animals, secretary-treasurer, 1924-68; Scottish Community Drama Association, secretary-treasurer, 1939-68. *Military service:* British Army, 1916-19; became lieutenant. *Member:* Institute of Chartered Accountants of Scotland, Royal Musical Association, American Musical Instrument Society. *Awards, honors:* Honorary fellow, Trinity College of Music, London, 1950, for services to music; M.A., University of Edinburgh, 1964; Order of British Empire, 1968.

WRITINGS: Index of Musical Wind Instrument Makers, privately printed, 1960, 2nd edition, Heinman, 1963, 3rd edition, 1972; *The Bassoon and Contrabassoon*, Norton, 1965; (with Noel Boston) *Church and Chamber Barrel-Organs: Their Origin, Makers, Music and Location*, Heinman, 1967, 2nd edition, 1970. Contributor to *Grove's Dictionary of Music and Musicians*, and to *Musical Times, Music and Letters, Musik in Geschichte und Gegenwart*, and other music journals.

WORK IN PROGRESS: Fourth edition of *Index of Musical Wind Instrument Makers*.

SIDELIGHTS: Langwill has working knowledge of French and German, and knows some Dutch, Italian, and Spanish. He plays cello, bassoon, and contrabassoon.

* * *

LANSING, Alfred 1921-

PERSONAL: Born July 21, 1921, in Chicago, Ill.; son of Edward Heaton and Ruth (Henderson) Lansing; married Barbara Conningham, February 23, 1955; children: Angus, Holly. *Education:* Attended North Park College, 1946-48, Northwestern University, 1948-50. *Home:* Sea Cliff, N.Y.

CAREER: United Press, Chicago, Ill., overnight bureau manager, 1948-51; *Collier's*, New York, N.Y., staff writer, 1951-54; free-lance writer, 1954-63; Time, Inc. Books, New York, N.Y., editor, 1963—. Scott Polar Research Institute, Cambridge, England, member, 1957—. *Military service:* U.S. Navy, 1940-46; became ensign; received Purple Heart. *Awards, honors:* Christopher Award and Secondary Education Board Book Award, both for *Endurance, Shackleton's Incredible Voyage*, 1960.

WRITINGS: Endurance, Shackleton's Incredible Voyage, McGraw, 1959; *Shackleton's Valiant Voyage*, Whittlesey House, 1960, abridged edition, University of London Press, 1963; (with Walter Modell) *Drugs*, Time, Inc., 1967. Adapter of *Endurance* for a forthcoming motion picture. Contributor to magazines.

WORK IN PROGRESS: Three books.

SIDELIGHTS: Lansing told *CA:* "I have a great many opinions about writing, but I'm afraid that all of them are unprintable. Furthermore, it's been my experience that most writers don't talk about their craft—they just do it." *Avocational interests:* Japanese gardening.†

* * *

LANTIS, David W(illiam) 1917-

PERSONAL: Born April 13, 1917, in Fort Thomas, Ky.; son of Vernon and Janet (Brown) Lantis; married Helen E. Fisher (a junior high school librarian), April 9, 1954. *Education:* Adams State College, A.B., 1939; University of California, Berkeley, graduate study, 1947-48; University of Cincinnati, M.A., 1948; Ohio State University, Ph.D., 1950; University Nacional de Mexico, additional study, 1951. *Politics:* Independent. *Religion:* Unitarian. *Home:* Rt. 2, 1616 Oak Park Ave., Chico, Calif. 95926.

CAREER: Morning News, Alamosa, Colo., editor, 1939; Adams State College, Alamosa, Colo., instructor, summers 1947 and 1949; University of Southern California, Los Angeles, assistant professor, 1949-53; taught at Los Angeles City College, 1953-55, and at Compton College, Compton, Calif., 1955-57; California State University, Chico, 1957—, now professor of geography. *Military service:* U.S. Navy, 1941-45; became lieutenant. *Member:*

Royal Geographic Society, Association of American Geographers, American Geographical Society, National Geographic Society, National Council for Geographic Education (member of executive board, 1962-65), American Meteorological Society, Association de Geographie Francais, Gesellschaft fuer Erdkunde zu Berlin, California Council of Geography Teachers (president, 1953), Los Angeles Geographic Society (co-founder and president, 1953 and 1957), Sigma Xi, Gamma Theta Upsilon (president, 1968-70). *Awards, honors:* Adams State College, outstanding alumnus award, 1969; California State University, Chico, Distinguished Teacher, 1970; National Council for Geography Education, Outstanding Teacher of Geography—college level, 1971.

WRITINGS: Alaska, Doubleday, 1957; *California*, Doubleday, 1958; *Los Angeles*, Doubleday, 1960; (with R. Steiner and A. E. Karinen) *California, Land of Contrast*, Wadsworth, 1963, 3rd edition, Kendall Hunt, 1973. Contributor to *Focus, Geographic Review*, and *Journal of Geography*.

WORK IN PROGRESS: Geography of the United States, and a revision of *California, Land of Contrast*.

SIDELIGHTS: Lantis has limited competence in German, French, and Spanish. He has traveled extensively in all fifty States and all Canadian provinces, Mexico, Europe, and Pacific Basin. *Avocational interests:* Gardening, photography, reading, stamp collecting, and hiking.

* * *

LARDAS, Konstantinos 1927-

PERSONAL: Born August 3, 1927, in Steubenville, Ohio; son of Nick Dimitrios and Constantina (Moraitis) Lardas; married Sofia Lacios, June 9, 1951; children: Nicholas Orestes, George Alexander, Stefan Jason. *Education:* University of Pittsburgh, B.A., 1950; Columbia University, M.A., 1951; University of Michigan, Ph.D., 1966. *Religion:* Greek Orthodox. *Home:* 68 Wakefield, Yonkers, N.Y. 10704. *Office:* City College of the City University of New York, New York, N.Y. 10031.

CAREER: Partner in an industrial painting and roofing company in Pittsburgh, Pa., 1951-60; University of Michigan, Ann Arbor, teaching fellow in English, 1961, instructor in English, 1964-66; City College of the City University of New York, assistant professor, 1966-70, associate professor of English, 1971-72. *Military service:* U.S. Army, 1946-47. *Member:* Modern Language Association, Academy of American Poets. *Awards, honors:* Fulbright student grant to University of Athens, 1962; Borestone Mountain Poetry Award, 1962, 1965; Rockefeller grant-in-aid fellowship, 1963; Major Hopwood Award in Fiction, University of Michigan; *Atlantic Monthly* "first" for short story.

WRITINGS: And in Him, Too; In Us (poems), Generation, University of Michigan, 1964; *A Tree of Man*, Hunter Press, 1968. Poems and short stories have appeared in sixty literary journals, including *Atlantic Monthly, Charioteer, Dalhousie Review, Harper's Bazaar, Krikos, Prairie Schooner, Antioch Review*, and other publications.

WORK IN PROGRESS: Poetry; translations from the *Folk Poetry of Modern Greece*.

SIDELIGHTS: Lardas is interested in modern Greek poetry.

LARKIN, Emmet J. 1927-

PERSONAL: Born May 19, 1927, in New York, N.Y.; son of Emmet Joseph and Annabell (Ryder) Larkin. *Education:* New York University, B.A., 1950; Columbia University, M.A., 1951, Ph.D., 1957; London School of Economics and Political Science, London, graduate study, 1955-56. *Home:* 50 Massachusetts Ave., Cambridge, Mass. *Office:* Massachusetts Institute of Technology, Cambridge, Mass.

CAREER: Brooklyn College, Brooklyn, N.Y., part-time instructor in history, 1954-55, full-time instructor, 1956-60; Massachusetts Institute of Technology, Cambridge, assistant professor of history, 1960—. Columbia University, executive secretary, Labor Seminar, 1956-60. *Military service:* U.S. Army, 1944-46. *Member:* American Committee for Irish Studies (treasurer, 1961—). *Awards, honors:* Fulbright scholar, University of London, 1955-56; grants-in-aid from American Philosophical Society, 1958, 1959, 1963, Social Science Research Council, 1958, 1961, American Council of Learned Societies, 1962, Massachusetts Institute of Technology, 1964, 1965; Dominion fellowship, Massachusetts Institute of Technology, 1962-63; Howard Foundation fellowship, Brown University, 1964-65.

WRITINGS: James Larkin, Irish Labour Leader, 1876-1947, M.I.T. Press, 1965, revised edition, New English Library, 1968; (contributor) *The Celtic Cross*, edited by Ray B. Browne, William John Roscelli, and Richard J. Loftus, Purdue University Press, 1965. Contributor of articles to *Victorian Newsletter, Victorian Studies, Review of Politics*, and historical periodicals.

WORK IN PROGRESS: A History of the Roman Catholic Church in Ireland in the Nineteenth Century, in five volumes for joint publication by M.I.T. Press and Routledge & Kegan Paul.†

* * *

LARSEN, Erling 1909-
(Peter Brand)

PERSONAL: Born September 7, 1909, in Cresco, Iowa; son of Lauritz (a clergyman) and Charlotte (Haugen) Larsen; married Eileen Dilley, June 10, 1933; children: Sigrid (deceased), Borghild (Mrs. John Tollefson), Eric. *Education:* St. Olaf College, B.A., 1930; University of Iowa, M.A., 1932. *Politics:* Democrat. *Home address:* Route 3, Box 243, Northfield, Minn. 55057. *Agent:* Carolyn W. Stagg, 15 East 48th St., New York, N.Y. 10017.

CAREER: Theater manager in Northfield, Minn., 1932-47; free-lance photographer, 1938—; farmer, Northfield, Minn., 1947—; Carleton College, Northfield, Minn., instructor, 1956-58, assistant professor, 1959-67, associate professor, 1968-69, professor of English, 1970-74. *Military service:* U.S. Navy, 1942-44; received Asiatic-Pacific Theater Ribbon with two battle stars, Philippine Liberation Ribbon with two battle stars, Navy Unit Commendation. *Member:* U.S. Naval Institute.

WRITINGS: Minnesota Trails: A Sentimental History, Denison, 1958; *The Educations of Laird Bell*, Carleton, 1967; *James Agee*, University of Minnesota Press, 1971. Contributor of short stories, essays, and reviews to periodicals.

WORK IN PROGRESS: The Superior Country: A Geographical Autobiography.

* * *

La SORTE, A(ntonio) Michael 1931-

PERSONAL: Born September 24, 1931, in Endicott, N.Y.;

son of Vitantonio and Rose (Giacovelli) LaSorte; married Diane Emenhiser, August 29, 1964; children: two. *Education:* Harpur College, State University of New York (now State University of New York at Binghamton), B.A., 1958; Rutgers University, M.A., 1962; Indiana University, Ph.D., 1967. *Home:* 8235 Ridge Rd., Brockport, N.Y. 14420. *Office:* Department of Sociology, State University of New York College at Brockport, Brockport, N.Y. 14420.

CAREER: Knox College, Galesburg, Ill., instructor in sociology and anthropology, 1964-66; Hofstra State University, Hempstead, N.Y., assistant professor of sociology, 1967-71; State University of New York College at Brockport, associate professor of sociology, 1971—. *Military service:* U.S. Marine Corps, 1951-54. *Member:* American Sociological Association, Population Association of America.

WRITINGS: (With L. L. Geisman) *Understanding the Multi-Problem Family*, Association Press, 1964. Contributor to *Social Work, Journal of Marriage and the Family, American Sociologist*, and *Sociological Quarterly*.

* * *

LAURENTS, Arthur 1920-

PERSONAL: Born July 14, 1920, in Brooklyn, N.Y.; son of Irving (a lawyer) and Ada (Robbins) Laurents. *Education:* Cornell University, B.A., 1939. *Residence:* Quogue, N.Y. *Agent:* Shirley Bernstein Paramuse, 1414 Sixth Ave., New York, N.Y. 10019.

CAREER: Playwright, writing primarily for radio, 1939-40, and for stage and screen, 1945—. Director of Broadway productions, "Invitation to a March," 1960, "I Can Get It for You Wholesale," 1962; "Anyone Can Whistle," 1965; director of London productions of "Gypsy" and "The Enclave," 1973; and National Company production of "Gypsy," 1974. Director, Dramatists Play Service. *Military service:* U.S. Army, 1941-45; became sergeant. *Member:* Dramatists Guild (member of council), P.E.N., National Motion Picture Academy. *Awards, honors:* Variety Radio Award, 1945, for "Assignment Home" series; National Institute of Arts and Letters grant in literature, 1946; co-winner of Sidney Howard Award, 1946, for "Home of the Brave"; Antoinette Perry (Tony) Award, 1967, for "Hallelujah, Baby."

WRITINGS: The Way We Were (novel), Harper, 1972.

Plays: *Home of the Brave* (produced in 1945), Random House, 1946; *The Bird Cage* (two-act; produced in 1950), Dramatists Play Service, 1950; *The Time of the Cuckoo* (two-act comedy; produced in 1952), Random House, 1953, acting edition, Samuel French, 1954; *A Clearing in the Woods* (two-act; produced in 1957), Random House, 1957, revised edition, Dramatists Play Service, 1960; *West Side Story* (musical; score by Leonard Bernstein and Stephen Sondheim; produced in 1957). Random House, 1958; *Gypsy* (musical; score by Jule Styne and Sondheim; produced in 1959), Random House, 1960; *Invitation to a March* (comedy; produced in 1960), Random House, 1961; *Anyone Can Whistle* (musical; score and lyrics by Sondheim; produced in 1964), Random House, 1967; *Do I Hear a Waltz?* (musical; based on *The Time of the Cuckoo*; score by Richard Rogers and Sondheim; produced in 1965), Random House, 1966.

Unpublished plays: "Hallelujah, Baby" (two-act musical; score by Styne, lyrics by Betty Comden and Adolph Green), produced on Broadway at Martin Beck Theatre,

April 26, 1967; "The Enclave," produced in Washington, D.C., at Theatre Club, February, 1972.

Screenplays: "The Snake Pit," 1948; "Rope," 1948; "Caught," 1948; (co-author) "Anna Lucasta," 1949; "Anastasia," 1956; "Bonjour Tristesse," 1958; "The Way We Were," 1973.

Plays anthologized in collections, including: *Best One-Act Plays of 1944-45*, edited by M. G. Mayora, Dodd, 1945; *Best One-Act Plays of 1945-46*, edited by Mayora, Dodd, 1946; *Best Plays of 1945-46*, edited by Burns Mantle, Dodd, 1946; *Best Plays of the Modern American Theatre, 1939-1946*, edited by John Gassner, Crown, 1947; *Best Plays of 1956-57*, edited by Louis Kronenberger, Dodd, 1957; *Broadway's Best, 1958*, edited by John A. Chapman, Doubleday, 1958; *Broadway's Best, 1959*, edited by Chapman, Doubleday, 1959.

* * *

LAUTER, Paul 1932-

PERSONAL: Born July 25, 1932, in New York, N.Y.; son of Herman and Lillian (Miller) Lauter; married, 1953 (divorced); children: David, Daniel. *Education:* New York University, B.A., 1953; Indiana University, M.A., 1955; Yale University, Ph.D., 1958. *Politics:* Radical Socialist. *Office:* American Friends Service Committee, 431 South Dearborn, Chicago, Ill.

CAREER: Instructor in English at Dartmouth College, Hanover, N.H., 1957-59, University of Massachusetts, Amherst, 1959-60; Hobart and William Smith Colleges, Geneva, N.Y., assistant professor of English, 1960-63; American Friends Service Committee, Philadelphia, Pa., director of peace studies, 1963-64; Smith College, Northampton, Mass., assistant professor of English, 1964-65; American Friends Service Committee, Chicago, Ill., peace education secretary, 1965—. Teacher in Mississippi Freedom Schools, summers, 1964-65. *Member:* Modern Language Association of America, American Association of University Professors.

WRITINGS: (Editor) *Theories of Comedy*, Anchor Books, 1964; (editor) *Teaching About Peace Issues*, American Friends Service Committee, 1965; (with Florence Howe) *The Conspiracy of the Young*, World Publishing, 1970; (editor) *The Politics of Literature*, Vintage Books, 1973. Contributor to *Nation, New Republic, New Leader*, and other periodicals.

WORK IN PROGRESS: A book on Vladimir Nabokov; co-editing a book on violence in America.†

* * *

LAUWERYS, Joseph (Albert) 1902-

PERSONAL: Born November 7, 1902, in Brussels, Belgium; son of Henri (a businessman) and Louise (Nagels) Lauwerys; married Waltraut Dorothy Bauermeister, November 5, 1931; children: Michael, Peter, John. *Education:* King's College, London, B.Sc. General (first class honors), 1927, B.Sc., Chemistry (first class honors), 1928, B.Sc. Physics (second class honors), 1929. *Politics:* "The rational man whose vote sways elections." *Religion:* Christian rationalist and scientific humanist. *Home:* Aston House, Chilworth, Surrey, England. *Office:* Atlantic Institute of Education, 5244 South St., Halifax, Nova Scotia, Canada.

CAREER: Christ's Hospital, Horsham, England, senior physics master, 1928-32; University of London, Institute of Education, London, England, lecturer in methods of science, 1932-41, reader in education, 1941-45, professor of comparative education, 1945-70; Atlantic Institute of Education, Halifax, Nova Scotia, director, 1970—. Visiting professor at Columbia University, 1939, 1951, University of Indiana, 1952, University of Southern California, 1953, 1955, 1957, 1959, 1961, University of Michigan, 1954, and at other universities in South Africa, Japan, and Chile, 1958-63. Consultant to Rockefeller Foundation, 1937, and to UNESCO, 1947-48; chairman of International New Education Fellowship; chairman of education committee, Parliamentary Group for World Government; member of Good Offices Commission, UNESCO. *Member:* Royal Institute of Chemistry (fellow). *Awards, honors:* D.Sc., University of Ghent, 1946; D.Lit., University of London, 1958; Commander, Ordre des Palmes Academiques, 1961.

WRITINGS: (With F. S. Baker) *Education and Biology*, Sands & Co., 1934; *Introductory Science*, three books, Edward Arnold, 1934-35; (with John Ellison) *Chemistry, with Some Geology*, University of London Press, 1937; (with Otto Raum) *Arithmetic in Africa*, Evans, 1938; *Film and Radio as Educational Media*, [London], 1939; *The Content of Education*, English Universities Press, 1944; *Educational Problems in the Liberated Countries*, 1946.

The Roots of Science, Evans, 1951; (contributor) M. Domnitz, *Education in Human Relations*, Woburn Press, 1951; *The Idea of Europe*, Jewish Historical Society of England, 1951; *History Textbooks and International Understanding*, UNESCO, 1953; *The Enterprise of Education*, Ampersand, 1955; *Morals, Democracy and Education* (Japanese-English parallel texts), Institute for Democratic Education (Tokyo), 1957.

(With Howard Barnard) *A Handbook of British Educational Terms*, Harrap, 1963; (with Irenee Lussier and Donald Huenen) *Desenvolvimento da educacao superior na Universidade Federal da Bahia*, Departamento Cultural de Reitoria, Universidade Federal da Bahia, 1968; *Man's Impact on Nature*, Aldus, 1969, American Museum of Natural History Press, 1970.

Contributor to series: (With Marie Neurath) "Visual Science," juvenile, edited by Lancelot Hogben, published by Parrish; (with Otto and Marie Neurath) "Visual History of Mankind," juvenile, edited by Hogben, published by Parrish; (with A. H. T. Glover) "Background Science Series," published by Thomas Nelson; "Primary Science Series," juvenile, published by Harrap. Also contributor to *Encyclopaedia Britannica*, *Chambers's Encyclopaedia*, and to journals and newspapers, including *Nature*, *New Era*, *Times Educational Supplement*, and *Educational Forum*.

Editor: *The Film in the School*, Christophers, 1935; *Odhams' Encyclopaedia for Children*, Odhams, 1954; *Scandinavian Democracy*, Danish Institute, 1958; *The Sciences: Understanding Natural Forces* (juvenile), Grolier Society, 1967. Editor, at various times with George Bereday, David Scanlon, and Robert K. Hall, of *Year Book of Education*, published by Evans and World Book for Institute of Education (University of London) and Teachers College (Columbia University), annually, 1947—. General editor of "Essays in Comparative Education" series, published by Evans.

WORK IN PROGRESS: Textbooks in comparative education and in philosophy of education.

SIDELIGHTS: Lauwerys is competent in most western European languages. *Avocational interests:* Walking and chess.

LAWLER, Lillian B.   1898-

PERSONAL: Born June 30, 1898, in Pittsburgh, Pa.; daughter of Thomas Joseph (an electrical worker) and Ellen (Nuttridge) Lawler. *Education:* University of Pittsburgh, B.A., 1919; University of Iowa, M.A., 1921, Ph.D., 1925; additional study at American Academy in Rome, 1925-26, American School of Classical Studies, Athens, 1955. *Politics:* Republican. *Home:* 1133 Howell St., Iowa City, Iowa 52240.

CAREER: University of Iowa, Iowa City, instructor in classics and history of art, 1923-25; University of Kansas, Lawrence, assistant professor of classics, 1926-29; Hunter College (now Hunter College of the City University of New York), New York, N.Y., instructor, 1929-30, assistant professor, 1930-43, associate professor, 1943-55, professor of classics, 1955-59, professor emeritus, 1959—. Traveling lecturer, Archaeological Institute of America, 1928-35; visiting professor, University of Iowa, 1961-67.

MEMBER: American Philological Association, American Classical League (vice-president, 1957-64; honorary vice-president, 1964—), Classical Association of the Middle West and South, Classical Association of the Atlantic States (member of executive committee, 1945-51; president, 1946-49), Classical Society of the American Academy in Rome (vice-president, 1945, 1948), Phi Beta Kappa, Eta Sigma Phi (member of national board of trustees, 1949-55), Pi Lambda Theta, Mortar Board. *Awards, honors:* Prix de Rome fellowship, 1925-26.

WRITINGS: *Latin Playlets for High Schools*, University of Iowa Press, 1925; *The Latin Club*, American Classical League, 1929, 10th edition, 1968; *Easy Latin Plays*, Macmillan, 1929; (with Mary L. Riley and R. H. Tanner) *Adventures in Language*, Prentice-Hall, 1941; (editor with D. M. Robathan and W. C. Korfmacher) *Studies in Honor of Ullman*, St. Louis University Press, 1960; *The Dance in Ancient Greece*, A. & C. Black, 1964, Wesleyan University Press, 1965; *The Dance of the Ancient Greek Theatre*, University of Iowa Press, 1964, revised edition, 1973.

Author of a number of teaching playlets for Latin students published by American Classical League and in *Auxilium Latinum*. Contributor of about one hundred articles (and a dozen reviews annually) to classical, philological, and dance journals in America and abroad. Associate editor, *Auxilium Latinum*, 1931-68; editor, *Classical Outlook*, 1936-57.

WORK IN PROGRESS: Research for an eventual book with working title, *The Dance in Ancient Rome*.

SIDELIGHTS: Miss Lawler has traveled on all continents observing dances, and has visited classical sites in a number of countries. She is competent in Greek, Latin, German, French, and Italian.

*   *   *

LAXALT, Robert P(eter)   1923-

PERSONAL: Born September 24, 1923, in Alturas, Calif.; son of Dominique (a sheepman) and Theresa (Alpetche) Laxalt; married Joyce Nielsen (a schoolteacher), May 29, 1949; children: Bruce, Monique, Kristin. *Education:* Santa Clara University, student, 1941-43; University of Nevada, B.A., 1947. *Politics:* Republican. *Religion:* Roman Catholic. *Home:* 650 Cardinal Way, Reno, Nev. *Agent:* Curtis Brown, Ltd., 575 Madison Ave., New York, N.Y. 10022. *Office:* University of Nevada, Reno, Nev.

CAREER: U.S. Consular Service, Belgian Congo, 1943-45;

United Press Associations, correspondent in Reno, Nev., 1948-53; University of Nevada, Reno, director of University Press, 1954—. U.S. Library of Congress, consultant on Basque history and culture. *Member:* Sigma Delta Chi. *Awards, honors:* Fulbright research fellow in Basque history and culture.

WRITINGS: Sweet Promised Land, Harper, 1957 (title in England, *Dominique*); *A Man in the Wheatfield*, Harper, 1964; *Nevada*, Coward, 1970; *In a Hundred Graves: A Basque Portrait*, University of Nevada Press, 1972. Contributor of articles and short stories to *Atlantic Monthly, Cosmopolitan, Saturday Evening Post, Mademoiselle, True, Bluebook, American Weekly*, and other periodicals.

SIDELIGHTS: Laxalt speaks French and Basque.†

* * *

LEARMONTH, Andrew Thomas Amos 1916-

PERSONAL: Surname is pronounced Lur-month; born December 17, 1916, in Edinburgh, Scotland; son of George Sanderson (a solicitor) and Mary (Amos) Learmonth; married Agnes Moffit Maxwell (a teacher and writer), April 8, 1950; children: two sons, two daughters. *Education:* Attended Heriot-Watt College, Edinburgh, Scotland, 1933-39, University of Edinburgh, 1945-49. *Religion:* Presbyterian. *Home:* 39 Endeavour St., Red Hill, Canberra, Australian Capital Territory, Australia. *Office:* School of General Studies, Australian National University, P.O. Box 4, Canberra, Australian Capital Territory, Australia.

CAREER: University of Liverpool, Liverpool, England, lecturer, 1949-62; Australian National University, Canberra, Australian Capital Territory, Australia, professor of geography, 1962-69; Open University, Buckinghamshire, England, professor of social sciences, 1970—. Colombo Plan consultant, Indian Statistical Institute, 1956-58; chairman, Commission on Medical Geography, International Geographical Union. *Military service:* British Army, Medical Corps, 1939-45; served in India, 1942-45; became warrant officer second class.

WRITINGS: (Contributor) *Scientific Survey of Merseyside*, Liverpool University Press for British Association, 1953; (contributor) *Geographical Essays in Memory of Alan G. Ogilvie*, edited by R. Miller and J. W. Watson, Nelson, 1959; *An Atlas of Resources of Mysore State*, 1960, and *Mysore State: A Regional Synthesis*, 1962 (two volumes of a pilot project regional survey in south India), India Statistical Institute and Asia Publishing House; (with wife, A. M. Learmonth) *The Eastern Lands* (textbook for children), 2nd edition, Oxford University Press, 1963; (contributor) *Geographers and the Tropics: Liverpool Essays*, edited by R. W. Steel and R. M. Prothero, Longmans, Green, 1964; *Health in India Sub-Continent, 1955-1964*, Australian National University, 1965; *Sample Villages in Mysore State, India*, Department of Geography, University of Liverpool, 1966; (with I. D. Reid) *Applications of Statistical Sampling to Geographical Studies*, Australian National University, 1966; (O.H.K. Spate) *India and Pakistan*, 3rd revised edition, Methuen, 1967; (compiler with A. M. Learmonth) *Encyclopedia of Australia*, F. Warne, 1968; (with A. M. Learmonth) *Regional Landscapes of Australia*, Angus and Robertson, 1971.

Contributor to *Encyclopaedia Britannica* and *Chambers's Encyclopaedia*; contributor of articles and occasional reviews to *Annals of Tropical Medicine and Parasites, Indian Geographical Journal, Erdkunde*, and other geographical journals.†

LEAVITT, Hart Day 1909-

PERSONAL: Born December 29, 1909, in Concord, N.H.; son of Ashley Day and Myrtle R. (Hart) Leavitt; married Caroline W. Parker, June 25, 1938; children: Sally (Mrs. John T. Blackburn), Edward, Judith. *Education:* Yale University, A.B., 1932; Bread Loaf School of English, summer study, 1941, 1943, 1950; graduate study, University of California at Berkeley, 1955-56. *Politics:* Democrat. *Religion:* Protestant. *Home:* 15 School St., Andover, Mass. *Office:* Phillips Academy, Andover, Mass.

CAREER: Salesman in Newark, N.J., professional jazz musician, and reporter in Concord, N.H., in period 1932-36; Phillips Academy, Andover, Mass., instructor in English, 1937—. Free-lance photographer. Former clarinetist in San Francisco Conservatory Orchestra and Andover Community Symphony Orchestra. Technical adviser to Andover Children's Theatre Workshop. *Member:* Permanent Peace Society (Boston; trustee), Amateur Chamber Music Players (New York), Andover Skating Club (founder).

WRITINGS: (Editor) *Looking Glass Book of Stories* (juvenile), Random House, 1960; (editor) *The Comic Looking Glass* (juvenile), Random House, 1961; (with David Sohn) *Stop, Look and Write*, Bantam, 1964; (editor) *Short Stories of H. G. Wells*, Bantam, 1965; (editor) Herman Melville, *Billy Budd*, Bantam, 1965; (contributor) Edward Gordon, editor, *Writing and Literature in the Secondary School*, Holt, 1965; *The Writer's Eye*, Bantam, 1968; *Pictures for Writing*, Bantam, 1969; *An Eye for People*, Bantam, 1970; *A Visual Dictionary of the Humanities* (tentative title), Bantam, in press.

SIDELIGHTS: As a professional musician during the thirties, Leavitt earned his way to Cuba, the Scandinavian countries, and twice to Moscow. Now music is his avocation and he plays regularly every summer at Squirrel Island, Me., as a member of "the oldest unincorporated jam session in America." He is the founder and director of "The Righteous Jazz Band," working in the Boston area.

* * *

LECKIE, Robert (Hugh) 1920-
(Roger Barlow, Mark Porter)

PERSONAL: Born December 18, 1920, in Philadelphia, Pa.; son of John Joseph (an advertising executive) and Marion Eugenie (Flood) Leckie; married Vera Keller, November 23, 1946; children: Geoffrey, Joan, David. *Education:* Attended New York University and Fordham University. *Politics:* Independent. *Religion:* Roman Catholic. *Home:* 281 Morris Ave., Mountain Lakes, N.J.

CAREER: Began newspaper career at age of sixteen as sportswriter for *Bergen Record*, Bergen County, N.J.; later worked variously as reporter, rewriteman, feature writer, financial editor, and on telegraph desk, for Associated Press, *Buffalo Courier-Express*, Buffalo, N.Y., *New York Journal-American*, New York, N.Y., *Newark Star-Ledger*, Newark, N.J., and *New York Daily News*, New York, N.Y.; full-time free-lance writer, 1957—. Sometime editor of Metro-Goldwyn-Mayer theater newsreel, "News of the Day," of "Telenews Weekly," and of other television newsfilm features; writer of television documentaries. *Military service:* U.S. Marines, machine gunner and scout, 1941-45; served in Pacific theater; received five battle stars, Naval Commendation Medal with Combat V, Purple Heart. *Member:* Lambs Club (New York). *Awards, honors:* Marine Corps Combat Correspondents Association Award.

WRITINGS: Helmet for My Pillow, Random House, 1957; *Lord, What a Family!*, Random House, 1958; *The March to Glory*, World Publishing, 1959; *Marines* (short stories), Bantam, 1960; *Strong Men Armed: The United States Marines Against Japan*, Bonanza Books, 1962; *Conflict: The History of the Korean War, 1950-1953* (juvenile), Putnam, 1962, published as *The War in Korea, 1950-1953*, Random House, 1963 (published in England as *The Korean War*, Pall Mall Press, 1963); (editor with Quentin J. Reynolds) *With Fire and Sword: Great War Adventures*, Dial Press, 1963; *The Story of World War II*, Random House, 1964; *These Are My Heroes: A Study of the Saints*, Random House, 1964; *Challenge for the Pacific*, Doubleday, 1965; *The Story of Football* (juvenile), Random House, 1965; (editor) Samuel L. A. Marshall, *The Story of World War I* (juvenile), Random House, 1965; *The Wars of America*, Harper, 1967; *The Battle of Iwo Jima*, Random House, 1967; *Great American Battles*, Random House, 1968; *Ordained* (novel), Doubleday, 1969; *American and Catholic*, Harper, 1970; *Warfare*, Harper, 1970; *The World Turned Upside Down: The Story of the American Revolution*, Putnam, 1972; *The War Nobody Won*, Putnam, 1974.

Under pseudonym Roger Barlow; all juvenile, all published by Simon & Schuster: *Black Treasure*, 1959; *Danger at Mormon Crossing*, 1959; *Fire at Red Lake*, 1959; *Secret Mission to Alaska*, 1959; *Stormy Voyage*, 1959; *Troubled Waters*, 1959; *The Big Game*, 1965.

Under pseudonym Mark Porter; all juvenile; all published by Simon & Schuster; all published in 1960: *Duel on the Cinders*; *"Keeper" Play*; *Overtime Upset*; *Set Point*; *Slashing Blades*; *Winning Pitcher*.

Contributor of short stories and articles to *Saturday Evening Post*, *True*, and other magazines. Columnist, *Country Beautiful*.

SIDELIGHTS: Leckie's books have had British and other European editions, and have been translated into several Asiatic languages. *Avocational interests:* Handball in the morning, drink and debate in the evening.

*   *   *

LEE, Dorris M(ay Potter)   1905-

PERSONAL: Born May 16, 1905, in Gowanda, N.Y.; daughter of Herbert (a teacher) and Margaret (Barnaby) Potter; children: Lawrence Keith, Lorna Jean (Mrs. Porter B. Lombard). *Education:* Occidental College, B.A., 1926; Columbia University, M.A., 1928, Ph.D., 1932. *Home:* 7226 Southwest Corbett Ave., Portland, Ore. 97219. *Office:* Portland State University, P.O. Box 751, Portland, Ore. 97207.

CAREER: Elementary schoolteacher in Glendale, Calif., 1926-27, 1928-31; Washington State College (now University), Pullman, acting assistant professor, 1952-53; Portland State College (now University), Portland, Ore., associate professor, 1956-59, professor of education, 1959-72, professor emerita, 1972—. Visiting professor at University of Utah, University of Alaska, Stanford University, and Montana State College; director of workshops at University of Hawaii, Arizona State College, and Portland public schools. *Member:* National Education Association, National Society for the Study of Education, National Society of College Teachers of Education, American Educational Research Association, Association for Childhood Educa-

tion International, American Association of Elementary, Kindergarten, Nursery Educators (member of executive committee, 1971-74; publications chairman, 1971-75; publications director, 1974-75), Association for Student Teaching, Association for Supervision and Curriculum Development, American Association of University Professors, Oregon Association for Higher Education, Oregon Education Association, Phi Beta Kappa.

WRITINGS: Lee's Maintenance Drills and Tests in Arithmetic, California Testing Bureau, 1930; *Importance of Reading for Achieving in Grades Four, Five, and Six*, Teachers College, Columbia University, Bureau of Publicatios, 1933; (with J. M. Lee) *Guide to Measurement in Secondary Schools*, Appleton, 1936; (with Lillian Lamoreaux) *The Dairy Farm*, Lyons & Carnahan, 1939; (with L. Lamoreaux) *Good Times in the City*, Lyons & Carnahan, 1940; (with Lee) *The Child and His Curriculum*, Appleton, 1940, 3rd edition, 1960; (with L. Lamoreaux) *Learning to Read Through Experience*, Appleton, 1943, 2nd edition with R. V. Allen, 1963; (with others) *Spelling Today*, seven volumes, Scribner, 1948, revised edition, 1954; (with J. M. Lee) *The Child and His Development*, Appleton, 1958; *Diagnostic Teaching*, National Education Association, 1963; (with A. Bingham and S. Woelfel) *Critical Reading Develops Early*, International Reading Association, 1968; *Diagnostic Teaching*, American Association of Elementary, Kindergarten, Nursery Educators, 1970. Contributor of articles to professional periodicals.

WORK IN PROGRESS: Pre-research exploration in diagnostic teaching, individualizing instruction, and open education. A book for pre-service and in-service teachers, *Language Learning: Reading, Writing, Speaking, Listening, Thinking*, with Helen Dunis and Joseph Rubin for Wadsworth.

*   *   *

LEE, Gordon C(anfield)   1916-

PERSONAL: Born February 26, 1916, in New York, N.Y.; son of Edwin A. (an educator) and Edna (Canfield) Lee; married Grace Marietta Eaton, June 22, 1940; children: Marshall MacDowell, Gordon Tamalon. *Education:* University of California. Berkeley, B.A., 1937; Columbia University, M.A., 1938, Ph.D., 1948. *Home:* 600 McGilvra Blvd. East, Seattle, Wash. 98102. *Office:* College of Education, 210 Miller Hall, University of Washington, Seattle, Wash. 98105.

CAREER: High school teacher in California, 1938-43; Pomona College, Claremont, Calif., assistant professor, 1948-52, associate professor, 1952-57, professor of education, 1957-58, chairman of department, 1948-58. Columbia University, Teachers College, New York, N.Y., professor of education, 1958-61; University of Washington, College of Education, Seattle, dean and professor, 1961—. Fulbright Conference on American Studies at Cambridge University, visiting lecturer, summer, 1952; British Summer School Program, honorary adviser, 1954-58. Helen Bush-Parkside School, board member, 1963—. *Military service:* U.S. Army, 1943-46; became technical sergeant.

MEMBER: National Education Association (adviser, educational policies commission, 1955—), American Historical Association, National Society of College Teachers of Education, American Association of University Professors, Washington Education Association, Phi Delta Kappa. *Awards, honors:* Fulbright research fellowship to England, 1953-54.

WRITINGS: The Struggle for Federal Aid: First Phase: 1870-1890, Bureau of Publications, Teachers College, Columbia University, 1949, reprinted, AMS Press, 1972; An Introduction to Education in Modern America, Henry Holt, 1953, revised edition, 1957; (editor with Henry Ehlers) Crucial Issues in Education (anthology), Henry Holt, 1959, 3rd edition, 1964; Crusade Against Ignorance: Thomas Jefferson on Education, Bureau of Publications, Teachers College, Columbia University, 1963; Education and Democratic Ideals, Harcourt, 1965. Contributor to British Journal of Educational Studies, and other journals.†

* * *

LEE, (Nelle) Harper 1926-

PERSONAL: Born April 28, 1926, in Monroeville, Ala.; daughter of Amasa Coleman (a lawyer) and Frances (Finch) Lee. Education: Attended Huntington College, 1944-45; studied law at University of Alabama, 1945-49; studied one year at Oxford University. Politics: Republican. Religion: Methodist. Home: Monroeville, Ala. Office: c/o McIntosh & Otis, Inc., 18 East 41st St., New York, N.Y. 10017.

CAREER: Airline reservation clerk with Eastern Air Lines and British Overseas Airways, New York, N.Y., during the fifties; left to devote full time to writing. Member, National Council on Arts, 1966-72. Awards, honors: Pulitzer Prize, 1961, Alabama Library Association award, 1961, Brotherhood Award of National Conference of Christians and Jews, 1961, Bestsellers' paperback of the year award, 1962, all for To Kill a Mockingbird.

WRITINGS: To Kill a Mockingbird (Literary Guild selection, Book-of-the-Month Club alternate, Reader's Digest condensed book), Lippincott, 1960, Popular Library, 1962, large print edition, National Aid to Visually Handicapped, 1965. Contributor to Vogue.

WORK IN PROGRESS: A second novel.

SIDELIGHTS: To Kill a Mockingbird, a first novel, received almost unanimous critical acclaim. It is a story narrated by a six-year-old Southern girl whose father, an attorney, defends a Negro accused of the rape of a white woman. Told with "a rare blend of wit and compassion" (Booklist), it moves "unconcernedly and irresistibly back and forth between being sentimental, tough, melodramatic, acute, and funny," according to the New Yorker. Keith Waterhouse, a British novelist, believes that "Miss Lee does well what so many American writers do appallingly: she paints a true and lively picture of life in an American small town. And she gives freshness to a stock situation." Richard Sullivan writes: ". . . the unaffected young narrator uses adult language to render the matter she deals with, but the point of view is cunningly restricted to that of a perceptive, independent child. . . . Casually, on the side, as it were, To Kill a Mockingbird is a novel of strong contemporary national significance. . . . But first of all it is a story so admirably done that it must be called both honorable and engrossing." Miss Lee considers the novel to be a simple love story.

Miss Lee, whose family is related to Robert E. Lee, writes slowly from noon until evening, completing a page or two a day. She considers the law, with its emphasis on logical thought, an excellent training for a writer.

To Kill a Mockingbird has been translated into ten languages. A screenplay adaptation by Horton Foote was filmed in 1962.

AVOCATIONAL INTERESTS: Golf and music.

BIOGRAPHICAL/CRITICAL SOURCES: New York Times Book Review, July 10, 1960, April 8, 1962; New York Herald Tribune Book Review, July 10, 1960; Chicago Sunday Tribune, July 17, 1960; Saturday Review, July 23, 1960; Atlantic, August, 1960; Booklist, September 1, 1960; New Yorker, September 10, 1960; New Statesman, October 15, 1960; Times Literary Supplement, October 28, 1960; Commonweal, December 9, 1960; Newsweek, January 9, 1961.*†

* * *

LEE, John Michael 1932-

PERSONAL: Born March 29, 1932, in Sheffield, Yorkshire, England; son of John Ewart (a bank manager) and May (Humber) Lee; married Mary Joy Bowman, June 23, 1962; children: Matthew, Helen. Education: Attended Christ Church, Oxford, 1950-54. Office: Department of Government, University of Manchester, Manchester 13, England.

CAREER: Schoolmaster and part-time research student, Oxford, England, 1954-57; University of Manchester, Manchester, England, lecturer, 1958-66, senior lecturer in government, 1966-68; Her Majesty's Treasury, temporary principal, 1968-69; University of London, Institute of Commonwealth Studies, senior lecturer, 1969—. Makerere College, Uganda, lecturer, 1962-63; University of Ghana, visiting summer lecturer, 1963.

WRITINGS: Social Leaders and Public Persons, Oxford University Press, 1963; (co-editor) Victoria County History of Leicestershire, Volume V, Oxford University Press, 1964; (contributor) The Making of Stamford, edited by A. Rogers, Leicester University Press, 1965; Colonial Development and Good Government, Clarendon Press, 1967; African Armies and Civil Order, Praeger, 1969.†

* * *

LEE, (Enoch) Lawrence 1912-

PERSONAL: Born January 1, 1912, in Wilmington, N.C.; son of Enoch Lawrence (a government employee) and Anna Jane (Reilly) Lee; married Mary Borden Wallace (an organist), October 19, 1940; children: Lawrence Borden, James Reilly. Education: University of North Carolina, B.S., 1934, M.A., 1951, Ph.D., 1955. Politics: Democrat. Religion: Roman Catholic. Home: The Citadel, Charleston, S.C.

CAREER: Accountant and auditor for various firms, 1934-42; Certified Public Accountant, 1941—; Shore Acres Co. (real estate developers), Wilmington, N.C., president, 1946—. University of North Carolina, Chapel Hill, instructor in social science, 1952-55; The Citadel, Charleston, S.C., assistant professor, 1956-60, associate professor, 1960-65, professor of history, 1965—. North Carolina Department of Archives and History, director of excavations at Brunswick Town State Historical Site, 1958; director of excavations on site of what is now Old Dorchester Historical Park, S.C., 1959. Military service: U.S. Army, Ordnance, 1942-46; became captain; received Commendation Medal. Member: American Historical Association, Southern Historical Association, South Carolina Historical Society (president, 1964—), Cape Fear Country Club (Wilmington, N.C.), Carolina Yacht Club, (Charleston, S.C.).

WRITINGS: Indian Wars in North Carolina, 1663-1763, Carolina Charter Tercentenary Commission, 1963; The Lower Cape Fear in Colonial Days, University of North

Carolina Press, 1965; *New Hanover County: A Brief History*, North Carolina State Department of Archives and History, 1971. Contributor to *Encyclopaedia Britannica*. Contributor of articles on history and colonial archaeology to newspapers and periodicals.

WORK IN PROGRESS: Research on colonial trade and shipping.

*   *   *

LEED, Richard L.   1929-

PERSONAL: Born January 31, 1929, in Lititz, Pa.; son of Jacob M. and Ada Leed; married Gretel E. Reinhold; children: Andrew, Noah, Jessica. *Education:* Oberlin College, B.A., 1954; Cornell University, Ph.D., 1958. *Home:* Garrett Rd., Ithaca, N.Y. *Office:* Cornell University, Ithaca, N.Y.

CAREER: Cornell University, Ithaca, N.Y., assistant professor, 1958-65, associate professor of linguistics, 1965—. *Member:* Linguistic Society of America, American Association of Teachers of Slavic and East European Languages, Linguistic Circle of New York.

WRITINGS: (Editor with A. L. Jaryc and Gordon H. Fairbanks) *Russian Readings in Popular Science*, Columbia University Press, 1963; (with Fairbanks) *Basic Conversational Russian*, Holt, 1964.

WORK IN PROGRESS: Research in Russian linguistics; pedagogical materials in Russian.

*   *   *

LEEDHAM, Charles   1926-

PERSONAL: Born June 14, 1926, in Cedar Rapids, Iowa; son of Charles L. (a medical doctor) and Esther (Gearhart) Leedham. *Education:* University of Iowa, B.A., 1949, M.A., 1951. *Agent:* Curtis Brown, Ltd., 60 East 56th St., New York, N.Y. 10022.

CAREER: Former television performer with animals, procuring and handling animals for "Birthday House", National Broadcasting Co. children's television program, 1961-66; consultant on training and care of dogs and other animals; commercial pilot and aviation consultant; commissioner, New York City Department of Marine and Aviation, 1968-74. *Member:* Society of Magazine Writers, Wings Club (member of board of directors). *Awards, honors: Care of the Dog* was named best dog book of 1961 by Dog Writer's Association of America; American Legion Air Service Post Medal of Merit for Civil Aviation contributions.

WRITINGS: (With Milo Pearsall) *Dog Obedience Training*, Scribner, 1958; *Care of the Dog*, Scribner, 1961; *Our Changing Constitution*, Dodd, 1964. Regular contributor to *New York Times Sunday Magazine*.

WORK IN PROGRESS: A nonfiction book on private flying; motion picture scripts, both documentary and fiction.

*   *   *

LEEDS, Morton (Harold)   1921-

PERSONAL: Born May 15, 1921, in New York, N.Y.; married Ingrid Leeds (an artist), June 25, 1948; children: Wendy, Karen, Lori. *Education:* City College (now City College of the City University of New York), New York, N.Y., B.Sc. (cum laude), 1944; New School for Social Research, M.A., 1948, Ph.D., 1950. *Religion:* Jewish. *Home:* 6219 Lone Oak Dr., Bethesda, Md. 20034.

CAREER: Sephardic Home for Aged, New York, N.Y., acting director, 1951-52; Borinstein Home for Aged, Indianapolis, Ind., director, 1953-62; Department of Housing and Urban Development, Washington, D.C., director of Senior Citizens Housing Loan Program, 1962-67, director of Plans, Programs, Evaluation Staff, 1967-72, special assistant to the assistant secretary for Housing Management, 1972—. Secretary, Indiana State Commission on Aging, 1955-62. *Military service:* U.S. Army, 1943-46. *Member:* National Association of Social Workers (charter), Gerontological Society (fellow), International Poetry Society (fellow).

WRITINGS: (Editor) *Aging in Indiana: Readings in Community Organization*, Bookwalters, 1959; *The Aged, The Social Worker and the Community*, Howard Allen, 1961; (editor with Herbert Shore) *Geriatric Institutional Management*, Putnam, 1964; (editor) *Washington Colloquium on Science and Society*, Mono Book Corp., 1967; *Jackstones* (poetry), Mono Book Corp., 1970; (with Gardner Murphy) *Self-Deception*, Basic Books, 1974. Contributor of over fifty articles, booklets, and chapters of books on social process.

SIDELIGHTS: Morton Leeds speaks French, German, and Italian.

*   *   *

LEEMAN, Wayne A(lvin)   1924-

PERSONAL: Born January 27, 1924, in Beloit, Wis.; son of Orville C. (a salesman) and Ella (McCray) Leeman. *Education:* University of Wisconsin, B.A., 1948, Ph.D., 1950. *Home:* 702 Crescent Dr., Columbia, Mo. *Office:* University of Missouri, Columbia, Mo.

CAREER: University of Missouri, Columbia, assistant professor, 1950-55, associate professor, 1955-59, professor of economics, 1959—. *Military service:* U.S. Army Air Forces, 1943-45; became sergeant; received Air Medal. *Member:* American Economic Association, Midwest Economic Association.

WRITINGS: The Price of Middle East Oil: An Essay in Political Economy, Cornell University Press, 1962; (editor) *Capitalism, Market Socialism, and Central Planning: Readings in Comparative Economic Systems*, Houghton, 1963. Contributor to economics journals.

WORK IN PROGRESS: Further research on capitalism, central planning, socialism, and communalism.

*   *   *

LEFTWICH, Richard Henry   1920-

PERSONAL: Born February 1, 1920, in Burden, Kan.; son of Rush Floyd (a farmer) and Nellie (Bailiff) Leftwich; married Maxine Ellen Dieterich, March 11, 1945; children: Judith, Gregory, Bradley. *Education:* Southwestern College, Winfield, Kan., B.A., 1941; Fort Hayes Kansas State College, graduate study, 1941-42; University of Chicago, M.A., 1948, Ph.D., 1950. *Religion:* Methodist. *Home:* 818 West Knapp Ave., Stillwater, Okla. 74074. *Office:* Department of Economics, Oklahoma State University, Stillwater, Okla. 74075.

CAREER: Oklahoma State University of Agriculture and Applied Science, Stillwater, assistant professor of economics, 1948-51, associate professor, 1951-55, professor, 1955—. Consultant to Oklahoma Department of Commerce and Industry, 1957-60, to the faculty of economics, Catholic University of Chile, 1962-63; visiting professor, University of Chicago, 1962-63. Licensed commercial pilot. *Military service:* U.S. Army Air Forces, 1942-45; became master sergeant; received Bronze Star Medal. *Member:* American Economic Association, Midwest Economic Association (vice-president, 1972-73), Rocky Mountain Social Science Association (president, 1973). Southern Economic Association (president, 1964-65). *Awards, honors:* Ford Foundation faculty research fellowship, 1960-61.

WRITINGS: The Price System and Resource Allocation, Holt, 1955, 5th edition, 1973; (with Richard W. Poole, John J. Klein, and Rudolph W. Trenton) *The Oklahoma Economy,* Oklahoma State University Press, 1962; (contributor) Julius Gould and William L. Kolb, editors, under UNESCO auspices, *A Dictionary of the Social Sciences,* Free Press of Glencoe, 1964; *An Introduction to Economic Thinking,* Holt, 1969; *Elementary Analytics of a Market System,* General Learning Press, 1972; (with Ansel M. Sharp) *The Economics of Social Issues,* Business Publications, 1974.

AVOCATIONAL INTERESTS: Aviation.

* * *

LEGER, (Marie-Rene) Alexis Saint-Leger 1887- (Saintleger Leger, Saint-John Perse)

PERSONAL: Born May 31, 1887, in Saint-Leger-les Feuilles, French West Indies; brought to France at age of eleven; son of Amedee (a lawyer) and Mme. Leger (*nee* Dormoy); married Dorothy Milburn Russell, 1958. *Education:* Attended Universities of Bordeaux and Paris, studied medicine, law, and literature, licencie en Droit; holds a diploma from the Ecole des Hautes Etudes Commerciales, and a licence in law. *Home:* 1621 34th St., Washington, D.C.; and Les Vigneaux, Giens (Var), France.

CAREER: French Foreign Office, deputy diplomat in the political and commercial division, 1914-16, served as secretary of the French Embassy in Peking, China, 1916-21; collaborator with French Foreign Minister, Aristide Briand, 1921-32; chef de cabinet, Ministry of Foreign Affairs, 1925-32, counsellor, 1925, minister, 1927; secretary-general of Ministry of Foreign Affairs, and Ambassador of France, 1932-40, removed from this post as a result of his firm stand against the appeasement of Germany; lost his French citizenship, October 29, 1940; fled to Arachon (France), to England, Canada, and finally arrived in Washington, D.C., in January, 1941; consultant on French poetry at the Library of Congress, 1941-45; his French citizenship was restored in 1945; he returned to France, 1957, and now maintains a home in Washington and Giens. *Member:* American Academy of Arts and Sciences (honorary), American Academy of Arts and Letters, National Institute of Arts and Letters of America, Modern Language Association of America (honorary fellow), Bayerischen Akademie der Schoenen Kuenste. *Awards, honors:* Knight Commander of Royal Victorian Order; Grand Officer of Legion of Honor; Knight Commander of the Bath; Knight of the Grand Cross of the British Empire; Commander des Arts et des Lettres; honorary degree from Yale University; American Academy of Arts and Letters Award of Merit, 1950; Grand Prix National des Letters, 1959; Grand Prix International de Poesie (Belgium), 1959; Nobel Prize for Literature, 1960.

WRITINGS—All under pseudonym St.-John Perse, except as noted: *Eloges* (poetry, under name Saintleger Leger), Gallimard, 1911, (under pseudonym St.-John Perse), Gallimard, 1925, translation by Louise Varese published as *Eloges, and Other Poems,* introduction by Archibald MacLeish, Norton, 1944, revised bilingual edition, without introduction, Pantheon Books, 1956; *Anabase* (poem), Gallimard, 1924, bilingual edition with English translation by T. S. Eliot published as *Anabasis,* Faber, 1930, 2nd edition, revised and corrected, Harcourt, 1949; (under name Alexis Leger) *La Publication francaise pendant la guerre, bibliographie restreinte (1940-1945),* four volumes, 1940's; *Exil* (poetry), Gallimard, 1942; (under name Alexis Leger) *Briand,* Wells College Press, 1943; (under name Alexis St. Leger Leger) *A Selection of Works for an Understanding of World Affairs Since 1914* [Washington], 1943; *Pluies* (poetry), Editions des Lettres Francaises (Buenos Aires), 1944; *Quatre Poemes (1941-1944),* Editions des Lettres Francaises, 1944, published as *Exil, suivi de Poeme a l'etrangere, Pluies, Neiges,* Gallimard, 1945, revised and corrected edition published as *Exil, suivi de Poemes a l'etrangere, Pluie, Neiges,* Gallimard, 1946, bilingual edition with English translation by Denis Devlin published as *Exile, and Other Poems,* Pantheon Books, 1949, 2nd bilingual edition, Pantheon Books, 1953; *Vents* (epic poem), Gallimard, 1946, bilingual edition with English translation by Hugh Chisholm published as *Winds,* Pantheon Books, 1952, 2nd bilingual edition, 1961; *Oeuvre poetique de Saint-John Perse,* two volumes, Gallimard, 1953, revised edition, 1960; *Amers* (poetry), NRF, 1953, Gallimard, 1957, bilingual edition with English translation by Wallace Fowlie published as *Seamarks,* Pantheon Books, 1958, Harper, 1961; *Etroits sont les vaisseaux* (later published as part of *Amers*), NRF, 1956; *Chronique* (poem), Gallimard, 1960, bilingual edition with English translation by Robert Fitzerald published as *Chronique,* Pantheon Books, 1960; *On Poetry* (Nobel Prize acceptance speech; also see below), bilingual edition with English translation by W. H. Auden, Pantheon Books, 1961; *L'ordre des oiseaux* (poems), Au vent d'Arles, 1962, published as *Oiseaux,* Gallimard, 1963, bilingual edition with translation by Robert Fitzgerald published as *Birds,* Pantheon Books, 1966; *Pour Dante* (address; also see below), Gallimard, 1965; *Two Addresses: On Poetry* [*and*] *Dante* (includes Auden's translation *On Poetry* and Fitzgerald's translation of *Pour Dante*), Pantheon Books, 1966; *Eloges, suivi de la Gloire des rois, Anabase, Exil,* Gallimard, 1967; *Vents, suivi de Chronique,* Gallimard, 1968; *Chante par celle qui fut la. . .* (bilingual edition), translation by Richard Howard, Princeton University Press, 1970; *Collected Poems,* translations by W. H. Auden and others, Princeton University Press, 1971.

Contributor to *Nouvelle Revue Francaise, Poetry, transition, Commerce, Mesa, Partisan Review, Intentions, Sewanee Review, Briarcliff Quarterly, Atlantic, Berkeley Review,* and other publications.

SIDELIGHTS: Diplomatic service and the writing of poetry were dual preoccupations during the greater part of Leger's life. It was the poet Paul Claudel, whom Leger met in 1905, who first suggested that Leger enter government service. For twenty-six years he served as a highly distinguished diplomat. At the same time he was writing poetry in secret in his spare time. His early writings were for the most part ignored, though *Anabase* was translated into German by Rainer Maria Rilke (1925), into English by T. S. Eliot (1930), and into Italian by Giuseppe Ungaretti (1931). (Wallace Fowlie recalls the story of Leger's recognition by Marcel Proust, who, in *Cities of the Plain,* published in 1922, includes an episode wherein he mentions a book of poems by a Saintleger Leger.)

From 1924 until 1942 Leger published no poetry, but he continued to write, accumulating five volumes of poems. When he fled Paris in 1940 he left his manuscripts (fifteen years of work) behind. The poems were destroyed by the Nazi police.

Even today the bulk of his work is by many standards small. He writes carefully and is reluctant to publish in haste. However, he has, as Wallace Fowlie maintained, "taken his place beside the four or five major poets of modern France: Baudelaire, Mallarme, Rimbaud, Valery, Claudel." Fowlie considers *Anabase* to be "one of the key poems of our age. It represents the poet as conqueror of the word...." Eliot thought it as important as James Joyce's later work.

To conceal his diplomat's identity Leger published under the pseudonym St.-John Perse. Some of the very early poems, however, were published without his consent (especially in *Nouvelle Revue Francaise* and *Commerce*, 1909-10) under the name Saintleger Leger. The name St.-John Perse, perhaps chosen because of Leger's admiration for the Roman poet Persius, was first used for the publication of "Anabase" in *Nouvelle Revue Francaise*, January, 1924.

Solitude and exile are Perse's themes. Principally he is interested in the unity and totality of things. Fowlie wrote: "To man and to every aspiration of man he ascribes some eternal meaning. Everything precarious and ephemeral appears less so in the condition of his poetry ..." "He is the contemporary poet who comes perhaps closest to considering himself the instrument of superior revelation." His poems praise and celebrate the entire cosmos.

His style is dazzling, opulent, set forth in nontraditional stanzas in which, as Fowlie writes, one finds "language brought back, almost by force, to its essential rhythm, language which uses myths and symbols, language which does not describe but which suggests." Transition between images is often nonexistent. Perse believes that the poet relies on his subconscious, but a subconscious that has been mastered by reason. His literary forebears are Persius, Tacitus, Racine, and Claudel.

He is noted for his brilliant and spellbinding conversations. His knowledge of botany, zoology, geology—anything concerned with nature—is encyclopedic. His avowed passions are horses and boats. His childhood and youth (indeed his entire life) have given his name an almost legendary quality: His nurse on the island of his birth was a secret priestess of Shira; his friends in China were the philosophers of the East; in his spare time he traveled to the Gobi Desert and the South Sea Islands; and he was at one time one of the most powerful men in France. He recalls his diverse experiences with ease, wrote Pierre Geurre, and speaks "a language of surprising diversity and exactitude, occasionally stopping to find an even more precise word to accurately define his thought. While listening to him, one gets the impression that something in the flow of time or being becomes immobilized and that the magic of word and thought creates a pause around itself."

Perse says he is not a professional writer, and he can hardly be considered bookish. Guerre noted Leger's "instinctive" distrust of books, and recalled an anecdote: "When during the war he worked at the Library of Congress in Washington, American critics, curious about the books he himself read, vainly ransacked the card files trying to find what he had taken out. But for five years Perse had not borrowed one book from the famous national library. As he wrote to a poet friend: 'My hostility to culture springs from homeopathy. I believe that culture should be carried to the utmost limit, at which point it disclaims itself, and ungrateful to itself, cancels itself out.'"

Although he has spent much of his time since 1941 in America, his allegiance belongs entirely to France. In 1942 he wrote to Archibald MacLeish: "I have nothing to say about France: it is myself and all of myself.... For me it is the holy kind, and the only one, in which I can communicate with anything universal, anything essential. Even were I not an essentially French animal, an essentially French clay (and my last breath, as my first, will chemically be French), the French language would still be my only imaginable refuge, the shelter and retreat par excellence, the only locus in this world where I can remain in order to understand, desire, or renounce anything at all."

BIOGRAPHICAL/CRITICAL SOURCES: Saint-John Perse: Poete de Gloire, by Maurice Saillet, Mercure de France, 1952; *Saint-John Perse*, by Alain Bosquet, Seghers, 1953, revised edition, 1967; *Christian Science Monitor*, October 26, 1960; *Yale Review*, December 2, 1960; *Poetry*, January, 1961; *Reporter*, February 2, 1961; *Contemporary Review*, March, 1961.*†

* * *

LEGGETT, Glenn 1918-

PERSONAL: Born March 29, 1918, in Ashtabula, Ohio; son of Glenn H. (a newspaper editor) and Celinda (Sheldon) Leggett; married Doris Ruth James, June 14, 1941 (deceased); married Russelle Seeberger Jones, March 11, 1973; children: Leslie Ann (Mrs. David Leonard), Susan Cady (Mrs. Michael Jones), Celinda Sheldon (Mrs. Raymond Riecke), Joanna Ruth; stepchildren: Brian Jones, Sarah Jones. *Education:* Middlebury College, A.B., 1940; Ohio State University, M.A., 1941, Ph.D., 1949. *Politics:* Independent. *Religion:* Congregational. *Home:* 1600 Park Street, Grinnell, Iowa 50112. *Office:* Office of the President, Grinnell College, Grinnell, Iowa 50112.

CAREER: Massachusetts Institute of Technology, Cambridge, instructor in English, 1942-44; Ohio State University, Columbus, instructor, 1946-49, assistant professor of English, 1949-52; University of Washington, Seattle, associate professor of English, 1952-58, special assistant to the president, 1958-61, vice provost, 1961-63, provost, 1963-65; Grinnell College, Grinnell, Iowa, president and professor of English, 1965—. Chairman, Conference on College Composition, 1959; chairman, National Conference of Teachers of English, 1964; College Entrance Examination, vice-chairman, 1970-72, chairman, 1972-74, trustee; Director of Great Grinnell Development Corp., and General Telephone Company of the Midwest. *Military service:* U.S. Navy, 1944-46, yeoman. *Member:* Modern Language Association, American Association of University Professors, National Council of Teachers of English, Association of American Colleges, Association Associated Colleges of the Midwest (chairman, 1971-73), Iowa Association of Private Colleges and Universities. *Awards, honors:* L.H.D. from Rockford College, 1967, and Ripon College, 1968; D.Litt., Lawrence University, 1968; LL.D., Middlebury College, 1971.

WRITINGS: (With David Mead and William Charvat) *Prentice Hall Handbook for Writers*, Prentice-Hall, 1951, 6th edition, 1974; (with Donald Lee) *Prentice Hall Workbook for Writers*, Prentice-Hall, 1954, 4th edition, 1967; (with Elinor Yaggy) *Writing Your Paper*, Ronald Press,

1955; (editor with Robert Daniel and Monroe Beardsley) *Theme and Form: An Introduction to Literature*, Prentice-Hall, 1956, 4th edition, 1974; (editor) *Twelve Poets*, Holt, 1958, alternate edition with Henry-York Steiner, 1967; (editor with Robert Daniel) *The Written Word*, Prentice-Hall, 1960; (contributor) R. O. Bowen, editor, *The New Professors*, Holt, 1960; (with Gregory Cowan and Elizabeth McPherson) *Plain English Please*, Random House, 1966. Contributor of essays and reviews to *Liberal Education*, *College English*, *Journal of Higher Education*, *Centennial Review*, and other journals.

WORK IN PROGRESS: Essays on poetry, and higher education.

SIDELIGHTS: Leggett told *CA:* "I think my interest in rhetoric was focused for me by a freshman-literature instructor who almost persuaded me that an understanding of words was central to an understanding of my self. I spent the rest of my undergraduate career alternately escaping and strengthening this persuasion, and though I enjoyed the difficult but tidy two-dimensional world of scientific courses, I found myself getting more and more committed to the slippery, three-dimensional world of rhetorical and literary studies, chiefly because the human personality was always at the center of it, qualifying and confusing my understanding, but enriching it, too."

*   *   *

LEHMAN, John F(rancis), Jr. 1942-

PERSONAL: Born September 14, 1942, in Philadelphia, Pa.; son of John Francis (an executive) and Constance (Cruice) Lehman. *Education:* St. Joseph's College, B.S., 1964; Cambridge University, B.A. (honors), M.A., 1967; University of Pennsylvania, M.A., Ph.D., 1974. *Politics:* Republican. *Religion:* Catholic. *Home:* 349 Roslyn Ave., Glenside, Pa.

CAREER: Intercollegiate Review, Philadelphia, Pa., assistant editor, 1964-66; Bendix-University of Pennsylvania Third International Arms Control Symposium, executive director, 1966; University of Pennsylvania, Philadelphia, Foreign Policy Research Institute, staff member, 1967-69; National Security Council, Washington, D.C., staff member, 1969-71, senior staff member and special counsel, 1971-74; Member of U.S. Delegation to Mutual Balance Force Reduction Talks, Vienna, Austria, 1974—. *Military service:* U.S. Navy Reserve. *Member:* Tau Omega Delta, University Club (Washington, D.C.), Cambridge Union Society, Vesper Rowing Club, Bedford Rowing Club (England).

WRITINGS: (Editor with James E. Dougherty) *The Prospects for Arms Control*, MacFadden, 1965; (editor with Dougherty) *Arms Control for the Late Sixties*, Van Nostrand, 1967.

WORK IN PROGRESS: A book, *Congress and the Presidency in National Security Affairs.*

*   *   *

LEIGH, Michael 1914-

PERSONAL: Surname originally Meryon-Leigh; born May 22, 1914, in Dublin, Ireland; son of Peter and Elizabeth (Johnstone) Meryon-Leigh; married Anne-Veronica McCann (a medical secretary); children: Margot, Michele. *Education:* Educated in schools in Ireland and England; Warrington Technological College, student, 1930-33. *Politics:* Liberal. *Religion:* Humanist. *Home:* 516-C Chestnut,

Santa Cruz, Calif. 95060. *Agent:* Harold Ober Associates Inc., 40 East 49th St., New York, N.Y. 10017.

CAREER: Pensacola News-Journal, Pensacola, Fla., chief editorial writer, geopolitical columnist, and literary editor, 1948-58; *San Francisco Progress*, San Francisco, Calif., editor, 1964—. Instructor in creative writing and contemporary world literature at Pensacola-Tulane University Center, Pensacola, Fla., 1950-51, at Pensacola Junior College, 1950-52. *Military service:* British Army, King's regiment, 1940-41; received Battle of Britain Star. *Member:* Florida Society of Editors, P.E.N. (London). *Awards, honors:* Honorary life Zionist; travel fellowship from American Christian Palestine Committee to report on Middle East, 1954-55.

WRITINGS: The Dark One, Stockwell, 1939; *Men Die Alone*, Eyre & Spottiswoode, 1946; *Comrade Forest*, Whittlesey House, 1949; *He Couldn't Say Amen*, Laurie, 1950; *Cross of Fire*, Laurie, 1952; *Warrior's Trail*, Crowell, 1954; *Rogue Errant*, Crowell, 1956; *The Velvet Underground*, MacFadden, 1962.

WORK IN PROGRESS: The Velvet Underground Revisited; a collaborative study of naturism-nudism and the infiltration of sexual psychopaths.

BIOGRAPHICAL/CRITICAL SOURCES: Fact, May-June, 1964.†

*   *   *

LEITHAUSER, Gladys Garner 1925-

PERSONAL: Born February 11, 1925, in Detroit, Mich.; daughter of Herbert Neil and Carolyn (Speer) Garner; married Harold Leithauser; children: Lance, Mark, Brad, Neil. *Education:* Wayne (now Wayne State) University, B.S., 1946, M.A., 1969, graduate study, 1969-74, Ph.D. candidate, 1974—. Michigan State University, graduate student, 1946. *Politics:* Democrat. *Religion:* Presbyterian. *Home:* 122 Elm Park, Pleasant Ridge, Mich. 48069.

CAREER: Substitute teacher, 1956-60; Detroit Institute of Cancer Research, Detroit, Mich., biology research assistant, 1961-66; Highland Park Community College (now Highland Park College), Highland Park, Mich., teacher of English, 1967-68. Part-time member of English department faculty, Wayne State University, 1969-72. *Member:* Detroit Women Writers. *Awards, honors:* Wayne State University graduate fellow, 1972-74.

WRITINGS: (With Lois Breitmeyer) *The Dinosaur Dilemma*, Golden Gate Junior Books, 1964. Contributor of articles to *English Language Notes*, and *Modern Fiction Studies*.

*   *   *

LEMARCHAND, Rene 1932-

PERSONAL: Born April 3, 1932, in Nantes, France; son of George and Simone (Marinier) Lemarchand; married Irene Giersing, December 23, 1959. *Education:* Studied at Sorbonne, University of Paris, 1949-51; Southwestern at Memphis, B.A., 1953; University of California, Los Angeles, M.A., 1957, Ph.D., 1963. *Home:* 2822 Southwest 14th Dr., Gainesville, Fla. *Office:* Political Science Department, University of Florida, Gainesville, Fla.

CAREER: Institut de Sociologie Solvay, Brussels, Belgium, research assistant, 1961-62; University of Florida, Gainesville, instructor, 1962-63, assistant professor, 1963-66, associate professor, 1966-71, professor of political science, 1971—, director, African Studies Center, 1965-66. *Member:* American Political Science Association, African Studies Association, American Association of University Professors. *Awards, honors:* Ford Foundation grant to University of Lovanium, 1960; Social Science Research Council grant for travel in Africa, 1964; Fulbright Hays fellow in central Africa, 1966; Herskovits Award, 1971; national fellow of Hoover Institution, 1972-73.

WRITINGS: Political Awakening in the Congo, University of California Press, 1964; *Rwanda and Burundi*, Pall Mall, 1970; (editor and contributor) *African Kingships in Perspectives*, Cass & Co., 1974; *Selective Genocide in Burundi*, Minority Rights Group Pamphlet (London), 1974.

WORK IN PROGRESS: A comparative study of dependency relationships in black Africa.

*   *   *

LENNON, Florence Becker (Tanenbaum) 1895-
(Florence Becker)

PERSONAL: Born February 20, 1895, in New York, N.Y.; daughter of Leon (a real estate man) and Johanna (Beran) Tanenbaum; married Samuel Becker (divorced); married John Lennon (divorced); children: (first marriage) Heloise Becker Colby, Isadora Becker. *Education:* Child Education Foundation Training School for Montessori Teachers, diploma, 1921; Columbia University, B.S., 1925; University of Colorado, M.A., 1947. *Politics:* Independent. *Religion:* Jewish ("non-practicing"). *Home:* 1074 Rose Hill Dr., Boulder, Colo. 80302.

CAREER: Teacher in Montessori schools, 1922-23. Poet. Freelance writer, *Boulder Daily Camera*, Boulder, Colo., for twenty-five years, and *Town & Country Review*, Boulder, Colo., for four years; conductor of radio program, "Enjoyment of Poetry," on WEVD, New York, N.Y., 1956-64. *Member:* Authors Guild of Authors League of America, Poetry Society of America, American Newspaper Guild, Overseas Press Club, National Association for the Advancement of Colored People, American Civil Liberties Union, Wilderness Society, Women's International League for Peace and Freedom, New England Poetry Society, Denver Women's Press Club. *Awards, honors:* Poetry prize, Bread Loaf Writers' Conference, 1938; MacDowell Colony fellowship, 1963; Huntington Hartford Foundation fellowship, 1963.

WRITINGS: (Under name Florence Becker) *Farewell to Walden* (sonnet sequence), Exile Press, 1939; (under name Florence Becker Lennon), *Victoria Through the Looking-glass: The Life of Lewis Carroll*, Simon & Schuster, 1945, revised edition published as *The Life of Lewis Carroll*, Collier, 1962, 3rd revised edition, Dover, 1972 (published in England as *Lewis Carroll*, Cassell, 1947); (under name Florence Becker Lennon) *Forty Years in the Wilderness* (poems), Linden Press, 1961. Poetry is published in magazines and reprinted in anthologies.

WORK IN PROGRESS: The Embattled Farmer, a biography of George William Curtis; *Riding the Hypotenuse*, a book about poets and poetry; *The Good Green Footstool*, a collection of poems; *The Heart in Twain*, a novel.

SIDELIGHTS: Mrs. Lennon told *CA* she dropped out of college, 1913, to marry, raise children, and write poetry, and returned eight years later "to find 'man's place in nature' (Thomas H. Huxley). . . . My central preoccupation is Global Housekeeping—how can we learn to live with one another and take care of earth, air, water, creatures?"

LEONARD, John 1939-

PERSONAL: Born February 25, 1939, in Washington, D.C.; son of Daniel D. and Ruth (Woods) Leonard; married Christiana Morison, June 13, 1959; children: Andrew Warren. *Education:* Harvard University, student, 1956-58; University of California, Berkeley, B.A., 1962. *Office: New York Times Book Review, New York Times*, New York, N.Y. 10036.

CAREER: National Review, Boston, Mass., editorial apprentice, 1959-60; Station KPFA, Pacifica FM Network, book reviewer, and drama and literature program producer, 1963-64; publicity writer in Boston, Mass., 1964-67; *New York Times*, New York, N.Y., 1967—, book reviewer, 1969-70, book review editor, 1971—.

WRITINGS: The Naked Martini, Delacorte, 1964; *Wyke Regis*, Delacorte, 1966; *Crybaby of the Western World*, Doubleday, 1969; *Black Conceit*, Doubleday, 1973; *This Pen For Hire*, Doubleday, 1973. Contributor to little literary magazines.

WORK IN PROGRESS: A satiric spy story set in southern California.

SIDELIGHTS: Leonard told *CA*: "I am interested in: The Boston Celtics, Marshall McLuhan, ex-Trotskyites, Georgia Brown, Bobby Kennedy, and, of course, the reconciliation of Marxist-Freudian-typographic-existential-Man-as-the-child-of-Cain-and-the-spawn-of-killer-apes—as well as money, all lunatics of one idea, Raul Castro, Gary Wood, and manners."

BIOGRAPHICAL/CRITICAL SOURCES: Newsweek, November 2, 1970; *Time*, November 2, 1970.†

*   *   *

LERNER, Marguerite Rush 1924-

PERSONAL: Born May 17, 1924, in Minneapolis, Minn.; daughter of Harry Harold (a salesman) and Sophia (Goldstein) Rush; married Aaron Lerner (a physician), June 21, 1945; children: Peter, Michael, Ethan, Seth. *Education:* University of Minnesota, B.A. (summa cum laude), 1945; graduate study at Barnard College, 1945-46, and Johns Hopkins University, 1946-48; Western Reserve University (now Case Western Reserve University), M.D., 1950. *Office:* 333 Cedar St., New Haven, Conn. 06510.

CAREER: University of Michigan Hospital, Ann Arbor, intern, 1951-52; resident at University of Michigan Hospital, Ann Arbor, and Multnomah Hospital, Portland, Ore., 1952-54; practicing physician, specializing in dermatology, New Haven, Conn., 1955—. Yale University, New Haven, Conn., 1966—, now professor of clinical dermatology at Medical School, and physician at University Health Service; staff member at Yale-New Haven Hospital.

WRITINGS: Dear Little Mumps Child, Lerner, 1959; *Michael Gets the Measles*, Lerner, 1959; *Peter Gets the Chickenpox*, Lerner, 1959; *Doctor's Tools*, Lerner, 1960; *Lefty*, Lerner, 1960; *Red Man, White Man, African Chief*, Lerner, 1960; (with husband, Aaron Lerner) *Dermatologic Medications*, Year Book, 1960; *Twins*, Lerner, 1961; *Fur, Feathers, Hair*, Lerner, 1962; *Who Do You Think You Are?*, Prentice-Hall, 1963; *Horns, Hoofs, Nails*, Lerner, 1966; *Where Do You Come From?*, Lerner, 1967; *Color and People: The Story of Pigmentation*, Lerner, 1971. Contributor of articles to medical journals.

LERNER, Max 1902-

PERSONAL: Born December 20, 1902, in Ivenitz, Minsk, White Russia; brought to United States, 1907; son of Benjamin (a teacher) and Bessie (Podell) Lerner; married Anita Marburg, July 20, 1928 (divorced, 1940); married Genevieve Edna Albers (a clinical psychologist), August 16, 1941; children: (first marriage) Constance (Mrs. Richard Russell), Pamela (Mrs. Joseph Schofield; deceased), Joanna (Mrs. Peter Townsend); (second marriage) Michael, Stephen, Adam. *Education:* Yale University, B.A., 1923, law student, 1923-24; Washington University, St. Louis, Mo., M.A., 1925; Brookings Graduate School of Economics and Government, Ph.D., 1927. *Politics:* Democratliberal. *Religion:* Jewish. *Home:* 445 East 84th St., New York, N.Y. 10028. *Office:* New York Post, 210 South St., New York, N.Y. 10002.

CAREER: Encyclopedia of Social Sciences, New York, N.Y., 1927-32, began as assistant editor, became managing editor; Sarah Lawrence College, Bronxville, N.Y., member of social science faculty, 1932-35; Harvard University, Cambridge, Mass., lecturer in government, 1935-36; *Nation*, New York, N.Y., editor, 1936-38; Williams College, Williamstown, Mass., professor of government, 1938-43; *PM* (newspaper), New York, N.Y., editorial director, 1943-48; *New York Star*, columnist, 1948-49; Brandeis University, Waltham, Mass., professor of American civilization, 1949-73, professor emeritus, 1973—, dean of Graduate School, 1954-56; *New York Post*, New York, N.Y., syndicated columnist, 1949—. Chairman of faculty, Wellesley Summer Institute, 1933-35; visiting professor, Harvard University, summers, 1939-41, University of Florida, 1974—, U.S. International University, 1974, and Pomona College, 1974-75; Ford Foundation Professor of American Civilization, New Delhi University, 1959-60. *Awards, honors:* LL.D., Wilberforce University, 1962; Ford Foundation grant to study European civilization, 1963-64.

WRITINGS: It Is Later Than You Think, Viking, 1938, revised edition, 1943; *Ideas Are Weapons*, Viking, 1939; *Ideas for the Ice Age*, Viking, 1941, reprinted, Greenwood, 1974; *The Constitution and the Crisis State* (address), College of William and Mary Press, 1941; (editor, and author of introduction and commentary) *The Mind and Faith of Justice Holmes*, Little, Brown, 1943; (with wife, Edna Lerner) *International Organization After the War: Roads to World Security*, National Council for Social Studies, 1943; *Public Journal*, Viking, 1945; *The Third Battle for France*, Union for Democratic Action Educational Fund, 1945; *The World of the Great Powers*, Foreign Policy Association, 1947; (editor and author of introduction) Thorstein Veblen, *The Portable Veblen*, Viking, 1948; *Actions and Passions: Notes on the Multiple Revolution of Our Time*, Simon & Schuster, 1949, reprinted, Kennikat, 1969.

America as a Civilization: Life and Thought in the U.S. Today, Simon & Schuster, 1957; *The Unfinished Country* (selections from *New York Post* columns), Simon & Schuster, 1959; (editor and author of introduction) *Essential Works of John Stuart Mill*, Bantam Classics, 1961; *The Age of Overkill: A Preface to World Politics*, Simon & Schuster, 1962; *Education and a Radical Humanism*, Ohio State University Press, 1962; (editor with J. P. Mayer and author of introduction) Alexis de Tocqueville, *Democracy in America*, two volumes, Harper, 1965 (Lerner's introduction published separately as *Tocqueville and American Civilization*, Harper, 1966); (contributor) Thomas R. Ford, editor, *The Revolutionary Theme in Contemporary America*,

University of Kentucky Press, 1965; (author of introduction) Max Nicholson, *The System: The Misgovernment of Modern Britain*, McGraw, 1969; *America and Its Discontents*, Simon & Schuster, in press; *Education and Value Systems*, Phi Delta Kappa Educational Foundation, in press.

SIDELIGHTS: Work as a journalist and scholar has taken Lerner to almost every part of the world. His thrice-weekly newspaper column is syndicated throughout the United States and in many foreign countries.

* * *

LeSHAN, Eda J(oan) 1922-

PERSONAL: Born June 6, 1922, in New York, N.Y.; daughter of Max (a lawyer) and Jean (Schick) Grossman; married Lawrence L. LeShan (a psychologist), August 19, 1944; children: Wendy Jean. *Education:* Columbia University, B.S., 1944; Clark University, M.A., 1947. *Religion:* Member of Ethical Culture Society. *Home and Office:* 263 West End Ave., New York, N.Y. 10023. *Agent:* Ann Elmo, 52 Vanderbilt Ave., New York N.Y. 10017.

CAREER: Worcester Child Guidance Clinic, Worcester, Mass., diagnostician and play therapist, 1947-48; Association for Family Living, Chicago, Ill., parent education discussion leader, 1949-51; Guidance Center, New Rochelle, N.Y., director of education, 1955-60; Manhattan Society for Mental Health, New York, N.Y., educational director, 1960-62, consultant, 1962—; Pengilly Country Day School, New Rochelle, N.Y., consulting psychologist, 1962—. New York State Regent's Committee on Parent Education, member 1963—. *Member:* American Psychological Association, Association for Humanistic Psychology, Author's League.

WRITINGS: How to Survive Parenthood, Random House, 1965; *The Conspiracy Against Childhood*, Atheneum, 1967; *Sex and Your Teen-ager: A Guide for Parents*, McKay, 1969; *Natural Parenthood: Raising Your Child Without a Script*, New American Library, 1970; *How do Your Children Grow?*, McKay, 1971; *On "How do Your Children Grow?": A Dialogue with Parents*, McKay, 1972; *What Makes Me Feel This Way?: Growing Up With Human Emotions*, Macmillan, 1972; *The Wonderful Crisis of Middle Age: Some Personal Reflections*, McKay, 1973. Author of Public Affairs pamphlets. Contributor to *Parents' Magazine* and *New York Times Sunday Magazine*.

SIDELIGHTS: Mrs. LeShan told *CA*: "[I] have a basically humanistic point of view." She has completed two television series for WNET-TV entitled "How do Your Children Grow?" *Avocational interests:* Theatre, opera, travel, and living at the seashore.

* * *

LESSER, Milton 1928-
(Andrew Frazer, Stephen Marlowe, Jason Ridgway, C. H. Thames)

PERSONAL: Born August 7, 1928, in New York, N.Y.; son of Norman (a broker) and Sylvia (Price) Lesser; married second wife, Ann Humbert; children: Deirdre, Robin. *Education:* College of William and Mary, B.A., 1949. *Agent:* Scott Meredith Literary Agency, Inc., 580 Fifth Ave., New York, N.Y. 10036.

CAREER: Fiction writer; now dividing time between Europe and America, with Switzerland, France, and Spain most frequent homebases abroad; College of William and

Mary, Williamsburg, Va., writer-in-residence, 1974-75. *Military service:* U.S. Army, 1952-54. *Member:* Mystery Writers of America (regional vice-president of New York, 1961-63; former member of board of directors).

WRITINGS: Earthbound, Winston, 1952; (editor) *Looking Forward* (science fiction anthology), Beechhurst Press, 1953; *The Star Seekers*, Winston, 1953; *Stadium Beyond the Stars*, Holt, 1961; *Lost Worlds and Men Who Found Them*, Whitman, 1962; *Walt Disney's Strange Animals of Australia*, Whitman, 1963; *Secret of the Black Planet*, Belmont Books, 1965.

Under pseudonym Andrew Frazer: *Find Eileen Hardin—Alive*, Avon, 1960; *The Fall of Marty Moon*, Avon, 1961.

Under pseudonym Stephen Marlowe: *Catch the Brass Ring*, Ace Books, 1952; *Model for Murder*, Graphic, 1954; *Dead on Arrival*, Ace Books, 1954; *Turn Left for Murder*, Ace Books, 1955; *Blond Bait*, Avon, 1959; *Passport to Peril*, Crest, 1961; *The Shining*, Trident, 1963; *The Search for Bruno Heidler*, Macmillan, 1966; *Come Over Red Rover*, Macmillan, 1968; *The Summit*, Geis, 1970; *Colossus*, Macmillan, 1972; *The Man with No Shadow*, Prentice-Hall, 1974.

Chester Drum series; under pseudonym Stephen Marlowe; all published by Gold Medal: *The Second Longest Night*, 1955; *Mecca for Murder*, 1956; *Trouble Is My Name*, 1956; *Murder Is My Dish*, 1957; *Killers Are My Meat*, 1957; *Terror Is My Trade*, 1958; *Violence Is My Business*, 1958; *Homicide Is My Game*, 1959; *Double in Trouble*, 1960; (with Richard S. Prather) *Danger Is My Line*, 1960; *Peril Is My Pay*, 1960; *Jeopardy Is My Job*, 1961; *Death Is My Comrade*, 1961; *Manhunt Is My Mission*, 1963; *Francesca*, 1963; *Drumbeat—Berlin*, 1964; *Drumbeat—Dominique*, 1965; *Drumbeat—Madrid*, 1966; *Drumbeat—Erica*, 1967; *Drumbeat—Marianne*, 1968.

Under pseudonym Jason Ridgway: *Adam's Fall*, Pocket Books, 1960; *People in Glass Houses*, Pocket Books, 1961; *Hardly a Man Is Now Alive*, Pocket Books, 1961.

Under pseudonym C. H. Thames: *Violence Is Golden*, Bouregy, 1956.

WORK IN PROGRESS: Two novels, one set in Mexico, the other in the United States, both for Prentice-Hall.

SIDELIGHTS: Lesser told *CA:* "Am an avid skier and history-buff, speak and write Spanish well enough to think in it, and French considerably less well. In both suspense fiction and historical fiction . . . I put particular emphasis on making backgrounds as authentic as possible."

*   *   *

LeSTOURGEON, Diana E. 1927-

PERSONAL: Born April 6, 1927, in Covington, Ky.; daughter of Percy E. (an army officer) and Mollie (Chapman) LeStourgeon. *Education:* Attended Alabama Polytechnic Institute (now Auburn University), 1944-45, and University of Oklahoma, 1945-46; University of Pennsylvania, A.B., 1949, A.M., 1950, Ph.D., 1960. *Home:* 336 West Fifth St., Media, Pa. 19063.

CAREER: Instructor in English, Auburn University, Auburn, Ala., 1954, University of Missouri, Columbia, 1954-55, and University of Pennsylvania, Philadelphia, 1960-63; Widener College, Chester, Pa., assistant professor, 1963-68, associate professor of English, 1968—. *Member:* Modern Language Association of America, American Association of University Professors.

WRITINGS: Rosamond Lehmann, Twayne, 1965. Contributor to *Encyclopedia of World Literature in the Twentieth Century*.

WORK IN PROGRESS: A study of the novels of Iris Murdoch.

AVOCATIONAL INTERESTS: Travel, art, and music.

*   *   *

LEVARIE, Siegmund 1914-

PERSONAL: Surname is accented on first syllable; born July 24, 1914, in Austria; came to United States, 1932, naturalized, 1942; son of Josef and Sofie; married Norma Cohn (a graphic designer), March, 1945; children: Janet. *Education:* Attended Northwestern University, 1932-33; Vienna Conservatory, Conductor's Diploma, 1935; University of Vienna, Ph.D. (summa cum laude), 1938. *Home:* 624 Third St., Brooklyn, N.Y. 11215. *Office:* Music Department, Brooklyn College of the City University of New York, Brooklyn, N.Y. 11210.

CAREER: University of Chicago, Chicago, Ill., member of music faculty, conductor of university orchestra, and director of university concerts, 1938-52; Chicago Musical College, Chicago, Ill., dean, 1952-54; Brooklyn College of the City University of New York, professor of music, 1954—, department chairman, 1954-62, Fromm Music Foundation, executive director, 1952-54, director, 1954-57; conductor, Brooklyn Community Symphony Orchestra, 1954-58. *Military service:* U.S. Army, Adjutant General's Department, 1941-46; became captain. *Member:* American Musicological Society (member of council, 1957-60, 1961-64).

WRITINGS: Mozart's Le Nozze di Figaro, University of Chicago Press, 1952; *Fundamentals of Harmony*, Ronald, 1954; *Guillaume de Machaut*, Sheed, 1954; *Musical Italy Revisited*, Macmillan, 1963; (with Ernst Levy) *Tone: A Study in Musical Acoustics*, Kent State University Press, 1968. Contributor to periodicals; author of music editions.

WORK IN PROGRESS: A book with Ernst Levy, *A Dictionary of Musical Morphology*.

SIDELIGHTS: Levarie speaks French, German, Italian; he reads Latin, Hebrew, Greek.

*   *   *

LEVER, Tresham (Joseph Philip) 1900-

PERSONAL: Second baronet; born September 3, 1900, in Leicester, England; son of Sir Arthur Lever and Beatrice (Falk); married Frances Yowart, 1930 (died, 1959); married Pamela Bowes Lyon, March 5, 1962; children: (first marriage) Tresham Christopher Arthur Lindsay. *Education:* Attended Harrow School; University College, Oxford, M.A. *Politics:* Conservative. *Religion:* Church of England. *Home:* Cullerne House, Findhorn, Forres, Morayshire, England.

CAREER: Called to bar, 1925; high sheriff of Leicestershire, 1962-63. Member of court, University of Leicester. *Member:* Bronte Society (member of council, 1963—), Carlton Club, St. James Club, Beefsteak Club.

WRITINGS: Profit and Loss: A Brief Consideration of Some Aspects of Modern Politics, Thornton Butterworth, 1933; *The Life and Times of Sir Robert Peel*, Norton, 1942; *The House of Pitt: A Family Chronicle*, J. Murray, 1947, new edition, 1952; *Godolphin: His Life and Times*, J. Murray, 1952; (editor) *The Letters of Lady Palmerston*, J. Murray, 1957; *The Herberts of Wilton*, J. Murray, 1967; *Lesudden House: Sir Walter Scott and the Scotts of Raeburn*, Rowman, 1971; *Clayton of Toc H*, J. Murray, 1971. Contributor of articles to *Times Literary Supplement* and *History Today*.

AVOCATIONAL INTERESTS: Fishing and shooting.

BIOGRAPHICAL/CRITICAL SOURCES: Observer Review, December 17, 1967; *Times Literary Supplement*, March 7, 1968.†

* * *

LEVEY, Martin 1913-

PERSONAL: Born May 18, 1913, in Philadelphia, Pa.; married Mary McGlinchy, 1944; children: Susan, Peter. *Education:* Temple University, A.B., 1934; University of Pennsylvania, graduate student, 1934-37; Dropsie College, Ph.D., 1952. *Home:* 229 West Hortter St., Philadelphia, Pa.

CAREER: Instructor at Pennsylvania State University, University Park, 1955-56, at Temple University, 1956-59; Institute for Advanced Study, Princeton, N.J., National Science Foundation fellow, 1959-60; Yale University, New Haven, Conn., research associate, School of Medicine, 1960-64; with Rockefeller University, 1964-65, Institute for Advanced Study, 1965-66; Rutgers University, New Brunswick, N.J., professor of the history of science, 1966—. *Wartime service:* U.S. Merchant Marine, 1940-43. *Member:* American Chemical Society, History of Science Society, Oriental Society, Mediaeval Academy of America.

WRITINGS: Chemistry and Chemical Technology in Ancient Mesopotamia, Elsevier Publishing, 1959; *Medieval Arabic Bookbinding*, American Philosophical Society, 1962; (editor and translator) *The Alegebra of Abu Kamil*, University of Wisconsin Press, 1965; (editor and translator) *Medical Formulary or Agrabadhin of al-Kindi*, University of Wisconsin Press, 1965; (editor and translator) Kushyar ibn Labban, *Principles of Hindu Reckoning*, University of Wisconsin Press, 1965; (editor) *Archaeological Chemistry: A Symposium*, University of Pennsylvania Press, 1966; (with N. al-Khaledy) *Medical Formulary of Al-Samarqandi*, University of Pennsylvania Press, 1966; *Ibn Wahshiya's Medieval Arabic Toxicology*, 1966; *Medical Ethics of Medieval Islam, with Special Reference to Al-Ruhawi's Practical Ethics of the Physician*, American Philosophical Society, 1967; *Abu Kamil's "On the Pentagon and Decagon"*, History of Science Society of Japan, 1971.

* * *

LEVI, Anthony H. T. 1929-

PERSONAL: Born May 30, 1929, in Ruislip, England; son of Herbert Simon (a merchant) and Edith Mary (Tigar) Levi. *Education:* Studied philosophy for three years in Munich, modern languages for three years at Oxford University, and theology for four years; Oxford University, B.A., 1958, D.Phil., 1963; Heythrop College, S.T.L., 1963. *Home:* Craigrothie House, Craigrothie, Cupar, Fife KY15 5P2, Scotland. *Office:* Department of French, Buchanan Building, University of St. Andrews, St. Andrews, Fife, Scotland.

CAREER: Engaged in business in England, 1946-49; member of Society of Jesus (Jesuits), 1949-71; Oxford University, Christ Church, Oxford, England, lecturer in French, 1966-71; University of St. Andrews, St. Andrews, Fife, Scotland, Buchanan Professor of French Language

and Literature, 1971—. University of Warwick, reader in French, 1966, personal chair in French, 1970. Spent 1963-64 in France.

WRITINGS: French Moralists: The Theory of the Passions, 1585-1649, Oxford University Press, 1964; *Religion in Practice*, Harper, 1966; (editor) *Humanism in France at the End of the Middle Ages and in the Early Renaissance*, Manchester University Press, 1971; (author of introduction and notes) Erasmus, *The Praise of Folly*, Penguin, 1971. Contributor of numerous articles and reviews to journals.

WORK IN PROGRESS: A book, *The Classical Dilemma*; general editor of a volume of *Complete Works of Erasmus in English*; research in the literature of the French Renaissance.

* * *

LEVI, Primo 1919-

PERSONAL: Born July 31, 1919, in Turin, Italy; son of Cesare (a civil engineer) and Ester (Luzzati) Levi; married Lucia Morpurgo (a teacher), September 8, 1947; children: Lisa, Renzo. *Education:* University of Turin, degree in chemistry, 1941. *Religion:* Jewish. *Home:* Corso Re Umberto 75, Turin, Italy. *Office:* SIVA, via Leyni 84, Settimo, Torino, Italy.

CAREER: Partisan in Italian Resistance, 1943; deported to Auschwitz Concentration Camp in Poland and imprisoned there, 1943-45; SIVA (paints, enamels, synthetic resins), Settimo, Torino, Italy, technical executive, 1948—. *Awards, honors:* Premio Campiello (Venice literary prize), 1963, for *La Tregua*; Premio Bagutta (Milan literary prize), 1967, for *Storie Naturali*.

WRITINGS: Se Questo e un Uomo, F. de Silva (Torino), 1947, 11th edition, Einaudi, 1967, translation by Stuart Woolf published as *If This Is a Man*, Orion Press (New York), 1959, new edition, Bodley Head, 1966, reissued as *Survival in Auschwitz: The Nazi Assault on Humanity*, Macmillan, 1966, dramatic version in original Italian with Pieralberto Marche, Einaudi, 1966; *La Tregua*, Einaudi, 1958, 8th edition, 1965, translation by Stuart Woolf published as *The Reawakening*, Little, Brown, 1965 (published in England as *The Truce: A Survivor's Journey Home From Auschwitz*, Bodley Head, 1965); *Storie Naturali*, Einaudi, 1967; (with Carlo Quartucci) *Intervista Aziendale* (radio script), Radiotelevisione Italiana, 1968; *Vizio di Forma*, Einaudi, 1971.

SIDELIGHTS: Levi told *CA:* "My uncommon experience of a concentration camp inmate and of a survivor has deeply influenced my later life, and has turned me into a writer. The two books [*Se Questo e un Uomo* and *Le Tregua*] . . . are a chronicle of my exile, and an attempt to understand its meaning."

BIOGRAPHICAL/CRITICAL SOURCES: "Journey Out of Hell," *Observer*, January 26, 1965; "Auschwitz: The Final Choice," *Guardian*, February 12, 1965.

* * *

LEVIN, Alfred 1908-

PERSONAL: Born November 25, 1908, in Colchester, Conn.; son of Michael and Anna (Schlossberg) Levin; married Fannie Wener, October 18, 1932. *Education:* Brown University, A.B., 1931; Yale University, Ph.D., 1937. *Office:* Department of History, Kent State University, Kent, Ohio 44240.

CAREER: City College (now City College of the City University of New York), instructor in history, 1941-42; U.S. Department of State, Washington, D.C., research analyst, 1945-46; Oklahoma State University, Stillwater, associate professor, 1946-48, professor of Russian history, 1948-68; Kent State University, Kent, Ohio, professor of history, 1968—. Fellow at Center for International Studies, Massachusetts Institute of Technology, 1951-52; visiting professor of history, University of Michigan, 1964-65. *Military service:* U.S. Army, Office of Strategic Services, 1942-45; became staff sergeant. *Member:* American Historical Association, American Association for the Advancement of Slavic Studies (member of executive committee, Midwestern branch), Council on Slavic Studies, Phi Beta Kappa. *Awards, honors:* Publication grant from Kingsley Trust Association Fund of Scroll and Key, Yale University, 1940, for *The Second Duma;* Fulbright grant to Finland, 1956-57; Interuniversity travel grant to U.S.S.R., 1960; Interuniversity Research and Exchanges Grant to U.S.S.R., 1970.

WRITINGS: *The Second Duma,* Yale University Press, 1940; (with Walt W. Rostow and others) *Dynamics of Soviet Society,* Norton, 1953; (editor with Alan D. Ferguson) *Essays in Russian History,* Archon Books, 1964; *The Third Duma: Elections and Profile,* Shoe String, 1973. Editor, Oklahoma State University "Arts and Sciences Studies," 1958—.

*   *   *

LEVIN, Marcia Obrasky 1918-
(Marcia Martin; Jeremy Martin, joint pseudonym)

PERSONAL: Born October 29, 1918, in Philadelphia, Pa.; daughter of Abraham N. (a dentist) and Elizabeth (Lauter) Obrasky; married Martin P. Levin (president of book group of Times Mirror Co., Inc.), April 2, 1939; children: Jeremy, Wendy, Hugh. *Education:* Philadelphia Normal School, certificate, 1939; additional courses at Temple University, 1939-40, 1949, and Indiana University, 1941-43. *Home:* 370 Grace Church St., Rye, N.Y. 10580.

CAREER: Philadelphia (Pa.) public schools, elementary teacher, 1939-40, teacher of remedial subjects, 1947-50; Beth Jacob Schools, Philadelphia, Pa., elementary teacher, 1945; writer for children.

WRITINGS: *Adventures from the Original Alice in Wonderland and Through the Looking Glass* (adapted and abridged for little children), Grosset, 1951; *Christmas Is Coming,* Wonder Books, 1952; *Tom Corbett's Wonder Book of Space,* Wonder Books, 1953; *The Merry Mailman,* Treasure Books, 1953; *Let's Take a Ride,* Treasure Books, 1953; *Johnny Grows Up,* Wonder Books, 1954; *The Merry Mailman around the World,* Treasure Books, 1955; (with Jeanne Bendick) *Take a Number,* Whittlesey House, 1961; (with Bendick) *Take Shapes, Lines and Letters,* Whittlesey House, 1962; (with Bendick) *Pushups and Pinups,* McGraw, 1963; (with Bendick) *Mathematics Illustrated Dictionary,* Whittlesey House, 1965; (with Bendick) *New Mathematics Practice Workbook,* Books I, II, III, and IV, Wonder Books, 1965-66; *New Mathematics Workbook,* Grosset, 1966.

Under pseudonym Marcia Martin: *How the Clown Got His Smile,* Wonder Books, 1951; *A Little Cowboy's Christmas,* Wonder Books, 1951; *Black Beauty, Retold for Little Children,* Wonder Books, 1951; *Sonny the Bunny,* Wonder Books, 1952; *Peter Pan, Retold for Little Children,* Wonder Books, 1952. Also author of *Donna Parker at Cherrydale,*

Donna Parker: Special Agent, Donna Parker on Her Own, Donna Parker: A Spring to Remember, Donna Parker in Hollywood, Donna Parker at Arawak, Donna Parker Takes a Giant Step (all published by Whitman).

With husband, Martin P. Levin, under joint pseudonym Jeremy Martin: *How to Prepare for Your Draft Test,* Crown, 1951; *Selective Service Draft Deferment Test,* Bantam, 1966.

*   *   *

LEVIN, Saul 1921-

PERSONAL: Born July 13, 1921, in Chicago, Ill.; son of Nathan Samuel (an insurance salesman) and Rose (Finkel) Levin; married Ruth Eleanor Harris, March 17, 1951; children: Nathaniel, Eve, Margaret, Anne, Daniel, Victoria. *Education:* University of Chicago, A.B., 1942, Ph.D., 1949; Harvard University, graduate study, 1946-49. *Religion:* Jewish. *Home:* 517 Harvard St., Vestal, N.Y. 13850. *Office:* State University of New York, Binghamton, N.Y. 13901.

CAREER: University of Chicago, Chicago, Ill., instructor in history and humanities, 1949-51; Washington University, St. Louis, Mo., assistant professor, 1951-55, associate professor of classics, 1955-61; State University of New York at Binghamton, professor of classics, 1961—. Has made a documentary film on chironomy in Bible reading. *Military service:* U.S. Army, 1942-45; became sergeant. *Member:* American Philological Association, National Association of Professors of Hebrew, American Oriental Society, Society of Biblical Literature, Classical Association of the Atlantic States, Linguistic Circle of New York, Phi Beta Kappa. *Awards, honors:* Faculty fellowship, Fund for the Advancement of Education, 1953-54.

WRITINGS: (Translator) Aelius Aristides, *To Rome,* Free Press of Glencoe, 1950; *The Linear B Decipherment Controversy Re-examined,* State University of New York Press, 1964; *Hebrew Grammar: An Objective Introduction to the Biblical Language,* State University of New York at Binghamton, 1966; *The Indo-European and Semitic Languages,* State University of New York, 1971. Contributor of articles and reviews to classical and linguistic journals.

WORK IN PROGRESS: *The Father of Joshua-Jesus;* other books on Hebrew scrolls and on dialect words in Greek literature.

SIDELIGHTS: Levin is most competent in Latin, Greek, Hebrew; he has studied several other ancient and modern languages.

*   *   *

LEVINE, Daniel 1934-

PERSONAL: Born December 31, 1934, in New York, N.Y.; son of Morris Simeon (a sculptor) and Margaret (Hirsch) Levine; married Susan Rose (a teacher), July, 1954; children: Timothy, Karen. *Education:* Antioch College, B.A., 1956; attended University of Edinburgh, 1954-55; Northwestern University, M.A., 1957, Ph.D., 1961. *Politics:* Democrat. *Home:* Mere Point Rd., Brunswick, Me. 04011. *Office:* Department of History, Bowdoin College, Brunswick, Me. 04011.

CAREER: Earlham College, Richmond, Ind., assistant professor of history, 1960-63; Bowdoin College, Brunswick, Me., assistant professor, 1963-66, associate professor, 1966-72, professor of history, 1972—. *Member:* American Historical Association, American Association of University Professors, Organization of American Historians, National Association for the Advancement of Colored People, Brunswick Democrats (member of executive committee).

WRITINGS: Varities of Reform Thought, State Historical Society of Wisconsin, 1964; *Jane Addams and the Liberal Tradition*, State Historical Society of Wisconsin, 1971.

WORK IN PROGRESS: A study of the development of the welfare state in Denmark.

* * *

LEVINE, Irving R(askin) 1922-

PERSONAL: Born August 26, 1922, in Pawtucket, R.I.; son of Joseph and Emma (Raskin) Levine; married Nancy Cartmell Jones, July 12, 1957; children: Jeffrey, Daniel Rome, Jennifer Jones. *Education:* Brown University, B.S., 1944; Columbia University, M.S. in Journalism, 1947. *Religion:* Jewish. *Office:* 4001 Nebraska Ave. N.W., Washington, D.C. 20016.

CAREER: International News Service, foreign news editor, New York, N.Y., 1947-48, foreign correspondent in Vienna and Paris, 1948-50; National Broadcasting Co., New York, N.Y., war correspondent in Korea, 1950-52, commentator on "World News Roundup" and "Monitor," New York, 1953-55 (with some intervals spent in Far East), foreign correspondent in Moscow, 1955-59, in Rome, 1959-67, London, 1967-68, Rome, 1968-70, Washington D.C., 1971—. First U.S. television correspondent to be accredited to Moscow, and for a time, the only radio correspondent, broadcasting a series, "This Is Moscow." *Military service:* U.S. Army, Signal Corps, 1943-46; headed news-photo group in Japan and Philippines; first lieutenant. *Member:* Overseas Press Club, Association of Radio-Television News Analysts, Phi Beta Kappa. *Awards, honors:* Council on Foreign Relations fellowship at Columbia University, 1952-53; named one of ten outstanding young men in America, U.S. Junior Chamber of Commerce, 1956; Headliners Award and Overseas Press Club Award, 1957; Columbia Alumni Award for distinctive service to journalism, 1959; New York Emmy Television Award, 1966; L.H.D., Brown University, 1969; named to Rhode Island Hall of Fame, 1972.

WRITINGS: Main Street, USSR, Doubleday, 1956 (published in England as *The Real Russia*, W. H. Allen, 1959); *Travel Guide to Russia*, Doubleday, 1959; *Main Street, Italy*, Doubleday, 1963; *The New Worker in Soviet Russia*, Macmillan, 1973. Contributor to national magazines, including *Collier's, Saturday Evening Post, Ladies' Home Journal, Saturday Review*, and *This Week*.

SIDELIGHTS: Levine's manuscripts of various writings and personal papers are kept in the Irving R. Levine Manuscript Collection at Syracuse University.†

* * *

LEVINE, Isaac Don 1892-

PERSONAL: Born February 1, 1892, in Mozyr, Russia; came to United States in 1911; son of Don and Sarah (Maloff) Levine; married Mary Leavitt; married second wife, Ruth Newman, December 14,1936; children: (first marriage) Robert V. *Education:* Educated at schools in Russia and Kansas City, Mo. *Residence:* Waldorf, Md. 20601.

CAREER: Began newspaper career with *Kansas City Star*, Kansas City, Mo., 1914; *New York Tribune*, New York, N.Y., foreign news editor, 1917; foreign correspondent for *Chicago Daily News*, Chicago, Ill., 1919-21, for Hearst Newspaper Syndicate, 1922-24; Book League of America (first paperback book club), New York, N.Y., managing editor, 1928-29; *Plain Talk* (monthly review), New York, N.Y., editor, 1946-50; writer and tobacco farmer in Waldorf, Md. Radio Liberty Committee, trustee, 1951—. *Member:* Overseas Press Club (founder member). *Awards, honors:* Freedoms Foundation Award, 1950.

WRITINGS: The Russian Revolution, Harper, 1917; *The Resurrected Nations*, Stokes, 1918; (with M. Botchkareva) *Yashka*, Stokes, 1919; (editor) *Letters from the Kaiser to the Czar*, Stokes, 1920; *The Man Lenin*, Seltzer, 1924; (compiler) *Letters from Russian Prisons*, Boni, 1924; *Stalin*, Cosmopolitan, 1931; (with V. Zenzinov) *The Road to Oblivion*, McBride, 1931; *Red Smoke*, McBride, 1932; (editor) Jan Valtin, *Out of the Night*, Alliance, 1941; *Mitchell: Pioneer of Air Power*, Duell, Sloan & Pearce, 1943; *Stalin's Great Secret*, Coward, 1956; *The Mind of an Assassin*, Farrar, Straus, 1959; *I Rediscover Russia*, Duell, Sloan & Pearce, 1964; *Intervention*, McKay, 1969; *Eyewitness to History: Memoirs and Reflections of a Foreign Correspondent for Half a Century* (autobiography), Hawthorn Books, 1973.

Collaborator with Oksana Kosenkina, Russian school teacher detained by Soviet agents against her will, in publication of her story. Editor, Macaulay "Drama Library," 1927. Writer of motion picture script, "Jack London"; translator with H. Alsberg of play, "Princess Turandot," 1925, produced by Provincetown Playhouse. Correspondent on special assignments for *Life*.

WORK IN PROGRESS: Research in the political motivations of Oswald's assassination of President Kennedy; began work on this project in January, 1964, in Dallas, Tex., where he met and repeatedly conferred with Marina Oswald prior to, and following, her appearance before the Warren Commission.

BIOGRAPHICAL/CRITICAL SOURCES: Isaac Don Levine, *Eyewitness to History*, Hawthorn Books, 1973.†

* * *

LeVINE, Victor T(heodore) 1928-

PERSONAL: Born December 6, 1928, in Berlin, Germany; became U.S. citizen, 1950; son of Maurice and Gilda (Hirschberg) LeVine; married Nathalie Christian (a ballet teacher), July 19, 1958; children: Theodore, Nicole Jeannette. *Education:* University of California, Los Angeles, B.A., 1950, M.A., 1958, Ph.D., 1961. *Office:* Department of Political Science, Washington University, St. Louis, Mo. 63130.

CAREER: Washington University, St. Louis, Mo., assistant professor, 1961-64, associate professor, 1965-70, professor of political science, 1970—. Professor of political science and head of department, University of Ghana, 1969-71. Consultant to U.S. Department of State and Peace Corps. *Military service:* U.S. Army, 1951-54. *Member:* American Political Science Association, African Studies Association, American Association for the United Nations (member of board of St. Louis chapter, 1963-65), American Civil Liberties Union, Midwest Political Science Association, Missouri Political Science Association.

WRITINGS: (Contributor) Helen A. Kitchen, editor, *The Educated African*, Praeger, 1961; (contributor) James S. Coleman and Carl G. Rosberg, editors, *Political Parties and National Integration in Tropical Africa*, University of

California Press, 1964; (contributor) Gwendolyn M. Carter, editor, *Five African States*, Cornell University Press, 1964; *The Cameroons from Mandate to Independence*, University of California Press, 1964; (contributor) William H. Lewis, editor, *French-Speaking Africa*, Walker & Co., 1965; *Political Leadership in Africa*, Hoover Institution, 1967; (contributor) Robert I. Rotberg and Ali A. Mazrui, editors, *Protest and Power in Black Africa*, Oxford University Press, 1970; *The Cameroon Federal Republic*, Cornell University Press, 1971; (contributor) Mazrui and Hasu H. Patel, editors, *Africa in World Affairs*, Third Press, 1973; *Political Corruption and Ghana*, Hoover Institution, 1974; *An Historical Dictionary of Cameroon*, Scarecrow, 1974. Book review editor, *American Political Science Review*, 1962-63. Contributor to *West Africa*, *African Digest*, *Africa Report*, *International Affairs*, and other political science journals.

WORK IN PROGRESS: An analysis of politics in French-speaking Africa.

SIDELIGHTS: LeVine has traveled widely in west, central, and east Africa since 1955. He is proficient in French, German, and Russian.

*   *   *

LEVINTHAL, Israel Herbert   1888-

PERSONAL: Born February 12, 1888, in Wilna, Lithuania; son of Bernard L. (a rabbi) and Minna (Kleinberg) Levinthal; married May R. Bogdanoff, August 12, 1908; children: Helen Hadassah (Mrs. Lester Lyons), Lazar E. *Education:* Columbia University, B.A., 1909, M.A., 1910; Jewish Theological Seminary of America, Rabbi, 1910, D.H.L., 1920; New York University, J.D., 1914. *Home:* 120 Rose Hill Ave., New Rochelle, N.Y. 10804. *Office:* 667 Eastern Parkway, Brooklyn, N.Y. 11213.

CAREER: Rabbi of Jewish temples in Brooklyn, N.Y., 1910-19; Brooklyn Jewish Center, Brooklyn, N.Y., rabbi, 1919—. Jewish Theological Seminary of America, New York, N.Y., lecturer, 1937-38, visiting professor of homiletics, 1947-62. Member of advisory committee on burial survey, Metropolitan Life Insurance Co., 1926-28; U.S. chairman of Jerusalem Synagogue Center Campaign, 1928-30; member of council of Jewish Agency for Palestine, 1929-33; president of Brooklyn Jewish Community Council, 1924-44, honorary president, 1944—. Trustee of Israel MATZ Foundation for Hebrew Writers, 1925—. *Member:* Jewish Academy of Arts and Sciences, American Academy for Jewish Research, Rabbinical Assembly of America (president, 1930-32), Brooklyn Board of Rabbis (first president, 1929-31). *Awards, honors:* D.D., Jewish Theological Seminary of America, 1940; D.J.T., Jewish Institute of Religion, 1948.

WRITINGS: Jewish Law of Agency, with Special Reference to Roman and Common Law, Jewish Theological Seminary, 1923; *Steering or Drifting—Which?*, Funk, 1928; *Judaism—An Analysis and an Interpretation*, Funk, 1935; *A New World Is Born*, Funk, 1943; *The Hour of Destiny*, 1949; *Point of View—An Analysis of American Judaism*, Abelard, 1958; *Judaism Speaks to the Modern World*, Abelard, 1963; *The Message of Israel*, Lex Printing Co., 1973. Contributor to *Jewish Quarterly Review* and other periodicals.

SIDELIGHTS: In 1948, the Jewish community of Brooklyn had a forest of twenty-thousand trees planted in Jerusalem in Levinthal's honor.

LEVY, David   1913-

PERSONAL: Born January 2, 1913, in Philadelphia, Pa.; son of Benjamin and Lillian (Potash) Levy; married Lucile Alva Wilds (an executive assistant), July 25, 1941; children: Lance, Linda. *Education:* University of Pennsylvania, B.S., 1934, M.B.A., 1935. *Home:* 9268 Robin Dr., Los Angeles, Calif. 90069. *Agent:* Annie Laurie Williams, Inc., 18 East 41st St., New York, N.Y. 10017. *Office:* Wilshire Productions, 10530 Wilshire Blvd., Los Angeles, Calif. 90024.

CAREER: Young & Rubicam, Inc. (advertising agency), New York, N.Y., began 1938, vice-president, 1950-59, associate director of radio and television department, 1958-59; National Broadcasting Co., New York, N.Y., vice-president in charge of network programs and talent, 1959-61; Filmways Television Productions, Los Angeles, Calif., executive producer, beginning, 1964; Four Star International, Inc., executive vice-president in charge of television activities, 1970-72; producer, Paramount Television, 1972-73; Wilshire Productions, Inc., Los Angeles, Calif., president. Executive producer, Universal Studios, 1971-72. Member of faculty, California State University, Northridge, 1973-74. U.S. Treasury Department, chief of radio section, War Finance Division, and consultant to Secretary of Treasury, 1945-46. Consultant to Hanna-Barbera Productions, 1973-74, and to National Broadcasting Co. and Logos Ltd. Citizens for Eisenhower-Nixon, senior adviser, 1952-56, director of radio-television, 1956. *Military service:* U.S. Naval Reserve, 1944-46; became lieutenant. *Member:* American Society of Composers, Authors and Publishers, National Academy of Television Arts and Sciences, Dramatists Guild, Writers Guild, Producers Guild, Hollywood Radio-Television Society (president, 1969-70).

WRITINGS: The Chameleons, Dodd, 1964; *Against the Stream* (poems), Outposts, 1970; *The Gods of Foxcroft*, Arbor House, 1970. Writer of television plays for "Goodyear-Alcoa Theatre," "Robert Montgomery Presents," and other television programs. Contributor of short stories to *Collier's* and *Good Housekeeping*.

SIDELIGHTS: Levy was the creator and executive producer of the television series "The Addams Family" and "The Pruitts of Southampton." He was also executive producer of "The Double Life of Henry Phyfe."†

*   *   *

LEWELLEN, T(heodore) C(harles)   1940-

PERSONAL: Born June 26, 1940, in Redding, Calif.; son of Lowell F. (a structural steel worker) and Dianne (Carmen) Lewellen. *Education:* Attended San Jose State College (now University), 1959-60; Alaska Methodist University, B.A. (magna cum laude), 1963. *Politics:* Independent. *Religion:* Atheist (non-messianic).

CAREER: Fired from first job as U.S. Forest Service firefighter (1959) for running off to Tijuana on standby time; from 1959-63 held a series of short-term and summer jobs, working as auto plant assemblyman and theater doorman in California, and as a gandy dancer, hod carrier, game warden, and film researcher in Alaska; made two trips to Cuba during the revolution ("luckily ran out of money the second time before I could be arrested for being a stupid Gringo"), hitchhiked from Key West to San Jose, Calif., on $11, was jailed there for vagrancy, and headed for Alaska, which he now considers home. *Military service:* U.S. Army, 1963-65.

WRITINGS: The Ruthless Gun, Gold Medal Books, 1964; *The Billikin Courier*, Random House, 1968.

WORK IN PROGRESS: A horror novel, *A Room for Children*; three Westerns, *A Long Night's Ride*, *The Drifter*, and *A Code for Dying*; epic novel, *The Solitary Way*; "an honest fictionalized dream-fantasy-realistic-stream of consciousness-satirical autobiography," titled *Coeur D'Alene*.

SIDELIGHTS: Lewellen on his theory of writing: "There is no free will in fiction, no accidents, no real choice which is not determined by the character's past. In other words I write about obsessions in conflict. Since I must know my character's subconscious motives, write him from the inside-out, so to speak, I never use characters from my own experience, whose cultural facade would impose certain limitations. A piece of earth also has a personality determined by its history just as a person does, so I have so far had a tendency to 'create' my own settings. The word 'create' here is misleading, since I do not believe that honest writing is an act of creation so much as discovery—breaking through our little moral facades to the actual drives. Thus I seldom try to think out a story or plot. That's something I just let happen over a period of years. By the time logic is ready to take over at the typewriter, the story is fully enough developed that I need not write in sequence. In other words I may begin with the middle chapter, then do the epilogue, then back to chapter one. I do not like moralistic, inspirational or sociological writing unless it is tongue in cheek (such as James Bond books). Thus I write no-holds-barred, and deal, perhaps excessively, with insanity, obsession, perversion, etc."

Special interests include the motion picture (Resnais, Kurosawa, Antonioni, Fellini, in that order); psychology of religion, myth, art, and dream ("which I see as inextricably linked"); modern art (Pollock, Albright). His prejudices are "soldiers, pop art, Texans, Barry Goldwater and prejudiced people."†

*   *   *

LEWENSTEIN, Morris R.   1923-

PERSONAL: Born October 30, 1923, in Duluth, Minn.; son of Sam (a merchant) and Gertrude (Flint) Lewenstein; married Ida Jenkins, August 17, 1958; children: Jay, Daniel. *Education:* University of Chicago, B.A., 1944, M.A., 1947; University of Illinois, Ph.D., 1953. *Home:* 3029 Rivera Dr., Burlingame, Calif. 94010. *Office:* Social Science Department, San Francisco State University, San Francisco, Calif. 94132.

CAREER: High school social studies teacher in Momence, Ill., 1944-46, Joliet, Ill., 1947-50, and Urbana, Ill., 1952-53; San Francisco State University, San Francisco, Calif., instructor, 1953-55, assistant professor, 1955-59, associate professor, 1959-63, professor of social science, 1963—, chairman of department, 1959-69. Illinois Curriculum Program, staff member, 1950-53. *Member:* National Council for the Social Studies, American Academy of Political and Social Science, California Council for the Social Studies (co-founder), Phi Beta Kappa, Phi Delta Kappa.

WRITINGS: (With Edith E. Starratt) *Our American Government Today*, Prentice-Hall, 1958, 2nd edition, 1966; *Teaching Social Studies in Junior and Senior High Schools*, Rand McNally, 1963. Contributor to "National Forum Guidance Series," 1948.

WORK IN PROGRESS: A study of political education and participation in the United States.†

LEWIS, Allan   1905-

PERSONAL: Born June 30, 1905, in New York, N.Y.; son of Ben (a cigar manufacturer) and Rebecca (Ehrlich) Lewis; married Matilda Ross (divorced, 1942); married Brooke Waring (a writer), June 20, 1944; children: Anita (Mrs. Roy Sorrels), Lanny (daughter). *Education:* City College (now City College of the City University of New York), A.B., 1927; Columbia University, A.M., 1929; graduate study at Columbia University, University of California, and New School for Social Research; Stanford University, Ph.D., 1943; National University of Mexico, D.Litt., 1954. *Office:* Shakespeare Institute, University of Bridgeport, Bridgeport, Conn.

CAREER: High school teacher and junior college instructor in drama and English, New York and California, 1927-42; Actors Theatre, Hollywood, Calif., lecturer on history of drama, 1946-47; Bennington College, Bennington, Vt., chairman of drama department, 1948-49; National University of Mexico, Mexico City, professor of theater history, 1950-58; Briarcliff College, Briarcliff Manor, N.Y., member of English faculty, 1958-60; New School for Social Research, New York, N.Y., lecturer on drama, 1958—; University of Bridgeport, Bridgeport, Conn., professor of English, 1965—. Director of New Dramatists Committee, 1960-61, of Shakespeare Institute, Stratford, Conn., 1965—. Director and actor, stage, films, and television; drama critic, *Bridgeport Sunday Herald*, 1963—.

MILITARY SERVICE: U.S. Army Air Forces, 1941-46; served in China-Burma-India Theater; became first lieutenant. *Member:* American National Theatre and Academy, American Educational Theatre Association, International Association of University Professors of English, American Association of University Professors, American Society for Aesthetics.

WRITINGS: The Contemporary Theatre, Crown, 1962; *American Plays and Playwrights of the Contemporary Theatre*, Crown, 1965; *Ionesco*, Twayne, 1973.

Stage plays: "Good Hunting"; "A Special Occasion." Screenplays: "Big Thunder"; "Canasta"; "The Tigress"; and others.

Contributor to *Educational Forum*, *Texas Quarterly*, *La Revista Universitaria*, and other professional journals.

WORK IN PROGRESS: Shakespeare's World and Ours, a two-year project.

SIDELIGHTS: Lewis is fluent in Spanish, French, and Russian; he is an extensive traveler in Europe, conducting student tours there, 1958-62. *Avocational interests:* Tennis, swimming, hiking.

*   *   *

LEWIS, Geoffrey (Lewis)   1920-

PERSONAL: Born June 19, 1920, in London, England; son of Ashley and Jeanne Muriel (Sintrop) Lewis; married Rafaela Bale-Seideman (a teacher), July 26, 1941; children: Lalage Anna, Jonathan Lewis. *Education:* St. John's College, Oxford, B.A. (classics), 1941, M.A., 1945, B.A. (oriental studies), 1947, D.Phil., 1950. *Religion:* Jewish. *Home:* Boar's Hill, Oxford, England. *Office:* Oriental Institute, Oxford University, Oxford, England.

CAREER: Oxford University, Oxford, England, lecturer, 1950-56, senior lecturer in Turkish, 1956—, fellow of St. Antony's College, 1961—. Robert College, Istanbul, Turkey, director of Humanities Program, 1959-60, visiting professor of humanities, 1960-68. Visiting professor at Princeton University, 1970-71, 1974. *Military service:* Royal Air Force, Radar Branch, 1940-45; received Africa Star and clasp.

WRITINGS: Teach Yourself Turkish, English Universities Press, 1953; *Turkey*, Benn, 1955, 4th revised edition, Praeger, 1974; *Katib Chelebi's Balance of Truth*, Allen & Unwin, 1957; (contributor) Paul Henry and Hans-Rudolf Schwyzer, editors, *Plotini Opera*, Volume II, Desclee de Brouwer, 1959; (contributor) Ragliavan Iyer, editor, *The Glass Curtain Between Asia and Europe*, Oxford University Press, 1965; *Turkish Grammar*, Oxford University Press, 1967; (with Martin S. Spink) *Albucasis on Surgery and Instruments*, University of California Press, 1973; (contributor) Peter Mansfield, editor, *The Middle East*, 4th edition, Oxford University Press, 1973; *The Book of Dede Korkut*, Penguin, 1974. Contributor to *Encyclopaedia Britannica*, *Encyclopaedia of Islam*, and *Cassell's Encyclopaedia of World Literature*.

WORK IN PROGRESS: A book, *Turkish Reader*, for Oxford University Press; an autobiographical book, *Death on "M" Deck.*

SIDELIGHTS: Lewis told *CA*: "My best languages are Turkish, French, Arabic, Latin, and Greek, in that order. I can cope with Persian and the Romance languages and German, and, using a dictionary for every other word, Russian. I consider language the most fascinating manifestation of human genius, used as it is as a vehicle, a cloak, and a substitute, for thought."

*   *   *

LEWIS, Mildred D. 1912-
(James DeWitt)

PERSONAL: Born February 4, 1912, in Battle Creek, Mich.; daughter of J. Newton and Gertrude (Harrison) Decker; married Kent W. Lewis (a U.S. treasury agent; deceased), April 28, 1934; children: James Kent. *Education:* Attended University of Michigan, 1931-32. *Politics:* Democrat. *Religion:* Protestant. *Home:* 7650 North 14th St., Phoenix, Ariz. 85020. *Agent:* Scott Meredith Literary Agency, Inc., 580 Fifth Ave., New York, N.Y., 10036.

CAREER: Lewis Bookstore (new and used), Santa Monica, Calif., owner, 1940-41; writer for young people.

WRITINGS: The Honorable Sword, Houghton, 1960; (under pseudonym James DeWitt) *In Pursuit of the Spanish Galleon*, Criterion, 1961. Contributor to *Jack and Jill, Children's Friend, Teen Talk, Twelve-Fifteen, Highlights for Children, Venture*, and *Teen Times*.

WORK IN PROGRESS: A novel for teen-age girls, not yet titled; research on the Aztecs and the Spanish Conquest.

AVOCATIONAL INTERESTS: Golf, knitting (often knits while writing).†

*   *   *

LEWIS, W(alter) David 1931-

PERSONAL: Born June 24, 1931, in Towanda, Pa.; son of Gordon C. (a correctional official) and Eleanor E. (Tobias) Lewis; married Carolyn Wyatt Brown, June 12, 1954; children: Daniel Kent, Virginia Lorraine, Nancy Ellyn. *Education:* Attended Juniata College, 1948-49; Pennsylvania State University, B.A., 1952, M.A., 1954; Cornell University, Ph.D., 1961. *Religion:* Episcopalian. *Home:* 816 Heard

Ave., Auburn, Ala. 36830. *Office:* 7008 Haley Center, Auburn University, Auburn, Ala. 36830.

CAREER: Hamilton College, Clinton, N.Y., instructor in public speaking, 1954-57; University of Delaware, Newark, part-time instructor, 1959-61, lecturer in history, 1961-65; Eleutherian Mills-Hagley Foundation, Wilmington, Del., fellowship coordinator, 1959-65; State University of New York at Buffalo, associate professor, 1965-71, professor of history, 1971; Auburn University, Auburn, Ala., Hudson Professor of History and Engineering, 1971—. Director of Auburn Project on Technology, Human Values, and the Southern Future. *Member:* Society for the History of Technology (program chairman, 1973), American Historical Association, American Society for Engineering Education, H. G. Wells Society International, Phi Beta Kappa, Phi Kappa Phi, Delta Sigma Rho, Phi Delta Theta. *Awards, honors:* Two grants from National Endowment for the Humanities; summer grants from State University of New York Research Foundation, Eleutherian Mills Historical Library, and Auburn University Research Foundation.

WRITINGS: From Newgate to Dannemora: The Rise of the Penitentiary in New York, 1796-1848, Cornell University Press, 1965; (editor with David T. Gilchrist) *Economic Change in the Civil War Era*, Eleutherian Mills-Hagley Foundation, 1965; (contributor) Kenneth S. Lynn, editor, *The Professions in America*, Houghton, 1965; (contributor) Melvin Kranzberg and Carroll W. Pursell, editors, *Technology in Western Civilization*, Oxford University Press, 1967; (contributor) Stanley Coben and Lorman Ratner, editors, *The Development of an American Culture*, Prentice-Hall, 1970; (contributor) Edward T. James and others, editors, *Notable American Women*, Harvard University Press, 1971. Contributor to *Dictionary of American Biography*, *Encyclopedia of American History*, *Encyclopedia of Southern History*; also contributor of articles and reviews to *Technology and Culture*, *Pennsylvania Magazine of History and Biography*, and to national and state journals.

WORK IN PROGRESS: A short history of the American iron and steel industry for Eleutherian Mills-Hagley Foundation; a short history of interaction between man, technology, and the environment for Elek; a history of Delta Air Lines, with Wesley P. Newton; a chapter on the career of William Henry, nineteenth-century ironmaster, for a book to be published by Texas Christian University Press.

*   *   *

LEWIS, William Hubert 1928-

PERSONAL: Born June 4, 1928, in New York, N.Y.; son of John S. and Lillian (Rome) Lewis; married Kathleen Moran (a research specialist), August 20, 1949. *Education:* Attended University of Arizona, 1947-48; George Washington University, B.A., 1952, M.A., 1953; Johns Hopkins University, graduate student, 1954-55; American University, Ph.D., 1960. *Religion:* Roman Catholic. *Home:* 1200 North Nash St., Arlington, Va. *Office:* Bureau of Political-Military Affairs, U.S. Department of State, Washington, D.C.

CAREER: U.S. Department of State, Washington, D.C., 1952—, chief of North and East Africa Division, 1961—, office director of Bureau of Political-Military Affairs, 1970—. Associate professor of history, Georgetown University, 1960—; visiting lecturer, Johns Hopkins University, 1962—. *Military service:* U.S. Army, 1946-47. *Member:* American Historical Association, African Studies Association, American Anthropological Association, Pi Gamma Mu.

WRITINGS: (With others) *Modern Middle East and Muslim Africa*, Praeger, 1962; (editor) *New Forces in Africa*, Public Affairs, 1963; (editor) *Emerging Africa*, Public Affairs, 1964; (with others) *Communist Revolution and Theory*, Princeton University Press, 1964; (with others) *Development Revolution in the Middle East*, Middle East Institute, 1964; (editor) *French-Speaking Africa: The Search for Identity*, Walker & Co., 1965; (editor with James Kritzeck) *Islam in Africa*, Van Nostrand, 1969. Contributor to political science journals. Reviewer, *St. Louis Post-Dispatch*.

WORK IN PROGRESS: History of the Horn of Africa, for Prentice-Hall.

SIDELIGHTS: Lewis speaks French, Spanish, Arabic; he has traveled extensively in Africa since 1954. *Avocational interests:* Tennis, golf.

* * *

LEY, Alice Chetwynd 1915-

PERSONAL: Surname rhymes with "day"; born October 12, 1915, in Halifax, Yorkshire, England; daughter of Frederick George (a journalist) and Alice Mary (Chetwynd) Humphrey; married Kenneth James Ley (a journalist), February 3, 1945; children: Richard James Humphrey, Graham Kenneth Hugh. *Education:* University of London, Diploma in Sociology, 1962. *Politics:* Liberal. *Religion:* Church of England. *Home:* 42 Cannonbury Ave., Pinner, Middlesex, England. *Agent:* Curtis Brown Ltd., 1 Craven Hill, London W2 3EW, England.

MEMBER: Romantic Novelists' Association, Society of Women Writers and Journalists, Jane Austen Society.

WRITINGS—Novels; all published by R. Hale: *The Jewelled Snuff Box*, 1959, Beagle Books, 1974; *The Georgian Rake*, 1960, Beagle Books, 1974; *The Guinea Stamp*, 1961; *Master of Liversedge*, 1966; *Clandestine Betrothal*, 1967; *Toast of the Town*, 1969; *Letters for a Spy*, 1970; *A Season at Brighton*, 1972; *Tenant of Chesdene Manor*, 1974.

WORK IN PROGRESS: Another historical romance set in London in the late eighteenth century.

AVOCATIONAL INTERESTS: History, literature, sociology, gardening.

BIOGRAPHICAL/CRITICAL SOURCES: Birmingham Post, Birmingham, England, July 10, 1961.

* * *

L'HEUREUX, John Clarke 1934-

PERSONAL: Born October 26, 1934, in South Hadley, Mass.; son of Wilfred (a civil engineer and artist) and Mildred (an artist; maiden name, Clarke) L'Heureux; married Joan Polston, June 26, 1971. *Education:* Attended National Academy of Theatre Arts, 1952, and College of the Holy Cross, 1952-54; Boston College, A.B., 1959, M.A. (philosophy), 1960, M.A. (English), 1963; Woodstock College, S.T.L., 1967; Harvard University, M.A. (English), 1968. *Office:* Department of English, Stanford University, Stanford, Calif. 94305.

CAREER: Entered Society of Jesus (Jesuits), 1954; ordained priest, 1965; laicized, 1971. Writer-in-residence, Georgetown University, Washington, D.C., 1964-65, Regis College, Weston, Mass., 1968-69; *Atlantic*, Washington, D.C., staff editor, 1968-69, contributing editor, 1969—; Stanford University, Stanford, Calif., assistant professor of English, 1973—. Visiting professor of American literature,

Hamline University, 1971, and Tufts College, 1971-73; visiting assistant professor, Harvard University, 1973.

WRITINGS: Quick as Dandelions (poems), Doubleday, 1964; *Rubrics for a Revolution* (poems), Macmillan, 1967; *Picnic in Babylon: A Jesuit Priest's Journal, 1963-67* (autobiography), Macmillan, 1967; *One Eye and a Measuring Rod* (poems), Macmillan, 1968; *No Place for Hiding* (poems), Macmillan, 1971; *Tight White Collar* (novel), Doubleday, 1972; *The Clang Birds* (novel), Macmillan, 1972; *Family Affairs* (short stories), Doubleday, 1974.

SIDELIGHTS: L'Heureux is competent in French and Latin; he reads German, Italian, Greek. *Avocational interests:* Painting.

* * *

LI, David H(siang-fu) 1928-

PERSONAL: Surname is pronounced Lee; born October 7, 1928, in Ningpo, China; son of Y. C. (a manufacturer) and S. C. (Lin) Li; married Liu (a medical technologist), November 30, 1957; children: Philip, Leslie. *Education:* St. John's University, China, A.B., 1949; University of Pennsylvania, M.B.A., 1950; University of Illinois, Ph.D., 1953. *Office:* College of Business Administration, University of Washington, Seattle, Wash. 98105.

CAREER: Mutual of Omaha Insurance Co., Chicago, Ill., controller, 1953-55; St. Mary's College, Winona, Minn., associate professor of economics, 1955-56; University of Southern California, Los Angeles, assistant professor of accounting, 1956-60; California State College at Fullerton (now University), professor of accounting, 1960-65; University of Washington, Seattle, professor of accounting, 1965—. Eagle Development Co., secretary-treasurer; Terra Titan, Inc., secretary-treasurer. International Communications Foundation, consulting comptroller, 1961-62. *Member:* American Institute of Certified Public Accountants, American Accounting Association, National Association of Accountants (associate director of programs, 1964-65), California Society of Certified Public Accountants, Rotary Club. *Awards, honors:* Professorial research fellow, Westinghouse Electric Corp., 1957; Sperry Rand grant in programmed learning, 1961-63.

WRITINGS: Accounting for Management Analysis, C. E. Merrill, 1964; *Cost Accounting for Management Applications*, C. E. Merrill, 1966; *Accounting, Computers, Management Information Systems*, McGraw, 1968; (compiler) *Design and Management of Information Systems*, Science Research Associates, 1972. Contributor to business journals.

WORK IN PROGRESS: Research monographs on accounting theory under the entity concept and on international accounting.

AVOCATIONAL INTERESTS: Bridge, photography, and travel.†

* * *

LIBLIT, Jerome

HOME: 3044 Wallace Ave., Bronx, N.Y. 10467.

CAREER: New York (N.Y.) Juvenile Delinquency Evaluation Project, research associate, 1956-61; Fund for Urban Improvement, Inc., New York, N.Y., director of research, 1961-64; New School for Social Research, program director, Center for New York City Affairs, 1964—. City University of New York, New York, N.Y., lecturer in political science, 1951—. Jewish Theological Seminary of America, New York, N.Y., lecturer on community planning, Institute for Religious and Social Studies, 1961-62, 1963-64. Housing consultant, Agency for International Development. Member of Borough of Manhattan Community Planning Board, New York City Citizens Union, and Citizens Housing and Planning Council of New York.

WRITINGS: (Editor) *Housing the Cooperative Way,* Twayne, 1964; (contributor) R. M. MacIver, *Assault on Poverty,* Harper, 1965. Contributor to *Cooperative Housing Quarterly, New York Herald Tribune,* and *Political Science Quarterly.†*

*   *   *

LICHELLO, Robert 1926-

PERSONAL: Surname originally Lichiello; born September 12, 1926, in Parkersburg, W. Va.; son of Carmine Antonio and Stella (Camerota) Lichiello. *Education:* West Virginia University, B.A., 1951. *Office:* Volitant Publishing, 21 West 26th St., New York, N.Y.

CAREER: Sometime disc jockey and radio announcer; magazine editor, New York, N.Y., beginning, 1959, editing *Real Men,* 1959-60, *Escape to Adventure,* 1961-63, *Man-to-Man,* 1964-65; free-lance writer and editor, 1965—. *Military service:* U.S. Army Air Forces, 1945-47; served in Pacific Theater; became sergeant. *Awards, honors:* Third prize, Audio Devices International Sound Recording Contest, for creative use of the tape recorder; Golden Quill Award for magazine article, 1964.

WRITINGS: Ju-Jitsu Self-Defense for Teen-agers, Messner, 1961 (published in England as *Ju-Jitsu,* Jenkins, 1963); *Cancer and Controversy,* London Press, 1962; *Sin Paradise,* Brandon House, 1963; *Pioneer in Blood Plasma: Dr. Charles Richard Drew,* Messner, 1968; *Dag Hammarskjold: A Giant in Diplomacy,* Sam-Har Press, 1971; *Edward R. Murrow: Broadcaster of Courage,* Sam-Har Press, 1971; *Enrico Fermi: Father of the Atomic Bomb,* Sam-Har Press, 1971. About one thousand articles and stories on medicine, show business and finance have been published in magazines.

WORK IN PROGRESS: A novel, *A Wind Is Rising;* a film play, "Mondo Chaic."†

*   *   *

LICHTENBERG, Elisabeth Jacoba 1913-
(Liesje van Someren)

PERSONAL: Born September 9, 1913, in Groningen, Netherlands; daughter of Engel (an army officer) and Sietske Lichtenberg; married Alexander Richard Putland, December 13, 1935; children: Alexandrina Elisabeth (Mrs. Michael Arthur). *Education:* University of Amsterdam, B.A., 1935. *Home:* Flat 4, 42 Castelnau, London S.W. 13, England. *Agent:* Christine Campbell Thomson, D. C. Benson & Campbell Thomson Ltd., Cliffords Inn, Fleet St., London E.C. 4, England.

CAREER: Author, 1942—. Associated Country Women of the World, vice-chairman, 1947-50, 1953-57, and press officer for international conferences, 1950, 1953. Broadcaster in England, Canada, Netherlands; lecturer for Royal Netherlands Embassy in London. *Member:* P.E.N. (English center), Society of Women Writers and Journalists, Society of Authors.

*WRITINGS—*Under pseudonym Liesje van Someren: *Escape from Holland,* Jenkins, 1942; *The Young Traveller in Holland,* Phoenix House, 1948, Dutton, 1953; *Ann and Peter in Holland,* Muller, 1959; *Ann and Peter in Belgium,* Muller, 1962; *Holland,* Weidenfeld & Nicolson, 1962; *Erica* (historical novel), Vrouw en Huis, 1962; *Grotius: Umpire to the Nations* (biography), Dobson, 1965; *Continental Cookbook,* Pitman, 1970. Contributor to *Nieuwe Rotterdamse Courant,* and to magazines in England and the Netherlands.

WORK IN PROGRESS: Research for biography of Bertha von Suttner, stressing her influence on Alfred B. Nobel, founder of the Nobel Prizes; research on Dutch Old Masters; research on the Kaiser in exile.

SIDELIGHTS: Elisabeth Lichtenberg is competent in Dutch, German, French, and English; she understands Flemish, Afrikaans, and a bit of the Scandinavian languages.

*   *   *

LIDDELL, (John) Robert 1908-

PERSONAL: Surname is pronounced to rhyme with "middle"; born October 13, 1908, in Tunbridge Wells, Kent, England; son of John Stewart (a major, Royal Engineers) and Anna Gertrude (Morgan) Liddell. *Education:* Corpus Christi College, Oxford, B.A. (first class honors), 1931, B.Litt., 1933, M.A., 1935. *Politics:* Anti-left. *Religion:* Roman Catholic.

CAREER: Oxford University, Bodleian Library, Oxford, England, senior assistant, 1933-38; University of Helsinki, Helsinki, Finland, lecturer, 1939; British Council lecturer in Greece, 1940-41; University of Alexandria, Alexandria, Egypt, and University of Cairo, Cairo, Egypt, lecturer, 1941-51; British Council lecturer in Greece, 1951—; University of Athens, Athens, Greece, acting head of department of English, 1963-68. *Member:* Society of Authors, Royal Society of Literature (fellow).

WRITINGS: The Almond Tree, J. Cape, 1938; *Kind Relations,* J. Cape, 1939, published as *Take This Child,* Greystone, 1939; *The Gantillons,* J. Cape, 1940; *Watering Place,* J. Cape, 1945; *A Treatise on the Novel,* (also see below) J. Cape, 1947; *The Last Enchantments,* J. Cape, 1948; *Unreal City,* J. Cape, 1952; *Some Principles of Fiction,* J. Cape, 1953, Indiana University Press, 1954 (published with *A Treatise on the Novel* as *Robert Liddell on the Novel,* University of Chicago Press, 1969); *The Novels of Ivy Compton-Burnett,* Gollancz, 1953; *Aegean Greece,* J. Cape, 1954; *Byzantium and Istanbul,* J. Cape, 1956; *The Morea,* J. Cape, 1958; *The Rivers of Babylon,* J. Cape, 1959; *The Novels of Jane Austen,* Longmans, Green, 1963; *Mainland Greece,* Longmans, 1965; *An Object for a Walk,* Longmans, 1966; *The Deep End,* Longmans, 1968; *Stepsons,* Longmans, 1969; *Cavafy: A Critical Biography,* Duckworth, 1974. Contributor to *Horizon, London Magazine, Encounter.*

Translator: D. Sicilianos, *Old and New Athens,* Putnam, 1960; Linos Politis, *A History of Modern Greek Literature,* Oxford University Press, 1973.

WORK IN PROGRESS: A book on George Eliot's novels.

SIDELIGHTS: Reviewing *The Deep End,* David Williams notes that it is "a novel which is subtle, lucid and highly personal in tone." Liddell is fluent in French and modern Greek, reads Italian. *Avocational interests:* European history, art, and architecture; cookery (practical and theoretical).

LIDDY, James (Daniel Reeves) 1934-
(Brian Lynch, Liam O'Connor)

PERSONAL: Born July 1, 1934, in Kilkee, Ireland; son of James Gonzaga (a doctor) and Clare (Reeves) Liddy. *Education:* University College, Dublin, M.A., 1959; King's Inns, Dublin, barrister, 1959. *Politics:* Labour. *Religion:* Ex-Catholic. *Residence:* Coolgreany, Gorey, County Wexford, Ireland.

CAREER: Poet-in-residence, San Francisco State University, 1967-68, Harpur College; visiting professor, State University of New York, Lewis and Clark College, and Denison University. *Military service:* Conscientious objector.

WRITINGS: Esau, My Kingdom for a Drink: Homage to James Joyce on His Eightieth Birthday (booklet), Dolmen Press, 1962; *In a Blue Smoke* (poems), Dufour, 1964; *Blue Mountain* (poems), Dufour, 1968; (with Jim Chapson and Thomas Hill) *Blue House: Poems in the Chinese Manner,* White Rabbit Press, 1968; *A Life of Stephen Dedalus* (booklet), White Rabbit Press, 1969; *A Munster Song of Love and War* (booklet), White Rabbit Press, 1971; (editor) *Nine Queen Bees,* White Rabbit Press, 1971. Work represented in anthologies, including *New Poets of Ireland,* edited by Donald Carroll, Alan Swallow, 1963. Contributor to *New York Times, Dublin Magazine.* Editor of *Arena.*

WORK IN PROGRESS: James Liddy '66, poems; *Tee-Hee-Mutt,* a novel; *Passion's Slave,* a dythirambic novel.

SIDELIGHTS: Liddy writes: "I believe, with Robert Graves, that the poet is not employed in a job, nor belongs to any organization.†

*   *   *

LILLIBRIDGE, G(eorge) D(onald) 1921-

PERSONAL: Born July 20, 1921, in Mitchell, S.D.; son of Charles Bradley (a pharmacist) and Neva (Soule) Lillibridge; married Florence Belson (a high school teacher of English), January 5, 1943; children: Michael, Linda, Jennifer, Catherine. *Education:* University of South Dakota, B.A., 1942; University of Wisconsin, M.A., 1948, Ph.D., 1950. *Politics:* Democrat. *Home:* 26 Cottage Ave., Chico, Calif. *Office:* Department of History, California State University, Chico, Calif.

CAREER: California State University, Chico, 1952—, now professor of U.S. history. *Military service:* U.S. Marine Corps, 1942-45; became first lieutenant. *Member:* American Historical Association, American Studies Association, Organization of American Historians.

WRITINGS: Beacon of Freedom, University of Pennsylvania Press, 1955; *The American Image: Past and Present,* Heath, 1970; *The Americans—Then and Now,* Houghton, in press.

*   *   *

LINDAY, Ryllis Elizabeth Paine 1919-

PERSONAL: Born June 3, 1919, in Mountain Iron, Minn.; daughter of Paul J. Paine; married Charles A. Linday (an electrician), September 14, 1940; children: James, Michael. *Education:* Attended Superior State College (now Wisconsin State University). *Home:* 660 Tenth St., Lake Oswego, Ore.

CAREER: Former nursery school teacher; now doing secretarial work at Forest Hills School, Lake Oswego, Ore. *Member:* Alpha Kappa.

WRITINGS—Picture books for children: *Look at Me,* Broadman, 1959; *Now I Am Two,* Broadman, 1963. Wrote monthly "Litterbug or Neaterbug," with Helen Berry Moore as artist, in *Wee Wisdom,* 1963-64.

AVOCATIONAL INTERESTS: Mountain camping with family, knitting, and bridge.

BIOGRAPHICAL/CRITICAL SOURCES: Growing, January-March, 1964.

*   *   *

LINDGREN, Astrid 1907-

PERSONAL: Born November 14, 1907, in Vimmerby, Sweden; daughter of Samuel August and Hanna (Jonsson) Ericsson; married Sture Lindgren, April 4, 1931 (died, 1952); children: Lars, Karin (Mrs. Carl Olof Nyman). *Home:* Dalagatan 46, Stockholm, Sweden.

CAREER: Writer of children's books, 1944—; Raben Sjogren (publishers), Stockholm, Sweden, children's book editor, 1946-70. *Member:* Union of Swedish Writers, League of the Nine, P.E.N. *Awards, honors:* Nils Nolgersson Medal, 1950, for *Nils Karlsson-Pyssling;* Swedish State Award, 1957, for high literary standards; International Hans Christian Andersen Award, 1958, for *Rasmus Pa Luffen,* and Boys' Clubs of America Junior Book Award, 1961, for American edition of same book, *Rasmus and the Vagabond; New York Herald Tribune* Children's Spring Book Festival Award (shared with Anna Riwkin-Brick), 1959, for *Sia Lives on Kilimanjaro;* Swedish Academy's Gold Medal, 1971; Doctor Honoris Causa, 1973.

WRITINGS—All Swedish books published by Raben & Sjogren, all translations published in America by Viking, except where noted: *Britt-Mari lattar sitt hjarta,* 1944, 3rd edition, 1959; *Pippi Langstrump,* 1945, new edition, 1968, translation by Florence Lamborn published as *Pippi Longstocking,* 1950; *Kerstin och jag,* 1945; *Masterdetektiven Blomkvist,* 1946, 11th edition, 1967, translation by Herbert Antoine published as *Bill Bergson Master Detective,* 1952; *Pippi Langstrump gar ombord,* 1946, translation by Marianne Turner published as *Pippi Longstocking Goes Aboard,* Oxford University Press, 1956, translation by Lamborn published as *Pippi Goes on Board,* Viking, 1957; *Alla vi barn i Bullerbyn,* 1947, 16th edition, 1967, translation by Lamborn published as *The Children of Noisy Village,* 1962 (published in England as *Cherry Time at Bullerby,* Methuen, 1964); *Pippi Longstrump i Soderhavet,* 1948, 14th edition, 1968, translation by Gerry Bothmer published as *Pippi in the South Seas,* Oxford University Press, 1957, Viking, 1959; *Mera om oss barn i Bullerbyn,* 1949, translation by Lamborn published as *Happy Times in Noisy Village,* 1963 (published in England as *Happy Days at Bullerby,* Methuen, 1965); *Nils Karlsson-Pyssling,* 1949, 9th edition, 1957.

Kaisa Kavat, 1950, 11th edition, 1967; *Kati i Amerika,* Bonniers, 1950, translation by Turner published as *Kati in America,* Brockhampton, 1964; *Masterdetektiven Blomkvist lever farligt,* 1951, translation by Antoine published as *Bill Bergson Lives Dangerously,* 1954; *Bara roligt i Bullerbyn,* 1952; *Kati pa Kaptensgatan,* Bonniers, 1952, reissued as *Kati i Italien,* Raben & Sjogren, 1971, published as *Kati in Italy,* Grosset, 1961; *Kalle Blomkvist och Rasmus,* 1953, 4th edition, 1965, translation by Lamborn published as *Bill Bergson and the White Rose Rescue,* 1965; *Mio, min Mio,* 1954, translation by Turner published as *Mio My Son,* 1956; *Kati i Paris,* Bonniers, 1954, published as *Kati in Paris,* Grosset, 1961; *Lillebror och*

Karlsson pa Taket, 1955, 4th edition, 1965, translation by Turner published as *Eric and Karlsson-on-the-Roof*, Oxford University Press, 1958, published as *Karlsson-on-the-Roof*, Viking, 1971; *Rasmus pa luffen*, 1956, translation by Bothmer published as *Rasmus and the Vagabond*, 1960; *Korea, ofredens land*, 1956; *Barnen pa Brakmakargatan*, 1956, translation by Bothmer published as *The Children on Troublemaker Street*, Macmillan, 1964; *Rasmus, Pontus och Toker*, 1957; *Bullerbybarnen*, Ehlins-Folkbildnings (Stockholm), 1957; *Pjaser for barn och ungdom*, 1959; *Sunnanang*, 1959; *Mina svenska kusiner*, 1959.

Madicken, 1960, translation by Bothmer published as *Mischievous Meg*, 1962; *Lotta pa Brakmakargatan*, 1961, translation by Bothmer published as *Lotta on Troublemaker Street*, Macmillan, 1963; *Karlsson pa Taket flyger igen*, 1962; *Emil i Lonneberga*, 1963, 5th edition, 1967, translation by Lilian Seaton published as *Emil in the Soup Tureen*, Follett, 1970; *Jul i Bullerbyn*, 1963, translation by Lamborn published as *Christmas in Noisy Village*, 1964; (with Anna Riwkin-Brick) *Jackie bor i Holland*, 1963, published as *Dirk Lives in Holland*, Macmillan, 1963; *Vi pa Saltkrakan*, 1964, translation by Evelyn Ramsden published as *Seacrow Island*, 1969; *Var i Bullerbyn*, 1965, published as *Springtime in Noisy Village*, 1966; (with Riwkin-Brick) *Randi bor i Lofoten*, Gyldendal (Oslo), 1965, published as *Randi Lives in Norway*, Macmillan, 1965 (published in England as *Gerda Lives in Norway*, Methuen, 1965); *Jag vill inte ga och lagga mej*, 6th edition, 1965; *Nya hyss av Emil i Lonneberga*, 1966, published as *Emil's Pranks*, Follett, 1971; *Noy bor i Thailand*, 1966, published as *Noy Lives in Thailand*, Macmillan, 1967; *Skrallan och sjorovarna*, 1967, translation by Albert Read and Christine Sapieha published as *Skralien and the Pirates*, Doubleday, 1969; *Karlsson pa Taket smyger igen*, 1968; *Matti bor i Finland*, 1968, published as *Matti Lives in Finland*, Macmillan, 1969; (with Ingrid V. Nyman) *Pippi flytar in*, 1969; (with Nyman) *Pippi ordnar allt*, 1969.

An lever Emil i Lonneberga, 1970, translation by Michael Heron published as *Emil and Piggy Beast*, Follett, 1973; *Visst kan Lotta cykla*, 1971; *Mina pahitt*, 1971; *Broderna Lejonhjarta*, 1973.

Translated from the Swedish: *Sia Lives in Kilimanjaro*, Macmillan, 1959; *My Swedish Cousins*, Macmillan, 1960; *Lilibet, Circus Child*, Macmillan, 1961; (with Riwkin-Brick) *Marko Lives in Yugoslavia*, Macmillan, 1963; *All the Bullerby Children*, Methuen, 1970; *Of Course Polly Can Ride a Bike*, Follett, 1972.

Also author of *Noriko-san, Girl of Japan*, Methuen, 1958; *The Tomten*, Coward, 1961; *Christmas in the Stable*, Coward, 1962; *Christmas at Bullerby*, Methuen, 1964; *The Tomten and the Fox*, Coward, 1966.

Has also written plays for children's theater, and scripts for television and motion pictures.

*   *   *

LINDSAY, J(ohn) Robert 1925-

PERSONAL: Born April 23, 1925, in Greenville, S.C.; son of J. Robert and Helen (Morgan) Lindsay; married Helen Poland, March 26, 1951; children: John Robert IV, David Allen, John Selman. *Education:* University of North Carolina, A.B., 1949; Harvard University, A.M., 1951, Ph.D., 1955. *Home:* 129 Sherwood Rd., Ridgewood, N.J. 07450. *Office:* Schools of Business, New York University, 100 Trinity Pl., New York, N.Y. 10006.

CAREER: Federal Reserve Bank of New York, New York, N.Y., 1954-64, began as economist, became division chief, special assistant, and senior economist; New York University, New York, N.Y., visiting associate professor, 1957-58, adjunct associate professor, Graduate School of Business Administration, 1960-61, professor of finance and faculty research adviser, Schools of Business, 1964—. Lecturer at Bernard M. Baruch School of Business and Public Administration of the City College (now Bernard M. Baruch College of the City University of New York), 1955-56; lecturer in banking, Columbia University, 1959; visiting lecturer in economics and business, University of California, 1963-64. Executive director, New York State Council of Economic Advisers, 1971—. President, Unitarian Society of Ridgewood, N.J., 1968—. *Military:* U.S. Navy, 1943-46. *Member:* American Economic Association, American Finance Association, American Association for the Advancement of Science, Regional Science Association, Phi Beta Kappa.

WRITINGS: (With Arnold W. Sametz) *Financial Management—An Analytical Approach*, Irwin, 1963, revised edition, 1967; *The Economics of Interest Rate Ceilings*, Institute of Finance, New York University. Contributor to economics journals.

*   *   *

LINDSAY, R(obert) Bruce 1900-

PERSONAL: Born January 1, 1900, in New Bedford, Mass.; son of Robert (a gas engineer) and Eleanora E. (Leuchsenring) Lindsay; married Rachel Tupper Easterbrooks, July 29, 1922; children: Robert III, Evelyn Tupper (Mrs. Richard Calvin Roberts). *Education:* Brown University, A.B. and M.S., 1920; University of Copenhagen, advanced study in theoretical physics, 1922-23; Massachusetts Institute of Technology, Ph.D., 1924. *Home:* 91 Indian Ave., Portsmouth, R.I. 02871. *Office:* Department of Physics, Brown University, Providence, R.I. 02912.

CAREER: Massachusetts Institute of Technology, Cambridge, instructor in physics, 1920-22; Yale University, New Haven, Conn., instructor, 1923-27, assistant professor of physics, 1927-30; Brown University, Providence, R.I., associate professor of theoretical physics, 1930-36, Hazard Professor of Physics, 1936-71, professor emeritus, 1971—, chairman of department, 1934-54, director of ultrasonics laboratory, 1946-60, dean of the Graduate School, 1954-66. *Military service:* U.S. Navy, 1918-21.

MEMBER: American Academy of Arts and Sciences (vice-president, 1957-59), Acoustical Society of America (president, 1956-57), American Institute of Physics (member of governing board, 1956-71; member of executive committee, 1959-71), American Association for the Advancement of Science (vice-president and section chairman, 1958, 1968), American Physical Society (chairman of New England section, 1935-36; member of council, 1943-46), American Association of Physics Teachers (member of executive committee, 1945-47), Philosophy of Science Association (member of governing board, 1958-59), History of Science Society, Society of Rheology, American Mathematical Society, Association of Graduate Schools in Association of American Universities (president, 1965-66), American Association of University Professors (U.S. representative on International Commission on Acoustics, 1963-69), Phi Beta Kappa, Sigma Xi. *Awards, honors:* Ed.D., Rhode Island College, 1959; Gold Medal of Acoustical Society of America, 1963; Distinguished Service

Citation, American Association of Physics Teachers, 1963; Sc.D., Southeastern Massachusetts University, 1968.

WRITINGS: (With George W. Stewart) *Acoustics*, Van Nostrand, 1930; *Physical Mechanics*, Van Nostrand, 1933, 3rd edition, 1961; (with Henry Margenau) *Foundations of Physics*, Wiley, 1936; *General Physics*, Wiley, 1940; *Physical Statistics*, Wiley, 1941; *Handbook of Elementary Physics*, Dryden Press, 1943; *Concepts and Methods of Theoretical Physics*, Van Nostrand, 1951; (editor) *International Dictionary of Physics and Electronics*, Van Nostrand, 1956; *Mechanical Radiation*, McGraw, 1960; *The Role of Science in Civilization*, Harper, 1963; *The Nature of Physics*, Brown University Press, 1968; *Lord Rayleigh: The Man and His Work*, Pergamon, 1970; *Basic Concepts of Physics*, Van Nostrand, 1971; *Julius Robert Mayer: Prophet of Energy*, Pergamon, 1973; (editor) *Acoustics: Historical and Philosophical Development*, Dowden, Hutchinson & Ross, 1973; (editor) *Physical Acoustics*, Dowden, Hutchinson & Ross, 1974; *Energy: Early Historical Development of the Concept*, Dowden, Hutchinson & Ross, in press.

Section editor, *American Institute of Physics Handbook*, McGraw, 1957; series editor, "Benchmark Papers in Acoustics," and "Benchmark Papers in Energy" series; editor, *Proceedings of the Third International Congress on Acoustics*, American Institute of Physics, 1957; editor, *Journal of the Acoustical Society of America*, 1957—.

Contributor to *Encyclopaedia Britannica*; also contributor of more than 100 papers on theoretical physics, acoustics, and the history and philosophy of physics to professional journals, 1924—, and more than 170 reviews of scientific books to various journals, 1940—.

WORK IN PROGRESS: A book, *The First Law of Thermodynamics*, for "Benchmark Papers in Energy" series.

AVOCATIONAL INTERESTS: Collecting books on the history of science and biographies of scientists; walking, sawing wood, cutting grass.

BIOGRAPHICAL/CRITICAL SOURCES: Journal of the Acoustical Society of America, Volume XXXV, Number 1298, 1963; *Physics Today*, Volume XVI, Number 8, 1963; *American Journal of Physics*, Volume XXI, Number 455, 1963.

*　　*　　*

LINDSELL, Harold 1913-

PERSONAL: Born December 22, 1913, in New York, N.Y.; son of Leonard Anthony and Ella (Harris) Lindsell; married Marion Joanne Bolinder, June 12, 1943; children: Judith Ann Lindsell Wood, Joanne Marjorie Lindsell Buffam, Nancy Jean Lindsell Sharp, John Harold. *Education:* Wheaton College, Wheaton, Ill., B.S., 1939; University of California, Berkeley, M.A., 1939; Harvard University, graduate study, 1939-40; New York University, Ph.D., 1942; Fuller Theological Seminary, D.D., 1964. *Politics:* Republican. *Home:* 704N 1600 South Eads St., Arlington, Va. 22202. *Office: Christianity Today*, Washington Building, Washington, D.C. 20005.

CAREER: Columbia Bible College, Columbia S.C., professor of history of missions, 1942-44; ordained Baptist minister, 1944; Northern Baptist Theological Seminary, Chicago, Ill., professor of missions and church history, 1944-47; Fuller Theological Seminary, Pasadena, Calif., professor of missions and church history, 1947-64, also dean and vice-president. *Christianity Today*, Washington, D.C.,

associate editor, 1964-67, editor, 1968-72, editor and publisher, 1972—. *Member:* American Historical Association, American Society of Church History, American Academy of Political and Social Science, National Association of Evangelicals, National Association of Biblical Instructors, American Association for Medieval History, Pi Kappa Delta, Pi Gamma Mu.

WRITINGS: Abundantly Above, Eerdmans, 1944; *A Christian Philosophy of Missions*, Van Kampen Press, 1949; *The Thing Appointed*, Van Kampen Press, 1949; *Park Street Prophet*, Van Kampen Press, 1951; (with Charles J. Woodbridge) *A Handbook of Christian Truth*, Revell, 1953; *Missionary Principles and Practice*, Revell, 1955; *The Morning Altar*, Revell, 1956; (editor) *Daily Bible Readings from the Revised Standard Version*, Harper, 1957; *Christianity and the Cults*, Gospel Light, 1963; (editor) *Harper Study Bible*, Harper, 1964; *When You Pray*, Tyndale, 1969; *The World the Flesh and the Devil*, Canon Press, 1973. Contributor of articles to religious periodicals.

WORK IN PROGRESS: A book, *The Battle of the Bible*.

*　　*　　*

LINGENFELTER, Richard Emery 1934-

PERSONAL: Born April 5, 1934, in Farmington, N.M.; son of Roy E. and Frances (Berry) Lingenfelter; married Naomi J. Brefka, December 27, 1957; children: Andrea, Kendale. *Education:* University of California, Los Angeles, A.B., 1956. *Office:* University of California, Los Angeles, Calif. 90024.

CAREER: Lawrence Radiation Laboratory, Livermore, Calif., physicist, 1957-62; University of California, Los Angeles, research geophysicist, 1962-68, professor of geophysics and planetary physics, 1969—. Visiting fellow, Tata Institute of Fundamental Research, Bombay, India, 1968-69. *Member:* American Physical Society, American Geophysical Union.

WRITINGS: (With Richard A. Dwyer) *The "Nonpareil" Press of T. S. Harris*, Dawson's, 1957; *First through the Grand Canyon*, Dawson's, 1958; (editor) *The Cement Hunters*, Dawson's, 1960; (editor) *Washoe Rambles*, Westernlore, 1963; *The Newspapers of Nevada, 1858-1958*, John Howell, 1964; (editor with Dwyer and David Cohen) *The Songs of the Gold Rush*, University of California Press, 1964; *The Pacific Island Presses, 1817-1867*, Plantin, 1965; (editor with Dwyer and Cohen) *The Songs of the American West*, University of California Press, 1968; *The Hardrock Miners*, University of California Press, 1974; (with Dwyer) *"Lying Jim" Townsend*, Plantin, in press; *Steamboats on the Colorado*, Howell-North Books, in press. Contributor to professional journals.

*　　*　　*

LINK, Mark J(oseph) 1924-

PERSONAL: Born April 21, 1924, in Coldwater, Ohio; son of Alois P. and Caroline (Antony) Link. *Education:* University of Cincinnati, B.S. in Architecture, 1950; West Baden College, licentiate in philosophy and theology, 1960; Lumen Vitae, Brussels, Belgium, advanced study in catechetics, 1961-62. *Home:* 3441 North Ashland Ave., Chicago, Ill. 60657.

CAREER: Entered Society of Jesus (Jesuits), 1950, ordained priest, 1960. St. Ignatius High School, Chicago, Ill., instructor in religion, 1963; Loyola University, Chicago, Ill., religion editor of Loyola University Press, 1963—, instructor in religion, 1964—. *Military service:* U.S. Army Air Forces, 1943-46; received Asiatic-Pacific Theater Ribbon with three Bronze Stars.

WRITINGS: Christ Teaches Us Today, Loyola University Press, 1964; (editor) *Faith and Commitment*, Loyola University Press, 1964; *We Live in Christ*, Loyola University Press, 1965; (editor) *Teaching the Sacraments and Morality*, Loyola University Press, 1965; *We Are God's People*, Loyola University Press, 1966; *Man in the Modern World: Perspectives, Problems, Profiles*, Loyola University Press, 1967; *Youth in the Modern World: Literature, Friends, Christ, Action*, Loyola University Press, 1969; *Life in the Modern World: Home, Parish, Neighborhood, School*, Loyola University Press, 1970; *He Is the Still Point of the Turning World*, Argus Communications, 1971; *In the Stillness Is the Dancing*, Argus Communications, 1972; *Take Off Your Shoes*, Argus Communications, 1972; *The Merriest Christmas Book*, Argus Communications, 1974. Scriptwriter for filmstrip, "Behold This Heart."†

*   *   *

LINTON, Calvin D(arlington)   1914-

PERSONAL: Born June 11, 1914, in Kensington, Md.; son of Irwin H. (a lawyer) and Helen (Grier) Linton; married Jeanne LeFevre (a government employee), August 1, 1951. *Education:* Attended Erskine College, 1931-32; George Washington University, A.B., 1935; Johns Hopkins University, M.A., 1939, Ph.D., 1940. *Politics:* Independent. *Religion:* Presbyterian. *Home:* 5216 Farrington Rd., N.W., Washington, D.C. 20016. *Office:* George Washington University, Washington, D.C. 20006.

CAREER: Johns Hopkins University, Baltimore, instructor in English, 1939-40; Queens College, Charlotte, N.C., associate professor of English and chairman of department, 1940-41; George Washington University, Washington, D.C., assistant professor, 1945-46, associate professor, 1946-48, professor of English literature, 1948—, dean of Columbian College of Arts and Sciences, 1957—. Consultant on report writing to Central Intelligence Agency, Federal Reserve Board, Internal Revenue Service, and other U.S. government agencies; lecturer at various times to more than forty thousand government employees; lecturer on literary topics, WGMS, Washington, D.C., 1953-54. *Military service:* U.S. Naval Reserve, active duty, 1941-45; became lieutenant commander. *Member:* International Association of University Professors of English, American Council of Academic Deans, Modern Language Association of America, Modern Humanities Research Association (American secretary, 1961—), Association of University Professors of English, Conference on Christianity and Literature (president, 1964-66), Council on Basic Education, Eastern Association of Deans and Advisers of Students (vice-president, 1964-65, president, 1965-66), Literary Society of Washington (Washington, D.C.; president, 1973-75), Cosmos Club (Washington, D.C.; president, 1973).

WRITINGS: How to Write Reports, Harper, 1954; *Effective Writing*, U.S. Government Printing Office, 1958, revised edition, 1962; *Educated Gullibility*, George Washington University Press, 1961. Articles anthologized in *Rhetoric*, Random House, and *Focus: A Book of College Prose*, Houghton, 1963. Writer of scripts for several Federal Aviation Agency training films. Contributor to *American Scholar*, *Shakespeare Quarterly*, *Christianity Today*, and *Southwest Review*.

WORK IN PROGRESS: A study of religious themes in T. S. Eliot's writings; other studies on materialistic existentialism and modern drama.

SIDELIGHTS: About 100,000 copies of *Effective Writing* have been sold.

*   *   *

LISTER, Raymond (George)   1919-

PERSONAL: Born March 28, 1919, in Cambridge, England; son of Horace (an engineer) and Ellen (Arnold) Lister; married Pamela Brutnell, June 6, 1947; children: Rory Brian George, Delia Fionnuala. *Education:* Attended Cambridge schools until fifteen. *Home:* Windmill House, Linton, Cambridgeshire, CB1 6NS, England. *Agent:* A. S. Knight, Chansitor House, Chancery Lane, London W.C. 2, England. *Office:* George Lister & Sons Ltd., 26 Abbey Rd., Cambridge, England.

CAREER: George Lister & Sons Ltd. (architectural metalworkers), Cambridge, England, director, 1939—; Golden Head Press Ltd., Cambridge, England, managing director and editor, 1952-72. Honorary senior member, University College, 1971—. Miniature painter, with work exhibited each summer at one-man shows in Federation of British Artists Galleries, London. *Member:* Royal Society of Arts, Royal Geographical Society, Royal Society of Miniature Painters, Sculptors and Gravers (treasurer, beginning, 1958; president, 1970—), Federation of British Artists (governor, 1972—), Private Libraries Association (president, 1971—), Liveryman of Worshipful Company of Blacksmiths, College Art Association of America, Sette of Odd Volumes (president, 1960), Savile Club. Royal Automobile Club, City Livery Club.

WRITINGS: Decorative Wrought Ironwork in Great Britain, G. Bell, 1957, Tuttle, 1970, 2nd edition, David & Charles, 1970; (translator from the French) V. I. Stepanov, *Alphabet of Movements of the Human Body*, Golden Head Press, 1958; *Decorative Cast Ironwork in Great Britain*, G. Bell, 1960; *The Craftsman Engineer*, G. Bell, 1960; *Private Telegraph Companies of Great Britain and Their Stamps*, Golden Head Press, 1961; *Great Craftsmen*, G. Bell, 1962; *Edward Calvert*, G. Bell, 1962; *The Miniature Defined* (booklet), Golden Head Press, 1963; *How to Identify Old Maps and Globes*, Archon Books, 1965; *Beulah to Byzantium: A Study of Parallels in the Works of W. B. Yeats, William Blake, Samuel Parker and Edward Calvert*, Dolmen Press, 1965; *College Stamps of Oxford and Cambridge*, Golden Head Press, 1966; *The Craftsman in Metal*, G. Bell, 1966, A. S. Barnes, 1968; *Victorian Narrative Paintings*, C. N. Potter, 1966; *Great Works of Craftsmanship*, G. Bell, 1967, A. S. Barnes, 1968; *William Blake: An Introduction to the Man and to His Work*, G. Bell, 1968, Ungar, 1970; *Samuel Palmer and His Etchings*, Watson-Guptill, 1969; *Hammer and Hand: An Essay on the Ironwork of Cambridge* (booklet), privately printed, 1969; *Antique Maps and Their Cartographers*, Archon Books, 1970; *British Romantic Art*, G. Bell, 1973. Also author of numerous pamphlets.

Contributor to *Connoisseur, Apollo, Journal of Royal Society of Arts, Irish Book, Blake Studies, Blake Newsletter*, and *Shell Book of Gardens*.

SIDELIGHTS: Lister is competent in French. *Avocational interests:* Book collecting, mountaineering in the fens.

BIOGRAPHICAL/CRITICAL SOURCES: Simon Lissim, *The Art of Raymond Lister*, Gray, 1958; C. R. Cammell and others, *Raymond Lister: Five Essays*, Golden Head Press, 1963.†

* * *

LISTOWEL, Judith (de Marffy-Mantuano) 1904-

PERSONAL: Born July 12, 1904, in Kaposvar, Hungary; daughter of Raoul and Irma (de Maar) de Marffy-Mantuano; children: Deirdre (Lady Grantley). *Education:* Attended private schools and University of Economic Science in Budapest; London School of Economics and Political Science, University of London, B.Sc., 1929. *Religion:* Roman Catholic. *Home:* 9 Halsey St., London S.W. 3, England. *Agent:* Bolf & Watts, 8 Storey's Gate, London SW1, England.

CAREER: London correspondent for *Nemzeti Ujsag* and *Peter Lloyd* (Hungarian daily newspapers), 1931-39; civilian lecturer for British Armed Forces, 1939-45; *East Europe* (anti-Communist weekly), London, England, publisher and editor, 1945-54; free-lance writer, and broadcaster, 1954—. Lecturer in United States and Canada on annual tours, 1954-60. *Member:* Royal Institute of International Affairs, Royal Commonwealth Society, P.E.N.

WRITINGS: This I Have Seen, Faber, 1943; *Crusaders in the Secret War*, C. Johnson, 1952; *The Golden Tree*, Odhams, 1958; *Manual of Modern Manners*, Odhams, 1960; *The Modern Hostess*, Odhams, 1961; *The Making of Tanganyika*, London House, 1966; *Amin*, Irish University Press, 1973; *The Other Livingstone*, Julian Friedman, 1974. Contributor to *Times*, *Tablet*, and other periodicals and newspapers.

SIDELIGHTS: Mrs. Listowel makes annual trips to Africa, usually visiting eight to ten countries.

* * *

LITTLE, Thomas Russell 1911-
(Tom Little)

PERSONAL: Born May 8, 1911, in Tynemouth, England; son of Joseph (an accountant) and Isabella (Reddy) Little; married Vera Turner, May 22, 1937; children: Judith Lesley, Anna Mary. *Education:* Attended grammar school in Tynemouth, England. *Home:* Manor College, Whitchurch, Oxfordshire, England. *Agent:* Alec Harrison and Associates, 118 Fleet St., London E.C. 4, England. *Office:* Saudi Press Agency, International Press Centre, 76 Shoe Lane, London EC4A 3JB, England.

CAREER: Reporter, *Shields Daily News*, *Northeastern Daily Gazette*, and *Newcastle Chronicle*, 1929-41; Arab News Agency (British-owned, reformed as Regional News Service Ltd., 1964), editor in Cairo, Egypt, 1943, diplomatic and special correspondent in London, New York, and Paris, 1946-49, general manager, 1949-69, managing director, 1964-69; Saudi Press Agency, London, England, correspondent, 1969—. Deputy correspondent, *The Times*, 1949-53, *The Economist* and *The Observer*, 1953-56 (all London). Does current affairs broadcasts for British Broadcasting Corp. *Military service:* British Army, Royal Corps of Signals, 1941-43; became captain. *Member:* Royal Institute of International Affairs, Press Club, and Wig and Pen Club (both London). *Awards, honors:* Order of the British Empire; Commander, Order of the Cedars (Lebanon); Order of the Star (Jordan); Order of Merit (Syria).

WRITINGS—All under name Tom Little: *Egypt*, Praeger, 1958; (contributor) *The Middle East: A Political and Economic Survey*, Oxford University Press for Royal Institute

of International Affairs, 2nd edition, 1954, 3rd edition, 1958; *The High Dam at Aswan*, Methuen, 1965; *Modern Egypt*, Praeger, 1967; (with Pierre Janssen and Terence Blunsum) *Egypt*, Follett, 1967; *South Arabia: Arena of Conflict*, Praeger, 1968; *The Arab World in the Twentieth Century*, John Day, 1972. Contributor to *Annual Register of World Events*, Longmans, Green, and to *Times* (London), *Observer*, *Economist*, *World Today*, and other journals and newspapers.

WORK IN PROGRESS: Modern Saudi Arabia, for Benn; a revision of *Modern Egypt*.

* * *

LITVAK, Isaiah A(llan) 1936-

PERSONAL: Born October 1, 1936, in Shanghai, China; son of Matthew and Basia (Daitch) Litvak; married Marilyn Kenigsberg (a teacher), September 21, 1958; children: Matthew. *Education:* McGill University, B.Comm., 1957; Columbia University, M.S., 1959, Ph.D., 1964. *Home:* 33 Thorndale North, Hamilton, Ontario, Canada. *Office:* McMaster University, Hamilton, Ontario, Canada.

CAREER: McMaster University, Hamilton, Ontario, associate professor of marketing and international business, 1961—. Consultant to Canadian Department of Labour, Department of Trade and Commerce, and to industry in Canada and abroad. Lecturer at foreign universities. *Member:* Canadian Economic Association, Canadian Institute of International Affairs, American Marketing Association, American Slavic Association, American Economic Association, Society for International Economic Development.

WRITINGS: Trading With The Communists, Baxter, 1963; (editor with Bruce E. Mallen) *Marketing: Canada*, McGraw, 1964, 2nd edition, 1968; (compiler and editor with Mallen) *A Basic Bibliography on Marketing in Canada*, American Marketing Association, 1967; (editor) *The Nation Keepers: Canadian Business Perspectives*, McGraw, 1967; (with Peter M. Banting) *Canadian Cases in Marketing*, McGraw, 1968; (editor) *Marketing Management for the Middleman*, Queen's Printer, 1968; (editor with Christopher J. Maule) *Foreign Investment: The Experience of Host Countries*, Praeger, 1970; (with Maule and Richard D. Robinson) *Dual Loyalty: Canadian-U.S. Business Arrangements*, McGraw, 1971; *Foreign Investment in Mexico: Some Lessons for Canada*, Canadian Institute of International Affairs, 1971; (with Maule) *Cultural Sovereignty: The Time and Reader's Digest Case in Canada*, Praeger, 1974. Contributor to *Business Quarterly, Cost and Management*. Associate editor of *Marketer*.

SIDELIGHTS: Litvak is competent in Russian and German.†

* * *

LITZINGER, Boyd (A., Jr.) 1929-

PERSONAL: Born April 2, 1929, in Johnstown, Pa.; son of Boyd A. and Sara (Ignoffo) Litzinger; married Nancy Curry, January 28, 1952 (died, 1959); married Maria Antonia Letro, June 10, 1961; children: Michael Boyd, Gretchen Maria. *Education:* St. Francis College, Loretto, Pa., student, 1947-49; University of South Carolina, B.S., 1951, M.A., 1952; University of Tennessee, Ph.D., 1956. *Religion:* Roman Catholic. *Office:* St. Bonaventure University, St. Bonaventure, N.Y. 14778.

CAREER: University of Tennessee, teaching assistant,

later instructor in English, 1952-56; Texas Technological College (now Texas Tech University), Lubbock, instructor in English, 1956-57; Lander College, Greenwood, S.C., head of English department, 1957-58; University of South Carolina, Columbia, assistant professor of English, 1958-59; St. Bonaventure University, St. Bonaventure, N.Y., associate professor, 1959-65; professor of English, 1965—, dean of School of Arts and Sciences, 1969—. Visiting associate professor of English, University of Tennessee, 1962-63; visiting professor, University of Wisconsin, summer, 1964. *Military service:* U.S. Naval Reserve, 1947-52. *Member:* Modern Language Association of America, South Atlantic Modern Language Association, New England Modern Language Association, American Association of University Professors, Delta Epsilon Sigma (president, 1971-73).

WRITINGS: Robert Browning and the Babylonian Woman, Armstrong Browning Library, 1962; *Time's Revenges: Browning's Reputation as a Thinker, 1889-1962,* University of Tennessee Press, 1964; (editor with K. L. Knickerbocker) *The Browning Critics,* University of Kentucky Press, 1967; (editor with Donald Smalley) *Browning: The Critical Heritage,* Barnes & Noble, 1970. Contributor to literary periodicals. Member of editorial board, *Victorian Poetry, Cithara, Studies in Browning and His Circle.*

WORK IN PROGRESS: A critical study of Gerard Manley Hopkins, publication for Routledge & Kegan Paul; studies on Victorian literature and of higher education.

* * *

LIU, Wu-chi 1907-
(Hsiao Hsia)

PERSONAL: Born July 27, 1907, in Wu-chiang, Kiangsu, China; came to U.S., 1946; naturalized U.S. citizen, 1972; son of Ya-tzu (a poet) and Pei-ni (Cheng) Liu; married Helen Gaw (a librarian), April 20, 1932; children: Shirley (Mrs. Raymond Clayton). *Education:* Tsing Hua College, Peking, China, graduate, 1927; Lawrence College (now Lawrence University), B.A., 1928; Yale University, Ph.D., 1931; University of London, postdoctoral study, 1931-32. *Home:* 521 Pleasant Ridge Rd., Bloomington, Ind. 47401. *Office:* Indiana University, Bloomington, Ind. 47401.

CAREER: Professor of Western language and literature in Chinese universities and editor of two literary journals and a literary supplement to a Chinese newspaper, 1932-46; Rollins College, Winter Park, Fla., visiting professor of English and Chinese culture, 1946-48; Yale University, New Haven, Conn., visiting professor of Chinese, 1951-53, associate director of research, Human Relations Area Files, 1955-60; Hartwick College, Oneonta, N.Y., chairman of department of Chinese studies, 1953-55; University of Pittsburgh, Pittsburgh, Pa., professor of Chinese language and literature, and director of Chinese Language and Area Center, 1960-61; Indiana University, Bloomington, professor of East Asian languages and literature, 1961—, chairman of department, 1962-67. Director of Far Eastern Language Institute of Committee on Institutional Cooperation (CIC), 1964. Consultant to National Endowment for the Humanities, 1969—, and *Funk & Wagnalls Encyclopedia,* 1969—; research consultant to National Science Council, Republic of China, 1975—. *Member:* American Oriental Society, Association for Asian Studies. *Awards, honors:* Bollingen Foundation fellowship, 1948-51; National Endowment for the Humanities senior fellowship, 1967-68.

WRITINGS: (Editor with Tien-yi Li) *Readings in Contemporary Chinese Literature,* five volumes, Far Eastern Publications, Yale University, 1953-58, revised edition, three volumes, 1964-68; *A Short History of Confucian Philosophy,* Penguin, 1955, Dell, 1964; *Confucius: His Life and Time,* Philosophical Library, 1955, Greenwood Press, 1972; (editor under pseudonym Hsiao Hsia) *China, Its People, Its Society, Its Culture,* Human Relations Area File Press, 1960; *Introduction to Chinese Literature,* Indiana University Press, 1966; (contributor) H. A. Giles, *A History of Chinese Literature,* Ungar, 1967; *Su Man-shu,* Twayne, 1972; (editor with Irving Y. C. Lo) *Sunflower Splendor: Three Thousand Years of Chinese Poetry,* Indiana University Press, 1975. Author of more than ten books written in or translated into Chinese, published in China, 1927-46. Contributor to *Biographical Dictionary of Republican China, Dictionary of Oriental Literature, Encyclopedia of World Biography, Encyclopedia of World Literature in the 20th Century, The Encyclopedia of Philosophy,* and *Funk & Wagnalls Encyclopedia.* Former contributor to Chinese periodicals. Member of editorial board, *Tsing-Hua Journal of Chinese Studies,* 1956—, *K'uei Hsing: A Journal of Translations from East and Central Asian Literature,* 1975; contributing editor, *Books Abroad,* 1964-66.

WORK IN PROGRESS: A translation, *Sharpened Sword and Resounding Strings: Poems of Two Southern Society Friends,* completion expected in 1976; a book, *Chinese Literature in the Twentieth Century,* 1978; *A History of Chinese Drama,* 1980; *Survey of Chinese History,* 1982.

SIDELIGHTS: Liu told *CA:* "It has been my ambition and guiding interest since coming to the United States in 1946 to teach and write about Chinese philosophy, literature, and history. Most of my writing and translation efforts, therefore, are directed towards this goal. Rather than doing scholarly works which reach only a small segment of the academic community, I consider it more useful to write for a larger public in the areas of Chinese culture, in which China's major contributions lie."

* * *

LIVINGS, Henry 1929-

PERSONAL: Born September 20, 1929, in Prestwich, Lancashire, England; son of George and Dorothy (Buckley) Livings; married Judith Francis Carter, April 2, 1957; children: Toby, Maria. *Education:* Attended University of Liverpool, 1948-50. *Politics:* Socialist (Labour Party). *Home:* 33 Woods Lane, Dobcross, Oldham, Lancashire, England. *Agent:* Harvey Unna Ltd., 14 Beaumont Mews, Marylebone High St., London W1, England.

CAREER: Formerly full-time professional actor in England; now mainly playwright, but still acts locally in repertory, and on radio and television; associated with British Broadcasting Corp. program, "Northern Drift." *Military service:* Royal Air Force, 1950-52. *Member:* Writers' Guild of Great Britain, British Actors' Equity Association. *Awards, honors: Evening Standard* Drama Award, 1961, for "Stop It Whoever You Are"; Britannica Award, from *Encyclopaedia Britannica,* 1965, for "Kelly's Eye"; Obie Award from *Village Voice,* 1967, for "Eh?"

WRITINGS—Plays; published and produced: "Stop It Whoever You Are" (produced in London at London Arts Theatre, 1961), published in *New English Dramatists 5,* Penguin, 1962; "Nil Carborundum" (produced in London at London Arts Theatre, 1962), published in *New English Dramatists 6,* Penguin, 1963; "Big Soft Nellie" (produced as "Thacred Nit" in Keswick, 1961; produced under original title in London at Theatre Royal, 1961), published in *Kelly's Eye and Other Plays*, Hill & Wang, 1964; "Kelly's Eye" (produced in London at the Royal Court Theatre, 1963), published in *Kelly's Eye and Other Plays*, Hill & Wang, 1964; *Eh?* (produced in London, 1964; produced in Cincinnati at Cincinnati Playhouse in the Park, July, 1966; produced Off-Broadway at Circle in the Square, October 16, 1966), Methuen, 1965, Hill & Wang, 1967, acting edition, Dramatists Play Service, 1968; "The Day Dumbfounded Got His Pylon" (produced in Stoke on Trent, 1965), published in *Worth a Hearing: A Collection of Radio Plays*, edited by Alfred Bradley, Blackie & Son, 1967; *Good Grief!* (includes "After the Last Lamp," "You're Free," "Variable Lengths," "Pie-Eating Contest," "Does It Make Your Cheeks Ache?," and "The Reasons for Flying"; produced in Manchester, 1967), Methuen, 1968; *Honour and Offer* (produced in Cincinnati, December, 1968; produced in London at Fortune Theatre, May, 1969), Methuen, 1969; *The Little Mrs. Foster Show* (produced in Liverpool, 1966), Methuen, 1969.

"The Gamecock" (produced in Manchester, 1969), published in *Pongo Plays 1-6*, Methuen, 1971; "Rattel" (produced in Manchester, 1969), published in *Pongo Plays 1-6*, Methuen, 1971; "The Boggart" (produced in Birmingham, 1970), published in *Pongo Plays 1-6*, Methuen, 1971; "Conciliation" (produced in Lincoln, 1970; produced in London, 1971), published in *Pongo Plays 1-6*, Methuen, 1971; "The Rifle Volunteer" (produced in Birmingham, 1970; produced in London, 1971), published in *Pongo Plays 1-6*, Methuen, 1971; "Beewine" (produced in Birmingham, 1970; produced in London, 1971), published in *Pongo Plays 1-6*, Methuen, 1971; *This Jockey Drives Late Nights* (first produced in Birmingham at Midlands Arts Centre, January 27, 1972), Methuen, 1972; *The Ffinest Ffamily in the Land* (produced in Lincoln at Theatre Royal, June 16, 1970; produced in London, 1972), Methuen, 1973; "Brainscrew" (produced in Birmingham, 1971), published in *Second Playbill 3*, edited by Alan Durband, Hutchinson, 1973.

Plays; produced only: "Tiddied," produced in Birmingham, 1970; "Mushrooms and Toadstools," produced in London, 1970; "You're Free," produced in London, 1970; "GRUP," produced in York, 1971; "Cinderella" (adaptation of the work by Perrault), produced in Stoke on Trent, 1972; "The Rent Man," produced in Stoke on Trent, 1972.

Collections: *Kelly's Eye and Other Plays* (includes "Kelly's Eye," "Big Soft Nellie," and "There's No Room for You Here for a Start"), Hill & Wang, 1964; *Pongo Plays 1-6* (includes "The Gamecock," "Rattel," "The Boggart," "Beewine," "The Rifle Volunteer," and "Conciliation"), Methuen, 1971.

Television plays: "The Arson Squad," 1961; "Jack's Horrible Luck," 1961; "Nil Carborundum" (adaptation from the stage play), 1962; "There's No Room for You Here for a Start," 1963; "A Right Crusader," 1963; "Brainscrew," 1966; "GRUP," 1970; "Honour and Offer" (adaptation from the stage play), 1970; "Big Soft Nellie" (adaptation from the stage play), 1971; "Daft Sam," 1972.

Radio Plays: "After the Last Lamp," 1961; adaptation of Hauptmann's "The Weavers," 1972; "The Day Dumbfounded Got His Pylon," 1963; adaptation of Ibsen's "An Enemy of the People," 1964; "Herr Kant Requests the Pleasure," 1967; "The Government Inspector," 1969; "The Dobcross Silver Band," 1971.

WORK IN PROGRESS: Six more pongo plays, including two for children.

SIDELIGHTS: Livings writes: "Traveled a little as a student. Spain, France, Austria. French hectic, Spanish limps. Still act locally in rep. (stock) and on radio and T.V., about the same as when I wasn't writing. Have worked all sides of the business, including variety, culminating in a vital spell with Joan Littlewood in the first production of "The Quare Fellow" and the Paris festival version of "The Good Soldier Schweik." Made first writing sale in T.V. [Livings sold "Jack's Horrible Luck" to B.B.C. in 1959], and have been able since to settle in Yorkshire industrial village just below the Pennine Moors. Thoroughly enjoy time spent in towns co-operating in the production of own plays, but have no interest in living in the smoke or mixing in exclusively artistic circles. Can't and won't lecture; and throw away manuscripts on the principle that it's a swindle to sell half-finished work."

Of Joan Littlewood he says: "Miss Littlewood's influence on my work would be hard to define; as a person and a theatre-worker she opened out my understanding of the art more than any other has done. Her illuminations of the relevance of theater to life and society (they coincide), and of the basic teaching of Stanislavsky, are still fundamental to me."

John Russell Taylor believes Livings to be "essentially the sort of dramatist who should come to critical approval by way of popular success rather than the other way round...." His plays, for the most part, lack a plot; "like so many of the new dramatists," writes Taylor, "he seeks just to show people together, interacting, existing."

"Stop It, Whoever You Are" was the source of considerable critical controversy; according to Taylor, "some found it both profound and riotously funny, others determinedly found it neither. It is certainly uneven, and still rather undisciplined, but at least it implies a powerful individuality at work, and as it progresses it gradually gathers a wealth of subsidiary meanings without ever (and herein lies the author's artfulness) departing from the farcical tone in which it began, so that by the time we reach its extraordinary final scene we suddenly discover that the apparently simple artless North Country farce has taken on the force and intensity of a parable." Plotless or not, Taylor is convinced that "there is no escaping the force and conviction of Living's writing...."

Honour and Offer was made into the film "Work Is a Four-Letter Word."

BIOGRAPHICAL/CRITICAL SOURCES: "Have been thoroughly chewed-over in all manner of glossy, tabloid, or heavyweight magazines, mainly due to editor's astonishment that I don't choose to live in London; but also attempts to categorize my work ('angry', 'New Wave', 'Kitchen Sink', 'Absurdist', 'Cruelty').... Happily these attempts don't work. John Russell Taylor has some sensible comments in *Anger and After* [Methuen, 1962]."†

* * *

LIVINGSTONE, Douglas (James) 1932-

PERSONAL: Born January 5, 1932, in Kuala Lumpur, Malaya; son of Douglas Nicol and Charlotte Anne (McPhail) Livingstone. *Education:* Attended Kearnsey College, Natal, South Africa; Pasteur Institute, Salisbury, Southern Rhodesia, Diploma in Bacteriology. *Address:* c/o Council of Scientific and Industrial Research, P.O. Box 17001, Congella, 4013, Natal, South Africa.

CAREER: Bacteriologist in pathological laboratories in

Northern and Southern Rhodesia, 1958-63; senior bacteriologist primarily involved in research on pathogenic microorganisms in the sea, 1964—. Poet. Former professional scuba diver. *Awards, honors:* English Association of South Africa award for poems, "Tales from the Tower of Babel"; winner of first United Kingdom science fiction poetry competition; Federal Broadcasting Corp. (Rhodesia) award for verse play, "The Sea My Winding Sheet"; Guiness Poetry Prize, 1965.

WRITINGS: The Skull in the Mud, Outposts Publications, 1960; *Sjambok and Other Poems from Africa*, Oxford University Press, 1964; (with Thomas Kinsella and Anne Sexton) *Poems*, Oxford University Press, 1968; *Eyes Closed Against the Sun* (poems), Oxford University Press, 1970; *The Sea My Winding Sheet* (verse play; broadcast by Rhodesian Broadcasting Corp., January, 1964), Theatre Workshop, 1970; *A Rosary of Bone* (poems), Mantis Books, 1975.

Also author of radio play, "A Rhino for the Boardroom," broadcast by the South African Broadcasting Corp., December, 1974.

Work represented in several anthologies, including *Penguin Book of South African Verse*, Penguin Books, 1968; *New Voices of the Commonwealth*, Evans Brothers, 1968; *Inscapes*, Oxford University Press, 1969. Other poems published in pamphlet form and in periodicals, including *London Magazine*, *Southern Review*, and *Encounter*.

*   *   *

LLEWELYN-DAVIES, Richard 1912-

PERSONAL: Born December 24, 1912; son of Crompton and Moya (O'Connor) Llewelyn-Davies; married Patricia Parry, June 3, 1943; children: Melissa, Harriet Lydia Rose, Rebecca. *Education:* Trinity College, Cambridge, M.A., 1933; additional study at Ecole des Beaux Arts, Paris, France, and Architectural Association, London, England. *Politics:* Labour. *Home:* 36 Parkhill Rd., London N.W. 3, England. *Office:* Llewelyn-Davies, Weeks, Forestier-Walker & Bor, 4 Fitzroy Square, London W1P 6JA, England.

CAREER: London, Midland and Scottish Railway, architect, 1942-48; consulting architect and planner in private practice, London, England, 1960—, now senior member of firm of Llewelyn-Davies, Weeks, Forestier-Walker & Bor; University College, London, England, professor of architecture and head of Bartlett School of Architecture, University College, 1960-69, professor of urban planning, 1969—, head of School of Environment Studies, 1971—. Consulting architect, with John R. Weeks, for rebuilding of London Stock Exchange, offices of Times Publishing Co. Ltd., and for other public buildings, hospitals, and villages. Member of House of Lords. Created Baron, 1964. Director of Division for Architectural Studies, Nuffield Foundation, 1953-60; member of Royal Fine Arts Commission, 1961-72; chairman of Center for Environmental Studies, 1967—. *Member:* Royal Institute of British Architects (fellow), Royal Town Planning Institute (fellow), American Institute of Architects (honorary fellow), World Society for Ekistics (president, 1965). Brooks's Club (London). *Awards, honors:* Leverhulme grant for research in building construction, 1948; Royal Institute of British Architects Bronze Medal (with John R. Weeks), 1957, for design of Diagnostic Centre, Corby, Northamptonshire; West Suffolk Award to Architects (also with Weeks), 1957, for design of Rushbrooke Village.

WRITINGS: (With others) *Studies in the Functions and Design of Hospitals*, Oxford University Press, 1955; (with D. J. Petty) *Building Elements* (textbook of building construction), Architectural Press, 1956; (with A. Baker and P. Sivadon) *Psychiatric Services and Architecture*, World Health Organization, 1959; (with others) *Design of Research Laboratories*, Oxford University Press, 1961; (with others) *Children in Hospital*, Oxford University Press, 1963. Contributor to professional journals.

*   *   *

LLOYD, Dennis 1915-
(Baron Lloyd of Hampstead)

PERSONAL: Born October 22, 1915, in London, England; son of Isaac (a company director) and Betty (Jaffa) Lloyd; married Ruth Tulla, September 15, 1940; children: Naomi Katharine Lloyd Hodges, Corinne Deborah Lloyd Newman. *Education:* Attended University College, London, and Gonville and Caius College, Cambridge; received LL.B., 1935, B.A., 1937, M.A., 1941, LL.D., 1956. *Home:* 18 Hampstead Way, London N.W. 11, England. *Office:* 6 Pump Ct., Temple, London E.C. 4, England.

CAREER: Barrister-at-law, Inner Temple, London, England, 1936—, practicing in London, 1937-39, 1946—; University of London, London, England, reader in English law at University College, 1947-56, Quain Professor of Jurisprudence at University College, 1956—, dean of Faculty of Laws, 1962-64, head of department of law. Member of House of Lords. Created Baron, 1965. Member of Lord Chancellor's Law Reform Committee, Consolidation Bills Committee, Joint Committee on Theatre Censorship, Conseil de la Federation Britannique de l'Alliance Francaise; chairman of British Film Institute, National Film School; chairman of governing council, University College School. *Military service:* British Army, Royal Artillery and Royal Army Ordnance Corps, 1939-46; liaison officer with Free French Forces in Syria and Lebanon, 1944-45; became captain. *Member:* International P.E.N. Club (honorary member), Athenaeum Club.

WRITINGS: Unincorporated Associations, Sweet & Maxwell, 1938; (with John Montgomerie) *Rent Control*, Butterworth & Co., 1939, 2nd edition, 1955; *Public Policy: A Comparative Study of English and French Law*, Athlone Press, 1953; *United Kingdom: Development of Its Laws and Constitution*, Stevens & Sons, 1955; (with John Montgomerie) *Business Lettings*, Butterworth & Co., 1956; *Introduction to Jurisprudence*, Stevens & Sons, 1959, 3rd edition, published under name Baron Lloyd of Hampstead, 1972; *Idea of Law*, Penguin, 1964; (under name Baron Lloyd of Hampstead) *Law*, Humanities, 1968; (editor under name Lord Lloyd of Hampstead, with G. Schwarzenberger) *Current Legal Problems*, Stevens & Sons, Volume 24 (Lloyd not associated with earlier volumes), 1971, Volume 25, 1972. Contributor to periodicals.

SIDELIGHTS: Lloyd's book, *Idea of Law*, has been translated into Japanese. *Avocational interests:* Painting and listening to music.

*   *   *

LLOYD, J. Ivester 1905-
(Jack Ivester Lloyd, John Ivester Lloyd)

PERSONAL: Born February 17, 1905, in England; son of Thomas Ivester (an artist) and Florence Mary (Bunting) Lloyd; divorced; children: Delphine Ivester (Mrs. Robert

O. Ratcliff). *Education:* Educated in English schools. *Politics:* Conservative. *Religion:* Christian. *Home and office:* Daneshill, Duloe, St. Neots, Huntingdonshire, England. *Agent:* A. P. Watt & Son, Hastings House, 10 Norfolk St., Strand, London W.C. 2, England.

CAREER: Writer. Linslade Urban District Council, councillor, 1947-52, vice-chairman, 1951-52. *Military service:* Royal Naval Volunteer Reserve, 1937-59; active duty, 1939-45; became lieutenant commander; received Distinguished Service Cross, mentioned in dispatches. *Member:* British Field Sports Society, British Deer Society, Naval Club (London).

WRITINGS—Under name John Ivester Lloyd: *Scrap, the Terrier Dog*, J. Murray, 1938; *Joey, the Tale of a Pony*, Scribner, 1938, 2nd edition, 1950; *Flash, the Gipsy Dog*, J. Murray, 1939; *Full Cry*, Duckworth, 1939; *People of the Valley*, Country Life, 1944; *Adventures of Tip the Terrier*, Duckworth, 1946; *Johhny Rides Out*, Citadel, 1948; *Well Ridden!*, Duckworth, 1949; *Moon Maiden's Treasure*, Duckworth, 1950; (with E. Samuel) *Rabbitting and Some Ratting*, British Field Society, 1950; *Riders of the Heath*, Country Life, 1951; *Ginger*, Country Life, 1951; *Come Hunting!*, Vinton, 1952; *Beagling*, Jenkins, 1954; *Happy the Hare*, Dolphin Books, 1960; *Otter's Path*, University of London Press, 1961.

Under name Jack Ivester Lloyd: *Beaglers: Harehunting with Harriers, Beagles, and Bassetts*, A. & C. Black, 1971; (and illustrator with James R. Mead) *Hounds of Britain, With Notes on Their Quarry*, A. & C. Black, 1973; *When All the Trees Were Green*, Roundwood Press, 1973.

Also author, with Basil Webster and others, of "Official Handbooks of Various Hunts," Hunts Association (London), 1952—. Contributor to *Horse and Hound*, *Shooting Times*, *The Field*, *Gamekeeper*, and other periodicals.

AVOCATIONAL INTERESTS: Ships, sailormen, and the sea; field sports, particularly fox hunting and beagling; young people, the English countryside, English village life, and natural history.

*　　*　　*

LLOYD-JONES, Esther McDonald 1901-

PERSONAL: Born January 11, 1901, in Lockport, Ill.; daughter of Leon and Claire A. (Rudd) McDonald; married Silas Lloyd-Jones (head of management consultant firm), June, 1924 (died, 1966); children: Joanne (Mrs. Calvin Cheek; died, 1968), Donald. *Education:* Northwestern University, A.B. (summa cum laude), 1923; Columbia University, A.M., 1924, Ph.D., 1929. *Religion:* Episcopalian. *Office:* 430 West 116th St., New York, N.Y. 10027.

CAREER: Northwestern University, Evanston, Ill., assistant director of personnel, 1924-26; Columbia University, Teachers College, New York, N.Y., 1928-66, started as instructor, professor of education and chairman of department of guidance and student personnel administration, 1941-66, professor emeritus, 1966—, head of guidance laboratory, 1933-59, associate director of personnel, 1939-46; professor of human behavior at United States International University, 1967—. Diplomate in counseling, American Psychological Association. Consultant to U.S. Secretary of War in selecting first group of Women's Army Corps (WAC) officer candidates, and consultant to U.S. Office of Education, 1960-72; member of Defense Advisory Committee on Women in the Services, 1954, of President's Commission on the Status of Women, 1961-63; member of

National Personnel Committee, Girl Scouts of America, 1939-44; chairman of Commission on the Education of Women, American Council on Education, 1953-58; chairman of Committee on College and University Relations, American National Red Cross, 1961-64. Trustee of Briarcliff College, 1945-51, Pratt Institute, 1946—, Elmira College, 1956-62.

MEMBER: American Personnel and Guidance Association, American College Personnel Association (secretary, 1933-35; president, 1935-37), Association for Counselor Education and Supervision, American School Counselors Association, Student Personnel Association for Teacher Education, National Vocational Guidance Association, National Association of Women Deans, Administrators, and Counselors, American Sociological Association, International Council of Psychologists, New York State Guidance and Personnel Association (president, 1943-45), Phi Beta Kappa, Pi Lambda Theta, Psi Chi, Kappa Delta Pi, Mortar Board.

AWARDS, HONORS: Award of Merit, Northwestern University, 1945, University of Arizona, 1960; L.L.D., Elmira College, 1955, Bridgeport University, 1966; Sc.D., Boston University, 1961; L.H.D., Long Island University, 1963.

WRITINGS: Student Personnel Work at Northwestern University, Harper, 1929; (with Margaret Ruth Smith) *A Student Personnel Program for Higher Education*, McGraw, 1938; (with Goodwin Watson and Donald Cottrell) *Redirecting Teacher Education*, Teachers Press, Teachers College, Columbia University, 1938.

Social Competence and College Students, American Council on Education, 1940; (with Ruth Fedder) *Coming of Age*, McGraw, 1941; *Orientacao Educacional*, Rio de Janeiro Instituto Brasil-Estados Unidos, 1952; (editor with Smith, and contributor) *Student Personnel Work as Deeper Teaching*, Harper, 1954; (editor with Ruth Barry and Beverly Wolf) *Case Studies in Human Relationships in Secondary School*, Teachers Press, Teachers College, Columbia University, 1956; (editor with Barry and Wolf) *Case Studies in College Student-Staff Relationships*, Teachers Press, Teachers College, Columbia University, 1956; (editor with Barry and Wolf) *Guidance in Elementary Education: A Case Book*, Teachers Press, Teachers College, Columbia University, 1956; (contributor) M. E. Hilton, editor, *Guidance in the Age of Automation*, Syracuse University Press, 1957.

(Editor with Esther Westervelt) *Behavioral Sciences and Guidance*, Teachers Press, Teachers College, Columbia University, 1963; (with Herman Estrin) *The American Student and His College*, Houghton, 1967; (editor with Norah Rosenau) *Social and Cultural Foundations of Guidance*, Holt, 1968; (with Estrin) *How Many Roads: The Seventies*, Glencoe Press, 1971.

Author of foreword: Randall W. Hoffmann and Robert Plutchik, *Small-Group Discussion in Orientation and Teaching*, Putnam, 1959; Irvin Faust, *Entering Angel's World: Case Studies in Cross-Cultural Communication*, Teachers Press, Teachers College, Columbia University, 1963; Kathryn S. Phillips, *My Room in the World*, Abingdon, 1963; Gordon Klopf and others, *Interns in Guidance: A New Dimension in Counselor Education*, Teachers Press, Teachers College, Columbia University, 1963.

Contributor to other books and yearbooks, to *Encyclopedia of Educational Research*, and about fifty articles to education journals. Associate editor, *Understanding the Child*, 1938-58.

LOBSENZ, Amelia

PERSONAL: Born in Greensboro, N.C.; daughter of Leo (a furniture manufacturer) and Florence Freitag; married Norman Lobsenz, June 2, 1947 (divorced, 1952); married Harry H. Abrahams (chief of surgery, Syosset Hospital), 1958; children: Michael, George, Kay. *Education:* Attended Agnes Scott College. *Home:* The Columns, Red Ground Rd., Old Westbury, N.Y. *Office:* Lobsenz Public Relations Co., Inc., 745 Fifth Ave., New York, N.Y. 10022.

CAREER: Edward Gottlieb and Associates, New York, N.Y., director of magazine and book department, 1949-56; Lobsenz Public Relations Co., Inc., New York, N.Y., president, 1956—. Free-lance writer for magazines. Long Island chairwoman, National Cultural Center; council member, Hofstra University. *Member:* Public Relations Society of America, National Association of Science Writers, Society of Magazine Writers, American Women in Radio and Television, Mystery Writers of America, Overseas Press Club, Long Island Public Relations Association, Publicity Club of Chicago.

WRITINGS: Kay Everett Calls CQ (Junior Literary Guild selection), Vanguard, 1951; *Kay Everett Works DX* (Junior Literary Guild selection), Vanguard, 1952. Some of her "How to Write . . ." articles have been anthologized including "How to Write the 'How to' Article," originally published in *Scribner's*, and "How to Write the Medical Article" and "How to Write the Personality Profile," first published in *Writer's Digest*. Contributor of some three hundred articles to *Coronet, Reader's Digest, This Week, Pageant, Nation's Business, Parade, American Weekly, McCall's, Better Living, Collier's, Woman's Home Companion*, and other magazines.

*   *   *

LOCKE, Edwin A. III   1938-

PERSONAL: Born May 15, 1938, in New York, N.Y.; son of Edwin Allen (a businessman) and Dorothy (Clark) Locke, Jr.; married second wife, Anne Hassard, June 13, 1968. *Education:* Harvard University, B.A., 1960; Cornell University, M.A., 1962, Ph.D., 1964. *Politics:* Objectivist. *Religion:* Atheist. *Home:* 10869 Deboral Dr., Potomac, Md. 20854. *Office:* Department of Business Administration, University of Maryland, College Park, Md. 20742.

CAREER: American Institutes for Research, Silver Spring, Md., 1964-70, began as associate research scientist, became research scientist; University of Maryland, College Park, assistant professor, 1967-69; associate professor, 1969-73; professor, 1973—. *Member:* American Psychological Association, Maryland Psychological Association, New York Academy of Sciences, Sigma Xi, Phi Kappa Phi.

WRITINGS: (With P. E. Breer) *Task Experience as a Source of Attitudes*, Dorsey, 1965. Contributor to *Journal of Applied Psychology* and other professional periodicals.

WORK IN PROGRESS: Research on study skills, job attitudes, and motivation.

*   *   *

LOCKE, Frederick W.   1918-

PERSONAL: Born June 16, 1918, in Jamaica Plain, Mass.; son of William J. (a master steamfitter) and Frances (Anderer) Locke; married Mary R. Keefe, August 6, 1942; children: Christopher, Beatrice, Elizabeth, Joseph. *Educa-*tion: Harvard University, A.B., 1948, A.M., 1948, Ph.D., 1953. *Politics:* Democrat (liberal). *Religion:* Roman Catholic. *Home:* 1009 Park Ave., Rochester, N.Y. 14610. *Office:* University of Rochester, 416 Morey Hall, Rochester, N.Y. 14627.

CAREER: Catholic University of America, Washington, D.C., instructor in French, 1951-55; Stanford University, Palo Alto, Calif., 1955-60, began as assistant professor, became associate professor of French; State University of New York, Harper College, Binghamton, N.Y., professor of French, 1960-64; University of Rochester, Rochester, N.Y., professor of medieval literature, 1964—. *Military service:* U.S. Army, medical department, 1942-46; became technician fifth class. *Member:* Medieval Academy of America, Dante Society of America, Modern Language Association of America.

WRITINGS: (Editor and author of introduction) Andre de Chapelain, *The Art of Courtly Love*, Ungar, 1957; (translator with R. W. Ackerman) Chrestien de Troyes, *Ywain, The Knight of the Lion*, Ungar, 1957; *The Quest for the Holy Grail*, Stanford University Press, 1960. Contributor of articles on medieval, French, and English literature to scholarly journals.

WORK IN PROGRESS: A literary study of *Chanson de Roland*; a book on Dante.

SIDELIGHTS: Locke knows Latin, Greek, French, and Italian.†

*   *   *

LOCKHART, (Jeanne) Aileene Simpson   1911-

PERSONAL: Born March 18, 1911, in Atlanta, Ga.; daughter of Thomas Ellis and Aileen Reeves (Simpson) Lockhart. *Education:* Texas Woman's University, B.S., 1932; University of Wisconsin, M.S., 1937, Ph.D., 1942. *Politics:* Democrat. *Religion:* Presbyterian. *Home:* 1314 Windsor Dr., Denton, Tex. 76201. *Office:* Texas Women's University, Denton, Tex. 76204.

CAREER: University of Southern California, Los Angeles, professor of physical education, 1949-73; Texas Woman's University, Denton, College of Health, Physical Education, and Recreation, dean, 1973—. Editor for physical education books, William C. Brown Co., Dubuque, Iowa, 1952—. *Member:* American Academy of Physical Education (fellow), American Association for Health, Physical Education and Recreation (fellow), American College of Sports Medicine (fellow). *Awards, honors:* Amy Morris Homans fellowship, Wellesley College, 1964.

WRITINGS: Modern Dance: Building and Teaching Lessons, W. C. Brown, 1951, 4th edition with Elizabeth Pease (Pease associated with 3rd and 4th editions), 1973; (with Jane A. Mott) *How to Organize Teams and Tournaments*, National Sports Equipment, 1954; (editor) *Selected Volleyball Articles*, American Association for Girl's and Women's Sports, 1960; (with Pia Gilbert) *Music for the Modern Dance*, W. C. Brown, 1961; (with Earl V. Pullias) *Toward Excellence in College Teaching*, W. C. Brown, 1964; (editor with Howard S. Slusher) *Anthology of Contemporary Readings: An Introduction to Physical Education*, W. C. Brown, 1966, 2nd edition, 1970; (with Joann M. Johnson) *Laboratory Experiments in Motor Learning*, W. C. Brown, 1970; (compiler with Betty Spears) *Chronicle of American Physical Education: Selected Reading, 1855-1930*, W. C. Brown, 1972. Contributor to *Aerospace Medicine, British Medical Journal, Research Quarterly*, and physical education journals.

WORK IN PROGRESS: Collaborating on compilation of anthology; a text on motor learning and motor performance.

AVOCATIONAL INTERESTS: Music, photography, poetry, and dance.

* * *

LOCKWOOD, Mary 1934-

PERSONAL: Born March 14, 1934, in Brooklyn, N.Y.; daughter of Edward Towne and Ann (Hamilton) Lockwood; married James B. Spelman, January 17, 1959; children: two daughters. *Education:* Smith College, B.A. (summa cum laude), 1955.

CAREER: Scholastic Magazines, Inc., New York, N.Y., 1955-57, copywriter, later assistant editor; Helen Bush School, Seattle, Wash., teacher of English, 1957-58. Fairfield County (Conn.) Symphony Chorus, member. *Member:* Authors League of America.

WRITINGS: Child of Light (novel), Morrow, 1963; *The Accessory*, Random House, 1968.

WORK IN PROGRESS: A novel.

SIDELIGHTS: Mary Lockwood told *CA:* "I hope to spend some time experimenting, in a modest way, with a variety of forms and subject matter. I think too many novelists tend to aim for the jackpot (whether critical or commercial) too soon, and then—if they hit it—subside into self-imitation." *Avocational interests:* Music, tennis, swimming, long walks; trips to the West Indies, where she and her husband have some property.

BIOGRAPHICAL/CRITICAL SOURCES: Westport Town Crier, Westport, Conn., April 2, 1964.†

* * *

LOFTUS, Richard J. 1929-

PERSONAL: Born June 22, 1929, in New York, N.Y.; son of Joseph Thiel Loftus (a telegrapher); children: Richard Gilmore. *Education:* Iona College, A.B., 1951; University of Wisconsin, M.A., 1954, Ph.D., 1962. *Home:* Apartment 1-S, 804 South Locust St., Champaign, Ill. *Office:* Department of English, University of Illinois, Urbana, Ill.

CAREER: University of Florida, Extension Division, Gainesville, director of public relations, 1955-57; United Press, Madison, Wis., staff writer, 1958; Purdue University, Lafayette, Ind., instructor in English, 1961-62; University of Illinois, Urbana, assistant professor of English, 1962—. *Military service:* U.S. Army, 1951-53. *Member:* Modern Language Association of America, American Committee for Irish Studies (member of conference planning committee, 1963—). *Awards, honors:* James Campbell Goodwill traveling fellowship, University of Wisconsin alumni research grant, University of Illinois faculty summer fellowship, and American Philosophical Society grant, all for research in Ireland.

WRITINGS: Nationalism in Modern Anglo-Irish Poetry, University of Wisconsin Press, 1964; (editor with William Roscelli) Ray Browne, *The Celtic Cross*, Purdue University Studies, 1964. Contributor of articles and reviews to scholarly journals.

WORK IN PROGRESS: A book on the mature poetry and aesthetic of Robert Graves.

SIDELIGHTS: Loftus spent a year and a summer doing research in Dublin, Ireland. He speaks French and Spanish moderately well and reads German.†

LOMUPO, Brother Robert 1939-

PERSONAL: Born November 8, 1939, in New York, N.Y.; son of Carmine (a truck driver) and Mary (DiFillipo) Lomupo. *Education:* St. Edward's University, Austin, Tex., B.A., 1962; Rhode Island College, graduate study. *Home:* 800 Maiden Lane, Rochester, N.Y. 14615.

CAREER: Roman Catholic religious, member of Congregation of Brothers of the Holy Cross, 1961—. Cardinal Mooney High School, Rochester, N.Y., chairman of English department, 1965.

WRITINGS: Fire Is His Name (biography of St. Vincent de Paul), Holy Cross Press, 1964.†

* * *

LONG, John H(enderson) 1916-

PERSONAL: Born April 8, 1916, in Carthage, Miss.; son of John Audley (a civil engineer) and Jeffie-Lytte (Williams) Long; married Bertie Louise October 20, 1940; children; Donald F., Barbara Elizabeth. *Education:* University of Florida, B.A., 1938, M.A., 1948, Ph.D., 1951; Georgetown University, graduate study, 1939. *Religion:* Episcopal. *Home:* 1703 West Friendly Rd., Greensboro, N.C. 27403.

CAREER: Morehead State College (now Morehead State University), Morehead, Ky., associate professor of English, 1950-59; Greensboro College, Greensboro, N.C., professor of English, 1959—. Lecturer, Piedmont University Center, 1964-65; Panelist, World Shakespeare Congress, 1971. *Military service:* U.S. Army, Ordnance, 1942-45; became technical sergeant. *Member:* Renaissance Society of America, American Musicological Association, South Atlantic Modern Language Association, Southeast Renaissance Conference. *Awards, honors:* Reading fellowship to Folger Shakespeare Library, 1955; Guggenheim fellowship, 1958.

WRITINGS: Shakespeare's Use of Music: Seven Comedies, University of Florida Press, 1955; *Shakespeare's Use of Music: The Final Comedies*, University of Florida Press, 1961; (editor) *Music on the Renaissance English Stage*, University of Kentucky Press, 1968; *Shakespeare's Use of Music: The Histories and Tragedies*, University of Florida Press, 1971. Contributor of articles to literary and musical journals.

WORK IN PROGRESS: "Survey of English Literature" for a tape cassette lecture series and "Shepherd Song," a television musical comedy.

SIDELIGHTS: Long is competent in French and Spanish.

* * *

LONGENECKER, Richard N(orman) 1930-

PERSONAL: Born July 21, 1930, in Mishawaka, Ind.; son of Ward F. (a masonry contractor) and Ruth (Steinback) Longenecker; married Frances Lee Wilson, August 5, 1955; children: Elizabeth Lee, David Norman, Bruce Ward. *Education:* Wheaton College, Wheaton, Ill., B.A., 1953, M.A., 1956; studied at Faith Theological Seminary, 1953-54, Northern Baptist Theological Seminary, 1954-56; University of Edinburgh, Ph.D., 1959. *Home:* 31 Mollard Rd., Agincourt, Ontario, Canada. *Office:* Wycliffe College, Toronto, Ontario, Canada.

CAREER: Wheaton College, Wheaton, Ill., instructor, 1956-57, assistant professor of Bible and theology, 1960-63; Trinity Evangelical Divinity School, Deerfield, Ill., assistant professor, 1963-65, associate professor, 1965-67, professor of New Testament history and theology, 1967-73; University of Toronto, Wycliffe College, Toronto, Ontario, professor of New Testament, 1973—. *Member:* Society of Biblical Literature, Evangelical Theological Society (secretary, 1962-63; treasurer, 1964-65; vice-president, 1973; president, 1974), Studiorum Novi Testamenti Societas. *Awards, honors:* Tyndale fellowship from Institute for Biblical Research.

WRITINGS: Paul, Apostle of Liberty, Harper, 1964; *The Christology of Early Jewish Christianity*, S.C.M. Press, 1970; *The Ministry and Message of Paul*, Zondervan, 1971; *Biblical Exegesis in the Apostolic Period*, Eerdmans, 1974. Contributor to Bible encyclopedias and dictionaries, symposia volumes, festschriften, and journals. Member of editorial, supervisory, and Bible translation committees of *The New International Version of the Bible*.

WORK IN PROGRESS: The Jerusalem Church, completion expected in 1976, *Paul and Jesus*, 1976, and *The Acts of the Apostles*, a commentary, 1978.

*   *   *

LONSDALE, Adrian L.   1927-

PERSONAL: Born November 9, 1927, in Port Angeles, Wash.; son of Carl A. (a lieutenant, U.S. Coast Guard) and Helen J. (Burdick) Lonsdale; married Jane H. Swett (an organist and piano teacher), June 4, 1950; children: Darcy J., Karl P., Ross B. *Education:* U.S. Coast Guard Academy, B.S., 1950; attended Armed Forces Staff College, 1965. *Politics:* Republican. *Religion:* Episcopalian. *Address:* Cutter Vigilant, U.S. Coast Guard, New Bedford, Mass.

CAREER: Enlisted in U.S. Coast Guard, 1945, commissioned officer, 1950; currently lieutenant commander. Commanding officer of Coast Guard Loran Station, Attu, Aleutian Islands, 1954, and of Coast Guard Cutter General Greene, Gloucester, Mass., 1959-60; press officer, U.S. Coast Guard Headquarters, Washington, D. C., 1961-65; Massachusetts Civil Defense, regional operations officer, 1957-61; currently commanding officer, Cutter Vigilant, New Bedford, Mass. *Member:* Masons.

WRITINGS: (With H. R. Kaplan) *A Guide to Sunken Ships in American Waters*, Compass Publications, 1964; (with Kaplan) *Voyager Beware*, Rand McNally, 1966. Contributor to *True Boating* and *Motor Boating*.

WORK IN PROGRESS: Contributing writer for a McGraw handbook on underwater engineering.†

*   *   *

LOPER, William C.   1927-

PERSONAL: Born August 21, 1927, in Riverside, Calif.; son of William Bryan (an electrical engineer) and Ruby (Campbell) Loper; married Carol Fagstad, August 17, 1957; children: John William. *Education:* Stanford University, B.S. in E.E., 1949, M.A. in Ed., 1950; San Francisco Theological Seminary, B.D., 1953; University of Manchester, Ph.D., 1955. *Address:* P.O. Box 357, San Juan Capistrano, Calif. 92675.

CAREER: Ordained minister of United Presbyterian Church in the U.S.A., 1953; assistant pastor, interim minister of Christian education, and interim pastor at churches in Los Angeles and Burbank, Calif., 1955-59; Community Presbyterian Church, San Juan Capistrano, Calif., pastor, 1960—. Teacher at Southern California Presbyterian Leadership Schools and Lay Academy.

WRITINGS: The Lord of History, Westminster Press, 1965.

*   *   *

LOPEZ, Felix Manuel, Jr.   1917-

PERSONAL: Born July 3, 1917, in Brooklyn, N.Y.; son of Felix Manuel (a stockbroker) and Loretta E. (Quinlan) Lopez; married Regina E. Powell, December 31, 1943; children: Virginia Alison, Felix Edward. *Education:* St. John's University, Brooklyn, N.Y., A.B., 1939; New York University, M.P.A., 1950; Columbia University, Ph.D., 1962. *Religion:* Roman Catholic. *Home:* 22 Plymouth Rd., Port Washington, N.Y. 11050. *Office:* Port of New York Authority, New York, N.Y.

CAREER: Port of New York Authority, New York, N.Y., 1947—, became manager of manpower planning and research; New York University, New York, N.Y., adjunct assistant professor of management, 1960—. American Management Association, lecturer in management course. *Military service:* U.S. Army, Corps of Engineers, 1942-46; became first lieutenant. *Member:* American Psychological Association, American Personnel and Guidance Association, Public Personnel Association, American Society for Public Administration, National Vocational Guidance Association, American Association for the Advancement of Science, American Catholic Psychological Association, New York Personnel Management Association (vice-president, 1965-66), New York State Psychological Association, Executive Study Conference (chairman, 1963-65).

WRITINGS: Selection and Placement in the Port of New York Authority (monograph), Port of New York Authority, 1950; *A Psychological Analysis of the Relationship of Role Consensus and Personality Consensus to Job Satisfaction and Job Performance*, Port of New York Authority, 1962; *The Ama Company In-Basket Exercise* (test), American Management Association, 1962; *Personnel Interviewing: Theory and Practice*, McGraw, 1965; *Evaluating Executive Decision Making: The In-Basket Technique*, American Management Association, 1966; *Evaluating Employee Performance*, Public Personnel Association, 1968; *The Making of a Manager: Guidelines to His Selection and Promotion*, American Management Association, 1970. Contributor to personnel and management periodicals. Editor, *New York Personnel Management Association Bulletin*, 1960-62.

WORK IN PROGRESS: Performance Appraisal in the Public Service, for Public Personnel Association; *Public Personnel Administration*, with Mailick and Henderson, for Macmillan.

BIOGRAPHICAL/CRITICAL SOURCES: New York Personnel Management Association Bulletin, March, 1961.†

*   *   *

LORD, Clifford L(ee)   1912-

PERSONAL: Born September 4, 1912, in Mount Vernon, N.Y.; son of Charles Clifford (a salesman) and Bertha Eunice (Lee) Lord; married Elizabeth Sniffen Hubbard, June 12, 1937; children: Charles Hubbard, Helen Patricia. *Education:* Amherst College, A.B., 1933, A.M., 1934; Columbia University, graduate student, 1934-36, Ph.D., 1943. *Home:* 8 Holbrook Lane, Briarcliff Manor, N.Y. 10510. *Office:* Hudson Institute, Croton-on-Hudson, N.Y. 10520.

CAREER: Columbia University, New York, N.Y., instructor in American history, 1936-41; consultant, Historical Records Survey, Works Progress Administration, New York, N.Y., 1935-39, New Jersey, 1940-42; director of State Historical Association, Cooperstown, N.Y., 1941-46 (organized Farmers' Museum, 1942), of State Historical Society, Madison, Wis., 1946-58; Columbia University, School of General Studies, New York, N.Y., dean and professor of history, 1958-64; Hofstra University, Hempstead, Long Island, N.Y., president, 1964-72, chancellor, 1972-73; Hudson Institute, Croton-on-Hudson, N.Y., president, 1973—. Director of Circus World Museum, 1952-58, honorary director, 1958—; vice-president of National Railroad Museum, 1958-62, honorary director, 1962—. Member of the board of American Heritage, Inc., 1956-60, Hudson Tersesquicentennial Commission, 1959, and Columbia University Press, 1959-62; member of council, Smithsonian Institution, 1966-72, honorary member of council, 1972—; member of advisory bodies, National Union Catalog and Manuscript Collections, 1957—, New Jersey Tercentenary Commission, 1961-64, and New Jersey State Museum, 1964. Consultant, Western Heritage Center, 1960-64, National Archives, 1962-64. *Military service:* U.S. Naval Reserve, active duty, 1942-46; administrative historian, Bureau of Aeronautics, 1943-45, head of Naval Aviation History Unit, 1945-46; became lieutenant commander.

MEMBER: American Association of Museums (member of council, 1944-48), American Historical Association, Organization of American Historians, American Association for State and Local History (member of council, 1950-52, 1960-64; chairman of advisory council of American History Research Center, 1950-59; vice-president, 1952-56; president, 1956-60; chairman of research and publications committee, 1960-64), Regional Plan Association (member of board of directors, 1967—), New Jersey Historical Society (member of board, 1963-64), Phi Beta Kappa, Century Club (New York). *Awards, honors:* LL.D., Lawrence College (now Lawrence University), 1948, University of Buffalo, 1962, Adelphi University, 1965, Rider College, 1970; L.H.D., Amherst College, 1953.

WRITINGS: Handbook of the Museum and Art Gallery of the New York State Historical Association, New York State Historical Association, 1942; *Atlas of Congressional Roll Calls, 1777-1789*, New York State Historical Association, 1943; (with wife, Elizabeth H. Lord) *Historical Atlas of the United States*, Holt, 1944, 2nd edition, 1954; (compiler and author of introduction) *The State Historical Society of Wisconsin: A Century of Service*, State Historical Society of Wisconsin, 1948; (with Archibald D. Turnbull) *History of United States Naval Aviation*, Yale University Press, 1949; (with Turnbull) *History of U.S. Ideas in Conflict: A Colloquium on Certain Problems in Historical Society Work*, 1958; (editor with Henry Graff) John Allen Krout, *American Themes*, Columbia University Press, 1963; *Teaching History With Community Resources*, Teachers College Press, 1964, 2nd edition, 1967, (editor) *Keepers of the Past*, University of North Carolina Press, 1965; (with Carl Ubbelohde) *Clio's Servant: The State Historical Society of Wisconsin, 1846-1954*, State Historical Society of Wisconsin, 1967. Author, with Charles E. Baker and Joseph E. Vaughan, of *Presidential Executive Orders*, unnumbered series, 1943, numbered series, 1944; also author of historical monographs.

General editor, "Localized History Series," Teachers College Press, Columbia University, 1964—. Editor of *New York History* (quarterly), 1942-43, *Wisconsin Magazine of History* (quarterly), 1946-53; member of advisory board, *America: History and Life*, 1964-68.

WORK IN PROGRESS: Statistical Handbook of the United States, for Harper.

BIOGRAPHICAL/CRITICAL SOURCES: Time, Volume 60, Number 55; *Milwaukee Journal*, July 1, 1956; *History News*, August, 1958, September, 1960; *New York Times*, April 8, 1964; *Columbia Owl* (Columbia University), April 15, 1964; *Hofstra Chronicle*, April 16, 1964; *Newsday*, April 30, 1964.†

* * *

LOTT, Arnold S(amuel) 1912-

PERSONAL: Born July 17, 1912, in Sac City, Iowa; married Nellie L. Reilly (an editor), November 29, 1934; children: Marilyn Harbin (Mrs. William Sutcliffe), Lowell Freyer. *Religion:* Presbyterian. *Home:* 20 Romar Dr., Annapolis, Md. *Office:* U.S. Naval Institute, Annapolis, Md.

CAREER: U.S. Navy, 1931-61; enlisted as apprentice seaman, promoted through enlisted ranks to chief yeoman, then commissioned ensign during World War II; now lieutenant commander (retired). Served as assistant personnel officer with Service Force of Seventh Fleet, personnel adviser to Republic of Korea Navy, and special assistant to Deputy Chief of Information, Department of the Navy. Self-taught painter, exhibiting at three one-man shows in Maryland, 1963—; art teacher in adult education classes. *Awards, honors:* Order of Chung Mu for work in augmenting Korean naval strength.

WRITINGS: A Long Line of Ships, U.S. Naval Institute, 1954; *Most Dangerous Sea*, U.S. Naval Institute, 1959; *Brave Ship, Brave Men*, Bobbs-Merrill, 1964; *The Bluejacket's Manual*, U.S. Naval Institute, 1973. Contributor on naval and military subjects to *Encyclopaedia Britannica* and *Britannica Junior*. General editor of Leeward Publications.

AVOCATIONAL INTERESTS: Piloting light planes.

* * *

LOVE, Thomas Teel 1931-

PERSONAL: Born October 14, 1931, in Springfield, Mo.; son of Robert William and Ruby (Teel) Love; married Shirley Ann Chestnut, August 28, 1955; children: Lynne Ann, Thomas Teel, Jr. *Education:* Drury College, student, 1949-51; University of Oklahoma, B.A., 1954; Perkins School of Theology, B.D., 1957; Princeton University, M.A., 1960, Ph.D., 1964; post doctoral study at Oxford University, 1966-67, and Southern Methodist University, 1967-68. *Home:* 18341 Minnehaha, Northridge, Calif. 91324. *Office:* Department of Religious Studies, California State University, 18111 Nordhoff, Northridge, Calif. 91324.

CAREER: Ordained Methodist minister, 1957. Cornell College, Mount Vernon, Iowa, assistant professor of Christian ethics, 1961-65, associate professor, 1965-67; Southern Methodist University, Dallas, Tex., lecturer in law, 1967-68; California State University, Northridge, professor of religious studies, 1968—. Visiting professor, Southern Methodist University, 1965. *Member:* American Society of Christian Social Ethics, American Academy of Religion (vice-president, 1970-71; president, 1971-72), Society for Religion in Higher Education (fellow), American Association of University Professors, Society for the Scientific Study of Religion, Iowa Philosophical Association.

Awards, honors: Woodrow Wilson fellowship, 1959; Cornell College research grants, 1963-66; Ford Foundation fellowship, 1964; American Council of Learned Societies grant-in-aid, 1964-65; Society for Religion in Higher Education fellowship, Oxford University, 1966-67; Council of Humanities Faculty research fellowship, 1967-68.

WRITINGS: John Courtney Murray: Contemporary Church-State Theory, Doubleday, 1965; (contributor) Thomas Bird, editor, *Theologians of Our Time*, volume II, University of Notre Dame Press, 1967; (with Richard Longaker) *Moral Guidelines Handbook*, California State Board of Education, 1973. Contributor to *Religion and the Public Order*, Number 4, 1968, and to theology journals.

WORK IN PROGRESS: Religious Freedom in the Modern World: Vatican II; Christian Ethics and Contemporary Society; a casebook in contemporary ethical issues; a series of case studies for a book *Morality in a Free Society*; editing series of volumes in *Man's Religions* for Harper.

*   *   *

LOVELL, (Alfred Charles) Bernard 1913-

PERSONAL: Born August 31, 1913, in Oldland Common, England; son of G. Lovell; married Mary Joyce Chesterman, 1937; children: three daughters, two sons. *Education:* University of Bristol, B.Sc., and Ph.D. *Home:* The Quinta, Swettenham, near Congleton, Cheshire, England. *Office:* Nuffield Radio Astronomy Laboratories, Jodrell Bank, Macclesfield, Cheshire, England.

CAREER: University of Manchester, Manchester, England, asst. lecturer in physics, 1936-39, lecturer in physics at Physical Laboratories and at Jodrell Bank Experimental Station, Cheshire, 1945-47, senior lecturer, 1947-49, reader in physics at Physical Laboratories and Jodrell Bank Experimental Station, 1949-51, university professor of radio astronomy, and director of Nuffield Radio Astronomy Laboratories, Jodrell Bank, Cheshire, 1951—. Member of staff, Telecommunications Research Establishment, 1939-45, Reith Lecturer, 1958; Condon Lecturer and Guthrie Lecturer, 1962; Halley Lecturer, 1964; Queen's Lecture, Berlin, 1970. Visiting Montague Burton Professor of International Relations, University of Edinburgh, 1973.

Member: International Astronomical Union (vice-president, 1970—), Royal Astronomical Society (president, 1969-71), Royal Society (fellow), Institute of Physics (fellow), American Academy of Sciences (honorary foreign member), New York Academy of Science (honorary life member), Royal Swedish Academy (honorary member), Institute of Electrical Engineers (fellow), Society of Engineers (fellow), Athenaeum Club. *Awards, honors:* Order of the British Empire, 1946; Duddell Medal of Physical Society, 1954; Royal Medal of Royal Society, 1960; knighted, 1961; honorary LL.D. from University of Edinburgh, 1961 and University of Calgary, 1966; D.Sc. from University of Leicester, 1961, University of Leeds, 1966, University of London, 1967, University of Bath, 1967, and University of Bristol, 1970; Daniel and Florence Guggenheim International Astronautics Award, 1961; L'Orde due Merite pour la Recherche et l'Invention, 1962; Churchill Gold Medal of Society of Engineers, 1964.

WRITINGS: Science and Civilization, Nelson, 1939; *World Power Resources and Social Development*, Pilot Press, 1945; *Electronics and Their Application in Industry and Research*, Pilot Press, 1947; (with J. A. Clegg) *Radio Astronomy*, Wiley, 1952; *Meteor Astronomy*, Clarendon Press, 1954; (with Robert Hanbury Brown) *The Exploration of Space by Radio*, Wiley, 1958; *The Individual and the Universe* (Reith lectures), Harper, 1959; *The Exploration of Outer Space* (Gregyog lectures), Harper, 1962; (with Joyce Lovell) *Discovering the Universe*, Harper, 1963; (with Tom Margerison) *The Explosion of Science: The Physical Universe*, Meredith Press, 1967; *Our Present Knowledge of the Universe*, Harvard University Press, 1967; *The Story of Jodrell Bank*, Harper, 1968; *The Origins and International Economics of Space Exploration*, Edinburgh University Press, 1973; *Out of the Zenith: Jodrell Bank, 1957-70*, Oxford University Press, 1973, Harper, 1974.

SIDELIGHTS: Sir Bernard Lovell is the creator of a 250-foot radio telescope at Jodrell Bank. Originally Lovell had not intended the telescope to be so large, but he soon noticed that this spot was perfect for the study of ionized trails left by meteors. So began the ten year struggle for the building and finally the completion of the telescope. Public sentiment was not always with Lovell, and missing also was the expected funding for the project. Lovell faced a prison term (he could not give the chairman of the University Council a writ for one million pounds) and was subjected to social ostracism before the telescope was completed. A New York Times reviewer estimated that "The process made Lovell one of the great scientist-adventurers, staking his career on a project involving great financial risk." *Avocational interests:* Cricket, gardening, and music.

*   *   *

LOWNDES, William 1914-

PERSONAL: Born August 16, 1914, in Victoria, British Columbia, Canada; son of Arthur and Emily (Fitzpatrick) Lowndes; married Enid Alicia Barham, 1945; children: Stephen William Hope. *Education:* Attended Manchester Grammar School, Manchester, England, 1927-31. *Home:* Beaumont House, Patching Hall Lane, Chelmsford, Essex, England.

CAREER: John Rylands Library, Manchester, England, assistant, 1931-38; Public Library, Preston, Lancashire, England, reference librarian, 1938-45; Public Library, Dukinfield, Cheshire, England, chief librarian, 1945-46; Public Library, Bebington, Cheshire, England, chief librarian, 1947-58. Regular broadcaster on soccer for British Broadcasting Corp., covering games throughout the season. *Member:* Library Association, Royal Society of Arts (fellow).

WRITINGS: The Story of Football, Thorsons Publishers, 1952, revised edition, Dent, 1964; *The Story of Bebington*, Bebington Corp., 1953. Contributor to library journals and popular magazines.

SIDELIGHTS: Lowndes told *CA*: "I like watching football (soccer) and getting paid for it. I enjoy playing badminton without getting paid for it. General dislikes include do-it-yourself carpentry jobs and—regretfully—most television programmes."†

*   *   *

LOWREY, Janette Sebring 1892-

PERSONAL: Born March 2, 1892, in Orange, Tex.; daughter of Ruluph R. (a teacher and school superintendent) and Janette (Scurry) Sebring; married Fred Vestal Lowrey (an attorney), August 3, 1922 (died, 1962); children: Alfred Sebring. *Education:* University of Texas,

B.A. 1929. *Politics:* Democrat. *Religion:* Episcopalian. *Agent:* McIntosh & Otis, Inc., 18 East 41st St., New York, N.Y. 10017.

CAREER: Teacher of English in Texas high schools, 1913-18; advertising manager of Houston Land & Trust Co., Houston, Tex., 1918-22; author of books and short stories for young people, 1938—. *Member:* San Antonio Art League, San Antonio Conservation Society, Theta Sigma Phi. *Awards, honors:* Theta Sigma Phi Headliner Award, 1953; Communicating Arts Award, Bexar County (Tex.) Library Committee, 1963; Texas Institute of Letters Award for best youth book of the year, for *Love, Bid Me Welcome*, 1964.

WRITINGS: Annunciata and the Shepherds, Gentry, 1938; *The Silver Dollar*, 1940; *Rings on Her Fingers*, Harper, 1941; *Tap-a-tan*, Harper, 1942; *The Poky Little Puppy*, Golden Books, 1942; *Baby's Book*, Golden Books, 1942; *Bible Stories*, Golden Books, 1943; *A Day in the Jungle*, Golden Books, 1943; *The Lavender Cat*, Harper, 1944; *In the Morning of the World*, Harper, 1944; *The Bird*, Harper, 1947; *Margaret* (Junior Literary Guild selection), Harper, 1950; *Mr. Heff and Mr. Ho*, Harper, 1952; *Where Is the Poky Little Puppy?*, Golden Books, 1962; *Love, Bid Me Welcome*, Harper, 1964; *Six Silver Spoons*, Harper, 1971. Contributor of short stories to children's magazines.

WORK IN PROGRESS: A juvenile book and an adult novel, both still untitled.

SIDELIGHTS: Janette Lowrey wrote her first story, based on the annual Christmas pageant presented in San Antonio, in 1938; it was released (as *Annunciata and the Shepherds*) at Thanksgiving time and sold out before Christmas. An interviewer later wrote that the first book had been "dashed off." Mrs. Lowrey says that she has never dashed off anything, believing that it is important for children to hear and see words which are put together well and that train the senses. One of her favorite examples: "And down they went to see, roly-poly, pell-mell, tumble-bumble, till they came to the green grass" (from *The Poky Little Puppy*).

BIOGRAPHICAL/CRITICAL SOURCES: Horn Book, February, 1947; *San Antonio Light*, San Antonio, Tex., April 17, 1963.†

* * *

LOWRY, Joan (Catlow) 1911-
(Joanna Catlow)

PERSONAL: Born July 17, 1911, in Kendal, Westmoreland, England; daughter of Edward Smith (a stockbroker) and Annie (Buckley) Catlow; married Colin Courtenay Lowry, 1933; children: Patricia Vivien. *Education:* Attended schools in Scotland and England. *Religion:* Church of England. *Home:* Buckleigh House, Westward Ho!, North Devonshire, England. *Agent:* Anthony Shiel Associates, 52 Floral St., Covent Garden, London W.C.2, England.

CAREER: Novelist. *Member:* International P.E.N., West Country Writers.

*WRITINGS—*Under name Joanna Catlow; all published by Hutchinson: *Sisters to Simon*, 1955; *The Sapphire Smoke*, 1957; *The Night of the High Wind*, 1960; *The Enchanted Land*, 1963.

WORK IN PROGRESS: A novel, *The Huntercombe Beauties*.

SIDELIGHTS: Joan Lowry has spent nearly twenty years traveling with her navy husband, and has lived in the West Indies, Bermuda, Australia, New Zealand, the Pacific Islands, Sarawak, and Hong Kong.

* * *

LUBELL, Samuel 1911-

PERSONAL: Born November 3, 1911, in Poland; came to United States in 1913; son of Louis and Mollie (Reitkop) Lubell; married Helen Sopot, March 22, 1941; children: Bernard, Walter. *Education:* Attended City College (now City College of the City University of New York), 1927-31; Columbia University, B.S., 1933. *Politics:* Independent Democrat. *Home:* 3200 New Mexico Ave. N.W., Washington, D.C. 20016.

CAREER: Member of editorial staff of newspapers, Long Island, N.Y., Richmond, Va., and Washington, D.C., 1925-38; free-lance writer for national magazines, most frequently for *Saturday Evening Post*, 1938-41; U.S. Office of Facts and Figures (later Office of War Information), writer, 1941; general secretary of Baruch Rubber Survey Committee, 1942; assistant to James F. Byrnes, director of Office of Economic Stabilization, and to Bernard M. Baruch, Advisory Unit on War and Post War Mobilization, 1942; *Saturday Evening Post*, war correspondent in China-Burma-India Theater, 1944; *Providence Journal* and North American Newspaper Alliance, European correspondent, 1946; election commentator for Columbia Broadcasting System or National Broadcasting Co., on radio and television, 1952-60; political analyst, 1952-72; Columbia University, Graduate School of Journalism, New York, N.Y., director of opinion reporting workshop, 1958-68.

MEMBER: National Press Club. *Awards, honors:* Pulitzer traveling scholarship from Columbia University for European travel, 1934; Guggenheim fellowship, 1951, 1954; Woodrow Wilson Foundation Award of American Political Science Association for best book of the year on government democracy, 1952, for *The Future of American Politics*.

WRITINGS: The Future of American Politics, Harper, 1952, 3rd edition, 1965; *Revolution in World Trade and American Economic Policy*, Harper, 1955; *Revolt of the Moderates*, Harper, 1956; *White and Black: Test of a Nation*, Harper, 1964, 2nd edition, 1965; *The Hidden Crisis in American Politics*, Norton, 1970; *The Future While It Happened*, Norton, 1973. Author of syndicated feature, "The People Speak." Contributor to *Look, Reader's Digest, Harper's, Commentary*, and other magazines.

SIDELIGHTS: Lubell is particularly well known for his unorthodox and generally very accurate opinion polls in national elections. His technique involves, basically, travelling widely and talking informally with a large number of people, and reporting his results in narrative summaries rather than in statistical analyses.

BIOGRAPHICAL/CRITICAL SOURCES: Newsweek, October 18, 1954; *Time*, October 15, 1956.†

* * *

LUCIA, Salvatore Pablo 1901-

PERSONAL: Born March 9, 1901, in San Francisco, Calif.; son of David and Julia Irene (Casino) Lucia; married Marilyn Matys (a psychiatrist), June 4, 1959; children: Salvatore Pablo, Jr., Darryl Reed. *Education:* University of California, A.B., 1926, M.D., 1930. *Home:* 20 Mercedes

Way, San Francisco, Calif. *Office:* School of Medicine, University of California, Third and Parnassus, San Francisco, Calif.

CAREER: Diplomate, National Board of Medicine and American Board of Internal Medicine. University of California, San Francisco, member of medical faculty, 1931—, professor of preventive medicine and medicine, 1947—, chairman of the department of preventive medicine, 1938-64. Consulting physician in oncology at University of California Cancer Research Institute, and at San Francisco Medical Center. Founder member of Universidad de los Andes, Bogota, Colombia; member of medical mission to Colombia for Unitarian Service Commission, 1948, and medical mission to Japan for Unitarian Service Commission and Supreme Commander, Allied Powers, 1951.

MEMBER: American Medical Association, American College of Physicians (fellow), American Society of Hematology, International Society of Hematology, American Federation for Clinical Research (San Francisco branch), Association of Teachers of Preventive Medicine, American Geriatric Society, Pan American Medical Association (past president), California Medical Association, California Academy of Medicine, New York Academy of Science (honorary), San Francisco County Medical Society, Hollywood Academy of Medicine, Phi Beta Kappa, Sigma Xi, Phi Sigma, Alpha Omega Alpha, Delta Omega. *Awards, honors:* D.Sc., University of Antioquia, 1948; Certification of Merit, Colombian Society of Internal Medicine, 1952; Biennial Award ($1,000) of Society of Medical Friends of Wine, 1964, for outstanding achievement.

WRITINGS: (With Paul Michael Aggeler) *Hemorrhagic Disorders,* University of Chicago Press, 1949; *Wine as Food and Medicine,* Blakiston Co., 1954; *History of Wine as Therapy,* Lippincott, 1963; (editor and contributor) *Alcohol and Civilization: A Symposium,* McGraw, 1963; *Wine and Health,* Fortune House, 1969; *Wine and the Digestive System,* Fortune House, 1970; *Wine and Your Well-Being,* Popular Library, 1971.

WORK IN PROGRESS: A bibliographic study of wine and wine components; a study of the correlation of maternal antibodies with the blood of the offspring; *The Religious and Festive Uses of Wine.*

SIDELIGHTS: Salvatore Lucia is competent in Italian, Spanish, and French.

*   *   *

LUCIE-SMITH, Edward   1933-

PERSONAL: Born February 27, 1933, in Jamaica; son of John Dudley (a civil servant with British Colonial Service) and Mary Frances (Lushington) Lucie-Smith. *Education:* Merton College, Oxford, B.A., 1954. *Home:* 24 Sydney St., London S.W.3, England.

CAREER: Advertising copywriter for a London agency, 1956-66; free-lance writer, 1966—. Founder of Turret Books, 1965, a private press to publish poetry and some background documentation. *Member:* Royal Society of Literature (fellow), P.E.N. (English committee), Societe Europeenne de la Culture. *Awards, honors:* Shared John Llewellyn Rhys Memorial Prize, 1961, and Arts Council Triennial Award for best first or second book of poems, 1961, both for *A Tropical Childhood.*

WRITINGS: (Author of introduction and notes) Raffaele Sanzio, *Raphael,* Batchworth Press (London), 1961; (author of introduction and notes) Sir Peter Paul Rubens, *Rubens,* Marboro Books (New York), 1961; *Rubens,* Spring Books, 1961; (editor with Philip Hobsbaum) *A Group Anthology,* Oxford University Press, 1963; (editor) *The Penguin Book of Elizabethan Verse,* Penguin, 1965; *What Is a Painting?,* Macdonald & Co., 1966; *Gallipoli, Fifty Years After,* limited edition, Turret Books, 1966; (editor and author of introduction) *A Choice of Browning's Verse,* Faber, 1967; (editor and author of introduction) *The Penguin Book of Satirical Verse,* Penguin, 1967; (translator from the French) Paul Claudel, *Five Great Odes,* Rapp & Carroll, 1967, Dufour, 1970; (translator from the French) Paul Claudel, *The Muses,* Turret Books, 1967; *Borrowed Emblems,* Turret Books, 1967; (translator from the French) Jean Paul de Dadelsen, *Jonah: Selected Poems,* Swallow Press, 1967; (translator from the French) Andre Pieyre de Mandiargues, *Hyacinths,* limited edition, Collection Paroles Peintes (Paris), 1967; (editor) *The Liverpool Scene,* Rapp & Carroll, 1967, Doubleday, 1968; (author of introduction) *Poetry Catalogue,* [London], 1968; *Thinking About Art: Critical Essays,* Calder & Boyars, 1968; (author of introduction) *Short-Title Catalogue,* 4th edition revised and enlarged, Arts Council of Great Britain, Poetry Library, 1969; *Movements in Art Since 1945,* Thames and Hudson, 1969; *Late Modern: The Visual Arts Since 1945,* Praeger, 1969; (compiler) *Holding Your Eight Hands: An Anthology of Science Fiction Verse,* Doubleday, 1969.

(With Patricia White) *Art in Britain, 1969-70,* Dent, 1970; (editor and author of introduction) *British Poetry Since 1945,* Penguin, 1970; (compiler) *Primer of Experimental Poetry,* Bobbs-Merrill, 1971; (compiler) *A Garland From the Greek: Poems From the Greek Anthology in Versions,* Turret Books, 1971; *A Concise History of French Painting,* Praeger, 1971; (editor and author of introduction with Simon W. Taylor) *French Poetry Today: A Bilingual Anthology,* Schocken, 1971; *Eroticism in Western Art,* Praeger, 1972; *Symbolist Art,* Praeger, 1972; (with Donald Carroll) *Movements in Modern Art,* Horizon Press, 1973.

Poetry: *A Tropical Childhood, and Other Poems,* Oxford University Press, 1961; (with Jack Clemo and George MacBeth) *Jack Clemo, Edward Lucie-Smith [and] George MacBeth,* Penguin, 1964; *Confessions and Histories,* Oxford University Press, 1964; *Jazz for the N.U.F.,* limited edition, Turret Books, 1965; *Three Experiments,* limited edition, Turret Books, 1965; *Silence,* limited edition, Trigram Press, 1967; *Towards Silence,* Oxford University Press, 1968; (with Christopher Logue, MacBeth, Erich Fried, and Georg Rapp) *Jupiter and Turret at the Wigmore,* Turret Books, 1968; *Egyptian Ode,* limited edition, Daedalus Press (Norfolk, Va.), 1969; *Six Kinds of Creature,* limited edition, Turret Books, 1969; *Lovers: A Poem,* limited edition, Sceptre Press, 1970; *Six More Beasts,* limited edition, Turret Books, 1970; *Two Poems of Night,* limited edition, Turret Books, 1972.

Also author of prefaces and introductions to catalogs for museum exhibits in New York and London, including *Animal Drawings From the XV to XX Centuries,* 1962, and *The Little Press Movement in England and America,* 1968. Contributor to *Critical Quarterly.*

SIDELIGHTS: Reviewing *Towards Silence,* Julian Symons notes that Lucie-Smith "is a very accomplished and observant poet with a fine sense of time, place, history." Symons describes one series of poems in the book as confirming Lucie-Smith's "unusual power as a writer of dramatic narrative, in a kind faintly reminiscent of Browning, but always original, well-ordered, elegant."

LUCK, G(eorge) Coleman 1913-

PERSONAL: Born May 21, 1913, in Augusta, Ga.; son of Felix Adolphus (a businessman) and Emma (Hill) Luck; married May Heldenbrand, May 31, 1942; children: G. Coleman, Jr., William F., Virginia May. *Education:* Austin College, A.B., 1945; Dallas Theological Seminary, Th.M., 1945, Th.D., 1949. *Home:* 818 East Indiana St., Wheaton, Ill. 60187. *Office:* Moody Bible Institute, 820 North La-Salle St., Chicago, Ill.

CAREER: Fellowship of Independent Evangelical Churches, ordained minister, 1942. Moody Bible Institute, Chicago, Ill., member of faculty, 1947—, chairman of department of theology, 1963-68, chairman of department of Bible, 1968—.

WRITINGS—All published by Moody: *The Bible, Book by Book*, 1955; *James—Christian Faith in Action*, 1955; *Zechariah*, 1957; *Daniel*, 1958; *First Corinthians*, 1958; *Second Corinthians*, 1959; *Luke—The Gospel of the Son of Man*, 1960; *Ezra—Nehemiah*, 1961; *Comfort for Suffering Christians*, 1961; *Thrilling Days in the Early Church*, 1962; *Widening Horizons in the Early Church*, 1962; *Salvation Through Faith*, 1963; *Trials and Triumphs in the Early Church*, 1964; *What It Means to Be Saved*, 1964. Book review editor, *Moody Monthly*, 1949-69.

AVOCATIONAL INTERESTS: Music, literature.

* * *

LUCKHARDT, Mildred Corell 1898-

PERSONAL: Born November 20, 1898, in New York, N.Y.; daughter of Philip George (an importer and artist) and Mildred (McCaffrey) Corell; married Gustav George Luckhardt (a consulting engineer), September 20, 1921; children: Jean (Mrs. Lewis M. Robbins), Mildred Mary (Mrs. David E. Kenney), Philip George. *Education:* Various courses in education, library science, and theology over a period of years at Columbia University and Union Theological Seminary, New York, N.Y. *Religion:* Presbyterian. *Home:* 121 Argonne St., Fairfield, Conn. 06432. *Office:* Rye Library, Rye, N.Y. 10580.

CAREER: Secretary to bank president, New York, N.Y., 1918-20, and editor of Wall Street bank house organ, 1920-21; Presbyterian Church, Rye, N.Y., director of Christian education, 1941-48; Rye Library, Rye, N.Y., part-time assistant in children's room, 1957-65. Wainright House (layman's retreat house), Rye, N.Y., volunteer librarian, 1961-66. Writer. Lecturer on the Bible, religious education, and children's literature; storyteller at libraries, schools, and at several interracial settlement houses and residences. Consultant on religious education for several churches, 1949—. *Member:* Authors Guild of America, National League of American Pen Women, American Library Association, Association of United Presbyterian Educators, Hymn Society of America, National Story League, Westchester County Storytellers Guild, Westchester Library Association, Rye Historical Society, Yarmouth Historical Society, Delta Kappa Gamma (honorary member).

WRITINGS: Light on our Path, Association Press, 1945; *Guide to Old Testament Study*, Association Press, 1945; *Walk in the Light*, Association Press, 1947; *Guide to New Testament Study*, Association Press, 1947; *The Church Through the Ages*, Association Press, 1951; *The Bells Ring Out*, Westminster, 1952; *Merrily We Roll Along*, Messner, 1953; *Coast Guard to the Rescue*, Messner, 1954; *Remember All the People*, Seabury, 1958; *Mission in Mexico*, Seabury, 1960; *The Story of Saint Nicholas*, Abingdon, 1960; *Christmas Comes Once More*, Abingdon, 1962; *Good King Wenceslas*, Abingdon, 1964; *The Church at Work and Worship*, Westminster, 1965; *Thanksgiving—Feast and Festival*, Abingdon, 1966; *Spring World, Awake: Stories, Poems, and Essays*, Abingdon, 1970; (compiler) *Spooky Tales About Witches, Ghosts, Goblins, Demons, and Such*, Abingdon, 1972; (compiler) *Funny Stories to Read or Tell*, Abingdon, 1974. Also author of *Brave Journey*, 1974.

Librettist for two published cantatas, *Job*, Willis Music Co., 1925, and *Vision of Deborah*, Theodore Presser, 1938. Also wrote lyrics for eight choral numbers, including *How Shall We Speak, O God?*, and for several hymns, including *Great Ruler Over Time and Space*. Other writings include a series of stories on the prophets for Methodist magazines, beginning, 1963, and curriculum material for three Protestant denominations.

WORK IN PROGRESS: A book, *Almanac of Holy Days and Holidays Celebrated by Different Faiths*, with Margueritte H. Bro; two books, *Candelas' Candle*, and *Cheers, Tears, Fun, Fears*.

AVOCATIONAL INTERESTS: Vacations on a Maine island, boating, hiking, travel, bridge, reading.

* * *

LUEDERS, Edward (George) 1923-

PERSONAL: Surname rhymes with "readers"; born February 14, 1923, in Chicago, Ill.; son of Carl G. (a businessman) and Vera (Simpson) Lueders; married Julia Demaree, June 5, 1946; children: Kurt, Joel, Julia Anne. *Education:* Hanover College, A.B., 1947; Northwestern University, M.A., 1948; University of New Mexico, Ph.D., 1952. *Home:* 3840 San Rafael Ave., Salt Lake City, Utah 84109. *Office:* Department of English, University of Utah, Salt Lake City, Utah 84112.

CAREER: University of New Mexico, Albuquerque, instructor, 1950-53, assistant professor of English and speech, 1953-57; Long Beach State College (now California State College at Long Beach), assistant professor, 1957-60, associate professor of English, 1960-61; Hanover College, Hanover, Ind., professor of English and chairman of department, 1961-66; University of Utah, Salt Lake City, professor of English, 1966—, chairman of department, 1969-71. Voluntary specialist in poetry for United States Information Service, and director of seminar on American poetry at American Studies Research Centre, both in India, spring, 1971; poet-in-residence, School of the Ozarks, spring, 1972; writer-in-residence, Pennsylvania State University, fall, 1972. *Military service:* U.S. Army Air Forces, 1943-46; served in China-Burma-India Theater; became sergeant. *Member:* National Council of Teachers of English, American Studies Association.

WRITINGS: (Editor with Jane Kluckhohn) *Through Okinawan Eyes*, University of New Mexico Press, 1951; *Carl Van Vechten and the Twenties*, University of New Mexico Press, 1955; (editor) *College and Adult Reading List of Books in Literature and the Fine Arts*, Washington Square Press, 1962; *Carl Van Vechten*, Twayne, 1965; (compiler with Stephen Dunning and Hugh L. Smith, Jr.) *Reflections on a Gift of Watermelon Pickle . . . and Other Modern Verse*, Scott, Foresman, 1966; (compiler with Dunning and Smith) *Some Haystacks Don't Even Have Any Needle, and Some Other Complete Modern Poems*, Scott, Foresman, 1969; (with Brewster Ghiselin and Clarice Short)

Images and Impressions: Poems by Brewster Ghiselin, Edward Lueders, and Clarice Short, University of Utah, 1969; *The Gang from Percy's Hotel and Other Poems*, American Studies Research Centre (Hyderabad, India), 1971. Contributor of articles, poetry, and reviews to *New Republic*, *College English*, and other professional journals. Editor, *Western Humanities Review*, 1969-72.

WORK IN PROGRESS: Editing, with Primus St. John, an anthology of poetry from many cultures, for Scott, Foresman; *The Clam Papers*, a personal, speculative miscellany; a new book of poems.

AVOCATIONAL INTERESTS: Jazz piano (played occasional professional engagements, 1940-66).

* * *

LUND, A. Morten 1926-
(Ted Borch)

PERSONAL: Born December 23, 1926, in Plattsburgh, N.Y.; son of Anton M. (a paper company executive) and Helga (Rorholt) Lund; married Beatrice B. Williams, May, 1972. *Education:* Bowdoin College, B.A. (cum laude), 1950; attended Harvard University, 1950-51. *Home:* 377 Bleecker St., New York, N.Y. 10014.

CAREER: Reporter, *Laconia Citizen*, Laconia, N.H., and *New Britain Herald*, 1951-53; *Sports Illustrated*, New York, N.Y., writer, 1953-59; *Show Magazine*, New York, N.Y., television editor, 1960-61; documentary film producer for Drew Associates, 1961-62; free-lance writer, 1962—.

WRITINGS: Inside Passage to Alaska, Lippincott, 1965; *Skier's Paradise*, Putnam, 1967; *Cruising the Maine Coast*, Walker & Co., 1967; *Skier's Bible*, Doubleday, 1968, revised edition, 1972; *Ski GLM*, Dial, 1970; *Eastward on Five Sounds*, Walker & Co., 1971; *The Pleasures of Cross Country Skiing*, Outerbridge & Lazard, 1972; *The Skier's World*, Random House, 1973; (with Bea Williams) *The Snowmobiler's Bible*, Doubleday, 1974.

WORK IN PROGRESS: A book, *The Expert Skier*, for Doubleday.

* * *

LUNDGREN, William R. 1918-

PERSONAL: Born October 4, 1918, in Chicago, Ill.; son of Ralph E. and Elsa (Fischer) Lundgren; married Martha Ward, December 3, 1949; children: Trudy C., James M. *Education:* Brown University, B.A., 1942; University of California, Los Angeles, graduate study, 1949-50; University of Southern California, General Secondary Teaching Credential, 1961. *Home:* 3 Shetland Court, Rockville, Md.

CAREER: Newspaper reporter, editor, and photographer in Illinois, Texas, and California, 1946-52; civilian employee of U.S. Army as public information officer in Riverside, Calif., 1952-55, of U.S. Air Force as publications writer in San Bernardino, Calif., 1955-58, and screenwriter in Los Angeles, Calif., 1958-61; Los Angeles (Calif.) city schools, teacher, 1961-62; free-lance writer, Los Angeles, Calif., and Washington, D.C., beginning 1962. *Military service:* U.S. Army, 1942-46; became first lieutenant.

WRITINGS: Across the High Frontier, Morrow, 1955; *The Primary Cause*, Morrow, 1963. Writer of some forty documentary filmscripts for U.S. government agencies.

WORK IN PROGRESS: An autobiographical novel.†

LUNT, Richard D(eForest) 1933-

PERSONAL: Born October 24, 1933, in New Haven, Conn.; son of Herbert Arthur (an agronomist) and Pearl (Collins) Lunt; married Ruth Bainton (a librarian), June 12, 1955. *Education:* Oberlin College, B.A., 1955; University of New Mexico, M.A., 1959, Ph.D., 1962. *Home:* 71 Bellevue Dr., Rochester, N.Y. 14680. *Office:* Rochester Institute of Technology, One Lomb Memorial Dr., Rochester, N.Y. 14623.

CAREER: Rochester Institute of Technology, Rochester, N.Y., instructor, 1961-63, assistant professor, 1963-65, associate professor of history, 1965—. *Military service:* U.S. Army, 1955-57. *Member:* American Historical Association, American Association of University Professors.

WRITINGS: The High Ministry of Government: The Political Career of Frank Murphy, Wayne State University Press, 1965.

WORK IN PROGRESS: A book, tentatively entitled *Law and Order vs. The Miners: The Struggle of the United Mine Workers of America to Organize the Miners of West Virginia, 1907-1932.*

* * *

LUTZ, Jessie Gregory 1925-

PERSONAL: Born September 6, 1925, in Halifax, N.C.; daughter of Arthur W. and Ruth (Shaw) Gregory; married Rolland Ray Lutz, Jr. (a college teacher), April 3, 1948. *Education:* University of North Carolina, B.A., 1946; University of Chicago, M.A., 1948; Cornell University, Ph.D., 1955. *Home:* 20 Messler St., East Brunswick, N.J. 08816. *Office:* Douglass College, New Brunswick, N.J. 08903.

CAREER: Rutgers University, Douglass College, New Brunswick, N.J., assistant professor, 1959-65, associate professor, 1965-71, professor of history, 1971—, chairman of department, 1972—. Visiting professor, Cornell University, summer, 1965. *Member:* Association for Asian Studies, Phi Beta Kappa. *Awards, honors:* Fulbright scholarship, 1962; American Association of University Women fellowship, 1963-64; Lindback Award for excellence in teaching, 1968; Social Science Research Council-American Council of Learned Societies fellowship, 1970-71; Berkshire Award for best historical work by a woman, 1971-73, for *China and Christian Colleges, 1850-1950.*

WRITINGS: (Editor) *Christian Missions in China*, Heath, 1965; *China and the Christian Colleges, 1850-1950*, Cornell University Press, 1971.

WORK IN PROGRESS: Research on educational rights and anti-Christian movements in China during the 1920's.

* * *

LUVAAS, Jay 1927-

PERSONAL: Born June 15, 1927, in Erie, Pa.; son of Morten J. (a teacher and composer) and Agnes (Olsen) Luvaas; married Vera Lee Hampson, June 19, 1949; children: John Randall, Karen Dawn, Susan Diane, Amy Jayne, Norman Eric. *Education:* Allegheny College, A.B., 1949; Duke University, M.A., 1951, Ph.D., 1956. *Politics:* Democrat. *Religion:* Unitarian Universalist. *Home:* 583 Highland Ave., Meadville, Pa. 16335. *Office:* Department of History, Allegheny College, Meadville, Pa. 16335.

CAREER: Duke University, Durham, N.C., director of George Washington Flowers Memorial Collection of Southern Americana, 1952-57; Allegheny College, Meadville, Pa., assistant professor, 1957-61, associate professor, 1961-66, professor of history, 1966—. Visiting professor of military history, United State Military Academy, 1972-73. *Military service:* U.S. Navy, 1945-46. *Member:* American Military Institute. *Awards, honors:* Monaco Prize, 1963, for article in *Military Affairs;* Outstanding Civilian Service Medal, 1973.

WRITINGS: (Editor) G. F. R. Henderson, *The Civil War, A Soldier's View,* University of Chicago Press, 1958; *The Military Legacy of the Civil War,* University of Chicago Press, 1959; *The Education of an Army,* University of Chicago Press, 1964; (contributor) Michael Howard, editor, *The Theory and Practice of War,* Cassell, 1965; (editor, translator, and author of introduction) *Frederick the Great on the Art of War,* Free Press, 1966; (editor) *Dear Miss Em: General Eichelberger's War in the Pacific, 1942-45,* Greenwood Press, 1972. Contributor to military texts. Co-editor of "Contributions of Military History" series, and "West Point Military Library" series, both for Greenwood Press. Contributor of articles and reviews to scholarly and military journals. Member of advisory board, *Civil War Times Illustrated,* and *Military Affairs.*

WORK IN PROGRESS: Editing and translating selections from Napoleon's *Correspondence* for a volume comprising his thoughts on war; a book on the military revolution within the American Civil War; a biography of Frederick the Great, for Batsford; a reader on war and society in the nineteenth century; co-authoring an interdisciplinary survey of World War I.

SIDELIGHTS: Luvaas has reading competence (for military treatises) in French, German. *Avocational interests:* Tramping Civil War and World War I battlefields, collecting and painting military miniatures, building a personal library, fishing.

* * *

LUYTENS, David (Edwin) Bulwer 1929-

PERSONAL: Born July 2, 1929, in London, England; son of Robert (a painter and architect) and Eva (Lubryznska) Luytens; married, now separated. *Education:* Oxford University, B.A., 1950, B.Litt., 1952; Yale University, graduate study, 1952-53. *Politics:* "Radical conservative." *Religion:* Roman Catholic. *Home:* 2 Teignmouth Lodge, Teignmouth Rd., Willesden N.W. 2, England. *Agent:* Rosica Colin, 4 Hereford Sq., London S.W. 3, England.

CAREER: Writer; extramural lecturer on subjects ranging from Byzantine history to psychology and culture. *Awards, honors:* Bernard Van Lear fellowship, Yale University, 1952-53.

WRITINGS: Judas Iscariot, Eyre & Spottiswoode, 1950; *Mary Stuart,* Eyre & Spottiswoode, 1952; *Lorenzo the Magnificent,* Eyre & Spottiswoode, 1952; *The Winged Avengers* (play), Harvill, 1954; *The Ode to the Shadows,* Secker & Warburg, 1960; *The Creative Encounter,* Secker & Warburg, 1961. Contributor of reviews and poems to journals, including *Twentieth Century, Tablet, Time and Tide, Times Literary Supplement.*

WORK IN PROGRESS: A long poem, using the basic myth of *Divina Commedia* as a means toward the interrelation of different elements of personal experience; research on the expansion of energy in terms of the application of certain aspects of the relativity theory to the structure of matter and to a variety of biogenic and psychogenic problems.†

LYALL, Leslie T(heodore) 1905-

PERSONAL: Born November 14, 1905, in Chester, England; son of James (a Presbyterian minister) and Edith A. (Thompson) Lyall; married Kathryn Judd, December 30, 1937; children: Sibelle, Gillian, Michael, Merilyn. *Education:* Cambridge University, B.A., 1927, M.A., 1960. *Religion:* Baptist. *Home:* 54 A Crown St., Redbourn, St. Albans, Hertfordshire AL3 7PF, England.

CAREER: China Inland Mission, missionary in China, 1929-51, men candidates secretary, London, England, 1952-65, editorial secretary, 1966-70.

WRITINGS: John Sung, China Inland Mission, 1955, 5th edition, revised, Moody, 1964; *Come Wind, Come Weather,* Moody, 1960; *Urgent Harvest: Partnership with the Church in Asia,* China Inland Mission, 1962, Moody, 1964; (with J. E. L. Newbigin) *The Church: Local and Universal,* World Dominion Press, 1962; (editor) *Missionary Opportunity Today: A Brief World Survey,* Inter-Varsity Fellowship, 1963; *A Passion for the Impossible: The China Inland Mission,* Moody, 1965; *The Church in Mao's China,* Moody, 1969; *Red Sky at Night: Communism Confronts Christianity in China,* Hodder & Stoughton, 1969, Moody, 1970; *A World to Win,* Inter-Varsity Fellowship, 1972; *Three of China's Mighty Men,* Overseas Missionary Fellowship, 1973.

SIDELIGHTS: Come Wind, Come Weather was translated into four European and six Asian languages, and sold more than 20,000 copies in England and 40,000 in United States; all of Lyall's books except one have been published in German. Lyall speaks French, German, and Chinese; he returned to the Far East for an extended tour in 1960.

* * *

LYDOLPH, Paul E. 1924-

PERSONAL: Born January 4, 1924, in Bonaparte, Iowa; son of Guy (a farmer) and Pauline (Ruschke) Lydolph; first wife deceased; married Mary Klahn, 1966; children: (first marriage) Edward, Donald, Paul, Thomas, Andrew. *Education:* University of Iowa, B.A., 1948, graduate study, 1949; study at Harvard University and Massachusetts Institute of Technology, 1944-45; University of Wisconsin, M.S., 1951, PhD., 1955; University of California, postdoctoral study, 1956-57. *Address:* Box 208, Rt. 2, Elkhart Lake, Wis. 53020. *Office:* University of Wisconsin-Milwaukee, Milwaukee, Wis. 53201.

CAREER: Packwood (Iowa) public schools, secondary teacher, 1947-49; Los Angeles State College (now California State University, Los Angeles), assistant professor, 1952-57, associate professor of geography, 1957-59; University of Wisconsin, Milwaukee, associate professor, 1959-62, professor of geography, 1962—, department chairman, 1963-72. *Military service:* U.S. Army Air Forces, 1943-47; became first lieutenant. *Member:* Association of American Geographers, American Geographical Society, American Association for the Advancement of Science, American Association for the Advancement of Slavic Studies, American Association of University Professors, Sigma Xi. *Awards, honors:* Ford Foundation fellowship, 1956-57.

WRITINGS: (With Barbara Borowiecki) *Physical Geography* (laboratory manual), W. C. Brown, 1963; *Geography of the U.S.S.R.,* Wiley, 1964, 2nd edition, 1970. Contributor of articles on climatology and geography of U.S.S.R. to *Compton's Encyclopedia, Geopaedia,* and to professional journals.

WORK IN PROGRESS: Continuing research on climatology and on the Soviet Union and writing *Climate of the U.S.S.R.*, Volume VII of *World Survey of Climatology*.

SIDELIGHTS: Lydolph travelled extensively in Soviet Union in 1960, 1964, and 1965.

*   *   *

LYLE, Jack   1929-

PERSONAL: Born March 27, 1929, in Pine Bluff, Ark.; son of John Knox (an aviator) and Eula (Taylor) Lyle. *Education:* Baylor University, B.A., 1951; Stanford University, M.A., 1956, Ph.D., 1959. *Politics:* Democrat. *Religion:* Episcopalian. *Home:* 1552 Chatham Colony, Reston, Va. 22090.

CAREER: Stanford University, Stanford, Calif., research associate, 1959-60; University of California, Los Angeles, began as assistant professor, became professor of journalism, 1960-72; Corporation for Public Broadcasting, Washington, D.C., 1972—. Deputy project director of International Institute for Educational Planning, 1965-66. *Military service:* U.S. Air Force, 1951-55; became staff sergeant. *Member:* American Association for Public Opinion Research (past officer of Pacific chapter), Association for Education in Journalism (member of research council).

WRITINGS: (With Wilbur Schramm and Edwin B. Parker) *Television in the Lives of Our Children*, Stanford University Press, 1961; (with Schramm and Ithiel de Sola Pool) *The People Look at Educational Television*, Stanford University Press, 1963; (with Schramm, Philip Coombs, and Frederick Kahnert) *The New Media: Memo to Educational Planners*, UNESCO, 1967; *The News in Megalopolis*, Chandler Publishing, 1967; (editor) *The Black American and the Press*, Ritchie, 1968. Contributor to *Journalism Quarterly*, *Journal of Broadcasting*, and *Human Relations*. Editor, *Communications Abstracts*.

WORK IN PROGRESS: (With others) *Television and the Florida Legislature*, *The People Look at Public Television, 1974*, and with Hidetoshi Kato and Kazuhiko Goto, *Television and Children in Japan and the U.S.*

AVOCATIONAL INTERESTS: Marine biology, scuba diving, birdwatching, gardening, and enology.

*   *   *

LYON, William Henry   1926-

PERSONAL: Born March 14, 1926, in Warrensburg, Mo.; son of William H. (a teacher and recreation superintendent) and Laura (Eubank) Lyon; married Marylin Stewart; children; Laurinda, Peggy, Marc, Matthew. *Education:* Central Missouri State College, B.S. in Education, 1947; University of Chicago, A.M., 1949; University of Missouri, Ph.D., 1958. *Office:* Department of Social Science, Northern Arizona University, Flagstaff, Ariz.

CAREER: Virginia Polytechnic Institute, Blacksburg, assistant professor of history, 1949-56; Arizona State College at Flagstaff (now Northern Arizona University), associate professor of history and chairman of department, 1958—.

WRITINGS: *The Pioneer Editor in Misouri, 1808-1860*, University of Missouri Press, 1965.

WORK IN PROGRESS: *The Pioneer Editor in Arizona, 1859-1900*.

*   *   *

LYONS, Joseph   1918-

PERSONAL: Born January 21, 1918, in Scranton Pa.; son of Goodman Israel (a merchant) and Sarah (Groh) Lyons; married Mildred Ruth Rubin, December 22, 1946; children: Ricki Jeanne. *Education:* City College (now City College of the City University of New York), B.A., 1938; University of Kansas, Ph.D., 1952. *Religion:* Jewish. *Office:* Veterans Administration Hospital, Lexington, Ky.

CAREER: U.S. Veterans Administration Hospital, Lexington, Ky., psychologist, beginning 1956. University of Kentucky, Lexington, lecturer on psychology, beginning 1958. *Military service:* U.S. Army Air Forces, World War II. *Member:* American Psychological Association, Sigma Xi.

WRITINGS: *Psychology and the Measure of Man*, Free Press of Glencoe, 1963; *A Primer of Experimental Psychology*, Harper, 1965; *Experience: An Introduction to a Personal Psychology*, Harper, 1973.†

*   *   *

LYONS, Sister Jeanne Marie   1904-

PERSONAL: Born April 1, 1904, in Baltimore, Md.; daughter of William Patrick and Mary (Carroll) Lyons. *Education:* College of Notre Dame of Maryland, B.A., 1926; Catholic University of America, M.A., 1938, Ph.D., 1940. *Home:* Maryknoll, N.Y.

CAREER: Roman Catholic nun, order of Maryknoll Missionary Sisters. Mary Rogers College, Maryknoll, N.Y., president, 1956—. *Member:* Delta Epsilon Sigma.

WRITINGS: (Translator from French) Reginald Garrigou-Lagrange, *The Love of God*, Herder, 1951; (translator) Garrigou-Lagrange, *The Cross of Jesus*, Herder, 1951; *Maryknoll's First Lady* (biography), Dodd, 1964; (translator from French) Marie France Jassy, *Basic Community in the African Churches*, Orbis Books, 1973. Contributor to *Catholic School Journal, Field Afar, Thomist, Sign*, and *Commonweal*; contributor of translated articles to *World Parish*.

WORK IN PROGRESS: Translation of *La Singularite Chretienne*, by Rene Marle, publication by Abbey Press expected as *Has Christianity Something Specific to Offer?*

SIDELIGHTS: Sister Lyons made a fifteen-month tour of Maryknoll Sisters' institutions and activities in Africa, Ceylon, Hong Kong, Formosa, Japan, Korea, Philippines, Caroline and Marshall Islands, and Hawaii, 1956-57, and an educational tour of order's schools in Lima, Peru, and Middle America, 1963. Her interests since 1964, have been in the areas of education and translation.

*   *   *

LYSTAD, Robert A(rthur)   1920-

PERSONAL: Born August 10, 1920, in Milwaukee, Wis.; son of Arthur Frederick and Lulu Marion (Lunde) Lystad; married Anita E. Firing, June 11, 1945 (died, 1952); married Mary Haneman, June 20, 1953; children: Lisa, Anne, Mary, Robert, James. *Education:* University of Wisconsin, B.A., 1941; Drew Theological Seminary, B.D., 1944; Northwestern University, Ph.D., 1951. *Home:* 4900 Scarsdale Rd., Washington, D.C. 20016. *Office:* School of Advanced International Studies, Johns Hopkins University, Washington, D.C.

CAREER: Tulane University of New Orleans, New Orleans, La., assistant professor, 1951-54, associate professor, 1954-59, professor of anthropology, 1959-61, chairman of sociology and anthropology departments, 1959-61; Johns

Hopkins University, School of Advanced International Studies, Washington, D.C., associate professor, 1961-64, professor of African studies, 1964—. Visiting lecturer, Foreign Service Institute, 1961—; director of Carnegie Endowment Foundation and Rockefeller Foundation seminars in diplomacy, 1961—; chairman, Africa screening committee, Foreign Area Fellowship Program, 1962-65. *Member:* African Studies Association, American Anthropological Association, International African Institute, International Congress of Africanists (member of permanent council, 1962-67). *Awards, honors:* Social Science Research Council, fellow, 1949-50; Carnegie Corporation grant, 1957-58.

WRITINGS: The Ashanti: A Proud People, Rutgers University Press, 1958; (editor) *The African World: A Survey of Social Research*, Praeger, 1965. Contributor to other books. Editor, African Studies Association.

WORK IN PROGRESS: Anthropology in Africa: A Case Study of the Nupe, for the American Anthropological Association Curriculum Development Project; a comparative study of the development of political institutions in West Africa, in connection with the West African Comparative Analysis Project.

SIDELIGHTS: Robert Lystad lived in Ghana and the Ivory Coast for two years while doing research on the processes of social change in sub-Saharan Africa.†

* * *

MABBOTT, John David 1898-

PERSONAL: Born November 18, 1898, in Duns, Scotland; son of Walter John (a schoolmaster) and Elizabeth (Davies) Mabbott; married Sheila Doreen Keith Roach, June 30, 1934. *Education:* University of Edinburgh, M.A., 1919; St. John's College, Oxford, B.Litt., 1923, M.A., 1926. *Home:* Wing Cottage, Mill St., Islip, Oxford, England.

CAREER: Oxford University, St. John's College, Oxford, England, fellow and lecturer in philosophy, 1924-63, president, 1963-69. *Military service:* British Army, 1917-18; became second lieutenant. *Member:* Mind Association (treasurer, 1946-63). *Awards, honors:* Companion of Order of St. Michael and St. George, 1946, for work in Foreign Office, 1940-45, Honorary Fellow of St. John's College, Oxford, 1969.

WRITINGS: The State and the Citizen, Hutchinson, 1948; *An Introduction to Ethics*, Hutchinson, 1966, Doubleday, 1969; *John Locke*, Macmillan, 1973. Contributor to philosophical periodicals.

* * *

MACDONALD, Robert S. 1925-

PERSONAL: Born July 20, 1925, in Manlius, N.Y.; son of Robert C. (a school superintendent) and Grace L. (Stevenson) Macdonald; married Jo An Burns, August 15, 1953; children: Nancy, Robert, William. *Education:* Syracuse University, B.S., 1948, M.S., 1949. *Politics:* Democrat. *Religion:* Methodist. *Home:* RFD 3, Elmendorf Heights, Kingston, N.Y. 12401. *Office:* International Business Machines Corp., Kingston, N.Y.

CAREER: Mathematics teacher, Ludlowville, N.Y., 1949-55; Kingston (N.Y.) city schools, assistant superintendent, 1955-59; International Business Machines Corp., Kingston, N.Y., industrial engineer, 1959, technical writer, 1963-64, publications manager, beginning 1964. *Military service:* U.S. Army, 1943-45; served in three European campaigns; wounded in action, 1945. *Member:* Lions Club (Hurley, N.Y.).

WRITINGS: Write Me at Lavaca, Humphries, 1964.

WORK IN PROGRESS: A yet unnamed book, a follow-up to *Write Me at Lavaca*, which was about Stephen Saunders, captain of a coastal trading schooner before the Civil War. The second book is about Saunders' brother, William, also a schooner captain.

SIDELIGHTS: Macdonald told *CA:* "My writing began as a result of finding, among my grandmothers effects, a packet of letters written by Stephen Saunders (her grandfather). The letters were all directed to his wife and children when he was at sea. My writings are based upon an expansion of these letters and supplemented by newspaper accounts of maritime news of that time."†

* * *

MACESICH, George 1927-

PERSONAL: Surname is pronounced May-sitch; born, May 27, 1927, in Cleveland, Ohio; son of Walter (Vaso) and Milka (Tepavac) Macesich; married Susana Sonia Svorkovich (a professor), February 20, 1955; children: Maja Susana Radmila, Milka Milena Milica, George Milan Peter. *Education:* George Washington University, A.A., 1951, B.A., 1953, M.A., 1954; University of Chicago, Ph.D., 1958. *Politics:* Independent. *Religion:* Serbian Orthodox. *Home:* 2401 Delgado, Tallahassee, Fla. *Office:* Center for Slavic and East European Studies, 610 Keen Building, Florida State University, Tallahasee, Fla. 32306.

CAREER: U.S. Navy, 1944-53; Illinois Institute of Technology, Chicago, instructor in economics, 1956-57; University of Chicago, Chicago, Ill., research associate, 1956-58; Chamber of Commerce of the United States, research economist, 1958-59; Florida State University, Tallahassee, assistant professor, 1959-61, associate professor, 1961-63, professor of economics, 1963—, director of Center for Slavic and East European Studies, 1965, director of institute in Yugoslavia (summers), 1969—. Professor of economics, University of Belgrade, Belgrade, Yugoslavia, 1971—, consultant to Council of Graduate Schools in the U.S., Washington, D.C., member of national advisory council, University of Montenegro, Yugoslavia, State Council on Economic Development, Tallahassee, Fla., director, 1961-63. Consultant, U.S. Department of Commerce, 1961-64. *Member:* American Economic Association, American Academy of Political and Social Science, American Statistical Association, Southern Economic Association.

WRITINGS: Statistical Abstract for Florida, State Council on Economic Development, 1963; (editor) *Essays on Florida's Economic Development*, State Council on Economic Development, 1963; *Yugoslavia: Theory and Practice of Development Planning*, University Press of Virginia, 1964; (contributor) *Essays in Southern Economic Development*, M. L. Greenhut and Tate Whitman, editors, University of North Carolina Press, 1964; *Commercial Banking and Regional Developments in the U.S., 1950-1960*, Florida State University Press, 1965; (contributor) Stanley Coben and Forest Hill, editors, *American Economic History: Essays in Interpretation*, Lippincott, 1966; *Money and the Canadian Economy*, National Bank of Yugoslavia (Belgrade), 1967; (contributor) Milton Friedman and David Mieselman, editors, *Varieties of Monetary Experience*, University of Chicago Press, 1969; (contributor) Wayne S. Vuvinich, editor, *Contemporary Yugoslavia: Twenty Years of Socialist Experiment in Socialism*, University of California Press, 1969.

Money in a European Common Market Setting, Nomos Verlagsgesellschaft, 1972; *Financing Industrial and Regional Development: American Experience with the Small Business Administration 1955-1965*, Institute for Industrial Economics (Belgrade), 1972; *Monetary and Financial Organization for Growth and Stability: The U.S. and Yugoslavia*, Institute for Economic Sciences (Belgrade), 1972; *Monetary Theory and Policy: Theoretical and Empirical Issues*, National Bank of Yugoslavia, 1973; *Economic Stability: A Comparative Analysis*, Bedogradshi Graficki Zavod (Belgrade), 1973; (with D. Dimitrijevic) *Money and Finance in Contemporary Yugoslavia*, Praeger, 1973. Author of pamphlets. Contributor of more than seventy articles and reviews to professional journals in the United States, Canada and Europe. Member of editorial board: *Southern Economic Journal*, 1961-63, 1973—, *The F.S.U. Slavic Papers*, 1967—, *Journal of Political Economy*, 1968—, *Foreign Trade and Cycles* (Belgrade), 1969—.

WORK IN PROGRESS: Articles and reviews for international professional journals.

SIDELIGHTS: Macesich is competent in Serbo-Croatian and French.

* * *

MACGREGOR, James (Murdoch) 1925-
(J. T. McIntosh)

PERSONAL: Born February 14, 1925, in Paisley, Scotland; son of Murdoch and Marion (Dracup) Macgregor; married Margaret Murray, July 28, 1960. *Education:* University of Aberdeen, M.A. (honors), 1947. *Home:* 63 Abbotswell Dr., Aberdeen, Scotland. *Agent:* Lurton Blassingame, 60 East 42nd St., New York, N.Y. 10017; John McLaughlin, 80 Chancery Lane, London, England.

CAREER: Former professional musician, schoolteacher, photographer, and newspaper sub-editor; writer, 1954—.

WRITINGS: Glamour in Your Lens, Focal Press, 1958; *When the Ship Sank*, Doubleday, 1959; *Incident Over the Pacific*, published in England as Doubleday, 1960; *A Cry to Heaven*, Heinemann, 1960; *The Iron Rain*, Heinemann, 1962; *The Million Cities*, Pyramid, 1963; *Wine Making for All*, Faber, 1966; *Beer Making for All*, Dover, 1967.

Under pseudonym J. T. McIntosh: *World Out of Mind*, Doubleday, 1953; *Born Leader*, Doubleday, 1954; *One in 300*, Doubleday, 1954; *The Fittest*, Doubleday, 1955, published as *The Role of the Pagbeasts*, Fawcett, 1956; *Time for a Change*, M. Joseph, 1967, published as *Snow White and the Giants*, Avon, 1968; *Six Gates from Limbo*, M. Joseph, 1968, Avon, 1969; *Take a Pair of Private Eyes* (based on television play by Peter O'Donnell), Doubleday, 1968; *A Coat of Blackmail*, Muller, 1970, Doubleday, 1971; *Transmigration*, Avon, 1970; *The Cosmic Spies*, R. Hale, 1972; *The Space Sorcerers*, R. Hale, 1972; *Flight from Rebirth*, R. Hale, 1972; *Galactic Takeover Bid*, R. Hale, 1973; *The Suiciders*, Avon, 1974. Contributor to *Galaxy, Fantasy and Science Fiction, Analog*, and other periodicals. Author of television play, "Danger Zone." 1963.

* * *

MACHIN, G(eorge) Ian T(hom) 1937-

PERSONAL: Surname is pronounced *May*-chin; born July 3, 1937, in Liverpool, England; son of George Seville (a Congregational minister) and Mary (Thom) Machin; married Jane Pallot, April 2, 1964; children: Jonathan Bruce, Anna Jane, Raoul Patrick Paul. *Education:* Jesus College,

Oxford, B.A., 1958, M.A., 1961, D.Phil., 1961. *Religion:* Congregational. *Office:* Department of History, University of Dundee, Dundee, Scotland.

CAREER: University of Singapore, assistant lecturer in history, 1961-63, lecturer, 1963-64; University of St. Andrews, Queen's College, Dundee, Scotland, lecturer in modern history, 1964-67; University of Dundee, Dundee, Scotland, lecturer in modern history, 1967—. *Member:* Royal Historical Society (fellow).

WRITINGS: The Catholic Question in English Politics, 1820-1830, Oxford University Press, 1964; *History of the English Speaking Peoples*, Purnell, 1971. Contributor to professional journals.

WORK IN PROGRESS: Books on religion and politics in nineteenth-century Britain.

AVOCATIONAL INTERESTS: Music, hill-climbing.

* * *

MACK, Raymond (Wright) 1927-

PERSONAL: Born July 15, 1927, in Ashtabula, Ohio; son of Wright R. and Hazel E. (Card) Mack; married Barbara Leonard, 1948 (divorced, 1953); married Ann Hunter, (a teacher) October 16, 1953; children: (first marriage) Donald Gene; (second marriage) Meredith, Julia, Margaret. *Education:* Baldwin-Wallace College, A.B. (with honors), 1949; University of North Carolina, M.A., 1951, Ph.D., 1953. *Home:* 2233 Orrington Ave., Evanston, Ill. 60201.

CAREER: University of Mississippi, University, assistant professor of sociology and anthropology, 1953; Northwestern University, Evanston, Ill., assistant professor, 1953-57, associate professor, 1957-59, professor of sociology and chairman of department, 1967, director of Center for Urban Affairs, 1968-71, vice-president and dean of faculties, 1971—. Faculty research fellow, Social Science Research Council, 1962-63; visiting scholar, Russell Sage Foundation, 1967-68. Surgeon General's Committee on Behavioral Science. *Member:* American Sociological Association (fellow), American Association for the Advancement of Science, Society for the Study of Social Problems, (president, 1969-70), American Association of University Professors, Sociological Research Association Midwest Sociological Society (president, 1967-68), Alpha Kappa Delta (president, 1966-68).

WRITINGS: (With Linton Freeman and Seymour Yellin) *Social Mobility: Thirty Years of Research and Theory*, Syracuse University Press, 1957; (with Kimball Young) *Sociology and Social Life*, American Book Co., 1959, 5th edition (with John Pease), 1973; (editor with Young) *Principles of Sociology: A Reader in Theory and Research*, American Book Co., 1960, 4th edition, 1968; (with George W. Barker) *The Occasion Instant*, National Academy of Science, 1961, *Race, Class, Power*, American Book Co., 1963, 2nd edition, 1968; (with Herbert R. Barringer and George I. Blanksten) *Social Change in Developing Areas: A Reinterpretation of Evolutionary Theory*, Schenkman, 1965; *Transforming America: Patterns of Social Change*, Random House, 1967; *Our Children's Burden: School Desegregation in Ten American Communities*, Random House, 1968. Contributor to *World Book Encyclopedia* and *Encyclopaedia Britannica*. Also contributor to *American Sociological Review, Social Forces, Trans-action*, and other journals. Editor, *The American Sociologist*, 1968-70, associate editor, *The Sociological Quarterly* and *Trans-action*.

MacKENZIE, Christine Butchart 1917-

PERSONAL: Born April 8, 1917, in Cleveland, Ohio; daughter of Franklin David (a minister) and Mary (Beckwith) Butchart; married Harry G. MacKenzie (a sales executive); children: Bonnie, Bruce, Douglas. *Education:* Hiram College, B.A., 1938. *Politics:* Republican. *Religion:* Disciples of Christ (Christian Church). *Home:* 45 Ground Pine Rd., Wilton, Conn.

CAREER: Cleveland Press, Cleveland, Ohio, reporter and columnist, 1938-41; Bell Aircraft Corp., Niagara Falls, N.Y.,instrument technician, 1943-44; U.S. government, civil service employee (instrument repair) at Air Force bases, 1944-45; Christian Board of Publication, St. Louis, Mo., curriculum writer, 1948—. Free-lance writer.

WRITINGS: Jesus Came Teaching (teacher's edition), Christian Board of Publication, 1957; *Principles to Live By*, Christian Board of Publication, 1959; *A Year Is Forever*, Bethany, 1964; *Safe at Home*, Bethany, 1964; *Out at Home*, Bethany, 1967. Currently columnist for *Flagship News* (American Airlines), photo-journalist for *The Hour*, Norwalk, Conn., and public relations writer for the town of Wilton. Author of short stories (adult and juvenile) and articles.

AVOCATIONAL INTERESTS: Travel and color photography for exhibit.

* * *

MacLAINE, Allan H(ugh) 1924-

PERSONAL: Born October 24, 1924, in Montreal, Quebec, Canada; son of Allan (a banker) and Lillian (Renshaw) MacLaine; married Sara Briden Hurdis, April 1, 1949; children: Nancy Goodwin. *Education:* McGill University, B.A., 1945; Brown University, Ph.D., 1951. *Home:* 109 Smithfield Rd, North Providence, R.I. 02904. *Office:* University of Rhode Island, Kingston, R.I.

CAREER: Brown University, Providence, R.I., instructor in English, 1947-50; University of Massachusetts, Amherst, instructor in English, 1951-54; Texas Christian University, Fort Worth, assistant professor of English, 1954-56, associate professor, 1956-62; University of Rhode Island, Kingston, professor of English, 1962—, dean of Division of University Extension, 1967-71. *Member:* Modern Language Association of America, College English Association (president, 1965-66).

WRITINGS: The Student's Comprehensive Guide to the Canterbury Tales, Barron's, 1964; *Robert Fergusson*, Twayne, 1965; *Robert Burns*, Twayne, in press. Also writer of book-length monograph, "The Christis Kirk Tradition: Its Evolution in Scots Poetry through Burns," which appeared in four installments in *Studies in Scottish Literature*, 1964-65. Contributor of more than a dozen articles on various aspects of Scots poetry to other literary journals.

WORK IN PROGRESS: A critical study of Allan Ramsay; an anthology of Scottish poetry, with G. Ross Roy.

* * *

MacRAE, Donald G. 1921-
(Clive Campbell)

PERSONAL: Born April 20, 1921, in Cathcart, Scotland; son of Donald (an engineer) and Elizabeth (Gunn) MacRae; married Helen Grace McHardy (a mathematician); children: Mairi, Helen. *Education:* University of Glasgow, M.A., 1942; Balliol College, Oxford, M.A., 1945. *Home:* 17 Fitzwarren Gardens, London N. 19, England.

CAREER: Formerly university lecturer in sociology at Oxford; London School of Economics and Political Science, London, England, formerly lecturer and reader, now professor of sociology; Heinemann Educational Books Ltd., London, England, editor of books on sociology, 1956—. Visiting professor in Germany, United States, and West Africa.

WRITINGS: Ideology and Society, Heinemann, 1961, Free Press of Glencoe, 1963; *Ages and Stages*, Athlone Press, 1973; *Max Weber*, Fontana, 1974.

WORK IN PROGRESS: Research on social theory, history of social thought, comparative institutions, and the advertising industry.

* * *

MacVICAR, Angus 1908-

PERSONAL: Born October 28, 1908, in Arygll, Scotland; son of Angus John (a minister) and Marsali (Mackenzie) MacVicar; married Jean Smith McKerral, June 24, 1936; children: Jock. *Education:* University of Glasgow, M.A., 1930. *Religion:* Protestant. *Home:* Achnamara, Southend, Campbeltown, Argyll, Scotland. *Agent:* A. M. Heath & Co. Ltd., 40-42 William IV St., London WC2N 4DD, England.

CAREER: Campbeltown Courier, Cambeltown, Argyll, Scotland, assistant editor, 1930-32; free-lance writer, 1932—. *Military service:* British Army, 1939-45; became captain; mentioned in dispatches. *Member:* Society of Authors, Dunaverty Players Drama Club, Dunaverty Golf Club (Southend).

WRITINGS—Adult fiction, all published by Stanley Paul: The Purple Rock, 1933; *Death by the Mistletoe*, 1934; *The Screaming Gull*, 1935; *The Temple Falls*, 1935; *Cavern*, 1936; *The Crooked Finger*, 1936; *The Ten Green Brothers*, 1936; *Flowering Death*, 1937; *Crime's Masquerader*, 1939; *Eleven for Danger*, 1939; *The Singing Spider*, 1939; *Strangers from the Sea*, 1939; *The Crouching Spy*, 1941; *Death on the Machar*, 1946; *Greybreek*, 1947; *Fugitives Road, 1949.*

All published by John Long, except as indicated: *Escort to Adventure*, Stanley Paul, 1952; *The Dancing Horse*, 1961; *The Killings on Kersivay,*, 1962; *The Hammers of Fingal*, 1963; *The Grey Shepherds*, 1964; *Life-Boat—Green to White*, Brockhampton Press, 1965; *Murder at the Open*, 1965; *The Canisbary Conspiracy*, 1966; *Night on the Killer Reef*, 1967; *Maniac*, 1969; *Duel in Glenfinnan*, 1970; *The Golden Venus Affair*, 1972; *The Painted Doll Affair*, 1973.

Adult non-fiction: *Rescue Call*, Kaye & Ward, 1966; *Salt in My Porridge*, Jarrolds, 1971; *Heather in My Ears*, Hutchinson, 1974.

Children's fiction, all published by Burke, except as indicated: *The Crocodile Men*, Art & Educational, 1947; *The Black Wherry*, Foley House Press, 1948; *Faraway Island*, Foley House Press, 1949; *King Abbie's Adventure*, 1950; *The Grey Pilot*, 1951; *Stubby Sees It Through*, 1951; *Tiger Mountain*, 1952; *The Lost Planet* (Children's Book Club choice), 1954; *Secret of the Lost Planet*, 1955; *Dinny Smith Comes Home*, 1955; *The Atom Chasers*, 1956; *The Atom Chasers in Tibet*, 1957; *Satellite 7*, 1958; *Red Fire on the Lost Planet*, 1959.

Peril on the Lost Planet, 1960; *Space Agent from the Lost Planet*, 1961; *Space Agent and the Isles of Fire*, 1962; *Kilpatrick—Special Reporter*, 1963; *Space Agent and the Ancient Peril*, 1964; *The High Cliffs of Kersivay*, Harrap, 1964; *The Kersivay Kraken*, Harrap, 1965; *The Cave of the Hammers*, Kaye & Ward, 1966; *Super Nova and the Rogue Satellite*, Brockhampton Press, 1969; *Super Nova and the Frozen Man*, Brockhampton Press, 1970.

Children's non-fiction: (With John C. Caldwell) *Let's Visit Scotland*, Burke, 1966, revised edition, John Day, 1967.

Adapted four adult books, *The Singing Spider*, *Strangers from the Sea*, *The Canisbary Conspiracy*, and *Night on Killer Reef*, and 17 of his juvenile books for radio serials in Britain, most of them also broadcast in United States, Germany, Malaya, and the Scandinavian countries; adapted *The Lost Planet* and *Return to the Lost Planet* for television serials. Other radio and television writing includes features and documentaries for both adults and children, a weekly radio comedy series, "The Glens of Glendale," which ran from 1954-59, and a television talks series, "Confessions of a Minister's Son," 1965-70.

Regular contributor to *Daily Express* (London); contributor of articles, short stories and serials to adult and juvenile magazines.

SIDELIGHTS: MacVicar was once a professional athlete, earning money that way for his university education; now golfs with a handicap of six. He writes and produces one-act plays for a local drama club, which has won awards in several national competitions. Most of his books have been translated into other languages.

BIOGRAPHICAL/CRITICAL SOURCES: Scottish Field, April, 1957.

* * *

MADDI, Salvatore R(ichard) 1933-

PERSONAL: Born January 27, 1933, in New York, N.Y.; son of Peter Anthony and Jennie (Benigno) Maddi; married Dorothy Linder (a research associate), September 11, 1954; children: Karen Lisa, Christopher David. *Education:* Brooklyn College (now Brooklyn College of the City University of New York), B.A., 1954; M.A., 1956; Harvard University, Ph.D., 1960. *Home:* 5559 South Blackstone Ave., Chicago, Ill. *Office:* Department of Psychology, University of Chicago, Chicago, Ill.

CAREER: University of Chicago, Ill., 1959—, began as lecturer, now professor of psychology, member of governing committee, Social Science College, 1966-68, 1972—. Clinical consultant in research, Chicago, 1959—. Distinguished visiting scholar, Educational Testing Service, 1963-64; visiting professor, Harvard University, 1969-70. *Member:* American Psychological Association, Midwestern Psychological Association, Illinois Psychological Association, Sigma Xi.

WRITINGS: (With Donald W. Fiske) *Functions of Varied Experience*, Dorsey, 1961; *Personality Theories: A Comparative Analysis*, Dorsey Press, 1968, revised edition, 1972; (compiler) *Perspectives on Personality: A Comparative Approach*, Little, Brown, 1971; (with Paul T. Costa) *Humanism In Personology: Allport, Maslow, and Murray*, Aldine-Atherton, 1972.

WORK IN PROGRESS: Research on need for variety as a characteristic of personality and on curiosity in children.

AVOCATIONAL INTERESTS: Cinema, sculpture.†

MADDISON, Angus 1926-

PERSONAL: Born December 6, 1926, in Newcastle upon Tyne, England; came to United States, 1949; son of Thomas and Jane (Walker) Maddison. *Education:* Selwyn College, Cambridge, B.A., 1947, M.A., 1951; postgraduate study at McGill University, 1949-50, and Johns Hopkins University, 1950-51. *Home:* Greensleeves, Kingswood Ave., Tyler's Green, Bucks, England. *Office:* Development Centre, Organization for Economic Co-operation and Development, 2 Rue Andre Pascal, Paris XVIe, France.

CAREER: University of St. Andrews, St. Andrews, Scotland, lecturer in economics, 1951-52; Organization for European Economic Co-operation and successor, Organization for Economic Co-operation and Development, Paris, France, 1953—, head of Economics Division, 1958-62, director of technical cooperation, 1963, fellow of Development Centre, 1964-66; director, Twentieth Century Fund Study on development, 1966-69; visiting professor, University of California, Berkeley, 1968; Development Advisory Service, (Pakistan and Ghana), Harvard University, 1969-71; Organization for European Co-operation and Development, Paris, 1971—. Consultant to United Nations Food and Agriculture Organization, 1952, Twentieth Century Fund, 1956-58, and United Nations Commission for Asia and the Far East, 1962. *Military service:* Royal Air Force, 1948-49; pilot officer.

WRITINGS: (Contributor) *Europe's Needs and Resources*, Twentieth Century, 1961; (contributor) *Problems of Long-Term Economic Projections*, United Nations Commission for Asia and the Far East, 1963; (contributor) *Planning Education for Economic and Social Development*, Organization for Economic Co-operation and Development, 1963; *Economic Growth in the West*, Twentieth Century, 1964; (contributor) *Labor Productivity*, edited by J. T. Dunlop and V. P. Diatchenko, McGraw, 1964; (contributor) *Motivations and Methods in Development and Foreign Aid*, Society for International Development (Washington, D.C.), 1964; *The Contribution of Foreign Skills, Training, and Technical Assistance to Economic Development*, Development Centre, Organization for Economic Co-operation and Development, 1965; (with A. D. Stavrianopoulos and Benjamin Higgins) *Technical Assistance and the Economic Development of Greece*, Development Centre, Organization for European Co-operation and Development, 1965; *Economic Growth in Japan and the U.S.S.R.*, Allen & Unwin, 1969; *Economic Progress and Policy in Developing Countries*, Allen & Unwin, 1970; (editor) *Myrdal's Asian Drama: An Interdisciplinary Critique*, Ciriec (Brussels), 1971; *Class Structure and Economic Growth*, Allen & Unwin, 1972; *Economic Performance and Policy in Europe, 1913-70*, Fontana, 1973.

Contributor of articles and reviews to economic and banking journals.

WORK IN PROGRESS: A study of the future of capitalism.

* * *

MADELUNG, A. Margaret (Arent) 1926-

PERSONAL: Born August 3, 1926, in Evanston, Ill.; daughter of Lynton E. (a commercial artist) and Alice (Sheffer) Arent; married Wilferd F. Madelung (a professor); children: Michael. *Education:* Carleton College, B.A., 1948; University of Chicago, M.A., 1951, Ph.D., 1961. *Home:* 547 Keystone, River Forest, Ill., 60305.

CAREER: Instructor in German at Carleton College, Northfield, Minn., 1952-54, University of Chicago, Chicago, Ill., 1955-58; University of Texas, Austin, instructor, 1960-61, assistant professor of Germanic languages, 1961-64. *Awards, honors:* Germanistic Society of America fellowship to Zurich, Switzerland, 1948-49; City of Oslo award for summer study, 1957; Fulbright grant to Iceland, 1958-59; University of Texas Research Institute grants, 1961, 1963.

WRITINGS: (Translator) *The Laxdoela Saga*, University of Washington Press and American Scandinavian Foundation, 1964; (contributor) Edgar C. Polome, editor, *Old Norse Literature and Mythology: A Symposium*, University of Texas Press, 1969; *The Laxdoela Saga: Its Structural Patterns*, University of North Carolina Press, 1972; (contributor) John Weinstock, editor, *Snorri Sturluson and Laxdoela: The Hero's Accoutrements*, Jenkins, 1972.

WORK IN PROGRESS: Two books, *Snorri Sturluson's Mirror of the Thirteenth Century*, and *Snorri Sturluson's Philosophy of History*.

SIDELIGHTS: Ms. Madelung has traveled in the interior of Iceland in 1959, 1961, and 1963 and spent eight months in Persia in 1972-73. She reads and understands Icelandic, French, Swedish, Danish, and Norwegian. *Avocational interests:* Fine arts, geology, photography, and travelogues with slides.

*   *   *

MAGGS, Will(iam) Colston 1912-

PERSONAL: Born March 19, 1912, in Bristol, England; son of Thomas William (a market gardener) and Alice Maud (Hayes) Maggs; married Doreen Elnora Dunnings, December 18, 1944; children: Robert, Penelope, Paul, Jennifer. *Education:* Studied at Tyndale Hall, 1934-37. *Home:* Bedworth Rectory, near Nuneaton, Warwickshire, England.

CAREER: Clergyman of Church of England. Missionary in Burma, 1937-42; chaplain in Madras, India, 1942-45; rector of Bedworth, Nuneaton, Warwickshire, England, beginning 1952; rural dean of Bedworth Deanery, beginning 1963. Chairman of Coventry Diocese Prison-Gate Mission. *Member:* Rotary Club (Bedworth).

WRITINGS: *Head Hunters' Moon*, Pathfinder Press, 1958; *Jewel of Destiny*, Pathfinder Press, 1961. Author of plays on Bible themes; contributor of serials to *Church of England Newspaper.*†

*   *   *

MAGLOIRE-SAINT-AUDE, Clement 1912-

PERSONAL: Born April 2, 1912, in Port-au-Prince, Haiti; son of Clement (a journalist) and Leonie (Saint-Aude) Magloire; divorced; children: Helene (Mrs. Daniel Holly). *Education:* Institution Saint-Louis de Gonzague, Port-au-Prince, Haiti, baccalaureate, 1930. *Address:* c/o *Le Nouvelliste*, Rue du Centre, Port-au-Prince, Haiti.

CAREER: Employed by Service d'Information et de Documentation (SID), beginning 1958.

WRITINGS—In French: *Dialogue de mes lampes* (poems), Presses Nationales d'Haiti (Port-au-Prince), 1941, 3rd edition, [Paris], 1970; *Tabou* (poems), Seminaire Adventiste (Port-au-Prince), 1941; *Parias* (documentary), Presses Nationales d'Haiti, 1949; *Ombres et reflets* (chronicles), Le Reveil (Port-au-Prince), 1952; *Veillee* (fiction),

Renelle (Port-au-Prince), 1956; *Dechu* (poems), Renelle, 1956. Contributor to *Le Nouvelliste* and *Haiti-Journal*.

In English: (Contributor) *From the Green Antilles*, edited by Barbara Howes, Macmillan, 1966.

WORK IN PROGRESS: Le Bistrot, fiction.

BIOGRAPHICAL/CRITICAL SOURCES: Andre Breton, *La Clef des champs*, Edition du Sagittaire (Paris), 1952; *Le Surrealisme, Meme*, Number 1, 1956.†

*   *   *

MAHAR, J. Michael 1929-

PERSONAL: Born August 21, 1929, in Portland, Ore.; son of James Francis and Irene (Hayward) Mahar; married Mary A. Gooch, June 8, 1961 (divorced); married Carolyn McWhorter, 1973; children: (first marriage) James Daniel; (second marriage) Eve Elizabeth. *Education:* Reed College, B.A., 1953; Cornell University, Ph.D., 1966. *Politics:* Socialist. *Home:* 2404 East 2nd, Tucson, Ariz.

CAREER: University of Arizona, Tucson, assistant professor beginning 1958, professor of Oriental studies, 1967—. Participant in Cornell University study of a village in North India, 1954-56. *Member:* American Anthropological Association, American Ethnological Society, Association for Asian Studies, American Civil Liberties Union (president of Arizona affiliate, 1962, 1964).

WRITINGS: India: A Critical Bibliography, University of Arizona Press, 1964; (editor and contributor) *The Untouchables in Contemporary India*, University of Arizona Press, 1972.

WORK IN PROGRESS: Patterns of employment in the northern Gangetic plain of India.

*   *   *

MAHONEY, Robert F. 1914-

PERSONAL: Born September 22, 1914, in West Bridgewater, Mass.; son of Francis A. (a shoe stitcher) and Margaret (May) Mahoney; married Clara Locke (a nurse), June 8, 1939; children: Roberta Locke (Mrs. W. Norman Pulaski). *Education:* McLean Hospital School of Nursing, Waverley, Mass., R.N., 1936; Boston University, B.S.N., 1950, Ed.M., 1955. *Home:* 157 Hersey St., Hingham, Mass. 02034.

CAREER: Worcester County Health Association, Worcester, Mass.,1948-56, became executive director; U.S. Veterans Administration Hospitals, associate chief of nursing service for education, Rutland Heights, Mass., 1956-60, Boston, Mass., 1960—. *Military service:* U.S. Army, 1945-46. *Member:* National League for Nursing, American Nurses Association, Massachusetts Nurses Association, Massachusetts League for Nursing, Massachusetts Lung Association.

WRITINGS: Emergency and Disaster Nursing, Macmillan, 1965, 2nd edition, 1968. Contributor to professional journals.

*   *   *

MAHONEY, Thomas H(enry) D(onald) 1913-

PERSONAL: Born November 4, 1913, in Cambridge, Mass; son of Thomas Henry, Jr. (with U.S. Department of Agriculture) and Frances (Lucy) Mahoney; married Phyllis Norton, July 14, 1951; children: Thomas H. D. IV, Linda, David, Peter, Philip. *Education:* Boston College, A.B., 1936, A.M., 1937; George Washington University, Ph.D.,

1944; Harvard University, M.P.A., 1967. *Politics:* Democrat. *Religion:* Roman Catholic. *Office:* Office 14N-333, Massachusetts Institute of Technology, Cambridge, Mass. 02139.

CAREER: Instructor at Gonzaga School, 1937-39, and Dunbarton College, 1938-39, both Washington, D.C.; Boston College, Boston, Mass., assistant professor of history, 1939-44; College of the Holy Cross, Worcester, Mass., assistant professor of history, 1944-46; Massachusetts Institute of Technology, Cambridge, Mass., 1945—, now professor of history and chairman of history section. Visiting lecturer in history and government at Smith College, 1944-45, Wellesley College, 1947-48; summer professor at University of Southern California, 1950. Lowell Lecturer, Boston, Mass., 1957. Carnegie Fellow in Law and History, Harvard Law School, 1965-66. Member of Cambridge School Committee, 1948-54, Cambridge Planning Board, 1960-64, Cambridge City Council, 1964—. Member of Massachusetts State Fulbright Commission, 1952—; trustee of Cambridge Library, 1948-54, Massachusetts State Library, 1950—; member of corporation of Mount Auburn Hospital, 1952—, Cambridgeport Savings Bank, 1955—, Cambridge Savings Bank, 1964—; representative, Massachusetts General Court, 1971—.

MEMBER: American Historical Association, American Catholic Historical Association (president, 1957), Conference on British Studies, Catholic Commission on Cultural and Intellectual Affairs, Royal Historical Society (fellow). *Awards, honors:* American Council of Learned Societies Fellow; Carnegie Fellow; Guggenheim Fellow.

WRITINGS: (With J. B. Rae) *The United States in World History*, McGraw, 1948, 3rd edition, McGraw, 1964; (with Rae) *Readings in International Order*, Massachusetts Institute of Technology Press, 1951; (with M. E. Cameron and G. E. McReynolds) *China, Japan and the Powers*, Ronald, 1952, 2nd edition, Ronald, 1960; (editor) *Burke's Reflections on the Revolution in France*, Bobbs, 1955; *Edmund Burke and Ireland*, Harvard University Press, 1960; (editor) *Selected Writings and Speeches on America by Edmund Burke*, Bobbs, 1964. Also contributor to *Edmund Burke: The Enlightenment and the Modern World*, 1967.

WORK IN PROGRESS: A book on Edmund Burke and the American Revolution.

*   *   *

MAIR, George Brown   1914-
(Robertson MacDouall)

PERSONAL: Born May 27, 1914, in Troon, Scotland; son of Alexander (a businessman) and Catherine (Robertson) Mair; married Geertruide van der Poest Clement, February 21, 1940; children: Alexander Craig van der Poest Clement, George Leonard Robertson. *Education:* University of Glasgow, M.B. and Ch.B., 1936, M.D. and F.R.C.S. (Edinburgh), 1939, F.R.F.P.S. (Glasgow), 1943. *Religion:* Theist. *Home:* Upper Kinneil House, Old Polmont, Stirlingshire, Scotland. *Agent:* Scottish Lecture Agency, Brisbane Street, Greenock, Scotland; Lawrence Pollinger Ltd., 18 Maddox St., Mayfair, London.

CAREER: University of Durham, Durham, England, assistant professor of surgery, 1945-46; Law Hospital, Lanarkshire, Scotland, surgeon, 1946-53; director of medical clinic in central Scotland, 1954-68. Celebrity lecturer on Pacific and Orient Lines summer cruises, 1953-72. Leader of Royal Scottish Geographical Society expeditions to Greece, Turkey, and Anatolia. Former examiner, General Nursing Council, Scotland; former demonstrator-lecturer in anatomy, University of Glasgow. *Member:* British Medical Association, Crime Writers Association, Mystery Writers of America, Guild of Travel Writers, P.E.N. (Scotland), Society of Authors, National Book League.

WRITINGS: Surgery for Abdominal Hernia, E. J. Arnold, 1948; *Surgeon's Saga*, Heinemann, 1950; *Doctor Goes East*, P. Owen, 1952; *Doctor Goes North*, P. Owen, 1958; *Doctor Goes West*, P. Owen, 1958.

Destination Moscow, Jenkins, 1960; *Doctor in Turkey*, R. Hale, 1961; *The Day Khrushchev Panicked*, Random, 1962; *Death's Foot Forward*, Random, 1963; *Miss Turquoise*, Random, 1964; *Live Love and Cry*, Jarrolds, 1965; *Kisses from Satan*, Jarrolds, 1965; *The Girl from Peking*, Jarrolds, 1967; *Black Champagne*, Jarrolds, 1968; *Goddesses Never Die*, Jarrolds, 1969.

A Wreath of Camellias, Jarrolds, 1970; *Crimson Jade*, Jarrolds, 1971; *Paradise Spells Danger*, Jarrolds, 1973; *Confessions of a Surgeon*, Luscombe, 1974; *Arranging and Enjoying Your Package Holiday*, New English Library, in press. Contributor to medical journals and to travel and popular magazines.

WORK IN PROGRESS: Escape From Surgery, to be a sequel to *Confessions of a Surgeon* and the second book of a proposed trilogy.

SIDELIGHTS: Mair has researched seventy-six countries and has lectured on thirty-seven. He is one of the few travelers in the past several decades to visit the Spanish Sahara (Rio de Oro), and Karakorum in the Himalayan state of Hunaz (Shangri-la). Mair and his wife traveled to the seldom visited matriarchal society of the Trobriand Islands. He is currently working on establishing international Faculties of Tourism for the training of guides serving tourists. *Avocational interests:* Collecting Georgian and earlier antiques, Sevres porcelain, and symbols of religious worhsip in pre-history, with emphasis on Minoan, Hittite, Buddhist, and Athenian civilizations.

BIOGRAPHICAL/CRITICAL SOURCES: Glasgow Evening Citizen, February 13, 1963.

*   *   *

MAJOR, John M(cClellan)   1918-

PERSONAL: Born October 20, 1918, in Rochester, N.Y.; son of George Alexander and Della (Page) Major. *Education:* Syracuse University, A.B., 1939, M.A., 1940; Harvard University, Ph.D., 1954. *Politics:* Democrat. *Home:* 950 Sixth St., Boulder, Colo. *Office:* Department of English, University of Colorado, Boulder, Colo. 80302.

CAREER: Oberlin College, Oberlin, Ohio, instructor in English, 1950-53; Duke University, Durham, N.C., instructor in English, 1954-57; University of Colorado, Boulder, associate professor, beginning 1957, now professor of English. *Military service:* U.S. Army, 1941-45; became captain; received Purple Heart and Air Medal. U.S. Army Reserve, 1945-64; now lieutenant colonel in Retired Reserve. *Member:* Modern Language Association of America, Renaissance Society of America, Milton Society of America.

WRITINGS: Sir Thomas Elyot and Renaissance Humanism, University of Nebraska Press, 1964. Contributor of articles on English literature of Renaissance period to scholarly journals; book review editor of *English Language Notes*.

WORK IN PROGRESS: Writing on Milton and other poets of the English Renaissance, and on the humanism of the period.

AVOCATIONAL INTERESTS: Politics, civil liberties, gardening, tennis, swimming, ice skating.

* * *

MALIN, Irving 1934-

PERSONAL: Born March 18, 1934, in New York, N.Y.; son of Morris and Bertha (Silverman) Malin; married Ruth Lief; children: Mark Charles. Education: Queens College (now Queens College of the City University of New York), B.A., 1955; Stanford University, Ph.D., 1958. Home: 96-13 68 Ave., Forest Hills, N.Y. 11375. Office: City College of the City University of New York, New York, N.Y. 10031.

CAREER: Stanford University, Stanford, Calif., acting instructor in English, 1955-56, 1957-58; Indiana University, Bloomington, instructor in English, 1958-60; City College of the City University of New York, New York, N.Y., assistant professor, 1960-69, associate professor, 1969-72, professor of English, 1972—. Member: Modern Language Association of America, Melville Society, American Jewish Historical Society, Society for the Study of Southern Literature, P.E.N., Authors' Guild, English Institute, American Studies Association, American Association of University Professors, Phi Beta Kappa. Awards, honors: Yaddo fellowship, 1963; National Foundation for Jewish Culture fellowship, 1963-64.

WRITINGS: William Faulkner: An Interpretation, Stanford University Press, 1957; New American Gothic, Southern Illinois University Press, 1962; (co-editor) Breakthrough: A Treasury of Contemporary American Jewish Literature, McGraw and Jewish Publication Society, 1964; Jews and Americans, Southern Illinois University Press, 1965; (editor) Psychoanalysis and American Fiction, Dutton, 1965; (editor) Saul Bellow and the Critics, New York University Press, 1967; (editor) Truman Capote's "In Cold Blood": A Critical Handbook, Wadsworth, 1968; (editor) Critical Views of Isaac Bashevis Singer, New York University Press, 1969; Saul Bellow's Fiction, Southern Illinois University Press, 1969; (editor with Melvin J. Friedman) William Styron's "The Confessions of Nat Turner": A Critical Handbook, Wadsworth, 1970; Nathanael West's Novels, Southern Illinois University Press, 1972; Isaac Bashevis Singer, Ungar, 1972; (editor) Contemporary American Jewish Literature: Critical Essays, Indiana University Press, 1973; (editor) The Achievement of Carson McCullers, Everett/Edwards, 1974; (co-editor) The Achievement of William Styron, University of Georgia Press, 1974.

Contributor: Neil D. Isaacs and Louis Leiter, editors, Approaches to the Short Story, Chandler Publishing, 1963; Frederick Utley, Lynn Bloom, and Arthur Kinney, editors, Bear, Man, and God: Eight Approaches to Faulkner's "The Bear," Random House, 1963; Lily Edelman, editor, Jewish Heritage Reader, Taplinger, 1965; Charles Shapiro, editor, Contemporary British Novelists, Southern Illinois University Press, 1965; Melvin J. Friedman and Lewis A. Lawson, editors, The Added Dimension, Fordham University Press, 1966; David Madden, editor, Tough Guy Writers of the Thirties, Southern Illinois University Press, 1968; M. T. Inge, editor, William Faulkner: "A Rose for Emily," Bobbs-Merrill, 1970; Madden, editor, American Dreams, American Nightmares, Southern Illinois University Press, 1970; Friedman, editor, The Vision Obscured, Fordham University Press, 1970; James L. Green, editor, John Hawkes, Everett/Edwards, 1974; Earl Kovit, editor, Saul Bellow, Prentice-Hall, 1974.

Contributor to Encyclopedia Judaica and to Books Abroad, London Magazine, Kenyon Review, Shenandoah, Jewish Heritage, Reconstructionist, Saturday Review, Nation, New Republic, Commonweal, American Scholar, Midstream, and others.

WORK IN PROGRESS: A book on Elie Wiesel.

* * *

MANDLER, Jean Matter 1929-

PERSONAL: Born November 6, 1929, in Oak Park, Ill.; daughter of Joseph Allen (an attorney) and May (Finch) Matter; married George Mandler (a professor), January 19, 1957; children: Peter Clark, Michael Allen. Education: Attended Carleton College, 1947-49; Swarthmore College, B.A. (with highest honors), 1951; Harvard University, Ph.D., 1956. Office: Department of Psychology, University of California at San Diego, La Jolla, Calif. 92037.

CAREER: Harvard University, Cambridge, Mass., U.S. Public Health Service postdoctoral fellow, 1956-57, research associate in psychology, 1957-60; University of Toronto, Toronto, Ontario, research associate in psychology, 1960-65; University of California at San Diego, La Jolla, associate research psychologist, 1965-73, lecturer, 1967-73, associate professor of psychology, 1973—. Member: American Psychological Association, Psychonomic Society, Society for Research in Child Development, Phi Beta Kappa. Awards, honors: American Association for University Women honor fellow, 1971-72.

WRITINGS: (With husband, George Mandler) Thinking: From Association to Gestalt, Wiley, 1964; (contributor) Donald Fleming and Bernard Bailyn, editors, The Intellectual Migration, Harvard University Press, 1969. Contributor to professional journals. Associate editor, Psychological Review, 1970—.

WORK IN PROGRESS: Research on cognitive development.

* * *

MANGIONE, Jerre 1909-

PERSONAL: Born March 20, 1909, in Rochester, N.Y.; son of Gaspare (a house painter and paperhanger) and Giuseppina (Polizzi) Mangione; married Patricia Anthony (an artist), February 18, 1957. Education: Syracuse University, B.A., 1931. Home: 1901 Walnut St., Philadelphia, Pa. 19103. Agent: Russell & Volkening, Inc., 551 Fifth Ave., New York, N.Y. 10017.

CAREER: Time, New York, N.Y., staff writer, 1931; Robert M. McBride & Co. (publishers), New York, N.Y., book editor, 1934-37; Federal Writers Project, Washington, D.C., national coordinating editor, 1937-39; public relations specialist, Census Bureau, U.S. Department of Commerce, 1939; U.S. Department of Justice, information specialist, 1940, member of public relations staff, 1941-42; U.S. Immigration and Naturalization Service, Washington, D.C., and Philadelphia, Pa., special assistant to commissioner, 1942-48, editor-in-chief of official publication, Monthly Review, 1945-47; writer for advertising and public relations offices, including N. W. Ayer & Son, Inc., and Columbia Broadcasting System Television, New York, N.Y., and Philadelphia, Pa., 1948-61; University of Pennsylvania, Philadelphia, director of freshman composition, 1961-63, associate professor, 1963-68, professor of English, 1968—, director of creative writing program, 1967—. Visiting lecturer, Bryn Mawr College, 1966-67; visiting professor, Trinity College, Rome, Italy, summer, 1973. Lecturer at Smith College, Le Moyne College, La Salle College, Ursinus College, Haverford College, Pennsylvania State University, Moore College of Art, Queens College of the City University of New York, and Barnard College. Judge, National Book Award in fiction, 1969. Member of board, Institute of Contemporary Art, University of Pennsylvania, 1964—.

MEMBER: Authors Guild, American Association of University Professors, P.E.N., Society of American Historians (fellow), American Friends of Danilo Dolci (president, 1969-72), America-Italy Society (member of Board, 1959—), American Institute of Italian Studies (member of board, 1975—), Philadelphia Art Alliance, Pi Delta Epsilon. *Awards, honors:* Yaddo creative writing fellowships, 1939, 1944, 1946, 1962, 1964, 1965, 1972; Guggenheim fellowship, 1945; MacDowell Colony creative writing fellowships, 1957, 1958, 1959, 1960, 1964, 1967, 1971, 1974; received key to city of Rochester, N.Y., 1963; Fulbright research fellowship in Sicily, 1965; Friends of the Rochester Public Library award, 1966, for *Night Search*; Rockefeller Foundation research grant, 1968-69; Commendatore decoration from Italian Republic, 1971; M.A., University of Pennsylvania, 1971; American Philosophical Society research grant, 1972; National Book Award in history nomination, for *The Dream and the Deal*; Philadelphia Athenaeum award for literature, 1973.

WRITINGS: Mount Allegro, Houghton, 1943, 2nd edition (introduction by Dorothy Canfield Fisher), Knopf, 1952, 4th edition (introduction by Maria Cimino), Crown, 1972; *The Ship and the Flame*, Current Books, 1948; *Reunion in Sicily*, Houghton, 1950; *Night Search*, Crown, 1965 (published in England as *To Walk the Night*, Muller, 1967); *Life Sentences for Everybody* (satiric fables), Abelard, 1965; *A Passion for Sicilians: The World Around Danilo Dolci*, Morrow, 1968, published as *The World Around Danilo Dolci*, Harper, 1972; *America Is Also Italian*, Putnam, 1969; *The Dream and the Deal: Federal Writers Project, 1936-43*, Little, Brown, 1972; *Mussolini's March on Rome*, F. Watts, 1975.

Work is represented in anthologies, including *Children of the Uprooted*, edited by Oscar Handlin, Braziller, 1966, and *Nation of Nations: The Ethnic Experience and the Racial Crisis*, edited by Peter I. Rose, Random House, 1971.

Contributor of articles and short stories to *Esquire, Holiday, Saturday Review, Mademoiselle, Harper's Bazaar*, and other magazines. Regular book reviewer for *New York Herald Tribune Books*, 1931-35, *New Republic*, 1931-37, *Pennsylvania Traveler*, 1959-60, and occasional reviewer for *New York Times Book Review, Washington Post Book World, Philadelphia Inquirer*, and *Philadelphia Bulletin*. Editor-in-chief, *WFLN Philadelphia Guide*, 1960-62. Advisory editor, *Italian Americana*, 1974—.

WORK IN PROGRESS: An Ethnic at Large, a combination memoir and history dealing with the thirties and forties, completion expected in 1976.

SIDELIGHTS: Mangione visited Sicily in 1965 and worked with Danilo Dolci for six months before writing *A Passion for Sicilians*. "Mangione," writes Walter Guzzardi in *Saturday Review*, "has done a sound, creditable, straight-forward report on Dolci and the people around him.... His style is direct and blessedly unadorned, in the

tradition of good journalism . . . , and he has undoubtedly caught the spirit of Dolci." Gavin Maxwell finds *A Passion for Sicilians* "utterly absorbing and permeated with the very spirit of Sicily as I know it. The apparently artless construction is craftsmanship of the highest order, and the dialogues are so convincing that I was amazed to be assured that the Professor Mangione carried no tape recorder."

Mangione told *CA* "I write to please myself. For this reason I prefer writing books to short stories and articles, and shun magazine editors as much as possible. Whether it be a book of fiction or nonfiction, I write each one as though it were going to be my last. One more observation: when I am writing fiction I can hardly wait to write nonfiction, and vice versa. In that respect I am like Italo Svevo's character Zeno, who when he was with his mistress yearned to be with his wife, and vice versa."

Mount Allegro was published in Argentina and Italy, and *The Ship and the Flame* in Sweden.

BIOGRAPHICAL/CRITICAL SOURCES: Olga Peragallo, *Italian-American Authors and Their Contributions to American Literature*, S. F. Vanni, 1949; *Saturday Review*, July 1, 1950; Lawrence Frank Pisani, *The Italian in America*, Exposition, 1957; *Pennsylvania Gazette* (University of Pennsylvania), December, 1963; *Philadelphia Evening Bulletin*, May 25, 1965; *Delaware Valley Calendar* (Philadelphia, Pa.), November, 1965; *Metropolitan Magazine* (Philadelphia), December, 1972; *Upstate New York Magazine* (Rochester), March 4, 1973; *Today Magazine (Philadelphia Inquirer)*, April 15, 1973; Rose Basile Green, *The Italian-American Novel*, Fairleigh Dickinson University Press, 1974.

* * *

MANKIEWICZ, Don M(artin) 1922-

PERSONAL: Surname is pronounced *Mank*-uh-witz; born January 20, 1922, in Berlin, Germany; son of American nationals, Herman J. and Sara (Aaronson) Mankiewicz; married Ilene Korsen, March 26, 1946 (divorced, 1972); married Carol Bell Guidi, July 1, 1972; children: (first marriage) Jane, John. *Education:* Columbia University, B.A., 1942, additional study at Law School. *Poltics:* Democrat. *Home and office:* 2 Prospect Ave., Sea Cliff, L.I., N.Y. 11579. *Agent:* Harold Ober Associates, 40 East 49th St., New York, N.Y. 10017.

CAREER: New Yorker, New York, N.Y., reporter, 1946-48; free-lance writer, 1948—. Active in New York Democratic Party politics, 1948—; Democratic-Liberal candidate for New York Assembly, 1952; vice-chairman, Nassau County Democratic Committee, 1953-72. Delegate-At-Large, New York State Constitutional Convention, 1967. *Military service:* U.S. Army, 1942-46; became staff sergeant. *Member:* Writers Guild, National Academy of Television Arts and Sciences. *Awards, honors:* Harper Prize Novel Award ($10,000) for *Trial*, 1954; Academy of Motion Picture Arts and Sciences nomination, 1959, for "I Want to Live", Television Academy Award nominations, 1966, for "Ironside," and 1968, for "Marcus Welby, M.D."

WRITINGS: See How They Run, Knopf, 1950; *Trial*, Harper, 1955; *It Only Hurts a Minute*, Putnam, 1967.

Motion pictures: "Trial," 1956; (with Nelson Giddings) "I Want to Live," 1959. Author of television plays for "Studio One," "Playhouse 90," Kraft Theatre," "Armstrong Theatre," "Profiles in Courage," and other programs. Also author of television pilot films, "Ironside," "Marcus Welby, M.D.," and "Sarge: The Badge or the Cross." Contributor of articles and stories to *Collier's, Cosmopolitan, Esquire, Saturday Evening Post*, and other national magazines.

*   *   *

MANNING, Bayless Andrew   1923-

PERSONAL: Born March 29, 1923, in Bristow, Okla; son of Raphael Andrew and Helen Mahala (Guffy) Manning; married Marjorie Jolivette, July 10, 1945; children: Bayless, Jr., Elizabeth, Lucia, Matthew. *Education:* Yale University, A.B., 1943, LL.B., 1949. *Office:* School of Law, Stanford University, Stanford, Calif.

CAREER: Member of District of Columbia, Ohio, and Connecticut bars. Law clerk to Supreme Court Justice Stanley F. Reed, 1949-50; Jones, Day, Cockley & Reavis, Cleveland, Ohio, attorney, 1950-56; Yale University, School of Law, New Haven, Conn., associate professor, 1956-60, professor, 1960-64; Stanford University, School of Law, Stanford, Calif., dean, beginning 1964. Special assistant to U.S. Under Secretary of State, 1962-63; member of President's Advisory Panel on Ethics and Conflict of Interest in Government, 1961; consultant to U.S. Department of Commerce on Trade Expansion Act of 1962. *Military service:* U.S. Army, Signal Corps, Intelligence, Japanese translator, 1943-46. *Member:* Phi Beta Kappa, Order of the Coif.

WRITINGS: (Staff director) *Conflict of Interest and Federal Service*, Harvard University Press, 1960; *Federal Conflict of Interest Law*, Harvard University Press, 1964. Also author of *A Short Textbook on Legal Capital*, 1968. Editor-in-chief, *Yale Law Journal*, 1949. Contributor to law journals, mainly articles on aspects of corporation law.†

*   *   *

MANNIX, Edward   1928-

PERSONAL: Born July 26, 1928, in Jersey City, N.J.; son of Edward (a contractor) and Marie (Bingle) Mannix; divorced; children: Lauren. *Agent:* McIntosh & Otis, Inc., 18 East 41st St., New York, N.Y. 10017.

CAREER: Writer. *Military service:* U.S. Navy, 1945-49.

WRITINGS: An End to Fury (novel), Dial, 1959; *A Journal of Love* (novel), Dial, 1964; *The Widow* (novel), World Publishing, 1970. Also author of a screen adaption of *A Journal of Love.*

WORK IN PROGRESS: A novel entitled *The Lovewright.*

*   *   *

MANTEL, Samuel J(oseph), Jr.   1921-

PERSONAL: Surname is pronounced Man-*tell*; born November 17, 1921, in Indianapolis Ind.; son of Samuel Joseph (a lawyer) and Beatrice (Talmas) Mantel; married Dorothy Jean Friedland, June 28, 1950; children: Michael L., Samuel J. III, Margaret I., Elizabeth B. *Education:* Attended Harvard University, 1940-42, 1946-48, A.B., 1948, M.P.A., 1950, Ph.D., 1952. *Religion:* Jewish. *Home:* 608 Flagstaff Dr., Cincinnati, Ohio 45215.

CAREER: Georgia Institute of Technology, Atlanta, assistant professor of social science, 1953-56; Case Institute of Technology (now Case Western Reserve University), Cleveland, Ohio, assistant professor of economics, 1956-59,

director of Economics-in-Action program, 1956-68, associate professor, 1959-69; University of Cincinnati, Cincinnati, Ohio, professor of management and quantitative analysis, 1969—, Joseph S. Stern Professor of Management, 1973—. Life member of board, Cleveland Hillel Foundation, member of board, Jewish Hospital, Jewish Family Service Bureau. *Military service:* U.S. Marine Corps, pilot, 1942-46, 1951-53; became major; received Distinguished Flying Cross and three oak leaf clusters, Air Medal and eleven oak leaf clusters, Presidential Unit Citation, and Navy Citation.

MEMBER: American Economic Association, American Academy of Political and Social Science, American Association of University Professors, Midwest Economic Association, Econometric Society, Sports Car Club of America, Gamma Alpha, Sigma Xi, Sigma Iota Epsilon. *Awards, honors:* Economics-in-Action fellowship, 1955; Outstanding Educator of America, 1972; Delta Sigma Pi Professor of the Year, 1974.

WRITINGS: (Contributor) *Principles of Economics*, Pitman, 1959; *Cases in Managerial Decisions*, Prentice-Hall, 1964; (contributor) Alfandry-Alexander, editor, *Analysis and Program Planning Budgeting*, Washington Operations Research Council, 1968; (contributor) Mearovic and Reisman, editors, *Systems Approach and the City*, North-Holland, 1972; (contributor) Cetron, Davidson, and Rubenstein, editors, *Quantitative Decision Aiding Techniques for Research and Development Management*, Gordon & Breach, 1972; (contributor) Reisman and Kiley, editors, *Health Care Delivery Planning*, Gordon & Breach, 1973. Contributor to *Journal of Engineering Education, World Reporter, Ohio State Medical Journal, Technology and Culture, Journal of Jewish Communal Services*, and other periodicals.

WORK IN PROGRESS: Systems analysis and evaluation of social service systems.

*   *   *

MANTLE, Winifred (Langford)
(Anne Fellowes, Frances Lang, Jane Langford)

PERSONAL: Born in Merry Hill, Staffordshire, England; daughter of Joseph Langford and Florence (Fellows) Mantle. *Education:* Lady Margaret Hall, Oxford, B.A. (first class honors), and M.A.; also studied at University of Strasbourg. *Religion:* Church of England. *Home:* 51 Spring Hill Park, Penn, Wolverhampton, England.

CAREER: St. Katharine's Training College, Liverpool, England, lecturer in French, 1938-41; University of St. Andrews, St. Andrews, Scotland, assistant lecturer in French, 1941-46; full-time writer of novels and short stories, 1954—. *Member:* Society of Authors, Romantic Novelists' Association. *Awards, honors:* Award for best historical novel from Romantic Novelists' Association, 1961, for *A Pride of Princesses.*

WRITINGS: Happy is the House, Chatto & Windus, 1951; *Country Cousin*, Chatto & Windus, 1953; *Five Farthings*, Hurst & Blackett, 1958; *Kingsbarns*, Hurst & Blackett, 1959; *Lords and Ladies*, Hurst & Blackett, 1959; *The Hiding-Place* (juvenile), Gollancz, 1962, Holt, 1963; *Griffin Lane*, Hurst & Blackett, 1962; *Sandy Smith* (juvenile), Benn, 1963; *Bennet's Hill*, Hurst & Blackett, 1963; *Tinker's Castle* (juvenile), Gollancz, 1963, Holt, 1964; *The Chateau Holiday* (juvenile), Gollancz, 1964; *The River Runs*, Hurst & Blackett, 1964; *A View of Christowe*, Collins, 1965; *The Painted Cave*, Gollancz, 1965; *The Same*

Way Home, Collins, 1966; *The Penderel House* (juvenile), Holt, 1966; *Summer at Temple Quentin*, Collins, 1967; *The Admiral's Wood* (juvenile), Gollancz, 1967; *Winter at Wycliffe*, Collins, 1968; *Piper's Row* (juvenile), Gollancz, 1968; *The May Tree*, Collins, 1969; *A Fair Exchange*, Collins, 1970; *The House in the Lane*, R. Hale, 1972; *Jonnesty* (juvenile), Chatto & Windus, 1973; *Jonnesty in Winter* (juvenile), Chatto & Windus, in press; *The Inconvenient Marriage*, R. Hale, in press.

Under pseudonym Anne Fellowes; all published by Mills & Boon: *The Morning Dew*, 1957; *Green Willow, 1958;* The Keys of Heaven, *1958.*

Under pseudonym Frances Lang: *Marriage of Masks*, Hurst & Blackett, 1960; *A Pride of Princesses*, Hurst & Blackett, 1961; *The Sun in Splendour*, Hurst & Blackett, 1962; *The Leaping Lords*, Hurst & Blackett, 1963; *Blind Man's Buff*, Collins, 1965; *The Marrying Month*, Collins, 1965; *The Well-Wisher*, Collins, 1967; *The Duke's Daughter*, Collins, 1967; *The Malcontent*, Collins, 1968; *Double Dowry*, Collins, 1970; *The Tower of Remicourt*, R. Hale, 1971; *Milord Macdonald*, R. Hale, 1973; *The Marquis's Marriage*, R. Hale, in press; *Stranger at the Gate*, R. Hale, in press.

Under pseudonym Jane Langford; all published by Mills & Boon: *Haste to the Wedding*, 1955; *The Secret Fairing*, 1956; *King of the Castle*, 1956; *Half-Way House*, 1957; *Promise of Marriage*, 1957; *One Small Flower*, 1958; *Strange Adventure*, 1958; *Weather House*, 1958; *Change of Tune*, 1959; *Happy Return*, 1960.

Writer of short stories under pseudonyms Anne Fellowes and Jane Langford.

WORK IN PROGRESS: A book *The Beckoning Maiden.*

SIDELIGHTS: Winifred Mantle's books have been serialized in many countries, including England, South Africa, Australia, France, Sweden, Canada, and Denmark. She is competent in French and German.

*   *   *

MARCH, James Gardner   1928-

PERSONAL: Born January 15, 1928, in Cleveland, Ohio; son of James H. (a professor, University of Wisconsin) and Mildred (MacCorkle) March; married Jayne Dohr, September 23, 1947; children: Kathryn S., Gary C., James C., Roderic G. *Education:* University of Wisconsin, B.A., 1949; Yale University, M.A., 1950, Ph.D., 1953. *Home:* 837 Tolman Dr., Stanford, Calif. 94305. *Office:* Stanford University, Stanford, Calif. 94305.

CAREER: Carnegie Institute of Technology, Pittsburgh, Pa., senior research fellow, 1953-55, assistant professor, 1955-57, associate professor, 1957-62, professor of industrial administration, 1962-64; University of California, Irvine, professor of psychology and sociology and dean of social sciences, 1964-70; Stanford University, Stanford, Calif., David Jacks Professor of Higher Education, Political Science, Sociology, and Business, 1970—. Visiting Distinguished Behavioral Scientist, Purdue University, 1965. Consultant to numerous companies and foundations, including Ford Foundation, National Science Foundation. *Military service:* U.S. Army, 1946-47; became staff sergeant. *Member:* American Political Science Association, American Sociological Association, American Psychological Association, American Economic Association, National Academy of Education, National Academy of Public Administration, National Academy of Sciences, National

Science Board, Phi Beta Kappa, Sigma Xi. *Awards, honors:* Fellow, Center for Advanced Study in the Behavioral Sciences, 1955-56; Ford Faculty Research fellow, 1961-62.

WRITINGS: (With Herbert A. Simon) *Organizations*, Wiley, 1958; (with Richard M. Cyert) *A Behavioral Theory of the Firm*, Prentice-Hall, 1963; (editor) *Handbook of Organizations*, Rand McNally, 1965; (with B. R. Gelbaum) *Mathematics for the Social and Behavioral Sciences*, Saunders, 1968; (with M. D. Cohen) *Leadership and Ambiguity*, McGraw, 1974.

Contributor: Heinz Eulau and others, editors, *Political Behavior*, Free Press of Glencoe, 1956; (with Cyert) Mason Haire, editor, *Modern Organization Theory*, Wiley, 1959; (with Cyert) *Contributions to Scientific Research in Management*, University of California at Los Angeles, 1960; (with Cyert) Bernard C. Lemke and J. D. Edwards, editors, *Administrative Control and Executive Action*, Prentice-Hall, 1961; (with Cyert) Beverly van Haller Gilmer, editor, *Industrial Psychology*, McGraw, 1961; Austin Rammey, editor, *Essays on the Behavioral Study of Politics*, University of Illinois Press, 1962; (with Cyert and C. Moore) Ronald E. Frank and others, editors, *Quantitative Techniques in Marketing Analysis*, Irwin, 1962; Lynton K. Caldwell, editor, *Politics and Public Affairs*, Institute of Training for Public Affairs, Indiana University, 1962; Glendon A. Schubert, editor, *Judicial Behavior*, Rand McNally, 1964; (with Cyert) William W. Cooper and others, editors, *New Perspectives in Organization Research*, Wiley, 1964; Paul F. Lazarsfeld and Neil W. Henry, editors, *Readings in Mathematical Social Science*, Science Research Associates, 1966; David Easton, editor, *Varieties of Political Theory*, Prentice-Hall, 1966.

Co-editor, Prentice-Hall monographs on the mathematical analysis of social behavior. Contributor to professional journals, including *Public Opinion Quarterly, Quarterly Journal of Economics, Stanford Law Review, Econometrica*, and *Behavioral Science*. Editorial associate, *American Political Science Review*, 1957-58; editorial consultant, *Sociometry*, 1958-61; member of editorial advisory board, *Journal of Politics*, 1961—, and *Interaction*, 1963—.

*   *   *

MARCH, William J.   1915-

PERSONAL: Born June 26, 1915, in Newfoundland, Canada; son of Abram (an inspector) and Sarah (Baker) March; married Effie Waye, 1935; children: Cecil Lawrence, William James, Raymond Lloyd. *Education:* Theological College, Queen's University, Kingston, Ontario, Canada, student, 1944-49; St. Andrews College, London, England, M.A., and D.T.H. *Home:* 32 Lakeshore Dr., Moonsburg, Ontario, Canada.

CAREER: Clergyman, United Church of Canada. Lecturer on industrial safety; broadcaster on religion and psychology. *Member:* Masons, Lions Club.

WRITINGS: Look Up! Lift Up, Eerdmans, 1959; *Christian Belief and Christian Practice*, Eerdmans, 1964. Author of newspaper articles on religion and life.

WORK IN PROGRESS: The Christian's Task in a Nuclear Age.†

*   *   *

MARCHAM, Frederick George   1898-

PERSONAL: Born November 20, 1898, in Reading, England; came to United States in 1923, naturalized in 1945; son of Frederick (a laborer) and Emma (Wheeler) Marcham; married Mary Cecilia Deacon, August 10, 1925; children: John, David, Ann. *Education:* Oxford University, B.A., 1923; Cornell University, Ph.D., 1926. *Home:* 112 Oak Hill Rd., Ithaca, N.Y. 14850.

CAREER: Cornell University, Ithaca, N.Y., instructor, 1923-28, assistant professor, 1928-30, professor of English history, 1930-42, Goldwin Smith Professor of English History, 1942-68, professor emeritus, 1968—, chairman of department, 1964-68. Mayor of Village of Cayuga Heights, N.Y., 1957—. *Military service:* British Army, 1917-20. *Member:* American Historical Association, Phi Beta Kappa, Phi Kappa Phi.

WRITINGS: History of England, Macmillan, 1937, 2nd edition, 1950; (with Carl Stephenson) *Sources of English Constitutional History,* Harper, 1937, 2nd edition, 1971; (contributor) D. C. Bryant, editor, *Rhetorical Idiom,* Cornell University Press, 1958; *A Constitutional History of Modern England,* Harper, 1960; (editor) *Louis Agassiz Fuertes and the Singular Beauty of Birds,* introduction by Roger Tory Peterson, Harper, 1971.

WORK IN PROGRESS: A study of the mind of Oliver Cromwell.

SIDELIGHTS: For twenty years, until 1959, Marcham also was boxing instructor at Cornell University. *Avocational interests:* Photography, collecting prints and drawings of the Old Masters, particularly the work of the seventeenth-century Dutch etcher, A. V. Ostade.

* * *

MARCHANT, Anyda 1911-

PERSONAL: Name is pronounced *Annee*da *Mar*-chant; born January 27, 1911, in Rio de Janeiro, Brazil; daughter of U.S. citizens, Langworthy (an educator and editor) and Maude Henrietta (Annett) Marchant. *Education:* National University, Washington, D.C., A.B. (with distinction), 1931, M.A., 1933, LL.B., 1936. *Politics:* Democrat. *Religion:* Episcopalian.

CAREER: Admitted to practice before bars of Virginia, District of Columbia, and U.S. Supreme Court; formerly attorney with law firms of Schuster & Feuille, New York, N.Y., and Covington & Burling, Washington, D.C.; Library of Congress, Washington, D.C., staff of law section, 1940-45; Light & Power Co., Rio de Janeiro, Brazil, legal staff, 1947-48; U.S. Department of Commerce, Washington, D.C., with Bureau of Foreign and Domestic Commerce, 1951-53; International Bank for Reconstruction and Development, Washington, D.C., legal staff, 1954—.

WRITINGS: (Contributor) T. Lynn Smith and Alexander Marchant, editors, *Brazil: Portrait of Half a Continent,* Dryden Press, 1951, revised edition, University of Florida Press, 1966; *Viscount Maua and the Empire of Brazil,* University of California Press, 1965. Contributor to *Hispanic American Historical Review, Frontiers, Americas, Southwest Review,* and other journals.

WORK IN PROGRESS: A social and horticultural history of the introduction of the tea rose from China into England and the United States.

SIDELIGHTS: Anyda Marchant speaks French, Portuguese, and Spanish; she knows some Italian. She has traveled extensively in Latin America, western Europe, and the Far East. *Avocational interests:* Popular horticulture and the history of horticultural research in South America.

MARCHANT, R(ex) A(lan) 1933-

PERSONAL: Born May 2, 1933, in Hastings, Sussex, England; son of Albert (a dairyman) and Lilian (Warren) Marchant; married Patricia Anne Buckland, April 9, 1958 (divorced, 1973). *Education:* Attended College of St. Mark and St. John, Chelsea, England, 1954-56. *Politics:* Conservative. *Religion:* Church of England. *Home:* 2 Eversfield Pl., St. Leonards on Sea, Sussex, England. *Agent:* A. M. Heath & Co. Ltd., 40-42 William IV St., London WC2N 4DD, England.

CAREER: Church of England Junior School, Bexhill of Sea, England, class teacher, 1958-73; Down Secondary School, Bexhill on Sea, English teacher, 1973—. *Military service:* Royal Air Force, interpreter, 1956-58; served in Iraq and Kurdistan. *Member:* Society of Authors, Fauna Preservation Society, Sussex Archeological Society, Sussex Trust for Nature Conservation, Old Hastonians Football Club (honorary secretary, 1964—).

WRITINGS: Beasts of Fact and Fable, Roy, 1962; *Nature on the Move,* G. Bell, 1965; *Man and Beast,* Bell, 1966, Macmillan, 1968; *Where Animals Live,* Macmillan, 1970; *Dogs,* Macdonald & Co., 1974. Contributor to *Encyclopaedia Brittanica* reading program; also contributor to *Railway, Schoolmaster,* regional periodicals.

SIDELIGHTS: Marchant writes to *CA:* "I have always wanted to write and during ... childhood illnesses would often amuse myself by ... compiling whole magazines—stories, articles and even advertisements. I would never show these to anyone and this reluctance to expose my work has continued even today and has probably slowed down my progress considerably." Marchant claims "some competence" in Russian. He hopes to begin writing fiction soon.†

* * *

MARDON, Michael (Claude) 1919-

PERSONAL: Born October 9, 1919, in Clifton, Gloucestershire England; son of Arthur Claude (a colonel, British Army) and Isabel Mary (Deans) Mardon; married Pia Denise Cowalr, August 15, 1957. *Education:* Attended Pembroke College, Cambridge, 1938-40. *Religion:* Roman Catholic. *Home:* Merlins Cottage, Motts Mill, Groombridge, Tunbridge Wells, England. *Agent:* Diana Crawford, Noel Gay Artists Ltd., 24 Denmark St., London W.C. 2, England.

CAREER: Circus clown in England, 1946-51; researcher in animal psychology and behavior.

WRITINGS: A Circus Year, Putnam, 1961. Writer of pantomime script, "Jack and the Beanstalk," 1959, and documentary film, "Sport in Britain." Contributor to *Spectator, Time and Tide,* and *Tablet.*

WORK IN PROGRESS: Research in circus history for book, *Come to the Circus!*†

* * *

MAREK, Hannelore M(arie) C(harlotte) 1926-

PERSONAL: Born June 2, 1926, in Hamburg, Germany; came to United States, 1954; daughter of Franz F. J. (a businessman) and Margarethe (Koenig) Schipmann; married Kurt W. Marek (a writer, under pseudonym, C. W. Ceram) December 30, 1952 (died April 12, 1972); children: Max Alexander. *Education:* Educated in German schools. *Home:* 2057 Reinbek, Gleisners Park 1, West Germany.

CAREER: Set and costume designer, Hamburg, Germany, 1947—, intermittently since 1954. Staatl Musikhochschule, Hamburg, Germany, teacher of history of costumes, 1952.

WRITINGS: The History of the Theater, Odyssey, 1964.

AVOCATIONAL INTERESTS: Making eight millimeter movies.

* * *

MARITANO, Nino 1919-

PERSONAL: Born August 29, 1919, in Turin, Italy; son of Carlo and Rosa (Kolando) Maritano. *Education:* University of Louvain, M.A. in Economics and M.A. in Political Science, 1952; Georgetown University, Ph.D., 1958. *Religion:* Roman Catholic. *Home:* 2115 Summit Ave., St. Paul, Minn. *Office:* St. Thomas College, St. Paul, Minn.

CAREER: St. Thomas College, St. Paul, Minn., assistant professor of economics, 1959—. Researcher and writer on Latin American problems in economic development. *Member:* American Economic Association, Catholic Economic Association, Midwest Economic Association, Minnesota Economic Association. *Awards, honors:* Grants for research in Latin America from Louis and Maud Hill Family Foundation, 1961 and 1962; Rockefeller Foundation research grant, 1963.

WRITINGS: (With Antonio Obaid) *Alliance for Progress: The Challenge and the Problem*, Denison, 1963; *Latin American Economic Integration*, Holt, 1965; *Latin American Economic Community: History, Policies, and Problems*, University of Notre Dame Press, 1970. Contributor to journals.

WORK IN PROGRESS: Teoria Economica, in Spanish; *The Economics of Developing Countries; Population and Economic Development.*

SIDELIGHTS: Maritano is competent in French, German, Portuguese, Spanish, and Italian, and can read Latin and Greek. He has made annual research trips to western European countries, 1947-54, and to Latin American countries annually since 1955.

BIOGRAPHICAL/CRITICAL SOURCES: U.S. Congressional Record, March 16, 1962; *Washington Post*, March 8, 1964.†

* * *

MARKMANN, Charles Lam 1913-

PERSONAL: Born April 16, 1913, in Philadelphia, Pa.; son of M. Jacob (a lawyer) and Julia (Lam) Markmann; children: Sonya, Julie; *Education:* Attended Friends' Select School, Philadelphia, Pa., 1926-29; University of Pennsylvania, A.B., 1933; New York University, LL.B., 1942. *Agent:* Seligmann & Collier, 280 Madison Ave., New York, N.Y. 10016.

CAREER: Author, editor, and consultant in New York, N.Y., 1935-65, 1967-73, in Federal Republic of Germany, 1966-67. Associate foreign editor of *New York Times*, 1942-47; New York correspondent for *Samedi-Soir* (Paris), 1945-47. Consultant to publishers and television; public relations consultant to New York Civil Liberties Union, 1964-65. Assistant professor of English, Middlesex Community College, 1969-70. Executive director (voluntary) of Citizens' Newspaper Committee working for settlement of the New York newspaper strike and lockout, 1962-63. *Member:* P.E.N. American Center, Authors Guild.

WRITINGS: (With Robert Goffin) *The White Brigade*,

Doubleday, 1944; (with Francis Trevelyan Miller) *History of World War II*, John C. Winston, 1945; (with William L. Terrell) *Reporter's Handbook*, Newsmen, 1953; (with Mark Sherwin) *The Book of Sports Cars*, Putnam, 1959; (with Sherwin) *One Week in March*, Putnam, 1961; (with Sherwin) *John F. Kennedy: A Sense of Purpose*, St. Martins, 1961; (editor) Sherwin, *The Extremists*, St. Martins, 1963; *The Noblest Cry*, St. Martins, 1965; *The Buckleys: A Family Examined*, Morrow, 1973.

Translator: Roger Caillois, *Pontius Pilate*, Macmillan, 1963; Deena Boyer, *The 200 Days of 8½*, Macmillan, 1964; Joseph Kessel, *The Bernan Affair*, St. Martins, 1965; Marcello Craveri, *The Life of Jesus*, Grove, 1967; Frantz Fanon, *Black Skin, White Masks*, Grove, 1967; Maurice Andrieux, *Rome*, Funk, 1968; Albertine Sarrazin, *Runaway*, Grove, 1968; Anovar Abdel-Malek, *Egypt: Military Society*, Random House, 1968; Josue de Castro, *The Black Book of Hungar*, Funk, 1968; Albert Thibaudet, *French Literature: From 1795 to Our Era*, Funk, 1968; Alfred A. Hasler, *Lifeboat Is Full*, Funk, 1969; Tibor Meray, *That Day in Budapest*, Funk, 1969; Pierre Do-Dinh, *Confucious and Chinese Humanism*, Funk, 1969; Vittorio Gorresio, *New Mission of Pope John Twenty-Third*, Funk, 1970; Rene Barjauel, *The Ice People*, Hart-Davis, 1970; Roger Mucchielli, *Introduction to Structural Psychology*, Avon, 1972; Arrigo Petacco, *Joe Petrosino*, Macmillan, 1974. Also translator of Daniel Gilles, *Checkhov: Observer Without Illusion*, Funk, and Paul Miliukov and others, editors, *The History of Russia*, 3 volumes, Funk.

Formerly regular contributor on the arts, economics, and national and world affairs to *Knickerbocker Weekly*; contributor to *Nation, Saturday Review/World.*

WORK IN PROGRESS: A book on the fall of the second German republic.

SIDELIGHTS: Markmann is bilingual in French and English, fluent in Italian, and has a practical command of German. *Avocational interests:* Human behavior, music and films.

* * *

MARKSBERRY, Mary Lee

PERSONAL: Born in Blairstown, Mo.; daughter of James A. and Mary Florence (McDonald) Marksberry. *Education:* Central Missouri State College (now University), B.S., 1935; University of Missouri, M.A., 1939; University of Chicago, Ph.D., 1951. *Home:* Route 1, Blairstown, Mo. 64726. *Office:* School of Education, University of Missouri, Kansas City, Mo. 64110.

CAREER: Teacher in Minnesota, 1942-46, and Hawaii, 1947-49; Wayne University (now Wayne State University), Detroit, Mich., assistant professor, 1951-53; University of Missouri, Kansas City, lecturer in education, 1953-56, associate professor, 1956-62, professor of education, 1962—, chairman of division of elementary education, 1964—. Teacher at University of Wyoming, summers, 1945, 1946, 1947, University of Mississippi, summer, 1951; visiting professor, University of British Columbia, summer, 1968, and University of Sydney, summer, 1973. *Member:* Association for Supervision and Curriculum Development, American Association of University Professors, National Council of Teachers of English, National Society for the Study of Education.

WRITINGS: Foundation of Creativity, Harper, 1963. Contributor to education journals.

WORK IN PROGRESS: Journal articles.

MARLOWE, Kenneth 1926-
(Mr. Kenneth, Leslie Stuart)

PERSONAL: Born November 26, 1926, in Des Moines, Iowa; son of Leonard (an auditor) and Mabel (Stewart) Marlowe. *Education:* Graduate of Thompson's Beauty School, Des Moines, Iowa; attended Central Bible Institute, Springfield, Mo., three years; attended Theresa and Arthur Mahoney Dance Studios, Carnegie Hall, New York, N.Y. *Politics:* Democrat. *Religion:* Protestant. *Home and office:* 8500 Cole Crest Dr., Los Angeles, Calif. 90046.

CAREER: For eight years was night club entertainer in Cincinnati, Calumet City (Ill.), Chicago, Newport (Ky.), and San Francisco; personal hair stylist to celebrities, including Gypsy Rose Lee, Phyllis Diller, Hedda Hopper, Joan Blondell, Imogene Coca, Lita Baron, and Bobo Lewis. *Military service:* U.S. Army. *Member:* Mattachine Society, Daughters of Bilitis, Tavern Guild of San Francisco. *Awards, honors:* Silver and Gold Award from Women's Christian Temperance Union.

WRITINGS: Mr. Madam, Sherbourne Press, 1964; *Speaking of Sex*, Sherbourne Press, 1965; *A Madam's Memoirs*, three volumes, Novel Books, 1965; *The Male Homosexual*, Sherbourne Press, 1965. Author of "A Madam's Memoirs," a weekly column in *National Tattler*, 1964-65. Contributor to *Confidential, Nugget, One*, and other publications.†

*   *   *

MARQUARDT, Dorothy Ann 1921-

PERSONAL: Surname is pronounced Mar-quart; born August 21, 1921, in Edina, Mo.; daughter of John A. and Beatrice M. (Franz) Marquardt; children: Nicholas L. Davis. *Education:* Took library courses at Washington University, St. Louis, Mo., and Quincy College. *Politics:* Democrat. *Religion:* Catholic. *Home:* 3421 Lawrence Rd., Quincy, Ill. *Office:* Quincy Free Public Library, Quincy, Ill. 62301.

CAREER: Topographer with Army Map Service and secretary in Department of the Navy, Quincy, Ill., during World War II; department store credit manager; Quincy Free Public Library, Quincy, Ill., junior library assistant, 1947-60, senior library assistant in children's department, 1960—.

WRITINGS: (With Martha E. Ward) *Authors of Books for Young People*, Scarecrow, 1965, first supplement, 1967, 2nd edition, 1971; (with Ward) *Illustrators of Books for Young People*, Scarecrrow, 1970.

WORK IN PROGRESS: Supplements for *Authors of Books for Young People*; a revision of *Illustrators of Books for Young People*; a preschool book.

AVOCATIONAL INTERESTS: Puppetry; collecting John F. Kennedy memorabilia.

*   *   *

MARR-JOHNSON, Diana (Maugham) 1908-
(Diana Maugham)

PERSONAL: Born September 16, 1908, in England; daughter of Viscount Frederic Maugham (former Lord Chancellor of Great Britain) and Helen (Romer) Maugham; married Kenneth Marr-Johnson (a chartered surveyor); children Frederick, Simon, William. *Education:* King's College, University of London, Diploma in Journalism.

Politics: Conservative. *Religion:* Church of England. *Home:* 14 Onslow Sq., Flat 3, London S.W. 7, England. *Agent:* A. P. Watt & Son, Hastings House, 10 Norfolk St., London W.C. 2, England.

CAREER: Writer. *Member:* P.E.N.

WRITINGS: (Under name Diana Maugham) *Rhapsody in Gold*, Nicholson & Watson, 1935; (under name Diana Maugham) *Bella North*, Chatto & Windus, 1954, St. Martin's, 1958; (under name Diana Maugham) *Goodnight Pelican* (Book Society recommendation), Chatto & Windus, 1957, St. Martin's, 1958; *Face of a Stranger*, Chatto & Windus, 1963; *Faces My Fortune*, David Bruce & Watson, 1970; *Take a Golden Spoon*, R. Hale, 1972.

Plays: *Never Say Die*, Samuel French, 1958; "Marriage Unlimited" (three-act comedy), first produced in London at Richmond Theatre, March, 1971.

Contributor of short stories and articles to periodicals.

WORK IN PROGRESS: A non-fiction book.

SIDELIGHTS: Diana Maugham's brother, the present Viscount Maugham, also is an author, under the name of Robin Maugham. Their uncle was W. Somerset Maugham.

*   *   *

MARSH, Robert C(harles) 1924-

PERSONAL: Born August 5, 1924, in Columbus, Ohio; son of Charles Lehman (an educational administrator) and Jane (Beckett) Marsh; married Kathleen Carmody Moscrop, July 4, 1956. *Education:* Northwestern University, B.S., 1945, A.M., 1946; graduate study at Cornell University, 1946-47, University of Chicago, 1948; Harvard University, Ed.D., 1951; postdoctoral research study at Oxford University, 1952-53, Cambridge University, 1953-56. *Politics:* Democrat. *Religion:* Episcopalian. *Office: Chicago Sun-Times*, 401 North Wabash Ave., Chicago, Ill. 60611.

CAREER: University of Illinois, Chicago, instructor in social science, 1947-49; Chicago City Junior College, Chicago, Ill., lecturer in humanities, 1950-51; University of Kansas City (now University of Missouri, Kansas City), assistant professor of education, 1951-52; State University of New York at New Paltz, visiting professor of education, 1953-54; University of Chicago, Chicago, Ill., member of humanities faculty, 1956-58; *Chicago Sun Times*, Chicago, Ill., music critic, 1956—. Broadcaster on British Broadcasting Corp. Third Programme, 1955, and on special programs, WFMT, Chicago, 1956—. Member of faculty and of national advisory committee, Rockefeller Foundation Project for the Training of Music Critics (at University of Southern California), 1965-72. *Member:* Sigma Delta Chi (life). *Awards, honors:* Ford Foundation fellowship, 1965-66.

WRITINGS: Toscanini and the Art of Orchestral Performance, Lippincott, 1956, revised edition published as *Toscanini and the Art of Conducting*, Collier, 1962; (editor) Bertrand Russell, *Logic and Knowledge* (essays), Macmillan, 1956; *The Cleveland Orchestra*, World Publishing, 1967. Contributing editor of *High Fidelity* 1955—, and regular contributor to *Christian Science Monitor*, 1958-72; also contributor to other periodicals.

WORK IN PROGRESS: A book, *Thirty Years of Music in Chicago*.

SIDELIGHTS: Marsh's book on Toscanini has been published in England, Germany, and Switzerland.

MARSH, Ronald (James) 1914-

PERSONAL: Born August 7, 1914, in Broadstairs, Kent, England; son of Donald Alfred Sackett and Helen Cicely (Perkins) March; married Phyllis Glenice Higgins; children: Valerie, David, Rosalind. *Education:* Educated in private and public schools in England, 1918-30. *Home:* 13 Farm Hill Ave., Rochester, Kent, England.

CAREER: Public Library, Margate, England, assistant, 1930-40; Public Library, Oxford, England, branch librarian, 1940-46; Public Library, Hornsey, London, England, lend librarian, 1946-50; Public Library, Rochester, England, city librarian, 1950-74. *Member:* Library Association (fellow), Society of Authors.

WRITINGS: Family Jigsaw (three-act comedy), Samuel French, 1943; *Irene* (novel), Chatto & Windus, 1948, Houghton, 1950; *Your Brother Still* (Novel), Chatto & Windus, 1953; *The Quarry* (novel), Macdonald & Co., 1962; *The Conservancy of the River Medway 1881-1969*, Medway Conservancy Board (England), 1971; *Rochester: the Evolution of the City and its Government*, Rochester City Council (England), 1974.

WORK IN PROGRESS: The Glad Season, a novel of small town life in England in the 1930's; a novel on the making of a juvenile delinquent; a crime novel studying corruption; research for a biographical and critical book on Charles Dickens.

*   *   *

MARSHALL, Burke 1922-

PERSONAL: Born October 1, 1922, in Plainfield, N.J.; son of Henry P. and Dorothy (Burke) Marshall; married Violet Person, June 20, 1946; children: Josephine Holcomb, Catherine Cox, Jane Montgomery. *Education:* Yale University, B.A., 1944, LL.B., 1951. *Politics:* Democrat. *Home:* Poverty Hollow Rd., Newtown, Conn. 06470.

CAREER: Admitted to District of Columbia bar, 1951; Covington & Burling (law firm), Washington, D.C., associate partner, 1951-61; U.S. Department of Justice, Washington, D.C., an assistant attorney general, 1961-65; Covington & Burling, Washington, D.C., partner, 1965; International Business Machines Corp., Armonk, N.Y., vice-president and general counsel, 1965-69; Yale University, New Haven, Conn., professor and dean of department of law, 1970—. *Military service:* U.S. Army, 1942-45; became first lieutenant. *Member:* Federal City Club (Washington, D.C.).

WRITINGS: Federalism and Civil Rights, Columbia University Press, 1964; (with Seymour Whitney North) *The Lawyers' Committee for Civil Rights Under Law*, Washington, 1966. Contributor of articles to legal journals.†

*   *   *

MARTEKA, Vincent (James) 1936-

PERSONAL: Born January 29, 1936, in Uxbridge, Mass.; son of Vincent James and Genevieve (Ramien) Marteka; married Janet Littler (a geologist), May 26, 1962; children: Andrew, Peter, Katherine. *Education:* University of Massachusetts, B.S. 1958; Rensselaer Polytechnic Institute, M.S., 1959. *Home:* Jobs Pond Rd., Portland, Conn. 06480. *Agent:* Marie Rodell, 145 East 49th St., New York, N.Y. 10017. *Office:* Xerox Education Publications, 55 High St., Middletown, Conn. 06458.

CAREER: U.S. Geological Survey, Washington, D.C., editor, 1959-60; Science Service (National wire service for newspapers), Washington, D.C., science writer and news editor, 1961-62; free-lance science writer, Washington, D.C., 1963; Xerox Education Publications, Middletown, Conn., science editor of *My Weekly Reader*, 1964, writer-editor of *Current Science* (weekly science newspaper for junior high school students), 1965—. *Military service:* U.S. Army Reserve; active duty, 1959-60. *Member:* American Association for the Advancement of Science, National Audubon Society.

WRITINGS: Bionics, Lippincott, 1965. Contributor to *Book of Knowledge* and other reference works, and to periodicals and newspapers, including *Science Digest, Sea Frontiers, New York Times, Baltimore Sun*, and *Child and Family*.

WORK IN PROGRESS: Periodical articles on recent journeys to Antarctica and Russia, and on natural history.

AVOCATIONAL INTERESTS: White-water canoeing, gourmet cooking, rare books, natural history, and nature photography.

*   *   *

MARTIN, John Bartlow 1915-

PERSONAL: Born August 4, 1915, in Hamilton, Ohio; son of John Williamson (a building contractor) and Laura (Bartlow) Martin; married Frances Rose Smethurst, August 17, 1940; children: Cynthia (Mrs. Joseph Coleman), Daniel Bartlow, John Frederick. *Education:* De Pauw University, B.A., 1937. *Politics:* Democrat. *Religion:* Protestant. *Home:* 185 Maple Ave., Highland Park, Ill. *Agent:* Harold Ober Associates, 40 East 49th St., New York, N.Y. 10017.

CAREER: Free-lance writer, 1938-62; consultant on Caribbean Affairs to the Department of State, 1961; special envoy of U.S. President to Dominican Republic, 1961 and 1965; U.S. Ambassador to Dominican Republic, 1962-64; free-lance writer, 1964—. Wesleyan University, Center for Advanced Studies, Middletown, Conn., senior fellow, 1964-65; Princeton University, Princeton, N.J., visiting fellow in public affairs, 1966-67; Graduate School and University Center of the City University of New York, N.Y., visiting professor, 1968; Northwestern University, Medill School of Journalism, Evanston, Ill., professor of journalism, 1970—. Staff member for Adlai Stevenson, 1952-56, John F. Kennedy, 1960, Lyndon B. Johnson, 1964, and Hubert H. Humphrey, 1968. Member of board of directors, Chicago Institute for Psychoanalysis. *Military service:* U.S. Army, 1944-46. *Member:* Authors Guild, Society of Magazine Writers, Sigma Delta Chi, Federal City Club (Washington, D.C.), Century Association (New York). *Awards, honors:* Sigma Delta Chi Magazine Award, 1950, 1957; Benjamin Franklin Magazine Award, 1954, 1956, 1957, and 1958; Indiana Authors' Day Award from Indiana University Writers' Conference, 1967, for *Overtaken By Events*.

WRITINGS: Call It North Country, Knopf, 1944; *Indiana: An Interpretation*, Knopf, 1947; *Butcher's Dozen*, Harper, 1950; *Adlai Stevenson*, Harper, 1952; *My Life in Crime*, Harper, 1952; *Why Did They Kill?*, Ballantine, 1953; *Break Down the Walls*, Ballantine, 1954; *The Deep South Says 'Never'*, Ballantine, 1957; *Jimmy Hoffa's Hot* (reprint of "The Struggle to Get Hoffa," *Saturday Evening Post*), Dell, 1959; *The Pane of Glass*, Harper, 1959; *Overtaken by Events*, Doubleday, 1966. Contributor to *Harper's, Reader's Digest, Saturday Evening Post*, and other magazines.

WORK IN PROGRESS: An oral history project for Kennedy Memorial Library; a biography of Adlai Stevenson, for Doubleday.

SIDELIGHTS: Of *Pane of Glass*, a study of mental illness in America, N. L. Browning wrote: "Martin knows how to transform historical data, statistics, clinical case histories, and psychiatric terms into real life drama—in laymen's language...." F. J. Braceland added that the book "cannot be pleasant reading but it is required reading, for it is an authoritative statement, a documentary." Kenneth Robinson wrote: "His publisher describes Mr. Martin as "the greatest American reporter in the field of social service,' and for once such a claim may well be valid."

Martin belives his outstanding magazine article was "The Blast in Centralia #5," *Harper's*, March, 1948. He has had a singularly diverse career as a writer and has managed to serve on the staffs of two presidents and a presidential candidate in addition to producing nearly a dozen highly praised books. John Fischer wrote of Stevenson's speechwriting crew during the 1952 campaign: "At one time or another four of the ghosts collapsed from nervous exhaustion.... Of the survivors, the best was John Bartlow Martin; he works under extreme pressure better than any writer I have ever known, and he has the ulcers to prove it."

BIOGRAPHICAL/CRITICAL SOURCES: Chicago Sunday Tribune, February 22, 1959; *New York Times*, May 31, 1959; *New Statesman*, February 6, 1960; *Harper's*, November, 1965.

* * *

MARTINDALE, Don (Albert) 1915-

PERSONAL: Born February 9, 1915, in Marinette, Wis.; son of Don Lucian (a laborer) and Elsie (Tetzloff) Martindale; married Edith (a social worker), February 2, 1943. *Education:* University of Wisconsin, B.A. (summa cum laude), 1939, M.A., 1940, Ph.D., 1948. *Home:* 2900 West Owasso Blvd., St. Paul, Minn. 55112. *Office:* Department of Sociology, University of Minnesota, Minneapolis, Minn. 55455.

CAREER: University of Wisconsin, Madison, instructor in sociology, 1946-48; University of Minnesota, Minneapolis, assistant professor, 1948-52, associate professor, 1952-54, professor of sociology, 1954—. *Military service:* U.S. Army, 1942-46; became captain. *Member:* American Sociological Association, American Academy of Political and Social Science, American Association of University Professors, Phi Beta Kappa.

WRITINGS: (With Elio D. Monachesi) *Elements of Sociology*, Harper, 1951; *The Nature and Types of Sociological Theory*, Houghton, 1960; *American Social Structure*, Appleton, 1960; *American Society*, Van Nostrand, 1960; *Social Life and Cultural Change*, Van Nostrand, 1962; *Community, Character and Civilization*, Free Press of Glencoe, 1963; *Functionalism in the Social Sciences*, American Academy of Political and Social Sciences, 1965; *Institutions, Organizations, and Mass Society*, Houghton, 1966; (editor) *National Character in the Perspective of the Social Sciences*, American Academy of Political and Social Sciences, 1967; *Small Town and the Nation: The Conflict of Local and Translocal Forces*, Greenwood, 1969; (with wife, Edith Martindale) *The Social Dimensions of Mental Illness, Alcoholism and Drug Dependence*, Greenwood, 1971; (with Edith Martindale) *Social Psychiatry in Minnesota: Coping with Mental Illness, Alcoholism, and Drug*

Dependence, Windflower Publishing, 1972; *American Society*, Krieger, 1972; (with Edith Martindale) *Psychiatry and the Law: The Crusade Against Involuntary Hospitalization*, Windflower, 1973; *Sociological Theory and the Problem of Values*, Merrill, 1974; *Prominent Sociologists Since World War II*, Merrill, 1975.

Translator and editor: (With Hans Gerth) Max Weber, *Ancient Judaism*, Free Press of Glencoe, 1952; (with H. Gerth) Max Weber, *Religions of India*, Free Press of Glencoe, 1958; (with Gertrud Neuwirth) Max Weber, *The City*, Free Press of Glencoe, 1958; (with G. Neuwirth and Johannes Riedel) Max Weber, *Rational and Social Foundations of Music*, Southern Illinois University Press, 1958.†

* * *

MARTINO, Rocco L(eonard) 1929-

PERSONAL: Born June 25, 1929, in Toronto, Ontario, Canada; son of Domenic (an executive) and Josephine (DiGiulio) Martino; married Barbara Italia D'Iorio, September 2, 1961; children: Peter Dominic. *Education:* University of Toronto, B.A. (honors), 1951, M.A. (mathematics), 1952, Ph.D. (aerospace engineering), 1955. *Religion:* Roman Catholic. *Residence:* Ithan, Pa. *Office:* Martino & Co., 130 West Lancaster Ave., Wayne, Pa. 19087.

CAREER: Adalia Ltd., Montreal, Quebec, Canada, director of Aerophysics Division, 1955-56; Sperry Rand Corp., Toronto, Ontario, director of UNIVAC Centres, 1956-59; Mauchly Associates, Toronto, Ontario, president, 1959-62; Olin Mathieson Chemical Corp., New York, N.Y., advanced systems manager, 1962-64; New York University, New York, N.Y., professor of mathematics, 1962—. Martino & Co., Philadelphia, Pa., and Toronto, Ontario, president, 1964—.

WRITINGS—All published by Management Development Institute except as indicated: *Finding the Critical Path*, American Management Association, 1964; *Applied Operational Planning*, American Management Association, 1964; *Allocating and Scheduling Resources*, American Management Association, 1965; *Critical Path Networks*, 1967; *Dynamic Costing*, 1968; *Information Management: The Dynamics of MIS*, 1968; *MIS: Management Information Systems*, 1968; *Project Management*, 1968; *Resources Management*, 1968; *Decision Patterns*, 1969; *MIS Methodology*, 1969; *PMS—Personnel Management Systems*, 1969; *Integrated Manufacturing Systems*, McGraw, 1972. Also author of *Dynamic Network Analysis*, and *Modern Techniques of Business Planning*. Contributor of more than sixty articles to business and technical periodicals. Editor, *Total Systems Newsletter*.

AVOCATIONAL INTERESTS: Photography, chess, hiking.

BIOGRAPHICAL/CRITICAL SOURCES: Chemical Week, May 25, 1963; *Executive Digest*, June, 1964; *Chemical Engineering*, September 14, 1964; *Data Processing Magazine*, October, 1964.†

* * *

MARTZ, Louis L(ohr) 1913-

PERSONAL: Born September 27, 1913, in Berwick, Pa.; son of Isaiah Louis Bower and Ruth Alverna (Lohr) Martz; married Edwine Montague, June 30, 1941; children: Frederick, Montague, Ruth Anne. *Education:* Lafayette College, A.B., 1935; Yale University, Ph.D., 1939. *Home:* 46 Swarthmore St., Hamden, Conn. 06517. *Office:* 994 Yale Station, New Haven, Conn.

CAREER: Yale University, New Haven, Conn., instructor, 1938-44, assistant professor, 1944-48, associate professor, 1948-54, professor of English, 1954-57, Douglas Tracy Smith Professor of English and American Literature, 1957-71, Sterling Professor of English, 1971—, chairman of department, 1956-62, director of Division of Humanities, 1959-62, director of Beinecke Rare Book and Manuscript Library, 1972—, fellow of Saybrook College. *Member:* Modern Language Association of America, Renaissance Society of America, Connecticut Academy of Arts and Sciences, Phi Beta Kappa, Kappa Delta Rho, Elizabethan Club (New Haven). *Awards, honors:* Guggenheim fellow, 1948-49; Christian Gauss Award from Phi Beta Kappa, 1955, for *The Poetry of Meditation: A Study in English Religious Literature of the Seventeenth Century*; D.Litt., Lafayette College, 1960.

WRITINGS: *The Later Career of Tobias Smollett*, Yale University Press, 1942; (editor) John Bunyan, *Pilgrim's Progress*, Rinehart, 1949; *The Poetry of Meditation: A Study in English Religious Literature of the Seventeenth Century*, Yale University Press, 1954, revised edition, 1962; (compiler) *The Meditative Poem* (anthology of seventeenth-century verse), New York University Press, 1963; *The Paradise Within: Studies in Vaughan, Traherne, and Milton*, Yale University Press, 1964; *The Poem of the Mind: Essays on Poetry, English and American*, Oxford University Press, 1966; (editor) *Milton: A Collection of Critical Essays*, Prentice-Hall, 1966; (editor with Richard Sylvester) *Thomas More's Prayer Book*, Yale University Press, 1969; *The Wit of Love: Donne, Carew, Crashaw, Marvell*, University of Notre Dame Press, 1969; (editor) Christopher Marlowe, *Hero and Leander*, Folger Shakespeare Library, 1972. Contributor of articles and reviews to British and American journals. Editorial chairman, "Yale Edition of the Works of Thomas More."

*   *   *

MARUYAMA, Masao 1914-

PERSONAL: Born March 22, 1914, in Osaka, Japan; married March 24, 1944; children: Akira, Takeshi (both sons). *Education:* Tokyo Imperial University, graduate, 1937. *Home:* 2-44-5, Higiashicho, Kichijoji, Musashino, Tokyo, Japan. *Office:* Faculty of Law, Tokyo University, Tokyo, Japan.

CAREER: Tokyo University, Tokyo, Japan, faculty of law, professor of political theory (specializing in the history of Japanese political thought), 1950—. Visiting professor, Harvard University, Cambridge, Mass., 1961-62, and St. Antony's College, Oxford, England, 1962-63. *Military service:* Japanese Army, 1944-45. *Member:* Association of Japanese Political Science (director), Shiso no Kagaku Kenkyukai (Association for the Study of Ideas). *Awards, honors:* Mainichi Shuppan Bunka Sho (prize awarded by the newspaper *Mainichi Shinbun*) for *Nippon Seiji Shisoshi Kenkyu*; Rockefeller Foundation fellowship for travel in western Europe, 1962.

WRITINGS: *Nippon Seiji Shisoshi Kenkyu* (title means "Studies in the History of Japanese Political Thought"), Tokyo University Press, 1952; *Seiji no Sekai* (title means "The World of Politics"), Ochanomizu, 1952; *Gendai Seiji no Shiso to Kodo*, Miraisha, 1956, 2nd edition, 1964; *Nihon no Shiso* (title means "Considerations on Japanese Thought"), Iwanami, 1961; *Thought and Behaviour in Modern Japanese Politics* (translation of nine essays included in *Gendai Seiji no Shiso to Kodo*; edited by Ivan

Morris), Oxford University Press, 1963, expanded edition, 1969; *Studies in the Intellectual History of Tokugawa Japan* (translated from Japanese) Princeton University Press, 1974.

WORK IN PROGRESS: Orthodoxy and heresy in the history of modern Japanese thought; problems of the grafting of western political ideas on traditional concepts in Japan.†

*   *   *

MARVIN, David Keith 1921-

PERSONAL: Born April 8, 1921; son of Henry Howard (a teacher) and Alma (Wright) Marvin; married Frances Cash, December 14, 1946; children: Margaret, Keith, Martha. *Education:* University of Nebraska, B.A., 1943; Northwestern University, M.A., 1955, Ph.D., 1957. *Office:* Department of International Relations, California State University, San Francisco, Calif. 94132.

CAREER: United Nations Relief and Rehabilitation Administration, administrative officer, Austrian Mission, 1946; U.S. Foreign Service, Washington, D.C., foreign service officer, 1946-53; San Francisco State College (now University), San Francisco, Calif., assistant professor, 1958-62, associate professor, 1962-67, professor of international relations, 1967—, chairman of department 1964-70. Visiting professor, University of California, Berkeley, 1967. Assistant chairman of social science division, 1960-64. *Military service:* U.S. Army, 1943-46; became sergeant. *Member:* African Studies Association (fellow), International Studies Association, Phi Beta Kappa.

WRITINGS: (Editor) *Emerging Africa in World Affairs*, Chandler Publishing, 1965. Editor, San Francisco International Studies Project Series, 1959.†

*   *   *

MARY FRANCIS, Mother 1921-
(Francis D. Clare)

PERSONAL: Born February 14, 1921, in St. Louis, Mo.; daughter of John Wolkiewicz and Anne Marie (Maher) Aschmann, *Education:* Attended Notre Dame Junior College and St. Louis University. *Home:* Poor Clare Monastery, 809 East 19th St., Roswell, N.M. 88201.

CAREER: Roman Catholic nun, member of order of Poor Clares; Poor Clare Monastery, Roswell, N.M., abbess, 1964—. *Member:* Catholic Poetry Society of America, National Catholic Theatre Conference.

WRITINGS: *Where Caius Is*, Franciscan Institute, 1955; *A Right to Be Merry*, Sheed, 1956; *Francis*, Sheed, 1959; *Walled in Light*, Sheed, 1960; *Spaces for Silence*, Franciscan Herald, 1964; *Strange Gods Before Me*, Sheed, 1965; *Marginals*, Franciscan Herald, 1967; *But I Have Called Your Friends*, Franciscan Herald, 1974.

Plays: *Candle in Umbria*, privately printed, 1953; *Smallest of All*, Samuel French, 1957; *Christmas at Greccio*, Samuel French, 1959; *La Madre*, Samuel French, 1959; *Counted as Mine*, Samuel French, 1959; *Road to Emmaus*, Samuel French, 1962; *Lady of Mexico*, Gregorian Institute of America, 1962.

Contributor to *New Mexico Quarterly* and to Catholic periodicals, formerly publishing poetry under pseudonym Francis D. Clare.

WORK IN PROGRESS: *Come Alive*, a book of essays on Christian renewal; a book of poems; studies on the religious life of women in the church.

SIDELIGHTS: Mother Mary Francis is competent in French and Latin. Avocational interests: Art, music, poetry.

* * *

MASON, Herbert Molloy, Jr. 1927-

PERSONAL: Born October 24, 1927, in Lockney, Tex; son of Herbert Molloy (a colonel in the U.S. Air Force) and Maude (Cheney) Mason; married Rigmor Aase Hansen (a painter); children: Berit Lynne. Education: Studied at American University of Beirut, 1947-48, L'Alliance Francaise, Paris, France, 1949; Trinity University, San Antonio, Tex., A.B. in Journalism, 1951. Agent: Paul R. Reynolds, Inc., 599 Fifth Ave., New York, N.Y. 10017.

CAREER: Radio Station KONO, San Antonio, Tex., news department, 1951-52; True (magazine), New York, N.Y., aviation editor, 1953-62; free-lance writer, 1962—. Military service: U.S. Marine Corps, 1944-46.

WRITINGS: The Lafayette Escardrille, Random, 1964; High Flew the Falcons, Lippincott, 1965; The Commandos, Duell, Sloan & Pearce, 1966; Bold Men, Far Horizons, Lippincott, 1966; The Texas Rangers, Meredith, 1967; Famous Firsts in Explorations, Putnam, 1967; The New Tigers, McKay, 1967; The Great Pursuit, Random House, 1970; Duel for the Sky, Grosset, 1970; Death from the Sea, Dial, 1972; The Rise of the Luftwaffe, Dial, 1973; Missions of Texas, Oxmoor House, 1974.

WORK IN PROGRESS: Air Force, for Mason & Lipscomb.

SIDELIGHTS: Mason has flown in numerous types of historical aircraft, from World War I vintage to 1000-miles-per-hour Air Force jets. He has lived and traveled in thirty countries, and wrote his first two books while spending two years in Norway. He is proficient in Spanish, Norwegian, and basic Arabic.

* * *

MASON, Ronald (Charles) 1912-

PERSONAL: Born July 30, 1912, in Thames Ditton, Surrey, England; son of Charles (a government official) and Mary (Canter) Mason; married Margaret Violet Coles, September 8, 1936; children: Nicholas Charles Sheppard, George Humphrey Paul, Elizabeth Mary. Education: University of London, B.A. (first class honors), 1947. Politics: Socialist. Home: Woodmans Cottage, Park Rd., Banstead, Surrey, England. Agent: David Higham Associates Ltd., 5-8 Lower John St., London WIR 4HA, England.

CAREER: H. M. Inland Revenue, Estate Duty Office, London, England, 1931-69, became senior examiner. University of London, London, England, part-time tutor, 1948-69, staff tutor in literature, extra-mural department, 1969—. Member: Marylebone Cricket Club, Surrey County Cricket Club, Cricket Society.

WRITINGS: Timbermills (novel), Sampson Low, Marston & Co., 1938; The Gold Garland (novel), Sampson Low, Marston & Co., 1939; Cold Pastoral (novel), Sampson Low, Marston & Co., 1946; The House of the Living (novel), Sampson Low, Marston & Co., 1947; The Spirit Above the Dust: A Study of Herman Melville, Lehmann, 1951; Batsman's Paradise, Hollis & Carter, 1955; Jack Hobbs, Hollis & Carter, 1960; Walter Hammond, Hollis & Carter, 1962; Sing All a Green Willow, Epworth, 1967; Plum Warner's Last Season, Epworth, 1971; Warwick Armstrong's Australians, Epworth, 1971. Contributor to Penguin, New Writing, Horizon, Voices, The Wind and the Rain, Adelphi, Friend, and other anthologies and periodicals; regular contributor to Cricketer.

AVOCATIONAL INTERESTS: Reading; playing, watching, and studying cricket; travel.

* * *

MAST, Russell L. 1915-

PERSONAL: Born August 23, 1915, in Walnut Creek, Ohio; son of William Robert (a merchant) and Beulah (Wettrick) Mast; married Alma Hilty; children: Thomas, James. Education: Bluffton College, A.B., 1937; Hartford Theological Seminary (now Hartford Seminary Foundation), B.D., 1940. Home: 11 Cherry Lane, Souderton, Pa. 18964.

CAREER: Mennonite minister. Pastor of Mennonite churches in Bedminister, Pa., Wadsworth, Ohio, and Freeman, S.D., 1940-57; Bethal College, North Newton, Kan., pastor, beginning, 1957. Board member, Prairie View Psychiatric Hospital. Member: Newton Rotary Club (vice-president, 1962).

WRITINGS: Christianity and Communism, Faith & Life, 1962; Lost and Found, Herald, 1963; Preach the Word, Faith & Life, 1968. Contributor of articles to Mennonite periodicals.

* * *

MASTERS, Nicholas A. 1929-

PERSONAL: Born February 8, 1929, in Carbondale, Ill.; son of A. N. and Pearl (Ebbs) Masters; married Marilyn J. Nelson, September 4, 1949; children: Marick F., Charissa L. Education: Southern Illinois University, B.A., 1950, M.A., 1951; University of Wisconsin, Ph.D., 1955. Politics: Democrat. Home: 150 Harris Dr., State College, Pa. Office: Department of Political Science, Pennsylvania State University, University Park, Pa.

CAREER: Wayne State University, Detroit, Mich., with Institute of Political Science, 1955-57, assistant professor, 1957-60; Washington University, St. Louis, Mo., visiting associate professor, 1960-63; research associate, James Bryant Conant, New York, N.Y., 1963-64; with Pennsylvania State University, University Park, 1964—. Military service: U.S. Navy. Member: American Political Science Association, Midwest Political Science Association, Pi Sigma Alpha.

WRITINGS: (With Robert Salisbury and Thomas H. Eliot) State Politics in the Public Schools, Knopf, 1964; (with Mary E. Balus) The Growing Powers of the Presidency, Parents' Magazine Press, 1968. Articles published in social science journals.

WORK IN PROGRESS: Senate campaign finance.†

* * *

MATCHETT, William H(enry) 1923-

PERSONAL: Born March 5, 1923, in Chicago, Ill.; son of James Chapman (a heating engineer) and Lucy (Jipson) Matchett; married Judith Wright, June 11, 1949; children: David Hammond, Katherine Cox, Stephen Chapman. Education: Swarthmore College, B.A., 1949; Harvard University, M.A., 1950, Ph.D., 1957. Religion: Society of Friends (Quaker). Office: Department of English, University of Washington, Seattle, Wash. 98195.

CAREER: University of Washington, Seattle, instructor, 1954-56, assistant professor, 1956-61, associate professor,

1961-66, professor of English, 1966—. Chairman of executive committee of Pacific Northwest office of American Friends Service Committee, 1959-62, 1964—. *Wartime service:* Conscientious objector; Civilian Public Service, 1943-46. *Member:* Modern Language Association of America, American Association of University Professors. *Awards, honors:* Hayes Prize, 1948; *Furioso* poetry prize, 1952, for "*Ruby-Throat.*"

WRITINGS: Water Ouzel, and Other Poems, Houghton, 1955; *The Phoenix and the Turtle*, Mouton, 1965; (with Jerome Beaty) *Poetry: From Statement to Meaning*, Oxford University Press, 1965; (editor) William Shakespeare, *King John*, Signet, 1966. Member of editorial board of *Poetry Northwest*, 1961—; editor, *Modern Language Quarterly*, 1963—. Contributor of poems to *Harper's*, *New Yorker*, *Harper's Bazaar*, of short stories to *Arizona Quarterly* and *Moderator*, and of articles to *PMLA*, *Essays in Criticism*, and other publications.

* * *

MATHEWS, Eleanor Muth 1923-

PERSONAL: Born August 10, 1923, in New York, N.Y.; daughter of Harry E. (a tradesman) and Paula (Fingerle) Muth; married William J. Mathews, Jr. (a chemical engineer), June 21, 1952; children: John, Patricia, Paul. *Education:* Hunter College (now Hunter College of the City University of New York), B.A. (magna cum laude), 1945; Columbia University, M.A., 1950. *Politics:* Republican. *Religion:* Lutheran. *Home:* 169 Circle Dr., Millington, N.J. 07946.

CAREER: Story Parade (magazine), New York, N.Y., editorial assistant, 1945-47; Hunter College High School, New York, N.Y., teacher of German, 1948-50; Hunter College (now Hunter College of the City University of New York), lecturer in education, 1950-54; Watchung Hills Regional High School, Warren, N.J., public relations coordinator. *Member:* Phi Beta Kappa.

WRITINGS: God's Way in the Old Testament (juvenile), Fortress, 1964; *The Trouble Is . . .* (juvenile), Fortress, 1966; *Lives That Praise God* (juvenile), Fortress, 1967. Poetry represented in anthology, *Sing a Song of Seasons*, edited by Sara and John Brewton, Macmillan, 1955. Contributor of articles to *Resource*, *Today*, and *These Days*.

* * *

MATLOFF, Maurice 1915-

PERSONAL: Born June 18, 1915, in New York, N.Y.; son of Joseph and Ida (Glickhouse) Matloff; married Gertrude Glickler (a teacher), October 25, 1942; children: Howard Bruce, Jeffrey Lewis, Jody Lynn. *Education:* Columbia University, B.A., 1936; Harvard University, M.A., 1937, Ph.D., 1956; Yale University, Certificate in Russian Area and Language, 1944. *Home:* 4109 Dewmar Ct., Kensington, Md. *Office:* Center of Military History, Department of the Army, Washington, D.C. 20315.

CAREER: Brooklyn College, Brooklyn, N.Y., instructor, 1939-42, associate professor of history, 1946; Department of the Army, Office of the Chief of Military History, Washington, D.C., senior historian in Historical Section, Operations Division, 1946-49, chief of Strategic plans section, 1949-60, deputy and acting chief of Post-World War II Branch, 1960-62, senior historical adviser and chief of Current History Branch, 1962-66, senior historical adviser and chief of General History Branch, 1966-68, deputy chief historian, 1969-70, chief historian, 1970—. Professorial lecturer at University of Maryland, 1957-71. Lecturer for adult education classes, Young Women's Christian Association, Washington, D.C., 1948-51; has lectured at Columbia University, and at U.S. Air Force Academy and other service schools and universities; visiting professor, San Francisco State College, University of California, Davis; Distinguished Visiting Professor, University of Georgia; adjunct professor, American University. *Military service:* U.S. Army, 1942-46.

MEMBER: American Historical Association, International Institute of Strategic Studies (London), Organization of American Historians, American Military Institute, Society for Historians of American Foreign Relations, American Committee on the History of the Second World War (member of executive board), Phi Beta Kappa. *Awards, honors:* Department of the Army Award for outstanding performance, 1958; Secretary of the Army fellowship for study and research, 1959-60; Department of the Army meritorious civilian service award, 1965.

WRITINGS: (With E. M. Snell) *Strategic Planning for Coalition Warfare, 1941-42*, U.S. Government Printing Office, 1953; *Strategic Planning for Coalition Warfare, 1943-44*, U.S. Government Printing Office, 1959; (general editor) *American Military History*, U.S. Government Printing Office, 1969.

Contributor: *Washington Command Post*, U.S. Government Printing Office, 1951; (and member of editorial panel) *Command Decisions*, revised edition (Matloff not associated with earlier edition), U.S. Government Printing Office, 1961; Harry Coles, editor, *Total War and Cold War*, Ohio State University Press, 1962; A. Eisenstadt, editor, *Recent Interpretations of U.S. History*, Crowell-Collier, 1962; S. Harcave, editor, *Readings in Russian History*, Crowell-Collier, 1962; Michael Howard, editor, *Theory and Practice of War*, Cassell, 1965; *D-Day: The Normandy Invasion in Retrospect*, University Press of Kansas, 1971; *Soldiers and Statesmen*, U.S. Government Printing Office, 1973.

Contributor of articles and reviews to *Encyclopaedia Britannica*, *School and Society*, *Military Affairs*, *U.S. Naval Institute Proceedings*, *Air University Review*, *Journal of Modern History*, and *American Historical Review*. Member of editorial staff, *Dictionary of Everyday Usage, German—English, English—German*, Army Information and Education Division and American Council of Learned Societies, 1945.

WORK IN PROGRESS: Development of Modern Strategic Thought.

SIDELIGHTS: Matloff is competent in German, French, and Russian. He spent a year abroad doing research in eleven countries of the North Atlantic Treaty Organization, 1959-60.

* * *

MATSON, Floyd W(illiam) 1921-

PERSONAL: Born August 31, 1921, in Honolulu, Hawaii; son of Floyd Emerson and Esther (Gould) Matson; divorced; children: Catherine Anne, Stephen Dale. *Education:* University of California, Berkeley, A.B., 1950, M.A., 1953, Ph.D., 1960. *Politics:* Independent. *Home:* 4557 Kolohala St., Honolulu, Hawaii 96816. *Office:* Department of American Studies, University of Hawaii, Honolulu, Hawaii 96822.

CAREER: Newspaperman in Honolulu, Hawaii, Salinas, Calif., and Lodi, Calif., 1940-42; Adel Precision Products Corp., Burbank, Calif., editor of technical publications, 1942-43; U.S. Army, Civil Information and Education Section, General Headquarters, Tokyo, Japan, civilian press and propaganda analyst, 1946-48; University of California, Far East Program, Japan, instructor in speech, 1951-52, resident administrator, 1955-56; University of California, Berkeley, lecturer in speech, 1952-65; University of Hawaii, Honolulu, visiting associate professor of political science, 1965-66, professor of American studies, 1966—. Consultant to National Federation of the Blind, 1953, Stanford Research Institute, 1968, Ford Foundation, 1973. Military service: U.S. Army Air Forces, information specialist, 1943-46.

MEMBER: American Association for Humanistic Psychology (president, 1969-70), American Academy of Political and Social Science, Phi Beta Kappa. Awards, honors: Woodrow Wilson Award, American Political Science Association, 1955, for Prejudice, War, and the Constitution.

WRITINGS: (With J. Ten Broek and E. N. Barnhart) Prejudice, War and the Constitution, University of California Press, 1954; (with Ten Broek) Hope Deferred: Public Welfare and the Blind, University of California Press, 1959; The Broken Image: Man, Science and Society (Book Find Club selection), Braziller, 1964; (editor with Ashley Montagu) The Human Dialogue: Perspectives on Communication, Free Press, 1966; (editor) Voices of Crisis: Significant Speeches on Contemporary Issues (anthology), Odyssey, 1966; (editor) Being, Becoming, and Behavior, Braziller, 1967; (editor) Without-Within: Behaviorism and Humanism, Brooks-Cole, 1973; The Idea of Man, Delacorte, 1975; The Human Persuasion, Gordon & Breach, 1975; The Psychology of Humanism, Knopf, 1975.

Contributor to Antioch Review, Social Research, Progressive, The Humanist, Journal of the History of Ideas, Pacific Spectator, Journal of Politics, and psychology journals.

* * *

MATSON, Wallace I(rving) 1921-

PERSONAL: Born June 18, 1921, in Portland, Ore.; son of Henry Irving (a railway engineer) and Nelle (Newton) Matson; married Olga Matveyenko, January 30, 1953; children: Alexander, Philip, Education: University of California, Berkeley, A.B., 1942, Ph.D., 1949. Politics: Reluctant Democrat. Home: 2511 Hill Ct., Berkeley, Calif. 94708. Office: Department of Philosophy, University of California, Berkeley, Calif. 94720.

CAREER: Pomona College, Claremont, Calif., visiting assistant professor of philosophy, 1949-50; University of Washington, Seattle, assistant professor of philosophy, 1950-55; University of California, Berkeley, assistant professor, 1955-58, associate professor, 1958-65, professor of philosophy, 1965—, chairman of department, 1968-71. Summer lecturer at University of Alberta, 1955, University of Rochester, 1964; visiting professor, University of Hawaii, spring, 1965. Military service: U.S. Army, 1942-46; became sergeant. Member: American Philosophical Association, Mind Association, Aristotelian Society, American Civil Liberties Union, Phi Beta Kappa. Awards, honors: Guggenheim fellow at Cambridge University, 1961-62; National Endowment for the Humanities senior fellow, 1971-72.

WRITINGS: The Existence of God, Cornell University Press, 1965; A History of Philosophy, Van Nostrand, 1968. Contributor to American and British philosophical journals.

WORK IN PROGRESS: Sentience, on philosophy of mind.

AVOCATIONAL INTERESTS: Music, especially baroque keyboard, and apple growing.

* * *

MATTESSICH, Richard V(ictor) 1922-

PERSONAL: Born August 9, 1922, in Trieste, Italy (now Free Territory of Trieste); son of Victor (a ship purser) and Gerda (Pfaundler) Mattessich; married Hermine, April 12, 1952. Education: Attended Engineering College, Vienna, Austria, 1936-40; Hochschule fuer Wethandel, Vienna, Dipl. Kfm., 1944, Dr. rer. pol., 1945. Home: 1194 Spruce St., Berkeley, Calif. 94707. Office: University of California, Berkeley, Calif. 94720.

CAREER: Austrian Institute for Economic Research, research associate, 1945-47; instructor at Rosenberg College, Switzerland, 1947-52, at McGill University, Montreal, Quebec, Canada, 1952-53; Mount Allison University, Sackville, New Brunswick, Canada, head of department of commerce, 1953-59; University of California, Berkeley, associate professor of business administration, 1959—. Certified Public Accountant. Member: American Economic Association, American Accounting Association, Institute of Management Science, Econometric Society, Association for Computing Machinery, Schmalenbach Gesellschaft. Awards, honors: Ford Foundation fellow, 1961-62.

WRITINGS: Accounting and Analytical Methods—Measurement and Projection of Income and Wealth in the Micro- and Macro-Economy, Irwin, 1964; Simulation of the Firm through a Budget Computer Program, Irwin, 1964.

Contributor: N. L. Enrick, Management Operations Research, Holt, 1965; Morton Backer, Handbook of Modern Accounting Theory, 2nd edition, Prentice-Hall, 1965. Contributor of more than thirty papers to professional journals.

WORK IN PROGRESS: Two books in German; research on the economic aspects of knowledge creation.

SIDELIGHTS: Mattessich was photographer, producer, and director of two 16 mm. films, "White City at the Golden Gate" and "Between Pacific and Sierra Nevada."†

* * *

MATTHEWS, J(ohn) H(erbert) 1930-

PERSONAL: Born September 11, 1930, in Swansea, Glamorganshire, Wales; son of John Oswald (a manufacturer) and Elizabeth Mabel (Morgan) Matthews; married Jeanne Brooks, July 23, 1955; children: Annette Elizabeth, Jonathan Gregory, Sian Adrienne. Education: University College of Swansea, University of Wales, B.A., 1949, B.A. in French (honors), 1951; University of Montpellier, Docteur d'Universite, 1955. Home: 123 Pine Ridge Rd., Fayetteville, N.Y. 13066. Office: Department of Romance Languages, Syracuse University, Syracuse, N.Y. 13210.

CAREER: University College of Swansea, University of Wales, Swansea, tutor in French, 1955; University of Exeter, Exeter, England, assistant lecturer in French, 1956-57; University of Leicester, Leicester, England, assistant lecturer, later lecturer in French, 1957-63; University of Minnesota, Minneapolis, assistant professor, later associate professor of Romance languages, 1962-65; Syracuse University, Syracuse, N.Y., professor of Romance languages, 1965—. Visiting professor, Williams College, 1960-61. *Military service:* British Army, Educational Corps, 1951-53. *Member:* Societe litteraire des Amis d'Emile Zola, Association des Amis de Benjamin Peret, Association pour l'etude du Mouvement Dada et Surrealisme, Modern Language Association of America, Centro Studie Scambi Internazionali. *Awards, honors:* Fulbright grant, 1960; American Council of Learned Societies grant, 1967 and 1970.

WRITINGS: Les Deux Zola, Lettres Modernes, 1957; (editor) Guy de Maupassant, *Selected Short Stories,* University of London Press, 1959; (editor) *Albert Camus devant la Critique anglo-saxonne: Configuration critique,* Lettres Modernes, 1961; (editor) *Un Nouveau Roman?,* Lettres Modernes, 1964; (translator) *Peret's Score: Vingt Poemes de Benjamin Peret,* Lettres Modernes, 1965; *An Introduction to Surrealism,* Pennsylvania State University Press, 1965; (editor) *An Anthology of French Surrealist Poetry,* University of Minnesota Press, 1966; *Surrealism and the Novel,* University of Michigan Press, 1966; *Andre Breton,* Columbia University Press, 1967; *Surrealist Poetry in France,* Syracuse University Press, 1969; *Surrealism and Film,* University of Michigan Press, 1971; *Theatre in Dada and Surrealism,* Syracuse University Press, 1974; *The Customhouse of Desire: Stories by Surrealists,* University of California Press, 1975; *Benjamin Peret,* Twayne, 1975.

American correspondent for *Phases, Cahiers internationaux de documentation sur la poesie et l'art d'avantgarde,* and *Sud* (all France), for *Edda* and *Gradiva* (both Belgium). Editor of *Symposium,* 1965—; member of editorial board, *Kentucky Studies in Romance Languages,* 1968—, *Books Abroad,* 1968—, and *Dada/Surrealism,* 1971—.

*   *   *

MAXWELL, James A.   1912-

PERSONAL: Born April 7, 1912, in Cincinnati, Ohio; son of Albert C. and Margaret (Dunican) Maxwell; married Genevieve Ludwig (an executive secretary), January 30, 1943 (deceased). *Education:* Attended evening classes at University of Cincinnati, 1932-37. *Home and office:* 300 W. 55th St., New York, N.Y. 10019. *Agent:* Curtis Brown Ltd., 60 East 56 St., New York, N.Y. 10022.

CAREER: Scripps-Howard Radio, Cincinnati, Ohio, news editor, 1934-37; Union Central Life Insurance Co., Cincinnati, Ohio, magazine editor, 1937-42; University of Cincinnati, Evening College, Cincinnati, Ohio, lecturer, 1948-52; full-time free-lance writer, mainly for magazines, 1946-65; Time-Life Books, New York, N.Y., text editor, 1965-1970; Reader's Digest Press, New York, N.Y., general books senior editor, 1970—. Member of Cincinnati City Charter Committee, 1962—; board member in Cincinnati of Children's Theatre, 1956-63, Summer Opera Association, 1960-64, Playhouse in the Park, 1963-65. *Military service:* U.S. Army, Counter Intelligence Corps, 1942-45; became master sergeant (special agent).

WRITINGS: I Never Saw an Arab Like Him (short stories), Houghton, 1948.

Contributor: John P. Frank, *Cases and Materials on Constitutional Law,* Callaghan, 1950; Paul H. Landis, *Social Living,* 3rd edition (Maxwell not associated with earlier editions), Ginn, 1958; Margaret B. Matson, *Workbook for Use with Sociology,* McGraw, 1958; P. H. Landis, *Sociology,* Ginn, 1964.

Articles and short stories have been anthologized in *55 Short Stories from the New Yorker, The O'Henry Awards: Prize Stories, The Baseball Reader,* and *Baseball Stories,* and have appeared in *Holiday, Saturday Evening Post, Reporter, Saturday Review, Esquire, Atlantic Monthly, New Republic, Reader's Digest, Sports Illustrated, Pageant, Portfolio, Town and Country, American Heritage,* and other periodicals. Author of scripts for television documentaries and for United Artists dramatic series.

*   *   *

MAXWELL, Sister Immaculata   1913-

PERSONAL: Born June 4, 1913, in Buffalo, N.Y.; daughter of John L. (a dentist) and Elizabeth (Dwyer) Maxwell. *Education:* Mount St. Joseph College, Buffalo, N.Y., B.S. in Ed., 1940, M.A., 1952; Rosary College, River Forest, Ill., B.A. in L.S., 1945. *Home and office:* Mount St. Joseph College, 2064 Main St., Buffalo, N.Y. 14214.

CAREER: Roman Catholic religious, member of order of Sisters of St. Joseph; Mount St. Joseph College, Buffalo, N.Y., 1945—, librarian and professor of English. *Member:* National Council of Teachers of English (member of book evaluation committee), New York State English Council, Buffalo Diocesan English Council. *Awards, honors:* Catholic Librarians Council of Western New York, citation.

WRITINGS: Like a Swarm of Bees, Daughters of St. Paul, 1957; *Witness to Christ,* Newman, 1964. Contributor of poetry, articles, and short stories to educational magazines.

WORK IN PROGRESS: A book on saints for children.†

*   ,   *   *

MAY, Georges Claude   1920-

PERSONAL: Born October 7, 1920, in Paris, France; came to United States, 1942, naturalized citizen, 1943; son of Lucien (a businessman) and Germaine (Samuel) May; married Martha Corkery, February 19, 1949; children: Anne Charlotte, Catherine Ellen. *Education:* University of Paris, B.A. and B.S., 1937; Licence-es-Lettres, 1941; University of Montpellier, Diplome d'Etudes Superieures, 1941; University of Illinois, Ph.D., 1947. *Home:* 177 Everit Street, New Haven, Conn. 06511. *Office:* Yale University, New Haven, Conn. 06520.

CAREER: Yale University, New Haven, Conn., instructor, assistant professor, associate professor, 1946-56, professor of French, 1956-71, dean of Yale College, 1963-71, Sterling professor of French, 1971—. Summer guest professor at University of Illinois, 1946, University of Minnesota, 1948, Middlebury College, 1951 and 1954, University of Michigan, 1952, University of California at Berkeley, 1959. *Military service:* French Army, 1939-40; U.S. Army, 1943-45. *Member:* Modern Language Association, Association Internationale des Etudes Francaises, Association of American Teachers of French, Societe d'Histoire Litteraire de la France, Societe d'Etudes du XVIIe Siecle, American Society for 18th Century Studies (president, 1974-75), Phi Beta Kappa. *Awards, honors:* Guggenheim fellow, 1950-51; Chevalier, French Legion d'Honneur, 1971.

WRITINGS: Tragedie cornelienne, tragedie racinienne, University of Illinois Press, 1948; *D'Ovide a Racine,* Yale University Press, 1949; *Quatre Visages de Denis Diderot,* Boivin-Hatier, 1951; *Diderot et La Religieuse,* Yale University Press, 1954; *Rousseau par lui-meme,* Editions du

Seuil, 1961; *Le Dilemme du roman au XVIIIe siecle: Etude sur les rapports du roman et de la critique, 1715-1761*, Yale University Press, 1963; (editor, author of introduction and notes) Pierre Corneille, *Polyeucte and Le Menteur*, Dell, 1964; (editor, annotator, and author of introduction) Franciscus Hemsterhuis, *Lettere sur l'homme et ses rapport: Avec le commentaire inedit de Diderot*, Yale University Press, 1964; *Diderot et Baudelaire*, Librairie Droz, 1967. Contributor of articles on French literature to professional journals.

WORK IN PROGRESS: Research in French literature of the 17th and 18th centuries, especially fiction and drama.

*   *   *

MAY, H(enry)J(ohn)   1903-
(H. J. Schlosberg)

PERSONAL: Adopted, 1912, by maternal grandfather and used his name, Hershel Joshua Schlosberg; reverted to use of family name, 1936; born on March 11, 1903, in Bulawayo, Rhodesia; married Olga Blaiberg, February 2, 1939; children: Daryl Norman. *Education:* Studied at University of Edinburgh, 1921-22, Gray's Inn, London, England, 1922-25. *Politics:* Conservative. *Residence:* Channel Islands, England. *Agent:* Peter Janson-Smith Ltd., 31 Newington Green, London, N16 9PU, England.

CAREER: Admitted to English bar, London, and to South African bar, 1925; engaged in private practice of law in Johannesburg and Durban, becoming a specialist in insurance law, 1925-65; Queen's Counsel, 1955. Examiner to universitites in constitutional law and the law of evidence. Lecturer on U.S. tour, 1950-51. *Military service:* South African Army Services, 1940-45; became captain. *Member:* Honourable Society of Gray's Inn.

WRITINGS: (Under name H. J. Schlosberg) *King's Republics*, Stevens, 1929; (under name H. J. Schlosberg) *South African Cases and Statutes on Evidence*, Juta, 1929, 4th edition, under name H. J. May, 1962, co-author, under name H. J. May, of supplement, *Ten Years' Leading Cases on Evidence, 1936-46*, 1947; (under name H. J. Schlosberg; with W. P. M. Kennedy) *The Law and Custom of the South African Constitution*, Oxford University Press, 1935, sole author, under name H. J. May, of 2nd and 3rd editions, published as *South African Constitution*, Juta, 1949 and 1955; (with J. Grenfell Williams) *I Am Black: The Story of Shabala*, Cassell, 1936; *Little Yellow Gentlemen*, Cassill, 1937; *Red Wine of Youth*, Shooter, 1947.

(With Iain Hamilton) *The Foster Gang*, Heinemann, 1966; *Murder by Consent: The Facts in the Tragedy of Baron von Schauroth*, Hutchinson, 1968; *Wolf by the Ears* (novel), Hutchinson, 1969; (editor) *Music of the Guns* (two journals of the Boer War), Hutchinson, 1970.

AVOCATIONAL INTERESTS: Gardening.

*   *   *

MAYER, Michael F.   1917-

PERSONAL: Born September 8, 1917, in White Plains, N.Y.; son of Arthur L. (a teacher and writer) and Lillie (Stein) Mayer; married Janet Claster, August 15, 1943; childern: Doe, Arthur, Aline L., Shelley B. *Education:* Harvard University, B.S., 1939; Yale University, LL.B., 1942. *Politics:* Democrat. *Religion:* Jewish. *Home:* 9 Inverness Rd., Scarsdale, N.Y. *Office:* 111 West 57th St., New York, N.Y. 10019.

CAREER: Kingsley International Picture Corp. (film dis-

tributors), New York, N.Y., secretary, 1956-62; Spring & Mayer (attorneys), New York, N.Y., partner, 1958-67; Independent Film Importers and Distributors of America, Inc., New York, N.Y., executive director, 1959-67; Mayer & Bucher (attorneys), New York, N.Y., 1968—. U.S. Special council, French Society of Authors, Composers, and Publishers, 1961—; lecturer on film topics at New School of Social Research, Columbia University Institute of Mass Communication, Dartmouth College, and University of Pennsylvania. *Military service:* U.S. Army Air Forces; served in China-Burma-India Theater, 1944; received Air Medal. *Member:* Westchester County Bar Association, Bar Association of City of New York, Variety Club, Yale Club of New York.

WRITINGS: Foreign Films on American Screens, Arco, 1965; *Divorce and Annulment in the Fifty States*, Arco, 1967; *What You Should Know About Libel and Slander*, Arco, 1968; *Rights of Privacy*, Law-Arts, 1972; *The Film Industries*, Hastings House, 1973.

WORK IN PROGRESS: Amnesty?

*   *   *

MAYERSON, Charlotte Leon

PERSONAL: Born in New York, N.Y.; daughter of Victor and Hilda (Weisman) Leon; married Burton Mayerson, April 8, 1951; children: Robert Henry. *Education:* Queen's College (now of the City University of New York), Flushing, N.Y., B.A., 1949. *Residence:* New York, N.Y. *Office:* Holt, Rinehart & Winston, Inc., 383 Madison Ave., New York, N.Y. 10017.

CAREER: Holt, Rinehart & Winston, Inc., New York, N.Y., now a general book editor.

WRITINGS: Shadow and Light: The Life, Friends and Opinions of Maurice Sterne, Harcourt, 1965; *Two Blocks Apart: Juan Gonzales and Peter Quinn*, Holt, 1965.†

*   *   *

MAYFIELD, Julian   1928-

PERSONAL: Born June 6, 1928, in Greer, S.C.; son of Hudson and Annie Mae (Prince) Mayfield; married Ana Livia Cordero (a physician); children: Rafael Ariel, Emiliano Kwesi. *Education:* Attended Lincoln University, Lincoln University, Pa. *Politics:* Blackist-Marxist. *Religion:* Atheist. *Address:* African Review, P.O. Box 2052, Accra, Ghana. *Agent:* Ruth Aley, Maxwell Aley Associates, 145 East 35th St., New York, N.Y. 10016.

CAREER: Puerto Rico World Journal, onetime editor and theater reveiwer; now editor, *African Review*, Accra, Ghana. *Member:* Actors' Equity Association, Writers Guild of America East, Ghanian Association of Journalists and Writers.

WRITINGS—Novels: The Hit, Vanguard, 1957; *The Long Night*, Vanguard, 1958; *The Grand Parade*, Vanguard, 1961, published as *Nowhere Street*, Paperback Library, 1968; (compiler) *Ten Times Black: Stories From the Black Experience*, Bantam, 1972. Co-author of filmscript "Uptight." Contributor of political articles to *Nation, Commentary, New Republic*, and other periodicals.

WORK IN PROGRESS: Look Pretty for the People, a novel; with Leslie A. Lacy, *The Living Ghana*, a historical, political, and cultural survey.

SIDELIGHTS: Mayfield's books have been translated into French, German, Czechoslovakian, and Japanese.†

MAYNE, Richard (John) 1926-

PERSONAL: Born April 2, 1926, in London, England; son of John William and K. H. (angus) Mayne; *Education:* Trinity College, Cambridge, B.A. (first class honors, with distinction), 1950, M.A., 1953, Ph.D., 1955. *Home:* 67 Harley St., London W.1., England.

CAREER: New Statesman, London, England, Rome correspondent, 1953-54; Cambridge Institute of Education, Cambridge, England, assistant tutor, 1954-56; European Coal and Steel Community, Luxembourg, staff member of High Authority, 1956-58; Commission of European Economic Community, Brussels, Belgium, staff member, 1958-68; Action Committee for United States of Europe, Paris, France, director of Documentation Center, 1963-66; Federal Trust for Education and Research, London, England, director, 1970-73; Commission of the European Communities, London, England, head of London office, 1973—. *Military service:* British Army Royal Signals, 1944-47; became lieutenant. Army Officers' Emergency Reserve, 1947—.

WRITINGS: The Community of Europe, Gollancz, 1962, Norton, 1963; *The Institutions of the European Community*, Political & Economic Planning (London), 1968; *The Recovery of Europe*, Harper, 1970; *The Europeans*, Weidenfeld & Nicolson, 1972; *Europe Tomorrow*, Fontant Books, 1972.

WORK IN PROGRESS: A portrait of Jean Monnet.

SIDELIGHTS: Mayne's books have been translated into six languages. He speaks French, Italian, German. *Avocational interests:* Travel, sailing, and inertia.

*   *   *

MAZOUR, Anatole G. 1900-

PERSONAL: Born May 24, 1900, in Kiev, Russia (now Ukrainian Soviet Socialist Republic); came to United States in 1922, naturalized in 1932; son of Gregory A. (a pomologist) and Sophie (Katova) Mazour; married Lucille Jackson, January 7, 1932; married second wife, Josephine Lurie, September 15, 1944; children: Alexander, Natasha. *Education:* University of Nebraska, A.B., 1929; Yale University, M.A., 1931; University of California, Berkeley, Ph.D., 1934. *Politics:* Democrat. *Religion:* Greek Orthodox. *Home:* 781 Frenchman's Rd., Stanford, Calif. 94305.

CAREER: Member of faculty at University of Chicago, University of Oregon, University of Wyoming, and University of Nevada, 1938-47; Stanford University, Stanford, Calif., professor of Russian history, 1947-66, professor emeritus, 1966—. Hill Foundation lecturer, Carleton College, 1956; Distinguished visiting professor, University of Nebraska, 1966-67. *Military service:* Russian Imperial and Russian White Army, 1917-20. *Member:* American Historical Society, Phi Beta Kappa, Phi Alpha Theta, Phi Kappa Phi, Commonwealth Club (San Francisco). *Awards, honors:* LL.D., University of Nebraska, 1963.

WRITINGS: The First Russian Revolution, 1825: The Decembrist Movement, its Origins, Development, and Significance, University of California Press, 1937, Stanford University Press, 1961; *An Outline of Modern Russian Historiography*, University of California Press, 1939, 2nd edition, revised and enlarged, published as *Modern Russian Historiography*, Van Nostrand, 1958; *Russia: Past and Present*, Van Nostrand, 1951; *Finland Between East and West*, Van Nostrand, 1956; (with John M. Peoples) *Men and Nations: A World History*, World Book, 1959, 2nd edition, Harcourt, 1968; *Rise and Fall of the Romanovs*, Van Nostrand, 1960; *Russia: Tsarist and Communist*, Van Nostrand, 1962; *Soviet Economic Development: Operation Outstrip, 1921-1965*, Van Nostrand, 1967; *The Writing of History in the Soviet Union*, Hoover Institution Press, 1971.

WORK IN PROGRESS: The Wives of the Decembrists.

*   *   *

MAZZE, Edward M(ark) 1941-

PERSONAL: Born February 14, 1941, in New York, N.Y.; son of Harry A. (a corporation president) and Mollie (Schneider) Mazze; married Sharon Sue Hastings, September 9, 1967; children: Candace Elizabeth. *Education:* City College (now City College of the City University of New York), B.B.A., 1961, M.B.A., 1962; Pennsylvania State University, Ph.D., 1966. *Address:* P.O. Box 873, Blacksburg, Va. 24060. *Office:* Department of Marketing, Virginia Polytechnic Institute and State University, Blacksburg, Va. 24060.

CAREER: University of Detroit, Detroit, Mich., associate professor of marketing, 1966-68; West Virginia University, Morgantown, associate professor of marketing and director of special programs, 1968-70; Virginia Polytechnic Institute and State University, Blacksburg, professor of business administration and coordinator of marketing program, 1970—, director of business extension of College of Business, 1971-72. Consultant to business and government, 1963—; advisory editor, Holt, Rinehart & Winston, 1963-69; visiting professor, University of Pittsburgh, 1970, University of Puerto Rico, 1974. *Member:* American Marketing Association, Academy of Management, American Institute for Decision Sciences, Association for Education in International Business. *Awards, honors:* European Association of Sales Consultants prize, 1965, for *Sales Management*.

WRITINGS: (With Conrad Berenson) *How to Organize for International Marketing in the Chemical Industry*, Corporate Publications, 1962; (editor with Huxley Madeheim and Charles Stein) *Readings in Organization and Management*, Holt, 1963; (editor with Madeheim and Stein) *International Business: Articles and Essays*, Holt, 1963; (editor with William Schultz) *Marketing in Action: Readings*, Wadsworth, 1963; (editor with Milton Alexander) *Sales Management: Theory and Practice*, Pitman, 1965, *Teacher's Manual*, 1965; (with Alexander) *Case Histories in Sales Management*, Pitman, 1965; *International Marketing Administration*, Chandler Publishing, 1967; (compiler) *Introduction to Marketing: Readings in the Discipline*, Chandler Publishing, 1970; *The Management of Retail Enterprises: Decision Exercises*, College of Business, Virginia Polytechnic Institute and State University, 1971; (contributor) Gerald Rudolph, editor, *The Academic Community Looks at Library Management*, Virginia Polytechnic Institute and State University, 1972.

General editor of "Basic Management Series," published by Holt, 1964-69; contributor of articles, and book reviews to *Management, Apparel Manufacturer*, and other professional journals; member of editorial staff of marketing abstracts section, *Journal of Marketing*, 1971-75.

WORK IN PROGRESS: Personal Selling: Choice vs. Chance, publication by West expected in 1976.

McAULAY, John D(avid) 1912-

PERSONAL: Born June 12, 1912, in Calgary, Alberta, Canada; son of Ewen Gould (a businessman) and Ruby (Tuggey) McAulay; married Vera Elizabeth Claxton, June 12, 1945; children: Thomas Ewen. *Education:* University of Alberta, B.A. and B. Ed., 1938; University of British Columbia, M.A., 1946; Stanford University, Ed.D., 1948. *Politics:* Democrat. *Religion:* Methodist. *Home:* 309 Hillcrest, State College, Pa. *Office:* Chambers 145, Pennsylvania State University, University Park, Pa.

CAREER: Teacher in rural and city elementary and junior high schools, 1948-58; Southern Oregon College, Ashland, director of education, 1958; Pennsylvania State University, University Park, 1958—, began as associate professor, became professor. Summer school instructor at Universities of Texas, Tennessee, California, and British Columbia. Fulbright scholar to Australia and New Zealand as consultant on teacher education, 1956-58; U.S. Department of State consultant on education in Central America and Venezuela, 1962. *Military service:* Canadian Army, 1940-45; became sergeant.

MEMBER: National Education Association, National Association of Geographers, National Commission on Teacher Education and Professional Standards, National Council for Social Studies, Association for Supervision and Curriculum Development, Association of Geography Teachers, Phi Delta Kappa, Phi Kappa Phi. *Awards, honors:* Journal of Geography award, 1962, for research in the geographic understandings of primary grade children.

WRITINGS: (With Regan) *Social Studies for Today's Children* (college textbook), Appleton, 1964, 2nd edition, 1973. (With Carls and Sorenson) *Knowing Our Neighbors in Canada and Latin America*, Holt, Rinehart & Winston, 1964; *This is Canada*, Grosset, 1965; (contributor) *Education Index*, Prentice-Hall, 1965 (with Burdin) *Elementary School Curriculum and Instruction* (college textbook), Ronald, 1971. Also principal author of "Sadlier Social Studies Series, Kindergarten-9th Grade," 1972. Contributor to professional journals.

WORK IN PROGRESS: Development of competency-based social studies modules for preparation of elementary teachers, construction of individualized socialization kits for pre-school and primary grade children.

*   *   *

McBRIDE, Alfred 1928-

PERSONAL: Born December 12, 1928, in Philadelphia, Pa.; son of Charles and Mary (Shannon) McBride. *Education:* St. Norbert College, B.A., 1950; Lumen Vitae, Brussels, Belgium, diploma, 1963; Catholic University of America, Ph.D. *Home:* 1737 Corcoran St. N.W., Washington, D.C. 20009. *Office:* NCEA, Suite 350, One Dupont Circle, Washington, D.C. 20036.

CAREER: Ordained Roman Catholic priest, member of Norbertine Fathers, 1953. Taught Latin and religion in parochial high school and then served in a parish, De Pere, Wis., 1953-59; St. Norbert Abbey, De Pere, Wis., master of novices, beginning 1959; now with NCEA, Washington, D.C., director of National Forum for Religious Educators. Lecturer on teaching of religion to educators in midwest; conductor of seminar on religious education in Montreal, 1965, member, St. Norbert Abbey. *Member:* Society for American Archaeology, Catholic Homiletic Society.

WRITINGS: Bible Themes for Modern Man, St. Norbert Abbey, 1964; *Homilies for the New Liturgy*, Bruce, 1965; *Cathechetics: A Theology of Proclamation*, Bruce, 1966; *The Human Dimensions of Catechetics*, Bruce, 1967; *Growing in Grace*, Gastonia Press, 1969; *The Pearl and the Seed*, Allyn & Bacon, 1971; *Heschel: Religious Educator*, Dimension Press, 1973; *The Gospel of the Holy Spirit*, Arena Lettres, 1974. Contributor to *Worship, Today, Ave Maria, American Ecclesiastical Review, Hi Time, America*, and *Pastoral Life.*

*   *   *

McCABE, Herbert 1926-

PERSONAL: Born August 2, 1926, in Middlesbrough, England; son of Francis Andrew (a headmaster) and Catharine (Buckley) McCabe. *Education:* University of Manchester, B.A. (honors in philosophy), 1949; Blackfriars, Oxford, England, S.T.L., 1957. *Politics:* Socialist. *Home:* Blackfriars, Oxford, England.

CAREER: Roman Catholic priest, member of Order of Preachers (Dominicans). Hawkesyard Priory in England, lecturer in philosophy, beginning 1964; now at Blackfriars, Oxford, lecturer in theology. Occasional lecture, theology and philosophy for extramural departments, University of Manchester, Oxford University, University of Birmingham, and other universities in England. *Member:* Society for the Study of Theology, Newman Association.

WRITINGS: (Contributor) *Theology of Work* (symposium), edited by John Todd, Darton, Longman & Todd, 1960; *The People of God: The Fullness of Life in the Church*, Sheed, 1964, published in England as *The New Creation: Studies on the Living Church*; (translator and editor) Thomas Aquinas, *Summa Theologiae*, Volume III, Eyre & Spottiswoode, 1964; (contributor) *Theology in the University* (symposium), edited by John Coulson, Darton, Longman & Todd, 1964; *Law, Love and Language*, Sheed, 1968, published as *What is Ethics All About?*, Corpus Books, 1969. Also author of *Liturgy and Community*, Darton, Longman & Todd. Contributor to journals, mainly Catholic.

WORK IN PROGRESS: A study of developments in moral theology and a book for Penguin, *Roman Catholicism.*

*   *   *

McCALLUM, Ian R. M. 1919-

PERSONAL: Born November 28, 1919, in London, England; son of Robert More (a businessman) and Jane (Taylor) McCallum. *Education:* Architectural Association School of Architecture, diploma, 1941. *Politics:* Anarchist. *Religion:* Agnostic. *Home:* 16 Kylestrome House, Ebury Sq., London S.W.1, England.

CAREER: Architects' Journal, London, England, associate editor, 1944-49; *Architectural Review*, London, England, executive editor, 1949-59; American Museum in Britain, near Bath, England, director, beginning 1959. National Trust, member of executive committee of Georgian Group and regional committee of Historic Buildings Council; Royal West of England Academy, member of council. *Member:* Royal Institute of British Architects (associate).

WRITINGS: (Editor) *Physical Planning: The Groundwork of a New Technique*, 1945; *A Guide to Modern Buildings in London*, 1951; *Architecture USA*, Reinhold, 1959.

SIDELIGHTS: Ian McCallum is competent in French.†

McCALLUM, Neil 1916-

PERSONAL: Born 1916, in Edinburgh, Scotland; married Marie Veitch; children: two sons, one daughter. Education: Attended University of Edinburgh. Politics: Democratic. Agent: Curtis Brown Ltd., 60 East 56th St., New York, N.Y. 10022.

CAREER: Author. Member: P.E.N., Scottish Arts Club.

WRITINGS: Half-way House, Cassell, 1949; My Enemies Have Sweet Voices (stories), Cassell, 1951; It's an Old Scottish Custom, Dobson, 1951, Vanguard, 1952; Fountainfoot, Cassell, 1952; Journey with a Pistol, Gollancz, 1958; A Scream in the Sky, Cassell, 1964. Contributor to New Statesman.†

* * *

McCARTHY, Cormac 1933-

PERSONAL: Born July 20, 1933, in Providence, R.I.; son of Charles Joseph and Gladys (McGrail) McCarthy. Education: Attended University of Tennessee four years. Agent: A. Watkins, Inc., 77 Park Ave., New York, N.Y. 10016.

CAREER: Author. Awards, honors: Ingram-Merrill Foundation grant for creative writing, 1960; American Academy of Arts and Letters traveling fellowship to Europe, 1965-66; William Faulkner Foundation award, 1965, for The Orchard Keeper.

WRITINGS: The Orchard Keeper, Random House, 1965; Outer Dark, Random House, 1968; Child of God, Random House, 1974. Contributor to Yale Review and Sewanee Review.

WORK IN PROGRESS: Two novels.

BIOGRAPHICAL/CRITICAL SOURCES: America, June 12, 1965; Saturday Review, June 12, 1965; Harper's, July, 1965; Book Week, July 4, 1965; Carolyn Riley, editor, Contemporary Literary Criticism, Volume IV, Gale, 1975.†

* * *

McCARTHY, Thomas P. 1920-

PERSONAL: Born May 12, 1920, in Boston, Mass.; son of Thomas P. (an engineer) and Rose (McKernan) McCarthy. Education: Loyola University, Chicago, Ill., Ph.B., 1950; Catholic University of America, M.A., 1953. Politics: Democrat. Home: 10 Artemesia Way, Reno, Nev. 89503.

CAREER: Roman Catholic priest of Clerics of St. Viator order. Teacher in Catholic high schools in Rock Island, Ill., 1953-59, in Peoria, Ill., 1959-64, at Bishop Gorman High School, Las Vegas, Nev., beginning 1964. Our Lady of Wisdom Catholic Church, Reno, Nev., pastor, 1973—.

WRITINGS: (Compiler) Guide to the Catholic Sisterhoods in the U.S., Catholic University of America Press, 1952, 5th edition, revised, Catholic University of America Press, 1964; Guide to the Diocesan Priesthood in the U.S., Catholic University of America Press, 1956; Total Dedication for the Laity, St. Paul Editions, 1964; Challenge for Now, privately printed, 1974. Editorial consultant, Catholic Youth Encyclopedia, McGraw, 1966.

* * *

McCLUNG, Robert M. 1916-

PERSONAL: Born September 10, 1916; son of Frank A. (a banker) and Mary A. (Goehring) McClung; married Gale Stubbs (editor of Mount Holyoke Alumnae Quarterly), July 23, 1949; children: William Marshall, Thomas Cooper. Education: Princeton University, A.B., 1939; Cornell University, M.S., 1948. Religion: Protestant. Home: 91 Sunset Ave., Amherst, Mass. 01002.

CAREER: McCann, Erickson, Inc. (advertising agency), New York, N.Y., copywriter, 1940-41, 1946-47; New York Zoological Park, New York, N.Y., assistant in animal departments, 1948-52, curator of mammals and birds, 1952-55; National Geographic Society, Washington, D.C., editor, 1958-62; free-lance writer and illustrator of children's books, 1955-58, 1962—. Military service: U.S. Naval Reserve, active duty as deck officer and naval aviaitor, 1941-46; became lieutenant commander.

WRITINGS—All self-illustrated, except as noted; all published by Morrow, except as noted: Wings in the Woods, 1948; Sphinx: The Story of a Caterpillar, 1949.

Ruby Throat: The Story of a Hummingbird, 1950; Stripe: The Story of a Chipmunk, 1951; Spike: The Story of a Whitetail Deer, 1952; Tiger: The Story of a Swallowtail Butterfly, 1953; Bufo: The Story of a Toad, 1954; Vulcan: The Story of a Bald Eagle, illustrated by Lloyd Sandford, 1955; Major: The Story of a Black Bear, 1956; Green Darner: The Story of a Dragonfly, 1956; Leaper: The Story of an Atlantic Salmon, 1957; Luna: The Story of a Moth, 1957; Little Burma, illustrated by Hord Stubblefield, 1958; All about Animals and Their Young, Random House, 1958; Buzztail: The Story of a Rattlesnake, 1958; Whooping Crane, illustrated by Sandford, 1959; Otus: The Story of a Screech Owl, illustrated by Sandford, 1959.

Shag: Last of the Plains Buffalo, illustrated by Louis Darling, 1960; Whitefoot: The Story of a Woodmouse, 1961; Mammals and How They Live (illustrated with photographs), Random House, 1963; Possum, 1963; Screamer: Last of the Eastern Panthers, illustrated by Sandford, 1964; Spotted Salamander, 1964; Honker: The Story of a Wild Goose, illustrated by Bob Hines, 1965; Caterpillars and How They Live, 1965; The Swift Deer (illustrated with photographs), Random House, 1966; Ladybug, 1966; Moths and Butterflies and How They Live, 1966; The Mighty Bears (illustrated with photographs), Random House, 1967; Horseshoe Crab, 1967; Black Jack: Last of the Big Alligators, illustrated by Sandford, 1967; Redbird: The Story of a Cardinal, 1968; Lost Wild America: The Story of Our Extinct and Vanishing Wildlife, illustrated by Hines, 1969; Blaze: The Story of a Striped Skunk, 1969.

Aquatic Insects and How They Live, 1970; Thor: Last of the Sperm Whales, illustrated by Hines, 1971; Bees, Wasps, and Hornets, and How They Live, 1971; Scoop: Last of the Brown Pelicans, illustrated by McClung and Sandford, 1972; Samson: Last of the California Grizzlies, illustrated by Hines, 1973; Mice, Moose, and Men: How Their Populations Rise and Fall, 1973; Gypsy Moth: Its History in America, 1974.

Editor and contributor, Wild Animals of North America, Song and Garden Birds of North America, Water, Prey, and Game Birds of North America, and Vacationland U.S.A., all published by National Geographic Society. Contributor to Grolier's New Book of Knowledge, and to magazines.

WORK IN PROGRESS: Lost Wild Worlds: The Story of Earth's Vanishing Wildlife, for Morrow.

McCOLLEY, Robert (McNair) 1933-

PERSONAL: Born February 2, 1933, in Salina, Kan.; son of Grant (a professor of literature) and Alice (McNair) McColley; married Diane Kelsey, August 30, 1958; children: Rebecca Diane, Susanna Antonia, Teresa Lelah Fay, Margaret Elizabeth, Carolyn Alice, Robert Lauren. Education: Harvard University, B.A., 1954, M.A., 1955; University of California, Berkeley, Ph.D., 1960. Religion: Episcopal. Home: 1101 South Orchard St., Urbana, Ill. 61801. Office: History Department, 309 Gregory Hall, Urbana, Ill. 61801.

CAREER: University of Illinois, Champaign, (now located in Urbana), instructor, 1960-62, assistant professor 1962-67; associate professor of history, 1967—. Member: Organization of American Historians Southern Historical Association.

WRITINGS: Slavery and Jeffersonian Virginia, University of Illinois Press, 1964; Federalists, Republicans, and Foreign Entanglements, Prentice-Hall, 1969.

WORK IN PROGRESS: Black Virginians: The Colonial Era, United States History Survey, with others, for Dorsey Press, completion expected in 1975, and Jefferson and Hamilton, a Reconsideration, completion expected in 1976.

* * *

McCOLLOUGH, Celeste 1926-

PERSONAL: Born September 12, 1926, in Boulder, Colo; daughter of Byron G. and Faye (Pevoto) McCollough. Education: Rice University student, 1943-44; Oberlin College, B.A., 1947; University of Michigan, M.A., 1949; Columbia University, Ph.D., 1955. Office: Oberlin College, Oberlin, Ohio.

CAREER: Olivet College, Olivet, Mich., 1954-56, began as assistant professor, became associate professor; Oberlin College, Oberlin, Ohio, member of faculty, beginning 1956.

WRITINGS: (With Loche van Atta) Statistical Concepts: A Program for Self-Instruction, McGraw, 1963; (with van Atta) Introduction to Descriptive Statistics and Correlation, McGraw, 1965; An Introductory Course in Statistical Analysis: A Semiprogrammed Approach, McGraw, 1974.†

* * *

McCOMB, K(atherine Woods) 1895-
(Constance Woods)

PERSONAL: Born June 8, 1895, in Clarksville, Tex.; daughter of William N. H. (a farmer) and Isabelle (Grantham) Woods; married Robert L. McComb, August 3, 1912. Education: Attended business college and took extension courses in writing from University of California. Religion: Methodist. Home: 3914 Herndon St., Corpus Christi, Tex. 78411.

CAREER: Employed by banks as a bookkeeper in Corpus Christi, Tex., 1918-23, Los Angles, Calif., 1924-32, as transit clerk in Los Angles, 1940-43; free-lance writer. Member: National Federation of Press Women, Southern California Women's Press Club (recording secretary, 1938-40), Texas Press Women, Byliners of Corpus Christi (vice-president, 1957-58, 1964-65), Awards, honors: Southwest Texas Writers Conference, first prize for juvenile books, 1959, 1960.

WRITINGS: G. for Gunsmoke, Arcadia House, 1957; Conestoga Campfire, Arcadia House, 1959; Death in a Downpour, Arcadia House, 1960; A Day for Murder, Avalon, 1963; Princess of White Starch, Ace Books, 1963; Nurse April, Avalon, 1967; Detour to Romance, Lancer, 1969; Night Duty Nurse, Avalon, 1970; Hollywood Nurse, Avalon, 1971; Nurse on Trial, Avalon, 1973.

Under pseudonym Constance Woods: Passport to Adventure, Avalon, 1967. Contributor of short stories to western pulp magazines, and to Practical English, Co-Ed, Teen, Hollywood, and religious periodicals.

WORK IN PROGRESS: A book, Frontier Nurse.

AVOCATIONAL INTERESTS: Reading about early America, fishing, travel.

* * *

McCONNELL, Virginia (McCorison) 1928-

PERSONAL: Born January 27, 1928, in Nashua, Iowa; daughter of Joseph Lyle (a clergyman) and Ruth (Mink) McCorison; married John Creston McConnell (owner of retail hardware store), July 29, 1950; children: Thomas Creston, Susan Ruth. Education: Oberlin College, A.B., 1949; Colorado College, graduate study. Politics: Democrat. Home: 1112 North Meade Ave., Colorado Springs, Colo.

CAREER: Colorado Springs Symphony Association, Colorado Springs, Colo., publicity, beginning 1962; Colorado Department of Education, Denver, writer on Western States Small Schools Project, beginning 1963. Member: National Federation of Press Women, American Association of University Women (member of board of directors, Lorain, Ohio, 1953-54), League of Women Voters (member of board of directors, Lorain, Ohio, 1953-54, Colorado Springs, Colo., 1958-61), Colorado State Historical Society, Junior League (Colorado Springs); Colorado Springs Ghost Town Club, Historical Society of the Pikes Peak Region (member of executive board, 1965).

WRITINGS: Ute Pass: Route of the Blue Sky People, Sage Books, 1963; (with Bettie Marie Daniels) The Springs of Manitou, Sage Books, 1964; Bayou Salado: The Story of South Park, Sage Books, 1966. Also author of An Experiment with Rural Students, Colorado Department of Education. Contributor to Trailer Life, Methodist Woman, and to newspapers in Denver, Cleveland, and Colorado Springs.

AVOCATIONAL INTERESTS: Music, poetry, skiing.†

* * *

McCOY, Iola Fuller
(Iola Fuller)

PERSONAL: Born in Marcellus, Mich.; daughter of Henry and Clara (Reynolds) Fuller; married twice; children: (first marriage) Paul Goodspeed. Education: University of Michigan, A.B., 1935, A.M. in English, 1940, A.M.L.S., 1962. Religion: Episcopalian. Home: 2756 Wisteria Place, Sarasota, Fla. 33579.

CAREER: Experience includes setting up new school libraries, college teaching, and writing and research; Ferris State College, associate professor of English, 1964-69; now engaged in full time writing. Member: American Association of University Professors, Phi Beta Kappa. Awards, honors: Avery Hopwood Award for Creative Writing, 1939; University of Michigan Distinguished Alumni Award, 1967.

WRITINGS—Under name Iola Fuller; all historical novels: *The Loon Feather*, Harcourt, 1940; *The Shining Trail*, Duell, Sloan & Pearce, 1943; *The Gilded Torch*, Putnam, 1957; *All the Golden Gates*, Putnam, 1966.

WORK IN PROGRESS: A historical novel set in seventeenth-century Quebec.

SIDELIGHTS: Iola McCoy told *CA:* "The late Professor Roy W. Cowden of the University of Michigan was my greatest writing influence, in his courses in creative writing. Important to me: accuracy in historical material used, a theme of universal importance, a carefully constructed plot, and careful character development. Good craftsmanship is a major goal. No formulas except the excellent old one: 'An *appealing* character strives against great odds to attain worthwhile goal.'"Iola McCoy has traveled extensively throughout Canada, Mexico, the United States and Europe in connection with research for her novels. She speaks French and German.†

*   *   *

McCOY, J(oseph) J(erome)   1917-

PERSONAL: Born January 4, 1917, in Philadelphia, Pa.; son of Joseph J. (a civil engineer) and Clara (Tinaro) McCoy; married Barbara Kocyan (an actress and teacher), April 13, 1948; children: Tara Irene, Liza Marie. *Education:* Pennsylvania State University, Associate degree in Agriculture. *Agent:* Bertha Klausner, International Literary Agency, 71 Park Ave., New York, N.Y. 10016.

CAREER: Radio producer-director in Philadelphia, Pa., 1946-47; Children's Aid Society, New York, N.Y., instructor in agriculture and nature, 1947-48; farm manager in Connecticut, 1948-50; New York (N.Y.) Humane Society, manager, 1950-56; Gaines Dog Research Center, New York, N.Y., assistant to director, 1956-60; General Features Corp., syndicated columnist, 1965-68; full–time writer, 1960—. *Military service:* U.S. Army, Veterinary Service, 1942-46; became technical sergeant. *Member:* Authors Guild, Hawk Mountain Sanctuary. *Awards, honors:* New York Herald Tribune Spring Book Festival, Honor Book, 1966, and National Association of Independent Schools Award, 1967, for *The Hunt for the Whooping Crane;* National Science Teachers Association and the Childrens Book Council, outstanding science book for children, 1973, for *Our Captive Animals.*

WRITINGS—Adult: (With H. J. Deutsch) *How to Care for Your Cat*, Cornerstone, 1961; *The Complete Book of Dog Training and Care*, Coward, 1962; *The Complete Book of Cat Health and Care*, Putnam, 1966; *Saving Our Wildlife*, Macmillan, 1970.

Juvenile: *Lords of the Sky*, Bobbs-Merril, 1963; *Animal Servants of Man*, Lothrop, 1963; *The World of the Veterinarian*, Lothrop, 1964; *The Hunt for the Whooping Crane*, Lothrop, 1966; *Swans*, Lothrop, 1967; *House Sparrows: Ragamuffins of the City*, Seabury, 1968; *The Nature Sleuths: Protectors of Our Wildlife*, Lothrop, 1969; *Shadows Over the Land*, Seabury, 1970; *To Feed a Nation*, Nelson, 1971; *Our Captive Animals*, Seaburg, 1972; *Wild Enemies*, Hawthorn, 1974; *A Sea of Troubles*, Seabury, 1975; *The Sacred Land*, Hawthorn, in press. Contributor to *Grolier Encyclopedia International* and *Encyclopedia America.*

WORK IN PROGRESS: Two plays for children and a book for adults entitled *Pets or Pests,* completion expected in 1976.

SIDELIGHTS: J. J. McCoy told *CA:* "One doesn't write down to children today; one is lucky to be able to keep up with them. Children want their intelligence to be respected and demand accuracy and clarity. The criticism of juvenile readers is blunt, unadorned, and pragmatic—and I would like to see juvenile books reviewed by children!" *Avocational interests:* Gardening, scouting, theater, hiking.

*   *   *

McDONALD, Eva (Rose)

PERSONAL: Born in London, England; daughter of Edgar William Jary and Louisa Harriet (Roberts) McDonald. *Education:* Attended South London Commerical College. *Religion:* Christian. *Home:* Wyldwynds, 105 Bathurst Walk, Iver, Buckinghamshire SL0 9EF, England.

CAREER: Novelist. *Member:* Society of Authors.

WRITINGS—All Published by R. Hale: *Lazare the Leopard*, 1959; *Dark Enchantment*, 1960; *The Rebel Bride*, 1960; *The Prettiest Jacobite*, 1961; *The Captive Lady*, 1962; *The Maids of Taunton*, 1963; *The Black Glove*, 1964; *The Reluctant Bridegroom*, 1965; *The Runaway Countess*, 1966; *The Gretna Wedding*, 1967; *The Austrian Bride*, 1968; *Lord Byron's First Love*, 1968; *The Lost Lady*, 1969; *The Wicked Squire*, 1970; *The French Mademoiselle*, 1970; *Shelley's Springtime Bride*, 1970; *The White Petticoat*, 1971; *The Spanish Wedding*, 1971; *The Lady from Yorktown*, 1972; *Regency Rake*, 1973; *The Revengeful Husband*, 1974; *Lament for Lady Flora*, 1974; *Lord Rochester's Daughters*, 1974.

SIDELIGHTS: Miss McDonald writes to *CA:* "I adore traveling, having been to Scandinavia and Europe, . . . in Switzerland, France, Italy, Germany, and Yugoslavia. I also adore cats but alas lost two, Smokey and Pinto, both dear little creatures: one followed me like a dog and Pinto used to meet me when I came off my train in the evening: he was so clever that he knew at what time I would come. As to my writing, my first book, *Lazare the Leopard*, was written when I was 21, but it was published many years later: I always meant to be a writer but I must confess to great despondency. Both my mother and grandmother . . . encouraged me tremendously: to them both I owe a tremendous debt: it was my Grandmother who arranged for me to be taught the piano and when I was in my twenties and thirties it was my darling mother who so encouraged me and always took in the melancholy returning manuscripts."

*   *   *

McDONALD, Nicholas   1923-

PERSONAL: Born October 24, 1923, in Gary, Ind.; son of John (a steelworker) and Pearl (Orlich) McDonald; married Elaine Hronkin, February 23, 1946; children: James, Jean, Jill. *Education:* Indiana University, student, 1947-49, 1957-60; Loyola University, Chicago, Ill., B.S. in Ed., 1952; Roosevelt University, M.A. in Ed., 1957. *Politics:* Democrat. *Religion:* Roman Catholic. *Home:* 942 East 53rd Ave., Gary, Ind. *Office:* Bailly Junior High School, 4621 Georgia St., Gary, Ind.

CAREER: Gary (Ind.) public schools, teacher, 1952-58, assistant principal, 1958-59, elementary supervisor, 1959-61, principal of Brunswick School, 1961-65, principal of Bailly Junior High School, beginning 1965. *Military service:* U.S. Army, 1943-45; served in Africa and Europe; became technical sergeant; received Bronze Star Medal. *Member:* National Association of Secondary School Principals, National Education Association, American Council on Education, International Reading Association.

WRITINGS: *English, Your Language,* Book 7 (text and workbook), Allyn & Bacon, 1964.†

* * *

McGANN, Thomas F.   1920-

PERSONAL: Born March 25, 1920, in Cambridge, Mass.; son of Thomas F. and Margaret (Chisholm) McGann; married Dorothy Rich, February 27, 1943; children: Margot, Wendy, Duncan, Mark. *Education:* Harvard University, A.B., 1941, A.M., 1949, Ph.D., 1952. *Politics:* Democrat. *Religion:* Roman Catholic. *Home:* 4615 Crestway Dr., Austin, Tex. *Office:* Department of History, University of Texas, Austin, Tex.

CAREER: U.S. Department of State, junior management assistant, 1941-42; Harvard University, Cambridge, Mass., instructor, 1952-54, assistant professor, 1954-58; University of Texas, Austin, associate professor, 1958-61, professor of Latin American history, 1961—. Stanford University, visiting professor, 1962-63. Town of Bellingham, Mass., member of finance committee, 1949-54. *Military service:* U.S. Naval Reserve, active duty, 1942-46, Ready Reserve, 1946—; now captain. *Member:* American Historical Association (general committee, Conference on Latin American History, 1965-67; chairman, 1971), American Association of University Professors, Texas Institute of Letters, Bidou Club of the World, Phi Beta Kappa. *Awards honors:* Lowery fellow, 1949; Clark fellow, Harvard University 1956-57; University of Texas Research Institute grants, 1961, 1964; Fulbright research fellow (Spain), 1966-67.

WRITINGS: *Argentina, the United States, and the Inter-American System, 1880-1914,* Harvard University Press, 1957; (translator, and author of introduction) Jose Luis Romero, *A History of Argentine Political Thought,* Stanford University Press, 1963; (editor with A. R. Lewis) *The New World Looks at Its History,* University of Texas Press, 1963; (editor) *Portrait of Spain; British and American Accounts of Spain in the Nineteenth and Twentieth Centuries,* Knopf, 1963; *Argentina, the Divided Land,* Van Nostrand, 1966. Contributor to *American Heritage, Hispanic American Historical Review,* and other periodicals. Editor, *Latin American Research Review,* 1969-74.

* * *

McGANNON, J(ohn) Barry   1924-

PERSONAL: Born April 18, 1924, in Humboldt, Kan.; son of Patrick Joseph (a banker) and Jane Clare (Barry) McGannon. *Education:* St. Louis University, A.B. (magna cum laude), 1947, Ph.L. and M.A., 1952, S.T.L., 1956, Ph.D., 1963. *Home:* 5225 Troost Ave., Kansas City, Mo. 64110.

CAREER: Entered Society of Jesus, 1942; ordained Roman Catholic priest, 1955. Marquette University High School, Milwaukee, Wis., instructor in English and classical languages, 1949-52; St. Louis University, St. Louis, Mo., administrative assistant to the president, 1957-63, instructor in education, 1963-65, assistant professor, 1965-68, associate professor, 1968-72, professor of education, 1972-73, and dean of College of Arts and Sciences, 1963-73; Rockhurst College, Kansas City, Mo., vice-president, 1973—. North Central Association of Colleges and Secondary Schools, examiner and consultant, 1960—, associate in Leadership Training Program, 1960-61; Center for Research Libraries (formerly Midwest Inter-Library Center), member of board of directors, 1963-73; Missouri College Union, member of executive committee, 1963—. *Member:* American Association for Higher Education, National Catholic Educational Association, American Council on Education, Association of Jesuit Colleges and Universities.

WRITINGS: (Editor) William Connell, *The Adolescent Boy,* Fides, 1958; *Patterns in the Teaching of Philosophy and Theology in American Jesuit Colleges and Universities,* Jesuit Educational Association, 1962; (editor) *The Role of Philosophy and Theology in American Jesuit Colleges and Universities,* Jesuit Educational Association, 1962; (editor and contributor) *Christian Wisdom and Christian Formation,* Sheed, 1964.

* * *

McGAVRAN, Donald   1897-

PERSONAL: Born December 15, 1897, in Damoh, India; son of John Grafton (a missionary) and Helen (Anderson) McGavran; married Mary Elizabeth Howard, August 29, 1922; children: Elizabeth Jean (Mrs. John Davis), Helen (Mrs. C. M. Corneli), Malcolm H., Winifred (Mrs. K. W. Griffen), Patricia (Mrs. Scribner Sheafor). *Education:* Butler University, B.A., 1920; Yale Divinity School, B.D. (cum laude), 1922; Columbia University, Ph.D., 1936. *Office:* School of Missions, Fuller Seminary, Pasadena, Calif. 91101.

CAREER: Minister of Christian Churches (Disciples of Christ). United Christian Missionary Society, Indianapolis, Ind., missionary in India, 1923-57; College of Missions, Indianapolis, Ind., professor of missions, 1957-60; Northwest Christian College, Institute of Church Growth, Eugene, Ore., director, 1961-65; Faller Theological Seminary, Pasadena, Calif., dean of School of World Mission, 1965-71, senior professor of missions, 1971—. Director, Lilly Endowment Research in Church Growth in Latin America, 1965-67. *Military service:* U.S. Army, American Expeditionary Forces, 1917-19. *Member:* National Association of Professors of Missions, American Society of Missiology.

WRITINGS: *How to Teach Religion in Mission Schools,* Mission Press (India), 1929; *Bridges of God,* Friendship, 1955; (with Pichett and Warnshuis) *Church Growth and Group Conversion,* Lucknow Publishing House, 1956; *Multiplying Churches in the Philippines,* United Church of Christ (Manila), 1957; *How Churches Grow,* Friendship, 1959; *Church Growth in Jamaica,* Lucknow Publishing House, 1961; *Church Growth in Mexico,* Eerdmans, 1963; *Church Frowth and Christian Mission,* Harper, 1965; *Understanding Church Growth,* Eerdmans, 1970; *Crucial Issues in Missions Tomorrow,* Moody Press, 1972; *The Eye of the Storm: The Great Debate in Missions,* Word Books, 1972; *The Clash Between Christianity and Cultures,* Canon Press, 1974. Also author of numerous articles in *International Review of Missions, Missiology, Evangelical Missions Quarterly, Christianity Today,* and other periodicals. Writer of news and views column in *United Church Review,* India, 1943-47. Editor, *Church Growth Bulletin,* 1964—.

WORK IN PROGRESS: Director of research for church growth studies for seven books by other writers; other church growth investigations in Southeast Asia, Africa, and Central America.

McGIFFERT, Michael 1928-

PERSONAL: Born October 5, 1928, in Chicago, Ill.; son of Arthur Cushman and Elisabeth (Eliot) McGiffert; married Genevieve Mischel (an opera director), August 13, 1960. *Education:* Harvard University, B.A. (cum laude), 1949; Union Theological Seminary, New York, N.Y., student, 1949-50; Yale University, B.D., 1952, Ph.D., 1958. *Home:* 5 Cole Lane, Williamsburg, Va. 23185. *Office:* William and Mary Quarterly, Box 220, Williamsburg, Va. 23185.

CAREER: Colgate University, Hamilton, N.Y., instructor in history, 1954-55, 1956-60; University of Maryland, College Park, instructor in history, 1955-56; University of Denver, Denver, Colo., associate professor beginning 1960, became professor of history; College of William and Mary, professor of history, 1972—. *Member:* American Historical Association, American Studies Association (president, Rocky Mountain chapter, 1962-63), American Association of University Professors, Organization of American Historians, American Civil Liberties Union.

WRITINGS: The Higher Learning in Colorado: An Historical Study, 1860-1940, Sage Books, 1964; (editor) *The Character of Americans: A Book of Readings*, Dorsey, 1964 revised edition, 1970; (editor) *Puritanism and the American Experience*, Addison-Wesley, 1969; (editor with R. A. Skotheim) *American Social Thought: Sources and Interpretations*, two volumes, Addison-Wesley, 1972; (editor) *God's Plot: The Paradoxes of Puritan Piety, Being the Autobiography and Journal of Thomas Shepard*, University of Massachusetts Press, 1972. Editor, *William and Mary Quarterly*, 1972—.

* * *

McKAY, Robert W. 1921-

PERSONAL: Born June 4, 1921, in Mayville, N.Y.; son of S. H. and Ebba (Stark) McKay; divorced; children: Robert W., Jr. *Education:* Attended University of Massachusetts. *Home:* 30 Academy St., Mayville, N.Y. *Agent:* Ann Elmo Agency, Inc., 52 Vanderbilt Ave., New York, N.Y. 10017.

CAREER: Free-lance writer. *Military service:* U.S. Army Air Forces, 1943-46; became second lieutenant. *Member:* Nu-Color Bird Association.

WRITINGS: The Way Things Are, Pyramid Books, 1964; *Canary Red*, Meredith, 1968; *Dave's Song*, Meredith, 1969; *Troublemaker*, Nelson, 1971. Contributor of short stories and articles to magazines.

WORK IN PROGRESS: A novel showing the impact of automation on an old-line manufacturing plant and the man who runs it.

AVOCATIONAL INTERESTS: Breeding canaries.†

* * *

McKEAN, Robert C(laud) 1920-

PERSONAL: Born November 28, 1920, in Valentine, Neb.; son of Floyd C. and Susa (Meyer) McKean; married Lora Myra Hobson, July 29, 1944; children: Michael Craig, Mark Douglas, Matthew Carl. *Education:* Reed College, A.B., 1948; Lewis and Clark College, M.Ed. 1950; University of Colorado, Ed.D., 1954. *Politics:* Democrat. *Religion:* Presbyterian. *Home:* 2265 Dartmouth Ave., Boulder, Colo. 80302. *Office:* Department of Education, University of Colorado, Boulder, Colo. 80302.

CAREER: High school teacher in Oregon, 1950-54; Tulare County (Calif.) schools, curriculum coordinator, 1954-55; San Francisco State College (now University), San Francisco, Calif., assistant professor of education, 1955-57; Indiana University, Bloomington, associate professor of education, 1957-58; University of Colorado, Boulder, professor of education, beginning, 1958. *Military service:* U.S. Marine Corps, fighter pilot, 1942-46; became captain; received Air Medal. *Member:* National Society for the Study of Education, Association for Supervision and Curriculum Development, National Council of Teachers of English, National Education Association, National Association of Secondary School Principals, Association for Student Teaching.

WRITINGS: Principles and Methods in Secondary Education, C. E. Merrill, 1962, 2nd edition, 1971; (with H. H. Mills) *The Supervisor*, Center for Applied Research in Education, 1964; (with Bob L. Taylor) *The Teacher in Colorado: A Handbook for New Teachers*, Preutt Press, 1965. Contributor to education journals.†

* * *

McKELWAY, Alexander J(effrey) 1932-

PERSONAL: Born December 8, 1932, in Durham, N.C.; son of Alexander J. (a minister) and Alice (Gibbon) McKelway; married Adelaide Bullard, September 17, 1960; children: Alexander J. VI, Daniel. *Education:* Davidson College, A.B., 1954; Princeton Theological Seminary, B.D. (cum laude), 1957; University of Basel, Th.D. (magna cum laude), 1963. *Office:* Department of Religion, Davidson College, Davidson, N.C.

CAREER: Clergyman, Vienna Community Church, Vienna, Austria, pastor, 1958-60; Dartmouth College, Hanover, N.H., instructor in religion, 1963-65; Davidson College, Davidson, N.C., assistant professor of religion, beginning, 1965. Fulbright Commission for Austria, member in charge of student affairs, 1958-60. *Member:* American Society of Church History, American Academy of Religion.

WRITINGS: The Systematic Theology of Paul Tillich: A Review and Analysis, John Knox, 1964; (with E. David Willis) *The Context of Contemporary Theology: Essays In Honor of Paul Lehmann*, John Knox, 1974.

WORK IN PROGRESS: A historical and systematic investigation of Christian anthropology.†

* * *

McKEOWN, James E(dward) 1919-

PERSONAL: Surname is pronounced Mc*Cue*-en; born September 3, 1919, in Detroit, Mich.; son of Francis Joseph and Grace Margaret (Ruddon) McKeown; married Mary McNamara (supervisor of high school department of American School of Correspondence), August 6, 1955. *Education:* Wayne (now Wayne State) University, B.A., 1941, M.A. 1945; University of Chicago, Ph.D., 1949. *Politics:* Independent Democrat. *Religion:* "Religious outlook, Ecumenical." *Home:* 1469 N. Sheridan Rd., Kenosha, Wis. 53140. *Office:* Division of Social Science, University of Wisconsin-Parkside, Kenosha, Wis. 53140.

CAREER: St. Xavier College, Chicago, Ill., instructor in social science, 1945-48; New Mexico Highlands University, Las Vegas, assistant professor of sociology, 1948-52; DePaul University, Chicago, Ill., assistant professor, 1952-55, associate professor, 1955-57, professor of sociology, 1957-70, chairman of department, 1962-70, director of inter-departmental programs in the social sciences, 1963-70; University of Wisconsin-Parkside, Kenosha, professor of Sociology, 1970—. Visiting professor, Emory University, 1952, Escuela Nacional de Asistancia Publica, La Paz, Bolivia, 1958, Concordia Teachers College, River Forest, Ill., 1965, Northwestern University, 1965, and Universidad Catolica de Chile, Santiago, 1968. Sociological consultant in part-time practice, 1959-70. State of Illinois Youth Commission, consultant to Division of Community Services, 1961-70.

MEMBER: American Sociological Association, Illinois Sociological Association (co-founder), City Club and Quadrangle Club (both Chicago). *Awards, honors:* Fund for Advancement of Education fellow, 1954-55; Social Science Research Council grant, 1958.

WRITINGS: (Editor with Frederick I. Tietze) *The Changing Metropolis*, Houghton, 1964, 2nd edition, 1971. Contributor to professional journals and encyclopedias.

WORK IN PROGRESS: Experimentation with community programs for rehabilitation of juvenile and adult offenders.

* * *

McKNIGHT, Gerald 1919-

PERSONAL: Born October 21, 1919, in Wraysbury, Buckinghamshire, England; son of Herbert (a captain, Indian Army) and Winifred (Pim) McKnight; married Barbara Eve Fraser, April 19, 1952; children: Sally Mark (U.S. citizen), Rayne John, Anna. *Home and office:* Oakleigh Park Ave., Chislehurst, Kent, England. *Agent:* Julian Back, 3 East 48th St., New York, N.Y. 10017.

CAREER: Journalist with Associated Newspapers, London, England, for thirteen years, starting as reporter on Paris edition of *Daily Mail* and becoming deputy editor of *Weekend Mail*; U.S. correspondent working in New York for *Daily Sketch* and *Sunday Dispatch*, 1955-57, covering (among other assignments), race conflict stories in the South; assistant editor of *Sunday Dispatch*, London, England, 1957-61; when *Sunday Dispatch* ceased publication in 1961, became full-time free-lance writer. *Military service:* Royal Air Force, 1939-45.

WRITINGS: (With Wally Thompoon) *Time Off My Life* (Thompson autobiography), Rich & Cowan, 1956; *The Compleat After-Dinner Speaker*, Souvenir Press, 1962; *The Compleat Gambler*, Souvenir Press, 1964; *Verdict on Schweitzer*, Day, 1964; *The English at Love*, New English Library, 1967; *The Fortunemakers*, M. Joseph, 1972; *Computer Crime*, M. Joseph, 1973, Walker, 1974; *The Mind of the Terrorist*, M. Joseph, 1974. Contributor to British and American magazines, writing both alone and in collaboration with Richard Gehman, for *McCall's, Cosmopolitan, Good Housekeeping, American Weekly, TV Guide, Saga*, and other U.S. periodicals.

WORK IN PROGRESS: Scandal in the Winterhouse, for M. Joseph, expected in 1976.

SIDELIGHTS: Gerald McKnight told *CA:* "Have spent my life in search of the sun, and a place in it; ... have a small holiday house in an ancient and beautiful village three miles inland from the crowded shore down in southern France where we drink local wine at 45 cents a bottle and live the lives of tanned Rileys."

* * *

McKUSICK, Marshall Bassford 1930-

PERSONAL: Born January 13, 1930, in Minneapolis, Minn.; son of James G. Blaine (a lawyer) and Marjorie (Chase) McKusick; married Charity Koeper, August 21, 1954; children: Blaine, Lucy. *Education:* University of Minnesota, B.A., 1952, M.A., 1954; Yale University, Ph.D., 1960. *Religion:* Unitarian Universalist. *Home:* 338 Rocky Shore Dr., Iowa City, Iowa.

CAREER: University of California, Los Angeles, lecturer in anthropology and research archaeologist, 1958-60; University of Iowa, Iowa City, 1960—, currently associate professor of anthropology and state archaeologist. *Member:* American Anthropological Association, Society for American Archaeology.

WRITINGS: Men of Ancient Iowa; As Revealed by Archaeological Discoveries, Iowa State University Press, 1964; (editor and author of introduction) Ellison Orr, *Reminiscences of a Pioneer Boy*, [Iowa City], 1971. Also author of evaluation and index for *Iowa Archaelogical Reports, 1934-1939*, [Madison, Wis.], 1963.†

* * *

McLARRY, Newman R(ay) 1923-

PERSONAL: Born July 11, 1923, in Sulphur Springs, Tex.; son of C. Burt (a state agricultural department employee) and Jessie Anna (Carpenter) McLarry; married Sue Freeman, August 17, 1947; children: Sharon, Deena. *Education:* Texas A & M University, B.A. and B.S., 1947; Baylor University, graduate study, 1948; Southwestern Baptist Theological Seminary, B.D., 1951, advanced study, 1955. *Home:* 3200 Northwest 20th St., Oklahoma City, Okla. *Office:* P.O. Box 75001, Oklahoma City, Okla.

CAREER: Accountant before studying for Baptist ministry; pastor in Texas, Arkansas, and Georgia, 1951-62; Southern Baptist Convention, Home Mission Board, Nashville, Tenn., associate director of Division of Evangelism, 1962-65, director of Philippine New Life Movement, 1963; Northwest Baptist Church, Oklahoma City, Okla., pastor, beginning 1965. Arkansas Baptist Hospital, former trustee. *Military service:* U.S. Army, Infantry, 1943-46; served in Europe; became captain (battlefield promotion); received Silver Star, Purple Heart with oak leaf clusters.

WRITINGS: When Shadows Fall, Broadman, 1959; *His Good and Perfect Will*, Broadman, 1965; (editor) *Handbook on Evangelism*, Broadman, 1965. Contributor to *Family Digest* and religious periodicals.

WORK IN PROGRESS: Cloud Over Our Heads—A Dallas Family, Nov. 21-25, 1963, with foreword and introduction by the two original attorneys for Jack Ruby; a historical novel; Sunday school lessons for Baptist Sunday School Board.†

* * *

McLAUGHLIN, Ted J(ohn) 1921-

PERSONAL: Born December 23, 1921, in Elkhart, Ind.; son of Frederick Luther (a railroad clerk) and Fern Agnes (McBride) McLaughlin; married Helen Frances Myers, August 24, 1946. *Education:* Manchester College, North Manchester, Ind., B.A., 1947; University of Wisconsin, M.A., 1948, Ph.D., 1952. *Religion:* Unitarian Universalist. *Office:* University of Wisconsin—Milwaukee, Milwaukee, Wis. 53211.

CAREER: University of Wisconsin, Milwaukee, instructor, 1949-53, assistant professor, 1953-57, associate professor, 1957-65, professor of speech, 1965-67, professor of communication, 1967—, associate dean of humanities and communication, 1962-65, 1967-69, associate dean of graduate school, 1971—. Louis Allis Co., Milwaukee, communication consultant, 1956-57. Friends of Art, gallery operations co-chairman, Milwaukee Art Center, 1962. *Military service:* U.S. Army, 1943-46; became sergeant. *Member:* American Business Writing Association, National Society for the Study of Communication, Speech Association of America, American Association of University Professors, Central States Speech Association, Wisconsin Speech Association (secretary-treasurer, 1953-56), Wisconsin Academy of Sciences, Arts and Letters (secretary, 1950-63; vice-president for arts, 1963-64), Delta Sigma Rho.

WRITINGS: (With Lawrence P. Blum and David M. Robinson) *Communication,* C. E. Merrill, 1964; (with Blum and Robinson) *Cases and Projects in Communication,* C. E. Merrill, 1965. Contributor to speech journals. Associate editor, *Wisconsin Academy of Sciences, Arts and Letters Review.*

WORK IN PROGRESS: Research of publications on the rhetoric of agitation and the ceremonial function of speech.†

*   *   *

McLEAN, George F(rancis)   1929-

PERSONAL: Born June 29, 1929, in Lowell, Mass.; son of Arthur William and Agnes Veronica (McHugh) McLean. *Education:* Oblate College, Newburgh, N.Y., 1946-48; Gregorian University, Rome, Italy, Ph.B., 1951, Ph.L., 1952, S.T.B., 1954, S.T.L., 1956; Catholic University of America, Ph.D., 1958. *Politics:* Democrat. *Home:* 391 Michigan Ave., N.E., Washington, D.C. 20017. *Office:* Catholic University of America, Washington, D.C. 20017.

CAREER: Roman Catholic priest of Oblate Fathers of Mary Immaculate. Oblate College, Washington, D.C., professor of philosophy, 1956—; Catholic University of America, Washington, D.C., instructor, 1958-61, assistant professor, 1961-64, associate professor of philosophy, 1964—, director of philosophy workshop, 1961—. *Member:* World Union of Catholic Philosophical Societies (Secretary General, treasurer, 1972—), American Catholic Philosophical Association (secretary, 1963—), American Philosophical Association, American Catholic Theological Society, Metaphysical Society of America.

WRITINGS: Man's Knowledge of God According to Paul Tillich: A Thomist Critique, Catholic University of America Press, 1958; (with Patrick J. Aspell) *Ancient Western Philosophy: The Hellenic Emergence,* Appleton, 1971; *Traces of God in a Secular Culture,* Alba, 1973.

Editor: *Philosophy and the Integration of Contemporary Catholic Education,* Catholic University of America Press, 1962; *Teaching Thomism Today,* Catholic University of America Press, 1963; *Philosophy in a Pluralistic Society,* American Catholic Philosophical Association, 1964; *The History and Philosophy of Science,* American Catholic Philosophical Association, 1964; *Philosophy in Technological Culture,* Catholic University of America Press, 1964; *Christian Philosophy and Religious Renewal,* Catholic University of America Press, 1964; *Philosophy and the Arts,* American Catholic Philosophical Association, 1965; *Index of the Proceedings of the American Catholic Philosophical Association,* American Catholic Philosophical Association, 1966; (and compiler) *Philosophy in the Twentieth Century: Catholic and Christian,* Ungar, Volume I: *An Annotated Bibliography of Philosophy in Catholic Thought 1900-1964,* 1967, Volume II: *A Bibliography of*

Christian Philosophy and Contemporary Issues, 1967; *Philosophy and the Future of Man,* Catholic University of America Press, 1968; *Philosophy and Contemporary Man,* Catholic University of America Press, 1968; *Truth and the Historicity of Man,* American Catholic Philosophical Association, 1969; *Current Issues in Modern Philosophy: New Departures in Colleges and Seminaries,* Catholic University of America Press, 1969; *Myth and Philosophy,* American Catholic Philosophical Association, 1971; *Religion and Contemporary Thought,* Alba, 1973.

Also author of *Perspectives on Reality: Readings on Metaphysics from Classical Philosophy to Existentialism,* volume II of the "Harbrace Series in Philosophy," 1966. Area editor, *New Catholic Encyclopedia,* 1960—. Compiler of "Chronicle of Philosophy," a quarterly report in *New Scholasticism,* 1963—. Also compiler of index to volumes I-XL of *New Scholasticism.*

*   *   *

McLOUGHLIN, William G.   1922-

PERSONAL: Born June 11, 1922, in Maplewood, N.J.; son of William G. (a lawyer and teacher) and Florence M. (Quinn) McLoughlin; married Virginia Ward Duffy; children: Helen, Gail, Martha. *Education:* Princeton University, A.B., 1947; Harvard University, A.M., 1948, Ph.D., 1953. *Home:* 204 Bowen St., Providence 6, R.I. *Office:* Department of History, Brown University, Providence, R.I.

CAREER: Harvard University, Graduate School of Arts and Sciences, Cambridge, Mass., assistant dean, 1950-53; Brown University, Providence, R.I., assistant professor of history, 1954-60, associate professor, 1960-63, professor, 1963—, American Civilization Program, co-chairman, 1973—. Member of executive committee, Institute of Early American History and Culture (Williamsburg), 1973—. *Member:* American Historical Association, American Studies Association, American Association of University Professors, Phi Beta Kappa. *Awards, honors:* Fulbright scholarship to England, 1953-54; Guggenheim fellow, 1960-61; fellow, Harvard Center for the Study of the History of Liberty, 1960-62; senior fellow, National Endowment for the Humanities, 1968-69; Frederick G. Melcher Book Award, 1972, for *New England Dissent, 1630-1833: The Baptists and the Separation of Church and State;* fellow, American Council of Learned Societies, 1972-73.

WRITINGS: Billy Sunday Was His Real Name, University of Chicago Press, 1955; *Modern Revivalism: Charles Grandison Finney to Billy Graham,* Ronald, 1958; *Billy Graham; Revivalist in a Secular Age,* Ronald, 1960; (editor) Charles Grandison Finney, *Lectures on Revivals of Religion,* Harvard University Press, 1961; (contributor) Daniel Boorstin, editor, *An American Primer,* University of Chicago Press, 1966; *Isaac Backus,* Little, Brown, 1967; *The Meaning of Henry Ward Beecher,* Knopf, 1967; (contributor) Henning Cohen, editor, *The American Experience,* Houghton, 1968; (editor) *The American Evangelicals,* Harper, 1968; (editor with Robert N. Bellah) *Religion in America,* Beacon, 1968; (editor) Isaac Backus, *Pamphlets on Church, State and Calvinism,* Harvard University Press, 1968; (contributor) D. R. Cutler, editor, *The Religious Situation,* Beacon, 1969; *New England Dissent, 1630-1833: The Baptists and the Separation of Church and State,* two volumes, Harvard University Press, 1971; (contributor) S. G. Kurtz and J. H. Hutson, editors, *Essays on the American Revolution,* Norton, 1973. Also contributor to *Dictionary of Notable American Women*, Harvard University Press, 1973. Editor, *American Quarterly*, 1962-64; member of editorial board, *William and Mary Quarterly*, 1972-73.

WORK IN PROGRESS: Editing a multi-volume edition of the papers of Isaac Backus, for Brown University Press, and a history of the slaveholding Indians in the South, 1790-1870, with special reference to missionary activities.

* * *

McMILLION, Bonner 1921-

PERSONAL: Born November 8, 1921, in Lott, Tex.; son of Charlie Adair (a merchant and publisher) and Nellie (Perteet) McMillion; married Virginia Womack, November 16, 1948; children: Charles Mark, Melissa, Roberta. *Education:* Baylor University, student, 1939-41. *Politics:* Democrat. *Religion:* Unitarian Universalist. *Agent:* Maurice Crain, Inc., 18 East 41st St., New York, N.Y. 10017. *Office:* Fayette County Record, LaGrange, Tex.

CAREER: Dallas Times Herald, Dallas, Tex., sports writer, 1945-48; *Elgin Courier*, Elgin, Tex., publisher, 1950-52; *Brazos Press*, Marlin, Tex., publisher, 1952-55; *Waco Tribune-Herald*, Waco, Tex., news editor, 1955-65; Fayette County Record, LaGrange, Tex., publisher, 1965—. *Military service:* U.S. Army Air Forces, 1942-45; served in Africa and Middle East; became staff sergeant. *Member:* Texas Institute of Letters.

WRITINGS: The Lot of Her Neighbors, Lippincott, 1953; *The Long Ride Home*, Lippincott, 1955; *So Long at the Fair*, Doubleday, 1964.

* * *

McMULLIN, Ernan 1924-

PERSONAL: Born October 13, 1924, in Donegal, Ireland; son of Vincent (a lawyer) and Carmel (a doctor; maiden name, Farrell) McMullin. *Education:* Maynooth College, B.Sc., 1945, B.D., 1949; Institute of Advanced Studies, Dublin, Ireland, graduate study, 1949-50; University of Louvain, Ph.D., 1954. *Address:* Box 36, Notre Dame, Ind.

CAREER: Roman Catholic priest. University of Notre Dame, Notre Dame, Ind., instructor, 1954-59, assistant professor, 1959-64, associate professor, 1964-67, professor of logic and philosophy of science, 1967—, chairman of department of philosophy, 1965-72. Research fellow, Yale University, 1957-59; visiting lecturer and research associate, University of Minnesota, 1964-65. Visiting professor or lecturer, Georgetown University, Immaculate Heart College, and Cape Town University. U.S. delegate to International Congress for Logic and Methodology, Amsterdam, 1967, Bucharest, 1971. Member of advisory panel on philosophy of science, National Science Foundation. *Member:* International Philosophy of Science Association (member of executive council, 1970-73), American Catholic Philosophical Association (president 1966-67), Philosophy of Science Society, Metaphysical Society of America (member of executive council; president, 1973-74), Society for Religion in Higher Education (fellow), Council for Philosophical Studies (member of executive committee, 1970—), Sigma Xi. *Awards, honors:* Doctor of Humane Letters, Loyola University (Chicago), 1969.

WRITINGS: (Translator) A. Dondeyne, *Contemporary European Thought and Christian Faith*, Dusquesne University Press, 1958; (editor and author of introduction) *The Concept of Matter*, Notre Dame University Press, 1963, 2nd edition published as *The Concept of Matter in Modern Philosophy*, 1974; (contributor) J. C. Steinhardt, editor, *Science and the Modern World*, Plenum, 1966; (editor and author of introduction) *Galileo: Man of Science*, Basic Books, 1967; (contributor) C. Singleton, *Art, Science and History in the Renaissance*, Johns Hopkins Press, 1968; (contributor) J. Roslansky, editor, *The Uniqueness of Man*, North-Holland, 1968; (contributor) P. Kuntz, editor, *The Concept of Order*, University of Washington Press, 1970; (contributor) A. G. Karczmar and J. C. Eccles, editors, *Brain and Human Behavior*, Springer Verlag, 1972.

Contributor to *Catholic Encyclopedia for School and Home*, 1966; *New Catholic Encyclopedia*, 1966, and *Dictionary of Scientific Biography*, 1970. Also contributor of articles to *Boston Studies in the Philosophy of Science, New Scholasticism, International Philosophy Quarterly*, and other journals.

Editor, Prentice-Hall's "Fundamentals of Logic" Series; member of editorial board, "Kansas Logic Series"; editorial consultant to Bobbs-Merrill Reprint Series and *New Catholic Encyclopedia*. Associate editor, *American Philosophical Quarterly*; editorial consultant, *New Scholasticism*; member of editorial board, *History and Philosophy of Science*.

WORK IN PROGRESS: A memorial volume, *Galileo Galilei*, and research into the theory of evidence.

* * *

McPHERSON, James Lowell 1921-

PERSONAL: Born January 25, 1921, in Cincinnati, Ohio; son of C. Lowell (a teacher) and Carolyn (Mohorter) McPherson; married Gertrude Huntington Wright (a professor), July 25, 1947 (divorced 1973); children: Karen Sue, Christopher Wright. *Education:* Middlebury College, student, 1938-40; West Virginia University, B.A., 1942; Columbia University, graduate study, 1946-48. *Politics:* "Nominal Democrat; basic dissenter." *Religion:* Post-Christian. *Home:* 33 Riverside Drive, New York, N.Y. 10023. *Agent:* Toni Strassman, 130 East 18th St., New York, N.Y. 10003.

CAREER: Instructor in sociology at Northeastern University, Boston, Mass., 1948-49, at Boston University, Boston, Mass., 1949-52, and at Smith College, Northampton, Mass., 1952-55; U.S. Post Office, Marble Dale, Conn., postmaster, 1961-1968; "exile and pilgrim," 1968-1970; writer, 1970—. *Military service:* U.S. Army, Infantry, 1942-45. *Member:* Authors Guild. *Awards, honors:* Poet laureate of West Virginia, 1944-46; First Appearance Prize, *Poetry* (magazine), 1948.

WRITINGS: Goodbye Rosie (novel), Knopf, 1965. Contributor of poetry to magazines.

WORK IN PROGRESS: A novel; poetry.

* * *

McWHIRTER, Norris Dewar 1925-

PERSONAL: Born August 12, 1925, in London, England; son of William Allan (former editor, *London Daily Mail*) and Margaret (Williamson) McWhirter; married Carole Eckert, December 28, 1957; children: Jane, Alasdair. *Education:* Trinity College, Oxford, B.A. and M.A., 1948. *Politics:* Conservative. *Religion:* Church of England. *Home:* Willoughby, Camlet Way, Hadley Common, Hertsford, England. *Office:* Guinness Superlatives Ltd., 8 Baker St., London W. 1, England.

CAREER: Athletics correspondent for *Observer*, London, England, 1949, *Star*, London, 1950; McWhirter Twins Ltd., London, England, managing director, beginning 1951; Guinness Superlatives Ltd., London, England, managing director, beginning 1955, assistant vice-president of New York branch, 1955. Dreghorn Publications Ltd., London, England, director, beginning 1962. British Broadcasting Corp., commentator, beginning 1951 (announced first four-minute mile by Roger Bannister, 1954), television commentator of Olympic track and field events, beginning 1952, guest, as "memory man" on facts and figures, on other radio and television programs. Contested 1964 general election for Conservatives. *Military service:* Royal Naval Volunteer Reserve, 1943-46; became sub-lieutenant. *Member:* Royal Institution, Association of Track and Field Statisticians, Society of Genealogists, Achilles Club, Vincent's Club (Oxford).

WRITINGS—With twin brother, Ross McWhirter: *Get to Your Marks*, Kaye, 1950; (editor) *Guinness Book of Records*, Guinness Superlatives, 1954, 15th edition, 1968; (editor) *Guinness Book of World Records*, Sterling, 1956, 5th edition, 1975; (editor) *Guinness Book of Olympic Records*, Sterling Publishing Co., 1964; *Dunlop Book of Facts*, Dreghorn Publications, 1964, 2nd edition, 1966; *The 1966 Guinness Book of British Empire and Commonwealth Games Records*, Guinness Superlatives, 1966; (editor) *Mexico '68*, Holland-Breumelhof, 1968; (compiler) *Dunlop Illustrated Encyclopedia of Facts*, Doubleday, 1969; *Guinness Sports Record Book*, Sterling, 1972. Contributor to *Encyclopaedia Britannica*, *Encyclopaedia Britannica Year Book*, *Modern Athletics*, and *Encyclopaedia of Sport*. Statistics editor, *News of World Almanac*, 1950; editor, *Athletics World*, 1952.

WORK IN PROGRESS: Two secret projects.

SIDELIGHTS: Sales of the *Guinness Book of Records* passed the million mark in 1964.

BIOGRAPHICAL SOURCES: Time, January 19, 1963; *Sports Illustrated*, February 8, 1965; *Reader's Digest*, May, 1965.†

*   *   *

MEBANE, John (Harrison)   1909-
(Harold Heartman, Philip DeVilbiss)

PERSONAL: Surname is pronounced Mebbin; born September 20, 1909, in Greensboro, N.C.; son of Cornelius and Minnie (Clark) Mebane; married Hannah Price Kallam (a hospital dietitian), July 22, 1944; children: Sister Mary William, David Clark, John Spencer. *Education:* University of North Carolina, A.B., 1930. *Politics:* Democrat. *Religion:* Presbyterian. *Home:* 7859 Mount Vernon Rd., Dunwoody, Ga. 30038. *Office: The Antiques Journal*, Dunwoody, Ga. 30038.

CAREER: High Point Enterprise, High Point, N.C., managing editor, 1930-42; *Atlanta Journal*, Atlanta, Ga., editorial writer, 1942-51; Dudley-Anderson-Yutzy (public relations counselors), New York, N.Y., Atlanta regional representative, 1951-1968, *The Antiques Journal*, Dunwoody, Ga., editor, 1968—. *Member:* Authors Guide. *Awards, honors:* Awards for outstanding achievement in journalism from Southern Association of Science and Industry and Georgia State College for Women.

WRITINGS: Books Relating to the Civil War, Yoseloff, 1963; *Treasure at Home*, A. S. Barnes, 1964; *New Horizons in Collecting*, A. S. Barnes, 1966; *The Coming Collecting Boom*, A. S. Barnes, 1968; *What's New That's Old*, A. S. Barnes, 1970; *The Poor Man's Guide to Antique Collecting*, Doubleday, 1971; *The Complete Book of Collecting Art Nouveau*, Coward-McCann, 1970; (with Donald Cowie) *How to Deal in Antiques*, Babka Publishing, 1972; *Collecting Nostalgia*, Arlington House, 1972. Contributor to *Better Homes and Gardens, Yankee*, and *Hobbies*. Regular Sunday columnist, "Treasure at Home," *Atlanta Journal and Constitution*, 1962, columnist, *Early American Life*, 1972—.

WORK IN PROGRESS: A book, *The Rewards of Sin*.

SIDELIGHTS: John Mebane's hobby of collecting books, early inkwells, lap desks, and other items (begun in 1948), led to his Sunday column, "Treasure at Home," and the book with the same title. He now writes articles on antiques and collectors' items, and their adaptation for use in the modern home, for several periodicals.

*   *   *

MEDLEY, (Rachel) Margaret   1918-

PERSONAL: Born March 6, 1918, in London, England; daughter of Charles Douglas (a solicitor) and Ann G. (Owen) Medley. *Education:* School of Oriental and African Studies, University of London, B.A. (honors), 1950. *Home:* 75 Carlton Hill, London N.W.8, England. *Office:* Percival David Foundation of Chinese Art, 53 Gordon Sq., London W.C. 1, England.

CAREER: University of London, London, England, Chinese art librarian, Courtauld Institute of Art, 1950-55, Eastern art librarian, School of Oriental and African Studies, 1956-60, lecturer in Chinese art, Extension Division, 1953-63, Percival David Foundation of Chinese Art, London, England, curator, 1959—. Victoria and Albert Museum, guide lecturer in Oriental Art, 1952-63. *Member:* Royal Asiatic Society (fellow), Museums Association, Japan Society, Oriental Ceramic Society, International Institute of Conservation, Society of Antiquaries (fellow).

WRITINGS: Catalogue of the Underglaze Blue Decorated Porcelains in the Percival David Foundation, School of Oriental and African Studies, University of London, 1963; *Handbook of Chinese Art*, International Publications Service, 1964; (contributor) *World Furniture*, Hamlyn, 1965; *Catalogue of Ming and Ch'ing Monochrome*, 1973; *Yuan Porcelain and Stoneware*, 1974; *Oxford Companion to the Useful Arts*, Oxford University Press, 1974. Contributor to *Oriental Art, Antique Collector, Ars Orientalis*, and *Transactions of the Oriental Ceramic Society*.

WORK IN PROGRESS: Ceramic Techniques and Wares of China; research in Chinese ceramic history.

SIDELIGHTS: Ms. Medley has working knowledge (in her field of studies) of French, German, Chinese, and Japanese. She visited Japan in 1960, United States and Canada, in 1964, the Far East in 1968, and the Near East, including Iran, Turkey, Syria, Lebanon, and Egypt, in 1973. *Avocational interests:* Gardening, photography, music, good food and drink with friends.

*   *   *

MEEKS, Wayne A.   1932-

PERSONAL: Born January 8, 1932, in Aliceville, Ala.; son of Benjamin LaFayette (a stationmaster) and Winnie (Gavin) Meeks; married Martha Fowler (a free-lance artist), June 10, 1954; children: Suzanne, Edith, Ellen. *Education:* University of Alabama, B.S., 1953; Austin Presbyterian Theological Seminary, B.D., 1956; University of Tuebingen, graduate study, 1956-57; Yale University, M.A., 1963, Ph.D., 1965. *Office:* Department of Religious Studies, Indiana University, Bloomington, Ind.

CAREER: Ordained Presbyterian minister, 1956; Presbyterian Campus Christian Life, Memphis, Tenn., university pastor, 1957-61; Dartmouth College, Hanover, N.H., instructor in religion, 1964-65; United Ministry to Yale, New Haven, Conn., university pastor, 1965-66; Indiana University, Bloomington, assistant professor, 1966-68, associate professor, 1969-73, professor of religious studies, 1973—, chairman of department, 1972-75. *Member:* American Academy of Religion, Studorium Novi Testamenti Societas, Society of Biblical Literature, Society for Religion in Higher Education, Phi Beta Kappa. *Awards, honors:* Fulbright fellowship to University of Tuebingen, 1956-57.

WRITINGS: Go From Your Father's House, John Knox, 1964; *The Prophet-King*, Brill, 1967; (contributor) J. Neusner, editor, *Religions in Antiquity*, Brill, 1968; (editor) *The Writings of St. Paul*, Norton, 1972; (editor with F. O. Francis) *Conflict at Colossae*, Society of Biblical Literature, 1973; (contributor) Neusner, editor, *Judaism, Christianity, and Other Greco-Roman Religions*, Brill, 1974; (contributor) M. de Jong, S. Safrai and others, editors, *Compendia Rerum Judaicarum ad Novum Testamentum*, Nijhoff, 1975. Also contributor of articles to *Journal of Biblical Literature: History of Religions.*

* * *

MEGGITT, M(ervyn) J(ohn) 1924-

PERSONAL: Born August 20, 1924, in Warwick, Queensland, Australia; son of Reginald Arthur (a businessman) and Susan (Brodie) Meggitt; married Joan Lillistone, January 1, 1949. *Education:* University of Sydney, B.A., 1953, M.A., 1955, Ph.D., 1960. *Office:* Department of Anthropology, Queens College of the City University of New York, Flushing, N.Y.

CAREER: University of Sydney, Sydney, Australia, lecturer in anthropology, 1954, 1956-60, research fellow, 1955, senior lecturer, 1961-65; University of Michigan, Ann Arbor, professor of anthropology, 1965-67; Queens College of the City University of New York, Flushing, N.Y., professor of anthropology, 1967—. Simon fellow at University of Manchester, 1963; visiting professor at University of Michigan and University of Chicago, 1964. Has done anthrop.ological fieldwork in central Australia and New Guinea; travelled in the Pacific, Spain, and Mexico, for anthropological reconnaissance. *Military service:* Royal Australian Navy, 1942-46. *Member:* Royal Anthropological Institute (London; fellow), British Association of Social Anthropologists (Australian branch), Anthropological Society of New South Wales (council member, 1958-62).

WRITINGS: Desert People: A Study of the Walbiri Aborigines of Central Australia, Angus & Robertson, 1962; *The Lineage System of the Mae Enga of New Guinea*, Barnes & Noble, 1965; (editor with P. Lawrence) *Gods, Ghosts and Men in Melanesia*, Oxford University Press, 1965; *Gadjari Among the Walbiri of Central Australia*, Oceania, 1966; (editor with R. M. Glasse) *Pigs, Pearl–Shells, and Women*, Prentice-Hall, 1969. Contributor to professional journals.

WORK IN PROGRESS: Continuing research on tribal life of Australian aborigines, on highland natives of New Guinea, and on rural life in Southern Spain.

MEHROTRA, S(ri) Ram 1931-

PERSONAL: Born June 23, 1931, in Etawah, Uttar Pradesh, India; son of Hari Narain and Manno Devi (Tandon) Mehrotra; married Eva Ganguli (a teacher), July 24, 1957. *Education:* Allahabad University, B.A. (first class honors), 1948, M.A., 1950; School of Oriental and African Studies, University of London, Ph.D., 1960. *Religion:* Hindu. *Home:* 19 Frognal, London N.W. 3, England. *Office:* School of Oriental and African Studies, University of London, London W.C. 1, England.

CAREER: Saugar University, Saugar, Madhya Pradesh, India, lecturer in history, 1950-58; University of London, London, England, research fellow, Institute of Commonwealth Studies, 1960-61, research fellow, School of Oriental and African Studies, 1961-62, lecturer in politics, School of Oriental and African Studies, 1962—.

WRITINGS: India and the Commonwealth, 1885-1929, Praeger, 1965; *The Emergence of the Indian National Congress*, Vikas Publications (Delhi), 1971. Contributor to *India Quarterly, Journal of Commonwealth Political Studies*, and *Journal of Development Studies.†*

* * *

MEIDEN, Walter 1907-

PERSONAL: Born July 12, 1907, in Grand Haven, Mich. *Education:* University of Michigan, A.B., 1931; Ohio State University, M.A., 1933, Ph.D., 1945. *Home:* 2949 Neil Ave., Apartment 301-C, Columbus, Ohio 43202.

CAREER: Ohio State University, Columbus, 1931—, began as graduate assistant, now professor of Romance languages. *Military service:* U.S. Naval Reserve, 1943-46. *Member:* Modern Language Association of America, U.S. Chess Federation.

WRITINGS: (With W. S. Hendrix) *Beginning French*, Houghton, 1940, 4th edition, 1970; (with Richard Armitage) *Beginning Spanish*, Houghton, 1953, 3rd edition, 1972; (with Olin Mo ore) *Onze Contes*, Houghton, 1957; (with Max Euwe) *Chess Master vs. Chess Amateur*, McKay, 1963, 2nd edition, 1971; (with Euwe) *Contes de Michelle Maurois*, Houghton, 1966; (with Euwe) *The Road to Chess Mastery*, McKay, 1966; (with Charles Carlut) *French for Oral and Written Review*, Holt, 1968; (editor with Diane Birckbichler and Ann Dube) Jean Anouilh, *Le voyageur sans bagage*, Holt, 1973; (with Mario Iglesias) *Spanish for Oral and Written Review*, Holt, 1975. Writer of monthly column with Norman Cotter, "Back to Basics," *Chess Life and Review*, 1973—.

WORK IN PROGRESS: Master vs. Master, with Max Euwe, and a second edition of *French for Oral and Written Review*, with Charles Carlut.

* * *

MEISELMAN, David I(srael) 1924-

PERSONAL: Born May 21, 1924, in Boston, Mass.; son of Samuel (a merchant) and Sarah (Bovarnick) Meiselman; children: Ellen, Nina, Samuel, Adam. *Education:* Boston University, B.A., 1947; University of Chicago, M.A., 1951, Ph.D., 1961. *Religion:* Jewish. *Home:* 2346 Centreville Rd., Herndon, Va. 22070. *Office:* Department of Economics, Virginia Polytechnic Institute and State University, Blacksburg, Va.

CAREER: Instructor at Illinois Institute of Technology, Chicago, Ill., 1950-55, at Northwestern University, Evanston, Ill., 1955; National Bureau of Economic Research, New York, N.Y., research associate, 1955-58; University of Chicago, Chicago, Ill., instructor in economics, 1959-60, assistant professor, 1960-62; U.S. government, Washington, D.C., economist, Office of the Secretary of the Treasury, 1962-63, senior economist, Banking and Currency Committee, U.S. House of Representatives, 1963; Johns Hopkins University, Baltimore, Md., lecturer in political economy, 1963-64; U.S. government, Washington, D.C., research fellow, Comptroller of the Currency, 1964-66; Macalester College, St. Paul, Minn., Frederick R. Bigelow professor of economics, 1966-71, acting chairman of department, 1968-69; Virginia Polytechnic Institute and State University, Blacksburg, professor of economics, director, Reston economics program, research associate at Center for Public Choice, 1971—. Chairman, Presidential Task Force on Inflation, 1968-69. Senior economist on Organization of American States and Inter-American Development Bank fiscal mission to Peru, 1964. *Military service:* U.S. Army, 1942-46. *Member:* American Econometric Society, Royal Economic Society, American Finance Association, Mont Pelerin Society. *Awards, honors:* Ford Foundation doctoral dissertation competition, 1960; Georgia Institute of Technology, named Miles B. Lane Lecturer, 1968.

WRITINGS: The Term Structure of Interest Rates, Prentice-Hall, 1962; (contributor) *Stabilization Policies,* Prentice-Hall, 1963; (with Eli Shapiro) *The Measurement of Corporate Sources and Uses of Funds,* National Bureau of Economic Research, 1964; (editor) *Varieties of Monetary Experience,* University of Chicago Press, 1970. Contributor of articles to professional journals.†

*   *   *

MELLINKOFF, David   1914-

PERSONAL: Born September 29, 1914, in McKeesport, Pa.; son of Albert (a businessman) and Helen (Mussoff) Mellinkoff; married Ruth Weiner, July 10, 1949; children: Daniel. *Education:* Stanford University, A.B., 1935; Harvard University, LL.B., 1939. *Politics:* Democrat. *Religion:* Jewish. *Home:* 744 Holmby Ave., Los Angeles, Calif. 90024. *Office:* School of Law, University of California, Los Angeles, Calif.

CAREER: Admitted to California bar, 1939. Lawyer in private practice in Beverly Hills and Los Angeles, Calif., 1939—. University of California, School of Law, Los Angeles, lecturer in law, 1964-65, professor of law, 1965—. *Military service:* U.S. Army, Field Artillery, World War II; became captain; received battle star (New Guinea). *Member:* American Bar Association, Los Angeles Bar Association, Beverly Hills Bar Association, Selden Society, Phi Beta Kappa. *Awards, honors:* Scribes Award for book best conveying the true spirit of the legal profession, 1963, for *The Language of the Law.*

WRITINGS: The Language of the Law, Little, Brown, 1963; *The Conscience of a Lawyer,* West Publishing, 1973. Contributor to legal journals.

WORK IN PROGRESS: Lawyers and the System of Justice for West.

*   *   *

MELONE, Joseph J(ames)   1931-

PERSONAL: Born July 27, 1931, in Pittston, Pa.; son of Dominick William (an insurance agent) and Beatrice (Pignone) Melone; married Marie J. DeGeorge, January 23,

1960; children: Lisa Jane, Carol Ann. *Education:* University of Pennsylvania, B.S. in Economics, 1953, M.B.A., 1954, Ph.D., 1961. *Politics:* Independent. *Religion:* Roman Catholic. *Home:* 86-1 Ferne Blvd., Drexel Hill, Pa.

CAREER: Chartered Life Underwriter and Chartered Property and Casualty Underwriter. National City Bank of Cleveland, Cleveland, Ohio, investment analyst, 1953-54; University of Pennsylvania, Wharton School, Philadelphia, assistant professor of insurance, 1959—. *Military service:* U.S. Army, 1955-57. *Member:* American Risk and Insurance Association (editor, committee on pension and profit sharing terminology).

WRITINGS: Collectively-Bargained Multi-Employer Pension Plans, Irwin, 1963; (with others) *Risk and Insurance,* Prentice-Hall, 1964; (contributor) *Life and Health Insurance Handbook,* edited by Gregg, Irwin, 1964; (with Everett T. Allen, Jr.) *Pension Planning: Pensions, Profit Sharing, and Other Deferred Compensations,* Irwin, 1966, revised edition, 1972; (with Helen L. Schmidt) *Insurance Courses in Colleges and Universities Outside the United States,* McCahan Foundation, 1968.†

*   *   *

MELTZER, Milton   1915-

PERSONAL: Born May 8, 1915, in Worchester, Mass.; son of Benjamin and Mary (Richter) Meltzer; married Hilda Balinsky (a college counsellor), June 22, 1941; children: Jane, Amy. *Education:* Attended Columbia University, 1932-36. *Politics:* Independent. *Religion:* Jewish. *Home:* 263 West End Ave., New York, N.Y. 10023. *Agent:* Raines and Raines, 244 Madison Ave., New York, N.Y. 10016.

CAREER: Pfizer, Inc., New York, N.Y., assistant director of public relations, 1955-60; Science & Medicine Publishing Co., Inc., New York, N.Y., editor, 1960-68; Thomas Y. Crowell Co., New York, N.Y., consulting editor, 1962—; Doubleday & Co., Inc., consulting editor, 1963-73; Scholastic Book Services, New York, N.Y., consulting editor, 1968-72. Lecturer at universities in U.S. and England, and at professional meetings and seminars. *Military service:* U.S. Army Air Forces, 1942-46; became sergeant. *Member:* Authors Guild (member of national council), P.E.N. (member of national council), Organization of American Historians, American Historical Association.

WRITINGS: (With Langston Hughes) *A Pictorial History of the Negro in America,* Crown, 1956, 4th edition, with C. Eric Lincoln, published as *A Pictorial History of Black Americans,* 1973.

Mark Twain Himself, Crowell, 1960; (editor) *Milestones to American Liberty,* Crowell, 1962, revised edition, 1965; (with Walter Harding) *A Thoreau Profile,* Croweland, reprinted, Thoreau Lyceum, 1970; (editor) *Thoreau: People, Principles and Politics,* Hill & Wang, 1963; *A Light in the Dark: The Life of Samuel Gridley Howe,* Crowell, 1964; (editor) *In Their Own Words: History of the American Negro,* three volumes, Crowell, 1964-67; *Tongue of Flame: The Life of Lydia Maria Child,* Crowell, 1965; (with August Meier) *Time of Trial, Time of Hope: The Negro in America, 1919-1941,* Doubleday, 1966; *Thaddeus Stevens and the Fight for Negro Rights,* Crowell, 1967; *Bound for the Rio Grande: The Mexican War, 1946-48,* Knopf, 1967; (with Langston Hughes) *Black Magic: A Pictorial History of the Negro in American Entertainment,* Prentice-Hall, 1967; *Bread and Roses: The Struggle of American Labor, 1865-1915,* Knopf, 1967; *Langston Hughes: A Biography,*

Crowell, 1968; *Brother, Can You Spare a Dime? The Great Depression, 1929-1933*, Knopf, 1969; (with Lawrence Lader) *Margaret Sanger: Pioneer of Birth Control*, Crowell, 1969.

Freedom Comes to Mississippi: The Story of Reconstruction, Follett, 1970; *Slavery: From the Rise of Western Civilization to Today*, two volumes, Cowles, 1971-72; *To Change the World: A Picture History of Reconstruction*, Scholastic Books, 1971; *Underground Man* (novel), Bradbury Press, 1972; *Hunted Like a Wolf: The Story of the Seminole War*, Farrar, 1972; *The Right to Remain Silent*, Harcourt, 1972; *Remember the Days: A Short History of the Jewish American*, Doubleday, 1974; (with Bernard Cole) *The Eye of Conscience: Photographers and Social Change*, Follett, 1974; *World of Our Fathers: The Jews of Eastern Europe*, Farrar, 1974.

Editor of "Women of America" series, Crowell, 1962—, "Zenith Books" series, Doubleday, 1963-73, and "Firebird Books" series, Scholastic Book Services, 1968-72. Author of scripts for radio, television, and documentary films. Contributor to magazines. Founder and editor-in-chief of *Pediatric Herald*, 1960-68; member of editorial board of *Children's Literature in Education*, 1973—.

WORK IN PROGRESS: Books on the Work Projects Administration (WPA) arts projects; *The Holocaust, The Migration of the East European Jews to America, Dorothea Lange: The Photographer.*

* * *

MENDEL, Arthur P. 1927-

PERSONAL: Born July 17, 1927, in Chicago, Ill.; son of Joseph (a furrier) and Mae (Toppel) Mendel; married Sara Pinsky (a teacher), February 1, 1951; children: Ruth, Aaron, Matthew, Joanna. *Education:* Roosevelt University, B.A., 1950; Harvard University, M.A., 1952, Ph.D., 1956. *Religion:* Jewish. *Home:* 1113 Olivia St., Ann Arbor, Mich.

CAREER: University of Michigan, Ann Arbor, associate professor of Russian history, 1961—. *Military service:* U.S. Army, 1945-47. *Member:* American Association for the Advancement of Slavic Studies, American Historical Association.

WRITINGS: (Contributor) *Russian Thought and Politics*, Harvard University Press, 1957; (editor and translator) *Short Stories of Tolstoy*, Bantam, 1960; (editor) *Essential Works of Marxism*, Bantam, 1961; *Dilemmas of Progress in Tsarist Russia*, Harvard University Press, 1961; (editor) *The Twentieth Century*, Free Press of Glencoe, 1964; (editor) *The Extraordinary Decade: Political Memoirs of Pavel Nikolaevich Miliukov, 1905-1917*, University of Michigan Press, 1967. Contributor to *American Slavic and East European Review.*

WORK IN PROGRESS: *Soviet Mind in Transition*; a second book, *History as Art*; a study of creative Russian art in thought in the closing decades of Tsarist Russia.†

* * *

MERIWETHER, James B. 1928-

PERSONAL: Born May 8, 1928, in Columbia, S.C.; son of Robert L. (a teacher) and Margaret (Babcock) Meriwether; married Nancy Callcott, July 29, 1955; children: Rebecca, Robert, George, Nicholas, Margaret. *Education:* University of South Carolina, B.A., 1949; Princeton University, M.A., 1952, Ph.D., 1958. *Home:* 1400 Devonshire Dr., Columbia, S.C.

CAREER: University of Texas, Austin, assistant professor of English, 1958-59; University of North Carolina, Chapel Hill, assistant professor, 1959-61, associate professor of English, 1961-64; University of South Carolina, Columbia, professor of English, 1964-70, McClintock Professor of Southern Letters, 1970—. *Military service:* U.S. Army, 1953-56. *Member:* American Studies Association, Modern Language Association of America, Bibliographical Society of America. *Awards, honors:* American Council of Learned Societies fellow, 1960-61; Guggenheim fellow, 1963-64.

WRITINGS: (Editor) Joyce Cary, *Memoir of the Bobotes*, University of Texas Press, 1960; *The Literary Career of William Faulkner*, Princeton University Library, 1961, reissued with new preface, 1971; (editor) William Faulkner, *As I Lay Dying*, Random House, 1964; (editor) *Essays, Speeches, and Public Letters of William Faulkner*, Random House, 1966; (editor with Michael Millgate) *Lion in the Garden: Interviews with Faulkner, 1926-1962*, Random House, 1968; (contributor) Jackson R. Bryer, editor, *Fifteen Modern American Authors: A Survey of Research and Criticism*, Duke University Press, 1969, supplemented contribution in enlarged edition, *Sixteen Modern American Authors: A Survey of Research and Criticism*, Norton, 1973; (editor and author of preface) *The Merrill Studies in The Sound and the Fury*, C. E. Merrill, 1970; *James Gould Cozzens: A Checklist*, introduction by James Gould Cozzens, Gale, 1973.

Established texts of two books by William Gilmore Simms, *Voltmeier; or, The Mountain Men*, University of South Carolina Press, 1969, and *As Good as a Comedy, and Paddy McGann*, University of South Carolina Press, 1972.

WORK IN PROGRESS: Various textual and critical studies of Faulkner and other southern writers.

AVOCATIONAL INTERESTS: Badminton and gardening.

* * *

MERRELL, Karen Dixon 1936-

PERSONAL: Born December 19, 1936, in Payson, Utah; daughter of Jack V. (a steel worker) and Jean Dixon; married V. Dallas Merrell (a university teacher), June 8, 1959; children: Ann, Kay, Joan, Paul Dixon. *Education:* Brigham Young University, B.S., 1959. *Religion:* Mormon. *Home:* 3247 Hollypark Dr., #1, Inglewood, Calif.

CAREER: Elementary school teacher in Provo, Utah, 1959-60. Summer lecturer at Brigham Young University. *Member:* White Key.

WRITINGS: *Prayer* (juvenile), Brigham Young University Press, 1964; *Tithing*, Extension Publications (Brigham Young University), 1966.

WORK IN PROGRESS: *Women in Mormon History*, with husband V. Dallas Merrell; *Great Women in World History.*†

* * *

MERRICK, Gordon 1916-

PERSONAL: Born August 3, 1916, in Cynwyd, Pa.; son of King Rodney (an investment broker) and Mary (Gordon) Merrick. *Education:* Princeton University, B.A., 1939. *Home:* 1 Ave. de Tourville, Paris 7, France. *Office:* McIntosh & Owen, 18 East 41st St., New York, N.Y. 10017.

CAREER: An actor, 1938-41, appeared in New York company of "The Man Who Came to Dinner," 1939-40; a journalist, 1941-44, with the *Washington Star, Baltimore Evening Sun, PM, New York Post. Wartime service:* Office of Strategic Services in France, 1944-45; civilian employee, rank equaling captain.

WRITINGS: The Strumpet Wind, Morrow, 1947; *The Demon of Moon,* Messner, 1954; *The Vallency Tradition,* Messner, 1955 (published in England as *Between Darkness and Day,* R. Hale, 1957); *The Hot Season,* Morrow, 1957 (published in England as *The Eye of One,* R. Hale, 1959); *The Lord Won't Mind,* Geis, 1970; *One for the Gods,* Geis, 1971; *Forth Into Light,* Avon, 1974. Contributor of book reviews and articles to *New Republic, Ikonos,* and others. Author of television script adapted from James Purdy's *The Nephew,* scheduled for production by British Broadcasting Corp.

WORK IN PROGRESS: A novel, *A Day With Leighton;* several television projects.

SIDELIGHTS: Merrick speaks French and Greek and divides his residence between those two countries. His first three novels have been published in French by Flammarion.†

*   *   *

MERRIL, Judith 1923-
(Ernest Hamilton, Rose Sharon, Eric Thorstein; Cyril Judd, a joint pseudonym)

PERSONAL: Name originally Josephine Judith Grossman; born January 21, 1923, in New York, N.Y.; daughter of Schlomo S. and Ethel (Hurwitch) Grossman; children: (first marriage) Merril Zissman (Mrs. Howard MacDonald); (second marriage) Ann Pohl. *Education:* Attended City College (now City College of the City University of New York), 1939-40. *Politics:* "Favor world government." *Religion:* Jewish. *Agent:* Virginia Kidd, Box 278, Milford, Pa. 18337.

CAREER: Research assistant and ghost-writer, 1943-47; Bantam Books, New York, N.Y., editor, 1947-49; free-lance writer and editor, specializing in science fiction, 1949-68; free-lance writer, lecturer, broadcaster, and radio documentarist, 1971—. Teacher of professional fiction writing, Port Jervis (N.Y.) Adult Education Program, 1963-64; consultant, Rochdale College, 1968-69, Spaced Out Library (Toronto), 1970—; lecturer in science fiction, University of Toronto, 1971-72; associate of department of humanities of science at Sir George Williams University, 1972—; director or participant in a number of science fiction writers' workshops and conferences. *Member:* Science Fiction Research Association (founding member), Writers Union of Canada, Institute for 21st Century Studies, Association of Canadian Television and Radio Actors, Voice of Women, Mensa, Hydra Club (founding member), 21 McGill Women's Club (Toronto; founding member), Elves, Gnomes and Little Men Chowder & Marching Society (honorary member), Witchdoctors' Club (New York; member of Witch's Auxiliary).

WRITINGS—Under name Judith Merril: Shadow on the Hearth (novel), Doubleday, 1950; (with others) *The Petrified Planet* (three short novels), Twayne, 1953; *The Tomorrow People* (novel), Pyramid Books, 1960; *Out of Bounds* (short stories), Pyramid Books, 1960; (with others) *Six Great Short Science Fiction Novels,* Dell, 1960; *Daughters of Earth* (three novellas), Gollancz, 1968, Doubleday, 1969; (author of introduction) *Path into the Unknown,* Delacorte, 1968; (author of introduction) E. L.

Fermin, editor, *Once and Future Tales from the Magazine of Fantasy and Science Fiction,* Harris-Wolfe, 1968; *Survival Ship,* Kakabeka, 1973.

Editor of anthologies: *Shot in the Dark,* Bantam, 1950; *Beyond Human Ken,* Random House, 1952; *Human?,* Lion Press, 1952; *Beyond the Barriers of Space and Time,* Random House, 1954; *Galaxy of Ghouls,* Lion Press, 1955, reissued as *Off the Beaten Orbit,* Pyramid Books, 1958; *The Year's Best Science Fiction,* Volumes I-IV, Gnome Press, 1956-59, Volumes V-IX, Simon & Schuster, 1960-64, Volumes X-XII, Delacorte, 1965-68; *SF: The Best of the Best,* Delacorte, 1967; *England Swings SF,* Doubleday, 1968 (published in England as *Space-Time Journal,* Granada, 1972); *Science Fiction Sukiyaki,* Bantam, in press.

Short stories and novelettes anthologized in *World of Wonder,* edited by Fletcher Pratt, Twayne, 1951; *Journey to Infinity,* edited by Martin Greenberg, Gnome Press, 1951; *Children of Wonder,* edited by William Tenn, Simon & Schuster, 1952; *Tomorrow the Stars,* edited by Robert Heinlein, Doubleday, 1952; *Beyond the End of Time,* edited by Frederik Pohl, Permabooks, 1952; *Star Science Fiction,* edited by Pohl, Ballantine, 1952; *The Damned,* edited by Daniel Talbot, Lion Press, 1954; *Best American Short Stories,* edited by Martha Foley, Houghton, 1955; *A Treasury of Great Science Fiction,* edited by Anthony Boucher, Doubleday, 1959.

Fantastic Universe Omnibus, edited by H. S. Santesson, Prentice-Hall, 1960; *World of Psychology,* edited by G. B. Levitas, Braziller, 1963; *Escape to Earth,* Belmont Books, 1963; *First Flight,* edited by Damon Knight, Lancer, 1963; *Transformations,* edited by D. Roselle, Fawcett, 1963; *Seventh Galaxy Reader,* edited by Frederik Pohl, Doubleday, 1964; *13 Above the Night,* edited by Groff Conklin, Dell, 1965; *The Saint Magazine Reader,* edited by Santesson, Doubleday, 1966; *Rod Serling's Devils and Demons,* Bantam, 1967; *Crime Prevention in the 30th Century,* edited by Santesson, Walker & Co., 1969.

Science Fiction Hall of Fame, Volume I, edited by Robert Silverberg, Doubleday, 1970; *SF: The Other Side of Realism,* edited by T. D. Clareson, Bowling Green University Press, 1971; *Speculations,* edited by T. Sanders, Glencoe Press, 1973; *Science Fiction,* edited by H. Katz and others. Rand McNally, 1974.

Radio documentaries: "How to Think Science Fiction," 1971-72; "Women of Japan," 1972; "What Limits?," 1973; "Growing Up in Japan," 1973; "How to Face Doomesday Without Really Dying," 1974.

With C. M. Kornbluth under joint pseudonym Cyril Judd: *Outpost Mars,* Abelard, 1952, reissued as *Sin in Space,* Beacon, 1961 (first published in serial form as "Mars Child" in *Galaxy Science Fiction,* 1951); *Gunner Cade,* Simon & Schuster, 1952 (serialized in *Astounding Science Fiction,* 1952).

Short stories have appeared in sports, western, and detective magazines under pseudonyms Ernest Hamilton, Rose Sharon, and Eric Thorstein, in sixteen science fiction magazines in America, and in periodicals published in England, France, Mexico, Japan, and other countries; also translator of science fiction short stories from the Japanese. Contributor of short stories to *Toronto Star* and *New York Post.* Book editor and reviewer for *Magazine of Fantasy and Science Fiction,* 1965-69.

SIDELIGHTS: Judith Merril settled on the science fiction genre because "it is closely concerned with my interest in the essential relationship between modern man and the modern environment.''

Her novel, *Shadow on the Hearth*, was televised as ''Atomic Attack'' on ''Motorola Playhouse,'' and a short story, ''Whoever You Are,'' was dramatized on C.B.C. Radio.

* * *

MERRILL, James (Ingram) 1926-

PERSONAL: Born March 3, 1926, in New York, N.Y. *Education:* Amherst College, B.A., 1947. *Home:* 107 Water St., Stonington, Conn.

CAREER: Poet, novelist, and playwright. *Military service:* U.S. Army, 1944-45. *Member:* National Institute of Arts and Letters. *Awards, honors:* Oscar Blumenthal Prize, 1947; *Poetry* magazine's Levinson Prize, 1949, and Harriet Monroe Memorial Prize, 1951; Morton Dauwen Zabel Memorial Prize, 1965, for ''From the Cupola''; National Book Award in poetry, 1967, for *Nights and Days*; D.Litt., Amherst College, 1968; Bollingen Prize in Poetry, 1973.

WRITINGS: Jim's Book: A Collection of Poems and Short Stories, privately printed, 1942; *The Black Swan* (poems), Icarus (Athens), 1946; *First Poems*, Knopf, 1951; *The Seraglio* (novel), Knopf, 1957; *The Country of a Thousand Years of Peace* (poems), Knopf, 1959, revised edition, Atheneum, 1970; *Selected Poems*, Chatto & Windus, 1961; *Water Street* (poems), Atheneum, 1962; *The (Diblos) Notebook* (novel), Atheneum, 1965; *Nights and Days* (poems), Atheneum, 1966; *The Fire Screen* (poems), Atheneum, 1969; *Braving the Elements* (poems), Atheneum, 1972.

Plays: ''The Immortal Husband,'' published in *Playbook*, New Directions, 1956; ''The Bait,'' published in *Artists Theatre*, Grove, 1960.

Poetry represented in anthologies, including *Poetry for Pleasure*, edited by I. M. Parson, Doubleday, 1960; *Contemporary American Poetry*, edited by Donald Hall, Penguin, 1962; *New Poets of England and America*, edited by Hall, Meridian, 1962; *Poet's Choice*, edited by Paul Engle and J. T. Langland, Dial, 1962; *Modern Poets*, edited by J. M. Brinnin and Bill Read, McGraw, 1963; *Poems on Poetry*, edited by Robert Wallace and J. G. Taaffe, Dutton, 1965; *Poems of Our Moment*, edited by John Hollander, Pegasus, 1968; *New Yorker Book of Poems*, Viking, 1970.

Contributor to *Hudson Review, Poetry*, and others.

SIDELIGHTS: Graham Martin wrote of Merrill in the *Listener*: ''James Merrill is an accomplished writer with a beautifully expert command of modern poetic idiom, its interplay of high and low styles, its tragicomic tone, its self-awareness, and its rhythmic subtlety, a speech stress continually moving towards and away from some traditional measure. He also has a rarer gift, imaginative power of the nightmarish kind which turns familiar domestic properties—a cat, laundry, your hand on the pillow at night—into the fearsome shapes that swarm in the early hours.'' A *Harper's* reviewer wrote of *The Fire Screen*: ''Each of James Merrill's books of poetry has been better than the previous one, and such a spectacle, in the case of one of our very best poets, is more than refreshing. *The Fire Screen* is an extraordinarily beautiful book in its total organization, as well as in its individual poems.''

BIOGRAPHICAL/CRITICAL SOURCES: Carolyn Riley, editor, *Contemporary Literary Criticism*, Gale, Volume II, 1974, Volume III, 1975.

MERWIN, W(illiam) S(tanley) 1927-

PERSONAL: Born September 30, 1927, in New York, N.Y., son of a Presbyterian minister; grew up in Scranton, Pa.; married Diana Whalley, 1954. *Education:* Princeton University, A.B., 1947, one year of graduate study in modern languages. *Residence:* Currently living in France.

CAREER: Tutor in France and Portugal, 1949; tutor of Robert Graves's son in Majorca, 1950; lived in London, England, 1951-54, supporting himself largely by doing translations of Spanish and French classics for the British Broadcasting Corporation Third Programme; returned to America in 1956 to write plays for the Poets' Theatre, Cambridge, Mass.; lived in New York, N.Y., 1961-63; associated with Roger Planchon's Theatre de la Cite, Lyon, France, ten months during 1964-65. *Member:* National Institute of Arts and Letters. *Awards, honors:* Kenyon Review fellowship in poetry, 1964; Rockefeller fellowship, 1956; National Institute of Arts and Letters grant, 1957; Arts Council of Great Britain playwriting bursary, 1957; Rabinowitz Foundation grant, 1961; Ford Foundation grant, 1964-65; fellowship from Chapelbrook Foundation, 1966; Harriet Monroe Memorial Prize, 1967; Rockefeller Foundation grant, 1969; Pulitzer Prize for poetry for *The Carrier of Ladders*, 1971.

WRITINGS: A Mask for Janus (poems), Yale University Press, 1952; *The Dancing Bears* (poems), Yale University Press, 1954; *Green With Beasts* (poems), Knopf, 1956; *The Drunk in the Furnace* (poems), Macmillan, 1960; (editor) *West Wind: Supplement of American Poetry*, Poetry Book Society (London), 1961; *The Moving Target* (poems), Atheneum, 1963; *Collected Poems*, Atheneum, 1966; *The Lice* (poems), Atheneum, 1969; *Animae* (poems), Kayak, 1969; *The Miner's Pale Children*, Atheneum, 1970; *The Carrier of Ladders* (poems), Atheneum, 1970; (with A. D. Moore) *Signs*, Stone Wall Press, 1970; *Asian Figures* (poems), Atheneum, 1973; *Writings to an Unfinished Accompaniment*, Atheneum, 1973. Contributor to numerous anthologies.

Translator: Lope Felix de Vega Carpio, *Punishment Without Vengeance*, microfilm at Columbia University, 1958; *The Poem of the Cid*, Dent, 1959, New American Library, 1962; *The Satires of Persius*, Indiana University Press, 1961; *Some Spanish Ballads*, Abelard, 1961, also published as *Spanish Ballads*, Doubleday Anchor, 1961; *The Life of Lazarillo de Tormes: His Fortunes and Adversities*, Doubleday Anchor, 1962; (with Denise Levertov, William Carlos Williams, and others) Nicanor Parra, *Poems and Antipoems*, New Directions, 1968; Jean Follain *Transparence of the World*, Atheneum, 1969; *W. S. Merwin: Selected Translations 1948-1968*, Atheneum, 1969; (and author of introduction) S. Chamfort, *Products of the Perfected Civilization: Selected Writings of Chamfort*, Macmillan, 1969; Antonio Porchia, *Voices: Selected Writings of Antonio Porchia*, Follett, 1969; Pablo Neruda, *Twenty Poems and a Song of Despair*, Cape, 1969; (with others) Pablo Neruda, *Selected Poems*, Cape, 1970. Also translator of Lope de Rueda, ''Eufemia,'' in *Tulane Drama Review*, December, 1958; Lesage, ''Turcaret,'' and Marivaux, ''The False Confessions,'' both in *The Classic Theatre*, edited by Eric Bentley, Doubleday, 1961; Lesage, ''Crispin,'' in *Tulane Drama Review*; ''The Song of Roland,'' in *Medieval Epics*, Modern Library, 1963, and, Garcia Lorca, ''Yerma,'' 1969.

Plays: (with Dido Milroy) ''Darkling Child'', produced, 1956; ''Favor Island,'' produced at Poets' Theatre, Cambridge, Mass., 1957, and on British Broadcasting Corporation Third Programme, 1958; "The Gilded West," produced at Belgrade Theatre, Coventry, England, 1961.

Contributor to *Nation, Botteghe Oscure, Encounter, Listener, Times Literary Supplement, Hudson Review, Partisan Review, Harper's, Sewanee Review, Poetry, New Yorker, Atlantic, Kenyon Review, Paris Review, San Francisco Review, Evergreen Review, New World Writing*, and *New York Review of Books*. Poetry editor of *The Nation*, 1962.

SIDELIGHTS: Merwin writes: "I started writing hymns for my father almost as soon as I could write at all, illustrating them. I recall some rather stern little pieces addressed, in a manner I was familiar with, to backsliders, but I can remember too wondering whether there might not be some liberating mode. In Scranton there was an anthology of *Best Loved Poems of the American People* in the house, which seemed for a time to afford some clues. But the first real writers, that held me were not poets: Conrad first, and then Tolstoy, and it was not until I had received a scholarship and gone away to the university that I began to read poetry steadily and try incessantly, and with abiding desperation, to write it. I was not a satisfactory student; ... I spent most of my time either in the university library, or riding in the country: I had discovered that the polo and ROTC stables were full of horses with no one to exercise them. I believe I was not noticeably respectful either of the curriculum and its evident purposes, nor of several of its professors, and I was saved from the thoroughly justified impatience of the administration, as I later learned, by the intercessions of R. P. Blackmur, who thought I needed a few years at the place to pick up what education I might be capable of assimilating, and I did in fact gain a limited but invaluable acquaintance with a few modern languages. While I was there, John Berryman, Herman Broch, and Blackmur himself, helped me, by example as much as by design, to find out some things about writing; of course it was years before I began to realize just what I had learned, and from whom.

"I am not, I believe, a teacher. I have not evolved an abstract aesthetic theory and am not aware of belonging to any particular group of writers. I neither read nor write much criticism, and think of its current vast proliferation chiefly as a symptom, inseperable from other technological substitutions. I do not admire government processes nor the necessities they reveal, and I put no faith in material utopias whether socialist or capitalist; they too, like much criticism, seem to me to be projections of a poverty that is not in itself material. Not that I think them impossible. But I imagine that a society whose triumphs one after the other emerge as new symbols of death, and that feeds itself by poisoning the earth, may be expected, even while it grows in strength and statistics, to soothe its fears with trumpery hopes, refer to nihilism as progress, dismiss the private authority of the senses as it has cashiered belief, and of course find the arts exploitable but unsatisfying.

"Writing is something I know little about; less at some times than at others. I think, though, that so far as it is poetry it is a matter of correspondances; one glimpses them, pieces of an order, or thinks one does, and tries to convey the sense of what one has seen to those to whom it may matter, including, if possible, one's self." *A Mask for Janus* established Merwin as a poet who could write in a variety of forms. He is technically assured, eloquent, and inventive, and easily employs perhaps the most startling imagery in contemporary poetry. Alonzo Gibbs notes that Merwin "presents a 'first morning' look at the world. And there is something unhurried about his poems as if he had an infinite amount of time to appraise what he saw and thought." Even his detractors admit that part of their dissatisfaction with his poetry stems from envy.

When Merwin's first book was published, W. H. Auden hailed him as a new "mythological" poet who spoke in universal and impersonal terms. Keith Gunderson, in a review of *The Moving Target* in *Kayak*, has refined this observation, noting that the "we," the "you," and even the "I" in Merwin's poems "all lack definite referents. That is not their point. They are not meant to be names ... nor personal pronouns in any usual sense. They are extended uses of these linguistic conventions and quasipersonifications which are used to write about something else. To this extent they are myth-*like* creatures without any myth ... other than Merwin's imagination, feelings and reactions. When we come to see how and why these conventions have been extended we see that they are descriptively indifinite suggestions or associations on which to hang moods and attitudes, and that they are designed to invoke or proscribe ranges of emotions, memory, feeling, apprehension, anxiety, fantasy and fear. Or they involve a radically 'subjective' ... interpretation of this or that aspect of Merwin's world.... The actions are not the literal actions of real people; they are the metaphorical actions of surreal people."

X. J. Kennedy once wrote that Merwin's best poems "do not attack the subject but graciously seduce it." Such poetry is often difficult. Gunderson admits that "Merwin at times does write at the very margins of intelligibility.... [Yet] this kind of writing can provide a poet with a mobility not easily obtained otherwise; a liberty to utilize the emotional and even descriptive effects which bizarre juxtapositions and unexpected associations can produce—effects not harnessed to the ordinary demands of thematic or descriptive accuracy...."

Merwin's abiding interest in animals is not unlike that of Edwin Muir, a poet he admires. In a review of Muir's *Collected Poems*, Merwin writes: "The ambiguous power of the animals' presence in his writing is due in part to the fact the world beyond time in which Muir's animals exist is at once the region from which man rose by virtue of his intelligence, and the Eden from which he fell and still falls." Similarly, through implied contrasts between animals and men, Merwin, as Roche has noted, paints "the dead landscape of our present despair."

BIOGRAPHICAL/CRITICAL SOURCES: Kayak, number 3; *Voices*, January-April, 1953, May-August, 1957, September-December, 1961; *Furioso*, spring, 1953; *Poetry*, May, 1953, May, 1961, February, 1963, June, 1964; *Western Review*, spring, 1955; *Prairie Schooner*, fall, 1957, fall, 1962, winter, 1962-63; *New Mexico Quarterly*, autumn, 1961; *Princeton University Library Chronicle*, autumn, 1964; *Shenandoah*, winter, 1970; Carolyn Riley, editor, *Contemporary Literary Criticism*, Gale, Volume I, 1973, Volume II, 1974, Volume III, 1975.†

*   *   *

MESSNER, Fred(rick) R(ichard) 1926-

PERSONAL: Born July 1, 1926, in Teaneck, N.J.; son of Frederick (an economist) and Beatrice (Bennett) Messner; married Violet Anderson, April 8, 1950; children: Steven Fredrick, Lynne, Kenneth Richard, Katherine. *Education:* Columbia University, A.B., and B.S. in Chemical Engineering, 1948. *Politics:* Independent. *Religion:* Lutheran. *Home:* 30 Ravine Dr., Woodcliff Lake, N.J. *Office:* Michel-Cather, 2 Park Ave., New York, N.Y.

CAREER: G. M. Basford Co. (advertising agency), New York, N.Y., 1948-61, became vice-president and account manager; McCann-Erickson, Inc. (advertising agency), New York, N.Y., vice-president and account director, Industrial, Technical and Scientific Marketing Division, 1961-65; Michel-Cather (advertising), New York, N.Y., vice-president and creative director, beginning 1965. New York University, former instructor in direct mail advertising. Ridgefield Park (N.J.) Community Chest, president, 1959; Ridgefield Park Board of Education, member, 1957-58. *Military service:* U.S. Naval Reserve, 1944-46. *Member:* Association of Industrial Advertisers (president, New Jersey chapter, 1962-63), Direct Mail Advertising Association (co-chairman, education committee, 1961-62), Chemists Club.

WRITINGS: Industrial Advertising: Planning, Creating, Evaluating, and Merchandising It More Effectively, McGraw, 1963. Weekly columnist, "Messner on Business Paper Ads," in *Printers' Ink* (also contributing editor); contributor to *Industrial Marketing* and *Journal of Marketing*.

SIDELIGHTS: Messner speaks and reads German. *Avocational interests:* Plays piano and writes songs.†

* * *

METCALF, Thomas R. 1934-

PERSONAL: Born May 31, 1934; son of George F. (a business executive) and May (Carroll) Metcalf; married Barbara Daly, October 17, 1964. *Education:* Amherst College, B.A., 1955; Cambridge University, B.A., 1957, M.A., 1961; Harvard University, Ph.D., 1960. *Home:* 719 Wellesley Ave., Berkeley, Calif. 94708. *Office:* History Department, University of California, Berkeley, Calif. 94720.

CAREER: University of Wisconsin, Madison, instructor, 1959-60; University of California, Santa Barbara, assistant professor of history, 1961-62; University of California, Berkeley, assistant professor of history, beginning 1962. *Member:* American Historical Association, Association for Asian Studies, American Institute of Indian Studies, Phi Beta Kappa. *Awards, honors:* American Institute of Indian Studies faculty fellow, 1964-65.

WRITINGS: Aftermath of Revolt: India 1857-1870, Princeton University Press, 1964; *Land Tenure and Rural Class Consciousness*, Center for South Asian Studies, 1964; *Modern India: An Interpretive Anthology*, Macmillan, 1971. Contributor to *Journal of Asian Studies, Journal of Modern History, Historical Journal* (Cambridge, England).

SIDELIGHTS: Thomas Metcalf traveled in India for study, 1960-61, 1964-65. He has knowledge of Hindi-Urdu.†

* * *

METHOLD, Kenneth (Walter) 1931-
(Alexander Cade)

PERSONAL: Born December 23, 1931, in Sussex, England; son of Walter Herbert and Winifred (Elliot) Methold; married Chuntana Chulasathira (a physician), July, 1962. *Education:* University of London, teacher's certificate. *Politics:* Independent. *Address:* c/o Longman Group Ltd., Harlow, Essex, England. *Agent:* International Famous Agency, London, England.

CAREER: Former teacher in England and for British Council in Thailand; established own publishing and bookselling company in Thailand; joined Longman Group Ltd., part-time consultant to Longman Group Ltd.; author.

WRITINGS: Broadcasting with Children, University of London Press, 1959; (compiler) *Modern Tales of Mystery and Detection*, Hamish Hamilton, 1959; *All Suspect* (fiction), Macdonald & Co., 1960; *The Man on His Shoulder* (fiction), Macdonald & Co., 1962; *Vital English*, four books, University of London Press, 1963-64; (with Vernor C. Bickley) *English Language Practice for Malaysia*, Hulton Educational Publications, 1964; (with Bickley) *Twentieth Century English*, University of London Press, Books I and II, 1965, Book III, 1967, Book IV, 1969; (editor with Bickley) *Progressive English Exercises*, University of London Press, 1965; *English Idioms at Work*, University of London Press, Books I and II, 1965, Book III, 1969; (with Bickley) *Systematic Composition: A Controlled Approach for Students of English as a Foreign Language*, University of London Press, 1966; *English Expression Practice*, Books IV and V, Longmans, Green, 1969; (under pseudonym Alexander Cade) *Turn Up a Stone*, Bles, 1969.

Editor of three anthologies of short stories for school use. Author of two radio plays for British Broadcasting Corp. Contributor of articles on education to journals and magazines.

WORK IN PROGRESS: Texts on English as a second language; materials for developing language skills in native English speakers; a collection of short stories; a radio play.

* * *

MEUDT, Edna Kritz 1906-

PERSONAL: Born September 14, 1906, in Wyoming Valley, Wis.; daughter of John William (a farmer) and Kristin (Neilsen) Kritz; married Peter J. Meudt (a farmer), October 10, 1924 (died May 2, 1972); children: Richard, Howard, Kathleen (Mrs. George Ott), Christine (Mrs. Daniel Parkinson). *Education:* Attended rural schools in Wisconsin and Sacred Heart Academy. *Politics:* Predominantly Democrat. *Religion:* Roman Catholic. *Home:* Rural Route 3, Dodgeville, Wis. 53533.

CAREER: Poet. Teacher of poetry course at annual summer Rhinelander Seminar and Festival of Arts, sponsored by University of Wisconsin extension; conductor of poetry workshop at Deep South Writer's Conference, Lafayette, La., 1965, and in Wisconsin high schools; judge in state and national poetry contests; lecturer on poetry to colleges and writers' conferences. *Member:* International Poetry Society, Academy of American Poets, National Federation of State Poetry Societies (president, 1963-64; now vice-president), Catholic Poetry Society of America, Wisconsin Fellowship of Poets (president, 1952-54, 1960-61), Wisconsin Regional Writers Association (member of board of directors, 1950-54), Wisconsin Arts Board (member of creative writers panel), Wisconsin State Historical Society, Wisconsin Academy of Sciences, Arts and Letters. *Awards, honors:* Wisconsin Regional Writers Association Bard's chair and jade ring award, 1958; American Poetry League first prize, 1959; National League of American Pen Women honors award, 1963, for *Round River Canticle*; Theta Sigma Phi's Wisconsin Writer's Cup award, 1965, for *In No Strange Land*; Wisconsin Arts Council's Governor's Award, 1970.

WRITINGS—Poetry: Round River Canticle, Wake-

Brook, 1960; *In No Strange Land*, Wake-Brook, 1964; *No One Sings Face Down*, Wisconsin House, 1970; *The Ineluctable Sea*, Edco-Vis Publishers, 1974. Also author of play, "A Case of Semantics." Poetry included in anthologies published by Wisconsin Fellowship of Poets. Contributor of poems to *American Weave, Beloit Poetry Journal, National Wildlife, American Forests, Sign, Christian Century, Creative Wisconsin*, and other journals. Co-editor, *Hawk & Wippoorwill Recalled*; editorial consultant, *Orbis*.

WORK IN PROGRESS: A novel, *Valley of the Hackmatacks*; a fifth volume of poetry.

BIOGRAPHICAL/CRITICAL SOURCES: Capital Times, May 17, 1965.

* * *

MEYER, Howard N(icholas) 1914-

PERSONAL: Born October 8, 1914, in Brooklyn, N.Y.; son of Richard (a manufacturer) and Minnie (Teitelbaum) Meyer; married Sylvette Engel (an artist), August 30, 1942; children: Andrew, Franklin, Jonathan. *Education:* Columbia University, A.B., 1934, LL.B., 1936. *Politics:* Independent. *Home:* 76 Tarence, Rockville Centre, N.Y. 11570.

CAREER: Lawyer in private practice, New York, N.Y., 1937—. Special assistant to U.S. Attorney General, New York, N.Y., 1942-48; member of advisory committee of Rockville Centre (N.Y.) Board of Education, 1954-56; panel arbitrator of New York State and New Jersey Boards of Mediation, 1971—; member of Nassau County Public Employment Relations Board. *Awards, honors:* Nominated for Pulitzer Prize, 1974, for *The Amendment that Refused to Die.*

WRITINGS: (Editor, and author of introduction) T. W. Higginson, *Army Life in a Black Regiment*, Collier, 1962; *Let Us Have Peace: A Biography of U. S. Grant*, Macmillan, 1965; (editor and author of introduction) Angelo Herndon, *Let Me Live*, Arno, 1969; (editor) *Integrating America's Heritage*, McGrath, 1970; *Colonel of the Black Regiment: A Biography of Thomas Wentworth Higginson*, Norton, 1970; *The Amendment that Refused to Die*, Chilton, 1973. Contributor of essays on historical distortions of race relations to *Commonweal, Midwest Quarterly, Book Week, Crisis, Negro Digest, New South*, other periodicals. Editor, *Columbia Law Review*, 1934-36.

* * *

MEYER, John Robert 1927-

PERSONAL: Born December 6, 1927, in Pasco, Wash.; son of Philip Conrad and Cora (Kempter) Meyer; married Helen Lee Stowell, December 17, 1949; children: Leslie Karen, Ann Elizabeth, Robert Conrad. *Education:* Pacific University, Forest Grove, Ore., student, 1945-46; University of Washington, Seattle, A.B., 1950; Harvard University, Ph.D., 1955. *Home:* 138 Brattle St., Cambridge, Mass. 02138. *Office:* National Bureau of Economic Research, Inc., 575 Technology Square, Cambridge, Mass. 02139.

CAREER: Harvard University, Cambridge, Mass., junior fellow, 1953-55, assistant professor, 1955-58, associate professor, 1958-59, professor of economics, 1959-68, 1973—; National Bureau of Economic Research, president, 1967—; Yale University, New Haven, Conn., professor of economics, 1968-73. Director of Charles River Association, Dun & Bradstreet, and Marine Bancorp.; consultant to U.S. Department of Commerce, RAND Corp., Council of Economic Advisors, Agency for International Development, and government of Israel. *Military service:* U.S. Navy, 1946-48. *Member:* American Economic Association, American Statistical Association, Econometric Society (program chairman, 1960), Economic History Association, Phi Beta Kappa. *Awards, honors:* Guggenheim Fellow, 1958-59; Ford Foundation research professorship, 1962-63.

WRITINGS: (With Edwin Kuh) *The Investment Decision: An Empirical Inquiry*, Harvard University Press, 1957; (with M. J. Peck, C. Zwick, and J. Stenason) *Economics of Competition in the Transportation Industries*, Harvard University Press, 1959; (with Robert Glauber) *Investment Decisions, Economic Forecasting and Public Policy*, Harvard University Press, 1964; (with A. Conrad) *The Economics of Slavery and Other Essays on the Qualitative Studies of Economic History*, Aldine, 1964; (with M. Wohl and J. F. Kain) *The Urban Transportation Problem*, Harvard University Press, 1965; (with Conrad) *Studies in Econometric History*, Chapman & Hall, 1965; (with David Denoon) *Technological Change, Migration Patterns and Some Issues of Public Policy*, Harvard University, 1967; (with Kain) *Interrelationships of Transportation and Poverty*, Harvard University, 1968; (with Paul O. Roberts) *An Analysis of Investment Alternatives in the Colombian Transport System*, Harvard University, 1968; (with Donald Eugene Farrar) *Managerial Economics*, Prentice-Hall, 1970; (with Mahlon R. Straszheim) *Pricing and Project Evaluation*, Brookings Institute (Washington), 1971; (with Gerald Kraft) *The Role of Transportation in Regional Economic Development*, Lexington Books, 1971; (compiler with Kain) *Essays in Regional Economics*, Harvard University Press, 1971; (editor) *Techniques of Transport Planning*, Brookings Institution, 1971.

Contributor: *The Public Stake in Union Power*, University of Virginia Press, 1959; *Technological Change and the Future of the Railways*, Northwestern University Press, 1961; *Digital Computers and Their Applications*, Harvard University Press, 1962; (with Kuh) *Impacts of Monetary Policy*, Prentice-Hall, 1964. Contributor of about twenty articles to economics journals in United States and abroad.

WORK IN PROGRESS: On the Theory and Measurement of Business Motivation, for publication by Graduate School of Business Administration, Harvard University; *Transportation Economics and Policy*, for McGraw.†

* * *

MEYER, Leonard B. 1918-

PERSONAL: Born January 12, 1918, in New York, N.Y.; son of Arthur S. and Marion (Wolff) Meyer; married Lee F. Malakoff, August 15, 1945; children: Marion Leslie, Carlin, Erica Cecile. *Education:* Bard College, student, 1936-38; Columbia University, B.A., 1940, M.A., 1948; University of Chicago, Ph.D., 1954. *Office:* Department of Music, University of Chicago, Chicago, Ill. 60637.

CAREER: University of Chicago, Chicago, Ill., 1946—, began as instructor, professor of music, 1961-73, Phyllis Fay Horton Distinguished Service Professor, 1973—, head of humanities section, 1958-60, chairman of music department, 1961-70. Fellow of Center for Advanced Study, Wesleyan University, 1960-61; member of board of directors, Institute for Cultural Development, 1963-70; Ernest Bloch Professor, University of California at Berkeley, 1970. *Military service:* U.S. Army, 1942-45; became second lieutenant; received Bronze Star. *Member:* American Musicological Society (executive board member, 1962-63), American Society for Aesthetics (executive board member, 1961-64), Society for Ethnomusicology (council member, 1962-63), American Association for the Advancement of Science, American Association of University Professors, Phi Beta Kappa. *Awards, honors:* L.H.D., Grinnell College, 1967, Loyola University, Chicago, 1970; Gordon J. Laing Prize from University of Chicago Press, 1968, for *Music, the Arts, and Ideas*; Guggenheim fellow, 1971-72.

WRITINGS: Emotion and Meaning in Music, University of Chicago Press, 1956; (with Grosvenor W. Cooper) *The Rhythmic Structure of Music*, University of Chicago Press, 1960; *Music, the Arts, and Ideas: Patterns and Predictions in Twentieth-Century Culture*, University of Chicago Press, 1967; *Explaining Music: Essays and Explorations*, University of California Press, 1973.

WORK IN PROGRESS: Research in style analysis of baroque and classical minuets, a methodological study; *Music as a Model for History*, a study of temporal patterns; a study of the nature of musical phrasing in performance.

SIDELIGHTS: Theodore Ziolkowski said of *Music, the Arts, and Ideas*: "Occasionally a book comes along that fundamentally shapes our entire critical thinking. Meyer's brilliant and profound analysis of contemporary culture and its reflection in the creative arts is such a work. I would suggest that the author . . . has written here the first significant post-modern aesthetics." Gordon Epperson noted, "I found myself taking issue with the author on almost every page," however, he continued: "I liked the book; it is the work of a lively and original intelligence. The range of Meyer's thought has increased enormously in the decade since *Emotion and Meaning in Music* appeared, and his gains in clarity and readability are equally impressive. The concluding essays . . . are among the most penetrating (and sometimes devastating) analyses of contemporary composition I have seen." *Avocational interests:* Contemporary painting.

* * *

MEZVINSKY, Shirley Shapiro   1936-

PERSONAL: Surname is accented on second syllable; born November 18, 1936, in Des Moines, Iowa; daughter of Philip and Helen (Davidson) Shapiro; married Norton Mezvinsky (a professor), July 22, 1956; children: Andrea. *Education:* Northwestern University, B.S. (cum laude), 1956; University of Wisconsin, M.A., 1958. *Politics:* Democrat. *Religion:* Jewish. *Residence:* New York, N.Y. *Agent:* Curtis Brown Ltd., 60 East 56th St., New York, N.Y. 10022.

CAREER: University of Wisconsin, Madison, teacher of drama and literature, 1959; professional actress in films, television, and on stage, in New York, Boston, Detroit, Chicago, and Wisconsin, beginning 1959; writer, 1961—. *Member:* Institute for the Advanced Study of Theater Arts, Actors' Equity Association.

WRITINGS: The Edge (novel), Doubleday, 1965. Contributor of short stories to *Jewish Horizon* and *New Idea*.

WORK IN PROGRESS: A collection of short stories, tentative title, *The Betrayed*, publication by Doubleday, and a novel.†

* * *

MICHAEL, S(tanley) T(heodore)   1912-

PERSONAL: Born January 20, 1912, in Pittsburgh, Pa.; son of Anthony and Albina (Dubsky) Michael; married, second wife; children: (first marriage) Faidon, Robert; (second marriage) Eloise. *Education:* University of Prague, M.D., 1937. *Religion:* Protestant. *Office:* Cornell University Medical College, 535 East 68th St., New York, N.Y. 10021.

CAREER: Diplomate of National Board of Medical Examiners, 1947, of American Board of Psychiatry and Neurology, 1949. Massachusetts General Hospital, Boston, Mass., research fellow in medicine, 1940-41; Yale University, School of Medicine, New Haven, Conn., instructor in psychiatry, 1946-48; New York State Psychiatric Institute, New York, N.Y., associate clinical psychiatrist, 1949-53; Institute of Living, Hartford, Conn., coordinator of clinical research, 1953-54; Cornell University Medical College, New York, N.Y., research associate, 1955-65; associate professor, 1969—. *Member:* American Medical Association, American Psychiatric Association, Association for Research in Nervous and Mental Diseases, World Federation for Mental Health, Society for Biological Psychiatry, New York State Medical Society, Westchester County Medical Society.

WRITINGS: (With others) *Mental Health in the Metropolis*, McGraw, 1962; (with Thomas S. Langner) *Life Stress and Mental Health*, Free Press of Glencoe, 1963. Contributor of thirty articles to scientific journals.

WORK IN PROGRESS: Research in social psychiatry.

* * *

MICKEN, Charles M.   1918-

PERSONAL: Born April 16, 1918, in Lancaster, Pa.; son of Charles and Della (Buckwatter) Micken; married Mary W. Kreider, July 31, 1939. *Education:* Millersville State College, B.S., 1938; University of Pennsylvania, M.S., 1949, Ed.D., 1958. *Religion:* Methodist. *Home:* 2 Larchwood Rd., West Chester, Pa. *Office:* West Chester State College, West Chester, Pa.

CAREER: Teacher and principal in Pennsylvania schools, 1938-42, 1946-50, 1954-57; Atlantic Highlands (N.J.) public schools, superintendent, 1957-59; West Chester State College, West Chester, Pa., professor of education, beginning 1959. Justice of the peace, 1946-50. Atlantic Highlands (N.J.) Library, member of board, 1950-59. *Military service:* U.S. Naval Reserve, active duty, 1942-46, 1950-54; now captain. *Member:* National Education Association, Association for High Education, National Organization on Legal Problems of Education, Pennsylvania State Education Association, Phi Delta Kappa.

WRITINGS: (Contributor) *Law and the School Superintendent*, H. W. Anderson Co., 1958; (with Lee O. Garber) *The Commonwealth, the Law and the Teacher*, Interstate, 1963; (with H. Halleck Singer) *The Law of Purchasing*, Interstate, 1964; *The Law of the Student: A Manual of Student Rights*, [West Chester, Pa.], 1966; (with Garber) *The Law and the Teacher in Pennsylvania*, Interstate, 1968, 2nd edition, 1971.

AVOCATIONAL INTERESTS: Gardening.†

* * *

MIDDLETON, Christopher   1926-

PERSONAL: Born June 10, 1926, in Truro, Cornwall, England; son of Hubert Stanley (a professor of music) and Dorothy (Miller) Middleton; married Mary Freer, April 11, 1953; children: Sarah, Miranda, Benjamin. *Education:*

Merton College, Oxford, B.A., 1951, D.Phil., 1954. *Residence:* Austin, Tex.

CAREER: Instructor in German literature at various universities. Zurich University, Zurich, Switzerland, lecturer in English, 1952-55; University of Texas, Austin, visiting professor, 1961-62 and 1966, professor of German literature, 1966—; King's College, University of London, London, England, senior lecturer, 1965-66. *Military service:* Royal Air Force, 1944-48; became sergeant. *Awards, honors:* Sir Geoffrey Faber poetry prize, 1964.

WRITINGS: Poems, Fortune Press, 1944; *Nocturne in Eden* (poems), Fortune Press, 1945; *Ohne Hass und Fahne*, Rowohlt Verlag, 1959; (editor with William Burford) *Poet's Vocation: Selections from the Letters of Hoelderlin, Rimbaud, and Hart Crane*, University of Texas Press, 1962; *Torse 3: Poems, 1949-1961*, Harcourt, 1962; *The Metropolitans* (comic opera; music by Hans Vogt), Alkor Editions, 1964; *Nonsequences/Selfpoems*, Longmans, Green, 1965, Norton, 1966; (compiler with William Burford) *The Poets' Vocations*, University of Texas Press, 1967; *Der Taschenelefant*, Neue Rabenpresse, 1969; *Our Flowers and Nice Bones* (poems), Horizon Press, 1969; *The Fossel Fish*, Burning Deck, 1970; *Wie wir Grossmutter zum Markt bringen*, Eremiten-Press, 1970; *Briefcase History*, Burning Deck, 1972.

Translator: Robert Walser, *The Walk and Other Stories*, J. Calder, 1957; (with others) Gottfried Benn, *Primal Vision*, New Directions, 1960; (with others) Hugo von Hofmannsthal, *Poems and Verse Plays*, Pantheon, 1961; (and editor with Michael Hamburger) *Modern German Poetry, 1910-1960*, Grove, 1962; (with Hamburger) Guenter Grass, *Selected Poems*, Harcourt, 1966; (and editor) *German Writing Today*, Penguin, 1967; (with others) Georg Trakl, *Selected Poems*, J. Cape, 1968; (and editor) *Selected Letters of Friedrich Nietzche*, University of Chicago Press, 1969; Robert Walser, *Jakob von Gunten*, University of Texas Press, 1970; Christa Wolf, *The Quest for Christa T.*, Farrar, Straus, 1970; *Selected Poems of Friedrich Hoelderlin and Eduard Moerike*, University of Chicago Press, 1972.

BIOGRAPHICAL/CRITICAL SOURCES: New Statesman, December 24, 1965; *Observer*, January 2, 1966; *Times Literary Supplement*, February 17, 1966.

* * *

MIKESELL, Arthur M. 1932-

PERSONAL: Born July 3, 1932, in Ovid, Mich.; son of Arthur Lee Roy and Sheila (Cronin) Mikesell; married Carol F. Butler, January 3, 1955; children: Stacey Lynn, Emily Sayre. *Education:* Michigan State University of Agriculture and Applied Science (now Michigan State University), B.A., 1957. *Home:* 24 Oak St., Westport, Conn. *Office:* National Association of Mutual Savings Banks, 200 Park Ave., New York, N.Y. 10017.

CAREER: Michigan State University Press, East Lansing, assistant editor, 1957-58; *Popular Mechanics*, New York, N.Y., associate editor, 1958-68; The American Bankers Association, New York, N.Y., speechwriter, 1968-71; National Association of Mutual Savings Banks, New York, N.Y., assistant director of information, 1971—. *Military service:* U.S. Army, 1954-56. *Member:* Sigma Delta Chi.

WRITINGS: The Popular Mechanics Home Book of Refinishing Furniture, Hawthorn, 1963. Contributor of articles to encyclopedias and to magazines.

WORK IN PROGRESS: A children's fantasy, as yet untitled.

* * *

MILES, Leland (Weber, Jr.) 1924-

PERSONAL: Born January 18, 1924, in Baltimore, Md.; son of Leland Weber (a stockbroker) and Marie (Fitzpatrick) Miles; married Virginia Geyer (a musician), July 9, 1947; children: Christine Marie, Gregory Lynn. *Education:* Juniata College, A.B. (cum laude), 1946; University of North Carolina, M.A., 1947, Ph.D., 1949; Duke University, post-doctoral study in religion, 1949. *Politics:* Independent. *Religion:* Episcopalian. *Home:* 332 North Cedar Rd., Fairfield, Conn. *Agent:* (Lectures) Robert Keedick, 475 Fifth Ave., New York, N.Y. *Office:* Office of the President, University of Bridgeport, Bridgeport, Conn.

CAREER: Hanover College, Hanover, Ind., associate professor of English, 1949-50, professor and chairman of department of English, 1950-60; University of Cincinnati, Cincinnati, Ohio, associate professor, 1960-63, professor of English, 1963-64; University of Bridgeport, Bridgeport, Conn., dean of College of Arts and Sciences, 1964-67; Alfred University, Alfred, N.Y., president, 1967-74; University of Bridgeport, Bridgeport, Conn., president, 1974—. Shipboard director of forums, Council on Student Travel, 1953, 1955. Lecturer in major cities of United States, 1956—; producer and moderator of regular weekly program, "Casing the Classics," WHAS-TV, Louisville, Ky., 1958-61. Vice-president of Bridgeport Area Cultural Council, 1964—; trustee, Western New York Nuclear Research Center, 1967-73, Commission on Individual Colleges, 1972—, Carborundum Museum of Ceramics, 1973—; chairman of board of trustees, College Center of Finger Lakes, 1968-71; Empire State Foundation, vice-chairman of board of directors, 1969-71, chairman, 1971-73. *Military service:* U.S. Army Air Forces, 1943-45; navigator with 14th Air Force (Flying Tigers), China, 1944-45; became first lieutenant; received Distinguished Flying Cross with oak leaf cluster.

MEMBER: Modern Humanities Research Association, Modern Language Association of America, College English Association, Renaissance Society of America, American Academy of Political and Social Science, Amici Thomae Mori, Conference on British Studies, Royal Society of Literature, English-Speaking Union of the United States, International Platform Association, Association for Higher Education, Phi Kappa Phi. *Awards, honors:* Danforth scholar, Union Theological Seminary, New York, N.Y., 1957; Lilly fellow, Indiana University School of Letters, 1959; Rosa and Samuel Sachs Prize, Cincinnati Institute of Fine Arts, 1962; American Council of Learned Societies fellow at Harvard University, 1963-64; senior Fulbright research scholar at Kings College, University of London, 1964, visiting scholar, 1972; D.Litt., Juniata College, 1969; L.H.D., Rosary Hill College, 1970.

WRITINGS: Guide to Writing Term Papers, W. C. Brown, 1955, revised edition, 1959; *Americans Are People*, Twayne, 1956; *John Colet and the Platonic Tradition*, Open Court, 1961; *Where Do You Stand on Linguistics?*, College English Association, 1964, revised edition, 1968; (editor) Thomas More, *Dialogue of Comfort against Tribulation*, Indiana University Press, 1966. Senior editor with Stephen Graubard of "Studies in British History and Culture" series, Conference on British Studies, 1968—; founder of journal, *Studies in Burke and His Times*, 1967;

contributor of articles and poetry to professional journals and to popular magazines.

WORK IN PROGRESS: Research on the thought and literary technique of Thomas More.

* * *

MILES, Mary Lillian (Brown) 1908-

PERSONAL: Born January 12, 1908, in Johannesburg, South Africa; daughter of Henry Frederick (an engineer) and Martha (Gowan) Brown; married Kenneth LeRoy Miles (a Baptist clergyman), August 21, 1936; children: Maragaret Ruth Miles Doell, Dorothy Jean Miles Hurt, Marilyn Jane Miles Olson, Wendell Kenneth. *Education:* University of British Columbia, student, 1928-29; Gordon College of Theology and Missions, Th.B., 1934. *Religion:* Baptist. *Home:* 7621 Simonds Rd., N.E., Bothel, Wash. 98011.

CAREER: Taught college typing and shorthand in Seattle, Wash., for one year; has done women's radio work in the past, including a weekly program of poetry and music, "Mount Up With Wings"; library technician at University of Washington Library, Seattle, 1965—.

WRITINGS: Devotions for Preteens, No. 1, 2, 3, 4, 5, 6, Moody, 1959-74, variously published under titles *Quiet Moments with God, My Quiet Time with God, Listening to God,* and *God Speaks to Me.* Author of tracts, "My Baby" and "In His Keeping"; also author of several published poems.

WORK IN PROGRESS: Devotions for Preteens, No. 7, on the Biblical book of *Numbers.*

* * *

MILLAR, Fergus 1935-

PERSONAL: Born July 5, 1935, in Edinburgh, Scotland; son of John Sidney Lawrence (a lawyer) and Jean Burtholme (Taylor) Millar; married Susanna Friedmann, November 2, 1959; children: Sarah Elizabeth, Andrew David, Jonathan Bruce Alexander. *Education:* Oxford University, D.Phil., 1962. *Home:* 80 Harpes Rd., Oxford, England. *Office:* Queen's College, Oxford, England.

CAREER: Oxford University, Oxford, England, fellow of All Souls College, 1958-64, fellow of Queen's College and tutor in ancient history, 1964—. *Military service:* Royal Navy, 1953-55. *Member:* Society for the Promotion of Roman Studies. *Awards, honors:* Conington Prize, Oxford University, 1963, for *A Study of Cassius Dio.*

WRITINGS: A Study of Cassius Dio, Clarendon Press, 1964; (editor and contributor) *Das Roemische Reich und seine Nachbarn,* Fischer-Buecherei, 1966, translation published as *The Roman Empire and Its Neighbours,* Weidenfeld & Nicolson, 1967, Delacorte, 1968; (editor with G. Vermes of revised edition) Emil Schuerer, *History of the Jewish People in the Age of Jesus Christ, 175 B.C.-135 A.D.,* Volume I, T & T. Clark, 1973. Contributor of articles and reviews to classical journals in England, Germany, Switzerland, and Italy; editor, *Journal of Roman Studies,* 1975—.

WORK IN PROGRESS: Volumes II and III of Schuerer's *History of the Jewish People* and *The Emperor in the Roman World, 31 B.C.-337 A.D.*

* * *

MILLAR, Margaret (Sturm) 1915-

PERSONAL: Surname is pronounced Miller; born February 5, 1915, in Kitchener, Ontario, Canada; daughter of Henry William (a businessman) and Lavinia (Ferrier) Sturm; married Kenneth Millar (a writer), June 2, 1938; children: Linda Jane (Mrs. Joseph J. Pagnusat; deceased). *Education:* Attended University of Toronto, 1933-37. *Politics:* Democrat. *Religion:* Protestant. *Home:* 4420 Via Esperanza, Santa Barbara, Calif. 93110. *Agent:* Harold Ober Associates, Inc., 40 East 49th St., New York, N.Y. 10017.

CAREER: Writer. *Member:* Writers Guild of America, West; Mystery Writers of America (president, 1957-58), National Audubon Society, Sierra Club. *Awards, honors:* Mystery Writers of America Edgar Allen Poe Award, 1956, for *Beast in View; Los Angeles Times* Woman of the Year, 1965.

WRITINGS—All published by Random House, except as indicated: *The Invisible Worm,* Doubleday, Doran, 1941; *The Weak-Eyed Bat,* Doubleday, Doran, 1942; *The Devil Loves Me,* Doubleday, Doran, 1942; *Wall of Eyes,* 1943; *Fire Will Freeze,* 1944; *The Iron Gates,* 1945; *Experiment in Springtime,* 1947; *It's All in the Family,* 1948; *The Cannibal Heart,* 1949; *Do Evil in Return,* 1950; *Vanish in an Instant,* 1952; *Rose's Last Summer,* 1952; *Wives and Lovers,* 1954; *Beast in View,* 1955; *An Air that Kills,* 1957; *The Listening Walls,* 1959; *A Stranger in My Grave,* 1961; *How Like an Angel,* 1962; *The Fiend,* 1964; *The Birds and the Beasts Were There,* 1967; *Beyond This Point Are Monsters,* 1970.

SIDELIGHTS: The critic Raymond A. Sokolov notes that Margaret Millar works on her novels in the afternoon, sitting in the old maple chair in which she has composed all her books. She keeps in touch with the underground by attending local trials with her husband, who writes detective novels under the pseudonym Ross Macdonald. *Avocational interests:* Birds.

* * *

MILLARD, Joseph (John) 1908-
(Joe Millard)

PERSONAL: Born January 1, 1908, in Canby, Minn.; son of Frank Earnest (a rancher) and Alice (Lake) Millard; married Amy Leone Lee, February 14, 1931; children: Michael Harrington. *Education:* Pioneer School of Business, St. Paul, Minn., graduate, 1926. *Politics:* "Mostly anti—currently Democrat." *Religion:* Baptist. *Home and office:* 9421 Beck St., Dallas, Tex. 75228.

CAREER: Started as space buyer with an advertising agency in St. Paul, Minn., 1926, subsequently working (in ten-year period), as advertising manager of *Northwest Furniture Digest,* Minneapolis, Minn., as account executive with Kraff Advertising Agency, Minneapolis, and Industrial Advertising Associates, Chicago, Ill., as editor of *How to Sell* (magazine), Chicago, and as editor and publisher of *National Mortician,* Chicago; full-time free-lance writer, 1936—.

WRITINGS: The Wickedest Man, Gold Medal Books, 1954; *Edgar Cayce,* Gold Medal Books, 1956; (editor and contributor) *True Civil War Stories,* Crest Books, 1961; *No Law but Their Own,* Regency, 1963; *The Cheyenne Wars,* Monarch Books, 1964; *The Gods Hate Kansas,* Monarch Books, 1964; *Cut-Hand the Mountain Man,* Chilton, 1964; *The Incredible William Bowles,* Chilton, 1965.

Under name Joe Millard: *For A Few Dollars More,* Award, 1967; *The Good, The Bad, The Ugly,* Award, 1967; *The Good Guys and the Bad Guys,* Award, 1970;

The Last Rebel, Award, 1970; *Macho Callahan*, Award, 1970; *Chato's Land*, Award, 1971; *The Hunting Party*, Award, 1971; *Coffin Full of Dollars*, Award, 1971; *Devil's Dollar Sign*, Award, 1972; *Blood for a Dirty Dollar*, Award, 1973; *Cahill U.S. Marshall*, Award, 1973; *Million-Dollar Bloodhunt*, Award, 1973; *The Hunted*, Award, 1974; *Thunderbolt and Lightfoot*, Award, 1974.

Contributor to about one hundred fiction and general magazines, and some twenty-five trade and technical journals, with the national magazines including *Holiday, True, Reader's Digest, Redbook, Good Housekeeping, American, Argosy, Real*, and *Saga*.

WORK IN PROGRESS: Captain Dickison's War with the Union, a young adult book, and third in a continuing series of fictionized historial biographies for Chilton; magazine nonfiction on science, world affairs, and other contemporary subjects; research in off-trail American history.

SIDELIGHTS: Millard told *CA*: "One day I read an old newspaper account of a washer-woman whose clothesline was ripped down and clothing dropped into the mud by a skirmish between Union and Confed. cavalry during Civil War. Her plight taught me more than anything else what history really is—the unwilling involvement of little people. I've tried never to lose that perspective." *Avocational interests:* Collecting stamps, maps, items of Americana.

*   *   *

MILLER, Elizabeth Kubota   1932-

PERSONAL: Born August 9, 1932, in Dairen, Union of Soviet Socialist Republics (city on northeast Asia coast); daughter of Yoshio (in shipping business) and Shizu (Miyajima) Kubota; married Ronald Keith Miller (a dentist), September 15, 1956; children: Theodosia Whitney. *Education:* Wheaton College, Wheaton, Ill., B.A., 1954; University of Minnesota, M.A., 1957; Harvard University, graduate study, 1958. *Religion:* Episcopalian. *Home:* 9406 Linden Ave., Bethesda, Md.

CAREER: Bethel College, St. Paul, Minn., instructor in English literature, 1956-59; Tachikawa Air Force Base, San Francisco, Calif., base librarian, 1960-63; Fairchild Hiller Corp., Rockville, Md., chief librarian, beginning, 1964. Visiting lecturer in English, Tokyo Woman's Christian College, Tokyo, Japan, 1960. *Member:* National Council of Teachers of English, American Library Association, American Association of University Professors, American Association of University Women, Lambda Iota Tau.

WRITINGS: Tell Me About Tokyo, Tuttle, 1964; *Seven Lucky Gods and Ken-chan*, Tuttle, 1969. Contributor to *Minneapolis Star, Minneapolis Tribune*, and *Women's Journal* (Tokyo).

*   *   *

MILLER, Heather Ross   1939-

PERSONAL: Born September 15, 1939, in Albemarle, N.C.; daughter of Fred E. (a novelist and newspaper editor) and Geneva (Smith) Ross; married Clyde H. Miller (a park superintendent), February 14, 1960; children: Melissa Martha, Kirk Alexander. *Education:* University of North Carolina at Greensboro, B.A., 1961, M.F.A., 1969. *Residence:* Badin, N.C.

CAREER: Pfeiffer College, Misenheimer, N.C., instructor in creative writing, 1965-67; Southeastern Community College, Whiteville, N.C., instructor in English, 1969-72; teacher and consultant to North Carolina's "Poetry in the Schools" program, 1972-74; Stanly Technical Institute, Albemarle, N.C., writer-in-residence, 1974—. *Member:* Phi Beta Kappa. *Awards, honors:* National Association of Independent Schools Best Book Award, 1964, for *The Edge of the Woods*; National Endowment on the Arts, fellowship, 1968-69, 1973-74.

WRITINGS: The Edge of the Woods (novel), Atheneum, 1964; *Tenants of the House* (novel), Harcourt, 1966; *The Wind Southerly* (poems), Harcourt, 1967; *Gone a Hundred Miles* (novel), Harcourt, 1968; *Horse Horse, Tyger Tyger* (poems), Red Clay Books, 1973. Contributor to *Impetus, Southern Poetry Review, Reflections, New York Times, Carolina Quarterly, American Scholar, Raleigh News and Observer, Red Clay Reader*, and *Vogue*.

WORK IN PROGRESS: Delphi, a collection of stories.

SIDELIGHTS: Mrs. Miller writes: "I am competent in nothing but telling stories; but I am competent in 'interests' and have many. My shelves are full of books on everything. But my biggest interests are Clyde and Melissa and Kirk. They are my satisfaction and my torment. Without them I could never write or would never care to. My biggest contribution will be in teaching others to write and read as I was taught by poet-friend-teacher Randall Jarrell."

In the *New York Review of Books*, Bernard Bergonzi writes of *Gone a Hundred Miles*: "Mrs. Miller's great virtue is her feeling for ordinary life, and the tangibility of the world she describes, which is never undercut by any symbolic pattern. If anything, her stress on clinical detail and the processes of primitive medicine is somewhat unrelenting, though they fit easily into the narrative. In spite of the remoteness and rawness of her material this is a fascinating and original work."

*   *   *

MILLER, Lyle L.   1919-

PERSONAL: Born August 20, 1919, in Deer Lodge, Mont.; son of Birl O. and Anna E. (Oakley) Miller; married Grace E. Moore (a professional consultant), September 12, 1942; children: Thomas O., Patricia Ann. *Education:* Montana State College, B.S., 1940; University of Southern California, M.S., 1944; Ohio State University, Ph.D., 1949. *Religion:* Presbyterian. *Home:* 1944 Sheridan, Laramie, Wyo. *Office:* Room 35, Education Hall, University of Wyoming, Laramie, Wyo.

CAREER: Gallatin County High School, Bozeman, Mont., teacher, 1940-42; Douglas Aircraft & California Flyers, Los Angeles, Calif., industrial personnel worker, 1942-44; Flathead County High School, Kalispell, Mont., teacher, 1944-46; Ohio State University, Columbus, Ohio, college of education, assistant junior dean, 1946-49; University of Wyoming, Laramie, Wyo., professor of education, 1949—, supervisor of student employment and study skills center, 1949-53, chairman of guidance and special education, 1953-65, director of reading research center, 1971—. Consultant to Wyoming State Department of Education, U.S. Office of Education, U.S. Social Security Agency; member of national executive board, Boy Scouts of America; member of executive board, Wyoming Mental Health Association, 1963-68. Member of Laramie Chamber of Commerce. *Member:* International Council for Exceptional Children, International Reading Association, National Education Association (life member), American School Counselors Association, American College Personnel Association, American Psychological Association, Association for Group Psychodrama and Psychotherapy, American Personnel and Guidance Association, Association for Counselor Education and Supervision (president, 1963-64), National Vocational Guidance Association, American Association of University Professors (chapter president, 1965-67), Wyoming Personnel and Guidance Association, Wyoming Education Association, Phi Delta Kappa. *Awards, honors:* Educational Service Award of the Wyoming Personnel and Guidance Association, 1964, 1972; National Service Award, Association for Counselor Education and Supervision, 1968.

WRITINGS: (With Alice Z. Seeman) *Guidebook for Prospective Teachers*, Ohio State University Press, 1948; *Increasing Reading Efficiency*, Holt, 1956, 3rd edition, 1970; *Maintaining Reading Efficiency*, Holt, 1959, 3rd edition, Developmental Reading Distributors, 1973; *Developing Reading Efficiency*, Pruett, 1963, 3rd edition, Burgess, 1972; (compiler) *Counseling Leads*, Pruett, 1962, 2nd edition, Developmental Reading Distributors, 1970; (editor) *Teaching Reading Efficiency*, Pruett, 1963, 2nd edition published as *Accelerating Growth in Reading Efficiency*, Burgess, 1967, revised edition published as *Teaching Efficient Reading Skills*, Burgess, 1972; (editor) *Challenge for Change in Counselor Education*, Burgess, 1969; (editor with Jasbir M. Singh and Harbans Lal) *Drug Addiction*, Futura, 1972—; *Personalizing Reading Efficiency*, Burgess, 1975. Contributor of articles to *Journal of Developmental Reading, Journal for Counselor Education and Supervision, School Counselor*, and others. One-time editor of *Wyoming Personnel and Guidance Newsletter*.

WORK IN PROGRESS: Continued research on developmental reading material.

* * *

MILLER, Melvin H(ull) 1920-

PERSONAL: Born April 19, 1920, in Flushing, Mich.; son of Melvin L. (a machinist) and Dorothy (Hull) Miller; married Shirley Lou Mershon, September 11, 1952; children: Pamela, Mark. *Education:* Albion College, A.B., 1942; Michigan State University, M.A., 1949; University of Wisconsin, Ph.D., 1957; additional study at University of Birmingham, 1952, and Oxford University, 1953. *Home:* 7332 Harwood Ave., Wauwatosa, Wis. 53213. *Office:* Department of Communication, University of Wisconsin-Milwaukee, Milwaukee, Wis. 53211.

CAREER: Grinnell College, Grinnell, Iowa, instructor in speech, 1949-51; University of Maryland, Overseas Program, instructor in England, Germany, French Morocco, Greece, and Turkey, 1951-54; University of Wisconsin-Milwaukee, instructor, 1956-58, assistant professor, 1958-63, associate professor, 1963-66, professor of communication, 1966—, chairman of department, 1963-66. *Military service:* U.S. Navy, 1942-47; became lieutenant commander; received Presidential Unit Citation and fourteen battle stars.

MEMBER: Speech Association of America, National Society for the Study of Communication, American Association of University Professors, United States Naval Institute, Central States Speech Association, Wisconsin Academy of Science, Art, and Letters, Wisconsin Historical Society, Delta Sigma Rho, Theta Alpha Phi. *Awards, honors:* Research grants, University of Wisconsin Graduate School, 1960, 1963.

WRITINGS: (With Myers) *Syllabus for Public Speaking*, W. C. Brown, 1962; (with Buys, Cobin, Hunsinger, and Scott) *Contest Speaking Manual*, National Textbook Corp., 1964. Contributor to professional journals.

MILLER, Stanley S. 1924-

PERSONAL: Born November 4, 1924; son of Eli (a businessman) and Bertha Miller; married Elaine Stone, August 29, 1955; children: Cindy Ellen, Jon Brian. *Education:* Harvard University, B.A., 1946, M.B.A., 1950, D.C.S., 1954. *Politics:* Liberal Republican. *Home:* 3 Compton Circle, Lexington, Mass.

CAREER: Harvard University, School of Business Administration, Boston, Mass., beginning 1950, now associate professor of business administration. Keio University, Tokyo, Japan, visiting professor, 1961; co-founder of Keio Business School. *Military service:* U.S. Army Air Forces, meteorologist, 1943-45; became first lieutenant.

WRITINGS: Manufacturing Policy, Irwin, 1957, revised edition (with D. C. D. Rogers), 1964; *Management Problems of Diversification*, Wiley, 1963. Contributor to business journals.

WORK IN PROGRESS: Computer applications in operations management; Japanese and western European management and culture; relations between business and the intellectuals.†

* * *

MILLER, Warren E. 1924-

PERSONAL: Born March 26, 1924, in Hawarden, Iowa; son of John C. (an educator) and Mildred O. (Lien) Miller; married Mildred Kiplinger, June 21, 1948; children: Jeffrey, Jennifer. *Education:* University of Oregon, B.S., 1948, M.S., 1950; Syracuse University, D.S.S., 1954. *Religion:* Unitarian Universalist. *Home:* 1511 Hillridge, Ann Arbor, Mich. *Office:* 3032 Institute for Social Research, University of Michigan, Ann Arbor, Mich.

CAREER: University of Michigan, Ann Arbor, assistant study director, 1951-53, then study director, Survey Research Center, 1953-54; University of California, Berkeley, assistant professor of political science, 1954-56; University of Michigan, assistant professor, 1956-58, associate professor, 1958-63, professor of political science, 1963—, research associate, 1956-59, then program director, Survey Research Center, 1959-70, director, Center for Political Studies, 1970—. Executive director, Inter-university Consortium for Political Research, 1962-70. Consultant, President's Commission on Registration and Voting Participation, 1963-64. *Military service:* U.S. Army Air Forces, 1943-46.

MEMBER: American Political Science Association, International Political Science Association, Society for the Psychological Study of Social Issues, Midwest Political Science Association. *Awards, honors:* Fellow, Center for Advanced Study in the Behavioral Sciences, 1961-62; honorary doctorate, University of Goeteborg, 1972.

WRITINGS: (With Angus Campbell and Gerald Gurin) *The Voter Decides*, Row, Peterson & Co., 1954; (with Campbell, P. Converse, and D. Stokes) *The American Voter*, Wiley, 1960; (with Campbell, Converse, and Stokes) *Elections and the Political Order*, Wiley, 1966. Contributor of chapters to *Twenty-Eighth Yearbook of 1958*, National Council for the Social Studies, and *American Government Annual, 1960-61*. Contributor of about twenty articles to *Scientific American, Labor Law Journal, Editor and Publisher, Public Opinion Quarterly*, and political science journals.

* * *

MILLER, William D. 1916-

PERSONAL: Born December 3, 1916, in Jacksonville,

Fla.; son of Frank Hoten (a businessman) and Verna (Sharp) Miller; married Rhea Bond (a teacher), August 27, 1944; children: William D., Jr., Francis Lloyd, Matthew Jenkins, Christopher Paul, Robert Holt, Carol Maria, Richard Gerard, Edmund Bond. *Education:* University of Florida, B.A., 1939, Ph.D., 1953; Duke University, M.A., 1943. *Politics:* Democrat. *Religion:* Roman Catholic. *Home:* Genessee Depot Village, Wis.

CAREER: High school teacher and assistant principal in Jacksonville, Fla., 1940-43; U.S. Department of State, Washington, D.C., vice-consul, 1945; Upsala College, East Orange, N.J., assistant professor of history, 1946-47; Memphis State University, Memphis, Tenn., associate professor of history, 1948-57; Marquette University, Milwaukee, Wis., professor of history, beginning, 1958. Member of Milwaukee Catholic Interracial Council; president of Marquette Faculty Association for Interracial Justice. *Member:* American Catholic Historical Association, Southern Historical Association, Organization of American Historians.

WRITINGS: Memphis During the Progressive Era, 1900-1917, Memphis State University Press, 1957; *Mr. Crump of Memphis*, Louisiana State University Press, 1964; *A Harsh and Dreadful Love: Dorothy Day and the Catholic Worker Movement*, Liveright, 1973.†

*   *   *

MILLWARD, John S(candrett)   1924-

PERSONAL: Born May 6, 1924, in Swansea, Wales; son of Arnold Manley (a sales superintendent) and Doris (Smith) Millward; married Margaret Grove, August 27, 1949; children: Alison Margaret, Richard Geoffrey. *Education:* Merton College, Oxford, B.A. and M.A., both 1949. *Religion:* Church of England. *Home:* 18 Witley Ave., Solihull, Warwickshire, England.

CAREER: Magdalen College School, Oxford, England, senior history master, 1949-59; Bristol Grammar School, Bristol, England, senior history master, 1960-64; Tudor Grange Grammar School, Solihull, England, headmaster, beginning 1964. *Military service:* Royal Air Force, pilot, 1943-46; became flying officer. *Member:* Historical Association.

WRITINGS: (Editor) *Portraits and Documents: 16th Century*, Hutchinson Educational, 1959, 2nd edition, revised and expanded, 1968; *Portraits and Documents: 17th Century*, Hutchinson Educational, 1959; (editor with H. P. Arnold-Craft) *Portraits and Documents: 18th Century*, Hutchinson Educational, 1961.†

*   *   *

MINOR, Andrew Collier   1918-

PERSONAL: Born August 17, 1918, in Atlanta, Ga.; son of Herbert Andrew and Annie Lou (Collier) Minor; married Catherine Hogan, August 1, 1952; children: Anne Collier, Madge Meredith. *Education:* Emory University, B.A., 1940; University of Michigan, M. Mus., 1947, Ph.D., 1951. *Home:* 919 Timberhill, Columbia, Mo. 65201. *Office:* Graduate School, University of Missouri, Columbia, Mo.

CAREER: University of Missouri, Columbia, assistant professor, 1950-55, associate professor, 1955-58, professor of music history and theory, 1958—. Guest lecturer in musicology, University of Michigan, summer, 1964, winter, 1965. *Military service:* U.S. Army, Signal Corps, 1942-46. *Member:* American Musicological Society (secretary-treasurer of Midwest chapter, 1963-65), Music Teachers National Association.

WRITINGS: (Editor) *Music in Medieval and Renaissance Life*, University of Missouri Press, 1964; (compiler with Bonner Mitchell) *A Renaissance Entertainment: Festivities for the Marriage of Cosimo I, Duke of Florence, in 1539*, University of Missouri Press, 1968. General editor, *Opera Omnia of Jean Mouton (1470-1522)*.

WORK IN PROGRESS: Recordings.

*   *   *

MINOT, Stephen   1927-

PERSONAL: Born May 27, 1927, in Boston, Mass.; son of William (a real estate manager) and Elizabeth (Chapman) Minot; married second wife, Virginia Stover; children: (first marriage) Stephen Reid; (second marriage) Nicholas William, Christopher Bailey. *Education:* Harvard University, A.B., 1953; Johns Hopkins University, M.A., 1955. *Politics:* Democrat. *Home:* 69 Hickory Hill Rd., Simsbury, Conn. 06070. *Agent:* Emilie Jacobson, Curtis Brown Ltd., 60 East 56th St., New York, N.Y. 10022. *Office:* Department of English, Trinity College, Hartford, Conn. 06106.

CAREER: Bowdoin College, Brunswick, Me., instructor, 1955-57, assistant professor of English, 1957-58; University of Connecticut, Hartford, visiting assistant professor of English, 1958-59; Trinity College, Hartford, Conn., 1959—, began as visiting lecturer, now associate professor of English. Writer-in-residence, Johns Hopkins University, 1974-75. *Military service:* U.S. Army Air Forces, 1945-46. *Member:* Authors Guild, American Civil Liberties Union, National Association for the Advancement of Colored People, National Committee for an Effective Congress, American Association of University Professors, American Veterans Committee. *Awards, honors:* "Atlantic First" award from *Atlantic Monthly*, 1962, for short story, "Sausage and Beer"; Saxton Memorial Foundation fellowship, 1963-64; "Mars Revisited" was included in *O. Henry Prize Stories, 1971*.

WRITINGS: Chill of Dusk (novel), Doubleday, 1964; *Three Genres: The Writing of Fiction, Poetry, and Drama* (college text), Prentice-Hall, 1965, 2nd edition, 1972; (editor with Robley Wilson, Jr.) *Three Stances in Modern Fiction*, Winthrop, 1972; *Crossings and Other Stories*, University of Illinois Press, 1974. Author of radio scripts for Voice of America, including "Nathanael West and Tragic Farce," and "The Vibrant World of Saul Bellow."

Short fiction is represented in anthologies, including: *The Story; A Critical Anthology*, edited by Mark Schorer, Prentice-Hall, 2nd edition, 1967; *Phase Blue*, edited by James Burl Hogins and Robert E. Yarber, Science Research Associates, 1970; *O. Henry Prize Stories*, Doubleday, 1971; *Mirrors: An Introduction to Literature*, edited by Christopher Reaske and John Knott, Canfield Press, 1972; *The Fact of Fiction: Social Relevance in the Short Story*, edited by Cyril Gulassa, Canfield Press, 1972.

Contributor of short stories to *Atlantic Monthly, Kenyon Review, Virginia Quarterly Review, Harper's, Redbook, Ladies' Home Journal, North American Review, Quarterly Review of Literature, Carleton Miscellany*, and *Playboy*; contributor of articles to *Poet and Critic, North American Review*, and other periodicals. Contributing editor, *North American Review*, 1969—.

WORK IN PROGRESS: Playing the Lyre.

SIDELIGHTS: Minot writes to *CA:* "I share with Camus and Sartre the conviction that no man—and particularly no writer—is 'whole' without having first become politically committed. It is primarily through political and social *action*—not mere contemplation—that a man begins to define himself. But one must balance these activities with periods of withdrawal, and for this reason I go with my family to Maine each summer. There we live in an old farm house far from tarred roads, classrooms, committee meetings, membership drives, and the perpetual lack of sleep which accompanies the active life. In my writing, I draw almost equally from both worlds."

* * *

MINOW, Newton N(orman) 1926-

PERSONAL: Born January 17, 1926, in Milwaukee, Wis.; son of Jay A. and Doris (Stein) Minow; married Josephine Baskin; children: Nell, Martha, Mary. *Education:* Northwestern University, B.S., 1949, LL.B., 1950. *Politics:* Democrat. *Religion:* Jewish. *Home:* 375 Palos Rd., Glencoe, Ill. 60022. *Office:* One First National Plaza, Chicago, Ill. 60670.

CAREER: Admitted to Illinois and Wisconsin bars, 1950; Mayer, Brown & Platt (law firm), Chicago, Ill., associate, 1950-51, 1953-55; U.S. Supreme Court, Washington, D.C., law clerk to Chief Justice Fred M. Vinson, 1951-52; administrative assistant to Governor Adlai E. Stevenson, Springfield, Ill., 1952-53; Stevenson, Rifkind & Wirtz (law firm), Chicago, Ill., partner, 1955-61; U.S. Federal Communications Commission, Washington, D.C., chairman, 1961-63; *Encyclopaedia Britannica*, Chicago, Ill., vice-president and general counsel, 1963-65; Leibman, Williams, Bennett, Baird & Minow (now Sidley & Austin; law firm), Chicago, Ill., partner, 1965—. Former chairman and member of board of trustees, Rand Corp., 1965—; member of board of trustees of Notre Dame University and Mayo Foundation; honorary chairman and member of board of trustees, Chicago Educational Television; member of board of directors, Adlai E. Stevenson Institute of International Affairs; member of advisory board of Peabody Awards; professorial lecturer, Northwestern University, Medill School of Journalism. *Military service:* U.S. Army, 1944-46; became sergeant.

MEMBER: American Bar Association (fellow), Illinois Bar Association, Chicago Bar Association, Economic Club, Legal Club, Standard Club, Law Club, Federal City Club, Northmoor Country Club. *Awards, honors:* George Foster Peabody Award for achievement in radio and television, 1961; Lee DeForest Award of National Association for Better Radio and Television; LL.D. from University of Wisconsin, and Brandeis University, 1963, Northwestern University, 1965.

WRITINGS: Equal Time: The Private Broadcaster and the Public Interest, Atheneum, 1964; (contributor) E. P. Doyle, editor, *As We Knew Adlai*, Harper, 1966; (with others) *Presidential Television*, Basic Books, 1973.

* * *

MINSHALL, Vera (Wild) 1924-

PERSONAL: Born August 23, 1924, in Stockport, Cheshire, England; daughter of Joseph W. and Elizabeth (Warren) Wild; married Allen Minshall (a storekeeper), August 28, 1946; children: Pauline Margaret, Peter Leslie. *Education:* Educated in convent school in England. *Religion:* Baptist. *Home:* 17 Fenton Ave., Stepping Hill, Stockport, Cheshire, England.

CAREER: Stenographer, 1939-46; writer. *Awards, honors:* First prize for film synopsis, Religious Films Ltd., 1964.

WRITINGS: I Was a Stranger, Pickering & Inglis, 1962; *The Doctor's Secret*, Zondervan, 1966; *Call of the High Road*, Zondervan, 1967; *This Stony Ground*, Zondervan, 1969. Author of four serials published in *Christian Herald*, one in *Sunday Companion*, and contributor of short stories to both periodicals.

WORK IN PROGRESS: A serial for *Christian Herald*.

AVOCATIONAL INTERESTS: Gardening, walking in the country, work with children, and church work.

* * *

MINTZ, Morton A. 1922-

PERSONAL: Born January 26, 1922, in Ann Arbor, Mich.; son of William (a merchant) and Sarah (Solomon) Mintz; married Anita I. Franze, August 30, 1946; children: Margaret, Elizabeth, Roberta, Daniel. *Education:* University of Michigan, A.B., 1943. *Home:* 3022 Macomb St., N.W., Washington, D.C. 20008. *Office: Washington Post*, 1515 L St., N.W., Washington, D.C. 20005.

CAREER: St. Louis Star-Times, St. Louis, Mo., reporter 1946-50; *St. Louis Globe-Democrat*, St. Louis, Mo., reporter, then assistant city editor, 1951-58; *Washington Post*, Washington, D.C., reporter, 1958—, covering U.S. Supreme Court, 1964-65. *Military service:* U.S. Naval Reserve, 1945-46; became lieutenant junior grade. *Awards, honors:* Heywood Broun, George Polk, and Raymond Clapper Memorial awards, all 1963, for breaking story of how Frances Kelsey kept the baby-deforming drug thalidomide off the American market; Nieman fellow at Harvard University, 1963-64.

WRITINGS: The Therapeutic Nightmare: A Report on the Roles of the United States Food and Drug Administration, the American Medical Association, Pharmaceutical Manufactures, and Others in Connection with the Irrational and Massive Use of Prescription Drugs that May Be Worthless, Injurious or Even Lethal, Houghton, 1965, 2nd edition published as *By Prescription Only*, 1967; *The Pill: An Alarming Report*, Fawcett, 1969; (with Jerry S. Cohen) *America, Inc.: Who Owns and Operates the United States*, introduction by Ralph Nader, Dial, 1971.

BIOGRAPHICAL/CRITICAL SOURCES: New York Times, November 28, 1965.†

* * *

MINTZ, Ruth Finer 1919-

PERSONAL: Born November 25, 1919, in Russia; daughter of Nathan (a cantor) and Sarah (Lederman) Finer; came to the United States, 1920; married Yale Mintz (a professor of meteorology, University of California, Los Angeles), 1944; children: Rena, Aviva and Shalom (twins). *Education:* Attended University of Omaha; Jewish Theological Seminary of America, B.H.L., 1942; graduate study at Hebrew University, Jerusalem, 1956-57, Oxford University, 1964; University of California, M.A., 1965. *Politics:* "Uneasy Democrat." *Religion:* Jewish. *Home:* 10765 Cushdon Ave., Los Angeles, Calif. 90064; and Neve Granot Block 3 Ent 5, Jerusalem, Israel.

CAREER: Teacher of Hebrew in New York, N.Y., and Los Angeles, Calif., 1940-55; writer, 1955—. *Awards, honors:* Charles Brown fellowship, Los Angeles Jewish Community Council, 1956; Harry and Florence Kovner Memorial Awards, Jewish Book Council of America, 1966, for *The Darkening Green*, 1971, for *Traveler Through Time*.

WRITINGS: *The Darkening Green* (poetry), Big Mountain Press, 1965; (editor and translator) *An Anthology of Modern Hebrew Poetry*, University of California Press, 1966; *Traveler Through Time*, (poetry), Jonathan David, 1970. Poetry has appeared in *Beloit Poetry Journal, Poetry, Inferno, Trace, Reconstructionist, Midstream, Recall, Coastlines, ETC, Accent, Views, Westwind, Antioch Review, Encounter, Moznayim* (Israel), *Keshet* (Israel), *Israel Argosy, Focus* (Israel), *Jerusalem Post, Lamerhav, Delphica Tetradia* (Greece), and *Poet* (India).

WORK IN PROGRESS: *Jerusalem Poems*, a third volume of poetry; *Bless Him for Lightning*, a novel about Ruth Mintz's Nebraska childhood.

SIDELIGHTS: Ruth Mintz is competent in Yiddish, Hebrew, French, and German. She has traveled in Israel, Greece, Italy, England, and France.

*   *   *

MISCHKE, Bernard Cyril   1926-

PERSONAL: Born March 18, 1926, in Little Falls, Minn.; son of Joseph Francis (an accountant) and Margaret Helen (Theis) Mischke. *Education:* Studied at Crosier seminaries, 1942-51; University of Notre Dame, M.A., 1957. *Home:* Crosier Seminary, Onamia, Minn.

CAREER: Entered Order of the Holy Cross (Roman Catholic), 1944, ordained priest, 1951. Crosier Seminary, Onamia, Minn., instructor in German and world history, 1951-55, in English, 1951—, spiritual director, 1957-66. St. Joseph Church, Browerville, Minn., pastor, 1973—.

WRITINGS: *Odilia* (novel), Crosier Press, 1955; *Meditations on the Psalms*, Sheed, 1963; *Bible and Rosary*, St. Paul Editions, 1964; *Meditations on the Mass*, Sheed, 1964; (with Fridolin P. Mischke) *Spreading the Word*, Joseph F. Wagner, 1972. Wrote lyrics for modern hymnal, *The Psalms*, published by World Library of Sacred Music. Editor, *Crosier*, 1951-55; book review editor, *Today's Family*; monthly columnist for *Sacred Heart Messenger*, 1957—, and for Canadian *Messenger*, 1960—.

WORK IN PROGRESS: *The Habit of Prayer*; two novels, *The Long Long Wilderness*, and *The Enemies*; lyrics for new hymns composed by Eugene Lindusky; a volume of liturgical meditations.

*   *   *

MITCHELL, J(ames) Clyde   1918-

PERSONAL: Born June 21, 1918, in Pietermaritzburg, South Africa; son of George S. and Rose K. (Jones) Mitchell; married Edna Grace Maslen, 1943 (deceased); married Hilary Ward-Hancock Klegg (a medical sociologist), August 24, 1963; children: (first marriage) Donald, Gillian, Kerr, Alan; (stepchildren) Erica Flegg. *Education:* Natal University College, B.A., 1941; University of South Africa, B.A. (honors), 1948; Oxford University, D.Phil., 1950. *Home:* 24 Coltman Rd., Mount Pleasant, Salisbury, Southern Rhodesia. *Office:* University College of Rhodesia and Nyasaland, Private Bag 167 H, Salisbury, Southern Rhodesia.

CAREER: Rhodes-Livingstone Institute, Lusaka, Zambia, assistant anthropologist, 1946-50, sociologist, 1950-52, director, 1953-55; University College of Rhodesia and Nyasaland, professor of African studies, 1955-64, professor of sociology, beginning 1964, vice-principal, 1961-62. University of Manchester, Simon Research Fellow, 1953; Johns Hopkins University School of International Studies, vis-

iting professor, 1960. Participant in United Nations and UNESCO conferences, and other international conferences in London, Paris, Uganda, Ethiopia, Egypt, and Nigeria. Associate member, Scientific Council for Africa. *Military service:* South African Air Force, navigator, 1942-45; became lieutenant.

MEMBER: British Sociological Association, American Sociological Association, Association of Social Anthropologists of the Commonwealth, International Population Union, Africa Studies Association (United States), other organizations in Rhodesia. *Awards, honors:* Rivers Memorial Medal of Royal Anthropological Institute for distinguished field work in central Africa, 1960.

WRITINGS: (With J. A. Barnes) *The Lamba Village*, School of African Studies, University of Cape Town, 1950; *The Yao Village*, Manchester University Press, 1956; *The Kalela Dance*, Rhodes-Livingstone, 1957; *Tribalism and the Plural Society* (lecture), Oxford University Press, 1960; *The Sociological Background to African Labour*, Ensign Publications, 1961; (editor) *Social Networks In Urban Situations*, Manchester University Press, 1969.

Contributor: E. Colson and M. Gluckman, editors, *Seven Tribes of British Central Africa*, Oxford University Press, 1951; W. V. Brelsford, *The Tribes of Northern Rhodesia*, Government Printer (Lusaka), 1956; *The Development of a Middle Class in Tropical and Sub-Tropical Countries*, [Brussels], 1956; W. V. Brelsford, editor, *Handbook of Rhodesia and Nyasaland*, Cassell, 1960; K. M. Barbour and R. M. Prothero, editors, *Essays on African Population*, Routledge & Kegan Paul, 1961.

Contributor of articles to other books, about twenty papers to published proceedings of international and African conferences, and some twenty articles to journals, including *Civilisations, African Studies, Africa, Human Problems, British Journal of Sociology, Central African Journal of Medicine*.

WORK IN PROGRESS: Studies of urbanization in Zambia, 1950-53, based on social surveys; studies of occupational prestige among Africans in Southern Rhodesia.†

*   *   *

MITCHELL, James   1926-
   (James Munro)

PERSONAL: Born March 12, 1926, in South Shields, England; son of James William (a fitter) and Mina Mitchell; married Norma Halliday (a teacher), August 1, 1953; children: Simon John, Peter James. *Education:* Saint Edmund Hall, Oxford, B.A., 1948, M.A., 1949. *Home:* 62 Marsden Rd., South Shields, England. *Agent:* Hughes Massie Ltd., 18 Southampton Pl., London W.C.1, England. *Office:* College of Art, Backhouse Park, Sunderland, England.

CAREER: Actor and travel agent in United Kingdom and Paris, France, 1948-50; Technical College, South Shields, England, lecturer in English, 1950-59; television writer in London, England, 1959-63; College of Art, Sunderland, England, lecturer in liberal studies, 1963—. *Member:* Screen Writers' Guild, Society of Film and Television Arts. *Awards, honors:* British Crime Writers' Association Award for *A Way Back.*

WRITINGS: *Here's a Villain*, Morrow, 1958; *A Way Back*, Morrow, 1959; *Steady Boys Steady*, P. Davies, 1961; *Among African Sands*, P. Davies, 1963; *Tales of Sagittarius*, Hoddypoll Press, 1968; *Tales of Thorn*, Hoddypoll Press, 1968; *A Magnum for Schneider*, Jenkins, 1969, published as *A Red File for Callan*, Simon & Schuster, 1971; *Ilion Like a Mist*, Cassell, 1969; *The Winners*, Cassell, 1970; *Russian Roulette*, Hamish Hamilton, 1973.

Under pseudonym James Munro: *The Man Who Sold Death*, Barrie & Jenkins, 1964, Knopf, 1965; *Die Rich, Die Happy*, Barrie & Jenkins, 1965, Knopf, 1966; *Money That Money Can't Buy*, Barrie & Jenkins, 1967, Knopf, 1968; *Innocent Bystanders*, Barrie & Jenkins, 1969, Knopf, 1970.

Contributor to reviews to *New Statesman, Books and Art, John O'London's*. Author of twelve television plays, and of film scripts, "Steady Boys Steady" and "Innocent Bystanders."

WORK IN PROGRESS: Research on mass media, eighteenth-century life in England, and the writing skills of painters and sculptors.

SIDELIGHTS: Mitchell speaks fair French and Spanish. He commented to *CA:* "I am interested in the novel, which I rate far higher than all television and most films. I like writing thrillers, and reading thrillers which read like latterday Gothic novels, i.e., I like reading Chandler. Teaching and writing are the two things I like doing best. I'm lucky to be able to do both."

The film "Innocent Bystanders" was adapted by Mitchell from his James Munro spy thriller. The film released by Paramount in 1973 is to be followed by film adaptions of the other three novels in the series.†

* * *

MITCHELL, Stephen O. 1930-

PERSONAL: Born May 11, 1930, in Muncie, Ind.; son of Omer M. (a high school principal) and Euva Mitchell; married Barbara Anthony; children: Leslie, Stephen, Judith. *Education:* Purdue University, B.S., 1952; University of Michigan, M.A., 1955; Indiana University, Ph.D., 1960. *Office:* Department of English, Syracuse University, Syracuse, N.Y.

CAREER: Syracuse University, Syracuse, N.Y., 1960—, associate professor of English, 1964—. *Military service:* U.S. Army, 1952-54; became first lieutenant. *Member:* Modern Language Association of America. *Awards, honors:* American Council of Learned Societies grant, 1964.

WRITINGS: (Editor with Summer Ives) *Language, Style, and Ideas*, Harcourt, 1964; (editor) Joshua Reynolds, *Discourses on Art*, Bobbs-Merrill, 1965. Contributor to professional journals.

WORK IN PROGRESS: Johnson's Philosophy of Science.†

* * *

MIZNER, Elizabeth Howard 1907-
(Elizabeth Howard)

PERSONAL: Surname is pronounced with long *i*; born August 24, 1907, in Detroit, Mich.; daughter of Walter Ingersoll and Agnes (Roy) Mizner. *Education:* University of Michigan, A.B., 1930, A.M., 1935; Wayne State University, graduate study, 1930-32. *Politics:* Independent. *Religion:* Presbyterian. *Home:* 9692 West Bay Shore Rd., Traverse City, Mich. 49684.

CAREER: Shorter College, Rome, Ga., instructor in history, 1935-36; writer of historical novels for young people, 1941—. *Member:* Anti-Cruelty Association, Cherryland Humane Society.

WRITINGS: Under name Elizabeth Howard: *Sabina*, Lothrop, 1941; *Adventure for Alison*, Lothrop, 1942; *Dorinda*, Lothrop, 1944; *Summer Under Sail*, Morrow, 1947; *North Winds Blow Free*, Morrow, 1949; *Peddler's Girl*, Morrow, 1951; *Candle in the Night*, Morrow, 1952; *A Star to Follow*, Morrow, 1954; *The Road Lies West*, Morrow, 1955; *A Girl of the North Country*, Morrow, 1957; *The Courage of Bethea*, Morrow, 1959; *Verity's Voyage*, Morrow, 1964; *Winter on her Own*, Morrow, 1968; *Wilderness Venture*, Morrow, 1973. Contributor to *Story Parade*.

SIDELIGHTS: Miss Mizner majored in history at the University of Michigan and has based most of her historical novels (aimed at the junior high group) on her favorite period, the mid-1800's. She writes on a fixed daily schedule, starting each book with a heroine, a definite time in history, and only a vague notion of what's going to evolve. "All sorts of things happen as you go along," she told an interviewer for the *Detroit News*, "and if I knew how my books were going to end, I'd never bother to finish them." *Avocational interests:* Dogs, all small animals, and birds; gardening, the theater.

* * *

MOELLERING, Ralph L(uther) 1923-

PERSONAL: Born February 10, 1923, in Snyder, Neb.; son of Herman Carl (a clergyman) and Anna Louise (Albrecht) Moellering; married Clarice Evonne Leite (a musician), December 31, 1953; children: Daniel Luther, Timothy Jerome, Jonathan Tobias, Aaron Christopher. *Education:* St. John's College, Winfield, Kan., A.A., 1942; Concordia Seminary, St. Louis, Mo., A.B., 1944, B.D., 1946, M.S.T., 1954; Washington University, St. Louis, Mo., M.A., 1949; Harvard University, Ph.D., 1964. *Politics:* Democrat. *Home:* 2018 Marin, Berkeley, Calif. 94707.

CAREER: Ordained to Lutheran ministry, 1946; Concordia Teachers College, Seward, Neb., instructor in religion and social studies, 1948; University of South Dakota, campus pastor, 1948-53; Chicago Medical Center, Chicago, Ill., inner-city pastor and campus pastor, 1953-58; University of California, Berkeley, campus pastor, 1960-67; pastor for special ministries, 1968-74. Guest professor, Johann Wolfgang Goethe University, Germany, 1971-72. *Member:* American Society for Reformation Research, American Church History Society, Lutheran Academy for Scholarship. *Awards, honors:* James M. Yard Brotherhood Award for interracial work in Chicago.

WRITINGS: Christianity and Communism, Commission on College and University Work, 1953; *Modern War and the American Churches*, American Press, 1957; *Christianity, Communism, and Race Relations*, Valparaiso University Press, 1961; *Christian Conscience and Negro Emancipation*, Fortress, 1965; *Modern War and the Christian*, Augsburg, 1969; (contributor) Daniel Martensen, editor, *Christian Hope and the Secular*, Augsburg, 1969. Contributor of articles and reviews to *American Lutheran, Concordia Theological Monthly, Cresset, Christian Century*, and *Dialog*.

WORK IN PROGRESS: The Missouri Synod: A Study in the Social and Religious History of the United States, for University of California Press; *Ethics for a World of Future Shock*, for Concordia; an essay for *Seek Peace and Pursue It*, for Fortress.

SIDELIGHTS: Moellering is competent in Spanish, German, Greek, Hebrew, and Latin.

BIOGRAPHICAL/CRITICAL SOURCES: Christian Century, December, 1956.

* * *

MOFFAT, Gwen 1924-

PERSONAL: Born 1924, in Brighton, Sussex, England; married Johnnie Lees (a mountain guide); children: Sheena. Education: Educated in English schools. Home: Bloan Farm, Brough Sowerby, Kirkby Stephen, Westmorland, England. Agent: Innes Rose, John Farquharson Ltd., 15 Red Lion Sq., London W.C.1, England.

CAREER: Mountain guide; first woman receiving guides' certificates of British Mountaineering Council, 1953, and Association of Scottish Climbing Clubs, 1957; specializes in English Lake District, North Wales, and Glencoe and Ben Nevis areas. Military service: Women's Royal Army Corps, 1943-47. Member: Society of Authors, Radiowriters Association, Sail Association, Alpine Climbing Club, Pinnacle Club.

WRITINGS: Space Below My Feet (autobiographical), Houghton, 1961; Two Star Red (R.A.F. Mountain Rescue Service), Hodder & Stoughton, 1964; On My Home Ground, Hodder & Stoughton, 1968. Contributor to British Broadcasting Corp. programs, to Daily Express and Sunday Express (both Scottish editions), Glasgow Herald, She, Woman, and other newspapers and journals.

WORK IN PROGRESS: A novel, Strike Force; another novel.

AVOCATIONAL INTERESTS: Skiing, travel and the cinema.

BIOGRAPHICAL SOURCES: Christian Science Monitor, December 6, 1961.†

* * *

MOHRT, Michel 1914-

PERSONAL: Born April 28, 1914, in Morlaix, France; son of Fernand and Amelie (Gelebart) Mohrt; married Francoise Jarrier; children: Francois. Education: Attended College St. Louis, Brest, France. Faculte de Droit, Rennes, France, licence en droit, 1936. Religion: Catholic. Home: 4 bis, rue du Cherche-Midi, Paris VI, France. Office: Librairie Gallimard, 5 rue Sebastien-Bottin, Paris VII, France.

CAREER: Lawyer in Marseilles, France, 1940-42; Yale University, New Haven, Conn., instructor, 1947-48; Librairie Gallimard (publisher), Paris, France, advisor for Anglo-Saxon literature. Visiting professor at University of California, Smith College, and Middlebury College, 1949-60. Military service: French Army, ski troops, 1937-40; became lieutenant; received croix de guerre. Awards, honors: Academie Francaise, grand prix du roman, 1962, for La Prison maritime, and grand prix de la critique litteraire, 1970, for L'Air du large.

WRITINGS: Les Intellectuels devant la defaite de 1870, Correa, 1942; Montherlant, "Homme libre," N.R.F., 1943; Le Repit (novel) Albin Michel, 1944; Mon Royaume pour un cheval (novel), Albin Michel, 1949; Les Nomades (novel), Albin Michel, 1951; Le Serviteur fidele (novel), Albin Michel, 1953; Le Nouveau roman americain, N.R.F., 1955; La Prison maritime (novel), N.R.F., 1961, translation by Xan Fielding published as Mariners' Prison, Viking, 1963; La Campagne d'Italie (novel), N.R.F., 1965, translation by Patrick O'Brien published as The Italian

Campaign, Viking, 1967; L'Ours des Adirondacks (novel), N.R.F., 1970; Un Jeu d'eufer (play), N.R.F., 1970; Deux Indiennes a Paris (novel), N.R.F., 1974. Contributor to Nouvelle Revue Francaise, Le Monde, La Revue des Deux Mondes, Figaro Litteraire, and other French periodicals.

WORK IN PROGRESS: A novel, Les Moyens du bord.

AVOCATIONAL INTERESTS: Sailing.

* * *

MOLLOY, Anne Baker 1907-

PERSONAL: Born October 4, 1907, in Boston, Mass.; daughter of Lawrence Wills (an orthodontist) and Lila (Nichols) Baker; married Paul Edward Molloy (a teacher), March 13, 1928; children: John Stearns, Jane (Mrs. Eliot F. Porter, Jr.). Education: Attended Mount Holyoke College, 1925-28. Religion: Unitarian Universalist.

CAREER: Writer of books for children. Exeter (N.H.) Public Library, trustee, 1957.

WRITINGS: Coastguard to Greenland, Houghton, 1942; Decky's Secret, Houghton, 1944; Bird in Hand, Houghton, 1945; Shooting Star Farm, Houghton, 1946; The Pigeoneers, Houghton, 1947; Celis's Lighthouse, Houghton, 1949; Uncle Andy's Island, Houghton, 1950; Lucy's Christmas, Houghton, 1950; Where Away?, Houghton, 1952; The Monkey's Fist, Houghton, 1953; The Secret of the Old Salem Desk, Farrar, Straus & Cudahy, 1955; Captain Waymouth's Indians, Hastings, 1957, published as Five Kidnapped Indians: A True Seventeenth Century Account of Five Early Americans, 1968; The Tower Treasure, Hastings, 1958; The Christmas Rocket, Hastings, 1958; Blanche of the Blueberry Barrens, Hastings, 1959; Three-Part Island, Hastings, 1960; A Proper Place for Chip, Hastings, 1963; The Mystery of the Pilgrim Trading Post, Hastings, 1964; Shaun and the Boat, Hastings, 1965; The Girl From Two Miles High, Hastings, 1967; The Years Before the Mayflower: The Pilgrims in Holland, Hastings, 1972.†

* * *

MONAS, Sidney 1924-

PERSONAL: Born September 15, 1924, in New York, N.Y.; son of David Joseph (a labor leader) and Eva (Kiener) Monas; married Carolyn Munro (a teacher), September 5, 1948; children: Erica, Deborah, Stephen. Education: Princeton University, A.B., 1948; Harvard University, Ph.D., 1955. Office: History Department, University of Rochester, Rochester, N.Y.

CAREER: Member of faculty, Amherst College, Amherst, Mass., 1955-57, Smith College, Northampton, Mass., 1957-62, University of Rochester, Rochester, New York, 1962—. Military service: U.S. Army, 1942-45; became sergeant. Member: American Historical Association, American Association for the Advancement of Slavic Studies.

WRITINGS: The Third Section, Harvard University Press, 1961; (translator, and author of introduction) M. Zoshchenko, Scenes from the Bath House, selected by M. Slonin, University of Michigan Press, 1961; (translator) Fedor Dostoevski, Crime and Punishment, New American Library, 1968; (translator) Complete Poetry of Osip Emilevich Mandelstam, State University of New York Press, 1973.

WORK IN PROGRESS: A study of the family and the state in classical Russian literature.†

MONKHOUSE, Francis John 1914-

PERSONAL: Born May 15, 1914, in Workington, Cumberland, England; son of Joseph (a docks manager) and Edith (Lowe) Monkhouse; married Bertha Greensmith, December 31, 1938; children: Laurence John, Rachel Frances. *Education:* Emmanuel College, Cambridge, B.A. (first class honors), 1935, M.A., 1937; Institute of Education, University of London, Teacher's Diploma, 1936. *Home:* North Lodge, Bassett Wood Rd., Southampton, England; and, Crag Farm House, Ennerdale, Cleator, Cumberland, England.

CAREER: University of Liverpool, Liverpool, England, lecturer in geography and education, 1945-54; University of Southampton, Southampton, England, professor of geography and chairman of department, 1954-66. Visiting professor, Miami University, Ohio, 1960-61, University of Southern Illinois, 1965-66, University of Maryland, 1968. *Military service:* Intelligence Division, British Admiralty, 1940-45. *Member:* Royal Geographical Society, Institute of British Geographers, Geographical Association. *Awards, honors:* D.Sc., Miami University, Oxford, Ohio.

WRITINGS: The Belgian Kempenland, Liverpool University Press, 1949.

(With H. R. Wilkinson) *Maps and Diagrams,* Methuen, 1952, 3rd edition, revised and enlarged, 1971; *Principles of Physical Geography,* University of London Press, 1954, Philosophical Library, 1963, 7th edition, American Elsevier, 1970; (contributor) H. C. Darby, editor, *The Domesday Geography of Midland England,* Cambridge University Press, 1954; *A Study Guide in Physical Geography,* University of London Press, 1956, and subsequent editions; *Landscape from the Air,* Cambridge University Press, 1959, 2nd edition, 1962; *A Regional Geography of Western Europe,* Longmans, Green, 1959, 4th edition, Praeger, 1974.

The English Lake District, Geographical Association, 1960; *Europe: A Geographical Survey,* Longmans, Green, 1961, new edition, 1964; (contributor) J. Mitchell, editor, *Great Britain: Geographical Essays,* Cambridge University Press, 1962; (with A. V. Hardy) *The Physical Landscape in Pictures,* Cambridge University Press, 1964; (editor) *A Survey of Southampton and Its Region,* Southampton University Press, 1964; (with A. V. Hardy) *The North American Landscape,* Cambridge University Press, 1965; *A Dictionary of Geography,* Arnold, 1965, Aldine, 1965, 2nd edition, Aldine, 1970; *The Countries of North-Western Europe,* Longmans, Green, 1965, Praeger, 1966, 2nd edition, Longman, 1971; (with H. R. Cain) *North America: A Geographical Survey,* Longman, 1970; *The Material Resources of Britain: An Economic Geography of the United Kingdom,* Longman, 1971; (with J. S. Williams) *Climber and Fellwalker in Lakeland,* David & Charles, 1972; (with Hardy) *Man-Made Landscape,* Cambridge University Press, 1974. Contributor to *Encyclopaedia Britannica, Chambers's Encyclopaedia,* and *Reader's Digest Great Encyclopedic Dictionary.*

WORK IN PROGRESS: America: A Regional Geography.

SIDELIGHTS: Monkhouse is competent in German and has reading knowledge of French. He lived in India and Ceylon for one year; other extensive travels in United States, Canada, Far East, and Middle East. *Avocational interests:* Mountaineering.†

MONROE, Elizabeth 1905-

PERSONAL: Born January 16, 1905, in Great Malvern, England; daughter of Horace (an Anglican clergyman) and Alice (Stokes) Monroe; married Humphrey Neame, September 23, 1938 (died, 1968). *Education:* Attended St. Anne's College, Oxford, 1923-26. *Religion:* Church of England. *Home:* 56 Montague Sq., London W1, England.

CAREER: League of Nations, Geneva, Switzerland, Information Section staff, 1931-33; Royal Institute of International Affairs, London, England, Information Section staff, 1933-38; Ministry of Information, London, England, Middle East division staff, 1940-44; *Economist,* London, England, Middle East desk, 1945-58; Oxford University, St. Antony's College, Oxford, England, senior research fellow, 1958-72, emeritus fellow. *Member:* Royal Institute of International Affairs, Royal Geographical Society (fellow). *Awards, honors:* Rockefeller traveling fellowship in the Middle East, 1936-37; fellow of St. Anne's College, Oxford University; Companion of St. Michael and St. George, 1973, for services to Middle Eastern studies.

WRITINGS: (With Alton Jones) *A History of Ethiopia,* Oxford University Press, 1935; *The Mediterranean in Politics,* Oxford University Press, 1938; *Britain's Moment in the Middle East,* Johns Hopkins Press, 1963; *The Changing Balance of Power in the Persian Gulf,* American Universities Field Staff, 1972; *Philby of Arabia,* Faber, 1973.

* * *

MONTAGU, Ivor (Goldsmid Samuel) 1904-

PERSONAL: Born April 23, 1904, in London, England; son of Louis, second Baron of Swaythling and Gladys (Goldsmid) Montagu; married Eileen Hellstern, January 10, 1927. *Education:* Attended Westminster School, London, England, and Royal College of Science, London; King's College, Cambridge, M.A. *Home:* Old Timbers, Verdure Close, Garston, Watford, Hertfordshire, England.

CAREER: British Museum, London, England, zoological researcher, 1920-25; founder and chairman, Film Society, 1925-39; *Daily Worker,* London, England, foreign correspondent and assistant editor, 1936-37; film writer and director for Gainsborough, Paramount, Gaumont-British, and Ealing, and writer for television. Member, World Peace Council, 1949—; president, Society for Cultural Relations with U.S.S.R., 1973—. *Member:* Association of Cine and Television Technicians (member of executive committee, 1933-62), Screen and Television Writers Guild (honorary member), International Table Tennis Federation (founder; president, 1926), English Table Tennis Association (life vice-president). *Awards, honors:* Order of Liberation, first class (Bulgaria), 1950; Lenin Peace Prize, 1960; Order of the Pole Star (Mongolia), 1961.

WRITINGS: Table Tennis Today, Heffer, 1923; *The Political Censorship of Films,* Gollancz, 1929; (translator) *Pudovkin on Film Technique,* Gollancz, 1929; (translator, with Sergei Nalbandov) Valerii I. Briusov, *The Fiery Angel,* Cayme Press, 1930; (translator) Isaak Babel, *Benia Krik,* Collet's Bookshop, 1935; *Table Tennis,* Pitman, 1936; *Traitor Class,* Lawrence & Wishart, 1940; *Plot Against Peace,* Lawrence & Wishart, 1952; *Land of Blue Sky,* Dobson, 1956; (editor and translator with Jay Leyda) V. B. Nizhny, *Lessons with Eisenstein,* Allen & Unwin, 1962, Hill & Wang, 1969; (translator) Eisenstein, *Ivan the Terrible,* Simon and Schuster, 1962; (editor) Vsevolod Illarionovich Pudovkin, *Film Technique and Film Acting,*

Wehman, 1963; *Film World*, Penguin, 1964; *Germany's New Nazis*, Panther Books, 1967; *Vietnam: Stop America's Criminal War*, Communist Party of Great Britain, 1967; *With Eisenstein in Hollywood*, Seven Seas (Berlin), 1968, International Publishers, 1969; *NATO-No! Defence or Danger?*, Communist Party (London), 1969; *The Youngest Son* (autobiography), Lawrence & Wishart, 1970; *Wild Horses and Asses*, David & Charles, 1974. Translator of other work from the French, German, and Russian. Writer of film scenarios, including "Scott of the Antarctic." Contributor to newspapers and periodicals, including *Daily Worker, Labour Monthly, Marxist Review, Times, Weekend Review, New Statesman, Observer, Sunday Graphic, Times Literary Supplement*.

*   *   *

MONTEIRO, Luis (Infante de la Cerda) de Sttau 1926-

PERSONAL: Born April 3, 1926, in Lisbon, Portugal; son of Armindo Sttau and Lucia (Infante de la Cerda) Monteiro; married June Goodyear, September 27, 1951; children: Carol, Ana Lucia, Digo, Tomaz. *Education:* Attended University of Lisbon Law School. *Politics:* "Not interested." *Religion:* "Not interestsed." *Home:* Quinta do Bom Sucesso, Barro, Loures, Portugal.

CAREER: Lived in England and raced motor cars for a few years; creative director of a publicity agency in Portugal, now director of the literary supplement of *Diario de Lisboa* (newspaper). *Military service:* Portuguese Army; became lieutenant. *Awards, honors:* First National Theatre Award for play, "Happily the Moon Is Out," 1961.

WRITINGS: Um homem nao chora (title means "A Man Should Never Cry"), Atica, 1960; *Angustis para o jantar*, Atica, 1961, translation by Ann Stevens published as *The Rules of the Game*, Putnam, 1964, published as *A Man of Means*, Knopf, 1965.

WORK IN PROGRESS: A novel, *Grab the Summer, Girl*.

SIDELIGHTS: Monteiro told *CA:* "I am interested in most things—too many things for my own good—but mainly in history, psychology, and all things connected with the sea. I am also interested especially in the theater.... I hate armies, soldiers, and everything connected with them. I was in the army against my will and a lieutenant against my will." Monteiro was imprisoned by the Fascist government in Portugal for his play "The Holy War." Some of his plays were banned by the official censors.

*   *   *

MONTGOMERY, Albert A. 1929-

PERSONAL: Born August 10, 1929, in Des Moines, Iowa; son of Albert A. and Grace (Wright) Montgomery; married Betty K. Russell, February 7, 1953; children: Stephen, Christine, Matthew. *Education:* University of Iowa, B.A., 1953, M.A., 1955, Ph.D., 1960. *Office:* 10 Pryor St. Bldg., Atlanta, Ga. 30303.

CAREER: Washington State University, Bureau of Economic and Business Research, Pullman, research economist, 1958-73; Georgia State University, Atlanta, senior research associate, 1973—. *Military service:* U.S. Army, 1947-49, 1953; became second lieutenant. *Member:* American Economic Association, Association for University Business and Economic Research, Regional Science Association, Phi Eta Sigma, Beta Gamma Sigma.

WRITINGS: (With Clark C. Bloom) *State and Local Tax Differentials and the Location of Manufacturing*, Bureau of Business and Economic Research, University of Iowa, 1956; *Washington Municipal Expenditures 1941-1957, An Economic Analysis*, Washington State University Press, 1963; (contributor with R. D. Towsley) *Trends in Distribution, Services and Transportation*, Washington State University, 1966; (contributor with Eldon C. Weeks) *Food Goals, Future Structural Changes, and Agricultural Policy: A National Basebook*, Iowa State University Press, 1969; (with W. Butcher and others) *Irrigation in the Horse Heaven Hills: A Study of Impacts and Potentials*, Research Center for the Washington State University College of Agriculture, 1970; (with P. Bourque and others) *An Input-Output Study of the 1967 Washington Economy*, University of Washington Press, 1970; (with W. Butcher and others) *Land Development and Water Use: Yakima River Basin*, Research Center for the Washington State University College of Agriculture, 1972; *National Forests of the Southeast: Economic Survey of Wildlife Recreation*, 2 volumes, Environmental Research Group, Georgia State University, 1974. Also author of numerous papers and reports for industrial and economic conferences. Contributor to *Iowa Business Review*, and *Iowa Economic Quarterly*.

WORK IN PROGRESS: A book, *Economic Management Model of Georgia's Forests*.

*   *   *

MOODY, Ernest A(ddison) 1903-

PERSONAL: Born September 27, 1903, in Cranford, N.J.; son of John (an author and publisher) and Anna (Addison) Moody; married Josephine Lane, October 11, 1928; children: Anne Elizabeth (Mrs. Walter J. Frank), Jean Farrington (Mrs. Halford E. Maninger). *Education:* Williams College, B.A., 1924; Columbia University, M.A., 1933, Ph.D., 1936; also studied piano in New York and Paris, 1927-29. *Home:* 673 Calle del Norte, Camarillo, Calif. 93010. *Office:* University of California, Los Angeles, Calif. 90024.

CAREER: Moody's Investors Service, New York, N.Y., economist, later salesman, 1925-26, 1930-31; Columbia University, New York, N.Y., 1939-53, started as lecturer, became associate professor of philosophy; owner and operator of cattle ranch in LaSalle County, Tex., 1953-58; University of California, Los Angeles, professor of philosophy, 1958-69, professor emeritus, 1969—, chairman of department, 1961-64. *Member:* American Philosophical Association (president of Pacific division, 1963), Mediaeval Academy of America (member of council, 1963-66; fellow, 1964), History of Science Society, Centro per la storia della tradizione aristotelica (University of Padua; corresponding member). *Awards, honors:* Haskins Medal of Mediaeval Academy of America, and Nicholas Murray Butler Medal in Silver of Columbia University, both for *Truth and Consequence in Medieval Logic*, 1956.

WRITINGS: The Logic of William of Ockham, Sheed, 1935, reprinted, 1965; (editor) Jean Buridan, *Quaestiones super libris quattuor de caelo et mundo*, Mediaeval Academy of America, 1942, reprinted, 1970; (editor and translator with Marshall Clagett) *The Medieval Science of Weights*, University of Wisconsin Press, 1952; *Truth and Consequence in Medieval Logic*, North-Holland Publishing Co., 1953; (editor) Guilielmi Ockham, *Expositio in librum Porphyrii* (critical edition), Franciscan Institute, 1965; (contributor) *Galileo Reappraised*, University of California

Press, 1966; *Studies in Medieval Philosophy, Science, and Logic* (collection), University of California Press, in press. Contributor to *Collier's Encyclopedia, Encyclopedia of Philosophy, Dictionary of Scientific Biography*, and contributor of articles and monographs to *Franciscan Studies, Philosophical Review, Scientific Monthly*, and other journals.

* * *

MOODY, T(heodore) W(illiam) 1907-

PERSONAL: Born November 26, 1907, in Belfast, Northern Ireland; son of William John (an engineer) and Ann Isabel (Dippie) Moody; married Margaret Robertson, July 6, 1935; children: David Robertson, Ann Sheila, Catherine Margaret, Janet Lucy, Susan Rosemary. *Education:* The Queen's University of Belfast, B.A., 1930; University of London, Institute of Historical Research, Ph.D., 1934. *Religion:* Society of Friends. *Home:* 14 Healthfield Rd., Dublin 6, Ireland. *Office:* 40 Trinity College, Dublin 2, Ireland.

CAREER: The Queen's University of Belfast, Belfast, Northern Ireland, assistant in history department, 1932-35, lecturer in history, 1935-39; University of Dublin, Trinity College, Dublin, Ireland, professor of modern history and fellow, 1939—, senior tutor, 1952-58, senior lecturer, 1958-64, Leverhulme Research Fellow, 1964-66. Member, Institute for Advanced Study, Princeton, N.J., 1965. Member of Irish Manuscripts Commission, 1943—, Cultural Relations Committee of Ireland, 1949-63, Council of Radio Eireann, 1953-60, Irish Broadcasting Authority, 1960-1972. Commission on Higher Education in Ireland, 1960-67. *Member:* Royal Historical Society (fellow), Royal Irish Academy. *Awards, honors:* D.Lit., The Queen's University of Belfast, 1959, for published work in Irish history.

WRITINGS: The Irish Parliament Under Elizabeth and James I: A General Survey, Royal Irish Academy, 1939; *The Londonderry Plantation, 1609-41*, Mullan, 1939; *Thomas Davis, 1815-45*, Hodges, Figgis & Co., 1945; (editor with others, and contributor) *Essays in British and Irish History in Honour of J. E. Todd*, Muller, 1949; (with J. C. Beckett) *Queen's, Belfast, 1845-1949: The History of a University*, Faber, 1959; (editor with F. X. Martin, and contributor) *The Course of Irish History*, Mercier Press, 1967; (editor and contributor) *The Fenian Movement*, Mercier Press, 1968; (editor and contributor) *Irish Historiography, 1936-70*, Irish Committee of Historical Sciences, 1971; *The Ulster Question, 1603-1973*, Mercier Press, 1974.

Joint editor and contributor, *Irish Historical Studies* (biannual), Hodges, Figgis & Co., 1937-67, Dublin University Press, 1968—; editor, *Studies in Irish History*, Faber, 1943-56, Routledge & Kegan Paul, 1960—. Contributor to historical journals.

WORK IN PROGRESS: The Life of Michael Davitt (1846-1906); with R. B. McDowell, the autobiography, diaries, letters and other writings of Theobald Wolfe Tone (1763-1798), a new edition from the original manuscripts, many hitherto unpublished; editor, with F. X. Martin and F. J. Byrne, of a cooperative history of Ireland in nine volumes, under the auspices of the Royal Irish Academy.

* * *

MOONEYHAM, W(alter) Stanley 1926-

PERSONAL: Born January 14, 1926, in Houston, Miss.; son of Walter Scott and Mary (Sullivan) Mooneyham; married LaVerda M. Green, December 13, 1946; children: Carol Gwen, Eric Scott, Robin Anne, Mark Randall. *Education:* Oklahoma Baptist University, B.S., 1950. *Home:* 2227 Canyon Dr., Arcadia, Calif. 91006. *Office:* 919 West Huntington Dr., Monrovia, Calif. 91016.

CAREER: Ordained Baptist minister, 1947. Pastor of Baptist churches in Oklahoma, 1948-52; National Association of Free Will Baptists, Nashville, Tenn., public relations and editorial work, 1953-59; National Association of Evangelicals, Wheaton, Ill., public relations, and editor of *United Evangelical Action*, 1959-64; Billy Graham Evangelistic Association, Atlanta, Ga., public relations, 1964-69; World Vision International, Monrovia, Calif., 1969—. *Military service:* U.S. Navy, 1943-45; became petty officer second class. *Member:* National Association of Evangelicals, Evangelical Foreign Missions Association (member of board of directors), Jesus People. *Awards, honors:* Litt.D., Houghton College, Houghton, N.Y., 1964.

WRITINGS: (Editor) *The Dynamics of Christian Unity: A Symposium on the Ecumenical Movement*, Zondervan, 1963; (editor) *One Race, One Gospel, One Task*, Worldwide Books, 1967; (editor) *Christ Seeks Asia*, Rock House (Hong Kong), 1969. Former editor of *Contact*; consulting editor, Word Books, Inc., Waco, Tex., and *Decision* (magazine), Minneapolis, Minn.

WORK IN PROGRESS: Research in the field of communication, especially as it relates to the Christian message.†

* * *

MOORE, (David) Harmon 1911-

PERSONAL: Born October 21, 1911, in Wedowee, Ala.; son of Thomas David (a farmer) and Ada (Smith) Moore; married Margaret Stone, December 12, 1945; children: Joyce E., David H., Steven L., James H. *Education:* Asbury College, student, 1933-34; Kentucky Wesleyan College, B.A., 1937; Emory University, B.D., 1940, graduate study, 1941; Columbia University, M.A., 1948. *Address:* Box 33, Wedowee, Ala.

CAREER: Minister in Kentucky and Alabama, 1935-42; ordained to ministry of The Methodist Church, 1942; U.S. Army, chaplain, 1942—, now colonel and senior chaplain, Berlin, Germany. Third U.S. chaplain to qualify as paratrooper, 1942; served in Panama, 1942, Southwest Pacific, 1943-44, Japan, 1950-53, Alaska, 1956-59, Germany, 1963—. *Awards, honors—Military:* Decorations include Legion of Merit, Bronze Star Medal, with oak leaf cluster, Army Commendation Ribbon with oak leaf cluster and medal pendant, and Korean Service Medal.

WRITINGS: Commander-Chaplain Guidelines, U.S. Army, 1964; (editor with Ernest A. Ham and Clarence E. Hobgood) *And Our Defense Is Sure: Sermons and Addresses from Pentagon Protestant Pulpit*, Abingdon, 1964. Writer of other manuals on chaplain's activities.

WORK IN PROGRESS: Compiling a book of sermons, *Freedom's Holy Light: Sermons and Addresses from the Berlin Free Pulpit.*†

* * *

MOORE, Katherine Davis 1915-

PERSONAL: Born October 8, 1915, in Knoxville, Tenn.; daughter of James Richard and Lucile (Lones) Davis; married Kyle C. Moore (lieutenant commander, U.S. Naval Reserve), July 23, 1942 (killed in action). *Education:* University of Tennessee, B.A., 1936; University of Michigan,

M.A., 1951; Syracuse University, student at art workshop in Mexico, 1951. *Home:* 1240 Weisgarber Rd., Knoxville, Tenn. *Office:* 210 McChung Tower, University of Tennessee, Knoxville, Tenn.

CAREER: Rule High School, Knoxville, Tenn., teacher of senior English, 1937-67; University of Tennessee, Knoxville, instructor in English, 1967—. Fulbright teacher to Invernessshire, Scotland, 1952-53, to Anatolia College, Thessaloniki, Greece, 1962-63; member of summer staff, American Symphony Orchestra League, 1956, 1959, 1960, 1963. First staff administrator, President's Music Committee of People to People Program, 1957. Knoxville Symphony Orchestra, member of board of directors, 1942-64, vice-president, 1960-61. Member of advisory committee of Juvenile Court of Knox County, 1954-65, secretary, 1958-64. *Member:* National Education Association, American Symphony Orchestra League (member of board, 1961-62), Daughters of the American Revolution, Tennessee Education Association, East Tennessee Education Association.

WRITINGS: (With David Van Vactor) *Every Child May Hear*, University of Tennessee Press, 1960. Assistant editor, American Symphony Orchestra League *Newsletter*, 1963-64.

*   *   *

MOORE, Patrick (Alfred) 1923-

PERSONAL: Born March 4, 1923, in Pinner, Middlesex, England; son of Charles (an army officer) and Gertrude (White) Moore. *Education:* Educated at private schools in England. *Politics:* Conservative. *Home and office:* Farthings, West St., Selsey, Sussex, England. *Agent:* Hilary Rubinstein, A.D. Watt & Son, 26-28 Bedford Row, London WC1, England.

CAREER: Author, mainly of scientific books. Lecturer in Europe and United States on astronomical topics. Regular broadcaster on British Broadcasting Corporation television, with "The Sky at Night" (monthly program), 1957—; Armagh Planetarium, Armagh, Northern Ireland, director, 1965-68. *Military service:* Royal Air Force, Bomber Command, 1940-45; became flight lieutenant. *Member:* International Astronomical Union, Royal Astronomical Society (fellow), British Astronomical Association (director of lunar section, 1965—; director of Mercury and Venus section, 1954-63), Royal Society of Arts (fellow), Children's Writers Group of London (chairman, 1964-65). *Awards, honors:* Lorimer Gold Medal, 1962, for services to astronomy; Goodacre Gold Medal, 1968; Officer Order of the British Empire, 1968; Guido Horn d'Arturo Medal, 1969; Amateur Astronomers' Medal, New York City, 1970; D.Sc., University of Lancaster, 1974.

WRITINGS: (Translator from the French) Gerard de Vaucouleurs, *Planet Mars*, Macmillan, 1950; *Master of the Moon*, Museum Press, 1952; *A Guide to the Moon*, Norton, 1953, revised edition, Collins, 1973; *Suns, Myths, and Men*, Muller, 1954, revised edition, 1968, Norton, 1969, published as *The Story of Man and the Stars*, Norton, 1955; (with A. L. Helm) *Out Into Space*, Museum Press, 1954; *Island of Fear*, Museum Press, 1954; *Frozen Planet*, Museum Press, 1954; *The True Book About Worlds Around Us*, Miller, 1954, published as *The Worlds Around Us*, Abelard, 1956; *A Guide to the Planets*, Norton, 1954, revised edition, 1960, published as *The New Guide to the Planets*, 1972; *Destination Luna*, Lutterworth, 1955; (with Hugh Percival Wilkins) *The Moon*, Macmillan, 1955, 2nd edition, Faber, 1961; *Quest of the Spaceways*, Muller,

1955; *Mission to Mars*, Burke Publishing Co., 1955; (with Irving Geis) *Earth Satellite: The New Satellite Projects Explained*, Eyre & Spottiswoode, 1955, published as *Earth Satellites*, Norton, 1956, revised edition, 1958; *World of Mists*, Muller, 1956; *Domes of Mars*, Burke Publishing Co., 1956; *The Boys' Book of Space*, Roy Publishers, 1956, 6th edition, Burke Publishing Co., 1963; *Wheel in Space*, Lutterworth, 1956; *The Planet Venus*, Faber, 1956, Macmillan, 1957, 3rd edition, 1961; (with Wilkins) *How to Make and Use a Telescope*, Norton, 1956 (published in England as *Making and Using a Telescope*, Eyre & Spottiswoode, 1956); *True Book About the Earth*, Muller, 1956; *Guide to Mars*, Muller, 1956, new edition, Macmillan, 1960, revised edition, Muller, 1965; *Voices of Mars*, Burke Publishing Co., 1957; *The True Book About Earthquakes and Volcanoes*, Muller, 1957; *Isaac Newton*, A. & C. Black, 1957, Putnam, 1958; *Science and Fiction*, Harrap, 1957, Folcroft, 1970; *The Amateur Astronomer*, Norton, 1957, 5th revised edition, Lutterworth, 1964, revised edition, Norton, 1966, published as *Amateur Astronomy*, 1968, 7th revised edition, Lutterworth, 1974; *The Earth, Our Home*, Abelard, 1957; *Peril on Mars*, Burke Publishing, 1958, Putnam, 1965; *Your Book of Astronomy*, Faber, 1958, 2nd edition, 1964; *The Solar System*, Methuen, 1958, Criterion, 1961; (editor with David R. Bates) *Space Research and Exploration*, Sloane, 1958; *The Boys' Book of Astronomy*, Roy Publishers, 1958; *The True Book About Man*, Muller, 1959; *Rockets and Earth Satellites*, Muller, 1959, 2nd edition, 1960; *Raiders of Mars*, Burke Publishing Co., 1959.

Astronautics, Methuen, 1960; *Captives of the Moon*, Burke Publishing Co., 1960; *Guide to the Stars*, Norton, 1960; *Stars and Space*, A. & C. Black, 1960, 3rd edition, 1969; (with Henry Brinton) *Navigation*, Methuen, 1961; *Astronomy*, Oldbourne, 1961, 3rd revised edition, 1967, 4th revised edition published as *The Story of Astronomy*, Macdonald & Co., 1972, published as *The Picture History of Astronomy*, Grosset, 1961, 3rd edition, 1967; *Wanderer in Space*, Burke Publishing Co., 1961; *The Stars*, Weidenfeld & Nicolson, 1962; (with Brinton) *Exploring Maps*, Odhams, 1962, Hawthorn, 1967; (with Paul Murdin) *The Astronomer's Telescope*, Brockhampton Press, 1962; (with Francis L. Jackson) *Life in the Universe*, Norton, 1962; *The Planets*, Norton, 1962; *The Observer's Book of Astronomy*, Warne, 1962; *Crater of Fear*, Harvey, 1962; *Telescopes and Observatories*, Weidenfeld & Nicolson, 1962; *Invader from Space*, Burke Publishing Co., 1963; *Survey of the Moon*, Norton, 1963; *Space in the Sixties*, Penguin, 1963; (editor) *Practical Amateur Astronomy*, Lutterworth, 1963, published as *A Handbook of Practical Amateur Astronomy*, Norton, 1964; *Exploring the Moon*, Odhams, 1964; *The True Book About Roman Britain*, Muller, 1964; (with Brinton) *Exploring Weather*, Odhams, 1964; *Caverns of the Moon*, Ulverscroft, c.1964; *The Sky at Night*, Volume I, Eyre & Spottiswoode, 1964, Norton, 1965, Volume II, Eyre & Spottiswoode, 1968; (with Jackson) *Life on Mars*, Routledge & Kegan Paul, 1965, Norton, 1966; *Exploring the World*, Oxford University Press, 1966, F. Watts, 1968; (with Hiliary Rubinstein) *The New Look of the Universe*, Norton, 1966; *Exploring the Planetarium*, Odhams, 1966; *Legends of the Stars*, Odhams, 1966; *Naked-Eye Astronomy*, Norton, 1966; *Basic Astronomy*, Oliver & Boyd, 1967; (with Brinton) *Exploring Other Planets*, Hawthorn, 1967; (with Brinton) *Exploring Earth History*, Odhams, 1967; (with Peter J. Cattermole) *The Craters of the Moon*, Norton, 1967; *The Amateur Astronomer's Glossary*, Norton, 1967; *Armagh Observatory: A History*,

1790-1967, Armagh Observatory, 1967; *Exploring the Galaxies*, Odhams, 1968; *Exploring the Stars*, Odhams, 1968; *Space: The Story of Man's Greatest Feat of Exploration*, Lutterworth, 1968, Natural History Press, 1969, 3rd edition, Lutterworth, 1970; (author of revision) Mervyn A. Ellison, *The Sun and Its Influence*, 3rd edition (Moore was not associated with earlier editions), American Elsevier, 1968; *The Sun*, Norton, 1968; *Moon Flight Atlas*, Rand McNally, 1969 revised edition, Philip & Son, 1970; *Astronomy and Space Research*, National Book League (London), 1969; *The Development of Astronomical Thought*, Oliver & Boyd, 1969.

The Atlas of the Universe, Rand McNally, 1970, 3rd edition, Mitchell Beazley, 1974; *Astronomy for O Level*, Duckworth, 1970, 2nd edition, 1974; *Seeing Stars*, Rand McNally, 1971; (author of introduction) Arthur C. Clarke, *Islands in the Sky*, Sidgwick & Jackson, 1971; *The Astronomers of Birr Castle*, Mitchell Beazley, 1971; *Can You Speak Venusian?*, David & Charles, 1972, Norton, 1973; (with David A. Hardy) *Challenge of the Stars*, Mitchell Beazley, 1972; (with Desmond Leslie) *How Britain Won the Space Race*, Mitchell Beazley, 1972; (with Laurence T. Clarke) *How to Recognize the Stars*, Corgi Books, 1972; *The Southern Stars*, Rigby, 1973; *Color Star Atlas*, Crown, 1973; *The Starlit Sky*, South African Broadcasting Co., 1973; *Man the Astronomer*, Priory, 1973; (with Charles A. Cross) *Mars*, Crown, 1973; (editor and contributor) *Astronomical Telescopes and Observatories for Amateurs*, David & Charles, 1973; (author of revision) James S. Pickering, *1001 Questions Answered About Astronomy*, Dodd, 1973; (translator from the French) E. M. Antoniadi, *The Planet Mercury*, Keith Reid, 1974; *The Comets*, Keith Reid, 1974; *Watchers of the Stars*, Putnam, 1974.

Editor, *Yearbook of Astronomy*, Norton, 1962—.

WORK IN PROGRESS: Rewriting *A Guide to the Moon*.

SIDELIGHTS: Moore told *CA:* "I speak French as well as the average schoolboy, but otherwise I believe in speaking English! I particularly like Scandinavia, notably Iceland, which I know well. I have done an eclipse television broadcast from Yugoslavia." *Avocational interests:* Cricket, tennis, chess, and work with Boy Scouts.

* * *

MOORE, Robert L(owell), Jr. 1925-
(Robin Moore)

PERSONAL: Born October 31, 1925, in Concord, Mass.; son of Robert Lowell and Eleanor (Turner) Moore; married third wife, Mary Olga Troshkin, February 17, 1973; children: (first marriage) Margo. *Education:* Harvard University, A.B., 1949. *Home:* Fairy Hill, Jamaica, West Indies; and 375 Park Ave., New York, N.Y. 10022. *Agent:* John Cushman, William Morris Agency, 1350 Ave. of the Americas, New York, N.Y.

CAREER: Independent package producer of television shows, 1949-53; Sheraton Corporation of America, advertising manager, 1953-55, vice-president of advertising and public relations, 1955-65. *Military service:* U.S. Army Air Forces, nose gunner, bombardier, 1944-46. *Member:* American Hotel Association, Association of National Advertisers, Overseas Press Club, Lambs Club, Athletic Club, Harvard Club, Metropolitan Club (all New York).

WRITINGS—All under pseudonym Robin Moore: *Pitchman*, Coward, 1956; (with Jack Youngblood) *The Devil to Pay*, Coward, 1961; *The Green Berets*, Coward, 1965; *The*

Country Team, Crown, 1966; *Fiedler, The Colorful Mr. Pops: The Man and His Music*, Little, Brown, 1968; *The French Connection*, Little, Brown, 1969; (with Henry Rothblatt) *Court-Martial*, Doubleday, 1971; (with June Collins) *The Khaki Mafia*, Crown, 1971; (with Henry Lowenberg) *Until Proven Guilty*, Little, Brown, 1971; *The Fifth Estate*, Doubleday, 1973; *The Making of a Happy Hooker*, New American Library, 1973; (with Al Dempsey) *The London Switch*, Pinnacle Books, 1974; (with Howard Jennings) *The Treasure Hunter*, Prentice-Hall, 1974; (with Milt Machlin) *The Family Man*, Pyramid Publications, 1974; *Phase of Darkness*, Third Press, 1974.

Also author of two screenplays, "The Awakening" and "Encounter." Wrote series of articles for *Boston Globe*, 1947.

SIDELIGHTS: Moore trained with the Green Berets as a civilian and went into battle with them in Viet Nam in order to gain first-hand information for *The Green Berets*, which later became a film. The film adaption of *The French Connection* won five Academy Awards, including the award for best picture, 1971.

BIOGRAPHICAL/CRITICAL SOURCES: Time, June 25, 1965; *New York Times Book Review*, July 11, 1965; *Nation*, August 2, 1965; *Commonweal*, August 6, 1965; *National Observer*, August 9, 1965; *Saturday Night*, November, 1965; *Social Education*, November, 1965; *Book Week*, November 7, 1965.†

* * *

MORAN, William E(dward), Jr. 1916-

PERSONAL: Born January 8, 1916, in Herkimer, N.Y.; son of William Edward (a restaurateur) and Esther (Henry) Moran; married Phyllis Duffy, May 17, 1941; children: William Edward III, Patricia. *Education:* Syracuse University, A.B., 1937, LL.B., 1940. *Religion:* Roman Catholic. *Home:* 4515 Hawthorne St., N.W., Washington, D.C. 20016. *Office:* Georgetown University, Washington, D.C. 20007.

CAREER: U.S. Government, 1940-59, starting as agent for Federal Bureau of Investigation, 1940-45, then with Department of State and Atomic Energy Commission, 1945-49, assistant director of Economic Cooperation Mission to Belgium, 1949-52, Chief of Dependent Overseas Territories Branch, Economic Cooperation Administration and Mutual Security Agency, 1952-53, director of African Division of Foreign Operations Agency, 1952-57, deputy director of International Cooperation Administration Mission to Morocco, 1957-59; Stanford Research Institute, Menlo Park, Calif., head of African program, 1959-61; Georgetown University, Washington, D.C., dean of School of Foreign Service, 1961—. Population Reference Bureau, member of board. *Member:* Catholic Association for International Peace (president), African Studies Association, Council on Foreign Relations, Eastern Association of College Deans, Washington Institute for Foreign Affairs.

WRITINGS: (With Guy Benveniste) *Handbook of African Economic Development*, Praeger, 1964; (editor) *Population Growth: Threat to Peace?*, P. J. Kenedy, 1965.†

* * *

MORGAN, John S. 1921-

PERSONAL: Born March 20, 1921, in Cleveland, Ohio; son of Clyde Spencer (a chemical engineer) and Mariem (Smith) Morgan; married Virginia L. Willis (a medical librarian), February 15, 1947; children: Penelope W., Patricia M., Madeleine S. *Education:* Yale University, B.A., 1943; Western Reserve University (now Case Western Reserve University), graduate study, 1945-49. *Politics:* Republican. *Religion:* Protestant. *Home:* 5 Oval Ct., Bronxville, N.Y. 10708.

CAREER: Steel (magazine), Cleveland, Ohio, associate managing editor, 1947-62; General Electric Co., New York, N.Y., consultant on management communication, 1962—. *Military service:* U.S. Army, Medical Department, 1943-45; became sergeant. *Awards, honors: Industrial Marketing* annual editorial competition awards, 1957, for series on need for federal tax depreciation reform, and 1960, for series on foreign competition.

WRITINGS: Getting Across to Employees, McGraw, 1964; (editor) *Welfare and Wisdom*, University of Toronto Press, 1966; *Practical Guide to Conference Leadership*, McGraw, 1966; *Managing the Young Adults*, American Management Association, 1967; *Improving Your Creativity on the Job*, American Management Association, 1968; *Business Faces the Urban Crisis*, Gulf Publishing, 1969; (with Richard L. Van Dyke) *White-Collar Blacks: A Breakthrough?*, American Management Association, 1970; *Managing Change: The Strategies of Making Change Work for You*, McGraw, 1972; *Aesop's Fables in the Executive Suite*, Van Nostrand, 1974. Writer of General Electric Co. publications on management communication.

* * *

MORGAN, Kenneth Owen 1934-

PERSONAL: Born May 16, 1934, in London, England; son of David James (a schoolmaster) and Margaret Morgan; married Jane Keeler, January 4, 1973. *Education:* Attended University College School, London, England, 1944-52; Oriel College, Oxford, M.A., 1958, D.Phil., 1958. *Politics:* Labour. *Home:* Stonecroft, East End, Oxford, England.

CAREER: University College of Wales, Swansea, senior lecturer in history, 1958-66; Oxford University, Queen's College, Oxford, England, fellow in modern history and political science, 1966—. Columbia University, New York, N.Y., visiting fellow, 1962-63, visiting summer professor, 1965; frequent television and radio broadcaster on political topics. *Member:* Royal Historical Society (fellow), Honourable Society of Cymmrodorion, British Association for American Studies, Historical Association, Oxford Union (life). *Awards, honors:* American Council of Learned Societies fellow, 1962-63.

WRITINGS: David Lloyd George, University of Wales Press, 1963; *Wales in British Politics, 1868-1922*, University of Wales Press, 1963, revised edition, 1970; (contributor) David Butler and Anthony King, *The British General Election of 1964*, Macmillan, 1965; *Freedom or Sacrilege? A History of the Campaign for Welsh Disestablishment*, Church in Wales Publications, 1966; *Keir Hardie*, Oxford University Press, 1967; *The Age of Lloyd George*, Barnes & Noble, 1971; *Lloyd George: Family Letters*, Oxford University Press, 1973; *Lloyd George*, Widenfeld and Nicolson, 1974; *Keir Hardie: Radical-Socialist*, Weidenfeld and Nicolson, in press. Editor, contributor to history journals. Editor, *Welsh History Review*, 1965—.

WORK IN PROGRESS: Studies of British political history since 1918, and of modern Wales since 1885.

SIDELIGHTS: Morgan speaks French and Welsh. *Avocational interests:* Sports, music, the theater, films, motoring in rural France, and Inca archaeology.

MORGAN, Kenneth R(emsen) 1916-

PERSONAL: Born June 3, 1916, in New London, Conn.; son of George K. (a stockbroker) and Katherine (McKim) Morgan; married Joan Caron, June 8, 1938; children: George, Diana, John, Matthew, Elizabeth, Katherine. *Education:* Yale University, B.A., 1938, M.D., 1942. *Politics:* Republican. *Religion:* Episcopalian. *Home:* 1488 Brookside Dr., Fairfield, Conn. *Office:* 325 Reef Rd., Fairfield, Conn.

CAREER: Physician and surgeon, specializing in obstetrics and gynecology, in New Haven, Conn., 1948-50, in Fairfield, Conn., 1950—. *Member:* American Board of Obstetricians and Gynecologists, American College of Abdominal Surgeons, College of Obstetrics and Gynecology. Authors Guild.

WRITINGS: Bed, Breakfast, and Bottled Water: A Cautionary Travel Guide to Europe, Morrow, 1963; *A Little Stork Told Me*, Morrow, 1965; *Speaking You English: A Light Hearted Guide to World Travel*, Fielding, 1973. Contributor of articles and short stories to *Argosy, Horizon*, and other magazines.

WORK IN PROGRESS: A book of travel anecdotes, *The Gay Girls of Europe*; a humorous novel.

SIDELIGHTS: Morgan writes for relaxation (his only hobby besides travel), and sometimes takes a clip board and pencil to the hospital when he suspects a baby is going to be slow about being born. He says his first and third books are aimed at "An utterly ignored segment of the traveling population, the middleaged bird . . . who has saved enough money to go abroad and wants to do it up brown without being broke, bored, or embarrassed—and is secretly afraid of being all three." Morgan, his wife, children, and a basset hound live in an oversized house (in Fairfield) that resembles a Norman castle.

* * *

MORGAN, Thomas Bruce 1926-
(Nicholas David, Nicholas Morgan)

PERSONAL: Born July 24, 1926, in Springfield, Ill.; son of David Edward (a merchant) and Mabel (Wolfe) Morgan; married Joan Zuckerman, October 1, 1950 (divorced); children: Katherine, Nicholas. *Education:* University of Illinois, student, 1944; Carleton College, B.A., 1949. *Politics:* Democrat. *Religion:* Jewish. *Home:* 1 West 67th St., New York, N.Y. 10023. *Office:* City Hall, New York, N.Y. 10007. *Agent:* Carl Brandt, Jr., Brandt & Brandt, 101 Park Ave., New York, N.Y.

CAREER: Esquire, New York, N.Y., associate editor, 1949-53; *Look*, New York, N.Y., senior editor, 1953-58; free-lance writer, 1958-69; Office of the Mayor, New York, N.Y., press secretary, 1969—. West Village Community Committee, New York, N.Y., vice-president, 1963-64. *Military service:* U.S. Army Air Forces, 1945; U.S. Air Force Reserve, 1945-48. *Awards, honors:* Awards for articles in *Look* include Freedoms Foundation Medal, 1945, School Bell Award of National Education Association, 1960, Blakeslee Award of American Heart Association, 1963, American Bar Association Award, 1964.

WRITINGS: Friends and Fellow Students, Crowell, 1956; (editor) *Creative America*, Ridge Press, 1964; *Self-Creations: Thirteen Impersonalities*, Holt, 1965; *This Blessed Shore*, Shorecrest, 1966; *Among the Anti-Americans*, Holt, 1967 (published in England as *The Anti-Americans*, M. Joseph, 1967). Author of screenplays. Contributor of about

250 articles to *Esquire, Look, Holiday, Harper's, Redbook, Good Housekeeping, Cosmopolitan, Think*, and *TV Guide*.

SIDELIGHTS: Morgan told *CA*: "My major recreation is movie-going. My greatest pleasure as a writer has been research on every continent, including Antarctica, and in *finishing* an assignment. Like most writers I live too extravagantly and fear success more than failure."

BIOGRAPHICAL/CRITICAL SOURCES: Thomas B. Morgan, introduction to *Self-Creations*, Holt, in press.†

* * *

MORISON, David Lindsay 1920-

PERSONAL: Born October 15, 1920, in Roslin, Midlothian, Scotland; son of Ernest Frederick (a clergyman) and Constance (Warne-Browne) Morison; married Alison Campbell Dawson, August 22, 1952; children: Patricia, James. *Education:* Attended Marlborough College, 1934-39; Merton College, Oxford, M.A., 1947. *Religion:* Church of England. *Home:* Clayhill House, Knott Park, Oxshott, Surrey, England. *Office:* Central Asian Research Centre, 66 King's Rd., London S.W.3, England.

CAREER: With British Broadcasting Corporation monitoring service, 1948-58; with Central Asian Research Centre, London, England, 1958—; editor of *Mizan* (journal dealing with Soviet policy in Africa, Middle East, and South-East Asia), in association with Soviet Affairs Study Group of St. Anthony's College, Oxford. *Military service:* British Army, 1941-45; served in East Africa, Burma, and India; became sergeant. *Member:* Royal Institute of International Affairs, African Studies Association of the United Kingdom, Association of British Orientalists.

WRITINGS: The USSR and Africa, Oxford University Press, 1964; (contributor) Hamrell and Widstrand, editors, *The Soviet Block, China and Africa*, Scandinavian Institute of Africa Studies, 1964; (translator) Teobaldo Filesi, *China and Africa in the Middle Ages*, International Scholars Book Service, 1972. Contributor to *Middle East Forum, Race, Afrika Forum, Problems of Communism*, and other journals.

SIDELIGHTS: Morison attended the First International Congress of Africanists in Ghana, 1962. He is competent in Swahili, Italian, French, Spanish, Russian, Arabic, Hausa.†

* * *

MORLEY, James William 1921-

PERSONAL: Born July 12, 1921, in Trenton, N.J. *Education:* Harvard University, A.B., 1943; Fletcher School of Law and Diplomacy, graduate study, 1943-44; Johns Hopkins University, M.A., 1945; Columbia University, Ph.D., 1954. *Home:* 145 Piermont Rd., Closter, New Jersey. *Office:* East Asian Institute, 915 International Affairs, Columbia University, New York, N.Y. 10027.

CAREER: Union College, Schenectady, N.Y., 1948-54, started as assistant professor, became associate professor of history; Columbia University, New York, N.Y., associate professor, 1954-66, professor of government, 1966—, director of East Asian Institute, 1970-73. *Military service:* U.S. Naval Reserve, Naval Intelligence, 1943-46; became lieutenant. *Member:* Council on Foreign Relations, Phi Beta Kappa. *Awards, honors:* Honorable mention in George Louis Beer Prize award of American Historical Association, 1958, for *The Japanese Thrust into Siberia, 1918*.

WRITINGS: (Contributor) Osgood Hardy and Glenn S. Dumke, *A History of the Pacific Area in Modern Times*, Houghton, 1949; (contributor) Matthew A. Fitzsimons, editor, *The Development of Historiography*, Stackpole, 1954; *The Japanese Thrust in Siberia, 1918*, Columbia University Press, 1957; *Soviet and Communist Chinese Policies Toward Japan*, Institute of Pacific Relations, 1958; *Japan and Korea: America's Allies in the Pacific*, Walker, 1965; (editor) Kuo Ting-yee, compiler, *Sino-Japanese Relations, 1862-1927*, East Asian Institute, Columbia University, 1965; (editor) *Dilemmas of Growth in Prewar Japan*, Princeton University Press, 1971; (editor) *Forecast for Japan: Security in the 1970's*, Princeton University Press, 1971; (editor) *Forecast for Japan: Security in the 1970's*, Princeton University Press, 1972. Contributor to *Information Please Almanac, Journal of Asian Studies, Challenge, Pacific Affairs*, other journals in America and Japan.

WORK IN PROGRESS: A translation, *Japan's Road to the Pacific War*, for Columbia University Press.

* * *

MORRIS, Alton C(hester) 1903-

PERSONAL: Born February 6, 1903, in Forest City, Fla.; son of Claude Chester (a farmer) and Mary Jane (Ingram) Morris; married Hazel Ruby Thornton, September 3, 1928; children: Alton Chester Jr., Kenneth Dale. *Education:* University of Florida, A.B.E., 1927, M.A., 1928; University of North Carolina, Ph.D., 1941. *Politics:* Democrat. *Religion:* Methodist. *Home:* 1516 Northwest 14th Avenue, Gainesville, Fla. *Office:* University of Florida, University Station, Gainesville, Fla.

CAREER: Agricultural and Mechanical College of Texas (now Texas A & M University), College Station, instructor in English, 1928-29; University of Florida, Gainesville, instructor, 1929-35, assistant professor of English, 1935-39; University of North Carolina, Chapel Hill, instructor in English, 1939-40; University of Florida, associate professor, 1940-46, professor of English, 1946-73, professor emeritus, 1973—. Visiting summer professor at University of Denver, 1942, Appalachian State Teachers College, 1945, Harvard University, 1950, 1951. Former member of executive committee, National Folk Festival; former consultant, Library of Congress Folklore Archives. *Member:* Modern Language Association of America, American Folklore Society, Dialect Society, American Name Society, South Atlantic Modern Language Association, Phi Beta Kappa, Phi Kappa Phi, Kappa Delta Pi, Phi Eta Sigma, Sigma Phi Epsilon, Florida Blue Key.

WRITINGS: (With Herman E. Spivey) *Essentials of Correctness in the Use of English*, Prentice-Hall, 1931; (editor) *The Meaning in Reading*, Harcourt, 1943, 4th revised edition, 1961; (editor) *Folksongs of Florida*, University of Florida Press, 1950; (editor with others) *College English: The First Year*, Harcourt, 1952, 6th edition, 1973; (with Biron Walker and Philip Bradshaw) *The Modern Essay: A Program for Reading and Writing*, Harcourt, 1965, 2nd edition, 1968; (with Walker and Bradshaw) *Imaginative Literature: Fiction, Drama, Poetry*, Harcourt, 1968, 2nd edition, 1972. Also author of *The Place Names of Florida*. Editor, *Southern Folklore Quarterly*, 1937-67.

AVOCATIONAL INTERESTS: American folk materials and their preservation.

MORRIS, Charles (William) 1901-

PERSONAL: Born May 23, 1901, in Denver, Colo.; son of Charles William and Laura (Campbell) Morris; married Gertrude E. Thompson, 1925; married second wife, Ellen Ruth Allen (a psychologist), October 25, 1951; children: (first marriage) Sara Morris Petrilli. *Education:* University of Wisconsin, student, 1918-20; Northwestern University, B.S., 1922; University of Chicago, Ph.D., 1925. *Address:* P.O. Box 14245, University Station, Gainesville, Fla.

CAREER: Rice University, Houston, Tex., instructor in philosophy, 1925-30; University of Chicago, Chicago, Ill., associate professor of philosophy, 1931-47, lecturer in philosophy, 1947-58; University of Florida, Gainesville, research professor of philosophy, 1958-71, professor emeritus, 1971—. Visiting lecturer in social relations, Harvard University, 1951-53; fellow, Center for Advanced Study in the Behavioral Sciences, 1956-57. *Military service:* U.S. Naval Reserve, 1918. *Member:* American Philosophical Association (president of western division, 1937), American Association for the Advancement of Science (fellow), American Academy of Arts and Sciences (fellow), Delta Upsilon. *Awards, honors:* Guggenheim fellow, 1942; Rockefeller fellow, 1943.

WRITINGS: Six Theories of Mind, University of Chicago Press, 1932; (editor) George H. Mead, *Mind, Self, and Society,* University of Chicago Press, 1934; *Logical Positivism, Pragmatism, and Scientific Empiricism,* Hermann et cie (Paris), 1937; (editor) George H. Mead, *The Philosophy of the Act,* University of Chicago Press, 1938; *Foundations of the Theory of Signs,* University of Chicago Press, 1938; *Paths of Life,* Harper, 1942; *Signs, Language, and Behavior,* Prentice-Hall, 1946; *The Open Self,* Prentice-Hall, 1948; *Varieties of Human Value,* University of Chicago Press, 1956; *Signification and Significance,* Massachusetts Institute of Technology Press, 1964; *Festival,* Braziller, 1966; *The Pragmatic Movement in American Philosophy,* Braziller, 1970; *Writings on the General Theory of Signs,* Mouton & Co., 1971. Associate editor, *International Encyclopedia of Unified Science,* 1936—.

AVOCATIONAL INTERESTS: Poetry.

* * *

MORRIS, John W(esley) 1907-

PERSONAL: Born November 14, 1907, in Billings, Okla.; son of Henry L. and Lillian M. (Knowles) Morris; married Mary Elizabeth Russell, February 19, 1932; children: Carroll June (Mrs. Harvey Wilson), Russell A. *Education:* University of Oklahoma, B.S., 1930; Oklahoma State University, M.S., 1934; George Peabody College for Teachers, Ph.D., 1941. *Home:* 833 McCall Dr., Norman, Okla. 73069.

CAREER: Seminole Junior College, Seminole, Okla., instructor in geography, 1931-38; Southeastern State College, Durant, Okla., associate professor 1939-42, professor of geography, 1946-48; University of Oklahoma, Norman, associate professor, 1948-50, 1952-54, professor of geography and head of department, 1954-73. Summer visiting professor at University of Florida, 1949, George Peabody College for Teachers, 1957, 1958, Western Washington College, 1962, Michigan State University, 1964, Moorhead State College, 1969, University of British Columbia, 1971, University of Wyoming, 1973. Consultant to National Park Service, 1952-53, Southern Appalachian Studies Program, 1958-60; consulting editor, Harlow Publishing Corp., Oklahoma City, 1940-68. *Military service:* U.S. Navy, 1942-46,

1950-51; became commander; received Pacific Ribbon with five battle stars, and Commendation Ribbon.

MEMBER: National Council for Geographic Education (fellow; secretary, 1955-58; president, 1960; director of publications, 1961-63). Association of American Geographers (chairman, Southwestern division, 1955-56, 1961-63), American Geographical Society (fellow), Southwestern Social Science Association (president, 1964), Oklahoma Education Association (chairman of geography section, 1940, 1947, 1949, 1954; board of directors, 1963), Oklahoma Academy of Science (fellow; chairman of geography section, 1953), Sigma Xi, Phi Beta Sigma, Phi Delta Kappa, Pi Gamma Mu, Phi Alpha Theta, Gamma Theta Upsilon, Lions Club. *Awards, honors:* Grants from U.S. Office of Naval Research, 1952-54, National Park Service, 1954, Ford Foundation, 1959, University of Oklahoma Faculty Research Fund; Distinguished Former Student Award, Central Oklahoma State College; Distinguished Service Award, National Council for Geographic Education.

WRITINGS: A Preliminary Index to the Source Materials of Oklahoma Geography, Oklahoma Council of Geography Teachers, 1929; *Comprehensive Guidebook for Commercial and Industrial Geography,* Harlow Publishing, 1931; *Population Projections for Oklahoma Towns and Cities of 2500 or More,* Arkansas-White-Red River Basin Authority, 1951; *Oklahoma Geography,* Harlow Publishing, 1952, 3rd edition, 1962; *An Analysis of the Tourist Industry in Selected Counties of the Ozark Area,* National Park Service, 1952; *Boreal Fringe Areas of Marsh and Swampland: A General Background Study,* Office of Naval Research, 1954; *Boreal Fringe Areas of Marsh and Swampland: Photoidentification Key for the Summer (Foliage) Season,* Office of Naval Research, 1954; *Boreal Fringe Areas of Marsh and Swampland: Photoidentification Key for the Winter (Non-Foliage) Season,* Office of Naval Research, 1954; (editor with Otis Freeman) *World Geography,* with study guide and instructor's manual, McGraw, 1958, 3rd edition, 1972; (with Harry E. Hoy) *Know Your America—Oklahoma,* American Geographical Society, 1965; (with Edwin C. McReynolds) *Historical Atlas of Oklahoma,* University of Oklahoma Press, 1965, 2nd edition, in press; (editor) *Methods of Geographic Instruction,* Blaisdell, 1968; *Southwestern United States,* Van Nostrand, 1970.

Contributor: Kent Ruth, editor, *Oklahoma, a Guide to the Sooner State,* University of Oklahoma Press, 1957; William H. Cartwright, editor, *Teaching American History in High School,* National Council for the Social Studies, 1961; Thomas R. Ford, editor, *The Southern Appalachian Region: A Survey,* University of Kentucky Press, 1962.

Author of thirty workbooks and laboratory manuals on geography of the United States, Canada, Latin America, and other parts of the world, for use in elementary, junior high, and high schools. Co-compiler of "Oklahoma History Maps" series of ten wall maps. Contributor to *World Book Encyclopedia, Student Merit Encyclopedia,* and professional journals.

WORK IN PROGRESS: Two books, *Historical Geography of the United States* and *Ghost Towns of Oklahoma.*

SIDELIGHTS: Morris's travels span four continents. *Avocational interests:* Photography and cartography.

* * *

MORRISON, Clinton (Dawson, Jr.) 1924-

PERSONAL: Born November 8, 1924, in Oklahoma City,

Okla.; son of Clinton Dawson and Margaret (Connor) Morrison; married Jean Constance Langley, June 3, 1947; children: Clinton Dawson III, Gregory Alan, Amy Jean. *Education:* Park College, B.A., 1945; McCormick Theological Seminary, B.D., 1948; University of Basel, D.Theol., 1960. *Home:* 1706 Gresham Rd., Louisville, Ky. 40205.

CAREER: Ordained minister of United Presbyterian Church, 1948; minister in Altamont, Ill., 1948-49; McCormick Theological Seminary, Chicago, Ill., instructor, 1951-56, assistant professor, 1956-59, associate professor, 1959-62, professor of New Testament, 1962-68; Louisville Presbyterian Theological Seminary, Louisville, Ky., professor of New Testament, and dean of faculty, 1968—. Consultant, Church Peace Mission, 1962-69; moderator, Presbytery of Chicago, 1965. Member of Drew-McCormick Archaeological Expedition at Shechem (Jordan), 1960. *Member:* Society of Biblical Literature, Chicago Society of Biblical Research (president, 1967-68).

WRITINGS: The Powers that Be, S.C.M. Press, 1960; *The Mission of the Church*, Herald Press, 1964; (with D. H. Barnes) *New Testament Word Lists*, Eerdmans, 1966. Contributor to dictionaries and professional journals. Editor, *Biblical Research*, 1962-64; member of editorial council, *Interpretation*, 1963-72.

WORK IN PROGRESS: Analytical Concordance of the R.S.V. New Testament.

*   *   *

MORRISON, N. Brysson

PERSONAL: Daughter of Arthur Mackay (an engineer) and Agnes Brysson (Inglis) Morrison. *Politics:* Conservative. *Religion:* Church of Scotland. *Address:* c/o The Caledonian Club, 112 Princes St., Edinburgh E H 4, Scotland.

CAREER: Writer. *Awards, honors:* First Frederick Niven Award for finest work written by a Scot, 1950, for *The Winnowing Years*; Literary Guild award (U.S.), 1961, for *Life of Mary Queen of Scots*.

WRITINGS: Breakers, J. Murray, 1930; *Solitaire*, J. Murray, 1932; *The Gowk Storm* (Book Society choice), Collins, 1933; *The Strangers*, Collins, 1935; *When the Wind Blows*, Collins, 1937; *These Are My Friends*, Bles, 1946; *The Winnowing Years*, Hogarth, 1950; *The Hidden Fairing* (Book Society choice), Hogarth, 1951; *The Keeper of Time,* Church of Scotland, 1954; *The Following Wind*, Hogarth, 1954; *They Need No Candle*, John Knox, 1957; *The Other Traveller*, Hogarth, 1957; *Life of Mary Queen of Scots*, Vista Books, 1960, Vanguard, 1961; *Thea*, Vanguard, 1962; *Life of Henry VII*, Vanguard, 1964; *Haworth Harvest: The Story of the Brontes*, Vanguard, 1969; *King's Quiver*, Dent, 1972, St. Martin's Press, 1974; *True Minds*, Dent, 1974.

SIDELIGHTS: The Gowk Storm was made into a movie, a play, and produced on radio; *The Hidden Fairing, The Other Traveller*, and *Thea* also were dramatized for radio. *The Following Wind* and *Life of Mary Queen of Scots* have been translated into Italian.

*   *   *

MORSE, Richard M(cGee)   1922-

PERSONAL: Born June 26, 1922, in Summit, N.J.; son of William Otis and Marie (Zimmerman) Morse; married Emerante de Pradines (a dancer), December 30, 1954; children: Marise, Richard. *Education:* Princeton University, B.A., 1943; Columbia University, M.A., 1947, Ph.D.,

1952. *Address:* Fundacao Ford Caixa, Postal 49-ZC-00, Rio de Janeiro GB, Brazil.

CAREER: Columbia University, New York, N.Y., lecturer, 1949-50, instructor, 1950-54, assistant professor of history, 1954-58; University of Puerto Rico, Rio Piedras, director, Institute of Caribbean Studies, 1958-61; State University of New York at Stony Brook, professor of history and chairman of department, 1961-62; Yale University, New Haven, Conn., associate professor, 1962-63, professor of history, 1963—, chairman of Council on Latin American Studies, 1963-64, 1965-70, fellow of Silliman College, 1963—. Visiting lecturer at Harvard University, 1960, Brooklyn College (now of the City University of New York), 1962, Columbia University, 1966, Stanford University, 1971; advisor, University of Nuevo Leon, 1958-60; Latin American consultant, Ford Foundation, 1958-64; secretary, Inter-American Foundation for the Arts, 1963-68. *Military service:* U.S. Naval Reserve, 1943-46; became lieutenant.

MEMBER: Latin American Studies Association, Conference on Latin American History (vice-chairman of general committee, 1968), Phi Beta Kappa. *Awards, honors:* First prize, National Theatre Conference Soldier Contest, for one-act play, "The Narrowest Street," 1945; essay prize, Conference on Latin American History, 1962; Guggenheim and Social Science Research Council fellowships, 1964-65.

WRITINGS: From Community to Metropolis: A Biography of Sao Paulo, Brazil, University of Florida Press, 1958; (with Louis Hartz and others) *The Founding of New Societies*, Harcourt, 1964; (editor, and author of introduction) *The Bandeirantes*, Knopf, 1965. Also author of Latin American historical studies in Spanish.

Co-editor of "Columbia Volumes on Contemporary Civilization," 1954-55. Contributor to *Encyclopaedia Britannica, American Oxford Encyclopedia*, and to periodicals and newspapers. Member of editorial board, *Hispanic American Historical Review*, 1960-65, *Latin American Urban Research*, 1970—; advisory editor, *Caribbean Studies*, 1961—, *Inter-American Review*, 1971.

WORK IN PROGRESS: A book on comparative history of Latin American cities.

SIDELIGHTS: Morse is fluent in French, Spanish, and Portuguese.†

*   *   *

MORTIMER, John Clifford   1923-

PERSONAL: Born April 21, 1923, in London, England; son of Clifford (a barrister) and Kathleen May (Smith) Mortimer; married Penelope Ruth Fletcher (a writer), 1949 (divorced, 1972); married Penelope Gollop, 1972; children: Sally, Jeremy; stepchildren: Madelon Lee Mortimer Howard, Caroline, Julia Mortimer Mankowitz, Deborah Mortimer Rogers. *Education:* Attended Brasenose College, Oxford. *Home:* 16a Blomfield Road, London W.9, England. *Agent:* A. D. Peters, 10 Buckingham St., Adelphi, London W.C. 2, England.

CAREER: Barrister-at-law, London, England, 1948—. Novelist and playwright. *Member:* Garrick Club. *Awards, honors:* Italia Prize, 1957, for play, "The Dock Brief"; Writers Guild of Great Britain award for best original teleplay, 1969, for "Voyage Round My Father"; Golden Globe award nomination, 1970, for screenplay "John and Mary."

WRITINGS—Novels, except as indicated: Charade,

Lane, 1948; *Rumming Park*, Lane, 1949; *Answer Yes or No*, Lane, 1950, published as *Silver Hook*, Morrow, 1950; *Like Men Betrayed*, Collins, 1953, Lippincott, 1954; *Three Winters*, Collins, 1956; *Narrowing Stream*, Collins, 1956; (with first wife, Penelope Ruth Mortimer) *With Love and Lizards* (travel), M. Joseph, 1957.

Plays: *Three Plays: The Dock Brief; What Shall We Tell Caroline?*; [*and*] *I Spy*, Elek, 1958, Grove, 1962; *The Wrong Side of the Park* (three-act), Heinemann, 1960; *Lunch Hour, and Other Plays* (contains "Collect Your Hand Baggage," "David and Broccoli," and "Call Me a Liar"), Methuen, 1960; *Lunch Hour* (one-act), Samuel French, 1960; *What Shall We Tell Caroline?* (three-acts), Heinemann, 1960; *Collect Your Hand Baggage* (one-act), Samuel French, 1960; *I Spy*, Samuel French, 1960; *Two Stars for Comfort*, Methuen, 1962; *The Judge* (first produced in London at Cambridge Theatre, March 1, 1967), Methuen, 1967; (translator) Georges Feydeau, *A Flea in Her Ear: A Farce* (first produced in London at Old Vic Theatre, February 8, 1966), Samuel French, 1968.

(Translator) Georges Feydeau, *Cat Among the Pigeons* (three-act; first produced in Milwaukee at Milwaukee Repertory Theatre, November, 1971), Samuel French, 1970; *Five Plays* (contains "The Dock Brief," "What Shall We Tell Caroline?," "I Spy," "Lunch Hour," and "Collect Your Hand Baggage"), Methuen, 1970; *Come As You Are* (contains four one-act comedies, "Mill Hill," "Bermondsey," "Gloucester Road," and "Marble Arch"; first produced, under combined title, in London at New Theatre, January 27, 1970), Methuen, 1971; *A Voyage Round My Father* (first produced in New York at Greenwich Theatre, November 24, 1970), Methuen, 1971; (translator) Carl Zuckmayer, *The Captain of Koepenick* (first produced in London at Old Vic Theatre, March 9, 1971), Methuen, 1971; "I, Claudius" (two-acts; adapted from Robert Graves's novels *I, Claudius* and *Claudius the God*), first produced in London at Queen's Theatre, July 11, 1972; *Knightsbridge*, Samuel French, 1973; "Collaborators" (two-act), first produced in London at Duchess Theatre, April 17, 1973.

Also author of plays for television, including "Married Alive," produced by Columbia Broadcasting System, January 23, 1970; "Only Three Can Play," Independent Broadcasting Authority, June 6, 1970; "Alcock and Gander," Thames Television Ltd., June 5, 1972.

Author of film scripts, "Bunny Lake is Missing," released by Columbia Pictures, 1965; and "John and Mary," Twentieth Century-Fox, 1969; and of a scenario for ballet, "Home," 1968. Work represented in anthologies, including *English One-Act Plays of Today*, edited by Donald Fitzjohn, Oxford University Press, 1962.

SIDELIGHTS: Writing about *The Dock Brief*, Mortimer once said: " The play is intended as comedy, comedy being, to my mind, the only thing worth writing in this despairing age, provided the comedy is truly on the side of the lonely, the neglected, the unsuccessful, and plays its part in the war against established rules and against the imposing of an arbitrary code of behaviour upon individual and unpredictable human beings.

"There may, for all I know, be great and funny plays to be written about successful lawyers, brilliant criminals, wise schoolmasters, or families where the children can grow up without silence and without regret. There are many plays that show that the law is always majestic or that family life is simple and easy to endure. Speaking for myself I am not

on the side of such plays and a writer of comedy must choose his side with particular care. He cannot afford to aim at the defenseless, nor can he, like the more serious writer, treat any character with contempt."

Mortimer's translation of "A Flea in Her Ear" was produced at Expo 67 in Montreal and was the basis for the film released by Twentieth Century-Fox in 1968.†

*   *   *

MORTON, Henry W(alter)   1929-

PERSONAL: Born October 6, 1929, in Vienna, Austria; son of Frank and Rose (Ungvari) Morton; married Lois Wasserman (educator and author), September 12, 1956; children: Philip, Amy. *Education:* City College (now City College of the City University of New York), B.A., 1952; Columbia University, M.A., 1954, Ph.D., 1959. *Home:* 12 Francis Terrace, Glen Cove, N.Y. 11542. *Office:* Queen's College, Flushing, N.Y. 11367.

CAREER: City College of New York (now City College of the City University of New York), lecturer, 1955-60; Queens College, Flushing, N.Y., assistant professor, 1960-69, professor of political science, 1970—. Visited Soviet Union under Cultural Exchange Program, 1964. *Member:* American Political Science Association, American Association for the Advancement of Slavic Studies. *Awards, honors:* Fellowship, Inter-University Committee on Travel Grants, 1964.

WRITINGS: Soviet Sport, Mirror of Soviet Society, Collier, 1963; (contributor and editor with Peter Henry Juviler) *Soviet Policy-Making: Studies of Communism in Transition*, Praeger, 1967; *The U.S.S.R. and Eastern Europe*, Macmillan, 1971; (contributor and editor with Rudolf L. Tokes) *Soviet Politics and Society in the 1970's*, Free Press, 1974. Contributor of articles to *New Leader, Survey, Problems of Communism*, and *Columbia University Forum*.

WORK IN PROGRESS: Studies in comparative housing policies of industrialized societies.

*   *   *

MOSER, Reta C(arol)   1936-

PERSONAL: Born July 22, 1936, in Waterloo, Iowa; daughter of Merle Roosevelt and Elizabeth (Eighmey) Moser. *Education:* Southern Illinois University, B.S., 1958, graduate study; graduate study at University of California, Los Angeles, and University of Southern California, 1959. *Home:* 1129 Harrison Ave., Venice, Calif.

CAREER: Former newspaper editor and reporter in central and southern Illinois; free-lance technical writer, mainly in space industry field, California, 1958—. *Member:* Angels' Flight, Sigma Beta Gamma, Theta Sigma Phi.

WRITINGS: Space-Age Acronyms, Plenum, 1964, revised edition, 1969.

WORK IN PROGRESS: A compilation of technical designation systems; children's stories.

SIDELIGHTS: Ms. Moser told *CA*: "*Space-Age Acronyms* was the outgrowth of my wasting half a day and the time of many others trying to find the meaning of an acronym vital to a crash project." *Avocational interests:* Real estate, reading, hi-fi, three dogs, travel, people, daydreaming, and (when there is time) sleeping.

MOTT, George Fox 1907-

PERSONAL: Born June 4, 1907, in Riverside, Calif.; son of George F. (a merchant) and Alice Yolande (Way) Mott; married Dorothy Hale Williams, February 12, 1944; children: David Edward Way, Jonathan Loren Gould. *Education:* Stanford University, A.B., 1929, A.M., 1931; University of Minnesota, Ph.D., 1938. *Religion:* Protestant. *Home:* 3745 Kanawha St. N.W., Washington, D.C. 20015. *Office:* Dupont Circle Building, Washington, D.C. 20036.

CAREER: San Diego Army and Navy Academy and Junior College, San Diego, Calif., dean and head of English department, 1929-33; Emerson Junior College, Chicago, Ill., dean and teacher of political science, 1933-34; Hancher Organization (philanthropic fund-raising), Chicago, Ill., assistant to president, 1935-36; University of Minnesota, Minneapolis, vice-principal of University High School, 1936-38; New Mexico College of Agriculture and Mechanic Arts (now New Mexico State University), Las Cruces, dean of students and director of publicity, 1938-39; Griffhagen & Associates, Chicago, Ill., consultant, 1939-40; U.S. War Assets Administration, Washington, D.C., chief analyst and staff director of advisory council, 1946-48; Mott of Washington & Associates (management consultants), Washington, D.C., partner, 1948—, chairman of Mott Research group, 1954—. Adjunct professor of journalism, The American University, 1963-68; visiting summer professor at other universities. Special consultant, American-Korean Foundation, 1962-69; consultant, Office of the Chief of Military History, U.S. Army, 1970-71. *Military service:* U.S. Army Reserve, commissioned, 1928; on active duty, Inspector General's Department, 1940-46; ad interim active duty tours, 1949-63; became colonel; received Bronze Star with oak leaf clusters, Pacific Theater Medal with three battle stars, Commendation Medal.

MEMBER: American Institute of Management (charter member of presidents' council), National Defense Transportation Association, American Political Science Association, American Academy of Political and Social Science, Reserve Officers Association (national council member, 1958, 1959), Military Order of the World Wars (perpetual member and past commander), American Legion (past post commander), American-Korean Foundation (founding member), United Board for Christian Higher Education in Asia (member of board of directors; chairman), Greater Washington Council (chairman, 1970—) American Symphony Orchestra League, Phi Delta Kappa, Army and Navy Club. *Awards, honors:* National Defense Transportation Association Service Award, 1957; decorated by Republic of Korea, 1963; Educational Hall of Fame Wisdom Award, 1970.

WRITINGS: San Diego Politically Speaking, Frye and Smith, 1931; (with Harold M. Dee) *History of the Middle Ages*, Barnes & Noble, 1933, 4th edition, revised, 1950; (editor and principal author) *Survey of Journalism*, Barnes & Noble, 1937; *Housing of College Students in the United States*, privately printed, 1938; *A Training Approach to Public Personnel Classification*, privately printed, 1938; (contributor) Seba Eldridge, editor, *Development of Collective Enterprise*, University of Kansas Press, 1943.

(Editor and principal author) *New Survey of Journalism*, Barnes & Noble, 1950, 5th revised edition, 1963; *Teaching—A Dynamic Process, Its Operation and Supervisory Requirements in the Public Schools*, Florida State University Press, 1950; *Survey of United States Ports*, Arco, 1951; *Miami's Marine Destiny*, Mott of Washington & Associates, 1955; *Korea and Koreans* (monograph), American-Korean Foundation, 1960, revised edition, 1962.

Editor and contributor: *Fraternity Manual of Training and Practice*, two volumes, University of Minnesota Press, 1937; *The Plan—The Johnson Method of Training Infantry Soldiers for Combat*, privately printed, 1945; *Improved Method for Withdrawing Manpower from Industry*, privately printed, 1962; *Transportation Century*, Louisiana State University Press, 1967; *Historical Record and 50 Years Who's Who of Military Order of the World Wars*, Batt, Bates, 1969; (with Richard D. Lambert) *Urban Changes and the Planning Syndrome*, American Academy of Political and Social Science, 1973.

Author of "Military Engineering Series," seven manuals and handbooks, U.S. Government Printing Office, 1952-54. Writer of monographs and radio and television scripts. Contributor to *Encyclopedia of Modern Education* and *Collier's Encyclopedia*. Contributor of articles and reviews to *Washington Star, San Francisco Chronicle, Sacramento Bee, Korean Report*, and to educational, military and business journals.

WORK IN PROGRESS: As a Man Teaches, studies in comparative education; *Mass Media in Society—The Role of Contemporary Communication*; *International Public Relations—The Image We Create*; *New Korea—Eastern Legacy and Western Keystone*; (with Po Sung Kim) *The Korean Press*; *Busing—And The Equality of Ignorance*; *Under Our Command: The Search for Urban Reformation*. Also writing on college administration, manpower utilization and training, international politics, economic systems, educational programs in Latin America and the Far East.

SIDELIGHTS: Mott once said: "Although described in 1951 by a reviewer as 'by all odds, the most entertaining technical writer of our time,' my effort has been not so much to entertain as to avoid writing with such lack of spriteliness as to have to hide behind technical competence for readership."

* * *

MOUNT, Charles Merrill 1928-

PERSONAL: Born May 19, 1928, in New York, N.Y.; married Sarah Long; children: Judith, Charles Merrill, Paul Harris, Anna Sarah, Eva Sarah. *Education:* Studied at Columbia University, University of California, Los Angeles, and at Art Student's League, New York, N.Y. *Home:* 425 Beach 133 St., Bell Harbor, N.Y. 11694.

CAREER: Portrait painter. Corcoran Gallery of Art, Washington, D.C., European agent, 1963-64. Lecturer on art in United States and Europe. *Member:* Irish Portrait Society (Dublin; founder and president), The Burr Artists (president and director). *Awards, honors:* Guggenheim fellowship, 1956; research grant from Archives of American art, 1962.

WRITINGS: John Singer Sargent: A Biography, Norton, 1955, 3rd revised and expanded edition, Kraus Reprint Co., 1969; *Gilbert Stuart: A Biography*, Norton, 1964; *Monet: A Biography*, Simon & Schuster, 1967. Contributor of more than a hundred articles on artists and art to *New York Times, Irish Independent, Country Life, Art Quarterly*, other publications in United States, France, Ireland, and Spain. Reviewer of books on art.

WORK IN PROGRESS: An exposition of fraudulent importation and sale of paintings attributed to John Singer Sargent.

SIDELIGHTS: Mount has worked with the FBI investigating art forgeries.

* * *

MOUSSA, Pierre L(ouis) 1922-

PERSONAL: Born March 5, 1922, in Lyons, France; married Anne-Marie Trousseau, August 14, 1957. *Education:* Ecole Normale Superieure, Paris, France, student, 1940-45, agrege des lettres, 1943; further study at Institut d'Etudes Politiques de Paris; inspecteur des finances, 1946. *Home:* 27 rue de Constantine, Paris, France.

CAREER: Ministry of Overseas Territories, Paris, France, director of economic affairs and planification, 1954-59; Ministry of Public Works and Transport, Paris, France, director of civil aviation, 1959-62; World Bank, Washington, D.C., director of Africa department, 1962-64; French Federation of Insurance Companies, president, 1965-69; Banque de Paris and des Pays-Bas, president, 1969—. Professor of problems of underdeveloped countries, Institut d'Etudes Politiques de Paris, Paris, France, 1959—. *Member:* Association Francaise de Sciences Economiques. *Awards, honors:* Chevalier de la Legion d'Honneur.

WRITINGS: Les Chances Economiques de le Communaute franco-africaine, Armand Colin, 1957; *Les Nations Proletaires*, Presses Universitaires de France, 1959, translation by Alan Braley published as *The Underprivileged Nations*, Sidgwick & Jackson, 1962, Beacon, 1963; *L'Economie de la Zone Franc*, Presses Universitaires de France, 1960; *Les Etats-Unis et les nations proletairs*, Editions du Seuil, 1965.

SIDELIGHTS: Les Nations Proletaires has been translated into four other languages besides English.†

* * *

MROZEK, Slawomir 1930-

PERSONAL: Born June 26, 1930, in Borzecin, Poland; son of Antoni (a post office clerk) and Zofia (Keozior) Mrozek; married Maria Obremba, 1959. *Education:* Studied architecture, oriental culture, and painting, in Krakow, Poland, for a few semesters. *Home:* Ul. Piekarska 4/5, Warsaw, Poland.

CAREER: Worked as a caricaturist for various newspapers and magazines, and as a journalist, in Krakow, Poland. Full-time writer

WRITINGS: Polska w Obrazach, [Krakow], 1957; *Slon* (satire), Wydawnictwo Literackie (Krakow), 1958, translation by Konrad Syrop published as *The Elephant*, McDonald, 1962, Grove, 1963; *Wesele w Atomicach* (stories), Wydawnictwo Literackie, 1959; *Postepowiec*, Iskry (Warsaw), 1960; *Ucieczka na Poludnie* (novel), Iskry, 1961, 2nd edition, 1965; *Deszcz* (stories), Wydawnictwo Literackie, 1962; *Opowiadania* (stories), Wydawnictwo Literackie, 1964; *Utwory Sceniczne* (plays), Wydawnictwo Literackie, 1964; *Six Plays*, Grove, 1967; *Prez Okulary Slawomira Mrozka*, Iskry, 1968; *The Ugupu Bird*, Macdonald, 1968; *Dwa listy i inne Opowiadania*, Instytut Literacki, 1970; *Vatzlav: A Play in 77 Scenes*, Grove, 1970; *Three Plays*, Grove, 1972.

Plays: "Policja," 1958; "Meczenstwo Piotra O'Heya," 1959; "Indyk," 1961; "Na Pelnym Morzu," 1962; "Karol," 1962; "Striptease," 1962; "Zabawa," 1962; "Kynolog w Rozterce," 1962; "Czarowna Noc," 1962; "Smierc Prucznika," 1963; "Tango," 1964.

WORK IN PROGRESS: Short stories and plays.

SIDELIGHTS: Mrozek's German publisher describes him as a thin, quiet man, gentle-voiced, withdrawn, rarely smiling. Mrozek, who is mentioned in most analyses of contemporary Polish literature as a notable talent, views his position as an author thus: "The more I travel around and speak in different countries with . . . those who know about the literary situation and the present and future possibilities, the greater becomes my self-confidence. I do not hope for any brilliant, thundering, effective public career, but the chance remains for a less sensational but solid position, and, more important in my opinion, for continuously growing success."

While living in Paris, Mrozek became a stateless person when his passport was cancelled by the Polish government for his outspoken opposition to his country's policy concerning the 1968 Soviet invasion of Czechoslovakia.

Translations of his various works have been published in the United States, and in all the European languages except Portuguese and Greek.

He is fluent in English, French, Italian, and Russian.

BIOGRAPHICAL/CRITICAL SOURCES: Carolyn Riley, editor, *Contemporary Literary Criticism*, Gale, Volume III, 1975.†

* * *

MUDD, Emily Hartshorne 1898-

PERSONAL: Born September 6, 1898, in Merion, Pa.; daughter of Edward Yarnall and Clementina (Rhodes) Hartshorne; married Stuart Mudd, September 12, 1922; children: Emily Borie (Mrs. James Mitchell), Stuart Harvey, Margaret Clark, John Hodgen. *Education:* University of Pennsylvania, M.S.W., 1936, Ph.D., 1950. *Home:* 734 Millbrook Lane, Haverford, Pa. *Office:* Room 1023, 1000 Courtyard Bldg., University Hospital, 34th and Spruce Sts., Philadelphia, Pa. 19104.

CAREER: Marriage Council of Philadelphia, Philadelphia, Pa., director, 1936-66, consultant to board of directors, 1967—; University of Pennsylvania Medical School, Philadelphia, assistant professor, 1952-56, professor of family study in psychiatry, 1956-67, professor emeritus, 1967—. Lecturer at Temple University and other universities in Philadelphia area, 1940-55; member of faculty for resident training program in neuropsychiatry, U.S. Veterans Administration (Philadelphia, Pa.), 1947-64. Principal investigator of research and training projects for U.S. Public Health Service, 1947-55, Commonwealth of Pennsylvania, 1955—, National Institute of Mental Health, 1964—; associate director, Continuing Education, Reproductive Biology Research Foundation (St. Louis, Mo.), 1970-72; co-chairman (appointed by Governor Sharp), Pennsylvania Abortion Law Commission, 1972-73. Member of family life advisory committee, Public Affairs Committee (New York), 1937—; consultant to U.S. Department of Health, Education and Welfare, 1956-58, Family Service Association of America, 1959-61; vice-chairman of Advisory Council on Alcohol, Pennsylvania Department of Health, 1963—; consultant to Division of Human Reproduction, Behavioral Sciences, Department of Obstetrics and Gynecology, School of Medicine, University of Pennsylvania, 1970—. Member of board of National Council on Family Relations, 1963—, Sex Information Education Council of the United States, 1964.

MEMBER: American Association of Marriage Counselors (fellow; vice-president 1950-52; president, 1952-54), American Association of Psychiatric Social Workers, American Association of Social Workers, American Group Psychotherapy Association, American Orthopsychiatric Association, American Sociological Association (fellow), Social Science Research Council, Social Work Research Group, Society for the Scientific Study of Sex, Academy of Social Workers, Royal Society for Promotion of Health (London), World Academy of Arts and Sciences (fellow), Delaware Valley Group Psychotherapy Society, University of Pennsylvania Women's Faculty Club (president, 1962-63), Cosmopolitan Club (Philadelphia). *Awards, honors:* Gimbel Philadelphia Award, 1958; named Pennsylvania Mother of the Year, 1961; woman of the year award, Women's Division, American Friends of the Hebrew University, 1965; Second Annual Award of the Philadelphia Society of Clinical Psychologists, 1968; honorary fellow, College of Physicians of Philadelphia, 1973. Honorary D.Sc., Hobart and William Smith College, 1958, and University of Pennsylvania, 1972; D.H.L., Washington and Jefferson College, 1973. Recipient of numerous other awards.

WRITINGS: The Practice of Marriage Counseling, Association Press, 1951; (contributor) Arthur Robert Olsen, editor, *Readings on Marriage and Family Relations*, Stackpole, 1953; (with Howard E. Mitchell and Sara B. Taubin) *Success in Family Living*, Association Press, 1955; (editor with A. M. Krich) *Man and Wife: A Sourcebook on Family Attitudes, Sexual Behavior and Marriage Counseling*, Norton, 1957; (editor with Abraham Stone, Maurice J. Karpf, and Janet F. Nelson) *Marriage Counseling: A Casebook*, Association Press, 1958; (editor with Robert C. Leslie) *Professional Growth for Clergymen: Through Supervised Training in Marriage Counseling and Family Problems*, Abingdon, 1970. Contributor to magazines and professional journals. Editor, "Public Affairs Pamphlets," 1960—. *Marriage and Family Living*, 1962-64.

*   *   *

MUELLER, Charles S(teinkamp) 1929-

PERSONAL: Born April 6, 1929, in Springfield, Ill.; son of Walter H. (an advertising man) and Aurelia (Steinkamp) Mueller; married Audrey Mae Prange, January 28, 1953; children: Sarah, Charles, Jr., Amy, Juliane. *Education:* St. John's College, Winfield, Kan., student, 1947-49; Concordia Seminary, St. Louis, Mo., B.D. and Ecclesiastical Diploma, 1953. *Home:* 3808 Littleton St., Silver Spring, Md. *Office:* Lutheran Church of St. Andrew, 12247 Georgia Ave., Silver Spring, Md.

CAREER: Lutheran Church of St. Andrew, Silver Spring, Md., pastor, 1957—. *Military service:* U.S. Air Force Reserve, chaplain with current rank of captain. *Member:* Kiwanis Club.

WRITINGS: God's Wonderful World of Words: Devotions for Families With Children Ages 9-13, Concordia, 1963; *The Christian Family Prepares for Christmas*, Concordia, 1965; *The Strategy of Evangelism: A Primer for Congregational Evangelism Committees*, Concordia, 1965; *What's This I Hear About Our Church: An Action Guide for Congregation Leaders*, Augsburg, 1974.

WORK IN PROGRESS: Wanted Men, a book on evangelism; two other devotional works.†

*   *   *

MUELLER, Gerald F(rancis) 1927-
(Brother Roberto)

PERSONAL: Born March 8, 1927, in Hillsboro, N.D.; son of Alvin F. (a farmer) and Agnes (Hanrahan) Mueller. *Education:* University of Notre Dame, A.B., 1950; VanderCook College of Music, Chicago, Ill., M.M.Ed., 1959. *Home:* 323 West Woodlawn Ave., San Antonio, Tex. 78212.

CAREER: Entered Congregatio Sanctae Crucis (Brothers of the Holy Cross), 1945; Catholic High School, teacher and band director in Long Beach, Calif., 1950-55, and New Orleans, La., 1955-64; Notre Dame High School, Sherman Oaks, Calif., teacher of English, Latin, and religion, and band director, 1964-68; Holy Cross High School, San Antonio, Tex., music director, 1969—. Author of biographies for young people, 1953—. Past president of "Mastersingers" chorale of San Antonio Symphony. *Member:* Texas Music Educators.

WRITINGS—All biographies; all under name Brother Roberto and published by Dujarie Press, except as noted: *The Man Who Limped to Heaven: St. Ignatius Loyola*, 1954; *I Serve the King: St. Francis Borgia*, 1954; *The Martyr Laughed: Father Pro of Mexico*, 1954, new edition, under name Gerald F. Mueller, published as *With Life and Laughter: The Life of Miguel Agustin Pro*, 1969; *Music from the Hunger Pit: Fr. Maximilian Kolbe*, 1954; *The Soldier Died Twice: St. Sebastian*, 1955; *I Saw an Angel: St. Frances of Rome*, 1955; *Kitty Come Quickly: Mother McAuley*, 1955; *A Crown for the Butcher's wife: Blessed Margaret Clitherow*, 1955; *The Flame Still Burns: St. Margaret of Cortona*, 1956; *The Girl Who Laughed at Satan: St. Rose of Lima*, 1956; *Now Comes the Hangman: Blessed Oliver Plunkett*, 1956; *Peter Laughed at Pain: St. Peter Alcantara*, 1956; *Angel of the Ragpickers: Father Lamy*, 1956; *A Torch in the Darkness: St. John Capistran*, 1956; *The Rock Cannot be Moved: Blessed Pope Innocent XI*, 1957; *The Family That Never Died: St. Felicitas and Seven Sons*, 1957; *The Heart in the Desert: Charles de Foucauld*, 1957; *With Fire, Sword and Whips: St. Andrew Bobola*, 1957; *A Tomb for the Living: Fr. Maximilian Kolbe* (high school level), 1957; *Dawn Brings Glory: Fr. Pro of Mexico*, 1957; *Trial by Torture: St. John Nepomucene* (high school level), 1957; *Our Lady Comes to New Orleans*, 1957; *The Broken Lamp: Edith Stein*, 1957; *The King's Trumpeter: St. Vincent Ferrar*, 1957; *Secrets of the Silent Tongue: St. John Nepomucene*, 1957; *A Crown for the School Boy: St. John Berbhmans*, 1957; *The Girl Who Worked Wonders: Philomena*, 1958; *No Tears for the Bride: St. Perpetua*, 1958; *Flames for the Bride: St. Agnes*, 1958; *The Brave Never Die: Frederic Ozanam*, 1958; *The Forgotten Madonna* (high school level), 1958; *Don't Turn Back: St. Ignatius Loyola* (high school level), 1958; *Out of the Darkness: Louis Martin* (high school level), 1958; *A King Without a Crown: St. Wenceslaus*, 1958; *And the Thunder Roared: St. Norbert*, 1958; *Follow the Setting Sun: Columbus*, 1959; *Please Bring the Children: Blessed Elizabeth Ann Seton*, 1959; *A Search for the Shepherd: Father Paul of Graymoor*, 1959; *No Wings for Nine Angels: Zelie Martin*, 1959; *Lead My Sheep: Pope John XXIII*, 1959; *Face in the Flames: St. Bridget of Sweden*, 1959; *More Than Money Can Buy: Mother Katherine Drexel*, 1959; *No Jewels for Jane: St. Jane de Chantal*, 1959; *There Are No Bad Boys: Father Flanagan of Boy's Town*, 1959; *We Sail at Dawn: Magellan*, 1959; *The Merry Watch Maker: Louis Martin*, 1959; *The Man Who Tamed a Monster: Andre Ampere*, 1959.

Stairway to the Stars: St. Germaine of Pibrac, 1960; *Cry Mutiny!: Magellan* (high school level), 1960; *Let Edward be King: St Edward the Confessor*, 1960; *So Much for So*

Many: St. Margaret of Scotland, 1960; *Throw Him to the Lions: St. Cyprian*, 1960; *Blue Angels with White Hats: St. Louise de Marillac*, 1960; *Tell My People: St. Bridget of Sweden* (high school level), 1960; *Miracles for the Asking: St. Germaine of Pibrac* (high school level), 1960; *Let Him Live: St. John Gaulbert*, 1960; *Break Down the Doors!: Pope Pius VII*, 1961; *A Rose for Rita: St. Rita of Cascia*, 1961; *My Friends, the Bandits: St. Paul of the Cross*, 1961; *A Light on the Mountain: St. Paul of the Cross* (high school level), 1961; *Man Without Fear: de Soto*, 1961; *The Rambling Rebel: John Banister Tabb*, 1961; *I Come to Conquer: Pizzaro*, 1961; *The Sea Is My Highway: Vasco de Gama*, 1961; *A Roar from the Cave: St. Jerome*, 1961; *The Ax Must Fall: St. John Fisher*, 1961; *Prince on a Galloping Horse: St. Charles Borromeo*, 1961; *Treasures at My Fingertips: Louis Braille*, 1962; *I Fight for Freedom: Thaddeus Kosciuszko*, 1962; *Let There Be Radio: Marconi*, 1962; *Who Will Believe Me?: Marco Polo*, 1962; *The Great Mistake: John and Sebastian Cabot*, 1962; *Lion of Bethlehem: St. Jerome* (high school level), 1962; *Hide the Children!: St. Bernard*, 1962; *King of Colors: Fra Angelico*, 1962; *Let Them Sing: Charles Gounod*, 1962; *Don't Push!: Cesar Franck*, 1962; *Drop the Dagger: St. Anthony Claret*, 1962; *The Killer Comes: St. Anthony Claret* (high school level), 1962; *Music for Millions: Paderewski*, 1962; *The Golden Gift: Rubens*, 1962; *No More Shall I Wander: von Weber*, 1962; *He Walks with Giants: Botticelli*, 1962; *The Girl and the Grotto: St. Bernadette*, 1966; *Boy in a Hurry: Dominic Savio*, 1966; (under name Gerald F. Mueller) *Martin Luther King, Jr., Civil Rights Leader*, Denison, 1971.

WORK IN PROGRESS: A biography of St. Germaine of Pibrac, for adults; other junior biographies of Camille Corot, Millet, Delacroix, Correggio, Rossini, and Blessed Therese.

*   *   *

MUIR, (Charles) Augustus (Austin Moore)

PERSONAL: Son of Walter (a clergyman) and Elizabeth (Carlow) Muir; married Jean Murray Dow Walker. *Education:* University of Edinburgh, M.A. *Politics:* Generally right-wing. *Religion:* Church of Scotland. *Home:* Parkhill, Stansted Mountfitchet, Essex, England.

CAREER: Author. *World*, London, England, former assistant editor and editor. Royal Scots, regimental historian. *Military service:* Royal Scots and King's Own Scottish Borderers, 1914-19. *Member:* Savage Club, Saintsbury Club (both London); Scottish Arts Club, Royal Scots Club (both Edinburgh).

WRITINGS: The Third Warning, Bobbs-Merrill, 1925; *The Blue Bonnet*, Bobbs-Merrill, 1926; *The Black Pavilion*, Methuen, 1926 published as *The Ace of Danger*, Bobbs-Merrill, 1927; *The Shadow on the Left*, Bobbs-Merrill, 1928; *The Silent Partner*, Methuen, 1929, Bobbs-Merrill, 1930; (under pseudonym Austin Moore) *Birds of the Night*, Hodder & Stoughton, 1930, Richard Smith, 1931; *Beginning the Adventure*, Methuen, 1932 published as *The Dark Adventure*, Putnam, 1933; (under pseudonym Austin Moore) *The House of Lies*, Hodder & Stoughton, 1932, Doubleday, 1933; *The Green Lantern*, Methuen, 1933; *The Riddle of Garth*, Methuen, 1933; *Scotland's Road of Romance*, Methuen, 1934; *Raphael M.D.*, Methuen, 1935; *The Crimson Crescent*, Methuen, 1935; *Satyr Mask*, Methuen, 1936; *The Bronze Door*, Methuen, 1936; *The Red Carnation*, Methuen, 1937; *The Man Who Stole the Crown Jewels*, Methuen, 1937; *Castles in the Air*, Methuen, 1938.

The Intimate Thoughts of John Baxter, Bookseller, Methuen, 1942; *Joey and the Greenwings*, M. Joseph, 1943; *Heather-Track and High Road*, Methuen, 1944; (co-editor) *George Saintsbury: The Memorial Volume*, Methuen, 1945 published as *Saintsbury Miscellany*, Oxford University Press, 1947; *Scottish Portrait*, Hopetoun Press, 1948; (co-editor) *A Last Vintage*, Methuen, 1950; *The Story of Jesus*, Odhams, 1952, Greystone, 1953; (editor) *How to Choose and Enjoy Wine*, Odhams, 1953; *Candlelight in Avalon*, Bles, 1954; *John White C. H.* (official biography), Hodder & Stoughton, 1958; *The First of Foot* (history of the Royal Scots), Blackwood, 1961.

Industrial histories: *The Fife Coal Company*, Heffer, 1953; *The Shotts Iron Company*, Heffer, 1954; *Nairns of Kirkaldy*, Heffer, 1956; *75 Years: The History of Smith's Stamping Works and Smith-Clayton Forge*, privately printed, 1958; *Blyth, Greene, Jourdain*, Newman Neame, 1963; *Churchill & Sim*, Newman Neame, 1963; *The Kenyon Tradition*, Heffer, 1964; *In Blackburne Valley: The History of Bowers Mills*, Heffer, 1969; *The History of the British Paper and Board Makers Association*, Heffer, 1972.

WORK IN PROGRESS: History of United Dominions Trust.

*   *   *

MUIRHEAD, Ian A(dair)   1913-

PERSONAL: Born August 16, 1913, in Falkirk, Stirlingshire, Scotland; son of John (a clergyman) and Isabel (Cumming) Muirhead; married Margaret Knox Napier, July 12, 1940; children: John Ninian Adair, Robin James Napier, Andrew Thomas Napier. *Education:* University of Glasgow, M.A. (first class honors), 1934, B.D. (with distinction), 1937. *Home:* 9 Hillhead St., Glasgow G12, Scotland.

CAREER: Minister of Church of Scotland (Presbyterian), 1937—. Parish minister of St. James' Church, Forfar, Scotland, 1940-48, of Brandon Church, Motherwell, Scotland, 1948-64; University of Glasgow, Glasgow, Scotland, lecturer, 1964-73, senior lecturer in ecclesiastical history, 1973—. Trinity College, Glasgow, Scotland, Kerr Lecturer, 1960-63. Church of Scotland, honorary secretary of Panel on Doctrine, 1960—, member of Special Commission on Baptism, Special Committee on Religious Education, and Committee on Anglican-Presbyterian Relations. *Member:* Society for the Study of Theology, Scottish Church History Society (vice-president).

WRITINGS: Education in the New Testament, Association Press, 1965. Contributor of articles and reviews to *Innes Review*, *Scottish Journal of Theology*, and other journals.

WORK IN PROGRESS: Research in the Scottish Church in the fifteenth and sixteenth century, and in Andrew Melville, the Presbyterian eldership, and Moody and Sankey's Scottish campaigns.

AVOCATIONAL INTERESTS: Archaeology, family history.

*   *   *

MULGREW, Peter David   1927-

PERSONAL: Born November 21, 1927; son of William John and Edith Mulgrew; married June Anderson, September 20, 1952; children: Robyn Mary, Susan Elisabeth. *Education:* Royal Naval College, Greenwich, England, A.M., I.R.E. *Home:* 50 Bay View Rd., Browns Bay, Auckland, New Zealand.

CAREER: With Royal New Zealand Navy as electrical officer, now lieutenant (retired); Pye Electronics Ltd., Auckland, New Zealand, manager of telecommunications division; Abilities Inc., director. *Member:* Royal Geographical Society (fellow). *Awards, honors*—Military: British Empire Medal, Polar Medal.

WRITINGS: No Place for Men, A. H. & A. W. Reed, 1964, published as *I Hold the Heights*, Doubleday, 1965.

WORK IN PROGRESS: Research on Antarctica.†

* * *

MUNK, Arthur W. 1909-

PERSONAL: Born April 26, 1909, in Kingsbury, Tex.; son of Walter Herman and Lydia (Stautzenberger) Munk; married Margaret Caldwell, June 10, 1933; children: Joe Byron. *Education:* Southwestern University, Georgetown, Tex., B.A., 1931; Southern Methodist University, B.D., 1933; Boston University, Ph.D., 1945. *Politics:* Independent ("in protest against bombings in Viet Nam I left the Democratic Party"). *Home:* 1216 East Porter St., Albion, Mich. 49224. *Office:* Albion College, Albion, Mich. 49224.

CAREER: Ordained Methodist minister, 1933; pastor of churches in Texas, 1933-42, and Massachusetts, 1942-46; Wesley College (affiliate of University of North Dakota), Grand Forks, N.D., associate professor of religion, 1946-51; Albion College, Albion, Mich., associate professor, 1951-60, professor of philosophy, 1960-69, professor of philosophy and resident scholar, 1969—, chairman of philosophy department, 1951-69. *Member:* International Social Science Society, Society for Asian and Comparative Philosophy, American Philosophical Association, American Association of University Professors, Metaphysical Society of America, Religious Education Association, Detroit Methodist Conference. *Awards, honors:* Distinguished Alumnus Award, Southwestern University, Georgetown, Texas, 1972.

WRITINGS: History and God, Ronald, 1952; *A Way of Survival*, Bookman Associates, 1954; *Perplexing Problems of Religion*, Bethany, 1954; (contributor) Edwin P. Booth, editor, *Religion Ponders Science*, Appleton, 1964; *A Synoptic Philosophy of Education*, Abingdon, 1965; *Roy Wood Sellars as Creative Thinker and Critic*, Sadhna Prakashan (Meerut, India), 1972. Contributor of articles and reviews to journals and newspapers, including *Philosophical Forum, Christian Century, Personalist, Hibbert Journal, Calcutta Review, Journal of Bible and Religion, Ethics, Michigan Christian Advocate, Religious Education, Social Science*, and *Philosophy & Phenomenological Research*.

WORK IN PROGRESS: The Riddle of Existence.

SIDELIGHTS: Munk told *CA*, "My philosophy is life-centered and personalistic rather than formalistic or purely academic. Moreover, I am deeply interested in the problem of world peace—indeed, I have been working for peace for over thirty years. During the Second World War, I was persecuted for my pacifism—a pacifism which is both realistic and idealistic.

"Although I am a conscientious objector, I am as much against the New Left as I am against the old Right. In short, I take a *moderate, middle of the road position . . .* The greatest danger to America today is a *strong rightist reaction* against the extremes of the *irrational* New Left. We need *reason* and *sanity.*"

* * *

MUNTZ, (Isabelle) Hope 1907-

PERSONAL: Born July 8, 1907, in Toronto, Ontario, Canada; daughter of Rupert Gustavus and Lucy Elsie (Muntz) Muntz. *Education:* Attended private schools, Central School of Arts and Crafts, and Westminster Polytechnic in England, and School of Art, Toronto, Ontario. *Politics:* "Confused!" *Religion:* Roman Catholic. *Address:* c/o Chatto & Windus Ltd., 40 William IV St., London W2, England.

CAREER: Set out to be an artist, and practiced commercial art and journalism as a free-lance; has done aircraft, precision engineering, office, and civil defense work. Historical researcher, writer, and artist. *Member:* Royal Historical Society (fellow), Society of Antiquaries of London (fellow), Historical Association, Ancient Monuments Society (fellow), Battle Historical Society (vice-president; honorary life member), Kent Archaeological Society, Sussex Archaeological Society, East Yorkshire Archaeological Society, University Women's Club (London; associate member).

WRITINGS: The Golden Warrior, Chatto & Windus, 1948, Scribner, 1949; *Battles for the Crown*, Chatto & Windus, 1966; (editor with Catherine Morton) *The Carmen de Hastingae Proelio of Guy Bishop of Amiens*, Clarendon Press, 1972. Contributor of articles to *Graya* and book reviews to other periodicals. Wrote a libretto from *The Golden Warrior*. Also author of script for documentary film *"The Norman Conquest in the Bayeux Tapestry."*

WORK IN PROGRESS: Historical research for nonfiction work with E. Morton; a revision of *The Golden Warrior*.

* * *

MUNZ, Peter 1921-

PERSONAL: Born May 12, 1921, in Chemnitz, Germany; married Keelah Anne Vickerman (a painter); children: Jacob. *Education:* University of Canterbury, Christchurch, New Zealand, M.A., 1944; Cambridge University, Ph.D., 1948. *Home:* 128 Ohiro Rd., Wellington, New Zealand.

CAREER: Victoria University of Wellington, Wellington, New Zealand, senior lecturer, 1948-61, associate professor, 1961-66, professor of history, 1966—.

WRITINGS: The Place of Hooker in the History of Thought, Routledge & Kegan Paul, 1952; *Problems of Religious Knowledge*, S.C.M. Press, 1959; *The Origin of the Carolingian Empire*, Leicester University Press, 1959; *Relationship and Solitude*, Wesleyan University Press, 1964; *Frederick Barbarossa: A Study in Medieval Politics*, Eyre & Spottiswoode, 1969; *Life in the Age of Charlemagne*, Batsford, 1969; *The Concept of the Middle Ages as a Sociological Category*, Victoria University (Wellington, New Zealand), 1969; (editor) *The Feel of Truth*, A. H. & A. W. Reed for Victoria University, 1969; (contributor) F. Heer, editor, *Milestones of History*, Volume II, Weidenfeld & Nicolson, 1970; *Reflections on the Theory of Revolution in France*, Victoria University, 1972; (with G. Ellis) *Boso's Life of Pope Alexander III*, Basil Blackwell, 1973; *When the Golden Bough Breaks: Structuralism of Typology*, Routledge & Kegan Paul, 1973. Contributor to *English Historical Review, American Historical Review, Philosophical Quarterly, History and Theory, Journal of Religious History*, and other journals.

WORK IN PROGRESS: Two books on the philosophy of history, *Time Into History* and *Incest, Gresham's Law, and the Fear of Judgement.*

* * *

MURDOCH, (Jean) Iris 1919-

PERSONAL: Born July 15, 1919, in Dublin, Ireland; daughter of Wills John Hughes and Irene Alice (Richardson) Murdoch; married John Oliver Bayley (novelist, poet, critic), 1956. *Education:* Somerville College, Oxford, awarded degree, 1942; Newman College, Cambridge, Sarah Smithson studentship in philosophy, 1947-48. *Home:* Cedar Lodge, Steeple Aston, Oxfordshire, England.

CAREER: Assistant principal with British Treasury, 1942-44; administrative officer with United Nations Relief and Rehabilitation Administration (UNRRA), London, Belgium, and Austria, 1944-46; St. Anne's College, Oxford, fellow, 1948-63, honorary fellow, 1963—, also university lecturer in philosophy. Lecturer at Royal College of Art, 1963-67. Member of Formetor Prize Committee.

WRITINGS—Novels; all published by Viking, except as noted: *Under the Net,* 1954, published with introduction and notes by Dorothy Jones, Longmans, Green, 1966; *The Flight From the Enchanter,* 1956; *The Sandcastle,* 1957; *The Bell,* 1958; *A Severed Head,* 1961; *An Unofficial Rose,* 1962; *The Unicorn,* 1963; *The Italian Girl,* 1964; *The Red and the Green,* 1965; *The Time of the Angels,* 1966; *The Nice and the Good,* 1968; *Bruno's Dream,* 1969; *A Fairly Honourable Defeat,* 1970; *An Accidental Man,* 1971; *The Black Prince,* 1973; *The Sacred and Profane Love Machine,* 1974.

Nonfiction: *Sartre: Romantic Rationalist,* Yale University Press, 1953; (contributor) *The Nature of Metaphysics,* Macmillan, 1957; (author of foreword) Wendy Campbell-Purdie and Fenner Brockaway, *Woman against the Desert,* Gollancz, 1964; *The Sovereignty of Good over Other Concepts* (Leslie Stephen lecture, 1967), Cambridge University Press, 1967, published with other essays as *The Sovereignty of Good,* Routledge & Kegan Paul, 1970, Schocken, 1971.

Plays: (Author of adaptation, with J. B. Priestley) *A Severed Head* (three-act; based on her novel; first produced in London at Royale Theatre, October 28, 1964; produced in New York, 1964), Chatto & Windus, 1964, acting edition, Samuel French, 1964; (author of adaptation, with James Saunders) *The Italian Girl* (based on her novel; first produced at Bristol Old Vic, December, 1967), Samuel French, 1968; *The Three Arrows* [and] *The Servants and the Snow* (both original plays; *The Servants and the Snow* first produced in London at Greenwich Theatre, September 29, 1970; *The Three Arrows* first produced in Cambridge at Arts Theatre, October 17, 1972), Chatto & Windus, 1973, Viking, 1974.

Contributor to periodicals in United States and Great Britain, including *Listener, Yale Review, Chicago Review, Encounter, New Statesman, Nation,* and *Partisan Review.*

SIDELIGHTS: William Van O'Connor believes that "Miss Murdoch is a kind of twentieth-century Congreve. Her characters are interesting puppets and interesting symbols, and she can make them dance or place them erect in an eerie green light. An intellectual game is going on. . . . The real game is between Miss Murdoch and her reader, not between the reader and the characters. This is her strength and her limitation."

She is one of the most accomplished of contemporary novelists. Her prose, writes James Gindin, is "rich, imagistic, highly suggestive." Her novels have found favor with most critics, although John Bowen in the *New York Times* writes that "her books are meringues—skillfully confected, delightful to eat, and not meant for nourishment." Mentioned at times as part of the Wain-Amis school, she once said: "I don't think we have any tenets in common, except being all left-wing. I belong to a slightly older generation than Wain and Amis, which gives even our politics a different flavor."

The human situations she portrays are similar to those found in the novels and plays of Jean-Paul Sartre. Notes O'Connor: "Man, a lonely creature in an absurd world, is impelled to make moral decisions, the consequences of which are uncertain. Unlike Sartre, however, Miss Murdoch can create living characters. . . . And she has what Sartre lacks completely, a sense of humor." A sense of mystery also pervades her existentialism. In a review of *The Italian Girl,* *Harper's* wrote: "She is primarily interested in prescientific dimensions of experience, in magic and enchantment and possession. In the best of her work the predictable everyday world offers at most a kind of surface tension that will bear up only those who are extraordinarily light and sure of foot; one misstep and it's down, down into depths and abysses where the light is strange and the distances are immeasurable and unblinking creatures float slowly by without a sound. Or eat you up."

"A Severed Head" (based on her novel and play), was filmed by Columbia Pictures, 1971; the film rights to *A Fairly Honourable Defeat* were sold in 1972.

BIOGRAPHICAL/CRITICAL SOURCES: Kenneth Allsop, *The Angry Decade,* P. Owen, 1958; James Gindin, *Postwar British Fiction,* University of California Press, 1962; William Van O'Connor, *The New University Wits, and the End of Modernism,* Southern Illinois University Press, 1963; *Times Literary Supplement,* September 10, 1964; *New York Times Book Review,* September 13, 1964; *Books and Bookmen,* October, 1964, April, 1971; *Harper's,* October, 1964; *Critique,* Volume X, number 1, and spring, 1964; Richard Kostelanetz, editor, *On Contemporary Literature,* Avon, 1964; A. S. D. Byatt; *Degrees of Freedom,* Barnes & Noble, 1965; Peter Wolfe, *The Disciplined Heart,* University of Missouri Press, 1966; Rubin Rabinowitz, *Iris Murdoch,* Columbia University Press, 1968; *Shenandoah,* winter, 1968; *Listener,* April 4, 1968; Carolyn Riley, editor, *Contemporary Literary Criticism,* Volume IV, Gale, 1975.†

* * *

MURPHEY, Robert W(entworth) 1916-

PERSONAL: Born October 4, 1916, in Winfield, Kan.; son of J. Ernest and Pearle (Wentworth) Murphey; married Betty L. Reick, 1952; children: Gregory. *Education:* DePauw University, B.A., 1936; Washington State University graduate student, 1936-37. *Home:* 735 Foxdale Ave., Winnetka, Ill.

CAREER: World Book Encyclopedia, Chicago, Ill., department editor, 1946-47; U.S. Army, Austria, intelligence staff member, 1948-50; Consolidated Book Publishers, Chicago, Ill., editor-in-chief, 1950-57; J. J. Little & Ives Co. Inc., New York, N.Y., editorial director, 1957-60; Encyclopaedia Britannica, Inc., Chicago, Ill., managing editor, *Britannica Book of the Year,* 1960-63; now owner of travel agency. *Military service:* U.S. Naval Reserve, 1941-46; became lieutenant. *Member:* Society of Midland Authors, Cliff Dwellers Club (Chicago).

WRITINGS: (Contributor) G. B. de Huszar, editor, *Soviet Power and Policy*, Crowell, 1955; (compiler) *How and Where to Look It Up*, McGraw, 1958; *Travel Agency Ownership and Operation*, McGraw, 1975.

WORK IN PROGRESS: Revision of *How and Where to Look it Up*.

* * *

MURPHY, Earl Finbar 1928-

PERSONAL: Born November 1, 1928, in Indianapolis, Ind.; son of Joseph Finbar (a builder) and Carroll (Cox) Murphy. *Education:* Butler University, A.B. (magna cum laude), 1949, M.A., 1954; Indiana University, J.D. (with high distinction), 1952; Yale University, LL.M., 1955, J.S.D., 1959. *Politics:* Democrat. *Religion:* Unitarian. *Office:* College of Law, Ohio State University, 1659 North High St., Columbus, Ohio 43210.

CAREER: Admitted to Indiana bar, 1952. Earl R. Cox & Associates (attorneys), Indianapolis, Ind., general practice of law, 1952-54; State University of New York, Harpur College (now State University of New York at Binghamton), assistant professor of law and jurisprudence, 1955-57; Temple University, School of Law, Philadelphia, Pa., assistant professor, 1958-60, associate professor, 1960-65, professor, 1965-69; Ohio State University, College of Law, professor, 1969—. Member of board, Messiah Universalist Home for the Aged, 1962-64; vice-chairman, Council of Liberal Churches of the Delaware Valley, 1963-65; board member, Joseph Priestly House for the Aged, 1966-69; chairman, Ohio Environmental Board of Review, 1972-74.

MEMBER: American Society for Legal History (secretary, 1957-59; treasurer, 1959-60), International Law Association, International Legal Philosophy Association, American Bar Association, Inter-American Bar Association, Indiana Bar Association, Societe d'Histoire de Droit de francais et etrangers.

WRITINGS: *Water Purity: A Study in the Legal Control of Natural Resources*, University of Wisconsin Press, 1961; *Governing Nature*, Quadrangle Books, 1967; *Man and His Environment: Law*, Harper, 1971. Assistant editor, *American Journal of Legal History*, 1959-69, acting editor, 1963-64.

WORK IN PROGRESS: General study in the legal control of the life-cycle resources (water, soil, air, trees, grass).

* * *

MURPHY, Francis 1932-

PERSONAL: Born March 13, 1932, in Springfield, Mass.; son of Frank E. and Sarah (O'Connor) Murphy. *Education:* American International College, B.A., 1953; University of Connecticut, M.A., 1955; Harvard University, Ph.D., 1960. *Home:* 7 Tekoa Ter., Westfield, Mass.

CAREER: Smith College, Northampton, Mass., professor of English language and literature, 1959—.

WRITINGS—Editor: *Poetry: Form and Structure*, Heath, 1964; *Diary of Edward Taylor*, Connecticut Valley Historical Society, 1964; *Major American Poets*, Heath, 1967; *Penguin Critical Anthologies: Walt Whitman*, Penguin, 1969; *Edwin Arlington Robinson*, Prentice-Hall, 1970; *Uncollected Essays of Yvor Winters*, Swallow Press, 1973; *Complete Poems of Walt Whitman*, Penguin, 1974; (co-editor) *Norton Anthology of American Literature*, Norton, 1975.

MURPHY, J(ohn) Carter 1921-

PERSONAL: Born July 17, 1921, in Fort Worth, Tex.; son of Joe P. (an architectural draftsman) and Elsie (Carter) Murphy; married Dorothy Elise Haldi, May 1, 1949; children: Douglas Carter, Barbara Elise. *Education:* Texas Christian University, student, 1939-41; North Texas State University, A.B., 1943, B.S., 1946; University of Chicago, A.M., 1949, Ph.D., 1955; University of Copenhagen, graduate study, 1952-53. *Religion:* Protestant. *Home:* 10530 Somerton Dr., Dallas, Tex. 75229. *Office:* Department of Economics, Southern Methodist University, Dallas, Tex. 75275.

CAREER: Illinois Institute of Technology, Chicago, instructor in business and economics, 1947-50; Washington University, St. Louis, Mo., instructor, 1950-55, assistant professor, 1955-57, associate professor of economics, 1957-62; Southern Methodist University, professor of economics, 1963—. Visiting professor, Southern Methodist University, spring, 1961, John Hopkins University, School of Advanced International Studies, 1961-62; United Nations technical assistance expert, United Arab Republic, summer, 1964; Special Field Staff of Rockefeller Foundation at Thammasat University, Thailand, 1966-67; senior staff economist of Council of Economic Advisors, 1971-72. *Military service:* U.S. Naval Reserve, 1943-55; became lieutenant; received Silver Star.

MEMBER: Society for International Development, American Economic Association, American Finance Association, American Association of University Professors, Royal Economic Society, Peace Research Society, Southern Economic Association, Midwest Economic Association, Southwestern Economic Association. *Awards, honors:* Fulbright fellow, Denmark, 1952-53, Italy, 1961-62; Ford Foundation faculty research fellow, 1957-58.

WRITINGS: (Editor) *Money in the International Order*, Southern Methodist University Press, 1964. Contributor to *International Encyclopedia of the Social Sciences* and to professional journals in United States and Europe.

WORK IN PROGRESS: Research on international economic policy and on the theory of international investment.

* * *

MURPHY-O'CONNOR, Jerome James 1935-

PERSONAL: Born April 10, 1935, in Cork, Ireland; son of Kerry (a wine wholesaler) and Mary (McCrohan) Murphy-O'Connor. *Education:* Attended Castleknock College and Christian Brothers College in Ireland; University of Fribourg, Th.L., 1961, Th.D., 1962; Ecole Biblique et Archeologique Francaise, Jerusalem, eleve titulaire, 1964; Pontifical Biblical Commission, Rome, Italy, S.S.L., 1965; advanced study at University of Heidelberg, 1965-66, and University of Tuebingen, 1966-67. *Address:* Ecole Biblique, P.O.B. 178, Jerusalem, Israel.

CAREER: Roman Catholic priest, member of the Irish Province of the Dominican order (O.P.), assigned to study and teach Sacred Scripture; Ecole Biblique et Archeologique Francaise, Jerusalem, Palestine, professor of New Testament, 1965—. Visiting professor, University of San Francisco, 1971, Aquinas Institute of Theology, 1969 and 1974; Boylan Lecturer, Dublin, Ireland, 1973; Macdonald Lecturer, University of Sydney, 1976.

WRITINGS: *Paul on Preaching*, Sheed, 1964; *Paul and Qumran*, Geoffrey Chapman, 1968; *What is Religious Life?*, Dominican Publishing, 1973; *Les directives morales selon saint Paul*, Editions du Cerf, 1974. Contributor to *Revue Biblique*, *Harvard Theological Review*, *Bible Today*, *Doctrine and Life*, *New Blackfriar*, *Revue de Qumran*, *Dictionnaire de la Bible: Supplement*.

WORK IN PROGRESS: Books on the methodology of New Testament literary criticism and on the origins and theology of the *Damascus Document*.

* * *

MURRAY, Edward J(ames) 1928-

PERSONAL: Born May 6, 1928, in Brooklyn, N.Y.; son of Enoch J. and Margaret (Conboy) Murray; married Louisa May Urey, September 11, 1954; children: Susan, Martha, Sarah. *Education:* Columbia University, A.B., 1949; Duke University, M.A., 1951; Yale University, Ph.D., 1955. *Office:* Department of Psychology, Syracuse University, Syracuse, N.Y.

CAREER: U.S. Army, 1953-58, becoming lieutenant, and serving as intern in clinical psychology, Walter Reed Army Hospital, Washington, D.C., 1953-54, chief clinical psychologist, Fort Belvoi Army Hospital, Fort Belvoi, Va., 1954-56, associate in psychology, George Washington University, Washington, D.C., 1955-57, and research psychologist, Walter Reed Army Institute of Research, 1956-58; Syracuse University, Syracuse, N.Y., assistant professor of psychology, 1958-62, associate professor, 1962—. Consultant to Veterans Administration, 1959—. *Member:* American Psychological Association, Eastern Psychological Association, New York State Psychological Association, Syracuse Psychological Association (president, 1960-61).

WRITINGS: Motivation and Emotion, Prentice-Hall, 1964; *Sleep, Dreams, and Arousal*, Appleton, 1965. Contributor to professional journals. Consulting editor, *Contemporary Psychology*, 1959-64.

WORK IN PROGRESS: Research in motivational patterns in families of normal and neurotic boys.

SIDELIGHTS: Began as an experimental psychologist interested in animal learning and motivation; now research and writing are concentrated on personality, psychopathology, and psychotherapy.†

* * *

MURRAY, Peter (John) 1920-

PERSONAL: Born April 23, 1920, in London, England; son of John Knowles (an agricultural merchant) and Dorothy (Catton) Murray; married Linda Bramley (a writer and teacher), July 1, 1947. *Education:* Slade School of Fine Art, University of London, 1937-40; Courtauld Institute of Art, University of London, B.A. (honors), 1947, Ph.D., 1956. *Religion:* Catholic. *Office:* Birkbeck College, University of London, London W.C.1, England.

CAREER: University of London, London, England, Courtauld Institute of Art and Birkbeck College, lecturer, 1948-67, Birkbeck College, professor of art history, 1967—, Witt Librarian, 1952-64. *Member:* Society of Antiquaries (fellow), Society of Architectural Historians of Great Britain, Walpole Society. *Awards, honors:* Senior research fellow, Warburg Institute, University of London, 1961.

WRITINGS: An Index of Attributions Made in Tuscan Sources Before Vasari, Olschki, 1959; (with wife, Linda Murray) *A Dictionary o*ꞌ *Art and Artists*, Penguin, 1959, illustrated and enlarged edition, 1965; (with P. Kidson) *A*

History of English Architecture, Harrap, 1962; (with L. Murray) *The Art of the Renaissance*, Praeger, 1963; *Italian Renaissance Architecture*, Batsford, 1963; *Renaissance Architecture*, Abrams, 1972.

Translator with wife, Linda Murray: Wolfflin, *Classic Art*, Phaidon, 1952; A Morassi, *G. B. Tiepolo: His Life and Work*, 2 volumes, Phaidon, 1955, 1962; E. F. Sekler, *Wren and His Place in European Architecture*, Macmillan, 1956; A. Chastel, *Italian Art*, Yoseloff, 1963. Contributor to periodicals.

WORK IN PROGRESS: A monograph on Bramante.

SIDELIGHTS: Murray is competent in French, German, and Italian.

* * *

MURRAY, Ralph L(a Verne) 1921-

PERSONAL: Born May 28, 1921, in Waterloo, Iowa; son of Harry N. and Elsie (Huber) Murray; married Bea Blunt (an educational therapist), December 19, 1942; children: Joseph Paul, Kathryn Elizabeth. *Education:* Iowa State Teachers College (now University of Northern Iowa), student, 1939-41; Carson Newman College, B.A., 1943; Southern Baptist Theological Seminary, B.D., 1947, Th.M., 1948. *Home:* 3407 Kesterwood Rd., Knoxville, Tenn. 37918. *Office:* Smithwood Baptist Church, P.O. Box 5288, Knoxville, Tenn. 37918.

CAREER: Ordained Baptist minister, 1942; Smithwood Baptist Church, Knoxville, Tenn., minister, 1948—. University of Tennessee, School of Religion, Knoxville, associate professor, 1960—. Tennessee Baptist Convention, chairman of education committee; Tennessee Baptist Foundation, trustee. *Member:* Knoxville County Baptist Association (moderator, 1955), Knoxville Ministerial Association (president, 1958), Kiwanis Club.

WRITINGS: From the Beginning, Broadman, 1964; *The Other Dimension*, Broadman, 1966; *Plumb-lines and Fruit Baskets*, Broadman, 1966; *Can I Believe in Miracles?*, Broadman, 1967; *Christ and the City*, Broadman, 1970; *The Biblical Shape of Hope*, Broadway, 1971.†

* * *

MUSA, Mark 1934-

PERSONAL: Born May 27, 1934, in Parma, Italy; son of Bruno and Ida (Berni) Musa; married Isabella Silva, October 9, 1960; children: Marco, Massimo, Marc'Andrea. *Education:* Rutgers University, B.A., 1956; University of Florence, graduate study, 1956-58; Johns Hopkins University, M.A., 1960, Ph.D., 1961. *Office:* Department of French and Italian, Indiana University, Bloomington, Ind.

CAREER: Indiana University, Bloomington, assistant professor, 1961-63, associate professor, 1963-64, professor of French and Italian, 1965—. *Member:* Modern Language Association of America, Phi Beta Kappa. *Awards, honors:* Fulbright fellow in Florence, Italy, 1956-58, Guggenheim fellow, 1971.

WRITINGS: (Translator) Dante, *La Vita Nuova*, Rutgers University Press, 1957, new edition, Indiana University Press, 1973; (translator) Machiavelli, *The Prince*, St. Martins, 1964; (editor) *Essays on Dante*, Indiana University Press, 1964; *The Poetry of Panuccio del Bagno*, Indiana University Press, 1965; (with Ilene Olken) *Strada Facendo: Speaking and Reading Italian*, St. Martins, 1966; (translator) Dante, *The Inferno*, Indiana University Press,

1971; *Advant at the Gates: Dante's Comedy*, Indiana University Press, 1974.

WORK IN PROGRESS: Dante's *Purgatory*; Boccaccio's *Decameron: Viking Portable Machiavelli*; Provencal lyrics.

*   *   *

MUSGROVE, Frank   1922-

PERSONAL: Born December 12, 1922, in Nottingham, England; son of Thomas (a mining engineer) and Fanny (Swain) Musgrove; married Dorothy Nicholls, September 12, 1948; children: Gail. *Education:* Magdalen College, Oxford, B.A., 1947; University of Nottingham, Ph.D., 1958. *Home:* 11 Ookwood Dr., Prestbury, Cheshire, England.

CAREER: Colonial Education Service, Uganda, East Africa, education officer, 1950-53; University of Leicester, Leicester, England, lecturer, 1957-62; University of Leeds, Leeds, England, senior lecturer, 1963-65; University of Bradford, Bradford, England, professor of research in education, 1965-70; University of Wellington, Wellington, New Zealand, Chancellor's lecturer, 1970; University of Manchester, Manchester, England, Sarah Fielden Professor of Education, 1971—. Visiting professor, University of British Columbia, 1965, University of California, 1969. *Military service:* Royal Air Force, Bomber Command, 1942-45; became flying officer. *Member:* Royal Society of Arts (fellow).

WRITINGS: The Migratory Elite, Heinemann, 1963; *Youth and the Social Order*, Routledge & Kegan Paul, 1964, University of Indiana Press, 1965; *The Family, Education, and Society*, Routledge & Kegan Paul, 1966; (with Philip Taylor) *Society and the Teacher's Role*, Routledge & Kegan Paul, 1969; *Patterns of Power and Authority in English Education*, Methuen, 1971; *Ecstasy and Holiness: Counter Culture and the Open Society*, Indiana University Press, 1974.†

*   *   *

MUTH, John F(raser)   1930-

PERSONAL: Born September 27, 1930, in Chicago, Ill.; son of Merlin Arthur (a tax accountant) and Margaret (Ferris) Muth. *Education:* Washington University, St. Louis, Mo., B.S.I.E., 1952; Carnegie Institute of Technology (now Carnegie-Mellon University), M.S., 1954, Ph.D., 1962. *Office:* School of Business, Indiana University, Bloomington, Ind.

CAREER: Carnegie Institute of Technology (now Carnegie-Mellon University), Pittsburgh, Pa., 1955-64; Michigan State University, East Lansing, 1964-69; Indiana University, Bloomington, professor of production management, 1969—. *Member:* American Economic Association, Econometric Society, American Statistical Association, Institute of Management Science.

WRITINGS: (With C. C. Holt, F. Modigliani, and H. A. Simon) *Planning Production, Inventories and Work Force*, Prentice-Hall, 1960; (with G. K. Groff) *Operations Management*, Irwin, 1972.

WORK IN PROGRESS: Research in production management and analysis, and in dynamic economic models and individual choice under uncertainty.

*   *   *

MUTH, Richard F(erris)   1927-

PERSONAL: Born May 14, 1927, in Chicago, Ill.; son of Merlin Arthur (an attorney and tax specialist) and Margaret (Ferris) Muth; married Helene Louise Martin, December 23, 1955; children: Lisa Helene. *Education:* U.S. Coast Guard Academy, student, 1945-47; Washington University, St. Louis, Mo., A.B., 1949, M.A., 1950; University of Chicago, Ph.D., 1958. *Politics:* "Nineteenth-century liberal." *Religion:* Congregational. *Home:* 801 South Fairfax St., Alexandria, Va. *Office:* Institute for Defense Analysis, 400 Army Navy Dr., Arlington, Va.

CAREER: Johns Hopkins University, Baltimore, Md., lecturer in political economy, 1955-56; Resources for the Future, Washington, D.C., research associate, 1956-58; University of Chicago, Graduate School of Business, Chicago, Ill., associate professor of urban economics, 1959-64, professor, 1964—. Vanderbilt University, Nashville, Tenn., visiting associate professor, 1958-59; Institute for Defense Analysis, Arlington, Va., economist, 1964-65. *Military service:* U.S. Coast Guard Reserve, ensign, 1951-52. *Member:* American Economics Association, American Statistical Association, Econometric Society, Regional Science Association, Phi Beta Kappa.

WRITINGS: (With Harvey S. Perloff, Edgar S. Dunn, Jr., and Eric E. Lampard) *Regions, Resources, and Economic Growth*, Johns Hopkins Press, 1960; (contributor) Arnold C. Harberger, editor, *The Demand for Durable Goods*, University of Chicago Press, 1960; *The Evaluation of Selected Present and Potential Poverty Programs*, Institute for Defense Analyses, Economic and Political Studies Division, 1966; *Differential Growth Among Large U.S. Cities*, Institute for Urban and Regional Studies, Washington University, 1968; *Cities and Housing: The Spatial Pattern of Urban Residential Land Use*, University of Chicago Press, 1969; *Public Housing: An Economic Evaluation*, American Enterprise Institute for Public Policy Research, 1973. Contributor of articles to professional journals.

WORK IN PROGRESS: A monograph on the spatial pattern of demand and supply of housing in cities.†

*   *   *

MYERS, Alexander Reginald   1912-

PERSONAL: Born November 3, 1912, in England; son of John William (an insurance manager) and Edith (Moon) Myers; married Christabel Ruth Owen, June 29, 1940; children: Ruth Eleanor, Rosalind Elizabeth, Christabel Edith. *Education:* University of Manchester, B.A., 1934, M.A., 1935; University of London, Ph.D., 1956. *Religion:* Church of England. *Home:* 3 Cholmondeley Rd., West Kirby, Wirral, Cheshire, England. *Office:* School of History, University of Liverpool, P.O. Box 147, Liverpool L69 3BX, England.

CAREER: University of Liverpool, Liverpool, England, senior tutor for men in Faculty of Arts, 1950-65, reader in medieval history, 1959, director of general studies, 1964-67, professor of medieval history, 1967—. *Military service:* Royal Navy, 1942-45; became lieutenant commander; received Africa Star and Atlantic Star. *Member:* Historical Association (national president, 1973-76), Royal Historical Society (fellow), Society of Antiquaries (fellow), Record Society of Lancashire and Cheshire (president, 1967—). *Awards, honors:* Mark Hovall book prize and Jones Fellowship.

WRITINGS: A History of England in the Late Middle Ages, Pelican, 1952, 8th edition, 1971; *The Household of Edward IV*, Manchester University Press, 1959; (editor)

English Historical Documents, 1327-1485, Eyre Methuen, 1969; *London in the Age of Chaucer*, University of Oklahoma Press, 1972; (author of introduction) George Buck, *History of Richard III*, EP Publishing, 1973. Contributor to *Encyclopaedia Britannica, Chambers's Encyclopaedia*, and to historical and other journals in Britain, Canada, and Germany.

WORK IN PROGRESS: Parliaments and Estates in Europe in 1789, to be published by Thames & Hudson; *Edward III*, to be published by Eyre Methuen.

SIDELIGHTS: Myers is competent in Latin, French, German, Italian, and Dutch.

*   *   *

MYERS, Robert J(ulius)   1912-

PERSONAL: Born October 31, 1912, in Lancaster, Pa.; son of Laurence B. (an engineer) and Edith (Hirsh) Myers; married Ruth McCoy (a program specialist), December 20, 1938; children: Jonathan, Eric. *Education:* Lehigh University, B.S., 1933; University of Iowa, M.S., 1934. *Religion:* Lutheran. *Home:* 9610 Wire Ave., Silver Spring, Md. 20901.

CAREER: U.S. government, various actuarial positions, Washington, D.C., 1934-47, chief actuary, U.S. Social Security Administration, 1947-70; Temple University, Philadelphia, Pa., professor of actuarial science, 1970—. Consultant to congressional committees and the federal judiciary; member of technical assistance missions (in connection with social security programs) to Colombia, Israel, Japan, West Germany, and other countries of Europe, South America, and Middle East. International Labour Office, member of committee of social security experts, 1948-51, 1957-70; United Nations, member of committee of actuaries, Joint Staff Pension Fund. *Military service:* U.S. Army, 1942-45; became captain.

MEMBER: International Social Security Association (vice-chairman, committee of social security actuaries), Permanent Committee for International Congresses of Actuaries (council), International Union for the Scientific Study of Population, Inter-American Association of Social Security Actuaries, Society of Actuaries (fellow), Casualty Actuarial Society (fellow), American Statistical Association (fellow), American Association for the Advancement of Science (fellow), Population Association of America, Royal Statistical Society (fellow), Spanish Institute of Actuaries (corresponding), Institute of Actuaries (England; associate). *Awards, honors:* Distinguished Service Award from U.S. Department of Health, Education, and Welfare; Career Service Award from National Civil Service League; honorary LL.D. from Muhlenberg College, 1964, and Lehigh University, 1970.

WRITINGS: Social Insurance and Allied Government Programs, Irwin, 1965; *Medicare*, Irwin, 1970.

SIDELIGHTS: In addition to his travels on technical assistance missions to sixteen nations, Myers has visited ten other countries, ranging from the Soviet Union to Ceylon, to study their social security systems.

*   *   *

MYKLE, Agnar   1915-

PERSONAL: Born August 8, 1915, in Trondheim, Norway; married three times; children: Arne (son), Mette (daughter), Moa (daughter), Jo (son). *Education:* Norwegian School of Economic and Political Sciences, civil economist, 1941; l'Academie des Compagnons de la Marionette, Paris, student, 1947-48. *Residence:* Asker, Norway. *Agent:* Maurice Michael, 3-4 Fox Ct., London E.C. 1, England.

CAREER: Writer. *Awards, honors:* Fulbright grant to study theater in United States, 1951-52.

WRITINGS: Tyven, Tyven Skal du Hete (novel), Tiden Norsk Forlag, 1951, translation by Maurice Michael published as *The Hotel Room*, Dutton, 1963; *Morgen i Appelsingult*, Tiden Norsk Forlag, 1951; *"Jeg er Like Glad," sa Gutten* (novel), Gyldendal, 1952; *Lasso rundt fru Luna* (novel), Gyldendal, 1954, translation by Maurice Michael published as *Lasso Round the Moon*, Dutton, 1960; *Sangen om den roede Rubin* (novel), Gyldendal, 1956, translation by Maurice Michael published as *The Song of the Red Ruby*, Dutton, 1961; *Kors pa halsen; Historier i Utvalg* (stories), Gyldendal, 1958; *Roman*, Gyldendal, 1965, translation by Maurice Michael published as *Rubicon*, Barrie & Rockliff, 1966, Dutton, 1967; (with wife, Jane Mykle) *Dukketeater* (puppet plays), Gyldendal, 1967; *Largo*, Gyldendal, 1967; *A Man and His Sink and Other Stories*, translated by Maurice Michael, Panther, 1968.

SIDELIGHTS: The Song of the Red Ruby was filmed by Palladium Studios as "Den roede rubin" in 1969.†

*   *   *

MYRICK, David F.

PERSONAL: Born in Santa Barbara, Calif.; son of Donald and Charlotte W. (Porter) Myrick. *Education:* Attended University of California, Santa Barbara, and Babson Institute (now Babson College). *Home:* 263 Filbert St., San Francisco, Calif. 94133. *Office:* One Market St., San Francisco, Calif. 94105.

CAREER: Southern Pacific Transportation Co., San Francisco, Calif., 1944—, special assistant to vice-president and treasurer, 1962-73, assistant to vice-president, 1973—. Editor and publisher, *Telegraph Hill Bulletin*, 1956-60; vice-president and director, *The Dakota Farmer Co.*, 1961-67; chairman of advisory board, Josephine D. Randall Junior Museum, 1971-73. *Member:* Railway and Locomotive Historical Society, Arizona Historical Society, California Historical Society, Nevada Historical Society, Santa Barbara Historical Society, Eastern California Museum Association, San Francisco Museum of Art, Book Club of California, Roxburghe Club of San Francisco, Bohemian Club.

WRITINGS: Railroads of Nevada and Eastern California, Volume I, Howell-North, 1962, Volume II, 1963; *San Francisco's Telegraph Hill*, Howell-North, 1972; *Rails Along the Bohemian Grove*, Lawton Kennedy, 1973; *Rails and Mines of Arizona, Sonora and Baja California*, Howell-North, 1974.

Author of introduction: Thompson and West, *History of Nevada*, Howell-North, 1958; Lord, *Comstock Mining and Miners*, Howell-North, 1959; Lingenfelter, *The Newspapers of Nevada*, 1964; Chappell, *Rails to Carry Copper*, 1973. Contributor of articles to magazines and historical society publications.

WORK IN PROGRESS: Volume III of *Railroads of Nevada and Eastern California*.

*   *   *

MYRON, Robert   1926-

PERSONAL: Born March 15, 1926, in Brooklyn, N.Y.;

son of Joseph (a manufacturer) and Sophie (Cantor) Myron; married Marie-Rose Henrietta Gansois (an assistant professor of French), October 28, 1954; children: Daniel, Jacques. *Education:* New York University, B.A., 1950, M.A., 1951; Ohio State University, Ph.D., 1953. *Home:* 130 Duncan Rd., Hempstead, Long Island, N.Y. *Agent:* Malcolm Reiss, Paul R. Reynolds, Inc., 599 Fifth Ave., New York, N.Y. 10017.

CAREER: Hofstra University, Hempstead, Long Island, N.Y., 1954—, started as instructor, now associate professor of fine arts. St. John's University, Jamaica, Long Island, N.Y., part-time assistant professor of fine arts, 1955-59; Michigan State University, East Lansing, visiting professor of fine arts, 1959. Instructor in Long Island adult education programs, 1955—. Painter, exhibiting at several shows. *Military service:* U.S. Army Air Forces, 1944-45. *Member:* American Archaeological Association, American Association of University Professors, Societe des Americanistes (Paris). *Awards, honors:* Belguim-American Foundation postdoctoral fellowship at Ohio State University, 1955.

WRITINGS: Prehistoric Art, Pitman, 1964; *Shadow of the Hawk*, Putnam, 1965; (with Ralph Fanning) *Italian Renaissance Art*, Pitman, 1965; *Mounds, Towns, Totems: Indians of North America*, World Publishing 1966; (with Fanning) *The Putnam Collegiate Guide to History of Art*, Putnam, 1966, published as *Art History: College Level*, R.D.M. Corp., 1968; (with Abner Sundell) *Two Faces of Asia: India and China*, World Publishing, 1967; (with Sundell) *Art in America From Colonial Days Through the Nineteenth Century*, Crowell-Collier, 1969; (with Sundell) *Modern Art in America*, Crowell-Collier, 1971. Editor of Pitman's "New Art History" series, 1965—. Writer of scripts for thirteen-program television series, "Art Around Us," 1965. Contributor to *Journal* of Societe de Americanistes.

WORK IN PROGRESS: Two books with Ralph Fanning, a biography of Andre Verrocchio and a history of Spanish art.

SIDELIGHTS: Robert Myron has reading knowledge of French and Spanish.

* * *

NADLER, Harvey 1933-

PERSONAL: Born June 30, 1933, in Brooklyn, N.Y.; son of Abe and Fay (Fleischman) Nadler; married Marilyn Kohl, January 12, 1958; children: Daniel Drew, Jeffrey Neil. *Education:* New York University, A.B., 1953, M.A., 1960, Ph.D., 1967. *Home:* 90-50 Union Turnpike, Glendale, N.Y.

CAREER: New York University, New York, N.Y., instructor in American Language Institute, 1959-72, professor of education, 1972—. Director of recruitment of Spanish speaking teachers for Board of Education, New York, N.Y. *Military service:* U.S. Army, 1954-56. *Member:* National Association for Foreign Student Affairs, National Council of Teachers of English, American Association of University Professors, Teachers of English to Speakers of Other Languages, New York State English to Speakers of Other Languages and Bilingual Educators Association (president), Phi Delta Kappa, Kappa Delta Pi.

WRITINGS: (Editor with W. R. Grindell and L. Marelli) *American Readings*, McGraw, 1964; (editor and contributor) *American English: An Integrated Series for Interna-*

tional Students, five volumes (includes tapes and laboratory scripts), Librarie Marcel Dider, 1969, revised edition, fourteen volumes (includes ninety tapes), Rand McNally, 1971; *The Teaching of ESL in the Public Schools*, Office of Field Research and School Services, 1969; *An Evaluation: Improvement of the Teaching of English as a Second Language*, Center for Educational Research and Field Services, 1973.

* * *

NAHM, Milton C(harles) 1903-

PERSONAL: Born December 12, 1903, in Las Vegas, N.M.; son of Sigmund and Ella (Kohn) Nahm; married Elinor Amram, April 3, 1933. *Education:* University of Pennsylvania, B.A., 1925, M.A., 1926, Ph.D., 1933; Oxford University, B.A., 1928, B.Litt., 1929. *Home:* 1102 Old Gulph Rd., Rosemont, Pa. *Office:* Bryn Mawr College, Bryn Mawr, Pa.

CAREER: University of Pennsylvania, Philadelphia, instructor in philosophy, 1929-30; Bryn Mawr College, Bryn Mawr, Pa., 1930—, began as lecturer, professor of philosophy, 1945-70, Leslie Clark professor in the humanities, 1970-72, professor emeritus, 1972—, head of department, 1946-72. Lecturer and broadcaster on creativity and aesthetics; speaker at International Congresses of Philosophy abroad. *Member:* American Philosophical Association (Eastern division secretary-treasurer, 1946-50, vice-president, 1954; national secretary-treasurer, 1950-52), American Society for Aesthetics (trustee, 1958-64, 1967-70), Metaphysical Society of America, Institut d'Esthetique de l'Universite d'Amsterdam, Fullerton Club (president, 1936-37, 1971-72), Phi Beta Kappa. *Awards, honors:* Rhodes scholar, 1926-29; Bollingen Foundation fellow, 1950, 1958; American Council of Learned Societies fellow, 1960; National Endowment for the Humanities senior fellow, 1972-73.

WRITINGS: (Editor) *Selections from Early Greek Philosophy*, Crofts, 1934, 4th edition, revised, and with new introduction, Appleton, 1964; (editor) John Wilson, *The Cheats*, Basil Blackwell, 1935; (with R. Bernheimer, Rhys Carpenter, and K. Koffka) *Art: A Bryn Mawr Symposium*, Lancaster Press, 1940; (editor with F. P. Clarke, and contributor) *Philosophical Essays in Honor of Edgar A. Singer, Jr.*, University of Pennsylvania Press, 1942; *Aesthetic Experience and Its Presuppositions*, Harper, 1946; (contributor) Lyman Bryson and others, editors, *Approaches to Group Understanding*, Harper, 1947; *Aristotle on Poetry and Music*, Liberal Arts Press, 1948; (contributor) Elizabeth Wilder, editor, *Studies in Latin American Art*, American Council of Learned Societies, 1949.

(Contributor) Lyman Bryson, L. Finklestein, and R. M. McIver, editors, *Perspectives on a Troubled Decade: Science, Philosophy and Religion 1939-49: A Symposium*, Harper, 1950; (editor with Leo Strauss) Isaac Husik, *Philosophical Essays, Ancient, Mediaeval and Modern*, Basil Blackwell, 1952; *The Artist as Creator*, Johns Hopkins Press, 1956; *Las Vegas and Uncle Joe: The New Mexico I Remember*, University of Oklahoma Press, 1964; *Genius and Creativity*, Torchbooks, 1965; (contributor) Philip P. Wiener, editor, *Dictionary of the History of Ideas*, Scribner, 1973; *Readings in Philosophy of Art and Aesthetics*, Prentice-Hall, in press.

Editor, *Proceedings of the American Philosophical Association*, Antioch, 1953. Contributor of more than sixty articles, papers, reviews, and abstracts to *Journal of Philoso-*

phy, *Review of English Studies, Philosophy of Science, Panamericanismo, American Journal of Archaeology, Kant-studien, Journal of the History of Ideas, Journal of Aesthetics and Art Criticism*, and other journals.

WORK IN PROGRESS: *The Fine Art of Criticism*, a third book devoted to systematic investigation of aesthetics; a book in which the author analyzes factual criticism and the criteria for criticism as a fine art, and discusses aesthetic criticism in its relation to the aesthetic values—the tragic, the ugly, and the comic.

AVOCATIONAL INTERESTS: Trout fishing in New Mexico, looking at Greek vase paintings.

*   *   *

NAMBIAR, O. K.   1910-

PERSONAL: Born August 19, 1910, in Tellicherry, Malabar, India; son of M. Kannan (an advocate) and O. Lakshmi (Amma) Nambiar; married Janaki Amma, November 17, 1939; children: Prema and Prabha (daughters), Jeevan (son). *Education:* Presidency College, B.A. (honors) and M.A. *Religion:* Hindu. *Home:* 22 Cunningham Rd., Bangalore-52, India. *Office:* 39/9 Lal Bagh Rd., Bangalore-27, India.

CAREER: Mysore University, Bangalore, India, assistant professor of English, 1940-51; D.R.M. College, Davangere, India, principal, 1951-52; Mysore University, professor of English language and literature, 1952-62; Bangalore University, Bangalore, India, professor of English and American literature, 1962-66. President, University Depressed Classes Hostels; commanding officer, National Cadet Corps (India); founder, Youth Hostels Association of India; vice-president, India Cultural Centre, Bangalore. *Member:* Indian Institute of World Culture, Indo American Association, Indo German Association, Board of Studies in English (Mysore), Mythic Society, English Teachers Association (Bangalore), Bangalore Fulbright Alumni Association (president), Free Mason. *Awards, honors:* Fulbright visiting scholar at Columbia University for research on Walt Whitman, 1959-60; Award for Outstanding Retired Teachers from the University Grants Commission, three terms.

WRITING: *The Last Perumal*, P. K. Brothers, 1946; *Portuguese Pirates and Indian Seamen*, Bhaktavatsalam, 1954; *Kunjalis—Admirals of Calicut*, Asia Publishing House, 1963; *Walt Whitman and Yoga*, Jeevan, 1966; (contributor) S. Mukherjee, editor, *Indian Essays in American Literature*, Verry, 1969; (contributor) M. K. Naik, editorial committee chairman, *Indian Response to Poetry in English*, Macmillan, 1970; (contributor) J. P. Strelka, editor, *Yearbook of Comparative Criticism*, Volume IV: *Anagogic Qualities of Literature*, Pennsylvania State University Press, 1971. Contributor of reviews and articles to *Saturday Review, Mysore University Journal*, and to Malayalam journals.

WORK IN PROGRESS: *Walt Whitman: The Prophet of Yoga*, a revised and enlarged edition of *Walt Whitman and Yoga*; *Yoga in the Temple*; *Indian Seafaring in the Indian Ocean*; short stories dealing with India in transition.

AVOCATIONAL INTERESTS: History, geography, religion and psychology, scientific examination of the occult, and collecting antiques.

*   *   *

NANDA, B(al) R(am)   1917-

PERSONAL: Born October 11, 1917, in Rawalpindi, India;

son of P. D. and Shrimati Maya (Devi) Nanda; married Janak Khosla, May 24, 1946; children: Naren and Biren (sons). *Education:* Educated in India at Gordon College, 1933-34, Khalsa College, 1934-35, Government College, Lahore, 1935-39. *Religion:* Hindu. *Address:* 11/63 Wellesley Rd., New Delhi 11, India.

CAREER: Joined Indian Railways in 1942, becoming joint director of Ministry of Railways, New Delhi, Indian Institute of Public Administration, New Delhi, project director, 1964—.

WRITINGS: *Mahatma Gandhi*, Allen & Unwin, 1958, Beacon, 1959; *The Nehrus*, Allen & Unwin, 1962, Day, 1963; *Motilal Nehru*, Publications Division, Government of India, 1964; (editor) *Selected Works of Jawaharlal Nehru*, Orient Longman, 1972; (editor) *Socialism in India*, Vikas Publications (Delhi), 1972; *Gandhi: A Pictorial Biography*, Ministry of Information and Broadcasting, 1972; *Gandhi and the Nehrus: Studies in Indian Nationalism*, St. Martin, 1974.

WORK IN PROGRESS: A biography of the Indian statesman, Gopal Krishna Gokhale, 1866-1915.

AVOCATIONAL INTERESTS: Visiting universities and institutions (in India and abroad) specializing in research in Indian history.†

*   *   *

NATHAN, Robert (Gruntal)   1894-

PERSONAL: Born January 2, 1894, in New York, N.Y.; son of Harold and Sarah (Gruntal) Nathan; married Dorothy Michaels, 1915 (divorced, 1922); married Nancy Wilson, 1930 (divorced, 1936); married Lucy Lee Hall Skelding, 1936 (divorced, 1939); married Janet McMillen Bingham, 1940 (divorced); married Clara May Blum Burns, 1951 (divorced); married Shirley Keeland, December 14, 1955 (died, 1969); married Joan Boniface Winnifrith, 1970; children: (first marriage) Joan (Mrs. M. Bergstrom). *Education:* Attended private schools in United States and Switzerland and Harvard University, 1912-15. *Home:* 1240 North Doheny Dr., Los Angeles, Calif. *Agent:* Curtis Brown Ltd., 575 Madison Ave., New York, N.Y. 10022.

CAREER: Novelist, playwright, and poet. New York University School of Journalism, New York, N.Y., lecturer, 1924-25; Metro-Goldwyn-Mayer, Hollywood, Calif., screen writer, 1943-49. Member of literary committee, Huntington Hartford Foundation. *Member:* National Institute of Arts and Letters (vice-president, 1939), Academy of American Poets (chancellor), Dramatists Guild, Writers Guild of America (West), Academy of Motion Picture Arts and Sciences, American Society of Composers, Authors, and Publishers (ASCAP), P.E.N. (charter member; president, 1940-43), Screen Writers Guild. *Awards, honors:* U.S. Treasury Department Silver Medal, World War II; California Writer's Guild Award of Honor.

WRITINGS: *Peter Kindred*, Duffield, 1919; *Autumn*, McBride, 1921; *The Puppet Master*, McBride, 1923; *Jonah*, McBride, 1925 (published in England as *Son of Amittai*, Heinemann, 1925), 2nd U.S. edition, Knopf, 1934; *The Fiddler in Barly*, McBride, 1926; *The Woodcutter's House*, Bobbs-Merrill, 1927; *The Bishop's Wife*, Bobbs-Merrill, 1928; *There Is Another Heaven*, Bobbs-Merrill, 1929.

The Orchid, Bobbs-Merrill, 1931; *One More Spring*, Knopf, 1933; *Road of Ages*, Knopf, 1935; *The Enchanted Voyage*, Knopf, 1936; *The Barly Fields* (collection of five earlier novels), Knopf, 1938; *Journey of Tapiola*, Knopf, 1938; *Winter in April*, Knopf, 1938.

The Concert, House of Books, 1940; *Portrait of Jennie*, Knopf, 1940; *They Went On Together*, Knopf, 1941; *Tapiola's Brave Regiment*, Knopf, 1941; *The Sea-Gull Cry*, Knopf, 1942; *Journal for Josephine*, Knopf, 1943; *But Gently Day*, Knopf, 1943; *Mr. Whittle and the Morning Star*, Knopf, 1947; *Long After Summer*, Knopf, 1948; *The River Journey*, Knopf, 1949.

The Married Look, Knopf, 1950 (published in England as *His Wife's Young Face*, Staples, 1951); *The Innocent Eve*, Knopf, 1951; *The Adventures of Tapiola* (includes *Journey of Tapiola* and *Tapiola's Brave Regiment*), Knopf, 1952; *Nathan Three* (includes *The Sea-Gull Cry*, *The Innocent Eve*, and *The River Journey*), Staples, 1952; *Jezebel's Husband* [and] *The Sleeping Beauty* (two plays), Knopf, 1953; *The Train in the Meadow*, Knopf, 1953; *Sir Henry*, Knopf, 1955; *The Rancho of the Little Loves*, Knopf, 1956; *So Love Returns*, Knopf, 1958; *The Snowflake and the Starfish*, Knopf, 1959.

The Color of the Evening, Knopf, 1960; *The Weans*, Knopf, 1960; *The Wilderness-Stone*, Knopf, 1961; *A Star in the Wind*, Knopf, 1962; *The Married Man*, Knopf, 1962; *The Devil With Love*, Knopf, 1963; *The Fair*, Knopf, 1964; *So Love Returns*, Knopf, 1964; *Mallot Diaries*, Knopf, 1965; *Juliet in Mantua* (play), Knopf, 1966; *Stonecliff*, Knopf, 1967; *Mia*, Knopf, 1970; *The Elixir*, Knopf, 1971; *The Summer Meadows: A Fictional Memoir*, Delacorte, 1973.

Poetry: *Youth Grows Old*, McBride, 1922; *A Cedar Box*, Bobbs-Merrill, 1929; *Selected Poems of Robert Nathan*, Knopf, 1935; *A Winter Tide*, Knopf, 1940; *Dunkirk*, Knopf, 1942; *Morning in Iowa*, Knopf, 1844; *The Darkening Meadows*, Knopf, 1945; *The Green Leaf: The Collected Poems of Robert Nathan*, Knopf, 1950; *Evening Song*, Capra Press, 1973.

Films: "The White Cliffs of Dover," 1944; "The Clock," 1945; "Wake Up and Dream," 1947; "Pagan Love Song," 1950.

Unpublished plays: "Music at Evening," 1935; "A Family Piece," 1947; "The Sea Gull," 1952; "Susan and the Stranger," 1954.

Magazine writer in the 1920's and 1930's, contributing to *New Yorker*, *Atlantic*, *Harper's*, *Scribner's*, *Century*, *Red Book*, *Cosmopolitan*, and other periodicals. Writer of songs and a violin sonata. Illustrator of *Tina Mina Tales*.

WORK IN PROGRESS: Plays, poems, and a screenplay.

SIDELIGHTS: A writer for more than fifty years, Nathan has not only been highly praised throughout his career, he has also, in a limited sense, defined his own literary genre. Edmund Fuller noted that "Robert Nathan has created a particular kind of literary product for a particular audience. In a sense, judging his work is like judging a master rifleman's. When 'ready, aim, fire' has been said, he hits his mark." He has successfully experimented with every traditional literary form—novel, poetry, plays, satire, and juvenile books—infusing all with his peculiar and enchanting imagery.

As early as 1935, Nathan's talent was recognized. One *Christian Science Monitor* reviewer wrote: "Such finished writing as [Nathan's] may, because of its very refinement and workmanship, be with us for some time before its power is generally felt, but it will endure. It will endure because it has the essence of poetry, because above and beyond its musical expression it possesses a spiritual quality characteristic of the ancient literature of Judaism." W. R. Benet said of *Road of Ages*: "[The novel] springs from so large an imaginative conception, involves such richness of material with so great an economy of means, is written throughout in so consistently fine a style that it deserves literary permanence.... It is one of those subtle and wise books, sometimes of an exquisite beauty, that makes one proud of the mind of man."

One of Nathan's favorite themes concerns "the power of love to transcend time and place," and he has employed this idea in several fantasies which, however fantastic, carry more than the expected weight of philosophical implication. Virgilia Peterson commented that "Nathan—seemingly so remote from his characters—is always present on the page." His expansive vision and lucid style produce poetry and prose that "evidence ... the human spirit at its most eloquent best," but the magical quality of his work is never sacrificed.

Nathan has also successfully adapted the fantasy form for children. M. S. Libbey compared Nathan's *The Snowflake and the Starfish* to the stories of Hans Christian Andersen, citing the "enchanting musical spells and the supple, graceful style that have great beauty when read aloud...."

If Nathan's work has not received the approbation of today's young adults, it is not because Nathan's skill has deteriorated. M. P. Brody wrote: "Indeed his delicacy of observation and quiet charm of expression may make him anachronistic in the eyes of young moderns accustomed to writers of the 'angry young men' school. Nathan is not angry; if anything, he is wistful."

BIOGRAPHICAL/CRITICAL SOURCES: L. Bromfield, *The Work of Robert Nathan*, Bobbs-Merrill, circa 1930; *Saturday Review of Literature*, February 2, 1935; *Christian Science Monitor*, November 13, 1935, June 30, 1945, June 27, 1970; *Springfield Republican*, June 11, 1945; *Catholic World*, October, 1958, January, 1962; *New York Herald Tribune Book Review*, October 5, 1958, November 1, 1959, April 10, 1960; *New York Times Book Review*, December 14, 1958, December 19, 1965, May 17, 1970; *Booklist*, December 1, 1960, July 1, 1961; Dan H. Laurence, *Robert Nathan: A Bibliography*, Yale University Library, 1961.

*   *   *

NATWAR-SINGH, K. 1931-

PERSONAL: Born May 16, 1931, in India; son of Govind-Singh. *Education:* St. Stephen's College, Delhi University, B.A. (first class honors), 1952; Corpus Christi College, Oxford, graduate study, 1952-54. *Religion:* Hindu. *Home:* Govind Niwas, Bharatpur, Rajasthan, India. *Agent:* William Morris Agency, 1940 Broadway, New York, N.Y. 10019. *Office:* New India House, 3 East 64th St., New York, N.Y. 10021.

CAREER: Indian Foreign Service, career diplomat, 1953—, serving in Peking, China, with Permanent Mission of India to the United Nations, New York, N.Y., 1961—. United Nations Committee on Decolonisation, rapporteur, 1963—. *Member:* Indian Council of World Affairs (New Delhi), Delhi Gymkhana Club.

WRITINGS—Editor: *E. M. Forster: A Tribute*, Harcourt, 1964; *Legacy of Nehru*, Day, 1965; *Tales from Modern India*, Macmillan, 1966; *Stories from India*, Hodder & Stoughton, 1971.

WORK IN PROGRESS: A novel set in India, pre-1947.

SIDELIGHTS: Natwar-Singh speaks, reads, and writes Chinese. He traveled around the world in 1964, adding to previous travels ranging from Chile to Mongolia.†

*   *   *

NEAL, Ernest G(ordon)   1911-

PERSONAL: Born May 20, 1911, in Boxmoor, Hertfordshire, England; son of F. (a Baptist minister) and Margaret Ower (Keith) Neal; married Helen Elizabeth Thomson, April 30, 1937; children: Keith Robert Cameron, David Alastair, Andrew Graham. *Education:* University of London, M.Sc., and Ph.D. *Religion:* Nonconformist. *Home:* Willis East, Taunton School, Taunton, Somersetshire, England.

CAREER: Rendcomb College, Cirencester, England, senior biologist, 1934-44; Taunton School, Taunton, England, head of science department, 1945-60, second master, 1960—. Somerset Trust for Nature Conservation, chairman, 1964—. *Member:* Society of Authors, Ecological Society, Mammal Society of British Isles (council).

WRITINGS: Exploring Nature with a Camera, Elek, 1942; *The Badger*, Collins, 1948, 2nd edition, 1962; *Woodland Ecology*, Heinemann, 1956; *Topsy & Turvey: My Two Otters*, Heinemann, 1961; *Uganda Quest: African Wildlife After Dark*, Taplinger, 1971. Wrote film script, "Woodland Ecology," for television and educational distribution, and booklets on otters and badgers for *Sunday Times* (London).

WORK IN PROGRESS: Continuing research in reproduction in the European badger.

AVOCATIONAL INTERESTS: Natural history photography, including motion pictures.†

*   *   *

NELSON, E(ugene) Clifford   1911-

PERSONAL: Born August 13, 1911, in Butler, S.D.; son of Martin and Gunhild (Anderson) Nelson; married Lois Jensen, July 21, 1936; children: Dagmar (Mrs. Richard Melin), David, Naomi (Mrs. G. Theo. Colburn). *Education:* St. Olaf College, B.A., 1933; Luther Theological Seminary, B.D., 1936; Yale University, Ph.D., 1952; post-doctoral study at University of Copenhagen, 1962, Heidelberg University, 1962-63, and at University of Oslo, 1971. *Home:* 320 Cherry St., Northfield, Minn. 55057. *Office:* St. Olaf College, Northfield, Minn. 55057.

CAREER: Ordained to Lutheran ministry, 1936. Pastor in Chicago, Ill., 1936-38, Ellendale, Minn., 1938-42, Minneapolis, Minn., 1942-50; St. Olaf College, Northfield, Minn., instructor, 1950-51; Office of the High Commissioner for Germany, Frankfurt, adviser, 1951-52; Luther Theological Seminary, St. Paul, Minn., professor of church history and dean, 1952-66. Director of Third Assembly, Lutheran World Federation, Minneapolis, Minn., 1955-57; member of board of regents, Augsburg College. *Member:* American Society of Church History, Norwegian-American Historical Association, Lutheran Historical Conference, Blue Key, Phi Beta Kappa. *Awards, honors:* Distinguished Alumnus Award, St. Olaf College, 1957; fellow, American Association of Theological Schools, 1962-63; honorary fellow, American-Scandinavian Foundation.

WRITINGS: This Is Life Eternal, Augsburg, 1949; (with E. L. Fevold as co-author of Volume I) *The Lutheran Church among Norwegian-Americans*, two volumes, Augsburg, 1960; *Lutheranism in North America, 1914-70*, Augsburg, 1972; *A Pioneer Churchman: J. W. C. Dietrichson in Wisconsin 1844-1850*, Twayne, 1973; *Lutherans in North America*, Fortress, 1975. Member of editorial board, *Lutheran World* (Geneva, Switzerland); contributing editor, *Dialog* (Minneapolis).

WORK IN PROGRESS: Pre-History of the Lutheran World Federation: The American Contribution, tentative title.

*   *   *

NELSON, F(rancis) William   1922-

PERSONAL: Born February 19, 1922, in St. Louis, Mo.; son of Hal and Florence (Signaigo) Nelson; married Susan Austin (a teacher), April 2, 1958; children: James Henry, William Paul, Antonya, David Hal, Juliet. *Education:* Texas Technological College, student, 1939-42; University of Texas, A.B., 1943; Columbia University, M.A., 1948; University of Oklahoma, Ph.D., 1957. *Politics:* Democrat. *Home:* 155 North Roosevelt, Wichita, Kan. *Office:* Wichita State University, Wichita, Kan.

CAREER: Wichita State University, Wichita, Kan., 1947—, started as instructor, professor of English, 1963—. *Military service:* U.S. Navy, 1942-46; became lieutenant. *Member:* American Association of University Professors.

WRITINGS: (Editor) *William Golding's Lord of the Files*, Odyssey, 1963.

WORK IN PROGRESS: American Criticism of the 1920's.

AVOCATIONAL INTERESTS: Fishing (during summer vacations at Telluride, Colo.).

*   *   *

NELSON, Walter Henry   1928-

PERSONAL: Born March 23, 1928, in Munich, Germany; son of U.S. diplomat; married Rita L. Christoffersen, June 30, 1962; children: Roger Stuart, Gregory Eugene, Victoria Eugenie. *Education:* Attended New York University, 1944, Norwich University, 1944-46, Columbia University, 1949-50. *Politics:* Independent. *Agent:* McIntosh, McKee & Dodds, 30 East 60th St., New York, N.Y. 10022. *Office:* c/o S. Korsh, 666 Fifth Ave., New York, N.Y. 10019.

CAREER: American Petroleum Institute Quarterly, New York, N.Y., editor, 1955-57; Reach, McClinton & Co., Inc., New York, N.Y., public relations director, 1957-59; vice-president and general manager, Candy Gram, Inc., and assistant to the president, Candy Kitchens, Inc., Chicago, Ill., 1959-60; Herbert M. Kraus & Co., Inc., Chicago, Ill., vice-president and director of operations, 1960-61; Fred Rosen Associates, Inc., New York, N.Y., associate, 1961-62; privately employed as public relations, advertising, and sales promotion consultant, New York, N.Y., 1962-64; free-lance writer, 1964—. *Military service:* U.S. Army, Military Intelligence, special agent in Germany, 1946-49. *Member:* Overseas Press Club of America (New York).

WRITINGS: Small Wonder: The Amazing Story of the Volkswagen, Little, Brown, 1965, revised edition, 1970; *The Great Discount Delusion*, McKay, 1965; *The Berliners: Their City and Their Saga*, McKay, 1969 (published in England as *The Berliners: Portrait of a People and Their City*, Harlow, 1969); *The Soldier Kings: The House of Hollernzollern*, Putnam, 1970; (editor and translator with Christopher Risso-Gill) *Ernest Hemingway: 100 Blitzlichter aus seinem Leben redektier*, Bechtle, 1971; *Germany*

Rearmed, Simon & Schuster, 1972; *The Londoners: Life in a Civilized City*, Random House, 1974. Contributor to *Atlantic Monthly, Saturday Evening Post*, and other national magazines; syndicated columnist for North American Newspaper Alliance, Spadea Syndicate, and Women's News Syndicate.

WORK IN PROGRESS: Three books under contract.

SIDELIGHTS: On the day that *The Great Discount Delusion* was published, Isadore Barmash wrote in the *New York Times:* "A bomb is due to burst today at the feet of the nation's discounters. It will probably not be fatal, but discount retailing will probably be painfully picking pieces of shrapnel out of its 'face' for weeks and months to come." At the time of publication, several leading discounters had already read the book. They were "indignant, frustrated and disgusted." One discount chain president told the *Times* that "the great delusion is not really discounting, but Nelson's book itself.... Any excesses charged in the book are due to the businessman's normal enthusiasm to push business."

Nelson claimed that his writing was subsidized by no one. He was convinced that discounters "were misleading the public. I wanted to open a lot of people's eyes to the reality behind the glitter."

BIOGRAPHICAL/CRITICAL SOURCES: New York Times, July 12, 1965.†

* * *

NETTEL, Reginald 1899-

PERSONAL: Born August 27, 1899, in Leek, Staffordshire, England; son of James Reginald (an electrical engineer) and Harriet E. (Clowes) Nettel; married Gwynneth Mary Davies, October 25, 1949. *Education:* Attended Manchester College, Oxford, and St. Catherine's Society (now St. Catherine's College), Oxford. *Home:* Caxton House, Lechlade, Gloucestershire, England.

CAREER: Music critic and writer on music. *Member:* P.E.N. (English section), Royal Musical Association.

WRITINGS: Music in the Five Towns, Oxford University Press, 1944; *Ordeal by Music*, Oxford University Press, 1945; *The Orchestra in England*, J. Cape, 1946; *While the Orchestra Assembles*, J. Cape, 1949; *To Soothe a Savage Breast*, Evans, 1951; *The Englishman Makes Music*, Dobson, 1952; *Sing a Song of England*, Phoenix House, 1955; *Seven Centuries of Popular Song*, Phoenix House, 1957; *Carols: 1400-1950*, Fraser Gallery, 1957; *Santa Claus*, Fraser Gallery, 1958; *Great Moments in Music*, Roy Publishers, 1959; *Christmas and Its Carols*, Faith Press, 1960; *Folk Dancing*, Arco Publications, 1962; (translator) Carl Philip Moritz, *Journeys of a German in England in 1782*, Holt, 1965; *Havergal Brian and His Music*, Dobson, 1974. Writer of about twenty radio scripts. Contributor to *Chambers's Encyclopaedia, Musik in Geschicht und Gegenwart*, and to periodicals, including *Listener, Gramaphone Record Review, Musical Times*.

WORK IN PROGRESS: A biography of Sir George Grove.

SIDELIGHTS: Nettel's special interests are opera, orchestra, and folk music in Europe, German literature not available in English translation, and the theater.

* * *

NEURATH, Marie (Reidemeister) 1898-

PERSONAL: Surname is pronounced Noy-raat; born May 27, 1898, in Brunswick, Germany; daughter of Hans (a civil servant) and Sophie (Langerfeldt) Reidemeister; married Otto Neurath (a sociologist and philosopher), February 26, 1941 (died, 1945). *Education:* Studied at Brunswick Technical University, University of Munich, University of Berlin, and University of Gottingen. *Politics:* Labour. *Home and office:* 3a Eldon Grove, London N.W. 3, England.

CAREER: Gesellschafts und Wurtschaftsmuseum, Wien, Austria, scientific assistant, 1925-34; Mundaneum, Hague, Netherlands, general secretary, 1935-40; International Foundation for Visual Education, Hague, Netherlands, general secretary, 1933—; Isotype Institute Ltd., London, England, secretary and director of studies, 1942—. Has done visual education work in developing countries, including Nigeria, 1953-54.

WRITINGS: Visual History, three volumes, Parrish, 1948-49; *Visual Science*, six volumes, Parrish, 1950-53; *Living With One Another: An Introduction to Social Studies*, Parrish, 1965, F. Watts, 1966; (editor with Robert S. Cohen) Otto Neurath, *Empiricism and Sociology*, D. Reidel (Dordrecht), 1973.

Wonder World of Nature series, published by Parrish: *The Wonder World of Animals*, 1952, *...of Insects*, 1952, *...of Birds*, 1953, *...of the Seashore*, 1953, *...of Long Ago*, 1954, *...of the Deep Sea*, 1955, *...of Strange Plants*, 1955, *Too Small to See*, 1956, *The Wonder World of Land and Water*, 1957, *...of Earth and Sky*, 1958, *...of Animal Travellers*, 1958, *...of Trees and Flowers*, 1960, *A New Life Begins*, 1960, *The Wonder Book of Snow and Ice*, 1961, *...of the Jungle*, 1961, *...of the Desert*, 1962.

"Wonders of the Modern World" series, published by Parrish: *If You Could See Inside*, 1948, *I'll Show You How It Happens*, 1948, *Railways Under London*, 1948, *Fire!*, 1950, *Rockets and Jets*, 1951, *Let's Look at the Sky*, 1952, *Speeding Into Space*, 1953, *A Message Round the World*, 1953, *Machines Which Seem to Think*, 1954, *Inside the Atom*, 1955, *What's New in Flying*, 1956, *Building Big Things*, 1957, *Exploring Under the Sea*, 1958, *This Is How It Works*, 1959, *Man-Made Moons*, 1959, *The Wonders of the Universe*, 1961.

"Junior Colour Books" series, published by Parrish: *Many Homes*, 1963, *Growing*, 1963, *All Sorts of Dress*, 1963, *Many Foods*, 1963, *Keeping Clean*, 1964, *Keeping Well*, 1964, *Friends and Enemies*, 1966, *Walking, Running, Climbing*, 1966.

"A New Look at Science" series, published by Parrish: *Living Things*, 1962, *About the Earth*, 1962, *What Is Electricity?*, 1964, *From Telegraph to Telstar*, 1964, *Heat and Power*, 1964.

"A New Look at History" series, published by Parrish: *How the First Men Lived*, 1950, *The First Great Inventions*, 1950, *How the World was Explored*, 1950.

"They Lived Like This" series, published by Parrish: *They Lived Like This in Ancient Egypt*, 1964, *...in Ancient Mesopotamia*, 1964, *...in Ancient Palestine*, 1965, *...in Ancient Crete*, 1965, *...in Ancient China*, 1966, *...in Old Japan*, 1966, *They Lived Like This: The Ancient Maya*, 1966, *They Lived Like This in Ancient Peru*, 1966, *...in Ancient India*, 1967, *...in Ancient Africa*, 1967, *...in Chaucer's England*, 1967, *...in Shakespeare's England*, 1968, *...in Ancient Greece*, 1968, *...in Ancient Rome*, 1968, *...in the Roman Empire*, 1969, *...in Ancient Britain*, 1969, *...in Ancient Persia*, 1970, *They Lived Like This: The Vikings*, 1970, *They Lived Like This in the Old Stone Age*, 1970, *...in Ancient Mexico*, 1971.

Author of filmstrips on various subjects.

SIDELIGHTS: Mrs. Neurath commented: "In our historical series, we are trying to let the ancient civilizations speak about themselves as much as possible, by using their own representations. The Egyptian wall pictures, the Sumerian cylinder seals, and the Chinese characters were most exciting subjects for such an approach. More than any other material, pictures address themselves to people of all ages, languages, levels of education. That may be why I never think of any special age group when I prepare a book. I hardly think of the readers as separate from myself. The books are for myself as well as for them, though I do not like to re-read them when they are printed, in fear of discovering flaws. If they please anybody at all, this is an extra reward—not expected, but most welcome."

* * *

NEUSCHEL, Richard F(rederick) 1915-

PERSONAL: Born March 3, 1915, in Buffalo, N.Y.; son of Percy J. and Anna M. (Becker) Neuschel; married Jean Fuller, October 16, 1943; children: Robin, Debra. *Education:* University of Colorado, student, 1932-33; Denison University, A.B., 1936; Harvard University, M.B.A. (cum laude), 1941. *Home:* 14 Woodacres Rd., Brookville, Glen Head, N.Y. *Office:* McKinsey & Co., Inc., 270 Park Ave., New York, N.Y. 10017.

CAREER: Sperry Gyroscope Co., Great Neck, N.Y., general procedures director, 1941-45; McKinsey & Co., Inc. (management consultants), New York, N.Y., 1945—, became director. Member of business advisory council and board of trustees, Denison University. *Member:* Associates of the Harvard Business School, Harvard Club and Sky Club (New York).

WRITINGS: How to Take Physical Inventory, McGraw, 1946; *Streamlining Business Procedures*, McGraw, 1950; *Management by System*, McGraw, 1960; (contributor) H. B. Maynard, *Industrial Engineering Handbook*, McGraw, 1961; (contributor) W. Alderson and S. J. Shapiro, editors, *Marketing and the Computer*, Prentice-Hall, 1963; (contributor) H. Koontz, editor, *Toward a Unified Theory of Management*, McGraw, 1964; (contributor) Roland Mann, editor, *The Arts of Top Management: McKinsey Anthology*, McGraw, 1971; *Management Systems and Organization Effectiveness*, McGraw, 1975. Writer of "Computer-Based Management Information Systems for Marketing," a video tape presentation. Contributor to business periodicals, including *Controller, Nation's Business, Harvard Business Review, Management Review*, and *Management and Business Automation*.

* * *

NEUSNER, Jacob 1932-

PERSONAL: Born July 28, 1932, in Hartford, Conn.; son of Samuel (publisher of *Connecticut Jewish Ledger*) and Lee (a publisher; maiden name, Green) Neusner; married Suzanne Richter (an artist), March 15, 1964; children: Samuel Aaron, Eli Ephraim, Noam Mordecai Menahem, Margalit Leah Berakhah. *Education:* Harvard University, A.B. (magna cum laude), 1953; graduate study at Oxford University, 1953-54, The Hebrew University of Jerusalem, 1957-58; Jewish Theological Seminary of America, M.H.L., 1960; Columbia University, Ph.D., 1960; Harvard University, postdoctoral study, 1962-64. *Religion:* Jewish. *Office:* Department of Religion, Dartmouth College, Hanover, N.H. 03755.

CAREER: Columbia University, New York, N.Y., instructor in religion, 1960-61; University of Wisconsin, Milwaukee, assistant professor of Hebrew, 1961-62; Brandeis University, Waltham, Mass., research associate in Jewish history, 1962-64; Dartmouth College, Hanover, N.H., assistant professor, 1964-66, associate professor of religion, 1966-68; Brown University, Providence, R.I., professor of religious studies, 1968—. Member of Kent Fellowship Advisory Council of Danforth Foundation, 1964-66.

MEMBER: Society for Religion in Higher Education, Rabbinical Assembly of America, American Society for Study of Religion, American Oriental Society, American Academy for Jewish Research (fellow), American Jewish Historical Society, American Academy of Religion (vice-president, 1967-68; president, 1968-69), Association for Jewish Studies (founding member; member of board), Royal Asiatic Society (fellow), Phi Beta Kappa. *Awards, honors:* Abraham Berliner Prize in Jewish History of the Jewish Theological Seminary of America for *A Life of Rabban Yohanan ben Zakkai*, 1962. Awarded fifteen fellowships, including American Council of Learned Societies Fellowship, 1970-71, and Guggenheim Fellowship, 1973-74.

WRITINGS: Learning With the Living Talmud (study guide), Mentor, 1957; *Study Guide to Tradition and Change*, National Academy for Adult Jewish Studies, 1959; *A Life of Rabban Yohanan ben Zakkai*, Brill, 1962, revised edition, 1970; *Fellowship in Judaism: The First Century and Today*, Vallentine, Mitchell, 1963; *History of Judaism*, Data Guide, 1963; *A History of the Jews in Babylonia*, Brill, Volume I: *The Parthian Period*, 1965, Volume II: *The Early Sasanian Period*, 1966, Volume III: *From Shapur I to Shapur II*, 1968, Volume IV: *The Age of Shapur II*, 1969, Volume V: *Later Sasanian Times*, 1970; *History and Torah: Essays on Jewish Learning*, Schocken, 1965; (contributor) David Weinstein and Michael Yizhar, editors, *Modern Jewish Educational Thought*, College of Jewish Studies Press, 1965; (editor) *Religions in Antiquity: Essays in Memory of Erwin Ramsdell Goodenough*, Brill, 1968.

Development of a Legend: Studies on the Traditions Concerning Yohanan ben Zakkai, Brill, 1970; *Way of Torah: An Introduction to Judaism*, Dickenson, 1970; *Judaism in the Secular Age: Essays on Fellowship, Community, and Freedom*, Vallentine, Mitchell, 1970; *Formation of the Babylonian Talmud: Studies in the Achievements of Late Nineteenth and Twentieth Century Historical and Literary-Critical Research*, Brill, 1970; *Aphrahat and Judaism: The Christian Jewish Argument in Fourth Century Iran*, Brill, 1971; *The Rabbinic Traditions About the Pharisees Before 70*, Brill, Volume I: *The Masters*, 1971, Volume II: *The Houses*, 1971, Volume III: *Conclusions*, 1971; *There We Sat Down: Talmudic Judaism in the Making*, Abingdon, 1972; *American Judaism: Adventure in Modernity*, Prentice-Hall, 1972; (editor) *Contemporary Judaic Fellowship, in Theory and Practice*, Ktav, 1972; *Eliezer ben Hyrcanus: The Tradition and the Man*, Brill, Volume I: *The Tradition*, 1973, Volume II: *The Man*, 1973; *The Idea of Purity in Ancient Judaism*, Brill, 1973; *From Politics to Piety: The Emergence of Pharisaic Judaism*, Prentice-Hall, 1973; (editor) *The Modern Study of the Mishnah*, Brill, 1973; (editor) *Soviet Views of Talmudic Judaism: Five Papers by Yu A. Solodukho*, Brill, 1973; *Invitation to the Talmud: A Teaching Book*, Harper, 1973; (editor) *Understanding Jewish Theology: Classical Themes and Modern Perspectives*, Ktav, 1973; *A History of the Mishnaic Law of Purities*, five volumes, Brill, 1974; (editor) *The Life of*

Torah: A Reader of Jewish Piety and Spirituality, Dickenson, 1974; (editor) *Understanding Rabbinic Judaism: From Talmudic to Modern Times*, Ktav, 1974.

Contributor to *American Oxford Encyclopedia* and *American Jewish Yearbook*. Contributor of more than one hundred articles and reviews to *Commentary*, *London Jewish Chronicle*, *New York Herald Tribune*, *Judaism*, and other general and scholarly journals. Columnist, *Jewish Digest*, 1955-59.

WORK IN PROGRESS: Christianity, Judaism and Other Greco-Roman Cults: Essays in Honor of Morton Smith, in four volumes.

*   *   *

NEWBIGIN, (James Edward) Lesslie 1909-

PERSONAL: Born December 8, 1909, in Newcastle upon Tyne, England; son of Edward Richmond and Ellen (Affleck) Newbigin; married Helen Stewart Henderson, August 20, 1936; children: Margaret (Mrs. David Beetham), Alison, Janet, John. *Education:* Queen's College, Cambridge, M.A., 1931; Westminster College, Cambridge, England, theological study, 1933-36. *Politics:* Labour. *Home:* Bishop's House Cathedral, Madras 86, South India.

CAREER: Ordained minister, Church of Scotland, 1936. Missionary in India, 1936-59, and bishop of Church of South India in Madura, 1947-59; International Missionary Council, general secretary, 1959-61; World Council of Churches, Geneva, Switzerland, associate general secretary, 1961-65; Bishop in Madras, India, 1965—. *Awards, honors:* D.D. from The Chicago Theological Seminary, 1954, University of St. Andrews, 1958, University of Hamburg, 1964.

WRITINGS: Christian Freedom in the Modern World, S.C.M. Press, 1937; *The Reunion of the Church*, S.C.M. Press, 1948; *South India Diary*, S.C.M. Press, 1951, published as *That All May Be One*, Association Press, 1952; *The Household of God*, S.C.M. Press, 1953; *Sin and Salvation*, S.C.M. Press, 1956; *A Faith for This One World?*, S.C.M. Press, 1961; *The Relevance of Trinitarian Doctrine for Today's Mission*, Edinburgh House Press, 1963, published as *Trinitarian Faith and Today's Mission*, John Knox, 1964; *Honest Religion for Secular Man*, Westminster Press, 1966; *The Finality of Christ*, John Knox, 1969; *Journey Into Joy*, Eerdsmans, 1973. Editor, *International Review of Missions*, 1959.†

*   *   *

NEWELL, Peter F(rancis) 1915-

PERSONAL: Born August 31, 1915, in Vancouver, British Columbia, Canada; son of Peter Francis and Alice E. (Heffron) Newell; married Florence O'Connor; children: Peter, Jr., Thomas, Roger, Gregory. *Education:* Loyola University of Los Angeles, A.B., 1940. *Religion:* Roman Catholic. *Home:* 1409 Gran Via Altamira, Palos Verdes Estates, Calif. 90274.

CAREER: University of California, Berkeley, director of intercollegiate athletics, 1960-68. San Diego Rockets, San Diego, Calif., general manager, 1968-72; Los Angeles Lakers, Los Angeles, Calif., general manager, 1972—. U.S. basketball coach at Olympic Games in Rome, 1960; conductor of basketball clinics. *Military service:* U.S. Naval Reserve, became lieutenant. *Member:* National Association of Basketball Coaches of the United States. *Awards, honors:* National Association of Basketball Coaches Metropolitan Award, 1968.

WRITINGS: (With John Benington) *Basketball Methods*, Ronald, 1961.

SIDELIGHTS: Newell has done coaching and conducted clinics in Guatemala, Brazil, and Japan.

*   *   *

NEWHAFER, Richard L. 1922-

PERSONAL: Born March 6, 1922, in Chicago, Ill.; son of Lewis P. and Mary (Dwyer) Newhafer; married Frederica Barker, 1965. *Education:* Attended University of Notre Dame, 1939-41, DePaul University, 1941-42. *Religion:* Roman Catholic. *Home and office address:* Box 1255-Rancho, Santa Fe, Calif. 92067. *Agent:* Gordon Molson, 10889 Wilshire Blvd., Los Angeles, Calif. 90024.

CAREER: U.S. Navy, naval aviator, 1942-55, became lieutenant commander; professional civilian pilot, 1955-60; full-time writer, 1960—. *Member:* Writers Guild of America (West), Authors League of America. *Awards, honors*—Military: Navy Cross, Distinguished Flying Cross and two oak leaf clusters, Air Medal and eleven oak leaf clusters, Presidential Unit Citation (twice), Navy Citation.

WRITINGS—All novels: *The Last Tallyho*, Putnam, 1964; *No More Bugles in the Sky*, New American Library, 1966; *The Golden Jungle*, New American Library, 1968; *On the Wings of the Storm*, Morrow, 1969; *The Frightful Sin of Cisco Newman*, Prentice-Hall, 1973; *Seven Days to Glory*, Pyramid, 1973.

Television scripts include episodes for "77 Sunset Strip," "Combat," and "Twelve o'Clock High."

WORK IN PROGRESS: The Flight of Jehovah One, a novel; "Rackley," a screenplay.

SIDELIGHTS: "My travel has been exclusively in the Far East, where in 1950 I had the dubious distinction of being the first American to fire a shot in the Korean War. It was no act of heroism—merely reflex action." *Avocational interests:* Golf ("fierce dedication and terrible score").

*   *   *

NEWMAN, Charles L. 1923-

PERSONAL: Born September 22, 1923, in New York, N.Y.; son of Harry and Rosetta (Nareff) Newman; married Della Scott, February 11, 1961; children: Mark, Scott, Lowell. *Education:* New York University, B.A., 1949, M.P.A., 1950, D.P.A., 1970; graduate study at University of North Dakota Law School, 1953, University of Minnesota, summers, 1954-56. *Politics:* Democrat. *Religion:* Presbyterian. *Home:* 1151 Westerly Parkway, State College Park, Pa. 16801. *Office:* Pennsylvania State University, 106 Human Development Bldg., University Park, Pa. 16802.

CAREER: New York (N.Y.) Department of Welfare, social investigator, 1950-51; Fairleigh Dickinson University, Rutherford, N.J., instructor in sociology, 1950-51; University of North Dakota, Grand Forks, instructor in sociology and social work, 1952-55; Florida State University, School of Social Welfare, Tallahassee, assistant professor of criminology and corrections, 1955-59; University of Louisville, Kent School of Social Work, Louisville, Ky., associate professor and director of program of correctional training, 1959-66; University of Louisville Law School, lecturer, 1962-66; Pennsylvania State University, University Park, professor and coordinator of law enforcement and corrections services, 1966—. Kentucky Citizens for Correctional

Research, director, 1961—; Kentucky Governor's Task Force on Criminal Justice, member, 1964-66; member, vice-president, Pennsylvania Governor's Justice Commission, Central Regional Planning Council, 1969—. Consultant to juvenile courts and correctional institutions; lecturer at conferences in United States and Canada. *Military service:* U.S. Army, 1943-46; New York National Guard, 1946-48; became second lieutenant.

MEMBER: International Society of Criminology, American Society of Criminology (fellow; national secretary-treasurer, 1962-66; president, 1971-72), National Association of Social Workers, American Correctional Association, American Association for the Advancement of Science (fellow), American League for the Abolition of Capital Punishment, National Council on Crime and Delinquency (Kentucky president, 1963-64.

WRITINGS: (Co-author) *Indiana Probation Survey*, three volumes, National Probation and Parole Association, 1957; *Educational Aspects of Delinquency, Illegitimacy, and Crime among Negroes in Florida*, State of Florida, 1957; *Sourcebook on Probation, Parole, and Pardons*, C. C Thomas, 1958, 3rd edition, 1968; (contributor) Vedder and Kay, editors, *Penology*, C. C Thomas, 1964; (editor with William Hewitt) *Police-Community Relations*, Foundation Press, 1970; *Personnel Practices in Adult Parole Systems*, C. C Thomas, 1971; (contributor) R. M. Carter and L. T. Wilkins, editors, *Probation and Parole*, Wiley, 1971; (contributor) *Crime and Punishment* (Turkish language), Mustafa Yucel, 1973; (editor with William Amos) *Parole: Legal Aspects, Predicitions, Research*, Aberdeen Press, 1974.

Contributor to *Indian Journal of Social Work, Police Film News, Police Chief, Federal Probation, Crime and Delinquency*, and to other legal, probation, and education journals. Editor of published symposia, *Criminologica* (journal of American Society of Criminology), 1962-65, and *Criminology: An Interdisciplinary Journal*, 1973—.

*   *   *

NEWMAN, Thelma R(ita)   1925-

PERSONAL: Born April 24, 1925, in Brooklyn, N.Y.; daughter of Allie H. and S. Kitty (Greenfield) Siegel; married Jack Newman, August 6, 1945; children: Jay Hartley, Lee Scott. *Education:* City College (now City College of the City University of New York), B.B.A., 1946; New York University, M.A., 1948; Columbia University, Ed.D., 1963. *Home:* 1101 Prospect St., Westfield, N.J.

CAREER: Instructor in art and art education at Jersey City State College, Jersey City, N.J., 1947-48, 1950-52, and at North Texas State College (now University), Denton, 1948-49; Union Township (N.J.) public schools, art specialist for elementary grades, 1957-61, for secondary grades, 1963-64, director of art, 1964-68; Classroom Renaissance, State of New Jersey, 1968-71; Project Open Classroom, Wayne, N.J., 1971—. Poly-Dec Co., Inc., Bayonne, N.J., president; operator of plastics studio, and exhibitor of sculpture in plastics throughout United States. Art consultant to Milton Bradley Co., 1961-62. *Member:* Society of Plastics Engineers (senior member). Museum of Contemporary Crafts (craftsman member).

WRITINGS: Plastics as an Art Form, Chilton, 1964, revised edition, 1968; *Wax as an Art Form*, A. S. Barnes, 1966; *Plastics as Design Form*, Chilton, 1972; *Creative Candlemaking*, Crown, 1972; *Contemporary Decoupage*, Crown, 1972; *Paper as Art and Craft*, Crown, 1973; *Leather as Art and Craft*, Crown, 1973; *The Frame Book*,

Crown, 1974; *Contemporary African Arts and Crafts*, Crown, 1974; *Plastics as Sculpture*, Chilton, 1974; *Plastics as Crafts*, Chilton, 1975; *Miniatures as Art and Craft*, Crown, 1975; *Wood as Craft Form*, Chilton, 1975; *Wood as Art Form*, Chilton, 1975; *Printforming Without a Press*, Crown, 1976. Contributor to *Craft Horizons, Instructor, Popular Imported Cars, Arts and Activities*, and other art and education journals.

*   *   *

NEWQUIST, Roy   1925-

PERSONAL: Born July 25, 1925, in Ashland, Wis.; son of Arvid and Faye (Horn) Newquist; married Ruth Strasen, January 7, 1948; children: Karen, Karl, Greta. *Education:* Attended Marquette University, 1943-46, University of Wisconsin, 1946-49. *Politics:* Independent. *Religion:* Protestant. *Home:* 428 Tomahawk, Park Forest, Ill. *Office: Chicago's American*, Chicago, Ill.

CAREER: Copy supervisor for various advertising agencies in Minneapolis and Chicago, 1951-63; *Chicago's American*, Chicago, Ill., literary editor, 1963—. Syndicated book review columnist; critic, for *New York Post*, 1963—. One-time host of radio program "Counterpoint," WQXR, New York.

WRITINGS: Counterpoint, Rand McNally, 1964; *Showcase*, Morrow, 1965; *Conversations*, Rand McNally, 1967; *Fielding's Guide to Chicago*, Fielding Publications, 1970; *A Special Kind of Magic*, Pyramid, 1972. Writes interview features for *Show*.

WORK IN PROGRESS: The official biography of Ben Hecht.

SIDELIGHTS: Newquist's first book covers more than sixty writers out of the 252 he interviewed on tape in New York (mainly), London, Paris, Edinburgh, and other points. The tapes ran about an hour on the average, and portions from them were culled for his radio program. In the introduction to *Counterpoint* he says that only three of the writers contacted refused to be interviewed, and only two interviews ended unhappily. For the rest the writers were "so cooperative, so congenial, that I finished up the series ten pounds heavier and a bit alcoholic."†

*   *   *

NICHOLS, Roger L(ouis)   1933-

PERSONAL: Born June 13, 1933, in Racine, Wis.; son of George Calvin (a tool and die worker) and Antoinette (Zegerius) Nichols; married Marilyn Jane Ward, July 11, 1959; children: Cynthia Margaret, Sarah Elizabeth, Martha Catherine, Jeffrey Robert. *Education:* Wisconsin State College (now University of Wisconsin at LaCrosse), B.S., 1956; University of Wisconsin, M.S., 1959, Ph.D., 1963. *Politics:* Liberal Democrat. *Religion:* Protestant. *Office:* History Department, University of Arizona, Tucson, Ariz.

CAREER: Junior high school teacher of history and English in Evergreen Park, Ill., 1956-57; Wisconsin State University (now University of Wisconsin at Oshkosh), assistant professor of history, 1963-65; University of Georgia, Athens, associate professor of history, 1965-69, University of Arizona, Tucson, associate professor, 1969-70, professor of history, 1970—. *Military service:* National Guard, 1951-59, *Member:* American Historical Association (Pacific Coast Branch), Organization of American Historians, Western Historical Association, Arizona Historical Society.

WRITINGS: General Henry Atkinson: A Western Military Career, University of Oklahoma Press, 1965; *The Missouri Expedition, 1818-1820*, University of Oklahoma Press, 1969; (editor with George R. Adams) *The American Indian: Past and Present*, Xerox College Publishing, 1971. Contributor of articles to *Annals of Iowa, Nebraska History, Wisconsin Magazine of History, Agricultural History, Kansas Quarterly, Military Affairs*, and other historical journals.

WORK IN PROGRESS: Stephen H. Long and American Frontier Exploration; American Frontier and Western Cities, publication by Putnam expected in 1977; *American Attitudes Toward the Indians*, expected in 1978.

* * *

NICHOLSON, Hubert 1908-

PERSONAL: Born January 23, 1908, in Hull, England; son of Samuel and Amy (Beckworth) Nicholson; children: two sons, one daughter. *Home:* Kertch Cottage, 3 Albert Road, Epsom, England.

CAREER: Journalist on various English newspapers and employee in aluminum foundry prior to 1945; Reuters News Agency, London, England, sub-editor, 1945-68; novelist and poet. *Member:* P.E.N., National Union of Journalists (fellow), Institute of Arts and Letters (fellow).

WRITINGS: Date (poetry), Coleridge Bookshop, 1935; *New Spring Song* (poetry), Fortune Press, 1943; *Half my Days and Nights* (autobiography), Heinemann, 1947; *A Voyage to Wonderland, and other Essays*, Heinemann, 1947; *Port and a Pistol* (drama), Heinemann, 1954; *The Mirage in the South* (poetry), Heinemann, 1955.

Novels—All published by Heinemann except as indicated: *Face your Lover*, Holt, 1935; *Here Where the World is Quiet*, 1944; *No Cloud of Glory*, Progress House, 1946; *The Sacred Afternoon*, 1949; *Little Heyday*, 1954; *Sunk Island*, 1956, Coward, 1957; *Mr. Hill and Friends*, 1960; *Patterns of Three and Four*, 1965; *Duckling in Capri*, 1966; *The Lemon Tree*, 1970; *Dead Man's Life*, 1971; *Ella*, 1973, Popular Library, 1974.

Poems represented in anthologies, including *Best Poems of 1955*, Stanford University Press, and in several P.E.N. collections.

* * *

NICOLE, Christopher Robin 1930-
(Peter Grange, Andrew York)

PERSONAL: Born December 7, 1930, in Georgetown, British Guiana; son of Jack (a police officer) and Jean Dorothy (Logan) Nicole; married Regina Amelia Barnett, March 31, 1951; children: Bruce, Jack, Julie. *Education:* Attended Harrison College, and Barbados, and Queen's College, British Guiana. *Home:* South Grange de Beauvoir, St. Peter Port, Guernsey, Channel Islands. *Agent:* Richmond Towers & Benson Ltd., 14 Essex St., London W.C. 2, England.

CAREER: Employed by Royal Bank of Canada in West Indian branches, 1947-56; author, now living on Guernsey, Channel Islands, England.

WRITINGS: West Indian Cricket, Phoenix Sports Books, 1957; *Off White* (novel), Jarrolds, 1959; *Shadows in the Jungle* (novel), Jarrolds, 1961; *Ratoon* (historical novel), Jarrolds, 1962; *Dark Noon* (historical novel), Jarrolds, 1963; *Amyot's Cay* (historical novel), Jarrolds, 1964; *Blood Amyot* (historical novel), Jarrolds, 1964; *The Amyot Crime* (historical novel), Jarrolds, 1965; *The West Indies*, Hutchinson, 1965; *White Boy*, Hutchinson, 1966; *The Self Lovers*, Hutchinson, 1968; *Operation Destruct*, Holt, 1969; *The Thunder and the Shouting*, Doubleday, 1969; *Operation Manhunt*, Holt, 1970; *The Longest Pleasure*, Hutchinson, 1970; *Where the Cavern Ends* (juvenile thriller), Holt, 1970; *Operation Neptune*, Holt, 1972; *Ratoon*, Bantam, 1973.

Under pseudonym Peter Grange: *King Creole*, Jarrolds, 1966; *The Devil's Emissary*, Jarrolds, 1968; *The Tumult at the Gate*, Jarrolds, 1970.

Under pseudonym Andrew York: *The Eliminator*, Hutchinson, 1966, Lippincott, 1967; *The Coordinator*, Lippincott, 1967; *The Predator*, Lippincott, 1968; *The Denominator*, Hutchinson, 1969; *The Doom Fisherman*, Hutchinson, 1969; *The Deviator*, Lippincott, 1969; *The Infiltrator*, Doubleday, 1971; *Appointment in Kiltone*, Hutchinson Junior Books, 1972; *The Expurgator*, Hutchinson, 1972, Doubleday, 1973; *The Captivator*, Doubleday, 1974.†

* * *

NICOLSON, (Lionel) Benedict 1914-

PERSONAL: Born August 6, 1914, in Sevenoaks, England; son of Sir Harold George and Victoria (Sackville-West) Nicolson; married Luisa Vertova (an art historian), August 8, 1955; children: Vanessa. *Education:* Attended Eton College, 1928-32, Balliol College, Oxford, 1933-36. *Home:* 45 B Holland Park, London W. 11, England. *Office:* Elm House, 10-16 Elm St., London W.C.1, England.

CAREER: Deputy surveyor of the King's Pictures, 1939-47; editor of *Burlington Magazine*, London, England, 1947—. *Military service:* British Army, Intelligence, 1939-45; served in Italy and Middle East; became captain. *Member:* Brooks's Club. *Awards, honors:* Member of the Royal Victorian Order, 1947.

WRITINGS: The Painters of Ferrara, Elek, 1950; *Hendrick Terbrugghen*, Lund, Humphries, 1958, *Wright of Derby*, 2 volumes, Pantheon, 1968; (with Christopher Wright) *Georges de la Tour*, Phaidon, 1974. Contributor to *New Statesman, Observer, Listener*, and *Art de France*.

SIDELIGHTS: Nicolson is competent in French and Italian. *Avocational interests:* Reading.

* * *

NIMMO, Dan D(ean) 1933-

PERSONAL: Born June 23, 1933, in Springfield, Mo.; son of James Wesley and Elizabeth (Baker) Nimmo; married Joan Jeanine Leimer, October 27, 1956; children: Gregory Phillip, Victoria Jeanine, Laurence Wesley. *Education:* University of Missouri, A.B., 1955; Vanderbilt University, M.A., 1956, Ph.D., 1962. *Home:* 7931 Corteland Dr., Knoxville, Tenn. 37919.

CAREER: University of Wichita, Wichita, Kan., assistant professor of political science, 1961-62; Texas Technological College (now Texas Tech University), Lubbock, assistant professor of political science, 1962-64; University of Houston, Houston, Tex., assistant professor, 1964-65, associate professor of political science, 1965-68; University of Missouri, Columbia, professor of political science, 1968-72; University of Tennessee, Knoxville, professor of political science, 1972—. *Military service:* U.S. Army, 1956-59; served in Europe; became first lieutenant. *Member:* American Political Science Association, International Communication Association, International Society for General Semantics, Southern Political Science Association, Southwestern Political Science Association. *Awards, honors:* Woodrow Wilson fellow, 1955-56; Ford Foundation grant for research in public affairs, 1960; visiting fellow, Brookings Institution, 1960-61; Atherton Press-American Political Science Association award, 1962, for *Newsgathering in Washington.*

WRITINGS: Newsgathering in Washington, Atherton, 1964; (with T. D. Ungs) *American Political Patterns: Conflict and Consensus,* Little, 1967, 3rd edition, 1973; *The Political Persuaders: The Techniques of Modern Election Campaigns,* Prentice-Hall, 1970; (with W. E. Oden) *The Texas Political System,* Prentice-Hall, 1971; (editor with C. M. Bonjean) *Political Attitudes and Public Opinion,* McKay, 1972; *Popular Images of Politics,* Prentice-Hall, 1974.

WORK IN PROGRESS: The Images of Political Candidates, publication by Goodyear expected in 1976; *Political Communication and Behavior,* publication by Goodyear expected in 1977.

*   *   *

NIMS, John Frederick 1913-

PERSONAL: Born November 20, 1913, in Muskegon, Mich.; son of Frank McReynolds and Anne (McDonald) Nims; married Bonnie Larkin, September 11, 1947; children: John, Frank, George (deceased), Sarah, Emily. *Education:* Attended DePaul University for two years: University of Notre Dame, A.B., 1937, A.M., 1939; University of Chicago, Ph.D., 1945. *Politics:* Democrat. *Religion:* Roman Catholic. *Office:* Department of English, University of Florida, Gainesville, Fla. 32611.

CAREER: Taught English and Latin in a prepatory school in Portland, Ore., 1936; University of Notre Dame, Notre Dame, Ind., 1939-45, 1946-62, began as instructor, became professor of English, 1955-62; University of Illinois, Urbana, visiting writer, 1961-62, professor of English, 1962-65, professor of English at Chicago Circle campus, 1965-73; University of Florida, Gainesville, professor of English, 1973—. Poetry judge, National Book Awards, 1969; visiting professor, University of Toronto, 1945-46, Bocconi University, 1952-53, University of Florence, 1953-54, University of Madrid, 1958-60, Harvard University, 1964, 1968-69, Breadloaf School of English, 1965-69. *Awards, honors:* Harriet Monroe Memorial Prize, 1942; Friends of Literature Award, 1947, for *The Iron Pastoral;* National Foundation for the Arts and Humanities grant, 1967-68; American Academy of Arts and Letters award, 1968; Brandeis University citation for poetry, 1974.

WRITINGS: (Contributor) *Five Young American Poets: Third Series,* New Directions, 1944; *The Iron Pastoral* (poems), Sloane, 1947; *A Fountain in Kentucky* (poems), Sloane, 1950; (translator) *Poems of St. John of the Cross,* Grove, 1959, revised edition, 1968; (contributor of translations) *Complete Greek Tragedies,* University of Chicago Press, 1959; *Knowledge of the Evening* (poems), Rutgers University Press, 1960; (associate editor and contributor) *The Poem Itself,* Holt, 1960; (editor) Ovid, *Metamorphoses,* Macmillan, 1965; *Of Flesh and Bone* (poems), Rutgers University Press, 1967; (compiler) *Sappho to Valery: Poems in Translation,* Rutgers University Press, 1971; *Western Wind: An Introduction to Poetry,* Random House, 1974.

Contributor to *Poetry, Accent, Partisan Review, Saturday Review, Harper's, Kenyon Review,* and to other publications. Member of editorial board, *Poetry,* 1945-48, visiting editor, 1960-61.

WORK IN PROGRESS: Poems and translations; an anthology of lyric poetry.

SIDELIGHTS: Robert Lewis Weeks calls Nims' poetry "highly individual, ... somewhat difficult because of a compressed intellectuality, ... [but] also full of emotional power." He has, writes J. P. Clancy, "a very real gift for irony, for colloquial wit.... But his finest talent is his pure sweet lyricism...." He is, according to some critics, never sentimental, not even in the masterful elegy to his dead son, which has been called one of the finest elegies in the language.

BIOGRAPHICAL/CRITICAL SOURCES: Commonweal, November 11, 1960; *New York Times Book Review,* November 13, 1960; *Nation,* November 26, 1906; *Epoch,* fall, 1960; *Saturday Review,* February 11, 1961; *Christian Century,* February 28, 1961; *Prairie Schooner,* winter, 1961-62; *Times Literary Supplement,* September 14, 1967; *Kenyon Review,* November, 1967; *Poetry,* August, 1968, January, 1969.

*   *   *

NIN, Anais 1903-

PERSONAL: Surname is pronounced *Neen;* born February, 1903, in Paris, France; came to United States in 1914, now an American citizen; daughter of Joaquin (a pianist and composer) and Rosa (a singer; maiden name Culmell) Nin; married Hugh Guiler (a banker; later, under the name Ian Hugo, a filmmaker and illustrator of Miss Nin's books) 1920. *Education:* Attended public schools in New York; self-educated after grammar school. *Agent:* Gunther Stuhlmann, 65 Irving Place, New York, N.Y. 10003.

CAREER: After leaving school at fifteen, worked as a fashion and artist's model; studied Spanish dance, giving one recital in Paris in the thirties; studied psychoanalysis, then practiced under Otto Rank in Europe, and briefly in New York, in the mid-1930's, returning to France in 1935; established Siana Editions with Villa Seurat group (Henry Miller, Alfred Perles, Michael Fraenkel), about 1935; returned to United States in 1940; published her own books for four years; more recently, has been a frequent lecturer at colleges and universities, including Harvard University, University of Chicago, Dartmouth College, University of Michigan, University of California, Berkeley, and Duke University. Has also taught creative writing, and acted in films. Member of advisory board, Feminist Book Club, Los Angeles, and Women's History library, Berkeley, Calif. *Member:* National Institute of Arts and Letters. *Awards, honors:* Prix Sevigne, 1971.

WRITINGS: D. H. Lawrence: An Unprofessional Study, E. W. Titus (Paris), 1932, Spearman, 1961, A. Swallow, 1964; *The House of Incest,* Siana Editions (Paris), 1936, [Ann Arbor, Mich.], 1958, Anais Nin Press, 1959, A. Swallow, 1961; *The Winter of Artifice,* Obelisk Press (Paris), 1939, A. Swallow, 1961; *Under a Glass Bell* (collected stories), Gemor Press (New York), 1944, Dutton, 1948, A. Swallow, 1961; *This Hunger,* Gemor Press, 1945; *Ladders to Fire,* Dutton, 1946; *On Writing,* O. Baradinsky, 1947; *Children of the Albatross* (novel), Dutton, 1947; *The Four-Chambered Heart* (novel), Duell, Sloan & Pearce, 1950; *A Spy in the House of Love,* British Book Centre, 1954; *Solar Barque,* [Ann Arbor], 1958.

Cities of the Interior (collection of previously-published novels), A. Swallow, 1961; *Seduction of the Minotaur*, A. Swallow, 1961; *Collages* (novel), A. Swallow, 1964; *The Diary of Anais Nin*, edited by Gunther Stuhlmann, Harcourt (first two volumes published in conjunction with Swallow Press), Volume I: *1931-1934*, 1966, Volume II: *1934-1939*, 1967, Volume III: *1939-1944*, 1969, Volume IV: *1944-1947*, 1971, Volume V, *1947-1955*, 1974 (published in England as *The Journals of Anais Nin*, P. Owen, Volume I, 1966, Volume II, 1967, Volume III, 1970); *Unpublished Selections from the Diary* (excerpts from Volume I), edited by Duane Schneider, D. Schneider Press, 1968; *The Novel of the Future*, Macmillan, 1968; *Nuances*, San Souci Press, 1970; *Paris Revisited*, Capra Press, 1972; (contributor) Rochelle Holt, editor, *Eidolons* (contains diary excerpts written in 1971), Ragnarok Press, 1973; *Anais Nin Reader*, edited by Philip K. Jason, Swallow Press, 1973.

Author of introduction: Henry Miller, *Tropic of Cancer*, Obelisk Press, 1934; Bettina L. Knapp, *Antonin Artaud: A Man of Vision*, David Lewis, 1969; John Pearson, *The Sun's Birthday*, Doubleday, 1973.

Work is represented in anthologies, including: *Affinities: A Short Story Anthology*, edited by John Tytell and Harold Jaffe, Crowell, 1970; *Woman: An Issue*, edited by Lee R. Edwards, Mary Heath, and Lisa Baskin, Little, Brown, 1972; *Images of Women in Literature*, edited by Mary Anne Ferguson, Houghton, 1973.

Contributor to periodicals and newspapers, including *Massachusetts Review, Books Abroad, New York Times, Village Voice, Saturday Review, New York Times Book Review, Open City, Matrix, Trace* (London), *Voyages*, and *Studies in the Twentieth Century. Booster and Delta* (both Paris), society editor, 1937, associate editor, 1937-38, member of editorial board, 1939; *Two Cities*, general editor, 1959, honorary editor, 1960; *Voyages*, member of advisory board, 1967—.

WORK IN PROGRESS: Editing further volumes of her journal, which now consists of over 150 volumes, or an estimated 15,000 typewritten manuscript pages.

SIDELIGHTS: Miss Nin once remarked: "I have wanted in my writing to unmask the deeper self that lies hidden behind the self that we present to the world. I have written about artists because they have a greater internal freedom. Despite their neuroses, they know how to *create* their lives and transform reality." "It is necessary to travel *inwardly*," she has said, "to find the levels at which we carry on, in a free-flowing, immensely rich vein, the uninhibited inner monologue in distinction to the controlled manner in which we converse with others." And, she writes, "We are going to the moon. That is not very far. Man has so much farther to go within himself."

She says she has been a writer since the age of eleven. In 1934 she wrote the preface to the first edition of Henry Miller's *Tropic of Cancer*, showing a perceptive appreciation for an author whose orientation was not necessarily her own. It was Miller who first brought her to the attention of American readers 30 years ago when he published *Un Etre Etoilique* ("A Luminous Being"). (Miller's letters to Miss Nin have been published.) Her poetic prose has always been associated with the vanguard of contemporary literature. For many years, unable to find an American publisher, she called herself an "underground writer." She bought a second-hand, foot-operated press, and began to print her own books. The books found a small though international audience. Later, her earlier works were reprinted in hard cover and paperback by Alan Swallow.

The central vision in her stories is always that of a woman. She explores a feminine character in great detail and defines other characters in relation to this woman. Harriet Zinnes in *Books Abroad* writes: "She is tremendously in tune with life and has that indestructible passion of one who lives and knows life fearlessly. She conceals nothing (nothing that is vital, that is), knows no taboos, yet there is nothing unlovely even in her relating of the crudest moments.... She exults in life and in being a woman ... she distrusts the object. She has no use for what has been called *l'ecole du regard*. It is the interior world that she trusts, and unashamedly she allows her 'feminine spirit—labyrinthine, elusive, and mobile' to dominate her perceptions."

Critics have claimed that by this predisposition for the interior world she neglects the "real" world to write about dreams and fantasies. But her intent has always been to remove the barriers which exist between our outer and inner selves, and to show the reality of the world of dreams. Her writing has been influenced by the surrealists, by psychoanalysis, by writers like D. H. Lawrence, Djuna Barnes, and Isak Dinesen, and by painters like Klee and Varda.

In a review of *Collages* in the *Los Angeles Free Press*, Deena P. Metzger writes: "... although *Collages* is a novel about people with dreams they are people who are connected to the world through a thousand sensual links and whose dreams are made manifest by a multiplicity of acts and gestures.... Certainly this is a frightening book. The characters and the reader stand naked." And the *Times Literary Supplement* called *Collages* "An insider's game, in both literary and biographical senses, but one which offers even to the outsider some excellent moments of comedy and beauty, a handful of perfectly told fables, and prose which is so daringly elaborate, so accurately timed, that even if one is mystified by the author's distinguished reputation it is not entirely surprising to hear her compared with Proust."

Henry Miller once remarked that Miss Nin's diary will "take its place beside the revelations of St. Augustine, Petronius, Abelard, Rousseau, and Proust," an enthusiasm that with the publication of five volumes, has not gone unconfirmed. Critics have called it "one of the most ambitious undertakings in modern writing," "singularly potent," "among the outstanding literary works of this century." While the diary is a highly personal record, it is also seen by some as "proof that by being one's self to the extreme, one may penetrate to the core of universality," or as "a remarkably complete assessment of an era." Daniel Stern writes that the intention and scope of the diary "evoke Proust, Gide, and their poetic siblings—those artists of the first person who took their own sensibility as the refracting mirror, placed their friends and the history of their time before it, and captured the reflections in crystals of light that will illumine long after ordinary 'memoirs' and 'diaries' have lost their temporary, temporal interest."

Miss Nin's recordings of her own work include: "Anais Nin Reading Her Own Novel *House of Incest*: A Prose-Poem Fantasy," and "Anais Nin Reading Her Own Short Stories from *Under a Glass Bell*," both released by Contemporary Classics, 1949; she has recorded selections from her diary for a record entitled "The Diary of Anais Nin," two discs, Spoken Arts, 1969. Walter Carroll adapted *Under a Glass Bell* for a film of the same title; the film was presented in New York at Headquarters Theatre, St. Mark's Place, 1967. John McLean and Sharon Bunn adapted Volume I of the *Diary* for a play entitled "The Voice of a Woman," first produced in Dallas, Tex. at Poverty Playhouse, 1970. Danielle Suissa acquired film rights to *A Spy in the House of Love* in 1970.

Much of Miss Nin's published and unpublished material has been collected at Northwestern University Library.

BIOGRAPHICAL/CRITICAL SOURCES: Outcast Chapbooks, No. 11; *Nation*, July 24, 1954; *Prairie Schooner*, fall, 1962; *L'Express*, February 28, 1963; *Books Abroad*, summer, 1963; *Times Literary Supplement*, April 30, 1964; *Los Angeles Free Press*, November 26, 1964; *New York Times Book Review*, November 29, 1964; *Mademoiselle*, March, 1965; O. W. Evans, *Anais Nin*, Southern Illinois University Press, 1968; Duane Schneider, *An Interview with Anais Nin*, D. Schneider Press, 1970; *Under the Sign of Pisces: Anais Nin and Her Circle* (quarterly published through Ohio State University Libraries), all issues, 1970—; *Southern Review*, spring, 1970; *Oz* (London), July, 1970; *The Second Wave* (Boston), summer, 1971; *Vogue*, October 15, 1971; E. J. Hinz, *The Mirror and the Garden*, Harcourt, 1973; Valerie Harms, editor, *Celebration with Anais Nin*, Magic Circle Press, 1973; *Anais Observed* (film), Robert Snyder, 1973; Carolyn Riley, editor, *Contemporary Literary Criticism*, Gale, Volume I, 1973, Volume IV, 1975.†

*   *   *

NITSKE, W(illiam) Robert   1909-

PERSONAL: Born March 29, 1909, in Germany; came to United States, 1929; became U.S. citizen, 1936; son of Robert and Emma Nitske; married Betty L. Fugatt, June, 1939. *Education:* Educated in German schools. *Home:* 7750 Arundel Dr., Tucson, Ariz.

CAREER: Manager, F. W. Woolworth Co. store and owner, Ben Franklin store prior to World War II; because of a war-connected disability, began free-lance writing, contributing to automobile magazines and doing a regular column on European automotive affairs for *Motoracing*; now regular columnist and feature editor for *Mercedes-Benz Star*, traveling (to Europe mainly) to report on automobile racing and rallying and on manufacturing trends. *Military service:* U.S. Army, 1943-46. *Member:* Mercedes-Benz Club of America (regional director, 1957), Channel City Club (Santa Barbara).

WRITINGS: The Complete Mercedes Story, Macmillan, 1955; *The Amazing Porsche and Volkswagen Story*, Autobooks, 1958; (with Charles Morrow Wilson) *Rudolf Diesel: Pioneer of the Age of Power*, University of Oklahoma Press, 1965; *The Life of Wilhelm Conrad Roentgen*, University of Arizona Press, 1971; (editor and translator from the German) Paul Wilhelm, *Travels in North America, 1822-24*, University of Oklahoma Press, 1973. Contributor to automotive magazines.

WORK IN PROGRESS: A biography of a German aviation pioneer.

*   *   *

NOEL HUME, Ivor   1927-

PERSONAL: Born 1927 in London, England; married Audrey Baines. *Education:* Attended Framingham College, Suffolk, England, and St. Lawrence College, Kent, England. *Office:* Department of Archaeology, Colonial Williamsburg, Va.

CAREER: Guildhall Museum, London, England, archaeol-

ogist responsible for recovery of antiquities in postwar London, 1949-57; Colonial Williamsburg, Va., chief archaeologist, 1957-64, director of department of archaeology, 1964—. Honorary research associate, Smithsonian Institution, 1959—. *Military service:* Indian Army, 1944-45; invalided out. *Member:* American Association of Museums, Zoological Society of London (fellow), Society of Antiquaries of London (fellow), Kent Archaeological Society, Virginia Archeological Society. *Awards, honors:* Society of Colonial Wars in the State of New York best book award and American Association for State and Local History award of merit, both 1964, for *Here Lies Virginia*.

WRITINGS: Archaeology in Britain, Foyle, 1953; (with A. Noel Hume) *Handbook of Tortoises, Terrapins and Turtles*, Foyle, 1954; *Treasure in the Thames*, Muller, 1956; *Great Moments in Archaeology*, Phoenix House, 1957; *Here Lies Virginia* (American Heritage selection), Knopf, 1963; *1775, Another Part of the Field*, Knopf, 1966; *Historical Archaeology*, Knopf, 1968; *A Guide to Artifacts of Colonial America*, Knopf, 1969; *All the Best Rubbish*, Harper, 1974.

Author of two pseudonymous novels in England, 1971 and 1972. Also author of pamphlets and more than forty archaeological reports, studies and articles on glass and ceramics published in British and American journals, including *Archaeologia Cantiana, Illustrated London News, Antiques, Journal of Glass Studies, Connoisseur, Apollo, Country Life.*

*   *   *

NOLAN, Winefride (Bell)   1913-

PERSONAL: Born November 12, 1913, in Bagillt, North Wales; daughter of James (an engineer) and Sarah (Williams) Bell; married James Joseph Nolan (a farmer), August 5, 1939; children: Brian Patrick. *Education:* University College of North Wales, B.A. (honors) and Higher Diploma in Education, 1935. *Religion:* Roman Catholic. *Home:* Tinnakilly Upper, Aughaim, County Wicklow, Ireland.

CAREER: Primary and secondary school teacher in Britain, 1933-45. Writer. *Member:* Soroptimists Club.

WRITINGS: Rich Inheritance, 1952, *Exiles Come Home*, 1955, and *David and Jonathan*, 1955 (historical trilogy for juniors), Macmillan; *The New Invasion* (autobiography), Macmillan, 1953; *The Flowing Tide* (novel), Macmillan, 1957; *Seven Fatkine*, Talbot, 1966; *The Night of the Wolf* (autobiography), Talbot, 1969. Writer of short stories for magazines and radio, and of articles, mostly for farming papers.

AVOCATIONAL INTERESTS: Agricultural community activities and youth work.†

*   *   *

NOONAN, John T., Jr.   1926-

PERSONAL: Born October 24, 1926, in Boston, Mass.; son of John T. and Marie (Shea) Noonan. *Education:* Harvard University, A.B., 1947, LL.B., 1954; Cambridge University, graduate study; Catholic University of America, M.A. and Ph.D., 1951. *Religion:* Catholic. *Home:* 2599 Buena Vista Way, Berkeley, Calif. 94708. *Office:* Law School, University of California, Berkeley, Calif.

CAREER: National Security Council, Washington, D.C., member of special staff, 1954-55; Herrick, Smith, Donald, Farley and Ketchum (law firm), Boston, Mass., attorney,

1955-61; University of Notre Dame Law School, Notre Dame, Ind., professor of law, 1961-66; University of California, Berkeley, professor of law, 1967—, chairman of religious studies, 1970-73, and director of Natural Law Institute. Brookline (Mass.) Redevelopment Authority, chairman, 1958-62. Papal Commission on the Family, Population, and Natality, consultant, 1965-66; secretary-treasurer, Institute for Research in Medieval Canon Law, 1970—. Trustee, Population Council, 1969—, Phi Beta Kappa foundation, 1970—. Oliver Wendell Holmes, Jr. lecturer, Harvard Law School, 1972. Member of board of directors, Center for Human Values in Health Sciences, 1969-71, Institute for the Study of Ethical Issues, 1971-73. Fellow, Center for Advanced Studies in Behavioral Sciences, 1973-74. *Member:* American Association for Legal and Political Philosophy (vice-president). *Awards, honors:* Guggenheim fellow, 1965; John Gilmary Shea Prize, 1965, for *Contraception: A History of Its Treatment by the Catholic Theologians and Canonists.*

WRITINGS: The Scholastic Analysis of Usury, Harvard University Press, 1957; *Contraception: A History of Its Treatment by the Catholic Theologians and Canonists*, Harvard University Press, 1965; *The Church and Contraception: The Issues at Stake*, Paulist Press, 1967; (editor) *The Morality of Abortion: Legal and Historical Perspectives*, Harvard University Press, 1970; *Power to Dissolve: Lawyers and Marriages in the Courts of the Roman Curia*, Harvard University Press, 1972. Editor, *Natural Law Forum*, 1961-70, *American Journal of Jurisprudence*, 1970.†

*　　*　　*

NORD, Ole C. 1935-

PERSONAL: Born December 24, 1935, in Oslo, Norway; son of Karl C. and Karen (Thinn) Nord. *Education:* Norwegian Institute of Technology, Siv. ing., 1959; Massachusetts Institute of Technology, S.M., 1962. *Office:* Informatics Inc., Western Systems Company, 21050 Vanowen St., Canoga Park, Calif. 91303.

CAREER: Massachusetts Institute of Technology, Cambridge, was staff member of industrial dynamics research group, 1960-64; Parsons & Williams, Los Angeles, Calif., and Copenhagen, Denmark, management consultant, 1974-74; Informatics Inc., Canoga Park, Calif., 1974—. *Member:* Institute of Management Science, Norwegian Engineers Association, Norwegian Economists Association.

WRITINGS: Growth of a New Product; Effects of Capacity-Acquisition Policies, M.I.T. Press, 1963; (contributor) W. Edwin Jarmain, editor, *Problems in Industrial Dynamics*, M.I.T. Press, 1963; (with David W. Packer and others) *Management Science: A Primer for Managers*, Management Science Associates, 1964; (editor) *Integrated Manufacturing Planning*, Student Literature (Sweden), 1967.

BIOGRAPHICAL/CRITICAL SOURCES: Business Week, December 28, 1963.

*　　*　　*

NORDBERG, Robert B. 1921-

PERSONAL: Born December 25, 1921, in Denver, Colo.; son of George G. and Esther M. (Lloyd) Nordberg; married Beverly Schulte, August 29, 1946; children: Paul, Peter. *Education:* University of Denver, B.A., 1948,

Ed.D., 1954; University of Colorado, M.A., 1949. *Religion:* Catholic. *Home:* 4129 North Farwell, Shorewood, Wis. *Office:* School of Education, Marquette University, 502 North 15th St., Milwaukee, Wis.

CAREER: Catholic University of America, Washington, D.C., assistant professor of education, 1954-61; Marquette University, Milwaukee, Wis., associate professor, 1961-66, professor of education, 1966—, director of graduate education, 1970—. Part-time teacher at various periods at University of Colorado, University of Alaska, University of Denver, Trinity College, Washington, D.C., Loyola College, Baltimore, Md., and University of Minnesota. *Military service:* U.S. Army Air Forces, 1942-45; served in Africa and Italy. U.S. Air Force, 1950-51; served in Alaska. *Member:* Psychologists Interested in Religious Issues, American Personnel and Guidance Association, Association for Counselor Education and Supervision, National Catholic Guidance Conference (member of board of directors, 1967-70), Wisconsin Personnel and Guidance Association.

WRITINGS: (With A. M. Dupuis) *Philosophy and Education: A Total View*, Bruce, 1964, 3rd edition, Benziger, Bruce & Glencoe, 1973, (with A. M. Dupuis) *The School and Society*, University of Minnesota Press, 1964; (with J. E. Wise and D. Reitz) *Methods of Research in Education*, Heath, 1967; *Guidance: A Systematic Introduction*, Random House, 1970; *The Teenager and the New Mysticism*, Rosen Press, 1973.

Contributor: J. W. Stafford, editor, *Counseling in the Secondary School*, Catholic University Press, 1962; H. W. Hildebrandt, editor, *Issues of Our Time: A Summons to Speak*, Macmillan, 1963; M. M. Redmond and R. B. Hayes, editors, *Training for Clinical Research in Mental Health Nursing*, Catholic University Press, 1963; W. B. Kolesnik and E. J. Power, editors, *Catholic Education: A Book of Readings*, McGraw, 1965.

Contributor of articles and reviews to professional journals. Director of miscellaneous workshops and tele-lecture series. Consulting editor, *Counseling and Values*, former editor, *Educational Research Monographs.*

*　　*　　*

NORDSTROM, Ursula

PERSONAL: Born in New York, N.Y.; daughter of William and Marie (Nordstrom) Litchfield. *Education:* Attended Northfield School for Girls and Scudder Preparatory School. *Politics:* Democrat. *Home:* 155 East 50th St., New York, N.Y. *Office:* Harper & Row, Publishers, Inc., 49 East 33rd St., New York, N.Y. 10016.

CAREER: Harper & Row, Publishers, Inc., New York, N.Y., assistant to children's book editor, 1936-40, director of boys and girls book department, 1941—, vice-president, 1960, senior vice-president and publisher, 1967—. *Member:* Children's Book Council (president, 1954), American Association of School Libraries, Children's Library Association, American Library Association, Cosmopolitan Club. *Awards, honors:* Harper and Row, Gold Medal Award for outstanding editorial achievement, 1967; Constance Lindsay Skinner Award, 1972.

WRITINGS: The Secret Language, Harper, 1960.†

*　　*　　*

NORTH, Joan 1920-

PERSONAL: Born February 15, 1920, in Hendon, London, England; daughter of Frank Wevil Gordon (a metallurgist) and Gladys May (Paybody) North; married C. A. Rogers (Astor Professor of Mathematics at University College, University of London), February 24, 1952; children: Jane Petronelle Rogers, Petra Nell Rogers. *Education:* Attended schools in England prior to 1932, in China, 1932-35, Lowther College, Wales, 1935-36, King's College, University of London, 1938-39. *Home:* 8 Grey Close, London NW. 11, England.

CAREER: Variously employed for brief periods in social work, nursing, with British Broadcasting Corp., and in publications department of Tate Gallery, London, England; now free-lance writer. *Military service:* British Woman's Auxiliary Air Force, 1940-45; became leading aircraftswoman. *Member:* Society of Authors, Buddhist Society, College of Psychic Science, Churches Fellowship for Spiritual and Psychic Studies.

WRITINGS: Emperor of the Moon, Bles, 1956; *The Cloud Forest,* Hart-Davis, 1965, Farrar, Strauss, 1966; *The Whirling Shapes,* Farrar, Straus, 1967, Hart-Davis, 1968; *The Light Maze,* Farrar, Straus, 1971. Contributor to *Guardian, Lady, Family Doctor,* and other periodicals and newspapers.

SIDELIGHTS: Ms. North told *CA:* "[I] am very lazy and take a long time to write a book—finding it difficult to plan ahead . . . usually have to rewrite a good deal. Interested in books—especially children's books—religions, anything fantastic and odd."

*   *   *

NORTHWOOD, Lawrence K(ing)   1917-

PERSONAL: Born April 16, 1917, in Detroit, Mich.; son of John Lawrence (a dentist) and Mabeth Eleanor (Richmond) Northwood; married Olga Remer (a social researcher), August 9, 1953. *Education:* Wayne (now Wayne State) University, B.A., 1947; University of Michigan, Ph.D., 1953. *Politics:* Independent. *Religion:* Protestant. *Home:* 3112 Fuhrman E., Seattle, Wash. *Office:* School of Social Work, University of Washington, Seattle, Wash. 98105.

CAREER: Drake University, Des Moines, Iowa, assistant professor of sociology, 1953-54; Council of Social Agencies, Grand Rapids, Mich., director of agencies evaluation project, 1955-56; Rutgers University, Newark, N.J., assistant professor of sociology, 1956-58; Columbia University, School of Social Work, New York, N.Y., lecturer in social research and social sciences, 1958-59; University of Washington, Seattle, 1960—, began as associate professor, became professor of social work. Consultant in research methods and community organization to Menninger Foundation, 1963-68, Stanford Research Institute, 1971, and other government and private agencies. Visiting lecturer, Cultural Institute of Guadalajara, 1973. *Military service:* U.S. Army Air Forces, 1942-45; became sergeant; received four Bronze Stars for campaigns in South Pacific.

MEMBER: International Conference of Social Work, (chairman of U.S. report committee, 1965), Society for the Study of Social Problems (chairman of social work and social problems committee, 1961-62), National Association of Social Workers, American Sociological Association (fellow), Academy of Certified Social Workers, Society for the Psychological Study of Social Issues, National Conference on Social Welfare, Northwest Committee for Applied Social Research (chairman, 1960-61). *Awards, honors:* Research grants from Field Foundation, Division Fund, Anti-

Defamation League of B'nai B'rith, and National Institute of Mental Health, Anti-Poverty Program.

WRITINGS: (Contributor) Nathan Cohen, editor, *Social Work and Social Problems,* National Association of Social Workers, 1964; (with Robert Leik and Robert Reed) *Outdoor Recreation in the Puget Sound Area,* Puget Sound Governmental Conference, 1964; (with Ernest A. T. Barth) *Urban Desegregation—Negro Pioneers and Their White Neighbors,* University of Washington Press, 1965, *Urban Development: Implications for Social Welfare,* International Conference for Social Welfare, 1966; *The Uses of Block Organization in the Anti-Poverty Program,* University of Washington Press, 1967. Contributor to *Social Problems, Phylon, Journal of Health and Human Behavior,* and half a dozen other sociology journals.

WORK IN PROGRESS: Strengthening the Components of Urban Planning and *One Man Armies: A Solution to Urban Violence.*

SIDELIGHTS: Northwood has some knowledge of French. *Avocational interests:* Playing piano and composing tunes; water sports.

*   *   *

NORTON, Perry L.   1920-

PERSONAL: Born August 18, 1920, in Marquette, Mich.; son of Perry L. (an architect) and Mildred (Peterson) Norton; married Harriet Stott Davis, December 20, 1947; children: Ann, Arthur, Elizabeth. *Education:* Northern Michigan College of Education (now Northern Michigan University), student, 1938-39; University of Michigan, B.L.A., 1949, M.C.P., 1950. *Politics:* Liberal Republican. *Religion:* Episcopalian. *Home:* 223 Leonia Ave., Leonia, N.J. *Office:* New York University, 4 Washington Sq., North, New York, N.Y. 10003.

CAREER: Chicago Housing Authority, Chicago, Ill., associate planner, 1950; Association of State Planning and Development Agencies, Chicago, assistant director, 1950-51; Regional Planning Commission, Cleveland, Ohio, principal planner, 1951-52; American Institute of Planners, Cambridge, Mass., executive director, 1952-57; self-employed urban planning consultant, Lexington, Mass., 1957-63; New York University, New York, N.Y., professor of urban planning, 1963—. Founder and editor-in-chief of Chandler-Davis Publishing Co., 1957-70. Senator, New York University, 1969-72. *Military service:* U.S. Army, 1942-45. *Member:* American Institute of Planners, American Society of Planning Officials. *Awards, honors:* American Institute of Planners, New York Metropolitan Chapter, Certificate of Merit, 1971.

WRITINGS: (Editor) *Urban Problems and Techniques,* Chandler-Davis, 1959; *Search,* National Council of Churches, 1960; *The Churches' Concern for the Urban Renaissance,* National Council of Churches, 1960; *The Relevant Church,* National Council of Churches, 1960; (editor) Frederick Bair, *Bair Facts,* Chandler-Davis, 1960; *Church and Metropolis,* Seabury, 1964; *Introduction to the Study of Urban Planning,* New York University Graduate School of Public Administration, 1973. Contributor to professional journals. Editor, *Journal of the American Institute of Planners,* 1952-57.

WORK IN PROGRESS: A textbook, *Community Psychology for Urban Planners,* completion expected in 1976, and a play commemorating American Revolution events of April, 1775.

NORTON, Peter (John) 1913-

PERSONAL: Born January 9, 1913, in Buriton, Hampshire, England; son of John Herbert (British Army) and Margery (Waterlow) Norton; married Olive Mary Deacon (a teacher of ballet, music and kindergarten), April 29, 1944; children: Sarah Katherine, John William Beauchamp. Education: Attended Winchester College, 1926-30. Religion: Church of England. Home: 1 The Square, Compton, Chichester, Sussex, England.

CAREER: Royal Navy, career service, 1930-58, retiring as captain; now artist and teacher of painting and art history. Co-director with wife of Cubertou Art Centre, Lot Valley, France. Member: Society for Nautical Research. Awards, honors—Military: Distinguished Service Cross; mentioned in dispatches.

WRITINGS: The Special Train, chatto & Windus, 1951; The End of the Voyage, Marshall & Co., 1959; Figureheads, National Maritime Museum, 1972; State Barges; National Maritime Museum, 1972.

WORK IN PROGRESS: Ships Figureheads for David & Charles.

SIDELIGHTS: Norton has lived and traveled extensively in Middle East, Africa, and continental Europe, with other travel in South America, West Indies, Canada, India. Avocational interests: The arts, sailing vessels and craft.

*   *   *

NOVAK, Robert D(avid) 1931-

PERSONAL: Born February 26, 1931, in Joliet, Ill.; son of Maurice Pall (a chemical engineer) and Jane (Sanders) Novak; married Geraldine Williams. Education: Attended University of Illinois, 1948-52. Home: 6417 Tilden Lane, Rockville, Md. 20852. Office: Room 1312, 1750 Pennsylvania Ave., N.W., Washington, D.C. 20006.

CAREER: Reporter for newspapers in Joliet, Ill., 1948-50, Urbana, Ill., 1950-51; Associated Press, correspondent in Lincoln and Omaha, Neb., Indianapolis, Ind., and Washington, D.C., 1954-58; Wall Street Journal, New York, N.Y., Washington correspondent, 1958-63; New York Herald Tribune Syndicate, New York, N.Y., columnist, "Inside Report," Washington, D.C., 1963-66; Publisher's Hall Syndicate, columnist, 1966—. Member: National Press Club, Sigma Delta Chi.

WRITINGS: The Agony of the GOP 1964, Macmillan, 1965; (with Rowland Evans, Jr.) Lyndon B. Johnson: The Exercise of Power, New American Library, 1966; (with Evans) Nixon in the White House: The Frustration of Power, Random House, 1971. Contributor to Saturday Evening Post, Reporter, New Republic, Esquire, National Observer, Economist (London), and other periodicals and newspapers.†

*   *   *

NSARKOH, J. K(wasi) 1931-

PERSONAL: Born September 20, 1931, in Akrokerri, Ghana; son of Kwasi Nsarkoh and Ammah Benemfaah; divorced; children: Ambrose, Gifly, Alex, Frank, Maxwell, Fred. Education: Local Government Training School, Accra, Ghana, Local Government Certificate, 1957; Karl Marx University, Leipzig, East German Democratic Republic, D.Jur., 1964. Politics: Convention People's Party (Ghana). Religion: Methodist. Address: University of Ghana, School of Administration, P.O. Box 48, Achimota, Ghana.

CAREER: Kwame Nkrumah Ideological Institute, Winneba, Ghana, senior lecturer in government, beginning 1958; currently with University of Ghana, School of Administration, Achimota, lecturer in government. Former member of National Advisory Panel on Local Government and National Advisory Panel on Labor; member of UNESCO Committee on Adult Education; member of steering committee of Radio Farm Forum Project. Member: Royal Economic Society (London; fellow), Royal Economic History Society (London; fellow), Institute of Public Administration (Ghana and London), Corporation of Secretaries (London; fellow).

WRITINGS: Local Government in Ghana, Oxford University Press, 1964. Writer of radio and television scripts. Contributor to magazines.

WORK IN PROGRESS: Current Local Government Problems.†

*   *   *

NUGENT, John Peer 1930-
(Barry Exall)

PERSONAL: Born October 5, 1930, in Brooklyn, N.Y.; son of Frank Zavier (an exporter) and Loretta Sabina (Baldwin) Nugent; married Phyllis Babbitt, May 6, 1961; children: Jamie, John Peer Bordenet, Tana. Education: Villanova University, B.A., 1952; graduate study at Fordham University, 1952-53. Religion: Roman Catholic. Agent: McIntosh & Otis, Inc., 18 East 41st St., New York, N.Y. 10017. Home: 443 Ocean Front, Santa Monica, Calif. 90402. Office: 1320 Second St., Santa Monica, Calif. 90401.

CAREER: Newsweek correspondent in New York, Chicago, Los Angeles, 1956-61, chief African correspondent, 1961-64, Los Angeles correspondent, 1964-70; David Wolper Productions, Metromedia, and own production company, writer, producer and director of public service documentaries, 1960—. Lecturer on Africa. Military service: U.S. Navy, correspondent in Caribbean, 1953-55.

WRITINGS: Call Africa 999, Coward, 1965; Black Eagle, Stein & Day, 1971. Contributor to Atlantic Monthly, True, Argosy, Catholic Digest, and Saga.

WORK IN PROGRESS: Research on Ethiopia and California projects; a novel with African setting.

AVOCATIONAL INTERESTS: Wines, pipes.†

*   *   *

NURNBERG, Walter 1907-

PERSONAL: Born April 18, 1907; married Rita Kern; children: Monica, Andrew. Education: Attended schools in Germany, including Reiman Art School, Berlin. Religion: Roman Catholic. Home: 18 Cornwood Close, London N. 2, England. Agent: Robert Harben, 3 Churchvale, London N. 2, England.

CAREER: Free-lance industrial photographer and consultant serving British firms. Author and lecturer. Guildford School of Photography, London, England, director, 1968-74. Military service: 1940-44. Member: Institute of Incorporated Photographers (fellow), Royal Photographic Society of Great Britain (fellow). Awards, honors: Hood Medal, Royal Photographic Society.

WRITINGS: The Science and Technique of Advertising Photography, Studio Publications, 1939; Lighting for Photography, Focal Press, 1940, 17th edition, 1971; Baby, the Camera and You, Chapman & Hall, 1946; Lighting for

Portraiture, Focal Press, 1947, 7th edition, Chilton, 1969; *Pocket Wisdom of Photography*, Press Centre, 1950; *Hands at Mass*, Sheed, 1951; (with Beatrice L. Warde) *Words in Their Hands*, privately printed, 1964. Contributor to journals.

SIDELIGHTS: Nurnberg's books have been translated into Danish, German, French, Spanish, and Dutch.

* * *

NUTTALL, Geoffrey Fillingham 1911-

PERSONAL: Born November 8, 1911, in Colwyn Bay, Denbighshire, Wales; son of Harold (a doctor of medicine) and Muriel Fillingham (Hodgson) Nuttall; married Mary (Preston) Powley, September 5, 1944. *Education:* Balliol College, Oxford, M.A., 1933; Mansfield College, Oxford, D.D., 1945. *Home:* 2 Brim Hill, London N. 2, England.

CAREER: Ordained minister of Congregational Church, 1938. New College, University of London, London, England, lecturer in church history, 1945—, dean of Faculty of Theology, 1960-64. Dr. Daniel Williams' Charity, trustee, 1948—. *Member:* London Society for the Study of Religion (honorary secretary, 1958-64), Congregational Historical Society (president, 1965—).

WRITINGS: (Editor) John Pinney, *Letters, 1679-1699*, Oxford University Press, 1939; *The Holy Spirit in Puritan Faith and Experience*, Basil Blackwell, 1947; *Visible Saints: The Congregational Way 1640-1660*, Basil Blackwell, 1957; *The Welsh Saints 1640-1660*, Verry, 1957; *Christian Pacifism in History*, Basil Blackwell, 1958; (joint editor) *From Uniformity to Unity 1662-1962*, S.P.C.K., 1962; *Richard Baxter*, Nelson, 1965; (contributor) *The Beginnings of Nonconformity*, J. Clarke, 1965; *Howel Harris: The Last Enthusiast*, University of Wales Press, 1965; *The Holy Spirit and Ourselves*, Epworth, 1966; *The Puritan Spirit: Essays and Addresses*, Epworth, 1967; *The Faith of Dante Alighieri*, Society for Promoting Christian Knowledge, 1969; *The Significance of Trevecca College, 1768-91*, Epworth, 1969. Contributor to theological journals.

SIDELIGHTS: Nuttall has reading knowledge of Hebrew, Greek, Latin, French, German, Dutch, Italian, and Welsh. *Avocational interests:* Medieval art and architecture.†

* * *

OAKES, John Bertram 1913-

PERSONAL: Born April 23, 1913, in Elkins Park, Pa.; son of George Washington and Bertie (Gans) Ochs-Oakes; married Margery C. Hartman, October 24, 1945; children: Andra, Alison, Cynthia, John. *Education:* Princeton University, A.B. (magna cum laude), 1934; University of Dijon, diploma in French, 1933; Queen's College, Oxford, Rhodes Scholar, 1934-36, A.B. and A.M., 1936. *Office:* New York Times, 229 West 43rd St., New York, N.Y. 10036.

CAREER: Trenton State Gazette, Trenton, N.J., reporter, 1936-37; *Washington Post*, Washington, D.C., political reporter and special feature writer, 1937-41; *New York Times*, New York, N.Y., editor, "Review of the Week," Sunday edition, 1946-49, member of editorial board, 1949-61, editor of editorial page, 1961—. Member of National Parks Advisory Board, U.S. Department of the Interior, 1955-62. Trustee and vice president of Temple Emanu-El, New York, N.Y.; trustee of Fisk University. *Military service:* U.S. Army, 1941-46; became major; received Bronze

Star, Order of the British Empire, Croix de Guerre, Medaille de Reconnaisance. U.S. Army Reserve, now colonel. *MEMBER:* Council on Foreign Relations, Rochester Museum of Arts and Sciences (fellow), Association of American Rhodes Scholars (director, 1957—), American Society of Newspaper Editors, National Conference of Editorial Writers, Phi Beta Kappa, Wilderness Society, Sierra Club, Nassau Club (Princeton), Cosmos Club (Washington, D.C.), Century Association (New York), Metropolitan Club (Washington, D.C.), Tower Club (Princeton). *Awards, honors:* Carnegie Corp. grant for study and travel in Europe and Africa, 1959; Columbia-Catherwood Award for journalism, 1960; LL.D., University of Hartford, 1960; Columbia-Catherwood Award for Distinguished Journalism, 1961; Department of Interior Conservation Service Award, 1963; Princeton Distinguished Service Award, 1964; George Polk Memorial Award for Editorial Comment, 1965; Silurian Society Award for Editorial Writing, 1969; L.H.D., Chatham College, 1969; Woodrow Wilson Award, Princeton University, 1970.

WRITINGS: The Edge of Freedom, Harper, 1961.

BIOGRAPHICAL/CRITICAL SOURCES: New York Times, April 26, 1961; *American Oxonian*, January, 1962.†

* * *

OAKESHOTT, Walter (Fraser) 1903-

PERSONAL: Born November 11, 1903, in England; son of Walter Field (a doctor) and Kathleen (Fraser) Oakeshott; married Noel Rose Moon, 1928; children: Helena Oakeshott Wakefield, Evelyn and Robert (twins), Rose Oakeshott Grant. *Education:* Balliol College, Oxford, B.A., M.A. *Home:* The Old School House, Eynsham, Oxford, England.

CAREER: Schoolteacher in England, 1926-36; Pilgrim Trust, London, England, member of committee conducting inquiry into unemployment, 1936-37; St. Paul's School, London, England, headmaster, 1938-46; Winchester College, Winchester, England, headmaster, 1946-54; Oxford University, Oxford, England, rector of Lincoln College, 1954-72, vice-chancellor of university, 1962-64. Trustee of Pilgrim Trust, 1949—. *Member:* British Academy (fellow), Society of Antiquaries (fellow). *Awards, honors:* LL.D., University of St. Andrews.

WRITINGS: Commerce and Society: A Short History of Trade and Its Effects on Civilization, Clarendon Press, 1936; (with others) *Men Without Work*, Cambridge University Press, 1937; *Founded Upon the Seas: A Narrative of Some English Maritime and Overseas Enterprises During the Period 1550-1616*, Cambridge University Press, 1942; (author of introduction) *The Artists of the Winchester Bible*, Faber, 1945; *The Sequence of English Medieval Art*, Faber, 1950; *The Sword of the Spirit: A Meditative and Devotional Anthology*, Beacon Press, 1952; *Classical Inspiration in Medieval Art*, Chapman & Hall, 1959, Praeger, 1960; *The Queen and the Poet*, Faber, 1960, Barnes & Noble, 1961; *The Mosaics of Rome: From the Third to the Fourteenth Centuries*, New York Graphic Society, 1967; *Sigena: Romanesque Paintings in Spain and the Winchester Bible Artists*, New York Graphic Society, 1972.

WORK IN PROGRESS: A handbook to the Winchester Bible.

* * *

OAKLEY, Francis (Christopher) 1931-

PERSONAL: Born October 6, 1931, in Liverpool, England; son of Joseph Vincent (a businessman) and Julia (Curran) Oakley; married Claire-Ann Lamenzo, August 9, 1958; children: Deirdre, Christopher, Timothy, Brian. *Education:* Corpus Christi College, Oxford, B.A., 1953, M.A., 1957; Pontifical Institute of Mediaeval Studies, Toronto, Ontario, graduate study, 1953-55; Yale University, M.A., 1958, Ph.D., 1960. *Religion:* Roman Catholic. *Residence:* Williamstown, Mass. *Office:* Department of History, Williams College, Williamstown, Mass. 01267.

CAREER: Yale University, New Haven, Conn., instructor in history, 1959-61; Williams College, Williamstown, Mass., 1961—, began as lecturer, became associate professor, professor of history, 1970—. *Military service:* British Army, Royal Corps of Signals, 1955-57; became second lieutenant. British Army Reserve, 1957-63; became first lieutenant. *Member:* Mediaeval Academy of America, American Historical Association, American Catholic Historical Association, Conference on British Studies, Ecclesiastical History Society. *Awards, honors:* Social Science Research Council fellowship in political theory, 1963; Weil Institute Research fellowship, 1965; American Council of Learned Societies fellowship, 1969-70.

WRITINGS: The Political Thought of Pierre d'Ailly: The Voluntarist Tradition, Yale University Press, 1964; *Council over Pope? Toward a Provisional Ecclesiology,* Herder & Herder, 1969; (with Daniel O'Connor) *Creation: The Impact of an Idea,* Scribner, 1969; *The Medieval Experience: Foundations of Western Cultural Singularity,* Scribner, 1974. Contributor to scholarly journals, including *Past and Present, American Historical Review, Church History, Natural Law Forum, Journal of British Studies, Journal of Ecumenical Studies, Harvard Theological Review, Mediaeval Studies,* and *Speculum.*

WORK IN PROGRESS: A short book on the later medieval church to be published by Basil Blackwell.

SIDELIGHTS: Francis Oakley is competent in Latin, French, and German.

* * *

OBER, Warren U(pton) 1925-

PERSONAL: Born May 2, 1925, in Smackover, Ark.; son of Andrew Clifton and Delilah (Upton) Ober; married Mary Rae Kemper, September 1, 1951; children: Christopher Kemper, Henry Upton, Robert Edmond. *Education:* Washington and Lee University, B.A. (magna cum laude), 1948; Indiana University, Ph.D., 1958. *Office:* University of Waterloo, Waterloo, Ontario, Canada.

CAREER: Kentucky Military Institute, Lyndon, instructor in English, 1948-50; Southern State College, Magnolia, Ark., instructor in English, 1953-55; Northern Illinois University, DeKalb, assistant professor, 1955-59, associate professor, 1959-62, professor of English, 1962-65, acting head of department of English, 1961-62, acting dean of Graduate School, 1964; University of Waterloo, Waterloo, Ontario, professor of English and chairman of department, 1965-69, 1973—, acting dean, Faculty of Arts, 1969-70, director, Inter-Faculty Programme Board, 1970-72. *Military Service:* U.S. Naval Reserve, 1943-46; became ensign. *Member:* Modern Humanities Research Association, International Association of University Professors of English, Association of Canadian University Teachers of English, Canadian Council of Teachers of English, Phi Beta Kappa.

WRITINGS: (Editor with Paul S. Burtness and William R. Seat) *The University Reader,* American Book Co., 1960;

(editor with Burtness and Seat) *The Enigma of Poe,* Heath, 1960; (with Burtness and Seat) *The Close Reading of Factual Prose,* Row, Peterson & Co., 1962; (editor with Burtness) *The Puzzle of Pearl Harbor,* Row, Peterson & Co., 1962; (editor with Burtness and Seat) *The Contemporary University Reader,* American Book Co., 1963; (editor with Burtness and Seat) *Young Coleridge,* Heath, 1963; (editor with Burtness and Seat) *The New University Reader,* American Book Co., 1966. Contributor to *The Yearbook of English Studies,* and to *Germano-Slavica, The Wordsworth Circle, Journal of English and Germanic Philology, Notes and Queries, Slavic and East European Journal, Dalhousie Review, Military Affairs, Virginia Cavalcade,* and *Clearing House.*

WORK IN PROGRESS: Studies of translations of English poetry into Russian, in collaboration with Kenneth H. Ober; studies in the poetry of Samuel Taylor Coleridge and research into his literary association with Robert Southey; studies in the poetry of John Keats, in collaboration with W. K. Thomas.

* * *

O'BRIEN, J(ohn) W(ilfrid) 1931-

PERSONAL: Born August 4, 1931, in Toronto, Ontario; son of Wilfred Edmond (a teacher) and Audrey (Swain) O'Brien; married Joyce Helen Bennett, August 4, 1956; children: Margaret Anne, Catherine Audrey. *Education:* McGill University, B.A., 1953, M.A., 1955, Ph.D., 1962; Institute of Political Studies, Paris, France, graduate study, 1953-54. *Home:* 62 Nelson St., Montreal, Quebec, Canada. *Office:* 1435 Drummond St., Montreal, Quebec PQ 107, Canada.

CAREER: Sir George William University, Montreal, Quebec, Canada, lecturer, 1954-57, assistant professor, 1957-61, associate professor, 1961-65, professor of economics, 1965—, assistant dean of the university, 1961-63, dean of Faculty of Art, 1963-68, vice principal, 1968-69, principal, vice chancellor, and president, 1969—. *Member:* Canadian Political Science Association, Canadian Economic Association, American Economic Association, American Association of Higher Education.

WRITINGS: Canadian Money and Banking, McGraw, 1964, 2nd edition (with G. Lerner), [New York], 1969.†

* * *

O'BRIEN, William V(incent) 1923-

PERSONAL: Born July 9, 1923, in Washington, D.C.; son of William Colomba and Theresa (Matthews) O'Brien; married Madge Roberts, September 19, 1951. *Education:* Georgetown University, B.S.F.S., 1946, M.S.F.S., 1948, Ph.D., 1953. *Politics:* Democrat. *Religion:* Roman Catholic. *Home:* 1432 44th St., N.W., Washington, D.C. 20007. *Office:* Institute of World Polity, Georgetown University, Washington, D.C. 20007.

CAREER: Georgetown University, Washington, D.C., instructor, 1950-53, assistant professor, 1953-59, associate professor of international law, 1959—, chairman of Institute of World Policy, 1957—. Max Planck-Institut fuer Auslandisches Offentliches Recht und Volkerrecht, visiting professor, 1963. Consultant, Council on Religion and International Affairs, Washington, 1965—. *Military service:* U.S. Army, 1943-46; served in Asiatic-Pacific Theater, U.S. Army Reserve, beginning 1946; now major. *Member:* International Law Association, American Society for International Law, American Political Science Association, Catholic Association for International Peace (president, 1961-62; chairman of international law and juridical institutions committee), Association of the United States Army, American Association of University Professors, American Peace Society (board member), Association for International Social Justice (Louvain), Council on Religion and International Affairs, National Citizens' Commission for the International Cooperation Year (member, disarmament committee), Delta Phi Epsilon, Pi Sigma Alpha. *Awards, honors:* Fulbright fellowship to Paris, 1951-52.

WRITINGS: (With H. F. Jaeger) *International Law: Cases, Text-Notes and Other Materials*, two volumes, Georgetown University Press, 1959; (with Ulrich S. Allers) *Christian Ethics and Nuclear Warfare*, Institute of World Polity, 1961; (with Jean-Robert Leguey-Feilleux) *International Law*, Georgetown University Press, 1965; (editor) *The Law of Limited International Conflict*, Institute of World Polity, 1965; (editor) *The New Nations in International Law and Diplomacy*, Praeger, 1965; *War and/or Survival*, Doubleday, 1969.

Editor of *World Polity I: Yearbook of Studies in International Law and Organization*, Spectrum, 1957, *World Polity II*, Spectrum, 1960, and *World Polity III*, Praeger, 1965.

Contributor to encyclopedias, and to *Military Law Review*, *Commonweal*, *Yale Law Journal*, and other journals. Associate editor, *World Justice* (periodical published at Louvain, Belgium).

WORK IN PROGRESS: A book, *The International Law of Nuclear War and Deterrence.*

BIOGRAPHICAL/CRITICAL SOURCES: Sign, April, 1963.†

*   *   *

O'CONNELL, Jeremiah Joseph 1932-

PERSONAL: Born August 5, 1932, in New York, N.Y.; son of Jerry Quinlan (a retail store manager) and Mary (Maloney) O'Connell; married M. Patricia O'Connell, September 2, 1959. *Education:* Mary Immaculate College, A.B., 1956; Dartmouth College, M.B.A., 1961; Columbia University, Ph.D., 1965. *Politics:* Republican. *Religion:* Roman Catholic. *Home:* 17 Black Friar Rd., Rosemont, Pa. 19010. *Office:* Wharton School, University of Pennsylvania, Philadelphia, Pa.

CAREER: Columbia University, New York, N.Y., preceptor in management, 1962-63, research associate, Graduate School of Business, 1962-64; University of Pennsylvania, Wharton School of Finance and Commerce, Philadelphia, Pa., lecturer in management and business policy, 1964—. Management consultant. *Member:* American Academy of Political and Social Science, Beta Gamma Sigma.

WRITINGS: (Editor with Charles E. Summer, Jr.) *The Managerial Mind: Science and Theory in Policy Decisions*, Irwin, 1964, 3rd edition, 1973; *Managing Organizational Innovation*, Irwin, 1968.

WORK IN PROGRESS: "Managing change—planning and controlling organizational change," a two-year study of the relationship between a large insurance company and a large management consultant firm.†

*   *   *

ODAJNYK, Walter 1938-

PERSONAL: Surname is pronounced O-*dine*-ik; born

April 10, 1938, in Ostrava, Czechoslovakia. *Education:* Hunter College, B.A., (cum laude), 1961; University of California, Berkeley, M.A., 1963; Columbia University, Ph.D., 1970. *Home:* 147-08 33rd Avenue, Flushing, N.Y. 11354.

CAREER: Department of Social Service, New York, N.Y., social investigator, 1963-64; Columbia University, New York, N.Y., instructor, 1968-70, assistant professor of political science, 1970—. *Member:* American Society for Political and Legal Philosophy, Conference for the Study of Political Thought, Phi Beta Kappa. *Awards, honors:* Swiss National Science Foundation, 1973-74.

WRITINGS: Marxism and Existentialism, Anchor Books, 1965; (contributor) E. Fromm, editor, *Socialist Humanism*, Doubleday, 1965; (contributor) John Somerville and Howard L. Parsons, editors, *Dialogues on the Philosophy of Marxism*, Greenwood Press, 1974. Contributor to *Encyclopedia Americana*, and to journals in his field.

Founding editor, *Political Theory: An International Journal of Political Philosophy*; member of advisory committee, *Soviet Studies in Philosophy*, and *International Journal of Politics.*

WORK IN PROGRESS: A book, *The Political Ideas of C. G. Jung.*

*   *   *

OGDEN, (John) Michael (Hubert) 1923-

PERSONAL: Born April 5, 1923, in Mombasa, Kenya; son of John (a shipping exporter) and Louise (Clark) Ogden; married second wife, Ivy Doreen Naish; children: (first marriage) Carol Yvonne, Simon Lewis Anthony; (second marriage) Julian Grenville Lewis. *Education:* Educated privately and at schools in England; The Polytechnic, London, England, School Certificate, 1939. *Politics:* "Antipolitician." *Religion:* Agnostic. *Home:* 129 Rydens Rd., Walton-on-Thames, Surrey KT12 3AP, England.

CAREER: Pilot in Royal Air Force, 1941-45, in Royal Navy, 1945-58, retiring as lieutenant commander; author, 1958—. Lecturer in creative writing, South Dorset Technical College, 1960-63; first chief flying instructor of Singapore Air Defence Command, 1969-70; freelance military aviation training advisor. *Member:* Association of Retired Naval Officers, Fleet Air Arm Officers' Association, Society of Authors, Royal Naval Volunteer Reserve Club.

WRITINGS: No Calm in the Morning, Kimber & Co., 1960; *The Battle of North Cape*, Kimber & Co., 1962. Contributor of short stories to *Chamber's Journal*, *Fighting Forces*, *Sheffield Weekly Telegraph*, other journals.

WORK IN PROGRESS: A biographical novel, *The Infidel.*

SIDELIGHTS: Ogden retired with 3,500 hours of flying time in the British forces, was in the first air detail over Inchon beachhead in 1950, and flew support missions for U.S. Marines in the Korean War.

*   *   *

OGILVIE, Robert Maxwell 1932-

PERSONAL: Born June 5, 1932, in Edinburgh, Scotland; son of Sir Frederick and Lady Mary (Macaulay) Ogilvie; married Jennifer Roberts, July 4, 1959; children: Isobel, Alexander, Charles. *Education:* Attended Balliol College, Oxford, 1950-54. *Home:* Errachd, Fort William, Scotland. *Office:* School House, Tonbridge School, Kent, England.

CAREER: Clare College, Cambridge University, Cambridge, England, fellow in classics, 1955-57; Balliol College, Oxford University, Oxford, England, fellow in classics, 1957-70; Tonbridge School, Kent, England, headmaster, 1970—. Visiting professor, University of Toronto, 1965-66; governor, Blundell's School. *Member:* Athenaeum Club (London), British Academy (fellow). *Awards, honors:* D.Litt., Oxford University, 1967.

WRITINGS: Latin and Greek, Shoe String, 1964; *Commentary on Livy Books, 1-5*, Oxford University Press, 1965; (editor with Sir Ian Richmond) Cornelius Tacitus, *De Vita Agricolae*, Oxford University Press, 1967; *The Romans and Their Gods*, Chatto & Windus, 1970. Contributor to *Journal of Roman Studies, Journal of Hellenic Studies, Classical Quarterly, Listener.*

WORK IN PROGRESS: A new text of Livy's "Fragments" for Oxford Classical Texts.

SIDELIGHTS: Robert Ogilvie is competent in French, German, and Italian. *Avocational interests:* Mountaineering in Scotland, field archaeology in Italy.

* * *

OGUL, Morris S(amuel) 1931-

PERSONAL: Born April 15, 1931, in Detroit, Mich.; son of Jack M. (a machinist) and Sarah (Zimmerman) Ogul; married Eleanor Simon (a teacher and supervisor), August 26, 1954. *Education:* Wayne State University, B.A., 1952; University of Michigan, M.A., 1953, Ph.D., 1958. *Home:* 309 Sharon Dr., Pittsburgh, Pa. 15221. *Office:* Department of Political Science, University of Pittsburgh, Pittsburgh, Pa. 15260.

CAREER: University of Pittsburgh, Pittsburgh, Pa., instructor, 1957-59, assistant professor, 1959-64, associate professor of political science, 1964—. *Member:* American Political Science Association, American Association of University Professors, Midwest Conference of Political Scientists, Pennsylvania Political Science and Public Administration Association.

WRITINGS: (With William J. Keefe) *The American Legislative Process*, Prentice-Hall, 1964, 3rd edition, 1973.

WORK IN PROGRESS: Research in political leadership, the American presidency, and legislative process.

* * *

OHMANN, Richard (Malin) 1931-

PERSONAL: Born July 11, 1931, in Cleveland, Ohio; son of Oliver Arthur (in industrial relations) and Grace (Malin) Ohmann; married Carol Burke (a teacher and writer), June 25, 1955; children: Sarah Malin, William Burke. *Education:* Oberlin College, B.A., 1952, Harvard University, M.A., 1954, Ph.D., 1960. *Office:* Wesleyan University, Middletown, Conn.

CAREER: Wesleyan University, Middletown, Conn., assistant professor, 1961-63, associate professor, 1963-66, professor of English, 1966—, associate provost, 1966-69, chancellor pro tempore, 1969-70. *Member:* Modern Language Association of America, National Council of Teachers of English, Linguistic Society of America. *Awards, honors:* Junior fellow, Society of Fellows, Harvard University, 1958-61; Guggenheim fellow, 1964-65.

WRITINGS: (Editor with Harold C. Martin) *Inquiry and Expression*, Rinehart, 1958, revised edition, Holt, Rinehart & Winston, 1963; *Shaw: The Style and the Man*, Wesleyan University Press, 1962; (editor) *The Making of Myth*, Putnam, 1962; (with Harold C. Martin and James H. Wheatley), *The Logic and Rhetoric of Exposition*, 3rd edition, Holt, 1969. Editor, *College English*, 1966—.

WORK IN PROGRESS: A book on the theory of literary language; a book on institutions in the profession of literary scholar and teacher.

* * *

OLDFIELD, Ruth L(atzer) 1922-

PERSONAL: Born June 2, 1922, in New York, N.Y.; daughter of Frederick (an electrical engineer) and Bessie (Cohen) Latzer; married Daniel G. Oldfield (a professor of biology), June 2, 1950; children: Elizabeth I., Frederic M. *Education:* Attended Radio Corp. of America Institutes, 1940-42. *Home:* 1200 East Madison Park, Chicago, Ill. 60615.

CAREER: American Technical Society, Chicago, Ill., technical writer, 1959-60; Britannica Schools, Chicago, Ill., supervisor of communications course, 1961-64; Gardner, Jones & Cowell (public relations), Chicago, Ill., technical writer, 1965—; R. L. Oldfield & Associates (public relations), Chicago, Ill., president, 1972—. Free-lance writer. *Member:* Institute of Electrical and Electronics Engineers (national publicity chairman for committee on engineering writing and speech), Society of Technical Writers and Publishers (senior member), Society of Women Engineers, Society of Programmed and Automated Learning (secretary, 1964-65), American Women in Radio and Television.

WRITINGS: Radio-Television and Basic Electronics, American Technical Society, 1956, 2nd edition, 1960; *Practical Dictionary of Electricity and Electronics*, American Technical Society, 1958; *True Story of Albert Einstein* (juvenile), Childrens Press, 1964; *Theory and Applications of Silicon Photovoltaic Cells*, Solar Systems, Inc., 1964; *Albert Einstein*, Childrens Press, 1968; *Fundamentals of Electronics*, La Salle Extension University Book Div., 1973; *Automation*, La Salle Extension University Book Div., 1974. Contributor to *Above and Beyond: The Encyclopedia of Aviation and Space Sciences.*

Physical sciences consultant to Childrens Press, Inc., for *Childrens Science Encyclopedia* and *Childrens Science Dictionary.*

* * *

OLIVA, L(awrence) Jay 1933-

PERSONAL: Born September 23, 1933, in Walden, N.Y.; son of Lawrence Joseph and Catherine (Mooney) Oliva; married Mary Ellen Nolan, June 3, 1961; children: Lawrence Jay II, Edward Nolan. *Education:* Manhattan College, B.A., 1955; Syracuse University, M.A., 1957, Ph.D., 1960; University of Paris, graduate study, 1957-59, *Religion:* Roman Catholic. *Residence:* Sparkill, N.Y. 10976.

CAREER: Syracuse University, Syracuse, N.Y., instructor and research associate, 1959-60; New York University, New York, N.Y., assistant professor, 1960-64, professor of Russian history, 1968—, vice chancellor, 1973—. Visiting professor, University of California, Los Angeles, 1963. *Member:* American Historical Association, American Association for the Advancement of Slavic Studies, American Catholic Historical Association, Society for French Historical Studies, Phi Alpha Theta. *Awards, honors:* Lindback Foundation Award for Distinguished Teaching, 1964.

WRITINGS: *Misalliance: A Study of French Policy in Russia During the Seven Years' War*, New York University Press, 1964; (editor) *Russia and the West From Peter to Kruschev*, Heath, 1965; *Russia in the Era of Peter the Great*, Prentice-Hall, 1969; (editor) *Peter the Great: Great Lives Observed*, Prentice-Hall, 1970; (editor) *Catherine the Great: Great Lives Observed*, Prentice-Hall, 1971. Contributor to *Journalism Quarterly, Journal of Negro History, Polish Review, Ukrainian Quarterly*, and other journals. Contributing editor, *Report*.

WORK IN PROGRESS: Volume I of *A History of Russia* for Praeger.

SIDELIGHTS: Oliva visited Soviet Union in 1958 and 1959 for research in special field—foreign influences on Russian history in the eighteenth century. Oliva is competent in Russian, French, Latin, and Irish.

* * *

OLIVER, A. Richard 1912-

PERSONAL: Born September 24, 1912, in Waterbury, Conn.; son of Salvatore and Maria (Galluzzo) Oliver; married Margaret Dorsey, February 7, 1948. *Education:* Columbia University, B.A. (honors in French), 1935, M.A., 1936, Ph.D., 1947. *Office:* Washington and Jefferson College, Washington, Pa.

CAREER: tutor in French, New York, N.Y., 1935-38; U.S. Coordinator of Information, New York, N.Y., multilingual monitor and propaganda analyst, 1941-42; Washington and Jefferson College, Washington, Pa., assistant professor, 1947-53, associate professor, 1953-58, Isabel McKennan Laughlin Foundation Professor of French, 1958—. Broadcaster on art and education for Station KDKA, Pittsburgh, Pa., 1961-62. *Military service:* U.S. Army, Counter Intelligence Corps, 1942-46; special agent and officer in New York, London, France, and Germany. *Awards, honors:* Fellow of Newberry Library, 1954.

WRITINGS: *The Encyclopedists as Critics of Music*, Columbia University Press, 1947; (contributor of sections on music, opera, and ballet) Cabeen, *A Critical Bibliography of French Literature*, Volume III, *The Seventeenth Century*, Syracuse University Press, 1961; *Charles Nodier, Pilot of Romanticism*, Syracuse University Press, 1964. Contributor of articles on French Romanticists to *A Dictionary of Music and Musicians*. Contributor of articles and reviews to *Musical Quarterly, Newberry Library Bulletin, Romanic Review, Gourmet, Orbis Litterarum, Studies in Romanticism*, and other journals.

WORK IN PROGRESS: A section on Charles Nodier for Volume VI, *A Critical Bibliography of French Literature*.

* * *

OLNEY, Ross R. 1929-

PERSONAL: Born April 9, 1929, in Lima, Ohio; son of Ross Nelan and Elizabeth (Bowers) Olney; married Patricia Wilson; children: Ross David, Scott Hunter, Eric Paul. *Education:* Studied journalism through U.S. Armed Forces Institute courses, University of Wisconsin, 1948-53. *Politics:* Independent. *Religion:* Protestant. *Home and office:* 7944 Capistrano, Canoga Park, Calif. 91304. *Agent:* Larry Sternig, 2407 North 44th St., Milwaukee, Wis. 53210.

CAREER: U.S. Air Force, 1947-53, with overseas service in Korea; *Science and Mechanics*, Chicago, Ill., managing editor, 1962-63; full-time free-lance writer, 1958—. Member of Southern California Council on Literature for Children

and Young People. *Member:* Authors Guild, American Auto Racing Writers and Broadcasters Association, Science Fiction Writers of America, Society of Magazine Writers, Society of Children's Book Writers, Greater Los Angeles Press Club (member of board of directors). *Awards, honors*—Military: Distinguished Flying Cross, Air Medal with four oak leaf clusters, two battle stars.

WRITINGS: *The Case of the Naked Diver* (fiction), Epic Books, 1961; *Lost Planet* (fiction), International Book, 1962; (with Robert D. Howard) *Skin Diver's Pocket Reference*, Better Books, 1963; *The Young Sportsman's Guide to Surfing*, Nelson, 1965; *Americans in Space: Five Years of Manned Space Travel*, Nelson, 1966, revised edition published as *Americans in Space: A History of Manned Space Travel*, 1970; *Daredevils of the Speedways*, Grosset, 1966; *The Young Sportsman's Guide to Water Safety*, Nelson, 1966; *The Inquiring Mind: Astronomy*, Nelson, 1967; *Sound All Around*, Prentice-Hall, 1967; *Light Motorcycle Riding*, Macmillan, 1967; *The Story of Traffic Control*, Prentice-Hall, 1968; *Let's Go Sailing*, Prentice-Hall, 1968; *Internal Combustion Engines*, Nelson, 1969; *The Inquiring Mind: Oceanography*, Nelson, 1969; *Kings of the Dragstrip*, Putnam, 1969; *Men Against the Sea*, Grosset, 1969; *Tales of Time and Space*, Western Publishing, 1969; *Great Moments in Speed*, Prentice-Hall, 1970; *Kings of Motor Speed*, Putnam, 1970; (with Richard W. Graham) *Kings of the Surf*, Putnam, 1970; *Great Dragging Wagons*, Putnam, 1970; *The Incredible A. J. Foyt*, Arco, 1970; *The Indianapolis 500*, Four Winds, 1970; *Simple Gasoline Engine Repair*, Doubleday, 1972; *Air Traffic Control*, Nelson, 1972; *Shudders*, Western Publishing, 1972; *Drag Strip Danger*, Western Publishing, 1972; *Simple Bicycle Repair and Maintenance*, Doubleday, 1973; *How to Keep Your Car Running, Your Money in Your Pocket, and Your Mind Intact!*, Regnery, 1973; *Great Auto Racing Champions*, Garrard, 1973; (with Ron Grable) *The Racing Bugs: Formula Vee and Super Vee*, Putnam, 1974; *Driving: How to Get a License (and Keep It!)*, F. Watts, 1974; *Quick and Easy Magic Fun*, Western Publishing, 1974; *Motorcycles*, F. Watts, 1974; *Motorcycle Repair*, F. Watts, 1975; *Superstars of Auto Racing*, Putnam, in press. Author of twelve automotive repair manuals; also author of over one hundred short stories and three hundred articles in magazines, including *True, Argosy, Popular Science*, and *Popular Mechanics*. Associate editor, *Skin Diver*, 1960-62.

WORK IN PROGRESS: A series of sports books for juveniles, for Western Publishing.

* * *

OLSEN, Donald J(ames) 1929-

PERSONAL: Born January 8, 1929, in Seattle, Wash.; son of Iver John (a factory manager) and Anna Marie (Lungdahl) Olsen. *Education:* Yale University, B.A., 1949, M.A., 1951, Ph.D., 1954; University of London, graduate study, 1951-52. *Office:* Department of History, Vassar College, Poughkeepsie, N.Y.

CAREER: University College, Hull, England, acting lecturer in history, 1952-53; University of Massachusetts, Amherst, instructor in history, 1954-55; Vassar College, Poughkeepsie, N.Y., instructor, 1955-58, assistant professor, 1958-65, associate professor, 1965-70, professor of history, 1970—, Eloise Ellery Professor of History, 1972—, chairman of the department, 1971-74. Visiting professor, Victorian Studies Centre, University of Leicester, 1970. *Member:* American Historical Association, Conference on

British Studies, American Society for Eighteenth-Century Studies (member of executive board, 1973—), American Association of University Professors, Society of Architectural Historians, Phi Beta Kappa. *Awards, honors:* Vassar College faculty fellowship, 1959-60; Guggenheim fellowship, 1967-68.

WRITINGS: Town Planning in London: The Eighteenth and Nineteenth Centuries, Yale University Press, 1964; (contributor) H. J. Dyos and Michael Wolff, editors, *The Victorian City*, Routledge & Kegan Paul, 1973. Contributor to *Victorian Studies*.

WORK IN PROGRESS: The Growth of Victorian London, for Batsford; studies of the Duke of Norfolk's estate in Sheffield, 1770-1870, and the Eton College estate in London in the nineteenth century.

* * *

OLSON, Mancur, Jr. 1932-

PERSONAL: Given name is pronounced Man-sir; born January 22, 1932, in Grand Forks, N.D.; son of Mancur (a farmer) and Clara (Fugleston) Olson; married Alison Gilbert (a university lecturer), August 29, 1959; children: Ellika Leslie Page, Mancur Severin, Sander Brandt. *Education:* North Dakota State University, B.Sc., 1954; Oxford University, B.A., 1956, M.A., 1960; Harvard University, Ph.D., 1963. *Home:* 4316 Clagett-Pineway, University Park, Md. 20782. *Office:* Department of Economics, University of Maryland, College Park, Md. 20740.

CAREER: Princeton University, Princeton, N.J., 1960-67, became assistant professor of economics; Department of Health, Education and Welfare, deputy assistant secretary, 1967-69; University of Maryland, College Park, professor of economics, 1969—. Consultant to RAND Corp., Santa Monica, Calif., and to Institute of Defense Analysis, Washington, D.C. *Military service:* U.S. Air Force, 1961-63; became first lieutenant. *Member:* American Economic Association, American Association of University Professors, Econometric Society, Economic History Society, American Farm Economics Association. *Awards, honors:* Rhodes Scholar, 1954-56.

WRITINGS: The Economics of the Wartime Shortage: A History of British Food Shortages in the Napoleonic Wars and World Wars I and II, Duke University Press, 1963; *The Logic of Collective Action: Public Goods and the Theory of Groups*, Harvard University Press, 1965, revised edition, 1971. Contributor to economic journals.

WORK IN PROGRESS: A book, *The Pattern of Economic Development*.†

* * *

O'MAHONY, Patrick 1911-
(Patrick Mahony)

PERSONAL: Born February 11, 1911, in London, England; brought to United States as a child; son of Frederick Henry Mahony (an army officer killed in World War I) and Ethel (Paterson) Mahony Bliss. *Education:* Educated mainly in California schools. *Politics:* Republican. *Religion:* Protestant. *Home:* 5885 Locksley Pl., Los Angeles, Calif. 90068. *Agent:* Multi Media Agency, 9507 Santa Monica Blvd., Beverly Hills, Calif.

CAREER: Literary assistant to Maurice Maeterlinck, New York, N.Y., 1941-47, and to Lord Dunsany, Santa Barbara, Calif., 1953-55; author, and lecturer in United States and Canada, 1947—. *Member:* P.E.N.

WRITINGS: Out of the Silence (psychic adventures), Storm, 1948; *Unsought Visitors* (psychic adventures), Devin, 1949; *You Can Find a Way*, Storm, 1950; *Magic of Maeterlinck* (biography), House-Warren, 1951, reprinted, Krauss Reprints, 1966; *Barbed Wit and Malicious Humor*, Citadel, 1956; *Breath of Scandal* (novel), Marvin Miller, 1957; *It's Better in America*, House of Words, 1964; *Who's There?*, Manor Books, 1970; *How to Build Your Inner Kingdom*, House of Words, in press. Contributor to magazines and journals.

SIDELIGHTS: Mahony told *CA*: "My career has two mountain slopes: before I met Maeterlinck and after, when my life became lit with better understanding of man's true destiny. I was literary assistant to Maeterlinck for five years when he was a refugee from the Nazis in the U.S.A. Being Irish, I am intensely absorbed with supernatural themes, and have used them in almost all my books."

BIOGRAPHICAL/CRITICAL SOURCES: William Oliver Stevens, *The Mystery of Dreams*, Dodd, 1950; Elsa Maxwell, *I Married the World*, Heinemann, 1955; W. H. Halls, *Maurice Maeterlinck: The Story of a Genius*, Oxford University Press, 1961.

* * *

O'MEARA, Walter (Andrew) 1897-

PERSONAL: Born January 29, 1897, in Minneapolis, Minn.; son of Michael (a logger) and Mary (Wolfe) O'-Meara; married Esther Molly Arnold, August 18, 1922; children: Donn, Ellen O'Meara Woolf, Deirdre O'Meara Humphrey, Wolfe. *Education:* Attended University of Minnesota, 1914-15; University of Wisconsin, B.A., 1920. *Politics:* Democrat. *Residence:* Nogales, Arizona.

CAREER: Started as reporter in Duluth, Minn., 1918; J. Walter Thompson Co. (advertising), Chicago, Ill., copywriter, 1920-31; Benton & Bowles, Inc. (advertising), New York, N.Y., creative director, 1932-40; J. Walter Thompson Co., New York, N.Y., creative director, 1940-50; Sullivan, Stauffer, Colwell & Bayles, Inc. (advertising), New York, N.Y., creative consultant, 1951-69; author of historic novels and non-fiction. U.S. government, chief of planning staff, Office of Strategic Services, 1942-43, deputy price administrator for information, Office of Price Administration, 1943-44. Director, National Conference of Christians and Jews. *Military service:* U.S. Army, 1918; became sergeant. *Member:* Phi Beta Kappa, Sigma Delta Chi, Deadline Club and The Players (both New York). *Awards, honors:* Award from American Association for State and Local History, 1951, for *The Grand Portage*; citation for distinguished services to journalism, University of Wisconsin, 1957.

WRITINGS: The Trees Went Forth (novel), Crown, 1947; *The Grand Portage* (novel), Bobbs-Merrill, 1951; *Tales of the Two Borders* (collection of short stories), Bobbs-Merrill, 1952; *The Spanish Bride* (novel), Putnam, 1954; *Minnesota Gothic* (novel), Henry Holt, 1956, reissued as *Castle Danger*, Manor Books, 1966; *The Devil's Cross* (novel), Knopf, 1957; *The Savage Country* (nonfiction), Houghton, 1960; *The First Northwest Passage* (youth book), Houghton, 1960; *The Last Portage* (nonfiction), Houghton, 1962, reissued as *In the Country of the Walking Dead*, Universal Publishing & Distributing, 1972; (contributor) *The Golden Book on Writing*, Viking, 1964; *Guns at the Forks* (nonfiction), Prentice-Hall, 1965; *The Duke of War* (novel), Harcourt, 1966; *Daughters of the Country: The Women of the Fur Traders and Moutain Men* (nonfiction), Harcourt,

1968; *The Sioux Are Coming* (youth book), Houghton, 1971; *We Made it Through the Winter* (memoirs), Minnesota Historical Society, 1974.

Author of column, "Just Looking," in *Advertising Age*. Short stories have appeared in *Saturday Evening Post* and other magazines; also contributor of articles and critical reviews to periodicals.

SIDELIGHTS: A. L. Rosenzweig describes *Daughters of the Country: The Women of the Fur Traders and Mountain Men* as an "excellent and engrossing survey of a forgotten corner of American frontier history." *Avocational interests:* Watercolor painting, canoeing, camping, and cross-country motoring.

BIOGRAPHICAL/CRITICAL SOURCES: Wilson Library Bulletin, January, 1958.

*   *   *

OMMANNEY, F(rancis) D(ownes) 1903-

PERSONAL: Born April 22, 1903, in England; son of Francis Frederick (a lawyer) and Olive Caroline (Owen) Ommanney. *Education:* Royal College of Science, London, England, A.R.C.Sc. and B.Sc. (honors), 1926; Ph.D. (London), 1934. *Home:* Ashleigh, Weekmoor, Milverton, Somerset, England. *Agent:* Curtis Brown Ltd., 1 Craven Hill, London W2 3EW, England.

CAREER: University of London, East London College, London, England, assistant lecturer in zoology, 1926-29; Colonial Office, London, England, scientific officer on "Discovery" Committee, 1929-39; British Council, London, England, science editor, 1946-47; Colonial Office, scientific officer on Mauritius-Seychelles Fisheries Survey in Indian Ocean, 1947-50; Marine Fisheries Research Organization, chief scientific officer, Zanzibar, 1951-52; Singapore Regional Fisheries Research Station, Singapore, principal scientific officer, 1952-57; University of Hong Kong, Hong Kong, reader in marine biology, 1957-60. UNESCO, adviser in oceanography, Pusan, South Korea, 1964. *Military service:* Royal Naval Volunteer Reserve, 1940-46; became lieutenant commander.

MEMBER: Marine Biological Association, Institute of Biology, Royal Society of Literature (fellow), Linnean Society (fellow), Challenger Society, Travellers' Club (London). *Awards, honors:* Bronze Polar Medal, 1942, for work in the Antarctic, 1929-39.

WRITINGS: Below the Roaring Forties, Longmans, Green (New York), 1938 (published in England as *South Latitude*, Longmans, Green [London], 1938); *North Cape*, Longmans, Green (London), 1939; *The House in the Park* (autobiographical), Longmans, Green (London), 1944; *The Ocean*, Oxford University Press, 1949; *The Shoals of Capricorn*, Harcourt, 1952; *Isle of Cloves*, Longmans, Green (London), 1954; *Eastern Windows*, Doubleday, 1957; *Fragrant Harbour*, Hutchinson, 1957; (with editors of *Life*) *The Fishes*, Time-Life, 1963; *A Draught of Fishes*, Crowell, 1965; *The River Bank*, Longmans, Green, 1966; *Lost Leviathan*, Dodd, 1971. Writer of scientific articles and reports.

SIDELIGHTS: Ommanney took part in three Antarctic expeditions with Research Ship, "Discovery II," from 1929-36; on the third expedition he went to the assistance of Explorer Lincoln Ellsworth at Little America after Ellsworth's Antarctic transcontinental flight and took him to Australia; during 1947-50 Ommanney participated in a fishing survey covering more than 25,000 miles of the western Indian Ocean. Ommanney speaks some French and German.

*   *   *

O'NEILL, Joseph Harry 1915-

PERSONAL: Born June 8, 1915, in Hamilton, Ontario, Canada. *Education:* Attended St. Augustine's Seminary; Niagara University, B.A., 1945, M.A., 1946; University of Ottawa, S.T.L., 1947. *Home:* 55 Church St., Pickering, Ontario, Canada.

CAREER: Ordained Roman Catholic priest, 1939. Pastor of St. Francis de Sales Church, Pickering, Ontario. *Member:* Catholic Homiletic Society (member of board of directors).

WRITINGS: A Pastor's Point of View, Bruce, 1963. Contributor to *Homiletic and Pastoral Review, Pastoral Life, Priest.*

WORK IN PROGRESS: A Pastor Writes for People.†

*   *   *

O'NEILL, Michael J. 1913-

PERSONAL: Born March 1, 1913, in Dublin, Ireland; son of Patrick J. (a sales manager) and Anne J. O'Neill; married Bridget Reidy. *Education:* Fordham University, A.B., 1937; University College of Dublin, National University of Ireland, A.M. (first honors), 1950, Ph.D., 1952. *Religion:* Roman Catholic. *Home:* 759 Eastbourne Ave., Ottawa 7, Ontario, Canada. *Office:* Faculty of Arts, University of Ottawa, Ottawa 2, Ontario, Canada.

CAREER: St. Louis University, St. Louis, Mo., assistant professor of English, 1946-58; Bellarmine College, Louisville, Mo., associate professor of English and chairman of department of English, 1958-63; University of Ottawa, Ottawa, Ontario, professor of English, 1963—. Assistant to director of Abbey Theatre, 1950-52. Member of committee, Junior Great Books Program, Louisville, Ky., 1959-60. *Military service:* U.S. Army Air Forces, Meteorological Service, 1942-46; became staff sergeant. *Member:* Royal Society of Antiquarians of Ireland (fellow), Society for Theatre Research (London), Association of Canadian Teachers of English, Canadian Association of University Teachers, American Association of University Professors. *Awards, honors:* Canada Council Award, 1965; Canada Council leave fellowship, 1966.

WRITINGS: (With others) *James Joyce Miscellany*, Southern Illinois University Press, 1959; *English Department Handbook*, Bellarmine College Press, 1961; *Lennox Robinson*, Twayne, 1964; (editor with Robert Hogan) *Joseph Holloway's Abbey Theatre*, Southern Illinois University Press, 1966; (editor with Hogan) *Joseph Holloway's Irish Theatre*, three volumes, Proscenium Press, 1968-70. Contributor to *Abstracts of English Studies*, 1959—, and to *Dublin Magazine, Commonweal, Modern Drama, Irish Digest, Shaw Review*, and other American and Irish literary journals.

SIDELIGHTS: O'Neill is competent in French. *Avocational interests:* Gardening, drama, travel, swimming, and music.

*   *   *

OPPEN, George 1908-

PERSONAL: Born April 24, 1908, in New Rochelle, N.Y.; son of George A. and Elsie (Rothfeld) Oppen; married

Mary Colby, August 11, 1928; children: Linda (Mrs. Alexander Mourelatos). *Education:* Attended public schools in California. *Home:* 2811 Polk St., San Francisco, Calif. 94109.

CAREER: Has worked as a tool and die maker, cabinet maker, experimental mechanic, production manager, and building contractor. Went to France in 1929, and operated the Objectivist Press with Louis Zukofsky. Fled to Mexico to escape the harassment of the McCarthy Committee, and owned and managed a small shop in Mexico City, designing and building furniture. Returned to United States in 1958. *Military service:* U.S. Army; served as combat infantryman during World War II; awarded the "normal 'decorations' and condolences." *Awards, honors:* Pulitzer Prize for poetry, 1969, for *Of Being Numerous.*

WRITINGS: Discrete Series, Objectivist Press, 1934; *The Materials*, New Directions, 1962; *This in Which*, New Directions, 1965; *Of Being Numerous*, New Directions, 1968; *Seascape: Needle's Eye*, Sumac Press, 1973. Work included in many anthologies, including *An Objectivists Anthology*, edited by Louis Zukofsky, Le Beausset, 1932; *Active Anthology*, edited by Ezra Pound, Faber, 1933; and *Mark in Time: Portraits and Poetry/San Francisco*, edited by Robert E. Johnson and Nick Harvey, Glide, 1971. Contributor to *Poetry, Hound and Horn, San Francisco Review, Massachusetts Review, New Yorker, The Nation*, and other periodicals.

WORK IN PROGRESS: Myth of the Blaze.

SIDELIGHTS: Paul Zweig writes that the award to Oppen of the 1969 Pulitzer Prize for poetry was "a tribute not to one book, but to a lifetime of achievement in poetry." Analyzing his work, Zweig says: "Oppen is not an easy poet to read. His poems are tightly wrought meditations which do not so much define as surround their subject with tentative thrusts of meaning. Abstractions and carefully observed details mingle to produce a line that is almost sculptural in its precision.... Statement lies outside the delicate structure of Oppen's style. Statement is a boundary line, a landmark. The poem itself has the elusiveness of growth and pure movement.... Ideas are presented not only to be understood, but to be experienced suggestively, musically, so to speak.... [Of Being Numerous] is one of the most important single poems to be written in recent years."

L. S. Dembo has said: "Still rigorously reporting only what he has 'seen' or truly sensed, [Oppen] begins to describe a world of alienation and loss—a world lethal and unknowable yet offering moments of intense aesthetic vision ..., Oppen reveals the human, if stark, struggle that underlies the perceptions of the objectivist.... 'The life of the mind,' which Oppen believes to be the only life for humanity, coexists with *Angst*, boredom, and despair. Yet underlying these opposing responses is the idea that reality in all its manifestations must be respected as truth. Nontruth [for Oppen], is represented by the invented ethic, detached from the actual feeling, or in objects, by the hollow decorations of an affluent civilization."

Oppen has said of his work: "I'm really concerned with the substantive, with the subject of the sentence, with what we are talking about, and not rushing over the subject-matter in order to make a comment about it. It is still a principle with me, of more than poetry, to notice, to state, to lay down the substantive for its own sake.... I'm trying to describe how the test of images can be a test of whether one's thought is valid, whether one can establish in a series of images, of

experiences ... whether or not one will consider the concept of humanity to be valid, something that is, or else have to regard it as being simply a word."

BIOGRAPHICAL/CRITICAL SOURCES: The Review, January, 1964; *Contemporary Literature*, Volume X, number 2, spring, 1969; *The Nation*, November 24, 1969; *Partisan Review*, Volume XL, number 2, 1973.

* * *

OPPENHEIMER, George 1900-

PERSONAL: Born February 7, 1900, in New York, N.Y.; son of Julius (a diamond and pearl wholesaler) and Ida (Adler) Oppenheimer. *Education:* Williams College, B.A., 1920; Harvard University, graduate study, 1921. *Politics:* Democrat. *Religion:* Jewish. *Home and office:* 15 East 64th St., New York, N.Y. 10021. *Agent:* Robert Lantz, 114 East 55th St., New York, N.Y.

CAREER: Alfred A. Knopf (publisher), New York, N.Y., advertising and publicity manager, 1921-25; Viking Press, New York, N.Y., co-founder, 1925-33; *Newsday*, Garden City, N.Y., writer and Sunday drama critic, 1955—. Writer of filmscripts, and stage, radio, and television plays. *Military service:* U.S. Army Air Forces, South East Asia Command, 1943-44; became captain. *Member:* New York Drama Critics Circle (past vice-president; president, 1970-72), Coffee House, Players Club.

WRITINGS: (Editor) *The Passionate Playgoer: A Personal Scrapbook*, Viking, 1958; *The View from the Sixties: Memories of a Spent Life* (autobiographical), McKay, 1966; (editor) *Frank Sullivan Through the Looking Glass*, Doubleday, 1970, 2nd edition published as *Well, There's No Harm in Laughing*, 1972; (editor with John K. Hutchens) *The Best of the World: A Selection of News & Feature Stories, Editorials, Humor, Poems & Reviews, 1921-28*, Viking, 1973.

Plays: "Here Today"; (with Arthur Kober) "A Mighty Man Is He"; "The Manhatters" (a revue).

Films: "Libeled Lady"; "A Day at the Races"; "Roman Scandals"; "I Love You Again"; "Decameron Nights"; "Yank at Oxford," and thirty others.

Writer of twenty-nine episodes for "Topper" television series. Also writer of other television scripts and of short stories. New York theatre correspondent, *Financial Times* (London).

* * *

ORENSTEIN, Henry 1924-

PERSONAL: Born May 29, 1924, in New York, N.Y.; son of Nathan (a merchant) and Hannah Orenstein. *Education:* University of California, Berkeley, A.B., 1950, Ph.D., 1957. *Politics:* Democrat. *Religion:* Jewish. *Home:* 7109 Walmsley Ave., New Orleans, La. *Office:* Department of Sociology and Anthropology, Tulane University, New Orleans, La. 70118.

CAREER: Syracuse University, Syracuse, N.Y., instructor, 1957-58; Tulane University, New Orleans, La., assistant professor, 1958-64, associate professor of anthropology, 1964—. *Military service:* U.S. Army, 1943-46. *Member:* American Anthropological Association, American Ethnological Society, Association for Asian Studies, American Association of University Professors, Indian Sociological Society, American Civil Liberties Union, Phi Beta Kappa, Sigma Xi. *Awards, honors:* National Science

Foundation grant, 1959-61; American Council of Learned Societies grant, 1959.

WRITINGS: Gaon: Conflict and Cohesion in an Indian Village, Princeton University Press, 1965; (editor with Mario D. Zamora and J. Michael Mahar) *Themes in Culture: Essays in Honor of Morris E. Opler*, Kayumangii Publishers (Philippines), 1971. Contributor to journals of sociology, anthropology, and ethnology.

WORK IN PROGRESS: Study of Hindu sacred law for a book emphasizing values and the problem of moral relativity.†

* * *

ORLICH, Donald C(harles) 1931-

PERSONAL: Born December 28, 1931, in Butte, Mont.; son of Sam (a miner) and Mary E. (Mihelich) Orlich; married E. Patricia Rend (a home economist) June 8, 1957; children: Michael James, Laura Anne. *Education:* University of Montana, B.A., 1953, Ed.D., 1963; University of Utah, Master of Science Education, 1959. *Religion:* Roman Catholic. *Home:* South East 435 Crestview, Pullman, Wash. 99163. *Office:* Department of Education, Washington State University, Pullman, Wash. 99163.

CAREER: Elementary and junior high school teacher in Butte, Mont., 1955-58, 1959-60; Idaho State University, Pocatello, assistant professor, 1962-65, associate professor of education, 1965-67, chairman of department, 1966-67; Washington State University, Pullman, associate professor, 1967-70, professor of education, 1970—. Visiting instructor in education, Montana State University, summer, 1961, 1962. *Military service:* U.S. Army, active duty, 1953-55; became first lieutenant; received Army Commendation Ribbon. U.S. Army Reserve; captain. *Member:* National Association for Research in Science Teaching, American Association of University Professors (member of executive board, 1964-65; president, 1965-67), Montana Academy of Sciences (chairman of teaching of science section, 1960-61; director, 1961-62), Washington Science Teachers Association (president, 1973-74), Phi Delta Kappa, Phi Sigma.

WRITINGS: (With S. Samuel Shermis) *Conspectus of American Education*, Edwards, 1964; (editor with Shermis) *The Pursuit of Excellence: Introductory Readings in Education*, American Book Co., 1965; (with Evelyn Craven and Robert D. Rounds) *The Development of an Information System for Teacher Turnover in Public Schools*, Idaho State University, 1968; (with Craven and Round) *Teacher Mobility in Idaho*, Idaho Education Association, 1968; (editor with C. Hilen) *Telecommunications for Learning*, Washington State University, 1969; *Institute for Training Directors of Teacher Education Reform*, U.S. Office of Education, 1973.

Writer and producer of forty-tape introductory education course for educational television. Contributor to *Elementary School Journal, Journal for Research in Science Teaching*, other education and library journals, and to *American School Board Journal.*

WORK IN PROGRESS: A monograph on teacher mobility; textbooks on teaching.

AVOCATIONAL INTERESTS: Photography, skiing and camping, computers.

* * *

ORLOVSKY, Peter 1933-

PERSONAL: Born July 8, 1933, in New York, N.Y.; son of Oleg (a silk screen printer for neckties) and Katherine (Schworten) Orlovsky. *Education:* Attended San Francisco Junior College for two and one half years. *Politics:* Pacifist. *Religion:* Buddhist. *Home:* 408 East Tenth St., New York, N.Y.

CAREER: Poet, singer, ambulance attendant, mental hospital attendant, farmer's helper, dishwasher in a hospital, secretary for Allen Ginsberg (whom he claims to have "married, Crismiss 1954", and with whom he has traveled in India, Morocco, Spain, France, England, Holland, Istanbul, Greece, East Africa, Pakistan, Yugoslavia, and Bulgaria); collater and sweeper at Peace Eye Bookstore, New York, N.Y., 1963; adviser to League for Sexual Freedom, and to LEMAR (a society supporting the legalization of marijuana); singer and walker for peace in New York, San Francisco, and Washington, D.C. *Military service:* U.S. Army, "bed pan medic," November, 1953-July, 1954.

WRITINGS—All poetry: (Contributor) *The Beat Scene*, edited by E. Wilentz, Centaur Press, 1960; (contributor) *New American Poetry: 1945-1960*, edited by Donald M. Allen, Grove, 1960. Contributor of poetry to *Beatitude Anthology*, City Lights Press, and to *Yugen, Outsider*, and *F—— You: A Magazine of the Arts.*

WORK IN PROGRESS: "Collecting & Bakeing my First Book of Poems & Sex Experiments; Something like Embarased Traveling Dream Poems of Look Rain Delight; Useing Tape machine & Fast Pen to record conversations of Allen Ginsberg."

SIDELIGHTS: Orlovsky's activities include distributing "countless birth poems all over, trying to learn Indian Raggs, [and] careing for 2 [of my] brothers who have been partly cattle treeted driven into state Mental Hospitals, one brother for almost 13 years & my younger brother for 2½ years." He was a devotee of "Hinduism-Lord Ganesh" in 1962. With Ginsberg, he often plays his zils (oriental finger cymbals) and leads Indian chants at public demonstrations. He has given poetry readings, most recently at Berkeley during "Vietnam Day." He wrote for *The New American Poetry*: ". . . Trouble in school: always thinking dreaming sad mistry problems. . . . Love pretzles & cant remember dreams anymore. . . . Did weight lifting with bus stops. Got to enjoy burnt bacon with mothers help. Stare at my feet to much & need to undue paroniac suden clowds. Enjoy mopping floors, cleaning up cat vommit. Enjoy swinning underwater. . . . Getting to enjoy blank mind state, especially in tub. . . . got to like flies tickleing nose & face. . . . I.Q. 90 in school, now specialized I.Q. is thousands."

Orlovsky has appeared in two films: Andy Warhol's "Couch," 1965, and "Me and My Brother," 1969.

BIOGRAPHICAL/CRITICAL SOURCES: The New American Poetry: 1945-1960, edited by Donald M. Allen, Grove, 1960.†

* * *

ORMONT, Louis Robert 1918-

PERSONAL: Born June 16, 1918, in Philadelphia, Pa.; married Joan Connor (a writer), August 27, 1959; children: Marian Amanda, Michael Llewellyn. *Education:* Temple University, B.S., 1941; graduate study at Washington and Jefferson College, 1943, Washington and Lee College, 1944; Western Reserve University (now Case Western Reserve University), M.S., 1946; Yale University, M.F.A., 1949; Columbia University, Ph.D., 1960. *Office:* 55 Central Park W., New York, N.Y. 10023.

CAREER: Psychologist in private practice, New York, N.Y., 1950—; Columbia University, New York, N.Y., instructor in group psychotherapy, 1958—; psychological director of Center for Career Planning, 1963—. Clinical professor of psychology, Institute of Advanced Psychological Studies, postdoctoral program in psychotherapy. Faculty member at Center for Modern Psychoanalytic Studies, National Psychological Institute for Psychoanalysis, New York Center for Psychoanalytic Training, California Institute of Graduate Studies, Philadelphia School of Psychoanalysis, and Boston Center for Psychotherapeutic Studies. Conducts training groups for psychotherapists in the technique of group treatment. *Military service:* U.S. Army, 1942-45. *Member:* American Psychological Association (fellow), American Group Psychotherapy Association, Interamerican Society of Psychology, New York Society of Clinical Psychologists, New York State Psychological Association.

WRITINGS: (With Rena Corman and Morton Hunt) *The Talking Cure*, Harper, 1964. Contributor to *Marriage and Family Living, British Journal of Medical Psychology*, other psychotherapy and psychoanalytic journals.

WORK IN PROGRESS: Modern Group Psychoanalysis, a book on conjoint and group psychotherapy.

AVOCATIONAL INTERESTS: The theater (writing, directing, and acting), archeology of Greece, Italy, and Asia Minor.

* * *

OSBORN, Robert (Chesley) 1904-

PERSONAL: Born October 26, 1904, in Oshkosh, Wis.; son of Albert LeRoy (a lumberman) and Alice Lydia (Wycoff) Osborn; married Elodie Courter, March 18, 1944; children: Nicolas Courter, Eliot Wycoff. *Education:* University of Wisconsin, student, 1922-23; Yale University, Ph.B., 1928; also studied at British Academy, Rome, Italy, 1928, and at Academie Scandinav, Paris, France, 1929. *Politics:* Democrat. *Residence:* Salisbury, Conn.

CAREER: Hotchkiss School, Lakeville, Conn., teacher of art, Greek philosophy, and football, 1929-35; free-lance artist and illustrator of books and magazine articles. Chairman of art and architecture committee, Yale Council, 1952-54, 1956-60; member, Salisbury (Conn.) Central School Board, 1954-60. *Military service:* U.S. Navy, 1941-45; became lieutenant commander; received Legion of Merit. *Member:* American Civil Liberties Union, The Century Association (New York City), Scroll and Key Club and Elizabethan Club (both New Haven). *Awards, honors:* Distinguished Public Service Award, Secretary of the Navy, 1958; fellow of Berkeley College, Yale University, 1958; Gold Medal of the Society of Illustrators, 1959; Wisconsin Governor's Council on the Arts Medal, 1964; honorary Doctor of Arts from The Maryland Institute, College of Art, 1964.

WRITINGS—Self-illustrated: *How to Shoot Ducks*, Coward, 1939; *How to Shoot Quail*, Coward, 1939; *How to Catch Trout*, Coward, 1939; *Aye Aye Sir*, Coward, 1942; *Dilbert*, Coward, 1943; *War Is No Damn Good*, Doubleday, 1946; *How to Ski*, Coward, 1947; *How to Play Golf*, Coward, 1948; *How to Shoot Pheasant*, Coward, 1948; *Low and Inside*, Farrar, Straus, 1954; *Osborn on Leisure*, Squibb & Sons, 1957; *The Vulgarians*, New York Graphic Society, 1961; *Dying to Smoke*, Houghton, 1964; *Mankind May Never Make It*, New York Graphic Society, 1969; (with Eve Wengler) *An Osborn Festival of Phobias*, Liveright, 1971.

Illustrator: Russell Lynes, *Snobs*, Harper, 1949; Fred Reader, *Safe for Solo*, Harper, 1950; Rice E. Cochran, *Be Prepared*, Sloane, 1951; John McDonald, *Strategy in Poker, Business and War*, Norton, 1952; S. J. Perelman, *Acres and Pains*, Reynal & Hitchcock, 1952; W. H. Whyte, Jr., *Is Anybody Listening?*, Simon & Schuster, 1953; Parke Cummings, *I'm Telling You Kids . . .*, Henry Schuman, 1953; Aguste C. Spectorsky, *The Exurbanites*, Lippincott, 1955; T. Whiteside, *The Relaxed Sell*, Oxford University Press, 1956; Michael Straight, *Trial by Television*, Beacon, 1957; T. N. Parkinson, *Parkinson's Law*, Houghton, 1959; John Keats, *The Insolent Chariot*, Lippincott, 1959.

The Decline of the American Male, Random, 1960; Russell Lynes, *Guests*, Harper, 1960; T. N. Parkinson, *The Law and the Profits*, Houghton, 1960; Marya Mannes, *SubVerse*, Braziller, 1961; Eve Merriam, *Basics*, Macmillan, 1961; *Book of Limericks*, Doubleday, 1962; T. N. Parkinson, *In-Laws and Outlaws*, Houghton, 1962; John Ciardi, *I Met a Man*, Houghton, 1962; Frank Getlein, *A Modern Demonology*, C. N. Potter, 1963; F. Birmingham, *How to Succeed at Touch Football*, Macmillan, 1963; E. Raskin, *Architecturally Speaking*, Reinhold, 1963; P. Reiss, *The Song of Paul Bunyan*, Pantheon, 1964; Peter Blake, *The Everlasting Cocktail Party . . .*, Dial, 1964; George R. Stewart, *Not So Rich as You Think*, Houghton, 1968; Herbert Scoville, *Missile Madness*, Houghton, 1970.

Contributor of illustrations to *Life, Harper's Magazine, Fortune, Look, New Republic*, and many other magazines. Also illustrator of sixty-two "Sense" books for the U.S. Navy and U.S. Army, 1942—. Producer and publisher of seven thousand "Dilbert" posters for U.S. Naval Aviation.

WORK IN PROGRESS: To Kill, a book about man killing his fellow man and the effect it has upon him.

SIDELIGHTS: Osborn told *CA*, "[I] enjoy most of all my marvelous wife. Living with this superb woman for 27 years has been the real meaning of my life." *Avocational interests:* Trout fishing, gardening, cross country skiing, swimming; making kites and light, transparent wing airplanes; France and Spain.

* * *

OSBORN, Ronald E(dwin) 1917-

PERSONAL: Born September 5, 1917, in Chicago, Ill.; son of G. Edwin (a clergyman and educator) and Alma E. (Lanterman) Osborn; married Naomi Elizabeth Jackson, September 10, 1940; children: Virginia Elizabeth (deceased). *Education:* Attended Lynchburg College, 1934-35, and Union Theological Seminary, Richmond, Va., 1936; Phillips University, Enid, Okla., B.A., 1938, M.A., 1939, B.D., 1942; University of Oklahoma, graduate study, 1940-41; University of Oregon, Ph.D., 1955. *Politics:* Democrat. *Office:* School of Theology at Claremont, 1325 North College, Claremont, Calif. 91711.

CAREER: Clergyman, Disciples of Christ (Christian Churches); minister in Lahoma, Okla., 1936-38, Geary, Okla., 1938-42, and Jonesboro, Ark., 1942-43; Christian Board of Publication, St. Louis, Mo., editor of youth publications, 1943-45; Northwest Christian College, Eugene, Ore., professor of church history, 1946-50; minister in Creswell, Ore., 1946-50; Christian Theological Seminary (formerly Butler University School of Religion), Indianapolis, Ind., associate professor, 1950-53, professor of church history, 1953-73, dean, 1959-70; School of Theology at Claremont, Claremont, Calif., professor of church history, 1973—. Lecturer, Graduate School of Ecumenical Studies, Ecumenical Institute, Geneva Switzerland, 1954-55; visiting professor of church history, Union Theological Seminary, Manila, Philippines, 1965; visiting professor, School of Theology at Claremont, 1970-71. Member of staff, Assembly of World Council of Churches, Evanston, Ill., 1954. Moderator, Disciples of Christ (Christian Churches), 1968.

MEMBER: American Historical Association, Renaissance Society of America, Mediaeval Academy of America, American Society of Church History, Phi Kappa Phi, Theta Phi. *Awards, honors:* Litt.D., Phillips University, 1969.

WRITINGS: Ely Vaughn Zollars: A Biography, Christian Board of Publication, 1947; *The Spirit of American Christianity*, Harper, 1957; (with Cynthia Pearl Maus, A. T. DeGroot, and others) *The Church and the Fine Arts*, Harper, 1960; (editor) *The Reformation of Tradition*, Bethany, 1963; *Toward the Christian Church*, Christian Board of Publication, 1964; *A Church for These Times*, Abingdon, 1965; *In Christ's Place*, Bethany, 1967; (contributor) Paul A. Crow and William J. Boney, editors, *Church Union at Midpoint*, Association Press, 1972; (contributor) George G. Beazley, Jr., editor, *The Christian Church: An Interpretative Examination in the Cultural Context*, Bethany, 1973. Contributor to *Encyclopaedia Britannica*, 1973. Editor of *Encounter*, 1952-60, 1972-73.

WORK IN PROGRESS: Folly of God, a work on the history of preaching.

SIDELIGHTS: Osborn has reading competence in Greek, Latin, French, German, and Italian. He has visited centers of theological education in Southeast Asia, 1965-66.

*   *   *

OSBORNE, Charles   1927-

PERSONAL: Born November 24, 1927, in Brisbane, Australia; son of Vincent Lloyd and Elsa (Raumer) Osborne. *Education:* Attended University of Queensland, 1944-45. *Politics:* Un-doctrinaire liberal. *Home:* 7 Paultons House, London S.W. 3, England. *Agent:* A. D. Peters, 10 Buckingham St., London W.C. 2, England.

CAREER: Began career as writer and actor in Australia; writer and editor in London, England, 1953—. Assistant editor, *London Magazine*, 1957-66; chief editor for Alan Ross Ltd. (publishers), 1965—; Arts Council of Great Britain, assistant literature director, 1966—. Writer on European musical events for *New York Times. Member:* P.E.N.

WRITINGS: (Editor) *Australian Stories of Today*, Faber, 1962; (with Brigid Brophy and Michael Levy) *Fifty Works of English and American Literature We Could Do Without*, Kapp & Carroll, 1967, Stein & Day, 1968; (editor) *Twelve Poets*, Poetry Book Society (London), 1967; *Kafka*, Oliver & Boyd, 1967, Barnes & Noble, 1968; *Swansong: Poems*, Shenval, 1968; *The Complete Operas of Verdi*, Gollancz, 1969, Knopf, 1970; *Ned Kelly*, Anthony Blond, 1970; (editor) *Australia, New Zealand and the South Pacific: A Handbook*, Praeger, 1970; (editor) *Letters of Giuseppe Verdi*, Gollancz, 1971, Holt, 1972; (editor and author of introduction) *Richard Wagner—Stories and Essays*, Library Press, 1973.

Plays include "Actor by Moonlight," and "Platonov." Contributor of poems to anthologies, including *Oxford Book of Australian Verse*. Contributor to journals and periodicals including *New Statesman*, *Spectator*, and *Observer*. Editor of *Opera*, 1966—.

WORK IN PROGRESS: A book on twentieth century opera.

SIDELIGHTS: Charles Osborne is competent in German and French.†

*   *   *

OSBORNE, Harold   1905-

PERSONAL: Born in 1905, in London, England; son of Owen John (a teacher) and Dulcibella Eden (Greville) Osborne. *Education:* Cambridge University, M.A. *Home:* 63 The Drive, London N.W. 11, England. *Agent:* Curtis Brown Ltd., 13 King St., London W.C. 2, England.

CAREER: Attached to staff of British Embassy, La Paz, Bolivia, 1947-52; now retired from British Civil Service. Permek Enterprises Ltd., director. *Member:* Mind Association, Aristotelian Society.

WRITINGS: Foundations of the Philosophy of Value, Cambridge University Press, 1933; *A Mirror of Character*, University Tutorial Press, 1935; *Indians of the Andes*, Routledge & Kegan Paul, 1952; *Theory of Beauty*, Routledge & Kegan Paul, 1952; *Bolivia: A Land Divided*, Oxford University Press for Royal Institute of International Affairs, 1954, 3rd edition, 1964; *Aesthetics and Criticism*, Routledge & Kegan Paul, 1955; *Aesthetics and Art Theory*, Longmans, Green, 1968, Dutton, 1970; *Aesthetics in the Modern World*, Weybright & Talley, 1968; *South American Mythology*, Feltham, Hamlyn, 1968; (editor) Francis Bacon, *New Atlantis*, University Tutorial Press, 1969; *The Art of Appreciation*, Oxford University Press, 1970; (editor) *The Oxford Companion to Art*, Clarendon Press, 1970; *Aesthetics*, Oxford University Press, 1972. Editor, *British Journal of Aesthetics*.

SIDELIGHTS: Harold Osborne is competent in French, Spanish, German, and Polish; knows ancient Greek and Latin. *Avocational interests:* South American art and culture.†

*   *   *

OSBORNE, John (James)   1929-

PERSONAL: Born December 12, 1929, in London, England; son of Thomas Godfrey (a commercial artist) and Nellie Beatrice (a barmaid; maiden name, Grove) Osborne; married Pamela Elizabeth Lane (an actress), 1951 (divorced, 1957); married Mary Ure (an actress), November 8, 1957 (divorced, 1963); married Penelope Gilliatt (a drama critic and novelist), May 24, 1963 (divorced, 1967); married Jill Bennett (an actress), April, 1968; children: (third marriage) Nolan Kate. *Education:* "Worth no mention," writes Osborne, who left school at sixteen. *Home:* The Water Mill, Hellingly, Sussex, England. *Agent:* Margery Vosper Ltd., 53A Shaftesbury Ave., London W. 1, England. *Office:* Woodfall Films, 27 Curzon St., London W. 1, England.

CAREER: Worked on trade journals, *Gas World* and *Miller*, for six months; was a tutor to juvenile actors in a touring group, later the group's assistant stage manager, and finally an actor specializing in characterizations of old men; made first stage appearance at Lyceum, Sheffield, England, in "No Room at the Inn," 1948; has appeared in "Don Juan," "Death of Satan," "Cards of Identity," "Good Woman of Setzuan," "The Apollo de Bellac," "The Making of Moo," and "A Cuckoo in the Nest." Playwright and producer; produced his first play at Theatre Royal, Huddersfield, England, 1949; for two seasons he co-managed a small theatrical company at seaside resorts (it proved unsuccessful); founder-director of Woodfall Films, 1958—; Oscar Lewenstein Plays Ltd., London, England, director, 1960—. Has appeared in films and television productions. Member of council, English Stage Co., 1968—. *Member:* Writers' Guild of Great Britain, Savile Club, Garrick Club. *Awards, honors: Evening Standard* Drama Award, 1956, 1965, for "A Patriot for Me," 1968, for "The Hotel in Amsterdam"; New York Drama Critics Circle Award, 1958, for "Look Back in Anger," and 1965, for "Luther"; Tony Award, 1963, for "Luther"; Academy Award, 1963, for script for "Tom Jones"; honorary doctorate, Royal College of Art, 1970.

WRITINGS—Plays; published and produced: *Look Back in Anger* (produced in London, 1956, New York, 1957), Criterion, 1957; *The Entertainer* (produced in London, 1957, New York, 1958), Faber, 1957, Criterion, 1958; (with Anthony Creighton) *Epitaph for George Dillon* (produced in Oxford, 1957, London and New York, 1958), Criterion, 1958; *The World of Paul Slickey* (produced in London, 1959), Faber, 1959, Criterion, 1961; *A Subject of Scandal and Concern* (televised as "A Matter of Scandal and Concern," 1960; produced as "A Subject of Scandal and Concern" in Nottingham, 1962, New York, 1965), Faber, 1961; *Luther* (produced in London, 1961, New York, 1963), Dramatic Publishing, 1961; *Plays for England: The Blood of the Bambergs* [and] *Under Plain Cover* (both produced in London, 1963, New York, 1965), Faber, 1963, Criterion, 1964; *Inadmissible Evidence* (produced in London, 1964, New York, 1965), Grove, 1965; *A Bond Honoured* (adaptation of play by Lope de Vega; produced in London, 1966), Faber, 1966; *A Patriot for Me* (produced in London, 1965, New York, 1969), Faber, 1966, Random House, 1970; *Time Present* [and] *The Hotel in Amsterdam* (both produced in London, 1968), Faber, 1968; *West of Suez* (produced in London, 1971), Faber, 1971; *Hedda Gabler* (adaptation of play by Henrik Ibsen; produced in London, 1972), Faber, 1972; *A Sense of Disenchantment* (produced in London, 1972), Faber, 1973.

Plays; produced only: "The Devil Inside Him," produced in Huddersfield, 1950; (with Anthony Creighton) "Personal Enemy," produced in Harrogate, 1955.

Television plays: *The Right Prospectus: A Play for Television* (televised, 1970), Faber, 1970; *Very Like a Whale* (televised, 1970), Faber, 1971; *The Gifts of Friendship* (televised, 1972), Faber, 1972. Also author of television plays "Billy Bunter," 1952, and "Robin Hood," 1953; author of television adaptation of stage play "The Hotel in Amsterdam," 1971.

Screenplays: *Tom Jones: A Film Script*, Faber, 1964, revised edition, Grove, 1965. Also author of screenplays based on stage plays, including "Look Back in Anger," 1959; "The Entertainer," 1960; "Inadmissible Evidence," 1968.

Other: (Contributor) Tom Maschler, editor, *Declaration*, Dutton, 1958; *The Naturalist Drama in Germany*, Rowman & Littlefield, 1971; *A Place Calling Itself Rome* (adaptation of Shakespeare's "Coriolanus"), Faber, 1973; *The Picture of Dorian Gray: A Moral Entertainment* (adaptation of novel by Oscar Wilde), Faber, 1973.

Plays represented in anthologies, including *Modern English Plays*, Progress Publishers (Moscow), 1966; *The Best Short Plays of the World Theatre, 1958-1967*, edited by Stanley Richards, Crown, 1968. Contributor to *Encounter, Observer, Sunday Telegraph, Sunday Times* (London), and other newspapers and journals.

SIDELIGHTS: Osborne became an "overnight success" when *Look Back in Anger* opened in London in 1956, running for 18 months in spite of a bad press. It drew huge audiences even though, as Osborne recalls, some people walked out yelling things like "Keep quiet." Critics attacked its rasping tone, its attacks on the establishment, and its uncompromising vulgarity. But the play thrived, and still remains the manifesto of the theater of protest on two continents.

Arthur Miller saw the play as an oasis of reality in "a theatre hermetically sealed off from life." Its protagonist, Jimmy Porter, is what Kenneth Tynan calls "politically a liberal and sexually a despot." With the production of *Look Back*, Osborne became the outstanding spokesman of the classless, of those lacking a cause, a purpose, or a leader. Tynan believes that "no germinal play of comparable strength has emerged since the war." And, for a first play, he considers it "a minor miracle."

The play even made some impression on the Establishment. When Osborne's second play, *The Entertainer*, was to be produced, Osborne was approached by Sir Laurence Olivier who wanted a part in the play. The leading role which Olivier got marked his return to the Royal Court after 29 years.

In *The Entertainer* the commentator, Jean, says: "Here we are, we're alone in the universe, there's no God, it just seems that it all began by something as simple as sunlight striking on a piece of rock. And here we are. We've only got ourselves. Somehow, we've got to make a go of it. *We've only ourselves.*" In his fifth play, *Luther*, the young Martin Luther cries out: "I am alone. I am alone and against myself." The rebellious diatribes Jimmy Porter had hurled against his wife and society in general (in *Look Back*) are gone. In *Luther*, Osborne masterfully dramatizes the complex struggle within one man.

Once again, with "A Patriot for Me," Osborne caused somewhat of a stir. Five of its scenes deal with homosexuality and were, therefore, banned by the Lord Chamberlain. The play was performed only before private audiences composed of members of the English Stage Society, June 30-August 14, 1965. The *New York Times* reported that an offer from New York to stage the premiere was refused.

Osborne's childhood in the London suburb of Fulham was by no means easy. He and his mother at one time subsisted on less than a pound a week. He was defiant even then. Tynan reports that "when a master slapped his face at school, he at once riposted by slapping the master; and this, in Britain, takes preternatural guts." Today Tynan describes him as a "disconcerting, rather impenetrable person to meet: tall and slim, wearing his shoulders in a defensive bunch around his neck; gentle in manner, yet vocally harsh and cawing; sharp-toothed, yet a convinced vegetarian. He looks wan and driven. . . . Sartorially he is something of a peacock, and his sideburns add a sinister touch of the Apache. A dandy, if you like: but a dandy with a machine-gun."

Osborne, who said he prefers writing at night, noted that "Whenever I sit down to write, it is always with dread in my heart." He feels he has "a great fund of violence. . . . But I've also got a fund of detachment. I think you can't write unless you have a certain amount of that." Believing that "All art is organized evasion," Osborne refuses to offer explanations about his plays; instead, he attempts "to make people feel, to give them lessons in feeling. They can think afterwards."

Osborne admires the work of Tennessee Williams, D. H. Lawrence, and Jean Anouilh, and likes to read, listen to music, go to the opera, and, occasionally, to watch television. He also likes, he told *CA*, "riding and boozing with friends."

In October, 1964, Osborne appeared in a revival of Ben Travers' farce, "A Cuckoo in the Nest," at the Royal Court Theater, and in 1965 he directed Charles Wood's "Meals on Wheels" there. In 1957 he told a *New Yorker* interviewer: "I don't act in my own plays, though; one gets enough slung at one's head without inviting it two ways. I find acting a great relief from writing. When you're with actors, you have some sense of community. When you're writing, you're on your own."

Osborne has produced a number of his plays, including "Look Back in Anger," "The Entertainer," "Epitaph for George Dillon," "The World of Paul Slickey," "A Subject of Scandal and Concern," "Plays for England," "Luther," "Inadmissible Evidence," and "A Patriot for Me." His plays have been translated into French, German, Russian, and Italian.

BIOGRAPHICAL/CRITICAL SOURCES: Vogue, April 1, 1957, February 15, 1959; *New Yorker*, October 26, 1957; *Maclean's Magazine*, December 7, 1957; *Saturday Review*, November 22, 1958; Woodrow Lyle Wyatt, *Distinguished for Talent*, Hutchinson, 1958; Tom Maschler, editor, *Declaration*, Dutton, 1958; Kenneth Allsop, *The Angry Decade*, British Book Centre, 1958; John Gassner, *Theatre at the Crossroads*, Holt, 1960; Kenneth Tynan, *Curtains*, Atheneum, 1961; John Russell Taylor, *Anger and After*, Methuen, 1962, Penguin, 1963; William A. Armstrong, editor, *Experimental Drama*, G. Bell, 1963; *Modern Drama, Volume VI*, 1963; Mary McCarthy, *Theatre Chronicles, 1937-62*, Farrar, Straus, 1963; *New York Times Magazine*, October 25, 1964; Kenneth Tynan, *Tynan on Theatre*, Penguin, 1964; *New York Times*, May 12, 1965; *Village Voice*, August 5, 1965; *Partisan Review*, spring, 1966; Walter Wager, editor, *The Playwrights Speak*, Dial, 1967; Frederick Lumley, *New Trends in Twentieth Century Drama*, 3rd edition, Oxford University Press, 1967; John Russell Taylor, editor, *Look Back in Anger*, Macmillan, 1968; Martin Banham, *Osborne*, Oliver & Boyd, 1969; Simon Trussler, *The Plays of John Osborne*, Gollancz, 1969; Alan Carter, *John Osborne*, Oliver & Boyd, 1969, 2nd edition, 1973; Ronald Hayman, *John Osborne*, Ungar, 1972; Carolyn Riley, editor, *Contemporary Literary Criticism*, Gale, Volume I, 1973, Volume II, 1974.

*   *   *

OSBORNE, Margaret 1909-

PERSONAL: Born October 12, 1909, in Wimbledon, England; daughter of Walter Horace (a company director) and Marguerite Anne (Young) Osborne. *Education:* Educated privately in England and in Switzerland. *Politics:* Conservative. *Religion:* Church of England. *Home:* Shiel, Stockbury Vale, Sittingbourne, Kent, England.

CAREER: Dog show judge and consultant on dogs in Britain, Continental Europe, and North and South America. Spent 1940-45 in Australia as escort to children evacuated from England. *Member:* Kennel Club (ladies branch).

WRITINGS: The Popular Collie, Popular Dogs Publishing, 1957, 4th edition published as *The Collie*, 1965; *The Popular Shetland Sheepdog*, Popular Dogs Publishing, 1959, revised edition published as *The Shetland Sheepdog*, 1970; *Collies*, W. & G. Foyle, 1961; *Know Your Welsh Corgi*, Pet Library, 1970. Breed correspondent for *Dog World* (England); staff writer for *Shetland Sheepdog Magazine* (California).

SIDELIGHTS: Miss Osborne is competent in French.

*   *   *

OSBORNE, Milton Edgeworth 1936-

PERSONAL: Born April 17, 1936, in Sydney, Australia; son of George Davenport (a university professor) and Gwynneth J. (Love) Osborne; married Rhondda M. McGown, March 18, 1959. *Education:* University of Sydney, B.A. (first class honors), 1958; Cornell University, graduate study in Southeast Asia Program. *Home:* 8 Karuah Rd., Turramurra, New South Wales, Australia.

CAREER: Australian Diplomatic Service, 1958-62, serving on embassy staff, Phnom Penh, Cambodia, 1959-61. *Member:* Australian Institute of International Affairs, Association for Asian Studies.

WRITINGS: Singapore and Malaysia, Cornell University Press, 1964; *Strategic Hamlets in South Viet-Nam*, Cornell University Press, 1965; *The French Presence In Cochinchina and Cambodia: Rule and Response (1859-1905)*, Cornell University Press, 1969; *Region of Revolt: Focus on Southeast Asia*, Pergamon Press, 1970; *Politics and Power in Cambodia*, Longman, 1974. Contributor to scholarly journals.†

*   *   *

OTCHIS, Ethel (Herberg) 1920-

PERSONAL: "O" in surname is pronounced as in "hot"; born July 29, 1920, in New York, N.Y.; daughter of Max and Sadie (Kopf) Herberg; married Jack Otchis (a jeweler), April 12, 1945; children: Maxine Ann, Susan Dale. *Education:* San Fernando Valley State College (now California State University, Northridge; cum laude), 1959; California State University, M.A., 1969. *Religion:* Jewish. *Home:* 4132 Ellenita Ave., Tarzana, Calif.

CAREER: Los Angeles (Calif.) city schools, elementary teacher, and master and demonstration teacher, 1959—. *Member:* International Reading Association (San Fernando Valley chapter).

WRITINGS: (With Bee Winkler) *The Boy Who Shook Hands with the President*, Golden Gate Junior Books, 1964; (with Winkler) *At the Top of the Hill*, Y. E. S. Books, 1970.

WORK IN PROGRESS: A children's adventure story.

*   *   *

OWEN, (William) Harold 1897-

PERSONAL: Born September 5, 1897, in Shrewsbury, England; son of Tom and Susan Harriet (Shaw) Owen; married Phyllis de Pass, April 30, 1927. *Education:* Attended Shrewsbury School of Art, 1908-13, Byam Shaw School of Painting, 1921, and Royal Academy Schools of Painting. *Politics:* "Not politically minded. Vote Conservative." *Religion:* Agnostic. *Home:* Rodgarden Shaw, Ipsden, Oxfordshire, England. *Agent:* Curtis Brown Ltd., 1 Craven Hill, London W.2, England.

CAREER: Painter, occasionally subsidized by doing agricultural work. Has exhibited at Claridge Galleries, the Royal Academy, Colnaghi, and Bond Street (all in London, England). *Military service:* Merchant Service, 1913-16; junior officer; Royal Naval Reserve, 1916-19; served as midshipman and sub-lieutenant; Royal Naval Volunteer Reserve, 1943-45; served as sub-lieutenant. *Member:* Royal Society of Literature (fellow). *Awards, honors:* Royal Society of Literature Award, 1964, for *Journey From Obscurity: Youth* (Volume II).

WRITINGS—All published by Oxford University Press: *Journey From Obscurity: Childhood* (Volume I), 1963; *Journey From Obscurity: Youth* (Volume II), 1964; *Journey From Obscurity: War* (Volume III), 1965; (editor) Wilfred Owens, *Collected Letters*, 1967; *Aftermath*, 1970.

* * *

OWENS, Joan (Margaret) Llewelyn 1919-

PERSONAL: Born September 27, 1919, in Prestatyn, Flintshire, Wales; daughter of Llewelyn Arthur (a lawyer) and Margaret (Leyshon) Owens; married Desmond Anthony Venner (a chartered civil engineer and company director), October 2, 1954. *Education:* Attended Cheltenham Ladies' College, 1933-37. *Home:* Ashley Cottage, Linden Grove, Walton on Thames, Surrey, England. *Agent:* Winaw Towers Ltd., 14 Clifford's Inn, London E.C. 4, England.

CAREER: News reporter for *West Sussex County Times* and *Grantham Journal*, 1940-45; Women's Royal Naval Service, educational and vocational training instructor, then education officer, 1945-49; writer, 1949—. Careers consultant to *Daily Telegraph*, 1970—. *Member:* Society of Authors, National Book League, Institute of Journalists, Walton on Thames Central Conservative Association (committee).

WRITINGS—Career books for young people: *Sally Grayson: Wren*, Bodley Head, 1954; *A Library Life for Deborah*, Chatto & Windus, 1957; *Margaret Becomes a Doctor*, Bodley Head, 1957; *Sue Takes Up Physiotherapy*, Bodley Head, 1958; *Diana Seton: Veterinary Student*, Bodley Head, 1960; *Hospital Careers for Girls*, Bodley Head, 1961; *Working with Children*, Bodley Head, 1962; *Travel While You Work*, Bodley Head, 1963; *Work in the Theatre*, Bodley Head, 1964; *Careers in Social Work*, Bodley Head, 1965; *Writing as a Career*, Bodley Head, 1967; *The Graduate's Guide to the Business World*, Leviathan House, 1973. Author of official recruiting brochures for Women's Royal Naval Service, Women's Prison Service, and Queen Alexandra's Royal Army Nursing Corps.

Contributor of articles and short stories to *She, Times*, (London), *Daily, Telegraph, Look and Learn, Birmingham Post*, and more than fifty periodicals and newspapers in Great Britain, United States, Belgium, and Scandinavia.

WORK IN PROGRESS: Collecting information for a factual book on the law courts, for Dent; writing the official recruiting brochure for Probation and After-Care Service; articles for *Daily Telegraph*.

SIDELIGHTS: Joan Owens outlined her background from which she draws ideas for her work: "I have flown to Majorca in the galley of a plane with an air hostess, accompanied a veterinary surgeon on her rounds, watched surgical operations on both human beings and animals, and sampled a variety of courses on probation, child care, youth leadership, medicine, and so forth. . . . Most years my husband and I travel abroad and have visited Canada, France, Italy, Spain, Germany, Austria, Belgium, and Scandinavia. . . . My conversational French is passable, my Spanish rather better." *Avocational interests:* Reading, gardening, discussing current affairs, and learning languages.

* * *

OXENHANDLER, Neal 1926-

PERSONAL: Born February 3, 1926, in St. Louis, Mo.; son of Joseph (an insurance broker) and Billie (Lutsky) Oxenhandler; married Jean Romano, June 23, 1951; children: Noel, Daniel, Alica. *Education:* University of Chicago, A.B., 1948; University of Paris, graduate study, 1948-49; Columbia University, M.A., 1950; University of Florence, graduate study, 1953-54; Yale University, Ph.D., 1955. *Religion:* Roman Catholic. *Agent:* Gunther Stuhlmann, 65 Irving Pl., New York, N.Y. 10003. *Office:* Dartmouth College, Hanover, N.H. 03755.

CAREER: St. Louis University, St. Louis, Mo., lecturer in French, 1950-51; Yale University, New Haven, Conn., assistant instructor, 1951-53, instructor in French, 1954-57; University of California, Los Angeles, assistant professor, 1957-60, associate professor of French, 1960-65; University of California, Santa Cruz, associate professor, 1965-66, professor of French, 1966-69; Dartmouth College, Hanover, N.H., professor of French, 1969—. *Member:* Society for Religion in Higher Education, Modern Language Association of America. *Awards, honors:* Fulbright fellow, 1953-54; Guggenheim fellow 1961-62; disciplinary fellowship of Society for Religion in Higher Education, 1966-67.

WRITINGS: Scandal and Parade: The Theatre of Jean Cocteau, Rutgers University Press, 1957; (with Robert J. Nelson) *Aspects of French Literature: An Anthology Along Critical Lines*, Appleton, 1961; *A Change of Gods* (novel), Harcourt, 1962; *Max Jacob and Les Feux de Paris* (monograph), University of California Press, 1964; (editor and author of introduction) *French Literary Criticism* (anthology in French), Prentice-Hall, 1966. Contributor of prose poem to *New Directions Anthology*, 1953, and articles on seven authors to *Lexikon der Weltliteratuer*. Writer of more than twenty articles, poems, and reviews appearing in journals, including *Perspective, Yale Review, French Review, Chicago Review*, and *L'Esprit createur*. Advisory editor, *Film Quarterly*.

WORK IN PROGRESS: A biographical novel.

* * *

PACK, S(tanley) W(alter) C(roucher) 1904-

PERSONAL: Born December 14, 1904, in Portsmouth, England. *Education:* Imperial College of Science and Technology, University of London, B.Sc. in Engineering (first class honors), 1926, M.Sc., 1927. *Home:* Blossom's Pasture, Strete, Dartmouth, Devonshire, England.

CAREER: Royal Navy, regular officer, 1927-60, retiring as captain. Assignments included naval meteorological liaison officer, Toronto, Ontario, Canada, 1939-40, secretary, Combined Meteorological Committee, Washington, D.C., 1941-43, director of current affairs course, Royal Naval College, Greenwich, England, 1946, deputy director, Naval Weather Service, Admiralty, London, England, 1951-54, deputy director, Naval Education Service, Admiralty, 1956-58, aide-de-camp to Her Majesty, Queen Elizabeth, 1957-60. *Member:* Royal Meteorological Society (London; fellow), Royal Ocean Racing Club (London). *Awards, honors:* Boyle Somerville Memorial Prize, British Admiralty, 1938; Legion of Merit (United States), 1948; Commander, Order of the British Empire, 1957.

WRITINGS: *Weather Forecasting*, Longmans, Green, 1948; *Anson's Voyage*, Penguin, 1948; *Admiral Lord Anson*, Cassell, 1960; *The Battle of Matapan*, Batsford, 1961; *Windward of the Caribbean*, Redman, 1964; *The Wager Mutiny*, Redman, 1964; *"Britannia" at Dartmouth*, Redman, 1967; *Sea Power in the Mediterranean*, Barker, 1971; *Night Action Off Cape Matapan*, Ian Allen, 1972; *The Battle for Crete*, Ian Allen, 1973; *Cunningham the Commander*, Batsford, 1974; *The Battle of Sirte*, Ian Allen, 1974; *Operation TORCH*, Ian Allen, in press. Contributor of stories and articles to *Blackwood's Magazine, Field, Navy, Daily Telegraph* (London), *Sunday Times* (London).

* * *

PACKARD, William 1933-

PERSONAL: Born September 2, 1933, in New York, N.Y.; son of Arthur Worthington and Mary (Moody) Packard; divorced. *Education:* Haverford College, student, 1952-55; Stanford University, A.B. (with honors in philosophy), 1956, graduate study, 1960-61. *Residence:* New York, N.Y.

CAREER: Playwright and poet. With Institute for Advanced Studies in the Theatre Arts, New York, N.Y., 1962-64, playwright-in-residence, 1964, teacher, 1965; also teaching at the Clark Center for the Performing Arts, and at New York University, 1965. *Member:* American National Theatre and Academy, Poetry Society of America, Dramatists Guild of Authors League of America. *Awards, honors:* Robert Frost Poetry Award, Bread Loaf School of English, 1957.

WRITINGS: *In the First Place* (play; produced, 1961), Experiment Press, 1958; *Once and For All* (play), Experiment Press, 1962; *On the Other Hand* (play), Experiment Press, 1963; *To Peel an Apple* (poetry), Experiment Press, 1963; *From Now On* (play), Acadia Press, 1964; (translator) Jean Baptiste Racine, *Phedre*, Samuel French, 1966; *The Creation Epic: A New English Adaptation of the Enuma Elish*, Dasein-Jupiter Hammon, 1967; *Voices/I Hear/Voices*, Barlenmir House, 1972; *The Craft of Poetry*, Doubleday, 1974. Also author of "Sandra and the Janitor" (play) first produced at the H. B. Playwrights Foundation, New York, October 11, 1968. Poems published in *Beloit Poetry Review, Transatlantic Review*, and other literary magazines.

WORK IN PROGRESS: *Iasta/Macbeth Log*, an account of John Blatchley's production of "Macbeth."

SIDELIGHTS: Packard's plays have been produced at the White Barn, New Haven, Conn., and at the Theatre de Lys. He has recorded his poetry and excerpts from his plays for the Library of Congress.†

* * *

PAGE, Ellis Batten 1924-

PERSONAL: Born April 29, 1924, in San Diego, Calif.; son of Frank Homer (an engineer) and Dorothy Mae (Batten) Page; married Elizabeth Latimer Thaxton, June 21, 1952; children: Ellis Batten, Jr., Elizabeth Latimer, Richard Leighton. *Education:* Pomona College, A.B., 1947; San Diego State University, M.A., 1955; University of California, Los Angeles, Ed.D., 1958; postdoctoral study, University of Michigan, 1959, Massachusetts Institute of Technology, 1966-67. *Religion:* Episcopalian. *Home:* 14 Willowbrook Rd., Storrs, Conn. 06268. *Office:* Department of Educational Psychology, University of Connecticut, Storrs, Conn. 06268.

CAREER: High school teacher, Grossmont, Calif., 1952-56; San Diego City College, San Diego, Calif., faculty of psychology department and counselor, 1957-58; Eastern Michigan University, Ypsilanti, director of guidance and testing, and lecturer in Graduate Division, 1958-60; Texas Woman's University, Denton, professor of education and psychology, and dean of College of Education, 1960-62; University of Connecticut, Storrs, professor of educational psychology, 1962—, director, Bureau of Educational Research and Service, 1962-70. University of Wisconsin, consultant in measurement and research design, Wisconsin Improvement Program, summer, 1960, visiting lecturer, summer, 1962; visiting professor, Stanford University, summer, 1964, Harvard University, 1968-69. Ministries of Education, head of research advisory team, Venezuela, 1969-70, consultant, Spain, summer, 1972, and Brazil, summer, 1973.

MEMBER: American Association for the Advancement of Science (fellow), American Psychological Association (fellow), Philosophy of Education Society (fellow), American Statistical Association, American Educational Research Association, American Personnel and Guidance Association (life member), National Council on Measurement in Education, Psychometric Society, National Society for the Study of Education, National Conference on Research in English (fellow), Sociedad Interamericana de Psicologia, Psi Chi, Phi Delta Kappa, Kappa Delta Pi. *Awards, honors:* National Science Foundation fellow, 1959; New England Visiting Scientist, 1966.

WRITINGS: (Editor) *Readings for Educational Psychology*, Harcourt, 1964. Author of "Teacher Comments and Student Performance: A Seventy-Four Classroom Experiment in School Motivation," originally published in *Journal of Educational Psychology*, and reprinted in fourteen books of readings edited by others; contributor to other books, yearbooks, reports on education studies, and journals, including *Journal of the American Statistical Association, Educational Psychologist, American Psychologist*, and *Educational Researcher*. Abstracter, *Psychological Abstracts*, 1959-63. Editor, *Educational Psychologist*, 1963-66; associate editor, *Journal of Educational Measurement, Psychology in the Schools, Educational and Psychological Measurement, Computer Studies in the Humanities*.

WORK IN PROGRESS: Operations research applied to education, and the sociology of the nature-nurture debate in psychology.

SIDELIGHTS: Page speaks Spanish and Portuguese.

* * *

PAHLEN, Kurt 1907-

PERSONAL: Born May 26, 1907, in Vienna, Austria; son of Richard (a musician) and Rosina (Kuhn) Pahlen; children: Ivonne. *Education:* University of Vienna, Dr.Phil., 1929; also studied at New Vienna Conservatory. *Religion:* Roman Catholic. *Home:* Soca 1916, Montevideo, Uruguay.

CAREER: "Wiener Volksoper", Vienna, Austria, conductor, 1934-37; migrated to South America in 1939; Filarmonica Metropolitana, Buenos Aires, Argentina, chief-conductor, 1939-45; University de la Republica, Montevideo, Uruguay, professor of musicology, 1949-59; Chorus-Organization, Montevideo, Uruguay, president, chief-conductor, 1950—. Manager, Theatre Colon (Opera House), 1957; guest conductor and visiting professor in South America, Europe and United States, 1961—. *Awards, honors:* Great Cross of Honor (Austria), 1959.

WRITINGS: *Historia Universal de la Musica*, Centurion, 1945, 4th edition, Carlos Lohle, 1964, translation by James A. Galston published as *Music of the World*, Crown, 1949; *El Nino y la Musica*, Ateneio, 1947, and three subsequent editions, translation by Oliver Coburn published as *The Magic World of Music*, W. H. Allen, 1959; *Sudamerka, Eine Neue Welt*, Orell Fussli (Zurich), 1949, and later editions; *Sintesis del Saber Musical*, Emece, 1949.

Manuel de Falla, Otto Walter, 1953; *Pedritos Heimfahrt*, Orell Fussli, 1954; *Kleines Sudamerikabuch*, Classen (Zurich), 1955; *Musiklexikon der Welt*, Orell Fussli, 1956; *Verworfen und Auserwahlt*, Otto Walter (Olten), 1956; *Que es la Musica?*, Columba, 1956; *Johann Strauss*, Melhoramentos, 1957; *Verdi*, Melhoramentos, 1957; *La Opera*, Emece, 1958; *Tschaikowsky*, Peuser, 1958; *Mein Engel, Mein Alles, Mein Ich*, Orell Fussli, 1959; *La Sinfonia*, Orpheus (Rome), 1959.

Que es la Sinfonia?, Columba, 1960; *So Sahen Wir Sie Spielen* (illustrated by Willy Dreifuss), Orell Fussli, 1961; *La Musica en la Educacion Moderna*, Ricordi Americana, 1961; *De Falla*, J. H. Gottmer, 1961; *Der Walzerkoenig Johann Strauss*, Orell Fussli, 1961, translation by Theodore McClintock published as *The Waltz King: Johann Strauss, Jr.*, RandMcNally, 1965; *La Musica*, Atlantica, 1962; *Que es la Opera?*, Columba, 1963; *La Musica Sinfonica*, Emece Editores, 1963; *Oper der Welt*, Schweizer Verlagshaus, 1963; *La Opera*, Emece Editores, 1963; *Musik*, Deutsche Buch-Gemeinshcaft, 1965; *Sinfonie der Welt*, Schweizer Verlaghaus, 1967; (with Juan B. Grosso) *Musica y canciones para los mas pequenos*, Editorial Kapelusz, 1967; *Wir entdecken das Wunderland der Musik*, Sudwest Verlag, 1968; *Grosse Meister der Musik*, Orell Fussli, 1968; *Musik hoeren: Musik verstchen*, Sudwest Verlag, 1969; (compiler) *Das Mozart-Buch*, Gunther, 1969.

Denn es ist kien land wie dieses, Benteli Verlag, 1971; *Grosse Saenger unserer Zeit*, Bertelsmann Sachbuchverlag, 1971, translation by Oliver Coburn published as *Great Singers from the Seventeenth Century to Present Day*, W. H. Allen, 1973; *Que es la musica moderna?*, Columba, 1972; *Grandes cantantes de nuestro tiempo*, Emece Editores, 1973; (compiler) *Musik-Therapie: Behandlung u Hulung gelstiger u seel*, Heyne, 1973.

SIDELIGHTS: Pahlen's first book, *Historia Universal de la Musica*, has been published in ten languages, his second in seven, and most of the others in several translations.†

* * *

PALLE, Albert 1916-

PERSONAL: Born September 14, 1916, in Le Havre, France; son of Sosthene and Odette (de Heyder) Palle; married Denise Jallais (a poet, journalist, and writer), December, 1960; children: Nathalie, Christophe, Sebastien Albertine. *Education:* University of Paris, Sorbonne, licence en philosophie, 1937. *Home:* 21 rue du Vieux-Colombier, Paris VI, France.

CAREER: Journalist, currently free-lance; has worked for *Combat* (with Albert Camus), *Figaro*, and as editor and reporter for *Elle*. *Military service:* French Army during World War II; received Croix de guerre. *Awards, honors:* Prix Theophraste Renaudot, 1959, for *L'Experience*.

WRITINGS: *L'Experience* (novel), Julliard, 1959, translation by Roger Senhouse published as *Experience*, Doubleday, 1961; *Les Marches* (novel), Julliard, 1962; *Les Chaudieres et la lune* (novel), Julliard, 1965.

WORK IN PROGRESS: A book tentatively entitled *Les Points cardinaux*; short novels.

* * *

PALLENBERG, Corrado 1912-

PERSONAL: Born October 31, 1912, in Rome, Italy; son of Franz (a painter) and Eleonora (Gojorani) Pallenberg; married Margaret Sommer; children: Richard. *Education:* University of Rome, law degree. *Politics:* "If American, would vote Democrat." *Religion:* Epicurean. *Home:* Pimprinnacolo, Porto Ercole, Italy. *Office:* Stampa Estera, Via della Mercede 55, Rome, Italy.

CAREER: London correspondent for Italian newspapers, 1937-39, and Rome correspondent for English newspapers, 1945-66; writer for *Reader's Digest*, 1966. *Military service:* Italian Army, Artillery and Intelligence, 1939-44; served in Ethiopian and Russian campaigns; became lieutenant.

WRITINGS: *Inside the Vatican*, Hawthorn, 1960; *The Art of Seduction*, Pyramid Books, 1963; *The Making of a Pope*, Macfadden, 1964; *Pope Paul VI*, Putnam, 1968; *Vatican Finances*, P. Owen, 1971.

WORK IN PROGRESS: A novel, *Murder in the Vatican*.

SIDELIGHTS: Pallenberg writes in English although Italian is his native tongue; he also speaks French and German, and reads Spanish. *Inside the Vatican* has been published in England, France, Germany, Italy, and Austria, *The Making of a Pope* in Germany and France, and *Vatican Finances* in Germany, Italy, Holland, Denmark, Spain, and Brazil.

* * *

PALMER, Alan Warwick 1926-

PERSONAL: Born September 28, 1926, in Ilford, Essex, England; son of Warwick Lindley and Edith (Perriam) Palmer; married Veronica Mary Cordell, September 1, 1951. *Education:* Oriel College, Oxford, M.A. and B.Lit., 1951. *Home:* 4 Farm End, Woodstock, Oxford, England. *Agent:* Peter Janson-Smith Ltd., 31 Newington Green, London N16 9PU, England.

CAREER: Highgate School, London, England, assistant master, 1951-53, senior history master, 1953-69. *Military service:* Royal Navy, 1944-47.

WRITINGS: *Dictionary of Modern History, 1789-1945*, Cresset, 1962; (with C. A. Macartney) *Independent Eastern Europe: A History*, Macmillan, 1962; *Yugoslavia*, Oxford University Press, 1964; *The Gardeners of Salonika*, Simon & Schuster, 1965; *Napoleon in Russia*, Simon & Schuster, 1967; *The Lands Between*, Weidenfeld & Nicolson, 1970; *Metternich*, Harper, 1972; *The Life and Times of George IV*, Weidenfeld & Nicolson, 1972; *Russia in War and Peace*, Macmillan, 1972; *Alexander I*, Harper, 1974; *Frederick the Great*, Weidenfeld & Nicolson, 1974.

WORK IN PROGRESS: A biography of Bismarck; a dictionary of historical quotations, with wife, Veronica Palmer.

AVOCATIONAL INTERESTS: Travel.

* * *

PALMER, Archie M(acInnes) 1896-

PERSONAL: Born May 9, 1896, in Hoboken, N.J.; son of Robert K(ennedy Kelty) and Sarah Grace (MacInnes) Palmer; married Elizabeth Cheatham, June 24, 1930; children: Elizabeth Reynolds, Archie MacInnes, Jr. *Educa-*

tion: Attended Cornell University, 1914-17, 1920, A.B., 1920; Columbia University, graduate study, 1925-33, M.A., 1927. *Religion:* Episcopalian. *Home:* 3321 Runnymede Pl., N.W., Washington, D.C. 20015. *Office:* 2101 Constitution Ave., N.W., Washington, D.C. 20418.

CAREER: Cornell University, Ithaca, N.Y., secretary and acting dean of College of Arts and Sciences, 1920-23; Procter & Gamble Co., Cincinnati, Ohio, sales and personnel research, 1923-25; Columbia University, New York, N.Y., alumni secretary and managing editor of *Columbia Alumni News*, 1925-27; Institute of International Education, New York, N.Y., assistant director, 1927-29; Association of American Colleges, New York, N.Y., associate secretary, 1929-34; Cornell University, executive secretary of Cornellian Council, 1934-38; University of Chattanooga, Chattanooga, Tenn., president, 1938-42; U.S. Government, Washington, D.C., served with Office of Price Administration, 1942-43, War Production Board, 1943-44, Department of State, 1944-46, Department of Defense, 1948-49; National Academy of Sciences-National Research Council, Washington, D.C., director, Office of Patent Policy Survey, 1946—. U.S. Government Patents Board, chairman, 1950-55. Lasdon Foundation, director of Washington office, 1957-60; Gale Research Center, director, 1965—. *Military service:* U.S. Army, 1917-20; served with American Expeditionary Forces in France and Germany. Tennessee National Guard, 1941—; colonel.

MEMBER: American Association for the Advancement of Science, American Historical Association, National Academy of Sciences-National Research Council (member of committee on patent policy, 1933—), Military Order of Foreign Wars of the United States, Phi Beta Kappa, Phi Delta Kappa, Delta Sigma Rho, Pi Gamma Mu, American Legion, Rotary, Free and Accepted Masons, Chattanooga Executives Club (president, 1940-42), Half Century Club (Tennessee), Torch Club (Washington, D.C.; president, 1946-47), The Inquirendo (Washington, D.C.; president, 1954-55), Cornell Club. *Awards, honors:* Officer, Order of the White Lion (Czechoslovakia), 1930; D.C.L., University of the South, 1941.

WRITINGS: (Editor) *The Liberal Arts College Movement*, privately printed, 1930; (with J. Fredrick Larson) *Architectural Planning of the American College*, McGraw, 1933; (with Grace Holton) *College Instruction in Art*, Association of American Colleges, 1934; *University Patent Policies*, Research Corp., 1934.

Survey of University Patent Policies, National Research Council, 1948; *Medical Patents*, American Medical Association, 1948; *University Research and Patent Problems*, National Research Council, 1949.

University Patent Policies and Practices, National Research Council, 1952, supplement, 1955; *Administration of Medical and Pharmaceutical Patents*, National Research Council, 1955; *Nonprofit Research and Patent Management*, four volumes, National Research Council, 1955-65; *Patents and Nonprofit Research*, U.S. Government Printing Office, 1957; (contributor) Albert S. Davis, Jr., editor, *Patent Licensing*, Practicing Law Institute, 1958.

University Research and Patent Policies, Practices and Procedures, National Research Council, 1962, with supplement; (editor) *Research Centers Directory*, Gale, 1965, revised editions, 1968, 1970, 1972, 1974. Also author of *Nonprofit Research Institutes*, and *Nonprofit Patent Management*.

Contributor of more than two hundred articles and book reviews to popular magazines and to educational and scientific journals. Contributing editor, *Association of American College Bulletin*, 1929-34. Editor, *New Research Centers*, Gale, 1965—.

AVOCATIONAL INTERESTS: Hiking, travel, gardening, reading historical novels.†

*   *   *

PALMER, C(edric) King 1913-

PERSONAL: Born February 13, 1913, in England; son of Henry William Hetherington (an architect) and Lilian (Whitehouse) Palmer; married Winifred Henry, May 2, 1947 (deceased); children: Roger Lindsey, Jane Hetherington. *Education:* Royal Academy of Music, London, England, L.R.A.M. (in orchestral conducting), 1922, A.R.A.M., 1930. *Home:* Clovelly Lodge, 2 Popes Grove, Twickenham, TW2 5TA, England.

CAREER: Conductor and composer. Conductor of Euphonic Symphony Orchestra, London, England, 1932-36, Sevenoaks Choral Society, 1934-38, North London Orchestra, 1937-39, King Palmer Light Orchestra (British Broadcasting Corp.), 1939—. Also conductor for London theatrical productions and films. Lecturer on music, City Literary Institute, London, England, 1939—. *Member:* Royal Society of Arts (fellow), Guild of Freemen of the City of London, Incorporated Society of Musicians, Performing Right Society, Royal Musical Association, Galpin Club, Savage Club.

WRITINGS—All published by English Universities Press, except as indicated: *Teach Yourself Music*, 1944; *Teach Yourself to Compose Music*, 1947; *The Musical Production*, Pitman, 1953; *Teach Yourself to Play the Piano*, 1957; (with Cossar Turfery) *Teach Yourself Orchestration*, 1964; (with Stephen Rhys) *The ABC of Church Music*, Hodder & Stoughton, 1967.

WORK IN PROGRESS: Writing on the psychology of creative musical art and the evolution of orchestral musical instruments.

*   *   *

PALMER, Charles Earl 1919-

PERSONAL: Born December 18, 1919, in Wiggins, S.C.; son of William David (a lumberman) and Theodosia (Yarborough) Palmer; married Sarah Rebecca Maull, September 30, 1950; children: Faye, Charles, Jr., John Clifford, Sarah Rebecca. *Education:* Rice Business College, Charleston, S.C., accounting diploma, 1937; also studied at Princeton University, 1943, University of Minnesota, 1944, and The Citadel, 1949. *Religion:* Methodist. *Home address:* Route 7, Box 270, Murray Forest on Lake Murray, Lexington, S.C. 29072.

CAREER: Worked for business firm in Charleston, S.C., 1937-41; Charleston Port of Embarkation, Charleston, S.C., post exchange manager, 1941-42; Northwest Airlines, St. Paul, Minn., treasury representative, based in Tokyo, Japan, 1947-49; Certified Public Accountant, state of South Carolina, 1949, and accountant in private practice in South Carolina, 1949-52; Palmer Colleges (junior colleges of business in Charleston and Columbia, S.C. and schools of business in North Charleston, S.C., and Augusta, Ga.), president, 1949—. Norfolk College, Norfolk, Va., founder and owner, 1953-58, chairman of board of trustees, 1958-60. President, Palmer College Corp., 1954—. Accrediting Commission of Association of Independent Colleges and

Schools, commissioner, 1961-66, vice-chairman, 1962-63, chairman, 1964-65, consultant, 1966. Vice-president, South Carolina Technical Centers Study Committee, 1966-67. Member, South Carolina Junior College Study Committee, 1959-61, Sweetland Education and Research Foundation advisory board, 1964—, South Carolina Conference Urban Work Committee, 1967-68, and South Carolina Conference Board of Education, 1968—. Chairman of board of trustees, Georgia-Carolina Foundation, Inc., 1966—. Director, Charleston Trident Chamber of Commerce, 1964-67. *Military service:* U.S. Army Air Forces, Finance Department, 1942-47; became captain.

MEMBER: American Institute of Certified Public Accountants, National Association and Council of Business Schools (now Association of Independent Colleges and Schools; president, 1958-59), American Association of Junior Colleges, National Association of Independent Junior Colleges (secretary, 1970-72), National Office Management Association (president of Charleston chapter, 1956-57), Southern Association of Business Colleges, Southeastern Business College Association (president, 1952-53), South Carolina Association of Certified Public Accountants, South Carolina Association of Business Colleges (president, three terms), Rotary Club. *Awards, honors:* Named Man of the Year in Private Business Schools by National Association and Council of Business Schools, 1959; Commendation Award for outstanding work in private business education, Southeastern Business College Association, 1964; honorary Doctor of Commercial Science, Fort Lauderdale University, 1967.

WRITINGS—All published by McGraw: (With Robert H. Van Voorhis and Fred C. Archer) *College Accounting Theory and Practice*, three volumes, with three workbooks and four practice sets, 1963, expanded edition, with Horace R. Brock and Archer, 1968; (with Brock and Archer) *Cost Accounting Theory and Practice*, with workbook and practice set, 1964; (with Brock and Archer) *College Accounting: Intermediate/Advanced*, with three workbooks, 1965; (with Brock, Archer, and Binnion) *College Accounting for Secretaries*, 1971; (with Brock and Archer) *Accounting: Principles and Applications*, with two study guides and two practice sets, 1974; (with Brock and Archer) *Accounting: Basic Principles*, with study guide and practice set, 1974; (with Brock and Archer) *Accounting: Intermediate*, with study guide, 1974; (with Brock, Archer, and Moretz) *Sight-Sound Tutorial Accounting*, 1974; (with Brock and Archer) *Accounting: Basic Computer Applications*, 1975. Contributor to professional periodicals.

*   *   *

PALMER, R(obert) R(oswell)   1909-

PERSONAL: Born January 11, 1909, in Chicago, Ill.; son of Roswell Roy and Blanche (Steere) Palmer; married Esther Howard, December 19, 1942; children: Stanley Howard, Richard Roswell, Emily Steere. *Education:* University of Chicago, Ph.B., 1931; Cornell University, Ph.D., 1934. *Politics:* Democrat. *Religion:* Presbyterian. *Home:* 46 Cliff St., New Haven, Conn. 06511. *Office:* Department of History, Yale University, New Haven, Conn. 06520.

CAREER: Princeton University, Princeton, N.J., faculty member, 1936-63, 1966-69, professor of history, 1946-52, Dodge Professor of History, 1952-63; Washington University, St. Louis, Mo., professor of history and dean of Faculty of Arts and Sciences, 1963-66; Yale University, New Haven, Conn., professor of history, 1969—. Visiting

summer professor at University of Chicago, 1947, University of Colorado, 1951, University of California, Berkeley, 1962, University of Michigan, 1969. U.S. Army Ground Forces, staff of Historical Division, 1943-45. *Member:* American Historical Association, American Philosophical Society, American Academy of Arts and Sciences, Society for French Historical Studies (president, 1961), Massachusetts Historical Society. *Awards, honors:* Bancroft Prize of Columbia University ($3,000; for best work in American history), 1960, for *The Age of the Democratic Revolution*; American Council of Learned Societies Prize for work in humanities, 1960; Litt.D., Washington University, St. Louis, Mo., 1962; L.H.D., Kenyon College, 1963; LL.D., University of Chicago, 1963; Dr. Honoris Causa, Toulouse, France, 1965.

WRITINGS: Catholics and Unbelievers in Eighteenth Century France, Princeton University Press, 1939; *Twelve Who Ruled*, Princeton University Press, 1941; *History of the Modern World*, Knopf, 1950, 4th edition (with Jol Colton), 1971; (editor) *Rand McNally Historical Atlas*, Rand McNally, 1957; *The Age of the Democratic Revolution: A Political History of Europe and America, 1760-1800*, Princeton University Press, volume I, 1959, volume II, 1964 (translator) G. Lefebvre, *The Coming of the French Revolution*, Princeton University Press, 1967; *The World of the French Revolution*, Harper, 1971. Co-author of two books on ground combat troops published by U.S. Government Printing Office, 1947-1948.†

*   *   *

PANAGOPOULOS, Epaminondas Peter   1915-

PERSONAL: Born February 26, 1915, in Athens, Greece; became U.S. citizen, 1955; son of Peter P. (a forester) and Vassiliki (Papathanassiou) Panagopoulos; married Beata-Maria Kitsikis (an instructor in art history, Foothill College); children: Peter, Beata-Domenica. *Education:* University of Athens, LL.B., 1941, M.A., 1946; University of Chicago, Ph.D., 1952. *Politics:* Democrat. *Religion:* Greek Orthodox. *Home:* 98 Blake Ave., Santa Clara, Calif. *Office:* California State University, San Jose, Calif.

CAREER: Attorney-at-law in Athens, Greece, 1941-44; U.S. Information Service, Athens, Greece, assistant editor, 1944-46; Wayne State University, Detroit, Mich., instructor in American history, 1952-56; California State University, San Jose, professor of American history, 1956—. *Military service:* Greek Army, World War II; became major; received Golden Cross for Bravery, Silver Cross with Swords. *Member:* American Historical Association, American Studies Association, Florida Historical Society, St. Augustine Historical Society.

WRITINGS: Alexander Hamilton's Pay Book, Wayne State University Press, 1961; *New Smyrna: An Eighteenth Century Greek Odyssey*, University of Florida, 1966. Contributor to *Encyclopedia Americana, Collier's Encyclopedia, New International Yearbook*, and to historical journals.

WORK IN PROGRESS: The Impact of Classicism on the United States Constitution; a second book, *The Growth of National Consciousness in America, 1775-1836*.

SIDELIGHTS: Epaminondas Panagopoulos speaks German and French. *Avocational interests:* Modern Greek literature, art, music, architecture, theater, and thought.†

PARATORE, Angela 1912-

PERSONAL: Born January 6, 1912, in Madison, Wis.; daughter of Teodoro and Antonina (Di Lorenzo) Paratore. *Education:* University of Wisconsin, B.A., 1934, M.A., 1936; Cornell University, Ph.D., 1950. *Office:* Department of Linguistics, Ballantine 542, Indiana University, Bloomington, Ind.

CAREER: High school teacher of languages in Wisconsin and Illinois, 1936-41; University of Michigan, Ann Arbor, instructor at English Language Institute, 1943-46; Cornell University, Ithaca, instructor in Spanish and English-for-foreigners, 1946-50; American Institute for Foreign Trade, Phoenix, Ariz., assistant professor of Spanish, 1951-52; Indiana University, Bloomington, associate professor of linguistics, 1952—. U.S. Department of State specialist in Nicaragua, 1960; senior research associate, English for Cubans Project, Miami, Fla., 1961-62; National Defense Education Act Institutes (summer), instructor at University of Notre Dame, 1961, 1962, Sonoma State College, 1963, University of Florida, 1964; visiting professor at University of Hawaii, 1963-64. *Member:* Linguistics Society of America, Modern Language Association of America, National Association for Foreign Student Affairs of directors, 1959-63). *Awards, honors:* Institute of International Education Fellow in Mexico, 1942-43; Fulbright fellow in Italy, 1950-51.

WRITINGS: (With Agard and Willis) *Speaking and Writing Spanish*, Henry Holt, 1951; *English Dialogues for Foreign Students*, Rinehart, 1956; *English Exercises: English as a Foreign Language*, Rinehart, 1958; *Written Exercises: English as a Foreign Language*, Holt, 1960; *Conversational English*, Prentice-Hall, 1961.†

* * *

PARKER, Edwin B(urke) 1932-

PERSONAL: Born January 19, 1932, in Berwyn, Alberta, Canada; son of Harry Ernest (a clergyman) and Margaret (Palmer) Parker; married Shan Greenwood, June 22, 1957; children: Karen, David. *Education:* McGill University, student, 1950-52; University of British Columbia, B.A., 1954; Stanford University, M.A., 1958, Ph.D., 1960. *Home:* 325 Princeton Rd., Menlo Park, Calif. 94026. *Office:* Institute for Communication Research, Stanford University, Stanford, Calif.

CAREER: Vancouver Sun, Vancouver, British Columbia, staff reporter, 1954-55; University of British Columbia, Vancouver, information officer, 1955-57; University of Illinois, Urbana, assistant professor of communication, 1960-62; Stanford University, Stanford, Calif., assistant professor, 1962-63, associate professor of communication, 1963—. UNESCO, director of training course for African government information officers at Makerere College, Kampala, Uganda, 1964. *Member:* American Psychological Association, American Sociological Association, American Statistical Association, American Association for Public Opinion Research, Association for Education in Journalism.

WRITINGS: (With Wilbur Schramm and Jack Lyle) *Television in the Lives of Our Children*, Stanford University Press, 1961; (editor with Bradley S. Greenberg) *The Kennedy Assassination and the American Public*, Stanford University Press, 1965; *Patterns of Adult Information Seeking*, Institute for Communicative Research, 1966; (with David A. Lingwood and William J. Paisley) *Communication and Research Productivity in an Interdisciplinary Behavioral Science Research Area*, Institute for Communi-

cative Research, 1968. Contributor of articles to scholarly journals.†

* * *

PARKER, Franklin D(allas) 1918-

PERSONAL: Born January 7, 1918, in Baltimore, Md.; son of Milton Augustus (a minister) and Josephine (Griffin) Parker; married Jennie Borden, July 20, 1940; children: Virginia (Mrs. Joseph Collier, Jr.), Jeannie (Mrs. Fred D. Blackwelder). *Education:* Attended Roberts College, 1934-36; Greenville College, B.A., 1939; graduate study at National University of Mexico, 1946, and University of Arizona, 1947; University of Illinois, M.A., 1949, Ph.D., 1951. *Politics:* Independent. *Religion:* Methodist. *Home:* 2009 Wright Ave., Greensboro, N.C. 27403. *Office:* Department of History, University of North Carolina, Greensboro, N.C. 27412.

CAREER: University of North Carolina, Greensboro, assistant professor, 1951-59, associate professor, 1959-64, professor of history, 1964—. Fulbright lecturer at universities in Peru and Colombia. *Member:* Conference on Latin American History, Latin American Studies Association, Southeast Conference on Latin American Studies, Sociedad de Geografia e Historia de Guatemala.

WRITINGS: Jose Cecilio del Valle and the Establishment of the Central American Confederation, University of Honduras, 1954; *The Central American Republics*, Oxford University Press, 1964; *Travels in Central America, 1821-1840*, University of Florida Press, 1970. Contributor to historical journals.

WORK IN PROGRESS: A history of the world since 1945, with emphasis on Asia, Africa, Europe, Latin America, and North America.

* * *

PARKER, Wyman W(est) 1912-

PERSONAL: Born October 31, 1912, in Woburn, Mass.; son of Austin Wilbur (an engineer) and Elizabeth (West) Parker; married Jane Kingsley (an editorial assistant, Wesleyan University Press), August 21, 1941; children: Christopher West, Kingsley Wyman, Andrew Duff. *Education:* Middlebury College, A.B., 1934, M.A., 1939; Columbia University, B.L.S., 1936. *Politics:* Democrat. *Religion:* Episcopalian. *Home:* 330 Pine St., Middletown, Conn. 06457. *Office:* Olin Library, Wesleyan University, Middletown, Conn. 06457.

CAREER: New York Public Library, reference division, stack superintendent, 1935-36; Middlebury College, Middlebury, Vt., acting librarian, 1936-37, librarian, 1938-41; Kenyon College, Gambier, Ohio, librarian, 1946-51; University of Cincinnati, Cincinnati, Ohio, director of libraries, 1951-56; Wesleyan University, Middletown, Conn., librarian, 1956—. U.S. Works Progress Administration, member of advisory board for historical record survey in Vermont, 1941-42; Midwest Inter-Library Center, director, 1951-56; Columbia University Library School, member of advisory council, 1960-66; Ohio College Association, director of survey on possibilities of academic library cooperation, 1963. *Military service:* U.S. Navy, Intelligence and Operations, 1941-46; served in Australia and New Guinea; served as lieutenant commander.

MEMBER: Association of College and Research Libraries (president, 1959-60), American Library Association (chairman of awards committee, 1957-59), Bibliographical

Society of America, American Association of University Professors, Connecticut Library Association, Bibliographical Society (London), Columbia Club, Grolier Club, Acorn Club, Archons of Colophon.

WRITINGS: Henry Stevens of Vermont, N. Israel (Amsterdam), 1963. Contributor to library and bibliographical periodicals. Member of editorial board, *Choice*, 1963-67.

BIOGRAPHICAL/CRITICAL SOURCES: College and Research Libraries, April, 1951; *Library Quarterly*, April, 1951, October, 1954.†

* * *

PARKS, Edna D(orintha) 1910-

PERSONAL: Born October 7, 1910, in Wakefield, Mass.; daughter of T. Fulton (a dentist) and Lillian E. (Mansfield) Parks. *Education:* Yale University, Mus.B., 1935; Boston University, M.A., 1944, Ph.D., 1957. *Home:* 212 Forest St., Winchester, Mass. *Office:* Wheaton College, Norton, Mass.

CAREER: Wakefield (Mass.) public schools, teacher of music, 1937-47; Western College for Women, Oxford, Ohio, instructor in music and college organist, 1947-48; Green Mountain College, Poultney, Vt., faculty of music department, 1948-56; Wheaton College, Norton, Mass., assistant professor, 1957-61, associate professor, 1961-64, professor of music, 1964—, chairman of department, 1962—. *Member:* American Guild of Organists (secretary of Vermont chapter; sub-dean of Brockton chapter), American Musicological Society, College Music Society (member of council, 1966-69; secretary, 1972-74).

WRITINGS: Hymns and Hymn Tunes Found in the English Metrical Psalters, Coleman-Ross, 1965; *Early English Hymns: An Index*, Scarecrow, 1972. Contributor to *Diapason* and *Notes*.

* * *

PARRY, Hugh J(ones) 1916-
(James Cross)

PERSONAL: Born March 10, 1916, in London, England; brought to United States in 1919, naturalized in 1924; son of John (an international patent attorney) and Jane Myfanwy (Jones) Parry; married Helen Mason Weston, May 30, 1941 (divorced, 1960); married Betty Widder Brawer, March 10, 1961; children: (first marriage) John W.; (second marriage) Brian Michael; (stepchildren) Roberta Brawer, Stephen Brawer. *Education:* Yale University, A.B., 1937, graduate study, 1937-38; Columbia University, M.S., 1939; University of Southern California, Ph.D., 1949. *Politics:* Democrat. *Home:* 4814 Falstone Ave., Chevy Chase, Md. 20015. *Agent:* Robert P. Mills, 527 Lexington Ave., New York, N.Y. 10017. *Office:* 2401 Virginia Ave., Washington, D.C. 20037.

CAREER: University of Denver, Denver, Colo., associate director of Opinion Research Center and professor of sociology, 1947-50; U.S. Army, Europe, assistant director of Troop Attitude Research, 1950-52; U.S. High Commission for Germany, project director, 1952-53; U.S. Information Agency, project director and research officer in Paris, France, 1955-62, chief of Survey Research Division, Office of Research and Analysis, 1962-63, director of Western European research, 1963-66; George Washington University, Washington, D.C., professor of sociology and associate director of Social Research Group, 1966—. Member of board of directors, Washington (D.C.) Chamber Or-

chestra. *Military service:* U.S. Naval Reserve, 1942-46; became lieutenant senior grade. *Member:* World Association for Public Opinion Research (membership chairman, 1956-58), American Association for Public Opinion Research, American Sociological Association, American Historical Association, Phi Beta Kappa, Phi Delta Theta.

WRITINGS: (With Leo P. Crespi) *Public Opinion in Western Europe*, U.S. Government Printing Office, 1953.

Under pseudonym James Cross: *Root of Evil*, Messner, 1957; *The Dark Road*, Messner, 1959; *The Grave of Heroes*, Heinemann, 1961; *To Hell for Half-a-crown*, Random House, 1967.

Contributor under own name to *Scientific Monthly*, *International Journal of Opinion and Attitude Research*, and other professional journals; contributor under pseudonym James Cross, to *Saturday Evening Post*, *Cavalier*, and other popular magazines.

WORK IN PROGRESS: A novel, *The King of the Dead*; short stories.

SIDELIGHTS: Hugh Parry is fluent in French; knows some Spanish, Italian, and German. *Avocational interests:* Travel, reading, tennis.†

* * *

PARRY-JONES, Daniel 1891-

PERSONAL: Born October 12, 1891, in Carmarthenshire, Wales; married Gladys Murgatroyd, 1920; children: one son, two daughters. *Education:* St. David's College, University of Wales, B.A., 1913. *Home:* 18 Allt-Yr-Yn-Crescent, Newport, Monmouthshire, Wales.

CAREER: Clergyman, Church of England. Vicar of Llanfihangel Rhydithon, Wales, 1926-36; rector of Llanelly, Brecons, Wales, 1936-62. Rural dean of Crickhowell, 1957; honorary canon of Swansea and Brecon, 1958.

WRITINGS: Welsh Country Upbringing, Batsford, 1948, 2nd edition, British Book Centre, 1949; *Welsh Country Characters*, British Book Centre, 1952; *Welsh Legend and Fairy Lore*, Batsford, 1952; *Welsh Children's Games and Pastimes*, Gee & Son, 1964; *My Own Folk*, Gwasg Gomer, 1972; *Welsh Country Parson*, Batsford, in press.

* * *

PARSON, Ruben L(eRoy) 1907-

PERSONAL: Born May 3, 1907, in Battle Lake, Minn.; son of Nels (a farmer) and Anna (Nelson) Parson; married Mary Louise Miller, July 20, 1940; children: Ronal, Charles, Luanne. *Education:* Moorehead State College, B.S. in Ed., 1932; Clark University, Worcester, Mass., M.A., 1934, Ph.D., 1943. *Politics:* Republican. *Religion:* Protestant. *Residence:* Battle Lake, Minn. 56515.

CAREER: Tennessee Valley Authority, junior geographer, 1935-36; National Resources Committee and Mississippi State Planning Commission, Jackson, Miss., land planner, 1937-39; Troy State College, Troy, Ala., chairman of geography department, 1939-41; East Tennessee State University, Johnson City, chairman of geography and geology department, 1946-58; Northern Illinois University, DeKalb, resource geographer, 1958-64, professor of geography, 1964-67; St. Cloud State College, St. Cloud, Minn., professor of geography, 1967-72, professor emeritus, 1973—, chairman of department, 1967. Coordinator, Civilian Pilot Training Program, Troy, Ala., 1940-41. *Military service:* U.S. Army Reserve, 1932-46; served in India and

Burma; became lieutenant colonel; received two battle stars for Burma campaigns. U.S. Air Force Reserve, 1946-1960; retired with rank of lieutenant colonel, 1960.

MEMBER: National Council for Geographic Education (fellow), Soil Conservation Society of America (chairman, Tennessee Upper Valley section, 1958), Conservation Education Association (chairman of curriculum development committee, 1957-64), Association of American Geographers (fellow). *Awards, honors:* Certificate of Appreciation, American Forest Products Industries, Inc., 1966; appointed Kentucky Colonel, 1966; Distinguished Service Award, Northern Illinois University, 1967; Certificate of Recognition, Delta Delta chapter, Phi Delta Kappa, 1968.

WRITINGS: (With others) *Conserving American Resources* (text), Prentice-Hall, 1956, 3rd edition, 1972. Contributor of articles and papers on conservation and geography to proceedings of learned societies and professional journals. Editor, *Illinois Geographical Society Bulletin*, 1965-67.

WORK IN PROGRESS: Story of grandfather's homesteading in Minnesota in 1869.

SIDELIGHTS: Parson told *CA*: "I mourn the passing of the small farm in America, and would like to write about it—from personal experience. I am reading book after book dealing with 'How to Write'." Parson is fluent in Swedish and calls himself an "avid gardener and tree planter," and a "persistent, though crude, painter of landscapes, in oil."

*   *   *

PARSONS, Denys   1914-

PERSONAL: Born March 12, 1914, in London, England; son of Alan (a dramatic critic) and Viola (daughter of British actor-manager, Sir Herbert Beerbohm Tree) Parsons; married Frances Burke (a bio-statistician), May 28, 1962; children: two sons. *Education:* University of London, B.Sc., University College, 1936, M.Sc., Imperial College of Science and Technology, 1938. *Home:* 6 The Vale, Golders Green, London N.W. 11, England.

CAREER: Revertex Sales Co. Ltd., London, England, rubber and plastics research, 1939-45; Realist Film Unit Ltd., London, England, director of educational and industrial films, 1945-51; National Research Development Corp. (development and exploitation of new inventions), London, England, manager of information and public relations services, 1952—. *Member:* Royal Institute of Chemistry (associate), Society for Psychical Research.

WRITINGS: It Must Be True, Macdonald & Co., 1952; *Can It Be True?*, Macdonald & Co., 1953; *All Too True*, Macdonald & Co., 1954; *True to Type*, Macdonald & Co., 1955; *Nothing Brightens a Garden Like Primrose Pants*, Hanover House, 1955; *Many a True World*, Macdonald & Co., 1958; *Never More True*, Macdonald & Co., 1960; *Say It Isn't So*, A. S. Barnes, 1962; *Funny Ha Ha and Funny Peculiar*, Pan Books, 1965; *Funny Convulsing and Funny Confusing*, Pan Books, 1971; (with Betty James) *London For You*, Pan Books, 1973.

Compiler of *Musical Appreciation* (listing of audio and visual aids), British Films Institute, 1948, and *What's Where in London* (shopping guide), Mason Publications, 1961, 6th edition, 1967. Contributor to *Journal of Society for Psychical Research* and *Venture*.

WORK IN PROGRESS: A dictionary of musical themes on a new system.

SIDELIGHTS: Six of Parson's books (the "True" group) are collections of newspaper boners; he also collects news clippings of freak or ludicrous events. Denys Parsons has language competency in Spanish and German.†

*   *   *

PARSONS, Kitty

PERSONAL: Born in Stratford, Conn.; daughter of Henry Chapman and Catherine Davis (Leavitt) Parsons; married Richard Henry Recchia (a sculptor), June 30, 1927; stepchildren: Richard Edmund, Anita Felicia (deceased). *Education:* Attended Pratt Institute, 1910; also attended Columbia University, and American Academy of Dramatic Art; took special courses at Boston University and University of Chicago. *Politics:* Republican. *Religion:* Episcopalian. *Home:* 6 Summer St., Rockport, Mass. 01966.

CAREER: Writer and watercolor painter. Paintings exhibited in one-man shows at Berkshire Museum, Pittsfield, Mass., Argent Galleries, New York, N.Y., Bennington Museum, Bennington, Vt., Milwaukee Public Library, Milwaukee, Wis., Bowdoin College, Brunswick, Me., and elsewhere, and in group shows. Maine Writers' Conference, poetry chairman, 1959-61, conference director, 1961-64. American Artists Professional League, former Massachusetts state director of Art Week.

MEMBER: National Association of Women Artists, National League of American Pen Women (vice-president of Boston chapter, 1964-65), American Poetry League, Poetry Society of Virginia, Poetry Society of Kentucky, Poetry Society of New Hampshire, League of Vermont Writers, Poetry Society of Pennsylvania, Sandy Bay Historical Society, Rockport Art Association (charter and life member), North Shore Arts Association, Rockport Garden Club, Rockport Women's Club (honorary), Boston Authors Club. *Awards, honors: American Weave* Poetry Chapbook Award, 1961; Rockport Art Association, Certificate of merit; other awards for poetry, watercolors, and plays.

WRITINGS: Do You Know Them?, Revell, 1922; *Stories of People Worthwhile*, Revell, 1924; *As the Wind Blows* (sonnets), Dierkes Press, 1951; *Ancestral Timber* (historical ballads), Golden Quill, 1957; *Down to Earth* (humorous verse), Golden Quill, 1964; *Up and Down and Round About* (juvenile verse), Golden Quill, 1967; *Your Husband or Mine* (humorous verse), Golden Quill, 1970. Author of three privately printed booklets and of fifteen plays published for amateur production. Contributor of humorous essays and verse to newspapers and magazines, including *Saturday Evening Post, Boston Transcript, Boston Post, Saturday Review, Christian Science Monitor*, and *Washington Star*.

WORK IN PROGRESS: A collection of own published juvenile verse, and a collection of short humorous articles previously published in periodicals.

AVOCATIONAL INTERESTS: Gardening, knitting, reading, music, earrings and hats, cooking and entertaining.

*   *   *

PASSMORE, John (Arthur)   1914-

PERSONAL: Born September 9, 1914, in Manly, New South Wales, Australia; son of Frederick Maurice (a pay clerk) and Ruby (Moule) Passmore; married Annie Doris Sumner, December 16, 1936; children: Helen Katherine (Mrs. Paul Hoffmann), Diana Margaret. *Education:* University of Sydney, B.A., 1933, M.A., 1940. *Office:* Australian National University, Canberra, Australian Capital Territory, Australia.

CAREER: University of Sydney, Sydney, New South Wales, Australia, successively tutor, lecturer, and senior lecturer in philosophy, 1935-49; University of Otago, Dunedin, New Zealand, professor of philosophy, 1950-55; Australian National University, Institute of Advanced Studies, Canberra, reader, then professor of philosophy, 1956—. Brandeis University, Ziskind Visiting Professor, 1960. Australian Elizabethan Theatre Trust, director, 1958—. Visiting fellow, All Souls College, Oxford, 1970, and Clare Hall, Cambridge, 1973. *Member:* Australian Academy of the Humanities (president, 1974—), Australian Academy of the Social Sciences, American Academy of Arts and Sciences (foreign honorary member), Australian Association of Psychology and Philosophy, Institut International de Philosophie.

WRITINGS: T. S. Eliot, Sydney University Literary Society, 1934; *Reading and Remembering,* Melbourne University Press, 1942; *Talking Things Over,* Melbourne University Press, 1945, 4th edition, 1969; *Ralph Cudworth,* Cambridge University Press, 1951; *Hume's Intentions,* Cambridge University Press, 1952, revised edition, Duckworth, 1968; *A Hundred Years of Philosophy,* Duckworth, 1957, 2nd edition, 1966.

Philosophical Reasoning, Duckworth, 1961, 2nd edition, 1970; (contributor) *The Pattern of Australian Culture,* Cornell University Press, 1963; (contributor) *Princeton Studies,* Prentice-Hall, 1964; (editor and author of introduction) *Joseph Priestley: Writings on Philosophy, Science, and Politics,* Macmillan, 1965; *The Perfectibility of Man,* Duckworth, 1970, Scribner, 1971; *Man's Responsibility for Nature,* Scribner, 1974. Also author of *Teaching in the Australian Universities,* 1965. Contributor to collections of essays; author of introductions to various books. Contributor to *Encyclopaedia Britannica, Encyclopedia Americana, Collier's Encyclopedia, Encyclopedia of Philosophy, Encyclopedia of the History of Ideas,* and to philosophical journals. Editor, *Australian Journal of Philosophy,* 1947-49.

WORK IN PROGRESS: Essays on twentieth century philosophies, and a book on the philosophy of teaching.

SIDELIGHTS: Passmore speaks French, Italian, and German. He has made ten trips to Great Britian and Europe for conferences. He has also visited the United States three times.

*   *   *

PATAKY, Denes 1921-

PERSONAL: Born August 3, 1921, in Budapest, Hungary; son of Joseph (an actor) and Gabrielle (Sailer) Pataky; married Susan Molnar (curator at Hungarian National Gallery), September 23, 1959; married second wife, Elisabeth Borzsak (curator at museum of Fine Arts), 1973; children: (first marriage) Susan. *Education:* University of Budapest, doctorate in history of art and literature, 1944. *Religion:* Catholic. *Home:* Deres-u. 7/a, Budapest XII, Hungary. *Office:* Department of Modern Art, Museum of Fine Arts, Budapest, Hungary.

CAREER: Museum of Fine Arts, Budapest, Hungary, curator in graphical department, 1945-59; Hungarian National Gallery, Budapest, Hungary, curator in graphical department, 1959-66; Museum of Fine Arts, director of modern art department, 1966—.

WRITINGS: A magyar rezmetszes tortenete (title means "The History of Hungarian Engraving"), Kozoktatasugyi Kiado (Budapest), 1951; *A rajzmuveszet mesterei XIX. es XX. szazad,* Kepzomuveszeti Alap Kiadovallalata (Budapest), 1958, 3rd edition Corvina (Budapest), 1965, translation published as *Master Drawings from the Collection of the Budapest Museum of Fine Arts, 19th and 20th Centuries,* Abrams, 1959; *A magyar rajzmuveszet,* Kepzomuveszeti Alap Kiadovallalata, 1960, translation published as *Hungarian Drawings and Water-Colours,* Corvina, 1961; (editor) *Magyar Nemzeti Galeria: A Nylocak es Aktivistak,* Hungarian National Gallery, 1961; (editor) *Stephan Szonyi: Malerei-Graphik,* National Gallery of Berlin, 1963; *Szinyei Merse Pal,* Kepzomuveszeti Alap Kiadovallalata, 1964, English translation by Edna Lenart published as *Pal Szinyei Merse,* Corvina, 1965; *Claude Monet,* Corvina, 1966; (editor) *Modern szoborkiallitas: XIX-XX. szazad,* Szepmuveszeti Museum, 1969; *Farkas Istvan,* Corvina, 1970; *Szonyi Istvan,* Corvina, 1971; *Pissarro,* Corvina, 1972; *Bernath Aurel,* Corvina, 1972; *A francia impresszionizmus tortenete* (title means "History of French Impressionism"), Kepzomuveszeti Alap Kiadovallalata, 1973; (with Imre Marjai) Hungarian title, *Hajo a muve-szetben,* translation published as *Ships in Art,* Corvina, 1973; (with Marjai) *A hajo tortenete* (title means "History of the ship"), Corvina, 1973.

WORK IN PROGRESS: Studies of French impressionism and postimpressionism, and Hungarian art of the twentieth century.

SIDELIGHTS: Pataky speaks French and German. His works have been published in German, French, Italian, Hungarian, and Russian, as well as in English. *Avocational interests:* Literature and music; history of ships of the seventeenth and eighteenth centuries.

*   *   *

PATERSON, (James Edmund) Neil 1916-

PERSONAL: Born 1916, in Greenock, Scotland; son of James Donaldson and Nicholas Kennedy (Kerr) Paterson; married Rosabelle Mackenzie, July 6, 1939; children: Lindsay (daughter), Kerr, John (sons). *Education:* University of Edinburgh, M.A. *Home:* St. Ronans, Crieff, Perthshire, Scotland. *Agent:* Curtis Brown Ltd., 1 Craven Hill, London W.2, England. H. N. Swanson, Inc., 8523 Sunset Blvd., West Hollywood, Calif. 90069.

CAREER: Author and film writer. Grampian Television, director. Films of Scotland, committee member, 1954—. British Film Institute, governor, 1958-60. Founder chairman of British Broadcasting Corp. radio program, "A Matter of Opinion," and of television program, "Compass." *Military service:* Royal Naval Volunteer Reserve, served in mine sweepers, 1940-46; lieutenant. *Member:* Scottish Arts Club (Edinburgh), R.N.V.R. Club, Royal and Ancient Club (St. Andrews). *Awards, honors:* Atlantic Award in Literature, 1946; Academy of Motion Picture Arts and Sciences Award for screenplay, "Room at the Top," 1960.

WRITINGS: The China Run, Hodder & Stoughton, 1948; *Behold Thy Daughter,* Hodder & Stoughton, 1950; *And Delilah,* Hodder & Stoughton, 1951; *Man on the Tight-Rope,* Hodder & Stoughton, 1953. Also author of *A Candle to the Devil.*

Screenplays: "The Little Kidnappers"; "High Tide at Noon"; "The Shiralee"; "Room at the Top"; "The Golden Fool"; "The Forty Days of Musa Dagh"; *The Spiral Road;* and others. †

PATRIDES, C(onstantinos) A(postolos) 1930-

PERSONAL: Surname is pronounced Pat-*rid*-es; born April 20, 1930, in New York, N.Y.; son of Apostolos C. and Helen (Michaelides) Patrides. *Education:* Kenyon College, B.A., 1952; Oxford University, D. Phil., 1957. *Religion:* Greek Orthodox. *Office:* Langwith College, University of York, York, England.

CAREER: University of California, Berkeley, instructor, 1957-59, assistant professor of English, 1959-64; Langwith College, University of York, York, England, lecturer, 1964-66, senior lecturer, 1966-70, reader, 1970—. *Military service:* U.S. Army, 1952-54; became sergeant, received Commendation Ribbon with medal pendant. *Member:* Modern Language Association of America, Modern Humanities Research Association, Renaissance Society of America, Milton Society of America (executive officer, 1962-64), The English Association, Society for Renaissance studies in Great Britain. *Awards, honors:* Guggenheim fellow, 1960-61, 1963-64; American Council of Learned Societies grant, 1963-64.

WRITINGS: Milton's "Lycidas": The Tradition and the Poem, Holt, 1961; *Milton and the Christian Tradition*, Oxford University Press, 1966; *Milton's Epic Poetry*, Penguin, 1967; (editor) *The Cambridge Platonists*, Harvard University Press, 1969; *Approaches to "Paradise Lost,"* University of Toronto Press, 1969; (editor) Sir Walter Ralegh, *The History of the World*, Temple University Press, 1971; (co-author) *Bright Essence: Studies in Milton's Theology*, Utah University Press, 1971; *The Grand Design of God: The Literary Form of the Christian View of History*, University of Toronto Press, 1972; (editor) *Milton: Selected Prose*, Penguin, 1974; (editor) *The English Poems of George Herbert*, Everyman Library, 1974. Contributor of more than forty articles on Renaissance literature to professional journals.

WORK IN PROGRESS: Research on Patristic, Byzantine, and Renaissance literature.

*   *   *

PATTERSON, Henry 1929-
(Martin Fallon, Hugh Marlowe, Harry Patterson, Jack Higgins, James Graham)

PERSONAL: Born July 27, 1929, in England; son of Henry and Henrietta Higgins (Bell) Patterson; married Amy Margaret Hewitt, December 27, 1958; children: two daughters, one son. *Education:* Leeds Training College for Teachers, Certificate in Education, 1958; University of London, B.Sc., 1961. *Politics:* "Slightly right of centre." *Religion:* Presbyterian. *Home:* 15 The Avenue, Leeds 8, Yorkshire, England. *Agent:* David Higham Associates Ltd., 76 Dean St., London W.1, England. *Office:* Leeds College of Commerce, Leeds 1, England.

CAREER: Worked at a variety of commercial and civil service posts before resuming his education in 1956; Allerton Grance Comprehensive School, Leeds, England, history teacher, 1958-64; Leeds College of Commerce, Leeds, England, lecturer in liberal studies, 1964—. Writer. Former member of Leeds Art Theatre. *Military service:* British Army, Royal Horse Guards, 1947-49. *Member:* Royal Economic Society (fellow), Royal Society of Arts (fellow), Crime Writers' Association.

WRITINGS: Pay the Devil, Barrie & Rockliff, 1963; *A Phoenix in the Blood*, Barrie & Rockliff, 1964.

Under pseudonym Martin Fallon: *The Testament of Caspar Shultz*, Abelard, 1962; *Year of the Tiger*, Abelard, 1964; *Keys of Hell*, Abelard, 1965; *Midnight Never Comes*, John Long, 1966; *Dark Side of the Street*, John Long, 1967.

Under pseudonym Hugh Marlowe: *Seven Pillars to Hell*, Abelard, 1963; *Passage by Night*, Abelard, 1964; *A Candle for the Dead*, Abelard, 1966.

Under name Harry Patterson—all published by John Long: *Sad Wind from the Sea*, 1959; *Cry of the Hunter*, 1960; *The Thousand Faces of Night*, 1961; *Comes the Dark Stranger*, 1962; *Hell Is Too Crowded*, 1962; *The Dark Side of the Island*, 1963; *Thunder at Noon*, 1964; *Wrath of the Lion*, 1964; *The Graveyard Shift*, 1965; *The Iron Tiger*, 1966.

Under pseudonym Jack Higgins: *East of Desolation*, Hodder & Stoughton, 1968, Doubleday, 1969; *In the Hour Before Midnight*, Doubleday, 1969; *Night Judgment at Sinos*, Hodder & Stoughton, 1970; *The Last Place God Made*, Collins, 1971, Holt, 1972; *The Savage Day*, Holt, 1972.

Under pseudonym James Graham: *A Game for Heroes*, Doubleday, 1970; *The Wrath of God*, Doubleday, 1971; *The Khufra Run*, Macmillan, 1972, Doubleday, 1973.

WORK IN PROGRESS: A Prospect of Gallows, a police crime novel.

SIDELIGHTS: Patterson told *CA:* "I look upon myself primarily as an entertainer. Even in my novel, *A Phoenix in the Blood*, which deals with the colour-bar problem in England, I still have tried to entertain, to make the events interesting as a story—not just the ideas [and] ethics of the situation. I believe that at any level a writer's only success is to be measured by his ability to communicate. . . ."

All of Patterson's books have been translated into Swedish, some into German, Italian, Norwegian, Dutch, and French. He spends his holidays on the continent "whenever possible," is interested in the theater.†

*   *   *

PAULU, Burton 1910-

PERSONAL: Born June 25, 1910, in Pewaukee, Wis.; son of Emanuel M. Paulu; married Frances Brown, 1942; children: Sarah Leith, Nancy Jean, Thomas Scott. *Education:* Attended Northern State Teachers College (now Northern State College), Aberdeen, S.D., 1926-28; University of Minnesota, B.A., 1931, B.S., 1932, M.A., 1934; New York University, Ph.D., 1949. *Home:* 5005 Wentworth, Minneapolis, Minn. 55419. *Office:* University of Minnesota, Minneapolis, Minn. 55455.

CAREER: With University of Minnesota, Minneapolis, 1938—, began as manager of university radio station, became professor, 1956, director of radio and television, 1957—, director of University Media Resources, 1972—. Summer teaching at New York University, 1943-44, 1947-48, University of Southern California, 1958, Los Angeles State College, 1961. Member of Radio Division, U.S. Office of War Information, 1944-45; member of U.S. delegation of radio and television broadcasters visiting Soviet Union, 1958. *Member:* National Association of Educational Broadcasters (president, 1957-58), University of Minnesota Campus Club, Phi Beta Kappa. *Awards, honors:* Fulbright senior research scholar, 1953-54, and Ford Foundation grant, 1958-59, both for study of broadcasting in England;

Ford Foundation grant, 1964-65, and 1970, for study of broadcasting on European continent.

WRITINGS: British Broadcasting: Radio and Television in the United Kingdom, University of Minnesota Press, 1956; *British Broadcasting in Transition*, University of Minnesota Press, 1961; *Radio and Television Broadcasting on the European Continent*, University of Minnesota Press, 1967; *Radio and Broadcasting in Eastern Europe*, University of Minnesota Press, 1974. Contributor to *Journalism Quarterly, NAEB Journal,* and *EBU Review.*

WORK IN PROGRESS: Research on comparative European broadcasting.

AVOCATIONAL INTERESTS: Music and photography.

*   *   *

PAYNE, Donald Gordon   1924-
(Ian Cameron, Donald Gordon, James Vance Marshall)

PERSONAL: Born January 3, 1924, in London, England; son of Francis Gordon and Evelyn (Rogers) Payne; married Barbara Back, August 20, 1947; children: Christopher, Nigel, Adrian, Alison, Robin. *Education:* Corpus Christi College, Oxford, M.A., 1949. *Religion:* Church of England. *Home:* Pippacre, Westcott Heath, near Dorking, Surrey, England. *Agent:* David Higham Associates Ltd., Golden Square, London W. 1, England; Harold Ober Associates, Inc., 40 East 49th St., New York, N.Y. 10017.

CAREER: Christopher Johnson Publishers Ltd., London, England, trainee, 1949-52; Robert Hale Ltd. (publishers), London, England, editor, 1952-56; full-time writer. *Military service:* Royal Naval Volunteer Reserve, Fleet Air Arm pilot, 1942-46; became lieutenant.

WRITINGS: The Heavies, Shudio Vista, 1967.

Under pseudonym Ian Cameron: *The Midnight Sea,* Hutchinson, 1958; *Red Duster, White Ensign* (story of Malta convoys), Muller, 1959, Doubleday, 1960; *The Lost Ones,* Hutchinson, 1961, Morrow, 1968; *Wings of the Morning* (story of Fleet Air Arm in World War II), Hodder & Stoughton, 1962, Morrow, 1963; *Lodestone and Evening Star* (history of sea exploration), Hodder & Stoughton, 1965, Dutton, 1966; *The Impossible Dream: Building of the Panama Canal,* Morrow, 1971; *The Mountains at the Bottom of the World: Novel of Adventure,* Morrow, 1972; *Magellan and the First Circumnavigation of the World,* Saturday Review Press, 1973; *Antarctica: The Last Continent,* Little, Brown, 1974.

Under pseudonym Donald Gordon: *Star-Raker,* Morrow, 1962; *Flight of the Bat,* Hodder & Stoughton, 1963, Morrow, 1964; *The Golden Oyster,* Hodder & Stoughton, 1967, Morrow, 1968; *Leap in the Dark,* Morrow, 1971.

Under pseudonym James Vance Marshall: *My Boy John that Went to Sea,* Hodder & Stoughton, 1966, Morrow, 1967; *A Walk to the Hills of the Dreamtime,* Morrow, 1970; *The Wind at Morning,* Morrow, 1973, new edition, G. K. Hall, 1974.

SIDELIGHTS: It has been stated that since James Vance Marshall's death, Payne is "using the name by permission of [Marshall's] family."†

*   *   *

PAYNTER, William Henry   1901-

PERSONAL: Born January 3, 1901, in Callington, Cornwall, England; son of William Henry (with Royal Navy) and Elizabeth (Bowhay) Paynter; married Doris Mary Roberts; children: Anne (Mrs. Henry Stafford Tucker). *Education:* Attended county school in Callington, England. *Home:* Janola, Miners Meadow, Addington, Liskeard, Cornwall, England.

CAREER; Curator of Cornish Museum, Looe, Cornwall, England. Liskeard Borough, archivist; bard of the Cornish Gorsedd, bardic name, Whyler Pystry, "Searcher-out of Witchcraft." Official lecturer for women's institutes, townswomens' guilds, and other groups; part-time tutor of adult education, Devon and Cornwall. *Member:* Society of Authors, Museums Association.

WRITINGS: History of St. Mary's Church, Callington, Underhill, 1933; *Daniel Gumb, the Cave-Man Mathematician,* George Philip & Son, 1936; *Guide to Callington,* Vicary Kyrle, 1939; *Guide to Liskeard and District,* Century Press, 1959; (editor of new edition) *Primitive Physic: John Wesley's Book of Old Fashioned Cures and Remedies,* Parade Printing, 1961; *History of Bishop Trelawny,* Quintrell, 1962; *Our Old Cornish Mines,* Snell & Cowling, 1965; (editor of revised edition) John Allen, *History of Liskeard, 1856,* Wordens of Cornwall, 1967; *Love, History and Guide,* Parade Printing Works, 1970. Contributor to London and provincial press, and to magazines and journals. Author of television scripts.

WORK IN PROGRESS: Charms and Charming and Old Time Cures and Remedies; Folklore of Devon and Cornwall.

*   *   *

PEARCE, Donn   1928-

PERSONAL: Born September 28, 1928, in Croydon, Pa.; son of George I. and Margaret B. (Mott) Pearce; married Christine Frede, December 15, 1961; children: Hawser, Anker, Rudder. *Education:* Attended high school in New York, N.Y. *Politics:* None. *Religion:* None. *Home:* 2443 Whale Harbor Lane, Ft. Lauderdale, Fla. 33312. *Agent:* Knox Burger, 39 1/2 Washington Square S., New York, N.Y. 10012.

CAREER: U.S. Merchant Marine, officer, 1945-65, except for a period in Florida State Prison, 1949, where he began writing. *Military service:* U.S. Army, 1944-45. *Awards, honors:* Breadloaf Writers' Conference scholarship, 1965; Academy Award nomination, 1967, for screenplay, "Cool Hand Luke."

WRITINGS: Cool Hand Luke (novel), Scribner, 1965; *Pier Head Jump* (novel), Bobbs-Merrill, 1972; *Dying in the Sun* (nonfiction), Charterhouse, 1974. Also author of Screenplay, "Cool Hand Luke," filmed by Warner Brothers, 1967. Frequent contributor to *Playboy, Esquire, Penthouse,* and other magazines.

*   *   *

PEARL, Arthur   1922-

PERSONAL: Born April 23, 1922, in New York, N.Y.; married Margaret Norie (a librarian), November 9, 1946; children: James Delevan, Henry Andrew, Daniel Joseph. *Education:* Attended San Francisco Junior College; University of California, Berkeley, B.A., 1947, M.A., 1949, Ph.D., 1960. *Home:* 3901 Livingston St., N.W., Washington, D.C. *Office:* Department of Education, 161 Education Bldg., University of Oregon, Eugene, Ore. 97403.

CAREER: Howard University, Washington, D.C., with Center for Youth and Community Studies; University of

Oregon, Eugene, Ore., professor of education, 1965—. Consultant to Urban Studies Center, Rutgers University, to Action for Boston Community Development, to National Committee for Children and Youth, Congress of Racial Equality, to National Cross-Cultural Study, University of Notre Dame, and to Lavenberg-Corner Foundation. Member of research advisory committee, National Council on Crime and Delinquency. *Member:* American Psychological Association, Sigma Xi.

WRITINGS: (Contributor) Putnam and Snyder, editors, *Society, Culture, and Drinking Patterns*, Wiley, 1962; (with Riessman and Cohen) *Mental Health for the Poor*, Free Press of Glencoe, 1964; (with Riessman) *New Careers—A Way Out of Poverty*, Free Press of Glencoe, 1965; (contributor) Sherif and Sherif, editors, *Fifth Symposium of Social Psychology*, Aldine Press, 1965; (with L. A. Ferman) *Poverty in America*, University of Michigan Press, 1968; *Teachers in the Real World*, American Association of Colleges of Teacher Education, 1968; (contributor) *Among the People: Encounters with the Poor*, Basic Books, 1968; *The Atrocity of Education*, New Critics, 1970; *Landslide*, Citadel, 1973. Writer of monographs on alcoholism, narcotic treatment, and school dropout problem. Member of editorial board of *Excerpta Criminologica* and *Journal of Crime and Delinquency*.†

*   *   *

PEARSON, Ronald Hooke   1915-

PERSONAL: Born December 22, 1915, in London, England; son of George Sherwin Hooke (in foreign service) and Adela (Woods) Pearson; married Kathleen Emily Francis Smith, May 1, 1946; children: Julian Hooke, Angela Winifred. *Education:* Educated at Marlborough College and at Magdalen College, Oxford. *Politics:* Conservative. *Religion:* Church of England. *Home:* Baynton House, Coulston, Westbury, Wiltshire, England. *Agent:* Anthony Shiel Associates Ltd., 6 Grafton St., London W. 1, England.

CAREER: Company director, agriculture worker, 1946-63; currently a teacher. Broadcaster on radio and television. *Military service:* British Army, Intelligence, 1939-45; became captain. *Member:* Society of Authors.

WRITINGS: Baynton House, Putnam, 1955; *A Seal Flies By*, Hart-Davis, 1959, Walker, 1961. Television films include "The Underwater Horse," produced by British Broadcasting Corp. Contributor of articles on aquatic diving with seals and dolphins to magazines.

WORK IN PROGRESS: Establishing artificial reef off Cornwall to attract marine life and provide material for television work and a book; other aquatic diving adventures for nonfiction and fiction writing.

SIDELIGHTS: A Seal Flies By was also published in Canada, and in Swedish, German, Swiss, and Norwegian editions.†

*   *   *

PECK, Merton J(oseph)   1925-

PERSONAL: Born December 17, 1925, in Cleveland, Ohio; son of Kenneth Richard and Charlotte (Hart) Peck; married Mary McClure Bosworth, June 13, 1949; children: Richard, Katherine, Sarah, David. *Education:* Oberlin College, A.B., 1949; Harvard University, A.M., 1951, Ph.D., 1954. *Home:* 415 Humphrey St., New Haven, Conn. 06511. *Office:* Department of Economics, Yale University, New Haven, Conn. 06520.

CAREER: Harvard University, Cambridge, Mass., teaching fellow and instructor in economics, 1951-55; University of Michigan, Ann Arbor, assistant professor of economics, 1955-56; Harvard University, assistant professor, 1956-60, associate professor of business administration, 1960-61; Office of the Secretary of Defense, Washington, D.C., director of Systems Analysis, 1961-63; Yale University, New Haven, Conn., professor of economics, 1963—; chairman of department, 1967—. Brookings Institution, Washington, D.C., senior staff member, 1963—. Part-time consultant. Member of Council of Economic Advisors to the Executive Office of the President, 1968-69. *Military service:* U.S. Army, 1944-46. *Member:* American Economic Association, American Association of University Professors. *Awards, honors:* A.M., Yale University, 1963.

WRITINGS: (With J. Meyer, J. Stenason, and C. Zwick) *The Economics of Competition in the Transportation Industries*, Harvard University Press, 1959; *Competition in the Aluminum Industry, 1945-1958*, Harvard University Press, 1961; (with Frederick Scherer) *The Weapons Acquisition Process: An Economic Analysis*, Division of Research, Graduate School of Business Administration, Harvard University, 1962; *Competitive Policy for Transportation?*, Brookings Institution Press, 1965; (with Richard R. Nelson and Edward D. Kalachek) *Technology, Economic Growth and Public Policy*, Brookings Institution Press, 1967; (with others) *Federal Regulation of Television*, Brookings Institution Press, 1973. Author of articles in his field.

BIOGRAPHICAL/CRITICAL SOURCES: Time, August 3, 1962.†

*   *   *

PECK, Robert F.   1919-

PERSONAL: Born September 22, 1919; son of Charles R. and Jessie (Kelley) Peck; married Tina Casillas, April 9, 1946; children: Joanne, Brian. *Education:* State University of New York College at Buffalo, B.Sc. in Ed., 1941; State University of New York at Albany, M.Sc., 1942; University of Chicago, Ph.D., 1951. *Politics:* Independent. *Religion:* Episcopalian. *Home:* 3304 Glen Rose Dr., Austin Tex. *Office:* EdA3.203, University of Texas, Austin, Tex. 78712.

CAREER: Social Research, Inc., special consultant on executive assessment, 1947-50; University of Chicago, Chicago, Ill., 1949-60, began as instructor, became research associate, Committee on Human Development; Worthington Associates, vice-president and research director, 1950-54; University of Texas, associate professor, 1954-59, professor of educational psychology, 1959—, director of Personality Research Center, 1962—. Management Development Service, executive director, 1957—: Development Center for Teacher Education, director, 1965-68, co-director, 1968—.

MEMBER: International Society for the Study of Behavioral Development, American Psychological Association (fellow, divisions of developmental psychology and educational psychology), Interamerican Society of Psychology, Society for Research in Child Development, Sigma Xi.

WRITINGS: (Contributor) J. Anderson, editor, *Psychological Aspects of Aging*, American Psychological Association, 1956; (with Robert J. Havighurst and others) *The Psychology of Character Development*, Wiley, 1960; (contributor) *Personality Factors on the College Campus*, Hogg Foundation for Mental Health, University of Texas,

1962; *Personality in Middle and Late Life*, edited by B. Neugarten and others, Atherton, 1964; (contributor with James Tucker) Robert Travers, editor, *Second Handbook of Research on Teaching*, Rand McNally, 1973. Contributor to *Genetic Psychology Monographs*, and of more than sixty articles to other publications, including *Life, Personnel, Armed Forces Management*, and psychology, education, and geriatrics journals.

WORK IN PROGRESS: The Cross National Study of Coping Styles and Achievement; "The Teaching-Learning Interaction" project, studying the differential effects of different kinds of teaching on pupils with different learning styles.

*   *   *

PEEL, Edwin A(rthur) 1911-

PERSONAL: Born March 11, 1911, in Liverpool, England; son of Arthur (a teacher) and Mary Ann (Miller) Peel; married Nora Kathleen Yeadon, October 4, 1939; children: John, Susan, Elizabeth, Timothy. *Education:* University of Leeds, B.Sc. (honors in chemistry), 1931; University of London, M.A., 1938, Ph.D., 1944, D.Litt., 1961. *Politics:* Liberal. *Religion:* Church of England. *Home:* 47 Innage Rd., Birmingham 31, England. *Office:* School of Education, The University, Birmingham 15, England.

CAREER: Schoolmaster and lecturer in science and mathematics, London, England, 1933-40; British Ministry of Supply, experimental officer in Scotland and England, 1940-45; University of Durham, Newcastle upon Tyne, England, lecturer in education at King's College, 1946, university reader in educational psychology, 1946-48, university professor, 1948-50; University of Birmingham, Birmingham, England, professor of education and head of department, 1950—. Consultant and examiner for educational bodies. *Member:* British Psychological Society (council, 1950-63; president, 1961-62), National Liberal Club. *Awards, honors:* Fellow, Center for Advanced Study in the Behavioral Sciences, Stanford, Calif., 1963-64.

WRITINGS: The Psychological Basis of Education, Oliver & Boyd, 1956; *The Pupil's Thinking*, Oldbourne, 1960; (contributor) *Handbook of Programmed Learning*, Cunningham, 1964; *The Nature of Adolescent Judgment*, Staples Press, 1971. Author of educational monographs; contributor of articles to education and psychology journals. Editors, *Educational Review*.

WORK IN PROGRESS: Research into the adolescent's cognitive and language development, relating particularly to judgment, thinking, concept formation, abstracting and generalizing, devising methods to assess the semantic, linguistic and logical components in textual problem solving situations.

AVOCATIONAL INTERESTS: Painting (Sunday painter when time permits), and aesthetics.

*   *   *

PEERMAN, Dean G(ordon) 1931-

PERSONAL: Born April 25, 1931, in Mattoon, Ill.; son of Stanley Jacob (a coal miner) and Irene (Monen) Peerman. *Education:* Northwestern University, B.S. (with highest distinction), 1953; Cornell University, graduate study, 1953-54; Yale University Divinity School, B.D., 1959. *Politics:* Democrat. *Religion:* American Baptist. *Home:* 1123 Maple Ave., Evanston, Ill. 60202. *Office: Christian Century*, 407 South Dearborn St., Chicago, Ill. 60605.

CAREER: Christian Century Foundation (publisher of *Christian Century* magazine), Chicago, Ill., copy editor, 1959-61, associate editor, 1961-64, managing editor, 1964—. *Wartime service:* Conscientious objector, working as psychiatric aide in a hospital, 1954-56. *Member:* Fellowship of Reconciliation, American Civil Liberties Union, National Association for the Advancement of Colored People, Phi Beta Kappa. *Awards, honors:* Honorary D.D., Kalamazoo College, 1967.

WRITINGS: (With Martin E. Marty) *Pen-ultimates*, Holt, 1963; (editor with Marty) *New Theology No. 1-10*, Macmillan, 1964-73; (editor with Marty) *Handbook of Christian Theologians*, World Publishing, 1965; (editor) *Frontline Theology*, John Knox, 1967; (editor with Alan Geyer) *Theological Crossings*, Eerdmans, 1971. Contributor to *Frontier, Theology Today, Religious Education, Modern Age*, and *Christian Century*. Contributing editor, *Year*, 1957.

AVOCATIONAL INTERESTS: Poetry (reading and writing), classical music, the theater, travel (especially in Spain and Mexico).

*   *   *

PEERS, William R. 1914-

PERSONAL: Born June 14, 1914, in Stuart, Iowa; son of Harry D. and Milfred (Stigers) Peers; married Rose Mary Rau, January 1, 1953; children: Barbara Anne Peers Hicks, Christina Peers, Neely. *Education:* Attended University of California, Los Angeles, 1933-37. *Religion:* Protestant. *Home:* 120 McAllister Ave., Kentfield, Calif. 94904.

CAREER: Career service in U.S. Army, 1938-73, with present rank of lieutenant general (retired); assignments have included: commanding officer in Northern Burma 1943-45, China Theater, 1945, of 4th Infantry Division, Vietnam, 1967, of First Field Force, 1968, of 8th U.S. Army, Korea, 1971-73; work in Washington, D.C., with Central Intelligence Agency, Office of the Secretary of Defense, and Department of the Army, 1949-65; Joint Chiefs of Staff, Washington, D.C., special assistant, 1965-66; received Distinguished Service Medal with three oak leaf clusters, Silver Star, Legion of Merit, Distinguished Flying Cross, Bronze Star with oak leaf cluster, Air Medal with oak leaf cluster, Joint Service Commendation Medal, Army Commendation Medal, Presidential Unit Citation. *Member:* American Ordnance Association, Association of the United States Army, Sigma Pi. *Awards, honors:* Honorary LL.D., Myongju University, Seoul, Korea, 1973; Eisenhower Distinguished Membership award, People to People International, 1973.

WRITINGS: (With Brelis) *Behind the Burma Road*, Little, 1963. Contributor to military journals on subjects relating to guerrilla warfare and counterinsurgency.

*   *   *

PEET, C(harles) Donald, Jr. 1927-

PERSONAL: Born July 8, 1927, in St. Louis, Mo.; son of Charles Donald and Queenie Marion (Evans) Peet. *Education:* Princeton University, A.B., 1948, Ph.D., 1956; Washington University, St. Louis, Mo., A.M., 1949. *Office:* 442 Ballantine Hall, Indiana University, Bloomington, Ind.

CAREER: Indiana University, Bloomington, 1956-66, associate professor of English, 1964-66, and director of freshman literature, 1960-66. *Military service:* U.S. Army, 1954-55. *Member:* Modern Language Association of America, Malone Society.

WRITINGS: (Editor) *Representative Poems*, Allyn & Bacon, 1964.

WORK IN PROGRESS: Studies in Elizabethan poetry, drama, and rhetoric.

*   *   *

PENNIMAN, Howard R(ae)   1916-

PERSONAL: Born January 30, 1916, in Steger, Ill.; son of Rae Ernest (a merchant) and Alethea (Bates) Penniman; married Morgia Anderson, December 30, 1940; children: Barbara Jean, Ruth Mary, William Howard, Catherine Clara, Matthew Francis. *Education:* Louisiana State University, B.A., 1936, M.A., 1938; University of Minnesota, Ph.D., 1941. *Religion:* Episcopal. *Home:* 1409 Red Oak Dr., Silver Spring, Md. *Office:* Georgetown University, Washington, D.C.

CAREER: University of Alabama, University, instructor in political science, 1941-42; Yale University, New Haven, Conn., instructor in department of government, 1942-45, assistant professor, 1945-48; U.S. Central Information Agency, Washington, D.C., staff member, 1948-49; U.S. Department of State, Washington, D.C., assistant chief of External Research Staff, 1949-52, chief, 1953-55, staff member of Psychological Strategy Board, 1952-53; U.S. Information Agency, chief of Overseas Book Division, 1955-57; Georgetown University, Washington, D.C., professor of government, 1957—, head of department, 1959-63. Adjunct scholar, American Enterprise Institute, 1971. Visiting lecturer in political science at Connecticut College for Women (now Connecticut College), 1944-45, University of Minnesota, 1947, New School for Social Research, 1947-48, University of Puerto Rico, 1950. Trustee, Montgomery College, 1971—. *Military service:* U.S. Army, 1945-46.

MEMBER: American Political Science Association, International Political Science Association, Pi Gamma Mu, Pi Sigma Alpha, Sigma Delta Chi. *Awards, honors:* Social Science Research Council field fellow, 1940-41; Fulbright research fellow in France, 1964-65.

WRITINGS: Editor, and author of introduction) *John Locke on Politics and Education*, 1947; (editor) *Sait's American Parties and Elections*, Appleton, 1948, revised edition, 1952; (with H. Zink and G. Hathorn) *American Government and Politics: National, State and Local*, Van Nostrand, 1958 (with H. Zink and G. Hathorn) *Government and Politics in the United States*, Van Nostrand, 1961, revised edition (with Ferber and G. Hathorn), 1965; *The American Political Process*, Van Nostrand, 1962; *Decision in Vietnam*, 1967; (with Ralph W. Winter, Jr.) *Campaign Finances: Two Views of the Political and Constitutional Implications*, American Enterprise Institute for Public Policy Research, 1971; *Elections in South Vietnam*, American Enterprise Institute for Public Policy Research, 1972. Contributor to professional journals. Columnist, *America*, 1958—.

WORK IN PROGRESS: Studies on French political parties and on American institutions.†

*   *   *

PENROSE, Harald

PERSONAL: Married Nora Sybil; children: Sybil Anne, Ian. *Education:* University of London, Diploma in Engineering, 1926. *Home:* Nether Compton, Sherborne, Dorsetshire, England.

CAREER: Westland Aircraft Ltd., Yeovil, England,

1925—, variously designer, production manager, test pilot, and group sales manager, also special director. Director of several marine companies. *Military service:* Royal Air Force Reserve, 1927-31. *Member:* Royal Aeronautical Society (fellow), Royal Institute of Naval Architects, Royal Motor Yacht Club. *Awards, honors:* Order of the British Empire.

WRITINGS: I Flew with the Birds, Scribner, 1949; *No Echo in the Sky*, Cassell, 1958; *Airymouse*, Vethon & Yates, 1965; *British Aviation: The Pioneer Years*, Putnam, 1967; *British Aviation: Great War and Armistice*, Putnam, 1969; *British Aviation: The Adventuring Fears*, Putnam, 1973. Author of marine, aeronautical, historical, and natural history articles, and of reviews.

WORK IN PROGRESS: Airs and Graces; *British Aviation: Flight Path to World War II*.

AVOCATIONAL INTERESTS: Sailing, flying, archaeology, yacht design, art, music, countryside conservation.

*   *   *

PERKINS, George (Burton, Jr.)   1930-

PERSONAL: Born August 16, 1930, in Lowell, Mass.; son of George Burton and Gladys (Jones) Perkins; married Barbara Miller, May 9, 1964; children: Laura, Suzanne, Alison. *Education:* Tufts College (now Tufts University), A.B. (magna cum laude), 1953; Duke University, M.A., 1954; Cornell University, Ph.D., 1960. *Home:* 1316 King George Blvd., Ann Arbor, Mich. 48104. *Office:* Department of English, Eastern Michigan University, Ypsilanti, Mich. 48197.

CAREER: Washington University, St. Louis, Mo., instructor in English, 1957-60; Baldwin-Wallace College, Berea, Ohio, assistant professor of English, 1960-63; Fairleigh Dickinson University, Rutherford, N.J., assistant professor of English, 1963-66; University of Edinburgh, Edinburgh, Scotland, lecturer in American Literature, 1966-67; Eastern Michigan University, Ypsilanti, associate professor, 1967-70, professor of English, 1970—. *Member:* Modern Language Association of America, American Association of University Professors, The English Association, American Civil Liberties Union, Phi Kappa Phi. *Awards, honors:* Fellow, Duke University, 1953-54; fellow, Cornell University, 1954-55.

WRITINGS: Writing Clear Prose, Scott, Foresman, 1964; (editor) *Varieties of Prose*, Scott, Foresman, 1966; (editor) *The Theory of the American Novel*, Holt, 1970; (editor) *Realistic American Short Fiction*, Scott, Foresman, 1972; (editor) *American Poetry Theory*, Holt, 1972; (contributor) James Vinson, editor, *Contemporary Novelists*, St. Martin's, 1972; (editor with Bradley, Beatty, and Long) *The American Tradition in Literature*, 4th edition, Grosset & Dunlap, 1974. Writer of play produced at Baldwin-Wallace College, 1963. Contributor of essays, fiction, and reviews to *Nineteenth-Century Fiction, Journal of American Folklore, New England Quarterly, Descant, Choice*, and other journals. General editor, *The Journal of Narrative Techniques*, 1971—.

WORK IN PROGRESS: Fiction; a book on the novel.

AVOCATIONAL INTERESTS: Folklore, folk song.

*   *   *

PERKINS, Ralph   1913-

PERSONAL: Born February 10, 1913, in Mount Ayr,

Iowa; son of Bert Willis (a farmer) and Blanche Olive (Randall) Perkins; married Flossie Leighton (a teacher and librarian), June 3, 1935; children: Larry, Gail (Mrs. Merlyn K. Walter), Donald. *Education:* Fort Hays Kansas State College, B.S., 1937; Colorado State College (now University of Northern Colorado), A.M., 1939; graduate study at four other universities and colleges; University of Denver, M.A.L.S., 1960. *Politics:* Democrat. *Religion:* Methodist. *Home:* 2316 Seventh Ave., North, Grand Forks, N.D. 58201.

CAREER: Public school administrator and librarian in Kansas schools and colleges, 1933-62; University of North Dakota, Grand Forks, director of library education, 1962—. School library consultant. *Member:* American Library Association.

WRITINGS: Prospective Teacher's Knowledge of Library Fundamentals, Scarecrow, 1965; *Guide to Reference Books*, New Concept Press, 1965; *Guide to Reference in Education*, New Concept Press, 1965; *Book Selection Media*, National Council of Teachers of English, 1965, revised edition, 1967; *Guide to Libraries and Reference Books*, 1966, 4th revised edition, 1970. Contributor to professional journals.

WORK IN PROGRESS: Three books, *Guide to Reference in the Humanities, Guide to Reference in the Social Sciences*, and *Guide to Reference in the Sciences.*†

* * *

PERLMUTTER, Nathan 1923-

PERSONAL: Born March 2, 1923, in New York, N.Y.; son of Hyman (a tailor) and Bella (Finkelstein) Perlmutter; married Ruth Osofsky, April 2, 1943; children: Nina, Dean. *Education:* Attended Georgetown University, 1942-43, and Villanova College (now University), 1943-44; New York University, LL.B., 1949. *Politics:* Variable. *Religion:* Jewish. *Office:* American Jewish Committee, New York, N.Y.

CAREER: Civil rights and human relations education executive with Anti-Defamation League of B'nai B'rith in Denver, Colo., 1949-52, Detroit, Mich., 1952-53, New York, N.Y., 1953-56, and Miami, Fla., 1956-64; American Jewish Committee, New York, N.Y., executive, 1964—. *Military service:* U.S. Marine Corps, 1943-46; became second lieutenant. *Member:* International League for the Rights of Man, American Civil Liberties Union, National Association of Intergroup Relations Officials.

WRITINGS: How to Win Money at the Races, Crowell-Collier, 1964; *A Bias of Reflections: Confessions of an Incipient Old Jew*, Arlington House, 1972. Contributor of articles to *Frontier, Nation, Progressive, New Leader, Commentary, National Jewish Monthly, Florida Historical Quarterly, Midstream.*

AVOCATIONAL INTERESTS: Horses, when they're racing, birds not in cages, flowers and trees anywhere, anytime.

BIOGRAPHICAL/CRITICAL SOURCES: Miami News, March 22, 1964; *Miami Herald*, April 22, 1964; *Jewish Floridian*, May 22, 1964.†

* * *

PERRIN, Noel 1927-

PERSONAL: Born September 18, 1927, in New York, N.Y.; son of Edwin Oscar (an advertising executive) and Blanche (Chenery) Perrin; married Nancy Hunnicutt, November 26, 1960; children: Elisabeth, Margaret. *Education:* Williams College, B.A., 1949; Duke University, M.A., 1950; Trinity Hall, Cambridge, M.Litt., 1958. *Religion:* Episcopalian. *Home:* Thetford Center, Vt. *Office:* Department of English, Dartmouth College, Hanover, N.H.

CAREER: Woman's College, University of North Carolina, Chapel Hill, instructor, 1956-59; Dartmouth College, Hanover, N.H., assistant professor of English, 1959—. *Military service:* U.S. Army, Artillery, 1945-46 and 1950-51; became first lieutenant; served in Korea; received Bronze Star. *Member:* Phi Beta Kappa.

WRITINGS: A Passport Secretly Green (essays), St. Martin's, 1961; *Dr. Bowlder's Legacy: A History of Expurgated Books in England and America*, Atheneum, 1969, Macmillan, 1970; *Amateur Sugar Maker*, University Press of New England, 1972; *Vermont: In All Weathers*, Viking, 1973. Contributor to *New Yorker.*†

* * *

PERRIN, (Horace) Norman 1920-

PERSONAL: Born November 29, 1920, in Willingborough, Northamptonshire, England; came to United States in 1956; U.S. citizenship pending; son of Horace (a factory worker) and Dorothy May (Healey) Perrin; married Rosemary Watson, July 2, 1949. *Education:* University of Manchester, B.A., 1949; University of London, B.D., 1952, M.Th., 1955; Kirchliche Hochschule, Berlin, Germany, graduate study, 1956-57; University of Gottingen, D.Theol., 1959. *Politics:* Liberal Democrat. *Home:* 6019 South Ingleside, Chicago, Ill. 60637.

CAREER: Ordained minister of Baptist Union of Great Britain and Northern Ireland, 1949, serving churches in London, England, and Swansea, South Wales, 1949-56; Emory University Theology School, Atlanta, Ga., assistant professor and later associate professor of New Testament, 1959-64; University of Chicago Divinity School, Chicago, Ill., associate professor of New Testament, 1964—. *Military service:* Royal Air Force, 1940-45. *Member:* American Association of University Professors, Society of Biblical Literature, Studiorum Novi Testamenti Societas.

WRITINGS: The Kingdom of God in the Teaching of Jesus, Westminster, 1963; *Rediscovering the Teaching of Jesus*, Harper & Row, 1967; *The Promise of Bultmann*, Lippincott, 1969; *What is Redaction Criticism?*, Fortress Press, 1969; *A Modern Pilgrimage in New Testament Christology*, Fortress Press, 1974; *The New Testament: An Introduction*, Harcourt, 1974.

Translator of works of J. Jeremias: *The Lord's Prayer in Modern Research*, Expository Times, 1959-60; *The Sermon on the Mount*, Athlone Press, 1961; *The Question of the Historical Jesus*, Facet Books, 1964; *The Eucharistic Words of Jesus*, revised edition, Westminster, in press.

Contributor of articles and reviews to theological journals.

SIDELIGHTS: Perrin has competence in classical and Biblical languages, and German, French, and knows some Syriac and Coptic. *Avocational interests:* Formerly cricket and chess; now travel through America by car.†

* * *

PERRY, Dick 1922-

PERSONAL: Born June 13, 1922, in Cincinnati, Ohio; son

of Robertson (a railroad engineer) and Gertrude (Willman) Perry; married Jean Jobes, September 18, 1948; children: Michael, Matthew, Ann. *Education:* Attended Oberlin College and University of Chicago. *Address:* Post Office Box 270, Oxford, Ohio. *Agent:* A. Watkins, Inc., 77 Park Ave., New York, N.Y. 10016.

CAREER: Worked in advertising radio, television, and other fields; now working as full-time free-lance writer. Formerly employed by Roche, Richerd, Henri, Hurst, Chicago, Ill., and as radio and television director at Wesco Advertising, Clearwater, Fla., creative director at WCPO-TV, Cincinnati, Ohio. *Military service:* U.S. Marine Corps.

WRITINGS: Raymond and Me That Summer, Harcourt, 1964; *The Roundhouse, Paradise, and Mr. Pickering*, Doubleday, 1966; *Vas You Ever in Zinzinnati?*, Doubleday, 1966; *Ohio: A Personal Portrait of the 17th State*, Doubleday, 1969; *Reflections of Jesse Stuart on a Land of Many Moods*, McGraw, 1971; *Not Just a Sound: The Story of WLW*, Prentice-Hall, 1971; (with Paul Ilyinsky) *Goodbye, Coney Island, Goodbye . . .* , Prentice-Hall, 1972. Author of plays produced in community and summer theaters and on Columbia Broadcasting System Television. Contributor to *Reader's Digest*, *McCall's*, and other periodicals.

WORK IN PROGRESS: A book, *The Briefcase Bohemian of the 7:54*; a three-act play, short stories, and articles.†

* * *

PERRY, James M(oorhead) 1927-

PERSONAL: Born August 21, 1927, in Elmira, N.Y.; son of James W. (an insurance agent) and Margaret (Moorhead) Perry; married Margaret Pancoast, September 18, 1954; children: Margaret, Katherine. *Education:* Trinity College, Hartford, Conn., B.A. *Religion:* Episcopalian. *Home:* 5002 Jamestown Rd., Washington, D.C. 20016. *Office: National Observer*, 11501 Columbia Pike, Silver Spring, Md.

CAREER: Member of editorial staff of *Hartford Times*, Hartford, Conn., 1950-53, *Philadelphia Bulletin*, Philadelphia, Pa., 1953-63; *National Observer*, political writer, Washington, D.C., 1963—. *Military service:* U.S. Marine Corps, 1945-46; writer for *Leatherneck*, 1946.

WRITINGS: Barry Goldwater: A New Look at a Presidential Candidate, Dow Jones, 1964; *The New Politics: The Expanding Technology of Political Manipulation*, C. N. Potter, 1968; *Us & Them: How the Press Covered the 1972 Election*, C. N. Potter, 1972.

* * *

PERRY, Milton F(reeman) 1926-

PERSONAL: Born August 14, 1926, in Bertie County, N.C.; son of Rosewell Westley and Etta May (Holloman) Perry; married Barbara Lee Posivak, April 7, 1949; children: Carolyn Diane, Julia Anne, Linda Hope. *Education:* College of William and Mary, A.B., 1950, graduate study, 1951. *Home:* 11803 Markham Rd., Independence, Mo. 64052. *Office:* Harry S Truman Library, Independence, Mo. 64050.

CAREER: Colonial Williamsburg, Inc., Williamsburg, Va., craft shops and archaeological assistant, 1947-51; Fort Macon State Park, Atlantic Beach, N.C., curator, 1952-53; U.S. Military Academy, West Point Museum, West Point, N.Y., curator of history, 1953-58; Harry S Truman Library, Independence, Mo., curator, 1958—. Counselor for Fort Leavenworth Museum, Fort Leavenworth, Kan.; adviser to Jackson County Historical Society, Independence, Mo.; creator of initial displays at Dwight D. Eisenhower Library, Abilene, Kan., developed Civil War Museum of Jackson County, Lone Jack, Mo. Speaker on historical preservation and restoration; instructor in museum appreciation, Penn Valley College.

MEMBER: American Association of Museums, Company of Military Historians (fellow), Museums Council of Mid-America (founder and charter chairman), Mountain Plains Museums Conference, Midwest Museums Conference, Missouri Council on Historic Sites, 35th Division Historical Association (curator).

WRITINGS: (With Barbara W. Parke) *Patton and His Pistols: The Favorite Sidearms of General George S. Patton, Jr.*, Stackpole, 1957; *Infernal Machines: The Story of Confederate Submarine and Mine Warfare*, Louisiana State University Press, 1965; *Mulkey Square, 1869-1973*, [Kansas City], 1973. Contributor to *American Rifleman, True West, Guns, Gun Report*, and to museums publications and historical journals. Member of editorial board, Midwest Museums Conference, 1959.

WORK IN PROGRESS: Research on the American Civil War and American social history.

BIOGRAPHICAL/CRITICAL SOURCES: College of William and Mary Alumni Gazette, Spring, 1960.

* * *

PERRY, Richard S. 1924-

PERSONAL: Born February 9, 1924, in Los Angeles, Calif.; son of Louis H. (a restaurant owner) and Julia (Stoddard) Perry; married Vera Terkelsen (a teacher), January 29, 1955; children: Julie Anne, Janet Marie, Johnathan Richard. *Education:* University of California, Los Angeles, B.S., 1947, M.E., 1949, Ed.D., 1956. *Politics:* Republican. *Religion:* Protestant. *Home:* 3240 Inglewood Blvd., Los Angeles, Calif. *Office:* School of Business Administration and Economics, California State University, Northridge, 18111 Nordhoff St., Northridge, Calif.

CAREER: Oceanside-Carlsbad College (now Mira Costa College), Oceanside Calif., instructor in business administration, 1949-50; Mount San Antonio Junior College, Walnut, Calif., instructor in business administration and counselor, 1950-55; University of California, Los Angeles, assistant professor of office management and business education, 1955-60; California State University, Northridge, professor of business and economics and chairman of department of office administration and business education, 1960—. C. F. Braun Co., Engineers, manager of presentation, 1960-62. Communications consultant to corporations. *Military service:* U.S. Army, Infantry, 1943-46; became first lieutenant; received Bronze Star and Purple Heart. *Member:* American Business Writing Association (vice-president, western region, 1964—; national board of directors, 1964—), National Business Education Association, California Business Education Association, Pi Omega Pi.

WRITINGS: (With brother, Louis B. Perry) *A History of the Los Angeles Labor Movement, 1911-1941*, University of California Press, 1963. Contributor of fifteen articles to professional journals. Member of editorial staff, *American Business Writing Association Bulletin*, 1961-64.

WORK IN PROGRESS: Devices for predicting success in education for business at the secondary school and collegiate levels.†

PETERS, Robert L(ouis) 1924-

PERSONAL: Born October 20, 1924, in Eagle River, Wis.; son of Samuel (a welder and farmer) and Dorothy (Keck) Peters; married Jean Louise Powell, October 22, 1950 (divorced, 1972); children: Robert II, Meredith Jean, Richard Nathaniel (deceased), Jefferson Marlowe. *Education:* University of Wisconsin, B.A., 1948, M.A., 1949, Ph.D., 1952. *Home:* 433 Locust St., Laguna Beach, Calif. *Office:* Department of English, University of California, Irvine, Calif.

CAREER: University of Idaho, Moscow, instructor in English, 1951-52; Boston University, Boston, Mass., assistant professor of humanities, 1952-54; Ohio Wesleyan University, Delaware, assistant professor of English, 1954-57; Wayne State University, Detroit, Mich., associate professor of English, 1957-63; University of California, Riverside, associate professor, 1963-66, professor of Victorian literature, 1966-68; University of California, Irvine, professor of English and comparative literature, 1968—. Visiting professor, University of California, Los Angeles, summer, 1965, University of Utah, summer, 1967. Member of board, Wayne State University Press, 1969-62. *Military service:* U.S. Army, 1943-46; became technical sergeant.

MEMBER: Modern Language Association of America, Poetry Society of America, American Society for Aesthetics (trustee and member of board, 1965-68). *Awards, honors:* Grant-in-aid, American Council of Learned Societies, 1963; Hilberry Publication Prize of Wayne State University Press, 1965, for *The Crowns of Apollo;* Guggenheim fellow, 1966-67; poems selected for Borestone Mountain Awards, 1967; fellowship to Yaddo, The MacDowell Colony, and Ossabaw Island Project, 1973-74.

WRITINGS: (Editor) *Victorians on Literature and Art,* Appleton, 1961; *The Crowns of Apollo: Swinburne's Principles of Literature and Art: A Study in Victorian Criticism and Aesthetics,* Wayne State University Press, 1965; (editor with David Halliburton) *Edmund Gosse's Journal of his Visit to America,* Purdue University Press, 1966; (editor with George Hitchcock) *Pioneers of Modern Poetry,* Kayak, 1967; *Songs for a Son* (poems), Norton, 1967; *Fourteen Poems,* privately printed, 1967; (editor with Herbert M. Schueller) *The Letters of John Addington Symonds* three volumes, Wayne State University Press, 1967-69; *The Sows Head and Other Poems,* Wayne State University Press, 1968; *Eighteen Poems,* privately printed, 1973; *Byron Exhumed* (poems), Windless Orchard Press, 1973; *Connections: In the English Lake District* (poems), Anvil Press, 1974; *Cool Zebras of Light* (poems), Christopher Press, 1974; *Red Midnight Moon* (poems), Empty Elevator Shaft Press, 1974; *Holy Cow: Parable Poems,* Red Hill Press, 1974; *The Gift to be Simple* (poems), Liveright, in press; *Selected Poems,* Crossing Press, in press; *The Great American Poetry Bake-Off* (essays), Crossing Press, in press.

Author of a play produced at the Cubiculo Theatre, 1971. Poems anthologized in *Best Poems of 1967: Borestone Mountain Poetry Awards,* edited by Lionel Stevenson and others, Pacific Books, 1968. Contributor to *Victorian Studies, Prairie Schooner, Fiddlehead, Kayak, The Little Square Review,* and other magazines and professional journals. *English Literature in Transition,* bibliographer, 1958-68, member of editorial board, 1962-68; associate editor, *Criticism: A Quarterly of Literature and the Arts,* 1961-63; assistant editor and bibliographer, *Journal of Aesthetics and Art Criticism,* 1963-65; American poetry editor, *Ikon.*

SIDELIGHTS: In reference to *The Letters of John Addington Symonds,* Lawrence Poston III writes: "The appearance of the Symonds' letters in this handsome edition is an important publishing event." G. S. Rousseau comments: "The editors, both eminent authorities on their subject, have superbly prepared this volume, printing the original manuscripts of Symonds' letters and annotating everything the reader, from amateur to scholar, could wish to know." Peters has given readings of his poetry across the U.S. and in Europe.

* * *

PETERSEN, Donald 1928-

PERSONAL: Born November 11, 1928, in Minneapolis, Minn.; son of Arthur William and Dorothy (Scholl) Petersen; married Jeanine Ahrens, February 2, 1952; children: James, Eric, Catherine, Christian. *Education:* Attended the Sorbonne, University of Paris, 1948-49; Carleton College, B.A., 1950; graduate study at the Indiana University School of Letters, summer, 1951 and 1952; State University of Iowa, M.F.A., 1952. *Office:* State University of New York College at Oneonta, Oneonta, N.Y.

CAREER: Western Review, assistant editor, 1950-55; State University of Iowa, Iowa City, instructor, 1954-56; State University of New York College at Oneonta, 1956—, began as assistant professor, now associate professor of English.

WRITINGS: The Spectral Boy (poems, 1948-64), Wesleyan University Press, 1964. Poems have appeared in *Poetry, Furioso, Paris Review, Western Review, Perspective, Carleton Miscellany,* and *New York Times.* Poems have been anthologized in *Midland,* edited by Paul Engle, Random House, 1961, *New Poets of England and America,* edited by Donald Hall and Robert Pack, Meridian Books, 1962, *Decade,* edited by Norman Holmes Pearson, Wesleyan University Press, 1969, *The Contemporary American Poets: American Poetry Since 1940,* edited by Mark Strand, New American Library, 1971. Has translated poems from Latin, French, German, and Russian.

WORK IN PROGRESS: Poems and translations.

SIDELIGHTS: Petersen writes to *CA:* "In a time when partly-formed verse is being widely published and praised, the attempt to write a finished poem may not be fashionable, but it is still worth making. Poetry must present not merely what one has observed with interest or amusement, not merely a bright array of words, but the things that a man has loved and hated and feared in his lifetime." *Avocational interests:* Cooking, reading sports pages, and looking at old houses. He says he is "quite possibly the only American poet to have played on a French basketball team."

* * *

PETERSON, Norma Lois 1922-

PERSONAL: Born December 22, 1922, Roseau, Minn.; daughter of E. J. and Alma (Odegard) Peterson. *Education:* Attended The American University, 1946-47; Colorado College, B.A. (magna cum laude), 1949; University of Missouri, M.A., 1951, Ph.D., 1953. *Politics:* Democrat. *Home:* 13 Bell, Alamosa, Colo. 81101. *Office:* Adams State College, Alamosa, Colo. 81102.

CAREER: University of Missouri, Columbia, instructor in history, 1951-53; Adams State College, Alamosa, Colo., assistant professor, 1953-55, associate professor, 1955-57, professor of history and chairman of Division of Social Studies, 1957-71, chairman of Division of History, Government, and Philosophy, 1971—. *Military service:* U.S. Naval Reserve, Women's Reserve (WAVES), 1943-46. *Member:* American Historical Association, Organization of American Historians, Southern Historical Association, Phi Beta Kappa. *Awards, honors:* Florence Sabin fellowship of American Association of University Women, 1957-58.

WRITINGS: Freedom and Franchise: The Political Career of B. Gratz Brown, University of Missouri Press, 1965; *The Defense of Norfolk, 1807*, Norfolk County Historical Society, 1970. Contributor to *Missouri Historical Review* and *Virginia Calvalcade.*

WORK IN PROGRESS: A biography of Littleton Waller Tazewell; a volume of the Harrison-Tyler Administration, to be published by University Press of Kansas.

* * *

PETERSON, Robert E(ugene) 1928-
(Peter Saya)

PERSONAL: Born December 7, 1928, in Eugene, Ore.; son of Orval Douglas (a clergyman) and Mary E. (Graybill) Peterson; married Dorothy Jean Gangnath (a teacher), June 15, 1950; children: Bobbi Jeanne, Conni Alayne, Steven Scott. *Education:* Yakima Valley Junior College, student; University of Oregon, B.A., 1951; Northwest Christian College, B.Th., 1951; Texas Christian University, B.D., 1954. *Home:* 215 Voorhees St., Teaneck, N.J. *Office:* National Council of Churches, 465 Riverside Dr., New York, N.Y. 10027.

CAREER: Ordained minister of Disciples of Christ (Christian) Church, 1954; pastor in Alpine, Tex., 1954-55; associate pastor in Odessa, Tex., 1955-56; West Hills Christian Church, San Antonio, Tex., organizing pastor, 1957-65; National Council of Churches, Department of Stewardship, New York, N.Y., associate executive director, 1965—. KXOL, Fort Worth, Tex., copy director, 1953-54, announcer, 1954; KOSA, Odessa, Tex., announcer and program director, 1955-56, announcer, and director of KOSA-TV, 1956-57; KTSA, San Antonio, Tex., conductor of "Church School of the Air," 1958-65. Member of public relations committee, International Convention of Christian Churches, 1954-58, of executive committee, 1965-68; Joint Boards of Christian Churches, vice-chairman, 1964-65.

WRITINGS: (Author of introduction) *The Living Bible*, Joseph W. Cain, 1959; *Handling the Church's Money*, Bethany, 1965; *Are Demons for Real?*, Moody, 1972. Writer and producer of audiovisual tapes for International Convention of Christian Churches and Texas Convention of Christian Churches. Contributor to *Christian, Christian Century*, and *Pulpit*. Editor of *Steward* (quarterly paper), and *Stewardship Facts* (annual magazine).

WORK IN PROGRESS: Articles, and scripts for movies and filmstrips.†

* * *

PFEFFER, Leo 1910-

PERSONAL: "P" in surname is silent; born December 25, 1910, in Hungary; son of Alter (a rabbi) and Honi (Yaeger) Pfeffer; married Freda Plotkin, September 18, 1937; children: Alan Israel, Susan Beth. *Education:* City College (now City College of the City University of New York), B.S.S., 1930; New York University, J.D., 1933. *Politics:* Independent. *Religion:* Jewish. *Home:* 191 Willoughby St., Brooklyn, N.Y. 11801.

CAREER: Admitted to New York bar, 1933; practice of law, New York, N.Y., 1933—; American Jewish Congress, New York, N.Y., general counsel, 1945-64, special counsel, 1964—. Lecturer at New School for Social Research, New York, N.Y., 1954-58, at Mount Holyoke College, South Hadley, Mass., 1958-60; Yeshiva University, New York, N.Y., David Petegorsky Professor of Constitutional Law, 1962-63; Long Island University, Brooklyn, N.Y., professor of political science and chairman of department, 1964—. Visiting professor of constitutional law, Rutgers University, 1965. Lawyers Constitutional Defense Committee, president, 1964-66, member of general counsel, 1966—; Horace Mann League, counsel; American Civil Liberties Union, consultant; committee for Public Education and Religious Liberty, counsel, 1966—; National Coalition for Public Education and Religious Liberty, counsel, 1974—; National Project Center for Film and the Humanities, member of advisory committee, 1974—. Member of panel arbitrators, American Arbitration Society. *Member:* National Association of Intergroup Relations Officials, American Political Science Association, American Academy of Religion, American Judicature Society, American Society for Legal History, Society for the Scientific Study of Religion, American Association of University Professors, New York University Law Review Association (president, 1962-66), Authors League.

WRITINGS: Church, State and Freedom, Beacon, 1953, revised edition, 1967; *The Liberties of an American*, Beacon, 1956, 2nd edition, 1963; *Creeds in Competition*, Harper, 1958; (with Anson Phelps Stokes) *Church and State in the United States*, Harper, 1964; *This Honorable Court*, Beacon, 1965; *God, Caesar and the Constitution*, Beacon, 1974.

Contributor: *Religion in the State University*, Burgess, 1950; *Cultural Pluralism and the American Idea*, University of Pennsylvania Press, 1956; *Religion in America*, Meridian, 1958; *Jews in the Modern World*, Twayne, 1962; *Religious Conflict in America*, Anchor, 1964; *Church State Relations in Ecumenical Perspective*, Duquesne University Press, 1966; *The Religious Situation*, Beacon, 1968; *The Rights of Americans*, Pantheon, 1971; *Religious Movements in Contemporary America*, Princeton University Press. Also contributor to encyclopedias. Member of editorial board, *Journal of Church and State*, 1958—; member of editorial board, *Judiasm*, 1964—.

WORK IN PROGRESS: The American Judicial System.

AVOCATIONAL INTERESTS: Biblical criticism.

* * *

PFEIFFER, Eric 1935-

PERSONAL: Born September 15, 1935, in Rauental, Germany; now United States citizen; son of Fritz and Emma (Saborovski) Pfeiffer; married Natasha Maria Emerson (a psychiatric social worker), March 21, 1964; children: Eric Alexander, Michael David, Mark Armin. *Education:* Washington University, St. Louis, Mo., A.B. (with honors), 1956, M.D. (with honors), 1960. *Home:* 1705 Beacon Hill Rd., Lexington, Ky. 40504.

CAREER: University of Rochester, School of Medicine and Dentistry, Rochester, N.Y., instructor in psychiatry, 1963-64; U.S. Public Health Service Hospital, Lexington, Ky., staff psychiatrist, 1964-66; University of Kentucky, College of Medicine, Lexington, clinical instructor in psychiatry, 1964-66; Duke University Medical Center, Durham, N.C., associate in psychiatry, 1966, assistant professor, 1967-69, associate professor, 1969-72, professor of psychiatry, 1973—, associate director, Center for the Study of Aging and Human Development, 1974—. Consultant in Student Health (psychiatry), Berea College, Berea, Ky., 1964-66. Project director, Older Americans Resources and Services Program. *Military service:* U.S. Public Health Service, 1964—; lieutenant commander. *Member:* American Psychiatric Association, American Geriatrics Society, Gerontological Society, Southern Psychiatric Association, North Carolina Neuropsychiatric Association, Phi Beta Kappa, Alpha Omega Alpha. *Awards, honors:* Charioteer Poetry Award, 1963, for *Take With Me Now That Enormous Step*; Markle Scholar in Academic Medicine, 1968-73.

WRITINGS: Take With Me Now That Enormous Step (poetry), Charioteer Press, 1964; *Disordered Behavior: Basic Concepts in Clinical Psychiatry*, Oxford University Press, 1968; (editor with E. W. Busse) *Behavior and Adaptation in Late Life*, Little, Brown, 1972; (with others) *Behavioral Science: A Selective View*, Little, Brown, 1972; (editor) *Alternatives to Institutional Care for Older Americans: Practice and Planning*, Duke University, 1973; (editor) *Successful Aging*, Duke University, 1974. Contributor of numerous articles to psychiatric and gerontological journals. Co-founder and editor of *Compass Review*, a quarterly of poetry, St. Louis, Mo., 1960-61.

* * *

PFLAUM, Irving Peter 1906-

PERSONAL: Born April 9, 1906, in Chicago, Ill.; son of Herbert Seligman and Claudia (Baum) Pflaum; married Melanie S. Loewenthal, February 11, 1930; children: John Herbert, Peter Edward, Thomas Martin. *Education:* University of Chicago, Ph.D., 1928, J.D., 1930; De Paul University, postdoctoral study, 1930; University of Madrid, certificate, 1934. *Office:* Chalet Windfall, El Tosalet 323, Javea (Alicante), Spain.

CAREER: Admitted to Illinois bar, 1930; practicing attorney, reporter, and foreign correspondent, 1930-34; United Press Associations, correspondent in Madrid, Spain, 1935-39; *Chicago Times* (later *Chicago Sun-Times*), foreign editor, 1939-63; syndicated columnist, radio and television commentator, 1939-63; Inter-American University, San German, Puerto Rico, professor and chairman, department of history and political science, 1961-70; Peace Corps, Latin American Study Center, San German, Puerto Rico, professor of social science, 1962-71; Associate, U.S. Office of Strategic Services, 1941-44; professor of journalism, Northwestern University, 1944-46; associate of American Universities Field Staff at American colleges and universities and in Cuba, 1960-61; visiting professor of history and American studies, Canterbury University, New Zealand, 1969-70.

MEMBER: American Association of University Professors, National Press Club, Overseas Press Club, Press Veterans (Chicago), University Club (Evanston, Ill.), Political Science Association (Puerto Rico). *Awards, honors:* Anglo-American Press Award, 1939; Marshall Field Award for journalism, 1958; Field Foundation of New York annual award for Latin American seminars, 1964, 1965.

WRITINGS: Tragic Island: Communism in Cuba, Prentice-Hall, 1961; *Arena of Decision: Latin America in Crisis*, Prentice-Hall, 1963; (with Rufo Lopez-Fresquet) *My Fourteen Months With Castro*, World Publishing, 1966. *WORK IN PROGRESS: The Iberians: A Study of Spain and Portugal in the Twentieth Century*; and an autobiography.

PFLAUM, Melanie L(owenthal) 1909-

PERSONAL: Born April 12, 1909; daughter of Edward and Judith (Weill) Loewenthal; married Irving Peter Pflaum (a professor of Latin American studies), February 11, 1930; children: John, Peter, Thomas. *Education:* Studied at Goucher College, 1926-27, University of Wisconsin, 1927-28; University of Chicago, Ph.B., 1929; other study at Sorbonne, University of Paris. *Home and office:* El Tosalet 323, Javea, (Alicante), Spain.

CAREER: American Medical Association, Chicago, Ill. manuscript editor, 1930-33; Scripps Howard Syndicate, foreign correspondent in Paris, Rome, Budapest, Athens, Warsaw, Madrid, 1933-39; manuscript editor for medical yearbooks, Chicago, Ill., 1939; Board of Economic Warfare, Washington, D.C., chief, Iberian Division, 1940-43; United States Office of Censorship, Chicago, Ill., 1943-45; free-lance writer for educational films, radio series, and magazines, 1945-55, novelist, 1955—; Northwestern University, Evanston, Ill., teacher of creative writing, 1958-59; Inter-American University of Puerto Rico, San German, teacher of literature and creative writing, 1960-65. *Member:* Society of Women Geographers, Society of Midland Authors, American Association of University Professors, Theta Sigma Phi, Arts Club (Chicago).

WRITINGS: Bolero, Heinemann, 1956, St. Martins, 1957; *Windfall*, Cassell, 1962; *The Insiders*, Cassell, 1963; *The Gentle Tyrants*, Carlton, 1965; *Ready by Wednesday*, Carlton, 1970; *Second Conquest*, Univers, 1971; *The Maine Remembered*, Pegasus, 1972; *Costa Brava*, Ediciones Juan Ponce de Leon, 1972; *Lili*, Pegasus, 1974. Contributor of stories and articles to *Vogue, American Mercury, Reporter, Canadian Home Journal*, and *Interamerican Review*. Writer of radio series on science.

WORK IN PROGRESS: A novel with a New Zealand background.

SIDELIGHTS: As the wife of a foreign correspondent, foreign editor, radio and television commentator, and university professor, Melanie Pflaum has lived in several countries of Europe, and in South America, Cuba, and other Latin America lands. She speaks, reads, and writes Spanish, French, and Italian.

* * *

PHILLIPS, Cecil R(andolph) 1933-

PERSONAL: Born July 30, 1933, in Birmingham, Ala.; son of Cecil R. and Alberta (Smith) Phillips; married Sarah Lee Kirby, August 25, 1956; children: Taylor, Leslie, Daniel. *Education:* Georgia Institute of Technology, B.I.E., 1955, M.S.I.E., 1960; Federal Institute of Technology, Zurich, Switzerland, graduate study, 1955-56. *Office:* The Georgia Conservatory, 3376 Peachtree Rd., Atlanta, Ga. 30326.

CAREER: General Electric Co., Schenectady, N.Y., technical editor, 1956-58; Operations Research, Inc., Silver Spring, Md., project leader, 1960-63; Management Science Atlanta, Inc. (management consultants), Atlanta, Ga., executive vice-president, 1963-67; Kurt Salmon Associates, vice-president, 1967-74; The Georgia Conservatory, Atlanta, executive director, 1974—. *Member:* Sierra Club, National Wildlife Federation, Common Cause, National Audubon Society.

WRITINGS: (With Joseph J. Moder) *Project Management with CPM and PERT*, Reinhold, 1964, 2nd edition, 1970. Contributor to *Operations Research* and *Journal of Industrial Engineering*.

PHILLIPS, D(ennis) J(ohn Andrew)   1924-
(Peter Chambers, Peter Chester)

PERSONAL: Born August 17, 1924, in London, England; son of John and Catherine (Rock) Phillips; married June Blake, February 17, 1954; children: Mark, Dudley, Alexandra. *Education:* Attended Westminster City School, London, England. *Politics:* Conservative. *Religion:* Church of England. *Home:* Preston Lodge, Shoppenhangers Rd., Maidenhead, Berkshire, England.

CAREER: Onetime entertainer; now full-time writer. *Military service:* Royal Air Force, 1942-47. *Member:* Crime Writers Association (England), Mystery Writers of America.

WRITINGS: Revenge Incorporated, R. Hale, 1970.

Under pseudonym Peter Chambers: *Murder Is for Keeps*, R. Hale, 1961, Abelard, 1962; *Wreath for a Redhead*, Abelard, 1962; *The Big Goodbye*, R. Hale, 1962; *Dames Can be Deadly*, R. Hale, 1963, Abelard, 1964; *Down-Beat Kill*, R. Hale, 1963, Abelard, 1964; *Lady, This Is Murder*, R. Hale, 1963; *This'll Kill You*, R. Hale, 1964; *Nobody Lives Forever*, R. Hale, 1964; *You're Better Off Dead*, R. Hale, 1965; *Always Take the Big Ones*, R. Hale, 1965; *The Bad Die Young*, Roy, 1967; *The Blonde Wore Black*, Roy, 1968; *No Peace for the Wicked*, Roy, 1968; *Speak Ill of the Dead*, Roy, 1969.

Under pseudonym Peter Chester: *Killing Comes Easy*, Jenkins, 1958, Roy Publishers, 1960; *Murder Forestalled*, Jenkins, 1960, Roy Publishers, 1961; *The Pay-Grab Murders*, Jenkins, 1962; *The Traitors*, Jenkins, 1964; *Blueprint for Larceny*, Jenkins, 1964.

WORK IN PROGRESS: Several books.

SIDELIGHTS: Phillips writes about four books a year, most of them with an American background. Three have been published in nine countries, most of the others have gone into at least four translations (European languages). *Avocational interests:* Old gangster movies, cricket, conversation, steak.†

*   *   *

PHILLIPS, Herbert P.   1929-

PERSONAL: Born July 4, 1929, in Boston, Mass.; married Barbara Haxo, August 3, 1973; children: (previous marriage) Katherine Anne, Elizabeth Belle, Frederick Jonathan. *Education:* Harvard University, A.B., 1952; Cornell University, Ph.D., 1962. *Office:* Center for Southeast Asia Studies, Department of Anthropology, University of California, Berkeley, Calif. 94720.

CAREER: Harvard University, Cambridge, Mass., research analyst, Russian Research Center, 1952-53; Cornell University, Ithaca, N.Y., research analyst on Thailand Project, 1955, acting director of Cornell Research Center, Bangkok, Thailand, 1958; Michigan State University, East Lansing, assistant professor of anthropology, 1960-63; University of California, Berkeley, assistant professor, 1963-65, associate professor, 1965-72, professor of anthropology, 1972—, acting chairman, Center of South Asia Studies and Center for Southeast Asia Studies, 1964-65, chairman, Center for Southeast Asia Studies, 1965—, chairman, Committee for the Protection of Human Subjects, 1973—. Member, National Security Council, The White House, 1969.

MEMBER: American Anthropological Association, American Ethnological Society, Society for Applied Anthropology, Association for Asian Studies, Kroeber Anthropological Society, Siam Society, Phi Kappa Phi. *Awards, honors:* Fellowships from Ford Foundation foreign area research program, 1956-58, Fels Foundation, 1959-60, Rockefeller Foundation, 1965-66, National Science Foundation, 1969.

WRITINGS: (Contributor) *HRAF Thailand Handbook*, Human Relations Area File Press, 1956; (contributor) Richard N. Adams and Jack Preiss, editors, *Human Organization Research*, Dorsey, 1960; (contributor) Bert Kaplan, editor, *Studying Personality Cross-Culturally*, Row, Peterson & Co., 1961; (with David A. Wilson) *Certain Effects of Culture and Social Organization on Internal Security in Thailand*, RAND Corp., 1964; *Thai Peasant Personality*, University of California Press, 1965; (contributor) Jack M. Potter, May N. Diaz, and George M. Foster, editors, *Peasant Society: A Reader*, Little, Brown, 1967; (contributor) Hans Dieter-Evers, editor, *Loosely Structured Social Systems: Thailand in Comparative Perspective*, Yale University Southeast Asia Studies, 1969; (contributor) S. Siwark, editor, *Banyaachon Siam* (in Thai language, title means "Siamese Intellectuals"), Krungisam Press (Bangkok), 1970; (contributor) G. William Skinner, editor, *Aspects of Culture in Thailand and Laos: Homage to Lauriston Sharp*, Cornell University Press, 1974. Contributor to *Far Eastern Survey, Journal of Social Issues, Human Organization, American Anthropologist*, and other periodicals.

WORK IN PROGRESS: Field research on Siamese intellectuals; study of scholarly ethics and government research in Thailand.

*   *   *

PHILLIPS, Margaret Mann   1906-

PERSONAL: Born January 23, 1906, in Kimberworth, Yorkshire, England; daughter of Francis Arthur (a clergyman) and Martha Hannah (Haigh) Mann; married Charles William Phillips (an archaeology officer) July 3, 1940; children: John, Penelope. *Education:* Somerville College, Oxford, B.A., 1927, M.A., 1931; Sorbonne, University of Paris, Doctorat d'Universite, 1934. *Religion:* Anglican. *Home:* 103 Ditton Rd., Surbiton, Surrey, England. *Office:* King's College, Strand, London W.C.2, England.

CAREER: University of Bordeaux, Bordeaux, France, lectrice d'anglais, 1929-30; University of Manchester, Manchester, England, assistant lecturer in French, 1934-36; Newnham College, Cambridge University, Cambridge, England, director of studies in modern languages, 1936-45; University of London, King's College, London, England, lecturer in French, 1959-60, 1963-64, reader in French, 1964-68, honorary lecturer, University College, 1971—. *Member:* Modern Humanities Research Association, British Federation of University Women, Society of French Studies, Society of Renaissance Studies, Teilhard de Chardin Society. *Awards, honors:* Prix Bordin of Academie de Belles Lettres for *Erasme et les debuts de la Reforme francaise*; College de France, Medal, 1969.

WRITINGS: Erasme et les debuts de la Reforme francaise, H. Champion (Paris), 1933; *Outgoing*, Shakespeare Head Press, 1936; *Within the City Wall*, Cambridge University Press, 1943; *Erasmus and the Northern Renaissance*, English Universities Press, 1949, Collier, 1965; (contributor) *Courants religieux et Humanisme*, Presses Universitaires de France, 1959; (editor and translator) *The Adages of Erasmus*, Cambridge University Press, 1964;

Erasmus on His Times, Cambridge University Press, 1967; (contributor) John Olia, editor, *Luther, Erasmus, and the Reformation*, Fordham University Press, 1969; (contributor) T. Dorey, editor, *Erasmus*, Routledge & Kegan Paul, 1970. Contributor to scholarly periodicals in England and France.

WORK IN PROGRESS: Two studies on Erasmus, a work on the *Adagia*, and a collected works.

* * *

PIERCE, E(ugene) 1924-

PERSONAL: Born April 30, 1924, in Chickasha, Okla; son of Velner Pierce; married Gwendolyn Harris (a clinical psychologist), April 29, 1944; children: Carol Jean, David Brian. *Education:* University of Oklahoma, B.S., 1950; Indiana University, M.S. 1952, Ph.D., 1957. *Religion:* Congregationalist. *Home:* 512 Southwest Maplecrest Dr., Portland, Ore. *Office:* Portland State College, Portland, Ore.

CAREER: Georgetown University, Washington, D.C., assistant professor of linguistics, 1955-61; Portland State College, Portland, Ore., associate professor, 1961-65, professor of anthropology, 1965—. Reviser of English teaching program for Turkish Ministry of Education, and administrator and researcher for mass literacy program in Turkish Armed Service, 1955-61. *Military service:* U.S. Army, active duty, 1942-46, 1950-51; became second lieutenant. National Guard, 1946-50. *Member:* American Anthropological Association, Linguistic Society of America, American Oriental Society, American Academy of Political and Social Science, Northwestern Anthropological Association, New York Academy of Science, Sigma Xi.

WRITINGS: Life in a Turkish Village, Holt, 1964; *A Frequency Count of Turkish Words*, Turkish Ministry of Education, 1964; *The Development of a Mass Literacy Project in the Turkish Armed Services*, Center for Applied Linguistics, 1965; *Understanding the Middle East*, Tuttle (Tokyo), 1972. Contributor of articles to linguistic and anthropological journals.

WORK IN PROGRESS: A book, *Fuzzy Sets and Linguistic Theory*. Also, machine handling of human speech research, and the development of language skills in children under two years of age.

AVOCATIONAL INTERESTS: Writing novels and short stories (unpublished).

* * *

PIERCE, Willard Bob 1914-

PERSONAL: Born October 8, 1914, in Fort Dodge, Iowa; son of Fred and Flora Belle (Harlow) Pierce; married Ruth Lorraine Johnson; children: Sharon (Mrs. David Harfman), Marilee, Robin Lynn. *Education:* Attended Pasadena College. *Home:* 1310 Santa Margarita Dr., Arcadia, Calif. *Office:* 117 East Colorado Blvd., Pasadena, Calif.

CAREER: Ordained minister of Baptist Church. Served as war correspondent during Korean conflict. Associated with World Vision; co-founder, with Billy Graham and others, of Youth for Christ.

WRITINGS: This Way to Harvest, Zondervan, 1949; *The Untold Korea Story*, Zondervan, 1951; *Orphans of the Orient*, Zondervan, 1964; *Emphasizing Missions in the Local Church*, Zondervan, 1964.†

PILLAR, James Jerome 1928-

PERSONAL: Born April 26, 1928, in St. Paul, Minn.; son of Harry Martin and Gertrude D. (Swifka) Pillar. *Education:* Attended Oblate College, Washington, D.C., 1949-54; Catholic University of America, S.T.L., 1955; Pontifical Gregorian University, Rome, Italy, Ph.D., 1962; studied English literature at University of Ottawa, and French at Institute Catholique, Paris, France. *Home:* Loyola University, New Orleans, La. 70118.

CAREER: Roman Catholic priest, member of Oblate Fathers of Mary Immaculate; Our Lady of the Snows Scholasticate, Pass Christian, Miss., professor of church history, 1955-59, 1963-65; Loyola University, New Orleans, La., assistant professor of history, 1965—. Historian, Catholic Diocese of Natchez-Jackson, Miss.

WRITINGS: The Catholic Church in Mississippi, 1837-1865, Hauser Press, 1964.

WORK IN PROGRESS: A second volume of history of the Catholic Church in Mississippi, covering period 1865-1890.†

* * *

PIMSLEUR, Meira Goldwater

PERSONAL: Daughter of Michael (a designer) and Ada (Levenson) Goldwater; married Solomon Pimsleur (a composer-pianist) July 8, 1925 (died April 22, 1962); children: Paul, Joel. *Education:* Hunter College (now of the City University of New York), B.A., 1946; attended Columbia University School of Library Service, 1946-47. *Home:* 535 Cathedral Pkwy., New York, N.Y. 10025. *Office:* Oceana Publications Inc., Dobbs Ferry, N.Y.

CAREER: Columbia University, Law Library, New York, N.Y., acquisitions librarian, 1930-73. Cataloger for Brooklyn Law School Library, 1957-73, and Institute of Judicial Administration, 1952-60. *Member:* American Association of Law Libraries (chairman, foreign law committee, 1964-65), Law Library Association of Upstate New York (board of directors, 1964-65), Law Library Association of Greater New York (president, 1956-57), Phi Beta Kappa.

WRITINGS—Editor: (With J. M. Jacobstein) *Law Books in Print*, Volume I, Oceana, 1957, Volume II, 1959, Volume III, 1961, consolidated edition, 1965, 1969 (volumes published quarterly with annual cumulations, 1970—.) *Checklists of Basic American Legal Publications*, Rothman, 1962, supplements annually, 1963—.

WORK IN PROGRESS: Free-lance index preparation for law and other books.

* * *

PINCHER, H(enry) Chapman 1914-

PERSONAL: Born March 29, 1914, in Ambala, Punjab State, India; son of Richard Chapman (an army officer) and Helen (Foster) Pincher. *Education:* Attended University of London, 1932-36. *Home:* Lowerhouse Farm, Ewhurst, Surrey, England. *Office: Daily Express*, Fleet St., London E.C. 4, England.

CAREER: Daily Express, London, England, 1946—, assistant editor, chief defense correspondent. *Military service:* British Army, specialist on rocket weapons, 1940-46; became staff captain.

WRITINGS: Into the Atomic Age, Hutchinson, 1946; *Breeding of Farm Animals*, Penguin, 1946; *A Study of Fishes*, Doubleday, 1948; *Evolution*, Jenkins, 1950; *Spot-*

light on Animals, Hutchinson, 1950; *Not with a Bang* (novel), New American Libarary, 1965; *The Giantkiller*, Weidenfeld & Nicolson, 1967; *The Penthouse Conspirators*, M. Joseph, 1970; *Sex in Our Time*, Weidenfeld & Nicolson, 1973; *The Skeleton at the Villa Wolkonsky*, M. Joseph, 1974.

* * *

PINE, Leslie Gilbert 1907-
(Henry Moorshead)

PERSONAL: Born December 22, 1907, in Bristol, England; son of Henry Moorshead (a tea merchant) and Lilian Grace (Beswetherick) Pine; married Grace Violet Griffin, August 7, 1948; children: Richard Leslie. *Education:* University of London, B.A., 1931; Inner Temple, London, England, barrister-at-law, 1953. *Politics:* Liberal. *Religion:* Roman Catholic. *Home:* Bodiam, High St., Petworth, Sussex, England. *Agent:* Rupert Crew Ltd., King's Mews, Gray's Inn Rd., London W.C. 1, England.

CAREER: Burke's Peerage Ltd. (publishers), London, England, assistant editor, 1935-40, executive director, 1946-60; *Shooting Times*, London, managing editor, 1960-64; currently proprietor of grocery and provisions business, Petworth, Sussex, England. Conservative Parliamentary candidate, Bristol Central, 1959-1962; Liberal Parliamentary candidate, South Croydon, 1963, resigned as candidate, 1964. Church of England, diocesan lay reader, 1939-64. Lecturer on genealogy and heraldry. Freeman of City of London; liveryman of Glaziers' Company. *Military service:* Royal Air Force, 1942-46; served in North Africa, Italy, Greece, and India; became squadron leader.

MEMBER: Institute of Journalists (fellow; member of council, 1953; chairman of London district, 1957), Royal Society of St. George, Zoological Society of London (associate), Ancient Monuments Society (fellow), Society of Antiquaries (Scotland; fellow), Honorable Society of Cymmrodorion.

WRITINGS: The Middle Sea, Edward Stanford, 1950, revised edition, David & Charles, 1973; *The Story of Heraldry*, Country Life, 1952, revised edition, 1963; *The Golden Book of the Coronation*, Daily Mail, 1953; *Trace Your Ancestors*, Evans, 1953, 3rd edition, 1964; *They Came with the Conqueror*, Evans, 1954; *The Story of the Peerage*, Blackwood, 1956; *Tales of the British Aristocracy*, Burke Publishing Co., 1956; *Teach Yourself Heraldry and Genealogy*, English Universities Press, 1957; *The Twilight of Monarchy*, Burke Publishing Co., 1958; *Prince of Wales*, Jenkins, 1959; *A Guide to Titles*, Elliot, 1959.

Orders of Chivalry and Decorations of Honour of the World, 1960; *American Origins*, Doubleday, 1960; *Ramshackledom, A Critical Appraisal of the Establishment*, Secker & Warburg, 1962; *Your Family Tree*, Jenkins, 1962; *Questions and Answers*, Elliot, 1965; *Heirs of the Conqueror*, R. Hale, 1965; *The Story of Surnames*, Country Life, 1965, Tuttle, 1967; *After Their Blood: A Survey of Sports in Britain*, Kimber, 1966; *Tradition and Custom in Modern Britain*, Whiting & Wheaton, 1967; (translator) Jaques Maher, *Adam*, Editions du belier (Montreal), 1967; *The Genealogist's Encyclopedia*, Weybright, 1969; *The Story of Titles*, David & Charles, 1969, Tuttle, 1970; *Princes of Wales*, Tuttle, 1970; *The Highland Clans*, David & Charles, 1972; *The New Extinct Peerage, 1884-1971*, Heraldry Today, 1972, Genealogical Publishing, 1973. Also writer of four privately printed family histories.

Former editor: *Burke's Peerage*; *Burke's Landed Gentry* (Great Britain); *Burke's Landed Gentry of Ireland*; (and founder) *International Year Book and Statesman's Who's Who, Author's and Writer's Who's Who*; *Who's Who in Music*; *Who's Who in the Free Churches*; and various business books.

Contributor of more than two thousand articles, mainly historical, to English and worldwide press, including *Toronto Globe*, *Dominion* (New Zealand), *South African Argus*, *Melbourne Argus*, and *Svenska Dagbladet* (Sweden); articles on industry have appeared in *British Trades Journal*, *New Commonwealth*, and *Leather*.

WORK IN PROGRESS: A book on hunting.

AVOCATIONAL INTERESTS: Politics, gardening, motoring, and travel abroad.†

* * *

PINES, Maya

PERSONAL: Daughter of Joseph and Rachela Pines (now Mrs. Maurice Burawoy); married Joseph Froomkin (an economist), 1959; children: Michael, Daniel. *Education:* Attended Lycee Francais de Londres, London, England, Barnard College, B.A., 1947; Columbia University, M.A., 1949. *Office:* 4724 32nd St. N.W., Washington D.C. 20008.

CAREER: Women's National News Service, New York, N.Y., reporter, 1950-52; *Life*, New York, N.Y., reporter, 1952-60; now free-lance writer.

WRITINGS: (With photographer, Cornell Capa) *Retarded Children Can Be Helped*, Channel Press, (Manhasset, N.Y.), 1957; (with Rene Dubos) *Health and Disease*, Life Science Library, 1965; *Revolution in Learning: The Years From Birth to Six*, Harper, 1967; *The Brain Changers: Scientists and the New Mind Control*, Harcourt, 1973. Contributor to periodicals and newspapers, including *Harper's, McCall's, The New York Times Magazine*.

SIDELIGHTS: "A handful of creative psychologists, linguists, social scientists, maverick teachers and interested lay persons have been trying to discover how children learn and how they can be helped to learn more easily. *Revolution in Learning* is a passionate, intriguing report on a few of the discoveries made by some of these educational innovators. Its author, Maya Pines, is a perceptive observer who combines fluency with a sense of outrage at the irreparable damage done to millions of children by the system's failure to recognize the need for early intellectual stimulation," wrote Gloria Levitas in her review for *Book World*.

* * *

PITKIN, Walter, Jr. 1913-

PERSONAL: Born June 29, 1913, in Dover, N.J.; son of Walter Boughton (a writer and educator) and Mary (Gray) Pitkin; married Susan Kobbe (a librarian), August 5, 1940; children: Ann (Mrs. Ray Teitelbaum), John Richard, Stephen. *Education:* Columbia University, A.B., 1938. *Politics:* Democrat. *Home:* Good Hill Rd., Weston, Conn.

CAREER: Penguin Books, Inc., New York, N.Y., editor-in-chief, 1941-45; Bantam Books, Inc., New York, N.Y., vice-president and editor-in-chief, 1945-52, executive vice-president, 1952-54; The Map and Book Store, Westport, Conn., owner and manager, 1955-62; New York University, New York, N.Y., lecturer on paperback book publishing, 1962—. Consultant to book publishers. Chairman of Westport (Conn.) Democratic Town Committee, 1958-60, and of Friends of the Weston Public Library, 1963—. *Member:* Phi Beta Kappa.

WRITINGS: What's That Plane?, Penguin, 1942; *Life Begins at Fifty*, Simon & Schuster, 1965.

WORK IN PROGRESS: Continuous research in book publishing and in gerontology.

SIDELIGHTS: The title of Pitkin's 1965 book has a link to a best-seller of 1932, *Life Begins at Forty*, written by Walter Pitkin, Sr.†

*   *   *

PLAMENATZ, John Petrov   1912-

PERSONAL: Born May 16, 1912, in Cetinje, Montenegro (now Yugoslavia); son of Peter (a lawyer) and Liubitza (Matanovitch) Plamenatz; married Marjorie Hunter, September 21, 1943. *Education:* Oriel College, Oxford, B.A., 1934, M.A., 1937. *Religion:* Serbian Orthodox. *Home:* Scotland Mount, Hook Norton, Banbury, England. *Office:* Nuffield College, Oxford, England.

CAREER: Oxford University, Oxford, England, fellow of All Souls College, 1936-51, university lecturer in social and political theory, 1950-67, Chichele Professor of Social and Political Theory, 1967—, fellow of All Souls College, 1967—. Fellow of Nuffield College, 1951-67. *Member:* British Academy.

WRITINGS: Consent, Freedom and Political Obligation, Oxford University Press, 1938, 2nd edition, 1968; *The English Utilitarians*, Basil Blackwell, 1949, 2nd edition, 1958; *The Revolutionary Movement in France 1815-1871*, Longmans, Green, 1951; *German Marxism and Russian Communism*, Longmans, Green, 1954, Harper, 1965; *Alien Rule and Self-Government*, Longmans, Green, 1960; *Man and Society*, two volumes, Longmans, Green, 1963, McGraw, 1963; (editor) *Readings from Liberal Writers: English and French*, Barnes & Noble, 1965; *Ideology*, Praeger, 1970; *Democracy and Illusion: An Examination of Certain Aspects of Modern Democratic Theory*, Longman, 1973. Contributor to political journals.

SIDELIGHTS: Plamenatz is competent in French and Serbian, and knows some Italian and German.†

*   *   *

PLIMPTON, Ruth Talbot   1916-

PERSONAL: Born June 17, 1916, in Boston, Mass.; daughter of Fritz Bradley and Beatrice (Bill) Talbot; married Calvin Hastings Plimpton (president of Amherst College), September 6, 1941; children: David, Thomas, Anne, Edward. *Education:* Radcliffe College, B.S., 1939; Simmons College, M.A. in Social Work, 1941. *Religion:* Protestant. *Home:* 175 South Pleasant St., Amherst, Mass.

WRITINGS: Operation Crossroads Africa, Viking, 1962.†

*   *   *

PLOSS, Sidney I.   1932-

PERSONAL: Born August 19, 1932, in Brooklyn, N.Y.; son of Reuben (a physician) and Frieda (Busch) Ploss. *Education:* Syracuse University, A.B., 1953; University of London, Ph.D., 1957. *Home:* 5533 Dunsmore Rd., Alexandria, Va. *Office:* U.S. Department of State, Washington, D.C.

CAREER: Brooklyn College (now of the City University of New York), Brooklyn, N.Y., lecturer, 1958; University

of Oklahoma, Norman, visiting assistant professor, 1959; U.S. government, research specialist, 1960-61; Princeton University, Princeton, N.J., visiting associate, Center of International Studies, 1962-64; University of Pennsylvania, Philadelphia, assistant professor of political science, 1964-66; George Washington University, Washington, D.C., associate professor of political science, 1966-71; Harvard University, research fellow, 1971-72; U.S. Department of State, research specialist, 1972—. *Military service:* U.S. Army, 1957; second lieutenant. *Member:* Phi Beta Kappa.

WRITINGS: Conflict and Decision-making in Soviet Russia: A Case Study of Agricultural Policy, 1953-63, Princeton University Press, 1965; *The Soviet Political Process*, Ginn, 1971. Contributor to *New Leader, World Politics, Problems of Communism, Survey, Osteuropa*, and other publications.

WORK IN PROGRESS: A History of the Komsomol; research in Soviet policy analysis.

*   *   *

PLOWMAN, E(dward) Grosvenor   1899-

PERSONAL: Born December 16, 1899, in Brookline, Mass.; son of George T. (an artist) and Maude Houston (Bell) Plowman; married Genifred Homer, May 24, 1924; children: Nancy (Mrs. Robert Lawthers), Jeanne (Mrs. Roger Deschner). *Education:* Dartmouth College, B.S. (magna cum laude), 1921; Harvard University, part-time graduate study, 1921-22; University of Denver, M.S., 1936; University of Chicago, Ph.D., 1937. *Home:* 48 Partridge Circle, Portland, Me. 04102.

CAREER: Teacher in the business schools of Massachusetts Institute of Technology, Cambridge, 1921-23, Boston University, Boston, Mass., 1923-24, Babson Institute, Babson Park, Mass., 1924-30, University of Denver, 1930-32; Denver Municipal Water Utility, Denver, Colo., manager, 1933-36; Colorado Fuel and Iron Corp., Denver, Colo., traffic manager, 1937-43; U.S. Steel Corp., Pittsburgh, Pa., vice-president in charge of traffic, 1944-63; University of Maine, Portland, appointed lecturer, 1965—; Maine Transportation Commission, chairman, 1965-68; Maine Aeronautics Commission, chairman, 1967-68; Transportation Research Foundation, president, 1968-70, chairman, 1970-73; U.S. Department of Transportation, consultant, 1972—. U.S. government, traffic manager, Steel Division, War Production Board, 1942-43, director of Military Traffic Service, Department of Defense, 1950-52; deputy under-secretary for transportation policy, Department of Commerce, 1963-64. Vice-chairman of Denver Planning Commission, 1934-42, of Pittsburgh Port Authority, 1959-61. Visiting professor, Stanford University and Ohio State University.

MEMBER: American Statistical Association (fellow), American Association for the Advancement of Science (fellow), American Society of Traffic and Transportation (certified member; president, 1951-52), National Defense Transportation Association (president, 1953-54; chairman, 1955-57), Phi Beta Kappa (associate). *Awards, honors:* U.S. Department of Defense Award for Exceptional Civilian Service, 1952; Salzberg Transportation Medal, University of Syracuse, 1955; Seley Medal, Transportation Association of America, 1962; Sheahan Award, National Council of Physical Distribution Management, 1967; D.Sc., University of Maine, 1971.

WRITINGS: Municipal Water Utility Management, University of Chicago Press, 1937; (with Elmore Petersen)

Business Organization and Management, Irwin, 1942, 5th edition (with Joseph M. Trickett), 1963; *Elements of Business Logistics*, Stanford University Press, 1964; (editor) *Coordinated Transportation*, Cornell Maritime Press, 1969. Also editor of *Dartmouth Drawings*, 1970.

WORK IN PROGRESS: A study of his father's etchings and lithographs of New England Subjects.

BIOGRAPHICAL/CRITICAL SOURCES: Traffic World, November 3, 1953.

*   *   *

POLEMAN, Thomas T(heobald)   1928-

PERSONAL: Born November 28, 1928, in St. Louis, Mo.; son of Thomas Theobald (a businessman) and Georgia (Riddle) Poleman; married Charlotte Mallery, September 5, 1955; children: Carol, Clare, Walter, Thomas. *Education:* University of Missouri, B.S., 1951, M.S., 1952; Stanford University, M.A., 1957, Ph.D., 1960. *Home:* 155 North Sunset Dr., Ithaca, N.Y. *Office:* Department of Agriculture Economics, Cornell University, Ithaca, N.Y.

CAREER: National Research Council, Washington, D.C., professional associate, 1959-60; Stanford University, Stanford, Calif., research associate, 1959-61; U.S. government, Washington, D.C., senior economist, 1961-63; Cornell University, Ithaca, N.Y., professor of international agricultural economics, 1963—. Consultant to Food and Agriculture Organization of the U.N., U.S. Department of Agriculture, and Peace Corps. *Military service:* U.S. Air Force, 1952-54; became first lieutenant. *Member:* American Economic Association, American Farm Economic Association, African Studies Association.

WRITINGS: The Food Economics of Urban Tropical Africa: The Case of Ghana, Food Research Institute, 1961; *The Papaloapan Project: Agricultural Development in the Mexican Tropics*, Stanford University Press, 1964; (contributor) V. F. Amann and D.G.R. Belshaw, editors, *Nutrition and Food in an African Economy*, Makere University (Uganda), 1972; (editor with D. K. Freebairn) *Food, Population, and Employment: The Impact of the Green Revolution*, Praeger, 1973; (with W. M. Beeghly, Peter Matlon, and Andrew McGregor) *Bio-Economics: Applications of Vital-Rate Monitoring in Developing Countries*, Praeger, 1974. Also author of monographs and articles on the food economies of developing nations. Co-editor, *East Africa Journal of Rural Development*.

WORK IN PROGRESS: Studies on evaluation and improvement of agricultural statistics in tropical countries, on economics of pioneer settlement in the tropics, on economics of tropical agricultural commodities, and on agricultural implications of rapid urbanization in the tropics.

SIDELIGHTS: Poleman has traveled on professional research in Central America, eastern and western Africa, and in eight Asian countries.

*   *   *

POLISH, David   1910-

PERSONAL: Born January 15, 1910; son of Morris (a merchant) and Mollie (Feinberg) Polish; married Aviva (a teacher), June 26, 1938. *Education:* Attended Western Reserve University (now Case Western Reserve University), 1926-28; University of Cincinnati, B.A., 1931; Hebrew Union College-Jewish Institute of Religion, Cincinnati, Ohio, Rabbi, 1934, D.H.C., 1941. *Home:* 1200 Lee St., Evanston, Ill. *Office:* 1200 Dempster St., Evanston, Ill.

CAREER: Rabbi, 1934—; Beth Emet Synagogue, Evanston, Ill., founding rabbi, 1950—. Visiting lecturer, Garrett Theological Seminary, 1955—; former president, Central Conference of American Rabbis; founder and former president, Chicago Board of Rabbis.

WRITINGS: (With Frederick Dippell) *A Guide for Reform Jews*, Bloch, 1957; *Eternal Dissent: A Search for Meaning in Jewish History*, Abelard, 1959; *The Higher Freedom: A New Turning Point in Jewish History*, Quadrangle Books, 1965; *A S'lichot Service*, Ktav, 1973. Contributor of articles to various periodicals. Member of editorial board, Central Conference of American Rabbis.

*   *   *

POLITELLA, Dario   1921-
(Tony Granite, David Stewart)

PERSONAL: Surname is pronounced Paul-ih-*tel*-ah; born August 12, 1921, in Lawrence, Mass.; son of Antonio (a salesman) and Caterina (Ionta) Politella; married Frances Charlotte O'Neal, October 5, 1942; children: Darian Susan, Dario Anthony, Daria Kay. *Education:* University of Massachusetts, A.B., 1947; Syracuse University, M.A., 1949, Ph.D., 1965. *Politics:* Independent. *Religion:* Episcopalian. *Home:* 2009 Lincolnshire Dr., Muncie, Ind. 47304. *Office:* Ball State University, Muncie, Ind. 47306.

CAREER: Geneva Daily Times, Geneva, N.Y., bureau manager, 1949-50; Kent State University, Kent, Ohio, assistant professor of journalism, 1950-55; Syracuse University, Syracuse, N.Y., instructor in journalism, 1955-57; *Flying*, New York, N.Y., associate editor, 1957-58; O. S. Tyson & Co., Inc., New York, N.Y., publicity account executive, 1958-60; Lockheed Aircraft Service Co., New York, N.Y., public relations representative, 1960-62; Ball State University, Muncie, Ind., assistant professor of journalism, 1962—. Summer work as an industrial publicist, managing editor of *Skyways*, and as television writer for Columbia Broadcasting System. Correspondent, *Lawrence Evening Tribune*, Lawrence, Mass., 1938-39, *Boston Herald*, 1946-47. *Military service:* U.S. Army, field artilleryman and army aviator, 1942-46, 1951-52; became first lieutenant; received Bronze Star, Air Medal with cluster, European Theater Medal with two battle stars, Korea Service Medal with battle star.

MEMBER: National Council of College Publications Advisers (founder, 1954; national vice-chairman, 1956), Aviation/Space Writers Association, Army Aviation Association of America, Future Journalists of America (honorary), Sigma Delta Chi, Alpha Phi Gamma, Correspondents' Club (Seoul).

WRITINGS: Operation Grasshopper (history of army light plane operations in Korea), Robert R. Longo Co., 1958; (editor) *Directory of the College Student Press in America*, Taylor, 1967, 2nd edition, Oxbridge, 1970; *My Sunderland: Quarter-millennial Souvenir*, two volumes, The 250 Years of Sunderland Committee, 1968; *The Illustrated Anatomy of Campus Humor*, Syllabus Publications, 1971.

Co-author of aviation section, *Book of Knowledge*, 1964, and author of three booklets, including an epic poem. Writer for radio shows and television. Contributor, sometimes under pseudonyms, to more than twenty-five magazines and newspapers, among them *Car Life, Reader's Digest, American Mercury, Editor and Publisher, The Quill, Air Facts, U.S. Army Aviation Digest, Collegiate*

Journalist. Editor, *Black and White* (Alpha Phi Gamma magazine), 1962-63, *Collegiate Journalist*, 1963—.

WORK IN PROGRESS: Make It a Feature; *Patterns of Student Press Freedom in America.*†

* * *

POLLACK, Norman 1933-

PERSONAL: Born May 29, 1933, in Bridgeport, Conn.; son of Benjamin and Mary (Beimel) Pollack; married Nancy Bassing, February 2, 1957; children: Peter Franklin. *Education:* University of Florida, B.A., 1954; Stanford University, graduate study, 1954-56; Harvard University, A.M., 1957, Ph.D., 1961. *Religion:* Jewish. *Office:* Department of History, Yale University, New Haven, Conn.

CAREER: Yale University, New Haven, Conn., assistant professor of history, 1961—. *Member:* American Federation of Teachers. *Awards, honors:* Morse Faculty Fellow, Yale University, 1964-65.

WRITINGS: The Populist Response to Industrial America, Harvard University Press, 1962; (editor with Frank Freidel) *Builders of American Institutions*, Rand McNally, 1962, 2nd edition, 1972; (editor with Freidel) *American Issues in the Twentieth Century*, Rand McNally, 1966; (editor) *The Populist Mind*, Bobbs-Merrill, 1967. Contributor to national and regional history journals.

WORK IN PROGRESS: A book on southern Populism; a book on sources of authoritarianism in American society.†

* * *

POLLARD, William G(rosvenor) 1911-

PERSONAL: Born April 6, 1911, in Batavia, N.Y.; son of Arthur Lewis (a mycologist and sales engineer) and Ethel (Hickox) Pollard; married Marcella Hamilton, December 27, 1932; children: William Grosvenor III, Arthur Lewis II, James H. (deceased), Frank H. *Education:* University of Tennessee, B.A., 1932; Rice Institute (now Rice University), M.A., 1934, Ph.D., 1935. *Politics:* Democrat. *Home:* 191 Outer Dr., Oak Ridge, Tenn., 37830. *Office:* Oak Ridge Associated Universities, P.O. Box 117, Oak Ridge, Tenn. 37831.

CAREER: University of Tennessee, Knoxville, assistant professor, 1936-41, associate professor, 1941-43, professor of physics, 1943-46; Oak Ridge Institute of Nuclear Studies (now Oak Ridge Associated Universities), Oak Ridge, Tenn., incorporator, 1946, and executive director, 1947—. The Protestant Episcopal Church, ordained deacon, 1952, priest, 1954; priest associate of St. Stephen's Church, Oak Ridge, Tenn., 1954—; priest in charge of St. Alban's Chapel, Clinton, Tenn., 1959-65. Columbia University, research scientist, 1944-45; University of the South, member of faculty, Graduate School of Theology, 1956, 1960, 1961, trustee, 1955-70.

MEMBER: American Physical Society (fellow; chairman of southeastern section, 1951-52), American Association for the Advancement of Science (fellow), American Nuclear Society (fellow; member of first board of directors, 1955-60), Tennessee Academy of Science, Phi Beta Kappa, Sigma Xi, Phi Kappa Phi, Sigma Pi Sigma, Beta Gamma Sigma. *Awards, honors:* Distinguished Service Award, Southern Association of Science and Industry, 1950; Semicentennial Medal of Honor, Rice University, 1962. Honorary D.Sc. from Ripon College, 1951, University of the South, 1952, Kalamazoo College, 1955; D.D. from Hobart College, 1956, Grinnell College, 1957; LLD. from Univer-

sity of Chattanooga, 1958, Kenyon College, 1964; L.H.D., Keuka College, 1962, Long Island University, 1965; Seattle Pacific College, 1969; Westminister College, 1969.

WRITINGS: (Author of introductions) *The Hebrew Iliad*, translated by R.H. Pfeiffer, Harper, 1957; (principal author) *The Christian Idea of Education* (Kent School Anniversary seminar) Part I, edited by Edmond Fuller, Yale University Press, 1957; *Chance and Providence*, Scribner, 1958; *Physicist and Christian*, Seabury, 1962; *Atomic Energy and Southern Science*, Oak Ridge Associated Universities, 1966; *Man on a Spaceship*, Claremount University Center, 1967; *Science and Faith: Twin Mysteries*, Nelson, 1970.

Contributor: James Pike, editor, *Modern Canterbury Pilgrims*, Morehouse, 1956; Edmund Fuller, editor, *Schools and Scholarship*, (Part II of *The Christian Idea of Education*), Yale University Press, 1962; Stephen Bayne, editor, *Space Age Christianity*, Morehouse, 1963; Frank Cellier, editor, *Liturgy Is Mission*, Seabury, 1964; *Religion and the University*, University of Toronto Press, 1964; Michael Hamilton, editor, *This Little Planet*, Scribner, 1970; E. Berkeley Tompkins, editor, *Peaceful Change In Modern Society*, Hoover Institution Press, 1971; Ian G. Barbour, editor, *Earth Might Be Fair*, Prentice-Hall, 1972. Contributor to university centennial publications.

BIOGRAPHICAL/CRITICAL SOURCES: "A Deacon in Oak Ridge," *New Yorker*, February 7, 1943 (reprinted in Daniel Lang's *The Man in the Thick Lead Suit*, Oxford University Press, 1954, and *From Hiroshima to the Moon*, Simon & Schuster, 1959).

* * *

POLNER, Murray 1928-

PERSONAL: Surname is pronounced *Pole*-ner; born May 15, 1928, in Brooklyn, N.Y.; son of Alex (a salesman) and Rebecka (Meyerson) Polner; married Louise Greenwald, June 16, 1950; children: Beth, Alex, Robert. *Education:* City College (now City College of the City University of New York), B.S.S., 1950; University of Pennsylvania, M.A., 1951; Columbia University, graduate study, 1951-53, 1955-57; Columbia University, certificate, 1967; Antioch College, Ph.D., 1972. *Politics:* Independent. *Religion:* Jewish. *Home:* 50-10 Concord Ave., Great Neck, N.Y. *Agent:* Nannine Joseph, 200 West 54th St., New York, N.Y. 10019.

CAREER: Queens College (now of the City University of New York), Flushing, N.Y., lectures in history and contemporary civilization. Associate professor of history at: Suffolk Community College, Lake Ronkonkoma, N.Y.; University of Maine; and University of Prince Edward Island, Charlottetown. New York Public Schools, executive assistant to chancellor. Vice-president and executive editor of Teachers Practical Press, Inc., and of Schain & Polner, Inc. (trade publishers). *Military service:* U.S. Naval Reserve, 1947-52. U.S. Army, 1953-55.

WRITINGS: Enriching Social Studies, Prentice-Hall, 1961; (with Arthur Barron) *Where Shall We Take the Kids?*, Doubleday, 1961; (with Barron) *The Questions Children Ask*, Macmillan, 1964; (with Robert Schain) *The Use of Effective Discipline*, Prentice-Hall, 1964; *Reflections of a Russian Statesman*, University of Michigan Press, 1965; (editor) *The Conquest of Spain and Other Essays of William Graham Sumner*, Regnery, 1965; *No Victory Parades: The Return of the Vietnam Veteran*, Holt, 1971; *When Can I Come Home: A Debate on Am-*

nesty for Exiles, Antiwar Prisoners and Others, Doubleday, 1972. Contributor to New Republic, New York Times Book Review, Commonweal, Christian Century, South Atlantic Quarterly, New York Herald Tribune, and other journals and newspapers. Editor, Present Tense.

WORK IN PROGRESS: Writing a biography of Dorothea Dix.

* * *

POND, Grace (Isabelle) 1910-

PERSONAL: Born May 20, 1910, in London, England; children: Ian Allan, Robin Allan. Education: Educated in English schools. Religion: Church of England. Home: Barbeeches, Buchan Hill, Crawley, Sussex, England.

CAREER: Cat breeder, specializing in Persians; organizer of National Cat Clubs Show in England, and cat show judge in England, Scotland, and Continental Europe. Member: Zoological Society (fellow).

WRITINGS: Observer Book of Cats, Warne, 1959; Cats, Arco, 1962; Persian Cats, Foyle, 1963; The Perfect Cat Owner, Museum Press, 1966; The Long-haired Cats, A. S. Barnes, 1968; Pet Library's Complete Cat Guide, Pet Library, 1968; The Batsford Book of Cats, Batsford, 1969, published as The Arco Book of Cats, Arco, 1970; The Complete Cat Encyclopedia, Crown, 1972; (with Catherine Mill Ing) Champion Cats of the World, St. Martin's Press, 1972; (with Alison Ashford) Rex, Abyssinian and Turkish Cats, Arco, 1974. Editor, Cat Lovers' Diary (annual), Collins. Contributor to Chambers's Encyclopaedia, Sunday Times (London), Our Cats, and other periodicals.†

* * *

PONSONBY, Frederick Edward Neuflize 1913-
(Tenth Earl of Bessborough)

PERSONAL: Born March 29, 1913, in London, England; son of ninth Earl of Bessborough and Roberte (de Neuflize); married Mary Munn (an American), 1949; children: Lady Charlotte Ponsonby. Education: Attended Eton College; Trinity College, Cambridge, M.A. Home: Stansted Park, Rowlands Castle, Hampshire, England. Agent: A. D. Peters, 10 Buckingham St., Adelphi, London W.C. 2, England.

CAREER: Tenth Earl of Bessborough, succeeding father to title, 1956. Actor in theatrical productions, 1928-38; League of Nations High Commission for Refugees, secretary, 1936-39; British Embassy, Paris, France, second, later first, secretary, 1944-49; director of music and television companies, including Associated Television Ltd., London, England, 1955-63; member of House of Lords, 1956—, serving as undersecretary for Science and Education, 1963-64, spokesman for Conservative party on science, technology, energy, foreign, and commonwealth affairs, 1964-70, deputy chairman of Metrication Board, 1969-70, Minister of State for Technology, 1970, chairman of committee of enquiry into research associations, 1972-73, vice-president of European Parliament and deputy leader of European Conservative group, 1972—. British Society for International Understanding, chairman of board of governors, 1939-70; International Atlantic Committee, chairman, 1952-55. Chichester Festival Theatre Trust Ltd., chairman of trustees, 1960—. Military service: British Army, 1939-43; served in France, Flanders, at Dunkirk, and in Africa; became major.

MEMBER: Royal Geographical Society (fellow), Royal Institution, English Stage Society (president), Men of the Trees, Turf Club, Garrick Club. Awards, honors: Officer of Order of St. John of Jerusalem; Chevalier of the Legion of Honor (France).

WRITINGS: (With Muriel Jenkins) Nebuchadnezzar (play), 1939; The Four Men (play; an adaptation after Hilaire Belloc), 1951; Triptych (plays; comprising "Like Stars Appearing," 1953, "The Noon Is Night," 1954, and "Darker the Sky") Theatre Arts, 1955; A Place in the Forest, Batsford, 1958; Return to the Forest, Weidenfeld & Nicolson, 1962. Contributor of articles and reviews to journals.

* * *

POOLER, Victor H(erbert), Jr. 1924-

PERSONAL: Born February 10, 1924, in Brewer, Me.; son of Victor Herbert and Mary (Luosey) Pooler; married Anne Mehlhorn, June 23, 1951; children: David, Steven, Kevin, Thomas. Education: University of Cincinnati, student, 1943; University of Maine, B.S. in Mechanical Engineering, 1949; special courses at other universities. Home: 1 North Ridge, DeWitt, N.Y. 13214. Office: Carrier Air Conditioning Co., Carrier Pkwy., Syracuse, N.Y. 13201.

CAREER: Professional engineer, licensed in state of New York, 1957. Ingersoll-Rand Co., Painted Post, N.Y., variously engineering estimator, designer, and buyer, 1949-57, plant senior buyer, 1957-59; Carrier Air Conditioning Co., Syracuse, N.Y., purchasing agent, 1959-61, purchasing manager, 1961-67, director of purchasing, 1967—. Civic Music Association, Corning, N.Y., director, 1950-51. Military service: U.S. Army Air Forces, 1943-45; became first lieutenant. Member: National Association of Purchasing Agents (director of Elmira chapter, 1956-59; president of Syracuse and Central New York chapter, 1963-64; national vice-president, 1971), National Management Association, Carrier Management Club, American Management Association. Awards, honors: Erlicher Award for outstanding service to purchasing profession.

WRITINGS: Developing the Negotiating Skills of the Buyer, American Management Association Bulletin, 1964; The Purchasing Man and His Job, American Management Association, 1964; (editor and contributor) Purchasing Handbook, revised edition, McGraw, 1973. Also co-author of Fundamentals of Effective Buying; writer of movie script and LP recording. Contributor to Purchasing. Associate editor, National Association of Purchasing Agents's Journal of Purchasing and Materials Management.

* * *

POPESCU, Christine 1930-
(Christine Pullein-Thompson; Christine Keir, pseudonym)

PERSONAL: Born October 1, 1930, in Surrey, England; daughter of H. J. (an army officer) and Joanna (an author; maiden name, Cannan) Pullein-Thompson; married Julian John Hunter Popescu (an author and journalist); children: Philip Hunter, Charlotte Vivien, Mark Cannan, Lucy Joanna. Education: Attended English schools. Religion: Church of England. Home: Highfield, Middle Assendon, Henley on Thames, England. Agent: Rosica Colin, 4 Hereford Square, London S.W.7, England.

CAREER: Grove Riding Schools Ltd., Peppard and Oxford, England, director, 1945-55.

WRITINGS—Children's books; all under name Christine

Pullein-Thompson, except as indicated: (With sisters, Josephine and Diane Pullein-Thompson) *It Began with Picotee*, A. & C. Black, 1946; *We Rode to the Sea*, Collins, 1948; *We Hunted Hounds*, Collins, 1949, Armada, 1964.

I Carried the Horn, Collins, 1951; *Goodbye to Hounds*, Collins, 1952, Armada, 1965; *Riders From Afar*, Collins, 1954; *Phantom Horse*, Collins, 1955; *A Day to Go Hunting*, Collins, 1956; *The First Rosette*, Burke Publishing Co., 1956; *Stolen Ponies*, Collins, 1957; (under pseudonym Christine Keir) *The Impossible Horse*, Evans Brothers, 1957, reissued under name Christine Pullein-Thompson, Granada, 1972; *The Second Mount*, Burke Publishing Co., 1957; *Three to Ride*, Burke Publishing Co., 1958; *The Lost Pony* (also see below), Burke Publishing Co., 1959.

Ride by Night, Collins, 1960; *The Horse Sale*, Collins, 1960; *Giles and the Elephant*, Burke Publishing Co., 1960; *For Want of a Saddle*, Burke Publishing Co., 1960, Granada, 1972; *The Empty Field*, Burke Publishing Co., 1961; *Giles and the Greyhound*, Burke Publishing Co., 1961; *The Open Gate*, Burke Publishing Co., 1962; *Bandits in the Hills*, Hamish Hamilton, 1962; *The Gipsy Children*, Hamish Hamilton, 1962; *Giles and the Canal*, Burke Publishing Co., 1962; *Homeless Katie*, Hamish Hamilton, 1963; *The Doping Affair*, Burke Publishing Co., 1963, Atlantic Book, 1968; *No One at Home*, Hamish Hamilton, 1964; *The Eastmans in Brittany*, Burke Publishing Co., 1964; (with others) *Triple Adventure*, contains *The Lost Pony*, Burke Publishing Co., 1964; *Granny Comes to Stay*, Hamish Hamilton, 1964; *The Eastmans Move House*, Burke Publishing Co., 1964; *The Boys from the Cafe*, Hamish Hamilton, 1965; *The Eastmans Find a Boy*, Burke Publishing Co., 1966; *The Stolen Car*, Hamish Hamilton, 1966; *A Day to Remember*, Hamish Hamilton, 1966; *The Lost Cow*, Hamish Hamilton, 1966; *Little Black Pony*, Hamish Hamilton, 1966; *Robbers in the Night*, Hamish Hamilton, 1967; *Room to Let*, Hamish Hamilton, 1968; *Dog in a Pram*, Hamish Hamilton, 1969; *Nigel Eats His Words*, Burke Publishing Co., 1969.

(Compiler) *Horses and Their Owners*, Nelson, 1970; *Phantom Horse Comes Home*, Collins, 1970; *Riders on the March*, Armada, 1970; *They Rode to Victory*, Armada, 1972; (editor) *The First Pony Scrap Book*, Pan Books, 1972; *Phantom Horse Goes to Ireland*, Collins, 1972; (editor) *The Second Pony Scrap Book*, Pan Books, 1973; *I Rode a Winner*, Collins, 1973; *The Follyfoot Horse and Pony Quiz Book*, Pan Books, 1974; *A Pony to Love*, Pan Books, 1974; *The Black Beauty Clan*, Brockhampton Press, 1974.

WORK IN PROGRESS: A book on riding horses.

*   *   *

POPPINO, Rollie E(dward)   1922-

PERSONAL: Surname is accented on first syllable; born October 4, 1922, in Portland, Ore.; son of Rollie B. and Greta (McFeron) Poppino; married Lois Lamberson, June 17, 1950; children: Richard Rollie, Margaret Lois, Steven Lamberson. *Education:* Attended Multnomah Junior College, Portland, Ore., 1941-42, and Oregon State College (now University), 1942-44, 1946; Stanford University, A.B., 1948, M.A., 1949, Ph.D., 1953. *Religion:* Protestant. *Home:* 1221 Eureka Ave., Davis, Calif. *Office:* Department of History, University of California, Davis, Calif. 95616.

CAREER: Stanford University, Stanford, Calif., instructor in history, 1953-54; U.S. Department of State, Washington,

D.C., intelligence research specialist, 1954-61; University of California, Davis, professor of history, 1961—. *Military service:* U.S. Army, 1942-45; served in Europe. *Member:* American Historical Association, Conference on Latin American History, Pacific Coast Council of Latin American Studies, Instituto Historico e Geografico Brasileiro. *Awards, honors:* Social Science Research Council-American Council of Learned Societies, fellowship, 1963, travel grant, 1967-68; National Endowment for the Humanities fellowship, 1967-68; Colar D. Pedro I (Brazil), 1972; Fulbright lectureship in Brazil, 1974.

WRITINGS: International Communism in Latin America: A History of the Movement, 1917-1963, Free Press of Glencoe, 1964; (contributor) Jose Marie Bello, *A History of Modern Brazil, 1889-1964*, Stanford University Press, 1966; *Feira de Santana*, Editora Itapua (Brazil), 1968; *Brazil: The Land and People*, Oxford University Press, 1968, 2nd edition, 1973; (contributor) W. S. Sworakowski, editor, *World Communism: A Handbook, 1918-1965*, Hoover Institution, 1973. Contributor of articles and reviews to historical journals.

WORK IN PROGRESS: A book, *The Vargas Era in Brazil*.

SIDELIGHTS: Poppino has traveled in Latin America since 1950. He is competent in Portuguese, Spanish, and French.

*   *   *

POSIN, Jack A.   1900-

PERSONAL: Surname is pronounced *Pose*-in; born February 4, 1900, in Askhabad, Russia; son of Abram D. (a clerk) and Anna (Isretz) Posin; married Frances Perstein. *Education:* University of California, Berkeley, A.B., 1933, M.A., 1935, Ph.D., 1939. *Politics:* Democrat. *Home:* 698 Matadero Ave., Palo Alto, Calif. 94306.

CAREER: Cornell University, Ithaca, N.Y., instructor in Russian language and literature, 1939-42; University of Iowa, Iowa City, assistant professor of Russian, 1942-44; University of Colorado, Boulder, associate professor of Russian and head of Russian department of U.S. Navy Language School, 1944-46; Stanford University, Stanford, Calif., associate professor, 1946-56, professor of Russian, 1956-65, professor emeritus, 1965—; University of Massachusetts, Amherst, professor and head of department of Slavic Languages and Literatures, 1966-68. Visiting summer professor, University of California, Los Angeles, 1948. *Member:* Modern Language Association of America, American Association of Teachers of Slavonic and East European Languages (vice-president, 1950-51), American Association of University Professors, Philological Association of the Pacific Coast, Stanford Philological Association.

WRITINGS: (Contributor) E. Simmons, editor, *Slavic Studies*, Cornell University Press, 1953; (contributor) C. Laird, editor, *The World Through Literature*, Appleton, 1951; *Beginners' Russian*, Heath, 1964; (annotator, and author of introduction) Turgenev, *Fathers and Sons* (in Russian), Bradda Books, 1970. Contributor of essays and articles to *Russian Review, Slavonic Review*, and other professional periodicals.

SIDELIGHTS: Posin is bilingual in Russian and English, competent in French and German, and knows some Italian. He has traveled in European and Asiatic Russia, western Europe, Japan, and China.

POSPISIL, J(aroslav) Leopold 1923-

PERSONAL: Born April 26, 1923, in Olomouc, Czechoslovakia; came to United States in 1949, naturalized in 1954; son of Leopold and Ludmila (Petrlak) Pospisil; married Zdenka Smydova (a college teacher of art), January 30, 1945; children: Zdenka, Miraslava. Education: Real-Gymnasium, Olomouc, Czechoslovakia, Mat.Ex. (B.A.), 1942; Charles University, J.U.C., 1947; Masaryk's University, advanced study, 1948-49; Willamette University, B.A., 1950; University of Oregon, M.A., 1952; Yale University, Ph.D., 1956. Home: 554 Orange St., New Haven, Conn. Office: Department of Anthropology, Yale University, Hillhouse 51, New Haven, Conn.

CAREER: Practiced law in Olomouc, Czechslovakia, 1947-48; Yale University, New Haven, Conn., instructor in anthropology, 1956-57, assistant professor, 1957-60, associate professor, 1960—, assistant curator of Peabody Museum, 1956-60, associate curator, 1960—. Field investigations in anthropology in Arizona, 1952, in West New Guinea, 1954-55, 1959, 1962, in Alaska, 1957, in North Tirol, Austria, 1962-63, 1964. Member: American Anthropological Association (fellow), Czechoslovak Academy of Arts and Sciences (Washington, D.C.), National Geographic Society, Archeological Society of Connecticut (secretary, 1956-60), Sigma Xi. Awards, honors: Grant-in-aid from Arctic Institute of America, 1957, from Social Science Research Council, 1959, 1962, National Science Foundation, 1962, 1964; Ford Foundation fellowship, 1954-55; Senior Sterling fellowship, 1955; American Philosophical Society fellowship, 1959, 1962; Guggenheim fellowship, 1962.

WRITINGS: Kapauku Papuans and Their Law, Yale University Publications in Anthropology, Volume LIV, 1956; Kapauku Papuan Economy, Yale University Publications in Anthropology, Volume LXVII, 1963; The Kapauku Papuans of West New Guinea, Holt, 1963; (contributor) W. H. Goodenough, editor, Explorations in Cultural Anthropology: Essays in Honor of George Peter Murdock, McGraw, 1964; (contributor) James Clifton, editor, Introduction to Cultural Anthropology: Essays in the Scope and Methods of the Science of Man, Houghton, 1968; Anthropology of Law, Harper, 1971. Contributor to Encyclopedia of Social Sciences and of more than thirty articles and reviews to American Anthropologist, Oceania, Nature, Pacific Affairs, other journals.

WORK IN PROGRESS: Tiroleau Peasant Economy and continuing investigations of culture change among the Kapauku Papuans in New Guinea and of law and social control in a Tirolean peasant village.

SIDELIGHTS: Pospisil escaped from Czechoslavakia for political reasons after the Communist coup in 1948, and once in the U.S. he went through seven more years of study with the aid of scholarships and fellowships, 1949-56. He speaks, reads, and writes Czech, Slovak, German, English, French, Kapauku Papuan; reads Spanish and Latin; understands Polish and Russian.

Pospisil expected to wind up his study of the effects of western civilization on the Kapauku Papuans with a field session in 1974. He spent the summer of 1965 on his other field study in Austria.

*   *   *

POSTER, Cyril D(ennis) 1924-

PERSONAL: Surname rhymes with "foster"; born September 5, 1924, in London, England; son of Harry (a businessman) and Anna (Solomons) Poster; married Doreen Hoyle, June 6, 1947; children: Jeremy, Lyn,, Sara, Zoe, David. Education: Pembroke College, Cambridge, B.A. (honors), 1948, M.A., 1951; Institute of Education, University of London, Postgraduate Teachers Certificate, 1949, Academic Diploma in Education, 1952. Religion: Quaker. Residence: Isle of Sheppey.

CAREER: Cambridgeshire Village College, Bottisham, Cambridgeshire, England, schoolmaster, 1949-55; Willenhall School, Willenhall, Staffordshire, England, deputy headmaster, 1955-59; Lawrence Weston School, Bristol, England, headmaster, 1959-69. Southwest Examinations Board, chairman of examining committee, 1964-65, chairman of governing council, 1965—. Military service: Indian Army, 1943-47; became major. Member: National Union of Teachers, School Libraries Association, Bristol Head Teachers' Association.

WRITINGS: Read, Write, Speak, two books and teacher handbook, Cambridge University Press, 1964; (reviser) E. Albert, The Story of English Literature, Collins, 1965; The School and the Community, Macmillan, 1971. Author of one-act plays and adapter of a seventeenth-century play, "Knight of the Burning Pestle." Contributor of articles and reviews to educational press, especially Use of English.

WORK IN PROGRESS: A book with proposed title To Everything a Season, for Collins.

SIDELIGHTS: Poster speaks French and Hindustani.†

*   *   *

POTTER, A(lfred) Neal 1915-

PERSONAL: Born March 22, 1915, in Arlington, Va.; son of Alden A. (a farmer) and Charlotte (Waugh) Potter; married Marion Esch, July 6, 1940; children: Joanne, Freda May. Education: Johns Hopkins University, student, 1933-35; University of Minnesota, B.A., 1937, M.A., 1940; University of Chicago, graduate study 1940. Politics: Democrat. Religion: Methodist. Home: 6801 Brookville Rd., Chevy Chase, Md. 20015. Office: Resources for the Future, Inc., 1755 Massachusetts Ave., N.W., Washington, D.C. 20036.

CAREER: U.S. Office of Price Administration, Washington, D.C., head of Income Analysis Unit, 1941-46; Washington State College (now University), Pullman, assistant professor of economics, 1947-51; United World Federalists, Richland, Wash., field director, 1951-54; Resources for the Future, Inc., Washington, D.C., research associate, 1956—. President of Washington chapter, United World Federalists, 1957, of Montgomery County Citizens Planning Association, 1965, of Montgomery County Council, 1973; chairman of Transportation Planning Board, Metropolitan Washington Council of Governments. Member: Society for International Development, Adult Education Association of the U.S.A., Phi Beta Kappa.

WRITINGS: (With Francis T. Christy, Jr.) Trends in Natural Resource Commodities, 1870-1957, Johns Hopkins Press, 1962; (with Joseph L. Fisher) World Prospects for Natural Resources, Johns Hopkins Press, 1964; (contributor) Philip Houser, editor, The Population Dilemma, Prentice-Hall, 1963; (contributor) Goals, Priorities, and Dollars, National Planning Association, 1966; Natural Resource Potentials of the Antarctic, American Geographic Society, 1969; (contributor) Rapid Population Growth, two volumes, Johns Hopkins Press for National

Academy of Science, 1971. Managing editor, *Federal Union World*, 1943-45.

WORK IN PROGRESS: An update of *Trends in National Resource Commodities.*

AVOCATIONAL INTERESTS: Peace through world government, politics.

* * *

POTTER, Margaret (Newman) 1926-
(Anne Betteridge)

PERSONAL: Born June 21, 1926, in London, England; daughter of Bernard and Marjory (Donald) Newman; married R. Jeremy Potter (a publisher), 1950; children: Jocelyn, Jonathan. *Education:* St. Hugh's College, Oxford, M.A. *Home:* London, England.

CAREER: King's Messenger (children's magazine), England, editor, 1950-55; novelist. Citizens Advice Bureau, London, former staff member. *Awards, honors:* Romantic Novel Major Award, 1967, for *The Truth Game.*

WRITINGS—Novels; all under pseudonym Anne Betteridge; all published by Hurst & Blackett: *The Foreign Girl*, 1960; *The Young Widow*, 1961; *Spring in Morocco*, 1962; *The Long Dance of Love*, 1963; *The Younger Sister*, 1964; *Return to Delphi*, 1964; *Single to New York*, 1965; *The Chains of Love*, 1965; *The Truth Game*, 1966; *A Portuguese Affair*, 1966; *A Little Bit of Luck*, 1967; *Shooting Star*, 1968; *Love in a Rainy Country*, 1969; *Sirocco*, 1970; *The Girl Outside*, 1971; *Journey From a Foreign Land*, 1972; *The Sacrifice*, 1973; *A Time of Their Lives*, 1974; *The Stranger on the Beach*, 1974.

Children's Books—All under name Margaret Potter: *The Touch-And-Go Year*, Dobson, 1968; *The Blow-And-Grow Year*, Dobson, 1970; *Sandy's Safari*, Dobson, 1971; *The Story of the Stolen Necklace*, Dobson, 1974; *Trouble on Sunday*, Methuen, 1974.

WORK IN PROGRESS: David in Delhi, for children; *Shiva Dancing*, for adults.

AVOCATIONAL INTERESTS: Tennis, gardening, travel abroad.

* * *

POULET, Georges 1902-

PERSONAL: Born November 29, 1902, in Chenee, Belgium; son of Georges Francois and Anne (Lion) Poulet; married Elsa Gregoire. *Education:* Universite de Liege, D. Law, 1925, Ph.D., 1927. *Home:* 38 Boulevard de Cimiez, Nice, France.

CAREER: University of Edinburgh, Edinburgh, Scotland, professor of French, 1928-51; Johns Hopkins University, Baltimore, Md., professor of French, 1951-57; University of Zurich, Zurich, Switzerland, professor of French, 1957-73. *Member:* Phi Beta Kappa (honorary), *Awards, honors:* Prix Sainte-Beuve, 1950, for *Etudes sur le temps humain*; Prix de Critique Litteraire, 1952, and Prix Durchon, 1953, both for *La Distance interieure*; Doctor honoris causa, University of Geneva, 1959.

WRITINGS: Etudes sur le temps humain, Plon, 1950, translation by Elliott Coleman, published as *Studies in Human Time*, John Hopkins Press, 1956; *La distance interieure*, Plon, 1952, translation by Elliott Coleman, published as *The Interior Distance*, John Hopkins Press, 1959; *Les Metamorphoses du cercle*, Plon, 1961, translation by Carley Dawson and Elliott Coleman, published as *The*

Metamorphoses of the circle, John Hopkins Press, 1967; *L'Espace proustein*, Gallimard, 1963; *Le Point de depart*, Plon, 1964; (editor) Henri Frederic Amiel, *Journal intime: L'annie, 1857*, Union generale d'editions, 1965; (compiler and author of introduction) Joseph Joubert, *Pensees*, Michel-Claude Jalard, 1966; *Trois essais de mythologie romantique*, Corti, 1968; *Benjamin Constant par lui-meme*, Editions du Sevil, 1968; *Mesure de L'Instant*, Plon, 1968; (editor with Gerald Antoine, Serge Doubrovsky, Gerard Genette, and Rene Gerard) *Les Chemins actuels de la critique*, Union generale d'editions, 1968; (with Robert Kopp) *Qui etait Baudelaire?*, Skira, 1969, translation by Robert Allen and James Emmons, published as *Who Was Baudelaire?*, World Publishing Co., 1969; *La conscience critique*, Corti, 1971.

* * *

POWELL, Donald M. 1914-

PERSONAL: Born May 25, 1914, in Yonkers, N.Y.; son of Jay D. and Theresa G. Powell. *Education:* Swarthmore College, A.B., 1936; Duke University, M.A., 1938; University of Michigan, A.B. in L.S., 1942. *Politics:* Independent Democrat ("if there is such a thing"). *Home:* 5318 East Sixth St., Tucson, Ariz.

CAREER: University of Arizona Library, Tucson, head of reference department, 1946-64, chief public services librarian, 1964, assistant librarian, 1965-73, head of special collections, 1973—. Library Consultant, College of Agriculture, Abu Ghrabe, Iraq, 1957. *Military service:* U.S. Army, 1942-45; became master sergeant. *Member:* American Library Association, American Association of University Professors, Western History Association, Arizona State Library Association (president, 1950), Phi Kappa Phi.

WRITINGS: The Peralta Grant, University of Oklahoma Press, 1960; *An Arizona Gathering*, Arizona Pioneers' Historical Society, 1960; *Arizona Fifty*, Northland, 1961; (editor) John Marion, *Notes of Travel Through the Territory of Arizona*, University of Arizona Press, 1965; *New Mexico and Arizona in the Serial Set, 1846-1861*, Dawsons, 1970; *Arizona Gathering II*, University of Arizona Press, 1973; (editor) John Ross Browne, *Adventures in the Apache Country*, University of Arizona Press, 1974. Compiler of some two dozen book indexes published mainly by University of Arizona Press and of an Arizona bibliography published semi-annually in *Arizona Quarterly*, 1952—. Editor, *Arizona Librarian*, 1948-49; editor, *Books of the Southwest*, 1966—.

WORK IN PROGRESS: Continuation of Serial Set bibliography.

* * *

POWERS, Patrick W(illiam) 1924-

PERSONAL: Born March 21, 1924, in Honolulu, Hawaii; son of Patrick Francis (a U.S. Army officer) and Margaret (Thompson) Powers; married Doris Mildred Hurt, November 12, 1950; children: Robert Warren, Patricia Joanne, Laura Suzanne. *Education:* U.S. Military Academy, B.S., 1945; University of Southern California, M.S. in M.E., 1950; graduate of U.S. Army Command and General Staff College, 1958, Naval War College, 1965. *Religion:* Protestant. *Address:* RR3, Box 36, Indianapolis, Ind.

CAREER: U.S. Army, career service, 1945—. Commissioned second lieutenant, 1945; served in Philippines and Japan, 1945-48; Fort Bliss, Tex., 1950-57, instructor at

Army Guided Missile School, later missile unit commander and range officer; staff assignments with Army General Staff, Washington, D.C., 1958-61, and Eighth U.S. Army in Korea, 1961-62; commander of first Pershing Missile Battalion, Fort Sill, Okla., 1962-63; now lieutenant colonel. *Member:* American Institute of Aeronautics and Astronautics, American Ordnance Association, Association of the United States Army, Military Order of the World Wars. *Awards, honors:* Army Commendation Medal.

WRITINGS: A Guide to National Defense, Praeger, 1964. Contributor and reviewer on military technology for *Collier's Encyclopedia*; contributor of articles and reviews on guided missiles, space projects, and military technology to technical journals and magazines.

SIDELIGHTS: Powers wrote one of the first technical papers published (1952) in America on construction of a miniature supersonic wind tunnel. He has participated in more than 140 guided missile firings.†

* * *

PRABHU, Pandharinath H. 1911-

PERSONAL: Born November 15, 1911, in Vengurla, Maharashtra, India; son of Hari Kanoba (a clerk) and Bhagirathi (Awsare) Prabhu; married Tarubala Ajogaonkar, 1934; children: Shobhana (daughter), Bhoosan (son). *Education:* Bombay University, B.A. (honors), 1930, LL.B., 1933, Ph.D., 1937; Government of India Scholar for Advanced Studies Abroad and postdoctoral fellow at University of Michigan, Columbia University, University of Pennsylvania, Ohio State University, and University of Minnesota, 1948-49; other postdoctoral study at Cambridge University, National Institute of Industrial Psychology, London, and Centre d' Etudes et Recherches Psychotechniques, Paris, 1949. *Religion:* Hindu. *Office:* Department of Humanities and Social Sciences, Indian Institute of Technology, Bombay 400 076, India.

CAREER: With Bombay Educational Service (state), 1937-50; Tata Institute of Social Sciences, Bombay, India, head of department of psychology, 1950-58; UNESCO Research Center, New Delhi, India, senior research officer, 1956-57; Gujarat University, Ahmedabad, India, director of University School of Psychology, Education and Philosophy, and professor of psychology, 1958-67; Transylvania University, Lexington, Ky., Title III Distinguished Visiting Professor of Psychology, 1968-69; State University of New York College at Oswego, N.Y., professor of psychology, 1969-71; Indian Institute of Technology, Bombay, India, senior professor of psychology and head of department of humanities and social sciences, 1972—. Maharaja Sayaji Rao Memorial lecturer, University of Baroda, India, 1942; senior research officer, UNESCO Research Center, New Delhi, India, 1956-57; president of psychology and educational sciences division, Indian Science Congress, 1963; Fulbright professor at Pennsylvania State University, and University of California, 1964; Leverhulme Professor of Psychology, Australian National University, 1970; member, International Planning Conference on Opportunities for Advanced Training and Research in Psychology.

MEMBER: International Council of Psychologists (fellow), American Psychological Association (fellow), American Association for the Advancement of Science (fellow), International Committee on Sociometry, International Council of Group Psychotherapy, Gujarat Psychological Association (president). *Awards, honors:* Honorary fellow, University of Minnesota and Ohio State University, 1949;

International Visiting Scientist Award of American Psychological Association, 1962.

WRITINGS: Lectures on the Psychology of Indian Social Institutions (Maharaja Sayaji Rao Memorial Lectures), Baroda State Government, 1945; (contributor) *A Survey of Research in Indian Sociology During Twenty-five Years, 1917-42*, Bhandarkar Oriental Research Institute (Poona), 1945; *The Problem of Monotony in Industry: A Psychological Study*, University of Michigan Press, 1948; (contributor) *Five Studies in Asia*, UNESCO Research Center (New Delhi), 1956; *Hindu Social Organization: Socio-Psychological and Ideological Foundations*, 5th edition Popular Book Depot, 1972; *Perception, Personality and Indian Approach* (University Lectures), Annamalai University, 1964; *Psychology in India* (monograph), American Psychological Association, 1964; *Psychology in Relation to Allied Natural Sciences*, Gujarat University, 1965; *Changing Motivation Through Changes in Attitudes*, Central Family Planning Institute (New Delhi), 1967; (contributor) *The Concept of Mind*, Popular Prakashan, 1972; (contributor) *Psychology Around the World Today*, Brooks-Cole, in press.

Contributor to *Socio-Economist, Eastern Anthropologist, Indian Journal of Social Work* and other professional journals. Consulting editor of *Psychologia, International Journal of Sociometry and Sociatry, Group Psychotherapy, Indian Journal of Psychology, Journal of Psychological Researches*, and *Journal of Indian Academy of Applied Psychology, International Review of Sociology, International Journal of Sociology of the Family*, and *Journal of Transpersonal Psychology*.

WORK IN PROGRESS: Reorganizing and developing the department of humanities and social sciences with a view to providing a broader perspective to the education of the professional engineer, adding suitable courses and faculty in order to play a more active role in the master's and doctoral programmes of the department also. Instituting interdisciplinary courses and research jointly with the technology faculty.

AVOCATIONAL INTERESTS: Music (Indian); flute and tabla.

* * *

PRATT, John Clark 1932-

PERSONAL: Born August 19, 1932, in St. Albans, Vt.; son of John Lowell (a publisher) and Katharine (Jennison) Pratt; married second wife, Doreen K. Goodman, June 28, 1968; children: Karen, Sandra, Pamela, John Randall; (stepchildren) Lynn Goodman, Christine Goodman. *Education:* Attended Dartmouth College, 1950-53; University of California, Berkeley, B.A., 1954; Columbia University, M.A., 1960; Princeton University, Ph.D., 1965. *Politics:* Variable. *Office:* Department of English, Colorado State University, Ft. Collins, Colo. 80521.

CAREER: U.S. Air Force, regular officer; commissioned second lieutenant. U.S. Air Force Adacemy, Colorado Springs, Colo., assistant professor, 1960-68, associate professor, 1968-73, professor of English, 1973-74; served in Vietnam, 1969-70; retiring as lieutenant colonel, 1974. Colorado State University, Ft. Collins, chairman of department of English, 1974—. Fulbright lecturer, University of Portugal, 1974-75; consultant in remedial English, United States Industries, Inc. *Member:* Coffee House (New York).

WRITINGS: The Meaning of Modern Poetry, Doubleday, 1962; *John Steinbeck*, Eerdmans, 1970; (editor) Ken Kesey, *One Flew Over the Cuckoo's Nest*, Viking, 1973; *The Laotian Fragments*, Viking, 1974; (contributor) *Hemingway in Our Time*, Oregon State University, 1974. Contributor of articles, poems, and reviews to journals in his field.

WORK IN PROGRESS: A novel, *Silence: A True History*; a musical; *The Middlemarch Notebooks: A Critical Edition.*

SIDELIGHTS: John Pratt is competent in French, German, and Latin.

* * *

PRATT, William C(rouch, Jr.) 1927-

PERSONAL: Born October 5, 1927, in Shawnee, Okla.; son of William Crouch (owner of shoe store) and Irene (Johnston) Pratt; married Anne Cullen Rich, October 2, 1954; children: Catherine Cullen, William Stuart, Randall Johnston. *Education:* University of Oklahoma, B.A., 1949; Vanderbilt University, M.A., 1951, Ph.D., 1957; University of Glasgow, graduate study, 1951-52. *Politics:* Relublican. *Religion:* Episcopalian. *Home:* 212 Oakhill Dr., Oxford, Ohio 45056.

CAREER: Vanderbilt University, Nashville, Tenn., instructor in English, 1955-57; Miami University, Oxford, Ohio, 1957—, began as instructor, associate professor and director of freshman English, 1964-68, professor of English, 1968—. *Military service:* U.S. Naval Reserve, active duty, 1945-46, 1953-55; became lieutenant. *Member:* Modern Language Association of America, National Council of Teachers of English, Ohio English Association, Phi Beta Kappa. *Awards, honors:* Rotary fellowship to University of Glasgow.

WRITINGS: (Editor) *The Imagist Poem*, Dutton, 1963; *The Fugitive Poets*, Dutton, 1965; *The College Writer*, Scribner, 1969; (contributor) *Bibliographical Guide to the Study of Southern Literature*, Louisiana State University Press, 1969.

WORK IN PROGRESS: A translation of a book on French origins of modern poetry; a translation of the poetry of Rainer Maria Rilke.

* * *

PREMINGER, Alex 1915-

PERSONAL: Born July 29, 1915, in Berlin, Germany; son of Saly (a businessman) and Lea (Sprechman) Preminger; married Augusta Friedman (a teacher), August 7, 1960. *Education:* New York University, B.A., 1950; Columbia University, M.S.L.S., 1952. *Politics:* Democrat. *Religion:* Jewish. *Home:* 1311 Decker St., Valley Stream, N.Y. 11580. *Office:* Brooklyn College Library, Brooklyn, N.Y. 11201.

CAREER: Bag and Burlap Co., Berlin, Germany, assistant sales manager, 1935-38; Somerset Tool Co., Newark, N.J., sales correspondent, 1940-41; New York University, New York, N.Y., library assistant, Law Library, 1946-51; Brooklyn College of the City University of New York, periodicals and documents librarian, 1952-59, social science librarian, 1959-60, humanities librarian, 1960-65, deputy chief of Humanities Division, 1963-65, assistant professor and chief of Humanities Division, 1965-68, associate professor, 1969—. Honorary consultant to the Folger Shakespeare Library. Educational Broadcasting Corp., chairman of Flushing affiliates, 1963-66. Director, Columbia University School of Library Service Alumni Association, 1964-67. *Military service:* U.S. Army, 1942-45. *Member:* American Library Association, Association of College and Research Libraries, American Association of University Professors, American Comparative Literature Association, Modern Language Association of America, Phi Beta Kappa, Beta Phi Mu, New York Library Club. *Awards, honors:* Bollingen Foundation fellow.

WRITINGS: (Editor and contributor) *Encyclopedia of Poetry and Poetics*, Princeton University Press, 1965; (editor) Harry D. Gideonse, *Against the Running Tide*, Twayne, 1970; (co-author) *Urban Educator,* Twayne, 1970; (editor) *Classical and Medieval Literary Criticism*, Ungar, 1974; (editor) *Princeton Encyclopedia of Poetry and Poetics*, Princeton University Press, 1975. Contributor to *Books Abroad, Library Journal, Modern Language Review, and Library Trends*. Member of editorial board, *Encyclopedia of Twentieth Century World Literature*, 1965-71.

AVOCATIONAL INTERESTS: Educational television, philosophy, languages, and psychology.

* * *

PRESS, (Otto) Charles 1922-

PERSONAL: Born September 12, 1922; son of Otto and Laura (Irion) Press; married Nancy Miller, June 10, 1950; children: Edward, William, Thomas, Laura. *Education:* Attended Elmhurst College, 1939-43; University of Missouri, B.J., 1948; University of Minnesota, M.A., 1951, Ph.D., 1953. *Politics:* Independent. *Religion:* Protestant. *Home:* 334 Marshall, East Lansing, Mich. 48823. *Office:* Department of Political Science, Michigan State University, East Lansing, Mich., 48824.

CAREER: North Dakota Agricultural College (now North Dakota State University), Fargo, instructor in political science, 1956-57; University of Wisconsin, Madison, assistant professor, 1957-58; Michigan State University East Lansing, assistant professor, 1958-62, associate professor, 1962-65, professor of political science, 1965—. Director, Grand Rapids Metropolitan Area Study, 1956-57. *Military service:* U.S. Army, 1943-45. *Member:* American Political Science Association, National Municipal League, Midwest Political Science Association (president, 1974-75), Michigan Conference of Political Scientists (president, 1972-73).

WRITINGS: (With Oliver Williams) *Democracy in Urban America*, Rand McNally, 1962, 2nd edition, 1970; *Main Street Politics*, Institute for Community Development, Michigan State University, 1962; (with Charles Adrian) *The American Political Process*, McGraw, 1965, 2nd edition, 1969; *Democracy in the Fifty States*. Rand McNally, 1966; (with Alan Arian) *Empathy and Ideology*, Rand McNally, 1966; (with Walter C. Adrian) *Governing Urban America*, 4th edition, McGraw, 1972.

* * *

PRESSEISEN, Ernst L(eopold) 1928-

PERSONAL: Surname is pronounced like "precise" with an "n" added; born July 13, 1928, in Rotterdam, Netherlands; son of Moritz Heinrich and Flora (Speelman) Presseisen; married Barbara Lenore Zemboch (a teacher and lecturer), June 30, 1963; children: Joshua William. *Education:* University of California, Berkeley, B.A. (cum laude), 1951; Harvard University, Ph.D., 1955. *Religion:* Jewish. *Home:* 1943 Pine St., Philadelphia, Pa. 19103. *Office:* Department of History, Temple University, Philadelphia, Pa. 19122.

CAREER: University of Akron, Akron, Ohio, instructor in history, 1955; U.S. Air Force, civilian historian, 1956; Stanford University, Stanford, Calif., instructor in history, 1956-60; Williamette University, Salem, Ore., assistant professor of history, 1960-61; Stanford University, Hoover Institution on War, Revolution, and Peace, research associate, 1961-63; Northern Illinois University, De Kalb, Ill., associate professor of history, 1963-66; Temple University, Philadelphia, Pa., professor of history, 1966—, chairman of department of history, 1967-68, 1971-74. *Member:* American Historical Association, American Association of University Professors, Conference Group for Central European History. *Awards, honors:* Research grants from American Philosopical Society, 1957, 1958, and from Hoover Institution, 1961.

WRITINGS: Germany and Japan: A Study in Totalitarian Diplomacy, 1933-41, Martinus Nijhoff, 1958; *Before Agression: Europeans Prepare the Japanese Army*, University of Arizona Press, 1965. Contributor to *Journal of Modern History*.

WORK IN PROGRESS: Engaged in comparative study of appeasement, examining British domestic motivations in appeasing Napoleon in 1891, and Hitler in 1938.

SIDELIGHTS: Presseisen writes, speaks, and reads German and French.

*   *   *

PRESTON, Ralph C(lausius)   1908-

PERSONAL: Born April 12, 1908, in Philadelphia, Pa.; son of Gilbert Kent and Anna E. (Clausius) Preston; married Madeline Perry, October 18, 1952; children: Kathleen, Elizabeth Ann (Mrs. Arthur U. Ayres, Jr.), John Nicholas. *Education:* Attended Antioch College, 1928-30; Swarthmore College, A.B., 1932; Columbia University, M.A., 1934, Ph.D., 1941. *Religion:* Society of Friends. *Home:* 51-6 Revere Rd., Drexel Hill, Pa. 19026. *Office:* Graduate School of Education, University of Pennsylvania, Philadelphia, Pa. 19104.

CAREER: Teacher in public and private schools in Pennsylvania, New York, and Connecticut, 1931-41; University of Pennsylvania, Philadelphia, 1941—, began as assistant professor, professor of education, 1953—, director of reading clinic, 1946—, vice-dean of Graduate School of Education, 1963-67. Consultant to Young America Films, and Cornet Instructional Films. *Member:* American Educational Research Association, American Psychological Association, National Council for the Social Studies, International Reading Association. *Awards, honors:* Fulbright research scholar in Germany, 1959.

WRITINGS: Children's Reactions to a Contemporary War Situation, Teachers College, Columbia University, Bureau of Publications, 1942; *Teaching Social Etudiesin the Elementary School*, Rinehart, 1950, 4th edition, revised, Holt, 1974; (editor and contributor) *Teaching World Understanding*, Prentice-Hall, 1955; (with Morton Botel) *How to Study*, Science Research Associates, 1956, 3rd edition, revised (with Wayne L. Herman, Jr.), 1974; *Teaching Study Habits and Skills*, Rinehart, 1959; (with J. Wesley Schneyer and Franc J. Thyng) *Guiding the Social Studies Reading of High School Students*, National Council for the Social Studies, 1963; (with Elizabeth A. Cox and Ardra S. Wavle) *A New Hometown*, Heath, 1964; (with FrancesV. Nichols and A. S. Wavle) *In School and Out*, Heath, 1964; (with Martha McIntosh and Mildred M. Cameron) *Greenfield, U.S.A.*, Heath 1964; (with Eleanor Clymer) *Com-*

munities at Work, Heath, 1964; (with John Tottle) *In These United States*, Heath, 1965; (with Jean C. Bernstein) *Families. Near and Far*, Heath, 1969; (with Caroline Emerson, and Arthur and Elizabeth Schrader) *Four Lands, Four Peoples*, Heath, 1969; (with Tottle) *In These United States and Canada*, Heath, 1969; (with Tottle) *In Latin American Lands*, Heath, 1969; (with McIntosh and Cameron) *Greenfield and Far Away*, Heath, 1969; (with Tottle, Marion Murphy, and James Flannery) *Culture Regions in the Eastern Hemisphere*, Heath, 1971. Contributor to education journals.

WORK IN PROGRESS: A Biography of Erich Hylla, a German educator; a series of books to develop reading and study skills, with Morton Botel.

*   *   *

PRICE, Stanley   1931-

PERSONAL: Born August 12, 1931, in London, England; son of Morris (a doctor) and Gertrude (White) Price; married Judy Fenton; children: Munro. *Education:* Caius College, Cambridge, M.A., 1954. *Home:* 21 Hillside Gardens, London N.6, England. *Agent:* Creative Management Associates, 600 Madison Ave., New York, N.Y. 10022; and A.L.S., 46 Brook St., London, W.1, England.

CAREER: Life, New York, N.Y., reporter, 1956-60; staff member of *Sunday Telegraph* and of *Observer*, London, England, 1961-66. *Town*, London, England, editor, 1963. *Military service:* British Army, 1949-51; became sergeant.

WRITINGS: Crusading for Kronk, Putnam, 1960; *Me for Posterity*, Vanguard, 1961; *A World of Difference*, Penguin, 1962; *The Biggest Picture*, M. Joseph, 1964.

Plays: "Horizontal Hold," produced in London, 1967; (with Lee Minoff) "Come Live with Me" (two-act comedy), first produced in New York at Billy Rose Theatre, January 26, 1967; "The Position Grotesque" (one-act comedy), first produced in London at Basement Theatre, May 17, 1971; "The Starving Rich" (comedy), first produced in London at Windsor Royal Theatre, May 16, 1972. Also author of "Exit Laughing" and "The Two of Me," not yet produced.

Filmscripts: (With Julian Mitchell) "Arabesque," produced by Stanley Doner, 1967; "Gold," produced by Michael Klinger, 1974; "Shout at the Devil," produced by Michael Klinger, 1974.

Contributor to magazines and periodicals in Great Britain and America.

AVOCATIONAL INTERESTS: Playing squash, watching rugby football, and cultivating his garden.

*   *   *

PRICHARD, James W(illiam)   1925-

PERSONAL: Born January 8, 1925, in St. Louis, Mo.; son of Leslie Elridge (an advertising censor) and Ann (Schoenemann) Prichard; married Christine McFarlane Alexander, June 29, 1946; children: John Stewart, William Robert. *Education:* Yale University, B.A. (physics), 1944. *Politics:* Republican. *Religion:* Presbyterian. *Home:* 3252 Brandy Ct., Falls Church, Va. 22042. *Office:* Bureau of Supplies and Accounts, Department of the Navy, Washington, D.C.

CAREER: U.S. Navy, Electronics Supply Office, Great Lakes, Ill., organization and methods examiner (civilian), 1946-51; U.S. General Services Administration, Washington, D.C., cataloger, 1951-52; U.S. Electronics Production

Resources Agency, Washington, D.C., industrial analyst, 1952-56; U.S. Department of the Navy, Bureau of Supplies and Accounts, Washington, D.C., supply officer (civilian), 1956-60, operations researcher, 1960-63, general supply officer, 1963—. *Military service:* U.S. Navy, 1943-46; became ensign. *Member:* American Production and Inventory Control Society.

WRITINGS: (With R. H. Engle) *Modern Inventory Management*, Wiley, 1965.†

* * *

PRINCE, Thomas Richard 1934-

PERSONAL: Born December 7, 1934, in New Albany, Miss.; son of James Thompson (a contractor) and C. Florence (Howell) Prince; married Eleanor Carol Polkoff, July 14, 1962; children: Thomas Andrew, John Michael, Adrienne Carol. *Education:* Mississippi State University, B.S., 1956, M.S., 1957; University of Illinois, Ph.D., 1962. *Religion:* Unitarian Universalist. *Home:* 303 Richmond Rd., Kenilworth, Ill. 60043.

CAREER: University of Illinois, Urbana, instructor, 1960-62; Northwestern University, Evanston and Chicago (Ill.) campuses, assistant professor, 1962-65, associate professor, 1965-69, professor of accounting, 1969—, chairman of department of accounting and information systems, 1968—. Consultant on information systems to private industry. *Military service:* U.S. Army, Finance Corps, 1957-60; became first lieutenant; received special citation for contribution to U.S. Army financial management. *Member:* Institute of Management Sciences, American Institute of Certified Public Accountants, American Accounting Association, National Association of Accountants, Systems and Procedures Association, Illinois Society of Certified Public Accountants, Phi Kappa Phi, Omicron Delta Kappa, Delta Sigma`Pi, Beta Alpha Psi.

WRITINGS: Extension of the Boundaries of Accounting Theory, South-Western Publishing, 1963; (with Thomas C. Hillard) *Analytical Accounting Case Problems*, South-Western Publishing, 1964; *Information Systems for Management Planning and Control*, Irwin, 1966, revised edition, 1970. Contributor to professional journals.

* * *

PRINGLE, J(ohn) M(artin) Douglas 1912-

PERSONAL: Born June 28, 1912, in Hawick, Scotland; son of John Douglas (a manufacturer) and Muriel (Martin) Pringle; married Celia Carroll, December 19, 1937; children: Caroline, Margaret, John. *Education:* Lincoln College, Oxford, M.A. (first class honors), 1934. *Home:* 27 Bayview St., McMahon's Point, Sydney, New South Wales, Australia.

CAREER: Manchester Guardian, Manchester, England, reporter and leader-writer, 1934-39, deputy editor, 1944-49; *Times*, London, England, special writer, 1949-52; *Sydney Morning Herald*, Sydney, Australia, editor, 1952-57; *Observer*, London, England, deputy editor, 1958-63; *Canberra Times*, Canberra, Australia, managing editor, 1964-65; *Sydney Morning Herald*, Sidney, New South Wales, Australia, editor, 1965-70. *Military service:* British Army, 1940-44; became acting major. *Member:* Travellers' Club.

WRITINGS: China Struggles for Unity, Penguin, 1938; *Australian Accent*, Chatto & Windus, 1958; *Australian Painting Today*, Thames & Hudson, 1963; *On Second Thoughts*, Angus & Robertson, 1972; *Have Pen: Will*

Travel, Chatto & Windus, 1973. Contributor to *Encounter, Times Literary Supplement.*

AVOCATIONAL INTERESTS: Literature, the arts; wildlife, especially birds; Gaelic.

* * *

PROSCH, Harry 1917-

PERSONAL: Born May 4, 1917, in Logansport, Ind.; son of Harry John and Clara (Rehwald) Prosch; married Doris Becker, August 22, 1948; children: Michael, Christine. *Education:* University of Chicago, A.B., 1948, A.M., 1950, Ph.D., 1955. *Home:* RD No. 6, Saratoga Springs, N.Y.

CAREER: Idaho State College (now University), Pocatello, instructor in philosophy, 1953-55; Shimer College, Mount Carroll, Ill., head of humanities staff, 1955-56; Southern Methodist University, Dallas, Tex., associate professor, later professor of philosophy, 1956-62; Skidmore College, Saratoga Springs, N.Y., professor of philosophy and chairman of department, 1962—. Willett Visiting Professor, University of Chicago, spring, 1970. *Military service:* U.S. Army, 1942-45; became staff sergeant. *Member:* American Philosophical Association, American Association of University Professors. *Awards, honors:* Danforth fellow at Southern Methodist University, 1961-62; National Endowment for the Humanities senior fellow, 1973.

WRITINGS: The Genesis of Twentieth Century Philosophy, Doubleday, 1964; *Cooling the Modern Mind: Polanyi's Mission*, Skidmore College, 1971; (contributor) Donald Hanson & Robert Fowler, editors, *Obligation and Dissent*, Little, Brown, 1971; (contributor) Joan Bondurant, editor, *Conflict: Violence and Nonviolence*, Aldine, 1971. Articles in professional journals.

WORK IN PROGRESS: A critical exposition of Michael Polanyi's thought; a book with Michael Polanyi, *Meaning.*

* * *

PRYCE-JONES, David 1936-

PERSONAL: Born February 15, 1936, in Vienna, Austria; son of Alan (a writer) and Therese (Fould-Springer) Pryce-Jones; married Clarissa Caccia, July 29, 1959; children: Jessica, Candida, Adam. *Education:* Magdalen College, Oxford, B.A., 1959, M.A., 1963. *Address:* c/o A. D. Peters, 10 Buckingham St., London W.C. 2, England. *Agent:* Harold Matson Co., 30 Rockefeller Plaza, New York, N.Y.

CAREER: Writer. Teacher of the writers workshop at University of Iowa, 1964-65, California State College at Hayward, 1968 and 1970, and at University of California at Berkeley, 1972. *Military service:* British Infantry, 1954-56.

WRITINGS: Owls and Satyrs (novel), Longmans, Green, 1960; (translator) *The Traveller*, a novel by G. Prassinos, Harvill Press, 1962; (translator) *Art on the Market*, by M. Rheims, Athenaeum, 1962; *The Sands of Summer* (novel), Holt, 1963; *Graham Greene* (critical study), Oliver and Boyd, 1963; (contributor) M. Sissons and P. French, editors, *The Age of Austerity*, Hodder & Stoughton, 1963; *Next Generation: Travels in Israel*, Weidenfeld & Nicolson, 1964, Holt, 1965; *Quondam* (novel), Holt, 1965; *The Stranger's View* (novel), Weidenfeld & Nicolson, 1967, Holt, 1968; *The Hungarian Revolution* (history), Bonn, 1969, Horizon Press, 1970; *Running Away* (novel), Weidenfield & Nicolson, 1971; *The Face of Defeat* (contemporary history), Holt, 1972; *E. D. Evelyn Waugh Waugh and His World* (literary essays), Little, Brown, 1973; *The England*

Commune (novel), Quartet, 1975. Literary editor, *Time and Tide*, 1960-61; drama critic, *Spectator*, 1963-64.

WORK IN PROGRESS: A novel.

* * *

PULZER, Peter George Julius 1929-

PERSONAL: Born May 20, 1929, in Vienna, Austria; son of Felix (a consultant engineer) and Margaret (Breiner) Pulzer; married Gillian Mary Marshall; children: Matthew, Patrick. *Education:* King's College, Cambridge, B.A. (first class honors), 1950, Ph.D., 1960; University of London, B.Sc. (first class honors), 1954. *Office:* Christ Church, Oxford University, Oxford, England.

CAREER: Oxford University, Oxford, England, lecturer in politics, 1957—, tutor in modern history and politics at Christ Church, 1962—. *Military service:* Royal Air Force, 1950-54; became flight lieutenant. *Member:* Political Studies Association of the United Kingdom.

WRITINGS: The Rise of Political Anti-Semitism, Wiley, 1964; (contributor) Peter Hall, editor, *Labour's New Frontier*, Deutsch, 1964; (contributor) E. K. Scheuch and R. Wildemann, editors, *Zur Soziologie der Wahl*, Westdeutscher Verlag, 1965: *Political Representation and Elections in Britain*, Allen & Unwin, 1967, 2nd edition, 1972; (contributor) J. M. S. Pasley, editor, *Germany: A companion to German Studies*, Methuen, 1972. Author of scripts for British Broadcasting Corp. Contributor to *The Times* (London), *Daily Telegraph*, *Economist*, *Time and Tide*, and other journals.

* * *

PUMPHREY, H(enry) George 1912-

PERSONAL: Born April 11, 1912, in Flint, North Wales; son of Alfred (a garage proprietor) and Emily (Warrington) Pumphrey; married Marion Susan Darling (a teacher), August 24, 1944; children: Peter Henry, Jane Ann, Judith Mary. *Education:* Bangor Normal Training College, diplomat. *Home:* 10 Rose Ave., Retford, Nottinghamshire, England.

CAREER: Headmaster of primary school, Horsham, Sussex, England, 1945-47; Wymondham Teachers Training College, Norfolk, England, lecturer, 1947-49; Powell County Primary School, Dover, Kent, England, headmaster, 1949-60; Teachers Training College (now College of Education), Eaton Hall, Retford, Nottinghamshire, England, 1960—, began as senior lecturer in education, became principal lecturer. *Member:* Society of Authors, Royal Institute of Public Health and Hygiene, National Union of Teachers, Association for Teachers in Colleges and Departments of Education.

WRITINGS: Look After Yourself, E. J. Arnold, 1939; *The Story of Liverpool's Public Services*, Liverpool University Press, 1939; *Look After Others*, E. J. Arnold, 1945; *Trouble at the Grange*, Schofield & Sims, 1946; *Good Manners*, Pitman, 1947; *Juniors*, Livingstone Press, 1950; *Children's Folk Tales*, Harrap, 1955; *Comics and Your Children*, Comics Campaign Council, 1954; *Children's Comics*, Epworth, 1955; *Grenfell of Labrador*, Harrap, 1958, Dodd, 1959; *What Children Think of Their Comics*, Epworth, 1964; *Conquering the English Channel*, Abelard, 1965. Contributor to education journals in England.

AVOCATIONAL INTERESTS: Fell and mountain walking, skiing, swimming, squash, badminton, tennis.

PURDOM, Thomas E. 1936-
(Tom Purdom)

PERSONAL: Born April 19, 1936, in New Haven, Conn.; son of Orlando Jackson and Inez (Tigna) Purdom; married Sara Wescoat (a development writer), November 19, 1960; children: Christopher William. *Education:* Attended Lafayette College, 1952-54. *Home and office:* 4734 Cedar Ave., Philadelphia, Pa. 19143. *Agent:* Scott Meredith Literary Agency, Inc., 580 Fifth Ave., New York, N.Y. 10036.

CAREER: United Airlines, part-time reservation clerk, Philadelphia, Pa., 1957-59, 1961—; University of Pennsylvania, Philadelphia, Moore School of Electrical Engineering, script writer (two computer-animated educational films), 1967-69, News Bureau, science writer, 1968-69; now full time free lance writer. Visiting assistant professor of English at Temple University, 1970 and 1971; publicity chairman, H. C. Lea School Open Classroom Parents Group, 1972-74. *Military service:* U.S. Army, Medical Corps, 1959-61. *Member:* World Future Society, Science Fiction Writers of America (vice-president, 1970-72), American Civil Liberties Union, American Time Travel Society (secretary), Philadelphia Science Fiction Society (president, 1962-64). *Awards, honors:* New Republic Young Writers Contest award, 1958, for essay, "In Praise of Science Fiction."

*WRITINGS—*All under name Tom Purdom: *I Want the Stars* (novel), Ace Books, 1964; *Tree Lord of Imeten*, Ace Books, 1966; *Five Against Arlane*, Ace Books, 1967; (editor) *Adventures in Discovery*, Doubleday, 1969; *Reduction in Arms*, Berkley, 1971; *The Barons of Behavior*, Ace Books, 1972. Stories included in *Star Science Fiction*, number six, edited by Frederik Pohl, Balantine, 1959; *World's Best Science Fiction, 1965*, Ace Books; *The Future is Now*, edited by William F. Nolan, Sherbourne Press, 1970; *Crime Prevention in the Thirteenth Century*, edited by Hans Santesson, Walker, 1970; *This Side of Infinity*, edited by Terry Carr, Ace Books, 1972; *Future Quest*, edited by Roger Elwood, Avon Books, 1973. Contributor of short stories to *Fantastic Universe, Galaxy, Analog, Amazing, Kiwanis, American Libraries*, and other science fiction magazines; articles to *Worlds of Tomorrow* book reviews for the *Philadelphia Bulletin*.

WORK IN PROGRESS: A series of adventure books for new science fiction line to be published by Harlequin Books; a novel about society where humans may develop on the moon in next century.

* * *

PURDY, Susan Gold 1939-

PERSONAL: Born May 17, 1939, in New York, N.Y.; daughter of Harold A. (a dentist) and Frances (Joslin) Gold; married Geoffrey Hale Purdy (a computer programmer), September 29, 1963; children: Cassandra Heather. *Education:* Attended Vassar College, 1957-59; Ecole des Beaux Arts and Sorbonne, University of Paris, 1959-60; New York University, B.S., 1962. *Home:* Wilton, Conn.

CAREER: Wamsutta Mills, New York, N.Y., textile designer, 1962-63; full-time writer and illustrator mainly for children; CBS-TV, New York, N.Y., teacher of cooking on "Patchwork Family", a children's program, 1973-1974. Co-director, Wilton Music and Art Day Camp (for girls six to twelve), summers, 1964, 1965; demonstrator of crafts for children and adults on various television shows, 1968—.

*WRITINGS—*Author and illustrator; all published by Lippincott: *My Little Cabbage*, 1965; *Christmas Decorations for You to Make*, 1965; *If You Have a Yellow Lion*, 1966; *Be My Valentine*, 1967; *Holiday Cards for You to Make*, 1967; *Festivals for You to Celebrate*, 1969; *Jewish Holidays*, 1969; *Costumes for You to Make*, 1972; *Books for You to Make*, 1973. Illustrator: Irene Bowen, *Suddenly, A Witch!*, Lippincott, 1970; Dr. Lydia Duggins, *Developing Children's Perceptual Skills in Reading*, Mediax, 1971. Contributor of articles on crafts and decorating to *Family Circle, Ladies Home Journal*, 1968—.

SIDELIGHTS: Ms. Purdy speaks French and Italian. *Avocational interests:* Painting.

* * *

PYKE, Magnus 1908-

PERSONAL: Born December 29, 1908, in England; son of Robert and Clara (Lewis) Pyke; married Dorothea Vaughan (a chartered accountant), 1937; children: John, Elizabeth. *Education:* McGill University, Diploma in Agriculture, 1929, B.Sc., 1933; University College, London, Ph.D., 1936. *Home:* 3 St. Peters Villas, London W6 9BQ, England. *Office:* Fortress House, 23 Savile Row, London W1X 2AA, England.

CAREER: Vitamins Ltd., London, England, chief chemist, 1934-40; Ministry of Food, Scientific Adviser's Division, London, England, principal scientific officer (nutrition), 1940-45, 1946-48; Allied Commission for Austria, British Element, Vienna, Austria, nutritional adviser, 1945-46; Distillers Co., Ltd., Glenochil Research Station, Menstrie, Scotland, manager, 1948-73; British Association for the Advancement of Science, secretary and chairman of council, 1973—.

WRITINGS: Manual of Nutrition, H.M.S.O., 1945, 2nd edition, 1947; *Industrial Nutrition*, Macdonald & Evans, 1950; *Townsman's Food*, Turnstile Press, 1952; *Automation: Its Purpose and Future*, Hutchinson, 1956; *Nothing Like Science*, J. Murray, 1957; *Slaves Unaware*, J. Murray, 1958; *About Chemistry*, Oliver & Boyd, 1959, Macmillan, 1960; *The Boundaries of Science*, Harrap, 1961; *The Science Myth*, Macmillan, 1962; *Nutrition*, English Universities Press, 1962; *Food Science and Technology*, J. Murray, 1964, 3rd edition, 1970; *What Scientists Are Up To*, Zenith, 1966; *The Science Century*, J. Murray, 1967; *The Human Predicament*, Collins, 1967; *Food and Society*, J. Murray, 1968; *Man and Food*, Weidenfeld & Nicolson, 1970; *Synthetic Food*, J. Murray, 1970; *Food Glorious Food*, Ginn, 1971; *Technological Eating*, J. Murray, 1972; *Catoring Science and Technology*, J. Murray, 1974; *Success in Nutrition*, J. Murray, 1975.

Contributor of chapters: *Industrial Medicine and Hygiene*, Butterworth & Co., 1954; *Yeasts*, Junk, 1957; *The Chemistry and Biology of Yeast*, Academic Press, 1958; *What the Human Race is Up To*, Gollancz, 1962.

Writer of radio scripts. Contributor to *Listener*.

WORK IN PROGRESS: A book on the material and intellectual contributions of chemistry for J. Murray.

* * *

PYLES, Thomas 1905-

PERSONAL: Born June 5, 1905, in Frederick, Md.; son of Joseph Thomas and Charlotte (Bowers) Pyles; married Bessie Alice Yort, December 21, 1929; children: Thomas, Jr. *Education:* University of Maryland, B.A., 1926, M.A., 1927; Johns Hopkins University, Ph.D., 1938. *Religion:* Episcopalian. *Home:* 629 NE Boulevard, Gainesville, Fla. 32601.

CAREER: University of Maryland, College Park, instructor in English, 1927-29, instructor, then assistant professor of English, Baltimore division, 1929-44, instructor in German, Baltimore division, 1943-44; Johns Hopkins University, Baltimore, Md., instructor in English, 1938-44; University of Oklahoma, Norman, professor of English, 1944-48, associate dean of Graduate School, 1948; University of Florida, Gainesville, professor of English, 1948-65, professor emeritus, 1972—, Northwestern University, Evanston, Ill., professor of English and linguistics, 1965-71, professor emeritus, 1971—. Visiting professor, University of Goettingen, 1956-57; visiting professor, New York University, summer, 1965. *Member:* International Association of University Professors of English, Modern Language Association of America, Linguistic Society of America, American Dialect Society (secretary-treasurer, 1952-56; executive council, 1957-58; vice-president, 1958-60; president, 1960-62), American Name Society, Modern Humanities Research Association, Phi Beta Kappa.

WRITINGS: (Editor with S. V. Larkey) *An Herbal, 1525*, Scholars' Facsimiles, 1941; *Words and Ways of American English*, Random, 1952, revised edition, Andrew Melrose, 1954; *The Origins and Development of the English Language*, Harcourt, 1964, 2nd edition, 1971; *The English Language: A Brief History*, Holt, 1968; (with John Algeo) *English: An Introduction to Language*, Harcourt, 1970.

Contributor of over fifty articles and about the same number of reviews to learned journals. Member of editorial committee, *ELH, Journal of English Literary History*, 1942-44, *Publication of the ADS* (semi-annual), 1952-56, 1960-72; member of editorial advisory board, *Funk & Wagnalls College Standard Dictionary*, 1963; member of editorial advisory committee, *World Book Encyclopedia Dictionary*, 1963, *American Speech*, 1970-71, *Thorndike-Barnhart College Dictionary*, and *Dictionary of American Regional English*.

WORK IN PROGRESS: Change and Continuity, to be published by University of Florida Press.

BIOGRAPHICAL/CRITICAL SOURCES: Saturday Review, August 2, 1952.

* * *

PYM, Christopher 1929-

PERSONAL: Born January 13, 1929, in London, England; son of Thomas Wentworth (a clerk in Holy Orders) and Dora Olive (Ivens) Pym; married Clemency N. Luce, May 28, 1960; children: John Luce, Catherine Mary, Victoria, Nicholas. *Education:* Trinity College, Cambridge, M.A., 1956. *Home:* 132 Bromley Rd., Beckenham, Kent, England. *Agent:* Stephen Aske, 39 Victoria St., London SW1H OEE, England.

CAREER: Parliamentary candidate at Blyth, 1960; Hansard Society for Parliamentary Government, elected to council, 1972. *Military service:* British Army, 1947-49; became second lieutenant.

WRITINGS: The Road to Angkor, R. Hale, 1959; *Mistapim in Cambodia*, Hodder & Staughton, 1960; (contributor) E. Bacon, editor *Vanished Civilisations*, Thames & Hudson, 1963; (editor) *Henri Mouhot's Diary*, Oxford University Press, 1966; *The Ancient Civilization of Angkor*, Mentor Books, 1968.

WORK IN PROGRESS: Revised edition of *Angkor* book.

BIOGRAPHICAL/CRITICAL SOURCES: R. Guthrie and T. Watts, editors, *Outlook Two*, Macdonald & Co., 1965.

* * *

QUANTRILL, Malcolm 1931-

PERSONAL: Born May 25, 1931, in Norwich, Norfolk, England; son of Arthur William (a factory worker) and Alice (Newstead) Quantrill; married Arja Irmeli Nenonen (a textile designer), November 2, 1958; children: Christopher George, Jan Robert. *Education:* University of Liverpool, B.Arch., 1954; University of Pennsylvania, M.Arch., 1955. *Agent:* David Higham Associates, Ltd., 76 Dean St., London W.1, England. *Office:* 21 Llwyn-Y-Grant Ter., Cardiff, Wales.

CAREER: Auburn University, School of Architecture, Auburn, Ala., assistant professor, 1955-56; Louisiana State University, Baton Rouge, assistant professor, department of architecture, 1956-59; free-lance work as architect, Helsinki, Finland, and London, England, 1959-61; Barbour Index Ltd., London, England, consulting architect, 1961-62; University of Wales, Welsh School of Architecture, Cardiff, senior lecturer, 1962—. Consulting architect to Richard Thomas & Baldwins Ltd., and Pilkington Brothers Ltd. Artist, exhibiting drawings and paintings in United States and Great Britain, currently showing regularly at Howard Roberts Gallery, Cardiff. *Member:* Royal Institute of British Architects (associate), Society of Architectural Historians of Great Britain.

WRITINGS: Gotobed Dawn, Barrie & Rockliff, 1962; *Gotobedlam*, Barrie & Rockliff, 1962; *John Gotobed Alone*, Barrie & Rockliff, 1964; *Ritual and Response in Architecture*, International Publications Service, 1974.

Plays—produced only: "Honeymoon", produced in London at Hampstead Theatre Club, 1967; "A Crucial Fiction", produced in London at Soho Lunch-time Theatre, 1970.

Radio plays: "Tea and Yesterday," 1963, "The Fence," 1964, "Return to Mustard Town," 1964 (all produced by British Broadcasting Corp.); "Saturday Night," 1964, "Monday Early," 1964 (both produced by Swedish Radio). Resident writer for literary section of *Western Mail*, 1964—.

WORK IN PROGRESS: A novel, *Ninepins*; two stage plays, "Pigeons on the Grass" and "The Statue in the Square"; a libretto for English composer Elizabeth Lutyen's *The Abbott Dies*.†

* * *

QUAY, Herbert C. 1927-

PERSONAL: Born August 27, 1927, in Portland, Me.; son of George J. and Susannah Fay (Bankerd) Quay; married E. Lorene Childs (a college professor), June 13, 1953; children: Jonathan, Jennifer. *Education:* Florida State University, B.S., 1951, M.S., 1952; University of Illinois, Ph.D., 1958. *Office:* Department of Psychology, University of Miami, Miami, Fla.

CAREER: Florida Industrial School for Boys, Marianna, Fla., clinical psychologist, 1952-53; Milledgeville State Hospital, Milledgeville, Ga., clinical psychologist, 1953-55; U.S. Veterans Administration Hospital, Danville, Ill., psychologist, 1955-56; Vanderbilt University, Nashville, Tenn., assistant professor of psychology, 1958-61; Northwestern University, Evanston, Ill., associate professor,

1961-63, became professor of psychology; University of Illinois, Urbana, research director of Children's Research Center, 1963-68; Temple University, Philadelphia, Pa., chairman of Division of Educational Psychology, 1968-74; University of Miami, Miami, Fla., director of program in applied social sciences and professor of psychology, 1974—. Consultant, U.S. Bureau of prisons, 1967—. *Military service:* U.S. Army, 1946-47; became sergeant. *Member:* American Psychological Association, Council for Exceptional Children (chairman of research committee, 1962—), Midwestern Psychological Association, Sigma Xi.

WRITINGS—Editor: *Research in Psychopathology*, Van Nostrand, 1963; *Juvenile Delinquency*, Van Nostrand, 1965; *Children's Behavior Disorders*, Van Nostrand, 1968; *Psychopaths: Logical Disorder of Childhood*, Wiley, 1972. Regular contributor to psychological journals. Assistant editor, *Exceptional Children*.

* * *

QUINN, James 1919-

PERSONAL: Born April 21, 1919, in Glasgow, Scotland; son of Thomas and Roseann (McCormick) Quinn. *Education:* University of Glasgow, M.A. (honors in classics), 1939; Heythrop College, theological studies, 1941-44, 1948-52. *Home:* 28 Lauriston St., Edinburgh EH3 9DJ, Scotland.

CAREER: Entered Roman Catholic order, Society of Jesus (Jesuits), 1939, ordained priest, 1950. Taught classics at Catholic College, Preston, Lancashire, England, 1944-48; on staff of Sacred Heart Church, Edinburgh, Scotland, 1953-54, 1955-63; editor of a Scottish Catholic publication, *Mercat Cross*, 1958-62; vice-postulator, cause of canonization of Blessed John Ogilvie, Society of Jesus, 1960—. Was one of the two observers, on behalf of the Secretariate for Promoting Christian Unity, at nineteenth general council of World Alliance of Reformed Churches, Frankfurt-am-Main, August, 1964.

WRITINGS: Our Lady in Scripture and Tradition, Taplinger, 1960; *New Hymns for all Seasons*, Chapman, 1969; *Theology of the Eucharist*, Fides, 1973. Contributor to *A Catholic Dictionary of Theology*, and to *Bodleian Library Record, Month, Tablet, Scotsman*, and *Downside Review*.†

* * *

QUINN, James Brian 1928-

PERSONAL: Born March 18, 1928, in Memphis, Tenn.; son of Clarence A. and Henriette (Rhein) Quinn; married Allie Brady James, February 9, 1950; children: James, John, Virginia. *Education:* Yale University, B.S., 1949; Harvard University, M.B.A., 1951; Columbia University, Ph.D., 1958. *Home:* 22 Rayton Rd., Hanover, N.H. 03755. *Office:* Amos Tuck School, Dartmouth College, Hanover, N.H.

CAREER: Allen B. DuMont Laboratories, Inc., Passaic, N.J., assistant head of research services and new products analyst, 1951-54; University of Connecticut, Storrs, assistant professor of marketing, 1954-57; Dartmouth College, Amos Tuck School of Business Administration, Hanover, N.H., 1957—, began as assistant dean and assistant professor, professor of business administration, 1964—; James Brian Quinn & Associates (consultants in research and development), president, 1961—. Consultant in long-range planning and research management to U.S. Congress, U.S.

Department of Defense, and private industry. *Awards, honors:* McKinsey Management Foundation Award, 1963, for article, "Transferring Research Results to Operations"; Ford Foundation grant for study in Europe on the planning of science and technological change, 1963-64; Sloan Foundation, fellow, 1967-68; Fulbright fellow, 1973.

WRITINGS: Yardsticks for Industrial Research Management, Ronald, 1959; (contributor) *Handbook of Industrial Research Management*, Reinhold, 1959; (contributor) *New Opportunities for Accounting in the 1960's*, American Institute of Certified Public Accountants, 1961; (contributor) *Technological Planning*, edited by J. Bright, Harvard University Press, 1962. Contributor to business and accounting journals.†

*   *   *

QUINTAL, Claire   1930-

PERSONAL: Born April 28, 1930, in Central Falls, R.I.; daughter of Armand (a businessman) and Helene (Messier) Quintal. *Education:* Anna Maria College, Paxton, Mass., B.A. (summa cum laude), 1952; University of Montreal, M.A. (magna cum laude), 1958; Sorbonne, University of Paris, Doctorat d'Universite (mention tres honorable), 1961. *Home:* 1279 High St., Central Falls, R.I. 02863. *Office:* 1, Place du Pantheon, Paris 5, France.

CAREER: American College in Paris, professor of French history, 1965—. Summer professor of contemporary French literature, Assumption College, Worcester, Mass., 1966—. Lecturer in modern French history, American Women's Club of Paris, 1965—. Lecturer on France, French literature, and Joan of Arc, throughout United States, 1964-65. *Member:* Federation Feminine Franco-Americaine (member of board of directors, 1952-58), Kappa Gamma Pi. *Awards, honors:* First recipient of Joan of Arc Award from Anna Maria College, 1965.

WRITINGS: Critique francaise de l'oeuvre de Theodore Dreiser, Sorbonne, University of Paris, 1961; (editor and translator) *The First Biography of Joan of Arc*, University of Pittsburgh Press, 1964; (with Daniel Rankin) *Letters of Joan of Arc*, Pittsburgh Diocesan Council of Catholic Women, 1969. Contributor of articles on the French language and methods of teaching to *L'Union*, 1957-58.

WORK IN PROGRESS: A biography of Joan of Arc's judge, Pierre Cauchon, bishop of Beauvais.

SIDELIGHTS: Claire Quintal is fluent in French, Spanish, German, and Latin. She has lived and traveled in Europe since 1958. *Avocational interests:* Poetry and painting.†

*   *   *

RACK, Henry D(enman)   1931-

PERSONAL: Born August 24, 1931, in Bishop Auckland, Durham, England; son of Henry Tong (a Methodist minister) and Annie (Watson) Rack; married Judith Mary Mills (a high school teacher), July 29, 1964. *Education:* Magdalen College, Oxford, B.A., 1955, M.A., 1959; Wesley House, Cambridge, England, B.A., 1957; University of Tuebingen, advanced theology study, 1959-60. *Home:* 40 Springbridge Rd., Manchester 16, England.

CAREER: Methodist minister, 1960—; Hartley Victoria College, Manchester, England, tutor in church history, 1965—.

WRITINGS: The Future of John Wesley's Methodism, Knox, 1965; *Twentieth Century Spirituality*, Epworth Press, 1969.

WORK IN PROGRESS: A study of German Pietism.†

*   *   *

RADER, Melvin (Miller)   1903-

PERSONAL: Born November 8, 1903, in Walla Walla, Wash.; son of Cary Melvin Rader; married Virginia Baker, March 27, 1935; children: Gordon, Miriam, Barbara Rader Boerner, Cary, David. *Education:* University of Washington, Seattle, A.B., 1925, A.M., 1927, Ph.D., 1929. *Politics:* Democrat. *Home:* 1719 Northeast Ravenna Blvd., Seattle, Wash. *Office:* Department of Philosophy, University of Washington, Seattle, Wash.

CAREER: University of Idaho, Moscow, instructor in English, 1927-28; Western Reserve University (now Case Western Reserve University), Cleveland, Ohio, assistant professor of English, 1929-30; University of Washington, Seattle, assistant professor, 1930-44, associate professor, 1944-48, professor of philosophy, 1948-71, professor emeritus, 1971—. Visiting associate professor, University of Chicago, 1944-45; visiting professor, University of South Florida, spring, 1972. *Member:* American Philosophical Association (president of Pacific division, 1953), American Society for Aesthetics (trustee, 1955-57; vice-president, 1971-72; president, 1973-74), American Civil Liberties Union (Washington State president, 1957, 1961-62). *Awards, honors:* Rockefeller Foundation research grant, 1948-49.

WRITINGS: Presiding Ideas in Wordsworth's Poetry, University of Washington Press, 1931; (editor and author of introduction) *A Modern Book of Esthetics*, Holt, 1935, 4th edition, 1973; *No Compromise*, Macmillan, 1939; *Ethics and Society*, Holt, 1950; *The Enduring Questions*, Holt, 1956, 2nd edition, 1969; *Ethics and the Human Community*, Holt, 1964; *Wordsworth: A Philosophical Approach*, Oxford University Press, 1967; *False Witness*, University of Washington Press, 1969. Contributor of articles and reviews to philosophical journals.

WORK IN PROGRESS: Art and the Human Community, to be published by Prentice-Hall.

SIDELIGHTS: Rader lived in Mexico, 1957-58, and has spent several summers there (and in Guatemala) since, studying native arts and archaeological remains. Also an explorer of the mountains and waterways of the Pacific Northwest.

A reviewer for *The Times Literary Supplement* commented in reference to *Wordsworth: A Philosophical Approach:* "This is the most comprehensive account of Wordsworth's debts to English and continental philosophers and it will prove invaluable to anyone interested in the Romantic period."

*   *   *

RADER, Ralph Wilson   1930-

PERSONAL: Born May 18, 1930, in Muskegon, Mich.; son of Ralph McCoy (a minister) and Nelle Emily (Fargo) Rader; married June Willadean Warring, September 3, 1950; children: Lois Jean, Eric Conrad, Michael William, Nancy Anne, Emily Rose. *Education:* Purdue University, B.S., 1952; Indiana University, Ph.D., 1958. *Politics:* Democrat. *Religion:* Protestant. *Home:* 465 Vassar Ave., Berkeley, Calif. 94708.

CAREER: University of California, Berkeley, instructor, 1956-58, assistant professor, 1958-63, associate professor, 1963-67, professor of English, 1967—, vice chairman of

English department, 1965-68. Visiting professor, University of Chicago, 1970. *Member:* Modern Language Association of America. *Awards, honors:* American Council of Learned Societies grant-in-aid, 1959; Guggenheim fellow, 1972-73.

WRITINGS: Tennyson's "Maud": The Biographical Genesis, University of California Press, 1963; (editor with Sheldon Sacks) *Essays: An Analytic Reader,* Little, Brown, 1964. Contributor of articles to literary and philological journals.

WORK IN PROGRESS: A book on Fielding's novels.†

*   *   *

RADLER, D(on) H. 1926-

PERSONAL: Born May 22, 1926, in New York, N.Y.; married Jean Dowell (an interior decorator), December 8, 1945; children: Scott, Philip, Judith. *Education:* Attended Kenyon College and the University of Chicago.

CAREER: Purdue Research Foundation, Lafayette, Ind., director of public relations. Democratic State Committee, Indianapolis, Ind., director of information. *Military service:* U.S. Army, 1944-46.

WRITINGS: (With H. H. Remmers) *The American Teenager,* Bobbs-Merrill, 1957; (with N. C. Kephart) *Success Through Play,* Harper, 1960; *El Gringo—The Yankee Image in Latin America,* Chilton, 1962. Writer of television and film scripts on medical subjects. Contributor of more than 150 articles to magazines, including *Harper's, Reporter, Scientific American, Industrial Research,* and *Science Digest.*†

*   *   *

RAE, John B(ell) 1911-

PERSONAL: Born March 21, 1911, in Glasgow, Scotland; son of James Bell (a painter) and Agnes (MacNaught) Rae; married Florence A. Urquhart, April 18, 1936; children: Helen U., James A. *Education:* Brown University, A.B., 1932, A.M., 1934, Ph.D., 1936; Yale University, graduate study, 1932-33. *Religion:* Congregational. *Home:* 437 West 11th St., Claremont, Calif. 91711. *Office:* Harvey Mudd College, Claremont, Calif. 91716.

CAREER: Brookings Institution, Washington, D.C., research assistant, 1936-37; Brown University, Providence R.I., administrative assistant, 1937-39; Massachusetts Institute of Technology, Cambridge, 1939-59, began as assistant professor, became associate professor of history; Harvey Mudd College, Claremont, Calif., professor of history, 1959—. Exchange professor of history, Case Institute of Technology, 1956-57; visiting professor, University of Manchester, Institute of Science and Technology, 1965-66; senior resident scholar, Eleutherian Mills-Hedley Foundation (Williamston, Del.), 1974. Director, Lincoln Educational Foundation. *Member:* Aemrican Historical Association, Economic History Association, Society for the History of Technology (president, 1973-74), American Society for Engineering Education (chairman, humanities and social science division, 1962-63, 1968-69), American Aviation Historical Society (director, 1963—), NASA (historical advisory committee, 1970-72). *Awards, honors:* Thomas McKean Memorial Trophy of Antique Automobile Club of America, 1960, for research in automotive history for *American Automobile Manufacturers: The First Forty Years.* National Science Foundation senior postdoctoral fellowship, 1965-66; Willard Keith, Jr. fellow in Humanities, Harvey Mudd College.

WRITINGS: (With T.H.D. Mahoney) *The United States in World History,* McGraw, 1949, 3rd edition, 1964; (editor with S. G. Morse and Laurence Foster) *Readings on the American Way,* Stackpole, 1954; *American Automobile Manufacturers: The First Forty Years,* Chilton, 1959; *The American Automobile,* University of Chicago, 1965; *Climb to Greatness: The American Aircraft Industry, 1920-60,* M.I.T. Press, 1968; *Henry Ford,* Prentice-Hall, 1969; *The Road and the Car in American Life,* M.I.T. Press, 1971. Contributor to economic, business, engineering, and technology journals. Advisory editor, *Technology and Culture,* 1959—, and *Business History Review,* 1954-58.

WORK IN PROGRESS: The Engineer as an Historical Failure.

*   *   *

RAEBECK, Lois 1921-

PERSONAL: Surname is pronounced Ray-beck; born October 2, 1921, in West Chicago, Ill.; daughter of Charles and Mae (Peterson) Rupp; married Albert Raebeck (an economist), December 19, 1959 (deceased). *Education:* Attended Cornell College, Mount Vernon, Iowa, 1939-43; Columbia University, B.S., 1946, M.A., 1948. *Home:* 31 Joralemon St., Brooklyn, N.Y. 11201.

CAREER: North Merrick (N.Y.) public schools, music teacher and music consultant, 1947-61; folk singer (in more than nine languages), 1961—; Classroom Materials, Inc., Great Neck, N.Y., script writer and performing artist for records, 1961—. *Member:* Music Educators National Conference, New York State Music Teachers Association.

WRITINGS: (With Lawrence Wheeler) *New Approaches to Music in the Elementary School,* W. C. Brown, 1964, 3rd edition, 1974; *Who am I?,* Folle H. Publishing, 1970; (with Lawrence Wheeler) *Orff and Kodaly Adapted for the Elementary School,* W. C. Brown, 1972; *An Elizabethan Songbag,* E. B. Marks Publishing, 1974. Scripts for recordings include "Johnny Can Sing Too," "Introduction to Music Reading," "Exploring the Rhythm Instruments," and 10 others.

*   *   *

RAGAN, Sam(uel Talmadge) 1915-

PERSONAL: Born December 31, 1915, in Raleigh, N.C.; son of William Samuel and Emma Clare (Long) Ragan; married Marjorie Usher (a free-lance writer), August 19, 1939; children: Nancy (Mrs. Kenneth Smith), Ann Talmadge. *Education:* Atlantic Christian College, B.A., 1936. *Politics:* Democrat. *Religion:* Presbyterian. *Home:* 255 Hill Rd., Southern Pines, N.C. 28387. *Office:* 145 West Pennsylvania Ave., Southern Pines, N.C. 28387.

CAREER: Newspaperman in North Carolina and Texas, 1936-48; *Raleigh News and Observer,* Raleigh, N.C., managing editor, 1948-57, executive editor, 1956-69; Sunday columnist, "Southern Accents," 1948—; *Raleigh Times,* Raleigh, N.C., executive editor, 1957—. North Carolina State University at Raleigh, lecturer on social studies and literature, 1959-68, director of writers workshop, 1964—; Sandhills College, instructor in creative writing, 1969—; St. Andrews College, instructor in creative writing, 1970—. Moderator of North Carolina Literary Forum, 1956—; trustee of North Carolina School of the Arts and of North Carolina Arts Council, 1963-72; member of North Carolina Government Reorganization, commissioner, 1970—. *Military service:* U.S. Army, Military Intelligence, 1934-46;

served in Pacific Theater; received Philippine Liberation Medal, Bronze Star.

MEMBER: Associated Press Managing Editors Association, American Society of Newspaper Editors (director and chairman, 1968), North Carolina Arts Council (chairman, 1967-72), North Carolina Literature and History Association (vice-chairman), North Carolina Writers Conference, North Carolina Press Association, North Carolina News Council (past president), Raleigh Sandwich Club, Raleigh History Club, Raleigh Country Club (director, 1957-59). *Awards, honors:* North Carolina Tercentenary Poetry award, 1963; D.Litt., Atlantic Christian College, 1972.

WRITINGS: The Democratic Party—Its Aims and Purposes, 1961; *The Tree in the Far Pasture* (collected poems), Blair, 1964; (editor) *The New Day,* Davis Publishing (Zebulon, N.C.), 1964; (with Elizabet S. Ives) *Back to Beginnings: Adlai E. Stevenson and North Carolina,* [Charlotte, N.C.], 1969; *To the Water's Edge* (poems), Moore Publishing, 1971. Contributor of articles to *American Scholar, Reader's Digest, Saturday Evening Post, Progressive, Journalism Review.* Contributing editor, *World Book Encyclopedia,* 1964—; editor, *The Pilot* (North Carolina), 1969—.†

* * *

RAINES, Robert A(rnold) 1926-

PERSONAL: Born July 12, 1926, in Newton, Mass.; son of Richard C. (a Methodist bishop) and Lucile M. (Arnold) Raines; married Margaret Gordon; children: Catharine, Barbara, Nancy. *Education:* Yale University, B.A., 1950; Yale Divinity School, B.D., 1953; Cambridge University, graduate study, 1954. *Home:* 8130 Winston Rd., Philadelphia, Pa. *Office:* First Methodist Church, 6023 Germantown Ave., Philadelphia, Pa. 19144.

CAREER: Ordained Methodist minister, 1953. Aldersgate Methodist Church, Cleveland, Ohio, minister, 1954-61; First Methodist Church, Germantown, Pa., minister, 1961—.

WRITINGS: New Life in the Church, Harper, 1961; *Reshaping the Christian Life,* Harper, 1964; (editor) *Creative Brooding,* Macmillan, 1966; *The Secular Congregation,* Harper, 1968; *Soundings,* Harper, 1970; *Lord, Could You Make It a Little Better?,* Word Books, 1972.

* * *

RAJAN, M. S. 1920-

PERSONAL: Born August 4, 1920, in Andhra Pradesh, India; son of M. V. and Rangamma Bhatrachar; married Padma Chellapilliengar, April, 1946; children: Pushpa and Vani (daughters), Venkatesan (son). *Education:* Mysore University, B.A. (honors), 1942, M.A., 1943; Columbia University, M.A., 1952. *Office:* Indian School of International Studies, Sapru House, New Delhi 1, India.

CAREER: Asian Relations Organization, New Delhi, India, assistant secretary, 1947-48; Indian Council of World Affairs, New Delhi, 1948-59, became research secretary; Indian School of International Studies, New Delhi, 1959—, professor of commonwealth studies, 1962—, director, 1965—; currently director of international studies, Jawaharlal Nehru University, New Delhi. *Member:* Indian Council of World Affairs (New Delhi). *Awards, honors:* D.Litt., Mysore University, 1963.

WRITINGS: United Nations and Domestic Jurisdiction, Orient Longmans, 1958, 2nd edition, Asia Publishing House, 1961; *The Post-war Transformation of the Commonwealth,* Asia Publishing House, 1962; *India in World Affairs, 1954-56,* Asia Publishing House, 1964; *Non-Alignment: India and the Future,* University of Mysore, 1970; (editor) *Studies in Politics,* Vikas Publications, 1971; *Eleven Analytical Studies of India's Diplomatic Relations Under Nehru (1947-64),* Asia Publishing House, 1974.†

* * *

RAMATI, Alexander 1921-

PERSONAL: Born December 20, 1921, in Poland; came to America in 1951; son of Solomon and Fania (Jakubowicz) Grynberg; married Didi Sonnenfeld (an actress). *Education:* Attended University of Warsaw and University of Rome, holds J.D. degree; University of California, Los Angeles, B.A., M.A. *Address:* c/o Shiffrin-Hyland, 315 South Beverly Hills Dr., Beverly Hills, Calif.

CAREER: With World News Agency, 1948-51; *Los Angeles Daily Journal,* Los Angeles, Calif., law editor, 1953-58; David Productions Ltd. (film producers), writer, director, and producer, 1963—. At one time was a writer under contract to Paramount Studios. *Military service:* Polish Army, 1941-47; Received Award of Merit with Swords, Cassino Medal, Italian Campaign Star. *Member:* Writers Guild of America. *Awards, honors:* Canadian Drama Guild Award, 1956, for "Survival."

WRITINGS: Chwedkowicki Las (title means "Forest of Chwedkowice"), 1944; *Armata Silenziosa* (title means "Silent Army"), 1946; *Beyond the Mountains* (novel; Book of the Month in Great Britain), Eyre & Spottiswoode, 1958, published as *The Desperate Ones,* New American Library, 1968; *Rebels Against the Light* (novel), Eyre & Spottiswoode, 1960, Farrar, Straus, 1961; *Israel Today,* Eyre & Spottiswoode, 1962; *Buenos Aires,* Plaza & Janes, 1965.

Plays include: "Survival," produced, 1956; "Rebels Against the Light," produced by David Productions, 1965; and several television plays. Author of screenplay *The Desperate Ones,* based on his novel *Beyond the Mountains,* American International, 1968. Contributor to *Life, Time.*

WORK IN PROGRESS: A novel, *Journey into the Past.*

SIDELIGHTS: Ramati is fluent in Russian, Polish, Italian, French, German, Hebrew, and English (learned since coming to United States). His first book was written in Polish, the second in Italian, and he also has written in Russian. *Beyond the Mountains* (about Russia), was published in Italian, Spanish, Hebrew, German, French, Dutch, and Portuguese; *Rebels Against the Light* (about Israel), was published in Spanish and German; and *Israel Today,* which is non-fiction, in Spanish.†

* * *

RAMAZANI, Rouhollah K(aregar) 1928-

PERSONAL: Born March 21, 1928, in Tehran, Iran; son of Ali K. (an architect) and Azam (Sultani) Ramazani, married Nesta Shahrokh, February 22, 1952; children: Vaheed, David, Jahan, Sima. *Education:* University of Tehran, LL.M., 1951; University of Virginia, S.J.D., 1954. *Office:* 232 Cabell Hall, University of Virginia, Charlottesville, Va.

CAREER: University of Virginia, Charlottesville, 1954—, research associate, Soviet Foreign Economic Relations Project, 1956-59, lecturer on Middle Eastern affairs, 1957, assistant professor of international law, 1957-60, associate professor of foreign affairs, 1960-64, professor of government and foreign affairs, 1964—, Edward R. Stettinius, Jr. professor of government and foreign affairs, 1972—. *Member:* American Political Science Association, American Society of International Law, Middle East Institute, British Institute of International and Comparative Law, Southern Political Science Association. *Awards, honors:* American Association for Middle East Studies prize, 1964, for manuscript of *The Foreign Policy of Iran, 1500-1941: A Developing Nation in World Affairs.*

WRITINGS: The Middle East and the European Common Market, University Press of Virginia, 1964; (contributor) Thomas T. Hammond, *Soviet Foreign Relations and World Communism*, Princeton University Press, 1965; *The Foreign Policy of Iran, 1500-1941*, University of Virginia Press, 1966; *The Northern Tier: Afghanistan, Iran and Turkey*, Van Nostrand, 1966; *The Persian Gulf: Iran's Role*, University Press of Virginia, 1972. Contributor of about twenty articles and more than thirty reviews to journals and newpapers, including *Middle East Journal, Free World Forum, Quarterly Review* (London), *Swiss Review of World Affairs, American Behavioral Scientist.*

*   *   *

RAMSAY, William M(cDowell)   1922-

PERSONAL: Born August 3, 1922, in Huntsville, Tex.; son of Charles Summer (a minister) and Catherine (McKay) Ramsay; married DeVere Maxwell, April 27, 1954; children: William McDowell, Jr., John Alston. *Education:* Southwestern at Memphis, A.B., 1946; Union Theological Seminary in Virginia, B.D.; University of Edinburgh, Ph.D. *Politics:* Democrat. *Home:* 7206 Vernon Rd., Richmond, Va. 23228. *Office:* Prebyterian Board of Christian Education, Box 1176, Richmond, Va. 23209.

CAREER: Ordained Presbyterian minister; pastor of churches in Knoxville, Tenn., 1950-54, and Paducah, Ky., 1954-59; Presbyterian Board of Christian Education, Richmond, Va., associate director of adult education, 1959—. Virginia Council of Human Relations, member; National Council of Churches, member of committee on adult work. *Military service:* U.S. Army, Infantry, rifleman. *Member:* American Academy of Religion.

WRITINGS: The Christ of the Earliest Christians, John Knox, 1959; *The Meaning of Jesus Christ*, Christian Literature Crusade, 1964; (with John Leith) *The Church, a Believing Fellowship*, Christian Literature Crusade, 1965; *Cycles and Renewal Trends in Protestant Lay Education*, Abingdon, 1969. Writer of articles, church school materials, and other educational materials for Presbyterian Board of Christian Education. Contributor of weekly page to *Outlook.*†

*   *   *

RAMSEY, Charles E(ugene)   1923-

PERSONAL: Born April 23, 1923, in Paragon, Ind.; son of S. Dodson (a painter) and Stella M. (Goss) Ramsey; married Alberta M. Jordan, July 19, 1943; children: James D., Charles W., Jane E., Suzanne. *Education:* Indiana State College, B.S., 1947; University of Wisconsin, 1948, Ph.D., 1952. *Home:* 1162 Autumn St., Roseville, Minn. 55113. *Office:* Department of Sociology, University of Minnesota, Minneapolis, Minn.

CAREER: University of Wisconsin, Madison, instructor, 1951-52; University of Minnesota, Minneapolis, assistant professor of sociology, 1952-54; Cornell University, Ithaca, N.Y., associate professor of rural sociology, 1954-62; Colo-

rado State University, Fort Collins, professor of sociology and chairman of department, 1962-65; University of Minnesota, Minneapolis, professor of Sociology, 1965—. Visiting professor at University of Puerto Rico, Rio Piedras, 1960-61. Research consultant to Inter-American Institute of Agricultural Science, Turrialba, Costa Rica, 1960, New York State Department of Education, 1961. *Military service:* U.S. Army Air Forces, 1943-46. *Member:* American Sociological Association, Rural Sociological Society, Sigma Xi, Phi Kappa Phi, Alpha Kappa Delta.

WRITINGS: (With Lowrie Nelson and Coolie Verner) *Community Structure and Change*, Macmillan, 1960; (with David Gottlieb) *The American Adolescent*, Dorsey, 1964; *Problems of Youth*, Dickenson Press, 1967; (with Gottlieb) *Understanding Children of Poverty*, Science Research Association, 1967; (with Donald J. McCarty) *The School Managers: Power and Conflict in American Public Education*, Greenwood Press, 1970. Contributor of about thirty articles to professional journals. Managing editor, *Rural Sociology*, 1959-60; consulting editor, F. A. Davis Publishing Co., 1967—.

*   *   *

RAND, Ayn   1905-

PERSONAL: First name rhymes with "pine"; born February 2, 1905, in St. Petersburg (now Leningrad), Russia; came to America in 1926, naturalized, 1931; married Frank O'Connor (an artist), 1929. *Education:* Attended private school in St. Petersburg; University of Leningrad, graduated in history, 1924. *Politics:* Radical for capitalism. *Religion:* Atheist. *Agent:* Curtis Brown Ltd., 60 East 56th St., New York, N.Y. 10022. *Office: The Ayn Rand Letter*, 183 Madison Ave., New York, N.Y. 10016.

CAREER: Cecil B. De Mille Studio, Hollywood, Calif., movie extra and junior screenwriter, 1926-28; RKO Pictures, New York, N.Y., 1929-32, began as filing clerk, became office head in wardrobe department; worked as screenwriter for Universal Pictures, Paramount Pictures, and Metro-Goldwyn-Mayer, 1932-34; worked as free-lance reader for RKO Pictures, then for Metro-Goldwyn-Mayer, both New York, N.Y., 1934-35; worked without pay as a typist for Eli Jacques Kahn, an architect, New York, N.Y. doing research work for *The Fountainhead*, 1937; Paramount Pictures, New York, N.Y., script reader, 1941-43; Hal Wallis Productions, Hollywood, Calif., screen writer (worked under special contract which committed her to work only six months of each year; during the other six months she pursued her own writing), 1944-49; full-time writer and lecturer, 1951—. Visiting lecturer at Yale University, 1960, Princeton University, 1960, Columbia University, 1960 and 1962, University of Wisconsin, 1961, Johns Hopkins University, 1961, Ford Hall Forum, Boston, mass., once each year, beginning 1961, Harvard University, 1962, Massachusetts Institute of Technology, 1962, United States Military Academy, 1974. *Awards, honors:* Doctor of Humane Letters, Lewis and Clark College, 1963.

WRITINGS: We the Living (novel), Macmillan, 1936; *Anthem* (novel), Cassell, 1938, revised edition, Pamphleteers, Inc., 1946, Caxton, 1953; *The Fountainhead* (novel), Bobbs-Merrill, 1943; *Atlas Shrugged* (novel), Random House, 1957; *For the New Intellectual: The Philosophy of Ayn Rand*, Random House, 1961; *The Virtue of Selfishness: A New Concept of Egoism*, New American Library, 1964; *Capitalism: The Unknown Ideal*, New American Library, 1966; *Introduction to Objectivist Epistemology*,

Objectivist, 1967; *The Romantic Manifesto: A Philosophy of Literature*, World Publishing, 1969; *The New Left: The Anti-Industrial Revolution*, New American Library, 1971. Co-editor and co-publisher, *The Objectivist*, a monthly journal (originally *The Objectivist Newsletter*, adopted magazine format, 1966), 1962-71; writer and publisher, *The Ayn Rand Letter*, 1971—.

Other writings: *Night of January 16th* (play; originally titled "Penthouse Legend"; produced in Hollywood, 1934, as "Woman on Trial," and on Broadway, 1935, as "Night of January 16th"), Longmans, Green, 1936, World Publishing, 1968; "The Unconquered" (play; adaptation of *We the Living* by the author), produced on Broadway, 1940; "Love Letters" (screenplay), Paramount, 1945; "You Came Along" (screenplay), Paramount, 1945; "The Fountainhead" (filmscript; adaptation of the novel by the author), Warner Bros., 1949.

SIDELIGHTS: When *The Fountainhead* was published in 1943, Lorine Pruette wrote: "Ayn Rand is a writer of great power. She has a subtle and ingenious mind and the capacity of writing brilliantly, beautifully, bitterly.... Good novels of ideas are rare at any time. This is the only novel of ideas written by an American woman that I can recall." In 1964, a *Playboy* editor wrote: "Ayn Rand ... is among the most outspoken—and important—intellectual voices in America today." Miss Rand's novels, then, are philosophical novels. Presented in her novels and non-fiction works, her ideas form the organized and consistent philosophy known as Objectivism.

Miss Rand states: "Objectivism holds that existence, the external world, is what it is, independent of man's consciousness; that reason, the faculty that identifies and integrates the material provided by man's senses, is man's only means of knowledge, and, therefore, his primary means of survival; that man's perception of the facts of reality must constitute the basis of his value judgments; that man is an end in himself, not a means to the ends of others; he must live for his own sake, neither sacrificing himself to others nor others to himself; that no man has the right to seek values from others by the initiation of physical force; that the politico-economic expression of these principles is laissez-faire capitalism, a system based on the inviolate supremacy of individual rights." Miss Rand wrote: "My philosophy, in essence, is the concept of man as a heroic being, with his own happiness as the moral purpose of his life, with productive achievement as his noblest activity, and reason as his only absolute." In *The Virtue of Selfishness*, she defines the virtue of Rationality as "the recognition and acceptance of reason as one's only guide to action.... The Objectivist ethics proudly advocates and upholds *rational selfishness*—which means: the values required for man's survival *qua* man—which means: the values required for *human* survival—not the values produced by the desires, the emotions, the 'aspirations,' the feelings, the whims or the needs of irrational brutes, who have never outgrown the primordial practice of human sacrifices, have never discovered an industrial society and can conceive of no self-interest but that of grabbing the loot of the moment."

Miss Rand told Alvin Toffler: "My views on charity are very simple. I do not consider it a major virtue and, above all, I do not consider it a moral duty." She added: "I am profoundly opposed to the philosophy of hedonism. Hedonism is the doctrine which holds that the good is whatever gives you pleasure and, therefore, pleasure is the standard of morality. Objectivism holds that the good must be defined by a rational standard of value, that pleasure is not a first cause, but only a consequence, that only the pleasure which proceeds from a rational value judgement can be regarded as moral, that pleasure, as such, is not a guide to action nor a standard of morality."

Romantic love is also explained in a manner consistent with Objectivist ethics: "Love is not self-sacrifice," she told Toffler, "but the most profound assertion of your own needs and values. It is for your *own* happiness that you need the person you love, and that is the greatest compliment, the greatest tribute you can pay to that person."

Miss Rand has stressed that Objectivism is not a philosophy to be defined in negatives, and it will not tolerate the compromise of an ideal. She told Toffler: "I most emphatically advocate a black-and-white view of the world.... What is meant by the expression 'black and white'? It means good and evil. Before you can identify anything as gray, as middle of the road, you have to know what is black and what is white, because gray is merely a mixture of the two. And when you have established that one alternative is good and the other is evil, there is no justification for the choice of a mixture. There is no justification ever for choosing any part of what you know to be evil."

Explaining the implications of Objectivism for politics, Miss Rand told *CA*: "[My] basic political principle is that no man or group has the right to *initiate* the use of physical force against others. 'In a civilized society, force may be used only in retaliation and only against those who initiate its use.... A government is the means of placing the retaliatory use of physical force under objective control—i.e., under objectively defined laws'." (*The Virtue of Selfishness*)

The two fundamental premises of religion—that there is an all-powerful being, and that man must come to accept this existence through faith rather than logic—are rejected by Miss Rand's philosophy. At the age of thirteen, Miss Rand concluded that she was an atheist. Miss Rand explained to *CA*: "First, there are no *reasons* to believe in God, there is no *proof* of the belief (she held); second, that the concept of God is insulting and degrading to man—it implies that the highest possible is not to be reached by man, that he is an inferior being who can only worship an ideal he will never achieve. Objectivists are uncompromising atheists, but atheism as such is not a *central* principle of the philosophy. The central principle is the advocacy of reason; the rejection of any form of mysticism, including theism, is a consequence to this principle."

When asked by Toffler if she believed that "Objectivism as a philosophy will eventually sweep the world," she replied: "Nobody can answer a question of that kind. Men have free will.... If you say, do I think that Objectivism will be the philosophy of the future, I would say yes, but with this qualification: if men turn to reason, if they are not destroyed by dictatorship and precipitated into another Dark Ages, if men remain free long enough to have time to think, then Objectivism is the philosophy they will accept."

Despite the influence of Miss Rand's ideas in intellectual circles, she regards herself primarily as a novelist (she told *CA*: "I'm not a propagandist, believe it or not") and, although she prefers not to be labeled in any conventional manner, she wrote: "As far as literary schools are concerned, I would call myself a Romantic Realist." In an essay in *The Romantic Manifesto*, entitled "The Goal of My Writing," she notes: "My purpose is *not* the philosophical enlightenment of my readers, it is *not* the beneficial influence which my novels may have on people. My purpose, first cause and prime mover is the portrayal of Howard Roark or John Galt *as an end in himself*—not as a means to any further end. Which, incidentally, is the greatest value I could ever offer a reader.''

She told a *Newsweek* reviewer: "One cannot write about life without discussing philosophy. Most novelists today try to be as vague as possible in order to be misunderstood by the greatest number of people. I want to be understood, so I present my philosophy openly and consciously.''

Discussing her method of characterization, Miss Rand has written: "Readers have asked me whether my characters are 'copies of real people in public life' or 'not human beings at all, but symbols.' Neither is true.... What I did was to observe real life, analyze the reasons which make people such as they are, draw an abstraction and then create my own characters out of that abstraction. My characters are persons in whom certain human attributes are focused more sharply and consistently than in average human beings. In 'The Goal of My Writing' since my purpose is the presentation of an ideal man, I had to define and present the conditions which make him possible and which his existence requires.... It was Aristotle who said that fiction is of greater philosophical importance than history, because history represents things only as they are, while fiction represents them 'as they *might be* and *ought to be.*' Why must fiction represent things 'as they might be and ought to be'? My answer is in one statement of *Atlas Shrugged*—and in the implications of that statement: 'As man is a being of self-made wealth, so he is a being of self-made soul'.''

As might be expected, Miss Rand approves of neither contemporary literature nor modern art. Toffler asked: "What is your appraisal of contemporary literature in general?'' She replied: "Philosophically, immoral. Aesthetically, it bores me to death. It is degenerating into a sewer, devoted exclusively to studies of depravity. And there's nothing as boring as depravity.'' She names Victor Hugo and Dostoevsky as her favorite novelists, and admires the early works of Mickey Spillane as belonging among the finest examples of popular literature, "which,'' she explains, "is today's remnant of Romanticism.'' She abhors the preoccupation of modern art with depravity and evil. "That which is not worth contemplating in life,'' she wrote, "is not worth re-creating in art.... The picture of an infected ruptured appendix may be of great value in a medical textbook—but it does not belong in an art gallery. And an infected soul is a much more repulsive spectacle.''

Analyzing her own work with respect to that of her contemporaries, she wrote: "It is a significant commentary on the present state of our culture that I have become famous—and also have become the object of hatred, smears, denunciations—as virtually the only novelist who has declared that *her* soul is *not* a sewer, and neither are the souls of her characters, and neither is the soul of man.''

In the introduction to an interview with Miss Rand, a *Playboy* editor summarized critical opinion toward her work, as represented by the reaction to *Atlas Shrugged*: "Despite [the] success [of the novel], the literary establishment considers her an outsider. Almost to a man, critics have either ignored or denounced the book. She is an exile among philosophers, too, although *Atlas* is as much a work of philosophy as it is a novel. Liberals glower at the very mention of her name; but conservatives, too, swallow hard when she begins to speak. For Ayn Rane, whether anyone

likes it or not, is sui generis: indubitably, irrevocably, intransigently individual. She detests the drift of modern American society: She doesn't like its politics, its economics, its attitudes toward sex, women, business, art or religion. In short, she declares, with unblinking immodesty, 'I am challenging the cultural tradition of two-and-a-half-thousand years.' She means it.''

In 1964, Miss Rand accepted the invitation of L. Quincy Mumford, Librarian of Congress, to place her manuscripts and personal papers in the Library of Congress.

BIOGRAPHICAL/CRITICAL SOURCES: New York Times Book Review, May 16, 1943, October 13, 1957; *Saturday Review of Literature*, May 29, 1943; *House and Garden*, August, 1949; *Newsweek*, October 14, 1957; *For the New Intellectual*, Random House, 1961; *Saturday Evening Post*, November 11, 1961; *Christian Century*, December 13, 1961; *Mademoiselle*, May, 1962; *Objectivist Newsletter*, October, 1963, November, 1963, December, 1965; *Playboy*, March, 1964; *New Statesman*, March 11, 1966; Carolyn Riley, editor, *Contemporary Literary Criticism*, Volume III, Gale, 1975.

*   *   *

RANDALL, Mercedes M.   1895-

PERSONAL: Born September 11, 1895, in Guatemala; daughter of Albert and Elsie Moritz; married John Herman Randall, Jr.; children: John H. III, Francis Ballard. *Education:* Barnard College, B.A., 1916; Columbia University, M.A., 1930, graduate study. *Home:* 15 Claremont Ave., New York, N.Y. 10027; (summer) Peacham, Vt. 05862.

MEMBER: Women's International League for Peace and Freedom, Fellowship of Reconciliation, War Resisters League, Wider Quaker Fellowship.

WRITINGS: The Voice of Thy Brother's Blood; a Plea for Jewish Rescue, Women's International League for Peace and Freedom, 1944; (editor) Jane Addams, *Peace and Bread*, Anniversary edition, King's Crown Press, 1945; *Highlights in W. I. L. P. F. History From the Hague to Luxembourg, 1915-1946*, Women's International League for Peace and Freedom, 1946; (editor) Emily Greene Balch, *Vignettes in Prose*, Women's International League for Peace and Freedom, 1952; *Pan, the Logos and John Dewey*, Women's International League for Peace and Freedom, 1959; *Improper Bostonian: Emily Green Balch*, Twayne, 1964; (editor) *Beyond Nationalism: The Social Thought of Emily Greene Balch*, Twayne, 1972.

*   *   *

RANDALL-MILLS, Elizabeth West   1906-

PERSONAL: Born September 15, 1906, in St. Louis, Mo.; daughter of Walter H. (a banker) and May (Scott) West; married Horace A. W. Randall-Mills, August 30, 1929 (deceased). *Education:* Vassar College, A.B., 1928. *Politics:* Independent. *Religion:* Episcopalian. *Home:* R.F.D. 2, Old Lyme, Conn. 00371.

CAREER: Poet. *Member:* Poetry Society of America, Catholic Poetry Society of America, Women Poets, Phi Beta Kappa.

WRITINGS: Country of the Afternoon (poetry), Golden Quill, 1964; *All Is Salutation* (poetry), Golden Quill, 1973. Lyric writer and collaborator with composer, Arnold Franchetti; also co-author of a devotional work, "Servants of the Altar.''

WORK IN PROGRESS: A book of poems.

SIDELIGHTS: Elizabeth Randall-Mills told CA: "My two areas of activity are religion and poetry. A poem gives value to life—life from which a poem is made and life in which the completed peom is read. Take the first, a poem is not a transcription of experience, but a celebration. The worlds of nature and events, of feelings and thought and spiritual insights are intuited in words (language being part of the experience) and held together in a musical, ordered relationship possible only through the power of the imagination. A unity is ignited by its components. These are given values as they illuminate each other in the formal world of the poem. Then as one looks from the poem to the outside world (and let the poem be read aloud) one finds the poem a measure of light by which life in the outside world is enhanced or diminished, is understood. A poem, being communication, bears responsibility for what it gathers and what it says with this. It is of the world and under divine jurisdiction. It exists to be harmonious to the divine, an epiphany declaring the spiritual infused in the material. A poem must celebrate whole reality."

* * *

RANDEL, William (Peirce) 1909

PERSONAL: Born January 7, 1909, in New York, N.Y.; son of William Adonijah (a surgeon) and Mabel Lucy (Peirce) Randel; married Janet Hosmer Belknap (a librarian), July 3, 1931; children: William Peirce, Jr., Elizabeth Peirce. Education: Attended Denison University, 1927-30; Columbia University, B.S., 1932, Ph.D., 1945; University of Michigan, A.M., 1933. Home: Peirce Farm, RFD 1, Alfred, Me. 04002. Agent: Bertha Klausner, International Literary Agency, Inc., 130 East 40th St., New York, N.Y. 10016. Office: Department of English, University of Maine, Orono, Me.

CAREER: University of Minnesota, Minneapolis, instructor in English, 1936-45; University of Missouri, Missouri School of Mines and Metallurgy, Rolla, assistant professor of English, 1945-47; Florida State University, Tallahassee, associate professor, 1947-53, professor of English, 1953-64; University of Maine, Orono, professor of English, 1965-72, Lloyd H. Elliott professor, 1972—. Visiting professor at University of Helsinki, 1950-51, University of Athens, 1955-56, University College of the West Indies, 1957-58, and University of Bologna, 1965; visiting summer professor at University of Minnesota, 1950, Duke University, 1952, and University of Wyoming, 1959.

MEMBER: Modern Language Association of America, American Studies Association, American Dialect Society, American Name Society, International Association of University Professors of English, Modern Humanities Research Association, North East Modern Language Association, Minnesota Historical Association (life member), Maine Historical Society, Phi Delta Theta.

WRITINGS: Bronson Alcott's Orphic Sayings, Golden Eagle Press, 1940; Edward Eggleston: Author of the Hoosier School-Master, King's Crown Press, 1945; Edward Eggleston, Twayne, 1963; Ku Klux Klan: A Century of Infamy, Chilton, 1965; Centennial: American Life in 1876, Chilton, 1969; (editor) Edward Eggleston, The Circuit Rider: A Tale of the Heroic Age, University Press of Kentucky, 1970; American Revolution: Mirror of a People, Hammond, Inc., 1973. Contributor of some fifty articles to literary and other journals.

WORK IN PROGRESS: White House Families: Biography of John Hancock.

RANOUS, Charles A. 1912-

PERSONAL: Surname is pronounced Ray-nus; born July 18, 1912, in Ann Arbor, Mich.; son of Adelbert (a farmer) and Cora (Sink) Ranous; married Dorothy Diefendorf, June 7, 1940; children: Karl E. Education: University of Michigan, A.B., 1936, M.A., 1938; graduate study at University of North Carolina, 1940-41, and at Columbia University. Politics: Republican. Religion: Protestant. Home address: Route #1, Edgerton, Wis. 53534. Office: University of Wisconsin, Madison, Wis. 53706.

CAREER: Instructor at University of Tennessee, Knoxville, 1938-41, University of North Carolina, Chapel Hill, 1941-42, Memphis State College, Memphis, Tenn., 1942-43, University of Oregon, Eugene, 1943-44, and Drake University, Des Moines, Iowa, 1944-47; Northern Illinois University, DeKalb, assistant professor of English, 1947-49; Fairleigh Dickinson University, Rutherford, N.J., assistant professor of English and chairman of freshman English, 1949-53; Federal Telecommunication Laboratories, Nutley, N.J., technical writer, 1953-57; Burroughs Corp., Military Electronic Computer Division, Detroit, Mich., engineering technical editor, 1957-60; University of Wisconsin, Madison, associate professor of technical writing in electrical engineering, 1960—. Visiting lecturer and conductor of workshops at other universities and colleges. Member: Institute of Electrical and Electronics Engineers, American Business Communications Association, Madison Technical Club.

WRITINGS: (Editor with Thomas Dunn) Our World in Words, W. C. Brown, 1946; (with Dunn) Learning Our Language, W. C. Brown, 1946, 2nd edition (with Dunn and Harold Allen), Ronald, 1950; Engineering Professional Expression, W. C. Brown, 1962; Communication for Engineers, Allyn & Bacon, 1964; (with Dorothy Ranous) The Inner Zone, College Publishing (Madison, Wis.), 1968; The Engineer's Interfaces, Xer-Lith (Madison, Wis.), 1974.

Writer of technical manuals and instruction books for International Telephone and Telegraph Laboratories, and reports for Burroughs Military Electronic Computer Division. Contributor to Educational Forum, College English, Wisconsin Engineer, and other journals. Editor of University of Wisconsin Electrical Engineering Staff Directory, 1961—, Research in Electrical Engineering, 1961—, Engineering Experiment Station Newsletter, 1961-63, and University of Wisconsin College of Engineering Catalog, 1962-64.

BIOGRAPHICAL/CRITICAL SOURCES: Institute of Electrical and Electronic Engineers Transactions on Education, June-September, 1964.

* * *

RAO, R(anganatha) P(admanabha) 1924-

PERSONAL: Born January 4, 1924, in Bidar (now in Mysore State), India; son of S. R. and Namagiri Amma Rao. Education: Loyola College, Madras University, B.A., 1942; Allahabad University, M.A., 1943. Politics: "Unshakable faith in democracy and its institutions." Religion: Hindu. Home: 3-5-272 Vithalwadi, Narayanguda, Hyderabad 29, Andhra Pradesh, India.

CAREER: Press Trust of India (national news agency), chief reporter in Hyderabad, 1948-56, senior reporter in Bombay, 1956-61; free-lance writer, and correspondent of North American Newspaper Alliance in New Delhi, India, 1961-63; Hindustan Times, New Delhi, India, correspondent in Hyderabad, 1964—. Also represented *Deccan Herald* (English daily published in Bangalore) in Hyderabad, in 1950's.

WRITINGS: Portuguese Rule in Goa, Asia Publishing House, 1963; *The Helping Hand*, Eurasia Publishing House, 1964; *Andhra Steel: Industrial Dawn for South*, [Hyderabad], 1965, 2nd edition, 1966; *Three General Elections: A Statistical Analysis*, [Hyderabad], 1966; *The Congress Splits*, Lalvani Publishing House, 1971. Writing for North American Newspaper Alliance includes feature stories carred in American and Canadian newspapers.

WORK IN PROGRESS: A book on Sino-Indian relations since 1947, with particular reference to Communist China's aggression against India and occupation of chunks of its territory.†

* * *

RATNER, Stanley C(harles)   1925-

PERSONAL: Born August 13, 1925, in Pittsburgh, Pa.; married Anita Sikov, September 5, 1950; children: Eric H., Keith A. *Education:* Attended Stanford University, 1943; University of Pittsburgh, B.S., 1948; Kent State University, M.A., 1950; Indiana University, Ph.D., 1954. *Office:* Department of Psychology, Michigan State University, East Lansing, Mich. 48824.

CAREER: Indiana University, Bloomington, instructor in psychology, 1953-55; Michigan State University, East Lansing, assistant professor, 1955-60, associate professor 1960-64, professor of psychology, 1964—. *Military service:* U.S. Army, 1943-46. *Member:* American Psychological Association, American Association for the Advancement of Science, Ecological Society of America, Sigma Xi. *Awards, honors:* National Science Foundation faculty fellow at Cambridge University, 1959-60.

WRITINGS: (With M. R. Denny) *Comparative Psychology*, Dorsey, 1964, revised edition, 1970; (with W. C. Corning) *Chemistry of Learning*, Plenum, 1968. Contributor of chapters to other books. Author of research articles.

WORK IN PROGRESS: Continued study of behavior of animal forms and the logic of comparative method.

* * *

RAUSCH, Edward N.   1919-

PERSONAL: Born November 8, 1919, in Dayton, Ohio; son of Leonard J. (a salesman) and Margaret (Schmidt) Rausch; married Eloise Sieck, April 24, 1943; children: Suzanne, Elizabeth. *Education:* University of Cincinnati, B.S., 1943. *Religion:* Lutheran. *Home:* 617 Mapleside Dr., Trotwood, Ohio 45426. *Office:* National Cash Register Co., Main and K Sts., Dayton, Ohio.

CAREER: National Cash Register Co., Dayton, Ohio, manager of methods department, 1962—. Sinclair College, Dayton, Ohio, instructor in management, 1955—. Village of Trotwood, member of board of Public Affairs, 1960-65, president of Board of Public Affairs, 1961-64, member of Village Council, 1965, mayor, 1966-68. *Military service:* U.S. Army, 1943-46. *Member:* Beta Gamma Sigma.

WRITINGS: Principles of Office Administration, C. E. Merrill, 1964.

WORK IN PROGRESS: Analysis of Data Processing Systems and Procedures.†

READ, Bill   1917-

PERSONAL: Born September 6, 1917, in Hutchinson, Kan.; son of Benjamin Thomas and Mary Golden (Nebel) Read. *Education:* University of Kansas, A.B., 1939; Harvard University, M.A., 1947; Boston University, Ph.D., 1959; summer study at National University of Mexico, 1940, Alliance Francaise, Paris, France, 1948. *Home:* 267 King Caesar Rd., Duxbury, Mass. 02332. *Agent:* Laurence Pollinger Ltd., 18 Maddox St., Mayfair, London W. 1, England. *Office:* Boston University, 855 Commonwealth Ave., Boston, Mass. 02215.

CAREER: University of Kansas, Lawrence, instructor in English, 1939-41; Suffolk University, Boston, Mass., assistant professor of English, 1947-48; Boston University, Boston, Mass., 1948—, began as instructor, professor of English, 1962—, acting chairman of the department of humanities, 1974—. *Member:* College English Association, Phi Beta Kappa.

WRITINGS: The Critical Reputation of Thomas Love Peacock, Boston University, 1959; (editor, with John Malcolm Brinnin) *The Modern Poets: An American-British Anthology*, McGraw, 1963; *The Days of Dylan Thomas: A Pictorial Biography*, McGraw, 1964; (editor with J. M. Brinnin) *Twentieth Century Poetry: American and British*, McGraw, 1970. Contributor to journals in field.

WORK IN PROGRESS: A book with working title of *Expressionism in Literature and Art.*

AVOCATIONAL INTEREST: Travel in Europe.

* * *

READ, Gardner   1913-

PERSONAL: Born January 2, 1913, in Evanston, Ill.; son of Gardner (an insurance broker) and Letitia (Hebert) Read; married Vail Payne, September 17, 1940; children: Cynthia Anne. *Education:* Eastman School of Music, B.Mus., 1936, M. Mus., 1937; private study of piano, organ, conducting, and orchestration; studied composition with Ildebrando Pizzetti in Italy and Jan Sibelius in Finland, 1939, and with Aaron Copland, summer, 1941. *Politics:* Independent. *Home:* Forster Rd., Manchester, Mass. *Office:* Boston University, Boston, Mass. 02215.

CAREER: Composer, teacher of music theory and composition, and conductor. Started as boy soloist with Episcopal church choir, Evanston, Ill., 1921; head of composition department at St. Louis Institute of Music, St. Louis, Mo., 1941-43, Kansas City Conservatory of Music, Kansas City, Mo., 1943-45, Cleveland Institute of Music, Cleveland, Ohio, 1945-48; Boston University, School of Fine and Applied Arts, Boston, Mass., professor of composition and music theory and composer-in-residence, 1948—, chairman of department of theory and composition, 1950-52. Visiting professor, University of California, Los Angeles, 1966. Commissioned orchestral works premiered by Chicago Symphony Orchestra, 1938, Indianapolis Symphony Orchestra, 1943, Cleveland Orchestra, 1946, and Louisville Orchestra, 1954; composer of other commissioned works for music festivals, string quartet, and stage. Major works also performed by the Boston, New York Philharmonic, Cincinnati, Indianapolis, San Francisco, Rochester, St. Louis, and Pittsburgh symphony orchestras, and other orchestras in United States, Europe, and South America. Guest conductor with Boston Symphony Orchestra, 1943, 1954, St. Louis Philharmonic Orchestra, 1943, 1944, Kansas City Philharmonic Orchestra, 1944, and Philadelphia Orchestra, 1964. Originator and commentator, weekly educational radio series, "Our American Music," Boston, 1953-60. Member of board of trustees, Boston Arts Festival, 1959-61.

MEMBER: American Society of Composers, Authors, and Publishers, MacDowell Colonists. *Awards, honors:* Summer fellowships to MacDowell Colony, 1936, 1937, 1946, 1950, to Berkshire Music Center, 1941; Cromwell traveling fellowship, 1938-39; U.S. Department of State grant to lecture on American music and conduct in Mexico, summers, 1957 and 1964; Huntington Hartford Foundation Fellowship, 1960 and 1965; honorary D. Mus., Doane College, 1962. Awards for compositions include first prize ($1,000 in each case) for symphonies, New York Philharmonic Symphony Society, 1937, and Paderewski Fund Competition, 1943; co-winner of $1,000 prize for "Suite for Organ," Pennsylvania College for Women, 1950; a number of awards for chamber works.

WRITINGS: Thesaurus of Orchestral Devices, Pitman, 1953; *Music Notation–A Manual of Modern Practice*, Allyn & Bacon, 1964, 2nd edition, Crescendo, 1972. Editor of "Birchard-Boston University Contemporary Music Series," 1950-60. Correspondent for *Musical Courier* (New York) and *Musical Leader* (Chicago); contributor of articles and reviews to music journals and to *New York Times, Arts in Society, Boston Globe*, and *Christian Science Monitor*.

WORK IN PROGRESS: Style and Orchestration; Contemporary Instrumental Techniques; Twentieth Century Notation; musical compositions.

SIDELIGHTS: Gardner is competent in French, German, and Spanish. *Avocational interests:* Chess, photography, wildlife.

* * *

RECK, Andrew J(oseph) 1927-

PERSONAL: Born October 29, 1927, in New Orleans, La.; son of Andrew Gervais and Katie (Mangiaracina) Reck. *Education:* Tulane University of Louisiana, B.A., 1947, M.A., 1949; Yale University, graduate study, 1949-52, Ph.D., 1954; University of St. Andrews, graduate study, 1952-53; Sorbonne, University of Paris, postdoctoral study, summers, 1962, 1964. *Office:* Department of Philosophy, Tulane University, New Orleans, La.

CAREER: Yale University, New Haven, Conn., instructor in philosophy, 1955-58; Tulane University of Louisiana, New Orleans, 1958—, started as assistant professor, now professor of philosophy, and chairman of department. *Military service:* U.S. Army, 1953-55; served in Berlin, Germany. *Member:* American Philosophical Association, Metaphysical Society of America (member of Council, 1971—), American Association of University Professors, Southern Society for Philosophy and Psychology, (treasurer, 1969-72), Southwestern Philosophical Society (president, 1972-73), Phi Beta Kappa. *Awards, honors;* Fulbright Fellowship, 1952-53; American Council of Learned Societies grant, 1961; Howard Foundation fellowship, 1962-63; American Philosophical Society grant, 1972; Huntington Library Fellowship, 1973.

WRITINGS: (Contributor) Irwin Lieb, editor, *Experience, Existence and the Good: Essays in Honor of Paul Weiss*, University of Southern Illinois Press, 1961; *Recent American Philosophy*, Pantheon, 1964; (editor) *Selected Writings of George Herbert Mead*, Bobbs-Merrill, 1964; (contrib-

utor) Sidney and Beatrice Rome, editors, *Philosophic Interrogations*, Holt, 1964; (contributor) *Spirit as Inquiry: Essays in Honor of Bernard Lonergan*, Continuum, 1964; *Introduction to William James*, Editions Seghers (Paris), 1966, Indiana University Press, 1967; *New American Philosophers*, Louisana State University Press, 1968; *Speculative Philosophy*, University of New Mexico Press, 1972; *Knowledge and Value*, Martinus-Nyhoff, 1972. Contributor of articles to professional journals.

WORK IN PROGRESS: Books on the philosophical background of the American Revolution, on metaphysics, and on William James.

SIDELIGHTS: Reck is competent in French and German.

* * *

RECORD, Jane Cassels 1915-

PERSONAL: Born December 16, 1915, in Fort Gaines, Ga.; daughter of G. E. Tucker and Josephine (Kaylor) Cassels; married Wilson Record (a university professor), July 24, 1938; children: Jeffrey. *Education:* University of California, Berkeley, Ph.D., 1954. *Home:* 2397 Hillside Lane, Lake Oswego, Ore. 97034. *Agent:* Curtis Brown Ltd., 60 East 56th St., New York, N.Y. 10022. *Office:* 4610 Belmont St., Portland, Ore. 97215.

CAREER: National War Labor Board, Atlanta, Ga., assistant director, later director of wage stabilization, 1943-47; Sacramento State College (now California State University, Sacramento), lecturer, 1954-55; University of California, Davis, assistant professor, and lecturer, 1956-63; University of Portland, professor of economics, 1965-70; Kaiser Foundation Research Institute, Health Services Research Center, Portland, Ore., senior economist and director of manpower studies, 1970—. British Hong Kong Imports, Sacramento, Calif., founder and sole owner, 1959-65. Industrial relations consultant. *Member:* American Economic Association, Industrial Relations Research Association, American Sociological Association. *Awards, honors:* Guggenhein fellow, 1968.

WRITINGS: (With husband, Wilson Record) *Little Rock, U.S.A.*, Chandler Publishing, 1960. Writer of social satire and travel pieces for magazines and newspapers, and articles for professional journals, with work appearing in *New Yorker, Antioch Review, Harper's, American Scholar, Library Journal*, and in sociology, economics, and medical journals.

WORK IN PROGRESS: Various research projects in ideologies, protest movements, social change, and leadership roles.

SIDELIGHTS: Mrs. Record is a world traveler; longest single trip was around-the-world tour largely via motor scooter in 1958. She visited the People's Republic of China in 1973.

* * *

REDDAN, Harold J. 1926-

PERSONAL: Born December 4, 1926, in Queens, New York, N.Y.; son of Harold B. (an electrical and chemical technician) and Catherine G. (Kelly) Reddan; married Margaret M. Byrne, October 12, 1952; children: Harold J., Patricia A., James J., Kathleen M. *Education:* St. Francis College, St. John's University, New York, N.Y., M.S., 1957, Ph.D., 1961. *Politics:* Democrat. *Religion:* Roman Catholic. *Home:* 96 Fifth St., Garden City Park, Nassau County, N.Y.

CAREER: New York (N.Y.) Department of Welfare, social investigator, 1950-58; St. John's University, New York, N.Y., 1958—, associate professor of sociology, 1964-69; Kings County Hospital Medical Center, School of Nursing, Brooklyn, N.Y., lecturer in sociology, 1961—; Manhattan College, New York, N.Y., professor and head of department of managerial sciences, 1969-73; Long Island University, C. W. Post Center, visiting professor of medical sociology, 1973—. Family relations consultant in private practice. Republic of Panama, sociological survey trips, 1961; Arco Publishing Co., consultant for sociology series. Coordinator, Citizens for Kennedy, New Hyde Park, N.Y.; local Democratic campaign manager, 1964. Director, Jamaica VI Peace Corps Training Project, 1965. *Military service:* U.S. Army, 1945-46; served in Pacific Theater. *Member:* American Sociological Association, Archaeological Institute of America, American Academy of Political and Social Science, National Geographic Society, Association for Psychiatric Treatment of Offenders, Garden City Park Historical Club (president), Zeta Sigma Pi, Alpha Kappa Delta, Delta Mu Delta, Delta Sigma Pi, Veterans of Foreign Wars, American Legion.

WRITINGS: Sociology, Medical Examination Publishing, 1964; (with John Saal) *Sociology: Its Scope and Purpose,* Sadlier, 1965, revised edition, 1974. *Advanced Test Series: G.R.E.: Sociology,* Arco, 1965. Editor, "Social Science" series, Sadlier, 1964-65.

WORK IN PROGRESS: Research on effects of group activities upon patient recovery. Analysis of special college programs for police and health care professionals.

*   *   *

REDMOND, Howard A(lexander)   1925-

PERSONAL: Born January 6, 1925, in Los Angeles, Calif.; son of Harold Alexander (an accountant) and Ada (Hansen) Redmond; married Lois Ann Wagner (a teacher), July 31, 1953; children: Colleen Linda, Calvin David. *Education:* University of California, Los Angeles, A.B., 1946; Princeton Theological Seminary, B.D., 1947; University of Southern California, M.A., 1950, Ph.D., 1953. *Politics:* Republican. *Home:* Route 1, Box 62-G, Colbert, Wash. 99005.

CAREER: Ordained Presbyterian minister, 1947; pastor in New Castle, Pa., 1947-49; Davis and Elkins College, Elkins, W.Va., associate professor of religion and philosophy, 1950-54; pastor in Sanger, Calif., 1954-57; Whitworth College, Spokane, Wash., professor of religion and philosophy, 1957—. Chamber of Commerce, Sanger, Calif., member of board of directors, 1957. *Member:* American Society for Aesthetics, Presbytery of Spokane.

WRITINGS: The Omnipotence of God, Westminster, 1964.

WORK IN PROGRESS: Research on books dealing with Christianity and the occult; also on the second advent of Christ.

AVOCATIONAL INTERESTS: Classical music (plays, and sometimes teaches, string bass); tennis, water sports, and skiing.

*   *   *

REED, Howard Alexander   1920-

PERSONAL: Born February 26, 1920, in Izmir, Turkey; son of U.S. citizens Cass Arthur (a college president) and Rosalind (MacLachlan) Reed; married second wife, Mary

A. Marshall, July 6, 1963; children: Seth Olcott, Heather MacLachlan, Deborah Lamont, Michael Azeltine, Nancy Lynn. *Education:* Yale University, B.A. (with high orations), 1942; Princeton University, M.A., 1949, Ph.D., 1951. *Politics:* Independent. *Religion:* Society of Friends. *Home:* 37 Northridge Rd., Old Greenwich, Conn. 06870. *Office:* Department of History, University of Connecticut, Storrs, Conn. 06268.

CAREER: Educational welfare officer, United Nations Relief and Rehabilitation Administration, Athens, Greece, and concurrently director of national relief and cultural programs for World Student Relief in Greece, 1946-47; Yale University, New Haven, Conn., instructor in history and resident director, International Student Center, 1950-52; McGill University, Montreal, Quebec, Canada, assistant professor of Islamic history and languages and assistant director of Institute of Islamic Studies, 1952-55; Ford Foundation, program specialist in international training and research, New York, N.Y., and Near East, 1955-57; Pendle Hill, Wallingford, Pa., lecturer and researcher on Islam and Middle East, 1957-58; American Friends Service Committee, Philadelphia, Pa., national director of college and projects programs, 1958-60; Danforth Foundation, St. Louis, Mo., associate director, 1960-64, consultant on non-Western studies, 1964—; Education and World Affairs, Inc., New York, N.Y., executive associate, 1964-67. Consultant to the Agency for International Development in India, and several colleges, universities, and educational agencies, 1964—; University of Connecticut, Storrs, director of International and Intercultural Studies, 1967-71, professor, 1967—. U.S. Foreign Service examiner, 1947-49; Association of American Colleges, director of national survey of non-Western studies in United States, 1963-64. Chief rapporteur for Islam, Colloquium at Princeton University and Washington, D.C., 1953. Member of board of Lisle Fellowship, Inc., 1948-52, 1958-60, 1965-70, School for Creative Work, Hartford, Conn., 1951-52, Pendle Hill, 1958-73, Association of Princeton Graduate Alumni, 1961-64; consultant, Campus Christian Foundation, 1969-73, American Research Institute, Turkey, 1969—; member of executive council, Conference on Peace Research in History, 1972—. *Military service:* U.S. Naval Reserve, 1942-56; active duty, 1942-46; became lieutenant; received Legion of Merit with Combat V (twice) and Distinguished Service Cross (British).

MEMBER: International Society for Oriental Research, American Historical Association, Middle East Institute, American Academy of Political and Social Science, Association for Asian Studies, Society for Religion in Higher Education (fellow), Phi Beta Kappa, British-American Alumni, Old Wellingtonian Society. *Awards, honors:* Rockefeller fellowships, 1947-50, 1952; Middle East Institute fellowship, 1947-50; Ford Foundation fellowship for research in Middle East, 1954; Fulbright fellow, 1970.

WRITINGS: (Principal author) *Non-Western Studies in the Liberal Arts College,* Association of American Colleges, 1964; (with Stephen Drance) *Essentials of Peremitry,* Oxford University Press, 2nd edition, 1972. Also author of *The Emergence of the Modern Middle East,* 1970.

Contributor: *Colloquium on Islamic Culture,* Princeton University Press, 1953; *Foreign Affairs Bibliography 1942-52,* edited by Henry L. Roberts, Council on Foreign Relations and Harper, 1955; *Doktor Abdulhak Adnan Adivar,* compiled by Halide Edib Adivar, [Istanbul], 1956; *Islam and the West,* edited by Richard N. Frye and others, Mouton, 1957; *Guide to Historical Literature,* edited by George

F. Howe and others, Macmillan, 1961; *General Education: Current Ideas and Concerns*, edited by James G. Rice, Association for Higher Education and National Education Association, 1964; *The University Looks Abroad: Approaches to World Affairs at Six American Universities*, edited by Allan A. Michie, 1965.

Contributor to *Encyclopaedia of Islam*, Luza, 1954, to *Encyclopedia Americana*, 1965, and to *Current Issues in Higher Education* (annual), 1964. Also contributor of articles and reviews to scholarly journals and newspapers in United States, Turkey, Germany, Lebanon, and India. Advising editor, *Muslim World*, 1970—.

WORK IN PROGRESS: Research on concepts and means to introduce international and intercultural dimensions of education more effectively into mainstream of American education; research on enhancing the continuing learning process for teachers and students with special attention to cross-cultural learning; collecting and analyzing data on the international dimensions of education.

SIDELIGHTS: "As I was born in Turkey," Reed writes, "and lived there, elsewhere in the Near East and Europe for many years, I grew up speaking French, Modern Greek, Turkish and English with almost equal facility. Since then I've learned German, Spanish, and some Arabic, and have done much study of the Islamic world, especially in Turkey and India.... My work with EWA offers unique, strategic opportunities to think, study and act at significant points in the world-wide effort to improve education and human resource development with a focus on the basic values, assumptions and beliefs of all concerned interacting with their rising hopes."†

*   *   *

REED, John F(ord) 1911-

PERSONAL: Born June 25, 1911, at Fort Sheridan, Ill.; son of Harrie F. (a captain, U.S. Army) and Eleanor (Painter) Reed; married Lydonia V. Robinson, June 21, 1941. *Education:* Attended Duke University, 1934-35, Temple University, 1935. *Home:* 418 Allendale Rd., King of Prussia, Pa. 19406.

CAREER: Formerly engaged in manufacturing business; now retired. Freedoms Foundation at Valley Forge, national historian. *Member:* Manuscript Society.

WRITINGS: Campaign to Valley Forge, University of Pennsylvania Press, 1965; *Valley Forge Crucible of Victory*, Philip Freneau Press, 1969. Writer of articles for *Manuscripts* (quarterly); contributor to local historical society publications.

WORK IN PROGRESS: Research on the Revolutionary War.

AVOCATIONAL INTERESTS: Reed collects historical manuscripts.

*   *   *

REEDY, William James 1921-

PERSONAL: Born July 26, 1921, in New York, N.Y.; son of James Leo (an accountant) and Grace (Freutel) Reedy; married Margaret Mary Maher; children: Marianne Joan. *Education:* Fordham University, M.S. in Ed., 1952. *Religion:* Roman Catholic. *Home:* 2200 East Temont Ave., New York, N.Y. 10462. *Office:* William H. Sadlier, Publishers, 11 Park Pl., New York, N.Y. 10007.

CAREER: William H. Sadlier (publishers), New York,

N.Y., director of catechetics. Lecturer in catechetics at seminaries, religious houses, and other Catholic institutions throughout America. *Member:* American Catholic Theological Society, American Catechetical Forum, Society of Catholic College Teachers of Sacred Doctrine, National Catholic Liturgical Conference, Religious Teachers Council of Archdiocese of New York (member of executive board).

WRITINGS: (With Flynn, Loretto, Simeon) *Way, Truth, Life*, Sadlier, 1956; (with Flynn, Loretto, Simeon) *The Triumph of Faith*, Sadlier, 1958; *Living Our Faith*, Sadlier, 1958; *Faith in Action*, Sadlier, 1960; (with Leland J. Boyer) *God's Plan for Us*, Sadlier, 1961; (with Boyer) *God's Life in Us*, Sadlier, 1962; (with Boyer) *God's Law of Love*, Sadlier, 1963; (with Boyer) *The Life of Faith*, Sadlier, 1964.

Editor: (And co-author) *Modern Challenge to Religious Education: The Good News Yesterday and Today*, (and co-author) *The ABC's of Modern Catechetics*.

Also author of *The Story of Salvation*, 1967, and *The Friendship of Christ*, 1968.

Author of "Catholic High School Religion Series" and "Catholic High School Confraternity Series." Also writer of a pamphlet-brochure, "About the Kerygma," and contributor of twenty-five articles on kerygmatic theology to magazines.

SIDELIGHTS: Sale of the four books in the "Catholic High School Religion Series" is near the 400,000-mark, and more than 100,000 copies of Reedy's pamphlet, "About the Kerygma," have been distributed in English-speaking countries.†

*   *   *

REESE, Jim E(anes) 1912-

PERSONAL: Born May 29, 1912, in Comanche, Tex.; son of Francis Jefferson (a pharmacist) and Martha (Eanes) Reese; married Sarah Burton (a teacher), September 1, 1936; children: Carolyn (Mrs. Peter Morris), John William, Margaret Gail, James Bassett. *Education:* University of Texas, B.A., 1933, M.A., 1935, Ph.D., 1941. *Home:* 802 South Pickard St., Norman, Okla. 73069. *Office:* Department of Economics, University of Oklahoma, Norman, Okla.

CAREER: Assistant professor of economics at Texas College of Arts and Industry, Kingsville (now Texas Arts and Industries University), 1939-42, Southern Methodist University, Dallas, 1942-43, 1946; University of Oklahoma, Norman, 1946—, associate professor, 1946-49, professor, 1949-61, David Ross Boyd Professor of Economics, 1962—, chairman of department, 1948-54. Regional representative, Economist Joint Council on Economic Education, 1957-58. *Military service:* U.S. Navy, 1943-46; became lieutenant junior grade. *Member:* American Economic Association, Economic History Association, American Association of University Professors, Southern Economic Association, Southwest Social Science Association (vice-president, 1973). *Awards, honors:* Teacher of the Year, University of Oklahoma, 1953.

WRITINGS: The American Economy, Houghton, 1953; (with Gilbert Fite) *An Economic History of the United States*, Houghton, 1959, 3rd revised edition, 1973; *Cowboys, Cattle and Commerce*, Joint Council on Economic Education, 1960; *Resource Use Policies (Historical Impact of Resource Decisions)*, Joint Council on Economic Education, 1960. Contributor to *Collier's Encyclopedia* and *Cowle's Encyclopedia*.

WORK IN PROGRESS: Economics, publication by Harper; *Urban Economics*, Irwin; *The Old West*.

AVOCATIONAL INTERESTS: Firearms and Western history.†

*   *   *

REEVE, G. Joan (Price) 1901-

PERSONAL: Born September 28, 1901, in Ilfracombe, Devonshire, England; daughter of Eustace Dickinson (a missionary) and Mary (Lillingston) Price; married Warren Scott Reeve (a minister and missionary; died, 1961); children: Evelyn Joan. *Education:* Westfield College, London, B.A., 1924; London Day Training College, Teacher's Diploma, 1925. *Residence:* Burnsville, N.C. 28714

CAREER: Church of England missionary teacher in Osaka, Japan,1927-32; Presbyterian missionary in Osaka, Japan, 1933-40; teacher of piano and church choir director, 1947-55, and released-time Bible school teacher, 1949-55, all in Shippenburg, Pa.; church choir director, 1955—, and teacher of piano, 1956—, in Burnsville, N.C. *Member:* Delta Kappa Gamma, Burnsville Women's Club (president, 1963-65), Burnsville Garden Club.

WRITINGS: The Mystifying Twins, Pageant, 1960, 2nd edition, Moody, 1964; *The Secret of the Mystifying Twins*, Moody, 1964; *Jerry and the Missing Cuckoo*, Moody, 1971; *Strange Boy of the Island*, Moody, 1972. Writer of Sunday school papers for Scripture Press. Editor of *Delta Kappa Gamma Newsletter*, 1963-64.

WORK IN PROGRESS: Chris of the Understanding Heart, a story of a young teacher in Japan; a second book, *Deep Waters*.

SIDELIGHTS: G. Joan Reeve lived in India with missionary parents for five years, and has traveled across Siberia, Russia and Europe, and then to Africa, to visit missionary members of her family. She is fluent in Japanese.

*   *   *

REEVES, Majorie E(thel) 1905-

PERSONAL: Born July 17, 1905, in Bratton, Westbury, Wilshire, England; daughter of Robert J. (an agricultural engineer) and Edith S. (Whitaker) Reeves. *Education:* St. Hugh's College, Oxford, B.A. (first class honors), 1926; Westfield College, London, Ph.D., 1931. *Home:* 38 Norham Rd., Oxford, England.

CAREER: Roan School for Girls, London, England, assistant mistress of history 1927-29; St. Gabriel's College, London, England, lecturer in history, 1931-38; Oxford University, St. Anne's College, Oxford, England, 1938—, began as tutor, became fellow in history, then vice-principal, honorary fellow, 1972—. Member of Central Advisory Council, British Ministry of Education, 1947-59; academic planning boards of University of Canterbury, University of Surrey, School Broadcasting Council British Broadcasting Corp., and Education Council of Independent Television Authority. Lecturer on four U.S. tours. *Member:* Royal Historical Society (fellow), Historical Association, Christian Frontier Council, University Teachers Group (chairman). *Awards, honors:* D.Litt., Oxford University, 1972.

WRITINGS: (With John Drewett) *What is Christian Education?*, Macmillan, 1942; *Growing Up in a Modern Society*, University of London Press, 1946, 4th edition, 1956; (with Leone Tondelli and Beatrice Hirsch-Reich) *Il Libro delle Figure dell' Abate Gioachino*, Societe Editrice Internazionale, 1953; (contributor) William Roy Niblett, editor, *Moral Education in a Changing Society*, Faber, 1963; (editor) *Eighteen Plus: Unity and Diversity in Higher Education*, Faber, 1965; *The Influence of Prophecy in the Later Middle Ages: A Study in Joachimism*, Clarendon Press, 1969; (contributor) G. J. Cuming and Derek Baker, editors, *Studies in Church History: Popular Belief and Practice*, Cambridge University Press, 1971; (with Hirsch-Reich) *The Figures of Joachim of Fiore*, Clarendon Press, 1972.

Editor of "Then and There" series for schools, Longmans, Green, and author of nine books in series, *Elizabethan Court*, 1956, *The Mediaeval Town*, 1958, *The Mediaeval Monastery*, 1958, *The Mediaeval Village*, 1959, *The Norman Conquest*, 1959, *Alfred and the Danes*, 1960, (with Paule Hodgson) *Elizabethan Citizen*, 1961, *The Mediaeval Castle*, 1963, *A Mediaeval King Governs*, 1971.

Contributor of articles on historical topics to *Times Educational Supplement, New Era, Speculum, Medieval and Renaissance Studies, Traditio, Recherches de Theologie, Medievalia et Humanistica*, and other journals.

WORK IN PROGRESS: A short book on Joachim of Fiore and his influence; a book on higher education, tentatively titled *The Limits of Analysis*.

SIDELIGHTS: Majorie Reeves is competent in Latin, French, and Italian; and knows some German.

*   *   *

REICHERT, Victor Emanuel 1897-

PERSONAL: Surname is pronounced *Rye*-kert; born March 17, 1897, in Brooklyn, N.Y., son of Isidor (a rabbi) and Mirian (Pakas) Reichert; married Louise Feibel, December 22, 1928; children: David, Jonathan. *Education:* City College (now City College of City University of New York), B.A., 1919; Columbia University, B.Litt. in journalism, 1921; Hebrew Union College B.H., 1923, Rabbi, 1926, D.D., 1932. *Politics:* Independent Republican. *Home:* 752 Red Bud Ave., Cincinnati, Ohio 45229. *Office:* Rockdale Temple, Cincinnati, Ohio 45236.

CAREER: Rockdale Temple Congregation B'nai Israel, Cincinnati, Ohio, rabbi, 1926-62, rabbi emeritus, 1962—. University of Cincinnati, Cincinnati, Ohio, lecturer on literature of Old Testament, 1942—. Visiting summer teacher at University of Virginia, 1938, and Middlebury College, Bread Loaf School of English, 1949; visiting lecturer at Hebrew Union College, 1959-62; visiting faculty member, Washington University, St. Louis, Mo., 1968-69; also affiliated with Temple Emanu-El, St. Louis, Mo., 1968-69. Preacher in London, Paris, Dublin, and Geneva; conducted religious retreat in Berchtesgaden, Germany. *Military Service:* U.S. Army, 1918-19.

MEMBER: Central Conference of American Rabbis, McDowell Society, Vermont Poetry Society, Sigma Alpha Mu, Honorable Order of Ten Batlanim (founder), Honorable Order of Kentucky Colonels, Literary Club (Cincinnati, honorary member; president, 1973). *Awards, honors:* Citation from U.S. Army for retreat at Berchtesgaden; D.H.L. from Hebrew Union College–Jewish Institute of Religion, Cincinnati, Ohio, 1955; D.Litt. from University of Cincinnati, 1965.

WRITINGS: Highways Through Judaism, Soncino Press, 1936; *The Tower of David and Other Poems*, privately printed, 1946, Vermont Books, 1964; (author of commentary) Abraham Cohen, editor, *Job*, Soncino Press, 1946;

(with Abraham Cohen) *Commentary on the Book of Ecclesiastes-The Five Megilloth*, Soncino Press, 1946; (with Moses Zalesky) *On Ben Peleh*, [Israel], 1963; (editor and translator from the Hebrew) Judah Ben Solomon al-Harizi, *The Fourteenth Gate of Judah al-Harizi's Tahkemoni*, R. H. Cohen Press, 1963; (translator) *The Tahkemoni of Judah al-Harizi*, Volume I, R. H. Cohen Press, 1965, Volume II, Bloch, in press.

Former editor of *Octagonian*; member of editorial board, *Journal* of the Central Conference of American Rabbis.

WORK IN PROGRESS: The Cantos of Immanuel of Rome.

SIDELIGHTS: Reichert has traveled in Eurpoe, Israel, and Turkey doing research, preaching, and tracing the footsteps of Harizi. He was a summer neighbor of Robert Frost in Vermont and long a personal friend of the late poet.

BIOGRAPHICAL/CRITICAL SOURCES: Lawrence Thompson, editor, *Selected Letters of Robert Frost*, Holt, 1964.

* * *

REICKE, Bo I(var) 1914-

PERSONAL: Born July 31, 1914, in Stockholm, Sweden; son of Ivar (a furniture merchant) and Esther (Danielsson) Reicke; married Ingalisa Ahstroem, July 6, 1941; children: Agnes, Daniel. *Education:* University of Uppsala, Dr.Theol., 1946. *Religion:* Lutheran. *Home:* Spalentorweg 24, Basel, Switzerland.

CAREER: University of Uppsala, Uppsala, Sweden, docent in New Testament studies, 1946-53; University of Basel, Basel, Switzerland, professor of New Testament studies, 1953—. Visiting professor in Vienna, Austria, 1948, and Richmond, Va., 1959; summer visiting professor in Berkeley, Calif., and at St. Olaf College, Northfield, Minn., 1962.

WRITINGS: The Disobedient Spirits and Christian Baptism, Munksgaard, 1946; *Diakonie, Festfreude und Zelos*, Lundequist, 1951; *Glaube und Leben der Urgemeinde*, Zwingli-Verlag, 1957; (editor with L. Rost) *Biblisch-historisches Handwoerterbuch*, three volumes, Vandenhoeck & Rupecht, 1962-66; *The Epistles of James, Peter, and Jude*, Doubleday, 1964; *Neutestamentliche Zeitgeschichte*, Toepelmann, 1964; *The Gospel of Luke*, John Knox, 1964; *Die zehn Worte*, Siebeck, 1973. Contributor of more than one hundred articles to dictionaries and theological journals. Editor of *Theologische Zeitschrift* (Basel), 1955—.

* * *

REID, Eugenie Chazal 1924-

PERSONAL: Born December 21, 1924, in Woodbury, N.J.; daughter of Philip Maxwell and Mabel (Batten) Chazal; married George K. Reid (a college professor), July 23, 1949; children: Louise, Philip. *Education:* Florida State University, A.B., 1945; University of North Carolina, B.S. in L.S., 1947. *Religion:* Presbyterian. *Home:* 2928 DeSoto Way South, St. Petersburg, Fla. *Agent:* Bertha Klausner, International Literary Agency, Inc., 130 East 40th St., New York, N.Y. 10016.

CAREER: Jacksonville (Fla.) public library, librarian, 1947; University of Florida Library, Gainesville, librarian. 1947-52.

WRITINGS: Mystery of the Carrowell Necklace (juvenile), Lothrop, 1965; *Mystery of the Second Treasure* (juvenile), Lothrop, 1967.

REID, Meta Mayne

PERSONAL: Born in England; daughter of Marcus Andrew (a farmer) and Elvina (Moody) Hopkins; married Ebenezer Mayne Reid (chairman, Ulster Museum), August 7, 1935; children: Mark McClean, David Mayne. *Education:* University of Manchester, B.A. (honors), 1926. *Religion:* Presbyterian. *Home:* Coolnean, Ballymullan Rd., Crawfordsburn, Northern Ireland.

CAREER: Author of children's books (ages nine-twelve). Broadcaster of own tales, poems, and talks on British Broadcasting Corp. programs. *Member:* P.E.N. (president of Irish branch, 1970-72).

WRITINGS—All for children: *Carrigmore Castle*, Faber, 1954; *All Because of Dawks*, Macmillan, 1955; *Tiffany and the Swallow Rhyme*, Faber, 1956; *Dawks Does It Again*, Macmillan, 1956; *Dawks on Robbers' Mountain*, Macmillan, 1957; *The Cuckoo at Coolnean*, Faber, 1957; *Strangers in Carrigmore*, Faber, 1958; *Dawks and the Duchess*, Macmillan, 1958; *McNeils at Rathcapple*, Faber, 1959.

Storm on Kildoney, Macmillan, 1961; *Sandy and the Hollow Book*, Faber, 1961; *With Angus in the Forest*, Faber, 1963; *The Tinkers' Summer*, Faber, 1965; *Silver Fighting Cocks*, Faber, 1966; *House at Spaniard's Bay*, Faber, 1967; *Glen Beyond the Door*, Faber, 1968; *The Two Rebels*, Faber, 1969.

Beyond the Wide World's End, Lutterworth, 1972; *Plotters at Pollnachee*, Lutterworth, 1973; *Snowbound at the Whitewater*, Grasshoppers Press, in press; *No Ivory Tower* (verse), Outposts Press, in press.

WORK IN PROGRESS: A book about children and the Northern Irish "troubles."

AVOCATIONAL INTERESTS: Anything Irish (but especially the country), gardening, walking, looking at mountains (and climbing them if possible).

* * *

REISS, Ira L(eonard) 1925-

PERSONAL: Born December 8, 1925, in New York, N.Y.; son of Philip (a clothing manufacturer) and Dorothy (Jacobs) Reiss; married Harriet M. Eisman, September 4, 1955; children: David Stephen, Pamela Faye, Joel Alan. *Education:* Syracuse University, B.S., 1949; Pennsylvania State University, M.A., 1951, Ph.D., 1953. *Politics:* Democrat. *Religion:* Jewish. *Home:* 5932 Medicine Lake Rd., Minneapolis, Minn. 55422.

CAREER: Bowdoin College, Brunswick, Me., instructor in sociology, 1953-55; College of William and Mary, Williamsburg, Va., assistant professor of sociology, 1955-59; Bard College, Annandale, N.Y., assistant professor of sociology, 1959-61; University of Iowa, Iowa City, associate professor 1961-64, professor of sociology, 1964-69; University of Minnesota, Minneapolis, professor of sociology, and director of the Family Study Center, 1969—. *Military service:* U.S. Army, 1944-46. *Member:* American Sociological Association, American Association of University Professors, American Civil Liberties Union, Midwest Sociological Association (president, 1971-72). *Awards honors:* Three National Institute of Mental Health research grants, 1960-64.

WRITINGS: Premarital Sexual Standards in America, Free Press of Glencoe, 1960; *The Social Context of Premarital Sexual Permissiveness*, Holt, 1967; *The Family System in America*, Holt, 1971.

WORK IN PROGRESS: A book tentatively titled *Emerging Family Forms*, and a theory paper on heterosexual permissiveness.

* * *

RESSNER, Phil(ip) 1922-

PERSONAL: Born October 29, 1922, in Brooklyn, N.Y.; son of Charles (a binder) and Jane (Kerensky) Ressner; married Lydia Ehrlich, August 13, 1957; children: Simon, Alice, Anabel. *Education:* Attended Brooklyn College (now of the City University of New York), 1942, University of Wyoming, 1943, University of Chicago, 1949; New York University, B.A., 1956. *Home:* 42 Montgomery Pl., Brooklyn, N.Y.

CAREER: New York (N.Y.) City Transit System, motorman, 1950-54; *Journal of American Water Works Association*, New York, N.Y., assistant editor, 1956-57; New York Academy of Sciences, New York, N.Y., associate editor, 1958-59; Harper & Row, Publishers, Inc., New York, N.Y., assistant editor, 1959—. *Military service:* U.S. Army, 1943-46.

WRITINGS—All juvenile: *August Explains*, Harper, 1963; *Dudley Pippin*, Harper, 1965; *At Night*, Dutton, 1967; *Jerome*, Parent's Magazine Press, 1967; *The Park in the City*, Dutton, 1971. Contributor of short stories to *Epoch*.

WORK IN PROGRESS: An adult novel; writing on preservation of historic buildings.

SIDELIGHTS: Ressner is competent in French, German, and Ashkenazi.†

* * *

REYNOLDS, Barrie (Gordon Robert) 1932-

PERSONAL: Born July 8, 1932, in London, England; son of Robert and Emma Amelia (Bettridge) Reynolds; married Ena Margaret Foster (a teacher), December 28, 1953; children: Julian Robert, Jill. *Education:* Fitzwilliam House, Cambridge, B.A. (honors), 1954, M.A., 1958, M.Sc., 1962; Oxford University, D.Phil., 1968. *Home:* 6 Redena Cres., Ottawa, K26 ON6, Canada. *Office:* Canadian Ethnology Service, National Museum of Man, Ottawa, K1A OM8, Canada.

CAREER: Rhodes-Livingstone Museum (now Livingston Museum), Livingstone, Republic of Zambia, keeper of ethnography, 1955-64, director, 1964-66; Centennial Museum, Vancouver, chief curator, 1968-69; National Museums of Canada, Ottawa, chief ethnologist, 1969—. *Member:* Royal Anthropological Society (fellow), Museums Association (associate), American Anthropological Association (fellow), Canadian Ethnology Society (secretary-treasurer, 1973—), International Committee for Museums of Ethnography (chairman, 1971—). *Awards, honors:* Diploma of Museums Association.

WRITINGS: Magic, Divination and Witchcraft Among the Barotse of Northern Rhodesia, University of California Press, 1963; *The African, His Position in a Changing Society*, Rhodes-Livingstone Museum, 1963; *Somalia Museum Development*, Unesco, 1966; *The Material Cultures of the Peoples of the Gwembe Valley*, Humanities Press, 1968; (contributor) Robert J. Charleston, editor, *World Ceramics*, Hamlyn, 1968. Contributor of fifty scientific, technical, and semi-popular articles to journals, mainly anthropological.

WORK IN PROGRESS: An ethnographic monograph on Kwandu craftsmen; an ethnohistory of Angola/Zambia border; an ethnography of the Beothuk, Newfoundland, and various aspects of museology.

* * *

REYNOLDS, Ernest 1910-

PERSONAL: Born September 13, 1910, in Northampton, England; son of Alfred and Fanny (Roddis) Reynolds. *Education:* University of Nottingham, B.A. (London; first class honors in English language and literature), 1930; Cambridge University, Ph.D., 1934. *Home:* 43 Wantage Rd., Abington Park, Northampton, England. *Agent:* Curtis Brown Ltd., 1 Craven Hill, London, W.2., England.

CAREER: Lecturer and writer, London, England, 1934-39; King Faisal College, Baghdad, Iraq, principal, 1940-41; British Council lecturer in Portugal, 1942-44; University of Birmingham, Birmingham, England, lecturer in English, 1946-55; full-time literary work, 1955—. Sometime professional actor in English theaters.

WRITINGS: Early Victorian Drama, 1830-1870, Heffer, 1936; *Mephistopheles and the Golden Apples* (poetic fantasy), Heffer, 1943; *Modern English Drama (1900-1950)*, Harrap, 1949, University of Oklahoma Press, 1951; *The Plain Man's Guide to Antique Collecting*, M. Joseph, 1963, published as *Guide to European Antiques*, A. S. Barnes, 1964; *The Plain Man's Guide to Opera*, M. Joseph, 1964; *Collecting Victorian Porcelain*, Arco, 1966; *Northamptonshire Treasures*, Ruth Bean, 1972; *Northampton Town Hall*, Northampton Corp., 1974. Also author of five short verse plays, published in Lisbon, and a verse drama, "Candlemas Night," broadcast by British Broadcasting Corp. "Third Programme."

WORK IN PROGRESS: A long poetic drama, in progress for many years (*Mephistopheles and the Golden Apples* is the first part), with working title of "Martinsmoon."

SIDELIGHTS: Ernest Reynolds told *CA:* "I regard myself as primarily a poet and my poetic work is what I most hope to be able to go on with. In my opinion, the production of one fine poem is worth a dozen books in prose."

AVOCATIONAL INTERESTS: Collecting antiques, especially antique porcelain and French clocks.

* * *

REYNOLDS, (Arthur) Graham 1914-

PERSONAL: Born January 10, 1914, in London, England; son of Arthur Thomas and Eva (Mullins) Reynolds; married Daphne Dent (an artist), February 6, 1943. *Education:* Attended Highgate School, London, England; Queens' College, Cambridge, B.A. (honors), 1935; University of Cologne, graduate study, 1935-36. *Home:* 14 Airlie Gardens, London W8, England. *Office:* Victoria and Albert Museum, London S.W. 7, England.

CAREER: Victoria and Albert Museum, London, England, assistant keeper of prints and drawings, 1937-39, deputy keeper of paintings, 1945-59, keeper of department of prints, drawings and paintings, 1959—. Ministry of Home Security, assistant principal, 1939-42, principal, 1942-45. University of London, member of Board of Studies in the History of Art, 1963—. *Member:* Walpole Society (member of executive committee, 1959-61, 1963—).

WRITINGS: Twentieth Century Drawings, Pleiades Books, 1947; *Van Gogh*, Lindsay Drummond, 1947; *Nicholas Hilliard and Isaac Oliver* (Victoria and Albert Museum Handbook), H.M.S.O., 1947; *Nineteenth Century Drawings*, Pleiades Books, 1949; *Thomas Bewick*, Art and Technics, 1949; *An Introduction to English Water-Colour Painting*, Country Life, 1950; *Gastronomic Pleasures*, Art and Technics, 1950; *Elizabethan and Jacobean Costume*, Harrap, 1951; *English Portrait Miniatures*, A. & C. Black, 1952; *Painters of the Victorian Scene*, Batsford, 1953; *Catalogue of the Constable Collection in the Victoria and Albert Museum*, H.M.S.O., 1960, revised edition, 1972; (editor) *Handbook to the Department of Prints and Drawings and Paintings, Victoria and Albert Museum*, H.M.S.O., 1964; *Constable: The Natural Painter*, McKay, 1965; *Victorian Painting*, Studio Vista, 1966, Macmillan, 1967; (editor) *The Engravings of S. W. Hayter*, H.M.S.O., 1967; *Turner*, Abrams, 1969; *A Concise History of Water Colour Painting*, Abrams, 1972.

Editor of series, "English Masters of Black and White," Art and Technics, 1948-50, and of museum picture books on British water colors, French paintings, Victorian paintings, and other collections.

Writer of verse in experimental forms, with palindromes published in *New Departures 1960*, and in *Listener* and *Times Literary Supplement*; contributor of articles to encyclopedias and to *Burlington Magazine, Connoisseur*, and *Apollo*. Member of editorial committee, Walpole Society, 1959-61, 1963—.

WORK IN PROGRESS: Catalogue of Portrait Miniatures in the Collection of Her Majesty the Queen, for Phaidon Press.

BIOGRAPHICAL/CRITICAL SOURCES: Apollo, July, 1964.†

* * *

REYNOLDS, Harry W., Jr. 1924-

PERSONAL: Born November 24, 1924, in Pottsville, Pa.; son of Harry W. and Elizabeth (Houser) Reynolds; married Beverly Brown; children: Nancy Elaine, Susan Louise. *Education:* Pennsylvania State University, B.A., 1947; Harvard University, M.A., 1949; University of Pennsylvania, Ph.D., 1954. *Religion:* Protestant. *Home:* 5101 Hamilton Street, Omaha, Neb. 68132.

CAREER: University of Pennsylvania, Philadelphia, instructor in political science, 1951-56; University of Southern California, Los Angeles, assistant professor of political science and director of city planning program, 1956-61; State University of New York at Buffalo, associate professor of political science, 1962-64; Municipal University of Omaha (now University of Nebraska at Omaha), associate professor and director of urban studies program, 1964-68, professor of political science, 1968—. Consultant on personnel training to U.S. Civil Service Commission. *Military service:* U.S. Army, 1943-45. *Member:* American Political Science Association, American Society for Public Administration, American Academy of Political and Social Science, Western Political Science Association.

WRITINGS: (Editor) *Urban Characteristics of the Niagara Frontier*, University of Buffalo Foundation, 1964; (editor) *Intergovernmental Relations in the United States*, American Academy of Political and Social Science, 1965. Contributor to public administration, personnel, and political science journals.

WORK IN PROGRESS: A book on politics and administration in the United States.

RHODES, Arnold Black 1913-

PERSONAL: Born September 21, 1913, in Rocky Point, N.C.; son of Arnold Nicholson (a merchant) and Lessie (Black) Rhodes; married Lela Nelson, June 8, 1938; children: Lessie Anne (Mrs. James Edwin King), Priscilla Nelson (Mrs. Carl Hurst Schmitt), Katharine Nelson. *Education:* Davidson College, A.B. (summa cum laude), 1935; Louisville Presbyterian Theological Seminary, B.D., 1941, Th.M., 1942; Southern Baptist Theological Seminary, Th.D., 1947; University of Chicago, Ph.D., 1951; University of Goettingen, postdoctoral study, 1965-66. *Politics:* Democrat. *Home:* 1576 Parsons Pl., Louisville, Ky. 40205. *Office:* Louisville Presbyterian Seminary, 1044 Alta Vista Rd., Louisville, Ky. 40205.

CAREER: Chamberlain-Hunt Academy, Port Gibson, Miss., instructor in Latin and history, 1935-38; ordained minister of Presbyterian Church, 1941; pastor in Lawrenceburg, Ky., 1941-42, and Hanover, Ind., 1942-44; Louisville Presbyterian Theological Seminary, Louisville, Ky., associate professor, 1944-48, professor of Old Testament, 1948—. New Albany (Ind.) Presbytery, moderator, 1944-45. Member of board of managers of Children's Agency, Louisville, Ky., 1952-58, and of Family and Children's Agency, 1958-62. Member of council on Theological Education of the United Presbyterian Church in the U.S., 1968-70.

MEMBER: Society of Biblical Literature, American Schools of Oriental Research, American Academy of Religion, Phi Beta Kappa, Eta Sigma Phi. *Awards, honors:* Advanced Religious Study Foundation fellowship, 1957, 1965-66, 1972-73; honorary D.D., Centre College of Kentucky, 1958; faculty fellowship, American Association of Theological Schools, 1965-66.

WRITINGS: (Editor and co-author) *The Church Faces the Isms*, Abingdon, 1958; (associate editor, contributor to Volume I, and author of Volume IX) *The Layman's Bible Commentary*, twenty-five volumes, John Knox, 1959-64; *The Mighty Acts of God*, two books (student's and teacher's), Covenant Life Curriculum Press, 1964; (contributor) *The Interpreter's One-Volume Commentary on the Bible*, Abingdon, 1971. Contributor to *Twentieth Century Encyclopedia of Religious Knowledge*, Baker Book, 1955, and to *Encyclopedia Britannica*. Also contributor of articles and reviews to theological and religious periodicals.

WORK IN PROGRESS: Work on the miracles of the Old Testament, and Biblical Theology and medical science.

SIDELIGHTS: The Layman's Bible Commentary has been published in England and Canada, translated into Japanese and Korean; *The Mighty Acts of God* has been published in Spanish.

BIOGRAPHICAL SOURCES: Presbyterian Survey, September, 1964; *Presbyterian Outlook*, September 21, 1964.

* * *

RHODES, Dennis Everard 1923-

PERSONAL: Born March 14, 1923, in Stourbridge, England; son of Nelson (a schoolmaster) and Ida Victoria (Sutton) Rhodes. *Education:* Attended Sidney Sussex College, Cambridge, 1941-43, 1946-47; Cambridge University, M.A., 1948; University of London, Ph.D., 1956. *Politics:* Conservative. *Religion:* Church of England. *Home:* Blantyre, Bois Lane, Chesham Bois, Buckinghamshire, England. *Office:* British Museum, London W.C. 1, England.

CAREER: British Museum, London, England, assistant

keeper of department of printed books, 1950—. *Military service:* British Army, Intelligence Corps, 1943-46; served mainly in Italy. *Member:* Bibliographical Society, Cambridge Bibliographical Society, Society for Italian Studies.

WRITINGS: The Writings of Edward Hutton, Hollis & Carter, 1955; (editor with Anna E. C. Simoni) Samuel Halkett and John Laing, *Dictionary of Anonymous and Pseudonymous English Literature*, Barnes & Noble, Volume VIII, 1956, Volume IX, 1962; *La Stampa a Viterbo, "1488"-1800*, Olschki (Florence), 1963; *La Vita e le Opere di Castore Durante e della Su a Famiglia*, Agnesotti, 1968; (editor) *In an Eighteenth Century Kitchen*, Woolf, 1968; (editor) *Essays in Honour of Victor Scholderer*, Pressler, 1970; (editor) *Studi Offerti a Roberto Ridolfi*, Olschki (Florence), 1973; *Dennis of Etruria: The Life of George Dennis*, Woolf, 1973.

WORK IN PROGRESS: Catalogue of incunabula at Oxford University, except the Bodleian Library, and a catalogue of incunabula in the libraries of Greece.

AVOCATIONAL INTERESTS: Italian literature, India, music, gardening.

* * *

RICHARDS, John Marvin 1929-

PERSONAL: Born August 19, 1929, in Dodge City, Kan.; son of W. Marvin (a superintendent of schools) and Anna (Gwinner) Richards; married Joanne Wofford, November 27, 1967. *Education:* University of Kansas, B.A., 1955; Kansas State Teachers College of Emporia, M.S., 1957; Louisiana State University, Ph.D., 1961. *Politics:* Democrat. *Religion:* Methodist. *Home:* 3349 Jamacia, Corpus Christi, Tex., 78419. *Office:* Texas A & I University, Corpus Christi, Tex. 78411.

CAREER: Instructor at Kansas State Teachers College of Emporia, 1956-57, and Louisiana State University, Baton Rouge, 1957-59; McNeese State College, Lake Charles, La., assistant professor of economics, 1961-62; Texas Western College, (now University of Texas, El Paso), 1963-73, began as an associate professor and head of department of economics, became professor of economics and dean of College of Business Administration; Texas A and I University at Corpus Christi, dean of College of Business Administration, 1973—. *Military service:* U.S. Navy, 1948-52. *Member:* American Economic Association, Regional Science Association, Alpha Kappa Lambda, Delta Sigma Pi, Beta Gamma Sigma.

WRITINGS: Highway Economics, State of Louisiana, 1961; (with W. M. Richards and B. Isley) *We the People*, Benefic, 1964; *Economic Growth in El Paso, Texas*, Texas Western Press, 1964; (with Robert Carter) *Of, By and For the People*, Benefic, 1972. Writer of monographs and articles. Editor of *El Paso Economic Review*, 1963-73.

* * *

RICHARDSON, Elmo 1930-

PERSONAL: Born April 6, 1930, in Chicago, Ill.; son of Ray Alphonso and Irene (Presley) Richardson. *Education:* University of Illinois, A.B. and M.A., 1952; University of California, Los Angeles, Ph.D., 1958. *Office:* Center for the Study of Popular Education and Recreation, Wallpacks Village, New Jersey 07881.

CAREER: University of Kansas, Lawrence, instructor in history, 1957-60; Washington State University, Pullman, assistant professor, 1961-64, associate professor of history,

1964-72; Center for the Study of Popular Education and Recreation, Delaware Water Gap National Recreational Area, New Jersey, director, 1972—. *Member:* Western History Association, Organization of American Historians, Forest History Society.

WRITINGS: (Compiler) *The Papers of Cornelius Cole and the Cole Family*, University of California (Los Angeles) Library, 1956; (co-author), *John Palmer Usher: Lincoln's Secretary of the Interior*, University of Kansas Press, 1960; *The Politics of Conservation: Crusades and Controversies, 1897-1913*, University of California Press, 1962; *Dams, Parks and Politics: Resource Development and Preservation in the Truman-Eisenhower Era*, University Press of Kentucky, 1973. Contributor of articles and reviews to historical journals on the subject of national parks and resources.

WORK IN PROGRESS: A study of the Eisenhower presidency.

AVOCATIONAL INTERESTS: Sailing, painting, cooking, camping, Vedanta, biography, and fiction.

* * *

RICHARDSON, Joanna

PERSONAL: Born in London, England; daughter of Frederick and Charlotte (Benjamin) Richardson. *Education:* St. Anne's College, Oxford, B.A. (honors), and M.A. *Politics:* Conservative. *Home:* 55 Flask Walk, London N.W. 3, England. *Agent:* Curtis Brown Ltd., 1 Craven Hill, London W.2, England.

CAREER: Biographer and critic. *Member:* Royal Society of Literature (fellow; member of council, 1961—).

WRITINGS: Fanny Brawne: A Biography, Vanguard, 1952; *Rachel*, Reinhardt, 1956, Putnam, 1957; *Theophile Gautier: His Life and Times*, Reinhardt, 1958, Coward, 1959; *Sarah Bernhardt*, Reinhardt, 1959; *Edward Fitzgerald*, Longmans, Green, 1960; *The Disastrous Marriage: A Study of George IV and Caroline of Brunswick*, J. Cape, 1960; *My Dearest Uncle, A Life of Leopold I of the Belgians*, J. Cape, 1961; *The Pre-Eminent Victorian: A Study of Tennyson*, J. Cape, 1962; (editor) *Fitzgerald: Selected Works*, Hart-Davis, 1962; *The Everlasting Spell: A Study of Keats and His Friends*, J. Cape, 1963; (editor) *Essays by Divers Hands: The Transactions of the Royal Society of Literature*, Oxford University Press, 1963; (author of introduction) Victor Hugo, *Things Seen*, Oxford University Press, 1964; *Edward Lear*, Longmans, Green, 1965; *George the Magnificent: A Portrait of King George IV*, Harcourt, 1966; *The Courtesans: The Demi-monde in Nineteenth-Century France*, World Publishing Co., 1967; *The Bohemians: La Vie de Boheme in Paris, 1830-1914*, Macmillan (London), 1969, A. S. Barnes, 1971; *Princers Mathlide*, Scribner, 1969; *Verlaine*, Viking, 1971; *La Vie Parisienne 1852-1870*, Viking, 1971; *Enid Starkie*, Macmillan, 1973; *Stendhal*, Gollancz, 1974; (editor) *Verlaine: Selected Poems in Translation*, Penguin, 1974.

WORK IN PROGRESS: A critical biography of Victor Hugo.

* * *

RICHARDSON, Robert Galloway 1926-

PERSONAL: Born October 2, 1926, in London, England; son of George (a medical practitioner) and Helen (Leslie) Richardson; married Stella Mary Whiting, August 30, 1952. *Education:* Brasenose College, Oxford, 1944-47, awarded

B.A.; attended Middlesex Hospital Medical School, University of London, 1947-51, M.A., B.M., B.Ch., and L.M.S.S.A., 1951. *Religion:* Church of England. *Home:* The Old Cottage, 258 Bromley Rd., Shortlands, Kent BR2 OBW, England.

CAREER: West Kent General Hospital, Maidstone, Kent, England, house physician and surgeon, 1951-52; Eaton Hall Officer Cadet School, Chester, Cheshire, England, medical officer, 1952-54; Butterworth & Co. (publishers), London, England, medical editor, 1955-63; *Medical News*, London, England, assistant editor, 1963-65, features editor, 1965-67; *Abbottempo* (medical periodical), London, England, editor, 1967-72, consultant medical editor, 1972—; *Spectrum International* (medical periodical), London, England, editor, 1974—. *Military service:* British Army, Royal Medical Corps, 1952-54; became captain. *Member:* Royal Society of Medicine (fellow), British Medical Association, International Society of the History of Medicine, World Medical Association, British Society of the History of Medicine, Medical Journalists Association, Society of Authors.

WRITINGS: The Surgeon's Tale, Allen & Unwin, 1958, Scribner, 1959, revised edition (under title *The Story of Modern Surgery*), Collier, 1964, 3rd edition published as *Surgery: Old and New Frontiers*, Scribner, 1968; (author of historical introduction) *Modern Trends in Cardiac Surgery*, Butterworth, 1960; *The Surgeon's Heart*, Heinemann, 1969, published as *The Scapel and the Heart*, Scribner, 1970; (editor) *The Second World Conference on Smoking and Health*, Pitman Medical, 1972; *The Menopause: A Neglected Crisis*, Abbott & Abbott, 1973; *The Abominable Stoma*, Abbott & Abbott, 1973; (editor) *The Fetus at Risk*, Abbott & Abbott, 1973; *The Hairs of Your Head are Numbered*, Abbott & Abbott, 1974; *Lorrey: Surgeon to Napoleon's Imperial Guard*, Murray, 1974; *Attitudes to Aging*, Abbott & Abbott, 1974. Editor of *British Journal of Physical Medicine*, 1955-57. Contributor to *Collier's Encyclopedia*, and *Encyclopaedia Britannica*.

SIDELIGHTS: Richardson told *CA*: "No man and no subject can be an island. In these days of increasing emphasis on science, specialization, and materialism generally the human, cultural, and artistic relationship of medicine need our attention as never before." *Avocational interests:* Swimming, and gramophone records.

* * *

RIDAY, George E(mil) 1912-

PERSONAL: Born January 16, 1912, in Philadelphia, Pa.; son of Howard Stewart (a bricklayer) and Alberta (Jensen) Riday; married Phyllis Hewson; children: Mary Beth (Mrs. Tom G. Hull), George Eric, Loralee, Martha Jane. *Education:* Eastern Baptist Theological Seminary, Th.B., 1937; Eastern Baptist College, A.B., 1941; Wayne State University, M.Ed., 1952; University of Michigan, Ph.D., 1956. *Residence:* Seminary Knolls, Covina, Calif.

CAREER: Baptist minister; California Baptist Theological Seminary, Covina, 1959—, became professor of pastoral psychology. Certified as psychologist by California State Board of Medical Examiners; licenced marriage, family, and child counselor. *Military service:* U.S. Army, chaplain, 1941-46; became captain; received Bronze Star. *Member:* American Psychological Association, National Council on Family Relations, California State Association of Marriage Counselors.

WRITINGS: Understanding the Learner, Judson, 1964; *God Speaks Through His Word*, American Baptist Board of Education and Publication, 1967.†

RIDLEY, Jasper (Godwin) 1920-

PERSONAL: Born May 25, 1920, in West Hoathly, Sussex, England; son of Geoffrey William (an architect) and Ursula (King) Ridley; married Vera Pollakova (a translator), October 1, 1949; children: Barbara Susan (Mrs. David Miler), Benjamin Nicholas, John Simon. *Education:* Studied at Sorbonne, University of Paris, 1937, and Magdalen College, Oxford, 1938-39. *Politics:* Labour. *Home:* The Strakes, West Hoathly, East Grinstead, Sussex, England. *Agent:* Curtis Brown Ltd., 1 Craven Hill, London, W2 3EW, England.

CAREER: Barrister-at-law, Inner Temple, London, England. Private practice of law, London, England, 1946-52; full-time writer, 1953—. Parliamentary candidate, 1955, 1959; St. Pancras Borough Council, councillor, 1945-49. *Military service:* British Army, anti-aircraft gunner, 1940-41. *Member:* Royal Society of Literature (fellow), Royal Society of International Affairs, Hardwicke Society, Sussex County Cricket Club. *Awards, honors:* James Tait Black Memorial Prize for biography, 1970, for *Lord Palmerston.*

WRITINGS: Nicholas Ridley, Longmans, Green, 1957; *The Law of Carriage of Goods*, Shaw Publishing Co., 1957; *Thomas Cranmer*, Oxford University Press, 1962; *John Knox*, Oxford University Press, 1968; *Lord Palmerston*, Constable, 1970, Dutton, 1971; *Mary Tudor*, Weidenfeld and Nicolson, 1973; *Garibaldi*, Constable, 1974; (contributor) *The Prime Ministers*, Allen & Unwin, 1974. Writer of radio scripts on historical subjects for British Broadcasting Corp., 1963-74, including the series "Dear and Honored Lady", 1973-74.

WORK IN PROGRESS: A biography of Gandhi.

SIDELIGHTS: Jasper Ridley speaks French and German, and reads Italian, Spanish, and Dutch. *Avocational interests:* Study of power politics of the sixteenth and twentieth centuries, walking, tennis, chess.

* * *

RIES, John C(harles) 1930-

PERSONAL: Born January 8, 1930, in Marysville, Calif.; son of John Charles (a machinist) and Elizabeth (Finegan) Ries; married Rita Kathryn Breen, January 22, 1955; children: Kathyrn L., John C. Paula, Mary E., James D. *Education:* University of Santa Clara, B.A., 1951; University of Detroit, M.A., 1953; University of California, Los Angeles, Ph.D., 1962. *Home:* 20859 Miranda St., Woodland Hills, Calif. 91364. *Office:* Department of Political Science, University of California, Los Angeles, Calif. 90024.

CAREER: U.S. Air Force, 1954-65, leaving service as captain; member of political science faculty at the Air Force Academy, Colorado Springs, Colo., 1958-65, starting as instructor and becoming associate professor; University of California, Los Angeles, assistant professor of political science, 1965—, acting director, Institute of Government and Public Affairs, 1973-74, assistant vice chancellor, 1974—. Consultant to cost analysis department, RAND Corp., Santa Monica, Calif., 1965—. *Member:* American Political Science Association, American Society of Public Administration, Western Political Science Association.

WRITINGS: The Management of Defense, Johns Hopkins Press, 1964; (editor with Wesley W. Posvor) *American Defense Policy*, Johns Hopkins Press, 1965; (with John C. Bollens) *The City Manager Profession: Myths and Realities*, Public Administration Service, 1969; *Executives in the*

American Political System, Dickenson Press, 1969. Contributor to *Western Political Quarterly, Rocky Mountain Social Science Journal*, and *Military Affairs*.

WORK IN PROGRESS: A political and economic analysis of contracting for municipal services in California, sponsored by the National Science Foundation.

*   *   *

RIGDON, Walter 1930-

PERSONAL: Born September 2, 1930, in Crossville, Tenn.; son of Arthur F. (a construction worker) and Vera (Rector) Rigdon. *Education:* University of Alabama, B.A., 1950; Sorbonne, University of Paris, graduate study, 1953. *Home:* 24 West 79th St., New York, N.Y. 10024. *Agent:* Mary Abbot, McIntosh & Otis, Inc., 18 East 41st St., New York, N.Y. 10017. *Office:* James H. Heineman, Inc., 60 East 42nd St., New York, N.Y. 10017.

CAREER: James H. Heineman, Inc. (publishers), New York, N.Y., writer and editor. Free-lance consultant on theater books and projects. *Military service:* U.S. Army, 1951-53. *Member:* International Federation for Theatre Research, American National Theatre and Academy.

WRITINGS: (Editor) *The Biographical Encyclopaedia and Who's Who of the American Theatre*, James Heineman, 1965.

WORK IN PROGRESS: Several works relating to the theater; editing annual supplement to *The Biographical Encyclopaedia and Who's Who of the American Theatre*.

SIDELIGHTS: Rigdon speaks French.†

*   *   *

RIGGS, Robert E. 1927-

PERSONAL: Born June 24, 1927, in Mesa, Ariz.; son of Lyle Alton (a lawyer) and Goldie (Motzkus) Riggs; married Hazel Dawn Macdonald , September 1, 1949; children: Robert Macdonald, Richard Edwon, Russel Owen, Rodney Lyle, Raymond David, Reisa Dawn. *Education:* Brigham Young University, student, 1947; University of Arizona, B.A., 1952, M.A., 1953, LL.B., 1963; Oxford University graduate study, 1952-53; University of Illinois, Ph.D., 1955. *Politics:* Democrat. *Religion:* Church of Jesus Christ of Latter-day Saints (Mormon). *Home:* 6453 Westchester Circle, Golden Valley, Minn. 55427.

CAREER: Brigham Young University, Provo, Utah, instructor, 1955-57, assistant professor of political science, 1957-60; University of Arizona, Tucson, government research associate, 1960-63; Riggs & Riggs (law firm), Temple Ariz., attorney in private practice, 1963-64; University of Minnesota, Minneapolis, associate professor 1964-68, professor of political science, 1968—. Mayor, Golden Valley, Minn., 1972—. *Military service:* U.S. Army, 1945-47; became technical sergeant. *Member:* American Political Science Association, American Bar Association, International Studies Association, Midwest Political Science Association, State Bar of Arizona. *Awards, honors:* Ford Foundation fellow, 1957; Rockefeller Foundation research fellow at Columbia University, 1957-58.

WRITINGS: Politics in the United Nations, University of Illinois Press, 1958; *The Movement for Administrative Reorganization in Arizona*, Bureau of Business and Public Research, University of Arizona, 1961; *Arizona State Personnel Policies*, Bureau of Business and Public Research,

University of Arizona, 1962; *Vox Populi: The Battle of 103*, University of Arizona Press, 1964; (with Jack C. Plano) *Forging World Order*, Macmillan, 1967; *U.S./U.N.: Foreign Policy and International Organization*, Appleton, 1971; (with Plano) *Dictionary of Political Analysis*, Dryden Press, 1973; (with Plano, Milton Greenburg, Roy Olton) *Political Science Dictionary*, Dryden Press, 1973. Contributor of articles and reviews to law and political science journals.

WORK IN PROGRESS: Impact of international organization on national policy making; revision of *Forging World Order*.

SIDELIGHTS: Riggs reads Spanish and French.

*   *   *

RIGONI, Orlando (Joseph) 1897-
(Leslie Ames, Carolyn Bell, James Wesley)

PERSONAL: Born December 27, 1897, in Mercur, Utah; son of Christian Joseph (a contractor) and Emma (Elseman) Rigoni; married Carolyn Broadhurst, July 16, 1946 (deceased); married Stella Marie Gondolfo, July 28, 1972; children: Patricia Margaret Rigoni Epperly, Orlando Patrick. *Education:* Attended high school and business college in Salt Lake City, Utah. *Politics:* Democrat. *Religion:* Realist. *Home and Office:* 2900 Dogwood Ave., Morro Bay, Calif. 93442.

CAREER: Formerly worked in railroading, construction, mining, and business including a term as forest clerk in the forest service, writing at the same time for pulp magazines; now realtor and writer. *Military Service:* U.S. Army and Navy.

WRITINGS: Brand of the Bow, Arcadia House, 1965; *Twisted Trails*, Arcadia House, 1965; *Massacre Ranch*, Arcadia House, 1966; *Showdown at Skelton Flat*, Arcadia House, 1967; *Six-Gun Song*, Arcadia House, 1967; *Ambuscade*, Arcadia House, 1968; *A Nickel's Worth of Lead*, Arcadia House, 1968; *The Pikabo Stage*, Arcadia House, 1968; *Headstone for a Trail Boss*, Arcadia House, 1969; *Close Shave at Pozo*, Lenox Hill, 1970; *Hunger Range*, Lenox Hill, 1970; *Drove Rider*, Lenox Hill, 1971; *Guns of Folly*, Lenox Hill, 1971; *Bullet Breed*, Lenox Hill, 1972, (published in England as *Brand of the Bullet*, R. Hale, 1972); *The Big Brand*, Crown, 1972; *Muskeg Marshal*, Lenox Hill, 1973; *Brand X*, Lenox Hill, 1974.

Under pseudonym Leslie Ames: *Bride of Donnybrook*, Arcadia House, 1966; *Journey to Romance*, R. Hale, 1966; *The Angry Wind*, Arcadia House, 1967; *The Hungry Sea*, Arcadia House, 1967; *The Hidden Chapel*, Arcadia House, 1967; *The Hill of Ashes*, Arcadia House, 1968; *To Shadow Our Love*, R. Hale, 1968; *Sinister Love*, R. Hale, 1968; *Castle on the Island*, Arcadia House, 1969; *King's Castle*, Lenox Hill, 1970; *Wind Over the Citadel*, Lenox Hill, 1971, 1973; *The Phantom Bride*, Lenox Hill, 1972.

Under pseudonym Carolyn Bell: *House of Clay*, Lenox Hill, 1971.

Under pseudonym James Wesley: *Showdown in Mesa Bend*, Avalon, 1972; *Maverick Marshal*, Bouregy, 1974.

WORK IN PROGRESS: The Temple of the Cats, a Gothic novel concerning cat worshipers; *The Gallows Tree*, a novel concerning the events in the life of a librarian on a bookmobile route.

RIKHOFF, James C. 1931-
(Jim Cornwall, Joe Fargo, Alan Kincaid)

PERSONAL: Born May 8, 1931, in Chicago, Ill.; son of Harold Franklin (an executive) and Blanche Marie (Bowlus) Rikhoff; married Janet M. Finlay, February 1, 1956; children: Erika Viktoria, Christina Anne, James, Jr. *Education:* Culver Military Academy, graduate, 1949; Denison University, student, 1949-51; The Ohio State University, B.A., 1956; American Institute for Foreign Trade, B.F.T., 1957. *Politics:* Independent. *Religion:* Roman Catholic. *Home:* 49 Dewey Rd., High Bridge, N.J. *Office:* Olin Mathieson Chemical Corp., 460 Park Ave., New York, N.Y. 10022.

CAREER: Olin Mathieson Chemical Corp., New York, N.Y., 1959—, public relations manager. Free-lance writer on outdoor life. *Military service:* U.S. Army, 1952-54. *Member:* National Rifle Association, National Skeet Shooting Association, Delta Phi Epsilon (vice-president, 1956-57), Phi Delta Theta, Campfire Club of Ameica, Midtown Turf, Polo, and Yachting Association, Kingwood Fox Hounds Club.

WRITINGS: (Editor and contributor) *The Compact Book of Hunting*, J. Lowell Pratt, 1964; (with Eric Peper) *Fishing Moments of Truth*, Winchester Press, 1973. Contributor, sometimes under pseudonyms, to *Esquire*, *True*, *Argosy*, *Sports Afield*, *Ourdoor Life*, *Sport Age*, *Gunsport*, *Guns and Hunting*, and other periodicals.

WORK IN PROGRESS: A novel.

SIDELIGHTS: Rikhoff speaks Spanish and Portuguese, has hunted in Kenya, Mozambique, Mexico, Canada, and all over the United States, and has traveled in Europe, Asia, and Cuba. He writes both fiction and non-fiction, specializing in hunting, antique and modern guns, ballistics, fishing and tackle, horses, camping, and other outdoor lore.†

*   *   *

RILEY, (Thomas) Nord 1914-

PERSONAL: Born May 7, 1914, in Wyndmere, N.D.; son of Thomas Edward and Hilda (Nord) Riley; married Betty L. Gardner, September 30, 1952; children: Elizabeth, Kathleen, Jan. *Education:* University of Chicago, B.A., 1936. *Religion:* Christian. *Home:* 645 31st St., Manhattan Beach, Calif. *Agent:* Curtis Brown Ltd., 575 Madison Ave., New York, N.Y. 10022.

CAREER: Free-lance writer. *Military service:* U.S. Army, 1942-46; became sergeant. *Member:* Chi Psi.

WRITINGS: *The Armored Dove*, Gold Medal Books, 1964. Also author of *Peter, Peter*, Gold Medal Books. Author of play, *The Armored Dove*, (produced in stock, 1962) Dramatists Play Service, 1968; and of television plays for "G.E. Theatre," "Dobie Gillis," "Colgate Playhouse," "Schlitz Playhouse," "My Favorite Husband," and other half-hour shows. Contributor of short stories and articles to magazines, including *Collier's*, *Saturday Evening Post*, *American*, *Cosmopolitan*, *Maclean's*, *Esquire*, *Outdoor Life*, *Field and Stream*, *Writer*.

WORK IN PROGRESS: A stage play; short stories; outdoor articles.

SIDELIGHTS: Riley has lived in Mexico and Europe; speaks Spanish and French. *Avocational interests:* Hunting and fishing.†

RIMLAND, Bernard 1928-

PERSONAL: Born November 15, 1928, in Cleveland, Ohio; son of Meyer (a carpenter) and Anna (Lansky) Rimland; married Gloria Belle Alf, August 28, 1951; children: Mark, Helen, Paul. *Education:* San Diego State College (now San Diego State University), B.A., 1950, M.A., 1952; Pennsylvania State University, Ph.D., 1953. *Home:* 4758 Edgeware Rd., San Diego, Calif. 92116. *Office:* U.S. Navy Personnel Research Laboratory, San Diego, Calif. 92152.

CAREER: U.S. Navy Personnel Research Laboratory, San Diego, Calif., department director, 1953—. Part-time lecturer in psychology, San Diego State University; director, Institute for Child Behavior Research, San Diego, Calif. *Member:* American Psychological Association, American Educational Research Association, National Council on Measurement in Education. *Awards, honors:* Century Award for distinguished contribution to psychology, for *Infantile Autism;* fellow, Center for Advanced Study in the Behavioral Sciences, 1964-65.

WRITINGS: Infantile Autism: The Syndrome and Its Implications for a Neural Theory of Behavior, Appleton, 1964. Contributor to psychology and psychiatry journals.

WORK IN PROGRESS: Three books—on unfortunate effects of psychoanalysis on contemporary life, on biological approaches to human thought and nature, and on nature and cause of mental illness.

*   *   *

RITCHIE, G(eorge) Stephen 1914-

PERSONAL: Born October 30, 1914, in Burnley, Lancashire, England; son of Sir Douglas and Peggy (Allan) Ritchie; married Disa Elizabeth Beveridge; children: John Paul, Tertia (daughter), Mark. *Education:* Attended Royal Naval College, Dartmouth, England, 1928-32. *Religion:* Church of England. *Home:* St. James, Avenue Princesse Alice, Monte Carlo, Monaco. *Agent:* A. M. Heath & Co. Ltd., 35 Dover St., London W. 1, England. *Office:* International Hydrographic Bureau, Avenue President Kennedy, Monte Carlo, Monaco.

CAREER: Career officer in Royal Navy, 1932-71. Commissioned, 1932, transferred to Royal Naval Surveying Service, 1936, hydrographer, 1966-71; International Hydrographic Bureau, Monte Carlo, Monaco, president of the directing committee, 1972—. *Member:* Royal Institution of Chartered Surveyors (fellow), Royal Institution of Chartered Surveyor (fellow), Royal Institution of Navigation (fellow), Royal Geographical Society (fellow), West Country Writers Association, Reform Club (London). *Awards, honors:* Distinguished Service Cross, 1942; Companion of the Bath, 1967; Gold Medal, Royal Geographical Society, 1972; Silver Medal, Royal Society of Arts, 1972.

WRITINGS: Challenger (story of a survey ship), Hollis & Carter, 1957; *The Admirality Chart*, Hollis & Carter, 1967. Contributor of articles to geographical and maritime journals.

WORK IN PROGRESS: A book, *A History of European Hydrography.*

AVOCATIONAL INTERESTS: Historical development of hydrography.

*   *   *

RIVE, Richard 1931-

PERSONAL: Surname rhymes with "leave"; born March

1, 1931, in Cape Town, South Africa; son of Nancy (Ward) Rive. *Education:* Hewat Training College, Teacher's Diploma, 1951; University of Cape Town, B.A., 1962; Columbia University, graduate study. *Address:* (Permanent) 2 Selous Ct., Rosmead Ave., Claremont, Cape Town, South Africa; (temporary) 345 Whittier Hall, 1230 Amsterdam Ave., New York, N.Y. 10027.

CAREER: South Peninsula High School, Cape Town, South Africa, teacher of English and Latin. *Awards, honors:* Farfield Foundation fellowship to travel and study contemporary African literature in English and French, 1963; Fulbright scholar and Heft scholar, 1965-66.

WRITINGS: African Songs (short stories), Seven Seas, 1963; (editor) *Quartet*, Crown, 1963; *Emergency* (novel), Faber, 1964, Collier Books, 1970; (compiler) *Modern African Prose*, Heinemann, 1964. Member of editorial board, *Contrast*.

WORK IN PROGRESS: A South African Abroad.

SIDELIGHTS: Rive is a former South African hurdling champion. *Avocational interests:* Mountain climbing, spear fishing.†

*   *   *

ROBBINS, Brother Gerald 1940-

PERSONAL: Born December 8, 1940, in Worcester, Mass.; son of Ewart Ainslie and Aline (Lamoureux) Robbins. *Education:* St. Edward's University, Austin, Tex., B.A., 1963; also attended Fordham University. *Home:* St. Joseph Faculty Residence, St. Edward's University, Austin, Tex. 78704. *Office:* Holy Cross Press, St. Joseph Noviate, Valatie, N.Y.

CAREER: Roman Catholic religious, member of Congregation of the Holy Cross; Vincentian Institute, Albany, N.Y., teacher of Latin and French, 1963—. Illustrator of books for children; paper sculptor, showing in local and state shows. *Member:* American Classical League, Empire State Classical Association, Alpha Chi.

WRITINGS: Figs From Thistles (biography of St. John Baptist De La Salle), Holy Cross Press, 1964.

Illustrator: *Brother Andre of Mount Royal*, Theodore Gaus, 1964; *Eagle of God* (John the Evangelist), Theodore Gaus, 1964.

WORK IN PROGRESS: More Than a Prophet, a biography of John the Baptist with emphasis on the ancient Essenes community.†

*   *   *

ROBERTS, Francis Warren 1916-

PERSONAL: Born December 3, 1916, in Menard, Tex.; son of William Clyde and Exie (Frazier) Roberts; married Patricia Lomasney (a student adviser, University of Texas), January 1, 1943; children: Jeffrey Warren, Victoria Anne. *Education:* Southwestern University, Georgetown, Tex., A.B., 1938; University of Texas, Ph.D., 1956. *Home:* 2305 Windsor Rd., Austin, Tex. 78703. *Office:* The Humanities Research Center, University of Texas, Box 7219, University Station, Austin, Tex. 78712.

CAREER: University of Pisa, Pisa, Italy, Fulbright lecturer, 1956-58; University of Texas, Austin, special instructor in English, 1954-56, assistant professor, 1958, associate professor of English, 1959-66, professor of English, 1967—, director of Humanitites Research Center, 1962—. Member of Board of directors, Southwestern Alumni Asso-

ciation. *Military service:* U.S. Naval Reserve, active duty, 1940-45, 1950-54; retired as commander. *Member:* Modern Humanites Research Association of American, South Central Modern Language Association (vice-president, 1972-73; president, 1973-74), Texas State Historical Association Collector's Institute, Texas Institute of Letters, Texas Folklore Society, Grolier Club (New York), The American Club (London). *Awards, honors:* Theta Sigma Chi Roundup Award, 1963, for *Bibliography of D. H. Lawrence;* D.Litt., Southwestern University, 1965.

WRITINGS: (Editor) D. H. Lawrence, *Look! We Have Come Through!* (poems), Ark Press, 1958; (editor) Helen Corke, *Songs of Autumn* (poems), University of Texas Press, 1960; *Bibliography of D. H. Lawrence*, Hart-Davis, 1963; (editor with Vivian de Sola Pinto) *The Complete Poems of D. H. Lawrence*, Viking, 1964; (editor and author of introduction) Helen Corke, *D. H. Lawrence: The Croydon Years*, University of Texas Press, 1965; (with Harry T. Moore) *D. H. Lawrence and His World*, Viking, 1966; (editor with Moore) *Phoenix II: Uncollected, Unpublished and Other Prose Work by D. H. Lawrence*, Viking, 1968; Member of editorial board, *The Letters of D. H. Lawrence.*

*   *   *

ROBERTS, Irene 1926-
(I. Roberts, I. M. Roberts; pseudonyms: Roberta Carr, Elizabeth Harle, Ivor Roberts, Iris Rowland, Irene Shaw)

PERSONAL: Born September 27, 1926, in London, England; daughter of Charles Harry and Ivy (Carpenter) Williamson; married Terence Granville Leonard Roberts (an artist), December 26, 1947; children: Paul Trevor, Peter John, Tracey Lynn. *Education:* Attended schools in London, England. *Religion:* Church of England. *Home:* Alpha House, Higher Toun, Malborough, Kingsbridge, Devon TQ7 3RL, England.

CAREER: Held varied jobs in England, working as chain store assistant, seller of plants on market stall, typist "of sorts," saleswoman in clothing stores; now writer of novels. *Member:* Writers Club (West Essex branch), Rosicrucian Order.

WRITINGS: Squirrel Walk, Gresham, 1960; *Love Song of the Sea*, Fleetway Publications, 1960; *Beloved Rascals*, Gresham, 1961; *The Shrine of Marigolds*, Gresham, 1961; *Come Back Beloved*, Gresham, 1961; *Only to Part*, Fleetway Publications, 1961; *Sweet Sorrel*, Gresham, 1962; *The Dark Night*, Fleetway Publications, 1962; *Laughing Is for Fun* (girls' book), Micron, 1962; *Tangle of Gold Lace*, Gresham, 1962; *Cry of the Gulls*, Fleetway Publications, 1963; *Holiday for Hanbury* (girls' book), Micron, 1963.

All published by R. Hale: *Whisper of Sea-Bells*, 1964; *Echo of Flutes*, 1965; *The Mountain Sang*, 1965; *Where Flamingoes Fly*, 1965; *Shadows on the Moon*, 1966; *A Handful of Stars*, 1966; *Jungle Nurse*, 1967; *Love Comes to Larkswood*, 1967; *Alpine Nurse*, 1968; *Nurse in the Hills*, 1968; *The Lion and the Sun*, 1968; *Thunder Heights*, 1968; *Surgeon in Tibet*, 1969; *Birds without Bars*, 1969; *The Shrine of Fire*, 1970; *Gull Haven*, 1970; *Sister at Sea*, 1971; *Moon over the Temple*, 1972; *The Golden Pagoda*, 1972.

Under name I. Roberts: *Green Hell* (war story), Micron, 1961.

Under name I. M. Roberts: *The Throne of Pharaohs*, R. Hale, in press.

Under pseudonym Roberta Carr: *Red Runs the Sunset*, Gresham, 1962; *Sea Maiden*, Gresham, 1963; *Fire Dragon*, Gresham, 1966; *Golden Interlude*, Gresham, 1970.

Under pseudonym Elizabeth Harle: *Golden Rain*, Gresham, 1963; *Gay Rowan*, Gresham, 1964; *Sandy*, Gresham, 1966; *The Silver Summer*, R. Hale, 1970; *Spray of Red Roses*, Gresham, 1970; *Buy Me a Dream*, Gresham, 1970.

Under pseudonym Ivor Roberts: *Jump Into Hell* (war story), Brown, Watson, 1960; *Trial by Water* (war story), Micron, 1960.

Under pseudonym Iris Rowland; all published by Gresham, except as noted: *The Tangled Web*, 1961; *Island in the Mist*, 1961; *The Morning Star*, 1962; *With Fire and Flowers*, 1962; *Golden Flowers*, 1964; *A Fountain of Roses*, 1965; *Valley of Bells*, 1965; *Blue Feathers*, 1966; *A Veil of Rushes*, 1966; *To Be Beloved*, 1967; *Rose Island*, 1968; *Cherries and Candlelight*, 1968; *Nurse at Kama Hall*, 1968; *Moon over Moncrieff*, 1968; *The Knave of Hearts*, R. Hale, 1969; *Star Drift*, 1969; *Rainbow River*, 1969; *The Wild Summer*, 1969; *Orange Blossom for Tara*, 1970; *Blossom in the Snow*, 1970; *Sister Julia*, 1971.

Under pseudonym Irene Shaw: *The House of Lydia*, Wright & Brown, 1965; *Moonstone Manor*, Wright & Brown, 1967; *The Olive Branch*, Wright & Brown, 1968.

Contributor of short stories and serials to magazines in England, United States, Belgium, Norway, Denmark, Netherlands, Sweden, and Italy.

WORK IN PROGRESS: Death of a Pharoah, Hatshepsut, Queen of the Nile, and *The Achaemian Eagle*, all under name I. M. Roberts.

SIDELIGHTS: Mrs. Roberts told *CA*: "Spent years studying Indian religions, Egyptology, and philosophy. Deeply interested in all facets; lots and lots yet to learn.... Find languages beyond me. In Italy, trying to purchase milk by sign language was offered half side of beef."

As a very young member of the Womans Land Army, she came to the conclusion that war apparently was a masculine effort full of glory—"but digging up potatoes! Ugh!"

* * *

ROBINSON, Cecil 1921-

PERSONAL: Born July 19, 1921, in Greenwich, Conn.; son of Watson Bryant (a lawyer) and Dorita Frances (MacElhinny) Robinson; married Madeleine Hale; children: Cecilia Hale, Daniel Hale. *Education:* Harvard University, B.A., 1943; Columbia University, M.A., 1949, Ph.D., 1960. *Home:* 3543 North Jackson Ave., Tucson, Ariz.

CAREER: Instituto Chileno-Norteamericano de Cultura, Concepcion, Chile, director, 1951-52; University of Arizona, Tucson, 1953—, began as assistant professor, now associate professor of English. Visiting professor in Brazil under auspices of Columbia University, 1963-64. *Military service:* U.S. Army Air Forces, 1942-45; became sergeant. *Member:* American Association of University Professors, Arizona Bi-Lingual Council, Pima Council of English Teachers. *Awards, honors:* Award of Ohio State University Institute for Education through Radio-Television, for radio teaching to the Spanish-speaking, 1957.

WRITINGS: With the Ears of Strangers: The Mexican in American Literature, University of Arizona Press, 1963.

WORK IN PROGRESS: A book tentatively titled *The Big House, Plantation, Rise and Fall in the Literature of North and Hispanic America*.†

ROBINSON, Chaille Howard (Payne)
(Jean Kirby, Kathleen Robinson)

PERSONAL: Given name is pronounced Shelly; daughter of Benjamin Howard (a railroad manager) and Chaille (Hyde) Payne; married Philip Carey Robinson (manager of Robinson Oil Equipment); children: William Payne. *Education:* Studied at Hamilton Hall. *Politics:* Republican. *Religion:* Episcopalian. *Home:* 944 Chelsea Ave., Glendale, Mo. 63122.

CAREER: Writer.

WRITINGS: (Under name Chaille Payne Robinson) *Manon's Daughter*, Cloud, 1947.

Under pseudonym Jean Kirby: *A Career for Kelly*, Whitman, 1962; *Nurses Three: First Assignment*, Whitman, 1963; *On Call for Trouble*, Whitman, 1964.

Under pseudonym Kathleen Robinson: *When Sara Smiled*, Whitman, 1962; *When Debbie Dared*, Whitman, 1963; *Designed by Suzanne*, Lothrop, 1968. Also author of *Runaway Heart* published by Whitman.

Author of radio dramas for St. Louis Art museum, articles on early St. Louis for *St. Louis Globe-Democrat*, and serials and stories for American, English, and Canadian periodicals.

WORK IN PROGRESS: A Deeper Song, the story of Sacajawea and William Clark.

AVOCATIONAL INTERESTS: Reading, gourmet cooking, music, French, horse, and travel (particularly in Canada).

* * *

ROBINSON, Godfrey Clive 1913-

PERSONAL: Born October 2, 1913, in Murree Hills, India; son of H. J. (a soldier) and K. M. (Killmer) Robinson; married Gladys H. Webber, March 28, 1942; children: Anne Katharine, Elizabeth Jane. *Education:* Attended Spurgeon's College, London; University of London, B.A., 1941, B.D. (with honors), 1946. *Home:* 32 Wendover Rd., Bromley, Kent, England.

CAREER: Baptist minister. Baptist Missionary Society, youth secretary, 1947-52; Main Road Baptist Church, Romford, England, minister, 1952—. North Africa Mission, British chairman. *Member:* Baptist Union Council, Evangelical Alliance Council, Essex Baptist Association (president, 1961-62).

WRITINGS—All with S. F. Winward: *The Way*, Scripture Union & C.S.S.M., 1945; *Here Is the Answer*, Marshall, Morgan & Scott, 1949, Judson, 1970; *The Art of Living*, Walter, 1951; *Colony of Heaven*, Walter, 1954; *The King's Business*, Scripture Union & C.S.S.M., 1957; *The Christian's Conduct*, Scripture Union & C.S.S.M., 1960; *Our Returning King*, Walter, 1962; *Companions of the Way*, Scripture Union & C.S.S.M., 1962; *In the Holy Land*, Scripture Union & C.S.S.M., 1963, Eerdmans, 1968; *A Practical Guide for Christian Life*, Moody, 1971; *Church Worker's Handbook*, Judson, 1973. Contributor of articles to *Life of Faith*, *Christian*, and *Baptist Times*.

WORK IN PROGRESS: A book of prayers for schools.†

* * *

ROBINSON, Helen Mansfield 1906-

PERSONAL: Born May 28, 1906, in Athens, Ohio; daughter of Merwin G. and Mabel (Butts) Mansfield; married Daniel W. Robinson, August 18, 1933 (deceased). *Education:* Ohio University, A.B., 1926; Ohio State University, A.M., 1927; University of Chicago, Ph.D., 1944. *Home:* 3710 Gulf of Mexico Dr., Sarasota, Fla. 33577.

CAREER: Miami University, Oxford, Ohio, instructor, later assistant professor of education, 1928-31; University of Chicago, Chicago, Ill., superintendent and psychologist at orthogenic school, 1931-43, director of Reading Clinic, 1944-58, successively instructor, assistant professor, associate professor, professor, 1944-60, William S. Gray Research Professor of Reading, 1961—, director of Reading Research Center, 1964-68. *Member:* International Reading Association (member of board of directors, 1958-61), National Conference on Research in English (president, 1960), American Educational Research Association, American Association for the Advancement of Science, National Council of Teachers of English. *Awards, honors:* D.O.S. from Illinois College of Optometry, 1957; Apollo Award of American Optometric Association for research on vision and reading, 1963.

WRITINGS: Why Pupils Fail in Reading, University of Chicago Press, 1946; (editor) *Clinical Studies in Reading,* University of Chicago Press, Volume I, 1949, Volume II, 1953, Volume III, 1968; (editor) *Corrective Reading in Classroom and Clinic,* University of Chicago Press, 1953; *Developing Permanent Interest in Reading,* University of Chicago Press, 1956; *Evaluation of Reading,* University of Chicago Press, 1958; *Sequential Development of Reading Abilities,* University of Chicago Press, 1960; *Innovation and Change in Reading Instruction,* University of Chicago Press, 1968; (editor) *Coordinating Reading Instruction,* Scott, Foresman, 1971. Senior author of "Curriculum Foundation Readers," for Scott. Editor, *Proceedings of Annual Reading Conference,* 1953-64.

WORK IN PROGRESS: Sociology of Reading; Visual and Auditory Perception in Beginning Reading.†

*   *   *

ROBINSON, Helene M.

PERSONAL: Born in Eugene, Ore.; daughter of Kirkman K. (a teacher) and Emily Agnew (Lackey) Robinson. *Education:* University of Oregon, B.A. (music), 1935; Northwestern University, M. Mus., 1942; University of Southern California, graduate study, summers, 1958-61, 1963, 1965. *Politics:* Republican. *Religion:* Methodist. *Residence:* Tempe, Arizona.

CAREER: Roseburg (Ore.) public schools supervisor of music education, 1936-42; Arizona State College, Flagstaff, assistant professor and head of piano and music education departments, 1942-50; Southern Oregon College, Ashland, associate professor of music and head of piano and music education departments, 1950-67; Arizona State University, Tempe, professor and coordinator of piano classes, 1967—. Visiting teacher at California State College (now California State University, Fullerton), 1961-62, University of California, Santa Barbara, 1963-64. *Member:* Music Educators National Conference, Music Teachers National Association, Arizona State Music Teachers Association (president, 1974-76).

WRITINGS: Basic Piano for Adults, Wadsworth, 1964; (editor) *Teaching Piano in Classroom and Studio,* Music Educators National Conference, 1967; *Intermediate Piano for Adults,* Wadsworth, 1970. Contributor to *Piano Quarterly.*

WORK IN PROGRESS: Revision of *Basic Piano for Adults.*

*   *   *

ROBINSON, James M(cConkey) 1924-

PERSONAL: Born June 30, 1924, in Gettysburg, Pa.; son of William Childs (a professor of ecclesiastical history at Columbia Theological Seminary) and Mary (McConkey) Robinson; married Marianne Schaeffer, March 10, 1951; children: Francoise Mary Anne, James Claude, Joy Odile. *Education:* Davidson College, A.B. (summa cum laude), 1945; Columbia Theological Seminary, B.D. (magna cum laude), 1946; studied at University of Marburg, 1950-51, University of Strasbourg, 1951, Ecole des hautes Etudes, 1952; University of Basel, D. Theol. (summa cum laude), 1952; Princeton Theological Seminary, Th.D., 1955. *Home:* Villa Padova, 3560 Padua Ave., Claremont, Calif.

CAREER: Ordained minister, Presbyterian Church in the U.S.A., 1953. Davidson College, Davidson, N.C., assistant professor of Greek and Bible, 1946-47; Emory University, Atlanta, Ga., instructor, later assistant professor of biblical theology at Candler School of Theology, 1952-53, associate professor, 1956-58, member of faculty of Institute of Liberal Arts, Graduate School, 1955-58; Southern California School of Theology, Claremont, associate professor, 1958-61, professor of theology and New Testament, 1961-64; Claremont Graduate School and University Center, Claremont, Calif., affiliate member of faculty, 1959-64, professor of religion, 1964—. Visiting professor at University of Goettingen, summer, 1959, University of Zurich, summers, 1960, 1962; lecturer at German universities, 1959-60, and at a number of American universities and theological schools, including Duke University, Harvard University, Notre Dame University, Columbia University, and Atlanta University. Lecturer in Japan, Korea, and Burma, 1965. Annual Professor, American School of Oriental Research, Jerusalem, Jordan, 1965-66. Member of Faith and Order Advisory Committee of National Council of Churches of Christ in America, 1964—.

MEMBER: Society of Biblical Literature (associate in council, 1962-64; vice-president of Western section, 1962; president of Western section, 1963), American Academy of Religion, Studiorum Novi Testamenti Societas, American Society for the Study of Religion, New Testament Colloquium, Pacific Coast Theological Group, Phi Beta Kappa. *Awards, honors:* Research grants from American Council of Learned Societies, Fulbright Commission, and American Association of Theological Schools, 1959-60.

WRITINGS: Das Problem des Heiligen Geistes bei Wilhelm Herrmann, Karl Gleiser, 1952; *Das Geschichtsverstandnis des Markus-Evangeliums,* Zwingli-Verlag, 1956 (English translation, somewhat revised, published as *The Problem of History in Mark,* Allenson, 1957); *A New Quest of the Historical Jesus,* Allenson, 1959.

(Contributor) *Reflection Book: New Directions in Biblical Thought,* edited by Martin E. Marty, Association Press, 1960; (contributor) *The Old Testament and Christian Faith,* edited by Bernhard W. Anderson, Harper, 1963; (editor with John B. Cobb, Jr.) *The Later Heidegger and Theology,* Harper, 1963; (editor with Cobb, and contributor) *New Frontiers in Theology; Discussions among Continental and American Theologians,* Volume I, Harper, 1963, Volume II, *The New Hermeneutic,* 1964; (contributor) *Ecumenical Dialogue at Harvard: The Roman Catholic-Protestant Colloquium,* edited by Samuel H.

Miller and G. Ernest Wright, Belknap Press, 1964; (contributor) *Zeit und Geschichte* (Bultmann festschrift), edited by Erich Dinkler, J. C. B. Mohr, 1964; (contributor) *Apophoreta* (Haenchen festschrift), edited by Walter Eltester, Verlag Alfred Topelmann, 1964; *The Bultmann School of Biblical Interpretation*, Harper, 1965; (editor with John B. Cobb, Jr.) *Theology as History*, Harper, 1967; (author of introduction) Albert Schweitzer, *Kerygma und historischer Jesus*, 2nd revised edition, Zwingli Verlag, 1967 (translation published as *The Quest of the Historical Jesus*, Macmillan, 1968); (editor with Cobb) *Theologie als Geschichte*, Zwingli Verlag, 1967; (editor) *The Beginnings of Dialectic Theology*, John Knox, 1968; *Americanski Journalist*, Westernlore, 1969.

(Editor) *The Future of Our Religious Past*, S.C.M. Press, 1971; (with Helmut Koester) *Trajectories Through Early Christianity*, Fortress Press, 1971; *West from Fort Pierre: The World of Scotty Philip*, Westernlore, 1974.

Contributor to *The Interpreter's Dictionary of the Bible*, Volumes I, III, and V, *Biblisch-Historisches Handworterbuch*, Volumes I and II. Contributor of about fifty articles and reviews to *Journal of Biblical Literature*, *Christian Century*, *Interpretation*, *Theology Today*, and other journals in America and Germany.

Member of editorial board of *Theologische Forschung*, Evangelischer Verlag, and *Journal for Theology and the Church*.†

*   *   *

ROBINSON, Joseph Frederick   1912-

PERSONAL: Born June 28, 1912, in New York, N.Y.; son of Albert Sewell (a ship's master) and Rose (Gange) Robinson; married Marion Morrell (a high school teacher), June 29, 1940; children Frederick Morrell, Rosemary. *Education:* Studied at Polytechnic Institute of Brooklyn and Pace College. *Politics:* Democrat. *Religion:* Episcopal. *Home:* 210 Longview Rd., Staten Island, N.Y. 10301. *Office:* Bureau of Plant Operation, Board of Education, 49 Flatbush Ave. Extension, Brooklyn, N.Y. 11201.

CAREER: Licensed chief marine engineer, oceans steam unlimited horsepower; stationary engineer; commissioned boiler and pressure vessel inspector. U.S. Merchant Marine, 1928-36; worked in various engineering capacities in New York, N.Y., and Washington, D.C., for Royal Indemnity Insurance Co., E. F. Drew & Co., Fall River Navigation Co., and P. Ballantine & Co., 1937-53; New York (N.Y.) Board of Education, borough supervisor, 1953—, now in charge of operation of three hundred school buildings. U.S. Navy, technical adviser and writer, 1962, 1964. Grymes Hill Civic Association, Staten Island, N.Y., president, 1964. *Military service:* U.S. Navy, 1940-46; became lieutenant commander. *Member:* Rotary International, Free and Accepted Masons, Richmond Borough Gun Club (president, 1962).

WRITINGS: (With Elonka) *Standard Plant Operators Questions and Answers*, McGraw, 1959. Author of various U.S. Navy books, pamphlets, and curriculum studies in engineering, and script writer for Navy training films, 1943-44, and 1962, 1964.

WORK IN PROGRESS: Engineering Problems; revision of *Standard Plant Operator's Questions and Answers*.

*   *   *

ROBINSON, Norman H(amilton) G(alloway)   1912-

PERSONAL: Born October 7, 1912, in Troon, Ayrshire, Scotland; son of George (a marine officer) and Barbara (Fraser) Robinson; married Mary Elizabeth Johnston, March 3, 1936; children: Norman Frazer, Gordon George Christopher, Catherine Barbara Elizabeth, Maureen Patricia Margaret. *Education:* University of Glasgow, M.A. (honors), 1934; Queen's College, Oxford, graduate study, 1934-36; University of Edinburgh, B.D., 1939. *Politics:* Uncommitted. *Home:* Arcan, Tay St., Newport-on-Tay, Fife, Scotland. *Office:* St. Mary's College, University of St. Andrews, St. Andrews, Fife, Scotland.

CAREER: Ordained minister, Church of Scotland, 1939. Minister in Shetland Islands, 1939-43, Fraserburgh, Aberdeenshire, 1943-48, Rothesay, Island of Bute, 1948-54; Rhodes University, Grahamstown, South Africa, professor of divinity, 1954-56; University of St. Andrews, St. Andrews, Fife, Scotland, professor of systematic theology, 1956-67, professor of divinity, 1967—. Dean of Faculty of Divinity, 1958-62. *Member:* Society for Study of Theology, Royal Institute of Philosophy, Societas Ethica. *Awards, honors:* D.Litt., University of Glasgow, 1948; D.D., University of Edinburgh, 1964.

WRITINGS: Faith and Duty, Gollancz, 1950; *The Claim of Morality*, Gollancz, 1952; *Christ and Conscience* Nisbet & Co., 1956; *The Groundwork of Christian Ethics*, Collins, 1971.

Contributor: E. Hastings, *Theologians of Our Time*, T. & T. Clark, 1966; A. Richardson, *Dictionary of Christian Theology*, S.C.M. Press, 1969; G.N.A. Vesey, *Talk of God*, Macmillan, 1969; P. G. Healey, *Preface to Christian Studies*, Lutterworth, 1971. Contributor to philosophy and theology journals.

WORK IN PROGRESS: A book, *The Logic of Christian Faith*.

*   *   *

ROBINSON, O(liver) Preston   1903-

PERSONAL: Born June 25, 1903, in Farmington, Utah; son of James Henry and Romina (Chaffin) Robinson; married Christine Hinckley, September 16, 1929; children: Miriam (Mrs. Richard P. Rebholz), Bruce Hinckley, Christine Carol (Mrs. Thomas M. Burton). *Education:* University of Utah, student, 1922-24; special courses at University of Grenoble and University of Munich, 1927; Brigham Young University, B.A., 1928; New York University, M.S., and Doctor of Commercial Science. *Politics:* Independent. *Religion:* Church of Jesus Christ of Latter-day Saints. *Home:* 670 East Three Fountains Dr., Apt. 196, Murray, Utah 84107.

CAREER: New York University, New York, N.Y., 1929-47, became professor and department head in Graduate School of Retailing, assistant director of War Training Center and co-director of personnel specialist program, 1942-44; Hofstra College, Hempstead, N.Y., head of retailing courses, 1934-37; National Institute of Credit, New York, N.Y., head of marketing instruction, 1935-44; University of Utah, Salt Lake City, head of department of marketing and founder and director of Bureau of Merchandising Services, 1947-50; Deseret News Publishing Co., Salt Lake City, Utah, 1950-73, began as special consultant, became general manager and editor of *Deseret News*, board chairman, 1971—. Teacher of special courses at University of Toronto, University of Southern California, other universities and colleges. U.S. Department of Defense, civilian aide to Secretary of the Army, 1956-64. President of British Mission of Church of Jesus Christ of Latter-day

Saints, 1964-67. Member of board of directors of Utah Association for Gifted Children, National Safety Council; president and member of board, Utah Safety Council; member and past president, Utah Symphony.

MEMBER: National Council on Alcoholism (board member), Utah Association for the United Nations (board member), Utah Association for Mental Health (board member), Utah Manufacturers Association (board member; chairman of public relations committee), Salt Lake City Chamber of Commerce (advisory council member), Salt Lake City Rotary Club (vice-president). *Awards, honors:* Distinguished Service Award of Brigham Young University Alumni Association, 1961.

WRITINGS: (Co-author) *Store Salesmanship*, Prentice-Hall, 1932, 5th revised edition, 1965; (co-author) *Store Organization and Operation*, Prentice-Hall, 1938, 2nd revised edition, 1957; *Retail Personnel Relations*, Prentice-Hall, 1940; (co-author) *Successful Retail Salesmanship*, Prentice-Hall, 1942, 2nd revised edition, 1961; (co-author) *How to Establish and Operate a Retail Store*, Prentice-Hall, 1946, 2nd revised edition, 1961; *Retail Business Operation*, International Correspondence Schools, 1947; *Retail Buying and Pricing*, International Correspondence Schools, 1947; *The Dead Sea Scrolls and Original Christianity*, Deseret, 1958; *The Challenge of the Scrolls: How Old Is Christ's Gospel*, Deseret, 1963; (co-author) *Biblical Sites in the Holy Land*, Deseret, 1963; *Israel's Bible Lands*, Deseret, 1973. Also author of booklet, *Must We Lose the Middle East*. Contributor to *Encyclopaedia Britannica* and to technical and specialized journals in marketing, retailing, and related subjects.

WORK IN PROGRESS: A book, *Origins of Christianity*.

* * *

ROBY, Mary Linn 1930-

PERSONAL: Born March 31, 1930, in Bangor, Me.; daughter of Robert Wilson and Annie (French) Linn; married Kinley E. Roby (a professor of English), February 2, 1951; children: Linn Kinley, Kinley Christopher. *Education:* University of Maine, B.A., 1951. *Residence:* Sudbury, Mass. *Agent:* Curtis Brown Ltd., 60 East 56th St., New York, N.Y. 10022.

CAREER: Orono High School, Orono, Me., teacher of history, 1957-67; Concord/Carlisle High School, Concord, Mass., teacher of English, 1972—. *Member:* Maine Teachers Association, League of Women Voters, Phi Kappa Phi.

WRITINGS—Novels: *Still as the Grave*, Dodd, 1964; *Afraid of the Dark*, Dodd, 1965; *Before I Die*, R. Hale, 1966; *Cat and Mouse*, R. Hale, 1967; *In the Dead of the Night*, New American Library, 1969; *Pennies on Her Eyes*, New American Library, 1969; *All Your Lovely Words Are Spoken*, Ace Books, 1970; *Some Die in Their Beds*, New American Library, 1970; *If She Should Die*, New American Library, 1970; *Lie Quiet in Your Grave*, New American Library, 1970; *That Fatal Touch*, New American Library, 1970; *Dig a Narrow Grave*, New American Library, 1971; *This Land Turns Evil Slowly*, New American Library, 1971; *Reap the Whirlwind*, New American Library, 1972; *And Die Remembering*, New American Library, 1972; *When the Witch Is Dead*, New American Library, 1972; *Shadow Over Grove House*, New American Library, 1973; *Speak No Evil of the Dead*, New American Library, 1973; *The White Peacock*, Hawthorn, 1973; *The House at Kilgallen*, New American Library, 1973; *The Broken Key*,

Hawthorn, 1973; *Marsh House*, Hawthorn, 1974; *The Tower Room*, Hawthorn, 1974.

WORK IN PROGRESS: A novel, *Shadow of the Dream*.

AVOCATIONAL INTERESTS: Travel.

* * *

ROCKAS, Leo 1928-

PERSONAL: Born October 12, 1928, in Rochester, N.Y.; son of John Constantine and Crystal (Tsychlas) Rockas; married Virginia Rouvina, June 25, 1960; children: Nia, Anastasia. *Education:* State University of New York College at Brockport, student, 1945-46; University of Rochester, A.B. (with honors), 1951, A.M., 1952; University of Michigan, Ph.D., 1960. *Home:* 89 Highridge Rd., West Simsbury, Conn. 06092. *Agent:* Gunther Stuhlmann, 65 Irving Pl., New York, N.Y. 10003. *Office:* University of Hartford, West Hartford, Conn. 06117.

CAREER: Wayne State University, Detroit, Mich., instructor, 1957-61; Rochester Institute of Technology, Rochester, N.Y., assistant professor, 1960-61; State University of New York College at Geneseo, 1961-67, began as assistant professor, became associate professor of English language and literature; Briarcliff College, Briarcliff Manor, N.Y., associate professor, 1967-71; University of Hartford, West Hartford, Conn., associate professor, 1971—. *Military service:* U.S. Army, 1946-48. *Member:* Modern Language Association of America, English Institute, National Council of Teachers of English, College Conference on Composition and Communication, American Association of University Professors, Phi Beta Kappa. *Awards, honors:* Avery Hopwood Award from University of Michigan.

WRITINGS: Modes of Rhetoric, St. Martins, 1964. Contributor to professional journals.

WORK IN PROGRESS: Writing on analysis of literature, parallels in Shakespeare, and notes on style.

* * *

RODES, John E(dward) 1923-

PERSONAL: Born May 3, 1923, in Frankfurt am Main, Germany; son of Charles Anthony and Olivia (Veit) Rodes; married second wife, Louise C. Bridgeforth, September 5, 1973; children: (first marriage) Elizabeth Ann, Jennifer Harriet. *Education:* University of Southern California, B.A., 1943, M.A., 1948; Sorbonne, University of Paris, Certificat d'etudes superieures, 1947; Harvard University, M.A., 1949, Ph.D., 1954. *Politics:* Democrat. *Home:* 416 East Mendocino St., Altadena, Calif. *Office:* Occidental College, Los Angeles, Calif.

CAREER: U.S. War Department, Washington, D.C., French interpreter, 1946-47; Simmons College, Boston, Mass., instructor in German, 1948-50; Occidental College, Los Angeles, Calif., instructor, 1950-51, assistant professor, 1951-56, chairman of department of history of civilization, 1953-62, associate professor, 1956-61, professor of history, 1961—. Visiting professor, University of Southern California, 1955 and 1973, University of British Columbia, 1970, and University of Hawaii, 1972. Organizer (and sometime leader) of European history study tours, annually, 1956—. *Military service:* U.S. Army, active duty, 1943-46. U.S. Army Reserve, 1946-70; became major. *Member:* American Historical Association, American Association of University Professors, Phi Beta Kappa, Phi Kappa Phi, Phi Alpha Theta.

WRITINGS: Germany, a History, Holt, 1964; *A Short History of the Western World*, Scribner, 1970; *The Quest for Unity*, Holt, 1971.

WORK IN PROGRESS: History of Western Civilization.

SIDELIGHTS: Rodes is fluent in French and German, fair in Spanish and Italian, knows some Russian. *Avocational interests:* Skiing.

*   *   *

RODRIGO, Robert 1928-
(Bob Rodney)

PERSONAL: Born April 11, 1928, in Newmarket, Suffolk, England; son of Robert (a journalist) and Hilda (Drackett-Case) Rodrigo; married Violet Michie; children: Robert, Mercedes Clair, Peter. *Education:* Educated in England at Perse School, Worksop College, and St. Joseph's College, Blackpool. *Home:* 14 Oaklands Rd., Groombridge, Tunbridge Wells TN3 QSB, England. *Office: Daily Mirror*, 33 Holborn, London EC1P 1DQ, England.

CAREER: Daily Mirror, London, England, sports writer under name Bob Rodney, 1952—. Associated with British Broadcasting Corp. "Grandstand" program (television), working as sub-editor, script writer, etc., 1958-72; public relations consultant. *Member:* National Union of Journalists, Society of Authors, Sports Writers' Association, Association of Golf Writers.

WRITINGS: The Racing Game, Phoenix House, 1958; *Search and Rescue*, Kimber & Co., 1958; *Peter May*, Phoenix House, 1960; *Berlin Airlift*, Cassell, 1960. Ghost writer of other books. Contributor to magazines.

WORK IN PROGRESS: A novel; golf books.

AVOCATIONAL INTERESTS: Gardening, golf, and horse racing.

*   *   *

RODWAY, Allan 1919-

PERSONAL: Born October 25, 1919, in Hayfield, Derbyshire, England; son of Edwin (a clerk) and Maud (Edwards) Rodway; married Kathleen Harrop, August 16, 1946; children: Christine Jennifer, Janice Pauline. *Education:* Emmanuel College, Cambridge, B.A., 1949; University of Nottingham, Ph.D., 1951. *Politics:* Liberal Socialist. *Home:* The White House, Radford Bridge Rd., Nottingham, Nottinghamshire, England. *Agent:* Harold Ober Associates, Inc., 40 East 49th St., New York, N.Y. 10017; Hughes Massie Ltd., 18 Southampton Pl., London W.C. 1, England.

CAREER: University of Nottingham, Nottingham, England, lecturer, later senior lecturer, 1952-63, reader in English, 1964—. Visiting professor at University of Oregon, 1960-61; lecturer on literature and criticism at Universities of Sarajevo and Zagreb (under British Council), 1958, Cambridge Summer School, 1959, universities in Oregon, Washington, and California, 1960-61. *Member:* Association of University Teachers.

WRITINGS: Godwin and the Age of Transition, Harrap, 1952; (editor with V. de S. Pinto) *The Common Muse*, Chatto & Windus, 1957; *Post-War English Short Stories*, Svtlost, 1961; *The Romantic Conflict*, Chatto & Windus, 1963; *Science and Modern Writing*, Sheed & Ward, 1964; (contributor) R. Fowler, editor, *Essays on Style and Language*, Routledge & Kegan Paul, 1966; (with Malcolm Bradbury) *Two Poets: Poems*, Byron Press, 1967; (editor)

Poetry of the 1930's, Longmans, Green, 1967; (editor) William Shakespeare, *Midsummer Night's Dream*, Blackie & Son, 1969; (contributor) A. O. Aldridge, editor, *Comparative Literature*, University of Illinois Press, 1969; (contributor) Bradbury and O. Palmer, editors, *Contemporary Criticism*, Edward Arnold, 1970; *The Truths of Fiction*, Chatto & Windus, 1970; *English Comedy: Its Role and Nature from Chaucer to the Present Day*, Chatto & Windus, in press.

Contributor to *Pelican Guide to English Literature*, 1958, *Literature-Lexikon*, 1959, and *Encyclopedia of World Literature in the 20th Century*. Also contributor of more than forty articles and reviews to *Essays in Criticism, Enquiry, Texas Quarterly, Listener, London Magazine, Saturday Review, Encounter, Times Literary Supplement* (London), and other literary periodicals, and poetry to British Broadcasting Corp. programs and half a dozen literary journals.

*   *   *

ROGERS, James Allen 1929-

PERSONAL: Born February 26, 1929, in Oregon City, Ore.; son of John Carl and Ruth (Jorgenson) Rogers. *Education:* University of California, Berkeley, B.S., 1952; Harvard University, M.A., 1955, Ph.D., 1957. *Office:* Claremont Men's College, Pitzer South 228, Claremont, Calif.

CAREER: Harvard University, Cambridge, Mass., fellow, Russian Research Center, 1957-58; Claremont Men's College, Claremont, Calif., assistant professor, 1958-60, associate professor, 1960-66, professor of history, 1966—, member of faculty of Claremont Graduate School, 1967—.

WRITINGS: (Editor) *Kropotkin's Memoirs of a Revolutionist*, Doubleday, 1962. Contributor to *Slavic Review, Russian Review, Jahrbuecher fuer Geschichte Osteuropas, Cahiers du Monde Russia et Sovietique, Race, Journal of the History of Ideas*, and *Isis*.

WORK IN PROGRESS: A book, *Darwinism and Russian Thought*.

SIDELIGHTS: Rogers is competent in French, German, and Russian.

*   *   *

ROGERS, Kate Ellen 1920-

PERSONAL: Born December 13, 1920, in Nashville, Tenn.; daughter of Raymond Louis and Louise (Gruver) Rogers. *Education:* George Peabody College for Teachers, B.A., 1946, M.A., 1947; Columbia University, Ed.D., 1954. *Politics:* Independent. *Religion:* Baptist. *Office:* 140 Stanley Hall, University of Missouri, Columbia, Mo.

CAREER: Texas Technological College (now Texas Tech University), Lubbock, instructor, 1947-53; Design Today, Inc., Lubbock, Tex., co-owner and vice-president, 1951-54; University of Missouri, Columbia, 1954—, now professor and chairman of department of housing and interior design. American National Red Cross, Nashville, Tenn., crafts instructor, 1946-47; Community Playhouse, Lubbock, Tex., set designer, 1947-48. *Military service:* U.S. Navy Women's Reserve (WAVES), 1944-46; became specialist second class. *Member:* American Institute of Interior Designers, National Society of Interior Designers, Foundation for Interior Design Education Research, Interior Design Educators Council (chairman of board of directors), American Home Economics Association, Delta Delta Delta, Phi Lambda Theta, Kappa Delta Pi, Gamma Sigma Delta,

Texas Tech University Faculty Club (secretary, 1952). *Awards, honors:* University of Missouri Faculty Alumni Award, 1968.

WRITINGS: The Modern House, U.S.A., Its Design and Decoration, Harper, 1962.

AVOCATIONAL INTERESTS: Travel in Europe and United States, "collecting" houses on photographic slides; painting.

* * *

ROLFE, Eugene (Edward Musgrave) 1914-

PERSONAL: Born September 12, 1914, in Bedford, England; son of Eugene Alfred (a schoolmaster) and Rose (Sansom) Rolfe; married Ilse Gostynski, March 31, 1945; children: Marlene. *Education:* Keble College, Oxford, student, 1933-37, M.A., 1945. *Politics:* "Keen on Europe." *Religion:* Church of England. *Home:* 44 Brampton Rd., St. Albans, Hertfordshire AL1 4PT, England. *Agent:* Anthony Sheil Associates Ltd., 52 Floral St., Covent Garden, London W.C. 2, England.

CAREER: British Department of Employment, London, England, translator, 1949-73. *Military service:* British Army, interpreter, 1944-47; became sergeant. *Member:* Oxford Union Society (life member), Analytical Psychology Club (London; associate member), English-Speaking Union.

WRITINGS: The Intelligent Agnostic's Introduction to Christianity, Skeffington & Sons, 1959, Macmillan, 1961.

Translator: (With David Cox) Edgar Herzog, *Psyche and Death*, Hodder & Stroughton, 1966, Jung Foundation Books, 1967; Erich Newmann, *Depth Psychology and a New Ethic*, Jung Foundation Books, 1969; Toni Wolff, *Studies in the Psycology of C. G. Jung*, Jung Foundation Books, 1974.

Contributor to *Hibbert Journal* and *Prism* (Anglican monthly).

WORK IN PROGRESS: Encounter with Jung, an account of Jung's impact on the author's thought and life; translating *Empirical Aspects of the Unconscious* by C. A. Meier.

SIDELIGHTS: Rolfe has an all-around knowledge of German and a good translator's knowledge of French, Italian, and Spanish.

* * *

ROLLIN, Betty

PERSONAL: Born in New York, N.Y.; daughter of Leon (a businessman) and Ida Rollin. *Education:* Sarah Lawrence College, B.A.

CAREER: Former actress on stage and television, with last stage appearance in national company of "Advise and Consent"; *Look Magazine*, New York, N.Y., senior editor; National Broadcasting Co., New York, N.Y., network news correspondent. Writer.

WRITINGS: I Thee Wed, Doubleday, 1961; (with others) *Mothers Are Funnier Than Children*, Doubleday, 1964; *The Non-Drinker's Drink Book*, Doubleday, 1966. Contributor of articles to *Vogue, McCall's, Look*, and the *New York Times*.

* * *

ROMANELLI, Charles S. 1930-

PERSONAL: Born October 26, 1930, in Staten Island,

N.Y.; son of Charles J. (a mail carrier) and Clara (Antonelli) Romanelli; married Mary Elizabeth Thompson, July 28, 1956; children: Katherine Anne, Theresa Anne, Stephen, Mary Claire, Paul. *Education:* University of Chicago, B.A., 1956; Fordham University, M.A., 1959. *Politics:* Liberal Democrat. *Religion:* Roman Catholic. *Home:* 154 Bard Ave., Staten Island, N.Y. 10310.

CAREER: New York (N.Y.) Board of Education, teacher of English, 1956-58; Kingston (N.Y.) Board of Education, teacher of English, 1959-60; New York Board of Education, teacher of English, 1961—. President, Catholic Interracial Council of Staten Island, 1963-64. *Military service:* U.S. Army, 1952-54. *Member:* Catholics United for Racial Equality, United Federation of Teachers. *Awards, honors:* Menn Foundation creative writers award, 1955.

WRITINGS: How to Make Money in One Day at the Track, Doubleday, 1965.

WORK IN PROGRESS: A theological work for laymen.†

* * *

ROMANS, J(ohn) Thomas 1933-

PERSONAL: Born December 26, 1933, in Yonkers, N.Y.; son of William M. A. and Alice (Thomas) Romans; married Joanne Fielding Jacobson, March 29, 1959. *Education:* Cornell University, B.S., 1955; University of Tennessee, M.S., 1957; Brown University, Ph.D., 1963. *Home:* 70 MacArthur Dr., Williamsville, N.Y. 14221. *Office:* Department of Economics, State University of New York at Buffalo, Buffalo, N.Y. 14260.

CAREER: Brown University, Providence, R.I., Ford Foundation research fellow in economics, 1957-60; State University of New York at Buffalo, 1960—, began as assistant professor, became associate professor of economics. *Member:* American Economic Association, American Association of University Professors. *Awards, honors:* New England Council publications prize for *Capital Exports and Growth Among U.S. Regions*.

WRITINGS: Capital Exports and Growth Among U.S. Regions, Wesleyan University Press, 1965. Contributor to professional journals.

WORK IN PROGRESS: Economic welfare indices, measurements of regional income, and alternate formulations of the social rate of discounts.

* * *

ROME, Beatrice K(aufman) 1913-

PERSONAL: Born January 21, 1913, in Russia; daughter of Abraham M. (a rabbi) and Marion (Sandberg) Kaufman; married Sydney C. Rome (a social scientist), October 21, 1934; children: Dina S. (Mrs. Martin C. Spechler). *Education:* Radcliffe College and Harvard University, B.A. (magna cum laude), 1935, Ph.D., 1953; Sorbonne and College de France, graduate study in philosophy, 1937-38. *Politics:* Democrat. *Religion:* Jewish. *Home:* 1300 Monument St., Pacific Palisades, Calif. 90272.

CAREER: College of William and Mary, Williamsburg, Va., instructor, 1947-53, assistant professor of philosophy, 1953-55; RAND Corp., Santa Monica, Calif., research scientist, 1956-57; System Development Corp. (formerly division of RAND Corp.), Santa Monica, Calif., research scientist, 1957-67, currently principal investigator with husband, Sydney C. Rome, on Leviathan Project (concerned with the theory of very large social organizations and computer-based laboratory experimentation on such organizations); Syntality, Inc., president, 1967—. Lecturer at U.S. Air Force Summer Science Seminar, 1964; chairman of working group on limited war research, Eleventh Military Operations Research Symposium, U.S. Naval Academy, 1963; visiting professor, Leon Recanati Graduate School of Business Administration, Tel-Aviv, 1972—. *Member:* American Philosophical Association, Metaphysical Society of America, Phi Beta Kappa, Mortar Board (honorary).

WRITINGS: (Contributor) *Information Retrieval and Machine Translation*, Volume III, edited by Allen Kent, Interscience, 1960-61; *Leviathan: An Experimental Study of Large Organizations with the Aid of Computers*, System Development Corp., 1962; (contributor) *Computer Applications in the Behavioral Sciences*, edited by H. Borko, Prentice-Hall, 1962; *The Philosophy of Malebranche: A Study of His Integration of Faith, Reason and Experimental Observation*, Regnery, 1963; (editor and author of introduction with Sydney C. Rome) *Philosophical Interrogations*, Holt, 1964; (contributor) *Studies in Organizational Behavior*, edited by Raymond Bowers, University of Georgia Press; (contributor) *Electronic Information Handling*, edited by Allen Kent, Science Press; (with husband, S. C. Rome) *Organizational Growth Through Decision-making*, American Elsevier Publishing, 1971. Author or co-author of scientific documents and technical memoranda for Leviathan Project. Contributor of monographs and articles to *Philosophy and Phenomenological Research*, *Business Week*, *Behavioral Science*, and other professional journals.

WORK IN PROGRESS: *The Leviathan Studies* and *The Philosophy of Social Organization*, both co-authored with husband, Sydney C. Rome.

SIDELIGHTS: Beatrice Rome is competent in French, Hebrew, German, and Russian. *Avocational interests:* Theater, music, travel, lecturing.†

*   *   *

ROMULO, Carlos P(ena) 1899-

PERSONAL: Born January 14, 1899, in Manila, Philippines; son of Gregorio (a politician) and Maria (Pena) Romulo; married Virginia Llamas, July 1, 1924; children: Gregorio, Ricardo, Carlos P., Jr., Roberto. *Education:* University of the Philippines, A.B., 1918; Columbia University, M.A., 1921. *Politics:* Nationalist Party. *Home:* 74 McKinley Rd., Forbes Park, Makati, Rizal, Philippines. *Agent:* Harold Matson Co., Inc., 30 Rockefeller Plaza, New York, N.Y. 10020. *Office:* Department of Foreign Affairs, Padre Faura St., Manila, Philippines.

CAREER: University of the Philippines, Diliman, Quezon City, faculty member, 1923-30, associate professor and head of English department, 1926-30, member of board of regents, 1931-41; TVT Publications, Manila, Philippines, editor-in-chief, 1931; DMHM Newspapers, Manila, Philippines, publisher, 1937-41; President Manuel Quezon's War Cabinet, Washington, D.C., Secretary of Information and Public Relations, 1943-44; resident commissioner of the Philippines to United States, 1944-46; President Sergio Osmena's Cabinet, acting Secretary of Public Instruction, 1944-45; United Nations, chief of Philippine Mission, 1945-54, president of Fourth General Assembly, 1949-50; President Elpidio Quirino's Cabinet, Secretary of Foreign Affairs, 1950-52; Philippines Ambassador to United States, 1952-53, 1955-62; special and personal envoy (with rank of ambassador) of President of the Philippines to United States, 1954-55; President Diosdado Macapagal's Cabinet, Secretary of Education, 1962-65, adviser on foreign affairs, 64-65; University of the Philippines, president, 1962-68; President Ferdinand Marcos's Cabinet, Secretary of Education, 1966-68, Secretary of Foreign Affairs, 1968—. Head of Philippine delegations to United Nations Conference in San Francisco, 1945, London Conference on Devastated Areas, 1946, New Delhi Conference on Indonesia, 1949, Japanese Peace Treaty Conference, San Francisco, 1951, Asian-African Conference, Indonesia, 1955, United Nations General Assembly, 1955, 1957. *Military service:* U.S. Army, 1941-44; General MacArthur's aide de camp in Bataan, Corregidor and Australia; accompanied MacArthur's liberating forces in the invasion of Leyte and the recapture of Manila; became brigadier general; received Distinguished Service Star of the Philippines, Gold Cross, Silver Star, Purple Heart, Presidential Unit Citation with two oak leaf clusters, Philippine Legion of Honor.

MEMBER: Philippine Academy of Sciences and Humanities (founding member), National Research Council of the Philippines, Veterans of Foreign Wars, Military Order of the Carabao, Military Order of the World Wars, Caballeros de Rizal (Manila), Pan Zenia, Alpha Phi Omega, Omicron Delta Kappa, Sigma Delta Chi, Tau Kappa Alpha, Phi Kappa Phi, National Press Club (Washington, D.C.), Rotary Club (Manila), Bohemian Club (San Francisco), Cosmos Club and Metropolitan Club (both Washington, D.C.).

AWARDS, HONORS: Pulitzer Prize in journalism, 1942, for series on the Far East; Gold Medal Award of Woodrow Wilson Memorial Foundation, 1947; International Benjamin Franklin Society Gold Medal for distinguished world statesmanship, 1948; Philippine Congressional Gold Medal of Honor, 1950; Grand Cross of Order of the Phoenix (Greece); Commander, U.S. Legion of Merit, 1950; Grand Cross of Order of Queen Isabella (Spain), 1950; One World Award for international statesmanship, 1950; Cardinal Gibbons Gold Medal of Catholic University of America, 1950; Order of Sikatuna (Philippines), 1953; Golden Heart Presidential Award from President Ramon Magsaysay, 1954; Gran Cordon of La Orden del Libertador (Venezuela), 1955; Christopher Literary Award, 1955; Four Freedoms Award, 1958; Special Freedom Leadership Award of Freedoms Foundation, 1959; Munha Medal (Republic of Korea), 1961; Grand Cordon of Order of the Brilliant Star (Republic of China), 1962; Grand Cross of the Military Order of Christ (Portugal), 1962; Medallion of Valor (Israel), 1962, and many other honors from public and private groups. Honorary degrees from University of Notre Dame, 1935, University of Athens, 1948, University of the Philippines, 1949, Harvard University, 1950, University of Hawaii, 1955, Georgetown University, 1960, Nihon University and Sophia University, 1963, Delhi University and University of Indonesia, 1964, and thirty-two other universities and colleges, mainly American, 1946-64.

WRITINGS: I Saw the Fall of the Philippines, Doubleday, 1942; *Mother America*, Doubleday, 1943, reprinted, Greenwood Press, 1974; *My Brother Americans*, Doubleday, 1945; *I See the Philippines Rise*, Doubleday, 1946; *The United* (novel), Crown, 1951; *Crusade in Asia*, Day, 1955, reprinted, Greenwood Press, 1973; *The Meaning of Bandung*, University of North Carolina Press, 1956; (with Marvin M. Gray) *The Magsaysay Story*, Day, 1956; (with Pearl Buck) *Friend to Friend*, Day, 1958.

Walked with Heroes (autobiography), Holt, 1961; *Contem-*

porary Nationalism and the World Order (Azad Memorial lectures), Asia Publishing House, 1964; *Mission to Asia: The Dialogue Begins*, University of the Philippines, 1964; *Academic Excellence and the Nature of the University*, University of the Philippines, 1964; *Identity and Change: Towards a National Definition*, Solidaridad Publishing House, 1965; *Evasions and Response: Lectures on the American Novel, 1890-1930* (introduction by Norman Cousins), Phoenix Publishing House (Quezon City), 1966; *Rejoining Our Asian Family*, Office of Public Affairs, Department of Foreign Affairs (Manila), 1969; *Clarifying the Asian Mystique*, Solidaridad Publishing House, 1970.

SIDELIGHTS: Carlos Romulo once said in a speech: "My dream is the unity of all nations, as it is embodied in the charter of the United Nations, which it was my privilege in 1945 to help write. On the way to it, as a prior condition, is the unity of Southeast Asian peoples; beyond this, the whole of Asia. . . . This is what makes it so crucial to hammer out a bond which is more lasting than the emotional, and this can only be one which is based on mutual understanding, on intellectual kinship."

Gladys Zehnpfennig writes: "In Romulo's books, his phrases live and breathe; he is a scholar with deep human compassion and an exuberant sense of humor. As General Douglas MacArthur's aide-de-camp after the World War II fall of Corregidor, [he demonstrated] sublime eloquence as a spokesman for freedom. During a farewell chat early in 1962, President John F. Kennedy said to retiring Ambassador Romulo, 'I understand we're losing the best speaker in America.' 'Why, Mr. President,' replied the Philippine diplomat, 'Are you leaving?'"

BIOGRAPHICAL/CRITICAL SOURCES: Cornelia Spencer, *Romulo: Voice of Freedom*, Day, 1953; Carlos P. Romulo, *I Walked with Heroes*, Holt, 1961; Evelyn Wells, *Carlos P. Romulo: Voice of Freedom*, Funk, 1964; Gladys Zehnpfennig, *General Carlos P. Romulo: Defender of Freedom*, Denison, 1965.

*   *   *

RONDTHALER, Edward   1905-

PERSONAL: Surname is pronounced Rahn-tahler; born June 9, 1905, in Bethlehem, Pa.; son of Howard E. (a college president) and Katharine (Boring) Rondthaler; married Dorothy Reid, April 12, 1930; children: Edward, David Lee, Timothy. *Education:* University of North Carolina, A.B., 1929; also studied two years at Westminster Choir College. *Politics:* Independent. *Home:* Croton-on-Hudson, N.Y. *Office:* Photo-Lettering, Inc., 216 East 45th St., New York, N.Y. 10017.

CAREER: Lee & Phillips, Typographers, New York, N.Y., designer, 1929-33; Rutherford Machinery Co., New York, N.Y., inventor, 1933-36; Photo-Lettering, Inc., New York, N.Y., president, 1936—. Electrographic Corp., vice-president, 1963-74. International Typeface Corp., chairman, 1970—. Croton-on-Hudson Recreation Commission, chairman, 1961-64. *Member:* American Institute of Graphic Arts, International Center for the Typographic Arts, Phi Beta Kappa, Type Directors Club of New York (vice-president, 1959-60), Phonemic Spelling Council. *Awards, honors:* Named Man of the Year in Croton-on-Hudson for civic service, 1962.

WRITINGS: Berlitz Money Converter, Grosset, 1958; (editor) *Alphabet Thesaurus*, Reinhold, Volume I, 1960, Volume II, 1965, Volume III, 1972; *Traveler's Instant Money Converter*, Grosset, 1962. Contributor to *Penrose*

Annual and *Art Direction* and *Graphics U.S.A.* Editorial director of *U&lc*, 1973—.

WORK IN PROGRESS: Research on type nomenclature, on copywright protection for typefaces, and on conversion of alphabet designs to keyboard typesetting; development of SoundSpel orthography for simplified English spelling and computerized transliteration.

AVOCATIONAL INTERESTS: Development of municipal parks and recreational facilities, conservation of natural resources, preservation and restoration of historic sites (particularly Old Salem in Winston-Salem, N.C.), music, European travel.

*   *   *

ROPPOLO, Joseph Patrick   1913-

PERSONAL: Surname is pronounced Row-*poe*-low; born March 17, 1913, in Shreveport, La.; son of Michael A. and Josephine (Corolla) Roppolo. *Education:* Attended University of Missouri, 1930-32; Centenary College, Shreveport, La., B.A., 1946; Tulane University, M.A., 1948, Ph.D., 1950. *Home:* 7447 Hampson St., New Orleans, La. 70118. *Office:* Tulane University, New Orleans, La. 70118.

CAREER: Reporter and editor on newspapers in Minden, La., 1928-31, and Shreveport, La., 1933-41; Tulane University, New Orleans, La., 1946—, began as teaching fellow, professor of English, 1964—. Onetime actor with Shreveport Little Theatre. *Military service:* U.S. Army Air Forces, 1942-45; became sergeant. *Member:* Modern Language Association of America, American National Theatre Academy, American Educational Theatre Association, American Comparative Literature Association, American Studies Association (president of Lower Mississippi Valley branch), Conference of Louisiana Colleges and Universities (president, 1965).

WRITINGS: Phillip Barry, Twayne, 1965. Writer of articles and short stories appearing in *Louisiana Folklore Miscellany, New England Quarterly, American Speech, Modern Language Notes*, and other journals.

WORK IN PROGRESS: Two books, a critical study of Poe's tales, and Shakespeare in New Orleans.

AVOCATIONAL INTERESTS: Music, travel, gardening, photography.

BIOGRAPHICAL/CRITICAL SOURCES: Shreveport Journal, August 24, 1963.

*   *   *

RORIPAUGH, A(lan) Robert   1930-

PERSONAL: Surname is pronounced *Roar*-a-paw; born August 26, 1930, in Oxnard, Calif.; son of Charles Clifford (a rancher and petroleum engineer) and Marion (Abbott) Roripaugh; married Yoshiko Horikoshi, August, 1956; children: Lee Ann. *Education:* Attended University of Texas, 1947-50; University of Wyoming, B.A., 1952, M.A., 1953, graduate study, 1955-56; University of New Mexico, graduate study, 1956-58. *Office:* Department of English, University of Wyoming, Laramie, Wyo. 82070.

CAREER: University of Wyoming, Laramie, instructor, 1958-62, assistant professor, 1962-67, associate professor, 1967-72; professor of English, 1972—. From time to time has worked as geological laboratory technician, oilfield roustabout, carpenter's helper, horse wrangler for a pack outfit, clerk-typist, and ranch hand. *Military service:* U.S. Army, 1953-55; served in Japan. *Member:* Authors League of America, Western Literature Association (member of executive council, 1968-71), The Wilderness Society. *Awards, honors:* Western Heritage Award of National Cowboy Hall of Fame for outstanding Western novel of 1963, *Honor Thy Father.*

WRITINGS: A Fever for Living (novel), Morrow, 1961; *Honor Thy Father* (novel), Morrow, 1963. Contributor of stories, poetry, and reviews to *Atlantic Monthly, Descant, South Dakota Review, West Coast Poetry, Western American Literature,* and other literary journals. Assistant editor, *Writing at Wyoming,* 1958-65; editorial associate, *Sage,* 1966-68.

WORK IN PROGRESS: Various projects in short and long fiction, and a volume of poetry utilizing modern Western experience and backgrounds.

SIDELIGHTS: Roripaugh has spent most of his life in the West and Southwest, with the exception of some time spent in Japan, both in and out of the military. He studied writing in college with the poet Joseph Langland. Roripaugh told *CA*: "In general, I believe an author must commit himself completely to the problems and demands of each work he attempts, whether a poem or novel—and not become too dogmatic about anything else connected with writing." *Avocational interests:* Nature and wildlife, problems related to conservation, population control, environmental sanity.

*   *   *

ROSA, Joseph G. 1932-

PERSONAL: Born November 20, 1932, in Chriswick, England. *Education:* Educated in England. *Home:* 17 Woodville Gardens, Ruislip, Middlesex, England.

CAREER: Employed as a copyholder and proofreader with firm of government printers in England, 1947-51, and as teletype operator with Cable & Wireless (British overseas telegraph service), London, England, 1954-58; Salvage Association, London, England, 1958—, began as communications executive, now manager. Writer and broadcaster on the old American West, and occasional commentator on British Broadcasting Corp. telecasts of "The Virginian" series. *Military service:* Royal Air Force, 1951-54; served on Malta. *Member:* Arms and Armour Society, Westerners International, Western Writers of America, Historical Breech Loaders Association, British Film Institute, English Westerners' Society, Westerners (Chicago corral; corresponding member), Kansas State Historical Society.

WRITINGS: They Called Him Wild Bill, University of Oklahoma Press, 1964, revised edition, 1974; *Alias Jack McCall,* Kansas City, 1966; *The Gunfighter: Man or Myth?,* University of Oklahoma Press, 1974; (with Robin May) *The Pleasure of Guns,* Octopus Books, 1974; *Address: Colonel Colt–the Story of Colt's London Armoury, 1853-57,* Arms and Armour Press, 1975. Contributor of stories and articles on the American West and on guns to *English Westerners' Brand Book, Guns Review, Lloyd's Log,* and other periodicals. Contributor to *Western Film and T.V. Annual,* 1956-62, and sometime associate editor.

WORK IN PROGRESS: A biography of Joseph "Rowdy Joe" Lowe, and a project on Joseph Alfred Slade.

AVOCATIONAL INTERESTS: Collecting old pistols, specializing in the early Colt and other cap and ball arms, target shooting, and collecting old photographs and early English and American pocket watches.

ROSAGE, David E. 1913-

PERSONAL: Born February 19, 1913, in Johnstown, Pa.; son of John V. (a steel worker) and Lena (Sellman) Rosage. *Education:* The Pontifical College Josephinum, Worthington, Ohio, B.A., 1937; Pontifical Seminary, M.A., 1943. *Home:* Immaculate Heart Retreat, Route 3, Box 653, Spokane, Wash. 99203.

CAREER: Roman Catholic priest. Diocese of Spokane, Spokane, Wash., former youth director, parish priest and pastor; Immaculate Heart Retreat House, Spokane, Wash., retreat director, 1957—.

WRITINGS: Letters to an Altar Boy, Bruce, 1952; *Crumbs from the Master's Table,* Immaculate Heart Retreat, 1961; *At Mass with Mary,* Immaculate Heart Retreat, 1962; *One Way, His Way,* Immaculate Heart Retreat, 1970; *Mary: The Model Charismatic,* Immaculate Heart Retreat, 1971; *Retreats and the Charismatic Renewal,* Dove, 1972; *Speak Lord, Your Servant Is Listening,* Immaculate Heart Retreat, 1974.

WORK IN PROGRESS: A series of essays.

*   *   *

ROSE, Jerome G. 1926-

PERSONAL: Born July 4, 1926, in New York, N.Y.; son of Robert (a businessman) and Ida (Lippman) Rose; married Naomi Lichtman; children: Patricia, Elizabeth, Theodore. *Education:* Cornell University, A.B., 1948; Harvard University, LL.B. (cum laude), 1951; New York University, current study toward doctorate. *Home:* 10 Pell Ter., Garden City, N.Y. 11535. *Office:* 200 Hudson St., New York, N.Y. 10013.

CAREER: Attorney-at-law, 1951—; Institute of Legal Knowledge, Inc. (publishers), Garden City, N.Y., director, 1964—. *Military service:* U.S. Navy, 1944-46. *Member:* American Society for Public Administration, Phi Beta Kappa, Harvard Law School Club of Long Island.

WRITINGS: The Legal Adviser on Home Ownership, Institute of Legal Knowledge, 1964; *Landlords and Tenants: A Complete Guide to the Residential Rental Relationship,* Dutton, 1973. Contributor of articles to *Modern Bride* and *House and Garden Plans Guide.*

WORK IN PROGRESS: The Legal Adviser for the Small Business.†

*   *   *

ROSE, Peter I(saac) 1933-

PERSONAL: Born September 5, 1933, in Rochester, N.Y.; son of Aaron E. and Lillian Rose; married Hedwig Hella Cohen, March 25, 1956; children: Elisabeth Anne, Daniel Eric. *Education:* Syracuse University, A.B., 1954; Cornell University, M.A., 1957, Ph.D., 1959. *Home:* 66 Paradise Rd., Northampton, Mass. *Office:* 103 Wright Hall, Smith College, Northampton, Mass.

CAREER: Goucher College, Baltimore, Md., began as instructor, became assistant professor of sociology, 1958-60; Smith College, Northampton, Mass., 1960—, began as assistant professor, now Sophia Smith professor of sociology and anthropology. Visiting lecturer, University of Massachusetts, 1961. Fulbright lecturer in sociology at University of Leicester, 1964-65, and at Flinders University (Australia), Kyoto University, and Doshina University (both Japan). Camp Chateaugay, Merrill, N.Y., director. Consultant to Anti-Defamation League, Puerto Rican Department of Health, Time-Life Books and to Random House. *Member:* American Sociological Association (fellow), Society for the Study of Social Problems, American Anthropological Association, Society for Applied Anthropology, American Association of University Professors, Phi Beta Kappa, Phi Kappa Phi, Alpha Kappa Delta.

WRITINGS: They and We: Racial and Ethnic Relations in the U.S., Random House, 1964, revised edition, 1974; (editor) *The Study of Society*, Random House, 1967, 2nd revised edition, 1973; *The Subject is Race*, Oxford University Press, 1968; *The Ghetto and Beyond*, Random House, 1969; *Americans from Africa*, Atherton Press, 1970; *Nation of Nations*, Random House, 1972; (editor) *Seeing Ourselves*, Knopf, 1972; *Through Different Eyes*, Oxford University Press, 1973.

General Editor, Random House *Ethnic Groups in Comparative Perspective* series. Editor, *Research Bulletin on Intergroup Relations*, 1958-63; co-editor, "The Threat of War," special issue of *Social Problems*, 1963.

WORK IN PROGRESS: Three books, *Society and Culture; Academic Sojourn;* and *Views from Abroad.*

* * *

ROSE, Willie Lee (Nichols) 1927-

PERSONAL: Born May 18, 1927, in Bedford, Va.; daughter of Grady Lee (a businessman) and Willie (Chafin) Nichols; married William George Rose (a free-lance photographer), June 18, 1949. *Education:* Mary Washington College, B.A., 1947; Johns Hopkins University, Ph.D., 1962. *Home:* 310 Northfield Place, Baltimore, Md.

CAREER: High school teacher of English and history in Howard County, Md., 1947-49, in Attleboro, Mass., 1949-50, in Baltimore County, Md., 1950-53; Towson State College, Towson, Md., instructor in American history, 1959; Goucher College, Baltimore, Md., instructor in European history, 1963; University of Virginia, Charlottesville, Va., professor of history, 1965-72; Johns Hopkins University, Baltimore, Md., professor of history, 1972—. *Member:* American Historical Association, Southern Historical Association, Organization of American Historians, Phi Beta Kappa. *Awards, honors:* Social Science Research Council Fellow, 1960-61; Parkman Prize of the Society of American Historians, 1964, for *Rehearsal for Reconstruction;* Charles Sydnor Award of the Southern Historical Association, 1966, for *Rehearsal for Reconstruction.*

WRITINGS: Rehearsal for Reconstruction; The Port Royal Experiment, Bobbs-Merrill, 1964; (contributor) *Anti-Slavery Vanguard*, edited by Martin Duberman, Princeton University Press, 1965.

WORK IN PROGRESS: The Fields of Stockbridge, Massachusetts.

SIDELIGHTS: Dr. Rose speaks French, German.

* * *

ROSELLE, Daniel 1920-

PERSONAL: Born August 11, 1920, in Brooklyn, N.Y.; son of Saul and Malvina (Escoll) Roselle; married Lois Jane Mitchell, August 30, 1954; children: David, Lynn. *Education:* City College (now City College of the City University of New York), Bachelor of Social Science, 1940; Columbia University, M.A., 1947, Ph.D., 1950. *Home:* 8714 Postoak Road, Potomac, Md.

CAREER: State University of New York College at Fre-

donia, 1950-68, started as assistant professor, professor of history and social science, organizer and director of Junior Semester in Belgium Program, 1959; *Social Education*, Washington, D.C., editor, 1968—. Fulbright research professor to France, 1952-53. Sometime editorial consultant to *Book of Knowledge. Military service:* U.S. Army, 30th Infantry Division, 1942-45; served in five major European campaigns; became sergeant. *Member:* American Historical Association, National Council for the Social Studies, American Association of University Professors, New York Association of European Historians, Kappa Delta Pi. *Awards, honors:* Faculty Research Summer Award, 1963; Educational Press Association of America Award for Editorial Writing; Eleanor Fishburn Award.

WRITINGS: A World History, Ginn, 1963; (contributor) *High School Topics*, Ginn, 1964; *Samuel Griswold Goodrich*, Antioch Press, 1968; *Our Western Heritage*, Ginn, 1972; *Transformations: Understanding History Through Science Fiction*, Fawcett, 1973.

Contributor to a school reader in "Think-and-Do" series and to *Book of Knowledge.* Adapter of a French folktale for a television script, "The Flying Beret." Contributor of a series of vignettes on life in France to *Social Education*, 1955-57, of historical fiction to *Ellery Queen's Magazine*, poetry to *Driftwood Poetry Magazine, Stars and Stripes*, and *New York State Education*, and articles to academic journals. Book review editor, *Social Education*, 1957-59, member of executive board, 1964-68.

WORK IN PROGRESS: Research in European folklore and French history.

SIDELIGHTS: Daniel Roselle has lived and traveled in most European countries; competent in French and Spanish.

* * *

ROSENBAUM, Kurt 1926-

PERSONAL: Born December 10, 1926, in Witten, Germany; married Shirley Feinstein, June 21, 1953; children: Beth Ellen, Jonathan David. *Education:* State University of New York at Albany, B.A. (cum laude), 1954, M.A., 1955; Syracuse University, Ph.D., 1961. *Home:* 531 Woodland Circle, Morgantown, W.Va. 26505. *Office:* 305 Woodburn Hall, West Virginia University, Morgantown, W.Va. 26506.

CAREER: State University of New York College at Oswego, assistant professor of history, 1960-61; University of New Hampshire, Durham, instructor in history, 1961-62; West Virginia University, Morgantown, assistant professor, 1962-66, associate professor, 1966-72, professor of history, 1972—. *Member:* American Historical Association, American Association for the Advancement of Slavic Studies, Southern Conference on Slavic Studies. *Awards, honors:* Central University Research Fund grant, University of New Hampshire, 1961.

WRITINGS: Community of Fate: German-Soviet Diplomatic Relations, 1922-28, Syracuse University Press, 1965; (translator) Martin Broszat, *Nationalsocialism*, Clio Press, 1965. Contributor to professional journals.

WORK IN PROGRESS: Co-author of *The Polish Campaign;* writing *Twentieth Century European Diplomacy.*

* * *

ROSENBAUM, S(tanford) P(atrick) 1929-

PERSONAL: Born March 17, 1929, in Vancouver, British

Columbia, Canada; married Susan Black (an assistant professor), May 23, 1958; children: two. *Education:* University of Colorado, B.A. (cum laude), 1951; Rutgers University, M.A., 1955; Pembroke College, Oxford, graduate study, 1956-57; Cornell University, Ph.D., 1960. *Office:* Department of English, Erindale College, University of Toronto, Toronto, Ontario, Canada.

CAREER: Cornell University, Ithaca, N.Y., instructor in English, 1958-60; Indiana University, Bloomington, assistant professor of English, 1960-62; Brown University, Providence, R.I., Carnegie Foundation interdisciplinary fellow in philosophy and literature, 1962-64; Erindale College, University of Toronto, Toronto, Ontario, associate professor of English, 1964—. *Member:* Modern Language Association of America.

WRITINGS: (Editor) Henry James, *The Ambassadors*, Norton, 1964; *A Concordance to the Poems of Emily Dickinson*, Cornell University Press, 1964; *English Literature and British Philosophy*, University of Chicago Press, 1971. Contributor of articles on American and modern British literature to scholarly journals.

WORK IN PROGRESS: Literary history of the Bloomsbury group.

* * *

ROSENBERG, Edgar 1925-

PERSONAL: Born September 21, 1925, in Fuerth, Bavaria, Germany; son of Otto and Lilly (Arnstein) Rosenberg; married Birthe Terp-Johansen, 1965. *Education:* Cornell University, B.A., 1949, M.A., 1950; University of Illinois, graduate study, 1950-51; Stanford University, Ph.D., 1958. *Religion:* Jewish. *Home:* 201 Forest Dr., Ithaca, N.Y. 14850. *Office:* Cornell University, Ithaca, N.Y. 14850.

CAREER: Stanford University, Stanford, Calif., acting instructor in English, 1952-53, 1954-57; San Jose State College, (now California State University, San Jose), instructor, 1953-54; Harvard University, Cambridge, Mass., instructor in English, 1957-60, Briggs-Copeland Assistant Professor of English, 1960-65; Cornell University, Ithaca, N.Y., associate professor, 1965-69, professor of English, 1969—. *Military service:* U.S. Army, Infantry, 1944-45; served in European theater. *Member:* Modern Language Association of America, American Comparative Literature Association, Jewish Historical Society of England, Dickens Society, Phi Beta Kappa. *Awards, honors:* Stanford Fiction Fellow, 1951-52; Bread Loaf Fellow, 1953; Guggenheim Fellow, 1973-74.

WRITINGS: From Shylock to Svengali: Jewish Stereotypes in English Fiction, Stanford University Press, 1960; *Tabloid Jews and Fungoid Scribblers*, Ktav, 1970; (editor) Dickens, *Great Expectations*, Norton, in press. Contributor of short fiction, articles, and translations to periodicals, including *Esquire, Commentary, Epoch, Judaism, The Dickensian*, and *English Language Notes*.

SIDELIGHTS: Rosenberg is interested in comparative literature and Anglo-Judaic studies.

* * *

ROSENBERG, James L. 1921-

PERSONAL: Born May 19, 1921, in Sheridan, Wyo.; son of James LeRoy (an editor) and Emily (MacPherson) Rosenberg; married Dorothy Ayre, June 12, 1949; children: Shelley, Robert, Susan. *Education:* University of Califor-

nia, Berkeley, A.B., 1951; University of Denver, M.A., 1952, Ph.D., 1954. *Home:* 3230 Beechwood Blvd., Pittsburgh, Pa. 15217.

CAREER: Kansas State University, Manhattan, 1953-61, became associate professor of English; Tulane University, New Orleans, La., visiting professor, 1961-62; Carnegie Institute of Technology, Pittsburgh, Pa., professor of drama, 1962—. *Military service:* U.S. Army, Infantry, 1942-46. *Awards, honors:* William Rose Benet Memorial Award of Poetry Society of America for best poem published in *Saturday Review* (1952), 1953; Alan Swallow New Poetry Series Award, 1961, for *A Primer of Kinetics*.

WRITINGS: (Translator) *Sir Gawain and the Green Knight*, Rinehart, 1959; (translator) Max Frisch, *The Chinese Wall*, Hill & Wang, 1961; *A Primer of Kinetics* (poetry), A. Swallow, 1961; (co-editor) *The Art of the Theatre*, Chandler Publishing, 1964; (co-editor) *The Context and Craft of Drama*, Chandler Publishing, 1964.

WORK IN PROGRESS: A novel, as yet untitled, several plays, and a new collection of poetry.

* * *

ROSKAMP, Karl Wilhelm 1923-

PERSONAL: Born August 19, 1923, in Leer, Germany; son of Jan and Anna (Witt) Roskamp; married Jacqueline Odette Labesse (a medical doctor), 1957; children: Eric Jan, Jeannette Anne. *Education:* Attended University of Goettingen, Free University of Berlin, and University of Frankfurt, 1952-54; University of Michigan, M.A., 1955, Ph.D., 1959. *Office:* Department of Economics, Wayne State University, Detroit, Mich.

CAREER: Massachusetts Institute of Technology, Cambridge, research assistant, Center for International Studies, 1955-56; Brandeis University, Waltham, Mass., visiting assistant professor of economics, 1959-60; Wayne State University, Detroit, Mich., associate professor, 1960-65, professor of economics, 1965—. *Member:* American Economic Association, American Association of University Professors. *Awards, honors:* Ford Foundation faculty fellow, 1961.

WRITINGS: (With Wolfgang F. Stolper) *The Structure of the East German Economy*, Harvard University Press, 1960; *Capital Formation in West Germany*, Wayne State University Press, 1965; *Die Amerikanische Wirtschaft* (title means "The American Economy"), Kroner Verlag, 1975. Contributor to economic journals in United States and abroad.

WORK IN PROGRESS: Problems of portfolio management and taxation.

SIDELIGHTS: Roskamp speaks French.

* * *

ROSKILL, Stephen W(entworth) 1903-

PERSONAL: Born August 1, 1903, in London, England; son of John Henry (a barrister) and Sybil (Dilke) Roskill; married Elizabeth Van den Bergh, August 12, 1930; children: Nicholas, Mark, Theresa (Mrs. Michael Till), Mary (Mrs. Martin Caroe), Thomas, Clare, Christopher. *Education:* Attended Royal Naval College, Osborne, England, and Royal Naval College, Dartmouth; Cambridge University, M.A., 1961, Litt.D., 1971. *Politics:* Independent Liberal. *Religion:* Church of England. *Home:* Frostlake Cottage, Malting Lane, Cambridge, CB3 9HF, England. *Office:* Churchill College, Cambridge, England.

CAREER: Royal Navy, career service, 1917-48, invalided out as captain, 1948; Cabinet Office, London, England, official naval historian, 1949-60; Cambridge University, Cambridge, England, Lees Knowles Lecturer, 1961, fellow of Churchill College, 1961-70, life fellow, 1970—. Distinguished visiting lecturer, U.S. Naval Academy, Annapolis, Md., 1965; Richmond lecturer, Cambridge, 1967. Served at sea as commander of H.M.S. Warspite, 1939, and H.M.N.Z.S. Leander, 1941-44; on Naval Staff, 1939-41; senior observer, Bikini Atomic Tests, 1946; deputy director, Naval Intelligence, 1946-48; received Distinguished Service Cross (British; 1944), Legion of Merit (United States). *Member:* Royal Historical Society (fellow), British Academy (fellow), Navy Records Society (vice-president, 1964; member of council, 1974), Travellers' Club (London).

WRITINGS: The War at Sea (official history), H.M.S.O., Volume I, 1954, Volume II, 1957, Volume III, Part 1, 1960, Volume III, Part 2, 1961; *H.M.S. Warspite*, Collins, 1957; *The Secret Capture*, Collins, 1959; *White Ensign*, U.S. Naval Institute, 1960; *The Strategy of Sea Power*, Collins, 1962; *A Merchant Fleet in War*, Collins, 1962; *The Art of Leadership*, Collins, 1964; *Naval Policy Between the Wars*, Collins, 1968; (editor) *Documents Relating to the Naval Air Service 1908-1918*, Navy Records Society, 1969; *Hankey, Man of Secrets*, Collins, Volume I, 1969, Volume II, 1972, Volume III, 1974. Regular contributor to *Sunday Times, Sunday Telegraph, Economist* and *Proceedings of U.S. Naval Institute.*

WORK IN PROGRESS: A history of naval policy, 1930-39.

SIDELIGHTS: Roskill speaks French and German. *Avocational interests:* Country life, painting.

*   *   *

ROSKOLENKO, Harry 1907-
(Colin Ross)

PERSONAL: Born September 21, 1907, in New York, N.Y.; son of Barnett (a tailor, presser, and farmer) and Sara (Goldstein) Roskolenko; married Diana Chang, May 10, 1948 (divorced August, 1955); children: Deborah Crozier. *Education:* Roskolenko writes: "No scholastic education worth mentioning. Self educated via hoboing and extensive travel as a sailor between 1920-1927." *Religion:* Pantheist. *Home:* 463 West St., New York, N.Y. 10014.

CAREER: Went to work in a factory at age of nine; at thirteen, swearing he was eighteen, he shipped as a seaman on an oil tanker bound for Mexico; worked on a WPA Writers Project during the Depression; has been a law clerk, patent researcher, second mate in the Merchant Marine, and a drawbridge operator; correspondent in China, Japan, Indochina, and East Asia, 1946-47; traveled extensively via scooter, motorcycle, and station wagon for material for his books; traveled the Nile River from source to mouth. *Military service:* U.S. Army, 1942; became sergeant. U.S. Army Transport Service, 1942-45; became second officer. *Member:* P.E.N.

WRITINGS: (Editor with Helen Neville) *Exiles Anthology: British and American Poets*, Press of James A. Decker, 1940; *Baedeker for a Bachelor* (travel book), Padell Books, 1952; *Black Is a Man* (novel), Padell Books, 1954; *Poet on a Scooter* (travel book), Dial, 1958; *Lan-Lan* (novel), New American Library, 1962; *White Man Go* (travel book), Regency, 1962; *When I Was Last on Cherry Street* (autobiography), Stein & Day, 1965; *The Terrorized: 1945-1950* (autobiography), Prentice-Hall, 1968; *The Time*

That Was Then: The Lower East Side, 1900-1914 (autobiography), Dial, 1971; (contributor) Thomas C. Wheeler, editor, *The Immigrant Experience*, Dial, 1971; (editor) *SOLO—Great Adventures Alone*, Playboy Press, 1973; (editor) *Great Battles and Their Great Generals*, Playboy Press, 1974.

Poetry: *Sequence on Violence*, Signal Press, 1938; *I Went Into the Country*, Decker Press, 1940; *A Second Summary*, Reed & Harris (Australia), 1944; *Notes From a Journey, and Other Poems*, Meanjin Press (Australia), 1946; *Paris Poems* [France], 1950; *American Civilization*, National Press (Melbourne, Australia), 1971; *Is*, National Press, 1971.

Also author of radio serial on Chinese-American relations for Voice of America, 1950. Contributor to *Prairie Schooner, New Republic, New York Times Book Review, Partisan Review, Sewanee Review*, and others. Editor, *Quadrant* (American edition), 1973.

WORK IN PROGRESS: A novel, *The Life and Death of a Building.*

SIDELIGHTS: The thirteenth of fourteen children, eight of whom died before his parents moved from the Ukraine to New York, Roskolenko is well acquainted with the poverty of the lower east side of New York City (see *When I Was Last on Cherry Street*). He finally ran away to become a poet and a Trotskyite, and later gave up both. Of his life as a radical he writes: 'We were so serious we couldn't tolerate each other's views." He now refers to his politics as a "private affair."

He told *CA*: "I travel—and usually in odd ways, to odd places. I prefer the wilderness to the City. I need wild green places, deserts, mountains, etc. The City will kill all of us, soon enough. The pollutions are as physical as they are social and spiritual. My books stem from this situation. We are over-gadgeted and breathless, incapable of free-wheeling anymore. We are locked in by highways going to a place called NOWHERE, U.S.A. Any attempt by the U.S. Government to beautify this country—can only be as disastrous as our current duplicity. Doomsday, U.S.A., is a permanent program called Progress. We have abdicated all the way home.

"I gave up poetry because it no longer is a valid art in our society. It is as empty as the American way of non-life." He later expanded on this statement: "Poetry is not valid *for me* because my world, our world, this world, this inhuman society—has *consciously* eradicated every moral and sensual basis for poetry as an art form. A simple example is a quote from my recent book, *When I Was Last on Cherry Street*: 'The new Barbarians, circa 1964, were at work on the City . . . and even the symbols of poetry were demolished. Whitman's house on Cranberry and Fulton Streets, where Whitman had set the type for *Leaves of Grass*, was torn down one bright day in June by the Able Demolition Company.'

"What is valid for me is one's natural irony and the continual criticism of the New Barbarism. That is my poetry—to expose the terror of bureaucratic stupidity; the mechanisms that rob all of us of basic human dignity; the City, now re-made, that encases us, dulls us, pollutes us. We are boxed in by skies without air, in cities without water, and a pastoral scene that has killed NATURE. It may make some sort of poetry for some poets; but God and Pantheism save me from that sort of poetry." (Despite the above comments, Roskolenko continues to write poetry.)

Of *The Time That Was Then*, Sanford Pinsker wrote in the *Saturday Review*: "Roskolenko's book is a valuable addition to the growing number of American Jewish memoirs which revisit the Cherry Streets of the imagination. His is a guided tour into a past that no longer exists—that 'time that was then'—and if the ghosts seem particularly lively, that is because Roskolenko writes out of experiences sincerely felt and a love which strikes the heart as true."

BIOGRAPHICAL/CRITICAL SOURCES: New York Times Book Review, September 28, 1958, May 23, 1965; *New York Herald Tribune*, May 12, 1965; *Washington Evening Star*, May 13, 1965; *New York Times*, May 14, 1965.

* * *

ROSS, Ralph 1911-

PERSONAL: Born August 27, 1911, in New York, N.Y.; son of Arthur Leonard (an attorney) and Mathilda (Burston) Ross; married Alicia Johnson, July 6, 1957; children: Allen, Penelope. *Education:* University of Arizona, B.A., 1933; Columbia University, M.A., 1935, Ph.D., 1940. *Office:* Department of Philosophy, Scripps College, Claremont, Calif. 91711.

CAREER: University of Newark, Newark, N.J., instructor in philosophy, 1935-40; City University of New York, New York, N.Y., instructor in philosophy at Queens College, 1940-45; New York University, New York, N.Y., assistant professor, 1945-47, associate professor of philosophy, 1947-51; University of Minnesota, Minneapolis, professor of philosophy and chairman of humanities program, 1951-66; Scripps College, Claremont, Calif., Hartley Burr Professor of Humanities and professor of philosophy, 1966—. Research associate in international relations, Princeton University, 1962. Lecturer at University of Texas, University of Miami, Carnegie Institute of Technology (now Carnegie-Mellon University), and Center for the Study of Liberal Education for Adults; Distinguished Visiting Professor, New York University, 1957-58. Alternate member, Committee on Business Ethics, U.S. Department of Commerce, 1961.

MEMBER: American Philosophical Association, American Political Science Association, American Sociological Association, Mind Association of Great Britain, American Society for Aesthetics, P.E.N., American Association of University Professors, British Society for Aesthetics. *Awards, honors:* Bollingen Fellow in aesthetics, 1958; Minneapolis Society of Fine Arts fellowship in aesthetics, 1958, 1959; Distinguished Teacher award, University of Minnesota, 1963.

WRITINGS: Scepticism and Dogma, privately printed, 1940; (editor and author of introduction) F. H. Bradley, *Ethical Studies*, Liberal Arts Press, 1951; (with Ernest van den Haag) *The Fabric of Society*, Harcourt, 1957; (with John Berryman and Allen Tate) *The Arts of Reading*, Crowell, 1960; (editor and author of introduction with Louis I. Bredvold) *The Philosophy of Edmund Burke*, University of Michigan Press, 1961; (editor and author of introduction) Bernard Bosanquet, *Three Lectures on Aesthetic*, Bobbs-Merrill, 1963; (with van den Haag) *Passion and Social Contraint*, Stein & Day, 1963; *The Nature of Communism*, Paul Amidon Associates, 1963; *Symbols and Civilization*, Harcourt, 1963; (author of introduction) George Santayana, *Soliloquies in England*, University of Michigan Press, 1967; (author of introduction) D. W. Prall, *Aesthetic Judgment*, Apollo, 1967; (author of introduction) Samuel Alexander, *Beauty and Other Forms of Value*, Apollo, 1968; (author of introduction) William James, *The Meaning of Truth*, University of Michigan Press, 1970; *Obligation: A Social Theory*, University of Michigan Press, 1970; (editor and author of introduction with Harry Girvatz) *Literature and the Arts: The Moral Issues*, Wadsworth, 1971.

Contributor: J. H. Wise and others, editors, *The Meaning in Reading*, 4th edition, 1956; Wise and others, editors, *College English: The First Years*, Harcourt, 1956; A. W. Gouldner and S. M. Miller, editors, *Applied Sociology*, Free Press, 1964; H. N. Revlin and others, editors, *The First Years in College*, Little, Brown, 1965; Paul Kurtz, editor, *Sidney Hook and the Contemporary World*, John Day, 1968. Contributor to *Funk & Wagnall's Universal Standard Encyclopedia*, *World Scope Encyclopedia*. Also contributor to *Ethics*, *Journal of Philosophy*, *American Political Science Review*, *American Sociological Review*, *New Republic*, *New Leader*, *Journal of Human Relations*, *New York Times Book Review*, and many other periodicals and journals. Adviser, Apollo Editions and University of Michigan Press; advisory editor, *Journal of Existentialism*; book review editor, *Journal of the History of Philosophy*.

WORK IN PROGRESS: A book, *Politics: A Moral Theory*.

AVOCATIONAL INTERESTS: Conversation, art, music, travel, "above all, friends, family."

* * *

ROSS, Robert H(enry), Jr. 1916-

PERSONAL: Born July 16, 1916, in Germantown, Ohio; son of Robert Henry and Marie C. (Deem) Ross; married Mary Bishop (an editor), August 3, 1940; children: Susan (Mrs. David H. Steingass), Robert H. III, Carolyn B. *Education:* Dartmouth College, A.B., 1938; Columbia University, M.A., 1940; Harvard University, graduate study, 1940-42; Ohio State University, Ph.D., 1958. *Politics:* Democratic. *Religion:* Presbyterian. *Office:* Department of English, Bowling Green State University, Bowling Green, Ohio 43403.

CAREER: Ohio Wesleyan University, Delaware, instructor, 1946-49, assistant professor, 1949-54, associate professor, 1954-60, chairman of department of humanities, 1959-61, professor of English, 1960-65; Washington State University, Pullman, professor of English and director of graduate studies in English, 1966-70; Bowling Green State University, Bowling Green, Ohio, professor of English, 1970—, chairman of department, 1970-71. *Military service:* U.S. Army Air Forces, 1942-45; became captain. *Member:* Modern Language Association of America, American Association of University Professors.

WRITINGS: The Georgian Revolt: Rise and Fall of a Poetic Ideal, Southern Illinois University Press, 1965, revised edition, Faber, 1967; (editor with William E. Stafford) *Poems and Perspectives*, Scott, Foresman, 1971; (editor) *In Memorium*, Norton, 1973. Contributor to *PMLA*, *American Literature*, *Victorian Poetry*, and *Victorian Studies*. Member of editorial board, *Victorian Poetry*.

WORK IN PROGRESS: Major Victorian Poems.

AVOCATIONAL INTERESTS: Victorian literature and literature of the early twentieth century.

* * *

ROSS, Sam 1912-

PERSONAL: Surname originally Rosen; born March 10,

1912, in Kiev, Russia (now in Ukranian Socialist Republic); son of Morris (a newsdealer) and Sophia (Freidman) Rosen; married Charlotte Bergman (an artist), May 3, 1941; children: Steve. *Education:* Northwestern University, B.S. (journalism), 1934. *Religion:* Jewish. *Home:* 2923 Grayson, Venice, Calif.

CAREER: Writer. *Military service:* U.S. Army, 1942-43, U.S. Merchant Marine, 1943-45; became ensign. *Member:* Writers Guild of America (West).

WRITINGS: He Ran All the Way, Farrar, Straus, 1947; *Someday, Boy*, Farrar, Straus, 1948; *The Sidewalks are Free*, Farrar, Straus, 1950; *Port Unknown*, World Publishing, 1951; *This, Too, is Love*, Gold Medal Books, 1953; *You Belong to Me*, Popular library, 1955; *The Tight Corner*, Farrar, Straus, 1956; *The Hustlers*, Popular Library, 1956; *Ready for the Tiger*, Farrar, Straus, 1964; *Hang-Up*, Coward, 1968; *The Fortune Machine*, Delacorte, 1970; *The Golden Box*, Dell, 1971; *Solomon's Palace*, Delacorte, 1973.

(With Lee Loeb) "My House is Your House" (first produced in New York at Players Theater, May, 1970). Adapted *He Ran All the Way* for film released as "He Ran All the Way," starring John Garfield. Writers of episodes for "Ben Casey," "Rawhide," "Adventures in Paradise," "Naked City," "The FBI," "Mannix," "Get Christie Love," and other television programs.

*　　*　　*

ROSSI, Nicholas Louis, Jr. 1924-
(Nick Rossi)

PERSONAL: Born November 14, 1924, in San Luis Obispo, Calif.; the son of Nicholas A. (a public accountant) and Lillian A. (McCurry) Rossi. *Education:* Glendale College, A.A., 1942; studied at Muskingum College, 1942-43, at Conservatoire de Musique, Marseille, France, 1946; University of Southern California, B.Mus., 1948, M.Mus., 1951. *Politics:* Republican. *Religion:* Protestant. *Home:* 6907 Camrose Drive, Hollywood, Calif. *Office:* Los Angeles City Schools, P.O. Box 3307, Terminal Annex, Los Angeles, Calif.

CAREER: Los Angeles (Calif.) City School Districts, music consultant, 1948—. Composer of more than thirty-five arrangements for choral ensembles. Glendale Council of Churches, music chairman, 1959-60; Community Concert Association, member of executive board, 1960—. *Military service:* U.S. Army, Corps of Engineers, 1942-46; became staff sergeant. *Member:* American Musicological Society, Music Educators National Conference (life member), National Association of American Composers and Conductors (member of executive board), Choral Conductors Guild (honorary), California Music Educators Association, Southern California Vocal Association, Los Angeles Secondary Music Teachers Association, Phi Mu Alpha, Pi Kappa Lambda.

WRITINGS: (With Sadie Rafferty) *Music Through the Centuries*, Humphries, 1963; (compiler with R. A. Choate) *Music of Our Time*, Century, 1970; *Musical Pilgrimage*, Branden, 1970; *The Realm of Music*, Crescendo, 1974. Author of monographs on contemporary composers. Contributor to music and music educators' journals.

WORK IN PROGRESS: Master Songs for Male Chorus.

SIDELIGHTS: Rossi has done research for his books in museums and archives in Norway, Sweden, Italy, Germany, Switzerland, and Austria.†

ROSTOW, Walt Whitman 1916-

PERSONAL: Born October 7, 1916, in New York, N.Y.; son of Victor Aaron (a metallurgical engineer) and Lillian (Helman) Rostow; married Elspeth Vaughan Davies, June 26, 1947; children: Peter Vaughan, Ann Larner. *Education:* Yale University, B.A., 1936, Ph.D., 1939; Balliol College, Oxford, M.A., 1938. *Home:* 1 Wildwind Point, Austin, Tex. 78746. *Office:* Department of Economics, University of Texas at Austin, Austin, Tex. 78712.

CAREER: Columbia University, New York, N.Y., instructor in economics, 1940-41; U.S. Department of State, Washington, D.C., assistant chief of German-Austrian Economic Division, 1945-46; Oxford University, Oxford, England, Harmsworth Professor of American History, 1946-47; United Nations Economic Commission for Europe, Geneva, Switzerland, assistant to executive secretary, 1947-49; Cambridge University, Cambridge, England, Pitt Professor of American History, 1949-50; Massachusetts Institute of Technology, Cambridge, professor of economic history, 1950-61, member of staff of Center for International Studies, 1951-61; Office of the President, Washington, D.C., deputy special assistant for national security affairs, 1961; U.S. Department of State, Washington, D.C., counselor and chairman, Policy Planning Council, 1961-66; Inter-American Committee on the Alliance for Progress, member, with rank of ambassador, 1964-66; special assistant to the President, 1966-69; University of Texas at Austin, professor of economics and history, 1969—. Consultant to Eisenhower Administration, and chairman of Quantico Panel that evolved President Eisenhower's open skies proposal at Geneva conference, 1955. Lecturer at Cambridge University, 1958, on U.S. lecture tour, 1959.

MILITARY SERVICE: U.S. Army, Office of Strategic Services, 1942-45; became major; received Legion of Merit and Order of the British Empire (military). *Awards, honors:* Rhodes Scholar, 1936-38; Presidential Medal of Freedom, with distinction, 1969; LL.D., Carnegie Institute of Technology, 1962, University of Miami, 1965, University of Notre Dame, 1966, Middlebury College, 1967.

WRITINGS: The American Diplomatic Revolution, Oxford University Press, 1947; *Essays on the British Economy of the Nineteenth Century*, Oxford University Press, 1948.

The Process of Economic Growth, Norton, 1952, revised edition, 1962; (with A. D. Gayer and A. J. Schwartz) *The Growth and Fluctuation of the British Economy, 1790-1850*, Oxford University Press, 1953; (with A. Levin and others) *The Dynamics of Soviet Society*, Norton, 1953, revised edition, 1967; (with others) *The Prospects for Communist China*, M.I.T. Press, 1953; (with R. W. Hatch) *An American Policy in Asia*, M.I.T. Press, 1955; (with M. F. Millikan) *A Proposal: Key to an Effective Foreign Policy*, Harper, 1957.

The Stages of Economic Growth: A Non-Communist Manifesto, Cambridge University Press, 1960, 2nd edition, 1971; *The United States in the World Arena: An Essay in Recent History*, Harper, 1960; (contributor) Max F. Millikan and Donald L. M. Blackmer, editors, *The Emerging Nations: Their Growth and United States Policy*, Little, Brown, 1961; (editor) *The Economics of Take-Off into Sustained Growth* (proceedings of International Economic Association conference), St. Martins, 1964; *View From the Seventh Floor*, Harper, 1964; *A Design for Asian Development* (speeches), Japan Council for International Understanding, 1965; (with William E. Griffith) *East-West Rela-*

tions: Is Detente Possible?, American Enterprise Institute for Public Policy Research, 1969.

Politcs and the Stages of Growth, Cambridge University Press, 1971; *The Diffusion of Power*, Macmillan, 1972.

SIDELIGHTS: Rostow was a close friend and trusted advisor to the late President Kennedy, and he is credited with many of the key ideas operative in Kennedy's 1960 campaign. David Wise called Rostow the originator of the slogan, the "New Frontier."

Rostow's books have been extremely well-received, by literary critics and politicians alike. According to the *Time Literary Supplement*, Rostow "writes the best kind of American prose. As is to be expected, [*The United States in the World Arena*] is a masterly account of the subject defined in the title: even the historical overtones of the word 'arena' are not to be missed." H. H. Brent found Rostow to be a "creative thinker and though some readers may disagree at times with his point of view, he has given us a thought-provoking and valuable work [*The United States in the World Arena*] which every educated American interested in our country's future should read."

Perhaps Rostow's greatest achievement was his book entitled *The Stages of Economic Growth: A Non-Communist Manifesto*. Of this original theory, phasing economic development into five stages, the *Times* (London) noted that "the implications were profound, and have influenced the Administration's policies in many fields, including foreign aid, the alliances, the Common Market, and above all in its relations with the Soviet Union." Harry Schwartz, calling the work "an impressive achievement," said: "[Rostow] has sent a shaft of lightning through the murky mass of events which is the stuff of history." For all his political and literary influence, however, Rostow still claims to be primarily a teacher. "I don't pose as a philosopher," he told the Washington *Post and Times Herald*; "I'm a working stiff."

BIOGRAPHICAL/CRITICAL SOURCES: New York Times Book Review, May 8, 1960; *Post and Times Herald*, August 7, 1960; *Times Literary Supplement*, February 17, 1961; *Times* (London), June 28, 1962; *New York Times Magazine*, July 8, 1962.

*   *   *

ROTBERG, Robert I. 1935-

PERSONAL: Born April 11, 1935, in Newark, N.J. *Education:* Oberlin College, A.B., 1955; Princeton University, M.P.A., 1957; Oxford University, Rhodes Scholar, 1957, D.Phil., 1960.

CAREER: Harvard University, Cambridge, Mass., 1961-68, began as instructor, became assistant professor, research associate, Center for International Affairs, 1961—; Massachusetts Institute for Technology, Cambridge, 1968—, began as associate professor, became professor of political science and history, Research director, Twentieth Century Fund, 1968-70. *Member:* African Studies Association, Conference on British Studies, American Historical Association. *Awards, honors:* Rockefeller Foundation grant; Ford Foundation grant; Guggenheim fellow.

WRITINGS: Christian Missionaries and the Creation of Northern Rhodesia, Princeton University Press, 1965; *The Rise of Nationalism in Central Africa*, Harvard University Press, 1965; *A Political History of Africa*, Harcourt, 1965; (editor) *Strike a Blow and Die*, Harvard University Press, 1967; (editor) *Africa and Its Explorers*, Harvard University Press, 1970; (editor) *Protest and Power in Black Africa*, Oxford University Press, 1970; (with C. K. Clague) *Haiti: The Politics of Squalor*, Houghton, 1971; (editor) *Rebellion in Black Africa*, Oxford university Press, 1971; *Joseph Thompson and the Exploration of Africa*, Oxford University Press, 1971; (editor) *The Family in History*, Harper, 1973; (editor) *East Africa and the Orient: Cultural Syntheses*, Africana Publications, 1974.

Editor, *Journal of Interdisciplinary History*, 1970—; senior consulting editor, Harvard University Press, 1973—.

*   *   *

ROTTENBERG, Isaac C. 1925-

PERSONAL: Born July 11, 1925, in Harrow on the Hill, England; son of naturalized American citizens, John Alter Mendel (a clergyman) and Cornelia (Boender) Rottenberg; married Malwina Tabaksblatt, March 5, 1948; children: John, Irene, Judith, Paul, Marcia. *Education:* University of Leyden, Candidate of Law, 1947; Hope College, B.A., 1952; Western Seminary, divinity studies, 1952-54; New Brunswick Theological Seminary, B.D., 1955; University of Utrecht, graduate study, 1958. *Home:* 95 Glenwood Dr., New Shrewsbury, N.J. *Office:* Reformed Church of New Shrewsbury, 62 Hance Ave., New Shrewsbury, N.J.

CAREER: Ordained minister of Reformed Church in America, 1955. Reformed Church of New Shrewsbury, New Shrewsbury, N.J., minister, 1958—. Theological Commission of Reformed Church in America, secretary and coordinator, 1959-62, chairman, 1962—. Shore Citizens for Better Human Relations (fair housing organization in Monmouth and Ocean counties, N.J.), president, 1965-66.

WRITINGS: Redemption and Historical Reality, Westminster, 1964; (translator) I. Hoekendijk, *Protestant-Catholic Marriages*, Westminster, 1967. Contributor to theological journals.

WORK IN PROGRESS: The Church Inside Out, a translation from the Dutch of a book by J. C. Hoekendyk.†

*   *   *

ROUTH, Francis John 1927-

PERSONAL: Born January 15, 1927, in Kidderminster, England; son of Richard John (a teacher) and Mildred Hilary (Barlow) Routh; married Virginia Raphael, September 1, 1956; children: Simon Christopher, Christina Phoebe, Belinda Rosalind, Alexander Francis. *Education:* Attended Malvern College, 1940-44; King's College, Cambridge, B.A. (honors), 1951; Royal Academy of Music, London, England, M.A., 1954. *Politics:* Liberal. *Religion:* Church of England. *Home:* Arlington Park House, London W4, England.

CAREER: Battersea College of Technology, London, England, instructor, 1959-66; Redcliffe Concerts of British, founder and artistic director, 1963—; work as composer, editor, and researcher. *Military service:* Royal Navy, 1945-48; became lieutenant. *Member:* Performing Rights Society (associate), Royal College of Organists (fellow), Composers Guild of Great Britain.

WRITINGS: Playing the Organ, English Universities Press, 1959; *Contemporary Music*, English Universities Press, 1968; (editor) *The Patronage and Presentation of Contemporary Music*, Redcliffe Concerts, 1970; *Contemporary British Music*, Macdonald, 1972; *Early English Organ Music*, Barri & Jenkins, 1973; *Stravinsky*, Dent, 1974. Contributor of articles to music periodicals.

WORK IN PROGRESS: Several musical compositions; a book, *The Aesthetics of Music*.

* * *

ROUX, Edward R(udolph)   1903-

PERSONAL: Born April 24, 1903, in Pietersburg, Transvaal, South Africa; son of Philippus Rudolf (a pharmacist) and Edith May (Wilson) Roux; married Winifred Lunt (a teacher), 1933; children: Alison Margaret Roux Pineschi. *Education:* University of the Witwatersrand, M.Sc., 1926; Cambridge University, Ph.D., 1929. *Politics:* Liberal Party. *Religion:* Atheist-humanist. *Home:* 72 Third Ave., Melville, Johannesburg, South Africa. *Office:* Department of Botany, University of the Witwatersrand, Johannesburg, South Africa.

CAREER: Low Temperature Research Laboratory, Cape Town, South Africa, scientist, 1929-30; Vitamin Oils (Pty) Ltd., Cape Town, South Africa, chemist, 1940-46; University of the Witwatersrand, Johannesburg, South Africa, senior lecturer, 1946-62, professor of botany and head of department, 1962—. *Member:* South African Association for the Advancement of Science (president of botany section, 1950), Rationalist Association of South Africa (chairman).

WRITINGS: Harvest and Health in Africa, Nelson, 1942; *S. P. Bunting, a Political Biography*, 1944; *The Cattle of Kumalo*, 1944; (with L. Lerner) *AB Adult Reader*, African Bookman, 1945; *The Easy English Handbook*, African Bookman, 1945; *The Veld and the Future*, Perkins, 1946; *Time Longer Than Rope—a History of the Black Man's Struggle for Freedom in South Africa*, Gollancz, 1948, 2nd edition, 1964; *Botany for Medical Students*, Juta, 1951; *A First-Year Plant Physiology*, Juta, 1962; *Grass: A Story of Frantenwald*, Oxford University Press, 1969; (with wife, Win Roux) *Rebel Pity: The Life of Eddie Roux*, Rex Collings Ltd., 1970. Contributor to *South African Rationalist, Humanist, Freethinker*, and scientific journals.†

* * *

ROWE, Margaret (Kevin)   1920-
(Sister Teresa Margaret)

PERSONAL: Born December 19, 1920, in Roma, Queensland, Australia; daughter of Arthur Thomas and Catherine (le Tuche) Rowe. *Education:* Attended Catholic schools in Australia, and University of Brisbane, 1939. *Home:* 441 Juniper St., Nanaimo, British Columbia, Canada.

CAREER: Roman Catholic nun, name in religion Sister Teresa Margaret; entered cloistered order of Discalced Carmelites at Bridell, near Cardigan, Wales, 1951, professed, 1953; began writing occasional articles for Carmelite publications, expanded area of writing to fill requests of the Catholic press for a cloistered nun's opinions on various questions related to religious doctrine. In 1969 left cloister to begin an experimental community, without cloister, living contemplative life with three other sisters in parish setting. Presently working with the handicapped of the Nanaimo area on Vancouver Island.

WRITINGS—Under name Sister Teresa Margaret: *God Is Love* (biography of St. Teresa Margaret), Spiritual Life Press, 1964; *I Choose All* (about St. Therese of Lisieux), Newman, 1964; *Fragments of the Spirit* (autobiography), Sorrento Press, 1972. Occasional contributor of articles and short stories to magazines under secular name. Also contributor to religious publications in Britain, Ireland, United States, and Canada.

ROWLAND, Arthur Ray   1930-

PERSONAL: Born January 6, 1930, in Hampton, Ga.; son of Arthur and Jennie (Goodman) Rowland; married Jane Thomas (a professor of biology at Paine College), July 5, 1955; children: Dell Ruth, Anna Jane. *Education:* Mercer University, A.B., 1951; Emory University, Master of Librarianship, 1952. *Religion:* Baptist. *Home:* 1339 Winter St., Augusta, Ga. 30904. *Office:* Augusta College Library, 2500 Walton Way, Augusta, Ga. 30904.

CAREER: Georgia State College (now University) Library, Atlanta, circulation assistant, 1952, circulation librarian, 1952-53; Armstrong College of Savannah (now Armstrong State College), Savannah, Ga., librarian, 1954-56; Auburn University Library, Auburn, Ala., head of circulation department, 1956-58; Jacksonville University, Jacksonville, Fla., librarian and associate professor, 1958-61; Augusta College, Augusta, Ga., librarian and associate professor, 1961—. Business manager of *Florida Libraries*, 1959-61; lecturer, University of Georgia Extension in Augusta, 1962-66; chairman of academic committee on libraries, University System of Georgia, 1969-71; trustee of Historic Augusta, Inc., 1969—.

MEMBER: American Library Association, Association of College and Research Libraries, American Association for State and Local History, National Trust for Historic Preservation, Southeastern Library Association (executive board member, 1971-72), Georgia Association of Junior Colleges (chairman of library section, 1964), Georgia Library Association (2nd vice-president, 1965-67 and 1971-73; 1st vice-president, 1973-75; president, 1975-77), Georgia Historical Society, Georgia Trust for Historic Preservation, Georgia Baptist Historical Society, Georgia Genealogical Society, Florida Library Association (secretary of reference services division, 1960-61), Central Savannah River Area Library Association (vice-president, 1962-64; president, 1964-65), Richmond County Historical Society (curator, 1964—; director, 1965-67; president, 1967-70), Duval County Library Association (vice-president, 1960-61).

WRITINGS: (Editor) *Reference Service: Contributions to Literary Literature*, Shoe String, 1964; *A Bibliography of the Writings on Georgia History*, Shoe String, 1965; (editor) *Historical Markers of Richmond County, Georgia*, Richmond County Historical Society, 1967, revised edition, 1971; *A Guide to the Study of Augusta and Richmond County, Georgia*, Richmond County Historical Society, 1967; (editor) *The Catalog and Cataloging*, Shoe String Press, 1969. Contributor of articles to literary and historical publications. Founder and editor of *Richmond County History* (journal of Richmond County Historical Society), 1969—.

WORK IN PROGRESS: Three books, *Early Printing in Augusta, Georgia; Printing in Georgia*; and *Georgia Place Names*.

AVOCATIONAL INTERESTS: Antiques and genealogy.

* * *

ROWLAND, Stanley J., Jr.   1928-

PERSONAL: Surname rhymes with "hoe-land"; born October 18, 1928, in New York, N.Y.; son of Stanley J. (an artist) and Harriet (Bailey) Rowland; married Lois Ruth Best, October 18, 1952; children: Michael Page, Martha Best, Peter Chapin. *Education:* Carleton College, A.B., 1952; graduate study at Union Theological Seminary, New

York, N.Y., and New York University. *Religion:* Protestant. *Home:* Lower Shad Rd., Pound Ridge, N.Y. 10576. *Agent:* American Literary Exchange, 325 East 53rd St., New York, N.Y. 10022. *Office:* 475 Riverside Dr., New York, N.Y.

CAREER: New York Times, New York, N.Y., reporter, 1954-58; United Presbyterian Church in the U.S.A., Commission on Ecumenical Mission and Relations, New York, N.Y., editor and writer, 1960—. Academy of Religion and Mental Health, New York, N.Y., consultant on public relations. *Member:* Authors Guild, Phi Delta Epsilon.

WRITINGS: Land in Search of God, Random House, 1958; (editor) *Assignment Overseas*, Crowell, 1959, revised edition, 1966; *Ethics, Crime, and Redemption*, Westminster, 1963; *Choose This Day* (play), Friendship, 1964; (with Bernard Ikeler) *Mission as Decision*, Friendship, 1965; *Men for Others*, Friendship, 1965; *Hurt and Healing*, Friendship Press, 1969. Contributor of articles and poetry to anthologies and to *American Scholar, Christian Century, Literary Review*, and other journals.

AVOCATIONAL INTERESTS: Woodcutting, gardening, swimming, mountain climbing, and trout fishing.†

* * *

ROYCE, Kenneth 1920-

PERSONAL: Born December 11, 1920, in Croydon, Surry, England; son of John Mathew and Ethel (Saunders) Gandley; married Stella Amy Parker, March 16, 1946. *Religion:* Church of England. *Home and office:* Tree Tops, Beech Grove, Amershan, Buckinghamshire, England. *Agent:* Harold Ober Associates, 40 East 49th St., New York, N.Y. 10017; David Higham Associates Ltd., 5-8 Lower John St., Golden Square, London N1R 4HA, England.

CAREER: Business and Holiday Travel Ltd. (travel agent), London, England, founder, managing director, beginning 1947; full-time author. *Military service:* British Army, 1939-46; became captain. *Member:* Skal Club of London, Safari Club.

WRITINGS: My Turn to Die, Barker, 1958; *The Soft Footed Moor*, Barker, 1959; *The Long Corridor*, Cassell, 1960; *No Paradise*, Cassell, 1961; *The Night Seekers*, Cassell, 1962; *The Angry Island*, Cassell, 1963; *The Day the Wind Dropped*, Cassell, 1964; *Bones in the Sand*, Cassell, 1967; *A Peck of Salt*, Cassell, 1968; *A Single to Hong Kong*, Hodder & Stoughton, 1969; *The XYY Man* (book club selection), McKay, 1970; *The Concrete Book* (book club selection), McKay, 1971; *The Miniatures Frame* (book club selection), Simon & Schuster, 1972; *The Masterpiece Affair* (book club selection), Simon & Schuster, 1973; *Spider Underground*, Hoddar & Stoughton, 1973; *The Woodcutter Operation*, Simon & Schuster, 1975.

WORK IN PROGRESS: Get Me the President for Simon & Schuster.

SIDELIGHTS: Royce's travels cover most countries of Europe and northern and central Africa. *Avocational interests:* Jazz.

* * *

ROYCE, Patrick M(ilan) 1922-

PERSONAL: Born May 3, 1922, in Casper, Wyo.; son of Pat William and Catherine (O'Shaughnessy) Royce; married Hilda E. Giannuzzi, November 18, 1945; children: Tina, Richard. *Education:* Woodbury College, B.S. (com-

mercial art), 1942; The Art Center School, Los Angeles, Calif., completion certificate in technical art. *Home:* 548 El Modena, Newport Beach, Calif. 92660. *Office:* Box 1967, Newport Beach, Calif. 92663.

CAREER: Technical and commercial artist, variously employed in New York, Los Angeles, Calif., and vicinity, 1945-58; full-time artist and writer on marine subjects with own firm, Royce Publications, Newport Beach, Calif., 1957—. Consultant to manufacturers for testing and evaluating new and potential marine products; conductor of sail instruction classes, 1960—; producer of courses for public instruction in sail and outboard.

WRITINGS—Self-illustrated: *Royce's Sailing Illustrated*, Royce Publications, 1956, 5th edition, 1971; *Royce's Trailer Boating Illustrated*, Royce Publications, 1960; *Junior Sailing Illustrated: The Dinghy Sailor's Bible*, Royce Publications, 1971. Columnist, *Popularboating*, and contributor to other magazines.

WORK IN PROGRESS: Continuing research in marine subjects, including powerboating, diving, sharks, and oceanography.

* * *

RUBINSTEIN, Amnon 1931-

PERSONAL: Born September 5, 1931, in Tel Aviv, Palestine (now Israel); son of Aaron and Rachel (Vilozny) Rubinstein; married Ronny Havatseleth (a lawyer), 1958; children: Tal (daughter), Nir (son). *Education:* Hebrew University of Jerusalem, LL.M. and B.A., 1956; London School of Economics and Political Science, Ph.D., 1961. *Religion:* Jewish. *Home:* 30 Alumim St., Afeka, Tel Aviv, Israel. *Office:* Faculty of Law, Tel Aviv University, Ramat Aviv, Israel.

CAREER: Hebrew University of Jerusalem, Faculty of Law, Tel Aviv, Israel, lecturer in constitutional law, 1961-64, senior lecturer, 1964-68; Tel Aviv University, Ramat Aviv, Israel, senior lecturer, 1968-70, associate professor of law, 1970—, dean of faculty of law, 1969—. *Member:* Institute de la Vie, International Society for the Study of Comparative Public Law (president).

WRITINGS: Jurisdiction and Illegality: A Study in Public Law, Oxford University Press, 1965; *The Constitutional Law of Israel*, Schocken (Tel Aviv), 1968, 2nd edition, 1974; *Here, Now*, Schocken (Tel Aviv), 1969; (contributor) Yoram Dinstein, editor, *Israel Yearbook on Human Rights*, Israel Press, Volume II, 1972, Volume III, 1973; *The Enforcement of Morality in a Permissive Society*, Schocken (Tel Aviv), 1974. Also author of published lectures. Contributor to periodicals in United States, Canada, England, and Israel. Member of editorial board of *Ha'aretz* (Israel independent daily newspaper) and *Israel Yearbook on Human Rights*.

WORK IN PROGRESS: Research on state and religion in Israel.

* * *

RUBSAMEN, Walter H. 1911-

PERSONAL: Born July 21, 1911, in New York, N.Y.; son of Karl A. (an engineer) and Pauline (Beutenmueller) Rubsamen; married Gisela Roth, May 1, 1955; children: Valerie, Glen, Eric, Hope. *Education:* Columbia University, A.B., 1933; studied music in Europe, 1934-36; University of Munich, Ph.D., 1937. *Home:* 3057 Lake Hollywood Dr., Los Angeles, Calif. 90068. Department of Music, University of California, 405 Hilgard Ave., Los Angeles, Calif. 90024.

CAREER: University of California, Los Angeles, instructor, 1938-42, assistant professor, 1942-48, associate professor, 1948-55, professor of music, 1955—, chairman of music department, 1965—. Visiting professor at University of Berne, 1948, Columbia University, 1950, and University of Chicago, 1957-58; director of summer music and art tours of Europe, 1960-62. *Member:* International Musicological Society, American Musicological Society, Societa Italiana di Musicologia, Verenigning v. Nederlandse Muziek Geschiedenis, Dante Alighieri Society (president of Southern California chapter, 1969-70), Gesellschaft fuer Musikforschung, Mediaeval Academy of America. *Awards, honors:* Guggenheim fellow, 1947-48, 1957-58; grants from Ford Foundation, 1954-55; National Endowment for the Humanities Senior fellowship, 1973.

WRITINGS: Literary Sources of Secular Music in Italy (circa 1500), University of California Press, 1943; *Music Research in Italian Libraries*, Music Library Association (Los Angeles), 1951; (with Howard M. Brown and Daniel Heartz) *Chanson and Madrigal, 1480-1530*, edited by James Haar, Harvard University Press, 1964. Editor, *The Ballad Opera Series*, Garland, 1974. Contributor to *Acta Musicologica*, *Annales Musicologiques*, and *Musical Quarterly*.

WORK IN PROGRESS: Music and Politics, from Plato to Mao; an edition, *The Taitt Manuscript of Scottish, English, and French Song*; an edition, *The Choirbooks of St. Aegidien in Nuernberg: Music and Poetry in 15th Century Italy*.

SIDELIGHTS: Rubsamen told *CA:* "My chief fields of research interest are the Renaissance in Italy and Northern Europe, and theatrical music of the British Isles and America in the 18th century. Most of my writings have emerged from some personal experience. For example, my participating in the performance of ''The Beggar's Opera'' at Columbia (1934) eventually led to my research into the entire corpus of the ballad operas; the acquisition of microfilmed frottole in Munich (1935) was to be the point of departure for my book on *Literary Sources*." Walter Rubsamen is competent in German, Italian, and French.

* * *

RUCKER, W(infred) Ray 1920-

PERSONAL: Born April 13, 1920, in Stamford, Tex.; son of John Lewis and Lou Jean (Rae) Rucker; married Norma Ruth Johnston, January 31, 1947. *Education:* Attended Southwest Texas State College (now University), San Marcos, 1938-40; Texas Christian University, B.A. and M.A., 1947; Harvard University, Ed.D., 1952. *Politics:* Democrat. *Religion:* Disciples of Christ. *Home:* 17863 Mirasol Dr., San Diego, Calif. 92128.

CAREER: Texas Christian University, Fort Worth, instructor in speech and education, 1946-47; Air University, Maxwell Air Force Base, Ala., educational consultant and instructor in academic instructor course, 1948-49; State University of New York College at Geneseo, supervision teacher, 1950-52; East Texas State College (now University), Commerce, assistant professor, later associate professor of education, 1952-56; University of Arizona, Tucson, chairman of Division of Elementary Education, 1956-58; National College of Education, Evanston, Ill., dean, 1958-61; East Texas State College (now University), dean of School of Education, 1961-67; U.S. International Uni-

versity, San Diego, Calif., dean of Graduate School Leadership and Human Behavior, 1967—. Chicago Value-Sharing Project, consultant, 1959-63. Commerce Community Fund, director. *Military service:* U.S. Army, 1942-45.

MEMBER: Association for Supervision and Curriculum Development, National Society of College Teachers of Education, American Educational Research Association, National Society for the Study of Education, John Dewey Society, Texas State Teachers Association, Texas Society of College Teachers of Education (president, 1964-65), Phi Delta Kappa, Kappa Delta Pi.

WRITINGS: Curriculum Development in the Elementary School, Harper, 1960; (editor) *Young People's Science Encyclopedia*, Childrens, 1962; (with Arthur J. Brodbeck and V. Clyde Arnspiger) *The Democratic Classroom*, Blaisdell. Also author of *Human Values Series of Readers*, *Human Values in Education*, *Personality in Social Process*, *Value Sharing*, *Human Value and Natural Science*. Author of monograph published by Hogg Foundation for Mental Hygiene, University of Texas, and contributor to *Harvard Educational Review*, *Science Education*, *Phi Delta Kappan*, *Journal of Teacher Education*, and other education journals. Editor, *Young People's Science Encyclopedia*, 1962.

WORK IN PROGRESS: Research on effectiveness of personality foundations course for college students.†

* * *

RUESCH, Hans 1913-

PERSONAL: Born May 17, 1913, in Naples, Italy; son of Arnold (a philosopher and archaeologist) and Ginevra (Buchy) Ruesch; married Marialuisa De la Feld, June 14, 1949; children: Hans, Jr., Peter, Viviane. *Education:* Attended schools in Naples, Italy, and Zuoz, Switzerland. *Home:* Chalet Ivalu, Klosters, Switzerland.

CAREER: Auto race driver in Europe, 1932-38; came to United States in 1938 and started writing in English; returned to Europe in 1950, and has been writing there since, doing most of work in English and own translations into Italian, French, and German.

WRITINGS—Novels, except as noted: *Gladiatoren*, Hallwag, 1939; *Top of the World*, Harper, 1950; *The Racer*, Ballantine, 1953; *South of the Heart*, Coward, 1957; *The Game*, Hutchinson, 1961; *The Stealers*, Hutchinson, 1962; ''Papers'' (play), first produced in New York at Provincetown Playhouse, December 1, 1968; *Back to the Top of the World*, Scribner, 1973. Contributor of short stories to *Collier's*, *Redbook*, *Esquire*, *Liberty*, *Saturday Evening Post*, *Argosy*, *American Mercury*, and publications in Great Britain, France, Italy, Germany, Switzerland, Sweden, Argentina, Spain, and Israel.

WORK IN PROGRESS: An autobiography, *Fragments in a Mirror*, and a book on modern scientific research.

SIDELIGHTS: Translations of his books have been published in twenty countries. Has traveled in Arabia and Africa for background material. *Avocational interests:* Tennis, skiing.

BIOGRAPHICAL SOURCES: Annabelle (Switzerland), September, 1954; *Schweizer Illustrierte*, September 14, 1959; *Tribune de Geneve*, July 25, 1962; *La Notte* (Milan, Italy), January 10, 1963; *Momento Sera* (Rome, Italy), February 13, 1963; *Corriere della Sera* (Milan, Italy), February 11, 1967; *Messaggero* (Rome), February 26, 1967.

RUMBLE, Thomas C(lark) 1919-

PERSONAL: Born January 1, 1919, in Deckerville, Mich.; son of Stilson A. and Lillian (Yakes) Rumble; married Audrey Ruth Shubert, January 15, 1946; children: Clayton Thomas, Bruce Borden. *Education:* Tulane University, B.A., 1949, M.A., 1951, Ph.D., 1955. *Home:* 32019 North Marklawn, Farmington, Mich. 48024. *Office:* Office for Graduate Studies, Wayne State University, Detroit, Mich. 48002.

CAREER: University of Mississippi, University, instructor in English, 1951-53; Tulane University, New Orleans, La., part-time instructor in English, 1953-55; Louisiana State University, Baton Rouge, instructor, 1955-57, assistant professor of English, 1957-59; Wayne State University, Detroit, Mich., assistant professor, 1959-62, associate professor, 1962-63; University of North Carolina at Greensboro, professor, 1964-65; Wayne State University, Detroit, Mich., associate professor, 1965-66, professor of medieval literature, 1966—, graduate chairman, 1966-68, assistant dean, 1968-70, associate dean, 1970-71, dean of graduate studies, 1971—. *Military service:* U.S. Army Air Forces, 1940-45; became staff sergeant.

MEMBER: Societe Internationale Arthurienne, Modern Language Association of America, Mediaeval Academy of America, South-Central Modern Language Association (chairman of medieval section, 1960), Michigan Academy of Sciences, Arts, and Letters (chairman of language and literature section, 1962-63), Kappa Delta Pi, Phi Beta Kappa. *Awards, honors:* Carnegie fellowship, 1955; Louisiana State University Research Council grant, 1957; Wayne State University faculty research fellowship, 1963.

WRITINGS: (Contributor) W. McNeir, editor, *Louisiana State University Studies in American Literature*, Louisiana State University Press, 1960; (contributor) R. M. Lumiansky, editor, *Malory's Originality: A Critical Study of le Morte d'Arthur*, Johns Hopkins Press, 1964; (editor) *The Breton Lays in Middle English*, Wayne State University Press, 1965, 2nd edition, 1967. Contributor of articles and reviews to *Annuale Mediaevale*, *Speculum*, other professional journals. Book review editor, *Criticism*, 1962-64.

*   *   *

RUSKIN, Ariane 1935-

PERSONAL: Born September 18, 1935; daughter of Simon L. (a physician) and Frances (Reder) Ruskin; married Michael Batterberry, May 15, 1968. *Education:* Barnard College, B.A., 1955; New Hall College, Cambridge, M.A., 1957. *Home:* 1100 Madison Ave., New York, N.Y. 10028.

CAREER: Dancer with Marquis de Cuevas Ballet, Paris, 1955; editorial work with United Nations, New York, N.Y., 1961; free-lance writer. *Member:* Phi Beta Kappa.

WRITINGS: The Pantheon Story of Art for Young People, Pantheon, 1964 (published in England as *The Pantheon Story of Art*, Heinemann, 1965); *Spy for Liberty: The Adventurous Life of Beaumarchais, Playwright and Secret Agent for the American Revolution*, Pantheon, 1965; *Nineteenth Century Art*, McGraw, 1969; *Seventeenth and Eighteenth Century Art*, McGraw, 1969; (with husband, Michael Batterberry) *Greek and Roman Art*, McGraw, 1970; *Art of the High Renaissance*, McGraw, 1970; *Prehistoric Art and Ancient Art of the Near East*, McGraw, 1971; (with Batterberry) *A Children's Homage to Picasso*, Abrams, 1971; (with Batterberry) *Primitive Art*, McGraw, 1972; (with Batterberry) *On the Town in New York*, Scrib-

ner, 1973; (with Batterberry) *Pantheon Story of American Art*, Pantheon, in press.

Contributor to *School and College*, and *Wine and Food*. Contributing editor, *Harper's Bazaar*.

WORK IN PROGRESS: A book on the history of clothing, with husband, Michael Batterberry.

SIDELIGHTS: Miss Ruskin speaks French and has a reading knowledge of Greek and Latin.

*   *   *

RUSSEL, Robert R(oyal) 1890-

PERSONAL: Born September 27, 1890, in Galva, Kan.; son of Robert Breckinridge (a farmer) and Emily (Smith) Russel; married Ethel Marie Hale, December 25, 1924; children: Robert Hale, James Matthew. *Education:* McPherson College, A.B., 1914; University of Kansas, M.A., 1915; University of Illinois, Ph.D., 1922; London School of Economics and Political Science, University of London, postdoctoral study, 1928-29. *Home:* 2120 Sheffield Dr., Kalamazoo, Mich. 49008.

CAREER: McPherson County (Kan.) public schools, teacher, 1908-09, 1910-12; Ottawa University, Ottawa, Kan., professor of history, 1919-22; Western Michigan University, Kalamazoo, professor of history, 1922-60, chairman of department, 1956-60, professor emeritus of history, 1960—. *Military service:* U.S. Army, 1917-18; became second lieutenant. U.S. Army Air Forces, 1943-45; became captain. *Member:* Organization of American Historians, Economic History Association, Michigan Historical Association, Southern Historical Association, Michigan Academy of Sciences, Arts, and Letters, Phi Beta Kappa. *Awards, honors:* Charles W. Ramsdell Award of Southern Historical Association for article, "What Was the Compromise of 1850?" in *Journal of Southern History*, 1956.

WRITINGS: Economic Aspects of Southern Sectionalism, 1840-1861, University of Illinois Press, 1924, 2nd edition, Russell, 1960; *Improvement of Communication with the Pacific Coast as an Issue in American Politics, 1783-1864*, Torch Press, 1948; *Ante-Bellum Studies in Slavery, Politics, and Railroads* (collection of articles), Graduate School, Western Michigan University, 1960; *A History of the American Economic System*, Appleton, 1964; (compiler) *Critical Studies in Antebellum Sectionalism*, Greenwood Press, 1972. Contributor to historical journals.

*   *   *

RUSSELL, D(avid) S(yme) 1916-

PERSONAL: Born November 21, 1916, in Whitburn, Scotland; son of Peter and Janet (Syme) Russell; married Marion Campbell, July 23, 1943; children: Douglas Campbell, Helen Marion. *Education:* Studied at University of Glasgow and Trinity College, Glasgow, Scotland, 1935-41, M.A., 1939, B.D., 1941; studied at Oxford University and Regent's Park College, Oxford, England, 1941-45, B.A., 1943, B.Litt., 1945, M.A., 1946. *Home:* 33 Friars Walk, Southgate, London N14 5LL, England.

CAREER: Ordained Baptist minister, 1939; minister in Oxford and London, England, 1943-53; Rawdon College, Leeds, England, principal and lecturer in Old Testament language and literature, 1953-64; Northern Baptist College, Manchester, England, joint principal and lecturer in Old Testament language and literature, 1965-67. Lecturer in United States and England, and preacher. *Member:* British Society for Old Testament Studies. *Awards, honors:* D.Litt., University of Glasgow, 1965.

WRITINGS: Between the Testaments, S.C.M. Press, 1960, Fortress Press, 1960, revised edition, Fortress Press, 1971; (with M. R. Bielby) *Two Refugees*, S.C.M. Press, 1962; *The Method and Message of Jewish Apocalyptic*, Russell, 1964; *The Jews from Alexander to Herod*, Oxford University Press, 1967. Contributor to *Encyclopaedia Britannica*, 1963.

WORK IN PROGRESS: Writing on biblical eschatology.†

*   *   *

RUSSELL, John   1919-

PERSONAL: Born January 22, 1919, in Fleet, England; married Alexandrine Apponyi, 1945 (divorced, 1950); married Vera Poliakoff, 1956 (divorced, 1971); children: (first marriage) Lavinia. *Education:* Magdalen College, Oxford, B.A., 1940. *Home:* 5 Westmoreland St., London W1, England. *Office: Sunday Times*, London W.C. 1, England.

CAREER: British Admiralty, Naval Intelligence Division, 1942-45; *Sunday Times*, London, England, member of editorial staff, 1946—, art critic, 1950—. London representative of *Art News* and *Art in America*, 1957—. Member of art panel, Arts Council, 1958-68. Organized Arts Council exhibitions: Modigliani, 1964, Rouault, 1966, and Balthus, 1966 (all at Tate Gallery, London); (with Suzi Gablik) Pop Art, 1969 (at the Hayward Gallery, London).

WRITINGS: Modern English, four books, Gibson, 1934-40; *Shakespeare's Country*, Batsford, 1942, revised edition, 1961; *British Portrait Painters*, Collins, 1944; *From Sickert to 1948*, Lund Humphries, 1948; *Switzerland*, Batsford, 1950, revised edition, 1962; (editor, and author of introduction) *Portrait of Logan Pearsall Smith*, Dropmore, 1950; *Erich Kleiber*, Deutsch, 1957; *History of Music for Young People*, Harrap, 1957; *Braque*, Phaidon Press, 1959; *Paris*, Batsford, 1960; (with F. W. Halliday) *Matthew Smith*, Allen & Unwin, 1962; (author of introduction) *Oskar Kokoschka: Watercolours, Drawings, Writings*, Thames, 1962; *Francis Bacon*, Methuen, 1964, New York Graphic Society, 1971; *Seurat*, Praeger, 1965; (with Lord Snowdon and Bryan Robertson) *Private View*, Nelson, 1965; *Max Ernst: Life and Work*, Abrams, 1967; *Henry Moore*, Putnam, 1968; (author of introduction) *Ben Nicholson: Drawings, Paintings and Reliefs*, Thames & Hudson, 1969; (with Suzi Gablik) *Pop Art Redefined*, Praeger, 1969; (with editors of Time-Life Books) *The World of Matisse, 1869-1954*, Time-Life, 1969; *Edouard Vuillard, 1868-1940*, Art Gallery of Ontario, 1971.

Translator: Andre Gide, *Oedipus and Theseus*, Knopf, 1950; Jules Supervielle, *Survivor*, Secker & Warburg, 1951; Andre Bay, *Holiday School*, Secker & Warburg, 1952; Paul Caludel and Andre Gide, *Correspondence, 1899-1926*, Pantheon, 1952; Raymond Maufrais, *Journey Without Return*, Kimber, 1953; Gilbert Cesbron, *Saints in Hell*, Secker & Warburg, 1953, Doubleday, 1954; (with Anthony Rhodes) Roger Nimier, *Blue Hussar*, MacGibbon & Kee, 1953; (with Robert Kee) Roger Nimier, *Children of Circumstance*, MacGibbon & Kee, 1954; Jacques Feschotte, *Albert Schweitzer: An Introduction*, Beacon, 1954; Martin du Gard, *Postman*, Viking; Claude Levi-Strauss, *Tristes Tropiques*, Criterion, 1961 (also published as *A World on the Wane*, Hutchinson, 1961); (with Patricia Russell) May Pellaton and Henry Larsen, *Black Sand*, Oliver, 1961; (with Jean Stewart) Eugene Ionesco, *The Colonel's Photograph and Other Stories*, Grove Press, 1970.

WORK IN PROGRESS: A book on travels in the Soviet Union.

SIDELIGHTS: Russell is competent in French, German, and Italian. *Avocational interests:* Late nineteenth-and twentieth-century music.

BIOGRAPHICAL/CRITICAL SOURCES: Washington Post, October 1, 1969.†

*   *   *

RUSSELL, John L(eonard)   1906-

PERSONAL: Born June 22, 1906, in Wye, Kent, England; son of Edward John (a scientist) and Elnor (Oldham) Russell. *Education:* Attended Oundle School, 1917-25; Christ's College, Cambridge, B.A., 1928, M.A., 1932, Ph.D., 1935. *Home:* Heythrop College, Cavendish Square, London W1M 0AN, England.

CAREER: Gresham's School, Holt, Norfolk, England, chemistry master, 1929-31; research in soil science at Cambridge University, Cambridge, England, 1931-35, Oxford University, Oxford, England, 1935-37; entered Roman Catholic order, Society of Jesus, 1937, ordained priest, 1945; University of London, Haythrop College (formerly Haythrop College in Oxfordshire), London, England, lecturer in philosophy, 1947—. *Member:* British Society for the History of Science, British Society for the Philosophy of Science, Newman Association of Great Britain.

WRITINGS: Science and Metaphysics, Sheed, 1958; (with E. Nemesszeghy) *Theology and Evolution*, Mercier Press, 1972; (contributor) J. Dobrzycki, editor, *The Reception of Copernicus' Heliocentric Theory*, Reidel (Dordrecht), 1973. Author of scientific papers published in learned journals and of articles in *Scrutiny, Month, Clergy Review*, and other periodicals.

WORK IN PROGRESS: Research in the historical relations of science and religion and in the philosophy of Teilhard de Chardin.

*   *   *

RUST, Doris (Dibblin)

PERSONAL: Daughter of Malcolm Hedley and Eva Grace (Crockford) Dibblin; married Leslie Richard Rust (deceased). *Education:* Attended City of London School, London, England. *Home:* 1 Seymour Ct., Hampton Wick, Kingston on Thames, England.

CAREER: Writer of children's books. *Member:* New Arts Theatre Club.

*WRITINGS—*All published by Faber, except as indicated: *A Week of Stories*, 1953; *A Story a Day*, 1954; *All Sorts of Days*, 1955; *Animals at Number Eleven*, 1956; *Animals at Rose Cottage*, 1957, A. S. Barnes, 1959; *Mixed-Muddly Island*, 1958; *Simple Tales for the Very Young*, 1960; *A Dog Had a Dream*, 1961; *Secret Friends*, 1962; *A Melon for Robert, and Other South Sea Tales*, 1963; *Tales from the Pacific*, 1966; *A Tale of Three Rivers and Other Stories from Wales*, 1966; *Tales from the Australian Bush*, 1968; *Tales of Magic from Far and Near*, 1969. Writer of radio scripts for British Broadcasting Corp., Australian Broadcasting Commission, and New Zealand Broadcasting Commission.

AVOCATIONAL INTERESTS: Music, ballet, theater, and travel.†

*   *   *

RUST, Eric C(harles)   1910-

PERSONAL: Born June 6, 1910, in Gravesend, England;

son of Charles Henry (Royal Naval dockyard officer) and Ruth (Wiles) Rust; married Helen M. Kenn, April 4, 1936; children: Margaret Rust Smith, Christine E., David C. *Education:* Royal College of Science, University of London, B.Sc. (first class honours), 1930, M.Sc., 1932, Associateship, Royal College of Science, 1930, Diploma of Imperial College, 1932; Oxford University, B.A., 1934, M.A. (first class honours, school of Theology), 1935, B.D., 1946. *Politics:* Democrat. *Home:* 213 Bramton Rd., Louisville, Ky. *Office:* Southern Baptist Theological Seminary, 2825 Lexington Rd., Louisville, Ky.

CAREER: Pastor of Baptist churches in Bath, England, 1935-39, Birmingham, England, 1940-42, Huddersfield, England, 1942-46; Rawdon Baptist Theological College, University of Leeds, England, professor and senior tutor, 1946-52; Crozer Theological Seminary, Chester, Pa., professor of biblical theology, 1952-53; Southern Baptist Theological Seminary, Louisville, Ky., professor of Christian philosophy, 1953—. *Member:* Society of Biblical Literature, Society for Old Testament Study, Kentucky Philosophical Association, Rotary Club. *Awards, honors:* Litt.D., University of Richmond.

WRITINGS: The Christian Understanding of History, Lutterworth, 1947; *Nature and Man in Biblical Thought,* Lutterworth, 1953; *Judges, Ruth, 1 and 2 Samuel* ("Layman's Bible Commentary"), John Knox, 1961; *Salvation History,* John Knox, 1963; *Salvation History,* John Knox, 1963; *Towards a Theological Understanding of History,* Oxford University Press, 1963; *Science and Faith: Toward a Theological Understanding of Nature,* Oxford University Press, 1967; *Evolutionary Philosophies and Contemporary Theology,* Westminster Press, 1969; *Positive Religion in a Revolutionary Time,* Westminster Press, 1970; *Nature: Garden or Desert?,* Word Books, 1971; *Covenant and Hope,* Word Books, 1972. Contributor to several volumes of essays; contributor of articles and reviews to professional journals.

WORK IN PROGRESS: Research on the relationship of the Christian faith to modern science and contemporary naturalism.

*   *   *

RUTMAN, Darrett B(ruce) 1929-

PERSONAL: Born March 4, 1929, in New York, N.Y.; son of Laurence (a newspaperman) and Jane (Saville) Rutman; married Anita Helen Greiff, April 30, 1954; children: James Morgan, Elizabeth Whitney. *Education:* University of Illinois, A.B., 1950; University of Virginia, Ph.D., 1959. *Politics:* Independent. *Religion:* Society of Friends. *Home:* 2634 Crosby Rd., Wayzata, Minn. 55391. *Office:* Department of History, University of Minnesota, Minneapolis, Minn. 55455.

CAREER: Newsday, Long Island, N.Y., 1950-55, began as reporter, became promotion manager; University of Minnesota, Minneapolis, instructor, 1959-61, assistant professor, 1961-64, associate professor of history, 1964—. University of Virginia, summer instructor, 1959. *Military service:* U.S. Army, Counter-Intelligence Corps, 1951-53.

MEMBER: American Historical Association, Conference of Early American Historians, Society for the History of Discoveries, Organization of American Historians, Southern Historical Association, Hakluyt Society, Phi Beta Kappa, Phi Alpha Theta, Raven Society (University of Virginia). *Awards, honors:* McKnight Foundation Humanities Award in American military history, 1960; American

Council of Learned Societies grant, 1961; grants-in-aid of research from University of Minnesota, 1961, 1962, 1964, and 1965; McKnight Foundation Humanities Award in American history and biography for manuscript of *Winthrop's Boston,* 1963; P. D. McMillan travel fellowship, 1965.

WRITINGS: (Editor) *The Old Dominion: Essays for Thomas Perkins Abernethy,* University Press of Virginia, 1964; *Winthrop's Boston: Portrait of a Puritan Town, 1630-1649,* University of North Carolina Press for Institute of Early American History and Culture, 1965; (contributor) *Law and Authority in Colonial America,* edited by George Billias, Barre, 1965; *The Farms and Villages of New Plymouth Colony, 1620-1692,* Plimoth Plantation, Inc., 1966; *Husbandsmen of Plymouth: Farms and Villages in the Old Colony, 1620-1692,* Beacon Press, 1967; (compiler) *The Great Awakening,* Wiley, 1970; *American Puritanism: Faith and Practice,* Lippincott, 1970; *The Morning of America, 1603-1789,* Houghton, 1971.

Contributor to *Collier's Encyclopedia;* also contributor of articles and reviews to *American Heritage, New York Times, William and Mary Quarterly,* and to historical journals.

WORK IN PROGRESS: Studies of various facets of seventeenth-century America and the Atlantic world of the seventeenth century.

SIDELIGHTS: Rutman told *CA:* "My research and writing is concentrated on the seventeenth century—the 'watershed' century in which, I firmly believe, modern western society had its origins." Has lived in Germany and knows some German and Dutch. *Avocational interests:* Water (not to fish or indulge in water-sports, but to be on water), gardening.†

*   *   *

RYAN, John K.   1897-

PERSONAL: Born October 29, 1897, in Caledonia, Minn.; son of Thomas Francis (a judge) and Mary (Kelly) Ryan. *Education:* College of the Holy Cross, B.A., 1920; Urban University, Rome, Italy, S.T.B., 1922; Catholic University of America, M.A., 1931, Ph.D., 1933. *Home:* 3133 Connecticut Ave. N.W., Washington, D.C. 20008. *Office:* Catholic University of America, Washington, D.C. 20017.

CAREER: Ordained Roman Catholic priest, 1924, appointed domestic prelate with title of right reverend monsignor, 1947. Instructor in philosophy at St. Mary's College, Winona, Minn., 1924-30, at College of St. Teresa, Winona, Minn., 1925-30; Catholic University of America, School of Philosophy, Washington, D.C., member of faculty, 1931-68, professor emeritus, 1968—, dean, 1956-67. *Military service:* U.S. Army, 1918. *Member:* American Catholic Philosophical Association, Renaissance Society of America, Pi Gamma Mu. *Awards, honors:* Medal Benemerenti from Pope John XXIII; LL.D. from St. Mary's College, Winona, Minn.

WRITINGS: Modern War and Basic Ethics, Catholic University of America Press, 1933, 2nd edition, revised, Bruce, 1940; *Reputation of St. Thomas Aquinas Among English Protestant Thinkers of the Seventeenth Century,* Catholic University of America Press, 1949; *The Most Reverend Francis M. Kelly, D.D., A Memoir, and a Tribute,* privately printed, 1951; *Philosophical Essays in Honor of the Very Reverend Ignatius Smith, O.P.,* Newman, 1952; *Holy Trinity Book of Prayers,* Kenedy, 1953; (translator and editor) St. Francis de Sales, *Introduction to the Devout Life*, Doubleday, 1954; *Basic Principles and Problems of Philosophy*, new edition, revised, Newman, 1954; (translator and editor) *The Confessions of St. Augustine*, Doubleday, 1960; (translator and editor) St. Francis de Sales, *On the Love of God*, Doubleday, 1963; (translator and editor) St. Francis de Sales, *On the Preacher and Preaching*, Regnery, 1964.

Founder and editor, *Studies in Philosophy and the History of Philosophy*, Catholic University of America Press, Volume I, 1961, Volume II, 1963, Volume III, 1965, Volume VI, 1973. Advisory editor, *Encyclopedia Americana*, 1945—. Contributor of articles on philosophy and related subjects to *New Scholasticism, Commonweal, Thought, America*, other journals.

* * *

RYAN, Neil Joseph 1930-

PERSONAL: Born March 20, 1930, in Manchester, England; son of James Joseph (a bank manager) and Alice (Ashbrook) Ryan; married Clare Baggs, 1963. *Education:* University of Bristol, B.A. (honors), 1952; University of London, Diploma in Education, 1953. *Politics:* Liberal. *Religion:* Roman Catholic. *Home:* Malay College, Kuala Kangsar, Perak, Malaysia.

CAREER: Joined British Colonial Education Service, 1952, posted to Malaya, 1953, as teacher of history at Anderson School, Perak, Malaysia; Malay College, Kuala Kangsar, Perak, Malaysia, teacher of history, 1955—, and principal, 1959—. *Military service:* British Army, 1947-49. *Member:* Royal Commonwealth Society, Historical Association.

WRITINGS: Malaya Through Five Centuries, Oxford University Press, 1959; *The Cultural Background of the People of Malaya*, Longmans, Green, 1962, 2nd edition, published as *The Cultural Heritage of Malaya*, Longman Malaysia, 1971; *The Making of Modern Malaya*, Oxford University Press, 1963, 4th edition, 1969; (joint editor) *Story of Malay College*, Straits Times Press (Singapore).

SIDELIGHTS: Ryan is competent in Malay language. *Avocational interests:* Sports (rugby football and motor racing), classical music, and photography.†

* * *

RYDBERG, Ernest E(mil) 1901-

PERSONAL: Born August 9, 1901, in Central City, Neb.; son of Frank Emil and Laura (Brouillette) Rydberg; married Louisa Hampton (an executive secretary and writer); children: Sonya (Mrs. Terry Cuclis). *Education:* University of Arizona, A.B., 1927. *Home:* 3742 Tennyson, San Diego, Calif. 92107.

CAREER: Along with free-lance writing, has worked in many fields—in sales, collections, banking, and in aircraft and shipbuilding plants; case reviewer, researcher, and writer for San Diego (Calif.) Department of Public Welfare, 1949—. Began writing for magazines and now concentrates on juvenile books.

WRITINGS—Juvenile books: Bright Summer, Longmans, Green, 1953; *Sixteen Is Special*, Longmans, Green, 1954; *The Silver Fleet*, Longmans, Green, 1955; *The Golden Window*, Longmans, Green, 1956; *Conquer the Winds*, Longmans, Green, 1957; *The Mystery in the Jeep*, Longmans, Green, 1959; *The Day the Indians Came*, McKay, 1964; *The Dark of the Cave*, McKay, 1965; *The Yellow Line*, Meredith, 1969; *Footsy*, Bobbs-Merrill, 1973, large-type edition, G. K. Hall, 1973.

Co-author of "Granville Bayse" (three-act play), produced, 1944, and of "The Third Monkey." Writer of about four hundred short stories for magazines and several radio scripts.

WORK IN PROGRESS: Two books completed but not yet sold; a juvenile novel, with wife, Louisa Rydberg.

SIDELIGHTS: Rydberg is a descendent on paternal side from Victor Rydberg, the Swedish writer, and on maternal side from John Watson (Ian Mclaren), a Scottish writer. Of his hopes to surpass his writing ancestors, Rydberg says: "So far it hasn't worked out quite that way."

* * *

RYERSON, Martin 1907-

PERSONAL: Born January 28, 1907, in New York, N.Y.; son of Frank Stephen (a mortician) and Ethel (Vinicombe) Smith; married Marilyn Reiss (in sales promotion), December 9, 1936; children: Lois Jean. *Education:* Attended schools in Brooklyn, N.Y., including Brooklyn Art School. *Politics:* Republican. *Religion:* Protestant. *Home and office:* 525 South Sierra Madre Blvd., Pasadena, Calif. 91107. *Agent:* Jay Garon-Brooke Associates, Inc., 415 Central Park West, 17D., New York, N.Y. 10025.

CAREER: Radio writer and director of several stage shows, New York, N.Y., in 1930's; free-lance writer for pulp magazines, 1940-43; associate editor, McCann-Erickson Advertising Agency, New York, N.Y., and writer of network radio and television scripts, 1945-53; copy director at KMJ-TV and KFRE-TV, Fresno, Calif., 1953-59; editor of *Fresno Star* (weekly newspaper), Fresno, Calif., 1959-64; editor of *Pasadena Courier*, Pasadena, Calif., 1965-70. Actor in television series, "O'Henry from Brooklyn," 1955, in other radio and television programs, and in Fresno Community Theatre productions. *Military service:* U.S. Army, 1943-45; news editor, and broadcaster, American Forces Network, London, 1943-45; became technical sergeant.

WRITINGS—Novels: Thunder in the Badlands, Bouregy, 1964; *Sudden Rage at War's Rim*, Sunset Books, 1964; *Showdown at Devil's Fork*, Sunset Books, 1964; *Press Agent for Murder*, Sunset Books, 1964; *Gunfire at Big Needles*, Sunset Books, 1964; *Doctor vs. Murder*, Sunset Books, 1964; *Star-Studded Murder*, Playtime Books, 1965; *No Time for Angels*, Novel Books, 1965; *Border Justice*, Bouregy, 1965; *Golden Venus*, Award Books, 1968; *Gunfighter*, Award Books, 1970; *Sex Goddess*, Award Books, 1970; *Gamecock*, Midwood, 1970; *Baseball Playboy*, Midwood, 1971; *Sugar Baby*, Greenleaf Books, 1973; *Mafia Mistress*, Midwood, 1973; *Fantasy Girl*, Liverpool, 1973; *Beauty in Bondage*, Manchester, 1974; *Freestyle Bunny*, Midwood, 1974. Also author of over 100 other novels under various pseudonyms.

Author of three one-act plays, produced at Attic Theatre, New York, N.Y., two three-act plays, "Old Mother Hubbard's" and "Revenge Without Music," produced in New York and New Jersey, 1936-37, and "First Stop to Nowhere," produced in Fresno, Calif., 1959. Writer of more than one hundred network radio and television scripts for such programs as "Suspense," "Lights Out," "Gangbusters," "Molle Mystery Theatre," "Grand Central Station," "Stars Over Hollywood," and "Death Valley Days," 1945-53. Also writer of two weekly dramatic shows for WEVD, New York, N.Y., 1936-39, and of radio scripts for British Broadcasting Corp., 1945.

Regular contributor to Standard Magazines, Columbia Publications, and Popular Publications, 1940-43, with stories in *Thrilling Magazine*, *Exciting Detective*, *Black Mask*, *Detective Tales*, *Thrilling Sports*, and other magazines.

WORK IN PROGRESS: An historical novel; a television play, "Nightstick."

* * *

RYWKIN, Michael 1925-

PERSONAL: Born November 23, 1925, in Wilno, Poland; came to United States in 1953; son of Solomon and Marie (Resnikoff) Rywkin; divorced; children: Richard, Monique, Robert. *Education:* Attended Uzbek State University in Uzbek Soviet Socialist Republic; University of Lodz in Poland, and Ecole des Haute Etudes Internationale and Ecole des Haute Etudes Sociale in France; City College (now City College of the City University of New York), M.A., 1955; Columbia University, Ph.D., 1960. *Religion:* Jewish. *Home:* 245 Fort Washington Ave., New York, N.Y. 10032. *Office:* City College of the City University of New York, New York, N.Y. 10031.

CAREER: Columbia University, New York, N.Y., special lecturer, U.S. Air Force Specialists Training Program at Russian Institute, 1954-57; New York University, New York, N.Y., instructor, 1958-59; Colgate University, Hamilton, N.Y., instructor in Russian studies, 1959-60; New York University, assistant professor of Russian and government, 1960-62; City College of the City University of New York, New York, N.Y., 1963—, began as assistant professor, became associate professor of Russian and Russian studies and chairman of department of Germanic and Slavic languages and literature, and of Russian Studies graduate program. U.S. Department of State, sometime escort and interpreter, 1960—; consultant on Russian affairs to various organizations, 1956-60. Alumni Association, International House, New York, N.Y., member board of directors. *Member:* American Association for the Advancement of Slavic Studies. *Awards, honors:* Fellow, Russian Research Center, Harvard University, 1962-63.

WRITINGS: Russia in Central Asia, Collier, 1963. Contributor to several professional journals in the field of Soviet affairs.

WORK IN PROGRESS: The Prikaz of Kazan: An Introduction.

SIDELIGHTS: Rywkin spent 1941-46 in Soviet Union, returning to Poland for one year before going to France, 1947-51, and Haiti, 1951-53. He is fluent in Russian, Polish, and French.

* * *

SAINT, Dora Jessie 1913-
(Miss Read)

PERSONAL: Born April 17, 1913, in Surrey, England; daughter of Arthur Gunnis and Grace (Read) Shafe; married Douglas Edward John Saint (a schoolmaster), July 26, 1940; children: one daughter. *Education:* Homerton College, student, 1931-33. *Address:* c/o Michael Joseph Ltd., 26 Bloomsbury St., London W.C. 1, England.

CAREER: Writer. Justice of the peace for Newbury Borough, Berkshire, England. *Member:* Society of Authors.

WRITINGS—All under pseudonym Miss Read: *Village School*, M. Joseph, 1955, Houghton, 1956; *Village Diary*, Houghton, 1957; *Hobby Horse Cottage*, M. Joseph, 1958; *Storm in the Village*, M. Joseph, 1958, Houghton, 1959; *Thrush Green*, Houghton, 1959; *Fresh From the Country*, M. Joseph, 1960, Houghton, 1961; *Winter in Thrush Green*, M. Joseph, 1961, Houghton, 1962; *Miss Clare Remembers*, M. Joseph, 1962, Houghton, 1963; (compiler) *Country Bunch*, M. Joseph, 1963; *Over the Gate*, M. Joseph, 1964; *Chronicles of Fairacre*, M. Joseph, 1964; *The Little Red Bus*, Nelson, 1964; *The New Bed*, Nelson, 1964; *No Hat!*, Nelson, 1964; *Over the Gate*, M. Joseph, 1964, Houghton, 1965; *Plum Pie*, Nelson, 1964; *Hob and the Horse-Bat*, M. Joseph, 1965; *Village Christmas*, Houghton, 1966; *The Market Square*, M. Joseph, 1966, Houghton, 1967; *The Howards of Caxley*, M. Joseph, 1967, Houghton, 1968; *The Fairacre Festival*, M. Joseph, 1968, Houghton, 1969; *Miss Read's Country Cooking or To Cut a Cabbage-Leaf*, M. Joseph, 1969; *Emily Davis*, Houghton, 1971; *News from Thrush Green*, M. Joseph, 1970, Houghton, 1971; *Tyler's Row*, Houghton, 1973; *The Christmas Mouse*, Houghton, 1973. Author of school scripts for British Broadcasting Corp.

WORK IN PROGRESS: A children's book, *Animal Boy*, for Pelham Books; *Farther Afield* for M. Joseph and Houghton.

AVOCATIONAL INTERESTS: Theater, music, reading, wildlife of the countryside.

* * *

SALE, Kirkpatrick 1937-
(J. Kirkpatrick Sale)

PERSONAL: Born June 27, 1937, in Ithaca, N.Y.; son of William M. and Helen (Stearns) Sale; married Faith Apfelbaum (an editor), 1962. *Education:* Attended Swarthmore College, 1954-55; Cornell University, B.A., 1958.

CAREER: New Leader, New York, N.Y., associate editor, 1959-61; *San Francisco Chronicle*, San Francisco, Calif., and *Chicago Tribune*, Chicago, Ill., foreign correspondent, 1961-62; University of Ghana, Legon, lecturer in history, 1963-65; *New York Times Magazine*, editor, 1965-68; author and lecturer, 1968—.

WRITINGS: (Under name J. Kirkpatrick Sale) *The Land and People of Ghana*, Lippincott, 1963, revised edition, 1972; (contributor) Howard Freeman and Norman Kurtz, editors, *America's Troubles*, Prentice-Hall, 1969; *SDS*, Random House, 1973; (contributor) *Espionagem Politica*, Dom Quixote Press, 1973; (contributor) David C. Saffell, editor, *Watergate*, Winthrop, 1974. Contributor to *Nation*, *New Republic*, *Dissent*, *Village Voice*, *New York Review of Books*, *Ramparts*, *Southern Exposure*, *University Review*, *New York Times Magazine*, *Evergreen Review*, and *WIN*. Editor, *Transactions of Ghana Historical Society*, 1963-65.

* * *

SALMON, John Tenison 1910-

PERSONAL: Born June 28, 1910, in Wellington, New Zealand; son of Charles Tenison and Marie Salmon; married Pamela Naomi Wilton, December, 1948; children: Guy W., Ian R., Roy W., Scott C. *Education:* Attended Wellington College, 1922-27; Victoria University of Wellington, B.Sc., 1932, M.Sc. (first class honors), 1934, D.Sc., 1945. *Religion:* Church of England. *Home:* 139A Seatoun Heights Rd., Wellington 3, New Zealand. *Office:* Zoology Department, University of Wellington, Wellington, New Zealand.

CAREER: Dominion Museum, Wellington, New Zealand, entomologist and photographer, 1934-48; Victoria University of Wellington, Wellington, New Zealand, senior lecturer in biology, 1948-58, associate professor of biology, 1958-64, head of zoology department, 1964-74, chairman of department, 1974—, dean of science, 1971-73. Member: Royal Society of New Zealand (fellow; member of council), Royal Entomological Society (fellow), Royal Photographic Society (fellow). Awards, honors: Nuffield traveling fellowship in natural sciences, 1950-51; Carnegie fellowship, 1958-59.

WRITINGS: Heritage Destroyed, A. H. & A. W. Reed, 1960; New Zealand Flowers and Plants in Colour, A. H. & A. W. Reed, 1963, 2nd edition, 1967; An Index to the Collembola, three volumes, Royal Society of New Zealand, 1964; Butterflies of New Zealand, A. H. & A. W. Reed, 1968; Field Guide to the Alpine Plants of New Zealand, A. H. & A. W. Reed, 1968; (with Guy Salmon) New Zealand Wild Flowers, A. H. & A. W. Reed, 1968; (contributor) Business and New Zealand Society, Hicks, 1973; (contributor) Natural History of New Zealand, A. H. & A. W. Reed, 1974. Contributor to Britannica Book of the Year, Oxford New Zealand Encyclopaedia, and An Encyclopaedia of New Zealand. Also contributor of more than eighty scientific papers to journals in New Zealand and abroad, and of articles on biology, photography, and conservation to magazines.

WORK IN PROGRESS: A book on New Zealand trees; a book on New Zealand insects.

AVOCATIONAL INTERESTS: Photography, swimming, tramping.

*   *   *

SALOMONE, A(rcangelo) William   1915-

PERSONAL: Born August 18, 1915, in Guardiagrele, Italy; came to United States in 1927, became U.S. citizen in 1942; son of Michael and Italia (Scioli) Salomone; married Lina Palmerio, September 13, 1941; children: Ilia. Education: LaSalle College, Philadelphia, Pa., B.A., 1938; University of Pennsylvania, M.A., 1940, Ph.D., 1943. Office: Department of History, University of Rochester, Rochester, N.Y. 14627.

CAREER: Instructor in history at Haverford College, Haverford, Pa., 1943-44, at University of Pennsylvania, Philadelphia, 1944-45; New York University, New York, N.Y., instructor, 1945-47, assistant professor, 1947-49, associate professor, 1949-57, professor of history, 1957-62; University of Rochester, Rochester, N.Y., Wilson Professor of European History, 1962—. Member of final selection committee, Italian government awards and fellowships; former consultant to Fulbright Committee and Institute of International Education; consultant on Italian history, Collier's Encyclopedia.

MEMBER: American Association of Teachers of Italian, American Historical Association, Renaissance Society of America, Society for Italian Historical Studies (president, 1958-60), Institute of the Italian Risorgimento (honorary member; president of American division, 1959-60), America-Italy Society, Sons of Italy, Italian Cultural Institute, New York Association of European Historians. Awards, honors: Herbert B. Adams Prize of American Historical Association, 1946; Guggenheim fellow to Italy, 1951-52; Social Science Research Council fellow, 1955-56; Order of Merit (Republic of Italy), 1960; LaSalle College Centennial Award in history, 1963.

WRITINGS: Italian Democracy in the Making, University of Pennsylvania Press, 1945; L'Eta giolittiana, DeSilva-La Nuova Italia, 1949 (English translation, with new selections added, published as Italy in the Giolittian Era, University of Pennsylvania Press, 1960); (editor with A. Baltzly) Readings in Twentieth-Century European History, Appleton, 1950; (editor and author of introduction) Italy from the Risorgimento to Fascism, Anchor Books, 1970. Contributor to Journal of Central European Affairs, American Historical Review, Journal of Modern History, Italica, and other periodicals. Member of editorial board, Journal of Modern History.

WORK IN PROGRESS: Prelude to a Great Rebellion, a nineteenth and twentieth-century cultural and intellectual history; Risorgimento Studies, two volumes on modern Italian history; A History of Italy since the Renaissance, for Scribner; Mazzini and the Culture of the Risorgimento.

SIDELIGHTS: Salomone is competent in Italian, French, German, and Spanish. Avocational interests: Music and drawing.

BIOGRAPHICAL/CRITICAL SOURCES: H. S. Hughes, Rassegna Storica del Risorgimento, Volume XLV, 1958; Charles F. Delzell, Italy in Modern Times, American Historical Association, 1964.

*   *   *

SAMBROOK, Arthur James   1931-

PERSONAL: Born September 5, 1931, in Nuneaton, Warwickshire, England; son of Arthur (a carpenter) and Constance Elizabeth (Gapper) Sambrook; married Patience Ann Crawford, March 25, 1961; children: John, William, Robert, Thomas. Education: Worcester College, Oxford University, B.A. (first class honors), 1955, M.A., 1959; University of Nottingham, Ph.D., 1957. Home: 36 Bursledon Rd., Hedge End, Southampton, England.

CAREER: St. David's College, Lampeter, Wales, lecturer in English, 1957-64; University of Southampton, Southampton, England, lecturer, 1964-71, senior lecturer in English, 1971—. Military service: Royal Air Force, 1950-52. Awards, honors: Killam Senior Research Fellow, Dalhousie University, Nova Scotia, 1968-69; Leverhulme Research Fellow, 1974-75.

WRITINGS: A Poet Hidden (life of Richard Watson Dixon), Athlone Press, 1962; (editor) The Scribleriad (1742), Augustan Reprint Society, 1967; (editor) James Thomson, The Seasons and The Castle of Indolence, Clarendon Press, 1972; William Cobbett, Routledge, 1973; (editor) Pre-Raphaelitism, University of Chicago Press, 1974. Contributor to The Victorians, edited by Arthur Pollard, Sphere Books, 1970; Alexander Pope, edited by Peter Dixon, Bell, 1972. Contributor of articles to Notes and Queries, English, Review of English Studies, Etudes Anglaises, Church Quarterly Review, Eighteenth Century Studies, English Miscellany, Forum, Modern Philology, Studies in Bibliography, Studies in Burke and his Time, Studies on Voltaire and the Eighteenth Century, Times Literary Supplement, Trivium, and Journal of the Warburg and Courtauld Institutes.

WORK IN PROGRESS: A variorum edition of Thomson's The Seasons in the Oxford English text series; a volume of studies in English pastoral.

*   *   *

SAMUELS, Harry   1893-

PERSONAL: Born November 18, 1893, in Liverpool, England; son of Morris (a jeweler) and Rose (Hyams) Samuels; married Celine Aronowitz, September 11, 1918; children: Michael L. (a professor), Miriam Karlin (an actress). *Education:* Liverpool College, student, 1907-12; Wadham College, Oxford, M.A. (honors), 1919. *Home:* 28 Exeter Rd., London N.W. 2, England. *Office:* 5 Paper Buildings, Temple, London, E.C. 4, England.

CAREER: Barrister-at-law, London, England, beginning 1923. East London Rent Tribunal, chairman, beginning 1946. *Member:* Reform Club (London). *Awards, honors:* Officer, Order of the British Empire, 1958.

WRITINGS: Industrial Law, Pitman, 1929, 7th edition, 1967; *Factory Law,* Knight & Co., 1937, 8th edition, 1969; *Industrial Workers' Guide,* Pitman, 1944; *Trade Union Law,* Stevens & Sons, 1946, 7th edition, Knight & Co., 1966; (with R. Pollard) *Industrial Injuries,* Stevens & Sons, 1947; (with R. Chope) *Rent Tribunals,* Stevens & Sons, 1949; *Law Relating to Shops,* Knight & Co., 1952, 3rd edition, Knight & Co., 1964; *The Offices (etc. Act 1963),* Knight & Co., 1963, 2nd edition, 1971; (with N. Stewart-Pearson) *Redundancy Payments: An Annotation and Guide to the Redundancy Payments Act, 1965,* Knight & Co., 1965. Contributor to *Encyclopaedia Britannica.*

SIDELIGHTS: Trade Union Law was translated into Japanese, and *Industrial Workers' Guide* was published (in part), in Hebrew and Czech.†

* * *

SAND, George X.

PERSONAL: Born in New Jersey; married Phyllis Philibert; children: Gail, Karen. *Home:* 1412 Winkler Ave., Ft. Myers, Fla. 33901.

CAREER: Free-lance writer and photo-journalist for more than twenty years, concentrating on fiction and articles for American and European magazine markets before turning to books. *Awards, honors:* First Florida recipient of Governor's Outstanding Conservationist award.

WRITINGS: Skin and Scuba Diving, Hawthorn, 1964; *Salt Water Fly Fishing,* Knopf, 1970; *The Everglades Today,* Four Winds Press, 1971; *Iron-Tail,* Scribner, 1971; *The Complete Beginner's Guide to Fishing,* Doubleday, 1974.

BIOGRAPHICAL/CRITICAL SOURCES: "Twenty Years of Wonderful Uncertainty," *Writer's Digest,* July, 1961.

* * *

SANDEEN, Ernest (Emanuel)   1908-

PERSONAL: Born December 15, 1908, in Warren County, Ill.; son of William and Mabel (Nelson) Sandeen; married Eileen Bader, September 12, 1936; children: Eric John, Evelyn Elaine. *Education:* Knox College, B.A., 1931; Oxford University, B.Litt., 1933; University of Iowa, Ph.D., 1940. *Politics:* Democrat. *Religion:* Catholic. *Home:* 17831 Ponsha St., South Bend, Ind. 46635.

CAREER: Instructor in English at Knox College, Galesburg, Ill., 1935-37, and University of Iowa, Iowa City, 1937-43; University of Notre Dame, Notre Dame, Ind., assistant professor, 1946-47, associate professor, 1947-60, professor of English, 1960—, head of department, 1965—. Summer instructor, University of Minnesota, 1961. *Military service:* U.S. Naval Reserve, 1943-46; became lieutenant. *Member:* Modern Language Association of Amer-

ica, College English Association, American Association of University Professors, Phi Beta Kappa. *Awards, honors:* Fulbright fellowship to Denmark, 1957-58.

WRITINGS: (Contributor) *Fifty Years of the American Novel,* Scribner, 1951; *Antennas of Silence* (poems), Contemporary Poetry, 1954; (contributor) *American Classics Reconsidered,* Scribner, 1958; *Children and Older Strangers* (poems), University of Notre Dame Press, 1961. Contributor to *New Yorker, Poetry, Commonweal, Critic, Nation, Scribner's, Hudson Review,* and other literary journals.

WORK IN PROGRESS: Nineteenth-century American literature studies.†

* * *

SANDERLIN, George   1915-

PERSONAL: Born February 5, 1915, in Baltimore, Md.; son of George Bismarck (a translator) and Charlotte (Brady) Sanderlin; married Owenita Harrah (a teacher and writer), May 30, 1936; children: Frea Sanderlin Sladek, Mary Sanderlin Buska, David, Johnny. *Education:* The American University, B.A., 1935; Johns Hopkins University, Ph.D., 1938. *Office:* San Diego State University, San Diego, Calif.

CAREER: University of Maine, Orono, associate professor of English, 1938-55; San Diego State University, San Diego, Calif., professor of English, 1955—. Member, San Diego Tennis Patrons. *Member:* American Association of University Professors, Mediaeval Academy of America.

WRITINGS: College Reading: A Collection of Prose, Plays and Poetry, Heath, 1953, revised edition, 1958; *St. Jerome and the Bible,* Farrar, Straus, 1961; (with J. I. Brown) *Effective Writing and Reading,* Heath, 1962; *St. Gregory the Great, Consul of God,* Farrar, Straus, 1964; *First Around the World: A Journal of Magellan's Voyage,* Harper, 1964; *Eastward to India: Vasco da Gama's Voyage,* Harper, 1965; *Effective Writing,* Heath, 1966; *Across the Ocean Sea: A Journal of Columbus's Voyage,* Harper, 1966; *1776: Journals of American Independence,* Harper, 1968; *The Sea-Dragon: Journals of Francis Drake's Voyage Around the World,* Harper, 1969; *Benjamin Franklin: As Others Saw Him,* Coward, 1971; *Bartolome de Las Casas: A Selection of His Writings,* Knopf, 1971; *The Settlement of California,* Coward, 1972; *A Hoop to the Barrel: The Story of the American Constitution,* Coward, 1973. Contributor to *Speculum, English Literary History, Chaucer Review, Classical World, Renaissance News,* and other journals.

WORK IN PROGRESS: Writing on medieval history, and lectures.

SIDELIGHTS: Sanderlin reads Latin, French, German, Italian, and Spanish. *Avocational interests:* Tennis—in 1962 he and his son David ranked ninth in the United States in father-and-son doubles.

* * *

SANDERS, Ed   1939-
(Black Hobart)

PERSONAL: Born August 17, 1939, in Kansas City, Mo.; son of Lyle David (a traveling salesman) and Mollie (Cravens) Sanders; married Miriam Kittell, October 5, 1961; children: Michael, Deirdre, Zak. *Education:* New York University, B.A., 1963. *Religion:* "Ra [Egyptian sun god] is hip to all." *Home and office:* 383 East Tenth St., New York, N.Y. 10009.

CAREER: Formerly clerk in a cigar store. Editor and publisher of F—— You Press, 1962-66, and of *F—— You/A Magazine of the Arts* (quarterly), 1962-66; Peace Eye Bookstore, New York, N.Y., owner, 1965—; Free University of New York, New York, N.Y., professor of revolutionary Egyptology, 1965—; organizer of, and lead singer with, "The Fugs," a literary folk-rock group. Member of steering committee, LEMAR (committee to legalize marijuana), 1964-65. Poet, editor, and moviemaker.

WRITINGS: Poem From Jail, City Lights Books, 1963; *A Valorium Edition of the Entire Extant Works of Thales! The Famous Milesian Poet-Philosopher, Physicist, Astronomer, Mathematician, Cosmologist, Urstoff-Freak, Absent-Minded Professor, and Madman*, introduction by Aristotle, F—— You Press, 1964; (compiler) *Bugger: An Anthology*, [New York], 1964; (compiler and contributor) *Despair: Poems to Come Down By*, [New York], 1964; *King Lord-Queen Freak*, Renegade Press, 1964, 2nd edition, 1965; *The Toe-Queen Poems*, F—— You Press, 1965; *Peace Eye*, Frontier Press (Buffalo, N.Y.), 1965, 2nd enlarged edition, 1967; *The Complete Sex Poems of Ed Sanders*, Fug-Press (New York, N.Y.), 1965; *Banana: An Anthology of Banana-Erotic Poems*, F—— You Press, 1965; with Ken Weaver and Betsy Klein) *The Fugs' Song Book*, Fug-Press, 1965; *Shards of God*, Grove, 1970; *The Family: The Story of Charles Manson's Dune Buggy Attack Battalion*, Dutton, 1971.

WORK IN PROGRESS: A translation of Hesiod's *Theogony*, bilingual edition to be published by Frontier Press; *Shards of Ra*, poems.

SIDELIGHTS: Sanders' publication, which has become a collector's item, is mimeographed on pastel paper. It was originally published in the offices of *The Catholic Worker*, and numbers among its contributors Robert Creeley, Allen Ginsberg, Norman Mailer, and William Burroughs. Sanders was tried for the possession of obscene literature, found in his bookstore, and was successfully defended in court by the New York Civil Liberties Union. He also was jailed for attempting to board a submarine during a peace demonstration in Rhode Island and his Egyptian hieroglyphics text was seized as a Russian codebook. Sanders walked 800 miles from Nashville to Washington, D.C. and stood, without eating, in front of the Pentagon for three days and nights, to protest American involvement in Indochina.

A *Village Voice* interviewer reports that Sanders says his goal is "a total assault on culture." But, says the interviewer, "it is a good-natured assault. Consistent with his purpose, he will print anything.... But the most hostile thing Sanders said in our interview was that he hates Plato."

Richard Duerden wrote that Sanders, for him, is one of the poets "in the front of American Verse *now*.... Sanders' language is not simply colloquial. He has swallowed the colloquial entirely, and the language is released—released into the informed by the life within his vision. It is a vision of life as an invisible net, a plexus, that is 'freaky' simply because it includes all things plus all persons.... Vision and compassion are as real as chemistry."

He has been called "the Tom Sawyer of Tompkins Square." His folk-rock group in which he played maracas and tambourine, has set William Blake to music, but also specialized in songs of protest, and in "a literate, loony, love-happy, psychedelic rock 'n' roll." They recorded for Broadside and on Bernard Stollman's ESP label.

Sanders first studied hieroglyphics in order to read Ezra Pound's *Cantos*. He wrote to *CA*: "I grew up on Ezra Pound, Allen Ginsberg, Hesiod, and my final form is governed by those great men, Pindar, Herodotus, and Charles Olson, Three years of my movie work was confiscated by the New York City police in August, 1965."

BIOGRAPHICAL/CRITICAL SOURCES: Village Voice, January 27, 1966; *Poetry*, May, 1966, June, 1966.†

*   *   *

SANDERS, Herbert H(arvey) 1909-

PERSONAL: Born April 29, 1909, in New Waterford, Ohio; son of Ernest R. (a farmer) and Zora (Chamberlain) Sanders; married Marion Clarke, September 3, 1946. *Education:* Ohio State University, B.S. in Ed., 1932, M.A., 1933, Ph.D., 1951. *Home:* 65 Mariposa Court, Los Gatos, Calif. 95030. *Office:* San Jose State University, San Jose, Calif.

CAREER: High school teacher of industrial arts in Ohio, 1934-38; San Jose State University, San Jose, Calif., 1938—, professor of art, 1952—. School for American Craftsmen, Alfred, N.Y., instructor and director, 1946-48; University of Hawaii, Honolulu, visiting professor of ceramic art, summer, 1957. Ceramic artist, with work in permanent collections of Metropolitan Museum of Art, San Diego Art Museum, Oakland Art Museum, and other museums and collections in United States, Yugoslavia, Italy, and Japan; exhibitor at ten one-man shows in San Francisco, San Diego, and Oakland, Calif., and Charlotte, N.C., Columbus, Ohio, 1942-66; also exhibitor in more than thirty other shows in major American cities, in France, Belgium, and Switzerland, and in State Department traveling exhibition to Europe and Near East, 1957.

MEMBER: American Ceramic Society (fellow), American Craftsmen's Council, International Ceramics Association, Designer Craftsmen of California, Association of San Francisco Potters, Montalvo Association (Saratoga, Calif.). *Awards, honors:* Second prize for pottery, National Ceramic Show, 1938; first prize in Pacific Ceramic Show, 1946; Canadian Guild of Potters Prize in Ceramic National, 1962; $500 prize, Ceramic Arts U.S.A., 1966; distinguished teaching award, 1966; Tau Delta Phi professor of the year, 1967; represented in Objects U.S.A., 1969; 24th Ceramic National-Syracuse China Company Award.

WRITINGS: Sunset Ceramics Book, Lane, 1953 (published in England as *The Practical Pottery Book*, Blandford Press, 1955), 2nd revised edition, published as *How to Make Pottery and Ceramic Sculpture*, Lane, 1964, 3rd revised edition, published as *How to Make Pottery*, Watson-Guptill, 1973; (with Kenkichi Tomimoto) *The World of Japanese Ceramics: Historical and Modern Techniques*, Kodansha, 1967. Contributor of more than thirty articles to *Ceramic Age* and *Craft Horizons*. Photographs and descriptions of work included in *Decorative Art-The Studio Year Book*, 1948, 1949, 1952, 1953, 1954, in the *Studio Year Book of Furniture and Decoration*, 1954-64.

WORK IN PROGRESS: Glazes for Special Effects, to be published by Watson-Guptill.

AVOCATIONAL INTERESTS: Camping and fishing, gardening.

*   *   *

SANDERS, J. Oswald 1902-

PERSONAL: Born October 17, 1902, in Invercargill, New

Zealand; son of Alfred (an accountant) and Margaret (Miller) Sanders; married Edith M. Dobson, December 19, 1931; children: J. Wilbur. *Education:* Attended University of Otago, 1920-23. *Religion:* Baptist. *Home and office:* 1285 A Dominion Rd., Mt. Roskill, Auckland, New Zealand.

CAREER: Onetime solicitor of Supreme Court of New Zealand; New Zealand Bible Training Institute Auckland, principal, 1933-45; China Inland Mission, home director for Australia and New Zealand, 1946-54, general director of overseas missionary fellowship, 1954—. Managing director, Keswick Book Depot, Melbourne, Australia, 1950-54; principal, Christian Leaders Training College, New Guinea, 1973-74.

WRITINGS: Divine Art of Soul-Winning, Moody, 1937; *Christ Indwelling and Enthroned*, Marshall, Morgan & Scott, 1939, revised edition published as *The Pursuit of the Holy*, Zondervan, 1972; *Holy Spirit of Promise*, Marshall, Morgan & Scott, 1940; *Light on Life's Problems*, Marshall, Morgan & Scott, 1944, revised edition published as *Spiritual Problems*, Moody, 1971; *Heresies and Cults*, Marshall, Morgan & Scott, 1948; *Christ Incomparable*, Marshall, Morgan & Scott, 1952; *A Spiritual Clinic*, Moody, 1958; *On to Maturity*, Moody, 1962; *Cultivation of Christian Character*, Moody, 1965; *Robust in Faith*, Moody, 1965; *Men from God's School*, Marshall, Morgan & Scott, 1965; *Spiritual Leadership*, Moody, 1967; *Expanding Horizons*, Institute Press (New Zealand), 1971; *Real Discipleship*, Zondervan, 1973; *At Set of Sun*, Marshall, Morgan, & Scott, 1973; *Bible Studies in Matthew*, Zondervan, 1974; *Satan is No Myth*, Moody, 1975; *Just the Same Today*, Overseas Mission of Fellowship, in press.

Editor of *Reaper* (New Zealand), 1933-45.

WORK IN PROGRESS: Planting Men in Melanesia, the story of Christian Leaders Training College; *One Hundred Days with John*, studies in John's gospel.

* * *

SANDS, Donald B. 1920-

PERSONAL: Born August 12, 1920, in Waterbury, Conn.; son of Roy (an auditor) and Irene (Knott) Sands; married Ernestine Good, June 28, 1945 (died, August 28, 1961); married Isabel S. Onate, June 12, 1965; children: (first marriage) Susanna Mansfield, Erica Wesley; (second marriage) Rebecca Ernestin, Nathaniel Joseph. *Education:* Lehigh University, B.A., 1942; Harvard University, M.A., 1949, Ph.D., 1953. *Home:* 1518 Newport Rd., Ann Arbor, Mich. *Office:* English Department, 1618 Haven, University of Michigan, Ann Arbor, Mich.

CAREER: Instructor in English and German at University of Arkansas, Fayetteville, 1945, University of Maine, Brunswick Annex, 1945-46, Bowdoin College, Brunswick, Me., 1949-51; G. & C. Merriam Co. (publishers), Springfield, Mass., assistant editor, *Webster's New Third International Dictionary*, 1953-57; Boston College, Newton, Mass., associate professor of English, 1957-63; University of Michigan, Ann Arbor, associate professor, 1964-69, professor of English, 1969—. Chairman, National Place Name Survey (Lower Peninsula, Mich.), 1973—. *Military service:* U.S. Army, 1942-45; cryptographer and instructor in German in Europe, 1944-45. *Member:* Modern Language Association of America, American Name Society, American Dialect Society.

WRITINGS: (Editor) *Reynard the Fox*, translated by William Caxton, Harvard University Press, 1960; (with A. G. Kennedy) *A Concise Bibliography for Students of English*, 4th edition, Stanford University Press, 1960; (editor) *Middle English Verse Romances*, Holt, 1966.

WORK IN PROGRESS: Dialect in Main Place Names; *Gottfried Benn (German Poet 1886-1956): A Literary Biography*.

AVOCATIONAL INTERESTS: History of American firearms and hunting.

* * *

SANDS, John Edward 1930-

PERSONAL: Born February 5, 1930, in Toronto, Ontario, Canada; son of Edward A. (an accountant) and Gladys (Kerr) Sands; married Barbara Lee Carstead, May 16, 1952; children: Michael, Nancy, Lee-Erin, Stephen. *Education:* University of Toronto, Bachelor of Commerce. *Home:* 31 Kellythorne Dr., Don Mills, Ontario, Canada. *Office:* Suite 1902, Royal Trust Tower, Toronto Dominion Center, Toronto, Ontario, Canada.

CAREER: Chartered accountant, Institute of Chartered Accountants of Ontario, Woods, Gordon & Co., Toronto, Ontario, consultant, 1955-57; University of Manitoba, Winnipeg, assistant professor of commerce, 1957-58; University of Toronto, Toronto, Ontario, associate professor of commerce, 1958-63; Urwick, Currie Ltd., Toronto, Ontario, consultant, 1963-65; Sands, Ward & Associates (management consultants), Toronto, Ontario, partner, 1965-66; SKLAR Manufacturing Lmt., Whitby, Ontario, secretary-treasurer, 1966-70; Trucena Investments Lmt., Toronto, vice-president, 1970—. *Member:* Institute of Chartered Accountants of Ontario.

WRITINGS: Wealth, Income and Intangibles, University of Toronto Press, 1963. Contributor to accounting journals.

WORK IN PROGRESS: A textbook, *Accounting*.

* * *

SANIEL, Josefa M. 1925-

PERSONAL: Born March 23, 1925, in Manila, Philippine Islands; daughter of Isidoro and Vicenta (Lucero) Saniel. *Education:* University of the Philippines, B.S.E. (magna cum laude), 1949; University of Chicago, M.A., 1953; University of Michigan, Ph.D., 1962. *Religion:* Roman Catholic. *Home:* 4, S. Fuentebella, Diliman, Quezon City, Republic of the Philippines. *Office:* Institute of Asian Studies, University of the Philippines, Diliman, Quezon City, Republic of the Philippines.

CAREER: University of the Philippines, Quezon City, instructor, 1949-55, assistant professor of history, 1955-63, assistant professor, 1963-64, associate professor, 1964-69, professor of East Asian studies, 1969—, program co-ordinator of Institute of Asian Studies, 1964-67, secretary of Asian Center, 1968—. Guest lecturer at Philippine National Defense College; visiting Leverhulme fellow, University of New South Wales, 1967. Member of executive board, Social Science Research Center, University of the Philippines, 1955-57; member of screening committee for study and training in the United States, U.S. Educational Foundation in the Philippines, 1962-68; International Christian University, Tokyo, Japan, member of screening committee in Manila, 1962-65; member of panel advisers of history, Philippine National Museum, 1963—; National Research Council of the Philippines, associate member, 1963-68, member, 1969—, chairman of social science division, 1973-

74. Consultant on Japan affairs to Department of Foreign Affairs, Republic of the Philippines, 1969—.

MEMBER: International Association of Historians of Asia (chapter secretary-treasurer, 1964-68), American Historical Association, American Sociological Association, Philippine Historical Association, Philippine Sociological Society, Philippine Association of University Women, University of Philippines Rizal Center Honor Society, Phi Kappa Phi, Pi Gamma Mu. *Awards, honors:* Travel grant for survey of Southeast Asia, Board of Scholarship and Exchange of Professors for Southeast Asia, 1955; fellow, University of the Philippines, 1957-59; Rockefeller Foundation fellow for research and travel in Japan, 1959-60, and Rockefeller postdoctoral study grant, 1961.

WRITINGS: Japan and the Philippines, 1868-1898, University of the Philippines Press, 1963, Russell, 1973; (contributor) R. N. Bellah, editor, *Religion and Progress in Modern Asia*, Free Press, 1965; (contributor) Inoki Masamichi, editor, *Japan's Future in Southeast Asia*, Center for Southeast Asia Studies, Kyoto University, 1966; (contributor) D. Feria and P. Daroy, editors, *Jose Rizal: Contrary Essays*, Guro Books (Quezon City, Republic of the Philippines), 1968; (contributor) F. H. King, editor, *The Development of Japanese Studies in Southeast Asia*, Center of Asian Studies, University of Hong Kong, 1969; (contributor) B. Grossman, editor, *Southeast Asia in the Modern World*, Verlag Otto Harrossowitz (Germany), 1972. Contributor to *Asian Studies, Panorama, U.P. Today, Philippine Social Sciences and Humanities Review, Education Quarterly*, and other journals.

WORK IN PROGRESS: Japan and the Philippines, 1898-1941, a book giving special emphasis on the Japanese minority in the Philippines before the outbreak of World War II; research on contemporary Philippines-Japan relations, Japan in Southeast Asia, and contemporary Philippines.

*   *   *

SANN, Paul   1914-

PERSONAL: Born March 7, 1914, in New York, N.Y.; son of Harry (a garment worker) and Frieda (Spilton) Sann; married Bertha Pullman, July 28, 1934 (deceased); children: Eleanor Sann Luft, Howard. *Education:* Attended public schools and New York Preparatory School. *Religion:* Jewish. *Home:* 281 West Fourth St., New York, N.Y. 10014. *Agent:* Willis Kingsley Wing, 24 East 38th St., New York, N.Y. 10016. *Office: New York Post*, 210 South St., New York, N.Y. 10002.

CAREER: New York Post, New York, N.Y., 1931— (except for short period with *New York Journal American*), started as copy boy, Washington correspondent, 1945, city editor, 1948-49, executive editor, 1949—. *Member:* Newspaper Reporters Association.

WRITINGS: (With James D. Horan) *Pictorial History of the Wild West*, Crown, 1954; *The Lawless Decade*, Crown, 1957; (with Arnold Red Auerbach) *Red Auerbach: Winning the Hard Way*, Little, Brown, 1966; *Fads, Follies and Delusions of the American People*, Crown, 1967; *Kill the Dutchman: The Story of "Dutch" Schultz*, Arlington House, 1971; *Dead Heat*, Dial Press, 1974. Contributor to national magazines.

WORK IN PROGRESS: A book of nonfiction.

*   *   *

SAPPINGTON, Roger E(dwin)   1929-

PERSONAL: Born March 6, 1929, in Avon Park, Fla.; son of Ross Frazier (a businessman) and Beulah (Snader) Sappington; married LeVerle Hochstetler, June 5, 1949; children: Charlotte, David, Paul, Mark. *Education:* Manchester College, A.B., 1951; Bethany Theological Seminary, Oak Brook, Ill., B.D., 1954; Duke University, A.M., 1954, Ph.D., 1959.

CAREER: Ordained minister, Church of the Brethren, 1951; pastor in Lima, Ohio, 1955-58; Bridgewater College, Bridgewater, Va., assistant professor, 1958-61, associate professor, 1961-65, professor of history, 1965—. National Brethren Historical Committee, chairman, 1958-63, 1970-73. *Member:* American Historical Association, Organization of American Historians, American Society of Church History, Pennsylvania German Society. *Awards, honors:* Duke University–University of North Carolina–Ford Foundation combined fellowship, 1966-67.

WRITINGS: Brethren Social Policy: 1908-1958, Brethren Press, 1961; *Courageous Prophet: Chapters from the Life of John Kline*, Brethren Press, 1964; *The Brethren Along Snake River*, Brethren Press, 1966; (contributor) Donald F. Durnbaugh, editor, *The Church of the Brethren Past and Present*, Brethren Press, 1971; *The Brethren in the Carolinas*, privately printed, 1972; *Revel B. Pritchett: Churchman and Antiquarian*, Park View Press, 1972; *The Brethren in Virginia*, Park View Press, 1973. Contributor of articles to periodicals, including *Brethren Life and Thought*, and *North Carolina Historical Review*.

WORK IN PROGRESS: A documentary history of the Brethren in the nineteenth century, for Brethren Press.

*   *   *

SARASY, Phyllis Powell   1930-

PERSONAL: Surname rhymes with "heresy"; born April 8, 1930, in Cleveland, Ohio; daughter of Stanley G. and Kathryn (Semler) Powell; married Lewis Craigo Sarasy (vice-president of a real estate firm), March 28, 1953; children: Brian Powell, Graham Powell. *Education:* Miami University, Oxford, Ohio, B.S. in Ed.; Hunter College (now of the City University of New York), M.S. in Ed. *Politics:* Republican. *Religion:* Episcopal. *Home:* 52 Morton St., New York, N.Y. 10014.

CAREER: St. Luke's School, New York, N.Y., teacher, 1956-62.

WRITINGS: Winter Sleepers, Prentice-Hall, 1962.†

*   *   *

SARGENT, John Richard   1925-

PERSONAL: Born March 22, 1925, in Birmingham, England; son of Sir John Philip (an educator) and Ruth (Taunton) Sargent; married Anne Elizabeth Haigh (a company director), July 16, 1949; children: Sara, Simon, Victoria. *Education:* Christ Church, Oxford, B.A. (first class honors), 1948. *Politics:* Labour. *Office:* University of Warwick, Coventry, England.

CAREER: Oxford University, Worcester College, Oxford, England, fellow and lecturer in economics, 1951-62; H. M. Treasury and Department of Economic Affairs, London, England, economic consultant, 1963-65; University of Warwick, Coventry, England, professor, 1965-73, associate professor of economics, 1974—, pro-vice-chancellor, 1970—; group economic adviser, Midland Bank, 1974—. Government of British North Borneo, adviser on transport development, 1959. Member of review bodies on doctors' and dentists' researches, 1972—. *Military service:* Royal

Navy, 1943-46; became sub-lieutenant. *Member:* Royal Economic Society, Fabian Society. *Awards, honors:* Rockefeller Foundation fellow in United States, 1959-60; Leverhulme research fellow, 1962-63.

WRITINGS: British Transport Policy, Oxford University Press, 1958. Contributor to *Listener, New Statesman, Socialist Commentary*, and to economics journals.

WORK IN PROGRESS: Research on movement of technical progress.

* * *

SAUER, Muriel Stafford
(Muriel Stafford)

PERSONAL: Born in Hartford, Conn.; daughter of Charles J. (an insurance man) and Nellie (Flynn) Stafford; married Edward A. Sauer (a realtor), September 11, 1948. *Education:* Attended Columbia University and New Britain Normal School (now Central Connecticut State College). *Religion:* Roman Catholic. *Home and office:* 3100 Northeast 28th St., Fort Lauderdale, Fla. 33308.

CAREER: Former teacher; graphologist and free-lance newspaper and magazine writer. *Member:* American Graphological Society (former president).

WRITINGS—Under name Muriel Stafford: *X Marks the Dot*, Duell, Sloane & Pearce, 1943; *You and Your Handwriting*, Dell, 1963. Contributor of articles on graphology to magazines and newspapers, including *Chicago Tribune, Buffalo News, Los Angeles Times, Detroit News, Woman* (England), *Toronto Globe and Mail, Boston Herald-Traveler, Parade*, and *New York Journal-American*.

* * *

SAUL, George Brandon 1901-

PERSONAL: Born November 1, 1901, in Shoemakersville, Pa.; adopted son of Daniel Brandon and Mary E. (Stamm) Saul; married Dorothy M. Ayers, June 28, 1925 (died, 1937); married Eileen S. Lewis, July 3, 1937; children: (first marriage) George Brandon II; (second marriage) Michael Brandon, Barbara Brigid Brandon (Mrs. Johnson M. C. Townsend, Jr.). *Education:* University of Pennsylvania, A.B., 1923, A.M., 1930, Ph.D., 1932. *Religion:* Lutheran. *Home:* 136 Moulton Rd., Storrs, Conn. 06268.

CAREER: University of Connecticut, Storrs, instructor, 1924-29, assistant professor, 1929-32, associate professor, 1932-42, professor of English, 1942-72, professor emeritus, 1972—. Editorial consultant, Pratt & Whitney Aircraft, 1956-61. *Member:* Poetry Society of America, American Committee for Irish Studies, Modern Language Association, International Association for the Study of Anglo-Irish Literature. *Awards, honors:* Prizes for poetry appearing in *Contemporary Verse, Lyric*, and *Poet Lore*; research awards for study in Ireland from University of Connecticut, 1967, 1970.

WRITINGS: The Cup of Sand (poetry), Vinal, 1923.

Bronze Woman (poetry), Humphries, 1930; *A. E. Coppard: His Life and His Poetry*, [Philadelphia], 1932; (translator, and author of introduction and notes) *The Wedding of Sir Gawain and Dame Ragnell*, Prentice-Hall, 1934; *Major Types in English Literature*, Burgess, 1935; (editor and bibliographer) A. E. Coppard, *Cherry Ripe*, Hawthorn House, 1935; *Unimagined Rose* (poetry), Hawthorn House, 1937.

"Only Necessity ..." (poetry), privately printed, 1941; *King Noggin* (juvenile), privately printed, 1943, revised edition, Walton Press, 1971; *Selected Lyrics*, Decker, 1947; *The Elusive Stallion* (essays), Decker, 1948.

October Sheaf (poetry), Prairie Press, 1951; *Handbook of English Grammar and Writing Conventions*, Stackpole, 1953; *The Shadow of the Three Queens*, Stackpole, 1953, revised and expanded edition published as *Traditional Irish Literature and Its Backgrounds: A Brief Introduction*, Bucknell University Press, 1970. *Stephens, Yeats, and Other Irish Concerns*, New York Public Library, 1954; *Prolegomena to the Study of Yeats's Poems*, University of Pennsylvania Press, 1957; *Prolegomena to the Study of Yeats's Plays*, University of Pennsylvania Press, 1958.

(Editor) *Age of Yeats* (anthology), Dell, 1964; (editor) *Owl's Watch* (stories), Fawcett, 1965; *In ... Luminous Wind* (essays on Yeats), Dolmen Press, 1966; *The Wild Queen*, Blair, 1967; *Quintet: Essays on Five American Women Poets*, Mouton & Co., 1967; *Hound and Unicorn: Collected Verse—Lyrical, Narrative, and Dramatic*, Walton, 1969; *Rushlight Heritage* (essays), Walton, 1969; *Carved in Findruine* (short stories), Walton, 1969; *A Little Book of Strange Tales*, Walton, 1969; *Concise Introduction to Types of Literature in English*, Walton, 1969.

Candlelight Rhymes for Early-to-Beds, Walton, 1970; *Withdrawn in Gold* (essays), Mouton & Co., 1970; *In Mountain Shadow* (novel), Walton, 1970; *Seumas O'Kelly* (monograph), Bucknell University Press, 1971; *The Forgotten Birthday* (juvenile), Walton, 1971; *Liadain and Curithir* (Irish novella and short stories), Walton, 1971; *Postscript to Hound and Unicorn* (poetry), Walton, 1971; *A Touch of Acid* (satiric verse), Walton, 1971; *Advice to the Emotionally Perturbed* (parody), Walton, 1971; *Skeleton's Progress: Being a Second Postscript to Hound and Unicorn*, Walton, 1971; (editor) Seumas O'Kelly, *The Shuiler's Child*, DePaul University, 1971; *Daniel Corkery* (monograph), Bucknell University Press, 1973; (editor) Daniel Corkery, *Fohnam the Sculptor*, Procenium Press, 1973; *The Stroke of Light* (poetry), Golden Quill, 1974. Also author of two one-act plays and of short stories, and of musical composition, *Four Songs*, published by Brandon Press, 1965.

Contributor to *Collier's Encyclopedia* and scholarly collections. Contributor of poems, book reviews, and some seventy-five articles to periodicals.

WORK IN PROGRESS: Verse, fiction, and essays. *Avocational interests:* Composing music for piano and songs.

* * *

SAUTER, Edwin Charles Scott, Jr. 1930-

PERSONAL: Born August 3, 1930, in Schenectady, N.Y.; son of Edwin Charles (a commercial art director) and Mary Eugenia Sauter; married Evelyn Dixon, August 4, 1956; children: Leslie Ireys (daughter), Charles Scott. *Education:* Yale University, B.A., 1952; University of Louisville, M.A., 1956; University of Michigan, graduate study, 1957-58. *Home:* Hawley Rd., R.F.D. 1, Brewster, N.Y.; 46 Harwood Rd., Glenview Manor, Louisville, Ky. 40222. *Agent:* Theron Raines, 244 Madison Ave., New York, N.Y. 10016. *Office:* Bedford-Rippowam School, Cantitoe Rd., Bedford, N.Y.

CAREER: Bedford-Rippowam School, Bedford, N.Y., teacher of English, Latin, and drama, 1960—. Assistant to director of adult education, Bedford (N.Y.) Central School District, 1965-66. *Military service:* U.S. Army, 1952-54; served in Korea. *Member:* Chi Psi. *Awards, honors:* Views (magazine) second prize in fiction, 1955, for short story, "The Seventh Sense"; Avery and Jule Hopwood Award, 1958, for short story collection, "The Hours of a Longest Season."

WRITINGS: (With Maurice N. Hennessy) *A Crown for Thomas Peters* (boys' book), Washburn, 1964; (with Maurice N. Hennessy) *Sword of the Hausas* (boys' book), Washburn, 1964; (with Maurice N. Hennessy) *Soldier of Africa* (boys' book), Washburn, 1965. Story anthologized in *New Campus Writing 4*, Grove. Contributor of short stories to *Views* (Louisville literary magazine).

WORK IN PROGRESS: A book about a man's religious conflicts with proposed title *The Double-minded Man*.

AVOCATIONAL INTERESTS: Sports, plays, and reading.†

* * *

SAVAGE, Katharine James 1905-

PERSONAL: Born August 13, 1905, in Worcester, England; daughter of James John and Mary Sanford; married Oswald Savage (a physician); children: four. *Education:* Educated at schools in England, United States, and Switzerland. *Home:* Kouroussa, 83 La Garde, Freinet, France.

CAREER: Ministry of Information, London, England, staff of Middle East section and later head of Counter Propaganda Section, 1943-45; *Economist*, London, England, editorial staff, 1946-54; writer of youth books. London County Council, member of management committee; Remand Home, committee member, 1945-59. *Member:* Cosmopolitan Club.

WRITINGS: The Story of the Second World War, Oxford University Press, 1957, Walck, 1958; *People and Power: The Story of Four Nations*, Oxford University Press, 1959, published as *People and Power: The Story of Three Nations*, Walck, 1959; *The Story of Africa South of the Sahara*, Walck, 1961; *The Story of the United Nations*, Walck, 1962, revised and enlarged edition, 1970; *The United Nations*, Blond Educational, 1964; *A State of War: Europe, 1939-45*, Blond Educational, 1964; *The History of World Religions*, Bodley Head, 1966, published as *The Story of World Religions*, Walck, 1967; *Marxism and Communism*, Bodley Head, 1968, published as *The Story of Marxism and Communism*, Walck, 1969; *The History of the Common Market*, Longmans, Young, 1969, published as *The Story of the Common Market*, Walck, 1970.†

* * *

SAYWELL, John T(upper) 1929-

PERSONAL: Born April 3, 1929, in Weyburn, Saskatchewan, Canada; son of John Ferdinand Tupper and Vera Margaret Saywell; married Patricia Edna Knudsen, 1950; children: Elizabeth Lynn, John Stephen Tupper, Graham Anthony Tupper. *Education:* Attended Victoria College, 1946-48; University of British Columbia, B.A. (double first honors), 1950, M.A. (honors), 1951; Harvard University, Ph.D., 1956. *Home:* 70 Forest Hill Rd., Toronto, Ontario, Canada. *Office:* York University, 2275 Bayview Ave., Toronto 12, Ontario, Canada.

CAREER: University of Toronto, Toronto, Ontario, Canada, lecturer in history, 1954-57, assistant professor, 1957-61, associate professor, 1961-63; York University, Toronto, Ontario, Canada, associate professor of history, associate dean, and chairman of Social Science Division, 1963-64, professor of history and dean of the faculty, 1964—. University of California, Berkeley, visiting professor, 1958. Province of Ontario, chief examiner in history, 1959-62. Consultant to Canadian Broadcasting Corp., 1956-64, Clarke, Irwin Co., Ltd., 1958-64, Toronto Board of Education, 1960-62, Canadian Department of Trade and Commerce, 1961, National Film Board, 1963-64. *Awards, honors:* Fellowship from Social Science Research Council (two), Canadian Social Science Research Council, Humanities Research Council, Canada Council; President's Medal, University of Western Ontario, 1956.

WRITINGS: The Office of Lieutenant-Governor: A Study in Canadian Government and Politics, University of Toronto Press, 1957; (with John C. Ricker and others) *The British Epic*, Clarke, Irwin, 1959, revised edition, 1964; (with Ricker) *The Modern Era*, Clarke, Irwin, 1960; (with E. Koch and Vincent Tovell) *Success of a Mission—Lord Durham in Canada* (three-act television play), Clarke, Irwin, 1960; (with Ricker) *How Are We Governed?*, Clarke, Irwin, 1961, revised edition, 1966; (contributor) N. Frye, editor, *Design for Learning*, University of Toronto Press, 1962; (with Ricker) *Nation and Province: The History and Government of Canada and Manitoba Since Confederation*, Clarke, Irwin, 1963; (contributor) W. Townley, editor, *The Decisive Years*, Musson, 1964; (with Ramsay Cook) *Canada: A Modern Study*, Clarke, Irwin, 1971, revised edition, 1971; (with Ricker) *The British Heritage*, Clark, Irwin, 1965; (with Kenneth W. McNaught and others) *Manifest Destiny: A Short History of the United States*, Clarke, Irwin, 1965; (with Ricker) *The Emergence of Europe*, Clarke, Irwin, 1968; (with Ricker) *Europe and the Modern World*, Clarke, Irwin, 1969; *Canada Past and Present*, Clarke, Irwin, 1969; *Quebec Seventy: A Documentary Narrative*, University of Toronto Press, 1970.

Editor: (And author of introduction) *The Canadian Journal of Lady Aberdeen*, Champlain Society, 1960; Cook and McNaught, *Canada and the United States*, Clarke, Irwin, 1963; Duncan Fishwick and others, *Foundations of the West*, Clarke, Irwin, 1963; (with Ricker) *Nation-Making: Original Documents on the Founding of the Canadian Nation and the Settlement of the West, 1967-85*, Burns & MacEachern, 1967. Also editor of "Clarke Irwin Histories for Collegiates," Clarke, Irwin, 1958-64, and *Canadian Annual Review*, University of Toronto Press, 1960-64.

Teacher's manuals and study guides—all with John C. Ricker; all published by Clarke, Irwin: (And Kennet Mawson) *The Modern Era*, 1960, *The British Epic*, 1961, *Canada and the United States*, 1963, *The Foundations of the West*, 1964.

Author of, and performer in, several hundred dramatic and documentary programs for Canadian Broadcasting Corp. and the National Film Board, including television plays, "Success of a Mission," "The Fourteenth Colony," and "The War of 1812," television documentaries, "Portraits of the 30's," "The Press and the Public," and radio documentaries, "Vincent Massey," "The Senate of Canada," "The American Political System," "Back Into the Present," and "The Crisis of Canada."

Editor of *Canadian Annual Review of Politics and Public Affairs.* Contributor to *Encyclopaedia Britannica, Encyclopedia Americana, Americana Yearbook, Colliers Encyclopedia, Book of Knowledge, Encyclopedia Canadiana.* Also contributor of articles and reviews to historical journals, newspapers, and popular periodicals, including *Globe and Mail, Toronto Star, Toronto Telegram, Star Weekly, Saturday Night, Canadian Forum, Financial Times, Cana-*

dian Historical Review, Historian, American Historical Review, and *International Journal*.

WORK IN PROGRESS: A study of Canada in the 1890's; another book on Canada.†

* * *

SCAGLIONE, Aldo D(omenico) 1925-

PERSONAL: Born January 10, 1925, in Torino, Italy; son of Teodoro (a bank clerk) and Angela (Grasso) Scaglione; married Jeanne Mathilde Daman, June 28, 1952. *Education:* Ginnasio-Liceo Classico Cavour, Torino, Italy, Maturita Classica, 1944; Universita di Torino, Laurea di Dottore in Lettere Moderne, 1948. *Home address:* Route 4, Box 539, Chapel Hill, N.C. 27514. *Office:* Department of Romance Languages, University of North Carolina, Chapel Hill, N.C.

CAREER: University of Toulouse, Toulouse, France, lecturer, 1949-51; University of Chicago, Chicago, Ill., instructor in Italian, 1951-52; University of California, Berkeley, 1952—, began as instructor in Italian, became professor of Italian and comparative literature, 1963-68; University of North Carolina, Chapel Hill, W. R. Kenan Professor of Romance Languages and Comparative Literature, 1968—. Visiting professor, Yale University, 1965-66. *Military service:* Italian Partisan Army, 1944-45. *Member:* Renaissance Society of America, Modern Language Association of America, Dante Society of America, Medieval Academy of America, American Association of Teachers of Italian, Renaissance Society of Northern California (president, 1962). *Awards, honors:* Fulbright fellowship, 1951; Guggenheim fellowship, 1958-59; Newberry Library senior fellowship, 1964-65; senior fellow, Southeastern Institute for Medieval and Renaissance Studies, 1968; senior fellow, Cini Foundation, Venice, Italy, 1973.

WRITINGS: (Editor) M. M. Boiardo, *Orlando Innamorato-Amorum Libri*, two volumes, Utet, 1951, revised edition, 1963; *Nature and Love in the Late Middle Ages*, University of California Press, 1963; *Ars grammatica*, Mouton, 1970; *The Classical Theory of Composition*, University of North Carolina Press, 1972. Contributor of thirty articles and fifty-odd book reviews on Italian and French literature to periodicals.

WORK IN PROGRESS: Research on themes of European Latin humanism, in particular, the development of style theories, language theories, and rhetoric.

SIDELIGHTS: Scaglione is competent in Italian, French, Spanish, Latin, and German.

BIOGRAPHICAL/CRITICAL SOURCES: Yale Review, Spring 1964, pages 468-472.

* * *

SCANLON, David G. 1921-

PERSONAL: Born October 2, 1921, in Leominster, Mass.; son of David L. and Marie (Beaudin) Scanlon; married Mary Janeth Smith (a librarian and teacher), December 29, 1945; children: Judith Ann. *Education:* Fitchburg Teachers College (now Fitchburg State College), B.S.E., 1946; Columbia University, M.A., 1947, Ed.D., 1951. *Office:* Teachers College, Columbia University, 525 West 120th St., New York, N.Y.

CAREER: UNESCO, consultant in Liberia, West Africa, 1951-52; Newark State College, Union, N.J., 1952-57, became professor; Columbia University, Teachers College,

New York, N.Y., professor of international education, 1957—. *Member:* African Studies Association, Comparative Education Society (president).

WRITINGS: (Editor) *International Education: A Documentary History*, Teachers College, Columbia University, Bureau of Publications, 1960; *Traditions of African Education*, Teachers College, Columbia University, Bureau of Publications, 1964; *Education in Uganda*, U.S. Office of Education, 1965; (editor with L. Gray Cowan and James O'Connell) *Education and Nation Building in Africa*, Praeger, 1965; (editor) *Church, State and Education in Africa*, Teachers College, Columbia University, Bureau of Publications, 1966; (compiler with James Shields) *Problems and Prospects in International Education*, Teachers College Press, 1968; (editor) Joseph Lauwerys, *Education in Cities*, Evans Brothers for University of London Institute of Education and Teachers College, 1970.

WORK IN PROGRESS: A history of education in Africa.

SIDELIGHTS: Scanlon has lived in East as well as West Africa, and has traveled extensively on the African continent and in Asia.†

* * *

SCHARLEMANN, Martin H(enry) 1910-

PERSONAL: Born December 28, 1910, in Nashville, Ill.; son of Ernst Karl (a clergyman) and Johanna (Harre) Scharlemann; married Dorothy Hoyer (a staff writer), June 18, 1938; children: Edith Louise, Ernst Theodor, Martin George, John Paul. *Education:* Concordia College, St. Paul, Minn., A.A., 1930; Concordia Seminary, St. Louis, Mo., M.Div., 1934; Washington University, St. Louis, Mo., M.A., 1936, Ph.D., 1938; Union Theological Seminary, New York, N.Y., Th.D., 1964; Air War College, distinguished graduate, 1964. *Politics:* Independent. *Home:* 1 Seminary Ter. N., St. Louis, Mo. 63105.

CAREER: Ordained minister of Lutheran Church-Missouri Synod, 1934. U.S. Army Air Forces and U.S. Air Force, chaplain on active duty, 1941-52; Concordia Seminary, St. Louis, Mo., professor of New Testament interpretation, 1952-64, director of graduate studies, 1954-60, graduate professor of exegetical theology, 1965-72, acting president, 1974. Served overseas with U.S. Army Air Forces in Europe during World War II, leaving active duty in 1952 with rank of colonel; U.S. Air Force Reserve, assigned to Office of Chief of Chaplains, (retired as Brigadier General, 1970); special lecturer for Air Force throughout the Pacific and Europe, and regular guest lecturer at Air University, Maxwell Air Force Base, Ala., 1953-73. Official commentator for Metropolitan Church on KMOX-TV, St. Louis, Mo., 1964-65; guest lecturer, Waldensian Seminary, Rome, Italy, 1966; ecumenical guest, Pontifical Biblical Institute, Rome, Italy, 1966; visiting professor, Nairobi University, Kenya, 1972-73; guest lecturer at Martin Luther Seminary, Lae, New Guinea and at Luther Seminary, Adelaide, Australia, 1973.

MEMBER: Lutheran Academy for Scholarship (president), Society of Biblical Literature, Societas Novi Testamenti Studiorum, Society for Music, Worship and the Arts, American Philosophical Society, Phi Beta Kappa. *Awards, honors—Military:* Legion of Merit, two battle stars for European campaigns. Civilian: Lutheran Brotherhood faculty fellowship, 1959-60; Air University award, 1965; Martin of Tours Silver Medal, 1968.

WRITINGS: Honor-Duty-Country, six volumes, Government Printing Office, 1951; *Toward Tomorrow*, Concordia, 1961; *Proclaiming the Parables*, Concordia, 1963; (contributor) Albert Huegli, editor, *Church and State Under God*, Concordia, 1964; *Redemption and Healing*, Concordia, 1965; *Stephen: A Singular Saint*, Pontifical Biblical Institute, 1968; *The Church's Social Responsibilities*, Concordia, 1971; *The Ethics of Revolution*, Concordia, 1971. Writer of professional and technical articles.

WORK IN PROGRESS: Commentary on First Peter.

*   *   *

SCHATTEN, Fritz (Max Robert) 1930-

PERSONAL: Born February 18, 1930, in Guben, East Germany; son of Max (a textile designer) and Emma Schatten; married Lore Peckhold (a free-lance journalist), August 6, 1956; children: Esther-Beate. *Education:* Attended Freie Universitat Berlin. *Home:* Haupstrasse 58a, Rheinbreitbach, West Germany. *Office:* c/o Radio Deutsche Welle, Bruederstrasse, Cologne, West Germany.

CAREER: Worked as free-lance press and radio correspondent in West, Berlin, West Germany, reporting on East European affairs, 1954-59, on African affairs, 1959-62; Radio Deutsche Welle, Cologne, West Germany, head of African department, 1962-64, head of Central Research Unit and foreign affairs roving correspondent, 1965—. *Member:* German Journalists Association (West Germany).

WRITINGS: Afrika—Schwartz oder rot?: Revolution eines Kontinents, Piper (Munich), 1961; (contributor) W. Z. Laqueur and L. Labedz, editors, *Polycentrism*, Praeger, 1962; *Der Konflikt Moskau-Peking: Analyse und Dokumente des roten Schisma*, Piper, 1963; *Communism in Africa*, Praeger, 1965; (with Oskar Splett) *Das Afrika der Gegenwart*, Bundeszentrale fuer politische Bildung, 1964. Regular contributor to newspapers and radio.

WORK IN PROGRESS: Three books: *Chinese Communism and Africa, The Ideology of the Third World From Bandung to Algiers, Communist Parties of the Developing Countries.*

SIDELIGHTS: Schatten, as one of the first newspaper correspondents to specialize in African affairs, has traveled extensively throughout Africa, attended most Afro-Asian conferences, and has twice covered United Nations General Assembly sessions, interviewing "dozens of Afro-Asian top politicians."†

*   *   *

SCHEER, George F(abian) 1917-

PERSONAL: Born October 21, 1917, in Richmond, Va.; son of George Fabian (a jeweler) and Hilda (Knopf) Scheer; married Genevieve Yost; children: George F. III. *Education:* Attended University of Richmond, 1936-40. *Home:* Kings Mill Rd., Chapel Hill, N.C. *Agent:* Phyllis Jackson, Ashley Famous Agency, Inc., 1301 Avenue of the Americas, New York, N.Y. 10019.

CAREER: University of North Carolina Press, Chapel Hill, salesman, 1945, sales and advertising manager, 1946-52; book publishers' representative, 1952—. *Member:* Company of Military Historians (fellow), Authors Guild, Manuscript Society, Players Club. *Awards, honors:* Thomas Alva Edison Foundation Children's Book Award for *Yankee Doodle Boy*, 1965.

WRITINGS: (With Hugh F. Rankin) *Rebels and Red-*

coats, World Publishing, 1957; (editor) Joseph P. Martin, *Private Yankee Doodle*, Little, Brown, 1962, published as *A Narrative of Some of the Adventures, Dangers, and Sufferings of a Revolutionary Soldier*, New York Times, 1968; (editor) *Yankee Doodle Boy*, W. R. Scott, 1964; (editor) *Cherokee Animal Tales*, Holiday House, 1968. General editor of "Meridian Documents of American History" series,World Publishing, 1959—. Contributor to *American Heritage* and *New York Times Book Review*.

WORK IN PROGRESS: A book for children on the beginning of the American Revolution; high school textbook in American history.

SIDELIGHTS: Scheer told *CA* that he came under the personal influence of Douglas Southall Freeman in his early writing days, and, thus trained, believes in "going to the original sources, to the letters, diaries, and journals of the men and women of the American past—and in quoting them in their own words as extensively as the art of story telling will allow.... I try to find everything they said for and of themselves, and what their contemporaries believed of them. And then I write, hewing as close to the facts as I know how. It's a tough, hard way, which I always approach with joy and achieve with agony."†

*   *   *

SCHELLENBERG, Helene Chambers

PERSONAL: Born in Saskatoon, Saskatchewan, Canada; daughter of Stanley Wilfred (a scientist) and Lillian (Lancaster) Chambers; married Carl E. Schellenberg (a Standard Oil Co. executive), February 25, 1938; children: Carl S., Gary E. (deceased). *Education:* Attended San Diego State College (now University), for three years; other study through extension and adult education courses. *Politics:* Democrat. *Religion:* Protestant. *Home and office:* 1014 Fassler Ave., Pacifica, Calif. 94044. *Agent:* Elyse M. Sommer, 25-50 Bessemund Ave., Far Rockaway, N.Y.

CAREER: Terra Nova (Calif.) High School, adult education teacher of creative writing, 1961—; *Pacifica Tribune*, Pacifica, Calif., women's page editor, 1962-63, feature writer, 1962—; with Storycraft (manuscript service), Pacifica, Calif., 1963—. *Member:* California Writers Club, Pacifica Writers Guild (charter); Press Club and Union League Club (both San Francisco); Pacifica Federated Women's Club (recording secretary).

WRITINGS: Song of the Ocean, Arcadia House, 1963; *Beth Adams, Private Duty Nurse*, Arcadia House, 1964; *Nurse's Journey*, Arcadia House, 1967; *Nurse in Research*, Bouregy, 1974. Contributor to short stories and articles to women's magazines.

WORK IN PROGRESS: Nurse Abroad.

AVOCATIONAL INTERESTS: Piano, gardening.†

*   *   *

SCHEPERS, Maurice B. 1928-

PERSONAL: Born October 5, 1928, in Holland, Mich.; son of Maurice H. and Minnie (Myaard) Schepers. *Education:* Aquinas College, Grand Rapids, Mich., A.B., Dominican Houses of Study, Somerset, Ohio, and Washington, D.C., S.T.L.; Angelicum (now University of St. Thomas), Rome, Italy, laurea in sacred theology. *Home:* 478 Michigan Ave., N.E., Washington, D.C. 20017.

CAREER: Roman Catholic priest of Dominican order.

Dominican House of Studies, Washington, D.C., professor of ecclesiology, 1959—. Catholic University of America, Washington, D.C., visiting lecturer in department of religious education, 1962—. *Member:* Catholic Theological Society of America.

WRITINGS: The Church of Christ, Prentice-Hall, 1963. Contributor to theological journals. Member of editorial staff, *Thomist*.

WORK IN PROGRESS: Writing on the mystery of the Catholic Church.†

*   *   *

SCHEYER, Ernst 1900-

PERSONAL: Born July 3, 1900, in Breslau, Germany; son of Nathan Norbert (a merchant) and Martha (Beuthner) Scheyer; married Evelyne Rodrigues Pereira (a pianist and harpsichordist), August 31, 1935; children: Ann B. Scheyer Harvey, Virginia Catherine Scheyer Markson. *Education:* University of Freiburg, Dr. Rer. Pol., 1922; University of Cologne, Dr. Phil., 1926. *Politics:* Democrat. *Religion:* Unitarian Universalist. *Home:* 201 Kirby Ave., Detroit, Mich. *Office:* Community Arts Building, Wayne State University, Detroit, Mich.

CAREER: Assistant curator in municipal museums in Koeln and Breslau, Germany, 1924-32; Detroit Institute of Arts, Detroit, Mich., research fellow, 1936-38; Wayne State Universtiy, Detroit, Mich., faculty member of department of art history, 1938—. Honorary research fellow, Detroit Institute of Arts, 1970—. Member of board of directors of Chamber Music Workshop, Detroit. *Awards, honors:* George Dehio Preis of Kunstgeschichte, 1970.

WRITINGS: Lyonel Feininger: Caricature and Fantasy, Wayne State University Press, 1964; *Malerei der Biedermeier-Zeit*, Verlag W. Weidlich (Frankfurt), 1965; *The Circle of Henry Adams: Art and Artist*, Wayne State University Press, 1970. Assistant editor, *Criticism* (Detroit).

SIDELIGHTS: Commenting on *The Circle of Henry Adams*, Viola Hopkins Winner states, "Continental in background, a prolific critic of the arts ranging from eighteenth-century chinoiserie to modern American painting, Mr. Scheyer lives up to his qualifications in tracing art influences and in evaluating these eclectic artists and connoisseurs [Henry Adams, John La Farge, Henry Hobson Richardson, and Augustus Saint-Gaudens] whose purview extended from the art of Archaic Greece to the contemporary South Seas."

*   *   *

SCHIFF, Michael 1915-

PERSONAL: Born March 4, 1915, in New York, N.Y.; son of Moses and Clara (Fleisher) Schiff; married Sylvia Schiffman, December 25, 1939; children: Janet, Allen, Jonathan. *Education:* City College (now City College of the City University of New York), B.B.A., 1936, M.B.A., 1939; New York University, Ph.D., 1947. *Home:* 466 Ocean Pkwy., Brooklyn, N.Y. 11218. *Office:* New York University, 100 Trinity Pl., New York, N.Y. 10003.

CAREER: Certified public accountant, New York, N.Y., 1939—; management consultant to industrial firms, including Union Carbide Co., Sylvania Electrical Products, and Dominion Bridge Co., General Electric Co., Celanese Corp., American Express Co., 1950—; New York University, New York, N.Y., Vincent C. Ross Professor of Ac-

counting, 1960—. *Member:* American Institute of Certified Public Accountants, Financial Executives Institute, National Association of Accountants, American Accounting Association, Beta Gamma Sigma.

WRITINGS: (With Longman) *Practical Distribution Cost Analysis*, Irwin, 1955; (with Lang and McFarland) *Cost Accounting*, Ronald, 1955, 2nd edition (with Benninger), 1963; (with Mellman) *Financial Management of the Marketing Function*, Financial Executives Institute, 1963; (with Schirger) *Control of Maintenance Cost*, National Association of Accountants, 1964; *Accounting and Control in Physical Distribution Management*, National Council for Physical Distribution Management, 1972; (with Lewin) *Behavioral Aspects of Accounting*, Prentice-Hall, 1974; *The Value Tax: The European Experience*, Financial Executives Research Foundation, 1974. Contributor to accounting and management journals.

*   *   *

SCHLUETER, Paul (George) 1933-

PERSONAL: Born May 10, 1933, in Chicago, Ill.; son of Paul George and Ruby (Browning) Schlueter; married Rosetta Van Diggelen, July 14, 1956 (divorced, 1971); children: Paul George III, Greta Renee, Laurie Ann. *Education:* Attended Bethel College, 1954-57; University of Minnesota, B.A., 1958; University of Denver, M.A., 1963; Southern Illinois University, Ph.D., 1968. *Office:* Department of English, Kean College of New Jersey, Union, N.J. 07083.

CAREER: College of St. Thomas, St. Paul, Minn., lecturer in English, 1959-60; Moorhead State College, Moorhead, Minn., instructor in English, 1960-62; University of Denver, Denver, Colo., teaching assistant in English, 1962-63; Southern Illinois University, Carbondale, instructor in English, 1963-66; Adrian College, Adrian, Mich., assistant professor of English, 1966-68; University of Evansville, Evansville, Ind., assistant professor of English, 1968-72; University of Hamburg, Hamburg, Germany, guest professor, 1973; Kean College of New Jersey, Union, assistant professor of English, 1973—. Visiting professor, Midwestern University, summer, 1964. *Member:* Modern Language Association of America, National Council of Teachers of English, American Association of University Professors, College English Association.

WRITINGS: (Contributor) Harry T. Moore, editor, *Contemporary American Novelists*, Southern Illinois University Press, 1964; (contributor) Charles Shapiro, editor, *Contemporary British Novelists*, Southern Illinois University Press, 1965; (contributor of check list) Alister Kershaw and F. J. Temple, editors, *Richard Aldington: An Intimate Portrait*, Southern Illinois University Press, 1965; (contributor) Wolfgang B. Fleischmann, editor, *Encyclopedia of World Literature*, Ungar, Volume I, 1967; *The Novels of Doris Lessing*, Southern Illinois University Press, 1973; (editor) *The Small Personal Voice: Essays, Reviews, Interviews*, Knopf, 1974; *Shirley Ann Grau*, Twayne, in press. Contributor to *Encyclopaedia Britannica*; also contributor to journals and newspapers, including *Studies in Short Fiction, Studies in American Fiction, Motive, Christian Century, Focus-Midwest, Chicago Daily News, Denver Post*, and *St. Louis Post-Dispatch*.

WORK IN PROGRESS: A study of twentieth-century women writers.

SIDELIGHTS: Schlueter told *CA*, "Particularly interested in relationships between the arts (especially literature) and religious faith (especially Christianity)."

SCHMIDT, J(akob) E(dward) 1906-

PERSONAL: Born June 16, 1906, in Riga, Latvia; came to United States in 1924, naturalized in 1929; son of Michael E. (a teacher) and Rachel I. (Goldman) Schmidt. *Education:* Attended Baltimore City College, 1926-29; University of Maryland, Ph.G., 1932, B.S., 1935, M.D., 1937. *Home:* Monroe at Park, Charlestown, Ind. 47111. *Office:* 934 Monroe St., Charlestown, Ind. 47111.

CAREER: Private practice of medicine in Baltimore, Md., 1940-53, Charlestown, Ind., 1953—; medical lexicographer, 1940—. Consultant in medical and medicolegal terminology. Inventor of iodine-pentoxide method for detection of carbon monoxide in medicinal oxygen; discoverer of effect of cesium on rate of oxidation of organic matter. *Member:* American Medical Association, Medical and Chirurgical Faculty of Maryland, National Association on Standard Medical Vocabulary (chairman), International Society for General Semantics, American Dialect Society, American Name Society, American Medical Writers' Association, Rho Chi, Owl Club. *Awards, honors:* D.Litt., 1939; award from New York chapter, American Medical Writers' Association, 1959.

WRITINGS—All published by C. C Thomas, except as indicated: *Sex Dictionary, and Lexicon of Related Emotions*, Hannah Publications, 1954; *Medical Terms Defined for the Layman*, 1958; *Reversicon: A Medical Word Finder*, 1958; *Dictionary of Medical Slang and Related Esoteric Expressions*, 1959; *Narcotics Lingo and Lore*, 1959; *Medical Discoveries: Who and When*, 1959.

Baby Name Finder, 1960; *Libido*, 1960, 2nd edition published as *Cyclopedic Lexicon of Sex: Erotic Practices, Expressions, Variations of the Libido*, Brussel & Brussel, 1967; *Attorney's Dictionary of Medicine*, Matthew Bender, 1962; *Attorney's Medical Word Finder*, Matthew Bender, 1964; *1000 Elegant Phrases and Expressions*, 1965; *The Medical Lexicographer*, 1966; *Police Medical Dictionary*, 1968; *Practical Nurses' Medical Dictionary: A Cyclopedic Medical Dictionary for Practical Nurses, Vocational Nurses, and Nurses' Aides*, 1968; *Structural Units of Medical and Biological Terms*, 1969; *Paramedical Dictionary: A Practical Dictionary for the Semi-Medical and Ancillary Medical Professions*, 1969.

English Word Power for Physicians and Other Professionals: A Vigorous and Cultured Vocabulary, 1971; *English Idioms and Americanisms for Foreign Students, Professionals, and Physicians*, 1972; *English Speech for Foreign Physicians, Scientists, and Students*; 1972; *Analyzer of Medical-Biological Words*, 1973; *English Speech for Foreign Students*, 1973; *Visual Aids for Paramedical Vocabulary*, 1973; *Index of Medical-Paramedical Vocabulary*, 1974. Also author of yearly supplements to *Attorney's Dictionary of Medicine*, Matthew Bender, 1966—.

Writer of vocabulary features for North American Newspaper Alliance; contributor of other articles on words and medical semantics to *Baltimore Sun, American Mercury, Modern Medicine, Police, Trauma, Medical Science*. Contributor to *Scientific American, Popular Mechanics*. Member of revision committee, *U.S. Pharmacopoeia*, Volume XI, 1933-43. Associate medical editor, *Trauma*; medical vocabulary editor, *Modern Medicine*.

WORK IN PROGRESS: Proof of God Through Human Anatomy.

SIDELIGHTS: Dr. Schmidt is competent in German, French, Russian, Greek, and Latin and, as he told *CA*, he is a "devoted student of English." He has invented the Reversicon, "a form of dictionary presentation which leads the reader from the concept of the word to the word itself," and introduced more than seven thousand new words into medical terminology. *Avocational interests:* Inventing labor-saving devices, making jewelry, and cultivating flowers.

* * *

SCHMIDT, Karl M. (Jr.) 1917-

PERSONAL: Born March 19, 1917, in Utica, N.Y.; son of Karl M. (a clothing manufacturer) and Jennie C. (Greenia) Schmidt; married Mary E. Murphy, April 3, 1943; children: Karl Michael, Jill Sheryl, Glen Mark. *Education:* Colgate University, A.B. (magna cum laude), 1948; Johns Hopkins University, M.A., 1950, Ph.D., 1951. *Politics:* Democrat. *Religion:* Unitarian Universalist. *Home:* 100 Cutler Dr., Syracuse, N.Y. 13219. *Office:* Maxwell School, Syracuse University, Syracuse, N.Y. 13210.

CAREER: Union College, Schenectady, N.Y., assistant professor of government and economics, 1951-57; Syracuse University, Syracuse, N.Y., associate professor of political science, 1957-70, professor of political science and public administration, 1971—. Pakistan Administrative Staff College, Lahore, senior resident adviser, 1960-62, 1967; visiting professor of political science at Colgate University, part time, 1962-63, University of Hawaii, 1964-65. New York State Department of Audit and Control, research consultant, 1956-57; Upstate New York Center for Education in Politics, director, 1962-66. Freedom Forum, Schenectady, N.Y., member, board of directors, 1953-57; American Association for the United Nations, chairman of Schenectady committee, 1956-57. *Member:* American Political Science Association, American Association of University Professors (chairman of regional committee on economic status, 1959-60), Association for Asian Studies, New York State Political Science Association (member of executive committee, 1956-58; secretary-treasurer, 1958-60), Phi Beta Kappa (president, Syracuse University chapter, 1968-70).

WRITINGS: Henry A. Wallace: Quixotic Crusade, 1948, Syracuse University Press, 1960; (editor) *Selected Papers from the Staff College*, Lion Art Press (Pakistan), 1962; (editor) *American National Government in Action*, Dickenson, 1965; (editor) *American State and Local Government in Action*, Dickenson, 1966; (editor) *American Government in Action: National, State and Local*, Dickenson, 1967. Upstate New York contributing editor, *National Civic Review*, 1959-60.

WORK IN PROGRESS: A book, *Pakistan Awaits Its Revolution.*

SIDELIGHTS: Schmidt has traveled extensively through the Indian sub-continent, 1960-62. He is competent in Spanish. *Avocational interests:* Photography, boating, and camping.

* * *

SCHMITT, Marshall L. 1919-

PERSONAL: Born January 23, 1919, in Rochester, N.Y.; son of John J. and Myrtle (Taverner) Schmitt; married Doris Miller, 1941; children: Marsha Jean. *Education:* State University of New York at Oswego, B.S., 1941; Ohio State University, M.S., 1946; Pennsylvania State University, Ed.D., 1953. *Religion:* Presbyterian. *Home:* 7440 Axton St., Springfield, Va. *Office:* U.S. Office of Education, 400 Maryland Ave., Washington, D.C.

CAREER: High school teacher in Red Creek, N.Y., 1941-42; U.S. Army Air Forces Technical Training Command, civilian instructor, 1942-43; Oswego State Teachers College (now State University of New York at Oswego), instructor in electricity and electronics, and in metals, 1946-49; North Carolina State College (now University at) Raleigh, associate professor of industrial arts education, 1949-57; U.S. Office of Education, Washington, D.C., researcher and educational specialist, 1957—, member of three-man team studying polytechnic education in Soviet Union, 1959. *Military service:* U.S. Naval Reserve, 1943-70, on active duty, 1943-46; became lieutenant commander. *Member:* American Industrial Arts Association, American Vocational Association, National Education Association, North Carolina Industrial Arts Association (life member; secretary-treasurer, 1956-57), Epsilon Pi Tau, Springfield Golf and Country Club. *Awards, honors:* Laureate Citation from Epsilon Pi Tau; Distinguished Alumnus Award, State University of New York at Oswego, 1968.

WRITINGS: Improving Industrial Arts Teaching, U.S. Government Printing Office, 1960; (with W. K. Medlin and Clarence B. Lindquist) *Soviet Education Programs*, U.S. Government Printing Office, 1960; (researcher) *Industrial Arts: An Analysis of 39 State Curriculum Guides, 1953-58*, U.S. Government Printing Office, 1961; (with Peter Buban) *Understanding Electricity and Electronics*, McGraw, 1962, 2nd edition, 1969; *Why the Industrial Arts?*, U.S. Government Printing Office, 1963; (with Albert L. Pelley) *Industrial Arts Education*, U.S. Government Printing Office, 1966; (with Buban) *Exploring Electricity and Electronics*, McGraw, 1967; (with Buban) *Technical Electricity and Electronics*, McGraw, 1972. Also author of *Planning and Designing Functional Facilities for Industrial Arts*. Regular contributor of articles to *Industrial Arts* and *Vocational Education*.

AVOCATIONAL INTERESTS: Amateur radio operator (call letters WA4PNP), golf.

*   *   *

SCHMUCK, Richard A(llen) 1936-

PERSONAL: Born June 13, 1936, in Chicago, Ill.; son of Walter A. (an insurance agent) and Myrtle (Grebe) Schmuck; married Patricia Halme (a teacher and author), June 13, 1959; children: Julie A., Allen R. *Education:* Attended Ohio Wesleyan University, 1954-55; University of Michigan, B.A. (with honors), 1958, M.A., 1959, Ph.D., 1962. *Office:* University of Oregon, Eugene, Ore. 97403.

CAREER: University of Michigan, Ann Arbor, study director, Institute for Social Research, 1962, assistant professor of psychology, 1963. University of California, Santa Barbara, assistant professor of psychology, 1964-65; Temple University, Philadelphia, Pa., associate professor of educational psychology, 1965-67; University of Oregon, Eugene, professor of educational psychology, 1967—, program director, Center for the Advanced Study of Educational Administration, 1967—. *Member:* International Association of Applied Social Scientists, American Psychological Association, Society for the Psychological Study of Social Issues, American Sociological Association, Society for the Study of Social Problems, National Training Laboratories (associate), Phi Beta Kappa, Phi Kappa Phi.

WRITINGS: (With D. Cartwright) *Bibliography on Dominance and Social Power*, Office of Research Administration, University of Michigan, 1964; (with Robert S. Fox and Ronald Lippitt) *Pupil-Teacher Adjustment and Mutual Adaptation in Creating Classroom Learning Environments*, U.S. Office of Education, 1964; *Strategies of Dominance and Social Power*, Office of Research Administration, University of Michigan, 1965; (with Mark Chesler and Lippitt) *Problem Solving to Improve Classroom Learning*, Science Research Associates, 1966; (with Fox and Luszki) *Diagnosing Classroom Learning Environments*, Science Research Associates, 1966; (with Philip J. Runkel) *Organizational Training for a School Faculty*, Center for the Advanced Study of Educational Administration, University of Oregon, 1970; (with wife, Patricia Schmuck) *Group Processes in the Classroom*, W. C. Brown, 1971; (compiler with Matthew B. Miles) *Organization Development in Schools*, National Press Books, 1971; (with others) *Handbook of Organization Development in Schools*, National Press Books, 1972; (with others) *Diagnosing Professional Climates in Schools*, Learning Resources, 1973; (with Patricia Schmuck) *A Humanistic Psychology of Education*, National Press Books, 1974. Co-author of four reports on Inter-Center Program on Children, Youth, and Family Life published by Institute for Social Research, University of Michigan. Contributor to *Child Development, Public Opinion Quarterly, Mental Hygiene, International Review of Education, Journal of Social Issues, American Journal of Sociology, Journal of Applied Behavioral Science*, and other journals.

*   *   *

SCHNECK, Stephen 1933-
(Ben Bite, Mack Fite, Larry Kite, James Knight, Jams Lite, Sam Spit)

PERSONAL: Born January 2, 1933, in New York, N.Y.; son of Samuel (a dress manufacturer) and Shirley (Lieberman) Schneck; reportedly married three times. *Education:* Attended Carnegie Institute of Technology (now Carnegie-Mellon University), for three months in 1950. *Home:* 622 Broadway, San Francisco, Calif. 94133.

CAREER: Entertainer. Writer-in-residence at The Committee, a San Francisco satirical review. *Awards, honors:* Olympia short story award (Paris, $1,000), 1963; Prix Formentor ($10,000), 1965, for *The Nightclerk*.

WRITINGS: The Nightclerk: Being His Perfectly True Confession, Grove, 1965; *Nocturnal Vaudeville*, Dutton, 1971.

SIDELIGHTS: Schneck's first book is, according to *Books*, about a "sleazy, surreal, whore-pervert-deviate-priested hotel's nightclerk who is ... the fattest man in American literature. 600 pounds." The author claims it is not a dirty book since none of the erotic scenes are consummated. 'It might be another kind of book," he said, "but it's certainly not dirty."

Schneck's work with The Committee, a cabaret theater created and developed in the improvisational mode, is "distinctive since, to the best of my knowledge, it makes me, officially, the one and only improvisational writer in the world," he told *CA*.

BIOGRAPHICAL/CRITICAL SOURCES: Books, June, 1965.†

*   *   *

SCHNEIDER, Herbert Wallace 1892-

PERSONAL: Born March 16, 1892, in Berea, Ohio; son of Frederick William (a professor of theology and vice-president of Baldwin-Wallace College) and Marie (Severinghaus)

Schneider; married Caroline Catherine Smith, 1921; married second wife, Grenafore Westphal, 1942; children: Edward, Frederick, Robert. *Education:* Columbia University, A.B., 1915, Ph.D., 1917. *Home:* 245 West 10th St., Claremont, Calif.

CAREER: Columbia University, New York, N.Y., instructor, 1918-24, assistant professor of philosophy, 1924-28, professor of philosophy and religion, 1929-57, professor emeritus, 1957—; Colorado College, Colorado Springs, distinguished service professor, 1958-59; Claremont Colleges of California, Claremont, director of affiliated Blaisdell Institute for Advanced Study in World Cultures and Religions, 1959-63, acting dean of Claremont Graduate School, 1960-62, professor emeritus of Claremont Graduate School, 1963—. Visiting professor at University of Illinois, 1926, University of Washington, 1946, University of Minnesota, 1946, University of Georgia, 1951, and Oregon State University, 1968-69. Fulbright lecturer at Universities of Paris, Toulouse, Bordeaux, and Marseilles, 1949-50; UNESCO, Paris, France, head of Division of Philosophy and Humanistic Studies, Department of Cultural Activities, 1953-56. *Military service:* U.S. Army, Medical Corps, 1917-18.

MEMBER: American Society of Church History (president, 1935), American Philosophical Association (president, Eastern division, 1947; chairman, committee on international cooperation, 1959-64), American Society for the Study of Religion, American Council of Learned Societies. *Awards, honors:* L.H.D. from Union College, 1947, Baldwin-Wallace College, 1960, Colorado College, 1968; LL.D. from Claremont Graduate School, 1962.

WRITINGS: Making the Fascist State, Oxford University Press, 1928; *The Puritan Mind*, Henry Holt, 1930; (with Horace L. Friess) *Religion in Various Cultures*, Henry Holt, 1932; *The Fascist Government of Italy*, Van Nostrand, 1936; *Meditations in Seasons on the Elements of Christian Philosophy*, Oxford University Press, 1938.

(With George Lawton) *A Prophet and a Pilgrim, Being the Incredible History of Thomas Lake Harris and Laurence Oliphant: Their Sexual Mysticisms and Utopian Communities*, Columbia University Press, 1942; *A History of American Philosophy*, Columbia University Press, 1946, 2nd edition, 1963; (editor) *Adam Smith's Moral and Political Philosophy*, Hafner, 1948; *Religion in Twentieth Century America*, Harvard University Press, 1952, revised edition, Atheneum, 1964; *Three Dimensions of Public Morality* (Mahlon-Powell Lectures, 1954), Indiana University Press, 1956.

(Editor with Irwin Edman) *Landmarks for Beginners in Philosophy*, Holt, 1960; *Morals for Mankind* (lectures) University of Missouri Press, 1960; *Ways of Being: Elements of Analytic Ontology* (Woodbridge Lectures), Columbia University Press, 1962; *Sources of Contemporary Philosophical Realism in America*, Bobbs-Merrill, 1964; *Civilized Religion: An Historical and Philosophical Analysis*, Exposition, 1972; *Readings from Hobbes*, Open Court, in press; (contributor) *Hobbes in His Times*, University of Minnesota Press, in press.

Author of pamphlets on philosophy and John Dewey. Contributor to philosophy and religion journals; contributor to University of Buffalo Studies. Editor, *Review of Religion*, 1933-39, *Journal of Philosophy*, 1938-49; book review editor, *Journal of the History of Philosophy*, 1962—.

SIDELIGHTS: A History of American Philosophy has been published in French, German, Italian, and Spanish.

SCHNEIDER, Robert W. 1933-

PERSONAL: Born May 28, 1933, in Loudonville, Ohio; son of Richard H. and Virginia Marie (Bernhard) Schneider; married Ann M. Stitzlein, June 12, 1955; children: Richard Jeffrey, Ronald Eric, Lynne Elisabeth. *Education:* College of Wooster, B.A., 1955; Western Reserve University (now Case Western Reserve University), M.A., 1956; University of Minnesota, Ph.D., 1959. *Office:* Department of History, Northern Illinois University, DeKalb, Ill.

CAREER: University of Minnesota, Minneapolis, instructor, 1958-59; College of Wooster, Wooster, Ohio, instructor in history, 1959-61; Northern Illinois University, DeKalb, assistant professor, 1961-65, associate professor, 1965—, professor of history, 1973—. *Member:* American Historical Association, American Studies Association, American Association of University Professors, American Civil Liberties Union, Organization of American Historians. *Awards, honors:* American Philosophical Society research grants, 1962, 1964.

WRITINGS: Five Novelists of the Progressive Era, Columbia University Press, 1965. Contributor to scholarly journals.

WORK IN PROGRESS: A biography of the American novelist-politician, Winston Churchill.

*   *   *

SCHOENSTEIN, Ralph 1933-

PERSONAL: Last syllable of surname rhymes with "keen"; born May 29, 1933, in New York, N.Y.; son of Paul and Miriam (Stahl) Schoenstein; married Judy Lois Greenspan, January 11, 1959; children: Jill Beth, Eve Lynn. *Education:* Hamilton College, student, 1949-51; Columbia University, A.B., 1953. *Home:* 164 Clover Lane, Princeton, N.J. 08540. *Agent:* Phyllis Jackson, Ashley-Steiner-Famous Artists, Inc., 555 Madison Ave., New York, N.Y. 10022.

CAREER: DuMont Television Network, New York, N.Y., writer-producer, 1955-56; *American Weekly*, New York, N.Y., staff writer, 1956-59; writer of humorous column, "Doubletake," for Newhouse Newspapers, Long Island City, N.Y., 1959-61, for *New York Journal-American*, New York, N.Y., 1962—; free-lance writer. Moderator of "Family Living," public service radio discussion show on National Broadcasting Co. network; performer of oral essays for National Broadcasting Co., and Columbia Broadcasting System. *Military service:* U.S. Army, 1953-55. *Member:* American Federation of Television and Radio Artists, Sierra Club. *Awards, honors:* Grantland Rice Memorial Award (Doubleday & Co.) for non-fiction sports story, for "A Giant Fan's Lament," published in *Sport*, 1962.

WRITINGS: The Block, Random House, 1960; *Time Lurches On*, Doubleday, 1965; *With T-Shirts and Beer Mugs for All*, Prentice-Hall, 1967; *My Year In the White House Doghouse*, David White, 1969; *Little Spiro*, Morrow, 1970; *I Hear America Mating*, St. Martin's, 1972; *Wasted on the Young*, Bobbs-Merrill, 1974; *Booze Book*, Playboy Press, 1974. Contributor of humorous essays to anthologies: *The Phoenix Nest*, Doubleday; *The Take Along Treasury*, Doubleday; *The Best of the Diners' Club Magazine*, Doubleday; *Grantland Rice Award Prize Sports Stories*, Doubleday; *Focus*, Houghton. Contributor of humerous articles to periodicals, including *Saturday Eve-*

ning Post, McCall's, Pageant, Saturday Review, and *Cosmopolitan.*

WORK IN PROGRESS: A comic novel and a musical play.

SIDELIGHTS: Schoenstein had six articles simultaneously accepted by national magazines. He speaks Spanish fluently. *Avocational interests:* Playing the piano, touch football, and tennis.

* * *

SCHOSBERG, Paul A. 1938-
(Paul Allyn)

PERSONAL: Born April 6, 1938, in New York, N.Y.; son of Eugene Louis and Thelma (Siegel) Schosberg; married Jane Mindlin, December 21, 1958; children: Jill Ernestine, Richard Eugene. *Education:* Middlebury College, A.B., 1959; Columbia University, law student, 1959-60. *Home:* 5142 Nebraska Ave. N.W., Washington, D.C.

CAREER: Reporter Dispatch, White Plains, N.Y., reporter, 1960-61, night editor, 1961-62, bureau manager, 1962-64; administrative assistant to U.S. congressman from New York, Richard L. Ottinger, 1965—.

WRITINGS: (Under pseudonym Paul Allyn, with Joseph Greene) *See How They Run*, Chilton, 1964.

WORK IN PROGRESS: A television series about politics, based on *See How They Run.*

AVOCATIONAL INTERESTS: Breeding, training, and exhibiting German shepherd dogs.†

* * *

SCHOTTLAND, Charles Irwin 1906-

PERSONAL: Born October 29, 1906, in Chicago, Ill.; son of Harry (a tailor) and Millie (Lustberg) Schottland; married Edna L. Greenberg, June 7, 1931; children: Richard Roy, Mary Elizabeth (deceased). *Education:* University of California, Los Angeles, A.B., 1927; University of Southern California, law student, 1929-33. *Politics:* Democrat. *Home:* 61 Fairgreen Pl., Chestnut Hill, Mass. 02167. *Office:* Heller School, Brandeis University, Waltham, Mass.

CAREER: Admitted to California bar, 1933. California Relief Administration, administrator, 1933-36; Federation of Jewish Welfare Organizations, Los Angeles, Calif., executive director, 1936-41; U.S. Department of Labor, Washington, D.C., assistant chief of Children's Bureau, 1941-42; private practice of law, Los Angeles, Calif., 1948-50; California Department of Social Welfare, Sacramento, director, 1950-54; U.S. Department of Health, Education and Welfare, Washington, D.C., Commissioner of Social Security, 1954-59; Brandeis University, Waltham, Mass., dean of Graduate School for Advanced Studies in Social Welfare, 1959-70, president, 1970-72, professor of law and social welfare in Heller School, 1972—. Lecturer, University of California, Los Angeles, 1949-54; member of board of directors, Microdot, Inc. *Military service:* U.S. Army, 1942-46; became lieutenant colonel; received Bronze Star, and decorations from Greece, Netherlands, Poland, Czechoslovakia, and France for services to their nations. *Member:* National Association of Social Workers (president, 1967-69), American Public Welfare Association, International Conference of Social Work (president, 1968-72), National Conference on Social Welfare (president, 1960). *Awards, honors:* Koshland Award of California Conference of Social Work as outstanding executive, 1954.

WRITINGS: (With Ewell T. Bartlett) *Federal Social Security: A Guide to Law and Procedure*, Joint Committee on Continuing Legal Education of American Law Institute and American Bar Association, 1959; *The Social Security Program in the United States*, Appleton, 1963, 2nd edition, 1970; (editor) *The Welfare State: Selected Essays*, Harper, 1967. Contributor of some one hundred articles to magazines.

* * *

SCHRAG, Peter 1931-

PERSONAL: Born July 24, 1931, in Karlsruhe, Germany; son of Otto (a businessman) and Judith (Haas) Schrag; married Jane Mowrer, June 9, 1953 (divorced, 1969); married Diane Diveky (a writer), May 24, 1969; children: Mitzi, Erin Andrew, David. *Education:* Amherst College, B.A., 1953; graduate study at Amherst College and University of Massachusetts, 1957-59. *Home:* 70 Palm Ave., San Francisco, Calif. 94118. *Agent:* Curtis Brown, Ltd., 60 East 56th St., New York, N.Y.

CAREER: El Paso Herald Post, El Paso, Tex., reporter, 1953-55; Amherst College, Amherst, Mass., assistant secretary, 1955-66, instructor in American studies, 1960-64; *Saturday Review*, New York, N.Y., associate education editor, 1966-68, executive editor, 1968-69; *Change Magazine*, New York, N.Y., editor, 1969-70; *Saturday Review*, contributing editor, 1970-73. Science Research Associates, Chicago, Ill., consultant, 1960-61. Member (elected) of Amherst Town Meeting, 1959—. Member, Committee on the Study of History. Consultant, U.S. Office of Education, U.S. Information Service. Lecturer, University of Massachusetts, 1970-72. *Awards, honors:* Guggenheim fellow, 1971-72; Professional Journalism fellow, Stanford University, 1973-74.

WRITINGS: (Editor) *The Ratification of the Constitution and the Bill of Rights*, Heath, 1964; *Voices in the Classroom—Public Schools and Public Attitudes*, Beacon, 1965; (editor) *The European Mind and the Discovery of a New World*, Heath, 1965; *Village School Downtown*, Beacon, 1967; *Out of Place in America*, Random House, 1970; *Decline of the WASP*, Simon & Schuster, 1972; *The End of the American Future*, Simon & Schuster, 1973; *Test of Loyalty*, Simon & Schuster, 1974.

Contributor to periodicals, including *Saturday Review, New Republic, Commonweal, Progressive, College Board Review*; also contributor to *New York Times Education Supplement, Nation*, and *Harpers.*

WORK IN PROGRESS: Currently engaged in research with wife, Diane Diveky, for book on psyche-social control of children (behavior modification, drugging, screening, testing of children "at risk").

SIDELIGHTS: Schrag speaks French and German. *Avocational interests:* Travel and sailing.

* * *

SCHRODER, Amund A. Schulze 1925-

PERSONAL: Born June 26, 1925, in Kragero, Norway; son of Amund and Karoline (Schulze) Schroder. *Education:* Oslo Handelsgymnasium, matriculation degree, 1944. *Religion:* Protestant. *Home:* Schives gt. 1 A, Oslo 2, Norway. *Office:* Norsk Rikskringkasting, Bj. Bjornsons pl. 1, Oslo, Norway.

CAREER: Vart Land (daily newspaper), Oslo, Norway, journalist, 1945-59; Norsk Rikskringkasting (Norwegian

Broadcasting Corp.), Oslo, Norway, announcer, 1959—. Author; scriptwriter for radio and television.

WRITINGS: Afrikafuglen, Gyldendal, 1955, translation by Evelyn Ramsden published as *The Bird That Got Left Behind*, Methuen, 1959; *Heia Olemann*, Gyldendal, 1957; *Olemann og Petter Vekkeklokke*, Gyldendal, 1958; *Snomannen, Kaffelars og andre viser*, Gyldendal, 1959; *Nils og Inger og Polly Papegoye*, Gyldendal, 1961; *Nils og Inger i tarnet*, Lutherstiftelsen, 1962; *Historien om juletreet*, Lutherstiftelsen, 1963. Author of about thirty radio and television plays for children's programs. Scriptwriter for special programs for small children and for educational broadcasting. Author and narrator of recording for children, "Historien om Glade jul" (The History of Silent Night).

WORK IN PROGRESS: A children's biography of Hans Christian Andersen.

SIDELIGHTS: Afrikafuglen has been translated into French, German, and Dutch.†

*   *   *

SCHULTZ, Edna Moore 1912-

PERSONAL: Born March 5, 1912, in Ellettsville, Ind.; daughter of Emerson E. and Anna M. (Hinshaw) Moore; married Charles S. Schultz (assistant chief of detectives, Buffalo, N.Y.); children: C. David, Nancy J. (Mrs. Raymond Morningstar), Janice E. (Mrs. Thomas J. Dalbo), Christine, Kathleen L. (deceased). *Education:* Attended public schools in Stinesville, Ind., and Buffalo, N.Y. *Politics:* Republican. *Religion:* Baptist. *Home:* 113 Zurbrick Rd., Depew, N.Y. 14043.

CAREER: One-time receptionist and typist in Buffalo, N.Y.; *Lancaster Enterprise* and *Depew Herald*, Lancaster, N.Y., feature writer, 1954—; broadcaster of regular poetry program, "Thoughts Along the Way," WDCX-FM, Buffalo, N.Y., 1964—. *Awards, honors:* First prize for light verse from Western New York Pen Women, for "Threading a Needle."

WRITINGS: Thoughts Along the Way (poetry), Rich & Bennett, Volume I, 1955, Volume II, 1959, Volume III, 1965, Volume IV, in press; *They Said Kathy Was Retarded*, Moody, 1963, published as *Kathy*, 1972; *Mother and Daughter Banquet Ideas*, Zondervan, 1969. Writer of poetry column, "Thoughts Along the Way," and about thirty poems for Lillenas Publishing Co.; also writer of pageants for Zondervan. Contributor of poems to *Ideals Magazine*, and articles to *Moody Monthly* and *Challenge*.

AVOCATIONAL INTERESTS: Sewing, cooking, travel, playing piano, church work.

*   *   *

SCHULZ, Clare Elmore 1924-

PERSONAL: Born April 12, 1924, in Lincoln, Neb.; daughter of Harry D. and L'Marie (Clare) Elmore; married William Gallagher Schulz, September 19, 1946; children: Eric Elmore, Douglas William, Stephanie Clare. *Education:* Washington University, St. Louis, Mo., B.F.A., 1946; University of Montana, M.Ed. Art, 1967. *Home address:* c/o U.N.D.P., P.O. Box 3041, Port Moresby, Papua, New Guinea.

WRITINGS: Peter, Anna, and the Little Lost Angel, Bruce, 1956; *Willi Weep, the Chimney Sweep*, Doubleday, 1964.

WORK IN PROGRESS: Kitsch Shoes; Ali Jalal and the Camels; Roro, the Atoll Cat; Number One Something.

*   *   *

SCHUMACHER, Alvin J. 1928-

PERSONAL: Born January 25, 1928, in Atchison, Kan.; son of Alvin B. (an insurance agent) and Agnes (Kramer) Schumacher; married Diane Boone, August 16, 1949; children: Michael, Gerald, Mark, Anne, Susan, James, Mary, Teresa. *Education:* Washburn University, A.B. and B.M., 1952; Kansas State Teachers College, M.S., 1953; Marquette University, Ed.D., 1968. *Religion:* Roman Catholic. *Home:* 7512 Fifth Ave., Kenosha, Wis. 53140.

CAREER: Topeka (Kan.) youth centers, executive director, 1951-54; Milwaukee (Wis.) public schools, elementary teacher, 1954-61, editorial assistant, 1961, supervisor of teacher personnel, 1961-67; Kenosha (Wis.) public schools, administrator of personnel services, 1967—. *Military service:* U.S. Navy, 1945-46; served in South Pacific. *Member:* American Association of School Personnel Administrators, Wisconsin Association of School Personnel Administrators.

WRITINGS: What Will I Be?, Bruce, 1957; *My Little Book of Feasts*, Bruce, 1958; *Thunder on Capitol Hill*, Bruce, 1964.

AVOCATIONAL INTERESTS: Church activities.

*   *   *

SCHUON, Karl Albert 1913-

PERSONAL: Born November 26, 1913, in Allentown, Pa.; son of Harold B. and Bessie M. (Weiler) Schuon; married Lucia Nelli (a teacher of guitar), October 6, 1950; children: Marshall, Joseph, Lucia, Marie. *Education:* Attended public schools in Allentown, Pa. *Politics:* Democrat. *Religion:* Lutheran. *Home:* 3846 Gallows Rd., Annandale, Va. 22003. *Office Address:* Box 1918, Quantico, Va. 22134.

CAREER: Leatherneck (Marine Corps magazine), Washington, D.C., managing editor, 1945—. *Military service:* U.S. Marine Corps, World War I.

WRITINGS: (With Earl Smith) *Marines and What They Do*, F. Watts, 1962; (with Philip N. Pierce) *John H. Glenn: Astronaut*, F. Watts, 1962; (editor) *The Leathernecks: An Anthology*, F. Watts, 1963; *Biographical Dictionary of the U.S. Marine Corps*, F. Watts, 1963; (with Ronald D. Lyons) *Servicewomen and What They Do*, F. Watts, 1964; *Biographical Dictionary of the U.S. Navy*, 1965; *The First Book of Acting*, F. Watts, 1965; *The First Book of Bowling*, F. Watts, 1966; *Home of the Commandants*, Leatherneck Association, 1966. Also author of short fiction pieces and articles.

WORK IN PROGRESS: Three books, *The First Book of Virginia, Encyclopedia of Virginia*, and *Directory of Government Agencies*, all for publication by F. Watts.

AVOCATIONAL INTERESTS: Fishing, opera, legitimate theater, playwriting, painting, bowling.†

*   *   *

SCHUR, Edwin M(ichael) 1930-

PERSONAL: Born October 18, 1930, in New York, N.Y.; son of Samuel John (an attorney) and Johanna (Bernhardt) Schur; married Joan Van Clute, December 20, 1953; children: Owen, David. *Education:* Williams College, A.B., 1952; Yale University, LL.B., 1955; New School for Social

Research, M.A., 1957; London School of Economics and Political Science, London, Ph.D., 1959. *Agent:* Virginia Rice, 301 East 66th St., New York, N.Y. 10021. *Office:* Department of Sociology, Tufts University, Medford, Mass.

CAREER: Wellesley College, Wellesley, Mass., instructor in sociology, 1959-61; Tufts University, Medford, Mass., 1961—, now associate professor of sociology. National Association for the Prevention of Addiction to Narcotics, member of advisory board. *Military service:* U.S. Army, 1955-57. *Member:* American Sociological Association, National Council on Family Relations, Society for the Study of Social Problems, Eastern Sociological Society.

WRITINGS: Narcotic Addiction in Britain and America: The Impact of Public Policy, Indiana University Press, 1962; (editor) *The Family and the Sexual Revolution: Selected Readings*, Indiana University Press, 1964; *Crimes Without Victims*, Prentice-Hall, 1965; *Law and Society: A Sociological View*, Random House, 1968; *Our Criminal Society: The Social and Legal Sources of Crime in America*, Prentice-Hall, 1969; *Labeling Deviant Behavior: Its Sociological Implications*, Harper, 1971; *Radical Nonintervention: Rethinking the Delinquency Problem*, Prentice-Hall, 1973; (with Hugo Bedau) *Victimless Crimes: Two Sides of a Controversy*, Spectrum Productions, 1974. Contributor of articles to *Nation, Journal of Criminal Law, Commentary, Dissent, Marriage and Family Living*, and other journals. Associate editor, *Social Problems* (journal of Society for the Study of Social Problems).†

* * *

SCHUSTER, Louis A. 1916-

PERSONAL: Born December 4, 1916, in Chicago, Ill.; son of George Nicholas (a storekeeper) and Susanna (Kayser) Schuster. *Education:* St. Mary's University, San Antonio, Tex., B.A., 1937; St. Louis University, M.A., 1945; Oxford University, B.A. 1954, M.A., 1957; University of Texas, Ph.D., 1962. *Home and office:* St. Mary's University, San Antonio, Tex. 78284.

CAREER: Roman Catholic brother, member of Society of Mary (Marianist); St. Mary's University, San Antonio, Tex., chairman of department of English, 1961-63, 1965-66, 1968-71. *Member:* Modern Language Association of America, Renaissance Society of America, National Council of Teachers of English, South-Central Renaissance Society (counselor, 1962-64; president, 1965), Texas Conference of Teachers of English (president, 1962), Malone Society. *Awards, honors:* Folger Shakespeare Library fellow, summer, 1956; Southern fellowship to Belgium, 1961; Henry Huntington Foundation research fellow, summer, 1964; postdoctoral fellowship, Yale University, summers, 1965-67, spring, 1968.

WRITINGS: (Translator, editor, and author of introduction) Nicolaus Vernulaeus, *Henry VIII, a Neo-Latin Drama*, University of Texas Press, 1964; *St. Thomas More's Confutation of Tyndale's Answer*, Volume III (in three parts), Yale University Press, 1973. Co-editor, "Catholic Author" series, 1945-47; editor, "Yale Series of St. Thomas More," 1963-73.

SIDELIGHTS: Schuster spent three years traveling and studying in Europe; he is competent in Latin, Italian, Spanish, French, and German. *Avocational interests:* Painting in watercolors, Renaissance Latin drama.

SCHWABER, Paul 1936-

PERSONAL: Born April 17, 1936, in Brooklyn, N.Y.; son of David (an accountant and lawyer) and Betty (Golding) Schwaber. *Education:* Wesleyan University, A.B., 1957, University of California, Berkeley, M.A., 1959; Columbia University, Ph.D., 1965. *Politics:* Liberal. *Religion:* Jewish. *Home:* 100 West 57th St., New York, N.Y.

CAREER: Columbia University, New York, N.Y., lecturer, 1960-64, associate in English, 1964-65; Wellesley College, Wellesley, Mass., instructor in English, 1965-66. *Member:* Modern Language Association of America, Phi Beta Kappa. *Awards, honors:* Woodrow Wilson fellowship, 1957-58.

WRITINGS: (Editor, with Erwin A. Glikes) *Of Poetry and Power: Poems Occasioned by the Presidency and by the Death of John F. Kennedy*, Basic Books, 1964. Contributor to *Criticism*.

WORK IN PROGRESS: The Style Book: A Guide to Writing Good Expository Prose, with Ronald P. Schreiber; *The Poetry of John Clare: A Critical Study.*†

* * *

SCHWARTZ, Alvin 1927-

PERSONAL: Born April 25, 1927, in Brooklyn, N.Y.; son of Harry (a taxi-driver) and Gussie (Younger) Schwartz; married Barbara Carmer (a teacher), August 7, 1954; children: John, Peter, Nancy, Elizabeth. *Education:* Attended City College (now City College of the City University of New York), 1944-45; Colby College, A.B., 1949; Northwestern University, M.S. in Journalism, 1951. *Politics:* Independent. *Home and office:* 50 Southern Way, Princeton, N.J. 08540. *Agent:* Marilyn Marlow, Curtis Brown Ltd., 60 East 56th St., New York, N.Y. 10022.

CAREER: Newspaper reporter, 1951-55; writer for nonprofit and commercial organizations, 1955-59; Opinion Research Corp., Princeton, N.J., director of communications, 1959-64; Rutgers University, New Brunswick, N.J., part-time teacher of English, 1962—; author, 1963—. Trustee, Joint Free Library of Princeton. Member of national council, Boy Scouts of America. *Military service:* U.S. Navy, 1945-46. *Member:* Authors League of America, Authors Guild. *Awards, honors:* Citation from *New York Times*, 1973, for *Tomfoolery*.

WRITINGS: A Parent's Guide to Children's Play and Recreation, Collier, 1963; *How to Fly a Kite, Catch a Fish, Grow a Flower*, Macmillan, 1965; *America's Exciting Cities*, Crowell, 1966; *The Night Workers* (juvenile), Dutton, 1966; *What Do You Think?*, Dutton, 1966; *The City and Its People* (juvenile), Dutton, 1967; *Museum*, Dutton, 1967; *The People's Choice*, Dutton, 1967; *To Be a Father*, Crown, 1968; *Old Cities and New Towns* (juvenile), Dutton, 1968; *The Rainy Day Book*, Simon & Schuster, 1969; *University*, Viking, 1969; *Going Camping*, Macmillan, 1969, revised edition, 1972; *A Twister of Twists, A Tangler of Tongues*, Lippincott, 1972; *Hobbies*, Simon & Schuster, 1972; *The Unions*, Viking, 1972; *Witcracks*, Lippincott, 1973; *Tomfoolery*, Lippincott, 1973; *Central City/Spread City* (juvenile), Macmillan, 1973; *Cross Your Fingers, Spit in Your Hat*, Lippincott, 1974.

WORK IN PROGRESS: Books for children dealing with American folklore and with social problems.

* * *

SCHWARTZ, Benjamin I. 1916-

PERSONAL: Born December 12, 1916, in Boston, Mass.;

son of Hyman and Jennie (Weinberger) Schwartz; married Bernice Cohen, July 5, 1947; children: Jonathan, Sara Ann. *Education:* Harvard University, A.B. (magna cum laude), 1938, A.M., 1940, A.M. (School of Education), 1948, Ph.D., 1950. *Home:* 3 Sedgwick Rd., Cambridge, Mass. 02138. *Office:* East Asian Research Center, 1737 Cambridge St., Cambridge, Mass.

CAREER: Harvard University, Cambridge, Mass., instructor in history and government, and in the Russian Research Center, 1950-51, assistant professor, 1951-56, associate professor, 1956-60, professor of history and government, 1960-61, with East Asian Research Center, 1961-74; Oxford University, Oxford, England, Eastman Professor, 1974—. *Military service:* U.S. Army, cryptanalyst in Intelligence Branch, Signal Corps, 1942-46, newspaper censorship officer in Japan, 1946-47; became captain. *Awards, honors:* Guggenheim fellow, 1953-54.

WRITINGS: Communism in China and the Rise of Mao, Harvard University Press, 1951; (with Conrad Brandt and J. K. Fairbank) *A Documentary History of Chinese Communism,* Harvard University Press, 1952; (contributor) H. Boorman, editor, *Moscow-Peking Axis,* Council on Foreign Relations, 1957; (author of foreword) *Intellectural Trends in the Ch'ing Period,* translated by Immanuel Hsu, Harvard University Press, 1957; (contributor) Fairbank, editor, *Chinese Thought and Institutions,* University of Chicago Press, 1957; (contributor) D. Nivison, editor, *Confucianism in Action,* Stanford University Press, 1959.

(Contributor) *The Russian Intelligentsia,* Columbia University Press, 1961; *In Search of Wealth and Power: Yen Fu and the West,* Belknap Press of Harvard University Press, 1964; *Chinese Communism and the Rise of Mao,* Harper, 1967; *Communism and China: Ideology in Flux,* Harvard University Press, 1968; (editor) *Reflections on the May Fourth Movement,* Harvard University, 1972. Contributor of articles and reviews to *New Republic, Saturday Review, Nation,* and other journals.

WORK IN PROGRESS: A book on the intellectual development of China in the twentieth century.†

*   *   *

SCHWARTZ, Charles W(alsh)   1914-

PERSONAL: Born June 2, 1914, in St. Louis, Mo.; son of Frederick O. (a physician) and Clara E. (Walsh) Schwartz; married Elizabeth Reeder (a biologist with Missouri Conservation Commission), December 22, 1938; children: Barbara (Mrs. Michael Miller), Carl Bruce, John Curtis. *Education:* University of Missouri, A.B., 1938, A.M., 1940. *Home:* 131 Forest Hill, Jefferson City, Mo.

CAREER: Missouri Conservation Commission, Jefferson City, biologist and wildlife photographer, 1940-45; Board of Agriculture and Forestry, Hawaii, biologist, 1946-47; Missouri Conservation Commission, biologist and wildlife photographer, 1948—. *Member:* American Ornithologists' Union, Wilson Ornithological Society, American Society of Mammalogists, Wildlife Society, Phi Beta Kappa. *Awards, honors:* Citations from Wildlife Society for *The Game Birds of Hawaii* as best publication in wildlife management and ecology, 1949-50, and from American Association for Conservation Information for *The Wild Mammals of Missouri* as outstanding wildlife book of 1959; awards for motion pictures include CONI Grand Medal at International Sports Film Festival, Cortina d'Ampezzo, Italy, for "Bobwhite Through the Year," and American Association for Conservation Information award for "The Story of the

Mourning Dove" as best North American wildlife movie, 1959.

WRITINGS: The Prairie Chicken in Missouri, Missouri Conservation Commission, 1945; (with wife, Elizabeth R. Schwartz), *The Game Birds of Hawaii* [Honolulu], 1949; (with Elizabeth Schwartz) *Cottontail Rabbit,* Holiday House, 1957; (with Elizabeth Schwartz) *Bobwhite,* Holiday House, 1959; (with Elizabeth Schwartz) *The Wild Mammals of Missouri,* Missouri Conservation Commission and University of Missouri Press, 1959; (with Elizabeth Schwartz) *Bobwhite From Egg to Chick to Egg,* Holiday House, 1959; (with Elizabeth Schwartz) *When Animal Are Babies,* Holiday House, 1964; (illustrator) Aldo Leopold, *A Sand County Almanac,* enlarged edition, Oxford University Press, 1966; (with Elizabeth Schwartz) *When Water Animals Are Babies,* Holiday House, 1970. Contributor of articles to periodicals. Writer and producer of wildlife films, including "Bobwhite Through the Year," "The Story of the Mourning Dove," and "This is the Mallard."†

*   *   *

SCHWARTZ, Elizabeth Reeder   1912-

PERSONAL: Born September 13, 1912, in Columbus, Ohio; daughter of Charles Wells (a professor) and Lydia (Morrow) Reeder; married Charles Walsh Schwartz (a biologist), December 22, 1938; children: Barbara Reeder (Mrs. Michael L. Miller), Carl Bruce, John Curtis. *Education:* Ohio State University, A.B., 1933; Columbia University, A.M., 1934; University of Missouri, Ph.D., 1938. *Home:* Route 1, Jefferson City, Mo. 65101.

CAREER: University of Missouri, Columbia, instructor in zoology, 1934-38; Sweet Briar College, Sweet Briar, Va., instructor in zoology, 1938-39; Stephens College, Columbia, Mo., instructor in biology, 1939-40; Board of Agriculture and Forestry, Honolulu, Hawaii, biologist, 1946-48; Missouri Conservation Commission, Jefferson City, biologist, 1950—. Wildlife photographer, and producer with husband of films on wildlife. *Member:* Phi Beta Kappa, Sigma Xi, Mortar Board, Alpha Phi. *Awards, honors:* North American Wildlife Society award, 1949-50; co-winner of American Association for Conservation Information award for outstanding wildlife book of the year, 1960, for *The Wild Mammals of Missouri*; other awards for motion pictures produced in collaboration with husband, including "Cottontail," "The Story of the Mourning Dove," and "This is the Mallard."

WRITINGS: Cottontail Rabbit, Holiday, 1957; (with husband, Charles W. Schwartz) *The Wild Mammals of Missouri,* University of Missouri Press, 1959; *Bobwhite from Egg to Chick to Egg,* Holiday, 1959; *When Animals Are Babies,* Holiday, 1964; *When Water Animals Are Babies,* Holiday, 1970; *When Flying Animals Are Babies,* Holiday, 1974. Contributor to popular magazines and scientific journals.

*   *   *

SCHWARTZ, Elliott S.   1936-

PERSONAL: Born January 19, 1936, in Brooklyn, N.Y.; son of Nathan (a physician) and Rose (Shelling) Schwartz; married Dorothy Feldman (an artist and instructor in art at University of Maine), June 26, 1960. *Education:* Columbia University, A.B., 1957, M.A., 1958, Ed.D., 1962; studied composition, piano, and theory privately. *Home:* 5 Atwood Lane, Brunswick, Me. 04011.

CAREER: University of Massachusetts, Amherst, instructor in music, 1960-64; Bowdoin College, Brunswick, Me., assistant professor, 1964-70; associate professor of music, 1970—. Visiting professor, Trinity College of Music, 1967, and University of California, Santa Barbara, 1970, 1974. Composer of symphonic, electronic, and chamber music works. *Member:* National Association for American Composers and Conductors, Music Teachers National Association, American Society of Composers, Authors and Publishers, American Music Center, American Society of University Composers (director, Region I). *Awards, honors:* MacDowell Colony fellowship, 1964 and 1965; American Society of Composers, Authors and Publishers Award, 1965; Ford Foundation travel grants, 1969, 1972; Gaudeamus Foundation Prize, 1970; National Endowment for the Arts grant, 1974.

WRITINGS: The Symphonies of Ralph Vaughan Williams, University of Massachusetts Press, 1965; (co-editor) *Contemporary Composers on Contemporary Music,* Holt, 1967; *Electronic Music: A Listener's Guide,* Praeger, 1973. Musical works published by General Music, Carl Fischer, Alexander Broude, Media Press, Bowdoin College Music Press. Contributor to *Yale Journal of Music Theory, Musical Quarterly, Massachusetts Review, Notes, Music and Musicians, Natida Musik, The Composer.*

WORK IN PROGRESS: Composing a large work for symphony orchestra; and an electronic work for a ballet production.

AVOCATIONAL INTERESTS: All sports, chess, travel, unusual cuisine, films, and the theater.

BIOGRAPHICAL/CRITICAL SOURCES: ASCAP Newsletter, fall, 1965; *Carl Fischer Newsletter,* No. 1, 1972.

*   *   *

SCHWARTZ, Eugene M.   1927-

PERSONAL: Born March 18, 1927, in Butte, Mont., son of Morris H. (a retailer) and Alice (Meyer) Schwartz; married Barbara Glicksman (an interior designer), May 6, 1951; children: Michael Holden. *Education:* University of Washington, Seattle, B.A., 1948; advanced study at New School for Social Research and Columbia University. *Religion:* Jewish. *Home:* 1160 Park Ave., New York, N.Y. 10028. *Office:* 200 Madison Ave., New York, N.Y. 10016.

CAREER: Eldorado Sales Corp., New York, N.Y., president, 1955-71; Certified Lists, Inc., New York, N.Y., president, 1956-73; Executive Research Institute, Inc., New York, N.Y., president, 1961—; Information, Inc., New York, N.Y., president, 1964-73, Mega-Man, Inc., consultant, 1973. Advertising and publishing consultant. New York University, guest lecturer in advertising. *Military service:* U.S. Navy, 1945-46.

WRITINGS: (With James Cato) *How to Repair Your Own TV Set,* Homecrafts, Inc., 1952; (with Ed Almquist) *How to Double the Performance of Your Car,* Eugene Stevens, Inc., 1954; *How to Double Your Child's Grades in School,* Executive Research, Inc., 1964; *Breakthrough Advertising,* Prentice-Hall, 1965; *How to Double Your Power to Learn,* Information, Inc., 1960.

WORK IN PROGRESS: Beyond Grammar; *Logical English*; *The Trojan Women.*

AVOCATIONAL INTERESTS: Travel, art, education.

SCHWARZ, Walter   1930-

PERSONAL: Born May 22, 1930, in Vienna, Austria; son of Theodor (a businessman) and Louise (Fischbein) Schwarz; married Dorothy Elisabeth Morgan, June 15, 1956; children: Daniella Habie, Benjamin Peter. *Education:* Queen's College, Oxford, B.A. (honors), 1951. *Home:* 27, The Park, London, N.W. 11, England. *Office: The Guardian,* 192 Gray's Inn Road, London W.C.1., England.

CAREER: Evening Standard, London, England, staff writer, 1953-56; *Jewish Observer and Middle East Review,* London, England, assistant editor, 1956-57; *West Africa,* London, England, assistant editor, 1959-63; African Universities Press, Lagos, Nigeria, manager, 1963-64; *The Guardian,* London, England, leader-writer, 1966—. West Africa correspondent for *Observer, Guardian,* British Broadcasting Corp., and *Economist. Military service:* British Army, 1952-53; served in Malaya; became lieutenant.

WRITINGS: The Arabs in Israel, Faber, 1959; *Nigeria,* Praeger, 1968.†

*   *   *

SCHWARZENBERGER, Georg   1908-

PERSONAL: Born May 20, 1908, in Heilbronn, Baden-Wuerttemberg, Germany; son of Ludwig and Ferry (Riesz) Schwarzenberger; married Suse Schwarz, August 30, 1931; children: Rolph Ludwig Edward. *Education:* University of Tubingen, Dr. Jr., 1930; University of London, Ph.D., 1936. *Home:* 4 Bowers Way, Harpenden, Hertfordshire, England. *Office:* Faculty of Laws, University College, Gower Street, London, W.C.1, England.

CAREER: London Institute of World Affairs (formerly New Commonwealth Institute), London, England, secretary, 1934-43, director, 1943—; University of London, London, England, lecturer in international law and relations at University College, 1938-45, sub-dean and tutor, Faculty of Laws of University College, 1942-49, vice-dean of Faculty of Laws, 1949-55, 1963-65, dean, 1965-67, university reader in international law, 1945-62, professor, 1962—. Barrister-at-law, Gray's Inn, 1955—. Visiting professor at law schools in Canada, and lecturer for Canadian Institute of International Affairs, 1958; lecturer at North Atlantic Treaty Organization Defense College, Paris, France, 1958, and at universities in several European, African, and Asian countries. *Member:* International Law Association (member of executive council, 1957-62; rapporteur, committee on the charter of the United Nations, 1954-62), Institute of Advanced Legal Studies (London).

WRITINGS: Das Voelkerbunds-Mandat fuer Palaestina (title means "The League Mandate for Palestine"), F. Enke, 1929; *Die Kreuger-Anleihen* (title means "The Kreuger Loans"), Duncker & Humblot, 1931; *Die Internationalen Banken fuer Zahlungsausgleich und Agrarkredite* (title means "The International Banks for Settlement and Agrarian Credits"), Junker & Dunnhaupt, 1932; *Die Verfassung der spanischen Republik* (title means "The Constitution of the Spanish Republic"), Graefe und Unzer, 1933; *William Ladd; An Examination of the American Proposal for an International Equity Tribunal,* Constable, 1935, 2nd edition, 1936; *The League of Nations and World Order,* Constable, 1936; (with G. W. Keeton) *Making International Law Work,* Peace Book, 1939, 2nd edition, Universal Distributors, 1946.

Power Politics: An Introduction to the Study of Interna-

tional Relations and Post-War Planning, J. Cape, 1941, 3rd edition, Stevens, 1964; *International Law and Totalitarian Lawlessness*, J. Cape, 1943; *International Law*, Stevens, Volume I: *International Law as Applied by International Courts and Tribunals*, 1945, 3rd edition, 1957, Volume II, 1968, Volume III, 1975; *A Manual of International Law*, Stevens, 1947, 6th edition, two volumes, 1975; (editor with Keeton) *Jeremy Bentham and the Law* (symposium), Stevens, 1948; *The Fundamental Principles of International Law*, Haueg Academy of International Law, 1955; *The Legality of Nuclear Weapons*, Stevens, 1958.

The Frontiers of International Law, Stevens, 1962; (editor with Keeton) *English Law and the Common Market*, Stevens, 1963; *The Inductive Approach to International Law*, Praeger, 1965; (editor with R. H. Code Holland) *Law, Justice, and Equity: Essays in Tribute to G. W. Keeton*, Pitman, 1967; *Foreign Investments and International Law*, Stevens, 1969; *Economic World Order? A Basic Problem of International Economic Law* (Melland Schill Lectures), Manchester University Press, 1970; *International Law and Order*, Stevens, 1971.

Editor with G. W. Keeton: "The Library of World Affairs," 1946; *Yearbook of World Affairs*, Universal Distributors, 1947, Stevens, 1948-49, Praeger, 1952—; *Current Legal Problems*, Stevens, annually, 1948—. Contributor to *Problems of War and Peace* (Grotius Society, London), *American Journal of International Law*, and to other law journals.

AVOCATIONAL INTERESTS: Swimming, gardening.

* * *

SCHWEIZER (-HANHART), Eduard 1913-

PERSONAL: Surname is pronounced *Schvietz*-er, second syllable to rhyme with "eye"; born April 18, 1913, in Basel, Switzerland; son of Eduard (a lawyer) and Hedwig (Boehni) Schweizer; married Elisabeth Hanhart (a teacher), July 8, 1940; children: Elisabeth, Ruth, Eva-Maria, Andreas. *Education:* Attended Universities of Basel, Marbur, and Zurich, 1932-36, Verbi Divini Minister, 1936; University of Basel, Dr.Theol., 1938. *Home:* 8 Pilgerweg, Zurich 44, Switzerland.

CAREER: Reformed Church of Switzerland, minister in Nesslau, St. Gallen, 1938-47; University of Mainz, Mainz, Germany, professor of New Testament, 1946-49; University of Zurich, Zurich, Switzerland, professor of New Testament, 1949—, rector (president), 1964-66. Summer professor at University of Bonn, 1949; guest lecturer at Colgate Rochester Divinity School, 1959-60, 1962, at San Francisco Theological Seminary, 1964, 1967, at Melbourne University (Australia), 1969, 1971. *Awards, honors:* Dr.theol., University of Mainz, 1950; D.D., University of St. Andrews, 1963; Dr.theol., University of Vienna, 1972.

WRITINGS: Ego Eimi, Vandenhoeck-Ruprecht, 1939, 2nd edition, 1965; *Der erste Petrusbrief*, Zwingli-Verlag, 1942, enlarged edition, 1949; *Das Leben des Herrn in der Gemeinde und ihren Diensten*, Zwingli-Verlag, 1946; *Gemeinde nach dem Neuen Testament*, Evangelischer Verlag, 1949.

Geist und Gemeinde in Neuen Testament und heute, Kaiser, 1952; *Erniedrigung und Erhoehung bei Jesus und seinen Nachfolgern*, Zwingli-Verlag, 1955, enlarged edition, 1962 (English translation, *Lordship and Discipleship*, S.C.M Press, 1960); *Gemeinde und Gemeindeordnung im Neuen Testament*, Zwingli-Verlag, 1959, 2nd edition, 1962 (English translation, *Church Order in the New Testament*, S.C.M. Press, 1961, 2nd edition, 1963); *Spirit of God*, A. & C. Black, 1960; *Neotestamentica*, Zwingli-Verlag, 1963; *The Church as the Body of Christ*, John Knox, 1964; *Jesus Christus*, Siebenstern-Verlag, 1968; *Neves Testament und Vertige Verkuendgung*, Neukirchner Verlag, 1969; *Beitrage zur Theologie des Neuen Testaments*, Theological Verlag, 1970; *God's Inescapable Nearness*, [Waco, Texas], 1971; *Gott versohnt*, Kreuz-Verlag, 1971; *Das Evangelium nach Markus, nach Matthaus*, Gottingen, 1967 and 1973.

Contributor of articles to *Kittel Theologisches Woerterbuch*, and essays to English and German periodicals. Co-editor, *Evangelische Theologie*; editor, *Evang-kath, Kommentar zum Neuen Testament*, Neukirchner Verlag.

WORK IN PROGRESS: A commentary on *Matthew*, to be published by Stuttgarten Bibelstudien.

* * *

SCOTT, Tirsa Saavedra 1920-

PERSONAL: Born June 21, 1920, in Guarare, Republic of Panama; became U.S. citizen; daughter of Jose del Carmen (a businessman) and Maria (Espino) Saavedra; married David Winfield Scott (director of National Collection of Fine Arts), July 10, 1947; children: Tirsa Margaret, Edith Elizabeth. *Education:* Pomona College, B.A., 1947; Claremont Graduate School, California teaching credential, 1960. *Home:* 3016 Cortland Pl. N.W., Washington, D.C.

CAREER: Claremont (Calif.) Unified School District, director of Spanish program for elementary schools, 1960-62; La Verne College, La Verne Calif., and Los Angeles State College of Applied Arts and Sciences (now California State University, Los Angeles), teacher of foreign language methodology, 1962-63. Consultant on foreign language teaching in elementary schools for the state of California. *Member:* Modern Language Association of Southern California.

WRITINGS: Somos Amigos, Ginn, 1963, manual, 1964; *Como se dice?*, with teachers' manual, Ginn, 1963; (with Annette Leblanc) *Nous sommes amis*, Ginn, 1963.

SIDELIGHTS: Tirsa Scott has traveled extensively in Europe and Latin America.†

* * *

SEAGOE, May V(iolet) 1906-

PERSONAL: Born February 17, 1906, in Pomona, Calif.; daughter of George Jacob and Ada (Phillips) Seagoe; children: Brent, Amy. *Education:* University of California, Los Angeles, B.Ed., 1929; Stanford University, M.A., 1931, Ph.D., 1934.

CAREER: Los Angeles, Calif., city and county public schools, teacher, 1925-28, counselor, 1928-31, special adviser, 1931-34; University of California, Los Angeles, beginning, 1934, as instructor, became professor of educational psychology, 1946, became assistant dean of academic affairs, School of Education, 1958, now retired. Diplomate of American Board of Examiners in Professional Psychology. Consultant to publishers; member of California State Advisory Commission for the Gifted, 1958-61. *Member:* American Psychological Association (president of division of school psychologists, 1958-59), Pi Lambda Theta (president, 1943-47). *Awards, honors:* Pi Lambda Theta fellowship; Distinguished Service Award of Association for the Gifted.

WRITINGS: A Teacher's Guide to the Learning Process, W. C. Brown, 1961; Yesterday Was Tuesday, All Day and All Night, Little, Brown, 1964; Learning Process and School Practice, Chandler Publishing, 1970. Contributor of more than two hundred articles to professional journals, and book reviews to Los Angeles Times.

WORK IN PROGRESS: A biography of Lewis M. Terman.

* * *

SEALTS, Merton M(iller), Jr. 1915-

PERSONAL: Born December 8, 1915, in Lima, Ohio; son of Merton Miller (a wholesale grocer) and Daisy (Hathaway) Sealts; married Ruth Louise Mackenzie, November 17, 1942. Education: College of Wooster, B.A. (honors), 1937; Yale University, Ph.D., 1942. Office: Department of English, University of Wisconsin, Madison, Wis. 53706.

CAREER: University of Missouri, Columbia, instructor in English, 1941-42; Wellesley College, Wellesley, Mass., instructor in English, 1946-48; Lawrence University, Appleton, Wis., assistant professor, 1948-51, associate professor, 1951-58, professor of English, 1958-65; University of Wisconsin, Madison, professor of English, 1965—. Military service: U.S. Army Air Forces, 1942-46; served in Brazil and India; became major; received Bronze Star. Member: Modern Language Association of America, National Council of Teachers of English, American Studies Association, American Association of University Professors, Emerson Society, Melville Society (president, 1953), Thoreau Society, Phi Beta Kappa. Awards, honors: Ford Foundation Fund for the Advancement of Education fellowship, 1953-54; John Simon Guggenheim Memorial Foundation fellowship, 1962-63; Edward and Rosa Uhrig Memorial Award for excellent teaching, 1965; American Council of Learned Societies grant-in-aid, 1970; National Endowment for the Humanities senior fellowship, 1975.

WRITINGS: Melville as Lecturer, Harvard University Press, 1957; (editor with Harrison Hayford) Herman Melville, Billy Budd, Sailor, University of Chicago Press, 1962; (editor) The Journals and Miscellaneous Notebooks of Ralph Waldo Emerson, Belknap Press, Volume V, 1965, Volume X, 1973; Melville's Reading: A Check-List of Books Owned and Borrowed, University of Wisconsin Press, 1966; (contributor) Max F. Schulz, editor, Essays in American and English Literature Presented to Bruce Robert McElderry, Jr., Ohio University Press, 1967; (editor with Alfred R. Ferguson) Emerson's "Nature": Origin, Growth, Meaning, Dodd, 1969; (contributor) Ray B. Browne and Donald Pizer, editors, Themes and Directions in American Literature: Essays in Honor of Leon Howard, Purdue University Studies, 1969; The Early Lives of Melville: Nineteenth-Century Biographical Sketches and Their Authors, University of Wisconsin Press, 1974. Contributor to American Literary Scholarship: Annual, for Duke University Press, 1967-73; also contributor to American Literature, Harvard Library Bulletin, New England Quarterly, PMLA, and other journals in field. Member of editorial board, American Quarterly, 1965-68.

WORK IN PROGRESS: A book, tentatively entitled Emerson on the Scholar; editing The Piazza Tales and Other Prose Pieces, 1839-1860, for the Northwestern-Newberry edition of The Writings of Herman Melville.

SEARLS, Henry Hunt, Jr. 1922-
(Hank Searls)

PERSONAL: Born August 10, 1922, in San Francisco, Calif.; son of Henry Hunt Searls; married Berna Ann Cooper; children: Courtney, Henry, Peter. Education: University of California, Berkeley, student, 1940; U.S. Naval Academy, B.S., 1944. Home and office: 33634 West Pacific Coast Hwy., Malibu, Calif. Agent: Scott Meredith Literary Agency, Inc., 580 Fifth Ave., New York, N.Y. 10036.

CAREER: U.S. Navy, 1941-54, became lieutenant commander; writer for Hughes Aircraft, Culver City, Calif., 1955-56, Douglas Aircraft, Santa Monica, Calif., 1956-57, Warner Brothers, Burbank, Calif., 1959; free-lance writer, 1959—. Member: Authors League of America, Writers Guild of America (West).

WRITINGS—All under name Hank Searls: The Big X, Harper, 1959; The Crowded Sky, Harper, 1960; Astronaut, Pocket Books, 1962; Pilgrim Project, McGraw, 1964; The Hero Ship, World Publishing, 1969; The Lost Prince: Young Joe, the Forgotten Kennedy, World Publishing, 1969; Pentagon, Geis, 1971.

AVOCATIONAL INTERESTS: Sailing, skiing, and skin diving.†

* * *

SEAT, William R(obert), Jr. 1920-

PERSONAL: Born November 9, 1920, in Lexington, Miss.; son of William R. (a Baptist minister) and Elizabeth (Rayner) Seat. Education: DePauw University, B.A., 1943; University of Chicago, M.A., 1949; Indiana University, Ph.D., 1957. Religion: Baptist. Office: Northern Illinois University, DeKalb, Ill. 60115.

CAREER: High school teacher of English in Glendale, Ind., 1946-47; DePauw University, Greencastle, Ind., instructor in English, 1949-50; Northern Illinois University, DeKalb, assistant professor, 1954-58, associate professor, 1958-61, professor of English, 1961—, chairman of department, 1974—. Conductor of students' classical tour in Europe, summer, 1963, 1969, 1971-72. Military service: U.S. Army Air Forces, pilot, 1943-45; became first lieutenant; received Air Medal. Member: National Council of Teachers of English, Modern Language Association of America, American Association of University Professors, Sigma Chi.

WRITINGS—All with Paul S. Burtness and Warren U. Ober: The University Reader, American Book Co., 1960; The Enigma of Poe, Heath, 1960; The Close Reading of Factual Prose, Row, Peterson & Co., 1962; Young Coleridge, Heath, 1963; The Contemporary University Reader, American Book Co., 1963; The Strategy of Prose, Van Nostrand, 1970.

WORK IN PROGRESS: A college freshman handbook; a book on Harriet Martineau in America.

* * *

SEEBER, Edward Derbyshire 1904-

PERSONAL: Born December 17, 1904, in Rochester, N.Y.; son of Edward J. (a businessman) and Sarah Carolyn (Gulick) Seeber; married Louise Combes, 1928; children: John W., Elizabeth C., Gilbert F. E. Education: Oberlin College, B.A., 1927; University of Rochester, M.A., 1931; Johns Hopkins University, Ph.D., 1934. Home: 506 Ballantine Rd., Bloomington, Ind. 47401.

CAREER: Instructor in French at Oberlin College, Oberlin, Ohio, 1929-30, and University of Rochester, Rochester, N.Y., 1930-31; Indiana University, Bloomington, associate professor, 1938-46, professor of French, 1946-67, professor emeritus, 1967—, chairman of graduate committee, comparative literature program. *Member:* Modern Language Association of America, American Association of Teachers of French, Academie des Sciences, Lettres et Beaux-Arts de Marseille (corresponding member), Rochester Historical Society, Phi Beta Kappa.

WRITINGS: Anti-Slavery Opinion in France during the Second Half of the Eighteenth Century, Johns Hopkins Press, 1937; (editor) *Choix de pieces huguenotes (1685-1756), publiees d'apres les manuscrits originaux recueillis par Alexandre Crottet*, Indiana University Press, 1942; (editor with Henry H. H. Remak) *Oeuvres de Charles-Michel Campion, poete marseillais du dix-huitieme siecle*, Indiana University Press, 1945.

(Contributor) H. J. Meessen, editor, *Goethe Bicentennial Studies*, Indiana University Press, 1950; (contributor) D. C. Cabeen, editor, *A Critical Bibliography of French Literature*, Vol. IV, Syracuse University Press, 1951, supplement, 1968; (translator) Edouard de Montule, *Travels in America, 1816-1817*, Indiana University Press, 1951; (translator) *On the Threshold of Liberty: Journal of a Frenchman's Tour of the American Colonies in 1777*, Indiana University Press, 1959; (contributor) Newton P. Stallknecht and Horst Frenz, editors, *Comparative Literature: Method and Perspective*, Southern Illinois University Press, 1961, revised edition, 1971; *A Style Manual for Students*, Indiana University Press, 1964, 2nd edition, revised, 1967; *A Style Manual for Authors*, Indiana University Press, 1965.

Contributor of more than twenty articles to language and other learned journals. Former editor of Indiana University "Humanities Series." Member of editorial committee, *Yearbook of Comparative and General Literature*.

*   *   *

SEGAL, Lore (Groszmann)   1928-

PERSONAL: Born March 8, 1928, in Vienna, Austria; daughter of Ignatz (an accountant) and Franzi (Stern) Groszmann; married David I. Segal (an editor), November 3, 1961. *Education:* Bedford College, University of London, B.A. (honors), 1948. *Religion:* Jewish. *Home:* 280 Riverside Dr., New York, N.Y. *Agent:* Lynn Nesbit, International Famous Agency, 1301 Avenue of the Americas, New York, N.Y.

CAREER: Writer. Taught English in the Dominican Republic for three years. Visiting professor, Bennington College, spring, 1973, Princeton University, spring, 1974; presently assistant professor of creative writing, Columbia University. *Awards, honors:* Guggenheim fellowship in creative writing, 1965-66; National Council of the Arts and Humanities grant, 1967-68; C.A.P.S. grant, 1972-73.

WRITINGS: Other People's Houses (autobiography), Harcourt, 1964; (translator with W. D. Snodgrass) Christian Morgenstern, *Gallows Songs*, University of Michigan Press, 1967; *Tell Me a Mitzi*, Farrar, Straus, 1970; *All the Way Home*, Farrar, Straus, 1973; (translator with Randall Jarrell) Wilhelm and Jacob Grimm, *The Juniper Tree and Other Tales*, Farrar, Straus, 1973. Contributor of short stories to *New Yorker, Saturday Evening Post, New Republic, Epoch, Commentary*, and other periodicals.

WORK IN PROGRESS: A novel, *Lucinella, N.Y.*

SIDELIGHTS: George A. Woods commented in reference to *Tell Me a Mitzi:* "Lore Segal's stories reflect the warmth and naturalness of family life with gentle mirth. Hers is seemingly effortless storytelling as though a tape recording were being replayed. But it is Mrs. Segal's skill to have recognized the purity and importance of the right mood and moment to select and play back to us."

BIOGRAPHICAL/CRITICAL SOURCES: Reporter, November 19, 1964; *New York Review of Books*, November 19, 1964; *Book Week*, November 29, 1964; *New Republic*, December 12, 1964; *Commonweal*, January 29, 1965; *Commentary*, March, 1965; *New Statesman*, March 19, 1965.

*   *   *

SEIDEL, Frederick (Lewis)   1936-

PERSONAL: Born February 19, 1936, in St. Louis, Mo.; son of Jerome Jay (a business executive) and Thelma (Cartun) Seidel; married Phyllis Munro Ferguson, June 7, 1960; children: Felicity Cutcheon Nelson. *Education:* Attended St. Louis Country Day School, 1948-53; Harvard College, A.B., 1957. *Politics:* Democrat. *Home:* 40 East 83rd St., New York, N.Y. 10028.

CAREER: Author. Writer-in-residence, Rutgers University, New Brunswick, N.J., fall, 1964.

WRITINGS: Final Solutions (poems), Random House, 1963. Work included in *A Controversy of Poets*, Doubleday, 1965. Poems have appeared in *Partisan Review, Paris Review, Hudson Review, Evergreen Review, Noble Savage*, and *Metamorphosis.*†

*   *   *

SEIDEL, George J(oseph)   1932-

PERSONAL: Surname rhymes with "bridle"; born April 25, 1932, in Tacoma, Wash.; son of George Frank (a manager) and Bernice C. (Herring) Seidel. *Education:* St. Martin's College, B.A., 1955; Collegio di Sant'Anselmo, Rome, Italy, graduate study, 1955-58; University of Toronto, M.A., 1960, Ph.D., 1962; University of Freiburg, Fulbright scholar, 1961-62. *Home:* St. Martin's College, Olympia, Wash. 98502.

CAREER: Roman Catholic religious, member of Order of St. Benedict. St. Martin's College, Olympia, Wash., chairman of philosophy department, 1962—. *Member:* Northwest Conference on Philosophy (president, 1971). *Awards, honors:* Organization of American States fellowship in Buenos Aires, 1965.

WRITINGS: Martin Heidegger and the Pre-Socratics: An Introduction to His Thought, University of Nebraska Press, 1964; *The Crisis of Creativity*, University of Notre Dame Press, 1966; *A Contemporary Approach to Classical Metaphysics*, Appleton, 1969; *Being Nothing and God: A Philosophy of Appearance*, Van Goreum, 1970.

WORK IN PROGRESS: Studies in nineteenth-century German philosophy and metaphysics.

SIDELIGHTS: Seidel is competent in German, Italian, French, Spanish, and Latin. *Avocational interests:* The organ music of J. S. Bach, jazz.

*   *   *

SEIDEN, Martin H.   1934-

PERSONAL: Surname is pronounced *Sigh*-den; born January 3, 1934, in Brooklyn, N.Y.; son of Burt (a businessman) and Julia (Herbach) Seiden; married Rosalie Schoenbrun. *Education:* City College (now City College of the City University of New York), B.A., 1954; Columbia University, M.A., 1955, Ph.D., 1962. *Religion:* Jewish. *Home:* 109 Williams Ave., Spring Valley, N.Y. 10977.

CAREER: New York State Department of Banking, economist, 1956-58; City College (now City College of the City University of New York), instructor in economics, 1958-62; National Bureau of Economic Research, New York, N.Y., project director, 1959-62. Consultant to American Broadcasting Co., Columbia Broadcasting System, National Broadcasting Corp., National Association of Broadcasters, Federal Communications Commission, Mississippi River Corp., and National Academy of Sciences. Lecturer, City University of New York, 1963-69. *Member:* American Economic Association, American Finance Association, Academy of Political Science.

WRITINGS: (Contributor) Lindsay and Sametz, *Financial Management—An Analytical Approach*, Irwin, 1963; *The Quality of Trade Credit*, National Bureau of Economic Research, 1964; *An Economic Analysis of Community Antenna Television Systems and the Television Broadcasting Industry*, U.S. Government Printing Office, 1965; *CATV Source Book*, Tab Publications, 1965; *Cable Television: U.S.A.*, Praeger, 1972; *Who Controls the Mass Media?*, Basic Books, 1974. Contributor to *Journal of Finance*.

WORK IN PROGRESS: A study of the mass communications industries, and mass communications by space satellite.

BIOGRAPHICAL/CRITICAL SOURCES: Fortune, February, 1963; *Bond Buyer*, April 20, 1964; *New York Herald Tribune*, April 20, 1964; *Wall Street Journal*, July 9, 1964; *Broadcasting Magazine*, March 8, 1965; *Variety*, March 10, 1965; *Television*, April, 1965.

* * *

SEITZ, Georg J(osef) 1920-

PERSONAL: Born May 27, 1920, in Cologne, Germany; son of Josef and Elisabeth Seitz; married Thea Hartel, July 31, 1948. *Education:* Attended Realgymnasium Koln-Lindenthal, Cologne, Germany. *Home:* Rua do Couto 74, Rio de Janeiro, Brazil.

CAREER: Received six years professional training in leather industry in German factories; Cortume Carioca, Rio de Janeiro, Brazil, leather expert, 1952—. *Member:* Clube dos correspondentes estrangeiros (Rio de Janeiro).

WRITINGS: Hinter dem Gruenen Vorhang, Brockhaus, 1960, translation by A. J. Pomerans published as *People of the Rain Forests*, Heinemann, 1963. Contributor of political and economics articles to German newspapers and radio. Writer of German television film on an Amazon expedition.

WORK IN PROGRESS: A series of plays about the Amazon region, for German broadcasting.

AVOCATIONAL INTERESTS: Enthnography.†

* * *

SELBY, Hubert, Jr. 1928-

PERSONAL: Born July 23, 1928, in Brooklyn, N.Y.; son of Hubert (an engineer) and Adalin (Layne) Selby; married (second marriage) Judith Lumino (a legal secretary), October 24, 1964; children: (by previous marriage) Claudia, Kyle; (by present marriage) two. *Education:* Attended Peter Stuyvesant High School, one year. *Religion:* Christian. *Home:* 205 East Tenth St., New York 3, N.Y. *Agent:* Sterling Lord Agency, 75 East 55th St., New York, N.Y. *Office: National Enquirer*, 655 Madison Ave., New York, N.Y.

CAREER: Oiler with Merchant Marine, 1944-46; hospital patient (with tuberculosis), 1946-50; clerk in various offices, insurance analyst, 1950-64; free-lance copy writer with *National Enquirer*, 1965—.

WRITINGS: Last Exit to Brooklyn (six stories), Grove, 1964; *The Room*, Grove, 1971. Contributor to *Black Mountain Review, Provincetown Review, New Directions* (number 17), and *Swank*.

WORK IN PROGRESS: A novel.

SIDELIGHTS: Selby's *Last Exit* caused a well publicized obscenity trial in England. The case was successfully prosecuted by a member of the House of Lords. It was banned in Italy as well as attacked in the United States. The book's characters are homosexuals, hoodlums, dope addicts, and prostitutes and the stories are frankly told.

Gilbert Sorrentino wrote of Selby's first book: "I would guess that Selby thinks of his reader as someone who might possibly want to know the truth about a real, living hell which exists in our own time, in the city of New York." Eliot Fremont-Smith believed that the degree of depression, violence, and grotesqueness "sometimes nullifies or engulfs belief. Yet that the author is able to make one believe at all in this sordid, hopeless world is an extraordinary achievement."

Sol Yurick perceived Selby's intent differently: "Hell implies just deserts.... Life appears at random: the structures that interrelate and organize the world and people are hidden.... Now the terrible and subversive thing Selby has done is to make us feel [the truth of] that [random] world by stimulating us sexually, and once straight people have been moved to react sexually in straight ways by descriptions of inversion the whole world ... begins to seem a little weird, itself inverted.... To sue for obscenity instead of subversion is a masked political countermove; the terms of the suit redefine Selby's work to render it nonsubversive."

Selby told Haskel Frankel of the *Saturday Review*: "I found in writing the only thing that gives me gratification, not that it's a joy to do." His literary idol is Isaac Babel, but he believes that his only influence is Beethoven. He told *Newsweek*: "I've known the people I write about all my life, and for a while when I was 21 I lived their life. I wasn't looking in. I *was* in."

BIOGRAPHICAL/CRITICAL SOURCES: Time, October 30, 1964; *New York Times Book Review*, November 8, 1964; *New York Review of Books*, December 3, 1964; *Nation*, December 7, 1964; *Book Week*, December 20, 1964; *Newsweek*, December 28, 1964; *Commentary*, January, 1965; *Playboy*, January, 1965; *Saturday Review*, January 23, 1965; *Negro Digest*, February, 1965; *Choice*, February, 1965; *Village Voice*, March 25, 1965; *Partisan Review*, spring, 1965; *Holiday*, June, 1965; Carolyn Riley, editor, *Contemporary Literary Criticism*, Gale, Volume I, 1973, Volume II, 1974, Volume IV, 1975.†

* * *

SELIGMAN, Lester George 1918-

PERSONAL: Surname is accented on first syllable; born February 6, 1918, in Chicago, Ill.; son of Samuel B. (a teacher) and Reva (Greenspahn) Seligman; married wife,

Judith, April 27, 1941; children: Susan Rena, David Hillel. *Education:* University of Chicago, B.A., 1939, Ph.D., 1947. *Religion:* Jewish. *Home:* 603 South Highland, Champaign, Ill. *Office:* Department of Political Science, University of Illinois, Urbana, Ill. 61801.

CAREER: University of Chicago, Chicago, Ill., instructor, 1947-49, assistant professor of political science, 1949-53; University of Oregon, Eugene, assistant professor, 1953-63, professor of political science, 1963-74, director of political studies program, 1957-63; University of Oregon, Eugene, professor of political science, 1974—. The Hebrew University of Jerusalem, Fulbright lecturer, 1960-61. Brookings Institution, member of Social Science Research Institute, summer, 1956. Visiting professor, Weizmann Institute Graduate School, University of Umeaa, 1970, University of Illinois, 1972, and University of Aarhus, 1973. Member of editorial board, General Learning Press, 1974—. *Military service:* U.S. Army, 1942-46; served in Philippines; became captain; received Bronze Star. *Member:* American Political Science Association (former member of executive council), Western Political Science Association (member of executive council; chairman of research committee). *Awards, honors:* Social Science Research Council fellowship, 1956-57; Ford Foundation travel and study award, 1968-70.

WRITINGS: Leadership in a New Nation, Atherton, 1964; (editor with Elmer E. Cornwell, Jr.) *New Deal Mosaic*, University of Oregon Press, 1965; (co-author) *Patterns of Recruitment*, Rand McNally, 1974. Contributor of articles to scholarly journals, including *American Political Science Review, Journal of Politics, Commentary, Western Political Science Quarterly, International Encyclopedia of the Social Sciences, Comparative Politics.*

WORK IN PROGRESS: Research on political elites and public policy in the United States.

*   *   *

SEMMELROTH, Otto   1912-

PERSONAL: Born December 1, 1912, in Bitburg, Germany; son of Otto and Margarete (Schmitz) Semmelroth. *Education:* Studied philosophy at Berchmanskolleg, Pullach bei Muenchen, Germany; attended Ignatiuskolleg, Valkenburg, Germany, Lizentiat, 1941; University of Bonn, Doctor theol., 1947. *Religion:* Roman Catholic. *Home:* Offenbacher Landstrasse 224, Frankfurt am Main, Federal Republic of Germany.

CAREER: Ordained Roman Catholic priest, September 19, 1939, member of Society of Jesus. Philosophisch-Theologische Hochschule Sankt Georgen, Frankfurt am Main, Germany, ordentlicher Professor fuer Dogmatik, 1949—. Theological adviser to the Bishop of Mainz and Peritus Concilii at the Vatican II Ecumenical Council.

WRITINGS—All published by Josef Knecht, unless otherwise indicated: *Urbild der Kriche*, Echter-Verlag, 1950, 2nd edition, 1954 (English translation published as *Mary, Archtype of the Church*, Sheed, 1963); *Die Kirche als Ursakrament*, 1953, 3rd edition, 1963; *Gott und Mensch in Begegnung*, 1956, 2nd edition, 1958; *Maria oder Christus?*, 1956; *Das geistliche Amt*, 1958; *Ich glaube an die Kirche*, Patmos-Verlag, 1959; *Vom Sinn der Sakramente*, 1960, 2nd edition, 1963; *Wirkendes Wort*, 1962; *Die Welt als Schoepfung*, 1962.

SENDREY, A(ladar) Alfred   1884-

PERSONAL: Born February 29, 1884, in Budapest, Hungary; came to United States in 1940; son of Henry Joachim and Johanna (Konigsbaum) Sendrey; married Eugenie Weiss, September, 1910 (deceased); children: Albert Richard, Lillian Felice Sendrey Swanson. *Education:* Studied at University of Budapest, 1900-04, Academy of Music, Budapest, 1902-05; University of Leipzig, Ph.D., 1931. *Home:* 524 North Laurel Ave., Los Angeles, Calif. 90048.

CAREER: Conductor and composer in Europe and United States. Operatic conductor in Chicago and New York, 1913-14, Berlin, 1914-15, Vienna, 1915-16, Leipzig, 1918-24; conductor of symphony orchestras in European capitals, 1924-33; teacher of musicology in the United States, beginning 1940; University of Judaism, Los Angeles, Calif., professor of musicology, 1958—. Compositions include orchestral, choral, operatic, and chamber music works.

WRITINGS: Rundfunk und Musikpflege, Kistner & Siegel, 1931; *Dirigierkunde*, Breitkopf & Haertel, 1932, 3rd edition, 1954; *Bibliography of Jewish Music*, Columbia University Press, 1951, reprinted, Kraus Reprint Co., 1969; (with Mildred Norton) *David's Harp: The Story of Music in Biblical Times*, New American Library, 1964; *Music in Ancient Israel*, Philosophical Library, 1969; *The Music of the Jews in the Diaspora, up to 1800*, Yoseloff, 1970; *Music in the Social and Religious Life of Antiquity*, Fairleigh Dickinson University Press, 1973.

WORK IN PROGRESS: Heresy and Superstition.

SIDELIGHTS: Professor Sendrey taught conducting to Charles Munch in Paris in 1934-39, and later to Henry Mancini and others in Hollywood. He speaks German, English, French, Hungarian, and Italian; he reads Hebrew, Latin, and Greek.

*   *   *

SERLE, (Alan) Geoffrey   1922-

PERSONAL: Born March 10, 1922, in Melbourne, Victoria, Australia; son of Percival (an author) and Dora Beatrice (Hake) Serle; married Jessie Catherine Macdonald, January 12, 1955; children: Donald Geoffrey, Oenone Catherine, James Farquhar, Richard Lachlan. *Education:* University of Melbourne, B.A., 1946; Oxford University, D.Phil., 1950. *Office:* Monash University, Melbourne, Victoria, Australia.

CAREER: University of Melbourne, Melbourne, Victoria, Australia, lecturer, later senior lecturer in history, 1950-60; Monash University, Melbourne, Victoria, Australia, 1961—, started as senior lecturer, now reader in history. *Military service:* Australian Army, 1941-44. *Awards, honors:* Rhodes Scholar, 1947; fellow, Australian Academy of the Humanities; fellow, Social Sciences Academy of Australia.

WRITINGS: (Editor with James Grant) *The Melbourne Scene, 1803-1956*, Melbourne University Press, 1957; *The Golden Age: A History of the Colony of Victoria 1851-1861*, Melbourne University Press, 1963; *The Rush to be Rich: A History of the Colony of Victoria, 1883-1889*, Melbourne University Press, 1971; (editor with Kathleen Thomson) *A Biographical Register of the Victorian Legislature, 1851-1900*, Australian National University Press, 1972; *From Deserts the Prophets Come: The Creative Spirit in Australia, 1788-1972*, Heinemann, 1973. Contributor to learned journals. Editor, *Historical Studies—Australia and New Zealand*, 1955-63; editor, *Meanjin*

Quarterly, 1957; section editor, *Australian Dictionary of Biography*.

WORK IN PROGRESS: History of Victoria, 1890's.

* * *

SESONSKE, Alexander 1917-

PERSONAL: Born November 19, 1917, in Gloversville, N.Y.; son of Charles (a film producer) and Esther (Goldberg) Sesonske; married Sarah Julia Schaden, April 7, 1947; children: Stephanie Alexandra. *Education:* Long Beach City College, student, 1946-48; University of California, Los Angeles, B.A., 1949, Ph.D., 1954. *Politics:* Democrat. *Home:* 3662 San Gabriel Lane, Santa Barbara, Calif. 93105. *Office:* Department of Philosophy, University of California, Santa Barbara, Calif. 93106.

CAREER: University of California, Los Angeles, instructor in philosophy, 1953-55; Columbia University, New York, N.Y., lecturer in philosophy, 1955-56; University of Washington, Seattle, assistant professor of philosophy, 1956-58; University of California, Santa Barbara, assistant professor, 1958-63, associate professor, 1963-68, professor of philosophy, 1968—, chairman of department, 1968-73. Wadsworth Publishing Co., Inc., Belmont, Calif., consulting editor. *Military service:* U.S. Army, 1942-45; received five battle stars. *Member:* American Philosophical Association, American Society for Aesthetics, British Film Institute.

WRITINGS: Value and Obligation, University of California Press, 1957; (editor with Noel Fleming) Plato, *Meno*, Wadsworth, 1964; (editor with Noel Fleming) *Meta-Meditations*, Wadsworth, 1964; (editor with Noel Fleming) *Human Understanding*, Wadsworth, 1964; (editor) *What is Art?*, Oxford University Press, 1965; (editor) Plato, *Republic*, Wadsworth, 1966; (contributor) D. Carr and E. Casey, editors, *Explorations in Phenomenology*, Martinus Nijhoff, 1973; *The Films of Jean Renoir*, University of California Press, 1974. Contributor to journals of philosophy.

* * *

SEVERSON, John H(ugh) 1933-

PERSONAL: Born December 12, 1933, in Los Angeles, Calif.; son of John Hughitt (a bookkeeper) and Dorothy (Flachman) Severson; married Louise Stier, December 4, 1959; children: Jenna Louise, Anna Marie. *Education:* Orange Coast College, A.A., 1953; Chico State College (now California State University, Chico), B.A., 1955; Long Beach State College (now California State University, Long Beach), M.A., 1956. *Religion:* Presbyterian. *Home:* 405 Alicia, San Clemente, Calif. *Office:* Severson Publications, Box 1028, Dana Point, Calif.

CAREER: Art teacher and coach in California high schools, 1956, 1958-59; Severson Films, Dana Point, Calif., producer and lecturer, 1958-64; Severson Publications, Dana Point, Calif., publisher, 1960—, editor of *Surfer*, 1960—, *Skateboarder*, 1964-65. Winner of international surfing championship in Peru, 1961. *Military service:* U.S. Army, 1956-58.

WRITINGS: Modern Surfing Around the World, Doubleday, 1964; (editor) *Great Surfing*, Doubleday, 1967.

AVOCATIONAL INTERESTS: Golf (has seven handicap), painting, fishing.†

SEYMOUR, Emery W. 1921-

PERSONAL: Born April 27, 1921, in Hackensack, N.J.; son of Malcolm Peters (an accountant) and M. Adeline (Stock) Seymour; married Norma Simmers, June 21, 1947; children: Paul, Scott, Jeffrey. *Education:* Colgate University, A.B. (cum laude), 1942; Springfield College, M.Ed., 1948, D.P.E., 1955; additional graduate study at New York University and Emory University. *Home:* 164 Fernwood Dr., East Longmeadow, Mass. *Office:* Springfield College, Springfield, Mass.

CAREER: Emory University, Atlanta, Ga., member of Division of Physical Education, 1948-56; Springfield College, Springfield, Mass., 1956—, became professor of physical education and assistant director of Division of Graduate Studies. College basketball and football official; consultant in physical training problems at U.S. Army Infantry Center, Fort Benning, Ga., 1951. East Longmeadow Scholarship Fund, co-chairman of grants committee. *Military service:* U.S. Army, Counter Intelligence Corps, World War II; served in Europe and North Africa. *Member:* American Association for Health, Physical Education and Recreation (fellow), National College Physical Education Association for Men.

WRITINGS: (With Richard C. Havel) *Administration of Health, Physical Education and Recreation for Schools* (textbook), Ronald, 1961. Contributor of articles to professional journals.

* * *

SEYMOUR, John 1914-

PERSONAL: Born June 12, 1914, in England; son of Albert and Christine (an American; maiden name, Owens) Turbayne; name changed to that of stepfather; married Sally Medworth (an artist and potter); children: Jane, Anne, Kate. *Home:* Fachongle Isaf, Pembrokeshire, Wales. *Agent:* David Higham Associates Ltd., 5-8 Lower John St., London, W1R 4HA, England.

CAREER: Formerly farm manager in southwest Africa, skipper of fishing vessel in southwest Africa and South Africa, miner in Northern Rhodesia, and government livestock officer in Barotseland; operator of a small farm, and free-lance writer. *Military service:* British Army, King's African Rifles, 1940-46; served in Ethiopia and Burma.

WRITINGS: The Hard Way to India, Eyre & Spottiswoode, 1951; *Round about India*, Eyre & Spottiswoode, 1953, published as *Around India*, Day, 1954; *One Man's Africa*, Eyre & Spottiswood, 1955, Day, 1956; *Boys in the Bundu* (juvenile), Harrap, 1955; *Sailing through England*, Eyre & Spottiswoode, 1956; *The Fat of the Land*, Faber, 1961, Taplinger, 1962; *On My Own Terms*, Faber, 1963; *Willynilly to the Baltic*, W. Blackwood, 1965; *Companion Guide to East Anglia*, Collins, 1970; *Self-Sufficiency*, Faber, 1973; *Companion Guide to the North East Coast of England*, Collins, 1974; *Companion Guide to the South West Coast of England*, Collins, 1974. Contributor to magazines.

WORK IN PROGRESS: Companion Guide to the Coast of East Anglia and the Thames Estuaries, for Collins.

SIDELIGHTS: Seymour's books have been translated into Norwegian and Spanish. Seymour writes: "We farm sixty-two acres, with a horse, cows, sows, and poultry, and grow nine-tenths of our own food and kill and cure our own meat." *Avocational interests:* Cruising in small open boats, travel, and topography.

SHACKLETON, Edward Arthur Alexander 1911-

PERSONAL: Born 1911, in London, England; son of Sir Ernest and Lady Emily Shackleton; married Betty Muriel Marguerite Homan, 1938; children: Charles, Alexandra. *Education:* Magdalen College, Oxford, M.A. *Politics:* Labour Party. *Home:* Long Coppice, Canford Magna, Wimborne, Dorset, England.

CAREER: Surveyor on Oxford University expedition to Sarawak, 1932, and organizer and surveyor on expedition to Ellesmereland, 1934-35; Labour candidate for Parliament for Epsom, in 1945; member of Parliament (Labour) for Preston, 1946-50, for Preston South, 1950-55, serving as parliamentary private secretary to Minister of Supply, 1949-50, to Lord President of Council, 1950-51, and to Foreign Secretary, 1951; Minister of Defense for the Royal Air Force, 1964-67; Minister without Portfolio and Deputy Leader of House of Lords, 1967-68; Lord Privy Seal, 1968-70; Paymaster General, 1968; Leader of House of Lords, 1968-70; Minister of Civil Service Department, 1968-70; Opposition Leader of House of Lords, 1970—. Member of British government committees and councils. Lecturer in Europe and United States; talks producer for British Broadcasting Corp. Director, John Lewis Partnership Ltd., 1940-45, RTZ Development Enterprises, Mercury Insurance Holdings. *Military service:* Royal Air Force, Intelligence, 1940-45; became wing commander; mentioned in dispatches twice and received Order of the British Empire (military).

MEMBER: Royal Geographical Society (former vice-president; president, 1971—), British Association of Industrial Editors (president, 1960-64), Association of Special Libraries and Information Bureaux (president, 1963-65), Arctic Club (president, 1960), Bath Club, Savile Club. *Awards, honors:* Cuthbert Peek Award of Royal Geographical Society, 1933; Ludwig Medallist, Munich Geographical Society, 1938; created baron, life peer of Burley, 1958; LL.D. from University of Newfoundland, 1970.

WRITINGS: Arctic Journeys, Hodder & Stoughton, 1937, Farrar & Rinehart, 1938; (contributor) *Borneo Jungle*, Drummond, 1938; *Nansen, the Explorer*, Witherby, 1959; (with others) *Heroes of Our Time*, Dutton, 1962. Contributor of articles on geographical and political subjects to periodicals and broadcasts.†

* * *

SHADBOLT, Maurice (Francis Richard) 1932-

PERSONAL: Born June 4, 1932, in Auckland, New Zealand; son of Francis Clement William and Violet (Kearon) Shadbolt; married Gillian Eve Muriel Heming (a free-lance journalist), November 21, 1953; married Barbara Magner, 1971; children: (first marriage) five. *Education:* Attended University of Auckland. *Politics:* Liberal Socialist. *Religion:* Christian. *Home:* 35 Arapito Rd., Titirangi, Auckland 7, New Zealand. *Agent:* Ursula Winanat, Richmond Towers & Benson Ltd., 14 Essex St., Strand, London W.C. 2, England.

CAREER: New Zealand National Film Unit, director, 1954-57; free-lance journalist, 1957—. Robert Burns Fellow in Literature, University of Otago, Dunedin, New Zealand, 1963. *Awards, honors:* Hubert Church Memorial Award, 1959, for *The New Zealanders*; New Zealand state literary scholar, 1960 and 1970; Katherine Mansfield Award, 1963 and 1967; National Association of Independent Schools Award, 1966, for *Among the Cinders*; Freda Buckland Award, 1969.

WRITINGS: The New Zealanders (short stories), Gollancz, 1959, Atheneum, 1961; *Summer Fires and Winter Country* (short stories), Eyre & Spottiswoode, 1963, Atheneum, 1966; (with Brian Brake) *New Zealand: Gift of the Sea* (nonfiction), Whitcombe & Tombs, 1963, East-West Press, 1964; *Among the Cinders* (novel), Atheneum, 1965; *The Presence of Music: Three Novellas*, Cassell, 1967; (editor) *The Shell Guide to New Zealand*, Whitcombe & Tombs, 1968; (with Olaf Ruhen) *Isles of the South Pacific*, National Geographical Society, 1968; *This Summer's Dolphin* (novel), Atheneum, 1969; *An Ear of the Dragon* (novel), Cassell, 1971; *Strangers and Journeys* (novel), St. Martin's, 1972. Writer-director of documentary films. Contributor to *National Geographic, New Yorker, New Zealand Listener, Landfall*. Regular columnist, *Sydney Bulletin*.

WORK IN PROGRESS: Search for Tim Livingstone (tentative title), a novel on New Zealand life, 1919-1959.

SIDELIGHTS: Shadbolt's major aim in writing is "to understand my country, my time—and myself."†

* * *

SHADEGG, Stephen C. 1909-

PERSONAL: Surname is accented on first syllable; born December 8, 1909, in Minneapolis, Minn.; son of Jacob (operator of a small business) and Katherine (Barden) Shadegg; married Eugenia Kehr, February 14, 1939; children: Cynthia, Eugenia, Stephen David, John Barden. *Education:* Attended California public schools, and studied at Pasadena Community Playhouse, 1931-32. *Politics:* Republican. *Religion:* Episcopalian. *Home:* 2045 East Missouri, Phoenix, Ariz. *Agent:* Oscar Collier, 299 Madison Ave., New York, N.Y. 10017. *Office:* 377 North 3rd Ave., Phoenix, Ariz. 85011.

CAREER: Free-lance writer for pulp magazines, radio, and motion pictures prior to 1941; S-K Research Laboratories (pharmaceutical manufacturers), Phoenix, Ariz., president, 1941—; Stephen Shadegg Associates, Inc. (advertising and public relations), Phoenix, Ariz., president, 1961—. Manager, Barry Goldwater's campaigns for U.S. Senate, 1952, 1958, Governor Jack Williams's campaigns, 1966, 1968, 1970, and Paul Fanin's campaigns for U.S. Senate, 1970; co-author of Goldwater newspaper column, "How Do You Stand Sir?" 1959-62; consultant, National Republican Senatorial Campaign Committee, 1959-60; chairman, Arizona Republican Party, 1960-62; western regional director, Goldwater for President Committee, 1964. Elected lay member of executive council (national), The Protestant Episcopal Church, 1961—; chairman of laymen's work in Eighth Province, 1958-61; speaker in more than fifty dioceses. President, Phoenix Little Theatre, 1949-52; fund chairman, State Cancer Crusade, 1957-59. *Member:* Press Club, Advertising Club, Kiwanis Club (all Phoenix); Phoenix Country Club (president, 1957).

WRITINGS: Barry Goldwater: Freedom in His Flight Plan, Fleet Publishing, 1962; *How to Win an Election*, Taplinger, 1964, revised edition published as *The New How to Win an Election*, 1972; *What Happened to Goldwater? The Inside Story of the 1964 Republican Campaign*, Holt, 1965; *The Remnant*, Arlington House, 1968; *Winning's a Lot More Fun*, Macmillan, 1969; *Clare Booth Luce: A Biography*, Simon & Schuster, 1971. Also author of five booklets for The Protestant Episcopal Church.

WORK IN PROGRESS: Upon What Meat, a political novel.

AVOCATIONAL INTERESTS: The amateur theater; golf, flying (pilot since 1927), politics.†

* * *

SHADI, Dorothy Clotelle Clarke 1908- (Dorothy Clotelle Clarke)

PERSONAL: Born July 16, 1908, in Los Angeles, Calif.; daughter of Thomas Tedford and Zilpha Jane (Dever) Clarke; married Sundar Singh Shadi, September 22, 1934; children: Zilpha Tedforda (Mrs. George Roland Paganelli), Ramona Rhea (Mrs. William Walter Miller), Verna Carol (Mrs. Allan Wayne Schindler). *Education:* University of California, Los Angeles, A.B., 1929; University of California, Berkeley, M.A., 1930, Ph.D., 1934. *Home:* 944 Arlington Ave., El Cerrito, Calif. 94530. *Office:* Department of Spanish and Portuguese, 4321 Dwinelle Hall, University of California, Berkeley, Calif. 94720.

CAREER: Dominican College of San Rafael, San Rafael, Calif., professor of Spanish, 1935-37; University of California, Berkeley, lecturer in Spanish and Portuguese, 1945-48, assistant professor, 1948-55, associate professor, 1955-61, professor of Spanish, 1961—, assistant dean, College of Letters and Science, 1963-66, and summers, 1964-70.

MEMBER: Modern Language Association of America, American Association of Teachers of Spanish and Portuguese, Modern Humanities Research Association, Hispanic Institute in the United States, Hispanic Society of America, Instituto Internacional de Literatura Iberoamericana, Mediaeval Academy of America, Dante Society of America, Renaissance Society of America, Societe Rencaevals, American Philological Association, American Society for Aesthetics, British Society of Aesthetics, National Historical Society, Smithsonian Associates, International Platform Society, Marquis Biographical Library Society, Medieval Association of the Pacific, Philological Association of the Pacific Coast, Foreign Language Association of Northern California, Sigma Delta Pi, Pi Delta Phi, Alpha Mu Gamma.

WRITINGS—Under name Dorothy Clotelle Clarke: *Una bibliografia de versificacion espanola*, University of California Press, 1937; *Romance Literature*, privately printed, 1948; *A Chronological Sketch of Castilian Versification Together with a List of Its Metric Terms*, University of California Press, 1952; (editor and author of introduction) Vicente Espinel, *Diversas rimas*, Hispanic Institute in the United States, 1956.

Morphology of Fifteenth-Century Castilian Verse, Duquesne University Press, 1964; (contributor) A. S. Preminger and others, editors, *Encyclopedia of Poetry and Poetics*, Princeton University Press, 1965; (contributor) E. H. Wilkins and others, editors, *A Concordance to "The Divine Comedy" of Dante Alighieri*, Harvard University Press, 1965; (translator) Juan Ventura Agudiez, *The Afternoons of Thereze Lamarck*, Las Americas, 1967; *Early Spanish Lyric Poetry: Essays and Selections*, Las Americas, 1967; *Allegory, Decalogue, and Deadly Sins in "La Celestina,"* University of California Press, 1968; *Agudiecism, Thematics, and the Newest Novel: A Study of Juan Ventura Agudiez's Heuristic Novel "Las tardes de Thereze Lamarck,"* Exposition, 1969; *Juan de Mena's "Laberinto de Fortuna": Classic Epic and "Mester de Clerecia"* (monograph), University of Mississippi, 1973.

Contributor of articles and review to professional journals, including *Hispanic Review*, *Revista de Filologia Espanola*, *Revista Iberoamericana*, *PMLA*, *Modern Language Journal*, *Romance Philology*, *Modern Philology*, *Renaissance News*, and *Idea and Experiment*.

WORK IN PROGRESS: An edition of the *Cancionero de Baena*, for publication by Castalia; essays on Spanish lyric poetry and modern Spanish drama.

SIDELIGHTS: Mrs. Shadi reads Spanish, French, Italian, and Portuguese.

* * *

SHAMON, Albert Joseph 1915-

PERSONAL: Born April 3, 1915, in Auburn, N.Y.; son of Asad Charles and Nettie (Mahfoud) Shamon. *Education:* Attended St. Andrew's Seminary, Rochester, N.Y.; St. Bernard Seminary, Rochester, N.Y., B.A., 1936; Canisius College, Buffalo, N.Y., M.A., 1951. *Home:* 115 Maple Ave., Victor, N.Y.

CAREER: Roman Catholic priest; assistant pastor in Rochester, N.Y., 1940-44; Aquinas Institute, Rochester, N.Y., English teacher, 1946-50; St. Andrew's Seminary, Rochester, N.Y., professor of English, 1950-61; St. Patrick's Church, Victor, N.Y., pastor, 1961—. National Council of Catholic Women, Rochester diocesan director, 1946-50.

WRITINGS: Behind the Mass, Christopher, 1950; *Treasure Untold*, Newman, 1955; *First Steps to Sanctity*, Newman, 1956; *The Only Life*, Bruce, 1961; *Come To Me*, Silver Burdett, 1964; *Catching Up On Catechetics*, Paulist Press, 1972.

WORK IN PROGRESS: Second Steps to Sanctity; and *Sanctity*.†

* * *

SHANNON, Robert C. 1930-

PERSONAL: Born September 1, 1930, in Corinth, Ky.; son of Charles (a farmer) and Gertrude (Marshall) Shannon; married Barbara Jean Adams, December 21, 1951; children: John Michael, Beth Ann. *Education:* Cincinnati Bible Seminary, A.B., 1952; attended Georgetown College, Tusculum College, and Lutheran Theological Seminary. *Politics:* Republican. *Home:* 3111 Honeysuckle Rd., Largo, Fla. *Office:* 1645 Seminole Blvd., Largo, Fla.

CAREER: First Christian Church, Greeneville, Tenn., minister, 1955-60; First Christian Church, Orlando, Fla., minister, 1963-67; First Christian Church, Largo, Fla., minister, 1967—. Southern Christian Convention, president, 1965—.

WRITINGS: The New Testament Church, Standard Publishing, 1965. Also author of *Broken Symbols*, published by Christian Restoration Association.

WORK IN PROGRESS: Commoners and Kings (sermons on Bible personalities).

* * *

SHAPIRO, David (Joel) 1947-

PERSONAL: Born January 2, 1947, in Newark, N.J.; son of Irving (a physician) and Fraida (Chagy) Shapiro; married Jean Lindsay Stamm (a designer), August 30, 1970. *Education:* Columbia University, B.A. (magna cum laude), 1968, Ph.D. (with distinction), 1974; Clare College, Cambridge, B.A., 1968, M.A. (first class honors), 1970. *Religion:* Jewish. *Home:* 915 West End Ave., New York, N.Y. 10025.

CAREER: Columbia University, New York, N.Y., instructor, 1972-73, assistant professor of English, 1973—. Has appeared as a violinist with New Jersey Symphony, Provincetown Symphony, and under Stokowski in Scranton, Pa. *Awards, honors:* Gotham Book Mart Avant Garde Poetry Award, 1962; Merrill fellowship, 1967; Kellett fellowship to Cambridge University, 1968-70; Book-of-the-Month Club grant, 1968; National Book Award nominee for poetry, 1971, for *A Man Holding an Acoustic Panel;* Columbia University Woodbridge Award for Academic Excellence, 1973; Creative Artists in Public Service award in poetry, 1974.

WRITINGS: January: A Book of Poems, Holt, 1965; *Poems from Deal,* Dutton, 1969; (editor with Ron Padgett) *An Anthology of New York Poets,* Random House, 1970; *The Page-Turner* (poems), Liveright, 1973. Contributor to *Antioch Review, Minnesota Review, Art and Literature, Beloit Poetry Journal, Art News, Craft Horizons, Saturday Review, Atlantic Monthly,* and others.

WORK IN PROGRESS: Editing *The Writings of Robert and Sonia Delaunay,* for Viking; *The Meaning of Meaninglessness: John Ashberry's Poetry,* for Columbia University Press; *Projects in Writing,* for Prentice-Hall.

*   *   *

SHAPIRO, Herman   1922-

PERSONAL: Born February 4, 1922, in New York, N.Y.; son of Simon and Esther (Teitelbaum) Shapiro; married Charlotte Bauer, December 4, 1956; children: Philip Samuel. *Education:* Hunter College, A.B., 1950; Columbia University, M.A., 1951, Ph.D., 1957. *Religion:* Jewish. *Office:* Department of Philosophy, San Jose State College (now California State University), San Jose, Calif.

CAREER: Instructor in philosophy at Queens College, New York, N.Y., 1956-57, Hunter College, New York, N.Y., 1957-58, and University of Connecticut, Storrs, 1958-60; San Jose State College (now California State University), San Jose, Calif., assistant professor, 1960-62, associate professor, 1963-67, professor of philosophy, 1967—. *Military service:* U.S. Coast Guard, 1943-45. *Member:* American Philosophical Association, Mediaeval Academy of America. *Awards, honors:* San Jose State College (now California State University, San Jose) research grant, 1964; Fulbright research grant, 1968-69.

WRITINGS: Motion, Time and Place, According to William of Ockham, Franciscan Institute (St. Bonaventure, N.Y.), 1957; (co-author) *In Quest of Value,* Chandler Publishing, 1963; *Medieval Philosophy,* Random House, 1964; (with E. Curley) *Hellenistic Philosophy,* Random House, 1965; *Renaissance Philosophy* (two volumes), Random House, 1967-69. Contributor to journals, including *Traditio, Speculum, Medievalia et Humistica, Franziskanische Studien.*

WORK IN PROGRESS: The Philosophy of Walter Burley, with F. Scott.

SIDELIGHTS: Shapiro is competent in Latin, French, German, and Italian.

*   *   *

SHARMA, Chandradhar   1920-

PERSONAL: Born January 31, 1920, in Kota, Rajasthan, India; son of Krishnadatt (a Rajpurohit) and Rama (Bai) Sharma; married Shanti Sharma, 1945. *Education:* Allahabad University, B.A., 1940, M.A., 1942, D.Phil., 1947, D.Litt., 1951. *Religion:* Hindu. *Home:* A/1 Sarasvati-Vihar, Jabalpur, Madhya Pradesh, India. *Office:* Jabalpur University, Jabalpur, Madhya Pradesh, India.

CAREER: Banaras Hindu University, Varanasi, Uttar Pradesh, India, assistant professor of philosophy, 1948-55, reader in philosophy, 1955-60; Jabalpur University, Jabalpur, Madhya Pradesh, India, professor of philosophy and chairman of department, 1960—. Whitney-Fulbright visiting professor in United States, 1963-64.

WRITINGS: Indian Philosophy, Nand Kishore, 1952; *Dialectic in Buddhism and Vedanta,* Nand Kishore, 1952; *Shraddhabharanam* (in Sanskirt), 1953; *Western Philosophy* (in Hindi), Nand Kishore, 1959, 5th edition, 1972; *A Critical Survey of Indian Philosophy,* Rider, 1960, Barnes & Noble, 1962.

Editor: *Surjana-charita-mahakavya,* privately printed, 1952; *Madhyanta-vibhaga-shastra,* [Jabalpur], 1963. Editor, *Journal of Philosophy,* Jabalpur University.

WORK IN PROGRESS: Writing on the spiritual experience in Indian and Western philosophical thought.

*   *   *

SHARP, Alan   1934-

PERSONAL: Born January 12, 1934, in Alyth, Scotland; adoptive son of Joseph Potts (a shipyard worker) and Margaret (Smart) Sharp; married (second marriage) Sarah Travers (an actress); children: (first marriage) Louise, Nola; (second marriage) Ruth. *Education:* Attended Greenock High School, three years. *Politics:* "Indeterminate. Vote Labour in conditioned reflex." *Home:* 15 Rothwell St., London N.W. 1, England. *Agent:* Sterling Lord Agency, 75 East 55th St., New York, N.Y. 10022.

CAREER: Apprentice in local shipyards; worked as assistant to a private detective, English teacher in Germany, construction laborer, dishwasher, night switchboard operator for burglar alarm firm, and a packer for a carpet company; worked for IBM; bummed around. Writer. *Military service:* British National Service, 1952-54. *Awards, honors:* Scottish Arts Council award, 1968, for *A Green Tree in Gedde.*

WRITINGS: A Green Tree in Gedde (novel), New American Library, 1965; *The Wind Shifts,* M. Joseph, 1967, Walker & Co., 1968. Author of television plays, including "A Sound from the Sea" and "The Long Distance Piano Player"; screenplays, including "The Last Run," released by Metro-Goldwyn-Mayer, 1971, and "The Hired Hand," released by Universal Pictures, 1971; and radio plays.

WORK IN PROGRESS: The third volume of the trilogy (of which *A Green Tree in Gedde* is the first and *The Wind Shifts* the second), *The Apple Pickers.*

SIDELIGHTS: Paul Pickrel called *A Green Tree in Gedde* "an original, independent, and beautiful piece of work." Its central character "recalls Lucky Jim, the Ginger Man, and Bellow's heroes, not because he derives from them but because he shares with them (though more of course with some than with others) a certain way of encountering experience and a certain strategy for survival: he lives the way a hen walks, by sticking his neck out and hoping that his legs will catch up with him."

It is "exhausting—and exhilarating," writes the *Newsweek* reviewer. Pickrel speaks of Sharp's extraordinary power over language: "He uses shocking episodes and words, yet without prurience, with, instead, decorum: they are necessary and right.'' Concerning the book, Sharp told Haskel Frankel: ''It's been called pornographic and excessively sexual. I admit the book is concerned with sex. I'm an obsessive writer about sex. It concerns me the way damnation concerned Kafka. . . . To accuse me of pornography is not even a relevant comment. Pornography has to do with marionettes who go through positions; it doesn't take into account landscape. Landscape is kind of crucial to me. People are made through environment.''

The *Hudson Review* believes that Sharp's picture on the book jacket ''makes him look like Britain's answer to Mailer.'' A mass of thick, shaggy curls hangs down his neck, accounting in part for his looking like what Frankel calls ''a slightly underfed lion.'' One of his childhood fantasies as an adopted child was ''that Humphrey Bogart was me father and Katherine Hepburn me mother.''

It took him four years to write his first novel, writing at night in longhand. He told *CA*: ''Messy life of somewhat guilty hedonism, interested in being a good writer. Protracted emotional immaturity, considerable interest in football (ours not yours), cats, swimming. Dislike travel, read history. Favorite authors, Wallace Stevens, Sir T. Browne, West (Nathaniel), Chandler, Joyce, Dos Passos, Beryl Bainbridge.''

BIOGRAPHICAL/CRITICAL SOURCES: Observer, March 21, 1965; *New Statesman*, April 2, 1965; *Punch*, April 14, 1965; *Spectator*, April 16, 1965; *New Leader*, April 26, 1965; *New York Times Book Review*, May 2, 1965; *Esquire*, June, 1965; *Harper's*, September, 1965; *Commentary*, October, 1965; *Hudson Review*, autumn, 1965.†

* * *

SHARP, Sister Mary Corona 1922-

PERSONAL: Born May 14, 1922, in Pasadena, Calif.; daughter of Louis Hovey (an artist) and Mary Elizabeth (Darenghy) Sharp. *Education:* University of Western Ontario, B.A., 1947; University of Notre Dame, M.A., 1956, Ph.D., 1962; University of Toronto, graduate study, 1957. *Home:* Brescia College, London, Ontario, Canada.

CAREER: Roman Catholic religious of Ursuline order. Entered Ursuline Convent, Chatham, Ontario, 1948; high school teacher in Windsor, Ontario, 1953-57; Brescia College, London, Ontario, assistant professor 1962-65, associate professor, 1965-66, professor of English and chairman of department, 1966—.

WRITINGS: The Gifts of God, Catechetical Guild, 1942; *The Confidante in Henry James*, University of Notre Dame Press, 1963. Contributor of articles to religious and literary periodicals.

WORK IN PROGRESS: A book on the comedies of Friedrich Durrenmatt.

SIDELIGHTS: Sister Sharp is fluent in German. *Avocational interests:* Makes puppets and marionettes and stages Shakespearean productions (and other classics).

BIOGRAPHICAL/CRITICAL SOURCES: Information, April, 1948.

* * *

SHAW, Irwin 1913-

PERSONAL: Born February 27, 1913, in New York, N.Y.; son of William and Rose (Tompkins) Shaw; married Marian Edwards, October 13, 1939; children: Adam. *Education:* Brooklyn College (now Brooklyn College of the City University of New York), B.A., 1934. *Residence:* Klosters, Switzerland. *Agent:* Irving P. Lazar, 211 South Beverly Dr., Beverly Hills, Calif.; and Max Wilkinson, 500 Fifth Ave., New York, N.Y.

CAREER: Began writing professionally immediately upon graduating from college; *New Republic*, Washington, D.C., former drama critic; New York University, New York, N.Y., former instructor in creative writing. Novelist, playwright, and short story writer. *Military service:* U.S. Army, 1942-45; became warrant officer. *Member:* Authors Guild, Dramatists Guild, Screen Writers Guild, P.E.N. *Awards, honors:* O. Henry Memorial Award first prize, 1944, for ''Walking Wounded,'' second prize, 1945; National Institute of Arts and Letters grant, 1946.

WRITINGS—Novels: *The Young Lions*, Random House, 1948; *The Troubled Air*, Random House, 1951; *Lucy Crown*, Random House, 1956; *Two Weeks in Another Town*, Random House, 1960; *Voices of a Summer Day*, Delacorte, 1965; *Rich Man, Poor Man*, Delacorte, 1969; *Evening in Byzantium*, Delacorte, 1973.

Plays: *Bury the Dead*, Random House, 1936; *The Gentle People*, Random House, 1939; *Sons and Soldiers*, Random House, 1943; *The Assassin*, Random House, 1945; *Children From Their Games*, Samuel French, 1965.

Unpublished plays: ''Siege,'' 1938; ''Quiet City,'' 1939; ''Retreat to Pleasure,'' 1940; (with Peter Viertel) ''The Survivors,'' 1948. Also author of ''Church, Kitchen, Children,'' and ''Salute.''

Short story collections: *Sailor Off the Bremen*, Random House, 1939; *Welcome to the City*, Random House, 1942; *Act of Faith*, Random House, 1946; *Mixed Company*, Random House, 1950; *Tip on a Dead Jockey*, Random House, 1957; *Love on a Dark Street*, Delacorte, 1965; *God Was Here, But He Left Early*, Arbor House, 1973.

Screenplays: ''This Angry Age,'' 1958; *In the French Style*, MacFadden, 1963; ''Survival,'' 1968.

Other writings: (With Robert Capa) *Report on Israel*, Simon & Schuster, 1950; *In the Company of Dolphins* (travel), Geis, 1964.

Contributor to *New Yorker*, *Esquire*, *Yale Review*, and others.

WORK IN PROGRESS: A travel book, *The Five Year Log*; a novel, *The Uncaged Man*; a new play, as yet untitled.

SIDELIGHTS: Criticism of Shaw's work seems to be peculiarly divided into two directly opposed schools of opinion. The one school, popular during the 'forties, expresses great admiration for Shaw's ability to realize characters both credible and familiar. William Peden, speaking for this group, wrote: ''Mr. Shaw's people seem wonderfully alive, even when the author descends to caricature and burlesque. Like Dickens, Mr. Shaw has created, prodigally, a crowded gallery of memorable people. Like Dickens, too, he handles scenes superbly; from the crummy atmosphere of a third-rate New York hotel to the oppressive heat of an Army newspaper office in Algiers, his stories are firmly anchored in time and space. And he communicates experience with a narrative felicity and sincerity which redeem even a frequently far-fetched sentimental or one-sided situation.'' Bergen Evans noted that ''he is essentially a master of episode. . . . Where his pity overcomes his self-restraint and still evades his indignation, he has produced some of the best short stories in contemporary literature.''

More recently, however, some critics believe that Shaw's fiction is "slick," "distorted," and "contrived," that his characters are incredible, and that his work is more properly "propaganda" than fiction. Richard Gilman dismissed him accordingly: "Nothing can be done for him; there is no cure for pseudo-creativeness." But there are a few who disregard the quality of Shaw's work as fiction and find value in his message alone. Lionel Trilling wrote: "I am inclined to believe that nothing Mr. Shaw might write could be wholly lacking in interest of one kind or another. For one thing, he always *does* observe and always *does* feel, and even when he is facile in observation and sentiment he is not insincere. And then he has established himself in a position which guarantees at least the historical or sociological or cultural interest of whatever he writes. He has undertaken the guidance of the moral and political emotions of a large and important class of people, those whom he once called 'the gentle people'.... In general and almost as a function of his good will Mr. Shaw has been content to tell his audience that decency is a kind of simplicity, that modern life is ghastly because it is an affront to simplicity, and that the simple virtues are all we have for our defense." Chester Eisinger concluded that "he is of inestimable value, without regard for the quality of his fiction, for the close way he works with the surface of his society and gives us so much of the range of its manners. He does not penetrate to its heart, but he knows its surface tensions and the ready conversational currency it exchanges for ideas."

Shaw himself dismisses critics in a body. In an interview with Roy Newquist he said: "My feeling about the criticism in America could be more or less wrapped up in one name: Edmund Wilson.... Aside from Wilson, I know of no critic of fiction who consistently makes any sense to me."

Speaking to Newquist of his own talents, Shaw said: "I like the movies as a medium to work in, when I'm my own boss. But when I had to worry about a studio or producers it became a troublesome medium. The dissatisfactions are tremendous, because the final thing is liable to bear very little resemblance to anything you actually wrote.... I'm too far gone as a short story writer and a novelist to be able to divide my time equally with the movies, but I would like to keep my hand in. I think that a writer is at his best, stimulated and keyed up and challenged, when he has a hand in many media. Even if subject matters never interact or interplay he's bound to grow, and growth is everything."

Shaw told *CA*: "Have lived in Europe since 1951, mostly in France [and] Switzerland, with frequent visits to [the] U.S. [I] ski and play tennis. Get to the Mediterranean whenever possible. Speak and read French."

A number of his novels and short stories have been filmed, including "Out of the Fog," 1941; "Act of Love," 1954; "Tip on a Dead Jockey," 1957; "The Young Lions," 1958; "Three," 1969.

BIOGRAPHICAL/CRITICAL SOURCES: New York Herald Tribune, January 25, 1942; Saturday Review, November 18, 1950, June 9, 1951; John W. Aldridge, After the Lost Generation, Noonday, 1951; English Journal, November, 1951; Kirkus, November 15, 1959; Atlantic, February, 1960; Commonweal, March 18, 1960, April 23, 1965; Chester E. Eisinger, Fiction of the Forties, University of Chicago Press, 1963; Roy Newquist, Counterpoint, Rand McNally, 1964; Books and Bookmen, July, 1965; Allan Lewis, American Plays and Playwrights of the Contemporary Theatre, Crown, 1965; Bestsellers, November 15, 1970.

SHAW, Leroy R(obert) 1923-

PERSONAL: Born January 15, 1923, in Medicine Hat, Alberta, Canada; came to United States, 1923; naturalized citizen, 1947; son of Roy A, (a trainman) and Ruby I. (Johnson) Shaw; married Ida Rosmarie Mannaberg (a college teacher), July 11, 1959. Education: University of California, Berkeley, A.B., 1944, M.A., 1946, Ph.D., 1954; graduate study at University of Zurich, 1949, and University of Vienna, 1950. Home: 1137 North Euclid Ave., Oak Park, Ill. 60302. Office: University Hall, University of Illinois, Chicago Circle, Chicago, Ill. 60680.

CAREER: University of Texas, Austin, 1953-65, became associate professor of German; University of Wisconsin, Milwaukee, professor of German, 1965-68; University of Illinois, Chicago, professor of German, 1968—. Fulbright professor, Trinity College, Dublin, Ireland, 1966-67. Military service: U.S. Army, 1942-45. Member: American Association of Teachers of German (executive council member, 1960-63), Modern Language Association of America, American Association of University Professors, Midwest Modern Language Association, Brecht Society. Awards, honors: American Philosophical Society fellowship, 1958; Alexander von Humboldt Stiftung fellowship, 1961-63.

WRITINGS: Witness of Deceit: Gerhart Hauptmann as Critic of Society, University of California Press, 1958; (with Lehmann, Rehder, and Werbow) Review and Progress in German, Holt, 1959; (with Winter) In einer deutschen Stadt, Holt, 1961; (editor) The German Theater Today, University of Texas Press, 1963; Focus on German for Beginners, Harper, 1965; Focus on German for Intermediates, Harper, 1965; The Playwright and Historical Change: Dramatic Strategies in Brecht, Hauptmann, Kaiser, and Wedekind, University of Wisconsin Press, 1970. Author of forty-five television scripts for "Focus on German," Texas Educational Microwave Project.

AVOCATIONAL INTERESTS: Attending concerts and the theater.†

*   *   *

SHAW, Priscilla Washburn 1930-

PERSONAL: Born September 25, 1930, in Boston, Mass.; daughter of George Ellery and Hildegarde (Shumway) Washburn; married Michael Shaw, January 22, 1955 (divorced). Education: Swarthmore College, B.A., 1952; Yale University, advanced study, 1952-53, 1954-60, Ph.D., 1960. Home: 150 Sunnyside Ave., Santa Cruz, Calif. 95062.

CAREER: Shipley School for Girls, Bryn Mawr, Pa., teacher of French and English, 1956-58; Haverford College, Haverford, Pa., part-time teacher of French, 1958-59; Rutgers University, Douglass College, New Brunswick, N.J., instructor in French, 1959-61; Yale University, New Haven, Conn., instructor, 1961-63, assistant professor, 1963-66, associate professor of literature, 1966-74; University of California, Santa Cruz, professor of English, 1974—. Member: Modern Language Association of America, Phi Beta Kappa. Awards, honors: Fulbright fellowship to Montpellier, France, 1953-54; Morse fellowship, 1965-66.

WRITINGS: The Domain of the Self: Rilke, Valery and Yeats, Rutgers University Press, 1964.

WORK IN PROGRESS: A book on Dylan Thomas' short stories.

SIDELIGHTS: Ms. Shaw is competent in French and German.

SHAWCROSS, John T. 1924-

PERSONAL: Born February 10, 1924, in Hillside, N.J.; son of Ernest Edward and Lillian (Kuncken) Shawcross. Education: Montclair State College, A.B., 1948; New York University, A.M., 1950, Ph.D., 1958. Home: 20 Vernon Ter., Bloomfield, N.J. 07003. Office: Department of English, Staten Island Community College, Staten Island, N.Y. 10301; and Graduate Center of the City University of New York, 33 West 42nd St., New York, N.Y. 10036.

CAREER: Newark College of Engineering, Newark, N.J., 1948-63, began as instructor, became associate professor of English; Rutgers University, New Brunswick, N.J., 1963-67, began as associate professor, became professor of English; University of Wisconsin, Madison, professor of English, 1967-70; Staten Island Community College, Staten Island, N.Y., and graduate center of the City University of New York, 1970—, began as professor, became distinguished professor of English. City College (now City College of the City University of New York), New York, N.Y., lecturer in English, 1960-63. Visiting professor of English, New York University, 1962 and 1965, C. W. Post College, 1963, University of Delaware, 1965-66, State University of New York at Stony Brook, 1974. Charles Pfizer, Inc., Brooklyn, N.Y., writing consultant, 1955-56. Military service: U.S. Naval Reserve, 1942-46; became lieutenant junior grade. Member: College English Association, Modern Language Association of America, National Council of Teachers of English, Milton Society (treasurer, 1962—). Renaissance Society of America, Bibliographical Society of America, Northeast Modern Language Association, New York Shavians, Bibliographical Society of the University of Virginia.

WRITINGS: (Editor) The Complete English Poetry of John Milton, New York University Press, 1963, revised edition, 1971; (editor with Ronald D. Emma) Language and Style in Milton, Ungar, 1967; (editor and author of introduction) The Complete Poetry of John Donne, Doubleday, 1967; Seventeenth-Century Poetry, Lippincott, 1969; Poetry and Its Conventions, Free Press, 1972; (editor) Milton: The Critical Heritage, Routledge & Kegan Paul, Volume I, 1970, Volume II, 1972; Myths and Motifs in Literature, Free Press, 1973; (editor with Michael J. Lieb) Achievements of the Left Hand: Essays on Milton's Prose, University of Massachusetts Press, 1974. Contributor of articles to professional journals.

WORK IN PROGRESS: A book, A Milton Bibliography, 1624-1799; editing English Prose and Criticism, 1660-1800, for Gale.

* * *

SHEARMAN, Hugh (Francis) 1915-

PERSONAL: Born August 17, 1915, in Belfast, Northern Ireland; son of John Nicholson (a teacher) and Margaret (Morrison) Shearman; married Mary Milligan, July 13, 1960; children: John Robert, Amanda Margaret. Education: The Queen's University of Belfast, B.A. (honors), 1938; University of Dublin, Ph.D., 1944. Home: 36 Cliftonville Rd., Belfast BT14 6JY, Northern Ireland. Agent: A. M. Heath & Co. Ltd., 35 Dover St., London W. 1, England.

CAREER: Writer, Confidential examiner for educational and public bodies, 1944—. Lecturer in Great Britain and in western Europe; radio broadcaster; newspaper columnist. Member: Society of Authors, Crime Writers Association, National Book League, Theosophical Society.

WRITINGS: Belfast Royal Academy, 1785-1935, Belfast Royal Academy, 1935; Not an Inch: A Study of Northern Ireland and Lord Craigavon, Faber, 1942; The Bishop's Confession (fiction), Faber, 1943; A Bomb and a Girl (fiction), Faber, 1944; Planning and Reconstruction in Northern Ireland, Royal Society of Ulster Architects, 1945; Northern Ireland, H.M.S.O., 1946, 3rd edition, 1962; Anglo-Irish Relations, Faber, 1948.

Ulster, R. Hale, 1950; Finland, Stevens & Sons for London Institute of World Affairs, 1950; How Northern Ireland Is Governed, H.M.S.O., 1951, 2nd edition, 1963; Modern Ireland, Harrap, 1952; Modern Theosophy, Theosophical Publishing House (Madras), 1952; The Purpose of Tragedy, Theosophical Publishing House (Madras), 1955; Purpose Beyond Reason, Theosophical Publishing House (London), 1955; Ireland Since the Close of the Middle Ages, Harrap, 1955; Desire and Fulfillment, Theosophical Publishing House (Madras), 1956; An Approach to the Occult, Theosophical Publishing House (Madras), 1959; To Form a Nucleus, Theosophical Publishing House (Madras), 1959; The Round of Experience, Theosophical Publishing House (Madras), 1962; The Passionate Necessity, Theosophical Publishing House (London), 1962; Northern Ireland 1921-71, H.M.S.O., 1971. Also author of fiction under pseudonym.

Writer of stories for children. Contributor to Encyclopaedia Britannica, Encyclopedia Americana, Chambers's Encyclopaedia, New Universal Encyclopaedia, Children's Encyclopaedia, Year Book of World Affairs, Commonwealth Annual. Also contributor to World Affairs, Times (London), Scotsman, Belfast News-Letter, and other journals.

WORK IN PROGRESS: Fiction; research in British, Irish, and European affairs, in local antiquities, in India, and in historic cases of conversion to or from religious bodies.

SIDELIGHTS: Shearman speaks French; reads German, Spanish, Latin, and Greek.

* * *

SHEARMAN, John 1931-

PERSONAL: Born June 24, 1931, in England; son of Charles E. G. (a brigadier, British Army) and Evelyn (White) Shearman; married Jane Smith, June 29, 1957; children: Juliet, Niccola, Sarah, Michael. Education: Courtauld Institute of Art, University of London, B.A., 1955, Ph.D., 1957. Home: Home Close, Long Lane, Rickmansworth, Herts., England.

CAREER: University of London, Courtauld Institute, London, England, lecturer, 1957-67, reader, 1967-74, professor of history of art, 1974—.

WRITINGS: (With Anthony Blunt) The Drawings of Nicolas Poussin, Volume IV, Warburg Institute, University of London, 1963; Andrea del Sarto, Oxford University Press, 1965; Mannerism, Penguin, 1967; Raphael's Cartoons, Phaidon, 1972. Contributor to Burlington Magazine and to other art journals in England, America, and Germany.

WORK IN PROGRESS: Catalogue of Italian Pictures in Royal Collection, 1300-1600.

SIDELIGHTS: Shearman is "variously competent" in Italian, French, German, Spanish. Avocational interests: Yacht racing, travel, music.

SHEATS, Mary Boney 1918-
(Mary Lily Boney)

PERSONAL: Born March 19, 1918, in Wallace, N.C.; daughter of Leslie Norwood (an architect) and Mary Lily (Hussey) Boney; married Francois L. Sheats, 1972. *Education:* Woman's College, University of North Carolina (now University of North Carolina at Greensboro), B.A., 1938; Emory University, M.A., 1949; Columbia University, Ph.D., 1956. *Politics:* Democrat. *Religion:* Presbyterian. *Home:* 363 S. Candler St., Decatur, Ga. 30030. *Office:* Agnes Scott College, Decatur, Ga. 30030.

CAREER: Director of religious education at Presbyterian churches in Knoxville, Tenn., 1939-41, Charleston, W. Va., 1941-44, Atlanta, Ga., 1944-49; Agnes Scott College, Decatur, Ga., 1949—, began as instructor, now professor of Bible. *Presbyterian Survey*, member of board of directors, 1961—, chairman, 1965-66. *Member:* American Academy of Religion (president of Southern section, 1960-61), Society of Biblical Literature, Phi Beta Kappa.

WRITINGS—Under name Mary Lily Boney: *God Calls*, John Knox, 1964.

* * *

SHELLY, Maynard W(olfe) 1928-

PERSONAL: Born November 21, 1928, in St. Louis, Mo.; son of Maynard Wolfe and Adele (Koch) Shelly; married Carolyn Jean Hall, September 14, 1956. *Education:* Westminster College, Fulton, Mo., B.A., 1950; University of Wisconsin, M.A., 1954, Ph.D., 1956. *Home:* 1919 Stratford Rd., Lawrence, Kan. 66044. *Office:* Department of Psychology, University of Kansas, Lawrence, Kan.

CAREER: U.S. Office of Naval Research, Washington, D.C., mathematician, 1958-65; University of Kansas, Lawrence, associate professor of psychology, 1965—. *Member:* American Association for the Advancement of Science, American Mathematical Society, American Psychological Association, Association for Symbolic Logic, Institute of Management Sciences, Psychometric Society, Sigma Xi. *Awards, honors:* Social Science Research Council fellow, 1955-56.

WRITINGS: (Editor with W. W. Cooper and H. J. Leavitt) *New Perspectives in Organization Research*, Wiley, 1964; (editor with G. L. Bryan) *Human Judgments and Optimality*, Wiley, 1964; (editor with E. Glatt) *The Research Society*, Gordon and Breach, 1968; (editor with Tina Z. Adelberg) *Recent Readings in Reinforcement and Satisfaction*, MSS Educational Publishing, 1969; (editor) *Analyses of Satisfaction*, three volumes, MSS Educational Publishing, 1969. Contributor of articles to professional journals.

WORK IN PROGRESS: Personal Structures: A Framework for the Analysis of Individual Behavior and research on interpersonal optimization and on management of pleasure.

SIDELIGHTS: Shelly reads technical French and speaks some French. *Avocational interests:* Painting, mostly abstractions or modified abstractions.†

* * *

SHEMIN, Margaretha (Hoeneveld) 1928-

PERSONAL: Born November 23, 1928, in Alkmaar, Netherlands; daughter of Gabe (a physician) and Jantje (Toxopeus) Hoeneveld; married Elias Ralph Shemin (a physi-

cian), January 5, 1954; children: Douglas, Barbara, Frances. *Education:* University of Leiden, law degree; Columbia University, M.L.S., 1971. *Religion:* Unitarian-Universalist. *Home:* 17 Otsego Rd., Pleasantville, N.Y.

CAREER: Children's librarian in White Plains, N.Y. *Awards, honors:* Child Study Association Award, 1969, for *The Empty Moat.*

WRITINGS: The Little Riders, Coward, 1963; *Mrs. Herring*, Lothrop, 1967; *The Empty Moat*, Coward, 1969.

WORK IN PROGRESS: A children's book.

SIDELIGHTS: Ms. Shemin speaks and reads German, French and Dutch. She came to United States right after she received her law degree and has never practiced as an attorney.

* * *

SHEPARD, Francis P(arker) 1897-

PERSONAL: Born Mary 10, 1897, in Brookline, Mass.; son of Thomas Hill and Edna (Parker) Shepard; married Elizabeth Buchner, June 12, 1920; children: Thomas Hill II, Anthony Lee. *Education:* Harvard University, A.B., 1920; University of Chicago, Ph.D., 1922. *Home:* 9090 La Jolla Shores Dr., La Jolla, Calif. *Office:* Scripps Institute of Oceanography, University of California, La Jolla, Calif.

CAREER: University of Illinois, Urbana, 1922-42, began as instructor, professor of geology, 1939-42; University of California, Scripps Institute of Oceanography, La Jolla, research associate in division of war research marine geology, 1942-45, principal geologist, 1945-48, professor of submarine geology, 1948-64, professor of oceanography, 1964—. Member of expeditions studying submarine canyons in various parts of the world, including Japan, Indian Ocean, Mediterranean, Gulf of Mexico, Hawaii, Atlantic Ocean. *Military service:* U.S. Naval Reserve, 1918. *Member:* Geological Society of America, International Association of Sedimentologists (president, 1958-63), Sigma Xi. *Awards, honors: Papers in Marine Geology*, Macmillan, 1964, was a commemorative volume written in honor of Shepard; Wollaston Medal, 1966; D.S.C., Beloit College, 1968; an award has been established in Shepard's name by the Society of Economic Paleontologists and Mineralogists.

WRITINGS: Submarine Geology, Harper, 1948, 3rd edition, 1973; *Earth Beneath the Sea*, Johns Hopkins Press, 1959; (editor) *Recent Sediments, Northwest Gulf of Mexico*, American Association of Petroleum Geologists, 1960; (with R. F. Dill) *Submarine Canyons and Other Sea Valleys*, Rand McNally, 1966; (with H. R. Wanless) *Our Changing Coastlines*, McGraw, 1971. Contributor of some 140 articles to scientific and semi-popular periodicals.

WORK IN PROGRESS: Investigating canyons of sea floor and currents in submarine canyons; studies on history of sea level and on marine sediments.

BIOGRAPHICAL/CRITICAL SOURCES: Preface, *Papers in Marine Geology*, Macmillan, 1964.

* * *

SHEPPARD-JONES, Elisabeth 1920-

PERSONAL: Born May 9, 1920, in Penarth, Glamorganshire, Wales; daughter of John Edwardd (a doctor) and Mary (Amphlett) Sheppard-Jones. *Home:* Draenen Wen, Meadow Lane, Penarth, Glamorganshire, Wales.

CAREER: Author.

WRITINGS: The Patchwork Quilt (juvenile novel), Edward Arnold, 1950; *I Walk on Wheels*, Bles, 1958; *Welsh Legendary Tales*, Nelson, 1959; *The Search for Mary* (juvenile novel), Nelson, 1960; *Scottish Legendary Tales*, Nelson, 1962; *The Empty House* (juvenile novel), Nelson, 1965; *The Byrd's Nest*, Brockhampton Press, 1968; *Emma and the Awful Eight*, Hamlyn, 1968; *Cousin Charlie*, Kaye & Ward, 1973. Regular contributor to British Broadcasting Corp. radio.

WORK IN PROGRESS: A juvenile novel, *The Reluctant Nurse*, publication expected by Hamlyn.

* * *

SHERMAN, D(enis) R(onald) 1934-

PERSONAL: Born December 20, 1934, in Calcutta, India; son of Denis Basil (a printer) and Marjorie (Clayton) Sherman; married Sylvaine Dingwall, November 6, 1961. *Education:* Received primary education in India, secondary education in England; British School of Wireless Telegraphy, London, P.M.G. Certificate, 1952. *Address:* Box 22, Palapye, Bechuanaland, Africa. *Agent:* A. M. Heath & Co. Ltd., 35 Dover St., London W.1, England.

CAREER: Marconi Marine, Chelmsford, Essex, England, radio officer, 1952-54; Rhodesia Railways, Africa, station foreman, 1956—. *Military service:* Royal Navy, 1954-56.

WRITINGS: Old Mali and the Boy (novel), Little, Brown, 1964; *Into the Noonday Sun* (novel), Little, Brown, 1966; *Brothers of the Sea*, Little, Brown, 1966; *Ryan*, Ace Books, 1973. Occasional contributor of short stories to magazines.

SIDELIGHTS: Sherman told *CA:* "[I] hope to be able to write well enough one day to earn my living at it. I really like to write, but most days it's an effort to make the start, and usually after two thousand words or so I get tired and begin to lose interest.... Enjoy horseriding, hunting, drinking. Used to speak Hindu well enough but have forgotten most of it."†

* * *

SHERMAN, Eleanor Rae 1929-
(Ellie Rae Fleuridas)

PERSONAL: Born January 31, 1929, in Boston, Mass.; daughter of Philip I. (a lawyer and judge) and Helen (Smith) Sherman; married second husband, Clark G. McGaughey (a physician), April 14, 1962; children: (first marriage) Colette L. Fleuridas, Lauren A. Fleuridas; (second marriage) Jodi C. *Education:* Vermont Junior College (now Vermont College), A.A., 1949; Rhode Island School of Design, B.A., 1952; Arizona State University, graduate study in education, 1963.

CAREER: Professional fashion and photographic model, 1950-53; Patricia Stevens School of Modeling, Boston, Mass., teacher, 1952-53; free-lance illustrator for *Vogue* and Hallmark Greeting Cards, New York, N.Y., 1953; *McCall's*, New York, N.Y., assistant in research study, 1958-60; Mildred Todhunter Sheet—Interiors West, Scottsdale, Ariz., interior decorator, 1961-62. Swimming instructor, American Red Cross, 1949-56. *Member:* Phoenix Symphony Guild, Scottsdale Hospital Auxiliary, Phoenix Executive Club. *Awards, honors:* Winner of *McCall's* Room Design Contest, 1955.

WRITINGS—Under name Ellie Rae Fleuridas: (Self-illustrated) *I Learn to Swim*, Macmillan, 1962.

WORK IN PROGRESS: Collected rhymes and stories of author and her daughter, Colette, self-illustrated; a children's book about Africa and pygmies.†

* * *

SHERMAN, Howard J. 1931-

PERSONAL: Born January 3, 1931, in Chicago, Ill.; son of Milton A. (an engineer) and Ida (Mayer) Sherman; married Ann Perlin, June 29, 1962; children: Paul Dylan. *Education:* University of California, Los Angeles, B.A., 1950; University of Chicago, Jur.D., 1953; University of Southern California, M.A., 1957; University of California, Berkeley, Ph.D., 1960. *Office:* University of California, Berkeley, Calif.

CAREER: Wayne State University, Detroit, Mich., assistant professor of economics, 1960-62; California Institute of Technology, Pasadena, assistant professor of economics, 1962-64; University of California, Berkeley, lecturer in economics, 1964—. *Member:* American Economic Association. *Awards, honors:* Research fellowship at Brookings Institution, 1960-61.

WRITINGS: Macrodynamic Economics, Appleton, 1964; *Introduction to the Economics of Growth, Unemployment, and Inflation*, Appleton, 1964; *Elementary Aggregate Economics*, Appleton, 1966; *Profits in the United States: An Introduction to a Study of Economic Concentration and Business Cycles*, Cornell University Press, 1968; *The Soviet Economy*, Little, Brown, 1969; (with E. K. Hunt) *Economics: An Introduction to Traditional and Radical Views*, Harper, 1972; *Radical Political Economy: Capitalism and Socialism from a Marxist-Humanist Perspective*, Basic Books, 1972. Contributor to *Proceedings of American Statistical Association* and to *Soviet Studies*.

SIDELIGHTS: Sherman is competent in Russian.†

* * *

SHERRARD, Philip (Owen Arnould) 1922-

PERSONAL: Born September 23, 1922, in Oxford, England; son of Raymond Nason and Brynhild (Olivier) Sherrard; married Anna Mirodia, 1947; children: Selga Maria, Liadain Olivier Alexandra. *Education:* Peterhouse, Cambridge, M.A., 1941; University of London, Ph.D., 1952; Oxford University, M.A. *Religion:* Orthodox Christian. *Home:* Katounia, Limni, Euboea, Greece.

CAREER: British School of Archaeology, Athens, Greece, assistant director, 1951-52, 1958-61. St. Antony's College, Oxford University, research fellow, 1957-58. *Military service:* British Army, 1941-46.

WRITINGS: Orientation and Descent: Poems, Saville Press, 1953; *The Marble Threshing Floor: Studies in Modern Greek Poetry*, Vallentine, Mitchell & Co., 1956; *The Greek East and the Latin West*, Oxford University Press, 1959; *Athos: The Mountain of Silence*, Oxford University Press, 1960; (with E. L. Keeley) *Six Poets of Modern Greece*, Knopf, 1960; *Constantinople: The Iconography of a Sacred City*, Urs Graf-Verlag, 1964, Oxford University Press, 1965; (editor with Keeley) *Four Greek Poets*, Penguin, 1966; *The Pursuit of Greece*, J. Murray, 1966; *Byzantium*, Time-Life, 1967; (editor and translator with Keeley) *George Seferis: Collected Poems*, Princeton University Press, 1967; (with J. C. Campbell) *Modern Greece*, Benn, 1968; *Studies in Neo-Hellenism*, Athens, 1971; (editor with Keeley) *C. P. Cavafy: Selected Poems*, Princeton University Press, 1973. Contributor to *Encounter, New Statesman, Sobornost, Studies in Comparative Religion*, and other periodicals and books.

WORK IN PROGRESS: Editing with E. L. Keeley, *C. P. Cavafy: Collected Poems*, for Princeton University Press and Hogarth Press.

* * *

SHERWOOD, John C(ollingwood) 1918-

PERSONAL: Born December 30, 1918, in Hempstead, N.Y.; son of George C. and Nettie (Allen) Sherwood; married Irma M. Zwergel (a teacher), December 23, 1944; children: Martha A., Jeremy C., Sarah R. *Education:* Lafayette College, B.A., 1941; Yale University, M.A., 1942, Ph.D., 1945. *Politics:* Democrat. *Religion:* Methodist. *Home:* 1981 Moss St., Eugene, Ore. *Office:* Department of English, University of Oregon, Eugene, Ore.

CAREER: Cornell University, Ithaca, N.Y., instructor in English, 1944-46; University of Oregon, Eugene, assistant professor 1946-55, associate professor, 1955-61, professor of English, 1961—. *Member:* Modern Language Association of America, National Council of Teachers of English, American Association of University Professors, Phi Beta Kappa. *Awards, honors:* American Council of Learned Societies fellowship, 1952-53.

WRITINGS: (Editor with Philip W. Souers and wife, Irma Z. Sherwood) *A Writer's Reader*, Harcourt, 1950; *Discourse of Reason*, Harper, 1960, 2nd edition, 1964. Contributor to literary and philological journals.

WORK IN PROGRESS: Research in literary criticism of John Dryden.

* * *

SHERWOOD, Morgan B(ronson) 1929-

PERSONAL: Born October 22, 1929, in Anchorage, Alaska; son of Jay Robert (a trainman) and Agnes (Banner) Sherwood; married Jeanie Woods, June 7, 1963. *Education:* San Diego State College (now University), A.B., 1953; University of California, Berkeley, M.A., 1958, Ph.D., 1962. *Office:* Department of History, University of California, Davis, Calif. 95616.

CAREER: University of California, Berkeley, research historian in Washington, D.C., 1961-64; University of Cincinnati, Cincinnati, Ohio, assistant professor of history, 1964-65; University of California, Davis, associate professor of history, 1965—. *Military service:* U.S. Army, 1953-54. *Member:* Organization of American Historians, Western History Association, Agricultural History Society, Society for the History of Technology.

WRITINGS: Exploration of Alaska, 1865-1900, Yale University Press, 1965; (editor with J. L. Penick, C. W. Pursell, and D. C. Swain) *The Politics of American Science*, Rand McNally, 1965, revised edition, M.I.T. Press, 1972; (editor) *Alaska and Its History*, University of Washington Press, 1967; (contributor) M. Kranzberg and C. W. Pursell, editors, *Technology in Western Civilization*, Oxford University Press, 1967; (contributor) C. J. Schneer, editor, *Toward a History of Geology*, M.I.T. Press, 1969. Contributor to professional journals. Editorial advisory board, *Pacific Northwest Quarterly*, 1966—; editorial advisory board, *Pacific Historical Review*, 1970-73; associate editor, *Agricultural History.*

WORK IN PROGRESS: Patent Nonsense in American Technology; and *Historiography of Alaska.*

SHETTY, C(handrashekar) M(ajur) 1927-

PERSONAL: Born March 9, 1927, in Udipi, Mysore, India; son of Uppoor Muthaya (a landlord) and Doddakka Shetty; married Vasanti, December 15, 1955; children: Uday, Binda. *Education:* Bombay University, B.A., 1952, M.A., 1958. *Office:* Industrial Credit and Investment Corp. of India Ltd., 163 Backbay Reclamation, Bombay 1, India.

CAREER: Government of India, economic research officer for Khadi and Village Industries Commission, 1954-55, field officer in economic investigation division of Central Small Industry Organization, Ministry of Commerce and Industry, 1956-60, research officer at Ministry of Agriculture, Agro-Economic Research Centre, 1961-63; Industrial Credit and Investment Corp. of India Ltd., Bombay, India, project officer, 1964—. Sardar Vallabhbhai University, Kaira, Gujarat, India, honorary postgraduate professor in industrial economics, 1961-63. Consultant to United Nations Industrial Development Organization, 1967; adviser and consultant to Asian Development Bank, Manila, 1969-72. *Member:* Society for International Development, Indian Economic Association.

WRITINGS: Small-Scale and Household Industries in a Developing Economy, Asia Publishing House, 1963; *Financing Small Industry Development*, United Nations Industrial Development Organization, 1968; *Dictionary of Development Banking*, Elsevier, 1972. Writer of more than twenty published research papers; contributor to proceedings; also contributor of articles and reviews to *Economic Weekly, Commerce, Bankers' Journal, Journal of Small and Cottage Industry*, and other journals in economic and financial fields.

WORK IN PROGRESS: Rural Industrialization: Its Pattern and Problems.

SIDELIGHTS: Shetty has traveled widely in Asia, Africa, Europe, the United States, and the Pacific countries.

* * *

SHIFFERT, Edith (Marcombe) 1916-
(Edith Marion Marcombe)

PERSONAL: Born January 9, 1916, in Toronto, Ontario, Canada; daughter of John Benjamin (an engineer) and Annie Marie (Drew) Marcombe; married Steven R. Shiffert (a technical writer), March 15, 1940 (divorced, 1970). *Education:* Attended University of Washington, Seattle, 1956-62. *Religion:* Presently non-formal. *Office:* Department of English, Kyoto Seika College, Iwakura-Kino, Sakyo-ku, Kyoto, Japan 606.

CAREER: Secretary in Seattle, Wash., and Los Angeles, Calif., employee of U.S. Weather Bureau in Anchorage, Alaska, and policewoman (briefly) in Hilo, Hawaii; Doshisha University, Koyota, Japan, instructor in English, 1963-69; Kyoto Seika College, Kyoto, Japan, professor of English, 1969—. Lecturer at Kyoto University, 1966-68; director of poetry readings on Seattle radio and television programs, 1958-62.

WRITINGS: In an Open Woods, A. Swallow, 1961; *For a Return to Kona*, A. Swallow, 1964; *The Kyoto Years*, Kyoto Seika Junior College Press (Japan), 1971; (translator and compiler with Yuki Sawa) *Anthology of Modern Japanese Poetry*, Tuttle, 1971; (translator with Sawa) *Chieko* (chapbook) Sinktree Press, 1973; (translator) Taeko Takaori, *When a Bird Rests and Other Tanka*, privately printed, 1974. Contributor of poetry, translations, articles, and reviews to journals in the United States, Canada, and

Japan. Contributions prior to 1939 under name Edith Marion Marcombe. A founder and former Far Eastern editor of *Poetry Northwest*; member of editorial staff of *East-West Review*, *Kyoto Seika English Papers*, and *Poetry Nippon*.

WORK IN PROGRESS: *Hermit, Lover, Cat*, a book of poems; *A Buson Reader*, translations from Buson, with Yuki Sawa; chapbooks.

SIDELIGHTS: Edith Shiffert was raised in eastern New York state and in Detroit, Mich. She has lived in Hawaii and Alaska, spending half her time in solitary mountain areas and half in large Japanese and American cities. She prefers a quiet life with a few friends, and a lot of walking.

* * *

SHINDELL, Sidney 1923-

PERSONAL: Born May 31, 1923, in New Haven, Conn.; son of Benjamin A. (a manufacturer) and Freda (Mann) Shindell; married Gloria Emhoff, June 17, 1945; children: Barbara Ann (Mrs. Marc D. Kaufman), Roger Mark, Lawrence Michael, Judith Lee. *Education:* Yale University, B.S., 1944; Long Island College of Medicine, State University of New York, M.D., 1946; Emory University, law studies, 1948-49; George Washington University, LL.B., 1951. *Home:* 9059 North Meadowlark, Bayside, Wis. 53217. *Office:* 1725 West Wisconsin Ave., Milwaukee, Wis. 53233.

CAREER: Licensed to practice medicine by National Board of Medical Examiners, 1947, in Georgia, 1947, Connecticut, 1950, Pennsylvania, 1960; U.S. Public Health Service, assigned to Georgia State Health Department, 1947-52; admitted to District of Columbia bar, 1952, Connecticut bar, 1954; Connecticut Commission on the Care and Treatment of the Chronically Ill, Aged and Infirm, medical director, 1952-57; American Joint Distribution Committee, overseas operations medical director, 1957-59; Allegheny County (Pa.) Health Department, director of health district, 1960-62; University of Pittsburgh, Pittsburgh, Pa., assistant clinical professor, department of preventive medicine and public health practice, 1960-61, assistant professor of preventive medicine, 1962-65; Hospital Utilization Project of Western Pennsylvania, director, 1965-66; Medical College of Wisconsin, Milwaukee, professor of preventive medicine and chairman of department, 1966—. Executive director of Health Service Data of Wisconsin, 1967—. Fellow of American College of Preventive Medicine and American College of Legal Medicine. Visiting lecturer at Harvard University and Smith College, 1954. Former member of medical-legal liaison committees in several states. *Member:* American Medical Association, American Bar Association, American Public Health Association (fellow), American Health Data Systems (secretary, 1972—), Association of Teachers of Preventive Medicine.

WRITINGS: *Statistics, Science and Sense*, University of Pittsburgh Press, 1964; *Law in Medical Practice*, University of Pittsburgh Press, 1965; (with M. London) *A Method of Hospital Utilization Review*, University of Pittsburgh Press, 1965. Contributor to *Encyclopedia International*. Writer of special surveys and reports for professional committees and commissions. Contributor of articles to law and medical journals.†

* * *

SHIPLEY, Joseph T(wadell) 1893-

PERSONAL: Born August 19, 1893, in Brooklyn, N.Y.; son of Jay R. (a law book salesman) and Jennie (Fragner) Shipley; married Helen Bleet; married second wife, Anne Ziporkes; children: (first marriage) Margaret (Mrs. Leslie Fiedler), Paul David; (second marriage) John Burke, Howard Thorne. *Education:* City College (now City College of the City University of New York), A.B., 1912; Columbia University, A.M., 1914, Ph.D., 1931. *Religion:* Society of Friends. *Agent:* Shirley Hector Agency, 29 West 46th St., New York, N.Y. 10036.

CAREER: Teacher, drama critic, author. Stuyvesant High School, New York, N.Y., instructor in English, 1914-57, senior adviser, 1940-57. Co-organizer of Yeshiva College (now University), New York, N.Y., 1926-28, assistant professor, and later associate professor of English and head of department, 1928-44; lecturer in Graduate Division, City College (now City College of the City University of New York), 1928-38, and Brooklyn College (now Brooklyn College of the City University of New York), 1932-38; conductor of seminar for playwrights, Dramatic Workshop, 1948-52; lecturer on American life and literature on world trip, 1957-58. Chairman, National Committee on Education in the Public Arts; U.S. director, Far East Research Institute; American advisor, Theatre des Nations, Paris; member of council of cultural advisors, American College in Paris; American correspondent, Association pour le Rencontre des Cultures; member of boards of Hwa Kiu University, Macao, and Canton University, Hong Kong. Editorial advisor, Philosophical Library; vocabulary consultant, Science Research Associates.

MEMBER: Association International des Critiques de Theatre (vice-president for United States), P.E.N., New York Drama Critics Circle (president, 1952-54; secretary, 1968—), Critics' Circle (London; honorary member), English Association (London; life member), Phi Beta Kappa (honorary member).

WRITINGS *King John* (fiction), Greenberg, 1925; *The Art of Eugene O'Neill*, University of Washington Press, 1928; *The Literary Isms*, University of Washington Press, 1931; *The Quest for Literature*, Richard R. Smith, 1931; *Auguste Rodin* (from notes by Rodin's assistant, Victor Frisch), Stokes, 1941; *Dictionary of Word Origins*, Philosophical Library, 1945, 2nd edition, Greenwood Press, 1969; *Trends in Literature*, Philosophical Library, 1949; *Dictionary of Early English*, Philosophical Library, 1955; *Dictionary of World Literary Terms*, Allen & Unwin, 1955, revised and enlarged edition, Writer, Inc., 1970; *Guide to Great Plays*, Public Affairs Press, 1956; *Playing With Words*, Prentice-Hall, 1960; *The Mentally Disturbed Teacher*, Chilton, 1961; *Word Games for Play and Power*, Prentice-Hall, 1962; *Ibsen: Five Major Plays*, American R.D.M., 1965; *Vocabulab*, Science Research Associates, 1970; *Word Play*, Hawthorn, 1972.

Editor: *Dictionary of World Literature: Criticism, Forms, Technique*, Philosophical Library, 1943, new edition, Littlefield, 1960; *Encyclopedia of Literature*, two volumes, Philosophical Library, 1946. Also editor of twelve books, and author of seven books, in "Study-Master Guides to Drama" series published by American R.D.M., 1963-65.

Translator from the French: Baudelaire, *Prose Poems and Diaries*, Modern Library, 1919; Paul Geraldy, *You and Me* (poems), Boni & Liveright, 1923; Albert Ades, *A Naked King* (novel), Boni & Liveright, 1924; (and compiler) *Modern French Poetry*, Greenberg, 1926, reprinted, Books for Libraries, 1972; Paul Eluard, *Pablo Picasso*, Philosophical Library, 1947.

Writer of television scripts for "Ford Hour," radio scripts for "Footlight Forum," WMCA, 1938-40, "Word Stories," WOR, 1949-51, and scenarios for forty-eight films of the work of New York City schools, 1938-40.

Author of poems and essays appearing in American, English, French, Indian, and Pakistani magazines, with the poems reprinted in fourteen anthologies in three countries.

Drama critic for *Call*, 1919-21, *Leader*, 1921-22, *New Leader*, 1922-62, and for radio station WEVD, 1940—. Foreign editor, *Contemporary Verse*, 1919-26; assistant editor, *Journal of the History of Ideas*, 1940-44; editor, *American Bookman*, 1944-50; member of editorial board, *Venture* (Pakistani literary quarterly); former member of editorial board, *Journal of Aesthetics*. Has covered the New York theater for the *Guardian* (Manchester, England), and *Theatre* (Paris).

WORK IN PROGRESS: More or Less Me (memoirs), and *Great Writers on Great Writers*, completion of both expected in 1975.

SIDELIGHTS: Various books have been translated into Hebrew, Spanish, German, French, and Japanese, and published in English in England and India. Since 1958, Shipley has spent three months annually observing the theater in Europe; on his world trip in 1957-58, he was the guest of eleven governments in Europe and Asia.

During his college days, Shipley was on swimming, tennis, and chess teams, and still plays chess when he can find the time.

BIOGRAPHICAL/CRITICAL SOURCES: Collier's, September 9, 1950.

*   *   *

SHIPP, Thomas J.   1918-

PERSONAL: Born January 3, 1918, in Nara Visa, N.M., son of Joel Thomas and Laura (Rowe) Shipp; married Dee Sparling, February 1, 1941; children: Thomas, Judy. *Education:* Drury College, B.A., 1941; Perkins School of Theology, Southern Methodist University, B.D., 1944; Texas Wesleyan College, D.D., 1964. *Home:* 8839 McCraw, Dallas, Tex. 75209.

CAREER: Ordained Methodist minister, 1944. Lovers Lane Methodist Church, Dallas, Tex., pastor, 1945. Lecturer on alcoholism throughout United States. The Methodist Church, former chairman of World Service Commission, North Texas Conference, fourteen years, became chairman of council on connectional ministries. Member of board of directors of Institute of Scientific Studies for Prevention of Alcoholism, Dallas Council of Social Agencies (former president), Dallas Rehabilitation Center, Methodist Hospital (vice-president of board), Bradford Memorial Hospital, other health and welfare agencies in Dallas. *Member:* Texas Social Welfare Association, Southern Methodist University Alumni Association (former president). *Awards, honors:* Award of Merit, Methodist General Board of Temperance, 1958; Distinguished Service Award, Drury College Alumni Association, 1958; Service to Mankind Award, Sertoma International, 1959; L.H.D. from Drury College.

WRITINGS: Helping the Alcoholic and His Family, Prentice-Hall, 1963. Contributor to magazines and journals.

AVOCATIONAL INTERESTS: Baseball, basketball, handball, bowling, swimming, golf, horseback riding.

BIOGRAPHICAL/CRITICAL SOURCES: Listen, January-February, 1962.

SHIRREFFS, Gordon D(onald)   1914-
(Gordon Donalds, Jackson Flynn, Stewart Gordon)

PERSONAL: Born January 15, 1914, in Chicago, Ill.; son of George and Rose (Warden) Shirreffs; married Alice Johanna Gutwein, February 8, 1941; children: Carole Alice, Brian Allen. *Education:* Attended Northwestern University, 1946-49; California State University, Northridge, B.A., 1967, M.A., 1973. *Home and office:* 17427 San Jose St., Granada Hills, Calif. 91344. *Agent:* Donald Mac-Campbell, Inc., 12 East 41st St., New York, N.Y. 10017; and Ruth Cantor, 156 Fifth Ave., New York, N.Y. 10010.

CAREER: Union Tank Car Co., Chicago, Ill., clerk, 1935-40, 1946; Brown & Bigelow, Chicago, Ill., salesman, 1946-47; Shirreffs Gadgets and Toys, Chicago, Ill., owner, 1948-52; professional writer, 1952—. *Military service:* U.S. Army, 1940-45, 1948; became captain. *Member:* Veterans of Foreign Wars, Disabled American Veterans, National Rifle Association, Western Writers of America. *Awards, honors:* Commonwealth Club of California Silver Medal Award, 1962, for *The Gray Sea Raiders*.

WRITINGS: Rio Bravo, Gold Medal Books, 1956; *Code of the Gun*, Crest Books, 1956; (under pseudonym Gordon Donalds) *Arizona Justice*, Avalon, 1956; *Range Rebel*, Pyramid Books, 1956; *Fort Vengeance*, Popular Library, 1957; (under pseudonym Stewart Gordon) *Gunswift*, Avalon, 1957; *Bugles on the Prairie*, Gold Medal Books, 1957; *Massacre Creek*, Popular Library, 1957; *Son of the Thunder People*, Westminster, 1957; (under pseudonym Gordon Donalds) *Top Gun*, Avalon, 1957; *Shadow Valley*, Popular Library, 1958; *Ambush on the Mesa*, Gold Medal Books, 1958; *Swiftwagon*, Westminster, 1958; *Last Train from Gun Hill*, Signet Books, 1958; *The Brave Rifles*, Gold Medal Books, 1959; *The Lonely Gun*, Avon, 1959; *Roanoke Raiders*, Westminster, 1959; *Fort Suicide*, Avon, 1959; *Trail's End*, Avalon, 1959; *Shadow of a Gunman*, Ace Books, 1959; *Renegade Lawman*, Avon, 1959.

Apache Butte, Ace Books, 1960; *They Met Danger*, Whitman, 1960; *The Mosquito Fleet*, Chilton, 1961; *The Rebel Trumpet*, Westminster, 1961; *The Proud Gun*, Avon, 1961; *Hangin' Pards*, Ace Books, 1961; *Ride a Lone Trail*, Ace Books, 1961; *The Gray Sea Raiders*, Chilton, 1961; *Powder Boy of the Monitor*, Westminster, 1961; *The Valiant Bugles*, Signet Books, 1962; *Tumbleweed Trigger*, Ace Books, 1962; *The Haunted Treasure of the Espectros*, Chilton, 1962; *Voice of the Gun*, Ace Books, 1962; *Rio Desperado*, Ace Books, 1962; *Action Front!*, Westminster, 1962; *The Border Guidon*, Signet Books, 1962; *Mystery of Lost Canyon*, Chilton, 1963; *Slaughter at Broken Bow*, Avon, 1963; *The Cold Seas Beyond*, Westminster, 1963; *The Secret of the Spanish Desert*, Chilton, 1964; *Quicktrigger*, Ace Books, 1964; *Too Tough to Die*, Avon, 1964; *The Nevada Gun*, World Distributors, 1964; *The Hostile Beaches*, Westminster, 1964; *The Hidden Rider of Dark Mountain*, Ace Books, 1964; *Blood Justice*, Signet Books, 1964; *Gunslingers Three*, World Distributors, 1964; *Judas Gun*, Gold Medal Books, 1964; *Last Man Alive*, Avon, 1964; *Now He Is Legend*, Gold Medal Books, 1965; *The Lone Rifle*, Signet Books, 1965; *The Enemy Seas*, Westminster, 1965; *Barranca*, Signet Books, 1965; *Bolo Battalion*, Westminster, 1966; *Southwest Drifter*, Gold Medal Books, 1967; *Torpedoes Away*, Westminster, 1967; *The Godless Breed*, Gold Medal Books, 1968; *Five Graves to Boothill*, Avon, 1968, revised edition, 1970; *The Killer Sea*, Westminster, 1968; *Mystery of the Lost Cliffdwelling*, Prentice-Hall, 1968; *Showdown in Sonora*, Gold Medal Books, 1969.

Jack of Spades, Dell Books, 1970; *The Manhunter*, Gold Medal Books, 1970; *Brasada*, Dell Books, 1972; *Bowman's Kid*, Gold Medal Books, 1973; *Mystery of the Haunted Mine*, School Book Service, 1973; (under pseudonym Jackson Flynn) *Sodbusters*, Universal Publishing, 1974.

Contributor of over 150 short stories and novelettes to periodicals.

WORK IN PROGRESS: The Apache Hunter; *The Man From Baja*.

SIDELIGHTS: Shirreffs's Western books have been published in Norway, Sweden, Denmark, Finland, Germany, France, Italy, Spain, England, Canada, and Australia. *Massacre Creek* was filmed as "Galvanized Yankee" for "Playhouse 90" (television), *Rio Bravo* as "Oregon Passage" by Allied Artists, *Silent Reckoning* as "The Lonesome Trail" by Lippert Productions, *Judas Gun* as "A Long Ride from Heel" by B.R.C. Productions, and *Blood Justice* by Jacques Bar Productions. *Avocational interests:* Arms collecting, model making, marksmanship (pistol, rifle, and bow), fishing, hunting, travel, Southwest legends, and sea lore.

*　　*　　*

SHOEMAKER, Robert John 1919-

PERSONAL: Born February 7, 1919, in Erie, Pa.; son of Robert Harrison (an electrical construction foreman) and Loraine Jane (Underhill) Shoemaker; married Mary Louise Altenbaugh, September 4, 1943 (died, September 1, 1965); married Gloria Lee Maruca, December 15, 1973; children: (first marriage) Suzanne (Mrs. Carl von Ende), Robert Harrison, Bonnie Louise, Jo Holland. *Education:* University of Pittsburgh, B.S., 1942, M.D., 1944; Pittsburgh Psychoanalytic Institute, specialized study, 1957-63. *Religion:* Presbyterian. *Home:* 825 Morewood Ave., Pittsburgh, Pa. 15213. *Office:* 121 University Pl., Pittsburgh, Pa. 15213.

CAREER: Intern, 1944-45, then resident in psychiatry, in Pennsylvania institutions, 1945-46, 1948-50; diplomate in psychiatry, American Board of Psychiatry and Neurology, 1950; private practice as psychiatrist, Pittsburgh, Pa., 1950—. University of Pittsburgh, Pittsburgh, Pa., instructor, 1950-55, clinical assistant professor, 1955-59, clinical associate professor of psychiatry, School of Medicine, 1959—, associate psychiatrist, Staunton Clinic, 1950-59. Consultant to Presbyterian-University Hospital, Woman's Magee Hospital, both Pittsburgh; also consultant to Blue Shield, 1973—, Pennsylvania State Office of Rehabilitation, and Metropolitan Life Insurance Co. Chairman of task force on religion and mental health, Pennsylvania Comprehensive Mental Health Planning; consultant to Atomic Energy Commission and Pittsburgh Theological Seminary. *Military service:* U.S. Army, Medical Corps, 1946-48.

MEMBER: American Medical Association, American Psychiatric Association (fellow), Pennsylvania Medical Society, Pennsylvania Psychiatric Society (fellow; president, 1971-72), Allegheny County Medical Society, Pittsburgh Neuropsychiatric Society (president, 1964-65).

WRITINGS: (Editor with Yale D. Koskoff) *Vistas in Neuropsychiatry*, University of Pittsburgh Press, 1964. Also author of introduction, *Prayer-Centered Listening*, by G. V. McCausland, [Pittsburgh], 1969. Contributor of papers to medical journals.

WORK IN PROGRESS: Papers on subjects in his field.

SHOEMAKER, William H(utchinson) 1902-

PERSONAL: Born March 21, 1902, in Norristown, Pa.; son of Edward C. (a manufacturer) and Margaret R. (Walker) Shoemaker; married Catharine K. Witherell, August 29, 1931; children: Edward C. II, Phillip W. *Education:* Princeton University, A.B., 1924, M.A., 1928, Ph.D., 1934; also studied at Centro de Estudios Historicos, Madrid, Spain, 1924, 1927, University of Pennsylvania, 1925, University of Chicago, 1928. *Religion:* Society of Friends (Quaker). *Home:* 602 Edgewood Ave., Columbia, Mo. 65201. *Office:* 16 Arts and Science, University of Missouri, Columbia, Mo. 65201.

CAREER: Lake Forest Academy, Lake Forest, Ill., Spanish master, 1924-26; Princeton University, Princeton, N.J., part-time instructor in Spanish, 1926-28, instructor, 1928-29, 1930-33, assistant professor, 1933-38; University of Kansas, Lawrence, professor and chairman of department of Romance languages and literatures, 1938-57; University of Illinois, Urbana, professor and head of department of Spanish, Italian, and Portuguese, 1957-69, professor and associate member of Center for Advanced Study, 1969-70, professor emeritus, 1970—. Visiting professor of Spanish at University of California, Los Angeles, 1954; guest lecturer at Ateneo de Madrid and University of Barcelona, 1963; visiting professor of Spanish, University of Missouri, 1970—. *Member:* Modern Language Association of America, American Association of Teachers of Spanish and Portuguese (president, 1950). *Awards, honors:* Grants from American Philosophical Society and University of Kansas Endowment Association for research in Spain, 1957, in London, 1961; William H. Shoemaker-Sigma Delta Pi annual scholarship award established in his honor by University of Kansas chapter of Sigma Delta Pi, 1957; Commander, Order of Civil Merit (Spain), 1959; Fulbright research scholar, 1963-64.

WRITINGS: The Multiple Stage in Spain during the Fifteenth and Sixteenth Centuries, Princeton University Press, 1935; (editor, and compiler of vocabulary and exercises) Jose Robles, *Tertulias espanolas*, Crofts, 1938; (with others) *Manual of Guides Part VI—Foreign Languages*, State of Kansas Department of Education, 1940; (editor) Alejandro Casona, *Nuestra Natacha*, Appleton, 1947; (editor) Benito Perez Galdos, *Cronica de la quincena*, Princeton University Press, 1948; *Spanish Minimum*, Heath, 1953; *Cuentos de la joven generacion*, Holt, 1959; *Los prologos de Galdos*, Ediciones de Andrea-University of Illinois Press, 1962; *Estudios sobre Galdos*, Castalia, 1970; *Los articulos de Galdos en "La Nacion": 1865-66, 1868*, Insula, 1972; *Las cartas desconocidas da Geldos en "La Prensa" de Buenos Aires*, Ediciones Cultura Hispanica, 1973. Contributor to language journals. Member of editorial committee, *Symposium*, 1946-52, Hispanofila, 1957—; consultant, PMLA.

WORK IN PROGRESS: Two books, *La critica literaria de Galdo's* and *The Novelistic Art of Galdos*.

*　　*　　*

SHORE, Wilma 1913-

PERSONAL: Born October 12, 1913, in New York, N.Y.; daughter of William J. and Viola (an author; maiden name Brothers) Shore; married Lou Solomon (a writer), June, 1935; children: Hilary (Mrs. Albert M. Bendich), Dinah (Mrs. Edward P. Stevenson). *Residence:* New York, N.Y. *Agent:* McIntosh & Otis, Inc., 18 East 41st St., New York, N.Y. 10017.

CAREER: Author. *Member:* Writers Guild of America (East).

WRITINGS: Women Should be Allowed, Dutton, 1965. Short stories published in a number of Magazines and anthologized in *Best Short Stories, Prize Short Stories: The O. Henry Awards*, and *The Best From Fantasy and Science Fiction.*†

*   *   *

SHORES, Louis 1904-

PERSONAL: Born September 14, 1904, in Buffalo, N.Y.; son of Paul (a painter) and Ernestine (Lutenberg) Shores; married Geraldine Urist, November 19, 1931. *Education:* University of Toledo, B.A., 1926; College of the City of New York, M.S., 1927; Columbia University, B.S. in L.S., 1928; attended University of Chicago, 1929-30; George Peabody College, Ph.D., 1934. *Politics:* Democrat. *Religion:* Baptist. *Home:* 2013 W. Randolph Circle, Tallahassee, Fla. 32303. *Office:* Room 304, Strozier Library, Florida State University, Tallahassee, Fla.

CAREER: New York Public Library, New York, N.Y., reference assistant, 1926-28; Fisk University, Nashville, Tenn., librarian and professor, 1928-33; George Peabody College, Nashville, Tenn., librarian, 1933-37; director of library school, 1933-46; Florida State University, Tallahassee, dean of library school and professor, 1946-67; professor, emeritus and dean emeritus, 1967—. Collier's Encyclopedia, New York, N.Y., advisor-designer, 1946-58, editor-in-chief, 1958—. Special lecturer in library science at McGill University, Montreal, Quebec, Canada, 1930, at University of Dayton, Dayton, Ohio, 1931, and at Colorado State College of Education (now University of Northern Colorado), Greeley, 1936. Compton's Pictured Encyclopedia, editorial advisor, 1934-41. Governor's Commission on Works Projects Administration Community Service Projects, chairman, 1939-41; Air University, Maxwell Air Force Base, Ala., library advisory board, 1952-56. Visiting professor, Southern Illinois University, University of Colorado, Dalhousie University, University of Georgia, Morehead State University, and Johnson C. Smith University. *Military service:* U.S. Army Air Forces, 1942-46; became major; Air Corps Reserve, 1946-53. Awarded Legion of Merit. *Member:* Association of College and Reference Librarians (director), American Library Association, American Library History Roundtable (a founder), National Education Association, Southeastern Library Association (president, 1950-52), Lions Club, Phi Kappa Phi, Phi Delta Kappa, Kappa Delta Pi, Pi Gamma Mu. *Awards, honors:* Senior Fulbright research fellow, 1951-52; Beta Phi Mu Award in Library Education, 1967; Isadore Gilbert Mudge Citation from Library-College Associates, 1967; D.H.L. from Dallas Baptist College, 1970.

WRITINGS: How to Use Your Library: A Series of Articles on Libraries for High School and College Students (pamphlet), Scholastic Publishing Co., 1928; *Origins of the American College Library, 1638-1800*, George Peabody College for Teachers, 1934; *The Library Arts College—A Possibility in 1954?* (pamphlet), School and Society, 1935; *Basic Reference Books; an Introduction to the Evaluation, Study, and Use of Reference Materials With Special Emphasis on Some 200 Titles*, American Library Association, 1937, 2nd edition, 1939; *Know Your Encyclopedia: A Unit of Library Instruction Based on "Compton's Pictured Encyclopedia"* (pamphlet), F. E. Compton, 1937; *Highways in the Sky: The Story of the AACS*, Barnes & Noble, 1947;

Libraries in Florida: A Survey of Library Opportunities in the State (pamphlet), Florida Library Association Survey Committee, 1948; *Not for Tourists* (pamphlet), Florida Library Association Library Action Committee, 1948; (editor) *Challenges to Librarianship*, Florida State University, c. 1953; *Basic Reference Sources: An Introduction to Materials and Methods*, American Library Association, 1954; *A Profession of Faith* (pamphlet), State University (Genesco, N.Y.), 1958; (editor) *Basic Materials for Florida Junior Colleges: Reference Books*, Florida State Department of Education, 1960; *Instructional Materials: An Introduction for Teachers*, Ronald, 1960; *Mark Hopkins' Log and Other Essays* (selected by John D. Marshall), Shoe String, 1965; (editor with Robert Jordan and John Harvey) *The Library-College: Contributions for American Higher Education at the Jamestown College Workshop, 1965*, Drexel Press, 1966; *Library-College USA: Essays on a Prototype for an American Higher Education*, South Pass Press, 1970; *Library Education*, Libraries Unlimited, 1972; *Looking Forward to 1999*, South Pass Press, 1972.

Co-author: (With Walter Scott Monroe) *Bibliographies and Summaries in Education to July 1935: A Catalog of More Than 4000 Annotated Bibliographies and Summaries Listed Under Author and Subject in One Alphabet*, H. W. Wilson, 1936; (with Joseph E. Moore) *Peabody Library Information Test: Elementary Level Form A* (pamphlet), Educational Publishers, 1940; (with Moore) *Peabody Library Information Test: High School Level Form A* (pamphlet), Educational Publishers, 1940; (with Moore) *Peabody Library Information Test: College Level Form A* (pamphlet), Educational Publishers, 1940; (editor with W. Hugh Stickler, James P. Stoakes) *General Education: A University Program in Action*, W. C. Brown, c. 1950; (editor with John D. Marshall and Wayne Shirley) *Books-Libraries-Librarians*, Shoe String, 1955.

Contributor: Samuel Smith, *Best Methods of Study*, Barnes & Noble, 1938, 3rd revised edition, 1958; *Education for Librarianship*, edited by Bernard Berelson, American Library Association, 1949; *The Wonderful World of Books*, edited by Alfred Stefferud, Houghton, c. 1952; (with Mary Alice Hunt) *Careers in Journalism*, edited by Laurence R. Campbell, Quill and Scroll Foundation, 1955; *A Collection of Readings for Writers: Book Three of a Complete Course in Freshman English*, edited by Harry Shaw, 4th edition, Harper, 1955; *Of, By, and For Librarians*, compiled by John D. Marshall, Shoe String, 1960; *An American Library History Reader*, compiled by John D. Marshall, Shoe String, 1961; *University of Tennessee Library Lectures*, edited by LaNelle Vandiver, University of Tennessee, 1961; (with Helen Danford, Lila Eubanks) *In Pursuit of Library History . . .*, edited by John D. Marshall, Library School, Florida State University, 1961; *Reference Services*, compiled by Arthur R. Rowland, Shoe String, 1963. Contributor to *The Library in General Education: National Society for the Study of Education Forty-Second Yearbook, Part II*, The Society, 1943.

Author of introduction: *SELA Directory of Member Libraries and Librarians in the Southeast*, edited by Mabel E. Wiloughby, Southeastern Library Association, 1952; Robert W. Murphey, *How and Where to Look It Up: A Guide to Standard Sources of Information*, McGraw, 1958; (with Loutrell Cavin) *Strategic Air Command Library Workshop*, Library School, Florida State University, 1959; *The Florida Handbook*, compiled by Allen Morris, Peninsula Publishing Co., 1962, 1963.

Editor, *Merit Students Encyclopedia*, Crowell-Collier,

1967—; editorial director, *Harvard Classics Home Study Program*, eleven volumes, Crowell-Collier, 1961. Editor, *Journal of Library History*, 1966—.

WORK IN PROGRESS: Quiet World, autobiography; *College Educate Yourself*; *Of Media and Man*, a book on communications; and *Speculation*, a dualistic interpretation of the struggle between God's order and primitive nature's chaos.

SIDELIGHTS: Shores told *CA:* "Steadily, a faith in librarianship as the profession of destiny grew mystically. Perhaps four years of war, especially the first two rough years in the CBI theatre away from library work, strengthened my belief in what I have titled my next book, 'The Quiet Force.' Possibly my growing concern with the meaning of death ... and a mounting concern that the devotion to research (a la the scientific method) may be a principal obstacle to coming to grips with the ultimate are lashing me to rouse my colleagues against the ancillary 'retriever' outlook that has shaped the librarian image of the past. In short, I long to balance our national passion for 'where the action is' with a bit of meditation and introspection, to rescue a few hours from the discotheque for reading in the bibliotheque.

"The quest continues for an extrasensory solution to the 'Riddle of the Universe.' Library quiet, I am convinced, is a necessary prelude—the climate that will enable us to devote ourselves to some ultimates. *Looking Forward to 1999* dissented with the activists of the sixties, the groovies, who despite their hypothetical claims of idealism were engaged in proximates. Their noise and bombast must be replaced with quiet; their corny 'explosions' with implosions.''

N. Orwin Rush writes: "As a librarian, teacher, dean, encyclopedist, lecturer, consultant, editor, soldier, and writer, Dr. Shores is probably the nearest the library profession has today to an international spokesman. He has performed in all these posts with distinction.... He has lectured on American library methods in three seminars before Italian librarians ... and was the first American, as well as the first librarian, to be invited to deliver the annual lecture before the Library Association of the United Kingdom."

BIOGRAPHICAL/CRITICAL SOURCES: Louis Shores: A Bibliography, by John David Marshall, Beta Phi Mu (Gamma Chapter), Florida State University Library School, 1964.

* * *

SHRIVER, Phillip Raymond 1922-

PERSONAL: Born August 16, 1922, in Cleveland, Ohio; son of Raymond Scott and Corinna Ruth (Smith) Shriver; married Martha Damaris Nye, April 15, 1944; children: Carolyn (Mrs. Richard B. Helwig), Susan, Melinda, Darcy, Raymond Scott II. *Education:* Yale University, B.A., 1943; Harvard University, M.A., 1946; Columbia University, Ph.D., 1954. *Religion:* United Church of Christ. *Home:* 310 East High St., Oxford, Ohio 45056.

CAREER: Kent State University, Kent, Ohio, 1947-65, began as assistant professor, became professor of history, assistant dean of College of Arts and Sciences, 1959-63, acting dean, 1963-64, dean, 1964-65; Miami University, Oxford, Ohio, president, 1965—. Member of advisory board of historians, Ohio Civil War Centennial Commission, 1959-65; member of board of directors, Cincinnati branch of Federal Reserve Bank, 1968—, Ohio College Library Center, 1968—; member of advisory board, Cincin-

nati Council of World Affairs, 1970—; council of presidents chairman, Mid-American Conference, 1971—. *Military service:* U.S. Navy, 1943-46; served in Pacific Theater; became lieutenant junior grade; received three battle stars.

MEMBER: American Historical Association, American Studies Association, American Association for State and Local History, American Indian Ethnohistorical Conference, American Association of University Professors (secretary-treasurer of Ohio state universities council, 1958-59), Organization of American Historians, Ohio Historical Society, Ohio Academy of History, Ohio Archaeological Society, Phi Beta Kappa. *Awards, honors:* Most Distinguished Faculty Member award, Kent State University, 1961; Distinguished Academic Service award from American Association of University Professors, 1965; Ohio Governor's Award, 1968. Litt.D., University of Cincinnati, 1966; LL.D., Heidelberg College, 1966, Eastern Michigan University, 1972, Ohio State University, 1973; H.H.D., McKendree College, 1973.

WRITINGS: (Contributor) *The Development of Historiography*, Stackpole, 1954; *The Years of Youth: Kent State University, 1910-1960*, Kent State University Press, 1960; *George A. Bowman: The Biography of an Educator*, Kent State University Press, 1963; (with Donald Breen) *Ohio's Military Prisons in the Civil War*, Ohio State University Press, 1964. Contributor to *Citizens' Research in Public Affairs*, 1962-65, and to *Dictionary of American Biography* and *Encyclopaedia Britannica*. Contributor of articles and reviews to historical journals.

* * *

SHROYER, Frederick B(enjamin) 1916-

PERSONAL: Born October 28, 1916, in Decatur, Ind.; son of Benjamin Franklin (an engineer) and Huldah (Mutschler) Shroyer; married Patricia Grace Connor (a poet), January 13, 1949; children: Madeline Gwynn. *Education:* Attended University of Michigan, 1935-36; University of Southern California, B.A., 1948, M.A., 1949, Ph.D., 1954. *Politics:* Independent. *Religion:* No preference. *Home:* 362 Coral View, Monterey Park, Calif. 91754. *Agent:* Russell & Volkening, Inc., 551 Fifth Ave., New York, N.Y. 10017. *Office:* Department of English, California State University, Los Angeles, 5151 State College Dr., Los Angeles, Calif. 90032.

CAREER: California State College (now California State University, Los Angeles), assistant professor, 1950-54, associate professor, 1954-59, professor of English and American literature, 1959—, chairman of department of language arts, 1951-53. Literary consultant for Columbia Broadcasting System Sylvania Award television series, "First Meeting," 1959; moderator and panelist for Peabody Award television series, "Cavalcade of Books," 1959-61, 1963-64; lecturer, KCOP-TV series on American novel, 1959-60; founder and director of Pacific Coast Writers Conference, 1953-55, and Idyllwild Writers Conference, 1956-57; novelist-in-residence, Pacific Coast Writers Conference, summers, 1965-67; visiting professor, University of Southern California, 1958, 1961; Bingham Professor of Humanities, University of Louisville, 1969-70; editorial consultant to various publishers; educational consultant, NBC-Bailey Educational Films, 1968-69. *Military service:* U.S. Army Air Forces, Intelligence, 1942-46; aide-de-camp to General Thomas D. White, commanding general of Seventh Air Force; became captain.

MEMBER: P.E.N. International, National Academy of

Television Arts and Sciences, American Federation of Television and Radio Artists, Authors Club, Phi Beta Kappa, Epsilon Phi (president, University of Southern California chapter, 1947-49), Southern California Cricket Association, Greater Los Angeles Press Club, Kent County Cricket Club (Canterbury, England), Shadow Mountain Country Club, Honorable Order of Kentucky Colonels. *Awards, honors:* Huntington Hartford Foundation resident fellowships, 1958, 1965; University of Southern California Alumnus of Distinction, 1961; California State University, Los Angeles outstanding professor award, 1967.

WRITINGS: (Editor with P. A. Jorgensen) *A College Treasury*, two volumes, Scribner, 1956, 2nd revised edition, 1965; *Wall Against the Night* (novel), Appleton, 1957; (with Jorgensen) *The Informal Essay*, Norton, 1961; (contributor) N. T. Boaz, compiler, *In Quest for Truth*, Scarecrow, 1961; *It Happened in Wayland* (novel), Ward, Lock, 1962, Reynal, 1963; (with Jorgensen) *The Art of Prose*, Scribner, 1964; (with Dorothy Parker) *Short Story: A Thematic Anthology*, Scribner, 1965; *There None Embrace* (novel), Ward, Lock, 1966; (author of introduction) J. S. LeFanu, *Uncle Silas*, Dover, 1966; (editor with L. G. Gardamal) *Types of Drama*, Scott, Foresman, 1970; (with H. E. Richardson) *Muse of Fire*, Knopf, 1971; (author of introduction) Ann Radcliffe, *Castles of Athlin and Dunboyne*, Arno, 1972. Literary editor, *Los Angeles Herald Examiner*, 1962—.

WORK IN PROGRESS: Biographical and critical preface for W. Child Green's *The Abbot of Montserrat*; *Flights of Angels*, a World War II novel about flight nurses; two novels, *Killed With Hunting Him* and *There Is a Season*.

SIDELIGHTS: Shroyer told *CA:* "Because I think truth is more important than facts, I write novels. I am especially interested in the Depression years, and three of my published novels have had some roots in the Thirties. I think, with Browning, that a country, a society—as well as individuals—reveals itself at a time of crisis. The Thirties were the crisis of America.

"I am increasingly convinced that we are entering a *new* Romantic Age, and thus I am doing more and more research and writing in the area of the Gothic novel. Moreover, I have been lecturing widely on this new Romanticism, my lecture being titled 'Come into the Castle, Maud: The New Romanticism!' Too, I have become a legal consultant in literature, researching and advising in cases which involve alleged plagiarism, etc. I have discovered, as have others, that the study of literature knows no boundaries, academic or otherwise, and that true 'literature' is synonymous with life."

Shroyer's first novel, *Wall Against the Night* was chosen as the initial title in Ward, Lock's Quadriga Press series of distinguished books (in England); his second, *It Happened in Wayland*, came out in two English editions. Off the literary track, he was the discoverer, with General Thomas D. White, of the *Pranesus Insularum Whitei* (a sub-species of tropical reef fish) in Saipan, now in the collection of the Smithsonian Institution.

* * *

SHUFORD, Cecil Eugene   1907-
(Gene Shuford)

PERSONAL: Born Feburary 21, 1907, in Fayetteville, Ark.; son of Eugene Wallace (a salesman) and Frances Elizabeth (Shelton) Shuford; married Catherine Brooks (a high school English teacher), June 27, 1937; children: Betty Grace (Mrs. Larry I. Crow), Thomas Eugene, Dan Brooks. *Education:* University of Arkansas, B.A., 1928; Northwestern University, M.S.J., 1929; further study at the University of Wisconsin, summer, 1941. *Home:* 12910 East McKinney, Denton, Tex. 76201. *Office:* Department of Journalism, North Texas State University, Denton, Tex.

CAREER: Fayetteville Daily Democrat, Fayetteville, Ark., reporter, 1926-28; Alabama Polytechnic Institute, Auburn, instructor in journalism, 1929-30; University of Arkansas, Fayetteville, instructor in English, 1934-36; Trinity University, Waxahachie, Tex., assistant professor of journalism and director of publicity, 1936-37; North Texas State University, Denton, assistant professor of journalism and director of publicity, 1937-42, director of journalism, 1945—, professor of journalism, 1961—. *Military service:* U.S. Army Air Forces, 1942-45; became first lieutenant. *Member:* American Society of Journalism School Administrators, Association for Education in Journalism, Poetry Society of America, Poetry Society of Texas, Texas Institute of Letters, Sigma Delta Chi, Sigma Chi. *Awards, honors:* Michael Sloane Fellowship Award from Poetry Society of America, 1962-63; William Marion Reedy Award from Poetry Society of America, 1966; Voertman Award from Texas Institute of Letters, 1973; twenty annual awards from Poetry Society of Texas, 1955-64.

WRITINGS: The Red Bull, and Other Poems, South and West, 1964; (under name Gene Shuford) *Selected Poems, 1933-1971*, North Texas State University Press, 1972. Contributor of poetry and of articles on journalism to *Scribner's, New Republic, Saturday Evening Post, Southwest Review, Frontier and Midland, Kaleidograph, New Mexico Quarterly, South and West, Voices, Best Articles and Stories, Quill, Journalism Educator*, and other publications.†

* * *

SHULVASS, Moses A.   1909-

PERSONAL: Born July 29, 1909, in Plonsk, Poland; son of Meyer (a merchant) and Rebecca (Michelson) Shulvass; married Celia A. Cemach, March 6, 1935; children: Phyllis (Mrs. Yoram Gelman), Ruth. *Education:* Tachkemoni Rabbinical Seminary, Warsaw, Poland, Rabbi, 1930; University of Berlin, Ph.D., 1934. *Home:* 2733 West Greenleaf Ave., Chicago, Ill. 60645. *Office:* Spertus College of Judaica, 618 South Michigan Ave., Chicago, Ill. 60605.

CAREER: Lecturer, author, and editor, in Jerusalem, Israel, 1935-47; Baltimore Hebrew College, Baltimore, Md., professor of rabbinic literature and Jewish history, 1948-51; Ner Israel Rabbinical College, Baltimore, Md., lecturer in Hebrew language, 1949-51; Spertus College of Judaica (formerly College of Jewish Studies), Chicago, Ill., distinguished service professor of Jewish history and chairman emeritus of department of graduate studies, 1951—. Yeshiva University, New York, N.Y., visiting lecturer in history, 1949; Emanuel Congregation, Chicago, Ill., scholar-in-residence, 1963-64. Member of National Board of License for Teaching and Supervisory Personnel in American Hebrew Schools, 1959-65.

MEMBER: American Jewish Historical Society, Conference on Jewish Social Studies, National Council for Jewish Education, Jewish Book Council of America (member-at-large of national committee), Jewish Historical Society of England, Historical Society of Israel (board member, 1945-48), Chicago Board of Rabbis, Hebrew P.E.N. Club of

America, Yiddish P.E.N. Club of America. *Awards, honors:* La Med Prize, 1956, for *Jewish Life in Renaissance Italy.*

WRITINGS: Bibliographical Guide to Jewish Knowledge, Torah Vaavodah (Warsaw), 1935; *Rome and Jerusalem,* Rabbi Kook Institute (Jerusalem), 1944; *Chapters From the Life of Samuel David Luzatto,* Yeshiva University (New York), 1951; *Jewish Life in Renaissance Italy,* Ogen Publishing House (New York), 1955; *In the Grip of Centuries,* Ogen Publishing House, 1960; *Between the Rhine and the Bosporus,* College of Jewish Studies Press, 1964; *From East to West: The Westward Migration of Jews from Eastern Europe During the Seventeenth and Eighteenth Centuries,* Wayne State University Press, 1971; *The Jews in the World of the Renaissance* (translated from the Hebrew by Elvin I. Kose), R. J. Brill (Leiden), 1973. Contributor to scholarly and literary journals published in English, Hebrew, and Yiddish.

* * *

SHWADRAN, Benjamin 1907-

PERSONAL: Born September 12, 1907, in Jerusalem, Palestine; came to United States in 1928; son of Mendel and Anna (Susman) Shwadran; married Dorothy Derman; children: Avivah. *Education:* Hebrew University, Jerusalem, Palestine, student, 1926-28; Clark University, Worcester, Mass., B.A., 1938, M.A., 1939, Ph.D., 1946. *Religion:* Jewish. *Home and office:* Rehov Yaakov Cohen 8, Jerusalem, Israel.

CAREER: American Zionist Council, New York, N.Y., director of research department, 1943-49; Council for Middle Eastern Affairs, New York, N.Y., secretary, 1950—. Lecturer in Middle East studies, New School for Social Research, 1947-50; head of Middle East Institute, Dropsie College, 1957-59; professor of Middle East studies, Yeshivah University, 1959-61; professor of political science, Hofstra University, 1970-73; professor of Middle Eastern history, Tel-Aviv University, 1968, 1969, 1973—.

WRITINGS: Palestine: A Study of Jewish, Arab and British Policies, Yale University Press, 1947; *The Middle East Oil and the Great Powers,* Praeger, 1955, 3rd edition, revised and enlarged, Wiley, 1973. *Jordan, A State of Tension,* Council for Middle Eastern Affairs Press, 1959; *The Middle East Oil and the Great Powers, 1959,* Council for Middle Eastern Affairs Press, 1959; *The Power Struggle in Iraq,* Council for Middle Eastern Affairs Press, 1960; (compiler) *General Index, Middle Eastern Affairs,* Council for Middle Eastern Affairs press, 1968. Contributor of articles to historical and political journals. Editor, *Middle Eastern Affairs,* 1950-63; Middle East editor, *Hadoar,* 1942-59; editor, *Palestine Affairs,* 1946-49.

WORK IN PROGRESS: A study of Israel's foreign policy; *Great Power Politics in the Middle East.*

* * *

SIEBER, Sam Dixon 1931-
(Norman D. Kerr)

PERSONAL: Born April 15, 1931, in Houston, Tex.; son of John E. (a realtor) and Adaleen (Dixon) Sieber; married Susan Reynaud (a market researcher), January 6, 1956. *Education:* Baylor University, student, 1949-50; New School for Social Research, B.A., 1953; Columbia University, M.A., 1954, Ph.D., 1963. *Politics:* Liberal. *Home:* 820 West End Ave., New York, N.Y. 10025. *Office:* Bureau of Applied Social Research, 605 West 115 St., New York, N.Y. 10025.

CAREER: Hunter College (now of the City University of New York), New York, N.Y., instructor in sociology, 1961-62; New York University, New York, N.Y., assistant professor of sociology, 1962-63; Columbia University, Bureau of Applied Social Research, New York, N.Y., research assistant, 1957-63, project director, 1963-64, research associate, 1964—. Consultant to school systems. *Military service:* U.S. Army, 1955-56. *Member:* American Sociological Association, American Educational Research Association, Eastern Sociological Society. *Awards, honors:* U.S. Office of Education research grant.

WRITINGS: (With Paul F. Lazarsfeld) *Organizing Educational Research,* Prentice-Hall, 1964; (with Lazarsfeld) *The Organization of Educational Research in the United States,* Bureau of Applied Social Research, Columbia University, 1966; (with Elisabeth Gemberling) *The Role of Secondary Education in the Development of Indigenous Leadership in Amercan Indian Communities,* U.S. Office of Education, 1970; (with Lazarsfeld) *Reforming the University: The Role of the Research Center,* Bureau of Applied Social Research, Columbia University, 1971, enlarged edition, Praeger, 1972; (with Karen Seashore Louis and Loya Metzger) *The Use of Knowledge: Final Report; Evaluation of the Pilot State Dissemination Program,* two volumes, Bureau of Applied Social Research, Columbia University, 1972; (editor with David Wilder) *The School in Society: Studies in the Sociology of Education,* Free Press, 1973. Contributor of articles to sociological journals. Associate editor, *Sociology of Education.*

WORK IN PROGRESS: Continuing studies in organizational problems of educational research; "Cabbages and Kings," a musical play.

AVOCATIONAL INTERESTS: Musical composition, playwriting, poetry.†

* * *

SIELAFF, Theodore J. 1920-

PERSONAL: Born December 11, 1920, in Livingston, Mont.; son of Otto R. and Nellie (Anderson) Sielaff; married Virginia Mae Finsand, November 26, 1948; children: John, James, Jeffrey. *Education:* University of Minnesota, B.S., 1942, M.A., 1944, Ph.D., 1951. *Politics:* Independent. *Religion:* Lutheran. *Home:* 2516 Lansford, San Jose, Calif. *Office:* San Jose State University, San Jose, Calif., and Lansford Publishing Co., 1088 Lincoln Ave., San Jose, Calif. 95125.

CAREER: Macalester College, St. Paul, Minn., professor of business, 1943-54; San Jose State College (now University), San Jose, 1954—, now professor of business; Lansford Publishing Co., San Jose, Calif., president.

WRITINGS: (With Aberle and Mayer) *General Business for Today and Tomorrow,* Prentice-Hall, 1959; (with Aberle) *Introduction to Business,* Wadsworth, 1961, revised edition, in press; *Statistics in Action,* Lansford, 1963; (with Wang) *Practical Problems in Business and Economic Statistics,* Holden-Day, 1968; *Application of Behavioral Control to Business,* Lansford, 1974.

AVOCATIONAL INTERESTS: Low-level gardening, talking, and behavioral psychology.

* * *

SIGWORTH, Oliver F(rederic) 1921-

PERSONAL: Born July 31, 1921, in Glendale, Ariz.; son

of Jay H. (a lawyer) and Bjorg (Fredericksson) Sigworth; married Alice Gibbs (died, 1959); married Heather Clarke, April 29, 1963; children: (first marriage) George Frederick, (second marriage) Rosalind Brooks. *Education:* Studied at Phoenix Junior College, 1940-42, University of Southern California, 1942-43; University of California, Berkeley, B.A., 1947, M.A., 1948, Ph.D., 1951. *Politics:* Democrat. *Home:* 3537 North Jackson Ave., Tucson, Ariz. 85719. *Office:* Department of English, University of Arizona, Tucson, Ariz. 85721.

CAREER: Instructor in English at University of Nevada, Reno, 1951-52, San Francisco State College (now University), San Francisco, Calif., 1952-53; University of Arizona, Tucson, instructor, 1953-57, assistant professor, 1957-62, associate professor, 1962-67, professor of English, 1967—, director of graduate studies in English, 1969—. *Military service:* U.S. Army, 1943-46; became technical sergeant. *Member:* Modern Language Association of America, American Society for Eighteenth Century Studies, American Association of University Professors, American Civil Liberties Union. *Awards, honors:* Ford Foundation fellow, 1955-56; best review award, *Arizona Quarterly*, 1962.

WRITINGS: Four Styles of a Decade (1740-1750), New York Public Library, 1960; *Nature's Sternest Poet: Essays on George Crabbe*, University of Arizona Press, 1965; *William Collins*, Twayne, 1965; *Criticism and Aesthetics, 1660-1800*, Rinehart, 1971. Editor, *Arizona English Bulletin*, 1958-62.

WORK IN PROGRESS: Studies in eighteenth-century literature.

AVOCATIONAL INTERESTS: Gardening, music, the outdoors, and eighteenth-century architecture.

*   *   *

SIIRALA, Aarne 1919-

PERSONAL: Born July 8, 1919, in Liperi, Finland; son of Martti Johannes (a doctor of medicine) and Siiri (Kononen) Siirala; married Katri Sipila, November 25, 1941; children: Helena, Lauri, Kari, Hanneli, Maarit. *Education:* University of Helsinki, Cand. Theol., 1943, Dr. Theol., 1956; University of Lund, Lic. Theol., 1950. *Religion:* Lutheran. *Home:* 310 Bridgeport Rd., Waterloo, Ontario, Canada.

CAREER: Minister in Finland in parishes of the Church of Finland, 1943-46; Church Institute, Jarvenpaa, Finland, teacher, 1946-52, director, 1952-60; Union Theological Seminary, New York, N.Y., visiting scholar, 1960-63; University of Helsinki, Helsinki, Finland, docent of systematic theology, 1962—; Waterloo Lutheran University, Waterloo, Ontario, professor of systematic theology, 1963—. Has participated in committee work of World Council of Churches, Lutheran World Federation, Directors Association of Evangelical Academies. *Wartime service:* Finnish Army, 1939-40; social worker at military hospitals in Helsinki, Finland, 1941-43. *Awards, honors:* Ford Foundation grant for study trip to the United States, 1958; University of Helsinki grant for postdoctoral research in New York, 1960-63; Rockefeller Foundation Grant, Harvard Divinity School, 1971-72.

WRITINGS: Gottes Gebot bei Martin Luther, Evangelisches Verlagshaus, 1956; (with Martti Siirala) *Elaman Ykseys* (title means "The Wholeness of Life"), Soderstrom, 1960; *Sairauden Sanottava*, Soderstrom, 1962 (translation published as *The Voice of Illness: A Study in*

Therapy and Prophecy, Fortress, 1964); *Divine Humanness*, Fortress, 1970. Contributor of numerous articles to Finnish, Swedish, German, and American theological periodicals.

*   *   *

SILVA, Ruth C.

PERSONAL: Daughter of Ignatius Dominic and Beatrice (Davis) Silva. *Education:* University of Michigan, A.B., 1943, A.M., 1943, Ph.D., 1948. *Politics:* Republican. *Religion:* Roman Catholic. *Office:* Department of Political Science, Pennsylvania State University, University Park, Pa.

CAREER: Wheaton College, Norton, Mass., instructor in government, 1946-48; Pennsylvania State University, University Park, 1948—, professor of political science, 1959—. Fulbright professor, Cairo University, Cairo, Egypt, 1952-53; Margaret Elliott Lecturer, University of North Carolina, Woman's College, 1956. Research consultant and speech writer for Paul H. Douglas, senator from Illinois, 1956; research consultant to U.S. Department of Justice, 1957, New York State Commission on Revision and Simplification of Constitution, 1959-60; commissioner, National Committee on Financing Post-Secondary Education, 1972-73. Visiting professor, Johns Hopkins University. *Member:* American Political Science Association (secretary, 1957-58; vice-president, 1972-73), National Municipal League, American Academy of Political and Social Science, Academy of Political Science, American Association of University Professors, Phi Kappa Phi.

WRITINGS: Presidential Succession, University of Michigan Press, 1951; *Legislative Apportionment*, two volumes, State of New York, 1960; (contributor) Alfred J. Junz, editor, *Present Trends in American National Government*, Hansard Society for Parliamentary Government, 1960, Praeger, 1961; *Rum, Religion, and Votes: 1928 Re-Examined*, Pennsylvania State University Press, 1962; (with William J. D. Boyd) *Selected Bibliography on Legislative Apportionment and Districting*, National Municipal League, 1963. Contributor of short sections to other books; also contributor to *New York Times Magazine* and to legal and political science journals.

*   *   *

SILVERMAN, Jerry 1931-

PERSONAL: Born March 26, 1931, in New York, N.Y.; son of William (a salesman) and Helen (Mindlin) Silverman. *Education:* City College (now of the City University of New York), B.S. (music), 1952; New York University, M.A. (musicology), 1953. *Home:* 30 Fifth Ave., New York, N.Y. 10011.

CAREER: Teacher of guitar, self-employed in own studio, New York, N.Y., 1950—. Performer at folk song concerts and writer on folk song subjects.

WRITINGS: Folk Blues, Macmillan, 1958, revised edition, 1971; *Folksingers Guitar Guide*, Volume I, with Pete Seeger, Oak, 1962, (sole author) Volume II, 1964; (translator and music editor) *A Russian Song Book*, Random House, 1962; *The Art of the Folk Blues Guitar*, Oak, 1964; *Beginning the Folk Guitar*, Oak, 1964; *Russian Songs—Old and New*, Oak, 1966; *A Folksinger's Guide to Note Reading and Music Theory: A Manual for the Folk Guitarist*, Oak, 1966; (compiler) *The Chord-1 Player's Encyclopedia*, Oak, 1967, also published as *A Folksinger's Guide to Chords and Tunings*, 1967; *How to Play the Guitar*, Doubleday,

1968; *The Liberated Woman's Songbook*, Macmillan, 1971; *How to Play Better Guitar*, Doubleday, 1972; *Beginning the Five-String Banjo*, Macmillan, 1974; *Jerry Silverman's Folk Guitar Method Book*, Grosset, 1974. Producer and recorder of supplementary Folkways long-playing records for all Oak books except *Folksingers Guitar Guide*, Volume I. Associate editor of *Sing Out* magazine.

WORK IN PROGRESS: The Flat-Picker's Guitar Guide.

SIDELIGHTS: Silverman travels extensively in Europe, collecting and recording folk music. He has translator's proficiency in Russian.†

* * *

SILVERT, Kalman H(irsch) 1921-

PERSONAL: Born March 10, 1921, in Bryn Mawr, Pa.; son of Henry Jacob (a furniture dealer) and Ida (Levine) Silvert; married Frieda Moskalik (a lecturer in sociology), July 24, 1942; children: Henry M., Benjamin B., Alexander M. *Education:* University of Pennsylvania, B.A., 1942, M.A., 1947, Ph.D., 1948. *Politics:* Democrat. *Religion:* Jewish. *Home:* Hopson Rd., Norwich, Vt.

CAREER: Tulane University, New Orleans, La., assistant professor, 1948-51, associate professor, 1951-56, professor of political science, 1956-60; Dartmouth College, Hanover, N.H., professor of government, 1960-67; New York University, New York, N.Y., professor of politics, 1967—, director of Ibero-American Center, 1967-72. Visiting professor at University of Delaware, 1948, University of Buenos Aires, 1958, 1960-61, Harvard University, summer, 1964, Brandeis University, spring, 1967, and Boston University, 1973. Staff associate to director of studies of American Universities Field Staff, 1955-67; program adviser in social sciences to Ford Foundation, 1967—. Consultant to Alliance for Progress.

MEMBER: Latin American Studies Association (founding president, 1965-67), Center for Inter-American Relations, Council on Foreign Relations. *Awards, honors:* Social Science Research Council grant for study in Guatemala, 1952-53; Middle American Research Institute fellowship, 1953; fellowships from Carnegie Corp., 1960-65, 1966-68 (through Brookings Institution); Faculdade Candido Mendes, Rio de Janeiro, Brazil, 1971.

WRITINGS: (With Leonard Reissman and Cliff Wing) *The New Orleans Registered Voter* (monograph), Tulane University, 1956; *A Study in Government: Guatemala*, Part I: *National and Local Government*, 1955, Part II: *The Constitutions of the State and Republic*, Middle American Research Institute, 1958; (with Frank Bonilla) *Education and the Social Meaning of Development: A Preliminary Statement*, American Universities Field Staff, 1961; *The Conflict Society: Reaction and Revolution in Latin America*, Hauser Press, 1961, revised edition, American Universities Field Staff, 1969; *Chile Yesterday and Today*, Holt, 1965; *La politica del desarrollo* (title means "The Politics of Development"), Editorial Paidos, 1966; *Man's Power: A Biased Guide to Political Thought*, Viking, 1970.

Editor and contributor: *Expectant Peoples: Nationalism and Development*, Random House, 1963, 2nd edition, Vintage, 1967; *Discussion at Bellagio: The Political Alternatives of Development*, American Universities Field Staff, 1964; *Churches and States: The Religious Institution and Modernization*, American Universities Field Staff, 1967; *The Social Reality of Scientific Myth*, American Universities Field Staff, 1969.

Contributor: *Integracion social en Guatemala* (title means "Social Integration in Guatemala"), Minis de Educacion, Volume III, 1955; R. N. Adams, editor, *Political Change in Guatemalan Indian Communities*, Middle American Research Institute, 1958; Herbert L. Matthews, editor, *The United States and Latin America*, American Assembly, 1959, revised edition, Prentice-Hall, 1963; William Manger, editor, *The Alliance for Progress: A Critical Appraisal*, Public Affairs Press, 1963; John J. Johnson, editor, *Continuity and Change in Latin America*, Stanford University Press, 1964; Werner Baer and Isaac Kerstenetsky, editors, *Inflation and Growth in Latin America*, Irwin, 1964; John D. Martx, editor, *The Dynamics of Change in Latin American Politics*, Prentice-Hall, 1965; W. H. Form and A. A. Blum, editors, *Industrial Relations and Social Change in Latin America*, University of Florida Press, 1965; Gene M. Lyons, editor, *America: Purpose and Power*, Quadrangle, 1965; Robert D. Thomasek, editor, *Latin American Politics: Twenty-Four Studies of the Contemporary Scene*, Doubleday, 1966; Peter G. Snow, editor, *Government and Politics in Latin America*, Holt, 1967; John Plank, editor, *Cuba and the United States*, Brookings Institution, 1967; Fredrick B. Pike, editor, *Latin American History: Select Problems*, Harcourt, 1969; Stanley R. Ross, editor, *Latin America in Transition: Problems in Training and Research*, State University of New York Press, 1970.

Author of reports for American Universities Field Staff, 1955—. Contributor to proceedings and annals, and *Encyclopaedia Britannica* and *International Encyclopaedia of the Social Sciences*. Contributor of about sixty articles and reviews to political science and social science journals, including *Social Change, American Journal of Sociology, International Journal, American Behavioral Scientist, Economic Development and Cultural Change*, and *Sociological Review Monograph*. Member of editorial advisory board of *Comparative Politics, American Behavioral Scientist, Transaction's* monograph series, and *Desarrollo Economico*. Consultant to *Encyclopaedia Britannica, World Book Encyclopedia*, and *Education and World Affairs*.

WORK IN PROGRESS: A book with Leonard Reissman, *Education and the Making of Social Fact: Dilemmas and Dynamics in Contemporary Chile and Venezuela*.

SIDELIGHTS: Silvert spent three years in Africa, and more than eight in Latin America, especially in Chile, Argentina, and Guatemala. He also did research in El Salvador, Mexico, Uruguay, Costa Rica, and Brazil.

* * *

SIM, Katharine (Thomasset) 1913-
(Nuraini)

PERSONAL: Born June 28, 1913, in Teddington, Surrey, England; daughter of Theodore Charles (a member of Stock Exchange) and Marjorie (Stringer) Thomasset; married Alexander Woodrow Stuart Sim, July 2, 1938; children: Jonathan Alexander Thomasset, Woodrow Sancroft Andrew. *Education:* Attended Heatherly's Art School, 1931-32, and Regent Street School of Art, 1932-35. *Politics:* Conservative. *Religion:* Church of England. *Home:* Maescanol, Pencarreg, Llanybydder, Dyfed. SA40 9QJ. United Kingdom.

CAREER: Portrait painter and exhibitor of pastels, watercolors, and oils in London, England; journalist. Broadcaster on British Broadcasting Corp. television. *Member:* Royal Geographical Society (fellow). *Awards, honors:* Ratna Kebudayan, a cultural award from Pure Life Society for interest and understanding of various communities as expressed in journalistic works in Malaysia.

WRITINGS: Malayan Landscape, M. Joseph, 1946; *These I Have Loved*, Wingate, 1947; *Malacca Boy*, Hodder & Stoughton, 1957; *The Moon at My Feet*, Hodder & Stoughton, 1958; *Black Rice*, Hodder & Stoughton, 1959; *Flowers of the Sun*, Eastern Universities Press, 1959; *The Jungle Ends Here*, Hodder & Stoughton, 1960; *Journey Out of Asia*, R. Hale, 1963; *Costumes of Malaya*, Eastern Universities Press, 1963; *Desert Traveller: The Life of Jean Louis Burckhardt*, Gollancz, 1969. Writer of scripts for British Broadcasting Corp. Schools Service. Contributor to *Times* (London), *Daily Telegraph* (London), *She, Homes and Gardens, English Digest, Cornhill, World Digest, The Guardian, Forum*, and other journals and periodicals.

WORK IN PROGRESS: Two new travel books, *Malayan Landscapes*, and its sequel.

SIDELIGHTS: Her specialized knowledge of Malaya includes its poetry and language. Travels include an overland journey from Calcutta, India, to Calais, France, the subject of *Journey Out of Asia*. She has also traveled to Turkey and Greece; and is interested in nineteenth century travel in the Middle East. She is interested in Wales and is learning the language.

*   *   *

SIMIRENKO, Alex   1931-

PERSONAL: Born September 6, 1931, in Kiev, Union of Soviet Socialist Republics; son of Wolodimir and Maria (Ul'ianchenko) Simirenko. *Education:* University of Minnesota, B.A., 1957, M.A., 1958, Ph.D., 1961. *Office:* 317 Liberal Arts Bldg., Pennsylvania State University, University Park, Pa. 16802.

CAREER: University of Nevada, Reno, 1960-69, began as assistant professor, became associate professor of sociology; Pennsylvania State University, University Park, professor of sociology, 1969—. *Member:* American Sociological Association, American Association for the Advancement of Slavic Studies, Pacific Sociological Association, Eastern Sociological Society, Society for the Study of Social Problems, Alpha Kappa Delta.

WRITINGS: Pilgrims, Colonists, and Frontiersmen: An Ethnic Community in Transition, Free Press of Glencoe, 1964; *Soviet Sociology: Historical Antecedents and Current Perspectives*, Quadrangle, 1966; *Social Thought in the Soviet Union*, Quadrangle, 1969.

WORK IN PROGRESS: A sociological analysis of the USSR entitled *Soviet Society*, for Random House, and a sociological analysis of American status and minority community studies entitled *Transplanted Worlds*, for Glendessary Press.

AVOCATIONAL INTERESTS: Chess.

*   *   *

SIMON, Edith   1917-

PERSONAL: Born May 18, 1917, in Berlin, Germany; daughter of Walter Frederick and Grete (Goldberg) Simon; married E. C. R. Reeve (a research geneticist), August 8, 1942; children: Antonia Mary, Simon Raynold, Jessica Carolyn. *Home:* 11 Grosvenor Crescent, Edinburgh, Scotland. *Agent:* Harold Ober Associates, Inc., 40 East 49th St., New York, N.Y. 10017.

CAREER: Artist, writer, and historian. Seven one-man shows of pictures and sculptures in many media, 1971-74.

WRITINGS: The Chosen, Bodley Head, 1940; *Biting the Blue Finger*, Bodley Head, 1942; *Wings Deceive*, Bodley Head, 1944; *The Other Passion*, Bodley Head, 1948; *The Golden Hand*, Putnam, 1952; *The House of Strangers*, Putnam, 1953 (English title, *The Pastmasters*); *The Twelve Pictures*, Putnam, 1955; *The Sable Coat*, Putnam, 1958; *The Piebald Standard* (history of Knights Templars), Little, Brown, 1959; *The Great Forgery*, Little, Brown, 1961; *The Making of Frederick the Great*, Little, Brown, 1963; *The Reformation*, Time-Life, 1967; *Luther Alive: Martin Luther and the Making of the Reformation*, Doubleday, 1968; *The Saints*, Dell, 1969; *The Anglo-Saxon Manner*, Cassell, 1972. Also author of plays, articles, and reviews.

WORK IN PROGRESS: Thrilleroyal, a novel; *A Landscape is the People in it*, an autobiography; and exhibitions in Paris, London, and Stuttgart.

SIDELIGHTS: Edith Simon is competent in German; French adequate for research. *Avocational interests:* History, the theater and cinema, people, clothes, reading.

*   *   *

SIMON, Herbert A.   1916-

PERSONAL: Born June 15, 1916, in Milwaukee, Wis.; son of Arthur (an engineer), and Edna (Merkel) Simon; married Dorothea Pye, (an educational researcher) December 25, 1937; children: Katherine, Peter, Barbara. *Politics:* Democrat. *Religion:* Unitarian. *Education:* University of Chicago, A.B., 1936, Ph.D., 1943. *Home:* 5818 Northumberland St., Pittsburgh, Pa. 15217. *Office:* Carnegie-Mellon University, Pittsburgh, Pa. 15213.

CAREER: International City Managers' Association, Chicago, Ill., staff member and assistant editor of *Public Management and Municipal Year Book*, 1938-39; University of California, Bureau of Public Administration, Berkeley, director of administrative measurement studies, 1939-42; Illinois Institute of Technology, Chicago, 1942-49, started as assistant professor, professor of political science, 1947-49, head of department of political and social science, 1946-49; Carnegie Institute of Technology, Pittsburgh, Pa., professor of administration, 1949-62, professor of administration and psychology, 1962-65, Richard King Mellon professor of computer service and psychology, 1965—, head of department of industrial management, 1949-59, associate dean, 1957-74. New York University, Ford Distinguished Visiting Professor, 1960; distinguished lecturer at Princeton University, Northwestern University, Massachusetts Institute of Technology, and Harvard University. U.S. Economic Cooperation Administration, acting director of Management Engineering Branch, and consultant, 1948; consultant to Cowles Foundation for Research in Economics, 1947—, to RAND Corp., 1952—, and to other agencies and organizations. Social Science Research Council, chairman of board of directors, 1961-65. Chairman, Division of Behavioral Sciences, National Research Council, 1967-69. Member, President's Science Advisory Committee, 1968-72.

MEMBER: Econometric Society (fellow), American Association for the Advancement of Science (fellow), American Academy of Arts and Sciences (fellow), American Psychological Association (fellow), American Society for Computing Machinery, American Sociological Association (fellow), National Academy of Science, Institute of Management Sciences (vice-president, 1954), American

Philosophical Society, American Political Science Association, American Association of University Professors, Operations Research Society of America, Psychonomic Society, Phi Beta Kappa, Sigma Xi (national lecturer, 1964). *Awards, honors:* Administrator's Award of American College of Hospital Administrators, 1958; honorary degrees from Yale University, 1963; Case Institute of Technology (now Case Western Reserve University), 1963; University of Chicago, 1964; Lund University, 1967; McGill University, 1971; Erasmus University of Rotterdam, 1974; American Psychological Association, Distinguished Scientific Contributions Award, 1969.

WRITINGS: (With C. E. Ridley) *Measuring Municipal Activities*, International City Managers Association, 1938, 2nd edition, 1943; (with Divine, Cooper, and Chernin) *Determining Work Loads for Professional Staff in a Public Welfare Agency*, Bureau of Public Administration, University of California, 1941; *Fiscal Aspects of Metropolitan Consolidation*, Bureau of Public Administration, University of California, 1943; (with Shepard and Sharp) *Fire Losses and Fire Risks*, Bureau of Public Administration, University of California, 1943; (with others) *Technique of Municipal Administration*, International City Managers' Association, 3rd edition, 1947; *Administrative Behavior*, Macmillan, 1947, 2nd edition, 1956; (editor) *Local Planning Administration*, International City Managers' Association, revised edition, 1948.

(With Smithburg and Thompson) *Public Administration*, Knopf, 1950; (with others) *Fundamental Research in Administration*, Carnegie Institute of Technology Press, 1953; (with Kozmetsky, Guetzkow, and Tyndall) *Centralization vs. Decentralization in Organizing the Controller's Department*, Controllership Foundation, 1954; *Models of Man*, Wiley, 1958; (with J. S. March) *Organizations*, Wiley, 1958; (with Holt, Modigliani, and Muth) *Planning Production, Inventories, and Work Force*, Prentice-Hall, 1960; *The New Science of Management Decision*, Harper, 1960; *The Shape of Automation*, Harper, 1965; *The Sciences of the Artificial*, M.I.T. Press, 1969 (with A. Newell) *Human Problem Solving*, Prentice-Hall, 1972; (editor and contributor with L. Silelossy) *Representation and Meaning*, Prentice-Hall, 1972.

Contributor: *Research Frontiers in Politics and Government*, Brookings Institution, 1955; *The State of the Social Sciences*, edited by L. D. White, University of Chicago Press, 1956; *Research in Industrial Human Relations*, edited by Arensberg and others, Harper, 1957; *Expectations, Uncertainty and Business Behavior*, edited by Mary Jean Bowman, Social Science Research Council, 1958; *The Axiomatic Method*, edited by Henkin, Suppes, and Tarski, North-Holland, 1959; George P. Schultz and John R. Coleman, *Labor Problems: Cases and Readings*, McGraw, 1959; *Industrial Man*, edited by Warner and Martin, Harper, 1959; *Analyses of Industrial Operations*, edited by Edward H. Bowman and Robert B. Fetter, Irwin, 1959.

Management Organization and the Computer, edited by Shultz and Whisler, Free Press of Glencoe, 1960; *Management and Corporations, 1985*, edited by Melvin Anshen and G. L. Bach, McGraw, 1960; Rubenstein and Haberstroh, *Some Theories of Organization*, Irwin, 1960; *Current Trends in Psychological Theory*, University of Pittsburgh Press, 1961; *Lernende Automaten*, edited by H. Billing, R. Oldenbourg, 1961; *Planning and the Urban Community*, edited by Harvey S. Perloff, Carnegie Institute of Technology and University of Pittsburgh Press, 1961; *Control of the Mint*, edited by S. M. Farber and

Roger H. L. Wilson, McGraw, 1961; *Management and the Computer of the Future*, edited by Martin Greenberger, Wiley, 1962; *Thought in the Young Child*, edited by William Kessen and Clementina Kuhlman, Society for Research in Child Development, 1962; *Automation: Implications for the Future*, edited by Morris Philipson, Vintage, 1962; (author of foreword) *Computer Applications in the Behavioral Sciences*, edited by Harold Borko, Prentice-Hall, 1962; *Contemporary Approaches to Creative Thinking*, Atherton, 1962; *Psychology: A Study of a Science*, Volume VI, edited by Sigmund Koch, McGraw, 1963; *Applications of Digital Computers*, edited by W. F. Freiberger and William Prager, Ginn, 1963; *Handbook of Mathematical Psychology*, Volume I, edited by Luce and others, 1963; *Essays on the Structure of Social Science Models*, Massachusetts Institute of Technology Press, 1963; (author of foreword) Timothy W. Costello and Sheldon S. Zalkind, *Psychology in Administration: A Research Orientation*, Prentice-Hall, 1963; *Toward a Unified Theory of Management*, edited by Harold Koontz, McGraw, 1964; *New Horizons of Economic Progress*, edited by Lawrence H. Seltzer (Franklin Memorial Lectures), Wayne State University Press, 1964; *Computer Augmentation of Human Reasoning*, edited by M. A. Sass and W. D. Wilkinson, Spartan Books, 1965; *Mind and Cosmos*, edited by R. G. Colodny, University of Pittsburgh Press, 1966; *Varieties of Political Theory*, edited by D. Easton, Prentice-Hall, 1966; *Problem Solving*, edited by B. Kleinmuntz, Wiley, 1966; *Contemporary Political Science*, edited by I. de Sola Pool, McGraw, 1967; *The Logic of Decision and Action*, edited by N. Rescher, University of Pittsburgh Press, 1967; *Formal Representation of Human Judgement*, edited by B. Kleinmuntz, Wiley, 1968; *Cognition in Learning and Memory*, edited by L. W. Gregg, Wiley, 1972; *Visual Information Processing*, edited by W. R. Close, Academic Press, 1973.

Contributor of lesser sections to other books and to published symposia, yearbooks, conference proceedings, and professional journals including *Public Management, British Journal of Psychology, Science, Management Science, Hospital Administration, Naval War College Review, Connaissance de L'Homme*, and journals in sociology and economic field.

SIDELIGHTS: Simon's books have been translated into a total of thirteen other languages, including Turkish, Persian, and Chinese; parts of two of them have been reprinted in four books by others.

*　　*　　*

SIMON, Hubert K. 1917-

PERSONAL: Born May 4, 1917, in Davenport, Iowa; son of Hugo M. (a merchant) and Corinne (Klein) Simon; married Betty Chuckrow, February 14, 1942; children: Molly Carol (Mrs. Peter J. Katz), Steven C. *Education:* Attended Northwestern University, 1935-37, Columbia University, 1937-38. *Residence:* White Plains, N.Y. 10607.

CAREER: H. K. Simon Advertising Agency, Hastings on Hudson, N.Y., owner, 1948—. *Military service:* U.S. Army, 1942-45; became staff sergeant. *Member:* Westchester Contract Bridge Association (former vice-president).

WRITINGS: Your Fortune in Mail Order Selling, Bantam, 1964. Also author of articles and monographs.

SIMON, Joan L. 1921-

PERSONAL: Born June 6, 1921, in New York, N.Y.; daughter of Sam A. and Margaret (Seligman) Levisohn; married Sidney Simon, 1945 (divorced, 1962); children: Mark, Teru, Rachel, Nora, Juno. *Education:* Bennington College, B.A., 1942; New York University, M.A., 1944. *Home:* 164 South Mountain Rd., New York, N.Y.

CAREER: Partisan Review, New York, N.Y., business manager, 1942-44; New York University, New York, N.Y., instructor in English, 1944-46. Rockland Country Day School, trustee, 1959-62.

WRITINGS: Portrait of a Father (novel), Atheneum, 1960.

WORK IN PROGRESS: A second novel; poems.†

* * *

SIMONS, Eric N(orman) 1896-

PERSONAL: Born January 12, 1896, in Birmingham, England; son of Frederick and Esther (Harris) Simons; married Lily Laybourn (a teacher); children: Audrey (Mrs. G. Webb), Martin. *Education:* Attended King Edward VI School, Birmingham, England, 1906-07, and Central Secondary School, Sheffield, England, 1908-11. *Politics:* Labour. *Religion:* Rationalist. *Home:* Flat 3, 3 St. John's Rd., Eastbourne BN20 7JA, Sussex, England.

CAREER: Publicity manager for Edgar Allen & Co. Ltd., 1923-59. Author. Director and executive chairman, Sheffield Repertory Co. Ltd., 1936-60. *Member:* Society of Authors, National Trust, Aslib, Rationalist Press Association, Readers' Union.

WRITINGS: The Amazing Sanders, Chatto & Windus, 1927; *Dear England,* Hodder & Stoughton, 1929; *A Lady of No Leisure,* Hodder & Stoughton, 1931; *Friendly Eleven: A Cricket Chronicle,* Laurie, 1950; *The Whistle Blew,* Laurie, 1951; *Lord of London,* Muller, 1963; *The Devil of the Vault: A Life of Guy Fawkes,* Muller, 1963; *The Queen and the Rebel: Mary Tudor and Wyatt the Younger,* Muller, 1964; *Into Unknown Waters: John and Sebastian Cabot,* Dobson, 1964; *Edward IV,* Muller, 1966; *The Story of Metals,* Dobson, 1967; *Henry VII,* Muller, 1968; *The Story of Trade,* Dobson, 1968; *The Story of Communication,* Dobson, 1970. Author of play, "A Lady of No Leisure."

Technical books: *Marketing the Technical Product,* Emmott, 1924; *Successful Buying,* Pitman, 1927; *The Structure of Steel Simply Explained,* Prentice-Hall, 1938, published as *The Structure of Steel,* Philosophical Library, 1958; (with Edwin Gregory) *Steel Manufacture Simply Explained,* Pitman, 1940; *Saws and Sawing Machinery,* Pitman, 1946; *Steel Castings,* P. Elek, 1946, Chemical Publishing Co., 1947; *Steel Files: Their Manufacture and Application,* Pitman, 1947; *Iron Simply Explained,* Stuyvesant, 1947; (with Edwin Gregory) *The Heat-Treatment of Steel,* Pitman, 1947, 2nd edition, 1958; (editor) William Francis Walker, *Form Tools: A Guide to Their Design, Manufacture and Use,* Hutchinson, 1947; (with Edwin Gregory) *Non-Ferrous Metals and Alloys,* P. Elek, 1948; (with W. D. Burnet) *Mechanics for the Home Student,* Iliffe, 1950; (with A. D. Romans) *Modern Welding Technique,* Pitman, 1950; (with William H. Salmon) *Foundry Practice,* Pitman, 1951, revised edition, 1957; *Cutting-Tool Materials,* Pitman, 1951; *The Grinding of Steel,* Odhams, 1954; (with Frederick C. Lea) *The Machining of Steel,* Odhams, 1960, 2nd edition, Macmillan, 1961; (with Peter d'Alroy Jones) *Story of the Saw,* Neame, for Spear & Jackson Ltd., 1961; *The Surface Treatment of Steel,* Pitman, 1962; *Machine Tools,* Muller, 1962; *Cement and Concrete Engineering,* Muller, 1964; (with Edwin Gregory) *Steel Working Processes,* Odhams, 1964; *Welding,* Muller, 1965; *Uncommon Metals,* Hart Publishing, 1967; *Outline of Metallurgy,* Muller, 1968; *Dictionary of Alloys,* Muller, 1969; *Dictionary of Ferrous Metals,* Muller, 1970; *Dictionary of Machining,* Muller, 1972; *Dictionary of Foundry Work,* Granada, 1972. Contributor to Encyclopaedia Britannica. Contributor of articles to *Sheffield Telegraph, Gramohone, Books,* and other periodicals and newspapers. Contributor to Ministry of Information, British Council.

WORK IN PROGRESS: Dictionary of Metal Heat-Treatment for Muller.

SIDELIGHTS: Simons has a working knowledge of French, German, Italian, and Spanish, and can translate from Swedish and Portuguese. *Avocational interests:* Travel, sports, literature, languages, history, cricket, English football.

* * *

SIMPSON, Jacqueline (Mary) 1930-

PERSONAL: Born November 25, 1930, in Worthing, Sussex, England; daughter of Walter Herbert and Yvonne (de Burlet) Simpson. *Education:* Bedford College, London, B.A. (first class honors), 1952; King's College, London, M.A. (with distinction), 1955. *Politics:* Liberal. *Religion:* Church of England. *Home:* 9 Christchurch Rd., Worthing, Sussex, BN11 1JH, England.

CAREER: Writer and researcher, mainly on medieval Icelandic literature, and folklore, and part-time teacher of English at Convent of Our Lady of Sion, Worthing, Sussex, England, 1955—. *Member:* Viking Society for Northern Research (member of council, 1960-63, 1965-68). Folklore Society (member of council, 1965—).

WRITINGS: (Author of new introduction, notes, and index, and of corrections to original translation by Samuel Laing) *Heimskringla Part 2, the Olaf Sagas,* two volumes, Dent, 1964; (translator, and author of introduction) *The Northmen Talk* (collection of Icelandic prose and poetry), University of Wisconsin Press, 1965; (with G. N. Garmonsway) *A Penguin Dictionary of English,* Penguin, 1965, revised and enlarged edition, 1969; *Everyday Life in the Viking Age,* Putnam, 1967, revised edition, 1969; (translator with Garmonsway) *Beowulf and its Analogues,* Dutton, 1968; (translator and author of introduction and notes) *Icelandic Folktales and Legends,* Batsford, 1972; *The Folklore of Sussex,* Batsford, 1973. Contributor to *Saga-Book, Folklore, Skirnir, Etudes Celtiques,* and other learned journals.

WORK IN PROGRESS: Translations of Icelandic folktales; research on English Folklore, and further enlargement of the *Penguin English Dictionary.*

SIDELIGHTS: Miss Simpson speaks French, reads German, Danish, and modern Icelandic. *Avocational interests:* Pottery, walking.

* * *

SIMPSON, N(orman) F(rederick) 1919-

PERSONAL: Born January 29, 1919, in London, England; son of George Frederick and Elizabeth (Rossiter) Simpson; married Joyce Bartlett, September 2, 1944; children: Judith. *Education:* University of London, B.A. (honors), 1954. *Agent:* International Famous Agency Ltd., 11-12 Hanover St., London W.1, England.

CAREER: Teacher, 1946-56; assistant lecturer to adult education groups, 1956-62. Teacher and lecturer, City of Westminster College. *Military service:* British Army, Royal Artillery and Intelligence Corps, 1941-46; became sergeant. *Member:* Society of Authors. *Awards, honors:* Observer (London) play competition third prize, 1957, for "A Resounding Tinkle."

WRITINGS—Plays: "A Resounding Tinkle," first produced in London, 1957, produced in Bloomington, Ind., 1961; *The Hole* (first produced in London, 1958), Samuel French, 1958; *One Way Pendulum* (first produced in London, 1959; produced in New York, 1961), Faber, 1960, Grove, 1961; (contributor) *One to Another* (first produced in London, 1959), Samuel French, 1960; (contributor) "You, Me and the Gatepost," first produced in Nottingham, England, 1960; (contributor) "On the Avenue," first produced in London, 1961; (contributor) "One Over the Eight," first produced in London, 1961; *The Form* (first produced in London, 1961), Samuel French, 1961; "Oh," first produced in London, 1961; *The Hole and Other Plays and Sketches* (includes a shortened version of "A Resounding Tinkle," *The Form*, "Gladly Otherwise," "Oh," "One Blast and Have Done"), Faber, 1964; *The Cresta Run* (first produced in London, 1965; produced in Louisville, Ky., 1968), Faber, 1966, Grove, 1967; (with Leopoldo Maler) "Playback 625," first produced in London, 1970; "How Are Your Handles" (includes "Gladly Otherwise," "Oh," "The Other Side of London"), first produced in London, 1971; *Was He Anyone?* (first produced in London, 1972), Faber, 1973.

Television plays: "Make a Man," 1966; "Three Rousing Tinkles" (includes "The Father by Adoption of One of the Former Marquis of Rangoon's Natural Granddaughters," "If Those Are Mr. Heckmonwick's Own Personal Pipes They've Been Lagged Once Already," and "The Best I Can Do by Way of a Gate-Leg Table Is a Hundredweight of Coal"), 1966; "Four Tall Tinkles" (includes "We're Due in Eastbourne in Ten Minutes," "In a Punt with Friends Under a Haystack on the River Mersey," "A Row of Potted Plants," and "At Least It's a Precaution Against Fire"), 1967; *Some Small Tinkles: Television Plays* (includes "We're Due in Eastbourne in Ten Minutes," "The Best I Can Do by Way of a Gate-Leg Table Is a Hundredweight of Coal," "At Least It's a Precaution Against Fire"), Faber, 1968; "World in Ferment" (series), 1969; "Charley's Grants" (series), 1970; "Thank You Very Much," 1971; "Elementary, My Dear Watson," 1973.

Screenplays: "One Way Pendulum," 1964; "Diamonds for Breakfast," 1968.

Radio play: "Something Rather Effective," 1972.

Plays anthologized in *Observer Plays*, Faber, 1958; *New English Dramatists II*, Penguin, 1960; *The Best One-Act Plays of 1960-61*, edited by Hugh Miller, Harrap, 1963; *Penguin Plays*, Penguin, 1964.

BIOGRAPHICAL/CRITICAL SOURCES: Revue de Paris, April, 1960; Martin Esslin, *The Theatre of the Absurd*, Doubleday, 1961; Kenneth Tynan, *Curtains*, Longmans, Green, 1961; Nigel Dennis, *Dramatic Essays*, Weidenfeld & Nicolson, 1962; *Contemporary Theatre*, Arnold, 1962; W. A. Armstrong, *Experimental Drama*, Bell, 1963; *Drama Survey* (Minnesota), winter, 1963; George Wellworth, *Theatre of Protest and Paradox*, New York University Press, 1964; Frederick Lumley, *New Trends in 20th Century Drama*, Oxford University Press, 1967.†

SIMS, Bernard John 1915-

PERSONAL: Born May 13, 1915, in London, England; married Elizabeth Margaret Eileen Endicott (a solicitor of the Supreme Court), April 27, 1963. *Education:* University of London and Law Society's School of Law, LL.B. (honors), 1937. *Religion:* Roman Catholic. *Home:* 89 Dovehouse St., Chelsea, London SW3 6JZ England. *Office:* Grindall House, 25 Newgate St., London, EC1A 7LH, England.

CAREER: Solicitor of the Supreme Court, London, England, 1937—. *Military service:* Royal Artillery, 1940-43; Royal Army Ordnance Corps, 1943-45; became captain. *Member:* Law Society, City of London Solicitors Company, City Livery Club.

WRITINGS: Controls on Company Finance, Sweet & Maxwell, 1957; (editor) *Sergeant on the Stamp Duties*, 3rd and 4th editions, Butterworth & Co., 1963, 5th and 6th editions, 1972. Taxation editor, *Encyclopaedia of Forms and Precedents*, 4th edition, Butterworth & Co., 1964-74. Member of editorial board, *Simon's Taxes*, 1970—.

*   *   *

SINGH, Karan 1931-

PERSONAL: Born March 9, 1931, in Cannes, France; son of Maharaja Sir Hari Singh of Jammu and Kashmir and Maharani Tara Devi; married Princess Yasho Rajya Lakshmi, March, 1950; children: Jyoti (daughter), Yuvaraj Vikramaditya (son), Ajatashatru (son). *Education:* Jammu and Kashmir University, B.A., 1951; Delhi University, M.A. (first class honors), 1957, and Ph.D. *Home:* (May-October) Karan Mahal, Srinagar, Jammu and Kashmir State, India; (November-April) Hari Niwas, Jammu Tawi, Jammu and Kashmir State, India.

CAREER: Appointed regent of Jammu and Kashmir by father, Maharaja Sir Hari Singh, 1949; elected first Sadari-Riyasat (head of state) by State Assembly when constitutional changes created this office, 1952, re-elected in 1957 and 1962; recognized hereditary successor to father by President of India, 1961; became first governor of Jammu and Kashmir when office of Sadar-i-Riyasat was so converted during further constitutional development, 1965. Chancellor of Jammu and Kashmir University, 1949—, and of Banaras Hindu University. Trustee of India International Centre, New Delhi, and of Jawaharlal Nehru Memorial Fund, and actively associated with other scholarly and cultural organizations. *Awards, honors:* Appointed honorary major general in Indian Army and honorary colonel of Jammu and Kashmir Regiment by President of India, 1962; honorary doctorate from Aligarth Muslim University, 1963.

WRITINGS: Varied Rhythms (essays and poems), Asia Publishing House (Bombay), 1960; *Shadow and Sunlight* (Dogra Pahari songs), Asia Publishing House (Bombay), 1962; *Prophet of Indian Nationalism: The Political Thought of Sri Aurobindo Ghosh, 1893-1910*, Allen & Unwin, 1963; *Selected Speeches and Writings*, Jammu and Kashmir Government, 1964; *Welcome, the Moonrise* (poems), Asia Publishing House (Bombay), 1965; *Post-Independence Generation—Challenge and Response* (lectures), Bharatiya Vidya Bhavan (Bombay), 1965.

AVOCATIONAL INTERESTS: Travel, music (particularly Indian classical music), tennis, badminton, golf, bridge, chess, and reading.†

SINGLETON, Jack 1911-

PERSONAL: Born February 3, 1911, in Barnsley, Yorkshire, England; son of Arthur (a policeman) and Ethel (Powell) Singleton; married Elsie Appleyard, August 26, 1937; children: Avril (Mrs. John James), Christopher Martin. *Education:* University of Leeds, B.A. (honors); additional study at Yorkshire United Independent College. *Politics:* Labour. *Home:* 35 Wimborne Dr., Pinner, Middlesex, England. *Office:* British Broadcasting Corp., Portland Pl., London W. 1, England.

CAREER: Congregational minister in Bradford, Bolton, England, 1934-39; Young Men's Christian Association, youth organizer, 1939-42; Wolstanton County Grammar School, Staffordshire, England, assistant master, 1942-44; Oxford University, Oxford, England, extramural lecturer in current affairs, 1944-49; British Broadcasting Corp., London, England, talks producer, 1949—. Justice of the peace, County of London Juvenile Bench. Lecturer on mass media and on juvenile delinquency.

WRITINGS: (With Tony Gibson) *The Spare-Time Book*, Gollancz, 1955; *Working for a Living*, S. C. M. Press, 1958; *Getting and Spending*, S. C. M. Press, 1960; *X Marks the Spot*, S. C. M. Press, 1964; (with R. G. Martin) *Epilogues for Youth*, Religious Education Press, 1964; (editor) *Home This Afternoon* (accompaniment to radio program), Lutterworth, 1966; (editor) *The Second Book of Home This Afternoon* (accompaniment to radio program), Lutterworth 1967. Author of radio scripts; contributor to periodicals.

AVOCATIONAL INTERESTS: Climbing.†

*   *   *

SINGLETON, Ralph Herbert 1900-

PERSONAL: Born May 25, 1900, in Cleveland, Ohio; son of George Herbert (in real estate) and Marie Ann (Strebel) Singleton; married Mercedes Greenwood Holden, July 23, 1924; children: Patricia Jane (Mrs. Michael Romanov), Mercedes Greenwood (Mrs. John R. Lichtwardt), Mary Ann. *Education:* Oberlin College, A.B., 1923, M.A., 1930; Western Reserve University (now Case Western Reserve University), Ph.D., 1939. *Politics:* Democrat. *Religion:* Protestant. *Home:* 2280 South West Seymour Dr., Portland, Ore. 97201. *Office:* Portland State University, P.O. Box 751, Portland, Ore. 97207.

CAREER: Iowa State wuniversity of Science and Technology, Ames, instructor in English, 1923-26; Oberlin College, Oberlin, Ohio, 1926-66, began as instructor, became professor of English, 1958; Portland State University, Ore., visiting professor of English, 1966-72, professor emeritus, 1972—, now teaching part time in department of continuing education. Teacher and lecturer at creative writing workshops. *Military service:* U.S. Army, 1918. *Member:* Modern Language Association of America, National Council of Teachers of English, Conference on College Composition and Communication (member of executive committee, 1956-58), Oberlin City Club (president, 1962-63), Portland City Club, University Club (Portland), Elks Club.

WRITINGS: (Editor) *Two and Twenty* (short stories), St. Martins, 1962; (editor) *Reviewing the Years: Memories of John Young-Hunter*, Crown, 1963; (author of introduction) Henry Fielding, *Tom Jones*, Washington Square Press, 1963; (author of introduction) Anthony Trollope, *Barchester Towers*, Washington Square Press, 1963; *Style: The Craft of Expository Prose*, Chandler Publishing, 1966; (editor with Stanton Millet) *Introduction to Literature*, World Publishing, 1966; (editor) *The Art of Prose Fiction*, World Publishing, 1967; (editor with Alexander Scharbach) *The Lively Rhetoric*, Holt, 1968, 2nd edition, 1972; (editor with Scharbach) *The New Lively Rhetoric*, Holt, 1970. Contributor to professional journals, such as *College English*; former contributor of sports articles to *Cleveland Plain Dealer* and *Cleveland Press*.

WORK IN PROGRESS: Diction, with Alexander Scharbach; a revision of *The Lively Rhetoric*.

SIDELIGHTS: Singleton reads French, Spanish, and German.

*   *   *

SINHA, Krishna N(andan) 1924-

PERSONAL: Born December 22, 1924, in India; son of Basudeo Narian and Sharda (Devi) Sinha; married Malti, May 2, 1943; children: Sanjiva (son), Rita (daughter). *Education:* Patna University, Patna, India, B.A. (honors), 1944, M.A., 1946; University of Arkansas, Ph.D., 1956. *Home:* West Jagjivan Rd., Gaya, Bihar, India. *Office:* Department of English, Bihar University, Muzaffarpur, Bihar, India.

CAREER: Gaya College, Gaya, Bihar, India, head of department of English, 1947-53; Panjab University, New Delhi, India, lecturer in English, 1957-59; Gaya College, head of department of English, 1959-61; Kurukshtera University, Kurukshtera, Panjab, India, lecturer in English, 1961-63; Bihar University, Muzaffarpur, Bihar, India, reader in English and head of department, 1963-70; Indian Institute of Advanced Study, Simla, India, visiting fellow, 1971-73; University of Bihar, Muzaffarpur, India, head of department of English, 1973—. *Member:* English Teachers Conference (India).

WRITINGS: Hardam Aag (in Hindi), Ajanta Press, 1951; *Nritya Ka Bulawa* (in Hindi), Asoka Press, 1953; *On Four Quartets of T. S. Eliot*, Stockwell, 1963; *Wait Without Hope*, Writers Workshop, 1967; *Mulk Raj Anand*, Twayne, 1972. Contributor of articles and reviews to *Literary Criterion, Quest, Thought, Illustrated Weekly of India, Preview* (United States), and other journals. Editor, *Gaya College Journal*, 1960-61. Also editor of *Consent*.

WORK IN PROGRESS: Symbolic Configurations in Five Modern Poets for the Indian Institute for Advanced Study; a novel, *When the Pale Moon Rages*; and stories, *The Rose City*; another novel, *Amar Kavita*, and stories, *Gulab Sahar*, both in Hindi; directing doctoral research on Graham Greene, Tennessee Williams, John Webster, R. Crashaw, William Wordsworth and other literary figures.

SIDELIGHTS: Sinha writes to *CA*: "Literature is, was and shall be my first love. But the pocation of teaching came my way, and I loved it. The universities proved to be the shrine where, devoted, concentrated in purpose, I began my journey. The quest seemed so unavailing—as all quests are—but over two years of work at the University of Arkansas, USA, and a journey through England and France—dispersed the clouds of unknowing.... Sensitive and intense, I have developed a sort of otherness which has nurtured my creative talent and given it its special flavour. Beginning with the romantic absorption of emblems and attitudes of a lost generation, I was swayed by the mainstream of the intellectual currents of the times; but [I] have now moved—or so it seems—toward a centrality which comes on account of a fair distribution of energy between experience and contemplation, journey and arrival. My works mirror—if I may say so—the stress and the glory of a sensitive understanding of life."

*   *   *

SINNIGEN, William G. 1928-

PERSONAL: Born September 12, 1928, in Paterson, N.J.; son of William Franklin (an insurance underwriter) and Lois Sinnigen. Education: University of Michigan, A.B., 1949, A.M., 1950, Ph.D., 1954; also studied at University of Munich, 1948, American Academy in Rome, 1952-54. Home: 1 West 67th St., New York, N.Y. 10023. Office: Department of History, Hunter College, 695 Park Ave., New York, N.Y. 10021.

CAREER: University of California, Berkeley, instructor, then assistant professor of history, 1956-62; Hunter College of the City University of New York, New York, N.Y., associate professor, 1962-65, professor of history, 1966—, chairman of department, 1971—. Military service: U.S. Army, 1954-56. Member: American Historical Association, Archaeological Institute of America, Classical Association of the American Academy in Rome, Phi Beta Kappa, Phi Eta Sigma, Phi Kappa Phi. Awards, honors: Fellow, American Council of Learned Societies, 1959-60.

WRITINGS: Officium of the Urban Prefecture, American Academy in Rome, 1957; (editor) Rome, Free Press of Glencoe, 1965; (with A. E. R. Boak) A History of Rome to A.D. 565, 5th edition, Macmillan, 1965. Contributor of articles and reviews to historical and classical journals in America and abroad.

WORK IN PROGRESS: The Roman Secret Service.

*   *   *

SIRJAMAKI, John 1911-

PERSONAL: Born May 9, 1911, in Chisholm, Minn.; son of John and Hannah (Karvala) Syrjamaki; married Verne Barbara, May 8, 1943; children: John Eric Maki. Education: Carleton College, A.B., 1934; Yale University, Ph.D., 1940. Politics: Democrat. Home: 9055 Cliffside Dr., Clarence, N.Y. 14031.

CAREER: New York University, New York, N.Y., instructor in sociology, 1940-41; assistant professor of sociology at University of Delaware, Newark, 1943-44, Vassar College, Poughkeepsie, N.Y., 1944-46, Yale University, New Haven, Conn., 1946-53; University of Minnesota, Minneapolis, associate professor, 1953-57, professor of sociology, 1957-63; State University of New York at Buffalo, professor of sociology, 1963—. Member: American Sociological Association.

WRITINGS: The American Family in the Twentieth Century, Harvard University Press, 1953; The Sociology of Cities, Random House, 1964; (co-author) Social Foundations of Human Behavior, Harper, 1965.

WORK IN PROGRESS: Research in comparative sociology of cities.

*   *   *

SISSON, Rosemary Anne 1923-

PERSONAL: Surname is pronounced to rhyme with "listen"; born October 13, 1923, in London, England; daughter of Charles Jasper (a professor) and Vera (Ginn) Sisson. Education: University College, London, B.A. (honors), 1946; Cambridge University, M.Lit., 1948. Politics: Conservative. Religion: Church of England. Home: 167 New King's Rd., London S.W. 6, England. Agent: Andrew Mann, Ltd., 32 Wigmore St., London W.1, England.

CAREER: University of Wisconsin, Madison, instructor in English, 1949-50; University College, University of London, London, England, assistant lecturer in American literature, 1950-54; University of Birmingham, Birmingham, England, assistant lecturer in English, 1954-55. Stratford-upon-Avon Herald, drama critic, 1955-57. Coventry Cathedral Drama Council, member. Military service: Royal Observer Corps, 1943-45. Member: Writers Guild of Great Britain, Writers Guild of America. Awards, honors: Repertory Players Award, 1964, for "The Royal Captivity."

WRITINGS—Children's books: The Adventures of Ambrose, Harrap, 1951, Dutton, 1952; The Impractical Chimney-Sweep, Macmillan, 1956, F. Watts, 1957; The Isle of Dogs, Macmillan, 1959; The Young Shakespeare, Parrish, 1959; The Young Jane Austen, Parrish, 1962; The Young Shaftesbury, Parrish, 1964; The Exciseman, R. Hale, 1973; The Killer of Horseman's Flats, R. Hale, 1973.

Plays: The Queen and the Welshman (acting edition), Samuel French, 1958; Fear Came to Supper (acting edition), Samuel French, 1959. Other plays produced: "The Splendid Outcasts"; "Home and the Heart"; "The Royal Capitivity"; "Bitter Sanctuary"; (with Robert Morley) "A Ghost on Tiptoe."

Television plays: "The Vagrant Heart"; "The Man from Brooklyn"; (adapter from the novel by Meredith) "The Ordeal of Richard Feverel"; (adapter from the novel by Eliot) "The Mill on the Floss"; "Catherine of Aragon" (Six Wives of Henry VIII" series); "The Marriage Game" ("Elizabeth R" series); "Beyond Our Means"; "Let's Marry Liz." Plays anthologized in Plays of the Year, Flek Books, 1958, 1959, and in "Heritage of Literature" series, Longmans, Green, 1962.

Script writer of episodes in British Broadcasting Corp. television series, "Compact," "Upstairs, Downstairs," and "Within These Walls." Contributor of poetry and short stories to magazines, and articles to Sunday Times.

WORK IN PROGRESS: A novel, The Stratford Story.

SIDELIGHTS: Miss Sisson speaks French "reasonably well."

*   *   *

SKELTON, Peter 1928-

PERSONAL: Born December, 1928, in Amsterdam, Holland; son of Major E. (an industrialist) and M. (Wilkins) Skelton. Education: Cambridge University, B.A. Home: St. Anthony, Hr. Woodfield, Torquay, England.

CAREER: Onetime reader with Faber & Faber Ltd., London, England; Hutchinson & Co., London, England, former art editor; editor of Go Travel Magazine and "Cherry Tree Books" (Sunday Times publications); editor and founder of "Fantasy Books"; Sunday Times, London, England, general production editor to Sunday Times Newspaper Group, 1950-53. Member: West Country Writers Association (founder), South Devon Literary Society (president). Awards, honors: The Charm of Hours was runner-up for Somerset Maugham Award (for travel) of Society of Authors; Compagnon Institute International des Arts et des Lettres.

WRITINGS: The Charm of Hours, Chatto & Windus,

1954, Morrow, 1955; *Animals All*, Collins, 1959, Day, 1960; *The Promise of Days*, William Holman, 1964; *The Blossom of Months*, Holland, 1973.

Also author of play, "Room of Overnight," 1958. Script writer for Government Crown Film Unit (later Central office of Information Film Unit). Contributor to *Daily Telegraph, Sunday Times, News of the World, Features*, and *Holland Herald*.

WORK IN PROGRESS: The Flowering of Seasons, the fourth volume of a continuous saga in six volumes.

BIOGRAPHICAL/CRITICAL SOURCES: Introduction, *The Promise of Days*, William Holman, 1964.

* * *

SKIDMORE, Rex A(ustin) 1914-

PERSONAL: Born December 31, 1914, in Salt Lake City, Utah; son of Charles H. (an educator) and Louise (Wangsgard) Skidmore; married Knell Spencer, August 31, 1939; children: Lee Spencer, Larry Rex. *Education:* University of Utah, B.A., 1938, M.S., 1939; University of Pennsylvania, Ph.D., 1941. *Religion:* Church of Jesus Christ of Latter-day Saints (Mormon). *Home:* 1444 South 20th East, Salt Lake City, Utah. *Office:* Graduate School of Social Work, University of Utah, Salt Lake City, Utah.

CAREER: Utah State University, Logan, instructor, 1941-42; Federal Bureau of Investigation, special agent in Miami, Fla., San Francisco, Calif., and San Antonio, Tex., 1943-45; University of Utah, Salt Lake City, associate professor, 1947-50, professor of social work, 1950—, director of bureau of student counsel, 1947-57, dean of Graduate School of Social Work, 1956—. President of Salt Lake area branch, Travelers Aid Society; member of board of Salt Lake Council, Boy Scouts of America, and of Salt Lake Community Services Council. *Member:* American Association of Marriage Counselors, National Association of Social Workers, Council on Social Work Education, Phi Kappa Phi, Pi Gamma Mu.

WRITINGS: Mormon Recreation: Theory and Practice, privately printed, 1941; (with A. S. Cannon) *Building Your Marriage*, Deseret, 1951, 3rd edition, 1964; *Youth, Love, and Marriage*, Deseret, 1955; (with C. J. Skidmore and Hulda Garrett) *Marriage Consulting*, Harper, 1955; *I Thee Wed*, Deseret, 1956; (with Milton G. Thackeray) *Introduction to Social Work*, Appleton, 1964, revised edition, Prentice-Hall, 1966. Contributor to scientific, sociological, and social work journals.

AVOCATIONAL INTERESTS: Tennis and camping.

* * *

SKILLING, H(arold) Gordon 1912-

PERSONAL: Born February 28, 1912, in Toronto, Ontario, Canada; son of William Watt (a shoe repairer) and Alice (Stevenson) Skilling; married Sara Bright, 1937; children: David Bright, Peter Conard. *Education:* University of Toronto, B.A., 1934; Oxford University, B.A., 1936, M.A., 1940; University of London, Ph.D., 1940. *Home:* 90 Cheritan Ave., Toronto, Ontario, Canada. *Office:* University of Toronto, 100 St. George St., Toronto 5, Ontario, Canada.

CAREER: University of Wisconsin, Madison, assistant professor of political science, 1941-47; Dartmouth College, Hanover, N.H., assistant professor, 1947-51, professor of government, 1951-59; Columbia University, New York,

N.Y., senior fellow, Russian Institute, 1949-51, visiting professor, 1952-53; University of Toronto, Toronto, Ontario, Canada, professor of political science, 1959—, and director of Centre for Russian and East European Studies, 1963—. Commentator for Czechoslovak Broadcasting Corp., 1938. Canadian Broadcasting Corp., 1944-45; research analyst for British Broadcasting Corp., 1940. *Awards, honors:* Rhodes Scholar, 1934; Social Science Research Council fellowships, 1948, 1961-62; M.A., Dartmouth College, 1951; Canada Council research fellowship, 1961-62.

WRITINGS: Canadian Representation Abroad, Ryerson, 1945; *Communism, National and International: Eastern Europe Since Stalin*, University of Toronto Press, 1964; *Governments of Communist East Europe*, Crowell, 1966.

Editor: (with Peter Brock) *The Czech Renascence of the Nineteeth Century: Essays Presented to Otakar Odlozilik*, University of Toronto Press, 1970; (with Franklyn Griffiths) *Interest Groups in Soviet Politics*, Princeton University Press, 1971.

Contributor: T. C. T. McCormick, editor, *Problems of the Postwar World*, McGraw, 1945; W. H. Bennett, editor, *Postwar Governments of the British Commonwealth*, [Gainesville, Fla.], 1947; Devere E. Pentony, editor, *Red World in Tumult: Communist Foreign Policies*, Chandler Publishing, 1962; Richard Pipes and others, *The Changing Communist World*, [Toronto], 1963; Edward McWhinney, editor, *Law, Foreign Policy, and the East-West Detente*, University of Toronto Press, 1964; Adam Bromke, editor, *The Communist States at the Crossroads: Between Moscow and Peking*, Praeger, 1965.

WORK IN PROGRESS: Czechoslovak Communism—A History, for University of Toronto Press.

SIDELIGHTS: Skilling speaks Czech, Russian, German, and French. He has traveled in Communist countries of eastern Europe, 1948, 1950, 1958, and 1961-62.†

* * *

SKINNER, Elliott P(ercival) 1924-

PERSONAL: Born June 20, 1924, in Port of Spain, Trinidad, West Indies Federation; became American citizen, 1943; married Thelma Garvin, December 15, 1946; children: Victor, Gale, Sopha, Touray. *Education:* Attended schools in Trinidad; University of Neutchatel, student, 1946; New York University, A.B., 1951; Columbia University, A.M., 1952, Ph.D., 1955. *Home:* 29 Claremont Ave., New York, N.Y. 10027.

CAREER: Columbia University, New York, N.Y., visiting assistant professor of anthropology, 1957-59; New York University, New York, N.Y., assistant professor, 1959-63, associate professor of anthropology, 1963; Columbia University, associate professor of anthropology, 1963-66; U.S. Ambassador to Upper Volta, 1966-69; Columbia University, associate professor of anthropology, 1968—. Field work in Sierra Leone, 1942, British Guiana, 1954, West Africa, 1955-57, 1964-65. Crossroad Africa Project, member of board. *Military service:* U.S. Army, World War II; served in European theater. *Member:* International African Institute, African Studies Association (fellow), American Anthropological Association (fellow), Royal Anthropological Association of Great Britain and Ireland (fellow), American Society of African Culture, National Association for the Advancement of Colored People.

WRITINGS: (Contributor) Paul Bohannan, editor, *African*

Trade and Market Systems, under auspices of National Science Foundation, Northwestern University Press, 1962; *The Mossi of the Upper Volta: An Analysis of the Political Development of a Sudanese People*, Stanford University Press, 1964; (contributor) Harwitz and Herskovitz, editors, *Economic Integration in Africa*, Northwestern University Press, 1965; (with Daniel Chu) *A Glorious Age in Africa*, Doubleday, 1965; (contributor) R. Cohen and J. Middleton, editors, *From Tribe to Nation in Africa*, Chandler, 1970; (contributor) Irving L. Markowitz, editor, *African Politics and Society*, Free Press, 1970; (contributor) J. Masserman and John J. Schwab, editors, *Man for Humanity*, C. C Thomas, 1972; (editor) *Peoples and Cultures of Africa: An Anthropological Reader*, Natural History Press, 1973; (with Margo Jefferson) *African Traditional Life*, Doubleday, 1973; *African Urban Life: The Transformation of Ouagadougou*, Princeton University Press, in press. Contributor to *American People's Encyclopedia*, 1964, and to *American Anthropologist, Journal of Negro History, Journal of Human Relations, Africa Report*, and many other professional journals.

SIDELIGHTS: Skinner is fluent in spoken and written French, also speaks More language of the Mossi of the Upper Volta.

* * *

SKINNER, Gordon S(weetland) 1924-

PERSONAL: Born November 9, 1924, in New Britain, Conn.; son of Dwight (a boys' club director) and Dorothy (Sweetland) Skinner; married Virginia M. Knodel, August 20, 1955; children: Michael Gordon, Jo Ann. *Education:* Boston University, B.S. (cum laude), 1948; University of Wisconsin, M.S., 1949, Ph.D., 1953. *Religion:* Presbyterian. *Home:* 547 Abilene Trail, Cincinnati, Ohio 45215. *Office:* University of Cincinnati, Cincinnati, Ohio 45221.

CAREER: Whitewater State College (now University of Wisconsin), Whitewater, instructor in economics, 1950-51; University of Wisconsin, Madison, instructor in economics, 1952-53; University of Cincinnati, Cincinnati, Ohio, 1953—, now professor of economics, head of department, 1963-74. Ohio State Employment Service, member of Cincinnati advisory council; Cincinnati Full Employment Commission, member, 1955—. *Military service:* U.S. Army Air Forces, navigator, 1943-46; became first lieutenant; received Air Medal with three oak leaf clusters and Distinguished Flying Cross. *Member:* American Economics Association, Industrial Relations Research Association, Econometric Society, Institute of Management Sciences, Midwest Economic Association, Alpha Kappa Psi, Beta Gamma Sigma, Phi Kappa Tau.

WRITINGS: (With J. M. Kuhlman) *The Economic System*, Irwin, 1959, revised edition, 1964; (with E. E. Herman) *Labor Law: Cases, Text and Legislation*, Random House, 1972.

WORK IN PROGRESS: A book on labor problems; research in labor market and unemployment.

* * *

SKOU-HANSEN, Tage 1925-

PERSONAL: Born February 12, 1925, in Fredericia, Denmark; son of Johannes (a businessman) and Martha (Skou) Hansen; married Ellen Porsgaard, July 1, 1950; children: Jens, Gerd, Jakob. *Education:* University of Aarhus, M.A., 1950. *Home:* Bredkaer Tvaervej 31, Egaa 8250, Denmark.

CAREER: Heretica (literary periodical), Copenhagen, Denmark, editor, 1952-53; Wivels Forlag, Copenhagen, Denmark, literary adviser, 1952-53; Gyldendalske Boghandel Nordisk Forlag (publisher), Copenhagen, Denmark, literary adviser, 1954-58; *Vindrosen* (literary periodical), Copenhagen, Denmark, editor, 1954-58; Askov Folk High School, Vejen, Denmark, teacher, 1958-67; free lance writer, 1967—. *Military service:* Danish Army, 1950-51. *Member:* Danish Film Foundation (member of board, 1970-72), Danish Author's Society (member of board, 1973), Danish State Art Foundation (member of board), Danish P.E.N. Club. *Awards, honors:* Louisiana Prize, 1963; Danish State Art Foundation scholarship, 1971; Anckerske travelling scholarship, 1972; Jeanne and Henri Nathansen's Memorial Scholarship, 1972.

WRITINGS: De nogne traeer, Gyldendal, 1957, translation from the Danish by K. John published as *The Naked Trees*, J. Cape, 1959; *Dagstjernen*, Gyldendal, 1962; (editor) *Den moderne roman*, Fremad, 1963; *Paa den anden side* (novel), Gyldendal, 1965; *Hjemkomst* (novel), Gyldendal, 1969; *Tredje halvleg* (novel), Gyldendal, 1971; *Det midlertidige faellesskab* (criticism), Gyldendal, 1972; *Tolvtemanden*, Broendums Forlag, 1972; *Medloeberen* (novel), Gyldendal, 1973.

WORK IN PROGRESS: A new novel.

* * *

SLADE, Peter 1912-

PERSONAL: Born November 7, 1912, in Fleet, Hampshire, England; son of John Godfrey (a medical practitioner) and May (Franks) Slade; married Barbara Mary Thompson, November 25, 1939; children: Imogen Anne Slade Whitmore, Clare Bernadette Slade Godolphin. *Education:* Lancing College, student, 1926-30; Central School of Speech Training and Dramatic Art, London, England, Certificate in Acting (honors), 1934. *Home:* Seafield House, 2 Seafield Lane, Beoley, Redditch, Worcestershire, England. *Office:* Education Office, Birmingham Education Authority, Birmingham, England.

CAREER: Actor and producer in repertory and other theater companies in London, England, 1930-36; producer for British Broadcasting Corp., youngest "uncle" in "Children's Hour," 1936; announcer and producer for western region B.B.C., 1937; social services secretary in Hereford, England, 1942-43; Staffordshire County Council, Staffordshire, England, drama adviser, 1943-47; Birmingham Education Authority, Birmingham, England, drama adviser, 1947—. Director of Educational Drama Association, 1948—, of Experimental Drama Centre, Birmingham, 1950—. Pioneer in children's theater, dramatherapy, and theater in the round; his methods have been adopted in Canada, West Indies, Scandinavia, Denmark, and South Africa. Member of British Ministry of Education Drama Working Party, 1948, of advisory committee, National Association of Mental Health, 1962. *Awards, honors:* Fellow of the College of Pheceptors, London.

WRITINGS: Drama in Religion, Education and Therapy, Guild of Pastoral Psychology, 1939; *Child Drama*, University of London Press, 1954; *Introduction to Child Drama*, University of London Press, 1958; *Dramatherapy as an Aid to Personal Development*, Guild of Pastoral Psychology, 1959; *Experience of Spontaneity*, Longmans, 1968. Regular contributor to *Creative Drama*; contributor to *Athene* and other periodicals. Author of radio play, "St. Patrick," 1939.

WORK IN PROGRESS: A book on natural improvised dance, guided action and developmental movement.

BIOGRAPHICAL/CRITICAL SOURCES: P. Coggin, Drama and Education, Thames & Hudson, 1956; Geraldine Brain Siks, Creative Dramatics, an Art for Children, Harper, 1958; H. F. N. McFarland, Psychology and Teaching, Harrap, 1958; Marjorie Batchelder and Virginia Lea Comer, Puppets and Plays, Faber, 1959; Tordis Orjasaeter, Med Barn i Teater, Gyldendal Norsk Forlag, 1959; Tansley and Gulliford, Education of Slow Learning Children, Routledge & Kegan Paul, 1960; C. V. Burgess, Discovering the Theater, University of London Press, 1960; Fishman, The Actor in Training, Jenkins, 1961; Bereiter and Engelmann, Teaching Disadvantaged Children in the Pre-School, Prentice-Hall, 1970; A. Wethered, Drama and Movement in Therapy, Macdonald & Evans, 1973.

*   *   *

SLATER, Leonard 1920-

PERSONAL: Born July 15, 1920, in New York, N.Y.; married Betty Moorsteen (a writer), February 2, 1946; children: Amy, Lucy. Education: University of Michigan, A.B., 1941. Home: 4370 Arista Drive, San Diego, Calif. 92103.

CAREER: Correspondent with National Broadcasting Co., Washington, D.C., 1941-45, Time, Washington, D.C., 1945; correspondent in United States, Europe, and Asia, for Newsweek, 1947-57, Western editor and founder of Los Angeles and San Francisco bureaus; editor and columnist with McCall's, New York, N.Y., 1957-62; now free-lance writer. Military service: U.S. Army, 1946. Member: Overseas Press Club.

WRITINGS: Aly, Random House, 1965; The Pledge, Simon & Schuster, 1970. Contributor of articles to national magazines.

WORK IN PROGRESS: The Roosevelt Connection for Simon & Schuster; a novel, tentatively titled The Island.

SIDELIGHTS: Slater's book The Pledge is a factual account of the arming of Israel to hold off an Arab invasion after the withdrawal of the British in 1948. The completion of this assignment was primarily the work of an underground movement, centered in the United States, which supplied the Palestinian armies with everything from planes for an Air Force to a special telescope for Moshe Dayan's good eye. The book, itself, has drawn numerous and diverse reviews. Hugh Nissenson said that Slater "has written an excellent popular history of an unusual event. 'The Pledge' is well-researched, dramatic, suspenseful and revelatory." However, Christopher Lehmann-Haupt calls the book "episodic, overdetailed, and repetitive."

BIOGRAPHICAL/CRITICAL SOURCES: Detroit Free Press, Sunday Magazine, April 25, 1965.

*   *   *

SLEIGH, Barbara 1906-

PERSONAL: Born January 9, 1906, in Worcestershire, England; daughter of Bernard (an artist) and Stella (Phillp) Sleigh; married David Davis (a free-lance broadcaster), January 29, 1936; children: Anthony, Hilary (daughter), Fabia. Education: Studied at art school, 1922-25, and took art teachers training, 1925-28. Religion: Church of England. Home: 18 Mount Ave., London W.5, England. Agent: Harvey Unna Ltd., 79 Baker St., London W.1, England.

CAREER: Smethwick High School, Staffordshire, England, art teacher, 1928-30; Goldsmiths' College, London, England, lecturer, 1930-33; British Broadcasting Corp., London, England, assistant on radio program, "Children's Hour," 1933-36; writer for children.

WRITINGS: Carbonel, Parrish, 1955, Bobbs-Merrill, 1958; Patchwork Quilt, Parrish, 1956; Singing Wreath, Parrish, 1957; The Seven Days, Parrish, 1958, Meredith, 1968; The Kingdom of Carbonel, Parrish, 1958, Bobbs-Merrill, 1960; No One Must Know, Collins, 1962, Bobbs-Merrill, 1963; North of Nowhere, Collins, 1964, Coward-McCann, 1966; Jessamy, Bobbs-Merrill, 1967; The Snowball, Brockhampton, 1969; Pen, Penny, Tuppence, Hamish Hamilton, 1968; West of Widdershins, Collins, 1971; The Smell of Privet (adult autobiography), Hutchinson, 1971; Stirabout Stories, Bobbs-Merrill, 1972; Ninety-Nine Dragons, Brockhampton Press, 1974; Funny Peculiar: An Anthology, David & Charles, 1974. Author of radio plays, stories, and talks for British Broadcasting Corp.

*   *   *

SLOBODKIN, Louis 1903-

PERSONAL: Born February 19, 1903, in Albany, N.Y.; son of Nathan (an inventor) and Dora (Lubin) Slobodkin; married Florence Gersh (an author), September 27, 1927; children: Laurence B., Michael E. Education: Beaux Arts Institute of Design, New York, N.Y., student, 1918-22. Politics: Democrat. Religion: Jewish. Home: 9341 East Bay Harbor Dr., Bay Harbor Islands, Fla. 33154 (winter); and Cottage Walk, Ocean Beach, N.Y. (summer).

CAREER: Sculptor; designer, illustrator, and author of children's books. Sculptor in studios in France and United States, 1931-35; head of sculpture division of New York City Art Project, 1941-42; executor of statues and panels for government buildings in Washington, D.C., New York, and other cities, including "Young Abe Lincoln" for U.S. Department of the Interior Building in the capital. Exhibitor and lecturer at museums. Member: Sculptors Guild (board of directors, 1939-41), National Sculpture Society, American Group (president, 1940-42), American Institute of Graphic Arts (chairman of artists committee, 1946), Authors Guild of Authors League of America. Awards, honors: Winner of various sculpture competitions; Caldecott Medal (for best illustrated book for children), 1944, for Many Moons, by James Thurber.

WRITINGS—Self-illustrated: Magic Michael, Macmillan, 1944; Friendly Animals, Vanguard, 1944; Clear the Track, Macmillan, 1945; Fo'castle Waltz, Vanguard, 1945; The Adventures of Arab, Macmillan, 1946; Seaweed Hat, Macmillan, 1947; Hustle and Bustle, Macmillan, 1948; Bixby and the Secret Message, Macmillan, 1948; Sculpture, Principles and Practice, World Publishing, 1949.

Mr. Mushroom, Macmillan, 1950; Dinny and Danny, Macmillan, 1951; Our Friendly Friends, Vanguard, 1951; The Space Ship under the Apple Tree, Macmillan, 1952; Circus April 1st, Macmillan, 1953; Mr. Petersham's Cats, Macmillan, 1954; The Horse with the High-Heeled Shoes, Vanguard, 1954; The Amiable Giant, Macmillan, 1955; Millions and Millions, Vanguard, 1955; The Mermaid Who Could not Sing, Macmillan, 1956; One Is Good but Two Are Better, Vanguard, 1956; Melvin, the Moose Child, Macmillan, 1957; Thank You, You're Welcome, Vanguard, 1957; The Space Ship Returns, Macmillan, 1958; The Little Owl Who Could not Sleep, Macmillan, 1958; The First Book of Drawing, F. Watts, 1958; Trick or Treat, Macmillan, 1959; Excuse Me, Certainly, Vanguard, 1959.

Up High and Down Low, Macmillan, 1960; *Gogo the French Sea Gull*, Macmillan, 1960; *Nomi and the Beautiful Animals*, Vanguard, 1960; *A Good Place to Hide*, Macmillan, 1961; *Picco*, Vanguard, 1961; *The Three-Seated Space Ship*, Macmillan, 1962; *The Late Cuckoo*, Vanguard, 1962; *Luigi and the Long-Nosed Soldier*, Macmillan, 1963; *Moon Blossom and the Golden Penny*, Vanguard, 1963; *The Polka-Dot Goat*, Macmillan, 1964; *Yasu and the Strangers*, Macmillan, 1965; *Colette and the Princess*, Dutton, 1965; *Read About the Policeman*, F. Watts, 1966; *Read About the Fireman*, F. Watts, 1967; *Read About the Busman*, F. Watts, 1967; *Round-Trip Space Ship*, Macmillan, 1968.

Space Ship in the Park, Macmillan, 1972; *Wilbur the Warrior*, Vanguard, 1972.

Collaborator, illustrator, and designer: Eleanor Estes, *The Sun and the Wind and Mr. Todd*, Harcourt, 1942; Estes, *The Hundred Dresses*, Harcourt, 1944; Jacob Blanck, *Jonathan and the Rainbow*, Houghton, 1948; Blanck, *The King and the Noble Blacksmith*, Houghton, 1950; Margarite Glendenning, *Gertie the Horse*, McGraw, 1951; Helen F. Bill, *The King's Shoes*, F. Watts, 1956; Florence Slobodkin, *Too Many Mittens*, Vanguard, 1958; Florence Slobodkin, *The Cowboy Twins*, Vanguard, 1960; Andrew Packard, *Mr. Spindles and the Spiders*, Macmillan, 1961; Florence Slobodkin, *Io Sono*, Vanguard, 1962; Florence Slobodkin, *Mr. Papadilly and Willy*, Vanguard, 1964.

Illustrator and designer: Eleanor Estes, *The Moffats*, Harcourt, 1941; Estes, *The Middle Moffat*, Harcourt, 1942; James Thurber, *Many Moons*, Harcourt, 1943; Estes, *Rufus M.*, Harcourt, 1943; Nina Brown Baker, *Peter the Great*, Vanguard, 1943; Baker, *Garibaldi*, Vanguard, 1944; Mabel Leigh Hunt, *Young Man of the House*, Lippincott, 1944; Baker, *Lenin*, Vanguard, 1945; Mark Twain, *Tom Sawyer*, World Publishing, 1946; J. Walter McSpadden, *Robin Hood*, World Publishing, 1946.

Edgar Eager, *Red Head*, Houghton, 1951; Charles Dickens, *The Magic Fishbone*, Vanguard, 1953; Edith Unnerstad, *The Saucepan Journey*, Macmillan, 1955; Washington Irving, *The Alhambra*, Macmillan, 1953; Irmengarde Eberle, *Evie and the Wonderful Kangaroo*, Knopf, 1955; Unnerstad, *Pysen*, Macmillan, 1955; Sara Kasdan, *Love and Knishes*, Vanguard, 1956; Eberle, *Evie and Cooky*, Knopf, 1957; Unnerstad, *Little O*, Macmillan, 1957; Robert Murphy, *The Warm-Hearted Polar Bear*, Little, Brown, 1957; F. Amerson Andrews, *Upside Down Town*, Little, Brown, 1958; Reda Davis, *Martin's Dinosaur*, Crowell, 1959; Priscilla and Otto Frederick, *Clean Clarence*, Lothrop, 1959; Priscilla and Otto Frederick, *Marshmallow Ghost*, Lothrop, 1960; Margaret Uppington, *The Lovely Culpeppers*, F. Watts, 1963; Sara Kasdan, *Mazel Tov Y'-all*, Vanguard, 1968; Florence Slobodkin, *Sarah Somebody*, Vanguard, 1970.

*   *   *

SLUSSER, Gerald H(erbert) 1920-

PERSONAL: Born June 13, 1920, in Willow Springs, Mo.; son of Herbert Fordyce and Carrie Louise (Thomas) Slusser; married Dorothy Mallett (a writer), November 24, 1943; children: Peter, Andrew. *Education:* Southwest Missouri State College (now University), student, 1938-40; Southern Methodist University, B.A. (magna cum laude), 1949; Austin Presbyterian Theological Seminary, B.D., 1952, Th.M., 1956; University of Texas, Ph.D., 1960; University of Glasgow, postdoctoral study, 1960-61. *Office:* Eden Theological Seminary, 475 East Lockwood Ave., Webster Groves, Mo. 63119.

CAREER: Braniff International Airways, Dallas, Tex., flight captain, 1941-48; ordained Presbyterian minister, 1952; pastor in Dallas, Tex., 1952-58; Hartford Seminary Foundation, Hartford, Conn., assistant professor of Christian education, 1961-65; Eden Theological Seminary, Webster Groves, Mo., professor of theology and education, 1965—. Visiting professor of Christian Education, Yale Divinity School, New Haven, Conn., 1963-64. *Member:* Religious Education Association, American Association of University Professors, History of Education Society, Connecticut Association for Mental Health, Phi Delta Kappa. *Awards, honors:* Faculty fellow, University of Glasgow, 1960-61.

WRITINGS: The Local Church in Transition: Theology, Education and Ministry, Westminster, 1964; (co-author) *The Jesus of Mark's Gospel*, Westminster, 1967; *A Christian Look at Secular Society*, Westminster, 1969; (co-author) *Technology: The God that Failed*, Westminster, 1971. Contributor to *American Journal of Psychology, Hartford Quarterly*, and to religious periodicals.

WORK IN PROGRESS: Research in function of language and symbols in education and religion, and in youth culture and its implications for education and religion.

*   *   *

SMART, J(ohn) J(amieson) C(arswell) 1920-

PERSONAL: Born September 16, 1920, in Cambridge, England; son of William Marshall (a professor) and Isabel (Carswell) Smart; married Janet Paine, August 9, 1956; children: Helen Carswell, William Robert. *Education:* University of Glasgow, student, 1938-40, 1945-46, M.A., 1946; The Queen's College, Oxford, B.Phil., 1948. *Home:* 9 Walsall St., Kensington Park, South Australia. *Office:* University of Adelaide, Adelaide, South Australia.

CAREER: Corpus Christi College, Oxford University, Oxford, England, junior research fellow, 1948-50; University of Adelaide, Adelaide, South Australia, 1950—, now Hughes Professor of Philosophy. Visiting professor of philosophy at Princeton University, 1957, Harvard University, 1963, Yale University, 1964. South Australian Hockey Association, president, 1960-61. *Military service:* British Army, Royal Corps of Signals, 1940-45; served in India and Burma; became lieutenant. *Member:* Australasian Association of Philosophy, Australian Humanities Research Council, Association for Symbolic Logic (council member, 1964), Mind Association, Aristotelian Society.

WRITINGS: An Outline of a System of Utilitarian Ethics, Melbourne University Press, 1961; *Philosophy and Scientific Realism*, Humanities, 1963; (editor) *Problems of Space and Time*, Macmillan, 1964; *Between Science and Philosophy: An Introduction to the Philosophy of Science*, Random House, 1968; (with Bernard Williams) *Utilitarianism: For and Against*, Cambridge University Press, 1973. Contributor of articles to philosophical journals.

AVOCATIONAL INTERESTS: Sports, especially cricket, field hockey, and squash.†

*   *   *

SMART, William (Edward, Jr.) 1933-

PERSONAL: Born February 28, 1933, in Jefferson City, Mo.; son of WIlliam E. (an engineer) and May Ferne (Whiteside) Smart; married Marymartha Kistenmacher (a social worker), August 27, 1955; children: Paul Whiteside, David Henry, Anne Fern. *Education:* Kenyon College,

A.B., 1955; University of Connecticut, M.A., 1960. *Home:* Chinnor Hill, Oxford, England.

CAREER: Harcourt, Brace & World, Inc., New York, N.Y., college representative, 1956-57; University of Connecticut, Storrs, lecturer in English, 1958-60; Skidmore College, Saratoga Springs, N.Y., instructor in English, 1960-64; University of Birmingham, Birmingham, England, Fulbright fellow, 1964-66.

WRITINGS: (Editor) *Eight Modern Essayists*, St. Martins, 1965. Contributor to *Kenyon Review, Reporter*, and *New York Times Book Review*.

WORK IN PROGRESS: A critical-biographical study of George Orwell; a thinly-disguised book of fiction.†

* * *

SMEETON, Miles (Richard)   1906-

PERSONAL: Born March 5, 1906, in England; son of Charles William (a physician) and Ethel (Kendal) Smeeton; married wife, Beryl, a writer, May 31, 1938; children: Clio. *Education:* Royal Military College, Sandhurst, 1924-25. *Politics:* Conservative. *Religion:* Church of England. *Residence:* Cochrane, Alberta, Canada.

CAREER: British Army, regular officer, 1925-47, retiring as brigadier. *Member:* Royal Cruising Club, Royal Victoria Yacht Club (Canada). *Awards, honors*—Military: Distinguished Service Order, Military Cross, Order of the British Empire. Civilian: Royal Cruising Club Challenge Cup for voyage from Singapore to Japan, 1964, and for voyage around Cape Horn, 1968; Blue Water Medal from the Cruising Club of America, 1974.

WRITINGS: Once Is Enough, Hart-Davis, 1960; *A Taste of the Hills*, Hart-Davis, 1961; *A Change of Jungles*, Hart-Davis, 1962; *Sunrise to Windward*, Hart-Davis, 1966; *The Misty Islands*, Nautical Publishing, 1969; *Because the Horn is There*, Nautical Publishing, 1972; *The Sea was Our Village*, Nautical Publishing, 1973; *Moose Magic*, Collins, 1974. Contributor to yachting and other magazines.

* * *

SMITH, Barbara Herrnstein   1932-
(Barbara Herrnstein)

PERSONAL: Born August 6, 1932, in New York, N.Y.; daughter of Benjamin (a post office clerk) and Ann (Weinstein) Brodo; married Richard J. Herrnstein, 1951 (divorced, 1961); married Thomas H. Smith, 1964 (separated, 1973); children: (first marriage) Julia Herrnstein, (second marriage) Deirdre Maud Smith. *Education:* Attended City College (now City College of the City University of New York), 1950-52; Brandeis University, B.A. (summa cum laude), 1954, M.A., 1955, Ph.D., 1965. *Office:* University of Pennsylvania, 3620 Walnut St., Philadelphia, Pa. 19104.

CAREER: Sanz School of Languages, Washington, D.C., instructor in English, 1956-57; Brandeis University, Waltham, Mass., graduate assistant, 1959-60, teaching and research assistant, 1960-61, instructor in English, 1961-62; Bennington College, Bennington, Vt., member of faculty of language and literature, 1962-74; University of Pennsylvania, Philadelphia, visiting lecturer, 1973-74, professor of English and communications, 1974—. *Member:* Modern Language Association of American, Phi Beta Kappa. *Awards, honors:* Christian Gauss Award, and Explicator Award, 1968, both for *Poetic Closure*; National Endowment for the Humanities Fellowship, 1971-72.

WRITINGS: (Editor, under name Barbara Herrnstein) *Discussions of Shakespeare's Sonnets*, Hetah, 1964; *Poetic Closure: A Study of How Poems End*, University of Chicago Press, 1968; (editor) *Shakespeares' Sonnets*, New York University Press, 1969; (contributor) Ralph Cohen, editor, *New Directions in Literary History*, Johns Hopkins University Press, 1974; *Fictive Discourse*, University of Chicago Press, in press.

* * *

SMITH, Bert Kruger   1915-

PERSONAL: Born November 18, 1915, in Wichita Falls, Tex.; daughter of Sam and Fania (Feldman) Kruger; married Sidney S. Smith (a realtor), January 19, 1936; children: Sheldon Stuart, Sarann. *Education:* University of Missouri, B.J., 1936; University of Texas, M.A., 1949. *Religion:* Jewish. *Home:* 5818 Westslope Dr., Austin, Tex. 78731. *Office:* Hogg Foundation for Mental Health, P.O. Box 7998, University of Texas, Austin, Tex. 78712.

CAREER: Former newspaperwoman in Wichita Falls, Tex.; with husband, published Coleman (Tex.) *Daily Democrat-Voice*; associate editor, *Junior College Journal*, 1952-55; Hogg Foundation for Mental Health, Austin, Tex., 1952-74, head of mental health education, 1955-74; writer. Member of medical-professional committee, United Cerebral Palsy Association of Texas; of planning committee, Texas Commission on Alcoholism; and of Texas Commission on Organizations for the Handicapped. Professional information committee chairman, Texas Association for Children with Learning Disabilities. President of Austin Council on Alcoholism, 1965. *Member:* National Association of Science Writers, Women in Communications, Delta Kappa Gamma (honorary member). *Awards, honors:* Winner of *Atlantic Monthly* Essay Contest, 1935; Southwest Writers Conference Novel Award for manuscript, "Far From the Tree," 1951; *Austin-American Statesman's* Outstanding Career Woman, 1966; Golden Key Award from Texas Association for Children with Learning Disabilities, 1970.

WRITINGS: (With Robert L. Sutherland, Wayne H. Holtzman, and Earl A. Koile) *Personality Factors on the College Campus*, Hogg Foundation for Mental Health, 1962; *No Language but a Cry*, Beacon Press, 1964; (with Sutherland) *Understanding Mental Health*, Van Nostrand, 1965; *Your Non-Learning Child: His World Upside Down*, Beacon Press, 1968; *A Teaspoon of Honey* (fiction), Aurora Publishing, 1970; *Insights for Uptights*, American Universal Artforms, 1973; *Aging in America*, Beacon Press, 1973. Author or co-author of twenty-one pamphlets published by Hogg Foundation and editor of thirty others. Author of filmscript, "In a Strange Land," produced by Hogg Foundation in cooperation with Texas Junior Chamber of Commerce, 1956; associate producer of "How to be Human" television series, KLRN-TV, 1967; interviewer, "The Human Condition" radio series, KUT-FM. Contributor to *Mental Hospitals, Chaplain, Lutheran, International Journal of Religious Education*, and other periodicals.

* * *

SMITH, Beulah Fenderson   1915-

PERSONAL: Born March 31, 1915, in Ogunquit, Me.; daughter of Archie Collins (a contractor) and Sarah (Clark) Fenderson; married Robert Morrill Smith, October 25, 1940; children: Kaaren (Mrs. Kenneth Cayer), Daniel

Thurston, Stephen Morrill, Susan Lee. *Education:* Colby College, B.A. and Secondary Teacher's Certificate, 1936. *Politics:* Republican ("mostly"). *Religion:* Protestant. *Home:* The Elmere, Route One, Wells, Me.

CAREER: Did advertising surveys for Lever Brothers, Cambridge, Mass., 1936-38, proofreading and advertising layouts for a newspaper in Bakersfield, Calif., 1938-40, and operated a kennel at the Smiths' Blueberry Hill Farm in Wells, Me., 1945-50; began to write professionally in 1953 when the *Ladies' Home Journal* accepted the first poem she sent out, and has since sold more than two thousand poems to magazines and newspapers; manager of campground and motor lodge in Wells, Me., 1967—. Adult education instructor in creative writing, Kennebunkport, Me., 1963-64. *Member:* Poetry Society of New Hampshire (charter member). *Awards, honors: Writer's Digest* Poetry Award, 1964; winner of Maine State Poetry Contest four times and Maine Writers' Conference Poetry Tournament, eight times; second prize, Poetry Society of New Hampshire Sonnet Contest, 1965; New England Press Association award, for column, "The Touchstone."

WRITINGS—Poetry: *Heartwood*, Wake-Brook House, 1964; *Pawprints on My Heart*, Star Press, 1972; *East from Tatnic Hill*, Star Press, 1974. Poems published in *Mc-Call's, Good Housekeeping, Ladies' Home Journal, New York Times, New York Herald Tribune* and in thirty-six other magazines and newspapers. Also contributor of short stories to periodicals, and writer of regular column, "The Touchstone," appearing in a Maine newspaper, *York County Coast Star.*

WORK IN PROGRESS: Cup of Wonder, poems about children; a New England historical novel; short stories.

SIDELIGHTS: Mrs. Smith now writes during the nine months her campground and motor lodge are not busy. She also raises Irish Setters for sale, but told *CA* she misses the wild animals she used to harbor—in all, forty baby raccoons, one fawn, and numerous birds. "I miss my wild animals," she writes, "but the last three orphan raccoons I had here went down to the campground at night and blew the horns in the campers' cars, causing much excitement."

*   *   *

SMITH, Charles W(illiam) (Frederick) 1905-

PERSONAL: Born July 16, 1905, in London, England, became U.S. citizen; son of William R. and Ellen R. (Munt) Smith; married Ivy Watkins, September 19, 1934; children: Anne Lee (Mrs. Richard Bugbee), Ellen G. (Mrs. A. Barrett Churchill), Ivy W. (Mrs. Stephen C. Prescott), Victoria G. *Education:* University of Virginia, B.A., 1933; Protestant Episcopal Theological Seminary in Virginia, B.D. (cum laude), 1933. *Politics:* Independent Democrat. *Home:* Bridgewater Hill, R.F.D. 2, Plymouth, N.H. 03264.

CAREER: Episcopal clergyman. Assistant minister at churches in University, Va., 1932-33, Richmond, Va., 1933-35; Christ Church, Exeter, N.H., rector, 1935-41; Phillips Exeter Academy, Exeter, N.H., instructor in Bible, 1939-41; Washington Cathedral, Washington, D.C., canon chancellor, 1941-45, and instructor at the Saint Alban's School for Boys, 1942-45; St. Andrew's Church, Wellesley, Mass., rector, 1945-51; Episcopal Theological School, Cambridge, Mass., lecturer in homiletics, and tutor, 1946-51, became professor, 1951, then Edmund Swett Rousmaniere Professor of Literature and Interpretation of the New Testament, professor emeritus, 1972—. Visiting

fellow, St. Augustine's College, Canterbury, England, 1955. Episcopal Church, chairman of department of Christian education, Diocese of Massachusetts, 1946-54, member of national Standing Liturgical Commission, 1955-73.

MEMBER: Society of Biblical Literature, Novi Testamenti Societas, American School of Oriental Research, Harvard Faculty Club. *Awards, honors:* D.D. from Protestant Episcopal Theological Seminary in Virginia, 1950.

WRITINGS: (Contributor) A. C. Zabriskie, editor, *Anglican Evangelicalism*, Church Historical Society, 1943; *The Jesus of the Parables*, Westminster, 1948, revised edition, Pilgrim Press, 1974; (contributor) Zabriskie, editor, *Doctor Lowrie of Princeton and Rome*, Seabury, 1957; *Biblical Authority in Modern Preaching*, Westminster, 1960; *The Paradox of Jesus in the Gospels*, Westminster, 1970. Contributor to *Interpreter's Dictionary of the Bible.* Author of booklets, contributor of lesson units to *Crossroads*, and articles to theological journals. Editor, *The Book of Offices*, 3rd edition, and of column, "Let Us Pray," in *Forth*, 1957-58.

WORK IN PROGRESS: A study of the Gospels, tentatively titled *Jesus and the Dispossessed.*

BIOGRAPHICAL/CRITICAL SOURCES: New Testament Abstracts, Volume VIII, number 1, page 142.

*   *   *

SMITH, Denison Langley 1924-

PERSONAL: Born February 2, 1924, in England; son of Arthur A. C. (a salesman) and Olive W. (Farmer) Smith; married Bernice Harper (a nurse), August 18, 1951; children: Gillian, William, Richard. *Education:* Trinity Hall, Cambridge, B.A. (honors), 1948, M.A., 1951; Leeds School of Librarianship, student, 1948-49. *Politics:* "Vague." *Religion:* "More or less Church of England." *Home:* 20 Eden Dr., Oxford, England. *Office:* Oxford College of Technology, Oxford, England.

CAREER: Gloucestershire County Library, branch librarian, 1948-52; Taunton Borough Library, reference librarian, 1953-56; Government Communications Headquarters, London, England, assistant librarian, 1956-58; Oxford College of Technology, Oxford, England, librarian, 1958—. *Military service:* Royal Navy, 1943-46; became lieutenant. *Member:* Library Association (fellow).

WRITINGS: (With E. G. Baxter) *College Library Administration in Colleges of Technology, Art, Commerce, and Further Education*, Oxford University Press, 1965; *How to Find Out in Architecture and Building: A Guide to Sources of Information*, Pergamon Press, 1967. Contributor to *Nature, Bookseller, Hindu Weekly*, and to library journals. Editor, *Bulletin* of Library Association's technical and further education colleges sub-section, 1962—.

SIDELIGHTS: Smith speaks French and German and reads Dutch and Swedish.†

*   *   *

SMITH, Donald G. 1927-

PERSONAL: Born December 1, 1927, in New York, N.Y.; son of Harry Cleveland (an engineer) and Marjorie (Mahon) Smith; married Theresa Redden (a technical librarian), November 11, 1950. *Education:* Attended New York University, 1948-49, and Columbia University, 1956-57. *Religion:* Roman Catholic. *Home:* 36-20 Bowne St., Flushing, N.Y.

CAREER: Newhouse Newspapers, Inc., New York, N.Y., feature writer and assistant sports editor, 1949-59; New York Giants (football), New York, N.Y., director of public relations, 1959—; Ivy Broadcasting Network, sports broadcaster, 1964—. Holder of Black Belt, and instructor in judo to high school and college students, members of armed forces, and police. Assistant athletic director at Flushing Young Men's Christian Association, 1950-59; coach of all sports at high school varsity level. *Military service:* U.S. Naval Reserve, Intelligence, World War II; cryptographer and Japanese translator; received Navy Unit Commendation. *Member:* National Football Writers Association.

WRITINGS: The New York Giants, Coward, 1960; *The Frank Gifford Story,* Putnam, 1961; *The Young Sportsman's Guide to Golf,* Nelson, 1961; (with Lynn Burke) *The Young Sportsman's Guide to Swimming,* Nelson, 1962; (with Sam Huff) *Defensive Football,* Ronald, 1963; (editor) *The Quarterbacks,* F. Watts, 1963; (with Y. A. Tittle) *I Pass,* F. Watts, 1964. Script writer for Columbia Broadcasting System Radio, and WNEW Radio, New York.

SIDELIGHTS: Smith reads and writes Japanese, Spanish, and Russian. *Avocational interests:* Amateur stereo; collecting and reading books on Pacific campaigns in World War II.†

* * *

SMITH, Edwin H. 1920-

PERSONAL: Born August 23, 1920, in Philadelphia, Pa. *Education:* University of Miami, B.Ed., 1950, M.Ed., 1951, Ed.D., 1962. *Office:* Florida State University, Tallahassee, Fla.

CAREER: University of Miami, Fla., assistant director of reading clinic, 1959-62; Florida State University, Tallahassee, director of reading clinic, and of Fundamental Education Center, 1964—. Consultant, National Education Association's Operation Alphabet, and to *Reader's Digest.* *Military service:* U.S. Army, Signal Intelligence, World War II; became sergeant. *Member:* International Reading Association, National Council of Teachers of English, National Association of Public School Adult Educators, American Education Association, Phi Delta Kappa. *Awards, honors:* Iron Arrow Award of University of Miami Graduate Alumni Association, 1962.

WRITINGS: (With Marie Smith) *Teaching Reading to Adults,* National Education Association, 1962; (with Florence Lutz) *My Country,* revised edition, Steck, 1964; (with Will McCall) *Test Lessons in Reading-Reasoning,* Bureau of Publications, Teachers College, Columbia University, 1964; *Teaching Reading in Adult Basic Education,* Florida State Department of Education, 1965; (with others) *Reading Development Kits, A, B, C,* Addisson-Wesley, 1968-69; (with Weldon Bradtmueller) *Individual Reading Placement Inventory,* Follett, 1969; *Literacy Education for Adolescents and Adults,* Boyd & Fraser, 1969; (with Glennon Rowell) *The Sound Spelling Program,* Boyd & Fraser, 1971; (with McKinnley Martin) *Guide to Curricula for Disadvantaged Adult Programs,* Prentice-Hall, 1972; (with Rowell and Lawrence Hafner) *The Sound Reading Program,* Educational Achievement Corp., 1972; (editor) *Creating Your Future,* Educational Achievement Corp., 1972; (with Rowell) *Mastering Decoding Skills,* Bell & Howell, 1973; (with Rowell) *Developing Sound Reading Skills: From Context to Concepts,* Educational Achievement Corp., 1974; (with Rowell and Morgan) *From Letters to Words,* Educational Achievement Corp., in press; (with

George Aker) *Building Adult Reading Skills,* Educational Achievement Corp., in press; (with Billy Guice and Nancy Frederick) *Learning and Teaching the Decoding Skills,* Educational Achievement Corp., in press; (with Guice and Frederick) *Informal Reading Diagnosis and Correction,* Educational Achievement Corp., in press. Contributor to education journals. Editor, *Florida Reading Quarterly.*

* * *

SMITH, Elton E. 1915-

PERSONAL: Born November 9, 1915, in New York, N.Y.; son of Elton Herbert (a theater owner-manager) and Christine (Conway) Smith; married Esther Marian Greenwell (a college instructor), October 17, 1942; children: Elton Greenwell, Esther Ruth, Stephen Lloyd. *Education:* New York University, B.S., 1937; Andover Newton Theological School and Harvard University, M.S.T., 1940; Syracuse University, M.A., 1958, Ph.D., 1961. *Residence:* Lakeland, Fla. *Office:* English Department, University of South Florida, Tampa, Fla.

CAREER: Baptist minister, 1940—. Pastor of churches in Massachusetts, Oregon, and New York, 1940-61; University of South Florida, Tampa, associate professor of English, Bible, and humanities, 1961—. Fulbright-Hays lecturer, University of Algiers, 1969-70. Baritone soloist, appearing in lieder and oratorio concerts in Oregon and New York. *Member:* Modern Language Association of America, American Association of University Professors, Conference on Christianity and Literature, South Atlantic Modern Language Association. *Awards, honors:* D.D. from Linfield College.

WRITINGS: The Two Voices: A Tennyson Study, University of Nebraska Press, 1964; (with wife, Esther G. Smith) *William Godwin: A Critical Study,* Twayne, 1965; *Louis MacNeice,* Twayne, 1970.

WORK IN PROGRESS: A book for Twayne's "English Authors" series, *Charles Reade;* a biblical novel based on the David-Absalom story, *My Son, My Son;* a teen-age murder mystery with wife, Esther G. Smith.

SIDELIGHTS: Smith has reading knowledge of Hebrew and Greek; some speaking knowledge of French.

* * *

SMITH, Julian W. 1901-

PERSONAL: Born July 18, 1901, in Leslie, Mich.; son of Frank M. and Rebecca (Warner) Smith; married Sadie Alderton, July 8, 1931; children: Juliane Susan (deceased), Gilman E. *Education:* Western Michigan College (now University), Life Teaching Certificate, 1923; University of Michigan, A.B., 1928, M.A., 1936. *Religion:* Protestant. *Home:* 2381 Hulett Rd., Okemos, Mich. *Office:* College of Education, Michigan State University, East Lansing, Mich.

CAREER: High school principal, Battle Creek, Mich., 1928-42; Michigan Department of Public Instruction, Lansing, state director of athletics, 1942-45; chief of health, physical education, and recreation, 1945-50, assistant superintendent of public instruction for health, physical education, and recreation, 1951-53; Michigan State University, East Lansing, 1953—, became professor of outdoor education. Member, Michigan Governor's Water Safety Commission, 1958-60, Michigan Governor's Recreation Study Commission, 1960-61.

MEMBER: American Association for Health, Physical Education and Recreation (fellow; director of Outdoor

Education project, 1955—), National Education Association (life member), National Recreation Association, American Academy of Physical Education (fellow), Outdoor Education Association, American Camping Association, American Institute of Park Executives, Society of State Directors of Health, Physical Education and Recreation, National Rifle Association (life member; member of board of directors, 1962—; member of executive committee, 1963—), Phi Delta Kappa. *Awards, honors:* National Association of Conservation Education and Publicity Award, 1953, for promoting school camping movement; Nash Conservation Award, 1953; Ed.D., Eastern Michigan University, 1955.

WRITINGS: Youth Love Thy Woods and Templed Hills, Michigan Department of Public Instruction, 1949, revised edition, 1950.

A Camping Experience for Older Youth, Michigan Department of Public Instruction, 1950; *A Work-Learn Program for Older Youth*, Michigan Department of Public Instruction, 1950; *Community School Camps*, Michigan Department of Public Instruction, 1951; (with others) *School and Community*, Prentice-Hall, 1954; (contributor) *Children in Focus*, American Association for Health, Physical Education and Recreation, 1956; (contributor) *Fitness for Secondary School Youth*, American Association for Health, Physical Education and Recreation, 1956; (editor) *Outdoor Education for American Youth*, American Association for Health, Physical Education and Recreation, 1957; (editor) *Casting and Angling*, American Association for Health, Physical Education and Recreation, 1958.

(Editor) *Shooting and Hunting*, American Association for Health, Physical Education and Recreation, 1960; (contributor) *Current Administrative Problems in Health, Physical Education and Recreation*, American Association for Health, Physical Education and Recreation, 1960; (editor) *Marksmanship for Young Shooters*, American Association for Health, Physical Education and Recreation, 1960; (with George W. Donaldson, Reynold E. Carlson, and Hugh B. Masters) *Outdoor Education*, Prentice-Hall, 1963, 2nd edition, 1972.

Contributor of about seventy articles to *Camping, Michigan Conservation, Canadian Camping, Baptist Leader, Sports Age*, and to educational journals. Contributor to American Association of Health, Physical Education and Recreation *Yearbook*, 1961, 1962. Editor of *Bulletin of Michigan Association for Health, Physical Education and Recreation*, 1945-53, and *Outdoor Education Newsletter*, 1954—.†

*   *   *

SMITH, Marie D.

PERSONAL: Born in Canton, Ga.; daughter of D. P. and Dessie (Marr) Smith. *Home:* 46 Laurel Dr., Fairfax, Va. *Agent:* Winzola McLendon, The Westchester, Cathedral Ave. N.W., Washington, D.C. *Office: Washington Post*, 1515 L St. N.W., Washington, D.C.

CAREER: Washington Post, Washington, D.C., staff writer, 1954—, covering White House from woman's angle, 1956—. *Member:* National League of American Pen Women, Women's National Press Club, American Newspaper Women's Club (Washington, D.C.; vice-president, 1964-65).

WRITINGS: The President's Lady: An Intimate Biography of Mrs. Lyndon B. Johnson, foreword by Harry S Truman, Random House, 1964; (with Louise Durbin) *White House Brides*, Acropolis Books, 1966; *Entertaining in the White House*, Acropolis Books, 1967, revised and updated edition, Macfadden/Bartell, 1970.†

*   *   *

SMITH, Mark (Richard)   1935-

PERSONAL: Born November 19, 1935, in Charlevoix, Mich.; son of Marcus Grey (a boat-builder) and Nellie (Van Eeuwen) Smith; married Anthea Eatough, May 22, 1963; children: Heidi, Matje, Maida, Gudrun. *Education:* Northwestern University, B.A., 1960. *Home:* Old Mountain Rd., Northwood, N.H. *Agent:* Russell & Volkening, 551 Fifth Ave., New York, N.Y.

CAREER: Has worked as a full-time author; University of New Hampshire, Durham, N.H., associate professor of English. Advisor to the Rockefeller Foundation, 1967-69. *Awards, honors:* Rockefeller Foundation grant, 1965-66; Guggenheim fellowship, 1968.

WRITINGS: Toyland (novel), Little, Brown, 1965; *The Middleman* (novel), Little, Brown, 1967; *The Death of the Detective* (novel), Knopf, 1974.

WORK IN PROGRESS: A novel, *The Delphinium Affair*; two completed novels, *Memorial Crumb*, and *The Moon Lamp*.

SIDELIGHTS: Peter Buitenhuis wrote in *The New York Times*, "In its sardonic and absurd humor, Mark Smith's writing is reminiscent of Faulkner, but the theme of this book is closer to Camus. In its uncompromising delineation of a deranged and yet highly analytical mind, 'The Middleman' is one of the best existential novels yet written in the United States."

BIOGRAPHICAL/CRITICAL SOURCES: Book Week, November 14, 1965.

*   *   *

SMITH, Paul B(rainerd)   1921-

PERSONAL: Born June 1, 1921, in Toronto, Ontario, Canada; son of Oswald Jeffrey (a minister) and Daisy (Billings) Smith; married Mary Anita Lawson, June 8, 1946; children: Oswald Glen, Jennifer Jann, Andrea Jill. *Education:* Attended Bob Jones University, 1939-41, University of British Columbia, 1941-42; McMaster University, B.A., 1945; University of Toronto, graduate study, 1945-46. *Home:* 34 Valloncliffe Rd., Thornhill, Ontario, Canada. *Office:* Peoples Church, 374 Sheppard Ave. E., Willowdale, Ontario.

CAREER: Peoples Church, Toronto, Ontario, associate pastor, 1952-58, minister, 1959—. Evangelistic crusader in Canada, Great Britain, United States, Australia, New Zealand, the Orient, South Africa, and Scandinavia. Speaker at conferences on world missions and at Bible conferences in United States and Canada.

WRITINGS: Candid Conclusions, Marshall, Morgan & Scott, 1947; *Church Aflame*, Marshall, Morgan & Scott, 1953; *After Midnight*, Marshall, Morgan & Scott, 1956; *Naked Truth*, Marshall, Morgan & Scott, 1957; *Eastward to Moscow*, Peoples Press Printing Society, 1959; *World Conquest*, Marshall, Morgan & Scott, 1960; *The Question of South Africa*, Peoples Press Printing Society, 1961; *Daily Gospel*, Zondervan, 1963; *Headline Pulpit*, Marshall, Morgan & Scott, 1964; *Perilous Times*, Attic Press, 1967; *Other Gospels*, Marshall, Morgan & Scott, 1970.†

SMITH, Ray 1915-

PERSONAL: Born May 1, 1915, Minneapolis, Minn.; son of Walter R. and Emily (Lundin) Smith; married second wife, Mara Kirk (a university librarian), February 23, 1969. *Education:* Hamline University, B.A., 1937; University of Minnesota, M.A. in American Studies, 1947, M.A.L.S., 1957. *Home:* 1811 Hammond Ave., Superior, Wis. 54880. *Office:* Superior Public Library, Superior, Wis. 54880.

CAREER: University of Minnesota, Minneapolis, instructor in English, 1946-52; truck farmer, graduate student, creative writing teacher, Minneapolis, Minnesota, 1953-56; Mason City Public Library, Mason City, Iowa, librarian, 1957-66; Mason City Community College, Mason City, Iowa, adult education advisory board, 1964-66; Dakota-Scott Library System, West St. Paul, Minn., director, 1966-68; Immaculate Heart College, Los Angeles, Calif., associate professor, 1968-71; Superior Public Library, Superior, Wis., director, 1971—. University of Chicago, Chicago, Ill., graduate library school, lecturer, August, 1962; University of Minnesota Library School, Minneapolis, visiting lecturer, summer sessions, 1963, 1964; University of Iowa, Iowa City, library workshop, lecturer, 1965. *Military service:* U.S. Army, 1941-45; became first lieutenant; awarded Silver Star. *Member:* American Library Association (Notable Books Council, member, 1964-68), Iowa Library Association (Intellectual Freedom Committee, chairman, 1959-60; vice president and director of district meetings, 1962-63; president, 1963-64). *Awards, honors:* Poetry magazine, Guarantors Prize, 1945.

WRITINGS: No Eclipse (poems), Prometheus Press, 1945; (contributor) *Lexicon of Contemporary Literature*, edited by Helmut Olles, Verlag Herder (Freiburg), 1960; (contributor) Carnovky and Winger, *The Medium-Sized Public Library: Its Status and Future*, University of Chicago Press, 1963; (contributor) *Kleines Lexikon*, edited by Helmut Olles, Verlag Herder, 1964; (contributor) *Poets of Today*, edited by Walter Lowenfels, International Publishers, 1964; *The Greening Tree* (poems), James D. Thueson (Minneapolis), 1965; *October Rain* (poems), Mary Bauer, 1969; *The Deer on the Freeway* (poems), University of South Dakota, Dakota Press, 1973; *Permanent Fires: Review of Poetry, 1958-1973*, Scarecrow, 1975.

Work represented in anthologies, including *From the Belly of the Shark*, edited by Walter Lowenfels, Random House, 1973; *For Nerduda/For Chile*, edited by Lowenfels, Beacon Press, 1975. Reviewer for *Library Journal*, 1958-69. Poetry editor, with wife, *North Country Anvil* (Minnesota bimonthly magazine). Contributor to *Library Quarterly*, *Wilson Library Bulletin*, *Poetry*, *Epoch*, and other periodicals.

WORK IN PROGRESS: A book on American utopian writing and a new collection of poems.

AVOCATIONAL INTERESTS: Fishing, camping.

*   *   *

SMITH, Rhoten A(lexander) 1921-

PERSONAL: Born January 17, 1921, in Dallas, Tex.; son of Rhoten Alexander (a hotel manager) and Ruth (Cooke) Smith; married Barbara Maria Okerberg, December 24, 1942; children: Susan Jane, Tyler Rhoten. *Education:* Attended Texas Wesleyan College, 1940, and University of Texas, 1940-42; University of Kansas, A.B., 1946, M.A., 1948; University of California, Berkeley, Ph.D., 1954. *Politics:* Democrat. *Home:* 717 Amberson Ave., Pittsburgh, Pa. 15232.

CAREER: University of Kansas, Lawrence, instructor, 1951-54, assistant professor, 1954-57, associate professor of political science, 1957-58, research associate, Governmental Research Center, 1951-58; Citizenship Clearing House, New York, N.Y., associate director, 1955-56, director, 1958-61; New York University, New York, N.Y., professor of politics, 1958-61, dean of College of Liberal Arts, 1961; Temple University, Philadelphia, Pa., dean of College of Liberal Arts, 1961-67; Northern Illinois University, DeKalb, president, 1967-71; University of Pittsburgh, Pittsburgh, Pa., provost, 1971—. National Center for Education in Politics, trustee and member of executive committee, 1962—. Consultant to Kansas Legislative Council, 1954 and 1957, Kansas Constitutional Revision Commission, 1957-58, Maurice and Laura Falk Foundation, 1958, Ford Foundation, 1960. *Military service:* U.S. Army Air Forces, 1942-45; heavy bomber pilot and crew commander with Eighth Air Force; became first lieutenant.

MEMBER: American Academy of Political and Social Science, American Association for the Advancement of Science (fellow), American Conference of Academic Deans, American Political Science Association, National Education Association, Eastern Association of Academic Deans, Midwest Conference of Political Scientists, Southern Political Science Association, Western Political Science Association, Kiwanis.

WRITINGS: The Life of A Bill, Bureau of Government Research, University of Kansas, 1946, revised edition, revised by William Hall, 1967; (contributor) *Presidential Nominating: Politics in 1952; The Middle West*, Volume IV, edited by Paul T. David, Malcolm Moos, and Ralph M. Goldman, Johns Hopkins Press, 1954; *The Citizenship Clearing House: Retrospect and Prospect*, Citizenship Clearing House, 1956; (with C. J. Hein) *Republican Primary Fight: A Study in Factionalism*, Henry Holt, 1958; (with Hein, J. Cabe, and C. Sullivant) *Kansas Votes: National Elections*, Governmental Research Center, University of Kansas, 1958. Contributor of articles on government to professional journals.

WORK IN PROGRESS: An American government text, with Currin V. Shields, for Random House; readings in parties and pressure groups, with John G. Grumm, for University of Kansas Press; *The Majesty of the Multitude: Majority Rule in America*, for University of California Press.†

*   *   *

SMITH, Robert W(illiam) 1926-

PERSONAL: Born December 27, 1926, in Richland, Iowa; son of William Edward (a farmer) and Gertrude (Orms) Smith; married Alice Langellier, February 1, 1951; children: Susan, David, Annette, Christine. *Education:* University of Illinois, B.S. (with highest honors), 1952; University of Washington, Seattle, M.A., 1953. *Politics:* Independent. *Religion:* Catholic. *Home:* 6412 Lone Oak Dr., Bethesda, Md.

CAREER: U.S. government, economist, 1955—. *Military service:* U.S. Marine Corps, 1944-46.

WRITINGS: (Editor) *Complete Guide to Judo*, Tuttle, 1958; *Bibliography of Judo*, Tuttle, 1959; (editor) *Secrets of Shaolin Temple Boxing*, Tuttle, 1963; (with Cheng Man-Ch'ing) *T'ai-chi*, Tuttle, 1963; *Pa-Kua: Chinese Boxing*, Kodansha, 1967; (with Donn F. Draeger) *Asian Fighting Arts*, Kodansha, 1969; *Chinese Boxing: Masters and Methods*, Kodansha, 1974; *Hsing-I: Chinese Mind-Body Box-*

ing, Kodansha, 1974. Contributor of articles on strength and health to U.S. and foreign magazines, 1949—.

WORK IN PROGRESS: A book, *The History of Wrestling*.

SIDELIGHTS: Smith is competent in Chinese, Japanese, and Russian.

* * *

SMITH, T(homas) E(dward) 1916-

PERSONAL: Born February 5, 1916, in Teddington, England; son of Thomas (a physicist) and Elsie M. (Elligott) Smith; married Margaret Thorven, November 29, 1947; children: Fern Katharine Thorven, Erica Helen Thorven. *Education:* Gonville and Caius College, Cambridge, B.A., 1938; Princeton University, graduate study, 1949-50. *Home:* 187 Coombe Lane, London S.W. 20, England. *Office:* Institute of Commonwealth Studies, University of London, London W.C.1, England.

CAREER: Malayan Civil Service, administrator, 1940-57, director of first election in Malaya, 1955, and of population census, 1957; Nuffield College, Oxford University, Oxford, England, research fellow, 1957-59; Institute of Commonwealth Studies, University of London, London, England, secretary, researcher in demography and academic administrator, 1960—. United Nations, European Office, Geneva, Switzerland, consultant in demography, Office of Social Affairs, 1965. *Military service:* British Army, 1941-45; became lieutenant. *Member:* International Union for the Scientific Study of Population, Royal Institute of International Affairs, Royal Commonwealth Society. *Awards, honors:* Commonwealth Fund fellowship to Princeton University, 1949-50; Officer of the Order of the British Empire, 1955.

WRITINGS: Population Growth in Malaya, Oxford University Press, 1952; *Elections in Developing Countries: A Study of Electoral Procedures Used in Tropical Africa, South-East Asia and the British Caribbean*, St. Martins, 1960; *The Background to Malaysia*, Oxford University Press, 1963; (with J. G. C. Blacker) *Population Characteristics of the Commonwealth Countries of Tropical Africa*, Oxford University Press, 1963; (with John Bastin) *Malaysia*, Oxford University Press, 1967; *Politics of Family Planning in the Third World*, Verry, 1973. Contributor to *World Today, Pacific Affairs, Public Administration*, and other journals.†

* * *

SMITH, Wendell I(rving) 1921-

PERSONAL: Born May 7, 1921, in Merrimac, Mass.; son of Irving Henry and Alberta (Hosford) Smith; married Mary Elizabeth Haupt (a teacher); children: Alex George Haupt. *Education:* Bucknell University, A.B., 1946, M.A., 1948; Pennsylvania State University, Ph.D., 1951. *Home:* 309 South 21st St., Lewisburg, Pa. *Office:* Office of the Provost, Bucknell University, Lewisburg, Pa.

CAREER: Bucknell University, Lewisburg, Pa., 1946—, began as instructor, professor of psychology, 1955—, chairman of department, 1958-70, provost, 1970—. Secretary-treasurer, Educational Services Lab., Inc., 1962—. *Military service:* U.S. Naval Reserve, 1942-45. *Member:* American Association for the Advancement of Science, American Psychological Association, American

Association of University Professors, Eastern Psychological Association, Pennsylvania Psychological Association (president), Phi Beta Kappa. *Awards, honors:* American Philosophical Society, grant, 1953; American Nurses' Foundation grant, 1956; Ford Foundation-National Science Foundation grant; National Institute for Mental Health, grant, U.S. Office of Education.

WRITINGS: (With J. W. Moore and M. McFadden) *Sets, Relations, and Functions*, McGraw, 1962; (with Moore) *Conditioning and Instrumental Learning*, McGraw, 1966; (with N. Rohrman) *Human Learning*, McGraw, 1969; *Multimedia Psychology*, McGraw, 1974.

Editor with J. W. Moore: *Programmed Learning*, Van Nostrand, 1962; B. Earl, *Groups and Fields*, McGraw, 1963; B. Earl, *Introduction to Probability*, McGraw, 1963. Also editor with J. W. Moore and M. McFadden, *Modern Trigonometry*. Contributor of twenty-five articles to psychology journals.

* * *

SMITH, Wilbur A(ddison) 1933-

PERSONAL: Born January 9, 1933, in Broken Hill, Northern Rhodesia; son of Herbert James and Elfreda (Lawrence) Smith; married Jewell Slabbert, August 28, 1964. *Education:* Rhodes University, Bachelor of Commerce, 1954. *Home:* 418 Liesbreck Gardens, Durban Rd., Mowbray, Cape, South Africa. *Agent:* Monica McCall, Inc., 667 Madison Ave., New York, N.Y. 10021.

CAREER: With Goodyear Tire & Rubber Co., Port Elizabeth, South Africa, 1954-58, and H. J. Smith & Son Ltd., Salisbury, Rhodesia, 1958-63, full-time writer, 1964—. *Member:* Chartered Institute of Secretaries, Rhodesian Wildlife Conservation Association, British Sub Aqua Club.

WRITINGS—Novels: When the Lion Feeds, Viking, 1964; *The Train From Katanga*, Viking, 1965 (published in England as *The Dark of the Sun*, Heinemann, 1965); *Shout at the Devil*, Coward, 1968; *Gold Mine*, Doubleday, 1970; *The Diamond Hunters*, Heinemann, 1971, Doubleday, 1972; *The Sunbird*, Heinemann, 1972, Doubleday, 1973; *Eagle in the Sky*, Doubleday, 1974. Contributor to *Argosy* (London) and to British Broadcasting Corp. programs.

SIDELIGHTS: Smith told *CA*: "I am essentially a writer of entertainment fiction. So far all my work is against the background of southern Africa. My interests are the history of this land, its wildlife, and its people. However, none of my work deals with present day politics or racial problems. I speak Afrikaans and some African dialects, including Zulu."

Dark of the Sun was filmed by MGM, released in 1968. Three other films based on Smith's novels are in various stages of production. *Avocational interests:* Golf, fishing, and hunting.†

* * *

SMITH, Wilfred Cantwell 1916-

PERSONAL: Born July 21, 1916, in Toronto, Ontario, Canada; son of Victor Arnold (a businessman) and Sarah (Cantwell) Smith; married Muriel Struthers, September 23, 1939; children: Arnold Gordon, Julian Struthers, Heather Patricia, Brian Cantwell, Rosemary Muriel. *Education:* University of Toronto, B.A. (honors), 1938; Cambridge University, research fellow, 1938-40; Westminster Theological College, Cambridge, England, theological study, 1938-40; Princeton University, M.A., 1947, and Ph.D., 1948.

Home: 6010 Inglis St., Halifax, Nova Scotia, Canada. *Office:* Department of Religion, Dalhousie University, Halifax, Nova Scotia, Canada.

CAREER: Ordained minister in United Church of Canada. Forman Christian College, Lahore, India, lecturer in Indian and Islamic history, 1941-44; McGill University, Montreal, Quebec, professor of comparative religion, 1949-63, and director of Institute of Islamic Studies, 1951-63; Harvard University, Cambridge, Mass., professor of world religions and director of Center for the Study of World Religions, 1964-73. Dalhousie University, Nova Scotia, McCulloch Professor of religion, and chairman of religion department, 1973—. *Member:* Royal Society of Canada (fellow; president, humanities and social sciences section, 1972-73), American Academy of Arts and Sciences (fellow), American Society for the Study of Religion (president, 1966-69), Canadian Society for the Study of Religion, Middle Eastern Studies Association, American Society for the Study of Religion (vice-president), American Oriental Society, Association for Asian Studies.

WRITINGS: Modern Islam in India, Minerva, 1943, revised edition, Gollancz, 1947; *Islam in Modern History,* Princeton University Press, 1957; *The Faith of Other Men,* New American Library, 1963; *The Meaning and End of Religion,* Macmillan, 1963; *Questions of Religious Truth,* Scribner, 1967. Contributor of articles to learned journals. Advisory editor, *Muslim World* and *Middle East Journal;* associate editor, *Journal of Religious Studies* (Cambridge, England); member of editorial board, *Studies In Religion* (Toronto).

WORK IN PROGRESS: Two books, *Faith and Belief: A Comparative Study* and *A Theology of Comparative Religion.*

*   *   *

SMITH, Wilfred R(obert)   1915-

PERSONAL: Born May 22, 1915, in Manitoba, Canada; son of Thomas James (a pipefitter) and Susan (Hazelgrove) Smith; married Marion Maysilles, 1954 (divorced, 1961); married Michelle Becker, 1965 (divorced, 1971); children: (first marriage) Anne (Mrs. Dennis Mayberry); (second marriage) Yvonne. *Education:* Wayne State University, B.A., 1948, Ed.D., 1959; University of Chicago, M.A., 1950. *Politics:* Democrat. *Religion:* Unitarian Universalist. *Home:* 23626 Irving, Taylor, Mich.

CAREER: Wayne State University, Detroit, Mich., special instructor in educational sociology, 1959-64; Henry Ford Community College, Dearborn, Mich., instructor in sociology and anthropology, 1959-64; Eastern Michigan University, Ypsilanti, associate professor of sociology and educational philosophy, 1964—. *Military service:* U.S. Army Air Forces, 1942-45; served as weather observer; became sergeant. *Member:* International Education Association (former vice-president; president, 1972), American Sociological Association, American Federation of Teachers, Society for Applied Anthropology, American Association of University Professors, Michigan Sociological Society. *Awards, honors:* Margaret Mead Award in Applied Anthropology from Henry Ford Community College staff, 1964; Educator of Year award from Internation Education Association, 1972.

WRITINGS: (With August Kerber) *Educational Issues in a Changing Society,* Wayne State University Press, 1962, 3rd edition, 1968; (with Kerber) *A Cultural Approach to Education,* Kendall/Hunt Publishing (Dubuque), 1972;

(with Robert Fisher) *Schools in an Age of Crisis,* Van Nostrand, 1972. Contributor to books and professional journals.

*   *   *

SMITH, William S.   1917-

PERSONAL: Born March 18, 1917, in Devil's Lake, N.D.; son of Leb F. and Mary Anne (Farmers) Smith; married Margaret E. Robinson (a registered nurse), 1947; children: Joelene Andra, Gregory Stephen. *Education:* Northern Illinois State College (now Northern Illinois University), B.Ed., 1941; Stanford University, M.A., 1949, Ph.D., 1952. *Home:* Rt. 1, Box 463, Dadeville, Ala. 36853.

CAREER: Northwestern State College of Louisiana (now Northwestern State University of Louisiana), Natchitoches, assistant professor of speech, 1950-52; Auburn University, Auburn, Ala., assistant professor and director of debate, 1952-54, associate professor, 1954-59, professor of speech, 1959-65, Alumni Professor of Speech, 1966-73. City of Auburn, chairman of parks and recreation board, 1963-64, member of city council, 1964-68, vice-chairman of city council, 1965-68. *Military service:* U.S. Army Air Forces, 1941-47; combat squadron commander in European Theater; became lieutenant colonel; received Purple Heart and twelve other medals. U.S. Air Force Reserve, 1941—; commander of 9978th Reserve Squadron, 1961-70. *Member:* American Speech Association, Southern Speech Association (first vice-president, 1960-61; president, 1961-62; member of legislative assembly), American Association of University Professors (chairman of committee on faculty participation in university government, 1964-65), American Forensic Association (governor, Southern region, 1954).

WRITINGS: (With Donald C. Canty) *Method and Means of Public Speaking,* Bobbs-Merrill, 1962; (with Paul D. Brandes) *Building Better Speech,* Noble, 1964, 2nd edition, 1965; *Group Problem-Solving Through Discussion,* Bobbs-Merrill, 1965. Contributor to speech journals.

WORK IN PROGRESS: Revision of *Group Problem-Solving Through Discussion.*

*   *   *

SMYTHE, Daniel Webster   1908-

PERSONAL: Born July 26, 1908, in Brockton, Mass.; son of Harry Wilson (a farmer) and Georgianna (Webster) Smythe; married Ruth Elizabeth Quantin (a teacher), March 31, 1956. *Education:* Union College and University, Schenectady, N.Y., B.A., 1950; University of Pennsylvania, M.A., 1952, Ph.D., 1957. *Home:* 1718 West Barker Ave., Peoria, Ill. 61606. *Office:* 430 Bradley Hall, Bradley University, Peoria, Ill.

CAREER: Chicken farmer, in business with his father, Plaistow, N.H., prior to 1933; assistant in a wildlife sanctuary, Delanson, N.Y., 1933-41; Skidmore College, Saratoga Springs, N.Y., instructor in English, 1953-55; Bradley University, Peoria, Ill., assistant professor, 1955-63, associate professor, 1963-65, professor of English, 1965—. *Military service:* U. S. Army, Infantry, 1941-45; became sergeant. *Member:* Poetry Society of America, National Wildlife Federation. *Awards, honors:* Annual Award, 1940, and Leonora Speyer Award, 1960, of Poetry Society of America; Idol Prize ($500) from Union College and University.

WRITINGS: Steep Acres (poems), Anderson House, 1941; *Only More Sure* (poems), Beacon, 1945; *Brief Inheri-*

tance (poems), Prarie, 1946; *Robert Frost Speaks*, Twayne, 1964; *Strange Element* (poems), Golden Quill, 1966; *Green Doors* (poems), Golden Quill, 1971; *Visits with Robert Frost*, Golden Quill, 1974; *Collected Poems*, Golden Quill, 1974. Contributor to about eighty periodicals and newspapers, including *New Yorker, Harper's, New York Times, Writer's Digest, Author and Journalist*.

WORK IN PROGRESS: A Bibliography of Articles and Books of the American Poetry Renaissance: 1912-1962; *An Outline of Versification*.

AVOCATIONAL INTERESTS: Chess, orinthology, astronomy, the Maine coast, botany, collecting Robert Frost materials.†

* * *

SNYDER, Graydon F. 1930-

PERSONAL: Born April 30, 1930, in Peru, Ind.; son of Clayton Fisher (an accountant) and Irene (Fisher) Snyder; married Lois Horning, June 13, 1953; children: Jonathan Edvard, Anna Christine, Stephen Daniel. *Education:* Manchester College, B.A., 1951; Bethany Biblical Seminary, Chicago, Ill., B.D., 1954; graduate study at University of Goettingen, 1954-55, University of Oslo, 1958-59; Princeton Theological Seminary, Th.D., 1961. *Home:* 1 S 110 Third St., Lombard, Ill. 60148. *Office:* Bethany Theological Seminary, Oak Brook, Ill.

CAREER: Minister, Church of the Brethren. Bethany Theological Seminary, Oak Brook, Ill., professor of biblical studies, 1959—. *Member:* Society of Biblical Literature, Chicago Society of Biblical Research. *Awards, honors:* Fulbright grant to University of Oslo, 1958-59.

WRITINGS: (Editor with William Klassen) *Current Issues in New Testament Interpretation*, Harper, 1962; *In His Hand*, Brethren, 1965; (editor) *The Shepherd of Hermas*, Nelson, 1968; (with Donald Eugene) *Using Biblical Simulations*, Judson, 1973. Member of editorial board, *Brethren Life and Thought*.

WORK IN PROGRESS: A study of the origins of early Catholicism in Rome.

AVOCATIONAL INTERESTS: Handball, photography, and crafts.†

* * *

SNYDER, William P(aul) 1928-

PERSONAL: Born August 30, 1928, in Columbus, Ohio; son of Samuel Paul (a railroad engineer) and Ruth Lillian (Davis) Snyder; married Elouie Farnsworth (a teacher), June 15, 1952; children: Marshal Kent, Morgan Clark, Murray Reed. *Education:* Miami University, Oxford, Ohio, student, 1945-46; U.S. Military Academy, B.S., 1952; Princeton University, Ph.D., 1963. *Politics:* Democrat. *Religion:* Protestant. *Home:* Quarters 555A, West Point, N.Y. 10996. *Office:* Department of Social Sciences, U.S. Military Academy, West Point, N.Y. 10996.

CAREER: U.S. Army, career service, 1952—, with current rank of major; U.S. Military Academy, West Point, N.Y., assistant professor of government and economics, 1962—. *Member:* American Political Science Association, Military Education Foundation (Highland Falls, N.Y.).

WRITINGS: The Politics of British Defense Policy: 1945-1962, Ohio State University Press, 1964; *Case Studies in Military Systems Analysis*, Industrial College of the Armed Forces, 1967.†

SODERHOLM, Marjorie Elaine 1923-

PERSONAL: Surname is pronounced *So*-der-holm; born May 3, 1923, in Holdrege, Neb.; daughter of Arthur (a farmer) and Minnie (Sauer) Soderholm. *Education:* Nebraska State Teachers College (now Kearney State College), B.A., 1948; Trinity College, Chicago, Ill., graduate study, 1950-51; Wheaton College, Wheaton, Ill., M.A., 1953. *Religion:* Evangelical Free Church of America. *Home:* 3001 Half Day Rd., Lake Forest, Ill. 60045.

CAREER: Teacher at elementary, junior high, and high school level in Nebraska schools, 1943-46, 1948-50; Trinity College, Deerfield (formerly in Chicago), Ill., assistant professor, 1953-62, associate professor, 1962-68, professor of Christian education, 1968-73, registrar, 1953-55, dean of women, 1962-64; Immanuel Baptist Church, Waukegan, Ill., consultant and instructor in Christian education, 1973—. Wheaton College, Wheaton, Ill., summer assistant in Christian education department, 1953-56. David C. Cook Publishing Co., Elgin, Ill., curriculum consultant, 1957-59. *Member:* National Sunday School Association, Chicago Christian Writers Club. *Awards, honors:* Alumni of the Year Award, Trinity College, Chicago, Ill., 1959.

WRITINGS: Understanding the Pupil, Part I, Baker Book, 1955, Part II, 1956, Part III, 1956; *The Junior: A Handbook for His Sunday School Teacher*, Baker Book, 1956; *Explaining Salvation to Children*, Beacon Press, 1962; *Salvation, Then What?*, Beacon Press, 1968; *A Study Guide to Bible Prayers*, Baker Book, 1968; (contributor) Roy Zuch and Roy Irving, editors, *Youth and the Church: A Survey of the Church's Ministry to Youth*, Moody, 1968; (contributor) Robert Clark, editor, *Christian Education for Early Childhood*, Moody, 1975. Contributor to books and magazines on Christian education.

SIDELIGHTS: Marjorie Soderholm's books have been published in Chinese, Dutch, and Japanese, and *Understanding the Pupil*, Part III has been adapted for use in India. *Avocational interests:* Sewing, millinery, and photography.

* * *

SOKOLSKI, Alan 1931-

PERSONAL: Born January 5, 1931, in New York, N.Y.; son of Irving (a realtor) and Pearl (Herzig) Sokolski; married Carol Stitt, July 27, 1956; children: Lynn, Lauren. *Education:* Cornell University, B.M.E., 1953; Columbia University, M.B.A., 1959, Ph.D., 1962. *Home:* 915 Hyde Rd., Silver Spring, Md.

CAREER: Western Union Telegraph, New York, N.Y., engineer, 1953-54, 1956; Foster Wheeler Corp., New York, N.Y., engineer, 1957-59; U.S. Federal Reserve Board, Washington, D.C., economist, 1962-63; U.S. Department of State, economist with Agency for International Development in Lagos, Nigeria, 1963-65, economist, Washington, D.C., 1965-70; Central Intelligence Agency, senior economic research officer, 1970—. *Military service:* U.S. Air Force, active duty in Chateauroux, France, 1954-56. U.S. Air Force Reserve, 1956—; now major. *Member:* African Studies Association (fellow), American Economic Association. *Awards, honors:* Eastman Kodak business fellowship; Carnegie travel fellowship.

WRITINGS: The Establishment of Manufacturing in Nigeria, Praeger, 1965.

SOLOMON, Morris J. 1919-

PERSONAL: Born March 22, 1919, in New York, N.Y.; son of Bene (a tailor) and Dora (Jacobson) Solomon; married Miriam Abramowitz, December 28, 1941; children: Eugene, Helen Mae, Norman, Aba. *Education:* Brooklyn College (now of the City University of New York), B.A., 1941; Columbia University, M.A., 1947; postgraduate study at New School for Social Research, 1947-48, The American University, 1950-53. *Office:* U.S. Bureau of the Census, Suitland, Md.

CAREER: Mathematical statistician with U.S. Air Force at the Pentagon, 1950-55, with U.S. Bureau of the Census, Suitland, Md., 1955-56; operations research analyst with American Greetings Corp., Cleveland, Ohio, 1956-58, with Atlas Chemical Co., Wilmington, Del., 1958-59; U.S. Bureau of the Census, consultant to government of India, Calcutta, 1959-61, chief of operations research, Suitland, Md., 1961—. University of Pittsburgh, visiting lecturer in development administration, 1962-63. Consultant, Agency for International Development, Ankara, Turkey, 1961-62, Ford Foundation, New Delhi, India, 1962, United Nations, 1963—; director of workshop on project analysis, Caracas, Venezuela, summer, 1964, for Central America, in Guatemala City, winter, 1964. *Military service:* U.S. Army, 1941-46; became first lieutenant. *Member:* Operations Research Society of America, American Statistical Association (fellow), Institute of Management Sciences, Econometric Society.

WRITINGS: Better Plant Utilization in India—a Blueprint for Action, Asia Publishing House, 1964; *Project Analysis: A System for Shaping and Appraising Projects With Special Application to Newly Developing Countries*, Department of Economic Affairs, Pan American Union, 1966, Spanish edition, with Osman Edin, published as *Analises de projetos: Um sistema de formulacao e avaliacao de projetos especialmente aplicavel a paises em vias de desenvolvimento*, APEC Editora, 1967; *Analysis of Projects for Economic Growth: An Operational System for Their Formulation, Evaluation, and Implementation*, Praeger, 1970. Writer of weekly column on consumer economics in *Greenbelt News*, Greenbelt, Md., 1954. Contributor to *Personnel Administration, Management Science, Indian Journal of Public Administration, Eastern Economist*, other journals in field.†

*   *   *

SOLOMONS, David 1912-

PERSONAL: Born October 11, 1912, in London, England; son of Louis and Hannah (Isaacs) Solomons; married Miriam Goldschmidt; children: Jane Naomi, Jonathan Peter. *Education:* London School of Economics and Political Science, London, Bachelor of Commerce, 1932. *Home:* 205 Elm Ave., Swarthmore, Pa. 19081. *Office:* Wharton School, University of Pennsylvania, Philadelphia, Pa. 19174.

CAREER: Chartered accountant in London, England, 1936-39, 1945-48; University of London, London, England, lecturer in accounting at London School of Economics and Political Science, 1946-48, university reader in accounting, 1948-55; University of Bristol, Bristol, England, professor of accounting, 1955-59, University of Pennsylvania, Wharton School, Philadelphia, professor of accounting, 1959-74, Arthur Young Professor of Accounting, 1974—. University of California, Berkeley, visiting associate professor, 1954; IMEDE (Institut pour l'Etude des Methodes de Direction de l'Entreprise), Lausanne, Switzerland, professor, 1963-64. *Military service:* British Army, Royal Army Service Corps, 1939-45; became captain. *Member:* Institute of Chartered Accountants in England and Wales (fellow), Royal Economic Society (fellow), Institute of Management Accounting (member of board of regents), American Accounting Association, National Association of Accountants (director, Philadelphia chapter, 1961-63).

WRITINGS: (Editor) *Studies in Costing*, Sweet & Maxwell, 1952, published as *Studies in Cost Analysis*, 1968; *Divisional Performance: Measurement and Control*, Financial Executives Research Foundation, 1961; *Prospectus for a Profession*, Gee & Co., 1974. Contributor of articles to professional journals.

*   *   *

SOMERS, Gerald G. 1922-

PERSONAL: Born August 6, 1922, in Toronto, Ontario, Canada; son of Joseph and Betty (Behr) Somers; married Rita Schacter, July 13, 1945; children: Eric, Jon, Laura. *Education:* University of Toronto, B.A., 1943, M.A., 1946; University of California, Berkeley, Ph.D., 1951. *Home:* 3311 Lake Mendota Dr., Madison, Wis. 53705. *Office:* University of Wisconsin, Madison, Wis. 53706.

CAREER: West Virginia University, Morgantown, associate professor of economics, and director of Institute of Industrial Relations, 1949-57; University of Wisconsin, Madison, associate professor, later professor of economics, and director of Industrial Relations Research Institute, 1957-59, 1964-68; chairman of economics department, 1968-71. Arbitrator of labor-management disputes; member, national panel of Federal Mediation and Conciliation Service and American Arbitration Association. *Military service:* Royal Canadian Air Force, 1942-45. *Member:* Industrial Relations Research Association, American Economic Association, American Association of University Professors. *Awards, honors:* Guggenheim Fellow, 1959-60; Social Science Research Council faculty research fellowship, 1961.

WRITINGS: Experience under National Wage Agreements, Bureau of Business Research, University of West Virginia, 1953; *Mobility of Chemical Workers in a Coal-Mining Area*, Bureau of Business Research, West Virginia University, 1954; *Grievance Settlement in Coal Mining*, Bureau of Business Research, West Virginia University, 1957.

Labor Supply and Mobility in a Newly-Industrialized Area, U.S. Bureau of Labor Statistics, 1960; (editor and contributor) *Labor, Management and Social Policy: Essays in the John R. Commons Tradition*, University of Wisconsin Press, 1963; (co-editor and contributor) *Adjusting to Technological Change*, Harper, 1963; (contributor) Arthur M. Ross, editor, *Unemployment and the American Economy*, Wiley, 1964; (contributor) Joseph Becker, editor, *In Aid of the Unemployed*, Johns Hopkins Press, 1964; *Retraining the Unemployed*, University of Wisconsin Press, 1968.

(With L. Sharp and T. Myint; editor) *The Effectiveness of Vocational and Technical Programs: A National Follow-up Survey*, Center for Studies in Vocational and Technical Education, University of Wisconsin, 1971; (with J. K. Little) *Vocational Education: Today and Tomorrow*, Center for Studies in Vocational and Technical Education, 1971; (with Myron Roomkin) *Training and Skill Acquisition: A Pilot Case Study*, Industrial Relations Research Institute, 1972; (with J. Kreps and R. Perlman) *Contemporary Labor Economics: Issues Analysis, and Policies*, Wadsworth Press, 1974.

Contributor to labor and economic journals in United States and to *Sociologie du Travail* (Paris). National editor, Industrial Relations Research Association, 1958—.

WORK IN PROGRESS: International Comparison of Labor Market Behavior; Evaluation of Manpower Policies; and *The Economics of Alcoholism in Industry.*

* * *

SOMMERFELD, Richard Edwin 1928-

PERSONAL: Born April 15, 1928, in Alpena, Mich.; son of Edwin and Beatrice (Serre) Sommerfeld; married Patricia Bradin, June 27, 1953; children: Susan, Gretchen, Eric. *Education:* Concordia Seminary, St. Louis, Mo., B.A., 1951, B.D., 1954; Washington University, St. Louis, Mo., M.A., 1953, Ph.D., 1957. *Home:* 7 Tyndale Pl., Fort Wayne, Ind. 46805. *Office:* 6600 North Clinton St., Fort Wayne, Ind. 46805.

CAREER: Ordained to Lutheran ministry, 1954. Richard Sommerfeld Associates (social research and development firm), Fort Wayne, Ind., director, 1956—; Concordia Senior College, Fort Wayne, Ind., associate professor of sociology, 1962—. Fort Wayne Mayor's Commission on Human Relations, consultant, 1964—; United Community Services, Fort Wayne, member of board of directors, 1965—. *Member:* American Sociological Association (fellow), Lutheran Academy for Scholarship, Society for Scientific Study of Religion, Religious Research Association.

WRITINGS: The Church of the Twenty-First Century, Concordia, 1965. Contributor to journals.

WORK IN PROGRESS: An introductory sociology text; a study of role concepts of Lutheran clergymen.†

* * *

SORENSEN, Virginia 1912-

PERSONAL: Born February 17, 1912, in Provo, Utah; daughter of Claud E. and Helen El Deva (Blackett) Eggertsen; married Frederick Sorensen (an English professor), August 16, 1933 (divorced); married Alec Waugh (a novelist), July 15, 1969; children: Elizabeth (Mrs. E. Christian Anderson), Frederick Walter. *Education:* Brigham Young University, B.S., 1934; Stanford University, graduate study. *Politics:* "I choose candidates, but mostly Democrats." *Religion:* Church of Jesus Christ of Latter-day Saints. *Residence:* Tangier, Morocco. *Agent:* Curtis Brown Ltd., 60 East 56th St., New York, N.Y. 10022.

CAREER: Author. *Member:* International P.E.N., National League of American Pen Women, Authors League, Delta Kappa Gamma (honorary member). *Awards, honors:* Guggenheim fellowship to Mexico, 1946-47, to Denmark, 1954-55; Children's Book Award of Child Study Association of America, 1955, for *Plain Girl;* John Newbery Medal of American Library Association for most distinguished contribution of the year to children's literature, 1957, for *Miracles on Maple Hill.*

WRITINGS—Novels, except as indicated: *A Little Lower Than the Angels,* Knopf, 1942; *On This Star,* Reynal & Hitchcock, 1946; *The Neighbors,* Reynal & Hitchcock, 1947; *The Evening and the Morning,* Harcourt, 1949; *The Proper Gods,* Harcourt, 1951; *Many Heavens,* Harcourt, 1954; *Kingdom Come,* Harcourt, 1960; *Where Nothing Is Long Ago* (short story collection), Harcourt, 1963; *The Man With the Key,* Harcourt, 1974.

Children's books: *Curious Missie,* Harcourt, 1953; *The*

House Next Door (for teen-agers), Scribner, 1954; *Plain Girl,* Harcourt, 1956; *Miracles on Maple Hill,* Harcourt, 1957; *Lotte's Locket,* Harcourt, 1964; *Around the Corner,* Harcourt, 1971.

Short stories have appeared in *Story, New Yorker, New Mexico Review, Arizona Quarterly,* and *Rocky Mountain Quarterly.* Writer of series of articles on current topics for *Denver Post.*

WORK IN PROGRESS: A children's book set in Morocco and a modern novel about the descendents of the Mormon emigrants who were characters in *Kingdom Come.*

SIDELIGHTS: Virginia Sorensen Waugh told *CA:* "For the past twenty years I have made traveling a way of life, with Morocco a kind of base, Tangier being a good 'jumping off place' to everywhere. [Since] married to Alec Waugh, an English novelist and travel writer, I have spent more time in Africa and London than in America, but twice a year return for visits with my children and three grandchildren, all now in Florida. My intention is to return to Utah for the 'declining years,' having found no place in the world more beautiful or satisfying."

BIOGRAPHICAL/CRITICAL SOURCES: Horn Book, summer, 1957.

* * *

SORGMAN, Mayo 1912-

PERSONAL: Born March 29, 1912, in Brockton, Mass.; son of Max (a businessman) and Lena Sorgman; married Eleanor Rashbaum (a speech therapist), December 28, 1948; children: Dara, Bram. *Education:* Massachusetts College of Art, B.S. in Ed., 1934; New York University, M.A., 1950; summer study at Parsons School of Design, 1945, Kansas City Art Institute, 1950, and in Paris. *Home:* Breezy Hill Rd., Stamford, Conn.

CAREER: Stamford (Conn) Board of Education, director of art, 1934—; Council for Continuing Education, Stamford, Conn., lecturer on art, 1940—. Free-lance commercial artist, 1936-60; painter (expressionist), exhibiting in one-man shows, and with American Watercolor Society, Allied Artists, and Audubon Artists; work shown in National Gallery of Art, St. Louis Art Museum, Rockhill-Nelson Gallery, and other museums and galleries. *Military service:* U.S. Army Air Forces, 1943-46; became sergeant. *Member:* National Commission on Art Education, National Art Education Association, Connecticut Education Association (president of Stamford branch, 1948), Connecticut Watercolor Society, Cape Ann Modern Artists, Silvermine Guild of Artists, Rockport Art Association. *Awards, honors:* Silvermine Guild Award for painting, 1956; Emily Lowe Award in watercolor, New York, N.Y., 1958.

WRITINGS: Brush and Palette: Painting Techniques for Young Adults, Reinhold, 1965.†

* * *

SOUSTER, (Holmes) Raymond 1921-
(John Holmes)

PERSONAL: Surname rhymes with "Gloucester"; born January 15, 1921, in Toronto, Ontario, Canada; son of Austin Holmes and Norma (Baker) Souster; married Rosalia Lena Geralde (a bank clerk), June 24, 1947. *Education:* Attended Humberside Collegiate Institute, 1938-39. *Politics:* New Democratic Party. *Religion:* United Church of Canada. *Home:* 39 Baby Point Rd., Toronto 325, Ontario,

Canada. *Office:* Canadian Imperial Bank of Commerce, Commerce Court, Toronto, Ontario M5L 1G9, Canada.

CAREER: Canadian Imperial Bank of Commerce, Toronto, Ontario, accountant, 1939—. *Military service:* Royal Canadian Air Force, 1941-45; leading aircraftsman. *Member:* League of Canadian Poets. *Awards, honors:* Canada's Governor-General Award, 1964, for *The Colour of the Times.*

WRITINGS: (Contributor) Ronald Hambleton, editor, *Unit of Five,* Ryerson, 1944; *When We Are Young* (poems), First Statement Press, 1946; *Go to Sleep, World* (poems), Ryerson, 1947; *City Hall Street* (poems), Ryerson, 1951; (compiler) *Poets 56: Ten Younger English-Canadians,* Contact Press, 1956; *Selected Poems,* Contact Press, 1956; *Crepe-hanger's Carnival: Selected Poems, 1955-58,* Contact Press, 1958; *Place of Meeting: Poems, 1958-60,* Gallery Editions, 1962; *A Local Pride: Poems,* Contact Press, 1962; *The Colour of the Times: The Collected Poems,* Ryerson, 1964; *12 New Poems,* Goosetree Press, 1964; *Ten Elephants on Yonge Street* (poems), Ryerson, 1965; (editor) *New Wave Canada,* Oberon Press, 1970; *As Is* (poems), Oxford University Press, 1967; *Lost & Found: Uncollected Poems by Raymond Souster,* Clarke, Irwin, 1968; (editor with John Robert Colombo) *Shapes and Sounds: Poems of W. W. E. Ross,* Longmans, Green, 1968; *So Far So Good: Poems 1938/68,* Oberon Press, 1969; (editor) *Made in Canada,* Oberon Press, 1970; *The Years* (poems), Oberon Press, 1971; *Selected Poems,* Oberon Press, 1972; (under pseudonym John Holmes) *On Target* (novel), Village Book Store Press, 1973; *Change-Up* (poems), Oberon Press, 1974; *Triple-Header* (poems), Oberon Press, in press; *Rain-Check* (poems), Oberon Press, in press.

Also author, under a pseudonym, of novel, *The Winter of Time,* 1949.

SIDELIGHTS: Fred Cogswell wrote of Souster in the *Fiddlehead:* "Souster differs from most poets in that from his early career to the present time, his outlook and style have remained almost unaltered. His first book is as good, if not as long, as his last; by and large, one Souster poem is as good as another. Souster's reputation has grown because of his persistence and the sheer bulk and uniform quality of his work rather than any development in excellence.... In technique, Souster is a master of the anecdote or description *with point.* He is a master as well of a diction which reproduces convincingly and seemingly without effort the rhymes and nuances of speech, and there is in all his poems hardly a trace of rhetoric or pretentiousness. His art as communication is as flawless as a mirror, and the poems stand or fall in the reader's attitude to their attitude and content."

AVOCATIONAL INTERESTS: Collecting airmail postal stationery of the world.

BIOGRAPHICAL/CRITICAL SOURCES: Canadian Literature, fall, 1964; *Canadian Forum,* December, 1968, February, 1969.

*   *   *

SOUTHAM, Brian Charles   1931-

PERSONAL: Born September 15, 1931, in London, England. *Education:* Lincoln College, Oxford, B.A., 1956, M.A., 1960, B.Litt., 1961. *Office:* Routledge & Kegan Paul Ltd., 68 Carter Lane, London E.C.4, England.

CAREER: Former member of English department, West-field College, University of London; Routledge & Kegan Paul Ltd. (publishers), London, England, editorial director, 1963—.

WRITINGS: (Editor) Jane Austen, *Volume the Second,* Oxford University Press, 1963; (editor) *Lord Tennyson: A Selection,* Chatto & Windus, 1964; *Jane Austen's Literary Manuscripts,* Oxford University Press, 1964; (editor) *Jane Austen: The Critical Heritage,* Barnes & Noble, 1968; (editor) *Critical Essays on Jane Austen,* Routledge & Kegan Paul, 1968, Barnes & Noble, 1969; *A Students Guide to the Selected Poems of T. S. Eliot,* Faber, 1968, Harcourt, 1969; (editor) Jane Austen, *Minor Works,* Oxford University Press, 1969; (contributor) G. Watson, editor, *New Cambridge Bibliography of English Literature,* Volume III: *1800-1900,* Cambridge University Press, 1969; *Tennyson,* Longman Group, 1971; (contributor) A. E. Dyson, editor, *The English Novel: Selected Bibliographic Guides,* Oxford University Press, 1974.

Contributor to *Encyclopaedia Britannica.*

*   *   *

SOYINKA, Wole   1934-

PERSONAL: Surname is pronounced Shoy-ink-a; given name, Akinwande Oluwole; born July 13, 1934, in Isata, Nigeria; married second wife, Olayide Idowu (a teacher), 1963. *Education:* Attended University of Ibadan; University of Leeds, B.A. (honors), 1959. *Agent:* Morton Leavy, 437 Madison Ave., New York, N.Y. 10022. *Office address: Transition,* P.O. Box 9063, Accra, Ghana.

CAREER: University of Ibadan, Nigeria, research fellow in drama, 1960-61; University of Ife, Ibadan, Nigeria, lecturer in English, 1962-63; University of Lagos, Lagos, Nigeria, senior lecturer in English, 1965-67; University of Ibadan, chairman of department of theatre arts, 1967-71; University of Ife, professor of drama, 1972; Cambridge University, Cambridge, England, fellow of Churchill College, 1973-74; *Transition,* Accra, Ghana, editor, 1974—; playwright, novelist, poet. Director of own theatre groups, Orisun Theatre and Maska, in Lagos and Ibadan, Nigeria. *Awards, honors:* Rockefeller grant, 1960; John Whiting Drama Prize, 1966; *New Statesman* Jock Campbell Award, 1968.

WRITINGS: The Interpreters (novel), Deutsch, 1965; (with D. O. Fagunwa) *The Forest of a Thousand Daemons* (novel), Nelson, 1967, Humanities, 1969; *Idanre and Other Poems,* Methuen, 1967, Hill & Wang, 1969; (contributor) D. W. Jefferson, editor, *The Morality of Art,* Routledge & Kegan Paul, 1969; (contributor) O. R. Dathorne and Willfried Feuser, editors, *African Prose,* Penguin, 1969; *Poems from Prison,* Rex Collings, 1969, published as *A Shuttle in the Crypt,* Hill & Wang, 1972; *Season of Anomy* (novel), Rex Collings, 1973; *The Man Died* (prison notes), Rex Collings, 1972, Harper, 1973; (editor) *Poems of Black Africa,* Hill & Wang, 1974.

Plays: "The Invention," first produced in London at Royal Court Theatre, 1955; *A Dance of the Forest* (first produced in London, 1960), Oxford University Press, 1962; *The Lion and the Jewel* (first produced at Royal Court Theatre, 1966), Oxford University Press, 1962; *Three Plays* (includes "The Trials of Brother Jero," one-act, produced Off-Broadway at Greenwich Mews Playhouse, November 9, 1967; "The Strong Breed," one-act, produced at Greenwich Mews Playhouse, November 9, 1967; "The Swamp Dwellers"), Mbari Publications, 1962, Northwestern University Press, 1963; *Five Plays* (includes "The Lion and the

Jewel," "The Swamp Dwellers," "The Trials of Brother Jero," "The Strong Breed," and "A Dance of the Forest"), Oxford University Press, 1964; *The Road* (produced in Stratford, England, at Theatre Royal, 1965), Oxford University Press, 1965; *Kongi's Harvest* (produced Off-Broadway at St. Mark's Playhouse, April 14, 1968), Oxford University Press, 1966; *Madmen and Specialists* (two-act; produced in Waterford, Conn., at Eugene O'Neill Memorial Theatre, August 1, 1970), Methuen, 1971, Hill & Wang, 1972; (editor) *Plays from the Third World: An Anthology*, Doubleday, 1971; *The Jero Plays* (includes "The Trials of Brother Jero," and "Jero's Metamorphosis"), Methuen, 1973; *Camwood on the Leaves*, Methuen, 1973; (adapter) *The Bacchae of Euripides* (first produced in London at Old Vic Theatre, August 2, 1973), Methuen, 1973; *Collected Plays*, Oxford University Press, Volume I, 1973, Volume II, 1974.

Also author of television script, "Culture in Transition." Co-editor, *Black Orpheus*, 1961-64.

SIDELIGHTS: Of *Idanre and Other Poems*, Martin Tucker wrote in the *Nation*: "In the past, Wole Soyinka has been lively, forceful, demonstrative, certainly playful. In this volume he is meditative and understated, willing to contemplate himself as well as grant others their expressions. This quiet dignity is a new center to Soyinka's work.

"Soyinka's plays, on one level, are about the conflict between past and present, between tribal beliefs and modern expediency. He was both critical and appreciative of both ways of life. What he was most attached to were those universal features of character that distinguish a man no matter *when* he was born. His work suggests an underlying animism: Soyinka allows for spirit in all things—in trees, in forests, in roads, even in jet planes.... [However, in *Idanre and Other Poems*] it is almost as if Soyinka's expansiveness has contracted. His spirit is not broken, but it has retrenched for watering. Though the poems are not the result of his prison experience, they are prophetic and reflective of it. Until the time of his imprisonment by his fellow Yoruba tribesmen and their powerful allies, the Hausas, he was a free spirit able to jibe and love all comers. Now the love remains but the stimulus for fulfillment, the desire for experience, has diminished."

BIOGRAPHICAL/CRITICAL SOURCES: New York Times, November 11, 1965, April 19, 1970; *Nation*, April 29, 1968, September 15, 1969; *New Statesman*, December 20, 1968; *Christian Science Monitor*, July 31, 1970, August 15, 1970; Carolyn Riley, editor, *Contemporary Literary Criticism*, Volume III, Gale, 1975.

*   *   *

SPACKMAN, Robert R., Jr.   1917-

PERSONAL: Born December 18, 1917, in Phoenixville, Pa.; son of Robert R. and Bessie (Schultz) Spackman; married Jane R. Garrison, June 10, 1950; children: Jill, Jan, Jenifer, Robert R. III. *Education:* West Chester State College, B.S., 1950; University of Pennsylvania, R.P.T., 1951; Southern Illinois University, M.S., 1960. *Religion:* Episcopalian. *Home:* 20 Hillcrest, Carbondale, Ill. 62901.

CAREER: Professional baseball player, 1940-50; St. Louis Browns, athletic trainer, 1952-53; Southern Illinois University, Carbondale, 1957—, began as head athletic trainer and assistant professor, became associate professor of physical education. Developer of isometric exercise equipment with Marvin A. Johnson and holder or co-holder of seven patents on such equipment. *Military service:* U.S. Army Air Forces, 1942-46; became staff sergeant.

WRITINGS: Baseball, U.S. Naval Institute, 1963; *Two-Man Isometric Exercise for the Whole Body*, W. C. Brown, 1964; *Conditioning for Baseball*, C. C Thomas, 1966; *Conditioning for Football*, C. C Thomas, 1966; *Exercise in the Office*, Southern Illinois University Press, 1968; *Physical Fitness in Law Enforcement*, Southern Illinois University Press, 1969; *Conditioning for Wrestling*, C. C Thomas, 1970; *Conditioning for Gymnastics*, C. C Thomas, 1970. Also author of nine other conditioning books published by Schwebel Printing, 1973-74.

WORK IN PROGRESS: Twelve more conditioning books to complete a sports library on conditioning for all sports.

*   *   *

SPARKS, Edgar H(erndon)   1908-

PERSONAL: Born December 12, 1908, in Lincoln, Calif.; son of William Martin, Jr. and Jessie (Hall) Sparks; married Ingrid Scherini. *Education:* San Francisco Conservatory of Music, certificate, 1932; University of California, Berkeley, A.B., 1939, Ph.D., 1950; Harvard University, M.A., 1942. *Home:* 1001 Alvarado Rd., Berkeley, Calif. 94705.

CAREER: San Francisco Conservatory of Music, San Francisco, Calif., faculty member, 1931-40, 1946-49; University of California, Berkeley, 1949—, became professor of music, professor emeritus, 1974—. *Military service:* U.S. Navy, 1942-45. *Member:* American Musicological Society, Vereniging vor Nederlandse Muziekgeschiedenis.

WRITINGS: Cantus Firmus in Mass and Motet: 1420-1520, University of California Press, 1963; *The Music of Noel Bauldeweyn*, The American Musicological Society, 1972.

WORK IN PROGRESS: The Complete Works of Noel Bauldeweyn.

*   *   *

SPEAIGHT, Robert W(illiam)   1904-

PERSONAL: Born January 14, 1904, at St. Margaret's Bay, Kent, England; son of Frederick William (a company director) and Emily Isabella (Elliot) Speaight; married Esther Evelyn Bowen, 1935; married Bridget Laura Bramwell Bosworth-Smith, May 28, 1951; children: Patrick William Ellis, Teresa Clare Davison, Crispin John. *Education:* Attended Haileybury and Imperial Service College, 1918-22; Lincoln College, Oxford, M.A. (honors), 1925. *Politics:* Conservative. *Religion:* Roman Catholic. *Home and office:* Campion House, Benenden, Kent, England. *Agent:* David Higham Associates Ltd., 76 Dean St., London W.1, England.

CAREER: British actor, author, and lecturer. Started theatrical career with Liverpool Repertory Theatre, 1926; toured Egypt with Shakespearina company, 1927; played leading Shakespearian roles at Old Vic, 1931-32; created role of Becket in T. S. Eliot's "Murder in the Cathedral," 1935; played St. Thomas More in Robert Bolt's "A Man for All Seasons" in Australia, 1962-63; has appeared in dozens of other roles in England, United States, Canada, France, Scotland, and Wales. Lecturer for British Council on tours abroad; lecturer in United States, 1961, 1962, 1965. Broadcaster and recording artist for English poetry on Argo and Spoken Arts records. *Member:* Royal Society of Literature (fellow), Beefsteak and Garrick Clubs. *Awards, honors:* Commander of Order of the British Empire, 1958; Legion of Honour, officer, 1969.

WRITINGS: Mutinous Wind, Davies, 1932; *The Lost*

Hero, Davies, 1934; *Legend of Helena Vaughan*, Putnam, 1936 (published in England as *The Angel in the Mist*, Cassell, 1936); *St. Thomas of Canterbury*, Putnam, 1938 (published in England as *Thomas Becket*, Longmans, Green, 1938, 2nd edition, 1949); *The Unbroken Heart*, Cassell, 1939; *Acting: Its Idea and Tradition*, Cassell, 1939; *Drama Since 1939*, Longmans, Green, 1948; (with others) *Drama, the Novel, Poetry, Prose Literature*, Dent, 1949; *George Eliot*, Roy, 1954; *William Poel and the Elizabethan Revival*, Harvard University Press, 1954; *Nature in Shakespearian Tragedy*, Macmillan, 1956; *The Life of Hilaire Belloc*, Farrar, Straus, 1957; (editor) Hilaire Belloc, *Letters*, Macmillan, 1958; *The Christian Theatre*, Hawthorn, 1960; *William Rothenstein*, Eyre & Spottiswoode, 1962; *Ronald Knox in His Writings*, Sheed, 1965; *The Life of Eric Gill*, Kenedy, 1965; *Teilhard de Chardin: A Biography*, Collins, 1967, published as *The Life of Teilhard de Chardin*, Harper, 1968; *Vanier: Soldier, Diplomat and Governor General: A Biography*, Collins, 1970; *The Property Basket: Recollections of a Divided Life* (autobiography), Collins, 1970; (with others) *Teilhard de Chardin: Remythologization*, Argus Communications, 1970; *Shakespeare on the Stage: An Illustrated History of Shakespearian Performance*, Little, Brown, 1973; *George Bernanos: A Biography*, Liveright, 1974.

Contributor to *Times Literary Supplement*, *Tablet*, *Shakespeare Quarterly*, and others.

WORK IN PROGRESS: Francois Mauriac; *Companion Guide to Burgundy*.

SIDELIGHTS: Of *The Life of Teilhard de Chardin*, Roger Hazelton wrote in the *New Republic*: "At this juncture, then, Mr. Speaight's biography is a welcome addition to the growing literature by and about this remarkable Jesuit scientist and seer. Though his book is by no means as monumental as Claude Cuenot's *Life* recently translated and published in England, and does not presume to be definitive, it is faithful to its subject, making Teilhard both accessible and comprehensible to a greatly expanded readership. That is a decided gain."

Speaight is competent in French. *Avocational interests:* Walking.

*   *   *

SPEARS, Woodridge 1913-

PERSONAL: Born January 22, 1913, in East Point, Johnson County, Ky.; son of George Kelley (a teacher) and Julia (Clark) Spears; married Mary Evalena Gilbert (a teacher), July 22, 1935; children: Philip, Richard, Sandra. *Education:* Attended Transylvania College (now University), 1931-32; Morehead State College (now University), A.B. in Education, 1935; University of Kentucky, A.M., 1947, Ph.D., 1935. *Home:* 905 Shoshoni, Georgetown, Ky. *Office:* College Station, Georgetown College, Georgetown, Ky.

CAREER: University of Kentucky, Lexington, instructor in English, 1948-51, 1953; Georgetown College, Georgetown, Ky., associate professor, 1953-63, professor of English, 1963—. Staff member, Morehead State College (now University) writers workshop. Deputy clerk, Greenup Circuit Court, Greenup, Ky., 1928-35. *Member:* Poetry Society of America, South Atlantic Modern Language Association, Phi Beta Kappa, Sigma Tau Delta.

WRITINGS: The Feudalist, Gustav Davidson, 1946; *River Island*, Morehead State College Press, 1963. Work

represented in *Diamond Anthology*, edited by Charles Angoff and others, A. S. Barnes, 1971. Poems and prose have appeared in magazines since 1936.

WORK IN PROGRESS: Poems; plays; studies in biography, the novel, and on Milton.

*   *   *

SPECTOR, Robert Donald 1922-

PERSONAL: Born September 21, 1922, in Bronx, N.Y.; son of Morris (a salesman) and Helen (Spiegel) Spector; married Eleanor Luskin (a teacher), August 19, 1945. *Education:* Long Island University, B.A., 1948; New York University, M.A., 1949; Columbia University, Ph.D., 1962. *Religion:* Jewish. *Home:* 1761 East 26th St., Brooklyn, N.Y. 11229. *Office:* Long Island University, Brooklyn, N.Y. 11201.

CAREER: Long Island University, Brooklyn, N.Y., instructor, 1949-59, assistant professor, 1959-61, associate professor, 1961-65, professor of English, 1965—. *Military service:* U.S. Coast Guard, 1942-46; served in European and African Theaters; became chief signalman. *Member:* Modern Language Association of America, National Council of Teachers of English, Society for the Advancement of Scandinavian Study, American-Scandinavian Foundation (member of committee on publications). *Awards, honors:* Swedish Institute travel grant, 1965; Huntington Library fellowship, 1974.

WRITINGS: English Literary Periodicals and the Climate of Opinion During the Seven Years' War, Mouton & Co., 1966; *Tobias Smollett*, Twayne, 1968; *Par Lagerkvist*, Twayne, 1973.

Editor: *Seven Masterpieces of Gothic Horror*, Bantam, 1963; Goldsmith, *Vicar of Wakefield*, Bantam, 1964; Dickens, *Hard Times*, Bantam, 1964; Hawthorne, *Scarlet Letter*, Bantam, 1965; *Essays on the Eighteenth-Century Novel*, Indiana University Press, 1965; Twain, *Tom Sawyer*, Bantam, 1966; *Great British Short Novels*, Bantam, 1968; *The Candle and the Tower*, Paperback Library, 1974.

Contributor of poetry, articles, and reviews to journals and newspapers, including *Scandinavian Studies*, *Saturday Review*, *New York Herald Tribune Book Week*, and *University of Kansas City Review*.

WORK IN PROGRESS: Arthur Murphy, publication by Twayne expected in 1977.

*   *   *

SPELLMAN, John W(illard) 1934-

PERSONAL: Born July 27, 1934, in Tewksbury, Mass.; children: Suzanne Bharati, John Gilligan. *Education:* Northeastern University, B.A., 1956; University of Wyoming, graduate study, summer, 1956; School of Oriental and African Studies, London, Ph.D., 1960. *Home:* Willard Rd., Asburnham, Mass. *Office:* University of Windsor, Windsor, Ontario, Canada.

CAREER: Wesleyan University, Middletown, Conn., visiting assistant professor of history, 1961-62; Kerala University, Trivandrum, Kerala, India, visiting assistant professor of politics, 1963-64; University of Washington, Seattle, assistant professor of history, 1964-67. University of Windsor, Windsor, Ontario, professor and head of department of Asian studies, 1967—. Lectured in Middle East, Pakistan, India, and Japan. *Member:* American Oriental Society, Association of Asian Studies, Royal Asiatic Society of

Great Britain and Ireland (fellow), Indian Political Science Association. *Awards, honors:* Ford Foundation fellowship, 1958-61; *Boston Globe—Horn Book* Award, 1967, for *The Beautiful Blue Jay.*

WRITINGS: (Author of introduction) *Kama Sutra of Vatsyayana,* Dutton, 1963; (co-author) *Studies in Social History* (modern India), edited by O. P. Bhatnagar, Allahabad, 1964; *Political Theory of Ancient India,* Clarendon Press, 1964; *The Beautiful Blue Jay and Other Tales of India,* Little, Brown, 1967. Contributor of articles to professional journals. Advisory editor, *International Review of Politics and History.*

WORK IN PROGRESS: Research on subjects concerned with ancient and contemporary India; Indian cultural values, witchcraft in Asia, indigenous medical systems.

AVOCATIONAL INTERESTS: Speaking, classical music, reading, auctions, and cooking.

*   *   *

SPENCER, Christopher   1930-

PERSONAL: Born April 14, 1930, in Cleveland, Ohio; son of Meade A. (an architect) and Emily (Stickney) Spencer; married Dorothy Groenendale; children: Andrew G., Abigail A., Duncan M. *Education:* Princeton University, A.B., 1952; Yale University, M.A., 1953, Ph.D., 1955. *Religion:* Episcopal. *Home:* 1809 Biscayne Dr., Greensboro, N.C. 27410.

CAREER: Duke University, Durham, N.C., instructor in English, 1955-58; Little Rock University, Little Rock, Ark., associate professor of English, 1958-1962, head of department of English, 1958-60, chairman of Division of Humanities, 1960-62; Illinois State University, Normal, associate professor, 1962-65; professor of English, 1965-70; University of North Carolina at Greensboro, professor of English, 1970—. *Member:* Modern Language Association of America, American Association of University Professors; South Atlantic Modern Language Association, Shakespeare Association of America. *Awards, honors:* Guggenheim fellowship, 1967.

WRITINGS: Davenant's Macbeth from the Yale Manuscript, Yale University Press, 1961; *Five Restoration Adaptations of Shakespeare,* University of Illinois Press, 1965; *Nahum Tate,* Twayne, 1972.

WORK IN PROGRESS: New variorum editions of Shakespeare's *Merchant of Venice* and *Macbeth.*

AVOCATIONAL INTERESTS: Reading, gardening, travel.

*   *   *

SPENCER, Elizabeth   1921-

PERSONAL: Born July 19, 1921, in Carrollton, Miss.; daughter of James L. (a farmer) and Mary J. (McCain) Spencer; married John Rusher (a language school director), September 29, 1956. *Education:* Belhaven College, B.A., 1942, Vanderbilt University, M.A., 1943. *Politics:* Democrat. *Religion:* Episcopalian. *Home:* 2300 St. Mathieu, Apt. 610, Montreal, Quebec, Canada.

CAREER: Writer. *Awards, honors:* Women's Democratic Committee award, 1949; National Institute of Arts and Letters award, 1953; Guggenheim fellowship, 1953; Rosenthal Foundation award, American Academy of Art and Letters, 1956; Kenyon College Fellow in Fiction, 1957; first McGraw-Hill Fiction award, 1960; Bryn Mawr College

Donnelly fellow, 1962; Henry Bellamann Award for Creative Writing, 1968; D.L., Southwestern University, 1968.

WRITINGS: Fire in the Morning, Dodd, 1948; *This Crooked Way,* Dodd, 1952; *The Voice at the Back Door,* McGraw, 1956; *The Light in the Piazza,* McGraw, 1960; *Knights and Dragons,* McGraw, 1965; *No Place for an Angel,* McGraw, 1967; *Ship Island and Other Stories,* McGraw, 1968; *The Snare,* McGraw, 1972. Contributor of stories to *Redbook, New Yorker, Virginia Quarterly Review, Texas Quarterly,* and to other publications.

WORK IN PROGRESS: A new collection of stories.

BIOGRAPHICAL/CRITICAL SOURCES: New York Times Book Review, October 22, 1967.†

*   *   *

SPIELMAN, Patrick E.   1936-

PERSONAL: Born March 17, 1936, in Shakopee, Minn.; son of Andrew (a laborer) and Della (Ince) Spielman; married Patricia R. Rogers, June 7, 1958; children: Robert P., Sherri L., Sandra J. *Education:* Stout State University, B.S., 1958. *Home and office address:* Box 188, Gibraltar Rd., Fish Creek, Wis. 54212.

CAREER: Industrial education instructor in public high schools in Fish Creek, Wis., 1958-62, Milwaukee, Wis., 1962-63, Tomah, Wis., 1963-65, and Coleman, Wis., 1965-66; owner of design and fabricating business in wood and plastics, 1972—. Free-lance writer for home workshop and craft magazines, 1957—, for technical publications and secondary education instruction texts, 1966—. Editorial consultant, Industrial Arts and Vocational Education Advisory Staff, 1967-68.

WRITINGS: Modern Projects in Wood, Metal and Plastics, Bruce, 1964; *How to Make Recurve Bows and Matched Arrows,* Bruce, 1964; (co-author) *Basic Mechanical Drawing,* Bruce, 1966, 2nd edition, Benziger, Bruce & GLencoe, 1974; (with D. F. Hackett) *Modern Wood Technology,* Bruce, 1968; *Make Your Sports Gear,* Bruce, 1970; *Design and Product Planning for Industrial Education,* DCA Educational Products, 1974. Also author of three teacher's manuals for transparency series produced by DCA Educational Products. Contributor to *Industrial Arts and Vocational Education, School Shop,* and *Popular Science.*

WORK IN PROGRESS: Another transparency series with teacher's manual for DCA Educational Products.

*   *   *

SPINAGE, Clive A(lfred)   1933-

PERSONAL: Born June 24, 1933, in Surrey, England; son of Alfred James and Clara Harriet (Lovell) Spinage. *Education:* Attended Chelsea College of Science and Technology, London, Ph.D., 1968. *Home:* The Bungalow, Steventon Rd., East Hanney, Wantage, Berkshire, England.

CAREER: Held various jobs; United Nations Food and Agriculture Organization Development Programme, wildlife ecologist. *Military service:* British Army, 1949-51. *Member:* Royal Photographic Society (fellow), Zoological Society of London (scientific fellow).

WRITINGS: Animals of East Africa, Houghton, 1963; *The Book of the Giraffe,* Houghton, 1968. Contributor of articles, photographs, and scientific papers to natural history magazines and journals.

WORK IN PROGRESS: Research on African wildlife.

SPITZ, Allan A(ugust) 1928-

PERSONAL: Born October 9, 1928, in Birmingham, Ala.; son of Peter George (a salesman) and Ann (Levinson) Spitz; married Mariko Shida, March 31, 1956; children: Peter Allan, Ann Rebecca. *Education:* University of New Mexico, B.A., 1952; Michigan State University, M.A., 1954, Ph.D., 1964. *Office:* University of Hawaii, Honolulu, Hawaii.

CAREER: Michigan State University, East Lansing, instructor in social science, 1960-62; University of Hawaii, Honolulu, government research, 1962—. *Military service:* U.S. Marine Corps, 1946-48. *Member:* American Political Science Association, Japan Society.

WRITINGS: (With Edward W. Weidner) *Development Administration: An Annotated Bibliography*, East-West Center Press, 1963; *Land Aspects of the Hawaiian Homes Program*, University of Hawaii Press, 1964; *Social Aspects of the Hawaiian Homes Program*, University of Hawaii Press, 1964; (editor) *Contemporary China*, Washington State University Press, 1967; *Developmental Change: An Annotated Bibliography*, University Press of Kentucky, 1969.

WORK IN PROGRESS: Personnel Systems and Hawaii's System of Public Education; an expansion of *Development Administration*.

SIDELIGHTS: Spitz is competent in Japanese and Chinese.†

* * *

SPRAGUE, Gretchen (Burnham) 1926-

PERSONAL: Born March 26, 1926, in Lincoln, Neb.; daughter of Archer L. (an educator) and Cecilia (Hoehne) Burnham; married Elmer D. Sprague, Jr. (a professor of philosophy), June 22, 1948; children: Emily, Jennifer, Timothy, Gilbert. *Education:* University of Nebraska, B.A., 1947. *Residence:* Brooklyn, N.Y.

CAREER: University of Nebraska, Lincoln, instructor in English, 1947-48. *Awards, honors:* Best Juvenile Mystery of the Year Award from the Mystery Writers of America, 1967.

WRITINGS—Teen-age novels: *A Question of Harmony*, Dodd, 1965; *Signpost to Terror*, Dodd, 1967; *White in the Moon*, Dodd, 1968.

* * *

SPRIGGE, Elizabeth (Miriam Squire) 1900-

PERSONAL: Born June 19, 1900; daughter of Sir Squire (editor of *Lancet*) and Mary Ada (Moss) Sprigge; married Mark Napier, July 23, 1921 (marriage dissolved, 1946); children: Julyan (Mrs. Cawthra Mulock), Ruth (Mrs. Timothy Lumley-Smith). *Education:* Attended Havergal College, Toronto, Ontario, Canada, and Bedford College, University of London. *Home:* 75 Ladbroke Grove, London, W11 2PD, England. *Agent:* Willis Kingsley Wing, 24 East 38th St., New York, N.Y. 10016.

CAREER: Author and translator. British Ministry of Information, London, England, Swedish specialist, 1941-44 (lived in Sweden, 1923-25). Co-founder of Watergate Theatre Club, London, England, 1949, and director, 1949-52. Lecturer and broadcaster on literature and the theater. *Member:* P.E.N.

WRITINGS—Novels: *A Shadowy Third*, Knopf, 1929; *Faint Amorist*, Knopf, 1930; *The Old Man Dies*, Macmillan, 1933; *Castle in Andalusia*, Heinemann, 1935; *The Son of the House*, Collins, 1937; *The Raven's Wing*, Macmillan, 1940.

Biographies: *The Strange Life of August Strindberg*, Macmillan, 1949; *Gertrude Stein: Her Life and Work*, Harper, 1957; (with Jean Jacques Kihm) *Jean Cocteau: The Man and the Mirror*, Gollancz, 1968; *Sybil Thorndike Casson*, Gollancz, 1971; *The Life of Ivy Compton-Burnett*, Gollancz, 1973.

Children's books: *Children Alone*, Eyre & Spottiswoode, 1935; *Pony Tracks*, Eyre & Spottiswoode, 1936; *Two Lost on Dartmoor*, Eyre & Spottiswoode, 1940; (with Elizabeth Muntz) *The Dolphin Bottle*, Gollancz, 1965.

Plays: (With Katriona Sprigge) "Elizabeth of Austria," produced at Garrick Theatre, 1939; (translator) Bjornsterne Bjornson, "Mary Stuart in Scotland," produced at Edinburgh Festival, 1960.

Translations: *Six Plays of Strindberg*, Anchor Books, 1955; *Five Plays of Strindberg*, Anchor Books, 1960; *Twelve Plays of Strindberg*, Constable, 1962; *August Strindberg, Plays*, Aldine, 1963; Jean Cocteau, *The Difficulty of Being*, P. Owen, 1966; August Strindberg, *The Red Room*, Dutton, 1967.

* * *

SQUIRE, Elizabeth 1919-

PERSONAL: Born April 24, 1919, in New York, N.Y.; daughter of William L. (an engineer) and Ethel May (Burrows) Archer; married Frederick Baekeland (a physician), April 20, 1962; children: (step-children) Scott, Heidi. *Education:* Smith College, B.A., 1940; Sorbonne, University of Paris, graduate study, 1948-49; Boston University, M.A., 1952. *Politics:* Independent. *Religion:* Episcopalian. *Agent:* Malcolm Reiss, Paul R. Reynolds, Inc., 599 Fifth Ave., New York, N.Y. 10017.

CAREER: C. Hansen-Moeller, Importers, Quayaquil, Ecuador, secretary and buyer, 1940-41; R. H. Macy & Co., New York, N.Y., assistant buyer, 1941-42; United Nations Relief and Rehabilitation Administration, Rome, Italy, executive secretary, 1946-47; American Community School, Paris, France, teacher, 1947-49; UNESCO, Beirut, Lebanon, reporter, 1949; State of New York Board of Higher Education, New York, research assistant, 1951-53; New Lincoln School, New York, N.Y., teacher, 1953.

WRITINGS: New York Shopping Guide, Barrows, 1961, revised edition, 1964; *Mail Order Shopping Guide*, Barrows, 1963; *New Fortune in Your Hand*, revised edition, Fleet, 1968; *Heroes of Journalism*, Fleet, 1973. Contributor of articles to *New York Herald Tribune, Sports Illustrated*, and *McCall's*.

WORK IN PROGRESS: A book on care of wild animals and birds.

SIDELIGHTS: Elizabeth Squire told *CA* that she "Traveled widely, using two skills, teaching and secretarial training, to get jobs in whatever country visited. Speaks French fairly well, a smattering of Italian. Started writing by accident after six months in a tuberculosis sanitarium. Was told to take part-time job with a lot of walking. Started checking shops in Manhattan for a now defunct magazine. Used collected material for first book."†

* * *

STAATS, Arthur (Wilbur) 1924-

PERSONAL: Born January 17, 1924, in Elmsford, N.Y.;

son of Frank and Jennie (Yollis) Staats; married Carolyn Kaiden, February 1, 1953; children: Jennifer, Peter. *Education:* University of California, Los Angeles, B.A., 1949, M.A., 1953, Ph.D., 1956. *Office:* University of Hawaii, Honolulu, Hawaii.

CAREER: Arizona State University, Tempe, 1955-64, started as assistant professor, became professor of psychology; University of California, Berkeley, visiting professor, 1964-65; University of Wisconsin, Madison, professor of educational psychology, 1965-67; University of Hawaii, Honolulu, professor of psychology and educational psychology, 1967—. University of London, National Science Foundation faculty fellow, 1961-62. Consultant in clinical psychology to Palo Alto Veterans Administration Hospital, 1965-66. *Military service:* U.S. Navy, 1942-45. *Member:* American Psychological Association, Averican Association for the Advancement of Science, Society for Research in Child Development, New York Academy of Sciences.

WRITINGS: (With wife, C. K. Staats) *Complex Human Behavior*, Holt, 1963; (editor) *Human Learning*, Holt, 1964; *Learning, Language and Cognition: Theory Research and Method for the Study of Human Behavior and Its Development*, Holt, 1968; (with Barbara A. Brewer and Michael C. Gross) *Learning and Cognitive Development*, University of Chicago Press, 1970; *Child Learning, Intelligence and Personality: Principles of a Behavioral Interaction Approach*, Harper, 1971. Contributor to professional journals.†

*   *   *

STACK, Nicolete Meredith   1896-
(Kathryn Kenny, a house pseudonym; Elleen Hill, Nicolete Meredith)

PERSONAL: Born February 22, 1896, in Des Moines, Iowa; daughter of Patrick Henry (a teacher) and Frances (Lynch) McGuire; married Edward Randolph Meredith, 1920 (died December 31, 1935); married Charles Monroe Stack, July 1, 1942 (died July 10, 1945). *Education:* Highland Park College, Des Moines, Iowa, B.A.; attended University of Colorado, one year, and H.M.S. "Franconia" Floating University Around the World, six months, 1930. *Politics:* Democrat. *Religion:* Roman Catholic. *Home:* 8 Colonial Village, C, Jamestown House, Webster Groves, Mo. 63119. *Agent:* Miss Ruth Cantor, 156 Fifth Ave., Room 1005, New York, N.Y. 10010.

CAREER: Social service activities in Iowa include volunteer worker in Ames, governor-appointed member of Iowa Old Age Assistance Board, member of Iowa State Board of Social Welfare; instructor in juvenile writing, McKendree College conference, 1961. *Member:* Authors League of America, National League of American Pen Women, Missouri Writers Guild, St. Louis Writers Guild (past president). *Awards, honors:* Missouri Writers Guild annual award for *Rainbow Tomorrow*; National League of American Pen Women award for poetry.

WRITINGS: Two to Get Ready, Caxton, 1953; *Pierre of the Island*, Bruce, 1954; *Rainbow Tomorrow*, Bruce, 1956; *Corky's Hiccups*, Golden Book, 1973; *Night Sounds*, Golden Press, in press; *A Friend for Katie*, Whitman, in press. Also author of eight picture books adapted from German, Milliken Publishing, 1966—.

Under name Nicolete Meredith: *Welcome Love*, Lothrop, 1959; *King of the Kerry Fair*, Crowell, 1960; *Milestone Summer*, Whitney, 1962.

Under pseudonym Kathryn Kenny: Author of five mystery books in the "Trixie Belden" series, Whitman, 1961-71.

Under pseudonym Elleen Hill: Author of "Robin Kane Mystery" series, five books, Whitman, 1966-71.

Contributor to *Atlantic, Reader's Digest, Franciscan Quarterly, Child Life, Humpty Dumpty, Jack and Jill, Highlights for Children.*

WORK IN PROGRESS: Mystery of Ming Toy, Flight to Camelot, Wrecked on Far Barbary, The Great Bronze Bell of Peking.

SIDELIGHTS: Mrs. Stack's book, *Two to Get Ready*, was written as a sequel to her mother's book, *Wagon to a Star.* Both books were illustrated by Gertrude Williamson, Mrs. Stack's sister, as was *Pierre of the Island*, which was also published in a braille edition.

*   *   *

STAMPP, Kenneth M.   1912-

PERSONAL: Born July 12, 1912, in Milwaukee, Wis.; son of Oscar M. and Eleanor (Schmidt) Stampp; married Katherine Mitchell, 1939; married second wife, Isabel M. Peebles Brown, July 4, 1962; children: (first marriage) Kenneth Mitchell, Sara Katherine; (second marriage) Jennifer Elizabeth. *Education:* University of Wisconsin, B.S., 1935, M.A., 1937, Ph.D., 1942. *Home:* 682 San Luis Road, Berkeley, Calif. 94707. *Office:* Department of History, University of California, Berkeley, Calif.

CAREER: University of Arkansas, Fayetteville, instructor in history, 1941-42; University of Maryland, College Park, assistant professor, 1942-45, associate professor of history, 1945-46; University of California, Berkeley, assistant professor, 1946-49, associate professor, 1949-51, professor of history, 1951-57, Morrison Professor of American History, 1957—, research professor in humanities, 1965. Harvard University, visiting professor, 1955; University of Munich, Fulbright lecturer at Amerika-Institut, 1957; University of London, Commonwealth Fund lecturer in American history, 1960; Oxford University, Harmsworth Professor of American History, 1961-62. Summer lecturer at University of Wisconsin and University of Colorado. Thomas Y. Crowell Co. (publishers), American history editor, 1960-70.

MEMBER: American Historical Association, Society of American Historians, American Civil Liberties Union (member of board of directors, Berkeley chapter), National Association for the Advancement of Colored People, Mississippi Valley Historical Association, Southern Historical Association, Phi Beta Kappa. *Awards, honors:* Guggenheim fellow, 1952-53.

WRITINGS: Indiana Politics During the Civil War, Indiana Historical Bureau, 1949; *And the War Came*, Louisiana State University Press, 1950; (contributor) *Problems in American History*, Prentice-Hall, 1952; *The Peculiar Institution*, Knopf, 1956; (editor) *The Causes of the Civil War*, Prentice-Hall, 1959, revised edition, 1974; (co-author) *The National Experience*, Harcourt, 1963, revised editions, 1968, 1973; (editor) *The McGraw-Hill Illustrated World History*, McGraw, 1964; *The Era of Reconstruction, 1865-1877*, Knopf, 1965; (editor with Leon F. Litwack) *Reconstruction: An Anthology of Revisionist Writings*, Louisiana State University Press, 1969. Contributor of articles to historical journals.

WORK IN PROGRESS: A volume for *The Oxford History of the United States*, for Oxford University Press.

* * *

STANFORD, Donald E(lwin) 1913-
(Don Stanford)

PERSONAL: Born February 7, 1913, in Amherst, Mass.; son of Ernest Elwood (a professor) and Alice (Carroll) Stanford; married Maryanna Peterson (a placement director), August 14, 1953. *Education:* Stanford University, B.A., 1933, Ph.D., 1953; Harvard University, M.A., 1934. *Home:* 776 Delgado Dr., Baton Rouge, La. 70808. *Office:* Department of English, Louisiana State University, Baton Rouge, La. 70803.

CAREER: Colorado State College, Fort Collins, instructor in English, 1935-37; Dartmouth College, Hanover, N.H., instructor in English, 1937-41; University of Nebraska, Lincoln, instructor in English, 1941-42; Louisiana State University, Baton Rouge, 1949—, began as instructor, became professor of English, 1963. Visiting associate professor, Duke University, 1961-62. *Member:* Modern Language Association of America, P.E.N., Melville Society, South-Atlantic Modern Language Association, South-Central Modern Language Association. *Awards, honors:* Guggenheim fellowship, 1959-60; National Endowment for the Humanities award, 1972; Louisiana State University Foundation distinguished faculty fellowship, 1973-74.

WRITINGS: (Under name Don Stanford) *New England Earth* (poems), Colt Press, 1941; (under name Don Stanford) *The Traveler* (poems), Cummington, 1955; (editor and author of introduction) *The Poems of Edward Taylor*, Yale University Press, 1960, paperback edition with new introduction, Yale University Press, 1963; (editor) *Nine Essays in Modern Literature*, Louisiana State University Press, 1965; *Edward Taylor*, University of Minnesota Press, 1965; (contributor) Everett Emerson, editor, *Chapters in Early American Literature*, University of Wisconsin Press, 1972; (editor) *Selected Poems of Robert Bridges*, Carcanet Press, in press; (editor) *Selected Poems of S. Foster Damon*, Cummington, in press.

Contributor to *Shakespeare Quarterly*, *Journal of Modern Literature*, and *Philological Quarterly*. Editor, Louisiana State University Humanities Series, 1962-67; editor, *Southern Review*, 1963—.

WORK IN PROGRESS: In the Classic Mode: The Achievement of Robert Bridges; *Edward Taylor: American Puritan Poet*.

AVOCATIONAL INTERESTS: Foreign travel.

* * *

STARR, Edward Caryl 1911-

PERSONAL: Born January 9, 1911, in Yonkers, N.Y.; son of Edward Charles (an electrician) and Mary (Reid) Starr; married Ruth Thomforde (a teacher), August 31, 1940; children: Caroline M. (Mrs. Norman C. Wehmer), E. Jonathan. *Education:* Colgate University, A.B. (cum laude), 1933; Columbia University, B.S. in L.S., 1939; Colgate Rochester Divinity School, B.D., 1940. *Politics:* Republican. *Home:* 299 Mulberry St., Rochester, N.Y. 14620.

CAREER: Ordained minister, American Baptist Convention, 1952; Colgate University, Hamilton, N.Y., curator of Samuel Colgate Baptist Historical Collection, 1935-48; Crozer Theological Seminary, Chester, Pa., librarian, 1948-54; American Baptist Historical Society, Chester, Pa., curator, 1948-55; American Baptist Historical Society, Rochester, N.Y., curator, 1955—; American Baptist Convention, archivist, 1961—. *Member:* Society of American Archivists, American Society of Church History, American Theological Library Association, Phi Beta Kappa.

WRITINGS: A Baptist Bibliography, Volumes I-XX, American Baptist, 1947-74. Contributor of articles to periodicals.

WORK IN PROGRESS: Additional volumes of *A Baptist Bibliography*; research on Baptist bibliography and origins of Baptist contributions to religious thinking.

AVOCATIONAL INTERESTS: Literature and gardening.

* * *

STARR, Isidore 1911-

PERSONAL: Born November 24, 1911, in Brooklyn, N.Y.; son of Nathan (a cabinetmaker) and Yetta (Lampert) Starr; married Kay Rubin, July 6, 1940; children: Lawrence. *Education:* City College (now City College of the City University of New York), New York, N.Y., B.A. (magna cum laude), 1932; St. John's University, Jamaica, N.Y., LL.B. (cum laude), 1936; Columbia University, M.A., 1939; Brooklyn Law School, D.J.S., 1942; New School for Social Research, Ph.D., 1957. *Home:* 44-59 Kissena Blvd., Flushing, N.Y. *Office:* Department of Education, Queens College of the City University of New York, Flushing, N.Y.

CAREER: New York (N.Y.) public schools, social studies teacher, 1934-61; Queens College of the City University of New York, Flushing, N.Y., visiting lecturer, 1961-62, associate professor, 1962-68, professor of education, 1968—. Consultant to U.S. Office of Education, Encyclopaedia Britannica Films, Grolier Society, and text-film department of McGraw-Hill Book Co. *Military service:* U.S. Army, Information and Education, 1943-46; received Commendation Medal. *Member:* American Bar Association, American Political Science Association, Council for the Study of Mankind, American Association of University Professors, National Council for the Social Studies (president, 1964-65), Phi Beta Kappa. *Awards, honors:* John Hay fellowship in the humanities, 1952-53.

WRITINGS: Human Rights in the United States, Oxford Book Co., 1951, 2nd revised edition, 1970; *The Federal Judiciary*, Oxford Book Co., 1957, published as *The American Judicial System*, 1972; (editor with Merle Curti and Lewis Paul Todd) *Living American Documents*, Harcourt, 1961, revised edition, 1972; (classroom editor and author of accompanying testbook, wordbook, and teacher's manual) Curti and Todd, *The Rise of the American Nation*, Harcourt, 1961; (editor with John Hope Franklin) *The Negro in Twentieth-Century America: A Civil Rights Reader*, Random House, 1968; *The Feiner Case*, Encyclopaedia Britannica, 1968; *The Gideon Case*, Encyclopaedia Britannica, 1968; *The Lost Generation of Prince Edward County*, Encyclopaedia Britannica, 1968; *The Supreme Court and Contemporary Issues*, Encyclopaedia Britannica, 1969; (with Howard Langer) *The Making of the President: Motion Picture Case Studies in the Nomination and Election of the President*, Simon & Schuster, 1972.

Contributor: *Great American Liberals*, edited by Gabriel Mason, Beacon Press, 1956; *The Day I Was Proudest to be an American*, edited by Donald Robinson, Doubleday, 1958; *Social Aspects of Education: A Casebook*, edited by Edward T. Ladd and William C. Sayres, Prentice-Hall,

1963; *Skill Development in Social Studies*, edited by Helen McCracken Carpenter, 33rd Yearbook of the National Council for the Social Studies, 1963. Contributor of an annual series of articles dealing with significant Supreme Court decisions to *Social Education*, 1951-63, to *Encyclopedia of Education*, and to other educational journals.

* * *

STATHAM, Jane 1917-

PERSONAL: Surname is pronounced *State*-ham; born November 28, 1917, in Norfolk, Va.; daughter of Leonidas A. (a chemist and rancher) and Hazel Marian (Snyder) Statham; married Alexander Burton Carver (a librarian), April 9, 1965. *Education:* University of Chicago, B.A., 1943, graduate student, 1961-62. *Home:* 112 Briarcliff Rd., Durham, N.C. 27707. *Office:* International Program of Laboratories for Population Statistics, University of North Carolina, Chapel Hill, N.C. 27514.

CAREER: Library of International Relations, Chicago, Ill., associate director, 1943-67; University of North Carolina, Chapel Hill, International Program of Laboratories for Population Statistics (POPLAB), editor, 1973—. *Member:* Illinois Library Club.

WRITINGS: (With Eloise G. ReQua) *The Developing Nations: A Guide to Information Sources*, Gale, 1965. Editor of Library of International Relations quarterlies, *World in Focus*, 1945-50, *International Information Service*, 1963-67.

SIDELIGHTS: Jane Statham has some competence in French, German, Spanish, Russian, and literary Chinese.

* * *

STEAD, Christina (Ellen) 1902-

PERSONAL: Born July 17, 1902, in Rockdale, Sydney, New South Wales, Australia; daughter of David George and Ellen (Butters) Stead; married William James Blake (an author; surname originally Blech; died, 1968). *Education:* Attended Teachers' College, Sydney University, received teacher's certification. *Residence:* Surrey, England. *Agent:* Cyrilly Abels, 597 Fifth Ave., New York, N.Y. 10017.

CAREER: Worked as a public school teacher, a teacher of abnormal children, and as a demonstrator in the psychology laboratory of Sydney University, all in Australia; grain company clerk, London, England, 1928-29; bank clerk in Paris, France, 1930-35; lived in the United States during the late thirties and the forties; was a senior writer for Metro-Goldwyn-Mayer, 1943; instructor in Workshop in the Novel, New York University, 1943-44. Full-time professional writer. *Awards, honors:* Paris Review Aga Khan Prize, 1966; Arts Council of Great Britain grant, 1967; Australian National University fellowship in the Creative Arts, 1969.

WRITINGS—Novels unless otherwise noted: *The Salzburg Tales* (stories), Appleton, 1934; (contributor) *The Fairies Return*, P. Davies, 1934; *Seven Poor Men of Sydney*, Appleton, 1935; *The Beauties and Furies*, Appleton, 1936; *House of All Nations*, Simon & Schuster, 1938; *The Man Who Loved Children*, Simon & Schuster, 1940, published with an introduction by Randall Jarrell, Holt, 1965; *For Love Alone*, Harcourt, 1944; *Letty Fox: Her Luck*, Harcourt, 1946; *A Little Tea, A Little Chat*, Harcourt, 1948; *The People With the Dogs*, Little, Brown, 1952; *Dark Places of the Heart*, Holt, 1966 (published in England as *Cotters' England*, Secker & Warburg, 1966); *The Puzzle-*headed Girl* (novellas), Holt, 1967; *The Little Hotel*, Holt, 1975.

Editor: (With William J. Blake) *Modern Women in Love*, Dryden Press, 1946; *South Sea Stories*, Muller, 1955.

Translator: Fernand Gigon, *Colour of Asia*, Muller, 1955; Jean Giltene, *The Candid Killer*, Muller, 1956; August Piccard, *In Balloon and Bathyscape*, Cassell, 1956.

Contributor of short stories to *Southerly, Kenyon Review,* and *Saturday Evening Post*, and of reviews to various papers.

WORK IN PROGRESS: A Fish in the Ocean of Story, an autobiography of her early years in Sydney; a novel, *I'm Dying Laughing*; and *The Huntress, and Other Stories*.

SIDELIGHTS: Miss Stead's novels and stories are all the competent work of a craftsman. Only one of these, however, has received any real notice, and that belatedly. *The Man Who Loved Children* was both a critical and a popular failure when it was first published in 1940. For 25 years it led an underground existence, read by and circulated among the cognoscenti. Its republication in 1965 was really a resurrection. Randall Jarrell, in a detailed introduction, states: "If I were asked to name a good book that we don't read but that people of the future will read, I'd answer, almost with confidence, *The Man Who Loved Children*." He goes on: "It seems to me as plainly good as *Crime and Punishment* and *Rememberance of Things Past* and *War and Peace* are plainly great. I call it a good book, but it is a better book, I think, than most of the novels people call great; perhaps it would be fairer to call it great. It has one quality that, ordinarily, only a great book has: it makes you a part of one family's immediate existence as no other book quite does. One reads the book," writes Jarrell, "with an almost ecstatic pleasure of recognition. You get used to saying, 'Yes, that's the way it is'; and you say many times, but can never get used to saying, 'I didn't know *anybody* knew that.' Henny, Sam, Louie, and the children are entirely real to the reader, and reality is rare in novels." Miss Stead has a "simple narrative power: she tells what happens so that it happens, and to you."

While an original, she is also a throwback to the nineteenth century. Christopher Ricks writes: "In its sense of growth and of generations, in its generality and specificity, above all in the central place which it accords to feelings of indignation and embarrassment, *The Man Who Loved Children* is in the best tradition of the nineteenth-century novel.... Like George Meredith at his best [Miss Stead] is fascinated by the way we speak to ourselves in the privacy of our skulls, and she is able to remind us of what we would rather forget—that we are all continually employing, to ourselves and to others, a false rhetoric, overblown, indiscriminately theatrical, and yet indisputably ours." Jose Yglesias observes that Miss Stead "is doggedly in the great tradition: she has not allowed political science, sociology or the various psychological schools to rob her of her material; she has not diminished the proper canvas of the novelist." She differs from the novelists of the previous century in that "she has no quietist messages and no comforting resolutions." "Everything in the book deserves notice," writes Ricks. "Its narrative skill; its sense of how much it matters to have money; its creation of locality (Washington, Baltimore); its pained insistence on the rights of women and children; its political acuteness, especially in its feeling for what underlies those people and those moments which protest that they are non-political; its presentation of a religious soft-soaping secularism: these are not extraneous but the fiber of the book." Eleanor Perry says much the same thing when she says that this novel is "not a slice of life. It *is* life." According to Jarrell, "There is a bewitching rapidity and lack of self-consciousness about Christina Stead's writing; she has much knowledge, extraordinary abilities, but is too engrossed in what she is doing ever to seem conscious of them, so that they do not cut her off from the world but join her to it." Most critics would now agree with Yglesias who believes that *The Man Who Loved Children* "is a funny, painful, absorbing masterpiece, obviously the work of a major writer."

BIOGRAPHICAL/CRITICAL SOURCES: Atlantic, March, 1965, June, 1965; *Nation*, April 5, 1965; *Saturday Review*, April 10, 1965; *Book Week*, April 18, 1965; *New York Review of Books*, June 17, 1965; *Southerly* (Sydney), 1962; R.G. Geering, *Christina Stead*, Twayne, 1969; Carolyn Riley, editor, *Contemporary Literary Criticism*, Volume IV, Gale, 1975.†

* * *

STEEN, John Warren, Jr. 1925-

PERSONAL: Born November 9, 1925, in Jackson, Miss.; son of John Warren (a post office supervisor) and Annabelle (Henry) Steen; married Dorothy Jean Lipham, September 2, 1952; children: John Warren III, Dorothy Annell, Lucinda Lipham. *Education:* Baylor University, B.A., 1948; Southern Baptist Theological Seminary, B.D., 1951, graduate study, 1952-53; Union Theological Seminary, New York, N.Y., S.T.M., 1952. *Home:* 6511 Currywood Dr., Nashville, Tenn. 37205. *Office:* Baptist Sunday School Board, 127 Ninth Ave. N., Nashville, Tenn. 37234.

CAREER: Baptist pastor in Peoria, Tex., 1946-47, Mount Vernon, N.Y., 1951-52; chaplain at Louisville General Hospital, Louisville, Ky., 1952-55; pastor in Milledgeville, Ga., 1955-60, Winston-Salem, N.C., 1960-63, and Clayton, N.C., 1963—; currently adult editor for Baptist Sunday School Board, Nashville, Tenn. *Military service:* U.S. Navy, chaplain's assistant, 1944-46. *Member:* Clayton Ministerial Association (president), Johnston Baptist Association (vice-president), Kiwanis Club (member of board), Rotary Club (member of board). *Awards, honors:* Freedoms Foundation at Valley Forge honor certificate, 1962, for sermon, "Take Atheism Seriously."

WRITINGS—All published by Broadman except as indicated: *Conquering Inner Space*, 1964; (contributor) *Is Christ for John Smith?*, 1968; (contributor) *Everyday, Five Minutes with God*, 1969; *Barnabas: Restless Fighter*, 1971; (editor) *Our Church in 1971-72*, Convention Press, 1971; (editor) *Our Church in Faith and Conquest*, Convention Press, 1972; (contributor) *Broadman Devotional Manual*, 1972; (editor) *A Study Guide to John*, Sunday School Board of Southern Baptist Convention, 1973; *Barnabas and Paul: Brothers in Conflict*, 1973; (contributor) *A Field of Diamonds*, 1974. Contributor of articles, book reviews, and lessons to periodicals and journals in his field.

WORK IN PROGRESS: Research into suicide motivation and prevention.

AVOCATIONAL INTERESTS: Piano playing, oil painting, greenhouse gardening, and architecture.

* * *

STEERE, Douglas V(an) 1901-

PERSONAL: Born August 31, 1901, in Harbor Beach, Mich.; son of Edward M. (a U.S. Postal employee) and Ruby (Monroe) Steere; married Dorothy MacEachron, June 12, 1929; children: Helen Weaver, Anne Steere Nash. *Education:* Michigan State University, B.S., 1923; Harvard University, M.A., 1925, Ph.D., 1931; Oxford University, B.A., 1927, M.A., 1953. *Politics:* Independent. *Religion:* Society of Friends (Quaker). *Address:* Haverford College, Haverford, Pa.

CAREER: High school teacher in Onaway, Mich., 1921-22; Haverford College, Haverford, Pa., assistant professor, 1928-31, associate professor, 1931-41, professor of philosophy, 1941-50, Thomas Wistar Brown Professor of Philosophy, 1950-64, professor emeritus, 1964—. Harry Emerson Fosdick Visiting Professor, Union Theological Seminary, New York, N.Y., 1961-62. Lecturer at universities and theological schools in the United States, 1939—; Nitobe Lecturer in Tokyo, 1954; Swarthmore Lecturer in London, 1955; Emily Hobhouse Memorial Lecturer in Johannesburg, 1957; Danforth Lecturer for Association of American Colleges, 1965-66. Society of Friends, chairman of Friends World Committee, 1964-70, member of missions to Europe, Africa, India, Japan, 1937-59; Quaker observer-delegate to the Vatican Council. Chairman of board of managers, Pendle Hill School of Religion and Social Studies, 1954-70; member of board of trustees, Wainwright House, John Woolman Memorial, Lewis M. Stevens Conference Foundation, East Ridge Community.

MEMBER: American Theological Society (president, 1946), American Philosophical Association, Association of American Rhodes Scholars, International Fellowship of Reconciliation (chairman of American section, 1953-64), Phi Beta Kappa. *Awards, honors:* Rhodes Scholar; D.D., Lawrence College, 1950; L.H.D., Oberlin College, 1954; D.H., Earlham College, 1965; S.T.D., General Theology Seminary, 1967; L.L.D., Haverford College, 1970.

WRITINGS: Prayer and Worship, Association Press, 1938; (translator from the Danish) Soren Kierkegaard, *Purity of Heart*, Harper, 1939; (editor, and author of biographical memoir) Thomas Kelly, *Testament of Devotion*, Harper, 1941; *On Beginning From Within*, Harper, 1943; *Doors Into Life*, Harper, 1948; *Time to Spare*, Harper, 1948; *On Listening to Another*, Harper, 1955; *Work and Contemplation*, Harper, 1957; *Dimensions of Prayer*, Harper, 1963; (editor, and author of introductory essay) *Spiritual Counsels and Letters of Baron von Huegel*, Harper, 1964; *God's Irregular: Arthur Shearly Cripps*, S.P.C.K., 1973. Author of five pamphlets for Pendle Hill, 1965-72. Contributor of chapters to books and articles to religious publications. Member of editorial board of *Religion in Life*.

WORK IN PROGRESS: Essays on nature of contemplation.

SIDELIGHTS: Steere speaks German and reads Scandinavian languages and French.

* * *

STEEVES, Frank Leslie 1921-

PERSONAL: Born September 17, 1921, in Kennebunkport, Me.; son of Frank Leslie and Gladys (MacCormack) Steeves; married Louise C. Patriarca, 1949; children: Helen Leslie, Frank Lloyd, Vincent Michael. *Education:* Boston University, B.S. and Ed.M., 1946, Ed.D., 1949. *Residence:* Waukesha, Wis. *Office:* Office of the Dean, School of Education, Marquette University, Milwaukee, Wis.

CAREER: St. Cloud State College, St. Cloud, Minn., supervisor of student teaching, 1949-52; University of North Dakota, Grand Forks, director of student teaching, 1952-57; Paterson State College (now William Paterson College of New Jersey), Wayne, N.J., director of placement and student teaching, 1957-58; University of Vermont, Burlington, professor of education, 1958-69; Marquette University, Milwaukee, Wis., dean of the school of education, 1969—. *Military service:* U.S. Army Air Forces, 1941-44; became staff sergeant. *Member:* National Education Association (life member), Association for Supervision and Curriculum Development, National Society for the Study of Education, Phi Delta Kappa.

WRITINGS: Fundamentals of Teaching in Secondary Schools, Odyssey, 1962; *Issues in Student Teaching*, Odyssey, 1963; (editor) *Readings in the Methods of Education*, Odyssey, 1964; (editor) *The Subjects in the Curriculum*, Odyssey, 1968. Contributor to education journals.

AVOCATIONAL INTERESTS: Outdoor activities.

* * *

STEIN, Edward V(incent) 1920-

PERSONAL: Born November 30, 1920; son of Charles (a physician) and Jean (Anderson) Stein; married Ruth Brainard, August 28, 1944; children: Lawrence, Karl, Laurel, Paula. *Education:* University of California, Los Angeles, B.A., 1943; Princeton Theological Seminary, B.D., 1946; University of Southern California, Ph.D., 1953; postdoctoral study at Mental Research Institute, Palo Alto, Calif., and Jung Institute, Zurich, Switzerland. *Home:* 7 Raven Rd., San Anselmo, Calif.

CAREER: Ordained Presbyterian minister, 1946; minister in Los Angeles, Calif., 1946-48, San Diego, Calif., 1948-53; University of California, Berkeley, director of Westminster House and chaplain for Presbyterian students, 1953-59; San Francisco Theological Seminary, San Anselmo, Calif., professor of pastoral psychology, 1959—; Graduate Theological Union, Berkeley, Calif., member of faculty. Union Theological Seminary, Philippine Islands, professor of psychology, 1957-58. *Member:* Academy of Religion and Mental Health, American Association of Pastoral Counselors, American Psychological Association, Alpha Mu Gamma, Pi Epsilon Theta.

WRITINGS: The Stranger Inside You, Westminster, 1965; *Guilt: Theory and Therapy*, Westminster, 1968; *Beyond Guilt*, Fortress, 1972. Contributor to *Discovery, Christian Century, Journal of Pastoral Care*, and other journals.

* * *

STEIN, Joseph

PERSONAL: Born in New York, N.Y.; son of Charles and Emma Stein; married Sadie Singer (died, 1974); children: Daniel, Harry, Joshua. *Education:* City College (now City College of the City University of New York), New York, N.Y., B.S.S., 1935; Columbia University, M.S.W., 1937. *Agent:* A. Horney, Alan V. Schwartz, Greenbaum, Wolf and Ernst, 437 Madison Ave., New York, N.Y.

CAREER: Consultation Center of Jewish Family Service, New York, N.Y., psychiatric social worker, 1939-44; Jewish Board of Guardians, New York, N.Y., public relations director, 1945-47; writer for radio, television, and then stage, 1947—, starting in radio ("Henry Morgan Show" and "Kraft Music Hall"), then writing television scripts for "Show of Shows" and "Sid Caesar Show" and specials for Phil Silvers, Debbie Reynolds, and other stars. *Member:*

Dramatists Guild of the Authors League of America. *Awards, honors:* Antoinette Perry Award (Tony) of American Theatre Wing for best musical, New York Drama Critics Award, and Newspaper Guild Award, all for "Fiddler on the Roof," 1965.

WRITINGS—Plays: (With Will Glickman) *Plain and Fancy* (produced, 1955), Random House, 1955; (with Glickman) *Mrs. Gibbon's Boys* (produced, 1949), Samuel French (London), 1958; (with Glickman) *The Body Beautiful* (produced, 1958), Samuel French, 1958; *Enter Laughing* (produced, 1963), Samuel French, 1963; *Fiddler on the Roof* (produced, 1964), Crown, 1965; *Zorba* (produced, 1968), Random House, 1969.

Also wrote musical books for three other Broadway productions, "Juno," 1960, "Take Me Along," 1961, and in collaboration with Will Glickman, "Mr. Wonderful," 1956. Adapted Carl Reiner's "Enter Laughing" for motion picture with same title released by Columbia Pictures, 1966; adapted *Fiddler on the Roof* for motion picture released by United Artists, 1972.

WORK IN PROGRESS: Musical version of "Enter Laughing," to be produced in 1974; screenplay based on Henry Roth's novel, *Call It Sleep*.

SIDELIGHTS: From Broadway all of Stein's plays have gone into stock, amateur, and foreign productions.

* * *

STEINBRUECK, Victor 1911-

PERSONAL: Born December 15, 1911, in Mandan, N.D.; son of John C. (a machinist) and Rose (Rittle) Steinbrueck; married Elaine P. Worden (divorced); married Marjorie Nelson (an actress), 1964; children: Matthew, Lisa, David, Peter. *Education:* University of Washington, Seattle, Bachelor of Architecture, 1935. *Home:* 2622 Franklin Ave., East, Seattle, Wash. 98102.

CAREER: University of Washington, College of Architecture and Urban Planning, Seattle, 1946—, now professor of architecture. Architect in private consultation practice, Seattle, Wash. *Military service:* U.S. Army, 1943-46.

WRITINGS: Guide to Seattle Architecture, 1851-1953, Reinhold, 1953; *Seattle Cityscape*, University of Washington Press, 1961; *Market Sketchbook*, University of Washington Press, 1968; *Seattle Cityscape #2*, University of Washington Press, 1973.

* * *

STEINER, George A(lbert) 1912-

PERSONAL: Born May 1, 1912, in Norristown, Pa.; married Jean E. Wood, September 19, 1937; children: John Frederick. *Education:* Temple University, B.Sc., 1933; University of Pennsylvania, M.A., 1934; University of Illinois, Ph.D., 1937. *Home:* 13943 Cumpston St., Van Nuys, Calif. *Office:* Center for Research and Dialogue on Business in Society, Graduate School of Business Administration, University of California, Los Angeles, Calif.

CAREER: Indiana University, Bloomington, instructor, 1937-39, assistant professor of finance, 1939-42, associate director, Bureau of Business Research, 1937-39; U.S. government, Washington, D.C., posts with War Production Board, 1942-43, with Civilian Products Administration, 1946-47; University of Illinois, Urbana, professor of economics, 1947-56; University of California, Graduate School of Business Administration, Los Angeles, professor of management theory, 1956—, director of division of research, Graduate School of Management, 1956-71, director, Center for Research and Dialogue on Business in Society, 1971—. Lockheed Aircraft Corp., Burbank, Calif., senior economic adviser in development planning, 1954-56; consultant to RAND Corp., Institute for Defense Analysis, and to government agencies, including Office of Emergency Planning; lecturer at Industrial College of the Armed Forces and other institutions. *Military service:* U.S. Army, 1943, U.S. Navy, 1943-46; became lieutenant senior grade.

MEMBER: International Council for Scientific Management (fellow), National Academy of Management (fellow; president, 1971-72), American Economic Association, American Management Association, American Association of University Professors, Society for Long Range Planning (Great Britain), Institute of Management Sciences, National Industrial Conference Board, Western Economic Association, Alpha Kappa Psi, Artus, Beta Gamma Sigma, Delta Tau Delta. *Awards, honors:* Litt.D. from Temple University, 1963; General Management Award, Society for Advancement of Management, 1963; Temple University, D.Litt., 1963; Distinguished Alumnus Award, Temple University, 1964; Office of Emergency Planning, Distinguished Service Award, 1968.

WRITINGS: (Editor and contributor) *Economic Problems of War*, Wiley, 1942; (editor and contributor) *Economics of National Defense*, Indiana University Press, 1942; (with David Novick) *Wartime Industrial Statistics*, University of Illinois Press, 1950; *Government's Role in Economic Life*, McGraw, 1953; *National Defense and Southern California*, Southern California Associates of Committee for Economic Development, 1961; (editor and contributor) *Managerial Long-Range Planning*, McGraw, 1963; (with Warren Cannon) *Multinational Corporate Planning*, Macmillan, 1966; (with William G. Ryan) *Industrial Project Management*, Macmillan, 1968; *Top Management Planning*, Macmillan, 1969; *Business and Society*, Random House, 1971, revised edition, 1974; *Instructor's Manual for Business and Society*, Random House, 1971; *Issues in Business and Society*, Random House, 1972; *Cases in Business and Society*, Random House, 1974. Also author of pamphlets. Contributor of numerous articles to *California Management Review, Business Horizons, Industry Week, Journal of Business Policy, Harvard Business Review*, and other professional periodicals.

Editor, *Indiana Business Review*, 1937-42; Managing editor, *California Management Review*, 1958-60. Member of editorial board, *California Management Review*, 1958-72; *Long Range Planning*, 1969—; *Journal of the Academy of Management*, 1970—. Editorial advisor, *Harvard Business Review*, 1971.

SIDELIGHTS: Some of Mr. Steiner's books have been translated into German, Finnish, and Japanese.

* * *

STEPHENS, J(ohn) M(ortimer) 1901-

PERSONAL: Born November 16, 1901, in Reston, Manitoba, Canada; son of John Mortimer and Rosa (McGregor) Stephens; married Olive McNeil, July 14, 1926; children: Dorothy G. (Mrs. H. M. Chase; deceased), F. Doreen (Mrs. Robert McElroy). *Education:* University of Manitoba, B.A., 1925; University of Toronto, graduate study, 1927-28; Columbia University, Ph.D., 1932. *Address:* P.O. Box 70, Shawnigan Lake, British Columbia, VOR 2WO, Canada.

CAREER: Johns Hopkins University, Baltimore, Md., assistant professor, 1930-37; associate professor, 1937-46; professor of education and psychology, 1946-65; professor emeritus, 1965—. Visiting professor, University of California, Berkeley, 1962-64, University of British Columbia, 1965-67; summer visiting professor at University of Saskatchewan, 1931, University of British Columbia, 1951, University of Southern California, 1953, University of California, Berkeley, 1956. *Military service:* U.S. Army Air Forces, 1943-45; became captain. *Member:* American Psychological Association.

WRITINGS: The Influence of Different Stimuli Upon Preceding Bonds, Teachers College, Columbia University, Bureau of Publications, 1932; *The Influence of the School on the Individual*, Edwards, 1933; *Educational Psychology*, Holt, 1951, revised edition, 1956; *The Psychology of Classroom Learning*, Holt, 1965; *The Process of Schooling*, Holt, 1967; (with E. D. Evans) *Development and Classroom Learning*, Holt, 1973.

* * *

STERNE, Richard S(tephen) 1921-

PERSONAL: Born May 9, 1921, in Philadelphia, Pa.; son of Leon T. and Elizabeth G. Sterne; married Mary L. Stowe (a social worker), May 30, 1948; children: Christopher S., Mary Elizabeth, John Stephen. *Education:* Swarthmore College, B.A. (with honors), 1942; Duke University, M.A., 1947; University of Pennsylvania, Ph.D., 1962. *Politics:* Democrat. *Religion:* Society of Friends. *Home:* 4062 Grenwich Road, Norton, Ohio 44203. *Office:* Department of Urban Studies, University of Akron, Akron, Ohio 44325.

CAREER: Instructor in sociology at Tufts College (now University), Medford, Mass., 1948-49, Northeastern University, Boston, Mass., 1949-50; Rhode Island Community Chests, Inc., Providence, R.I., budget director, 1951-55; Delaware Valley United Fund, Trenton, N.J., research and budget director, 1955-60; Social Service Council of Greater Trenton, Trenton, N.J., research director, 1960-62; University of Miami, Coral Gables, Fla., associate professor of sociology, 1962-68; Council of Social Agencies and Citizens Planning Council, Rochester, N.Y., director of research, 1968-73; University of Akron, Akron, Ohio, associate professor of urban studies and sociology, 1973—. Welfare Planning Council of Dade County, Miami, Fla., director of research, 1962-68. Research consultant to Massachusetts Committee for the Mid-Century White House Conference on Children and Youth, 1950. *Member:* National Association of Social Workers, American Sociological Association, Gerontological Society, Eastern Sociological Association, Pi Gamma Mu. *Awards, honors:* National Institute of Mental Health research grant, 1965.

WRITINGS: Delinquent Conduct and Broken Homes, College and University, 1964; (with James E. Phillips and Alvin Rabushka) *The Urban Elderly Poor*, Heath, 1974. Writer of professional monographs and research reports. Contributor to proceeding of learned organizations and to *Social Work, Urban Affairs Quarterly, Quaker Life, Sociology and Social Research*, and other periodicals.

WORK IN PROGRESS: Writing and research in the field of gerontology, criminology, and an analysis of the future of racial violence in the United States.

STEURT, Marjorie Rankin 1888-

PERSONAL: Born October 8, 1888, in Pennsylvania; daughter of a Presbyterian minister; married Roy Steurt. Education: Mount Holyoke College, graduate, 1911; Columbia University, M.A., 1928, Ph.D., 1929; studied engineering during World War II. Home address: P.O. Box 72, Hemet, Calif.

CAREER: Teacher in Negro school in Alabama, 1911-12; went to China in 1912, and remained as teacher and principal of mission high school, supervisor of forty country schools, and acting head of English department at Cheloo University, during period 1912-25; caught in communist uprising in 1925 after Nanking Massacre and escaped on last train out to the coast; after further study in America returned to China in 1929 as director of experimental education at Nankai University, Tientsin, and teacher of education methods at Normal College of Tientsin; driven out again by Japanese take-over in 1932, came back to United States and worked (during depression) as dog walker and operator of gas station, among other things, then became head of psychology department of Monmouth Junior College, West Long Branch, N.J., and later, school psychologist for Hawthorne (N.J) public schools; during World War II ran experimental engines in airplane factory; former teacher of creative writing in adult education program. Public lecturer.

MEMBER: American Association of University Women (president, 1958-60), National League of American Penwomen (vice-president, 1962-65), Phi Beta Kappa, National Writers Club, Sierra Club.

WRITINGS: The Kingdom of Mimus, Golden Gate Junior Books, 1964; (author of text) Bernie Crampton, Rocky and Sandy (juvenile book of photographs), Ritchie, 1967; Broken Bits of China, Nelson, 1973.

WORK IN PROGRESS: The End of the Rainbow; Through Paper Windows; and seven adventure books for children—The Centipede Seal, Hell's Gate, Desert Magic, Shadow of a War Lord, White Water, Oh-Hannah-By-Gosh, and Behind the Ranges.

SIDELIGHTS: Mrs. Steurt has traveled extensively throughout the world. Her trips have taken her to Antartica, Galapagos Islands, India, Sikim, Nepal, New Guinea, South Sea Islands, Philippines, Africa, Columbia, Argentina, New Zealand, Chile, Peru, Iceland, Baffin Island, North Pole, besides most of Europe. Her China papers have been filed in the library of the Claremont Colleges in California. Avocational interests: Running river rapids, camping, desert wood arrangements, travel (has crisscrossed the United States, Mexico, and Canada in a trailer).

*   *   *

STEVENS, Martin 1927-

PERSONAL: Surname originally Steinberg; born January 11, 1927, in Hamburg, Germany; son of Hans Siegfried (a manufacturer) and Hertha (Stern-Geiger) Steinberg; married Anne N. McGregor, December 27, 1947; children: Cynthia Jean, Mark Dane, David Paul. Education: Western Reserve University (now Case Western Reserve University), B.A., 1949, M.A., 1950; Michigan State University, Ph.D., 1956. Politics: Democrat. Home: 769 Kettering Dr., Columbus, Ohio.

CAREER: Michigan State University, East Lansing, instructor in communication skills, 1950-56; University of Louisville, Louisville, Ky., assistant professor, 1956-61, associate professor of English, 1961-64; Ohio State University, Columbus, associate professor of English, 1964—. Louisville Mayor's Advisory Committee, member, 1963. Military service: U.S. Navy, 1944-45; received two battle stars. Member: Modern Language Association of America, National Council of Teachers of English, American Association of University Professors, American Civil Liberties Union, Phi Beta Kappa, Phi Eta Sigma, Phi Kappa Phi.

WRITINGS: (With Charles H. Kegel) Communication: Principles and Practice, Wadsworth, 1959; (with Kegel) A Glossary for College English, McGraw, 1966; (editor with Jerome Mandel) Old English Literature: Twenty-two Analytical Essays, University of Nebraska Press, 1968; (compiler with John Lewis Bradly) Masterworks of English Prose, Holt, 1968. Contributor of articles to literary and philological periodicals.

WORK IN PROGRESS: Co-editing a new edition of Towneley Cycle, for Early English Text Society.

SIDELIGHTS: Stevens is fluent in German, and has some proficiency in Italian, Spanish, and French.†

*   *   *

STEVENSON, Janet 1913-

PERSONAL: Born February 4, 1913, in Chicago, Ill.; daughter of John C. (an investment banker) and Atlantis (McClendon) Marshall; married second husband, Benson Rotstein (an educator), 1964; children: (previous marriage) Joseph Stevenson, Edward Stevenson. Education: Bryn Mawr College, B.A. (magna cum laude), 1933; Yale University, M.F.A., 1937. Religion: Unitarian Universalist. Address: Route #1, Astoria, Oregon.

CAREER: University of Southern California, Los Angeles, lecturer in drama, 1951-53; Grambling College, Grambling, La., assistant professor of English, 1966-67; Portland State University, Portland, Oregon, lecturer, 1968. Member: Authors League, P.E.N. Awards, honors: Friends of American Writers awards for Weep No More and The Ardent Years; National Arts of the Theatre Award for "Weep No More," dramatic version of book; John Golden fellowship in playwriting.

WRITINGS: Weep No More, Viking, 1957; The Ardent Years, Viking, 1960; Painting America's Wildlife (biography of John James Audubon), Encyclopaedia Britannica, 1961; Singing for the World (biography of Marian Anderson), Encyclopaedia Britannica, 1963; Sisters and Brothers, Crown, 1966; Pioneers in Freedom, Reilly & Lee, 1967; Soldiers in the Civil Rights War, Reilly & Lee, 1968; Archibald Grimke, Crowell-Collier, 1968; Woman Aboard, Crown, 1969; First Book of American Women, F. Watts, 1972; The Montgomery Bus Boycott, F. Watts, 1972; The School Segregation Cases, F. Watts, 1973. Author of plays, "Declaration" and "Counter-attack," in collaboration with Philip Stevenson, and "Weep No More." Also author of motion picture scripts, short stories, and reading texts.

WORK IN PROGRESS: A novel with 1850 maritime background concerning a woman navigator, Right Ascension; a biography of Robert W. Kenny of California; an autobiographical account of a year spent on the faculty of a southern black university, Do Not Forgive Them; a biography of Denmark Vesey; a libretto for an opera, Lysistrata, in collaboration with composer Henry Leland Clarke.

SIDELIGHTS: Janet Stevenson told CA: "I have 'graduated' to the writing of historical novels and biographies from a foundation in the theater, for which I still have so strong a yearning that I would turn back to dramatic forms in a moment, if I could earn my living at that sort of writing. . . ."

* * *

STEVENSON, William 1925-
(Chen Hwei)

PERSONAL: Born June 1, 1925, in London, England; son of William (a master mariner) and Alida (Delaporte) Stevenson; married Glenys (an aviation draftswoman), July 28, 1948; children: Andrew, Jacqueline, Kevin, Sally. Education: Ruskin College, Oxford, B.A., 1948. Religion: Buddhist. Home: 5 Palace Gardens Ter., Kensington, London, England. Agent: Willis Kingsley Wing, 24 East 38th St., New York, N.Y. 10016. Office: Independent Television News, Television House, Kingsway, London, England.

CAREER: Foreign correspondent for Sunday Times, London, England, for Toronto Star, Toronto, Ontario, Canada, and for Canadian Broadcasting Corp., 1950-64, with headquarters in Peking, China, 1955-56, Hong Kong, 1956-61, New Delhi, India, 1961-63, Kenya, 1963-64; Independent Television News, London, England, editor, 1964—. War correspondent in Korea, Indochina, and Malaya, with other assignments in Moscow, Cairo, Tokyo, Warsaw, and Kabul, 1950-63. Five Continents Film Corp., Toronto, Ontario, Canada, director; filmer and producer of documentaries (including a three-part series on China) for National Broadcasting Co. American & Commonwealth Research and Development Corp. (ACRAND), aviation adviser. Pan-Africa Research Institute, president, 1963. Military service: Royal Navy Air Service, carrier fighter pilot, 1942-46; became lieutenant commander.

MEMBER: Aviation Writers Association, English-Speaking Union, London Press Club, Foreign Correspondents Club (Tokyo and Hong Kong), Indian Press Club (New Delhi), Underwater Explorers Club (Paris), Bindles of Mayfair.

WRITINGS: Saka the Seagull, Brockhampton Press, 1947; The Yellow Wind—Red China Explored, Houghton, 1957; After Nehru—What?, Toronto Globe Publishing, 1961; The World's Most Rugged Frontier, Toronto Globe Publishing, 1962; Birds' Nests in Their Beards, Houghton, 1964; The Bushbabies, Houghton, 1965; Strike Zion!, Bantam, 1967; Zanek!: A Chronicle of the Israeli Air Force, Viking, 1971; The Bormann Brotherhood, Harcourt, 1971. Editor, Wildlife in Africa.

WORK IN PROGRESS: The Arm'd Rhinoceros; Flutes of Zanzibar; The Snake Shop on Ice-House Street.

SIDELIGHTS: Peripatetic Stevenson recalls once trying to explain to Russian sailors on a Soviet line from Odessa to Yalta how he could be an Englishman, with a Canadian passport, working (on an assignment) for an American magazine, a resident of Hong Kong, and recently expelled from Egypt. The permanent interests that he has picked up poking into most corners of the globe include oceanography, marine biology and the "art of simplifying life in a complicated society." His novel The Bushbabies was filmed under the title "The Bushbaby," in 1970.†

STEWART, W(illiam) A(lexander) Campbell 1915-

PERSONAL: Born December 17, 1915, in Glasgow, Scotland; son of Thomas (a scientist) and Helen (Fraser) Stewart; married Ella Elizabeth Burnett, September 27, 1947; children: Lindsey Fraser (daughter), Ian Burnett Campbell. Education: University College, London, B.A., 1937; Institute of Education, London, diploma, 1938, M.A., 1941, Ph.D., 1947. Home: The Clock House, The University, Keele, Staffordshire, England. Office: The University, Keele, Staffordshire, England.

CAREER: Friends' School, Saffron Walden, Essex, England, senior English master, 1938-43; Abbotsholme School, Derbyshire, England, senior English master, 1943-44; University of Nottingham, Nottingham, England, assistant lecturer in education, 1944-47; University of Wales, Cardiff, lecturer in education, 1947-50; University of Keele, Keele, England, professor of education, 1950-67, vice-chancellor, 1967—, director of Institute of Education. Visiting professor at McGill University, 1957, University of California, Los Angeles, 1959. Simon Visiting Professor, University of Manchester, 1962-63. Chairman of national education committee, Young Mens Christian Association; Deputy-Lieutenant, County of Stafford, 1973. Member: British Psychological Society, British Association, Association of Teachers in Colleges and Departments of Education, Conference of Institute Directors (chairman). Awards, honors: D.Litt., University of Ulster, 1973.

WRITINGS: Quakers and Education, Epworth, 1953; (editor with J. S. Eroes) Karl Mannheim, Systematic Sociology, Routledge & Kegan Paul, 1959; (with Mannheim) Introduction to the Sociology of Education, Routledge & Kegan Paul, 1962; (contributor) The American College, Wiley, 1962; The Educational Innovators, Volumes I and II, Macmillan, 1968; Progressives and Radicals in English Education: 1750-70, Kelly's Directories, 1972. Contributor of articles to professional journals.

* * *

STINCHCOMBE, Arthur L. 1933-

PERSONAL: Born May 16, 1933, in Clare County, Mich.; son of Frank Homer (a high school counselor) and Christina (Stratton) Stinchcombe; married Barbara E. Bifoss, July 1, 1953; children: Maxwell Benjamin, Amy Lenore, Adam Michael. Education: Central Michigan University, A.B., 1953; University of California, Berkeley, Ph.D., 1960. Politics: Socialist. Office: Johns Hopkins University, Baltimore, Md.

CAREER: Johns Hopkins University, Baltimore, Md., assistant professor, 1959-65, associate professor of social relations, 1965—. Harvard University-Massachusetts Institute of Technology Joint Center for Urban Studies, member, did research in Venezuela and elsewhere, 1964-65. Military service: U.S. Army, Medical Corps, 1953-55. Member: American Sociological Association, American Civil Liberties Union.

WRITINGS: Rebellion in a High School, Quadrangle, 1965; Constructing Social Theories, Harcourt, 1968. Contributor to anthologies and professional journals.

WORK IN PROGRESS: Research on Latin-American steel bureaucracies, on local variations in civil rights movement, and on social embedding of American industries.†

* * *

STOBART, Thomas Ralph 1914-

PERSONAL: Born March 10, 1914, in Darlington, England; son of Ralph Forester (a scientist) and Aileen A. (Bowden) Stobart; married Jayne Garrod (an artist), May 3, 1956; children: Patrick Thomas, Gina Anne, Nicola Jayne. *Education:* University of Sheffield, B.Sc. (honors), 1936; Cambridge University, graduate study, 1936-37. *Politics:* "Cynical" Liberal. *Religion:* Agnostic. *Home:* 38 Via Pasteur, Bordighera, Italy. *Agent:* David Higham Associates Ltd., 76 Dean St., London W. 1, England. *Office:* T. S. Productions, Allgemeines Treuunternehmen, Vaduz, Liechtenstein.

CAREER: Dartington Hall Film Unit, Totnes, Devonshire, England, producer-director, 1947-49; free-lance film director and photographer, specializing in expeditions and in travel subjects for industrial films, 1949—. Member of Nun Kun Expedition, 1946, Norwegian-British-Swedish Antarctic Expedition, 1949-50, Armand Denis Central African and Northern Australian Expedition, 1951-52, British Mount Everest Expedition, 1953, *Daily Mail* "Abominable Snowman" Expedition, 1954, Pittard Ethiopian Expedition, 1957, other expeditions, 1960-64. *Military service:* Indian Army; became major. *Member:* Royal Geographical Society (fellow), Royal Photographic Society (honorary). *Awards, honors:* Officer, Order of the British Empire; Sykes Medal of Royal Central Asian Society; awards at international film festivals in Rome, Rouen, Berlin, Budapest, Turin, and other cities, and from British Film Academy.

WRITINGS: I Take Pictures for Adventure, Doubleday, 1957; *Herbs, Spices, and Flavorings*, International Publications Service, 1972. Author of screenplay, "Hazard." Adventure films include "Conquest of Everest," "The White Continent," "Adventure On," and many others.

WORK IN PROGRESS: Caviare in Bad Company, an adventure story; "North Wall," a film story.†

* * *

STOBBS, John L(ouis) N(ewcombe) 1921-

PERSONAL: Born August 4, 1921, in Potters Bar, Hertfordshire, England; son of John Louis (a bank manager) and May (Newcombe) Stobbs; married Anne M. B. Miller, April 5, 1950; children: Louisa, Amanda, Frances. *Education:* Pembroke College, Oxford, 1939-41, 1946-48, M.A. *Politics:* Liberal party. *Religion:* Church of England-Humanist. *Home and office:* Cherry Bounce, The Hamlet, Porten End, Berkhamsted, Hertfordshire, England.

CAREER: Picture Post, London, England, general staff writer, 1950-57; *Observer*, London, England, golf correspondent, 1956-60. Occasional professional photographer. Berkhamsted Liberal Association, committee member, 1953—, chairman, 1963-64; Berkhamsted Citizens Association, committee member, 1956-62. *Military service:* British Army, Royal Artillery, 1941-46; served in Gibralter and Italy; became captain. *Member:* Society of Authors, Association of Golf Writers, Soil Association, Association of Liberal Trade Unionists, Chiltern Society, Oxford Union Society (treasurer, 1948), Oxford Society, Oxford and Cambridge Golfing Society, Old Berkstedlands Golfing Society, Berkhamsted Golf Club.

WRITINGS: (Editor) *The World of Scouts*, Hulton Press, 1956; *Tackle Golf This Way*, S. Paul, 1961, revised edition, 1974, published as *The Anatomy of Golf*, Emerson, 1962; (with John Jacobs) *Golf*, S. Paul, 1963; *An A.B.C. of Golf*, S. Paul, 1964; *At Random Through the Green* (anthology), Pelham, 1966; (with Alistar Cochran) *The Search for the Perfect Swing*, Heinemann, 1967, Lippincott, 1968. Con-

tributor to *Golf World* (Brighton), and to other golf magazines, as well as to London daily newspapers and other publications. Editor, *Golfing* (London), 1957-60.

WORK IN PROGRESS: A book on political economics; a farce.

SIDELIGHTS: Stobbs was member of Oxford University golf team, 1948, Hertfordshire's team, 1948-62; student of golf courses and course architecture, and currently more interested in the technicalities and development of the game. *Avocational interests:* Everything to do with the countryside and country life, particularly in and around the Chiltern Hills; forestry, compost gardening, Hertfordshire pubs and beer, and town and country planning.

* * *

STOCKARD, James Wright, Jr. 1935-
(Jimmy Stockard)

PERSONAL: Born November 2, 1935, in Shreveport, La.; son of James Wright and Hazel (Alexander) Stockard; married Peggy Anne Murphey, January 25, 1958; children: Sandra Renee, Jennifer Leah, James Wright III. *Education:* Northwestern State College of Louisiana (now Northwestern State University of Louisiana), B.A., 1960, M.Ed., 1963; Louisiana State University, Ph.D., 1970. *Religion:* Baptist. *Home:* 2916 Independence Ave., Shreveport, La. *Office:* Caddo Parish School Board, Shreveport, La.

CAREER: Shreveport (La.) public schools, sixth grade teacher, 1960-64; Louisiana State Department of Education, Baton Rouge, state supervisor of elementary education, 1964-65; Shreveport (La.) public schools, supervisor of instructional materials, 1965—. Region I Science Fair, director, 1962-64. *Military service:* U.S. Army, paratrooper serving with Inter-American Geodetic Survey, mapping Central and South America, 1954-57. *Member:* International Reading Association, National Education Association, Association for Childhood Education, Association for Supervision and Curriculum Development, Louisiana Teachers Association, Louisiana School Supervisors Association.

WRITINGS: The New Math, Educational Research, 1963; *Experiments for Young Scientists*, Little, Brown, 1964; *Reading Exercises for Adults*, Educational Research, 1968; *Building Reading Skills in the Content Areas*, Webster's, 1970; *Individual Corrective Reading*, Educational Research, 1971. Also author of instructional tapes: *Story of Afro-American History*, Benefic Press, 1970; *Stories of the U.S. Presidents and Their Wives*, Rand-McNally, 1971; *Career Education Series*, Educational Research, 1973; *The Being Together Series*, Lerner Publications, 1973; *Individual Corrective Spelling*, Educational Research, 1973. Also author of filmstrip and recording, *Exploring Louisiana*, Educational Research, 1967. Contributor of articles on education to journals and periodicals. Columnist for *Louisiana Schools*, 1967-68; editor, *Caddo Teacher*, 1963-64.

SIDELIGHTS: James Stockard speaks Spanish. *Avocational interests:* College and professional football, bass fishing, and sport parachuting.

* * *

STOCKHAMMER, Morris 1904-

PERSONAL: Born June 5, 1904, in Austria; came to United States in 1939; son of Marcus (a jeweler) and Elsie (Seligmann) Stockhammer; married Frieda Rindner, June 19, 1932; children: Mona (Mrs. Elliott Drooker). *Educa-*

tion: University of Vienna, Dr. rer. pol., 1927; other study in Vienna and New York. *Politics:* "Free Enterprise System." *Religion:* Mosaic. *Home:* 1973 70th St., Brooklyn, N.Y.

CAREER: Rindner Baumaterialien, Vienna, Austria, executive, 1932-39; Estes Realty Co., New York, N.Y., president, 1952-58.

WRITINGS: Kants Zurechnungsidee und Freiheitsantinomie, Koelner Universitaets-Verlag (Cologne), 1961; *Platons Weltanschauung*, Koelner Universitaets-Verlag, 1962; *Das Buch Hiob: Versuch einer Theodizee*, Europaeischer Verlag (Vienna), 1963; (editor) *Plato Dictionary*, Philosophical Library, 1963; *Kant Essays*, Koelner Universitaets-Verlag, 1964; (editor) *Thomas Aquinas Dictionary*, Philosophical Library, 1965; (editor) *Karl Marx Dictionary*, Philosophical Library, 1965; (editor) *Kant Dictionary*, Philosophical Library, 1972. Regular contributor to *Philosophischer Literaturanzeiger* (journal published in Munich), 1957-65; also contributor of more than thirty essays in various languages to other journals.

WORK IN PROGRESS: Karl Marx: Capital, for Philosophical Library; *Popularwoerterbuch der Philosophie*; *Literarische Studien*.

SIDELIGHTS: Stockhammer knows German, Polish, Ukrainian, French, Latin, Czech, Slovak, Esperanto, Hebrew. *Avocational interests:* Chess, travel, music, poetry.†

*   *   *

STOCKS, Mary Danvers (Brinton)   1891-

PERSONAL: Born July 25, 1891, in London, England; daughter of Roland Danvers (a medical doctor) and Constance (Rendel) Brinton; married John Leofric Stocks, December, 1913 (died, 1936); children: Ann Stocks Patterson, John, Helen. *Education:* London School of Economics and Political Science, London, B.Sc., 1913. *Politics:* Labour. *Religion:* Church of England. *Home:* Aubrey Lodge, Aubrey Rd., London W.8, England.

CAREER: London School of Economics and Political Science, University of London, London, England, assistant lecturer, 1916-19; King's College for Women, London, lecturer in economics, 1918-19; University of Manchester, Manchester, England, extension lecturer and extramural tutor, 1924-37; London Council of Social Service, London, England, general secretary, 1938-39; Westfield College, University of London, London, England, principal, 1939-51. Justice of the peace, Manchester City, 1930-36. *Member:* Royal Society of Literature (fellow), Royal Society of Arts (fellow), Society of Authors, International P.E.N. *Awards, honors:* LL.D., from University of Manchester and University of Leeds; Lit.D. from University of Liverpool; created Baroness (life peeress), 1966.

WRITINGS: The Industrial State, Collins, 1921; *Hail Nero* (play), Sidgwick & Jackson, 1933; *Fifty Years in Every Street*, The Manchester University Press, 1945; *Eleanor Rathbone* (biography), Gollancz, 1949; *History of the Workers' Educational Association*, Allen & Unwin, 1953; *A Hundred Years of District Nursing*, Allen & Unwin, 1960; *Ernest Simon of Manchester* (biography), Manchester University Press, 1963; *Unread Best-Seller: Reflections on the Old Testament*, British Broadcasting Corporation, 1967; *Where is Liberty?*, Epworth, 1968; *My Commonplace Book* (autobiography), Davies, 1970.

Other plays: "Everyman of Every Street"; "King Herod"; "Dr. Scholefield." Writer of radio scripts and articles.

AVOCATIONAL INTERESTS: Crossword puzzles, reading, attending sessions of the House of Lords.†

*   *   *

STOCKTON, John R(obert)   1903-

PERSONAL: Born October 19, 1903, in Leon, Iowa; son of John Collins and Isabel (McCready) Stockton; married Beulah Vaughn, December 24, 1928; children: Joanne Beatrice (deceased), John Robert, Jr., Eileen Doris (Mrs. L. A. Hearn, Jr.). *Education:* Maryville College, Maryville, Tenn., A.B., 1925; University of Iowa, M.A., 1927, Ph.D., 1932. *Politics:* Democrat. *Religion:* Presbyterian. *Home:* 1010 Gaston Ave., Austin, Tex. 78703. *Office:* Business-Economics Bldg., University of Texas, Austin, Tex. 78712.

CAREER: Coe College, Cedar Rapids, Iowa, instructor in accounting, 1927-29; Drake University, Des Moines, Iowa, assistant professor of accounting, 1929-32; Meredith Publishing Co., Des Moines, Iowa, statistician, 1932-35; University of Texas, Austin, assistant professor, 1935-37, associate professor, 1937-39, professor of business statistics, 1939—, director of Bureau of Business Research, 1950-69. Member of board of directors, Federal Reserve Bank of Dallas, San Antonio branch; member of Texas Committee on State and Local Tax Policy, 1957-64. *Military service:* U.S. Army, Ordnance, 1942-46; became lieutenant colonel. *Member:* American Statistical Association (member of council, 1951-55, 1963-64; honorary fellow), American Economic Association, American Marketing Association, American Association of University Professors, Western Council for Travel Research (president), Phi Kappa Phi, Beta Gamma Sigma. *Awards, honors:* LL.D. from Maryville College, 1956; D.Litt. from Texas Christian University, 1971.

WRITINGS: An Introduction to Business Statistics, Heath, 1938, revised edition, 1947; (with Richard C. Henshaw and Richard W. Graves) *Economics of Natural Gas in Texas*, Bureau of Business Research, University of Texas, 1952; *Chart Book of Texas Business*, Bureau of Business Research, University of Texas, 1952; (with S. A. Arbingast) *Water Requirements Survey: Texas High Plains*, Bureau of Business Research, University of Texas, 1952; (with others) *Water Requirements Survey: Red River Basin*, Texas, Bureau of Business Research, University of Texas, 1953; (with others) *Economic Survey of Denton County, Texas*, Bureau of Business Research, University of Texas, 1953, revised edition, by Sylva M. Bowlby, 1957; (with others) *Economic Survey of Killeen, Texas*, Bureau of Business Research, University of Texas, 1954; *Business Statistics*, South-Western Publishing, 1958, 4th edition published as *Introduction to Business and Economic Statistics*, 1971; (with others) *Water for the Future*, Bureau of Business Research, University of Texas, 1959. Editor, *Texas Business Review*, 1949-62.

*   *   *

STOESSINGER, John G.   1927-

PERSONAL: Born October 14, 1927, in Austria; came to United States in 1947; son of Oscar and Irene Stoessinger. *Education:* Grinnell College, B.A., 1950; Harvard University, M.A., 1952, Ph.D., 1954. *Home:* 275 Central Park West, New York, N.Y. 10024. *Office:* Hunter College, New York, N.Y.

CAREER: Wellesley College, Wellesley, Mass., instructor, 1955-56; Massachusetts Institute of Technology, Cambridge, instructor, 1956-57; Hunter College, New York,

N.Y., assistant professor, 1957-60, associate professor, 1960-63, professor of political science, 1964—. Columbia University, New York, N.Y., visiting associate professor of international relations, 1964-67; United Nations, New York, N.Y., acting director of Political Affairs Division, 1967—. Director of Peace Corps Training Program in World Affairs and American Institutions, 1963-64. Conductor of radio and television courses on international affairs, including one network series; public lecturer on world events. *Awards, honors:* Bancroft Prize of Columbia University ($4,000) for *The Might of Nations: World Politics in Our Time,* as the best book on international relations published in 1962.

WRITINGS: The Refugee and the World Community, University of Minnesota Press, 1956; *The Might of Nations: World Politics in Our Time,* Random House, 1962; (with others) *Financing the United Nations System,* Brookings, 1964; (editor with A. F. Westin) *Power and Order,* Harcourt, 1964; *The United Nations and the Superpowers,* Random House, 1965; *Nations in Darkness: China, Russia, America,* Random House, 1971; *Why Nations Go to War,* St. Martin's, 1974.

SIDELIGHTS: Stoessinger left Nazi-occupied Austria at the age of eleven for refuge in Czechoslovakia, fled that country via Siberia to China in 1941, and made his third bid for Freedom (from Chinese Communists this time) in 1947. During his years in Shanghai, Stoessinger worked with the International Refugee Organization.

* * *

STOKES, Adrian Durham 1902-

PERSONAL: Born October 27, 1902, in London, England; married Ann Mellis, 1947; children: Tetter, Philip, Ariadne. *Education:* Magdalen College, Oxford, B.A. *Home:* 20 Church Row, London NW3, England.

CAREER: Author. Tate Gallery, trustee, 1960-67.

WRITINGS: The Thread of Ariadne, Kegan Paul, 1925; *Sunrise in the West,* Kegan Paul, 1926; *The Quattro Cento,* Faber, 1932; *Stones of Rimini,* Faber, 1934, Schocken, 1969; *Tonight the Ballet,* Faber, 1934; *Russian Ballets,* Faber, 1935; *Colour and form,* Faber, 1937; *Venice: An Aspect of Art,* Faber, 1945; *Cezanne,* Faber, 1946; *Inside Out,* Faber, 1947; *Art and Science,* Faber, 1949; *Smooth and Rough,* Faber, 1951; *Michelangelo: A Study in the Nature of Art,* Tavistock Publications, 1955; *Practical Landscape Painting,* Seeley Service, 1956; *Raphael,* Faber, 1956; *Greek Culture and the Ego,* Tavistock Publications, 1958; *Monet,* Faber, 1958; *Three Essays on The Painting of Our Time,* Tavistock Publications, 1961; *Painting and the Inner World,* Tavistock Publications, 1963; *The Invitation in Art,* Tavistock Publications, 1965, Chilmark, 1966; *Reflections on the Nude,* Tavistock Publications, 1967; *The Image in Form: Selected Writings of Adrian Stokes,* Harper, 1972.†

* * *

STOLL, Dennis G(ray) 1912-
(Denys Craig)

PERSONAL: Born May 25, 1912, in London, England; son of Sir Oswald (a theater impresario) and Millicent (Shaw) Stoll; married Patricia Ward Healey, January, 1950. *Education:* Christ's College, Cambridge, B.A., 1934, M.A., 1938. *Religion:* Christian. *Home:* 9 Heath Mansions, Putney Heath Lane, London S.W. 15, England.

CAREER: Composer, and writer on music. Onetime conductor of Ballets de Monte Carlo, and deputy conductor to Sir Thomas Beecham. Lecturer on Oriental music for Royal India and Pakistan Society. Sir Oswald Stoll Foundation, London, England, life member, member of governing council, 1946—; International Cultural Exchange, London, England, music and dance director, 1964. *Member:* English-Speaking Union Composers' Guild (London), Cambridge Union (life member), P.E.N.

WRITINGS: Music Festivals of Europe, John Miles, 1938; *Comedy in Chains,* Gollancz, 1944; *The Dove Found no Rest,* Gollancz, 1946, Doubleday, 1947; *The Doctor and the Dragon,* Doubleday, 1947; *Memory Is the Scar,* Gollancz, 1949; (under pseudonym Denys Craig) *Man in Ebony,* Gollancz, 1950; *Feed Him with Apricocks,* Muller, 1957; *Music Festivals of the World,* Macmillan, 1963. Writer of radio scripts for documentaries and talks. Critic, *Music Journal* (New York), contributor of articles on Oriental music to other music journals. Composer of "Persian Suite," 1958, and "Homage to Hafiz," 1959, both commissioned by British Broadcasting Corp., and "First String Quartet," performed by Tatrai Quartet, 1962.

WORK IN PROGRESS: An opera, "Napoleon in Egypt," in Arabic scales.†

* * *

STOLTZFUS, Ben F(rank) 1927-

PERSONAL: Born September 15, 1927, in Sofia, Bulgaria; son of B. Frank (a teacher) and Esther (Johnson) Stoltzfus; married Elizabeth R. Burton, August 20, 1955; children: Jan, Celia, Andrew. *Education:* Amherst College, B.A., 1949; Middlebury College, M.A., 1954; graduate study in Paris, France, as Fulbright scholar, 1955-56; University of Wisconsin, Ph.D., 1959. *Politics:* Democrat, "left wing liberal." *Religion:* Agnostic. *Home:* 5128 Queen St., Riverside, Calif. *Agent:* Harold Matson Co., Inc., 22 East 40th St., New York, N.Y. 10016. *Office:* Department of French and Italian, University of California, Riverside, Calif. 92502.

CAREER: Loomis Institute, Windsor, Conn., instructor in French, 1951-53; Choate School, Wallingford, Conn., instructor in French, 1954-55; Smith College, Northampton, Mass., instructor in French literature, 1958-60; University of California, Riverside, professor of French literature, 1960—, vice-chairman, division of humanities, 1962-63, chairman, interdisciplinary studies in the Humanities, 1972-75. *Member:* Association des Amis d'Andre Gide, Modern Language Association of America. *Awards, honors:* Fulbright research grant to Paris, 1963-64.

WRITINGS: Alain Robbe-Grillet and the New French Novel, Southern Illinois University Press, 1964; *Georges Chenneviere et l'unanimisme,* Michel Minard, Les Lettres Modernes, 1965; *The Eye of the Needle,* Viking, 1967; *Gide's Eagles,* Southern Illinois University Press, 1969; (contributor) Allen Belkind, editor, *The Critics and the Writer's Intention,* Southern Illinois University Press, 1971; *Black Lazarus,* Winter House, 1972; (contributor) Claude Martin, editor, *Andre Gide et la fonction de la Litterature,* Michel Minard, 1972; (contributor) Michel Esteve, editor, *Etudes Cinematographiques,* Michel Minard, 1974. Contributor of articles, mostly on modern and contemporary French literature, and of several poems to literary periodicals.

WORK IN PROGRESS: A monograph on Hemingway's *Old Man and the Sea,* a novel, *Valley of Roses,* and a book of criticism on death in modern literature.

SIDELIGHTS: In a statement about his book, *Black Lazarus*, Stoltzfus wrote, "Novel-writing is not so much a question of ideas as it is of language. Language has little to do with a writer's sex, or the color of his skin, and perhaps even less with his experience.... The issue is not ... whether a white man can or should write about the black experience, but that a white man should want to.... The order and harmony of a work of art are a way out from chaos—a solution to the tensions that divide men." Stoltzfus spent one year as an American citizen in German occupied Bulgaria. He has traveled extensively in Europe, the Balkans, and the Near East. *Avocational interests:* Skiing, tennis, scuba diving, and spear fishing.

*   *   *

STONE, Brian 1919-

PERSONAL: Born December 20, 1919, in Birmingham, England; son of Theodore Henry (a broker) and Emily Ida (Sellers) Stone; married Yvette Valensky, December 21, 1945; children: Robin, Jeremy, Merlin, Oren, Miriam. *Education:* Borough Road College, Teacher's Certificate, 1948; University of London, B.A. (honors), 1951, M.A. (honors), 1954. *Home:* 36 Harrington Rd., Brighton BN1 6RF, England.

CAREER: Shell Co., employee, 1937-39, 1943-45; teacher of English at grammar schools in Brighton and Middlesex, England, 1949-59; Loughborough Training College, Loughborough, England, senior lecturer in English, 1959-63; Brighton College of Education, Brighton, England, principal lecturer in English, 1963-69, head of department, 1965-69; Open University, Milton Keynes, England, reader in literature, 1969—. Lecturer in British Council courses for foreign teachers, 1960-64. Free-lance journalist for Israeli newspapers, especially *Jerusalem Post*, 1946-54. *Military service:* British Army, Royal Tank Regiment, 1939-42; became captain; wounded and taken prisoner, 1942; received Military Cross. *Member:* British Legion (life member). *Awards, honors:* Runner-up in English Festival of Spoken Poetry, 1951.

WRITINGS: Prisoner from Alamein, Witherby, 1944; (translator) *Sir Gawain and the Green Knight*, Penguin, 1959, 2nd edition, 1974; (translator) *Medieval English Verse*, Penguin, 1964; (translator) *The Owl and the Nightingale, Cleaness, Sir Erkenwald*, Penguin, 1971. Writer of series of articles on teaching of English in primary schools for *Teachers World*.

SIDELIGHTS: Stone wrote *CA*: "I am European-minded, speak some French, a Zionist since 1945.... Conclusively dedicated to the service of youth, and if I had to choose between teaching and writing, both of which I enjoy, I would choose teaching." *Avocational interests:* Adult education, theatre, and music.

*   *   *

STONE, Elna
(Elna Worrell Daniel)

PERSONAL: Born in Gattman, Miss.; daughter of Walter L. and Verna (Worrell) Burchfield; married Joseph E. Daniel (deceased); married Donald S. Stone (a junior college counselor), September 28, 1962; children: (first marriage) Thalia, Jane, Jeffery; (second marriage) Robert and Richard (twins). *Education:* University of Alabama, B.S., graduate study at Florida State University and University of West Florida. *Religion:* Baptist (Southern Baptist Convention). *Residence:* Pensacola, Fla.

CAREER: Former teacher; Florida State Employment Service, Pensacola, employment counselor, 1961-66; Pensacola Junior College, Pensacola, Fla., teacher, 1969—.

WRITINGS: (Under name Elna Worrell Daniel) *Speak Up!*, Zondervan, 1964; *How to Choose Your Work*, Macmillan, 1969; *How to Get a Job*, Macmillan, 1969; *Secret of the Willows* (novel), Belmont Publications, 1971; *Ghosts at the Wedding*, Belmont Publications, 1971; *Dark Masquerade*, Lancer Books, 1973; *Whisper of Fear*, Beagle Books, 1973. Also contributor to *Seven Steps to a Vital Faith*, Guideposts, Inc. Contributor to religious magazines, including *Guideposts*, *Christian Home*, and *This Day*.†

*   *   *

STONE, Harry 1928-

PERSONAL: Born September 9, 1928, in London, England; son of Gerald William and Celina (Poland) Stone. *Education:* Harrow School, student, 1942-46. *Home:* 12 Charlwood Pl., London S.W.1, England.

CAREER: Illustrated Newspapers, London, England, worked on *Sphere*, 1950-55; Leonard Hill Publications, London, England, assistant editor of *Pottery and Glass*, 1955-57; Princes Press, London, England, 1957-66, began as assistant editor, of *World Airports*, became group editorial manager, *H.A.P. Weekly*; MacIvan & Sons, London, England, editor, 1966—. Consulting engineer in heating and air conditioning. *Military service:* British Army, 1946-49. *Member:* Institute of Journalists.

WRITINGS: Winter Sports and Resorts, Mason Publications, 1961; *Day Outings*, Planned Action, 1974. Editor, *Ski-ing Monthly*, 1959-60.

AVOCATIONAL INTERESTS: Alpine skiing, semi-high diving, theater (especially musical comedy), literature published by resistance movements during World War II, alcoholism and vagrancy.

*   *   *

STONE, Lawrence 1919-

PERSONAL: Born December 4, 1919, in Epsom, Surrey, England; son of Lawrence Frederick (an artist) and Mabel (Reid) Stone; married Jeanne Caecilia Fawtier, July 24, 1943; children: Elizabeth C., Robert L. F. *Education:* Attended Sorbonne, University of Paris, 1938; Christ Church, Oxford, B.A., 1940, M.A., 1946, research student, 1946-47. *Politics:* Liberal. *Home:* 71 College Rd. W., Princeton, N.J. 08540. *Office:* Princeton University, Princeton, N.J. 08540.

CAREER: Oxford University, Oxford, England, lecturer in history, University College, 1946-50, fellow in history, Wadham College, 1950-63; Princeton University, Princeton, N.J., Dodge Professor of History, 1963—, chairman of department, 1967-70, director, Shelby Cullom David Center for Historical Studies, 1968—. Member, Institute for Advanced Study, 1960-61. *Member:* American Academy of Arts and Sciences (fellow), American Philosophical Association. *Military service:* Royal Navy, 1940-45; became lieutenant.

WRITINGS: An Elizabethan: Sir Horatio Palavicino, Oxford University Press, 1955; *Sculpture in Britain: The Middle Ages*, Penguin, 1955, 2nd edition, 1972; *The Crisis of the Aristocracy 1558-1641*, Oxford University Press, 1965, abridged edition, 1967; *Social Change and Revolution in 17th-Century England*, Longmans, Green, 1965; *Social Change and Revolution in England 1540-1640*, Barnes &

Noble, 1965; *The Causes of the English Revolution 1529-1642*, Harper, 1972; *Family and Fortune: Studies in Aristocratic Finance in the Sixteenth and Seventeenth Centuries*, Oxford Clarendon Press, 1973; (editor) *The University in Society*, Princeton University Press, Volume I: *Oxford and Cambridge from the 14th to the Early 19th Century*, 1974, *Europe, Scotland, and the United States from the 16th to the 20th Century*, 1974. Contributor of articles on history and the history of art to scholarly journals. Member of editorial board, *Past and Present*, 1959—.

WORK IN PROGRESS: Research on social structure and mobility in sixteenth-and seventeenth-century England, on the counter-revolution in England, 1629-40, and on English sculpture in the sixteenth and seventeenth centuries.†

*　*　*

STONE, William Sidney 1928-

PERSONAL: Born August 24, 1928, in Boston, Mass.; son of Roger P. and Carol (Rix) Stone; married Erika Klopfer (a photographer), 1954; children: Michael Roger, David William. *Education:* Dartmouth College, B.A., 1950. *Politics:* Democrat. *Home:* 160 East 48th St., New York, N.Y. 10017. *Office:* Batten, Barton, Durstine & Osborn, 383 Madison Ave., New York, N.Y. 10017.

CAREER: Free-lance photographer in New York, N.Y., 1952-54; Batten, Barton, Durstine & Osborn, New York, N.Y., copywriter, 1954-60, now vice-president and copy supervisor. Filmed motor racing events in Europe, 1957, 1964, for Tel-Ra Productions, Philadelphia, Pa. *Military service:* U.S. Army, 1950-52. *Member:* New England Trail Riders.

WRITINGS: (With Martin J. Dain) *Guide to American Sports Car Racing*, Doubleday, 1960, 4th edtion, 1971; *MG Sports Sedan Guide*, Sportscar Press, 1964; *Mustang Guide*, Sportscar Press, 1965; *Guide to Racing Drivers Schools*, Sports Car Press, 1972.

AVOCATIONAL INTERESTS: Automobiles, music, motorcycles, and travel.

*　*　*

STONEHOUSE, Merlin 1911-

PERSONAL: Born December 13, 1911; son of Clarence Marigold and Frances (Hendrickson) Stonehouse. *Education:* Attended Eveleth Junior College, Northwestern University, University of Iowa; University of California, Los Angeles, Ph.D., 1961. *Religion:* Unitarian Universalist. *Home:* 735 Oak Knoll Circle, Pasadena, Calif. 91106.

CAREER: Transradio News Features, New York, N.Y., director, 1938-39; Stonehouse News Agency, Washington, D.C., news correspondent covering (in particular) the White House and Department of State, 1939-59; Occidental College, Los Angeles, Calif., member of department of history, 1961-65; University of California, Los Angeles, member of department of history, 1965-66; University of Wyoming, Laramie, member of department of history, 1966-71. *Member:* American Historical Association, Organization of American Historians, Pacific Coast Historical Association, Western Historians, state and local historical societies.

WRITINGS: John Wesley North and the Reform Frontier, University of Minnesota Press, 1965.

WORK IN PROGRESS: Lincoln's Radical Reconstruction; a biography of Henry Douglas Bacon; editing *Dame North: The Letters of Ann Loomis North*, and *Down in Dgypt*, a collection of Lincoln's impolite stories.

*　*　*

STONESIFER, Richard James 1922-

PERSONAL: Born June 21, 1922, in Lancaster, Pa.; son of Paul Tobias and Esther (Wittlinger) Stonesifer; married Nancy Weaver, June 28, 1947; children: Pamela Ann. *Education:* Franklin and Marshall College, A.B., 1946; Northwestern University, M.A., 1947; University of Pennsylvania, Ph.D., 1953. *Home:* 95 Buttonwood Dr., Fair Haven, N.J. 07701. *Office:* Monmouth College, West Long Branch, N.J.

CAREER: Franklin and Marshall College, Lancaster, Pa., member of faculty of English, 1947-63, assistant to dean, 1957-60, assistant to president and director of public relations, 1960-63; University of Pennsylvania, Philadelphia, associate professor of communications in Annenberg School of Communications, assistant to provost, and director of College of General Studies, 1963-65; Drew University, Madison, N.J., dean of College of Liberal Arts, 1965-71; Monmouth College, West Long Branch, N.J., president, 1971—. Participant in educational and commercial television, 1953-61. Division chairman, Lancaster County Community Council, 1962-63; member of board of directors of Harrisburg Area Center for Higher Education and Pennsylvania Advisory Committee for Educational Broadcasting, 1963-65. *Military service:* U.S. Army Air Forces, 1943-46; served in photographic intelligence at 8th Air Force Headquarters, England; became staff sergeant. *Member:* National Association of Educational Broadcasters, College English Association, National Council of Teachers of English, Eastern Association of Deans, Phi Beta Kappa, Sigma Pi.

WRITINGS: W. H. Davies: A Critical Biography, J. Cape, 1963, Wesleyan University Press, 1965. Script writer for "New Books of Significance," discussion series on WGAL-TV, Lancaster, Pa., 1953-60. Contributor of newspaper column, "Campus and Classroom," to 122 papers, 1961-63.

WORK IN PROGRESS: A book on cultural, instructional, and educational aspects of American television; a book analyzing form in William Faulkner's novels.

AVOCATIONAL INTERESTS: Art, music, mass media analysis.†

*　*　*

STORER, Tracy I(rwin) 1889-

PERSONAL: Born August 17, 1889, in San Francisco, Calif.; son of Frank (a publisher) and Olietta (McDowell) Storer; married Ruth Charlotte Risdon (a part-time physician), June 16, 1917. *Education:* University of California, Berkeley, B.S., 1912, M.S., 1913, Ph.D., 1925. *Home:* 430 A St., Davis, Calif. *Office:* 171 Animal Science Building, University of California, Davis, Calif.

CAREER: University of California, Berkeley, museum curator and writer, 1914-23; University of California, Davis, 1923-56, began as assistant professor, professor of zoology, 1942-56, professor emeritus, 1956—. *Military service:* U.S. Army, Sanitary Corps, 1917-19; became first lieutenant. *Member:* American Association for the Advancement of Science, Ecological Society of America, American Society of Mammalogists (president, 1949; director, beginning 1950), American Society of Ichthyologists and Herpetologists, American Ornithologists Union, Cooper Ornithological Society, Herpetologists League, Wild Life Society (president, 1949), California Academy of Sciences, Wilson Ornithological Club. *Awards, honors:* LL.D. from University of California, 1960.

WRITINGS: (With J. Grinnell and H. C. Bryant) *Game Birds of California*, University of California Press, 1918; (with Grinnell) *Animal Life in the Yosemite*, University of California Press, 1924; *General Zoology*, McGraw, 1943, 5th edition (with Robert Usinger), 1972; *Laboratory Manual for Zoology*, McGraw, 1944, 4th edition, 1965; (with Usinger) *Elements of Zoology*, McGraw, 1955, 3rd edition, 1968; (with L. P. Tevis, Jr.) *The California Grizzly*, University of California Press, 1955; (with Usinger) *Laboratory Workbook for Zoology*, McGraw, 1959, 4th edition, 1965; (editor) Robert L. Strecker and others, *Pacific Island Rat Ecology: Report of a Study Made on Ponape and Adjacent Islands, 1955-58*, Bernice Pauahi Bishop Museum (Honolulu), 1962; (with Usinger) *Sierra Nevada Natural History: An Illustrated Handbook*, University of California Press, 1963.

Contributor of articles, mostly on economic relations of vertebrates in California and west North America, to scientific journals. Editor, *Journal of Wildlife Management*, 1942-46.

WORK IN PROGRESS: Miscellaneous writings.

AVOCATIONAL INTERESTS: Travel, photography, and music.†

*   *   *

STORR, Catherine (Cole)   1913-
   (Irene Adler, Helen Lourie)

PERSONAL: Born July 21, 1913, in London, England; daughter of Arthur Frederick (a lawyer) and Margaret (Gaselee) Cole; married Anthony Storr (a psychiatrist and writer), February 6, 1942; married Lord Balogh (an economist); children: Sophia, Cecilia, Emma. *Education:* Studied at Newnham College, Cambridge, 1932-36 and 1939-41, and West London Hospital, 1941-44. *Religion:* Agnostic. *Home:* 14 Hampstead High St., Hampstead, London N.W.3, England. *Agent:* A. D. Peters, 10 Buckingham St., London W.C.2, England.

CAREER: West London Hospital, London, England, assistant psychiatrist, 1948-50; Middlesex Hospital, London, England, assistant psychiatrist, 1950-62; now full-time writer. *Member:* Society of Authors.

WRITINGS: Ingeborg and Ruthy, Harrap, 1940; *Clever Polly*, Faber, 1951; *Stories for Jane*, Faber, 1952; *Clever Polly and the Stupid Wolf*, Faber, 1955; *Polly, the Giant's Bride*, Faber, 1956; *The Adventures of Polly and the Wolf*, Faber, 1957; *Marianne Dreams*, Faber, 1958; *Marianne and Mark*, Faber, 1960; *Magic Drawing Pencil*, A. S. Barnes, 1960; *Lucy*, Bodley Head, 1961; *Lucy Runs Away*, Bodley Head, 1962; (under pseudonym Helen Lourie) *A Question of Abortion*, Bodley Head, 1962; *Robin*, Faber, 1962; (under pseudonym Irene Adler) *Freud for the Jung*, Cresset, 1963; *The Catchpole Story*, Faber, 1965; *The Merciful Jew* (adult), Barrie & Rockcliff, 1968; *Polly and the Wolf*, Penguin, 1968; *Rufus*, Faber, 1969; Gambit, 1970; *Puss and Cat*, Faber, 1969; *Thursday*, Faber, 1971, Harper, 1972; *Black God, White God*, Barrie & Rockcliff, 1972; *Kate and the Island*, Faber, 1972; *The Painter and the Fish*, Faber, 1975; *Adolescence*, Hutchinson, 1975; *The Chinese Egg*, Faber, 1975. Contributor of articles to *Nova* and *Cosmopolitan*.

WORK IN PROGRESS: A book, *Unnatural Fathers*.

*   *   *

STOTT, D(enis) H(erbert)   1909-

PERSONAL: Born December 31, 1909, in London, England; son of Augustus Parker and Margaret (Smith) Stott; married Jane Brook (a teacher), July 30, 1937; children: Marion Stott Davidson, Peter. *Education:* Cambridge University, B.A., 1932, M.A., 1941; University of London, Ph.D., 1950. *Home:* 25 Ledcameroch Crescent, Bearsden, Glasgow, Scotland. *Office:* University of Glasgow, Glasgow W. 2, Scotland.

CAREER: Teacher of modern languages at schools in England, 1932-46; Carnegie United Kingdom Trust, Dunfermline, Scotland, research officer, 1946-51; University of Bristol, Bristol, England, research fellow, 1951-57; University of Glasgow, Glasgow, Scotland, lecturer in psychology, 1957—. Charles Russell Memorial Lecturer, 1957. *Member:* British Psychological Society (fellow).

WRITINGS: A School German Course Using Inductive and Other Active Methods, Methuen, 1944; *Language Teaching in the New Education*, University of London Press, 1946; *Delinquency and Human Nature*, Carnegie United Kingdom Trust, 1950; *Saving Children from Delinquency*, Philosophical Library, 1952; *Unsettled Children and Their Families*, Philosophical Library, 1956; (with E. G. Sykes) *The Bristol Society Adjustment Guides*, University of London Press, 1956, 4th edition (with N. C. Marston), 1971; *The Social Adjustment of Children* (manual to *The Bristol Society Adjustment Guides*), University of London Press, 1958, 4th edition, 1972; (contributor) M. F. A. Montague, editor, *Culture and the Evolution of Man*, Oxford University Press, 1962; *Studies of Troublesome Children*, Humanities, 1966; *The Parent as Teacher*, Fearon, 1974; (contributor) Maurice F. Freehill, editor, *Disturbed and Troubled Children*, Spectrum, 1974; (with N. C. Marston and S. D. Neill) *Taxonomy of Behaviour Disturbance*, University of London Press, in press.

Author of "Day-of-the-Week Books" and "Micky Books" series, Holmes McDougall, 1961. Also author of Programmed Reading Kit, 1962; Flying Start: Learn to Learn Kit, 1972; Flying Start Extension Kit, 1973; Learning about Numbers, 1973; Math Activity Kits, 1974; all Holmes McDougall. Script writer for film, "We Learn to Read." Contributor of more than thirty articles to *British Journal of Delinquency, New Scientist, Lancet*, other psychological and educational journals.

WORK IN PROGRESS: Research in learning disabilities, maladjustment, and the teaching of reading.

SIDELIGHTS: Stott is competent in French and German. *Avocational interests:* Ceramics.

*   *   *

STOW, (Julian) Randolph   1935-

PERSONAL: Born November 28, 1935, in Geraldton, Western Australia; son of Cedric Ernest (a barrister and solicitor) and Mary (Sewell) Stow. *Education:* University of Western Australia, B.A., 1956. *Religion:* Church of England. *Address:* c/o Richard Scott Simon Ltd., 36 Wellington St., London W.C.2, England.

CAREER: Novelist and poet. Worked at various times on a mission for aborigines in northwest Australia, and as assistant to the government anthropologist in New Guinea; has lived in East Anglia, Scotland, and Malta, teaching

English betweentimes in Australia at the University of Adelaide, 1957, and University of Western Australia, 1963-64, and in England at the University of Leeds, 1962, 1968-69. Harkness Fellow of the Commonwealth Fund, 1964-66.

WRITINGS: A Haunted Land (novel), Macdonald & Co., 1956; *The Bystander* (novel), Macdonald & Co., 1957; *Act One* (poems), Macdonald & Co., 1957; *To the Islands* (novel), Macdonald & Co., 1958; *Outrider* (poems), Macdonald & Co., 1962; *Tourmaline* (novel), Macdonald & Co., 1963; (editor) *Australian Poetry 1964*, Angus & Robertson, 1964; *The Merry-go-Round in the Sea* (novel), Macdonald & Co., 1965; *Midnite* (novel for children), Macdonald & Co., 1967, Prentice-Hall, 1968; *A Counterfeit Silence: Selected Poems*, Angus & Robertson, 1969.

Also author, with Peter Maxwell Davies, of "Eight Songs for a Mad King," 1969, and "Miss Donnithorne's Maggot," 1974, both for music theatre.

* * *

STRACHAN, T(ony) S(impson) 1920-

PERSONAL: Born May 10, 1920, in Mountsorrel, Leicestershire, England; son of James (a physician) and Olivia (Edmunds) Strachan; married Daphne Veronica Trew, March 21, 1951; children: Alexander Frederick. *Education:* Attended Uppingham School, 1934-37. *Politics:* Conservative. *Religion:* Church of England. *Home:* 505-1510 Harco St., Vancouver, British Columbia, Canada. *Office:* U.I.C., 750 Cambie St., Vancouver, British Columbia, Canada.

CAREER: Young & Rubicam (advertising agency), London, England, copywriter, 1958-59; Erwin Wasey, Rauthrauff & Ryan (advertising agency), London, England, copywriter, 1959-61; Pritchard Wood Ltd. (advertising agency), London, England, copywriter, 1961-65. Now employed by Canadian Federal Government in its publications. *Military service:* British Army, 1939-46; became lieutenant; prisoner of war in Germany, 1940-45. *Member:* P.E.N.

WRITINGS: No One to Worry Us, Laurie, 1949; *Fire Escape*, Laurie, 1950; *The Short Weekend*, Heinemann, 1953; *Key Major*, Heinemann, 1954; *No Law in Illyria*, Heinemann, 1957. Contributor of short stories and articles to British periodicals, and book reviews to Canadian periodicals.

WORK IN PROGRESS: Working Gorilla, a novel with a Lisbon background; a novel set in the Canary Isles.

SIDELIGHTS: Strachan speaks French and German. *The Short Weekend* has been published (as a serial) in Holland, broadcast over Australian and South African radio, and bought for a film production in Hollywood.

* * *

STRAKER, J(ohn) F(oster) 1904-
(Ian Rosse)

PERSONAL: Born March 26, 1904, in Farnborough, Kent, England; son of Leonard Herbert (an engineer) and Elizabeth (Foster) Straker; married Margaret Brydon, January 24, 1935; children: Ian Christopher. *Education:* Attended Framlingham College. *Politics:* Conservative. *Religion:* Church of England. *Home:* Lincoln Cottage, Horsted Keynes, Sussex, England.

CAREER: Kingsland Grange School, Shrewsbury, Shropshire, England, mathematics master, 1926-34; Blackheath Preparatory School, London, England, teacher, 1936-38; Cumnor House School, Danehill, Sussex, England, mathe-

matics master, 1944—. *Military service:* British Army, 1939-44; served as staff officer in Middle East; became major.

WRITINGS—All published by Harrap, except as noted: *Postman's Knock*, 1954; *Pick up the Pieces*, 1955; *The Ginger Horse*, 1956; *A Gun to Play With*, 1956; *Goodbye, Aunt Charlotte!*, 1958; *Hell Is Empty*, 1958; *Death of a Good Woman*, 1961; *Murder for Missemily*, 1961; *A Coil of Rope*, 1962; *Final Witness*, 1963; *The Shape of Murder*, 1964; *Ricochet*, 1965; *Miscarriage of Murder*, 1967; *Sin and Johnny Inch*, 1968; *A Man Who Cannot Kill*, 1969; *Tight Circle*, 1970; *A Letter For Obi*, 1971; *The Goat*, 1972; (under pseudonym Ian Rosse) *The Droop*, New English Library, 1972. Contributor of short stories to *Evening Standard*, *Evening News*.

SIDELIGHTS: Dust jackets of his books have been designed by his son, a commercial artist. *Avocational interests:* Travel, music, carpentry, gardening, all games and sports (now mostly as a spectator).

BIOGRAPHICAL/CRITICAL SOURCES: Smith's Trade News, April 14, 1956; *Books and Bookmen*, September 22, 1958.

* * *

STRASBERG, Lee 1901-

PERSONAL: Born November 17, 1901, in Budanov, Austria-Hungary (now in Union of Soviet Socialist Republics); brought to United States, 1909; became U.S. citizen, 1936; son of Baruch Meyer and Ida (Diner) Strasberg; married Nora Z. Krecaun (deceased); married Paula Miller, March 16, 1934 (deceased); married Anna Mizrahi, January 7, 1968; children: (second marriage) Susan (an actress), John; (third marriage) Adam Lee, David Lee. *Education:* Studied at American Laboratory Theatre under Richard Boleslavski and Maris Ouspenskaya. *Home:* 135 Central Park West, New York, N.Y. 10023.

CAREER: Began acting in productions at a New York settlement house; started Broadway career with the Theatre Guild, 1924, as assistant stage manager for the Lynn Fontanne and Alfred Lunt play, "The Guardsman," and appeared in "Red Rust" and several other Guild presentations, 1925-31; joined actors and directors interested in the "method" ideas of Constantin Stanislavski (Moscow Art Theatre) in founding the Group Theatre, 1931, and was co-director of the Group's first Broadway hit, "The House of Connelly," 1931, and director of the Pulitzer-Prize winning "Men in White," 1933, and "Johnny Johnson," 1936; resigned from the Group Theatre, 1937, staging plays independently before going to Hollywood in 1942; returned to Broadway in 1948 as director of "Skipper Next to God" and, later, "The Big Knife"; artistic director of Actors Studio, Inc., New York, N.Y., since its founding in 1947. Artistic director, Actor's Studio Theatre, Inc., 1962-66; artistic director for "The Silent Partner, Felix"; director for "The Three Sisters," 1964. Established Lee Strasberg Institute of Theatre in New York City and Los Angeles, 1969. Lecturer at Harvard University, Brown University, Yale University, Brandeis University, and Northwestern University. Made film debut in "The Godfather-Part II."

AWARDS, HONORS: Kelcey Allen award, New York, N.Y., 1961; Centenial Gold Medal award for excellence in dramatic arts, Boston College, 1963.

WRITINGS: (Editor) *Famous American Plays of the 1950's*, Dell, 1963; *Strasberg at the Actors Studio*, edited by Robert H. Hethmon, Viking, 1965; *Lee Strasberg on Acting*, Harper, 1973. Also author of articles on acting, contributed to *Encyclopaedia Britannica*, 15th edition.

AVOCATIONAL INTERESTS: Collecting books on the theater.

BIOGRAPHICAL/CRITICAL SOURCES: New York Times, July 20, 1958; *Strasberg at the Actors Studio*, Viking, 1965.

* * *

STRAUMANN, Heinrich 1902-

PERSONAL: Surname rhymes with "plowman"; born September 22, 1902, in Bellinzona, Switzerland; son of Karl and Marie (Fuchs) Straumann; married Ursula Gerber; children: Kathrin Platt, Ulrich Daniel, Matthias Dieter, Hans Peter Ernst. *Education:* Universities of Zurich, Aberdeen, and Berlin, 1921-27, Ph.D. *Religion:* Protestant. *Home:* Gfennstrasse 51, CH-8603, Schwerzenbach, Switzerland. *Office:* University of Zurich, Zurich, Switzerland.

CAREER: Teacher in Zuoz, Switzerland, 1927-28, in Aarau, Switzerland, 1928-39; University of Zurich, Zurich, Switzerland, lecturer in English literature, 1933-38, professor, 1939—, rector, 1960-62. Member of Board of Education, Canton of Zurich, 1955-63. *Military service:* Swiss Army. *Member:* International P.E.N. (president, Zurich chapter, 1942-46), Swiss Association of University Teachers of English (president), Swiss National Foundation of Scientific Research, Swiss-British Society (founder president, 1946-52), Swiss-American Society, Athenaeum Club (London).

WRITINGS: Justinus Kerner, Huber, Frauenfeld, 1928; *Newspaper Headlines*, Allen & Unwin, 1935; *Byron and Switzerland*, University of Nottingham Press, 1949; *American Literature in the Twentieth Century*, Hutchinson, 1951, Torchbooks, 1965; *Phoenix und Taube*, Artemis, 1953; *William Faulkner*, Athenaeum, 1968; (with Martin Bircher) *Shakespeare und die deutsche Schweiz*, Francke, 1971; *Contexts of Literature: An Anglo-Swiss Approach*, Francke, 1973. Contributor to *English Studies* (Amsterdam). Adviser to *Encyclopaedia Britannica*.

SIDELIGHTS: Straumann was one of the first to give regular lectures on contemporary American literature at a European university (in 1936), and his *American literature in the Twentieth Century* has gone into Spanish, Italian, and Japanese translations. He has made four extended visits to the United States since 1937, the last in 1963. *Avocational interests:* Music, walking, skiing, bowling.

BIOGRAPHICAL/CRITICAL SOURCES: English Studies, Straumann Anniversary Number, Volume XLIII, Number 5, October, 1962.

* * *

STRAUSS, Bert(ram) Wiley 1901-

PERSONAL: Born October 10, 1901, in Des Moines, Iowa; son of Leon (a wholesale milliner) and Bertha (Sheuerman) Strauss; married Frances Goetzmann (a teacher and writer), July 13, 1931; children: Helen Strauss Seitz, Emily Babette. *Education:* University of Pennsylvania, B.S., 1922. *Home:* 3129 Sleepy Hollow Rd., Falls Church, Va. 22042.

CAREER: Worked in millinery factory and department stores, 1922-29, for brokerage firm, 1930-33, and for a state emergency relief administration, 1934-35; U.S. government,

management posts with Farm Security Administration, 1935-44, Department of the Army, Washington, D.C., 1944-46, and Civil Aeronautics Administration, 1946-47; management analyst, Office of the Comptroller of the Army, Washington, D.C., 1948-60, adviser on public administration, Agency for International Development, U.S. Department of State, 1960-64, serving as adviser to governments of Northern and Southern Rhodesia, Nyasaland, West Pakistan, and Iran; self-employed consultant on management training, 1964—. Management consultant to Interim Commission, World Health Organization, 1947-48; former teacher of courses in group behavior at Department of Agriculture Graduate School, Catholic University of America, and the American University. *Awards, honors:* Meritorious Civilian Service Award, U.S. War Department, 1945.

WRITINGS: (With wife, Frances Goetzmann Strauss) *New Ways to Better Meetings*, Viking, 1951, 2nd edition, 1964; (with Frances Goetzmann Strauss) *Barcelona, Step by Step*, Editorial Teide (Barcelona), 1974; (with Mary E. Stowe) *How to Get Things Changed*, Doubleday, 1974. Contributor to management and public administration journals in United States and Pakistan.

WORK IN PROGRESS: Applications of research in group dynamics to management, management training, and community relations.

AVOCATIONAL INTERESTS: Travel and photography in Europe, Africa, and Asia.

* * *

STRAUSS, Erich 1911-

PERSONAL: Born June 1, 1911, in Vienna, Austria; British subject, residing in England since 1938. *Education:* Attended University of Vienna. *Home:* 20 Greenwood Rd., Thames Ditton, Surrey, England.

CAREER: Certified accountant; formerly chief economist, Milk Marketing Board, Thames Ditton, Surrey, England; United Nations Food and Agriculture Organization, consultant.

WRITINGS: Soviet Russia: Anatomy of a Social History, Bodley Head, 1941; *Bernard Shaw: Art and Socialism*, Gollancz, 1942; *George Bernard Shaw*, Longmans, Green, 1950; *Irish Nationalism and British Democracy*, Columbia University Press, 1951; *Sir William Petty: Portrait of a Genius*, Free Press of Glencoe, 1954; *Common Sense about the Common Market*, Rinehart, 1958; *The Ruling Servants: Bureaucracy in Russia, France—and Britain?*, Praeger, 1961; *European Reckoning*, Allen & Unwin, 1962; *Soviet Agriculture in Perspective*, Praeger, 1969. Contributor of articles to *Journal of Royal Statistical Society*, *Economic Journal*, and other periodicals.

* * *

STREET, Lucie

PERSONAL: Born in Sussex, England; daughter of John Peter and Lucie (Carver) Street; married Peter Penn (a retired Army officer and an economic adviser; deceased); children: two sons. *Education:* University of Manchester, B.A. (honors), M.A.; additional study at Sorbonne, University of Paris. *Religion:* Church of England. *Home:* Warminghurst, High Hurstwood, Uckfield, Sussex, England.

CAREER: Writer. Chairman of County Secondary School Governors, Uckfield, Sussex, England, and of Primary

School Managers, High Hurstwood, Sussex, England. Governor of Educational Trust. *Member:* P.E.N., Naval and Military Club (London), London Lancastrian Association.

WRITINGS: Penn of Pennsylvania (three-act play), Sidgwick & Jackson, 1942; *H. E. William Penn* (novel), Cassell, 1942; (editor) *I Married a Russian*, Allen & Unwin, 1944; (with husband, Peter Penn) *Tomorrow's Continent*, Sidgwick & Jackson, 1946; *Wind on the Morja* (novel), R. Hale, 1948; *Goodmorning! Miranda* (novel), R. Hale, 1950; *Spoil the Child*, Phoenix House, 1963; *The Tent Pegs of Heaven: A Journey through Afghanistan*, R. Hale, 1967; *Autumn Phoenix* (poems), Outposts Publications, 1972. Author of plays, including "The Fourth Wise King," and "A College Day."

WORK IN PROGRESS: Biography of William Penn's father; a novel about childhood; and a study of modern education.

SIDELIGHTS: Lucie Street speaks French and has travelled widely through the Middle East, Iran, Afghanistan, central Africa, Rhodesia, United States, and the Caribbean. She has a special interest in Philadelphia (late husband was a descendent of William Penn).

* * *

STRODE, Hudson 1892-

PERSONAL: Born October 31, 1892, in Cairo, Ill.; son of Thomas Fuller and Hope (Hudson) Strode; married Therese Cory, December 20, 1924. *Education:* University of Alabama, A.B., 1913; Columbia University, M.A., 1914; Harvard University, special study, 1916. *Politics:* Independent. *Religion:* Episcopalian. *Home:* 49 Cherokee Rd., Tuscaloosa, Ala.

CAREER: Syracuse University, Syracuse, N.Y., instructor in English, 1914-16; University of Alabama, University, associate professor, 1916-24, professor of English, 1924-63. Author and lecturer. *Member:* P.E.N., Newcomen Society, Phi Beta Kappa, Delta Kappa Epsilon. *Awards, honors:* First prize, National Little Theater Contest, for one-act play, "The End of the Dance," 1929; D.Litt. from University of Alabama, 1952, University of the South, 1960; knighted (Knight of the Royal Order of the North Star) by King Gustaf Adolf of Sweden, 1961.

WRITINGS: The Story of Bermuda, Smith & Haas, 1932; *The Pageant of Cuba*, Smith & Haas, 1934; *South by Thunderbird*, Random House, 1937; *Immortal Lyrics*, Random House, 1939; *Finland Forever*, Harcourt, 1941; *Timeless Mexico, a History*, Harcourt, 1944; *Now in Mexico, a Book of Travel*, Harcourt, 1947; *Sweden: Model for a World*, Harcourt, 1949, revised edition, 1965; *Denmark Is a Lovely Land*, Harcourt, 1951; *Jefferson Davis*, Harcourt, Volume I: *American Patriot*, 1955, Volume II: *Confederate President*, 1959, *Tragic Hero*, 1964; (editor) *Jefferson Davis: Private Letters 1823-1889*, Harcourt, 1967; *Ultimates in the Far East*, Harcourt, 1973.

Contributor of articles, stories, poetry, and reviews to *Forum, New Republic, Harper's Bazaar, Reader's Digest, New York Times Magazine*, and other periodicals in United States and abroad.

SIDELIGHTS: Strode lived in Italy for a year, has traveled elsewhere in Europe, throughout South America. *Avocational interests:* Gardening, reading, and collecting specimen pieces of Orrefors (Swedish) glass.

STROM, Ingrid Mathilda 1912-

PERSONAL: Born December 8, 1912, in Duluth, Minn.; daughter of John and Mary (Gregg) Strom. *Education:* Duluth State Teachers College (now University of Minnesota at Duluth), B.Ed., 1935; University of Minnesota, M.A., 1944, Ph.D., 1955. *Politics:* Democrat. *Religion:* Lutheran. *Home:* 3801 East Third St., Bloomington, Ind.; 3718 Grand Ave., Duluth, Minn.

CAREER: Teacher in public schools of Minnesota and Wisconsin, 1935-42; Indiana University, Bloomington, instructor and critic teacher in University High School, 1944-53, assistant director of student teaching, School of Education, 1953—, assistant professor, 1955-61, associate professor of education, 1961—. U.S. Armed Forces Institute, member of National Advisory Textbook Commission, 1949-50. *Member:* National Council of Teachers of English, National Education Association, Association for Student Teaching American Association of University Professors, American Association of University Women, National League of American Pen Women, Indiana Council of Teachers of English, Indiana State Teachers Association, Pi Lambda Theta, Delta Kappa Gamma, Delta Phi Lambda.

WRITINGS: (With Richard Carbin) *Practice in Modern English*, Scott, 1956; *The Teaching Load of Teachers of English in Indiana*, School of Education, Indiana University, 1956; (with others) *An Instructional Utility Analysis of 319 National Educational Television Programs*, Ford Foundation, 1958; *The Role of Literature in the Core Curriculum*, School of Education, Indiana University, 1958; *Implications of Research in Grammar and Usage for Teaching Writing*, School of Education, Indiana University, 1960; (editor) *Leadership Through Research*, Association for Student Teaching, 1961. Editor and author of department, "Summary of Investigations in the English Language Arts in Secondary Education," in *English Journal*, annually, 1957—. Member of advisory board, *Literary Cavalcade*, 1952-54.

WORK IN PROGRESS: Teaching Load of Teachers of English in United States, for National Council of Teachers of English; editing *Implications of the Findings of Research for the Improvement of Student Teaching*, for National Association for Student Teaching.

SIDELIGHTS: Ingrid Strom speaks Swedish and French, reads German.†

* * *

STRONG, Rupert 1911-

PERSONAL: Born May 10, 1911, in Hampstead, London, England; son of Rupert (a clergyman) and Norah (Strousberg) Strong; married Eithne O'Connell, 1942; children: Jennifer Strong Duncan, Brita, Sarah, Rachel, Helen, Kevin, Fionnuala, Lorraine, Philip. *Education:* Trinity College, University of Dublin, B.A. *Religion:* Church of England. *Home:* 17 Eaton Sq., Monkstown, Dublin, Republic of Ireland.

CAREER: Traveled in Europe, including Russia, as journalist between school and college; psychoanalyst, practicing in Dublin, Ireland, 1945—.

WRITINGS: Jonathan of Birkenhead, and Other Poems, Runa Press, 1953; *From Inner Fires*, Runa Press, 1962; *Poems of the Ordinary*, Dolmen Press, 1967; *The Challenger*, Runa Press, 1968; *Selected Poems*, Runa Press, 1974.

SIDELIGHTS: Strong wrote, "What a poem has to say is, to me, more important than how it is said; but the two go together and the most successful pieces are a combination of both. Economy of expression is much to my liking. We live in a world of ever-increasing verbiage and a good poem may say as much in a few words as a novel takes to unfold. The poet can pour a bucket into a thimble; his job is to compress the maximum into the minimum."

* * *

STROUP, Herbert H(ewitt) 1916-

PERSONAL: Born May 1, 1916, in Philadelphia, Pa.; son of William Valentine and Margaret (Hewitt) Stroup; married Grace Evelyn Guldin, May 20, 1939; children: Timothy Diener, Trudi Ann. *Education:* Muskingum College, A.B., 1937; Union Theological Seminary, B.D., 1940; New School for Social Research, Dr. of Social Science, 1942. *Home:* 171 Fairlawn Ave., West Hempstead, N.Y. *Office:* Brooklyn College of the City University of New York, Brooklyn, N.Y.

CAREER: Camp Gould, Bantam Lake, Conn., director, 1940-42; The Sheltering Arms, New York, N.Y., houseparent, 1940-42; Brooklyn College of the City University of New York, Brooklyn, N.Y., 1942—, began as tutor, became professor of sociology, 1954, department of student services, chairman, 1954-68, dean of students, 1954-68. Ripon College, Ripon, Wis., member of board of trustees, 1963—. Director for Greece, Congregational Christian Service Committee, 1953-54; member of board, Board of Homeland Ministries, United Church of Christ, 1962-74. *Member:* Association of Brooklyn Settlements (member of board), Society for Religion in Higher Education (fellow), Danforth Foundation (Personalization of Education, consultant), American Sociological Society, Church World Service (executive committee member), National Council of Churches (Division of Overseas Ministries, member of program board; Department of Higher Education, chairman), Christian Faith and Higher Education Projects (chairman of National Administration and Policy Committee).

WRITINGS: (Compiler) *Symphony of Prayer*, American Baptist Publication Society, 1944; *Jehovah's Witnesses*, Columbia University Press, 1945, Russell, 1947; *Social Work: An Introduction to the Field*, American Book Co., 1948, revised edition, 1960; *Community Welfare Organization*, Harper, 1952; *Toward a Philosophy of Organized Student Activities*, University of Minnesota Press, 1964; *Bureaucracy and Higher Education*, Free Press, 1966; *Church and State in Confrontation*, Seabury, 1967; *Four Religions of Asia*, Harper, 1968; (with others) *The Future of the Family*, Family Service Association of America, 1969; *Like a Great River: An Introduction to Hinduism*, Harper, 1972. Member of *Journal of Long Island* Consultation Center; member of committee on publication, *Lutheran Social Welfare Quarterly*.

SIDELIGHTS: Stroup has visited various Arab countries of the Middle East, Israel, and nearly all of the European countries on fifteen occasions. In 1959, he headed a study team to survey refugees in West Bengal, India, for the Church World Service.

* * *

STROUT, (Sewall) Cushing (Jr.) 1923-

PERSONAL: Born April 19, 1923, in Portland, Me.; son of Sewall C. (a banker) and Margaret (Deering) Strout; mar-

ried Jean Philbrick, June 12, 1948; children: Nathaniel, Benjamin, Nicholas. *Education:* Williams College, B.A., 1947; Harvard University, M.A., 1949, Ph.D., 1952. *Politics:* Democrat. *Home:* 204 Cayuga Heights Rd., Ithaca, N.Y. *Office:* Cornell University, Ithaca, N.Y.

CAREER: Williams College, Williamstown, Mass., instructor in history and literature, 1949-51; Yale University, New Haven, Conn., instructor, 1952-55, assistant professor of history, 1955-59; California Institute of Technology, Pasadena, associate professor, 1959-62, professor of humanities, 1962-64; Cornell University, Ithaca, N.Y., visiting professor, 1962-63, professor of English, 1964—. *Military service:* U.S. Army, 87th Infantry Division, 1943-46; became staff sergeant. *Member:* American Historical Association, American Studies Association, Phi Beta Kappa. *Awards, honors:* Morse fellowship, Yale University, 1956-57; American Philosophical Society grant, 1961; Society for the Humanities fellowship, 1971-72.

WRITINGS: The Pragmatic Revolt in American History: Carl Becker and Charles Beard, Yale University Press, 1958; *The American Image of the Old World*, Harper, 1963; (editor) *Conscience, Science, and Security: The Oppenheimer Case*, Rand McNally, 1963; (editor) J. Allen Smith, *The Spirit of American Government*, Belknap Press, 1965; (editor) *Hawthorne in England*, Cornell University Press, 1965; *The New Heavens and New Earth: Political Religion in America*, Harper, 1974.

WORK IN PROGRESS: Research in American intellectual history.

* * *

STRUGLIA, Erasmus Joseph 1915-

PERSONAL: Born June 26, 1915; son of Loreto and Vincenza (Bonavenia) Struglia; married Patricia Martin Hill, August, 1967; children: Rachel. *Education:* St. Francis College, Brooklyn, N.Y., B.S., 1936; Columbia University, M.L.S., 1938. *Religion:* Roman Catholic. *Home:* 148 West 54th St., New York, N.Y. 10019.

CAREER: Brooklyn (N.Y.) Public Libraries, branch librarian, 1946-49; Allied Chemical & Dye Corp., New York, N.Y., assistant librarian, 1949-51; Ortho Research Foundation, Raritan, N.J., research librarian, 1951-52; Consumers Union of United States, Inc., Mount Vernon, N.Y., librarian, 1952—, project supervisor for special report to National Bureau of Standards. *Military service:* U.S. Army, Infantry, 1941-45; became captain. *Member:* Special Libraries Association, Westchester Library Association.

WRITINGS: Standards and Specifications—Information Sources, Gale, 1965. Contributor to *Media & Consumer*.

SIDELIGHTS: Struglia is competent in French, Italian, Spanish, and German. *Avocational interests:* Horsemanship, playing piano, social dancing.

* * *

STRUMPEN-DARRIE, Robert L. 1912-

PERSONAL: Born January 14, 1912, in Antwerp, Belgium; son of Jacques (president of Berlitz Schools of Languages, 1933-53) and Aida (Fildes) Strumpen-Darrie; married Bae Carte, November 16, 1935; children: Jeanne, Michael, Jacqueline. *Education:* Received early education in Chicago, Ill.; Institut Saint Ignace, Antwerp, Belgium, Licence en Science Commerciales; other study at Georgetown University School of Foreign Service. *Politics:*

Republican. *Religion:* Roman Catholic. *Home:* 18 Walnut Ave., Larchmont, N.Y. *Office:* Berlitz Schools of Languages of America, Inc., 630 Fifth Ave., New York, N.Y., 10020.

CAREER: Berlitz Schools of Languages of Amèrica, Inc., · New York, N.Y., 1932—, beginning as a teacher at the Chicago School, Chicago, Ill., director of Chicago School, 1933-37, director of Brooklyn School, Brooklyn, N.Y., 1939-42, vice-president of firm, 1945-53, president (succeeding father), 1953—. Also president of Berlitz Publications, Inc., Berlitz Schools of Mexico, Berlitz Schools of Canada Ltd. *Military service:* U.S. Navy, 1942-46; served in European and Mediterranean theaters; became lieutenant. *Member:* New York Athletic Club, Larchmont Shore Club. *Awards, honors:* Medaille de la Ville de Paris, 1963.

WRITINGS—Editor, or co-director, of compilation with Charles F. Berlitz, all published by Grosset: "Self Teacher Courses"—*Berlitz Self-Teacher Spanish*, 1949, *Berlitz Self-Teacher Italian*, 1950, *Berlitz Self-Teacher French*, 1950, *Berlitz Self-Teacher Ingles*, 1951, *Berlitz Self-Teacher Russian*, 1951, *Berlitz Self-Teacher Portuguese*, 1953; *Berlitz Self-Teacher German*, 1953, *Berlitz Self-Teacher Hebrew*, 1953.

"Berlitz Phrase Books"—all published by Grosset: *Berlitz Spanish for Travelers*, 1954, 2nd edition, 1962, *Berlitz Italian for Travelers*, 1954, 2nd edition, 1962, *Berlitz German for Travelers*, 1954, 2nd edition, 1962, *Berlitz French for Travelers*, 1954, 2nd edition, 1962, *Berlitz Ingles para Viajeros*, 1958, *Berlitz Russian for Travelers*, 1959, 2nd edition, 1963, *Berlitz Scandinavian Languages for Travelers*, 1959, 2nd edition, 1962, *Berlitz World-Wide Phrase Book*, 1962.

"Berlitz Dictionaries"—all published by Grosset: *Berlitz Basic German Dictionary*, 1957, *Berlitz Basic Italian Dictionary*, 1957, *Berlitz Basic French Dictionary*, 1957, *Berlitz Basic Spanish Dictionary*, 1957, *Berlitz Diners' Dictionary*, 1961.

"Berlitz Language Books for children"—all published by Grosset: *Berlitz Spanish for Children*, Series I, 1959, Series II, 1961, Series III, 1963, *Berlitz French for Children*, Series I, 1959, Series II, 1961, Series III, 1963, *Berlitz Italian for Children*, Series I, 1960, Series II, 1962; *My First French Book*, 1965; *My Second French Book*, 1965; *My First Spanish Book*, 1965; *My Second Spanish Book*, 1965.

Also: "Berlitz Rotary Verb Finders," in French, Spanish, Italian, and German; "Berlitz Self-Teaching Record Courses," in French, Spanish, Italian, and German; "Berlitz Simplified Language Records," in French, Italian, and Spanish.

BIOGRAPHICAL/CRITICAL SOURCES: New York Times, September 13, 1953.†

*   *   *

STRYK, Lucien 1924-

PERSONAL: Born April 7, 1924, in Chicago, Ill.; married; children: two. *Education:* Indiana University, B.A., 1948; Sorbonne, University of Paris, M.F.S., 1950; University of Maryland, M.F.S., 1950; attended University of London, 1950-51; State University of Iowa, M.F.A., 1956. *Office:* Department of English, Northern Illinois University, DeKalb, Ill. 60115.

CAREER: Free-lance writer in England, 1952-54; Northern Illinois University, DeKalb, Ill., 1958—, began as assistant professor, now professor of English. Has given readings of his poetry on radio and at universities; visiting lecturer, Niigata University, 1956-58, Yamaguchi University, 1962-63, both in Japan. *Military service:* U.S. Army, 1943-45. *Member:* Asia Society. *Awards, honors:* Grove Press fellowship, 1960; Asia Society grant, 1961; Ford Foundation faculty fellowship, 1961; Fulbright grant for travel to Iran, 1961-62; *Chicago Daily News* New "Chicago" Poem Competition, shared first prize with John Berryman and Hayden Carruth, 1963; Isaac Rosenbaum Poetry Award, 1964; National Translation Center grant; Swallow Press new poetry series award; Northern Illinois University excellence in teaching award.

WRITINGS: Taproot (poems), Fantasy Press (Oxford, England), 1953; *The Tresspasser* (poems), Fantasy Press, 1956; (editor and translator with Takashi Ikemoto) *Zen: Poems, Prayers, Sermons, Anecdotes, Interviews*, Doubleday, 1965; *Notes for a Guidebook*, Swallow Press, 1965; (contributor) W. W. West, editor, *On Writing, By Writers*, Ginn, 1966; (contributor) *Developing Writing Skills*, Prentice-Hall, 1966; (editor) *Heartland: Poets of the Midwest*, Northern Illinois University Press, Volume I, 1967, Volume II, in press; (editor) *World of the Buddha: A Reader*, Doubleday, 1968; *The Pit and Other Poems*, Swallow Press, 1969; (editor and translator with Ikemoto) *Afterimages: Zen Poems of Shinkichi Takahashi*, Swallow Press, 1970; (translator with Ikemoto) *Twelve Death Poems of the Chinese Zen Masters*, Hellcoal Press, 1973; (translator with Ikemoto) *Zen Poems of China and Japan: The Crane's Bill*, Doubleday, 1973; *Awakening* (poems), Swallow Press, 1973.

Poetry represented in anthologies, including *Japanese Image*, Orient-West, 1965; *From the Hungarian Revolution*, edited by David Ray, Cornell University Press, 1966; *Stained the Water Clear*, Reed College, 1967; *Illinois Poets: A Selection*, edited by E. Earle Stibitz, Southern Illinois University Press, 1968; *A Book of Sonnets*, Twayne, 1969; *Southern Poetry Review Anthology*, North Carolina University Press, 1969; *New York Times Book of Verse*, edited by Thomas Lask, Macmillan, 1970.

Contributor to *American Poetry Review, Nation, Poetry, Saturday Review, Listener, London Magazine, New Statesman, Twentieth Century*, and others.

WORK IN PROGRESS: A volume of poetry.

SIDELIGHTS: Stryk told *CA:* "I have become strongly interested and rather actively involved in public poetry readings, feel that they are rarely done well and hope at last that with training it may be possible to make an art of poetry reading. As an exponent of Zen Buddhism, I am of course interested in reaching as many as possible so as to make them aware of its liberating possibilities. Travel has been enormously important to my life, and I hope that it will continue to be—especially in the Far East."

A collection of Stryk's worksheets has been established at the University of Buffalo and a manuscript collection at Boston University.

BIOGRAPHICAL/CRITICAL SOURCES: W. W. West, editor, *On Writing, By Writers*, Ginn, 1966; *Chicago Review*, June, 1967.

*   *   *

STUART, Alice V(andockum) 1899-

PERSONAL: Born December 16, 1899, in Rangoon, Burma; daughter of John (an editor and author) and Sarah

Augusta (McArthur) Stuart. *Education:* Somerville College, Oxford, student, 1919-22 (first class honors in English). *Home:* 57 Newington Rd., Edinburgh EH9 IQW, Scotland.

CAREER: Former teacher of English literature in schools in England and Scotland. Arranger of poetry recitals. *Member:* Society of Authors, International P.E.N. (Scottish Centre), Society of Teachers of Speech and Drama (honorary), Soroptimist Club (Edinburgh). *Awards, honors:* Lilian Bowes Lyon Award of Poetry Society, 1955, for *The Door Between*; Premium Award of The Poetry Society, 1966, for ''The Poet's Tale.''

WRITINGS—Poetry: The Far Calling, William & Norgate for Poetry Lovers' Fellowship, 1944; *The Dark Tarn,* George Ronald, 1953; *The Door Between,* H. T. Macpherson, 1963; *The Unquiet Tide,* Ramsay Head Press, 1971; (editor with Charles Graves) *Voice and Verse* (an anthology of poems by past and present members of the Scottish Association for the Speaking of Verse), Ramsay Head Press, 1974. Also author of booklet on David Gray, the poet of the Luggie.

Poems anthologized in *The Pattern of Verse* (verse-speaking anthology), edited by William Kean Seymour and John Smith, Burke Publishing Co., 1963, *An Anthology of Commonwealth Verse,* edited by Margaret J. O'Donnell, Blackie & Son, 1963, and *The Oxford Book of Scottish Verse,* edited by John MacQueen and Tom Scott, Oxford University Press, 1966. Translator of verse from the French and German. Contributor to *Poetry Review, Scotsman,* and other periodicals. One of founder-editors of *New Athenian Broadsheet* (quarterly of contemporary verse), 1947-51.

SIDELIGHTS: Selected poems have been produced by Plantagenet Productions Recorded Library, 1969.

BIOGRAPHICAL/CRITICAL SOURCES: The Burns Chronicle for 1958, the fourth in the series, ''Scots Poets of Today,'' published by Burns Federation.

*   *   *

STUART, Francis 1902-

PERSONAL: Born April 29, 1902, in Townsville, Australia; son of Henry Irwin and Elizabeth (Montgomery) Stuart; married, wife's maiden name Meissner, 1954; children: one son, one daughter. *Education:* Attended Rugby School in England. *Home:* 2 Highfield Park, Dublin 14, Ireland.

CAREER: Writer. *Member:* Irish Academy of Letters (founder member). *Awards, honors:* Royal Irish Academy Award.

WRITINGS: We Have Kept the Faith (poems), privately printed, 1923; *Pigeon Irish,* Gollancz, 1932, Macmillan, 1933; *Angel of Pity,* Grayson & Grayson, 1935; *Pillar of Cloud,* Gollancz, 1948; *Redemption,* Gollancz, 1949, Devin, 1950; *Victors and Vanquished,* Gollancz, 1958, Pennington Press, 1959; *Black List, Section H,* Southern Illinois University Press, 1970; *Memorial,* Martin, Brian & O'Keefe, 1973. Also author of play, ''Who Fears to Speak,'' neither produced nor published.

WORK IN PROGRESS: A novel.

SIDELIGHTS: Stuart's books have been translated into French and German.

BIOGRAPHICAL SOURCES: Envoy, July, 1951; *Critique,* July-August, 1954.

STUART, Vivian (Finlay) 1914-
(Barbara Allen, Fiona Finlay, Alex Stuart, V. A. Stuart)

PERSONAL: Born January 2, 1914, in Rangoon, Burma; daughter of Sir Campbell Kirkman (with Burma Oil Co.) and Lady Alice (Norton) Finlay; married third husband, Cyril William Mann (a banker), October 24, 1958; children: (previous marriages) Gillian Rushton, Jennifer Gooch, Vary and Valerie Stuart (twins). *Education:* Attended University of London; University of Budapest, pathologist qualification, 1938; Technical Institute, Newcastle, Australia, diploma in industrial chemistry and laboratory technique, 1942. *Politics:* Conservative. *Religion:* Church of England. *Home and office:* Hop Grove Farm Cottage, 461 Malton Rd., York, England.

CAREER: Romantic novelist; co-founder of Romantic Novelists Association, London, England, 1960, and chairman, 1960-63; Writers' Summer School, London, England, committee member, 1961-63, 1972—, vice-chairman, 1964, chairman, 1964-65, 1966-67, and 1969-71. Lecturer on writers and writing for Arts Council, Workers' Educational Association, and York Education Authority. *Military service:* During World War II served on non-combat duty with Australian Forces, 1942-43; as member of Women's Auxiliary Service with British XIV Army in Burma, 1944-45; became lieutenant; received Burma Star, Pacific Star, and other decorations. *Member:* Society of Authors, Institute of Journalists, Crime Writers' Association, Society of Women Writers and Journalists, Military Historical Society, Association of Yorkshire Bookmen (vice-president, 1960-74), Women's Press Club, Burma Star Association (president of York and North-Eastern Area branch, 1958—). *Awards, honors:* Romantic Novelists' Association awards for *Star of Oudh* (runner-up as best romantic novel of 1960), and *Like Victors and Lords* (best historical romantic novel), 1964.

*WRITINGS—*Titles published in United States under name V. A. Stuart: *Proud Heart,* Jenkins, 1953; *Along Came Ann,* Jenkins, 1953; *Eyes of the Night,* Jenkins, 1954; *Unlit Heart,* Jenkins, 1954; *Pilgrim Heart,* Jenkins, 1955; *Lover Betrayed,* Jenkins, 1955; *No Single Star,* R. Hale, 1956; *Life Is the Destiny,* R. Hale, 1958; *The Summer's Flower,* R. Hale, 1961; *Like Victors and Lords,* R. Hale, 1964, Pinnacle, 1972; *The Valiant Sailors,* R. Hale, 1964, Pinnacle, 1972; *The Beloved Little Admiral: The Life and Times of Admiral of the Fleet the Hon. Sir Henry Keppel,* Pinnacle, 1968; *The Brave Captains,* Pinnacle, 1968; *Black Sea Frigate,* R. Hale, 1971, published as *Hazard's Command,* Pinnacle, 1972; *Hazard of Huntress,* Pinnacle, 1972; *Hazard in Circassia,* Pinnacle, 1973; *Hazard: Victory at Sebastopol,* Pinnacle, 1973; *Mutiny in Meerut,* Pinnacle, 1974; *Massacre at Cawnpore,* Pinnacle, 1974; *Cannons of Lucknow,* Pinnacle, 1974; *The Heroic Garrison,* Pinnacle, 1975; *Hazard: Guns to the Far East,* Pinnacle, 1975.

Under pseudonym Barbara Allen: *Serenade on a Spanish Guitar,* Mills & Boon, 1956; *Dr. Lucy,* Mills & Boon, 1956; *Someone Else's Heart,* Mills & Boon, 1958; *The Gay Gordons,* Mills & Boon, 1961; *The Scottish Soldier,* R. Hale, 1965.

Under pseudonym Fiona Finlay: *Moon Over Madrid,* Mills & Boon, 1957.

Under pseudonym Alex Stuart; all published by Mills & Boon: *The Captain's Table,* 1953; *Ship's Nurse,* 1954; *Soldier's Daughter,* 1954; *Island for Sale,* 1955; *Gay Cavalier,*

1955; *Huntman's Folly*, 1956; *A Cruise for Cinderella*, 1956; *Bachelor of Medicine*, 1956; *The Last of the Logans*, 1957; *Queen's Counsel*, 1957; *Master of Guise*, 1957; *Garrison Hospital*, 1957; *Daughters of the Governor*, 1958; *Master of Surgery*, 1958; *Castle in the Mist*, 1959; *The Peacock Pagoda*, 1959; *Star of Oudh*, 1960; *Spencer's Hospital*, 1961; *Sister Margarita*, 1961; *Doctor Mary Courage*, 1961; *Doctor on Horseback*, 1962; *The Dedicated*, 1962; *The Piper of Laide*, 1963; *Maiden Voyage*, 1964; *Samaritan's Hospital*, 1965; *There But for Fortune*, 1966; *Strangers When We Meet*, 1967; *Random Island*, 1968; *Young Dr. Mason*, 1970; *Research Fellow*, 1971; *A Sunset Touch*, 1972.

Editor and publisher of a three-part series, *A Modern Writer's Guide*.

WORK IN PROGRESS: Hazard's Indian Mutiny and *Sheridan's First Afghan War*; foreword to *Crimean Casualty Rolls*.

SIDELIGHTS: Vivian Stuart is competent in French, Urdu, and knows some Hungarian, German, and Italian. She collects Victorian campaign medals.

* * *

STUBBS, Harry C(lement) 1922-
(Hal Clement)

PERSONAL: Born May 30, 1922, in Somerville, Mass.; son of Harry Clarence (an accountant) and Marjorie (White) Stubbs; married Mary Elizabeth Myers, July 19, 1952; children: George Clement, Richard Myers, Christine. *Education:* Harvard University, B.S., 1943; Boston University, M.Ed., 1947; Simmons College, M.S., 1963. *Politics:* Republican. *Religion:* Episcopalian. *Home:* 12 Thompson Lane, Milton, Mass. 02187.

CAREER: Milton Academy, Milton, Mass., teacher of science, 1949—. Science fiction writer. Milton (Mass.) Warrant (finance) Committee, member. Boy Scouts of America, chairman of district board of review. *Military service:* U.S. Army Air Forces, World War II; bomber pilot with 8th Air Force; received Air Medal and four oak leaf clusters. U.S. Air Force, technical instructor at Sandia Base, N.M., 1952-53. U.S. Air Force Reserve, 1953—; now lieutenant colonel. *Member:* American Association for the Advancement of Science, Authors Guild, Meteoritical Society, New England Association of Chemistry Teachers (division chairman, 1961-62).

WRITINGS—All science fiction, under pseudonym Hal Clement: *Needle*, Doubleday, 1950; *Iceworld*, Gnome Press, 1952; *Mission of Gravity*, Doubleday, 1954; *The Ranger Boys in Space*, L. C. Page & Co., 1956; *Cycle of Fire*, Ballantine, 1957; *Close to Critical*, Ballantine, 1964; *Natives of Space* (short stories), Ballantine, 1965; *Small Changes*, Doubleday, 1969; (editor) *First Flights to the Moon*, introduction by Isaac Asimov, Doubleday, 1970; *Starlight*, Ballantine, 1971.

WORK IN PROGRESS: A junior high school chemistry text; with Robert P. Fox, a paperback science study, tentative title, *Biography of a Mountain*; a science fiction novel.†

* * *

STUCKI, Curtis W(illiam) 1928-

PERSONAL: Surname rhymes with "cookie"; born October 28, 1928, in LaCrosse, Wis.; son of Frank Emmanuel (a minister) and Hulda (Kehrli) Stucki; married Yasuko Hirabayashi, December 20, 1952. *Education:* Cornell College, Mount Vernon, Iowa, B.A., 1950; University of Oregon, M.A., 1954; University of Illinois, M.S. in L.S., 1956. *Politics:* Democrat. *Religion:* United Church of Christ. *Home:* 9519 48th Ave., N.E., Seattle, Wash. 98115. *Office:* University of Washington Library, Seattle, Wash. 98105.

CAREER: State University of New York School of Industrial and Labor Relations at Cornell University, Ithaca, reference librarian and bibliographer, 1956-60; University of Iowa Library, Iowa City, head of special collections department, 1960-62, head of catalog department, 1961-63; University of Washington Library, Seattle, head of catalog division, 1964—. *Military service:* U.S. Army, Troop Education and Information, 1951-53. *Member:* American Library Association, Pacific Northwest Library Association, Puget Sound Mycological Society, Beta Phi Mu.

WRITINGS: American Doctoral Dissertations on Asia, 1933-58, Southeast Asia Program, Cornell University, 1959, revised edition (covering 1933-62), 1963, 2nd revised edition, 1966. Compiler of recent publications section for *Industrial and Labor Relations Review*, 1956-60; regular reviewer of books on Japan for *Library Journal*.

WORK IN PROGRESS: Editing "*Ethnic Studies*" series, for Gale.†

* * *

STUHLMUELLER, Carroll 1923-

PERSONAL: Born April 2, 1923, in Hamilton, Ohio; son of William and Alma (Huesing) Stuhlmueller. *Education:* Studied at Passionist Seminaries in St. Louis, Detroit, Chicago, and Louisville, 1936-50; Catholic University of America, S.T.L., 1952; Pontifical Biblical Institute, Rome, Italy, S.S.L., 1954, S.S.D., 1968. *Office:* Catholic Theological Union, 5401 S. Cornell Ave., Chicago, Ill. 60615.

CAREER: Roman Catholic priest of Passionist order; Passionist Seminary, Chicago, Ill., teacher of scripture and Hebrew, 1954-58; Viatorian Seminary, Evanston, Ill., assistant professor of scripture, 1955-58; Passionist Seminary, Louisville, Ky., professor of scripture, 1958-65; Loretto Junior College, Nerinx, Ky., assistant professor of scripture and history, 1959-65; St. Meinrad Seminary, St. Meinrad, Ind., professor of scripture and Hebrew, 1965-68; Catholic Theological Union, Chicago, Ill., professor of Old Testament, 1968—; St. John's University, New York, N.Y., 1970— (fall semester). Visiting professor, Ecole Biblique et Archeologique, Jerusalem, 1973, Winter Theological School, South Africa, summer, 1973. St. Mary's College, Notre Dame, Ind., member of summer faculty, Graduate School of Theology, 1957-64. *Member:* Catholic Biblical Association of America, Catholic Theological Society of America, Mariological Society of America, Society of Biblical Literature, College Theology Society; American Schools of Oriental Research, National Council of Churches (Catholic member of Faith and Order Commission, 1970-73).

WRITINGS: Gospel of St. Luke, Liturgical Press, 1960, 2nd edition, 1964; *Leviticus*, Paulist Press, 1960; *Postexilic Prophets*, Paulist Press, 1961; *The Prophets and the Word of God*, Fides, 1964, 2nd edition, 1966; (editor) Barnabas Ahern, *New Horizons*, Fides, 1963; *Book of Isaiah*, Liturgical Press, 1964; *Jerome Biblical Commentary*, Prentice-Hall, 1968; *Creative Redemption in Deutero-Isaiah*, Biblical Institute Press, 1970; *Prophets: Charismatic Men*, Argus, 1972; *Biblical Inspiration: Divine-Human Phenomenon*, Argus, 1972; (co-editor) *The Bible Today Reader*,

Liturgical Press, 1973. Contributor to *The New Catholic Encyclopedia*, McGraw, 1966. Contributor to Catholic journals. Co-editor, *Old Testament Reading Guide*, Liturgical Press; formerly assistant editor, *Magister*; member of editorial board, *Bible Today* and *Catholic Biblical Quarterly*.

WORK IN PROGRESS: A study of the poetical style of Isaiah 40-55; a book on Psalms.

* * *

STURGILL, Claude C(arol) 1933-

PERSONAL: Surname is pronounced *Stir*-jill; born December 9, 1933, in Glo, Ky.; son of Gomer C. (an attorney) and Luvenia (McComas) Sturgill; married Carrollton Sue Harrison (a teacher of mathematics), September 3, 1956; children: Bonnie Lou, Mary Elizabeth, Virginia Ann. *Education:* University of Kentucky, A.B., 1956, M.A., 1959, Ph.D., 1963. *Politics:* Republican. *Religion:* Episcopalian. *Office:* Department of History, University of Florida, Gainesville, Fla.

CAREER: University of Kentucky, Lexington, instructor in history, 1961; Western Kentucky State College, Bowling Green, instructor, 1962-63, assistant professor of history, 1963-64; Wisconsin State University, Oshkosh, assistant professor of French history, beginning, 1964; currently at University of Florida, Gainesville, professor of history. *Military service:* U.S. Army, 1956-58; became first lieutenant. *Member:* American Historical Association, Association for State and Local History, French Historical Association, American Association of University Professors, Southern Historical Association, Association of Wisconsin Teachers of College History, Wisconsin Library Association, Phi Alpha Theta, Phi Sigma Iota, Tau Kappa Delta. *Awards, honors:* Research grants from Kentucky Research Council, 1961, Western Kentucky State College, 1962, 1963, and Wisconsin State University Regents Fund, 1964.

WRITINGS: Marshal Villars and the War of the Spanish Succession, University Press of Kentucky, 1965; (editor with Lee Kennett) *The Consortium on Revolutionary Europe*, University of Florida Press, 1974; *Claude le Blanc: Civil Servant of the King*, University of Florida Press, in press. Also author with Donald W. Hensel of *Study Guide to Accompany History of the Western World*, 3 volumes, Heath, 1969. Contributor to *Journal of the West* and *French Historical Studies*. Abstractor for three French army journals for *Historical Abstracts* and *America: History and Life*.

WORK IN PROGRESS: Research in Europe and writing of second volume in a projected series of books covering French military history from the reign of Louis XIV to Napoleon; editing "The Diary of a French Officer in Canada during the Seven Years' War" for Institut d'-Histoire de l'Amerique Francaise.

SIDELIGHTS: Sturgill was a resident of France, 1961-62, 1965-66, while doing research in Paris, Vienna, London, and The Hague.†

* * *

STYCOS, J(oseph) Mayone 1927-

PERSONAL: Born March 27, 1927, in Saugerties, N.Y.; son of Steven (a businessman) and Clotilda (Mayone) Stycos; married Mary McCulloch (divorced); married Maria Nowakowska; children: Steven, Christina, Marek. *Education:* Princeton University, A.B., 1947; Columbia

University, Ph.D., 1952. *Home:* 28 Twin Glens Rd., Ithaca, N.Y. *Office:* Department of Sociology, Cornell University, Ithaca, N.Y.

CAREER: Columbia University, New York, N.Y., research associate, Bureau of Applied Social Research, 1949-51; Social Science Research Center, Puerto Rico, program director, 1951-54; Population Council, fellow in North Carolina, 1954-55; St. Lawrence University, Canton, N.Y., associate professor of sociology, 1955-57; Cornell University, Ithaca, N.Y., associate professor, 1957-63, professor of sociology, 1963—, director of Latin American Program, 1961-66, of International Population Program, 1962—, chairman of department of sociology, 1966-70. Consultant to International Planned Parenthood Federation, Population Council, and Population Reference Bureau. *Member:* National Academy of Sciences, American Sociological Society, Population Association of America.

WRITINGS: Family and Fertility in Puerto Rico, Columbia University Press, 1955; (with Reuben Hill and Kurt Back) *The Family and Population Control*, University of North Carolina Press, 1959; (with Judith Blake and Kingsley Davis) *Family Structure in Jamaica: Social Context of Reproduction*, Free Press of Glencoe, 1961; (with Back) *The Control of Human Fertility in Jamaica*, Cornell University Press, 1964; (editor with J. Arias) *Population Dilemma in Latin America*, Potomac Books, 1966; *Human Fertility in Latin America: Sociological Perspectives*, Cornell University Press, 1968; *Children of the Barriada: A Photographic Essay on the Latin American Population Problem*, Grossman, 1970; *Ideology, Faith, and Family Planning in Latin America: Studies in Public and Private Opinion on Fertility Control*, McGraw, 1971; *Clinics, Contraception, and Communication: Evaluation Studies of Family Planning Programs in Four Latin American Countries*, Appleton, 1973; *Margin of Life: Population and Poverty in the Americas*, Grossman, 1974.

AVOCATIONAL INTERESTS: Photography and jazz piano.

* * *

SULLIVAN, George Edward 1927-

PERSONAL: Born August 11, 1927, in Lowell, Mass.; son of Timothy J. (a salesman) and Cecilia (Shea) Sullivan; married Muriel Moran, May 24, 1952; children: Timothy. *Education:* Fordham University, B.S., 1952. *Home:* 330 East 33rd St., New York, N.Y. 10016. *Agent:* Lurton Blassingame, 10 East 43rd St., New York, N.Y. 10017.

CAREER: American Machine and Foundry Co., Inc., New York, N.Y., public relations manager, 1955-62; free-lance writer, 1962—. Instructor in nonfiction writing, Fordham University, Bronx, N.Y. *Military service:* U.S. Navy, 1945-48. *Member:* Authors Guild of Authors League of America.

WRITINGS: (With Frank Clause) *How to Win at Bowling*, Fleet, 1961; (with Dick Weber) *The Champions Guide to Bowling*, Fleet, 1963; (with Frank Clause and Patty McBride) *Junior Guide to Bowling*, Fleet, 1963; *The Story of the Peace Corps*, Fleet, 1964; (with Irving Crane) *The Young Sportsman's Guide to Pocket Billiards*, Nelson, 1964; *The Story of Cassius Clay*, Fleet, 1964; *Harness Racing*, Fleet, 1964; (with Luther Lassiter) *The Modern Guide to Pocket Billiards*, Fleet, 1964; *Boats*, Maco, 1964.

The Champions Guide to Golf, Fleet, 1965; *Better Ice Hockey for Boys*, Dodd, 1965; (with Finn Larsen) *Skiing*

for Boys and Girls, Follett, 1965; *How Do They Make It?*, Westminster, 1965; (with Larry Scott) *Teenage Guide to Skin and Scuba Diving*, Fell, 1965; *The Modern Guide to Softball*, Fleet, 1965; *Camping*, Maco, 1965; *How Do They Grow It?*, Westminster, 1966; *Seven Modern Wonders of the World*, Putnam, 1966; *Pro Football's Unforgettable Games*, Putnam, 1966; *Tennis*, Follett, 1966; *The Boom in Going Bust*, Macmillan, 1966; *The Personal Story of Luci and Lynda Johnson*, Popular Library, 1966; *The Complete Book of Family Skiing*, Coward, 1966; *Fighter Pilot*, Nelson, 1966; *Wilt Chamberlain Biography*, Grosset, 1966; *Nigeria*, Macmillan, 1967; *Bowling Secrets of the Pros*, Doubleday, 1967; *They Flew Alone*, Warne, 1967; *The Modern Guide to Skin and Scuba Diving*, Coward, 1967; (with John Fanning) *Work When You Want to Work*, Macmillan, 1968; *How Do They Make It?*, Westminster, 1968; *Pro Football's All-Time Greats*, Putnam, 1968; *Face-Off!*, Van Nostrand, 1968; *Bart Starr, Cool Quarterback*, Putnam, 1968; *More How Do They Make It?*, Westminster, 1969; *The Dollar Squeeze and How to Beat It*, Macmillan, 1969; *This is Pro Football*, Dodd, 1969; *The New World of Communications*, Dodd, 1969; *Soccer*, Follett, 1969.

(With Earl Morrall) *In the Pocket*, Grosset, 1970; *How Do They Run It?*, Westminster, 1970; *Understanding Architecture*, Warne, 1970; *The New World of Robots*, Warne, 1970; *Tom Seaver of the Mets*, Putnam, 1970; *The Complete Book of Autograph Collecting*, Dodd, 1970; *Inflation-Proof Your Future*, Walker, 1970; *Pitchers and Pitching*, Dodd, 1971; *Pro Football Plays in Pictures*, Grosset, 1971; *Great Running Backs*, Grosset, 1971; *Understanding Photography*, Warne, 1971; *By Chance a Winner: The History of Lotteries*, Dodd, 1971; *How Do They Build It?*, Westminster, 1971; *The Gamemakers*, Putnam, 1971; *The Rise of the Robots*, Dodd, 1971; *Backpacker's Handbook*, Grosset, 1972; *Pro Football's Kicking Game*, Dodd, 1972; *A Parent's Guide to Sports for Children*, Winchester, 1973; *How Does It Get There?*, Westminster, 1973; *Baseball's Art of Hitting*, Dodd, 1974; *Better Bicycling for Boys and Girls*, Dodd, 1974; *Pictorial Encyclopedia of Pro Football*, Winchester, 1975; *How Do They Find It?*, Westminster, 1975; *Pro Football's Winning Plays*, Dodd, 1975.

SIDELIGHTS: Sullivan wrote, "The first books that I wrote were for juveniles. I have a natural inquisitiveness about a world of subjects. Young people do, too. So I've written about a wide range of things, from aviation to electronics, from auto racing to scuba diving." Sullivan had become interested in photography and uses his own photographs to illustrate many of his books.

*   *   *

SULLIVAN, Mary B(arrett)   1918-

PERSONAL: Born December 5, 1918, in New York, N.Y.; daughter of Edward F. a lawyer and Elizabeth (Corcoran) Barrett; married Walter Sullivan (a journalist), August 17, 1950; children: Elizabeth, Catherine, Theodore. *Education:* Washington State University, B.A., 1940; Columbia University, M.S. (journalism), 1942. *Politics:* Democrat. *Religion:* Unitarian Universalist. *Home:* 66 Indian Head Rd., Riverside, Conn. 06878.

CAREER: Writer. Board member of Greenwich Community Council, Greenwich Center for Child and Family Service, and Greenwich Association for Public Schools.

WRITINGS: Careers in Government, Walck, 1964.

WORK IN PROGRESS: Careers in the Earth Sciences.†

SULLIVAN, Walter   1906-

PERSONAL: Born October 19, 1906, in Pepperell, Mass.; son of Jeremiah (an engineer) and Ann (Meehan) Sullivan. *Education:* College of the Holy Cross, A.B., 1929; Catholic University of America, S.T.B., 1935; Wayne University (now Wayne State University), graduate study, 1950. *Home:* 70 St. Stephen St., Boston, Mass.

CAREER: Roman Catholic priest, member of Congregation of St. Paul (Paulist Fathers); parish priest in New York, N.Y., and member of Paulist East Coast Mission Band prior to 1941; member of West Coast Mission Band, with headquarters in San Francisco, Calif., 1941-42; Paulist Mission House, Detroit, Mich., superior, 1947-52; Paulist Fathers, Boston, Mass., consultor-general, 1958-64; Paulist Mission House, Detroit, Mich., superior, 1964-68; Paulist Fathers, author-in-residence, 1971—. *Military service:* U.S. Army Air Forces, chaplain, 1942-46; became captain; received Bronze Star and Presidential Citation. U.S. Air Force, 1952-55; became lieutenant colonel. *Member:* Shakespeare Society of New York.

WRITINGS—All published by Paulist Press: *Thoughts for Troubled Times*, 1961; *Live in Hope*, 1964; *Shakespeare: His Times and His Problems*, 1968; *Like Yourself, For God's Sake*, Paulist Press, 1975.

*   *   *

SULLY, Kathleen M.   1910-

PERSONAL: Born April 14, 1910, in London, England; daughter of Albert (a mathematical engineer) and Kate (Bown) Coussell; children: three. *Education:* Studied dress design at Barrett Street Trade School, art at Taunton Art College and St. Alban's Art College, and attended various night colleges before enrolling at Gaddesden Teacher Training College, where she received a teaching certificate. *Politics:* Liberal ("if anything"). *Religion:* Christian ("not a church-goer"). *Home:* Munys, Penmenner Rd., The Lizard, Cornwall, England.

CAREER: Jobs have ranged from domestic to teacher of art and English, and include (not necessarily in order), dress model, professional swimmer and diver, cinema usherette, tracer in Admiralty, free-lance artist, bus conductor, owner of antique shop, and dress manufacturer; now full-time novelist, Cornwall, England.

WRITINGS: Small Creatures (juvenile), Ward, Lock, 1946; *Stoney Stream* (juvenile), Ward, Lock, 1946; *Canal in Moonlight*, Davies, 1955, published as *Bikka Road*, Coward, 1956; *Canaille*, Davies, 1956; *Through the Wall*, Davies, 1957; *Merrily to the Grave*, Davies, 1958; *Burden of the Seed*, Davies, 1958; *A Man Talking to Seagull*, Davies, 1959; *Shade of Eden*, Davies, 1960; *Skrine*, Davies, 1960; *The Undesired*, Davies, 1961; *A Man on the Roof*, Davies, 1961; *The Fractured Smile*, Davies, 1965; *Not Tonight*, Davies, 1966; *Dear Wolf*, Davies, 1967; *Horizontal Image*, Davies, 1968; *A Breeze on a Lonely Road*, Davies, 1969; *Island in Moonlight*, Davies, 1970; *A Look at Tadpoles*, Davies, 1970. Author of play, "The Waiting of Lester," produced 1957.

WORK IN PROGRESS: Two novels, tentatively titled *Someone's Got to Love Me* ("a kind of autobiography"), and *Not Forever*; a play, "Under the Yew."

SIDELIGHTS: Kathleen Sully told *CA:* "Main interest now and ever since I could think: Man—why and whence.... Have written since a child but stuff mostly too off-beat for publication. Interests in general: philosophy;

art; realistic literature; dancing; swimming and diving; teaching; diet and health—mental and physical; why the chicken crossed the road."

* * *

SULTAN, Stanley 1928-

PERSONAL: Born July 18, 1928, in Brooklyn, N.Y.; son of Jack (a merchant) and Bess (Leinwand) Sultan; married Betty Hillman; children: James, Lehman, Sonia Elizabeth. *Education:* Cornell University, A.B., 1949; Boston University, M.A., 1950; Yale University, Ph.D., 1955. *Politics:* "Economically collectivist, politically libertarian." *Religion:* Secularist. *Home:* 25 Hardwick St., Brighton, Mass. 02135. *Agent:* Gunther Stuhlmann, 65 Irving Pl., New York, N.Y. 10003. *Office:* Clark University, Worcester, Mass.

CAREER: National Lexicographic Board Ltd., New York, N.Y., assistant editor, 1952-55; Smith College, Northampton, Mass., instructor in English, 1955-59; Clark University, Worcester, Mass., assistant professor, 1959-62, associate professor, 1962-68, professor of English literature, 1968—. Director of National Defense Education Institute in English, 1965. *Member:* International Association for the Study of Anglo-Irish Literature, Malone Society. *Awards, honors:* Yaddo fellowship.

WRITINGS: The Argument of Ulysses, Ohio State University Press, 1965; (contributor) Maurice Harmon, editor, *The Celtic Master*, Dolmen Press, 1969; (editor) John Milington Synge, *The Playboy of the Western World*, Imprint Society, 1970. Story included in *Best American Short Stories*, 1953. Contributor to literary journals.

WORK IN PROGRESS: The Voice of the Jar: Eloquent Form in Modernist Drama, completion expected in 1975.

* * *

SUMMERS, Harrison B(oyd) 1894-

PERSONAL: Born March 19, 1894, in Stanford, Ill.; son of Zelotes Fisher (in insurance) and Alice Marian (Boyd) Summers; married Leda Pauline Pfeifer, March 8, 1917; children: Robert Edward, Dorothy May (Mrs. John W. Higgins). *Education:* Fairmount College (now University of Wichita), A.B., 1917; University of Oklahoma, M.A., 1921; University of Missouri, Ph.D., 1931. *Religion:* Presbyterian. *Home:* 2110 Avenue M, Huntsville, Tex. 77340.

CAREER: Park College, Kansas City, Mo., instructor in speech, 1922-23; Kansas State College (now Kansas State University of Agriculture and Applied Science), Manhattan, 1923-39, began as associate professor of speech, professor of radio, 1931-39; National Broadcasting Co., New York, N.Y., director of public service programs, Eastern Division, 1939-42; American Broadcasting Co., New York, N.Y., director of public service programs, 1942-46; Ohio State University, Columbus, professor of radio-television in department of speech, 1946-64. Visiting professor of radio and television programming at Michigan State University, 1964-65, and University of Southern California, summer, 1965. *Member:* Speech Communications Association, National Academy of Television Arts and Sciences, Association for Professional Broadcasting Education.

WRITINGS: (Contributor) Roy E. Curtis, editor, *Trusts and Economic Control*, McGraw, 1931; *Contest Debating*, Wilson, 1934, revised edition (with Forest L. Whan) published as *How to Debate*, 1940, 2nd revised edition (with Whan and Thomas A. Rousse), 1950, 3rd revised edition,

1963, new edition, 1975; *The Kansas Radio Audience*, Capper Publications, annually, 1937-42, (with Whan, 1941, 1942); *Iowa Radio Audience Survey*, Central Broadcasting Co., annually, 1938-42 (with Whan, 1941, 1942); (with Worth McDougald) *Programming on Radio and Television*, [Ohio], 1958, 2nd edition, 1959; *A Thirty Year History of Programs Carried on National Radio Networks in the United States, 1926-1956*, Ohio State University, 1958; (with Robert E. Summers) *Broadcasting and the Public*, Wadsworth, 1962, revised edition (with R. E. Summers and John Pennybacker), 1975; (contributor) John Lerch, editor, *Careers in Broadcasting*, Appleton, 1962.

Compiler—All published by Wilson, except as indicated: *Unicameral Legislatures*, 1936; *Unicameralism in Practice*, 1937; *Anglo-American Agreement*, 1938; (with R. E. Summers) *Dictatorships versus Democracies*, 1938; *Radio Censorship*, 1939; (with R. E. Summers) *The Railroad Problem*, 1939; (with R. E. Summers) *The Railroads: Government Ownership in Practice*, 1940; (with R. E. Summers) *Increasing Federal Power*, 1940; (with R. E. Summers) *Planned Economy*, 1940; (with R. E Summers) *Universal Military Service*, 1941; *Laws, Regulations, and Decisions affecting Broadcast Programs and Policies*, [Ohio], 1953.

Author of eight published monographs. Contributor of fifteen articles to periodicals, including *Journal of Broadcasting* and *Quarterly Journal of Speech*.

BIOGRAPHICAL/CRITICAL SOURCES: Broadcasting, August 10, 1964.

* * *

SUMMERS, James L(evingston) 1910-

PERSONAL: Born September 11, 1910, in Oshkosh, Wis.; son of Levingston Lee (a teacher) and Anna Louise (Pratt) Summers; married Vera Mae Elmquist (a teacher), June 4, 1932; children: Julie Anne (Mrs. Michael Marcus), Richard Lee. *Education:* Attended Chaffey College, 1928, University of Wisconsin, 1928-30; University of California, Los Angeles, A.B., 1939, Secondary Teaching Credential, 1940. *Politics:* Democrat. *Religion:* Episcopalian. *Home and office:* 5280 Olmeda Ave., Box 564, Atascadero, Calif. *Agent:* McIntosh & Otis, Inc., 18 East 41st St., New York, N.Y., 10017.

CAREER: Industrial Laboratory Supply Co., Los Angeles, Calif., owner, 1940-42; high school teacher of industrial arts at Lone Pine and Barstow, Calif., 1942-46, of U.S. history at Paso Robles, Calif., 1948-54; full-time writer, primarily for young people, 1954—. *Member:* California Writer's Club, Phi Delta Kappa, Masons. *Awards, honors:* New York Herald Tribune Children's Spring Book Festival honor book citation for *Girl Trouble*, 1953; prize from Bureau for Intercultural Education for "Boy in the Mirror."

WRITINGS: Open Season, Doubleday, 1951; *Girl Trouble*, Westminster, 1953; *Prom Trouble* (Junior Literary Guild selection), Westminster, 1954; *Operation ABC*, Westminster, 1955; *Off the Beam*, Westminster, 1956; *Trouble on the Run*, Westminster, 1956; *Ring Around Her Fingers* (Young Peoples Guild selection), Westminster, 1957; *Sons of Montezuma*, Westminster, 1957; *The Wonderful Time*, Westminster, 1958; *Wait for Private Black*, Westminster, 1958; *Heartbreak Hot Rod* (Junior Literary Guild selection), Doubleday, 1958; *The Limit of Love*, Westminster, 1959; *Tougher Than You Think*, Westminster, 1959.

This Random Sky, Westminster, 1960; *Trouble on Hogback Hill*, Westminster, 1960; *Gift Horse* (Junior Literary Guild selection), Westminster, 1961; *The Karting Crowd* (Junior Literary Guild selection), Westminster, 1961; *Muscle Boy*, Westminster, 1962; *The Shelter Trap*, Westminster, 1962; *The Trouble With Being in Love*, Westminster, 1963; *Tiger Terwilliger* (Junior Literary Guild selection), Westminster, 1963; *The Cardiff Giants*, Westminster, 1964; *The Amazing Mr. Tenterhook* (Junior Literary Guild selection), Westminster, 1964; *Wild Buggy Jordan*, McKay, 1965; *Senior Dropout* (Junior Literary Guild selection), Westminster, 1965; *The Long Ride Home*, Westminster, 1966; *Cumash Summer*, McKay, 1967; *The Shelter Trap*, Pflaum, 1967; *The Lucky Suzuki*, McKay, 1968; *The Iron Doors Between*, Westminster, 1968; *You Can't Make It by Bus*, Westminster, 1969.

Don't Come Back a Stranger, Westminster, 1970; *Change of Focus*, Westminster, 1972.

Contributor of short stories to *Southwest Review* and to other literary journals.

SIDELIGHTS: Summers told *CA*: "My juvenile writing has all been undertaken with the most serious literary intent and I find the work to be exacting. When I work on my books I do almost nothing else, preferring a sustained effort to other techniques of writing."†

* * *

SUMMERS, Ray 1910-

PERSONAL: Born February 21. 1910, in Allen, Tex.; son of Luther C. (a farmer) and Vertie Alice (Holley) Summers; married Jester Hilger, June 20, 1934; children: David Ray, Mary Lois, Sarah Nell. *Education:* Baylor University, B.A., 1933; Southwestern Baptist Theological Seminary, Th.M., 1938, Th.D., 1943; postdoctoral study at Garrett Biblical Institute, 1947, University of Edinburgh and University of Basel, 1954. *Home:* 213 Harrington Ave., Waco, Tex. 76703. *Office:* Department of Religion, Baylor University, Waco, Tex. 76703.

CAREER: Baptist minister, 1928—, serving churches in Texas, 1928-41; Southwestern Baptist Theological Seminary, Fort Worth, Tex., professor of New Testament, 1938-59, director of graduate studies, 1955-59; Southern Baptist Theological Seminary, Louisville, Ky., professor of New Testament, 1959-64, director of graduate studies, 1961-64; Baylor University, Waco, Tex., chairman of department of religion, 1964—. *Member:* International Society of New Testament Studies, American Academy of Religion, Society of Biblical Literature.

WRITINGS: Worthy Is the Lamb, Broadman, 1951; *Essentials of New Testament Greek*, Broadman, 1951; (contributor) J. E. Lambdin, editor, *Keeping the Faith*, Broadman, 1953; *The Life Beyond*, Broadman, 1959; *Ephesians: Pattern for Christian Living*, Broadman, 1960; (contributor) H. C. Brown, Jr., editor, *Southeastern Sermons*, Broadman, 1960; (contributor) E. J. Vardaman and J. L. Garrett, editors, *The Teacher's Yoke*, Baylor University Press, 1964; *The Secret Sayings of the Living Jesus: Studies in the Coptic Gospel According to Thomas*, Word Books, 1968; *First Peter, Second Peter, and Jude*, Broadman, 1972; *Commentary on Luke*, Word Books, 1973. Contributor of more than 130 articles to denominational and professional journals and more than 100 reviews to theological journals. Area editor and contributor, *Southern Baptist Encyclopedia*.

SIDELIGHTS: Summers is competent in Hebrew, Greek, Latin, German, French, and Spanish. *The Life Beyond* and *Worthy is the Lamb* have appeared in a total of four translations and both have been made into recordings for the blind. The latter book has been published in Braille.

* * *

SUPER, R(obert) H(enry) 1914-

PERSONAL: Born June 13, 1914, in Wilkes-Barre, Pa.; son of John Henry (a high school principal) and Sadie (Rothermel) Super; married Rebecca Ragsdale, January 25, 1953; children: David Allen, Paul Eric. *Education:* Princeton University, A.B., 1935, Ph.D., 1941; Oxford University, B.Litt., 1937. *Religion:* Lutheran. *Home:* 1221 Baldwin Ave., Ann Arbor, Mich. *Office:* Department of English, University of Michigan, Ann Arbor, Mich. 48104.

CAREER: Princeton University, Princeton, N.J., instructor in English, 1938-42; Michigan State Normal College (now Eastern Michigan University), Ypsilanti, assistant professor of English, 1942-47; University of Michigan, Ann Arbor, assistant professor, 1947-54, associate professor, 1954-60, professor of English, 1960—. Visiting professor at University of Chicago, summer, 1954, Rice University, 1965-66, University of California at Los Angeles, 1967, University of California at Berkeley, 1973. Foreign Economic Administration field intelligence officer, 1945. *Member:* Modern Language Association of America. *Awards, honors:* Fulbright research fellow, United Kingdom, 1949-50; American Council of Learned Societies fellow, 1959-60; Guggenheim fellow, 1962-63, and 1970-71.

WRITINGS: The Publication of Landor's Works, Bibliographical Society (London), 1954; *Walter Savage Landor: A Biography*, New York University Press, 1954; (editor) *The Complete Prose Works of Matthew Arnold*, ten volumes, University of Michigan Press, 1960-74; *The Time-Spirit of Matthew Arnold*, University of Michigan Press, 1970.

WORK IN PROGRESS: Editing the one remaining volume in Matthew Arnold series.

* * *

SURLES, Lynn 1917-

PERSONAL: Born July 23, 1917, in Milwaukee, Wis.; son of Pasco Clyde (president of Fidelity Appraisals Co.) and Gladys (Morgan) Surles; children: Mark, Laurie. *Education:* Northwestern University, M.A. *Office:* 1721 East Lake Bluff, Milwaukee, Wis. 53211.

CAREER: With Colgate University, Hamilton, N.Y., 1947-50; Marquette University, Milwaukee, Wis., instructor in speech and communication and creative writing, 1950-52; Lynn Surles Associates (communication training service), Milwaukee, Wis., president, 1954—. *Member:* Sales and Marketing Executives Club International, American Society of Training and Development, Wisconsin Council of Writers.

WRITINGS: (With W. G. Stanbury) *The Art of Persuasive Talking*, McGraw, 1960; *Ten Vital Abilities of the Successful Salesman*, Dartnell Corp. Also author of booklets on human relations and accident prevention, and on communication and other sales subjects. Contributor to sales and business journals.

WORK IN PROGRESS: A book on industrial alcoholism.

SUSKIND, Richard 1925-

PERSONAL: Born May 2, 1925, in New York, N.Y.; son of Herman R. (a furrier) and Ruth (Raphael) Suskind. *Education:* Attended University of Paris, University of Florence, Columbia University. *Religion:* Jewish. *Agent:* Willis Kingsley Wing, 24 East 38th St., New York, N.Y. 10016.

CAREER: Merchant seaman, 1950-53; Associate editor, *Cavalier*, 1959-60; senior technical writer, 1962; currently editor-in-chief, *Saga. Military service:* U.S. Army, 1943-46; received Combat Infantry Badge.

WRITINGS: The Crusades, Ballantine, 1962; *Do You Want To Live Forever?*, Bantam, 1964; *Cross and Crescent: The Story of the Crusades*, Norton, 1967; *Men in Armor: The Story of Knights and Knighthood*, Norton, 1968; *The Battle of the Belleau Wood: The Marines Stand Fast*, Macmillan, 1969; *Swords, Spears, and Sandals: The Story of the Roman Legions*, Norton, 1969; *The Barbarians: The Story of the European Tribes*, Norton, 1970; *The Sword of the Prophet: The Story of the Moslem Empire*, Grosset, 1971.

SIDELIGHTS: Suskind is fluent in French, Italian, and Spanish.†

*   *   *

SUTHERLAND, C(arol) Humphrey V(ivian) 1908-

PERSONAL: Born May 5, 1908, in London, England; son of G. H. V. (a civil servant) and Elsie (Foster) Sutherland; married Monica La Fontaine McAnally (an author). *Education:* Christ Church, Oxford, B.A., 1931, M.A., 1936, D.Litt., 1945. *Home:* Westfield House, Cumnor, Oxford, England.

CAREER: Oxford University, Oxford, England, assistant keeper of coins, Ashmolean Museum, 1932-52, deputy keeper, 1952-57, keeper, 1957—, university lecturer in numismatics, 1939—, fellow of Christ Church, 1945—, curator of pictures, Christ Church, 1947-55, and 1970—. Winslow Lecturer, Hamilton College, Clinton, N.Y., 1949, 1957. President, Commission Internationale de Numismatique, 1960-73. *Member:* Royal Numismatic Society (president, 1948-53), Roman Society, American Numismatic Society, British Academy (fellow). *Awards, honors:* Huntington Medal of American Numismatic Society, 1950; Silver Medal of Royal Numismatic Society, 1950, of Royal Society of Arts, 1955; Commander, Order of the British Empire, 1970.

WRITINGS: Coinage and Currency in Roman Britain, Oxford University Press, 1937; *The Romans in Spain*, Methuen, 1939; *Anglo-Saxon Gold Coinage*, Oxford University Press, 1948; (with J. G. Milne and J. D. A. Thompson) *Coin Collecting*, Oxford University Press, 1950; *Coinage in Roman Imperial Policy*, Methuen, 1951; *Art in Coinage*, Batsford, 1954; *Gold*, Thames and Hudson, 1959; *The Astophori of Augustus*, Royal Numismatic Society, 1970; *English Coinage 600-1900*, Barrie & Jenkins, 1973; *Roman Coins*, Barrie & Jenkins, 1974. Contributor and editor with others, "Roman Imperial Coinage" series, 1939—; editor, *Numismatic Chronicle*, 1953-66.

*   *   *

SUTHERLAND, H(erbert) W(arren) 1917-

PERSONAL: Born December 26, 1917, in South Shields, England; son of Laurence (a master mariner) and Ella (Mitchell) Sutherland; married Margaret Langham-Hobart (a librarian), July 29, 1950; children: Alexander Christian. *Education:* King's College, University of Durham, B.A. and Dip.Ed., 1949. *Politics:* Liberal. *Religion:* Church of England. *Home:* 3 Westlands, High Heaton, Newcastle upon Tyne 7, England. *Agent:* Curtis Brown Ltd., 1 Craven Hill, London W2 3EW, England.

CAREER: Teacher at various schools in Newcastle, 1949-61; Raby Street County Secondary School, Byker, Newcastle upon Tyne, England, deputy headmaster, 1961-1969; Newcastle Polytechnic, Newcastle, senior lecturer in communication, 1969—. *Military service:* British Army, Royal Signals, 1940-46; served in Libya, Greece, Syria, Iraq, Iran, India, Burma, and Germany. *Awards, honors:* Prize winner in *Observer* Short Story Competition, 1954; Northern Arts Award, 1966, for *Best Out of Three*.

WRITINGS: Fiddle Me Free, Putnam, 1958; *Best Out of Three*, Bles, 1960; *A Case of Knives*, Bles, 1964. Short stories appear in *A.D. 2500* (twenty-one prize *Observer* short stories), edited by Angus Wilson, Heinemann, 1955; and *Pick of Today's Short Stories*, edited by John Pudney, Putnam, 1958; *Magnie*, Bles, 1967. Contributor of short stories to *Chambers's Journal, Queen.*

WORK IN PROGRESS: Two plays, "Whatever Became of South Shields' Left Book Club?" and "Straight on for Bondi?".

AVOCATIONAL INTERESTS: Collecting violins and researching the origins of surnames for B.B.C. radio program.

*   *   *

SUTTLES, Shirley (Smith) 1922-
(Lesley Conger)

PERSONAL: Born March 25, 1922, in Seattle, Wash.; daughter of Walker Conger and Marie (Beidel) Smith; married Wayne Suttles, 1941; children: seven. *Education:* University of California, B.A., 1944. *Home:* 5750 S.W. Hewett Blvd., Portland, Oregon. *Agent:* Howard Moorepark, 444 East 82nd St., New York, N.Y. 10028.

CAREER: Free-lance writer.

WRITINGS—All under pseudonym Lesley Conger: *Love and Peanut Butter*, Norton, 1961; *Adventures of an Ordinary Mind*, Norton, 1963; *Three Giant Stories*, Four Winds, 1968; *Tops and Bottoms: Adapted from a Folk Tale*, Four Winds, 1970; *To Writers, With Love*, Writer, Inc., 1971. Writer of radio and television scripts for Canadian Broadcasting Corp. Contributor to popular magazines, including *Redbook, Cosmopolitan, Good Housekeeping*, and *Ladies' Home Journal*. Author of monthly column "Off the Cuff", *The Writer*, 1965—.

*   *   *

SUTTON, Horace (Ashley) 1919-

PERSONAL: Born May 17, 1919, in New York, N.Y.; son of Herman and Belle (Chodorov) Sutton; married Nancy Waring, May 7, 1950; married second wife, Patricia Anne Diamond, June 10, 1958; children: (first marriage) Andrew; (second marriage) Miranda, Patrick. *Education:* Lawrenceville School, graduate, 1936; studied at University of Pennsylvania, 1936-38, Columbia University, 1938-41. *Home:* 4634 Waipahee Place, Honolulu, Hawaii. *Office: Saturday Review/World*, 488 Madison Ave., New York, N.Y. 10020.

CAREER: New York Post, New York, N.Y., travel editor, 1946-47; *Saturday Review*, New York, travel editor, 1947-61, associate editor, 1961-72; *World Magazine*, New

York, editorial director, 1972-73; *Saturday Review/World*, New York, editorial director, 1973—. Contributing travel editor of *Sports Illustrated*, 1955-61, of *McCall's*, 1961-65; columnist, "Of All Places," Hall Syndicate, 1959—; editorial director, *Paradise of the Pacific*, 1963-66. Radio and television commentator and panelist. *Military service:* U.S. Army, Counter Intelligence Corps, 1941-46; served in European theater; became captain; received Bronze Star, Croix de Guerre with silver star (France). *Member:* Travel Writers Association, Overseas Press Club (member of board of governors, 1960-62). *Awards, honors:* Star of Solidarity first class (Italy); Travel Journalism Award, American Society of Travel Agents, 1951; Overseas Press Club Award, 1968; French Medaille du Tourisme, 1973.

WRITINGS: Footloose in France, Rinehart, 1948; *Footloose in Canada*, Rinehart, 1949; *Footloose in Switzerland*, Rinehart, 1949; (with Ewing Krainin) *Happy Holiday*, Simon & Schuster, 1949; *Footloose in Italy*, Rinehart, 1950; *Confessions of a Grand Hotel*, Henry Holt, 1951; *Sutton's Places*, Henry Holt, 1954; *Aloha, Hawaii: The New United Air Lines Guide to the Hawaiian Islands*, Doubleday, 1967. Contributor to most national magazines.

WORK IN PROGRESS: A pictorial social history of travel by Americans.

SIDELIGHTS: Sutton travels about one hundred thousand miles a year gathering material, commutes every three or four months between his home in Hawaii and his office in New York.†

* * *

SUTTON, Maurice Lewis 1927-
(Stack Sutton)

PERSONAL: Born February 9, 1927, in Vero Beach, Fla.; son of Daniel Lewis and Eva (Sheffield) Sutton; married Kay White; children: (previous marriage) Karen, Randolph. *Education:* Attended University of Miami, Coral Gables, Fla., 1954; University of Florida, B.A., 1963, M.Ed., 1964. *Religion:* Protestant. *Home:* 1225 Tangerine Park, Winterhaven, Fla.

CAREER: U.S. Border Patrol, inspector, 1952-58; Daytona Beach (Fla.) Fire Department, fireman, 1959-61; Polk County Junior College, Winter Haven, Fla., instructor in English, 1964—. Instructor in adult education classes, Gainesville, Fla., 1963-64. *Military service:* U.S. Marine Corps, 1945-47. U.S. Marine Corps Reserve, 1948-51; became sergeant. *Member:* Modern Language Association of America, Florida Education Association, Florida Historical Society, Gainesville Writing League, Scriptteasers.

WRITINGS: Joseph Conrad: Heart of Darkness—The Secret Sharer, Barnes & Noble, 1968; *Joseph Conrad: The Nigger of the Narcissus*, Barnes & Noble, 1968; *Joseph Conrad: Victory*, Barnes & Noble, 1969; (with Larry M. Sutton and W. Ronald Puckett) *A Simple Rhetoric*, Holbrook Press, 1969; (with others) *Now*, Free Press of Glencoe, 1969; (editor with Norman Small) *The Making of Drama: Idea and Performance*, Holbrook Press, 1972; (with Puckett) *College English*, Holbrook Press. Also author of Barnes & Noble study guides for Joseph Conrad novels.

Novels—under name Stack Sutton: *Circle R Range*, Arcadia House, 1963; *Tumbleweed*, Thomas Bourgey, 1965. Also author of *Leatherwood*, Powell. Contributor to men's magazines, automotive magazines, and Sunday supplements.

WORK IN PROGRESS: A book on the Seminole Indian chief Wild Cat, completion expected in 1978.

SIDELIGHTS: Sutton speaks, reads, and writes what he describes as "poor Spanish." *Avocational interests:* Jai-alai, professional football, fencing, golf, woodworking, tenor sax, and reading.

* * *

SWANSON, Don R(ichard) 1924-

PERSONAL: Born October 10, 1924, in Los Angeles, Calif.; son of Harry Windfield and Grace Clara (Sandstrom) Swanson; married Shirley Mae Sollenberger, June 30, 1951 (divorced, 1968); children: Douglas Alan, Richard Brian, Judith Ann. *Education:* California Institute of Technology, B.S. (with honor), 1945; Rice University, M.A. (physics), 1947; University of California, Berkeley, Ph.D., 1952. *Home:* 5550 Dorchester Ave., Chicago, Ill. 60637.

CAREER: Hughes Aircraft Co., Research and Development Laboratories, Culver City, Calif., researcher on computer design, 1952-55; Thompson Ramo-Wooldridge, Inc., Canoga Park, Calif., manager of synthetic intelligence department, 1955-63; University of Chicago, Chicago, Ill., dean of Graduate Library School, 1963-72, professor of library science, 1963—. National Science Foundation, member of science information council, Office of Science Information Service, 1960-65; Library of Congress, member of automation study committee, 1961-63; President's Science Advisory Committee, member of toxicological information panel, 1964-66. National Opinion Research Center, trustee, 1964-73. Member of Committee on Scientific and Technical Communication of the National Academy of Science, 1966-69. *Military service:* U.S. Naval Reserve, 1943-46; became lieutenant junior grade. *Member:* Sigma Xi, Tau Beta Pi.

WRITINGS: (Co-author) *Automation and the Library of Congress*, Library of Congress, 1964; (editor) *The Intellectual Foundations of Library Education*, University of Chicago Press, 1965; (co-editor) *Operations Research: Implications for Libraries*, University of Chicago Press, 1972; (co-editor) *Management Education: Implications for Libraries and Library Schools*, University of Chicago Press, 1974.

Contributor: Paul L. Garvin, editor, *Natural Language and the Computer*, McGraw, 1961; H. P. Edmundson, editor, *Proceedings of the National Symposium on Machine Translation*, McGraw, 1961; *Machine Indexing: Progress and Problems*, 3rd edition, American University, 1961; B. Markuson, editor, *Libraries and Automation*, Library of Congress, 1963. Also contributor of foreword to *Principles of Information Retrieved by M. Kochen*, Melville, 1974. Contributor to various other published conference proceedings. Contributor of articles and reviews to computing and documentation journals.

* * *

SWATRIDGE, Charles
(Theresa Charles, a joint pseudonym)

PERSONAL: Born in Norfolk, England; son of Charles (a clergyman) and Sarah (Hardy) Swatridge; married Irene Mossop. *Education:* Attended Norwich School and Cambridge University. *Politics:* Conservative. *Religion:* Church of England. *Home:* Ladygate, Heathfield Rd., Woking, Surrey, England. *Agent:* Curtis Brown Ltd., 1 Craven Hill, London W2 3EW, England.

CAREER: Author.

WRITINGS—All with wife Irene Swatridge, under joint pseudonym Theresa Charles: *The Distant Drum*, Longmans, Green, 1940; *My Enemy and I*, Longmans, Green, 1941; *Happy Now I Go*, Longmans, Green, 1947; *To Save My Life*, Longmans, Green, 1948; *Man-Made Miracle*, Longmans, Green, 1949.

Burning Beacon, Cassell, 1950; *At a Touch I Yield*, Cassell, 1952; *Fairer Than She*, Cassell, 1953; *My Only Love*, Cassell, 1954; *Kinder Love*, Cassell, 1955; *Ultimate Surrender*, R. Hale, 1958; *A Girl Called Evelyn*, R. Hale, 1959.

No Through Road, R. Hale, 1960; *House on the Rocks*, R. Hale, 1962; *Ring for Nurse Raine*, R. Hale, 1962; *Widower's Wife*, R. Hale, 1963; *Nurse Alice in Love*, R. Hale, 1964; *Patient in Love*, R. Hale, 1964; *The Man For Me*, R. Hale, 1965; *How Much You Mean to Me*, R. Hale, 1966; *The Way Men Love*, R. Hale, 1967; *Proud Citadel*, R. Hale, 1967; *The Shadowy Mind*, R. Hale, 1968; *From Fairest Flowers*, R. Hale, 1969.

Wayward as the Swallow, R. Hale, 1970; *Second Honeymoon*, R. Hale, 1970; *My True Love*, R. Hale, 1971; *Therefore Must Be Loved*, R. Hale, 1972; *Castle Kelpiesloch*, R. Hale, 1973; *Nurse by Accident*, R. Hale, 1974.

SIDELIGHTS: Happy Now I Go was filmed as "The Woman with No Name." Novels have been translated into sixteen languages and serialized throughout Europe. *Avocational interests:* Animal welfare, classical music, and art.

* * *

SWEETKIND, Morris 1898-

PERSONAL: Born December 8, 1898, in Odessa, Russia; son of Joseph (a painter) and Bella (Feldman) Sweetkind; married Betty Kauffman, September 11, 1927; children: David William, Judith Rose (Mrs. Lawrence Levey). *Education:* Yale University, Ph.B., 1920, M.A., 1923. *Religion:* Jewish. *Home:* 4 Birch Dr., New Haven, Conn.

CAREER: Cheshire Academy, Cheshire, Conn., teacher of English, 1920-64, head of department, 1940-65. Also taught at Southern Connecticut State College, 1940-50, University of Connecticut, 1950-55, and University of California, Los Angeles, 1966. *Member:* National Council of Teachers of English, Connecticut Council of Teachers of English.

WRITINGS: Basic English Grammar, Cheshire Press, 1960; (with John Gassner) *Introducing the Drama*, Holt, 1963; *Teaching Poetry in the High School*, Macmillan, 1964; (editor) Thomas Hardy, *Mayor of Casterbridge*, Macmillan, 1965; *Wonderful World* (poems for children), Mack & Co., 1967; (with Gassner) *Tragedy, History, and Romance*, Holt, 1968; (editor) *Ten Great One Act Plays*, Bantam, 1968; (editor) *15 International One Act Plays*, Washington Square Press, 1969; *Getting Into Poetry*, Holbrook, 1972. Also translator of Moliere's "Sganarelle."

* * *

SWINDLER, William F(inley) 1913-

PERSONAL: Born October 24, 1913, in St. Louis, Mo.; son of Merton Clay and Nona Pearl (Traller) Swindler; married Benetta Rollins, October 7, 1939; children: Elizabeth Pearl Henrietta, William Rollins Clayton. *Education:* Washington University, St. Louis, Mo., A.B. and B.S., 1935; University of Missouri, M.A., 1936, Ph.D., 1942; University of Nebraska, LL.B., 1958. *Politics:* Democrat. *Religion:* Episcopal. *Office:* Marshall-Wythe School of Law, College of William and Mary, Williamsburg, Va. 23185.

CAREER: St. Louis Star-Times, St. Louis, Mo., reporter and editorial writer, 1936-38; University of Missouri, Columbia, instructor in journalism, 1938-40; University of Idaho, Moscow, assistant professor, 1940-44, associate professor, 1944-45, professor of journalism, 1945-46, head of department, 1941-44; University of Nebraska, Lincoln, professor of journalism and dean, 1946-56; admitted to Nebraska bar, 1958; College of William and Mary, Williamsburg, Va., professor of legal history and director of development, 1958—. General counsel, Virginia Commission on Constitutional Revision, 1968-69; editor and director, Research Project on State Constitutions, 1968—; Chairman, ad hoc committee on Supreme Court History for the Judicial Conference of the U.S., 1972—; member, publications committee, Virginia Independence Bicentennial Committee. *St. Louis Post-Dispatch*, special correspondent, 1938-40; *Lincoln State Journal*, editorial writer, 1946-50; *Hastings Tribune*, editorial columnist, 1952; Columbia Broadcasting System, special correspondent, 1952; freelance magazine writer, 1939—. *Member:* American Bar Association, American Judicature Society (member of board of directors, 1972—), British Society of Public Teachers of Law (associate), American Law Institute, National Lawyers Club, American Society for Legal History (director, 1960—; vice-president, 1962-64), District of Columbia Bar Association, Nebraska Bar Association, Virginia Bar Association, Selden Society, Phi Delta Phi.

WRITINGS: A Bibliography of Law on Journalism, Columbia University Press, 1947; *Problems of Law in Journalism*, Macmillan, 1955; *Common Law in America*, Virginia State Bar, 1959; *Magna Carta: Legend and Legacy*, Bobbs-Merrill, 1965; *Magna Carta*, Grosset, 1968; *Government by the People: Theory and Reality in Virginia*, University Press of Virginia, 1969; *Court and Constitution in the 20th Century*, Bobbs-Merrill, Volume I: *The Old Legality, 1889-1932*, 1969, Volume II: *The New Legality, 1932-1968*, 1970, Volume III: *The Constitution of the United States; A 20th Century Interpretation*, 1973; *Justice in the States*, West, 1971; *Sources and Documents of United States Constituions*, ten volumes, Oceana, 1972-74; *The Course of Human Events: The Continental Congress, 1774-1789*, Mason & Lipscomb, 1974; *Principles of Constitutional Law*, Bobbs-Merrill, 1974.

Contributor to *Encyclopedia Americana*, 1968—. Also contributor of articles to scholarly journals, law reviews and magazines, including *American Heritage*, *Nebraska Law Review*, *American Bar Association Journal*, *Vanderbilt Law Review*, and *Georgetown Law Journal*. Founder and editor of journalism bulletin series, University of Idaho, 1944-46, University of Nebraska, 1947; member of editorial board, *Journalism Quarterly*, 1945-58; advisory editor, *Nebraska Foreign Service Review*, 1950-51.

WORK IN PROGRESS: Research in constitutional and legal history.

* * *

SWINTON, William E(lgin) 1900-

PERSONAL: Born September 30, 1900, in Kirkcaldy, Fife, Scotland; son of William Wilson (a civil engineer) and Rachel (Cargill) Swinton. *Education:* University of Glasgow, student, 1917-22, D.Sc., Ph.D. *Home:* 276 Saint George St., Toronto M5R 2P6, Ontario, Canada. *Office:* Massey College, University of Toronto, 4 Devonshire Pl., Toronto M5S 2E1, Ontario, Canada.

CAREER: University of Glasgow, Glasgow, Scotland, demonstrator in geology, 1922-24; British Museum (Natural History), London, England, paleontologist, 1924-61, became principal scientific officer; University of Toronto, Toronto, Ontario, professor of geology, 1961-68, fellow of Massey College, 1974. Royal Ontario Museum (Toronto), director, 1962-66, honorary trustee. Member of board of Ontario Science Centre. Visiting professor at Queen's University at Kingston (Ontario), 1974. Member of museum advisory board of London County Council, 1950-61. *Military service:* Royal Navy Volunteer Reserve, 1939-45; became lieutenant commander.

MEMBER: International Council of Museums, Museums Association (president, 1958-60), Royal Anthropological Institute (fellow), Linnaean Society (fellow), Royal Society of Medicine (fellow), Academy of Medicine (Toronto; honorary fellow), fellow of other scientific societies, Athenaeum Club (London), Arts and Letters Club, Royal Canadian Yacht Club, and University Club (all Toronto).

WRITINGS: On Fossil Reptilia From Sokoto Province [London], 1930; (author of foreword and descriptive notes) *Monsters of Primeval Days*, Figurehead, 1931; *The Dinosaurs: A Short History of a Great Group of Extinct Reptiles*, Murby & Co., 1934; *A Guide to the Fossil Birds, Reptiles and Amphibians in the Department of Geology and Paleontology*, British Museum (Natural History), 1934; (contributor) *The Science of Living Things*, Odhams, 1935; *The Crocodile of Maransart*, Bruxelles, 1937; (with F. J. North and C. F. Davidson) *Geology in the Museum*, Oxford University Press, 1941; *The Corridor of Life*, J. Cape, 1948; *Fossil Amphibians and Reptiles*, British Museum (Natural History), 1954, 6th edition, 1973; *Type Specimens in Botany and Zoology*, International Council of Museums, 1955; *The Leeds Collection of Fossil Reptiles*, Basil Blackwell, 1956; *Fossil Birds*, British Museum (Natural History), 1958, 2nd edition, 1966.

Animals Before Adam, Phoenix House, 1961; *The Wonderful World of Prehistoric Animals*, Garden City Books, 1961 (published in England as *The Story of Prehistoric Animals*, Rathbone Books, 1961, revised and enlarged edition, Macdonald & Co., 1970); *Fossils*, Museum Press, 1961; *Dinosaurs*, British Museum (Natural History), 1962, 4th edition, 1970; *Digging for Dinosaurs*, Doubleday, 1962; *Harry Govier Seeley and the Karroo Reptiles*, British Museum (Natural History), 1962; *Giants, Past and Present*, R. Hale, 1966; *The Earth Tells Its Story*, Bodley Head, 1967, 2nd edition, 1973; *The Dinosaurs*, Allen & Unwin, 1970. Also contributor to *Studies on Fossil Vertebrates*, 1962.

WORK IN PROGRESS: The Medical Founders of the Arts and Sciences.

SIDELIGHTS: Swinton reads German, French, and the Scandinavian languages. He has traveled widely in Europe, India, Africa, the Arctic, and America.

*   *   *

TABRAH, Ruth Milander   1921-

PERSONAL: Born February 28, 1921, in Buffalo, N.Y.; daughter of Henry and Ruth H. (Flock) Milander; married Frank L. Tabrah (a physician), May 8, 1943 (divorced, 1971); children: Joseph Garner, Thomas. *Education:* University of Buffalo, B.A., 1941; University of Washington, Seattle, graduate study, 1944-45. *Politics:* Democrat. *Religion:* Buddhist. *Home:* 108 Puako Beach Drive, Kamuela, Hawaii.

CAREER: Author, editor, and free-lance photojournalist; Hawaii School Advisory Council, elected member, 1962-66; chairman, 1964-66; Hawaii State Board of Education, elected member, 1966-74. National Association of State Boards of Education, vice-president of western division, 1968-72, director-at-large, 1971; consultant, U.S. Office of Education, 1969-72, The Consulting Organization, 1972—. *Member:* P.E.N., Author's League of America, Sierra Club (Big Island chairman, 1970-72), League of Women Voters, American Association of University Women, Phi Beta Kappa. *Awards, honors:* Distinguished Woman in Education Award from American Association of University Women, 1970.

WRITINGS: Pulaski Place, Harper, 1950; *The Voices of Others*, Putnam, 1959, published as *Town for Scandal*, Pocket Books, 1960; *Hawaiian Heart*, Follett, 1964; *Hawaii Nei*, Follett, 1967; *The Red Shark*, Follett, 1970; *Buddhism: A Modern Way of Life and Thought*, Jodo (Honolulu), 1970; *The Old Man and the Astronauts*, Island Heritage (Honolulu), 1974. Editor of Island Heritage's "Folktale Series," 1972-74. Contributor of magazine and feature articles nationwide.

WORK IN PROGRESS: Adult novel with working title, *The Territory of the Heart*; non-fiction book, *A Buddhist Experience*; and a children's book, *The Tricky Ghosts of Lanai*.

SIDELIGHTS: Mrs. Tabrah speaks French and German, and small amounts of Japanese and Spanish. She has travelled widely doing research for her books. *Avocational interests:* Painting, skin diving.

*   *   *

TAFT, William H(oward)   1915-

PERSONAL: Born October 24, 1915, in Mexico, Mo.; son of Raymond E. (an insurance man) and Ferrie (Dains) Taft; married Myrtle Adams, January 18, 1941; children: Marie, Bill, Alice. *Education:* Westminster College, Fulton, Mo., A.B., 1937; University of Missouri, B.J., 1938, M.A., 1939; Western Reserve University (now Case Western Reserve University), Ph.D., 1951. *Politics:* Republican. *Religion:* Methodist. *Home:* 107 Sondra Ave., Columbia, Mo. 65201. *Office:* School of Journalism, University of Missouri, Columbia, Mo. 65201.

CAREER: Hiram College, Hiram, Ohio, public relations man and teacher, 1939-40, 1947-48; Youngstown College (now Youngstown State University), Youngstown, Ohio, assistant professor of English and journalism, 1946-48; Defiance College, Defiance, Ohio, professor of English and journalism, 1948-50, head of department of English, 1949-50; Memphis State University, Memphis, Tenn., associate professor, 1950-56, head of department of journalism, 1955-56; University of Missouri, Columbia, member of journalism department, 1956—. *Commercial Appeal*, Memphis, Tenn., part-time copy editing, 1950-55. *Military service:* U.S. Army and U.S. Army Air Forces, 1941-45. U.S. Air Force Reserve, 1945-51; became captain. *Member:* American Historical Association, Association for Education in Journalism, Delta Tau Delta, Pi Delta Epsilon, Kappa Tau Alpha (national treasurer and chief of central office).

WRITINGS: Let's Publish that Top-Rated Yearbook, Lucas Brothers, 1961; (co-author) *Modern Journalism*, Pitman, 1962; *Missouri Newspapers*, University of Missouri Press, 1964; *Missouri Newspapers, When and Where, 1808-1963*, State Historical Society of Missouri, 1964; *American Journalism History: Outline*, Lucas Brothers,

1968, 3rd edition, 1973; *Newspapers as Tools for Historians*, Lucas Brothers, 1970; (co-author) *Mass Media and the National Experience*, Harper, 1971. Compiler of bibliography of books on American journalism, published by School of Journalism, University of Missouri, 1965; editor, *Kappa Tau Alpha Yearbook*. Contributor to *American People's Encyclopedia Yearbook*, *Encyclopedia Americana*, *Book of Knowledge*, and to newspapers and journalism journals.

WORK IN PROGRESS: Compiling *Mass Media and Society: A Documentary History*, projected three volumes, for Random House; biography of Bernarr Macfadden; history of Donrey Media and its founder, Donald Reynolds.

* * *

TALBOT, Carol Terry 1913-
(Carol Terry)

PERSONAL: Born February 24, 1913, in Los Angeles, Calif.; daughter of Vinal Smith and Wilhelmina (Reid) Terry; married Louis Thompson Talbot (chancellor of Biola College, The Bible Institute of Los Angeles), February 5, 1964. *Education:* Graduate of Woodbury Business College; The Bible Institute of Los Angeles, diploma, 1940; Los Angeles Theological Seminary (now Talbot Theological Seminary), Bachelor of Christian Education, 1947; Chapman College, B.A., 1953. *Politics:* Republican. *Religion:* Protestant. *Home:* Apartment 3C, 13560 St. Andrews Dr., Seal Beach, Calif. *Office:* Ramabai Mukti Mission, P.O. Box 4912, Clinton, N.J. 08809.

CAREER: Went as missionary to Ramabai Mukti Mission (orphanage and rescue home), Kedgaon, Poona District, India, in 1941; was captured by Japanese en route and spent three and one-half years as prisoner until rescued by U.S. forces; following release served as assistant superintendent and sometime superintendent of mission, and publicity director; presently Western U.S. representative of Ramabai Mukti Mission and lecturer. The Bible Institute of Los Angeles, teacher of missions. *Member:* Phi Kappa Chi.

WRITINGS—Under name Carol Terry: *Kept*, privately printed, 1945; *Let's Go to India*, Zondervan, 1964. Editor of *Prayer Bell* (India).

WORK IN PROGRESS: A biography of Louis T. Talbot, tentative title, *For This I Was Born*.

SIDELIGHTS: Carol Talbot is competent in Marathi language of India.

* * *

TALMON, Jacob L(aib) 1916-

PERSONAL: Born June 14, 1916, in Rypin, Poland; son of Abraham (a businessman) and Ziporah (Lichtenstein) Talmon; married Irene Anna Bugajer (a physician), November 24, 1961; children: Daniella-Josephine, Maya-Anath. *Education:* The Hebrew University of Jerusalem, M.A., 1939; Sorbonne, University of Paris, graduate student, 1939-40; London School of Economics and Political Science, London, Ph.D., 1943. *Religion:* Jewish. *Home:* 25 Shderot ben-Maimon, Jerusalem, Israel.

CAREER: The Hebrew University of Jerusalem, Jerusalem, Israel, 1949—, began as instructor, now professor of modern history. *Awards, honors:* Israel Prize, 1954, for *The Origins of Totalitarian Democracy*.

WRITINGS: The Origins of Totalitarian Democracy,

Secker & Warburg, 1952; *Political Messianism—The Romantic Phase*, Secker & Warburg, 1960; *The Unique and the Universal*, Secker & Warburg, 1965; *Romanticism and Revolt: Europe 1815-1848*, Thames & Hudson, 1967; *Israel Among the Nations*, Weidenfeld & Nicolson, 1970; *The Origins of Ideological Polarization in the Twentieth-Century*, Secker & Warburg, in press. Contributor to *Commentary*, *Midstream*, and *Encounter*.

* * *

TANCHUCK, Nathaniel 1912-

PERSONAL: Born December 2, 1912, in Brooklyn, N.Y.; son of Max (a sculptor) and Sadie (Tichtman) Tanchuck; married Rachel Mary Mason, November 12, 1945; children: Heather Natalie. *Education:* Attended New York University, 1931, University of Utah, 1933-34; University of Southern California, B.S. in Journalism, 1936; Cambridge University, certificate in modern drama, 1946. *Home:* 3620 Meier St., Los Angeles, Calif. 90066. *Agent:* William Morris Agency, Beverly Hills, Calif. *Office:* Suite 124, 1800 North Highland, Hollywood, Calif. 90028.

CAREER: Writer, director, and producer for radio, television, and motion pictures, 1936—. President, Arista Films. *Military service:* U.S. Army Air Forces, 1942-46; became captain; received five battle stars, Croix de Guerre avec Palme (France), Croix de Guerre (Belgium), George Medal (Great Britain), Presidential Citation; U.S. Air Force Reserve, 1946-72; retired as lieutenant colonel. *Member:* Writers Guild of America (West), American Institute of Journalists, Authors League, Dramatists Guild, Sigma Delta Chi, Los Angeles Press Club, Kittyhawk Club. *Awards, honors: Salt Lake City Tribune* Short Story Award, for "The Borzoi," "Pride and Fall," and "The Coward," 1933, 1934, and 1935.

WRITINGS: A Certain French Girl, Fawcett, 1964. Writer of radio scripts, "American Sketches," "Free French Series," "Great Loves." Television writer for network series, including "Bonanza," "Wagon Train," "Fury," "Flicka," and "Tugboat Annie." Contributor of short stories to periodicals.

WORK IN PROGRESS: There I Stood With My Croix de Guerre, based on actual happenings.

SIDELIGHTS: Tanchuck told *CA:* "To paraphrase John Dryden's definition of criticism, writing comes from drinking ass's milk, hating to punch clocks, and being too stiff-necked to be content with life as it is. Thus, I have retired from my career as a writer as often as Frank Sinatra. The last time, some three years ago. I started doing TV commercials just because I thought I could do a better job than most, and now it is a continuous sideline, which, incidently, has irritated me sufficiently to return to authoring another book, and also completing several screenplays which I refuse to sell unless I am permitted to direct. My purpose is not so much money, as a sort of last chance to film my way, and not some bank's." *Avocational interests:* Pursuing "little known facts of life, both historical and contemporary."

BIOGRAPHICAL/CRITICAL SOURCES: Reporter, August, 1952.

* * *

TANNER, James M(ourilyan) 1920-

PERSONAL: Born August 1, 1920, in Camberly, England; son of Frederick Charles (an army officer) and Ethelwyn

(Mourilyan) Tanner; married Bernice Alture (a physician), July 1, 1942; children: Helen, David. *Education:* Attended University of Exeter, 1938-39, St. Mary's Hospital Medical School, University of London, 1939-44, University of Pennsylvania Medical School, 1941-43; M.B., B.S., and M.D. Ph.D., and D.Sc. *Politics:* Radical. *Religion:* Humanist. *Home:* 21 Holland Villas Rd., London W. 14, England.

CAREER: Oxford University, Oxford, England, demonstrator in anatomy, 1946-48; St. Thomas's Hospital Medical School, University of London, lecturer and senior lecturer in physiology, 1948-55; University of London, London, England, 1955—, began as reader in Institute for Child Health, became professor of human growth and development. Consultant to Hospital for Sick Children, London, England. *Member:* Society for the Study of Human Biology, Biometric Society, Physiological Society, Anatomical Society, Genetical Society, Society for Research in Child Development.

WRITINGS: Growth at Adolescence, Blackwell Scientific Publications, 1955, 2nd edition, 1962; *Education and Physical Growth*, University of London Press, 1961; (with G. A. Harrison, J. S. Weiner, and N. A. Barnicolt) *Human Biology*, Oxford University Press, 1964; *The Physique of the Olympic Athlete*, Allen & Unwin, 1964. Author of filmscript, "The Growth and Development of Children." Editor of *Human Biology*.

WORK IN PROGRESS: Research on human and animal growth, pediatric endocrinology, and human biology.

SIDELIGHTS: Tanner speaks French and German. *Avocational interests:* Music, painting, athletics, skiing, and travel.

*   *   *

TAPPLY, H(orace) G(ardner)   1910-

PERSONAL: Born September 18, 1910, in Waltham, Mass.; son of George Sammuel and Gertrude (Dore) Tapply; married Muriel Langley Morgridge, September 28, 1938; children: William George, Martha Langley (Mrs. Mark Van Drunen). *Education:* Northeastern University, B.B.A., 1932. *Home:* Route 1, Box 81, East Alton, N.H. 03809.

CAREER: Reporter, *Boston Globe*, 1930; public relations assistant, Northeastern University, 1931; *Coronado Journal*, Coronado, Calif., editorial assistant, 1932-33; *National Sportsman* and *Hunting and Fishing*, Boston, Mass., editorial assistant, 1933-35, managing editor, 1935-36, editor, 1936-40; editor of *Hunting and Fishing*, 1940-42, *Outdoors*, Boston, Mass., 1942-50; *Field and Stream*, New York, N.Y., associate editor, 1950—; Reilly, Brown, Tapply & Carr, Inc. (advertising agency), Boston, Mass., executive vice-president and director, 1950—. Former director of Open Road Publishing Co. and Child Life Inc. Member of Alton (N.H.) Conservative Commission. *Member:* Outdoor Writers Association of America, New England Outdoor Writers Association (honorary life member). *Awards, honors:* Sportsman of the Year Award from New England Outdoor Writers Association, 1973.

WRITINGS: Tackle Tinkering, A. S. Barnes, 1946; *The Fly Tyer's Handbook*, Durrell, 1950; *The Sportsman's Notebook and Tap's Tips*, Holt, 1964; *Field and Stream's Secrets of Expert Outdoorsmen: The Best of Tap's Tips*, Holt, 1970. Editor, *Trout*, 1967-69.†

TARR, Herbert   1929-

PERSONAL: Surname originally Targovik; born September 10, 1929, in Brooklyn, N.Y.; son of Isidore and Anna (Rubinfeld) Targovik. *Education:* Brooklyn College (now of the City University of New York), B.A. (magna cum laude), 1949; Columbia University, M.A., 1951; Hebrew Union College-Jewish Institute of Religion, New York, N.Y., B.H.L., 1953, M.H.L. and Rabbi, 1955. *Home:* 31-11 New Hyde Park Rd., New Hyde Park, N.Y.

CAREER: Teacher at Temple Rodeph Sholom, New York, N.Y., 1953, and Temple Beth Sholom, Roslyn, N.Y., 1954-56; Temple Beth Zion, Buffalo, N.Y., rabbi, 1958-60; Westbury Temple, Westbury, N.Y., rabbi, 1960—. *Military service:* U.S. Air Force, chaplain, 1956-58. *Member:* Central Conference of American Rabbis, New York Board of Rabbis, Nassau-Suffolk Board of Rabbis.

WRITINGS: The Conversion of Chaplain Cohen (novel), Geis, 1963; *Heaven Help Us!*, Random House, 1968; *A Time for Loving*, Random House, 1973.

Musical: "Heaven Help Us!" (adaptation from novel), produced on Broadway, 1969.

WORK IN PROGRESS: Writing screenplay of *The Conversion of Chaplain Cohen* for 20th Century Fox.†

*   *   *

TATE, Marilyn Freeman   1921-

PERSONAL: Born April 25, 1921, in Ardmore, Okla.; daughter of William Fain and Bertha (Forbes) Freeman; married John C. Tate (a lieutenant colonel, U.S. Air Force), August 31, 1944; children: John William, Harry. *Education:* Studied journalism at University of Oklahoma. *Politics:* Democrat. *Religion:* Episcopal. *Home:* 6531 Abbington Dr., Washington, D.C. (Oxon Hill, Md.) 20021.

CAREER: Started out as a stenographer in an oil company in Ardmore, Okla., in 1938, and worked for other oil firms, in Civil Service jobs, with Gene Autry's Flying A Rodeo, and a pianist-organist on a sustaining radio program until 1944 (says she always meant to leave town and go into the Great World where things were happening, but it was too interesting at home); as an Air Force wife has lived at a number of locations in the United States and overseas (six years) since 1944, serving as organist for both Catholic and Protestant services at ten Air Force chapels, and "meddling in every kind of civic activity from symphony to dog shows." *Member:* Authors Guild of the Authors League of America, National League of American Pen Women (Chevy Chase, Md., branch).

WRITINGS: One Kiss for France (novel), Doubleday, 1963. Contributor to trade journals, religious magazines, and newspapers.

WORK IN PROGRESS: Novels.

SIDELIGHTS: Marilyn Tate writes: "My 'idol' authors are, of course, Flaubert, T. Wolfe and Jessamyn West. . . . I am too poor a writer to hope to embody The Great Message in any work of fiction I write. But if I could, it would concern the sad transition in the America I was raised up in—from The Moral to The Material. . . . I fight, as a mother, the infernal over-organization of children and their activities because I think the most important thing in the world we presently live in is to recognize (1) that the only place initiative *begins* is within *one* individual, and (2) to employ it, *without* aiming toward eccentricity."†

TATFORD, Frederick Albert 1901-

PERSONAL: Born February 22, 1901, in Southsea, England; son of Frederick and Emma (Adams) Tatford; married Grace Dorothy Vince, June 9, 1924; children: Brian Frederick Barrington. *Education:* Attended college in Portsmouth and London. *Religion:* Open Brethren. *Home:* 7 Pearl Ct., Devonshire Pl., Eastbourne, Sussex, England. *Office:* Prophetic Witness Movement, Upperton House, The Avenue, Eastburne, Sussex, England.

CAREER: Minister. Editor of *Harvester*, 1934-72, and *Prophetic Witness*, 1960—; Moorlands Bible College, president, 1950-66; United Kingdom Atomic Energy Authority, London, England, director of contracts and stores, 1954-66. Prophetic Witness Movement, general secretary, 1963-70, chairman and director, 1970—; Upperton Press, Eastburne, England, director, 1970—. *Member:* Institute of Public Supplies (president, 1960-62), National Institute of Governmental Purchasing (director, 1962).

WRITINGS: The Person and Work of the Devil, Ritchie, 1932; *British Israelism*, Ritchie, 1933; *Tabernacle and Temple*, Ritchie, 1933; *Is the Bible Reliable?*, Ritchie, 1934; *Christian Life in Practice*, Pickering & Inglis, 1940; *Early Steps*, Ritchie, 1942; *The Art of Preaching*, Ritchie, 1943; *Revival in Our Time*, Paternoster, 1946; *Prophecy's Last Word*, Pickering & Inglis, 1947; *In France Today*, Paternoster, 1949.

God's Prophetic Programme, A.T.P.M., 1950; *The Master*, Loizeaux, 1950; *The Judgment Seat of Christ*, A.T.P.M., 1951; *Background of the Epistles*, Victory Press, 1951; (editor) *The Faith*, Pickering & Inglis, 1952; *The Climax of the Ages*, Marshall, Morgan & Scott, 1953, Zondervan, 1964; *The Lighted Road*, Victory Press, 1954, Christian Literary Crusade, 1955; *In Bible Lands Today*, Parkinson, 1955; *The Silent Messenger*, Victory Press, 1956; *The Message of Sinai*, Victory Press, 1957; *The Coming Generation*, Ritchie, 1957; *What Think Ye of Christ?*, Walterick, 1958; *The Middle East in Prophecy*, A.T.P.M., 1959.

Are We Challenging God?, A.T.P.M., 1960, 2nd edition, 1961; *The Life Worth Living*, Evangelical Tract Society, 1960; *Preparation for Platform and Pulpit*, Stirling Tract Enterprise, 1960; *Heralds of His Coming*, A.T.P.M., 1963; *Gods Program of the Ages*, Kregel, 1970; *The Clock Strikes*, Marshall, Morgan & Scott, 1971; *Five Minutes to Midnight*, Victory Press, 1970; *Born to Burn*, Upperton Press, 1971; *Man Who Could Not Die*, Upperton Press, 1971; *Life Isn't All Honey*, Upperton Press, 1972.

Also author of religious booklets for Prophetic Witness Movement.

*   *   *

TATHAM, Laura (Esther) 1919-

PERSONAL: Surname is pronounced *Tay*-tham; born August 10, 1919, in London, England; daughter of Guy Thomas Percy (a research chemist) and Margaret Laura (Phipps) Tatham. *Education:* Royal College of Music, London, England, A.R.C.M., 1939. *Home and office:* 25 Remington St., London N1 8DH, England.

CAREER: Control Commission for Germany, in British occupation zone in Germany, clerical officer, 1946-48; secretary for various firms in London, England, 1949-51; *Canadian Business*, Montreal, Quebec, editorial assistant, 1951-55; *Office Equipment News*, London, England, editor, 1957-60; free-lance journalist, 1960—. *Military service:*

British Army, Auxiliary Territorial Service, 1942-46. *Member:* British Computer Society, Wig and Pen Club (London).

WRITINGS: Equipment and Methods for the Smaller Office, Business Publications, 1958; *The Efficiency Experts: An Impartial Survey of Management Consultancy*, Business Publications, 1964; *The Use of Computers for Profit: A Businessman's Guide*, McGraw, 1969; *Computers in Everyday Life*, Pelham Books, 1970. Contributor to data processing, trade, and technical publications.

AVOCATIONAL INTERESTS: Making own clothes, cooking, home decorating.

*   *   *

TAUBENFIELD, Howard J(ack) 1924-

PERSONAL: Born December 23, 1924, in New York, N.Y.; son of David (an attorney) and Rose (Oswald) Taubenfield; married Rita Falk (an economist), October 28, 1951; children: David, Marc, Robin. *Education:* Columbia University, A.B., 1947, LL.B., 1948, Ph.D., 1958. *Office:* Law School, Southern Methodist University, Dallas, Tex.

CAREER: Attorney in private practice in New York, N.Y., 1948-54, in San Francisco, Calif., 1954-61; Golden Gate College (now University), San Francisco, Calif., professor of law, 1954-61; Southern Methodist University, Law School, Dallas, Tex., professor of international law, 1961—. *Military service:* U.S. Army, 1943-46.

WRITINGS: (With P. C. Jessup) *Controls for Outer Space*, Columbia University Press, 1959; (editor and contributor) *Space and Society*, Oceana, 1964; (with wife, Rita F. Taubenfield) *Race, Peace, Law and Southern Africa*, Association of the Bar of the City of New York, 1966; *Weather Modification*, National Science Foundation, 1966; (with S. Houston Lay) *The Law Relating to the Activities of Man in Space*, two volumes, American Bar Foundation, 1968; (editor) *Weather Modification and the Law*, Oceana, 1968; (editor) *Controlling the Weather*, Dunellen, 1970. Contributor to law reviews.†

*   *   *

TAYLOR, Betty Jo 1933-

PERSONAL: Born February 10, 1933, in Dallas, Tex.; daughter of William Samuel and Donna M. (Lester) Taylor. *Education:* Attended Hockaday Junior College, Dallas, Tex., 1950-51; University of Texas, B.J., 1955; Vanderbilt Divinity School, graduate study. *Politics:* Democrat. *Religion:* Presbyterian. *Home:* 2117 Westwood Ave., Nashville, Tenn. 37202. *Office:* Presbyterian U.S. Board of World Missions, Box 330, Nashville, Tenn. 37202.

CAREER: Dallas Times Herald, Dallas, Texas, reporter, 1955-56; Republic National Life Insurance Co., Dallas Tex., magazine editor, 1957-59; Presbyterian U.S. Board of World Missions, Nashville, Tenn., director of information and publications, 1959—. National Council of Churches of Christ, chairman of early teens committee, Division of Education for Mission. Tennessee Council on Human Relations, member. *Member:* Fellowship of Concern, Theta Sigma Phi.

WRITINGS: Where the Clock Walks (documentary on Spanish Americans), Friendship, 1964. Regular contributor to *Presbyterian Survey*. Editor, *Today in World Missions* (Presbyterian quarterly).

WORK IN PROGRESS: Articles and booklets on overseas work of Presbyterian Church in the United States.†

TAYLOR, Charles 1931-

PERSONAL: Born November 5, 1931, in Montreal, Quebec, Canada; son of Walter M. (an industrialist) and Simone (Beaubien) Taylor; married Alba Romer, April 2, 1956; children: Karen, Miriam, Wanda, Gabriella, Gretta. *Education:* McGill University, B.A., 1952; Oxford University, B.A., 1955, M.A., 1960, D.Phil., 1961. *Politics:* New Democratic Party (Socialist). *Religion:* Roman Catholic. *Home:* 344 Metcalfe Ave., Montreal, Quebec, Canada.

CAREER: McGill University, Montreal, Quebec, 1961—, began as assistant professor now professor of philosophy and Political Science. New Democratic Party, member of both federal and provincial executives, 1963—. *Member:* Ligue des Droits de l'Homme, Society for the Abolition of the Death Penalty, Campaign for Nuclear Disarmament, Canadian Association of Philosophy, Movement Laique de League Francaise.

WRITINGS: Explanation of Behaviour, Humanities, 1964. Contributor of articles to political and philosophical journals. Founder and former editor, *New Left Review* (England).

WORK IN PROGRESS: A book on Hegel, and one on freedom of the will; research in field of philosophical anthropology.

SIDELIGHTS: Taylor is bi-lingual in French and English and he also speaks some German, Spanish, and Polish.

* * *

TAYLOR, Dawson 1916-

PERSONAL: Born November 14, 1916, in Detroit, Mich.; son of George M. and Florence (Dawson) Taylor; married Mary Ellen Connolly, May 21, 1941; children: Ellen Denise (Mrs. Patrick Martin), Mary Christine, Dawson. *Education:* University of Detroit, A.B., 1936, LL.B., 1939. *Residence:* Florida. *Office:* National Enquirer, Lantana, Fla. 33462.

CAREER: Admitted to Michigan bar, 1942. Practicing attorney in State of Michigan, 1942-43; Dawson Taylor Chevrolet, Inc., Detroit, Mich., president, 1957-69; *National Enquirer*, Lantana, Florida, book editor, 1969—. *Military service:* U.S. Navy, 1942-45; served in Pacific; became lieutenant, junior grade; received Navy Unit Commendation. *Member:* American Society of Composers, Authors, and Publishers, Michigan Bar Association, Detroit Bar Association. *Awards, honors:* Nathan Burkan Memorial Award from American Society of Composers, Authors, and Publishers, 1934.

WRITINGS: The Secret of Bowling Strikes, A. S. Barnes, 1959; *The Secret of Holing Putts*, A. S. Barnes, 1960; *The Making of the Pope*, A. S. Barnes, 1961; *Your Future in the Automotive Industry*, Rosen, 1962; (with James Bradley) *Your Future in Automotive Service*, Rosen Press, 1971; *The Masters: Profile of a Tournament*, A. S. Barnes, 1973; *St. Andrews: Cradle of Golf*, A. S. Barnes, 1974; *How to Break Ninety at the Masters*, A. S. Barnes, 1975; *Secrets of Top Tennis Play*, Wilshire, 1975. Composer of published and recorded songs.

* * *

TAYLOR, Don(ald) 1910-

PERSONAL: Born September 5, 1910, in Barrow-in-Furness, Lancashire, England; son of William John (an engine fitter) and Barbara (Wood) Taylor; married Kathleen Bell, April 8, 1939; children: John Stewart Cameron, Kathleen Janice. *Education:* Educated in English schools. *Politics:* Variable. *Religion:* Church of England. *Home:* 33 Manor Gardens, Hampton, Middlesex, England. *Office:* New Commonwealth, 4/5 Fitzroy Sq., London W.C.1, England.

CAREER: Was a shipyard worker and farm laborer in early youth; became a reporter on provincial newspapers; after war service became editor-in-chief of Manchester Weekly Newspapers, then commonwealth correspondent for London *Sunday Express*; Commonwealth Institute, London, England, editor of the Institute's journal and of *New Commonwealth*, and governor, 1963—. A. E. Morgan Publications, director. *Military service:* Royal Air Force, 1929-35, 1939-45; became flight sergeant. *Member:* Royal Commonwealth Society, Royal Overseas League.

WRITINGS: World Development, Verschoyle, 1951; *Rainbow on the Zambesi*, Museum Press, 1953; *The Rhodesian: The Life of Sir Roy Welensky*, Museum Press, 1955; *Ten Stars South of Asia—Australia and New Zealand in the Modern World*, R. Hale, 1957; *The Years of Challenge: The Commonwealth and British Empire, 1945-58*, R. Hale, 1959, Praeger, 1960; *The British in Africa*, R. Hale, 1962, Roy, 1962; (editor and contributor) *Development Means People*, Macmillan, 1964; *Africa: The Portrait of Power*, R. Hale, 1967. Contributor of articles to newspapers.

WORK IN PROGRESS: A Man and His Country, a biography of Sir Robert Menzies, prime minister of Australia.

SIDELIGHTS: Taylor has traveled in sixty countries, most extensively in Africa.†

* * *

TAYLOR, Elizabeth 1912-

PERSONAL: Born July 3, 1912, in Reading, Berkshire, England; daughter of Oliver and Elsie (Fewtrell) Coles; married John William Kendall Taylor (a director), March 11, 1936; children: Renny, Joanna (Mrs. David Routledge). *Education:* Attended the Abbey School, Reading. *Politics:* Labour. *Religion:* None. *Home:* Grove's Barn, Penn, Buckinghamshire, England. *Agent:* Brandt & Brandt, 101 Park Ave. New York, N.Y. 10017.

CAREER: Author. *Member:* P.E.N., Society of Authors.

WRITINGS: At Mrs. Lippincote's, P. Davies, 1945, Knopf, 1946, *Palladian*, P. Davies, 1946, Knopf, 1947; *A View of the Harbour*, Knopf, 1949; *A Wreath of Roses*, Knopf, 1949; *A Game of Hide-and-Seek*, Knopf, 1951; *The Sleeping Beauty*, Viking, 1953; *Hester Lilly: Twelve Short Stories*, Viking, 1954 (published in England as *Hester Lilly and Other Stories*, P. Davies, 1954); *Angel*, Viking, 1957; *The Blush and Other Stories*, P. Davies, 1958, Viking, 1959; *In a Summer Season*, Viking, 1961; *The Soul of Kindness*, Viking, 1964; *A Dedicated Man and Other Stories*, Viking, 1965; *Mossy Trotter* (juvenile), Harcourt, 1967; *The Wedding Group*, Viking, 1968; (contributor) J. Burnley, editor, *Penguin Modern Stories 6*, Penguin, 1970; *Mrs. Palfrey at the Claremont*, Viking, 1971; *The Devastating Boys and Other Stories*, Viking, 1972. Contributor of short stories to the *New Yorker*.

WORK IN PROGRESS: Short stories.

SIDELIGHTS: Books and Bookmen feels that Mrs. Taylor is "one of the great wasted talents of our age. Her prose is precise, delicate, very feminine. The style, considered in isolation, can bear favourable comparison with Jane Austen. But she seldom seems to use it to good purpose and her books are inclined to lack substance of characterisation and plot. She admits that her own reading preference is for 'books in which practically nothing ever happens' and this choice is all too often reflected in her own work.''

She has, however, received a good deal of critical acclaim. William Peden writes: "With admirable understanding Mrs. Taylor reveals the hearts and minds of her characters in a cool, disciplined prose, which is as good as any being written today on either side of the Atlantic." Alice McCahill notes that all of Elizabeth Taylor's novels show "the same keen understanding of people, the ability to share that understanding with her readers, a sense of humor, and a gift and feeling for words." And Kingsley Amis believes that "Comedy of a special kind—its attachments include a splendid relish and a sort of contemptuous charity—is one of Mrs. Taylor's leading talents."

AVOCATIONAL INTERESTS: Travel in Greece.

BIOGRAPHICAL/CRITICAL SOURCES: Spectator, November 21, 1958; *Saturday Review,* April 4, 1959; *Isis,* January 28, 1959; *Review of English Literature,* April, 1960; *Writer,* January, 1970; Carolyn Riley, editor, *Contemporary Literary Criticism,* Gale, Volume II, 1974, Volume IV, 1975.†

* * *

TAYLOR, Florence M(arian Tompkins) 1892-

PERSONAL: Born March 4, 1892, in Brooklyn, N.Y.; daughter of Edward Osborn and Ruth (Flandreau) Tompkins; married George Russell Taylor, December 18, 1916; children: Edward Osborn, Elizabeth Anne (Mrs. Willard B. Fernald), Margaret Flandreau (Mrs. Robert C. West, Jr.). *Education:* Graduated from Montclair State Normal School (now Montclair State College). *Religion:* Protestant. *Home:* 261 North Drexel Ave., Columbus, Ohio 43209.

CAREER: Kindergarten teacher at school for retarded children and in New Jersey public schools, 1909-17; Protestant Council of the City of New York, New York, N.Y., writer of textbooks for church schools, 1938—, associate in Christian education, 1942-57.

WRITINGS: Neighbors at Peace, Abingdon, 1938; *Child Life in Bible Times,* Bethany, 1939; *Their Rightful Heritage,* Pilgrim Press, 1942; *Thine is the Glory,* Westminster, 1948; *Growing Pains,* Westminster, 1948; *Good News to Tell,* Westminster, 1949; *Your Children's Faith: A Guide for Parents,* Doubleday, 1964; *The Autumn Years: Insights and Reflections,* Seabury, 1968; *A Boy Once Lived in Nazareth,* Walck, 1969; *From Everlasting to Everlasting: Promises and Prayers Selected from the Bible,* Seabury, 1973; *Hid in My Heart: The Word of God in Times of Need,* Seabury, 1974. Author with Imogene M. McPherson of series of interdenominational church school textbooks, six teacher's books and twelve pupil's books, for use in released-time classes in New York, N.Y., Abingdon-Cokesbury, 1947-49.

* * *

TAYLOR, Marion Ansel 1904-

PERSONAL: Born February 23, 1904, in Chicago, Ill.; daughter of Augustus Martin (a salesman) and Laura Catherine (Hormel) Ansel; married John E. Taylor (divorced); children: John Ansel. *Education:* University of Iowa, B.A., 1925, M.A., 1929, Ph.D., 1931. *Home:* 549 Nevada St., East Alton, Ill. *Office:* Humanities Division, Southern Illinois University, Alton, Ill.

CAREER: Illinois State Normal University, Normal, 1932-42, became associate professor of English; Southern Illinois University, Alton, associate professor of English, 1948-73, professor emeritus, 1973—; full-time writer, 1973—. Fulbright lecturer at Jammu and Kashmir University and Saugar University, in India, 1960-61; public lecturer on women of India and Japan. *Member:* Modern Language Association of America, Shakespeare Association, American Association of University Professors.

WRITINGS: Whiz: 850 on Your Radio Dial, Bles, 1954; *American Geisha,* Bles, 1956; *A New Look at the Old Sources of "Hamlet",* Mouton & Co., 1968; *Bottom! Thou Art Translated: Political Allegory in "A Midsummer Night's Dream" and Related Literature,* Editions Rodopi, 1973. Contributor of articles to *Shakespeare Quarterly;* one-act plays to *Plays;* short stories and articles to magazines, including *U.S. Lady, Teen, Parents' Magazine, Baby Talk.*

WORK IN PROGRESS: A teen novel on the Black Hawk War, *Dangerous Journey;* an adult mystery set in modern Turkey, *The Snow of Ararat;* a true account of faulty housing in California, *Reverse Gold Rush.*

AVOCATIONAL INTERESTS: The theatre, reading, travel.

* * *

TAYLOR, Peter (Hillsman) 1919-

PERSONAL: Born January 8, 1919, in Trenton, Tenn.; son of Matthew Hillsman (a lawyer) and Katherine (Taylor) Taylor; married Eleanor Lilly Ross (a poet), June 4, 1943; children: Katherine Baird, Peter Ross. *Education:* Attended Vanderbilt University, 1936-37, Southwestern at Memphis, 1937-38; Kenyon College, A.B., 1940. *Home address:* Box 357, Route 1, Earlysville, Va. 22936. *Office:* Department of English, Wilson Hall, University of Virginia, Charlottesville, Va. 22901.

CAREER: University of North Carolina, Chapel Hill, 1946-67, became professor of English; University of Virginia, Charlottesville, professor of English, 1967—. Visiting lecturer, Indiana University, 1949, University of Chicago, 1951, Kenyon College, 1952-57, Oxford University, 1955, Ohio State University, 1957-63, and Harvard University, 1964. *Member:* National Institute of Arts and Letters. *Military service:* U.S. Army, 1941-45; became sergeant. *Awards, honors:* Guggenheim fellowship in fiction, 1950; National Institute of Arts and Letters grant in literature, 1952; Fulbright fellowship to France, 1955; first prize, O. Henry Memorial Awards, 1959, for "Venus, Cupid, Folly and Time," and short stories included in O. Henry Award anthologies 1950, 1961, 1965; Ohioana Book Award, 1960, for *Happy Families Are All Alike;* Ford Foundation fellowship, to England, 1961; Rockefeller Foundation grantee, 1964; third prize, *Partisan Review-Dial* for "The Scoutmaster."

WRITINGS: A Long Fourth and Other Stories, Harcourt, 1948; *A Woman of Means* (novel), Harcourt, 1950; *The Widows of Thornton* (short stories and a play), Harcourt, 1954; *Tennessee Day in St. Louis* (play), Random House, 1959; *Happy Families Are All Alike: A Collection of Stories,* Astor Honor, 1959; *Miss Leonora When Last Seen and Fifteen Other Stories,* Astor Honor, 1963; (editor with Robert Lowell and Robert Penn Warren) *Randall Jarrell, 1914-1965,* Farrar, Straus, 1967; *The Collected Stories of Peter Taylor,* Farrar, Straus, 1969; *Presences: Seven Dramatic Pieces* (one-act plays), Houghton, 1973. Also author of *A Stand in the Mountains*, produced at Barter Theatre, 1971, published in Kenyon Review, 1965.

Work represented in more than twenty anthologies, including *The Best American Short Stories*, edited by Martha Foley, Houghton, 1945-46, 1950, 1959, 1965, edited by Foley and David Burnett, 1960, 1961; *Prize Stories of 1950: The O. Henry Awards*, edited by Herschell Bricknell, Doubleday, 1950; *The Literature of the South*, edited by R. C. Beatty and others, Scott, Foresman, 1952; *Stories from the Southern Review*, edited by Cleanth Brooks and Robert Penn Warren, Louisiana State University Press, 1953; *Prize Stories 1959: The O. Henry Awards*, edited by Paul Engle, Doubleday, 1959; *Prize Stories 1961: The O. Henry Awards*, edited by Richard Poirier, Doubleday, 1961; *Prize Stories 1965: The O. Henry Awards*, edited by Poirier and William Abrahams, Doubleday, 1965; *The Sense of Fiction*, edited by Robert L. Welker and Herschel Gover, Prentice-Hall, 1966.

Contributor of short stories to *Sewanee Review, Virginia Quarterly Review, Kenyon Review, New Yorker*, and numerous other journals.

WORK IN PROGRESS: A novel; short stories; a play, "The Girl From Forked Deer."

SIDELIGHTS: Gene Baro asks: "Does it need to be said that [Peter Taylor] is one of the most accomplished short-story writers of our time?" Morgan Blum calls Taylor's prose "a subtle instrument capable of rendering states of mind and feeling with great precision, of suggesting a character's point of view and even the 'tone of voice' of his thought without ever being confined by this tone or the character's horizons.... Mr. Taylor has, from the beginning of his career, been able to imagine with such great verisimilitude people very different from himself in every way ... that few of the usual pathways to growth were available to him. As a writer, he matured young." Taylor's is a world of observation rather than imagination. He writes of people he has known, only modifying his characterizations by the use of his imagination. Unlike the historical novelist, he writes only from his experience. Ashley Brown comments: "Mr. Taylor is essentially ironic about history, and many of his characters have accepted the world as it is. Indeed there is scarcely any Southern writer who depends less on the great myth of the South as it has been raised by Faulkner and his generation, and perhaps in forfeiting this advantage Mr. Taylor has lost something. But ... he has gained something, too, because he has a special insight into the way our society presents itself at this moment...." James Penny Smith notes: "The place of Peter Taylor in modern short fiction is secure.... His 'acceptable' subject matter, his quiet style, his indirection and understatement are profoundly unlike the sensationalism, contortion, and richly suggestive language of some of his fellow Southerners. His people are not grotesque, his action is not violent, his language is not flamboyant. Mr. Taylor's strongest impact comes through the quiet revelation of the unconscious complexity of human motivation, and his knowledge of the limited vision which determines our simplest actions." Blum sees in Taylor's work certain aspects of Tolstoy's talent: "(1) the ability to see in every act a man or woman performs some expression of that being's total history; (2) the ability to create real families and extremely moving scenes of family life. More than this, Mr. Taylor has achieved a third thing that we have no right to expect of a work as wide-ranging and inclusive as *War and Peace*: he has produced short stories that are perspicuous and unified gems." Richard Sullivan writes: "Because of their fine craftsmanship—their style, expert but never showy—these stories by Peter Taylor seem not so much written as remembered out into words."

Taylor has also been praised for his plays. Brainard Cheney notes that "few other contemporary published plays have had more literary recognition. Indeed, they had the unusual distinction to be published in book form, without having ever produced." Although Taylor's sense of drama is frequently recognized, many wonder if his plays "work" on the stage. Cheney remarks: "He is not a punster, a paragrapher, a verbalist. His talent is for true humor: humor that grows out of the human condition, the human predicament; that is perceptible to the senses, an imitation of life. This humor sustains and makes complex his sure sense of drama. But it is a drama best suited for fiction.... He espouses no mythology of experience. And it is Mr. Taylor's noncommittalism that seeks validation, seeks security, seeks meaning in the theater...."

BIOGRAPHICAL/CRITICAL SOURCES: Western Review, Volume XVIII, 1953; *Chicago Sunday Tribune*, December 6, 1959; Louis D. Rubin, Jr. and Robert D. Jacobs, *South: Modern Southern Literature in Its Cultural Setting*, Doubleday, 1961; *Sewanee Review*, Volume LXX, 1962; Charles E. Eisinger, *Fiction of the Forties*, University of Chicago Press, 1963; *New York Times Book Review*, March 29, 1964; *Critique*, Volume IX, number 3, 1967; *Georgia Review*, winter, 1970; Albert Griffith, *Peter Taylor*, Twayne, 1970; *Southern Review*, Volume VII, number 1, 1971; Carolyn Riley, editor, *Contemporary Literary Criticism*, Gale, Volume I, 1973, Volume IV, 1975.

*　　*　　*

TAYLOR, Rebe Prestwich 1911-

PERSONAL: Born April 10, 1911, in Southport, Lancashire, England; daughter of George Peter (a physician) and Ethel Forshaw (Whittaker) Taylor. *Education:* Attended schools in England. *Home:* 1136 Manchester Rd., Castleton Rochdale, Greater Manchester, England.

CAREER: Qualified as associate of the library Association, 1945. Rochdale Central Library, Rochdale, England, in charge of reference library, 1941-50; writer and free-lance journalist, 1950—. Rochdale County Borough, co-opted member of Education Committee, 1953-72; Rochdale College of Adult Education, member of governing committee, 1942—, governor of schools, 1953—. *Member:* Society of Authors, Library Association (associate), Soroptimist Club.

WRITINGS: Minky the Kitten (juvenile), Harrap, 1948; *Pyrenean Holiday* (travel), R. Hale, 1952; *Rochdale Retrospect*, County Borough of Rochsdale, 1956; *Muggins and Moke* (juvenile), Harrap, 1958; *The Concert by the Lake* (juvenile), Harrap, 1960; *Tatham: 1866-1966*, William Tatham, 1966.

*　　*　　*

TAYLOR, Rex 1921-

PERSONAL: Born March 21, 1921, in Brindle, Chorley, Lancashire, England; son of Thomas and Ellen (Hodkinson) Taylor; married Melna Halliwell, April 22, 1946; children: Glynnis Joanna, Stephen Edward Kenneth, Robin James, Christopher Michael. *Education:* Attended schools in Lancashire until fourteen. *Politics:* Independent ("being free to criticise all political parties and factions"). *Religion:* Methodist. *Home:* 10 Hardlands Ave., Torrisholme, Morecambe, Lancashire, England. *Agent:* A. P. Watt & Son, 26/28 Beford Row, London, WC1R 4HL, England.

CAREER: Civil Engineer. Poet. *Military service:* Royal Air Force, 1939-46; served in Africa and Middle East; became flight-sergeant pilot; received Africa Star and clasp. *Member:* Association of Surveyors in Civil Engineering.

WRITINGS: (With Terence Hards and Martin Seymour-Smith) *Poems*, Longmans & Dorchester, 1952; *Michael Collins*, Hutchinson, 1958; *Poems*, Hutchinson, 1959; *Assassination*, Hutchinson, 1961; (contributor) *Here Today* (anthology of poems), Hutchinson, 1963. Also author of monograph, *Italy in Libya*. Writer of scripts for British Broadcasting Corp. programs. Contributor to *Irish Times*, *Poetry Review*, *Tomorrow* (United States), *Encounter*, and other periodicals.

WORK IN PROGRESS: A history of the English civil wars in the northwest counties, provisionally titled, *Gentlemen at Arms*.

SIDELIGHTS: Taylor speaks Italian. He lived in Eire, 1959-62, and his interest in Irish politics led to *Michael Collins* and *Assassination*. Maintaining that the English poet, Edward Thomas (killed in 1917) has no equal, Taylor owns a complete collection of his first editions. He is a friend and admirer of Robert Graves.

*　　*　　*

TEGNER, Henry (Stuart)　1901-
(The Northumbrian Gentleman, The Ruffle)

PERSONAL: Born August 15, 1901, in Yokohama, Japan; son of Frederik May (a merchant) and Beatrix (Eldridge) Tegner; married Helen Elizabeth Henderson, February 25, 1924; children: Ann, Veronica, Alison, John. *Education:* Cambridge University, M.A., 1923. *Politics:* Conservative. *Religion:* Church of England. *Home:* Seven Stars, Whalton, Northumberland, England.

CAREER: With Anglo-American Oil Co. Ltd., 1924-34; with Scott & Turner Ltd. (pharmacists), 1934-59; Sherlock and Edmenson (stockbrokers), Newcastle upon Tyne, England, partner, 1964—. *Military service:* Royal Air Force, 1939-45; became wing commander; created Chevalier of the Belgian Crown, 1957. *Member:* Mammal Society of the British Isles, Fauna Preservation Society, Natural History Society of Northumberland, Durham and Newcastle upon Tyne (vice-president).

WRITINGS: (Under pseudonym The Ruffle) *Sporting Respite*, Lincoln Williams, 1935; *The Sporting Rifle in Britain*, Batchworth Press, 1951; *The Roe Deer*, Batchworth Press, 1951; *The White Foxes of Gorfenletch*, Hollis & Carter, 1954; *The Buck of Lordenshaw*, Batchworth Press, 1955; *A Border County*, R. Hale, 1955; *The Tale of a Deer Forest*, Bles, 1957; (under pseudonym The Northumbrian Gentleman) *The Old Man Hunts*, Hutchinson, 1959.

(Under pseudonym The Northumbrian Gentleman) *Across the Hills and Faraway*, Hutchinson, 1961; *Beasts of the North Country*, Galley Press, 1961; *The Sporting Rifle*, Jenkins, 1962; *Wild Cheviot*, Kimber & Co., 1962; *Game for the Sporting Rifle*, Jenkins, 1963; *Rhymeside*, Kimber & Co., 1964; *The Molecatcher Says*, Phoenix Press, 1964; *The Magic of Holy Island*, Frank Graham, 1969; *The Story of a Regiment: Being a Short History of the Northumberland Hussers Yeomanry, 1918-1969*, Frank Graham, 1969; *Wild Hares*, John Baker, 1969; *The Charm of the Cheviots*, Frank Graham, 1970; *Naturalist on Speyside*, Bles, 1971; *Natural History*, Frank Graham, 1972.

Contributor to *Times* and *Sunday Times* (London), *Punch*, *Field*, *Country Life*, and other outdoor and popular magazines.

*　　*　　*

TEIKMANIS, Arthur L.　1914-

PERSONAL: Born April 8, 1914, in Ranka, Latvia; came to United States following World War II; son of Robert Julius (a blacksmith and farmer) and Maria (Apsha) Teikmanis; married Austra V. Stikhevitz (a registered nurse), June 25, 1941; children: Sylvia Gundega (Mrs. Peter Douglas Scott), Mahra Linda, Nora Diana. *Education:* Latvian Baptist Seminary, diploma, 1940; University of Latvia, B.A. equivalent, 1944; Andover-Newton Theological School, B.D. (cum laude), 1949; Harvard University, Ph.D., 1953; Mansfield College, Oxford, postdoctoral study, 1964. *Politics:* Democrat. *Home:* 161 Alexander Pl., Winter Park, Fla. 32789. *Office:* First Congregational Church, 225 South Interlachen Ave., Winter Park, Fla. 32789.

CAREER: Ordained to Christian ministry, 1940; pastor of Baptist church in Priekule, Latvia, 1941-44, and of refugee Baptist church in Augsburg, Germany, 1945-46; minister of Congregational churches in West Peabody, Mass., 1950-52, Lowell, Mass., 1952-56, and Sayville, N.Y., 1956-61; First Congregational Church, Winter Park, Fla., senior minister, 1961—. Instructor in the history and philosophy of religion at Lowell Technological Institute, 1955-56, at Adelphi College, 1959-61, and at Rollins College, 1961—. Lecturer on life behind the Iron Curtain and related subjects. Social action chairman, Suffolk County Council of Churches, 1959-61, Florida Conference of United Church of Christ, 1962—; organizer and president of Winter Park Council of Churches, 1963—; chairman of Civil Rights Committee, Florida Council of Churches, 1962—. *Military service:* Latvian Army, 1934-35.

MEMBER: Society for Religion in Higher Education, Masons; Rotary Club, Harvard Club, and University Club (all Winter Park). *Awards, honors:* George Washington Honor Medal of Freedoms Foundation for achievement in bringing about better understanding of the American way of life, 1961, 1962.

WRITINGS: Preaching and Pastoral Care, Prentice-Hall, 1964. Scriptwriter for television series, "Moral Issues of Our Times," Orlando, Fla., 1963. Contributor to *Childhood Education*.

WORK IN PROGRESS: Two books, *Destination Freedom* and *God, Our Ultimate Concern*.

SIDELIGHTS: Teikmanis escaped from behind the Iron Curtain and was interned in a labor camp in Stargard, Germany, during World War II. He is competent in Latvian, German, Russian, French, Greek, and Latin.†

*　　*　　*

TEITELBAUM, Myron　1929-

PERSONAL: Born February 27, 1929, in New York, N.Y.; son of Milton (a draftsman) and Judith (Levowitz) Teitelbaum; married Audrey Fleischman, November 28, 1954; children: Bruce Randall, Linda Carol. *Education:* Ohio State University, B.S., 1951, LL.B., 1953; University of Dayton, graduate study, 1961-63; University of Miami, Coral Gables, Fla., M.D., 1967. *Home:* 13055 Keystone Ter., North Miami, Fla. 33161.

CAREER: Admitted to Ohio bar, 1953; also member of bar

of U.S. Supreme Court; Teitelbaum, Jacobson & Busch (lawyers), Dayton, Ohio, partner, 1954-63; private medical practice, Miami, Fla., 1969—. Diplomat of American Academy of Family Practice. *Member:* B'nai B'rith (international president of Aleph Zadik Aleph, 1947; president of Eshcol Lodge, 1962), American Medical Association, American Academy of Family Practice, Florida Medical Association, Florida Academy of Family Practice, Dade County Medical Association, Masons.

WRITINGS: Hypnosis Induction Technics, C. C Thomas, 1965. Contributor to legal and medical-legal journals.

* * *

TEMIN, Peter 1937-

PERSONAL: Born December 17, 1937, in Philadelphia, Pa.; son of Henry (an attorney) and Annette (Lehman) Temin. *Education:* Swarthmore College, B.A., 1959; Massachusetts Institute of Technology, Ph.D., 1964. *Office:* Sloan School of Management, Massachusetts Institute of Technology, Cambridge, Mass. 02139.

CAREER: Harvard University, Cambridge, Mass., junior fellow, Society of Fellows, 1962-65; Massachusetts Institute of Technology, Cambridge, assistant professor of industrial history, 1965—. *Member:* American Economic Association, Economic History Association, Phi Beta Kappa.

WRITINGS: Iron and Steel in Nineteenth-Century America: An Economic Inquiry, M.I.T. Press, 1964; *The Jacksonian Economy*, Norton, 1969; (editor) *New Economic History*, Penguin, 1973; *American Economic History in the Nineteenth Century*, Humanities, 1975. Contributor to scholarly journals.†

* * *

TENG, S(su)-Y(u) 1906-

PERSONAL: Born June 23, 1906, in Hunan, China; became U.S. citizen, 1953; son of Chieh-ching and Hsin-yin (Wu) Teng; married Margaret Henriques, August, 1949; children: Elizabeth, Dorothy, Patricia. *Education:* Yenching University, B.A., 1932, M.A., 1935; Harvard University, Ph.D., 1942. *Politics:* Democrat. *Religion:* Presbyterian. *Home:* 905 South Hawthorne Dr., Bloomington, Ind. *Office:* Department of History, Indiana University, Bloomington, Ind. 47401.

CAREER: University of Chicago, Chicago, Ill., instructor, 1941-43, assistant professor of Chinese history, 1943-45, 1947-49; National Peking University (China), professor, 1946-47; Harvard University, Cambridge, Mass., visiting lecturer, 1949-50; Indiana University, Bloomington, associate professor, 1950-57, professor of history, 1957—, university professor, 1966—. Visiting lecturer, Harvard, 1949-50; visiting summer professor at University of Minnesota, 1962, The American University, 1963, 1964. *Member:* American Historical Association, Far Eastern Association (director), Association for Asian Studies. *Awards, honors:* Fulbright professor in Japan, 1956-57; grants from American Council of Learned Societies, American Philosophical Society, and Social Science Research Council.

WRITINGS: (Compiler) *An Annotated Bibliography of Selected Chinese Reference*, Harvard-Yenching Institute, Yenching University, 1936, 3rd revised edition with Knight Biggerstaff, Harvard University Press, 1971; *Conversational Chinese*, University of Chicago Press, 1947. (With J. K. Fairbank) *China's Response to the West*, Harvard University Press, 1954; (editor and translator with Jeremy Ingalls) Li Chien-nung, *The Political History of China, 1840-1928*, Van Nostrand, 1956.

(With J. K. Fairbank) *Ching Administration, Three Studies*, Harvard University Press, 1960; *The Nien Army and Their Guerilla Warfare, 1851-1868*, Mouton, 1961; *Japanese Studies on Japan and the Far East*, Oxford University Press, 1961; *Historiography of the Taiping Rebellion*, Harvard University Press, 1962; *Advanced Conversational Chinese*, University of Chicago Press, 1965; (translator) Yen Chih-t'ui, *Family Instructions for the Yen Clan*, E. J. Brill, 1968; *The Taiping Rebellion and the Western Powers*, Clarendon Press, 1971. Contributor to professional journals. Editor of *Chinese Historical Annual*, 1934-37.

WORK IN PROGRESS: A short history of the People's Republic of China.

* * *

TERZIAN, James P. 1915-

PERSONAL: Born October 12, 1915, in Adana, Turkey, of Armenian parents; came to United States in 1924; son of Paul (a pharmacist) and Sirouhi (Kalousdian) Terzian; married Mary Brodney (a librarian), February 14, 1938; children: Kathryn, Elizabeth. *Education:* University of Wisconsin, B.A. cum laude, 1943. *Home:* 168 North Bedford Rd., Chappaqua, N.Y. 10514. *Agent:* Robert P. Mills, 20 East 53rd St., New York, N.Y. 10022. *Office:* Equitable Life Assurance Society of United States, 1285 Avenue of the Americas, New York, N.Y. 10019.

CAREER: Publicist and programmer for Madison (Wis.) Board of Education, 1939-41, and radio news editor and copywriter in Madison, Wis., 1941-43, while continuing education; U.S. Information Agency, Voice of America, New York, N.Y., 1946-54, began as news writer, then feature writer for documentary radio programs, and chief of World Wide English Service; Equitable Life Assurance Society of United States, New York, editor and writer, 1956—. *Military service:* U.S. Navy, Seabees, 1943-46; combat correspondent in Pacific Theater. *Awards, honors:* Prize for best college short story, *Story* (magazine), 1944; cited in added index of distinctive short stories in *Best American Short Stories*, 1961, 1964; best short story award, *Ararat* (magazine), 1964.

WRITINGS: Caravan from Ararat (novel), Muhlenberg Press, 1959; (with Jim Benagh) *The Jimmy Brown Story*, Messner, 1964; *Defender of Human Rights: Carl Schurz*, Messner, 1965; *The Many Worlds of Herbert Hoover*, Messner, 1966; (with Kathryn Terzian) *Glenn Curtiss: Pioneer Pilot*, Grosset, 1966; *The Kid From Cuba: Zoilo Versalles*, Doubleday, 1967; *Pete Cass: Scramber*, Doubleday, 1968; (with Kathryn Cramer) *Mighty Hard Road: The Story of Cesar Chavez*, Doubleday, 1970; *New York Giants*, Macmillan, 1970. Writer of scripts for documentary albums, "The Second Elizabeth" and "Ike from Abilene," Abbey Records, 1952; writer of more than one hundred radio and television scripts and of film scripts for United Nations, National Council of Churches, and educational groups.

WORK IN PROGRESS: Several books in juvenile biographical field.

SIDELIGHTS: Terzian told *CA*: "Am dividing my 16-hour working day between full-time job and outside writing. I've found congenial experience in juvenile biography field since it gives opportunity to set character development against events ... and to explore subjects and attitudes glossed over in grade and high school studies—at least in my youth.... On the third level of writing, there is my 'private' output—*the* completed, but unpublished novel, two chapters of which have been published in literary magazines (and cited in *Best American Short Stories*), yet drawing no publisher interest. 'Not commercial' is the reaction.''†

* * *

THACKER, Ernest W(ichman) 1914-

PERSONAL: Born March 29, 1914, in Santa Ana, Calif.; son of Joseph (a minister) and Ernestine (Wichman) Thacker; married Miriam Lorelei Ihrig, January 26, 1947; children: Joel Ernest, Alice Joanna, Elizabeth Lorelei. *Education:* Santa Ana College, A.A., 1933; University of Redlands, A.B. (with honors), 1935; Emory University, B.D., 1938; University of Southern California, Ph.D., 1952. *Politics:* Democrat. *Home:* 8800 Newcastle Ave., Northridge, Calif. *Office:* Los Angeles Valley College, 5800 Fulton Ave., Van Nuys, Calif.

CAREER: Ordained Methodist minister, 1938. Minister at churches in southern California, 1938-48, Los Angeles, Calif., 1951-53; University of Southern California, examiner in American civilization, 1946-51, lecturer in American civilization, 1951-53; Los Angeles Valley College, Van Nuys, Calif., 1953—, began as associate professor, became professor of history and political science. Professor, California State University at Northridge, 1963-73. *Member:* American Academy of Religion, National Educational Association, Phi Beta Kappa, Phi Alpha Theta.

WRITINGS: (With Russell L. Caldwell) *American and California Government*, Lucas Brothers, 1953; (with Bernard L. Hyink and Seyom Brown) *Politics and Government in California*, Crowell, 1959, 8th edition, 1973.

WORK IN PROGRESS: Research on Protestant missions in Latin America; research in the career of Adlai E. Stevenson.

SIDELIGHTS: Thacker spent part of his youth in Mexico and Cuba.

* * *

THACKERAY, Milton G. 1914-

PERSONAL: Born August 22, 1914, in Morgan, Utah; married Farol Hassell, June 5, 1941; children: Lenore (Mrs. David Young), Milton, Joan, John, David. *Education:* University of Utah, B.S. and M.S., 1941; Western Reserve University (now Case Western Reserve University), M.S.S.A., 1948. *Politics:* Independent. *Religion:* Church of Jesus Christ of Latter-Day Saints. *Home:* 54 South 12th E., Salt Lake City, Utah 84102. *Office:* University of Utah, Salt Lake City, Utah 84112.

CAREER: University of Utah, Salt Lake City, 1948—, began as assistant professor, professor of social work, 1962—. Utah State Department of Health, consultant, 1960—. Children's Service Society, member of board, 1951—, president of board, 1952-53. *Member:* National Council on Social Work Education (member of board of directors, 1963-66), National Association of Social Workers, Utah Association for Mental Health (president, 1951-52), Phi Delta Kappa, Phi Kappa Phi.

WRITINGS: (With Rex A. Skidmore) *Introduction to Social Work*, Appleton, 1964. Contributor to social work, mental hygiene, and educational journals.†

THADDEUS, Janice Farrar 1933-

PERSONAL: Born July 20, 1933, in New York, N.Y.; daughter of John (a publisher) and Margaret (a crossword puzzle editor; maiden surname Petherbridge) Farrar; married Patrick Thaddeus (a physicist), April 6, 1963; children: Eva, Michael. *Education:* Radcliffe College, student, 1950-52; Barnard College, A.B., 1955; Columbia University, A.M., 1959, Ph.D., 1965. *Politics:* Democrat. *Home:* 606 West 116 St., New York, N.Y. 10027. *Office:* Barnard College, New York, N.Y. 10027.

CAREER: Barnard College, New York, N.Y., instructor, 1956-65, assistant professor of English, 1965—. *Member:* Wilderness Society, Zero Population Growth, Phi Beta Kappa.

WRITINGS: (Editor with John A. Kouwenhoven) *When Women Look at Men*, Harper, 1963.

WORK IN PROGRESS: An edition of the notebooks of Lenore Marshall.

* * *

THALE, Jerome 1927-

PERSONAL: Born June 6, 1927, in Evanston, Ill.; son of Francis X. (an engineer) and Vera (Sparks) Thale; married Rose Marie Kelly, December 16, 1950; children: Christopher, Geoffrey, Brian, Margaret, John. *Education:* Loyola University, Chicago, Ill., B.A., 1949; Northwestern University, M.A., 1950, Ph.D., 1953. *Politics:* Democrat. *Religion:* Catholic. *Home:* 4525 North Bartlett, Milwaukee, Wis. 53211. *Office:* Marquette University, Milwaukee, Wis. 53233.

CAREER: University of Notre Dame, Notre Dame, Ind., instructor in English, 1952-56; Marquette University, Milwaukee, Wis., assistant professor, 1956-59, associate professor of English, 1959—. *Military service:* U.S. Navy, 1945-46. *Member:* Modern Language Association of America, American Association of University Professors.

WRITINGS: The Novels of George Eliot, Columbia University Press, 1959; (editor) George Eliot, *Silas Marner*, Holt, 1962; *C. P. Snow*, Oliver & Boyd, 1964, Scribner, 1965. Contributor to literary journals.

WORK IN PROGRESS: Research in nineteenth- and twentieth-century British literature.

* * *

THATCHER, Dora (Fickling) 1912-

PERSONAL: Born September 14, 1912, in Abertillery, Pembrokeshire, Wales; daughter of Harold Trevor and Alice Gertrude (Irving) Fickling: married Josiah Clayton Thatcher (a civil servant), October 28, 1939; children: Keith, Ann. *Education:* Attended schools in Wales. *Religion:* Church of England. *Home:* Craig-y-Mor, Parrog, Newport, Pembrokeshire, Wales.

CAREER: British Ministry of Labour, executive officer in Birmingham, England, and South Wales, 1929-39, 1941-44; author of children's books, 1956—. Town of Newport, mayor, 1960-62. *Member:* Women's Institute (Great Britain; county president, 1973-74).

*WRITINGS—*All published by Brockhamton Press: *Tommy the Tugboat*, 1956; *Henry the Helicopter*, 1956; *Tommy Joins the Navy*, 1957; *Tommy Gets a Medal*, 1958; *Henry to the Rescue*, 1959; *Ferryboat Tommy*, 1959; *Henry the Hero*, 1960; *Tommy's New Engine*, 1961; *Hovering with Henry*, 1961; *Henry in the News*, 1963; *Henry's*

Busy Winter, 1964; *The Coracle Builders*, 1964; *Tommy and the Onion Boat*, 1962; *Tommy and the Lighthouse*, 1965; *Henry Joins the Police*, 1966; *Tommy and the Gil Rig*, 1967; *Henry and the Astronaut*, 1968; *Tommy and the Spanish Galleon*, 1969; *Henry and the Traction Engine*, 1970; *Tommy and the Yellow Submarine*, 1971; *Henry in the Mountains*, 1972; *Henry in Iceland*, 1973; *Tommy in the Caribbean*, 1974; *Henry on Safari*, 1975. Writer of material for strip books (comic books) and of radio stories. Contributor of column for children to Newport newspaper.

WORK IN PROGRESS: A new "Tommy the Tugboat" book.

* * *

THEOCHARIS, Reghinos D(emetrios) 1929-

PERSONAL: Born February 10, 1929, in Nicosia, Cyprus; son of Demetrios (an advocate) and Florentia (Mylona) Theocharis; married Madeleine Loumbou, June 6, 1954; children: Charis, Eleni. *Education:* Graduate School of Economics and Commercial Science, Athens, Greece, Diploma in Economics, 1949; University of Aberdeen, Certificate in Economics, 1952; Garnett College, London, Teacher's Certificate, 1953; London School of Economics and Political Science, London, Ph.D., 1958. *Religion:* Greek Orthodox. *Home:* 10 K Anaxagoras St., Nicosia, Cyprus. *Office:* Bank of Cyprus Ltd., Nicosia, Cyprus.

CAREER: Inspector of secondary schools and secondary teacher of economics and commerce in Cyprus, 1949-51, 1953-56; Bank of Greece, Athens, Greece, research department, 1958-59; Minister of Finance, Cyprus, 1959-62; Bank of Cyprus Ltd., Nicosia, Cyprus, governor, beginning 1962. Honorary fellow, London School of Economics and Political Science. *Member:* Royal Economic Society (fellow).

WRITINGS: The Dynamic Stability of Equilibrium (in Greek), [Athens], 1959; *Early Developments in Mathematical Economics*, Macmillan, 1961. Contributor to economics journals.

WORK IN PROGRESS: A study of the theory of price particularly with respect to the dynamic oligopoly.

SIDELIGHTS: Theocharis speaks English, French, and German. *Avocational interests:* Reading and chess.

BIOGRAPHICAL/CRITICAL SOURCES: The Middle East, 1963, Europa Publications.†

* * *

THEODORE, Chris A(thanasios) 1920-

PERSONAL: Born April 21, 1920, in Athens, Greece; married Athena Rentoumis (an assistant professor of sociology), September 8, 1951; children: Arthur, Suzanne, Stuart. *Education:* University of Athens, M.A., 1947; Boston University, M.A., 1949, Ph.D., 1952. *Office:* Boston University, Boston, Mass.

CAREER: Boston University, Boston, Mass., instructor, 1953-57, assistant professor, 1957-60, associate professor, 1961-64, professor of business administration, 1965—. Visiting professor, University of Hawaii. Consultant to United Nations Food and Agriculture Organization, to federal and state agencies, and business organizations. *Member:* American Economic Association, American Statistical Association, American Sociological Association. *Awards, honors:* Ford Foundation fellowship to Harvard University Institute of Basic Mathematics for Application to Business, 1959-60.

WRITINGS: New England Economic Indicators, Boston University, College of Business Administration, 1955; (with W. C. Danforth) *Hull Insurance and Protection and Indemnity Insurance of Commercial Fishing Vessels*, U.S. Department of the Interior, 1957; (co-editor) *Mathematical Models and Methods in Marketing*, Irwin, 1961; (with F. Doody) *The Rutland Railroad Corporation*, U.S. Department of Commerce, 1964; (with W. Dymeza and F. Hung) *The Proposed Hawaii Inter-Island Sea Ferry System*, Economic Research Center, University of Hawaii, 1965; *Applied Mathematics: An Introduction*, Irwin, 1965, revised edition, 1971; *The Economic Importance of the Insurance Industry in Massachusetts*, Association of Insurance Companies in Massachusetts, 1968; *Boolean Algebra and Digital Computers*, C. E. Merrill, 1969; (contributor) *Proceedings of the Meeting on Investment in Fisheries*, Food and Agriculture Organization of the United Nations, 1969. Contributor to *Transportation Science*.

WORK IN PROGRESS: Probability and Statistics, publication by Irwin expected in 1976.

* * *

THERNSTROM, Stephan (Albert) 1934-

PERSONAL: Born November 5, 1934, in Port Huron, Mich.; son of Albert George (a railroad executive) and Bernadene (Robbins) Thernstrom; married Abigail Mann (a political scientist), January 3, 1959; children: Melanie Rachel, Samuel Altgeld. *Education:* Northwestern University, B.S., 1956; Harvard University, A.M., 1958, Ph.D., 1962. *Home:* 1445 Massachusetts Ave., Lexington, Mass. 02173. *Office:* Department of History, Harvard University, Cambridge, Mass. 02138.

CAREER: Harvard University, Cambridge, Mass., instructor in history and literature, 1962-65, assistant professor of history, 1965-67; Brandeis University, Waltham, Mass., associate professor of history, 1967-69; University of California, Los Angeles, professor of history, 1970-73; Harvard University, professor of history, 1973—. U.S. Department of Health, Education, and Welfare, historical consultant, 1965. *Member:* American Historical Association, Organization of American Historians, Society of American Historians. *Awards, honors:* American Council of Learned Societies fellowship, 1965-66; Guggenheim fellowship, 1969-70; Bancroft prize, 1974.

WRITINGS: Poverty and Progress: Social Mobility in a 19th-Century City, Harvard University Press, 1964; *Poverty, Planning and Politics in the New Boston*, Basic Books, 1968; *The Other Bostonians: Poverty and Progress in the American Metropolis, 1880-1970*, Harvard University Press, 1973. Co-editor of "Harvard Studies in Urban History." Contributor to professional journals. Member of editorial board, *Journal of Interdisciplinary History*, *Labor History*, and *Journal of Urban History*.

WORK IN PROGRESS: An analysis of the central themes of American history from the beginnings to the present.

* * *

THIMMESCH, Nick 1927-
(William Nicholas, joint pseudonym)

PERSONAL: Surname is pronounced Tim-esh; born November 13, 1927, in Dubuque, Iowa; son of Leo Nicholas (a salesman) and Victoria (a teacher; maiden name Glatzmaier) Thimmesch; married Susan Plum, April 18, 1953; children: Nicholas, Susan, Martha, Peter, Michael. *Educa-*

tion: University of Iowa, B.A. and graduate study. *Politics:* Independent. *Religion:* Roman Catholic. *Home:* 6301 Broadbranch Rd., Chevy Chase, Md. 20015. *Office:* *Newsday*, 1750 Pennsylvania Ave., Washington, D.C. 20006.

CAREER: Reporter for *Davenport Times*, 1950-52, *Des Moines Register*, 1952-55; *Time*, New York, N.Y., 1955-67, began as correspondent, became chief of New York bureau; *Newsday*, Garden City, Long Island, N.Y., chief of Washington bureau, 1967—. Instructor of communication skills, State University of Iowa, 1953-55. Syndicated columnist, 1969—. Onetime boxing judge in Michigan. *Military service:* U.S. Merchant Marine.

WRITINGS: (With William O. Johnson) *Robert Kennedy at Forty*, Norton, 1965; (with Johnson, under joint pseudonym William Nicholas) *The Bobby Kennedy Nobody Knows*, Fawcett, 1967; *The Condition of Republicanism*, Norton, 1968.

SIDELIGHTS: Thimmesch has appeared on the television programs "Meet the Press" and "Face the Nation"; he has also done commentaries for CBS-TV and CBS-radio. *Avocational interests:* International relations, politics, urban problems, race relations, labor-management confrontations, the Right to Life movement, boxing, bicycling, hiking, airplanes, reviving American railroads, the Mississippi River, and other Americana.

* * *

THIRKELL, John Henry 1913-

PERSONAL: Born November 14, 1913, in Leigh, Essex, England; son of Horace Vyse (a company director) and Ethel Mary (Lacey) Thirkell; married Barbara Lucie Baker, November 18, 1939; children: Nicholas John Vyse, Paul Michael Richard. *Education:* Attended King's College, London. *Religion:* Church of England. *Home:* 145 North End Rd., London N.W. 11, England.

MILITARY SERVICE: British Army, 1940-46; became staff captain. *Member:* Hampstead Golf Club.

WRITINGS: The End Product (novel), M. Joseph, 1961; *Four Hundred Glorious Pubs* (documentary), Imprint Co., 1973; *Sixty Glorious Restaurants* (documentary), Imprint Co., 1974; *Top of the Pubs* (documentary), Imprint Co., 1974. Author of radio play; contributor to *Punch*.

WORK IN PROGRESS: A novel, *The Tall City*.

SIDELIGHTS: Thirkell speaks French. *Avocational interests:* Conversation, music and golf.

* * *

THOMAS, Daniel H(arrison) 1904-

PERSONAL: Born December 6, 1904, in Wetumpka, Ala.; son of Walter Elihu (a merchant) and Lucy (McCoy) Thomas; married Margaret Mawhinney, May 28, 1939; children: Margaret Ann. *Education:* University of Alabama, A.B., 1925, M.A., 1929; University of Chicago, graduate study, summers, 1930, 1931; University of Pennsylvania, Ph.D., 1934. *Politics:* Democrat. *Religion:* Calvinist. *Home:* 12 Briar Lane, Kingston, R.I. 02881.

CAREER: History teacher in public and private schools in Alabama, 1925-30; member of history faculty of Butler University, Indianapolis, Ind., 1930-31, and University of Alabama, University, 1935-36; University of Pennsylvania, Philadelphia, Harrison research fellow, 1936-38; Temple University, Philadelphia, Pa., instructor in history, 1938-40; University of Rhode Island, Kingston, professor of his-

tory, 1940-74, head of the department of history and political science, 1940-61. Visiting summer professor, University of Alabama, Emory University, and University of Pennsylvania. Kingston Free Library, president of board of trustees, 1956-74.

MEMBER: American Historical Association, New England History Teachers Association (president, 1955-56), Phi Alpha Theta (member of national advisory board), Phi Beta Kappa, Phi Kappa Phi. *Awards, honors:* Officier, Ordre de Leopold II; Belgian-American Educational Foundation fellow, 1939, 1948-49; Fulbright research fellow in Belgium, 1960-61.

WRITINGS: (Editor with Lynn M. Case) *Guide to the Diplomatic Archives of Western Europe*, University of Pennsylvania Press, 1959, revised edition, 1975; *Fort Toulouse: The French Outpost at the Alibamos on the Coosa*, Alabama State Department of Archives and History, 1960; (contributor) Barker and Brown, editors, *Diplomacy in an Age of Nationalism*, Nijhoff, 1971. Contributor of articles on Belgian neutrality to historical journals in United States, Belgium, and England. Editor of chapter on history in *Good Reading*, New American Library, 1948-62.

WORK IN PROGRESS: Volume two of *Belgian Neutrality: Its History and Role in International Relations*; articles on Madame Juliette Adam and A. de La Guerionniere.

* * *

THOMAS, David A(rthur) 1925-

PERSONAL: Born February 6, 1925, in Wanstead, Essex, England; son of Edwin Gordon (a bank official) and Helen (Dawson) Thomas; married Joyce Petty, April 3, 1948; children: Valerie Ann. *Education:* Northampton College of Advanced Technology, diploma, 1951. *Politics:* Conservative. *Religion:* Church of England. *Home:* 18 Tennyson Ave., Wanstead, London, England. *Office:* W. Canning & Co. Ltd., Watford, Hertfordshire, England.

CAREER: W. Canning & Co. Ltd. (electro-plating plant manufacturers), Birmingham, England, technical representative, 1946—. Deputy chairman, Redbridge Sports Centre Trust. *Military service:* Royal Naval Volunteer Reserve, 1942-46; became sublieutenant. *Member:* Institute of Metal Finishing, Navy Records Society, West Essex Conservative Club.

WRITINGS: With Ensigns Flying, William Kimber, 1958; *Submarine Victory*, William Kimber, 1961; *What Do You Know?*, Tandem Books, 1964; *Battle of the Java Sea*, Deutsch, 1968, Stein & Day, 1969; *Crete 1941: The Battle at Sea*, Deutsch, 1972, published as *Nazi Victory: Crete 1941*, Stein & Day, 1973.

WORK IN PROGRESS: Research on Pacific carriers striking force, 1942, and Malta convoys, 1941-42.

AVOCATIONAL INTERESTS: Local, national, and international politics.

* * *

THOMAS, Leslie John 1931-

PERSONAL: Born March 22, 1931, in Newport, Monmouthshire, England; son of David (a seaman) and Dorothy (Court) Thomas; married Maureen Crane, March 27, 1955; married second wife Diana Miles, 1970; children: (first marriage) Lois Kendal, Mark David, Gareth. *Education:* "Very little." *Religion:* Anglican. *Home:* Old Manor

Cottage, Burchetts Green, Berkshire, England, *Agent:* Desmond Elliott, 15 Duke St., St. James's, London S.W.1, England.

CAREER: Evening News, London, England, 1957-66, writer, and special correspondent covering international assignments, including Eichmann trial in Israel and visits of Queen Elizabeth in Australia, 1963, and Germany, 1965; now a free-lance writer and director of Arlington Books, London, England. *Military service:* British Army, 1949-51; served in Malaya. *Awards, honors:* Award for the world's strangest stories, *Evening News*, 1956.

WRITINGS: This Time Next Week: The Autobiography of a Happy Orphan, Constable, 1964, Little, Brown, 1965; *The Virgin Soldiers*, Little, Brown, 1966; *Orange Wednesday*, Constable, 1967, Delacorte, 1968; *The Love Beach*, Constable, 1968, Delacorte, 1969; *Some Lovely Islands* (non-fiction), Arlington, 1968, Coward-McCann, 1969; *Come to the War*, Scribner, 1969; *His Lordship*, M. Joseph, 1970; *Onward Virgin Soldiers*, M. Joseph, 1971, New American Library, 1972; *Arthur McCann and all his Women*, M. Joseph, 1972. Writer of television play, "A Piece of Ribbon," for British Broadcasting Corp.; also writer of television documentaries and short stories.

AVOCATIONAL INTERESTS: Islands—maps, history, and visiting them.

BIOGRAPHICAL/CRITICAL SOURCES: This Time Next Week, Constable, 1964, Little, 1965; "Nostalgia for the Boss," *Books and Bookmen*, October, 1967.†

* * *

THOMPSON, Daniel (Calbert) 1916-

PERSONAL: Born March 3, 1916; son of William (a farmer) and Sarah J. (Barnett) Thompson; married Wilma Miller (a teacher), June 4, 1947; children: Danelle, Wilma Sarah. *Education:* Clark College, Atlanta, Ga., A.B., 1941; Gammon Theological Seminary, B.D., 1944; Atlanta University, M.A., 1945; Harvard University, A.M., 1950; Columbia University, Ph.D., 1955. *Politics:* Democrat. *Religion:* Methodist. *Home:* 3423 St. Anthony St., New Orleans, La. 70122.

CAREER: Clark College, Atlanta, Ga., instructor, 1941-42; Dillard University, New Orleans, La., 1945—, began as instructor, became professor of sociology. Howard University, Washington, D.C., visiting professor of sociology, 1962-63. Research associate at Columbia University Bureau of Applied Social Research, 1952, and at Tulane University Urban Life Research Institute, 1953-57. Consultant to Ford Foundation, U.S. Office of Economic Opportunity, U.S. Office of Education, and to civic and professional groups. Technical consultant and chairman of steering committee, New Orleans Anti-Poverty Program. Lecturer on race relations, education, and related issues. *Member:* American Sociological Association, Southern Sociological Association.

WRITINGS: (With others) *The Eighth Generation*, Harper, 1960; *The Negro Leadership Class*, Prentice-Hall, 1963; (contributor) Gordon J. Klopf, editor, *Integrating the Urban School*, Bureau of Publications, Teachers College, Columbia University, 1963; (contributor) Jackson Toby, editor, *Contemporary Society*, Wiley, 1964; (with Robin M. Williams and Oscar Cohen) *Social Action and the Social Scientist*, Public Affairs Research Center, University of Houston, 1964; (editor with Thomas F. Pettigrew) *Negro American Personality*, Society for the Psychological Study

of Social Issues, 1964; *Private Black Colleges at the Crossroads*, Greenwood Press, 1973; *Sociology of the Black Experience*, Greenwood Press, 1974. Contributor to professional journals and to proceedings of seminars and learned societies.

WORK IN PROGRESS: Contributing to *Readings on Professionalization*, being edited by Donald Mills and Howard M. Vollmer, publication expected by Prentice-Hall; a systematic study of students in Negro colleges.†

* * *

THOMPSON, Thomas Kirkland 1914-

PERSONAL: Born November 10, 1914, in Little Rock, Ark.; son of Earl Dare and Madeline (Dace) Thompson; married Elsie Press, September 3, 1939; children: Judith, Cynthia, Rosemary. *Education:* Baylor University, B.A., 1934; Southern Baptist Theological Seminary, B.D., 1937; Union Theological Seminary, New York, N.Y., S.T.M., 1939. *Politics:* Democrat. *Home:* Indian Ridge Rd., Contoocook, N.H. 03229. *Office:* 85 North State St., Concord, N.H. 03301.

CAREER: Minister, United Church of Christ. Assistant pastor of Congregational church in Brooklyn, N.Y., 1940-42; pastor of Congregational churches in Angola, N.Y., 1942-44, Chicago, Ill., 1944-45; Congregational Christian Churches (now part of United Church of Christ), secretary of Christian Stewardship Missions Council, 1945-50; United Church of Christ, Cranston, R.I., pastor, 1950-51; National Council of Christian Churches in the U.S.A., New York, N.Y., executive director of Commission on Stewardship and Benevolence, 1951—; Wagner College, Staten Island, N.Y., vice-president, 1965-67; American Bible Society, New York, N.Y., director of development, 1967-70; Eden Theological Seminary, Webster Groves, Mo., vice-president for development, 1970-72; United Church of Christ, 17/76 Achievement Fund, Montclair, N.J., area counsellor, 1972—. Union Theological Seminary, New York, N.Y., member of board of directors. *Awards, honors:* D.D., Hillsdale College, 1960.

WRITINGS: (Editor) *Stewardship in Contemporary Theology*, Association Press, 1960; *Handbook of Stewardship Procedures*, Prentice-Hall, 1964; (editor) *Stewardship Illustrations*, Prentice-Hall, 1965; (editor) *Stewardship in Contemporary Life*, Association Press, 1965.†

* * *

THOMPSON, Wilbur R(ichard) 1923-

PERSONAL: Born August 6, 1923, in Detroit, Mich.; son of Dell and Grace (Vosburgh) Thompson; married Margaret Elizabeth Lashinsky, September 7, 1951; children: Philip, Martha, Andrew. *Education:* Wayne State University, B.A., 1947; Brown University, graduate study, 1947-48; University of Michigan, M.A., 1949, Ph.D., 1953. *Home:* 15963 Warwick, Detroit, Mich. *Office:* Department of Economics, Wayne State University, Detroit, Mich.

CAREER: Wayne State University, Detroit, Mich., instructor, 1950-54, assistant professor, 1954-59, associate professor, 1959-63, professor of economics, 1963—. Resources for the Future, Inc., Washington, D.C., research associate, 1961-62, director of Committee on Urban Economics, 1964-65. Southfield (Mich.) Planning Commission, member, 1956-61. *Military service:* U.S. Army, 1943-46. *Member:* American Economic Association, Regional Science Association.

WRITINGS: (With John M. Mattila) An Econometric Model of Postwar State Industrial Development, Wayne State University Press, 1959; A Preface to Urban Economics, Johns Hopkins Press, 1965; Trends in the Detroit Area Economy, Wayne State University, 1966.

Contributor: The Rate and Direction of Inventive Activity, National Bureau of Economic Research, Princeton University Press, 1962; Philip M. Hauser and Leo F. Schnore, editors, The Study of Urbanization, Wiley, 1965; William Haber, W. Allen Spivey, and Martin R. Warshaw, editors, Michigan in the 1970's, Graduate School of Business Administration, University of Michigan, 1965. Contributor to professional journals.

WORK IN PROGRESS: Research on urban economic growth and development, and on urban managerial economics.†

*   *   *

THOMPSON, William E(llison), Jr.   1923-

PERSONAL: Born December 3, 1923, in Chapel Hill, N.C.; son of William Ellison (a banker) and Clemmie (Flowe) Thompson; married Edith Eppes Bass, November 18, 1944; children: William E. III, David C., Mark R., Sally A., Randall H. Education: University of North Carolina, B.S., 1943. Politics: Democrat. Religion: Episcopalian. Home: 135 Orchard Lane, Oak Ridge, Tenn. Office: Oak Ridge National Laboratory, P.O. Box X, Oak Ridge, Tenn.

CAREER: Oak Ridge National Laboratory (nuclear energy research center operated by Union Carbide Corp. for U.S. Atomic Energy Commission), Oak Ridge, Tenn., 1944—, began as chemist, became equipment and general plants projects manager. U.S. Atomic Energy Commission, consultant, Division of Technical Information. Boys' Club of Oak Ridge, secretary, 1960-61, president, 1961-63; Anderson County Community Chest, member of board of directors, 1963—. Military service: U.S. Army, 1945-46. Member: Alpha Chi Sigma, Oak Ridge Bridge Association (treasurer, 1964-65), Oak Ridge Tennis Club (treasurer, 1962). Awards, honors: Society for Advancement of Management award for contribution to solution of problem of technical personnel shortage, for Your Future in Nuclear Energy Fields.

WRITINGS: Industrial Careers in Nuclear Science and Technology (monograph), Institute for Research (Chicago), 1957; Career As a Physicist (monograph), Institute for Research, 1958; Your Future in Nuclear Energy Fields, Rosen, 1961, revised edition, Arco, 1971; Review of California's Regional Water Supply Systems and Possible Applications of Desalting, Oak Ridge National Laboratory, 1972. Also author of brochure on U.S. fusion research, 1958. Contributor to U.S. Atomic Energy Commission semi-annual reports to Congress, 1950-62.

WORK IN PROGRESS: A history of research and development progress at Oak Ridge National Laboratory from 1943 to present, covering contributions to nuclear energy development from first atomic bomb on.†

*   *   *

THORBURN, Hugh G(arnet)   1924-

PERSONAL: Born February 8, 1924, in Toronto, Ontario, Canada; son of Hugh and Delia (Jacobs) Thorburn; married Gwendolyn Montgomery, July 8, 1950; children: Janet Louise, Julie Alexandra, John Andrew, Alice Maria, Mal-

colm Bruce. Education: University of Toronto, B.A., 1949; Columbia University, A.M., 1950, Certificate of European Institute, 1951, Ph.D., 1958. Office: Queen's University, Kingston, Ontario, Canada.

CAREER: Mount Allison University, Sacksville, New Brunswick, lecturer, 1952-53, assistant professor of political science, 1953-54, 1955-56; University of Saskatchewan, Saskatoon, assistant professor of political science, 1954-55; Queen's University, Kingston, Ontario, assistant professor, 1956-63, associate professor, 1963-64, professor of political science and government, 1964—, head of department of political studies, 1968-71. President, Social Science Research Council of Canada, 1967-69. Military service: Canadian Army, Intelligence Corps, 1943-46; became captain. Awards, honors: Social Science Research Council of Canada, grant-in-aid, 1955; Canada Council grant for summer research, 1958, 1960, grants-in-aid of publication for Politics in New Brunswick and for Canadian Anti-Combines Administration 1952-1960; Canada Council fellowship, 1963, 1971-72.

WRITINGS: Politics in New Brunswick, University of Toronto Press, 1961; (with Gideon Rosenbluth) Canadian Anti-Combines Administration 1952-1960, University of Toronto Press, 1963; (editor) Party Politics in Canada, Prentice-Hall (Toronto), 1963, 2nd edition, 1967. Contributor to Canadian Journal of Political Science, Queen's Quarterly, Canadian Forum, other journals in Canada.

WORK IN PROGRESS: A book on the realignments of political parties in France since 1958; a study of the Canadian party system.

SIDELIGHTS: Thorburn speaks French and German; he spent 1963-64 and 1971-72 in France, studying and doing research.

*   *   *

THORELLI, Hans B(irger)   1921-

PERSONAL: Born September 18, 1921, in Newark, N.J.; son of Hans W. R. (an executive) and Hetty Thorelli; married Sarah V. Scott, May 14, 1948; children: Irene Margareta, Thomas Harold. Education: University of Stockholm, M.A., 1944, LL.B., 1945, Ph.D., 1954; Northwestern University, graduate study, 1946-47. Office: Graduate School of Business, Indiana University, Bloomington, Ind.

CAREER: United Nations Secretariat, New York, N.Y., consultant, 1952; Industrial Council for Social and Economic Studies, Stockholm, Sweden, executive director, 1953-56; General Electric Co., Marketing Services Division, New York, research consultant, 1956-59; University of Chicago, Chicago, Ill., professor of business administration, 1959-64; Indiana University, Bloomington, professor of business administration, 1964—, E. W. Kelley Professor of Business Administration, 1972—, chairman of marketing department, 1966-69. Visiting professor, Stanford University, 1962, Institut pour l'Etude des Methodes de Direction de l'Enterprise, 1964-65, University of South Africa, 1967, 1973, and London Graduate School of Business Studies, 1969-70. Consultant to industry, including LaSalle Steel Co., Tower Oil Co., Monsanto Co., and General Electric Co.; conductor of field survey of Latin American operations, Sears, Roebuck & Co., 1962. Member of consumer advisory committee, Federal Energy Office, 1973—.

MEMBER: American Economic Association, American Marketing Association (vice-president of public policy, 1972-73), Academy of Management, Association for Consumer Research. *Awards, honors:* Honorary docent, University of Stockholm, 1954; Fahlbeck Foundation of University of Lund Medal for outstanding treatise in field of political science; Ford Foundation faculty research fellowship, 1963; Consumer Research Institute research grant, 1970; Midwest Universities Consortium for International Affairs research grant, 1973.

WRITINGS: The Federal Antitrust Policy of the United States—Origination of an American Tradition, Johns Hopkins Press, 1955; (contributor) Wroe Alderson and S. J. Shapiro, editors, *Marketing and the Computer*, Prentice-Hall, 1963; (with Robert L. Graves) *International Operations Simulation, with Comments on Design and Use of Management Games*, Free Press of Glencoe, 1963; (contributor) Alderson and Reavis Cox, editors, *Theory in Marketing*, new edition, Irwin, for American Marketing Association, 1964; (editor) *International Marketing Strategy*, Penguin, 1973; (with wife, Sarah Thorelli) *Consumer Information Handbook*, Praeger, 1975. Writer of monographs and articles on industrial marketing and economic, political, and administrative problems in both English and Swedish. Member of editorial board, *Journal of Marketing Research*, 1966-72, *Industrial Marketing Management*, 1971—.

WORK IN PROGRESS: A book on organization theory and management and consumer policy, tentatively entitled *The Information Seekers: An International Study of Consumer Information and Advertising*, for Image Publishing.

SIDELIGHTS: Thorelli grew up in Stockholm, Sweden, and has traveled extensively in Europe and elsewhere. He speaks Swedish, German, French, and some Spanish.

*   *   *

THORP, Duncan Roy   1914-

PERSONAL: Born May 10, 1914, in Fish Creek, Wis.; son of Merle Roy and Edna (McLeod) Thorp; married Bernadette Langlois, October 5, 1937; children: Pamela, Duncan M., Jane. *Education:* Attended Chaffey Junior College (now College), 1932-33; University of Wisconsin, B.A. in Journalism, 1940. *Politics:* Independent. *Religion:* Protestant. *Home:* 2463 Century Dr., Columbus, Ohio. *Agent:* McIntosh & Otis, Inc., 18 East 41st St., New York, N.Y. 10017. *Office:* Ohio TB and Health Association, 1575 Neil Ave., Columbus, Ohio.

CAREER: Sometime guide, merchant sailor, and farmhand; Wisconsin Anti-TB Association, Milwaukee, public relations director, 1940-46; *Door County Advocate*, Sturgeon Bay, Wis., advertising manager, 1946-48; Door County Chamber of Commerce, Sturgeon Bay, Wis., executive secretary, 1948-50; with Ohio TB and Health Association, Columbus, 1954—. *Military service:* U.S. Naval Reserve, active duty aboard destroyers in Atlantic, 1944-46, communications officer in Tokyo, Japan, 1950-52; became lieutenant.

WRITINGS: Only Akiko, Little, Brown, 1958; *Thanks, Yer Honor*, Crown, 1963; *Over the Wall*, Pinnacle Books, 1972.

WORK IN PROGRESS: The Fish at the End of the Rainbow, a novel with a northern Wisconsin setting; *The Election*, a novel dealing with a Carribean Island dictatorship.

SIDELIGHTS: Thorp models his writing on pioneer Wisconsin story tellers he remembers, striving for lyric bluntness. He speaks and writes French and Spanish, and speaks Japanese. *Avocational interests:* Outdoor activities—hunting, fishing, and boating.†

THUMM, Garold W(esley)   1915-

PERSONAL: Born September 22, 1915, in Pinch, W.Va.; son of George Wesley (a minister) and Myrtle (Jarrett) Thumm. *Education:* Morris Harvey College, A.B., 1940; University of Pennsylvania, M.A., 1947, Ph.D., 1954. *Politics:* Republican. *Religion:* Congregationalist. *Home:* 15 Ware St., Lewiston, Me. 04240. *Office:* Bates College, Lewiston, Me. 04240.

CAREER: University of Pennsylvania, Philadelphia, instructor, 1947-54, assistant professor of political science, 1954-61; Bates College, Lewiston, Me., professor of government and chairman of Division of Social Sciences, 1961—. Visiting professor, National War College, 1966-68. *Military service:* U.S. Army, 1941-46, 1951-53; became major. *Member:* International Political Science Association, International Studies Association, American Political Science Association.

WRITINGS: (Editor with A. Z. Rubinstein) *The Challenge of Politics*, Prentice-Hall, 1961, 3rd edition, 1970; (editor with Edward Janosik) *Parties and the Government System*, Prentice-Hall, 1967; (contributor) Murray S. Stedman, editor, *Modernizing American Government: The Demands of Social Change*, Prentice-Hall, 1968. Contributor to *Current History*, *Social Education*.

WORK IN PROGRESS: Research on American foreign policy.

*   *   *

THURSTON, Jarvis   1914-

PERSONAL: Born April 20, 1914, in Huntsville, Utah; son of Christian Schade (a rancher) and Martha (Berg) Thurston; married Mona Van Duyn (a writer), August 31, 1943. *Education:* University of Utah, A.B., 1936; University of California, Berkeley, graduate study, 1940; University of Iowa, M.A., 1944, Ph.D., 1946. *Politics:* Independent. *Religion:* None. *Home:* 7505 Teasdale Ave., St. Louis, Mo. 63130. *Office:* Department of English, Washington University, St. Louis, Mo. 63130.

CAREER: High school mathematics teacher in Ogden, Utah, 1936-43; University of Louisville, Louisville, Ky., assistant professor of English, 1946-50; Washington University, St. Louis, Mo., professor of English, 1950—. *Member:* Modern Language Association of America, American Association of University Professors.

WRITINGS: (Editor) *Reading Modern Short Stories*, Scott, 1955; (with Hartman, Wright, and Emerson) *Short Fiction Criticism*, A. Swallow, 1960; (with Curt Johnson) *Short Stories from the Literary Magazines*, Scott, 1970. Short stories and articles have appeared in literary journals and have been anthologized in *Kafka Today*, *A Country in the Mind*, *Rocky Mountain Reader*, *Accent, 1940-1960*, and *Great Western Short Stories*. Book review editor, *Ogden Standard Examiner*, Ogden, Utah, 1938-43; editor with wife, Mona Van Duyn, of *Perspective* (quarterly journal of literature and arts), 1947—.

WORK IN PROGRESS: A critical study of the poetry of Wallace Stevens.

*   *   *

TIEDT, Iris M(cClellan)   1928-

PERSONAL: Surname is pronounced to rhyme with "neat"; born February 3, 1928, in Dayton, Ohio; daughter of Raymond Hill (an engineer) and Ermalene (Swartzel)

McClellan; married Sidney W. Tiedt (a college professor), September 17, 1949; children: Pamela Lynne, Ryan Sidney. *Education:* Northwestern University, B.S., 1950; University of Oregon, M.A., 1961; Stanford University, Ph.D., 1972. *Politics:* Democrat. *Home:* 1654 Fairorchard Ave., San Jose, Calif. 95125. *Office:* University of Santa Clara, Santa Clara, Calif. 95053.

CAREER: Elementary teacher at public schools in Chicago, Ill., 1950-51, in Kenai, Alaska, 1951-52, Anchorage, Alaska, 1953-57; University of Oregon, Eugene, teaching fellow and supervisor of student teaching, 1959-61; Roosevelt Junior High School, Eugene, Ore., librarian, 1961; University of Santa Clara, Santa Clara, Calif., director of teacher education, 1968-72, director of graduate reading program, 1972—. *Member:* American Association of University Women, Modern Language Association of America, National Council of Teachers of English, Pi Lambda Theta, Sigma Delta Pi.

WRITINGS—With husband, Sidney W. Tiedt, except where noted: *Unrequired Reading: An Annotated Bibliography for Teachers and School Administrators*, Oregon State University Press, 1963, 2nd edition, 1967; *Creative Writing Ideas*, Contemporary Press, 1963, revised edition, 1964; *Exploring Words*, Contemporary Press, 1963; (sole author) *Bulletin Board Captions*, Contemporary Press, 1964, revised edition, 1965; *Imaginative Social Studies Activities for the Elementary School*, Prentice-Hall, 1964; *Selected Free Materials*, Contemporary Press, 1964; *Elementary Teacher's Complete Ideas Handbook*, Prentice-Hall, 1965; *Contemporary English in the Elementary School*, Prentice-Hall, 1967, 2nd edition, 1975; (compilers) *Readings on Contemporary English in the Elementary School*, Prentice-Hall, 1967; (sole author) *Opening Classrooms and New Ways with Individualization*, National Council of Teachers of English, 1973; (sole author) *Women and Girls*, National Council of Teachers of English, 1973; (sole editor) *Drama in Your Classroom*, National Council of Teachers of English, 1974; (sole editor) *What's New in Reading?*, National Council of Teachers of English, 1974; (sole author) *Sexism in Education*, General Learning, 1974; (sole author) *Books/Literature/Children*, Houghton, in press. Co-editor, "Contemporary Classroom Series," Contemporary Press. Contributor to *Instructor*, *Childhood Education*, *Elementary English*, and other professional journals. Editor, *Elementary English*, 1972—.

WORK IN PROGRESS: Contemporary English Handbook, for Oxford University Press; *Twelve Faces of Eve*; *Words at Your Command*.

AVOCATIONAL INTERESTS: The arts, designing original contemporary rugs, writing poetry and stories; wordplay.

*   *   *

TIEDT, Sidney W. 1927-

PERSONAL: Surname rhymes with "neat"; born August 15, 1927, in Chicago, Ill.; son of Harry W. and Jeanette U. (Ryan) Tiedt; married Iris McClellan (a professor), September 17, 1949; children: Pamela Lynne, Ryan Sidney. *Education:* Northwestern University, B.S., 1950, M.A., 1953; University of Oregon, Ed.D., 1961. *Politics:* Democrat. *Home:* 1654 Fairorchard Ave., San Jose, Calif. 95125. *Office:* San Jose State University, San Jose, Calif. 95114.

CAREER: Teacher in Illinois and Alaska, 1950-56; commercial salmon fisherman in Alaska, summers, 1953-55; Anchorage (Alaska) Independent School District, princi-

pal, 1956-59; with University of Oregon, Eugene, 1959-61; San Jose State University, San Jose, Calif., professor of education, 1961—. Director, National Defense Education Act Contemporary English Institute, 1965. *Military service:* U.S. Navy, 1945-46. *Member:* American Educational Research Association, National Council of Teachers of English, Phi Delta Kappa.

WRITINGS—All with wife, Iris M. Tiedt, except where noted: *Unrequired Reading: An Annotated Bibliography for Teachers and School Administrators*, Oregon State University Press, 1963, 2nd edition, 1967; *Creative Writing Ideas*, Contemporary Press, 1963, revised edition, 1964; *Exploring Words*, Contemporary Press, 1963; *Imaginative Social Studies Activities for the Elementary School*, Prentice-Hall, 1964; (sole author) *Quotes for Teaching*, Contemporary Press, 1964; *Selected Free Materials*, Contemporary Press, 1964; *Elementary Teacher's Complete Ideas Handbook*, Prentice-Hall, 1965; (sole author) *The Role of the Government in Education*, Oxford University Press, 1966; *Contemporary English in the Elementary School*, Prentice-Hall, 1967, 2nd edition, 1975; (compilers) *Readings on Contemporary English in the Elementary School*, Prentice-Hall, 1967; (with Lowell G. Keith) *Contemporary Curriculum in the Elementary School*, Harper, 1968, 2nd edition, 1974; (sole editor) *Teaching the Disadvantaged Child*, Oxford University Press, 1968; (sole author) *Creativity in the Classroom*, General Learning, 1974. Co-editor, "Contemporary Classroom Series," Contemporary Press, "The Elementary Teacher's Ideas and Materials Workshop" series, Parker Publishing, 1968—, and "Contemporary Education Foundation Series," General Learning, 1974. Contributor to *Instructor*, *Clearing House*, and other professional journals.

*   *   *

TIMMS, Noel 1927-

PERSONAL: Born December 25, 1927, in London, England; son of Harold (a builder) and Josephine (Bogusz) Timms; married Rita Cadwell, July 1, 1957; children: Julie, Clare, Dominic, Mark. *Education:* King's College, London, B.A. (honors), 1949; Barnett House, Oxford, Diploma in Public and Social Administration, 1950; London School of Economics and Political Science, London, Diploma in Mental Health, 1955, M.A., 1960. *Religion:* Roman Catholic. *Home:* 4 Wilton Grove, London S.W. 19, England. *Office:* London School of Economics and Political Science, Houghton St., London W.C.2, England.

CAREER: Family Service Units in Birmingham and Liverpool, England, caseworker, 1952-54; Child Guidance Clinic, Surrey, England, psychiatric social worker, 1955-57; University of Wales, University College, Cardiff, lecturer, 1957-61; University of Birmingham, Birmingham, England, lecturer, 1961-63; University of London, London School of Economics and Political Science, London, England, lecturer in social casework and sociology, 1963—. College of Deaf Welfare and Social Studies, consultant in social studies. *Member:* Association of University Teachers, Association of Psychiatric Social Workers, Council for Social Work Training, Joint University Council for Public and Social Administration (honorary secretary).

WRITINGS: (With A. F. Philip) *The Problem of the Problem Family*, Family Service Units, 1957; *Casework in the Child Care Service*, Butterworth & Co., 1962, 2nd edition, 1969; *Psychiatric Social Work in Great Britain, 1939-1962*, Humanities, 1964; *Social Casework: Principles and*

Practice, Humanities, 1964; *The Christian Family in the Mid-Twentieth Century*, Darton, Longman & Todd, 1964; *A Sociological Approach to Social Problems*, Routledge & Kegan Paul, 1967; *The Language of Social Casework*, Humanities, 1968; *Rootless in the City*, National Council of Social Service, 1969; *Social Work: An Outline for the Intending Student*, Routledge & Kegan Paul, 1970; (with John E. Mayer) *Working Class Impressions of Casework*, Atherton Press, 1970; *Recording in Social Work*, Routledge & Kegan Paul, 1972; (editor) *The Receiving End: Consumer Accounts of Social Help for Children*, Routledge & Kegan Paul, 1973.

WORK IN PROGRESS: Research on child guidance clinics and on the philosophy of social work.†

* * *

TINSLEY, James Robert 1921-
(Jim Bob Tinsley)

PERSONAL: Born August 12, 1921, in Brevard, N.C.; son of Brance Thomas (a farmer) and Sallie Belle (Bryson) Tinsley; married Doris Eleanor Wilson (an educator), October 4, 1947. *Education:* University of Florida, B.S. (journalism), 1956; Arizona State College (now Northern Arizona University), M.A. in Ed., 1959. *Home:* 217 South East 31st Ave., Ocala, Fla.

CAREER: Ballad singer and guitar player since early teens, appearing at folk festivals throughout America, as member of the Horace Heidt organization on television, and with other television groups and personalities; Marion County Board of Public Instruction, Ocala, Fla., teacher of English and social studies, 1959-68, counselor, 1968—. Marion Players (little theater group), actor, director, and member of board of directors. *Military service:* U.S. Navy, 1942-45; aerial photographer in Africa, Sicily, and Italy. *Member:* National Education Association, Outdoor Writers Association of America, Florida Outdoor Writers Association (regional director), Florida Educational Association, Sigma Delta Chi.

WRITINGS—Under name Jim Bob Tinsley: (With E. Douglas DePew) *Land of Waterfalls*, Stephens Press, 1954; *The Sailfish: Swashbuckler of the Open Seas*, University of Florida Press, 1964; (editor) *The Florida Panther*, Great Outdoors Publishing, 1970. Editor, *Central Florida Outdoors*, and *Southeastern Outdoor World*.

WORK IN PROGRESS: Four books, *The Puma: Legendary Lion of the Americas*, *From Totopotomoy to Transylvania*, *Pennsylvania Panther Tales*, and *Traditional Songs of the American Cowboy*, in two volumes.

SIDELIGHTS: Tinsley's performances as a folk singer range from the musical debut of a small boy with a guitar at age thirteen in the Mountain Dance and Folk Festival, Asheville, N.C., to entertaining Franklin D. Roosevelt and Sir Winston Churchill with cowboy ballads at the Casablanca Conference. *Avocational interests:* Sailfishing, big game hunting, painting, collecting western Americana.

BIOGRAPHICAL/CRITICAL SOURCES: All-Florida (magazine), January 24, 1965.

* * *

TODD, Frances 1910-

PERSONAL: Born December 17, 1910, in San Francisco, Calif.; daughter of Frank Gregory (a bank clerk) and Ella (Mattingly) Todd. *Education:* University of California, Berkeley, A.B., 1930, M.A., 1931; Stanford University,

Ed.D., 1951; other study at Columbia University, Yale University, Stanford University, and University of Vienna. *Politics:* Republican. *Religion:* Episcopal. *Home:* 1932 Ptarmigan Dr. #1, Walnut Creek, Calif. 94595.

CAREER: San Francisco (Calif.) Unified School District, science teacher and high school counselor, and supervisor of health and family life education, 1931-72. Health education consultant, Department of Health, Education, and Welfare Project Teen Concern, and Harcourt, 1972—. San Francisco State College (now University), part-time associate professor of health education, 1959-62; other teaching at University of Nevada and Stanford University. American National Red Cross, served overseas, 1943-48. *Member:* American Association for Health, Physical Education and Recreation (fellow), American School Health Association (fellow), American National Council for Health Education of the Public, American Public Health Association (fellow), National Vocational Guidance Association, California Teachers Association, Delta Kappa Gamma (state regional director, 1957-59; state research chairman, 1960-62), Pi Lambda Theta. *Awards, honors:* National Honor Award, National Women's Association of Allied Beverage Industries, 1964; service awards from American Association for Health, Physical Education and Recreation, California Association for Health, Physical Education and Recreation, and National Retired Teachers Association.

WRITINGS: (With Maud L. Knapp) *Democratic Leadership in Physical Education*, National Press Publications, 1952; *Narcotics and Dangerous Drugs*, San Francisco Unified Schools, 1957; *Alcohol Education*, San Francisco Unified Schools, 1957; *Teaching About Alcohol*, McGraw, 1964; *Teacher's Guide to Health and Family Life Education*, San Francisco United Schools, 1968; *Teacher's Guide on Narcotics and Dangerous Drugs*, San Francisco United Schools, 1974; *Teacher's Guide to Venereal Disease Education*, Harcourt, 1974. Contributor of about twenty-five articles to education and health journals. Former consulting editor, *Journal of Health, Physical Education and Recreation*, and *Journal of California Association of Secondary School Administrators*; foreign correspondent, *L'Education Physique* (Paris).

WORK IN PROGRESS: Booklets on alcohol, drugs, venereal disease, and sex education for teenagers.

SIDELIGHTS: Frances Todd has traveled for pleasure and research in about one hundred countries, in all continents, interviewing educational and health authorities on health problems, particularly as related to young people.

* * *

TOFFLER, Alvin 1928-

PERSONAL: Born October 28, 1928, in New York, N.Y.; married Adelaide Farrell, April 29, 1950; children: Karen. *Education:* New York University, B.A., 1949. *Residence:* Ridgefield, Conn. 06877.

CAREER: Washington correspondent for various newspapers and magazines, 1957-59; *Fortune* magazine, New York, N.Y., associate editor, 1959-61; free-lance writer, 1961—. Member of faculty, New School for Social Research, 1965-67; visiting professor, Cornell University, 1969; visiting scholar, Russell Sage Foundation, 1969-70. Member of board of directors, Composers and Choreographers Theatre. Consultant to organizations, including Rockefeller Brothers Fund, American Telephone & Telegraph Co., Institute for the Future, and Educational Facilities Laboratories, Inc. *Member:* Society of Magazine Writers (vice-president, 1964), Society for the History of Technology (member of advisory council). *Awards, honors:* Award from National Council for the Advancement of Educational Writing, 1969, for *Schoolhouse in the City*; McKinsey Foundation Book Award, 1970, and Prix du Meilleur Livre Etranger (France), 1972, both for *Future Shock*; *Playboy* magazine best article award, 1970; Dr. of Laws from University of Western Ontario, D.Litt. from University of Cincinnati, D.Sc. from Rensselaer Polytechnic Institute, and D.Litt. from Miami University, all in 1972.

WRITINGS: The Culture Consumers (Literary Guild selection), St. Martin's, 1964; (editor) *The Schoolhouse in the City*, Praeger, 1968; *Future Shock*, Random House, 1970; (editor) *The Futurists*, Random House, 1972; (editor) *Learning for Tomorrow*, Random House, 1973.

Contributor: *Bricks and Mortarboards*, Educational Facilities Laboratories, Inc., 1966; B. M. Gross, editor, *A Great Society?*, Basic Books, 1968; K. Baier and N. Rescher, editors, *Values and the Future*, Free Press, 1969; B. M. Gross, editor, *Social Intelligence for America's Future*, Allyn & Bacon, 1969.

Work is represented in anthologies, including: *Politics: U.S.A.*, edited by A. M. Scott and E. Wallace, 2nd edition, Macmillan, 1965; *Essays Today*, edited by William Moynihan, Harcourt, 1968; *The Sociology of Art and Literature*, edited by M. C. Albrecht and others, Praeger, 1970.

Contributor to *Fortune, Life, Reader's Digest, Horizon, New York Times Book Review, Saturday Review, Playboy, Think, New Republic, Nation, Technology and Culture, Arts in Society, Book Week, London Observer, Annals of the Academy of Political and Social Science*, and other journals and periodicals.

SIDELIGHTS: "In the risky business of social and cultural criticism, there appears an occasional book that manages—through some happy combination of accident and insight—to shape our perceptions of its times," wrote Robert Gross, adding Toffler's *Future Shock* to the ranks of books by such notable analysts of the contemporary scene as David Reisman and John Kenneth Galbraith. "Even before reading the book," Gross continued, "one is ready to acknowledge the point of the title." Toffler's study of the effects of rapid technological and social change has been widely credited with astute observation and synthesis. P. M. Grady ascribed to *Future Shock* "the not inconsiderable merit of summarizing and updating an awful lot of futurist conjecture. . . . [It] might assist us not only in preparing for a softer landing into the future, but also in diagnosing more keenly some of today's social puzzles."

*   *   *

TOMALIN, Ruth

PERSONAL: Born in County Kilkenny, Ireland; daughter of Thomas Edward (a professional gardener and writer) and Elspeth Rutherford (Mitchell) Tomalin; divorced; married William N. Ross (a journalist), 1971; children: (first marriage) Nicholas Leaver. *Education:* King's College, London, Diploma in Journalism. *Address:* c/o Barclay's Bank, 15 Langham Pl., London W.1, England.

CAREER: Journalist and author. Began newspaper work in 1942 with *Portsmouth Evening News*, Portsmouth, Hampshire, England, and has since been a staff reporter, at various times, for other newspapers in England, and a press agency reporter in London law courts. *Member:* National Union of Journalists, Society of Authors.

WRITINGS: Threnody for Dormice (poems), Fortune Press, 1947; *The Day of the Rose* (essays and portraits), Fortune Press, 1947; *Deer's Cry* (poem), Fortune Press, 1952; *All Souls* (novel), Faber, 1952; *W. H. Hudson* (biography), Philosophical Library, 1954; *The Daffodil Bird* (juvenile novel), Faber, 1959, A. S. Barnes, 1960; *The Sea Mice* (juvenile novel), Faber, 1962; *The Garden House* (novel), Faber, 1964; *The Spring House* (novel), Faber, 1968; (editor) *Best Country Stories*, Faber, 1969; *Away to the West* (novellas), Faber, 1972; *A Green Wishbone* (juvenile novel), Faber, 1975; *A Stranger Thing* (juvenile novel), Faber, 1975.

WORK IN PROGRESS: Two more novels about country homes in England and Ireland (*The Garden House* was the first of the series); a juvenile textbook on ecology, for Faber.

AVOCATIONAL INTERESTS: Country life and wildlife preservation.

*   *   *

TOMKINS, Calvin   1925-

PERSONAL: Born December 17, 1925, in Orange, N.J.; son of Frederick (a manufacturer) and Laura (Graves) Tomkins; married Judy Johnston, November 11, 1961; children: (first marriage) Anne, Susan, Spencer. *Education:* Princeton University, A.B., 1948. *Home:* Snedens Landing, Palisades, N.Y. *Office: New Yorker*, 25 West 43rd St., New York, N.Y.

CAREER: Radio Free Europe, New York, N.Y., reporter, 1953-57; *Newsweek*, New York, N.Y., writer and editor, 1957-61; *New Yorker*, New York, N.Y., staff writer, 1961—. *Military service:* U.S. Navy, 1944-46. *Member:* Writers Guild of America (East), Century Association, Society of American Historians.

WRITINGS: Intermission, Viking, 1951; *The Bride and the Bachelors*, Viking, 1965; *The Lewis and Clark Trail*, Harper, 1965; *The World of Marcel Duchamp*, Time-Life, 1966; *Eric Hoffer: An American Odyssey*, Dutton, 1968; *Merchants and Masterpieces: The Story of the Metropolitan Museum of Art*, Dutton, 1970; *Living Well Is the Best Revenge*, Viking, 1971; (with wife, Judy Tomkins) *The Other Hampton*, Viking-Grossman, 1974. Writer of television documentary, "The Journals of Lewis and Clark," produced by National Broadcasting Co., 1965. Contributor to *Harper's, Life*, and other periodicals.

AVOCATIONAL INTERESTS: Contemporary art and music, with special attention to avant garde ideas.

*   *   *

TOWLER, Juby Earl   1913-

PERSONAL: Surname is pronounced *Toe*-ler; born February 4, 1913, in Pittsylvania County, Va.; son of John Henry (a farmer) and Emma (Keatts) Towler; married Louise Barbour, December 1, 1933; children: Joseph Alan, Michael Terry. *Education:* Attended public schools in Virginia. *Politics:* Variable (depending on principles of candidate). *Religion:* Baptist. *Home:* 885 Glendale Ave., Danville, Va.

CAREER: Danville (Va.) Police Department, member of force, 1940-72. Civil Defense coordinator, Danville, 1961—; president of Virginia Civil Defense Association,

1965; Virginia representative on U.S. Civil Defense Council, 1964-65; public speaker on civil defense and related topics. *Member:* Associated Public-Safety Communications Officers, F.B.I. National Academy Associates of Virginia, Southside Virginia Police Supervisory Training Association. *Awards, honors:* First prize, U.S. Civil Defense Council, for best civil defense news story of 1964; Flick award for outstanding service in civil defense, 1972.

WRITINGS: The Evil We Seek, privately printed, 1952; *Police Tests and Examinations*, privately printed, 1960; *Practical Police Knowledge*, C. C Thomas, 1962; *The Police Role in Racial Conflicts*, C. C Thomas, 1964; *Civil Defense Dictionary*, [Danville, Va.], 1966; *From the Fruit of the Garden*, privately printed, 1968. Also author of *Dixie Dictionary*, 1969, and *The Adventures of Ellardwishes*, 1969. Contributor to *Police*.

WORK IN PROGRESS: Poetry of the Psalms; *Memoirs of John Doe*; two novels, *The Lowlands* and *Blood, Guts and Thunder*; research on a single-fingerprint file system for small police departments.

*   *   *

TRACY, Michael 1932-

PERSONAL: Born October 22, 1932, in Preston, England; son of Cantrell (a veterinary surgeon) and Jean (Renton) Tracy; married Arpine Kludj, May 27, 1959; children: Anne, Moira, Eileen. *Education:* Attended Fettes College, Edinburgh, Scotland, 1945-50; Pembroke College, Cambridge, B.A., 1955, M.A., 1960. *Office:* Secretariat of the Council of the European Communities, 170 rue de la Loi, Brussels, Belgium.

CAREER: United Nations Economic Commission for Europe, Geneva, Switzerland, research assistant, 1955-57; United Nations High Commission for Refugees, Geneva, Switzerland, statistical officer, 1957-58; Political and Economic Planning, London, England, research assistant, 1958-60; Organization for Economic Co-operation and Development, Paris, France, head of agricultural policies division, 1960-73; Secretariat of the Council of the European Communities, Brussels, Belgium, director, 1973—. *Member:* Agricultural Economics Society (United Kingdom).

WRITINGS: Agriculture in Western Europe—Crisis and Adaptation since 1880, Praeger, 1964; *Japanese Agriculture at the Crossroads*, Trade Policy Research Centre (London), 1972. Contributor to professional journals.

WORK IN PROGRESS: Study of agricultural problems and policies, particularly in the European Economic Community.

SIDELIGHTS: Tracy is fluent in French and German. His Armenian wife is French-speaking and their children bilingual.

*   *   *

TREADGOLD, Mary 1910-

PERSONAL: Born April 16, 1910, in London, England; daughter of John R. W. (a stockbroker) and Hilda (Edwards) Treadgold. *Education:* Bedford College, London, M.A., 1934. *Politics:* Conservative. *Home:* 61 Swan Ct., Chelsea, London S.W. 3, England.

CAREER: British Broadcasting Corp., Overseas Service, producer, literary editor, 1941-60; Jonathan Cape Ltd. (publishers), London, England, literary adviser for children's books, 1963—. *Member:* P.E.N. (English center; member of executive committee, 1956—; chairman of program committee, 1959—). *Awards, honors:* Carnegie Medal of Library Association (London) for outstanding children's book of the year, 1941, for *We Couldn't Leave Dinah.*

WRITINGS: We Couldn't Leave Dinah, Doubleday, 1941; *No Ponies*, J. Cape, 1946; *The Polly Harris*, J. Cape, 1949, Nelson, 1970, published as *The Mystery of the Polly Harris*, Doubleday, 1951; *The Running Child* (Book Society recommendation), J. Cape, 1951; *The Heron Ride*, J. Cape, 1962; *The Winter Princess*, Van Nostrand, 1962; *Return to the Heron*, J. Cape, 1963; *The Weather Boy*, Van Nostrand, 1964; Maid's Ribbons, *Nelson, 1965;* Elegant Patty, *Hamish Hamilton, 1967;* Poor Patty, *Hamish Hamilton, 1968;* This Summer, Last Summer, *Hamish Hamilton, 1968;* The Humbugs, *Hamish Hamilton, 1968;* Rum Day of the Vanishing Pony, *Brockhampton Press, 1970.*

WORK IN PROGRESS: A book and short stories.

SIDELIGHTS: Mary Treadgold speaks some French and German; she has traveled in the Far East, the eastern United States, and nearly all countries of Europe. *Avocational interests:* Cooking, reading, and talking.

BIOGRAPHICAL/CRITICAL SOURCES: Margery Fisher, *Intent Upon Reading*, Brockhampton Press, 1963.†

*   *   *

TREFFTZS, Kenneth Lewis 1911-

PERSONAL: Surname is pronounced Trefs; born December 28, 1911, in Sparta, Ill.; son of John Sydney and Nora (Wright) Trefftzs; married Ellen Ryniker, August 7, 1937; children: Jeffrey Lewis, Ellen Sterling. *Education:* University of Illinois, B.S., 1936, M.S., 1937, Ph.D., 1939. *Home:* 5402 Weatherford Dr., Los Angeles, Calif. 90008.

CAREER: Carnegie Institute of Technology (now Carnegie-Mellon University), Pittsburgh, Pa., instructor in economics, 1939-41; University of Southern California, Graduate School of Business, Los Angeles, 1941—, began as assistant professor of finance, 1950—, chairman of department of finance, 1945-57, became chairman of department of finance and real estate, 1959, chairman of department of finance and business economics, 1966-71. Visiting professor at University of California, Los Angeles, 1947, University of Washington, Seattle, 1949-50; instructor at Pacific Coast Banking School, summers of 1949, 1950. Consultant under Agency for International Development, University of Karachi, 1962. Member of board of more than fourteen companies and investment corporations; economic consultant to firms and associations. Trustee, Lincoln Mortgage Investors.

MEMBER: American Economic Association, American Finance Association (vice-president, 1946-48), Western Economic Association (president, 1955-56), Western Finance Association (president, 1965-66), Phi Kappa Phi, Lambda Alpha, Rho Epsilon, Beta Gamma Sigma, Beta Alpha Psi, Omicron Delta Gamma, Skull and Dagger. *Awards, honors:* Dean's Award, University of Southern California, for outstanding services, 1963.

WRITINGS: (With E. J. Hills) *Mathematics of Business and Accounting*, Harper, 1947, 2nd edition published as *Mathematics of Business, Accounting, and Finance*, 1956; *What Put the Stock Market Where It Is?*, USCRIBE, 1962; (with Harold Dilbeck) *Some Current Practices in Capital Budgeting*, USCRIBE, 1963. Also author of *Mathematics of Banking and Finance*, 1944; editor of *Moving*

Production and Stabilizing Employment Through Consumer Credit, University of Southern California Press.

* * *

TRENHOLM, Virginia Cole 1902-

PERSONAL: Born March 12, 1902, in Columbia, Mo.; daughter of James B. (a doctor) and Virginia (Bedford) Cole; married Robert S. Trenholm (a rancher), September 1, 1932; children: James R., Virginia Trenholm Phillippi. *Education:* University of Missouri, B.J., 1925, M.A., 1926.

CAREER: Member of faculty at Stephens College, Columbia, Mo., 1926-28, and Park College, Parkville, Mo., 1928-31. Free-lance writer. *Member:* American Association for State and Local History, Western Writers of America, Wyoming Press Women, Wyoming Pioneer Association (president, 1961-62), Wyoming Mayflower Society (governor, 1955-57), Kappa Tau Alpha, Theta Sigma Phi.

WRITINGS: Footprints on the Frontier, Douglas Enterprise, 1945; (with Maurine Carley) *Wyoming Pageant*, Bailey School Supply (Casper, Wyo.), 1958; (with Carley) *The Shoshonis: Sentinels of the Rockies*, University of Oklahoma Press, 1964; *The Arapahoes: Our People*, University of Oklahoma Press, 1970. Contributor to newspapers and to historical periodicals.†

* * *

TREVELYAN, Raleigh 1923-

PERSONAL: Surname is pronounced Trevillian; born July 6, 1923, in Port Blair, Andaman Islands, India; son of Walter Raleigh Fetherstonhaugh (a colonel in the Indian Army) and Olive Beatrice (Frost) Trevelyan Ralston. *Education:* Attended Winchester College, Winchester, England, 1937-42. *Religion:* Church of England. *Home:* St. Cadix, St. Veep, Lostwithiel, Cornwall, England. *Agent:* A. M. Heath & Co. Ltd., 40-42 William IV St., London W.C.2, England. *Office:* Hamish Hamilton Ltd., 90 Great Russell St., London W.C.1, England.

CAREER: Samuel Montagu (merchant bankers), London, England, trainee, 1947-48; William Collins Sons & Co. Ltd. (publishers), London, England, editor, 1948-58; Hutchinson & Co. Ltd. (publishers), London, England, editor and director of Arrow Books Ltd. and New Authors Ltd., 1958-61; Penguin Books Ltd. (publishers), Harmondsworth, Middlesex, England, editor, 1961-62; Michael Joseph Ltd. (publishers), London, England, editorial director, 1962-73; Hamish Hamilton Ltd. (publishers), London, England, director, 1973—. Director of Anglo-Italian Society for the Protection of Animals. *Military service:* British Army, Rifle Brigade, Infantry, 1942-46; served with Military Mission to Italian Army in Rome, 1944-46; became captain; mentioned in dispatches. *Member:* Travellers Club, Garrick Club. *Awards, honors:* John Florio Prize, Translators Association, for *The Outlaws.*

WRITINGS: The Fortress: A Dairy of Anzio and After (Book Society recommendation), Collins, 1956, St. Martin's, 1957; *A Hermit Disclosed* (Book Society choice), Longmans, Green, 1960, St. Martin's, 1961; (translator) Giuliano Palladino, *Peace at Alamein*, Hodder & Stoughton, 1962; *The Big Tomato*, Longmans, Green, 1966; (editor) *Italian Short Stories*, Penguin, 1965; (editor) *Italian Writing Today*, Penguin, 1967; (translator from the Italian) Luigi Meneghello, *The Outlaws*, Morrow, 1967; *Princess Under the Volcano*, Morrow, 1972.

WORK IN PROGRESS: A book based on the papers of Pauline Lady Trevelyan, for Chatto & Windus; a book on Pompeii and Mt. Vesuvius, for Folio; a book on childhood in India.

SIDELIGHTS: Trevelyan is competent in Italian and French, and to a lesser degree, in Spanish and German. His travels include a visit to the United States as a member of a United Kingdom Goodwill Mission to Virginia for the Jamestown Festival in 1957. *Avocational interests:* Travel, gardening, collecting, and theatre.

* * *

TREVES, Ralph 1906-

PERSONAL: Born July 16, 1906, in Salamanca, N.Y.; son of Isador (a builder) and Rose Treves; married Estelle Hennefeld (a teacher), 1932; children: Suzanne, Joyce Leslie. *Education:* Attended New York University. *Home:* 184-29 Tudor Rd., Jamaica Estates, New York, N.Y. 11432. *Office:* Sumner Rider Associates, 355 Lexington Ave., New York, N.Y. 10017.

CAREER: Member of editorial staff of newspapers, New York, N.Y., including *New York Daily Mirror*, and *New York Journal-American*; medical writer, *Medical World News*, New York, N.Y.; free-lance writer. *Member:* American Medical Writers Association, National Association of Science Writers, National Association of Home Workshop Writers.

WRITINGS: Complete Book of Basement Improvement, Hill & Wang, 1953; *Early American Furniture You Can Build*, Fawcett, 1963; *How to Make Your Own Recreation and Hobby Rooms*, Popular Science, 1968; *Do-It-Yourself Home Protection: A Commonsense Guide*, Popular Science, 1972; (editor) *Family Handyman Improvement Book*, Scribner, 1972; *The Homeowner's Complete Guide*, Dutton, 1974. Author of weekly column on home maintenance in *Philadelphia Inquirer, Los Angeles Times*, and *Toronto Star*, 1949-63. Contributor of articles on workshop and tool skills to *Popular Science, Popular Mechanics, Workbench, Science and Mechanics, Better Homes and Gardens*, and *Mechanix Illustrated.*

* * *

TRIMBLE, Jacquelyn W(hitney) 1927-
(J.L.H. Whitney)

PERSONAL: Born October 21, 1927, in Portland, Ore.; daughter of Frederick Willis (a civil engineer) and Naomi (Groll) Whitney; married Louis Preston Trimble (a college teacher and writer), November 21, 1952; children: Victoria Rosemary (stepdaughter). *Education:* University of Washington, Seattle, B.A., 1951, M.L.S., 1959; further study at Eastern Washington State College, 1952-53, University of Pennsylvania, 1955-56. *Office:* King County Public Library, 1100 East Union, Seattle, Wash. 98122.

CAREER: Worked as secretary and clerk for commercial firms while continuing education; University of Pennsylvania, Philadelphia, secretary and librarian in microbiology department, 1955-56; Hartman's Books, Seattle, Wash., buyer of children's books, 1957-59; King County Public Library, Seattle, Wash., assistant to reference librarian, 1962-64, reference librarian, 1964—. *Member:* Mystery Writers of America.

WRITINGS: (Under name J.L.H. Whitney) *Whisper of Shadows*, Ace Books, 1964; (with husband, Louis Trimble) *Guardians of the Gate*, Ace Books, 1972.

WORK IN PROGRESS: A Novel.

AVOCATIONAL INTERESTS: Travel, gardening, collecting dolls, golf.†

*   *   *

TRIMBLE, Louis P. 1917-
(Stuart Brock, Gerry Travis)

PERSONAL: Born March 2, 1917, in Seattle, Wash.; son of Charles Louis (an artist) and Rose Alice (Potter) Trimble; married Renee Eddy, January 2, 1938 (died, 1951); married Jacquelyn Whitney (a librarian and author), November 21, 1952; children: (first marriage) Victoria Rosemary. *Education:* Eastern Washington State College, B.A., 1950, Ed.M., 1953; graduate study, University of Washington, Seattle, 1952-53, 1955, 1956-57, and University of Pennsylvania, 1955-56. *Home:* 12840 139th Ave., N.E., Kirkland, Wash. 98033. *Agent:* Scott Meredith Literary Agency, Inc., 580 Fifth Ave., New York, N.Y. 10036. *Office:* Humanities-Social Studies Department, College of Engineering, University of Washington, Seattle, Wash. 98105.

CAREER: High school teacher of English, Bonners Ferry, Idaho, 1946-47; Eastern Washington State College, Cheney, instructor in Spanish and English, 1950-54; University of Washington, Seattle, instructor, 1956-59, assistant professor, 1959-65, associate professor of humanities and social studies, 1965—. Free-lance writer, 1938—. Editor of architects division, U.S. Army, Corps of Engineers. *Member:* International Association of Teachers of English as a Foreign Language, Association of Teachers of English as a Second Language, Science Fiction Writers of America, Western Writers of America (member of executive board, 1963-64).

WRITINGS: Sports of the World, Golden West, 1938.

Fit to Kill, Phoenix Press, 1941; *Tragedy in Turquoise,* Phoenix Press, 1942; *Date for Murder,* Phoenix Press, 1942; *Murder Trouble,* Phoenix Press, 1945; *Design for Dying,* Phoenix Press, 1945; *Give Up the Body,* Superior, 1946; *You Can't Kill a Corpse,* Phoenix Press, 1946; *Valley of Violence,* Macrae Smith, 1948; *The Case of the Blank Cartridge,* Phoenix Press, 1949.

Gunsmoke Justice, Macrae Smith, 1950; *Blonds Are Skin Deep,* Lion Books, 1951; *Gaptown Law,* Macrae Smith, 1951; *Fighting Cowman,* Popular Publications, 1952; *Bring Back Her Body,* Wyn, 1953; *Crossfire,* Avalon, 1953; *Bullets on Bunchgrass,* Avalon, 1954; *The Virgin Victim,* Mercury, 1956; *Stab in the Dark,* Wyn, 1956; *Nothing to Lose But My Life,* Wyn, 1957; *Mountain Ambush,* Avalon, 1958; *The Smell of Trouble,* Wyn, 1958; *Corpse Without a Country,* Wyn, 1959; *Till Death Do Us Part,* Wyn, 1959; *Obit Deferred,* Ace Books, 1959.

Girl on a Slay Ride, Avon, 1960; *The Duchess of Skid Row,* Ace Books, 1960; *Love Me and Die,* Ace Books, 1960; *The Surfside Caper,* Ace Books, 1961; *Montana Gun,* Hillman, 1961; *Deadman's Canyon,* Ace Books, 1961; *Siege at High Meadows,* Ace Books, 1961; *Wild Horse Range,* Ace Books, 1963; *The Man from Colorado,* Ace Books, 1963; *The Dead and the Deadly,* Ace Books, 1963; *Trouble at Gunsight,* Ace Books, 1964; *The Desperate Deputy of Cougar Hill,* Ace Books, 1965; *Holdout in the Diablos,* Ace Books, 1965; *Showdown in the Cayuse,* Ace Books, 1966; *Standoff at Massacre Buttes,* Ace Books, 1967; *Marshal of Sangaree,* Ace Books, 1968; *Anthropol,* Ace Books, 1968; *West to the Pecos,* Ace Books, 1968; *Hostile Peaks,* Ace Books, 1969.

Trouble Valley, Ace Books, 1970; *The Lonesome Mountains,* Ace Books, 1970; *The Noblest Experiment in the Galaxy,* Ace Books, 1970; (with Tom West) *Lobo of Lynx Valley* [by Tom West and] *The Ragbag Army* [by Louis Trimble], Ace Books, 1971; (with wife, Jacquelyn Trimble) *Guardians of the Gate,* Ace Books, 1971; *The City Machine,* Daw Books, 1972; *The Wandering Variables,* Daw Books, 1972; *The Bodelan Way,* Daw Books, 1974.

Under pseudonym Stuart Brock: *Just Around the Coroner,* Morrow, 1948; *Death Is My Lover,* Morrow, 1948; *Double Cross Ranch,* Avalon, 1954; *Whispering Canyon,* Avalon, 1955; *Action at Boundary Peak,* Avalon, 1955; *Forbidden Range,* Avalon, 1956; *Killer's Choice,* Graphic Books, 1956; *Railtown Sheriff,* Avalon, 1957.

Under pseudonym Gerry Travis: *Tarnished Love,* Phoenix Press, 1942; *A Lovely Mask for Murder,* Mystery House, 1956; *The Big Bite,* Mystery House, 1957.

Editor: *Criteria for Highway Benefit Analysis,* National Academy of Sciences and College of Engineering, University of Washington, Volume I (interim report), 1964, Volumes I and II (final report), 1965, revised edition, with Robert G. Hennes, National Highway Research Board, 1966-67; *Incorporation of Shelter into Apartments and Office Buildings,* Office of Civil Defense, Department of the Army, 1965.

Contributor of about forty mystery, Western, sports, and juvenile stories to periodicals and newspapers, including *Toronto Star Weekly* and *Future Farmer.*

WORK IN PROGRESS: Science fiction novels; a Western novel; research on the rhetoric of scientific and technical English and its application to teaching English as a second or foreign language.

SIDELIGHTS: Trimble has a reading knowledge of Spanish, French, German, Hungarian, Latin, and Serbo-Croatian (varying from "without a dictionary to with dictionary and grammar aids"). *Avocational interests:* Golf, hiking, and traveling to collect story locales and information.

*   *   *

TRIPP, Miles (Barton) 1923-
(John Michael Brett, Michael Brett)

PERSONAL: Born May 5, 1923, in Ganwick Corner, near Barnet, England; son of Cecil Lewis and Brena Mary (Yells) Tripp. *Education:* Attended county school in Hertfordshire. *Address:* c/o Macmillan & Co. Ltd., Little Essex St., London W.C.2, England.

CAREER: Free-lance writer. *Member:* Society of Authors (England), Crime Writers Association (England; president, 1968-69).

WRITINGS—All published by Macmillan (London), except as indicated: *Faith Is a Windsock,* P. Davies, 1952; *The Image of Man,* Darwen Finlayson, 1955; *A Glass of Red Wine,* Macdonald & Co., 1960; *Kilo Forty,* 1963, Holt, 1964; (under pseudonym Michael Brett) *Diecast,* Fawcett, 1963, published under pseudonym John Michael Brett, Pan Books, 1966; *The Skin Dealer,* Holt, 1964; (under pseudonym Michael Brett) *A Plague of Dragons,* Arthur Barker, 1965, published under pseudonym John Michael Brett, Pan Books, 1966; *A Quartet of Three,* 1965; *The Chicken,* 1966; (under pseudonym John Michael Brett) *A Cargo of Spent Evil,* Arthur Barker, 1966; *The Fifth Point of the Compass,* 1967; *One is One,* 1968; *The Chicken* [and] *Zilla,* Pan Books, 1968; *Malice and the Maternal Instinct,* 1969; *The Eighth Passenger,* Heinemann, 1969; *A Man Without*

Friends, 1970; *Five Minutes with a Stranger*, 1971; *The Claws of God*, 1972; *Obsession*, 1973; *Woman at Risk*, 1974. Also author of television adaptation "A Man Without Friends" based on his novel, and broadcast in England, 1972.

* * *

TROMAN, Morley 1918-

PERSONAL: Born February 26, 1918, in Wednesbury, England; married Shulamith Przepiorka (a painter), February 12, 1946; children: Robin Henry, Nanda Mary. *Education:* Studied drawing and sculpture at Wolverhampton College of Art, Wolverhampton, England, 1935-40, and took external courses from University of London while prisoner in Germany, 1942-44. *Home and office:* Kerallary, Ploumillian, Cotes-du-Nord, Brittany, France. *Agent:* Richmond, Towers & Benson Ltd., 14 Essex St., Strand, London W.C. 2, England.

CAREER: Self-employed in a number of different fields since 1935 (when he worked briefly as an insurance clerk); free-lance occupations have ranged from furniture moving to acting, from fishing to painting houses, but main interests have always centered on sculpture and writing; sculpture has been exhibited in Paris salons and in several international shows. Civilian prisoner in Germany and France, 1942-44; volunteer, working with concentration camp victims in England and Germany, 1945-46; resided in Paris, 1946-56, then bought a farm in Britanny where he has lived since; producer and program director, French Radio, 1950—. *Member:* P.E.N. (London).

WRITINGS: The Hill of Sleep (novel), Chatto & Windus, 1960; *The Devil's Dowry* (novel), Chatto & Windus, 1961. Radio scripts: "The Leaf of Joy" (play), produced by British Broadcasting Corp., 1959; "My Street," weekly series of talks about Paris for English Language Section of French Radio—ORTF, 1952-54; "Breton Village," weekly series in English for French Radio, 1962-64; "Channel Nord-Sud," weekly series in French on diversified topics, 1964—.

WORK IN PROGRESS: The Standing Stone, a novel.

SIDELIGHTS: Troman told *CA:* "Still hope (after twenty years trying) to devote *all* my time to sculpture and writing." In the meantime Troman has been restoring his seventeenth-century farmhouse in Brittany, planting trees and cultivating strawberries. He is fluent in French, speaks "fairly good" Yiddish (picked up from concentration camp survivors), and a little Italian and German. A short television film about his Breton home and activities was shown on a French network in July, 1964.†

* * *

TROOP, Miriam 1917-

PERSONAL: Born April 27, 1917, in Philadelphia, Pa.; daughter of Abraham (a news dealer) and Fannie (Eisbart) Troop; married Bernard Zuger (a physician), January 28, 1954; children: Abigail Del. *Education:* Studied at Moore College of Art, 1936-40, Pennsylvania Academy of Fine Arts, 1940-42, and Art Students League of New York, 1944, 1954, 1963.

CAREER: Free-lance illustrator, 1940—, and writer. U.S. Army, Special Services, civilian service in Korea. *Member:* National Association of Women Artists, Society of Illustrators, Artists Equity Association. *Awards, honors:* Margaret Lowencorund Award, 1964.

WRITINGS: (Self-illustrated) *Children Around the World* (Junior Literary Guild selection), Grosset, 1958; (editor and illustrator) *The Limerick Book*, Grosset, 1964. Contributor of travel articles to *American* and *Woman's Day*.

WORK IN PROGRESS: A book, *An Introduction to the Artist in America.*†

* * *

TRUMP, Fred(erick Leonard) 1924-

PERSONAL: Born April 18, 1924, in Jamestown, N.Y.; son of Leonard J. (a farmer) and Clara (an English teacher; maiden name, Keopka) Trump; married Lois Stelson, September 8, 1951; children: Christine, Eric, Timothy, Sara. *Education:* Cornell University, B.S., 1949. *Religion:* Protestant. *Home:* 631 Wayland Ave., East Lansing, Mich. 48823.

CAREER: Michigan Farmer (magazine), East Lansing, Mich., assistant editor, 1949—. *Military service:* U.S. Army Air Forces, 1943-46; became sergeant. *Member:* American Association of Agricultural Editors, Sigma Delta Chi. *Awards, honors:* Spotlight on Dairying national award, National Milk Producers Federation, 1962, for dairy articles; certificate of merit for conservation articles, Michigan chapter of Soil Conservation Society of America, 1965.

WRITINGS: The Grange in Michigan, privately printed, 1963; *Buyer Beware!*, Abingdon, 1965; *Uphill Into the Sun*, Naylor, 1973.

AVOCATIONAL INTERESTS: History, meteorology, confidence schemes, farming, young people.†

* * *

TSCHEBOTARIOFF, Gregory P. 1899-

PERSONAL: Surname is pronounced Che-bo-ta-ri-off; born February 15, 1899, in Pavlovsk, Russia; son of Porphyry Grigorievich (an army officer) and Valentina (Doubiagsky) Chebotarioff; married Florence Dorothy Bill, April 2, 1939. *Education:* Studied at Imperial Law School, Petrograd, Russia, 1911-16, Mihailovsky Artillery School, Petrogard, 1916; Technische Hochschule, Berlin, Germany, Diplom Ingenieur, 1925; Technische Hochschule, Aachen, Germany, Doktor Ingenieur, 1952. *Politics:* Independent. *Religion:* Russian Eastern Orthodox. *Home and office:* 26 George St., Lawrenceville, N.J. 08648.

CAREER: Engineer with construction firms in France, Germany, and Egypt, 1924-29; Egyptian government, Cairo, engineer, 1929-37, research engineer at Egyptian University, 1933-37; Princeton University, Princeton, N.J., lecturer, 1937, assistant professor, 1937-43, associate professor, 1943-51, professor of civil engineering, 1951-64, professor emeritus, 1964-70. King & Gavaris (consulting engineers), New York, N.Y., associate, 1956-70. Director of research projects in applied soil mechanics for Civilian Aeronautics Administration, 1943-46, U.S. Navy, 1943-49, 1951-56. Official delegate of Egyptian University at First International Conference on Soil Mechanics and Foundation Engineering at Harvard University, 1936, and of Princeton University at second conference in Rotterdam, Netherlands, 1948, Chairman, special session of eighth conference in Moscow, 1973. *Military service:* Imperial Russian Army, 1916-17; became third lieutenant. Don Cossack Army (White Russians), 1918-20; became second lieutenant.

MEMBER: American Society of Civil Engineers, National Society of Professional Engineers, American Historical

Association, American Association for the Advancement of Slavic Studies, Sigma Xi. *Awards, honors:* Docteur honoris causa, Free University of Brussels, 1959; Author Award from New Jersey Association of Teachers of English for autobiography, *Russia, My Native Land.*

WRITINGS: Soil Mechanics, Foundations and Earth Structures, McGraw, 1951; (translation editor) Nikolai A. Tsytovich, *Bases and Foundations on Frozen Soil,* Highway Research Board, 1960; (contributor) *Foundation Engineering,* McGraw, 1962; (translation editor) *Dynamics of Bases and Foundations,* McGraw, 1962; *Russia, My Native Land* (autobiography), McGraw, 1964; *Foundations: Retaining and Earth Structures,* McGraw, 1973. Writer of historical-political articles on Russia; contributor of some one hundred articles on soil and foundation engineering to technical periodicals and to proceedings of national and international conferences.

SIDELIGHTS: Tschebotarioff speaks, reads, and writes Russian, French, and German fluently.

BIOGRAPHICAL/CRITICAL SOURCES: Gregory P. Tschebotarioff, *Russia, My Native Land,* McGraw, 1964.

*   *   *

TSCHUDY, James Jay   1925-

PERSONAL: Surname is pronounced *Chew*-dee; born July 27, 1925, in Moline, Ill.; son of Jacob Leopold and Marie (Montgomery) Tschudy; married Belva Worrell, October 2, 1946; children: James Jay II, Raymond Von, Katrina. *Education:* University of Utah, B.S., 1950; Brigham Young University, M.S., 1953; University of California, Berkeley, Ph.D., 1958. *Religion:* Church of Jesus Christ of Latter-day Saints. *Home:* 1451 Plumas, Seaside, Calif. 93955. *Office:* Monterey County Psychiatric Clinic, 1270 Natividad Rd., Salinas, Calif. 93904.

CAREER: Certified psychologist, California State Board of Medical Examiners, and licensed psychologist, State of Utah. Utah State University, Logan, associate professor of psychology, 1961-63; George Washington University, research scientist with Human Resources Research Office, Monterey, Calif., 1963-64. Monterey County Psychiatric Clinic, Salinas, Calif., chief clinical psychologist, 1964—. Church of Jesus Christ of Latter-day Saints, high councilman of Monterey Bay Stake, 1963—. *Military service:* U.S. Naval Reserve, on active duty, 1942-46, 1951-52; became lieutenant commander. *Member:* American Psychological Association.

WRITINGS: The Art of Counseling, Deseret, 1963. Contributor to *Instructor.*

WORK IN PROGRESS: The Struggle Within, a book dealing with inner and interpersonal conflicts, commonly experienced by ''normal'' people.†

*   *   *

TUNLEY, Roul   1912-

PERSONAL: First Name is pronounced *Rule*; born May 12, 1912, in Chicago, Ill.; son of Joseph H. (a broker) and Lillian (Boyd) Tunley. *Education:* Yale University, B.A., 1934. *Residence:* Stockton, N.J. *Agent:* Paul R. Reynolds & Son, 599 Fifth Ave, New York, N.Y. 10017.

CAREER: New York Herald Tribune, New York, N.Y., reporter, 1934-37; *Look* magazine, assistant circulation manager, 1937-39, director of editorial promotion, 1948-50; syndicated columnist, 1939-41; Yale University, New Ha-

ven, Conn., instructor in English, 1946-47; *American* magazine, New York, N.Y., writer and associate editor, 1951-56; *Woman's Home Companion,* assistant managing editor, 1956; *Saturday Evening Post,* Philadelphia, Pa., associate editor, 1961-63. *Military service:* U.S. Navy Air Force, 1942-45; lieutenant commander (Reserves). *Member:* Authors Guild, Elizabethan Club.

WRITINGS: Kids, Crime and Chaos, Harper, 1962; *The American Health Scandal,* Harper, 1966; *Ordeal By Fire,* World Publishing, 1966. Contributor to *Reader's Digest, Nation, Saturday Evening Post, Holiday, Woman's Day, New York Times,* and other publications.

*   *   *

TURCO, Lewis Putnam   1934-

PERSONAL: Born May 2, 1934, in Buffalo, N.Y.; son of Luigi (a minister) and May (Putnam) Turco; married Jean Houdlette, June 16, 1956; children: Melora Ann, Christopher Cameron. *Education:* University of Connecticut, B.A., 1959; State University of Iowa, M.A., 1962. *Home:* 54 West 8th St., Oswego, N.Y. 13126. *Office:* Sheldon Hall, State University of New York, College at Oswego, Oswego, N.Y. 13126.

CAREER: Fenn College (now Cleveland State University), Cleveland, Ohio, instructor in English, 1960-64, founder and director of Poetry Center, 1961-64; Hillsdale College, Hillsdale, Michigan, assistant professor of English, 1964-65; State University of New York, College at Oswego, assistant professor, 1965-68, associate professor, 1968-70, professor of English, 1970—, director of program in writing arts, 1971—. Founder and director, Conference of Midwestern Poets, 1965; visiting professor, State University of New York at Potsdam, 1968-69; honorary trustee, Theodore Roethke Memorial Foundation. *Military service:* U.S. Navy, 1952-56. *Awards, honors:* Yaddo Writer's Conference, resident fellowship, 1959; Academy of American Poets prize, 1960; Bread Loaf Poetry Conference fellowship, 1961; State University of New York Research Foundation fellowship, 1966, 1967, 1969, 1971, and 1973.

WRITINGS: First Poems, Golden Quill Press, 1960; *The Sketches of Lewis Turco and Livevil: A Mask,* American Weave Press, 1962; (contributor) Martha Foley and David Burnett, editors, *The Best American Short Stories of 1967,* Houghton, 1967; *The Book of Forms,* Dutton, 1968; *Awaken, Bells Falling* (poems), University of Missouri Press, 1968; *The Inhabitants* (poems), Despa, 1970; *Creative Writing in Poetry,* State University of New York, 1970; *The Literature of New York,* New York State English Council, 1970; *Pocoangelini: A Fantography and Other Poems,* Despa, 1971; *Poetry: An Introduction Through Writing,* Reston Publishing, 1973; *The Weed Garden,* Peaceweed, 1973; *Freshman Composition and Literature,* State University of New York, 1973; *The Book of Beasts,* Grey Heron Press, in press.

Poetry represented in anthologies, including *New Campus Writing 3,* Grove, 1959; *Poetry for Pleasure,* Doubleday, 1960; *Midland,* Random House, 1961; *Anthology of Contemporary American Poetry* (recording), Folkways, 1961; *Doors into Poetry,* Prentice-Hall, 1962; *Of Poetry and Power,* Basic Books, 1964; *Best Poems of 1965,* Pacific Books, 1966; *The New Yorker Book of Poems,* Viking, 1969; *Best Poems of 1971,* Pacific Books, 1972; *Contemporary Poetry in America,* Random House, 1973; *Journeys,* Ginn, 1973; *Shape,* Ginn, 1973.

Author of play, ''The Dark Man,'' produced in Stoors and

Coventry, Conn., 1959, also author of libretto for opera based on play, "The Dark Man," music by Walter Hekster, 1969.

Contributor to *Prairie Schooner, Carleton Miscellany, Antioch Review, Sewanee Review, Paris Review, Northwest Review, Kenyon Review, Poetry, American Scholar, Saturday Review, Nation, Commonweal, New Yorker, Atlantic Monthly, New York Quarterly, Tri-Quarterly Review, Poetry Northwest, Iowa Review, New Republic, New York Times Magazine, Michigan Quarterly Review*, and others.

WORK IN PROGRESS: The Familiar, Sarrazinois, Seasons of the Blood, Poems on the Tarot, The Compleat Melancholick, all poetry; a novel, *The Journal of Charles Ally; Good Grey Poets and Bad Old Bards*, a book of criticism; *The Putnams of Salem Village*.

SIDELIGHTS: Of *Awaken, Bells Falling*, a reviewer for the *Virginia Quarterly Review* wrote: "It is a full and varied book, showing off the range of Turco's talent and the variety of his mind. His view of things is quiet and dark; he accepts rather than affirms, acknowledges rather than celebrates. But the poems have a solidity beyond acceptance, for he knows the music of the day's events and remembers the way the ordinary can often glow and blaze. Whether he writes of a pumpkin, a Christmas tree, the death of a president or an ordinary evening in Cleveland, he writes with compassion and precision. If death too often overshadows life, and pain, life's joys, nevertheless Lewis Turco finds his singing voice in suffering, finds reason to live and love in despair. These are good poems by a poet of a real ability."

"While the Spider Slept," a ballet based on a Turco poem, by Brian Macdonald, was performed by the Royal Swedish Ballet in 1966. Turco has recorded his "Raceway and Other Poems" for the Library of Congress.

* * *

TURNER, George Allen 1908-

PERSONAL: Born August 28, 1908, in Willsboro. N.Y.; son of Charles Doyle (a carpenter and farmer) and Bertha Eunice (Hayes) Turner; married Lucile Marjorie McIntosh (a schoolteacher), October 8, 1938; children: Allen Charles, Carol Jean. *Education:* Greenville College, A.B., 1932, B.D., 1934; Biblical Seminary in New York, S.T.B., 1935, S.T.M., 1936; Harvard University, Ph.D., 1946. *Politics:* Republican. *Home:* 206 Asbury Ave., Wilmore, Ky. *Office:* Asbury Theological Seminary, Wilmore, Ky.

CAREER: Minister, Free Methodist Church. Asbury Theological Seminary, Wilmore, Ky., 1945—, now professor of Biblical literature. Associate director of Bible Land Seminars, Wilmore, Ky.; lecturer on Biblical theology in Japan, India, Formosa, and Egypt, 1961; teacher and researcher in Jerusalem and Jordan, 1964 and 1968. *Member:* National Association of Hebrew Instructors, Society of Biblical Literature, Evangelical Theological Society. *Awards, honors:* D.Litt. from Greenville College, 1964; distinguished alumnus award from Greenville College, 1973.

WRITINGS: The More Excellent Way, Light and Life Press, 1952; (with J. R. Mantey) *Evangelical Commentary on John's Gsopel*, Eerdmans, 1964; *The Vision Which Transforms: Is Christian Perfection Scriptural?*, Nazarene Publishing, 1964; (with Mantey) *The Gospel According to John*, Eerdmans, 1964; *Historical Geography of the Holy Land*, Baker Book, 1973; *The New and Living Way*, Bethany Fellowship, 1974. Also author of Aldersgate Study Guides to *John's Gospel*, 1963, *Isaiah*, 1966, *Revelation*, 1967, and *Books of the Exilic Period*, 1969, all published by Light and Life Press. Contributor to *Old Testament in Parallel Versions* and to *Pictorial Bible Encyclopedia*, both published by Zondervan. Also contributor of "The Sunday School Lesson" to *Herald*, Louisville, Ky., 1948—.

WORK IN PROGRESS: Followers of the Way, pen-portraits of some "saints," and *Relevance of the Wesleyan Message*, lectures on holiness, both for Beacon Hill Press; *The World of St. Paul: The Apostle's Travels from Damascus to Rome*, companion volume to *Historical Geography of the Holy Land*.

SIDELIGHTS: The More Excellent Way was published in Japanese. Turner has made ten study trips to the Near East since 1953. He is competent in Greek, German, and French.

* * *

TURNER, Howard M(oore), Jr. 1918-

PERSONAL: Born December 16, 1918, in Boston, Mass.; son of Howard Moore (a civil engineer) and Helen (Eustis) Turner; married Josephine Ross, September 2, 1944; children: Hope, Howard Ross. *Education:* Harvard University, A.B. *Politics:* Independent. *Religion:* Episcopalian. *Home:* 342 Woodbury Rd., Huntington, Long Island, N.Y. *Office:* D'Arcy Advertising Co., 430 Park Ave., New York, N.Y. 10022.

WRITINGS: Sales Promotion That Gets Results, McGraw, 1959; *The People Motivators: Consumer and Sales Incentives in Modern Marketing*, McGraw, 1973.†

* * *

TWEEDIE, Donald F(erguson), Jr. 1926-

PERSONAL: Born July 24, 1926, in Salem, Mass.; son of Donald Ferguson (a farmer) and Gladys (Sylvester) Tweedie; married Norma Smith, October 31, 1945; children: Donald F. III, Thomas T., Joel S., Andrew P., Peter F., Paula. *Education:* Gordon College, A.B., 1950; Boston University, Ph.D., 1954; University of Vienna, postdoctoral study, 1959-60. *Politics:* Republican. *Religion:* Protestant. *Home:* 4326 Oakwood, LaCanada, Calif. *Office:* Pasadena Community Counseling Center, 177 North Madison, Pasadena, Calif.

CAREER: Gordon College, Wenham, Mass., instructor in philosophy and psychology, 1952-54, assistant professor, 1954-57, associate professor, 1957-60, professor of psychology, 1961-64; Pasadena Community Counseling Center, Pasadena, Calif., director, 1964—. U.S. Veterans Administration Hospital, Lexington, Ky., resident specialist, 1962-63. *Military service:* U.S. Army Air Forces, 1943-45. *Member:* American Psychological Association, American Scientific Affiliation, American Society of Clinical Hypnosis, Christian Association for Psychological Studies. *Awards, honors:* Kentucky Colonel.

WRITINGS: Logotherapy and the Christian Faith, Baker Book, 1961; *The Christian and the Couch*, Baker Book, 1963; *Of Sex and Saints*, Baker Book, 1965; *Christian and Sex*, Baker Book, 1965; *Logotherapy*, Baker Book, 1972. Contributor to professional and academic journals.

WORK IN PROGRESS: Two books, *Faith and Feeling*, and *The Sick Soul*.

SIDELIGHTS: Tweedie is fluent in German.†

TYLER, Robert L(awrence) 1922-

PERSONAL: Born February 11, 1922, in Virginia, Minn.; son of Leon Meredith and Bessie (Carver) Tyler; married Molly Erlich, February 22, 1947 (divorced, 1971); married Gerry Sack Tyler (an assistant dean, University of Rhode Island); children: (first marriage) Deborah, Daniel. Education: University of Minnesota, B.A., 1948, M.A., 1949; University of Oregon, Ph.D., 1953. Office: Department of History, Southern Connecticut State College, New Haven, Conn. 06515.

CAREER: Taught at University of Oregon and at Oregon State University, 1950-54; University of North Dakota, Grand Forks, instructor in history, 1954-55; University of Colorado, Boulder, instructor in history, 1955-56; Ball State University, Muncie, Ind., assistant professor, 1961, associate professor, 1961-66; University of Guyana, Georgetown, Fulbright professor, 1966-67; Wagner College, Staten Island, N.Y., member of faculty, 1967-70; Southern Connecticut State College, New Haven, professor of history, 1970—. Military service: U.S. Army, medical department, 1942-46. Member: American Historical Association, Organization of American Historians, American Association of University Professors, American Civil Liberties Union, Mensa, Indiana Academy of the Social Sciences.

WRITINGS: Deposition of Don Quixote, and Other Poems, Golden Quill Press, 1964; Rebels of the Woods: The I.W.W. in the Pacific Northwest, University of Oregon Press, 1968; Walter Reuther, Eerdmans, 1972. Editor, Proceedings of the Indiana Academy of the Social Sciences. Contributor to Nation, Prairie Schooner, Antioch Review, Approach, and to historical journals. Contributing editor, Humanist.

SIDELIGHTS: Tyler writes: "I am interested in the culture of dissent, from the I.W.W., let's say, to SNCC, and in particular the literature it generates. In general, I am interested in history as a humanity rather [than as] a behavioral or social science."

*   *   *

TYNAN, Kenneth 1927-

PERSONAL: Born April 2, 1927, in Birmingham, England; son of Sir Peter Peacock and Letitia Rose Tynan; married Elaine Bundy (an American writer), January 25, 1951 (divorced, 1964); married Kathleen Halton (a writer), 1967; children: (first marriage) Tracy; (second marriage) Roxanna Nell, and a son. Education: Magdalen College, Oxford, B.A., 1948. Politics: Socialist. Religion: None. Home: 20 Thurloe Sq., London S.W.7, England. Agent: Curtis Brown Ltd., 60 East 56th St., New York, N.Y. 10022. Office: National Theatre, Aquinas St., London S.E.1, England.

CAREER: Director of weekly repertory company, Lichfield, Staffordshire, six months in 1949; directed "Man of the World," Lyric Theatre, 1950, and "Othello," for Arts Council Tour, 1950; drama critic, Spectator, 1950-51, Evening Standard, 1952-53, Daily Sketch, 1953-54, Observer, 1954-63 (all London), and New Yorker, 1958-60; film critic, Observer, 1964-66; head of script department, Ealing Films, 1954-56; television producer, 1961-62; literary manager, British National Theatre, 1963-69, literary consultant, 1969-73. Appeared in "Hamlet," at New Theatre, London, 1951; co-produced "Soldiers," New Theatre, 1968. Member of drama panel, British Council. Member: Royal Society of Literature (fellow).

WRITINGS: He That Plays the King, Longmans, Green, 1950; Persona Grata, (photographs by Cecil Beaton), Wingate, 1953, Putnam, 1954; Alec Guinness, Rockliff, 1953, Macmillan, 1955, 3rd edition, Macmillan, 1961; Bull Fever, Harper, 1955, enlarged edition, Atheneum, 1966; (contributor) Tom Maschler, editor, Declaration, MacGibbon & Kee, 1959; (with Harold Lang) The Quest for Corbett, Gabberbocchus, 1960; Curtains, Atheneum, 1961; Tynan on Theatre, Penguin, 1964; (editor) William Shakespeare, Othello (National Theatre production), Hart-Davis, 1966, Stein & Day, 1967; (author of introduction) Lenny Bruce, How to Talk Dirty and Influence People, P. Owen, 1966; (editor) George Farquhar, The Recruiting Officer, (National Theatre production), Hart-Davis, 1965; Tynan Right and Left, Atheneum, 1967; (deviser and contributor) Oh! Calcutta! An Entertainment with Music (first produced Off-Broadway at Eden Theatre, June 17, 1969; produced in London at The Roundhouse, July 27, 1970), Grove, 1969; (contributor) Douglas A. Hughes, editor, Perspectives on Pornography, St. Martin's, 1970.

Co-author of radio feature, "The Quest for Corbett," 1956; author of script for television documentary, "The Actors," broadcast in England by ITV, 1968; author of screenplay adaptation with Roman Polanski, Shakespeare's "Macbeth," 1972. Contributor to periodicals in England and United States.

SIDELIGHTS: "What makes Tynan that rare phenomenon, a genuine theatre critic," writes Harold Clurman, "is that he is disposed toward the theatre in the sense that we speak of certain people being naturally musical.... Tynan experiences the theatre with his nerves, body, mind, and spirit. He possesses in regard to the theatre something like absolute pitch."

Tynan, influenced by Brecht, feels that drama should be involved with society. Although he was at first attracted to the theatre of fantasy and shock, he came to believe "that art, ethics, politics, and economics were inseparable," and "that no theatre could sanely flourish until there was an umbilical connection between what was happening on the stage and what was happening in the world." He believes that the drama of protest will most likely come from the Left. "The trouble with most Socialist drama," he wrote in Declaration, "is its joylessness.... Socialism ought to mean more than progress for its own sake: it ought to mean progress towards pleasure."

"I'm not interested in the metaphysical, the abstract. I'm interested in the here and now." He wants to see plays "that are Brechtian in their internationalism, their loathing of hero-worship, their mordant rejection of verbal frills (leave them to bourgeois-decadent critics like myself, don't festoon human lips with their foolery), and their conviction that 'to talk of trees is almost a crime, since it implies silence about so many enormities.' I want plays that affirm candour, valour, grace and sensuality; and plays that recoil from determinism, because determinism denies free choice, and without free choice there can be no drama.... I don't mean, of course, that style is unimportant; nor that I could admire a shoddily-written play merely because I agreed with its content.... On the other hand, I could never cheer a play, no matter how well-written, the content of which I found wholly offensive...."

The New York Times reports that "Tynan's function as a critic has been to shock, to outrage, to stimulate." He can be "brutal to mediocrity." He reportedly left New York because of his weariness with the "light comedies and heavy musicals" offered regularly on Broadway. More recently he made news when he used the four-letter Anglo-Saxon word for sexual intercourse in a discussion of censorship on B.B.C. television, leading certain Conservative members of Parliament to ask for legal action as well as for his dismissal from the National Theatre. Most of his mail, however, supported him. Again, in the spring of 1966, he caused a stir when he reviewed Truman Capote's *In Cold Blood* for *The Observer*, condemning Capote for his failure to be more than an observer of the Clutter murder case. "For the first time," Tynan wrote, "an influential writer of the front rank has been placed in a position of privileged intimacy with criminals about to die, and—in my view—done less than he might have to save them." Capote, enraged by Tynan's quotations from an anonymous lawyer and psychiatrist, called his critic a bully and a coward. The following week Tynan revealed the sources of his quotations.

While at Oxford he produced plays and also acted. Among his teachers was C. S. Lewis, whom he admired, though he believes that the man who had the greatest influence on him was Orson Welles. One of Tynan's ambitions is to write about jazz. "I bought a trumpet once because I'd always wanted to play one. I went for lessons to a wonderful teacher but I found my face was the wrong shape."

AVOCATIONAL INTERESTS: Contriving and playing word or guessing games; good food; German white wine; bullfights.

BIOGRAPHICAL/CRITICAL SOURCES: Tom Maschler, editor, *Declaration*, MacGibbon & Kee, 1959; *New York Times Book Review*, March 19, 1961, *Spectator*, October 6, 1961; *Christian Century*, November 29, 1961; *New York Times*, November 16, 1965; *New Statesman*, letter, December 24, 1965; *New York Times Magazine*, January 9, 1966.†

* * *

UCHIDA, Yoshiko 1921-

PERSONAL: Surname is pronounced Oo-*chee*-dah; born November 24, 1921, in Alameda, Calif.; daughter of Dwight Takashi (a businessman) and Iku (Umegaki) Uchida. *Education:* University of California, Berkeley, A.B. (cum laude), 1942; Smith College, M.Ed., 1944. *Politics:* Democrat. *Religion:* Protestant. *Home:* 645 63rd St., Oakland, Calif. 94609.

CAREER: Grew up in Berkeley, Calif., but was evacuated with others of Japanese descent in 1942 to Utah, where she taught second grade at the relocation center; after receiving master's degree from Smith College (on a fellowship), taught at Frankford Friends' School, Philadelphia, Pa., 1944-45; moved to New York City and began writing Japanese folk tales, working meanwhile as membership secretary for Institute of Pacific Relations, 1946-47, and secretary of United Student Christian Council, 1947-52; went to Japan on a Ford Foundation research fellowship, 1952, and remained for two years collecting material; worked as a secretary at University of California, Berkeley, 1957-62, but has been a full-time writer except for that period, 1952—. *Awards, honors:* New York Herald Tribune Children's Spring Book Festival honor award, 1955, for *The Magic Listening Cap*; *Journey to Topaz* was named American Library Association Notable Book, 1972; Commonwealth Club of California Medal for Best Juvenile Book by a California Author, 1972, for *Samurai of Gold Hill*; Award of Merit, California Association of Teachers of English, 1973.

WRITINGS: *The Dancing Kettle and Other Japanese Folk Tales*, Harcourt, 1949; *New Friends for Susan*, Scribner, 1951; (self-illustrated) *The Magic Listening Cap—More Folk Tales From Japan*, Harcourt, 1955; (self-illustrated) *The Full Circle* (junior high school study book), Friendship, 1957; *Takao and Grandfather's Sword*, Harcourt, 1958; *The Promised Year*, Harcourt, 1959.

Mik and the Prowler, Harcourt, 1960; (translator of English portions) *Shoji Hamada*, edited by Soetsu Yanagi, Asahi Shimbun Publishing, 1961; *Rokubei and the Thousand Rice Bowls*, Scribner, 1962; *The Forever Christmas Tree*, Scribner, 1963; *Sumi's Prize*, Scribner, 1964; *The Sea of Gold, and Other Tales From Japan*, Scribner, 1965; *Sumi's Special Happening*, Scribner, 1966; *In-Between Miya*, Scribner, 1967; *Hisako's Mysteries*, Scribner, 1969; *Sumi and the Goat and the Tokyo Express*, Scribner, 1969.

Makoto the Smallest Boy, Crowell, 1970; *Journey to Topaz*, Scribner, 1971; *Samurai of Gold Hill*, Scribner, 1972; *The Birthday Visitor*, Scribner, 1975.

Writer of adult stories and articles for Woman's Day, Gourmet, Far East, and for newspapers. Regular columnist, "Letter from San Francisco," in Craft Horizons, 1958-61.

WORK IN PROGRESS: Two books, *The Rooster Who Understood Japanese* and *Desert Exile*.

SIDELIGHTS: Yoshiko Uchida's books have been translated into German and Dutch. She speaks Japanese and French, and has a special interest in fine arts and folk crafts.

* * *

ULAM, Adam Bruno 1922-

PERSONAL: Born April 8, 1922, in Lwow, Poland; son of Jozef and Anna (Auerbach) Ulam; married Mary Hamilton Burgwin, 1963; children: Alexander Stanislaw, Joseph Howard. *Education:* Brown University, A.B., 1943; Harvard University, Ph.D., 1947. *Politics:* Democrat. *Home:* 17 Lowell St., Cambridge 38, Mass. *Office:* Littaner Center, Harvard University, Cambridge, Mass.

CAREER: Harvard University, Cambridge, Mass., began as teaching fellow, 1947, professor of government, 1959—, Russian Research Center, research associate, 1948, director, 1973-74; Center for International Studies, Massachusetts Institute of Technology, research associate, 1953-55. *Member:* Signet Club (Cambridge), Boston Badminton and Tennis Club. *Awards, honors:* Guggenheim Fellow, 1956; Rockefeller Fellow, 1957,1960.

WRITINGS: *Philosophical Foundations of English Socialism*, Harvard University Press, 1951; *Titoism and the Cominform*, Harvard University Press, 1952; *The Unfinished Revolution*, Random House, 1960; (editor with Samuel Hutchinson Beer) *Patterns of Government*, 2nd edition, revised, Random House, 1962; *The New Face House of Soviet Totalitarianism*, Harvard University Press, 1963; *The Bolsheviks*, Macmillan, 1965; *Expansion and Coexistence: The History of Soviet Foreign Policy, 1917-1967*, Praeger, 1968; *The Rivals: American and Russia Since World War II*, Viking, 1971; *The Fall of the American University*, Library Press, 1972; *Stalin: The Man and His Era*, Viking, 1973; *Russian Political System*, Random House, 1974. Contributor to professional journals.

* * *

ULLAH, Najib 1914-

PERSONAL: Born February 14, 1914, Jalalabad, Afghanistan; son of Prince Mohammed Yunos Khan (a general in Afghan Army) and Princess Hajira; married Princess Sharifa, January 2, 1931; children: Wahid Najib and Yousof Najib (sons). *Education:* Isteqlal College, Kabul, Afghanistan, Bachelier es lettres, 1933; Institute of Political Science, Kabul, graduate study, 1935; Sorbonne, University of Paris, equivalent of Licencie es lettres, 1946; University of Lyon, Docteur es lettres, 1949. *Religion:* Islam. *Home:* 175 West 72nd St., New York, N.Y. *Office:* Fairleigh Dickinson University, Teaneck, N.J.

CAREER: Government of Afghanistan, Kabul, secretary and interpreter in Foreign Office, 1934-35, head of League of Nations Department of Foreign Office, 1935-37, general director of political affairs in Foreign Office, 1937-46, Minister of Education, 1946-49, ambassador to India, 1949-54, ambassador to England, 1954-57, ambassador to United States, 1957-58, resigned, 1958; Council on Islamic Affairs, Inc., New York, N.Y., research associate, 1958-60; Princeton University, Princeton, N.J., senior visiting lecturer and research associate, 1960-61; Fairleigh Dickinson University, Teaneck, N.J., adjunct professor, 1958, professor of history, 1961—. Head of Afghan delegation at UNESCO General Assembly, Beirut, Lebanon, 1948, and at United Nations General Assembly, 1957; Afghan representative at Asian Conference for Indonesia, New Delhi, India, 1949, and at Bandung Conference, 1955; member of other missions to Soviet Russia, 1937, Persia, 1938, India, 1938-39. *Member:* Afghan Academy, Royal Asiatic Society (London; fellow). *Awards, honors:* Commander, Legion of Honor (France); Commander, Order of Danenbrog (Denmark).

WRITINGS: Political History of Afghanistan, two volumes, [Kabul, Afghanistan], 1942-44; *Strabo and Aryana*, [Kabul], 1945; *Negotiations With Pakistan*, [Kabul], 1948; *Islamic Literature*, Washington Square, 1963. Also author of *A Short History of Afghanistan* and several booklets on political and literary subjects, published in England and India, 1949-55.

SIDELIGHTS: Ullah speaks Persian, Pushtu, French, Arabic, English; reads and understands Hindustani and Turkish.†

*   *   *

ULLAH, Salamat   1913-
(Salamatullah)

PERSONAL: Born August 4, 1913, in Sahayal, Etawah, Uttar Pradesh, India; son of Ibadullah (a tradesman) and Ruqayya (Begam) Salamatullah; married second wife Syeda, October 12, 1956; children: (first marriage) Saida (Mrs. Maqsood), Kamal, Najma; (second marriage) Zulfia, Asad, Salman, Zeba. *Education:* Aligarh Muslim University (India), B.Sc., 1936, M.Sc., 1938, B.T., 1939; Columbia University, Ed.D., 1948. *Religion:* Islam. *Office:* Teachers' College, Jamia Millia Islamia, New Delhi 25, India.

CAREER: Teachers' College, Jamia Millia Islamia, New Delhi, India, lecturer, 1939-57, director of Institute of Educational Research, 1953-63, principal, 1957—, dean of Faculty of Education, 1963—. Delhi University, member of Faculty of Education, 1960—; Muslim University, member of Faculty of Arts, 1964—. Chairman of Educational panel of Taraqqui Urud Board, 1974—. *Member:* All-India Association of Training Colleges (member of executive committee, 1963—), National Council of Educational Research and Training (member of advisory committee), Indian Psycho-

metric and Educational Research Association (member of governing council, 1973—), National Council of Teacher Education.

WRITINGS: Examinations in India, Orient Longmans, 1951; *Basic Way to Arithmetic*, Orient Longmans, 1955; (editor) *Handbook for Teachers of Basic Schools*, Government of India, 1956; *Can Education Do It?*, Punjabi Publishers, 1958; *Evaluation in Basic Education*, Government of India, 1961; *Thoughts on Basic Education*, Asia Publishing House, 1963; (contributor) S.D. Mukerji, editor, *Education of Teachers in India: Volume I*, S. Chand & Co., 1968; (editor) *The School and Community*, Ministry of Education, Government of India, 1970. Contributor to *Indian Yearbook of Education: Second Yearbook 1964*. Editor, *Nai Taleem*, ("New Education"), Urdu edition, 1941-43; editor and subject coordinator, Urdu Encyclopedia, 1973; member of editorial board: *Studies in Education*, 1973—.

WORK IN PROGRESS: Directing research groups on construction of curriculum for basic schools and development of teacher education programs for elementary schools.

*   *   *

ULRICH, Louis E., Jr.   1918-

PERSONAL: Born April 3, 1918, in Milwaukee, Wis.; son of Louis Emil (a school principal) and Annabel (Brandt) Ulrich; married Betty J. Garton, January 5, 1946; children: Barbara, James, Ruth, John, David. *Education:* University of Wisconsin, Milwaukee, B.S., 1941; Northwestern Lutheran Theological Seminary, B.D., 1948; University of Minnesota, M.A., 1949. *Home:* 2746 Vincent Ave. N., Minneapolis, Minn. *Office:* 1813 University Ave., S.E., Minneapolis, Minn.

CAREER: Lutheran minister. Senior pastor in Minneapolis, Minn., 1950-55; University of North Dakota, Grand Fords, faculty member and pastor to Lutheran students, 1955-58; senior pastor in Kenosha, Wis., 1958-64; University of Minnesota, Minneapolis, pastor to Lutheran students, 1964—. Chairman, Synodical Committee on Church Vocations; president, Kenosha Ministerium. *Military service:* U.S. Army, Corps of Engineers, 1941-45; became captain; received Bronze Star. *Member:* National Lutheran Council, Kappa Delta Pi.

WRITINGS: That I May Live in His Kingdom, Augsburg, 1963.

WORK IN PROGRESS: What About Heaven, What About Prayer, and other short books for laymen.

AVOCATIONAL INTERESTS: Art, hunting, fishing, photography.†

*   *   *

UNETT, John
(James Preston)

PERSONAL: Surname is pronounced Younet. *Education:* Attended school in Haileybury, England, and in France. *Residence:* Colwall, England.

CAREER: Chartered accountant, 1930—, never in practice. *Military service:* Royal Air Force, commissioned officer, 1940-46. *Member:* Institute of Chartered Accountants, Society of Authors, Society of Genealogists.

WRITINGS: Book-keeping for Small Traders, Iliffe, 1955; *Management for Small Traders*, Iliffe, 1955; *Fishing Days*,

Cassell, 1957; *Making a Pedigree*, Allen & Unwin, 1961, 2nd edition, Genealogical Publishing Co., 1971; (under pseudonym James Preston) *The Empty Years*, Cresset, 1962; *Garage Accounting and Administration*, Iliffe, 1964.†

* * *

UNGER, Henry F. 1912-

PERSONAL: Born December 22, 1912, in Cleveland, Ohio; son of Frank and Josephine (Mastny) Unger. *Education:* Attended John Carroll University, two years; University of Western Ontario, B.A. *Religion:* Roman Catholic. *Address:* P.O. Box 13366, Phoenix, Ariz. 85002.

CAREER: Social Reign Magazine, Washington, D.C., editor, 1947-52; publicity-advertising supervisor for Salt River Project, 1952-57; part-time writer and photographer, 1937-57, full-time, 1957—. Phoenix correspondent for Religious News Service, and for *Air Conditioning, Heating and Refrigeration NEWS*. Part-time public relations director for St. Vincent de Paul Society of Maricopa County, Ariz. *Military service:* U.S. Army, 1941; U.S. Navy, 1942-45. *Member:* Third Order of St. Francis, Friends of St. John's, St. Vincent de Paul Society, Phoenix Serra Club.

WRITINGS: Writing for the Catholic Market, Academy Guild Press, 1959; (contributor) *Skills for School Reading*, revised edition, Harcourt, 1974. Contributor to trade journals and popular magazines, including *Seventeen, Ford Times, Steelways, Popular Mechanics*.

WORK IN PROGRESS: Magazine articles, picture-stories.

SIDELIGHTS: Henry Unger understands and speaks "fairly well" Czech and Latin. *Avocational interests:* Playing piano.

* * *

URQUHART, Alvin W. 1931-

PERSONAL: Born June 8, 1931, in Portland, Ore.; son of Orin and Miriam (Cox) Urquhart; married Elizabeth Rodman, June 5, 1958; children: Sarah Elizabeth. *Education:* Oregon State College (now University), student, 1949-51; University of California, Berkeley, B.A., 1953, M.A., 1958, Ph.D., 1962. *Home:* 1960 Agate, Eugene, Ore. *Office:* Department of Geography, University of Oregon, Eugene, Ore.

CAREER: University of Oregon, Eugene, instructor in geography, 1960-61; Dartmouth College, Hanover, N.H., instructor in geography, 1961-63; University of Oregon, assistant professor of geography, 1963—. Taught at Ahmadu Bello University, Zaria, Nigeria, 1967-69. *Military service:* U.S. Army, 1953-55; became lieutenant. *Member:* Association of American Geographers, Phi Beta Kappa.

WRITINGS: Patterns of Settlement and Subsistence in Southwestern Angola, National Academy of Sciences, National Research Council, 1963.

WORK IN PROGRESS: Two books, *Settlement Patterns in Africa* and *Urban Planning in Nigeria*.

SIDELIGHTS: Alvin Urquhart did field research in geography in Jamaica, Nigeria, and Angola.

* * *

USTINOV, Peter (Alexander) 1921-

PERSONAL: Born April 16, 1921, in London, England; son of Iona (a journalist, professional name "Klop") and Nadia (a painter and scenic designer; maiden name Benios) Ustinov; married Isolde Delham, 1940 (divorced, 1950); married Suzanne Cloutier (an actress), 1953 (marriage ended, 1971); married Helen du Lau d'Allemans, June 17, 1972; children: (first marriage) Tamara, (second marriage) Pavla, Igor, Andrea. *Education:* Attended Westminster School, London, England, 1934-37, and London Theatre Studio, 1937-39. *Agent:* Christopher Mann Ltd., 140 Park Lane, London W.1, England.

CAREER: Actor and director in the the theatre, films, and television; playwright, filmscript writer, and author. Joint Director, Nottingham Playhouse, 1963—. First rector, University of Dundee, 1968—. Goodwill ambassador for UNICEF, 1969—. Has directed on the stage "The Man in the Raincoat," "No Sign of the Dove," "Photo Finish" (in Paris); directed the films "The Spies," "An Angel Flew Over Brooklyn," "Schools for Secrets," "Vice Versa," "Private Angelo," "Billy Budd," and "Lady L." Has played on the stage in "The Wood Demon," "The Bishop of Limpopoland," "White Cargo," "Rookery Nook," "Laburnam Grove," "First Night," "Swinging the Gate," "Threshold," "Hermione Gingold Revue," "Diversion 1," "Diversion 2," "Squaring the Circle," "Crime and Punishment," "Frenzy," "Love in Albania," "The Love of Four Colonels," "Romanoff and Juliet," "Photo Finish," and "The Unknown Soldier and His Wife." Played in films "Mein Kampf, My Crimes," "Let the wpeople Sing," "One of Our Aircraft is Missing," "The Way Ahead," "Private Angelo," "Odette," "The Goose Steps Out," "The True Glory," "School for Secrets," "Vice Versa," "Quo Vadis," Beau Brummel," "The Egyptian," "Hotel Sahara," "We're No Angels," "Lola Montez," "The Sundowners," "Spartacus," "Billy Budd," "Topkapi," "John Goldfarb," "Lady L," "The Comedians," "Blackbeard's Ghost," "Hot Millions," "Viva Max," and "Hammersmith Is Out." Participated in radio series "In All Directions" with Peter Jones; has also written for, and appeared in television productions, including "The Life of Samuel Johnson," 1957, and "Conversation with Lord North," 1971. Has directed productions of the Royal Opera at Covent Garden, 1962, and the Hamburg Opera, 1968. *Military service:* British Army, Royal Sussex Regiment, 1942-46; also served with Royal Army Ordnance Corps and Kinematograph Service.

MEMBER: Royal Society of Arts (fellow), British Actors' Equity, New York Dramatists Guild, London Society of Authors, British League of Dramatists, Societe des Auteurs (France), British Film Academy, British Screen Writers' Society, Hollywood Screen Actors' Guild, Garrick Club, Savage Club, Royal Automobile Club, Queen's Club.

AWARDS, HONORS: Golden Globe Award, 1952; New York Drama Critics Circle Award, 1953, for "The Love of Four Colonels"; *Evening Standard* Drama Award for best new play, 1956, for "Romanoff and Juliet"; Benjamin Franklin Medal, Royal Society of Arts, 1957; Academy Awards for acting, 1960, for "Spartacus," and 1965, for "Topkapi"; Emmy Awards for acting, three times, including 1958, for "The Life of Samuel Johnson"; Grammy Award for his recording of "Peter and the Wolf"; First prize of Syndicat des journalistes et ecrivains (France), 1964, for "Photo Finish"; Academy Award nomination for best story and screenplay, and British comedy screenplay award from Writers Guild, both 1969, for "Hot Millions"; Doctor of Law, University of Dundee, 1969; Mus.D., Cleveland Conservatory of Music, 1970; D.F.A., La Salle College, 1971; D.Litt., University of Lancaster, 1972.

WRITINGS: Add a Dash of Pity (short stories), Little, Brown, 1959; *Ustinov's Diplomats* (photographs and commentary), Bernard Geis Associates, 1960; *The Loser* (novel), Little, Brown, 1960; *We Were Only Human* (caricatures), Little, Brown, 1961; (illustrator) Paul Marc Henry, *Poodlestan: A Poodle's Eye View of History*, Reynal, 1965; *The Frontiers of the Sea* (short stories), Little, Brown, 1966; *The Wit of Peter Ustinov*, compiled by Dick Richards, Frewin, 1969; *Krumnagel* (novel), Little, Brown, 1971.

Plays: *House of Regrets* (three-act tragi-comedy; first produced in London at Arts Theatre, 1942), J. Cape, 1943; *Beyond* (one-act; first produced at Arts Theatre, 1943), English Theatre Guild, 1944; *The Banbury Nose* (four-act; first produced in London at Wyndham's Theatre, 1944), J. Cape, 1945.

Plays about People (includes: "Blow Your Own Trumpet," first produced in London at Old Vic Theatre, 1943; "The Tragedy of Good Intentions," first produced in Liverpool at Old Vic Theatre, 1945; "The Indifferent Shepherd," first produced in London at Criterion Theatre, 1948), J. Cape, 1950; *The Love of Four Colonels* (three-act; first produced at Wyndham's Theatre, 1951), English Theatre Guild, 1951, Dramatists Play Service, 1953; *The Moment of Truth* (four-act; first produced in London at Adelphi Theatre, 1951), English Theatre Guild, 1953; *Romanoff and Juliet* (three-act comedy; first produced in London at Piccadilly Theatre, 1956; produced in New York at Plymouth Theatre, 1957), English Theatre Guild, 1957, Random House, 1958, musical version, with libretto by Ustinov, produced as "R Loves J," at Chichester Festival Theatre, 1973.

Photo Finish: An Adventure in Biography in Three Acts (first produced in London at Saville Theatre, 1962), Heinemann, 1962, Little, Brown, 1963, revised acting edition, Dramatists Play Service, 1964; *Five Plays* (includes "Romanoff and Juliet," "The Moment of Truth," "Beyond," "The Love of Four Colonels," and "No Sign of the Dove"), Little, Brown, 1965; *The Unknown Soldier and His Wife* (two-act; first produced in New York at Vivian Beaumont Theatre, July 6, 1967), Random House, 1967 (published in England as *The Unknown Soldier and His Wife: Two Acts of War Separated by a Truce*, Heinemann, 1968); *Halfway Up the Tree* (three-act comedy; first produced in New York at Brooks Atkinson Theatre, November 7, 1967), Random House, 1968.

Other plays: "The Bishop of Limpopoland" (sketch), produced in London, 1939; (translator and adapter from the French) Jean Sarment, "Fishing for Shadows," produced in London, 1940; "Frenzy" (adapted from the Swedish of Ingmar Bergman), produced in London at St. Martin's Theatre, 1948; "The Man in the Raincoat," produced at Edinburgh Festival, 1949; "High Balcony," produced in 1952; "No Sign of the Dove," produced in London at Savoy Theatre, 1953; "The Empty Chair," produced in Bristol at Old Vic Theatre, 1956; "Paris Not So Gay," produced in Oxford, England, 1958; "The Life in My Hands," produced at Nottingham Playhouse, 1963.

Motion picture scripts: (With Eric Ambler) "The Way Ahead," 1943-44 (later released as "Immortal Battalion"); "School for Secrets," 1946; "Vice Versa," 1947; "Private Angelo," 1949; "Secret Flight," 1951; "School for Scoundrels," 1960; "Romanoff and Juliet," 1961; "Lady L," 1965; (with Robert Rossen) "Billy Bud," 1962; (with Ira Wallach) "Hot Millions," 1968; "Hammersmith Is Out," 1972.

Author of material for revues produced in London, "Diversion," 1940, and "Diversion 2," 1941. Author of material for BBC radio program, "In All Directions." Author of two unfinished novels, "The Secret Sky" and "Flight into Fiction." Contributor to *Atlantic*, *Listener*, and other publications.

WORK IN PROGRESS: A play, "Who's Who in Hell."

SIDELIGHTS: The *New Statesman* once wrote that Ustinov's greatest function is that of "unpaid, unlicensed court jester. The public will never see the cream of his great gifts of mimicry, which need the context of the small dinner-party or the saloon bar.... he will occupy a long car journey by an uncannily accurate pastiche of opera or folk-song from any language, any country, in nonsense-words so near to their original as to sound wholly convincing, sung in voice that accommodatingly reproduces soprano, alto, baritone, bass, 'cello, oboe, harp, tongs, bones and applause, separately or all at once." He has made a recording, "Mock Mozart," in which he imitates a full orchestra and a male quartet. He has also recorded "Peter and the Wolf," and "Baron Munchausen: Eighteen Truly Tall Tales," Caedmon, 1972.

Ustinov is competent in at least eight languages.

AVOCATIONAL INTERESTS: Reading voluminously, cars, music, collecting old masters' drawings, lawn tennis, and squash.

BIOGRAPHICAL/CRITICAL SOURCES: New Statesman and Nation, March 27, 1954; *Vogue*, October 1, 1957; Geoffrey Willans, *Peter Ustinov*, Copp, 1957, Transatlantic, 1958; *Time*, March 10, 1958; *Newsweek*, March 10, 1958; *Life*, April 14, 1958, April 19, 1963; *Look*, April 29, 1958; *Holiday*, July, 1958; *McCall's*, November, 1958; *New York Times Magazine*, January 29, 1961; *Atlantic*, July, 1964; *New York Times*, January 24, 1965; *Listener*, February 17, 1966, February 24, 1966; *New Yorker*, July 15, 1967; Tony Thomas, *Ustinov in Focus*, A. S. Barnes, 1971; Carolyn Riley, editor, *Contemporary Literary Criticism*, Volume I, Gale, 1973.

* * *

VALDES, Mario J. 1934-

PERSONAL: Born January 28, 1934, in Chicago, Ill.; son of Mario (a businessman) and Juanita (San Martin) Valdes; married Maria Elena Diaz Barriga, August 13, 1955; children: Mario Teotimo, Michael Jordi. *Education:* University of Illinois, B.A., 1957, M.A., 1959; Ph.D., 1962. *Home:* 80 Dale Ave., Toronto, Ontario, Canada. *Office:* Department of Hispanic Studies, University of Toronto, Toronto, Ontario, Canada.

CAREER: University of Michigan, Ann Arbor, instructor in Spanish, 1962-63; University of Toronto, Toronto, Ontario, assistant professor, 1963-66, associate professor, 1966-70, professor of Spanish literature, 1970—. Visiting professor, Columbia University, 1967, Transylvania College (now University), 1968, Odense University, Denmark, 1972. *Member:* Modern Language Association of America, Canadian Comparative Literature Association, Canadian Association of Hispanists.

WRITINGS: Death in the Literature of Unamuno, University of Illinois Press, 1964, 2nd edition, 1966; (editor and author of introduction) Miguel de Unamuno y Jugo, *Niebla*, Prentice-Hall, 1969; *An Unamuno Source Book*, University of Toronto Press, 1973; (editor) *San Manuel Bueno Martin*, Estudios de Hispanofila (Valencia), 1974. Contributor to *Hispanofila, New Literary History*, and *University of Toronto Quarterly*. Member of editorial boards, *Canadian Revue of Comparative Literature*, *Reflexion* (Canadian journal of Spanish culture), and *Twentieth-Century Journal of Spanish Studies*.

WORK IN PROGRESS: Disclosure of the Novel: An Inquiry into the Novelistic Reading Experience, A Concordance to the Philosophical and Ideological Concepts of Unamuno, and *Myth in Contemporary Mexican Literature*.

SIDELIGHTS: Valdes is bilingual in Spanish and English, with reading knowledge of French. He visits Spain and Mexico in alternate years.

* * *

VALTZ, Robert C. K.   1936-

PERSONAL: Born February 21, 1936, in Boston, Mass.; son of James John and Margaret (Curtin) Valtz; married Clare L. Casparis, June 8, 1961; children: James John II. *Education:* Harvard University, A.B., 1958, M.B.A., 1961. *Home:* 31 Linnaean St., Cambridge, Mass. 02138. *Office:* Arthur D. Little, Inc., Acorn Park, Cambridge, Mass. 02140.

CAREER: With Arthur D. Little, Inc. (management consultants), Cambridge, Mass.

WRITINGS: (With Edmund P. Learned and Francis J. Aguilar) *European Problems in General Management*, Irwin, 1963. Contributor to *Harvard Business Review* and *Metalworking*.

WORK IN PROGRESS: Study of corporate long-range planning.†

* * *

van den HEUVEL, Cornelisz A.   1931-
(corneliszavandenheuvel)

PERSONAL: Born March 6, 1931, in Biddeford, Me.; son of Dirk Jan (an electrician) and Lily (Yuill) van den Heuvel; married Kevin E. Mathias, September 4, 1962. *Education:* University of New Hampshire, B.A., 1957. *Residence:* New York, N.Y.

CAREER: Has worked as newspaperman, salesman, dishwasher, gardener, commercial fisherman, coffee house poet, editor, and magazine make-up man. *Military service:* U.S. Air Force, 1950-53; served as photographer.

WRITINGS—All poetry, published under name corneliszavandenheuvel; all published by Chant Press: *sun and skull*, 1961; *a bag of marbles*, 1962; *3 jazz chants*, 1962; *the window-washer's pail*, 1963; *EO7 (or christ should have carried a pearl-handled revolver)*, 1964; *Bang! you're dead*, 1966; *Water in a stone depression*, 1969; (editor) *The Haiku Anthology: English Language Haiku by American and Canadian Poets*, Doubleday, 1974.†

* * *

VANDER ZANDEN, James Wilfrid   1930-

PERSONAL: Born November 28, 1930, in Green Bay, Wis.; son of Wilfrid B. (a jeweler) and Martha (Van Susteren) Vander Zanden; married Marion J. Vangeli, August 23, 1960 (deceased); children: Bradley Tanner, Nels Blake. *Education:* University of Wisconsin, B.S., 1952, M.S., 1954; University of North Carolina, Ph.D., 1958; Univer-

sity of Michigan, postdoctural study, 1958. *Home:* 1678 Cardiff Rd., Columbus, Ohio 43221. *Office:* Ohio State University, 1775 South College Rd., Columbus, Ohio 43221.

CAREER: Paine College, Augusta, Ga., instructor in sociology, 1954-56; Duke University, Durham, N.C., instructor in sociology, 1958-60; Ohio State University, Columbus, assistant professor, 1960-65, associate professor, 1965-72, professor of sociology, 1972—. Consultant to American Sociological Association on sociological resources for secondary schools. *Member:* American Sociological Association, American Anthropological Association, Ohio Valley Sociological Association.

WRITINGS: American Minority Relations, Ronald, 1963, 3rd edition, 1972; *Race Relations in Transition*, Random House, 1965, 2nd edition, 1975; *Sociology: A Systematic Approach*, Ronald, 1965.

* * *

VANGER, Milton Isadore   1925-

PERSONAL: Born April 11, 1925, in New York, N.Y.; son of Max Manuel and Rose (Rothstein) Vanger; married Elsa Maria Oribe, September 10, 1956; children: John, Mark, Rachel. *Education:* Attended City College (now City College of the City University of New York), 1942-43; Princeton University, A.B., 1948; Harvard University, Ph.D., 1958. *Politics:* Democrat. *Religion:* Jewish. *Home:* 32 Gray St., Cambridge, Mass. 02138. *Office:* Brandeis University, Waltham, Mass.

CAREER: Oklahoma State University of Agriculture and Applied Science, Stillwater, instructor in history, 1956-58; Sacramento State College (now California State University, Sacramento), Sacramento, Calif., assistant professor of history, 1958-62; Brandeis University, Waltham, Mass., associate professor, 1962-74, professor of history, 1974—, chairman of Latin American Studies, 1971—. *Member:* American Historical Association Conference on Latin American History, New England Council of Later American Studies (secretary, treasurer), Phi Beta Kappa.

WRITINGS: Jose Batlle y Ordonez: The Creator of His Times, 1902-1907, Harvard University Press, 1963. Contributor to *Yale Review, American Political Science Review*, and *Encyclopaedia Britannica*.

WORK IN PROGRESS: Second volume on Jose Batlle y Ordonez and *Economic-Social History of Uruguay* for Oxford University Press.

* * *

VanSLYCK, Philip   1920-

PERSONAL: Born January 10, 1920, in New Orleans, La.; son of Philip Noyes (an accountant) and Edith G. (Conley) VanSlyck; divorced; children: Phyllis Elizabeth, Peter Wilson. *Education:* San Diego State College (now University), student, 1937-38; University of California, Berkeley, A.B. (honors), 1941. *Home:* 320 East 54th St., New York, N.Y. 10022.

CAREER: Philip VanSlyck & Associates (public relations and advertising), San Francisco, Calif., owner, 1948-53; Junior Chamber International, Miami Beach, Fla., secretary-general, 1953-55; Foreign Policy Association, Inc., New York, N.Y., editor of program materials, 1956-62; free-lance writer and editorial consultant, New York, N.Y., 1962—. Editorial consultant to Japanese government, Republic of Nigeria, Liberian government, and to private corporations, foundations, and associations. *Military service:* U.S. Army Air Corps, 1941-42. U.S. Army, Military Intelligence, 1942-46; became captain. *Member:* Asia Society (Philippines council).

WRITINGS: (With Warren Rovetch) *Land-Grant Resources in Latin America's Future*, [Washington], 1962; *Peace: The Control of National Power*, Beacon, 1963. Editor of Foreign Policy Association "Great Decisions" series, 1956-62, of "Headline" series, 1961-62.

WORK IN PROGRESS: A book on problems of stalemate and consensus in America politics, for Random House; a book on problems of constitutional structure in a stable or disarmed world.

SIDELIGHTS: VanSlyck speaks Spanish and French.†

*   *   *

VAN VLECK, Sarita 1933-

PERSONAL: Born January 13, 1933, in Montclair, N.J.; daughter of Joseph (an educator) and Mary (McLain) Van Vleck. *Education:* Vassar College, B.A., 1955. *Residence:* Montclair, N.J.

CAREER: American Museum of Natural History, New York, N.Y., researcher. Illustrator and author. Herpetologist and general assistant, Yale University expedition to Haiti, 1958.

WRITINGS: Growing Wings, Doubleday, 1963.

WORK IN PROGRESS: A book on a six-months camping trip through western United States and Canada, emphasizing man's relationship to his natural environment.†

*   *   *

VAN ZANTE, Helen Johnson 1906-

PERSONAL: Born June 29, 1906, in Denver, Colo.; daughter of H. and Clara (Johnson) Johnson; married Peter H. Van Zante (a physician; now deceased). *Education:* State College of Agriculture and Mechanic Arts (now South Dakota State University), B.S., 1928; Iowa State College of Agriculture and Mechanic Arts (now Iowa State University of Science and Technology), M.S., 1942, Ph.D., 1946. *Residence:* Pella, Iowa. *Office:* University of Wisconsin-Stout, Menomonie, Wis. 54751.

CAREER: Former teacher of science and mathematics in secondary schools; Iowa State University of Science and Technology, Ames, teacher, 1949-67; University of Wisconsin-Stout, Menomonie, professor of housing and equipment, 1967—. *Member:* American Home Economics Association, International Home Economics Association, Woman's Auxiliary to the American Medical Association, Des Moines Art Center, Sigma Xi, Phi Kappa Phi, Iota Sigma Pi. *Awards, honors:* Outstanding Educator of America, American Association of Housing Educators.

WRITINGS: Household Equipment Principles, Prentice-Hall, 1964; *The Microwave Oven*, Houghton, 1973. Also author of workbooks published by University of Wisconsin-Stout, *Consumer Economics*, and *Family History*. Contributor to home economics and farm journals.

AVOCATIONAL INTERESTS: Travel (studied housing and family life in Soviet Russia and other European countries, 1963), painting, growing flowers.

*   *   *

VARDYS, V(ytautas) Stanley 1924-

PERSONAL: Born September 2, 1924, in Berzoras, Lithu-ania; son of Stasys (a businessman) and Karolina (Budrys) Zvirzdys; married Nijole A. Rimkus, April 16, 1955; children: Ina M., Elizabeth R. *Education:* University of Tuebingen, student, 1945-49; Carroll College, Helena, Mont., B.A., 1951; University of Wisconsin, M.A., 1953, Ph.D., 1958. *Religion:* Roman Catholic. *Office:* Department of Political Science, University of Oklahoma, Munich Center, 455 West Lindsey, DHT 205, Norman, Okla. 73069.

CAREER: University of Wisconsin-Milwaukee, instructor 1955-58, assistant professor, 1958-1964, associate professor of political science, 1964-68; University of Oklahoma, Norman, professor of political science and director of Munich Center, 1968—. *Member:* American Political Science Association, American Association for the Advancement of Slavic Studies, American Association of University Professors, Association of Advanced Baltic Studies (president, 1970-71), Midwest Conference of Political Scientists, Baltic Research Institute (Bonn, Germany), World Affairs Council of Milwaukee.

WRITINGS: (Editor and contributor) *Lithuania Under the Soviets: Portrait of a Nation, 1940-1965*, Praeger, 1965; (editor and author of introduction) *Karl Marx: Scientist? Revolutionary? Humanist?*, Heath, 1971. Contributor to *Lithuanian Encyclopedia*; also contributor of articles to journals of political science and Slavic studies.

SIDELIGHTS: Vardys is competent in Lithuanian, German, Russian, and French.†

*   *   *

VATIKIOTIS, P(anayiotis) J(erasimos) 1928-

PERSONAL: Born February 5, 1928, in Jerusalem, Palestine; son of Jerassimos Y. (a civil servant) and Paraskevi (Meimarachi) Vatikiotis; married Patricia Mumford, March 22, 1956; children: Michael, Helen, Daphne. *Education:* The American University at Cairo, B.A., 1948; Louisiana State University, M.A., 1951; Johns Hopkins University, Ph.D., 1954. *Office:* Department of Economic and Political Studies, School of Oriental and African Studies, University of London, London WC1E 7HP, England.

CAREER: The American University at Cairo, Egypt, instructor in social sciences, 1948-49; Johns Hopkins University, School of Advanced International Studies, Washington, D.C., instructor in Arabic, 1952-53; Indiana University, Bloomington, 1953-65; started as instructor in government, now professor of government. University of London, School of Oriental and African Studies, lecturer in politics, 1964-65, professor of politics, 1965—. *Military service:* U.S. Army, 1954-56. *Member:* Reform Club (London). *Awards, honors:* Guggenheim Fellow, 1961-62.

WRITINGS: The Fatimid Theory of State, Orientalia Publications (Pakistan), 1957; (contributor) P. W. Thayer, editor, *Tensions in the Middle East*, Johns Hopkins Press, 1958.

The Egyptian Army in Politics, Indiana University Press, 1961; (contributor) Roy Macridis, editor, *Foreign Policy in World Politics*, 2nd revised edition, Prentice-Hall, 1962; (contributor) J. Proctor Harris, editor, *Islam and International Relations*, 1965; *Politics and the Military in Jordon: A Study of the Arab Legion, 1921-57*, Praeger, 1967; (contributor) Peter Holt, *Political and Social Change in Modern Egypt*, Oxford University Press, 1968; (editor) *Egypt Since the Revolution*, Praeger, 1968; *The Modern History of Egypt*, Praeger, 1969.

Conflict in the Middle East, Allen & Unwin, 1971; *Revolu-*

tion in the Middle East and Other Case Studies, Rowan & Littlefield, 1972; (contributor) Paul Hammond and Sidney Alexander, editors, *Political Dynamics in the Middle East*, Elsevier (Netherlands), 1972; (contributor) Alvin Cottrell & James Theberge, editors, *The Western Mediterranean: Its Political, Economic, and Strategic Importance*, Praeger, 1973; (contributor) Ivo Lederer and Wayne Vucinich, editors, *The Soviet Union and the Middle East: Post World War II Era*, Hoover Institution, 1974.

WORK IN PROGRESS: El Rayyes, a political portrait of Nasser of Egypt; and *The Political Experience of the Fertile Crescent, 1920-47.*

SIDELIGHTS: Vatikiotis told *CA*: "I prefer writing essays to books, partly because I am too skeptical to seek final solutions; another kind of writing I attempt in my spare time is short sketches on life amid Middle East foreign communities; these may be published someday under the title, *Mixed Upbringing.*" He speaks Greek, Arabic (three dialects fluently), French, some Italian.

*   *   *

VAUGHAN, Richard Patrick   1919-

PERSONAL: Born May 26, 1919, in Los Angeles, Calif.; son of Vincent B. and Elizabeth L. (Eichler) Vaughan. *Education:* St. Louis University, A.B., 1943, M.A., 1945; Alma Theological College, S.T.L., 1951; Fordham University, Ph.D., 1956. *Address:* Box 519, Los Gatos, Calif. 95030.

CAREER: Roman Catholic priest, member of Society of Jesus; McAuley Neuropsychiatric Institute, San Francisco, Calif., clinical psychologist, 1956-61; University of San Francisco, San Francisco, Calif., associate professor, 1958-67, professor of psychology, 1967-69, chairman of department, 1958-67, director of psychological services, 1960-65, dean of College of Arts and Letters, 1967-69; California Jesuit Province, Los Gatos, Calif., vice-provincial for education, 1969-71, regional provincial, 1971—.

WRITINGS: Mental Illness and the Religious Life, Bruce, 1962; *The Psychological Screening of Candidates in Religious Life in the Church Today*, University of Notre Dame Press, 1962; *An Introduction to Religious Counseling*, Prentice-Hall, 1969. Contributor to psychological, guidance, and religious journals.

*   *   *

VAUGHAN, Sam(uel)   1928-

PERSONAL: Born August 3, 1928, in Philadelphia, Pa.; son of Joseph (a lineman) and Anna Catherine (Alexander) Vaughan; married Josephine Vaughan, October 22, 1949; children: Jeffrey Marc, Leslie Jane, Dana Alexander, David Samuel. *Education:* Pennsylvania State College (now University), A.B., 1951. *Politics:* Independent. *Religion:* Episcopalian. *Home:* 23 Inness Rd., Tenafly, N.J. *Agent:* Sterling Lord Agency, 75 East 55th St., New York, N.Y. 10022. *Office:* Doubleday & Co., Inc., 245 Park Ave., New York, N.Y.

CAREER: Doubleday & Co., Inc., New York, N.Y., 1952—, successively advertising manager, sales manager, senior editor, executive editor, publisher and vice-president. *Military service:* U.S. Marine Corps, 1946-48.

WRITINGS—Juveniles: *Whoever Heard of Kangaroo Eggs?*, Doubleday, 1957; *New Shoes*, Doubleday, 1961; *The Two-thirty Bird*, Norton, 1965; *The Little Church*, Doubleday, 1969. Contributor to *New York Times Book Review, Wilson Library Bulletin, Famous Writers.*

VENN, Grant   1919-

PERSONAL: Born March 1, 1919, in Seattle, Wash.; son of Roy William (a farmer) and Vera (Masters) Venn; married Patricia Mildred Aiken, July 28, 1945; married second wife, Olga Montopoli, August 3, 1962; children: (first marriage) Victoria Susan, John Jeffry, Deborah Elizabeth; (second marriage) Diane Tobia. *Education:* University of Washington, Seattle, student, 1937-38; Washington State University, Pullman, B.S. and B.Ed., 1941, M.A., 1948, D.Ed., 1952; University of Minnesota, graduate study, 1949-50. *Politics:* Democrat. *Home:* 1 Valley View Dr., Vienna, W.Va. *Office:* Wood County Schools, 1210 13th St., Parkersburg, W.Va.

CAREER: Yakima (Wash.) public schools, director of guidance curriculum, 1948-49; Bellevue (Wash.) public schools, superintendent, 1949-51; Washington State University, Pullman, assistant professor of education, 1951-52; superintendent of schools in Othello, Wash., 1952-56, and Corning, N.Y., 1956-60; Western State College of Colorado, Gunnison, president, 1960-62; Wood County public schools, Parkersburg, W.Va., superintendent of schools, 1963-66; Department of Health, Education and Welfare, Washington D.C., U.S. Office of Education, associate commissioner of education, 1966-70; National Academy for School executives, Washington, D.C., director, 1970-72; Georgia State University, Atlanta, Calloway professor of education, 1972—. U.S. Peace Corps, Washington, D.C., director of field training, 1962—. Consultant to American Council on Education, 1962-63. *Military service:* U.S. Navy, pilot, 1942-46; became lieutenant junior grade. *Member:* National Education Association, American Association of School Administrators, Phi Kappa Phi, Phi Delta Kappa, Alpha Zeta, Psi Chi, Rotary.

WRITINGS: The Bellevue Story, Bellevue Schools, 1951; *Man, Education and Work*, American Council on Education, 1964; *Man, Education, and Manpower*, Association of School Administrators, 1970. Contributor to educational journals.†

*   *   *

VERNEY, Douglas Vernon   1924-

PERSONAL: Born January 21, 1924; son of John Henry (a minister) and Olive (Barritt) Verney; married Diana Robinson, June 24, 1950; children: Andrew, Jonathan. *Education:* Oriel College, Oxford, B.A., 1947, M.A., 1949; University of Liverpool, Ph.D., 1953. *Home:* 164 Lytton Blvd., Toronto 12, Ontario, Canada. *Office:* Department of Political Science, York University, 4700 Keele St., Downsview, Ontario, Canada.

CAREER: Lecturer in Helsinki, Finland, 1948-49; University of Liverpool, Liverpool, England, assistant lecturer, later lecturer, 1949-61; York University, Downsview, Ontario, associate professor, 1961-62, professor of political science, 1962—, chairman of department, 1962-67. Visiting professor, University of Florida, 1958-59, Columbia University, 1967; director, Social Science Research Council of Canada, 1972-74. *Military service:* Royal Artillery, 1942-45; became captain. *Member:* Political Science Association (England), Canadian Political Science Association (executive council member; president, 1969-70), American Political Science Association, Canadian Institute of Public Administration, Canadian Institute of International Affairs. *Awards, honors:* Commonwealth Fund fellowships at Columbia University, 1953, University of California, 1954; Canada Council Leave fellowships, 1967-68, 1974-75.

WRITINGS: Parliamentary Reform in Sweden 1866-1921, Clarendon Press, 1957; Public Enterprise in Sweden, Liverpool University Press, 1959; The Analysis of Political Systems, Free Press of Glencoe, 1959; Political Patterns in Today's World, Longmans, Green (Canada), 1963; (translator) Herbert Tingsten, The Problems of Democracy, Bedminster, 1965; British Government and Politics: Life Without a Declaration of Independence, Harper, 1966; (contributor) E. A. Goerner, editor, Democracy in Crisis: New Challenges to Democracy in the Atlantic Area, University of Notre Dame Press, 1971. Contributor to political journals. Editor, Canadian Public Administration, 1970-74.

WORK IN PROGRESS: Executive Crises in Canada and Sweden, completion expected in 1975; The Canadian Political Tradition, 1978.

SIDELIGHTS: Verney speaks Swedish.

* * *

VERNEY, Michael P(almer) 1923-

PERSONAL: Born February 17, 1923, in Gloucester, England; son of John Palmer Setters (an electrical engineer) and Dorothy (Davis) Verney; married Dora Reader, November 20, 1948; children: Stephen Palmer, Michael Lee. Education: Attended Crypt School, Gloucester, England, 1933-40. Home: 36 The Parkway, Rustington, Sussex, England.

CAREER: River Severn Catchment Board, Stratford on Avon, England, civil engineer, 1947-50; West Sussex River Board, Chichester, England, civil engineer, 1950-65; Sussex River Authority, Brighton, England, civil engineer, 1965—. Marine craft consultant. Inventor. Military service: British Army, Royal Engineers, 1944-47. Member: Institution of Civil Engineers (London), Institution of Water Engineers (London), British Institute of Management (London; associate member), Steamboat Association of Great Britain, Little Ship Club, Arun Yacht Club.

WRITINGS: Amateur Boat Building, J. Murray, 1948; Practical Conversions and Yacht Repairs, J. Murray, 1951; Lifeboat into Yacht, Yachting Monthly, 1953; Complete Amateur Boat Building, J. Murray, 1959; Building Chine Boats, Yachting Monthly, 1960; Yacht Repairs and Conversions, J. Murray, 1961; Boat Maintenance by the Amateur, Kaye & Ward, 1970; Boat Repairs and Conversations, J. Murray, 1972. Contributor of articles to Sunday Times (London), Look & Learn, Light Steam Power, and boating magazines, 1944-71.

* * *

Ver STEEG, Clarence L(ester) 1922-

PERSONAL: Born December 28, 1922, in Orange City, Iowa; son of John A. and Annie (Vischer) Ver Steeg; married Dorothy Ann De Vries, December 24, 1943; children: John Charles. Education: Morningside College, B.A., 1943; Columbia University, M.A., 1946, Ph.D., 1950. Politics: Democrat. Religion: Presbyterian. Home: 2619 Ridge Ave., Evanston, Ill. 60201. Office: Department of History, Northwestern University, Evanston, Ill. 60201.

CAREER: Columbia University, New York, N.Y., lecturer and instructor in history, 1946-48, 1949-50; Northwestern University, Evanston, Ill., instructor, 1950-52, assistant professor, 1952-55, associate professor, 1955-59, professor of history, 1959—. Visiting professor, Harvard University, 1959-60; visiting member, Institute for Advanced Study, Princeton, 1967-68. Adviser to Encyclo-

paedia Britannica Films. Military service: U.S. Army Air Forces, 1942-45; became first lieutenant; received Air Medal with three clusters, and five battle stars.

MEMBER: American Historical Association, Organization of American Historians, American Association of University Professors (president, Northwestern University chapter, 1963-64), Institute of Early American History and Culture (Williamsburg, Va.; member of council), Southern Historical Association. Awards, honors: Albert J. Beveridge Award ($1,500) of American Historical Association, 1952, for Robert Morris, Revolutionary Financier; George A. and Eliza Gardner Howard Foundation fellowship, 1954-55; Huntington Library research fellow, 1955; American Council of Learned Societies national fellow, 1958-59; Guggenheim fellow, 1964-65; National Endowment for the Humanities senior fellow, 1973.

WRITINGS: (Contributor) R. W. Leopold and A. S. Link, editors, Problems in American History, Prentice-Hall, 1953, revised edition, 1957; Robert Morris, Revolutionary Financier, University of Pennsylvania Press, 1954; (editor, and author of introduction) A True and Historical Narrative of the Province of Georgia, University of Georgia Press, 1960; The American People: Their History, Harper, 1961; (contributor) The Democratic Experience, Scott, 1963; The Formative Years, 1607-1763, Hill & Wang, 1964; The Story of Our Country, Harper, 1965; (editor with Richard Hofstadter) Great Issues in American History: From Settlement to Revolution, 1584-1776, Random House, 1969; (with Richard Hofstadter) A People and a Nation, Harper, 1971; (with others) Investigating Man's World, six volumes, Scott, Foresman, 1969; Southern Colonies in the Eighteenth Century: 1689-1763, Louisiana State University Press, 1975. Contributor to professional journals.

* * *

VICKERS, Douglas 1924-

PERSONAL: Born July 13, 1924, in Rockhampton, Australia; son of John William and Vera (Turner) Vickers; married Miriam Betts, October 12, 1946; children: Paul. Education: University of Queensland, B.Com., 1949; University of London, B.Sc., 1952, Ph.D., 1956. Office: Department of Finance, Wharton School, University of Pennsylvania, Philadelphia, Pa. 19104.

CAREER: With National Bank of Australasia, London, England, 1949-55; with Vauxhall Motors Ltd., England, 1955-57; University of Pennsylvania, Philadelphia, assistant professor, 1957-61, associate professor, 1961-67, professor of finance, 1967—, chairman of department of finance, 1971—. Military service: Royal Australian Air Force, 1942-46. Member: Royal Economic Society, American Economic Association, Econometric Society, American Finance Association. Awards, honors: Ford Foundation faculty research fellow, 1964-65.

WRITINGS: Studies in the Theory of Money 1690-1776, Chilton, 1959; (with Irwin Friend, F. E. Brown, and E. S. Herman) A Study of Mutual Funds, U.S. Government Printing Office, 1962; The Theory of the Firm: Production, Capital and Finance, McGraw, 1968; The Cost of Capital and Structure of the Firm, J. Finance, 1970. Contributor to economics, accounting, and finance journals.†

* * *

VIERTEL, Joseph 1915-

PERSONAL: Born August 13, 1915, in New York, N.Y.;

son of Jack Shapiro (a builder) and Daisy Viertel; married Janet Man (an underwater photographer), September 13, 1939; children: Thomas Man, Alice Susan, John Richard. *Education:* Staunton Military Academy, student, 1928-32; Harvard University, A.B., 1936; Yale University, student at Drama School, 1936-37. *Politics:* Democrat. *Religion:* Jewish. *Home:* Estate Green Cay, Christiansted, St. Croix, Virgin Islands. *Agent:* Brandt & Brandt, 101 Park Ave., New York, N.Y. 10017. *Office:* Presidential Realty Corp., 180 South Broadway, White Plains, N.Y.

CAREER: Presidential Realty Corp., White Plains, N.Y., chairman of finance committee, 1940—. Director of Trans-Lux Corp., 1948-53, F. D. Rich Construction Co., 1962-69, and Lanvin-Charles of the Ritz, 1961-70. Novelist and short story writer. United Fund of Stamford, vice-chairman, 1960-61; Stamford Human Rights Commission, secretary, 1964—; Stamford Anti-Poverty Committee, vice-president, 1963—. *Member:* Phi Beta Kappa, Harvard Club of New York.

WRITINGS: The Last Temptation (Literary Guild selection), Simon and Schuster, 1955; *To Love and Corrupt* (Reader's Digest Book Club selection), Random House, 1962; *Monkey on a String*, Trident, 1968. Author of play, "So Proudly We Hail," produced by James Ramsey Ullman at 46th Street Theatre, New York, 1936. Contributor of short stories to *McCall's, Story, Collier's,* and *American.*

WORK IN PROGRESS: A novel of four generations beginning in Minsk, Byelo-Russia and ending in Waterford, Connecticut, publication expected in 1977.

* * *

VIERTEL, Peter 1920-

PERSONAL: Born November 16, 1920, in Dresden, Germany; son of Berthold and Salomea (Steuerman) Viertel; married Deborah Kerr (an actress), July, 1960; children: Christine. *Education:* Attended University of California, Los Angeles, and Dartmouth College. *Politics:* Democrat. *Home:* Wyhergut, Klosters, Switzerland 7250. *Agent:* I. P. Lazar, 211 South Beverly Dr., Beverly Hills, Calif.

CAREER: Free-lance writer. *Military service:* U.S. Marine Corps Reserve, World War II; served in Pacific and European Theaters; received Bronze Star and three battle stars. *Member:* Authors League, Screen Writers Guild. *Awards, honors:* Christopher Award for screenplay, "The Old Man and the Sea."

WRITINGS: The Canyon (novel), Harcourt, 1940; *Line of Departure* (novel), Harcourt, 1947; *White Hunter, Black Heart* (novel), Doubleday, 1953; *Love Lies Bleeding* (novel), Doubleday, 1964; *Bicycle on the Beach* (novel), Delacorte, 1971. Author with Irwin Shaw of play, "The Survivors," 1948. Writer of screenplays, "Decision Before Dawn," "The Old Man and the Sea," and "The Sun Also Rises."

SIDELIGHTS: Film rights to *White Hunter, Black Heart* have been sold to Ted Richmond Productions.

* * *

VIGNESS, David M(artell) 1922-

PERSONAL: Born October 12, 1922, in La Feria, Tex.; son of Lewis Martell (a farmer) and Nina (Hegge) Vigness; married Winifred Woods, January 29, 1949; children: Margaret Ellen, Richard Martell. *Education:* University of Texas, B.A., 1943, M.A., 1948, Ph.D., 1951. *Politics:*

Democrat. *Religion:* Presbyterian. *Home:* 3523 58th St., Lubbock, Tex. 79413. *Office:* Department of History, Texas Tech University, Lubbock, Tex. 79409.

CAREER: University of Texas, Austin, instructor, 1951; Schreiner Institute, Kerrville, Tex., professor of history and head of department of social science, 1951-55; Texas Tech University, Lubbock, assistant professor, 1955-58, associate professor, 1958-61, professor of history and chairman of department, 1961—. Fulbright lecturer at University of Chile and at Catholic University, Santiago, Chile, 1957-58. Lubbock City-County Child Welfare Board, past chairman; South Plains Council, executive board; Lubbock United Fund, member. *Military service:* U.S. Naval Reserve, 1943-46; served in Pacific Theater; became lieutenant. *Member:* American Historical Association, Organization of American Historians, Conference on Latin American History, Western History Association, Southwestern Social Science Association (executive council, 1964-65), Southwestern Council of Latin American Studies (president, 1972-73), Texas State Historical Association (fellow), Phi Kappa Phi, Phi Alpha Theta, Pi Sigma Alpha, Sigma Delta Pi.

WRITINGS: (Staff writer and contributor) *Handbook of Texas History*, two volumes, Texas State Historical Association, 1952; (editor with Ernest Wallace) *Documents of Texas History*, Steck, 1963; *The Revolutionary Decades*, Steck, 1965; (co-author) *Estudios de historia del Noreste*, Sociedad Nuevoleonesa de Historia, Geografia y Estadistica, 1972. Contributor to historical journals.

* * *

VILLASENOR, David V. 1913-

PERSONAL: Born February 25, 1913, in Jalisco, Mexico; son of Refugio (a saddle-maker) and Maria (Villanueva) Villasenor; married Jean Gimlin, April 18, 1948. *Education:* Escuela Industrial y Artes Graficas, Hermosillo, Sonora, Mexico, student, two years. *Religion:* Baha'i World Faith. *Agent:* Vinson Brown, 8339 West Dry Creek Rd., Healdsburg, Calif. *Office:* 1138 La Flora Lane, Glendora, Calif. 91740.

CAREER: Artist, sculptor, and painter, specializing in interpreting Mexican and Indian cultures; perhaps best known for developing sand painting into a permanent art form. Teacher of arts and crafts and Indian lore to boys' clubs, Young Women's Christian Association classes, and other youth groups, 1937-50. *Military service:* U.S. Army, Medical Corps; became staff sergeant; received Commendation Ribbon for permanent contribution to medical science for medical mulages, now on exhibition at Medical Museum of Armed Forces Institute of Pathology, Washington, D.C.

WRITINGS—With wife, Jean G. Villasenor: *How To Do Nature Printing*, Walter Foster, 1949; *Tapestries in Sand*, Naturegraph, 1964; *How to Do Permanent Sandpainting*, Litho-Color, 1972. Also author with Jean G. Villasenor of "The 24th Night of the Long Night Moon," a Christmas story filmed by Joe Rock Productions.

SIDELIGHTS: Villasenor was first intrigued by the possibilities of sand painting at the age of sixteen. For years he attempted to find a way to preserve the ancient and highly ephemeral Indian art. When his methods proved successful, he made innovations. Whereas the Indians have used sand-like substances to provide color, Villasenor decided to create his paintings with sand only, obtaining red from the canyon walls of Zion National Park, the Grand Canyon, and the Painted Desert; yellow from Oak Creek Canyon in Arizona; copper sulphate from Arizona and Nevada; and black from iron magnatite deposits along the Merced River and from the ocean.

BIOGRAPHICAL/CRITICAL SOURCES: Pasadena Independent Star-News, June 24, 1962, August 18, 1964.

* * *

VINAVER, Eugene 1899-

PERSONAL: Surname is pronounced Vin-a-*ver*; born June 18, 1899, in St. Petersburg, Russia (now Leningrad); son of Maxime (a barrister) and Rosalie (Hichine) Vinaver; married Alice Elizabeth Vaudrey, September 23, 1939; children: One son. *Education:* Oxford University, B.Litt., 1922, M.A., 1927, D.Litt., 1950; University of Paris, Docteur es Lettres, 1925. *Home:* 27 Palace St., Canterbury, Kent, England. *Agent:* Curtis Brown Ltd., 13 King St., London W.C.2, England. *Office:* Northwestern University, Evanston, Ill. 60201.

CAREER: Oxford University, Oxford, England, lecturer in French language and literature at Lincoln College, 1924-28, university lecturer in French, 1928-31, university reader in French literature, 1931-33; University of Manchester, Manchester, England, professor of French language and literature, 1933-66; professor emeritus, 1966—. Zaharoff Lecturer, University of Oxford, 1960; Alexander White Professor, University of Chicago, 1960; visiting professor, Stanford University, 1962; University of Wisconsin, Herbert F. Johnson Professor, 1964-65, visiting professor, 1966-70, Phi Beta Kappa visiting scholar, 1967-68; visiting professor, Northwestern University, 1970—; Lord Northcliff Lecturer, University of London, 1971. *Member:* Modern Language Association of America (honorary member; president, 1961), Society for the Study of Medieval Language and Literature (president, 1939-48), Modern Humanites Research Association (president, 1966), International Arthurian Society (president, 1966-69; honorary president, 1969—), Belgian Royal Academy of French Language and Literature (foreign member). *Awards, honors:* Fellow, Lincoln College, Oxford University; honorary doctorates from University of Chicago and University of Hull; Chevalier, French Legion of Honor; Prix Broquette-Gonin, 1971.

WRITINGS: The Love Potion in the Primitive Tristan Romance, Velay, 1924; *Le Roman de Tristan et Iseut dans l'oeuvre de Malory*, Champion (Paris), 1925; *Etudes sur le Tristan en prose*, Champion, 1925; *Malory*, Clarendon Press, 1929, Folcraft, 1970; (editor, with T.B.L. Webster) Renan, *Prier sur l'Acropole*, Manchester University Press, 1934; *Principles of Textual Emendation*, Manchester University Press, 1939; *Hommage a Bedier*, Editions du Calame, 1942; (author of introduction) *Le Roman de Balain*, Manchester University Press, 1942; (author of critical edition) Racine, *Principes de la tragedie en marge de la Poetique d'Aristote*, 1944, 2nd edition, 1951; (editor) *The Works of Sir Thomas Malory*, three volumes, Clarendon Press, 1947, 2nd edition, 1967, one-volume edition, 1954, 2nd edition, 1971; *Racine et la poesie tragique*, Nizet (Paris), 1951, 2nd revised and enlarged edition, 1963, translation by P. Mansell Jones published as *Racine and Poetic Tragedy*, Manchester University Press, 1955; (editor) *The Tale of the Death of King Arthur*, Clarendon Press, 1955; (editor) *King Arthur and His Knights: Selected Tales*, Houghton, 1956, revised and enlarged edition, 1968; *L'-Action poetique dans le theatre de Racine*, Clarendon Press, 1960; *A la recherche d'une poetique medievale*, Nizet, 1970; *The Rise of Romance*, Oxford University Press, 1971.

Contributor to *French Studies, Medium Aevum*, and French-language journals. Editor of *Arthuriana*, 1929-31.†

* * *

VIZENOR, Gerald Robert 1934-

PERSONAL: Born October 22, 1934, in Minneapolis, Minn.; son of Clement William and LaVerne (Peterson) Vizenor; married Judith Helen Horns (an instructor, University of Minnesota), 1959; children: Robert Thomas. *Education:* Attended New York University, 1955-56; University of Minnesota, B.A., 1960, graduate study, 1962-65. *Address:* Box 436, Walker, Minn. 56484.

CAREER: Ramsey County Corrections Authority, St. Paul, Minn., group worker, 1957-58; Capital Community Center, St. Paul, Minn., roving group worker, 1958; Department of Corrections, Minnesota State Reformatory, St. Cloud, Minn., corrections agent, 1960-61; University of Minnesota, Minneapolis, with library services, 1962-64. *Military service:* Minnesota National Guard, 1950-51; U.S. Army, 1952-55, served in Japan. *Member:* Delta Phi Lambda.

WRITINGS— Poems: Born in the Wind, privately printed, 1960; *The Old Park Sleepers* (poem), Obercraft, 1961; *Two Wings the Butterfly* (Haiku in English), privately printed, 1962; *South of the Painted Stones* (poems), Obercraft, 1963; *Raising the Moon Vines* (Haiku in English), Callimachus, 1964; *Seventeen Chirps* (Haiku in English), Nodin Press, 1964; *Empty Swings* (Haiku in English), Nodin Press, 1967.

Other: (Editor) *Escorts to White Earth, 1868-1968: 100 Year Reservation*, Four Winds, 1968; *Thomas James White Hawk*, Four Winds, 1968; *The Everlasting Sky*, Crowell, 1972.

WORK IN PROGRESS: Rendering Ojibway songs into English tentative title *Summer in the Spring*; a novel, *The Humours of Benjamin*; editing a legendary history of the Ojibway Indians of Minnesota.

SIDELIGHTS: Vizenor wrote to *CA*: "I am too young to discuss what I think might be a philosophy gained from my travels and [from] books about the problems of mechanical impotency and [the] clash between the occult and archaic transcendence. I feel best walking along the river in the Spring and Autumn, or sleeping in a windy park, or talking with children and writing haiku for my friends. I emphasize my Indian blood (Ojibway, member of the Minnesota Chippewa Tribe) for my passion and humor and trickery, and my poor formal education as a youth for my originality and curiosity. Tranquillity and independence strengthen my breath. My romantic weakness is my loneliness to return to the place of my father's birth on the White Earth Reservation."

BIOGRAPHICAL/CRITICAL SOURCES: Minneapolis Sunday Tribune, January 24, 1965.†

* * *

VOEKS, Virginia (Wilna) 1921-

PERSONAL: Surname rhymes with "oaks"; born May 9, 1921, in Champaign, Ill.; daughter of B. Forrest (a high school mathematics teacher) and Dorothy (Wade) Voeks; married William McBlair (a professor of biology and oceanography), 1957. *Education:* University of Washington, Seattle, B.S. (summa cum laude), 1943, M.S., 1944; Yale University, Ph.D., 1947. *Home:* 4319 Explorer Rd., P.O. Box 877, La Mesa Calif. 92041. *Office:* San Diego State University, San Diego, Calif.

CAREER: University of Washington, Seattle, assistant professor of psychology, 1947-49; San Diego State University, San Diego, Calif., assistant professor, 1949-55, associate professor, 1955-58, professor of psychology, 1958—. U.S. Civil Service, constructor of tests, Personnel Research Section, 1945. Consultant, "Happy Hideaway" television series for children. *Member:* American Psychological Association (fellow; secretary-treasurer, Division 1, 1965—), Psychonomic Society (charter member), National Wildlife Federation, Association of American Indian Affairs, American Association of University Professors, Western Psychological Association, New York Academy of Sciences (fellow), San Diego Ballet Association (charter member), Phi Beta Kappa, Sigma Xi (life), Psi Chi, Sigma Epsilon Sigma, Alpha Delta Pi.

WRITINGS: On Becoming an Educated Person, Saunders, 1957, 3rd edition, 1970. Contributor to *International Encyclopedia of Social Sciences*; also contributor to professional journals and to United Features syndicated "Spotlight Series." Editor of American Psychological Association's *Newsletters*, 1965-74.

WORK IN PROGRESS: Research on relative freedom from hostility and academic success.

SIDELIGHTS: Ms.Voeks is competent in French, German, and Esperanto. *Avocational interests:* Cooking, chess, landscaping and gardening, music, embroidery, contract bridge, dress design, sewing, interior decorating, flower arranging, table tennis.

* * *

VOGEL, Ezra F. 1930-

PERSONAL: Born July 11, 1930, in Delaware, Ohio; son of Joseph and Edith (Nachman) Vogel; married Suzanne Hall (a psychiatric social worker), July, 1953; children: David, Steven. *Education:* Ohio Wesleyan University, B.A., 1950; Harvard University, Ph.D., 1958. *Home:* 46 Parker St., Cambridge, Mass. 02138.

CAREER: Harvard University, Cambridge, Mass., lecturer, 1958-60; Yale University, New Haven, Conn., assistant professor, 1960-61; Harvard University, research associate, 1961-67, professor of sociology, 1967—, director of East Asian Research Center, 1973—. *Military service:* 1951-53.

WRITINGS: (Editor with Norman W. Bell) *A Modern Introduction to the Family*, Free Press of Glencoe, 1960; *Japan's New Middle Class*, University of California Press, 1963; *Canton Under Communism: Programs and Politics in a Provincial Capital, 1949-1968*, Harvard University Press, 1969.

WORK IN PROGRESS: A study of Chinese society through its literature.

* * *

VOGEL, Ilse-Margret 1918-

PERSONAL: Born June 5, 1918, in Breslau, Germany; came to United States, 1950, naturalized, 1955; daughter of Sperling Erich and Margaret (Gaertner) Vogel; married Howard Knotts (an artist), June 1, 1959. *Education:* Edu-

cated in German schools; studied art in Berlin, Germany, prior to World War II, and in Basel, Switzerland, 1948. *Address:* Duell Rd., Bangall, N.Y. 12506.

CAREER: Co-founder and co-owner of Rosen Gallery, first gallery for modern art in Berlin, Germany, 1945-48; assistant to J. B. Neumann at New Art Circle (gallery), New York, N.Y., 1950-53; began designing toys and writing for *Humpty Dumpty* (magazine), 1954; head designer for Knickerbocker Toy Co., New York, N.Y., 1956-63; writer and illustrator of books for children, 1964—.

WRITINGS—Author and illustrator: *The Don't Be Scared Book*, Atheneum, 1964; *1 Is No Fun, But 20 Is Plenty*, Atheneum, 1965; *Willy, Willy, Don't Be Silly*, Atheneum, 1965; *Hello Henry*, Parents, 1965; *When I Grow Up*, Golden Press, 1968; *Come On Play Ball*, Golden Press, 1969; *Peek-A-Boo*, Golden Press, 1970; *1, 2, 3, Juggle With Me*, Golden Press, 1970; *My Little Dinosaur*, Golden Press, 1971; *The Bear in the Boat*, Golden Press, 1972; *Daisy Dog's Wake Up Book*, Golden Press, 1973.

Illustrator: *Bears Birthday*, Golden Press, 1964; *Little Plays for Little People*, Parents, 1965; *City Cats, Country Cats*, Golden Press, 1969.

Creator of activity books for children for Whitman & Dell. Regular contributor to *Parent's Magazine* and *Humpty Dumpty*.

WORK IN PROGRESS: The Rainbow Dress for Harper.

SIDELIGHTS: Ms. Vogel made extensive study trips to France, Germany, Italy, the Netherlands, Switzerland, and Spain, visiting museums, 1959-62. *Avocational interests:* Gardening, travel, watching cats (has ten), cooking, watching birds, reading, and seeing the seasons change.

* * *

VOIGT, Melvin J(ohn) 1911-

PERSONAL: Born March 12, 1911, in Upland, Calif.; son of Adolf Frank and Marie (Hirschler) Voigt; married Susie Warkentin, December 28, 1933; children: Marjorie (Mrs. Robert E. Huskins), Dolores (Mrs. Peter L. Scott), Paul Warren. *Education:* Bluffton College, A.B., 1933; University of Michigan, A.B. in L.S., 1936, A.M. in L.S., 1938. *Home:* 1209 Crest Rd., Del Mar, Calif. 92014. *Office:* San Diego State University, La Jolla, Calif. 92037.

CAREER: Buffton (Ohio) School District, teacher and librarian, 1933-35; University of Michigan, Ann Arbor, science librarian, 1935-43; General Mills, Inc., Minneapolis, Minn., director of library and publications, 1942-46; Carnegie Institute of Technology, Pittsburgh, Pa., librarian, 1946-52, associate professor, 1946-50, professor of library science, 1950-52; University of California at Berkeley, assistant librarian, 1952-59; Kansas State University, Manhattan, director of libraries and professor of library science, 1959-60; San Diego State University, La Jolla, university librarian, 1960—. University of Michigan, visiting summer professor, 1951; Georgia University Center, visiting scholar, 1965. UNESCO, member of International Advisory Committee on Bibliography, Documentation and Terminology, 1961-68. Consultant to government, business, and universities on library buildings, library collections, and on organization and use of data processing. Member of board of Musical Arts Society of La Jolla and Tuberculosis Association of San Diego, 1964—. President of Tuberculosis and Respiratory Disease Association of San Diego and Imperial Counties, 1969-70.

MEMBER: American Library Association (president of

resources and technical services division, 1960-61; president of library education division, 1964-65), Special Libraries Association (director, 1948-54), American Documentation Institute, American Association for the Advancement of Science (fellow), Pennsylvania Library Association (president, 1951-53), California Library Association, Phi Kappa Phi. *Awards, honors:* Fulbright research grant to University of Copenhagen, 1958-59.

WRITINGS: Subject Headings in Physics, American Library Association, 1944; *Scientists' Approaches to Information*, American Library Association, 1961; *Books for College Libraries*, American Library Association, 1967; (editor) *Advances in Librarianship*, Academic Press, Volume I, 1970, Volume II, 1971, Volume III, 1972, Volume IV, 1974. Contributor to *Scientific Monthly*, and to library journals.

WORK IN PROGRESS: Volumes five and six of *Advances in Librarianship.*

BIOGRAPHICAL/CRITICAL SOURCES: California Librarian, Number 22, 1961.

* * *

von ECKARDT, Ursula M(aria) 1925-

PERSONAL: Born February 24, 1925, in Hamburg, Germany; daughter of Hans (a professor) and Gertrud (Dannheisser) von Eckardt. *Education:* Hunter College (now of the City University of New York), B.A. (cum laude), 1946; University of Chicago, graduate study, 1946-48; New School for Social Research, M.A., 1950, Ph.D. (magna cum laude), 1953. *Politics:* Independent voter. *Religion:* Freethinker. *Home:* Rio Piedras Darlington 401, Rio Piedras, Puerto Rico 00925.

CAREER: University of Puerto Rico, Rio Piedras, assistant professor, 1956-59, professor of social science and philosophy, 1959-64. Puerto Rico Institute of Psychiatry, Rio Piedras, lecturer, 1961—. *San Juan Star*, feature columnist, 1959—.

WRITINGS: The Pursuit of Happiness in the Democratic Creed, Praeger, 1959; (with Ramon Fernandez-Marina) *Horizons of the Mind*, Philosophical Library, 1964. Also author of *The Sober Generation: A Portrait of Competent Adolescents.* Contributor to *Yale Law Review, Annals* of New York Academy of Sciences.

WORK IN PROGRESS: A collection of *San Juan Star* columns and essays (in Spanish); research at Puerto Rico Institute of Psychiatry under National Institute of Mental Health grant; *A Morphology of Values: Value Formation and Transformation.*†

* * *

von GLAHN, Gerhard E(rnst) 1911-

PERSONAL: Born May 26, 1911, in Wiesbaden, Germany; son of William Henry (a chemist) and Gertrude (Saelzer) von Glahn; married Dorothy Ellen Grant, October 27, 1942; children: Peter Grant, Karen Elizabeth. *Education:* Bucknell University, student, 1928-30; Columbia University, B.S. in B.A., 1932, M.A., 1935; Northwestern University, Ph.D., 1939. *Politics:* Republican. *Religion:* Presbyterian. *Home:* 2105 Vermilion Rd., Duluth, Minn. 55812.

CAREER: Clinch & Co. (investment counsel; now defunct), New York, N.Y., research statistician, 1932-37; Western Reserve University (now Case Western Reserve

University), Cleveland, Ohio, instructor in political science, 1939-41; Duluth State Teachers College (now University of Minnesota, Duluth) instructor, 1941-43, 1946-47, associate professor of political science, 1947; University of Minnesota, Duluth Campus, associate professor, 1947-51, professor of political science and head of department, 1951—. *Military service:* U.S. Army, 1943-46; served with Military Government, Germany, 1944-46; became first lieutenant; received Bronze Star. *Member:* American Political Science Association, American Society of International Law, Pi Gamma Mu.

WRITINGS: The Occupation of Enemy Territory, University of Minnesota Press, 1957; *Law Among Nations—An Introduction to Public International Law*, Macmillan, 1965, 2nd revised edition, 1970; (contributor) C. C. Havighurst, editor, *International Control of Propaganda*, Oceana, 1967. Contributor of articles and reviews to professional journals.

WORK IN PROGRESS: A two-volume work with tentative title of *Images of the Future: A History of American Utopian Literature since 1890*, completion expected in 1975; and *The Social Thought of Johann Gottlieb Fichte.*

SIDELIGHTS: von Glahn is fluent in German; reads French and Spanish. *Avocational interests:* Philately (Jugoslavia and modern Japan).

* * *

von MENDELSSOHN, Felix 1918-

PERSONAL: Born August 11, 1918, in Dresden, Germany; son of Georg R. (an artist) and Gerta (Clason) von Mendelssohn; married Hildegard Tammert, May 17, 1949; children: Constance, Thomas, Bettina. *Education:* University of Lausanne, M.D., 1943; also studied at University of Zurich. *Office:* 1330 New Hampshire Ave. N.W., Washington, D.C.

CAREER: Staff psychiatrist in a Swiss mental hospital, 1944-50; Cedars of Lebanon Hospital, Hollywood, Calif., intern, 1951-52; resident in psychiatry in state of New York, at University of Michigan, and in Delaware, 1952-55; National Institute of Mental Health, Washington, D.C., assistant clinical director, 1961-65; Georgetown University, School of Medicine, Washington, D.C., associate clinical professor, 1963—; psychiatrist in private practice, Washington, D.C., 1965—. *Military service:* U.S. Army, Medical Corps, 1955-60; became lieutenant colonel. *Member:* American Medical Association, American Psychiatric Association, Pan American Medical Association, District of Columbia Medical Society, District of Columbia Psychiatric Society.

WRITINGS: This Is Psychiatry, F. Watts, 1964, 2nd edition, Intercontinental Medical Book Corp., 1973. Contributor of papers and reviews on psychiatric and psychopharmacological subjects to professional journals.†

* * *

VRETTOS, Theodore 1919-

PERSONAL: Surname is accented on first syllable; born November 23, 1919, in Peabody, Mass.; son of Leonidas and Karabelas (Zacharoula) Vrettos; married Vassille Parianos, September 15, 1946. *Education:* Greek Theological School, student, 1940-45; Harvard University, graduate study. *Religion:* Greek Orthodox. *Home:* 75 Prospect St., Peabody, Mass.

CAREER: Teacher of world literature and creative writing at Salem State College, Salem, Mass.

WRITINGS: Hammer on the Sea (novel), Little, Brown, 1965; *A Shadow of Magnitude* (non-fiction), Putnam, 1974. Contributor to magazines, including *Literary Review, Audience, Catholic Digest*, and *Yankee*.

WORK IN PROGRESS: A novel about contemporary Greece, a non-fiction book about third-century Alexandria.

SIDELIGHTS: Vrettos is fluent in Greek.

* * *

VUCINICH, Wayne S.   1913-

PERSONAL: Born June 23, 1913, in Butte, Mont.; son of Spiro J. and Soka (Palikuca) Vucinich; married Serafina Stys (a teacher and counselor), January 31, 1942; children: Constance (Mrs. Clement Furlong), Annette (Mrs. Roger Davis). *Education:* University of California, Berkeley, A.B., 1936; M.A., 1937, Ph.D., 1941; also studied at Charles University, 1937-38. *Politics:* Democrat. *Religion:* Serbian Orthodox. *Home:* 13826 Page Mill Rd., Los Altos Hills, Calif. 94305. *Office:* Department of History, Stanford University, Stanford, Calif. 94022.

CAREER: Library of Congress and Office of Coordinator of Information, Washington, D.C., member of U.S.S.R. section, 1941-42; Office of Strategic Services, Washington, D.C., Balkan expert, 1942-45, liaison officer to Political Intelligence Division foreign office in London, 1943-44, head of research and analysis unit in Bari, Italy, 1944; U.S. Department of State, Washington, D.C., member of research and analysis department, 1945-46; Stanford University, Stanford, Calif., instructor, 1946-47, assistant professor, 1947-49, associate professor, 1950-56, professor of history, 1956—, chairman of Center for Russian and East European Studies, 1972—, curator for the Russian and east European collection and coordinator of studies on Russia and eastern Europe of Hoover Institution on War, Revolution, and Peace, 1974—. Liaison officer, interpreter, and Balkan expert for Allied Control Council, Sofia, Bulgaria, 1943-45. *Military service:* U.S. Naval Reserve, active duty, 1943-46; became lieutenant; received Bronze Star Medal.

MEMBER: American Historical Association (chairman of Conference on Slavic and East European History, 1972), American Association for the Advancement of Slavic Studies (member of board of directors, 1973—), Medieval Academy of America, American Committee to Promote Studies of the History of the Habsburg Monarchy (member of executive committee), Western Slavic Association (chairman, 1967-68).

WRITINGS: Serbia Between East and West, Stanford University Press, 1954; *The Ottoman Empire: Its Record and Legacy*, Van Nostrand, 1965; (editor) *The Peasant in Nineteenth Century Russia*, Stanford University Press, 1968; (editor and contributor) *Russia and Asia*, Hoover Institution, 1972; *Eastern Europe*, Ginn, 1973. Contributor of articles and reviews to history journals. Member of editorial board of *Austrian History Yearbook* and *Journal of Modern History*.

SIDELIGHTS: Vucinich speaks Serbo-Croatian, Russian, Czech, Bulgarian, Slovak, German, Italian, French, Polish, Ukrainian, and Slovene.

* * *

WADDINGTON, C(onrad) H(al)   1905-

PERSONAL: Born November 8, 1905, in Evesham, England; son of Hal (a tea planter in India) and Mary Ellen (Warner) Waddington; married Cecil Elizabeth Lascelles, 1926; married second wife, Margaret Justin Blanco White (an architect and town planner), 1936; children: (first marriage) Cecil Jacob; (second marriage) Caroline, Margaret Dusa. *Education:* Sidney Sussex College, Cambridge, B.A., 1927, Sc.D., 1938. *Home:* 15 Blacket Pl., Edinburgh, Scotland. *Office:* Institute of Animal Genetics, University of Edinburgh, West Mains Rd., Edinburgh, Scotland.

CAREER: Cambridge University, Cambridge, England, lecturer in zoology, and embryologist at Strangeways Research Laboratory, 1933-45; fellow of Christ's College, 1934-45; University of Edinburgh, Edinburgh, Scotland, Buchanan Professor of Animal Genetics, 1947—. Honorary director of animal genetics unit of Agricultural Research Council; honorary director of epigenetics group of Medical Research Council; vice-president of International Biological Program. *Military service:* Royal Air Force, officer in charge of Operational Research Section, Coastal Command, 1944-45.

MEMBER: International Union of Biological Sciences (president), Royal Society of London (fellow), Royal Society of Edinburgh (fellow), American Academy of Arts and Sciences (foreign member), World Academy of Arts and Sciences (fellow), Athenaeum Club (London). *Awards, honors:* Rockefeller Foundation traveling fellow, 1932, 1938; Albert Brachet Prize for embryology, Royal Academy of Belgium, 1936; commander, Order of the British Empire, 1958; D. Sc., University of Montreal, 1958.

WRITINGS: How Animals Develop, Norton, 1935, revised edition, Harper, 1962; *An Introduction to Modern Genetics*, Norton, 1939; *Organisers and Genes*, Cambridge University Press, 1940; *The Scientific Attitude*, Penguin, 1941, new edition, Hutchinson, 1968; (editor) *Science and Ethics*, Allen & Unwin, 1942; *The Epigenetics of Birds*, Cambridge University Press, 1952; (editor with E. C. R. Reeve) *Quantitative Inheritance*, H.M.S.O., 1952; *Principles of Embryology*, Allen & Unwin, 1956; *The Strategy of the Genes*, Allen & Unwin, 1957; (editor) *Biological Organisation*, Pergamon, 1959; *The Ethical Animal*, Atheneum, 1960; *The Nature of Life*, Atheneum, 1961; *New Patterns in Genetics and Development*, Columbia University Press, 1962; *Biology for the Modern World*, Barnes & Noble, 1962; *Principles of Development and Differentiation*, Macmillan, 1966; (editor) *Towards a Theoretical Biology: An International Union of Biological Sciences Symposium*, Edinburgh University Press, Volume I: *Prolegomena*, 1968, Volume II: *Sketches*, 1969, Volume III: *Drafts*, 1970, Volume IV: *Essays*, 1972; *Behind Appearance: A Study of the Relations between Painting and the Natural Sciences in This Century*, Edinburgh University Press, 1969, Massachusetts Institute of Technology Press, 1970; *O.R. in World War II: Operational Research against the U-Boat*, Elek, 1973, British Book Centre, 1974. Contributor of more than two hundred articles to scientific and popular journals.

SIDELIGHTS: Commenting on *Towards a Theoretical Biology*, P.B. Medawar wrote in the *New York Review of Books*, "These volumes may not inaugurate a theoretical biology . . . but they might well inaugurate a new authentic style of scientific literature, for the contributions are thoughtful, imaginative, sometimes illuminating, and always a delight to read."

Waddington's books have been translated into Russian, Spanish, Dutch, Japanese, and Swedish. *Avocational interests:* Painting.

WADDY, Lawrence H(eber) 1914-

PERSONAL: Born October 5, 1914, in Parramatta, Australia; son of Percival S. (a canon, Episcopal Church) and Etheldred (Spittal) Waddy. *Education:* Balliol College, Oxford, B.A., 1937, M.A., 1945. *Home:* 5910 Camino De La Costa, La Jolla, Calif. 92037. *Office:* 743 Prospect St., La Jolla, Calif. 92037.

CAREER: Clergyman, Church of England. Winchester College, Winchester, Hampshire, England, chaplain and teacher of classics, 1938-42, 1946-49; Tonbridge School, Tonbridge, Kent, England, headmaster, 1949-62; British Broadcasting Corp., London, England, education officer, religious broadcaster, and writer, 1962-63; The Bishop's School, La Jolla, Calif., chaplain, associate in administration, and teacher, 1963-67; University of California, San Diego, lecturer in classics, 1969—; Church of the Good Samaritan, vicar, 1970—. University of California, Berkeley, lecturer in classics, 1961. Honorary canon of Rochester, England, 1961-63; honorary chaplain to Bishop of Rochester, 1963-67. *Military service:* Royal Naval Volunteer Reserve, chaplain, 1942-46. *Member:* Royal Institute of International Affairs, English-Speaking Union, Society of Authors. *Awards, honors:* British Broadcasting Corp. production of his musical play, ''Job,'' was a prize-winner at Monte Carlo Film Festival, 1964.

WRITINGS: Pax Romana and World Peace, Chapman & Hall, 1950; *The Prodigal Son* (musical play), Samuel French, 1963.

Television plays broadcast in England: ''The Wedding Feast''; ''The Prodigal Son''; ''Job''; ''The Good Samaritan''; ''Jonah and the Whale.'' Also author of thirteen radio plays for Episcopal Church series, ''The Witness,'' 1964. Contributor to *American Journal of Archaeology* and other periodicals.

WORK IN PROGRESS: Musical plays for television, radio, and publication; also religious dramas with music (contemporary), to be acted in modern dress, for local production.

*   *   *

WADE, John Stevens 1927-
(Clysle Stevens)

PERSONAL: Original name Clysle Stevens; born December 8, 1927, in Smithfield, Me.; son of Earl Wade and Leanora May (Witham) Stevens; married Stella Rachel Taschlicky, June 13, 1954; children: Juanita, John Stevens. *Education:* Connecticut State Teachers College (now Central Connecticut State College), B.S., 1953. *Address:* P.O. Box 14, Mt. Vernon, Maine 04352.

CAREER: Formerly a hotel manager; now poet, painter, and farmer. Editor and founder, *Northeast Literary Magazine*, 1963-64, *Dimension*, 1964—. *Military service:* U.S. Army, 1945-47.

WRITINGS—All poetry: (Under name Clysle Stevens) *Loose Stones: First Poems*, E. R. Hitchcock Co., 1954; *Climbs of Uncertainty*, New Athenaeum Press, 1961; *Two From Where It Snows*, Northeast Chapbook Series, 1964; *Drowning In The Dark*, The Group (Holland), 1965; (translator) *Poems from the Lowlands*, Small Pond, 1967; *Gallery*, Poet & Printer (London), 1969; *The Cats in the Colosseum*, Crossing Press, 1973. Work represented in many anthologies, including *Man: In the Poetic Mode*, McDougal, Little, 1970; *It's Only A Movie*, Prentice-Hall, 1971; *An Anthology of Contemporary Poetry*, Peace &

Pieces Press, 1972. Contributor to over 350 magazines, reviews, and journals, world wide.

SIDELIGHTS: Wade's travels include most Western European nations. His poetry has been translated into French, Italian, Arabic, and Flemish.

*   *   *

WAGLEY, Charles (Walter) 1913-

PERSONAL: Born November 9, 1913, in Clarksville, Tex.; son of Walter Clarence and Sally (Riddling) Wagley; married Cecilia Roxo, September 12, 1941; children: Isabel Anne, Carlos William. *Education:* University of Oklahoma, student, 1931-34; Columbia University, A.B., 1936, Ph.D., 1941. *Home:* 1760 Northwest Eight Ave., Gainesville, Fla. 32611. *Office:* Center for Latin American Studies, University of Florida, Gainesville, Fla. 32611.

CAREER: Museu Nacional, Rio de Janeiro, Brazil, visiting lecturer and curator, 1941-42; U.S. government, member of Institute of Inter-America Affairs field party in Brazil, 1942-45; John Simon Guggenheim Foundation, New York, N.Y., member of staff, 1945-47; Columbia University, New York, N.Y., assistant professor of anthropology, 1946-49; Social Science Research Council, New York, N.Y., member of staff, 1948-49; Columbia University, associate professor, 1949-53, professor of anthropology, beginning 1953, director of Institute of Latin America Studies, 1961—; University of Florida, Gainesville, Graduate Research Professor of anthropology, 1971—. Fulbright professor to Brazil, 1962. Bahai State (Brazil)–Columbia University Research Program, director, 1950-53. National Research Council, member, 1948—. *Member:* American Anthropological Association (fellow; executive board, 1959-62), Social Science Research Council, American Ethnological Society (president, 1957-58). *Awards, honors:* Order of Southern Cross (Brazil), 1946; Fellow, Center for Advanced Study in the Behavioral Sciences, 1957-58; honorary doctorate, University of Bahia, 1962; honorary doctor in law, University of Notre Dame, 1964.

WRITINGS: Economics of a Guatemalan Village, American Anthropological Association, 1941; *Social and Religious Life of a Guatemalan Village*, American Anthropological Association, 1949; (with Eduardo Galvao) *Tenetehara Indians of Brazil*, Columbia University Press, 1949; (editor and contributor) *Race and Class in Rural Brazil*, UNESCO, 1952; *Amazon Town: A Study of Man in the Tropics*, Macmillan, 1953; (with M. Harris) *Minorities in the New World: Six Case Studies*, Columbia University Press, 1958; *An Introduction to Brazil*, Columbia University Press, 1963; (editor) *Man in the Amazon*, University of Florida Press, 1973. Contributor of articles and reviews to journals.

WORK IN PROGRESS: South American ethnology.

SIDELIGHTS: Charles Wagley is fluent in Spanish and Portuguese.

*   *   *

WAGNER, Harvey M. 1931-

PERSONAL: Born November 20, 1931, in San Francisco, Calif.; married Ruth G. Glesby, June 26, 1954; children: Caroline Beth, Julie Lynne. *Education:* Stanford University, B.S., 1953, M.S., 1954; King's College, Cambridge, research, 1954-55; Massachusetts Institute of Technology, Ph.D., 1960; other study at University of California, Los Angeles, 1950, 1951, at Oxford University, 1952. *Home:*

Tulip Tree Lane, Woodbridge, Conn. 06525. *Office:* Advanced Science Department, Yale University, 2 Hillhouse Ave., New Haven, Conn. 06520.

CAREER: Massachusetts Institute of Technology, School of Industrial Management, Cambridge, instructor, 1955-57; Stanford University, Graduate School of Business, Stanford, Calif., assistant professor, 1957-60, associate professor, 1960-63, professor of business administration, industrial engineering and statistics, 1963-67; Yale University, New Haven, Conn., director of doctoral, professor, administrative sciences, 1967—. Currently consultant to RAND Corp. and McKinsey & Co. San Mateo County (Calif.) United Fund, chairman of admissions and allocations committee, 1963-65.

MEMBER: American Economics Association, American Statistical Association, Econometric Society, Institute of Mathematical Statistics, The Institute of Management Science (president, Northern California chapter, 1961-62; American chairman, international meeting in Tokyo, 1963; member of council, 1969-71, 1972—; national president, 1973-74), Operations Research Society (chairman of education committee, 1963-64; vice-chairman of Western section, 1964; chairman of Western section, 1965-66; council member, 1972—), Phi Beta Kappa, Sigma Xi. *Awards, honors:* Marshall scholarship (British government grant) for research at Cambridge University, 1954-55; Ford Foundation faculty research fellowship, 1963-64; research grants from Western Management Science Institute, 1960-65, National Science Foundation, 1962-68; National Science Foundation travel grant, 1963-72, office of Naval Research grant, 1973—; Army Research Office grant, 1974—. Recipient, Lanchester prize, Operations Research Society of America, 1969; Maynard Book award, 1970.

WRITINGS: Statistical Management of Inventory Systems, Operations Research Society and Wiley, 1962; (with John Haldi) *Simulated Economic Models*, Irwin, 1963; (contributor) *Industrial Scheduling*, edited by Muth and Thompson, Prentice-Hall, 1963; (editor with C. Bonini and R. Jaedicke) *Management Controls: New Directions in Basic Research*, McGraw, 1964; *Principles of Operations Research with Applications to Managerial Decisions*, Prentice-Hall, 1969; *Principles of Management Science with Applications to Executive Decisions*, Prentice-Hall, 1970.

Author or co-author of technical reports published by Stanford Computation Center, Stanford University, and RAND Corp. Contributor of more than fifty articles, and reviews to *Harvard Business Review, American Economic Review, Management Science*, other economic, business, and statistical journals. Associate editor, *Journal of ASA*, 1963-69; departmental editor, *Management Science*, 1969-72.

*　　*　　*

WAINWRIGHT, J(oseph) Allan 1921-

PERSONAL: Born February 23, 1921, in London, England; son of Joseph (a civil servant) and Beatrice Mary (Morris) Wainwright; married Margaret Clark (a science teacher), April 10, 1951; children: Patricia, Rachel. *Education:* King's College, London, theological associateship and B.D. (first class honors), 1950. *Home:* 169 Hampstead Way, London, N.W.11, England. *Office:* British Council of Churches, 10 Eaton Gate, London S.W. 1, England.

CAREER: Ordained priest, Church of England, 1950. St. James' Church, Boston, Lincolnshire, England, priest-in-charge, 1950-53; St. Paul's College of Education, Cheltenham, Gloucestershire, England, head of divinity department, 1953-62; British Council of Churches, London, England, education secretary, 1962—. *Military service:* British Army, Royal Artillery, 1939-45; became acting captain. *Member:* Institute of Christian Education (member of council), Society for Old Testament Study.

WRITINGS: The Role of the Church Training Colleges for Teachers, 1960; *The Story of the English New Testament*, Hulton, 1961; *God and Man in the Old Testament*, S.P.C.K., 1962; (with M. Hardin) *The Fall of a City* (Jeremiah), S.C.M. Press, 1962; *Notes on Examinations in Religious Knowledge*, Hulton, 1963; *Church and School*, Oxford University Press, 1963. Contributor to *Learning for Living, School Librarian, View-Review, Times Educational Supplement*, and *Church Times*.

WORK IN PROGRESS: Research for experimental syllabuses in religious teaching in schools.†

*　　*　　*

WAITZMANN, Dorothea 1915-

PERSONAL: Born April 2, 1915, in Chicago, Ill.; daughter of Otto and Clara (Frerck) Waitzmann. *Education:* Attended Convent of the Sacred Heart, Chicago, Ill., 1933; St. Norbert College, B.S., 1963. *Religion:* Congregational. *Office: Green Bay Register*, Green Bay, Wis.

CAREER: Western Newspaper Union, Frankfort, Ky., free-lance feature writer, 1942-51; free-lance writer, and columnist for *Green Bay Register*, Green Bay, Wis., 1964—. *Member:* Business and Professional Women's Club, Christian Writers and Editors, Brown County Historical Society.

WRITINGS: (With Georgia Harkness) *A Special Way of Victory*, John Knox, 1964.

WORK IN PROGRESS: A second book; a historical series featuring documents, legislation, and judicial proceedings involved in the development of present day rights and procedures.

SIDELIGHTS: Ms. Waitzmann is competent in French and Latin, and knows some German. *Avocational interests:* Classical and light music, baseball, poetry.†

*　　*　　*

WAKEFIELD, Robert A. 1916-

PERSONAL: Born March 18, 1916, in Bridgeport, Conn.; married Donna M. Sinkey, February 12, 1940; children: Sandra Lillian, John Carter. *Education:* University of Southern California, A.B., 1940; University of California, Los Angeles, M.Ed. (with honors), 1958, Ed.D., 1964. *Politics:* Independent. *Religion:* Christian Science. *Home:* 295 Mabery Rd., Santa Monica, Calif. 90402.

CAREER: Santa Monica (Calif.) Unified School District, director of testing, counselor, 1955—; University of California Extension, Los Angeles, instructor, 1964—. *Member:* American Personnel and guidance Association, National Education Association, Council for Exceptional Children (president of Los Angeles County chapter, 1964-65), California Teachers Association, California Counseling and Guidance Association, Phi Delta Kappa.

WRITINGS: Basic Dictionary Skills, Scott, 1954; *Thinking and Driving*, Stanwix House, 1971; *Thinking and Driving Teachers Manual*, Stanwix House, 1971. Contributor to professional journals.

AVOCATIONAL INTERESTS: Gardening, bird watching.

WAKOSKI, Diane 1937-
(Diane Wakoski-Sherbell)

PERSONAL: Born August 3, 1937, in Whittier, Calif.; daughter of John Joseph and Marie (Mengel) Wakoski; married S. Shepard Sherbell (a magazine editor), October 22, 1965; *Education:* University of California, Berkeley, B.A., 1960. *Home:* 403 West 21st St., New York, N.Y. 10011.

CAREER: British Book Centre, New York, N.Y., bookstore clerk, 1960-63; Junior High School 22, New York, N.Y., English teacher, 1963—. *Awards, honors:* Robert Frost fellowship in poetry from Bread Loaf Writers Conference, 1966.

WRITINGS: Coins and Coffins, Hawk's Well Press, 1962; (with Rochelle Owens, Barbara Moraff, Carol Berge) *Four Young Lady Poets*, edited by LeRoi Jones, Totem-Corinth, 1962; *Discrepancies and Apparitions*, Doubleday, 1966; *The George Washington Poems*, Riverrun Press, 1967; *The Diamond Merchant*, Sans Souci Press, 1968; *Inside the Blood Factory*, Doubleday, 1968; *Talking from Christmas*, Black Sparrow Press, 1968; *Greed* (3 volumes), Black Sparrow Press, 1968-71; *The Lament of the Lady Bank Dick*, Sans Souci Press, 1969; *The Moon has a Complicated Geography*, Odda Tala, 1969; *Poems*, Key Printing Co., 1969; *Some Black Poems for the Buddha's Birthday*, Pierripont Press, 1969; *Thanking my Mother for Piano Lessons*, Perishable Press, 1969; *Black Dream Ditty for Billy "the Kid"*, Black Sparrow Press, 1970; *The Magellanic Clouds*, Black Sparrow Press, 1970; *The Motorcycle Betrayal Poems*, Simon & Schuster, 1971; *On Barbara's Shore: A Poem*, Black Sparrow Press, 1971; *The Nest*, Black Sparrow Press, 1971; *The Pumpkin Pie*, Black Sparrow Press, 1972; *Smudging*, Black Sparrow Press, 1972; *Dancing on the Grave of a Son of a Bitch*, Black Sparrow Press, 1973; *Trilogy*, Doubleday, 1974. Editor of *Dream Sheet* and *Software*.

AVOCATIONAL INTERESTS: Astrology.

BIOGRAPHICAL/CRITICAL SOURCES: Carolyn Riley, editor, *Contemporary Literary Criticism*, Gale, Volume II, 1974, Volume IV, 1975.†

*   *   *

WALDO, Willis H. 1920-

PERSONAL: Born September 27, 1920, in Detroit, Mich.; son of Howard Clelland (a civil engineer) and Helen (Kendall) Waldo; married Anna Lee Van Artsdale, August 27, 1949; children: Judith Ann, Sara Kendall, Dale Frederick, Patricia Gwyn, Richard Kirk. *Education:* Washington and Jefferson College, B.S., 1942; University of Maryland, M.S., 1950. *Politics:* Republican. *Religion:* Presbyterian. *Home:* 1471 Wilton Lane, Kirkwood, Mo. *Office:* Monsanto Co., 800 North Lindbergh Blvd., St. Louis, Mo.

CAREER: E. I. duPont de Nemours & Co., Inc., Wilmington, Del., control chemist, 1942-45; Socony-Vacuum Oil Co., Paulsboro, N.J., special analytical research assistant, 1945-46; American University, Washington D.C., lecturer in chemistry, 1947; Monsanto Chemical Co., technical editor, Miamisburg, Ohio, 1949-53, research group leader, St. Louis, Mo., 1953-61, information manager, St. Louis, 1961—. National Academy of Sciences-National Research Council, member of committee on modern methods of handling chemical information. American Chemical Society, Chemical Abstracts Service, member of advisory board. *Member:* American Chemical Society, American Documentation Institute, Research Society of America, Society of Technical Writers and Publishers, Sigma Xi, Alpha Chi Sigma.

WRITINGS: Better Report Writing, Reinhold, 1957, 2nd revised and enlarged edition, 1965. Contributor of over a dozen technical papers on report writing and reporting by computer to journals.

WORK IN PROGRESS: Reports by Computer; research on chemical information retrieval computer programs.†

*   *   *

WALDRON, Ann Wood 1924-

PERSONAL: Born December 14, 1924, in Birmingham, Ala.; daughter of Earl Watson (a bookkeeper) and Elizabeth (Roberts) Wood; married Martin O. Waldron (a newspaper reporter), October 18, 1947; children: Peter, Laura, Thomas William, Pennington. *Education:* University of Alabama, A.B., 1945. *Politics:* Democrat. *Religion:* Presbyterian. *Home:* 2225 Albans Rd., Houston, Tex. 77005. *Office: Houston Chronicle*, Houston, Tex. 77002.

CAREER: St. Petersburg Times, St. Petersburg, Fla., former Tallahassee correspondent and weekly columnist; currently book editor for *Houston Chronicle*, Houston, Tex. *Member:* Theta Sigma Phi, Alpha Delta Pi.

WRITINGS: (With Allen Morris) *Your Florida Government*, University of Florida Press, 1965; *The House on Pendleton Block*, Hastings House, 1974.

*   *   *

WALKDEN, George Brian 1923-

PERSONAL: Born May 28, 1923, in England; son of George Roland (a headmaster) and Gladys M. Walkden; married Mary Elizabeth Wilkie, November, 1947; children: Michael David, Rosemary Frances. *Education:* Attended Manchester Grammar School and took courses at University of Manchester. *Home:* 21 Millyard Crescent, Woodingdean, Brighton 7, Sussex, England. *Office: Amateur Gardening*, 2-10 Tavistock St., Covent Garden, London W.C. 2, England.

CAREER: Was in charge of a small nursery for a time, then became a lecturer and show organizer for a concern manufacturing cloches, in Surrey, England, 1945-47; *Amateur Gardening*, London, England, assistant editor, 1947—; *Modern Woman*, London, England, gardening correspondent, 1961—.

*WRITINGS—*All published by Collingridge: *Gardening in Pictures*, 1952; *Cloche Cultivation*, 1955; *Garden Making*, 1956; *Garden Carpentry*, 1960; *Vegetables*, 1961; *Aids to Better Gardening*, David & Charles, 1973. Editor of a 1964 and 1965 guide to new plants and equipment.

SIDELIGHTS: Walkden has produced 16mm. films on gardening for *Amateur Gardening*.†

*   *   *

WALKER, Alan 1911-

PERSONAL: Born June 4, 1911, in Sydney, Australia; son of Alfred Edgar (a clergyman) and Louise (Lavis) Walker; married Winifred Channon, March 26, 1938; children: Lynette, Bruce, David, Christopher. *Education:* University of Sydney, B.A. and M.A.; also studied at Leigh Theological College, Sydney, Australia. *Home:* 16 Corona Ave., Roseville, New South Wales, Australia. *Office:* Central Methodist-Mission, Wesley Centre, 210 Pitt St., Sydney, New South Wales, Australia.

CAREER: Methodist minister in Australia. Associate director of New South Wales Methodist Youth Department, 1936-38, minister in Cessnock, New South Wales, 1939-44; superintendent minister at Waverly Methodist mission, 1944-54; director of Australian Mission (Methodist) to the Nation, 1955-56; leader of mission to United States, 1956-57; superintendent of Central Methodist Mission, Sydney, New South Wales, 1958—. Founder of Sydney Life Line Centre. Adviser, Australian delegation to United Nations, 1949. Currently conductor of Australian television program, "I Challenge the Minister." *Awards, honors:* Officer, Order of the British Empire; honorary D.D. Bethany Theological Seminary, Chicago, Ill.

WRITINGS: Coal-Town: A Sociological Survey, Oxford University Press, 1945; *The Whole Gospel for the New World,* Abingdon, 1957; *A New Mind for a New Age,* Abington, 1958; *God Is Where You Are,* Lutterworth, 1961; *The Many-Sided Cross of Jesus,* Epworth, 1962, published as *How Jesus Helped People,* Abingdon, 1964; *A Ringing Call to Mission,* Abingdon, 1966; *God, The Disturber,* Word, 1973; *Jesus, The Liberator,* Abingdon, 1973.

WORK IN PROGRESS: A book, *The New Evangelism.*

* * *

WALKER, Elinor 1911-

PERSONAL: Born March 16, 1911, in Enderlin, N.D.; daughter of Charles Emerson (a barber) and Cora (Freeman) Walker. *Education:* Macalester College, B.A., 1933; University of Minnesota, B.S., 1944. *Home:* 625 Brummel St., Evanston, Ill. 60202. *Office:* American Library Association 50 East Huron St., Chicago, Ill. 60611.

CAREER: Librarian and high school teacher in Cottonwood, Minn., 1937-41, and Plainview, Minn., 1941-43; St. Paul (Minn.) Public Library, young adult librarian, 1943-46; American Library Association, Chicago, Ill., young adult editor of *ALA Booklist,* 1946-48; Carneigie Library of Pittsburgh, Pittsburgh, Pa., coordinator of work with young people, 1948-70; currently young adult book reviewer for American Library Association, Chicago, Ill. Moderator of programs with teen-age participants on KQV Radio, 1949-50, WQED-TV, 1956, and WJAS Radio, 1962-68. *Member:* American Library Association (president of Young Adult Services Division, 1949-50; president of Public Library Association, 1959-60), World Affairs Forum for Youth (head of bibliographic committee, 1951-56), Pittsburgh Library Club (president, 1964-65).

WRITINGS: (Editor) *Book Bait,* American Library Association, 1957, 2nd edition, 1969; (editor with Donald Allyn, Helen Lutton, and Alice Johnson) *Doors to More Mature Reading,* American Library Association, 1964. Associate editor, then editor, of *Top of the News,* 1952-54.

AVOCATIONAL INTERESTS: Travel, painting, kniting and other handicraft, cooking and baking.

* * *

WALKER, Leo

PERSONAL: Son of Edson L. (a farmer) and Margaret (McInerney) Walker; married Inez Margaret Lehrbach, June 5, 1936; children: Maurice Edward. *Education:* Creighton University, student, 1930-31. *Politics:* Republican. *Religion:* Catholic. *Home:* 1845 Fern Lane, Glendale, Calif. 91208.

CAREER: Professional musician, 1930-35; Littrell Supply Co., Grants Pass, Ore., salesman, 1935-41; E. I. du Pont Co., Seattle, Wash., salesman, 1941-45; Minnesota Mining and Manufacturing Co., salesman, San Francisco, Calif. 1945-52, division sales manager, St. Louis, Mo., 1952-58, Los Angeles, Calif., 1958—. *Member:* San Francisco Press Club, Hollywood Press Club.

WRITINGS: The Wonderful Era of the Great Dance Bands, Howell-North, 1964. Also writer of articles on people in the music business.

WORK IN PROGRESS: Profiles of the Big Band Era; a novel based on the career of a name band leader.†

* * *

WALKER, Peter F(ranklin) 1931-

PERSONAL: Born July 24, 1931, in Knoxville, Tenn.; son of Franklin Trenaby and Anna (Lansdell) Walker; children: Franklin Trenaby. *Education:* Mississippi College, A.B., 1951; Vanderbilt University, M.A., 1954, Ph.D., 1958. *Office:* Department of History, University of North Carolina, Chapel Hills, N.C.

CAREER: University of North Carolina, Chapel Hill, assistant professor of history, 1958—. *Military service:* U.S. Marine Corps, 1951-53; became major. *Member:* American Historical Association, Southern Historical Association, Organization of American Historians.

WRITINGS: Vicksburg: A People at War 1860-65, University of North Carolina Press, 1960. Contributor to *Encyclopaedia Britannica* and *Journal of Tennessee History.*†

* * *

WALKER, Robert H(arris) 1924-

PERSONAL: Born March 15, 1924, in Cincinnati, Ohio; married Grace V. Burtt, 1953; children: three. *Education:* Northwestern University, B.S., 1945; Columbia University, M.A., 1950; University of Pennsylvania, Ph.D., 1955; additional study at University of Colorado and Oklahoma State University, 1945-46, Universite de Montpellier and College de Cannes, 1950, University of Pittsburgh and University of Cincinnati, 1951. *Home:* 3915 Huntington St. N.W., Washington, D.C. 20006. *Office:* George Washington University, Washington, D.C. 20006.

CAREER: U.S. Military Government, Shizuoka, Japan, education specialist, 1946-47; instructor at Carnegie Institute of Technology (now Carnegie-Mellon University), Pittsburgh, Pa., 1950-51, University of Pennsylvania, Philadelphia, 1953-54, Haverford College, Haverford, Pa., 1954-55; University of Wyoming, Laramie, assistant professor of American studies, 1955-59, acting director of School of American Studies, 1956-59; George Washington University, Washington, D.C., associate professor of American literature, 1959-63, professor of American civilization, 1963—. Director of American Studies Program, 1959-66, 1968-70; director of education and public programs, National Endowment for the Humanities, 1966-68. Visiting summer professor at Jamestown College, 1961, Stetson University, 1965, and University of Hawaii, 1967. Consultant to U.S. Information Agency, 1959—, and to other government and private agencies. *Military service:* U.S. Naval Reserve, 1942-61; on active duty, 1943-46; became lieutenant junior grade.

MEMBER: American Studies Association (chairman of committee on research in humanities, 1963—; president of Chesapeake chapter, 1963-65; national president, 1970-71), Organization of American Historians, Phi Beta Kappa, Cosmos Club. *Awards, honors:* U.S. Department of State specialist grants to Japan, 1964, to Germany and Sweden, 1965; Fulbright grant, 1971; fellow Woodrow Wilson International Center, 1972-73.

WRITINGS: American Studies in the United States, Louisiana State University Press, 1958; *The Poet and the Gilded Age*, University of Pennsylvania Press, 1963; *Everyday Life in the Age of Enterprise*, Putnam, 1967; *Life in the Age of Enterprise*, Capricorn, 1971. Author of U.S. Information Service pamphlets, "Recent American Fiction," 1961, "The Literature of Social Protest in America: 1880-1915," 1965; editor of a series of monographs *Contributions in American Studies*, Greendwood Press. 1970—. Contributor of articles and reviews to literary and historical journals. Editor, *American Quarterly*, 1953-54.

WORK IN PROGRESS: "American Literature, 1775-1905," for UNESCO's *The History of the Scientific and Cultural Development of Mankind; The Reform Spirit in America*, a document collection, for Anchor Books.

* * *

WALLACE, Ernest 1906-

PERSONAL: Born June 11, 1906, in Daingerfield, Tex.; son of Thomas (a farmer) and Lula (Barber) Wallace; married Ellen Kegans, April 10, 1926; children: Ernesteen Wallace Barton. *Education*: East Texas State College (now University), B.S. in Ed., 1932; Texas Technological College (now Texas Tech University), M.A., 1935; University of Texas, Ph.D., 1942; Harvard University, postdoctoral study, 1952-53. *Religion*: Episcopalian. *Home*: 3117 45th St. Lubbock, Tex. *Office*: Texas Tech University, Lubbock, Tex. 79409.

CAREER: Texas Tech University, Lubbock, instructor, 1936-41, assistant professor, 1941-43, associate professor, 1943-45, professor of history and assistant dean of School of Arts and Sciences, 1945-55, professor of history, 1955-67, Horn Professor of History, 1967—. University of Texas, visiting summer instructor, 1938, 1939, 1942. U.S. Department of Justice, consultant on Indian Land Suits in the Southwest. Commission on the Coordination of Education in Texas, member, 1950-56; Lubbock Public Schools, member of advisory council, 1958-61.

MEMBER: American Historical Association, Organization of American Historians, Southern Historical Association, Texas State Historical Association (fellow; member of executive council, 1961-70), West Texas Historical Association (president, 1951-52), Texas Archaeological Society (secretary-treasurer, 1947-55; honorary life member), Western Historical Association, Masons, Rotary. *Awards, honors: The Comanches* won the American Institute of Graphic Arts Award for 1952 and was selected by *Western Corral* as one of the ten top books on the American West; Ford Foundation fellowship, 1952-53; West Texas Chamber of Commerce "Cultural Achievement Award for Contributions to the Field of Historical Literature" 1968; "Piper Professor of 1969 for Outstanding Scholarly and Academic Achievement," Minne Stevens Piper Foundation; "Action Award for Contributions to the Enrichment of Culture of the Great Plains," West Texas Museum Association, 1971.

WRITINGS: Charles DeMorse, Pioneer Editor and Statesman, Texas Technological College Press, 1943; (with E. A. Hoebel) *The Comanches*, University of Oklahoma Press, 1952; (contributor) *The Builders of the Southwest*, Texas Technological College Press, 1957; (editor with D. M. Vigness) *Documents of Texas History, 1528-1846*, Library, Texas Technological College, 1960; (editor with Vigness) *Documents of Texas History, 1528-1961*, Steck, 1963; *Ranald S. Mackenzie on the Texas Frontier*, West Texas Museum Association, 1965; *Texas in Turmoil, 1849-1876*, Steck-Vaughn, 1965; (editor) *Ranald S. Mackenzie's Official Correspondence Relating to Texas, 1871-1879*, West Texas Museum Association, 1967-68; (with R.N. Richardson and A. N. Anderson) *Texas: The Lone Star State*, Prentice-Hall, 1970. Contributor to *Handbook of Texas*, 1952, and *Encyclopaedia Britannica*, 1959—. Assistant editor, *West Texas Historical Association Year Book*, 1960—.

SIDELIGHTS: Wallace speaks Spanish, French, German.

* * *

WALLACE, Luther T(ompkins) 1928-

PERSONAL: Born August 16, 1928, in Evanston, Ill.; married Audrey Taylor, September 1, 1951; children: Carey B., Peter L., Barbara A. *Education*: Harvard University, B.A. (cum laude), 1949; Oregon State University, M.S., 1955; Purdue University, Ph.D., 1960. *Office*: University of California, Berkeley, Calif.

CAREER: Self-employed rancher in Crawfordsville, Ore., 1949-54; University of Nevada, Reno, assistant professor, 1955-57; Purdue University, Lafayette, Ind., instructor, 1957-60, assistant professor, 1960-62, associate professor of agricultural economics, 1962-63; Univeristy of California, Berkeley, agriculturist and professor of agricultual economics, 1963—. Senior staff economist on agriculture, President's Council of Economic Advisors, 1968-69. *Member*: American Agricultural Economics Association (member of board of directors, 1971-74), Western Farm Economics Association, Phi Kappa Phi.

WRITINGS: Agriculture, Economics, and Growth, Appleton, 1964, 3rd edition, Prentice-Hall, 1975. Contributor of some eighty articles to periodicals.

WORK IN PROGRESS: Research in local and regional economic growth, land use and water resource development, and the role of agriculture in economic growth.

* * *

WALLACE, Robert 1932-

PERSONAL: Born January 10, 1932, in Springfield, Mo.; son of Roy Franklin and Tincy (Stough) Wallace; married Janeen Ann Weaver (a painter), July 24, 1965. *Education*: Harvard College, B.A. (summa cum laude), 1953; Cambridge University, B.A., 1955, M.A. (honours), 1959. *Home*: 2440 Overlook Rd., Apt. 21, Cleveland, Ohio 44106. *Office*: English Department, Case Western Reserve University, Cleveland, Ohio 44106.

CAREER: Bryn Mawr College, Bryn Mawr, Pa., instructor in English, 1957-61; Sweet Briar College, Sweet Briar, Va., assistant professor of English, 1961-63; Vassar College, Poughkeepsie, N.Y., assistant professor of English, 1963-65; Case Western Reserve University, Cleveland, Ohio, associate professor, 1965-74, professor of English, 1974—. Reader for Book-of-the-Month Club and for Educational Testing Service. *Military service*: U.S. Army, 1955-57. *Awards, honors*: William Rose Benet memorial award, Poetry Society of America, 1957; Bragdon Prize, *Approach* Magazine, 1965.

WRITINGS: This Various World, and Other Poems, Scribner, 1957; (editor with J. G. Taaffe) *Poems on Poetry*, Dutton, 1965; *Views From a Ferris Wheel* (poems), Dutton, 1965; *Ungainly Things* (poems), Dutton, 1968. Poems have appeared in *New Yorker, Atlantic, Harper's, Poetry, Kenyon Review, Saturday Review, Approach, Epoch, Botteghe Oscure, Antioch Review, Chicago Review, Choice, Nation, Poetry Northwest, Wormwood Review, New York Times, New York Herald Tribune, Massachusetts Review, Ladies' Home Journal, Southern Review, Shenandoah, Transatlantic Review, Virginia Quarterly Review, New Republic, Christian Science Monitor*, and other periodicals.

*   *   *

WALLACE, Willard M(osher) 1911-

PERSONAL: Born October 11, 1911, in South Portland, Me.; son of Herbert Henry (a sea captain) and Gertrude (Mosher) Wallace; married Elizabeth Mueller (a supervisor), December 21, 1941; children: Joy (Mrs. Paul D. Wendehack), Pamela. (Mrs David B. Parker). *Education:* Wesleyan University, Middletown, Conn., B.A., 1934, M.A., 1935; University of Pennsylvania, Ph.D., 1940. *Politics:* Democrat. *Religion:* Congregational. *Home:* 840 Worthington Ridge, Berlin, Conn. *Office:* Public Affairs Center, Wesleyan University, Middletown, Conn.

CAREER: Lehigh University, Bethlehem, Pa., instructor in history, 1940; Wesleyan University, Middletown, Conn., assistant professor of history and dean of freshmen, 1946-49, became professor of history. Hartford College for Women, visiting professor of history, 1955-69; Woodrow Wilson Fellowship Committee, regional member, 1955-58. Berlin Free Library, president, 1961-68; Berlin Charter Commission, member, 1962-64. *Military service:* U.S. Army, Medical Administrate Corps, 1941-45; became captain; received Legion of Merit. *Member:* American Historical Association, Conference on British Studies, Historical Association, Conference on British Studies, Company of Military Collectors and Historians, Connecticut Academy of Arts and Sciences, Connecticut Historical Association, Berlin Choral Society (president, 1946-47). *Awards, honors:* Guggenheim Fellow, 1951-52.

WRITINGS: Appeal to Arms: A Military History of the American Revolution, Harper, 1951; *Traitorous Hero: The Life and Fortunes of Benedict Arnold*, Harper, 1954; *Friend William* (juvenile biography of William Penn), Nelson, 1958; *Sir Walter Raleigh*, Princeton University Press, 1959; (with Harold C. Syrett and Jean G. Cooke) *Interview in Weehawken: The Burr-Hamilton Duel Documents*, Wesleyan University Press, 1960; *Soul of the Lion: A Biography of General Joshua L. Chamberlain*, Nelson, 1960; *East to Bagaduce* (novel), Regnery, 1963; *Jonathan Dearborn, A Novel of the War of 1812*, Little, Brown, 1967; *The Raiders, A Novel of the Civil War at Sea*, Little, Brown 1970.

WORK IN PROGRESS: A study of the theory and practice of war, 1968; a history of Wesleyan University.

AVOCATIONAL INTERESTS: Choir and choral singing, gardening, roaming the coast of Maine, watching football.

*   *   *

WALLACE, William N. 1924-
(Bill Wallace)

PERSONAL: Born April 29, 1924, in Washington, D.C.; son of Lew (a businessman) and Josephine (Parrott) Wallace; married Carol Gardner, June 27, 1953; children: Eve, Carol, Josephine. *Education:* Yale University, B.A., 1949.

Home: 658 Pequot Rd., Southport, Conn. *Agent:* Theron Raines, 207 East 37th St., New York, N.Y. 10016. *Office:* New York Times, 229 West 43 St., New York, N.Y.

CAREER: Sportswriter for *New York World-Telegram & Sun*, 1949-57, *New York Herald Tribune*, 1957-62; *New York Times*, New York, N.Y., sportswriter, 1963—. *Military service:* U.S. Army, 1943-46; became technical sergeant. *Member:* Yale Club of New York City, Country Club of Fairfield (Conn.).

WRITINGS—Under name Bill Wallace, except where noted: *Boats and Outboards*, Maco Magazine Press, 1959; *Sailing:* Golden Press, 1960; *Golden Guide To Sailing*, Golden Press, 1961; *The Young Sportsman's Guide to Skiing*, Nelson, 1961; *Golden Guide to Power Boats*, Golden Press, 1962, revised edition, 1966; *Young People's Guide to Skiing*, Nelson, 1962; *Nelson's Encyclopedia of Pro Football*, Nelson, 1964; (under name William N. Wallace) *Macmillan Book of Boating*, Macmillan, 1964; *Nelson's Encyclopedia of Pro Football*, Nelson, 1964; (with Bob Beattie) *Golden Guide to Skiing*, Golden Press, 1966; (under name William N. Wallace) *Frank Gifford*, Prentice-Hall, 1969; *Fly Fishing Digest*, Follett, 1973; *Sailing*, Western Publishing, 1974.†

*   *   *

WALLACH, Michael A(rthur) 1933-

PERSONAL: Born April 8, 1933, in New York, N.Y.; son of Max and Wilma (Cheiker) Wallach; married Lise Wertheimer (a psychologist), July 26, 1959; children: Rachel Paula. *Education:* Swarthmore College, B.A. (highest honors), 1954; Harvard University, graduate student, 1954-55, 1956-58, Ph.D., 1958; Cambridge University, Westengard traveling fellow from Harvard, 1955-56. *Home:* Department of Psychology, Duke University, Durham, N.C. 27706.

CAREER: Harvard University, Cambridge, Mass., instructor in social psychology, 1958-59; Massachusetts Institute of Technology, Cambridge, assistant professor of psychology, 1959-62; Duke University, Durham, N.C., associate professor, 1962-66, professor of psychology, 1966—. Principal or co-principal investigator in research projects for National Institute of Mental Health, 1958-61, U.S. Office of Educaton, 1961-65, National Science Foundation, 1961-63, 1964-67; William S. Gray Professor of Education, University of Chicago, 1972-73. *Awards, honors:* Social Science Research Council research grant, 1962.

WRITINGS: (Contributor) *Psychopathology of Aging*, edited by P. H. Hoch and J. Zubin, Grune, 1961; (contributor) *Measurement in Personality and Cognition*, edited by S. Messick and J. Ross, Wiley, 1962; (contributor) *Child Psychology: The Sixty-Second Yearbook of the National Society for the Study of Education*, Part I, edited by H. W. Stevenson, University of Chicago Press, 1963; (with Kogan) *Risk Taking: A Study in Cognition and Personality*, Holt, 1964; (contributor) *Behavioral Science and Human Survival*, edited by M. Schwebel, Science and Behavior, 1965; (with Kogan) *Modes of Thinking in Young Children: A Study of the Creativity-Intelligence Distinction*, Holt, 1965; (contributor with Kogan) *New Directions in Psychology III*, Holt, 1967; (with C. W. Wing, Jr.) *The Talented Student: A Validation of the Creativity-Intelligence Distinction*, Holt, 1969; (contributor) *Carmichael's Manual of Child Psychology*, Volume I, edited by P. H. Mussen, Wiley, 3rd edition, 1970; (with Wing) *College Admission and the Psychology of Talent*, Holt, 1971; *The*

Intelligence/Creativity Distinction, General Learning Press, 1971. Author of monographs. Contributor of about thirty articles to psychological jouranls. Editor, *Journal of Personality*, 1963-72.

* * *

WALLOP, Lucille Fletcher 1912-
(Lucille Fletcher)

PERSONAL: Born March 28, 1912; daughter of Matthew Emerson (a marine draftsman) and Violet (Anderson) Fletcher; married John Douglass Wallop III (a writer), January 6, 1949; children: (previous marriage) Dorothy Louise Herrmann, Wendy Elizabeth Herrmann. *Education:* Vassar College, B.A., 1933. *Home and office:* Avon Light, Oxford, Md. 21654. *Agent:* William Morris Agency, 1740 Broadway, New York, N.Y. 10019.

CAREER: Author.

WRITINGS—Under name, Lucille Fletcher; all published by Random House, except as indicated: (With Allan Ullman) *Sorry, Wrong Number*, 1949; (with Ullman) *Night Man*, 1951; *The Daughters of Jasper Clay*, Henry Holt, 1958; *Blindfold*, 1960; *And Presumed Dead*, 1963; *The Strange Blue Yawl*, 1964; *The Girl in Cabin B54*, 1968; *Night Watch* (play, produced at Morosco Theatre, Broadway, February 28, 1972), 1972. Writer of radio and screen adaptions of *Sorry, Wrong Number* and *Night Man*, of twenty radio plays for "Suspense" series, and of television scripts for "Chrysler Theatre" and "Lights Out" programs.

SIDELIGHTS: Films of Lucille Wallop's books, *Blindfold* and *And Presumed Dead*, have also been produced.†

* * *

WARD, Dennis 1924-

PERSONAL: Born February 1, 1924, in Rotherham, England; son of Clifford (a steelworker) and Doris (Duke) Ward; married Doreen Mary Robinson, May 25, 1946; children: Ann-Mari, John Maxim, Adam Christopher. *Education:* Christ's College, Cambridge, B.A., 1948, M.A., 1950. *Home:* 21 Clermiston Rd., Edinburgh 12, Scotland. *Office:* Department of Russian, David Hume Tower, George Sq., Edinburgh 8, Scotland.

CAREER: University of Edinburgh, Edinburgh, Scotland, 1949—, began as lecturer, became professor of Russian, 1963—. *Military service:* British Army, 1943-47; became captain. *Member:* Association Phonetique Internationale, Linguistics Association of Great Britian, British Universities' Association of Slavists, Great Britain-USSR Association, Association of Teachers of Russian.

WRITINGS: Russian Pronunciation—A Practical Course, Oliver & Boyd, 1958; *Russian for Scientists*, University of London Press, 1960; *Keep Up Your Russian*, British Broadcasting Corp., 1961, 2nd edition, Harrap, 1963; (with M. Greene) *Graded Russian Readers*, Books 1-3, Oliver & Boyd, 1961-62; *Starting Russian*, British Broadcasting Corp., 1962; (editor) M. Yu. Lermontov, *Demon*, 2nd edition, Bradda Books, 1964; *Introduction to Russian*, British Broadcasting Corp., 1964; *The Russian Language Today*, Hutchinson, 1964; *Russian Pronunciation Illustrated*, Cambridge University Press, 1966; (with D. Jones) *The Phonetics of Russian*, Cambridge University Press, 1969; (contributor) D. S. Worth, editor, *The Slavic Word*, Mouton, 1972.

Writer of scripts for British Broadcasting Corp. Contributor

to Slavic studies and reviews. Editor, Cambridge University Press "Russian Language Series."

SIDELIGHTS: Dennis Ward is competent in Russian, French, German, Serbo-Croat, old Slavonic, and other Slavic languages. *Avocational interests:* Painting.

* * *

WARD, John Owen 1919-

PERSONAL: Born September 20, 1919, in London, England; son of John Dudley (an underwriter) and Betty (Snow) Ward; married Maya Riviere (a research consultant), August, 1954. *Education:* Oxford University, M.A., 1952. *Office:* Boosey & Hawkes, 30 West 57th St., New York, N.Y. 10019.

CAREER: Antiquarian music dealer in London, England, 1938-49; assistant to Percy Scholes in Switzerland and Oxford, England, 1949-56; Oxford University Press, New York, N.Y., manager of music department, 1957-72; Boosey & Hawkes, New York, N.Y., director of serious music, 1972—. *Military service:* British Army, Royal Artillery, 1940-46; became staff sergeant. *Member:* Royal Musical Association, International Musicological Association, American Musicological Association, Society for Italian Studies.

WRITINGS: (Editor) Percy Scholes, *Oxford Companion to Music*, 10th edition, Oxford University Press, 1970; (editor) *Junior Companion to Music*, Oxford University Press, 1954; (editor) *Concise Oxford Dictionary of Music*, 2nd edition, Oxford University Press, 1964; *Careers in Music*, Walck, 1968.

SIDELIGHTS: John Ward speaks Italian, German, French.

* * *

WARDEN, Lewis (Christopher) 1913-

PERSONAL: Born August 26, 1913, near St. Clairsville, Ohio; son of Christopher Militzer (an accountant) and Alice (Lewis) Warden; married Emma Wallace, August 26, 1939; children: Rebecca, Deborah. *Education:* Ohio State University, A.B., 1934; Harvard University, LL.B. (since converted to J.D.), 1969. *Home:* 1903 Northeast 15th St., Gainesville, Fla. 32601.

CAREER: Licensed to preach by The Methodist Church, 1931; pastor of country churches in Ohio, 1932-34; minister in Lowell, Mass., 1934-35; admitted to Ohio State bar, 1938; attorney in private practice in Columbus, Ohio, 1938-42, Gallipolis, Ohio, 1943-45; Lawyers Cooperative Publishing Co., Rochester, N.Y., writer and editor, 1950—, supervising editor, 1961-68, project editor, 1968—. Elected Republican county chairman, Gallia County, Ohio, 1943, common pleas judge, Gallia County, 1944. District chairman, United Service Organization, 1944-45. *Military service:* U.S. Army, 1942; discharged because of injury. *Member:* Phi Beta Kappa, Delta Sigma Rho, Pi Sigma Alpha, Phi Eta Sigma. *Awards, honors:* Presidential Certificate of Commendation for aid to Selective Service System, 1946.

WRITINGS: The New Crusade, R. G. Adams, 1934; *The Life of Blackstone*, Michie, 1938; *Torrent of the Willows* (novel), Vantage, 1954; *Murder on Wheels* (mystery novel), Bouregy, 1964. Also editor of *American Jurisprudence*, 2nd edition, 1972—.

Contributor; all published by Lawyers: *American Law*

Reports, 2nd edition, 1950-53; *Ohio Jurisprudence*, 2nd edition, 1953-56; *Florida Jurisprudence*, 1956-58; *New York Jurisprudence*, 1958-62; *American Jurisprudence*, 2nd edition, 1962—. Also contributor to *Columbus Dispatch, Case and Comment*, and *Harvard Law School Bulletin*.

WORK IN PROGRESS: Articles for jurisprudence volumes; a novel.

*   *   *

WARDROPPER, Bruce W(ear)   1919-

PERSONAL: Born February 2, 1919, in Edinburgh, Scotland; came to United States, 1945; son of Joseph B. and Edna (Bruce) Wardropper; married Joyce Vaz, December 15, 1942 (died March, 1959); married Nancy Palmer, July 19, 1960; children: (first marriage) Ian Bruce. *Education:* Cambridge University, B.A. (honors), 1939, M.A., 1942; University of Pennsylvania, Ph.D., 1949. *Home:* 3443 Rugby Rd., Hope Valley, Durham, N.C. 27707. *Office:* Duke University, Durham, N.C. 27706.

CAREER: Wolmer's School, Kingston, Jamaica, teacher of modern languages and head of department, 1940-45; University of Pennsylvania, Philadelphia, instructor, 1945-49; Johns Hopkins University, Baltimore, Md., assistant professor, 1949-53, associate professor of Romance languages, 1953-55, chairman of department, 1954-55; Ohio State University, Columbus, professor of Spanish, 1955-59; Johns Hopkins University, professor of Spanish, 1959-62; Duke University, Durham, N.C., W. H. Wannamaker Professor of Romance Languages, 1962—. Visiting professor of Romance languages at Pennsylvania State University, 1951, Harvard University, 1954, University of North Carolina, 1967-68, and California State University, Los Angeles, 1973. Visiting Andrew Mellon Professor of Romance Languages at University of Pittsburgh, 1965.

MEMBER: Modern Language Association of America, Asociacion Internacional de Hispanistas, Modern Humanities Research Association, Renaissance Society of America, Association of Hispanists of Great Britain and Ireland. *Awards, honors:* Guggenheim fellowships, 1952, 1959; grants-in-aid from American Philosophical Society, 1957, and American Council of Learned Societies, 1959.

WRITINGS: Introduccion al teatro religioso del Siglo de Oro, Revista de Occidente (Madrid), 1953; (editor) *Cancionero espiritual*, Castalia (Valencia), 1954; *Historia de la poesia lirica a lo divino*, Revista de Occidente, 1959; (editor) *Critical Essays on Calderon*, New York University Press, 1965; (editor) *Poesia elegiaca espanola*, Anaya (Salamanca, Spain), 1967; (contributor) Victor Lange, editor, *Modern Literature II*, Prentice-Hall, 1968; (editor) *Teatro espanol del Siglo de Oro*, Scribner, 1970; (editor) *Spanish Poetry of the Golden Age*, Appleton, 1971; (contributor) J. B. Avalle-Arce and E. Riley, editors, *Suma Cervantina*, Tamesis, 1972. Contributor of scholarly articles to periodicals. Editor, *Modern Language Notes*, 1960-62; member of editorial board, *PMLA*, 1962-69, 1973—.

WORK IN PROGRESS: The urban comedy of Lope de Vega.

SIDELIGHTS: Wardropper has speaking knowledge of French, Spanish, and Italian, and reading knowledge of Latin, German, and Portuguese. *Avocational interests:* Classical Spanish theater; lyric poetry in Spain, particularly folksong.

WARE, George W(hitaker)   1902-

PERSONAL: Born December 22, 1902, in Belen, Miss.; married; children: George W., Jr. *Education:* Mississippi Agricultural and Mechanical College (now Mississippi State University), student, 1920-22; University of Arkansas, B.S., 1924; Cornell University, M.S., 1935. *Politics:* Democrat. *Religion:* Methodist. *Home and office:* 4301 Columbia Pike, Apartment 506, Arlington, Va. 22204.

CAREER: University of Arkansas, Fayetteville, agricultural extension agent in Pine Bluff and Newport, 1925-27, head of horticultural branch experiment station at Hope, 1927-43; U.S. Department of the Army, agricultural institutions officer in Germany, 1946-48; U.S. Department of State, chief of vocational section, E and CR Division, Germany, 1948-52, program officer for Point-Four Agricultural Mission in Brazil, 1952-57, chief of International Cooperation Adninistration Agricultural Mission to Indonesia, 1957-59; Museum of Fine Arts, Little Rock, Ark., director, 1959-61; U.S. Department of Agriculture, Foreign Agricultural Service, Washington, D.C., staff member, 1961-67. *Military service:* With U.S. Army, Military Government officer in Germany, 1943-46; became major. *Member:* American Society of Appraisers, Alpha Zeta, Kappa Alpha.

WRITINGS: Southern Vegetable Crops, American Book Co., 1937, revised edition (with J. P. McCollum) published as *Raising Vegetables*, Interstate, 1959; *German and Austrian Porcelain*, Lothar Woeller Press, 1952, Crown, 1964; (with McCollum) *Producing Vegetable Crops*, Interstate, 1968, revised edition, in press; *The New Guide to Happy Retirement*, 1968. Contributor of articles on domestic and foreign agriculture and agriculture institutions to periodicals.

SIDELIGHTS: Ware's collection of European and Oriental porcelains (three hundred pieces) has been shown in several museums and art centers. The Wares have made liberal gifts of porcelains and/or glass to the Smithsonian Institution, University of Arkansas Museum, Campbell Museum, Tennessee Fine Arts Center, Museum of Science and Industry, and the Southeast Art and Science Center in Arkansas.

*   *   *

WARNE, Clinton L.   1921-

PERSONAL: Born September, 1921, in Binghamton, N.Y.; son of Colston E. (a professor) and Frances (Corbett) Warne; married Katharine, June, 1953; children: Frances, Clinton, Jr., Carolyn. *Education:* University of Colorado, A.B., 1947; Clark University, A.M., 1948; University of Nebraska, Ph.D., 1953. *Religion:* Methodist. *Office:* 1707 University Tower, Cleveland State University, Cleveland, Ohio 44115.

CAREER: Ohio State University, Columbus, associate professor of economics, 1960-65, 1966-67; Cleveland State University, Cleveland, Ohio, professor of economics, 1967—, acting chairman of economics department, 1968-70. Visiting professor at Northernwestern University, 1965-66, and University of Colorado, 1967. *Military service:* U.S. Army, served in the South Pacific, World War II. *Member:* Association Economic Association, Economic History Association, Transportation Association of America, American Council of Consumer Interests (treasurer, 1970-72; first vice-president, 1972-73).

WRITINGS: (With R. D. Patton) *The Development of the*

American Economy, Scott, Foresman, 1953; *Cement*, University of Kansas, 1955.†

* * *

WARNER, H(oyt) Landon 1911-

PERSONAL: Born May 22, 1911, in Cleveland, Ohio; son of Hoyt Landon and Caroline Fay (Wheeler) Warner; married Charlotte Collins, October 27, 1934; children: Hoyt Dinsmore, Charles Collins. *Education:* Harvard University, A.B., 1932, A.M., 1941, Ph.D., 1951. *Politics:* Democrat. *Religion:* Episcopal. *Address:* P.O. Box 390, Gambier, Ohio 43022. *Office:* Department of History, Kenyon College, Gambier, Ohio 43022.

CAREER: W. H. Warner & Co., Cleveland, Ohio, assistant secretary, 1932-37; Kanawha & Hocking Coal and Coke Co., Charleston, W.Va., assistant to general manager, 1937-39; Kenyon College, Gambier, Ohio, assistant professor, 1946-53, associate professor, 1953-56, professor of history, 1956-59, Henry M. Weaver Memorial Professor, 1959-73, professor emeritus, 1973—, chairman of department, 1953-64, 1965-66. Visiting professor in history, Yale University, 1968-69. Member of acquisitions committee, Rutherford B. Hayes Library, Fremont, Ohio, 1957—; member of advisory committee, Ohio Civil War Centennial Committee, 1960-65. *Military service:* U.S. Naval Reserve, 1942-45; became lieutenant commander; received Bronze Star. *Member:* American Historical Association, Organization of American Historians, Ohio Academy of History (president, 1957-58), Ohio Historical Society. *Awards, honors:* Social Science Research Council grant, 1951-53; Ohio Academy of History Achievement Award, 1960, and 1965, and Distinguished Service Award, 1973.

WRITINGS: The Life of Mr. Justice Clarke, Western Reserve University Press, 1959; *Progressivism in Ohio, 1897-1917*, Ohio State University Press and Ohio Historical Society, 1964; (editor and compiler) *Reforming American Life in the Progressive Era*, Jerome Ozer, 1971. Contributor to *The Dictionary of American Biography*.

WORK IN PROGRESS: A book, *Progressive Era in United States, 1900-1920*.

* * *

WARRACK, John 1928-

PERSONAL: Born February 9, 1928, in London, England; son of Guy (a conductor and composer) and Jacynth (Ellerton) Warrack; married second wife, Lucy Beckett; children: Simon, Nigel, Benedict. *Education:* Attended Winchester College, London, England, 1941-46, and Royal College of Music, 1949-52. *Religion:* Church of England. *Home:* Beck House, Rievaulx, Helmsley, York, England.

CAREER: Free-lance oboist in England, especially with the Boyd Neel and Sadler's Wells orchestras, 1950-54; *Daily Telegraph*, London, England, assistant music critic, 1954-61; *Sunday Telegraph*, London, England, chief music critic, 1961-72. Broadcaster on radio and television. City Literary Institute, London, member of governing board, 1964-72. Columnist for *Gramophone*, Harrow, Middlesex, England, 1968—. *Military service:* British Army, Royal Army Educational Corps, 1946-48; served in Greece and Egypt. *Member:* Royal College of Music (associate member), Royal Musical Association, Critics' Circle (chairman of music section, 1959).

WRITINGS: Six Great Composers, Hamish Hamilton, 1958; (with Harold Rosenthal) *Concise Oxford Dictionary of Opera*, Oxford University Press, 1964; *Carl Maria von Weber*, Hamish Hamilton, 1968; *Tchaikovsky*, Hamish Hamilton, 1973. Contributor to *Grove's Dictionary of Music*, 6th edition, and to periodicals and journals in his field, including *Musical Times* and *Music and Letters*. Assistant editor of *Opera*, 1956-61, member of editorial board, 1961—; member of editorial board of *New Berlioz Edition*.

WORK IN PROGRESS: Revision and a new edition of *The Concise Oxford Dictionary of Opera*.

SIDELIGHTS: Warrack told *CA*: "[My] main interests [are] Romanticism as a movement of European thought, especially its manifestation in music."

Warrack has traveled in most European countries, including Russia, as music critic. He is competent in French, German, and Italian; knows some modern Greek but has largely forgotten classical Greek and Latin; can read Spanish and attempts some other languages in connection with his work. *Avocational interests:* Domesticity, playing cricket, and cooking.

* * *

WARREN, Robert Penn 1905-

PERSONAL: Born April 24, 1905, in Guthrie, Ky.; son of Robert Franklin (a businessman) and Anna Ruth (Penn) Warren; married Emma Brescia, September 12, 1930 (divorced, 1950); married Eleanor Clark (a writer), December 7, 1952; children: Rosanna Phelps, Gabriel Penn. *Education:* Vanderbilt University, B.A. (summa cum laude), 1925; University of California, Berkeley, M.A., 1927; Yale University, graduate study, 1927-28; Oxford University, Rhodes Scholar, 1928-30, B.Litt., 1930. *Politics:* Democrat. *Home:* 2495 Redding Rd., Fairfield, Conn. 06430. *Agent:* Helen Strauss, William Morris Agency, 1740 Broadway, New York, N.Y. 10019. *Office:* Yale University, New Haven, Conn.

CAREER: Member of Fugitive Group of Poets (a Nashville group interested in poetry), 1923-25; Southwestern College, Memphis, Tenn., assistant professor of English, 1930-31; Vanderbilt University, Nashville, Tenn., acting assistant professor, 1931-34; Louisiana State University, Baton Rouge, assistant professor, 1934-36, associate professor, 1936-42; University of Minnesota, Minneapolis, professor of English, 1942-50; Yale University, New Haven, Conn., professor of playwrighting, 1950-56, professor of English, 1961-73, professor emeritus, 1973—. Visiting lecturer, State University of Iowa, 1941. Staff member of writers conferences, University of Colorado, 1936, 1937, 1940, Olivet College, 1940. Held chair of poetry, Library of Congress, 1944-45. *Member:* American Academy of Arts and Letters, Academy of American Poets (chancellor), Century Club (New York).

AWARDS, HONORS: Caroline Sinkler Award (poetry), 1936, 1937, 1938; Levinson Prize (*Poetry* magazine), 1936; Houghton Mifflin literary fellowship, 1939, for *Night Rider*; Guggenheim fellowship, 1939-40, 1947-48; Shelley Memorial Award, 1943; Pulitzer Prize (fiction), 1947, for *All the King's Men*; Southern Prize, 1947; Robert Meltzer Award, Screen Writers Guild, 1949; Union League Civic and Arts Foundation Prize (*Poetry* magazine), 1953; Sidney Hillman Prize, 1957, for *Segregation*; Edna St. Vincent Millay Memorial Award, American Poetry Society, 1958, for *Promises*; National Book Award, 1958, for *Promises*; Pulitzer Prize (poetry), 1958, for *Promises*; Herald Tribune Van Doren award, 1965, for *Who Speaks for the Negro?*; Bollingen prize in poetry, Yale University, 1967; Van

Wyck Brooks award for poetry, 1970; National medal for literature, 1970; award for literature, University of Southern California, 1973.

Honorary degrees: University of Louisville, 1949, Kenyon College, 1952, University of Kentucky, 1955, Colby College, 1956, Swarthmore College, 1958, Yale University, 1959, Bridgeport University, 1965, Fairfield University, 1969, Weslayan University, 1970.

WRITINGS: John Brown: The Making of a Martyr, Payson & Clarke, 1929; *Thirty-six Poems*, Alcestis, 1936; (contributor) Herbert Agar and Allen Tate, editors, *Who Owns America? A New Declaration of Independence*, Houghton, 1936; *Night Rider* (novel), Houghton, 1939; *Eleven Poems on the Same Theme*, New Directions, 1942; *At Heaven's Gate* (novel), Harcourt, 1943; *Selected Poems*, Harcourt, 1944; *All the King's Men* (novel), Harcourt, 1946; *Blackberry Winter*, Cummington Press, 1946; *The Circus in the Attic, and Other Stories*, Harcourt, 1948; *World Enough and Time* (novel), Random House, 1950; *Brother to Dragons* (poem), Random House, 1953; *Band of Angels* (novel), Random House, 1955; *Segregation: The Inner Conflict in the South*, Random House, 1956; *Promises: Poems 1954-1956*, Random House, 1957; *Remember the Alamo!*, Random House, 1958; *Selected Essays*, Random House, 1958; *The Cave* (novel), Random House, 1959; *The Gods of Mount Olympus*, Random House, 1959; *All the King's Men* (play), Random House, 1960, Piscator version produced, 1947, premiere as "Willie Stark: His Rise and Fall," Dallas, 1958; *You, Emperors and Others: Poems 1957-1960*, Random House, 1960; *The Legacy of the Civil War*, Random House, 1961; *Wilderness: A Tale of the Civil War* (novel), Random House, 1961; *Flood: A Romance for Our Time* (novel), Random House, 1964; *Who Speaks for the Negro?*, Random House, 1965; *A Plea in Mitigation: Modern Poetry and the End of an Era*, Weslayan College, 1966; *Selected Poems: New and Old, 1923-1966*, Random House, 1966; *Incarnations: Poems, 1966-1968*, Random House, 1968; *Audubon: A Vision*, Random House, 1969; *Homage to Theodore Dreiser*, Random House, 1971; *Meet Me in the Green Glen*, Random House, 1971; *Or Else: Poems, 1968-1974*, Random House, 1974.

With Cleanth Brooks: (Editor, also with John T. Purser) *An Approach to Literature*, Louisiana State University Press, 1936, 4th edition, Appleton, 1967; (editor) *Understanding Poetry*, Holt, 1938, 3rd edition, Holt, 1960; (editor) *Understanding Fiction*, Crofts, 1943, 2nd edition, Appleton, 1959, shorter version published as *Scope of Fiction*, Appleton, 1960; *Modern Rhetoric*, Harcourt, 1949, 3rd edition, Harcourt, 1970, shorter edition, Harcourt, 1972; *Fundamentals of Good Writing*, Harcourt, 1950, 2nd edition, Dobson, 1956; (editor) *Anthology of Stories From the Review* (from the *Southern Review*), Louisiana State University Press, 1953.

Other books edited: *A Southern Harvest: Short Stories by Southern Writers*, Houghton, 1937; (with Albert Erskine), *Short Story Masterpieces*, Dell, 1954, 2nd edition, 1958; (with Erskine) *Six Centuries of Great Poetry*, Dell, 1955; (with Erskine) *A New Southern Harvest*, Bantam, 1957; *Faulkner: A Collection of Critical Essays*, Prentice-Hall, 1966; *Randall Jarrell, 1914-1965*, Farrar, Straus, 1967; *John Greenleaf Whittier's Poetry*, University of Minnesota Press, 1971.

Founder-editor, with Cleanth Brooks, of the *Southern Review*, 1935-42; advisory editor, *Kenyon Review*, 1938-61; author of play, "Proud Flesh," produced, 1946. Contributor to *Virginia Quarterly Review, Southern Review, Mademoiselle, Sewanee Review, New Republic, Poetry, American Review, Harvard Advocate, Nation, American Scholar, New York Times Book Review, Holiday, Fugitive, Botteghe Oscure, Yale Review, Saturday Review*, and other publications.

SIDELIGHTS: Warren is America's man of letters—critic, poet, novelist, essayist, short story writer, and dramatist—a notable achievement for someone who began college with the intent of majoring in chemistry. But poor instruction in chemistry and good instruction in freshman English (John Crowe Ransom) influenced Warren's decision to turn to literature. He was also one of Donald Davidson's students at Vanderbilt, and for a time he roomed with Allen Tate and Ridley Wills, who began taking him to Fugitive meetings.

He is an accomplished artist in each of his chosen fields. *Brother to Dragons* assured Warren of a prominent position among contemporary poets. His novels, writes Cleanth Brooks, "are written with a kind of Elizabethan gusto. Though the school of criticism [the New Critics] with which he is sometimes associated is charged with being overintellectual, formal, and even Alexandrian, Warren's own creative work, in its color and strident action, calls in question that oversimple account. Neither his poetry nor his fiction wear a prim and chilly formalism." Leonard Casper notes that, as a critic, Warren evaluates literature with "Coleridgean brilliance and clarity."

The early influences on Warren included Eliot, Melville, Santayana, Dostoevski, Milton, and Emily Dickinson. Dudley Fitts, writing about *Selected Poems*, 1944, states that "even in responding to his influences Mr. Warren shows his strength. He does not 'write like' Marvell; he becomes Marvell in our time, as Yeats became Swift, as Eliot became Andrewes."

On his approaches to writing, Warren had this to say to his *Paris Review* interviewers: "You don't choose a story, it chooses you. You get together with that story somehow; you're stuck with it. . . . The business of researching for a book strikes me as a sort of obscenity. What I mean is, researching for a book in the sense of trying to find a book to write. Once you are engaged by a subject, are in your book, have your idea, you may or may not want to do some investigating. But you ought to do it in the same spirit in which you'd take a walk in the evening air to think things over."

All the King's Men was filmed, 1949, *Band of Angels*, 1956.

BIOGRAPHICAL/CRITICAL SOURCES: John Bradbury, *The Fugitives*, University of North Carolina Press, 1958; Donald Davidson, *Southern Writers in the Modern World*, University of Georgia Press, 1958; Malcolm Cowley, editor, *Writers at Work: The Paris Review Interviews*, Viking, 1959; Louise Cowan, *The Fugitive Group*, Louisiana State University Press, 1959; Leonard Casper, *Robert Penn Warren: The Dark and Bloody Ground*, University of Washington Press, 1960; Cleanth Brooks, *The Hidden God*, Yale University Press, 1963; Louis D. Rubin, Jr., *The Faraway Country*, University of Washington Press, 1963; Chester E. Eisinger, editor, *Fiction of the Forties*, University of Chicago Press, 1963; Charles H. Bohner, *Robert Penn Warren*, Twayne, 1964; John L. Stewart, *The Burden of Time*, Princeton University Press, 1965; Roy Newquist, editor, *Conversations*, Rand McNally, 1967; *New York Times*, February 6, 1967, December 16, 1969; *Washington Post*, December 2, 1970;

Frank Gado, editor, *A Conversation with Robert Penn Warren*, The Idol, 1972; Carolyn Riley, editor, *Contemporary Literary Criticism*, Gale, Volume I, 1973, Volume IV, 1975.†

* * *

WARREN, Virginia Burgess 1913-

PERSONAL: Born August 1, 1913, in St. Louis, Mo.; daughter of George and Florence (Hart) Burgess; married Frank E. Warren; children: Thomas B., Cynthia S. *Education:* Attended Convent of the Sacred Heart, Grosse Pointe, Mich., and University of Detroit. *Home:* 3700 Woodridge Ave., Silver Spring, Md. *Agent:* Julian Bach, Jr., 249 East 48th St., New York, N.Y. 10017. *Office:* National Education Association, 1201 16th St., Washington, D.C. 20006.

CAREER: Former writer for Harwood Martin Advertising Agency, Cities Service Co., and Lewis Edwin Byce Advertising Agency, all in Washington, D.C.

WRITINGS: How Adults Can Learn More—Faster, National Association of Public School Adult Educators, 1961; *Tested Ways to Help Your Child Learn*, Prentice-Hall, 1961; (editor) *A Treasuary of Techniques for Teaching Adults*, National Association for Public School Adult Education, 1964; *The Second Treasuary of Techniques for Teaching Adults*, National Association for Public School Adult Education, 1970. Contributor to *Parent's Magazine, McCall's, Better Homes and Gardens, Family Weekly, Redbook, Successful Farming, Woman*, and *Service*.†

* * *

WASSON, Chester R(eynolds) 1906-

PERSONAL: Born November 30, 1906, in Wilkinsburg, Pa.; son of Howard Bruce (a cabinetmaker) and Mary (McDowell) Wasson. *Education:* University of Pittsburgh, B.A., 1929; Cornell University, graduate study 1930-31; Oberlin College, M.A., 1931; University of Minnesota, Ph.D., 1938. *Politics:* Independent. *Religion:* Unitarian Universalist. *Home:* 1502 Dunstan Rd., Geneva, Ill. 60134. *Office:* Northern Illinois University, DeKalb, Ill. 60115.

CAREER: University of Minnesota, Minneapolis, instructor in sociology, 1931-33, assistant state supervisor of rural research, 1934-37; Virginia Polytechnic Institute, Blacksburg, assistant state supervisor of rural research, 1938-39; research consultant for public opinion studies, St. Paul, Minn., 1939-41; U.S. government, Washington, D.C., industrial economist for war agencies, 1941-43; Spiegel, Inc., Chicago, Ill., senior marketing analyst, 1946-49; U.S. government, Washington, D.C., marketing research specialist, Department of Agriculture, 1949-50, economic adviser, Metals Branch of Office of Price Stabilization, 1950-53; Leo Burnett, Inc., Chicago, Ill., marketing research analyst, 1953-54; Ag Products Co., Chicago, Ill., part-time sales and research director, 1954-58; Roosevelt University, Chicago, Ill., lecturer in marketing, 1955-58; Drexel Institute of Technology, Philadelphia, Pa., associate professor of marketing, 1958-60; Case Institute of Technology, Cleveland, Ohio, associate professor of economics, 1960-62; University of Tulsa, Tulsa, Okla., associate professor of marketing, 1962-64; California Western University, San Diego, professor of business and economics, 1964-65; University of Southern California, Los Angeles, visiting professor of business and economics, 1965-66; University of California, Los Angeles, lecturer, 1966-67; Northern Illinois University, DeKalb, professor, 1967—. *Military service:* U.S. Army, 1943-45; became sergeant.

MEMBER: American Marketing Association, American Economic Association, American Association of University Professors, Western Economic Association. *Awards, honors:* Ford Foundation fellowship, 1963.

WRITINGS: Strategy of Marketing Research: Text and Cases, Appleton, 1964; *Research Analysis for Marketing Decision*, Appleton, 1965; *Economics of Managerial Decision*, Appleton, 1965; *Understanding Quantitative Analysis*, Appleton, 1966; *Managerial Economics: Texts and Cases*, Appleton, 1966; *Product Management: Product Life Cycles and Competitive Marketing Strategy*, Challenge Books, 1971, revised edition published as *Dynamic Competitive Strategy and Product Life Cycles*, 1974; *Cases in Product Policy, Pricing Tactics, and Competitive Strategy*, Challenge Books, 1972.

Author of articles, "What is New About a New Product," originally published in *Journal of Marketing*, 1960, and reprinted in Kelley and Laser, *Managerial Marketing*, Irwin, 1963, Andersen and Cateers, *Marketing Insights*, Appleton, 1963, and Berg and Schuchman, *Product Strategy and Management*, Holt, 1964. Contributor to professional journals.

WORK IN PROGRESS: Consumer Behavior: A Managerial Viewpoint, for Lone Star.

SIDELIGHTS: Wasson reads French, Spanish, and German.

* * *

WASTI, Syed R(azi) 1929-

PERSONAL: Born September 17, 1929, in Peshawar, West Pakistan; son of Fakhruddin Syed Wasti; married Helen Chrystal-Smith, July 22, 1961; children: Syed Tariq. *Education:* University of the Punjab, M.A., 1951; University of London, B.A. (honors), 1959, Ph.D., 1962. *Religion:* Islam. *Home:* 92 Bengali Mohalla, Lahore, West Pakistan. *Office:* Historical Research Institute, University of the Punjab, Lahore, West Pakistan.

CAREER: Government College, Lyallpur, West Pakistan, lecturer in history, 1951-57; Government College, Lahore, West Pakistan, lecturer in history, 1962-65; University of the Punjab, Lahore, West Pakistan, director of Historical Research Institute, 1965—. *Member:* Royal Asiatic Society (Great Britain; fellow), Asiatic Society (Pakistan).

WRITINGS: Lord Minto and the Indian Nationalist Movement, 1905-1910, Clarendon Press, 1964; *Social Studies (History)*, West Pakistan Text Book Board, 1965; (editor) *Memoirs and Other Writings of Syed Ameer Ali*, People's Publishing House, 1968; *Syed Ameer Ali on Islamic History and Culture*, People's Publishing House, 1968. Contributor to *Pakistan Times* and to historical journals; author of short stories in Urdu.

WORK IN PROGRESS: History of Indo-Muslim Civilization, 1858-1958, in three volumes.

AVOCATIONAL INTERESTS: Travel, reading, photography.†

* * *

WATSON, George 1927-

PERSONAL: Born October 13, 1927, in Brisbane, Australia; son of Richard Grimes (a farmer) and Mary Lindsay (Dowrie) Watson. *Education:* University of Queensland, B.A., 1948; Trinity College, Oxford, B.A., 1950, M.A., 1954; Cambridge University, M.A., 1959. *Politics:* Liberal. *Home:* St. John's College, Cambridge, England.

CAREER: Council of Europe, Strasbourg, France, member of information staff, 1952-57; Cambridge University, Cambridge, England, lecturer in English, 1959—, and fellow of St. John's College. Lecturer at California universities, 1964, and in other parts of United States at earlier periods. *Member:* Bibliographical Society (London).

WRITINGS: (Editor) Coleridge, *Biographia Literaria*, Dent, 1956; (editor) *Cambridge Bibliography of English Literature*, Volume V, Cambridge University Press, 1957; (editor) *The Unservile State*, Allen & Unwin, 1957; *The British Constitution and Europe*, Sijthoff, 1958; (editor) *Concise Cambridge Bibliography of English Literature*, Cambridge University Press, 1958, revised edition, 1965; (editor) *Radical Alternative*, Eyre & Spottiswoode, 1962; (editor) Dryden, *Of Dramatic Poesy*, two volumes, Dent, 1962; *The Literary Critics*, Penguin, 1962; (editor) Maria Edgeworth, *Castle Rackrent*, Oxford University Press, 1964; (editor) *The English Mind*, Cambridge University Press, 1964; *Coleridge the Poet*, Routledge & Kegan Paul, 1966; *The English Petrachans*, Warburg Institute, 1967; *The Study of Literature*, Allan Lane, 1969; *The Literary Thesis*, Longmans, Green, 1970; *The English Ideology: Studies in the Language of Victorian Politics*, Allen Lane, 1973. General Editor, *The New Cambridge Bibliography of English Literature*, Volumes 1-3, 1969-74.

*   *   *

WATSON, Margaret G(oodrich) 1913-

PERSONAL: Born October 18, 1913, in Minot, N.D. *Education:* Colorado State College (now University), B.A., 1939; University of Nevada, M.A., 1940; attended Morehead State College (now University), Utah State Agricultural College (now University), San Jose State College (now University), University of California, University of Southern California, California State College (now University), Los Angeles and Long Beach; also studied in England, France, Austria, Germany, Italy, and Switzerland. *Politics:* Independent. *Religion:* "Respectful of nearly all religions." *Home:* 994 Forest St., Reno, Nev. 89502.

CAREER: Rural school teacher in Minnesota and Nevada, 1931-33; Palisade Grammar School, Palisade, Nev., principal and teacher, 1933-38; Reno and Sparks secondary schools, Nev., teacher, 1940-41; North Hollywood High School, North Hollywood, Calif., teacher of reading and social science, 1946; Amarillo High School, Amarillo, Tex., teacher of English, 1947; Rosemead High School, teacher of history, 1950-69, advisor to California Scholarship Federation, 1951-60, librarian, 1960. Master teacher for University of Nevada, Reno, 1940-41, Whittier College, Whittier, Calif., 1953-54, California State College (now University), Los Angeles, 1961-62. Coordinator of employed high school students, Los Angeles, Calif. J. N. Tedford and Tom Wheelwright Construction Companies, Nevada, chief cook, during the thirties; writing consultant, 1938-41; worked as bookkeeper with Farfers' Cooperative Creamery, Roseau County, Minn., and a peach grower in Antelope Valley, Calif.; Association to Advance Ethical Hypnosis, ethical hypnotist and certified hypnotechnician, 1969—. *Member:* International Society for Professional Hypnosis, American Historical Association, National Education Association, National Congress of Parents and Teachers, College Poetry Society of America (Beta Chapter, secretary, 1938-39), Nevada State Historical Society, Nevada Education Association, California Teachers Association, North Hollywood Faculty Club, El Monte Historical Society, Phi Alpha Theta, Kappa Delta Pi (national recording secretary, 1957-59, vice-president, 1966-67; Southern California chapter president, 1967-68), Sigma Phi Lambda, Rebecca Lodge.

WRITINGS: Silver Theatre, Arthur Clark, 1964. Contributor of scripts to such publications as *Real Heroes* and *Calling All Girls*. Contributor of articles, poems, and stories to *Grade Teacher, Instructor, American Childhood, Family Circle, Ranch Romances*, and other periodicals.

WORK IN PROGRESS: A children's book dealing with early California history; a biography of a northern spy of the Civil War; *Into Light*, a growing awareness.

SIDELIGHTS: Margaret Watson has travelled in the United States, Canada, Mexico, Europe, and South America. She is a frequent speaker for clubs and churches.

BIOGRAPHICAL/CRITICAL SOURCES: Santa Barbara News-Press, November 8, 1964; *Elko Daily Free Press*, November 14, 1964; *Westways*, December, 1964; *Pacific Historical Review*, August, 1965.

*   *   *

WATSON, William Alexander Jardine 1933- (Alan Watson)

PERSONAL: Born October 27, 1933, in Hamilton, Scotland; son of James Walker and Janet (Jardine) Watson; married Cynthia Balls (a university teacher), July 5, 1958; children: David Jardine, Eleanor Ann Jardine. *Education:* University of Glasgow, M.A., 1954, LL.B., 1957; Oxford University, M.A., 1958, D.Phil., 1961. *Office:* Department of Civil Law, University of Edinburgh, Edinburgh, Scotland.

CAREER: Oxford University, Oxford, England, lecturer in law at Wadham College, 1957-59, university lecturer in law, 1959-65, lecturer in law at Oriel College, 1959-60, fellow of Oriel College, 1960-65; University of Glasgow, Glasgow, Scotland, Douglas Professor of Civil Law, 1965-68; University of Edinburgh, Edinburgh, Scotland, professor of civil law, 1968—. *Member:* Society of Public Teachers of Law, Societe Internationale de l'Histoire des Droits de l'Antiquite, Stair Society. *Awards, honors:* D.C.L., Oxford University, 1973.

WRITINGS—All under pseudonym Alan Watson: *Contract of Mandate in Roman Law*, Clarendon Press, 1961; *The Law of Obligations in the Later Roman Republic*, Clarendon Press, 1965; *The Law of Persons in the Later Roman Republic*, Clarendon Press, 1967; *The Law of Property in the Later Roman Republic*, Clarendon Press, 1968; *The Law of the Ancient Romans*, Southern Methodist University Press, 1970; *The Law of Succession in the Later Roman Republic*, Clarendon Press, 1971; *Roman Private Law around 200 B.C.*, Edinburgh University Press, 1971; *Law Making in the Later Roman Republic*, Clarendon Press, 1974; *Legal Transplants*, Scottish Academic Press, 1974; (editor) *Daube Noster*, Scottish Academic Press, 1974. Contributor to British, Continental, and American law journals.

WORK IN PROGRESS: Law in an Early Society: The XII Tables, and *The Comparative Law of Damage by Animals*.

SIDELIGHTS: Watson is "almost fluent" in French, German, and Italian. He is also competent in Spanish and Dutch. *Avocational interests:* Literature, the theater.

WATT, Ian 1917-

PERSONAL: Born March 7, 1917, in Windermere, Westmoreland, England; son of Thomas (a schoolmaster) and Renee Jeanne Gabrielle (Guitton) Watt; married Ruth Mellinkoff (an American), July 14, 1947; children: George Hilary, Josephine. *Education:* St. John's College, Cambridge, B.A. (first class honors), 1938, M.A., 1946; graduate study at University of California, Los Angeles, 1946, Harvard University, 1947-48. *Office:* Department of English, Stanford University, Stanford, Calif.

CAREER: St. John's College, Cambridge University, Cambridge, England, research fellow and supervisor in English, 1948-52, lecturer in English, 1949-50; University of California, Berkeley, assistant professor, 1952-55, associate professor, 1955-59, professor of English, 1959-62; University of East Anglia, Norwich, England, professor of English and dean of School of English Studies, 1962-64; Stanford University, Stanford, Calif., faculty member of English department, 1964-71, Jackson Eli Reynolds Professor of Humanities, 1971—. Visiting summer professor at Stanford University, 1956, University of British Columbia, 1960, University of Hawaii, 1965, 1967, and 1968, and Williams College, 1970; Alexander Lecturer, University of Toronto, 1974. Public lecturer on English literature and modern fiction, and broadcaster on literary topics for British Broadcasting Corp. *Military service:* British Army, 1939-46; became lieutenant; wounded and captured by Japanese at Singapore, 1942; prisoner of war in Siam, 1942-45. *Awards, honors:* Commonwealth Fund fellow in United States, 1946-48; Guggenheim fellow in England, for work on Joseph Conrad, 1959 and 1972-73; American Academy of Arts and Sciences fellow, 1972.

WRITINGS: (Editor) *Wordsworth in Cambridge*, Cambridge University Press, 1950; *The Rise of the Novel: Studies in Defoe, Richardson and Fielding*, University of California Press, 1957; (editor) *Jane Austen: A Collection of Critical Essays*, Prentice-Hall, 1963; (editor, and author of introduction and notes) *Tristram Shandy*, Houghton, 1963; (editor) *The Victorian Novel: Modern Essays in Criticism*, Oxford University Press, 1971; (editor) Joseph Conrad, *The Secret Agent: A Casebook*, Macmillan, 1973; (compiler) *The British Novel: Scott through Hardy*, AHM Publishing, 1973.

Contributor: *The Age of Shakespeare*, Pelican, 1955; (author of introduction) Henry Fielding, *An Apology for the Life of Mrs. Shamela Andrews*, Augustan Reprint Society, 1956; *From Dryden to Johnson*, Pelican, 1957; *Harbrace College Reader*, Harcourt, 1959; *Eighteenth-Century Studies*, edited by James L. Clifford, Oxford University Press, 1959; Mark Schorer, *Modern British Fiction*, Oxford University Press, 1961; (author of introduction) *Sense and Sensibility*, Harper, 1961; Robert Scholes, *Approaches to the Novel*, Chandler Publishing, 1961; *Fielding, A Collection of Critical Essays*, edited by Paulson, Prentice-Hall, 1962.

Also contributor to *Encyclopaedia Britannica*, and of about forty articles and reviews to *Listener, New Republic, Partisan Review, Essays in Criticism*, and other literary and language journals. Editor, *Eagle* (magazine supported by members of St. John's College, Cambridge), 1949-52; advisory editor, *Nineteenth-Century Fiction*, 1959, *Eighteenth-Century Literature*, 1966—, *Novel*, 1966—, *Style*, 1967—.

WORK IN PROGRESS: Studies on current myths.

WAVELL, Stewart Brooke 1921-

PERSONAL: Born January 11, 1921, in Jeram, Selangor, Malaya; son of Horace Brooke (a planter) and Gladys (Longman) Wavell; married Molly Driscoll, June 20, 1941; children: Derek, Stuart, Stella. *Education:* Attended School of Oriental and African Studies, University of London. *Home:* Ulu Dong, 164 Coulsdon Rd., Old Coulsdon, Surrey, England. *Agent:* Mark Hamilton, A. M. Heath & Co., Ltd., 35 Dover St., London W.1, England.

CAREER: Lived and worked in Malaya, on and off, for sixteen years; British Broadcasting Corp., London, England, Burmese Programme organizer, 1960-65, and broadcaster. Public lecturer in Great Britain. Jungle explorer in Malaya; member of Cambridge expedition to Malaya and Thailand, 1962. *Military service:* Royal Air Force, served in Europe and Southeast Asia, 1942-46; became squadron leader. *Member:* Britain-Burma Society and Burma Association (both London), International Language Club (Croydon), Burma Research Society (Rangoon), Cambridge Explorers' and Travelers' Club. *Awards, honors:* Hamilton Holt Medal from Rollins College for interpreting Eastern cultures to the West, 1963.

WRITINGS: The Lost World of the East, Souvenir Press, 1958; *The Naga King's Daughter*, Allen & Unwin, 1964, Atheneum, 1965; (with Audrey Butt and Nina Epton) *Trances*, Allen & Unwin, 1966, Dutton, 1967; *The Art of Radio: A C.B.C. Training Manual*, Ceylon Broadcasting Corp., 1969. Editor, *International News*.

SIDELIGHTS: Wavell speaks Malay, Chinese, and Burmese.†

*   *   *

WEARIN, Otha Donner 1903-

PERSONAL: Born January 10, 1903, in Hastings, Iowa; son of Joseph Andrew (a farmer) and Mary Jane (Donner) Wearin; married Lola Irene Brazelton, January 2, 1931; children: Martha (Mrs. Robert Rasmussen), Rebecca. *Education:* Grinnell College, B.A., 1924; International Institute of Agriculture, Rome, Italy, graduate study. *Politics:* Democrat. *Religion:* Congregational. *Home:* Nishna Vale Farm, Hastings, Iowa 51540.

CAREER: Farmer, conservationist, and agricultural researcher in Iowa, 1924—. Iowa State Legislature, member, 1928-32; U.S. Congressman from 7th District of Iowa, 1933-40. Production Credit Association, Clarinda, Iowa, member of board of directors, 1950—; Grinnell College, member of advisory board, 1961—. Member of Enemy Hearing Board from southern district of Iowa during World War II. *Member:* Thomas Jefferson Memorial Association (life member), Iowa State Historical Society (life member), Westerners (Omaha corral), Ak-Sar-Ben. *Awards, honors:* Community Service Award, Grinnell College.

WRITINGS: An Iowa Farmer Abroad, Nishna Vale Book Co., 1928; *Old Montana and Her Cowboy Artist* (C. M. Russell), World Publishing, 1964; *Statues That Pour*, Sage Press, 1965; *I Remember Hastings*, World Publishing (Shenandoah, Iowa), 1965; *Clarence Ellsworth: Artist of the Old West*, World Publishing, 1967; *Before the Colors Fade*, Wallace-Homestead, 1974. Writer of brochures on local history. Contributor of articles to *Farmer, Successful Farming, Hobbies, Antiques Journal, Western Collector*, and *American Architecture*.

WORK IN PROGRESS: Country Roads to Washington, a story of rural politics and how they are played; *Farming the*

Middle-Border, about early day agriculture in Iowa; *Heinold's First and Last Chance Bar*, a Jack London rendezvous; research in western American and Iowa history and modern agricultural trends.

AVOCATIONAL INTERESTS: Collecting character or figural bottles; American primitives, Victorian glass, political advertising, western Americana and art.

* * *

WEATHERLY, (John) Max   1921-

PERSONAL: Born March 25, 1921, in Alco, La.; son of Obie Lee and Lilla (Givens) Weatherly. *Education:* Stetson University, student, 1946-48; Florida State University, A.B., 1949; University of Alabama, graduate student, 1950-51. *Politics:* Liberal Democrat, but votes independently. *Agent:* Cyrilly Abels, 119 West 57 St., New York, N.Y. 10019.

CAREER: Okaloosa County Veterans' School, Crestview, Fla., teacher of English, 1949-50; Arabian-American Oil Co., Dhahran, Saudi Arabia, secretary, 1951-54; secretarial jobs in New York, N.Y., 1954-64; New York University, New York, N.Y., instructor in writing, 1964-71; Lehigh County Community College, Schnecksville, Pa., instructor in writing, 1971; Cedar Crest College, Allentown, Pa., English teacher, 1972; Allentown Brake and Wheel, Allentown, Pa., billing clerk, 1972-73; *Journal of Commerce*, Phillipsburg, N.J., advertising department, 1973—. *Military service:* U.S. Army Air Forces, 1942-45; became staff sergeant. *Awards, honors:* Yaddo fellowship, 1964.

WRITINGS—Novels, except as noted: *The Long Desire*, Zenith, 1959; *Adultress*, Monarch Books, 1962; *The Mantis and the Moth*, Houghton, 1964; (contributor of non-fiction) Neil Postman, editor, *Language in America*, Pegasus, 1969.

WORK IN PROGRESS: A novel, *Morton*; a memoir of Carson McCullers, *The Black Widow*.

SIDELIGHTS: Weatherly writes: "Although born in the deep woods of Louisiana, I grew up in Alabama. At 12 I wrote a short 3-act play which was performed at my school. A junior in high school, I wrote a longer one which was performed. My people were merely embarrassed and discouraged my ambitions.... I have circled the globe as a passenger on various freighters and would very much like to spend a year in Japan which I found to be a completely charming and extremely civilized country. An Arabia similar to Lawrence Durrell's is very much in my blood.... Of all cultural interests, the theatre interests me most. I ... want to try my hand at professional play writing one day. Of all my novels, *The Mantis and the Moth* is the one I'd most like to dramatize.... None of my people are artistically inclined and they find it difficult, to this day, to understand what I do for a living. They think it's a hobby about which I'm destructively serious! In the last few years I have wanted very much to do some painting, but I find little time for this.... I don't give a tinker's dam for the cocktail circuit and/or glamorous clothes and/or things 'smart'."

Reviewing *The Mantis and the Moth*, H. H. Van Lenten found "a little Poe [and] a snatch of Faulkner" in the work. K. G. Jackson called the novel a "tour de force, and a good one.... Indeed it is almost too well done; one can't believe such dark doings wouldn't have exploded into the light long before they do.... It all seems so quietly reasonable...."

WEAVER, Anthony Frederick   1913-

PERSONAL: Born November 21, 1913, in London, England; son of Alfred Berry (a lawyer) and Muriel (Roberts) Weaver; married Alla Perepletnik (a picture researcher), September 5, 1939; children: Nicholas, Harriet. *Education:* Jesus College, Cambridge, B.A., 1937, M.A., 1953; Jesus College, Oxford, M.A., 1964, D.Phil., 1969. *Politics:* "Pacifist-anarchist." *Office:* 18 Campden Grove, London W8 4JG, England.

CAREER: Assistant teacher in independent and local authority schools, London, England, and Home counties, 1937-48; head teacher in Home counties schools for maladjusted children, 1949-54; senior lecturer in education, Whitelands College, London, England, 1956-64, Redland College, Bristol, England, 1965-71; University of London, Goldsmith's College, London, England, senior lecturer in education, 1971—. Conscientious objector to military service, 1940-45.

WRITINGS: They Steal for Love, Parrish, 1959; *War Outmoded*, Housmans Bookshop, 1960; (contributor) *World Questions: A Study Guide*, Methuen, 1963; (contributor) *Alternatives to War and Violence*, J. Clarke, 1963. Joint editor of *New Era*, 1972—.

* * *

WEAVER, Horace R.   1915-

PERSONAL: Born January 5, 1915, in Hardtner, Kan.; son of George Henry and Mary (McMahan) Weaver; married Margaret Lenore Fenner (a teacher), June 16, 1940; children: Cheryl Elaine, Heidi Diane. *Education:* Capital University, B.Sc., 1938, B.A., 1939; Boston University School of Theology, S.T.B., 1941; Boston University, Ph.D., 1949; postdoctoral study at New York University, summer, 1959, University of Pittsburgh, summer, 1961. *Home:* 1805 Laurel Ridge Dr., Nashville, Tenn. 37215. *Office:* 201 Eighth Ave., South, Nashville, Tenn. 37203.

CAREER: Ordained deacon in West Ohio Conference of The Methodist Church, 1941, elder, 1943; minister of music at church in Chelsea, Mass., and minister in Shawnee and Malta, Ohio; director of religious education and minister of music in Cincinnati, Ohio, 1946-47; The Board of Education of the Methodist Church, Nashville, Tenn., editor of adult publications, 1960—. *Military service:* U.S. Army, chaplain, 1943-45. *Member:* American Academy of Religion, Society of Biblical Literature, American Schools of Oriental Research, Adult Education Association of the U.S.A., Masons.

WRITINGS: (Editor) *International Lesson Annual*, Abingdon, 1963—; *The Everlasting Covenant*, Methodist Publishing House, 1965; (with Harold Fair) *Key to Luke*, Abington, Part I, 1972, Part II, 1973. Also co-author of *Channels of His Spirit*. Contributor of more than eight hundred articles to various periodicals of Editorial Division of Methodist Publishing House, 1950—.

SIDELIGHTS: Weaver made two study tours of Bible Lands, led three other tours to the same area, and has traveled in thirty-six countries.

* * *

WEAVER, Peter Malcolm   1927-

PERSONAL: Born June 10, 1927, in Southwark, London, England; son of Philip Roland (a train driver) and Gwendolin Maude Elizabeth (Flower) Weaver; married Felicity Rachel Lloyd (an artist and teacher of art), February 16,

1952. *Education:* Studied in London, England, at St. Martin's School of Art, 1948-50, at Camberwell School of Art and Crafts, 1950-52; Slade School of Fine Art and University College, University of London, diploma in Fine Arts, 1954. *Home:* 50 Wood Vale, London S.E. 23, England.

CAREER: Tool and gauge maker, 1943-46; Watford School of Art, Watford, England, teacher of drawing, painting, and lithography, 1955-64; Camberwell School of Art and Crafts, London, England, teacher of lithography, 1957—. Artist, lithographer, and free-lance graphic designer, with work in Victoria and Albert Museum and in private collections in England and America; exhibitor at University College of North Wales, and in group in England and Ireland. *Military service:* British Army, 1946-48. *Member:* Artists International Association, Association of Teachers in Technical Institutions, Printing Historical Society, Printmakers' Council (founder-member).

WRITINGS: The Technique of Lithography, Reinhold, 1964; *Printmaking: A Medium for Basic Design*, Reinhold, 1968.

WORK IN PROGRESS: Articles for *Artist's Proof*, (journal of the Pratt Graphic Art Center, New York), on rubbings, frottage, and transferring technique in lithography; a book on aesthetics and design techniques in lithography; research on the history of lithography in the nineteenth century, both commercial and fine art.†

*   *   *

WEBB, Kempton E.   1931-

PERSONAL: Born December 28, 1931, in Melrose, Mass.; son of Winthrop L. and Margaret (Evans) Webb; married Nancy Ann Boyd, September 3, 1955; children: Rachel Drake, Scott Winthrop. *Education:* Harvard University, A.B., 1953; Syracuse University, M.A., 1955, Ph.D., 1958. *Politics:* Democrat. *Religion:* Unitarian. *Home:* 468 Overbrook Rd., Ridgewood, N.J.

CAREER: Columbia University, New York, N.Y., assistant professor, 1961-65, associate professor, 1965-70, professor of geography, 1970—, assistant director, 1962-65, associate director, 1965-70, director of Institute of Latin American Studies, 1970-73, chairman of geography department, 1974—. *Military service:* U.S. Army Reserve, 1954-62; became sergeant. *Member:* Association of American Geographers, American Association of University Professors, American Geographical Society.

WRITINGS: Suprimento dos Generos Alimenticios Basicos para a Cidade de Fortaleza, Banco do Norderte do Brasil, 1957; *Geography of Food Supply in Central Minas Gerais*, National Academy of Sciences, 1959; *Brazil*, Ginn, 1964; (editor) *Latin America: A Geographical Commentary*, J. Murray, 1965; (with David Grossman) *Geography*, Littlefield, 1967; (contributor) Eric Baklanoff, editor, *The Modernization of Brazil*, Louisiana University Press, 1969; (contributor) W. Zelinsky and others, editors, *Geography and a Crowding World*, Oxford University Press, 1970; *Latin America*, Prentice-Hall, 1972; *The Changing Face of Northeast Brazil*, Columbia University Press, 1974. General editor of cultural geography series published by Sadlier, 1967-71. Contributing editor, *Handbook of Latin American Studies*, Library of Congress. Contributor to *Annals of the Association of American Geographers* and *Journal of Inter American Affairs*.

SIDELIGHTS: Webb speaks Portuguese, Spanish, and French. He spent three years in Brazil, another year in other sections of Latin America; has traveled throughout the Western Hemisphere, in Greenland, Africa, and western Europe.

*   *   *

WEBB, Lance   1909-

PERSONAL: Born December 10, 1909, in Boaz, N.M.; son of John Newton Shields (a clergyman) and Delia (Lance) Webb; married Mary Elizabeth Hunt, June 30, 1933; children: Jeanne (Mrs. David B. Davis), Mary (Mrs. Lee Edlond), Ruth (Mrs. Alan Lindstrom). *Education:* McMurry College, Abilene, Tex., B.A.; Southern Methodist University, B.D. and M.A.; Union Theological Seminary, New York, N.Y., graduate study. *Home:* 1949 Bates Ave., Springfield, Ill. 62704. *Office:* Illinois Area, The Methodist Church, 705 Myers Building, Springfield, Ill. 62701.

CAREER: Methodist minister, former pastor in Shamrock, Pampa, and Eastland, Tex.; McMurry College, Abilene, Tex., professor of Bible and chaplain, 1936-37; senior minister of churches in Dallas, Tex., 1942-52, Columbus, Ohio, 1953-64; The Methodist Church, bishop of Illinois area, 1964—. Chaplain to Ohio Senate, 1961-64. Conductor of preaching mission in South America, 1955; exchange preacher in England and Scotland, 1960; leader of People-to-People goodwill tour around the world, including conference of World Council of Churches in New Delhi, India, 1962. *Member:* Masons, International Civitan Club (chaplain). *Awards, honors:* D.D., McMurry College, 1948, Ohio Wesleyan University, 1960, MacMurray College, 1967, McKendree College, 1971; D.H., Illinois Wesleyan University, 1966; LL.D., Southern Methodist University, 1966.

WRITINGS—All published by Abington, except as noted: *Conquering the Seven Deadly Sins*, 1955; *Discovering Love*, 1959; *Point of Glad Return*, 1960; *The Art of Personal Prayer*, 1962; *On the Edge of the Absurd*, 1965; *When God Comes Alive*, 1968; *Disciplines for Life in the Age of Aquarius*, Word Inc., 1972.

*   *   *

WEBER, Brom   1917-

PERSONAL: Born May 14, 1917, in New York, N.Y.; son of Kalman (a contractor) and Nadia (Svonkin) Weber; married Nettie Held, March 21, 1939; children: Eden Elizabeth, Kyle Maxson. *Education:* City College (now City College of the City University of New York), B.S.S., 1938; University of Wyoming, M.A., 1955; University of Minnesota, Ph.D., 1957. *Home:* 23 Almond Lane, R.D.1, Davis, Calif. 95616. *Office:* Department of English, University of California, Davis, Calif. 95616.

CAREER: Works Progress Administration, Historical Records Survey, New York, N.Y., writer and editor, 1938-39; U.S. Government, Administrator and writer in agencies in Washington, D.C., and Jersey City, N.J., 1940-45; City College (now City College of the City University of New York), New York, N.Y., instructor in English, 1945-50; New School for Social Research, New York, N.Y., lecturer in literature and writing, 1948-54; Purdue University, West Lafayette, Ind., assistant professor of English, 1957-58; University of Minnesota, Minneapolis, assistant professor, 1958-60, associate professor of English, 1960-63; University of California, Davis, professor of English, 1963—, professor of American studies, 1969—, chairman of American studies program, 1969. Visiting summer professor at

DePauw University, 1958, University of Washington, Seattle, 1965, University of Wyoming, 1966, and University of Colorado, 1968; Fulbright-Hays lecturer at Conference on American Literature and History, Osmania University, Mussoorie, India, 1963, at University of Aix-Marseille, 1966-67, and at Seoul National University, Sogang Jesuit University, and Chonnam National University (all in Korea), 1973; has also lectured in Taiwan, Turkey, Italy, Germany, and England. Consultant to university presses.

MEMBER: Modern Language Association of America, Northern California American Studies Association (vice-president, 1968-70; president, 1971-72). *Awards, honors:* Yaddo fellowship, Trask Foundation, 1949; McKnight Foundation Humanities Award for Biography, 1962; senior non-resident fellowship, Canada Council, 1963; Humanities Institute fellow, University of California, 1966.

WRITINGS: Hart Crane: A Biographical and Critical Study, Bodley Press, 1948, new edition, Russell, 1970; *Sherwood Anderson*, University of Minnesota Press, 1964.

Editor: *The Letters of Hart Crane, 1916-1932*, Hermitage, 1952; (with Charles Glicksberg) *American Vanguard*, Dial, 1953; George W. Harris, *Sut Lovingood*, Grove, 1954; *An Anthology of American Humor*, Crowell, 1962, published as *The Art of American Humor*, Apollo, 1970; Edgar W. Howe, *The Story of a Country Town*, Holt, 1964; *The Complete Poems and Selected Letters and Prose of Hart Crane*, Liveright, 1966; (with Harrison Meserole and Walter Sutton) *American Literature: Tradition and Innovation*, three volumes, Heath, 1969; *Sense and Sensibility in Twentieth-Century Writing*, Southern Illinois University Press, 1970.

Contributor: Dorothy Norman, editor, *Stieglitz Memorial Portfolio*, Twice a Year Press, 1947; *New Directions 10*, New Directions, 1948; Robert F. Spencer, editor, *Many-Sided Language*, University of Minnesota Press, 1964; Jackson R. Bryer, editor, *Fifteen Modern American Authors*, Duke University Press, 1969; *William Faulkner, Eugene O'Neill, John Steinbeck*, Alexis Gregory, 1971; Malcolm Bradbury and David Palmer, editors, *The American Novel in the Nineteen Twenties*, Edward Arnold, 1971, Crane, Russak, 1972; L. D. Rubin, editor, *The Comic Imagination in America*, Rutgers University Press, 1973; Bryer, editor, *Sixteen Modern American Authors: A Survey of Research and Criticism*, Duke University Press, 1973.

Author of introduction: John Steinbeck, *Tortilla Flat* (in French), Rombaldi (Paris), 1965.

Contributor to annual, *American Literary Scholarship*, published by Duke University Press, and to *Encyclopaedia Britannica* and *Encyclopaedia Judaica*; contributor to literary journals and general periodicals. Assistant editor, *Twice A Year*, 1946-48; associate editor, *Tiger's Eye*, 1949-51; advisory editor of *Modern Fiction Studies*, 1957-58, and "Lovingood Papers," 1962-66; member of board of editors, *Hollins Critic*, 1965-66; member of advisory board, *Early American Literature*, 1966-69. Editorial consultant to *American Literature*, *PMLA*, and *American Quarterly*.

SIDELIGHTS: Weber has tape-recorded lectures, "Hart Crane I," and "Hart Crane II," for Everett, Edwards, Inc., 1973. *Avocational interests:* Still photography.

*   *   *

WEBSTER, Douglas   1920-

PERSONAL: Born April 15, 1920, in London, England; son of Robert and Anne (Ashwell) Webster. *Education:* Attended St. Peter's College, Oxford, 1939-42, Wycliffe Hall, 1942-43. *Home:* Wycliffe Hall, Oxford, England.

CAREER: Ordained deacon, Church of England, 1943, priest, 1944. Curate of St. Helens, Lancashire, England, 1943-46, at Crouch End, London, England, 1946-47; London College of Divinity, tutor, 1947-52; Church Missionary Society, education secretary, 1952-61, theologian-missioner, 1961—. Wycliffe Hall, Oxford, Chavasse Lecturer in World Mission, 1963—. Honorary canon of Chelmsford, 1962.

WRITINGS: (Editor) *Truly Called*, Highway Press, 1954; *What is This Church of South India?*, Highway Press, 1954; *What is a Missionary?*, Highway Press, 1955; *What is Spiritual Healing?*, Highway Press, 1955; *And Who is My Neighbor?*, Highway Press, 1955; *In Debt to Christ*, Highway Press, 1957, Fortress Press, 1964; *Listen to the Wind*, Highway Press, 1958; *What Is Evangelism?*, Highway Press, 1959; *Into All the World*, S.P.C.K., 1959.

Missionary Societies—One or Many?, Highway Press, 1960; *Local Church and World Mission*, S.C.M. Press, 1962; *The Ministry in the Middle East*, World Council of Churches, 1962; *The Continuing Missionary Task*, S.P.C.K., 1962; *The Healing Christ*, Highway Press, 1963; *Patterns of Part-Time Ministry*, World Dominion Press, 1964; *Our Image of Mission*, Prism, 1964; *Pentecostalism and Speaking with Tongues*, Highway Press, 1965; *Mutual Irresponsibility*, S.P.C.K., 1965; *Mission and the New Theology*, Prism, 1965; *Unchanging Mission: Biblical and Contemporary*, Fortress, 1965; *Yes to Mission*, Seabury, 1966; *Not Ashamed: Studies in Mission and Ministry*, Hodder & Stoughton, 1970. Also author of *Good News in John*.

Contributor: *Bicentenary Essays, 1759-1959*, edited by A. F. Pollard and M. M. Hennell, S.P.C.K., 1959; *The Parish Communion Today*, edited by D. M. Paton, S.P.C.K., 1962; *Mutual Responsibility: Questions and Answers*, edited by John Wilkinson, S.P.C.K., 1964.†

*   *   *

WEDGE, Bryant (Miner)   1921-

PERSONAL: Born May 21, 1921, in Coldwater, Mich.; son of Stanley E. (an attorney) and Edna (Miner) Wedge; married Dorothy A. Reed, May 30, 1943; children: Ann Kristen, Daniel Bryant. *Education:* Attended Kalamazoo College, 1939-42; University of Michigan, M.D., 1945; Chicago Institute for Psychoanalysis, candidate in training, 1949-52. *Home:* Moores Mill, Mount Rose Rd., Hopewell, N.J. *Office:* 240 Nassau St., Princeton, N.J. 08540.

CAREER: Queens' Hospital, Honolulu, Hawaii, intern and resident, 1945-48; University of Chicago, Chicago, Ill., resident and instructor in psychiatry, 1948-52; certified in psychiatry by American Board of Psychiatry and Neurology, 1952; Yale University, New Haven, Conn., psychiatrist-in-chief, department of university health, and associate clinical professor of psychiatry, 1954-60, fellow of Saybrook College, 1956—; Institute for the Study of National Behavior, Princeton, N.J., research associate, 1960-62, director and president of board, 1962—. Consultant to Armed Forces Epidemiologic Board, 1956-57, Peace Corps, 1961, 1963, Palestine Conciliation Commission of United Nations, 1961—, and to health and education organizations. Lecturer at U. S. Foreign Service Institute, 1962—, Menninger Foundation, 1963, and International Affairs Seminars of Washington, 1963. Participant in national and international conferences on health and education. Center for Cross-Cultural Communications, Washington, D.C., trustee, 1963—. *Military service:* U.S. Army Reserve, Medical Corps., chief of psychiatric consultation service, Valley Forge Army Hospital, 1952-54.

MEMBER: American Psychiatric Association (fellow), Group for the Advancement of Psychiatry, American Association for the Advancement of Science, American Academy of Political and Social Science, Federation of American Scientists, National Council of Scientists on Survival (trustee, 1962-63), Society for Psychological Study of Social Issues, National Research Council on Peace Strategy. *Awards, honors:* Eisenhower Exchange Fellow, 1959; grant for study of psychological factors in Soviet disarmament negotiations, U.S. Arms Control and Disarmament Agency, 1963.

WRITINGS: (Editor and contributor) *Psychosocial Problems of College Men*, Yale University Press, 1958; (contributor) *The Student and Mental Health; an International View*, edited by D. Funkenstein, World Federation for Mental Health, 1959; *Nation-to-Nation: A Study of International Communications*, Rutgers University Press, 1964; *Visitors to the United States and How They See Us*, Van Nostrand, 1965; *Problems in Dialogue: Brazilian University Students and the United States*, Institute for the Study of National Behavior, 1965. Contributor to published reports on mental health conferences and workshops, and to social psychology, psychiatry, and mental hygiene journals. Associate editor, *Journal of Conflict Resolution*.

WORK IN PROGRESS: *Soviet Political Psychology* (and negotiating behavior); studies on diplomacy.

SIDELIGHTS: "J. R. R. Tolkien said it in *The Return of the King*: 'It is not our part to master all the tides of the world, but to do what is in us for the succour of those years wherein we are set, uprooting the evil in the fields that we know, so that those who live after may have clean earth to till.' The fields I know are those of international understanding."†

* * *

WEEKES, Richard V. 1924-

PERSONAL: Born April 26, 1924, in Berea, Ky.; son of Ernest J. (a college professor) and Jessie Weekes; married Ava Smith (a writer and researcher), October 11, 1955; children: Annelise S. *Education:* Oberlin College, B.A., 1949; Columbia University, M.A., 1954. *Office:* Ford Foundation, 477 Madison Ave., New York, N.Y.

CAREER: Railway Progress (magazine), Washington, D.C., assistant editor, 1949-51; U.S. Information Service, information officer in Karachi, Pakistan, 1951-53; *Time*, New York, N.Y., foreign correspondent, London, England, 1954-57; The American University, Washington, D.C., editor, Human Relations Area Files, 1957-58; Cooperative for American Relief Everywhere (CARE), representative in Istanbul, Turkey, 1958-59; Iran Foundation, New York, N.Y., executive director, 1959-64; Ford Foundation, New York, N.Y., assistant representative in Rio de Janeiro, Brazil, 1964—. *Military service:* U.S. Navy, 1943-46; served in Pacific Theater. *Member:* Overseas Press Club.

WRITINGS: Pakistan: Birth and Growth of a Muslim Nation, Van Nostrand, 1964; (editor) *Contemporary Latin America: A Selection of Papers*, University of Houston, 1968.

WORK IN PROGRESS: A book on Brazil.†

WEEKS, Albert L. 1923-

PERSONAL: Born March 28, 1923, in Highland Park, Mich.; son of Albert Loren (a writer) and Vera (Jarvis) Weeks. *Education:* Attended University of Michigan, 1942-43; University of Chicago, M.A., 1949; Columbia University, graduate study, 1949-51, Ph.D., 1965. *Home:* 37 Washington Sq., New York, N. Y. 10011. *Office:* New York University, 1 Washington Sq. North, New York, N.Y. 10001.

CAREER: U.S. Department of State, New York, N.Y., political analyst, 1950-53; Columbia University, New York, N.Y., lecturer in Soviet government and American diplomatic history, 1951-53; Free Europe Committee, New York, N.Y., political analyst, 1953-56; New York University, New York, N.Y., assistant professor and lecturer in English and American history and Soviet politics, 1958—. *Newsweek*, editorial assistant, 1960-61; McGraw-Hill Book Co., Inc., technical translator, Russian-to-English, and glossary compiler, 1961-62. *Member:* American Association for Advancement of Slavic Studies.

WRITINGS: Reading American History, McGraw, 1963; *The First Bolshevik: A Political Biography of Peter Tkachev*, New York University Press, 1968; *The Other Side of Coexistence: An Analysis of Russian Foreign Policy*, Pitman, 1970. Contributor to *New Republic, New Leader, Sky and Telescope, East Europe*, other journals. Editorial adviser, *Current Digest of the Soviet Press*, 1963-64.

AVOCATIONAL INTERESTS: Astronomy.†

* * *

WEEKS, Robert Lewis 1924-

PERSONAL: Born July 9, 1924, in Huntington, W.Va.; son of Edwin F. and Josephine (Steckel) Weeks; married Joanne Parsons, June 7, 1950; children: Robin Ann, Hallam Parsons. *Education:* West Virginia University, A.B., 1948, M.A., 1949; Indiana University, Ph.D., 1956. *Politics:* Liberal Democrat. *Home:* 6767 East Dartmouth, Denver, Colo. 80222. *Office:* Department of English, Colorado Women's College, Denver, Colo. 20220.

CAREER: West Virginia University, Morgantown, instructor in English, 1949-51; Indiana University, Bloomington, teaching associate, 1951-54; Wisconsin State University, Eau Claire, instructor, 1954-56, assistant professor, 1956-58, associate professor, 1958-61, professor, 1961-63; Stephen F. Austin State College, Nacogdoches, Tex., professor of English, 1963-66; Colorado Women's College, Denver, professor of English, 1966—. Visiting professor, West Virginia University, Morgantown, 1970. *Military service:* U.S. Army Signal Corps, South Pacific, 1944-46; awarded five battle stars. *Member:* Modern Language Association of America, American Civil Liberties Union, Danforth Association.

WRITINGS: To the Maker of Globes, and Other Poems, introduction by Karl Shapiro, South & West, 1964; *For Those Who Waked Me*, South & West, 1969; *The Master of Clouds*, Juniper Books/Northeast, 1971. Contributor of poems, articles, short stories, and reviews to *New Yorker, Carleton Miscellany, Prairie Schooner, Poetry Northwest, Southwest Review, Beloit Poetry Journal*, and other publications.

WORK IN PROGRESS: Poems, articles, and other writings.

SIDELIGHTS: Weeks has published over 250 individual poems in over one hundred different magazines.

* * *

WEEKS, Robert P(ercy) 1915-

PERSONAL: Born September 22, 1915, in Detroit, Mich.; son of Albert L. (a writer) and Vera (Jarvis) Weeks; married Frances Wirtz, June 24, 1946; children: Thomas, Jane, Sarah. *Education:* University of Michigan, B.A., 1938, M.A., 1947, Ph.D., 1952. *Politics:* Democrat. *Home:* 2120 Needham Rd., Ann Arbor, Mich. *Office:* English Department, College of Engineering, University of Michigan, Ann Arbor, Mich.

CAREER: Detroit News, Detroit, Mich., reporter, 1940-41; University of Michigan, Ann Arbor, 1945—, began as teaching fellow, became professor of English, College of Engineering, 1962—. Member of Ann Arbor City Council, 1964-68. *Military service:* U.S. Army, 1941-45; became first lieutenant. *Member:* National Council of Teachers of English, American Civil Liberties Union. *Awards, honors:* Silver Medal for Merit, University of Graz, Austria; Fulbright lecturer in Europe, 1962-63 and 1970-71.

WRITINGS: (Editor) *Commonwealth vs. Sacco and Vanzetti,* Prentice-Hall, 1958; (editor) *Machines and the Man,* Appleton, 1961; (editor) *Hemingway: A Collection of Critical Essays,* Prentice-Hall, 1962; *King Strang,* Five Wives Press, 1970. Contributor of articles on modern literature to scholarly periodicals.

WORK IN PROGRESS: Studies on Hemingway and Dos Passos.

* * *

WEIDNER, Edward William 1921-

PERSONAL: Surname is pronounced *Wide*-ner; born July 7, 1921, in Minneapolis, Minn.; son of Peter Clifford (a purchasing agent) and Lillian (Halbe) Weidner; married Jean Elizabeth Blomquist, March 23, 1944; children: Nancy Louise, Gary Richard, Karen Jean, William Steven. *Education:* University of Minnesota, B.A. (magna cum laude), 1942, M.A., 1943, Ph.D., 1946; University of Wisconsin, graduate student, 1943-45. *Home:* 3015 Bay View Dr., Green Bay, Wis. 54301. *Office:* University of Wisconsin, Green Bay, Green Bay, Wis. 54302.

CAREER: University of Wisconsin, Madison, lecturer in political science, 1944-45; University of Minnesota, Minneapolis, instructor, 1945-47, assistant professor of political science, 1947-49, assistant director of research in intergovernmental relations, 1946-53; University of California, Los Angeles, assistant professor of political science, 1949-50; Michigan State University, East Lansing, associate professor, 1950-52, professor of political science, 1952-62, director of Governmental Research Bureau, 1951-57, coordinator of Vietnam Project, 1956-57, director of Institute of Research on Overseas Programs, 1956-60; University of Hawaii, Honolulu, vice-chancellor of Institute of Advanced Projects, East-West Center, 1962-66; University of Kentucky, Lexington, director of Center for Developmental Change, 1966; University of Wisconsin, Green Bay, chancellor, 1966—. Consultant to Foreign Operations Administration, Vietnam, 1954-55, Ford Foundation in Pakistan, 1956, Department of State, 1963, and Agency for International Development, 1964-65; member of national advisory board of Bolton Institute, 1973—.

MEMBER: International Political Science Association, International Institute of Administrative Sciences, American Association for Higher Education, American Political Science Association (member of national council, 1950-52), American Society for Public Administration (member of national council, 1947-50), Society for International Development, National Municipal League, American Civil Liberties Union, Asia Society, Phi Beta Kappa.

WRITINGS: County Boards and Commissions, U.S. Department of Commerce, 1947; (with William Anderson) *American City Government,* Henry Holt, 1950; (with William Anderson) *State and Local Government,* Henry Holt, 1951; (with William Anderson) *American Government,* Henry Holt, 1953; (with others) *The International Programs of American Universities,* Michigan State University Press, 1958.

(With Anderson and Clara Penniman) *Government in the Fifty States,* Holt, 1960; *Intergovernmental Relations as Seen by Public Officials,* University of Minnesota Press, 1960; (co-author) *Positive Contracting for AID,* President's Task Force on Foreign Assistance, 1961; *The World Role of Universities,* McGraw, 1962; (with Allan A. Spitz) *Development Administration: An Annotated Bibliography,* East-West Center Press, 1963; (with Cole Brembeck) *Education and Development in India and Pakistan: A Select and Annotated Bibliography,* Michigan State University Press, 1963; *Technical Assistance in Public Administration Overseas,* Public Administration Service (Chicago), 1964; *Prelude to Reorganization: The Kennedy Foreign Aid Message of March 22, 1961,* Inter-University Case Program, 1969; (editor) *Development Administration in Asia,* Duke University Press, 1970.

Contributor: *County Government Across the Nation,* edited by Paul W. Wager, University of North Carolina Press, 1950; *Rural Social Systems and Adult Education,* Michigan State University Press, 1953; *Capitol, Courthouse, and City Hall,* edited by Robert L. Morlan, Houghton, 1954, 2nd edition, 1960; *Federalism Mature and Emergent,* edited by Arthur W. Macmahon, Doubleday, 1955; *Current Issues in Higher Education,* Association for Higher Education, 1958.

Technical Assistance in Training Administrators, Institute of Training for Public Service, Indiana University, 1962; *Papers in Comparative Public Administration,* Institute of Public Administration, University of Michigan, 1962; *Models and Priorities in the Comparative Study of Public Administration,* American Society for Public Administration, 1963; *Education and Training in Developing Countries,* edited by W. Y. Elliott, Praeger, 1965; *Universities and Development Assistance Abroad,* edited by Richard A. Humphrey, American Council on Education, 1967.

Writer of pamphlets published by National Municipal League and Michigan State University Press; contributor to *Municipal Year Book,* 1953, 1955, 1957, and to *Book of States,* Council of State Governments, 1952, 1954. Contributor of about twenty articles and reviews to professional journals.

Editor, with W. Anderson, "Intergovernment Relation Series," University of Minnesota Press, ten titles, 1950-60; editor of "Governmental Research Bureau Series," six titles, 1953-55, and of "Institute of Research on Overseas Programs Series," eight titles, 1958-62 both published by Michigan State University Press. *National Municipal Review,* editor of local affairs abroad department, 1944-47, editor of county and township department, 1953-55.

WEIGAND, George R(obert) J(oseph) 1917-

PERSONAL: Surname is pronounced *Why*-gand; born April 4, 1917, in Trenton, N.J.; son of George J. (a contractor) and Mary (Berkenkopf) Weigand; married Dorris L. Lobell, December 20, 1939 (divorced); married Marvene Harris, December 27, 1972; children: (first marriage) George A., James P., Christopher R., John L. *Education:* Johns Hopkins University, A.B., 1938, graduate study, 1939-40; University of Maryland, Ph.D., 1951. *Home:* 201 Granville Dr., Greenville, N.C. *Office:* East Carolina University, Greenville, N.C.

CAREER: Certified psychologist, Maryland Board of Examiners of Psychologists and State Board of North Carolina. Instructor at Bordentown Military Institute, Bordentown, N.J., 1940-41, and West Nottingham Academy, summers, 1940-41; University of Maryland, College Park, instructor, later assistant professor, 1947-53, assistant dean of students, 1953-57, director of office of intermediate registration, 1957-63; East Carolina University, Greenville, N.C., director counseling center, 1963—. U.S. Department of Agriculture Graduate Schools, Washington, D.C., instructor, 1959-63; vocational expert for U.S. Department of Health, Education, and Welfare. Cavalier Co., Baltimore, Md., consultant and partner; Parks M. Adams, Towson, Md., vice-president. Ford Foundation adviser for U.S. National Student Association research project. Member of Pitt County Action Committee. *Military service:* U.S. Army, Infantry, 1941-46; assistant professor of military science and tactics, Virginia Military Institute, 1945-46; became major; received Bronze Star and Army Commendation Ribbon.

MEMBER: American Psychological Association, Maryland Psychological Association, Sigma Xi.

WRITINGS: (With Walter S. Blake, Jr.) *College Orientation*, Prentice-Hall, 1955; *How to Study and Like It*, Fieldcrest, 1963; *How to Pass Examinations*, Fieldcrest, 1963; *How to Succeed in High School*, Barron's, 1965. Contributor to *Personnel and Guidance Journal*.

*   *   *

WEINGARTNER, Rudolph H(erbert) 1927-

PERSONAL: Born February 12, 1927, in Heidelberg, Germany; son of Jacob (a businessman) and Grete (Kahn) Weingartner; married Fannia Goldberg-Rudkowski (a freelance editor), December 28, 1953; children: Mark H., Eleanor C. *Education:* Columbia University, A.B., 1950, A.M., 1953, Ph.D., 1959. *Politics:* Independent. *Religion:* Jewish. *Office:* Vassar College, Poughkeepsie, N.Y. 12601.

CAREER: Columbia University, New York, N.Y., instructor in philosophy, 1955-59; San Francisco State College (now University), San Francisco, Calif., assistant professor, 1959-63, associate professor of philosophy, 1968; Vassar College, Poughkeepsie, N.Y., professor of philosophy, 1968—, chairman of department, 1969—, Taylor Professor of philosophy, 1973—. *Military service:* U.S. Naval Reserve, 1945-46. *Member:* American Philosophical Association, American Association of University Professors, Society for Philosophy and Public Affairs, Phi Beta Kappa. *Awards, honors:* Guggenheim fellowship and Fulbright travel grant, 1965-66.

WRITINGS: Experience and Culture: The Philosophy of George Simmel, Wesleyan University Press, 1962; (editor with Joseph Katz) *Philosophy in the West*, Harcourt, 1965; *The Unity of the Platonic Dialogue: The Cratylus, the Protogoras, the Parmenides*, Bobbs-Merrill, 1973. Contributor to philosophical journals.

WORK IN PROGRESS: A book on the objectivity of history.

SIDELIGHTS: Weingartner commented to *CA*, ''On writing: It is work. On philosophy: It's hard. On staying rational: It is mandatory. Languages: German (good), French (OK), Italian (barbarically).'' Weingartner spent a year in Florence, 1965-66 and a year in Oxford, England, 1971-72. *Avocational interests:* Work in wood, including sculpting.

*   *   *

WEINSTEIN, Donald 1926-

PERSONAL: Born March 13, 1926, in Rochester, N.Y.; son of Harris (a tailor) and Rose (Shaywitz) Weinstein; married Anne Kingsley, January 20, 1954; children: Jonathan, Elizabeth. *Education:* University of Chicago, B.A., 1948, M.A., 1950; University of Iowa, graduate study, 1950-53, 1955-57, Ph.D., 1957; University of Florence, graduate study, 1953-55. *Religion:* Jewish. *Home:* 25 Grant Ave., Highland Park, N.J. 08904. *Office:* Department of History, Rutgers University, New Brunswick, N.J.

CAREER: University of Iowa, Iowa City, instructor in history, 1955-58; Roosevelt University, Chicago, Ill., assistant professor of history, 1958-59; Rutgers University, New Brunswick, N. J., assistant professor, 1960-61, associate professor of history, 1961—. *Military service:* U.S. Army, 1944-46; received Bronze Star Medal and Combat Infantryman's Badge. *Member:* American Historical Association, Renaissance Society of America, Society for the History of Discoveries.

WRITINGS: Ambassador from Venice, University of Minnesota Press, 1960; (editor) *The Renaissance and the Reformation, 1300-1600*, Free Press of Glencoe, 1965; *Savonarola and Florence: Prophecy and Patriotism in the Renaissance*, Princeton University Press, 1970. Contributor of articles and reviews to professional journals.

WORK IN PROGRESS: Research in religious movements in fifteenth-century Italy and in the history of Florence.†

*   *   *

WEINSTEIN, Sol 1928-

PERSONAL: Born July 29, 1928, in Trenton, N.J.; son of Samuel E. (a junk peddler) and Clara Sara (Sherman) Weinstein; married Ellie Eisner, May 29, 1955; children: David Meyer, Judith Miriam. *Education:* Attended Washington Square College, New York University, three years. *Politics:* ''Hollow centrist.'' *Religion:* Jewish, ''warmly, devotedly so.'' *Home:* 5410 Fenwood Ave., Woodland Hills, Calif. 91364.

CAREER: Trentonian, Trenton, N.J., newspaperman, 1952-60; *Camden Courier-Post*, Camden, N.J., newspaperman, 1960-62; ''Jerry Lester Show'' (television), New York, N.Y., comedy writer, 1962; ''That Was the Week That Was'' (television show), New York, N.Y., comedy writer, 1964. Writer of nightclub material for Joe E. Lewis, Totie Fields, Godfrey Cambridge, Dick Gregory, Jackie Kannon, Pat Henry, Paul Gray, Timmie Rogers, and others. Television credits include ''The Bobby Darin Show,'' ''Sammy Davis, Jr.'s NBC Follies,'' ''Friars Roast of Joe Namath and Sammy Davis, Jr.,'' ''How to Handle a Woman,'' several Alan King specials, and others. *Member:* American Society of Composers, Authors and

Publishers (ASCAP), American Guild of Authors and Composers, Writers Guild of America—West.

WRITINGS: (With Jackie Kannon) *Poems for the John*, Kanrom, 1962; *Loxfinger*, Pocket Books, 1965; *Matzoh-ball*, Pocket Books, 1966; *On the Secret Service of His Majesty, the Queen*, Pocket Books, 1966; *You Only Live Until You Die*, Trident, 1968; *Everything You Never Wanted to Know About Sex: But I'll Tell You Anyway*, Warner Press, 1971; (with Howard Albrecht) *The Odd-father*, Pinnacle Books, 1973; (with Albrecht) *Jonathan Segal Chicken*, Pinnacle Books, 1973; (with Albrecht) *Oh Henry!*, Pinnacle Books, 1973; (with Albrecht) *The Exer-ciser*, Ballantine, 1974.

Contributor to *Playboy, Mad, Metronome, Jazz, Down-beat, Julius Monk Plaza 9 Revue.*

SIDELIGHTS: Weinstein is interested in pop singing and jazz compositions. He wrote a pop ballad, "The Curtain Falls," which was recorded by Steve Lawrence and Eydie Gorme. Weinstein knows Yiddish and some Hebrew and Russian.

* * *

WEIR, Rosemary (Green) 1905-

PERSONAL: Born July 22, 1905, in Kimberley, South Africa; daughter of George Alfred Lawrence (editor of *Cape Argus*) and Katherine (Bell) Green; separated; children: Alison. *Education:* Educated privately and at schools in England. *Politics:* Conservative. *Religion:* Church of England. *Home:* The Old Lodge, Lodge Lane, Axminster, Devonshire, England. *Agent:* Charles Lavell Ltd., Mowbray House, Norfolk St., London W.C.2, England.

CAREER: Trained for stage in England and then became partner in a touring theatrical company, playing one-night stands in rural districts of England and Wales for three years; joined First Aid Nursing Yeomanry when World War II began (invalided out); after that, in partnership with a friend, Lelia Downes-Martin, farmed in North Wales and Devonshire, taught elocution and sewing in a school, ran a furniture renovating business, and worked as a domestic and cook, privately and in hotels and lodges; began writing short stories and articles "in sheer desperation, to dig myself out of tiring and boring jobs with my pen"; now full-time writer for children and young people.

WRITINGS—All youth books: *The Secret Journey*, Parrish, 1957; *The Secret of Cobbet's Farm*, Parrish, 1957; *No. 10 Green Street*, Parrish, 1958; *The Island of Birds*, Parrish, 1959; *The Honeysuckle Line*, Parrish, 1959, published as *Robert's Rescued Railway*, F. Watts, 1959.

The Hunt for Harry, Parrish, 1960; *Great Days in Green Street*, Parrish, 1960; *Pineapple Farm* (school reader), Parrish, 1960; *Little Lion's Real Island*, Harrap, 1960; *A Dog of Your Own* (nonfiction), Harrap, 1960; *The House in the Middle of the Road*, Parrish, 1961; *Albert the Dragon*, Abelard, 1961; *What a Lark*, Brockhampton Press, 1961; *Tania Takes the Stage*, Hutchinson, 1961; *Top Secret*, Parrish, 1962; *Soap Box Derby*, Brockhampton Press, 1962, Van Nostrand, 1965; *Black Sheep*, Criterion, 1963; *The Young David Garrick* (nonfiction), Parrish, 1963; *The Smallest Dog on Earth*, Abelard, 1963; *The Further Adventures of Albert the Dragon*, Abelard, 1964; *The Star and the Flame*, Farrar, Straus, 1964; *Mike's Gang*, Abelard, 1964; *A Patch of Green*, Parrish, 1965; *The Real Game*, Van Nostrand, 1965; *Soap-Box Derby*, Van Nostrand, 1965; *The Boy From Nowhere*, Abelard, 1966; *High Cour-*

age, Farrar, Straus, 1967; *Pyewacket*, Abelard, 1967; *No Sleep for Angus*, Abelard, 1969; *The Man Who Built a City: A Life of Sir Christopher Wren*, Farrar, Straus, 1971; *Boy on a Brown Horse*, Hawthorn, 1971; *Three Red Herrings*, T. Nelson, 1972; *Blood Royal*, Farrar, Straus, 1973.

Scripts for British Broadcasting Corp. include serialization of *The Secret Journey* and a series, "Strange Tales."

WORK IN PROGRESS: A historical novel for older children about the Monmouth rebellion.

SIDELIGHTS: Rosemary Weir's books for children have appeared in Holland, France, and Switzerland, as well as United States. *Avocational interests:* The theater, classical music, animals, gardening, and country life.

BIOGRAPHICAL SOURCES: Trade News, September 23, 1961.†

* * *

WEISS, David 1909-

PERSONAL: Born June 12, 1909, in Philadelphia, Pa.; son of Hyman (a painter) and Rebecca (Goldberg) Weiss; married Stymean Karlen (an artist and writer), November 25, 1945. *Education:* Temple University, B.Sc., 1933; New School for Social Research, graduate courses in drama, 1943-46. *Politics:* Liberal. *Home:* 235 West End Ave., New York, N.Y. 10023. *Agent:* Robert Lantz Ltd., 111 West 57th St., New York, N.Y. 10019.

CAREER: Full-time novelist in more recent years. Earlier jobs (about fifty) ranged from stevedore to story editor for David O. Selznick, and included meat-loader, actor, welfare worker, ghost writer, store clerk, and basketball and swimming instructor. Weiss also has held editorial posts with other major Hollywood studios besides Selznick—Paramount, 20th Century-Fox, RKO, and Columbia Pictures. *Awards, honors:* Frieder Literary Award ($5,000) for best novel on a Jewish theme published in America, 1953, for *The Guilt Makers.*

WRITINGS: The Guilt Makers, Rinehart, 1953; *The Spirit and the Flesh* (novel based on the life of Isadora Duncan), Doubleday, 1959; *Naked Came I: A Novel of Rodin* (Literary Guild selection), Morrow, 1963; *Justin Moyan*, Morrow, 1965; *The Great Fire of London*, Crown, 1968; *Sacred and Profane*, Morrow, 1968; *The Assassination of Mozart*, Morrow, 1970; *No Number is Greater than One*, Coward, 1972; *Myself, Christopher Wren*, Coward, 1974.

WORK IN PROGRESS: A novel.

SIDELIGHTS: Weiss' first novel won the Frieder award over nearly eight hundred other entries, but *Naked Came I* has been his major success to date. It was distributed by major U.S. book clubs (with a combined readership of 5,-000,000), and translated into twenty-five languages. John Barkham has called Weiss, "the most gifted biographical novelist writing today."

BIOGRAPHICAL/CRITICAL SOURCES: New York Times Book Review, November 15, 1959, November 24, 1963; *Newsweek*, November 25, 1963; *Book Week*, December 15, 1963; *America*, January 11, 1964.

* * *

WEISSMAN, Jack 1921-
(George Anderson)

PEAL: Born June 6, 1921, in Chicago, Ill.; son of Ben and Ida (Meyerson) Weissman; married Bernice Platt, November 13, 1949; children: Bruce, David, Ellen. *Education:*

Northwestern University, B.S., 1942, M.S. in Journalism, 1943; University of Chicago, graduate study, 1947. *Religion:* Jewish. *Home:* 8622 Keystone, Skokie, Ill. *Agent:* Donald MacCampbell, Inc., 12 East 41st St., New York, N.Y. 10017. *Office: Opportunity*, 1460 John Hancock Center, Chicago, Ill. 60611.

CAREER: Banker's Monthly (magazine), Chicago, Ill., assistant editor, 1943; *Practical Knowledge* (magazine), Chicago, Ill., managing editor, 1944-46; Roosevelt University, Chicago, Ill., member of publicity staff, 1947-50; *Opportunity* (magazine), Chicago, Ill., managing editor, 1950—. *Military service:* U.S. Army, 1945-46; received Army Commendation Medal. *Member:* Chicago Press Club, Sigma Delta Chi, Phi Delta Kappa.

WRITINGS—Under pseudonym George Anderson: *Make Money at Home*, MacFadden, 1962; *How to Make a Fast Buck*, MacFadden, 1963; *How to Make Correct Decisions*, MacFadden, 1964; *Money Making Businesses You Can Start for $500 or Less*, MacFadden, 1965.

* * *

WEITHORN, Stanley S. 1924-

PERSONAL: Born August 28, 1924, in New York, N.Y.; son of Louis W. (a corporate executive) and Florence (Mandel) Weithorn; married Corrine J. Breslow, December 26, 1949; children: Lois Ann, Michael Joshua. *Education:* Hofstra University, B.S., 1947; New York University, LL.B., 1954, LL.M., 1956. *Politics:* Democrat. *Religion:* Jewish. *Home:* 144 Woodhill Lane, Manhasset, N.Y. 11030. *Office:* Chrysler Bldg., New York, N.Y. 10017.

CAREER: Admitted to New York bar, 1955; engaged in practice of law, New York, N.Y., 1955—, as partner in firm of Wormser, Koch, Kiely & Alessandroni, 1964-66; private practice, 1967-68; Upham, Meeker, and Weithorn, senior partner, 1968—. Practicing Law Institute, lecturer and panel member, 1956—, panel chairman, 1962-64; lecturer on tax matters at New York University, DePaul University, and for other groups. Member of leadership council of United Jewish Appeal, 1966—, member of executive committee, Equal Opportunity Council, Inc., 1968—. *Military service:* U.S. Army, 1943-46; served in European Theater. *Member:* American Bar Association, National Social Welfare Assembly, Tax Discussion Group (New York; founder).

WRITINGS: Penalty Taxes on Accumulated Earnings and Personal Holding Companies, Practising Law Institute, 1963; *Tax Techniques for Foundations and Other Exempt Organizations*, Bender, 1964; (contributor) *Lasser's Income Tax Techniques*, Bender, 1965. Contributor of articles on tax law to journals. Contributing editor, *Tax Management*, 1959—.†

* * *

WELFORD, A(lan) T(raviss) 1914-

PERSONAL: Born January 27, 1914, in London, England. *Education:* Cambridge University, B.A., 1935; M.A., 1939, Sc.D., 1964; Princeton University, M.A., 1946. *Office:* Department of Psychology, University of Adelaide, Adelaide 5001, Australia.

CAREER: Cambridge University, Cambridge, England, Nuffield Unit for Research Into Problems of Ageing, director, 1946-56, university lecturer in experimental psychology, 1947-68, fellow and tutor of St. John's College, 1956-68; University of Adelaide, Adelaide, Australia, professor of psychology, 1968—. University of Adelaide, visiting professor, 1964. Ordained deacon of Church of England, 1937, priest, 1938. *Member:* British Psychological Society (fellow), Experimental Psychology Society, Gerontological Society (fellow), Ergonomics Research Society (chairman of council, 1954-57; honorary member), Ergonomics Society of Australia and New Zealand (fellow), Academy of the Social Sciences in Australia (fellow), Australian Psychological Society (fellow). *Awards, honors:* Kenneth Craik Award for physiological psychology, 1948; Vernon Prize for industrial psychology, 1958.

WRITINGS: Skill and Age: An Experimental Approach, Oxford University Press, 1951; (editor with W. F. Floyd) *Fatigue*, H. K. Lewis & Co., 1953; (editor with Floyd) *Human Factors in Equipment Design*, H. K. Lewis & Co., 1954; *Ageing and Human Skill*, Oxford University Press, 1958; *Ergonomics of Automation*, H.M.S.O., 1960; (editor with M. Argyle, D. V. Glass, and J. N. Morris) *Society: Problems and Methods of Study*, Routledge & Kegan Paul, 1962; (editor with J. E. Birren) *Behavior, Aging and the Nervous System*, C. C Thomas, 1964; *Fundamentals of Skill*, Methuen, 1968; (editor with Birren) *Decision Making and Age: Interdisciplinary Topics in Gerontology IV*, Karger, 1969; (editor with L. Houssiadas) *Contemporary Problems in Perception*, Taylor & Francis, 1970; *Christianity: A Psychologists Translation*, Hodder & Stoughton, 1971; (editor) *Man Under Stress*, Taylor & Francis, 1974. Editor of *Ergonomics*, 1957-64.

* * *

WELLS, Joel F(reeman) 1930-

PERSONAL: Born March 17, 1930, in Evansville, Ind.; son of William Jackson (an engineer) and Edith (Strassell) Wells; married Elizabeth Hein, June 5, 1952; children: William, Eugenia, Susan, Steven, Daniel. *Education:* University of Notre Dame, B.A. (journalism), 1952; Northwestern University, graduate study, 1963. *Religion:* Roman Catholic. *Home:* 827 Colfax St., Evanston, Ill. *Office:* Thomas More Association, 180 North Wabash, Chicago, Ill. 60601.

CAREER: Thomas More Association, Chicago, Ill., promotion director, 1955-64, editor of *Critic* (magazine), 1964—, editor of Thomas More Press, 1971—, vice-president and director. Rosary College, River Forest, Ill., lecturer, 1963—. *Military service:* U.S. Navy, 1952-55; became lieutenant junior grade.

WRITINGS: (Editor with Dan Herr) *Bodies and Souls*, Doubleday, 1961; (editor with Herr) *Blithe Spirits*, Doubleday, 1962; (editor with Herr) *Bodies and Spirits*, Doubleday, 1964; (editor with Herr) *Through Other Eyes*, Newman, 1965; *Grim Fairy Tales for Adults*, Macmillan, 1968; *A Funny Thing Happened to the Church*, Macmillan, 1969; *Second Collection*, Thomas More Press, 1973. Contributor of fiction, articles, and parodies to newspapers and periodicals including *New York Times*, *National Catholic Reporter*, and *Chicago Sun-Times*.

* * *

WELSCH, Glenn Albert 1915-

PERSONAL: Born April 1, 1915, in Woodward, Okla.; son of George Franklin (a farmer) and Minnie Melissa (Bowers) Welsch; married Irma Richards, April 5, 1942; children: Glenn Andrew, Linden Richards, Mary Ann. *Education:* Northwestern State College, Alva, Okla., B.S., 1935; Oklahoma State University, M.S., 1949; University of Texas, Ph.D., 1952; *Religion:* Methodist. *Home:* 3405 Taylors

Dr., Austin, Tex. *Office:* Graduate School of Business, University of Texas, Austin, Tex.

CAREER: Certified public accountant, Oklahoma, 1949, Texas, 1952. High school teacher in Alva, Okla., 1937-40; American National Life Insurance Co., Bartlesville, Okla., salesman, 1946-48; University of Texas, College of Business Administration, Austin, 1952—, started as assistant professor, professor of accounting, 1955—, John Arch White professor of accounting, 1968—, associate dean for graduate studies, 1962-67. Carman G. Blough Distinguished professor (visiting), University of Virginia, 1970-71. *Military service:* U.S. Army, Signal Corps, 1940-46; served in European and Pacific theaters; graduate of Command and General Staff College, 1944; became major. *Member:* American Accounting Association (vice-president, 1959; president, 1963-64), National Association of Cost Accountants, American Institute of Certified Public Accountants, Southwestern Social Science Association, Texas Society of Certified Public Accountants (vice-president, 1960), Financial Executives Institute, Planning Executives Institute, Beta Alpha Psi, Beta Gamma Sigma.

WRITINGS: (With B. H. Sord) *Business Budgeting—A Survey of Management Planning Control Practices*, Controllership Foundation, 1958; (with C. T. Zlatkovich and J. A. White) *Intermediate Accounting*, Irwin, 1963, revised edition, 1972; *Budgeting: Profit Planning and Control*, 3rd edition, Prentice-Hall, 1971; (with Sord) *Managerial Planning and Control as Viewed by Lower Levels of Supervision*, Bureau of Business Research, University of Texas, 1964; (with Charles H. Griffin) *Advanced Accounting*, Irwin, 1966; *Cases in Profit Planning and Control*, Prentice-Hall, 1970; *Programmed Learning Aid for Intermediate Accounting*, two volumes, Learning Systems Co., 1970. Writer of a manual on profit planning and control and of a U.S. Small Business Administration pamphlet. Contributor to accounting and other business journals.

WORK IN PROGRESS: A research project on the essential ingredients for effective management, for the Financial Executives Institute (New York), the results to be published as a book.

AVOCATIONAL INTERESTS: Philosophy, history, antique automobiles, sports.†

* * *

WELTHY, Soni Halstead 1933-

PERSONAL: Born August 11, 1933, in Ann Arbor, Mich.; daughter of Gordon B. (an educator) and Helen (Honsinger) Halstead; married Davendra K. Welthy, May 2, 1953; children: Shantnu Lauro (son), Rytra Karuna (daughter). *Education:* Attended Antioch College, 1951-52, Visva-Bharati, Santiniketan, West Bengal, 1952-53; Calcutta University, I.A., 1955; attended New School for Social Research, and Fairleigh Dickinson University; received B.A. *Home:* 108 Meadow Crest Rd., Bristol, Tenn.

CAREER: History teacher, Ridgewood, N.J., 1962-63. Ridgewood Committee for Experiment in International Living, chairman, 1962-63, 1964-65; Soni School, Bristol, Tenn., director, 1971—. *Awards, honors:* New Jersey Association of English Teachers Award; Named Outstanding Young Educator in State of California, 1969.

WRITINGS: Getting to Know the River Ganges, Coward, 1964.

WORK IN PROGRESS: A novel about a middle-class woman in changing India.

SIDELIGHTS: Ms. Welthy lived in India, 1952-57, returned there in 1962 as leader of a student-teacher tour.

* * *

WENGER, (Anna) Grace 1919-

PERSONAL: Born July 26, 1919, in Ronks, Pa.; daughter of Elam Musselman (a farmer) and Anna (Myer) Wenger. *Education:* Elizabethtown College, B.S. in Education, 1940; University of Pennsylvania, M.A., 1949. *Politics:* Independent. *Religion:* Mennonite. *Home:* 171 East Main St., Leola, Pa.

CAREER: Elementary teacher in public schools in Pennsylvania, 1940-43; Eastern Mennonite College, Harrisonburg, Va., English teacher, 1943-56; Lancaster Mennonite School, Lancaster, Pa., English teacher, 1956—; Mennonite Publishing House, Scottdale, Pa., missionary education editor, 1959—. *Member:* National Council of Teachers of English.

WRITINGS—All published by Herald: *God Leads Us to Witness at Home*, 1960; *God Builds the Church in Latin America*, 1961; *God Builds the Church Through Congregational Witness*, 1962; *God Builds the Church in South Asia*, 1963; *Stewards of the Gospel*, 1964.†

* * *

WERMUTH, Paul C(harles Joseph) 1925-

PERSONAL: Surname is pronounced Worm-*youth*; born October 28, 1925, in Philadelphia, Pa.; son of Paul C. (a railroad dispatcher) and Susan (Manga) Wermuth; married Barbara E. Braun (a registered nurse), August 26, 1951; children: Geoffrey, Paul, Jr., Alan, Stephen. *Education:* Boston University, A.B., 1951, M.A., 1951; Pennsylvania State University, Ph.D., 1955. *Home:* 73 Mostyn St., Swampscott, Mass. *Office:* Department of English, Northeastern University, Boston, Mass.

CAREER: Clarkson College of Technology, Potsdam, N.Y., instructor in English, 1951-52; Pennsylvania State University, University Park, part-time instructor in English, 1952-55; College of William and Mary, Richmond, Va., assistant professor of English, 1955-57; Central Connecticut State College, New Britain, began as assistant professor, became associate professor of English, 1957-68; Northeastern University, Boston, Mass., professor of English and chairman of department, 1968—. Visiting associate professor of American literature at Middlebury College, 1963-64. *Military service:* U.S. Army Air Forces, 1943-45. *Member:* Modern Language Association of America, American Studies Association, Mensa. *Awards, honors:* Danforth Foundation summer study grant, 1961.

WRITINGS: (Editor) *Modern Essays on Writing and Style*, Holt, 1964, 2nd edition, 1969; (editor) *Essays in English: Ascham to Baldwin*, Holt, 1967; *Bayard Taylor*, Twayne, 1973. Contributor of articles and reviews to *Virginia Cavalcade, New England Quarterly, Library Journal* and other periodicals; occasional writer of verse and children's stories.

WORK IN PROGRESS: A critical study of the Genteel Tradition, and associated authors.

* * *

WERNER, Eric 1901-

PERSONAL: Born August 1, 1901, in Vienna, Austria; came to United States in 1938; son of Julius (a professor) and Helen (Donath) Werner; married Elizabeth Mendelssohn, July, 1932. *Education:* Studied at Universities of Graz, Vienna, Prague, Berlin, Goettingen, and Strasbourg, receiving Ph.D., 1928; also studied at conservatories and academies of music in Vienna and Berlin. *Office:* Hebrew Union College-Jewish Institute of Religion, 40 West 68th St., New York, N.Y. 10023.

CAREER: Hebrew Union College-Jewish Institute of Religion, New York, N.Y., 1938—, now professor of musicology and comparative liturgy and head of graduate department; Tel Aviv University, Tel Aviv, Israel, chairman of department of musicology, 1966-71. Visiting professor at other universities. Composer and writer. *Member:* International Musicology Association (fellow), American Musicological Society, American Academy of Jewish Research, American Society of Ethnomusicology, American Association of University Professors, Central Conference of American Rabbis. *Awards, honors:* Guggenheim fellowship, 1957; American Council of Learned Societies fellowship; D.H.C., Hebrew Union College, 1967.

WRITINGS: In the Choir Loft, Union of American Hebrew Congregations, 1958; *The Sacred Bridge*, Columbia University Press, 1959; *Anthology of Hebrew Music*, A. Volk Verlag, 1962; *Mendelssohn: A New Image of the Composer and His Age*, Free Press of Glencoe, 1963; (editor) *Contributions to a Systematic Study of Jewish Music*, Ktav, 1972; *A Voice Still Heard*, Pennsylvania State University Press. Also editor of *Urtext: Selected Piano Music of Mendelssohn*, Henle Publishing, New York. Contributor of articles to journals in his field.

SIDELIGHTS: Eric Werner is competent in English, German, Italian, and Hebrew; reads French, Latin, and Greek. *Avocational interests:* Mountaineering, chess, travel.

*   *   *

WERNING, Waldo J.   1921-

PERSONAL: Born May 1, 1921, in Newhall, Iowa; son of George C. (a farmer) and Paula (Dornseif) Werning; married Ruth C. Kienow (a teacher), July 28, 1945; children: Sharon, Daniel, Charlotte, Jonathan, James. *Education:* Studied at Concordia College, St. Paul, Minn., 1939-41, Concordia Seminary, St. Louis, Mo., 1941-45, Concordia Teachers College, River Forest, Ill., 1943, 1946. *Home:* 3141 Prairie Rd., Lincoln, Neb. 68506. *Office:* Southern Nebraska District of the Lutheran Church, 733 South 13th St., Lincoln, Neb. 68508.

CAREER: Lutheran minister. Lutheran Church-Missouri Synod, St. Louis, Mo., associate stewardship counselor, 1952-56, executive secretary of stewardship and missions, Southern Nebraska District, Lincoln, 1956—. Also member of Synod's Board for European Affairs, 1962—. Leader of Orient mission tour, 1960, European tour, 1961, world tour, 1963. *Member:* Lutheran Academy of Scholarship, Lutheran Education Association, Lutheran Human Relations Association of America, People-to-People.

WRITINGS: Partners With God, Lockwood Luminary, 1948; *Investing Your Life*, Zondervan, 1955; *How to Raise Men and Money*, American Lutheran Publicity Bureau, 1956; *Your Pulpit in Life*, Church-Craft, 1962; *Come, Follow Me!*, Concordia, 1955; *Winning Them Back*, Augsburg, 1963; (editor) *Topics and Program Helps*, Lutheran Women's Missionary League, 1963; *Where Does the Money Go?*, Church-Craft, 1964; *Stewardship: Theology, Message and Method*, Concordia, 1965; *Managing Your*

Life for Christ, Concordia, 1965; (with Albert Miller) *Growing as a Christian* (teacher's and pupil's books), Concordia, 1967.

Writer of three filmstrips issued by Church-Craft Pictures, 1960-64. Evangelism columnist and contributor to *American Lutheran*, 1957—; contributor to other Lutheran periodicals. Member of editorial committee and topic editor, *Lutheran Woman's Quarterly*, 1957—.

WORK IN PROGRESS: Live!, a stewardship book for youth, and accompanying filmstrip, for Church-Craft.†

*   *   *

WESCOTT, Glenway   1901-

PERSONAL: Born April 11, 1901, in Kewaskum, Wis.; son of Bruce Peters (a farmer) and Josephine (Gordon) Wescott. *Education:* Attended University of Chicago, 1917-19. *Home:* Haymeadows, Rosemont, N.J.

CAREER: Full-time writer, 1921—. *Member:* Authors Guild (council), National Institute of Arts and Letters (president, 1959-62), American Academy of Arts and Letters. *Awards, honors:* Harper Prize, 1927, for *The Grandmothers*; D.Litt., Rutgers University, 1963.

WRITINGS: The Bitterns (poems), Monroe Wheeler, 1920; *The Apple of the Eye* (novel), Dial, 1924; *Natives of Rock* (poems), Francisco Bianco (New York), 1925; *The Grandmothers* (novel), Harper, 1927; *Good-buy Wisconsin* (stories), Harper, 1928; *The Babe's Bed* (novella), Harrison (Paris), 1930; *Fear and Trembling* (essays), Harper, 1932; *A Calendar of Saints for Unbelievers* (hagiography), Harrison, 1932; *The Pilgrim Hawk* (novella), Harper, 1940; *Apartment in Athens* (novel), Harper, 1945; (editor and author of introduction) *The Maugham Reader*, Doubleday, 1950; (editor and author of introduction) *Short Novels of Colette*, Dial, 1951; (narrator) *Twelve Fables of Aesop* (stories), Museum of Modern Art, 1954; *Images of Truth* (criticism), Harper 1962; *The Best of All Possible Worlds: Journals, Letters and Remembrances, 1914-1937*, Farrar, Straus, 1975.

SIDELIGHTS: Glenway Wescott, a contemporary of F. Scott Fitzgerald, lived for eight years in France. Before and after those years he traveled to Europe frequently with friends or family. Patricia Kane writes, ''A principal question for mankind, according to Glenway Wescott, is the way home, a theme recurring from Homer's *Odyssey*, to contemporary novels. Wescott's own fiction can be seen as illustrating this theme; from his stories about Americans in his home state of Wisconsin, to one of an American's experience in Europe, to a story of Greece and its traditions of heroic manhood, his work reflects a journey home, a movement from the place of birth to the place of affinity. Although Wescott has been praised more for his style than for this substance (he once called himself a fussy stylist), in his theme of going home, he has written a kind of Odyssey of an American that deserves attention for itself as well as for its embodiment in his fine prose.''

BIOGRAPHICAL/CRITICAL SOURCES: Edmund Wilson, *Classics and Commercials*, Farrar, Straus, 1950; *Time*, September 28, 1962; *New Yorker*, September 29, 1962; *Saturday Review*, October 6, 1962; *Commonweal*, October 12, 1962; *New York Times Book Review*, October 21, 1962; William H. Rueckert, *Glenway Wescott*, Twayne, 1965; Ira D. Johnson, *Glenway Wescott: The Paradox of Voice*, Kennikat Press, 1971.

WESSEL, Helen (Strain) 1924-

PERSONAL: Born January 9, 1924, in San Anselmo, Calif.; daughter of John Albert and Laura (Hammerli) Strain; married Walter W. Wessel (a Baptist minister), June 22, 1945; children: Margaret, Sharyl, Deborah, Dorothy, Daniel, Donald. *Education:* Sioux Falls College, B.A., 1960; University of Minnesota, currently graduate student. *Religion:* Baptist. *Home:* 3905 Rolling Hills Rd., St. Paul, Minn. 55112.

CAREER: Currently president of Bookmates International, Orange, Calif., and Bookmates Inc., Ossian, Indiana (publishers). *Member:* International Childbirth Education Association (president, 1964-66).

WRITINGS: Natural Childbirth and the Christian Family, Harper, 1963, revised edition published as *Natural Childbirth and the Family*, 1973; (editor with Harlan F. Ellis, M.D.) Grantly Dick Read, *Childbirth Without Fear*, 4th edition, Harper, 1972; (with Neil and Peggy Verwey) *Voice of Joy*, Bookmates, 1973.

WORK IN PROGRESS: Various book manuscripts.

*   *   *

WEST, D(onald) J(ames) 1924-

PERSONAL: Born June 9, 1924, in Liverpool, England. *Education:* University of Liverpool, M.B. and Ch.B., 1947, M.D., 1958; University of London, Diploma in Psychological Medicine, 1952. *Residence:* Cambridge, England.

CAREER: Cambridge University Institute of Criminology, Cambridge, England, assistant director of research, 1960—. Honorary consultant psychiatrist in the Cambridge Psychiatric Service, Cambridge, England. *Member:* College of Psychiatrists, Society for Psychical Research (president, 1964-65).

WRITINGS: Eleven Lourdes Miracles, Duckworth, 1957; *Homosexuality*, Penguin, 1960; *Psychical Research Today*, Penguin, 1962; *The Habitual Prisoner*, Macmillan, 1963; *Murder Followed by Suicide*, Heinemann, 1965; *The Young Offender*, Penguin, 1967; *Present Conduct and Future Delinquency*, Heinemann, 1969; *Who Becomes Delinquent*, Heinemann, 1973.

*   *   *

WEST, John Foster 1918-

PERSONAL: Born December 10, 1918, in Champion, N.C.; son of John Wilson (a farmer) and Elvira (Foster) West; married Nan Elizabeth Love, January 15, 1944 (deceased); children: Bettie Sue, Leah Clarice, John Kimrey. *Education:* Attended Mars Hill Junior College, 1940-42; University of North Carolina, A.B., 1947, M.A., 1949; State University of Iowa Writers Workshop, summer, 1952. *Politics:* Democrat. *Religion:* ex-Methodist. *Home:* Route #4, Box 379C, Boone, N.C. 28607. *Office:* Appalachian State University, Boone, N.C.

CAREER: Elon College, Elon College, N.C., professor of English, 1949-58; Old Dominion College, Norfolk, Va., assistant professor of English, beginning 1958; currently at Appalachian State University, Boone, N.C., associate professor of English, writer-in-residence. *Military service:* North Carolina National Guard (Engineers), 1938-40; U.S. Air Corps, 1943-46; served as aviation cadet. *Member:* Association for Education in Journalism, North Carolina Folklore Society (president), North Carolina Writer's Conference (chairman, 1970), North Carolina Literary and His-

torical Association, Sigma Delta Chi. *Awards, honors:* Dodd, Mead Intercollegiate Fellowship for Novels, runner-up, 1947; North Carolina Poetry Society state contest, first prize, 1951; Southern Fellowship Award, 1956.

WRITINGS: up ego! (poetry), privately printed by Payton, Paul Publishing Co., 1951; *Time Was* (novel), Random House, 1965; *The Ballad of Tom Dula*, Moore Publishing, 1970; *Appalachian Dawn*, Moore Publishing, 1973. Cofounder and member of first fiction staff, *Carolina Quarterly*. Frequent contributor of poems and short stories to *Red Clay Reader, Carolina Quarterly*, and other periodicals.

SIDELIGHTS: West told *CA* that he "started working toward career as writer at age of eight. Had seven novels rejected before *Time Was*.... I write only when I feel like it and then furiously.... I do all my own typing [and] editing." West reads French, German, and Latin. *Avocational interests:* Studying folklore, especially of the southern Appalachians, swimming, skiing, camping, and hiking.

BIOGRAPHICAL/CRITICAL SOURCES: North Carolina Folklore Journal, March, 1971.

*   *   *

WEST, Paul 1930-

PERSONAL: Born February 23, 1930, in Eckington, Derbyshire, England; son of Alfred Massick and Mildred (Noden) West; children: Amanda Klare. *Education:* University of Birmingham, B.A., 1950; Oxford University, graduate study, 1950-52; Columbia University, M.A., 1953. *Home:* 313 West Prospect Ave., State College, Pa. 16801. *Agent:* Helen Brann, 14 Sutton Place S., New York, N.y. 10022. *Office:* South 133 Burrowes, University Park, Pa. 16802.

CAREER: Memorial University of Newfoundland, St. John's, Newfoundland, began as assistant professor, associate professor of English, 1957-62; Pennsylvania State University, University Park, associate professor, 1963-69, professor of English and comparative literature, 1969—, senior fellow of Institute for Arts and Humanistics Studies, 1970—. Visiting professor, University of Wisconsin, 1956-66; Crawshaw Professor of English, Colgate University, 1972; Melvin Hill Distinguished Visiting Professor of Humanities, Hobart and William Smith Colleges, 1974. *Military service:* Royal Air Force, 1954-57; became flight lieutenant. *Member:* P.E.N., Authors Guild. *Awards, honors:* Canada Council senior fellowship, 1959; Guggenheim fellowship, 1962; Listed in "Books of the Year" by *New York Times*, 1969, for *Words for a Deaf Daughter*, 1970, for *I'm Expecting to Live Quite Soon*, and 1971, for *Caliban's Filibuster*; *Words for a Deaf Daughter* also included in "Best Books of the Year" list by *Time*, 1969; *Paris Review* Aga Khan Prize for fiction, 1974.

WRITINGS: The Fantasy Poets: Number Seven, Fantasy Press, 1952; *The Growth of the Novel*, Canadian Broadcasting Corp., 1959; *The Spellbound Horses* (poems), Ryerson, 1960; *Byron and the Spoiler's Art*, St. Martin's, 1960; *A Quality of Mercy* (novel), Chatto & Windus, 1961; *I, Said the Sparrow* (memoirs), Hutchinson, 1963; (editor) *Byron: A Collection of Critical Essays*, Prentice-Hall, 1963; *The Modern Novel* (two volumes), Hillary, 1963, 2nd edition, 1965; *Robert Penn Warren*, University of Minnesota Press, 1964; *The Snow Leopard* (poems), Hutchinson, 1964, Harcourt, 1965; *Tenement of Clay* (novel), Hutchinson, 1965; *The Wine of Absurdity: Essays on Literature and Consolation*, Pennsylvania State University Press, 1966; *Alley Jaggers* (novel), Harper, 1966; *Words for a Deaf Daughter*, Harper, 1969; *I'm Expecting to Live Quite Soon* (novel), Harper, 1970; *Caliban's Filibuster* (novel), Doubleday, 1971; *Bela Lugosi's White Christmas* (novel), Harper, 1972; *Colonel Mint* (novel), Dutton, 1973.

Regular contributor to *Book World* and *New York Times Book Review*. Also contributor of essays, poems, and reviews to *Botteghe Oscure, Times Literary Supplement, Nation, Kenyon Review, South Atlantic Quarterly, New World Writing, London Magazine, Sinn und Form, Twentieth Century, New American Review, Partisan Review, New Directions Literary Anthology, New Story, Paris Review, Harpers, Nova, New Literary History, Modern Occasions, Carleton Miscellany*, and other journals. Fiction critic, *New Statesman*, 1959-60.

WORK IN PROGRESS: A collection of short fiction and two new novels; also a volume of autobiography.

SIDELIGHTS: West is "a lyrical stringer together of invective, riposte and gossip," writes J. A. Cuddon, "The fluency is torrential; reminiscent of Anthony Burgess and Joyce Cary clinched in a pummelling fifteen round contest with a running commentary by William Faulkner, it is at once exhausting and curiously elating.... As long as there are writers like Mr. West the novel is far from moribund." Daniel Stern speaks of "the extraordinary gifts of [the] author," gifts that are displayed in *Words for a Deaf Daughter*, which is "brilliant and joyful," according to John Hollander, who continues: "Some of the words are really poems and fictions that flower in the richness of Mandy's father's awareness of her." It is the opinion of R. Z. Sheppard that "It is an act of love, not merely its expression.... It is also a work of art, the vision of the loved object widening beyond adoration into new ways of seeing the world."

AVOCATIONAL INTERESTS: Music, travel, and astronomy.

BIOGRAPHICAL/CRITICAL SOURCES: Paul West, *Caliban's Filibuster* (appendix), Doubleday, 1971.

* * *

WESTIN, Alan F(urman) 1929-

PERSONAL: Born October 11, 1929, in New York, N.Y.; son of Irving (a retail merchant) and Etta (Furman) Westin; married Bea Shapoff (a teacher), June 20, 1954. *Education:* University of Florida, A.B., 1948; Harvard University, LL.B., 1951, Ph.D., 1965. *Home:* 1092 Windsor Rd., Teaneck, N.J. *Office:* Fayerweather Hall, Columbia University, New York, N.Y. 10027.

CAREER: Cornell University, Ithaca, N.Y., assistant professor of government, 1957-59; Yale University, New Haven, Conn., visiting associate professor of political science, 1960-61; Columbia University, New York, N.Y., lecturer in Law School, 1962, lecturer in Teachers College, 1962-64, associate professor of public law and government, 1959—, and director of Center for Research and Education in American Liberties, 1965—. Salzburg Seminar in American Studies, lecturer, 1958; Brandeis University, Sidney Hillman Lecturer, 1959. Executive vice-president of National Assembly on Teaching the Principles of the Bill of Rights; member of national board of directors of American Civil Liberties Union, of national civil rights committee of Anti-Defamation League, of legal committee of American Committee for Cultural Freedom, and of commission on law and social action of American Jewish Congress. Expert witness at U.S. Senate Subcommittee on Constitutional Rights wiretap hearings, 1958, 1961. Has appeared on "Open End," "Open Mind," "Court of Reason," and other television programs.

AWARDS, HONORS: Rockefeller Foundation grant, 1959-60; research grants from Fund for the Republic and New World Foundation; Distinguished Alumnus Award from Delta Sigma Rho-Tau Kappa Alpha, 1965.

WRITINGS: The Anatomy of a Constitutional Law Case, Macmillan, 1958; *The Supreme Court: Views from Inside*, Norton, 1961; *The Uses of Power: Seven Cases in American Politics*, Harcourt, 1961; (editor of reprint edition, with introduction and bibliographies) Charles Beard, *The Supreme Court and the Constitution*, Prentice-Hall, 1962; (with C. Herman Pritchett) *The Third Branch of Government*, Harcourt, 1962; (with Louis Koenig and H. D. Price) *The Centers of Power*, Harcourt, 1963; *An Autobiography of the Supreme Court*, Macmillan, 1963; (with John Stoessinger) *Power and Order: Seven Cases in World Politics*, Harcourt, 1963; *Freedom Now! The Civil Rights Struggle in America*, Basic Books, 1964; (with E. Redford, D. Truman, A. Hacker, and R. Wood) *Politics and Government in the United States*, Harcourt, 1965; (with Gwendolyn Carter) *Politics in Europe: Five Cases in European Government*, Harcourt, 1965.

(Editor with others) *Views of America*, Harcourt, 1966; (editor with Alexander Dallin) *Politics in the Soviet Union*, Harcourt, 1966; *Privacy and Freedom*, Atheneum, 1967; *The Anatomy of a Constitutional Law Case*, Macmillan, 1968; (editor) *Information Technology in a Democracy*, Harvard University Press, 1971; (editor) *Databanks in a Free Society*, Quadrangle, 1972; (with Barry Mahoney) *Martin Luther King, Jr. and the Supreme Court*, T. Y. Crowell, 1973; *The Trial of Martin Luther King, Jr.*, T. Y. Crowell, 1974.

Contributor: Alfred Kelley, editor, *Foundations of Freedom in the American Constitution*, Harper, 1958; Daniel Bell, editor, *The Radical Right*, Doubleday, 1963; Dunham and Kurland, editors, *Mr. Justice*, University of Chicago Press, 1964; John A. Garrary, editor, *Quarrels That Have Shaped the Constitution*, Harper, 1964.

Contributor to *New York Times, Harper's, American Heritage, New Republic, Nation, New Leader, Saturday Review*, and other magazines, and to law journals. Political science editor, "Casebook Series," Harcourt.†

* * *

WESTON, Paul B(rendan) 1910-

PERSONAL: Born July 23, 1910, in Dobbs Ferry, N.Y.; children: Mary Ellen. *Education:* Studied writing at Columbia University; Sacramento State College (now California State University, Sacramento), B.A., 1961, M.A., 1963. *Agent:* Harold Altshuler, 225 West 86th St., New York, N.Y. 10024. *Office:* Department of Police Science, 6000 Jay St., California State University, Sacramento, Calif. 95819.

CAREER: New York (N.Y.) Police Department, 1936-58, began as rookie policeman, became deputy chief inspector; California State University, Sacramento, associate professor of government and of police science, and chairman of department of police science, 1959-71, professor of criminal justice, 1971—. Consultant to California Disaster Office, 1959-61, California State Police, 1962-63, California

Department of Mental Hygiene, 1963—. *Military service:* U.S. Navy, 1943-46. *Member:* International Association of Chiefs of Police, International Association of Police Professors, American Society of Criminology, Kiwanis Club.

WRITINGS: Target Shooting Today, Greenberg, 1951; (editor and collaborator) *The Handbook of Criminal Investigation*, Greenberg, 1952; (editor and collaborator) *Plainclothesman*, Greenberg, 1953; (with William F. Kessler) *The Detection of Murder*, Greenberg, 1954; (with Brendan P. Battle) *Arson*, Greenberg, 1956; *The Police Traffic Control Function*, C. C Thomas, 1958, 2nd edition, 1968; (editor and co-author) *Narcotics, U.S.A.*, Greenberg, 1958.

Combat Shooting for Police, C. C Thomas, 1960; *Hammer in the City*, Regency, 1962; *Muscle on Broadway*, Regency, 1962; *Mayor Mike* (three-act play), Sacramento State College Foundation, 1964; (contributor) *Interdisciplinary Problems in Criminology*, Ohio State University Press, 1964; *Supervision in the Administration of Justice: Police, Corrections, Courts*, C. C Thomas, 1965; (with Kenneth M. Wells) *The Administration of Justice*, Prentice-Hall, 1967, 2nd edition, 1973; *The Handbook of Handgunning: New Concepts in Pistol and Revolver Shooting*, Crown, 1968.

(With Wells) *Criminal Investigation: Basic Perspectives*, Prentice-Hall, 1970, 2nd edition, 1974; (with Wells) *Elements of Criminal Investigation*, Prentice-Hall, 1971; (with Wells) *Criminal Evidence for Police*, Prentice-Hall, 1971; *Criminal Justice and Law Enforcement: Cases*, Prentice-Hall, 1972; (with Wells) *Fundamentals of Evidence*, Prentice-Hall, 1972; *Law Enforcement and Criminal Justice: An Introduction*, Goodyear Publishing, 1972; (with Robert W. Cole) *Case Studies of Drug Abuse and Criminal Behavior*, Goodyear Publishing, 1973.

Contributor of articles on guns and shooting to *Field and Stream, Guns and Hunting*, and *Gun Digest*.

WORK IN PROGRESS: Three books, *Prison Lingo, How to Shoot*, and *Broadway Squad*; and a three-act play, "The Riding Academy."†

*   *   *

WESTWOOD, J(ohn) N(orton)   1931-

PERSONAL: Born September 18, 1931, in Solihull, England; son of Herbert Butler (an engineer) and Phyliss (Coleman) Westwood. *Education:* University of Birmingham, B.Com., 1953; graduate study at Sorbonne, University of Paris, 1953-54, and Cambridge University, 1955-56; University of Montreal, M.A., Ph.D., 1961. *Home:* 51 Oakleigh Close, Backwell, Bristol, England.

CAREER: Canadian National Railways, Montreal, Quebec, economist, 1957-59; McGill University, Montreal, Quebec, lecturer in Russian language and literature, 1959-64; Florida State University, Tallahassee, associate professor of history, 1967-69; University of Sydney, Sydney, Australia, senior lecturer in history, 1970-72. Qualified Russian interpreter. Photographer, doing films on transport for British Broadcasting Corp. *Awards, honors:* Canada Council Award, 1962.

WRITINGS: Soviet Railways Today, Citadel, 1963; *History of Russian Railways*, Allen & Unwin, 1964; *Russia 1917-1964*, Harper, 1967; *Witnesses of Tsushima*, Diplomatic Press, 1970; *Endurance and Endeavour*, Oxford University Press, 1973; *Railways of India*, David & Charles, 1974. Contributor to *Birmingham Post, Guardian, New Scientist, Trains, Modern Transport, Soviet Studies*, and other periodicals and newspapers.

WORK IN PROGRESS: A book, *The Monkey and the Bear: the Russo-Japanese War.*

SIDELIGHTS: J. N. Westwood is competent in French as well as Russian; and illustrates articles with own photographs.

*   *   *

WEVILL, David   1937-

PERSONAL: Surname rhymes with *devil*; born May 15, 1937, in Yokohama, Japan; son of George Frederick and Sylvia (Bryan) Wevill; married Assia Gutman (a copywriter), May 17, 1960. *Education:* Caius College, Cambridge, B.A., 1957.

CAREER: Writer. *Awards, honors:* E. C. Gregory Award for the manuscript of *Birth of a Shark*; Richard Hillary Prize, 1965; Arts Council Triennial Award, 1965; Arts Council Bursary, 1965, 1966.

WRITINGS: (With Christopher Middleton and David Holbrook) *Penguin Modern Poets IV*, Penguin, 1963; *Birth of a Shark* (poems), Macmillan (London), 1964; *A Christ of the Ice Floes*, St. Martin's, 1966; (translator) *Selected Poems of Terence Juhasz*, Penguin, 1969; *Firebreak*, St. Martin's, 1971; *Where the Arrow Falls*, Macmillan, 1973. Represented in anthologies including *New Poems*, Hutchinson, 1961; *A Group Anthology*, Oxford University Press, 1963; *New Poetry*, Penguin, 1966, *Penguin Book of Canadian Verse*, Penguin, 1967. Contributor to *Listener, Observer, New Yorker, Sewanee Review, New York Times*, and other periodicals.

BIOGRAPHICAL/CRITICAL SOURCES: New Statesman, November 27, 1964; *Pluck*, No. 1, 1967.†

*   *   *

WEYRAUCH, Walter O(tto)   1919-

PERSONAL: Born August 27, 1919, in Lindau, Germany; came to United States in 1952; son of Hans Ernst Winand (a writer) and Meta Margarete (Loenholdt) Weyrauch; married Jill White (an attorney), March 17, 1973; children: (previous marriage) Roman Kurt, Corinne Harriet Irene, Bettina Elaine. *Education:* University of Frankfurt, Dr. jur., 1951; Georgetown University, LL.B., 1955; Harvard University, LL.M., 1956; Yale University, J.S.D., 1962. *Religion:* Lutheran. *Home:* 3425 Southwest 2 Ave., Gainesville, Fla. 32607. *Office:* College of Law, University of Florida, Gainesville, Fla. 32611.

CAREER: Admitted to practice, German Bar Association, 1949, to bar of U.S. Court of Appeals, Allied High Commission, Germany, 1951. Practicing attorney in Frankfurt am Main, Germany, 1949-52; University of Florida, College of Law, Gainesville, associate professor, 1957-60, professor of law, 1960—. Visiting professor of law, Rutgers University, 1968; visiting professor of political science, University of California at Berkeley, 1968-69. *Member:* International Association for Philosophy of Law and Social Philosophy, Law and Society Association, American Association of University Professors, Order of the Coif. *Awards, honors:* Rockefeller Foundation grant, 1958-59.

WRITINGS: The Personality of Lawyers, Yale University Press, 1964; (contributor) Harrop A. Freeman, editor, *Legal Interviewing and Counseling*, West Publishing, 1964; (contributor) Ralph Slovenko, editor, *Sexual Behavior and the Law*, C. C Thomas, 1965; (contributor) Freeman and

Henry Weihofen, *Clinical Law and Training: Interviewing and Counseling*, West Publishing, 1972. Contributor to law journals.

WORK IN PROGRESS: A book, *Legal Regulation of the Family*, with Stanford N. Katz; contributing to *Issues of Law and Justice for Legal Socialization*, for Holt.   .

AVOCATIONAL INTERESTS: The behavioral sciences.

BIOGRAPHICAL/CRITICAL SOURCES: American Behavioral Scientist, December, 1963.

* * *

WHALEN, Richard J(ames) 1935-

PERSONAL: Born September 23, 1935, in New York, N.Y.; son of George Carroll (a business executive) and Veronica (Southwick) Whalen; married Joan Marie Guiffre, October 19, 1957; children: Richard Christopher, Laura Anne, Michael James. *Education:* Queens College (now Queens College of the City University of New York), B.A., 1957. *Politics:* Republican. *Religion:* Roman Catholic. *Residence:* Fort Sumner, Md. 20016. *Agent:* Owen Laster, William Morris Agency, 1740 Broadway, New York, N.Y. 10019. *Office:* Suite 400, 1720 Eye St., N.W., Washington, D.C. 20006.

CAREER: Richmond News Leader, Richmond, Va., reporter, 1957-58, associate editor, 1958-59; *Time*, New York, N.Y., contributing editor, 1959-60; *Wall Street Journal*, New York, N.Y., editorial writer, 1960-62; *Fortune*, New York, N.Y., associate editor, 1962-65, member of board of editors, 1965-66; Georgetown University, Center for Strategic and International Studies, Washington, D.C., writer-in-residence, 1966-69; State Department, Washington, D.C., consultant, 1969—. President, Worldwide Information Resources, Inc. *Member:* Cosmos Club (Washington, D.C.).

WRITINGS: The Founding Father: The Story of Joseph P. Kennedy, New American Library, 1964; *A City Destroying Itself: An Angry View of New York*, Morrow, 1965; *Catch the Falling Flag: A Republican's Challenge to His Party*, Houghton, 1972; *Taking Sides: A Personal View of America From Kennedy to Nixon to Kennedy*, Houghton, 1974. Contributing editor, *Harper's*, 1973—.

WORK IN PROGRESS: Research on the Kennedy family since 1963; research in pre-World War II Anglo-American diplomacy.

SIDELIGHTS: Whalen's first book, *The Founding Father*, hit the best-seller list shortly after publication and remained there for some months. *Avocational interests:* Thoreau, the Spanish Civil War, hiking, and fishing.

BIOGRAPHICAL/CRITICAL SOURCES: New York Post, March 22, 1965, June 2, 1972; *Book Week*, March 28, 1965; *Washington Evening Star*, May 4, 1972.

* * *

WHATMORE, Leonard Elliott 1912-

PERSONAL: Born 1912, in Birmingham, England; son of Leonard Worthing and Enid Winifred (Elliott) Whatmore. *Education:* Studied at Wadham College, Oxford, 1931-35, at St. John's Seminary, Wonersh, England, 1935-41. *Residence:* Hailsham, Sussex, England.

CAREER: Ordained Roman Catholic priest, Diocese of Southwark, England, 1941. Curate in South London and Canterbury prior to 1960; St. Anselm's Catholic Church, Hindhead, Surrey, England, parish priest, 1960-66; St. Wil-frid's Church, Hailsham, Sussex, England, parish priest, 1966—. *Member:* Royal Historical Society (fellow), Kent Archaeological Society, Sussex Archeological Association, Henry VI Society.

WRITINGS: Archdeacon Harpsfield's Canterbury Visitations, two volumes, Catholic Record Society, 1950, 1951; (translator) *A Cedar of Lebanon*, Browne & Nolan, 1958; *Blessed Carthusian Martyrs*, Vice-Postulation, 1962; *Blessed Margaret Ward*, Vice-Postulation, 1964. Also author of *The Story of Dockhead Parish*, 1960, and *Highway to Walsingham*, 1973. Contributor to *Pax, Clergy Review, Southwark Record*, other journals.

WORK IN PROGRESS: A book, *Venerable Thomas Pilcher, Martyr (1557-87)*; research on contraception and resurrection.

* * *

WHEELER, W(illiam) Lawrence 1925-

PERSONAL: Born March 4, 1925, in Eureka, Kan.; son of Perly Samuel (a salesman) and Edna Marion (Jacobs) Wheeler; married Mary Elizabeth Looper, June 20, 1946; children: Julie Lynne, Sandra Alisa. *Education:* Northwestern University, B.M., 1948, M.M., 1949; Columbia University, Ed.D., 1958. *Religion:* Episcopalian. *Home:* 122 Glen Cove Dr., Glen Head, Long Island, N.Y. 11545.

CAREER: Winthrop College, Rock Hill, S.C., assistant professor of music, 1949-55; Plainview (N.Y.) public schools, music teacher, 1956-58; Union Free School District 29, North Merrick, N.Y., music consultant, 1958—; Manhattan School of Music, New York, N.Y., member of faculty. Organist and choirmaster in various churches. Orff-Kodaly clinician. *Member:* Phi Mu Alpha Sinfonia.

WRITINGS: (With Lois Raebeck) *New Approaches to Music in the Elementary School*, W. C. Brown, 1964, 3rd edition, 1974; (with Gerald Burakoff) *Music Making in the Elementary School*, Hargail Music Press, 1968; *The Ensemble Recorder*, Consort Music, 1970; (with Raebeck) *Orff and Kodaly Adapted for the Elementary School*, W. C. Brown, 1972; (with Elizabeth Wheeler) *Comprehensive Recorder Method: Playing and Singing with Orff Instruments*, four volumes, Belwin Mills Publishing, 1974.

AVOCATIONAL INTERESTS: Antique collector, with a special interest in clocks, and amateur painter.

* * *

WHEELOCK, John Hall 1886-

PERSONAL: Born 1886, in Far Rockaway, Long Island, N.Y.; son of William Efner and Emily Charlotte (Hall) Wheelock; married Phyllis E. De Kay, August 25, 1940. *Education:* Harvard University, A.B., 1908; University of Goettingen, student, 1909; University of Berlin, student, 1910; Otterbein College, Dr. Humane Letters, 1954. *Home:* 350 East 57th St., New York, N.Y. 10022.

CAREER: Employed at Charles Scribner's Sons, New York, N.Y., 1911-57, editor, 1926-57, became senior editor upon the death of Maxwell Perkins in 1947, director and secretary, 1932-42, treasurer, 1942-46, assistant treasurer and assistant secretary, 1946-57. Honorary consultant in American letters to Library of Congress. *Member:* American Academy of Arts and Letters, Poetry Society of America (vice president, 1944-46), National Institute of Arts and Letters (vice-president), Academy of American Poets (chancellor, 1947-71; honorary fellow, 1974—). *Awards, honors:* Golden Rose, New England Poetry Society, 1937; Ridgely Torrence Memorial Award, 1956, and Borestone Mountain Poetry Award, 1957, both for *Poems Old and New*; Bollingen Prize, 1962; Signet Society Medal, Harvard University, 1965, for distinguished achievement in the arts; Gold Medal, Poetry Society of America, 1972, for notable achievement in poetry.

WRITINGS—Poetry: (With Van Wyck Brooks) *Verses by Two Undergraduates*, privately printed, 1905; *Human Fantasy*, Sherman, French, 1911; *Beloved Adventure*, Sherman, French, 1912; *Love and Liberation*, Sherman, French, 1913; *Dust and Light*, Scribner, 1919; *The Black Panther*, Scribner, 1922; *The Bright Doom*, Scribner, 1927; *Collected Poems, 1911-1936*, Scribner, 1936; *Poems Old and New*, Scribner, 1956; *The Gardener and Other Poems*, Scribner, 1961; *Dear Men and Women: New Poems*, Scribner, 1966; *By Daylight and in Dream: New and Collected Poems, 1904-1970*, Scribner, 1970; *In Love and Song: Poems*, Scribner, 1971.

Other books: *Alan Seeger; Poet of the Foreign Legion* (essay), Scribner, 1918; *A Bibliography of Theodore Roosevelt*, Scribner, 1920; (translator) *Happily Ever After* (fairy tales), Scribner, 1939; (compiler, editor, and author of introduction) *The Face of a Nation: Poetical Passages from the Writings of Thomas Wolfe*, Scribner, 1939; (editor and author of introduction) *Editor to Author: The Letters of Maxwell E. Perkins*, Scribner, 1950; *What is Poetry?*, Scribner, 1963. Editor, *Poets of Today, Volumes I-VIII*, Scribner, 1954-61. Contributor to *Dictionary of American History*, Scribner, 1940, and to numerous periodicals.

SIDELIGHTS: In a television interview with Davidson Taylor, Wheelock mentioned that he couldn't have helped being a poet. "You will find," he explained, "that at those times when life becomes most real, in the great moments of life, almost every man or woman becomes a poet at heart—as when in love or when experiencing a great loss or bereavement; in other words, when coming very close to reality. Because, you see, we have these two necessities here. One is the necessity of keeping alive and the other is the necessity which the first sometimes gets in the way of, and that is: to realize our whole situation, not just our own little private experience, but the whole significance of life, the realities around us that we forget about."

Wheelock emphasizes that it is the compulsion to rediscover the essence of reality for oneself that distinguishes poet from non-poet. "You have to sort of pretend you aren't really trying to do it; sort of walking around it, thinking of something else; because if you go at it too quickly and too hard, it gets away from you.... The poem gives back the reality that we've lost sight of because we've become so familiar with it. The poem gives it back to us with that sense of surprise.... A poem doesn't arise out of an impulse to communicate. A poem is what happens when a poet rediscovers, for himself, some phase of reality.... But you must not think that the process is one of rediscovery on the part of the poet and then transmittal in the poem. That, perhaps, *would* be communication. Rather, you have to think of it as communion within a potentially universal fellowship. And also, the poem itself is part of the rediscovery.... In the poem, the poet might be said to be talking to himself. He has finally established communication with his own being, and therefore potentially with others."

But, Wheelock explains, meaning in a poem is a dynamic, rather than a static, entity and the process of a poem's becoming meaningful must be shared by poet and reader.

"... Some poems," said Wheelock, "take a long time for the meaning to develop in them, by acquaintance with the poem.... A really good poem, a poem that means anything more than what is on the surface, takes a good deal of rereading, an almost living yourself into it, I think, to understand it." Wheelock concluded that "poetry, like all the arts, gets its meaning, perhaps principally, from the tragic nature of things—either as escape from it in play or as a celebration of it in the more exalted moments. Against the backdrop of fate, life shows at its noblest and most endearing. Its glory is in its doom. The inexorable truth is the music to which all the arts move, in rage or delight, with proud or dancing step."

It would seem that Wheelock's poetical convictions are admirably applied in his work. Godfrey John wrote: "Wheelock's poetry marries a serenity of movement with a clarity of impression that is no less than classical in its impact. He writes affirmatively, with an impassioned, yet innocent, delight in natural beauty. His language takes on the overtones of gesture, serving his ideas constantly and reverently to result in a clearly defined poetic wherein private imagery is carefully subordinated to truth of mood and consistency of theme." John Malcolm Brinnin said of *The Gardener and Other Poems*: "There is a radiance at the center of Wheelock's book, a warming light of awareness that humanizes even the ghastly realities of the modern world."

BIOGRAPHICAL/CRITICAL SOURCES: James Nelson, editor, *Wisdom*, Norton, 1958; *New York Times Book Review*, September 24, 1961; *Saturday Review*, November 4, 1961; *Christian Science Mointor*, December 14, 1961; *New Yorker*, April 14, 1962; *Book Week*, October 27, 1963; *New York Times Book Review*, February 2, 1964.

* * *

WHITAKER, Dorothy Stock 1925-

PERSONAL: Born March 30, 1925, in Chicago, Ill.; daughter of Charles W. and Martha (Utesch) Stock; married F. P. G. Whitaker (a university lecturer), December 21, 1963; children: Charles William Ashley. *Education:* University of Chicago, Ph.B., 1944, M.A., 1948, Ph.D., 1952. *Home:* The Blue House, Low Grantley, Ripon, Yorkshire, England.

CAREER: University of Chicago, Chicago, Ill., research associate in department of education, 1952-55, assistant professor, 1957-63, associate professor of psychology, 1963-64; Veterans Administration Research Hospital, Chicago, Ill., research psychologist, 1955-57; Northwestern University Medical School, Chicago, Ill., associate professor of psychology, 1955-57; University of Leeds, Leeds, England, lecturer in department of psychology, 1964-73; University of York, Heslington, England, professor of social work, 1973—. *Member:* American Psychological Association, American Group Psychotherapy Association, Group Analytic Society (London). *Awards, honors:* National Institute of Mental Health research grants, 1957-64.

WRITINGS: (With Herbert A. Thelen) *Emotional Dynamics and Group Culture*, New York University Press, 1958; (with Morton A. Lieberman) *Psychotherapy Through the Group Process*, Atherton, 1964. Contributor of articles on group psychotherapy and group dynamics to professional journals.

WORK IN PROGRESS: Further research in group psychotherapy.

WHITBREAD, Thomas (Bacon) 1931-

PERSONAL: Born August 22, 1931, in Bronxville, N.Y.; son of Thomas F. (a philatelist and realtor) and Nancy (Bacon) Whitbread. *Education:* Amherst College, B.A., 1952; Harvard University, A.M., 1953, Ph.D., 1959. *Home:* 1014 East 38th St., Austin, Tex. 78705.

CAREER: University of Texas, Austin, 1959—, began as instructor, assistant professor, 1962-65, associate professor, 1965-71, professor of English, 1971—. Visiting associate professor of English, Rice University, 1969-70. *Member:* Modern Language Association of America, American Amateur Press Association, National Amateur Press Association (vice-president, 1949-50; president, 1950-51, 1964-65; executive judge, 1951-52, 1959-60; chairman of bureau of critics, 1952-53, 1962-63), The Fossils, Phi Beta Kappa. *Awards, honors:* Third Aga Khan Award, *Paris Review*, for short story, "The Rememberer"; Texas Institute of Letters poetry award, 1965, for *Four Infinitives*; National Endowment for the Arts Award, for poem "pochet Island."

WRITINGS: Four Infinitives (poems), Harper, 1964; (editor and contributor) *Seven Contemporary Authors*, University of Texas Press, 1966. Articles included in *Six Contemporary Novels*, edited by William O. S. Sutherland, University of Texas Press, 1962, and *In Defense of Reading*, edited by Reuben A. Brower and William Richard Poirier, Dutton, 1962; short story, "The Rememberer," in *Prize Stories, 1962: The O'Henry Awards*, edited by Poirier, Doubleday, 1962. Poetry represented in anthologies, including *Of Poetry and Power*, edited by Erwin A. Glikes and Paul Schwaber, Basic Books, 1964; *Southwest Writers Anthology*, edited by Martin Shockley, Steck, 1967; *East of America: A Selection of Cape Cod Poems*, edited by John V. Hinshaw, Chatham Press, 1969; *The New Yorker Book of Poems*, Viking, 1969; *The New York Times Book of Verse*, edited by Thomas Lask, Macmillan, 1970; *Poetry Amherst*, compiled by Richard Aldridge, Amherst College Press, 1972.

WORK IN PROGRESS: Poems for a second collection; a book on contemporary poetry.

AVOCATIONAL INTERESTS: Handpress printing, travel, music (playing the piano, listening to records, attending concerts), drama, tennis and golf, and spectator sports.

*　　*　　*

WHITCOMB, Helen Hafemann

PERSONAL: Born in Oradell, N.J.; daughter of Frank E. (a jeweler) and Elizabeth (Buedinger) Hafemann; married John P. Whitcomb (a teacher), July 16, 1950; children: Claire, Jonathan. *Education:* Ursinus College, A.B., 1946; studied at Eastman Business School, 1946-47, Columbia University, 1947-50. *Religion:* Protestant. *Home:* 111 Timber Dr., Berkeley Heights, N.J. 07922.

CAREER: Chain Store Age, New York, N.Y., assistant editor in beauty field, druggist editions, 1947-51; McGraw-Hill Book Co., Inc., Gregg Publishing Division, New York, N.Y., managing editor of *Today's Secretary* (magazine), 1951-55; free-lance writer and editor. *Member:* American Association of University Women.

WRITINGS: (With husband, John P. Whitcomb) *Strictly for Secretaries*, Whittlesey House, 1957, 2nd edition, 1965; (with Rosalind Lang) *Charm: The Career Girl's Guide to Business and Personal Success*, Gregg Division, McGraw,

1964, revised edition, 1971; (with Lang) *A Portfolio of Activities for Charm* (workbook), McGraw, 1964, revised edition, 1971; (with Lang) *Manual for Charm* (teaching guide), McGraw, 1965, revised edition, 1971; (with Lang) *Charm for the Modern Woman* (textbook, activity guide, exercise booklet, and hair styling booklet), Gregg Division, McGraw, 1967; (with Lang) *Manual and Key for Charm for the Modern Woman* (teaching guide), Gregg Division, McGraw, 1967; (with Laura Cochran) *Charm for Miss Teen*, Gregg Division, McGraw, 1969; (with Cochran) *Teacher's Manual and Key for Charm for Miss Teen*, Gregg Division, McGraw, 1969.

WORK IN PROGRESS: With Laura Cochran, *The Modern Ms.*, to be published by Gregg Division, McGraw (accompanied by a teaching guide).

AVOCATIONAL INTERESTS: Reading, theater, travel, tennis.

*　　*　　*

WHITE, Carl M(ilton) 1903-

PERSONAL: Born August 12, 1903, in Burnet, Okla.; son of Josiah Milton (a farmer) and Jennie Anne (Patterson) White; married Ruth Bennett (a writer), August 5, 1928; children: Sherril Elizabeth (Mrs. Leland Stanford Spencer, Jr.), Caroline Lucretia (Mrs. John Buchanan). *Education:* Oklahoma Baptist University, A.B. (cum laude), 1925; Mercer University, M.A. (magna cum laude), 1928; University of Iowa, graduate study, 1929-30; Cornell University, Ph.D., 1933; Columbia University, B.S. in L.S., 1934. *Politics:* Independent. *Religion:* Protestant. *Home:* 5811 Beaumont Ave., La Jolla, Calif. 92037.

CAREER: Fisk University, Nashville, Tenn., librarian, 1934-38; University of North Carolina, Chapel Hill, university librarian and chairman of Division of Library and of School of Library Science, 1938-40; University of Illinois, Urbana, director of university library and of Library School, and professor of library science, 1940-43; Columbia University, New York, N.Y., director of libraries, 1943-53, dean of faculty of library service, 1943-54, professor of library service, 1943-62; Ford Foundation, New York, N.Y., program specialist in library development, 1962-67, served as library adviser to government of Nigeria in establishing a national library, 1962-64; University of California, San Diego, library specialist, 1967-71. University of Ankara, Ankara, Turkey, director of Institute of Librarianship, 1959-61 and holder of first chair of professor of library science, 1960-61. London Conference of Allied Ministers of Education, technical adviser on books and libraries, 1945; Friends of Columbia Libraries, organizer, 1951.

MEMBER: American Library Association (member of executive board, 1941-45), Association of College and Reference Libraries, Association of Research Libraries (member of advisory committee, 1943-47; chairman, 1946-47), American Geographical Society (member of council, 1951-53), Bibliographical Society of America.

WRITINGS: (Contributor) A. F. Kuhlman, editor, *College and University Library Service: Trends, Standards, Appraisal, Problems*, American Library Association, 1938; *Origins of the American Library School*, Scarecrow, 1961; (editor and contributor) *American Kutuphanecilik Tecrubeleri*, Faculty of Letters, University of Ankara, 1961; (editor and contributor) *Modern Kutuphaneciligin Esaslari*, Faculty of Letters, University of Ankara, 1961; (editor and contributor) *Bases of Modern Librarianship*, Pergamon, 1964; (editor and compiler with others) *Sources of Informa-*

tion in the Social Sciences: A Guide to the Literature, Bedminster, 1964, 2nd edition, American Library Association, 1973; *The National Library of Nigeria: Growth of the Idea, Problems and Progress*, Federal Ministry of Information (Nigeria), 1964; *A Survey of the University of Delhi Library*, University of Delhi, 1965; *Mexico's Library and Information Services*, Bedminster, 1969; (contributor) Melvin J. Voigt, editor, *Advances in Librarianship*, Academic Press, Volume I, 1970.

Contributor to *Saturday Review, Vital Speeches of the Day, American Library Association Bulletin*, and other journals. Editor, *College and Research Libraries*, 1941-48; chairman of council, *Who's Who in Library Service*, 1954-55.

*   *   *

WHITE, E(lwyn) B(rooks)   1899-

PERSONAL: Born July 11, 1899, in Mount Vernon, N.Y.; son of Samuel Tilly (a piano manufacturer) and Jessie (Hart) White; married Katharine Sergeant Angell (a *New Yorker* editor), November 13, 1929; children: Joel McCoun. *Education:* Cornell University, A.B., 1921. *Residence:* North Brooklin, Me. *Office: New Yorker*, 25 West 43rd St., New York, N.Y.

CAREER: Reporter with *Seattle Times*, Seattle, Wash., 1922-23; worked two years in advertising agency as production assistant and copywriter; *New Yorker*, writer, contributing editor, 1927—. Regular contributor of column, "One Man's Meat," to *Harper's*, 1938-43. *Military service:* U.S. Army, 1918. *Member:* National Institute of Arts and Letters, American Academy of Arts and Sciences (fellow), American Academy of Arts and Letters, Phi Beta Kappa, Phi Gamma Delta. *Awards, honors:* Litt.D., Dartmouth College, 1948, University of Maine, 1948, Yale University, 1948, Bowdoin College, 1950, Hamilton College, 1952, Harvard University, 1954; L.H.D., Colby College, 1954; Gold Medal Award, Limited Editions Club, 1944, for *One Man's Meat*; National Association of Independent Schools Award, 1955, for *The Second Tree From the Corner*; Gold Medal, Institute of Arts and Letters, 1960; Presidential Medal of Freedom, 1963; Laura Ingalls Wilder Award, American Library Association, 1970; National Medal for Literature, National Book Committee, 1971.

WRITINGS: The Lady is Cold (poetry), Harper, 1929; (with James Thurber) *Is Sex Necessary?* (essays), Harper, 1929; *Ho Hum*, Farrar & Rinehart, 1931; *Another Ho Hum*, Farrar & Rinehart, 1932; *Every Day is Saturday* (commentary), Harper, 1934; *Farewell to Model T*, Putnam, 1936; *The Fox of Peapack* (poetry), Harper, 1938; *Quo Vadimus?* (essays), Harper, 1939; (editor with K. S. White) *A Subtreasury of American Humor*, Coward, 1941; *One Man's Meat*, Harper, 1942, enlarged edition, 1944; *Stuart Little* (juvenile), Harper, 1945; *The Wild Flag*, Houghton, 1946; *Here is New York*, Harper, 1949; *Charlotte's Web* (juvenile), Harper, 1952; *The Second Tree From the Corner*, Harper, 1954; (editorial supervisor and contributor) William Strunk, Jr., *The Elements of Style*, revised edition, Macmillan, 1959; *The Points of My Compass*, Harper, 1962; *The Trumpet of the Swan* (juvenile), Harper, 1970. Contributor to periodicals.

SIDELIGHTS: Irwin Edman once wrote of the veritable spokesman for the *New Yorker:* "E. B. White is the finest essayist in the United States. He says wise things gracefully; he is the master of an idiom at once exact and suggestive, distinguished yet familiar. His style is crisp and ten-

der, and incomparably his own." In his acceptance remarks for the National Medal for Literature, White noted: "I fell in love with the sound of an early typewriter and have been stuck with it ever since. I believed then, as I do now, in the goodness of the published word: it seemed to contain an essential goodness, like the smell of leaf mold."

BIOGRAPHICAL/CRITICAL SOURCES: New York Times, January 17, 1954.

*   *   *

WHITE, Eugene E.   1919-

PERSONAL: Born October 31, 1919, in Denver, Colo.; son of Jacob and Atlanta Louise (McMachen) White; married Roberta Fluitt, April 23, 1943; children: Eugene Robert. *Education:* Oregon State University, B.S., 1942; Louisiana State University, M.A., 1944, Ph.D., 1947. *Politics:* Democrat. *Home:* 1402 South Garner St., State College, Pa. *Office:* Department of Speech, 313 Sparks Building, Pennsylvania State University, University Park, Pa.

CAREER: Louisiana State University, Baton Rouge, instructor in speech, 1946-47; Western Reserve University (now Case Western Reserve University), Cleveland, Ohio, assistant professor of speech, 1947-49; University of Miami, Coral Gables, Fla., associate professor, 1949-55, professor of speech, 1955-60; Pennsylvania State University, University Park, associate professor of speech, 1960—. *Member:* Speech Association of America (chairman, rhetorical and public address area; member of legislative assembly), American Association of University Professors, American Historical Association, Eastern Speech Association, Southern Speech Association (director of publications; member of executive council), Pennsylvania Speech Association. *Awards, honors:* Liberal Arts Research Scholar, Pennsylvania State University, 1962.

WRITINGS: (With Clair R. Henderlider) *Practical Public Speaking*, Macmillan, 1954, 2nd edition (sole author), 1964; *Practical Speech Fundamentals*, Macmillan, 1960; (editor with Robert T. Oliver) *Selected Speeches From American History*, Allyn & Bacon, 1966; *Puritan Rhetoric: The Issue of Emotion in Religion*, Southern Illinois University Press, 1972. Contributor of articles to speech and historical journals. Editor of *Southern Speech Journal*, 1960-61.

WORK IN PROGRESS: Rhetoric and Michael Wigglesworth: The Teaching of Rhetoric at Early Harvard; Persuasion and Revivalism: The Great Awakening; a revision of *Practical Speech Fundamentals*.

SIDELIGHTS: White is competent in French, German, and Latin.†

*   *   *

WHITE, Jon Manchip   1924-

PERSONAL: Born June 22, 1924, in Cardiff, Wales; son of Gwilym Manchip (a shipowner) and Eve Elizabeth (Ewbank) White; married Valerie Leighton; children: Bronwen, Rhiannon. *Education:* Cambridge University, M.A. (honours in English literature, prehistoric archaeology, and Egyptology), and Diploma in Anthropology. *Residence:* El Paso, Tex.

CAREER: British Broadcasting Corp. Television, London, England, story editor, 1950-51; H. M. Foreign Service, information research department in London, 1952-56; Hammer Film Productions Ltd., London, England, scenario editor, 1956-57; screenwriter in Paris and Madrid, under contract to Samuel Bronston Productions, 1960-64;

University of Texas, El Paso, associate professor, 1967—. Minsterworth Productions Ltd., director. *Military service:* Royal Navy and Welsh Guards, 1942-46.

WRITINGS—Novels: *Mask of Dust*, Hodder & Stoughton, 1953; *Build Us A Dam*, Hodder & Stoughton, 1955; *The Girl From Indiana*, Hodder & Stoughton, 1956; *No Home But Heaven*, Hodder & Stoughton, 1957; *The Mercenaries*, Hutchinson, 1958; *Hour of the Rat*, Hutchinson, 1962; *The Rose in the Brandy Glass*, Eyre & Spottiswoode, 1965; *Nightclimber*, Chatto & Windus, 1968; *The Game of Troy*, Chatto & Windus, 1971; *The Garden Game*, Chatto & Windus, 1974.

Verse: *The Rout of San Romane*, Hand & Flower Press, 1952; *The Mountain Lion*, Chatto & Windus, 1971.

Other books: *Ancient Egypt*, Wingate, 1952, Crowell, 1953, revised edition, Allen & Unwin, 1970; *Anthropology*, English Universities Press, 1952; (translator) Samivel, *The Glory of Egypt*, Thomes & Hudson, 1955; *Marshal of France*, Rand McNally, 1962; *Everyday Life in Ancient Egypt*, Batsford, 1963, Putnam, 1964; *Deige Velazquez*, Hamish Hamilton, 1969; *The Land God Made in Anger: A Journey Through South West Africa*, Allen & Unwin, 1969; *Cortes and The Downfall of the Aztec Empire*, Hamish Hamilton, 1971; (editor) Adolf Erman, *Life in Ancient Egypt*, Dover, 1971; (editor) E. W. Lane, *Manners & Customs of the Modern Egyptians*, Dover, 1971; *A World Elsewhere: The American Southwest*, Crowell, 1975.

Author of many motion picture scripts (including recent work for Walt Disney Productions), and radio and television plays produced in Britain and on "U.S. Steel Hour." Contributor to *Spectator, Financial Times, Listener*, and other British journals.

SIDELIGHTS: White speaks fluent French and Spanish. *Avocational interests:* Fishing, music and travel.

* * *

WHITE, Lonnie J(oe) 1931-

PERSONAL: Born February 12, 1931, in Knox City, Tex.; son of John Alexander (an irrigation farmer) and Fannie (Coates) White; married Nancy Evans, June 23, 1951; children: John Evans, Brenda Jo. *Education:* West Texas State University, B.A., 1950; Texas Technological College (now Texas Tech University), M.A., 1955; University of Texas, Ph.D., 1961. *Religion:* Baptist. *Home:* 3795 Christy Cove, Memphis, Tenn. 38111. *Office:* Memphis State University, Memphis, Tenn. 38111.

CAREER: Panoma Gasoline Corp., Hooker, Okla., operator, 1950-51, 1953-54; Memphis State University, Memphis, Tenn., assistant professor, 1961-63, associate professor of history, 1963—. *Military service:* U.S. Army, 1951-53. *Member:* American Historical Association, Organization of American Historians, Southern Historical Association, Western History Association, Arkansas Historical Association, Tennessee Historical Association, West Tennessee Historical Society, Phi Alpha Theta, Pi Sigma Alpha. *Awards, honors:* American Philosophical Society research grant, 1963.

WRITINGS: Politics on the Southwestern Frontier: Arkansas Territory, 1819-1836, Memphis State University Press, 1964; (editor) J. T. Marshall, *The Miles Expedition of 1874-1875: An Eyewitness Account of the Red River Ear*, Encino Press, 1971; *Hostiles and Horse Soldiers: Indian Battles and Campaigns in the West*, Pruett, 1972. Contributor of sixteen articles to regional historical journals.

WORK IN PROGRESS: Research for a book dealing with Indian raids on the Kansas frontier, 1865-1875.†

* * *

WHITE, Nancy Bean 1922-

PERSONAL: Born September 8, 1922, in Hartford, Conn.; daughter of George Edward McCormick and Adelaide B. Bean; married Theodore H. White (journalist and author), March 29, 1947; children: Ariana van der Heyden, David Fairbank. *Education:* Sweet Briar College, B.A., 1943. *Home:* 168 East 64th St., New York, N.Y. 10021. *Agent:* Julian Bach, Jr., 3 East 48th St., New York, N.Y. 10017.

CAREER: U.S. Office of War Information, New York, N.Y., assistant editor, 1943-45; *Life*, New York, N.Y., researcher and writer, 1945-48, special assignments, 1948-53; free-lance researcher and writer, 1953-59; *New York Times Sunday Magazine*, New York, N.Y., assistant editor, 1959-60; part-time free-lance journalist, New York, N.Y., 1960—. Town School, New York, N.Y., trustee, 1958-66.

WRITINGS: Meet John F. Kennedy, Random House, 1964.

WORK IN PROGRESS: Research for *Meet Theodore Roosevelt*.†

* * *

WHITE, W(illiam) J(ohn) 1920-

PERSONAL: Born March 30, 1920, in Cork, Ireland; son of William Luke (an accountant) and Mary (Tyler) White; married Edna B. McGuckin, June 16, 1943; children: Stephen L., Melissa C., Victoria R. *Education:* Trinity College, Dublin, B.A. and LL.B., 1942. *Religion:* Protestant. *Home:* 95 Booterstown Ave., Blackrock, County Dublin, Ireland. *Office:* Telefis Eireann, Dublin 4, Ireland.

CAREER: Irish Times, Dublin, Ireland, leader writer, 1942-45, London editor, 1946-52, features editor, 1952-61; Telefis Eireann (Irish Television), Dublin, Ireland, head of public affairs, 1961-63, assistant controller of programs, 1963—. Novelist. *Member:* Society of Authors (London).

WRITINGS: One for the Road, J. Cape, 1956; *The Hard Man*, J. Cape, 1958; *The Devil You Know*, J. Cape, 1962. Contributor to *Observer, Guardian, Spectator*, and other periodicals and newspapers. Writer of radio scripts.

WORK IN PROGRESS: A novel.

SIDELIGHTS: All of White's novels deal strictly with contemporary Ireland, but his journalistic interests center on foreign-background articles. He did a series for *Irish Times* on awakening of Africa in 1960, visited the Congo (for material) in 1961, Nigeria in 1963, and has traveled widely in Europe, Israel, and Cuba. White speaks French.†

* * *

WHITEHILL, Walter Muir 1905-

PERSONAL: Born September 28, 1905, in Cambridge, Mass.; son of Walter Muir (an Episcopal clergyman) and Florence Marion (Williams) Whitehill; married Jane Revere Coolidge, June 5, 1930; children: Jane C. (Mrs. William Rotch), Diana (Mrs. C. Christopher Laing). *Education:* Harvard University, A.B., 1926, A.M., 1929; University of London, Ph.D., 1934. *Religion:* Episcopalian. *Home:* 44 Andover St., North Andover, Mass.

CAREER: Did research in medieval history in Europe, 1930-36; Peabody Museum of Salem, Salem, Mass., assistant director, 1936-42; Boston Athenaeum, Boston, Mass., director and librarian, 1946-73. Harvard University, Cambridge, Mass., member of faculty of Peabody Museum of Archaeology and Ethnology, 1951-72. Allston Burr Senior Tutor in Lowell House, 1952-56, lecturer in history, 1956-57, Lowell Institute lecturer, 1958. Trustee of Museum of Fine Arts (Boston), Peabody Museum of Salem, Museum of Navajo Ceremonial Art, Fruitlands Museum, Eleutherian Mills Hagley Foundation, and Marlboro College. Director of Athenaeum of Philadelphia, and of University Press of Virginia; member of Massachusetts Historical Commission; president of Thomas Jefferson Memorial Foundation, Merrimack Valley Textile Museum, and Historic Boston, Inc.; honorary vice-president of Virginia Historical Society and of Naval Historical Foundation, Washington, D.C. *Military service:* U.S. Naval Reserve, active duty, 1942-46; commander (retired).

MEMBER: American Academy of Arts and Sciences (librarian), American Antiquarian Society (member of council), Hispanic Society of America, Massachusetts Historical Society (recording secretary), Colonial Society of Massachusetts, Phi Beta Kappa (president of Harvard chapter, 1959-61); Somerset Club, Tavern Club, and Old Volumes Club (all Boston); Century Association (New York), Army and Navy Club (Washington). *Awards, honors:* D.Litt., University of New Brunswick, 1959; LL.D., Washington and Jefferson College, 1959; L.H.D., Northeastern University, 1961, University of Delaware, 1967, Merrimack College, 1968, University of Massachusetts, 1971, College of William and Mary, 1974; D. Humanities, Suffolk University, 1970.

WRITINGS: Spanish Romanesque Architecture of the Eleventh Century, Oxford University Press, 1941; *The East India Marine Society and the Peabody Museum of Salem*, Peabody Museum of Salem, 1949; (with Ernest J. King) *Fleet Admiral King: A Naval Record*, Norton, 1952; *Boston Public Library: A Centenary History*, Harvard University Press, 1956; *Boston: A Topographical History*, Harvard University Press, 1959; *Independent Historical Societies*, Boston Athenaeum, 1962; (with Katharine Knowles) *Boston: Portrait of a City*, Barre, 1964; (with Knowles) *Cambridge*, Barre, 1965; *Boston in the Age of John F. Kennedy*, University of Oklahoma Press, 1966; *Dumbarton Oaks*, Harvard University Press, 1967; *Analecta Biographica*, Greene, 1969; *Museum of Fine Arts Boston: A Centennial History*, two volumes, Harvard University Press, 1970; *Boston Statues*, Barre, 1970.

Contributor to historical journals. Founding editor of *American Neptune: A Quarterly Journal of Maritime History*, 1941, and member of editorial board, 1941—; editor, Colonial Society of Massachusetts, 1946—; member of editorial board, *New England Quarterly*.

WORK IN PROGRESS: Guide Book to Boston, for Harvard University Press; *Boston: A State of Mind*, Athenaeum.

AVOCATIONAL INTERESTS: Historic preservation.

BIOGRAPHICAL/CRITICAL SOURCES: Walter Muir Whitehill: A Record Compiled by His Friends, [Minot, Mass.], 1958; *Bulletin of Bibliography and Magazine Notes*, July-September, 1973.

*   *   *

WHITELY, Oliver R.   1918-

PERSONAL: Born October 21, 1918, in Lebanon, Mo.;

children: John, Christopher. *Education:* Drake University, B.A., 1940, M.A., 1941; Yale University, B.D., 1944, Ph.D., 1952. *Home:* 2443 South Colorado #228, Denver, Colo. 80222. *Office:* Iliff School of Theology, 2201 South University, Denver, Colo. 80210.

CAREER: Ordained minister of Christian Churches (Disciples of Christ), 1944; Park College, Parkville, Mo., assistant professor of sociology, 1952-53; Phillips University, Enid, Okla., associate professor of sociology, 1953-56; Iliff School of Theology, Denver, Colo., associate professor, 1956-59, professor of the sociology of religion, 1959—. *Military service:* U.S. Naval Reserve, chaplain, 1944-47; became lieutenant. *Member:* American Sociological Association, Society for the Scientific Study of Religion, Religious Research Association. *Awards, honors:* Bethany Press Manuscript Award ($2,500), 1958, for manuscript of *Trumpet Call of Reformation*; American Association of Theological Schools fellowship, 1962-63.

WRITINGS: Trumpet Call of Reformation, Bethany, 1959; *Religious Behavior: Where Sociology and Religion Meet*, Prentice-Hall, 1964; *The Church: Mirror or Window*, Bethany, 1969. Contributor to religious and sociological journals.

WORK IN PROGRESS: Contributing, with Clarence Snelling, to *Social Research in the Contemporary Study of Religion*.

*   *   *

WHITNEY, Eleanor Noss   1938-

PERSONAL: Born October 5, 1938, in Plainfield, N.J.; daughter of Henry (a dean, New York University) and Edith (Tyler) Noss; married William R. Whitney III (a teacher), August 9, 1960; children: Lynn, William Russell IV. *Education:* Radcliffe College, A.B., 1960. *Politics:* Independent. *Religion:* Atheist.

WRITINGS: A Mah Jong Handbook: How to Play, Score, and Win the Modern Game, Tuttle, 1963.

WORK IN PROGRESS: Translation of a German diary, written during the early 1940's by a refugee from what is now Poland.†

*   *   *

WHITON, James Nelson   1932-
(Solomon Bolo; Boyd Boylan, a joint pseudonym)

PERSONAL: Born November 27, 1932, in Troy, N.Y.; son of Harry Finley (a lawyer) and Katherine (a librarian; maiden name Nelson) Whiton; married Dorothy Pugsley, 1952; married second wife, Vulnavia Matlock, 1960; married third wife, Antonia D'Artinconch, 1964; children: Deborah, Grant, Walter, Priscilla, Pealease. *Education:* Attended public schools in Troy, N.Y. *Religion:* Jewish. *Home:* 5 Euclid Ave., Troy, N.Y.

CAREER: President of Solomon Bolo Productions Ltd., a writing partnership for the public entertainment industry.

WRITINGS: (With Rex Lode, under pseudonym Boyd Boylan) *The Third Eye of America*, Lyle Stuart, 1963. Screen writer, under pseudonym Solomon Bolo, for "The Adventures of the Gold Giant," and "The Great Big Fat Train Robbery," both produced in 1964.

WORK IN PROGRESS: A new genre prose triptych, "The Hudson Trilogy," with subject titles of "Non Omnis Moriar," "Hudson Mirable," and "The Woe of Stylus"; a novel, *The Idols of Disenchantment*; collaborating with

Rex Lode on *The Sexual Propeller* and "The Pocket Goose" paperbacks.†

* * *

WHITTAKER, Kathryn Putnam 1931-

PERSONAL: Born February 18, 1931, in Detroit, Mich.; daughter of John Alfred (a carpenter-contractor) and Thelma Mary Francis (Donald) Whittaker; married; children: Gutav Franz, Christian Putnam. *Education:* Attended Valparaiso University, one year. *Politics:* Republican. *Religion:* Evangelical Lutheran. *Residence:* New York, N.Y. *Agent:* S. B. Lourie, 26 St. Mark's Pl., New York, N.Y. 10003.

MILITARY SERVICE: Women's Army Corps.

WRITINGS: Roll Your Tent Flaps, Girls!, Avon, 1963. Writer of religious plays.

WORK IN PROGRESS: A novelette about gamblers.

SIDELIGHTS: Kathryn Whittaker told *CA* that while working on a "naughty" novelette, she also is "stewing about a play on Martin Luther's wife (in my better moments)." She continued: "Love sports of all kinds; co-manager of boys' soccer team. Ride a bike, ride a horse when I see one. Understand German but can't speak it well. Enjoy most of all good books, good conversation, good wine and attractive men (although I'm a dyed-in-the-wool Bluestocking). Believe a writer must mentally live his material before it becomes real."†

* * *

WICKHAM, Thomas Frederick 1926-

PERSONAL: Born June 11, 1926, in Abersychan, Monmouthshire, England; son of Thomas Joseph (a company director) and Elizabeth (Prior) Wickham; married Brenda Patricia Alford, June 30, 1951; children: Stephen Thomas, Mark Simon. *Politics:* Socialist. *Home:* 24 Windrush Rd., Keynsham, Somersetshire, England.

CAREER: British Merchant Marine, 1942-56; began as cadet, served at sea, 1942-51, becoming first officer; seamanship instructor for B.T.S. "Formidable," 1951-56. Proctor & Gamble Ltd., traveling representative, 1956—.

WRITINGS: Teach Yourself Seamanship, English Universities Press, 1954; *A Dictionary of Nautical Terms*, Coles, 1965.

SIDELIGHTS: Wickham told *CA*: "Having divorced myself from all seagoing activities I have no further interest in the subject apart from taking the kids out in a small dinghy with a fishing rod. I have no further literary aspirations apart from the occasional article or short story to the local rag. I am however an avid reader of good fiction. . . ."†

* * *

WIEDNER, Donald L(awrence) 1930-

PERSONAL: Surname is pronounced *Weed*-ner; born November 17, 1930, in Oceanside, N.Y.; son of Frank Lawrence (an engineer) and Gladys (Cook) Wiedner; married Elsie Margaret Weigand (a professor), June 18, 1958; children: Pamela Jane, David Stephen. *Education:* Colgate University, A.B., 1952; Harvard University, A.M., 1953, Ph.D., 1958. *Religion:* Episcopalian. *Office:* Department of History, Temple University, Philadelphia, Pa. 19122.

CAREER: Instructor in history at University of Michigan, Ann Arbor, 1958-59, Mount Holyoke College, South Had-

ley, Mass., 1959-61; University of Alberta, Edmonton, associate professor of history, 1961-65; Temple University, Philadelphia, Pa., professor of history, 1965—. Canadian delegate, First International Congress of Africanists, 1962. *Military service:* U.S. Naval Reserve, active duty, 1953-55; became lieutenant junior grade. *Member:* American Historical Association, Canadian Historical Association, African Studies Association (fellow), Nigerian Historical Society, Committee on African Studies in Canada (president, 1963-65).

WRITINGS: A History of Africa South of the Sahara, Random House, 1962. Contributor to professional journals. Editor, *Bulletin of African Studies in Canada.*

WORK IN PROGRESS: A book, *Equatorial Guinea in History*; research in currency and accounting in early modern Europe and overseas.

SIDELIGHTS: Wiedner's book on Africa has been published in England, France, and Egypt. He is competent in German, French, Spanish, Portuguese, and Afrikaans.

* * *

WIENERS, John 1934-

PERSONAL: Born January 6, 1934, in Boston, Mass.; son of Albert Eugene and Anna Elizabeth (Laffan) Wieners. *Education:* Boston College, A.B., 1954; attended Black Mountain College, 1955-56, State University of New York at Buffalo, 1965-69. *Politics:* None. *Religion:* Catholic. *Home:* 44 Joy St., Boston, Mass. 02114.

CAREER: Poets Theatre, Boston, Mass., actor and stage manager, 1956; *Measure*, Boston, Mass., founder, and editor, 1957-62; Beacon Hill Free School, Boston, Mass., teacher, 1973—. *Member:* Academy of American Poets. *Awards, honors:* Awards from Poets Foundation, 1962, New Hope Foundation, 1963, and National Institute of Arts and Letters, 1968; National Endowment for the Arts grant, 1968-69.

WRITINGS: The Hotel Wentley Poems, Auerhahn Press, 1958, 2nd edition, 1965; *Ace of Pentacles* (poems), J. F. Carr (New York), 1964; *Chinoiserie*, Dave Haselwood (San Francisco), 1965; *Hart Crane, Harry Crosby, I See You Going Over the Edge* (poem), Artists' Workshop Press (Detroit), c. 1966; *Gardenias* (for Billie Holiday), Frontier Press, 1966; (author of preface) Gerrit Lansing, *The Heavenly Tree Grows Downward*, Matter Books, 1966; *King Solomon's Magnetic Quiz*, [Pleasant Valley, N.Y.], 1967; *Pressed Wafer* (poem), Gallery Upstairs Press (Buffalo), 1967; *A Letter to Charles Olson*, S. Charters, 1968; *Unhired*, Perishable Press (Mt. Horeb, Wis.), 1968; *Asylum Poems*, Angel Hair (New York), 1969; *Untitled Essay on Frank O'Hara*, Doubleday, 1969; *A Memory of Black Mountain College*, M.I.T. Press, 1969; *Invitation*, Unicorn Press (Santa Barbara), c. 1970; *Youth*, Phoenix Book Shop (New York), 1970; *Larders*, Restau Press (Cambridge), 1970; *Nerves*, Cape Goliard Press, 1970, Grossman, 1971; *Woman* (poems), Institute of Further Studies (New York), 1972; *Selected Poems*, Grossman, 1972; *We Were There!*, Good Gay Poets (Boston), 1972.

Also author of plays "Still Life," 1961, "In Hell's Despite," 1963, and "Jive Shoelaces and Anklesox," 1967. Two plays performed by Judson Poets' Theatre and American Theatre for Poets, New York, N.Y., 1962 and 1963.

Work represented in anthologies, including *New American Poetry*, Grove, 1960; *Junge Amerikanische Lyrik*, Carl Hanser Verlag, 1961; *A Controversy of Poets*, Doubleday, 1965; *New Writing in the U.S.A.*, Penguin, 1967.

Contributor to *Nation, Evergreen Review, Paris Review, Chicago Review*, and other journals.

WORK IN PROGRESS: A book of poetry, *An Unmade Bed*; a novel, *On Board*.

SIDELIGHTS: Wieners says that, through his poems, he is "engaged in taking away from God his sound." Robert Duncan in *The Nation* writes: "John Wieners may be related to Baudelaire, whose artificial paradise was raised in despair and yearning for, but also in accusation of, the Father, and more immediately to Rimbaud, whose illuminations also (fire stolen from Zeus or sound from God) were flashes, grains of light. . . ."

Wieners participated in the Spoleto Festival of Two Worlds, June 26-July 2, 1965, and the Berkeley Poetry Conference, July 12-26, 1965, and has read at Harvard, Princeton, Yale, Cornell, St. Lawrence, and Sir George Williams Universities, and Emerson College, New School for Social Research, Wheaton, San Francisco Poetry Centre.

BIOGRAPHICAL/CRITICAL SOURCES: Big Table, No. 4, 1960; *Book Week*, January 3, 1965; *Poetry*, February, 1965; *Nation*, May 31, 1965.

*   *   *

WIESNER, Jerome B(ert)   1915-

PERSONAL: Born May 30, 1915, in Detroit, Mich.; son of Joseph J. (a storekeeper) and Ida (Friedman) Wiesner; married Laya Wainger, September 1, 1940; children: Joshua, Lisa, Zachary, Stephen. *Education:* University of Michigan, B.S.E.E., 1937, M.S., 1939, Ph.D., 1950. *Home:* 61 Shattuck Rd., Watertown, Mass. 02172. *Office:* Massachusetts Institute of Technology, Cambridge, Mass. 02139.

CAREER: University of Michigan, Ann Arbor, associate director of broadcasting, 1937-40; Library of Congress, Washington, D.C., chief engineer, 1940-42; Massachusetts Institute of Technology, Cambridge, member of staff of Radiation Laboratory, 1942-45; University of California, member of staff and group leader at Los Alamos Scientific Laboratory, 1945-46; Massachusetts Institute of Technology, assistant professor, 1946-47, associate professor, 1947-50, professor of electrical engineering, 1950—, assistant director, 1947-49, associate director, 1949-52, director of Research Laboratory of Electronics, 1952-61, dean of science, 1964-66, provost, 1966-71, president, 1971—. Member of U.S. Army Science Advisory Committee, 1956-61; special assistant to the President on science and technology, and chairman of President's Science Advisory Committee, 1961-64. Consultant to RAND Corp. and Raytheon Manufacturing Co.; member of advisory board, Television Fund, Inc., and of technical advisory committee, American Foundation for the Blind.

MEMBER: Institute of Radio Engineers (fellow), American Academy of Arts and Sciences (fellow), Acoustical Society of America (member of advisory board), American Society for Engineering Education, American Geophysical Union, Institute of Electrical and Electronics Engineers (fellow), National Academy of Sciences, American Philosophical Society, American Association of University Professors, Sigma Xi, Phi Kappa Phi, Eta Kappa Nu, Tau Beta Pi. *Awards, honors:* Medal of Honor, Electronics Industries Association, 1961.

WRITINGS: (Contributor) Louis N. Ridenour, editor, *Modern Physics for the Engineer*, McGraw, 1954; (contributor) Donald G. Brennan, editor, *Arms Control, Disarmament, and National Security*, Braziller, 1961; (contributor)

Louis Henkin, editor, *Arms Control: Issues for the Public*, Prentice-Hall, 1961; (author of introduction) Hermann Volle, editor, *Sicherung vor ueberraschungsangriffen im Atomzeitalter*, Alfred Metzner, 1962; *Where Science and Politics Meet*, McGraw, 1965; (with Abram Chayes) *ABM: An Evaluation of the Decision to Deploy an Antiballistic Missile System*, Harper, 1969. Contributor of technical articles to periodicals.

BIOGRAPHICAL/CRITICAL SOURCES: New Yorker (profile), January, 1963.†

*   *   *

WIGAN, Bernard (John)   1918-

PERSONAL: Born June 8, 1918, in East Grinstead, Sussex, England; son of Cuthbert John (a priest, Church of England) and Helen (Soldi) Wigan; married Mary Young, November 13, 1944; children: Christina, Helen, Edmund, William. *Education:* St. Edmund Hall, Oxford, B.A., 1940, M.A., 1943. *Home:* Windrush, Blackness Rd., Crowborough, Sussex, England.

CAREER: Assistant editor of *Lexicon of Patristic Greek*, 1942-44; priest of Church of England, serving in various parishes, 1942—. Oxford Diocesan Council of Education, Oxford, England, assistant secretary, 1944-48; St. Augustine's College, Canterbury, England, lecturer in liturgy, 1953-57. Examining chaplain to Bishop of Rochester, 1963—; member of Church of England Liturgical Commission, 1955—. *Member:* Society of Genealogists, Kent Archaeological Society, Sussex Archaeological Society, Henry Bradshaw Society, Canterbury and York Society.

WRITINGS: (Editor) *The Liturgy in English*, Oxford University Press, 1962, 2nd edition, 1964.

WORK IN PROGRESS: Editing *Four Early Pontificals* for Henry Bradshaw Society, *The English Collects* for Oxford University Press, and *The Sacramentary of Sarapion* for Clarendon Press.†

*   *   *

WIGGINS, Robert A.   1921-

PERSONAL: Born February 8, 1921, in Columbus, Ga.; son of Alva Lee (a comptroller) and Ruby L. (Snell) Wiggins; married Lillian Katherine, April 1, 1944 (divorced, 1972); children: Roberta L., Julie A. *Education:* University of Maryland, A.B., 1942; University of California, Berkeley, M.A., 1949, Ph.D., 1953. *Politics:* Democrat. *Religion:* Episcopal. *Home:* 622 Elmwood Dr., Davis, Calif. 95616. *Office:* University of California, Davis, Calif. 95616.

CAREER: University of California, Davis, 1950—, professor of English, 1965—, chairman of department, 1966-70, associate dean, College of Letters and Science, 1963-64, 1972—, vice-chancellor, 1964-66. *Military service:* U.S. Army, 1942-46; became captain. *Member:* Modern Language Association of America, American Council of Teachers of English, American Studies Association, American Association of University Professors, Commonwealth Club (San Francisco).

WRITINGS: Mark Twain: Jackleg Novelist, University of Washington Press, 1964; *Ambrose Bierce*, University of Minnesota Press, 1964. Contributor of short stories to magazines.

WORK IN PROGRESS: A novel and other fiction projects; editing, with William Van O'Connor, and contributing to, *Religion in American Literature*, for University of Washington Press.†

WILDER, Thornton (Niven) 1897-

PERSONAL: Born April 17, 1897, in Madison, Wis.; son of Amos Parker (an editor, and with U.S. Foreign Service) and Isabella Thornton (Niven) Wilder. *Education:* Attended public and private schools in the United States and in Chefoo, China, graduating from Berkeley (California) High School, 1915; attended Oberlin College, 1915-17; Yale University, A.B., 1920; studied at the American Academy in Rome, 1920-21; Princeton University, A.M., 1926. *Politics:* Democrat. *Religion:* Congregationalist. *Home:* 50 Deepwood Dr., Hamden, Conn. 06517.

CAREER: Lawrenceville School, Lawrenceville, N.J., French teacher, and assistant master of Davis House, 1921-25, on leave to study for master's degree and tutor and write both in the United States and abroad, 1925-27, housemaster, 1927-28; engaged in writing and first cross-country lecture tour, 1928-29; University of Chicago, Chicago, Ill., lecturer in comparative literature, 1930-36 (two quarters each year); at other times during this period (1930-36), worked for several motion picture studios and made more lecture tours; University of Hawaii, Honolulu, visiting professor, 1935; American delegate to the Institut de Cooperation Intellectuelle, Paris, France, 1937; sent to three South American countries on an educational mission for the U.S. Department of State, 1941; International P.E.N. Club Congress delegate (with John Dos Passos) to meeting in England, 1941; Harvard University, Cambridge, Mass., Charles Eliot Norton Professor of poetry, 1950-51; chief of the U.S. delegation to the UNESCO Conference of Arts, Venice, 1952. His acting experience includes taking the leading role of stage manager in his play, "Our Town," in New York City when the star, Frank Craven, went on vacation, playing the same part in many summer stock theaters for several seasons beginning in 1939, and later playing the part of Mr. Antrobus in "The Skin of Our Teeth" in both stock and summer theaters (he recalls that he found it difficult to learn his own lines.) *Military service:* Coast Artillery Corps, 1918-19; became corporal; commissioned captain in U.S. Army Air Intelligence, and served 1942-45, advancing to lieutenant colonel; awarded Legion of Merit, Bronze Star; Legion d'Honneur, Honorary Member of the Order of the British Empire (M.B.E.).

MEMBER: American Academy of Arts and Letters, Modern Language Association of America (honorary), Authors Guild, Actors Equity Association, Hispanic Society of America, Bayerische Akademie (corresponding member), Akademie der Wissenschaften und der Literatur (Mainz), Bavarian Academy of Fine Arts (honorary), Century Association, Players (honorary), Graduate Club, Elizabethan Club, Alpha Delta Phi. *Awards, honors:* Pulitzer Prize, 1928, for *The Bridge of San Luis Rey*, 1938, for *Our Town*, and 1943, for *The Skin of Our Teeth*; Chevalier, Legion of Honor, 1951; Gold Medal for Fiction, American Institute of Arts and Letters, 1952; Friedenspreis des Deutschen Buchhandels (Frankfurt-am-Main), 1957; Sonderpreis des Oesterreichischen Staatspreises, 1959, Goethe-Plakette, 1959; Edward MacDowell Medal (first time presented), 1960; Brandeis University Creative Arts Award, 1960; Century Association Art Medal; Medal of the Order of Merit (Peru); Order Pour le Merite (Bonn); Presidential Medal of Freedom, 1963; National Book Committee's National Medal for Literature (first time presented), 1965; National Book Award, 1968, for *The Eighth Day*. Honorary degrees from New York University, Yale University, Kenyon College, College of Wooster, Harvard University, Northeastern University, Oberlin College, University of New Hampshire, Goethe-Frankfurt University, University of Zurich.

WRITINGS—Novels: *The Cabala*, Boni, 1926; *The Bridge of San Luis Rey*, Boni, 1927; *The Woman of Andros*, Boni, 1930; *Heaven's My Destination*, Harper, 1935; *The Ides of March*, Harper, 1948; *The Eighth Day*, Harper, 1967; *Theophilus North*, Harper, 1973, large print edition, G. K. Hall, 1974.

Plays: *The Angel That Troubled the Waters, and Other Plays*, Coward, 1928; *The Long Christmas Dinner, and Other Plays in One Act* (includes "Pullman Car," "Hiawatha," "The Happy Journey From Trenton to Camden," "Love and How to Cure It," "The Queens of France"), Yale University Press, 1931; (translator) Andre Obey, *Lucrece* (from *Le Viol de Lucrece*), Houghton, 1933 (produced in New York, 1932); *Our Town* (three-act play), Coward, 1938, acting edition, 1965 (one performance on January 22, 1938, in Princeton, N.J., then produced in Boston, January 24, 1938, then produced in New York, 1938); *The Merchant of Yonkers: A Farce in Four Acts*, Harper, 1939 (produced in Boston and New York, 1938); *The Skin of Our Teeth* (three-act play), Harper, 1942 (produced in New Haven, October 15, 1942, then in Baltimore, Philadelphia, Washington, and New York, 1942); *Our Century* (a play in three scenes), Century Association, 1947.

Omnibus volumes: *A Thornton Wilder Trio: The Cabala, The Bridge of San Luis Rey, The Woman of Andros*, Criterion, 1956; *Three Plays: Our Town, The Skin of Our Teeth, The Matchmaker* (the last-named is a rewritten version of *The Merchant of Yonkers* based on 19th century German farce of Johann Nestroy; produced in Boston and New York, 1938), Harper, 1938, rewritten version produced as "The Matchmaker" at Edinburgh Festival, 1954, and New York, 1955 (also see below); *The Cabala and The Woman of Andros*, Harper, 1968.

Other plays: "The Trumpet Shall Sound," written while an undergraduate, published in the Yale literary magazine, 1919-20, produced by the American Laboratory Theater, 1926; translator and adapter of Henrik Ibsen's "A Doll's House," produced in Colorado and New York, 1937; translator of Jean-Paul Sartre's "The Victors" ("Morts sans sepulture"), produced Off-Broadway, 1949; "The Alcestiad," first produced at Edinburgh Festival, 1955, as "A Life in the Sun," (German translation produced as *Die Alkestiad*, in Zurich, Switzerland, 1957, S. Fischer Verlag), later made into an opera, libretto by Wilder, music by L. Talma, produced in Frankfurt, Germany, March, 1962; author of libretto for opera, "The Long Christmas Dinner," adapted from his play, music by Paul Hindemith, translated into German by Hindemith, produced in Mannheim, Germany, 1961; "Plays for Bleecker Street" (three one-act plays: "Infancy"; "Childhood"; "Someone From Assisi") produced at The Circle in the Square, New York, January 11, 1962.

Contributor: *The Intent of the Artist*, edited by Augusto Centeno, Princeton University Press, 1941. Contributor to *Harper's, Hudson Review, Poetry, Atlantic, Yale Review*.

Author of prefaces for Gertrude Stein's *Narration*, University of Chicago Press, 1935, *The Geographical History of America*, Random House, 1936, *Four in America*, Yale University Press, 1947.

Wrote film script, "Shadow of a Doubt," for Alfred Hitchcock, 1942. "The Bridge of San Luis Rey" was filmed three times, the first time in 1929; also filmed were "Our Town," 1940, and "The Matchmaker," 1958. Wilder served as unofficial consultant to the script of "Our Town," but he had nothing to do with any of the other scripts based on his works. "Hello, Dolly," 1964, is a musical based on "The Matchmaker." There have also been radio and television versions of many of his works.

WORK IN PROGRESS: Two cycles of plays, "The Seven Ages of Man" and "The Seven Deadly Sins."

SIDELIGHTS: "Wilder occupies," writes Edmund Wilson, "a unique position, between the Great Books and Parisian sophistication one way, and the entertainment industry the other way, and in our culture this region, though central, is a dark and almost uninhabited no man's land." Louis Broussard notes that "In such company as O'Neill, Eliot, Anouilh, and many other post-war pessimists, Wilder emerges as a lone dissenter. Not because he was an optimist, . . . but because his optimism grows out of an indifference to his own period. . . . No other writer begins with so hopeful a premise: that this age is essentially no different from any other, that its problems, whatever they may be, . . . will resolve themselves in change which can only be better than the past. His is not the search for an exit from dilemma; there is no dilemma."

Wilder himself believes the theater consists of presenting experience's sake. "I regard the theater as the greatest of all art forms," he told the *Paris Review*, "the most immediate way in which a human being can share with another the sense of what it is to be a human being. This supremacy of the theater derives from the fact that it is always 'now' on the stage." Ignoring conflict, preferring comedy to tragedy, extolling traditional ideas, Wilder is "the artist of the anachronism," writes Malcolm Cowley. Broussard writes of *Our Town*: Wilder "can present the cycle of life without conflict because the foundations upon which his ideals rest have not yet been shaken. Romantic love, marriage, the concept of the 'Mind of God', . . . these remain safe behind the barrier of isolated time." *The Skin of Our Teeth*, which portrays a five thousand-year history of man and has some basis in Joyce's *Finnegans Wake* "is really a way of trying to make sense out of the multiplicity of the human race and its affections," says Wilder.

Harold Clurman finds that Wilder's plays are particularly American in "their benign humor, their old-fashioned optimism, their use of the charmingly homely detail, the sophisticated employment of the commonplace, their avuncular celebration of the humdrum, their common sense, popular moralism, and the simplicity—one might almost say simple-mindedness—behind a shrewdly captivating manipulation of a large selection of classic elements." Edmund Wilson believes "all of this works very well in the theater. . . . But if one happens to be feeling a little morose . . . or if one tries the experiment of reading [*The Skin of Our Teeth*] in cold blood, the marriage of Plato and Groucho Marx may fail to appeal." Wilder, however, believes the theater addresses itself to the group-mind and "partakes of the nature of festival." A play "presupposes a crowd." He once said: "I would love to be the poet laureate of Coney Island."

Originally Wilder had been somewhat ignored by serious critics. In fact, *Our Town* closed after one week in Boston (1938), because of bad notices; however, later that year it opened in New York. Now he is being praised for his experimentation and innovation, and *The Skin of Our Teeth* may become a modern classic. Travis Bogard calls Wilder "a man who, along with O'Neill, freed the American theater from its traditional forms through his experi-

ments in *Our Town* and *The Skin of Our Teeth*. . . . In a sense, perhaps, all of Wilder's plays are about the Day of Judgment, imaging human character as a bubble rising to burst on the surface of eternity. There undoubtedly were influences on his experimental style, but, in the last analysis, Wilder's innovations are important consequences of his point of view and of his way of commenting on experience." Some of the influences one could mention were Proust, Joyce, T. S. Eliot, Ezra Pound, Gertrude Stein, Gide, and Anatole France.

Wilder once told the *Paris Review*: "I'm the kind of man whom timid old ladies stop on the street to ask about the nearest subway station. News vendors in university towns call me 'professor,' and hotel clerks, 'doctor.'" Some of his best ideas, he claims come to him in the shower. He plays the piano and has composed a few pieces. He can speak French, German, Spanish, and Italian.

BIOGRAPHICAL/CRITICAL SOURCES: New Republic, August 8, 1928; Edward Wagenknecht, *Cavalcade of the English Novel*, Holt, 1943; *Nation*, September 3, 1955; *Saturday Review*, October 6, 1956; Edmund Wilson, *A Literary Chronicle: 1920-1950*, Anchor Books, 1956; Francis Fergusson, *The Human Image in Dramatic Literature*, Doubleday, 1957; Malcolm Cowley, editor, *Writers at Work: The Paris Review Interviews*, Viking, 1957; J. M. Edelstein, compiler, *Bibliographical Checklist of the Writings of Thornton Wilder*, Yale University Library, 1959; Toby Cole, editor, *Playwrights on Playwriting*, Hill & Wang, 1961; R. Burbank, *Thornton Wilder*, Twayne, 1961; Louis Broussard, *American Drama*, University of Oklahoma Press, 1962; *Twentieth Century Literature*, IX, 1963; Travis Bogard and William I. Oliver, editors, *Modern Drama: Essays in Criticism*, Oxford University Press, 1965; Walter Allen, *The Modern Novel*, Dutton, 1965; Malcolm Goldstein, *The Art of Thornton Wilder*, University of Nebraska Press, 1965; Donald Haberman, *The Plays of Thornton Wilder*, Wesleyan University Press, 1967; Helmut Papajewski, *Thornton Wilder*, translated by John Conway, Unger, 1969; Herman Stresau, *Thornton Wilder*, translated by Frieda Schultze, Unger, 1971; M. C. Kuner, *Thornton Wilder: The Bright and the Dark*, Crowell, 1972; Carolyn Riley, editor, *Contemporary Literary Criticism*, Volume I, Gale, 1973.†

*   *   *

WILDMAN, Louis Robert   1941-

PERSONAL: Born November 15, 1941, in Portland, Oreg.; son of John Adrian Harwood and Constance (Bougher) Wildman. *Education:* Lewis and Clark College, A.B., 1963; Portland University, M. Mus.Ed., 1964; University of Washington, Ed.D., 1971. *Religion:* Episcopalian. *Home:* 6335 North Delaware Ave., Portland, Ore. *Office:* Box 84, Lester, Wash. 98035.

CAREER: Portland Symphony Orchestra, Portland, Ore., solo timpanist, 1958-66; Portland State College (now University), Portland, Ore., instructor in mathematics, 1964-66; Green River Community College, Auburn, Wash., instructor in mathematics, 1966-68; University of Washington, Seattle, research associate, 1968-71; Institute for Quality in Human Life, founder and director, 1971—. *Member:* American Mathematical Society, American Musicological Society, American Association of University Professors, Phi Mu Alpha-Sinfonia.

WRITINGS: Practical Understanding of the Percussion Section, Humphries, 1964; *The University Community*,

Institute for Quality in Human Life, 1974. Contributor to *Diapason, Journal of the National Association of College Wind and Percussion Instructors, International Musician, College Student Survey Journal,* and *Chronicle of Higher Education.*

BIOGRAPHICAL/CRITICAL SOURCES: International Musician, December, 1964; *School Musician,* April 1965; *Portland University Review,* spring, 1965.

*   *   *

WILDS, Nancy Alexander 1926-

PERSONAL: Born March 7, 1926, in Little Rock, Ark.; daughter of George Ludovic (a banker) and Gladys (McCullough) Alexander; children: Ellen, Alexander, Stephanie. *Education:* Attended Southwestern at Memphis, for two years; University of Chicago, Ph.B. *Religion:* Episcopalian. *Home:* 245 Greenville St., N.W., Aiken, S.C.

CAREER: Ecclesiastical designer, with work including illumination of manuscripts, polychroming altars and chancel furnishings, and designing liturgical gardens, with own studio, Aiken, S.C.; Mead Hall Episcopal Day School, Aiken, S.C., teacher of sacred art.

WRITINGS: Church Grounds and Gardens, Seabury, 1964.

*   *   *

WILHELM, Kathryn Stephenson 1915-

PERSONAL: Born October 2, 1915, in Graysville, Tenn.; daughter of Claiborne Bell (a minister) and Edith (Hand) Stephenson; married John Arthur Wilhelm (a surgeon), March 25, 1936; children: David John, Charles Claiborne, Jerald Arthur. *Education:* Attended Southern Junior College (now Southern Missionary College), and Columbia Union College; also studied at Jacksonville College of Music, Jacksonville, Fla. *Address:* Box 544, Keystone Heights, Fla.

CAREER: Review & Herald Publishing Association, Washington, D.C., associate manager of periodical department, 1936-38; private secretary, nurse in doctor's office, and hospital admissions officer at other periods.

WRITINGS: Sally Roses and Other Stories from My Memory Chest (juvenile), Southern Publishing, 1963; *Butterfly Blue* (poems), Southern Publishing, 1966; *The Hot Brick and Other Stories,* Southern Publishing, 1966. Contributor of poetry to newspapers and magazines.

WORK IN PROGRESS: Spring Violets, adult poems; *Absolutely Not!,* humorous account of household pets.

AVOCATIONAL INTERESTS: Singing (contralto soloist), flying, boating, golf, rock collecting, nature study.†

*   *   *

WILKES-HUNTER, R(ichard)
(Dean Ballard, Marc Brody, Tod Conrad, Alex Crane, Shane Douglas, James Dunn, Peter Gordon, Kerry Mitchell, C. M. O'Niell, Kent Sanders, Alan Shulberg)

HOME: Sonning, 38 Careel Head Rd., Avalon Beach, New South Wales, Australia.

CAREER: Began his career on the *Sydney Daily Guardian,* Sydney, Australia, 1926-30; in the years between 1930 (when the *Guardian* ceased publication) and 1948, he prospected in Queensland and New Guinea, drove trucks and owned a small fleet of them, saw some army service, worked on ranches breaking in horses, did some professional boxing as a welterweight, drove a milk truck, started a factory for canning shrimps, and wrote about a thousand short stories, which were published in every English-speaking country of the world; Rural Newspapers Lt., Orange, New South Wales, Australia, reporter for *Western Stock and Station Journal,* 1947, editor and advertising manager, 1951-53, editor of *Poultryman,* 1948-51; Modern Illustrators Printery Ltd., director, 1952-54; full-time writer of pocket books 1954—.

WRITINGS—All published by Leisure Publishing, except as indicated: *Crusade into Crime* (novel), Australian Publishing Co., 1948; *Patient Is the Hunter,* 1953; *White Trails Over London,* 1953; *Run With the Weasel,* 1953; *Ride West of the Law,* 1953; *The Day I Stopped Running,* 1953; *Heritage of the Horned Steer,* 1954; *Five Came to Kill,* 1954; *Trail of the Hunted,* 1954; *Badge for a Gunfighter,* 1954; *Partisans Die Alone,* 1954; *Task Demolition,* 1954; *Violent Holiday,* 1954; *Take This Gun,* Cleveland Publishing, 1954; *Commandos Are Expendable,* 1954; *Fool from Down Under,* Cleveland Publishing, 1954; *Six Gun Empire,* Cleveland Publishing, 1955; *Train a Fast Gun,* 1955; *Fighter Pilot,* 1955; *Range Justice,* Cleveland Publishing 1955; *Hostage,* Cleveland Publishing, 1955; *Deserters Don't Come Back,* 1955; *Gunsmoke Haze,* Cleveland Publishing, 1955; *Kid With a Gun,* Cleveland Publishing, 1955; *Fast with a Gun,* Cleveland Publishing, 1955; *Ride West of the Law,* 1956; *Bank Robbery Hostage,* 1956; *Five Days to Kill,* Horwitz, 1956; *Death Date,* 1957; *A Tomb for Mr. Lee,* 1957; *Commando,* Webster Publishing, 1958; *Borneo Patrol,* Webster Publishing, 1958; *Kokoda Trail,* Webster Publishing, 1958.

All published by Horwitz: *Student Nurse,* 1960; *The Innocent Savage,* 1960; *The Doctor's Affair,* 1960; *Fighting Patrol,* 1961; *Operation Gunsight,* 1961; *Mata,* 1963; *Tikai,* 1964; *Chata,* 1964.

Under pseudonym Dean Ballard; all published by Horwitz: *Ride the Wide Trail,* 1956; *Range War,* 1956; *Fan a Fast Gun,* 1956; *Quick Finger Heritage,* 1956; *Gunslinger,* 1956; *Passion Branded,* 1956; *Vengeance Is a Woman,* 1956.

Under pseudonym Marc Brody: *Lady Don't Shroud Me,* Horwitz, 1958.

Under pseudonym Tod Conrad: *Rawhide Vixen,* Webster Publishing, 1958; *Kane and Miss Able,* Webster Publishing, 1958; *The Colonel and the Corpse,* Webster Publishing, 1958.

Under pseudonym Alex Crane: *Bushman,* Horwitz, 1959; *One Night of Fear,* Horwitz, 1959.

Under pseudonym Shane Douglas; all published by Horwitz, except as indicated: *Night Nurse,* 1959; *Doctor in Flight,* 1959; *Doctor Deceived,* 1959; *Emergency Call,* 1959; *My Love Is a Scalpel,* 1959; *Ship's Surgeon,* 1959; *Micheline,* 1959; *Psycho Ward,* 1960; *The Plastic Surgeon,* 1960; *Gae Bryant M.D.,* 1960; *Doctor Deceived,* 1960; *Crisis,* 1960; *Doctor on Call,* 1960; *Heart Surgeon,* 1961; *The Hospital Secret,* 1961; *Doctor in Doubt,* 1961; *The Flying Physicians,* 1961, New American Library, 1963; *Special Case,* 1961; *Assistant Surgeon,* 1961, New American Library, 1962; *The Doctor's Past,* 1962, New American Library, 1963; *Surgeon on Call,* 1962, New American Library, 1963; *The Doctor's Pledge,* New American Library, 1962; *Surgeon in Need,* New American Library, 1962; *Doctor in Danger,* New American Library, 1962; *Emergency Surgeon,* New American Library, 1962; *Doctor at*

Fault, 1962, New American Library, 1964; *Surgeon Unmasked*, 1963; *Prison Camp Doctor*, 1963; *Theatre Nurse*, 1963; *The Young Surgeon*, 1963; *Doctor in Action*, 1963, New American Library, 1964; *Dr. Glen Carew*, 1963.

Under pseudonym James Dunn: *The Adventures of Lawrence of Arabia*, Horwitz, 1963.

Under pseudonym Peter Gordon: *Commando Sortie*, Horwitz, 1963.

Under pseudonym Kerry Mitchell; all published by Horwitz, except as indicated: *Bush Nurse*, 1960; *Flying Doctor Overdue*, 1960; *Doctor on Trial*, 1960; *Condition Critical*, 1960; *The Doctor's Secret*, 1960; *Doctor in Darwin*, 1960; *Flying Doctor Emergency*, 1961; *The Doctor's Desire*, 1961; *The Doctor's Intrigue*, 1961; *Mercy Flight*, 1961; *Heartbeat*, 1961; *Duty Sister*, 1961; *Problem Patient*, 1961; *Surgeon Accused*, 1961; *Doctor at Bay*, 1962, Dell, 1963; *Special Nurse*, Dell, 1962; *The Doctor's Decision*, Dell, 1962; *The Doctor Who Dared*, 1963; *Operation Secret*, 1963; *Emergency Doctor*, Dell, 1963.

Under pseudonym C. M. O'Niell: *Flight into Romance*, Horwitz, 1960; *Rock-n-Roll RomaNce*, Horwitz, 1960; *Probationary Nurse*, Horwitz, 1960.

Under pseudonym Kent Sanders: *The Devil's Dossier*, Horwitz, 1959.

Under pseudonym Alan Shulberg: *Vendetta Valley*, Webster Publishing, 1959.

Also author of (under pseudonym Adrian Gray; all published by New American Library) *The Young Doctors, Doctors' Desires*, and *Doctors' Women*.

SIDELIGHTS: Wilkes-Hunter's books have been translated into Norwegian, Swedish, Flemish, German, French, Dutch, Israeli, Spanish, and Finnish. Resigned from business in 1954 "to concentrate on writing pocket books, in which form of mental torture I have indulged ever since."

* * *

WILKIE, Brian 1929-

PERSONAL: Born March 30, 1929, in Brooklyn, N.Y.; son of James William and Mary Ellen (Devine) Wilkie; married Ann Johnson, August 8, 1957; children: John, Brian Scott, Neil. *Education:* Columbia University, B.A., 1951; University of Rochester, M.A., 1952; University of Wisconsin, Ph.D., 1959. *Office:* English Department, University of Illinois, Urbana, Ill.

CAREER: University of Wisconsin, Madison, instructor in English, 1959; Dartmouth College, Hanover, N.H., instructor, 1959-61, assistant professor of English, 1961-63; University of Illinois, Urbana, assistant professor, 1963-65, associate professor, 1965-71, professor of English, 1971—. Associate, University of Illinois Center for Advanced Study, 1973. *Military service:* U.S. Army, 1952-54. *Member:* Modern Language Association of America. *Awards, honors:* University of Illinois Teacher Excellence Award, 1966.

WRITINGS: Romantic Poets and Epic Tradition, University of Wisconsin Press, 1965; (contributor) David V. Erdman and John E. Grant, editors, *Blake's Visionary Forms Dramatic*, Princeton University Press, 1970; (contributor) W. Paul Elledge and Richard L. Hoffman, editors, *Romantic and Victorian*, Fairleigh Dickinson University Press, 1971; (contributor with Mary Lynn Johnson) Stuart Curran and Joseph A. Wittreich, editors, *Blake's Sublime Allegory*, University of Wisconsin Press, 1973. Contributor

of articles to *College English, Soundings, Journal of English and Germanic Philology, Journal of Aesthetic Education*, and *Blake Studies*.

WORK IN PROGRESS: A study of Blake's *The Four Zoas*.

* * *

WILKINSON, (William) Roderick 1917-

PERSONAL: Born March 31, 1917, in Glasgow, Scotland; son of William (a carpenter) and Lily (McSwan) Wilkinson; married Jean Robertson (a teacher), September 28, 1945; children: Roderick, Sheila, Jane. *Education:* Attended secondary school in Glasgow, Scotland. *Religion:* Presbyterian. *Home:* 5 Dargarvel Ave., Glasgow S.1, Scotland. *Agent:* Austin Wahl, 21 East Van Buren St., Chicago, Ill. *Office:* Caterpillar Tractor Co. Ltd., Glasgow, Scotland.

CAREER: Rex Publicity Ltd. (advertising agency), Glasgow, Scotland, 1932—, became director in 1957; Caterpillar Tractor Co. Ltd., Glasgow, Scotland, employee relations manager, 1960—. Former director of Alexander Howie Research. *Member:* Advertising Association, Institute of Practitioners in Advertising, Institute of Marketing, Institute of Personnel Management, British Institute of Management, Author's Society.

WRITINGS: Murder Belongs to Me, Museum Press, 1956; *The Big Still*, John Long, 1958, British Book Center, 1959; *Everything Goes Dead*, R. Hale, 1967; *The Pressure Men*, R. Hale, 1967; *The Network*, R. Hale, 1969; *The Hallmarks of Antique Glass*, Richard Madley, 1969. Author of filmscript, "In the Picture," and of forty radio plays and documentaries aired in some twenty countries. Contributor of short stories and articles to periodicals.

WORK IN PROGRESS: Radio and television features for a series about a British family; a novel, an adventure story set in the Scottish Highlands; features and articles about bagpipes.

SIDELIGHTS: Wilkinson's first two books were published in Denmark, Italy, and Germany, and serialized on radio in ten countries.†

* * *

WILL, Frederick L(udwig) 1909-

PERSONAL: Born May 8, 1909, in Swissvale, Pa.; son of Frederick L. (a clergyman) and Katherine Dora (Graf) Will; married G. Louise Hendrickson, June 17, 1932; children: Katherine (Mrs. Joseph G. Jorgensen), George Frederick. *Education:* Thiel College, A.B., 1929; Ohio State University, M.A. 1932; Cornell University Ph.D. 1937. *Home:* 602 E. Harding Dr., Urbana, Ill. 61801. *Office:* University of Illinois, Urbana, Ill. 61801.

CAREER: High school instructor in Ohio 1932-33; Cornell University, instructor, 1937; instructor, 1938-41; assistant professor, 1941-46, associate professor, 1946-55, professor of philosophy, 1955—, chairman of department, 1961-63, associate member of Center for Advanced Studies, 1963-64. Cornell University, Ithaca, N.Y., visiting professor, 1955, 1964-65. *Member:* American Philosophical Association (president, Western division, 1968-69), American Association of University Professor. *Awards, honors:* Guggenheim fellow, 1945-46; Fulbright senior research scholar at Oxford University, 1961.

WRITINGS: Induction and Justification, Cornell University Press, 1974.

Contributor: *Essays in Political Theory*, edited by Konwitz and Murphy, Cornell University Press, 1948; *Philosophical Analysis*, edited by Max Black, Cornell University Press, 1950; *Logic and Language*, second series, edited by A. Flew, Basil Blackwell, 1953, Doubleday, 1965.

Contributor of articles and reviews to professional journals.

* * *

WILLETT, Brother Franciscus 1922-
(Brother Jeremy Premont, Brother Orrin Primm)

PERSONAL: Born July 24, 1922; son of Clyde Francis (a mechanic) and Helen (Kegel) Willett. *Education:* University of Notre Dame, B.A., 1945, M.A., 1950; St. John's University, New York, N.Y., M.L.S., 1955. *Home:* St. Joseph Novitiate, Valatie, N.Y. 12184. *Office:* Holy Cross Press, Valatie, N.Y. 12184.

CAREER: Roman Catholic religious, member of Congregation of the Holy Cross, 1940—. Has taught at Holy Trinity High School, Chicago, Ill., Vincentian Institute, Albany, N.Y., and Holy Cross High School, Flushing, N.Y.; Holy Cross Press, Valatie, N.Y., president, 1963—. Writer and editor. Supervisor of libraries for Holy Cross Brothers, Eastern Province.

WRITINGS—All published by Holy Cross Press, except as indicated: *The Fisherman Saint*, Dujarie Press, 1947; *The Tentmaker from Tarsus*, Dujarie Press, 1950; *The Merry Music Maker*, Dujarie Press, 1952; *The Thunder of Silence*, 1964; (under pseudonym Brother Jeremy Premont) *The Cardinal Said No!* 1964; *Tales of the California Missions*, 1964; *St. Matthew and His Gospel*, 1964; (under pseudonym Brother Orrin Primm) *The Mountain of God*, 1965; (under pseudonym Brother Jeremy Premont) *The Eagle of God*, 1965; *A Mountain for St. Joseph*, 1965; *The Promise to Angela*, 1966; *The Glorious Maccabees*, 1967; *Understanding the Inquisition*, 1968. Contributor of about fifty pieces of fiction, nonfiction and poetry to magazines.

WORK IN PROGRESS: A commentary on Acts of the Apostles; a group of stories about Indians in New York area; stories of the catacombs; a novel.

SIDELIGHTS: Brother Franciscus told *CA*: "As a religious, I was assigned this work [full-time publisher of young people's books] . . . but I had followed it from conviction for a period of time previously. I believe deeply in good reading for children. Each book is a time bomb that can explode into the lives of its young readers at any time."

As a publisher, Brother Franciscus looks for subjects neglected by other publishing houses and then tries to find someone to write the book. On his own part, he writes what he is interested in and what he thinks is needed. "Even if I don't think a book will sell I have to write it."†

* * *

WILLEY, Peter (Robert Everard) 1922-

PERSONAL: Born September 24, 1922, in London, England; son of Alfred Everard (a clergyman) and Anne (Watts) Willey. *Education:* Christ's College, Cambridge, M.A. (honors), 1947. *Politics:* Conservative. *Religion:* Church of England. *Home:* Wellington College, Crowthorne, Berkshire, England. *Agent:* John Farquharson Ltd., 15 Red Lion Sq., London, W.C.1, England.

CAREER: Wellington College, Crowthorne, Berkshire, England, senior language master and housemaster, 1947—. Lecturer at Oxford University, and lecturer throughout United Kingdom, 1959—. Leader of five archaeological expeditions to northern Iran, including one in 1965 to discover locations of more Assassin castles on the Iran-Afghan border. *Military service:* British Army, 1942-45; served in Sicily and Italy; became major; held as prisoner of war; mentioned in dispatches three times. *Member:* Royal Geographical Society (fellow), Royal Central Asian Society (fellow), Junior Army and Navy Club.

WRITINGS: Guten Tag, Harrap, 1961; *The Castles of Assassins*, Harrap, 1963. Contributor to *Illustrated London News, Times Educational Supplement*, and other periodicals.

WORK IN PROGRESS: A book on the history of the Assassins.

SIDELIGHTS: Willey speaks French, German.†

* * *

WILLGOOSE, Carl E. 1916-

PERSONAL: Born August 29, 1916, in Needham, Mass.; son of Samuel and Cora (Wood) Willgoose; married Ruth Terrell, May 25, 1946; children: Tom, Richard, Laura, James. *Education:* Boston University, B.S. in Ed., 1939, Ed.M., 1940; Syracuse University, Ed.D., 1951. *Politics:* Republican. *Religion:* Methodist. *Home:* Wakeland Rd., Dover, Mass.

CAREER: Director of health and physical education, North Reading, Mass., 1940-41; director of health and physical education, Andover, Mass., 1941-42; Syracuse University, Syracuse, N.Y., chairman, department of physical education, 1946-51; Oswego State Teachers College (now State University of New York College at Oswego), professor of health and physical education, 1951-58; Temple University, Philadelphia, Pa., professor of education, 1958-60; Boston University, Boston, Mass., associate professor, 1960-64, professor of education, 1964—. *Military service:* U.S. Army Air Forces, Air Transport Command, 1942-46. U.S. Air Force Reserve, 1946—; became lieutenant colonel. *Member:* American Association for Health, Physical Education and Recreation (fellow; vice-president, 1964-66), American Public Health Association (fellow), American College of Sports Medicine (fellow), American School Health Association (fellow), Westwood-Dover Conservation Club (president, 1963-65).

WRITINGS: (Co-author) *Selected Team Sports for Men*, Saunders, 1952; *Health Education in the Elementary School*, Saunders, 1959, 4th edition, 1974; *Evaluation in Health Education and Physical Education*, McGraw, 1961; (with Charles A. Bucher) *The Foundations of Health*, Appleton, 1967; *The Curriculum in Physical Education*, Prentice-Hall, 1969; *Health Teaching in Secondary Schools*, Saunders, 1972. Contributor of about sixty articles to health and education journals. Associate editor of *Research Quarterly*.

WORK IN PROGRESS: A health series for publication by Ginn.†

* * *

WILLIAMS, Bruce R(odda) 1919-

PERSONAL: Born January 10, 1919, in Warrigul, Victoria, Australia; son of William James (a parson) and Helen (Baud) Williams; married Roma Olive Hotten, July 25, 1942; children: Helen, Frances, Erica, Ruth, Julia. *Education:* Studied at Wesley College, Melbourne, Australia, 1932-35, Queen's College, University of Melbourne, 1936-

39. *Office:* University of Sydney, Sydney, New South Wales 2006, Australia.

CAREER: University of Adelaide, Adelaide, South Australia, lecturer in economics, 1939-46; The Queen's University of Belfast, Belfast, Northern Ireland, lecturer in economics, 1946-50; University of Keele, Keele, Staffordshire, England, professor of economics, 1950-59; University of Manchester, Manchester, England, Robert Otley Professor, 1959-63, Stanley Jevons Professor of Political Economy, 1963-67, dean of Faculty of Economics; University of Sydney, Sydney, Australia, vice-chancellor and principal, 1967—. Director, Centre for Business Research; secretary and co-director of research, science and industry committee, 1952-59. Visiting professor of economics, University of Melbourne, 1962. Economic advisor, Minister of Technology, 1966-67. Member of academic advisory committee, University of Lancaster; member, National Board for Prices and Incomes, 1966-67, Central Advisory Council on Science and Technology, 1967, and Reserve Bank Board, 1969—. *Member:* British Association for Advancement of Science (section president, 1964-65).

WRITINGS: The Socialist Order and Freedom, Reed & Harris, 1942; (with C. F. Carter) *Industry and Technical Progress*, Oxford University Press, 1957; (with Carter) *Investment in Innovation*, Oxford University Press, 1957; (with Carter) *Science in Industry*, Oxford University Press, 1959; *International Report on Factors in Investment Behaviour*, Organisation for Economic Cooperation and Development, 1962; *Science and Economic Growth in Australia*, Hassell Press, 1963; *Investment and Technology in Growth*, Manchester Statistical Society, 1964; (with W. P. Scott) *Investment Proposals and Decisions*, Allen & Unwin, 1965; *Technology, Investment and Growth*, Chapman & Hall, 1967; (editor) *Science and Technology in Economic Growth*, Wiley, 1973.

Contributor: G. L. Wood, editor, *Australia*, Angus & Robertson, 1949; G. L. S. Shackle, editor, *Uncertainty and Business Decisions*, Liverpool University Press, 1957; D. Burn, editor, *The Structure of British Industry*, Cambridge University Press, 1958; J. H. B. Tew and R.F. Henderson, editors, *Studies in Company Finance*, Cambridge University Press, 1959. Editor, *Manchester School*, 1949-67, *Sociological Review*, 1953-59.

WORK IN PROGRESS: Economic Growth and Research Strategies in Europe.†

*   *   *

WILLIAMS, Frances Leigh   1909-

PERSONAL: Born March 20, 1909, in Richmond, Va.; daughter of Francis Deane (president of F. D. Williams & Co., a tobacco firm) and Mary Mason (Anderson) Williams. *Education:* Attended Smith College, 1926-27. *Politics:* Independent. *Religion:* Episcopalian. *Home:* 103 West Franklin St., Richmond, Va.; and 1007 Harbor Dr., Delray Beach, Fla. 33444. *Agent:* Bliss Celebrity Bureau, Inc., 7615 Piney Branch Rd., Richmond, Va.

CAREER: Richmond News-Leader, Richmond, Va., reporter, 1927-35; historical research assistant to Douglas Southall Freeman, 1935-37; Winifred Hanigan Fashions, Washington, D.C., partner, 1947-51; Sea Horse Hotel, Virginia Beach, Va., executive manager, 1949-60; Sea Terrace, Delray Beach, Fla., executive manager, 1954-57. Consultant to Jamaica Square, Delray Beach, Fla. *Member:* Association for the Preservation of Virginia Antiquities, Virginia Historical Society, Confederate Memorial Literary Society; Woman's Club, Colony Club, Poe Foundation, and Junior League (all Richmond). *Awards, honors:* United Daughters of the Confederacy citation 1963, for *Matthew Fontaine Maury: Scientist of the Sea*.

WRITINGS: Historic Richmond: Her Story and Her Spirit, Whittet & Shepperson, 1936; *They Faced the Future*, Whittet & Shepperson, 1951; *Welcome to Dunecrest*, Messner, 1955; *The Shawnee Tomahawk*, Henry Holt, 1958; *Matthew Fontaine Maury: Scientist of the Sea*, Rutgers University Press, 1963; *A Century of Service, Prologue to the Future: A History of the First & Merchants Bank*, [Richmond], 1965; *Ocean Pathfinder: A Biography of Matthew Fontaine Maury*, Harcourt, 1966; *Plantation Patriot: A Biography of Eliza Lucas Pinckney*, Harcourt, 1967.

AVOCATIONAL INTERESTS: Designing and building Florida residences, and travel.†

*   *   *

WILLIAMS, George (Guion)   1902-

PERSONAL: Born May 1, 1902, in Rogers, Tex.; son of Thomas Nathaniel (a justice of the peace) and Virginia M. (Speer) Williams; married Marian Williams; children: Stephen G., Geoffrey N. *Education:* Rice University, B.A., 1923, M.A., 1925. *Politics:* Democrat. *Home:* 2732 University, Houston, Tex. 77005. *Agent:* Maurice Crain, Inc., 18 East 41st St., New York, N.Y. 10017. *Office:* Rice University, Houston, Tex. 77001.

CAREER: Rice University, Houston, Tex., 1927-70, started as instructor, professor of English, 1958-70. Houston Museum of Natural History, president, 1947-49, member of board of directors, 1947-55. Linda Scott Brown Lecturer in Ornithology, University of California at Los Angeles, 1958; distinguished scholar lecturer, Rice Alumni, 1965. Staff member of Southwestern Writers Conference, Writers' Round-up, and Corpus Christi Fine Arts Colony. *Member:* Texas Institute of Letters, American Ornithologists' Union, Houston Philosophical Society. *Awards, honors:* McMurray Bookshop Award of Texas Institute of Letters for best novel of the year by a Texan, 1952, for *The Blind Bull*.

WRITINGS: Creative Writing, Harper, 1935; (editor) *Readings for Creative Writers*, Harper, 1938; *The Blind Bull*, Abelard, 1952, published as *Flesh and the Dream*, Pocket Books, 1953; *Some of My Best Friends Are Professors*, Abelard, 1958; *Distribution and Migration of American Birds*, University of California Press, 1961; *A New View of Chaucer*, Duke University Press, 1965; *A Guide to Literary London*, Hastings House, 1973. Regular colomnist, *Audubon Magazine*, 1941-51; contributor to *Nation, Fact, Sewanee Review*, and other journals.

WORK IN PROGRESS: Modern British Poetry; a novel.

SIDELIGHTS: Convinced, in view of the wars and other world upheavals of his lifetime, Williams told *CA*: "that the only star worth following is compassion—for man and for beast." He is competent in French and Spanish.

*   *   *

WILLIAMS, Greer   1909-

PERSONAL: Born October 20, 1909, in Detroit, Mich.; son of Eugene Francis and Nellie (Brown) Williams; married Blanche Lusk, 1934 (divorced); married second wife, Lorna Doone Hughes, April 26, 1952; children: Deborah V., Kevin G., Julie N. *Education:* Attended William and

Mary College, 1929-30. *Politics:* Independent. *Home:* 55 Whiton Ave., Hingham, Mass. *Agent:* Henry Volkening, Russell & Volkening, Inc., 551 Fifth Ave., New York, N.Y. 10017. *Office:* Rockefeller Foundation, 111 West 50th St., New York, N.Y.

CAREER: Reporter or sports writer for newspapers in Michigan and Virginia, 1927-35; *Chicago Tribune*, Chicago, Ill., reporter and science writer, 1935-40; U.S. Public Health Service, Washington, D.C., information assistant, 1940-41; *Chicago Sun*, Chicago, Ill., science editor, 1941-42; free-lance writer and medical public relations consultant, 1945—. American College of Surgeons, public relations director, 1951-55; Joint Commission on Mental Illness and Health, director of information, 1956-60; Children's Hospital Medical Center, Boston, Mass., assistant director, 1960-62. Consultant to Veterans Administration, 1946-47, National Society for Crippled Children and Adults, 1947-48, American Cancer Society, 1949-50, Aero Medical Laboratory, Wright Patterson Air Force Base, 1951-52, Association of American Medical Colleges, 1952; consultant on medical and natural sciences, Rockefeller Foundation, 1963—. *Military service:* U.S. Army Air Forces, public relations officer, Headquarters, Air Surgeon, 1943-46; became captain. *Member:* National Association of Science Writers, American Association for the Advancement of Science.

WRITINGS: Virus Hunters, Knopf, 1959; (editor) *Action for Mental Health*, Basic Books, 1961; *The Plague Killers*, Scribner, 1969; *Kaiser-Permanente Health Plan: Why It Works*, [Oakland, Calif.], 1971. Contributor to *Saturday Evening Post, Atlantic Monthly, Modern Hospital*, other journals and newspapers.

WORK IN PROGRESS: A history of the international health activities of the Rockefeller Foundation.†

* * *

WILLIAMS, Guy R. 1920-

PERSONAL: Born August 23, 1920, in Mold, North Wales; son of Owen Elias (a physician) and Beatrice (Chadwick) Williams. *Education:* Attended St. Edward's School, Oxford, England, and several art schools; received art teacher's diploma, 1950. *Religion:* Church of England. *Home:* 8 The Mall, East Sheen, London SW14 7JH, England. *Agent:* Anthony Sheil Associates, 52 Floral St., London WC2E 9DA, England. *Office:* 1A Earl Rd., East Sheen, London SW14 7JH, England.

CAREER: Parmiter's School, London, England, master in charge of drama and careers, 1950—. Artist and illustrator, with work exhibited at Royal Academy, London, England, and at many galleries. *Awards, honors:* Saxon Barton Prize of Royal Cambrian Academy for an oil painting.

WRITINGS: Use Your Hands!, Chapman & Hall, 1956; *Use Your Eyes!*, Chapman & Hall, 1957; *Use Your Leisure!*, Chapman & Hall, 1958; *Use Your Head!*, Chapman & Hall, 1959; *Instructions to Young Collectors*, Museum Press, 1959.

Use Your Spare Time!, Chapman & Hall, 1960; *Instructions to Young Model-Makers*, Museum Press, 1960; *Use Your Legs!*, Chapman & Hall, 1961; *Use Your Playtime!*, Chapman & Hall, 1962; *Woodworking*, Museum Press, 1962; *Drawing and Sketching*, Museum Press, 1962; *Use Your Ears!*, Chapman & Hall, 1963; *Sketching in Pencil*, Pitman, 1963; *Tackle Leatherwork This Way*, Stanley Paul, 1963; (editor) *Enjoy Painting in Oils*, Gollancz, 1963; *In-*

structions in Handicrafts, Museum Press, 1964; *Making a Miniature House*, Oxford University Press, 1964; *Teach Your Child to be Handy*, Pearson, 1964; *Let's Look at Wales*, Museum Press, 1965; *Let's Look at London*, Museum Press, 1965; *Tackle Drawing and Painting This Way*, Stanley Paul, 1965; *The World of Model Trains*, Deutsch, 1970; *The World of Model Ships and Boats*, Deutsch, 1971; *The Hidden World of Scotland Yard*, Hutchinson, 1972; *The World of Model Aircraft*, Deutsch, 1973; *The Black Treasurers of Scotland Yard*, Hamish Hamilton, 1973.

Editor of "Enjoying Home and Leisure" series, Gollancz. Advisory editor, *Dramascripts* series, Macmillan.

WORK IN PROGRESS: The World of Model Cars, to be published by Deutsch.

SIDELIGHTS: Williams is interested in the problems of play production; has directed several Shakespearean productions, editing the texts and designing settings.

* * *

WILLIAMS, Hiram D. 1917-

PERSONAL: Born February 11, 1917, in Indianapolis, Ind.; son of Earl Boring (a Baptist minister) and Inez (Draper) Williams; married Avonell Baumunk, July 7, 1941; children: Curtis Earl, Kim Avonell. *Education:* Pennsylvania State University, B.S., 1950, M.Ed., 1951. *Religion:* Unitarian. *Home:* 2804 Northwest 30th Ter., Gainesville, Fla. 32601. *Office:* Art Department, University of Florida, Gainesville, Fla.

CAREER: University of Southern California, Los Angeles, assistant professor of art, 1953; University of Texas, Austin, assistant professor of art, 1954-60; University of Florida, Gainesville, associate professor of art, 1960—. Painter with work hung in national exhibitions, including shows at Whitney Museum of American Art, Corcoran Gallery, and Carnegie Institute. Member of Chancellor's Council, University of Texas. *Military service:* U.S. Army, Combat Engineers, 1941-45; received European Theater Ribbon with three battle stars. *Awards, honors:* Guggenheim fellowship, 1963-64.

WRITINGS: Notes for a Young Painter, Prentice-Hall, 1963; *Forms*, University of Texas Press, 1969. Former Florida correspondent, *Art in America*.

WORK IN PROGRESS: Further Notes for a Young Painter (essays).

SIDELIGHTS: Williams told *CA:* "My concern: humanism in art (painting)."

* * *

WILLIAMS, Howard Russell 1915-

PERSONAL: Born September 26, 1915, in Evansville, Ind.; son of Clyde Alfred (an engineer) and Grace (Preston) Williams; married Virginia Merle Thompson, November 3, 1942; children: Frederick. *Education:* Washington University, St. Louis, Mo., A.B., 1937; Columbia University, LL.B., 1940. *Politics:* Democratic. *Religion:* Protestant. *Home:* 811 Mayfield Ave., Stanford, Calif. 94305.

CAREER: Attorney-at-law; Root Clark, Buckner & Ballantine (law firm), New York, N.Y., associate, 1940-41; University of Texas Law School, Austin, associate professor, 1946-48, professor, 1948-51; Columbia University Law School, New York, N.Y., associate professor, 1951-52, professor 1952-59, Dwight Professor, 1959-63; Stanford

University Law School, Stanford, Calif., professor, 1963-68, Lillick professor, 1968—. President's Materials Policy Commission, oil and gas consultant, 1951; Rocky Mountain Mineral Law Foundation, trustee, 1963—; member of California Law Revision Commission, 1971—. *Military service:* U.S. Army, Field Artillery, 1941-46; became major.

WRITINGS: Cases and Materials on Property, Foundation, 1954; (with R. C. Maxwell and C. J. Meyers) *Cases and Materials on Oil and Gas*, Foundation, 1956, 3rd edition, 1974; (with C. J. Meyers) *Oil and Gas Terms*, Matthew Bender & Co., 1957, 3rd edition, 1971; (with C. J. Meyers) *Oil and Gas Law*, Matthew Bender & Co., Volumes I and II, 1959, Volumes III and IV, 1962, Volumes V and VI, 1964; *Cases on Decedents' Estates and Trust*, Foundation, 1968; *Cases on Future Interests*, Foundation, 1970; (with Meyers) *Oil and Gas Law* (abridged edition), Matthew Bender & Co., 1973. Contributor to law reviews and journals.

*   *   *

WILLIAMS, John (Herbert)   1908-

PERSONAL: Born July 16, 1908, in St. Leonards on Sea, Sussex, England; son of Sidney Herbert (a dental surgeon and a barrister) and Dorothy (Roth) Williams; married Sonia Kinahan, August 3, 1940; children: Deirdre Nicola, Vanessa June, Eve Melanie. *Education:* University College, London, Diploma in Librarianship, 1926; Birbeck College, B.A., 1936. *Politics:* Liberal. *Religion:* "Brought up in the Church of England." *Home:* 25 Filsham Rd., St. Leonards on Sea, Sussex, England. *Agent:* John Farquharson Ltd., 15 Red Lion Sq., London WCIR 46W, England.

CAREER: Reform Club, London, England, librarian, 1936-47; Administrative Staff College, Henley on Thames, England, librarian, 1947-56. Free-lance journalist, 1946—. *Military service:* British Army, Royal Artillery, 1940-46; became captain. *Member:* Library Association, Crime writers' Association (London), Savile Club (London).

WRITINGS: Suddenly at the Priory, British Book Service, 1957; *Heyday for Assassins*, British Book Service, 1958; *Hume: Portrait of a Double Murderer*, British Book Service, 1960; *Mutiny, 1917*, Heinemann, 1962; *The Ides of May: The Defeat of France, May-June, 1940*, Knopf, 1968; *France Summer 1940*, Ballantine, 1970; *The Home Fronts, Britain, France, Germany, 1914-1918*, Regnery, 1972.

Historical consultant and co-writer for British Broadcasting Corp. television series. "The Great War," 1963-64, and "The Lost Peace," 1965—; scriptwriter for Thames television series, "The World of War," 1972-73. Contributor to newspapers and periodicals, including *Everybody's, Chambers's Journal, World Review, Evening News, History Today*, and *Evening Standard*.

WORK IN PROGRESS: The Guns of Dakar (1940), to be published by Heinemann and Delacorte Press.

*   *   *

WILLIAMS, Miller   1930-

PERSONAL: Born April 8, 1930, in Hoxie, Ark.; son of E. B. (a Methodist minister) and Ann Jeanette (Miller) Williams; married Lucille Day (a pianist), December 29, 1951; children; Lucinda Gayl, Robert Miller, Karen Elizabeth. *Education:* Arkansas State College, B.S. (in biology), 1951; University of Arkansas, M.S. (in zoology), 1952. *Office:* English Department, Louisiana State University, Baton Rouge, La. 70803.

CAREER: Formerly taught biology at McNeece State College, Lake Charles, La., and Millsaps College, Jackson, Miss., intermittently, 1952-60; also worked as a fieldman with a New York publishing house, a projectionist in a movie house, a manager of a Sears Roebuck furniture department, a Montgomery Ward tire salesman, a stock car driver, and, he told *CA*, "for a while I was the person who put the sticks in the popsicles for all the hot little mouths in Arkansas"; Louisiana State University, Baton Rouge, member of English department, 1962—. Visiting professor, University of Chile, 1964. *Awards, honors:* Henry Bellaman Award for poetry, 1957; Breadloaf fellowship in poetry, 1961; Amy Lowell Travelling scholarship in poetry, 1963-64.

WRITINGS: (Editor) *19 Poets*, U.S. Information Service (Chile), 1964; *A Circle of Stone* (poetry), Louisiana State University Press, 1964; (contributor) *Nine Essays in Modern Literature*, Louisiana State University Press, 1964; *Recital* (a selection of poems from *A Circle of Stone*, in English and Spanish) Oceano (Chile), 1965; (editor with John William Corrington) *Southern Writing in the Sixties: Fiction*, Louisiana State University Press, 1966; (editor with Corrington) *Southern Writing in the Sixties: Poetry*, Louisiana State University Press, 1967; (editor) *Nicanor Parra, Poems and Antipoems*, New Directions, 1967; (compiler) *Chile: An Anthology of New Writing*, Kent State University Press, 1968; *So Long at the Fair* (poetry), Dutton, 1968; (editor) *The Achievement of John Ciardi*, Scott, Foresman, 1969; *The Only World There Is* (poetry), Dutton, 1971; (translator) *Nicanor Parra, Emergency Poems*, New Directions, 1972; *The Poetry of John Crowe Ransom*, Rutgers University Press, 1972; *Halfway from Hoxie* (poetry), Dutton, 1973; (compiler) *Contemporary Poetry in America*, Random House, 1973. Also translator of *The Poems of Nicanor Parra*, New Directions. Contributor to *Poetry, Saturday Review, American Scholar, Shenandoah, Oberlin Quarterly, Motive*, and *Prairie Schooner*. Advisory editor in poetry, Louisiana State University Press; contributing editor, *Oberlin Quarterly*.

WORK IN PROGRESS: Two novels.

SIDELIGHTS: Laurence Lieberman has described Miller Williams as "a poet who has entirely secured his own line and his own idiom. . . . He has a lively eye, wit, and an alert intelligence. His style is lean and spare, streamlined to add up a welter of fresh images and impressions at a remarkable velocity." Joel Conarroe noted: "Mr. Williams is unpretentious, perceptive, technically uninhibited, and funny as hell. He is that rare phenomenon, a teacher-critic whose humor is hardly ever literary, whose laughs derive from an unpredictable buffoonery that depends more on tone of voice than on allusive cleverness or syntactical poise." *Avocational interests:* Billiards, pool, and travel.†

*   *   *

WILLIAMS, Ned   1909-
(Robert Harbin)

PERSONAL: Born February 12, 1909, in Balfour, South Africa; son of John and Rosa (Kirk) Williams; married Edith Philp, March 23, 1934. *Education:* Attended government schools in South Africa. *Politics:* Liberal. *Religion:* Agnostic. *Home:* 65 Clarence Gate Gardens, London NW1 6QS, England.

CAREER: Magician, actor, and entertainer. *Military service:* British Army, 1941-47; became lieutenant colonel. *Member:* Magic Circle (London; honorary vice-president).

Awards, honors: Magician of the Year award from Magic Circle (London), 1970; Creative Fellowship from Academy of Magical Arts Inc., 1971.

WRITINGS—Under pseudonym Robert Harbin: *Paper Magic: The Art of Paper Folding*, Oldbourne, 1956, Branford, 1957; *How to Be a Wizard in Magic*, Oldbourne, 1957, Branford, 1958, published as *How to Be a Conjurer*, Sphere Books, 1969; *Paper Folding Fun*, Oldbourne, 1960, Branford, 1961; (author and illustrator) *Secrets of Origami Old and New: The Japanese Art of Paperfolding*, Oldbourne, 1963, published as *Secrets of Origami: The Japanese Art of Paper Folding*, Octopus Books, 1971; *Instant Memory: The Way to Success*, Corgi Books, 1968; *Teach Yourself Origami: The Art of Paper-Folding*, English Universities Press, 1968, published as *Origami: The Art of Paper Folding*, Funk, 1969; *Origami*, Hodder & Stroughton, Volume I, 1968, Volume II, 1971, Volume III, 1972; *Magic of Robert Harbin*, privately printed, 1970; *More Origami: The Art of Paper-Folding*, Hodder Paperbacks, 1971, published as *New Adventures in Origami: The Art of Paper-Folding*, Funk, 1973; *Waddingtons Family Card Games*, Drake Publishers, 1973; *Step by Step Origami*, Hamlyn, 1974.

WORK IN PROGRESS: Another book on origami, featuring the work of Neal Elias.

SIDELIGHTS: Williams speaks Afrikaans, has traveled to most parts of the world. He (along with Samuel Randlett in America) has popularized origami as a hobby in English-speaking countries. *Origami*, Volume I, has been translated into French, Dutch, German, Swedish, Danish, and Italian.

* * *

WILLIAMS, Robert L(ewis) 1903-

PERSONAL: Born December 3, 1903, in Hillsboro, Tex.; son of Edwin L. (a railroad conductor) and Janie (Webb) Williams; married Florence Ellzey, June 11, 1926; children: Florence June, Nancy Jean (Mrs. Fleet Senseman). *Education:* Millsaps College, A.B., 1925; Northwestern University, M.A., 1926, Ph.D., 1928. *Home:* 23 Harvard Pl., Ann Arbor, Mich. *Office:* Administration Building, University of Michigan, Ann Arbor, Mich.

CAREER: Mississippi State College for Women, Columbus, assistant professor of education and psychology, 1928-30, director of educational research, 1930-32, registrar, 1932-36; University of Michigan, Ann Arbor, assistant registrar, 1936-45, assistant to provost, 1945-51, assistant dean of faculties, 1951-58, administrative dean, 1958—, professor of education, 1955—. Member of Committee on Institutional Cooperation of Big Ten Universities and University of Chicago, 1957-68, of publication evaluation Committee for State Technical Services Act, U.S. Department of Commerce, 1968-69, of national advisory council, Western Interstate Commission of Higher Education, of U.S. Army Advisory Panel on Reserve Officers Training Corps (ROTC), and of Midwest Council of State Governments. *Member:* Association of American Universities, North Central Association of Colleges and Secondary Schools, Michigan Association of Collegiate Registrars (past president), Michigan Secondary School Association, Michigan Association for Higher Education (founder; past president; member of executive committee), Scabbard and Blade, Pi Kappa Alpha, Sigma Upsilon, Phi Delta Kappa.

WRITINGS: The Administration of Academic Affairs in Higher Education, University of Michigan Press, 1965; *Legal Bases of Coordinating Boards of Education in Thirty-Eight States*, University of Michigan, 1967; *Educational Alternatives for Colonized People: Models for Liberation*, Dunellen Publishing Co., 1974. Contributor of more than one hundred articles on administration in higher education to periodicals. Associate editor, American Association of College Registrars and Admissions Officers, 1943-46.

WORK IN PROGRESS: Continuing research on administration in higher education.†

* * *

WILLIAMS, Robin M(urphy), Jr. 1914-

PERSONAL: Born October 11, 1914, in Hillsboro, N.C.; son of Robin Murphy (a farmer) and Mable (Strayhorn) Williams; married Marguerite York, July 29, 1939; children: Robin M. III, Nancy E., Susan Y. *Education:* North Carolina State College (now North Carolina State University at Raleigh), B.S., 1933; University of North Carolina, M.S., 1935; Cornell University, graduate study, 1935-36; Harvard University, M.A., 1939, Ph.D., 1943. *Religion:* Protestant. *Home:* 414 Oak Ave., Ithaca, N.Y. *Office:* Cornell University, Ithaca, N.Y.

CAREER: University of Kentucky, Lexington, instructor and research assistant, 1939-42; U.S. War Department, research analyst and statistician, 1942-45, serving at Headquarters, European Theater of Operations, 1943-45; Cornell University, Ithaca, N.Y., associate professor, 1946-48, professor of sociology, 1949-54, Henry Scarborough Professor of Social Science, 1967—, director of social science research center, 1949-54. University of Oslo, Fulbright lecturer, 1954-55; University of Hawaii, Carnegie visiting professor, 1958. National Institute of Mental Health, consultant, 1949—; National Conference of Christians and Jews, member of council on religious freedom and public affairs; National Research Council, member of assembly on social and behavioral science. *Member:* American Sociological Association (first vice-president, 1955-56; president, 1958), Sociological Research Association (president, 1958), Rural Sociological Society, Society for the Study of Social Problems, American Philosophical Society, American Academy of Arts and Sciences, Eastern Sociological Society.

WRITINGS: The Reduction of Intergroup Tensions, Social Science Research Council, 1947; (with S. A. Stouffer and others) *The American Soldier*, Volumes I-II, Princeton University Press, 1949; *American Society*, Knopf, 1951, 3rd edition, 1970; (editor with Margaret W. Ryan) *Schools in Transition*, University of North Carolina Press, 1956; (with R. Goldsen and others) *What College Students Think*, Van Nostrand, 1960; (with John P. Dean, Edward A. Suchman, and others) *Strangers Next Door: Ethnic Relations in American Communities*, Prentice-Hall, 1964. Contributor to proceedings of Intergroup Relations Conference, 1964.

WORK IN PROGRESS: Writing on race and ethnic relations.†

* * *

WILLIAMS, Ronald Ralph 1906-

PERSONAL: Born October 14, 1906, in England; son of Ralph (a clergyman) and Mary (Sayers) Williams; married Cicely Maud Kay (a writer), June 9, 1934. *Education:* Studied at Gonville and Caius College, Cambridge, 1924-28, at Ridley Hall, 1928-29; M.A. *Home:* Bishop's Lodge, Springfield Rd., Leicester, England.

CAREER: Clergyman, Church of England, St. Aidan's College, Birkenhead, England, tutor, 1928-29; Leyton Parish Church, Leyton, England, curate, 1929-31; Ridley Hall, Cambridge, England, chaplain, 1931-34; Church Missionary Society, London, England, home education secretary, 1934-40; British Ministry of Information, Religious Division, staff member, 1940-45, director of division, 1943-45; examining chaplain to Bishop of Durham, 1945; St. John's College, Durham, England, principal, 1945-53; Bishop of Leicester, 1953—. Entered House of Lords, 1959. Chairman of The Church of England Board for Social Responsibility. *Member:* United University Club, Alpine Club, Leicestershire Club, Marylebone Cricket Club. *Awards, honors:* D.D. from Cambridge University.

WRITINGS: Religion and the English Vernacular, S.P.C.K., 1940; *The Strife Goes On*, Religious Tract Society, 1940; *The Christian Religion*, S.C.M. Press, 1941; *Authority in the Apostolic Age*, Macmillan, 1950; *The Perfect Law of Liberty*, 1952; *The Acts of the Apostles*, S.C.M. Press, 1953, Macmillan, 1954; (contributor) *Scripture and Tradition*, Seabury, 1955; (contributor) *Studies in Ephesians*, Mowbray, 1956; (contributor) *Studia Evangelica*, 1959, second edition, 1964; *Reading Through Hebrews*, Mowbray, 1960; *The Word of Life*, 1960; *Take Thou Authority: Ordination Charges*, Mowbray, 1961; *The Bible in Worship and Ministry*, Canterbury, 1962; *Commentary on Letters of John and James*, Cambridge University Press, 1965; *I Believe and Why*, Mowbray, 1971; *Faith and the Faith*, Mowbray, 1973.

AVOCATIONAL INTERESTS: Golf, walking, climbing.

*   *   *

WILLIAMS, Thomas Howard   1935-

PERSONAL: Born Setpember 4, 1935, in Cincinnati, Ohio; son of Paul Eugene (an administrator) and Lucile (Thomas) Williams; married Nancy Jane Martin, June 15, 1956; children: Pamela Jane, Paul Martin, Valerie Lucile, Charles Louis. *Education:* University of Cincinnati, B.B.A., 1958; University of Illinois, M.S., 1959, Ph.D., 1961. *Politics:* Independent. *Religion:* Protestant. *Home:* 7308 West Rim Dr., Austin, Tex. 78731. *Office:* University of Texas, Austin, Tex. 78712.

CAREER: Certified Public Accountant in Ohio, Illinois, and Indiana. University of Illinois, Urbana, 1959-63, began as instructor, became assistant professor of accounting; University of Texas, Austin, assistant professor, 1963-64, associate professor, 1964-66, professor of accounting, 1966—, chairman of accounting department, 1967-71. *Military service:* U.S. Army, Finance Corps, 1962-63; became first lieutenant. *Member:* American Institute of Certified Public Accountants, American Accounting Association, The Institute of Management Sciences.

WRITINGS: (With C. H. Griffin) *The Mathematical Dimension of Accountancy*, South-Western Publishing, 1964; (with C. H. Griffin and G. A. Welsch) *Advanced Accounting*, Richard D. Irwin, Inc., 1966, revised edition (with Griffin and K. D. Larson), 1971. Contributor to professional journals.

WORK IN PROGRESS: With R. G. May and G. G. Mueller, *A New Introduction to Accounting*, for Prentice-Hall.

*   *   *

WILLIAMS, Ursula Moray   1911-

PERSONAL: Born April 19, 1911, in Petersfield, Hampshire, England; daughter of A. Moray (an archaeologist) and Mable (Unwin) Williams; married Peter Southey John, September 28, 1935; children: Andrew, Hugh, Robin, James. *Education:* Privately educated at home by governess, followed by one year at finishing school in France and a year of art school at Winchester, England. *Religion:* Church of England. *Home:* Court Farm House, Beckford near Tewkesbury, Gloucestershire, England. *Agent:* Curtis Brown Ltd., 1 Craven Hill, London W2 3EW, England.

CAREER: Author of books for children, 1931—. Justice of the peace, Worcestershire-Evesham bench. Governor of County School, Evesham; manager of Beckford Junior School. *Member:* P.E.N. (London), National Book League, Cheltenham Literary Festival Society.

WRITINGS: Jeane-Pierre, A. & C. Black, 1931; *For Brownies: Stories and Games for the Pack and Everybody Else*, Harrap, 1932; *Grandfather* (verse), Allen & Unwin, 1933; *Pettabomination*, Search Publishing, 1933, new edition, Lane, 1948, (play) S. French, 1951; *Autumn Sweepers, and Other Plays for Children*, A. & C. Black, 1933; *More for Brownies*, Harrap, 1934; (author and co-illustrator) *Kelpie the Gipsies' Pony*, Harrap, 1934, Lippincott, 1935; *Sandy-on-the-Shore*, Harrap, 1936; *Elaine of La-Signe*, Harrap, 1937, published as *Elaine of the Mountains*, Lippincott, 1939; (with Peter John) *Adventures of Boss and Dingbatt*, Harrap, 1937; *Adventures of Puffin*, Harrap, 1939; *Adventures of the Little Wooden Horse*, Harrap, 1938, Lippincott, 1939.

Peter and the Wanderlust, Lippincott, 1940, revised edition published as *Peter on the Road*, Hamish Hamilton, 1963; *Gobbolino the Witch's Cat*, Harrap, 1942; *Pretenders Island*, Knopf, 1942; *The Good Little Christmas Tree*, Harrap, 1943, (play) S. French, 1951; *The House of Happiness*, Harrap, 1946, (play) S. French, 1951; *Three Toymakers*, Harrap, 1946, Nelson, 1971, new edition, Hamish Hamilton, 1970; *Malkin's Mountain*, Harrap, 1948, Nelson, 1972; *The Story of Laughing Dandino*, Harrap, 1948.

Jockin the Jester, Chatto & Windus, 1951, Nelson, 1973; *Binklebys at Home*, Harrap, 1951; *Binklebys on the Farm*, Harrap, 1953; *Secrets of the Wood*, Harrap, 1955; *Grumpa*, Brockhampton Press, 1955; (self-illustrated) *Goodbody's Puppet Show*, Hamish Hamilton, 1956; *The Golden Horse with a Silver Tail*, Hamish Hamilton, 1957; *Hobbie*, Brockhampton Press, 1958; *The Moonball*, Hamish Hamilton, 1958, Morrow, 1960; *The Noble Hawks*, Hamish Hamilton, 1959, published as *The Earl's Falconer*, Morrow, 1961; *The Nine Lives of Island Mackenzie*, Chatto & Windus, 1959, published as *Island Mackenzie*, Morrow, 1960.

Beware of This Animal, Hamish Hamilton, 1963, Dial, 1965; *Johnnie Tigerskin*, Harrap, 1964, Duell, Sloane & Pearce, 1966; (self-illustrated) *O For a Mouseless House!*, Chatto & Windus, 1964; *High Adventure*, Nelson, 1965; *Cruise of the "Happy-Go-Gay"*, Hamish Hamilton, 1967, Meredith Press, 1968; *A Crown for a Queen*, Meredith Press, 1968; *The Toymaker's Daughter*, Hamish Hamilton, 1968, Meredith Press, 1969; *Mog*, Allen & Unwin, 1969; *Boy in a Barn*, Nelson, 1970; *Johnnie Golightly and his Crocodile*, Chatto & Windus, 1970, Harvey House, 1971; *Hurricanes*, Chatto & Windus, 1971; *Castle Merlin*, Nelson, 1972; *A Picnic with the Aunts*, Chatto & Windus, 1972; *The Kidnapping of My Grandmother*, Heinemann, 1972; *Tiger Nanny*, Brockhampton, Press, 1973, Nelson, 1974.

"Milly-Molly-Mandy Series"; all published by Harrap: *Anders and Marta*, 1935; *Adventures of Ann*, 1935; *Twins and Their Ponies*, 1936; *Tales for the Sixes and Sevens*, 1936; *Dumpling*, 1937; *Castle for John Peter*, 1941.

WORK IN PROGRESS: A book on church mice, self-illustrated; a picture book for small children, also self-illustrated.

SIDELIGHTS: Ursula Williams's twin sister, Barbara Moray Williams, is also an artist (married Icelandic sculptor, Magnus Arnason) and exhibits in Paris and the United States. Their brother, Alan Moray Williams is a journalist in Copenhagen and the author of several published books of poetry. Ursula Williams is the niece of British publisher, Sir Stanley Unwin.

Gobbolino the Witch's Cat was recorded on Delyse Records, 1967.†

* * *

WILLIAMS, Willard F(orest) 1921-

PERSONAL: Born October 3, 1921, in Lubbock, Tex.; son of Willard E. (a farmer) and Emma (Nelson) Williams; married Damaris L. Robbins, June 1, 1945; children: Robert F., Gary W., Christine L., Willard B., Lynda L. *Education:* Oregon State University, B.S., 1947; University of California, Berkeley, M.S., 1948; Purdue University, Ph.D., 1952. *Religion:* Church of Jesus Christ of Latter-day Saints. *Home:* 2128 53rd St., Lubbock, Tex. *Office:* Department of Agricultural Economics, Texas Tech University, Lubbock, Tex.

CAREER: University of California and U.S. Department of Agriculture, Berkeley, Calif., cooperative agent, 1948-49; University of Nevada, Reno, assistant professor of agricultural economics, 1949-50; California Department of Agriculture, Sacramento, marketing economist, 1952-53; Federal Reserve Bank of San Francisco, San Francisco, Calif., senior agricultural economist, 1953-55; U.S. Department of Agriculture, Marketing Research Division, Washington, D.C., agricultural economist, 1955-60; Oklahoma State University, Stillwater, professor of agricultural economics, 1960-63; Texas Tech University, Lubbock, professor of agricultural economics, 1963—, chairman of department, 1963-71, Horn Professor, 1971-72. President, Texas Agricultural Research Associates, Inc., 1966—. *Military service:* U.S. Army Air Forces, 1943-45; received Air Medal with three oak leaf clusters and Distinguished Flying Cross. *Member:* American Agricultural-Economics Association, Western Agricultural-Economics Association, Southern Agricultural-Economics Association (vice-president, 1970-71), Sigma Xi, Alpha Zeta, Alpha Gamma Rho.

WRITINGS: (With Thomas T. Stout) *Economics of the Livestock-Meat Industry*, Macmillan, 1964; (contributor) *Market Structure Research*, edited by Paul L. Farris, Iowa State University Press, 1964. Writer of about fifteen marketing research reports for U.S. Department of Agriculture and Oklahoma Agricultural Experiment Station. Contributor to agricultural marketing and farm economics journals; columnist for *Beef* (magazine), *National Hog Farmer*, and *The Cattleman*. Editor of *Market Master Weekly* and monthly letter on the livestock industries.

WORK IN PROGRESS: Further research reports for U.S. Department of Agriculture and Oklahoma Agricultural Experiment Station.

* * *

WILLIAMS-ELLIS, Sir Clough 1883-

PERSONAL: Born May 28, 1883, in Northamptonshire, England; son of John Clough and Ellen Mabel (Greaves) Williams-Ellis; married Amabel Strachey (an author and journalist), July 29, 1915; children: Susan (Mrs. Ewan Cooper-Willis), Charlotte (Mrs. Lindsay Wallace), Christopher (killed in action, 1944). *Education:* Attended Oundle School and Trinity College, Cambridge. *Home:* Plas Brondanw, Penrhyndeudraeth, Merionethshire, North Wales.

CAREER: Architect, town planner, and landscape designer whose works include castles, monuments, public buildings, village and manor developments, churches, schools, and hotels in England, Wales, and Ireland, and residences in several countries abroad; designer, builder, and owner of Portmeirion (a model resort development) in North Wales. Chairman of Council for the Preservation of Rural Wales; member of advisory council for Welsh Reconstruction, and of Government Committee on Art and Industry, National Parks Committee, National Trust Committee for Wales, and Art Committee of University of Wales. Lecturer for British Council and Foreign Office on travels abroad; broadcaster on architecture, planning, and preservation of the countryside. *Military service:* British Army, Welsh Guards and Tank Corps, 1914-18; served in France and Belgium; became major; received Military Cross, mentioned in dispatches.

MEMBER: Royal Institute of British Architects (fellow), Institute of Landscape Architects (fellow; vice-president), Town Planning Institute, British Travel Association (member of grand council), Athenaeum Club, Lansdowne Club, Royal Welsh Yacht Club. *Awards, honors:* Commander of the British Empire, 1958; Knight Bachelor, 1972.

WRITINGS: *The Tank Corps*, Doran, 1919; *Cottage Building in Cob, Pise, Chalk and Clay*, Scribner, 1919, 3rd edition, revised and enlarged (with John and Elizabeth Eastwick-Field) published as *Building in Cob, Pise and Stabilized Earth*, Country Life, 1947; (with wife, Amabel Williams-Ellis) *The Pleasures of Architecture*, J. Cape, 1924, revised edition, 1954; *England and the Octopus*, Bles, 1928, revised edition, Blackie, 1974; *The Architect*, Bles, 1929; *Sir Lawrence Weaver*, Bles, 1933; (with Sir John Summerson) *Architecture Here and Now*, Nelson, 1934; (editor) *Britain and the Beast*, Dent, 1937; (with Lord Rosse) *The Protection of Ancient Buildings*, 1939.

Plan for Living; the Architect's Part, Faber, 1941; *The Adventure of Building*, Architectural Press, 1946; *On Trust for the Nation*, Volume I, Elek, 1947, Volume II, 1949; *Town and Country Planning*, Longmans, Green, 1951; *Royal Festival Hall; the Official Record*, Parrish, 1951; (with A. Williams-Ellis) *Headlong Down the Years*, Liverpool University Press, 1952; *Portmeirion: The Place and Its Meaning*, Faber, 1963, revised edition, Blackie, 1972; *Architect Errant* (autobiography), Constable, 1971.

AVOCATIONAL INTERESTS: Travel (has covered most of the world, except China, Japan, and South America).

BIOGRAPHICAL/CRITICAL SOURCES: New Yorker, January, 1962.

* * *

WILLIAMSON, Chilton 1916-

PERSONAL: Born November 11, 1916, in Granville, Ohio; son of Robert D. (an editor) and Mary Fitch (Parsons) Williamson; married Frances J. Philpotts (a teacher), June 24, 1944; children: Chilton, Jr., Jane Burnett, Peter Dawson. *Education:* Columbia University, B.A., 1938, M.A., 1939, Ph.D., 1948. *Home:* 29 Claremont Ave., New York, N.Y. 10027.

CAREER: Columbia University, Barnard College, New York, N.Y., 1942—, started as lecturer, professor of history, 1962—. Researcher in Great Britain, 1962. Member: Phi Beta Kappa, Alpha Delta Phi.

WRITINGS: Vermont in Quandary, Vermont Historical Society, 1949; American Suffrage from Property to Democracy: 1760-1860, Princeton University Press, 1960.

WORK IN PROGRESS: The Collapse of Representative Government in the British West Indies: 1834-1884.†

*   *   *

WILLIAMSON, Joanne Small   1926-

PERSONAL: Born May 13, 1926, in Arlington, Mass.; daughter of Floyd Emmon and Gertrude (Small) Williamson. Education: Studied at Barnard College, 1942-44, Diller Quaile School of Music, 1944-45. Politics: Registered Democrat. Religion: Congregational. Address: Box 491, Kennebunkport, Me.

CAREER: Bridgeport Sunday Herald, Bridgeport, Conn., feature writer, fashion editor, 1948-50; Columbia Presbyterian Medical Center, New York, N.Y., publicity writer, 1950-51; Retail Apparel Outlook, New York, N.Y., editor, 1951-54; Fairfield County Publications, Fairfield, Conn., production manager, 1955-56; writer for young people, 1956—. Member: Authors Guild of the Authors League of America. Awards, honors: New York Herald Tribune Children's Spring Book Festival honor award, 1956, for Jacobin's Daughter.

WRITINGS: Jacobin's Daughter, Knopf, 1956; The Eagles Have Flown, Knopf, 1957; Hittite Warrior, Knopf, 1960; The Glorious Conspiracy (American Library Association Notable Book), Knopf, 1961; The Iron Charm, Knopf, 1964; And Forever Free, Knopf, 1967; To Dream Upon a Crown, Knopf, 1968. Author of radio and television scripts.

WORK IN PROGRESS: A Black history for young people.

SIDELIGHTS: Ms. Williamson told CA: "History is my great fascination, and I try to get a little beneath its surface in my books. The piano is my avocation," she teaches piano part time.

*   *   *

WILLIS, F(rank) Roy   1930-

PERSONAL: Born July 25, 1930, in Prescot, England; married Mary K. Kroncke, October 2, 1959; children: Jane M., Clare G., Geoffrey H. Education: King's College, Cambridge, B.A. 1952; Stanford University, Ph.D., 1959. Office: Department of History, University of California, Davis, Calif.

CAREER: University of Washington, Seattle, 1960-64, began as instructor, became associate professor; University of California, Davis, associate professor; 1964-67, professor of history, 1967—.

WRITINGS: The French in Germany, 1945-1949, Stanford University Press, 1962; France, Germany and the New Europe, 1945-1967, revised edition, Stanford University Press, 1968; Europe in the Global Age, Dodd, 1968; Italy Chooses Europe, Oxford University Press, 1971; Western Civilization: An Urban Perspective, Heath, 1973.

WORK IN PROGRESS: The Two Europes: European Underdevelopment Since 1945.

WILLOCK, Colin   1919-

PERSONAL: Born January 13, 1919, in London, England; son of David and Kate (Dowdall) Willock; married Joan Bevan, 1946; children: Paul, Simon and Jane (twins). Education: Attended Tonbridge School. Politics: "Confused." Religion: Agnostic. Home: 17 Ashley Dr., Walton on Thames, England. Agent: Curtis Brown Ltd., 1 Craven Hill, London W2 3EW, England.

CAREER: Former editor, Hilliput, and assistant editor, Picture Post for Colin Willock Ltd., London, England; became Head of Anglia Television Natural Hsstory Unit, 1961; now Executive Director of Survival Anglia Ltd., maker of international wildlife films for television. Military service: Royal Marines, 1939-45.

WRITINGS: Come Fishing With Me, Muller, 1952; Come Fly Fishing with Me, Muller, 1953; Coarse Fishing, Faber, 1955; Death at Flight, Heinemann, 1956; Rod Pole or Perch, Parrish, 1958; The Gun Punt Adventure, Faber, 1959; Death at the Strike, Heinemann, 1959; The Angler's Encyclopaedia, Odhams, 1960; Death in Covert, Heinemann, 1961; Kenzie (biography), Deutsch, 1962; Duck Shooting, Vista Books, 1962; Look at African Animals, Hamish Hamilton, 1962; The Animal Catchers (novel), Deutsch, 1964; The Enormous Zoo, Longmans, Green, 1964; Landscape With Solitary Figure (autobiography), Longmans, Green, 1966; Hazanda (novel), Deutsch, 1968; The Coast of Loneliness (novel), Deutsch, 1971; Town Crier (autobiography), Deutsch, 1973; The Fighters (novel), Macmillan, 1973; The Great Rift Valley, Time-Life, 1974. Weekly Column, "Town Crier," for Shooting Time's.

WORK IN PROGRESS: ABC of Shooting, to be published by Deutsch.

AVOCATIONAL INTERESTS: Fishing, shooting, nature conservation, bird watching.

*   *   *

WILLOCK, Ruth

PERSONAL: Born in Brooklyn, N.Y.; daughter of Frederick James (an art director) and Mary (Nicklaus) Willock; divorced. Education: Northfield Seminary, Northfield, Mass., student; Pratt Institute, Graduation Certificate; additional courses at New York University. Agent: McIntosh & Otis, Inc., 18 East 41st St., New York, N.Y. 10017.

CAREER: Free-lance advertising designer and copywriter. Member: Mystery Writers of America, English Speaking Union.

WRITINGS: The Night of the Visitor, Ace Books, 1965; The Street of the Small Steps, Hawthorn, 1972; The Moonlit Trap, Hawthorn, 1973. Also author of 5:30 to Midnight, Harper; Bring Back the Spring, Macrae Smith; A Little Thing Like Love (play), Baker Co.; Continental Cans, Kanrom. Contributor to American, Woman's Home Companion, Reader's Digest, Ladies' Home Journal, Toronto Star, Mademoiselle, and to magazines and newspapers in Britain, Sweden, Norway, Finland, Holland, Germany, Italy, France, Chile, Union of South Africa.

WORK IN PROGRESS: A novel for Hawthorn.

SIDELIGHTS: The Night of the Visitor was serialized in seven European countries, and published in England, Stockholm, and Munich. The Night of the Visitor, The Street of the Small Steps, and The Moonlit Trap have been translated into several languages.

WILLSON, Robina Beckles (Ballard) 1930-

PERSONAL: Born September 26, 1930, in London, England; daughter of Robertson (a clergyman) and Dorothy (Cuss) Ballard; married Anthony Beckles Willson (an architect); children: Mark Robert, Rachel Clare Elizabeth. *Education:* University of Liverpool, B.A. (honors), 1948, M.A., 1952. *Religion:* Church of England. *Home:* 44 Popes Ave., Twickenham, Middlesex, England. *Agent:* A. M. Heath & Co. Ltd., 40-42 William IV St., London WC2N 4DD, England.

CAREER: Teacher of English and music at schools in Leeds, Liverpool, and London, England. *Member:* Galpin Society.

WRITINGS: Leopards on the Loire, Gollancz, 1961; *A Time to Dance*, Collins, 1962; *A Seraph in a Box*, Hart-Davis, 1963; *Pineapple Palace*, Hart-Davis, 1964; *Musical Instruments*, Oliver & Boyd, 1964; *Anchors Wharf*, Macmillan, 1971; *The Last Harper*, Macmillan, 1972; *The Shell on Your Back*, Heinemann, 1972.

WORK IN PROGRESS: The Voice of Music (non-fiction), to be published by Heinemann.

* * *

WILSON, John Stuart Gladstone 1916-

PERSONAL: Born August 18, 1916, in St. Kilda, Victoria, Australia; son of Herbert Gladstone and Mary Buchanan (Wylie) Wilson; married Beryl Margaret Gibson, July, 1943. *Education:* University of Western Australia, Diploma in Commerce, 1939, B.A. (honors), 1941, M.A., 1948. *Office:* Department of Economics, University of Hull, Hull, Yorkshire, England.

CAREER: With Commonwealth Bank of Australia, 1935-41; lecturer in economics at University of Tasmania, Hobart, Australia, 1941-43, University of Sydney, Sydney, Australia, 1944-45, University College, Canberra, 1946-47; University of London, London, England, lecturer in economics at London School of Economics and Political Science, 1948-49, university reader in economics, 1950-59; University of Hull, Hull, England, professor of economics and commerce, 1959—, dean of Faculty of Social Sciences and Law, 1962-65. Made comparative studies of banking and financial institutions in Europe, 1950-59, in India and Pakistan, 1950, 1968-69, 1973-74, United States and Canada, 1955-56, 1962, 1969, 1974; conducted economic survey of New Hebrides for British Colonial Office, 1958-59, 1963-66. Centre for South East Asian Studies, chairman; Institute of Commonwealth Studies, member of management committee; School of Oriental and African Studies, University of London, governor. *Member:* Royal Economic Society, American Economic Association, Economics Society of Australia and New Zealand. *Awards, honors:* Leverhulme Research Award to visit United States and Canada, 1955.

WRITINGS: (Contributor) R. S. Sayers, editor, *Banking in the British Commonwealth*, Oxford University Press, 1952; *French Banking Structure and Credit Policy*, Bell, for London School of Economics, 1957; (contributor) R. S. Sayers, editor, *Banking in Western Europe*, Oxford University Press, 1962; (contributor) W. B. Hamilton, K. Robinson, C. D. W. Goodwin, editors, *A Decade of the Commonwealth, 1955-1965*, Duke University Press, 1966; *Economic Survey of the New Hebrides*, HMSO, 1966; *Monetary Policy and the Development of Money Markets*, Allen & Unwin, 1966; (editor with C. R. Whittlesey) *Essays in Money and Banking*, Clarendon Press, 1968; *Availability of Capital and Credit to United Kingdom Agriculture*, HMSO, 1973; (editor with C. F. Scheffer) *Multinational Enterprises: Financial and Monetary Aspects*, Sijthoff, 1974. Editor, *Yorkshire Bulletin of Economic and Social Research*, 1964-67; member of editorial board, *Modern Asian Studies*, 1966—.

WORK IN PROGRESS: Report for European Economic Community on "Agricultural Credit in the New Member States—the Situation in the United Kingdom and Future Needs"; *Banking Policy and Structure: A Comparitive Analysis.*

SIDELIGHTS: Wilson has limited knowledge of French and German. *Avocational interests:* Gardening, squash, the theater, and art.

* * *

WILSON, R(oger) H(arris) L(ebus) 1920-
(Roger Harris)

PERSONAL: Born March 27, 1920, in San Francisco, Calif.; son of Julian M. (a physician) and Ethel (Lebus) Wolfsohn; married Nancy L. Hooper (a project analyst), February 28, 1955. *Education:* Cambridge University, B.A., 1941, M.A., 1950, M.B. and B.Chir., 1946; M.R.C.P. (London), 1948. *Home:* 130 Palm Ave., San Francisco, Calif. 94118. *Office:* 500 Spruce St., San Francisco, Calif. 94118.

CAREER: Postgraduate training in England, 1946-51, at Stanford University Medical School, Stanford, Calif., 1951-53; University of California Medical School, San Francisco, in charge of Pulmonary Physiology Research Laboratory, San Francisco General Hospital, 1953—, assistant clinical professor of medicine, 1955-72, associate director for continuing education, medicine and health sciences, 1962-72, lecturer in medicine, 1972—. Member of consulting staff at San Francisco hospitals. *Member:* American College of Physicians (fellow), American College of Chest Physicians (fellow), American Medical Association, British Medical Association, Council on Public Health (chairman of air pollution committee), California Medical Association, California Tuberculosis and Health Association, San Francisco Medical Association.

WRITINGS: (With R. Nissen) *Pages in the History of Chest Surgery*, C. C Thomas, 1960; (editor, with S. M. Farber) *The Air We Breathe*, C. C Thomas, 1961; (editor with Farber) *Control of the Mind*, McGraw, 1962; (editor with Farber) *Conflict and Creativity*, McGraw, 1963; (editor with Farber) *The Potential of Woman*, McGraw, 1963; (with Farber and P. Mustacchi) *California and the Challenge of Growth: Man Under Stress*, University of California Press (Berkeley), 1964; (editor with Farber and Mustacchi) *Man and Civilization: The Family's Search for Survival*, McGraw, 1965; (editor with Farber) *The Challenge to Women*, Basic Books, 1966; (editor with Farber and N. L. Wilson) *Food and Civilization*, C. C Thomas, 1967; (editor with Farber) *Sex Education and the Teenager*, Diablo Press, 1967; (editor with Farber) *Teenage Marriage and Divorce*, Diablo Press, 1967.

Contributor: H. C. Hinshaw and L. H. Garland, *Diseases of the Chest*, Saunders, 1956; B. Gordon, *Clinical Cardio-Pulmonary Physiology*, Grune, 1957, 2nd edition, 1960; B. M. Fried, *Tumors of the Lungs and Mediastinum*, Lea & Febiger, 1958; D. M. Greenberg and H. A. Harper, *Enzymes in Health and Disease*, C. C Thomas, 1960; A. L. Banyai, *Dyspnea—Diagnosis and Treatment*, Davis, 1963;

Wilson, *Obesity*, F. A. Davis, 1969; S. Margen and Wilson, *Progress in Human Nutrition*, Avi Publishing, 1971; H. F. Conn and Rex B. Conn, *Current Diagnosis*, W. B. Saunders, 1974.

Writer of weekly column of classical record reviews, under pseudonym Roger Harris, for *San Francisco Progress*, 1957-71. Contributor to scientific journals.

WORK IN PROGRESS: Research in lung disease.

* * *

WILSON, William H(enry)   1935-

PERSONAL: Born November 3, 1935, in St. Joseph, Mo.; son of William Harry (a wholesaler) and Margaret (Perrine) Wilson; married Katharine Lehr, June 18, 1960; children: Katharine Margaret, Margaret Johanne. *Education:* St. Joseph Junior College, St. Joseph, Mo., student, 1953-54; University of Missouri, B.J., 1957, M.A., 1958, Ph.D., 1962. *Religion:* Methodist. *Address:* P.O. Box 6324, North Texas Station, Denton, Tex. 76203.

CAREER: University of South Dakota, Vermillion, assistant professor of history, 1962-63; University of Alaska, College, assistant professor of history, 1963-67; North Texas State University, professor of history, 1968—. *Member:* American Historical Association, Organization of American Historians, Southern Historical Association, American Association of University Professors, Phi Alpha Theta.

WRITINGS: The City Beautiful Movement in Kansas City, University of Missouri Press, 1964; *Coming of Age: Urban America, 1915-1945*, Wiley, 1974. Contributor to historical journals.

WORK IN PROGRESS: Completed, but as yet unpublished, *A Study of the Alaska Railroad to 1945;* a study of the city beautiful movement, nationwide scope.

* * *

WINGENBACH, Father Gregory C(harles)   1938-
(Charles E. Wingenbach)

PERSONAL: Born February 1, 1938, in Washington, D.C.; son of Charles (a paperhanger and interior decorator) and Pearl Adeline (Stanton) Wingenbach; married Mary Ann Pearce, September 16, 1961; children: Mary Adele, Karl Eduard, John Clair. *Education:* Attended St. Charles College-Seminary, 1951-54; University of Florida, 1955-56; Georgetown University, 1958-61, summer, 1962; Goddard College, B.A., 1972; University of Thessaloniki, Greece, graduate study, 1973-74. *Politics:* Independent. *Religion:* "Greek Orthodox-Catholic". *Residence:* Louisville, Ky. *Agent:* Curtis Brown Ltd., 60 East 56th St., New York, N.Y. 10022. *Office:* Assumption Greek Orthodox Community, 932 South Fifth St., Louisville, Ky. 40203.

CAREER: Washington Star, Washington, D.C., reporter-trainee, 1957-58; *New York Herald Tribune*, Washington Bureau, researcher and editorial assistant, 1958-62; writer and research assistant to U.S. Senator Clair Engle of California, 1962-63; Kentucky State Government, Frankfort, senior publicity specialist, 1964-65; U.S. Office of Economic Opportunity, Executive Office of the President, Washington, D.C., community relations programs officer, 1965-69; Oak Ridge Associated Universities, Oak Ridge, Tenn., training and technology program development officer, 1970-73; ordained Greek Orthodox deacon, 1971, ordained priest, 1973; now affiliated with Assumption Greek Orthodox Community, Louisville, Ky. *Military service:*

U.S. Naval Reserve, 1955-63, special active duty, Berlin-Cuba crises, 1961-62. *Member:* Authors League of America, American Society for Public Administration (founder and council member of East Tennessee Chapter, 1972-73), International Fellowship of St. Alban and St. Sergius, Royal Stuart Society (life member; American secretary, 1955-58), Honorable Order of Kentucky Colonels.

WRITINGS: The Peace Corps: Who, How and Where, John Day, 1961, revised edition, 1963; *A Guide to the Peace Corps*, McGraw, 1965. Also author of unpublished works on American missions in East Africa, and on American Indians. Contributor of articles to current-events periodicals and religion journals.

BIOGRAPHICAL/CRITICAL SOURCES: Kentucky Standard, Bardstown, Ky., June 21, 1964; *Knoxville Journal*, Knoxville, Tenn., November 10, 1972; *Knoxville News-Sentinel*, Knoxville, Tenn., August 30, 1973; *CHANGE Magazine*, October 1973.

* * *

WINGER, Fred E.   1912-

PERSONAL: Born July 24, 1912, in Elwood, Neb.; son of Guy E. and Blanche Winger; married Beth Gavin, August 25, 1934; children: Michael, Timothy. *Education:* University of Nebraska, B.S., in Ed., 1934; University of Iowa, M.A., 1938; University of Oregon, D.Ed., 1951. *Politics:* Independent Republican. *Religion:* Congregational. *Home:* 1439 Northwest 13th St., Corvallis, Ore. 97330.

CAREER: High School teacher in Nebraska and Iowa, 1934-38; Stephens College, Columbia, Mo., instructor in typing and business education, 1939-43; Oregon State University, Corvallis, 1947—, professor of secretarial service, business education, and coordinator of Business and Distributive Education, 1951—. International Business Machines, workshop instructor. *Military service:* U.S. Army, 1943-45. *Member:* National Business Education Association, American Association of University Professors, Western Business Education Association, Oregon Business Education Association, Pi Omega Pi, Kappa Delta Phi. *Awards, honors:* Named one of three outstanding professors at Oregon State University, 1956.

WRITINGS: Tailored Timings, Allied Publishers (Portland, Ore.), 1955; (with Carpenter) *Type Right from the Start*, Allied Publishers, 1956.

With Alan Lloyd and John Rowe; all published by Gregg Publishing Division, McGraw: *Typing Power Drills*, 1956, 2nd edition, 1965; *Typing Power Drills*, 1956, 2nd edition, 1965; *Gregg Typewriting for Colleges*, 1957, 2nd edition, 1964; *Typing Skill Drives*, 1960; *Gregg Typing 1—Textkit for Adult Education*, 1965; *Gregg Typing 2—Textkit 2 for Adult Education*, 1966; *Typing 75-4 Boxes*, 1971; *Typing 300*, 1973. Also author of *Selective Practice Typing Drills; Manual and Electric Editions;* (with Weaver) *Gregg Tailored Timings*.

Author or co-author of four slide series for typewriting, shorthand, filing, and bookkeeping, issued by Keystone View Co. Contributor of more than forty articles to business education journals.

AVOCATIONAL INTERESTS: Sports, coin collecting.

* * *

WINGREN, Gustaf F(redrik)   1910-

PERSONAL: Born November 29, 1910, in Tryserum,

Sweden; son of Gustaf Fabian (a foreman) and Teresia (Sundman) Wingren; married Signhild Carlsson, April 4, 1943; children: Anna, Anders. *Education:* University of Lund, Dr. Theol., 1943. *Home:* Vintergatan 2c, Lund, Sweden.

CAREER: University of Lund, Lund, Sweden, 1949—, professor of systematic theology, 1951—. Deputy professor at University of Abo, Finland, and University of Basel, Switzerland, 1947, and at University of Goettingen, Germany, 1950; guest lecturer at Cambridge University, University of Edinburgh, University of Heidelberg, and other universities throughout Europe, and at Luther Theological Seminary, St. Paul, Minn., and Union Theological Seminary, Richmond, Va. World Council of Churches, member of Advisory Commission, 1951-54, member of International Commission on Faith and Order, 1952-68; adviser to Theological Commission of Lutheran World Federation, 1964-70. *Member:* Royal Society of Humanistic Studies (Lund; vice-president, 1972-73), Societas Ethica (president, 1968-72). *Awards, honors:* D.Th. from University of Kiel, 1965, St. Andrews College, 1966, and Universitaet Rostock, 1969.

WRITINGS: Luthers lara om kallelsen, Gleerup, 1942, translation published as *Luther on Vocation*, Muhlenberg Press, 1957 (published in England as *Christian's Calling: Luther on Vocation*, Oliver and Boyd, 1958); *Manniskan och inkarntionen enligt Irenaeus*, Gleerup, 1947, translation published as *Man and Incarnation: A Study in the Biblical Theology of Irenaeus*, Fortress, 1959; *Predikan*, Gleerup, 1949, translation published as *The Living Word: A Study of Preaching and the Church*, Fortress, 1960; *Teologiens metodfraga*, Gleerup, 1954, translation published as *Theology in Conflict*, Fortress, 1958; *Skapelsen och lagen*, Gleerup, 1958, translation published as *Creation and Law*, Fortress, 1961; *Evangeliet och Kyrkan*, Gleerup, 1960, translation published as *Gospel and Church*, Fortress, 1964; *The Main Lines of Development in Systematic Theology and Biblical Interpretation in Scandinavia*, Union Theological Seminary (Richmond, Va.), 1964; *An Exodus Theology*, Fortress, 1969; *The Flight from Creation*, Augsburg, 1971; *Vaexling och Kontinuitet*, Gleerup, 1972; *Credo*, Gleerup, 1974. Contributor to *Theologische Realenzyklopaedie* (Germany). Coeditor of *Kerygma und Dogma* (Germany).

WORK IN PROGRESS: Contributions to *Theologische Realenzyklopaedie*.

SIDELIGHTS: Wingren's books have been translated into German, Finnish, Chinese, and Japanese.

* * *

WINKLER, Bee (Finkelberg) 1919-

PERSONAL: Born April 29, 1919, in Chicago, Ill.; daughter of Benjamin and Lee (Schneiderman) Finkelberg; married Harry Winkler (a television and film writer), September 28, 1941; children: Roxane (Mrs. Michel Alkaslassy), David. *Education:* San Fernando Valley State College (now California State University, Northridge), B.A., 1959. *Religion:* Jewish. *Home:* 16800 Oak View Dr., Encino, Calif. 91316.

CAREER: Los Angeles (Calif.) city schools, kindergarten teacher, 1959—. *Member:* National Education Association, International Reading Association.

WRITINGS: (With Ethel Otchis) *The Boy Who Shook Hands with the President*, Golden Gate Junior Books, 1964.

WORK IN PROGRESS: A Bicycle Ride to Remember, a story on bicycle safety; *Mickey Meets the Mayor*, about children in a contemporary city.†

* * *

WINSBERG, Morton D. 1930-

PERSONAL: Born August 1, 1930, in Chicago, Ill.; son of David Bennett (a salesman) and Lucille (Walder) Winsberg. *Education:* University of Illinois, B.S., 1951, M.S., 1954; University of Florida, Ph.D., 1958. *Politics:* Democrat (most of the time). *Religion:* Jewish. *Home:* Route 1, Box 331B, Delray Beach, Fla. 33444. *Office:* Department of Geography, Florida State University, Tallahassee, Fla. 32306.

CAREER: East Carolina College (now University), Greenville, assistant professor of geography, 1958-63; Ohio University, Athens, assistant professor of geography, 1963-65; Florida State University, Tallahassee, assistant professor of geography, 1965—. *Military service:* U.S. Army Air Forces, Intelligence; became second lieutenant. *Member:* Association of American Geographers, American Geographical Society, National Council for Geographic Education. *Awards, honors:* Social Science Research Council postdoctoral fellowship.

WRITINGS: Colonia Baron Hirsch, a Jewish Agricultural Colony in Argentina, University of Florida Press, 1964. Contributor to geographical journals.

WORK IN PROGRESS: Agricultural geography of Latin America and U.S.

* * *

WINTER, Alice 1919-

PERSONAL: Born March 22, 1919, in Osage City, Kan.; daughter of William Caius (a railroad conductor) and Gladys (Guthrie) Greer; married Calvert J. Winter (a pediatrician), March 13, 1943; children: Calvert J. III, William Greer, Michael Henry. *Education:* University of Kansas, A.B., 1942. *Politics:* Democrat. *Religion:* Unitarian Universalist. *Home:* 2601 Wood, Kansas City, Kan. 66104. *Agent:* Margot Johnson Agency, 405 East 54th St., New York, N.Y. 10022.

CAREER: Secretary to an engineer, a lawyer, and a physician; began writing short stories in 1959, sold first novel in 1964. *Awards, honors:* First Morrow Honor Book Award ($500) for *The Velvet Bubble*.

WRITINGS: The Velvet Bubble (novel), Morrow, 1965. Contributor of short stories to *Kansas Magazine, Woman's Day, University of Kansas City Review*, and other periodicals.

WORK IN PROGRESS: A novel.

SIDELIGHTS: Her short story, "Only People Cry," has been reprinted thirty-five times and has appeared in five foreign publications. *The Velvet Bubble* has been published in Finland, Spain, and the Netherlands.†

* * *

WINTER, Elmer L(ouis) 1912-

PERSONAL: Born March 6, 1912, in Milwaukee, Wis.; son of Sigmund and May (Kraus) Winter; married Nannette Rosenberg, September 11, 1936; children: Susan (Mrs. Michael Freeman), Lynn (Mrs. Gruzen), Martha (Mrs. Michael Gross). *Education:* University of Wisconsin, B.A. and LL.B., 1935. *Home:* 8014 North Lake Dr., Milwaukee,

Wis. 53217. *Office:* Manpower, Inc., 5301 North Ironwood Rd., Milwaukee, Wis. 53201.

CAREER: Admitted to Wisconsin bar, 1935, to Illinois bar, 1942; Scheinfeld & Winter (attorneys), Milwaukee, Wis., partner, 1936-42; practicing attorney in Milwaukee, Wis., and Chicago, Ill., 1944-48; Manpower, Inc. (temporary help service with offices on five continents), Milwaukee, Wis., founder and president, 1948—. Speaker before business and professional groups throughout United States. Appointed by President Johnson to serve as the Metropolitan Milwaukee Chairman of the National Alliance of Businessmen.*Member:* The American Jewish Committee (president).

WRITINGS: A Woman's Guide to Earning a Good Living, Simon and Schuster, 1961; *A Complete Guide to Making a Public Stock Offering*, Prentice-Hall, 1962; *Cutting Costs Through the Effective Use of Temporary and Part-Time Help*, National Foremen's Institute, 1964; *How to be an Effective Secretary*, Pocket Books, 1965; *Your Future in Your Own Business*, Rosen Press, 1966; *Women at Work: Every Woman's Guide to Successful Employment*, Simon & Schuster, 1967; *1,015 Way's to Save Time: Trouble and Money in the Operation of Your Business*, Prentice-Hall, 1968; *Your Future as a Temporary Office Worker*, Rosen Press, 1969.

AVOCATIONAL INTERESTS: Amateur painter, sculptor, and mosaicist.

*   *   *

WISBEY, Herbert Andrew, Jr. 1919-

PERSONAL: Born April 29, 1919, in Boston, Mass.; son of Herbert Andrew (a school principal) and M. Marietta (Burgess) Wisbey; married Adelia May Wagner, November 26, 1945; children: Thomas B., Jane C., Susan M., Peter A. *Education:* University of Rhode Island, B.S., 1941; University of Arizona, M.A., 1946; Columbia University, Ph.D., 1951. *Home:* 4300 Fairway Lane, Horseheads, N.Y. 14845.

CAREER: Brown University, Providence, R.I., instructor in history, 1946-47; Monmouth Junior College, Long Branch, N.J., instructor in history, 1949-52; Keuka College, Keuka Park, N.Y., associate professor, 1952-53, professor of history and head of department, 1953-62; Corning Community College, Corning, N.Y., professor of history, 1962-65; Elmira College, Elmira, N.Y., professor of history, 1965—. *Military service:* U.S. Army, 1942-45; historian, Seventh Armored Division. *Member:* American Historical Association, American Association for State and Local History, American Studies Association, Association for Asian Studies, New York State Historical Association, New York Folklore Society, Phi Gamma Delta. *Awards, honors:* Fulbright grant, 1966, for summer Seminar in Chinese Culture in Taiwan.

WRITINGS: Soldiers Without Swords: A History of the Salvation Army in the United States, Macmillan, 1955; *A History of the Volunteers of America*, Volunteers of America, 1954; *Pioneer Prophetess: Jemima Wilkinson, the Publick Universal Friend*, Cornell University Press, 1964. Contributor to *Dictionary of American Biography* and *Notable American Women, 1607-1950*; contributor of more than seventy-five articles to *Grolier Encyclopedia International*; contributor of more than twenty articles and reviews to *New England Galaxy, Yankee, York State Tradition*, historical journals. *New York Folklore Quarterly*, editorial associate, 1957-59, 1963-72, associate editor, 1959-62.

WORK IN PROGRESS: New York State religious sects and their leaders; early American missionaries in Japan and China; the American-born inventor of the jinrikisha.

*   *   *

WISE, William 1923-

PERSONAL: Born July 21, 1923, in New York, N.Y. *Education:* Yale University, B.A., 1948. *Agent:* Curtis Brown, Ltd., 60 East 56th St., New York, N.Y. 10022.

CAREER: Free-lance writer.

WRITINGS—Juvenile: *Jonathan Blake*, Knopf, 1956; *Silversmith of Old New York: Myer Myers*, Farrar, Straus, and Jewish Publication Society, 1958; *Albert Einstein: Citizen of the World*, Farrar, Straus, and Jewish Publication Society, 1960; *The House with the Red Roof*, Putnam, 1961; *The Cowboy Surprise*, Putnam, 1961; *Alexander Hamilton*, Putnam, 1963; *The Story of Mulberry Bend*, Dutton, 1963; *In the Time of the Dinosaurs*, Putnam, 1964; *Detective Pinkerton and Mr. Lincoln*, Dutton, 1964; *The Two Reigns of Tutankhamen*, Putnam, 1964; *The World of Giant Mammals*, Putnam, 1965; *The Spy and General Washington*, Dutton, 1965; *Franklin D. Roosevelt*, Putnam, 1967; *Monsters of Today and Yesterday*, Putnam, 1967; *When the Saboteurs Came*, Dutton, 1967; *Sir Howard, the Coward*, Putnam, 1967; *Killer Smog* (adult nonfiction), Rand McNally, 1968; *Monsters of the Ancient Seas*, Putnam, 1968; *Aaron Burr*, Putnam, 1968; *Booker T. Washington*, Putnam, 1968; *Secret Mission to the Philippines*, Dutton, 1969; *Nanette: The Hungry Pelican*, Rand McNally, 1969; *Giant Birds and Monsters of the Air* (Junior Literary Guild selection), Putnam, 1969; *The Terrible Trumpet*, Norton, 1969; *The Amazing Animals of Latin America*, Putnam, 1969.

The Amazing Animals of Australia (Junior Literary Guild selection), Putnam, 1970; *The Lazy Young Duke of Dundee*, Rand McNally, 1970; *Fresh as a Daisy, Neat as a Pin*, Parents' Magazine Press, 1970; *From Scrolls to Satellites*, Parents' Magazine Press, 1970; *Giant Snakes and Other Amazing Reptiles*, Putnam, 1970; *Charles A. Lindbergh: Aviation Pioneer*, Putnam, 1970; *Monsters of the Middle Ages*, Putnam, 1971; *Amazing Animals of North America*, Putnam, 1971; *Fresh, Canned, and Frozen*, Parents' Magazine Press, 1971; *All on a Summer's Day*, Pantheon, 1971; *Off We Go!*, Parents' Magazine Press, 1972; *Cities, Old and New*, Parents' Magazine Press, 1973; *Leaders, Laws, and Citizens*, Parents' Magazine Press, 1973; *The Strange World of Sea Mammals*, Putnam, 1973.

Author of television scripts; contributor of fiction to *Harper's, Yale Review*, and other periodicals, and of reviews to *New York Times* and *Saturday Review*.

*   *   *

WITHAM, W(illiam) Tasker 1914-

PERSONAL: First syllable of surname rhymes with "myth"; born May 20, 1914, in Worchester, Mass.; son of Raymond Lee (an electrical engineer and college professor) and Marion (Tasker) Witham; married Drusilla Goodwin, May 25, 1940; children: Raymond Tasker, Suzanne May (deceased), Kathleen Louise (deceased), Lawrence Robert. *Education:* Drew University, A.B., 1936; Columbia University M.A., 1940; University of Illinois, Ph.D., 1961. *Religion:* Presbyterian. *Home:* 2323 Washington Ave., Terre Haute, Ind. 47803. *Office:* Indiana State University, Terre Haute, Ind. 47809.

CAREER: Newton School for Boys, Newton, N.J., teacher of English, science, French, and German, 1936-38; church parish hall receptionist, 1938-40, and Young Men's Christian Association activities secretary, 1940-42, both New York, N.Y.; Hiwassee College, Madisonville, Tenn., head of English department, 1942-43; Hartwick College, Oneonta, N.Y., assistant professor, 1943-49, associate professor of English, 1949-59; Indiana State University, Terre Haute, assistant professor, 1959-63, associate professor, 1963-67, professor of English, 1967—. Lay preacher, Presbyterian Church, 1953-57. Director of plays for community theaters, high schools, and colleges, 1944-57, 1965; president of community theater in Oneonta, N.Y., 1953-55; director for community theater in Terre Haute, 1967—. President of Terre Haute Peace Council, 1962-64.

MEMBER: Modern Language Association of America, Modern Humanities Research Association, College English Association, National Council of Teachers of English, American Association of University Professors, Midwest Modern Language Association, Society for the study of Midwestern Literature, Indiana College English Association, Indiana Council of Teachers of English, Phi Sigma Kappa, Alpha Psi Omega, Phi Kappa Phi, Sigma Tau Delta (regional director, 1970-72, 1973—). *Awards, honors:* Danforth summer study grant, 1961; Indiana State University research grant, 1961-62.

WRITINGS: Americans as They Speak and Live, Ungar, 1945; *Panorama of American Literature,* S. Daye, 1947; *Living American Literature,* S. Daye, 1947; *The Adolescent in the American Novel, 1920-60,* Ungar, 1964, revised edition, 1974. Contributing editor, *Annual Bibliography of English Language and Literature* (publication of Modern Humanities Research Association), 1964—.

WORK IN PROGRESS: A book, tentatively titled *The Adolescent in American Drama, 1920-1970,* completion expected in 1976; research for *Annual Bibliography of English Language and Literature.*

SIDELIGHTS: Witham is competent in French and German.

* * *

WITHERS, William 1905-

PERSONAL: Born December 21, 1905, in St. Louis, Mo.; son of John W. and Margaret C. (Mathews) Withers; married Irma Rittenhouse, May 29, 1931. *Education:* Columbia University, A.B., 1926, A.M., 1928, Ph.D., 1932. *Politics:* Democrat. *Religion:* Methodist. *Address:* R.D.1, Box 40A, Eatontown, N.J. 07724. *Office:* Queens College of the City University of New York, Flushing, N.Y. 11367.

CAREER: Lehigh University, Bethlehem, Pa., instructor in economics, 1927-29; New York University, New York, N.Y., instructor in economics, 1929-31; Columbia University, New York, N.Y., chairman of social science department, New College, 1932-37, assistant professor of education, Teachers College, 1935-37; Queens College of the City University of New York, Flushing, Long Island, N.Y., assistant professor, 1937-40, associate professor, 1940-51, professor of economics, 1951-73, professor emeritus, 1974—. Liberal Party of New York State, vice-chairman, 1945-46; formerly active on boards of other liberal organizations, including League for Industrial Democracy and Union for Democratic Action. President, Ricardo Associates, Inc., 1974—. *Member:* American Economic Association, Latin American Studies Association, Phi Beta Kappa.

WRITINGS: The Retirement of National Debts, 1932; *Current Social Problems,* Prentice-Hall, 1936; *Financing Economic Security,* Columbia University Press, 1939; *The Public Debt,* Day, 1945; *Public Finance,* American Book, 1948; (with Harold Rugg) *The Social Foundations of Education,* Prentice-Hall, 1955; *The Economic Crisis in Latin America,* Free Press of Glencoe, 1964; *Freedom Through Power,* Day, 1965; *Business in Society,* Appleton, 1966; *The Corporations and Social Change,* Barrons Educational Series, 1972. Contributor to *Industrial Gerontology* and business and economic journals.

WORK IN PROGRESS: The Economics of Upper-Aging.

SIDELIGHTS: Withers speaks Spanish, has traveled in Europe, Cuba, Mexico, and most South American countries.

* * *

WITTE, Glenna Finley 1925- (Glenna Finley)

PERSONAL: Born June 12, 1925, in Puyallup, Wash.; daughter of John Ford (a biologist) and Gladys de F. (Winters) Finley; married Donald Macleod Witte (a corporation official), May 19, 1951; children: Duncan. *Education:* Stanford University, B.A. (cum laude), 1945. *Religion:* Episcopalian. *Home:* 2645 34th Ave. West, Seattle, Wash. 98199. *Agent:* Ann Elmo Agency, Inc., 52 Vanderbilt Ave., New York, N.Y. 10017.

CAREER: National Broadcasting Co., New York, N.Y., producer in International Division, 1945-47; Time, Inc., New York, N.Y., Staff of *Life* News Bureau, 1947, film librarian for "March of Time," 1948-50; publicity and copywriter in Seattle, Wash., 1950-51. Free-lance writer. *Member:* National League of American Pen Women, Stanford Club.

WRITINGS—Under name Glenna Finley; *Death Strikes Out,* Arcadia House, 1957; *Career Wife,* Arcadia House, 1964; *Nurse Pro Tem,* Arcadia House, 1967; *A Tycoon for Ann,* Lancer, 1968; *Journey to Love,* Signet, 1970; *Love's Hidden Fire,* Signet, 1971; *Treasure of the Heart,* Signet, 1971; *Love Lies North,* Signet, 1972; *Bridal Affair,* Signet, 1972; *Kiss a Stranger,* Signet, 1972; *Love in Danger,* Signet, 1973; *When Love Speaks,* Signet, 1973; *The Romantic Spirit,* Signet, 1973; *Surrender My Love,* Signet, 1974; *A PromisiNg Affair,* Signet, 1974.

WORK IN PROGRESS: Love's Magic Spell.

* * *

WOHLGELERNTER, Maurice 1921-

PERSONAL: Born February 13, 1921, in Poland; son of Jacob Isaac (a rabbi) and Deborah (Yagoda) Wohlgelernter; married Esther Feinerman (a teacher), February 1, 1948; children: Debra, Elliot, Beth. *Education:* Yeshiva University, B.A., 1941, Rabbi, 1944; Columbia University, M.A., 1946, Ph.D., 1961. *Home:* 62 Park Terrace West, New York, N.Y. 10034.

CAREER: Yeshiva University, New York, N.Y., assistant professor of English, 1955-70; Bernard M. Baruch College of the City University of New York, New York, N.Y., associate professor of English, 1972—. Visiting assistant professor, City College (now City College of the City University of New York), summers, 1962-65; visiting professor at Bar-Ilan University, Israel, and at the New School for Social Research, 1966-68. Panelist on television programs, "Minorities in American Literature," WYNC-TV, and

"The American Novel: Voice of Minorities," WNBC, 1965. *Member:* Modern Language Association of America, National Council of Teachers of English, American Association of University Professors.

WRITINGS: Israel Zangwill: A Study, Columbia University Press, 1964; *Israel Zangwill: Selected Bibliography*, Jewish Book Council of America, 1964; (author of introduction) Israel Zangwill, *The King of Schnorrers*, Dover, 1965. Contributor to *Horizon, History of Ideas Newsletter, Midstream*, and *Congress Bi-Weekly*. Also contributing editor of *Tradition*.

WORK IN PROGRESS: A book, *Frank O'Connor: A Critical Introduction.*

* * *

WOLCOTT, Leonard Thompson

PERSONAL: Born in Buenos Aires, Argentina; son of Maynard (a minister) and Edna (Thompson) Wolcott; married Carolyn Muller, September 31, 1951; children: Joy (Mrs. Bruce Vaughan). *Education:* Asbury College, B.A.; Hartford Seminary Foundation, M.A.; Drew University, M.Div., Oxford University, D. Phil. *Home:* 3372 Mimosa Dr., Nashville, Tenn. 37211. *Office:* Scarritt College for Christian Workers, Nashville, Tenn.

CAREER: Methodist minister. Methodist Church, church worker in Bihar, India, 1945-50; Scarritt College for Christian Workers, Nashville, Tenn., Mabel K. Howell Professor of Missions, 1953—. Lecturer at universities and colleges in India, and lecturer throughout America. Consultant at Sat Tal Ashram, India, 1974. *Member:* Association of Professors of Missions (secretary-treasurer, 1960-62), American Oriental Society, Society of Biblical Literature, American Association of University Professors, American Society of Missiology, North American Academy of Ecumenists, Midwest Fellowship of Professors of Missions (president, 1973-74). *Awards, honors:* Grant from Dr. William's Trust (British) for research.

WRITINGS: Twelve Modern Disciples, Upper Room, 1964; *Meditations on Ephesians*, Abingdon, 1965; (co-author) *Religions Around the World*, Abingdon, 1967; *La Iglesia en El Mundo*, Centro de Estudios Teologicos, 1972. Writer of study-guide books and curriculum materials for church schools. Regular columnist, *Indian Witness* (Lucknow); contributor to *International Review of Missions*, other church magazines.

SIDELIGHTS: Leonard Wolcott spent a sabbatical in 1963, in research in rural and industrial India, and wrote for Centro de Estudios Teologicos in 1971 while on sabbatical. Wolcott has lived at other periods in England and Germany, and has traveled widely in Europe, Asia, Africa, and South America. He is competent in Hindi, French, German, and Spanish. *Avocational interests:* Folk dancing, bird study, drama, violon, Sanskrit and Greek.

* * *

WOLF, Donald J(oseph) 1929-

PERSONAL: Born June 6, 1929, in Torrance, Calif.; son of Walter Joseph and Martha (Burback) Wolf. *Education:* Gonzaga University, B.A., 1953, M.A., 1955; Georgetown University, Ph.D., 1960; University of Santa Clara, S.T.M., 1964.

CAREER: Roman Catholic priest, member of Society of Jesus. University of Santa Clara, instructor in American government, 1955-56; Georgetown University, Washington,

D.C., instructor in political theory, summers, 1961 and 1964. *Member:* Alpha Sigma Nu.

WRITINGS: (With James Schall) *American Society and Politics* (text with workbook), Allyn & Bacon, 1964; (editor with Schall, and contributor) *Current Trends in Theology*, Doubleday, 1965; *Toward Consensus: Catholic-Protestant Interpretations of Church and State*, Anchor Books, 1968. Contributor to *America, Social Order, Cithara, Review of Politics*, other journals.

WORK IN PROGRESS: Research for a study in the political philosophy of Walter Lippmann.†

* * *

WOLF, Harold A. 1923-

PERSONAL: Born February 10, 1923, in Lind, Wash.; son of Edward and Olga (Linert) Wolf; married Jeanette Elizabeth Dunn, March 24, 1961; children: Mark H., Suellen I. *Education:* University of Oregon, B.A., 1951; University of Michigan, M.A., 1952, Ph.D., 1958. *Home:* 7004 Edgefield Dr., Austin, Tex. *Office:* Department of Finance, University of Texas, Austin, Tex. 78712.

CAREER: Lehigh University, Bethlehem, Pa., instructor, 1955-57; University of Colorado, Boulder, assistant professor, 1958-60, associate professor of finance, 1960-65, professor of finance, 1965-67; University of Texas, Austin, professor of finance, 1968—. Consultant to banks and loan associations. *Military service:* U.S. Navy, 1941-47. *Member:* American Economic Association, American Finance Association, Pi Gamma Mu, Delta Phi Alpha.

WRITINGS: (With Maurice Unger) *Personal Finance*, Allyn & Bacon, 1964, 4th edition, 1975; (editor with Lee Richardson) *Readings in Finance*, Appleton, 1966; *Monetary and Fiscal Management*, C. E. Merrill, 1966; (editor with Conrad Doenges) *Readings in Money and Banking*, Prentice-Hall, 1968; *High School Economics*, 2nd edition, C. E. Merrill, 1971; *Consumer Education*, Allyn & Bacon, 1975. Contributor to professional journals.

* * *

WOLF, Herbert C(hristian) 1923-

PERSONAL: Born April 6, 1923, in Baltimore, Md.; son of Carl George (a minister) and Margaret (Umhau) Wolf; married Margaret Schroder, June 18, 1947; children: Gretchen, Gary, Martin, Allen, Miriam. *Education:* Johns Hopkins University, A.B., 1943; Lutheran Theological Seminary, Columbus, Ohio, B.D., 1947; University of Chicago, M.A., 1959; Harvard University, Th.D., 1968. *Politics:* Democrat. *Home:* 1126 North Fountain, Springfield, Ohio 45504. *Office:* Wittenberg University, Springfield, Ohio 45501.

CAREER: Capital University, Columbus, Ohio, instructor in religion, 1945-47; ordained to Lutheran ministry, 1947; Michigan State University, East Lansing, lecturer in religion and National Lutheran Council campus pastor, 1948-57; Wittenberg University, Springfield, Ohio, associate professor of religion, 1957—, chairman of department, 1969—. Friends of East Lansing Public Library, member of board, 1954-56, president, 1955. Clark County (Ohio) Democratic Central and Executive Committees, member, 1960—, chairman 1966—. *Member:* American Academy of Religion, American Theological Society, American Association of University Professors (chapter president, 1962-63). *Awards, honors:* Danforth teacher study grants and Martin Luther fellowships, 1961, 1963.

WRITINGS: Kierkegaard and Bultmann: The Quest of the Historical Jesus, Augsburg, 1965.

WORK IN PROGRESS: The Concept of God as Person—A Critical Study of Barth, Farmer, and Tillich.†

* * *

WOLFBEIN, Seymour L(ouis) 1915-

PERSONAL: Born November 8, 1915, in Brooklyn, N.Y.; son of Samuel and Fanny (Katz) Wolfbein; married Mae Lachterman (a counselor), March 1, 1941; children: Susan Lois (Mrs. William Morris), Deeva Irene (Mrs. Robert Garel). *Education:* Brooklyn College (now Brooklyn College of the City University of New York), B.A., 1936; Columbia University, M.A., 1937, Ph.D., 1941. *Home:* 6305 Crathie Lane, Washington, D.C. 20016. *Office:* Office of the Dean, School of Business Administration, Temple University, Philadelphia, Pa. 19122.

CAREER: U.S. Department of Labor, Washington, D.C., 1942-44, 1945-67, chief of Manpower and Employment, Bureau of Labor Statistics, 1950-59; deputy assistant secretary of labor, 1959-62, director of Office of Manpower, Automation and Training, 1962-65, economic advisor to secretary of labor, 1965-67; American University, Washington, D.C., adjunct professor of economics, 1947-67; Temple University, Philadelphia, Pa., professor of economics and dean of School of Business Administration, 1967—. Visiting professor of education, University of Michigan, 1950-70; Salzburg Seminar in American studies, Austria, lecturer, 1965, and dean of faculty, 1972; lecturer in the Far East, Greece and Asia, for the Bureau of Cultural Affairs, U.S. Department of State, 1970. Representative to International Association of Gerontology, Italy, 1957, Sweden, 1963; delegate to International Labor Office, Geneva, 1959-64, Organization for Economic Cooperation and Development, Paris, Lisbon, Venice, 1961-63, 1965, 1967, 1971, United Nations Industrial Development Organization, Athens, 1967. Member of advisory board to U.S. Secretary of Commerce, 1969-70; member of board of directors, Lincoln Bank, Philadelphia, Pa. Consultant and lecturer at many insurance firms and industrial companies. *Military service:* U.S. Army, 1944-45. *Member:* American Association for the Advancement of Science (fellow), American Statistical Association (fellow), American Personnel and Guidance Association (trustee), Washington Statistical Society (president, 1957-59). *Awards, honors:* Distinguished Service Award, U.S. Department of Labor, 1954, 1961; Alumni Award of Honor, Brooklyn College (now Brooklyn College of the City University of New York), 1954; Eminent Career Award, National Vocational Guidance Association, 1970.

WRITINGS: Decline of a Cotton Textile City, Columbia University Press, 1944; (with H. Goldstein) *The World of Work*, Science Research Associates, 1951; *Employment and Unemployment in the United States*, Science Research Associates, 1964; *Employment, Unemployment and Public Policy*, Random House, 1966; *Education and Training for Full Employment*, Columbia University Press, 1968; *Occupational Information*, Random House, 1969; *Emerging Sectors of Collective Bargaining*, edited by D. H. Marks, General Learning Corp., 1970; *Work in American Society*, Scott, Foresman, 1971. Contributor to statistical, labor, and personnel guidance journals.

* * *

WOLFE, Roy I. 1917-

PERSONAL: Born November 19, 1917, in Poland; married Rosemary Schawlow, June 26, 1949; children: Robert D., P. Richard, Judith D., Miriam R. *Education:* McMaster University, B.A. (honors), 1940; University of Toronto, M.A., 1947, Ph.D., 1956. *Home:* 203 Douglas Dr., Toronto, Ontario M4W 2B6, Canada. *Office:* Department of Geography, York University, Toronto, Ontario.

CAREER: High school teacher of physics and chemistry in Fort Frances, Ontario, 1941-43; Veterans' Rehabilitation Institute (now Ryerson Institute of Technology), Toronto, Ontario, 1945-47; Department of Highways, Ontario, began as statistician, became research geographer, 1952-67; R. I. Wolfe Associates, partner, 1967—. York University, Toronto, Ontario, associate professor, 1967-68, professor of geography, 1968—. Visiting lecturer in urban and transportation geography, University of Washington, Seattle, 1960-61; special lecturer at University of Toronto, 1969-70; member of commission on Transport, International Geographical Union, 1969-72. *Military service:* Canadian Army, 1943-45. *Member:* Canadian Association of Geographers, Regional Science Association, International Peace Research Society, World Society for Ekistics.

WRITINGS: Transportation and Politics, Van Nostrand, 1963; (contributor) W. A. Douglas Jackson, editor, *Politics and Geographic Relationships*, Prentice-Hall, 1964; *A Theory of Recreational Highway Traffic*, Ontario Department of Highways, 1967; (contributor) *Profiles of a Province*, Ontario Historical Society, 1967; (contributor) John Warkentin, editor, *Canada: A Geographical Interpretation*, Methuen, 1968; (contributor) *Essays on Mid-Canada*, MacLean-Hunter, 1970; (contributor) *Leisure and the Quality of Life: A New Ethic for the Seventies, and Beyond*, American Institute of Planners, 1972; (contributor) W. Peter Adams and Frederick M. Helleiner, *International Geography*, University of Toronto Press, 1972; (contributor) James Forrester and John N. Jackson, editors, *Practical Geography: Strategy for Study*, McGraw, 1972; *Technology and Canadian Society*, Canadian Studies Foundation, 1973.

* * *

WOLFE, Thomas Kennerly, Jr. 1931-
(Tom Wolfe)

PERSONAL: Born March 2, 1931, in Richmond, Va.; son of Thomas Kennerly (a scientist and business executive) and Helen (Hughes) Wolfe. *Education:* Washington and Lee University, B.A. (cum laude), 1951; Yale University, Ph.D., 1957. *Residence:* New York, N.Y. *Agent:* International Famous Agency, 1301 Avenue of the Americas, New York, N.Y. 10019.

CAREER: Reporter with *Springfield Union*, Springfield, Mass., 1956-59, and *Washington Post*, Washington, D.C., 1959-62; *New York Herald Tribune*, New York, N.Y., reporter and writer for *New York* Sunday magazine (later became *New York* Magazine), 1962-66; New York *World Journal Tribune*, New York, writer, 1966-67; *New York* Magazine, New York, contributing editor, 1968—. Has had one-man shows of drawings at Maynard Walker Gallery, 1965, and Tunnel Gallery, 1974 (both New York, N.Y.). *Awards, honors:* Two Washington Newspaper Guild awards, one for foreign news, one for humor, both 1961; Society of Magazine Writers award for excellence, 1970; D.F.A. from Minneapolis College of Art, 1971; D.Litt., Washington and Lee University, 1974.

WRITINGS—All under name Tom Wolfe: The Kandy-Kolored Tangerine-Flake Streamline Baby (essays), Farrar, Straus, 1965; (contributor) Alan Rinzler, editor, *The New York Spy*, David White, 1967; *The Electric Kool-Aid Acid Test*, Farrar, Straus, 1968; *The Pump House Gang* (essays), Farrar, Straus, 1968; *Radical Chic & Mau-Mauing the Flak Catchers* (two essays), Farrar, Straus, 1970; *The New Journalism* (essay by Wolfe, with anthology edited by Wolfe and E. W. Johnson), Harper, 1973; *The Painted Word*, Farrar, Straus, 1975; *The Right Stuff*, Farrar, Straus, 1975. Contributor to *Esquire, New York*, and other publications. One of co-founders of literary quarterly, *Shenandoah*, while an undergraduate.

SIDELIGHTS: For his free-wheeling style and attitude, Tom Wolfe (no relation to the earlier writer) has been called "supercontemporary," "parajournalistic," and "poet laureate of pop." *The Kandy-Kolored Tangerine-Flake Streamline Baby* is "a groove and a gas," writes Terry Southern. Wolfe has developed a new journalistic form by using a unique, irreverent jargon, scrambling his metaphors.

Dwight Macdonald notes that "elaboration rather than development is Wolfe's forte.... There is no space between writer and topic, no 'distancing' to allow the most rudimentary objective judgment...." C. H. Simonds believes that amid the rapid-fire delivery and slickness "Wolfe is able to preserve a hard core of perceptiveness ...; always he poses and bravely tries to answer the frustrating question 'What (if anything) does it all *mean?*' ... The evocation of organized insanity is excellent, and the conclusion worth a ponder." Kurt Vonnegut, Jr.'s verdict: "Excellent book by a genius who will do anything to get attention."

"Tom Wolfe is more than brilliant, which his first critics noted in full," estimates Karl Shapiro in reviewing *The Pump House Gang* and *The Electric Kool-Aid Acid Test*: "He is more than urbane, suave, trenchant and all those book review adjectives. He really understands his subjects, is really compassionate (when possible), really involved with what he says and clearly responsible to his judgments. Tom Wolfe is a goddam joy. Also, not to insult him, he writes like a master."

Wolfe's mode of expression originated with an *Esquire* article he hadn't time to complete. He was asked to simply type out his notes and return them to be rewritten. He writes: "I just started recording it all and inside of a couple of hours, typing along like a madman, I could tell that something was beginning to happen." The notes were printed as he originally wrote them, and what he calls "the wowie!" style, "a complex mixture of several vernaculars—teenage, jet set, academic and drugstore modern" (*Life*), came into existence. The *Newsweek* reviewer writes: "His cells simply rearranged themselves like Lon Chaney Jr., and he became the Wolfe-man."

His varied background (Ph.D., former semi-pro ballplayer) allows him to arrive "at zonky conclusions couched in scholarly terms," as Vonnegut notes. His most vigorous attack (*New York*, April 11 and 18, 1965) was directed at the respectable *New Yorker*, which, he wrote, "for forty years ... has maintained a strikingly low level of literary achievement." His criticism led to strong rebuttals, including one from J. D. Salinger, a *New Yorker* contributor, who had heretofore abstained from public comment of any kind.

Wolfe's dandified appearance, crowned with a floppy "pseudo-Mod" haircut, is as unique as his prose. One observer called him "resplendent in nubby suit and buckle-over bootlets." Wolfe told Haskel Frankel: "As a writer, I'm concerned with the liberation of thinking. At the moment, a sort of nineteenth-century pattern of thinking has a grip on the country.... Our thinking is dominated by a pattern from our Eastern universities, a pattern of European origin. The real story of our country has not been written.

The film rights to *The Kandy-Kolored Tangerine-Flake Streamline Baby* were sold to MGM in 1967.

BIOGRAPHICAL/CRITICAL SOURCES: New York Times Book Review, June 27, 1965; *Book Week*, June 27, 1965; *Life*, July 2, 1965; *Time*, July 2, 1965; *New Republic*, July 24, 1965; *Newsweek*, July 28, 1965, January 31, 1966; *Saturday Review*, July 31, 1965; *Esquire*, August, 1965; *Village Voice*, August 5, 1965; *Reporter*, August 12, 1965; *New York Review of Books*, August 26, 1965, February 3, 1966; *Virginia Quarterly Review*, autumn, 1965; *Commonweal*, September 17, 1965; *Critic*, October-November, 1965; *National Review*, November 2, 1965, January 12, 1971; Chicago Tribune *Book World*, August 18, 1968; *New York*, August 19, 1968, June 8, 1970; *Partisan Review*, number 3, 1969; *Writer's Digest*, January 1970; *Listener*, February 19, 1970; Carolyn Riley, editor, *Contemporary Literary Criticism*, Gale, Volume I, 1973, Volume II, 1974.

* * *

WOLL, Peter 1933-

PERSONAL: Born January 6, 1933, in Philadelphia, Pa.; son of John William (a business executive) and Ruth (Crowther) Woll; married Mary Louise Jobes, June 26, 1954; children: Robert, Lucinda. *Education:* Haverford College, A.B., 1954; Cornell University, Ph.D., 1958. *Home:* 43 Oxbow Rd., Weston, Mass. *Office:* Brandeis University, Waltham, Mass.

CAREER: University of California, Los Angeles, assistant professor of political science, 1960-64; Brandeis University, Waltham, Mass., associate professor of politics, 1965—. Lecturer, U.S. Civil Service Commission. *Member:* American Political Science Association, Phi Beta Kappa.

WRITINGS: American Government: Readings and Cases, Little, Brown, 1962, 4th edition, 1972; *Administrative Law: The Informal Process*, University of California Press, 1963; *American Bureaucracy*, Norton, 1963; *Public Policy*, Winthrop, 1974. Contributor to legal and political science journals.

WORK IN PROGRESS: Research in administrative law and administrative decision-making processes, attempting to assess attitudes of bureaucrats as well as private clients toward procedural and substantive issues.

* * *

WOLMAN, Benjamin B. 1908-

PERSONAL: Born October 27, 1908, in Warsaw, Poland; son of Jehuda Leib (a playwright) and Hinda Leah (Cukier) Wolman; divorced; children: Danielle. *Education:* University of Warsaw, M.A., 1932, Ph.D., 1935. *Religion:* Jewish. *Office:* 10 West 66th St., New York, N.Y. 10023.

CAREER: Director of mental health clinic, Tel-Aviv, Palestine, 1935-42; Columbia University, New York, N.Y., 1951-53; psychologist-psychoanalyst in private practice, New York, N.Y., 1952—; Adelphi University, Garden City, N.Y., clinical professor of psychology, 1962-68; Institute of Applied Psychoanalysis, New York, N.Y., dean of faculty, 1965-72; Long Island University, N.Y., professor of psychology, 1965—. *Member:* International Organization for the Study of Group Tensions (president), American Psychological Association (fellow), Association for Advancement of Psychotherapy (fellow), Association for Applied Psychoanalysis (co-chairman of committee on faculty).

WRITINGS: Contemporary Theories and Systems in Psychology, Harper, 1960; (editor with E. Nagel) *Scientific Psychology*, Basic Books, 1965; (editor) *Handbook of Clinical Psychology*, McGraw, 1965; *Vectoriasis Praecox or the Group Schizophrenias*, C. C Thomas, 1966; (editor) *Historical Roots of Contemporary Psychology*, Harper, 1966; (with others) *Psychoanalytic Techniques: A Handbook for The Practicing Psychoanalyst*, Basic Books, 1967; *The Unconscious Mind: The Meaning of Freudian Psychology*, Prentice-Hall, 1968; (with others) *Psychoanalysis as Art and Science*, Wayne University Press, 1968; *Children Without Childhood: A Study of Childhood Schizophrenia*, Grune, 1970; (with others) *Psychoanalytic Interpretation of History*, Basic Books, 1971; (with others) *Manual of Child Psychopathology*, McGraw, 1972; (with others) *Success and Failure in Psychoanalysis and Psychotherapy*, Macmillan, 1972; (with others) *Handbook of Child Psychoanalysis*, Van Nostrand, 1972; *Call No Man Normal*, International Universities Press, 1973; (with others) *Handbook of General Psychology*, Prentice-Hall, 1973; *Victims of Success*, Quadrangle Books, 1973; (with others) *Dictionary of Behavioral Science*, Van Nostrand, 1973. Editor, *International Journal of Group Tensions*.

SIDELIGHTS: Several of Wolman's books have been translated for publication in Europe, Asia, and South America.

*   *   *

WONG, Lin Ken   1931-

PERSONAL: Born July 31, 1931, in Penang, Malaysia; son of Choon San (a writer) and Siew Kam (Liew) Wong; married Lili Tan (an occupational therapist), September 23, 1961; children: Ch'iu-man, Ch'iu-yin, Yi-Lin. *Education:* University of Malaya, B.A., 1953, B.A. (first class honors), 1954, M.A., 1955; University of London, Ph.D., 1959. *Office:* History Department, University of Singapore, Cluny Rd., Singapore 10.

CAREER: University of Singapore, Singapore, lecturer, 1961-65, non-resident fellow of Dunearn Roads Hostel, 1963-64, senior lecturer, 1965-67, Raffles Professor of History, 1967—; Government of Singapore, permanent representative to United Nations, 1967-68, ambassador to United States and Brazil, 1967-68, member of Parliament, 1968—, minister of Home Affairs, 1970-72. Member of Advisory Commitee on Secret Societies, 1960-61, Film Censorship Appeal Committee, 1962-63, Permanent Examination Board of Civil Service, 1962-67; director of External Affairs Bureau, Peoples Action Party, 1963-68; chairman of Adult Education Board, 1964-67. *Member:* Royal Asiatic Society (vice president of Malaysia branch, 1969-72), Institute of Southeast Asian Studies (member of executive committee, 1968-70), The Pyramid. *Awards, honors:* Public Service Star, 1966.

WRITINGS: A Study of the Trade of Singapore 1819-1869, Malayan Branch, Royal Asiatic Society, 1960; (contributor) K. G. Tregonning, editor, *Papers on Malayan History*, [Singapore], 1962; (contributor) C. D. Cowan, editor, *The Economic Development of Southeast Asia*, [London], 1964; *The Malayan Tin Industry to 1914*, Association

for Asian Studies (United States), 1965. Contributor to *Journal of Economic History*, and *Solidarity: Current Affairs, Ideas and the Arts*. Member of editorial board, *Journal of Southeast Asian Studies*, and *Journal of the South Seas Society*.

*   *   *

WOOD, Fred M.

PERSONAL: Born in Memphis, Tenn.; son of Claude W. and Florence Wood; married Lillie Belle Johnson; children: Mitchell, David. *Education:* Union University, Jackson, Tenn., A.B., 1944; Southern Baptist Theological Seminary, B.D., 1947, Th.M., 1948, Th.D., 1949. *Home:* 537 Colonial Rd., Memphis, Tenn. 38117.

CAREER: Southern Baptist minister; Eudora Baptist Church, Memphis, Tenn., pastor, 1952—. Evangelist, Bible conference speaker, and Sunday School lesson writer. President of Memphis Pastor's Conference, 1970; president of Tennessee Baptist Convention, 1972-73. *Awards, honors:* D.D., Union University, 1962.

WRITINGS: Fire in My Bones, Broadman, 1959; *Bible Truth in Person*, Broadman, 1965; *Yesterday's Voice for Today's World*, Broadman, 1967; *Instant Bible*, Zondervan, 1968; *The Glory of Galatians*, Broadman, 1972; (editor with others) *Teacher's Bible Commentary*, Broadman, 1972; *Dynamic Living for Difficult Days*, Broadman, 1973. Contributor to *Pastor's Annual*, and to religion periodicals and journals.

SIDELIGHTS: Wood is a student of Hebrew and Greek. *Avocational interest:* Golf.

*   *   *

WOOD, Margaret (L. E.)   1910-

PERSONAL: Born March 4, 1910, in Great Yarmouth, Norfolk, England; daughter of Ernest Charles (a company director) and Ethelmary (Child) Bellamy; married Edward Rudolf Wood (a schoolteacher), April 27, 1937; children: Margaret Helen, Caroline. *Education:* University of London, B.A. (second class honors), 1933; Hughes Hall, Cambridge, Diploma in Education (first class). *Religion:* Church of England. *Home:* White House, Much Birch, Hereford, England.

CAREER: Playwright. Justice of the peace, City of Hereford, England. *Awards, honors:* First place in Amateur Stage Playwriting Competition for "Road to Damascus," 1956; British Drama League One-Act Play Award, and Geoffrey Whitworth Cup, both for "The Day of Atonement," 1962.

WRITINGS—Plays; all published by Samuel French except as indicated: *Instruments of Darkness*, 1955; *Women's Ward*, 1955; *The Road to Damascus*, 1956; *The Copper Kettle* (comedy), 1956; *Home is the Sailor* (comedy), 1957; *Withington Warrior* (comedy), 1958; *The Guilty Generation*, 1958; *Cato's Daughter*, 1958; *Dark Horses* (comedy), 1959; *Fools' Errand*, 1960; *Atalanta*, 1961; *Out-patients* (comedy), 1961; *A Dog's Life* (comedy), 1962; *The Primrose Path*, 1964; *Crying in the Wilderness*, 1964; *The Witches*, Evans, 1964; *The Third Windmill Book of One-Act Plays*, Heinemann, 1965; *A Kind of Justice*, 1966; *Plays for Christmas and Easter*, Heinemann, 1966; *The King and the Quaker*, 1968; *The Double Dealers*, 1968; *Covenant with Death*, Evans, 1970. Scriptwriter for British Broadcasting Corp. radio schools.

WORK IN PROGRESS: Educational scripts for television.

WOODARD, Christopher R. 1913-

PERSONAL: Born August 3, 1913, in Bury St. Edmunds, Suffolk, England; son of A. L. Woodard (a priest, Church of England); married Dorothy B. MacMurray, September 12, 1944; children: Christopher James Anthony, Nicolas Andrew. Education: Attended Lancing College, 1927-32; Trinity College, Cambridge, M.A. (honors), 1938; Middlesex Hospital Medical School, University of London, M.R.C.S. and L.R.C.P., 1942. Politics: Non-political. Religion: Church of England. Home and office: 31 Wimpole St., London W.1. England. Agent: A. P. Watt & Son, Hastings House, 10 Norfolk St., Strand, London W.C. 2, England.

CAREER: In private practice as specialist in psychosomatic medicine, London, England, 1948—. Ockenden Venture (refugee organization), chairman. Military service: Royal Navy Volunteer Reserve, 1943-1946; became surgeon-lieutenant. Member: Royal Society of Medicine (fellow), Pedal Club (president), Pickwick Cycle Club (president).

WRITINGS: A Doctor Heals by Faith, Parrish, 1948; Scientific Training for Cycling, 1952, 3rd edition, Temple Press, 1961; A Doctor's Faith Is Challenged, Parrish, 1954; A Doctor's Faith Holds Fast, Parrish, 1956; Sports Injuries, Parrish, 1956; Healing Words: An Anthology, Parrish, 1960.

WORK IN PROGRESS: The Challenge of Faith in Sickness and Suffering.

SIDELIGHTS: Woodard trains international athletes in all sports.†

*   *   *

WOODIN, Ann Snow 1926-

PERSONAL: Born June 27, 1926, in New York, N.Y.; daughter of John B. Snow and Catherine (Joralemon) Rollins; married William H. Woodin III, July 10, 1948; children: Peter, John, Michael, Hugh. Education: Wellesley College, B.A., 1948. Religion: Episcopalian. Home address: Route 2, Box 251, Tucson, Ariz.

CAREER: Summer School of World Affairs, Greece, staff member, 1964. Mayor's Committee for Urban Renewal, Tucson, Ariz., member, 1960-62. Member: League of Women Voters, Planned Parenthood (board member, Tucson, 1958-62).

WRITINGS: Home is the Desert, Macmillan, 1964; In the Circle of the Sun (autobiography), Macmillan, 1971.

WORK IN PROGRESS: A proposed series of children's books on natural history.

SIDELIGHTS: Ann Woodin speaks French and Spanish. She spends part of most summers in Europe and is particularly interested in student exchange programs.†

*   *   *

WOODS, John 1926-

PERSONAL: Born July 12, 1926, in Martinsville, Ind.; son of Jefferson Blount and Doris (Underwood) Woods; married Emily Newbury, December 1, 1951; children: David Warren, Richard William. Education: Indiana University, B.S., 1949, M.A.T., 1955; University of Iowa, graduate study, 1957-58. Home: 6411 Hampton St., Portage, Mich. 49081. Office: English Department, Western Michigan University, Kalamazoo, Mich. 49001.

CAREER: Western Michigan University, Kalamazoo, assistant professor, 1955-61, associate professor, 1961-65, professor of English, 1965—. Visiting professor, University of California at Irvine, 1967-68. Military service: U.S. Army Air Force, 1944-46. Member: American Association of University Professors, Modern Language Association of America. Awards, honors: Theodore Roethke Award from Poetry Northwest, 1969; Publication Award from National Endowment for the Arts, 1970.

WRITINGS—Poetry: The Deaths at Paragon, Indiana University Press, 1955; On the Morning of Color, Indiana University Press, 1961; The Cutting Edge, Indiana University Press, 1966; Keeping Out of Trouble, Indiana University Press, 1968; Turning to Look Back: Poems, 1955-70, Indiana University Press, 1972; (with James Hearst and Felix Pollack) Voyages to the Inland Sea, Wisconsin State University at LaCrosse, 1972; The Knees of Widows (broadsheet), Westigan Review, 1971; Alcohol, Pilot Press, 1973; Bone Flicker, Juniper Books, 1974.

Work represented in many anthologies including American Literary Anthology, Viking, 1970; Just What the Country Needs, Wadsworth, 1971; Contemporary American Poetry, Penguin, 1971.

Contributor of poems, stories, plays, and reviews to Poetry, Shenandoah, Folio, Kenyon Review, Chicago Review, Epoch, Western Review, Paris Review, Fresco, Calliope, Saturday Review, Prairie Schooner, Poetry Northwest, Massachusetts Review, Critic, Choice, CCC Journal, Western Humanities Review, and numerous other magazines. Has recorded his poetry for the Library of Congress and for Aural Press (where he was poetry editor, 1964-65).

*   *   *

WOODS, John A(ubin) 1927-

PERSONAL: Born February 25, 1927, in London, England; son of Albert Edward (a teacher) and Iris (McCrea) Woods. Education: Downing College, Cambridge, M.A., 1948; University of Rochester, Ph.D., 1952. Politics: Labour. Home: 37 Tytherton Rd., London, N. 19, England.

CAREER: The Correspondence of Edmund Burke, associate, 1955-61; University of Leeds, Leeds, England, lecturer in American history, 1961—.

WRITINGS: A Bibliography of Parliamentary Debates of Great Britain, H.M.S.O., 1956; Roosevelt and Modern America, English Universities Press, 1959, Collier, 1962; (editor) The Correspondence of Edmund Burke, University of Chicago Press, Volume IV, 1963, Volume VII, 1969; (editor, and author of notes) Harriet Beecher Stowe, Uncle Tom's Cabin, Clarendon Press, 1965.

WORK IN PROGRESS: A biography of Granville Sharp.

*   *   *

WOODS, Kenneth F. 1930-

PERSONAL: Born October 20, 1930, in Randolph, Mass.; son of E. and Marguerite (Phinney) Woods; married Elaine Wilson, June 7, 1957. Education: Ball State University, B.S., 1954; University of Maryland, M.A., 1959; The American University, Ph.D., 1962. Office: Department of History, San Diego State University, San Diego, Calif.

CAREER: San Diego State University, San Diego, Calif., assistant professor of Latin American history, 1962—. U.S. Peace Corps, regional officer for Ecuador and Peru, 1965-

66. *Military service:* U.S. Army, 1948. *Member:* American Historical Association, Association for Higher Education, Association for Latin American studies.

WRITINGS: (Contributor) *Area Handbook for Panama*, U.S. Department of the Army, 1963. Contributor of articles and reviews to *World Affairs* and *Southern California Quarterly.*

WORK IN PROGRESS: Research on Latin American history during national period.†

* * *

WORMSER, Rene A(lbert) 1896-

PERSONAL: Born July 17, 1896, in Santa Barbara, Calif.; son of David (a merchant) and Angeline (Boeseke) Wormser; married Ella Madge Ward August 7, 1945; children: Angele Boeseke, Elissa Ward. *Education:* Columbia University, B.S., 1917, LL.B., 1920. *Politics:* Republican. *Residence:* Ginkgo Lane, Greenwich, Conn.

CAREER: Admitted to bar of New York State, 1920; attorney with law firms and in private practice, New York, N.Y., 1920-30; partner in law firms bearing his name (and others), New York, N.Y., 1930-71; Wormer, Kiely, Alessandroni, Mahoney & McCann, New York, N.Y., senior partner, 1971—. New York University, member of faculty and planning committee, Federal Tax Institute, 1945-55, lecturer on estate planning, 1948-55; general counsel, U.S. House of Representatives Special Committee to Investigate Tax Exempt Foundations, 1953-54; chairman of advanced estate planning panels, Practicing Law Institute, 1956-68; chairman of advisory committee of University of Miami Estate Planning Institute, 1967—; member of committee on tax exempt organizations, Internal Revenue, 1970-71. Lecturer to bar associations. *Military service:* U.S. Navy, World War I. *Member:* American Bar Association, New York State Bar Association, Association of the Bar of the City of New York, Delta Upsilon, University Club and Union League Club (both New York), Belle Haven Club (Greenwich). *Awards, honors:* LL.D., Valparaiso University, 1964.

WRITINGS: Your Will and What Not to Do About It, Simon and Schuster, 1937; *Personal Estate Planning in a Changing World*, Simon and Schuster, 1942; *Collection of International War Damage Claims*, Alexander, 1944; *The Theory and Practice of Estate Planning*, Callaghan, 1944, *The Law*, Simon and Schuster, 1949, revised edition published as *The Story of the Law*, Regnery, 1962; *The Myth of the Good and Bad Nations*, Regnery, 1954; *Foundations: Their Power and Influence*, Devin, 1958; *Wormser's Guide to Estate Planning*, Prentice-Hall, 1958; (editor) *The Planning and Administration of Estates*, Practicing Law Institute, 1961; *Wills That Made History*, Newkirk Associates, 1974. Writer of brochures on taxes and planning. Contributor of articles to legal and other journals.

WORK IN PROGRESS: Journal articles.

SIDELIGHTS: Wormser is competent in German. *Avocational Interests:* Painting and wood carving.

* * *

WORTH, Helen 1913-

PERSONAL: Born July 17, 1913, in Cleveland, Ohio; daughter of Carol (an electrical engineer and head of own company) and Birdie (Stone) Levison; divorced. *Education:* Lake Erie College, student, 1931; University of Michigan, B.A., 1935; New School for Social Research, addi-

tional study, 1946, 1947. *Home and office:* Helen Worth Enterprises and Helen Worth Cooking School, 106 EAst 31st St., New York, N.Y. 10016.

CAREER: Scheel Advertising Agency, Cleveland, Ohio, editor of house organ, 1944-46; Helen Worth Enterprises and Cooking School, New York, N.Y., director, 1948—. Conductor of "Shopper's Matinee," Dumont Television, New York, N.Y., 1951; lecturer and food demonstrator; consultant to food and beverage firms and restaurants. Food consultant to National Association for the Specialty Food Trade, 1968-70; Judge of Professional Chef's Competition, 1967. *Member:* Author's Guild, Society of Magazine Writers, Sommelier Society, Culinary Institute of America (fellow), Compagnon de Bordeaux, Metropolitan Museum of Art, Friends of the New York Public Library.

WRITINGS: The Down-on-the-Farm Cook Book, Greenberg, 1943; *Shrimp Cookery*, Citadel, 1952; *Cooking Without Recipes* (Cook Book Guild selection), Harper, 1965; *Hostess Without Help* (Cook Book Guild selection), Westover Publishing, 1971; (contributor) Patricia Fink, editor, *Best Recipes from the Cook Book Guild*, Doubleday, 1972; *Damn Yankee in a Southern Kitchen*, Westover Publishing, 1973. Food editor, *Town and Village* (newspaper), 1947-60, *Girl Talk*, 1970—; columnist, "The Inspired Ingredient," for magazines in food management group, 1964-66; contributor to national magazines.

WORK IN PROGRESS: Books and articles on food, menus, wine, other spirits.

* * *

WOY, James Bayly 1927-

PERSONAL: Born May 19, 1927, in Moorefield, W. Va.; son of James Bayly (an automobile dealer) and Verna (Liller) Woy; married Sara Germon (a librarian), March 14, 1953; children: Susan, Patricia, Jeffrey. *Education:* West Virginia University, A.B., 1949; University of Illinois, M.S. in L.S., 1950. *Politics:* Democrat. *Religion:* Unitarian Universalist. *Home:* 405 West Stafford St., Philadelphia, Pa. 19144. *Office:* Mercantile Library (Free Library of Philadelphia), 1021 Chestnut St., Philadelphia, Pa. 19107.

CAREER: Brooklyn Public Library, Brooklyn, N.Y., reference assistant, 1950-52; University of Delware, Newark, head of circulation department, 1953; Free Library of Philadelphia, Philadelphia, Pa., 1954—, head of Mercantile Library, 1964—. *Member:* Special Libraries Association, American Library Association, Pennsylvania Library Association.

WRITINGS: (Editor) *Business Trends and Forecasting*, Gale, 1965; *Investment Information*, Gale, 1970; (editor with Paul Wasserman and others) *Encyclopedia of Business Information Sources*, two volumes, Gale, 1970; *Investment Methods*, Bowker, 1973; *Commodity Trading Methods*, Bowker, in press. Reviewer of business books for *Library Journal.*

AVOCATIONAL INTERESTS: Music and photography.

* * *

WOYCHUK, N(icholas) A(rthur) 1915-

PERSONAL: Born December 9, 1915, in Sky Lake, Manitoba, Canada; son of Max (a farmer) and Dorothy (Boyko) Woychuk; married Alice Gilham, February 19, 1956; children: Sharon Ruth, James Arthur. *Education:* Winnipeg Normal School, student, 1935; Baylor University, A.B., 1941, M.A., 1942; Dallas Theological Seminary, Th.M.,

1941, Th.D., 1943. *Politics:* Independent. *Office:* Bible Memory Association, 1298 Pennsylvania, St. Louis, Mo.

CAREER: Minister of United Presbyterian Church. Union High School, Dawson, Tex., principal, 1942; Bible Memory Association International, St. Louis, Mo., founder and executive director, 1943—.

WRITINGS: A Pattern of Good Works (biography of T. J. Tanner), Cumberland Presbyterian Publishing House, 1941; *Into the Fray Unafraid*, Moody, 1944; *Unconsidered Factors in Global Peace*, Moody, 1944; *The Faith of Experience*, Eerdmans, 1953; *Building Gold, Silver and Precious Stones*, Dunham, 1955 (now issued under title *For All Eternity*, Books, Inc.); (editor) *Beside the Still Waters*, Miracle Press, 1960; (editor and author of biography) John Bunyan, *Heart's Ease for Heart Trouble*, Miracle Press, 1963; *The Infallible Word*, Moody, 1964; *An Exposition of Second Timothy*, Revell, 1973. Also editor of *Making Melody*, a song book published by Bible Memory Association, 1949, and deviser of ten bible games issued by Zondervan, Cross Publishing, and Miracle Press.

*   *   *

WRIGHT, Constance Choate   1897-

PERSONAL: Born October 30, 1897, in Brooklyn, N.Y.; daughter of Jonathan (a doctor) and Susan Osgood (Choate) Wright. *Education:* Attended Brearley School; Vassar College, B.A., 1918; Columbia University, M.A., 1920; Sorbonne, University of Paris, graduate student, 1922. *Residence:* Pleasantville, N.Y. *Agent:* John Shaffner, 896 Third Ave., New York, N.Y. 10022.

CAREER: Writer. *Member:* Cosmopolitan Club (New York).

WRITINGS: Silver Collar Boy, Dent, 1934, Dutton, 1935; *Their Ships Were Broken*, Dent, 1937, Dutton, 1938; *A Chance for Glory*, Holt, 1957; *Madame de Lafayette*, Holt, 1959; *A Daughter to Napoleon*, Holt, 1961; *A Royal Affinity*, Scribner, 1965; *Beautiful Enemy*, Dodd, 1969; *Fanny Kemble and the Lovely Land*, Dodd, 1972.

WORK IN PROGRESS: A book on Moliere.

SIDELIGHTS: Ms. Wright's books have had German, French, and Dutch editions; she is competent in French, and "a great lover of French culture."

*   *   *

WRIGHT, Deil S(pencer)   1930-

PERSONAL: Born June 18, 1930, in Three Rivers, Mich.; son of William H. and Gertrude (Buck) Wright; married Patricia M. Jaffke, August 22, 1953; children: David C., Mark W., Matthew D., Lois L. *Education:* University of Michigan, B.A., 1952, M.P.A., 1954, Ph.D., 1957. *Politics:* Republican. *Religion:* Methodist. *Home:* 323 Burlage Circle, Chapel Hill, N.C. 27514. *Office:* Department of Political Science, University of North Carolina, Chapel Hill, N.C.

CAREER: Wayne State University, Detroit, Mich., instructor, 1955, 1956-58, assistant professor of political science, 1958-59; University of Iowa, Iowa City, assistant professor, 1959-62, associate professor, 1962-67; University of North Carolina, Chapel Hill, professor of political science, 1967—. Visiting professor, University of California, Berkeley, 1965-66. Consultant to local government units in Detroit area, 1956-59, Cleveland Metropolitan Services Commission, 1958, Southwestern Pennsylvania Regional Planning Commission, 1964, Institute on State Programming for the 1970's, 1967-68; member of advisory committee to the director of National Institute of Health, 1970-74; member of North Carolina Council on Goals and Policies, 1973-77. *Member:* American Political Science Association, American Society for Public Administration, National Municipal League, American Association of University Professors, American Association for the Advancement of Science, Policy Studies Organization, Southern Political Science Association, Midwest Conference of Political Scientists, Phi Eta Sigma, Pi Sigma Alpha, Phi Kappa Phi.

WRITINGS: (Co-author) *Public Administration and the Public—Perspective Trends Toward Government in a Metropolitan Community*, Institute of Public Administration, University of Michigan, 1958; (co-author) *Profile of a Metropolis: A Casebook*, Wayne State University Press, 1962; *Trends and Variations in Local Finances: The Case of Iowa Counties*, Institute of Public Affairs, University of Iowa, 1965; *Federal Grants-in-Aid: Perspectives and Alternatives*, American Enterprize Association, 1968. Author of monographs. Contributor of more than forty articles and reviews to journals on government, public policy, and public administration.

WORK IN PROGRESS: Research on American state administrators; policy studies on general revenue sharing and health policy-making; articles, essays, and a monograph on intergovernmental relations.

*   *   *

WRIGHT, Dorothy   1910-

PERSONAL: Born January 4, 1910, in Derbyshire, England; daughter of Godfrey Fitzherbert (an ironmaster) and Maud F. B. Wright; married Charles Beattie Dix, 1971. *Education:* Studied at Abbey School, Malvern Wells, England, four years, and at art school, two years. *Home:* Long Whitstone, Bovey Tracey, Devon, England. *Agent:* Curtis Brown Ltd., 1 Craven Hill, London W2 3EW, England.

CAREER: London County Council, London, England, instructor in crafts, 1948-64; University of Reading, Museum of English Rural Life, Reading, England, attached for research, 1964-71. British War Office, junior civil assistant, 1943-46. *Member:* P.E.N.

WRITINGS: Gentle Phoenix, Heinemann, 1938; *Queen's Wilde*, Heinemann, 1950; *Advance in Love*, Heinemann, 1953; *Laurian and the Wolf*, Macmillan 1956; *Among the Cedars*, Macmillan 1959; *Baskets and Basketry* (nonfiction), Batsford, 1959, 3rd edition, David & Charles, 1972; *Beginning Patchwork*, Dryad Press, 1971. Also author of *A Caneworker's Book*, 1971.

Plays: *Cradle of Willows*, Evans Plays, 1952; *The Nightingale*, Evans Plays, 1956. Contributor to *Good Work* and *Crafts Review*.

WORK IN PROGRESS: Baskets Yesterday and Today, for David & Charles.

*   *   *

WRIGHT, Judith   1915-

PERSONAL: Born May 31, 1915, in Armidale, New South Wales, Australia; daughter of Phillip Arundell and Ethel (Bigg) Wright; married Jack Philip McKinney (a philosophical writer); children: Meredith Anne. *Education:* Attended New South Wales Correspondence School and New England Girls' School; University of Sydney, arts degree. *Politics:* Swing voter. *Home:* Long Rd., North Tamborine, Queensland, Australia.

CAREER: J. Walter Thompson (advertising agency), Sydney, Australia, secretary, 1938-39; University of Sydney, Sydney, Australia, secretary, 1940-42; Australian Universities Commission, Brisbane, Australia, clerk, 1944-46; University of Queensland, Brisbane, Queensland, Australia, statistician, 1946-49. Part time lecturer in Australian literature at various Australian universities. President, Wildlife Preservation Society of Queensland, 1962-63, 1963-64, 1964-65. *Member:* Society of Authors (Australia; council member), Australian Academy of the Humanities (fellow). *Awards, honors:* Grace Leven Prize, 1953; D.Litt., University of Queensland, 1962, University of New England, 1963; *Encyclopaedia Britannica* Award, 1964.

WRITINGS—Poetry: *The Moving Image*, Meanjin, 1946, revised edition, 1953; *Woman to Man*, Angus & Robertson, 1949, 2nd edition, 1955; *The Gateway*, Angus & Robertson, 1953; *The Two Fires*, Angus & Robertson, 1955; *Birds*, Angus & Robertson, 1962; *Five Senses*, Angus & Robertson, 1963, revised edition, 1972; *City Sunrise*, limited edition, Shapcott Press, 1964; *The Other Half*, Angus & Robertson, 1969; *Collected Poems*, Angus & Robertson, 1971.

Editor: *Australian Poetry*, Angus & Robertson, 1948; *A Book of Australian Verse*, Oxford University Press, 1956, 2nd revised edition, 1969; *New Land, New Language: An Anthology of Australian Verse*, Oxford University Press, 1957; *Judith Wright* (poetry), Angus & Robertson, 1963; *Shaw Neilson* (biography and selected poetry), Angus & Robertson, 1963; (with Andrew Kilpatrick) *The Poet's Pen*, Jacaranda, 1965.

Other: *The Generations of Men*, Oxford University Press, 1959, new edition, 1966; *Kings of the Dingoes* (juvenile), Oxford University Press, 1959; *Charles Harpur* (biography and criticism), Lansdowne Press, 1963; *The Day the Mountains Played* (juvenile), Angus & Robertson, 1963; *Range the Mountains High* (juvenile), Lansdowne Press, 1963; *Country Towns* (juvenile), Oxford University Press, 1964; *Preoccupations in Australian Poetry* (history and criticism), Oxford University Press, 1965, new edition, 1967; *The River and the Road* (juvenile), Lansdowne Press, 1966.

WORK IN PROGRESS: Completion of a book of verse; work on wildlife conservation in Australia.

* * *

WRIGHT, Theodore P(aul), Jr. 1926-

PERSONAL: Born April 12, 1926, in Port Washington, N.Y.; son of Theodore Paul (an aeronautical engineer) and Margaret (McCarl) Wright; married Susan J. Standfast (a physician), February 18, 1967; children: Henry Sewall, Margaret Standfast, Catherine Berrian. *Education:* Swarthmore College, B.A. (with high honors), 1949; Yale University, M.A., 1951, Ph.D., 1957. *Politics:* Conservative Democrat. *Religion:* Unitarian. *Office:* Graduate School of Public Affairs, State University of New York, Albany, N.Y.

CAREER: U.S. Department of Defense, research analyst, 1952-53; Bates College, Lewiston, Me., 1955-65, began as instructor, became associate professor of government; State University of New York, Albany, Graduate School of Public Affairs, associate professor, 1965-1972, professor of political science, 1971—. *Military service:* U.S. Navy,

1944-46. *Member:* American Political Science Association, Association for Asian Studies, American Association of University Professors, New England Political Science Association, Phi Beta Kappa. *Awards, honors:* Carnegie grant in Indian civilization, University of Chicago, 1961-62; Fulbright senior research grant for India, 1963-64; National Defense Foreign Language fellow, University of California, summer, 1967; American Institute of Indian Studies fellow, 1969-70; American Council of Learned Societies South Asia fellow, 1974-75.

WRITINGS: American Support of Free Elections Abroad, Public Affairs, 1964; (contributor) D. E. Smith, editor, *South Asian Politics and Religion*, Princeton University Press, 1966. Contributor of articles and reviews to political science journals in United States and India.

WORK IN PROGRESS: A book on politics of the Muslim minority in India since independence.

SIDELIGHTS: Wright traveled in Europe, 1948, 1951, 1953, Middle East, 1958, India and elsewhere in Southeast Asia, 1961, India, 1963-64 and 1969-70, Soviet Union, 1964. He has reading knowledge of French.

* * *

WRONSKI, Stanley P(aul) 1919-

PERSONAL: Born April 8, 1919, in Minneapolis, Minn.; son of John (a carpenter) and Katherine (Kotvis) Wronski; married Geraldine Breslin, May 27, 1943; children: Linda Ann, Mary Jo, Sandra Jean, John Stanley, Paul Stephen. *Education:* University of Minnesota, B.A., 1942, M.A., 1947, Ph.D., 1950. *Office:* College of Education, Michigan State University, East Lansing, Mich.

CAREER: Central Washington State College, Ellensburg, assistant professor, 1950-51; Boston University, Boston, Mass., assistant professor, 1951-54, associate professor of education, 1954-57; Michigan State University, East Lansing, associate professor, 1957-60, professor of education and social science, 1960—. Thai Ministry of Education, Bangkok, Thailand, adviser to Educational Planning Office, 1964-66; consultant to International Cooperation Administration, 1959, U.S. Office of Education, 1960-61. New England Economic Education Council, executive director, 1955-56. *Military service:* U.S. Navy, 1942-46, 1961-62; became commander.

MEMBER: American Academy of Political and Social Science, American Sociological Association, National Council for the Social Studies (board of directors, 1956-58), National Education Association, Michigan Council for the Social Studies (president, 1960), Phi Delta Kappa, Delta Sigma Rho.

WRITINGS: (Contributor) Roy O. Billett and J. Wendell Yeo, *Growing Up*, 2nd edition, Heath, 1958; (contributor) *Educating Citizens for Democracy*, edited by Richard E. Gross and Leslie D. Zeleny, Oxford University Press (New York), 1958; (with Carl H. Gross and John W. Hanson) *School and Society: Readings in the Social and Philosophical Foundations of Education*, Heath, 1962; (with Francis S. Doody and Richard V. Clemence) *Modern Economics*, Allyn & Bacon, 1964, teacher's manual and test questions with D. C. Davis; (with Edgar B. Wesley) *Teaching Social Studies in High Schools*, 5th edition, Heath, 1964.

Writer of bulletins for National Council for the Social Studies, for New England Economic Education Council, and for "American Industries Series." Contributor of articles and reviews to professional journals and yearbooks.

WORK IN PROGRESS: Working as educational adviser in Thailand, with plans for at least one publication based on this experience.

AVOCATIONAL INTERESTS: Golf (captain of University of Minnesota golf team, 1942, winner of Naval District I golf tournament, 1961).†

* * *

WYCOFF, Mary Elizabeth Jordan 1932-

PERSONAL: Born November 20, 1932, in Philadelphia, Pa.; daughter of Walter Edward (a clergyman) and Jeannette (Kinnear) Jordan; married William Randolph Wycoff (a clergyman), September 4, 1954; children: Walter Van-Kirk, Katharine Mary. *Education:* Baldwin School, graduate, 1950; College of Wooster, B.A., 1954; Princeton Theological Seminary, M.R.E., 1957. *Religion:* Protestant. *Home:* 1437 Stirling Dr., Wayne, Pa.

CAREER: George Washington Memorial Park, Plymouth Meeting, Pa., president, 1970—.

WRITINGS: Encounter with Early Teens, Westminster, 1965.

* * *

WYRICK, V(ictor) Neil, Jr. 1928-

PERSONAL: Born September 23, 1928, in Norfolk, Va.; son of Victor Neil (a pharmacist) and Dell (McCrary) Wyrick; married Mary Ann Cooke, December 16, 1950; children: Joy, Anne Lee, Dawn Elaine. *Education:* Hampden-Sydney College, B.A., 1950; Union Theological Seminary, Richmond, Va., B.D., 1954. *Home:* 5630 Southwest 64th Pl., Miami, Fla. 33143. *Office:* 6790 Southwest 56th St., Miami, Fla. 33155.

CAREER: Ordained Presbyterian minister, 1954; pastor of four churches near Brookneal, Va., 1954-55; Palmetto Presbyterian Church, Miami, Fla., founding pastor, 1955—. Founder of Biblical Miniatures, Inc., 1962; founder and director of Pageantry, Inc., 1963. Regular broadcaster of devotional programs on radio and television in Miami; conductor of Dial-A-Devotional service. Former chairman of drama department of Greater Miami Council of Churches; writer, director, and narrator of Easter Pageant in Orange Bowl, 1958—, and writer and director of Fourth of July Pageant in Orange Bowl, 1964, 1965.

WRITINGS: One-A-Day, Your Spiritual Vitamins, God's Power, 1963; *Boundaries Unlimited*, John Knox, 1965; *I Am*, Abingdon, 1966. Scriptwriter for film, "What Is a Minister?" and for two filmstrips produced by Miami Council of Churches. Columnist, "The Why of It All," in three Florida newspapers and *Trailer News*; contributor of twelve prayers annually to syndicated column, "Prayers for Today"; and contributor to *Family Circle, American Home, Rotarian*, and other general and religious periodicals.

WORK IN PROGRESS: God's Power for Man's Problems.

AVOCATIONAL INTERESTS: Freehand drawing, cartooning, flying (holds private pilot's license), bowling, skiing, tennis.†

* * *

YARROW, P(hilip) J(ohn) 1917-

PERSONAL: Born November 8, 1917, in Newcastle upon Tyne, Northumberland, England; son of Arthur John (a children's care officer) and Elvira Isabella (Truttmann) Yarrow; married Dorothy Fenton Joy; children: Anne Fenton, Anthony John. *Education:* Corpus Christi College, Cambridge, B.A., 1938. *Home:* 50 Moorside South, Newcastle upon Tyne, England. *Office:* Department of French Studies, University of Newcastle upon Tyne, Newcastle upon Tyne NE1 7RU, England.

CAREER: University of Exeter, Exeter, England, lecturer in French, 1947-63; University of Newcastle upon Tyne, Newcastle upon Tyne, England, professor of French, 1963—. *Military service:* British Army, Intelligence Corps, 1940-46; became captain. *Member:* Society for French Studies, Society for Italian Studies, Modern Humanities Research Association.

WRITINGS: (Editor) Moliere, *L'Avare*, University of London Press, 1958; (with J. Petit) *Barbey d'Aurevilly, Journaliste et Critique: Bibliographie*, Les Belles Lettres, 1959; *La Pensee politique et religieuse de Barbey d'Aurevilly*, Droz, 1961; *Corneille*, Macmillan, 1963; *A Literary History of France*, Benn, Volume II: *The Seventeenth Century*, 1967; (with Elizabeth Suddaby) *Lady Morgan in France*, Oriel Press, 1971; (editor) T. Corneille and D. de Vise, *La Devineresse*, University of Exeter, 1971; (editor) V. Hugo, *Chatiments*, Athlone Press, in press. Contributor of articles to *French Studies, Modern Language Review*, and other professional journals.

WORK IN PROGRESS: Racine.

SIDELIGHTS: Yarrow speaks French, German, and Italian.

* * *

YATES, Elizabeth 1905-
(Elizabeth McGreal)

PERSONAL: Born December 6, 1905, in Buffalo, N.Y.; daughter of Harry (a businessman) and Mary (Duffy) Yates; married William McGreal, November 6, 1929 (died, 1963). *Education:* Attended private school in Buffalo, N.Y., and studied abroad. *Home and office:* Shieling, Old Street Rd., Peterborough, N.H.

CAREER: Author. Staff member of writers' conferences at state universities; conductor of annual summer workshop at Christian Writers and Editors Conference, Green Lake, Wis. Member, State Library Commission; member of board of directors, New Hampshire Association for the Blind; trustee, Peterborough Town Library. *Member:* Delta Kappa Gamma. *Awards, honors: New York Herald Tribune* Spring Festival award, 1943, 1950; John Newbery Medal of American Library Association, 1951, and William Allen White Children's Book Award, 1953, both for *Amos Fortune, Free Man*; Annual Award of Women's International League for Peace and Freedom for *Rainbow Round the World*, a book about UNICEF; Litt.D., Aurora College, 1965; L.H.D., Eastern Baptist College, 1966, Keene State College, 1967, Ripon College, 1970, New England College, 1972; Sarah Josepha Hale Award, 1970.

WRITINGS: High Holiday, A. & C. Black, 1938; *Gathered Grace*, Heffer, 1938; *Hans and Frieda*, Nelson, 1939; *Climbing Higher*, A. & C. Black, 1939, published as *Quest in the Northland*, Knopf, 1940.

Haven for the Brave, Knopf, 1941; *Under the Little Fir*, Coward, 1942; *Around the Year in Iceland*, Heath, 1942; *Patterns on the Wall*, Knopf, 1943; *Mountain Born*, Coward, 1943; *Wind of Spring*, Coward, 1945; *Nearby*, Coward, 1947; *Once in the Year*, Coward, 1947; *The Young*

Traveller in the U.S.A., Phoenix House, 1948; *Beloved Bondage*, Coward, 1948.

Amos Fortune, Free Man, Aladdin Books, 1950; *Guardian Heart*, Coward, 1950; *Children of the Bible*, Aladdin Books, 1950; *Brave Interval*, Coward, 1952; *David Livingstone*, Row, Peterson & Co., 1952; *A Place for Peter*, Coward, 1952; *Hue and Cry*, Coward, 1953; *Your Prayers and Mine*, Houghton, 1954; *Rainbow Round the World*, Bobbs-Merrill, 1954; *Prudence Crandall, Woman of Courage*, Aladdin Books, 1955; *The Carey Girl*, Coward, 1956; *Pebble in a Pool: The Widening Circles of Dorothy Canfield Fisher's Life*, Dutton, 1958, published as *The Lady from Vermont: Dorothy Canfield Fisher's Life and World*, Greene, 1971.

The Lighted Heart, Dutton, 1960; *The Next Fine Day*, Day, 1962; *Someday You'll Write*, Dutton, 1962; *Sam's Secret Journal*, Friendship, 1964; *Carolina's Courage*, Dutton, 1964; *Howard Thurman: Portrait of a Practical Dreamer*, Day, 1964; *Up the Golden Stair*, Dutton, 1966; *Is There a Doctor in the Barn?*, 1966; *An Easter Story*, Dutton, 1967; *With Pipe, Paddle, and Song*, Dutton, 1968; *On That Night*, Dutton, 1969; *New Hampshire*, Coward, 1969.

Sarah Whitcher's Story, Dutton, 1971; *Skeezer: Dog with a Mission*, Harvey House, 1973; *The Road through Sandwich Notch*, Greene, 1973.

Editor: Enys Tregarthen, *Piskey Folk*, Day, 1940; Tregarthen, *The Doll Who Came Alive*, Day, 1942; (and author of foreword) *Joseph*, Knopf, 1947; Tregarthen, *The White Ring*, Harcourt, 1949; (and author of foreword) *The Christmas Story*, Knopf, 1949; George Macdonald, *Sir Gibbie*, Dutton, 1963.

SIDELIGHTS: Mrs. McGreal lived in London (where her husband's business was based) for ten years. Her first four books were published in England during that period; five others have had English editions since. The most widely translated are *The Young Traveller in the U.S.A.*, which appeared in Dutch, Japanese, and Israeli, and *Rainbow Round the World*, in German, Bengali, and Sinhalese.

* * *

YEARLEY, Clifton K(rebs), Jr. 1925-

PERSONAL: Born March 8, 1925, in Baltimore, Md.; son of Clifton Krebs and Fannye (Van Sant) Yearley; married Carlyn Prichett, August 24, 1946; children: Michael, Thomas, Scott. *Education:* Johns Hopkins University, A.B., 1950, Ph.D., 1953. *Politics:* Democrat. *Home:* 1 Fox Chapel Rd., Williamsville, N.Y. 14221. *Office:* Joseph Elliott Complex Room B 482, State University of New York, Amherst Campus, Buffalo, N.Y. 14261.

CAREER: Johns Hopkins University, Baltimore, Md., instructor in history, 1950-53; University of Delaware, Newark, instructor in History, 1953-54, assistant professor, 1955; University of Florida, Gainesville, instructor, 1954-57, assistant professor, 1957-62, associate professor of economic and social history, 1962-66; State University of New York, Buffalo, professor, 1966—, director of graduate studies, 1967-74, chairman of department, 1973—. Johns Hopkins University, McCoy College, summer assistant professor, 1955-62, associate professor of history, 1963. Fulbright lecturer in American history at University of Rome and University of Bologna, 1963-64. *Military service:* U.S. Navy, 1942-46; received two bronze stars. *Member:* American Historical Association, Economic History Associa-

tion, American Academy of Political Science, American Association of University Professors (member of executive board), Organization of American Historians, Phi Alpha Theta. *Awards, honors:* Fulbright-Hayes lectureship in Italy, 1963-64; Guggenheim fellowship, 1972-73; grants from American Philosophical Society and American History Research Center.

WRITINGS: Britons in American Labor, Johns Hopkins Press, 1957; *Enterprise and Anthracite*, Johns Hopkins Press, 1961; *The Money Machines*, State University of New York Press, 1971. Contributor of about thirty-five articles to national journals.

WORK IN PROGRESS: London, Paris, and New York: A Comparative Study, 1820-1940.

* * *

YECK, John D(avid) 1912-

PERSONAL: Born November 11, 1912, in Akron, Ohio; son of Augustus (a retail merchant) and Bertha Elizabeth (Schell) Yeck; married Willa Sanger, December 27, 1948; children: Joanne Louise. *Education:* Miami University, Oxford, Ohio, A.B., 1934. *Religion:* Presbyterian. *Home:* 3017 Locust Camp Rd., Dayton, Ohio 45419.

CAREER: Boy Scouts of America, Dayton, Ohio, assistant executive, 1934-38; Yeck Brothers Company (direct mail agency), Dayton, Ohio, partner, 1938—; Yeck & Yeck (sales and advertising counseling), Dayton, Ohio, partner, 1946—. *Member:* Direct Mail Educational Foundation (chairman of board, 1966—), Direct Mail/Marketing Association (board member, 1953-56, 1969—), Mail Advertising Service Association International (president, 1954-55, 1966—), Dayton Council on World Affairs (chairman, 1954-55), Dayton Advertising Club (president, 1941-42), Kiwanis Club. *Awards, honors:* Bishop Award from Miami University, 1961; Advertising Federation of America Silver Medal Award, 1961.

WRITINGS: (Contributor) *Copywriter's Guide*, Harper, 1959; (with John T. Maguire) *Planning and Creating Better Direct Mail*, McGraw, 1961; *How to Get Profitable Ideas*, McGraw, 1965.

* * *

YODER, John H(oward) 1927-

PERSONAL: Born December 29, 1927, in Smithville, Ohio; son of Howard Christian and Ethel (Good) Yoder; married Anne Marie Guth, July, 1952; children: Rebecca, Marthe, Daniel, Elisabeth, Esther, John David. *Education:* College of Wooster, student, 1944-45; Goshen College, B.A., 1947; University of Akron, graduate study, 1947-48; University of Basel, Ph.D., 1962. *Religion:* Mennonite. *Home:* 3100 Benham, Elkhart, Ind. 46514. *Office:* Associated Mennonite Biblical Seminaries, 3003 Benham, Elkhart, Ind. 46517.

CAREER: Mennonite Central Committee, director of postwar relief and social work for France, 1949-54; Associated Mennonite Biblical Seminaries, Elkhart, Ind., professor of theology, 1958—. Mennonite Board of Missions, administrative assistant for overseas, 1959-65. *Wartime service:* Conscientious objector, with alternative service, 1951-53. *Member:* American Society of Church History, Chicago Society for Biblical Research.

WRITINGS: (Translator) A. L. E. Verheyden, *Anabaptism in Flanders*, Herald, 1961; *The Christian and Capital Punishment*, Faith & Life, 1961; (translator) Hendrik Bekhof, *Christ and the Powers*, Herald, 1962; *The Christian Witness to the State*, Faith & Life, 1964; *The Original Revolution*, Herald, 1972; *Nevertheless*, Herald, 1972; *The Politics of Jesus*, Eerdmans, 1972. Editor of series of pamphlets, "Concern," 1957-61.

* * *

YOLEN, Jane H. 1939-

PERSONAL: Born February 11, 1939, in New York, N.Y.; daughter of Will Hyatt (a public relations man) and Isabelle (Berlin) Yolen; married David W. Stemple (a computer expert), September 2, 1962; children: Heidi Elisabet, Adam Douglas, Jason Frederic. *Education:* Smith College, B.A., 1960; New School for Social Research, graduate courses, 1960-63. *Politics:* Liberal Democrat. *Religion:* Quaker. *Home:* Phoenix Farm, 31 School St., Hartfield, Mass. 01038. *Agent:* Marilyn Marlowe, Curtis Brown Ltd., 60 East 56th St., New York, N.Y. 10022.

CAREER: Saturday Review (magazine), New York, N.Y., production assistant, 1960-61; Gold Medal Books (publishers), New York, N.Y., assistant editor, 1961-62; Rutledge Books (publishers), New York, N.Y., associate editor, 1962-63; Alfred A. Knopf, Inc. (publishers), New York, N.Y., assistant juvenile editor, 1963-65; full-time professional writer, 1965—. *Member:* Society of Childrens Book Writers (member of board of directors), Childrens Literature Association, American Civil Liberties Union, American Friends Service Committee, Central Committee for Conscientious Objectors, Citizens for Participation Politics.

WRITINGS—All juveniles: *See This Little Line*, McKay, 1963; *Pirates in Petticoats*, McKay, 1963; *The Witch Who Wasn't*, Macmillan, 1964; *Gwinellen, The Princess Who Could Not Sleep*, Macmillan, 1965; *Trust a City Kid*, Lothrop, 1966; *The Emperor and the Kite*, World Publishing, 1967; *The Minstrel and the Mountain*, World Publishing, 1967; *Isabel's Noel*, Funk, 1967; *The Longest Name on the Block*, Funk, 1968; *Greyling*, World Publishing, 1968; *World on a String*, World Publishing, 1968; *It All Depends*, Funk, 1969; *The Inway Investigators*, Seabury, 1969; *The Wizard of Washington Square*, World Publishing, 1969.

The Seventh Mandarin, Seabury, 1970; *Hobo Toad and the Motorcycle Gang*, World Publishing, 1970; *The Bird of Time*, Crowell, 1971; *The Fireside Song Book of Birds and Beasts*, Simon & Schuster, 1972; *Friend: The Story of George Fox and the Quakers*, Seabury, 1972; *The Girl Who Loved the Wind*, Crowell, 1972; *Zoo 2000*, Seabury, 1973; *The Wizard Islands*, Crowell, 1973; *The Adventures of Eera Mouse*, Weekly Reader Books, 1974; *The Girl Who Cried Flowers and Other Tales*, Crowell, 1974; *The Boy Who Had Wings*, Crowell, 1974; *The Rainbow Rider*, Crowell, 1974; *Ring Out! A Book of Bells*, Seabury, 1974; *The Magic Three of Solatia*, Crowell, 1974; *The Little Spotted Fish*, Seabury, 1974; *The Seeing Stick*, Crowell, in press; *Soul Fisher and Other Tales*, Crowell, in press; *An Invitation to the Butterfly Ball*, Parents' Magazine Press, in press.

Nonfiction: *Writing Books for Children*, Writer Inc., 1973.

Author of column "Children's Bookfare," in *Daily Hampshire Gazette*. Contributor of articles to *The Writer* and *Wilson Library Journal*, and book reviews to *New York Times*.

SIDELIGHTS: Jane Yolen told *CA:* "I generally write books for children ... because it is the one medium in which honesty must be the motivating force. Through fantasy, I feel I can say all I want to say about the real world and make myself understood—even by grown-ups." On penning children's books, Yolen wrote: "So, when you write for children, you must write as well as you would for an adult audience. Only better.... To me, a poet turned fantasist, each word, each sentence, each paragraph in a picture book must be polished. I write a sentence and then read it out loud before going on to the next. Then the paragraph is read aloud. Finally, the entire book is read and reread to the walls, to the bathtub, to the blank television, to my long-suffering husband." *Avocational interests:* Folk music and dancing, folk literature, politics, and the Elizabethan Age.

* * *

YOUNG, Charles R(obert) 1927-

PERSONAL: Born October 12, 1927, in Howard, Kan.; son of James Howard (a baker) and Gladys (Moffit) Young; married Betty Irene Osborne, March 7, 1946; children: Philip Howard, Janet Irene. *Education:* University of Kansas, A.B., 1949, M.A., 1950; Cornell University, Ph.D., 1954. *Religion:* Methodist. *Home:* 2929 Welcome Dr., Durham, N.C. 27705.

CAREER: Duke University, Durham, N.C., 1954—, began as instructor, associate professor, 1962-70, professor of history, 1970—. *Military service:* U.S. Naval Reserve, 1945-46. *Member:* American Historical Association, Mediaeval Academy of America, American Association of University Professors, Conference on British Studies, Southern Historical Association, Phi Beta Kappa.

WRITINGS: The English Borough and Royal Administration 1130-1307, Duke University Press, 1961; *Hubert Walter: Lord of Canterbury and Lord of England*, Duke University Press, 1968; (editor) *The Twelfth-Century Renaissance*, Holt, 1969. Contributor to *South Atlantic Quarterly*, *Church History*, *Journal of British Studies*, and *American Journal of Legal History*.

WORK IN PROGRESS: A book, *Royal Forests in Medieval England*.

SIDELIGHTS: Young spent 1961-62 in England doing research.

* * *

YOUNG, Donald 1933-

PERSONAL: Born June 29, 1933, in Indianapolis, Ind.; son of Thomas F. and Lucile (Boston) Young. *Education:* Indiana University, B.A., 1955; Butler University, M.A., 1964. *Home:* 166 East 61st St., New York, N.Y. 10021. *Office: Encyclopedia Americana*, 575 Lexington Ave., New York, N.Y. 10022.

CAREER: Indianapolis Star, Indianapolis, Ind., copy editor, 1955-63; *Encyclopedia Americana*, New York, N.Y., member of editorial staff, 1963-66; American Heritage Publishing Co., New York, N.Y., editorial staff, 1966-67; *Encyclopedia Americana*, senior editor, 1967—. *Military service:* U.S. Army, 1956-58. *Awards, honors:* Indiana University Author Award, 1965; Award of Merit, State Historical Society of Wisconsin, 1971.

WRITINGS: American Roulette: The History and Dilemma of the Vice-Presidency, Holt, 1965, 2nd revised edition, Viking, 1974; (contributor) Kenneth W. Leish, editor, *The American Heritage Pictorial History of the Presidents of the United States*, Simon & Schuster, 1968; (editor)

Adventure in Politics: The Memoirs of Philip La Follette, Holt, 1970. Assistant editor, "Smithsonian Library" series, American Heritage, 1967—. Contributor to *Encyclopedia Americana* yearbooks; also contributor to *Saturday Review*.

* * *

YOUNG, Dorothea Bennett 1924-
(Dorothea Bennett)

PERSONAL: Born January 28, 1924, in Burma; married Terrence Young (a film director). *Home:* Ferme des Roses, Huemoz sur Ollon, Vaud, Switzerland. *Agent:* Curtis Brown Ltd., 1 Craven Hill, London W2 3EW, England.

WRITINGS—Under name Dorothea Bennett: *Dry Taste of Fear*, Barker, 1960; *Under the Skin*, Barker, 1961, Mill, 1962. Writer of screen scripts.

AVOCATIONAL INTERESTS: Skiing, sailing, gardening.†

* * *

YOUNG, M(erwin) Crawford 1931-

PERSONAL: Born November 11, 1931, in Philadelphia, Pa.; son of Ralph Aubrey (an economist) and Louise M. (Merwin) Young; married Rebecca Conrad (a county board supervisor), August 17, 1957; children: Eva, Louise, Estelle, Emily. *Education:* University of Michigan, B.A., 1953; studied at Institute of Historical Research, University of London, 1955-56; Institut d'Etudes Politiques, University of Paris, 1956-57; Harvard University, Ph.D., 1964. *Home:* 639 Crandall St., Madison, Wis. *Office:* Department of Political Science, University of Wisconsin, Madison, Wis.

CAREER: Coordinating Secretariat of National Unions of Students, Leiden, Netherlands, associate secretary, 1957-59; University of Wisconsin, Madison, assistant professor, 1963-66, associate professor, 1966-69, professor of political science, 1969—. U.S. Department of State, consultant. *Military service:* U.S. Army, Infantry, 1953-55; became first lieutenant. *Member:* American Political Science Association, African Studies Association (member of board, 1969-73), Midwest Political Science Association.

WRITINGS: Politics in the Congo: Decolonization and Independence, Princeton University Press, 1965; (contributor) Gerhard Leibholz, editor, *Jahrbuch des Offentlichen Rechts der Gegenwart*, 1966; (contributor) Gwendolen M. Carter, editor, *Politics in Africa*, Harcourt, 1966; (with Charles W. Anderson and Fred R. Von der Mehden) *Issues of Political Development*, Prentice-Hall, 1967; (contributor) J. Kritzek and W. H. Lewis, editors, *Islam in Africa*, Van Nostrand, 1969; (contributor) A. A. Mazrui and R. I. Rotberg, editors, *Protest and Power in Black Africa*, Oxford University Press, 1970; (contributor) L. H. Gann and P. J. Dunigan, editors, *Colonialism in Africa*, Cambridge University Press, 1970; (contributor) M. F. Lofchie, editor, *The State of the Nations*, University of California Press, 1971. Contributor of chapters to books. Also regular contributor to *Africa Report*.

* * *

YOUNG, Percy M(arshall) 1912-
(Percy Marshall)

PERSONAL: Born May 17, 1912, in Northwich, England; son of William Joseph (a clerk) and Annie (Marshall) Young; married Anna Letitia Carson, August 7, 1937 (deceased); married Renee Morris, February 10, 1969. *Education:* Selwyn College, Cambridge, B.A. and Mus. D., 1937. *Politics:* Labour. *Religion:* Church of England. *Home:* 72 Clark Rd., Wolverhampton, WV3 9PA, England. *Agent:* A. P. Watt & Son, 26 Bedford Row, London W.C. 1R 4HL, England.

CAREER: Stranmillis Teacher's Training College, Belfast, Northern Ireland, director of music, 1934-37; musical adviser to city schools, Stoke on Trent, England, 1937-44; College of Technology, Wolverhampton, Staffordshire, England, director of music, 1944-65. Writer and composer. Visiting scholar, University Center, Georgia, 1971; visiting lecturer, Bucknell University, 1972. Member, Wolverhampton Borough Council, and Dolmetsch Foundation. International Society of Musicology, Royal Musical Association (associate member) Royal College of Organists, Incorporated Society of Musicians, Performing Rights Society, Gesellschaft fuer Musik-forshung, Society of Authors, National Book League, Royal Commonwealth Society, British-Caribbean Association, Hungarian Friendship Society, Hallische Haendel-Gesellschaft, Goettinger Haendel-Gesellschaft, Ernst Thaelmann Brigade (honorary member), Selwyn College Association, Grand Theatre Club, Old Blues, Wolverhampton Cricket Club, Wine Society. *Awards, honors:* Handel Prize, Halle, Germany, 1961.

WRITINGS: Pageant of England's Music, Heffer, 1939; *Handel*, Dutton, 1947, revised edition, Collier, 1963; *Music Is for You: A Guide to Music for Young People*, Lutterworth, 1948; *Introduction to the Music of Mendelssohn*, Dobson, 1949; *The Oratorios of Handel*, Dobson, 1949, Roy, 1950.

Music Makers, Dobson, 1951, Roy, 1953; *Messiah: Study in Interpretation*, Dobson, 1951; (compiler) *Carols for the Twelve Days of Christmas*, Dobson, 1952, Roy, 1954; *Vaughan Williams*, Dobson, 1953; *A Handbook of Choral Technique*, Dobson, 1953; *Biographical Dictionary of Composers, with Classified List of Music for Performance and Study*, Crowell, 1954 (published in England as *A Critical Dictionary of Composers and Their Music*, Dobson, 1954); *More Music Makers*, Roy, 1955; *Elgar, O.M.: A Study of a Musician*, Collins, 1955; *Instrumental Music*, Methuen, 1955, Roy, 1958; *The Story of Song*, Methuen, 1956, Roy, 1958; *In Search of Music*, Lutterworth, 1956; (editor and annotator) Edward W. Elgar, *Letters and Other Writings*, Bles, 1956; *Tragic Muse: The Life and Works of Robert Schumann*, Hutchinson, 1957, enlarged edition, Dobson, 1961; *Symphony*, Phoenix House, 1957, Crescendo, 1968; *Music and the Young Child*, McDougall's Educational Co., 1957; *Concerto*, Phoenix House, 1957; *Ding Dong Bell*, Dobson, 1957; *Read and Sing*, two books, Allen & Unwin, 1958; *Music Makers of Today*, Roy, 1958, 2nd edition, 1966.

Johann Sebastian Bach: The Story of His Life and Work, Boosey & Hawkes, 1960; *Music and Its Story*, Lutterworth, 1960, Roy, 1962, revised edition, 1970; *The Young Musician*, Nelson, 1961; *Musical Composition for Pleasure*, Hutchinson, 1961; *The Choral Tradition: An Historical and Analytical Survey from the Sixteenth Century to the Present Day*, Norton, 1962; (under pseudonym Percy Marshall) *Masters of the English Novel*, Dobson, 1962; *Music*, Nelson, 1963; *Zoltan Kodaly: A Hungarian Musician*, Benn, 1964; *Handel* (juvenile), Benn, 1965, David White, 1966; *Mozart*, Benn, 1965, David White, 1966; *The Current Tradition*, Roy, 1965; (editor) Edward Elgar, *Letters to Nimrod*, Dobson, 1965; *Music for Children*, Record

Books, 1965; *Beethoven*, David White, 1966; *World Composers*, Abelard, 1966; (under pseudonym Percy Marshall) *Masters of English Poetry*, Dobson, 1966; *World Conductors*, Abelard, 1966; *Britten*, David White, 1966; *Keyboard Musicians of the World*, Abelard, 1967; *A History of British Music*, Norton, 1967; *Great Ideas in Music*, Maxwell, 1967, David White, 1968; (editor) Edward Elgar, *A Future for English Music*, Dobson, 1968; *The Enjoyment of Music*, E.M.I. Records (London), 1968; *Debussy*, David White 1968; *Tchaikovsky*, David White, 1968; *Haydn*, David White, 1969; *Choral Music of the World*, Abelard, 1969; *Stravinsky*, David White, 1969.

Dvorak, David White, 1970; *Schubert*, David White, 1970; *The Bachs, 1500-1850*, Crowell, 1970; *Sir Arthur Sullivan*, Dent, 1971, Norton, 1972; *A Concise History of Music*, David White, 1974.

Sports books: *Football: Facts and Fancies: or The Art of Spectatorship*, Dobson, 1950; *Appreciation of Football*, Dobson 1951; *Football Year*, Phoenix House, 1956; *Football Through the Ages*, Methuen, 1957; *The Wolves: The First Eighty Years*, Stanley Paul, 1959; *Manchester United*, Heinemann, 1960; *Bolton Wanderers*, Stanley Paul, 1961; *Football in Sheffield*, Stanley Paul, 1962; *Football on Merseyside*, Stanley Paul, 1963; *A History of British Football*, Stanley Paul, 1968.

Editor, "Student Music Library" series, Dobson, 1951—. Contributor to *Grove's Dictionary of Music and Musicians*, *Book of Association Football*, and *Football Yearbook*; also contributor to *Encyclopaedia Britannica*, *Collier's Encyclopedia*, *World Book Encyclopedia*, *Children's Encyclopaedia*, and other publications in Germany and the United States.

WORK IN PROGRESS: Editing two collections, for Broude, *The Madrigal in the Romantic Era*, and *Music of the Great Churches*.

SIDELIGHTS: Young has traveled widely in Europe and North America in connection with research and lecturing. *Avocational interests:* Traveling, gardening, sports.

*   *   *

YOUNG, Peter   1915-

PERSONAL: Born July 28, 1915, in London, England; son of Dallas H. W. and Barbara (Mellor) Young; married Joan Duckworth, 1950. *Education:* Trinity College, Oxford, M.A., 1938; Staff College, Camberley, England, P.S.C. *Politics:* Royalist. *Home:* Bank House, Ripple, Tewkesbury, Gloucestershire GL20 6EP, England.

CAREER: British Army, 1937-59, retiring as brigadier; Royal Military Academy, Sandhurst, England, head of military history department, beginning, 1959. Served with British Expeditionary Force at Dunkirk, 1940 (wounded); with Commandos in raids on Norwegian coast, 1941, Dieppe, 1942, Sicily and Italy, 1943, Normandy, 1944, Burma, 1944-45; commander of First Commando Brigade, 1944-45, of Ninth Regiment, Arab Legion, 1953-56. *Member:* Royal Historical Society (fellow), Royal Archaeological Society, Society of Antiquaries of London (fellow). *Awards, honors*—Military: Distinguished Service Order, 1942; Military Cross, 1942, with two bars, 1943; Order of El Istiqlal (Jordan), 1954.

WRITINGS: Bedouin Command, Kimber & Co., 1956; *Storm From the Sea*, Kimber & Co., 1958; (with A. H. Burne) *The Great Civil War*, Eyre & Spottiswoode, 1959; *Cromwell*, Batsford, 1962; (with John Adair) *From Has-*

tings to Culloden, G. Bell, 1964; (contributor) *Great Military Battles*, Weidenfeld and Nicolson, 1964. Military editor of *Chambers's Encyclopaedia*.

WORK IN PROGRESS: A concise history of World War II; a history of the Royalist Army in the Great Civil War, 1642.

SIDELIGHTS: Young is an interpreter in French, has fair knowledge of Arabic and Italian, and knows some German. *Avocational interests:* Equitation, and collecting military books, pictures, and models.

*   *   *

YOUNG, Richard Knox   1913-

PERSONAL: Born 1913, in Roxboro, N.C.; married Mary Frances Vickers; children: Vicki Rose, Richard Knox, Jr., David. *Education:* Wake Forest College, B.A., 1943; Southern Baptist Theological Seminary, B.D., 1946, Th.D., 1952. *Home:* 414 North Stratford Rd., Winston-Salem, N.C. 27104. *Office:* North Carolina Baptist Hospital, Box 90, Winston-Salem, N.C. 27103.

CAREER: Ordained Baptist minister, 1946. North Carolina Baptist Hospital and Bowman Gray School of Medicine, Winston-Salem, N.C., 1946—, currently director of department of pastoral care; Southeastern Baptist Theological Seminary, Wake Forest, N.C., associate professor of pastoral care. *Member:* American Medical Association (medicine and religion committee), National Conference on Clinical Pastoral Education (executive committee), Chaplains' Division of the American Protestant Hospital Association (past president), Southwide Baptist Hospital Chaplains' Association (past president).

WRITINGS: The Pastor's Hospital Ministry, Broadman, 1954; (with Albert L. Meiburg) *Spiritual Therapy*, Harper, 1960.†

*   *   *

YOUNG, Virginia G(arton)   1919-

PERSONAL: Born January 16, 1919, in Mountain View, Mo.; daughter of Charles Clinton (an insurance executive) and Mattie Belle (Cartwright) Garton; married Raymond Arthur Young (executive vice-president of MFA Oil Co.), June 18, 1940; children: David Bruce. *Education:* Attended University of Missouri, 1936-37; Southwest Missouri State College (now University), A.B. (with high distinction), 1939; University of Oklahoma, library science degree, 1940. *Religion:* Protestant. *Home:* 10 East Parkway Dr., Columbia, Mo. 65201.

CAREER: Library consultant and writer. U.S. Department of Health, Education, and Welfare, member of advisory committee to U.S. Commissioner of Education, Library Services Branch, 1960-63; U.S. Department of Defense, member of Defense Advisory Committee on Women in the Services, 1963-65. Missouri State Library Commission, member, 1955—, and past president; Columbia (Mo.) Public Library Board, trustee, 1951-54, 1956-59, 1962-65, president, 1957-58, 1962-64. *Member:* American Library Trustee Association (president, 1956-61), Missouri Library Association (vice-president and membership chairman, 1953-55; president of trustees and citizens division, 1955-57; co-chairman of legislative committee, 1956-57), Friends of University of Missouri Library (board, 1960-64; president, 1964-66), Academy of Missouri Squires. *Awards, honors:* Citation for meritorious achievement, Missouri Library Association, 1956; American Library Association trustee citation of merit, 1962.

WRITINGS: (Contributor) Winser, *Handbook for Library Trustees*, Bowker, 1959; *The Trustee of a Small Public Library*, American Library Association, 1962; (editor) *The Library Trustee: A Practical Guidebook*, Bowker, 1964, 2nd edition, 1969. Contributor to *Library Journal, Wilson Library Bulletin*, and a number of other national and state library periodicals.†

*   *   *

YOUNG, Warren C(ameron) 1913-

PERSONAL: Born December 25, 1913, on Prince Edward Island, Canada; son of Walter Burns (a farmer) and Margaret (Bruce) Young; married Alda Helena Jones (a teacher), June 9, 1943; children: Judith Ann, Karen Alane, Lynn Adele. *Education:* Gordon College, A.B., 1942; Boston University, A.M., 1944, Ph.D., 1946; Northern Baptist Theological Seminary, B.D., 1948; graduate study at University of Heidelberg. *Home:* 1490 Briar Cove, Wheaton, Ill. 60187.

CAREER: Ordained Baptist minister, 1944. Northern Baptist Theological Seminary, Oak Brook, Ill., professor of Christian theology and philosophy, 1946—. *Member:* American Theological Society, American Philosophical Association, American Academy of Religion, Society for Scientific Study of Religion, Evangelical Theological Society, Chicago Society of Biblical Research.

WRITINGS: A Christian Approach to Philosophy, Baker Book, 1954; (contributor) C.F.H. Henry, editor, *Christian Faith and Modern Theology*, Channel Press, 1964. Contributor of articles and reviews to religious journals.

SIDELIGHTS: Young speaks and reads German; he reads French.

*   *   *

YOUNG, Wayland 1923-

PERSONAL: Born August 2, 1923, son of Edward Hilton (first Lord Kennet) and Kathleen (Bruce) Young; married Elizabeth Adams (a writer), 1948; children: Easter, Emily, Mopsa, Thoby, Louise, Zoe. *Education:* Trinity College, Cambridge, B.A., 1946; additional study at University of Perugia and Harvard University. *Politics:* Labour Party. *Home:* 100 Bayswater Rd., London W2 3HJ, England. *Agent:* A. P. Watt & Son, 26-28 Bedford Row, London WC1R 4HL England.

CAREER: Writer; succeeded father to title as Lord Kennet, 1960. With British Foreign Office, 1946-47, 1949-51; *Observer*, London, England, correspondent in Rome and North Africa, 1953-55; member of parliamentary delegations to Council of Europe and Western Europe Union, 1962-65; *Manchester Guardian Weekly*, Manchester, England, columnist, 1966-70; British Government, London, England, minister responsible for environment and planning, 1970—. Chairman, International conferences on the Human Environment. Director, European Community Project. *Military service:* Royal Navy, 1942-45; became sub-lieutenant. *Member:* Institute of Strategic Studies.

WRITINGS: The Italian Left, Longmans, Green, 1949; *The Deadweight*, Cresset, 1952; *Now or Never*, Cresset, 1953; (with wife, Elizabeth Young) *Old London Churches*, Faber, 1956; *The Montesi Scandal*, Doubleday, 1957; *Still Alive Tomorrow*, Cresset, 1958; *Strategy for Survival*, Penguin, 1959; (with Elizabeth Young) *The Socialist Imagination*, Fabian Society, 1960; (with Elizabeth Young) *Disarmament: Finnegan's Choice*, Fabian Society, 1961; *The*

Profumo Affair, Penguin, 1963; *Eros Denied*, Grove Press, 1964; *Thirty-Four Articles*, Weidenfeld & Nicolson, 1965; *Existing Mechanisms of Arms Control*, Pergamon, 1965; *Preservation*, Maurice T. Smith, 1972. Television writer for British Broadcasting Corp. and Granada Television. Editor, *Disarmament and Arms Control*.

SIDELIGHTS: Young speaks French and Italian.

*   *   *

YOUNGS, Robert W(ells) 1913-

PERSONAL: Born March 10, 1913, in Auburn, N.Y.; son of Lewis Brooks (a teacher) and Florence (Wells) Youngs; married Adele Buckwalter, March 28, 1936; children: Ruth (Mrs. Charles McCaslin), Edwin B., Martha (Mrs. Stephen Fuller), Elizabeth H. *Education:* College of Wooster, B.A., 1935; Auburn Theological Seminary, B.Th., 1938. *Home:* 235 Patton Dr., Wichita, Kan. 67208. *Office:* 525 North Broadway, Wichita, Kan. 67214.

CAREER: Presbyterian minister, 1938—; First Presbyterian Church, Wichita, Kan., senior minister, 1959—. Parsons College, member of board of trustees. *Military service:* U.S. Naval Reserve, chaplain, World War II. *Awards, honors:* Freedoms Foundation Award.

WRITINGS: (Contributor) *Golden Moments of Religious Inspiration*, McGraw, 1954; *What It Means to Be a Christian*, Farrar, Straus, 1960; (contributor) *How to Get What You Want Out of Life*, edited by Mel Hickerson, Appleton, 1962; *Renewing Your Faith Day by Day*, Doubleday, 1965.†

*   *   *

YOXALL, Harry W(aldo) 1896-
(F. H. Partington)

PERSONAL: Born June 4, 1896, in Richmond, Surrey, England; son of Sir James Henry (an educator and member of Parliament) and Lady Elizabeth (Coles) Yoxall; married Josephine Fairchild Baldwin, June 29, 1918; children: Lindsey Elizabeth Yoxall Pietrzak, Nicholas Baldwin. *Education:* Balliol College, Oxford, Diploma in Economics and Political Science. *Religion:* Church of England.

CAREER: Conde Nast Publications, Inc., New York, N.Y., promotion writer, 1921-24; Conde Nast Publications Ltd., London, England, business manager and director, 1924-37, managing director, 1937-57, chairman of board, 1957-64. Justice of the Peace, Richmond, Surrey, England, 1941—. Periodical Proprietors' Association, president, 1956-59, vice-president, 1959-65; International Federation of the Periodical Press, vice-president, 1960-65. *Member:* Savile Club, Royal Automobile Club, Richmond Golf, Saintsbury Club.

WRITINGS: Modern Love, Faber & Gower, 1927; *All Abroad*, Faber & Gower, 1928; *A Respectable Man*, Barker, 1935; *Journey Into Faith*, Mowbray, 1963; *Forty Years in Management*, British Broadcasting Corp., 1964; *A Fashion of Life* (autobiography), Heineman, 1966, Taplinger, 1967; *The International Wine and Food Society's Guide to the Wines of Burgundy*, M. Joseph, 1968, Stein & Day, 1970; *Retirement a Pleasure: Or Out but Not Down*, Hamilton, 1971; *The Enjoyment of Wine*, M. Joseph, 1972, Drake Publishers, 1973. Contributor of articles to journals, some under pseudonym F. H. Partington.

AVOCATIONAL INTERESTS: Travel, wine, golf, and bridge.†

YUDKIN, John 1910

PERSONAL: Born August 8, 1910, in London, England; son of Louis (a merchant) and Sarah (Itkin) Yudkin; married Milly Himmelweit, December 17, 1933; children: Michael David, Jonathan, Jeremy. *Education:* Studied at Chelsea College of Science and Technology, 1927-29, Christ's College, Cambridge, 1929-34, 1938-43, London Hospital Medical College, 1934-38; B.Sc. (London), B.A., M.A., M.B., M.D., and Ph.D. (Cambridge). *Home:* 16 Holly Walk, Hampstead, London N.W. 3, England.

CAREER: Cambridge University, Christ's College, Cambridge, England, director of medical studies, 1940-43; University of London, Queen Elizabeth College, London, England, professor of physiology, 1945-53, professor of nutrition, 1953-71, professor emeritus, 1971—. *Military service:* Royal Army Medical Corps, 1943-45; became captain. *Member:* Royal Institute of Chemistry (fellow), Royal Society of Medicine (fellow), Royal College of Physicians, other scientific societies. *Awards, honors:* William Julius Mickle Fellow, University of London, 1961-62, for most important contribution to medicine over a five-year period.

WRITINGS: This Slimming Business, MacGibbon & Kee, 1958; (with Gweneth M. Chappel) *The Slimmer's Cookbook*, MacGibbon & Kee, 1961; *The Complete Slimmer*, MacGibbon & Kee, 1964; (editor with John C. McKenzie) *Changing Food Habits*, MacGibbon & Kee, 1964; (editor with McKenzie and Theodore C. Barker) *Our Changing Fare*, MacGibbon & Kee, 1966; *Pure, White and Deadly: The Problem of Sugar*, Davis-Poynter, 1972. Contributor of scientific and medical articles to *British Medical Journal, Lancet*, and other journals, and popular articles to *Family Doctor* and other magazines.

WORK IN PROGRESS: Nutritional research, particularly with regard to food habits and coronary thrombosis.

*   *   *

YURICK, Sol 1925-

PERSONAL: Born January 18, 1925, in New York, N.Y.; son of Samuel and Florence (Weinstein) Yurick; married Adrienne L. Lash, November, 1958; children: Susanna. *Education:* New York University, B.A., 1950; Brooklyn College of the City University of New York, M.A., 1961. *Home:* 949 President St., Brooklyn, N.Y. 11215. *Agent:* Georges Borchardt, Inc., 145 East 52nd St., New York, N.Y. 10022.

CAREER: New York University, New York, N.Y., librarian, 1945-53; New York City Department of Welfare, social investigator, 1954-59; writer, 1961—. *Military service:* U.S. Army, 1944-45.

WRITINGS: The Warriors (novel), Holt, 1965; *Fertig* (novel), Trident, 1966; *The Bag* (novel), Trident, 1968; *Someone Just Like You* (short stories), Harper, 1972; (editor) *Voices of Brooklyn* (anthology), American Library Association, 1973. Work is represented in anthologies, including *Literature of Revolution*, edited by G. White and C. Newman, Holt, 1971. Contributor to *Nation, Evergreen Review, Tri-Quarterly,* and *Transatlantic Review.*

WORK IN PROGRESS: A novel, *Sound Money Kill*; a nonfiction work, *Burning the Bank of America.*

SIDELIGHTS: "Rage is the fuel that makes Sol Yurick's fiction burn," notes Christopher Lehmann-Haupt, "—a revolutionist's rage at the urban bureaucratic machine that flattens people into forgotten file drawers," an analysis in keeping with Yurick's own contention that writing should

"define the screams of the people." John Leonard writes that Yurick's achievement in *The Bag* is "stunning because it is multiple; he has created real characters, from every social stratum; mastered their life-styles and their prose styles; resisted caricature and risked sympathy.... With rare responsibility he has brilliantly conceived and powerfully executed a portrait of the sight, sound, smell and taste of Urban Now, beneath the plastic; and he has renewed the novel as a social transaction."

*   *   *

YZERMANS, Vincent Arthur 1925-

PERSONAL: Born December 2, 1925, in St. Paul, Minn.; son of Alfons A. and Katherine (Fahey) Yzermans. *Education:* Crosier Seminary, Onamia, Minn., student, 1939-45; St. Paul Seminary, St. Paul, Minn., B.A., 1951; Fordham University, graduate study, summers of 1955, 1956. *Home:* 4001 14th St., N.E., Washington, D.C. *Office:* National Catholic Welfare Conference, 1312 Massachusetts Ave., N.W., Washington, D.C. 20005.

CAREER: Roman Catholic priest; National Catholic Welfare Conference, Washington, D.C., director of Bureau of Information, 1964—. *Member:* Catholic Theological Society, Catholic Historical Society, Minnesota Newspaper Association, National Press Club. *Awards, honors:* Frank Murray journalism award, 1964.

WRITINGS: The Popes Speak of Mary, 1854-1954, Continental Press, 1954; *All Things in Christ*, Newman, 1955; *Pius XII and the American People*, Helicon, 1958; *Major Addresses of Pius XII*, North Central Publishing, 1962; *Death and Resurrection: Meditations on Holy Week from the Church Fathers*, Liturgical Press, 1963; *A New Pentecost*, Newman, 1964; *Our Lady of the Runestone*, Franciscan Herald Press, 1964; (editor) *American Participation in the Second Vatican Council*, Sheed, 1968. Contributor to Catholic magazines and journals.

WORK IN PROGRESS: Research for a book on Pope Vigilius.†

*   *   *

ZATURENSKA, Marya 1902-

PERSONAL: Born September 12, 1902, in Kiev, Russia; came to United States, 1909, naturalized citizen, 1912; daughter of Avram Alexander and Johanna (Lupovska) Zaturensky; married Horace Gregory (poet and critic), August 21, 1925; children: Joanna (Mrs. Samuel Howell Zeigler), Patrick. *Education:* Attended Valparaiso University, 1922-23, University of Wisconsin, 1923-25. *Home:* Palisades, Rockland County, N.Y.

CAREER: Writer, 1919—. *Awards, Honors:* John Reed Memorial Award (*Poetry* magazine), 1922; Shelley Memorial Award, 1935; Guarantors Award (*Poetry* magazine), 1937; Pulitzer Prize in Poetry, 1938, for *Cold Morning Sky.*

WRITINGS: Threshold and Hearth (poems), Macmillan, 1934; *Cold Morning Sky* (poems), Macmillan, 1937; *Listening Landscape* (poems), Macmillan, 1941; *Golden Mirror* (poems), Macmillan, 1943; (with husband, Horace Gregory) *A History of American Poetry*, Harcourt, 1946; *Christina Rossetti* (biography), Macmillan, 1949; *Selected Poems*, Grove, 1951; (editor with Horace Gregory) *The Mentor Book of Religious Verse*, New American Library, 1957; *Terraces of Light* (poems), Grove, 1960; (editor with Horace Gregory) *The Crystal Cabinet*, Holt, 1962; (author of introduction) A. C. Swinburne, *Love's Cross Currents,*

New American Library, 1964; *Collected Poems*, Viking, 1965; (compiler with Horace Gregory) *The Silver Swan: Poems of Romance and Mystery*, Holt, 1966; *The Hidden Waterfall* (poems), Vanguard, 1974. Contributor to *New Republic, Poetry, Virginia Quarterly Review, Atlantic*, and other publications.

* * *

ZAWODNY, J(anusz) K(azimierz) 1921-

PERSONAL: Born December 11, 1921, in Warsaw, Poland; naturalized American citizen; married La Rae Koppit; children: Roman Janusz. *Education:* London School of Foreign Trade, diploma, 1948; University of Iowa, B.S., 1950, M.A., 1951; Stanford University, Ph.D., 1955, postdoctoral study in psychology, 1958-59. *Office:* Political Science Department, Wharton School, University of Pennsylvania, Philadelphia, Pa. 19104.

CAREER: Princeton University, Princeton, N.J., instructor, 1955-57, assistant professor, 1957-58; University of Pennsylvania, Philadelphia, associate professor, 1962-63; Washington University, St. Louis, Mo., professor, 1963-65; University of Pennsylvania, Wharton School, professor of international relations, 1965—. Research associate, Harvard University Center for International Affairs, 1968; senior associate, St. Anthony's College, Oxford University, 1968-69; member of Institute for Advanced Study, 1971-72. *Military service:* Polish Underground Forces, 1940-44; became 2nd lieutenant; 2nd Polish Corps, attached to Eighth British Army, 1945-48; lieutenant; holds orders of Virtuti Militari, Commander Polona Restituta, Krzyz Walecznych. *Awards, honors:* Fellow, Social Science Research Council, 1953-54; fellow, Center for Advanced Study in the Behavioral Sciences, 1962-63.

WRITINGS: Death in the Forest: The Story of the Katyn Forest Massacre, University of Notre Dame Press, 1962; *Guide to The Study of International Relations*, Chandler Publishing, 1966; (editor and contributor) *Man and International Relations: Contributions of the Social Sciences to the Study of Conflict and Integration*, two volumes, Chandler Publishing, 1967. Contributor to *International Encyclopedia of Social Sciences*, and to scholarly journals, including *Annals of American Academy of Political and Social Science, American Scholar, Soviet Studies, Industrial and Labor Relations Review*.

WORK IN PROGRESS: Uprising of Warsaw, 1944.

* * *

ZEIGLER, L(uther) Harmon 1936-

PERSONAL: Surname is pronounced *Zeeg*-ler; born March 9, 1936, in Savannah, Ga.; son of Luther Harmon (a lawyer) and Sarah (Betts) Zeigler; married Patricia Duffy, December 16, 1956; children: Michael, Amanda. *Education:* Emory University, A.B., 1957; University of Illinois, M.A., 1958, Ph.D., 1960. *Politics:* Democrat. *Religion:* Episcopal. *Home:* 1950 Graham Dr., Eugene, Ore. 97405. *Office:* Department of Political Science, University of Oregon, Eugene, Ore. 97403; C.A.S.E.A., 1472 Kincaid, University of Oregon, Eugene, Ore. 97401.

CAREER: Assistant professor of political science at Florida State University, Tallahassee, 1960-61, Emory University, Atlanta, Ga., 1961-63, University of Georgia, Athens, 1963-64; University of Oregon, Eugene, associate professor, 1964-67, professor of political science, 1967—, Center for the Advanced Study of Educational Administra-

tion, research associate, 1964-67, program director, 1967—, director of Institute of Policy Studies, 1973—. Visiting professor, University of Washington, 1966, University of Oslo, 1972; visiting lecturer, University of Gothenburg, 1972. *Member:* American Political Science Association. *Awards, honors:* Ford Foundation faculty research fellowship, 1969; Guggenheim Foundation fellowship, 1969-70; International Research and Exchanges Board grant, for work at Soviet Academy of Sciences, U.S.S.R., 1972.

WRITINGS: The Politics of Small Business, Public Affairs, 1961; *Interest Groups in American Society*, Prentice-Hall, 1964, 2nd edition, 1972; (with Alvin Boskoff) *Voting Patterns in a Local Election*, Lippincott, 1964; (editor with Kent Jennings) *The Electoral Process*, Prentice-Hall, 1966; *The Political World of the High School Teacher*, Center for the Advanced Study of Educational Administration, University of Oregon, 1966; *The Political Life of American Teachers*, Prentice-Hall, 1967; (with Michael Baer) *Lobbying: Interaction and Influence in American State Legislatures*, Wadsworth, 1969; (with Thomas R. Dye) *The Irony of Democracy*, Wadsworth, 1970, 3rd edition, in press; (editor with Dye) *The Few and the Many*, Duxbury Press, 1972; (with Karl Johnson) *The Politics of Education in the States*, Bobbs-Merrill, 1972; (with Jennings and Wayne Peak) *Governing American Schools: Political Interaction in Local School Districts*, Duxbury Press, 1974. Contributor to numerous political science, social science, and educational journals.

WORK IN PROGRESS: School Boards and the Politics of Education, based on interviews with members of school boards and superintendents in ninety-seven school districts, for the Center for the Advanced Study of Educational Administration; *The Superintendent: Politician or Manager*, a continuation of the research mentioned above; *Past, Present, and Future: A New Introduction to Political Science*, an application of Delphi techniques to the estimations of the probability of various political events; *The Responsiveness of Public Schools to Their Clientele*, for the National Institute of Education, 1972-76, a longitudinal study of demands and responses in twelve school districts; and a basic introduction text to political science.

SIDELIGHTS: Zeigler has traveled extensively in South America and Europe. He is proficient in French and German.

* * *

ZEITLIN, Maurice 1935-

PERSONAL: Born February 24, 1935, in Detroit, Mich.; son of Albert Joseph and Rose (Goldberg) Zeitlin; married Marilyn Geller, March 1, 1959; children: Michelle Deborah, Carla Simone. *Education:* Wayne State University, B.A., 1957; University of California, Berkeley, M.A., 1960, Ph.D., 1964. *Politics:* Independent. *Religion:* Jewish. *Home:* 2437 Allied Dr., Madison, Wis. 53711.

CAREER: Princeton University, Princeton, N.J., instructor in sociology and anthropology, 1961-63, research associate of Center of International Studies, 1962-64; University of Wisconsin, Madison, assistant professor, 1964-67, associate professor, 1967-70, professor of sociology, 1970—. Visiting professor, University of California, Santa Barbara, 1970-71, Hebrew University, Jerusalem, Israel, 1971-72. *Member:* American Sociological Association, Monthly Review Associates, American Historical Association, American Civil Liberties Union, American Association of University Professors. *Awards, honors:* Woodrow

Wilson Foundation fellowship in sociology, 1959-61; Ford Foundation postdoctoral fellowship in Latin American studies, 1965-67; Louis M. Rabinowitz Foundation Grant, 1969-70; Ford Foundation research fellowship and American Philosophical Society grant, 1970-71.

WRITINGS: (With Robert Scheer) *Cuba: Tragedy in Our Hemisphere*, Grove, 1963, revised edition published as *Cuba, An American Tragedy*, Penguin, 1964; *Revolutionary Politics and the Cuban Working Class*, Princeton University Press, 1967; (compiler with James Petras) *Latin America: Reform or Revolution?*, Fawcett, 1968; (with Petras) *El radicalismo politico de la clase trabajadora chilena*, Centro Editor de America Latina, 1969, revised edition, 1970; (compiler) *American Society, Inc.: Studies of the Social Structure and Political Economy of the United States*, Markham, 1970. Contributor of articles to *Sociological Review, Blaetter fuer Deutsche und Internationale Politik, New University Thought, Liberation*, and *Nation*, and reviews to other journals. Co-editor, *Root and Branch: A Journal of Politics and Culture.*

WORK IN PROGRESS: Research in Chile and Argentina for book on workers and peasants in politics.

SIDELIGHTS: Zeitlin speaks Spanish and Hebrew and reads French and German.

BIOGRAPHICAL/CRITICAL SOURCES: Realist, September, 1963; "America from Inside," *Shiso No Kagaku*, Volume I, Number 10, 1963.†

* * *

ZELINSKY, Wilbur 1921-

PERSONAL: Born December 21, 1921, in Chicago, Ill.; son of Louis and Esther (Mastoon) Zelinsky; married Gladys Florence Epstein, July 5, 1944; children: Karen Jay, Hollis Gay. *Education:* Studied at Wright Junior College, 1939-40, University of Chicago, 1939-40, 1943, Columbia Technical Institute, Washington, D.C., 1941-42, George Washington University, 1942, University of North Carolina, 1943; University of California, Berkeley, B.A. (with honors), 1944, Ph.D., 1953; University of Wisconsin, M.A., 1946. *Home:* 467 Martin Ter., State College, Pa. 16801. *Office:* Pennsylvania State University, University Park, Pa. 16802.

CAREER: Map draftsman for firms in Washington, D.C., 1942-43, Chicago, Ill., 1943, and New York, N.Y., 1944-45; U.S. Army, Corps of Engineers, terrain analyst in American Occupation Zone of Germany, 1946; University of Georgia, Athens, assistant professor of geography, 1948-52; University of Wisconsin, Madison, project associate in geography, 1952-54; Chesapeake & Ohio Railway Co., Detroit, Mich., industrial analyst, 1954-59; Southern Illinois University, Carbondale, professor of geography, 1959-63; Pennsylvania State University, University Park, professor of geography, 1963—. Wayne State University, special instructor in geography, 1955-59.

MEMBER: Association of American Geographers (chairman of West Lakes Division, 1959-61; national president, 1972-73), American Geographical Society, Population Association of America, American Name Society, Society for the History of Discoveries, International Union for the Scientific Study of Population.

WRITINGS: (Contributor) Robert S. Platt, editor, *Field Study in American Geography*, Department of Geography, University of Chicago, 1959; (contributor) G. H. T. Kimble, *Tropical Africa*, Volume I, Twentieth Century Fund, 1960; (contributor) *Readings in Cultural Geography*, edited by Marvin W. Mikesell and Philip L. Wagner, University of Chicago Press, 1962; *A Bibliographic Guide to Population Geography*, Department of Geography, University of Chicago, 1962; (editor with Martha Church and Robert E. Huke) *A Basic Geographical Library: A Selected, Annotated List for American Colleges*, Association of American Geographers, 1965; *A Prologue to Population Geography*, Prentice-Hall, 1966; *The Cultural Geography of the United States*, Prentice-Hall, 1973.

Contributor to proceedings and annals of geographical societies and to journals, with more than twenty articles in *Journal of Negro History, Focus, Social Forces, Economic Geography*, and other related periodicals.

SIDELIGHTS: Zelinsky reads French, German, and Spanish; has partial command of Portuguese, Russian, Latin, and Greek. He is an amateur violinist.

* * *

ZIEGLER, Raymond J. 1922-

PERSONAL: Born August 28, 1922, in Toledo, Ohio; son of John M. and Elsa A. (Jacobs) Ziegler; married Ella Sue Garrett, September 26, 1955; children: James G. *Education:* University of Toledo, B.B.A., 1946, M.B.A., 1948; University of Florida, Ph.D., 1957. *Office:* Merrimack College, North Andover, Mass.

CAREER: Assistant professor at University of North Dakota, Grand Forks, 1952-54, Marquette University, Milwaukee, Wis., 1954-55; associate professor at Washington State University, Pullman, 1955-58, Kent State University, Kent, Ohio, 1958-60, University of Illinois, Urbana, 1960-64; Merrimack College, North Andover, Mass., professor of management and director of Division of Business, 1964-66; Cleveland State University, Cleveland, Ohio, professor, 1966-68, associate dean of College of Business Administration, 1968-71; Florida Southern College, Lakeland, professor of management, 1972—. Visiting professor, University of Oregon, 1962-63, Northwestern University, 1966-67. Employed in management posts at various times with Libbey-Owens-Ford Glass Co., Keuhmann Foods, Inc., Nordmann Roofing Corp., and Flourney & Gibbs (publicity and public relations). *Member:* American Economic Association, American Statistics Association, Society for Advancement of Management, Academy of Management, American Association of University Professors, Delta Sigma Pi.

WRITINGS: Principles of Industrial Management Casebook (with solutions manual), Macmillan, 1961; *Casebook in Production Management*, Wiley, 1962; (with Hodges) *Managing the Industrial Concern*, Houghton, 1963; *Current Cases in Business*, C. E. Merrill, 1964; *Business Policies and Decision Making*, Appleton, 1966. Contributor to business and management periodicals.

WORK IN PROGRESS: Introduction to Production Management, for Irwin; research on policy issues facing some fifty corporations.†

* * *

ZIFF, Larzer 1927-

PERSONAL: Born October 2, 1927, in Holyoke, Mass.; son of Isadore Menden (a manufacturer) and Sara (Rosenbloom) Ziff; married Linda Geisenberger, March 21, 1951; children: Joshua, Oliver, Joel, Abigail. *Education:* Middlebury College, student, 1945-47; University of Chicago,

M.A., 1950, Ph.D., 1955. *Office:* Exeter College, Oxford University, Oxford, England.

CAREER: University of Chicago, Chicago, Ill., director of academic programs at University College, 1954-56; University of California, Berkeley, professor of English, 1965-73; Oxford University, Exeter College, Oxford, England, university lecturer and fellow, 1973—. Fulbright Professor at University of Copenhagen, 1959-60, University of Warsaw, 1963, and University of Sussex, 1964. Consultant in English to Miles College, Birmingham, Ala.; member of State of California Commission on Teachers' Professional Standards. *Member:* Modern Language Association of America (chairman, literature and society section, 1965), American Studies Association. *Awards, honors:* Huntington Library fellow, 1958; Newberry Library fellow, 1964; American Council of Learned Societies fellow, 1964-65; National Endowment for the Humanities senior research fellow, 1968-69; Christian Gauss Award from Phi Beta Kappa, 1967, for *The American 1890s*; National Book Award nominee, 1974.

WRITINGS: (Editor) *Writings of Benjamin Franklin*, Rinehart, 1959; (editor) Thoreau, *Walden*, Holt, 1961; *The Career of John Cotton*, Princeton University Press, 1962; (editor) Hawthorne, *The Scarlet Letter*, Bobbs-Merrill, 1963; *The American 1890s: Life and Times of a Lost Generation*, Viking, 1966; (editor) *John Cotton on the Churches of New England*, Harvard University Press, 1968; *Puritanism in America*, Viking, 1973. Contributor to *Encyclopaedia Britannica*. Also contributor of essays to *Saturday Review* and to scholarly journals.

WORK IN PROGRESS: An edition of Puritan writings, for Harvard University Press.

* * *

ZIM, Herbert S(pencer) 1909-

PERSONAL: Born July 12, 1909, in New York, N.Y.; son of Marco (a painter and sculptor) and Minnie (Orlo) Zim; married Sonia Elizabeth Bleeker (an author), January 16, 1934 (died, 1971); married Irmgard Baker, April 1, 1972; children: (first marriage) Aldwin H., Roger S. *Education:* Attended City College (now City College of the City University of New York), 1927-29; Columbia University, B.S., 1933, M.A., 1934, Ph.D., 1940. *Religion:* Society of Friends. *Home:* Plantation Key, Box 34, Tavernier, Fla. 33070.

CAREER: Did first science teaching at summer play schools, New York, N.Y., while a high school student; Ethical Culture Schools, New York, N.Y., instructor in science, 1932-50, head of science department, 1937-45; University of Illinois, Urbana, associate professor, 1950-54, professor of education (science), 1954-57; full-time writer and editor on science subjects, and consultant, 1957—. Columbia University, instructor, summers, 1935, 1936, and conductor of summer field trips through North America, 1937-41. Educational consultant, U.S. Fish and Wildlife Service, 1947-51, Western Publishing Co., 1967-70, American Friends Service Committee, 1968—; educational director, Artists and Writers Press, 1957-69; editorial consultant for Massachusetts Institute of Technology Physical Science Study Program. Conductor of Study of Science Interests of Adolescents for Progressive Education Association, 1934-37; member of steering committee for Biological Sciences Curriculum Study, and participant in Elementary Science Study. Adjunct professor of education, University of Miami, Miami, Florida, 1968—. *Wartime service:* Conscientious objector working on Pre-induction Training Program, U.S. War Department, 1942-43, and in Civilian Public Service, 1943-45.

MEMBER: International Union for the Conservation of Nature, American Institute of Biological Sciences, American Association for the Advancement of Science (fellow), American Nature Study Society (director, 1968-70), American Anthropological Association, National Science Teachers Association, National Association for Research in Science Teaching, National Association of Biology Teachers, Audubon Society, Association for Supervision and Curriculum Development, Nature Conservancy, Isaac Walton League, John Dewey Society, American Orchid Society. *Awards, honors:* D.Sc. from Beloit College, 1967.

WRITINGS: Science Interests and Activities of Adolescents, Ethical Culture Schools, 1940; *Mice, Men and Elephants*, Harcourt, 1942; *Submarines*, Harcourt, 1942; *Parachutes*, Harcourt, 1942; *Air Navigation*, Harcourt, 1943; *Man in the Air*, Harcourt, 1943; (with E. K. Cooper) *Minerals*, Harcourt, 1943; *Rockets and Jets*, Harcourt, 1945, Armed Forces edition, 1945; *Elephants*, Morrow, 1946; *Goldfish*, Morrow, 1947; *Plants*, Harcourt, 1947; *Rabbits*, Morrow, 1948; (with R. W. Burnett and B. Jaffe) *New World of Science*, Silver Burdett, 1948, 2nd edition, 1953; *Codes and Secret Writing*, Morrow, 1948; *Homing Pigeons*, Morrow, 1949; (with A. C. Martin and I. N. Gabrielson) *American Birds and Wildflowers*, Simon and Schuster, 1949; *Snakes*, Morrow, 1949; (with I. N. Gabrielson) *Birds*, Golden Press, 1949, revised edition, 1956.

(With A. C. Martin) *Flowers*, Golden Press, 1950; *Frogs and Toads*, Morrow, 1950; *Owls*, Morrow, 1950; *The Great Whales*, Morrow, 1951; *Golden Hamsters*, Morrow, 1951; (with C. Cottam) *Insects*, Golden Press, 1951, revised edition, 1964; (with A. C. Martin and A. Nelson) *American Wildlife and Plants*, McGraw, 1951, Dover, 1961; (with R. H. Baker) *Stars*, Golden Press, 1951, revised edition, 1956; *Lightning and Thunder*, Morrow, 1952; (with A. C. Martin) *Trees*, Golden Press, 1952, revised edition, 1956; *Alligators and Crocodiles*, Morrow, 1952; *What's Inside of Me?*, Morrow, 1952; *What's Inside of Plants?*, Morrow, 1952; *The Sun*, Morrow, 1953; *What's Inside of Engines?*, Morrow, 1953; *What's Inside of Animals?*, Morrow, 1953; *What's Inside the Earth?*, Morrow, 1953; *Parakeets*, Morrow, 1953; (with H. M. Smith) *Reptiles and Amphibians*, Golden Press, 1953, revised edition, 1956; *Dinosaurs*, Morrow, 1954; *Things Around the House*, Morrow, 1954; *Monkeys*, Morrow, 1955; (with N. Dodge) *The Southwest*, Golden Press, 1955; (with D. F. Hoffmeister) *Mammals*, Golden Press, 1955; (with L. Ingle) *Seashores*, Golden Press, 1955; *The Big Cats*, Morrow, 1955; *Our Senses*, Morrow, 1956; (with R. W. Burnett) *Photography*, Golden Press, 1956, revised edition (with R. W. Burnett and W. B. Brummitt), 1964; (with H. H. Shoemaker) *Fishes*, Golden Press, 1956; (with R. W. Burnett and P. E. Lehr) *Weather*, Golden Press, 1957; *Comets*, Morrow, 1957; *Your Food and You*, Morrow, 1957; (with P. R. Schaffer) *Rocks and Minerals*, Golden Press, 1957; *Ostriches*, Morrow, 1958; *Shooting Stars*, Morrow, 1958; (with R. W. Burnett and H. I. Fisher) *Zoology*, Golden Press, 1958; *Diamonds*, Morrow, 1959; *The Southeast*, Golden Press, 1959; *Giant Little Golden Book of Fish*, Golden Press, 1959; (with N. N. Dodge) *The Pacific Northwest*, Golden Press, 1959; *Your Heart and How It Works*, Morrow, 1959.

Guide to Everglades National Park and Nearby Florida Keys, Golden Press, 1960; *How Things Grow*, Morrow,

1960; *The Universe*, Morrow, 1961, revised edition, 1970; *Rocks and How They Were Formed*, Golden Press, 1961; (with A. Sprunt IV) *Gamebirds*, Golden Press, 1961; (with F.H.T. Rhodes and P. R. Shaffer) *Fossils*, Golden Press, 1962; *The Rocky Mountains*, Golden Press, 1964; (with R. T. Mitchell) *Butterflies and Moths*, Golden Press, 1964; *Sharks*, Morrow, 1966; *Corals*, Morrow, 1966; (with Chandler Robbins) *Birds of North America*, Golden Press, 1966; *Waves*, Morrow, 1967; (with Floyd Shuttleworth) *Non-Flowering Plants*, Golden Press, 1967; *Blood*, Morrow, 1968; (with wife, Sonia Bleeker Zim) *Mexico*, Golden Press, 1969; *Bones*, Morrow, 1969; (with James Skelly) *Hoists, Cranes, and Derricks*, Morrow, 1969; (with Skelly) *Machine Tools*, Morrow, 1969.

(With Shuttleworth) *Orchids*, Golden Press, 1970; (with Skelly) *Trucks*, Morrow, 1970; (with Sonia Bleeker Zim) *Life and Death*, Morrow, 1970; (with Taylor Alexander) *Botany*, Golden Press, 1970; (with Skelly) *Cargo Ships*, Morrow, 1970; *Armored Animals*, Morrow, 1971; *Your Brain and How It Works*, Morrow, 1972; (with Skelly) *Tractors*, Morrow, 1972; *Your Stomach and Digestive Tract*, Morrow, 1973; (with Lucretia Krantz) *Commercial Fishing*, Morrow, 1973; (with Krantz) *Crabs*, Morrow, 1974; (with Skelly) *Pipes and Plumbing Systems*, Morrow, 1974; *Medicine*, Morrow, 1974; (with Skelly) *Metric Measure*, Morrow, 1974; (with Skelly) *Eating Places*, Morrow, 1975; (with Krantz) *Snails*, Morrow, 1975.

Contributor: (Compiler of science sections) *Bibliography of Books for Children*, Association for Childhood Education, 1942, 1945, 1946, 1948, 1950, 1952; *Collecting Science Literature for General Reading*, Graduate School of Library Science, University of Illinois, 1961; *Man/Problem Solver*, International Design Conference, 1961.

Editor-in-chief: "Golden Guide" series, Golden Press, 1947-70; *Our Wonderful World*, eighteen volumes, Spencer Press (Chicago), 1955-60; *What Is Happening in Our Wonderful World*, Spencer Press (Chicago), 1958, 1960, 1961; "Fact and Fiction" series, three books, Spencer Press, 1958-61; *The Golden Book Encyclopedia of Natural Science*, sixteen volumes, Golden Press, 1962; "Golden Bookshelf of Natural History," three books, Golden Press, 1963-64.

Editor—All published by Golden Press, except as indicated: (With O. L. Austin Jr. and A. Singer) *Birds of the World*, 1961; R. T. Abbott, *Sea Shells of the World*, 1962; J.F.G. Clarke, *Butterflies*, 1963; "Quiz Me" series, fourteen books, 1963-65; R. E. Smallman, *Washington*, 1964; H. Gasser, *Painting*, 1964; G. W. Sharpe, *A Guide to Arcadia National Park and the Nearby Coast of Maine*, 1968; (with James Skelly) *Telephone Systems*, Morrow, 1971.

Contributor of articles and reviews on science and natural history subjects to magazines.

SIDELIGHTS: All but three of the books Zim has written are still in print, with sales exceeding sixty million copies. They have appeared in more than sixty-five foreign editions, with translations in Arabic, Japanese, and seven European languages, and Navajo; *Birds of the World* currently is circulating in six languages. Many of the books stem from findings in his study on science interests of adolescents. The report, published in 1940, indicated that children's interests in science are very specific, and much stronger in certain areas than in others.

BIOGRAPHICAL/CRITICAL SOURCES: Lee Bennett Hopkins, *Books Are By People*, Citation Press, 1969.

ZIMMER, Basil G(eorge)   1920-

PERSONAL: Born June 29, 1920, in Smith Creek, Mich.; son of Walter N. (a carpenter) and Mary A. (Martin) Zimmer; married Janet M. Jackson, November 3, 1942; children: Basil George, Jr., Linda Jean. *Education:* Port Huron Junior College, student, 1939-41; University of Michigan, B.A., 1947, M.A., 1949, Ph.D., 1954. *Religion:* Roman Catholic. *Home:* 10 Bridgham Farm Rd., Rumford, R.I. *Office:* Department of Sociology, Brown University, Providence, R.I.

CAREER: Eastern Michigan University, Ypsilanti, instructor in sociology, 1950-51; University of Michigan, Ann Arbor, instructor in sociology, 1951-52; Florida State University, Tallahassee, assistant professor of sociology, 1952-53; University of Michigan, Flint Campus, resident director of social science research project, 1953-59, associate professor of sociology, 1956-59; Brown University, Providence, R.I., associate professor, 1959-61, professor of sociology, 1961—. University of Kerala, consultant to Demographic Program, summer, 1964; attached worker, Medical Research Council, Aberdeen, Scotland, 1972—; visiting scholar, Australian National University, 1973; director, Center for Urban Studies, 1974—. *Military service:* U.S. Army, 1941-45; became staff sergeant. *Member:* American Sociological Association, National Academy of Sciences (highway research board), International Union for Scientific Study of Population, Population Association of America, Eastern Sociological Association.

WRITINGS: Rebuilding Cities, Quadrangle, 1964; *Metropolitan Area Schools: Resistance to District Reorganization*, Sage Publications, 1968; *The Metropolitan Community: Its People and Government*, Sage Publications, 1970; *Migration Within the United States*, Allyn & Bacon, 1972.

Contributor: *Reader in Urban Sociology*, Free Press of Glencoe, 1957; *Community Political Systems*, Free Press of Glencoe, 1961; *Readings in Human Ecology*, Row, Peterson, 1961; *Urban Renewal: The Record and the Controversy*, M.I.T. Press, 1966; *Urban Sociology: Selected Readings*, Appleton, 1968; *Community Politics: A Behavioral Approach*, Free Press, 1971; *Readings in Sociology of Migration*, Pergamon, 1972; *The City is People*, University of Western Australia, 1973; *Urbanization: State of Knowledge*, National Academy of Sciences, 1974.

Contributor to professional journals.

WORK IN PROGRESS: Writing on the problems of political structure in the suburbs and the impact of social mobility on fertility behavior in Aberdeen, Scotland.

*   *   *

ZIMMERMAN, Franklin B.   1923-

PERSONAL: Born June 20, 1923, in Wauneta, Kan.; married Rachel M. Phillip; children: Eve, Guy, Claire, Grace. *Education:* University of Southern California, B.A., 1949, M.A., 1952, Ph.D., 1958; Oxford University, B.Litt., 1956. *Religion:* Protestant. *Office:* Department of Music, University of Pennsylvania, Philadelphia, Pa. 19143.

CAREER: State University of New York College at Potsdam, assistant professor of music, 1958-59; University of Southern California, Los Angeles, visiting associate professor, 1960, associate professor of music and chairman of department of music history and literature, 1961-64; Dartmouth College, Hanover, N.H., professor of music, 1964-68; University of Pennsylvania, Philadelphia, professor of music and chairman of department, 1968—. French horn player with Tucson (Ariz.) Symphony Orchestra, 1938-40, 1945-46, with Sinfonia Nacional de Panama, 1941-42; conductor of concerts at Dartmouth College, and in Los Angeles, Oxford, and London; lecturer on music in United States, London, Cologne. Founder and director of Pennsylvania Pro Musica.

MEMBER: International Musicological Society, American Musicological Society, Royal Music Society (London), Renaissance Society of America, College Music Society, American Association of University Professors, Plainsong and Medieval Music Society (London), Gesellschaft fuer Musikforschung. *Awards, honors:* Fulbright scholar, 1953-55; American Council of Learned Societies fellowship, 1959-60, grant, 1963; International Gold Medal for Musicology, Arnold Bax Foundation, 1960.

WRITINGS: (Contributor) *Henry Purcell: Essays on His Music*, Oxford University Press, 1959; (editor) Henry Purcell, *I Will Love Thee, O Lord* (edition of anthem), University of Pittsburgh Press, 1961; *Henry Purcell, 1659-1695: An Analytical Catalogue of His Music*, Macmillan (London), 1963; (contributor) *Festschrift for O. E. Deutsch*, Barenreiter, 1963; *Henry Purcell: His Life and Times*, Volume I, Macmillan, 1967. Also contributor to *Hinrichsen's Yearbook*, 1958, 1959, *Anuario Musical*, Instituto de Musicologia (Barcelona), 1959. Contributor of about forty articles and reviews to music journals.

WORK IN PROGRESS: Volume II of biography of Henry Purcell.

*   *   *

ZIMMERMAN, Gordon G(lenn)   1922-

PERSONAL: Born March 8, 1922, in Flanagan, Ill.; son of Joseph H. and Ida (Slagle) Zimmerman; married Ruth Steiner, June 9, 1946; children: Roger, Charles. *Education:* Moody Bible Institute, pastor's course diploma, 1942; Sterling College, B.A., 1945; Bowling Green State University, M.A., 1950; University of Michigan, Ph.D., 1961. *Office:* Speech Department, Greenville College, Greenville, Ill. 62246.

CAREER: Minister of Mennonite churches in Sterling, Kan., 1943-48, and Wauseon, Ohio, 1948-57; University of the Pacific, Stockton, Calif., 1957-65, began as assistant professor, became associate professor, served as dean of men, 1961-65; Taylor University, Upland, Ind., professor of speech and director of development, 1965-67; Taylor University, Upland, Ind., vice-president for academic affairs, 1967-73; Greenville College, Greenville, Ill., professor of speech and chairman of department, 1973—. *Member:* Pi Kappa Delta, Phi Kappa Phi, Phi Eta Sigma. *Awards, honors:* Named outstanding faculty member, University of the Pacific, 1960.

WRITINGS: (With Donald Duns) *A Guidebook to Public Speaking: Philosophy and Practice*, Allyn & Bacon, 1964.

WORK IN PROGRESS: Research in the works of T. S. Eliot, and in the preaching and writings of Edgar DeWitt Jones.

AVOCATIONAL INTERESTS: Collecting books on homiletics.

*   *   *

ZIOLKOWSKI, Theodore (Joseph)   1932-

PERSONAL: Born September 30, 1932, in Birmingham, Ala.; son of Mieclaw (a pianist) and Cecilia (Jankowski)

Ziolkowski; married Yetta Goldstein, March 26, 1951; children: Margaret Cecilia, Jan Michael, Eric Joseph. *Education:* Duke University, A.B., 1951, A.M., 1952; University of Innsbruck, graduate study, 1952-53; Yale University, Ph.D., 1957. *Politics:* Democrat. *Home:* 101 Broadmead West, Princeton, N.J. *Office:* Department of Germanics, Princeton University, Princeton, N.J.

CAREER: Yale University, New Haven, Conn., instructor, 1956-60, assistant professor of German, 1960-62; Columbia University, New York, N.Y., associate professor, 1962-64; Princeton University, Princeton, N.J., professor of German, 1964-69, Class of 1900 Professor of Modern Languages, 1969—, chairman of German department, 1973—. Visiting professor, Rutger University, 1966, Yale University, 1968, City College of the City University of New York, 1971; visiting lecturer, University Center of North Carolina, 1971. *Member:* Authors Guild, Internationale Vereinung der Germanisten, Modern Language Association of America, American Association of Teachers of German, American Comparative Literature Association. *Awards, honors:* Guggenheim fellow, 1964-65; Fulbright Research fellow in Germany, 1958-59; American Philosophical Society grant, 1959; American Council of Learned Societies fellow, 1972-73; James Russell Lowell Prize in Criticism, 1973.

WRITINGS: Hermann Broch, Columbia University Press, 1964; *The Novels of Hermann Hesse*, Princeton University Press, 1965; *Hermann Hesse*, Columbia University Press, 1966; (translator) Herman Meyer, *The Poetics of Quotation in the European Novel*, Princeton University Press, 1968; *Dimensions of the Modern Novel*, Princeton University Press, 1969; *Fictional Transfigurations of Jesus*, Princeton University Press, 1972; (editor) Hermann Hesse, *Autobiographical Writings*, Farrar, Straus, 1972; (editor) Hermann Hesse, *Stories of Five Decades*, Farrar, Straus, 1972; (editor) *Hesse: A Collection of Critical Essays*, Prentice-Hall, 1973; (editor) Hermann Hesse, *My Belief: Essays on Life and Art*, Farrar, Straus, 1974.

Contributor of articles to literary journals in United States and Germany. Member of editorial board, of *Germanic Review, Books Abroad, PMLA*, and Princeton University Press.

WORK IN PROGRESS: Disenchanted Images and *A History of the German Elegy Since 1795.*

SIDELIGHTS: Ziolkowski is convinced that literature cannot be studied from a national point of view alone, and that criticism is by its very nature essentially comparative literature. He is competent in German, French, Italian, and Dutch.

*   *   *

ZOLLITSCH, Herbert G(eorge)   1916-

PERSONAL: Born May 3, 1916, in Buffalo, N.Y.; son of Frank J. (a heating engineer) and Marion (Klipfel) Zollitsch; married Donna Trice, October 27, 1945; children: Jay, Sharon, Michael, Stephen. *Education:* State Teachers College at Buffalo (now State University of New York College at Buffalo), B.S., 1940; University of Buffalo, graduate student (evenings), 1947-50; State University of New York School of Industrial and Labor Relations at Cornell University, M.S., 1951; Cornell University, Ph.D., 1954. *Home:* 11225 North Country View Dr., Mequon, Wis. 53092. *Office:* Marquette University, 606 North 13th St., Milwaukee, Wis.

CAREER: High school industrial arts instructor, Angola, N.Y., 1940-42; U.S. Navy Teacher Training Center, Chicago, Ill., teacher-trainer, 1942-43; Niagara Frontier Transit Co., Buffalo, N.Y., assistant to superintendant of employment and instruction, 1946-50; Cornell University, Ithaca, N.Y., supervisory instructor, 1951-53; Marquette University, Milwaukee, Wis., 1954—, now professor of management. Personnel management consultant to business firms, 1954—. Milwaukee Mayor's Special Committee to Study the Salaries of Top Elected Officials, member, 1960. Military service: U.S. Naval Reserve, active duty, 1943-46; became lieutenant senior grade; later promoted to lieutenant commander.

MEMBER: Industrial Relations Research Association (vice-president of Wisconsin chapter, 1962-63; president, 1963-64), Academy of Management (midwest division vice-president, 1969-70; national president, 1970-71), American Production and Inventory Control Society, Wisconsin Training Directors, Beta Gamma Sigma, Phi Delta Kappa, Kappa Delta Pi, Epsilon Pi Tau. Awards, honors: Ford Foundation fellowship to study new developments in behavioral science as they apply to business administration, 1962; Business Administration Faculty Award, 1965.

WRITINGS: (With Adolph Langsner) Wage and Salary Administration (text and instructor's manual), South-Western Publishing, 1961, 2nd edition, 1970. Contributor of articles and reviews to journals in field.

WORK IN PROGRESS: The third edition of Wage and Salary Administration, publication by South-Western Publishing expected in 1978.

AVOCATIONAL INTERESTS: Tennis, travelling, golf, making teaching aids.

*   *   *

ZOLLSCHAN, George K(arl)   1930-

PERSONAL: Surname is pronounced Tsoll-shun; born March 18, 1930, in Vienna, Austria. Education: London School of Economics and Political Science, London, B.Sc. (honors), 1952. Religion: Hebrew. Office: Department of Sociology, State University of New York, Stony Brook, N.Y.

CAREER: Held various research and teaching positions in England, 1952-56, and then in America; Purdue University, Lafayette, Ind., assistant professor of sociology, 1961-64; Bureau of Social Science Research, Washington, D.C., research associate, 1965—. Member: American Sociological Association, British Sociological Association.

WRITINGS: (Editor with Walter Hirsch) Explorations in Social Change, Houghton, 1964; Social Change: Conjectures, Explorations, and Diagnoses, Schenkman, 1974. Contributor to sociological journals and symposia.

WORK IN PROGRESS: Development of a theory of social change.

ZONIK, Eleanor Dorothy   1918-
(Eleanor Dorothy Glaser)

PERSONAL: Surname is pronounced Zone-ik; born March 11, 1918, in West Didsbury, Manchester, England; daughter of Herbert and Theodora Mary (Moon) Farrington; married V. Glaser, 1941; married second husband, Andrew Louis Zonik (a lecturer in catering), November 18, 1961; children: (first marriage) Henrietta Bennett, Natasha Douty. Education: Attended Harrogate College, 1930-35; extramural study, L.R.A.M. and L.G.S.M. Politics: Conservative. Religion: Church of England. Home: Childyke, Mill Lane, Harbury, Warwickshire, England.

CAREER: Speech teacher in English schools; drama tutor, lecturer, and adjudicator; actor and director, Loft Theatre, Leamington Spa, Warwickshire, England. Member of county executive committee, Warwickshire Federation Womens' Institutes. Member: Speech and Drama Teachers Association.

WRITINGS—Under name Eleanor Dorothy Glaser: Up the Brook (one-act play), J. Garnett Miller, 1955; Call the Selkie Home (one-act play), Heinemann, 1960; Parish Pump (one-act play), J. Garnet Miller, 1964. Also author of Mulligan's Sheebeen, published by Samuel French, and We're All Equal Aren't We, published by J. Garnett Miller. Other plays produced, mainly by clubs: "Circle of Love," 1956; "Saturday's Bread"; "Flowerin' of the Grass"; "Before Eve Was Lilith"; "Man Upon the Land." Contributor to Speech and Drama.

WORK IN PROGRESS: A novel.

AVOCATIONAL INTERESTS: Painting, dressmaking, and gardening.

*   *   *

ZUELKE, Ruth E.   1924-

PERSONAL: Surname is pronounced Zull-key; born December 20, 1924, in Minneapolis, Minn.; daughter of Charles Ludwig (an engineer) and Lydia (Sjhostrom) Zuelke. Education: University of Minnesota, B.S., 1952, M.A., 1961. Politics: Varies. Religion: Protestant. Office: Birmingham Public Schools, Birmingham, Mich. 48001.

CAREER: U.S. government, director of art-photo facilities, Germany, 1954-59; University of Minnesota, Minneapolis, instructor in art, 1959-64; St. Paul Gallery Art School, St. Paul, Minn., instructor in jewelry, 1962-63; Birmingham (Mich.) public schools, coordinator of art, 1963—. Member: National Art Education Association, Michigan Art Education Association, Metropolitan Detroit Bureau of School Studies (art committee).

WRITINGS: The Horse in Art, Lerner, 1964; (editor) A Broader Scope in Art Appreciation, Metropolitan Detroit Bureau of School Studies, 1965.

WORK IN PROGRESS: Working on layouts, writing, photos, and type, for four books on feelings and emotions.†